HISTORICAL
AND
STATISTICAL
GAZETTEER

OF

NEW YORK
STATE

HEART OF THE LAKES
PUBLISHING

INTERLAKEN, NY 14847

1980

This reprint is dedicated
to all those that work
to make available
the documents and records
from the past
to help us preserve our heritage
for the future.

We have for sale
to compliment this work
An Index of Personal Names
compiled by
Frank Place, II

Please see our ad on page 751

Printed in the United States
ISBN: 0-932334-31-8   (Hardcover edition)
0-932334-32-6   (Softcover edition)

Heart of the Lakes Publishing
Interlaken, New York 14847

NEW YORK AND BROOKLYN.
FROM
WILLIAMSBURGH.

HISTORICAL AND STATISTICAL GAZETTEER

OF NEW YORK STATE

R. P. Smith, Publisher.
8 Sth. Salina Street, Syracuse.

1860.

GAZETTEER

OF THE

STATE OF NEW YORK:

EMBRACING

A COMPREHENSIVE VIEW

OF THE

GEOGRAPHY, GEOLOGY, AND GENERAL HISTORY OF THE STATE,

AND

A COMPLETE HISTORY AND DESCRIPTION

OF

Every County, City, Town, Village, and Locality.

WITH FULL TABLES OF STATISTICS.

BY

J. H. FRENCH,

MEMBER OF THE AMERICAN ASSOCIATION FOR THE ADVANCEMENT OF SCIENCE; CORRESPONDING MEMBER OF THE NEW YORK
HISTORICAL SOCIETY; OF THE ALBANY INSTITUTE, ETC.

Illustrated by Original Steel Engravings,

AND ACCOMPANIED BY A NEW MAP OF THE STATE FROM ACCURATE SURVEYS.

SYRACUSE, N. Y.:
PUBLISHED BY R. PEARSALL SMITH.
1860.

LIST OF PERSONS EMPLOYED UPON THE CONSTRUCTION OF THE STATE MAP AND THE PREPARATION OF THE GAZETTEER.

This list includes the names of those only who have been employed for considerable lengths of time.

GENERAL SUPERINTENDENT.
J. H. FRENCH.

FOREMAN OF DRAFTING DEPARTMENT.
FRANCIS MAHLER.

FOREMEN OF STATISTICAL DEPARTMENT.
FRANKLIN B. HOUGH, M.D.,   JAMES JOHONNOT.

DRAFTSMEN.

FRANCIS MAHLER,	WM. E. WOOD,
FRANK FRENCH,	B. W. O'GRADY.

SURVEYORS AND STATISTICIANS.

G. R. BECHLER,	JAY GOULD,	EBENEZER MIX,
S. BEEMAN,	H. W. HARDY,	J. B. MOORE,
SILAS N. BEERS,	FRANKLIN B. HOUGH,	SAMUEL M. REA,
H. P. BENTON,	CHESTER HULL,	THOMAS W. RHODES,
LORIN BLODGET,	WM. JAY HUNT,	A. E. ROGERSON,
P. J. BROWNE,	J. W. HURLBUT,	ALPHONSE SCHOPPE,
L. H. CHENEY,	JAMES JOHONNOT,	J. C. SIDNEY,
GURDON EVANS,	GEO. P. JOHONNOT,	STEPHEN O. SLOSSON,
LAWRENCE FAGAN,	D. J. LAKE,	HOMER D. L. SWEET,
FRANK FRENCH,	A. D. LAMPKINS,	A. V. TRIMBLE,
CYRUS GATES,	MORRIS LEVY,	A. VAN NOSTRAND,
JOHN F. GEIL,	A. LIGOWSKY,	R. B. VAN PETTEN,
SAMUEL GEIL,	WM. LOREY,	CHARLES M. WILBUR,
FRANKLIN GIFFORD,	HORACE C. MANNING,	WM. E. WOOD,
WM. T. GIBSON,	DAVID E. E. MIX,	S. K. GODSHALK.

ENGRAVERS.
On Stone.

GEORGE WORLEY,	GUSTAVUS R. BECHLER,	CHARLES REEN.
WM. BRACHER,	BENJ. MATTHIAS,	

On Steel.

J. SARTAIN,	J. W. STEELE, D. L. GLOVER.

On Wood.
H. SEBALD.

ARTISTS.

GEORGE N. BARNARD,	B. W. O'GRADY,	WM. T. RICHARDS.

Entered according to Act of Congress, in the year 1859, by
R. PEARSALL SMITH,
in the Clerk's Office of the District Court of the United States for the Northern District of New York.

STEREOTYPED BY L. JOHNSON & CO.

COLLINS, PRINTER.

PREFACE.

THE map of Westchester County which was commenced about ten years since, and soon after published by Robert Pearsall Smith, was probably the first map of any county in the State of New York published from actual survey of roads and boundaries. This was followed by maps of other counties on a similar plan; and, about eight years since, Mr. Smith conceived the idea of publishing a series of maps from actual survey, embracing all the counties in the State, and, from these, of producing a State Map that should be more full, complete, and reliable than any ever before published. But, about four years since, upon careful trial, in reducing a large number of these county maps to a uniform scale, so many omissions and discrepancies were found in them, that a new survey of the State was deemed necessary to the construction of an accurate map of the State. An arrangement was accordingly made with the author to take the general superintendence of the new survey; the general plan for the works to be prepared was fixed upon; and the re-survey of the State and the collection of statistics were begun.

At the commencement of the re-survey, maps of fifty-one counties had been completed and published; six counties had been surveyed, but the maps were not yet published; and three counties were still unsurveyed. Of the fifty-one published maps, twelve were found to be so deficient in matters essential to the completion of the State Map according to the plan fixed upon, as to render entire new surveys of these counties necessary. Surveyors were sent into the remaining counties, with copies of the published or manuscript maps in hand, with instructions to visit every town, to correct every error that should be found upon the maps, to make additions of new roads, note changes in boundaries, and, in short, to return the maps properly revised and corrected for use in the preparation of the State Map. In many instances new surveys of parts of towns, town lines, roads, and streams were found necessary, and also countless changes in the location of boundary lines, roads, streams and bodies of water, and in the representation of the topographical features of the country. The surveyors were instructed to obtain copies of manuscript and other local maps, as far as practicable, as these were generally found to contain metes and bounds, and, being plotted to large scales, were of value in laying down boundary lines. Draftsmen were also sent to the several private Land Offices in the State, and to Albany, and all maps of any value in the offices of the State Engineer and Surveyor and the Secretary of State were copied, to be laid under contribution in the preparation of the State Map. The Superintendent of the United States Coast Survey and the Secretary of the Interior also furnished copies of all the maps in their Departments pertaining to the State. The number and variety of maps and plots, printed and manuscript, that have thus been collected is very great, and probably embraces more valuable matter than any similar collection in the State.

Not the least difficult part of the labor of constructing a map of a large extent of country is "making the projection." In surveys of small areas this difficulty does not occur, as the proportion of the curvature of the earth's surface to that part of its area contained in a rectangle of thirty to fifty miles, is so small that, when reduced to the scale of even an inch to the mile, it is scarcely perceptible. But in projecting a map of territory of as great extent as the State of New York, the curvature of the surface from a plane is so great as to make the departure of the lines of latitude and longitude from right lines plainly visible upon a map even when plotted to a scale of less than one-fourth of an inch to a mile.

The Flamstead Improved Projection, being the one best adapted to the correct representation of a large extent of country, was adopted for the State Map.

The maps of the State heretofore published embrace a large part of the New England States, Pennsylvania, and Canada. The space thus usually occupied is appropriated to plans of the cities, and to smaller maps illustrating particular features of the State. These marginal maps, it is believed, add to the value of the work. By placing a map of Long Island by itself,— at the same time showing its relative position to the rest of the State, by retaining a map of nearly one-third of the island in its proper place,—the map of the entire State is constructed

3

on a scale about twenty per cent. (linear scale) larger than can be done on a sheet of the same size with all of Long Island projecting eastward of New York City. This increased scale will be found to fully compensate for the change of place of the eastern portion of Long Island. The map of the State is plotted to the scale of $\frac{1}{300,000}$, which is $\frac{625}{132}$ or a small fraction more than 4.7 miles to an inch; and the city plans to the scale of $\frac{1}{50,000}$, which is $\frac{625}{792}$ or a small fraction more than .78 of a mile to an inch.

The longitude of several points in the eastern and western portions of the State having been accurately determined by the Coast Survey and the Department of the Interior, and the latitude of many points on the north and south borders and within the State from numerous and repeated observations, the projection of the parallels and meridians was first made with accurately constructed scales, using the most recent tables of latitude and longitude measurements as adopted by the Coast Survey and the U.S. Military Academy at West Point. The boundaries of the State were next projected, after which the lines of the counties were located on the map. The town lines were next laid out; and finally the roads, bodies of water, streams, topography, and all other details were filled in. This course could not fail to secure accuracy in all parts of the work; and, while the map does not agree, in many points, with previous maps of the State, the author feels confident that it will bear the closest scrutiny and criticism.

A prominent and distinctive feature of the State Map is the representation of all the roads, railroads, canals, and routes of travel, every mile of each of which has been run and every angle measured.

The city plans are all drawn to the same scale, thus presenting, at a glance, the comparative extent of the built-up portions of each. Albany, Brooklyn, and Buffalo have so great an extent of unoccupied or farm lands that it was not practicable to show the entire corporate limits of either on the city plans; but no built-up part of either city has been omitted. The plans of the other cities embrace their entire area.

In the construction of the Geological and Land Patent Map, the geology of the State according to the New York System has been followed; but the different strata or formations are represented by a system of shading in the engraving,—instead of by color, as is usually done in geological maps. This plan was adopted, as it was desirable to present two distinct features in the one map; and the engraved shading for the geology permits the use of colors for the land patents. The size of the map would not admit of the representation of tracts of land smaller than a township; but a complete list of all the grants will be found in this work.

In the year 1825 the Regents of the University established meteorological stations in various parts of the State, and reports were required to be made from these stations annually to the Board of Regents. At the expiration of twenty-five years the Regents caused these reports to be digested; and the mean averages of the summaries thus deduced—so far as relates to temperature, fall of rain, and direction of wind—are embraced in the Meteorological Map. On this map the several stations (including three established at military posts, and not subject to the direction of the Board of Regents) are at the centers of the small circles. In each of these circles are either two or three numbers: when two, the upper number is the mean annual temperature in degrees Fahrenheit, and the lower number is the mean annual fall of rain in inches; and when three, the upper and lower numbers indicate, respectively, temperature and rain, and the middle one the elevation of the station above tide, in feet. The diagram at the right represents the mean annual direction of wind at the several stations, the index in any case denoting the point of compass, and its length the number of days,— one inch in length of radius representing five days. Thus, taking the index for Canandaigua, the direction is S. 63° 37′ W., and the length of the radius is 3.4 inches. This indicates that the mean annual direction of the wind at this station was from the w. s. w. for 17 days in the year more than from all other directions. For the isothermal lines, or lines of equal temperature, and the shading representing the different depths of rain, we are indebted to LORIN BLODGET, author of American Climatology.

The Time Indicator has been prepared from minute calculations, and will be found correct in every case.

The diagram showing the capacity of the church edifices is constructed to a scale, and correctly represents the proportion of each to the whole.

An examination of the various Gazetteers heretofore published cannot fail to satisfy any one that a great part of the material from which they were compiled was furnished by corre-

spondents. This plan seemed to be the one most likely to secure accuracy, and with some modifications it was at first adopted in collecting materials for this work. Agents were sent into some portions of the State, furnished with printed instructions, questions, and blanks, to obtain the desired information, either by personal research, or through the assistance of such competent persons in the various localities visited as would undertake to fill the blanks and return them to the general office. While a few persons promptly responded to the request thus made of them, others delayed giving it immediate attention, and still others neglected it altogether. A large proportion of the matter received from correspondents was found to be irrelevant, devoted to specialties, or unreliable, and therefore of little value. Much matter was received which possesses a greater or less amount of local interest, but which could not be admitted without giving undue prominence to some subjects or localities at the expense of others. After a fair trial of the plan first adopted, it was found subject to so many objections that it was abandoned. The surveyors and agents were then instructed to visit every city, town, and village, to search records, examine documents, consult the best living, printed, and manuscript authorities, and to make returns to the general office of all the reliable matter and information obtained. They were instructed to take no statement on a single authority, and in cases where authorities were found to differ, to examine diligently and impartially, and report all the facts, so that in digesting and arranging them for the press, all the evidence might be at hand. They were particularly cautioned against taking mere hearsay or traditionary tales for truth, and not to seek wonders and marvels. A competent person was employed to examine records and documents in the State Library and State and other public offices at Albany and in New York City, for information that might be available in the preparation of this work. The Documentary History and the State Geology of New York, general and local histories, biographies, sketches, essays, reports, newspapers, manuscripts, and all other available authorities that were likely to contain any information of value, were collected, and in turn consulted, and their accuracy and value tested as the work progressed.

The plan for the work finally fixed upon, while it embraces a wider range than is usually taken by similar works, seems to be one that cannot fail to meet the wants and tastes of the people, as it presents the wealth, resources, present condition, and past history of the State in a form and style at once convenient, perspicuous, and concise.

The details of description of each county, city, town, and village, have been arranged, as far as practicable, according to a uniform plan or outline; as has been also the General Article embraced in the first 154 pages. The subjects embraced in this article seemed to cover all the ground that properly belongs to the work; and they are treated at as great length as their proportional importance to the limits of the volume would permit. A Gazetteer of a State should not be expected to contain, in a connected form, a complete compendium of knowledge upon whatever pertains to a State. But present condition, brief and comprehensive statements, short historical sketches of general interest, tables, facts and figures as connected with the wealth, prosperity, and resources of a State, should be considered to an extent sufficient for a work of reference, such as a Gazetteer is intended to be.

The general outline of the county descriptions is as follows: 1st. Date of formation of the county, from what taken, subsequent changes in boundaries, location in the State, and air-line distance of geographical center from the Capitol at Albany. 2d. Geology, topography, and drainage; embracing the general geological formations, general contour of the surface, lakes, rivers, and other watercourses. 3d. Soil, leading articles of production, and occupation of the people. 4th. Works of internal improvement. 5th. County seat, names of first county officers, and description of county buildings and institutions. 6th. History of the newspaper press. 7th. Brief historical sketch of the county from the date of first settlement to the present time. The descriptions of the towns are according to nearly the same general plan, and embrace, 1st. Date of formation, from what taken, subsequent changes in boundaries, and location in the county. 2d. Peculiarities in geological formations not mentioned in county description. 3d. Topography and drainage. 4th. Names and description of villages, hamlets, and localities, with their location in town, date of incorporation, institutions, leading branches of business, and population according to the most recent reliable enumeration. 5th. A brief historical sketch, embracing incidents of general and local interest, names of first settlers, first birth, marriage, and death, first church, school, mill, and factory, and number of churches

in 1855. After the towns in each county is a table compiled from the last State census, except the valuation and statistics of schools, which are from the returns for the year 1858. In many cases, the population of villages and the number of churches given are from enumerations taken since 1855; but the last State census has invariably been taken as authority on these two points, except in cases where later reliable enumerations have been taken. The acres of land as given in the tables fall short of the area of the county as given at the commencement of each county description. The reason of this is obvious: the acres of land as shown by the tables are from the returns of assessors, which seldom embrace marsh, swamp, and unproductive lands, and lands under water; while the area in square miles, as given in the county descriptions, has in every case been ascertained from actual measurements.

The steel plate illustrations are engraved from original views taken expressly for this work. The map has been engraved on stone, at great expense, by the best artists, and the mechanical execution of both works is highly creditable to the publisher.

The Index of Subjects at the commencement of the work, and the Index of Geographical Names at the close, cannot fail of being justly valued for their convenience. The uniform use of a bold-face letter for names of towns, villages, and hamlets will also be found to greatly facilitate rapid search for this class of geographical names.

To many of the officers in the several State Departments, and to numerous county, town, and city officers, local surveyors, civil engineers, land agents, members of the press, and others, the author is indebted for furnishing valuable materials for these works. To them, and to all who have in any way rendered him assistance in the preparation of either Map or Gazetteer, he desires to acknowledge his obligations. Many persons may feel disappointment at finding that information furnished by them has not been used. An examination of the work, however, must convince them that nothing has been omitted which was essential to the general plan of the work, and that whatever did not come within this plan could not be introduced.

The author would not be doing justice to himself nor to the public did he fail to acknowledge his obligations to those who have been associated with him in the preparation of these works. He desires to make particular mention of the valuable services of LIEUT. FRANCIS MAHLER, FRANKLIN B. HOUGH, M.D., and JAMES JOHONNOT. Lieut. Mahler was educated in a European Military Academy for a Topographical Engineer. Ten years of subsequent practice rendered him eminently qualified for the position he has occupied on the Survey. Dr. Hough is well known to the people of the State as the Superintendent of the last State census and as the author of several historical and statistical works. His services in searching records and documents at Albany, in New York City, and elsewhere, have been invaluable, and to his practical knowledge of the geology of the State the author is mainly indebted for whatever pertains to that subject in this work. Mr. Johonnot has devoted many years to the subject of Physical Geography. The topography of the State, its counties and towns, has been mainly written by him.

The intelligent citizens of the State of New York cannot fail to appreciate the liberality of the publisher in the great expenditures he has made in bringing out these works. The cost of the original surveys for the county maps was about $48,000, and the expenditures on the works from the commencement of the re-survey to the date of publication have reached about $46,000 more, making a total investment of $94,000. The whole time spent in surveys, collection of materials, writing, engraving, proof-reading, &c., has been equal to the time of one person 125 years. It is believed that no similar enterprise of equal extent, and involving the outlay of so large a capital, has ever been undertaken at private expense in this or any other country. Time, talents, and money have alike been devoted to the production of a Map and Gazetteer that it is hoped will be found every way worthy of the Empire State.

INDEX OF SUBJECTS.

Abeel, John, Indian trader, 414.
Abercrombie, Gen. James, 298.
Academies, general article on, 125.
  list of incorporated, 130.
  notices of, 48, 140, 160, 161, 169, 171, 172, 173, 175, 176, 180, 184, 193, 197, 200, 201, 202, 203, 205, 211, 212, 214, 216, 220, 228, 229, 230, 235, 237, 239, 243, 244, 246, 247, 248, 251, 252, 253, 259, 260, 261, 263, 265, 270, 272, 275, 277, 278, 282, 283, 286, 289, 300, 303, 305, 311, 312, 317, 324, 326, 327, 330, 331, 332, 333, 343, 346, 349, 355, 356, 357, 360, 361, 362, 363, 369, 372, 378, 383, 384, 385, 390, 391, 392, 393, 398, 399, 400, 401, 403, 405, 412, 414, 429, 430, 453, 456, 463, 464, 465, 466, 467, 468, 469, 471, 482, 484, 485, 486, 489, 495, 498, 505, 506, 508, 509, 510, 514, 515, 516, 522, 527, 528, 532, 536, 538, 546, 547, 548, 554, 556, 557, 558, 559, 560, 561, 575, 577, 580, 582, 587, 588, 590, 591, 592, 597, 598, 604, 606, 607, 616, 617, 625, 627, 628, 634, 637, 638, 640, 645, 647, 650, 652, 657, 658, 663, 665, 666, 674, 675, 679, 680, 682, 683, 684, 685, 686, 692, 694, 695, 698, 699, 700, 701, 704, 705, 707, 708, 713, 714, 715, 716.
  statistical summary of, 128.
Academy of Music, 436.
Accidents, steamboat, statistics, 115.
Acid springs, 320, 324, 325, 456, 593.
Acres of land, by cos., &c., 108.
  by towns, 167, 177, 185, 196, 207, 217, 222, 231, 240, 249, 256, 266, 278, 294, 306, 313, 319, 328, 335, 339, 350, 364, 373, 380, 387, 394, 406, 417, 457, 472, 491, 500, 511, 516, 529, 539, 543, 551, 562, 567, 571, 583, 594, 599, 608, 612, 618, 630, 640, 648, 653, 659, 669, 676, 687, 695, 709, 716, 721.
Adgate's Patent, 48, 341, 349.
Adjutant General, 43.
African Methodist Episcopal Church, 139.
Agrarian movement. See *Anti Rent*.
Agricultural College, 616.
  fairs, 101.
  Hall, 27, 160.
Agricultural Implement manufactory, 160, 166, 199, 200, 216, 244, 248, 260, 274, 286, 312, 362, 368, 384, 387, 400, 401, 405, 406, 407, 411, 416, 454, 466, 484, 488, 495, 509, 510, 536, 556, 559, 561, 571, 575, 598, 611, 617, 665, 681, 691, 693, 695, 699, 716.
  products, counties excelling in, 103.
  societies, town and county, 83, 102, 103, 575.
  Society, 27, 101, 495.
Agriculture, appropriations for, 106.
  statistics of, by cos., 104 to 107.
Albany Institute, 101, 161.
Aldermanic Districts, New York, 420.
Aliens, statistics of, by counties, 150.
Allen, Ebenezer, 384, 398, 402, 404, 406, 711.
  Capt. Ebenezer, 300, 301.
  Ethan, at Ticonderoga, 299, 305.
  family murdered, 679.
  Nathaniel, 498.
Almshouses, 161, 365, 393, 398, 422, 425, 426, 509, 553.
Ambuscade, 345, 411, 461, 604, 671, 672.
American Anti Slavery Society, 146.
  and Foreign Christian Union, 146.
  Bethel Society, 146.
  Bible Society, 144.
  Board Commissioners for Foreign Missions, 145.
  Colonization Society, 146.
  Home Missionary Society, 146.
  Institute, 435.
  Seamen's Friend Society, 146.
  Sunday School Union, 146.
  Tract Society, 145.
Amherst, Sir Jeffrey, 49, 298, 337, 574, 673, 674.
Analyses of Mineral Waters, 248, 383, 394, 470, 480, 497, 537, 592, 607.
Anchor manufactory, 297, 508, 510, 681.
André, Major J., 504, 541, 570, 603, 699, 700, 701, 703.
Andrustown plundered, 342, 349.

Angier, Sieur, surveys by, 298.
Anne, Queen, Germans settle under, 242, 245.
Anniversary Week, N. Y., 144.
Anti masonic movement, 147, 323.
  Mission Baptists, 139.
  rent troubles, 157, 210, 242, 258, 259, 269, 322, 360, 553, 602, 621, 643.
Anti Slavery Society, 146.
Antwerp Company, 353, 355, 375.
Appel Patent, 585.
Apples, statistics of, by counties, 105.
Appling, Major D., 355, 358, 525.
Appointing power, 31.
Aqueducts, 60, 165, 275, 397, 418, 424, 589, 597, 689, 714.
Ararat, or resting place for Jews, 291.
Arcade, 403.
Architecture, 436, 437.
Argyle Patent, 679.
Armories, 44, 369, 437, 489, 580.
Armstrong, Gen. John, 276.
Arnold, Benedict, 299, 333, 335, 338, 342, 410, 504, 541, 542, 570, 687, 699, 700.
Arsenals, 44, 45, 165, 286, 312, 325, 362, 369, 423, 437, 466, 495, 582, 602, 606.
Artesian wells, 25, 362, 392, 424.
Artillery Patent, 681.
Asia, man-of-war, 438.
Asparagus culture, 544.
Assay Office, 122, 437.
Assembly, 28.
  districts, 28.
Assessments, power of Supervisors in, 30.
Associate Presbyterians and Associate Reformed Presbyterians, 139.
Astor claim, Putnam co., 541.
  Library, 435.
Astronomical Instrument manufactory, 392.
  Observatories, 161, 423.
Asylums, 42, 149, 198, 275, 276, 365, 370, 396, 398, 403, 412, 419, 425, 432, 433, 434, 468, 483, 488, 518, 524, 566.
Atheneum, 368, 403.
Attainder. See *Forfeiture*.
Attorney General, 32.
Auditor of Canal Department, 54.
Auger manufactory, 286.
Avenues, New York City, plan of, 422.
Awl manufactory, 286.
Ax factories, 166, 220, 235, 286, 368, 402, 483, 484, 558, 593, 616, 668.
Axle manufactory, 235, 277, 668, 699.

Bakeries, statistics by counties, 109.
Bank note engraving, 90.
Banks, agencies of, 90.
  commissioners, 90.
  existing, list of, 90 to 95.
  general article on, 89.
  individual, 89.
  obsolete and closing, 95 to 99.
  savings, 99.
  suspension of, 90.
  United States, 90.
Baptists, 139, 140.
  Free Will, 140.
  Old School, 139.
  Seventh Day, 143.
Barley, counties where most raised, 101.
  statistics by counties, 104.
  trade, 159.
Barracks, 45, 239, 354, 358, 542, 555, 580.
Barrel manufactory, 220, 402, 488, 509, 518, 520, 522.
Barytes, sulphate of, 352, 356, 577, 600, 604, 698.
Basket manufactory, 286.
Batteries, 423, 437, 565.
Batting manufactory, 464.
Battles, 219, 233, 234, 297, 305, 316, 342, 343, 345, 355, 358, 371, 410, 411, 438, 461, 478, 521, 525, 554, 556, 569, 574, 575, 580, 586, 602, 604, 607, 633, 643, 645, 661, 667, 671, 681, 698, 701, 707.
Baum, Col., defeated, 586.
Bayard's Patent, 601.
Bay of New York, 437.
Beaches, 544, 547, 550, 631, 634, 635, 636, 638, 684.
Beacons. See *Lighthouses*.
Beacraft, a tory, 602.
Beans, statistics by counties, 105.

Beardsley, Purchase, 210.
Beck, Dr. T. Romeyn, 156, 160.
Becker's Patent, 603.
Bedini, Cardinal, 287.
Bedstead manufactory, 166, 291.
Beef, supply to New York City, 427, 428.
Beekman's Patent, 269, 270, 276, 277.
Bell, attempt to steal, 343.
  founderies, 166, 561.
Belletre, expedition of, 348.
Bellevue Hospital, 425.
Bellows manufactory, 286.
Belting manufactory, 199, 549.
Bemis Heights, 586, 679.
Benevolent Societies, 81, 144, 370, 371, 403, 432.
Bennington, battle of, 554, 556, 586, 680.
Bethel Society, 146.
Bible Societies, 144, 145, 370, 403, 434, 489.
Big Tree Council, 322.
Billiard Table manufactory, 286.
Billop House, 565.
  Manor, 564.
Bird, Col., 699.
Bituminous springs, 168, 173
Blackberry culture, 703.
Blacking manufactory, 716.
Black Lead, 302, 303, 304.
  manufactory, 297, 304.
Black River Navigation Co., 60.
  Tract, 375.
Blacksmith shops by counties, 109.
Blacksmiths, number by counties, 152.
Blackwells Island, 419, 425.
Blanchard, Col., 672.
Blank Book manufactory, 286.
Blenheim Patent, 602, 603.
Blind, Institution for the, 432, 433.
  statistics by counties, 150.
Blockhouses, 232, 297, 301, 310, 342, 343, 346, 356, 359, 467, 469, 470, 511, 549, 577, 582, 591, 596, 604, 646, 681, 682, 687, 691.
Block manufactory, 368.
Bloomer costume, origin of, 617.
Board of Agriculture, 102, 106.
  Education, New York, 430.
  Health, 116, 428.
Boatbuilding, 367, 402, 419, 616, 618, 657, 662, 686.
Bog iron ore, 25.
Boiler manufactory, 160, 286, 652.
Bolt manufactory, 166.
Bonaparte, Joseph, 363, 376.
Bonded warehouses, 111, 113.
Bone boiling, 372.
  manure, 368.
  pits, 361, 453, 522.
Bony fish, 124, 631.
Bookbinderies, 160, 246, 286.
Book manufactory, 199.
Boon, Gerrit, 462, 468.
Boot and Shoe Makers, number by counties, 152.
Boot and Shoe manufac., 286, 402, 488, 596.
  statistics by counties, 109.
Boroughs, 596, 598, 698, 706.
Boston Corner, 18.
  Ten Towns, 18, 180, 199, 479, 650.
Botanical gardens, 370, 423, 430.
Bouck's Patent, 605.
Bouck, William C., 59.
Boundaries, 17, 258, 290, 308, 418, 586.
Boundary commissions, 18, 677.
  controversies, 503, 545, 551, 700, 706.
Bourbon, reputed, 309.
Box manufactory, 286.
Boyd, Lieut. Wm., 384.
Boylston Tract, 375.
Braddock's defeat, 671.
Bradford, William, 431.
Bradstreet, Col., 519.
Brantingham Tract, 375.
Brant, Joseph, 219, 264, 265, 283, 315, 342, 343, 349, 409, 410, 412, 414, 454, 478, 503, 531, 538, 586, 604.
Brass foundery, 166, 286.
Breakwater, 280, 284.
Breathing well, so called, 190.
Breweries, 109, 160, 214, 237, 241, 275, 286, 367, 368, 383, 385, 399, 402, 406, 419, 468, 483, 488, 509, 556, 561, 563, 598, 617, 657, 662, 691.

Brick manufactory, by counties, 109.
  manufactory of, 110, 160, 246, 286, 330, 331, 332, 398, 505, 542, 550, 563, 566, 568, 569, 598, 632, 639, 662, 666, 691, 696, 698, 699.
Brine springs, 26, 178, 181, 186, 197, 203, 257, 325, 327, 392, 395, 400, 449, 456, 473, 474, 478, 479, 482, 483, 512, 514, 515, 517, 522, 532, 619, 688.
Britannia Ware manufactory, 163, 286.
Brockville captured, 574.
Brooklyn Institute, 369.
Broom Corn, statistics by counties, 107.
  culture of, 101, 220, 381, 407, 413, 595, 597, 600, 606.
Broom Handle manufactory, 590, 597.
  manufactory, 243, 282, 413, 595, 597.
Brothertown Indians, 465.
Brown, Col., 410, 416.
  John, settlement of, 349.
Brown's Tract, 341, 349, 375, 379.
Brush manufactory, 286, 556.
  plains, 631, 636.
Buckskin manufactory, 311, 317.
Buckwheat, quantity raised, 101, 104.
Building associations, 81, 366, 700.
Building stone, 26.
Buildings, public, New York City, 436, 437.
Bull, William, surveys by, 621.
Burgoyne, Gen., 164, 166, 233, 299, 461, 504, 554, 559, 586, 673, 679, 682, 685, 687.
Burial Case manufactory, 549.
Burial Places, New York City, 428.
  See Rural Cemeteries.
Burnetsfield Patent, 341, 344, 345, 346.
Burning of jail, Delaware county, 258.
  of steamer Sir Robert Peel, 360.
  springs, 208, 213, 214, 267, 491, 499, 691.
Burr, Aaron, 404.
Busti, Paul, 322.
Butler, Col. John, 409, 410, 411, 415.
  Walter N., 347, 409, 410, 411, 415, 531.
Butler's Patent, 317, 605.
Butt and Hinge manufactory, 166
Buttermilk Channel, 419.
  Falls, 505.
Butter, product by counties, 106.
Byrne's Patent, 605, 682.

Cabinet Making shops, by counties, 109.
Cabinet Ware manufactory, 203, 286, 368, 390, 402, 514, 515, 522, 523, 598, 618.
Cabinet of Natural History, 125, 126.
Calcareous tufa, 391, 717.
Calculating machine, 161.
Calico Printing, 293.
Cambridge Patent, 680.
Camden Tract, 685.
Campbell's Patent, 679, 683.
Camphene manufactory, 368.
Canada, expeditions against, 246, 311, 358. 408, 493, 681, 682.
Canada, fortifications in, 45.
Canadian canals, 119.
  railways, 119.
  trade, 117, 118.
Canal Appraisers, 54.
  Black River, history of, 60, 61.
  Board, 54.
  boats, 58.
  Cayuga & Seneca, history of, 62.
  Celebration, 58, 59.
  Champlain, history of, 60.
  Chemung, history of, 62.
  Chenango, history of, 60, 61.
  Clearances, 56.
  Commissioners, 54, 59.
  Companies, 64, 356, 632, 642, 661.
  Crooked Lake, history of, 62.
  Delaware & Hudson, 63, 502, 506.
  Department, Auditor of, 54.
  distances, 59.
  enlargement, 59, 60.
  Erie, history of, 58.
  feeders, 201, 218, 321, 389, 482, 484, 513, 620, 624, 645, 671.
  Fund, 54.
  general notice of, 54.
  Genesee Valley, history of, 62, 63.
  hydraulic, 359, 454, 455, 484, 524, 593, 637, 657.
  Manhattan Island, 418.
  natural, 575.
  Oneida Lake, history of, 61.

Canal Oswego, history of, 61, 62.
  reservoirs, 60, 61, 173, 389, 390, 393.
  statistics, 55, 56, 57, 58.
  structures, 58.
  tolls, 56, 57.
Canals, notices of, 156, 169, 171, 173, 179, 186, 187, 193, 198, 201, 203, 218, 220, 221, 224, 226, 228, 230, 279, 280, 288, 293, 330, 341, 346, 375, 381, 384, 385, 387, 388, 395, 397, 398, 401, 402, 403, 404, 407, 413, 420, 449, 451, 452, 455, 459, 466, 468, 469, 475, 482, 484, 488, 489, 492, 502, 491, 512, 513, 514, 515, 518, 520, 523, 524, 526, 574, 581, 585, 587, 593, 598, 609, 610, 611, 614, 617, 642, 624, 654, 689, 690, 691, 693, 714, 718.
Canastota Tract, 47, 389.
Capital, State, 26, 27.
Car manufactory, 286, 395, 509, 571.
  Wheel manufactory, 160, 273, 286, 509.
  Mills, 462, 516, 608, 694, 695.
Carding Machines introduced, 683.
Card manufactory, 199.
Carillon Fort, 298.
Carleton, Major, 300.
Caroline steamer destroyed, 453.
Carpenters, by counties, 109, 152.
Carpet Bag manufactory, 510.
Carpet manufactory, 199, 244, 275, 402, 407, 411, 468, 549, 686, 695, 707.
Carriage manufactory, 109, 160, 166, 228, 229, 237, 255, 275, 286, 346, 368, 399, 401, 402, 405, 411, 419, 463, 484, 487, 494, 496, 522, 548, 561, 575, 598, 657, 658, 683, 716.
Cartridge manufactory, 549.
Cary, Trumbull, and others, purchase by, 210.
Cascades, 20, 21, 22, 165, 203, 210, 227, 235, 239, 253, 255, 271, 300, 305, 310, 312, 320, 324, 326, 328, 333, 346, 352, 355, 360, 361, 374, 376, 377, 379, 383, 386, 390, 395, 401, 402, 419, 467, 474, 484, 486, 487, 505, 508, 514, 515, 517, 521, 523, 524, 526, 527, 532, 558, 560, 572, 579, 593, 597, 604, 605, 609, 611, 613, 616, 617, 618, 646, 654, 656, 657, 658, 664, 670, 674, 675, 715.
Cases before Court of Sessions, N.Y., 421.
Cassiltown Manor, 564.
Castle Garden, 117, 427.
Castles of the Mohawks, 408.
Catholic Schools, New York, 431. See Roman Catholics.
Catskill Mountain House, 333.
  Patent, 332.
Cattle market, 427.
  statistics by counties, 106.
  trade, 428.
Caughnawaga Indians 408.
Caves, 26, 155, 162, 163, 164, 302, 328, 351, 356, 360, 361, 362, 393, 416, 482, 570, 600, 604, 606, 607, 666, 674, 675, 684.
Cayuga Bridge, 199, 200.
  Marshes, 63, 474.
Cazenove, Theophilus, 322.
Cement manufactory.—See Waterlime.
Central American Educational Society, 146.
  Asylum for Deaf and Dumb, 412.
  Park, New York, 44, 423, 424.
Chain across the Hudson, 504, 505, 508, 509, 542.
  Lake Champlain, at Ticonderoga, 299.
Chain Cable manufactory, 681.
Chair manufactory, 275, 282, 286, 343, 402, 462, 487, 527, 610.
Chamber of Commerce, 116, 436.
Chambers, Thomas, 661, 662, 664.
Chambly Canal, 119.
Champlain Lake, 297.
  grants on, 298.
Champlain, Samuel, 233, 297, 477, 519.
Chandleries, 109, 286, 368, 419, 563, 567.
Channels of New York Harbor, 418.
Chapel, Queen Anne's, 413.
Charitable societies, 144, 247, 287, 403, 433, 434, 561.
Charity schools, 370, 431.
Charles III of Spain, grant to a New York church, 435.
Charters, New York City, 418, 438.
  to academies, 127.
Chase, Rev. Philander, 265.
Chasm, remarkable, in Clinton co., 238.
  in Lewis co., 378.

Chassanis, Peter, Purchase, 353, 375, 377.
Cheesebox manufactory, 343, 347, 348.
Cheesecock's Patent, 503, 508, 568.
Cheese manufactory, 175, 416, 537.
  product of, by counties, 107.
Chemical works. See Laboratories.
Chenango Tract, 47.
  Triangle, 224.
  Twenty Towns, 52, 224, 389.
Cherry Valley massacre, 410, 531.
  Patent, 532.
Chevaux de frise, 542.
Children's Aid Society, 370, 403, 434.
  Hospital, 432.
Chinese, early trade with, 162.
Cholera, 308.
Christian Association, 146.
  Connexion, 140.
  Unions, 146, 147.
Cryslers Field, 311.
Churches, general article on, 139 to 144.
  New York, 434, 435.
Church, John B., and Philip, 169.
  property controversy, 287.
  Tract, 321.
Cider, product by counties, 105
Cigar manufactory. See Tobacco.
Cincinnati, Society of, 434.
Ciscoes, fishery of, 359
Cities, officers of, 31.
City Courts, 34.
  Halls, 156, 160, 246, 275, 365, 369, 403, 423, 436, 468, 488, 524.
  Inspector's Department, N. Y., 427.
  Park, Brooklyn, 369.
  Railroads, 367, 368, 429.
  Schools, 160, 199, 246, 275, 286, 369, 403, 429, 430, 468, 488, 524, 560, 598.
Clark, Rev. Thomas, 685, 686.
  Willis and Lewis G., 486.
Clarke, Miss Sara J., 487.
Claus, Colonel Daniel, 315, 409, 412.
Clearances on Northern lakes, 118.
Clearing-House Association, N. Y., 436.
Clendening Valley Aqueduct, 424.
Clergymen, number by counties, 151.
  property of, exempt from taxes, 48.
Clerks' offices. See County Buildings.
Clermont, steamboat, 162, 521.
Clifton Park Patent, 585, 587.
  Mine, 572.
Clinton, Charles, 510.
  College, Fairfield, 343.
Clinton, De Witt, 58, 59, 102, 481, 506, 549.
  George, 274, 276.
  Sir Henry, 504, 664, 699.
  General James, 410, 412, 531, 536.
  Prison, 41, 238
  Purchase, 224.
  Township, 47.
Clock manufactory, 638.
Clover mill, 350.
Cloves of the Catskills, 329, 334.
Coachmakers, number by counties, 151.
Coal formations, 329, 619.
  mining for, 178, 407.
  Oil manufactory, 367.
  trade, 220, 488, 618, 624, 655, 657, 661, 662, 663, 664.
Coasting trade, statistics of, 115, 116.
Coast Survey, 23, 121.
Coffee and Spice manufactory, 368.
Colden, Cadwallader, 508, 546.
  Tract, 341, 343, 344, 345, 348.
Collar and Bosom manufactory, 657.
Collection districts, coasting trade by, 115.
  general article on, 111.
  Northern frontier, 117, 118.
  ship building by, 115
  tonnage by, 112.
Collectors on canals, 54.
Collect Pond, N. Y., 418.
Colleges, general article upon, 125.
  notices of, 48, 125, 126, 160, 161, 188, 220, 252, 343, 384, 391, 403, 419, 430, 431, 455, 464, 498, 546, 560, 564, 575, 598, 610, 616, 657, 707.
  tabular list and statistics of, 126, 127
Colonial history, 125.
Colonization Society, 146.
Colored Home, 425, 426.
  schools, 136.
  statistics of, by counties, 150.
Color manufactory, 272, 373.
Comb manufactory, 272, 286.
Commerce, foreign, 111, 112, 113, 114, 115, 162, 247, 367, 418, 436, 438, 639.

Commerce, lake, 118, 119, 208, 214, 237, 239, 280, 285, 352, 395, 399, 402, 403, 452, 517, 518, 520, 524, 525, 580, 582, 657.
river, 156, 246, 268, 274, 276, 285, 330, 332, 502, 509, 561, 580, 581, 620, 652, 661, 662, 663, 664, 666, 699.
Commercial colleges, 287, 431, 489.
Commissioners of Canal Fund, 54.
for taking acknowledgment of deeds, 35.
of Emigration, 117, 419, 420, 427, 549.
of Excise, 36.
of Health, 116.
of Highways, 39.
of Land Office, 46, 53.
Common Councils of cities, 31, 420.
Communities, 293, 405.
Comptroller, 32.
Confectioneries, 286.
Congregational Churches, 140.
Methodist Church, 140.
Congress, Continental, 565.
first meeting in New York, 438.
first Colonial, 162.
Connecticut Tract, 321, 513.
Constable's Towns, 375.
Contracting Board, 54.
Contributions to aid Schenectady, 599.
Controversy in Dutch Church, 275.
Convention for adopting U. S. Const., 276.
Hartford, 48, 52.
Hempstead, 544, 545.
Kingston, 664.
Provincial, 269, 272, 276.
Conventions at Syracuse, 488.
Convents, 419, 431, 434, 701.
Convictions, statistics of, 36, 421.
Cooper Institute, 435.
Cooper, J. Fenimore, 536.
Cooperages, 286, 514, 691.
Coopers, number by counties, 151.
Copperas, 305.
manufactory, 575.
Copper coinage, 509.
ores, 25, 267, 340, 575, 577, 579, 660, 704.
Corn, statistics of, 101, 104.
Cornplanter, an Indian chief, 410, 414.
Cornwall county, 18.
Coroners, 35, 427.
Cortland Manor, 705, 706, 708.
Corporations, general article on, 80.
Cosby's Manor and Patent, 341, 344, 348, 469.
Cotringer Tract, 321.
Cotton manufactory, 110, 166, 216, 228, 241, 247, 248, 253, 271, 274, 276, 293, 334, 346, 347, 348, 352, 356, 360, 362, 368, 402, 464, 465, 466, 468, 471, 504, 509, 510, 525, 527, 532, 533, 534, 535, 536, 538, 554, 556, 558, 559, 560, 561, 569, 571, 584, 590, 591, 598, 605, 634, 638, 662, 666, 682.
Councils, Indian, 322, 344, 414.
Council of Appointment, 31.
of Revision, 31.
of Safety, 601.
Country Roads, Suffolk co., 632.
Country seats, 272, 275, 276, 664, 696, 703, 704, 707, 708.
County buildings, 156, 160, 168, 179, 186, 198, 208, 218, 223, 232, 241, 251, 258, 268, 280, 297, 307, 314, 320, 330, 337, 341, 352, 365, 375, 381, 388, 396, 407, 451, 458, 475, 492, 502, 512, 518, 530, 540, 544, 553, 563, 568, 573, 584, 595, 600, 609, 614, 620, 632, 642, 649, 654, 661, 671, 678, 689, 697, 710, 717.
Clerk, 35.
courts, 34.
Superintendent, 137.
Treasurer, 36.
Courts of admiralty, 117.
of Appeals, 33.
for Trial of Impeachments, 33.
New York City, 428.
of oyer and terminer, 35.
of sessions, 35.
State, 33.
United States, 33.
of Wiltwyck, ancient, 663.
Courtenay, E. H., 368.
Coverlet manufactory, 695.
Cowbell manufactory, 283.
Cowboys, 551.
Cowen, Eseck., 592.
Cows, number by counties, 106.
Craigie Tract, 321.
Cranberry swamp, 528, 618.

Cratean lakes, Onon. co., 26, 474, 482, 484.
Cricket grounds, 423.
Crime of New York City, 421.
Criminal convictions, 35, 36.
courts, 35.
statistics, 425.
Crosby, Enoch, 541.
Croton Aqueduct, 418, 422, 424, 697, 706, 707, 708.
Valley surveyed, 424.
Crown Point, fort at, 297, 298, 299, 673.
Crumhorn Mountain Tract, 125.
Crystal palace, 423, 424.
Cuck, George, a tory, 414.
Cumberland Bay, naval victory in, 234.
Currents of rivers reversed, 304, 579.
Customhouses, 119, 120, 239, 247, 286, 355, 356, 436, 524, 580, 638.
Cutlery manufactory, 246, 508.

Dairying, product of. See Acres, &c.
Dakin Ore Bed, 273.
D'Alainville, seigniory of, 298
Dam, State, 678.
Deaf and dumb, statistics by counties, 150.
Asylum, 419, 432, 433.
Deane's Patent, 48, 235, 471.
Deaths, New York, totals, 428.
of Holland Co. proprietors, 322.
De Bruyn, John Hendrick, Patent of, 247.
Debt of N. Y. to U. S., Revolutionary, 45.
Debtors, imprisoned, 42.
De Courcelles, expedition of, 408.
Deep Spring, so called, 484.
Deeds, acknowledgment of, 35.
Degrees conferred by Regents, 125.
De Lancey's corps, 551.
De Lancey, James, 701, 705.
Patent of, 413.
De la Barre's expedition, 358.
Delaware & Hudson Canal, 63, 642, 661, 662, 664, 666, 668.
Delliu's Patent, 682.
De Nonville, expedition of, 493, 499.
Denton, Rev. Richard, 547.
Depots, 403, 561.
Deserters executed, 412, 536.
De Tracy's expedition, 408.
De Veaux, Samuel, 455.
Devendorf, Jacob, scalped, 416.
Devil's Hole, event at, 452, 453.
De Vries, D. P., 564.
Dewitt, Simeon, 58, 657.
Die manufactory, 593.
Dieskau, Baron, 298, 671, 672.
Dikes, 677.
Diluvial valleys, 361.
Dioceses of New York, 142, 143.
Dionondahowa Falls, 680, 683.
Disciples of Christ, 140.
Dise's Manor, 604.
Dispensaries, New York, 370, 432.
Distances by canals, 59 to 64.
by railroads, 66 to 73.
Distilleries, 160, 198, 199, 201, 213, 214, 286, 344, 367, 368, 384, 385, 391, 398, 401, 406, 454, 462, 467, 483, 484, 487, 497, 515, 535, 561, 593, 617, 618, 691, 693, 699.
Distributing post offices, 123, 652.
District attorneys, 35.
libraries, 135.
school meetings, 135.
Districts, aldermanic, 420.
Assembly, 28.
collection. See Customhouses.
judicial, 33, 34.
military, 43.
Senatorial, 28.
of Tryon co., early, 409.
Divisions, Colonial, Dutchess co., 269.
Docks, 367.
Dolomite, 41, 267, 699.
Domestic manufactures by counties. See Acres, &c.
Dongan, Governor, 564.
Dover Stone Church, so called, 271.
Door factory, 188.
Dorfs of Palatinates, 601.
Downie, Commodore, 234.
Downing, A. J., 708.
Doxtader, Tory, 411, 416, 602, 607.
Dressmakers, number by counties, 151.
Drouth, 352.
Drowned Lands, 501, 506, 507, 510, 511.
Drug manufactory, 275.
Dry docks, 45, 368, 618.

Dry goods, statistics of, 113.
Duane, Colonel, 410.
Dubois, Bishop, school founded by, 360.
Colonel, 410.
Dudley Observatory, 161.
Duel, 358.
Duerville Patent, 235.
Duke of Gloucester, 574.
Dukes county, 18.
Dutch, policy of, toward Indians, 408.
settlements by, 366, 408, 437, 503, 601, 663, 667.
Duties on salt, 54.
Duties, receipts from, 111, 113, 114.
Dwellings, number and kind of, 108.
Dwight, Francis, 137.
Dyed Stuffs manufactory, 373, 563.
works, 293, 465, 565, 706.

Earl of Moira, 574.
Earthen Ware manufactory, 198, 286, 499, 668.
Easton's Patent, 466.
Eaton, Amos, 24.
Ebenezer Society, 293
Edge Tool manufactory, 166, 235, 286, 300, 347, 393, 395, 402, 486, 590.
Edmeston, Col., 533.
Elections, New York, 420.
canvass of, 30.
Inspectors of, 40.
military, 44.
Electors, census of, 31.
Elephant, fossil remains of, 163.
Elevations above tide, 19 to 22.
Delaware co., 257.
Steuben co., 619.
Washington co., 677.
Elevators, 293, 356, 399, 525.
Eleven Towns on Black River, so called, 353, 355, 357, 358, 361, 362, 375.
Elias, officers of the ship, 564.
Elk, domestication of, 192.
Ellicott, Joseph, 322.
Embargo, 233, 247, 356, 357, 643.
Emery manufactory, 546.
Emigration. See Commissioners of Emigration.
Emigrant homes, 427.
Emmons, E., analysis by, 324.
geologist of Second District, 24.
Encroachment upon N. Y. Harbor, 46.
Endowment of Union College, 598.
Engineers, Canal, 54.
English conquest, 438.
Engraving, 286.
Entries of vessels at New York, 112.
Epidemic, 361, 579.
Erie Canal. See Canals.
Basin, 284.
Escheats, 48.
Esopus, enemy advance to, 504.
Evacuation Day, 437, 438.
Evangelical Lutheran Church, 140.
Evans, David E., 322.
Evan's Patent, 503.
Evans, William, bequest of, 393.
Evening schools, 430.
Exchange building, 160.
Excise, Commissioners of, 36.
Executive Department, N. Y. City, 420.
State, 179.
Expeditions against Canada. See Canada.
Exports, Canadian, 118.
total New York, since 1701, 112, 114.
Eye and Ear Infirmaries, 370, 432.

Fairs, Colonial, 101.
State, and other, 102, 269, 706.
Fall Hill Patent, 341, 343, 346.
Families, number of, by counties. See Acres, &c.
Fancy Goods manufactory, 455.
Fanning Mill manufactory, 618, 691, 692.
Farms, number of, by counties, 108, 151.
Farrett, James, agent of Earl of Stirling, 633, 635, 637, 639.
Federalist (the) newspaper articles, 276.
Feldspar, 267, 671, 674.
Females, Asylum for, 433, 488.
Female Guardian Society, 433.
Seminaries. See Academies.
Ferries, general act, and list of, 82.
notices of, 200, 245, 249, 271, 272, 275, 276, 277, 356, 367, 420, 428, 450, 509, 546, 555, 563, 570, 580, 636, 664, 666, 699, 700, 704.

Fertilizers, 631.
Feudal privileges, 242.
Fever, 425.
Field notes of Holland Land Co., 322.
File manufactory, 271, 275, 510, 571.
Fillmore, Millard, 203, 206, 283.
Finance Department New York City, 420.
Fire arms first known to Indians in New York, 297.
Fire Brick manufactory, 26, 468, 563, 567, 699.
  Departments, 275, 369, 422, 423, 424.
  destructive, 83, 162, 362, 438, 468, 561, 575, 593, 652, 682.
  Engine manufactory, 402, 593, 617.
  Insurance, 83, 436.
  Wardens, 423.
  in the woods, 631.
Fish Manures, 631, 632, 638, 639.
  preservation of, 124.
Fisher, Col. Frederick, 415.
Fisheries, 18, 46, 124, 232, 247, 357, 359, 427, 520, 544, 550, 632, 634, 636, 637, 641, 701.
Fitch, Dr. Asa, 27.
  John, 82, 418.
Five Dutch Towns of Kings co., 366.
Flagg, Azariah C., 137.
Flagging Stone, 26, 197, 204, 205, 223, 267, 329, 332, 381, 385, 449, 454, 491, 512, 515, 581, 660, 663, 664, 666, 717.
Flax culture, 555, 558, 680, 686.
  statistics of lint and seed, by cos., 106.
  mills, 368, 558, 569.
Floating battery, 45.
Flour manufactory, 160, 169, 170, 172, 173, 176, 193, 194, 199, 202, 203, 205, 211, 212, 213, 214, 216, 220, 221, 222, 226, 238, 246, 248, 259, 271, 272, 273, 274, 276, 286, 324, 325, 328, 346, 352, 357, 362, 385, 390, 392, 395, 400, 401, 402, 405, 406, 413, 454, 465, 468, 481, 482, 484, 497, 514, 516, 518, 520, 521, 522, 524, 525, 527, 528, 534, 536, 537, 538, 561, 622, 575, 593, 610, 611, 612, 617, 618, 623, 625, 626, 627, 629, 634, 651, 652, 655, 657, 658, 675, 682, 683, 685, 690, 691, 694, 695, 712, 713, 715.
Flower culture, 548, 549.
Floyd, Col. Richard, 634.
  Gen. William, 463, 471, 634.
Fonda, Douw, 415.
Foote, Stillman, 271.
Forrest, Edwin, 708.
Forfeitures, 48, 314, 316, 342, 347, 348, 540, 541, 602, 698, 700, 702, 704, 708.
Forges, 25, 235, 238, 239, 240, 297, 349, 360, 465, 482, 504, 508, 582, 681, 686, 694.
Fork manufactory, 229, 390, 416, 487, 535, 536, 575, 617.
Forman, Joshua, 58.
Fortifications, general notice of, 45.
  tabular list of, 45.
Fort Brewerton, 481, 522.
  Clinton, 503, 504.
  Columbus, 419.
  Dayton, 342, 345.
  Diamond, 373.
  Edward, 298, 682.
  Frederick, 297.
  Gibson, 419.
  Hamilton, 373.
  Herkimer, 342, 345.
  House, 417.
  Hunter, 408, 413.
  Independence, 699.
  Jay, 419.
  Johnson, 315, 412.
  La Fayette, 373, 699.
  Levi, 574.
  Lyman, 298, 671, 672.
  Miller, 591.
  Montgomery, 18, 45, 237, 503, 504, 505.
  Niagara, 452.
  Plain, 410, 414.
  Porter, 286.
  Putnam, 504, 505.
  Orange, 156.
  Richmond, 565.
  Schuyler, 345, 410, 461, 467, 469, 586, 706.
  Slongo, 638.
  Stanwix, 166, 461, 467.
  Sullivan, 219.
  Tompkins, 565.
  Wood, 419.
  William Henry, 298, 672.

Forts, Canadian, 45.
  notices of, 45,156,157, 162, 163, 166, 206, 219, 220, 221, 237, 264, 274, 275, 277, 286, 297, 298, 299, 301, 304, 305, 327, 342, 344, 353, 356, 358, 373, 393, 408, 409, 110, 412, 413, 414, 415, 416, 417, 419, 437, 452, 453, 460, 461, 467, 469, 478, 499, 503, 504, 505, 519, 525, 542, 546, 551, 559, 564, 565, 569, 574, 596, 598, 599, 601, 602, 604, 605, 634, 664, 673, 679, 681, 682, 700, 707.
Forty Thousand Acre Tract, 321.
Founderies, 160, 189, 193, 201, 206, 227, 237, 239, 240, 244, 246, 248, 272, 277, 286, 344, 356, 367, 391, 400, 401, 405, 454, 465, 466, 470, 484, 487, 488, 506, 509, 510, 515, 521, 525, 533, 534, 535, 536, 542, 549, 556, 557, 558, 569, 570, 591, 593, 604, 605, 606, 607, 610, 611, 615, 617, 618, 622, 625, 627, 647, 656, 657, 694, 702, 705, 707, 708, 715.
Fountains, 362, 423.
Fowling, 544, 634.
Fox, George, 546.
  Hall Manor, 49, 662, 663.
Franciscan College, 188.
Franklin Institute, Syracuse, 489.
Frauds, 308, 311, 362.
Free Academy, New York, 429, 430.
  colonization, 353.
  colonies, 224.
  defeat of, 409.
  fortifications, 297, 519.
  grants on Lake Champlain, 233, 298.
  missions, 477, 580.
  posts, 298.
  Protestants, 371, 546.
  settlements, 264, 301, 363, 375, 376, 377, 378, 454, 477, 478, 546.
  surrender, 574.
  traces of, 457, 477, 482.
  Tract, 224.
  War. See War, French.
Freshets, 157, 162, 165, 302, 329, 558, 613, 644, 682, 683.
Friends, 142, 360.
  cemetery, 371.
  mission established by, 187, 195.
Frigates on Lake Ontario, 358.
Frisnell's Patent, 50.
Frontiers, 297.
Frontenac, expedition of, 408, 478.
  Fort, 519.
Fruit culture, 198, 205, 327, 395, 402, 456, 464, 481, 497, 512, 546, 569, 570, 609, 661, 662, 688, 689, 696, 703, 706.
Fur Company, North Western, 525.
  dressing. 368,
  trade, 232.
Fulton, Robert, 83.
Funds, lands belonging to, 46, 47.
Furnaces, 109, 195, 198, 202, 211, 212, 214, 226, 228, 235, 238, 244, 245, 247, 270, 273, 282, 289, 291, 293, 325, 356, 360, 368, 382, 383, 385, 386, 390, 393, 398, 399, 400, 402, 406, 408, 462, 466, 471, 484, 508, 514, 515, 522, 538, 577, 657, 682, 690, 691, 692, 693, 695.
Furniture, 109, 286, 291, 362, 368, 402, 488, 514, 515, 522, 523, 618.
  makers, by counties, 152.

Gage's Patent, 50.
Game, protection of, 30.
Gananoqui, expedition against, 354.
Gansevoort, Col. Peter, 461, 478, 614.
Gardeau Tract, 711.
Gardening, 101, 365, 398, 399, 501, 544, 546, 547, 548, 549, 568, 571, 696, 706.
Garden Seeds, 214, 243, 686.
Gardner, Lyon, 635, 638.
Garlock, John Christian, 409.
Garnets, 407.
Gaslight manufactory, 80, 317, 368, 424, 563, 693.
  springs, 26, 186, 203, 208, 213, 214, 236, 267, 310, 325, 385, 386, 456, 462, 491, 499, 555, 569, 592, 607, 615, 691.720.
Gate rights, so called, 50.
Gauntlet, running of the, 452.
Gaylord, Willis, 486.
Geddes, James, 58, 59, 479, 483.
  George, 63, 474, 482.

General Assembly, 698.
  Court, 635, 640.
Genesee Falls Portage, 386, 710.
  Tariff, 322.
Genet, Edmund C., 555.
Geographical and Statistical Society, 436.
Geological survey, 24.
  Hall, 27, 100.
George III, statue of, 423, 438.
German Flats, 342, 344, 410.
  Methodists, 141.
Ghent, treaty of, 18.
Gibbs, the pirate, 419.
Gilliland, William, 299, 300, 301, 305.
Ginseng trade, 415, 469.
Glass manufactory, 164, 240, 291, 355, 368, 462, 470, 517, 521, 549, 558, 589, 641, 644, 668, 691.
Glebes, 344, 566, 571, 607, 699.
Glen's Purchase, 341, 343, 345, 346, 585.
Glove and Mitten manufactory, 286, 311, 314, 317, 318.
Glue manufactory, 286, 368, 398.
Goat Island, 455.
Gold Beating, 286.
Gold Island, 455.
Gold Pen manufactory, 368.
Gold and Silver Refining, 368.
Gore Tracts, 224, 263, 690.
Gospel and School Lands, 47, 135, 250, 574.
Governor, powers, qualifications, &c., 31.
Governors Island, forts on, 419.
  Purchase. See Chenango.
Grain, amount by towns. See Acres, &c.
  cradle manufactory, 484, 510.
  destroyed, 264.
  excellence of the several counties in, 101.
  trade, Buffalo, 285.
Grand Island Tract, 290.
Granger, Gideon, 495.
Grape culture, 101, 497, 628, 699.
Graphite, 26, 267, 297, 300, 301, 302, 303, 304, 337, 338, 340, 540, 670, 671, 685.
Grass Seed, Sullivan co., 641.
Great Nine Partners' Tract, 269, 277.
Green, Col., 708.
Griffin, first vessel on upper lakes, 452, 455.
Grindstone manufactory, 168, 223, 471.
Gristmills, number by counties, 109.
  See Flour manufactory.
Grocers, number by counties, 152.
Guano manufactory, 637, 639.
Gun manufactory, 246, 286, 699.
  barrel manufactory, 655.
Gunpowder explosion, 489.
Guthrie, Dr. Samuel, 359.
Gutta Percha Belting manufactory, 549.
Guy Park, 412.
Gypsum, 26, 110, 197, 203, 320, 326, 340, 388, 392, 393, 394, 395, 398, 406, 458, 469, 473, 480, 481, 482, 484, 485, 491, 497, 613, 614, 617, 688, 690.

Haile, Gen., 577.
Haldeman, Gen., 300.
Half-Moon Patent, 585.
  Point, 593.
  Orphan Asylum, N. Y., 433.
Hall, James, Paleontologist and Geologist of the Fourth District, 24.
Hall, N. K., 283.
Hall of Records N. Y., 423, 437.
Halls of Justice N. Y., 426, 437.
Hame manufactory, 229.
Hamilton, Alexander, 125, 276.
  College Telescope, 392.
Hammer manufactory, 228.
Hammond, Jabez D., 137.
Hampton, Gen. Wade, 234, 310.
Harbor at Black Rock, 288.
  Buffalo, 284.
  encroachment N. Y., 46, 418.
  Hill, Roslyn, 550.
  masters, 116.
  New York, 418.
Harbors on the lakes, 22.
Hardenburgh Patent, 258, 331, 600, 663.
Hardware manufactory, 216, 286, 471, 488.
Harlem Canal, 418.
Harness manufactory, by counties, 109.
Harper Patent, 50, 224.
Harper, Col., 316, 410, 624.
  Robert, 225.
Harpersfield burned, 410.
Harrisoff, Charles, 349.
Harrison's Patent, 50.
Hartford Convention, 18, 180.
Hartman, John A., 345.

Hartwick Patent, 533.
Hasenclever's Patent, 341, 345, 348.
Hat manufactory, 160, 198, 247, 286, 368, 510, 707.
　by counties, 109.
Hawley, Gideon, 137, 605.
　Jesse, 58.
Hay, 101, 163, 241, 331, 332, 547, 554, 665.
　product by counties, 104.
Head Quarters of Washington, Newburgh, 509.
Health Commissioner, 428.
　Officer, 116, 428.
　Public, 116, 427, 428.
Heathcote, Caleb, 701, 702, 703.
Height of mountains, table of, 19.
　lakes and rivers, 20, 22.
Hellgate, 548, 549.
Henderson's Patent, 341, 348.
Hendrick, King, 298, 343, 671.
Hennepin, Father, 452, 455.
Henry Clay steamer burned, 708.
Herkimer, Gen. N., 264, 343, 345, 409, 410, 461, 538.
High Bridge, 424, 707.
High Falls on Black River, 379.
Highlanders, Scotch, 316.
Highlands of the Hudson, 501, 542.
High Rock Spring, Saratoga, 592.
Highways, 39.
Historical Society N. Y., 435.
Hoe manufactory, 200, 229, 390, 537, 557, 571, 575, 590.
Hoffman, aged 118, 269.
Holland Land Co., 52, 169, 187, 210, 280, 288, 321, 322, 452, 468, 515, 516.
　agent of, 322, 390.
　co. buildings erected by, 320.
　names of members, 321.
　Patent, 467.
　Purchase, 280, 468, 513.
Holley, Myron, 59.
Home Association, 488.
Home Missions, 146.
Homeopathic Medical Societies, 149.
Homestead exemption, 48.
Honey, product by counties, 106.
Hoosick Patent, 556.
Hop culture, 101, 223, 230, 340, 388, 412, 414, 458, 530, 537, 600, 603, 606, 607
Hops, product by counties, 105.
Horse mill, 373.
　races, colonial, 546.
　Rake manufactory, 716.
　Shoe manufactory, 235, 300.
Horses, association for improving breed of, 83.
　killed by Sullivan, 221.
　statistics of, by counties, 107.
Horticultural Society, Brooklyn, 370.
Hosiery manufactory, 166, 561, 617.
Hospitals, 120, 161, 287, 356, 365, 368, 370, 404, 419, 420, 425, 426, 427, 432, 505, 524, 555, 561, 565, 702.
House of Industry, 433, 434.
　of Refuge, 42, 404, 420, 425.
　Lord, death of, 298.
Huddlestone executed as a spy, 276.
Hudson, Hendrick, 156, 437, 559, 564.
Huguenot settlements, 269, 503, 564, 661, 663, 705, 703.
Hunter Lodges, 354.
　Road, 642.
　grounds, 232, 636.
Huntersfield Patent, 607.
Hurley Patent, 663.
Hutchinson, Mrs. Anne, 704, 705.
Hypersthene rock, 296, 346.

Ice, 162, 180, 365, 419, 484, 569, 663, 703.
Idiotic, statistics of, by counties, 150.
　Asylum for the, 483, 488.
Illiterate, statistics of, by counties, 150.
Immigration, general statistics of, 122.
Impeachment, 33.
Imports, Canadian, 113.
　total, since 1700, 112, 114.
Inclined planes on rail roads, 67.
Independence, Declaration of, 244, 697.
Independent Order of Odd Fellows, 149.
India Rubber manufactory, 419, 546, 708.
Indian antiquities, 180, 181, 188, 194, 200, 202, 203, 206, 220, 253, 260, 264, 283, 293, 327, 355, 358, 359, 360, 361, 393, 412, 414, 453, 458, 482, 493, 494, 498, 499, 513, 516, 534, 551, 559, 588, 593, 605, 616, 643, 644, 679, 704, 705.

Indian disguise worn by anti-renters, 258.
　hung for murder, 198.
　invasions, 165, 180, 210, 260, 262, 264, 297, 331, 334, 342, 343, 344, 345, 346, 347, 349, 372, 408, 410, 411, 412, 414, 415, 416, 417, 461, 467, 477, 493, 503, 531, 533, 535, 564, 596, 597, 602, 604, 607, 608, 642, 661, 662, 664 668, 679, 705, 708.
Indian Purchases, 46, 48, 180, 187, 224, 233, 242, 243, 258, 261, 270, 322, 332, 389, 394, 398, 437, 478, 499, 545, 551, 596, 634, 635, 638, 639, 698, 700, 701, 703, 705, 707, 708.
　reservations, 48, 53, 187, 280, 308, 309, 311, 322, 324, 327, 353, 382, 384, 385, 389, 393, 452, 462, 469, 478, 483, 485, 580.
　Pass, 303.
　settlements, 180, 187, 210, 274, 287, 308, 322, 382, 389, 393, 408, 415, 452, 458, 465, 473, 476, 483, 493, 495, 498, 499, 557, 559, 574, 580, 601, 632, 633, 637, 638, 655, 678.
　statistics, 151.
　trade, 157, 162, 415, 452, 485, 682.
　tradition of, 458, 477, 482, 493.
　tribes on Long Island, 632, 634
Indians at Montauk, 635.
Industrial schools, 161, 370, 404.
Inebriate Asylum, 180.
Infirmaries, 370.
Ink manufactory, 593.
Inland Steam Nav. Companies, list of, 82.
Inman's Triangle, 375.
Inn Keepers, by counties, 152.
Insane, statistics of, by counties, 150.
　statistics of, 151.
　See Lunatic Asylum.
Insects in grain, 320.
Inspection of steamboats, 115.
　of vessels, 428.
Inspector, City, 427.
Insurance companies, 81, 83, 436.
　obsolete, list, 85 to 89.
　rates lowered by Croton, 424.
Intermitting spring, 310.
Invasions, hostile, 180, 209, 232, 234, 236, 260, 262, 264, 280, 288, 290, 297, 299, 308, 310, 311, 312, 316, 331, 334, 342, 344, 345, 346, 347, 349, 354, 355, 356, 358, 359, 365, 372, 404, 408, 410, 411, 412, 413, 414, 415, 416, 417, 452, 460, 461, 467, 477, 478, 503, 504, 513, 519, 525, 531, 554, 556, 564, 569, 574, 578, 579, 580, 587, 596, 597, 599, 602, 604, 607, 608, 624, 633, 634, 639, 642, 643, 661, 662, 671, 679, 681, 682, 694.
Iron bridge, 407.
　manufactory, 41, 110, 166, 220, 232, 235, 236, 238, 241, 243, 245, 246, 261, 270, 271, 273, 275, 276, 286, 296, 297, 300, 301, 302, 303, 304, 305, 310, 349, 352, 360, 361, 362, 363, 395, 419, 462, 464, 471, 501, 508, 510, 521, 533, 535, 549, 561, 573, 575, 577, 579, 580, 582, 617, 652, 666, 668, 681, 699.
　ores, 19, 21, 25, 155, 165, 186, 218, 232, 235, 236, 237, 241, 243, 245, 267, 270, 271, 273, 277, 296, 297, 300, 301, 302, 303, 304, 305, 307, 310, 311, 312, 337, 348, 349, 352, 355, 360, 361, 374, 376, 377, 378, 388, 392, 395, 458, 464, 470, 471, 501, 517, 521, 528, 540, 542, 543, 563, 572, 575, 577, 581, 582, 589, 600, 670, 674, 675, 680, 692, 693, 695, 717.
Iron sand, 297, 340, 349, 374.
Ives, L. S., 380.
Ivory Black manufactory, 368, 563.

Jail limits, Jefferson co., 352.
Jails. See County Buildings.
Japanned Cloth manufactory, 368.
　Ware manufactory, 286.
Jay Ore Bed, 581.
　Treaty, 519.
Jemison, Mary, the white woman, 711, 712.
Jersey City, relations with New York, 429.
Jerseyfield Patent, 341, 347, 348.
Jervis, John B., 423.
Jesuit missions, 408, 415, 477, 519.
Jews, attempt to collect, 290.
Jogues, Father, 435, 477.
Johnson Hall, 316, 318, 409.
　Guy, 315, 341, 346, 409, 412.
　Sir John, 300, 315, 316, 409, 410, 413, 415, 602, 605.

Johnson, Sir William, 298, 315, 317, 318, 343, 348, 409, 412, 452, 512, 592, 671, 672.
　Indian children of, 315, 348.
Johnston, Bill, 360.
Joncaire, ——, French adventurer, 452.
Jones, Samuel, charity fund, 549, 550.
Judicial Department, 33, 428.
　districts, 34.
Julia, encounter of the schooner, 574.
Junction Canal Company, 218.
Jurisdiction, 18, 33, 34, 418.
Justices' courts, 34.
Juvenile delinquents, 42, 420.
　Asylum, 433.

Kakiate Patent, 568.
Kane brothers, 412, 469.
Kaolin, 301, 675, 567.
Kast's Patent, 341, 348.
Kayaderosseras Patent, 585, 587.
Kidd, William, the pirate, 570.
Kinderhook Patent, 247.
Kingsborough Patent, 317, 318.
Kingsbury Patent, 685.
King's College. See Columbia College.
King's District, 241, 243.
King's Ferry, 569, 699.
King's Garden, 356.
Kirkland, Rev. Samuel, 461, 464, 485, 499
Kirkwood, James P., 369.
Klock's Field, battle of, 410, 417.
Knapp, Uzal, 509.
Knitting mills, 166, 558, 590.
Kortright Patent, 262.
Kosciusko, Thaddeus, 504, 586.

Laboratories, 248, 368, 419, 464, 505, 549.
Laborers, number by counties, 152.
La Cole surprised, 234.
La Fayette, Marquis de, 27, 410, 467.
La Hontan, Baron, 288, 404.
Lakes, general sketch of, 20.
Lake George Steamboat Companies, 82.
Lake ridges, 351, 355, 361, 395, 449, 453, 512, 514, 524, 688, 693.
Lallemant, Father, 477, 479.
Lamp and Lantern manufactory, 368.
Lampblack manufactory, 593.
Lancasterian schools, 125, 160, 246, 560, 599, 657.
Land Office, 322, 323.
　Commissioners of, 46, 494.
　attacked by a mob, 210, 322.
Land patents, list of, 49.
Landslides, 303, 413, 560.
Land, State, how sold, 46.
　tenure and title of, 46.
　under water, 46, 418, 419.
Lansing's Patent, 341, 343, 348.
Lantern manufactory, 286.
La Salle, visits Niagara Falls, 452, 455.
Last manufactory, 286, 705.
Lath manufactory, 289.
Law, George, 424, 684.
Law Department, New York, 427.
　Library & Institute, 435.
　libraries, 287, 369.
　schools, 161, 275.
Laws, 29, 30.
Lawyers, number by counties, 153.
Lay, Amos, 580.
Lead ore, 25, 241, 243, 267, 340, 355, 374, 378, 407, 506, 528, 573, 579, 581, 646, 660, 686, 704.
　Pipe manufactory, 362, 657
Leake & Watts Asylum, 433.
Lease, law respecting lands under, 46.
　tenure of, 273, 471.
　lands under, Delaware co., 258.
　Indian, 462.
Ledyard Canal, 484.
Legislature, 28.
　at Kingston, 662.
　at Poughkeepsie, 276.
　dispersed, 26.
　New York City, 420.
Leisler, Jacob, 700, 703.
Le Moyne, Father, 479.
Lery, M. de, 460, 467.
Le Roy's Patent, 603.
Le Roy, Bayard & McEvers, 321, 468.
Lewis, Governor Morgan, 272.
L'Hommedieu, Ezra, 125.
　Patent, 341, 343, 348.
Liancourt, Duke de, 498.
Liberty poles cut down, 344, 438.

Libraries, 27, 48, 102, 125, 126. 127, 139, 144, 145, 246, 287, 369, 383, 391, 403, 432, 434, 454, 475, 488, 489, 505, 524.
  school district, 135, 137.
License question, 147.
Lieutenant Governor, powers and duties of, 32.
Lifeboat manufactory, 367.
  stations, 121, 122, 365, 544, 550, 631.
Life leases, 242.
  and health insurance, 83.
Lighthouses, 120, 216, 271, 280, 284, 297, 355, 356, 358, 360, 399, 403, 419, 524, 527, 550, 567, 569, 577, 634, 635, 636, 638, 639, 662, 694. 706.
Lime manufactory, 109, 110, 186, 197, 250, 252, 279, 301, 305, 331, 346, 381, 383, 391, 394, 395, 462, 474, 484, 485, 512, 568, 569, 570, 590, 613, 615, 649, 654, 662, 666, 670, 683. 690, 693, 700.
Limestone terrace, 288, 292.
Lincklaen Purchase, 389.
Lincoln, General, 299.
Lindsey's Patent, 341, 343, 531.
Linen manufactory, 237, 559.
Line of Property, 257, 462.
Liquorice manufactory, 368.
Lispenard's Patent, 341.
Literary associations and societies, 144, 369, 385, 434, 489.
Literature Fund, 46, 125, 126.
  lands, 47.
Lithography, 286.
Little Beard, 384.
Little Nine Partners' Tract, 269, 272, 273.
Livingston Manor, 242, 687.
  Patent, 242, 244, 348, 603.
  Robert R., 82, 83, 147.
Lloyd's Neck Manor, 551.
Loans, State, statistics of, 38.
  when lands are sold under, 46, 48.
Lock manufactory, 286.
  navigation, 556, 579, 596.
Locks, canal, 451, 454.
Locomotive factory, 598.
Logan, an Indian chief, 200.
Log navigation, 297, 573.
Longee, a French partisan, 672.
Long Island farms, (New York city poor,) 549.
Lotbinière, grants to, 298.
Lotteries, 125, 425, 556.
Louis Philippe, travels in N. Y., 219, 404, 498.
Lovelace, Governor, 564.
Lumber, 110, 160, 165, 166, 168, 170, 171, 173, 176, 183, 186, 188, 189, 190, 193, 194, 195, 211, 214, 215, 218, 220, 221, 232, 235, 236, 238, 248, 257, 260, 262, 263, 264, 265, 286, 290, 293, 296, 301, 302, 303, 304, 305, 307, 309, 311, 312, 314, 316, 317, 337, 338, 347, 349, 356, 357, 360, 363, 367, 375, 377, 390, 392, 399, 402, 454, 468, 470, 502, 509, 518, 521, 522, 523, 525, 526, 527, 529, 573, 575, 576, 580, 581, 584, 588, 589, 590, 591, 593, 618, 620, 623, 624, 625, 626, 629, 641, 643, 644, 645, 647, 648, 649, 652, 661, 663, 665, 667, 668, 671, 675, 680, 685, 686, 692, 693.
Lunatic Asylums, 31, 42, 200, 247, 365, 396, 398, 419, 425, 426, 432, 468, 495. 518.
Lush's Patent, 347.
Lyceums, 275, 369, 436.
Lying in Asylum, 432.
Lynds, Elam, 41, 704.

McCrea, Jane, 682.
McDonald, D., 345.
McDonough, Commodore, 234, 239.
Machine shops, 109, 160, 166, 195, 199, 202, 206, 214, 227, 235, 237, 238, 240, 244, 246, 247, 248, 271, 272, 286, 289, 292, 293, 317, 356, 367, 368, 383, 385, 387, 390, 391, 400, 401, 402, 406, 462, 484, 487, 488, 506, 509, 510, 515, 522, 525, 536, 537, 548, 556, 557, 560, 569, 570, 591, 593, 606, 615, 617, 618, 625, 656, 657, 658, 682, 683, 685, 686, 691, 692, 693, 699.
Machinery manufactory, 109, 300, 362, 395, 411, 454, 465, 468, 488, 536, 556, 617, 652, 681, 686.
Machinists, number by counties, 153.
Machin's Patent, 48, 341, 347, 413, 468, 603.
McNeil's Patent, 342, 348.
Macomb, Alexander, 352, 579.

Macomb, General, 234.
Macomb's Purchase, 48, 308, 375, 458, 572, 574, 581.
Magazines, military, 44.
Magdalen Female Benevolent Society, 433.
Magnetic machine, 297.
Mail routes by railroad and steamboat, 123.
  early, 469.
  ocean, 124.
Mail service, general statistics, 122, 123.
Malignant fever, 428.
Malleable iron, 471.
Malt manufactory, 160, 166, 368, 618, 691.
Manganese, 26, 241, 267, 600, 704.
Manhattan Company, 89, 424.
Manor of Fox Hall, 662.
  Wm. Gilleland attempts to found, 305.
  Staten Island, 564.
  Westchester co., 698, 703, 706, 707.
  Fordham, 707.
  Rensselaerwyck. See Rensselaerwyck.
  Livingston. See Livingston.
  Cortland. See Cortland.
Manors, list of Colonial, 49.
Manual Labor Schools, 283.
Manufactures, statistics of, 109, 286, 436.
Maple sugar, 101.
Marble, 26, 41, 109, 267, 271, 273, 274, 286, 300, 301, 368, 376, 418, 577, 581, 590, 670, 671, 696, 699, 700, 702, 704, 708.
  cemeteries, 428.
Marine barracks, 368.
  clay, 572, 573, 580.
  court, 35, 117, 428.
  Family Asylum, 566.
  Fund, 117.
  Hospital, 117, 120, 368.
  railways, 286, 368, 525, 581.
  Society, 434.
Markets, 286, 427. 706.
Marl, 186, 218, 241, 250, 252, 267, 273, 274, 279, 292, 318, 320, 388, 391, 394, 395, 458, 474, 540, 614, 619, 688, 690, 691, 693, 710.
Marthas Vineyard, 18, 49.
Martial law, Delaware co., 410.
Marvin's Patent, 347.
Masons, number by counties, 153.
Massachusetts, attempt to settle on the Hudson, 242.
  claims, 242, 494.
  lands, 52.
  pre-emption, 18, 48.
  Ten Towns, 48, 180.
Massacre, Indian, 661, 664, 672, 685, 700.
Mastodon, skeleton of, 501, 548.
Matchbox manufactory, 377.
Mayors, 39, 420.
Mayville land office sacked, 322.
Mechanics' Association, 403.
  Institute, 435.
Mechanical trades, total number of persons engaged in, 153.
Medical Colleges, 126, 287, 343, 430, 498.
  Societies, 126, 149, 150, 287, 431.
Medicinal extracts, 241, 248.
Meigs, Colonel, 639.
Melodeon manufactory, 286.
Menageries, 706.
Mennonites, 141.
Mercantile Colleges, 139, 287.
  Library, 435.
Merchants, number by counties, 153.
Merchants' Exchange, 436.
Meteorological observations, 126.
Methodist African Church, 139.
  Congregational Church, 140.
  Episcopal Church, 141.
  German Church, 141.
  Primitive Church, 142.
  Protestant Church, 141.
  Reformed, 143.
  Wesleyan. 144.
Metropolitan Police, 366, 420, 564.
Midge, ravages by, 381, 383, 395, 512, 518, 717.
Millinery, by counties, 110.
Mile Strip, Niagara, 48.
Military Academy, 45, 505.
  districts, 43.
  organization, 43.
  Road, 45, 354.
  stations, 419.
  Tract, 47, 180, 199, 224, 473, 478, 610, 615, 655, 690, 691.
Militia called out, 259, 269, 437.
  laws, 43, 44.
  officers, 43.

Militia, services of, 565.
Milk market, 101, 268, 273, 277, 501, 502, 506, 510, 511, 540, 543, 544, 550, 554, 557, 568, 570, 696.
Miller, David C., 323.
  Rev. Wm., 683.
Millers, number of, by counties, 153.
Milliners, number of, by counties, 153.
Mill Iron manufactory, 297.
Millstone manufactory, 286, 355, 468, 641, 660.
Millyard Tract, 398.
Mineral localities, 26, 267, 296, 352, 361, 362, 374, 378, 407, 540, 563, 572, 573, 576, 577, 579, 582, 584, 600, 604, 606, 675, 698.
  springs, 26, 155, 159, 163, 164, 165, 168, 170, 173, 175, 178, 186, 188, 195, 213, 221, 229, 241, 244, 248, 257, 267, 279, 282, 301, 302, 305, 312, 320, 324, 325, 332, 343, 345, 347, 349, 355, 356, 357, 359, 360, 361, 363, 375, 377, 378, 379, 382, 386, 392, 393, 394, 402, 413, 455, 456, 458, 462, 469, 470, 481, 482, 484, 488, 491, 497, 503, 515, 532, 534, 537, 546, 552, 554, 557, 558, 579, 590, 591, 592, 593, 607, 620, 650, 664, 666, 679, 683, 688, 692, 696, 702, 704.
Mines, 25, 570, 660.
  Road, 503, 642.
Mining, Mechanical, & Chemical Cos., 80.
Minisink, battle of, 503.
  massacre, 503.
  Patent, 503.
Mint, 122, 509.
Minuet, Peter, 437.
Mirage, 352, 705.
Missions, 139, 142, 146, 187, 195, 273, 274, 308, 370, 393, 404, 431, 434, 477, 519.
Mitchell's Cave, 416.
Mobs, 210, 269, 322, 438, 549, 565, 601.
Mohegans, 697, 704.
Mohawk Indians, 408.
  River rifts, on, 23.
  settlements. See Herkimer and Montgomery cos.
Molang, a French Partisan, 686.
Molding mill, 707.
Montauk, 632, 633, 635, 638.
Montcalm, Marquis of, 298, 519, 672.
Montgomery, Richard, 276, 299.
Montour, Captain, 624.
Montour, Catharine, 610.
Montreal, expedition against, 408.
Monument to Herkimer voted, 343.
  to martyrs of prison ships, talked of, 372.
  to Paulding, 699.
  to Pike and others, disgraceful, 359.
  to shipwrecked persons, 547.
  to Van Wart, 700.
  to Washington, (corner stone,) 423.
  to Williams, 298.
  to Gen. Worth, 423.
Moody, Lady Deborah, 372.
Moose River Tract, 342, 349.
Moravian mission, 273, 274.
Morgan, William, 323, 452, 495.
Mormonism, 494, 497, 690, 693.
Morris, Chief Justice, 705.
  Gouverneur, 58, 375.
  Honorary Creditor Tract, 321.
  Lewis, 702.
  Reserve, 169, 321, 382, 494.
  Robert, 321, 621.
  Roger, 540, 541.
  title of, 494.
Morse, James O., 210.
Morse, S. F. B., 274.
Mosaic code, 640.
Mounds, Indian, 200. See Indian Antiquities.
Mount, murder of, 347.
Mountain Ridge, 395, 512.
  systems of the State, 19.
Mowers and Reapers, 405.
Muck, 186, 198, 279, 292, 320, 388, 394, 474, 518, 590, 614, 617, 618, 628, 688, 692, 683.
Mules, number by counties, 107.
Muller, Lewis A., 391.
Munro, Major, attack by, 587.
  Colonel, 672.
Museum, 27, 432.
Musical Association, 287, 489.
Mutual aid societies, 434.
Mutual Insurance companies, 83.
Myers Mine, 236.

Nail manufactory, 198, 235, 297, 300, 301, 302, 561.
Nantucket formerly in New York, 18.
Narrows, 365, 373, 563.
National societies, 434.
   Comp. Emancipation Society, 146.
Natural Bridge, 674, 704.
Nautical society, 434.
Naval Depôt, 368.
   Hospital, 45, 368.
   Lyceum, 369.
   stores, 245.
Navigation, 22, 156, 272, 279, 296, 297, 418.
   companies, 64, 82.
Navy Yard, 368.
Neander, Dr., library of, 403.
Necks of land, 544, 549, 550, 551, 631, 638, 703, 706.
Needle manufactory, 570.
Newburgh, discontent of troops at, 504.
   Patent, 509.
New Dorlach Patent, 603.
New England Alliance, L. I., 633.
Newgate Prison, so called, 41.
New Petersburgh Tract, 389.
Newspapers, 157, 169, 178, 187, 198, 209, 218, 224, 233, 241, 251, 258, 268, 280, 297, 307, 315, 321, 330, 337, 341, 352, 366, 375, 381, 389, 396, 407, 439, 451, 459, 475, 492, 502, 513, 518, 530, 540, 545, 553, 564, 568, 573, 585, 595, 602, 610, 614, 620, 632, 642, 650, 655, 661, 671, 678, 689, 697, 711, 718.
   discontinued, New York City, 442.
   New York, before Revolution, 431.
New York State Agricultural College, 126.
   Harbor encroachment, 46, 418.
   Library Society, 435.
   Society, 101.
   system, geological, 24.
Niagara River and Falls, 449, 450, 452, 455.
Nickel, 26.
Nicoll's Patent, 637.
Nitschman, Bishop David, 274.
Noah, Mordecai M., 290.
Noble, Arthur, 337, 339, 349.
Nobleboro' Patent, 342, 349.
Noble's Patent, 48.
Normal School, 125, 136, 137, 369, 429.
Northern Inland Lock Nav. Co., 60.
Notaries public, 35.
Nott, Rev. Eliphalet, 532, 598.
Noxious animals, 30.
Nurseries, 398, 402, 498, 544, 546, 694, 703.
   for children, 420, 425, 426, 433, 549.

Oakum manufactory, 286.
Oats, statistics of, 101, 104.
Oblong Tract, 18, 269, 540, 703.
Observatories, 423, 464, 505.
Ocean steamers, 82.
   mails, 124.
Ocher, 175, 377.
Odeltown, affair at, 234.
Officers, State, county, and town, 40.
Ogden Samuel, purchase by, 321.
   Tract, 321.
Ogdensburgh taken, 574.
Ohio Basin, 284.
Oil cask manufactory, 638.
   cloth manufactory, 368, 468, 556, 590, 657, 658.
   manufactory, 198, 286, 293, 357, 368, 390, 402, 515, 532, 549, 556, 567, 618, 632, 637, 639, 657, 691.
Old Fort, so called, 327.
   Military Tract, 235, 237, 240.
   Pre-emption Line, 494.
   School Baptist Church, 139.
Omnibus routes, New York City, 429.
Oneida Community, 392.
   Indians, friendly, 410, 596.
   Reservation, 389.
   River Improvement, 62.
   stone, 458.
Oothoudt's Patent, 48, 468.
Ophthalmic Hospital, 432.
Optical Instrument manufactory, 392.
Ordnance, summary of, 45.
Organ manufactory, 286, 468.
Oriskany, battle of, 342, 410, 412, 414, 461.
Orphan Asylums, 161, 200, 247, 275, 370, 403, 419, 425, 426, 433, 488, 518, 524, 561.
Oswegatchie District, 575.
Overseers of Highways, 39.
Owasco Lake Improvement, 63.
Oxen, statistics by counties, 106.

Oysters, 46, 544, 549, 550, 563, 567, 632, 636, 638, 704.

Page, David P., 137.
Pail manufactory, 286, 297, 301, 385, 482, 536, 570, 657.
Paine, John, 242.
   Thomas, 703.
Paint man'y., 312, 368, 402, 419, 549, 555.
Painted Post, 624.
Painters, by counties, 153.
Palatinates, 242, 245, 408, 409, 412, 415, 416, 509, 601, 603, 605, 606, 667.
Palisades, 21, 25.
Palisades, (military,) 372, 373, 437.
Palmer, Edmund, tory spy, 699.
   Erastus D., 487
   Mine, 236.
   Purchase, 585.
Paper Box manufactory, 317.
   manufactory, 110, 166, 199, 200, 215, 228, 241, 243, 244, 247, 248, 274, 277, 286, 297, 317, 330, 334, 345, 346, 352, 362, 375, 377, 384, 385, 390, 402, 407, 466, 484, 485, 487, 504, 510, 516, 527, 538, 550, 556, 557, 558, 561, 570, 584, 589, 590, 593, 605, 606, 610, 634, 657, 666, 704.
Pardoning power, 31.
Pardons, statistics of, 36.
Parish, David, 580.
Parker, Col., 266.
Parks, 369, 422, 423.
Parsonage, Queens, 413.
Passengers, statistics of, 117, 122.
Patchin, Gen., 603.
Patent Leather manufactory, 286, 368.
Patents, Land, 46, 48, 49, 53, 258, 341, 408.
Pathological Society, New York, 431.
Patriot "War," 235, 354, 357, 360, 452, 574, 575.
Patroon, title of, 159.
Paulding, John, 699.
Pauw, Michael, 564.
Peaches, quantity by counties, 107.
Pearling Mill, 593.
Pearl barley, 482, 484.
Pears, quantity by counties, 107.
Peas, statistics by counties, 105.
Peat, 232, 237, 241, 267, 337, 394, 458, 474, 505, 540, 570, 629, 671.
Peg manufactory, 317.
Pelham Manor, 703, 704.
Pell, Thomas, 700, 703, 704.
Pemaquoit, 18.
Pendergrast sentenced, 269.
Penet Square, 48, 353, 357, 360.
Penitentiaries, 156, 280, 365, 425, 475.
Peppermint, 689.
   Oil manufactury, 691.
Perache's Tract, 48.
Percentage of population, 151.
Perry, Commodore, gifts to, 423.
Personal liabilities of stockholders, 80.
Pestilence, 428, 601.
Petrie's Purchase, 342.
Petroleum springs, 168, 173, 186.
Pharmacy, College of, 431.
Phelps and Gorham Purchase, 321, 382, 398, 494.
Philippe, Louis, 404, 498.
Philipsburgh Manor, 700, 702, 704, 708.
Philipse Patent, 540, 541.
Philosophical Instrument man'y., 286.
Physicians, by counties, 153.
Piano manufactory, 160, 228, 286, 468, 509, 685.
Pickle manufactory, 707.
Picquet, Francis, 574.
Pictured Rocks, 380.
Pierrepont Estate, 376, 378.
Piers, 156, 280, 284, 356, 367, 419, 422, 524.
Pike, Z. M., monument to, 359.
Pilots, 115, 116.
Pine plains, 156, 312, 351, 638.
Pin manufactory, 275.
Pipe clay, 26.
Pistol manufactory, 699.
Pitcher, Lieutenant Governor, 685.
Pitt, statue of, 438.
Plains, Hempstead, 544, 547, 548.
Plane manufactory, 286.
Plan of union proposed, 162.
Planing mills, 160, 205, 220, 228, 235, 237, 239, 286, 289, 292, 293, 317, 347, 367, 368, 393, 399, 401, 402, 405, 406, 454, 466, 506, 514, 546, 590, 598, 604, 610, 617, 625.

Plank roads, 39, 80, 159, 179, 235, 236, 258, 284, 311, 321, 354, 459, 515, 518, 596, 601, 642.
Plaster mills, 110, 205, 221, 228, 229, 238, 244, 247, 271, 274, 367, 385, 393, 398, 400, 401, 406, 454, 468, 484, 559, 618, 652, 657, 682, 683.
Plate of Johnson family, 316, 400, 410.
Plattsburgh attacked, 234.
Plow manufactory, 244, 454, 466, 515, 699.
Plums, by counties, 107.
Pocket Book manufactory, 286.
Point au Fer, 233, 237.
Police Department, 420.
Political societies, 434.
Poor, associations for relief of, 287, 370.
   county and town, 161, 168, 179, 186, 198, 208, 211, 218, 223, 233, 241, 251, 258, 268, 280, 297, 307, 314, 320, 330, 341, 352, 375, 381, 388, 396, 407, 425, 427, 434, 451, 459, 475, 492, 502, 513, 518, 530, 546, 550, 553, 595, 600, 614, 634, 635, 636, 637, 638, 639, 642, 649, 654, 661, 671, 678, 689, 696, 711, 718.
   statistics of, 37, 38.
   Superintendents of, 30, 36.
Popham, Major Wm., 705.
Population, total, by counties, 150.
   by towns. See Acres, &c.
   comparative, 151.
   of cities, 371, 404, 435, 436, 469, 599.
Porcelain manufactory, 367, 368.
Portages, 22, 23, 460, 466, 519, 528.
Portage Falls, 386, 711, 713.
Porter Road, 642.
Port of New York, 438.
Portrait gallery, 495.
Portraits in Capitol, 27.
Ports of entry, 111, 216, 399, 438, 638, 694.
Port Wardens, 116.
Postal arrangements, 122, 123.
Post office, 123, 437.
Potash, 415, 518.
Potato culture, 101, 105, 639, 682.
Potsdam sandstone quarries, 312.
Potter, Rev. Alonzo, 137, 270.
Potteries, 286, 468, 691.
Potters' Field, 420, 423, 425, 426, 428.
Pouchot, M., surrender of, 574.
Powder mills, 504, 559.
Premiums for domestic manufacture, 102.
Presbyterian Church, 141, 142.
   United, 139.
Prevost Patent, 333.
Prideaux, Gen., 452.
Primitive Methodists, 142.
Printers' Library, 435.
   number by counties, 153.
Printing cloths, 509.
   offices by counties, 110.
Print manufactory, 272, 563, 565, 576.
Prison Association of New York, 42, 426, 433.
Prisoners sold as slaves, 661.
Prisons, 41, 200, 238, 425, 426, 427.
Prison ships, 371, 372.
Privateering on St. Lawrence, 355.
Prize fighting, Boston Corners, 243.
Protestant Episcopal Church, 142.
Provident and Mutual Aid Societies, 434.
Provincial Congress, 662.
   Patent, 684.
Provost, Sir George, 234.
Public health, 427.
   Schools, 135.
   School Society of New York, 430.
Pulteney, Sir William, 321, 384, 404, 621, 622.
Pump manufactory, 286, 368, 400, 405, 463, 598, 617.
Putnam, Gen. Israel, 298, 371, 450, 504, 540, 541, 672, 682, 685, 686.
Puts Rock, 686.
Pyroligneous Acid manufactory, 182.
Pyrotechny, 699.

Quackenboss, John, 685.
Quaker settlement, 366.
   Springs, 591.
Quarantine, 18, 31, 116, 117, 419, 427, 428, 563, 565, 566.
Quarries, 26, 41, 155, 165, 167, 168, 170, 172, 173, 175, 190, 191, 192, 197, 201, 204, 205, 208, 213, 214, 215, 218, 223, 243, 245, 267, 270, 271, 279, 282, 284, 301, 305, 312, 314, 318, 320, 331, 332, 340, 341, 343, 346, 347, 349, 359, 381, 383, 385, 393, 395, 400, 407, 411, 449, 454,

Quarries, continued.
458, 463, 464, 467, 470, 471, 473, 482, 483, 484, 485, 491, 497, 512, 515, 517, 528, 530, 532, 540, 542, 566, 572, 577, 581, 587, 590, 613, 615, 617, 660, 662, 663, 664, 666, 688, 692, 693, 696, 699, 700, 702, 704, 705, 708, 713, 714, 715.
Quarter Sales, 157.
Quartz crystals, 340, 343, 649.
Queensborough Patent, 585.
Quitman, General, 277.
Quitrents, 46, 242, 258, 699, 701, 704.
Quogue Purchase, 638.

Race courses, 548, 549, 550.
Rafting, 265, 352.
Rail Roads, Canadian, 119.
   Commissioners, 69.
   employees, by counties, 153.
   gauge, 74.
   general article on, 66.
   notices of, 71, 112, 156, 159, 169, 170, 172, 173, 174, 179, 180, 182, 184, 186, 187, 189, 191, 192, 193, 194, 201, 203, 204, 205, 208, 209, 214, 218, 219, 220, 224, 232, 235, 237, 238, 241, 244, 245, 246, 247, 248, 258, 265, 268, 270, 271, 276, 280, 282, 292, 293, 307, 310, 312, 321, 324, 325, 337, 341, 345, 346, 354, 356, 357, 366, 367, 381, 382, 383, 384, 385, 388, 392, 395, 397, 398, 399, 400, 401, 402, 403, 405, 407, 416, 451, 454, 455, 459, 462, 466, 467, 468, 470, 471, 475, 480, 482, 483, 484, 488, 495, 496, 498, 500, 502, 504, 505, 506, 507, 508, 510, 513, 514, 515, 518, 520, 521, 530, 540, 542, 544, 545, 546, 548, 549, 550, 552, 555, 557, 561, 563, 568, 569, 570, 571, 573, 575, 576, 577, 578, 579, 580, 581, 582, 585, 587, 590, 593, 596, 598, 600, 609, 610, 612, 614, 617, 618, 620, 622, 623, 624, 625, 626, 627, 628, 632, 636, 637, 639, 640, 641, 642, 650, 651, 652, 653, 654, 655, 657, 678, 689, 690, 691, 692, 693, 696, 697, 698, 699, 700, 701, 702, 703, 704, 705, 706, 707, 708, 711.
   projects, &c., 76 to 79.
   statistics of, 74, 75.
Rake manufactory, 260, 657.
Randall, Robert Richard, 566.
Randalls Island, 42, 420, 425.
Rangers, 242, 298, 305.
Rank of military officers, 43.
Rapelje, Sarah, 371, 437.
Raspberry culture, 498.
Ratan manufactory, 546.
Reaches on the Hudson, 542.
Real, Count, 356.
Reciprocity Treaty, 117, 524.
Record Commissioners, 365.
Recorder, 420, 428.
Records, State, 26.
Red Jacket, 615.
Reformed Methodists, 143.
   Presbyterians, 143.
   Protestant Dutch, 143.
Refugees, Canadian and Nova Scotian, 235, 237.
Refuge for Juvenile Delinquents, 432, 433.
Regalia manufactory, 286.
Regents of the University, 125, 126, 635.
Registers of Deeds, 35, 365, 697.
Registration of births, marriages, and deaths, 427.
Religious societies, 100, 144.
Remsenburgh Patent, 48, 342, 347, 349, 460.
Rensselaerwyck Manor, 155, 156, 157, 165, 553.
Reservations, gold and silver mines, 26, 46.
   Salt Springs, 478, 479, 480.
   See *Indian Reservations.*
Reservoirs. See *Canal Reservoirs.*
Resident Physician, 116.
Revenues, United States, 111.
Revolution. See *War of Revolution.*
Revolutionary claims, 419.
Rheimensnyders Bush, attack upon, 346.
Richmond College, 564.
Rideau Canal, 119.
Ridge Road. 512, 693.
Rifle manufactory, 344, 402.
Riots. See *Mobs.*
Rivers, general sketch, 20.
Roads, opening of, 39.
Robberies, 242.
Robert, Louis J., grant to, 298.

Robinson, Beverly, 540, 542, 699.
Rock City, so called, 173, 192.
Rocking stones, 701, 705.
Rogers, Platt, 300.
   Robert, 298, 674, 685, 701.
Rolling mills, 199, 235, 297, 569, 571, 666, 699, 708.
Roman Catholic Church, 143.
Roofing slates, 26, 243, 267, 555, 677, 682, 684.
Rope manufactory, 228, 286, 368, 376, 464, 556, 558, 634, 693.
Rosin Oil manufactory, 368.
Ross and Butler, 416.
Ross, Major, 316.
Rotunda, N. Y., 423, 437.
Royal Grant, 315, 342, 343, 345, 347, 348.
Rubber Toy manufactory, 272.
Rumbout's Patent, 269, 272.
Rural cemeteries, 100, 166, 200, 275, 371, 372, 373, 398, 404, 428, 549, 599, 703, 704.
Rye, where most raised, 101.
   statistics of, 104.

Sable Iron Co., 236.
Sackets Harbor, 525.
Sackett, Richard, 270.
Sacondaga Patent, 317.
Saddle & Harness manufactory, by cos., 153.
   Tree manufactory, 691.
Safe manufactory, 160, 368, 402, 561.
Safety fund, 89.
Sail manufactory, 286.
Sailors' Snug Harbor, 566.
St. Hilary, Count, 521.
St. Lawrence Canal, 119.
St. Leger, Gen., 166, 342, 410, 461, 467, 586.
St. Regis Indians, 233, 308.
Saleratus manufactory, 401.
Salisbury, Aaron, 290.
Salmon fisheries, 124, 520.
Salometer, 480.
Salt holes, so called, 488.
   manufactory, 110, 198, 203, 399, 405, 479, 483, 487, 488, 489, 512, 514, 515, 522, 532, 632, 692, 693.
   marshes and meadows, 365, 372, 373, 418, 544, 546, 547, 548, 550, 563, 566, 631, 633, 635, 636, 638, 696, 706.
   Springs Lands. 47.
   springs. See *Brine Springs.*
   wells, 479, 480, 483.
Salvage, 117.
Sandpaper manufactory, 546.
Sand plain, 584.
Sandstone terrace, 577.
Sandy Creek battle, 525.
Sandy Hook fort, 565.
   light, 419.
Sanger, W. P. S., 368.
Saratoga Patent, 585.
Sargent, Henry G., 59.
Sash & Blind manufactory, 110, 188, 228, 229, 244, 248, 255, 270, 286, 297, 301, 362, 368, 385, 386, 393, 407, 413, 454, 463, 484, 510, 515, 554, 575, 582, 590, 596, 603, 652, 686, 716.
Satinet manufactory, 261, 508.
Savings banks, 99, 100, 166, 436, 640.
Saw manufactory, 286, 506.
Sawmills, by counties, 110.
Saw Set manufactory, 348.
Scale manufactory, 402, 693.
Scarcity of provisions, 264.
Schaghticoke Indians, 559.
Schoharie invaded, 316.
School Commissioners, 38, 135, 137, 139.
   Districts, 31, 135, 138.
   Fund, 46, 47, 135.
   General Article on, 135.
   houses, 138.
   Indian, 412, 478.
   Lands, 47, 389.
   statistics, 138. See *Acres, &c.*
Schools, Common, 38, 135.
   See *City Schools.*
Schuyler, Han Yost, 342.
   Patent, 269, 342.
   Peter, 408.
   Philip, 316, 410, 591, 592.
Scott's Patent, 413, 602, 603.
Screw manufactory, 468.
Scriba, George, 519, 520, 528.
Scriba's Patent, 48, 519, 521.

Scythe manufactory, 274, 312, 466, 483, 590, 617.
Sealer of Weights and Measures, 30, 38.
Seal of Broome Co. presented, 178.
   Delaware Co. adopted, 257.
Seamen's Friend Society, 146.
   employed, 113.
   Hospital, 120, 434.
   Retreat, 566.
   tax upon, 117, 120, 566.
Seamless Bag manufactory, 590, 683.
   clothing, 271.
Seat of Government, 26, 438.
Secretary of State, 32, 125.
Secret Societies, 147.
Seigniories, French, 233, 298.
Select schools under Regents, 125.
Seminaries, 200, 453, 454, 498, 533, 602, 713.
   See also *Academies.*
Senate, 28.
   Districts, 28.
Seneca Indians, 397, 452, 493.
   Lock Navigation Company, 62.
   River Improvement, 61, 62.
   Turnpike, 469.
Serpentine, 670, 675.
Serpent, tradition of, 493.
Servis's Patent, 466, 468.
Seventh Day Baptists, 143.
Seward, William H., 200, 510.
Sewers, New York, 425.
Shad fisheries, 124.
Shakers, 143, 166, 243, 248, 384.
Shannandhoi Patent, 585, 587.
Shattuck, Artemas, 714.
Shawl manufactory, 508, 598, 618.
Shay, Daniel, 165, 603.
Sheep husbandry, 107, 637, 686.
Shell, John Christian, 345.
Sheriff murdered, 242.
   county, 35.
Shingle manufactory, 110, 286, 290, 291, 292, 293, 301, 338, 454, 470, 523, 526, 527, 575, 580, 590, 611, 625, 667, 694.
Shinnecock Indians, 638.
Ship building, 115, 213, 286, 297, 352, 356, 357, 358, 359, 367, 368, 399, 520, 525, 549, 569, 570, 632, 633, 634, 636, 639, 662, 686.
   canal, 284, 690.
   Timber Co., 291.
Shipments, Buffalo, 285.
Shoe manufactory, 346, 373, 402, 548, 568, 570, 705.
Shovel manufactory, 705.
Showmen, 706.
Sickness, 681.
Silk manufactory, 275, 286, 391, 566, 570, 657.
Silliman, Prof., analysis by, 324.
Silurian rocks, 155.
Silver Lake Tract. 711.
   mines. so called, 257, 337, 374.
   Plating, 286.
   traces of, 528.
   Ware manufactory, 110, 163, 368, 488, 652.
Simcoes Queen's Rangers, 551.
Skanandoa, Indian chief, 469.
Skene, Philip, 299, 686.
Skinners, 698.
Slack Water Navigation Co., 614.
Slate, 26.
Slate Cos., 267, 270, 273.
Slave rescue, 489.
Slaves, Indians sold as, 661.
Small Pox Hospital, 425.
Smallwood, Col., 701.
Smith, Col., 452.
   Gerrit, 393, 524.
   Joe, 494, 467.
   Peter, lease of, 462.
   purchase of, 389, 393.
   William, H., 634.
Smuggling, 233, 357.
Snell and Zimmerman's Tract, 342.
Soap manufactory, 109, 286, 368, 402, 509, 593.
Socialists, 392.
Societies, Agricultural, 102. See *New York State Agricultural Society.*
Society for Promoting Agricultural Arts and Manufactures, 101, 161.
   Promoting Useful Arts, 101.
Soda manufactory, 286.
Solar works, 479, 480.
Solitary confinement, 41.
Sons of Liberty, 423, 438.

Sons of Malta, 148.
Spanish Brown, 25.
  relic, 477.
  invasion, 478.
Spaulding, Solomon, 532.
Specie, 113, 122.
  payment suspended, 90.
Speculations, 366.
Spencer, John C., 137, 323.
Spies, 412.
Spiritual rappings, 690.
Spoke manufactory, 277, 590, 667.
Springs, copious, 205, 277, 522, 570, 615.
Spuytenduyvil Creek, 418.
Squatters, 242, 243, 269, 290, 291, 358, 360, 389, 394.
Stage boat, 469.
  licensed, 553.
  rights, 469.
  routes, early, 496.
Stair building, 110.
Stalactites, 164, 416, 600, 604, 606, 607.
Staley's Patent, 342, 344.
Stamp Act, 438.
Starch manufactory, 232, 237, 238, 240, 286, 297, 307, 346, 468, 518, 521, 525, 550, 581.
Stark, Gen. John, 298, 556.
State Engineer and Surveyor, 33, 54,'68, 69.
  Government, 28.
  Hall, 27.
  House, 26.
  Library, 27, 125, 126.
  Prisons, 36, 41, 42, 63, 200, 238, 704.
  officers, 41.
  reservations for villages, 288, 704.
  Roads, 322, 615, 655.
Statue of George III. and Pitt, 423, 438.
  Washington, 423.
Stave manufactory, 238, 262, 286, 290. 292, 363, 487, 514, 522, 526, 618.
Steamboat Companies, 82.
  mail routes, 123.
  statistics of, 115.
  tax, 54.
Steamboats, 115, 162, 200, 214, 247, 275, 286, 288, 307, 354, 356, 360, 368, 375, 399, 418, 429, 452, 489, 495, 526, 550, 551, 561, 573, 579, 584, 611, 615, 616, 620, 627, 628, 655, 657, 664, 673, 687, 696, 697, 699, 700, 703, 705, 708.
Steam Engine manufactory, 286, 525, 652, 685.
Stedman, William, 452, 455.
Steele, O. N., murder of, 259.
Steel manufactory, 270, 311, 508, 510, 540, 566, 571, 701.
Sterritt Tract, 321.
Steuben, Baron, 48, 467, 484.
Stevens, Ebenezer, 549.
  John C., 418.
Stewart, Alvan, 210.
Stilwellitos, 140.
Stirling, Earl of, 18, 550, 633, 635, 639.
Stirling, Lord, 510, 564, 637.
Stock, breeding of, 277.
  amount of. See Acres, &c.
Stockade, 469. See Forts.
Stone and Marble dressing, 153, 368, 663, 666.
Stone Arabia battle, 316.
  Patent, 317, 408, 416.
Stone Heap Patent, 413, 603, 605.
Stone heaps, 242, 605.
Stone Ware manufactory, 286, 468.
Stove manufactory, 160, 286, 561, 699.
Strang, Daniel, execution of, 699.
Straw, paper factory, 166.
Streets, arrangement, New York, 422.
  Department, 422.
  inspection, 427.
Stuart, Charles B., 368.
Sturgeon fisheries, 124.
Stuyvesant pear tree, 437.
  Peter G., 423.
Suburban population, 429.
Sugar Loaf Hill fortified, 299.
Sugar refineries, 419.
Sullivan, General, 219, 221, 371, 382, 410, 478, 493, 531, 536, 564, 602, 609, 614, 617.
Sunday schools, 146.
Superintendent Poor, 36.
Superintendent Public Instruction, 125, 135.
Supervisors, 30, 39, 420.
  Tryon County, 410.
Supreme Court, 34.

Surrogate, 34.
Survey Fifty, so called, 479.
Surveyor General, 33.
Surveys of Holland Land Co., 322.
Surveys of Lake Champlain, 298.
Suspension bridges, 235, 362, 412, 453, 455, 663.
Susquehanna Navigation, 619.
Swallow, steamer, wrecked, 331.
Swedenborgian Church, 139.
Swift, General John, 690.
Swine, statistics by counties, 107.

Taconic system, 24, 25.
Tailors, by counties, 153.
  shops, by counties, 110.
Tallmadge, Major, 634, 638, 701.
Tammany Society, 434.
Tanneries, 110, 153, 181, 183, 188, 193, 194, 195, 198, 202, 205, 213, 219, 225, 228, 230, 238, 239, 244, 248, 257, 259, 260, 262, 263, 265, 282, 283, 286, 289, 290, 291, 292, 293, 297, 302, 304, 305, 311, 314, 316, 317, 318, 319, 330, 331, 332, 333, 334, 338, 339, 342, 343, 346, 347, 348, 350, 352, 360, 362, 363, 375, 377, 385, 386, 390, 391, 392, 394, 400, 402, 454, 462, 463, 465, 466, 468, 469, 470, 483, 484, 505, 514, 515, 516, 520, 521, 522, 523, 525, 526, 527, 529, 532, 533, 534, 535, 536, 537, 538, 541, 554, 575, 576, 584, 589, 590, 591, 598, 603, 604, 605, 606, 607, 608, 610, 611, 612, 623, 625, 627, 628, 641, 643, 644, 645, 647, 649, 651, 652, 655, 657, 661, 663, 665, 667, 668, 671, 675, 690, 691, 693, 695, 699.
Tape manufactory, 706.
Tariffs, 111.
Tarleton, Gen., 700.
Tavern sign in verse, 222.
Taxation, 48, 422.
Tax sales, 48.
Teachers' classes, 126, 138.
  institutes, 137.
  statistics of, by counties, 153.
Tea destroyed in New York Harbor, 438.
Teamsters, number, by counties, 153.
Telegraph companies, list of, 81.
  Instrument manufactory.
Temperance Society, New York State, 147.
Ten Governors, 425.
Ten Towns on St. Lawrence, 47, 572, 574, 575, 576, 577, 578, 579, 580, 581, 582.
Tenure of lands, 46.
Tertiary clays, 237, 296.
Theater at Bath, 622.
Theller, E. A., 405.
Theological seminaries, 127, 200, 391, 403, 430, 431, 533, 575, 707.
Thermal springs, 26, 241, 247.
Thermometer manufactory, 248.
Thimble manufactory, 636.
Thorburn, Grant, 549.
Thousand Islands, 577.
Thread manufactory, 593, 597.
Threshing machine, 657.
Ticonderoga, 298, 299, 305, 671, 672, 673.
Tidal estuaries, 365, 367, 372, 544, 546, 547, 563, 696, 706.
Tide mills, 371, 544, 546, 640, 696, 701, 705.
Tides, 23, 156, 419.
Tile manufactory, 160, 398, 499, 691.
Tillier, Rodolph, 375, 377, 378.
Timber stealing, 309, 311, 360, 580.
Tin manufactory, 368, 546, 618.
Tinsmiths, by counties, 153.
Tinware manufactory, by counties, 110.
Titanium, 26.
Title, controversy about, 299, 357.
Tobacco and cigar manufactory, 110, 166, 276, 286, 368, 468, 488, 693, 699.
Tobacco culture, 101, 105, 219, 220, 221, 372, 487, 689.
  Indian tradition, 482.
Tompkins, Governor, 564, 705.
Tonawanda Swamp, 450.
Tonnage, American, compared with foreign, 112.
  Buffalo, 285.
  at different periods, 115, 116.
  by counties, 113.
  by districts, 112.
  coasting, 115.
  general article on, 115.
  on great lakes, 118.
  Oswego, 524.
  registered and enrolled, 111, 112, 115.

Tool manuf'y, 300, 391, 393, 527, 590, 598.
Topographical outline of State, 19.
Topping Purchase, 638.
Tories, 163, 180, 345, 346, 398, 602, 607, 636.
Tornado, 310.
Totten & Crossfield's Purchase, 47, 337, 342, 349.
Town Clock manufactory, 390.
  halls, 239, 700, 707.
  meeting days, 30.
    powers of people at, 31.
  officers, 30, 40.
  Purchase, 638.
Townsend Fund, Jamaica, 548.
Townships patented, Delaware county, 258.
Tract societies, 145, 404, 489.
Trading posts, 452, 519, 661.
Transit Line, 321, 322.
  storehouse, 322, 328.
Trap rock, 501, 568.
Treasure buried, 316.
Treasurer, State, 32.
Treaties, 18, 180, 224, 257, 290, 299, 344, 382, 461, 478, 479, 661.
Treaty, Reciprocity, 524.
Trial of Zenger, 431.
Triangular Tract, 321, 326, 398.
Tribunals of Conciliation, 34.
Trinity Cemetery, 428.
  Church, 434.
Triphammer manufactory, 347, 391, 393.
Trombois Mine, 236.
Trumbull, Col. John, 385.
Trustees of Academies, 126.
  school districts, 39
Tryon, Governor, 26.
  county, ravages in, 411.
Tub manufactory, 297, 466, 570, 590.
Tufa, 26, 186, 395, 592.
Tunnels, 68.
Turkish present to Com. Perry, 423.
Turner's Purchase, 705.
Turning, by counties, 110.
Turnpikes, 39, 182, 284, 601.
Tuscarora Indians, 410, 452, 596.
Twenty Towns on Chenango, 224
Twine manufactory, 571, 593, 597, 604.
Type manufactory, 160, 286.

Union College, 126, 549, 598.
  schools, 136, 138, 201, 214, 324, 346, 359, 401, 405, 454, 483, 484, 487, 495, 548, 580, 617, 618, 636, 691, 692, 712.
Unitarians, 143.
United Presbyterians, 139.
United States Courts, 33.
  Deposit Fund, 125.
Universal Friend, so called, 718, 719, 720, 721.
Universalists, 143.
Universities. See Colleges.
Upholstery, 286.
Upton, Paul, letter from, 269.

Vaccination, 432.
Valuation by towns. See Acres, &c.
Van Alstyne, Eva, 411.
Van Buren, Ex-President, 247.
Van Cortlandt, Jacob, 698.
  Stephen; 699.
Vander Donk, 708.
Vander Kemp, John J., 322.
Van Driessen's Patent, 342.
Van Horne's Patent, 342, 343.
Van Kleek House, 275, 276.
Van Rensselaer, Killian, 156.
  Patent, 603.
  Robert, 316, 410, 417.
  Stephen, 59, 157, 553.
Van Schaick, Col., 478.
  Myndert, 424.
Van Wart, Isaac, 700.
Varnish manufactory, 549.
Vaughan, Gen., 664.
Vaughan's Patent, 342, 343, 346, 348.
Verd Antique, 603.
Vermont controversy, 18.
  militia at Plattsburgh, 234.
  negotiations with the enemy, 300.
  Sufferers' Tract, 224, 225.
Verplancks Point, 504, 569.
Veto power, 30, 31.
Vice manufactory, 286, 598.
Villages, officers of, 39.
Vineyards, 205, 628, 699.
Vlaie, Sacondaga, 314, 316, 318, 337.
Voters, by counties, 150.

Vrooman's Land, 605.
　Patent, 48, 342, 343, 348, 349, 601.

Wadsworth, James, 137, 382.
Walk-in-the-Water, steamer, 288.
Walloomsac Patent, 556, 686.
Walloons, settlement of, 371, 437.
Walton's Patent, 52, 265, 342, 348.
　Tract, 489.
Walworth, Reuben H., 592.
Wampum, 635.
Wards, date of formation, New York, 420.
Wards Island, 117, 419, 420, 427.
War of 1812–15 noticed, 45, 233, 353, 354,
　355, 356, 358, 366, 372, 373, 398, 399,
　404, 437, 513, 520, 525, 555, 574, 579,
　581, 583, 633, 639, 687, 690, 694.
Warren, Sir Peter, 315, 409, 419.
Wars, French, 301, 305, 460, 461, 467, 503,
　519, 533, 554, 556, 558, 586, 672, 685,
　686.
　Indian, 408, 415, 416, 478, 493, 555, 556,
　559, 588, 597, 599, 661, 700.
　Revolutionary, 164, 180, 233, 242, 244,
　299, 331, 334, 366, 371, 415, 416, 531,
　437, 438, 461, 467, 503, 504, 508, 519,
　533, 535, 537, 538, 545, 548, 549, 550,
　551, 554, 586, 587, 601, 604, 624, 633,
　635, 636, 637, 638, 639, 642, 643, 646,
　662, 663, 664, 668, 698, 699, 701, 702,
　707, 708.
Washington College, 564.
Washington, General George, 273, 371, 467,
　503, 504, 509, 536, 570, 699, 700.
　inaugurated, 438.
Washington monument proposed, 423.
Water Cures, 180, 204, 220, 344, 385, 470,
　497, 498, 658.
Waterlime, 24, 26, 155, 197, 199, 204, 207,
　279, 282, 292, 305, 320, 340, 357, 374,
　388, 390, 393, 394, 395, 454, 458, 469,
　473, 482, 484, 485, 491, 497, 512, 514,
　600, 613, 660, 661, 662, 663, 664, 666,
　717.
Waterman's Society, 434.
Waterspouts, 352.
Waterworks, 160, 284, 312, 362, 363, 369,
　424, 488, 509, 548, 561, 697, 706.
Watkins & Flint, 219, 610, 655.
Watson's Tract, 342, 349, 375.

Wawayanda Patent, 503, 506, 568.
Wax, product by counties, 107.
Wayne, Anthony, 569.
Weavers, number by counties, 153.
Webb, General, the coward, 461, 467, 672.
Webster, Ephraim, 479, 485, 489.
Weeds, noxious, 39.
Weights and measures, 38, 39, 427.
Welland Canal, 119, 520, 525.
Well, remarkable, 271.
Wells family murdered, 531.
Wells in N. Y., 418, 424.
Welsh settlement, 466.
Wesleyan Methodists, 144.
Western House of Refuge, 42, 404.
　Inland Lock Navigation Co., 58, 346,
　461, 466, 596.
West India Co., 437.
West Patent, 702, 703.
West Point, 504.
Whalebone manufactory, 546.
Whale fisheries, 124, 247, 632, 636, 638, 639.
Whales, drift, 124, 635.
Wharves, New York, 422.
Wheat, statistics of, 101, 104.
Wheelbarrow manufactory, 482, 484, 665.
Wheeler, Silas, 629.
Whetstones, 223.
Whip manufactory, 286.
Whitehouse, Rev. Dr., 137.
White Lead manufactory, 286, 368, 563,
　566, 666.
Whiting manufactory, 368.
Wilbur, Hervey B., 488.
Wilkinson, General, expedition of, 310, 354,
　356, 357, 574.
　Jemima, 718, 719, 720, 721.
Wilkins Point, 45.
Willet's Patent, 345.
Willett, Colonel, 316, 411, 461, 607.
Williams College founded, 298.
Williams, David, 603, 700.
　Ephraim, 298, 671.
Williamson, Charles, 384, 621, 622, 690,
　692, 694.
Willis, N. P., 652.
Will of Sir Wm. Johnson, 315.
Windmill, battle of, 575.
Windmills, 635, 636, 637, 640.
Window Shade manufactory, 368.

Wire manufactory, 699, 708.
Wolf, 580, 581.
　bounty frauds, 308.
Woman's Hospital, 432.
Wooden Ware manufac., 573, 580, 581, 591.
Woodhull, General N., 371, 634.
Woodworth, Lieutenant Solomon, 345.
Woolen manufactory, 110, 166, 175, 194,
　199, 200, 203, 206, 212, 216, 220, 221,
　229, 244, 248, 255, 260 261, 263, 265,
　270, 272, 283, 289, 291, 292, 293, 301,
　332, 343, 344, 346, 356, 362, 379, 386,
　390, 391, 392, 393, 394, 400, 401, 402,
　406, 407, 411, 412, 413, 416, 454, 463,
　466, 468, 471, 485, 486, 487, 505, 510,
　514, 522, 535, 554, 561, 569, 584, 593,
　597, 610, 611, 617, 618, 636, 651, 655,
　658, 662, 663, 668, 681, 682, 683, 685,
　695, 703, 704, 713, 715.
Wool growing, 168, 178, 186, 198, 208, 218,
　223, 280, 320, 395, 492, 498, 609, 620,
　628, 688, 710.
Woolsey, Lieutenant 525.
Wooster, Ebenezer, 258.
Workhouses, 280, 398, 425, 426, 475.
Worth, General, monument to, 423.
Wreckmasters, 117, 544, 631.
Wright, Benjamin, 59, 70, 519.
　Silas, 576, 685.
Wyandance, Montauk sachem, 633, 634,
　638.
Wyoming massacre, 265, 410.

Yarn manufactory, 276, 346, 505, 569.
Yellow fever, 428.
Yeo, Sir James, 399, 525, 694.
Yorkshire, on Long Island, 365, 544, 545.
Young, Brigham, 495.
　John, 326.
　Samuel, 59, 137, 481.
Young Men's Association, 147, 161, 275,
　287, 369.
　Christian Association, 146.
　Christian Union, 147, 287.
Young's Patent, 342.

Zenger, Peter, trial of, 431.
Zinc ores, 26, 704.
Zinzendorf, Count, 274.
Zoological Garden, 423.

GAZETTEER

OF THE

STATE OF NEW YORK.

STATE BOUNDARIES.

THE STATE OF NEW YORK is situated between 40° 29′ 40″ and 45° 0′ 42″ N. latitude, and between 71° 51′ and 79° 47′ 25″ longitude W. of Greenwich. It is bounded on the N. by Canada, E. by Vermont, Massachusetts, and Connecticut, S. by the ocean, New Jersey, and Pennsylvania, and W. by Pennsylvania and Canada.

The Northern Boundary, commencing in the middle of Lake Ontario, N. of the mouth of Niagara River, extends eastward through the lake, midway between the opposite shores, to its E. extremity, thence north-easterly through the St. Lawrence River to the 45th parallel of N. latitude, and thence easterly in a gradually diverging line from the parallel, and terminating upon Lake Champlain 4,200 feet N. of it.

The Eastern Boundary extends S. through Lake Champlain to its S. extremity, thence a short distance S. E. along Poultney River, and thence in an irregular line, but in a generally southerly direction, to Lyons Point, at the mouth of Byram River, on Long Island Sound. From this point the line extends eastward through the Sound, very near the Connecticut shore, to the E. extremity of Long Island, including within the limits of the State nearly all the islands in the Sound.

The Southern Boundary extends from the E. extremity of Long Island along the ocean to the S. W. extremity of Staten Island, thence northward through the channel between Staten Island and New Jersey and through New York Bay and the Hudson to the 41st parallel of N. latitude, thence north-westerly to a point upon the Delaware at latitude 41° 20′ N., thence north-westerly along Delaware River to latitude 42° N., and thence W. along the 42d parallel to a meridian passing through the W. extremity of Lake Ontario.

The Western Boundary, commencing upon the 42d parallel, extends N. to the middle of Lake Erie, thence eastward to the E. extremity of the lake, and thence N. through Niagara River and to the middle of Lake Ontario.[1]

---

[1] The boundary through Lake Ontario is 175 mi.; through the St. Lawrence, 108 mi.; along the Canada frontier, E. of the St. Lawrence, 62.75 mi.; through Lake Champlain, 105 mi.; along Poultney River, 17.25 mi.; the Vt. line, S. of that river, 54.06 mi.; the Mass. line, 50.52 mi.; the Conn. line, to Lyons Point, on Long Island Sound, 81.20 mi.; through the Sound, 96 mi.; along the ocean to the N. J. shore, 150 mi.; through the Bay and Hudson River, to latitude 41° N., 44 mi.; along the N. J. line, W. of the Hudson, 48.50 mi.; through Delaware River, 78 mi.; along the Penn. line, on latitude 42°, 225.50 mi.; on the meridian to Lake Erie, 18.75 mi., and upon the meridian in Lake Erie, 22 mi.; through Lake Erie to Buffalo, 50 mi.; and through Niagara River, 34 mi.

2

17

The boundaries of the State have been settled from time to time by commissioners appointed by the several governments whose territories are contiguous. In several instances long and angry controversies have occurred, which have extended through many years and almost led to civil war. The boundaries are all now definitely fixed, except that of Conn., respecting which a controversy is now pending.[1]

---

[1] *Canada Boundary.*—By royal proclamation, issued in Oct. 1763, the line of 45° N. was fixed as the boundary between the provinces of Quebec and New York, and this was confirmed in council, August 12, 1768. The line was surveyed by Valentine and Collins, October 20, 1774. By the treaty of 1783 the 45th parallel was recognized as the N. boundary of the State from Lake Champlain to the St. Lawrence. By the treaty of Ghent the same line was recognized as the boundary, and provisions were made for a re-survey. In 1818–19, Gov. Van Ness and Peter B. Porter on the part of the U. S., and John Ogilvie on the part of Great Britain, ran the line with great care; and it was found that the old line coincided with the parallel only at St. Regis, and that from that point E. it diverged, until at Lake Champlain it was 4,200 feet too far N. The deepest channel of the St. Lawrence was not always adopted, as a mutual exchange of islands was made satisfactory to both parties. Before the N. line was re-surveyed, in 1818, the U. S. Government had commenced the erection of a fortress at Rouses Point, on Lake Champlain; and this was found to be within the British territory. By the treaty of August 9, 1842, the old line of Valentine and Collins was restored, and the strip of territory before taken off again came under the jurisdiction of the U. S. The commissioners to run the line under the treaty of 1842 were Albert Smith on the part of the United States, and J. B. B. Estcourt on the part of Great Britain.

Vermont Boundary.—The territory of Vermont was originally claimed by both New York and New Hampshire, and conflicting grants were made by the two governments. Most of the actual settlers holding title under N. H. resisted the claims of N. Y., and many actual collisions occurred. Jan. 15, 1777, the settlers declared themselves independent, and laid claim to the territory W. to the Hudson, N. of Lansingburgh, and along the W. shore of Lake Champlain. By an act of Congress passed Aug. 20, 1781, they were required to recede from this claim. A final agreement was entered into between Vt. and N. Y., Oct. 7, 1790, by which N. Y. surrendered all her claim to jurisdiction to the present territory of Vt., and Vt. paid $30,000 to certain persons who had been deprived of lands granted by N. Y. The boundary line was run by Robert Yates, Robert R. Livingston, John Lansing, jr., Gulian C. Verplanck, Simeon De Witt, Egbert Benson, Richard Sill, and Melancthon Smith on the part of N. Y., and Isaac Tichenor, Stephen R. Bradley, Nathaniel Chipman, Elijah Paine, Ira Allen, Stephen, Jacob, and Israel Smith on the part of Vt. The final line was established June 8, 1812.

Massachusetts Boundary.—The charter of Massachusetts embraced all the territory between 44° and 48° N. latitude "throughout the Maine lands from sea to sea." Grants made under this authority conflicted with those of N. Y., and angry controversies ensued, which in colonial times often resulted in violence and bloodshed. On the 18th of May, 1783, an agreement was entered into between John Watts, Wm. Smith, Robert R. Livingston, and Wm. Nicoll, commissioners on the part of N. Y., and Wm. Brattle, Joseph Hawley, and John Hancock, on that of Mass.; but the Revolution soon followed, and the line was never run. Commissioners appointed by both States in 1783 failed to agree; and December 2, 1785, Congress appointed Thomas Hutchins, John Ewing, and David Rittenhouse commissioners to run the line and finally end the controversy. The claims of Mass. to the lands westward were finally settled at Hartford, Conn., Dec. 16, 1786, by James Duane, Robert R. Livingston, Robert Yates, John Haring, Melancthon Smith, and Egbert Benson, commissioners on the part of N. Y., and John Lowell, James Sullivan, Theophilus Parsons, and Rufus King, on the part of Mass. By this agreement Mass. surrendered the sovereignty of the whole disputed territory to N. Y., and received in return the right of soil and pre-emptive right of Indian purchase W. of a meridian passing through the 82d milestone of the Penn. line, excepting certain reservations upon Niagara River. The title to a tract known as "The Boston Ten Towns," lying E. of this meridian, previously granted by Mass., was also confirmed. Nantucket, Marthas Vineyard, and the adjacent islands, were purchased from the Earl of Sterling by the Duke of York, and civil jurisdiction was exercised over them, under the name of "*Dukes County,*" by the governors of N. Y., until it was annexed to Mass. by the provincial charter of 1692. "Pemaquid and its dependencies," comprising a considerable part of the coast of Maine, was also bought from the Earl of Sterling, and governed by N. Y., as "*Cornwall County,*" until 1686, when it was transferred to Mass. Boston Corner, a small arable tract in

the town of Mount Washington, separated by a rugged mountain from the convenient jurisdiction of Mass. was surrendered by that State May 14, 1853, accepted by N. Y. July 21, 1853, and the transfer was confirmed by Congress, Jan. 3, 1855. Russell Dorr was appointed on the part of N. Y., and John Z. Goodrich by Massachusetts, to run and mark the line.

Connecticut Boundary.—By the charter of 1662 the territory of Conn. extended to the "South Sea;" and by patent granted in 1664 the territory of the Duke of York was bounded E. by Connecticut River. Commissioners sent over in 1664 settled upon a line 20 mi. E. of the Hudson as the boundary, fixing the starting point on Mamaroneck River. The decision proving grossly erroneous, the controversy was renewed, and in 1683 another commissioner was appointed to settle the matter. It was finally agreed to allow Conn. to extend her boundaries W. along the Sound, and N. Y. to receive a compensation in the N.; and the line was definitely established May, 1731. By this agreement a tract called the "Oblong," containing 61,440 acres, along the N. part of the W. border of Conn., was surrendered to N. Y. The exact line of Conn. has to the present day been a subject of controversy, and in 1856 commissioners were appointed by each State to effect a settlement, but without success. N. Y. owns all the islands in the Sound to within a few rods of the Conn. shore.

New Jersey Boundary.—The original patent of New Jersey was bounded N. by a line running directly from a point on the Delaware, latitude 41° 40′, to a point on the Hudson, latitude 41°, and E. by Hudson River. The N. line was run and marked in 1774, and the E. was claimed by N. Y. as extending only to low-water mark on the adjacent waters. N. J. claimed "full right and lawful authority to exercise jurisdiction in and over the said Hudson River and the said main sea," including Staten Island, and, by an act of Nov. 2, 1806, appointed Aaron Ogden, Wm. S. Pennington, James Parker, Lewis Condict, and Alexander C. McWhorter commissioners to settle her claims. The New York Legislature, on the 3d of April, appointed Ezra L'Hommedieu, Samuel Jones, Egbert Benson, Simeon De Witt, and Joseph C. Yates to meet the commissioners of N. J.; but their interviews led to no result. The question of jurisdiction was finally settled in 1833, by an agreement between Benj. F. Butler, Peter A. Gay, and Henry Seymour on the part of N. Y., and Theodore Frelinghuysen, James Parker, and Lucius Q. C. Elmer on the part of N. J.; confirmed by N. Y. Feb. 5, by N. J. Feb. 26, and by Congress June 28, 1834. The right of each State to land under water and to fisheries extends to the center of the channel. The State of N. Y. has sole jurisdiction over all the waters of the bay and of the river W. of New York City to low-water mark on the Jersey shore, except to wharves and vessels attached thereto. This jurisdiction covers the waters of Kil Van Kull and of Staten Island Sound to Woodbridge Creek, as for quarantine purposes. South of this, N. J. has exclusive jurisdiction over the waters of the Sound and of Raritan Bay westward of a line from Princes Bay Light to Manhattan Creek, subject to right of property in lands under water, of wharves, docks, and vessels aground or fastened to any wharf or dock, and the right of fishing to the center of the channel.

Civil process in each State may be executed upon the waters of the river and bay, except on board of vessels aground or attached to wharves in the other State, or unless the person or property are under arrest or seizure by virtue of authority of the other State. By the late survey of N. J. the point of departure of the boundary from the Delaware is 41° 20′.

Pennsylvania Boundaries.—The original boundary line between New York and Pennsylvania extended from the N. W. corner of New Jersey along the center of Delaware River to 42° N. latitude, and thence due W. to Lake Erie. Samuel Holland on the part of N. Y., and David Rittenhouse on the part of Penn., were appointed commissioners, Nov. 8, 1774, to run this boundary; but the Revolution soon after commenced, and nothing was done. In 1785–86 the line was run W. to the 90th milestone, and the survey was certified Oct. 12, 1786, by James Clinton and Simeon De Witt, of N. Y., and Andrew Elliott, of Penn. By authority of the State Legislature, the N. Y. delegates in Congress, March 1, 1781, released to the General Government all the lands to which they had claim W. of a meridian extending through the W. extremity of Lake Ontario. The triangular tract so surrendered was sold to Penn. for $151,640, and secured to that State 30 mi. of lake coast and an excellent harbor. The line was run by the U. S. Surveyor General in 1788–89.

TOPOGRAPHY.

Surface.—This State lies upon that portion of the Appalachian Mountain system where the mountains generally assume the character of hills and finally sink to a level of the lowlands that surround the great depression filled by Lake Ontario and the St. Lawrence River. Three distinct mountain masses or ranges enter the State from the s. and extend across it in a general N. E. direction. The first or most easterly of these ranges—a continuation of the Blue Ridge of Va.—enters the State from N. J. and extends N. E. through Rockland and Orange cos. to the Hudson, appears on the E. side of that river, and forms the highlands of Putnam and Dutchess cos. A northerly extension of the same range passes into the Green Mts. of Western Mass. and Vt. This range culminates in the Highlands upon the Hudson. The highest peaks are 1,000 to 1,700 feet above tide. The rocks which compose these mountains are principally primitive or igneous, and the mountains themselves are rough, rocky, and precipitous, and unfit for cultivation. The deep gorge formed by the Hudson in passing through this range presents some of the finest scenery in America, and has often been compared to the celebrated valley of the Rhine.

The second series of mountains enters the State from Penn. and extends N. E. through Sullivan, Ulster, and Greene cos., terminating and culminating in the Catskill Mts. upon the Hudson. The highest peaks are 3,000 to 3,800 feet above tide. The Shawangunk Mts., a high and continuous ridge extending between Sullivan and Orange cos. and into the s. part of Ulster, is the extreme E. range of this series. The Helderbergh and Hellibark Mts. are spurs extending N. from the main range into Albany and Schoharie cos. This whole mountain system is principally composed of the rocks of the New York system above the Medina sandstone. The summits are generally crowned with old red sandstone and with the conglomerate of the coal measures. The declivities are steep and rocky; and a large share of the surface is too rough for cultivation. The highest peaks overlook the Hudson, and from their summits are obtained some of the finest views in Eastern New York.

The third series of mountains enters the State from Penn. and extends N. E. through Broome, Delaware, Otsego, Schoharie, Montgomery, and Herkimer cos. to the Mohawk, appears upon the N. side of that river, and extends N. E., forming the whole series of highlands that occupy the N. E. part of the State and generally known as the Adirondack Mountain region. South of the Mohawk this mountain system assumes the form of broad, irregular hills, occupying a wide space of country. It is broken by the deep ravines of the streams, and in many places the hills are steep and nearly precipitous. The valley of the Mohawk breaks the continuity of the range, though the connection is easily traced at Little Falls, The Noses, and other places. North of the Mohawk the highlands extend N. E. in several distinct ranges, all terminating upon Lake Champlain. The culminating point of the whole system, and the highest mountain in the State, is Mt. Marcy, 5,467 feet above tide. The rocks of all this region are principally of igneous origin, and the mountains are usually wild, rugged, and rocky. A large share of the surface is entirely unfit for cultivation; but the region is rich in minerals, and especially in an excellent variety of iron ore. West of these ranges, series of hills forming spurs of the Alleganies enter the State from Penn. and occupy the entire s. half of the w. part of the State. An irregular line extending through the southerly counties forms the watershed that separates the northern and southern drainage; and from it the surface gradually declines northward until it finally terminates in the level of Lake Ontario.[1] The portion of the State lying s. of this watershed and occupying the greater part of

[1] TABLE
Of Heights of the Principal Summits in the State.

NAME OF MOUNT.	LOCATION.		FEET.	NAME OF MOUNT.	LOCATION.		FEET.
Mount Marcy	Essex	co	5,467	Pine Orchard	Greene	co	3,000
Dix Peak	"	"	5,200	Mount Pisgah	Delaware	"	3,400
Mount McIntyre	"	"	5,183	Rockland Mount	Sullivan	"	2,400
" McMartin	"	"	5,000	Walnut Hill	"	"	1,980
" Sandanoni	"	"	5,000	Mount Toppin	Cortland	"	1,700
" Nipple Top	"	"	4,900	Pompey Hill	Onondaga	"	1,743
" White Face	"	"	4,900	Beacon Hill	Dutchess	"	1,685
" Pharaoh	"	"	4,500	Old Beacon	Putnam	"	1,471
" Taylor	Hamilton	"	4,500	Bull Hill	"	"	1,586
" Seward	Franklin	"	5,100	Anthony's Nose	"	"	1,228
" Emmons	Hamilton	"	4,000	Butter Hill	Orange	"	1,529
" Crane	Warren	"	3,000	Crows Nest	"	"	1,418
Round Top	Greene	"	3,804	Bear Mount	"	"	1,350
High Peak	"	"	3,718	Break Neck	"	"	1,187

19

the two southerly tiers of counties is entirely occupied by these hills. Along the Penn. line they are usually abrupt and are separated by narrow ravines, but toward the N. their summits become broader and less broken. A considerable portion of the highland region is too steep for profitable cultivation and is best adapted to grazing. The highest summits in Allegany and Cattaraugus cos. are 2,000 to 2,500 feet above tide.

From the summits of the watershed the highlands usually descend toward Lake Ontario in series of terraces, the edges of which are the outcrops of the different rocks which underlie the surface. These terraces are usually smooth, and, although inclined toward the N., the inclination is generally so slight that they appear to be level. Between the hills of the s. and the level land of the N. is a beautiful rolling region, the ridges gradually declining toward the N. In that part of the State s. of the most eastern mountain range the surface is generally level or broken by low hills. In New York and Westchester cos. these hills are principally composed of primitive rocks. The surface of Long Island is generally level or gently undulating. A ridge 150 to 200 feet high, composed of sand, gravel, and clay, extends E. and w. across the island N. of the center.

Rivers and Lakes.—The river system of the State has two general divisions,—the first comprising the streams tributary to the great lakes and the St. Lawrence, and the second those which flow in a general southerly direction. The watershed which separates these two systems extends in an irregular line eastward from Lake Erie through the southern tier of counties to near the N. E. corner of Chemung; thence it turns N. E. to the Adirondack Mts. in Essex co., thence s. E. to the E. extremity of Lake George, and thence nearly due E. to the E. line of the State.[1]

The northerly division has 5 general subdivisions. The most westerly of these comprises all the streams flowing into Lake Erie and Niagara River and those flowing into Lake Ontario w. of Genesee River. In Chautauque co. the streams are short and rapid, as the watershed approaches within a few mi. of Lake Erie. Cattaraugus, Buffalo, Tonawanda, and Oak Orchard Creeks are the most important streams in this division. Buffalo Creek is chiefly noted for forming Buffalo Harbor at its mouth; and the Tonawanda for 12 miles from its mouth is used for canal navigation. Oak Orchard and other creeks flowing into Lake Ontario descend from the interior in a series of rapids, affording a large amount of water-power.

The second subdivision comprises the Genesee River and its tributaries. The Genesee rises in the N. part of Penn. and flows in a generally northerly direction to Lake Ontario. Its upper course is through a narrow valley bordered by steep, rocky hills. Upon the line of Wyoming and Livingston cos. it breaks through a mountain barrier in a deep gorge and forms the Portage Falls, —one of the finest waterfalls in the State. Below this point the course of the river is through a beautiful valley 1 to 2 mi. wide and bordered by banks 50 to 150 ft. high. At Rochester it flows over the precipitous edges of the Niagara limestone, forming the Upper Genesee Falls; and 3 mi. below it flows over the edge of the Medina sandstone, forming the Lower Genesee Falls. The principal tributaries of this stream are Canaseraga, Honeoye, and Conesus Creeks from the E., and Oatka and Black Creeks from the w. Honeoye, Canadice, Hemlock, and Conesus Lakes lie within the Genesee Basin.

The third subdivision includes the Oswego River and its tributaries and the small streams flowing into Lake Ontario between Genesee and Oswego Rivers. The basin of the Oswego includes most of the inland lakes which form a peculiar feature of the landscape in the interior of the State. The principal of these lakes are Cayuga, Seneca, Canandaigua, Skaneateles, Crooked, and Owasco,— all occupying long, narrow valleys, and extending from the level land in the center far into the highland region of the s. The valleys which they occupy appear like immense ravines formed by some tremendous force, which has torn the solid rocks from their original beds, from the general level of the surrounding summits, down to the present bottoms of the lakes.[2] Oneida and Onondaga

---

1 TABLE

Showing the height above tide of the passes between the principal river basins of the State.

BETWEEN	AT	FEET.	BETWEEN	AT	FEET.
Hudson River and Ramapo River......	Moncey.............	557	Susquehanna River and Cayuga Lake	Ithaca Summit...	969
" " " Delaware River.......	Otisville	900	" " " Seneca Lake.	Horseheads........	884
" " " Neversink River....	Wawarsing........		" " " Genesee Riv.	Alfred Summit...	1,780
" " " Lake Ontario.........	Rome	427	Genesee River and Allegany River....	Cuba.................	1,699
" " " Lake Erie..............	Tonawanda	557	Allegany River and Lake Erie.........	Little Val. Sum...	1,614
Delaware River and Susquehanna Riv.	Deposit Summit..	1,373	Mohawk River and Lake Ontario......	Kasoag.............	536
Susquehanna River and Mohawk Riv.	Bouckville..........	1,127	" " " Black River......	Boonville..........	1,120
" " " Oneida Lake..	Tully	1,247	Lake Champlain and St. Lawrence...	Chateangay Sum.	1,050

The most remarkable passes through the mountains are, first, that of the Hudson, through the eastern mountains; second, that of Wood Creek, from the Hudson to Lake Champlain; and, third, that of the Mohawk, through the central mountains.

[2] The ravines of these lakes, and the streams which flow down parallel to them, are usually bordered by steep hillsides, the strata of which lie in parallel layers nearly level E. and w., and slightly inclined toward the s. Upon the opposite banks the

Lakes occupy basins upon the level land in the N. E. part of the Oswego Basin. Mud Creek, the most westerly branch of Oswego River, takes its rise in Ontario co., flows N. E. into Wayne, where it unites with Canandaigua Outlet and takes the name of Clyde River; thence it flows E. to the w. line of Cayuga co., where it empties into Seneca River. This latter stream, made up of the outlets of Seneca and Cayuga Lakes, from this point flows in a N. E. course, and receives successively the outlets of Owasco, Skaneateles, Onondaga, and Oneida Lakes. From the mouth of the last-named stream it takes the name Oswego River, and its course is nearly due N. to Lake Ontario.

The fourth subdivision includes the streams flowing into Lake Ontario and the St. Lawrence E. of the mouth of the Oswego. The principal of these are Salmon, Black, Oswegatchie, Grasse, and Racket Rivers. These streams mostly take their rise upon the plateau of the great Northern wilderness, and in their course to the lowlands are frequently interrupted by falls, furnishing an abundance of water-power. The water is usually very dark, being colored with iron and the vegetation of swamps.

The fifth subdivision includes all the streams flowing into Lakes George and Champlain. They are mostly mountain torrents, frequently interrupted by cascades. The principal streams are the Chazy, Saranac, and Au Sable Rivers, and Wood Creek. Deep strata of tertiary clay extend along the shores of Lake Champlain and Wood Creek. The water of most of the streams in this region is colored by the iron over which it flows.

The second general division of the river-system of the State includes the basins of the Allegany, Susquehanna, Delaware, and Hudson. The Allegany Basin embraces the southerly half of Chautauqua and Cattaraugus cos. and the s. w. corner of Allegany. The Allegany River enters the State from the s. in the s. E. corner of Cattaraugus co., flows in nearly a semicircle, with its outward curve toward the N., and flows out of the State in the s. w. part of the same co. It receives several tributaries from the N. and E. These streams mostly flow in deep ravines bordered by steep, rocky hillsides. The watershed between this basin and Lake Erie approaches within a few miles of the lake, and is elevated 800 to 1,000 feet above it.

The Susquehanna Basin occupies about one-third of the s. border of the State. The river takes its rise in Otsego Lake, and, flowing s. w. to the Penn. line, receives Charlotte River from the s. and the Unadilla from the N. After a course of a few miles in Penn. it again enters the State, and flows in a general westerly direction to near the w. border of Tioga co., whence it turns s. and again enters Penn. Its principal tributary from the N. is Chenango River. Tioga River enters the State from Penn. near the E. border of Steuben co., flows N., receives the Canisteo from the w. and the Conhocton from the N. From the mouth of the latter the stream takes the name Chemung River, and flows in a s. E. direction, into the Susquehanna in Penn., a few miles s. of the State line. The upper course of these streams is generally through deep ravines bordered by steep hillsides; but below they are bordered by wide and beautiful intervales.

The Delaware Basin occupies Delaware and Sullivan and portions of several of the adjacent cos. The N. or principal branch of the river rises in the N. E. part of Delaware co. and flows s. w. to near the Penn. line; thence it turns s. E. and forms the boundary of the State to the line of N. J. Its principal branches are the Pepacton and Neversink Rivers. These streams all flow in deep, narrow ravines bordered by steep, rocky hills.

The Basin of the Hudson occupies about two-thirds of the E. border of the State, and a large territory extending into the interior. The remote sources of the Hudson are among the highest peaks of the Adirondacks, more than 4,000 feet above tide. Several of the little lakes which form reservoirs of the Upper Hudson are 2,500 to 3,000 feet above tide. The stream rapidly descends through the narrow defiles into Warren co., where it receives from the E. the outlet of Schroon Lake, and Sacondaga River from the w. Below the mouth of the latter the river turns eastward, and breaks through the barrier of the Luzerne Mts. in a series of rapids and falls. At Fort Edward it again turns s. and flows with a rapid current, frequently interrupted by falls, to Troy, 160 miles from the ocean. At this place the river falls into an estuary, where its current is affected by the tide; and from this place to its mouth it is a broad, deep, sluggish stream. About 60 miles from its mouth the Hudson breaks through the rocky barrier of The Highlands, forming the most easterly of the Appalachian Mt. Ranges; and along its lower course it is bordered on the w. by a nearly perpendicular wall of basaltic rock 300 to 500 feet high, known as "The Palisades." Above Troy the Hudson receives Hoosick River from the E. and the Mohawk from the w. The former stream rises in Western Mass. and Vt., and the latter near the center of the State.

---

dissevered edges of the strata exactly correspond, showing that the intermediate portions have been torn away. The force that effected these immense changes was probably great currents of water from the N.,—the direction being determined by the character of the boulders upon the hills, and by the peculiar nature of the drift deposits.

At Little Falls and "The Noses" the Mohawk breaks through mountain barriers in a deep, rocky ravine; and at Cohoes, about 1 mile from its mouth, it flows down a perpendicular precipice of 70 feet, forming an excellent water-power. Below Troy the tributaries of the Hudson are all comparatively small streams. South of the Highlands the river spreads out into a wide expanse known as "Tappan Bay." A few small streams upon the extreme E. border of the State flow eastward into the Housatonic; and several small branches of Passaic River rise in the s. part of Rockland co.

Lake Erie forms a portion of the w. boundary of the State. It is 240 miles long, with an average width of 38 miles, and it lies mostly w. of the bounds of the State. It is 334 feet above Lake Ontario, 565 feet above tide, and has an average depth of 120 feet. The greatest depth ever obtained by soundings is 270 feet. The harbors upon the lake are Buffalo, Silver Creek, Dunkirk, and Barcelona.

Niagara River, forming the outlet of Lake Erie, is 34 miles long, and, on an average, more than a mile wide.[1] About 20 miles below Lake Erie the rapids commence; and 2 miles further below are Niagara Falls.[2] For 7 miles below the falls the river has a rapid course between perpendicular, rocky banks, 200 to 300 feet high; but below it emerges from the Highlands and flows 7 miles to Lake Ontario in a broad, deep, and majestic current.

Lake Ontario forms a part of the N. boundary to the w. half of the State. Its greatest length is 130 miles and its greatest width 55 miles. It is 232 feet above tide, and its greatest depth is 600 feet. Its principal harbors on the American shore are Lewiston, Youngston, Port Genesee, Sodus and Little Sodus Bays, Oswego, Sackets Harbor, and Cape Vincent. St. Lawrence River forms the outlet of the lake and the N. boundary of the State to the E. line of St. Lawrence co. It is a broad, deep river, flowing with a strong yet sluggish current until it passes the limits of this State. In the upper part of its course it incloses a great number of small islands, known as "The Thousand Islands."[3]

The surfaces of the great lakes are subject to variations of level,—probably due to prevailing winds, unequal amounts of rain, and evaporation. The greatest difference known in Lake Erie is 7 feet, and in Lake Ontario 4¾ feet. The time of these variations is irregular; and the interval between the extremes often extends through several years. A sudden rise and fall, of several feet, has been noticed upon Lake Ontario at rare intervals, produced by some unknown cause.

Navigable Waters.—The natural internal navigation of the State is very extensive. Before the commencement of internal improvements, the rivers and lakes formed the most easy means of communication between distant portions of the State; and along these natural channels of commerce the early settlements were principally made.[4] The most important lines of early

---

1 TABLE
Of the heights above tide of the principal lakes in the State.

NAME OF LAKE.	LOCATION.		FEET:
Avalanche Lake	Essex	co	2,900
Lake Colden	"	"	2,851
" Henderson	"	"	1,936
" Sandford	"	"	1,826
" Eckford	Hamilton	"	1,791
Fulton Lakes, (6, 7, and 8)	"	"	1,776
Racket Lake	"	"	1,745
Forked "	"	"	1,704
Newcomb Lake	Essex	"	1,698
Cattaraugus Lake	Cattaraugus	"	1,665
Fulton Lakes, (3, 4, and 5)	Herkimer	"	1,645
Long Lake	"	"	1,575
Cranberry Lake	St. Lawrence	"	1,570
Upper Saranac Lake	Franklin	"	1,567
Tuppers "	"	"	1,545
Rich "	Essex	"	1,545
Lower Saranac "	Franklin	"	1,527
Lake Pleasant	Hamilton	"	1,500
Chautauqua Lake	Chautauqua	"	1,291
Tully "	Onondaga	"	1,200
Schuyler "	Otsego	"	1,200
Otsego "	"	"	1,193
Cazenovia "	Madison	"	900
Skaneateles "	Onondaga	"	860
Crooked "	Yates	"	718
Owasco "	Cayuga	"	670
Canandaigua "	Ontario	"	668
Seneca "			447
Cayuga "			387
Oneida "			369
Onondaga "	Onondaga co		361
Lake Erie			
" George			
" Ontario			232
" Champlain			93

[2] For a more full description of Niagara Falls, see page 450.

[3] The river scenery upon the St. Lawrence is unsurpassed. The water is perfectly pure and nearly transparent. In consequence of its being fed by the great lake reservoirs, it is never subject to sudden rises, but steadily pursues its majestic way to the ocean, unaffected by the changes of the seasons or other causes.

[4] The navigable waters N. of the great watershed before the completion of the Erie Canal were as follows:—

Cattaraugus Creek, about 1 mi. from its mouth.

Buffalo Creek, boatable 8 mi. from Lake Erie.

Tonawanda Creek, boatable 30 mi. from its mouth.

Niagara River, navigable for vessels of any size from Buffalo to Schlosser, at the head of the Rapids,—a distance of 22 mi.; also from Lewiston to Lake Ontario, a distance of 7 mi.

Oak Orchard Creek, boatable 4 mi. from its mouth.

Genesee River, to Carthage Landing, a distance of 5 mi.; and from Rochester to Mt. Morris for boats.

Oswego River was navigated with great difficulty by bateaux, with a portage at Oswego Falls, now Fulton.

Oneida Outlet and Lake were navigable for bateaux, and for many years constituted a portion of the great thoroughfare between the E. and w.

Seneca River was boatable to Cayuga Lake, and to Seneca Lake with one portage at Seneca Falls; *Clyde River* was boatable to Lyons.

The Interior Lakes, including Seneca, Cayuga, Canandaigua, Onondaga, Owasco, Skaneateles, Crooked, Chautauqua, and Otsego, are all navigable. Steamers have plied upon each of them.

Fish Creek was navigable to Rome with canoes. A portage of less than 1 mi. intervened between this stream and the Mohawk River.

Salmon River was navigable to Port Ontario.

Salmon Creek was navigable on each branch, for small vessels, about 1 mi. from the lake.

Black River was navigable for large vessels from the lake to Dexter, a distance of 6 mi., and for boats and small steamers from Carthage to Lyons Falls, a distance of 43 mi.

Lake Ontario, with all its bays and inlets, is navigable for vessels of all sizes.

inland navigation were, first, N. from Albany, through the Hudson to Fort Edward, thence a portage to Fort Ann, and thence by Wood Creek to Lake Champlain; and, second, W. from Albany, by way of the Mohawk, Wood Creek, Oneida Lake, and Oswego River, to Lake Ontario. Upon the latter route were portages at several of the rifts of the Mohawk, from the Mohawk to Wood Creek, and at Oswego Falls.

Tides.—The tides at New York Harbor and along the coast have been carefully observed, under the direction of the Coast Survey. The tidal wave from the Sound, as it moves forward in a wedge-shaped channel, becomes augmented, whilst that from Sandy Hook is slightly diminished. These two waves meet in East River, at points between Hell Gate and Throggs Neck.[1]

Cranberry and *French Creeks* were boatable about 2 mi. from their mouths.

Indian River and *Black Lake* were navigable from Rossie to the foot of the lake.

Oswegatchie River is navigable in high water for rafts from Ox Bow to Ogdensburgh.

Racket River was formerly boatable about 18 mi. from its mouth, but the navigation is now destroyed by dams. In the wilderness near the headwaters of this river are several miles of slack water navigation.

St. Regis River is navigable for steamboats 2 mi. from its mouth.

Salmon River, navigable to Fort Covington.

St. Lawrence River is navigable for vessels of any size from the lake to Ogdensburgh. Below that point rafts, arks, and boats could descend, but could ascend only by towing with horses and cattle up the principal rifts. Locks and canals have been constructed around the Rapids by the Canadian Government, so that the navigation for steamboats, sloops, and schooners is now uninterrupted from Lake Ontario to the ocean.

Wood Creek was boatable from Fort Ann to Lake Champlain.

Lake George is navigable for boats and steamers.

Lake Champlain is navigable for all kinds of vessels. Rafts were formerly sent down to the St. Lawrence; but vessels could not ascend the Richlieu until after the construction of a canal and locks around the Rapids.

Chazy River is navigable to Champlain Landing.

The navigable waters S. of the great watershed were as follows:

Allegany River, in high water, is navigable for small steamers up to Olean.

Connewango Creek and several of its tributaries are navigable for rafts in high water.

Susquehanna River was navigable for boats, in high water, to Otsego Lake.

Unadilla River was also boatable for a considerable distance.

Chenango River and several of its tributaries were boatable in high water.

Chemung River was boatable and navigable for rafts in high water.

Conhocton River was boatable to Bath.

Tioga River and the *Canisteo* were also boatable a considerable distance.

Delaware River is navigable for rafts in high water. Immense quantities of lumber have been floated down the Delaware and Susquehanna to the markets of Philadelphia and Baltimore.

Hudson River is navigable for ships to Hudson, and by sloops and steamers to Troy. Boats formerly ascended to Fort Edward, with portages around the Falls.

Rondout and *Wappinger Creeks* are navigable each about 2 mi. from their mouths.

Mohawk River was boatable from Schenectady to "Fort Stanwix," now Rome, with several interruptions. The principal obstructions were the "Six Flats Rift," 6 mi. above Schenectady; "Fort Hunter Rift;" "Caughnawaga Rift," at Canajoharie; "Ehles Rift," near Fort Plain; "Kneisherns Rift," near the Upper Indian Castle; and the "Little Falls," which was a complete bar to upward navigation and required a portage around it.

Sacondaga River is navigable for small steamers from Hadley to Northampton,—a distance of 20 mi. In and around New York and Long Island the bays, creeks, and inlets are nearly all navigable in high tide.

Peconic River is navigable to Riverhead.

Byram River is navigable to Port Chester.

Bronx River is navigable to West Farms, a distance of 3 mi.

Harlem River can be navigated by small craft from East River to High Bridge.

[1] TIDE TABLES.

The following table, prepared by A. D. Bache, Superintendent of the Coast Survey, shows the progress of the tidal wave up the Hudson. The time is that after the last preceding transit of the moon across the meridian at Sandy Hook. The plane of reference is mean low tide.

	Sandy Hook.	Governors Island.	Dobbs Ferry.	Verplanks Point.	West Point.	Poughkeepsie.	Tivoli.	Stuyvesant.	Castleton.	Greenbush.
	H. M.	H. M.	H. M.	H. M.	H. M.	H. M.	H. M.	H. M.	H. M.	H. M.
Time after last preceding transit at S. H.	7.29	8.14	9.24	10.10	11.5	13.0	13.50	15.41	16.54	17.45
Rise of highest tide above plane of reference.	7.1 ft.	6.1 ft.	5.0 ft.	4.7 ft.	4.9 ft.	5.6 ft.	6.4 ft.	6.0 ft.	4.9 ft.	6.4 ft.
Fall of lowest tide below " " "	1.4	2.2	0.9	0.8	0.8	1.1	1.5	1.6	0.8	1.7
Fall of mean low water of spring tides below plane of reference	0.5	0.5	0.3	0.2	0.4	0.4	0.5	0.2	0.3	0.4
Height of mean low water of neap tides above plane of reference	0.5	0.4	0.5	0.3	0.3	0.4	0.4	0.3	0.3	0.4
Mean rise and fall of tides	4.8	4.3	3.59	3.12	2.71	3.24	3.95	3.67	2.66	2.46
" " " " " spring tides	5.6	5.1	4.5	3.8	3.4	4.0	4.3	4.3	3.3	3.2
" " " " " neap tides	4.0	3.4	2.7	2.5	2.0	2.4	3.0	2.8	1.8	1.1
	H. M.	H. M.	H. M.	H. M.	H. M.	H. M.	H. M.	H. M.	H. M.	H. M.
Mean duration, reckoning from { of rise..	6.10	6.0	6.5	5.25	5.28	5.41	5.40	5.18	5.1	4.26
the middle of one stand { of fall..	6.15	6.25	6.18	7.12	7.10	6.44	6.54	7.02	7.23	8.4
to the middle of the next. { of stand..	0.21	0.28								

Tide table for the shores of Long Island and adjacent places in New York. Time after moon's transit and plane of reference as above.

	Montauk Point.	Little Gull Island.	Oyster Bay.	Sands Point.	New Rochelle.	Throggs Neck.
	H. M.	H. M.	H. M.	H. M.	H. M.	H. M.
Interval between time of moon's { Mean interval	8.20	9.38	11.7	11.13	11.22	11.20
transit and time of high water. { Diff. between greatest and least interval.	1.11	1.7	0.51	0.31	0.32	0.39
{ Spring tides	2.4 ft.	2.3 ft.	9.2 ft.	8.9 ft.	8.6 ft.	9.2 ft.
Rise and fall. { Neap tides	1.8	2.9	5.4	6.4	6.6	6.1
{ Mean	1.9	2.5	7.3	7.7	7.6	7.3
	H. M.	H. M.	H. M.	H. M.	H. M.	H. M.
{ Flood tide.	6.7	6.1	6.8	5.55	5.51	5.50
Mean duration. { Ebb tide.	6.7	6.21	6.24	6.30	6.35	6.33
{ Stand.	0.31	0.37		0.14	0.12	0.43

Report of Coast Survey, 1856, p. 122.

GEOLOGY.

Our knowledge of the geology of the State is derived from the survey made under State authority from 1836 to 1843, and from the investigations of several eminent geologists who have examined particular localities.[1]

Rocks.—The geological formations of the State include the igneous or primary rocks, and all the strata lying between them and the coal measures of Penn. The classification adopted by the State geologists, embracing all the rocks above the primary, is known as the "New York system," the rocks being identical with the Silurian and Devonian system of the English geologists. The igneous or primary rocks, including granite, gneiss, and other varieties destitute of organic remains, occupy the greater part of the mountainous region in the N. E. part of the State, the Highlands upon the Hudson, and a considerable portion of the country below, including Manhattan Island. A portion of these rocks are imperfectly stratified, and are generally found in broken and disrupted masses with the strata highly inclined. The remaining portions of the State are occupied by series of stratified rocks, generally extending E. and W. and varying in thickness from a few inches to several hundred feet. The strata overlie each other, and have a slight dip toward the s., so that a person in traveling from the N. border of the State to the Penn. line would successively pass over the exposed edges of the whole series. Toward the E. these strata all are bent, and appear to be arranged around the primitive region in the same order in which they lie elsewhere. The highest of the series of rocks found in the State forms the floor of the coal measures; so that it is perfectly futile to search for coal within the limits of the State. The rocks are distinguished by their color, quality, and situation, and by the fossils which they contain. In many instances a stratum disappears entirely, and in others strata of several hundred feet in thickness in one place are but a few feet thick in another. In places where many strata are wanting and two rocks usually widely separated are found in contact, the geologist is obliged to depend entirely upon the fossils which they contain to determine their classification.[2]

---

[1] In 1799, Dr. Samuel L. Mitchill, under the auspices of the "Society for Promoting Agriculture, Arts, and Manufactures," published an essay upon the rocks in the State. While the Erie Canal was in process of construction, Stephen Van Rensselaer employed Prof. Amos Eaton to prepare an account of the rocks along the canal route. This was published in 1824. Prof. Eaton's work was one of great merit; and to him we are indebted for the first accurate knowledge ever obtained of the general system of rocks in the State.

On the 15th of April, 1836, an act was passed authorizing a geological survey of the State. The State was divided into four districts, to each of which were appointed a geologist and an assistant. A zoologist, botanist, mineralogist, and paleontologist were appointed for the whole State.

The *First District* included the counties of Albany, Columbia, Delaware, Dutchess, Greene, Kings, New York, Orange, Putnam, Queens, Rensselaer, Richmond, Rockland, Saratoga, Schenectady, Schoharie, Suffolk, Sullivan, Ulster, Washington, and Westchester. Wm. W. Mather was appointed Principal Geologist, and Caleb Briggs, J. Lang Cassels, and —— Seymour, Assistants. The Report, in 1 vol. 4to, was published in 1843.

The *Second District*, consisting of the counties of Clinton, Essex, Franklin, Jefferson, St. Lawrence, and Warren, was placed under the charge of Dr. Ebenezer Emmons, Principal, and Jas. Hall and E. Emmons, jr., Assistants. The Report, in 1 vol., was published in 1842.

The *Third District*, consisting of the counties of Broome, Cayuga, Chenango, Cortland, Fulton, Herkimer, Lewis, Madison, Montgomery, Oneida, Onondaga, Oswego, Otsego, Tioga, and the E. half of Tompkins, was placed under charge of Lardner Van Uxem, Principal, and Jas. Eights and E. S. Can, Assistants. The Report, in 1 vol., was published in 1842.

The *Fourth District*, consisting of the counties of Allegany, Cattaraugus, Chautauqua, Chemung, Erie, Genesee, Livingston, Monroe, Niagara, Ontario, Orleans, Seneca, Steuben, the w. half of Tompkins, Wayne, Wyoming, and Yates, was assigned to Jas. Hall, Principal, and J. W. Boyd and E. N. Horsford, Assistants. The Report was published in 1 vol. in 1843.

The *Mineralogical Department* was assigned to Dr. Lewis C. Beck, Principal, and Wm. Horton and L. D. Gale, Assistants. The Report, in 1 vol., was published in 1842.

The *Zoological Department* was assigned to Dr. Jas. E. De Kay, Principal, and John W. Hill, Draftsman. The Report, in 5 vols., was published in 1842–43:—Vol. I, Mammalia, with General Introduction by Gov. Seward; Vol. II, Ornithology; Vols. III and IV, Reptiles and Fishes; Vol. V, Mollusca and Crustacea.

The *Botanical Department* was assigned to Dr. John Torry. The Report, in 2 vols., was published in 1843.

The *Agricultural Department* was assigned to Dr. Ebenezer Emmons. The Report, in 5 vols., was published from 1846 to 1854,—Vol. I, Soils and Climate; Vol. II, Analysis and Results of Experiments; Vols. III and IV, Fruits; Vol. V, Insects.

The *Paleontological Department* was assigned to T. A. Conrad in 1837. He resigned in 1843, and was succeeded by Prof. Jas. Hall. The Report, to consist of 5 vols., is in process of publication. Two vols. are already issued; and the third is in press. A geological map, accompanying the Reports, is issued with this work.

[2] The following is the classification of the New York system, with the position which the different strata occupy in the classification of English geologists. The order of the arrangement is from below upward:—

Primitive or Igneous Rocks.
Taconic System.

LOWER SILURIAN.
Potsdam Sandstone.
Calciferous Sandstone.
Chazy Limestone.
Birdseye Limestone.
Black River Limestone.
Trenton Limestone.
Utica Slate.
Hudson River Group, Lorraine Shales.

UPPER SILURIAN.
Oneida Conglomerate, Shawangunk Grit.
Medina Sandstone.
Clinton Group.
Niagara Group, Coraline Limestone in the east.
Onondaga Salt Group. { Red Shales. Green Shales. Gypsum.
Waterlime Group.
Pentamerus Limestone.
Delthyris Shaly Limestone.
Upper Pentamerus Limestone.
Oriskany Sandstone.
Cauda Galli Grit.
Schoharie Grit.
Onondaga Limestone.
Corniferous Limestone.
Marcellus Shales.

DEVONIAN.
Hamilton Group. { Ludlowville Shales. Encrinal Limestone. Moscow Shales.
Tully Limestone.
Genesee Slate.
Portage Group. { Coshaqua Shales. Gardeau Flag Stones. Portage Sandstone.
Chemung Group.
Old Red Sandstone.
Conglomerate of the Coal Measures.

24

The Catskill Mts. are composed principally of Old Red Sandstone; and the tops of some of the higher peaks are covered with the conglomerate of the coal measures. New Red Sandstone is found in a few localities along the Hudson, below the Highlands. Trap, a rock of volcanic origin, forms the Palisades upon the Hudson; and trap dikes are common in the primitive region of the N. Tertiary clay, in deep strata, extends along the valleys of Lake Champlain and St. Lawrence River. Drift, including loose deposits of boulders, gravel, sand, and clay, is found in most parts of the State, in some places covering the rocks beneath to the depth of several hundred feet. The character of this drift, the peculiar forms which it has assumed, and the position which it occupies, all give evidence of some great general moving power which existed after the stratified rocks were lifted from their original beds, and ages before the present order of things was instituted.

Within more recent periods, considerable changes have been wrought by the action of present streams of water and the wasting agencies of the atmosphere and frost. From these are derived marl, alluvium, and the greater part of the soils. The thickness of the rock strata is generally determined by its outcrop along the ravines of the streams, and by Artesian wells, which have been sunk to a great depth in different parts of the State.[1]

Metallic Minerals.—The principal metals in the State are iron and lead, the former only of which is found in sufficient quantity and purity to render its manufacture profitable. Iron ore is found in three distinct varieties, viz., magnetic oxide or magnetite, specular oxide or red hematite, and hydrous peroxide or limonite. Magnetic ore is widely diffused throughout the primitive region. It is usually found in beds between the rock strata, parallel to the mountain ranges; and sometimes it is blended with the rock. The beds in many places are immense in extent, and the ore is 75 to 95 per cent. pure iron.[2] Specular iron ore is found in narrow beds between the igneous and sedimentary rocks. It is principally found in St. Lawrence and Jefferson cos.[3] A variety of this ore, known as argillaceous iron ore or clay ironstone, is associated with the lower strata of the Clinton group, extending from Herkimer to Monroe co. It is found in beds 2½ feet thick and about 20 feet apart, and its general form is that of flattened grains. Limonite is found also associated with the igneous rocks and in various other localities. It is usually in the form of shot or bog ore, or yellow ocher. It is wrought to a considerable extent in Richmond, Orange, Putnam, Dutchess, Columbia, Washington, Franklin, St. Lawrence, Jefferson, and Lewis cos. Bog ore is probably found, to a greater or less extent, in every co. in the State. The iron made from it is usually tough and soft.[4]

Lead ore is found in St. Lawrence, Ulster, Dutchess, Westchester, Orange, Columbia, Lewis, Jefferson, and Sullivan cos.; and in several of them the mines have been worked to some extent. The Rossie Mines, of St. Lawrence, are the only ones now wrought.[5] Copper ore in the form of

---

New Red Sandstone.
Tertiary.
Diluvial or Drift.
Quaternary.
    The Taconic system is claimed by some as corresponding to the Cambrian system of Mr. Sedgwick, and by others to be newer formations changed by heat.

[1] TABLE

Showing the depths of the principal Artesian wells in the State.

County.	Locality.	Depth.	Product.
Albany.........	City................	128	Fresh water.
"	" Ferry St......	617	Mineral water.
Cayuga.........	Montezuma.......	200	Brine.
Columbia......	Hudson...........	228	Fresh water.
Delaware....	Elk Brook.........	394	Weak brine.
Jefferson......	Watertown........	127	Fresh water.
Livingston...	York..............	50	Weak brine and gas.
New York...	U. S. Hotel.......	626	Fresh water.
" " ...	Bleeker St........	448	" "
" " ...	By Manhatt'n co.	280	" "
Oneida.........	Utica.............	314	" "
Onondaga....	Syracuse.........	600	" "
"	"	400	" "
"	"	80 to 390	Brine.
Orleans.......	Oak Orchard......	140	Weak brine.
Wayne.........	Savannah..........	250	" "
"	Little Sodus and Clyde.............	400	" " and gas.

The deepest Artesian well in the U. S. is at St. Louis, Mo., and is 2199 feet deep. A well at Louisville, Ky., is 2086 feet deep; and another at Columbus, Ohio, 1900 feet deep.

[2] The principal mines which have been worked in the northern primitive region are in Warren, Essex, Clinton, St. Lawrence, and Franklin cos. So common are particles of iron in the rocks of this region that the iron sand upon the banks of the streams is sufficiently pure to repay the labor of collecting for the forge. Magnetic ores are also abundant in Orange co., and mines have there been worked since the earliest periods. This ore has also been found among the igneous rocks of Rockland, Westchester, Putnam, Washington, Saratoga, Hamilton, Herkimer, Jefferson, and Lewis cos.

[3] The principal mines in St. Lawrence and Jefferson cos. yield this variety of ore. It is most abundant in the towns of Gouverneur, Rossie, and Antwerp, and is there usually associated with crystaline sulphuret of iron, spathic iron, and quartz. The argillaceous ore supplies the furnaces in Oneida, Oswego, and Wayne cos. It is red, and imparts a dull red color to whatever it comes in contact with. In the region of mines and furnaces the clothing of the laborers, the trees, fences, and vehicles employed, are all colored by it. It is used as a paint, under the name of "Spanish Brown."

[4] Bog ore is deposited in swamps, the bottoms of which are clay, hardpan, or some other strata impervious to water. It is continually accumulating, so that it may be removed two or three times in a century. It has various shades of color, from yellow to a dark brown. In the primitive region it sometimes assumes a stalactital or botryoidal form, with a fibrous texture and a glossy black surface. A loamy variety, when used in high furnaces, is liable to blow up. This is caused by the mass melting away below, leaving a crust above, and, as the support at last gives away, the moisture contained in the mass is suddenly converted into steam by the intense heat, and the liquid iron below is thrown out with great force, sometimes destroying the furnace.

[5] A vein has recently been opened in Orange co. that promises great richness. Lead ore is usually found in the form of sulphurets, or galena. It is often associated with crystalized minerals of great beauty.

a sulphuret has been found in Washington, Jefferson, and St. Lawrence cos., but not in sufficient quantities to render mining profitable. Zinc ore in the form of a sulphuret, or blende, is found, associated with lead, in St. Lawrence co. Manganese, titanium, nickel, and several other metals, have been found in small quantities, though they have never been reduced except in the laboratories of the chemist.[1]

Non-Metallic Minerals.—The most valuable non-metallic minerals in the State are limestone, gypsum, waterlime, pipeclay, clay and sand suitable for common and fire brick and pottery, graphite, talc, and slate. Nearly every part of the State is well supplied with building stone; and in most of the counties extensive quarries have been worked. Lime, waterlime, and gypsum are also extensively quarried.[2]

Mineral Springs are numerous, and are found in nearly every co. in the State. The most celebrated of these are the salt springs of Onondaga, the medicinal springs of Saratoga, and the thermal springs of Columbia co. Sulphur and chalybeate springs are common, and many of them have considerable notoriety for medicinal properties.[3] In the w. part of the State springs emitting nitrogen and carburetted hydrogen gas are numerous. In the limestone regions of the State the water is generally more or less impregnated with carbonate and sulphate of lime; and in many places tufa is deposited in large quantities by the water. The slow dissolving of the limestone rocks has given a cavernous structure to several localities, and in others it has formed deep holes in the ground. The caves of Albany, Schoharie, and Jefferson cos. are doubtless formed in this manner; and the peculiar sink-holes and cratean lakes of Onondaga are probably formed by the breaking of the superincumbent mass into the caverns beneath.

SEAT OF GOVERNMENT.

THE SEAT OF GOVERNMENT was originally fixed at New York City, and remained there until the Revolution, with occasional adjournments of the General Assembly and Executive Department on account of prevailing sickness. Such of the public records as related to the immediate interests of the crown were removed, by order of Gov. Tryon, in Dec. 1775, to the armed ship *Duchess of Gordon*, and remained on board till Nov. 1781, when most of them were returned to the city.[4] In June, 1776, the other public records were removed to Kingston, and, on the approach of the enemy in Oct. 1777, they were hastily taken to Rochester, Ulster county.[5] They were soon afterward taken to Poughkeepsie, and in 1784 to New York. In 1797, commissioners were appointed to erect a building for the records in Albany, and an order dated July 31, 1798, authorized their removal thither[6] and the permanent location of the seat of Government at that place.

The State House was begun in 1803 and finished in 1807, at the joint expense of the city and county of Albany and the State of New York. The original cost exceeded $120,000, of which

---

[1] In many of the original patents of the mountainous regions upon the Hudson, reservations were made of all the gold and silver that might be found. To this day, however, these metals have not been found; though it is said that traces of silver have been discovered in several places.

[2] The following is a list of the most important quarries in the State:—

Gypsum is found in Cayuga, Madison, Onondaga, Wayne, Orleans, and Genesee.

Limestone is quarried in most of the counties of the State except those along the Penn. line.

Water-Limestone is quarried in Erie, Jefferson, Lewis, Madison, Montgomery, Niagara, Onondaga, and Ulster.

Flagging is found in most of the southern counties, and in various other localities. The thin bedded sandstone of the Portage group furnishes the best varieties.

Building stone of excellent quality is found in nearly every section of the State. Granite and gneiss are extensively quarried in New York and Westchester and in the N. E. cos. of the State. The Potsdam sandstone, Black River limestone, the gray and Medina sandstone, and the Onondaga limestone all furnish excellent building stone. Most of the locks upon the Erie Canal are built of the last named stone. The shales of the Portage and Chemung group are separated into strata by hard, compact sandstone, excellent for building or flagging.

Marble is found and quarried in Westchester, Putnam, Dutchess, and Orange cos.

Roofing slate is quarried in Washington, Rensselaer, Columbia, and Dutchess cos.

[3] The principal of these springs are those of Massena, St. Lawrence co.; Richfield, Otsego co.; Avon, Livingston co.; Sharon, Schoharie co.; New Lebanon and Stockport, Columbia co.; Chittenango, Madison co.; and Alabama, Genesee co.

[4] Six years' close confinement on shipboard damaged some of these records almost beyond remedy. The most valuable were transcribed in 1798, under the direction of commissioners appointed by law.

[5] The first State Legislature, then in session, hastily adjourned and met in Jan. at Poughkeepsie. The citizens of Goshen tendered the hospitalities of their village and the use of rooms, if the Legislature chose to remove thither. In March, 1778, a concurrent resolution directed the Secretary of State and the clerks of counties to put their records into strong and light inclosures, to be ready for instant removal in case of danger. The Legislature held its sessions at Poughkeepsie, Kingston, or Albany, as suited convenience, until 1784, when it removed to New York. Two sessions were afterward held at Poughkeepsie, and three at Albany, before the final removal to the latter place in 1797.

[6] Philip Schuyler, Abraham Ten Broeck, Jeremiah Van Rensselaer, Daniel Hale, and Teunis T. Van Vechten were appointed commissioners. The edifice stood on the site of the present Geological and Agricultural Hall, and was torn down in 1855.

$34,200 was paid by the city and $3,000 by the county of Albany. It continued to be used for city, county, and State offices and courts until about 1832, when the State became the exclusive owner and the Capitol was fitted up for legislative and other public purposes. It stands at the head of State Street, 130 feet above the Hudson, and has in front a park of three acres inclosed by an iron fence. It is substantially built of stone faced with Nyack red freestone.[1]

The State Library is a fireproof building in the rear of the State House and connected with it by a long corridor. It is built of brick and iron and faced on its two fronts with brown freestone. It is already nearly filled with books, manuscripts, and maps, which the State has been collecting for many years.[2]

The State Hall, situated upon Eagle Street, fronting the Academy Park, was finished in 1842. It is built of cut stone, with a colonnade in front, supported by six Ionic columns, and is surmounted by a dome.[3] It contains the offices of the Secretary of State, Comptroller, Treasurer, Auditor of Canal Department, Canal Appraisers, Canal Commissioners, State Engineer and Surveyor, Division Engineers, Clerk of Court of Appeals, Superintendent of Public Instruction, Superintendent of Bank Department, Attorney General, and State Sealer of Weights and Measures.

The State Geological and Agricultural Hall, corner of State and Lodge Sts., is the depository of the specimens collected during the geological survey, and also contains the cabinet of the State Agricultural Society.[4]

---

[1] It is 90 feet broad, 50 high, and was originally 115 feet long. In 1854, 15 feet were added to the w. end. The eastern front has an Ionic portico with four columns of Berkshire marble each 3 feet 8 inches in diameter and 33 feet high. The north and south fronts have each a pediment of 65 feet base; and the doorways are decorated with columns and angular pediments of freestone. The entrance hall is 40 by 50 feet and 16 feet high, the ceiling of which is supported by a double row of reeded columns, and the floor is vaulted and laid with squares of Italian marble. Upon the north side of the hall are the office of Adjutant General and the Assembly Library, and on the south side the Executive Chambers. The remainder of the first story is devoted to the Assembly Chamber with its lobbies and postoffice. This chamber is now 56 by 65 feet and 28 feet high. The Speaker's desk is on the w. side, and the desks of the clerks are upon each side and in front of it. Desks of members are arranged in semi-circles in front. Upon the E. side is a gallery supported by iron pillars. The ceiling is richly ornamented in stucco. Over the Speaker's seat is a copy by Ames of a full length portrait of Stewart's Washington. In the second story, over the entrance hall, is the Senate chamber, 40 by 50 feet and 22 feet high. The President's desk is upon the s. side, and the desks of the Senators are arranged in a circle in front. On the N. side are the library and cloak room of the Senate, and on the s. the postoffice and room of the Sergeant at Arms. Over the President's seat is a crimson canopy, and opposite are the portraits of Gov. Clinton and Columbus. The latter was presented to the Senate in 1784 by Mrs. Farmer, a grand-daughter of Gov. Leisler, and had been in her family 150 years. Over the Assembly lobbies is the room of the Court of Appeals, and in the third story are the consultation rooms of this court, committee rooms of both houses, and part of the Senate Library. The courtroom of the Court of Appeals contains portraits of Chancellors Lansing, Sandford, Jones, and Walworth, Chief Justice Spencer, Abraham Van Vechten, and Daniel Cady. The inner Executive Chamber has a full size portrait of Gen. La Fayette, painted when he was in the city in 1825.
The roof of the State house is pyramidal, and from the center rises a circular cupola 20 feet in diameter, supporting a hemispherical dome upon 8 insulated Ionic columns. Upon the dome stands a wooden statue of Themis, 11 feet high, holding in her right hand a sword and in her left a balance.
[2] The State Library was founded April 21, 1818, and for nearly forty years was kept in the upper rooms of the Capitol. Its growth was comparatively slow until 1844, when its supervision was transferred from the State officers who had been ex-officio trustees to the Regents of the University. Their Secretary, the late Dr. T. Romeyn Beck, was eminently fitted for the task of building up an institution of this character. The library at the time of the transfer contained about 10,000 volumes. The number has increased during the subsequent 15 years to about 53,000. The present building, erected in 1853-54, is 114 feet long by 45 broad, was built at a cost of $91,900, and opened to the public Jan. 2, 1855. The first floor is supported by stone pillars and groined arches, and the second floor and galleries by arched spans of iron filled with concrete. The roof, rafters, trusses, pillars, shelves, and principal doors are of iron, and the floors are paved with colored tile. The first story is devoted to the law department, and the second story to the general library, including a large number of costly presents from other Governments, a valuable series of MSS. and parchments relating to our colonial and early State history, and an extensive collection of medals and coins. The office of the Regents of the University is in the library building.
The library, formerly known as the "Chancellors' Library,"
was divided in 1849, and, with additions since made, now forms two public libraries, called the "Libraries of the Court of Appeals," one of which is located at Syracuse and the other at Rochester. They consist chiefly of law books, and are in charge of librarians appointed by the Regents and paid by the State. There is also a small library, for reference, in the consultation room of the Court of Appeals. Each of the judges of the Supreme Court and the Vice Chancellor of the Second District, under the late Constitution, held libraries owned by the State, which are for the use of the four judges of the Court of Appeals elected by the people of the State at large, and their successors in office. There is also a small library for the use of the Attorney General; and means are annually provided for the increase of each of these collections, chiefly from the income of moneys known as the "Chancellors' Library Fund" and "Interest Fund," which are kept invested by the Clerk of the Court of Appeals for this purpose.
[3] This building is 138 by 88 feet and 65 feet high. The ceilings of the basement and of the two principal stories are groined arches, and all the rooms, excepting in the attic story, are fireproof. The basement and attic are each 19 feet, and the two principal stories each 22 feet, high. The building cost about $350,000.
[4] In 1842 the old State Hall was converted into a geological hall, and rooms were assigned in the same building to the State Agricultural Society. The old building was torn down, and the present Geological and Agricultural Hall erected in its place, in the summer of 1855. The Agricultural Rooms were dedicated Feb. 12, 1857, and the Cabinet was opened to the public Feb. 22, 1858. The present building is of brick, and is 4 stories high, besides the basement. In the rear is a spacious wing, of the same height as the main building. It contains a lecture room, the spacious geological cabinet, and the rooms of the State Geological Society. The basement is occupied by a taxidermist and a janitor. The building itself is subject to the order of the Commissioners of the Land Office. The Cabinet originated in the Geological Survey, and in extent and value it ranks among the first in America. Within the past year a series of English fossils has been given to the State by the British Government; and a valuable collection of shells, embracing several thousand species, has been recently presented and arranged by Philip P. Carpenter, an English naturalist. The Museum is designed to embrace a complete representation of the geological formations of the State, with their accompanying minerals and fossils, and of its entire native flora and fauna. The birds and quadrupeds are preserved by a skilful taxidermist, with the attitudes and appearance of life; and the reptiles and fishes are principally preserved in alcohol. Connected with this cabinet is a historical and antiquarian department, embracing numerous aboriginal antiquities and specimens of modern Indian art, relics of battle fields, and other objects of historical interest. The whole is under the charge of a curator appointed by the Regents. The museum of the State Agricultural Society, in a separate department of the building, contains a large collection of obsolete and modern implements of husbandry, specimens of agricultural and mechanical products, models of fruits, samples of grains and soils, drawings illustrating subjects connected with the useful arts; and it is designed to include an extensive collection of insects, made with especial reference to showing their influence upon the fruit and grain crops of the State. The entomological department is in charge of Dr. Asa Fitch, who has been for several years employed by the society in studying the habits of destructive insects, with the view to ascertaining the means of preventing their ravages. The whole of these collections are open to the public on every weekday except holidays. The meetings of the Executive Committee of the State Agricultural Society, and the winter fairs, are held in their rooms in this building.

STATE GOVERNMENT.

The State Government consists of the Legislative, Executive, Judicial, and Administrative Departments; the powers and duties of the several officers being defined by the Constitution and regulated by law.

LEGISLATIVE DEPARTMENT.

The State Legislature is composed of a Senate and Assembly.

The SENATE consists of 32 members, chosen by single districts every two years, the whole number being chosen at once. The Lieut. Governor is *ex officio* President of the Senate, and has a casting vote in case of a tie. The Senate appoints a President *pro tem.*, who presides in the absence of the Lieut. Governor, and becomes *ex officio* Lieut. Governor in case of a vacancy in that office. The Senate with the Judges of the Court of Appeals forms a court for the trial of impeachments, and it ratifies or rejects the nominations of the Governor to a great number of offices.

The Senate elects the following officers: a clerk, sergeant-at-arms, assistant sergeant-at-arms, doorkeeper and assistants, librarian, and such other officers as may be deemed necessary.[1]

The ASSEMBLY consists of 128 members, elected annually by single districts. The districts are re-apportioned once in ten years, after the State census is taken. The Speaker, or Presiding Officer of the Assembly, is elected by the members from their number, and usually appoints all committees. All bills upon financial matters must originate in the Assembly.

The Assembly elects the following officers: a Speaker, clerk, sergeant-at-arms, doorkeeper and two assistants. The Speaker appoints an assistant sergeant-at-arms, a postmaster and assistant, a janitor, keeper of the Assembly chamber, and several doorkeepers and pages.[2]

---

[1] The sergeant-at-arms is also librarian. The clerk appoints his deputies and assistants, and the President appoints a janitor, superintendent of the Senate chamber, and pages. Committees are usually appointed by the Lieut. Gov. The appointments are made for two years. About half a dozen reporters are admitted to seats within the Senate chamber. Standing committees in the Senate consist of 3 members.

SENATE DISTRICTS.

1. Queens, Richmond, and Suffolk Counties.
2. 1st, 2d, 3d, 4th, 5th, 7th, 11th, 13th, and 19th Wards of Brooklyn.
3. 6th, 8th, 9th, 10th, 12th, 14th, 15th, 16th, 17th, and 18th Wards of Brooklyn, and the towns of Kings County.
4. 1st, 2d, 3d, 4th, 5th, 6th, 7th, 8th, and 14th Wards of New York.
5. 10th, 11th, 13th, and 17th Wards of New York.
6. 9th, 15th, 16th, and 18th Wards of New York.
7. 12th, 19th, 20th, 21st, and 22d Wards of New York.
8. Putnam, Rockland, and Westchester Counties.
9. Orange and Sullivan Counties.
10. Greene and Ulster Counties.
11. Columbia and Dutchess Counties.
12. Rensselaer and Washington Counties.
13. Albany County.
14. Delaware, Schenectady, and Schoharie Counties.
15. Fulton, Hamilton, Montgomery, and Saratoga Counties.
16. Clinton, Essex, and Warren Counties.
17. Franklin and St. Lawrence Counties.
18. Jefferson and Lewis Counties.
19. Oneida County.
20. Herkimer and Otsego Counties.
21. Oswego County.
22. Onondaga County.
23. Chenango, Cortland, and Madison Counties.
24. Broome, Tioga, and Tompkins Counties.
25. Cayuga and Wayne Counties.
26. Ontario, Seneca, and Yates Counties.
27. Chemung, Schuyler, and Steuben Counties.
28. Monroe County.
29. Genesee, Niagara, and Orleans Counties.
30. Allegany, Livingston, and Wyoming Counties.
31. Erie County.
32. Cattaraugus and Chautauqua Counties.

[2] The clerk appoints his assistants and deputies, a librarian and assistant, a bank clerk, and a clerk's messenger. These officers are appointed for the session, except pages, who are changed in the middle of each session. Standing committees of the Assembly consist of 5 members, except those upon Ways and Means, the Judiciary, and Canals, each of which has 7 members. About 20 reporters are admitted and provided with seats within the bar. They usually share with members in extra appropriations for books, and in the privilege of mailing documents at the public expense.

ASSEMBLY DISTRICTS.

[Those Counties not enumerated in this list form but one District. Fulton and Hamilton form one District.]

ALBANY COUNTY.—FOUR DISTRICTS.

1. 1st Ward of Albany, Bethlehem, Coeymans, New Scotland, Rensselaerville, and Westerlo.
2. 9th and 10th Wards of Albany, Bern, Guilderland, and Knox.
3. 2d, 3d, 4th, 5th, 6th, and 8th Wards of Albany.
4. 7th Ward of Albany and Watervliet.

ALLEGANY COUNTY.—TWO DISTRICTS.

1. Allen, Almond, Angelica, Belfast, Birdsall, Burns, Caneadea, Centerville, Granger, Grove, Hume, New Hudson, Rushford, and West Almond.
2. Alfred, Alma, Amity, Andover, Bolivar, Clarksville, Cuba, Friendship, Genesee, Independence, Scio, Ward, Wellsville, Willing, and Wirt.

CATTARAUGUS COUNTY.—TWO DISTRICTS.

1. Allegany, Ashford, Carrolton, Elgin, Farmersville, Franklinville, Freedom, Hinsdale, Humphrey, Ischua, Machias, Olean, Portville, and Yorkshire.

The sessions of the Legislature commence on the first Tuesday in January, and members can only receive pay for 100 days. The business of each year begins *de novo;* but if an extra session is called by the Governor, bills are taken up where they were left at the last previous adjournment. Each house decides upon the qualifications of its own members; and both houses must concur in the election of U. S. Senators, Regents of the University, and Superintendent of Public Instruction. Bills, except measures of finance, may originate in either house, and must be

2. Bucktooth, Coldspring, Connewango, Dayton, Ellicottville, East Otto, Great Valley, Leon, Little Valley, Mansfield, Napoli, New Albion, Otto, Perrysburgh, Persia, Randolph, and South Valley.

CAYUGA COUNTY.—Two Districts.

1. Brutus, Cato, Conquest, Ira, Mentz, Montezuma, Sennett, Sterling, Throop, Victory, and the 1st and 4th Wards of Auburn.
2. Aurelius, Fleming, Genoa, Ledyard, Locke, Moravia, Niles, Owasco, Scipio, Sempronius, Springport, Summer Hill, Venice, and the 2d and 3d Wards of Auburn.

CHAUTAUQUA COUNTY.—Two Districts.

1. Busti, Chautauqua, Clymer, Ellery, French Creek, Harmony, Mina, Portland, Ripley, Sherman, Stockton, and Westfield.
2. Arkwright, Carroll, Charlotte, Cherry Creek, Ellicott, Ellington, Gerry, Hanover, Kiantone, Poland, Pomfret, Sheridan, and Villenova.

CHENANGO COUNTY.—Two Districts.

1. Columbus, Lincklaen, New Berlin, North Norwich, Norwich, Otselic, Pharsalia, Pitcher, Plymouth, Sherburne, and Smyrna.
2. Afton, Bainbridge, Coventry, German, Guilford, Greene, McDonough, Oxford, Preston, and Smithville.

COLUMBIA COUNTY.—Two Districts.

1. Ancram, Claverack, Clermont, Copake, Gallatin, Germantown, Greenport, Hudson City, Livingston, and Taghkanick.
2. Austerlitz, Canaan, Chatham, Ghent, Hillsdale, Kinderhook, New Lebanon, Stockport, and Stuyvesant.

DELAWARE COUNTY.—Two Districts.

1. Colchester, Delhi, Franklin, Hamden, Hancock, Masonville, Sidney, Tompkins, and Walton.
2. Andes, Bovina, Davenport, Harpersfield, Kortright, Meredith, Middleton, Roxbury, and Stamford.

DUTCHESS COUNTY.—Two Districts.

1. Amenia, Beekman, Dover, East Fishkill, La Grange, Northeast, Pawling, Pine Plains, Stanford, Union Vale, and Washington.
2. Clinton, Hyde Park, Milan, Pleasant Valley, Poughkeepsie, City of Poughkeepsie, Red Hook, and Rhinebeck.

ERIE COUNTY.—Four Districts.

1. 1st, 2d, 3d, 4th, 5th, and 13th Wards of Buffalo.
2. 6th, 7th, 8th, 9th, 10th, 11th, and 12th Wards of Buffalo.
3. Alden, Amherst, Chicktawauga, Clarence, Elma, Grand Island, Hamburgh, Lancaster, Marilla, Newstead, Tonawanda, and West Seneca.
4. Aurora, Boston, Brandt, Colden, Collins, Concord, East Hamburgh, Eden, Evans, Holland, North Collins, Sardinia, and Wales.

HERKIMER COUNTY.—Two Districts.

1. Fairfield, Herkimer, Little Falls, Manheim, Newport, Norway, Ohio, Russia, Salisbury, and Wilmurt.
2. Columbia, Danube, Frankfort, German Flats, Litchfield, Schuyler, Stark, Warren, and Winfield.

JEFFERSON COUNTY.—Three Districts.

1. Adams, Brownville, Ellisburgh, Henderson, Hounsfield, Lorraine, Rodman, and Worth.
2. Antwerp, Champion, Le Ray, Philadelphia, Rutland, Watertown, and Wilna.
3. Alexandria, Cape Vincent, Clayton, Lyme, Orleans, Pamelia, and Theresa.

KINGS COUNTY.—Seven Districts.

1. Flatbush, Flatlands, Gravesend, New Lots, New Utrecht, and the 8th, 17th, and 18th Wards of Brooklyn.
2. 1st, 6th, and 12th Wards of Brooklyn.
3. 4th and 10th Wards of Brooklyn.
4. 2d, 3d, and 5th Wards of Brooklyn.
5. 9th and 11th Wards of Brooklyn.
6. 13th, 14th, and part of 19th Wards of Brooklyn.
7. 7th, 15th, 16th, and part of 19th Wards of Brooklyn.

LIVINGSTON COUNTY.—Two Districts.

1. Avon, Caledonia, Conesus, Geneseo, Groveland, Leicester, Lima, Livonia, and York.
2. Mount Morris, North Dansville, Nunda, Ossian, Portage, Sparta, Springwater, and West Sparta.

MADISON COUNTY.—Two Districts.

1. Brookfield, De Ruyter, Eaton, Georgetown, Hamilton, Lebanon, Madison, and Nelson.
2. Cazenovia, Fenner, Lenox, Smithfield, Stockbridge, and Sullivan.

MONROE COUNTY.—Three Districts.

1. Brighton, Henrietta, Irondequoit, Mendon, Penfield, Perinton, Pittsford, Rush, and Webster.
2. The City of Rochester.
3. Chili, Clarkson, Gates, Greece, Ogden, Parma, Riga, Sweden, Union, and Wheatland.

NEW YORK CITY AND COUNTY.—Seventeen Districts.

17 districts, corresponding to Aldermanic districts.

NIAGARA COUNTY.—Two Districts.

1. Lockport, Pendleton, Royalton, and Wheatfield.
2. Cambria, Hartland, Lewiston, Newfane, Niagara, Porter, Somerset, and Wilson.

ONEIDA COUNTY.—Four Districts.

1. Deerfield, City of Utica, and Whitestown.
2. Augusta, Bridgewater, Kirkland, Marshall, New Hartford, Paris, Sangerfield, Vernon, and Westmoreland.
3. Camden, Florence, Rome, Verona, and Vienna.
4. Amesville, Ava, Brownville, Floyd, Lee, Marcy, Remsen, Steuben, Trenton, and Western.

ONONDAGA COUNTY.—Three Districts.

1. Camillus, Clay, Elbridge, Lysander, Marcellus, Skaneateles, Spafford, and Van Buren.
2. Cicero, Salina, and Syracuse.
3. De Witt, Fabius, Geddes, La Fayette, Manlius, Onondaga, Otisco, Pompey, and Tully.

ONTARIO COUNTY.—Two Districts.

1. Farmington, Gorham, Hopewell, Manchester, Phelps, and Seneca.
2. Bristol, Canadice, Canandaigua, East Bloomfield, Naples, Richmond, South Bristol, Victor, and West Bloomfield.

ORANGE COUNTY.—Two Districts.

1. Blooming Grove, Chester, Cornwall, Monroe, Montgomery, Newburgh, and New Windsor.
2. Crawford, Deerpark, Goshen, Greenville, Hamptonburgh, Minisink, Mount Hope, Walkill, Warwick, and Wawayanda.

OSWEGO COUNTY.—Three Districts.

1. City of Oswego, Hannibal, Oswego, and Scriba.
2. Constantia, Granby, Hastings, Palermo, Schroeppel, Volney, and West Monroe.
3. Albion, Amboy, Boyleston, Mexico, Orwell, Parish, Redfield, Richland, Sandy Creek, New Haven, and Williamstown.

OTSEGO COUNTY.—Two Districts.

1. Cherry Valley, Decatur, Exeter, Maryland, Middlefield, Otsego, Plainfield, Richfield, Roseboom, Springfield, Westford, and Worcester.
2. Unadilla, Burlington, Butternuts, Edmeston, Hartwick, Laurens, Milford, Morris, New Lisbon, Otego, Oneonta, and Pittsfield.

QUEENS COUNTY.—Two Districts.

1. Flushing, North Hempstead, and Oyster Bay.
2. Hempstead, Jamaica, and Newtown.

RENSSELAER COUNTY.—Three Districts.

1. City of Troy.
2. Berlin, Grafton, Hoosick, Lansingburgh, Petersburgh, Pittstown, and Schaghticoke.
3. Brunswick, Clinton, Greenbush, Nassau, North Greenbush, Poestenkill, Sand Lake, Schodack, and Stephentown.

ST. LAWRENCE COUNTY.—Three Districts.

1. De Kalb, De Peyster, Fine, Fowler, Gouverneur, Macomb, Morristown, Oswegatchie, Pitcairn, and Rossie.
2. Canton, Colton, Edwards, Hermon, Lisbon, Madrid, Norfolk, Pierrepont, and Russell.
3. Brasher, Hopkinton, Lawrence, Louisville, Massena, Parishville, Potsdam, and Stockholm.

SARATOGA COUNTY.—Two Districts.

1. Ballston, Charlton, Clifton Park, Galway, Halfmoon, Malta, Milton, Stillwater, and Waterford.
2. Corinth, Day, Edinburgh, Greenfield, Hadley, Moreau, Northumberland, Providence, Saratoga, Saratoga Springs, and Wilton.

passed by both, and receive the signature of the Governor,—or, if vetoed by him, the votes of two-thirds of both houses,—to become laws. The original laws of the Legislature, bearing the signatures of the presiding officer of each house and of the Governor and Secretary of State, are bound, and preserved in the Secretary's office. All general laws are published in such newspapers in each county as may be designated by the Board of Supervisors.

Besides the State Legislature, a limited power of enacting laws is possessed by the boards of supervisors in the several counties, by the common councils of cities, and by citizens generally assembled in town and school district meetings.

The Board of Supervisors meets annually at the county seat, on the week following the general election, to canvass the votes for State and county officers; it may hold special meetings at any time. It has power to appoint a clerk of the board, a county sealer of weights and measures, special commissioners for laying out roads, printers for publishing the general laws, inspectors of turnpike and plank roads, and, in some counties, the Superintendent of the Poor, and other officers, and to fix the salaries of the county Judge and Surrogate, and of School Commissioners, (above $500, allowed by law,) and, in some counties, the salary of the District Attorney; to establish the bounds of assembly and school commissioner districts, to fix upon town meeting days,[1] to make orders concerning property owned by the county, and to repair or rebuild the county buildings; to audit and settle charges against the county, and the accounts of town officers; to equalize assessments and levy taxes to meet county expenses, and for such special purposes as may be directed by law. It also has power to alter the bounds of towns, and to erect new towns; to change the location of the county seat and purchase sites for the erection of new buildings; and to examine annually the securities held by loan commissioners. It may pass laws for the preservation of game or fish, and for the destruction of noxious animals, and perform such other duties as may be from time to time authorized by law.

STEUBEN COUNTY.—THREE DISTRICTS.

1. Avoca, Bath, Bradford, Conhocton, Prattsburgh, Pulteney, Urbana, Wayne, and Wheeler.
2. Addison, Cameron, Campbell, Caton, Corning, Erwin, Hornby, Lindley, Rathbone, Thurston, and Woodhull.
3. Canisteo, Dansville, Fremont, Greenwood, Hornellsville, Howard. Hartsville, Jasper, Troupsburgh, West Union, and Wayland.

SUFFOLK COUNTY.—TWO DISTRICTS.

1. East Hampton, Riverhead, Shelter Island, Southampton, and Southold.
2. Brookhaven, Huntington, Islip, and Smithtown.

ULSTER COUNTY.—THREE DISTRICTS.

1. Hurley, Kingston, and Saugerties.
2. Esopus, Gardiner, Lloyd, Marbletown, Marlborough, New Paltz, Plattekill. Rosendale, and Shawangunk.
3. Denning, Hardenburgh, Olive, Rochester, Shandaken, Wawarsing, and Woodstock.

WASHINGTON COUNTY.—TWO DISTRICTS.

1. Argyle, Cambridge. Easton, Fort Edward, Greenwich, Jackson, Salem, and White Creek.
2. Dresden, Fort Ann, Granville, Hampton, Hartford, Hebron, Kingsbury, Putnam, and Whitehall.

WAYNE COUNTY.—TWO DISTRICTS.

1. Butler, Galen, Huron, Lyons, Rose, Savannah, Sodus, and Wolcott.
2. Arcadia, Macedon, Marion, Ontario, Palmyra, Walworth, and Williamson.

WESTCHESTER COUNTY.—THREE DISTRICTS.

1. East Chester, Morrisania, Westchester, West Farms, and Yonkers.
2. Greenburgh, Harrison, Mamaroneck, Mount Pleasant, New Rochelle, North Castle, Pelham, Poundridge, Rye, Scarsdale, and White Plains.
3. Bedford, Cortlandt, Lewisboro, New Castle, North Salem, Ossining, Somers, and Yorktown.

[1] TOWN MEETINGS.

Town meetings are held on the same day throughout the county; and the time may be changed once in 3 years. The town meetings must come between the 1st day of Feb. and the 1st of May. They are at present all held on Tuesdays, as follows:—

COUNTIES.	Tuesdays upon which Town Meetings are held.	COUNTIES.	Tuesdays upon which Town Meetings are held.	COUNTIES.	Tuesdays upon which Town Meetings are held.
Albany.......	2d in April.	Herkimer....	1st in March.	Richmond ...	2d in Feb.
Allegany. ...	2d in March.	Jefferson	3d in Feb.	Rockland.....	2d in April.
Broome......	2d in Feb.	Kings.........	1st in April.	St. Lawrence	2d in Feb.
Cattaraugus	Last in Feb.	Lewis	3d in Feb.	Saratoga	1st in March.
Cayuga	1st after 1st Mon. in Mar.	Livingston...	1st in April.	Schenectady	1st in April.
Chautauqua	3d in Feb.	Madison......	1st in March.	Schoharie ...	3d in Feb.
Chemung....	2d after 1st Mon. in Feb.	Monroe......	1st after 1st Mon. in Mar.	Schuyler	2d in Feb.
Chenango...	1st in March.	Montgomery	2d in Feb.	Seneca	2d in March.
Clinton.......	1st in March.	New York...		Steuben......	2d in Feb.
Columbia....	1st in March.	Niagara	2d in April.	Suffolk........	1st in April.
Cortland	3d in Feb.	Oneida........	1st in March.	Sullivan......	1st after 1st Mon. in Mar.
Delaware.....	2d in Feb.	Onondaga....	3d in Feb.	Tioga	1st in Feb.
Dutchess.....	2d in March.	Ontario.......	1st after 1st Mon. in April.	Tompkins ...	1st in April.
Erie	1st in March.	Orange........	1st in March.	Ulster.........	1st in March.
Essex..........	1st in March.	Orleans.......	1st in April.	Warren........	1st in April.
Franklin.....	1st in Feb.	Oswego.......	1st in March.	Washington	1st in March.
Fulton........	2d in Feb.	Otsego........	1st in March.	Wayne........	1st in March.
Genesee......	1st in March.	Putnam......	1st after 1st Mon. in April.	Westchester	Last in March.
Greene........	1st in Feb.	Queens.......	1st in April.	Wyoming....	Last in Feb.
Hamilton ...	1st in Feb.	Rensselaer...	1st in March.	Yates	Last in Feb.

At these meetings are elected, by ballot, a supervisor, town clerk, 4 justices, (with exceptions named on page 34, 3 assessors, (for 3 years, 1 annually,) a collector, 1 or 2 overseers of poor, (at the option of the town, excepting Montgomery and Kings cos. that are not included in the general law,) 1 or 3 commissioners of highways, (if 3, one elected annually for 3 years,) not more than 5 constables and 2 inspectors of election for each election district, a third being appointed by the presiding officer of the town meetings from the two having the next highest vote. The town of Manlius elects 7 constables. Each town at its annual meeting also elects by ayes and noes, or otherwise, as many overseers of highways as there are road districts, and as many pound masters as the electors may determine.

The Common Council in each of the cities has jurisdiction over municipal affairs within limits fixed by law, and observes the usual formalities of legislative bodies in its proceedings. Two aldermen are generally elected from each ward, who, with the mayor, constitute the Common Council; but the organization of no two cities is in this respect exactly alike.[1] The enactments of the Common Council are usually termed "ordinances," and have the force of law. The council usually has the appointment of a large class of minor city officers, including the keepers of parks and public buildings, inspectors of various kinds, and in some instances the officers and members of the police and fire departments. These appointments are usually held at the pleasure of the appointing power.

Town Meetings may pass laws regulating roads and bridges, the height of fences, the support of the poor, the range of animals, the destruction of noxious weeds, the preservation of town property, and for such other purposes as may be directed by special acts. Every town is a corporate body, may sue and be sued, may hold and convey lands within its limits for purposes specified by law, and may appropriate moneys for public objects within the town.

School Districts, at regular meetings, may pass rules concerning the support of schools, employment of teachers, repairs, supplies, and similar affairs, which have the force of law.

EXECUTIVE DEPARTMENT.

The Governor is elected once in two years.[2] He is commander-in-chief of the military and naval forces of the State, and possesses the sole power of granting pardons and commutations of sentence after conviction.[3] He issues requisitions for the return of criminals in other States, and he is authorized to offer rewards for the arrest of criminals within this State. He annually communicates to the Legislature, at the commencement of each session, a statement of the condition of the public departments, and such other matters as he may deem necessary. On extraordinary occasions he may convene the Senate or Legislature.[4] Within ten days after its passage by the Legislature, he may veto any act, by returning it to the house in which it originated, with his objections; and such act can become a law only by the concurrence of two-thirds of both houses.[5]

The Governor nominates, for appointment by the Senate, a large class of State and county and a few military officers,[6] and may fill vacancies occurring in these offices during the recess of the Senate. Some other classes of officers are appointed by the Governor alone,—generally for specific terms, but in some cases during pleasure. He may also fill vacancies occurring in elective offices, and

---

[1] In New York, the Common Council consists of two branches,—the Board of Aldermen, consisting of 17 members, chosen for 2 years; and the Board of Councilmen, consisting of 24 members, chosen annually, 6 from each senatorial district. Each of these branches elects one of its own number president; and the mayor possesses a veto power upon their laws analogous to that of the Governor upon those of the State Legislature.

[2] To be eligible to the office of Governor a person must be a citizen of the U. S., a resident of the State for the last 5 years previous to election, and must have attained the age of 30 years. The colonial governors of N. Y. were appointed by the crown. Under the Constitution of 1777 they were elected for 3 years and were required to be freeholders. Under the Constitution of 1822, the governor was elected for 2 years, and, in addition to the present qualifications, was required to be a native of the U. S. and a freeholder.

Under the first State Constitution electors were classified, and only those owning freehold property worth $250 and upward were allowed to vote for Senators and Governor. The aggregate of the several classes at different periods has been as follows:—

YEARS.	Worth $250 and upward.	Worth $50 to $250.	Not Freeholders, but renting tenements worth $5.	Other electors.	Total.
1790........	19,369	23,425	14,674	138	57,606
1795........	36,338	4,838	22,598	243	64,017
1801........	52,058	5,264	28,522	63	85,907
1807........	71,159	5,800	44,330	88	121,289
1814........	87,491	5,231	59,104	20	151,846
1821........	100,490	8,985	93,035	20	202,510

[3] In cases of treason and impeachment the Governor can only suspend sentence until the next session of the Legislature, that body alone possessing the pardoning power in such cases. Under the Constitution of 1777, the same restriction was applied in cases of murder.

[4] He also possessed under the Constitution of 1777 the power to prorogue the Legislature for a period not exceeding 60 days in one year. This was once done by Gov. Tompkins, to defeat the passage of a bank charter, but without success.

[5] The first court created a council of revision, consisting of the Governor, Chancellor, and judges of the Supreme Court, who sat with closed doors and observed the usual formalities of legislative proceedings. During the continuance of this council it rejected 144 bills, several of which became laws notwithstanding.

[6] The following officers are appointed by the Governor and Senate: 1 Superintendent of Bank Department, 1 Auditor of Canal Department, 3 Canal Appraisers, 1 Superintendent of Onondaga Salt Springs, 6 Commissioners of Emigration, 5 Commissioners of Metropolitan Police, 11 Harbor Masters, 9 Wardens of the Port of N. Y., 2 Special Wardens to reside at Quarantine, 1 Harbor Master at Albany, 1 Health Officer at Quarantine, 1 Physician of Marine Hospital and not less than 4 assistants, 1 Resident Physician and 1 Health Commissioner for the city of New York, 1 Agent for the Onondaga Nation, 1 Attorney to Seneca Nation, directors in certain banks of which the State holds stock according to the amount held, as many Hellgate pilots as the Board of Wardens may recommend, 5 trustees of the Idiot Asylum, 9 trustees of State Lunatic Asylum, 2 commissioners in each co. for loaning moneys of the United States, as many notaries public as the law may allow or the Governor determine, and such other officers and special commissioners as are required from time to time by law. He appoints field officers of regiments and generals of brigades, when such regiments and brigades are not fully organized. Under the first constitution, almost every civil and military office was filled by the Council of Appointment, consisting of the Governor and 4 Senators, chosen annually by the Assembly. In 1821, 8,287

may remove, under limitations prescribed by statute, most State and county officers.[1] He has a private secretary, with a salary of $2000, a clerk and a doorkeeper.

The Lieutenant Governor is elected at the same time as the Governor, and must possess the same qualifications. He discharges the duties of Governor when a vacancy occurs in that office. He is President of the Senate, having the casting vote in that body, a Commissioner of the Canal Fund and of the Land Office, a member of the Canal Board, a trustee of the Idiot Asylum and of Union College, a Regent of the University, and a trustee of the Capitol and State Hall.

The Secretary of State[2] is keeper of the State archives; is a Regent of the University, a Commissioner of the Land Office and of the Canal Fund, a member of the Canal Board and of the Board of State Canvassers, a trustee of the State Idiot Asylum, of Union College, of the Capitol, and of the State Hall. He has specific duties in relation to the publication and distribution of the laws; the issuing of patents for land, of commissions, pardons, and peddlers' licenses; the filing of the declarations of aliens, and the articles of association of companies under general laws; issuing notices of elections, receiving and reporting statistics of pauperism and crime from sheriffs and county clerks, and furnishing certified copies of laws and other documents in his office. He administers the oath of office to members of the Assembly, and other State officers. His deputy is *ex officio* Clerk of the Commissioners of the Land Office.

The Comptroller[3] is the auditor of the public accounts, excepting those payable from the Canal and Bank Funds; a Commissioner of the Land Office and of the Canal Fund; a member of the Canal Board and of the Board of State Canvassers, and a trustee of the Idiot Asylum, of Union College, of the Capitol, and State Hall. He has responsible duties in relation to the payment of appropriations made by the Legislature, the collection of taxes, and sale of lands sold for taxes, the management of funds, supervision of fire and life insurance companies, loaning of moneys, and other duties connected with the finances of the State. He reports annually to the Legislature the condition of the public funds, the receipts and expenses of the State, the condition of insurance companies, and upon such other matters as he may from time to time be called upon by the Legislature for information. He has a deputy, an accountant, and about a dozen clerks.

The Treasurer[4] receives all moneys paid into the treasury, and pays all warrants of the Comptroller, Auditor of the Canal Department, Superintendent of the Bank Department, and Superintendent of Public Instruction. He is a Commissioner of the Land Office and of the Canal Fund, a member of the Canal Board and of the Board of State Canvassers, and a trustee of Union College. He has a deputy, and two or three clerks.

The Attorney General[5] is the legal prosecutor and adviser in behalf of the State. He is a

---

military and 6,663 civil officers held under this appointment, and most of them at will. From 1822 to 1846, the Governor and Senate appointed, in addition to most of those it now appoints, all judicial officers, except justices, Masters and Examiners in Chancery, Supreme Court Commissioners, inspectors for commercial purposes, Commissioners of Deeds, several city officers, and State Prison Inspectors.

[1] Representatives in Congress and members of the State Legislature can be elected only. The Governor appoints, on his own authority, Commissioners for taking acknowledgments of Deeds in other States and countries, wreck masters, and certain commissioners directed to be appointed for special purposes.

[2] The Secretary of State was formerly Clerk of the Council of Appointment and of the Council of Revision, and from 1823 to 1854 was Superintendent of Schools. In colonial times he was appointed by the crown; from 1777 to 1822, by the Council of Appointment; and from 1822 to 1846, by the Legislature.

[3] This office was created in 1797, in place of that of Auditor General, formed by the Provincial Convention; but it was not permanently organized until 1812. The Comptroller was appointed by the Council of Appointment until 1822, when the appointing power was changed to the Legislature and the tenure of the office fixed at 3 years.

[4] The office of Treasurer, under the colonial government and early years of State government, was a very important one; and for many years after 1777, the Treasurer was appointed by special act from year to year. About the beginning of the present

century, the defalcation of a Treasurer occasioned a revision of the law creating the department; and, from his being the principal financial officer of the government, the Treasurer became the most unimportant, and his powers were narrowed down to the payment of the drafts of other officers. For many years previous to 1822 he was appointed by the Council of Revision; and from 1822 to 1846, by the Legislature. The accounts of the Treasurer are annually compared with those of the Comptroller, Superintendent of Bank Department, and Auditor of the Canal Department, by a commissioner appointed for the purpose; and these officers thus become a check upon each other. The Treasurer may be suspended for cause, by the Governor, in the recess of the Legislature.

[5] This office has existed almost from the beginning of the Colonial Government. It was filled by the Council of Appointment from 1777 to 1822, and by the Legislature, with a term of 3 years, from 1822 to 1846. The Attorney General originally attended the circuits of Oyer and Terminer, as prosecutor in criminal suits, until 1796, when the State was divided into 8 districts, to each of which an assistant Attorney General was appointed, except in New York, where the head officer officiated personally. In 1818 each co. was made a separate district, and a District Attorney was appointed in each. The Attorney General still occasionally attends upon important criminal trials; but his time is chiefly occupied in civil suits in which the State is a party.

Commissioner of the Land Office and of the Canal Fund, a member of the Canal Board and of the Board of State Canvassers, and a trustee of Union College, of the Capitol, and State Hall. He has a deputy and a clerk.

The State Engineer and Surveyor[1] has charge of the engineering department of the canals and such land surveys as involve the interests of the State. He reports annually the statistics of these departments and of railroads. He is a Commissioner of the Land Office, a member of the Canal Board and Board of State Canvassers, and a trustee of Union College and the State Hall. He must be a practical engineer. He is assisted by a deputy and 3 clerks.

JUDICIAL DEPARTMENT.

United States Courts.—The second of the U. S. Courts comprises New York, Vermont, and Connecticut. A court is held twice a year in each State by a Justice of the Supreme Court and the District Judge of the district in which the court sits.

The State of New York is divided into two Judicial Districts, in each of which is held a District Court.[2] The officers of this court in each district are a District Judge, Attorney, Marshal, and Clerk. In the Southern District a term is held in each month, at New York; and in the Northern District one term is held each year at Albany, Utica, Auburn, and Buffalo, and one term annually in St. Lawrence, Clinton, or Franklin co., as the Judge may direct.[3] These courts have nearly concurrent original jurisdiction in all matters in which the United States is a party; and they take cognizance of offenses against the laws of the U. S. An appeal lies from the District to the Circuit Court, and thence to the Supreme Court.

State Courts.—The State Courts consist of a Court for the Trial of Impeachments, the Court of Appeals, the Supreme Court and Court of Oyer and Terminer, the County Court and Court of Sessions, Justices' Courts, and City Courts.

The Court for the Trial of Impeachments consists of the Senate and the Judges of the Court of Appeals. Its judgments extend only to removal of officials and to disqualification for holding office.[4] Parties impeached are liable to all the penalties of the civil and criminal laws. This court is a court of record; its meetings are held at Albany.

The Court of Appeals,[5] instituted in 1847, is composed of 8 judges, 4 of whom are elected, (one every 2 years,) and 4 of whom are the Judges of the Supreme Court having the shortest term to serve. The judge elected having the shortest term to serve is Chief Judge; and 6 judges constitute a quorum. This court has power to correct and reverse all proceedings of the Supreme Court, or of the former Supreme Court, and Court of Chancery. It holds 4 terms a year at the Capital; and every 2 years one term must be held in each Judicial District. Its clerk has an office in the State Hall, where the records of this and former State and Colonial Courts are preserved. The State Reporter prepares for the press and publishes the decisions of the court, copies of which are sent to each county, and franked, under the Governor's hand, to each of the other States and Territories of the Union.

---

[1] This office takes the place of that of "*Surveyor General*," which existed under the colony. In the earlier years of the State Government, numerous and responsible duties were imposed upon this officer, under acts for the sale and settlement of lands, the adjustment of disputed titles, boundaries, and Indian claims, laying out roads, and business relating to the salt springs, reserved village plats, and other State property. These duties were discharged from 1784 to 1834 by Simeon De Witt, with great integrity and success.

The Secretary of State, Comptroller, Treasurer, Attorney General, and State Engineer are elected biennially at the same time,—their election occurring on alternate years from those of the election of the Governor and Lieut. Governor.

[2] *United States District Courts.*—There are two Districts within this State. The Southern District embraces Columbia, Greene, Ulster, Sullivan, and the counties South. The Northern District embraces the remainder of the State.

[3] The United States has caused or ordered buildings to be erected in part for the accommodation of these courts at New York, Utica, Buffalo, Ogdensburgh, Canandaigua, and Plattsburgh. These edifices are of the most substantial kind, and generally fireproof.

[4] This court has assembled but once. In 1853 it was convened for the trial of impeachment of John C. Mather, Canal Commissioner. He was acquitted.

[5] *Constitution, Art. VI, Sec. 2.* This court takes the place of the former "*Court for the Correction of Errors,*" and in some respects fills that of the old Supreme Court and Court of Chancery.

3

The Supreme Court.—The State is divided into 8 Judicial Districts,[1] in each of which, except the first, 4 justices are elected. The clerks of counties are clerks of this court. It has general jurisdiction in law and equity, and power to review the judgments of the County Courts and of the former Court of Common Pleas. This court has three distinct branches,—General Terms, Special Terms, and Circuits. The *General Term* held by three or more of the Supreme Judges, including the presiding judge, is an appellate court for the review of cases from the courts below, and for deciding solely upon questions of law. *Special Terms* are held by one Supreme Judge, without a jury, for the decision of equity cases; and *Circuit Courts* are held by one Supreme Judge, with a jury, for the trial of issues of fact. At least four general terms of this court are held in each district every year. Every county (except Hamilton) has at least one special and two circuit courts annually. A general term of the Supreme Court is held at the Capital in January of each alternate year, for the purpose of arranging the terms of all the Circuit Courts and Courts of Oyer and Terminer, of assigning the business and duties of the justices, and revising the rules of the court.

County Courts are held by the County Judge,[2] assisted by two justices of the peace elected annually for the purpose. The judge performs the duty of surrogate, except in counties where the population exceeds 40,000, in which the Legislature may provide for the election of a separate officer as surrogate.[3] The Legislature may direct the election of local officers, not exceeding two in any county, to discharge the duties of judge and surrogate in case of inability or vacancy in that office, and to exercise such other powers as may be provided by law.[4] Judges and surrogates receive a salary fixed by the Supervisors, and which cannot be increased during their term of office.

County Courts have jurisdiction in civil cases when the real estate, or all the defendants, or all the parties interested are within the co., and where the action of debt assumpsit or covenant claimed is not above $2,000, or in actions for injury to the person, or trespass upon property, where the damage claimed does not exceed $500; or in replevin suits where the value claimed is not above $1,000. These courts have equity jurisdiction for the foreclosure of mortgages, the sale of the real estate of infants, the partition of lands, admeasurement of dower, the satisfaction of judgments over $75, and the care and custody of lunatics and habitual drunkards. Surrogate's Courts are held by the County Judge or Surrogate, (in counties where the latter is elected,) and have the ordinary jurisdiction of Courts of Probate.

Justices' Courts are held by justices of the peace, who have jurisdiction in civil suits where the sum claimed does not exceed $100 in value.[5] They have jurisdiction in criminal cases for imposing fines to the amount of $50, and of inflicting imprisonment in the county jail for a term not exceeding 6 months.[6]

Tribunals of Conciliation may be established, and their powers and duties prescribed by law; but their judgments are not obligatory unless the parties previously agree to abide by such decision.[7]

City Courts. In each of the cities and in several of the larger villages are courts of local jurisdiction organized under special laws.[8]

---

[1] *New York State Judicial Districts under the Act of May 8, 1847:*—
1. City and County of New York.
2. Dutchess, Kings, Orange, Putnam, Queens, Richmond, Rockland, Suffolk, and Westchester Counties.
3. Albany, Columbia, Greene, Rensselaer, Schoharie, Sullivan, and Ulster Counties.
4. Clinton, Essex, Franklin, Fulton, Hamilton, Montgomery, St. Lawrence, Saratoga, Schenectady, Warren, and Washington Counties.
5. Herkimer, Jefferson, Lewis, Oneida, Onondaga, and Oswego Counties.
6. Broome, Chemung, Chenango, Cortland, Delaware, Madison, Otsego, Schuyler, Tioga, and Tompkins Counties.
7. Cayuga, Livingston, Monroe, Ontario, Seneca, Steuben, Wayne, and Yates Counties.
8. Allegany, Cattaraugus, Chautauqua, Erie, Genesee, Niagara, Orleans, and Wyoming Counties.

[2] From 1777 to 1822 Judges were appointed by the Council of Appointment; and from 1822 to 1846, by the Governor and Senate. One in each co. was styled "*First Judge;*" and a fixed number (subsequently 4) of others were called Judges.

[3] Surrogates are elected in Albany, Cayuga, Chautauqua, Columbia, Dutchess, Erie, Jefferson, Kings, Monroe, New York, Oneida, Onondaga, Ontario, Orange, Otsego, Rensselaer, St. Lawrence, Saratoga, Ulster, Washington, Wyoming, and Yates cos.

[4] *Constitution, Art.* VI. *Sec.* 15. Special acts have been passed for this purpose, as follows:—*Special Judge and Special Surrogate* in Cayuga, Chautauqua, Jefferson, and Oswego, 1849; Washington, 1855. *Special Judge* in Oneida, Orange, St. Law-

rence, and Tioga, 1849; Ulster, 1850; Chenango, 1851; Sullivan, 1854; Essex, 1857; and Tompkins, 1858. The term for which these officers are elected is 3 years, except in Chenango, Tompkins, and Ulster, in which it is 4 years.

[5] There are 4 justices elected in each town except Champlain, Ellisburgh, Fort Ann, Hanover, Harmony, Hector, Lenox, Niagara, Pomfret, and Potsdam, which have each 5, and Brookhaven, which has 8. Justices were appointed by the Council of Appointment from 1777 to 1822, and by the Supervisors and Judges from 1824 to 1827, since which they have been elected.

[6] *Revised Statutes, Art.* I, *Title* 4, *Chap.* 2, *Part* 3.
[7] *Constitution, Art.* VI, *Sec.* 23.
[8] The principal City Courts are as follows:—

In Albany.—A *Mayor's Court,* held by the Mayor, Recorder, and Aldermen, or the Mayor and Recorder jointly, or either of them singly. It is practically held by the Recorder only; a *Court of Special Sessions,* held by the Recorder or County Judge, with one or more Justices; a *Justices' Court,* held by 3 Justices elected for the purpose. Two Police Justices elected.

In Auburn.—*Justices' and Police Courts.* Three Justices of the Peace elected.

In Brooklyn.—The *City Court,* held by the City Judge: *Police Courts* and *Justices' Courts,* for whose convenience the city is divided into 5 districts; a *Court of Special Sessions,* held by a Justice or Police Justice.

In Buffalo.—A *Superior Court,* held by 3 Justices; *Justices' and Police Courts.* Eight Justices of the Peace and one Police Justice elected.

The officers in each county, auxiliary to the judiciary, are as follows:—

The District Attorney,[1] who is the official prosecutor in all criminal cases coming before the county courts, and has general duties in relation to suits in which the county has an interest.

The Sheriff,[2] who is charged with the preservation of the public peace and the execution of the orders of the courts. He has charge of the jail and prisoners, and appoints as many deputies as he may deem necessary. He can hold no other office, and is ineligible to the same office for the next 3 years after his term expires. He is required to give bonds, in default of which the office becomes vacant.

The County Clerk, who is made the keeper of the county records. He attends the courts and records their proceedings, records deeds and mortgages, files papers and documents required by law to be preserved in his office, and is the medium of communication between State and town officers. He is the clerk of the Supreme Court for his county. He appoints a deputy, who, when duly sworn, may discharge all his duties.

Four **Coroners,** who are charged with the duty of inquiring into the cause of sudden deaths. Upon being notified, it is their duty to attend at the place where a dead body is found, summon a jury and witnesses, examine into the causes, and make a written report to the county clerk. They also have the sole power of issuing writs against sheriffs.

A **Register,** performing that part of the duties of county clerks relating to the recording of conveyances and mortgages, is elected in New York, Kings, and Westchester counties; and each of these appoints a deputy.

Commissioners of Deeds, to take acknowledgments of deeds and legal documents, are appointed by the Common Councils of cities in such numbers as they may decide, except in New York, where the number is limited to 300, and in Syracuse to 12.[3]

Notaries Public are appointed by the Governor and Senate for a term of 2 years, and have authority to demand and accept payment of foreign bills of exchange, and to protest the same for nonpayment, and to exercise the customary duties of this office. Their number is limited to 400 in New York, 25 in Troy, and in other cities and towns as many as the Governor may deem proper.

Criminal Courts. Courts for the trial of criminal cases consist of the Court of Oyer and Terminer connected with the circuit of the Supreme Court, the Court of Sessions connected with the County Court, City Criminal Courts, and Justices' Courts.[4]

Courts of Oyer and Terminer consist of a Justice of the Supreme Court associated with the County Judge and two Justices of the Sessions, (except in New York City,) the Supreme Judge and two of the others constituting a quorum for trials. This court has original and general jurisdiction.

Courts of Sessions are held by the County Judge and two Justices of Sessions. They have jurisdiction over cases in which the imprisonment in case of conviction is less than ten years. The inferior City Courts and Justices' Courts have jurisdiction over petty criminal cases.

In Hudson.—A *Mayor's Court,* held by the Mayor, Recorder, and Aldermen, or the Mayor and Recorder jointly or singly; a *Justices' Court,* held by 2 Justices. One Police Justice elected.

In New York.—The *Superior Court,* consisting of a Chief Justice and 6 Justices; the *Court of Common Pleas,* composed of 3 Justices; the *Marine Court,* composed of 3 Justices; the *Court of Oyer and Terminer,* held by a Justice of the Supreme Court; the *Court of General Sessions,* held by the Recorder or City Judge; the *Court of Special Sessions,* held by the Recorder or City Judge without a jury; *Police Courts,* held by Special Justices in 4 separate districts; and *Justices'* or *District Courts,* held in 6 separate districts.

In Oswego.—A *Recorder's Court,* held by the Recorder, or, in his absence, by the Mayor or any two Aldermen; a *Court of Special Sessions,* held by the Recorder. Two Justices elected.

In Poughkeepsie.—*Justices' and Police Courts.*

In Rochester.—*Justices' and Police Courts.* Three Justices of the Peace and 1 Police Justice elected.

In Schenectady.—*Justices' and Police Courts.* Four Justices elected.

In Syracuse.—*Justices' and Police Courts.* Three Justices of the Peace and 1 Police Justice elected.

In Troy.—A *Mayor's Court,* held by the Mayor, Recorder, and Aldermen, or the Mayor and Recorder jointly, or either singly. Practically it is held by the Recorder; a *Justices' Court,* held by 3 Justices elected for the purpose.

In Utica.—A *Recorder's Court,* held by the Recorder; a *Court of Special Sessions,* held by the Recorder and 2 Aldermen. Four Justices and 1 Police Justice elected.

[1] By an act passed April 14, 1852, the supervisors may determine whether this shall be a salaried office, and may fix the compensation. In the absence of such action, the District Attorney is paid by fees.

[2] *Constitution, Art.* X, *Sec.* 1. From 1777 to 1822 sheriffs were appointed annually by the Governor and Council, and could not hold the office more than 4 successive years. They have been elected since 1822.

[3] In towns the duties of the office are performed by justices of the peace. Special commissioners for this service were appointed in the several cos. by the Council of Appointment under the first Constitution, and by the Governor and Senate under the Constitution of 1821. The Governor may appoint, for a term of 4 years, any number of persons not exceeding 5, in any city or co. of other States and of Canada, to take acknowledgments of instruments or conveyances to be recorded in this State. The consuls, vice-consuls, and ministers of the U. S. in foreign countries, the mayors of London, Liverpool, and Dublin, the provost of Edinburgh, and persons appointed by the Governor, not exceeding 3 in each of the cities of London, Liverpool, Glasgow, Paris, and Marseilles, may also perform this duty, and administer oaths or affirmations substantiating proofs to documents requiring to be recorded or to be produced in evidence within this State.

[4] In 1829, co. clerks were required to report to the Secretary of State a transcript of all convictions and the sentences thereon. The intention of this act was to establish evidence in case of the trial of the same person for a second offense, in which the punishment for the same crimes is enhanced in severity. In 1837, the Secretary of State was required to report a statement of all convictions reported under this act, and annually afterward to lay before the Legislature a like summary. In 1839, sheriffs were also required to report the name, occupation, age, sex, and native country of every person convicted, and such other information as might indicate degree of education, the effect of home influences, and such other details as might be required. Under the administration of E. W. Leavenworth, the statistics of crime

ADMINISTRATIVE DEPARTMENT.

Under the head of the Administrative Department are classed the officers charged with the general administration of the affairs of canals, of State prisons, of the salt springs, of academic and common school education, and other public interests, each of which is particularly noticed elsewhere. It also includes a variety of other offices, the principal of which are as follows:—

The County Treasurer is charged with the duty of receiving all moneys collected by tax, or otherwise payable into the county treasury, of paying all orders issued by the Supervisors, and of accounting to the Comptroller of the State for such moneys as are due to the State treasury. He is required to give bonds; and in case of vacancy the office is filled by appointment of the Supervisors until the January following the next general election.

Superintendents of the Poor have charge of the county poor and of the poorhouses, unless otherwise provided by law. The Supervisors may elect to have 1 or 3 superintendents. In several of the counties, special laws exist with regard to this office.[1]

Commissioners of Excise are appointed by the County Judge and the two Associate Justices, except in New York, where the Chief Justice of the Superior Court, the presiding Judge of the Court of Common Pleas, and the Recorder, have the appointing power. They meet annually on the third Tuesday of May, to grant licenses for selling liquors and keeping inns under restrictions fixed by law. This office was created April 16, 1857. Twenty freeholders must unite in a petition for a license; and the same person can sign but one petition. Licenses cost $30 to $250 each.

---

from the first reports to, and including, 1854 were published, which gave the following results:—

New York State Prison received from 1798 to 1827 inclusive, 5,879 prisoners: died, 765; escaped, 25; sentence expiated, 1,262; pardoned, 3,160; removed, 348: natives of N. H., 99; Vt., 114; Mass., 392; R. I., 110; Ct., 391; N. Y., 2,426; N. J., 314; Penn., 234; Del., 21; Md., 75; Va., 69; other States, 43; B. A., 87; W. I., 141; S. A., 12; Eng., 247; Ire., 655; Scot., 79; Ger., 58; Hol., 22;

Fr., 49; Spain, 6; Italy, 13; Portugal, 6; Sweden, 10; Norway, 2; other European countries, 18; Africa, 26; E. I., 8; unknown, 152: crimes against the person, 280; against property, with violence, 291; without violence, 4,016; forgery, and against the currency, 728. Sentence varied from 7 mo. to life. the most being as follows: 1 year, 242; 2 years, 259; 3 years, 581; 3 years 1 day, 278; 4 years, 604; 5 years, 764; 7 years, 820; 10 years, 294; 14 years, 239; life, 603.

Convictions in Courts of Record from 1830 to 1856.

YEARS.	Against the Person.	Against Property, with violence.	Against Property, without violence.	Against the Currency, and Forgery.	Other offenses.	Total.	YEARS.	Against the Person.	Against Property, with violence.	Against Property, without violence.	Against the Currency, and Forgery.	Other offenses.	Total.
1830...	237	101	502	74	144	1,059	1845...	471	177	467	54	520	1,689
1831...	243	93	464	63	94	956	1846...	384	138	471	38	440	1,471
1832...	289	79	440	60	98	966	1847...	385	132	396	24	408	1,295
1833...	362	75	462	61	153	1,113	1848...	437	120	512	33	425	1,527
1834...	217	99	355	53	148	869	1849...	397	150	545	44	404	1,540
1835...	287	92	426	34	237	1,076	1850...	397	199	521	36	410	1,563
1836...	316	86	379	32	150	963	1851...	409	148	475	49	401	1,482
1837...	393	124	477	52	145	1,191	1852...	412	228	480	48	434	1,602
1838...	296	112	472	42	164	1,086	1853...	483	185	573	52	553	1,846
1839...	287	115	479	51	186	1,118	1854...	432	189	591	75	835	2,122
1840...	463	120	437	49	274	1,343	1855...	397	278	586	37	544	1,842
1841...	458	121	460	49	427	1,515	1856...	432	248	573	49	212	1,514
1842...	484	175	504	63	376	1,602	1857...	475	350	607	64	158	1,654
1843...	408	244	504	78	336	1,570	1858...	436	332	617	90	237	1,712
1844...	394	172	489	60	312	1,427							

Of the 1712 convicted in 1858, 1582 were males and 130 females. The number of convictions reported by sheriffs falls short of that by clerks for the obvious reason that many who are fined pay down their penalties and never come into the sheriff's hands. The excess reported by clerks from 1839 to 1854 varied from 172 to 1.000 annually. Males form about 94 per cent. of all convictions reported by clerks, 93½ per cent. of those reported by sheriffs, and 85 per cent. of those convicted in courts of special sessions. The results of trial compared with total indictments have varied in different years within the following limits:—

Ratio of convictions to indictments...................... 593 to 689.
"   acquittals   "   .... 249 to 380.
"   disagreement of juries "   .... .013 to .025.
"   convict'ns on confess'n "   .... .182 to .390.

The least number of convictions reported from 1829 to 1855, in proportion to population, was in 1834, when it was 1 to 2,444. The greatest number was in 1845, when it was 1 to 1,542.

Pardons.—The number of pardons granted from 1778 to 1854 inclusive, was 8,793; of which 160 were from fines, 160 from fines and imprisonment, 1,285 from jails and local prisons, 5,747 from State prison for term of years, and 559 from State prison for life. Of the whole number, 1,640 were conditioned mostly to leaving the State or U. S., 807 were restored to rights of citizens, 59 were respited from capital offenses. The pardoning power has been exercised as follows:—

George Clinton...............	308	Wm. L. Marcy...............	834
John Jay.......................	160	Wm. H. Seward............	377
Morgan Lewis................	213	Wm. C. Bouck............	279
Daniel D. Tompkins........	1,693	Silas Wright..............	282
John Taylor...................	223	John Young.................	268
De Witt Clinton.............	2,289	Hamilton Fish.............	97
Joseph C. Yates.............	291	Washington Hunt.........	346
Nathaniel Pitcher..........	228	Horatio Seymour.........	456
Martin Van Buren.........	34	Myron H. Clark..........	530
Enos T. Throop.............	415	John A. King.............	426

[1] The salary of these officers, where there is but one in a county, is fixed by the Supervisors; but in those counties where there are 3 they are usually paid for the time employed. Albany has none. Chemung, Clinton, Dutchess, Essex, Franklin, *Fulton*, Genesee, *Herkimer*, *Jefferson*, Montgomery, Orange, Orleans, Otsego, Putnam, Schenectady, *Schuyler*, Sullivan, and *Ulster*, have each one; and those in italic are appointed by Supervisors. In early times each town supported its own poor, and where persons who had not acquired residence became chargeable, they were sent from town to town back to the place where they had formerly resided. A very able report was presented to the Senate by J. V. N. Yates, Secretary of State, Feb. 9, 1824, upon the subject of the "laws for the relief and settlement of the poor," in which he advised the erection of one or more houses of employment in each co., in which paupers might

State Assessors.—The object of the office is to collect the necessary statistics among the several counties to enable the Board of Equalization to equalize the State tax among the several counties, and fix the amount of real and personal estate upon which the State tax shall be levied. The Assessors are appointed by the Government and Senate, and hold office for three years.

The Board of Equalization consists of the Commissioners of the Land Office, and the State Assessors. It meets at Albany on the first Tuesday of September of each year, for the purpose of equalizing the taxes, &c.

be maintained and employed at the county charge, and that children at suitable ages should be put out to some useful trade. An act was accordingly passed Nov. 27, 1824, authorizing the establishment of county poorhouses. In most of the counties such institutions were established within a few years. They were located upon farms, which were designed to be worked, as far as practicable, by the inmates. The towns in Queens and Suffolk counties have mostly town poorhouses, and in these there are no county establishments of this kind. The county of Albany supports its poor at the city almshouse.

In most counties a distinction is made between town and county poor, the former including those who have gained a residence; and this distinction may be made or not, at the option of the Board of Supervisors. Temporary relief may be extended in cases where the pauper cannot be removed, or for other causes satisfactory to the Superintendents. Towns may vote at town meetings the sum estimated to be necessary for the support of their own poor.

The following tables and summaries are from the last annual Report of the Secretary of State:—

Statistics of Poorhouses and of the Support of the Poor, for the year ending Dec. 1, 1858.

Counties.	*Acres of land attached to Poorhouse.*	*Estimated value of Poorhouse establishments.*	*Value of labor of paupers.*	*Weekly expenses of each person.*	*Number of county paupers relieved or supported.*	*Number of town paupers relieved or supported.*	*Number of persons temporarily relieved.*	*Expenses connected with the county Poorhouses.*	*Expenses of administering temporary relief.*	*Whole expense of support of county and town paupers for the year ending December 1, 1858.*
Allegany	183	$10,000 00	$250 00	$1 02	243	223	223	$5,879 68	$2,675 41	$8,555 09
Broome	130	8,000 00	200 00	59	1,335	....	1,178	3,727 01	8,250 01	11,977 02
Cattaraugus	200	6,500 00	200 00	1 12	160	219	271	2,725 44	6,136 14	8,861 58
Cayuga	96	20,000 00	800 00	83	2,778	....	....	9,393 21	16,968 47	26,361 68
Chautauqua	171.8	12,000 00	2,524 00	787	4,106	....	3,725	5,094 65	5,846 58	10,941 23
Chemung	175	13,000 00	....	894	245	....	....	2,850 48	6,513 53	9,364 01
Chenango	172	5,000 00	449 76	72	109	151	103	3,997 33	1,078 19	5,075 52
Clinton	90	3,000 00	250 00	89	2,738	....	2,585	3,076 02	6,362 84	9,438 86
Columbia	204¼	35,000 00	1,000 00	1 09	565	....	....	12,158 15	....	12,158 15
Cortland	118	6,800 00	180 00	72	250	....	172	2,950 52	2,422 61	5,373 13
Delaware	200	5,000 00	250 00	90	136	312	386	3,096 93	2,948 62	6,045 55
Dutchess	106	15,000 00	....	1 00	1,771	....	....	15,965 09	300 00	16,265 09
Erie	154	49,091 00	3,500 00	70	1,292	5,915	5,915	35,028 73	20,474 90	55,503 63
Essex	100	4,500 00	200 00	1 00	44	223	136	2,695 47	2,273 45	4,968 92
Franklin	162	4,639 75	200 00	42	84	....	56	1,315 79	1,489 11	2,804 90
Fulton	86	8,000 00	....	....	112	....	....	3,701 44	922 00	4,623 44
Genesee	134	8,000 00	500 00	662	175	66	....	3,079 68	2,192 46	5,272 14
Greene	130	10,000 00	600 00	685	97	117	66	3,178 46	250 00	3,428 46
Hamilton	......	....	....	....	21	....	17	400 00	100 00	500 00
Herkimer	65	10,000 00	742 90	1 10	4,908	....	4,656	7,399 10	15,219 04	22,618 14
Jefferson	107	14,000 00	500 00	76	1,464	....	1,015	6,440 95	11,960 67	18,401 62
Kings	......	400,000 00	1,500 00	2 22	37,730	....	29,881	146,499 66	32,110 47	178,610 13
Lewis	59	3,500 00	200 00	93	126	48	70	3,564 41	561 26	4.125 67
Livingston	118	18,000 00	700 00	74	286	....	....	4,630 62	4,094 01	8,724 63
Madison	172	16,500 00	....	1 035	....	....	....	6,954 37	11,781 23	18,735 60
Monroe	134	40,375 16	350 00	70	2,858	2,817	4,614	18,432 62	28,815 88	47,248 50
Montgomery	150	7,500 00	400 00	1 637	1,063	....	....	9,680 76	13,330 00	23.010 76
New York	......	....	....	....	....	....	110,822	351,152 10	139,731 54	490,883 64
Niagara	120	12,000 00	1,000 00	81	3.980	....	3,687	5,322 80	7,552 98	12,875 78
Oneida	150	8,100 00	....	1 00	8,102	....	7,062	13,271 67	31,298 65	44,570 32
Onondaga	36¼	16,000 00	1,380 00	915	2,460	1,733	3,538	10,159 82	40,384 84	50,544 66
Ontario	212	21,200 00	700 00	68	2,753	....	2,402	6,795 93	7,065 80	13,861 73
Orange	267	25,000 00	1,500 00	985	1,679	....	1,330	9,288 35	10,755 09	20,043 44
Orleans	107	10,113 75	375 00	1 07	865	....	510	3,781 97	4,140 10	7,922 07
Oswego	60	4,350 00	500 00	1 14	747	2,830	3,330	5,126 74	43,199 99	48,326 73
Otsego	170	15,350 00	....	42	63	492	342	4,702 40	3,974 70	8,677 10
Putnam	196	10,000 00	300 00	58	....	....	....	1,388 84	2,590 53	3,979 37
Queens	......	....	....	....	555	381	36	22,303 15	2,287 75	24,590 90
Rensselaer	144	29,000 00	500 00	1 48	966	3,578	3,986	16,172 00	30,754 00	46.926 00
Richmond	125	21,000 00	800 00	1 45	1,881	....	1,642	9,457 82	3,496 42	12,954 24
Rockland	47	11,000 00	700 00	805	384	449	636	3,099 07	2,417 21	5,516 28
St. Lawrence	130	7,200 00	500 00	737	2,931	....	2,499	6,990 24	13,944 38	20,943 62
Saratoga	200	6,000 00	300 00	94	505	....	....	7,460 42	....	7,460 42
Schenectady	113	8,000 00	128 00	94	403	206	868	7,174 72	2,156 49	9,331 21
Schoharie	110	5,000 00	100 00	77	57	359	297	2,471 70	4,510 44	6,982 14
Schuyler	......	....	....	....	144	113	160	3,547 87	1,400 00	4,947 87
Seneca	126½	16,000 00	300 00	855	1,535	....	1,164	3,918 89	4,019 73	7.938 62
Steuben	200	10,000 00	275 00	1 00	1,175	....	870	4,420 89	5,729 07	10,149 96
Suffolk	......	....	....	1 00	56	453	225	12,008 79	4,260 00	16,268 79
Sullivan	100	1,500 00	200 00	83	350	....	296	3,357 03	4,132 93	7.489 96
Tioga	60	6,000 00	750 00	84	240	417	657	3,046 81	6,452 06	9.498 87
Tompkins	100	6,000 00	500 00	72	99	49	148	3,271 15	647 51	3,918 66
Ulster	140	9,000 00	500 00	70	1,280	1,191	2,047	6,721 72	9,791 36	16.513 08
Warren	200	2,500 00	100 00	49	82	....	....	1,241 75	2,368 92	3.610 67
Washington	174	12,000 00	755 00	50	2,629	....	2,332	4.051 40	6.391 49	10,442 89
Wayne	193	7,620 00	325 00	1 275	1.335	666	1,163	8,887 78	8,280 36	17,168 14
Westchester	165	35.500 00	1,150 00	1 018	1,312	61	....	15,981 09	149 98	16.131 07
Wyoming	111	5,000 00	150 00	801	170	70	89	3,416 02	620 22	4,036 24
Yates	123	5,500 00	200 00	96	65	66	....	3,162 80	112 69	3.275 49
Total	7,208.8	$1,059,339 66	$29,484 66	$ 90.5	103,499	23,205	207,207	$884.119 78	$607.271 50	$1,491.391 28

During the year 1858, 38.582 were admitted, 38,400 were discharged, 1,007 absconded, 849 were born, 2,584 died, and 646 were bound out.

Supported in Poorhouse.—Males, 6,219; Females, 7,203; total, 13,422. Foreigners, 6,503; Lunatics, 1,838; Idiots, 437; Mutes, 36. *Temporarily Relieved.*—Foreigners, 58,709; Lunatics, 2,408; Idiots, 595; Mutes, 52.

Loan Commissioners[1] are appointed in each county by the Governor and Senate, except in Onondaga, where they are elected. They are paid ¼ to ¾ of one per cent. on all moneys loaned, and are obliged to give bonds and report annually to the Comptroller.

School Commissioners are elected one in each Assembly District, and under certain circumstances another may be added. They are required to examine and grant certificates to teachers, visit schools, apportion the public moneys, and report to the Superintendent of Public Instruction. The Board of Supervisors in the counties have the power of arranging the several commissioner districts and of increasing the salary of the commissioners above $500. All cities, and many villages, are under special laws with regard to schools, and are more or less exempt from the jurisdiction of County School Commissioners.[2]

Sealers of Weights and Measures are appointed for the State and for each county and town. The State Superintendent has an office at Albany, and he furnishes to the several counties and towns standard sets of weights and measures.[3] The County Sealer keeps the Standards

Children under 16,—Males, 2,776; Females, 3,045. Total, 5,821. Number of children instructed, 3,219. Average 8 months in the year.

Nativities of Persons relieved in 1858.	Males.	Females.	Total.
United States	45,174	59,570	104,744
Ireland	42,212	50,504	92,716
Germany	12,601	16,173	28,774
England	4,183	3,371	7,554
Canada	1,995	2,013	4,008
France	1,094	1,995	3,089
Scotland	1,268	1,068	2,336
Total	108,527	134,694	243,221

Causes of Pauperism, as far as ascertained.	Males.	Females.	Total.
Intemperance direct	16,669	9,164	25,833
Children of intemperate parents	5,133	3,140	8,273
Wives with intemperate husbands		3,140	3,140
Total intemperance	21,802	15,444	37,246
Debauchery	543	622	1,165
Debauchery of parents	392	375	767
Idleness	5,582	4,080	9,662
Vagrancy	1,417	904	2,321
Idiocy	431	441	872
Lunacy	1,206	1,533	2,739
Blindness	353	165	518
Lameness	1,329	662	1,991
Sickness	12,667	10,167	22,834
Decrepitude	668	447	1,115
Old age	1,948	2,077	4,025
Total from all causes reported	48,338	36,917	85,255

[1] The first State loan was made by an act passed April 18, 1786, creating bills of credit to the amount of $500,000, the most of which was apportioned among the counties in proportion to their supposed wants, and loaned by officers appointed for the purpose. These bills were of convenient denominations and circulated as money. They were receivable in payment of taxes, and for some purposes were legal tender. This loan was distributed among the counties then existing, as follows:—

Albany	$55,000	New York	$80,000	Suffolk	$25,000
Dutchess	42,500	Orange	25,000	Ulster	31,000
Kings	11,250	Queens	28,750	Washington	7,500
Montgomery	30,000	Richmond	11,250	Westchester	23,750

The sum of $79,447.53 remained due on the loan of 1786 at the beginning of 1810, and the whole was finally called in in 1830.

By an act of March 14, 1792, another loan of $500,000 was made and distributed among the counties, as follows:—

Albany	$41,000	New York	$48,250	Saratoga	$26,000
Clinton	3,500	Ontario	3,000	Suffolk	24,000
Columbia	40,750	Orange	27,250	Tioga	6,500
Dutchess	68,000	Otsego	7,500	Ulster	40,500
Herkimer	7,000	Orleans	21,500	Washington	33,500
Kings	4,750	Rensselaer	33,500	Westchester	35,250
Montgomery	23,500	Richmond	4,750		

A third loan of $400,000 was authorized to the several counties, excepting New York, Kings, Queens, Richmond, Suffolk, and Westchester, in proportion to the number of their electors. In case the Supervisors of these counties applied for a share, a further sum of $50,000 was authorized to be issued. In 1819 the above loan was transferred to the Common School Fund. In 1850 the office of Loan Commissioner for the loans of 1792 and 1808 was abolished, and the loans remaining in their hands were transferred to the custody of the commissioners for loaning the U. S. Deposit Fund.

The U. S. Deposit Fund originated as follows: An Act of Congress, passed June 23, 1836, directed the surplus in the treasury on the 1st day of Jan. 1837, excepting $5,000,000, to be deposited with the several States in proportion to their representation. The amount thus deposited was $37,468,859.97, of which N. Y. received $5,352,694.28. This was apportioned to the several counties according to population, as follows:—

Albany	$147,107.48	Oneida	$33,858.70
Allegany	86,681.22	Onondaga	40,699.36
Broome	49,698.81	Ontario	93,558.80
Cattaraugus	61,504.43	Orange	98,363.76
Cayuga	121,113.45	Orleans	29,622.36
Chautauqua	110,447.53	Oswego	96,803.13
Chemung	42,991.07	Otsego	93,017.26
Chenango	100,337.93	Putnam	95,483.74
Clinton	51,057.58	Queens	48,728.95
Columbia	100,298.54	Rensselaer	130,679.06
Cortland	59,491.87	Richmond	78,910.08
Delaware	84,165.51	Rockland	39,613.81
Dutchess	124,810.71	St. Lawrence	76,534.68
Erie	141,770.83	Saratoga	102,747.79
Essex	50,951.74	Schenectady	142,979.45
Franklin	30,771.91	Schoharie	119,038.36
Genesee	144,217.61	Seneca	664,839.06
Greene	74,272.51	Steuben	65,206.61
Herkimer	89,110.77	Suffolk	190,814.86
Jefferson	18,921.82	Sullivan	149,928.42
Kings	23,867.24	Tioga	100,603.77
Lewis	103,501.02	Tompkins	111,006.31
Livingston	93,568.65	Ulster	56,352.39
Madison	39,951.05	Warren	94,142.19
Monroe	70,174.02	Washington	124,131.32
Montgomery	55,697.62	Wayne	28,433.43
New York	101,994.55	Westchester	61,858.89
Niagara	69,598.02	Yates	136,653.25

[2] In Utica and Schenectady the care of schools is intrusted to "Commissioners of Common Schools;" in Buffalo and Hudson the Common Councils are *ex officio* Commissioners of Schools; and in Albany, Astoria, Auburn, Brooklyn, Castleton, and Southfield, (Clifton,) College Point, East Chester, Flushing, Jamaica, Lockport, Medina, Newburgh, New York, Oswego, Port Byron, Poughkeepsie, Pulaski, Rochester, Salem, Syracuse, Troy, Waterford, Westfarms, and Whitestown, schools are under a Board of Education, usually elected, but in some of the cities appointed by the Common Council. In most cities a Superintendent, who is clerk of the Board, is appointed by the Board of Education for the more immediate supervision of schools and inspection of teachers. In Buffalo the Superintendent is elected.

[3] A *County Standard* consists of—

1. A large balance, comprising a brass beam and scales, with stand and lever.
2. A small balance, with a drawer stand for small weights.
3. A set of large brass weights, namely, 50lb., 20lb., 10lb., 5lb.
4. A set of small brass weights, avoirdupois, namely, 4lb., 2lb., 1lb., 8oz., 4oz., 2oz., 1oz., ½oz., ¼oz.
5. A brass yard measure, graduated to feet and inches, and the first graduated to eighths of an inch, and also decimally; with a graduation to cloth measure on the other side; in a case.
6. A set of liquid measures made of copper, namely, 1 gallon, ½ gallon, 1 quart, 1 pint, ½ pint, 1 gill; in a case.
7. A set of dry measures of copper, namely, ½ bushel, 1 peck, ½ peck, 2 quarts, 1 quart; in a case.
There are also cases to contain the large brass weights and the necessary packing boxes included, etc. The cost of the set is $300.

A *Town Standard* differs in some particulars, as consisting of but one medium sized balance, the large weights being of iron in place of brass; the yard measure being a cast metallic square rod, without decimal graduation, etc.; and likewise without cases, in general. The cost of the set is $125.

furnished by the State, and is required to have them compared with the State Standard once in 3 years. The Town Sealer is required to examine all weights and measures in use once a year.[1]

The Mayors of cities are administrative officers of State laws and executive officers of city ordinances. They are elected annually, except in Albany and New York, where they hold their offices for two years.

The Supervisors of towns are administrators of the general laws relating to towns.

The President and Trustees of villages have charge of every thing pertaining to the welfare of their respective localities within the limits of the charter of incorporation.

Trustees of School Districts are the officers recognized by law to whom is intrusted the administration of the school laws within their districts.

Turnpike Inspectors are appointed in every county in which there are turnpikes, the acts of incorporation of which do not require the appointment of special inspectors. They are 3 to 5 in number, and must have no interest in any turnpike in the State.

Plank Road Inspectors are appointed in every county having plank roads. Their duties are analogous to those of the inspectors of turnpikes; and they are chiefly intended to protect the public against the collection of tolls when plank roads are unsafe or difficult to travel from neglect or other cause.

Commissioners of Highways have the power of directing repairs, laying out and altering roads, discontinuing old roads, and of ordering new bridges to be built and kept in repair.[2] They must annually divide the towns into road districts, and assign such inhabitants to work upon them as they may deem proper; and they must deposit an accurate description of all new roads in the Town Clerk's office for record.

Overseers of Highways, or "Pathmasters," have charge of road districts.[3]

---

[1] The statute defines the State Standard of Weights and Measures to be the same as that approved by Congress June 14, 1836, and furnished by the U. S. to the States in 1842. The set furnished consisted of a yard, sets of Troy and avoirdupois weights, the wine gallon and the half bushel and their subdivisions. The unit of length and surface, from which all other measures of extension are derived, whether linear, superficial, or solid, is the yard, which is divided into 3 feet of 12 inches each, except for cloths or other articles sold by the yard, when it may be divided into halves, eighths, and sixteenths. The rod contains 5½ yards, and the mile 1,760 yards; the acre is 160 square rods; the chain for land surveying is 22 yards long and subdivided into 100 links; the Troy pound is to the avoirdupois as 5,760 to 7,000, the one containing 12 and the other 16 ounces; 100lbs. avoirdupois form a hundredweight, and 2,000lbs. a ton. All measures of capacity not liquid are derived from the half bushel, the subdivisions of which are obtained by dividing repeatedly by 2. Coal, ashes, marl, manure, corn in the ear, fruit, and roots, are sold by heap measure.

The Standards now in use do not vary essentially from those established by the State Government before standards were furnished by the U. S. As formerly defined, the unit of linear measure was the yard, which bore the ratio of 1,000,000 to 1,086,140, to a pendulum beating seconds in a vacuum at the temperature of melting ice at Columbia College. A cubic foot of water at its maximum density in vacuo was declared equal to 1000 ounces avoirdupois. The liquid gallon to contain 8lbs., and the dry gallon 10lbs., of distilled water at its greatest density and mean pressure at sea level.

Weights of articles per bushel as fixed by Standard.

ARTICLES.	LBS.	ARTICLES.	LBS.	ARTICLES.	LBS.
Beans	62	Flaxseed	55	Rye	56
Cloverseed	60	Oats	32	Salt	56
Corn	58	Peas	60	Timothy	44
Buckwheat	48	Potatoes	60	Wheat	60
Barley	48				

[2] Roads extending through several towns may be laid out by commissioners appointed by the Supervisors; and those extending through several counties are usually laid out by special commissioners appointed by law. The commissioners of highways are required to report annually, at town meeting, their receipts and expenditures, and a statement of what improvements are necessary, and the cost of obtaining them. These estimates are referred to the Board of Supervisors, and assessed as other town charges. They may summon jurors and witnesses in opening and closing roads. Roads through improved lands must be certified as necessary by the oath of twelve respectable freeholders; and a like certificate to the contrary is required in closing roads. Every owner may obtain a road to his land.

New roads cannot be laid through orchards or gardens of more than four years' growth or use, or through buildings or yards, and inclosures of mills and factories, without the owner's consent. The law requires the commissioners of highways to erect mileboards along the line, and guideboards at the crossing of post and such other important roads as they may deem

proper; and the defacing of these is punishable as a misdemeanor. Every owner or occupant of lands in any town, and every male inhabitant above the age of 21, must be assessed for highway labor. The whole number of days' labor annually expended in the town must be at least three times the number of taxable inhabitants; and every male inhabitant over 21, except ministers, paupers, idiots, and lunatics, must be assessed at least one day. The residue is assessed upon the property of individuals and corporations. Labor may be commuted at the rate of 62½ cts. per day; and the moneys so paid must be expended in the district.

[3] Overseers of Highways are required by law to warn out to work all persons assessed for highway labor in their respective districts; keep their roads in order; superintend work; receive and apply commutation moneys; cause the noxious weeds upon the wayside to be cut down or destroyed once before July and once before Sept. of each year; remove obstructions; and collect all fines, whether for neglect of work, idleness, or putting up of gates contrary to law. They may require additional labor, to the amount of one-third of the first tax. All roads must be fenced by the owners of adjacent lands, unless liable to be overflowed by streams, when the overseers of highways must erect, and keep in repair, good swinging gates at the expense of the lands benefitted; and persons leaving such gates open are liable to triple damages. All rivers where the tide ebbs and flows are public highways, without special law. Many other streams have been so declared by acts, and obstructions in such streams and in highways are punished by fine, notwithstanding a plea of title. Such obstructions may be abated as nuisances; and the persons causing them are liable to actions for damage. Persons owning lands upon roads 3 rods wide, or more, may plant trees on the roadside adjacent to their line, and may prosecute for damages to such trees. They may also construct a sidewalk, with a railing. Trees falling into the road from inclosed lands must be removed by the occupant within 2 days, after notice by any person, under a fine of 50 cts. a day. Assessors and commissioners of highways are *ex officio* fence viewers in their several towns. In case of fires in the woods of any town, it is the duty of the supervisor, justices, and commissioners of highways to order such and so many inhabitants, liable to work upon the roads, as may be deemed necessary, and reside near, to assist in checking the fires, under penalty of $50, and liability to prosecution for misdemeanor, and further fine not over $100 or imprisonment not more than 60 days.

Persons aggrieved at the decision of commissioners may appeal to referees appointed by the county judge or justices of sessions. Kings, Queens, and Suffolk cos. have from an early colonial period had a road law peculiar to themselves. It differs by fixing the number of days at *twice* the number of persons assessed; in granting private roads for *limited periods,* in allowing roads through gardens and orchards of less than *ten* years' use or growth, by allowing appeals to the *county judge,* and in a few other minor details. Richmond co. has also a special law, which requires assessments in *money only,* to be collected with the general tax, and the repairs of roads to be let out at public auction by districts from year to year and to the lowest bidder. There are many other special laws, chiefly applicable to cities and villages, but too numerous to mention here.

SUMMARY OF THE SEVERAL STATE, COUNTY, AND TOWN OFFICERS.

	Total No. in State.	Years in Office.	Commencement of term of Office.	How filled.	Vacancies how filled.	Compensation.
United States Senators............	2	6	March 4.	Legislature.	Governor.	$3,000 and mileage.
Representatives in Congress....	33	2	"	Election.	Special election.	" "
STATE OFFICERS.						
LEGISLATIVE—						
State Senators....................	32	2	January 1.	"	"	$3 per day and mileage.
Members of Assembly............	128	1	"	"	"	" "
EXECUTIVE—						
Governor........	1	2	"	"	Lieut. Gov.	$4,000 and house rent.
Lieutenant Governor.............	1	2	"	"	Pres. p. t. of Sen.	$6 per day and mileage.
Secretary of State.................	1	2	"	"	Governor.	$2,500.
Comptroller ....,............	1	2	"	"	"	"
Treasurer..........................	1	2	"	"	"	$2,000.
Attorney General.................	1	2	"	"	"	$2,500.
State Engineer and Surveyor...	1	2	"	"	"	
JUDICIAL—						
Judges of the Court of Appeals[a]	8	8	"	"	"	$2,500 before 1857 ; $3,500 since.
Justices of the Supreme Court	33	8	"	"	"	Ditto.
Clerk of the Court of Appeals..	1	2	"	"	"	$2,000.
State Reporter......................	1	2	Date of appt.	{ Gov., Lt. Gov., & Atty. Gen.	Gov., Lt. Gov., & Atty. Gen. }	"
ADMINISTRATIVE—						
{ Supt. of Public Instruction...	1	3	"	Legislature.	Governor.	$2,500.
{ Regents of the University[b] ...	19	...	"	"	Legislature.	None.
Supt. of Banking Department..	1	3	"	Gov. & Senate.	Governor.	$5,000.
Inspectors of State Prisons......	3	3	January 1.	Election.	"	$1,600.
Canal Commissioners.............	3	3	"	"	"	$2,000.
Auditor of Canal Department..	1	3	Date of appt.	Gov. & Senate.	"	$2,500.
Canal Appraisers.................	3	3	"	"	"	$2,000.
Supt. of Weights and Measures	1	Indef.	"	{ Gov., Lt. Gov., & Sec. of State.	Gov., Lt. Gov., & Sec. of State. }	$500.
State Assessors....................	3	3	"	Gov. & Senate.		
COUNTY OFFICERS.	No. in each Co.					
County Judge.....................	1	4	January 1.	Election.	Governor.	Sal. fixed by Supervisors.
Surrogate (in certain counties)	1	4	"	"	"	
Special Judges and Surrogates[c]	1	1	"	"	"	Per diem.
Justices of Sessions	2	1	"	"	"	Fees or salary.
District Attorney..................	1	3	"	"	"	Fees.
Sheriff.............................	1	3	"	"	"	Per diem.
Coroners	4	3	1st Tues. Aug	"	Supervisors.	Percentage.
Treasurer..........................	1	3	January 1.	"	Governor.	Fees.
County Clerk......................	1	3	"	"	"	Percentage.
Commissioners for loaning moneys of the U. S..........	2	2	Date of Appt.	Gov. & Senate.	County Judge.	Not less than $500.
School Commissioners[d]		3	January 1.	Election.	Supervisors.	Per diem or salary.
Superintendents of the Poor....	1 or 3	3	"	{ Judges and Just. of Sess. }	Judge & Justices	Per diem.
Commissioners of Excise.........	3	6	"	"	"	
County Sealer of Weights and Measures.........................	1	Indef.	Date of Appt.	Supervisors.	Supervisors.	Fees.
Notaries Public...........{	Fixed by Gov.	} 2	"	Gov. & Senate.	Governor.	Fees.
Turnpike Inspectors[e].............	3	2	"	Supervisors.	Supervisors.	Per diem.
Plank Road Inspectors	3	2	"	"	"	"
TOWN OFFICERS.	No. in ea. town.					
Supervisor..........................	1	1	Date of Elec.	Election.	Specl. town meet.	Per diem.
Town Clerk.........................	1	1	"	"	....	Fees and per diem.
Inspectors of Election[f]...........	3 to 18	1	"	See note j.	{ Superv. town clerk, & jus. }	Per diem.
Justices of the Peace..............	4[g]	4	"	Election.	Governor.	Fees.
Constables[h]........................	1 to 5	1	January 1.	"	"	Fees.
Assessors[i].........................	3	3	Date of Elec.	"	Spec. town meet.	Per diem.
Collector............................	1	1	"	"	Superv. & 2 jus.	Percentage.
Overseers of the Poor[j]	1 or 2	...	"	"	Spec. town meet.	Per diem.
Commissioners of Highways...	1 or 3	3	"	"	"	"
Overseers of Highways..........{	1 to each road dis.	} 1	"	"	Com. highways.	"
Pound Masters.....................	Indef.	1	"	"	Justices.	Fees.
Town Sealer of Weights and Measures.......!...............	1	1	"	Superv. & j. p.	Superv. & j. p.	Fees.
SCHOOL DIST. OFFICERS.	No. in each dist.					
Trustees[k]........................	1 or 3	3	2d Tues. Oct.	Election.	Supervisor.	None.
District Clerk......................	1	1	"	"	Trustees.	"
Collector	1	1	"	"	"	"
Librarian	1	1	"	"	"	"

[a] 4 elected for 8 yrs., and 4 senior Justices of Supreme Court. [b] 4 others ex officio Regents. [c] Regulated by special acts. [d] One in each Assembly district. [e] In certain counties. [f] 2 inspectors are elected and 1 appointed from the next highest ticket, to each election dist. by the chairman of town meetings. In cities there is 1 such dist. if under 500 inhabitants; 2, if from 500 to 800; and there may be more if above 800. In towns of over 500, the supervisor, assessors, and clerk meet annually to designate or change these districts. If vacancies of supervisors, assessors. commissioners of highways, or overseers of the poor are not filled within 15 days, the justices may appoint; and, if from any cause there be less than 3, they may asso-

ciate justices of neighboring towns in making appointments. [g] Towns in Sullivan co. may have 1 or 3; and if 1, he is chosen annually. Oyster Bay, Oswegatchie, and Watervliet have 5, and Southold 6. [h] Towns may decide upon the number. Manlius has 7. [i] In Seneca co. 1 in each town. [j] See exceptions on p. 36. [k] Annual school meetings determine whether to elect 1 or 3.

Among the officers of local jurisdiction, not included in the foregoing lists, are harbor masters, wardens, health officers, and others connected with sanitary supervision, pilots, wreck masters, superintendent of Onondaga salt springs, and officers charged with duties relating to Indian affairs.

PRISONS.

For a great number of offenses criminals are sentenced to be confined at labor for different periods of time, and the State has provided prisons at several places for the security of these offenders against law.[1] The principal of these are the three State Prisons, an Asylum for Insane Convicts, two Houses of Refuge, and several penitentiaries and jails.

The Auburn State Prison is located upon a lot of 10 acres near the center of the city of Auburn. It consists of the prison proper, containing 800 cells and a large number of workshops, all surrounded by a high and strong wall. **The Sing Sing State Prison** is located upon a lot of 130 acres upon the Hudson, in the village of Sing Sing. It contains a prison for males and another for females, the latter the only one in the State. It has an aggregate of 1,000 cells and a great variety of workshops.[2] **The Clinton State Prison** is situated upon a lot of 250 acres in the town of Dannemora. About 25 acres are inclosed within the walls of the prison. It contains workshops, forges, and furnaces, and has an aggregate of 396 cells.[3]

The general supervision of the State Prisons is intrusted to a Board of 3 Inspectors, one of whom is elected each year for a term of three years.[4] They appoint all the officers of the several prisons and renew them at pleasure.[5] The discipline of the several prisons is rigid and uniform, and all convicts are treated alike, irrespective of their former standing in society or of the crimes of which they are convicted. The rules for the general conduct of prisoners are rigidly enforced. In the administration of discipline a leading object is to secure the reform of the criminal and his return to society with regular and industrious habits and correct moral principles.[6] All convicts in health are required to labor in shops by day, under rigid supervision, and without exchanging words or looks with each other or with those who may visit the prison. They observe strict silence upon all occasions when not addressed by some person allowed the privilege. In passing to and from the cells, shops, and dining rooms, they march in close single columns, with their

---

[1] By an act of March 26, 1796, John Watts, Matthew Clarkson, Isaac Sloatenburgh, Thomas Eddy, and John Murray, jr. were appointed commissioners to build a State prison in New York City. This prison, styled "*Newgate*," was located on a lot of 9 acres on the Hudson, at the foot of Amos St. with its principal front on Greenwich St. It was 204 feet long, and from each end a wing extended to the river. It had 54 rooms, each for 8 persons, and cost $208,846. It was opened Nov. 25, 1797, and continued in use until May, 1828, when it was sold. Convicts were employed in shoe and nail making and other work in leather and iron, and as carpenters, tailors, weavers, spinners, and gardeners. A second prison was ordered, in 1796, to be built at Albany, but the act was repealed in 1797. The limited accommodations and wretched moral influences of the New York prison led to the ordering of another prison, in 1816, which was located at Auburn. The south wing was completed in 1818, and in 1819 the north wing was ordered to be fitted up with single cells. The prison was enlarged in 1824.

[2] An act passed March 7, 1824, ordered a prison to be erected at Sing Sing. Work was begun May 14, 1825, and the prison was finished in 1829, with 800 cells, to which 200 were added in 1830. It was finally completed in 1831. The grounds here occupy 130 acres, and include marble quarries, upon which it was designed to employ the convicts. The State Hall at Albany is built of magnesian marble or dolomite quarried and dressed at this prison. The prison for females is built of rough marble in the Ionic style of architecture. It stands on elevated ground and is entirely distinct from the male prison in its offices and management. Previous to its erection, in 1835–40, female convicts were kept by the city of New York at their prison at Bellevue, at an annual cost to the State of $100 each.

[3] Clinton Prison was built, in 1844–45, under the direction of Ransom Cook, with the design of employing convicts in iron mining and manufacture.

[4] These Inspectors must visit all the State prisons four times a year, in company, inspect their management, discipline, and financial affairs, keep minutes of their proceedings, and report annually to the Legislature. They establish rules for the observance of the officers of the prisons, and may examine witnesses. One prison is assigned to each Inspector for three months, and he is required to spend at least one week in each month at the prison in special charge, and to inform himself minutely concerning its details. The Inspectors are successively changed to other prisons. Inspectors can make no appointments of relations within the 3d degree, and they can have no interest in contracts. Their salary is $1600.—*Constitution, Art.* V, *Sec.* 4.

[5] The officers of each prison consist of the following:—
1. *An Agent, or Warden,* who is the principal fiscal officer of

the prison. He receives a salary of $1,250 to $1,500, and is required to give a bond of $25,000.

2. *A Principal Keeper,* who has charge of police regulations and discipline of the prison, and must live upon the premises. He keeps a journal of every infraction of rules, records, punishments, complaints, &c., and reports monthly to the Inspectors. Salary, $——.

3. *Keepers* under the direction of the Principal are appointed, not to exceed 1 for every 25 prisoners. Salary, $——.

4. *A Clerk,* who records all commitments and discharges, keeps the accounts, and reports annually to the Secretary of State. Salary, $1,000 at Sing Sing and $900 at the other prisons.

5. *The Chaplain* visits prisoners in their cells, devotes a stated time each Sabbath to religious services, keeps the prison library, and allows the use of books, under proper regulations, and is expected to counsel and assist convicts in the formation of settled resolutions for reform upon leaving the prison. Through him they may obtain whatever is allowed of correspondence with friends. Salary, $900.

6. *A Physician and Surgeon,* who has charge of the Hospital and attends at all times when his services are required. Salary, $700 at Sing Sing and $600 at the other prisons.

7. *Instructors,* of which there are 2 each at Auburn and Sing Sing, 1 at Clinton, and 1 at the Female Prison, who give all necessary instruction to the prisoners in their several occupations.

8. *A Store Keeper,* who has general charge of the provisions and clothing and other property belonging to the prison.

9. *A Guard,* under the command of a sergeant, who are stationed in the prison and upon the walls to prevent escapes. The number of privates is 20 at Auburn, 25 at Clinton, and 30 at Sing Sing. They are armed and equipped from the State arsenals, and are held legally justified if they shoot down prisoners attempting to escape.

10. *A Matron,* who has charge of the Female Prison. Assistant matrons are appointed, not to exceed 1 for every 25 prisoners.

[6] Solitary confinement without labor was tried at Auburn in 1821, but with the most unhappy results, and in 1823 the present system was adopted upon the suggestion of Capt. Elam Lynds and John D. Cray. Capt. Lynds deserves particular notice from the energy and firmness with which he brought his favorite system into successful operation and to a degree of perfection scarcely conceivable to one who had not witnessed it. This plan has been adopted in many prisons and has received the name of the "Auburn System." The labor not required in the domestic affairs of these prisons is hired upon contract to manufacturers, who put up the requisite machinery and employ agents and foremen to superintend the work. Willful violation of the rules is punished by the lash, ball and chain, yoke, strait jacket, shower bath, dark cell, and similar means.

faces turned to the side on which their keeper walks. Their shops have narrow openings in the walls, through which they may be seen without the possibility of knowing it. They are confined at night in solitary cells; and guards with woolen socks tread silently around their cells at all hours of the night. The fare is abundant, but coarse; and all convicts are required to wear a costume peculiar to the prison.[1]

An Asylum for Insane Convicts is located at Auburn, in the rear of the prison. It is under the general charge of a medical superintendent.[2]

The New York House of Refuge, situated upon Randalls Island, near New York City, is an establishment for the reformation of juvenile offenders. It is partly a State and partly a city institution.[3] **The Western House of Refuge,** located upon a farm of 42½ acres in Rochester, is another juvenile establishment of a similar kind. It is entirely under State patronage. These institutions are under rigid discipline; and the inmates receive instruction in the elementary branches of education during certain hours of the day, and are required to labor during certain other hours. The New York institution was established in 1824, and receives both sexes. The Rochester institution was started in 1849, and receives boys only.[4]

The Prison Association of New York was formed Dec. 6, 1844, and incorporated May 9, 1846. It has for its objects the amelioration of the condition of prisoners, whether detained for trial or finally convicted, or as witnesses; the improvement of prison discipline and of the government of prisons, whether for cities, counties, or States; and the support and encouragement of reformed convicts after their discharge, by affording them the means of obtaining an honest livelihood and sustaining them in their efforts at reform.[5] The association is supported entirely by private contribution. The members pay $10 annually. The payment of $25 constitutes a member

STATISTICS OF STATE PRISONS.

YEARS.	AVERAGE NUMBER OF CONVICTS.					TOTAL YEARLY EARNINGS.				EXPENSES INCLUDING IMPROVEMENTS.			
	Auburn.	Sing Sing. Male.	Sing Sing. Female.	Clinton.	Total.	Auburn.	Sing Sing.	Clinton.	Total.	Auburn.	Sing Sing.	Clinton.	Total.
1848	497	664	80	146	1,387	$53,456.71	$51,652.77	$5,549.46	$110,658.94	$66,960.41	$97,221.41	$39,900.98	$204,082.80
1849	512	637	76	157	1,382	63,021.54	63,052.83	13,210.97	139,285.34	56,777.99	81,850.28	50,126.47	188,754.74
1850	661	661	84	119	1,525	68,737.31	71,178.99	18,451.95	158,368.25	71,164.07	95,828.64	37,698.97	204,686.68
1851	752	723	73	114	1,662	73,494.91	88,385.27	17,664.10	179,544.28	88,546.25	79,506.82	37,958.13	206,011.20
1852	759	788	81	125	1,753	64,986.29	99,380.12	29,736.20	194,102.61	86,291.73	85,414.42	39,825.20	211,531.35
1853	753	865	96	186	1,900	81,150.24	99,082.89	37,207.77	217,440.90	80,516.37	120,818.73	49,483.14	250,818.24
1854	747	933	110	199	1,989	81,994.74	95,345.34	41,674.04	219,014.12	72,417.82	136,142.24	61,088.75	269,648.81
1855	730	915	111	249	2,005	74,948.53	90,904.71	32,372.19	198,225.43	67,783.15	116,774.37	48,832.42	233,389.94
1856	686	862	101	304	1,953	72,763.48	86,440.89	38,100.76	197,305.13	69,915.46	100,523.39	55,032.74	225,471.57
1857	678	976	84	278	2,016	69,954.08	94,946.97	26,882.58	191,783.63	74,180.35	109,586.53	47,947.29	231,714.17

The surplus expenses of the State prisons are paid from the general fund. For a fuller account of these institutions, see *Introduction to Natural History of New York,* Vol. I, pp. 181–188.

2 Until 1859, persons charged with crime and proved insane were sent to the State Lunatic Asylum at Utica. An act for the erection of the present asylum was passed April 13, 1855, and the building was completed in 1858.

3 The New York Asylum is conducted by a close corporation, consisting of 30 managers, who serve without pay and report annually to the Common Council of New York and to the State Legislature. It is supported by the labor of its inmates, an annual appropriation from the Marine Hospital fund, theater and circus licenses, school moneys from the Board of Education, and grants from the City and State of New York. It can accommodate 1,000 inmates. In 1858 there were received 378; of which number 304 were boys and 74 were girls. The former are engaged in making shoes, chair-seats, wire cloth, weaving, &c.; the latter in needlework. Each day 7 hours are devoted to labor, 4¼ to school, 1½ to meals, 9½ to sleep, and 1½ to recreation.

4 *Statistics of Houses of Refuge for 1857.*

	New York.	Rochester.
Cost per capita	$85	$96
Officers employed	31	22
Aggregate salaries	$9,119	$8,345
Revenue from labor	$13,414	$12,000
Per cent. reformed	75	75
Average period of detention	16 mo.	24 mo.
Deaths since opening	59	14
" in last 12 months	3	1
Escapes since opening	97	9
" in last 12 months	4	0
Average age of inmates	13½	13½
Cost of location and buildings	$330,441	$110,000
Annual expenses	$42,005	30,000

The Western House of Refuge is supported by the labor of its inmates, the product of its farm, and an annual State appropriation. Its managers are appointed for a term of 3 years by the Governor and Senate, and are so classified that 5 are appointed annually. Its rules require half an hour more at labor and an hour less at school than is required at the New York Asylum; and 10 hours are allowed for sleep. In 1859, 508 boys were received at this institution. Of these, 128 were employed in making chains, 171 in making shoes, 37 in making brushes, 7 upon the farm, 20 in the sewing rooms, and 23 as domestics.

5 The condition of prisoners has from a remote period enlisted the sympathies of the benevolent and led to associated efforts for their relief. A society was formed in New York, soon after the Revolution, for the relief of imprisoned debtors. "The Philadelphia Society for alleviating the miseries of Public Prisons" was formed over 80 years since by the Friends; and the Prison Discipline Society of Boston is nearly 20 years older than that of similar objects in New York. The Prison Association of New York for some time issued a bulletin called the "Monthly Record." The female department for some years maintained a Home for the temporary residence of discharged female prisoners until other means of support could be found. This association has for several years appointed committees for visiting county jails; and the facts reported show abundant reason for continuing efforts for reform in their management. The aid furnished by this association to discharged convicts during the last three years reported has been as follows:—

	1854.	1855.	1856.
Number of discharged persons aided with money	230	439	282
Number supplied with clothing	131	147	138
Number provided with situations	52	155	112
Total	413	741	532

foi life; of $100, an honorary member of the Executive Committee for life, and $500 a life patron. A department, consisting of ladies, has in charge the interests of prisoners of their sex. The managers of the association receive no pay for their services. They usually report to the Legislature annually; but no reports were made in 1856 and 1858. Office, 15 Center Street, New York.

MILITARY.

THE Governor is Commander-in-Chief of the land and naval forces of the State. In time of peace the supervision of the militia and military establishments is intrusted to the Adjutant General, who has an office of record at the capital, issues, under his seal, all military commissions, keeps a register of the names and residences of the officers of militia throughout the State, issues all orders on behalf of the Commander-in-Chief, prescribes the manner of reporting from the several subordinate divisions, and reports the statistics thus obtained—through the Governor—to the Legislature annually.[1] He has the rank of brigadier general; and his assistant has the rank of colonel. The militia of the State is composed of 8 divisions, 26 brigades, and 62 regiments, embracing 220 companies of infantry, 126 of artillery, 41 of cavalry, 37 of rifles, and a total of 18,107 officers and privates.[2]

All able-bodied white male citizens between the ages of 18 and 45, not exempt by law, are

[1] OFFICERS OF THE NEW YORK STATE MILITIA.

GENERAL STAFF.			
GENERAL OFFICERS.	Major Generals	8
	Brigadier Generals	26
ADJUTANT GENERAL'S DEPART.	Adjutant General	1
	Assistant Adjutant General	1
	Division Inspectors (Colonels)	8
	Brigade Inspectors (Majors)	23
	Adjutants (Lieutenants)	57
	Inspector General	1
COMMISSARY GENERAL'S DEPART.	Commissary General	1
	Assistant Commissary General	1
DEPART. OF ENGINEERS.	Engineer-in-Chief	1
	Division Engineers (Colonels)	7
	Brigade Engineers (Majors)	25
	Regimental Engineers (Captains)	50
JUDGE ADV. GENERAL'S DEPART.	Judge Advocate General	1
	Division Judge Advocates (Colonels)	8
	Brigade Judge Advocates (Majors)	25
SURGEON GENERAL'S DEPART.	Surgeon General	1
	Hospital Surgeons (Colonels)	7
	Surgeons (Captains)	22
	Surgeon's Mates (Lieutenants)	52
Q'RMASTER GENERAL'S DEPART.	Quartermaster General	1
	Division Quartermasters (Lieut. Cols.)	5
	Brigade Quartermasters (Captains)	25
	Regimental Quartermasters (Lieutenants)	38
PAYMASTER GENERAL'S DEPART.	Paymaster General	1
	Division Paymasters (Majors)	5
	Brigade Paymasters (Captains)	21
	Regimental Paymasters (Lieutenants)	54
	Aids-de-Camp	41

LINE.			
FIELD OFFICERS.	Colonels	60
	Lieutenant Colonels	60
	Majors	58
COMPANY OFFICERS.	Captains	402
	First Lieutenants	379
	Second Lieutenants	460
	Non-Commissioned Staff	143
	Company Non-Commissioned Officers, Musicians, and Privates	15,874
STAFF CORPS.	Sappers and Miners (attached to Engineer Department)	103
	Total	18,107

The office of the Adjutant General was· made an office of record in 1827, previous to which commissions were issued by the Secretary of State, under the privy seal of the Governor.

[2] In Jan., 1859, the division districts were as follows:—

1. New York and Richmond cos.
2. Kings, Orange, Putnam, Queens, Rockland, Suffolk, and Westchester cos.
3. Albany, Columbia, Dutchess, Greene, Rensselaer, Saratoga, Sullivan, Ulster, and Washington cos.
4. Clinton, Essex, Franklin, Jefferson, Lewis, St. Lawrence, and Warren cos.
5. Broome, Chenango, Cortland, Delaware, Fulton, Hamilton, Herkimer, Madison, Montgomery, Otsego, Schenectady, and Schoharie cos.
6. Cayuga, Oneida, Onondaga, Oswego, Schuyler, Seneca, Tioga, and Tompkins cos.
7. Chemung, Livingston, Monroe, Ontario, Steuben, Wayne, and Yates cos.
8. Allegany, Cattaraugus, Chautauqua, Erie, Genesee, Niagara, Orleans, and Wyoming cos.

The estimated number of enrolled militia, at the beginning of 1859, was 350,000. Those included in regiments were as follows:—

Infantry.....7.490 privates, and 8.094 including officers.
Artillery....5,365   "   "   5,760   "   "
Cavalry....1.590   "   "   1.733   "   "
Rifles........1,429   "   "   1,528   "   "

liable to military duty. An enrolment is made annually by the assessors.[1] Militia officers are chosen by election;[2] excepting major generals and the Commissary General, who are appointed by the Governor and Senate. Staff officers are appointed by the commanding officer of the forces to which they are attached.[3] The Adjutant General, Judge Advocate General, Quartermaster General, Paymaster General, Surgeon General, Engineer-in-Chief, and one Instructor of Artillery and one of Cavalry to each division, are appointed by the Governor.[4]

Arsenals. An arsenal is provided for each division of the Militia, and an armory for each regiment. The general custody and supervision of the military property of the State is intrusted to the Commissary General, who has his office in New York, and reports annually through the Governor to the Legislature.[5]

---

[1] The laws of the U. S. exempt from military service the Vice President, the Judicial and Executive officers of the Government of the U. S., members and officers of both Houses of Congress, customhouse officers and clerks, post officers and stage drivers in carriage of mails, ferrymen on post roads, inspectors of exports, pilots and mariners in actual sea service. The State exempts, besides the above, persons in the army and navy and those honorably discharged therefrom, preachers of every sect, commissioned officers and privates of uniformed companies who have resigned after seven years' service, and certain firemen. All others may commute by paying 50 cts. annually, except in Kings and New York cos. and the cities of Albany and Buffalo, where the commutation is fixed at 75 cts.

These moneys are paid to the collectors of taxes and applied to the military fund, from which the officers and men of regiments are paid, from $1.25 to $4, according to rank, for every day's military service. Persons going to, remaining at, or returning from military duty are exempt from arrest upon civil process. Previous to the act of 1846, the State contained 33 divisions, 66 brigades, 272 regiments, and 1836 companies, and numbered 141,436 officers and men. The number of enrolled militia had been as follows, at different periods:—

Years.	Infantry.	Artillery.	Cavalry.	Light Artillery.	Riflemen.	Total.
1805	74,429	1,700	1,852	......	......	77,982
1810	86,673	2,619	3,385	......	......	92,677
1815	90,383	6,364	2,158	......	......	98,905
1820	112,760	6,538	3,132	123	......	122,553
				Horse Artill'y.		
1825	131,561	4,432	2,505	646	......	146,805
1830	166,514	12,803	5,814	1,763	......	188,610
1835	168,786	11,698	7,317	1,174	......	192,083
1840	163,300	9,082	7,336	......	......	183,100
1845	141,436	9,369	3,849	......	4,276	162,427

[2] Under the Constitution of 1777, nearly every military as well as civil officer in the State received his appointment from the Council of Appointment, and mostly held during their pleasure. The Constitution of 1822 introduced the following system, now in use:—"Militia officers shall be chosen or appointed, as follows: Captains, subalterns, and non-commissioned officers shall be chosen by the written votes of the members of their respective companies; field officers of regiments and separate battalions, by the written votes of the commissioned officers of the respective regiments and separate battalions; brigadier generals and brigade inspectors, by the field officers of their respective brigades; major generals, brigadier generals, and commanding officers of regiments or separate battalions shall appoint the staff officers to their respective divisions, brigades, regiments, or separate battalions."—*Constitution*, 1822, Art. IV, Sec. 1; *Constitution*, Art. XI, Sec. 2.

The above rule does not apply to regiments and brigades not fully organized. If the former contain less than 6 companies, the field officers are appointed by the Governor; and if the brigades are not within the requirements of the law, the brigadier generals are also appointed by the Governor. *Const.* 1846.

[3] The staff of the Commander-in-Chief consists of the Adjutant General, Inspector General, Commissary General, Engineer-in-Chief, Judge Advocate General, Surgeon General, Quartermaster General, Paymaster General, Aids-de-Camp, and Military Secretary, who severally rank in the order here given. The precedence and gradation of officers and non-commissioned officers in the militia is as follows:—

1. The Commander-in-Chief.	8. First Lieutenant.
2. Major General.	9. Second Lieutenant.
3. Brigadier General.	10. Sergeant-Major.
4. Colonel.	11. Quartermaster Sergeant.
5. Lieutenant Colonel.	12. First Sergeant.
6. Major.	13. Sergeant.
7. Captain.	14. Corporal.

In each grade precedence is given by priority in date of election, or appointment.

[4] The instructors, with the rank of colonel, are attached to the headquarters of the division, and hold by the same tenure as commissioned officers of the line. Instructors and division engineers must pass an examination as to special qualification before a board of not less than five officers, convened by the Commander-in-Chief. Appointments to this office have hitherto been made entirely from among the graduates of West Point.

[5] The Constitution of 1777 ordained that a proper magazine of warlike stores, proportionate to the number of inhabitants, should be established in every county of the State; but this provision was never fully carried out. An arsenal was built at New York at an early period, and another at Albany soon after, the latter on the site purchased for a State prison. Under an act of Feb. 12, 1808, entitled "An Act for the defense of the northern and western frontiers," and by subsequent acts, arsenals were erected at Canandaigua, Batavia, Onondaga Hollow, Rome, Watertown, Russell, Malone, Plattsburgh, and Elizabethtown.

The arsenal at Plattsburgh was burned in 1813 or '14, and the one at Rome, which occupied the present site of St. Peter's Church, was burned with its contents a few years since. Neither has been rebuilt. In 1844 the State leased the city of Buffalo a market building on Batavia St. for an arsenal. Magazines were also located at New York, at Albany, and on Staten Island. In 1850 these arsenals were mostly ordered to be sold, together with such arms and other property as had become unserviceable for military purposes. An arsenal occupying the site of an old powder magazine of the Dutch, between Center, Elm, Franklin, and White Streets, New York, was authorized to be sold in 1844, and a new one was directed to be built. The site was purchased by the city for $30,000, and a new city armory was built, on the corner of White and Elm Streets. In 1808 the city of New York conveyed to the State a tract of ground upon Fifth Avenue, between Sixty-Third and Sixty-Fifth Sts., upon which a magazine was erected. In 1844 the Legislature authorized a new arsenal to be erected on these premises with such moneys as might be paid by the U. S. for the military works upon Staten Island. The sale was completed in April, 1847, for $37,284.87, of which $33,284.87 was applicable to the arsenal. The work was commenced, but in March, 1848, was suspended by the Commissioners of the Land Office, to whose charge and that of the Commissary General the work had been intrusted. It was alleged that the latter officer had expended moneys most unwarrantably; and subsequent observation has proved that the structure was unfit for this or, in fact, for any other purpose.—*Assembly Doc.* 1856, No. 141. *Senate Doc.* 1848, No. 54.

In laying out the Central Park, the premises consisting of 152 building lots, valued in 1856 at $266,000, were included in the proposed improvement, and an act was passed, April 15, 1857, under which this property, which the State purchased in 1808 for $700, was conveyed back to the city for $275,000. Of this sum $100,000 was made applicable to the erection of an arsenal at New York; $45,000 for an arsenal at Buffalo; $40,000 for an arsenal in Brooklyn; $25,000 for the improvement of the arsenal at Albany and the erection of an armory; $17,000 for the purchase of the U. S. arsenal at Rome; $14,000 for an arsenal at Corning, and for armories; $5,000 at Rochester, $5,000 at Troy, $4,000 at Auburn, $4,000 at Syracuse, $4,000 at Utica, $3,000 at Ballston Spa, $3,000 at Dunkirk, $3,000 at Ogdensburgh, $3,000 at Oswego, and $3,000 for the purchase of a stone fort in Schoharie for an armory. The arsenal in Albany, by act of April 17, 1858, was exchanged with the city for a site on Hudson and Eagle Streets, and $5,000 toward an arsenal and armory buildings, which were erected in 1858–59. During the summer of 1858, buildings at Albany, Auburn, Ballston Spa, Brooklyn, Corning, Dunkirk, New York, Ogdensburgh, and Syracuse were put under contract and finished, or far advanced, the same year. The stone fort or church at Schoharie was purchased, but no steps were taken for the erections authorized at Troy, Rochester, Oswego, and Utica. The new arsenal built at New York in 1858 was located on Seventh Avenue, corner of Thirty-Fifth St., and was nearly completed, when the roof fell, on the morning of Nov. 13, 1858, greatly injuring the building.

Most of the structures erected under this act are of substantial workmanship and elegant architectural style. They were built under the direction of commissioners appointed by law. When completed, they will be placed in charge of the Commissary General, who also attends to the safe keeping of arms and

The fortifications within the State are owned and supported by the United States although several of them were built by the State of New York under an arrangement for the settlement of the Revolutionary debt.[1]

military equipments belonging to the State. He keeps his office in New York.

Summary of the ordnance arms in the hands of the troops and in the arsenals of the State on the 1st day of January, 1859.

Six pounders	101	Musquetoons	222
Nine pounders	3	Carbines	340
Twelve pound howitzers	5	Cavalry sabres	1,337
Twenty-four pound howitzers	7	Artillery sabres	1,188
Mountain howitzers	13	Artillery swords	1,344
Flint muskets and bayonets	671	Cartridge boxes and plates	10,744
Percussion muskets and bayonets	11,975	Cartridge box belts and plates	10,813
Flint rifles	563	Bayonet scabbard belts and plates	9,890
Percussion rifles	1,365	Waist belts and plates	9,258
Flint pistols	114	Cap pouches	7,155
Percussion pistols	2,254	Pistol holsters	1,553

[1] In Feb. 1801, there was due from the State of New York to the United States, on account of Revolutionary expenses, the sum of $2,074,846. An Act of Congress, passed February 15, 1799, allowed any State to discharge its debt by payment into the treasury before April, 1800, or by expending a like amount within five years in the erection of fortifications. New York was the only State that chose to extinguish its debt by erecting defenses upon its own soil; and a committee of Congress reported in February, 1801, that no other States had shown any disposition to pay the balances reported against them. The amount credited to New York was $891,129.31, and the remainder of the indebtedness was subsequently released.—*American State Papers, Finance*, I, 697.

The amount of moneys reduced to specie value received by, or paid to, the State of New York from the beginning of the Revolution to April, 1790, was as follows, in dollars :—

Received from State	$1,545,889
Paid to State	822,803

A descriptive and historical notice is given of the several fortifications in the localities where they occur. The latest official summary that has been published, dated in 1851, is given below :—

United States Fortifications.

FORTS.	LOCATION.	When commenced.	When finished.	Garrison in war.	Total number of guns.	Estimated cost of construction or repair.	Amount expended for construction or repair.	Amount required to complete or construct.	Estimated cost of armament, including 100 pounds of ammunition.
Fort Schuyler	Throggs Neck	1833	......	1,250	318	$873,013	$848,013	$25,000	$225,040
Fort Columbus	Governors Island	1831	......		105	....	....	....	103,749
Castle Williams		1831	......	} 800	78	269,467	259,467	10,000	79,332
South Battery		1831	1845		14	....	....	....	12,184
Fort Gibson	Ellis Island	1841	1844	80	15	5,096	5,096	....	18,672
Fort Wood	Bedloes Island	1841	......	350	77	245,689	213,000	32,689	76,540
Fort Richmond	Staten Island	1847	......		140	505,808	205,606	300,202	124,302
Fort Tompkins		......	1846	} 1,000	64	....	....	....	59,209
Battery, Hudson		1841	1846		50	20,081	20,081	....	57,060
Battery, Morton		1841	1846		9	3,508	3,508	....	10,665
Fort Lafayette	Reef, near Long Island	1812	......	370	76	348,573	341,941	6,632	75,778
Fort Hamilton	Long Island	1824	......	800	118	634,752	614,752	20,000	86,757
Fort Montgomery	Rouses Point	1841	......	500	164	411,497	187,355	224,142	132,384
Fort Ontario	Oswego	1839	......	300	30	83,013	78,013	5,000	18,610
Fort Niagara	Mouth of Niagara River	1840	......	300	21	84,027	59,027	25,000	12,961
Fort Porter	Black Rock	1842	......	300	64	150,000	116,500	33,500	51,208

The forts on Staten Island are being rebuilt on an extensive scale. Fort Schuyler, on Throggs Neck, has since been finished, a site purchased for a fort at Wilkins Point, directly opposite, and an immense fortress has been commenced on Sandy Hook, for the more effectual defense of New York Harbor. These works will effectually defend the approaches to New York by water, but would not prevent an attack by land should an enemy effect a landing upon Long Island. To guard against this, it has been proposed to erect a line of redoubts across the island from Wilkins Point to Fort Hamilton at such intervals as would secure this object.

The General Government has appropriated large sums of money during many years to the construction of a floating battery for the defense of New York Harbor. It is building at Hoboken, and is said to be nearly completed. It is of iron, of great strength and thickness, with its outer deck oval, and every part proof against cannon ball. It is to be mounted with heavy guns and propelled by steam. No official account of its construction has been published; and, for obvious reasons, the details of its plan are kept secret. It is reported that it has a capacity to accommodate 3000 men, with the necessary supplies of fuel and military stores; and it is thought that of itself it might oppose an effectual barrier against the approach of a hostile fleet in any passage which it might be brought to defend. This mighty engine of war was planned by the late John C. Stevens.

The other military establishments of the National Government in New York are,—

The Military Academy at West Point.

The Navy Yard, Dry Dock, Naval Hospital, and Laboratory at Brooklyn.

The Arsenal at Watervliet for the manufacture of gun carriages and other heavy furniture of artillery for the field and fort.

The Arsenal of Deposit, at Rome.

Plattsburgh Barracks.

Madison Barracks, at Sackets Harbor.

Buffalo Barracks.

A few years after the last war with Great Britain, a military road was surveyed and partly opened by the United States from Plattsburgh to Sackets Harbor; but this work from the first has been kept in repair by the towns as a common highway.

Fort Montgomery is the only work now under construction on the northern frontier. The Canadians have the following fortifications adjacent to New York :—

Fort Wellington, at Prescott, erected in 1812–15.

Fort Henry, at Kingston, with several Martello towers and batteries, for the protection of the harbor and town and defense of the north channel of the St. Lawrence. They were partly built in the War of 1812–15, and partly in 1837–40. Fort Carlton, now within the United States, commanded the south channel, and portions of the work, executed a century ago, (and since the Revolution entirely neglected,) might still be made available upon short notice.

Fort Massasauga, at Niagara, directly opposite the American fort, is of modern origin.

NOTE.—By the Militia Regulations of this State, the device at the head of this article is borne upon buttons and other insignia worn by military officers.

LANDS.

The absolute property of all the lands in the State is vested in the respective owners, liable only to escheat and to the reservation of gold and silver mines in such as derive title from Colonial patents.[1]

The law prohibits the leasing of agricultural lands for a longer period than twelve years.[2] The care and sale of lands belonging to the State are intrusted to the Commissioners of the Land Office. These commissioners have also the sole right of dealing with the Indians for the sale and surrender of reservations, excepting within the territory whereof the pre-emptive right of purchase was ceded to Massachusetts and is now held by the Ogden Company.

The Commissioners of the Land Office were created by an act of May 11, 1784, to carry into execution the promises of bounty lands for Revolutionary services which had been made by the Legislature in 1780. As now formed, this Board consists of the Lieutenant Governor of the State, Speaker of Assembly, Secretary of State, Comptroller, Treasurer, Attorney General, and State Engineer and Surveyor. The Deputy Secretary of State is *ex officio* Clerk of the Board, and the meetings are held in the Secretary's office, upon the call of the Secretary of State.

When State lands are to be sold, they are first surveyed, appraised, and advertised for sale at auction, and their minimum bid affixed. The lots that remain without a bid are liable to be taken by the first applicant upon payment of one-fourth of the price and giving bonds for the residue. If they remain unsold any considerable time, they are re-appraised and offered at a lower rate.[3]

The lands under water in the bays around Long Island are in most cases the property of the townships, by virtue of original patents; and the privilege of fishing and taking oysters and clams is by some towns held as exclusively belonging to their inhabitants.[4]

---

[1] The Dutch Government sometimes granted lands in the Colony without the formalities of Indian purchase; but it was the rule of the English to first extinguish the aboriginal title. It was customary to apply to the Governor and Council for leave to purchase. If granted, a treaty was held and an Indian deed obtained, a warrant was issued to the Surveyor General for a survey, and the map and field notes were reported. The Attorney General was then directed to prepare a draft of a patent, which was submitted to the Governor and Council, and, if approved, was engrossed upon parchment, recorded, sealed, and issued. The fees incident to procuring a patent were important sources of revenue to the officers concerned. Only 1,000 acres could be granted to one person; but this rule was evaded by associating great numbers of merely nominal parties; and the officers through whose hands the papers passed were often largely interested in the grants. The Colonial Government in this respect became exceedingly corrupt, and stood greatly in need of a reform like that wrought by the Revolution. In a few isolated cases grants of land were made directly by the crown, and no records appear in our offices. Of this class was the Royal Grant to Sir Wm. Johnson, N. of the Mohawk. Patents for land were generally very formal, and abounded in repetitions. The grants were "in fee and common socage," as in the manor of East Greenwich, in the co. of Kent, and included with the land all "houses, messuages, tenements, erections, and buildings, mills, milldams, fences, inclosures, gardens, orchards, fields, pastures, common of pastures, meadows, marshes, swamps, plains, woods, underwoods, timber, trees, rivers, rivulets, runs, streams, water, lakes, ponds, pools, pits, brachen, quarries, mines, minerals, (gold and silver [wholly or in part] excepted,) creeks, harbors, highways, easements, fishing, hunting, and fowling, and all other franchises, profits, commodities, and appurtenances whatsoever." This enumeration of rights, more or less varied, was embraced in all land patents. Colonial grants were usually conditioned to the annual payment of a *quitrent*, at a stated time and place named in the patent. This payment was sometimes due in money, and often in wheat or other commodity. Others were conditioned to the payment of the skins of animals or a merely nominal article, as simply an acknowledgment of the superior rights of the grantors. The quitrents formed an important source of revenue, and, after the Revolution, became due to the State. In 1786 it was provided that lands subject to these rents might be released upon payment of arrears, and 14 shillings to every shilling of the annual dues. Large amounts of land upon which arrears of quitrents had accumulated were sold from time to time; and laws continued to be passed at frequent intervals for the regulation of these rents until 1824, when an act was passed for the final sale of all lands which had not been released by commutation or remitted by law. Such lands as then remained unredeemed were allowed to be released by payment of $2.50 to each shilling sterling due. The last sale took place in March, 1826. The arrears for quitrents, then amounting to $53,380, were in 1819 taken from the general fund and given in equal portions to the Literature and School Funds.

[2] This feature was adopted to prevent the recurrence of anti-rent difficulties. The Legislature, in 1846, enacted a law providing that all lands previously rented for a life or lives, or for more than 21 years, should be taxed as the personal property of the persons receiving the rents, to an extent equal to a sum that at legal interest would produce the annual rent. Such taxes were made payable in the cos. where the lands lay; and this unpleasant encumbrance has largely contributed to reduce the amount of lands thus held.

[3] Unappropriated lands in the counties of Clinton, Essex, Franklin, Hamilton, Montgomery, Saratoga, St. Lawrence, Washington, and Warren may be sold by the commissioners in quantities of not less than 160 acres, if already surveyed, at such price as they may be found worth. If over 1,000 acres, they may be surveyed and sold for their value, and may not be assessed at a higher rate for five years. Lands sold under foreclosure of loan mortgages are bid in by the Loan Commissioners if liable to go for less than the sum due. They are then sold by auction, or otherwise, for the best interests of the State, under the regulations above stated. Land under water may be conveyed by the Commissioners of the Land Office, under regulations fixed by law. Notice of application for such grants must be advertised for six weeks in the co. newspaper where the lands lie, and posted on the courthouse door. These notices must describe the adjoining lands and give the names of their owners. Applicants must make affidavit that they intend to appropriate the lands applied for to commercial purposes. The co. judge, or supervisor and town clerk, or two assessors of the town where the lands lie, must make affidavit that the land is not more than is necessary for the purposes of commerce, and that the persons applying are believed to be *bona fide* applicants for the purposes stated. Applicants must also produce an accurate map of the proposed grant and the adjacent lands owned by them, certified by the oath of a surveyor; and also a correct description in writing, with courses and distances, and the soundings for every 50 feet on the exterior line. The map must show the general course of the shore for a mile each way, and the particular course at the point applied for, and include all docks, bulkheads, or other improvements, the names of owners of lands adjoining, and the width of the channel or river if less than two miles. The deduction of title and proof that the lands belong to the State must also be produced, with claim of ownership by the applicant, or by himself and those under whom he claims. The patent is conditioned to occupation in the mode agreed upon within —— years, and the fees are $5.00. Grants under the waters of navigable rivers and lakes can only be made to the owners of the land along the shores; and the commissioners are restricted in their powers so far as relates to New York City and the Hudson River R. R.

[4] Around Staten Island the owners of the shores possess the right of using or leasing the adjacent lands under water for planting oysters. The custom of granting lands under water without the restrictions here enumerated has led to serious encroachments upon the harbor of New York, the details of which are stated on pages 418, 419.

46

The public lands are greatly reduced in quantity, and belong to the several permanent funds to which they have from time to time been granted.[1]

Gospel and School Lands.—Under an act of 1782, a lot of 400 acres was to be reserved in each township of the Military Tract for the support of the gospel, and two lots of 200 acres for schools.[2]

In each of the Twenty Towns of the Chenango Tract a lot of 250 acres (usually Lot 45) was reserved for the gospel, and another (Lot 46) of like extent for schools; but these lots were sold with the lands, and the Canastota Tract, in Sullivan and Lenox, adjoining Oneida Lake, was in 1805–08 given in lieu, and apportioned among the Twenty Towns.[3]

In each of the Ten Towns on the St. Lawrence a mile square (usually Lot 55) was granted for gospel and schools, and in some towns was applied in early years to both these objects.[4]

Besides these grants for schools by the State, land proprietors have in some instances conveyed certain lots for this purpose, to encourage settlement. In nearly every instance these lands have been applied for the benefit of the original townships within which they were granted, and in their subdivision the local school fund has been equitably divided. Other lands were subsequently granted, as elsewhere noticed; and in 1822 the Constitution gave all the public lands not specially appropriated to the school fund.[5]

---

[1] The quantity now owned forms about 4½ per cent. of that held in 1823, and compares between the two periods as follows:—

	Jan. 1, 1823.	Jan. 1859.
Lands belonging to the School Fund......	991,659 A.	9,463 A.
" " Literature Fund	17,946 "	640 "
" " Canal	129,769 "	...... "
" " General	...... "	39,269 "
" " Salt	...... "	209 "
Total......	1,139,374 "	49,581 "

[2] These lots were designated by the supervisors of Onondaga and Seneca cos., under acts passed in 1796 and 1808, as follows:—

Gospel and School Lands of the Military Tract.

ORIGINAL TOWNSHIP AND ITS NUMBERS.	Gospel and School Lot.	Literature Lot.	Present Towns sharing in Profits of School Lot.
1. Lysander....	9	100	Lysander and part of Granby.
2. Hannibal....	5	14	Hannibal, Cicero. parts of Oswego City, and Granby.
3. Cato..........	25	89	Victory, Ira, and parts of Conquest and Cato.
4. Brutus	87	58	Brutus, and parts of Sennett, Mentz, Conquest, and Cato.
5. Camillus	72	15	Camillus, Elbridge, and Van Buren.
6. Cicero........	14	16	Clay and Cicero.
7. Manlius......	74	18	De Witt and Manlius.
8. Aurelius......	60	36	Owasco, Fleming, Auburn, and parts of Aurelius, Sennett, and Mentz.
9. Marcellus...	22	19	Marcellus, Skaneateles, and parts of Spafford and Otisco.
10. Pompey	67	30	Pompey, Lafayette, and part of Otisco.
11. Romulus....	50	55	Romulus, Varick, Fayette, and parts of Seneca Falls.
12. Scipio.........	1	82	Scipio, Venice, and part of Niles.
13. Sempronius	52	25	Sempronius, Moravia, and part of Niles.
14. Tully.........	76	69	Tully, Preble, Scott, and parts of Spafford and Otisco.
15. Fabius	3	36	Fabius and part of Truxton.
16. Ovid.........	30	23	Ovid, Lodi, and Covert.
17. Milton	24	56	Genoa and part of Lansing.
18. Locke........	15	94	Groton, Summer Hill, and Locke.
19. Homer.......	34	85	Homer and Cortlandville.
20. Solon........	22	41	Solon and part of Truxton.
21. Hector......	1	6	Hector.
22. Ulysses......	5	24	Ulysses, Enfield, Ithaca, and part of Lansing.
23. Dryden	29	63	Dryden.
24. Virgil........	36	20	Virgil.
25. Cincinnatus	53	49	Cincinnatus, Freetown, Marathon, and Willet.
26. Junius	78	79	Junius, Tyre, Waterloo, and part of Seneca Falls.
27. Galen........	45	33	Galen and Savannah.
28. Sterling......	73ᵃ	88	Sterling, Butler, Wolcott, Huron, and Rose.

ᵃ Exchanged for No. 17 by Chap. 177, Laws of 1812.

[3] In each of the following townships a lot of 640 acres was reserved for schools, viz.:—*Fayette,* now Guilford, and part of Oxford; *Clinton,* now Bainbridge, Afton, and part of Coventry; *Greene,* now parts of Greene, Smithville, and Coventry; *Warren,* now parts of Colesville, Sanford, and Windsor; *Chenango,* now parts of Port Crane, Conklin, Colesville, and Windsor; *Sidney,* now parts of Binghamton and Vestal; *Randolph,* now parts of Sanford, Windsor, and Conklin; and *Hamden,* now parts of Vestal, Owego, and Nichols.

[4] In Plattsburgh 640 acres was reserved for the gospel, and 460 for schools; and in Totten and Crossfield's Purchase 16 lots of 640 acres each. The latter have been selected under the Sackets Harbor and Saratoga R. R. Grant. In Benson Township (Hope and Lake Pleasant) 4 lots of 160 acres each were given for schools and literature.

[5] The lands of the school fund were, Jan. 1859, as follows:—4,270 acres in Hamilton, 2,861 in Essex, 1,680 in Clinton, 350 in Wayne, 105 in Schoharie, 75 in St. Lawrence, 30 in Washington, 28 in Oneida, 25 in Fulton, 16 in Montgomery, 12 in Herkimer, 6 in Dutchess, and 5 in Onondaga cos.

Literature Lands have been reserved as follows:—1 mi. square in each of the townships of Fayette, Greene, Clinton, Chenango, Warren, Sidney, and Hamden. Townships 1, 4, 5, 8, 13, 14, 17, 19, 31, 32, 33, 34, 35, 36, 38, 41, in Totten and Crossfield's Purchase. Lot No. 56 in each of the Ten Towns of St. Lawrence co. A lot of 550 acres (less 50 for survey) in each of the 28 towns of the Military Tract. These lots were appropriated as follows:—

Military Tract.—Townships 7, 8, 9, 10, 11, 12, 15, 16, 17, and 20, to Union College.

Township 13, to Oxford Academy, Chap. 112, Laws of 1800.

"	5, " Pompey	"	119,	"	1813.
"	3, " Cayuga	"	71,	"	1814.
"	1, " Onondaga	"	200,	"	1814.
"	19, " Cortland	"	10,	"	1822.
"	28, " Auburn	"	266,	"	1825.
"	22, " Ithaca	"	308,	"	1825.

The remainder were sold for the benefit of the Literature Fund.

Clinton Township, granted to the town of Jericho, Chap. 3, Laws of 1822. All other townships in Broome and Chenango cos. were sold for the benefit of the Literature Fund.

Ten Towns in St. Lawrence Co.—In Potsdam, granted to St. Lawrence Academy, Chap. 148, 1816. In Canton, granted to Lowville Academy, Chap. 134, Laws of 1818. The remainder was sold, and $1,000 given to Middlebury Academy in 1823; $1,000 to Redhook Academy in 1824; $2,500 to St. Lawrence Academy in 1825; and the remainder passed to the Literature Fund.

Totten and Crossfield's Purchase.—10,240 acres absorbed by S. H. & S. R. R. In Benson Township, 4 lots of 160 acres each remain unsold. Of the unsold lands of the State in Jan. 1859, there were 39,269 acres; of which 19,020 are in Clinton, 5,133 in Hamilton, 5,111 in Essex, 4,728 in Franklin, 1,643 in Warren, 1,147 in Delaware, and the same in Erie, 780 in Herkimer, 212 in Cortland, 175 in Seneca, 116 in Sullivan, and 57 in Washington cos.

The Salt Springs Lands are, by Article 7, Sec. 7 of the Constitution of 1846, declared as belonging inalienably to the State, and comprise the grounds upon which salt is manufactured, whether by solar evaporation or artificial heat. The Commissioners of the Land Office may sell, under authority of law, certain portions for the purpose of purchasing other lands, so that the amount shall not be diminished. Since 1846, 114.85 acres have been sold, for $153,039.50, and 543.12 acres purchased, for $154,161.79.

With certain exceptions[1] all property, both real and personal, is liable to taxation whether owned by individuals or corporations. Real estate is taxed in the town where it lies, unless adjacent to lands of the same owner or occupant in another town where he resides.

Personal property is taxed where the owner resides, and corporations in the towns where their property lies. Stocks of corporations are taxed to the company and not to the holders. Property may be sold for the payment of taxes, and lands upon which the taxes remain unpaid are returned by the co. treasurers to the comptroller, and so much of each parcel is sold at stated periods, as is necessary to pay the taxes, interest, and charges that accrue thereon.[2]

The pre-emptive title to the lands of the State w. of a meridian passing through the 82d mile-stone on the Penn. line, was conveyed to Massachusetts, (except a mile strip along the Niagara,) at a convention held at Hartford, Dec. 16, 1786. These lands amounted to about 6,000,000 acres. Ten towns of 234,400 acres, in Broome and Tioga cos., called "The Massachusetts Ten Towns," were also conveyed at the same time.

Large tracts of land remained in possession of the government when it became a State. These and other portions derived from forfeitures, escheats, tax sales, Indian purchases, and foreclosure of loan mortgages, have been sold in small parcels, as parts of large tracts, having a general name and system of survey. Sometimes as many patents have been issued for these tracts as they had lots, and in others many lots have been conveyed to the same person.

The largest grant ever made by the State to citizens was that of Macomb's Purchase, in Franklin, St. Lawrence, Jefferson, Lewis, Herkimer, and Oswego cos. It embraced 3,693,755 acres, and was patented to Daniel McCormick and Alexander Macomb in 1791–8. The State, in accordance with Indian treaties, has conveyed sundry tracts, the principal of which are Penet Square, (10 mi. sq.,) in Jefferson co., and Peraché's, Kirkland, and other minor tracts, in Oneida co. Others, for like cause, have been assigned for missions and other specific objects. The Legislature has also by acts directed the land commissioners to convey extensive tracts for the promotion of roads, railroads, and canals, colleges, academies, schools, and other institutions, and to reward military or other services to the State. Of the latter class was a grant of 16,000 acres in Oneida co. to Baron Steuben, in 1794.

Of patents to citizens not included in either of the preceding lists, the principal are Scriba's 500,000 acres in Oswego and Oneida cos.; Adgate's, Coxe's, Machin's, Oothoudt's, Remsen's, Dean's, and other tracts in Oneida; Vrooman's, Noble's, &c. in Herkimer; and Watkins & Flint's in Chemung and adjoining counties. Numerous grants of land to communities, with privileges of government, were made upon Long Island, and in the counties bordering upon the Hudson, which will be specially noticed in the localities to which they refer.

Several of the cities have special laws for the sale of real estate for taxes, and such sales are made under the direction of the fiscal officer of the corporation. All other tax sales occur at Albany once in three years, and are duly advertised by the Comptroller and in each co. by such newspapers as are designated by the supervisors.

---

[1] The real estate not subject to taxation comprises property belonging to the State and United States; buildings and grounds for public uses owned by counties, cities, villages, and towns; colleges, academies, and incorporated seminaries; churches, school houses, and the property of corporations for reform of offenders; public libraries; bank stock owned by State and by literary and charitable societies; Indian reservations, and the property of Indians living thereon; the property of clergymen to the extent of $1,500 each, and property not liable to sale under execution for debt. The last named includes (if owned by householders) a spinning wheel, a loom, stoves put up or in use, the family Bible, family pictures, and school books in use, books not exceeding $50 in value, a seat or pew in church, ten sheep with their fleeces, and the yarn or cloth made therefrom, one cow, two swine, and their necessary food, all necessary pork, beef, fish, flour, and vegetables provided for family use, and fuel for 60 days, all necessary wearing apparel, beds, bedsteads, and bedding for the family, arms and accouterments required by law to be kept for service in the militia, necessary cooking utensils, one table, six chairs, table furniture for six persons, one crane and its appendages, one pair of andirons, a shovel and tongs, tools of mechanics to the value of $25, a team worth $150, and land set apart for a private burying ground not more than ¼ acre. A building and lot worth $1,000 occupied as a dwelling by the owner and his family may be exempt by causing a description of the premises to be recorded in the co. clerk's office, but such record does not exempt from sale for taxes, and property generally is liable for debts contracted in its purchase. Where a homestead is exempted the privilege continues for the benefit of the widow and family after the death of the head. Such of the above articles as are movable continue exempt while the family to whom they belong are removing from one place of residence to another.

[2] Each parcel is held up at auction, and those persons competing at the sale name the least amount of land in a square, usually in the N.W. corner, that they will accept, and pay the taxes and charges due. The sale is declared in favor of the person naming the least quantity, and the purchaser receives a certificate naming the time when a deed will be due. If not paid, the Comptroller may in 3 months cancel the certificate and give to another upon payment of the same amount, and any person may redeem within 2 years by paying the taxes, charges, and 10 per cent. in addition. Specific or undivided parts of tracts of land may be sold. If not redeemed in 2 years the Comptroller issues a full deed to the purchaser. The portion sold to pay taxes is designated by the comptroller and varies with circumstances. If a village lot, it is located so as to front upon a street, and in long narrow tracts it is taken off from one end. A tax sale takes place in 1859, and triennally thereafter.

TABLES OF MANORS, COLONIAL PATENTS, PURCHASES, AND LAND GRANTS.

Manors of the Colonial Period in New York and its Dependencies.

NAMES.	PATENTEES.	DATES.	LOCATION AND REMARKS.
Bentley	Capt. Ch'r Billop	May 6, 1687	S. W. part of Staten Island, sometimes called "Billop Manor."
Cassiltown	John Palmer	Mar. 20, 1687	N. part of Staten Island.
Cortlandt	Col. Stephanus Cortlandt	June 17, 1697	N. part of Westchester co., had 1 Rep. in Gen. Assembly.
Fletcher	Capt. John Evans	Sept. 6, 1694	Canceled.
Fox Hall	Capt. Thos. Chambers	May 21, 1667	Annexed to Kingston, Mar. 12, 1787.
Gardners Island	Earl of Stirling	Mar. 10, 1639	With full power as an independent town.
Livingston	Robert Livingston	June 22, 1668	Columbia co., had 1 Rep. in Gen. Assembly.
Marthas Vineyard	Matthew Mayhew	April 20, 1685	Since annexed to Massachusetts.
Morrisania	Col. Lewis Morris	May 9, 1697	S. point of Westchester co.
Pelham	John Pell	Oct. 25, 1687	S. E. border of Westchester co.
Philipsburgh	Frederick Philipse	April 1, 1680	Putnam co.
Plumme Island	Samuel Willes	April 2, 1675	Plum and Gull Islands.
Rensselaerwyck	Killian Van Rensselaer	1630–37	Fully organized; represented in Gen. Assembly; confirmed Oct. 17, 1685, May 20, 1704.
St. George	Col. Wm. Smith	Oct. 5, 1693	In town of Brookhaven, Suffolk co.
Scarsdale	Caleb Heathcote	Mar. 21, 1701	Westchester co.
Sophy	John Paine	July 25, 1672	Prudence Island, R. I. Disallowed by R. I., and authority resisted.
Tysbury	Thos. Mayhew	July 8, 1761	Marthas Vineyard, now a part of Massachusetts.

Several of these existed only in name; perhaps a few other patents bore the name of Manors, upon which active settlement was not begun under the Colonial Government.

Table of the more important Patents

Granted under the English Colonial Government, in the eastern part of New York.

NAME OF PATENT.	County.	Date.	Extent in Acres.	Patentees.
Adaquataugie Patent	Otsego	May 8, 1770	26,000	Sir William Johnson and others.
Amherst Tracts	Hamilton	April 6, 1774	40,000	Sir Jeffery Amherst, (2 tracts.)
Anaquassacook Patent	Washington	May 11, 1762	10,000	R. J. F. & W. Schermerhorn and others.
Argyle Patent	"	March 13, 1764	47,450	Duncan Reid and others.
Arieskill Patent	Montgomery	Nov. 12, 1737	10,000	James De Lancey.
Artillery Patent	Washington	Oct. 24, 1764	24,000	Joseph Walton and others.
Babington's Patent	Delaware	May 22, 1770	2,000	Charles Babington.
Bagley's Patents	Schenectady	June 17, 1737	4,000	Timothy Bagley and others.
" "	Montgomery	Feb. 9, 1838	6,000	" "
Balfour's Patent	Ham. & Warren.	March 6, 1775	5,000	Henry Balfour, (Totten & Crossfield's Pur.)
Banyar's Patent	Otsego & Scho.	April 14, 1753	4,000	Goldsbrow Banyar and others.
Batavia Patent	Greene	April 24, 1736	4,200	Vincent Matthews and others.
Bayard's Patent	Oneida & Herk.	June 12, 1771	50,000	Wm. & Rob. Bayard and others, (Freemasons' Patent.)
Becker's Patent	Schoharie	March 19, 1754	6,000	Johannes Becker and others.
Bedlington Patent	Delaware	May 24, 1770	27,000	John Leake and others.
Beekman's Patent	Dutchess	June 25, 1703		Henry Beekman.
Beekmantown Patent	Clinton	March 27, 1769	30,000	William H. Beekman.
Belvidere Patent	Otsego & Scho.	July 6, 1769	100,000	George Croghan and others, (2 tracts.)
Bishop's Patent	Hamilton	April 6, 1774	14,000	Wm. Bishop, (T. & C. Pur.)
Bleecker's Patent	Montgomery	Sept. 22, 1729	4,300	Rutger Bleecker and others.
Blenheim Patent	Schoharie	Nov. 28, 1769	40,000	John Weatherhead and others.
Bradshaw's Patent	Washington	May 18, 1762	23,000	James Bradshaw.
Bradt's Patent	Schenectady	Feb. 14, 1738	4,000	Krent Bradt and others.
" "	" "	Dec. 16, 1737	3,870	" "
Buffington Patent	Schoharie	July 13, 1770	4,000	David Buffington.
Burnetsfield Patent	Herkimer	April 30, 1725	9,400	John Joost Petrie and others, (German Flats.)
Cambridge Patent	Washington	July 21, 1761	31,500	Colden, Smith, Banyar, and others.
Campbell's Patent	Essex	July 11, 1764	5,000	Allen Campbell.
" "	Hamilton	April 5, 1784	4,000	Duncan Campbell, (T. & C. Pur.)
Catskill Patent	Greene	July 11, 1767	35,500	Martin Garretson Van Bergen and others.
Caughnawaga Patent	Montgomery	Nov. 4, 1714	2,000	John & Margaret Collins.
Clarke's Patent	Delaware	May 22, 1770	2,000	James Clarke.
Claus's Patent	Fulton	Sept. 29, 1770	3,000	Daniel Claus.
Caterskill Patent	Greene	Nov. 1, 1695		Jacob Lockerman.
Cheesecock's Patent	Orange	March 25, 1707		Ann Bridges and others.
Cherry Valley Patent	Otsego	April 18, 1738	7,050	John Lindsey and others.
Clifton Park Patent	Saratoga	Sept. 23, 1708		N. Hermanse and others, (Shenondehowa Pat.)
Cobus Kill Patent	Schoharie	Jan. 15, 1770	40,000	Stephen Skinner and others.
Corry's Patent	Mont. & Scho.	Nov. 19, 1737	25,000	Wm. Corry and others.
Cosby's Manor	Oneida & Herk.	June 2, 1734	22,000	Joseph Worrell and others.
Cosby's Patent	Schenectady	Feb. 9, 1738	6,000	Alex., Ph. & Wm. Cosby.
Coxburgh & Carolina.	Oneida	May 30, 1770		
Coxe's Patent	"	May 30, 1770	47,000	Daniel Coxe and others, (s. w. of Mohawk.)
"	"	Jan. 5, 1775	29,000	" " " (E. of Susquehanna.)
Croghan's Patent	Otsego	June 29, 1770	18,000	Geo. Croghan and others, (s. of Mohawk.)
Dartmouth Patent	Hamilton	Oct. 4, 1774	18,036	Jeremiah Van Rensselaer.
Dean's Patent	Clinton	July 11, 1769	30,000	Elkanah Dean.
De Bernier's Patent	Delaware	May 22, 1770	2,000	John De Bernier.
De Lancey's Patent	Montgomery	Nov. 12, 1737	10,000	James De Lancey and others, (s. of Mohawk.)
" "	"	Aug. 23, 1737	5,426	" " " (N. of Mohawk.)
Edmeston's Patent	Otsego	July 21, 1770	5,000	Robert Edmeston.
" "	"	July 20, 1770	5,000	William Edmeston.
Franklin Patent	Otsego	June 20, 1770	9,000	Walter Franklin and others.

NAME OF PATENT.	County.	Date.	Extent in Acres.	Patentees.
Franklin Township	Delaware	Feb. 26, 1770	30,000	Thomas Wharton and others.
Frank's Patent	Herkimer	Sept. 6, 1765	5,000	Coenradt Frank and others.
Frazer's Patent	Greene	June 17, 1765	2,000	Hugh Frazer.
Freeman's Patent	Schenectady	July 3, 1736	5,000	Thomas Freeman.
Friswell's Patent	Clinton	May 7, 1765	3,000	John Friswell.
Gage's Patent	Oneida	July 6, 1769	18,000	Thomas Gage.
Glazier's Patent	Schoharie	Sept. 10, 1772	3,000	Beamsley Glazier.
Glen's Purchase	Saratoga	Aug. 24, 1770	45,000	John Glen, jr.
Goldsborough Township	Delaware	June 15, 1770	6,000	Edward Tudor and others.
Grant's Patent	Essex	Aug. 17, 1764	3,000	Robert Grant.
Greenwich Patent	Washington	Nov. 11, 1763	10,000	Donald Campbell.
Guerin's Patent	Montgomery	Aug. 29, 1735	4,000	Maynard & Elizabeth Guerin.
Half Moon Patent	Saratoga	Oct. 13, 1665	......	Petersen Philip Schuyler and others.
Hanson's Patent	"	July 17, 1713	2,000	Hendrick Hausen and others.
Hardenburgh Patent	Delaware & Sull.	April 20, 1708	......	Johannes Hardenburgh and others.
Harper's Patent	Delaware	Dec. 8, 1769	22,000	John Harper, jr.
Harrison's Patent	Montgomery	Oct. 11, 1735	4,000	Edward Harrison and others.
" "	"	March 18, 1722	12,000	Francis Harrison and others.
Hartwick Patent	Otsego	April 22, 1761	21,500	Christian John Hartwick.
Hasenclever's Patent	Herkimer	Feb. 27, 1769	18,000	Peter Hasenclever.
Henderson's Patent	"	1739	6,000	James Henderson and others.
Herkimer's Patent	"	April 13, 1752	2,324	Joost Johan Herkimer and others.
Holland Patent	Oneida	March 17, 1769	20,000	Lord Henry Holland.
Hoosick Patent	Rens. & Wash.	June 3, 1688	......	Maria Van Rensselaer and others.
Huntersfield Patent	Schoharie	Nov. 3, 1714	10,000	Myndert Schuyler and others, (Schoharie Pat.)
Hurley Patent	Ulster	Oct. 19, 1708	......	Cornelius Cool and others.
Huyk Patent	Columbia	Oct. 6, 1731	6,000	Burgar Huyk.
Hyde Township	Warren	Sept. 10, 1774	40,000	Edward Jessup & C. Hyde.
Ingoldsby's Patent	Schenectady	July 20, 1737	10,000	Geo. Ingoldsby and others.
Jerseyfield Patent	Herkimer & Fult.	April 12, 1770	94,000	Henry Glen and others.
Jessup's Purchase	Warren	March 21, 1768	11,650	Ebenezer Jessup and others, (2 tracts.)
" "	"	April 10, 1772	2,000	" "
Johnson's Patent	Herkimer	Sept. 27, 1765	2,000	Guy Johnson.
Judd's Patent	Essex	April 16, 1765	2,000	James Judd.
Kakiate Patent	Rockland	June 25, 1696	......	Daniel Honan and others, (Yachtaucke.)
Kayaderosseras Patent	Saratoga & War.	Nov. 2, 1708	......	Manning Hermanse and others, (Queensboro.)
Kellet's Patent	Essex	Aug. 7, 1764	2,000	Roger Kellet.
Kempe's Patent	Washington	May 3, 1764	10,200	John Tabor Kempe.
Kennedy's Patent	Essex	Aug. 7, 1764	2,000	John Kennedy.
" "	Warren	Aug. 26, 1774	2,000	Robert Kennedy.
Kinderhook Patent	Columbia	March 14, 1686	......	John Hendrik De Bruyn and others.
Kingsborough Patent	Fulton	June 23, 1753	20,000	Arent Stevens and others.
Kingsbury Patent	Washington	May 18, 1762	26,000	James Bradshaw and others.
Kingsfield Manor[a]	"	Dec. 12, 1695		
Klock's Patent	Montgomery	Dec. 21, 1754	16,000	George Klock and others.
Kortright Patent	Delaware	Feb. 24, 1770	22,000	Lawrence Kortright.
Lansing's Patent	Herkimer	June 23, 1753	6,000	Jacob Lansing and others.
Lawyer's Patent	Schoharie	Dec. 29, 1768	36,600	Johannes Lawyer and others.
" "	"	Feb. 6, 1753	2,640	" " "
" "	"	Aug. 14, 1761	7,000	" " "
Leake's Patent	Delaware	May 22, 1770	5,000	Robert Leake.
Legge's Patent	Essex	June 26, 1769	5,000	Francis Legge.
Lindsley's Patent	Otsego	Aug. 18, 1738	7,050	John Lindsley and others.
" "	"	Aug. 18, 1738	1,965	" " "
" "	"	Oct. 7, 1741	2,000	" " "
Lindsley & Livingston's Patent	Herkimer	Aug. 24, 1730	3,000	John Lindsley & Ph. Livingston.
Lispenard's Patent	Otsego	Sept. 6, 1770	9,000	Leonard Lispenard and others.
Livingston's Patent	Herk. & Mont.	Feb. 10, 1762	20,000	Philip Livingston and others.
" "	Fulton & Sara.	Nov. 8, 1760	4,000	" "
Lott's Patent	Fulton	Sept. 16, 1761	20,000	Abraham Lott, jr., and others.
Ludlow's Patent	Orange	Oct. 18, 1731	4,000	Gabriel Ludlow.
Lyne's Patent	Herkimer	Jan. 2, 1754	20,000	John Lyne and others.
" "	Montgomery	Aug. 12, 1736	2,000	" " "
McCullock's Patent	Washington	May 3, 1765	4,000	Nathaniel McCullock, (2 tracts.)
McIntosh's Patent	Essex	Aug. 7, 1765	3,000	Alexander McIntosh.
McKee's Patent	Delaware	Jan. 16, 1770	40,000	Alexander McKee and others.
" "	"	April 30, 1770	18,000	" " "
McLeod's Patent	Fulton	Sept. 29, 1770	3,000	Norman McLeod.
McNeile's Patent	Otsego	April 5, 1769	5,928	John McNeile.
" "	Herkimer	Aug. 15, 1761	4,000	" "
Magin's Patent	Fulton	March 31, 1761	6,000	Sarah Magin and others.
Markham's Patent	Hamilton	April 5, 1774	5,000	William Markham.
Matthews's Patent	Greene	April 24, 1736	4,200	Vincent Matthews and others, (3 tracts.)
Maunsell's Patent	Washington	March 7, 1771	5,000	John Maunsell.
Mawighunk Patent	Columbia	Aug. 4, 1743	......	Stephen Bayard and others.
Mayfield Patent	Fulton & Ham.	June 25, 1703	......	
Menzies's Patent	Washington	Sept. 11, 1764	2,000	Alexander Menzies.
" "	"	" "	2,000	Thomas Menzies.
Middlefield Patent	Otsego	April 18, 1761	29,000	Godfrey Miller and others.
Middleton's Patent	"	Feb. 24, 1770	5,000	Peter Middleton.
Minisink Patent	Sull. & Orange	Aug. 28, 1704	......	Matthew Ling and others.
Montresor's Patent	Essex	June 6, 1765	3,000	John Montresor and others.
Mooney's Patent	Washington	Oct. 28, 1765	2,000	David Mooney.
Morris's Patent	Montgomery	Oct. 23, 1722	6,000	Lewis Morris and others.
" "	"	June 30, 1723	6,000	" " "
" "	Schoharie	May 24, 1726	3,500	" " Jr. and others.
" "	Montgomery	" " "	6,000	" " "
" "	Otsego	1769	......	Staats Long Morris.
Munroe's Patent	Washington	Sept. 23, 1764	2,000	Harry Munroe.
Nestigione Patent	Saratoga	April 22, 1708	......	John Rosie and others.
Nettlefield Patent	Otsego	March 31, 1770	13,000	Richard Loudon and others.

a Twenty-four miles above Schenectady.

NAME OF PATENT.	County.	Date.	Extent in acres.	Patentees.
Nine Partners (Great, or Lower)	Dutchess	May 27, 1697	.....	Caleb Heathcote and others.
" " (Little, or Upper)	"	April 10, 1706	.....	Sampson Boughton and others.
Northampton Patent	Fulton	Oct. 17, 1741	6,000	Jacob Mase and others.
Oblong Patent	W. Chester, Put. & Dutch.	June 8, 1731, met seq.	50,000	Thomas Hawley and others.
Oothoudt's Patent	Otsego	Aug. 18, 1741	13,000	Volkert Oothoudt and others.
Ord's Patent	Essex	Jan. 31, 1775	5,000	Thomas Ord.
Oriskany Patent	Oneida	April 18, 1705	.....	Thomas Wenham and others.
Otsego Patent	Otsego	Feb. 3, 1770	69,000	Charles Read and others.
" "	"	Nov. 30, 1769	100,000	Geo. Croghan and 99 others.
Otsquaga Patent	Montgomery	Sept. 22, 1729	4,300	Rutger Bleecker and others.
Palmer's Patent	Richmond	March 31, 1687	5,100	Capt. John Palmer.
Panton Tract	Warren	Oct. 18, 1775	2,000	Francis Panton.
Pinefield Patent	Delaware	June 22, 1775	30,000	John Rapalje and others.
Preston Patent	Hamilton	June 27, 1770	14,000	Achilles Preston and others.
Prevost Patent	Greene	Aug. 15, 1765	5,000	Augustine Prevost.
" "	"	March 10, 1768	5,000	" "
" "	Delaware	1770	.....	" "
" "	Orange	Jan. 18, 1775	5,000	James Prevost.
Provincial Patent	"	May 2, 1764	26,000	William Cockroft and others.
Queensbury Patent	Warren	May 20, 1762	23,000	Daniel Prindle and others.
Rhinebeck Patent	Dutchess	June 8, 1703	.....	Henry Beekman.
Rightmeyer's Patent	Scho. & Greene	May 6, 1754	8,000	Ury Rightmeyer and others.
Roberts's Patent	Fulton	Sept. 29, 1770	2,000	Benjamin Roberts.
Rochester Patent	Ulster	June 25, 1703	.....	
Ross's Patent	Essex	April 16, 1765	2,000	James Ross.
Royal Grant	Herkimer	" "	93,000	Sir John Johnson.
Rumbout's Patent	Dutchess	Oct. 7, 1685	.....	Francis Rumbout.
Sacondaga Patent	Fulton & Ham.	Dec. 2, 1741	28,000	Lendert Gansevoort and others.
Sadachqueda or Saghquate Patent	Oneida	June 25, 1736	6,000	Frederick Morris and others.
Salem Patent	Washington	Aug. 7, 1764	25,000	Alexander and James Turner and others.
Saratoga Patent	Wash. & Sara.	Nov. 4, 1684	.....	Peter Schuyler and others.
Sawyer's Patent	Wash. & Sara.	Oct. 29, 1708	.....	Isaac Sawyer.
Schaghticoke	Wash & Rens	July 23, 1761	61,000	Cornelius Van Dyck and others.
Schermerhorn's Patent	Washington	May 11, 1762	10,000	Ryer Schermerhorn.
Schneider's Patent	"	Aug. 23, 1764	2,000	George Schneider.
" "	Rensselaer	March 24, 1762	10,000	Hendrick Schneider.
Schuyler's Patent	Herk. & Oneida	1755	43,000	David Schuyler and others.
Schuyler's Patent	Wash. & Rens.	May 19, 1737	11,250	Abm. David Schuyler and others.
" "	Otsego	June 3, 1755	43,000	David Schuyler and others.
" "	Washington	July 18, 1740	12,000	John Schuyler and others.
" "	Rensselaer	July 29, 1737	2,000	" " " "
Scott's Patent	Schoharie	Jan. 2, 1770	42,500	John Morin Scott and others.
Seaton's Patent	Greene	July 18, 1767	3,000	Sir Henry Seaton.
Servis's Patent	Oneida	Feb. 28, 1769	25,000	Peter Servis and others.
Sherriff's Patent	Warren	Oct. 18, 1775	4,000	Charles Sherriff.
Skeenesboro' Patent	Washington	March 31, 1765	25,000	Philip Skeene and others.
Skeene's Patent	Essex	July 30, 1771	3,000	Philip Skeene.
Skeene's Little Patent	Washington	July 6, 1771	9,000	" "
Skinner's Patent	Schoharie	Jan. 15, 1770	40,000	Stephen Skinner and others.
Small's Patent	Essex	April 6, 1774	5,000	John Small.
Spaight's Patent		Nov. 6, 1767	2,000	William Spaight.
Spornheyer's Patent	Schoharie	Aug. 23, 1764	2,000	Ernst William Spornheyer and others.
Springfield Patent	Otsego	Nov. 4, 1741	17,000	John Groesbeck and others.
Staley's Patents	Herkimer	June 14, 1755	34,000	Rudolph Staley and others.
Starnberg's Patent	Schoharie	Sept. 30, 1769	3,000	Jacob Starnberg and others.
" "	"	March 19, 1759	3,000	Lambert Starnberg and others.
Steward's Patent	Clinton	May 7, 1765	2,000	Peter Steward.
Stewart's Patent	Hamilton	May 27, 1755	24,000	James Stewart and others.
" "	Greene	Sept. 7, 1771	2,000	Walter Stewart.
Stone Arabia Patent	Mont. & Fult.	Oct. 19, 1723	12,700	John Chr. Garlock and others.
Stone Heap Patent	Mont. & Scho.	Sept. 15, 1770	15,500	John Bowen and others.
Stony Hill Tract	Schoharie	March 25, 1768	18,000	Michael Byrne and others.
Stony Point Tract	Rockland	July 13, 1743	.....	Richard Bradley and others.
Stoughton's Patent	Essex	July 25, 1764	2,000	John Stoughton.
Strasburgh Township	Delaware	Dec. 4, 1770	37,000	John Butler and others.
Stringer's Patent	Schoharie	Jan. 12, 1769	2,000	Samuel Stringer.
Sutherland's Patent	Washington	Sept. 5, 1764	2,000	Erick Sutherland.
" "	Essex	Aug. 7, 1764	3,000	Nicholas Sutherland.
Swallowfield Patent	Westchester	April 22, 1708	7,630	George Booth.
Ten Eyck's Patent	Schoharie	May 30, 1739	3,500	Hendrick Jacob Ten Eyck and others.
Timberman's Patent	Herkimer	May 30, 1755	3,000	Jacob Timberman and others.
Totten & Crossfield's Purchase[a]	Herk. Ham. Essex, Warren.			
Turloch Patent	Schoharie	Feb. 21, 1752	18,000	Jacob Borst and others.
Upton's Patent	Otsego	March 8, 1770	20,000	Clotworthy Upton and others.
Van Bergen's Patent	Greene	July 11, 1767	35,500	Martin Garretson Van Bergen and others.
Van Dam's Patent	Orange	March 23, 1709	3,000	Rip Van Dam.
Van Rensselaer Patent	Sara. & Fult.	Oct. 4, 1774	28,964	Jeremiah Van Rensselaer.
Van Slyck's Patent	Montgomery	Sept. 1, 1716	2,000	Harman Van Slyck.
Vaughan's Patent	Herkimer	April 24, 1770	8,000	John Vaughan and others.
Wallace Patent	Hamilton	April 11, 1770	6,365	Hugh Wallace and others.
Walloomsac Patent	Washington	June 15, 1739	12,000	Edward Collins and others.
Walter's Patent	Westchester	Feb. 14, 1701	5,000	Robert Walters.
Walton's Patent	Herkimer	Aug. 12, 1768	12,000	William Walton and others.
" "	Delaware	March 15, 1770	20,000	" " " "

[a] This tract, embracing 50 townships, was surveyed just before the Revolution, but small portions only were granted until after the war. Among those who received patents for large portions after that period were Robert G. Livingston, Isaac Norton, John G. Leake, Abijah Hammond, Frederick Rylander, Philip Livingston, John Thurman, Jacob Watson, Alexander Macomb, Ph. Rockafeller, White Matlack, Enos Mead, Zephaniah Platt, Goldsbrow Banyar, Peter V. B. Livingston, Joshua Mersereau, Jonathan Lawrence, Thomas Franklin, Effingham Lawrence, Stephen Crossfield, and others. Extensive tracts have been repeatedly sold for taxes.

NAME OF PATENT.	County.	Date.	Extent in Acres.	Patentees.
Watkins's Patent	Washington	March 2, 1775	2,000	John Watkins.
Wawayanda Patent	Orange	April 29, 1703	....	Dr. John Bridges.
Wawieghnuck Patent	Columbia	Aug. 4, 1743	4,380	William and Stephen Bayard.
Weir's Patent	"	Feb. 18, 1775	3,000	Archibald Weir and others.
Wharton's Patent	Essex	April 15, 1765	3,000	John Wharton.
Whiteboro Township	Delaware	March 10, 1770	38,000	Henry White and others.
Winne's Patent	Herkimer	Oct. 6, 1741	2,000	Peter Winne.
" "	Montgomery	Oct. 10, 1741	4,000	Peter Winne and others.
Williams Patent	"	Aug. 29, 1735	14,000	Charles Williams and others.
Wilmot Patent	"	Aug. 29, 1735	2,000	Anne Wilmot.
Windecker's Patent	"	Nov. 12, 1731	2,000	Hartman Windecker.
Wriesberg Patent	Essex	Feb. 18, 1775	3,000	Daniel Wriesberg.
Young's Patent	Otsego & Scho.	Oct. 11, 1752	20,000	Frederick Young.
" "	Herkimer	Aug. 25, 1752	14,000	Theobald Young and others.

SUBDIVISIONS OF THE MASSACHUSETTS PURCHASE

Of about 6,000,000 acres of Lands ceded to Massachusetts by the State of New York at the Hartford Convention, Dec. 16, 1786.

TRACTS.	Parties.	Date.	Acres.	Counties.
Phelps and Gorham*a*	Massachusetts to Phelps and Gorham...	Nov. 21, 1788	2,600,000	Allegany, Livingston, Monroe, Ontario, Schuyler, Steuben, Wayne, and Yates.
Morris Reserve	" to Robert Morris	May 11, 1791	500,000	Allegany.
Triangular Tract	Morris to Le Roy, Bayard, & McEvers.		87,000	Monroe.
Connecticut Tract*b*	" Watson, Cragie, & Greenleaf.		100,000	Orleans and Genesee.
Cragie Tract	" Andrew Cragie.		50,000	Genesee.
Ogden Tract	" Samuel Ogden		50,000	Wyoming.
Cottinger Tract	" Gerrit Cottinger		50,000	Wyoming and Allegany.
Forty Thousand Acre Tract	" Wilhelm and Jan Willink		40,000	Wyoming & Livingston.
Sterritt Tract	" Samuel Sterritt		150,000	Allegany.
Church Tract	" John B. Church		100,000	Allegany.
Morris Honorary Creditors' Tract..	" Creditors		58,570	Allegany & Livingston.
Holland Co.'s Purchase	" Agents of Holland Co.	1792–93	3,600,000	Chautauqua, Cattaraugus, Allegany, Wyoming, Erie, Genesee, Orleans, and Niagara.
Boston Ten Towns	Massachusetts to Settlers	Nov. 7, 1787	230,400	Broome and Tioga.

a Phelps and Gorham originally contracted for the whole tract at $1,000,000, payable in a kind of scrip called "Consolidated Securities," then much below par. A rise to par prevented them from fulfilling the agreement. *b* In 1801, conveyed in undivided halves to the State of Conn. and Sir Wm. Pulteney, the former using part of her School Fund in the purchase. Divided by alternate lots in 1811. *c* Conveyed in four tracts to the agents of the Holland Co.: viz., 1,500,000, Dec. 24, 1792, to Le Roy and Lincklaen; 1,000,000 Feb. 27, 1793, to Le Roy, Lincklaen, and Boon; 800,000, July 20, 1793, to the same; and 300,000, same date, to Le Roy, Bayard, and Clarkson.

SUBDIVISION OF MACOMB'S GREAT PURCHASE

In Franklin, St. Lawrence, Jefferson, Lewis, Oswego, and Herkimer Counties.

TRACTS.	Patentees.	Date of Patent.	Acres.	Remarks.
Great Tract No. 1	Daniel McCormick	May 17, 1798	821,879	Twenty-seven towns, Franklin co.
" " 2	" "	May 17, 1798	553,020	Eighteen towns, St. Lawrence co.
" " 3	" "	March 3, 1795	640,000	Fifteen " " "
" " 4 } " " 5 } " " 6 } Remainder }	Alexander Macomb	Jan. 10, 1792	{ 450,950 / 26,250 / 74,400 / 1,368,400 }	Antwerp and Jefferson cos. } Jefferson, Lewis, Oswego, and Herkimer cos.
	Purchasers.	*Date of Purchase.*		
Chassanis Tract	Pierre Chassanis & Co	April 12, 1793	210,000	Jefferson and Lewis cos.
Black River Tract	{ Harrison, Hoffman, } { Low, & Henderson }	July 15, 1795	290,376	" "
Boylston Tract	Samuel Ward	Dec. 18, 1792	817,155	Jefferson, Oswego, and Lewis, 13 towns.
Brantingham Tract	Wm. Inman	Feb. 20, 1793	74,400	Greig, Lewis co.
Constable's Towns	James Constable	....	....	Five towns, Lewis co.
Ellisburgh	Marvel Ellis	March 22, 1797	52,834	Lewis co.
Inman's Triangle	Wm. Inman	Feb. 20, 1793	25,000	Leyden and Lewis, Lewis co.
Watson's Tract	James Watson	April —, 1796	61,433	Lewis co.

Chenango Twenty Townships.

Tp.	Acres.	Date of Patent.	Patentees.	Tp.	Acres.	Date of Patent.	Patentees.
1	27,187	June 14, 1793	Alexander Webster.	11	26,200	Jan. 28, 1793	Leonard M. Cutting.
2	28,245	April 16, 1794	William S. Smith.	12	24,185	April 16, 1794	Wm. Matlack, sr.
3	24,624	" "	" "	13	24,218	March 2, 1793	Thos. Ludlow and J. Shipperly.
4	24,400	" "	" "	14	26,030	June 1, 1793	Leonard M. Cutting.
5	26,200			15	25,335	Dec. 29, 1792	" "
6	24,384	March 2, 1793	Thos. Ludlow, jr.	16	18,713	Feb. 14, 1793	John Taylor.
7	24,186	Jan. 31, 1793	Robert C. Livingston.	17	18,068	" "	" "
8	25,780	April 16, 1794	William S. Smith.	18	22,565	May 3, 1793	John J. Morgan.
9	24,205			19	20,750	" "	" "
10	24,200	Jan. 13, 1793	James Talmadge.	20	24,856	" "	" "

Table of the Principal Tracts

Which have been granted in small parcels by the State, under the Commissioners of the Land Office.

NAME OF TRACT.	County.	No. of Lots.	Remarks.
Adgate's 3,600 acre Tract............	Essex........................	7	West of Perou Bay.
Bedlington Tract......................	Delaware....................	77	Escheat of John G. Leake.
Benson Township....................	Hamilton...................	383	Named from Egbert Benson.
Bergen's Purchase..................	Hamilton and Fulton.......	13	
Black Rock Village.................	Erie	233	Part of Niagara Mile Strip.
Brant Lake Tract....................	Warren......................	254	Surveyed by Geo. Webster, 1803.
Bristol Tract........................	Schoharie	62	} Unappropriated lands remaining at close of Revolution.
Bulwagga Bay Tract.................	Essex........................	4	
Butler's Tract.......................	Delaware....................	7	Part of Hardensburgh Patent.
Canastota Tract.....................	Madison.....................	91	Gospel and Schools for Chenango Twenty Towns.
Chemung Township.................	Chemung	205	{ Laid out in 1788 by Jas. Clinton, J. Hathorn, and J. Cantine.
Chenango Township.................	Broome......................	......	49,710 acres to A. Hammond and others.
Chenango Twenty Towns............	Madison, Chenango, Oneida	......	Patented separately. See table preceding this.
Clinton Township...................	Chenango	......	Given to the Vermont sufferers.
Cookquago Tract....................	Delaware and Broome.......	144	
Cowasselon Tract...................	Madison.....................	25	
Crum Horn Mountain Tract........	Otsego......................	79	Given to schools and literature.
Delaware Tract......................	Broome......................	19	Town of Windsor.
Essex Tract..........................	Essex........................	248	Unappropriated lands remaining after Revolution.
Fayette Township...................	Chenango....................	100	
Fort Ann Tract......................	Washington	33	Mile Square Reservation.
Fort Covington Village..............	Franklin	......	Unappropriated lands remaining after Revolution.
French Mountain Tract.............	Warren......................	48	
Grand Island........................	Erie	117	Given to Canal Fund.
Greene co. Tract....................	Greene......................	108	To Walter Livingston, M. West, and W. Morris.
Greene Township....................	Chenango	......	In quarters.
Gore, Old Military, and Refugee Tract.	Clinton	68	
Gores, others in great number.			
Hambden Township.................	Tioga.......................	......	Robert Morris and Alexander Macomb.
Hague Tract.........................	Warren and Essex...........	62	
Iron Ore Tract......................	Essex	234	
Islands in great number.			
Jay Tract............................	Essex and Clinton...........	160	
Lake George Tract..................	Warren......................	93	
Lewis (South) Tract.................	Essex	33	
Lewiston Village....................	Niagara......................	421	House, out, and water lots.
Long Sault Island...................	St. Lawrence................	38	
Luzerne Tract.......................	Warren......................	173	
Masset[?] Township.................	St. Lawrence................	......	Small tracts upon Military Class rights.
Maul's [?] atent.....................	Essex	5	
Military Tract.......................	{ Cayuga, Cortland, Onondaga, Oswego, Schuyler, Seneca, Tompkins and Wayne. }	.....	{ Twenty eight townships—1,680,000 acres to soldiers of the Revolution.
Military Tract (Old).................	Clinton and Franklin........	......	{ Ten townships, 640,000 acres set apart to soldiers, not conveyed.
Moose River Tract..................	Hamilton and Herkimer....	......	Nine townships, mostly of modern grant.
Niagara River Tract................	Erie and Niagara............	107	Reserved in Massachusetts cession.
North River Head Tract............	Essex	140	
North West Bay Tract..............	Essex	133	
Oswego Falls Village...............	Oswego.....................	52	} Reserved by State in previous grants.
Oswego Village.....................	Oswego	......	
Ox Bow Tract......................	Hamilton....................	304	
Palmer's Purchase..................	Warren......................	......	State, Middle, Rear, and River Lots.
Paradox Tract.......................	Essex........................	428	Named from Paradox Lake.
Perou Bay Tract....................	Essex........................	130	
Refugee Tract.......................	Clinton	......	131,420 acres to Canada and Nova Scotia refugees.
Reservations, Indian:			
Cayuga...........................	Cayuga and Seneca...........	256	West, East, and Residence Tracts, Canoga Reservation.
Oneida...........................	Oneida and Madison........	......	Fish Creek, Oneida, Castleton, Oneida Creek, Otsequet, Pagan Purchase, and Wood Creek Tracts of the purchases of 1798, 1802, 1815, 1824, 1826, 1829, 1830, 1834, 1840, 1842.
Onondaga	Onondaga	......	Various, including plats of Salina, Geddes, Liverpool, Lodi, &c.
St. Regis.........................	Franklin	......	Various, including lands at Fort Covington and Hogansburgh Village.
Stockbridge......................	....	......	Various purchases, including E. Hill Tract of fifty, and W. Hill Tract of forty-two lots.
Roaring Brook Tract................	Essex	86	
Saddle Mountain Tract.............	Washington.		
St. Lawrence Ten Towns...........	St. Lawrence................	10 mi. sq. each	Sold at auction in quarter and mile squares,, but bid in by a small number. Cambray, De Kalb, and Hague, each 92,720 acres; Lisbon, Louisville, and Stockholm, each a little less, were conveyed to Alex. Macomb, Dec. 17, 1787.
Schroon Tract.......................	Essex	111	
Sidney Township....................	Broome......................	162	
Split Rock Tract....................	Essex........................	33	
Stedman Farm......................	Niagara.		
Trembleau Tract....................	Essex........................	17	
Tongue Mountain Tract............	Warren......................	52	
Warrensburgh Tract................	Warren......................	22	
Warren Township...................	Broome......................	......	61,440 acres to Robert Harper and others.
Watkins and Flint's Purchase......	Chemung and Schuyler.		
Westfield Tract......................	Washington	58	
West of Road Patent...............	Essex........................	174	
White Face Mountain Tract........	Essex and Clinton.		

Tables of many small grants, tracts, and purchases will be found in the descriptions of the counties in which such lands are located.

CANALS.

The Public Canals of the State are made, by the Constitution, inalienable. They were first constructed for the purpose of facilitating settlement and of opening an easy means of communication between the Atlantic and the great lakes. The canals are under the care of several State officers, the powers and duties of whom are as follows:—

The Canal Commissioners, three in number, are elected one each year and hold office for three years. They have the immediate supervision and management of the construction and repairs of canals, and are *ex officio* members of the Canal and Contracting Boards. They have their office in the State Hall, and report annually to the Legislature. The canals have three general divisions, each of which is under the special charge of a commissioner.[1]

The State Engineer and Surveyor has general charge of the engineering department of the canals, and is a member of the Canal and Contracting Boards. He has an office in the State Hall, and reports annually to the Legislature.[2]

The Canal Board consists of the Commissioners of the Canal Fund, the State Engineer, and the Canal Commissioners. It meets, during the session of the Legislature, at the office of the Canal Department, fixes the rates of toll, appoints collectors of tolls, their assistants and weighmasters, directs extraordinary repairs; hears appeals from the Canal Appraisers, remits penalties, and regulates the police of the canals.[3]

The Auditor of the Canal Department draws warrants on the Treasurer for all canal payments, audits accounts, instructs collecting and disbursing officers, and keeps account of canal receipts and expenditures. He is *ex officio* Secretary of the Commissioners of the Canal Fund and of the Canal Board, and a member of the Contracting Board. His office, known as the "Canal Department," is in the State Hall at Albany.

The Canal Appraisers, three in number, are appointed one each year, and hold office for three years. They appraise all damages arising from the canals, whether temporary or permanent in their nature. They have an office in the State Hall.

The Contracting Board consists of the State Engineer, the Auditor of the Canal Department, and the Canal Commissioners. It appoints all division, resident, and first assistant engineers.[4]

The Commissioners of the Canal Fund consist of the Lieutenant Governor, Secretary of State, Comptroller, Treasurer, and Attorney General. The Auditor of the Canal Department is *ex officio* Secretary of the Board. They have the general management of the funds and debts of the canal.[5]

---

[1] *The Eastern Division* embraces the Erie Canal as far w. as Oneida Lake Canal, 136 miles; Champlain Canal and Glens Falls Feeder, 78 miles; Pond above Troy Dam, 3 miles; Black River Canal and Improvement, 98 miles; making a total of 315 miles. *The Middle Division* embraces the Erie Canal from the E. bank of Oneida Lake Canal to the E. line of Wayne co., including feeders and reservoirs, 76 miles; Chenango Canal, 97 miles; Oneida Lake Canal, 7 miles; Oswego Canal, 38 miles; Baldwinsville Side Cut, 1 mile; Oneida River Improvement, 20 miles; Seneca River towing path, 5¾ miles; Cayuga & Seneca Canal, 23 miles; Crooked Lake Canal, 8 miles; Chemung Canal and Feeder, 39 miles; Oneida Creek Feeder, 2 miles; Seneca River Improvement, 12¼ miles; making a total of 331 miles. *The Western Division* embraces the remainder of the Erie Canal, 155 miles, and the Genesee Valley Canal and Dansville Side Cut, 118 miles, making a total of 273 miles.

[2] He prescribes the duties of engineers and assigns to them divisions, visits and inspects all the canals at least once in each year, and prepares plans, surveys, maps, and estimates for construction or improvement. He has other duties relating to railroads, lands belonging to the State; and other subjects are also assigned to him from time to time.

In the Engineering Department are the following subordinate officers:—

Division Engineers, one to each division, are appointed by the Contracting Board with the consent of the State Engineer. They have special supervision of the sections of canals in their respective divisions, and are obliged to frequently pass over the canal; and they prepare all maps, plans, and specifications for work to be put under contract. They make full reports annually to the State Engineer. The office of the Resident Engineer of the Eastern Division is at Albany, of the Middle Division at Syracuse, and of the Western Division at Rochester.

Resident Engineers, 12 in number, have immediate charge of certain sections under the supervision of resident engineers. They are assisted by:

First Assistant Engineers, appointed by the Contracting Board, and

Second Assistant Engineers, appointed by Resident Engineers. The number of these assistants is regulated by the amount of labor in progress. Levelers, surveyors, draftsmen, clerks, &c. are employed as the Department may require, and are appointed in the same manner as Second Assistant Engineers. No engineer or other public officer appointed upon the canals, or a clerk, foreman, or overseer of laborers, is allowed to have an interest in the boarding of laborers, or in furnishing teams, materials, or any other thing belonging to himself, for the use of the public.

[3] There are 20 collectors of tolls on the Erie, 3 on the Champlain, 3 on the Oswego, 3 on the Seneca & Cayuga, 3 on the Chemung, 1 on the Crooked Lake, 3 on the Chenango, 5 on the Genesee Valley, 1 on the Black River, and 1 on the Oneida Lake Canal. There are also 41 assistant collectors. Collectors may be removed by the Canal Commissioners or the Auditor.

[4] This Board was created April 15, 1854, and its powers were enlarged and defined May 14, 1857. Until May 1, 1859, it appointed superintendents of repairs; but since that time all repairs are made by contract. Repairs were formerly made by laborers, hired by the day or month, under the direction of superintendents; but in 1857 the Contracting Board was authorized to let the ordinary repairs upon contract for a term of years.

[5] The canal fund was derived from the following sources:—

1817–35. Auction duties, (in part,) amounting in all to	$3,592,039.05
" " Salt duties, amounting in all to	2,055,458.06
In 1835, these revenues were restored to the general fund, by a popular vote of 68,126 to 8,675.	
1817–23. Steamboat passenger tax, amounting in all to	73,509.99

Reports are annually made to the Legislature by the heads of the various Canal Departments concerning every thing pertaining to the Canal interests. These reports, embodying voluminous details and summaries, are printed, and are easily accessible to all.[1]

Loans for construction, at sundry times, secured by State stocks. The avails for Erie and Champlain Canals, up to Sept. 30, 1858, amounted to $8,271.831.00
Loans for enlargement, &c.............................. 11,828,000.00
Loans for deficiencies.................................. 10,203,844.10
Loans for enlargement and completion............... 10,500,000.00
Canal revenue certificates............................. 1,512,390.75
Temporary loans.. 1,700,000.00
Tolls.. 64,429,475.41
Tax (1844, '45, '46, '47, 1854, '55, '56, '57, '58)...... 2,936,623,21
Sale of lands for benefit of canals, viz.: 102,635 acres in Cattaraugus co., given by the Holland Land Co.; 3,000 acres, by John Hornby; 1,000 acres, by Gideon Granger; Grand Island, (17,381 1-5 acres,) and 8 small islands, (502½ acres,) given by the State for benefit of canals; and a tract of land on Wood Creek, bought with the rights of the Western Inland Lock N. Co......... 107,430.18
Interest on investment and deposits.................. 3,157,860.60
Surplus tolls, from lateral canals.................... 1,010,731.43
Miscellaneous.. 1,101,123.43
Total receipts Erie and Champlain Canals...........123,043,734.84
Receipts upon all the State canals....................143,607,002.91
Total payments upon the Erie and Champlain Canals...
Total payments upon all the State canals............141,627,845.85

The total premiums upon loans amounted to...... $2,295,744.12
The total discount upon loans amounted to......... 290,508.04
Special loans were made for most of the lateral canals. A tract of land from the Onondaga Salt Springs Reservation was sold for the benefit of the Oswego Canal Fund, and amounted to $160,000. Stock in the Western Inland Lock Navigation Co., amounting to $92,000, was canceled for the benefit of the canals, and the interests of individuals in that work were canceled by purchase. The amount appraised was $152,718.52.

The Constitution provides (Art. VII) that, after paying the expenses of collection, superintendence, and repairs, the sum of $1,300,000, and after 1855, $1,700,000, shall be applied annually, from the revenues of the canals, to a sinking fund, to pay the canal debt. In 1857, the surplus receipts of tolls failed, for the first time since 1846, to meet this, and it became necessary to raise by direct tax the money required to pay interest on the stock. The clause in the Constitution prohibiting the creation of a debt for any public work, without imposing a direct tax for its payment and a submission to the popular vote, was suspended by an amendment adopted Feb. 14, 1854, to allow of the raising of $9,000,000, by the issue of State stock, for the more speedy enlargement and completion of the canals. A measure was introduced in the Legislature of 1859, for the loan of a further sum for this object, and the submission of the question to the decision of a popular vote.

[1]SUMMARIES OF THE PRINCIPAL REPORTS.

Amount and value of property moved, and miles run, on all the State Canals, since 1835.

Year.	ESTIMATED VALUE OF PROPERTY TO AND FROM OTHER STATES, VIA BUFFALO, BLACK ROCK, TONAWANDA, AND OSWEGO.		Total value of property moved on all the canals.	Cleared at New York, Albany, and West Troy.	Cleared at Buffalo, Black Rock, and Tonawanda.	Cleared at all other offices.	Total number of tons moved on all the canals.	MILES RUN IN EACH YEAR BY ALL THE BOATS.	
	Products coming from.	Merchandise going to.						Packets.	Freight boats.
1836	$5,493,816	$9,723,250	$67,634.343	....	....	....	1,310,807	....	....
1837	4,813,626	6,322,750	55.809,288	$25,784.147	$3,286,128	$18,650.604	1,171,296	405,050	5,556,950
1838	6,369.645	8.657.250	65.746,559	33,062,858	4,854.927	19,209.858	1,333,011	400,250	5,126,800
1839	7,258,968	10 259,109	73.399.764	40,094.302	5,222.756	18,854.427	1,435,713	290,900	5,785,850
1840	7,877,358	7,057.600	66.403,892	36,398,039	6,200,829	15.204,936	1,417,046	258,880	5,952,300
1841	11,889,273	11.174.400	92 202,929	56,798,447	9,607,924	16.376,503	1,521,661	322,860	7,103.580
1842	9,215,808	7,218.900	60.016,608	32,314,998	7,541.793	12.466,736	1,236,931	354,300	6,173,200
1843	11,937,943	13,067,250	76,276.909	42,258,488	9,732.616	13,288,470	1,513,439	381,820	6,586,700
1844	15,875,558	14,845,250	90.921,152	53,142,403	9,561.146	15,822,504	1,816,586	427,740	7,841,750
1845	14,162,239	17,366,300	100,629,859	55,453,998	10,351.749	19,248,224	2,977,565	420,540	7,924,250
1846	20,471.939	20,415.500	115,612,109	64,628.474	15,819.314	18,815.639	2,268,662	414,340	9,065.450
1847	32.666,324	27,298.800	151.563,428	77.878.766	28,503,745	23,518.927	2,869,810	443,080	11,733.250
1848	23,245,353	30,553,920	140,086,157	77,477.781	19,621,700	11,544,421	2,796,230	542,300	9,633,850
1849	26,713,796	31,793,400	144,732,285	78,481,941	20,647.562	22,238.010	2,894,732	305,760	10,153,350
1850	25,539,605	41,272,491	156,397.929	74,826,999	20,991.462	31,335.526	3,076,617	343,475	10,718,100
1851	27,007,142	63,659.440	159,881,801	80,739,899	24,543.286	31,784.847	3,582,733	206,150	11,926,950
1852	37,041.380	79,127.640	196,603,517	121.087.312	25,674.776	22.219,056	3,863,441	71,725	12,306,950
1853	42,367.564	94,230,720	207,179.570	116,185,331	28,866,951	27,629,827	4,247.852	46,650	12,327,050
1854	39,346.283	83,476,440	210,284,312	116.772.966	29,745.555	30,613,260	4,165,862	24,675	11,244,200
1855	43,555,243	79,879,680	204,390,147	113.443.863	31,403,640	24,906,992	4,022,617	28,875	9,671,450
1856	38,043.813	66,064,680	218.327,062	134,131.707	22,873,866	21.749,502	4,116,082	21,175	9,656,700
1857	26,466,121	42,525,360	136,997.018	71,016,241	17,567,181	15,470.217	3,344,061	16,950	7,374,850
1858	36,182,405	27,680,400	138,568,844	57,983,123	25,039.901	20.570,577	3,665,192	18,725	7,886,100
Tot.	$513,541,202	$793,670,521	$2,929,665,482	$1,559,962,083	$377,659,507	$451,519,063	59,647,996	5,746,220	191,739,630

Total amount per cent., and averages of different classes.

CLASSES.	TOTAL FOR TWENTY-THREE YEARS.		PERCENTAGE OF EACH.		AVERAGES FOR PERIODS OF SEVEN YEARS.					
					From 1836 to 1842.		From 1843 to 1849.		From 1850 to 1856.	
	Tons.	Value.	T.ns.	Value.	Tons.	Value.	Tons.	Value.	Tons.	Value.
Products of forest	24,516.913	$207,472.053	41.11	7.08	634.922	$7.133,875	947.120	$7,200.900	1,549,378	$12,619.591
Agriculture.......	17,238.941	321,768,110	28.89	28.05	306.004	18,400,404	765,948	36,326,168	1,098,289	51,083.488
Manufactures.....	4,086.894	167,860.314	6.85	5.73	101,610	5.750,494	165,912	6,825.363	240,790	8,720.900
Merchandise......	5,233.933	1,594.938,801	8.78	54.44	119,108	34,687.389	189,170	61,888,015	380.654	111.862,964
Other articles.....	8,571,265	137,726,204	14.37	4.70	184,992	2,772,607	237,139	4,876,878	598,775	9,007.96
Total	59,647,946	$2,929,765,482	100.00	100.00	1,346.636	$68,744,769	2,305,289	$117,117,411	3,867,886	$193,294,905

Tolls collected at each office on the New York State Canals, from 1825 to 1858, both inclusive.

OFFICES.	1825.	1830.	1835.	1840.	1845.	1850.	1855.	1856.	1858.
New York						$285,595	$245,124	$290,280	$78,921
Albany	$126,652	$212,045	$357,595	$295,563	$340.667	312,654	253,234	116,973	67.965
West Troy	37,181	124,793	153,402	186,947	386,915	315,042	301,262	349,517	110.837
Schenectady	29,819	37,806	64,973	23,670	9,544	9,312	21,705	9,473	5.173
Fultonville	....	....	....	10,778	17,653	10,227	5,222	5,015	4,643
Little Falls	6,124	8,772	16,840	16,505	13,389	9,382	5,967	5,349	5,028
Utica	46,302	46,142	50,575	42,606	63,507	55,514	41,808	37,159	26,720
Rome	21,060	28,835	36,456	36,063	55,997	46,283	52,427	40,906	31,638
Syracuse	35,349	85,876	74,756	69,384	119,229	78,095	48,233	35,162	31,292
Jordan	....	....	....	....	....	....	55,470	65,378	38,464
Montezuma	a55,635	82,611	93,809	86,581	103,826	77,837	37,830	29,740	18,821
Lyons	11,197	24,229	23,018	21,855	17,432	19,197	10,553	10,172	9,898
Palmyra	21,466	48,338	40,180	61,199	58,021	53,798	19,594	12,357	14,994
Rochester	88,494	150,129	176,140	248,210	224,529	190,532	101,087	88,130	86,204
Brockport	7,517	12,314	24,982	7,587	10,897	65,932	6,304	18,180	101,171
Albion	b3,793	12,139	19,865	30,844	36,263	26,355	25,899	3,132	14,378
Medina	....	....	....	....	....	....	14,308	9,556	16,296
Lockport	10,514	21,553	52,129	23,227	106,413	181,973	23,467	14,015	30,503
Tonawanda	....	....	....	54......	....	55,642	23,685	34,901	30,291
Black Rockc	786	....	....	321,164	56,583	68,456	97,679	22,145	....
Buffalo	1,671	48,959	106.213	,417	482,635	703,498	755,575	783,906	719,683
Waterford	12,295	10,527	8,065	14,820	9,085	7,012	8,556	3,737	225
Schuylerville	....	11,766	16,201	2,262	15,371	7,379	9,164	8,806	37,494
Glens Falls	d17,318	....	....	....	....	8,955	10,568	12,030	132,023
Whitehall	33,106	41,052	63,924	48,160	55,911	71,356	54,367	55,364	8,923
Salina	....	8,662	51,214	30,653	53,812	44,655	21,184	20,412	17,950
Phœnix	....	....	....	....	....	....	22,092	22,241	5,626
Oswego	....	3,673	46,850	51,899	138,704	310,135	271,159	406,813	2,308
Seneca Falls	....	....	....	....	....	....	14,317	13,399	15,831
Geneva	....	36,701	35,879	33,350	44,336	47,473	27,765	21,669	32,302
Ithaca	....	....	....	....	....	....	....	13,079	....
Havana	....	....	6,256	6,574	16,132	11,376	14,485	13,765	8,365
Horseheads	....	....	15,133	14,595	26,747	32,853	29,584	30,272	....
Corning	....	....	....	....	82,466	54,060	65,860	44,610	....
Dresden	....	....	4,096	5,696	5,667	9,566	3,495	3,238	1,029
Penn Yan	....	....	8,958	16,787	26,734	21,192	15,376	15,827	2,482
Hamilton	....	....	....	2,767	3,012	3,177	4,735	5,658	4,594
Oxford	....	....	....	4,573	10,415	6,026	2,553	2,312	1,863
Binghamton	....	....	....	2,721	13,885	7,189	8,587	8,033	7,703
Scottsville	....	....	....	4,510	21,147	28,647	5,985	4,934	5,276
Mount Morris	....	....	....	....	....	....	14,470	15,542	4,450
Dansville	....	....	....	....	18,605	28,400	6,665	5,231	....
Oramel	....	....	....	....	....	....	17,120	11,290	20,383
Boonville	....	....	....	....	....	....	12,285	9,235	....
Higginsville	....	....	....	....	652	9,124	16,894	18,664	....
Baldwinsville	....	....	....	....	....	....	548	605	....
Olean	....	....	....	....	....	....	....	....	....
	$566,279	$1,066,922	$1,548,109	$1.775,967	$2,646,181	$3,273,899	$2.805,077	$2,748,212	$1,838,836

a Collected at Port Byron.   b At Newport.   c Office abolished in 1857.   d At Saratoga, Ft. Miller, Ft. Edward, and Ft. Ann.

Number of Clearances issued from 1833 to 1858, both inclusive, on the Several Canals.

YEAR.	Erie.	Champlain.	Oswego.	Cayuga and Seneca.	Chemung.	Crooked Lake.	Chenango.	Genesee Valley.	Black River.	Oneida Lake Canal.	Seneca River Towing Path.	Total.
1833	21,841	5,938	3,739	1,086	253	153	....	....	......	....	......	48,740
1834	29,441	7,159	6,867	1,891	1,247	896	....	....	......	....	......	63,726
1835	30,963	7,438	7,763	1,693	1,802	1,075	....	....	......	....	......	69.078
1836	31,837	6,752	6,870	1,730	1,951	1,179	....	....	......	....	......	67.255
1837	29,511	5,967	6,651	1,385	1,704	998	517	....	......	....	......	62,273
1838	30,282	5,582	7,864	1,361	1,629	958	1,069	....	......	....	......	64,796
1839	33,454	5,804	8,456	1,213	1,624	930	880	....	......	....	......	68,296
1840	35,231	5,871	7,472	1,223	1,553	814	762	478	......	....	......	69,133
1841	36,333	6,067	9,125	1,421	2,595	890	1,039	1,096	......	574	......	75,990
1842	31,529	4,709	6,877	1,397	8,361	731	815	1.595	......	1,101	......	67,515
1843	32,529	4,303	7,948	1,068	2,469	964	968	1,809	......	1,250	......	69,720
1844	32,216	4,911	10,204	1,249	3,050	976	1,128	2,045	......	1,237	......	76,409
1845	35,142	5,128	10,296	1,449	3,696	1,495	1,189	3,223	......	1,260	......	81,629
1846	93,276	6,605	11,067	1,881	3,699	1,278	1,207	2,366	......	1,089	......	89,936
1847	46,255	6,937	12,838	1,814	4,440	1,300	1,477	2,283	......	1,307	......	104,478
1848	43,829	6,454	12,406	1,932	4,569	1,184	1,545	2,389	......	1,677	......	98.325
1849	37,507	6,996	7,861	969	3,843	1,025	989	2,162	......	2,034	......	85,648
1850	39,115	6,958	7,751	886	3,839	1,042	1,295	2.225	......	393	......	89,124
1851	41,563	6,766	8,071	1,056	3,828	916	907	2,037	530	695	......	92,926
1852	39,177	7,714	7,844	954	3,999	827	1,603	2,014	609	1,187	......	93,842
1853	39,621	9,865	9,129	1,016	5.019	916	1,762	2,897	674	1,373	......	100,148
1854	41,462	7,781	13,316	1,857	6,630	705	1,899	2,968	817	2,563	491	104,902
1855	40,850	7,421	12,248	1,971	5,267	760	1,954	2,434	933	2,393	470	97,856
1856	35,514	7,625	14,827	2,439	5,982	752	1,923	2,333	834	3,177	494	98,214
1857	31,307	7,754	10,133	2,097	5,909	261	1,906	2,405	900	1,289	......	80,309
1858	28,849	8,807	13,538	1,740	5,105	534	1,532	2,314	868	1,339	......	80,985

TABLE OF TOLLS

Collected on, and applicable or belonging to, each Canal, in each year, from 1823 to 1858, both inclusive.

YEARS.	Erie Canal.	Champlain Canal.	Oswego Canal.	Cayuga & Seneca Canal.	Chemung Canal.	Crooked Lake Canal.	Chenango Canal.	Genesee Valley Canal.	Oneida Lake Canal.	Seneca River Towing Path.	Oneida River Improvement.	Cayuga Inlet.	Black River Canal.	Baldwinsville Canal.	Total.
1823a	$199,655.08														$199,655.08
1824	294,546.62	$46,214.45													340,761.07
1825	492,664.23	73,615.26													566,279.49
1826	687,976.68	74,191.19													766,190.82
1827	775,919.22	83,341.02													859,260.24
1828	727,650.20	107,757.08	$2,757.67												838,444.65
1829	707,888.49	87,171.03	9,439.44	$3,622.96											813,137.45
1830	943,545.35	89,063.78	12,335.18	11,987.81											1,056,922.12
1831	1,091,714.26	102,896.23	16,271.10	12,992.39											1,223,801.98
1832	1,056,012.28	110,191.95	12,335.18	13,893.04											1,229,483.47
1833	1,290,163.19	110,101.95	19,766.20	17,174.91	$279.70										1,614,329.06
1834	1,180,967.56	132,572.12	13,893.04	18,030.95	8,643.49	$694.00									1,341,329.06
1835	1,375,673.12	115,211.90	22,168.02	18,397.47	11,987.81	1,473.40									1,292,623.38
1836	1,440,539.87	116,131.10	23,015.84	20,523.43	12,992.39	1,833.76									1,548,986.48
1837	1,444,170.21	115,425.24	22,203.38	20,430.14	13,893.04	2,331.86	$200.84								1,463,820.90
1838	1,414,174.21	120,998.06	30,469.83	18,030.95	18,030.95	5,066.20	20,430.87								1,500,911.07
1839	1,427,031.53	103,522.88	21,092.92	18,397.47	20,523.43	1,521.15	16,778.33								1,616,382.00
1840	1,507,334.46	106,524.67	27,372.28	20,523.43	4,431.60	1,721.31	$10,812.72								1,775,147.57
1841	1,813,650.58	104,125.15	34,162.40	18,547.47	4,968.41	1,723.68	20,436.63								2,084,882.81
1842	1,568,946.50	113,753.60	29,522.93	18,397.47	9,396.42	2,017.32	14,001.53	$462.02							1,749,197.62
1843	1,850,314.55	104,196.93	38,244.22	20,523.43	7,702.05	989.39	13,815.48	9,927.69	$462.02						2,051,590.17
1844	2,190,147.34	102,427.74	31,222.19	23,583.37	4,394.60	1,328.18	13,204.11	13,291.78	462.63						2,446,374.52
1845	2,361,884.24	117,841.14	36,203.93	17,417.28	5,187.27	1,497.89	16,194.75	19,641.20	507.74						2,646,181.87
1846	2,301,147.32	95,967.54	56,164.93	19,417.38	9,762.56	1,962.73	22,177.96	23,173.98	621.45						2,756,120.89
1847	2,449,275.58	102,308.50	58,347.05	24,618.17	14,385.13	2,482.81	26,521.75	23,448.57	653.53						3,252,212.19
1848	2,361,347.36	116,739.32	58,185.43	22,520.14	11,503.44	1,912.81	23,492.86	28,570.33	542.43	$844.18	$14.52	$232.95	$2,629.89		3,298,826.03
1849	3,333,347.36	119,210.44	77,933.34	27,282.11	16,677.70	1,946.50	33,272.80	26,722.12	624.74	149.51	176.07	175.03	3,661.91		3,329,727.00
1850	2,947,881.76	108,094.67	79,793.22	28,925.95	16,191.25	1,821.70	21,296.45	25,567.42	688.97	296.80	9,483.14	189.14	4,628.67		3,118,244.02
1851	2,962,132.09	120,097.80	91,220.39	28,314.20	15,751.34	1,790.04	27,675.95	26,707.25	821.06	270.42	239.71	274.63	4,698.71		3,204,711.04
1852	2,953,125.93	117,500.66	98,528.42	27,192.71	15,997.74	1,696.75	19,908.72	27,722.12	688.07	469.72	236.89	263.17	5,880.07		3,329,727.00
1853	2,994,329.53	121,672.06	95,010.21	26,739.89	22,681.44	1,473.81	28,228.18	24,917.96	3,683.62	226.15		320.43	6,897.92		3,655,380.00
1854	2,799,849.88	183,969.43	88,690.42	23,681.32	22,266.70	1,363.01	20,228.18	26,881.07	7,593.84	187.18	25,680.08	274.53	5,585.06		2,805,076.10
1855	2,465,686.47	119,333.77	97,297.93	23,535.76	21,162.32	956.04	19,964.01	30,907.78	8,009.78	111.12	37,630.47	263.17	5,385.06	$864.25	2,743,211.67
1856	2,459,272.27	114,591.51	82,121.52	22,918.83	22,918.83	1,080.65	22,036.66	29,508.91	7,012.21	244.92	25,680.08	352.71	5,880.07	61.95	2,805,076.10
1857	1,709,179.09	111,229.15	82,565.63	20,462.31	17,117.52	635.36	20,294.61	25,203.81	1,265.53	145.99	3,546.37	313.81	6,131.57	13.12	2,045,640.75
1858	1,838,835.64	96,936.75	87,783.74	16,022.59	14,623.39	683.16	15,886.39	27,913.34	1,566.79	138.37	4,971.96	177.88	5,294.15	20.67	2,110,763.82

a To 1823 inclusive.

The Erie Canal, connecting the Hudson with Lake Erie, was commenced at Rome, July 4, 1817, and was completed Oct. 26, 1825. As first constructed, it was 363 mi. long, 28 ft. wide at the bottom, 40 ft. wide at the top, and 4 ft. deep. The locks were 90 ft. long between the gates, and 15 ft. wide. The original cost of the whole was $7,143,789. 86.[1]

The number of boats upon the canals at different periods has been—in 1843, 2,136; in 1844, 2,126; in 1847, 2,725; in 1853, 3,401; and in 1859, about 3,500. The following numbers of new boats have been registered:—

1844, 378	1847, 1,466	1850, 152	1853, 590	1856, 364
1845, 297	1848, 457	1851, 213	1854, 760	1857, 329
1846, 477	1849, 215	1852, 271	1855, 745	1858, 255

Some opinion may be formed of the class of boats used from the numbers built. These were, in 1857, of scows, 106; decked scows, 23; lake boats, 95; bullheads, 102; and packets, 3. None of the last named were built in 1858; and the day for traveling upon the canals may be considered as virtually passed, unless steam canal boats—now being introduced into use—prove successful competitors in speed with steam upon railroads.

The largest boat registered in 1844 was 90 tons. In 1849, some were as high as 135 tons; in 1850, 170 tons; in 1853, 250 tons; and in 1858, 300 tons. The average tonnage of boats has been as follows:—

1849	76
1850	80
1851	87
1852	88
1853	97
1854	105
1855	102
1856	107
1857	114
1858	109
General average	100

Structures upon the New York State Canals at the close of 1857.

	Erie Canal.	Champlain Canal and Feeder.	Chenango Canal.	Black River Canal and Improvement.	Oneida Lake Canal.	Oswego Canal.	Oneida River Improvement.	Seneca River Improvement.	Cayuga & Seneca Canal.	Crooked Lake Canal.	Chemung Canal and Feeder.	Genesee Valley Canal and Side Cut.	Total.
Lift Locks[a]	76	39	116	110	7	18	2	1	12	27	53	113	574
Guard Locks	4	6	1	1		5		1		1	1	3	23
Weigh Locks	5												5
Aqueducts	35	4	19	5							4	17	84
Waste Weirs	49	23	21	12		5			3	6	10	34	163
Culverts	243	27	52	18	2	5		1		2	2	103	455
Guard Gates	3												3
Road Bridges		52		36	2	11	1	3	13		27		103
Farm Bridges		75		40	1	1			1		16		102
Tow Bridges		13		1		11			27		16	9	
Total Bridges[b]	509	140	212	77	3	23	1	3	41	14	59	214	1,296
Dams[c]	10	8	12	1		8	1		5		1	5	51

^a Double locks, side by side, are counted as one. The number upon the Erie Canal, when completed, will be two less, by dispensing with those now at Montezuma.

^b Farm bridges are gradually lessening in number, as the claims of individuals are from time to time commuted, or the damages appraised from failure to rebuild them. The principal increase of bridges is in cities and villages, from the opening of new streets; and in these localities permanent iron bridges are now generally built upon the principal thoroughfares.

^c Of the 10 dams in the first column, 8 are feeder dams.

---

[1] Plans for improving the navigation of the Mohawk were proposed in 1725, but nothing was done to this end till March 30, 1792, when the "Western Inland Navigation Company" was incorporated, with powers to improve the channel and build canals and locks to Lake Ontario and Seneca Lake. The cost to Oneida Lake was estimated at £39,500. This work consisted mainly of the following:—

1st. A canal at Little Falls, 4,752 feet long, of which 2,550 feet were through solid rock. Upon it were 5 locks, with a total rise of 44½ feet. 2d. A canal 1¼ miles long, with a lock, at Wolf Rift, German Flats. 3d. A canal, 1¾ miles long, at Rome, connecting the Mohawk with Wood Creek; and, 4th, four locks upon Wood Creek, with a total depth of 25 feet. The work was begun at Little Falls, in 1793, but the want of funds delayed the work until 1794, when a subscription of 200 shares was obtained from the State. Boats first passed the canal and locks at this place Nov. 17, 1795, and on that day and the next 8 large and 102 small boats were passed, at a toll of £80 10s, exclusive of 9 that passed the first day. The chambers of the locks were 74 by 12 feet, and allowed boats of 32 tons to pass; but other impediments limited boats to a burden of 10 or 11 tons. Light boats could go from Schenectady to Fort Stanwix and back in 9 days; but the larger boats required 14 days to make the trip. In 1793, Wood Creek was cleared out, and 13 isthmuses were cut across, shortening the channel 7 miles. In 1796, boats passed through to Oneida Lake; and the work, in 1797, had cost $400,000, of which the State paid $92,000. The great cost required high tolls: and in 1812 but 300 boats passed, with 1,500 tons. at Little Falls. The company gave up its rights west of Oneida Lake in 1808, and sold out to the State, in 1820, for $152,718.52.—*Report of Weston, the Engineer*, 1796; *Spafford's Gazetteer*, 1813; *Hist. N. Y. Canals*, II, 40.

It is entirely uncertain who originated the first idea of constructing a chain of water communication through the State. All of the early efforts were directed to effecting a passage through the Mohawk, Wood Creek, Oneida Lake, and Oswego River to Lake Ontario. The Western connection was sought by locking around Niagara Falls. In 1800, Gouverneur Morris first suggested the idea of a direct canal from Lake Erie to the Hudson, through the center of the State. His plan was to tap Lake Erie, and have a continuous slope from the lake to the high land that borders upon the Hudson, and a series of locks thence to the river. In 1803 he stated the outline of his plan to the Surveyor-General, Simeon De Witt, who looked upon it as chimerical. The next year Mr. De Witt, in a conversation with James Geddes, then a land surveyor of Onondaga county, stated the plan of Mr. Morris as one of the impracticable schemes which had been advanced. Mr. Geddes, however, looked at the matter in a different light, and after some little reflection, he concluded that the plan, with some modifications, was by far the best that had yet been suggested. He counseled with Jesse Hawley upon the subject; and the latter, convinced of the feasibility of the project, wrote a series of papers which were published in the Genesee Messenger from Oct. 1807, to March, 1808. These essays were signed "Hercules," and were the first ever printed in favor of the Erie Canal. In 1808, Joshua Forman, an intimate associate of Mr. Geddes. then a member of the Assembly, introduced a resolution for the survey of a canal route, to the end that Congress might be led to grant moneys for the construction of a canal. The sum of $600 was granted for surveys under the direction of the Surveyor-General. James Geddes was intrusted with this service, and was directed to level down from Oneida Lake to the mouth of Salmon Creek, to ascertain whether a canal could be opened from Oswego Falls to Lake Ontario, and to survey the best route for a canal around Niagara Falls. He was also directed to survey a route eastward from Lake Erie to Genesee River, and thence to the waters flowing east into Seneca Lake. He finished this work, and made a report showing the practicability of the last named route and its great superiority over the others which had been proposed. This report at once excited general attention, and secured the influence of De Witt Clinton, then a member of the Senate, and many other prominent men. In 1810, commissioners, at the head of whom was De Witt Clinton. were appointed to explore a canal route through the center of the State. On the 8th of April, 1811. an act was passed to provide for the improvement of the internal navigation of the State. and efforts were made to obtain aid from the General Government. but without success. The report of the commissioners stated the importance of this measure with such force and eloquence that a law was passed the next year continuing the commissioners, and authorizing them to borrow and deposit money, and take cessions of land, for the proposed canal; but the war suspended active operations. The project. however, continued to be discussed, and an act was passed on the 17th of April, 1816. providing for a definite survey. The canal was begun at Rome, July 4, 1817, and on the 22d of October, 1819, the first boat passed from Utica to Rome.

The completion of the canal was celebrated by extraordinary

The enlargement of this canal was ordered May 11, 1835, and has been going on more or less rapidly since, except during a few years of suspension commencing under Gov. Wright's administration. It was estimated by the State Engineer and Surveyor, in Jan., 1859, that $1,565,077.75 would complete the enlargement upon the present plan, making the total cost of that work $23,000,000. The length of the Erie Canal when enlarged will be reduced to 349.74 mi. Its section gives a breadth of 70 ft. at the surface of the water, 52½ ft. at the bottom, and a depth of 7 ft.

civic and military ceremonies throughout the State, and especially in New York City, on the 4th of Nov. 1825. As the first boat, with Governor Clinton on board, entered the canal, at Buffalo, at 10 o'clock, (Oct. 26,) a line of cannon, previously arranged a few miles apart, passed a signal along to Albany, and down the Hudson to Sandy Hook, from whence it was returned in like manner. The signal was heard at New York, at 11.20. The flotilla with the Governor was everywhere greeted with enthusiastic rejoicing. Upon reaching New York it passed down to Sandy Hook, and the waters of the lake were mingled with those of the ocean with imposing ceremonies.

The Canal Commissioners under whom the Erie and Champlain Canals were constructed were Stephen Van Rensselaer, De Witt Clinton, Joseph Ellicott, Samuel Young, and Myron Holley. Henry Seymour was appointed in place of Ellicott in March, 1819, and William C. Bouck was added to the number in March, 1821. The chief engineers were James Geddes, of Onondaga co., and Benjamin Wright, of Rome, neither of whom had ever seen a canal, or enjoyed means of acquiring a practical knowledge of engineering other than that obtained from surveying land. The precision with which their canal surveys were executed, under the circumstances, may be regarded as truly wonderful. Among the assistant engineers were —— Peacock, David Thomas, Nathan S. Roberts, David S. Bates, Canvass White, Davis Hurd, Noah Dennis, Charles T. Whippo, William Jerome, Henry G. Sargent, Frederick C. Mills, Isaac J. Thomas, Henry Farnam, Alfred Barrett, John Bates, William H. Price, John Hopkins, and Seymour Skiff.

The Canal Board have adopted the following table of distances from place to place upon the Erie Canal. The elevations above tide are those shown by the lockages, and do not take into account the descent given to cause a flow of water between locks, which does not vary much from an inch to a mile. The long level is supposed to be perfectly uniform in elevation above tide.

Stations, Distances, and Elevations above Tide on the Erie Canal.

PLACES.	Miles from place to place.	Miles from Albany.	Miles from Buffalo.	Elevation above tide, in feet.	PLACES.	Miles from place to place.	Miles from Albany.	Miles from Buffalo.	Elevation above tide, in feet.
Albany	0	0	352		Weedsport	4	190	162	402
West Troy	7	7	345		Centerport	2	192	160	
Junction	0	7	345		Port Byron	2	194	158	
Cohoes	4	11	341		Montezuma	5	199	153	391
Crescent	3	14	338		Pitt Lock	6	205	147	
Upper Aqueduct	12	26	326		Clyde	5	210	142	397
Schenectady	4	30	322	188	Lock Berlin	4	214	138	
Hoffmans Ferry	10	40	312		Lyons	3	217	135	410
Port Jackson	6	46	306	269.5	East Arcadia	3	220	132	
Schoharie Creek	5	51	301		Lockville	3	223	129	
Auriesville	2	53	299		Newark	1	224	128	
Fultonville	3	56	296	295	Port Gibson	3	227	125	
Yatesville	6	62	290		Palmyra	5	232	120	445
Sprakers	3	65	287		Macedon	4	236	116	
Canajoharie	3	68	284	301	Wayneport	3	239	113	
Fort Plain	3	71	281		Knappville	2	241	111	
St. Johnsville	5	76	276	309	Fairport	3	244	108	462
Mindenville	2	78	274		Fullam's Basin	1	245	107	
East Canada Creek	4	82	270		Bushnell's Basin	3	248	104	
Little Falls	5	87	265	360	Cartersville	2	250	102	
Mohawk	8	95	257		Pittsford	1	251	101	
Ilion	3	98	254		Lock No. 65	2	253	99	
Frankfort	3	101	251	403	Brighton	3	256	96	471
Fergusons	5	106	246		Rochester	3	259	93	509
Utica	4	110	242	424	Greece (6-mile grocery)	7	266	86	
York Mills	3	113	239		Brockways	3	269	83	
Whitesboro	1	114	238		Spencerport	2	271	81	
Oriskany	3	117	235	427	Adams Basin	3	274	78	
Rome	8	125	227	427	Cooleys Basin	3	277	75	
New London	6	131	221		Brockport	2	279	73	
Higginsville	4	135	217		Holley	5	284	68	
Dunbarton	1	136	216		Hulberton	3	287	65	
Loomis	1	137	215		Brockville	1	288	64	
Durhamville	3	140	212		Hindsburgh	1	289	63	
Lenox	3	143	209		Albion	4	293	59	
Canastota	2	145	207		Gaines Basin	2	295	57	
New Boston Landing	4	149	203		Eagle Harbor	1	296	56	
Canaseraga Landing	1	150	202		Knowlesville	3	299	53	
Chittenango	1	151	201		Medina	4	303	49	
Bolivar	1	152	200		Shelbys Basin	3	306	46	
Pools Brook	2	154	198		Middleport	3	309	43	
Kirkville	1	155	197		Reynales Basin	4	313	39	
Manlius	3	158	194		Mabees	1	314	38	
Limestone Feeder	1	159	193		Gasport	1	315	37	
Orville Feeder	2	161	191		Orangeport	1	316	36	
Lodi	4	165	187		Millards	2	318	34	
Syracuse	1	166	186	400	Lockport	3	321	31	565
Geddes	2	168	184		Sulphur Springs, G. Lock	5	326	26	
Bellisle	4	172	180		Pendleton	2	328	24	
Nine Mile Creek	2	174	178		Pickardsville	5	333	19	
Camillus	1	175	177		Martinsville	3	336	16	
Canton	5	180	172		Tonawanda	4	340	12	
Peru	2	182	170		Lower Black Rock	8	348	4	
Jordan	3	185	167	407	Black Rock	1	349	3	
Cold Spring	1	186	166		Buffalo	3	352	0	

The number of locks will be 74, or 10 less than the original number.[1] The banks of the enlarged canal are protected from washing by slope walls, consisting of stone firmly packed upon the sloping sides. The canal will allow the passage of boats of 200 to 250 tons burden. Steam has been introduced to some extent in propelling boats, and the success of the experiment has been so great that probably steam power will ultimately supersede horse power.

The Champlain Canal, extending from the Erie Canal, near Cohoes, to Lake Champlain, was begun June 10, 1818, finished to Waterford Nov. 28, 1822, and completed Sep. 10, 1823, at an original cost of $875,000, exclusive of the feeder to Glens Falls. It is 64 mi. long and has a navigable feeder of 7 mi. to Glens Falls, with a slackwater navigation 5 mi. further upon the Hudson.[2]

The Chenango Canal,[3] connecting the Erie Canal at Utica with the Susquehanna River at Binghamton, was authorized Feb. 23, 1833. It is 97 mi. long, exclusive of 13¾ mi. of feeders, none of which are navigable.

The Black River Canal and Erie Canal Feeder extends from Rome up the valley of the Mohawk and of Lansing Kil to Boonville, and thence it descends the valley of Black River to a point below the High Falls. From the latter point is a river navigation 42½ mi. to Car-

---

1 The chambers of the enlarged locks are 110 by 18 feet, and their lift varies from 3 to 15½ feet. The canal leaves Lake Erie at Buffalo, follows the river bank to Black Rock, and communicates with the dam at that place. At a point 10 mi. below Buffalo it enters Tonawanda Creek, follows its channel 12 mi., and crosses thence, through a rock cutting, to the brow of the mountain ridge, at Lockport, where it descends 55.83 feet by 5 combined locks. It continues thence, eastward, from 1 to 3 mi. S. of the ridge road, to Rochester, crosses the Genesee upon a stone aqueduct, makes a circuitous sweep across the Irondequoit valley, along the top of a natural range of hills, and finally delivers the waters of Lake Erie into Seneca River, after supplying 153 mi. of the Erie Canal, and affording a large amount of water-power at various points along its course. It then rises by 2 locks, descends into the Onondaga valley by 1 lock, and then rises by 3 locks to the long level which extends from Syracuse to Utica, from whence it descends the Mohawk valley, mostly on its S. side, to the Hudson. Below Schenectady, it twice crosses the Mohawk, upon stone aqueducts. It is continued down the bank of the Hudson to Albany, where it terminates in a spacious basin. At West Troy it also opens into the Hudson. The total lockages going W. are 612.9 feet up, and 43.5 feet down, or a total of 656.4 feet. The canal is fed by numerous streams along its course, and by 9 reservoirs, all of which, with a single exception, are upon the middle division. They are as follows:

Reservoirs.	*Acres in area.*	*Elevation above canal, in feet.*	*Depth, in feet.*	*Length of feeders in mi.*
Erieville[a]	340	46	21½	20
Hatchs Lake	134	15	10	98[b]
Eatons Brook	254	60	50	8
Bradley Brook	134	30	25	3[c]
Leland Pond	173	13	8	½
Woodmans Lake	148	18	11	¼
Madison Brook	235	55	45	2
Skaneateles Lake	8,320	6	...	9
Cazenovia Lake	1,778	...	4½	10
Total	11,516	....	....	150¾

a Built in 1857, at a cost of $10,884.73. In Nelson, Madison co.

b Leads to Bradley Brook reservoir.

c Leads to Eaton Brook feeder.

Besides these are the reservoirs upon the Black River Canal, which is itself but a feeder to the long level of the Erie Canal. Several of the feeders to the middle and western divisions of the Erie Canal are navigable for short distances. Connected with the canal at Buffalo are Main and Hamburg street canals, the Clark and Skinner Canal, the Ohio basin, and several slips connected with the canal, and a ship-lock channel at Black Rock. At Tonawanda is a side-cut for a river-lock.

2 A company styled the "Northern Inland Navigation Co." was formed at the same time as the Western Co.; but failed to raise funds to accomplish its objects. A natural water communication, interrupted by portages, extended along the route of this canal, which was used by the natives with their canoes. The canal was built of the same dimensions as the Erie. It crosses the Mohawk in a pond formed by a dam 1,700 feet in length, and follows near the W. bank of the Hudson to Schuylerville, where it crosses into Washington co. by another dam 700 feet long, and continues near the east bank to Fort Edward. Here it leaves the river and crosses to the valley of Wood Creek, and thence, partly in the bed of that stream, to Whitehall. When this canal was first opened slackwater navigation upon the Hudson was used 8 miles above and 3 miles below Fort Miller, with a short canal and 2 locks around the falls at that place. It was fed from the Hudson by means of a high and costly dam near Fort Edward. The use of the channel of the Hudson is now entirely superseded by a canal along its bank, built in 1826–27; and the high dam has given place to a feeder to a point above Glens Falls, where there is a dam 770 feet long and 12 feet high. The feeder enters the canal at the summit level, 1½ miles N. E. from Fort Edward. The canal communicates with the Hudson above the State dam at Waterford by a side-cut with 3 locks. It has 7 locks between the lake and the summit, with 54 feet total lift, and 14 locks, with a total of 134 feet, between the Summit and the Hudson at Waterford. The locks on this canal are being enlarged to a capacity of 15¾ by 100 feet.

Stations, Distances, and Elevations upon the Champlain Canal.

Places.	*Miles from place to place.*	*Miles from Albany.*	*Miles from Whitehall.*	*Feet above tide.*
Albany	0	0	71	
West Troy	7	7	64	
Junction	0	7	64	25
Waterford	3	10	61	55
Mechanicsville	8	18	53	
Stillwater Village	4	22	49	
Bleeckers Basin	2	24	47	
Wilburs Basin	2	26	45	
Van Deusens Landing	5	31	40	
Schuylerville	3	34	37	100
Saratoga Bridge	2	36	35	110
Fort Miller	3	39	32	131
Moses Kil	3	42	29	
Fort Edward	5	47	24	140
Glens Falls Feeder	2	49	22	150
Bakers Basin	1	50	21	
Smiths Basin	5	55	16	
Fort Ann	4	59	12	
Comstocks Landing	4	63	8	
Whitehall	8	71	0	96

Glens Falls Feeder.

Places.	*Miles from place to place.*
Champlain Canal	0
Sandy Hill	2
Glens Falls	3
Head of the Feeder	2
Head of the Pond	5
Total	12

3 This canal is supplied by Chenango River and 6 reservoirs, viz.,—Madison Brook, Woodmans Pond, Lelands Pond, Bradleys Brook, Hatchs Lake, and Eaton Brook Reservoirs,—all of which are in the south part of Madison co. The canal extends across to and up the valley of Oriskany Creek to the summit level, and down the valley of Chenango River. It was begun in 1833 and finished in 1837, at a cost of $1,737,703. From Utica to the Summit it rises 706 feet by 76 locks, and from thence it descends 303 feet by 38 locks to the Susquehanna. Of its 114 locks, 2 are stone and the remainder composite. Upon the feeders are 12 road and 18 farm bridges.

thage, on the line of Jefferson co. At Boonville the canal receives a navigable feeder 12 mi. long, which derives its water from Black River. Length of main canal 36.62 mi., of feeders 12.48 mi., and of reservoirs 12.95 mi.[1]

The Oneida Lake Canal[2] connects the Erie Canal at Higginsville (3¾ mi.) with Wood Creek, and by slackwater, 2¼ mi. on that stream, with Oneida Lake, a total distance of 6 mi., and a descent of 56 ft.

The Oswego Canal, extending from Syracuse to Oswego, was authorized Nov. 20, 1824. A loan of $160,000 was allowed April 20, 1825; it was begun in 1826, and was completed in 1828, at a cost of $525,115.[3] It is 38 mi. long, and includes 19 mi. of slackwater navigation in Oswego and Seneca Rivers, with a towing path on the E. bank. Connected with this work are the **Oneida River Improvement,** extending the whole length of that stream from Three River Point to Fort Brewerton, at the outlet of Oneida Lake; the **Seneca River Improvement,** extending from Mud Lock, on the Oswego Canal, to Baldwinsville, by slackwater navigation; and

Stations, Distances, and Elevations upon the Chenango Canal.

PLACES.	Miles from place to place.	Miles from Utica.	Miles from Binghamton.	Feet above tide.
Utica	0	0	97	427
Road leading from New Hartford to Whitesboro	3	3	94	
Clinton	6	9	88	572
Deansville	5	14	83	775
Oriskany Falls	5	19	78	956
Solsville	3	22	75	1,109
Bouckville	2	24	73	1,128
Pecks Basin	2	26	71	
Hamilton	4	30	67	1,112
Lebanon Factory	2	32	65	
Earlsville	4	36	61	1,078
Sherburne	5	41	56	1,033
North Norwich	4	45	52	1,018
Plasterville	2	47	50	
Norwich	4	51	46	996
Oxford	9	60	37	958
Haynes Mill	10	70	27	
Greene	4	74	23	924
Forks	8	82	15	881
Pond Brook	2	84	13	
Port Crane	5	89	8	
Crockers Mills	1	90	7	
Binghamton	7	97	0	814

[1] This canal was authorized April 19, 1836, and began the next summer. The summit level is 693 feet above the canal at Rome, to which it descends by 70 locks. Northward the canal descends 386 feet, by 39 locks. The feeder has but one level. The State has caused reservoirs to be formed by damming the outlet of Woodhull, Chub, North and South Branch, and other lakes in Herkimer co. The Eight Lakes near the source of Moose River are available as reservoirs to supply Black River with water, withdrawn to feed the canal southward.

Table of the principal Lakes which are used or available as reservoirs.

LAKES.	Area in acres.	Feet above tide.
Chub Lake	530	1,599
Sand "	......	1,793
Mud "	......	1,799
Woodhull Lake	1,236	1,854
South Branch	518	2,019
North "	423	1,821
Jocks Lake	......	2,188
Moose "	......	1,772
First "	403	1,684
Second "	175	1,684
Third "	166	1,684
Fourth "	1,979	1,687
Fifth "	9	1,691
Sixth "	53	1,760
Seventh "	1,609	1,762
Eighth "	309	1,776

In September, 1857, the Canal Board abandoned its plans for improving the channel of Black River by wing-dams and piers, and ordered a dam and lock to be built at the mouth of Otter

Creek. The river has no towing path, and boats are towed by steamers. The State has built a dam and bridge at Carthage, and the piers of two other bridges, of which the superstructure is built by the towns.

Stations, Distances, and Elevations upon the Black River Canal.

PLACES.	Miles from place to place.	Miles from Rome.	Miles from Lyons Falls.	Feet above tide.
Rome	0	0	35	427
Ridge Mills	2	2	33	
Lock No. 7	3	5	30	
Walworth's Storehouse	1	6	29	
Westernville	3	9	26	
Wells Brook Aqueduct	2	11	24	595
Stringers Creek	2	13	22	643
Lansing Kil	1	14	21	683
Lock No. 31	2	16	19	
Lansing Kil Dam or Feeder	1	17	18	783
Lower Falls, Lansing Kil	2	19	16	
Upper Falls, Lansing Kil	2	21	14	
Lock No. 70	2	23	12	1,130
Boonville	2	25	10	1,120
Sugar River	3	28	7	
Little Falls, Black River	1	29	6	
Port Leyden	3	32	3	892
Lock No. 97	1	33	2	
Lyons Falls	2	35	0	734

Boonville Feeder.

Hawkinsville, on Feeder	"	3 miles from Boonville.	
A. Lee's, on	"	5 " " "	
R. B. Miller's, on	"	6 " " "	
State Dam, on	"	10 " " "	
Head of Reservoir		12 " " "	

[2] This canal was completed in the fall of 1835 by a company incorporated March 22, 1832, as the "Oneida Lake Canal Co." The company having to use the waters of the Erie Canal from the long level, were required to supply an equivalent amount. A feeder was constructed 5 miles west, drawing its waters from Oneida Creek. It is 2 miles long, and not navigable. The company had authority to extend its improvements 4 miles up Wood Creek, but nothing was ever done in that direction. By an act of May 11, 1840, the Canal Commissioners were authorized to purchase it at a cost not exceeding $50,000, which was done April 12, 1841, and State stock bearing 5 per cent. interest, and redeemable in 10 years, was issued in payment. The first cost of the canal and feeder was $78,824.85.

This canal forms an important link in the internal water communication of the State, extending navigation from the Erie Canal to Oneida Lake, and by the Oneida Outlet to the Oswego Canal and River. Before the Erie Canal was built the Oneida Lake route was the great thoroughfare for the transportation of goods westward.

[3] The act did not originally authorize a connection with the Erie Canal, but only a communication with Onondaga Lake. The connection was recommended by the commissioners in 1827, and it was authorized soon after. This canal has a fall of 123 feet by 18 locks.

The Oneida River Improvement has 2 steamboat locks, one of 3 and one of 3¼ feet lift, 120 feet long and 30 wide, passing boats drawing 4 feet of water. It also has one dam and one draw bridge at Oak Orchard and Brewerton.

thence by a canal three-fourths of a mile long, with one lift and one guard lock, and by slack-water on the Seneca River to Jacks Reef.

Cayuga and Seneca Canal connects the Erie Canal at Montezuma with Cayuga Lake at East Cayuga and with Seneca Lake at Geneva. About half of the canal is formed by slackwater navigation upon Seneca River, and the remainder is a channel parallel to the river. As enlarged, this canal admits the passage of large boats from the Erie Canal to the head of Cayuga and Seneca Lakes.[1]

Crooked Lake Canal connects Crooked Lake at Penn Yan with Seneca Lake at Dresden.[2]

Chemung Canal and Feeder connects Seneca Lake at Watkins with Chemung River at Elmira, with a navigable feeder from Knoxville on Chemung River to Horseheads, on the summit level of the Chemung Canal, including slackwater navigation from the dam and guard lock at Gibson to Knoxville.[3]

The Genesee Valley Canal extends from Rochester up the Genesee Valley to Olean upon the Allegany. The summit level is 978 ft. above Rochester and 86 ft. above the Allegany River, at Olean, and from it 97 locks descend toward the N. and 9 toward the S.[4]

Stations, Distances, and Elevations upon the Oswego Canal.

PLACES.	Miles from place to place.	Miles from Syracuse.	Miles from Oswego.	Feet above tide.
Syracuse	0	0	38	400
Salina	2	2	36	
Liverpool	3	5	33	368
Mud Lock	2	7	31	
Cold Spring	1	8	30	
New Bridge	5	13	25	
Three River Point	2	15	23	
Phœnix	2	17	21	358
Sweet's Lock	3	20	18	
Ox Creek	3	23	15	
Fulton	4	27	11	345
Braddock's Rapid	4	31	7	
Tiffany's Landing	4	35	3	306
High Dam	1	36	2	
Oswego	2	38	0	243

Oneida River Improvement.

PLACES.	Miles from place to place.
Three River Point	0
Peter Scott Creek	4
Oak Orchard	4
Caughdenoy	7
Brewerton	5
Total	20

Seneca River Improvement.

	Miles from place to place.
Mud Lock	0
Baldwinsville	6
Jack's Reef	12
Total	18

1 *Cayuga and Seneca Canal—Stations and Distances.*

PLACES.	Miles from place to place.
Montezuma	0
Seneca River	5
S. Dermont's	2
Seneca Falls	3
Chamberlain's Mills	2
Waterloo	2
Teal's	5
Geneva	2
Lateral Canal to East	
Cayuga	2
Total	23

The Seneca Lock Navigation Co. was incorporated April 6, 1813, for the purpose of improving the outlet of Seneca and Cayuga Lakes; and the Cayuga and Seneca Canal Co. was chartered April 20, 1815. Its capital was increased in 1816 to $60,000, and in 1817 a further call of 25 per cent. upon the original stock was authorized, including a like extension of payment on stock held by the State. The proposition for assuming this work by the State was approved in 1825, and the interest of the company was purchased for $33,867.18, exclusive of the amount owned by the State. The work was begun in 1826, and finished in 1828, at a

cost of $214,000. The inlet to Cayuga Lake is navigable 1¼ miles to Ithaca. The locks of this canal are all enlarged, excepting one at Chamberlain's Dam, which will be dispensed with so as to include the distance from Seneca Falls to Waterloo in one level. The descent from Geneva to Montezuma is 74 feet by 12 locks.

2 The survey of this canal was authorized by the Legislature in 1828. The canal was ordered to be built by an act of April 11, 1829. It was begun in 1830 and finished in 1833. It has a descent of 269 feet by 27 locks. It extends water communication to the various ports upon Crooked Lake.

Crooked Lake Canal—Stations and Distances.

PLACES.	Miles from place to place.
Dresden	0
Mallory's	3
Andrews and Ways	2
Penn Yan	2
Crooked Lake	1
Total	8

3 This canal was authorized April 15, 1829, and its construction was begun in that year and finished in 1833. The total lockages on both the canal and feeder are 516 feet by 53 locks, and the original cost was $344,000. From Corning, the Blossburg & Corning R. R. ascends into the bituminous coal region of Tioga co., Penn., and this article forms a very important item in the business of the canal. It also communicates with the Erie R. R. The Junction Canal, a private enterprise connecting the Chemung Canal at Elmira with the North Branch Canal of Penn. at Athens, 19 mi. s., promises to become an important tributary to the trade of this canal by opening access to the coal region. The diversion of Chemung River into our canals has been made a subject of complaint and remonstrance by the State of Penn. Plans have been proposed for using Mud Lake, (459 acres) and Little Lake, (708¼ acres,) in Tyrone, as reservoirs to relieve this canal from the inconvenience felt in dry seasons from low water.

Chemung Canal and Feeder—Stations and Distances.

PLACES.	MILES.	PLACES.	MILES.
Seneca Lake	0	*Feeder.*	
Havana	4	Horseheads	0
Millport	6	Miller's Basin	7
Horseheads	7	Dam at head of Feeder.	7
Elmira	6	Knoxville	2
Knoxville	22		
Total	47	Total	16

4 This canal was authorized by act of May 6, 1836, and was begun the same year. The portion from the Junction to Rochester and the Dansville side-cut, in all 52 miles, was finished in 1840; to Oramel, 36 miles further, with the Genesee Feeder at that place, in 1851; to Belfast, 2 miles, in 1853; to Rockville, 3 miles, in 1854, and to Olean, 24 miles, in 1856. A section of one mile, with 2 lift locks and 2 bridges, still remains to be finished.

The repairs of the first and second sections of this canal were put under contract for five years in Dec. 1855, the former for $8,440 and the latter for $13,900 per annum. In consequence of heavy freshets and unexpected damages, the contractor on the first section abandoned his contract in June, 1857.

An act passed, 1857, authorized the extension of this canal from Olean eastward across Olean Creek and the bottom lands along the N. bank of the Allegany to its entrance into Mill Grove Pond, 6.52 miles.

Besides the foregoing navigable improvements by the State, the following have been placed under the direction of the Canal Commissioner for construction :

The Owasco Lake Improvement, ordered in 1852, and designed to make this lake a reservoir for supplying a water power for the machinery in Auburn State Prison.[1]

The draining of Cayuga Marshes, for reclaiming a large amount of land, estimated at 40,000 acres, at the outlet of Cayuga Lake and along Seneca River. By an act of April 12, 1853, the channel of the river was ordered to be lowered, and the lands benefitted to be taxed for the expense. Surveys have been made and the work partly accomplished under the direction of the Canal Commissioners.[2]

Several companies have been incorporated for the purpose of constructing navigable canals, but, with two or three exceptions, none of these have at present a corporate existence.

The Delaware and Hudson Canal, extending from Rondout on the Hudson to Honesdale, Penn., is the most important of these. It is connected with the Lackawanna coal region by a R. R. 16 mi. long, and is one of the principal routes by which coal is brought to the market upon the Hudson.[3]

Stations, Distances, and Elevations upon the Genesee Valley Canal.

PLACES.	Miles from place to place.	Miles from Rochester.	Miles from Olean.	Feet above tide.
Rochester	0	0	107	507
Rapids (Lock No. 1)	2	2	105	
Tone's Basin	6	8	99	
Scottsville	4	12	95	537
Canawaugus (Avon road)	8	20	87	
Sackett's Basin	2	22	85	557
Fowlerville Road	2	24	83	
Barclay's Mill	2	26	81	
Piffardinia	3	29	78	
Spencer's Basin	1	30	77	
Tracy's Basin	2	32	75	
Cuylerville	1	33	74	564
Leicester, Moscow Landing	1	34	73	
Genesee River Dam	2	36	71	589
Mount Morris	1	37	70	600
Shaker Settlement	4	41	66	
Brushville	5	46	61	796
Nunda	5	51	56	947
Messenger's Hollow	2	53	54	
Genesee Falls (Tunnel section)	4	57	50	
Portageville	2	59	48	1,132
Lock No. 61	5	64	43	
Mixville Landing, Wiscoy Feeder	1	65	42	1,152
Fillmore	4	69	38	
Burrville	6	75	32	1,222
Caneadea Center	1	76	31	
Oramel	2	78	29	
Belfast	2	80	27	1,315
Rockville	3	83	24	1,410
Caseville	1	84	23	
Black Creek Corners	4	88	19	
Cuba	5	93	14	1,485
Ischua Feeder	6	99	8	
Hinsdale	1	100	7	
Olean	7	107	0	1,399

Dansville Branch.

PLACES.	Miles from place to place.
Shaker Settlement	0
Fitzhugh's Basin	2
Kysorville	1
Rock Spring	2
Sherwoods Landing	1
Steam Sawmill	1
McNairs Landing	1
Woodville	1
Commonsville	1
Dansville	1
Total	11

[1] This work was 2 years in charge of the Agent of the State Prison and the Mayor of Auburn, but in 1855 it was placed in the hands of the Canal Commissioners. The work, up to 1857, was greatly injured by a Spring flood. From 1852 to 1857 inclusive, $33,485 had been appropriated for this work.

[2] In 1824, and several times afterward. the drainage of these marshes was made the subject of legislative enactment, but without other results than surveys. A concise history of this movement is given in *Senate Doc.* 35. 1853. The work was placed in 1853 under the direction of George Geddes, and up to 1858, $175,000 had been appropriated and mostly expended.—*Report Canal Commissioners*, 1858, p. 110.

[3] The Delaware and Hudson Canal Company was incorporated April 23, 1823, with a capital of $1,500,000, with the right of using $50.000 in banking until 1844. The credit of the State was loaned for $800,000, in stock, bearing interest of 4½ or 5 per cent. The canal was begun in July, 1825, and opened for use in Oct. 1828. Its length from Rondout to Port Jervis, on the Delaware, is 59 miles; and from Port Jervis, up the Delaware to the mouth of the Lakawaxen, 24 miles. It crosses the river at the latter place, and extends 26 miles further to Honesdale. Its highest summit between the Hudson and Delaware Rivers is 585 feet above tide. Its descent to the Delaware is 80 feet; its rise along the Delaware is.148 feet; and its rise between the Delaware and Honesdale 187 feet. The aggregate number of locks is 107, and the total rise and fall is 950 feet. The railroad to the coal mines is also owned by the Canal Company. The original cost of the New York section of the canal was $1,424.994, and of the Penn. section $612,123. The company own most of the boats used upon the canal, and conduct the mining operations at Carbondale. Present capital, $7,500,000. The canal was originally constructed to afford 4 feet of depth, and to accommodate boats of 30 tons. In Sept., 1842, a plan of enlargement was adopted, and 5 feet of water was obtained, accommodating boats of 40 tons each. In 1851 a further enlargement was completed, obtaining 6 feet of water, and accommodating boats of 120 tons. The locks are now constructed with a single gate at the upper end, which turns down upon hinges like a door. It is found to be very serviceable, and much quicker to operate than the double gate.

Annual Receipts of Tolls on the Delaware and Hudson Canal since its completion.

1830	$16,422,44	1845	$25,880.92
1831	20,554,64	1846	26,068.65
1832	28,717,51	1847	38,971.34
1833	37,004,58	1848	46,548.54
1834	36,946.07	1849	34,817.95
1835	41,154.73	1850	97.999.15
1836	45,154.73	1851	158,441.96
1837	44,832.42	1852	293,174.67
1838	40,328.38	1853	378,479.83
1839	40,095.26	1854	587,349.52
1840	35,450.46	1855	652,362.94
1841	39,388.19	1856	583.737.86
1842	33,894.93	1857	435,198.44
1843	30,996.53	1858	
1844	33,525.61		

Distances on the Delaware and Hudson Canal.

Names of Places.	Nos. of Locks.	Miles from Eddyville.	Miles from Honesdale.	Names of Places.	Nos. of Locks.	Miles from Eddyville.	Miles from Honesdale.
Eddyville	No. 1	0	108	Graham's Basin	....	42	66
Greenkill	....	1	107	Manerza Smith's	....	43	65
Hornbeck's Bridge	....	2	106	Brown Haven	....	44	64
Head of Pond	2 to 4	3	105	Oak Brook Aqueduct	....	45	63
Hardenburgh's Basin	5	4	104	Indian Spring	....	46	62
Le Fever's Falls	6	5	103	Tunnel Hill	....	47	61
Rosendale	7	6	102	Westbrookville	....	48	60
Lawrence's Mills	8 and 9	7	101	Samuel Staunten's	....	49	59
Marble Quarries	10 and 11	8	100	Van Inweigen's Basin	....	50	58
High Falls	12 to 19	9	99	Cuddebackville	....	51	57
Hasbrouck's Basin	20 and 21	10	98	Neversink Aqueduct	55 to 59	52	56
Philip Hasbrouck's	....	11	97	Piersonville	60	53	55
Clove Church	....	12	96	Solomon Van Etten's Bridge	....	54	54
Alligerville	22	13	95	Canal Store	....	55	53
John S. Depuy's Basin	23	14	94	Hornbeck's Culvert	....	56	52
Enoch Freeland's	....	15	93	Bird's Nest Rock	....	57	51
Stony Hill Aqueduct	24	16	92	Stop Gate—Pine Woods	....	58	50
Port Jackson	....	17	91	Benjamin Cuddeback's	....	59	49
David Venooy's	....	18	90	Port Jervis	....	60	48
C. P. Hornbeck's	....	19	89	Stop Gate—Westfall's Basin	....	61	47
Mountain Brook	....	20	88	Sparrow Bush Brook	....	62	46
Middleport	25	21	87	Honesville	....	63	45
Bruyn's Basin	....	22	86	Bolton	....	64	44
Port Hyxson	26	23	85	Butler's Falls	61	65	43
Port Benjamin	27	24	84	Mongaup	62 and 63	66	42
Heirstard's Bridge	....	25	83	Dickerson's Eddy	....	67	41
Southwick's Brick Yard	28	26	82	Stairway Brook	64	68	40
Terwilliger's Feeder	29 and 30	27	81	Vanaukin's Bridge	65	69	39
Ellenville	31 and 32	28	80	Fish Cabin Brook	66	70	38
Cutler's Basin	33	29	79	Tucker's Aqueduct	....	71	37
Broadhead's Brickhill	34	30	78	Pond Eddy	67	72	36
Jared Ritche's	35 and 36	31	77	Van Tuyl's Brook	68	73	35
Penney's Basin	37 and 38	32	76	Van Tuyl's Basin	....	74	34
Red Bridge	39 to 41	33	75	Craigsville	69 and 70	75	33
Phillipsport	42 to 51	34	74	Buttermilk Falls	....	76	32
Davis—Summit Level	52 to 54	35	73	Handsome Eddy	71	77	31
Beatysburgh	....	36	72	David Johnston's	....	78	30
Log House in Swamp	....	37	71	Barrysville	72 and 73	79	29
South Side of Swamp	....	38	70	Panther Brook	....	80	28
Gumare's Brook	....	39	69	Beaver Brook	....	81	27
Wurtsboro'	....	40	68	Stop Lock	....	82	26
Sneed's Basin	....	41	67	Delaware Dam	G'nd L'k.	83	25

Table of Companies which have been organized for Constructing Canals and Extending Navigation in the State.

Names of Canals.	Date of Organization.	Capital.	Connections.	Remarks.
Allegany River Slackwater Navigation Co.	April 7, 1857	$30,000	....	To improve Allegany River below Olean.
Auburn Canal and R. R. Co.	April 24, 1832	150,000	Auburn and Erie Canal	Nothing done.
Auburn & Owasco Canal Co.	April 21, 1828	100,000	Auburn and Owasco Lake	Charter renewed in 1834; not finished.
Binghamton, Owego, & Penn. Slackwater Navigation Co.	April 9, 1855	100,000	....	Act amended in 1857.
Black River Canal Co.	March 20, 1828	400,000	Erie Canal and Black River	Nothing done.
Black River Navigation Co.	April 5, 1810	10,000	Brownville and Lake Ontario	Not constructed.
Cassadaga Navigation Co.	April 16, 1827	20,000	....	To improve Cassadaga Creek; not completed.
Cattatunk Dock Navigation Co.	March 3, 1815	70,000	....	To improve Cattatunk Creek from its mouth to N. W. branch. Nothing done.
Cayuga & Seneca Canal Co.	April 20, 1815	....	Montezuma and Seneca Lake	Rights purchased by the State.
Chenango Junction Canal Co.	May 12, 1846	....	Binghamton to State line	Nothing done.
Chittenango Canal Co.	March 1, 1818	....	Chittenango Village and Erie Canal.	Assumed by the State, and used as a navigable feeder to Erie Canal.
Delaware & Susquehanna Navigation Co.	April 20, 1825	....	Delaware and Susquehanna River.	Nothing done.
Ellicotts Creek Slackwater Navigation Co.	April 23, 1829	5,000	....	Nothing done.
Gowanus Bay & East River	April 24, 1837	....	City of Brooklyn may cause to be constructed.	Partially improved.
Great Chazy Navigation Co.	May 11, 1836	5,000	Lake and Lower Bridge at Champlain.	
Granville Canal Co.	April 18, 1825	....	Champlain Canal and Bishops Corners.	Nothing done.
Harlem Canal Co.	April 18, 1826	550,000	East River and Manhattanville.	Partly done and abandoned.
Harlem River Canal Co.	April 16, 1827	500,000	Spuyten Duyvil Creek and Harlem River.	Surveyed but not constructed.
Hudson River & Channel Co.	April 4, 1806	3,500	For raft navigation on upper water.	Nothing done.
Jefferson County Canal Co.	April 15, 1828	300,000	Carthage and Sackets Harbor	Nothing done.
Junction Canal Co.	April 21, 1828	100,000	From Erie Canal near Champlain Junction to Hudson River.	Nothing done.

Table of Companies which have been organized for Constructing Canals and Extending Navigation in the State, continued.

NAMES OF CANALS.	Date of Organization.	Capital.	Connection.	Remarks.
Junction Canal Co....................	May 11, 1845	....	From Chemung Canal at Elmira to State line to connect with North Branch Canal.	Completed in 1858.
Long Island Canal Co..............	April 15, 1828	$200,000	To connect Bays on s. side and to cross Canoe Place to Peconic Bay.	Nothing done but survey.
Long Island Canal & Navigation Co.	April 8, 1848	300,000	The same...............................	Nothing done.
Manlius Canal Co.....................	April 15, 1828	50,000	Erie Canal and Manlius Slackwater Navigation.	State Canal Feeder.
Mohawk & Hudson Lock Navigation Co.	April 17, 1816	500,000	Cohoes Falls and Schenectady...	Nothing done.
Neversink Navigation Co..........	April 16, 1816	50,000	....	The project failed. The State loaned its credit for $10,000 and lost the whole sum.
New York & Sharon..................	April 19, 1823	....	From Sharon, Conn., to tide water to any point on the Hudson or in the City of New York.	Surveyed nearly on the present line of the Hudson R. R.
Niagara Canal Co......................	April 5, 1798	....	Lake Erie and Lake Ontario......	Nothing done.
Northern Inland Lock Navigation Co.	March 30, 1792	....	Hudson River and Lake Champlain.	Work commenced but no part completed.
Northern Slackwater & Railway Co.	May 13, 1846	....	Port Kent and Saranac............	Nothing done.
Oneida Lake Canal Co..............	March 22, 1832	40,000	....	Finished in 1835, and purchased by the State in 1841.
Onondaga Canal Co..................	Nov. 25, 1824	....	Erie Canal and Onondaga Hollow.	Not constructed.
Ontario Canal Co......................	March 31, 1821	100,000	Canandaigua Lake and Erie Canal.	Nothing done.
Orange & Sussex Canal Co........	April 11, 1825	....	From Columbia, on the Delaware, through Orange co., to the Hudson.	The right granted in 1828 to build a R. R. on the line. Nothing done on either.
Oswegatchie Navigation Co.......	April 25, 1831	....	From the St. Lawrence to Black Lake and Canton.	Nothing done.
Owasco & Erie Canal Co...........	May 1, 1829	150,000	Owasco Lake and Erie Canal.....	Nothing done.
Peconic River Lock Navigation Co.	April 8, 1808	....	To construct Locks and Dams in Peconic River.	Nothing done.
Rochester Canal & R. R. Co.......	March 26, 1831	30,000	Rochester and Lake Ontario......	Railroad only constructed.
St. Lawrence Lock Co..............	April 1, 1808	....	For building Locks at Isle au Rapid.	Locks completed but too small for general use.
Salmon River Harbor Canal Co..	May 16, 1837	350,000	Lake Ontario and Port Ontario..	Never completed.
Scottsville Canal Co..................	April 30, 1829	15,000	Scottsville and Genesee River.	
Seneca Lock Navigation Co.......	April 6, 1813	50,000	For improving navigation between Seneca and Cayuga Lakes.	Merged in Cayuga & Seneca Canal.
Seneca & Susquehanna Lock Navigation Co.	March 31, 1815	300,000	From Seneca Lake to Chemung River near Elmira.	Nothing done.
Sodus Canal Co.......................	March 19, 1829	200,000	From Seneca River or Canandaigua outlet to Great Sodus Bay.	Partly constructed, but never used.
Susquehanna & Chenango.........	May 20, 1836	....	From river to Chenango Canal.	
Wallabout Canal Co..................	April 9, 1828	20,000	Wallabout Bay and Tillory St. Brooklyn.	Not constructed.
Wallabout Canal Co..................	April 18, 1838	25,000	Wallabout Bay to Kent Avenue, Brooklyn.	
Western Inland Lock Navigation Co.	March 30, 1792	....	To open navigation on the Mohawk, Wood Creek, Oneida, and Oswego Rivers to Lake Ontario.	Completed to Oneida Lake in 1797. The rights were afterward vested in the State, and such as were available were used for the Erie Canal.

RAIL ROADS.

The first rail road in the State, and the second in the U. S., was opened from Albany to Schenectady in 1831. Although rudely constructed, at great and much needless expense, the advantages of this means of communication became so apparent that within 3 years rail roads, duly chartered by law, were projected in every part of the State.[1] These early grants were generally limited to 50 years, and work was required to be commenced within 3 years, the State being allowed to become purchaser at the expiration of the charter. The charters contained the necessary provisions for the taking of property by appraisements, named the commissioners for opening subscriptions, and sometimes for locating and surveying the road, which in a few instances was done at the expense of the State.

At an early period the aid of the General Government was solicited, in view of the utility of these roads in the transportation of the mails, and, in case of war, of military supplies; but, with the exception of surveys made in two instances, no aid was obtained from this source. The State has

[1] **Albany, Vermont, & Canada Rail Road,** formerly the Albany Northern R. R. Company organized Feb. 12, 1851. Connects Albany and Eagle Bridge. Road opened through about the 1st of July, 1853. It was sold under foreclosure of mortgage Oct. 16, 1856, and assumed its present name Nov. 7, following.

Albany, Vermont, and Canada Rail Road.

Stations and Distances.

STATIONS.	DISTANCES IN MILES.		
	Between Stations.	From Albany.	From EagleB'dg.
Albany	0	0	33
Cemetery	4	4	29
West Troy	2	6	27
Cohoes	3	9	24
Waterford	2	11	22
Saratoga Junction............	1	12	21
Schaghticoke...................	10	22	11
Pittstown.....................	1	23	10
Johnsonville	3	26	7
Buskirks.....................	5	31	2
Eagle Bridge	2	33	0

Albany & West Stockbridge Rail Road, formerly Castleton & West Stockbridge R. R. Company organized April 19, 1830, but nothing was done under the first name. Present name assumed May 5, 1836. Road opened from Greenbush to Chatham Dec. 21, 1841, and to the State line Sept. 12, 1842. It was leased to the Western (Mass.) R. R. Nov. 18, 1841, for the term of its charter; and has since been operated as a part of that road, including the ferry at Albany. The city of Albany, at different times, issued its bonds for $1,000,000, to aid in building the road, the lessees paying the interest and $10,000 annually toward the sinking fund. It connects Albany with Springfield and Boston.

Western Rail Road.

Stations and Distances.

STATIONS.	DISTANCES IN MILES.		
	Between Stations.	From Albany.	From Boston.
Albany	0	0	200
Greenbush.....................	1	1	199
Schodack.....................	7	8	192
Kinderhook.....................	8	16	184
Chatham Center	3	19	181
Chatham Four Corners......	4	23	177
East Chatham.................	5	28	172
Canaan	5	33	167
State Line	5	38	162
Pittsfield, Mass..............	11	49	151
Springfield, "	53	102	98
Worcester, "	54	156	44
Boston, "	44	200	

Atlantic & Great Western Rail Road Co. was formed Dec. 9, 1858. The line extends from the New York & Erie R. R. at Little Valley to the s. line of Chautauque county.

Attica & Hornellsville Rail Road. Company incorporated May 14, 1845; capital $750,000. Time extended April 11, 1849. Other roads allowed to take stock April 9, 1851. Capital increased and company allowed to purchase the Buffalo & Rochester R. R., from Attica to Buffalo, and to change its name March 3, 1851. Name changed to Buffalo & New York City R. R., April 16, 1851.

Black River & Utica Rail Road. Company formed Jan. 29, 1853. Road opened to Trenton Jan. 1, 1855, and to Boonville Dec. 18, 1855. The city of Utica has issued its bonds for $250,000, to aid in the construction of road. It is designed to connect Utica and Clayton.

Black River & Utica Rail Road.

Stations and Distances. (Official.)

STATIONS.	DISTANCES IN MILES.		
	Between Stations.	From Utica.	From Boonville.
Utica.....................	0	0	35
Marcy.....................	6	6	29
Floyd Road	2	8	27
Stittsville.....................	2	10	25
Holland Patent...............	2	12	23
Trenton.....................	4	16	19
Trenton Falls...............	1½	17½	17¾
Prospect.....................	1	18½	16¾
Remsen.....................	2¾	21	14
Alder Creek	7	28	7
Boonville	7	35	0

Blossburg & Corning Rail Road, formerly the Corning & Blossburg R. R., and previously the Tioga Coal, Iron Mining, & Manufacturing Co.'s R. R. Was leased for a term of years to the Tioga (Pa.) R. R. Co. In 1854 it was sold for $250,000, subject to a mortgage of $245,000 and a ten years lease to the Tioga Co. It is operated at present by the lessees.

Blossburg and Corning Railroad.

STATIONS.	DISTANCES IN MILES.		
	Between Stations.	From Corning.	From Blossburg.
Corning	...	...	41
Erwin Center.................	...	...	...
Lindley Town.................	...	...	...
Blossburg.....................	...	41	...

Brooklyn City Rail Road. Company formed Dec. 16, 1853. Opened as follows:
Flushing Avenue Route. Fulton St. to Throop Avenue in... July, 1854
Fulton Avenue Route. Ferry to Washington Avenue in... July, 1854
Myrtle Avenue Route. Fulton St. to Nortram Avenue in... July, 1854
Greenwood Route. Fulton St. to Gowanus Creek in...................................... Aug. 1854
Washington Avenue to Brooklyn Avenue in...... Sept. 1854
Kent Avenue to Bushwick Creek in................. Oct. 1854
Gowanus Creek to 36th St. in........................ Nov. 1854
Nortram Avenue to Division Avenue in .... Nov. 1854

upon several occasions loaned its credit to R. R. companies by issuing stock and retaining a lien upon the roads, which in some cases was afterward relinquished, and in others sacrificed by sale at nominal prices.

Throop Avenue to Division Avenue in.............. April, 1855
Hamilton Avenue Route, Court St. to Ferry in May, 1855
This road is used for passengers only, and horse power is exclusively employed.
36th St. to City Line...................................... July, 1855
Bushwick Creek to Kent St. in........................ Oct. 1855
Kent St. to Furman St. in.............................. Dec. 1855
City Line to Yellow Hookland in.................... July, 1856

Brooklyn & Jamaica Rail Road. Company formed April 25, 1832. In 1836 the road was leased to the Long Island R. R. Co. for the term of its charter. The lessees built a tunnel 2,550 feet long under Atlantic St., bought access to the river, erected buildings and docks at a cost of over $300,000, and have since maintained and operated the road in connection with the Long Island R. R., of which it is virtually a part.

Buffalo, Bradford, & Pittsburgh Rail Road Co. was formed ——— 1859, by the consolidation of the Buffalo & Bradford and Buffalo & Pittsburgh R. R's.
Buffalo & New York City Rail Road, formerly Attica & Hornellsville R. R. Articles filed Jan. 22, 1851. 31 mi. sold to Buffalo, New York, & Erie R. R. Oct. 31, 1857, and name changed to

Buffalo, New York, & Erie Rail Road.
Stations and Distances. (Official.)

STATIONS.	DISTANCES IN MILES.		
	Between Stations.	From Buffalo.	From Corning.
Buffalo & Corning.			
Buffalo	0	0	141.57
Junction	1	1	140.57
Lancaster	9.45	10.45	131.12
Town Line.......................	4.05	14.5	127.07
Alden	4.95	19.45	122.12
Darien	5.47	24.92	116.65
Attica	6.14	31.06	110.51
Alexander	3.40	34.46	107.11
Batavia	7.20	41.66	99.91
Stafford	5.60	47.26	94.31
Le Roy............................	4.32	51.58	89.99
Caledonia........................	7.31	58.89	82.68
Avon	6.93	65.82	75.75
Hamiltons	9.05	74.87	66.7
Livonia	2.56	77.43	64.14
South Livonia	3.64	81.07	60.5
Conesus	3.71	84.78	56.79
Springwater	6.65	91.43	50.14
Wayland	4.76	96.19	45.38
Bloods	5.91	102.1	39.47
Liberty	4.36	106.46	35.11
Wallaces	4.87	111.33	30.24
Avoca	2.88	114.21	27.36
Kanona............................	3.64	117.85	23.72
Bath...............................	3.77	121.62	19.95
Savona	6.15	127.77	13.8
Campbell	4.71	132.48	9.09
Curtis	1.67	134.15	7.42
Coopers...........................	2.60	136.75	4.82
Painted Post.....................	3.22	139.97	1.6
Corning	1.60	141.57	0
New York		432.63	291.06

Rochester Division.		From Rochester.	From Avon.
Rochester.........................	0	0	18.25
Henrietta.........................	8.45	8.45	9.8
Scottsville........................	3.27	11.72	6.53
Rush...............................	2.27	13.99	4.26
Avon...............................	4.26	18.25	0

Hornellsville Division.		From Attica.	From Hornellsville.
Attica	0	0	60.26
Linden............................	6.87	6.87	53.39
Middlebury.......................	4.33	11.2	49.06
Warsaw...........................	5.78	16.98	43.28
Gainesville.......................	6.77	23.75	36.51
Castile............................	2.76	26.51	33.75
Portage...........................	3.61	30.12	30.14
Hunts Hollow	4.07	34.19	26.07
Nunda.............................	2.07	36.26	24
Swainville........................	7.17	43.43	16.83
Canaseraga	4.43	47.86	12.4
Burns..............................	4.10	51.96	8.3
Hornellsville	8.30	60.26	0

Buffalo & State Line Rail Road. Company formed June 6, 1849. Road opened from Dunkirk to the State Line Jan. 1, 1852, and to Buffalo Feb. 22 following. The Company purchased the North East (Penn.) R. R. under act of April 13, 1857, and now form one company from Buffalo to Erie, Penn. It is now operated under the name of

Buffalo and Erie Rail Road.
Stations and Distances. (Official.)

STATIONS.	DISTANCES IN MILES.		
	Between Stations.	From Buffalo.	From Erie, Penn.
Buffalo	0	0	88
Hamburg	10	10	78
18 Mile Creek	5	15	73
Evans Center....................	6	21	67
Saw Mill	5	26	62
Irving.............................	3	29	59
Silver Creek.....................	2	31	57
Dunkirk	7	40	48
Salem.............................	8	48	40
Portland..........................	2	50	38
Westfield.........................	7	57	31
Ripley.............................	5	62	26
Quincy............................	3	65	23
State Line	3	68	20
Erie, Penn	20	88	0

Canandaigua & Corning Rail Road. Company incorporated May 11, 1845; capital $1,600,000 Time extended April 15, 1847, and again March 24, 1849. Surveys were begun June, 1845, and the construction in Aug. 1850. Road opened from Canandaigua to "*Jefferson*" (now Watkins) 46 7/100 mi., Sept. 15, 1851, the New York & Erie R. R. furnishing engines, cars, &c., for a specific rate per mile. The road was allowed to connect with the Chemung R. R. at Jefferson, and to change name Sept. 11, 1852, to Canandaigua and Elmira R. R.
Canandaigua & Elmira Rail Road, changed from Canandaigua & Corning R. R. Sept. 11, 1852. Leased the Chemung R. R. 17 36/100 mi. and 4 mi. of Erie R. R. Sold to parties in Elmira, Penn Yan, and Providence, R. I. April 23, 1857, and possession given May 1. Price $35,000, subject to $500,000 due bondholders, and name changed to the Elmira, Canandaigua, & Niagara Falls R. R. the next day.
Canandaigua & Niagara Falls Rail Road. Company incorporated Dec. 10, 1850; capital $1,000,000. Road opened to Batavia, 50 mi., Jan. 1, 1853, to Niagara Falls 47 mi. July 1, 1853, and to Suspension Bridge 1½ mi. April 1, 1854. Sold March 22, 1857, to Jas. M. Brown and others, and name changed to Niagara Bridge & Canandaigua R. R. Now leased and run by New York Central R. R.

Cayuga & Susquehanna Rail Road, formerly the Ithaca & Owego R. R., was chartered Jan. 28, 1828,—the second R.R. charter granted in the State. The road was opened in April, 1834. An inclined plane at Ithaca rose 1 foot in 4 28/100 ft. and stationary steam power was used for drawing up the cars. Above this was another inclined plane, that rose one foot in 21 ft., on which horse power was used. The road was subsequently sold by the Comptroller on stock issued by the State, on which the company had failed to pay interest. A new company was organized and the present name assumed April 18, 1843; the road was reconstructed, the inclined planes were done away with, and Jan. 1, 1855, it was leased to the Delaware, Lackawanna & Western R. R. Co., and is operated by them as the Cayuga Division. This is an important route from the coal mines of Penn., and coal forms the principal item of business.

Delaware, Lackawanna and Western Rail Road.
Stations and Distances. (Official.)

STATIONS.	DISTANCES IN MILES.		
	Between Stations.	From Ithaca Pier.	From Owego.
Ithaca Pier......................	0	0	35
Ithaca............................	2	2	33
Pugsleys..........................	13	15	20
Willseyville	6	21	14
Candor	4	25	10
Catatunk	6	31	4
Owego............................	4	35	0

Champlain & St. Lawrence Rail Road. Company formed Feb. 26, 1851. The Road extends from Rouses Point to the Canada line 2¼ miles, and is leased to a road in Canada of the same name, which extends to St. Johns and La Prairie opposite Montreal.

By resolution of Assembly of Feb. 2, 1843, R. R. companies were required to report annually to the Secretary of State; and by an act of April 11, 1849, to the State Engineer and Surveyor; a

Chemung Rail Road. Company formed May 14, 1845. The road extends from Watkins, at the head of Seneca Lake, to the New York & Erie R. R., 4 mi. N. W. of Elmira. It was opened in Dec. 1849; leased to the New York & Erie R. R. Co. for ten years from Jan. 1, 1850, for $36,000 per annum; and sub-let to the Canandaigua and Elmira R. R. Co., for the same. It is now operated by the New York & Erie R. R. Co.

Chemung Rail Road.

Stations and Distances. (Official.)

Stations.	Distances in Miles.		
	Between Stations.	*From Watkins.*	*From Elmira.*
Jefferson (Watkins)	0	0	21.6
Havana	3.2	3.2	18.4
Groton Corners	3.7	6.9	14.7
Millport	2	8.9	12.7
Pine Valley	2.8	11.7	9.9
Horseheads	4.4	16.1	5.5
Junction	1.2	17.3	4.3
Elmira	4.3	21.6	0

Elmira, Canandaigua & Niagara Falls Rail Road. Changed from Canandaigua & Niagara Falls R. R. April 24, 1857. The name was changed to

Elmira, Jefferson & Canandaigua Rail Road Co. Feb. 18, 1859. The road is now leased and run by the New York & Erie R. R. Co.

Elmira, Jefferson & Canandaigua Rail Road.

Stations and Distances. (Official.)

Stations.	Distances in Miles.		
	Between Stations.	*From Canandaigua.*	*From Watkins, (Jefferson Station.)*
Canandaigua	0	0	46.9
Hopewell	6.4	6.4	40.5
Gorham	5.3	11.7	35.2
Halls Corners	2.8	14.5	32.4
Bellona	3.8	18.3	28.6
Benton Center	1.9	20.2	26.7
Penn Yan	4	24.2	22.7
Milo Center	4.1	28.3	18.6
Himrods	3.6	31.9	15
Starkey	3.9	35.8	11.1
Big Stream	2.6	38.4	8.5
Rock Stream	1.9	40.3	6.6
Jefferson (Watkins)	6.6	46.9	0
Elmira	21.6	68.5	21.6

Flushing Rail Road. Company formed Feb. 24, 1852. Opened June 26, 1854. The road extends from Flushing to Hunters Creek, and the Co. runs a steamer to Fulton street, New York.

Flushing Rail Road.

Stations and Distances. (Official.)

Stations.	Distances in Miles.		
	Between Stations.	*From New York.*	*From Flushing.*
New York[a]	0	0	12
Hunters Point	4	4	8
Penny Bridge	1	5	7
Winsfield	2½	7½	4½
Newtown	1	8½	3½
National Race Course	1½	10	2
Flushing	2	12	0

[a] By steamboat between New York and Hunters Point.

Hicksville & Cold Spring Branch Rail Road. Company formed June 28, 1851, and organized Nov. 3, 1853. The road was to extend from Hicksville to Cold Spring Harbor. It was opened to Syosset, July 3, 1854. Nothing has been done beyond there. It has been leased to the Long Island R. R. Co., and is operated by them.

Hudson & Boston Rail Road. Company allowed to organize Feb. 22, 1855; the organization took place Dec. 1, 1855. The company own and operate the road from Hudson to Chatham Four Corners, with a leased right to West Stockbridge.

Hudson & Boston Rail Road.

Stations and Distances. (Official.)

Stations.	Distances in Miles.		
	Between Stations.	*From Hudson.*	*From Chatham 4 Corners.*
Hudson	0	0	17
" Upper Station	1	1	16
Claverack	3	4	13
Mellenville	5	9	8
Pulvers	3	12	5
Ghent	3	15	2
Chatham Four Corners	2	17	0

Hudson River Rail Road. Company formed May 12, 1846. Opened from New York to Peekskill Sept. 29, 1849; to Hamburgh, Dec. 6, 1849; to Poughkeepsie, Dec. 31, 1849; from Albany to Hudson, June 16, 1851; to Tivoli, Aug. 4; and through, Oct. 1, 1851. The road extends from Albany to New York, along the east bank of the river. It has tunnels of 226, 60, 70, 358, 600, 518, 835, 124, 145, and 82 feet; in the whole 3,018 feet.

Hudson River Rail Road.

Stations and Distances. (Official.)

Stations.	Distances in Miles.		
	Between Stations.	*From New York.*	*From Albany.*
Chambers Street, N.Y.	0	0	143½
31st Street	2½	2½	141
52d Street	1	3½	140
Burnhams	1	4½	139
Strykers Bay	1¼	5¾	137¾
Manhattan	1¾	7½	136
152d Street	1	8½	135
Fort Washington	1½	10	133½
Tubby Hook	1½	11½	132
Spuyten Duyvil	¾	12¼	131¼
Riverdale	1¾	14	129½
Yonkers	2¼	16¼	127¼
Glenwood	¾	17	126½
Hastings	3½	20½	123
Dobb's Ferry	1¼	21¾	121¾
Irvington	2	23¾	119¾
Tarrytown	2½	26¼	117¼
Scarborough	4¼	30½	113
Sing Sing	1½	32	111½
Croton	3¼	35¼	108¼
Crugers	3½	38¾	104¾
Verplancks	1¾	40½	103
Peekskill	2	42½	101
Fort Montgomery	3¾	46¼	97¼
Garrisons	4¾	51	92½
Cold Spring	2½	53½	90
Cornwall	2¾	56¼	87¼
Fishkill	3½	59¾	83¾
Carthage	3½	63¼	80¼
New Hamburgh	2½	65¾	77¾
Milton Ferry	4½	70¼	73¼
Poughkeepsie	4	74½	69¼
Hyde Park	6	80¼	63¼
Staatsburgh	4	84¼	59¼
Rhinebeck	5¾	90	53½
Barrytown	5½	95½	48
Tivoli	4	99½	44
Germantown	4¾	104¼	39¼
Oak Hill	5¼	109½	34
Hudson	5¾	115¼	28¼
Stockport	5	120¼	23¼
Coxsackie	2½	122¾	20¾
Stuyvesant	2½	125¼	18¼
Schodack	6¾	132	11½
Castleton	3¾	135¾	7¾
East Albany	7¾	143½	0
Troy	6	149½	6

custom that has since been continued, except during the short period in which the office of R. R. Commissioners was in existence. This Board was created April 14, 1855, and abolished April 16, 1857. The expenses of the State Engineer and Surveyor's office chargeable to rail roads are assessed upon the several companies in proportion to their earnings. The general act to authorize the formation of R. R. companies was passed March 27, 1848. There are at present within the State 2,554¼ mi. of R. R., besides double tracks and turn outs. The rail roads give employment to about 18,000

Long Island Rail Road. Company organized June 15, 1835. Opened through in July, 1844. The road extends from Brooklyn to Greenport; $100,000 in State stocks was issued to aid in the construction. The company have leased the Brooklyn & Jamaica and the Hicksville & Cold Spring Branch R. Roads, which they operate as a part of this road.

Long Island Rail Road.

Stations and Distances. (Official.)

STATIONS.	DISTANCES IN MILES.		
	Between Stations.	*From Brooklyn.*	*From Greenport.*
South Ferry	0	0	95
Bedford	2½	2½	92½
East New York	3	5½	89½
Cypress Avenue.	1½	7	88
Union Course	½	7½	87½
Woodhaven	¾	8¼	86¾
Jamaica	2¾	11	84
Willow Tree	1	12	83
Queens (Brushville)	2	14	81
Hyde Park	3½	17½	77½
Hempstead Branch	2½	20	75
Hempstead	2½	2½	2½
Westbury	3	23	72
Hicksville	3	26	69
Syosset	4	4	4
Jerusalem	3	29	66
Farmingdale	2	31	64
Deer Park	6	37	58
Thompson	4	41	54
N. Islip (Suffolk)	2½	43½	51½
Lakeland	5½	49	46
Waverly	4	53	42
Medford	2	55	40
Bellport	2½	57½	37½
Yaphank	2½	60	35
Manor	6	66	29
Riverhead	8	74	21
Jamesport	5	79	16
Mattituck	4	83	12
Cutchogue	3	86	9
Hermitage	3	89	6
Southold	2	91	4
Greenport	4	95	0

Newburgh Branch of New York & Erie Rail Road. Branch allowed to Newburgh April 8, 1845. Opened Jan. 8, 1850.

New York Central Rail Road. Company formed by consolidating the several roads in operation, and some projected roads between Albany, Troy and Buffalo, and Niagara Falls. The act allowing the consolidation was passed April 2, 1853, and was carried into effect the 17th of May following. The consolidated capital amounted to $23,085,600, and debts were assumed to the amount of $1,947,815.72. The stock of the several companies was received at the following rates, viz.:—

Albany & Schenectady	117	Rochester & Syracuse	130
Syracuse & Utica Direct	150	Rochester, Lockport & Niagara Falls	125
Schenectady & Troy	75	Buffalo & Rochester	140
Utica & Schenectady	115	Buffalo & Lockport	125
Mohawk Valley	155		
Syracuse & Utica	160		

Each stockholder received a like amount of stock of the new company, at par, (the Troy & Schenectady upon payment of $25 per share,) and for the differences, certificates or premium bonds bearing six per cent. interest, semi-annually, and payable May 1, 1883. These certificates amounted to $8,892,600. The Rochester & Lake Ontario R. R., and the Buffalo & Niagara Falls R. R., have since been merged in this road.

Date of opening the several roads now forming the New York Central Rail Road.

Albany & Schenectady	1831	Batavia & Attica	1843
Schenectady & Troy	1843	Attica & Buffalo	1845
Utica & Schenectady	1835	Rochester & Buffalo	1852
Syracuse & Utica	1839	Rochester, Lockport & Niagara Falls	1852
Rochester & Syracuse	1853	Niagara Falls & Lewiston	1854
Auburn & Syracuse	1836	Lockport & Tonawanda	1853
Auburn & Rochester	1840	Rochester & Charlotte	1853
Tonawanda	1836		

New York Central Rail Road.

Stations and Distances. (Official.)

STATIONS.	DISTANCES IN MILES.		
	Between Stations.	*From Albany.*	*From Buffalo.*
Albany & Buffalo.			
Albany	0	0	296¼
West Albany	3¼	3¼	293
Center	5	8¼	288
Schenectady	8¾	17	279¼
Hoffmans	9¼	26¼	270
Cranes Village	3½	29¾	266½
Amsterdam	3¼	33	263¼
Tribes Hill	5½	38½	257¾
Fonda	5	43½	252¾
Yosts	5¼	48¾	247½
Sprakers	3¼	52	244¼
Palatine Bridge	3	55	241¼
Fort Plain	3	58	238¼
Palatine Church	2¾	60¾	235½
St. Johnsville	3	63¾	232½
East Creek	3¼	67	229¼
Little Falls	6½	73½	222¾
Herkimer	7¼	80¾	215½
Ilion	2¼	83	213¼
Frankfort	2¼	85¼	211
Utica	9½	94¾	201½
Whitesboro	3¾	98½	197¾
Oriskany	3	101½	194¾
Rome	7½	109	187¼
Greens Corners	4¼	113¼	183
Verona	4¼	117½	178¾
Oneida	4¼	121¾	174½
Wampsville	3¼	125	171¼
Canastota	2	127	169¼
Canaseraga	3¾	130¾	165½
Chittenango	2½	133¼	163
Kirkville	4	137¼	159
Manlius	2½	139¾	156½
Syracuse	7¾	147½	148¾
Warners	9½	157	139¼
Canton	2½	159½	136¾
Jordan	5¼	164¾	131½
Weedsport	4½	169¼	127
Port Byron	3¼	172½	123¾
Savannah	7	179½	116¾
Clyde	6	185½	110¾
Lyons	7¼	192¾	103½
Newark	5½	198¼	98
East Palmyra.	3½	201¾	94½
Palmyra	3¾	205½	90¾
Macedon	5	210½	85¾
Fairport	7¾	218¼	78
Rochester	10¼	228½	67¾
Coldwater	6¼	234¾	61½
Chili	4	238¾	57½
Churchville	4¼	243	53¼
Bergen	3¼	246¼	50
West Bergen	3¼	249½	46¾
Byron	3½	253	43¼
Batavia	7½	260½	35¾
Crofts	6	266½	29¾
Pembroke	5¼	271¾	24½
Alden	4½	276¼	20
Wende	2¾	279	17¼
Town Line	1¾	280¾	15½
Lancaster	5	285¾	10½
Forks	2¾	288½	7¾
Buffalo	7¾	296¼	0
Troy & Schenectady Branch.		*From Troy.*	*From Schenectady.*
Troy	0	0	21¼
Cohoes	3½	3½	17¾
Summit Bridge	2½	6	15¼
Niskayuna	5½	11½	9¾
Aqueduct	6	17½	3¾
Schenectady	3¾	21¼	0

men, and have an aggregate of $74,634,954.76 of stock paid in, and a capital of stocks and debts amounting to $149,262,311.81, or more than one-tenth of the total valuation of the property of the State.

Syracuse & Rochester, via Auburn.	*Between Stations.*	*From Syracuse.*	*From Rochester.*
Syracuse	0	0	102¾
Camillus	8½	8½	94¼
Marcellus	2¼	10¾	92
Halfway	3	13¾	89
Skaneateles Junction	3¾	17½	85¼
Sennett	3¼	20¾	82
Auburn	5½	26¼	76½
Cayuga	10¾	37	65¾
Seneca Falls	4¾	41¾	61
Waterloo	3¼	45	57¾
Geneva	6½	51½	51¼
Oaks Corners	4¾	56¼	46½
Phelps	3¼	59½	43¼
Clifton Springs	4¼	63¾	39
Shortsville	4½	68¼	34½
Canandaigua	6	74¼	28½
Milk Station	6	80¼	22½
Victor	3¾	84	18¾
Fishers	3¾	87¾	15
Pittsford	6¾	94½	8¼
Rochester	8¼	102¾	0

Rochester, Lockport, & Niagara Falls Branch.		*From Rochester.*	*From Niagara Falls.*
Rochester	0	0	77
Spencerport	10	10	67
Adams Basin	2½	12½	64½
Brockport	4½	17	60
Holley	4¾	21¾	55¼
Murray	3½	25¼	51¾
Albion	5½	30¾	46¼
Knowlesville	5½	36¼	40¾
Medina	4¼	40½	36½
Middleport	4½	45	32
Gasport	5	50	27
Lockport	6	56	21
Lockport Junction	3½	59½	17½
Pekin	6¾	66¼	10¾
Suspension Bridge	9	75¼	1¾
Niagara Falls	1¾	77	0

Lockport Junction to Tonawanda.		*From Lockport Junction.*	*From Tonawanda.*
Lockport Junction	0	0	11¼
Halls Station	6¼	6¼	5
Tonawanda	5	11¼	0

Buffalo & Lewiston.		*From Buffalo.*	*From Lewiston.*
Buffalo	0	0	27½
Black Rock	4	4	23½
Tonawanda	6¼	10¼	17¼
La Salle	6	16¼	11¼
Niagara Falls	5	21¼	6¼
Suspension Bridge	1¾	23	4½
Lewiston	4½	27½	0

Canandaigua & Niagara Bridge Branch.		*From Canandaigua.*	*From Tonawanda.*
Canandaigua	0	0	85.6
Gunns Crossing	4.2	4.2	81.4
East Bloomfield	3.8	8	77.6
Millers Corners	4.6	12.6	73
West Bloomfield	3	15.6	70
Honeoye Falls	3.1	18.7	66.9
West Rush	6.2	24.9	60.7
Genesee Valley R. R. Junc.	1.1	26	59.6
Canal	1.2	27.2	58.4
Caledonia	5.8	33	52.6
Le Roy	7.1	40.1	45.5
Stafford	4.1	44.2	41.4
Batavia	5.9	50.1	35.5
East Pembroke	6.2	56.3	29.3
Richville	6.6	62.9	22.7
Akron	3.4	66.3	19.3
Clarence Center	7	73.3	12.3
Transit	3.2	76.5	9.1
Getzville	3	79.5	6.1
Vincent	3	82.5	3.1
Tonawanda	3.1	85.6	0

Attica Branch.	*Between Stations.*	*From Batavia.*	*From Attica.*
Batavia	0	0	11
Alexander	8	8	3
Attica	3	11	0

Charlotte Branch.		*From Rochester.*	*From Charlotte.*
Rochester	0	0	8½
Charlotte	8½	8½	0

New York and Erie Rail Road. Company organized in July, 1833. The act authorizing the road was passed April 24, 1832. The first preliminary survey was made in 1832, by De Witt Clinton, jr., by order of the government. In 1834 the Governor appointed Benj. Wright to survey the route; who, assisted by Jas. Seymour and Charles Ellett, began the survey May 23d, and finished it the same year. In 1835 the Co. was reorganized, and 40 mi. were put under contract. In 1836 the Comptroller was directed to issue $3,000,000 State stock to aid in constructing the road. In 1845 the State released its lien on the road, and authorized the original stockholders to surrender two shares of old stock, and receive one share of new. April 8, 1845, a branch was allowed to be built from Chester to Newburgh, 19 mi. The road was opened as follows: from Piermont to Goshen, Sept. 22, 1841; to Middletown, June 7, 1843; to Port Jervis, Jan. 6, 1848; to Binghamton, Dec. 28, 1848; to Owego, June 1, 1849; to Elmira, Oct. 1849; to Corning, Jan. 1, 1850; and to Dunkirk, May 14, 1851. The Newburgh Branch opened Jan. 8, 1850. The road is compelled to pay a bonus of $10,000 annually to the State of Pennsylvania for the privilege of passing a short distance in that State. Ample details will be found in The New York & Erie R. R. Guide, the annual and special reports of the company, and especially that of Nov. 1853, and in the following documents of the New York Legislature: Senate Doc. No. 12, of 1836; Nos. 37, 38, of 1839; Nos. 18, 58, of 1842. Assem. Docs. Nos. 27, 171 of 1838; No. 47, of 1839; No. 215, of 1840; Nos. 113, 297, of 1841; and No. 50, of 1842. The Patterson & Ramapo (N. J.) R. R., 29½ mi., and the Union R. R., $\frac{79}{100}$ mi., the Chemung R. R., and the Elmira, Jefferson, & Canandaigua R. R. are leased and operated by the this company.

New York & Erie Rail Road.

Stations and Distances. (Official.)

STATIONS.	DISTANCES IN MILES.			
	Between Stations.	*From Piermont Pier.*	*From Jersey City.*	*From Dunkirk.*
New York	......	24.00	1.00	460.72
Pier	24.00	......	......	445.95
Piermont	1.00	1.00	......	444.95
Blauveltville	3.48	4.48	......	441.47
Clarkstown	4.25	8.73	......	437.22
Spring Valley	2.57	11.30	......	434.65
Monsey	1.30	12.60	......	433.35
15 Mile Turnout	2.47	15.07	......	430.88
Jersey City	.00	......	.00	459.72
Bergen	2.47	......	2.47	457.25
Germantown	2.28	......	4.75	454.97
Hackensack Br.	1.49	......	6.24	453.48
Boiling Spring	3.05	......	9.29	450.43
Passaic Bridge	1.80	......	11.09	448.63
Huylers	.83	......	11.92	447.80
Paterson	4.58	......	16.50	443.22
Gravel Switch	3.21	......	19.71	440.01
Godwinville	1.91	......	21.62	438.10
Hohokus	1.68	......	23.30	436.42
Allendale	2.20	......	25.50	434.22
Ramseys	1.94	......	27.44	432.28
Sufferns	4.23	17.90	31.67	428.05
Ramapo	1.95	19.85	33.62	426.10
Sloatsburg	1.70	21.55	35.32	424.40
Southfields	6.53	28.08	41.85	417.87
Greenwood	2.21	30.29	44.06	415.66
Turners	3.19	33.48	47.25	412.47
Monroe	2.15	35.63	49.40	410.32
Oxford	2.62	38.25	52.02	407.70
East Junction, N. B.	1.58	39.83	53.60	406.12
West " "	.46	40.29	54.06	405.66

New York & Erie Rail Road, continued.

Stations.	Distances in Miles.			
	Between Stations.	*From Piermont Pier.*	*From Jersey City.*	*From Dunkirk.*
Chester	.97	41.26	55.03	404.69
Goshen	4.43	45.69	59.46	400.26
Hampton	4.00	49.69	63.46	396.26
Middletown	3.37	53.06	66.83	392.89
Howells	3.88	56.94	70.71	389.01
Otisville	4.69	61.63	75.40	384.32
Shin Hollow	6.40	68.03	81.80	377.92
Port Jervis	6.31	74.34	88.11	371.61
McCluers Turnout	3.83	78.17	91.94	367.78
Rosa Switch	5.70	83.87	97.64	362.08
Pond Eddy	1.86	85.73	99.50	
Middaughs	2.07	87.80	101.57	358.15
Shohola	5.21	93.01	106.78	352.94
Lackawaxen	3.98	96.99	110.76	348.96
Mast Hope	5.35	102.34	116.11	343.61
Narrowsburg	6.01	108.35	122.12	337.60
Nobodys	3.74	112.09	125.86	333.86
Cochecton	4.76	116.85	130.62	329.10
Callicoon	5.19	122.04	135.81	323.91
Hankins	6.92	128.96	142.73	316.99
Basket	3.65	132.61	146.38	313.34
Lordville	6.92	139.53	153.30	306.42
Stockport	5.76	145.29	159.06	300.66
Hancock	4.58	149.87	163.64	296.08
Dickinsons	5.61	155.48	169.25	290.47
Hales Eddy	2.53	158.01	171.78	287.94
Deposit	4.91	162.92	176.69	283.03
Gulf Summit	7.28	170.20	183.97	275.75
Cascade Bridge	4.03	174.23	188.00	271.72
Canewacta Bridge	2.81	177.04	190.81	268.91
Susquehanna	1.38	178.42	192.19	267.53
Great Bend	8.28	186.70	200.47	259.25
Kirkwood	5.61	192.31	206.08	253.64
Binghamton	8.64	200.95	214.72	245.00
Union	8.55	209.50	228.27	236.45
Campville	6.57	216.07	229.84	229.88
Owego	6.82	222.89	236.66	223.06
Tioga	5.43	228.32	242.09	217.63
Smithboro'	4.42	232.74	246.51	213.21
Barton	2.42	235.16	248.93	210.79
Waverly	6.91	242.07	255.84	203.88
Chemung	4.78	246.85	260.62	199.10
Wellsburgh	5.77	252.62	266.39	193.33
Elmira	7.00	259.62	273.39	186.33
Junction Chemung Br	4.09	263.71	277.48	182.24
Big Flats	5.98	269.69	283.46	176.26
Noyes Switch	1.84	271.53	285.30	174.42
Corning	5.76	277.29	291.06	168.66
Painted Post	1.55	278.84	292.61	167.11
Addison	9.21	288.05	301.82	157.90
Rathboneville	5.11	293.16	306.93	152.79
Cameron	7.63	300.79	314.56	145.16
Crosbyville	8.19	308.98	322.75	136.97
Canisteo	4.92	313.90	327.67	132.05
Hornellsville	4.21	318.11	331.88	127.84
Almond	4.94	323.05	336.82	122.90
Alfred	4.17	327.22	340.99	118.73
Tip Top Summit	3.55	330.77	344.54	115.18
Andover	4.80	335.57	349.34	110.38
Elm Valley	2.68	338.25	352.02	107.70
Genesee	6.01	344.26	358.03	101.69
Scio	3.72	347.98	361.75	97.97
Phillipsville	4.14	352.12	365.89	93.83
Belvidere	3.55	355.67	269.44	90.28
Friendship	4.43	360.10	373.87	85.85
Cuba Summit	4.04	364.14	377.91	81.81
Cuba	4.81	368.95	382.72	77.00
Hinsdale	6.82	375.77	389.54	70.18
Olean	5.55	381.32	395.09	64.63
Allegany	3.41	384.73	398.50	61.22
Tunungwant	7.20	391.93	405.70	54.02
Great Valley	5.36	397.29	411.06	48.66
Bucktooth	3.81	401.10	414.87	44.85
Little Valley	6.27	407.37	421.14	38.58
Cattaraugus	7.31	414.68	428.45	31.27
Persia Turnout	6.11	420.79	434.56	25.16
Dayton	3.29	424.08	437.85	21.87
Perrysburgh	2.93	427.01	440.78	18.94
Smiths Mills	6.92	433.93	447.70	12.02
Forestville	3.87	437.80	451.57	8.15
Sheridan	3.49	441.29	455.06	4.66
Dunkirk	4.66	445.95	459.72	......

New York & Harlem Rail Road. Company formed April 2, 1831. Work was commenced Feb. 24, 1832, and the first mile opened in Oct. following. The company was allowed to extend the road north of Harlem River, to meet the New York & Albany R. R. at such point as might be agreed upon, in May, 1840; and to continue to Albany, May 14, 1845. The road was opened to Chatham 4 Corners Jan. 19, 1852, connecting at that place with the Albany & West Stockbridge R. R.

New York & Harlem Rail Road.

Stations and Distances. (Official.)

Stations.	Distances in Miles.		
	Between Stations.	*From New York.*	*From Chatham 4 Corners.*
White and Center Sts., N.Y.	0	0	130¾
26th Street	2¾	2¾	128
Yorkville	2¾	5½	125¼
Harlem	2¼	7¾	123
Mott Haven	½	8¼	122½
Melrose	1	9¼	121½
Morrisania	¾	10	120¾
Tremont	1¼	11¼	119½
Fordham	1¼	12½	118¼
Williams Bridge	1½	14	116¾
West Mt. Vernon	2¾	16¾	114
Bronxville	2	18¾	112
Tuckahoe	¾	19½	111¼
Scarsdale	3	22½	108¼
Harts Corners	1½	24	106¾
White Plains	2	26	104¾
Washingtons Quarters	2	28	102¾
Kensico	¾	28¾	102
Unionville	3	31¾	99
Pleasantville	2¼	34	96
Chappaqua	2	36	94¾
Mount Kisco	4¼	40¼	90½
Bedford	2¼	42½	88¼
Whitlockville	2¾	45¼	85½
Goldens Bridge	2	47¼	83½
Purdys	2	49¼	81½
Croton Falls	2	51¼	79½
Brewsters	4¼	55½	75¼
Dykemans	2¾	58¼	72½
Towners	3	61¼	69½
Paterson	2½	63¾	67
Pawlings	3½	67¼	63½
South Dover	6	73¼	57½
Dover Furnace	2¾	76	54¾
Dover Plains	4¼	80¼	50½
Wassaic	4½	84¾	46
Amenia	3¼	88	42¾
Sharon Station	3¼	91¼	39½
Millerton	4¾	96	34¾
Mount Riga	3¼	99¼	31½
Boston Corners	3¾	103	27¾
Copake	5¼	108¼	22½
Hillsdale	4	112¼	18½
Bains	2¾	115	15¾
Martindale	3¾	118¾	12
Philmont	3½	122¼	8½
Ghent	6	128¼	2½
Chatham Four Corners	2½	130¾	0
East Albany	23	153¾	23

New York & New Haven Railroad. This company was allowed to extend their road from the State line to the Harlem R. R. near Williams Bridge. The company run their trains 15 miles on the Harlem track for which they pay that company the net profits. The road was opened Dec. 28, 1848.

New York & New Haven Railroad.

Stations and Distances.

Stations.	Distances in Miles.		
	Between Stations.	*From New York.*	*From New Haven.*
Twenty-seventh St., New York	0	0	76
Thirty-second St	3	3	73
Harlem	4	7	69
Williams Bridge	6	13	63
Mount Vernon	4	17	59
New Rochelle	3	20	56
Mamaroneck	3	23	53
Rye	4	27	49
Port Chester	2	29	47
Greenwich	2	31	45
Cos Cob	2	33	43
Stamford (Conn.)	3	36	40
Norwalk "	8	44	32
Bridgeport "	14	58	18
New Haven "	18	76	0

Ogdensburgh Railroad. This company was formed by the second mortgage bondholders of the Northern R. R., from which its name was changed. The road extends from Ogdensburgh to Rouses Point, and includes a branch to Champlain Landing.

Ogdensburgh (Northern) Railroad.

Stations and Distances. (Official.)

Stations.	Distances in Miles.		
	Between Stations.	From Ogdensburgh.	From Rouses Point.
Ogdensburgh	0	0	118
Lisbon.	8¾	8¾	109¼
Madrid	8½	17¼	100¾
Potsdam	7½	24¾	93¼
Knapps	3	27¾	90¼
Brasher Falls & Stockholm	7¾	35½	82½
Lawrence	5¾	41¼	76¾
Moira	5¾	47	71
Brush's Mills	2½	49½	68½
Bangor	5¾	55¼	62¾
Malone	6	61¼	56¾
Burke	7½	68¾	49¼
Chateaugay	4½	73¼	44¾
Summit	7½	80¾	37¼
Brandy Brook	7½	88¼	29¾
Ellenburgh	1	89¼	28¾
Chazy	8	97¼	20¾
Centerville	5½	102¾	15¼
Mooers	3½	106¼	11¾
Perrys Mills			
Champlain	7¼	113½	4½
Rouses Point	4½	118	0

Oswego & Syracuse Railroad. Company formed April 29, 1839. Route surveyed during the summer of that year. The company was fully organized March 25, 1847, and the Road was opened in Oct. 1848.

Oswego & Syracuse Railroad.

Stations and Distances. (Official.)

Stations.	Distances in Miles.		
	Between Stations.	From Oswego.	From Syracuse.
Oswego	0	0	35½
Minetto	4½	4½	31
Fulton	6⅝	11⅛	24⅜
South Granby	4¾	15⅞	19⅝
Lamsons	2⅜	18¼	17¼
Baldwinsville	4¾	23	12½
Syracuse	12½	35½	0

Plattsburgh & Montreal Railroad. Company formed Feb. 25, 1850. Road commenced in Aug. 1851, and opened July 20, 1852. It connects with the Lake, St. Louis, & Province Line R. R. It crosses the Ogdensburgh R. R. at Mooers Junction.

Plattsburgh and Montreal Railroad.

Stations and Distances.

Stations.	Distances in Miles.		
	Between Stations.	From Plattsburgh.	From Montreal.
Plattsburgh	0	0	62
Beekmantown	5	5	57
West Chazy	5	10	52
Sciota	5	15	47
Mooers	5	20	42
Montreal (Canada)	42	62	0

Sackets Harbor & Ellisburgh Rail Road. Company formed May 23, 1850. Road opened June 1, 1853. It connects with W. R. & C. V. R. R. at Pierrepont Manor.

Sackets Harbor & Ellisburgh Rail Road.

Stations and Distances. (Official.)

Stations.	Distances in Miles.		
	Between Stations.	From Sackets Harbor.	From Pierrepont Manor.
Sackets Harbor	0	0	18
Smithville	5	5	13
Henderson	4	9	9
Belleville	4	13	5
Pierrepont Manor	5	18	0

Potsdam & Watertown Railroad. Company formed Jan. 8, 1852. Road opened through in Jan., 1857, and operated by contractors for construction to April 1 following.

Potsdam & Watertown Railroad.

Stations and Distances. (Official.)

Stations.	Distances in Miles.		
	Between Stations.	From Watertown.	From Potsdam.
Watertown Junction	0	0	76¼
Watertown	1	1	75¼
Sanfords Corners	5	6	70¼
Evans Mills	4¾	10¾	65½
Philadelphia	7	17¾	58½
Antwerp	6¼	24	52¼
Keene	5	29	47¼
Gouverneur	7	36	40¼
Richville	7¾	43¾	32½
De Kalb	4	47¾	28½
Hermans	4¼	52	24¼
Canton	7¼	59¼	17
Potsdam	10¾	70	6¼
Potsdam Junction	6¼	76¼	0

Rensselaer & Saratoga Rail Road. Company formed April 14, 1832. Fully organized in May, 1833, and surveys commenced the same year. Opened from Waterford to Ballston Aug 19, 1835, and to Troy in the spring of 1836. The Co. leases and runs the Saratoga and Schenectady R. R.

Rensselaer & Saratoga Rail Road.

Stations and Distances. (Official.)

Stations.	Distances in Miles.		
	Between Stations.	From Troy.	From Saratoga.
Troy Union Depot	0	0	32.3
Green Island	.877	.877	31.423
Waterford	3.676	4.553	27.747
A. Junction	1.402	5.955	26.345
Mechanicville	6.530	12.485	19.815
Ballston	13.108	25.593	6.707
Saratoga	6.707	32.3	0

Rochester & Genesee Valley Rail Road. Company formed June 7, 1851; allowed to extend their road to Portage. Work was commenced in 1852, and the road opened to Avon in 1854. It connects at Avon with the Buffalo, New York & Erie R. R.

Rutland & Washington Rail Road extends from Rutland to Eagle Bridge, 63 mi. We have not been able to obtain statistics of this road, as it has made no report for several years.

Rutland & Washington Rail Road.

Stations and Distances.

Stations.	Distances in Miles.		
	Between Stations.	From Eagle Bridge.	From Rutland.
Albany	0	0	95
Troy	10	10	85
Eagle Bridge	23	33	62
Cambridge	6	39	56
Shushan	5	44	51
Salem	7	51	44
Granville	18	69	26
North Granville	2	71	24
Poultney, Vt.	6	77	18
Castleton "	7	84	11
Rutland "	11	95	0

Saratoga & Schenectady Rail Road. Company formed Feb. 16, 1831. Work commenced in Sept. 1831. Road opened to Ballston July 12, 1832, and to Saratoga Springs in 1833. The road is leased and operated by the Rensselaer & Saratoga R. R. Co.

Saratoga & Schenectady Rail Road.

Stations and Distances. (Official.)

Stations.	Distances in Miles.		
	Between Stations.	From Schenectady.	From Saratoga.
Schenectady	0	0	22
Halfway House	8	8	14
Ballston	7½	15½	6½
Saratoga	6½	22	0

Saratoga & Washington Rail Road. Chartered May 2, 1834. Capital, $600,000. Company organized April 20, 1835. The work was begun and over $60,000 expended, when it was stopped in 1836. The time was extended April 13, 1840, May 4, 1844, and April 4, 1850, and the stock was increased $250,000 April 7, 1847. Company allowed to extend the road east to Vt., March 7, 1848. A new route in part adopted upon resuming work. Began laying rails April 10, 1848. Road opened to Gansevoort Aug. 15, 1848, to Whitehall Dec. 10, 1848, and to Lake Station April 9, 1851. Sold Feb. 27, 1855, on foreclosure of second mortgage, and name changed to **Saratoga & Whitehall Rail Road.** Company formed June 8, 1855. Capital $500,000. This company leases and runs the Rutland and Whitehall R. R. to Castleton, Vt.

Saratoga & Whitehall Rail Road.
Stations and Distances.

STATIONS.	DISTANCES IN MILES.		
	Between Stations.	From Saratoga.	From Whitehall.
Saratoga	0	0	39
Gansevoort	10.66	10.66	28.34
Moreau	5.3	15.96	23.04
Fort Edward	.8	16.76	22.24
Dunham's Basin	3.32	20.08	18.92
Smith's Basin	4.5	24.58	14.42
Fort Ann	3.91	28.49	10.51
Comstocks	3.91	32.4	6.6
Whitehall Junction	6.6	39	0
Lake Station	1.88	40.88	1.88
State Line	6.62	45.62	6.62
Fair Haven, Vt.	1.85	47.47	8.47
Hydeville "	1.75	49.22	10.22
Castleton "	3.28	52.5	13.5

Second Avenue Rail Road Company of the City of New York was formed Jan. 19, 1853. Road to extend from Harlem River to Peck Slip. In 1855 the company were allowed to bridge Harlem and Bronx Rivers, to discontinue the road from Chatham St. through Oliver and South Sts., and to lay a new track on Bowery to Pearl St.

Sixth Avenue Rail Road Company of the City of New York was formed Dec. 7, 1851. The road extends from Chambers St. to Harlem River, and was opened from Broadway to Forty-Fourth St. Aug. 19, 1852.

Syracuse, Binghamton, & New York Rail Road. Company originally formed July 2, 1851, as the Syracuse & Binghamton R. R. Road opened through Oct. 23, 1854. It was sold Oct. 13, 1856, on foreclosure of mortgage, and name changed to the Syracuse & Southern R. R. Its present name was assumed under act of March 31, 1857. In 1858 the company were authorized to purchase the Union R. R. to the canal at Geddes.

Syracuse, Binghamton, & New York Rail Road.
Stations and Distances. (Official.)

STATIONS.	DISTANCES IN MILES.		
	Between Stations.	From Syracuse.	From Binghamton.
Syracuse	0	0	79.33
Jamesville	6.69	6.69	72.64
La Fayette	7.67	14.36	64.97
Apulia	5.10	19.46	59.87
Tully	1.97	21.43	57.9
Preble	5.33	26.76	52.57
Little York	2.71	29.47	49.86
Homer	4.26	33.73	45.6
Cortland	2.67	36.4	42.93
Blodgets Mills	3.54	39.94	39.39
State Bridge	6.25	46.19	33.14
Marathon	3.90	50.09	29.24
Killawog	2.90	52.99	26.34
Lisle	3.65	56.64	22.69
Whitneys Point	2.14	58.78	20.55
Chenango Forks	9.28	68.06	11.27
Chenango	6.14	74.2	5.13
Binghamton	5.13	79.33	0

Third Avenue Rail Road Company of the City of New York was formed Oct. 6, 1853. The road extends from the intersection of Park Row and Broadway through Park Row, Chatham St., Bowery, and Third Avenue to Harlem River. It was opened from Ann to Sixty-First St. in 1853, and to Eighty-Sixth St. July 4, 1854.

Troy & Bennington Rail Road. Company formed May 15, 1851. Work commenced in June, 1851. Road opened Aug. 1, 1852. Connects the Troy & Boston R. R. with the Western Vt. R. R. It is leased to the Troy & Boston R. R. Co.

Troy & Boston Rail Road. Company formed Nov. 20, 1849. Work commenced in June, 1850. Road opened from Troy to Hoosick Falls in Aug. 1853. Most of the remainder to the State Line is graded. The company leases the Troy & Bennington R. R. and 7 mi. of the Vermont Western R. R.

Troy & Bennington Rail Road.
Stations and Distances.

STATIONS.	DISTANCES IN MILES.		
	Between Stations.	From Troy.	From
Troy	0	0	
Lansingburgh	3	3	
Junction	5	8	
Schaghticoke	4	12	
Pittstown	2	14	
Johnsonville	2	16	
Buskirks Bridge	5	21	
Eagle Bridge	2	23	
Hoosick Falls Junction	2	25	
Hoosick Falls	2	27	
Hoosick Corners	3	30	
Petersburgh	2	32	
North Adams, Mass.	15	47	

Western Vermont Rail Road.

STATIONS.	From North Hoosick.	From
North Hoosick	0	0
Walloomsac	2	2
North Bennington, Vt.	4	6
Rutland "	54	60

Troy & Greenbush Rail Road. Company organized May 14, 1845 under a lease from the New York & Albany R. R. The road had been commenced about 1842, and operations suspended. It was opened in June, 1845. It is operated by the Hudson River R. R. Co. under a lease.

Troy & Rutland Rail Road. Company formed March 6, 1851. The road extends from Hoosick near Eagle Bridge to Salem. It was opened June 28, 1852, and leased to the Rutland & Washington (Vt.) R. R., until March, 1855, when it was placed in the hands of a receiver, and run by the Albany Northern R. R.

Troy Union Rail Road. Company formed July 21, 1851. Road commenced in Feb. 1853, and opened Feb. 22, 1854. It is owned by parties representing the interests of the Troy & Greenbush, Troy & Boston, Rensselaer & Saratoga, and New York Central R. Roads, and is used by the above companies in common.

Union Rail Road. Company formed Jan. 10, 1851. The road extends from Patterson and Ramapo (N. J.) to the New York & Erie R. R. at Sufferns. It is operated by the latter road under a lease.

Union Rail Road. Company formed Nov. 13, 1856. The road extends from the 6th Ward in Syracuse to the Erie Canal in Geddes. By an act of April 16, 1858, the Co. were authorized to sell the road to the Syracuse, Binghamton, & N. Y. R. R. Co.

Watertown & Rome Rail Road. Company formed April 17, 1832. Work commenced at Rome in Nov. 1848. Road opened to Camden in 1849, to Pierrepont Manor in May, 1851, to Watertown in Sept. 1851, to Chaumont in Nov. 1851, and to Cape Vincent May 1, 1852.

Watertown, Rome, & Cape Vincent Rail Road.
Stations and Distances. (Official.)

STATIONS.	DISTANCES IN MILES.		
	Between Stations.	From Cape Vincent.	From Rome.
Cape Vincent	0	0	97
Three Mile Bay	8	8	89
Chaumont	3	11	86
Limerick	6	17	80
Brownville	4	21	76
Watertown	4	25	72
Adams Center	10	35	62
Adams	3	38	59
Pierrepont Manor	5	43	54
Mannsville	2	45	52
Sandy Creek	5	50	47
Richland	5	55	42
Albion	5	60	37
Kasoag	6	66	31
Williamstown	3	69	28
West Camden	5	74	23
Camden	5	79	18
McConnelsville	5	84	13
Taberg	2	86	11
Rome	11	97	0

Williamsport & Elmira Rail Road. Incorporated by Penn. April 9, 1850, and allowed to extend the road to the New York & Erie R. R. at Elmira. The village of Elmira was authorized to loan its credit for $100,000 toward the construction. Eight m'les of the road are in this State.

Official Summary of Rail Road Statistics

NAMES.	Length of track laid, in miles.	Length of second track and turn-outs.	Amount of capital stock authorized by law.	Amount of capital paid in.	Total amount of funded debt.	Total amount of funded and floating debt.
Albany, Vermont & Canada	32.95	3.39	$ 600,000	$ 439,004.97	$ 1,575,098.79	$ 1,625,098.79
Albany & West Stockbridge	38	34	1,000,000	1,000,000.00	1,289,933.98	1,289,933.98
Black River & Utica	34.94	....	1,500,000	804,647.99	662,500.00	715,070.60
Blossburg & Corning	14.81	1.60	250,000	250,000.00	220,000.00	220,000.00
Brooklyn City	20.15	19.95	1,000,000	1,000,000.00		
Buffalo, New York & Erie	142	11.33	1,500,000	680,000.00	2,409,593.88	2,574,532.19
Buffalo & State Line	68.34	18	1,300,000	1,913,000.00	1,049,000.00	1,221,378.49
Cayuga & Susquehanna	34.61	3.49	1,500,000	687,000.00	473,000.00	480,402.28
Chemung	17.36	2.06	380,000	380,000.00	70,000.00	70,000.00
Eighth Avenue	5	....	800,000	800,000.00		
Elmira, Canandaigua & Niagara Falls	46.84	2.90	300,000			
Flushing	7.80	.39	200,000	131,339.90	236,500.00	269,913.32
Hudson & Boston	17.33	.50	175,000	175,000.00		
Hudson River	144	106.50	4,000,000	3,758,466.59	8,842,000.00	9,297,003.04
Long Island	95	10.08	3,000,000	1,852,715.79	639,497.67	653,263.02
New York Central	555.88	311.80	24,182,400	24,182,400.00	14,402,634.69	14,402,634.69
New York & Erie	446	282.50	10,500,000	11,000,000.00	26,438,016.55	27,170,274.41
New York & Harlem	130.75	28.84	8,000,000	5,717,100.00	5,151,287.21	5,298,927.88
New York & New Haven	62.25	63.82	3,000,000	2,980,839.33	2,163,500.00	2,194,051.07
Ogdensburgh	118	17.75	4,571,900			
Oswego & Syracuse	35.91	2.21	350,000	396,340.00	197,000.00	213,414.94
Potsdam & Watertown	75.36	2	2,000,000	633,077.15	818,500.00	998,638.47
Rensselaer & Saratoga	25.22	2.01	610,000	610,000.00	140,000.00	140,000.00
Rochester & Genesee Valley	18.45	1.25	800,000	555,450.10	150,000.00	180,417.13
Sackets Harbor & Ellisburgh	18	1	175,000	167,485.89	278,400.00	306,810.47
Saratoga & Schenectady	21	1.57	300,000	300,000.00	86,500.00	86,500.00
Saratoga & Whitehall	40.86	3.87	500,000	500,000.00	395,000.00	400,455.94
Second Avenue	8	8	800,000	627,200.00	350,000.00	380,000.00
Sixth Avenue	4	4.38	750,000	750,000.00		
Syracuse, Binghamton & New York	81	7.09	1,201,300	1,200,130.00	1,500,000.00	1,763,486.80
Third Avenue	6	6.50	1,170,000	1,170,000.00	50,000.60	90,600.00
Troy & Bennington	5.38	.28	80,000	75,358.00	171,200.00	172,295.37
Troy & Boston	27.23	3.23	1,000,000	568,297.22	797,500.00	1,028,582.99
Troy & Greenbush	6	.04	275,000	275,000.00		
Troy & Rutland	17.27	2.75	325,000	249,939.50		
Troy Union	2.14	2.14	30,000	30,000.00	680,000.00	680,000.00
Watertown & Rome	96.76	11	1,500,000	1,498,400.00	688,500.00	769,250.76
Total	2,520.59	978.12	$79,625,600	$67,358,192.43	$71,925,162.77	$74,692,936.63

The Plattsburgh & Montreal R. R., 23.17 mi.; Champlain & St. Lawrence R. R., 2.5 mi. to Canada line; and Williamsport & Elmira R. R., 8 mi. to Pennsylvania line, are not included in the above table, from default in reports. The gauge of the New York & Erie R. R. and of the connecting roads is 6 ft., the same as that of several roads in Penn. The New York Central R. R.

General Summary of Rail Road Statistics for the year ending September 30, 1858.

Length of roads in miles..3,124.71
Length of roads laid..2,442.91
Length of roads in operation, excluding city roads.......2,397.62
Length of double track, including sidings.....................970.48
Length of branches owned by company and laid.........373.44
Length of double track on same............................6.37
Length of equivalent single track, exclusive of city roads...3,709.08
Number of engine houses and shops.........................183
Number of engines...738
Number of first-class passenger cars, rated as eight-wheeled...1,071
Number of second-class and emigrant cars..................175
Number of baggage, mail, and express cars.................239
Number of freight cars..9,014

Excluding City Roads.   Miles.

Average rate of speed of ordinary passenger trains, including stops..20.72
Average rate of same when in motion......................25.53
Average rate of speed of express passenger trains, including stops..25.44
Average rate of same when in motion......................29.39
Average rate of speed of freight trains, including stops.....10.69
Average rate of same when in motion......................13.95

Tons.

Average weight in tons of passenger trains, exclusive of passengers and baggage......................................73.09
Average weight in tons of freight trains, exclusive of freight..129.27

Miles run by passenger trains.........................11,578,745
The same, excluding city roads.........................6,145,862
Number of passengers of all classes carried in cars...43,786,579
The same, excluding city roads........................11,250,073
Number of miles traveled by passengers, or number of passengers carried one mile, city roads not included..373,159,179

Miles run by freight trains...................................5,417,456
Number of tons carried on freight trains..................3,473,725
Total movement of freight, or number of tons carried one mile...420,604,609

Classification of Freight.

	Tons.
Products of the forest	303,236
Products of animals	734,995
Vegetable food	914,206
Other agricultural products	77,174
Manufactures	325,596
Merchandise	562,378
Other articles	556,140
Total tonnage	3,473,725

Costs.

Repairs of road bed	$2,282,807.73
Cost of iron for repair	464,712.95
Repairs of buildings	207,846.56
Repairs of fences and gates	48,660.35
Taxes on real estate	290,771.47
Other road expenses	398,329.66
Total road expenses	$3,693,129.72
Repairs of engines	$ 930,627.16
Repairs of cars	1,003,906.26
Repairs of tools	82,975.15
Oil, waste, &c	112,518.64
Other costs	43,759.29
Total cost of repairs of machinery	$2,173,786.69
Office expenses, stationery, &c	$ 86,427.81
Agents and clerks	622,981.68
Labor, loading and unloading freight	449,060.96
Porters, watchmen, and switchmen attendance	420,180.66
Wood and water station attendance	96,958.14

for the year ending Sept. 30, 1858.

Total cost of road equipments and other expenses.	Earnings for the year ending Sept. 30, 1858.	Gross transportation expenses.	Dividends paid.	Passenger Transportation.		Freight Transportation, in Tons.		Accidents.	
				Number.	Mileage.	Number.	Mileage.	Killed.	Wounded.
$ 2,010,634.64	$ 84,119.86	$ 72,904.83		196,911	1,864,210	34,918	698,360	1	
2,289,933.98				171,046	5,094,681	226,035	7,511,341	3	1
1,234,514.64	60,524.33	28,091.92		53,647	1,121,012	13,136	316,660		3
496,661.28	23,554.24		$ 12,500.00	9,364	103,847	73,908	831,679		
1,038,839.97	395,026.80	288,771.22	80,000.00	7,505,859					5
2,975,325.66	429,753.89	301,632.09		185,876	8,192,000	143,709	14,360,000	3	1
2,772,987.09	840,116.71	480,507.05	108,000.00	296,194	17,854,082	290,532	19,809,225	4	14
1,183,012.71	97,151.68	77,285.40		26,253	623,885	85,556	2,674,375		2
400,000.00									
833,642.87	338,410.16	177,753.91	96,000.00	6,768,203				2	
200,000.00	17,989.46	11,947.28		15.852	479,841	4,293	175,969		
308,891.38	40,072.52	41,566.29		226,779	1,483,464	1,460	8,356		
175,000.00	58,207.21	47,367.60	10,500.00	37,110	413,356	50,806	880,466		1
11,328,989.96	1,636,412.28	1,041,773.43		1,415.339	56,658,109	160,197	18,416,865	14	4
2,566,270.07	320,588.93	174,215.05		360,130	7,380,760	89,480	2,236,990	7	2
30,732.517.54	6,528,412.70	3,487,292.67	1,919,564.00	2,124,439	136,091,023	765,407	142,691,178	33	87
34,058,632.63	5,151,616.43	3,791,457.62		793,662	64,931,456	816,965	165,895,636	25	53
7,948,116.35	975,853.86	617,061.47		720,070	17,940,971	122,371	7,446,561	6	5
5,324,527.09	836,612.14	532,477.85		953,819	32,908,957	64,058	3,715,364	11	4
4,788,791.26	410,806.66	283,793.93	2,108.75	71,764	2,767,920	150,432	13,210,357	1	2
761,380.11	115,996.68	54,649.63	37,097.93	92,492	2,131,962	42,810	1,375,557	2	
1,587,028.08	94,385.03	49,672.54		71,850	1,725,177	21,142	699,023		
900,550.58	208,222.86	110,982.77	18,300.00	151,576	3,662,026	59,903	1,580,757		1
653,539.64	37,280.57	3,514.02		43,948	703,184	27,700	470,900		
389,170.84	48,358.60			7,340	68,913	8,342	74,692		
480,684.15	30,150.00		7,500.00						
903,890.92	139,388.67	95,723.46		93,035	2,452,281	62,868	1,871,411		
1,005,403.71	227,457.70	119,704.37	12,544.00	4,504,645					
855,957.22	280,617.86	178,226.24	75,000.00	5,612,357					
2,837,607.66	177,627.85	100,700.61		107,504	2,753,962	73,410	5,058,890		3
1,378,090.74	403,055.08	242,811.53	93,600.00	7,945,462				1	6
253,931.19	3,164.88								
1,422,188.86	125,042.55	71,753.69		87,432	1,798,203	56,049	1,482,292		
294,731,43									
338,688.87									
732,114.72								1	2
2,159,295.04	391,973.40	232,667.41	44,952.00	127,285	4,100,132	123,599	9,899,128	3	8
$129,621,542.88	$20,527,951.53	$12,716,305.68	$2,517,667.08	40,977,229	375,335,441	3,569,082	423,362,032	117	204

and its connecting roads have a gauge of 4.71 ft., the same as New England roads generally. The Buffalo & State Line R. R. has a gauge of 4.83 feet, like the Ohio roads; and a few tracks near Suspension Bridge have a gauge of 5.5 feet, like that of the principal roads in Canada.

Conductors, baggagemen, and brakesmen	553,122.23
Enginemen and firemen	552,985.29
Fuel and cost of labor in preparing for use	1,598,250.16
Oil and waste for engines and tenders	204,078.43
Oil and waste for cars	54,202.29
Loss and damage to goods and baggage	98,939.98
Damages for injuries to persons	135,214.26
Damages for property and for cattle killed	18,519.15
General superintendence	203,301.81
Contingencies	545,259.03
Other costs	906,669.45
Total cost of operating roads	$6,636,051.33

Earnings.

From passenger business	$ 9,016,747.50
From freight business, city roads excluded	10,532,714.97
From other sources	759,591.38
Total earnings for all roads	$20,309,053.85
Payments for transportation expenses	$12,830,526.87
Payments for interest	4,156,997.05
Payments for dividends on stock	2,503,013.93
Amount carried to surplus fund	218,541.42
Total payment for all roads	$19,709,079.27

Accidents.

Number of passengers killed	20
Number of passengers injured	142
Number of employees killed	29
Number of employees injured	24
Number of others killed	68
Number of others injured	36
Total number killed	117
Total number injured	202
Total number killed, excluding city roads	114
Total number injured, excluding city roads	191

Cost of Construction and of Equipment.

Grading and masonry	$58,355,306.85
Bridges	2,396,300.42
Superstructure, including iron	28,165,443.55
Passenger and freight stations, buildings and fixtures	4,777,786.65
Engine and car houses, machine shops, machinery and fixtures	1,920,498.40
Land damages, and fences	9,047,417.34
Locomotives and fixtures and snow plows	6,884,506.70
Passenger and baggage cars	2,670,501.01
Freight and other cars	5,586,736.19
Engineering and agencies	12,102,948.10
Total cost of construction and equipment	131,907,445.21
Total cost of same, excluding city roads	126,873,010.70

Excluding City Rail Roads, the following deductions per Mile.

Average cost per mile	$52,916.23
Average cost single track per mile	34,206.05
Average number of miles traveled by each passenger	33.17
Average number of passengers to each train	60.72
Average distance each ton of freight is transported in miles	120.91
Average number of tons in each freight train	77.54
Average number of trains over each track daily	8.54

Average Cost per Mile of Road.

For maintaining of road way	$1,511.70
For repairs of machinery	892.47
For operating road	2,415.49

Average Cost per Mile of Single Track.

For maintaining of roadway	$ 677.19
For repairs of machinery	577.45
For operating road	1,561.42

Average amount received for passengers per mile, 1.98 cts.
Proportion of passengers killed to miles traveled, 1 to 18,657,959.
Proportion of passengers killed to passengers traveling, 1 to 562,504.
Proportion of expenses to earnings, 63 to 100.32.

Rail Roads Projected, Abandoned, and merged in other Roads.

NAMES OF RAIL ROADS.	Date of Organization.	Capital.	Connections.	Remarks.
Adirondack	April 1, 1839	$100,000	Adirondack Iron Works and Clear Pond......................	Nothing done.
Albany, Bennington & Rutland	April 23, 1850	400,000	Albany, Bennington, and Rutland......................	Merged in Albany Northern R.R.
Albany Northern......................	Feb. 12, 1851	335,000	Albany and Troy, and Rutland R. R. at Eagle Bridge.	Sold, and succeeded by Albany, Vermont, & Canada R. R.
Albany & Cohoes......................	Co. not organ'd	....	Albany and Cohoes................	Nothing done.
Albany & Saratoga	June 28, 1852	300,000	Albany and Green Island..........	Nothing done.
Albany & Saratoga Springs.......	Sept. 20, 1852	200,000	Albany Northern R. R. and Saratoga Springs............	Nothing done.
Albany & Schenectady.............	April 19, 1847	....	Albany and Schenectady...........	Changed from Mohawk & Hudson, and merged in the New York Central R. R., May 17, 1853.
Albany & Susquehanna............	April 2, 1851	4,000,000	Albany and Binghamton	Partly graded.
Albion & Tonawanda	April 17, 1832	200,000	Albion and Batavia...............	Nothing done.
Atlantic & Great Western........	Dec. 1, 1858	150,000	Buffalo & New York Central R. R. and Penn. State Line	Nothing done.
Attica & Allegany Valley........	Sept. 16, 1852	1,000,000	Attica to Penn. State Line.......	Partly graded.
Attica & Buffalo......................	May 3, 1836	350,000	Attica and Buffalo...............	Consolidated as Buffalo & Rochester, afterward as Buffalo & N. York City R. R., at present as Buffalo, New York, & Erie.
Attica & Hornellsville	May 14, 1845	750,000	Attica and Hornellsville..........	Consolidated, and is now the Buffalo & New York City R. R.
Attica & Sheldon.....................	May 21, 1836	50,000	Attica and Sheldon................	Nothing done.
Auburn & Canal......................	April 24, 1832	150,000	Auburn and Canal................	Nothing done.
Auburn & Ithaca.....................	May 21, 1836	500,000	Auburn and Ithaca...............	Nothing done.
Auburn & Rochester.................	May 13, 1836	2,000,000	Auburn and Rochester.............	Consolidated in New York Central R. R.
Auburn & Syracuse..................	May 1, 1834	400,000	Auburn and Syracuse.............	Consolidated in New York Central R. R.
Aurora & Buffalo.....................	April 14, 1832	300,000	Aurora and Buffalo...............	Not constructed.
Batavia & Cheektawaga............	Aug. 17, 1850	300,000	Batavia and Attica & Buffalo R.R.	Nothing done.
Bath & Coney Island.				
Bath & Crooked Lake..............	March 24, 1831	20,000	Bath and Crooked Lake...........	Nothing done.
Binghamton & Susquehanna.....	April 29, 1833	150,000	Binghamton and Penn. S. Line	Nothing done.
Black River............................	April 17, 1832	900,000	Rome or Herkimer and River St. Lawrence..................	Nothing done.
Black River............................	May 21, 1836	200,000	Clayton and Carthage.............	Nothing done.
Black River............................	Jan. 27, 1853	120,000	Clayton and Mohawk Village	Nothing done.
Brewerton & Syracuse	May 1, 1836	80,000	Outlet of Oneida Lake and Syracuse..................	Nothing done.
Broadway R. R. Co. of Brooklyn	Aug. 11, 1858	200,000	Through a part of Brooklyn.......	Not constructed.
Brooklyn, Fort Hamilton	May 12, 1836	150,000		Nothing done.
Buffalo International................	Feb. 25, 1857	150,000	Buffalo and proposed international bridge, opposite Squaw Island................	Nothing done.
Buffalo, New York & Erie.........	Sept. 1, 1857	1,500,000	Buffalo, New York & Erie R. R. at Corning................	Consolidation of the Buffalo, Corning, and New York R. R. and part of Buffalo & New York City R. R.
Buffalo & Allegany Valley........	May 21, 1853	300,000	Buffalo and Attica & Allegany R. R................	Partly done.
Buffalo & Batavia......................	April 18, 1838	500,000	Buffalo and Batavia................	Not constructed by this organization.
Buffalo & Black Rock..............	April 29, 1833	100,000	Buffalo and Black Rock............	Horse-power. Since abandoned.
Buffalo & Conhocton Valley......	June 26, 1850	1,400,000	Buffalo, New York & Erie R. R. at Corning.	Now the Buffalo, New York & Erie R. R.
Buffalo, Corning & New York.....	March 18, 1852	....		Name changed from Buffalo & Conhocton Valley R. R.
Buffalo & Erie........................	April 14, 1832	650,000	Buffalo and Erie, Penn...........	Surveyed and located.
Buffalo & Hinsdale..................	May 12, 1846	500,000	Buffalo and Hinsdale..............	Nothing done.
Buffalo & Lake Huron (Canada)	....	....		Allowed to purchase real estate in 1857.
Buffalo & Lockport..................	April 27, 1852	600,000	Buffalo and Lockport..............	Consolidated with New York Central R. R., 1853.
Buffalo & New York.................	Jan. 16, 1851	350,000	Buffalo and Attica..................	Connected with Attica & Hornellsville R. R., and name changed to Buffalo & New York City R. R.
Buffalo & New York City..........	April 8, 1851	....	Buffalo and Hornellsville..........	Consolidation of Attica & Buffalo R. R. and Buffalo & New York R. R.
Buffalo, Tonawanda & Niagara Falls..............................	June 23, 1853	250,000	Tonawanda and Black Rock......	Not constructed.
Buffalo & Niagara Falls............	May 3, 1834	110,000	Buffalo and Niagara Falls.........	Leased to New York Central R. R. Co. in 1853.
Buffalo & Pittsburg	Oct. 7, 1852	750,000	Buffalo and State Line near Olean..................	Reorganized as the Buffalo, Pittsburg & St. Louis R. R.
Buffalo, Pittsburg & St. Louis...	Oct. 11, 1852	....		Partly graded.
Buffalo & Rochester.................	Oct. 8, 1850	1,825,000	Buffalo and Rochester.............	Formed by union of Tonawanda and Attica & Buffalo R. Roads.
Canandaigua Railway & Transportation Co......................	April 12, 1828	50,000	Canandaigua and Watson.........	Connected with Chemung R. R. to Elmira.
Canandaigua & Corning	May 11, 1845	1,600,000	Canandaigua and Elmira..........	Formed from Canandaigua & Corning and Chemung R. Roads. Leased to New York & Erie R. R. Co.
Canandaigua & Elmira.............	Sept. 11, 1852	....	Canandaigua and Niagara Bdge.	Leased to New York Central R. R. Co. in 1858.

Rail Roads Projected, Abandoned, and merged in other Roads, continued.

NAMES OF RAIL ROADS.	Date of Organization.	Capital.	Connections.	Remarks.
Canandaigua & Niagara Falls....	Dec. 10, 1850	$1,000,000	Canandaigua and Erie Canal.....	Nothing done.
Canandaigua & Syracuse..........	Nov. 26, 1853	1,000,000	Canandaigua and Syracuse........	Nothing done.
Cassadaga & Erie......................	May 21, 1836	250,000	{ Cassadaga Creek and Penn. State Line...................... }	Nothing done.
Castleton & West Stockbridge...	May 5, 1834	300,000	Castleton and West Stockbridge	Nothing done under this organization.
Catskill & Canajoharie.............	April 19, 1830	600,000	Catskill and Canajoharie...........	Partly constructed, and afterwards abandoned.
Catskill & Ithaca.....................	April 21, 1828	1,500,000	Catskill and Ithaca..................	Nothing done.
Chautauque County	July 23, 1851	50,000	{ New York & Erie R. R. and Penn. State Line .... }	Not constructed.
Chemung & Ithaca....................	May 16, 1837	200,000	Head of Cayuga and Penn. Line	Nothing done.
Cherry Valley & Susquehanna...	May 10, 1836	500,000	{ Utica & Syracuse R. R. and New York & Erie R. R..... }	Nothing done.
Clifton & South Clifton............	March 8, 1853	350,000	{ Clifton and Vreeland Farm, on Lower Bay................ }	Nothing done.
Clyde & Sodus Bay	Jan. 22, 1853	150,000	Clyde and Lake Ontario...........	Nothing done but survey.
Coeymans............................	May 21, 1836	75,000	Landing and Moss Hill Quarries	Nothing done.
Cold Spring...........................	April 30, 1839	2,500	In Cattaraugus co...................	Nothing done. Intended for lumbering purposes.
Cooperstown & Cherry Valley...	May 15, 1837	150,000	{ Cooperstown and Canandaigua & Syracuse R. R..... }	Nothing done.
Corning & Blossburg................	April 5, 1851	....	{ Corning and Blossburg Coal Region in Penn. }	Changed in 1854 to Blossburg & Corning R. R.
Corning & Olean.....................	Feb. 5, 1853	850,000	Corning and Olean.................	Nothing done.
Coxsackie & Schenectady..........	May 15, 1837	500,000	Coxsackie and Schenectady	Nothing done.
Dansville & Rochester.............	March 22, 1832	300,000	Dansville and Rochester...........	Surveyed. Nothing further done.
Delaware	May 21, 1836	400,000	Delhi and Deposit..................	Nothing done.
Division Avenue	March 1, 1853	500,000	Brooklyn...........................	Not constructed.
Dunkirk & State Line..............	April 15, 1850	500,000	Dunkirk and State Line...........	Nothing done.
Dutchess.............................	March 28, 1832	600,000	Poughkeepsie and State Line.....	Nothing done.
Dutchess.............................	May 25, 1836	1,000,000	{ Poughkeepsie and Mass. or Conn. line .... }	Nothing done.
Elmira, Canandaigua & Niagara Falls.................. }	April 24, 1857	....	Elmira and Suspension Bridge...	{ Formed by connection of Canandaigua & Elmira and Canandaigua & Niagara Falls R. Roads. }
Elmira & Williamsport.............	April 21, 1832	75,000	Elmira and Williamsport, Penn.	Nothing done by this Corporation.
Erie & Cattaraugus.................	May 15, 1837	200,000	{ Attica & Buffalo R. R. and Genesee & Cattaraugus R.R. }	Nothing done.
Erie & New York City..............	July 11, 1851	750,000	{ Little Valley Creek and Penn. State Line .... }	Partly graded.
Fishhouse & Amsterdam...........	April 26, 1832	250,000	Fishhouse and Amsterdam........	Nothing done.
Fishkill Landing & State Line...	April 12, 1848	....		Company never organized.
Fredonia & Van Buren.............	May 21, 1836	12,000	Fredonia and Van Buren..........	Nothing done.
Genesee Valley......................	June 2, 1856	300,000	Avon and Mount Morris...........	Trains commenced in March 1859.
Genesee & Cattaraugus...........	May 15, 1837	400,000	{ Attica and New York & Erie R. R................... }	Nothing done.
Genesee & Hudson River..........	Dec. 11, 1852	7,000,000	Rochester and Albany.............	Nothing done.
Geneseo.............................	April 11, 1848	15,000	Geneseo and Canal in York	Nothing done.
Geneseo & Pittsford................	May 11, 1836	150,000	Geneseo and Pittsford.............	Nothing done.
Geneva & Canandaigua...........	April 21, 1828	100,000	Geneva and Canandaigua.........	Nothing done.
Gilboa...............................	April 15, 1839	150,000	Gilboa to Canajoharie.............	Nothing done.
Goshen & Albany....................	April 12, 1842	1,500,000	Albany and Goshen................	Nothing done.
Goshen & New York................	May 13, 1837	150,000	Goshen to New Jersey State line	Nothing done.
Great Ausable.......................	April 17, 1828	150,000	Port Kent and Ausable Forks....	Nothing done.
Greene..............................	April 18, 1838	20,000	{ Greene and New York & Erie R. R................... }	Nothing done.
Harlem & High Bridge.............	Aug. 25, 1853	150,000	East River and High Bridge......	Not constructed.
Herkimer & Trenton................	May 21, 1836	200,000	Herkimer and Trenton.............	Nothing done.
Honeoye.............................	May 21, 1836	250,000	Erie Canal and Honeoye Lake...	Nothing done.
Hudson & Berkshire................	April 21, 1858	350,000	Hudson and Berkshire.............	Merged in Hudson and Boston R. R.
Hudson & Delaware.................	April 19, 1830	500,000	Newburgh and Delaware River..	Graded, but nothing further done.
Ithaca & Geneva....................	April 9, 1832	800,000	{ Ithaca and Geneva & Canandaigua R. R.............. }	Not constructed.
Ithaca & Owego.....................	Jan. 28, 1828	150,000	Ithaca and Owego..................	Changed to Cayuga and Susquehanna R. R.
Ithaca & Port Renwick............	April 16, 1834	15,000	Ithaca and Cayuga Lake..........	Not constructed.
Jamesville...........................	May 21, 1836	25,000	Jamesville to Erie Canal	Not constructed.
Johnstown...........................	May 13, 1836	75,000	{ Johnstown and Utica & Syracuse R. R............... }	Nothing done.
Jordan & Skaneateles..............	May 6, 1837	20,000	{ Jordan and terminus Skaneateles R. R.............. }	Not constructed.
Kingston Turnpike & R. R.......	April 23, 1835	20,000	Esopus Creek and Kingston......	Not constructed.
Lake Champlain & Ogdensburgh	April 20, 1832	3,000,000	Ogdensburgh and L. Champlain..	Surveyed, but not constructed.
Lake Ontario, Auburn & New York................ }	April 15, 1851	1,500,000	{ Little Sodus Bay and Clyde & Sodus R. R. }	Grading commenced, but no part completed.
Lake Ontario, Auburn & New York................ }	May 9, 1856	1,500,000	The same.	{ Work resumed, but no part completed. }
Lake Ontario & Hudson River...	April 6, 1857	....		Name changed from Sackets Harbor & Saratoga R. R. No part completed.
Lake Ontario & New York........	Aug. 20, 1852	150,000	{ Lewiston and mouth of Niagara River................ }	Nothing done.
Lansingburgh & Troy..............	May 19, 1836	40,000	Lansingburgh and Troy..........	Nothing done.
Lansingburgh & Troy..............	Nov. 13, 1853	10,000	The same.	Nothing done.
Lebanon Springs....................	Dec. 1, 1851	500,000	Lebanon Springs and Chatham..	Grading commenced, but no part completed.
Lewiston..............................	May 6, 1836	200,000	Lewiston and Niagara Falls......	Leased to the New York Central R. R. Co.

Rail Roads Projected, Abandoned, and merged in other Roads, continued.

NAMES OF RAIL ROADS.	Date of Organization.	Capital.	Connections.	Remarks.
Lockport & Batavia	May 21, 1836	....	Lockport and Batavia	Nothing done.
Lockport & Niagara Falls	April 24, 1834	$ 175,000	Lockport and Niagara Falls	Merged in the New York Central R. R.
Lockport & Youngstown	May 21, 1836	350,000	Lockport and Youngstown	Nothing done.
Madison County	April 17, 1829	70,000	Chittenango and Cazenovia	Preliminary surveys made. Nothing else done.
Malden	May 13, 1837	350,000	Malden and junction of Smithbush and Esopus Roads	Nothing done.
Manhattan	Nov. 28, 1853	310,000	Manhattanville and South Ferry	Nothing done.
Manheim & Salisbury	April 28, 1834	75,000	Little Falls and Nicholville	Name changed to Mohawk & St. Lawrence R. R.
Mayville & Portland	March 29, 1832	150,000	Mayville and Portland	Nothing done.
Medina & Darien	May 15, 1834	100,000	Medina and Alexander	Nothing done.
Medina & Lake Ontario	May 13, 1836	200,000	Medina and Carlton	Nothing done.
Mohawk Valley	Jan. 11, 1851	2,000,000	Utica and Schenectady	Surveyed, but not constructed.
Mohawk & Hudson	April 17, 1826	300,000	Albany and Schenectady	Name changed to Albany & Schenectady R. R. First R. R. in the State.
Mohawk & Moose River	April 14, 1857	....	New York Central R. R. in Montgomery county and Moose River Lakes	Nothing done.
Mohawk & St. Lawrence R. R. & Navigation Co	May 11, 1837	1,000,000	Nicholville and Piseco Lake	Not constructed.
Newark	May 21, 1836	100,000	Vienna and Lake Ontario	Nothing done.
New York City	May 12, 1851	120,000	Lower part of the city and Macombs Bridge	Nothing done.
New York & Albany	April 17, 1832	3,000,000	New York and Albany	No part of the road completed by this Company.
New York & Connecticut	May 12, 1846	150,000	Ridgefield, Conn., and Harlem	Nothing done.
New York & Newburgh	March 27, 1854	500,000	Newburgh and New Jersey State line	Nothing done.
New York & New Rochelle	Feb. 18, 1852	1,000,000	New Rochelle and New York City	No part constructed..
New York & Troy	Jan. 30, 1852	1,000,000	New York & Harlem R. R. in Ghent and Troy	Nothing done.
New York & Western	June 10, 1853	12,000,000	State Line in Rockland Co. and Canandaigua	Surveyed, nothing further done.
Niagara Bridge & Canandaigua	Aug. 23, 1858	1,000,000	Niagara Bridge and Canandaigua	Changed from Canandaigua & Niagara Falls R. R. Leased to New York Central R. R.
Niagara Falls, Buffalo & New York	June 4, 1852	250,000	Suspension Bridge and Buffalo	Nothing done.
Niagara Falls & Lake Ontario	Sept. 3, 1852	100,000	Niagara Falls and Youngstown	Graded and rails laid, but not used.
Niagara Falls & Lewistown	Sept. 1, 1847	150,000	Niagara Falls and Lewiston	Nothing done.
Niagara River	July 3, 1852	175,000	Niagara Falls and Lewiston	Nothing done.
Northern	May 14, 1845	2,000,000	Rouses Point and Ogdensburgh	Since changed to Ogdensburgh R. R.
Northern (N. J.)	April 15, 1858	....	Piermont and Jersey City	Allowed to extend from State Line to Piermont. Constructed.
Northern Slackwater & Railway Co	May 13, 1846	2,000,000	Port Kent and Boonville	Route explored, nothing further done.
Ogdensburgh	Dec. 31, 1857	1,538,500		Name changed from Northern.
Ogdensburgh, Clayton & Rome.	Feb. 19, 1853	2,000,000	Ogdensburgh and Rome	Partly graded, and abandoned.
Orange & Sussex Canal Co	April 9, 1829	....		Allowed to build a R. R. on the line of their route. Nothing done.
Oswego, Binghamton & New York	Aug. 14, 1855	400,000	Oswego and Syracuse	Nothing done beyond surveys.
Oswego Northern & Eastern	Jan. 12, 1853	400,000	Oswego and Whitehall & Rutland R. R	Nothing done.
Oswego & Troy	Feb. 21, 1854	2,000,000	Oswego and Troy	Nothing done but survey.
Oswego & Utica	May 13, 1836	750,000	Oswego and Utica	Nothing done but survey.
Otsego	April 26, 1832	200,000	Cooperstown and Milford	Nothing done.
Owego & Cortland	May 21, 1836	500,000	Owego and Cortland or Homer	Nothing done.
Penfield & Canal	May 6, 1837	12,000	Penfield and Erie Canal	Nothing done.
Piermont West Shore	Dec. 4, 1857	40,000	Piermont and terminus of Northern R. R. (N. J.) at State Line	Superseded by extension of Northern R. R. to Piermont.
Plattsburgh & Rouses Point	March 17, 1851	500,000	Plattsburgh and Rouses Point	Nothing done.
Port Byron & Auburn	April 17, 1829	50,000	Auburn and Port Byron	Nothing done.
Rochester, Lockport & Niagara Falls	Dec. 10, 1850	....	Rochester and Niagara Falls	Consolidated in New York Central R. R.
Rochester & Canal Rail Road	March 26, 1831	30,000	Rochester and Lake Ontario	Completed to near the Landing in 1832.
Rochester & Lake Ontario	May 3, 1852	100,000	Rochester and Charlotte	Leased to New York Central R. R. Co. on consolidation.
Rochester & Lockport	May 15, 1837	400,000	Rochester and Lockport	Nothing done under this organization.
Rochester & Pittsburgh	July 18, 1853	1,000,000	Genesee Valley R. R. and Allegany Valley R. R.	Not constructed.
Rochester & Southern	Dec. 27, 1852	200,000	Rochester and Mendon	Not constructed.
Rochester & Syracuse	Aug. 1, 1850	4,200,000	Rochester and Syracuse	Consolidated with New York Central in 1855.
Rome & Port Ontario	May 13, 1837	350,000	Rome and Port Ontario	Nothing done.
Rutland & Whitehall	May 21, 1836	100,000	Whitehall and Rutland	Nothing done.
Sackets Harbor & Saratoga	April 10, 1848	2,000,000	Sackets Harbor and Saratoga	Partly graded. Name changed to Lake Ontario and Hudson R. R.
Sackets Harbor & Watertown	Aug. 25, 1855	110,000	Sackets Harbor and Watertown	Surveyed, but nothing further done.

Rail Roads Projected, Abandoned, and merged in other Roads, continued.

NAMES OF RAIL ROADS.	Date of Organization.	Capital.	Connections.	Remarks.
Salina & Port Watson...............	April 27, 1829	$ 375,000	Syracuse and Port Watson........	Nothing done.
Saratoga Springs & Schuylerville	April 6, 1832	100,000	{ Saratoga Springs and Schuy- lerville .... }	Nothing done.
Saratoga & Fort Edward...........	April 17, 1832	200,000	Saratoga and Fort Edward.......	Nothing done by this company.
Saratoga & Montgomery	May 6, 1836	150,000	{ Ballston Spa and W. branch of North River.............. }	Nothing done.
Saratoga & Washington............	May 2, 1834	600,000	Saratoga and Vt. State Line......	Name changed to Saratoga & Whitehall R. R.
Schenectady & Catskill............	May 13, 1846	1,000,000	Schenectady and Catskill..........	Nothing done.
Schenectady & Susquehanna	May 13, 1846	1,500,000	{ Schenectady and New York & Erie R. R................ }	Nothing done.
Schenectady & Troy................	May 21, 1836	500,000	Schenectady and Troy	Consolidated with New York Central R. R. in 1853.
Schoharie & Otsego	April 25, 1832	300,000	{ Catskill & Central R. R. and Susquehanna .... }	Nothing done.
Scottsville & Canandaigua.........	April 12, 1838	100,000	Scottsville and Canandaigua......	Nothing done.
Scottsville & LeRoy	May 21, 1836	200,000	Scottsville and LeRoy...............	Partly constructed but afterwards abandoned.
Sharon & Root........................	April 18, 1838	50,000	{ Branch of Catskill & Cana- joharie R. R................ }	Nothing done.
Skaneateles...........................	May 19, 1836	25,000	{ Skaneateles and some point on Skaneateles & Jordan R. R................. }	Constructed, but since abandoned.
Skaneateles & Jordan..............	March 13, 1838	....	Skaneateles and Jordan...........	Changed from Skaneateles R. R.
Sodus Point & Southern	March 8, 1852	350,000	{ Sodus Point and Catskill & Ithaca R. R. }	Partly graded; work stopped in 1854.
Staten Island........................	May 21, 1836	250,000	{ From near Quarantine to opposite Amboy............. }	Not constructed.
Staten Island........................	Aug. 2, 1851	300,000	Clifton and Tottenville.............	Not constructed.
Syracuse, Cortland & Bing- hamton..........................	May 21, 1836	500,000	Syracuse and Binghamton........	Surveyed. Nothing further done.
Syracuse Stone......................	May 13, 1836	75,000	Syracuse and Stone quarries......	Nothing done.
Syracuse & Binghamton...........	July 2, 1851	1,200,000	Syracuse and Binghamton........	Opened in 1854. Name changed to Syracuse & Southern R. R.
Syracuse & Southern	Oct. 13, 1856	1,201,300	Syracuse and Binghamton........	Successor of Syracuse & Bing- hamton R. R. Name changed to Syracuse, Binghamton & New York R. R.
Syracuse & Utica....................	May 11, 1836	1,000,000	Syracuse and Utica.................	Consolidated with New York Cen- tral R. R. in 1853.
Syracuse & Utica Direct............	Jan. 20, 1853	600,000	Syracuse and Utica.................	Not constructed.
Tioga Coal, Iron Mining & Manufacturing Co............	1841	....	{ Bituminous coal region and Chemung Canal............. }	{ Sold in 1852, and name changed to Corning & Blossburg R. R. }
Tonawanda...........................	April 14, 1832	500,000	Rochester and Attica...............	Consolidated with Attica & Buffalo R. R. in 1850.
Trenton & Sackets Harbor.......	May 15, 1837	500,000	Trenton and Sackets Harbor......	Nothing done.
Troy Turnpike & Rail Road......	April 18, 1831	100,000	Troy and Bennington, Vt..........	Not constructed.
Troy & Utica........................	Feb. 10, 1853	2,500,000	Troy and Utica.....................	Nothing done.
Troy & West Stockbridge.........	May 10, 1836	600,000	Troy and West Stockbridge.......	Nothing done.
Tyrone & Geneva	May 16, 1837	500,000	{ Geneva and New York & Erie R. R............... }	Nothing done.
Ulster County	May 21, 1836	500,000	{ Kingston and New York & Erie R. R............... }	Nothing done.
Unadilla & Schoharie..............	May 9, 1836	600,000	{ Mouth of Unadilla River and New York & Erie R. R... }	Nothing done.
Utica & Binghamton...............	May 18, 1853	1,000,000	Utica and Binghamton.............	Nothing done.
Utica & Schenectady...............	April 29, 1833	2,000,000	Utica and Schenectady.............	Consolidated with New York Central R. R. in 1853.
Utica & Susquehanna..............	April 25, 1832	1,000,000	Utica and Susquehanna...........	Not constructed.
Utica & Syracuse Straight Line..	Sept. 18, 1852	1,000,000	Utica and Syracuse.................	Not constructed.
Utica & Waterville.................	June 26, 1854	300,000	Utica and Waterville...............	Nothing done.
Warren County......................	April 17, 1832	250,000	Glens Falls and Caldwell..........	Not constructed.
Warsaw & LeRoy..................	May 5, 1834	100,000	Warsaw and LeRoy.................	Nothing done.
Warwick..............................	May 13, 1837	100,000	{ Branch of New York & Erie near Chester............ }	Nothing done.
Washington County Central......	Dec. 8, 1853	200,000	Pittstown and Greenwich	Surveyed and nothing further done.
Watertown & Cape Vincent......	May 13, 1836	50,000	Watertown and Cape Vincent...	Surveyed and nothing further done.
Watervliet & Schenectady........	May 21, 1836	500,000	West Troy and Schenectady.......	Nothing done.
Westchester County.................	Nov. 7, 1856	500,000	Harbor River and New Rochelle..	Nothing done.
West Side.............................	Feb. 1854	6,000,000	Albany and Sufferns...............	Nothing done.
Whitehall & Plattsburgh	Dec. 15, 1852	1,000,000	Whitehall and Plattsburgh.........	Surveyed, but not constructed.
Whitehall & Rutland...............	April 26, 1833	100,000	Whitehall and Rutland, Vt.......	Not constructed by this company.
Williamsburgh, Brooklyn, Bushwick & New Lots	June 29, 1853	....	Williamsburgh and New Lots....	Allowed to build Horse R. Road, for 21 years.

CORPORATIONS.

CORPORATIONS were generally formed under special acts until the adoption of the Constitution of 1846, which directed that general laws should be passed for this purpose, and forbade special legislation, except for municipal purposes and in cases where the purpose to be attained could not otherwise be effected. The Legislature has power to alter and repeal the powers of any corporation formed under the general laws. The articles of association or declaration of intention must in all cases be filed in some office of record specified in the general acts; and limitations of time, capital, and location must be specified. The stockholders of the more important classes of corporations are personally liable to an extent equal to the amount of stock owned. Under the present Constitution, general acts of incorporation have been passed for a variety of purposes, all of which belong to one of 4 general classes.[1]

Class I. includes those whose articles are filed in the office of the Secretary of State.

1. *"An Act to provide for the Incorporation of Companies to construct* **Plank Roads and Turnpikes."**[2]

2. *"An Act to authorize the formation of Companies for* **Mining, Mechanical, and Chemical Purposes"** was passed Feb. 8, 1848.[3]

3. *"An Act to authorize the formation of* **Gas Light Companies"** was passed Feb. 16, 1848.[4]

---

[1] *Constitution*, Art. VIII, *Revised Statutes.* Previous to 1846, general laws existed for the organization of religious societies, (1784;) colleges and academies, (1787;) public libraries, (1796;) medical societies, (1806;) manufacturing companies, (1811;) banks, (1838;) and agricultural societies, (1819, 1841.)

[2] Several hundred of these corporations were formed and several thousand miles of plank road built in 1848-52. It is probable that less than 5 per cent. of these are now in use, having mostly been abandoned and divided into road districts as public highways. The companies were required to report, but generally neglected to do so; and few general statistics are preserved concerning them.

[3] These companies, though quite numerous, were not required to report; and statistics concerning them cannot be obtained. Many companies that filed their articles never went into operation.

[4] *Gas Light Companies.*
A * indicates companies not in operation.

NAMES OF COMPANIES.	Date of Organization.	Original Capital.	Present Capital.
Albany Gas Light Consumers' Co.*	Feb. 18, 1856	$75,000	$75,000
Albion Gas Light Co.*	March 13, 1856	20,000	20,000
Albion Gas Light Co.	May 13, 1858	30,000	30,000
Astoria Gas Co.	Dec. 1, 1853	20,000	20,000
Auburn Gas Light Co.	Jan. 29, 1850	20,000	50,000
Batavia Gas Light Co.	June 11, 1855	32,000	32,000
Binghamton Gas Light Co.	June 25, 1853	50,000	50,000
Brockport Gas Light Co.	Jan. 17, 1859		
Brooklyn Gas Co.*	Oct. 21, 1848	200,000	200,000
Brooklyn Consolidated Gas Light Co.	Oct. 24, 1856	500,000	500,000
Buffalo City Gas Light Co.	March 12, 1853	150,000	150,000
Buffalo Gas Light Co.	Feb. 29, 1848	150,000	750,000
Canandaigua Gas Light Co.	Aug. 3, 1853	50,000	50,000
Catskill Gas Light Co.	July 13, 1855	40,000	40,000
Citizens' Gas Light Co.	Oct. 26, 1858	1,000,000	1,000,000
Citizens' Gas Light Co. of the City of Rochester	Jan. 22, 1852	50,000	50,000
Citizens' Independent Gas Co	June 13, 1859		
Cohoes Gas Light Co.	Sept. 13, 1852	50,000	50,000
Elmira Gas Light Co.	May 8, 1852	50,000	50,000
Fishkill Gas Light Co.	July 20, 1858	15,000	15,000
Flushing Gas Light Co.	July 18, 1855	40,000	61,000
Fulton Gas Light Co.	June 12, 1858	12,000	12,000
Gas Light Co. of Syracuse	Feb. 9, 1849	100,000	100,000
Geneva Gas Light Co.	Nov. 24, 1852	75,000	75,000
Glens Falls Gas Light Co.	June 17, 1854	35,000	35,000
Green Point Gas Light Co.	Nov. 29, 1853	100,000	40,000
Harlem Gas Light Co.	Feb. 5, 1855	120,000	350,000
Hempstead Gas Light Co.	April 18, 1857	15,000	15,000
Hempstead Gas Light Co.	April 9, 1859		
Hudson Gas Co.	Feb. 23, 1853	50,000	50,000
Hudson Gas Light Co.*	May 22, 1852	50,000	50,000
Ithaca Gas Light Co.	Oct. 28, 1852	75,000	75,000
Jamaica Gas Light Co.	June 2, 1856	30,000	20,000
Johnstown Gas Light Co.	March 16, 1857	18,000	18,000
Lansingburgh Gas Light Co.	Feb. 28, 1853	100,000	100,000
Lockport Gas Light Co.	March 17, 1851	17,000	40,000
Lyons Gas Light Co.	Jan. 25, 1859		
Manhattan Gas Light Co.	Oct. 4, 1855		2,000,000
Morrisania Gas Light Co.	Oct. 28, 1852	200,000	200,000
Newburgh Gas Light Co.	May 17, 1852	60,000	70,000
New York Mutual Saving Gas Light Co.*	Sept. 20, 1852	1,500,000	1,500,000
Ogdensburgh Gas Co.	Aug. 23, 1854	75,000	75,000
Ogdensburgh Gas Light Co.	June 15, 1853	100,000	100,000
Ogdensburgh Gas Light & Coke Co.	June 11, 1854	75,000	75,000
Oswego Gas Light Co.	April 22, 1852	65,000	65,000
Owego Gas Light Co.	March 24, 1856	40,000	40,000

4. *"An Act for the incorporation of* **Benevolent, Charitable, Scientific, and Missionary Societies"** was passed April 12, 1848.[1]

5. *"An Act to provide for the incorporation and regulation of* **Telegraph Companies"** was passed April 12, 1848, and amended June 24, 1853.[2]

6. *"An Act for the incorporation of* **Building, Mutual Loan, and Accumulating Fund Associations"** was passed April 10, 1851.[3]

7. *"An Act to provide for the formation of* **Insurance Companies"** was passed April 10, 1849.[4]

Gas Light Companies, continued.

NAMES OF COMPANIES.	Date of Organization.	Original Capital.	Present Capital.
Palmyra Gas Light Co.	Oct. 29, 1856	12,500	12,500
Peekskill Gas Light Co.	July 18, 1855	40,000	31,000
Plattsburgh Gas Light Co.	July 5, 1859		
Poughkeepsie Gas Light Co.	Dec. 18, 1850	70,000	70,000
Richmond County Gas Light Co.	April 26, 1856	200,000	350,000
Rochester Gas Light Co.	May 12, 1848	100,000	200,000
Rome Gas Light Co.	Dec. 28, 1850	20,000	30,000
Rondout & Kingston Gas Light Co.	May 27, 1854	65,000	65,000
Saratoga Gas Light Co.	Aug. 4, 1853	75,000	75,000
Schenectady Gas Light Co.	June 19, 1849	50,000	70,000
Seneca Falls Gas Light Co.*	July 17, 1856	50,000	50,000
Seneca Falls & Waterloo Gas Light Co.	Dec. 24, 1856	80,000	80,000
Sing Sing Gas Light Co.	May 3, 1854	80,000	80,000
Sing Sing Gas Manufacturing Co.	July 25, 1855	35,000	35,000
Staten Island Gas Light Co.	March 14, 1856	150,000	150,000
Syracuse Gas Light Co.	Nov. 30, 1848	100,000	100,000
Tarrytown and Irvington Union Gas Light Co.	March 4, 1859		
The Consumers' Gas Light Co. of Saratoga Springs.	Aug. 23, 1858	30,000	30,000
Troy Gas Light Co.	April 6, 1848	100,000	200,000
Utica Gas Light Co.	Nov. 23, 1848	100,000	80,000
Waterford Gas Light Co.	Oct. 4, 1858	12,000	12,000
Watertown Gas Light Co.	Feb. 28, 1852	20,000	20,000
West Farms Gas Light Co.	Nov. 18, 1852	200,000	200,000
West Troy Gas Light Co.	Jan. 31, 1853	100,000	100,000
Williamsburgh Gas Light Co.	July 5, 1850	80,000	449,500
Yonkers Gas Light Co.	May 12, 1854	70,000	70,000

[1] These companies are not required to report.
[2] These companies make no report; and there is no official knowledge concerning those now existing. Several of those formed never went into operation, and others have been consolidated. The N. Y. & Erie R. R. have a telegraph for regulating the trains upon that road. The N. Y. Central and some other roads have the exclusive or preferred use of telegraph wires along their route for like purposes.

Telegraph Companies.

A * indicates companies not in operation.

NAME.	Date of Organization.	Capital.	NAME.	Date of Organization.	Capital.
Albany, Springfield & Boston Direct Telegraph Co.	May 19, 1854	$ 35,000	New York & Montreal Telegraph Co.*	Oct. 23, 1852	$ 40,000
American Telegraph Co.*	Dec. 12, 1855	200,000	New York & New England Tel. Co.*..	April 26, 1849	42,300
Atlantic & Pacific Telegraph Co.*..	June 15, 1857	300,000	New York & New England Tel. Co.....	July 3, 1852	30,000
Baldwinsville Electro Magnetic Telegraph Co.*	Dec. 4, 1852	400	New York & Philadelphia Branch Telegraph Co.	April 24, 1848	15,000
Buffalo, Corning & New York Telegraph Co.	Jan. 25, 1856	15,000	New York & Sandy Hook Telegraph Co.	Aug. 13, 1852	25,000
Central & Southern Telegraph Co.*	Nov. 13, 1854	11,250	New York & Washington Printing Telegraph Co.	May 26, 1852	200,000
Eastern & Western Telegraph Co.*	May 30, 1855	20,000	New York & Western Union Telegraph Co.	Dec. 22, 1852	10,000
Erie & Central Junction Tel. Co.*..	April 24, 1852	11,250	New York, St. Louis & New Orleans Junction Telegraph Co.	Aug. 26, 1850	200,000
Erie & Central Junction Tel. Co.....	July 19, 1853	11,250	New York State Printing Telegraph Co.*	July 15, 1850	200,000
Genesee Valley Turnpike Co.	April 10, 1857	80,000	New York State Telegraph Co.*.......	May 15, 1850	25,000
Long Island, Marine & Inland Telegraph Co.	March 24, 1858	40,000	Otsego Telegraph Co.	Sept. 30, 1851	4,000
Merchants' Telegraph Co.*	Sept. 23, 1852	40,000	Syracuse, Oswego & Ogdensburgh Telegraph Co.	Sept. 22, 1855	20,000
New York, Albany & Buffalo Electro Magnetic Telegraph Co.	May 31, 1848		Transatlantic Telegraph Co.*	May. 19, 1857	100,000
New York, Albany & Buffalo Telegraph Co., incorp. by special act*	Jan. 25, 1856	250,000	Transatlantic & Submarine Telegraph Co.	Jan. 18, 1858	100,000
New York & Canada House's Printing Telegraph Co.	Nov. 19, 1855	40,000	Troy, Albany & Boston Telegraph Co..	July 25, 1857	50,000
New York & Mississippi Tel. Co.*..	April 8, 1851	360,000	Utica & Oxford Magnetic Telegraph Co.	Aug. 2, 1852	6,400
New York & Mississippi Valley Printing Telegraph Co.*	Feb. 21, 1854	170,000	West Troy, Lansingburgh, Waterford & Cohoes Telegraph Co.	July 14, 1855	3,000
New York & Montreal Printing Telegraph Co.*	Sept. 15, 1853	60,000			

[3] These associations were chiefly limited to the vicinity of New York, numbering 72 in New York co., about 40 in Kings co., with a few in Queens, Richmond, and Westchester. Their operations consisted in raising money by subscription of the members, to be loaned to that member who would allow the highest premium,—the avowed intention being to afford to people of humble means the opportunity of securing for each a home. This absurd fallacy found multitudes of dupes; and in the competition for loans the premiums paid in some instances ran as high as one half of the amount loaned. The mode of appropriating loans varied. It appeared in evidence before the legislative committee of 1855 that in one instance it was as follows:—"The names of all the shareholders who are not more than four weeks in arrear are put in the end of a quill, and all put into a bottle; the whole is then shaken, and the name which first comes out on reversing the bottle has the right to the appropriation." Nearly or quite all of these associations have been abandoned, a few only being kept together by the complexity of their interests and obligations, which are not readily adjusted. A statement showing the operation of these associations was reported by a special legislative committee in 1856.—*Assem. Doc.*, 1856, *No.* 46, *p.* 16.
[4] This act relates to Marine Insurance Companies which make no report. A list of them will be found in the general list of Insurance Companies, pp. 83 to 89.

8. "*An Act for the Incorporation of Companies formed to* **Navigate the Ocean by Steamships**" was passed April 12, 1852.[1]

9. "*An Act to authorize the formation of Companies for* **Ferry Purposes**" was passed April 9, 1853.[2]

10. "*An Act for the Incorporation of Companies formed to* **Navigate the Waters of Lake George by Steamboats**" was passed January 14, 1854.[3]

11. "*An Act for the Incorporation of Companies formed to* **Navigate the Lakes and Rivers**" was passed April 15, 1854. Cos. report annually to the State Engineer and Surveyor.[4]

[1] Previous to 1852, Steamship Cos. were incorp. by special acts; since that time they have organized under the general act.

Ocean Steam Navigation Companies.

NAMES OF COMPANIES.	Date of Organization.	Capital.	NAMES OF COMPANIES.	Date of Organization.	Capital.
Amazon Steamship Co.	Dec. 26, 1853	$55,000	N. Y. & Havre Steamship Co.	Jan. 13, 1855	$700,000
Amer. Atlantic Steam Nav. Co.	Feb. 23, 1839, & May 8, 1845	2,000,000	N. Y. & Matanzas Steamship Co.	Jan. 15, 1859	
Amsterdam Steamship Co.	Jan. 6, 1854	300,000	N. Y. & New Orleans Steamship Co.	Sept. 12, 1854	360,000
Atlantic Steamship Co.	May 26, 1855	686,000	N. Y. South American Steamboat Co	April 14, 1827	100,000
Cal., N.Y., & Europ. Steamship Co.	Oct. 1, 1858	500,000	N. Y. & Southern Steamship Co.	Sept. 29, 1853	500,000
Cal., N.Y., & Europ. Steamship Co.	Oct. 1, 1859		N. Y. & Virginia Steamship Co.	April 10, 1850	300,000
Cent. Amer. & Cal. Steamship Co.	July 7, 1852	400,000	North American Steam Nav. Co.	May 1, 1839	1,500,000
Mexican Ocean Mail & Inland Co.	Jan. 25, 1853	1,500,000	Ocean Steam Navigation Co.	May 8, 1846	1,000,000
N. Y., Balt. & Alex. Steamship Co.	Oct. 27, 1852	120,000	Ocean Steam Packet Co.	May 6, 1839	1,000,000
N. Y. & Boston Steamboat Co.	April 19, 1828	150,000	Ocean Steamship Co.	April 7, 1819	250,000
N. Y. & California Steamship Co.	March 15, 1853	1,500,000	Parker Vein Steamship Co.	Dec. 26, 1853	1,000,000
N. Y. & Galway Steamship Co.	Sept. 6, 1853	1,000,000	Staten Island & N.J. Steam Nav. Co.	March 17, 1853	50,000
N. Y. Harbor Steam Freight Co.	March 11, 1853	100,000	U. S. & Cent. American Transit Co.	June 25, 1859	
N. Y. & Havana Steamship Co.	Jan. 14, 1859		U. S. & Liberia Steamship Co.	March 13, 1854	100,000
			W. India & Venezuela Steamship Co	March 8, 1856	150,000

[2] The Ferry Companies are required to report annually to the Secretary of State; but the reports are not published.

Ferry Companies formed under the General Act.

NAMES OF COMPANIES.	Date of Organization.	Capital.	NAMES OF COMPANIES.	Date of Organization.	Capital.
Brooklyn Ferry Co.	Feb. 26, 1855	$100,000	People's Ferry Co. (N. Y. to Williamsburgh).	April 21, 1853	$300,000
Esopus & Hyde Park Ferry Co.	Nov. 7, 1854	3,000	Piermont & Dearman Ferry Co.	Sept. 5, 1853	50,000
Fort Montgomery Ferry Co.	April 19, 1853	500,000	Rhinebeck & Kingston Ferry Co.	May 7, 1853	8,000
Flushing, College Point & N. Y. Steam Ferry Co.	June 29, 1859		Rosevelt & Bridge St. Ferry Co. (N. Y. to Brooklyn).	April 26, 1853	250,000
Garrison & West Point Ferry Co.	Jan. 21, 1854	12,000	Sidney & Unadilla Ferry Co.	April 25, 1855	100
Long Island Ferry Co. (N. Y. & Brooklyn).	May 9, 1859		Staten Island & N. Y. Ferry Co.	Oct. 26, 1853	900,000
Navy Yard Ferry Co.	June 20, 1859		Union Ferry Co. of Brooklyn.	Nov. 9, 1854	800,000

[3] The only Company formed under this act is the Lake George Steamboat Co., incorp. Jan. 20, 1854. It has a capital of $20,000.

[4] Inland Steam Navigation Companies.

NAMES OF COMPANIES.	Date of Organization.	Capital.	NAMES OF COMPANIES.	Date of Organization.	Capital.
American Steamboat Co.	Feb. 3, 1858	$80,000	Lake Navigation Co.	Feb. 20, 1856	500,000
American Transportation Co.[a]	Jan. 11, 1855	540,000	New York Transportation Co.	April 15, 1854	100,000
Archimedean Propeller Co.	June 1, 1859	200,000	New York & Albany Propeller Line	Dec. 1, 1856	40,000
Black River Steamboat Co.	April 12, 1848	25,000	New York & Western Towing Co.	Sept. 21, 1857	55,000
Black River Steamboat Co.	April 24, 1856	10,000	Niagara Falls Steamboat Assoc.	Sept. 2, 1854	50,000
Blanchard Steamboat Co.	Feb. 25, 1856	25,000	Northern Transportation Co.	Feb. 6, 1855	300,000
Buffalo & Toledo Transportation Co.	May 6, 1856	120,000	Northern Transportation Line	April 6, 1857	59,500
Catskill Steamboat Transport. Co.	Aug. 15, 1854	20,000	North River Steamboat Co.[d]	March 10, 1820	600,000
Cayuga Lake & Inlet Steamboat Co.	Feb. 25, 1828	50,000	Old Oswego Line.	May 2, 1856	300,000
Chautauqua Steamboat Co.	May 4, 1829	10,000	Oneida Lake & River Steamboat Co.[e]	April 2, 1838	10,000
Crooked Lake Steamboat Co.	April 18, 1826	5,000	Ontario Steam & Canal Boat Co.[f]	1842	
Dutchess & Orange Steamboat Co.	April 20, 1825	100,000	Ontario Steamboat Co.	May 12, 1859	100,000
Essex Steam Navigation Co.	April 24, 1829	20,000	Ontario & St. Lawrence Steamboat Co.[g]	1848	
Flushing Steamboat Co.	April 21, 1829	15,000	Orangetown Point Steamboat Co.	April 16, 1830	10,000
Fulton Steamboat Co.	April 18, 1815	250,000	Poughkeepsie Steamboat Co.	March 30, 1827	50,000
Harlem & New York Nav. Co.	Jan. 14, 1856	27,000	St. Lawrence Steamboat Co.	1842	
Hudson River Steamboat Co.	April 20, 1825	200,000	Seneca Lake Steamboat Co.	April 6, 1825	20,000
Hudson River Steamboat Co.	Sept. 15, 1856	20,000	Suffolk Steamboat Co.	March 25, 1829	8,000
Lake Champlain Steamboat Co.[b]	March 12, 1813	200,000	Susquehanna Steam Navigation Co.	May 11, 1835	50,000
Lake Champlain Steamboat Navigation Co.	May 11, 1853	100,000	Troy Steamboat Co.	March 31, 1825	80,000
Lake Erie Steamboat Co.	March 10, 1820	114,000	United States Mail Steamship Co.	April 5, —	1,500,000
Lake Erie Transportation Co.	Nov. 20, 1856	100,000	Western Transportation Co.	Dec. 8, 1855	800,000
Lake Erie & Buffalo Steamboat Co.	March 23, 1859	50,000			
Lake Ontario Steamboat Co.[c]	Jan. 28, 1831	100,000			

[a] Capital reduced to $270,000 Jan. 15, 1859.
[b] Charter expired April 11, 1838. The first steamboat on Lake Champlain was in 1810.
[c] Merged in the Ontario & St. Lawrence Steamboat Co. in 1848.

[d] Charter expired April 11, 1838.
[e] Charter limited to 20 years. Reincorporated April 12, 1842.
[f] Merged in the Ontario & St. Lawrence Steamboat Co. in 1848.
[g] Merged in the American Steamboat Co. in 1858.

Exclusive individual and corporate rights for steam navigation upon the waters of this State have been granted under special acts, as follows:—An act was passed March 19, 1797, granting to John Fitch the sole right of steam navigation in the waters of the State for a period of fourteen years. Having done nothing for ten years, this act was repealed in 1798. An act was passed March 27, 1798, granting to Robert R. Livingston the sole right of navigating by steam for twenty years, conditioned to building a boat of at least 20 tons, capable of moving four miles per hour against the current of Hudson River. This

12. "*An Act for the Incorporation of* **Associations for Improving the Breed of Horses**" was passed April 15, 1854.[1]

13. "*An Act to facilitate the formation of* **Agricultural and Horticultural Societies**" was passed June 8, 1853, and amended April 15, 1855.[2]

Class II. includes all those whose certificates are required to be filed in the Comptroller's office.

1. "*An Act to provide for the Incorporation of* **Life and Health Insurance Companies,** *and in relation to Agencies of such Companies,*" was passed June 24, 1853.[3]

2. "*An Act to provide for the Incorporation of* **Fire Insurance Companies**" was passed June 25, 1853.[4]

[1] The following companies have been formed under this act:—

NAMES.	Place.	When formed.
Fashion Association	Newtown...	Nov. 26, 1855
National Association	Newtown...	May 29, 1854
Orange County Central Horse Co.	Goshen......	July 31, 1855
Union Association	Jamaica....	July 31, 1858

[2] For Table of Agricultural Societies, see pp. 102, 103.

privilege was extended two years, March 29, 1799, to enable Nicholas J. Rosevelt to complete experiments. By act passed in 1798, Robert R. Livingston and Robert Fulton secured the exclusive right of navigating by steam for a period of twenty years; and by an act passed April 11, 1808, an extension of five years was granted for each new boat—the whole time, however, not to exceed thirty years. This monopoly was contested in the State and Federal Courts, in a suit begun in 1819, and finally decided in the Supreme Court of the U. S. in Feb. 1824, as repugnant to the Constitution, which authorizes Congress to regulate commerce. So far as these acts prohibited vessels licensed by the laws of the United States from carrying on a coasting trade, they were void.—*Johnson's Reports,* IV, 148; *Cowan's Reports,* III, 713; *Wheaton's Reports,* IX, 1.

[3] These companies report annually to the Comptroller. A list of them is given in the general list of Insurance Companies.

[4] These companies were formerly created by special acts,—generally for periods of 20, 21, or 30 years. Until about 1834 they were almost invariably upon the joint stock principle. For many years this class of investments were considered extremely reliable, and large dividends were often paid to the stockholders. The great fire in New York in Dec. 1835, proved a heavy disaster to almost all the Insurance companies then formed, and many of them were prostrated by it. This event soon led to the formation of Mutual Insurance Companies in almost every county in the State: most of these companies have since become insolvent. A graphic and truthful statement of the operations that ruined these companies is given in the Comptroller's Report on Fire Insurance Cos. of 1854. A general law, passed April 10, 1849, provided for the incorporation of these companies, under which risks of every kind might be taken. The frauds perpetrated under this system rendered a revision indispensable; and in 1853 two general laws were enacted,—one for the formation of companies for insurance of life and health, and the other against loss by fire, or inland navigation, and transportation. The articles of association (under the law of 1849, required to be filed in the Secretary's office) were, by

these acts, filed in the Comptroller's office, and general powers were conferred upon the Comptroller, with the view of protecting the public from any frauds that might be attempted, and to secure the equal and uniform operation of the laws relating to insurance. Annual reports are made to the Comptroller, and by him to the Legislature, under each of these laws. Marine Insurance companies are still filed in the Secretary's office, but are required to make no report.

Insurance companies formed under the laws of other States or countries cannot establish agencies in this State without first depositing with the Comptroller a certified copy of their charters, and of the vote or resolution creating the agency, a statement of their condition, and proof that their capital is equal to that required by the laws of this State, and, if a Life Insurance company, securities to the amount of $100,000, for the benefit of policy holders. Foreign Marine Insurance companies are required to pay 2 per cent. upon all premiums received by any agent; and a bond in the penal sum of $1,000 is required of every agent of such companies for the payment of this tax. This tax was first collected in 1858, and amounted to $3,742.55. Several companies are not required to report their statistics to the Legislature. The aggregate reports of Fire Insurance Companies for 1857 show the following results:—

Capital invested	$16,731,010.00
Cash premiums received	6,051,304.87
Gross amount of income	7,577,872.62
Losses paid	2,898,166.11
Dividends paid	2,240,434.72
Taxes paid	243,062.79
Gross expenditures	6,855,953.88
Unpaid claims	968,683.00

The following tables comprise the companies which have been incorporated under special acts or the general laws of the State. Foreign companies authorized to transact business in the State are not included in the list:—

Insurance Companies in the State on 1st day of Jan. 1858.

NAME.	Location.	Date of Act, or of filing articles of association.	Expiration of charter.	Stock, or Mutual.	Nature of risks allowed.	Present capital of stock companies.
Ætna Fire Insurance Co. of New York.[a]	New York	March 31, 1824	March 31, 1878	S.	f.	$200,000
Adriatic Fire Insurance Co.	New York	Nov. 24, 1858	Nov. 24, 1888	S.	f. n.	150,000
Agricultural Mutual Insurance Co.[b]	Watertown	Sept. 25, 1851	Sept. 25, 1881	M.	f. n.	
Albany Insurance Co.[c]	Albany	March 8, 1811	Feb. 18, 1881	S.	f. n.	125,000
American Fire Insurance Co.	New York	April 21, 1857	April 21, 1887	S.	f. n.	200,000
Arctic Fire Insurance Co.	New York	July 16, 1853	July 16, 1883	S.	f. n.	250,000
Astor Fire Insurance Co.	New York	June 11, 1851	June 11, 1881	S.	f. n.	150,000
Astor Mutual Insurance Co.	New York	April 18, 1843		M.	m.	
Atlantic Fire Insurance Co.	Brooklyn	Feb. 20, 1851	Feb. 20, 1881	S.	f. n.	
Atlantic Mutual Insurance Co.	New York	April 11, 1842	April 11, 1872	M.	m. n.	150,000
Beekman Fire Insurance Co.	New York	March 4, 1853	March 4, 1883	S.	f. n.	
Brevoort Fire Insurance Co.	New York	Feb. 4, 1857	Feb. 4, 1887	S.	f. n.	200,000
Broadway Insurance Co.	New York	Oct. 2, 1849	Oct. 2, 1879	S.	f. n.	150,000
Brooklyn Fire Insurance Co.	Brooklyn	April 3, 1824	April 3, 1884	S.	f.	200,000
Chautauqua County Mutual Insurance Co.	Fredonia	April 1, 1836	April 1, 1876	M.	f	102,000
Citizens' Fire Insurance Co.[d]	New York	April 28, 1836	April 28, 1866	S.	f.	150,000
City Fire Insurance Co.	New York	April 26, 1833	April 26, 1863	S.	f.	210,000

[a] Reorganized Feb. 12, 1836, under act of Feb. 12, 1836.
[b] Removed from Evans Mills April 10, 1855.
[c] Reorganized Feb. 18, 1851. Capital, $100,000. Originally Albany Fire Insurance Co. Capital, $100,000, and allowed to take fire, marine, and life risks. Once extended. Expired June 1, 1851.
[d] Changed to Citizens' Fire Insurance Co. April 5, 1849.

Existing Insurance Companies, continued.

NAME.	Location.	Date of Act, or of filing articles of association.	Expiration of charter.	Stock, or Mutual.	Nature of risks allowed.	Present capital of stock companies.
Clinton Fire Insurance Co.............................	New York........ ...	July 9, 1850	July 9, 1880	S.	f. n.	$ 250,000
Columbia Fire Insurance Co..........................	New York............	March 9, 1853	March 9, 1883	S.	f. n.	200,000
Columbian Insurance Co...............................	New York...........	Aug. 8, 1857	Aug. 8, 1887	S.	m.	500,000
Commercial Insurance Co..............................	Albany.............	1858				
Commercial Fire Insurance Co......................	New York............	May 14, 1850	March 14, 1880	S.	f. n.	200,000
Commonwealth Fire Insurance Co..................	New York...........	1853	1883	S.	f. n.	250,000
Continental Fire Insurance Co......................	New York...........	March 9, 1853	March 9, 1883	S.	f. n.	200,000
Corn Exchange Fire & Inland Nav. Ins. Co.........	New York...........	Feb. 16, 1853	Feb. 16, 1883	S.	f. n.	200,000
Dividend Mutual Insurance Co.......................	Glens Falls........	April 15, 1850	April 15, 1880	M.	f. n.	
Dutchess Co. Mutual Insurance Co.................	Poughkeepsie.....	April 12, 1836	April 12, 1876	M.	f.	
Eagle Fire Company of New York.ᵃ.................	New York...........	April 4, 1806	Unlimited.	S.	f.	300,000
East River Insurance Co.ᵇ...........................	New York...........	April 24, 1833	....	S.	f.	150,000
Empire City Insurance Co............................	New York...........	Sept. 17, 1850	Sept. 17, 1880	S.		200,000
Empire Insurance Co.................................	Union Springs.....	Dec. 22, 1851	Dec. 22, 1881	M.		
Everett Fire Insurance Co...........................	Cayuga co. N. Y...	Dec. 15, 1858	Dec. 15, 1888	S.	f. n.	150,000
Excelsior Fire Insurance Co.........................	New York...........	July 25, 1853	July 25, 1883	S.	f.	200,000
Exchange Fire Insurance Co.........................	New York...........	May 20, 1853	May 20, 1883	S.	f. n.	150,000
Farmers' Fire Insurance Co..........................	Meridian............	April 28, 1853	April 28, 1883	M.	f. n.	
Farmers' Mutual Insurance Co.......................	Buffalo..............	May 14, 1845	May 14, 1865	M.	f.	
Firemen's Fund Insurance Co.......................	New York...........	May 1, 1858	May 1, 1888	S.	f. n.	150,000
Firemen's Insurance Co.ᵉ...........................	New York...........	April 18, 1825	....	S.	f.	204,000
Franklin Co. Mutual Insurance Co..................	Malone..............	May 12, 1836	May 12, 1876	M.	f.	
Fulton Fire Insurance Co.ᵈ..........................	New York...........	Feb. 23, 1853	Feb. 23, 1883	S.	f. n.	150,000
Gallatin Fire Insurance Co...........................	New York...........	Aug. 11, 1857	Aug. 11, 1887	S.	f. n.	150,000
Gebhard Fire Insurance Co..........................	New York...........	Aug. 6, 1857	Aug. 6, 1887	S.	f. n.	200,000
Glen Cove Mutual Insurance Co.....................	Glen Cove	March 29, 1857	March 29, 1877	M.	f. n.	
Globe Mutual Insurance Co..........................	New York...........	March 22, 1855	March 22, 1885	M.	m.	300,000
Goodhue Fire Insurance Co..........................	New York...........	Aug. 29, 1857	Aug. 29, 1887	S.	f. n.	200,000
Great Western Marine Insurance Co................	New York...........	Aug. 29, 1855	Aug. 29, 1885	S.	m.	1,000,000
Greenwich Insurance Co.............................	New York...........	May 5, 1834	May 5, 1864	S.	f.	200,000
Grocers' Fire Insurance Co..........................	New York...........	Jan. 16, 1850	Jan. 16, 1880	S.	f.	200,000
Hamilton Fire Insurance Co.ᵉ.......................	New York...........	May 22, 1852	May 22, 1882	S.	f.	150,000
Hanover Fire Insurance Co..........................	New York...........	April 1, 1852	April 1, 1882	S.	f.	200,000
Harmony Fire Insurance Co.........................	New York...........	Dec. 1853	Dec. 1883	S.	f. n.	150,000
Home Fire Insurance Co.............................	New York...........	April 11, 1853	April 11, 1883	S.	f. n.	500,000
Homestead Fire Insurance Co.......................	New York...........	Dec. 15, 1858	Dec. 15, 1888	S.	f. n.	150,000
Hope Fire Insurance Co. (The)......................	New York...........	June 16, 1856	June 16, 1886	S.	f. n.	150,000
Howard Insurance Co.ᶠ..............................	New York...........	March 9, 1825	June 16, 1866	S.	f. n.	250,000
Humboldt Fire Insurance Co........................	New York...........	May 5, 1857	May 5, 1887	S.	f.	200,000
Huntington Mutual Fire Insurance Co.ᵍ...........	Huntington........	April 2, 1838	April 2, 1858	M.	f. n.	
Income Insurance Co.................................	New York...........	April 17, 1858	....	S.		100,000
Indemnity Fire Insurance Co........................	New York...........	April 11, 1856	April 11, 1886	S.	f. n.	150,000
Irving Fire Insurance Co.............................	New York...........	Jan. 9, 1852	Jan. 9, 1882	S.	f. n.	200,000
Jamestown Farmers' Fire Insurance Co............	Jamestown........	Aug. 25, 1851	Aug. 25, 1881	M.	f. n.	
Jefferson Insurance Co...............................	New York...........	March 4, 1824	....	S.	f.	200,000
Kings County Fire Insurance Co.....................	New York...........	Oct. 19, 1858	....	S.	f. n.	150,000
Kingston Mutual Insurance Co.......................	Kingston............	March 12, 1836	March 12, 1876	M.		
Knickerbocker Life Insurance Co....................	New York...........	March 29, 1853	March 29, 1883	S.	l.	100,000
Knickerbocker Fire Insurance Co. of N. Y.ʰ.......	New York...........	March 23, 1798	....	S.	....	280,000
Lafarge Fire Insurance Co...........................	New York...........	May 9, 1853	May 9, 1883	S.	f. n.	150,000
La Fayette Fire Insurance Co........................	Brooklyn	Dec. 23, 1856	Dec. 3, 1886	S.	f. n.	150,000
Laman Fire Insurance Co............................	Brooklyn	Dec. 10, 1856	Dec. 10, 1886	S.	f. n.	200,000
Lenox Fire Insurance Co.............................	New York...........	April 1, 1853	April 1, 1883	S.	f. n.	150,000
Long Island Insurance Co............................	Brooklyn	April 26, 1833	April 26, 1863	S.	f.	200,000
Lorillard Fire Insurance Co..........................	New York...........	Jan. 16, 1852	Jan. 16, 1882	S.	f. n.	200,000
Manhattan Life Insurance Co........................	New York...........	May 17, 1850	May 17, 1880	S.	l.	112,000
Manhattan Fire Insurance Co.ⁱ.....................	New York...........	March 23, 1821	1866	S.	f. n.	250,000
Market Fire Insurance Co............................	New York...........	Jan. 26, 1853	Jan. 26, 1883	S.	f. n.	200,000
Mechanics' Mutual Insurance Co....................	Troy.................	May 14, 1836	May 14, 1876	M.	f.	
Mechanics' Fire Insurance Co.......................	Brooklyn	May 5, 1857	May 5, 1887	S.	f. n.	150,000
Mechanics' & Traders' Fire Insurance Co..........	New York...........	Feb. 4, 1853	Feb. 4, 1883	S.	f. n.	200,000
Mercantile Fire Insurance Co........................	New York...........	Dec. 24, 1851	Dec. 24, 1881	S.	f. n.	200,000
Mercantile Mutual Insurance Co.....................	New York...........	April 12, 1842	April 12, 1872	M.	m. n.	
Merchants' Insurance Co.............................	New York...........	Feb. 20, 1850	Feb. 20, 1880	S.	f. n.	200,000
Metropolitan Fire Insurance Co.....................	New York...........	Oct. 1, 1852	Oct. 1, 1882	S.	f. n.	300,000
Monroe Co. Mutual Insurance Co...................	Rochester...........	March 21, 1836	March 21, 1876	M.	f.	
Montauk Fire Insurance Co..........................	Brooklyn	May 19, 1857	May 19, 1887	S.	f. n.	150,000
Montgomery Co. Mutual Insurance Co.............	Canajoharie.......	March 30, 1836	March 30, 1876	M.	f.	
Mutual Ins. Co. of the City and Co. of Albany.....	Albany.............	May 3, 1836	May 3, 1886	M.	f.	
Mutual Life Insurance Co............................	New York...........	April 12, 1842	Till repealed.	M.	l.	135,000
Nassau Fire Insurance Co............................	Brooklyn	Oct. 31, 1851	Oct. 31, 1881	S.	f. n.	150,000
National Fire Insurance Co.ⱼ........................	New York...........	April 9, 1838	....	S.	f. n.	200,000
New Amsterdam Fire Insurance Co.................	New York...........	Feb. 28, 1853	Feb. 28, 1883	S.	f. n.	200,000
New World Fire Insurance Co........................	New York...........	Oct. 13, 1856	Oct. 13, 1886	S.	f.	200,000
New York Bowery Fire Insurance Co...............	New York...........	April 24, 1833	April 24, 1863	S.	f.	300,000
New York Equitable Insurance Co.ᵏ................	New York...........	April 23, 1823	1866	S.	f. l.	210,000

ᵃ Original capital $500,000. Special relief on account of fire of July 19, 1845, granted by act of May 12, 1846.

ᵇ Organized March, 1835. Allowed to take inland transportation risks April 29, 1840. Changed to East River Mutual Insurance Co. April 12, 1842.

ᶜ Original capital $300,000, reduced May 12, 1846, by the fire of July, 1845.

ᵈ Allowed to remove from Williamsburgh April 13, 1855. Changed from Williamsburgh City Fire Insurance Co.

ᵉ Changed from Building Association Fire Insurance Co. March 8, 1853.

ᶠ Reorganized 1836. Original capital $300,000.

ᵍ Organized March, 1840, under act March 12, 1840.

ʰ Changed from Mutual Insurance Co. of the City of New York, May 12, 1846, having been twice extended. Originally named the Mutual Insurance Co. of New York.

ⁱ Reorganized June 7, 1836.

ⱼ Changed May 24, 1841, from Seventeenth Ward Fire Insurance Co. Amended charter March, 1857.

ᵏ Reduced from $300,000 Feb. 18, 1848.

Existing Insurance Companies, continued.

NAME.	Location.	Date of act, or of filing articles of association.	Expiration of charter.	Stock, or Mutual.	Nature of risks allowed.	Present capital of stock companies.
New York Fire and Marine Insurance Co.ᵃ	New York	April 18, 1832	April 18, 1862	S.	f. m.	$200,000
New York Indemnity Insurance Co.ᵇ	Albany	July 29, 1851	July 29, 1881	M.	f. n.	
New York Life Insurance Co.ᶜ	New York	May 21, 1841	Unlimited	......	l.	108,800
New York Life Insurance & Trust Co.	New York	March 9, 1830	Unlimited	......	l.	100,000
New York Mutual Insurance Co.	New York	March, 1851	March, 1881	M.	m. n.	
New York & Erie Insurance Co.	Middletown	Nov. 29, 1852	Nov. 29, 1882	M.	f. n.	
Niagara Fire Insurance Co.	New York	June 22, 1850	June 22, 1880	S.	f. n.	200,000
North American Insurance Co.	New York	Jan. 1, 1836	....	S.	f.	250,000
Northern New York Mutual Insurance Co.	Plattsburgh	Sept. 18, 1852	Sept. 18, 1882	M.	f. n.	
North River Insurance Co.ᵈ	New York	Feb. 6, 1822	Feb. 6, 1862	S.	f. n.	350,000
North Western Insurance Co.ᵉ	Oswego	April 26, 1832	Jan. 1, 1877	S.	f. n.	150,000
Ocean Insurance Co.ᶠ	New York	Jan. 29, 1853	Jan. 29, 1883	S.	m.	300,000
Ocean Insurance Co.	New York	April 3, 1855	April 3, 1885	S.	f. m. n.	300,000
Ontario & Livingston Co. Mutual Insurance Co.	West Bloomfield.	March 21, 1836	March 20, 1876	M.	f.	
Orange Co. Mutual Insurance Co.	Goshen	March 15, 1837	March 15, 1877	M.	f.	
Orien Mutual Insurance Co.	New York	Jan. 18, 1859	Jan. 18, 1889	S.	m. n.	
Pacific Fire Insurance Co.	New York	April 17, 1851	April 7, 1881	S.	f. n.	200,000
Pacific Mutual Insurance Co.	New York	Dec. 18, 1854	Dec. 18, 1884	S.	m. n.	
Park Fire Insurance Co.	New York	Feb. 1, 1853	Feb. 1, 1883	S.	f. n.	200,000
People's Fire Insurance Co.	New York	April 22, 1851	April 11, 1881	S.	f. n.	150,000
Peter Cooper Fire Insurance Co.	New York	March 30, 1853	March 30, 1883	S.	f. n.	150,000
Phoenix Fire Insurance Co.	Brooklyn	March 14, 1853	March 14, 1883	S.	f. n.	200,000
Poughkeepsie Mutual Fire Insurance Co.	Poughkeepsie	July 30, 1850	July 30, 1880	M.	f. n.	100,000
Relief Fire Insurance Co.	New York	Dec. 17, 1855	Dec. 17, 1885	S.	f. n.	150,000
Republic Fire Insurance Co.	New York	March 22, 1852	March 22, 1882	S.	f. n.	150,000
Resolute Fire Insurance Co.	New York	July 10, 1857	July 10, 1887	S.	f. n.	200,000
Richmond County Mutual Insurance Co.	Richmond	March 30, 1836	March 30, 1876	M.	f.	
Rutgers Fire Insurance Co.	New York	Sept. 12, 1853	Sept. 12, 1883	S.	f. n.	200,000
St. Lawrence Co. Mutual Insurance Co.	Ogdensburgh	May 12, 1836	May 12, 1876	M.	f.	
St. Marks Fire Insurance Co.	New York	July 14, 1853	July 14, 1883	S.	f. n.	150,000
St. Nicholas Insurance Co.	New York	July 23, 1852	July 23, 1882	S.	f. n.	150,000
Schenectady Insurance Co.ᵍ	Schenectady	May 26, 1841	May 26, 1891	M.	f.	
Security Fire Insurance Co.	New York	June 20, 1856	June 20, 1886	S.	f. n.	200,000
Star Insurance Co.	Ogdensburgh	Nov. 30, 1853	Nov. 30, 1883	S.	f. n.	150,000
Stuyvesant Insurance Co.	New York	Jan. 7, 1851	Jan. 7, 1881	S.	f.	200,000
Suffolk County Mutual Insurance Co.	Southold	April 30, 1836	April 30, 1876	M.	f.	
Sun Mutual Insurance Co.	New York	May 22, 1841	May 22, 1861	M.	f. m. n.	
Tradesmen's Fire Insurance Co.	New York	Dec. 20, 1858	Dec. 20, 1888	S.	f. n.	150,000
Union Mutual Insurance Co.	New York	May 14, 1845	May 14, 1875	M.	f. m.	
United States Fire Insurance Co.	New York	March 31, 1824	April 1, 1884	S.	f.	250,000
United States Life Insurance Co.	New York	Jan. 26, 1850	Jan. 26, 1880	S.	l.	100,000
Wall St. Fire Insurance Co.	New York	Oct. 19, 1858	Oct. 19, 1888	S.	f. n.	200,000
Washington Insurance Co.	New York	Feb. 11, 1850	Feb. 11, 1880	S.	f. n.	200,000
Waterville Protection Insurance Co.	Waterville	Feb. 8, 1851	Feb. 8, 1881	M.	f. n.	
Wayne County Mutual Insurance Co.	Newark	April 1, 1853	April 1, 1883	M.	f. n.	
Westchester County Mutual Insurance Co.	New Rochelle	March 14, 1837	March 14, 1877	M.	f.	
Western Farmers' Mutual Insurance Co.	Batavia	April 23, 1844	April 23, 1864	M.	f.	
Williamsburgh City Fire Insurance Co.	Williamsburgh	Dec. 13, 1852	Dec. 12, 1882	S.	f.	150,000
Wyoming County Mutual Insurance Co.	Warsaw	Nov. 25, 1851	Nov. 25, 1881	M.	f.	

ᵃ Changed from New York Fire Insurance Co. May 10, 1847, and allowed to take marine risks.
ᵇ Removed from Broadalbin April 15, 1857.
ᶜ Changed from Nautilus Insurance Co. April 5, 1849, and limited to life risks. First organized April 12, 1845, and allowed m. n. and f. risks. Capital, $200,000.

ᵈ Reorganized July 18, 1852. Originally allowed marine risks.
ᵉ Organized Jan. 1834.
ᶠ Enjoinder.
ᵍ Changed from Schenectady County Mutual Insurance Co. April 7, 1858.

Obsolete Insurance Companies in the State, Jan. 1, 1859.

NAME.	Location.	Date of act of incorporation or of filing articles.	Stock or Mutual.	Remarks.
Ætna Insurance Co. of Utica	Utica	March 14, 1851	M.	
Albany County Mutual Ins. Co.	Albany	May 3, 1836	M.	Receiver appointed Jan. 1854.
Allegany Mutual Insurance Co.	Angelica	April 13, 1857	M.	Closed.
Allegany County Mutual Ins. Co.	Angelica	April —, 1857	M.	Closing business. No receiver.
Alliance Insurance Co.	New York	April 30, 1839	S.	Cap. $250,000.
Alliance Mutual Insurance Co.	New York	April 10, 1843	M. f. m.	
American Fire Ins. Co. of New York.	New York	April 18, 1825	S. f. n.	Cap. $300,000, 21 years; April 20, 1832, $200,000, 30 years.
American Ins. Co. of New York	New York	June 18, 1812	S.	Successor to Marine Ins. Co., 15 years, from May 12; cap. $250,000. In 1814, marine, not exceeding $1,000,000. Extended to May 12, 1857. Closed in 1845.
American Insurance Co. of the City of New York	New York	June 12, 1856	...... m.	
American Insurance Co.	Utica	Sept. 6, 1852	......	Receiver appointed April, 1855.
American Manufacturers' Mutual Assurance Co.	New York	March 30, 1832	M. f.	
American Mutual Insurance Co.	Amsterdam	April 23, 1850	M.	Receiver appointed Dec. 1854.
American Mutual Insurance Co.	New York	April 1, 1843	M. f. m.	
Anchor Insurance Co.	New York	April 5, 1826	S.	Changed from La Fayette Ins. Co. of the City of New York.
Atlantic Insurance Co. of New York.	New York	Feb. 27, 1824	S. m.	Cap. $500,000. Discon. in 1828; allowed to close up and reorganize new company.

Obsolete Insurance Companies, continued.

NAME.	Location.	Date of act of incorporation or of filing articles.	Stock or Mutual.		Remarks.
Atlas Insurance Co. of New York....	New York....	April 8, 1825	S.	m.	Cap. $300,000.
Atlas Marine Insurance Co..............	New York....	April 14, 1836	S.	m.	Cap. $350,000. Revived April 14, 1838.
Atlas Mutual Insurance Co..............	New York....	April 10, 1843	M.	m.	
Auburn Co...................................	Auburn	March 14, 1825	S.	f. n.	Cap. $150,000.
Bowery Fire Insurance Co..............	New York....	April 24, 1833	S.	f.	Cap. $300,000.
Broome County Mutual Ins. Co.		April 10, 1837	M.		
Brooklyn Firemen's Insurance Co. ...	Brooklyn...........	May 25, 1836	S.	f.	Cap. $150,000. Successor to Firemen's Insurance Co.
Buffalo Fire & Marine Insurance Co.	Buffalo	April 1, 1830	S.	f. m. n.	Cap. $100,000.
Buffalo Mutual Insurance Co..........	Buffalo	March 17, 1837	M.		
Building Association Fire Ins. Co....	New York...........	May 3, 1852	S.		Changed March 8, 1853, to Hamilton Fire Insurance Co.
Canal Insurance Co.	New York...........	March 14, 1825	S.	f. n.	Cap. $300,000. Revived April 21, 1828, cap. $150,000.
Canal Ins. Co. of the City of New York	New York....	May 25, 1836	S.		Cap. $300,000.
Cattaraugus County Mutual Ins. Co.	Ellicottville........	May 17, 1837	M.	f.	
Cayuga County Mutual Ins. Co........	Aurora	March 20, 1837	M.	f.	Closed business in 1852.
Chatham Fire Insurance Co. of the City of New York......................	New York...........	April 16, 1822	S.	f.	Cap. $400,000.
Chelsea Insurance Co.....................	New York...........	April 29, 1839	S.		Cap. $250,000.
Chemung County Mutual Ins. Co.....		April 2, 1838	M.		
Chenango County Mutual Ins. Co.....		May 3, 1838	M.		
Cherry Valley Mutual Ins. Co..........	Cherry Valley....	April 12, 1842	M.		
Clinton Fire Insurance Co. of the City of New York......................	New York...........	April 26, 1831	S.	f.	Cap. $300,000; time extended 1832–33.
Clinton Insurance Co. in the City of Albany	Albany	May 4, 1829	S.		Cap. $300,000.
Clinton & Essex Mutual Ins. Co.......	Keeseville..........	May 12, 1836	M.	f.	Receiver appointed Jan. 1854.
Columbia County Mutual Ins. Co.....	Hudson.............	May 12, 1836	M.		
Columbian Fire Insurance Co. of the City of New York .... }	New York...........	May 25, 1836	S.	{ f.	Cap. $300,000. Revived April 5, 1839, cap. $250,000.
Columbian Insurance Co.................	New York....	March 21, 1801	S.	f. l. m.	Cap. $500,000. Receiver appointed Jan. 1853.
Columbian Insurance Co.................	Amsterdam	June 4, 1851	......		
Commercial Insurance Co...............	New York...........	April 4, 1805	S.	f. l. n.	Cap. $250,000. Extended 21 years April 3, 1811.
Commercial Insurance Co...............	New York...........	April 12, 1842	S.	f. m. n.	Changed June 16, 1853, to Commercial Mutual Insurance Co.
Cortland County Mutual Ins. Co......	Cortlandville......	May 12, 1836	M.		Closed about 1852.
Croton Insurance Co......................	New York...........	April 10, 1849	M.		
Croton Mutual Insurance Co...........	New York...........	April 10, 1843	M.	f. m. n.	
Dunkirk Marine Insurance Co.........	Dunkirk............	May 9, 1837	S.	m.	Cap. $250,000.
Dutchess County Insurance Co........	Poughkeepsie.....	April 15, 1814	S.		Cap. $200,000.
Eighth Ward Fire Insurance Co......	New York...........	April 25, 1836	S.		Original cap. $300,000. Changed to Trust Fire Ins. Co. April 25, 1839.
Eighth Ward Mutual Insurance Co..	New York...........	April 30, 1836	M.	f.	
Emmet Fire Insurance Co...............	New York...........	April 6, 1839	S.	f.	Cap. $250,000.
Empire State Mutual Insurance Co..	Saratoga Springs	Dec. 8, 1849	M.		Receiver appointed June 1855.
Enterprise Insurance Co.................	New York...........	Aug. —, 1855	......		Enjoined Dec. 28, 1855; injunction removed Jan. 31, 1856. Closing.
Farmers' Fire Ins. & Loan Co.........	New York...........	Feb. 28, 1822	S.		Cap. $500,000.
Farmers' Ins. Co. of Oneida County..	Utica	June 26, 1851	......		Receiver appointed Nov. 1854.
Farmers and Merchants' Ins. Co. of Western New York........ }	Rochester	Oct. 29, 1850	......	{	Changed to Rochester Insurance Co. March 20, 1852.
Farmers' Mutual Insurance Co. of Sherburne	Sherburne	May 13, 1845	M.		Receiver appointed.
Fifth Ward Fire Insurance Co. of the City of New York .... }	New York...........	April 13, 1836	S.	{	Cap. $500,000; reduced to $200,000 April 21, 1837.
Firemen's Insurance Co. of the City of Albany........................ }	Albany	April 3, 1831	S.	{ f.	Cap. $150,000. M. risks allowed April 20, 1832. To expire June, 1861.
Firemen's Insurance Co.................	Brooklyn...........	April 29, 1833	S.	f.	Cap. $150,000. Changed to Brooklyn Firemen's Ins. Co. May 25, 1836.
Franklin Fire Insurance Co.............	New York...........	March 13, 1818	S.	f. l. ann.	Cap. $500,000. Reduced one-half, 1828. Continued in 1835 to '56. Reduced by the great fire of 1835.
Franklin Fire Insurance Co. in the City of New York......................	New York...........	April 2, 1819	S.		Cap. $500,000.
Franklin Fire Ins. Co. of New York..	Saratoga Springs	March 5, 1851	......		Receiver appointed June, 1855.
Franklin Marine & Fire Insurance Co. of New York	Saratoga Springs	April 12, 1852	M.		Receiver appointed Sept. 1854.
Fulton Fire Insurance Co. in the City of New York......................	New York...........	April 2, 1819	S.		Cap. $500,000.
Fulton Fire Insurance Co...............	New York...........	May 14, 1840	S.		Cap. $250,000.
General Mutual Insurance Co..........	New York...........	May 25, 1841	M.	f. m. n.	
Genesee Mutual Insurance Co.........	Le Roy	May 3, 1836	M.		Receiver appointed Oct. 1851.
Girard Fire Insurance Co. of the City of New York......................	New York...........	March 4, 1839	S.		Cap. $250,000.
Globe Fire Insurance Co.................	New York...........	May 2, 1837	S.	f. n.	Cap. $500,000. Company of like name incorp. July 24, 1851, cap. $200,000.
Globe Insurance Co.......................	New York...........	March 18, 1814	S.		Cap. $1,000,000. Reduced one-half March 17, 1836.
Globe Insurance Co.......................	Utica...............	June 5, 1852	M.		Receiver appointed August, 1855.
Granite Insurance Co.....................	Utica...............	Oct. 21, 1852	M.		Removed from Utica April, 1859. Receiver appointed Feb. 1856.
Greene County Mutual Insurance Co.	Catskill	March 30, 1836	M.		
Greenwich Fire Insurance Co..........	New York...........	March 31, 1824	S.		Cap. $250,000.
Good Hope Ins. Co. of New York.....	New York...........	April 25, 1852	S.	m.	Cap. $300,000.
Guardian Insurance Co..................	New York...........	April 24, 1833	S.	f.	
Hamilton Fire Insurance Co. of the City of New York......................	New York...........	April 25, 1836	S.	f.	Cap. $500,000.

Obsolete Insurance Companies, continued.

NAME.	Location.	Date of act of incorporation or of filing articles.	Stock or Mutual.		Remarks.
Hamilton Marine Insurance Co......	New York..........	April 4, 1838	S.	f. m.	Cap. $250.000.
Harmony Fire Insurance Co...........	New York..........	....	f.		Changed to Harmony Fire & Marine Insurance Co. April 17, 1858.
Harmony Fire & Marine Ins. Co......	New York..........	....	......	f. m. n.	Changed from Harmony Fire Insurance Co. April 17, 1858.
Henry Clay Fire Insurance Co........	New York..........	Dec. 29, 1855	S.		Receiver appointed Dec. 1855.
Herkimer County Mutual Ins. Co....	Little Falls........	April 28, 1836	M.		Receiver appointed 1853.
Hope Insurance Co........................	New York..........	Jan. 26, 1821	S.		Changed from New York Firemen's Insurance Co. Cap. $300,000.
Householders' Mutual Insurance Co.	New York..........	May 25, 1841	M.	f. (Pictures, furniture, &c.)	Repealed April 17, 1843. Changed to Merchants & Householders' Mutual Ins. Co.
Howard Life Insurance Co.............	New York..........	June 29, 1852	S.	l.	Discontinued issuing policies 1856 or '57. See Comp. Rep. 1859, p. 53.
Hudson Fire Insurance Co.............	New York..........	April 6, 1838	S.	f. n.	Cap. $200,000. Reduced to $150,000 April 17, 1843.
Hudson Insurance Co.....................	New York..........	April 4, 1811	S.	f.	Cap. $200,000.
Hudson Insurance Co. of the City of New York..........................	New York..........	April 8, 1825	S.	m.	Cap. $300,000.
Hudson River Marine & Fire Ins. Co.	Crescent.............	June 1, 1852	M.	f. m. n.	Receiver appointed Aug. 1854.
Hudson River Mutual Insurance Co. at Waterford....................	Waterford..........	Aug. 8, 1850	M.	{	Business transferred to Hudson River Marine & Fire Insurance Co.
Indemnity Fire Insurance Co. of the City of New York.....................	New York..........	April 13, 1836	S.		Cap. $500,000.
Insurance Company of Firemen......	New York..........	May 2, 1810			
International Insurance Co.............	....	April 11, 1855			Changed from Kings County Mutual Ins. Co.
Jackson Marine Ins. Co. of the City of New York............................	New York..........	April 23, 1831	S.	{ f. m.	Cap. $400,000. Reduced to $300,000 April 24, 1840. Reduced to $200,000 and fire risks allowed.
Jefferson County Mutual Ins. Co.....	Watertown	March 8, 1836	M.		
Kings County Mutual Insurance Co.	Brooklyn	April 15, 1844	M.		Changed to International Ins. Co. April 11, 1845.
Knickerbocker Insurance Co...........	Waterford..........	May 15, 1852	M.		Receiver appointed July, 1855.
La Fayette Ins. Co. of the City of New York...............................	New York..........	April 8, 1825	S.	{	Cap. $300,000. Changed to Anchor Ins. Co. of the City of New York, April 8, 1826.
Lewis County Mutual Insurance Co.	....	Feb. 27, 1837	M.	f.	Took but one insurance. Never fully organized.
Long Island Farmers' Ins. Co. in the Co. of Queens............................	Hempstead	April 29, 1833	S.		Cap. $50,000. Revived May 2, 1835.
Long Island Mutual Insurance Co...	Brooklyn	April 30, 1836	M.		
Madison Co. Mutual Ins. Co...........	Cazenovia	March 23, 1836	M.		Closed under act of Jan. 25, 1854.
Madison Marine Ins. Co. of the City of New York........................	New York..........	April 8, 1825	S.	m.	Cap. $300,000.
Marine Insurance Co. of New York..	New York..........	March 16, 1802	......	m.	Cap. $250,000. Closed up under act of June 18, 1812, by the American Ins. Co. of New York having become insolvent.
Mechanics' Fire Ins. Co. of the City of New York............................	New York..........	April 7, 1819	......	{	Original cap. $500,000. Reduced to $300,000 Jan. 12, 1828.
Merchants' Fire Insurance Co........	New York..........	April 2, 1819	......	f. l.	Cap. $300,000. Reduced to $250,000.
Merchants' Mutual Ins. Co. of Buffalo	Buffalo..............	Feb. 4, 1850	M.		Made assignment and diss. Jan. 1852.
Merchants & Householders' Mutual Ins. Co...................................	New York..........	April 17, 1843	M.	{	Changed from Householders' Mutual Ins. Co.
Merchants' Ins. Co. in the City of Albany	Albany	April 7, 1824	S.	f. m. n.	Cap. $250,000.
Merchants' Insurance Co................	Buffalo..............	Feb. 4, 1851	......		Closed.
Merchants' Marine Insurance Co....	New York..........	April 26, 1836	S.	f. m.	Cap. $400,000.
Merchants' Insurance Co...............	New York..........	April 10, 1843	M.	f. m. n.	
Metropolis Ins. Co. of the City of New York...............................	New York..........	Jan. 29, 1853	S.	{	Changed to Ocean Ins. Co. of the City of New York April 3, 1855.
Metropolis Insurance Co................	New York..........	April 29, 1839	S.		Cap. $250,000.
Metropolitan Insurance Co.............	New York..........	Oct. 2, 1852	S.		Cap. $500,000. Never organized.
Mohawk Insurance Co. of New York	New York..........	April 3, 1824	S.		Cap. $500,000.
Mohawk Valley Farmers' Ins. Co	Scotia	June 27, 1851	M.		Receiver appointed Oct. 1854.
Mohawk Valley Insurance Co..........	Amsterdam	June 6, 1851	M.		Receiver appointed Jan. 1855.
Monroe Fire Insurance Co	Rochester..........	March 9, 1825	S.		Cap. $250,000. Revived April 17, 1826.
Mutual Assurance Co. of New York.	New York..........	March 23, 1798	M.	f.	Renewed 1808 as Mutual Ins. Co. of New York. Cap. $350,000. To continue till repealed. Changed to Knickerbocker Fire Ins. Co. of New York May 12, 1846.
Mutual Insurance Co. of Buffalo.....	Buffalo..............	April 18, 1843	M.	f. m. n.	
Mutual Protection Insurance Co......	New York..........	May 25, 1841	S.	f. m. n.	Cap. $200,000.
Mutual Protection Ins. Co. of Rochester..................................	Rochester..........	May 7, 1844	......	f. n.	
Mutual Safety Insurance Co...........	New York..........	April 17, 1838	......	f. m.	Extended April 12, 1843.
National Exchange Insurance Co....	New York..........	May, 1855			Receiver appointed Sept. 1855.
National Insurance Co...................	New York..........	April 14, 1815	S.	l. m. n.	Original cap. $100,000.
National Insurance Co...................	New York..........	April 9, 1838	......		Cap. $150,000.
National Protection Insurance Co.....	Saratoga Springs.	Feb. 22, 1851	......		Receiver appointed Aug. 1855.
Nautilus Insurance Co....................	New York	....	......		April 5, 1849, changed to New York Life Ins. Co. and limited to life risks.
New York Central Insurance Co......	Cherry Valley....	Jan. 16, 1851	......		Closing up. No new policies issued.
New York City Insurance Co...........	New York..........	Nov. 13, 1852	......		Receiver appointed Sept. 1855.
New York City Insurance Co...........	New York..........	March 22, 1825	S.		Cap. $250,000.
New York Contributionship Ins. Co.a	New York..........	April 5, 1824	......	f. n.	Cap. $300,000. Similar act May 6, 1844.

a The New York Contributionship for the Insurance of Houses & Property from Loss by Fire, incorp. April 5, 1822. Changed to above.

Obsolete Insurance Companies, continued.

NAME.	Location.	Date of act of incorporation or of filing articles.	Stock or Mutual.		Remarks.
New York Fire Ins. Co. of the City of New York }	New York		......	{	Changed May 10, 1847, to New York Fire & Marine Ins. Co.
New York Protection Insurance Co.	Rome	July 23, 1849	......		Made assignment Jan. 1852, and closed up.
New York State Mutual Ins. Co.	Newark	Oct. 31, 1849	M.		Receiver appointed.
New York Union Mutual Ins. Co.	Johnstown	May 9, 1850	M.		Receiver appointed July, 1855.
New York Firemen Insurance Co.	New York	March 2, 1810	S.		Cap. $500,000. Closed by losses 1818 and reorganized. Changed to Hope Ins. Co. Jan. 26, 1821.
New York Guardian Insurance Co.	New York	April 6, 1838	S.		Cap. $300,000.
New York Insurance Co	New York	April 2, 1798	......		Expired 1820. Extended to Jan. 1860.
New York La Fayette Ins. Co	New York	April 14, 1825	S.	f. n.	Cap. $200,000.
New York Marine Insurance Co.	New York	April 2, 1798	......		Cap. $500,000.
New York Mechanics' Life Ins. & Coal Co }	New York	Feb. 28, 1822	......	{l.	Cap. $600,000. Changed April 15, 1823, to Life & Fire Ins. Co.
New York Mutual Insurance Co.	New York	March 28, 1809			
New York Northern Fire Ins. Co.		May 4, 1829	......		Changed from Sun Fire Ins. Co. Cap. $240,000.
New York State Marine Ins. Co	New York	April 8, 1825	......		Cap. $400,000. Revived April 25, 1831. Cap. $300,000.
New York Union Mutual Ins. Co.	Johnstown	May 9, 1850	M.	{ m.	Cap. $250,000. Changed to Neptune Bell Mutual Ins. Co. of New York, April 22, 1831.
Neptune Ins. Co. of the City of New York }	New York	April 11, 1825	......		
Neptune Bell Marine Ins. Co. of New York }	New York	April 22, 1831	......	{ m.	Changed from Neptune Ins. Co. Cap. $250,000. Revived April, 1832.
Niagara County Mutual Ins. Co	Lockport	April 13, 1837	M.		
North American Fire Insurance Co.	New York	April 8, 1836	S.	f.	Cap. $250,000. Changed from Phœnix Fire Ins. Co. Allowed to take inland navigation risks May 7, 1845.
North American Insurance Co	New York	April 13, 1826	S.		Cap. $300,000.
North American Mutual Ins. Co.	Brasher Falls	May 26, 1851	......		Receiver appointed June, 1855.
Northern New York Live Stock Ins.Co	Plattsburgh	July 8, 1851			
Northern New York Mutual Ins. Co.	Plattsburgh	Sept. 17, 1852			
Northern Protection Insurance Co.	Camden	Nov. 14, 1851	M.		Receiver appointed Oct. 1854.
Ocean Insurance Co	New York	March 2, 1810	S.	m. n.	Cap. $500,000. Extended to Jan. 1860. Capital reduced to $350,000.
Oneida County Mutual Ins. Co.	Utica	April 28, 1836	M.		Closed.
Oneida Insurance Co	Utica	March 23, 1832	S.	f. n.	Cap. $250,000.
Oneida Lake Mutual Insurance Co.	Cleveland	March 8, 1853	M.		Closed.
Onondaga County Mutual Ins. Co.	Baldwinsville	April 13, 1836	M.		Closing up.
Ontario Insurance Co.	Geneva	March 21, 1825	S.	f. n.	Cap. $250,000.
Orange Fire Insurance Co	Newburgh	April 7, 1819	S.		Cap. $400,000.
Orleans Insurance Co	Albion	June 1, 1850	......		Receiver appointed March, 1852.
Oswego County Mutual Ins. Co.	Mexico	April 28, 1836	M.		
Pacific Insurance Co. of New York	New York	April 14, 1815	S.		Cap. $500,000.
Palladium Fire Insurance Co.	New York	April 20, 1832	S.	f.	Cap. $300,000. Reincorporated May 3, 1839. Cap. $250,000.
Pelican Mutual Insurance Co	New York	April 10, 1843			
Phœnix Insurance Co. of New York	New York	Feb. 20, 1807	......	f. l. m. n.	Cap. $500,000.
Phœnix Fire Insurance Co	New York	March 29, 1823	S.		Original cap. $250,000. Changed to North America Fire Insurance Co. April 8, 1836.
People's Ins. Co. of the State of N. Y.	Kingston	May 14, 1851	......		Receiver appointed March, 1854.
Poughkeepsie Insurance Co	Poughkeepsie	April 8, 1825	S.	f. n.	Cap. $100,000.
Protection Fire Insurance Co.	New York	April 7, 1824			
Renovation Fire Insurance of the City of New York	New York	March 31, 1836	S.		Cap. $300,000.
Rensselaer County Mutual Ins. Co.	Lansingburgh	April 29, 1836	M.		Reorganized Oct. 11, 1851. Receiver appointed Feb. 1855.
Rensselaer Insurance Co	Lansingburgh	April 15, 1852	S.		Cap. $50,000.
Rensselaer & Saratoga Ins. Co.a	Troy	April 15, 1819	S.	f. l. n.	Cap. originally, $500,000. Closed up.
Rochester Insurance Co	Rochester	March 20, 1852	......	f.	Changed from Farmers & Merchants' Insurance Co. of Western N. Y.
Saratoga County Mutual Fire Ins. Co.	Saratoga Springs	May 5, 1834	M.	f.	Receiver appointed Jan. 1857.
Salem Fire Insurance Co.	Salem	July, 1852	......	f.	
Schenectady & Saratoga Ins. Co.		May 6, 1834	S.	f. n.	Cap. $500,000. Stopped issuing policies by act May 25, 1841.
Schenectady County Mutual Ins. Co.	Schenectady	May 26, 1841	M.		Changed by dropping "County Mutual" April 7, 1858. Extended 30 years.
Schoharie Mutual Insurance Co.	Schoharie	April 22, 1831	......		Revived May 9, 1836.
Schoharie County Mutual Ins. Co.	Cobleskill	Dec. 3, 1850	M.		Receiver appointed.
Sea Insurance Co	New York	May 5, 1834	S.	m. n.	Cap. $250,000. Time for final dividend extended 1840 to June 28, 1841.
Seneca County Mutual Ins. Co.	Waterloo	April 12, 1839	M.	f.	Cap. $250,000.
Seventh Ward Fire Insurance Co.	New York	April 29, 1839	S.	f.	
Seventeenth Ward Fire Ins. Co.	New York	April 9, 1838	S.	f. n.	Cap. $200,000. Changed to National Fire Insurance Co. May 24, 1841.
Steuben County Mutual Ins. Co.		March 29, 1837			
Steuben Farmers & Merchants' Insurance Co.	Bath	Sept. 29, 1851	......		Receiver appointed Nov. 1856.
Susquehanna Fire Insurance Co.b	Albany	Aug. 1854	S.		Changed from Cooperstown Feb. 1855. Receiver appointed.
Syracuse Insurance Co.	Syracuse	April 26, 1833	S.		Cap. $100,000.
Tioga County Mutual Insurance Co.	Owego	April 1, 1837	M.		

a Capital reduced from $199,880.90 to $87,536.45 by the great Troy fire of 1820. Life insurance taken away in 1831. Directed to close up by act of April 18, 1843.
b See Comptroller's Report, 1858, p. 45.

Class III. includes those whose certificates are filed in the Banking Department.

"*An Act to authorize the* **Business of Banking**" was passed April 18, 1838, and was modified April 12, 1851, upon the creation of a Bank Department. Reports previously made to the Comptroller are now made to this Department. In 1853 the articles of association previously filed in the Secretary's office were transferred to this department.[1]

Individuals or copartners may obtain bills from the department for circulation as individual bankers, and are liable to the full extent of their property for the redemption of the notes and the payment of the debts of such private banks. The name of individual banks must now be that of their owners; and the privilege cannot be sold, or the bills be signed by an agent. It may, however, be

Obsolete Insurance Companies, continued.

NAME.	Location.	Date of act of incorporation or of filing articles.	Stock or Mutual.		Remarks.
Tompkins County Mutual Ins. Co....	Ithaca................	April 25, 1840	M.		
Traders' Ins. Co. in the City of N. Y.	New York..........	March 9, 1825	S.	f. n.	Cap. $250,000.
Tradesmen's Insurance Co. in the City of New York....................	New York..........	March 14, 1825	S.	f. n.	Cap. $200,000.
Triton Insurance Co.....................	New York..........	April 4, 1838	S.	f. m. n.	Cap. $250,000. Reduced to $150,000 May 26, 1841.
Tontine Fire Insurance Co.............	New York..........	May, 1855	......		Receiver appointed Oct. 1856.
Troy Insurance Co........................	Troy.................	April 5, 1831	S.	f. m. n.	Cap. $200,000. Directed to close up by act of April 21, 1840.
Troy Mutual Safety Insurance Co....	Troy.................	May 7, 1844			
Trust Fire Insurance Co................	New York..........	April 25, 1830	S.		Cap. $150,000.
Tempest Insurance Co....................	Meridian............	Jan. 29, 1853	......		A committee appointed in 1855 could not find the books or Secretary of this Co.
Trust Fire Insurance Co................	New York..........	April 25, 1839	S.	f. n.	Changed from Eighth Ward Fire Ins. Co. Cap. may increase $200,000.
Unadilla Mutual Insurance Co.........	Unadilla............	May 12, 1836	M.	f.	
Union Fire Insurance Co. of the City of New York......................	New York..........	April 24, 1833	S.	f.	Cap. $400,000.
Union Insurance Co.......................	New York..........	March 18, 1818	S.	l. ann.	Cap. $500,000. In 1837 extended to Jan. 1, 1862.
Union Mutual Ins. Co. at Fort Plain	Fort Plain	May 21, 1850	M.		Changed to Union Insurance Co. July 8, 1851.
United Insurance Co......................	New York..........	May 14, 1840	S.	m. n.	Cap. $500,000.
United Ins. Co. in the City of N. Y...	New York..........	March 10, 1798	S.	f. l. m.	Cap. $500,000. Twice extended.
United States Insurance Co. of the City of New York.................	New York..........	March 31, 1837	S.	} m.	Cap. $1,000,000. Fire risks allowed May 5, 1840.
United States Mutual Insurance Co.	West Potsdam....	Nov. 8, 1850	M.		Receiver appointed Feb. 1855.
United States Insurance Co.............	Saratoga Springs	Feb. 22, 1851	M.		Receiver appointed Feb. 1859.
Utica Insurance Co	Utica................	March 29, 1816		f. m. n.	Receiver to be appointed by act of May 26, 1841.
Utica Live Stock Insurance Co.........	Utica	April 12, 1852	S.	(insured live stock.) Cap. $25,000.	
Washington County Mutual Ins. Co.	Granville...........	April 22, 1837	M.		Reorganized Dec. 13, 1849. Receiver appointed Sept. 1856.
Washington Insurance Co...............	New York..........	April 29, 1839	S.		Cap. $250,000.
Washington County Insurance Co...	....	April 24, 1832	S.	f.	Cap. $50,000.
Washington Marine Insurance Co. of the City of New York.........	New York..........	April 27, 1833	S.	} m.	Cap. $300,000. Reduced to $100,000, 1833, and changed to Marine Mutual Fire Insurance Co. Allowed to take fire risks April 27 1833.
Washington Mutual Assurance Co. of the City of New York..........	New York..........	March 30, 1802	S.	f.	
Washington Mutual Insurance Co.....	New York..........	April 11, 1842	M.		
Wayne County Mutual Ins. Co........	....	May 12, 1836			
Webster Fire Insurance Co.............	New York..........	March, 1855	......		Referee appointed Sept. 1855.
Western Fire Insurance Co.............	Canandaigua......	April 3, 1824	S.	f	Cap. $250,000.
Western Insurance Co. of Olean......	Olean	Jan. 22, 1853	......		Receiver appointed Dec. 1855.
Western Insurance Co. of the village of Buffalo.............................	Buffalo.............	April 7, 1817	......	f. m. n.	Cap. not over $400,000.
Western New York Agricultural Live Stock Insurance Co.	Cleveland, Oswego co.............	April 15, 1852			
Williamsburgh Fire Insurance Co....	Williamsburgh....	April 17, 1843	S.	f.	
Yates County Mutual Insurance Co...	....	March 9, 1837	M.	f.	

[1] The first bank organized in the State was the Bank of New York, which had existed several years previously as a private partnership. In many of the earlier banks the State reserved the right of subscribing stock, and of appointing directors to represent their interest in proportion to the amount held. Banking powers could only be enjoyed by special act of the Legislature, and were commonly limited to a period of 30 years. In 1838 a general law was enacted, allowing the organization of associations for banking, upon depositing the requisite securities with the Comptroller and filing articles of association in the Secretary's Office. Up to the date of the general law, 106 banks had been created,—of which 31 are still in existence, 36 have reorganized, and 39 have failed, closed, or changed their names. The Manhattan Co., created "for supplying the city of New York with pure and wholesome water," and the New York Dry Dock Co. possess perpetual banking powers. Other corporations for manufacturing or commercial purposes were allowed like privileges for limited periods, all of which have expired. In 1829 a "safety fund" was created, by requiring an annual contribution of ½ per cent. of its capital paid in from each bank formed or extended after that time, until each had paid 3 per cent. This fund was placed in charge of the Comptroller, and applied to the redemption of the bills of insolvent banks contributing to this fund, after their other means had been ex-

bequeathed.　All banks, excepting those in New York, Brooklyn, Albany, and Troy, must have an agency in New York, Albany, or Troy, for the redemption of their bills within one-fourth of one per cent. of par.

hausted. The bank fund has long since been exhausted, the draft upon it far exceeding the income. In 1848, 11 insolvent banks, which had contributed but $86,282 to this fund, had drawn from it $2,577,927.—*Comptroller's Report*, 1848, *p.* 55.

The same law provided for the appointment of 3 Bank Commissioners, who were required to visit the banks thrice annually, to ascertain their condition, take measures to secure the public against fraud or loss, and report annually to the Legislature. This office was abolished April 18, 1843, and the Comptroller was invested with general powers relating to banks, from which he was relieved by the creation of a special Bank Department in 1851. This department is under a superintendent appointed by the Governor and Senate for 3 years. It has the custody of all plates for printing bank bills; registers, numbers, and issues to banks such bills as their charters and securities entitle them to; destroys the same when withdrawn from circulation; and destroys the plates when the bank is closed. It appoints special agents for examining the condition of doubtful banks, directs prosecutions in behalf of the State, sells the securities of broken banks to redeem their circulation, and reports the condition of banks to the Legislature annually. Banks can only obtain bills for circulation by depositing New York State or United States stocks bearing interest equivalent to 6 per cent., or bonds and mortgages of not over $5,000 each upon unincumbered improved lands at two-fifths value, exclusive of buildings, and bearing 7 per cent. interest. Closing banks, after calling in 90 per cent. of their

circulation, may withdraw their stocks or mortgages, and substitute cash for the redemption of the remaining 10 per cent. of circulation. Stockholders of banking associations are personally liable to an extent equal to their capital stock. Experience has shown that under our free bank system bonds and mortgages have realized but about 88 per cent. on the sum for which notes were issued, while the aggregate securities, including stocks, have almost always sold for more than enough to redeem the circulation based upon them.—*Report*, 1859, *p.* 8.

Bank Note Engraving is now done by a company, formed in 1858 by the union of most of the establishments previously existing.

The Bank of the United States had branches for discount and deposit at New York, Utica, and Buffalo, in this State.

Specie payment has been generally suspended three times by the banks of New York State. In the fall of 1814 all the banks of the Union, except those of New England, suspended until the spring of 1817. In May, 1837, there was a second suspension, which continued until the spring of 1838. On the 13th of Oct. 1857, a third suspension took place in all the banks of New York City, with one exception, (Chemical Bank,) and this was soon followed by the banks of the State generally; but specie payment was resumed in about 60 days.

The following tables, derived from returns in the Bank Department, are corrected up to Jan. 1, 1859. The amount of capital is reported for Dec. 18, 1858:

Existing Banks in the State, Jan. 1, 1859.

CORPORATE NAME.	Location.	C.—Chartered by law. A.—Associated free bank. I.—Individual bank.	Of filing articles.	Of beginning business or of act of incorporation.	Of expiration of charter or privilege.	Original capital, in thousands of dollars.	Present capital.	S.—Stocks of N.Y. or U.S. S.E.—Stocks and real estate.
Addison Bank	Addison	I.		May 17, 1856	Jan. 1, 1864		$ 50,000	S. E.
Albany City Bank	Albany	C.		April 30, 1834	Jan. 1, 1854	500	500,000	
Albany Exchange Bank	Albany	A.	Dec. 12, 1838	Jan. 1, 1839	Jan. 1, 2500	100	311,100	S. E.
American Exchange Bank	New York	A.	Oct. 1, 1838	Sept. 14, 1838	Sept. 14, 1938	500	4,999,550	S.
Artisans' Bank[a]	New York	A.	Aug. 22, 1856	July 10, 1856	July 1, 1956	500	660,000	S.
Atlantic Bank	Brooklyn	C.		March 10, 1836	Jan. 1, 1866	500	500,000	
Atlantic Bank of the City of New York	New York	A.	May 27, 1853	July 2, 1853	July 2, 1953	400	400,000	S.
Auburn City Bank	Auburn	A.	July 6, 1853	July 25, 1853	July 5, 1953	200	200,000	S.
Auburn Exchange Bank	Auburn	A.	Feb. 16, 1856	Feb. 1, 1856	Jan. 1, 1956	150	200,000	S.
Ballston Spa Bank[b]	Ballston Spa	A.	Jan. 31, 1839	Dec. 10, 1838	Dec. 10, 1938	100	125,000	S. E.
Bank of Albany[b]	Albany	A.	Dec. 15, 1854	Dec. 30, 1854	Jan. 1, 1904	360	500,340	S.
Bank of Albion	Albion	A.	July 16, 1839	July 15, 1839	Jan. 2, 2039	100	100,000	S. E.
Bank of America[c]	New York	A.	Dec. 30, 1852	Dec. 1, 1852	Jan. 1, 1953	2,000	3,000,000	S.
Bank of Attica	Buffalo	A.	April 24, 1850	March 1, 1850	Jan. 1, 2000	160	250,000	S. E.
Bank of Auburn[d]	Auburn	A.	Jan. 2, 1850	Dec. 31, 1849	Jan. 1, 1950	200	200,000	S.
Bank of Bath	Bath	I.		April 11, 1854			50,000	S. E.
Bank of Binghamton	Binghamton	A.	Nov. 17, 1852	July 29, 1852	Jan. 1, 2000	150	200,000	S. E.
Bank of Canandaigua	Canandaigua	I.		April 4, 1854			26,000	S. E.
Bank of the Capitol	Albany	A.	Jan. 3, 1853	Feb. 1, 1853	Jan. 1, 2000	150	519,600	S.
Bank of Cayuga Lake[e]	Painted Post	I.	1847	Sept. 1847			10,000	S.
Bank of Cazenovia	Cazenovia	A.	Feb. 28, 1856	Feb. 21, 1856	Jan. 1, 1900	120	120,000	S. E.
Bank of Central New York	Utica	A.	Sept. 17, 1838	Sept. 8, 1838	Jan. 15, 1889	100	110,200	S.
Bank of Chemung	Elmira	A.	Dec. 11, 1852	Jan. 1, 1853	Jan. 1, 1893	100	50,000	S. E.
Bank of Chenango[f]	Norwich	A.	Dec. 28, 1855	Dec. 31, 1855	Jan. 1, 1956	120	150,000	S. E.
Bank of Cohoes	Cohoes	A.	March 18, 1859					
Bank of Commerce in New York	New York	A.	Feb. 15, 1839	Jan. 1, 1839	Jan. 1, 1889	5,000	8,851,760	S.
Bank of Commerce of Putnam County	Carmel	I.		April, 1853			63,012	S. E.
Bank of Cooperstown	Cooperstown	A.	Feb. 1, 1853	Jan. 1, 1853	Jan. 1, 1953	150	200,000	S. E.
Bank of the Commonwealth	New York	A.	March 22, 1853	March 1, 1853	March 1, 1953	750	750,000	S.
Bank of Corning	Corning	A.	Jan. 17, 1839	Jan. 12, 1839	Jan. 12, 1939	117	78,500	S. E.
Bank of Coxsackie	Coxsackie	A.	March 14, 1853	March 4, 1853	Jan. 1, 1900	120	142,000	S. E.
Bank of Dansville	Dansville	A.	June 10, 1839	June 10, 1839	June 10, 1539	100	150,250	S. E.
Bank of Fayetteville	Fayetteville	A.	Jan. 19, 1854	Jan. 9, 1854	Jan. 9, 1954	110	115,400	S. E.
Bank of Fishkill	Fishkill	A.	Feb. 28, 1850	June 1, 1850	Dec. 31, 1899	120	150,000	S.
Bank of Fort Edward	Fort Edward	A.	Oct. 3, 1851	Oct. 1, 1851	In year 1951	100	200,000	S. E.
Bank of Genesee[g]	Batavia	A.	Dec. 22, 1851	Dec. 1, 1851	Dec. 31, 1951	100	150,000	S. E.

[a] Articles amended May 11, 1857.
[b] First incorp. April 10, 1792; cap. $40,000; allowed to reduce two-fifths April 4, 1820, and shares reduced from $400 to $30 April 17, 1830; twice extended; expired Jan. 1, 1855; State reserved right to subscribe stock at first.
[c] First incorp. June 2, 1812; cap. $6,000,000, and late United States Bank allowed to take five-sixths of the stock; reduced to $4,000,000 March 20, 1813; once extended.
[d] First incorp. March 31, 1817; cap. $400,000; once extended; expired Jan. 1, 1850.
[e] Started at Ithaca.
[f] First incorp. April 21, 1818; cap. $200,000; once extended; expired Jan. 1, 1856.
[g] First incorp. April 29, 1829; cap. $100,000; expired Jan. 1, 1852.

Existing Banks, continued.

Corporate Name.	Location.	C.—Chartered by law. A.—Associated free bank. I.—Individual bank.	Dates			Original capital, in thousands of dollars.	Present capital.	Securities—S.—Stocks of N.Y. or U.S. S.E.—Stocks and real estate.
			Of filing articles.	Of beginning business or of act of incorporation.	Of expiration of charter or privilege.			
Bank of Geneva*a*	Geneva	A.	Nov. 20, 1852	Nov. 15, 1852	Jan. 1, 1900	205	$205,000	S. E.
Bank of Havana	Havana	I.		April 4, 1851			50,000	S. E.
Bank of the Interior	Albany	A.	June 4, 1857	June 1, 1857	May 1, 1957	700	251,550	S.
Bank of Kent	Ludingtonville	A.	March 15, 1856	Feb. 27, 1856	Feb. 27, 1955	100	111,940	S. E.
Bank of Kinderhook	Kinderhook	A.	Dec. 19, 1838	Dec. 15, 1838	Jan. 2, 1839	125	250,000	S. E.
Bank of Lansingburgh*b*	Lansingburgh	A.	June 22, 1855	June 1, 1855	July 1, 1955	120	150,000	S. E.
Bank of Lima	Lima	I.		Feb. 6, 1857			50,000	S. E.
Bank of Lowville	Lowville	A.	Dec. 26, 1838	Dec. 18, 1838	Nov. 1, 2301	100	102,450	S. E.
Bank of Malone	Malone	A.	Aug. 18, 1851	Aug. 6, 1851	Jan. 1, 1900	100	196,800	S. E.
Bank of Newark	Newark	A.	April 6, 1854	April 1, 1854	Dec. 31, 1900	100	100,000	S. E.
Bank of Newburgh*c*	Newburgh	A.	Dec. 17, 1850	Jan. 1, 1851	Jan. 1, 1951	200	300,000	S. E.
Bank of Newport	Newport	A.	April 2, 1858	March 28, 1858	March 25, 1908	100	50,025	S. E.
Bank of New York*d*	New York	A.	Dec. 21, 1852	Dec. 22, 1852	Jan. 1, 1953	2,000	2,838,975	S.
Bank of North America*e*	New York	A.	April 11, 1851	April 10, 1851	Jan. 1, 1951	1,000	1,000,000	S.
Bank of Norwich	Norwich	A.	Feb. 21, 1856	July 15, 1856	July 1, 2056	125	125,000	
Bank of Old Saratoga*f*	Schuylerville	A.	Jan. 23, 1858	Jan. 1, 1856	Jan. 1, 1958	110	105,850	S. E.
Bank of Orange County*g*	Goshen	C.		April 6, 1813	Jan. 1, 1862	*	105,660	
Bank of Owego	Owego	C.		May 21, 1836	Jan. 1, 1866	200	200,000	
Bank of Pawling	Pawling	A.	April 4, 1849	Sept. 3, 1849	Sept. 3, 1899	125	175,000	S. E.
Bank of Port Jervis	Port Jervis	A.	Feb. 4, 1853	March 1, 1853	March 1, 1953	120	130,000	S.
Bank of Poughkeepsie*f*	Poughkeepsie	A.	Dec. 31, 1857	Dec. 31, 1857	Jan. 1, 1958	200	200,000	S.
Bank of the Republic	New York	A.	Jan. 25, 1850	Feb. 1, 1851	Jan. 1, 1951	1,000	2,000,000	S.
Bank of Rhinebeck	Rhinebeck	A.	June 1, 1853	June 1, 1853	Dec. 31, 1899	125	125,000	S.
Bank of Rome	Rome	C.		April 16, 1832	Jan. 1, 1862	100	100,000	
Bank of Rondout	Rondout	A.	Oct. 5, 1848	Sept. 1, 1848	Sept. 5, 1898	100	150,000	S.
Bank of Salem	Salem	A.	May 17, 1853	May 10, 1853	Jan. 1, 1950	100	138,000	S. E.
Bank of Salina	Syracuse	C.		April 20, 1832	Jan. 1, 1862	150	150,000	
Bank of Saratoga Springs*h*	Saratoga Springs	A.	May 11, 1852	May 1, 1852	May 1, 1952	100	100,000	S.
Bank of Seneca Falls	Seneca Falls	I.		May, 1854			80,000	S. E.
Bank of Silver Creek	Silver Creek	A.	Oct. 25, 1839	Oct. 15, 1839	In year 2500	100	100,800	S. E.
Bank of Sing Sing	Sing Sing	A.	July 13, 1853	Aug. 1, 1853	Dec. 31, 1953	125	150,000	S.
Bank of the State of New York	New York	C.		May 18, 1836	Jan. 1, 1866	2,000	2,000,000	
Bank of Syracuse	Syracuse	A.	Sept. 26, 1838	Sept. 15, 1838	Sept. 15, 2338	100	200,000	S. E.
Bank of Tioga	Owego	A.	June 20, 1856	June 14, 1856	June 14, 1956	100	100,000	S.
Bank of Troy*i*	Troy	A.	Nov. 6, 1852	Dec. 1, 1852	Jan. 1, 1952	440	440,000	S. E.
Bank of Ulster	Ulster Village	A.	June 17, 1852	July 6, 1852	June 1, 1950	100	150,000	S. E.
Bank of Utica*j*	Utica	A.	Dec. 18, 1849	Dec. 1, 1849	Jan. 1, 1950	600	600,000	S. E.
Bank of Vernon	Vernon	A.	Jan. 14, 1839	Jan. 1, 1839	Jan. 1, 1939	100	100,000	S. E.
Bank of Watertown	Watertown	A.	Jan. 26, 1839	Jan. 17, 1839	Jan. 17, 2340	100	47,779	S. E.
Bank of Waterville	Waterville	A.	Dec. 10, 1838	Oct. 1, 1838	Oct. 1, 2838	100	120,000	S. E.
Bank of Westfield	Westfield	I.		April 12, 1848			50,000	S. E.
Bank of West Troy	West Troy	A.	April 26, 1852	May 1, 1852	May 1, 1900	200	250,000	S. E.
Bank of Whitehall*k*	Whitehall	A.	June 14, 1859					
Bank of Whitestown	Whitesboro	A.	Feb. 28, 1839	Feb. 25, 1839	Feb. 25, 2839	100	120,000	S. E.
Bank of Yonkers	Yonkers	A.	June 26, 1854	July 10, 1854	Dec. 31, 1953	150	150,000	S.
Black River Bank	Watertown	A.	June 16, 1851	June 1, 1851	Jan. 1, 1890	100	100,000	S. E.
Briggs Bank of Clyde	Clyde	I.		Sept. 21, 1855			62,611	S. E.
Broadway Bank	New York	A.	Aug. 15, 1849	Aug. 9, 1849	Aug. 9, 1950	500	1,000,000	S.
Brockport Exchange Bank.	Brockport	I.		July, 1852			50,000	S. E.
Brooklyn Bank	Brooklyn	C.		Feb. 24, 1832	Jan. 1, 1860	200	150,000	
Broome County Bank*l*	Binghamton	A.	Dec. 17, 1854	Dec. 31, 1854	Jan. 1, 1954	100	100,000	S.
Buffalo City Bank	Buffalo	A.	Feb. 22, 1853	March 1, 1853	Jan. 1, 2000	100	277,700	S. E.
Bull's Head Bank of the City of New York	New York	A.	July 18, 1854	1854	Dec. 31, 1953	300	173,300	S.
Burnet Bank	Syracuse	I.		Oct. 12, 1852			93,400	S. E.
Butchers & Drovers' Bank in the City of New York*m*	New York	A.	Dec. 16, 1852	Dec. 22, 1852	Dec. 31, 1953	600	800,000	S.
Cambridge Valley Bank at North White Creek	White Creek	A.	June 20, 1855	Sept. 3, 1855	Jan. 1, 1905	115	168,339	S. E.
Canajoharie Bank	Canajoharie	A.	Nov. 30, 1855	April 3, 1855	April 3, 1955	100	125,000	S. E.
Canastota Bank	Canastota	A.	Feb. 28, 1856	April 1, 1856	Jan. 1, 2000	110	110,000	S. E.
Cataract Bank	Lockport	A.	Sept. 16, 1858	Sept. 20, 1858	Sept. 1, 1958	100	40,000	S. E.
Catskill Bank*n*	Catskill	A.	Dec. 28, 1852	Dec. 31, 1852	Jan. 1, 1899	†	128,962	S.
Cayuga County Bank	Auburn	C.		March 14, 1833	Jan. 1, 1900	250	250,000	

a First incorp. March 28, 1817; cap. $400,000; once extended; expired Jan. 1, 1853.
b First incorp. March 19, 1813; cap. $200,000; once extended; expired July 1, 1855.
c First incorp. March 22, 1811.
d First bank in State; incorp. March 22, 1791; cap. $900,000; thrice extended; expired Jan. 1, 1853.
e A bank of similar name filed Jan. 7, 1839; cap. $100,000; did not organize.
f Begun as an individual bank.
g Once extended.
h Individual bank of this title begun 1847.
i First incorp. March 22, 1811; cap. $500,000; allowed to open offices of discount and deposit at Waterford and Lansinburgh; once extended; expired Jan. 1, 1853; State reserved right to take stock.
j First incorp. June 1, 1812; cap. $1,000,000; once extended; allowed to open a branch at Canandaigua April 10, 1815; State reserved right to take stock.
k Organized in place of Safety Fund Bank of same name whose charter expired June 13, 1859.
l First incorp. Apr. 18, 1831; cap. $100,000; expired Jan. 1, 1855.
m Butchers & Drovers' Bank incorp. April 8, 1830; cap. $300,000, increased to $500,000; expired Jan. 1, 1853.
n First incorp. March 26, 1813; cap. $400,000; once extended: expired Jan. 1, 1853.

* $105,660. † $110,007.

Existing Banks, continued.

| CORPORATE NAME. | Location. | C.—Chartered by law. A.—Associated free bank. I.—Individual bank. | DATES | | | Original capital, in thousands of dollars. | Present capital. | Securities— S.—Stocks of N. Y. or U. S. S. E.—Stocks and real estate. |
			Of filing articles.	Of beginning business or of act of incorporation.	Of expiration of charter or privilege.			
Central Bank of Brooklyn..	Brooklyn............	A.	April 9, 1853	Aug. 1, 1853	July 31, 1953	200	$200,000	S.
Central Bank at Cherry Valley*....................	Cherry Valley.....	A.	Dec. 13, 1854	Dec. 14, 1854	Jan. 1, 1955	200	200,000	S. E.
Central Bank of Troy	Troy	A.	Feb. 5, 1853	May 1, 1853	May 1, 2353	200	300,000	S. E.
Central City Bank*............	Syracuse............	A.	May 12, 1852	May 12, 1852	May 12, 1952	110	125,200	S. E.
Chatham Bank...................	New York..........	A.	Feb. 6, 1851	Feb. 20, 1851	Jan. 1, 1899	300	450,000	S.
Chautauqua County Bank..	Jamestown........	C.	....	April 18, 1831	Jan. 1, 1860	100	100,000	
Chemical Bank...................	New York..........	A.	Feb. 5, 1844	Feb. 24, 1844	Jan. 1, 1899	300	300,000	S.
Chemung Canal Bank.......	Elmira...............	C.	....	April 9, 1833	....	200	200,000	
Chester Bank.....................	East Chester	A.	May 11, 1846	May 1, 1846	May 1, 2500	100	125,500	S. E.
Chittenango Bank	Chittenango	A.	Feb. 4, 1853	April 1, 1853	Jan. 1, 2000	105	150,000	S. E.
Citizens' Bank*.................	Fulton	A.	Sept. 8, 1853	Aug. 20, 1853	Dec. 31, 1953	125	166,100	S. E.
Citizens' Bank...................	New York..........	A.	May 3, 1851	May 1, 1851	Jan. 1, 1951	300	400,000	S.
City Bank of Brooklyn.....	Brooklyn............	A.	Nov. 6, 1850	Dec. 14, 1850	Jan. 1, 1950	150	300,000	S.
City Bank of New York* ...	New York..........	A.	May 26, 1852	July 1, 1852	Jan. 1, 1952	800	1,000,000	S.
City Bank...........................	Oswego	A.	Dec. 17, 1849	Nov. 1, 1849	Nov. 1, 2049	125	276,400	S. E.
Clinton Bank of Buffalo.....	Buffalo	A.	July 3, 1856	Aug. 1, 1856	July 1, 2000	250	253,000	S. E.
Commercial Bank of Albany*...........................	Albany	A.	July 3, 1847	July 1, 1847	Jan. 1, 2000	300	500,000	S.
Commercial Bank of Clyde.	Clyde.................	I.	....	Nov. 1850	....	......	25,000	S. E.
Commercial Bank of Glens Falls...........................	Glens Falls........	A.	April 28, 1853	April 28, 1853	Jan. 1, 1954	150	136,400	S. E.
Commercial Bank of Rochester...........................	Rochester...........	A.	April 8, 1839	Nov. 7, 1838	Nov. 7, 1938	400	500,000	S. E.
Commercial Bank of Saratoga Springs.................	Saratoga Springs	A.	Feb. 18, 1856	Feb. 1, 1856	Feb. 1, 1956	125	125,000	S.
Commercial Bank of Troy..	Troy	A.	Jan. 8, 1839	Jan. 5, 1839	In year 2000	100	300,000	S. E.
Commercial Bank of Whitehall............................	Whitehall...........	A.	Aug. 5, 1849	Aug. 15, 1849	Jan. 1, 2500	*	108,200	S.
Continental Bank..............	New York..........	A.	Jan. 24, 1853	Jan. 24, 1853	Jan. 1, 1953	1,500	2,000,000	S.
Corn Exchange Bank..........	New York..........	A.	Dec. 21, 1852	Jan. 1, 1853	Jan. 1, 1950	500	1,000,000	S.
Croton River Bank............	Brewster Station	A.	March 21, 1856	March 15, 1856	March 15, 1956	100	107,500	S. E.
Cuba Bank........................	Cuba..................	A.	June 20, 1855	June 1, 1855	June 1, 1900	100	100,000	S. E.
Cuyler's Bank...................	Palmyra.............	A.	April 9, 1853	April 15, 1853	Jan. 1, 1900	100	74,000	S. E.
Delaware Bank..................	Delhi..................	A.	March 21, 1839	Jan. 1, 1839	Jan. 1, 1939	100	150,000	S.
Deposit Bank*...................	Deposit	A.	Nov. 12, 1856	Oct. 1, 1856	Jan. 1, 1959	125	125,000	S. E.
Dover Plains Bank.............	Dover	A.	Feb. 12, 1857	March 15, 1858	March 1, 2000	100	100,000	S.
East River Bank*..............	New York..........	A.	Sept. 11, 1852	Sept. 8, 1852	Sept. 18, 1952	300	206,525	S.
Elmira Bank.....................	Elmira	A.	April 22, 1854	Nov. 1, 1853	Jan. 1, 1953	200	100,000	S. E.
Essex County Bank*..........	Keeseville	C.	....	April 25, 1832	Jan. 1, 1862	100	100,000	
Exchange Bank at Lockport.............................	Lockport	A.	Nov. 12, 1851	July 1, 1851	In year 2000	150	150,000	S. E.
Fallkill Bank....................	Poughkeepsie.....	A.	June 17, 1852	April 1, 1852	July 1, 1952	150	200,000	S.
Farmers' Bank of Amsterdam.............................	Amsterdam	A.	April 26, 1839	April 10, 1839	April 10, 1939	100	118,000	S. E.
Farmers' Bank of Attica...	Attica	I.	....	May 7, 1856	....	......	54,533	S. E.
Farmers' Bank of Hudson..	Hudson..............	A.	Feb. 7, 1839	March 1, 1839	Dec. 31, 1900	100	300,000	S. E.
Farmers' Bank of Lansingburgh	Lansingburgh	A.	March 31, 1854	April 1, 1854	April 1, 1954	200	171,300	S. E.
Farmers' Bank of Saratoga County	....	A.	....	....	....	......	200,000	S. E.
Farmers' Bank of the City of Troy*......................	Troy	A.	Nov. 13, 1852	Dec. 1, 1852	Jan. 1, 1950	350	350,000	S.
Farmers' Bank of Washington County..................	Fort Edward......	A.	June 30, 1856	Jan. 1, 1856	Jan. 1, 1956	100	168,650	S. E.
Farmers & Citizens' Bank of Long Island*............	Williamsburgh...	A.	June 21, 1852	July 3, 1852	July 3, 2000	200	200,000	S.
Farmers & Drovers' Bank..	Somers	A.	July 16, 1839	March 16, 1839	In year 1950	†	111,150	S. E.
Farmers & Manufacturers' Bank	Poughkeepsie	C.	....	April 26, 1834	Jan. 1, 1864	300	300,000	
Farmers & Mechanics' Bank of Genesee*...................	Buffalo	A.	Dec. 13, 1838	Nov. 1, 1838	Nov. 1, 2000	100	150,000	S. E.
Farmers & Mechanics' Bank of Rochester...............	Rochester..........	A.	March 15, 1839	Feb. 12, 1839	Jan. 1, 3838	100	125,000	S. E.
Flour City Bank...............	Rochester...........	A.	March 4, 1856	March 1, 1856	Jan. 1, 1956	200	300,000	S. E.
Fort Plain Bank...............	Fort Plain	A.	Jan. 2, 1839	Jan. 1, 1839	Jan. 1, 2001	100	150,000	S. E.
Fort Stanwix Bank...........	Rome	A.	Nov. 5, 1847	Nov. 6, 1847	Nov. 3, 2347	110	150,000	S. E.
Frankfort Bank.................	Frankfort...........	A.	Feb. 6, 1854	May 15, 1854	May 15, 2354	105	105,000	S. E.
Fredonia Bank..................	Fredonia.............	A.	July 2, 1856	Aug. 1, 1856	May 1, 2000	100	100,000	S. E.
Frontier Bank..................	Potsdam.............	A.	April 29, 1854	April 30, 1854	Jan. 1, 1899	100	100,000	S. E.

---

a.Cherry Valley Bank incorp. April 21, 1818; cap. $200,000; changed to Central Bank; once extended; expired Jan. 1, 1855.
b Changed from Crouse Bank Feb. 3, 1857.
c Removed from Ogdensburgh.
d City Bank incorp. June 16, 1812; cap. $2,000,000; twice extended; expired July 1, 1852; cap. reduced one half March 24, 1820, and afterward to $720,000.
e Commercial Bank incorp. April 12, 1825; cap. $300,000; once extended; expired July 1, 1847.

f An individual bank merged in association.
g Allowed to reduce cap. to $313.918 March 7, 1836.
h Allowed to increase cap. to $400,000 May 10, 1836.
i Farmers' Bank incorp. March 31, 1801; cap. $250,000; State reserved right to take stock; twice extended; expired Jan. 1, 1853.
j Increased to $300,000 March 9, 1854; afterward reduced.
k Removed from Batavia June 3, 1852

　　　* $108,200.　　　　　　　　　　　　　† $111,150.

Existing Banks, continued.

Corporate Name.	Location.	C.—Chartered by law. A.—Associated free bank. I.—Individual bank.	Dates Of filing articles.	Dates Of beginning business or of act of incorporation.	Dates Of expiration of charter or privilege.	Original capital, in thousands of dollars.	Present capital.	Securities—S.—Stocks of N. Y. or U. S. S. E.—Stocks and real estate.
Fulton Bank, in the City of New York[a]	New York	A.	Jan. 15, 1844	March 1, 1844	Jan. 1, 1899	600	$600,000	S. E.
Fulton County Bank	Gloversville	A.	April 28, 1852	March 23, 1852	March 23, 1952	150	150,000	S. E.
Genesee County Bank	Le Roy	A.	Dec. 19, 1838	Jan. 1, 1839	Jan. 1, 2000	100	200,000	S. E.
Genesee River Bank	Mount Morris	A.	Oct. 1, 1853	Oct. 5, 1853	Oct. 5, 1919	130	130,000	S. E.
Genesee Valley Bank	Geneseo	A.	May 6, 1851	May 10, 1851	Jan. 1, 2000	120	150,000	S. E.
Geo. Washington Bank	Corning	I.			1854		50,000	
Glens Falls Bank	Glens Falls	A.	Oct. 31, 1851	Oct. 31, 1851	Sept. 1, 1952	150	112,000	S. E.
Goshen Bank	Goshen	A.	Sept. 25, 1850	Nov. 1, 1851	Nov. 1, 1951	110	110,000	S.
Greenwich Bank of the City of New York[b]	New York	A.	May 30, 1855	June 4, 1855	June 7, 1954	200	200,000	S. E.
Grocers' Bank in the City of New York	New York	A.	Aug. 15, 1851	Aug. 1, 1851	Jan. 1, 1950	150	240,000	S.
Hamilton Bank	Hamilton	A.	Feb. 19, 1853	March 1, 1853	Jan. 1, 2053	110	110,000	S. E.
Hanover Bank	New York	A.	April 2, 1851	April 2, 1851	April 2, 1951	500	1,000,000	S.
Herkimer County Bank	Little Falls	C.		March 14, 1833	Jan. 1, 1863	200	200,000	
Highland Bank	Newburgh	C.		April 26, 1834	Jan. 1, 1864	200	200,000	
H. J. Miner & Co.'s Bank	Dunkirk	I.		Feb. 24, 1859				
H. T. Miner's Bank		I.					25,000	S.
Hudson River Bank[e]	Hudson	A.	April 23, 1855	May 8, 1855	May 10, 1955	200	250,000	S.
Huguenot Bk. of New Paltz	New Paltz	A.	April 25, 1853	June 1, 1853	July 1, 1953	125	125,000	S. E.
Hungerford's Bank[d]	Adams	A.	Sept. 17, 1853	Sept. 1, 1853	July 1, 1953	125	125,000	S. E.
Ilion Bank	Ilion	A.	Feb. 6, 1852	Feb. 2, 1852	Feb. 3, 2352	100	100,000	S. E.
Importers & Traders' Bank	New York	A.	Nov. 28, 1855	Dec. 1, 1855	Jan. 1, 1955	1,000	1,500,000	S. E.
International Bank	Buffalo	A.	May 11, 1854	June 1, 1854	Jan. 1, 1954	400	400,000	S. E.
Iron Bank	Plattsburgh	I.		July, 1853			50,000	S. E.
Irving Bank in the City of New York	New York	A.	March 29, 1851	March 31, 1851	Jan. 1, 1950	500	500,000	S. E.
Jamestown Bank	Jamestown	I.		Feb. 1853			92,915	S. E.
Jefferson County Bank[e]	Watertown	A.	Oct. 21, 1853	Dec. 31, 1853	Jan. 1, 1900	200	2,000,000	S. E.
J. N. Hungerford's Bank	Corning	I.	Feb. 9, 1859	March 16, 1859				
J. T. Raplee's Bank	Penn Yan	I.		July 15, 1858			50,000	S. E.
Judson Bank[d]	Ogdensburgh	A.	Aug. 1, 1854	July 1, 1854	July 1, 1904	132	122,000	S. E.
Kingston Bank	Kingston	C.		May 18, 1836	Jan. 1, 1866	200	200,000	
Lake Mahopac Bank	Mahopac	I.		April 15, 1854			40,850	S.
Lake Ontario Bank	Oswego	A.	March 17, 1857	March 12, 1857	March 12, 1957	250	325,000	S. E.
Lake Shore Bank	Dunkirk	I.		Jan. 1855			39,200	S. E.
Leather Manufacturers' B'k	New York	C.		April 23, 1832	June 1, 1862	600	600,000	
Leonardsville Bank	Leonardsville	A.	April 25, 1856	Feb. 27, 1856	Feb. 27, 2356	100	100,000	S.
Lockport City Bank[f]	Lockport	A.	May 13, 1859					
Long Island Bank[g]	Brooklyn	A.	June 16, 1845	June 16, 1845	July 1, 1890	200	400,000	S. E.
Lyons Bank[h]	Lyons	I.		Dec. 1843			48,609	S. E.
Manhattan Company[i]	New York	C.		April 2, 1799	Unlimited	2,000	2,050,000	
Manufacturers' Bank of Brooklyn[j]	Brooklyn	A.	April 19, 1853	March 6, 1853	May 1, 1903	250	150,000	
Manufacturers' Bank of Troy	Troy	A.	Aug. 12, 1852	April 22, 1852	July 1, 1952	200	250,000	S. E.
Manufacturers & Traders' Bank	Buffalo	A.	June 26, 1856	July 1, 1856	Jan. 1, 2000	200	495,000	S. E.
Marine Bank of Buffalo	Buffalo	A.	July 15, 1850	Aug. 1, 1850	Jan. 1, 2000	170	300,000	S. E.
Marine Bank, at Oswego	Oswego	A.	June 25, 1856	Aug. 20, 1856	Aug. 20, 2856	125	186,000	S. E.
Marine Bank of the City of New York	New York	A.	March 23, 1853	Jan. 1, 1853	Jan. 1, 1953	500	659,100	S.
Market Bank	New York	A.	Oct. 19, 1852	Aug. 30, 1852	Aug. 30, 1951	650	1,000,000	S.
Market Bank of Troy	Troy	A.	July 5, 1853	Sept. 2, 1853	Jan. 1, 1953	200	300,000	S. E.
Mechanics' Bank of Brooklyn	Brooklyn	A.	Aug. 12, 1852	Aug. 10, 1852	Jan. 1, 1952	200	300,000	S.
Mechanics' Bank of the City of New York[k]	New York	A.	Dec. 18, 1854	Jan. 1, 1855	Jan. 1, 1955	2,000	2,000,000	S.
Mechanics' Banking Association[l]	New York	A.	Aug. 1, 1838	Aug. 1, 1838	Aug. 1, 1938		316,000	S.
Mechanics' Bank of Syracuse	Syracuse	A.	Sept. 29, 1851	Aug. 28, 1851	Jan. 1, 1950	140	140,000	S. E.
Mechanics & Farmers' Bank of Albany[m]	Albany	A.	Nov. 4, 1852	Dec. 1, 1852	Jan. 1, 1950	350	350,000	S. E.
Mechanics & Traders' Bank in the City of New York.	New York	A.	Dec. 30, 1856	Jan. 2, 1857	Jan. 1, 1957	400	400,000	S.

[a] Fulton Bank incorp. April 1, 1824; cap. $500,000; increased to $750,000 March 16, 1827; expired March 1, 1844.
[b] Greenwich Bank incorp. April 17, 1830; cap. $200,000; expired June 6, 1853.
[c] First incorp. March 29, 1830; cap. $100,000; increased to $150,000 April 16, 1832; expired June 12, 1855.
[d] Originally an individual bank.
[e] First incorp. April 17, 1816; cap. $400,000, and located at Adams; failed; removed to Utica Nov. 19, 1824, and cap. reduced to $100,000; increased to $200,000 May 19, 1836; once extended; expired Jan. 1, 1854.
[f] Niagara River Bank, Buffalo, removed to Lockport, and name changed May 13, 1859.

[g] First incorp. April 1, 1824; cap. $300,000; once extended; expired July 1, 1845.
[h] Begun under the name of Palmyra Bank; changed name March 31, 1857.
[i] Chartered for supplying city with water, with perpetual banking privileges.
[j] Changed from Mechanics' Bank of Williamsburgh, and cap. reduced April 15, 1858.
[k] Mechanics' Bank first incorp. March 23, 1810; cap. $1,500,000; reduced to $1,440,000; once extended; expired Jan 1, 1855; State reserved right to take stock.
[l] Under Chap. 183, laws of 1858; original cap. $128,175.
[m] First incorp. March 22, 1811; cap. $600,000; reduced one-fourth April 4, 1820; once extended; expired Jan. 1, 1853.

Existing Banks, continued.

CORPORATE NAME.	Location.	C.—Chartered by law. A.—Associated free bank. I.—Individual bank.	Of filing articles.	Of beginning business or of act of incorporation.	Of expiration of charter or privilege.	Original capital, in thousands of dollars.	Present capital.	Securities— S.—Stock of N.Y. or U.S. S.E.—Stocks and real estate.
Medina Bank	Medina	I.		May, 1854			$ 50,000	S. E.
Mercantile Bank^a	New York	A.	Jan. 8, 1850	Jan. 8, 1850	Jan. 1, 1950	200	1,000,000	S.
Mercantile Bank of Plattsburgh	Plattsburgh	A.	Jan. 24, 1856	Jan. 1, 1856	Jan. 1, 1956	100	100,000	S.
Merchants' Bank of Albany	Albany	A.	Jan. 22, 1853	March 21, 1853	March 1, 1953	250	400,000	S.
Merchants' Bank of Erie County	Lancaster	I.		May, 1844			50,000	S. E.
Merchants' Bank in the City of New York^c	New York	A.	Dec. 24, 1856	Jan. 2, 1857	Jan. 1, 1957	1,500	2,638,975	S.
Merchants' Bank in Poughkeepsie	Poughkeepsie	A.	Jan. 19, 1845	July 2, 1845	July 1, 1895	110	150,000	S.
Merchants' Bank	Syracuse	A.	Feb. 21, 1851	Dec. 31, 1850	Dec. 31, 1950	135	180,000	S. E.
Merchants' Bank of Westfield^b	Westfield	I.		April, 1853			40,000	S. E.
Merchants' Exchange Bank in the City of New York^b	New York	A.	April 24, 1849	June 1, 1849	Jan. 1, 1899	1,000	1,235,000	S.
Merchants & Farmers' Bank	Ithaca	A.	Oct. 24, 1838	Oct. 15, 1838	Jan. 1, 2040	150	80,000	S.
Merchants & Mechanics' Bank of Troy	Troy	A.	Dec. 15, 1853	Dec. 15, 1853	Jan. 1, 1954	300	300,000	S. E.
Metropolitan Bank	New York	A.	April 10, 1851	April 10, 1851	Jan. 1, 1950	250	4,000,000	S.
Middletown Bank	S. Middletown	A.	May 17, 1839	July 1, 1839	May 1, 2130	100	125,000	S. E.
Mohawk Bank of Schenectady^c	Schenectady	A.	Oct. 13, 1852	Dec. 1, 1852	Jan. 1, 1952	125	200,000	S.
Mohawk River Bank	Fonda	A.	Jan. 2, 1856	Jan. 1, 1856	Jan. 1, 1956	100	100,000	S.
Mohawk Valley Bank	Mohawk	A.	March 28, 1839	July 1, 1839	Jan. 1, 2839	100	150,000	S. E.
Monroe County Bank	Rochester	A.	May 26, 1857	May 23, 1857	May 23, 2557	100	100,000	S.
Montgomery County Bank^d	Johnstown	A.	Dec. 30, 1856	Dec. 31, 1856	Jan. 1, 1956	100	100,000	S. E.
Mutual Bank	Troy	A.	Jan. 3, 1853	Feb. 1, 1853	Feb. 1, 1953	200	234,500	S. E.
Nassau Bank	New York	A.	Oct. 28, 1852	Nov. 1, 1852	Nov. 1, 1952	500	979,200	S.
Nassau Bank of Brooklyn	Brooklyn	A.	Jan. 28, 1859	Jan. 12, 1859			150,000	
National Bank of Albany	Albany	A.	Feb. 8, 1856	Jan. 16, 1856	Jan. 16, 1956	600	600,000	S.
National Bank in the City of New York^e	New York	A.	Dec. 22, 1856	Jan. 2, 1857	Jan. 1, 1957	1,500	1,500,000	S.
New York County Bank of the City of New York	New York	A.	June 25, 1855	June 1, 1855	June 1, 1955	200	200,000	S.
New York Dry Dock Company^f	New York	C.		April 12, 1825	Unlimited	200	200,000	
New York & Erie Bank^g	Buffalo	A.	Aug. 12, 1852	Sept. 1, 1852	Jan. 1, 2000	120	300,000	S. E.
New York Exchange Bank in the City of New York	New York	A.	April 14, 1851	April 21, 1851	Jan. 1, 1900	250	130,000	S.
New York State Bank^h	Albany	A.	Oct. 26, 1850	Dec. 31, 1850	Jan. 1, 1950	250	350,000	S.
Niagara County Bank	Lockport	A.	May 7, 1856	May 1, 1856	Before 2500	200	100,000	S. E
North River Bank in the City of New York^i	New York	A.	July 1, 1842	June 1, 1842	Jan. 1, 1899	500	316,000	S.
Ocean Bank in the City of New York	New York	A.	Dec. 22, 1849	Dec. 10, 1849	Jan. 1, 1950	500	1,000,000	S.
Ogdensburgh Bank	Ogdensburgh	C.		April 30, 1829	Jan. 1, 1859	100	100,000	
Oneida Bank	Utica	C.		May 14, 1836	Jan. 1, 1866	400	400,000	
Oneida Central Bank	Rome	A.	Oct. 29, 1853	Sept. 19, 1853	Sept. 19, 2000	150	173,500	S. E.
Oneida County Bank	Utica	A.	May 2, 1853	May 10, 1853	Jan. 2, 2000	125	125,000	S. E.
Oneida Valley Bank	Oneida	A.	Sept. 27, 1852	Sept. 22, 1852	Sept. 2, 1902	105	105,000	S. E.
Onondaga Bank	Syracuse	A.	May 1, 1854	May 1, 1854	May 1, 1954	150	96,200	S.
Onondaga County Bank	Syracuse	A.					150,000	S.
Oriental Bank	New York	A.	July 6, 1853	July 11, 1853	July 11, 1953	300	300,000	S.
Oswegatchie Bank	Ogdensburgh	A.	Oct. 3, 1854	Oct. 10, 1854	Oct. 1, 1954	200	200,000	S. E.
Oswego Bank	Oswego	C.		March 14, 1831	Jan. 1, 1859	150	150,000	
Oswego River Bank	Fulton	A.	Oct. 3, 1855	Jan. 1, 1856	Dec. 31, 1955	125	114,500	S.
Otsego County Bank^j	Cooperstown	A.	Dec. 30, 1853	Dec. 31, 1853	Jan. 1, 1954	200	200,000	S. E.
Pacific Bank	New York	A.	Oct. 8, 1850	June 17, 1850	Jan. 1, 1950	500	422,700	S.
Park Bank	New York	A.	March 12, 1856	March 1, 1856	March 1, 1956	2,000	2,000,000	S.
People's Bank of the City of New York	New York	A.	Feb. 27, 1851	April 1, 1851	April 1, 1950	250	412,500	S. E.
Perrin Bank	Rochester	I.		Sept. 29, 1855			43,620	S. E.
Phœnix Bank of the City of New York^k	New York	A.	Dec. 27, 1853	Jan. 2, 1854	Jan. 2, 1954	1,200	1,800,000	S.
Pulaski Bank	Pulaski	A.	Sept. 16, 1853	Sept. 1, 1853	Dec. 31, 1899	100	100,000	S. E.
Quassaick Bank	Newburgh	A.	March 19, 1852	March 19, 1852	Jan. 1, 1952	130	300,000	S.
Randall Bank	Cortlandville	I.		Aug. 1853			50,000	S. E.

a Successor to Bank of Ithaca.

b First incorp. April 29, 1829; cap. $750,000.

c Mohawk Bank incorp. March 13, 1807; cap. $200,000; allowed to reduce April 4, 1820; twice extended; expired Jan. 1, 1853.

d First incorp. March 15, 1831; cap. $100,000; expired Jan. 1, 1857.

e National Bank incorp. April 30, 1829; cap. $1,000,000; expired Jan. 1, 1857.

f Dock Co., with perpetual banking powers.

g Removed from Dunkirk March, 1854.

h First incorp. March 19, 1803; cap. $460,000; once extended; expired Jan. 1, 1851; State reserved right to take stock.

i North River Bank incorp. March 23, 1821; cap. $500,000; expired July 1, 1842; judgment dissolving an injunction filed Sept. 25, 1858.

j First incorp. April 8, 1830; cap. $100,000; expired Jan. 1, 1854.

k Incorp. June 15, 1812, cap. $1,000,000, as New York Manufacturing Co., for making wire and cards; amended Sept. 26, 1814, with banking privileges to extent of $150,000 besides $350,000 in manufacturing; changed to Phœnix Bank, Feb. 2, 1817; once extended; expired Jan. 1, 1854; increased to $1,000,000 April 29, 1834, and reduced May 7, 1841.

Existing Banks, continued.

Corporate Name.	Location.	C.—Chartered by law. A.—Associated free bank. I.—Individual bank.	Dates — Of filing articles.	Of beginning business or of act of incorporation.	Of expiration of charter privilege.	Original capital, in thousands of dollars.	Present capital.	Securities— S.—Stocks of N.Y. or U.S. S.E.—Stocks and real estate.
Rensselaer County Bank	Lansingburgh	A.	Dec. 7, 1852	Jan. 1, 1853	Jan. 1, 1953	200	$ 200,000	S. E.
R. M. Goddard & Co.'s Bank	Canton	I.		April 29, 1859				
Rochester Bank	Rochester	A.	March 31, 1854	April 1, 1854	Jan. 1, 1954	100	200,000	S. E.
Rochester City Bank	Rochester	C.		May 18, 1836	Jan. 1, 1866	400	400,000	
Rome Exchange Bank	Rome	A.	Feb. 18, 1851	Feb. 18, 1851	Jan. 1, 1951	100	100,000	S. E.
St. Nicholas Bank	New York	A.	Nov. 25, 1852	Nov. 15, 1852	Nov. 15, 1952	500	750,000	S.
Salt Springs Bank	Syracuse	A.	Feb. 4, 1852	Jan. 3, 1852	Jan. 3, 1952	125	200,000	S. E.
Saratoga County Bank^a	Waterford	A.	Nov. 28, 1856	Dec. 1. 1855	Dec. 1, 1956	100	150,000	S. E.
Schenectady Bank	Schenectady	C.		April 16, 1832	Jan. 1, 1862	150	150,000	
Schoharie County Bank	Schoharie	I.		April, 1852			100,000	S. E.
Seneca County Bank	Waterloo	C.		March 12, 1833	Jan. 1, 1863	200	200,000	
Seventh Ward Bank	New York	C.		April 30, 1833	Jan. 1, 1863	500	500,000	
Shoe & Leather Bank	New York	A.	Dec. 30, 1852	Dec. 3, 1852	Dec. 2, 1952	600	1,500,000	S.
Smith's Bank of Perry	Perry	I.		Sept. 22, 1858			50,000	S. E.
Spraker Bank	Canajoharie	A.	May 31, 1853	June 1, 1853	June 1, 1953	100	100,000	S. E.
State Bank of Troy	Troy	A.	May 20, 1852	April 27, 1852	Jan. 1, 2000	250	250,000	S. E.
State of New York Bank	Kingston	A.	July 9, 1853	Sept. 6, 1853	Sept. 5, 1893	100	125,000	S.
Steuben County Bank	Bath	C.		March 9, 1832	Jan. 1, 1862	150	150,000	
Stissing Bank^b	Pine Plains	A.	June 8, 1858	May 29, 1858	Jan. 1, 1900	120	60,000	S. E.
Suffolk County Bank	Sag Harbor	I.		April, 1844			20,000	S.
Susquehanna Valley Bank	Binghamton	A.	Jan. 31, 1855	Jan. 10, 1855	Jan. 9, 1955	100	100,000	S. E.
Syracuse City Bank	Syracuse	A.	Dec. 21, 1849	Oct. 26, 1849	Oct. 26, 1949	100	160,250	S. E.
Tanners' Bank	Catskill	C.		March 14, 1831	Jan. 1, 1860	100	100,000	
Tompkins County Bank	Ithaca	C.		May 14, 1836	Jan. 1, 1866	250	250,000	
Tradesmen's Bank of the City of New York^c	New York	A.	Dec. 28, 1854	Jan. 2, 1855	Jan. 1, 1950	800	800,000	S.
Traders' Bank of Rochester^d	Rochester		June 1, 1859					
Troy City Bank	Troy	C.		April 19, 1833	Jan. 1, 1863	300	300,000	
Ulster County Bank	Kingston	C.		March 14, 1831	June 1, 1861	100	100,000	
Unadilla Bank	Unadilla	I.		July, 1844			125,550	S E.
Union Bank of Albany	Albany	A.	June 8, 1853	July 4, 1853	July 4, 1953	250	500,000	S.
Union Bank of Kinderhook	Kinderhook	A.	June 23, 1853	June 23, 1853	Jan. 1, 1900	125	200,000	S. E.
Union Bank of the City of New York^e	New York	A.	Dec. 21, 1852	Dec. 22, 1852	Jan. 1, 1952	1,000	1,500,000	S.
Union Bank of Rochester	Rochester	A.	Jan. 20, 1853	March 1, 1853	Jan. 1, 1953	400	500,000	S. E.
Union Bank of Sullivan County	Monticello	A.	March 3, 1851	March 1, 1851	Jan. 1, 1899	110	150,000	S. E.
Union Bank of Troy	Troy	A.	Jan. 20, 1851	Jan. 1, 1851	Jan. 1, 1951	250	300,000	S. E.
Union Bank of Watertown	Watertown	A.	June 14, 1852	July, 1852	July 1, 1952	100	187,900	S. E.
Utica City Bank	Utica	A.	Aug. 30, 1848	Sept. 1, 1848	Jan. 1, 1898	125	200,000	S. E.
Wallkill Bank	Middletown	A.	June 9, 1857	Aug. 3, 1857	Aug. 3, 1957	125	125,000	S.
Washington County Bank	Union Village	A.	March 8, 1839	July 1, 1839	In year 2050	100	200,000	S. E.
Watertown Bank & Loan Company	Watertown	A.	Jan. 21, 1839	Jan. 20, 1839	Jan. 1, 2839	100	100,000	S. E.
Waverly Bank	Waverly	A.	Aug. 20, 1855	Aug. 6, 1855	Aug. 6, 1955	100	106,100	S. E.
Weedsport Bank	Weedsport	A.	July 12, 1854	July 3, 1854	Jan. 1, 1954	100	100,000	S. E.
Westchester County Bank	Peekskill	C.		March 21, 1833	Jan. 1, 1863	200	200,000	
West Winfield Bank	West Winfield	A.	March 10, 1854	Feb. 16, 1854	Feb. 16, 2354	100	125,000	S. E.
White's Bank of Buffalo	Buffalo	A.	April 9, 1853	April 6, 1853	In year 1900	100	200,000	S. E.
Williamsburgh City Bank	Williamsburgh	A.	Feb. 25, 1852	Feb. 4, 1852	Feb. 4, 1952	200	500,000	S. E.
Wooster Sherman's Bank	Watertown	I.		Dec. 1841			50,000	S. E.
Worthington Bank	Cooperstown	I.		Dec. 1854			50,000	S. E.
Wyoming County Bank	Warsaw	I.		Nov. 1851			50,000	S. E.

a First incorp. March 29, 1830; cap. $100,000; expired Jan. 1, 1857.
b Successor to Pine Plains Bank.
c Tradesmen's Bank incorp. March 29, 1823; cap. $600,000; reduced to $400,000 March 26, 1827; once ext.; exp. Jan. 1, 1855.
d Formed by the consolidation of the Manufacturers' Bank and the Eagle Bank by special act of 1859.
e Union Bank incorp. March 8, 1811; cap. $1,800,000; once extended; expired Jan. 1, 1853; successor to Jersey Bank, incorp. by State of New Jersey.

Obsolete and Closing Banks.

(Those marked with a * are redeemed by the Banking Department.)

Name.	Location.	C.—Chartered. A.—Associated. I.—Individual.	Date of charter or beginning of business.	Capital.	Rate of redemption of circulation. S.—Stocks. S.E.—Stocks and mortgages on real estate.	Remarks.
Adams Bank	Ashford	I.	Aug. 1850			Redemption expires June 2, 1860. Geo. Jones, N. Y.
*Agricultural Bank of Herkimer	Herkimer	A.	Jan. 11, 1839	$ 100,000	Par	Failed June 4, 1858. Red. at New York State Bank, Albany.
Allegany County Bank	Angelica	I.	May 13, 1840		S. 36	
Aqueduct Association in Village of Catskill	Catskill	C.	April 21, 1818			Changed to Greene County Bank Feb. 5, 1819.

Obsolete and Closing Banks, continued.

NAME.	Location.	C.—Chartered. A.—Associate. I.—Individual.	Date of charter or beginning of business.	Capital.	Rate of redemption of circulation.—S.—Stocks. S. E.—Stocks and mortgages on real estate.	Remarks.
American Bank	Mayville	I.	June, 1847			Closing. Red. by Henry Keep until Nov. 16, 1861.
*Astor Bank	New York	A.	June 2, 1852	$200,000	Par	Closing.
Atlas Bank of New York	Clymer	I.	June, 1847		S. 97, S. E. 75	Failed 1847.
Amenia Bank	Leedsville	I.	1844		Par	Red. by Geo. Jones, N. Y., until Sept. 14, 1861.
Bank of America at Buffalo	Buffalo	A.	Sept. 26, 1839	100,000	S. 76, S. E. 78	Failed.
Bank of Bainbridge	Penn Yan	I.	April, 1847			Closing. Red. by H. B. Bennett until March 26, 1863.
Bank of Brockport	Brockport	A.	Nov. 13, 1839	150,000	80	Failed.
Bank of Buffalo	Buffalo	C.	March 14, 1831	200,000	Par	Failed.
Bank of Carthage	Carthage	I.	July, 1852			Closed. Red. until April 29, 1863.
Bank of Columbia	Hudson	C.	March 6, 1793	160,000		Failed 1829. Twice extended.
Bank of Commerce of Buffalo	Buffalo	A.	Aug. 27, 1839	100,000	S. 76	Failed.
Bank of the Empire State	Fairport	I.	June, 1848			Closing. Red. until Oct. 7, 1862.
*Bank of Hornellsville	Hornellsville	A.	March 1, 1856	100,000	Par	Closing. Originally individual.
Bank of Hudson	Hudson	C.	March 25, 1808	300,000		Failed 1820. Allowed office of discount at Catskill.
Bank of Lake Erie	Buffalo	I.	Sept. 1847			Closing. Red. until March 21, 1862.
Bank of Lodi	Lodi, (Seneca co.,)	A.	Jan. 8, 1839	100,000	S. 83, S. E. 97	Failed.
Bank of Lyons	Lyons	C.	May 14, 1836	200,000	Par	Failed.
Bank of the Metropolis	New York	A.	March 31, 1851	100,000		Scarcely began business. Got one plate engraved.
Bank of Monroe	Rochester	C.	April 22, 1829	300,000	Par	Charter expired Jan. 1, 1850.
Bank of New Rochelle	Bolivar	I.	Jan. 1846		S. par, S. E. 81	Failed Oct. 1, 1851. Time expired for redemp. Jan. 8, 1859.
Bank of Ithaca	Ithaca	C.	April 29, 1829	200,000	Par	Charter expired Jan. 1, 1850. Removed to N. Y., and now Mercantile Bank of New York.
Bank of Niagara	Buffalo	C.	April 17, 1816	400,000		Failed 1825.
Bank of Olean	Olean	A.	Feb. 13, 1840	100,000	S. 87, S. E. 74	Failed.
Bank of Orleans	Albion	C.	April 30, 1834	200,000		Failed. Elizur Hart receiver.
Bank of the People	Lowville	I.	Sept. 1852		Par	Closing. Red. until Oct. 28, 1862.
Bank of Plattsburgh	Plattsburgh	C.	April 7, 1817	300,000		Failed 1825.
Bank of Rochester	Rochester	C.	Feb. 19, 1824	250,000	Par	Charter expired July 1847.
Bank of Tonawanda	Wheatfield	A.	Dec. 15, 1838	100,000	S. 68	Failed 1840.
Bank of the Union	Belfast	I.	March, 1852			Closing. Red. until June 2, 1864.
*Bank of the Union in the City of New York	New York	A.	May 25, 1853	300,000	Par	Closing.
Bank of the United States in New York	New York	A.	Aug. 13, 1838	200,000	Par	Closed 1843.
Bank of Warsaw	Warsaw	A.	Jan. 1, 1839	100,000		
Bank of Washington & Warren	Sandy Hill	C.	April 7, 1817	400,000		Failed 1825.
Bank of Waterford	Waterford	A.	Jan. 1, 1839	100,000		Failed.
Bank of Western New York	Rochester	A.	July 4, 1838	180,000	S. 75	Failed.
Bank of Whitehall	Whitehall	C.	April 30, 1829	100,000		Charter expired June 13, 1859.
Binghamton Bank	Binghamton	A.	Dec. 26, 1838	100,000	S. 75, S. E. 74	Failed.
Bowery Bank of the City of New York	New York	A.	Aug. 16, 1847	300,000	Par	Failed. Jno. A. Stewart receiver.
Camden Bank	Camden	A.	Jan. 27, 1848	112,550	Par	Closing. Red. by Edwin Rockwell until Jan. 1, 1864.
Canal Bank	Albany	C.	May 2, 1829	300,000	40	Failed July 11, 1848.
*Canal Bank of Lockport	Lockport	A.	April 10, 1839	200,000	Par	Closing. (See Rep. Comp. 1848. p. 70.)
Cattaraugus County Bank	Randolph	A.	Jan. 23, 1840	100,000	S. 84, S. E. 77	Failed.
*Central Bank of the City of New York	New York	A.	Jan. 17, 1853	300,000	Par	Failed.
Chemical Manufacturing Co	New York	C.	April 21, 1824	400,000	Par	Charter expired. Merged in Chemical Bank.
Chemung County Bank	Horseheads	I.	Sept. 14, 1855		Par	Failed March 23, 1858. Red. by Bank Dept. until Sept. 23, 1864.
Chelsea Bank	New York	A.	Jan. 8, 1839	1,000,000	25	Failed in 1840.
City Bank of Buffalo	Buffalo	C.	May 21, 1836	400,000		Failed 1839. (See Comp. Rep. 1848, p. 75.)
City Trust & Banking Co	New York	A.	March 10, 1839	100,000	Par	Closed 1841.
Clinton Bank	New York	A.	Feb. 10, 1840	100,000		Failed 1844.
Commercial Bank of Buffalo	Buffalo	C.	April 26, 1834	400,000		Failed.
Commercial Bank of New York	New York	C.	April 28, 1834	500,000		Failed.
Commercial Bank of Oswego	Oswego	C.	May 19, 1836	250,000		Failed.
Cortland County Bank	Truxton	A.	Sept. 30, 1839	100,000		
Cortland County Bank	Cincinnatus	I.	Sept. 1848		Par	Closing. Red. until Dec. 2, 1859.
Crouse Bank	Syracuse	A.	May 12, 1852	100,000	Par	Changed to Central City Bank Feb. 3, 1857.
Champlain Bank	Ellenburgh	I.	Oct. 1846		Par	Closing. (See Rep. Comp. 1848, p. 75.) Red. until Nov. 16, 1861.
Commercial Bank	Lockport	I.	Aug. 1847		Par	Closing. Red. until Aug. 25, 1861.

Obsolete and Closing Banks, continued.

NAME.	Location.	C.—Chartered. A.—Associate. I.—Individual.	Date of Charter or beginning of business.	Capital.	Rate of redemption of circulation. S.—Stocks. S. E.—Stocks and mortgages on real estate.	Remarks.
Commercial Bank, Allegany County..............	Friendship.........	I.	July, 1847	....	Par	Closing. Red. until July 22, 1862.
Clinton County Bank........	Plattsburgh	C.	May 18, 1836	$200,000	....	Failed.
*Dairymen's Bank............	Newport............	A.	Nov. 1, 1855	100,000	Par	Failed May 1858. Red. at New York State Bank at Albany until Nov 6, 1864.
Delaware & Hudson Canal Co.....................	New York..........	C.	Nov. 19, 1824	600,000	Par	Banking privilege expired Nov. 19, 1844.
Dutchess County Bank......	Poughkeepsie.....	C.	April 12, 1825	150,000	Par	Charter expired July 1, 1845.
Dutchess County Bank......	Amenia	I.	Aug. 1849	....	Par	Closing. Red. until Nov. 6, 1863.
Drovers' Bank of St. Lawrence County..............	Ogdensburgh......	I.	Dec. 1843	....	....	Closed. Removed from Cattaraugus co.
Dunkirk Bank................	Dunkirk............	I.	July, 1851	....	....	Closed.
Eagle Bank....................	New York..........	A.	April 5, 1849	100,000	....	Failed.
Eagle Bank of Rochester...	Rochester..........	A.	March 27, 1852	200,000	S. E. 94........	Merged in the Traders' Bank of Rochester June, 1859.
Eighth Avenue Bank........	New York..........	A.	Sept. 1, 1853	100,000	Par	Failed Nov. 1854. Red. at Bank Dept.
*Empire City Bank..........	New York..........	A.	Jan. 1, 1852	500,000	....	Failed. Red. at North River Bank.
Erie County Bank	Buffalo	A.	Sept. 1, 1838	100,000	S. 62, S. E.72	Failed.
Excelsior Bank................	Meridian............	I.	Feb. 1851	....	Par	Closing. Red. until Nov. 16, 1861.
*Exchange Bank of Buffalo.	Buffalo	I	April, 1844	....	Par	Failed. Red. at Albany City Bank.
*Exchange Bank of Genesee	Batavia.............	A.	Jan. 8, 1849	100,000	Par	Closing. Removed from Alexander June 24, 1850.
Exchange Bank of Rochester............	Rochester	I.	Oct. 31, 1839	....	Par	Closed.
Farmers' Bank of Ovid......	Ovid	A.	Oct. 6, 1838	100,000	....	
Farmers' Bank of Hamilton County..................	Arietta..............	I.	April, 1850	....	Par	Closing. Red. until July 16, 1863.
Farmers' Bank of Geneva..	Geneva.............	A.	July 18, 1839	100,000	....	
Farmers' Bank of Malone..	Malone	I.	Oct. 1844	....	....	Closed. Worthless.
Farmers' Bank of Mina.....	Mina................	I.	May, 1847	....	Par	Closing. Red. until Mar. 9, 1864.
*Farmers' Bank of Onondaga.....................	Onondaga Valley,	I.	July, 1852	....	85..........	Failed May 1853. Red. at Bank Dept. at 85 until Nov. 12, 1859.
Farmers' Bank of Orange County	Warwick............	I.	Aug. 1842	....	....	Closed 1843.. Worthless. (See Comp. Rep. 1844, p. 61.)
Farmers' Bank of Orleans..	Gaines	A.	Oct. 29, 1838	200,000	....	Failed. Worthless.
Farmers' Bank of Penn Yan	Penn Yan	A.	Aug. 20, 1839	100,000	Par	Closed 1843.
Farmers' Bank of Seneca County..................	Romulus............	A.	April 20, 1839	100,000	S. par,S. E.74	Failed 1840.
Farmers & Drovers' Bank of Erie County	Buffalo	I.	Oct. 1843	....	....	Failed 1846. Worthless.
Farmers & Mechanics' Bank of Ogdensburgh.....	Ogdensburgh	A.	Aug. 28, 1843	100,000	Par	Closed.
Farmers & Mechanics' Bank of Onondaga........	Fayetteville........	A.	Aug. 24, 1839	250,000	Par	Closed 1841.
Franklin Bank of Chautauqua County.............	French Creek	I.	1847	....	Par	Closing. Red. until Aug.25, 1861.
Franklin Bank...............	New York..........	C.	April 21, 1818	500,000	....	Failed 1830.
Franklin County Bank......	Malone	I.	Aug. 1846	....	....	Closed 1852.
Farmers' Bank of Saratoga County	Crescent............	A.	April 1, 1851	200,000	Par	Still redeeming its own notes.
Freemen's Bank of Washington County............	Hebron.............	I.	Oct. 1850	....	....	Closing. Red. until Oct. 2, 1861.
Genesee Central Bank.......	Attica..............	A.	Dec. 11, 1838	100,000	....	
Globe Bank	Seneca Falls.......	I.	Dec. 23, 1839	....	....	Failed.
Globe Bank in the City of New York...................	New York..........	A.	April 11, 1840	100,000	....	
Greene County Bank........	Catskill............	C.	Feb. 5, 1819	....	....	Failed 1826.
*Hamilton Exchange Bank of Greene..........	Greene..............	I.	Aug. 1850	....	84..........	Redeemed at Bank Dept. at 84 until June 23, 1864.
Hartford Bank...............	Hartford	I.	June, 1849	....	Par	Closing. Red. until July 14, 1862.
H. J. Miner's Bank of Utica.	Fredonia............	I.	Feb. 1850	25,000	Par	Closing. Still redeems its own notes.
Henry Keep's Bank..........	Watertown.........	I.	Sept. 1847	....	Par	Closing. Red. until Sept. 17, 1859.
*Hollister Bank of Buffalo..	Buffalo.............	A.	Feb. 1, 1850	100,000	....	Failed. Red. at Commercial Bank at Albany.
Howard Trust & Banking Co.....................	Troy.................	A.	April 16, 1839	100,000	Par	Closed 1844.
Hudson River Bank..........	New York	A.	Dec. 6, 1838	100,000	....	
*Island City Bank...........	New York..........	A.	June 1, 1849	300,000	Par	Failed Oct. 1857. Red. at Manhattan Co. until April 22, 1864.
Ithaca Bank...................	Ithaca..............	A.	Dec. 31, 1838	250,000	....	
James Bank....................	Jamesville..........	A.	Feb. 7, 1839	106,000	91..........	Failed Oct. 1, 1851. Worthless.
Kinderhook Bank.............	Kinderhook........	I.	Jan. 25, 1839	....	....	
Knickerbocker Bank	Genoa	I.	Sept. 1848	....	Par	Closing. Red. until Nov. 16, 1861.
Knickerbocker Bank of the City of New York	New York	C	Oct. 1, 1851	200,000	Par	Failed. Red. at North River Bank.
Kirkland Bank................	Clinton	I.	Dec. 1845	....	Par	Closing. Red. until June 3, 1863.
La Fayette Bank..............	New York..........	C.	April 18, 1834	500,000	....	Failed.

Obsolete and Closing Banks, continued.

NAME.	Location.	C.—Chartered. A.—Associate. I.—Individual.	Date of charter or beginning of business.	Capital.	Rate of redemption of circulation. S.—Stocks. S. E.—Stocks and mortgages on real estate.	Remarks.
Leland Bank	New Lebanon	I.	July, 1852		Par	Closing. Red. until July 16, 1864.
Le Roy Bank of Genesee	Le Roy	A.	Jan. 1, 1839	$100,000		
Lewis County Bank	Martinsburgh	C.	April 30, 1833	100,000		Failed Nov. 4, 1854.
Livingston County Bank	Geneseo	C.	April 7, 1830	100,000	Par	Charter expired July 1, 1855.
Lockport Bank	Lockport	C.	April 22, 1829	100,000		Charter repealed May 15, 1837.
Lockport Bank & Trust Co.	Lockport	A.	Oct. 31, 1838	500,000	Par	Closing. Red. until Nov. 12, 1863.
Lumberman's Bank	Wilmurt	I.	March, 1851		Par	Closing. Red. until Oct. 24, 1861.
*Luther Wright's Bank	Oswego	A.	March 28, 1846	300,000	Par	Closing.
McIntyre Bank	Adirondac	I.	Sept. 1847		Par	Closing. Red. until Feb. 27, 1861.
Madison Co. Bank	Cazenovia	C.	March 14, 1831	100,000	Par	Charter expired Jan. 1, 1858.
Manhattan Exchange Bank	New York	A.	April 1, 1839	300,000		
Manufacturers' Bank of Ulster Co	Saugerties	I.	Sept. 10, 1840		Par	Closed.
Manufacturers' Bank of Rochester	Rochester	A.	July 28, 1856	200,000		{ Merged in The Traders' Bank of Rochester June, 1859.
Mechanics' Bank	Watertown	I.	Sept. 1851		Par	Closing. Red. until Sept. 23, 1861.
Mechanics' Bank of Buffalo	Buffalo	A.	Jan. 25, 1839	100,000	S. E. 63	Failed.
Mechanics' Bank of Williamsburgh	Williamsburgh	A.	March 1, 1853			{ Changed to Manufacturers' Bank of Brooklyn, 1858.
Mechanics & Farmers' Bank	Ithaca	A.	Oct. 24, 1838	100,000		
Mercantile Bank of Schenectady	Schenectady	A.	March 26, 1839	100,000	Par	Closed 1844.
Merchants' Bank	Mina	I.	Feb. 1847		Par	Closing. Red. until Oct. 17, 1861.
Merchants' Bank of Ontario County	Naples	I.	March 1846			Closed.
Merchants' Banking Co	New York	A.	Sept. 4, 1839	1,000,000		Closed.
Merchants' Exchange Bank of Buffalo	Buffalo	A.	Sept. 20, 1838	200,000	S. 81, S. E. 65	Failed 1840.
Merchants & Farmers' Bank	Carmel	I.	Oct. 1845		Par	Closing. Red. until May 30, 1862.
*Merchants & Mechanics' Bank of Oswego	North Granville	A.	July 1852		77	{ Failed March 1854. Red. at Bank Dept. at 77 until Sept. 28, 1860.
Middle District Bank	Poughkeepsie	C.	March 22, 1811	200,000		Failed 1829.
Millers' Bank of New York	Clyde	A.	Dec. 1, 1838	300,000	S. Par, S.E.94	Failed 1840.
*Monroe Bank of Rochester	Cuba	I.	Oct. 1852		Par	Closing.
New York Banking Co	New York	A.	March 23, 1839	100,000	S. 42	Failed.
New York Bank of Saratoga	Hadley	I.	Feb. 1851		Par	Closing. Red. until April 1, 1862.
New York City Bank	New York	A.	May 6, 1840	200,000		
New York Manufacturing Co	New York	C.	Sept. 26, 1814	150,000	Par	{ Merged in Phœnix Bank Feb. 21, 1817. Incorp. June 15, 1812, for manufacturing cards and wire.
New York City Trust & Banking Co	New York	I.			Par	Closed 1840.
New York Security Bank	Hope Falls	I.	Aug. 1848		Par	Closing. Red. until Aug. 16, 1864.
New York Stock Bank	Durham	I.	June 1846		Par	Closing. Red. until July 19, 1862.
*New York State Stock Security Bank	New York	I.	Nov. 30, 1838		Par	{ Closing. Red. at New York State Bank, Albany.
*New York Traders' Bank of Washington Co	North Granville	I.	Sept. 1851			{ Closing. Red. at New York State Bank, Albany.
Niagara River Bank[a]	Buffalo	A.	March 15, 1853	104,000		Removed to Lockport May 13, 1859, and name changed to Lockport City Bank.
North American Bank	New York	A.	Oct. 21, 1839	100,000	Par	Closed 1841.
North American Trust & Banking Co	New York	A.	Nov. 6, 1838	2,000,000		Failed.
Northern Bank of New York	Madrid	I.	Feb. 1847		Par	Closing. Red. until Nov. 1, 1860
Northern Exchange Bank	Brasher Falls	I.	July 1847		Par	Closing. Red. until March 1, 1862
Northern Canal Bank	Fort Ann	I.	Aug. 1848		Par	Closing. Red. until Oct. 13, 1862
North River Banking Co	New York	A.	Dec. 4, 1839	100,000		
*Oliver Lee & Company's Bank	Buffalo	A.	Jan. 1, 1844	100,000	Par	{ Failed. Red. at Albany City Bank.
Onondaga County Bank	Syracuse	A.	Jan. 1, 1854	150,000		Closed.
Ontario Bank	Canandaigua	C.	March 12, 1813	500,000		Charter expired Jan. 1, 1856. Allowed to establish Branch at Utica April 10, 1815, and this continued until charter expired as Ontario Branch Bank of Utica.
Ontario Bank, (President and Directors of)	Utica	A.	Dec. 29, 1855	500,000		Failed. E. A. Wetmore, receiver.
*Ontario County Bank	Phelps	I.	Nov. 1855		Par	Failed March, 1858. Red. at Union Bank, Albany, until Aug. 11, 1864.
Oswego County Bank	Meridian	I.	Oct. 1849		Par	Closing. (1854.) Red. until Sept. 5, 1860.
Palmyra Bank of Wayne County	Palmyra	I.	Dec. 1843			{ Changed to Lyons Bank March 31, 1857.
Pachin Bank	Buffalo	A.	Oct. 1, 1847	100,000	Par	Closed. Red. by A. D. Patchin until Feb. 28, 1862.
Phœnix Bank	Bainbridge	I.	June 1850			Closed.
Phœnix Bank at Buffalo	Buffalo	A.	Oct. 30, 1839	500,000	S. E. 73	Failed. Red. until Sept. 2, 1863.
*Pine Plains Bank	Pine Plains	A.	March 9, 1839	100,000	Par	Failed April 1858. Reorganized as Stissing Bank.

[a] Removed from Tonawanda, Sept. 24, 1857.

Savings Banks are institutions intended to receive in trust small sums of money, generally the surplus earnings of the laboring classes, and to return the same with moderate interest at a future time. They are banks of deposit only; their officers serve without pay, and the money received on deposit can be invested only in mortgages upon real estate, public stocks, or such other securities

Obsolete and Closing Banks, continued.

NAME.	Location.	C.—Chartered. A.—Associate. I.—Individual.	Date of charter or beginning of business.	Capital.	Rate of redemption of circulation. S.—Stocks. S. E.—Stocks and mortgages on real estate.	Remarks.
Powell Bank	Newburgh	A.	Dec. 27, 1838	$130,000	Par	Closing. Red. its own notes.
*Pratt Bank of Buffalo	Buffalo	I.	Oct. 1847		94	Failed Feb. 1858. Red. at Bank Dept. at 94.
Prattsville Bank	Prattsville	I.	Aug. 1843		Par	Closing. Red. until Dec. 15, 1860.
Putnam County Bank	Farmers' Mills	A.	Nov. 22, 1848	100,000	Par	Closing. Red. by David Kent until Oct. 1863.
Putnam Valley Bank	Putnam Valley	I.	May, 1849		Par	Closing.
Queen City Bank	Buffalo	I.	Sept. 1853		Par	Closing. Red. until Feb. 10, 1863.
Reciprocity Bank	Buffalo	C.	March 6, 1857	200,000		Changed from Sackets Harbor Bank March 6, 1851. Failed. Receiver app. Aug. 27, 1857.
Sackets Harbor Bank	Buffalo	C.	April, 28, 1834	200,000		Removed from Sackets Harbor March 25, 1852. Changed to Reciprocity Bank 1857.
St. Lawrence Bank	Ogdensburgh	A.	Jan. 8, 1839	100,000	S. 32, S. E. 50	Failed Dec. 3, 1841.
State Bank of New York	Buffalo	A.	Oct. 15, 1839	100,000	S. 31	Failed.
Silver Lake Bank of Genesee	Perry	A.	Jan. 5, 1839	100,000		
*State Bank at Sackets Harbor	Sackets Harbor	I.	May, 1852		Par	Failed Nov. 1, 1856. Red. at Union Bank, Albany, until Nov. 11, 1862.
*State Bank at Saugerties	Saugerties	I.	April, 1847		Par	Closing.
Staten Island Bank	Port Richmond	A.	Oct. 29, 1838	100,000	S. E. 56	Failed.
*Suffolk Bank	New York	A.	July 1, 1852	100,000	Par	Closing.
Sullivan County Bank	Monticello	I.	Oct. 1850		Par	Closing. Red. until Aug. 21, 1860.
Tenth Ward Bank	New York	A.	Dec. 1, 1838	100,000	S. 94	Failed 1840.
Troy Exchange Bank	Troy	A.	Jan. 1, 1838	100,000		
Union Bank at Buffalo	Buffalo	A.	Oct. 10, 1839	100,000	S. 81	Failed.
United States Bk. at Buffalo	Buffalo	A.	Dec. 13, 1838	100,000	S. E. 77	Failed.
Valley Bank of Boonville	Boonville	I.			Par	Closing. Red. by E. N. Merriam, of Ogdensburgh, until March 20, 1863.
Valley Bank of Lowville	Lowville	I.	Aug. 1851		Par	Removed to Boonville. See above.
Village Bank	Randolph.	I.	June, 1848		Par	Closing. Red. until June 3, 1859.
*Walter Joy's Bank	Buffalo	I.	Feb. 1848		Par	Failed 1850. Red. at Mechanics & Farmers' Bank, Albany.
Warren County Bank	Johnsburgh	I.	Dec. 1845		Par	Closing. Red. until Nov. 12, 1859.
Washington Bank in the City of New York	New York	A.	July 18, 1839	125,000	65, 35, & Par.	Failed 1843.
Watervliet Bank	West Troy	C.	May 21, 1836	250,000		Failed. (See Comp. Rep. 1848, p. 77.
Wayne County Bank	Palmyra	C.	April 30, 1829	100,000		Closed.
*White Plains Bank	Naples	I.	June, 1844			Closing.
Western Bank of Suffolk County	S. Huntington	I.	June, 1850		Par	Closing. Red. until June 17, 1862.
Williamsburgh Bank	Williamsburgh	A.	Jan. 12, 1839	100,000	Par	Closed.
Willoughby Bank	Brooklyn	A.	Nov. 1, 1839	100,000	Par	Closed 1840.
Wool Growers' Bank of the State of New York	New York	A.	Jan. 12, 1839	100,000	Par	Closed 1841.
Yates County Bank	Penn Yan	C.	April 2, 1831	100,000		Failed 1848. (See Comp. Rep. 1849, p. 35.)

Savings Banks in the State, Jan. 1, 1859.

NAME.	Location.	Date of incorporation.	Amount due depositors.	Resources.
Albany City Savings Institution	Albany	March 29, 1850	$ 168,181	$ 168,181
Albany Exchange Savings Bank	Albany	April 18, 1856	27,987	27,987
Albany Savings Bank	Albany	March 24, 1820	998,924	1,049,804
Auburn Savings Institution	Auburn	March 12, 1849	71,235	71,415
Bank for Savings in the City of New York	New York	March 26, 1819	8,701,923	9,259,996
Bloomingdale Savings Bank	New York	April 17, 1854	56,300	57,599
Bowery Savings Bank	New York	May 1, 1834	7,818,143	8,274,445
Broadway Savings Institution	New York	June 20, 1851	841,346	872,967
Brockport Savings Bank	Brockport	July 18, 1853	2,439	2,511
Brooklyn Savings Bank	Brooklyn	April 7, 1827	2,660,981	2,816,817
Buffalo Savings Bank	Buffalo	May 9, 1846	872,681	924,863
Central City Savings Institution	Utica	June 20, 1851	28,431	30,688
Central Savings Bank of Troy	Troy	April 15, 1857	25,712	25,712
Cohoes Savings Institution	Cohoes	April 11, 1851	34,734	34,734
Commercial Savings Bank of Troy	Troy	April 12, 1855	60,031	60,031
Dry Dock Savings Institution	New York	April 12, 1848	1,118,876	1,169,401
East River Savings Institution	New York		785,782	829,569
Elmira Savings Bank	Elmira	April 17, 1854	1,973	2,107
Emigrant Industrial Savings Bank	New York	April 10, 1850	1,628,754	1,695,951

as may be approved by law.   They can be organized by special act of the Legislature, and their charters are perpetual.   The total number of savings institutions incorp. prior to 1859 was 75, of which 57 reported their statistics in 1858.   They are placed under the care of the Superintendent of the Banking Department, who has general powers for the protection of the interests of depositors, and is required to report their condition annually to the Legislature.   Most of these institutions bear names closely resembling those of banks of discount and circulation, and are kept in the same building and have the same persons as officers of both.[1]

Class IV includes those whose certificates are filed in the County Clerks' offices.   Most of the corporations already described are required to file their articles in the clerk's office of their respective counties, in addition to depositing them in the departments of the State Government.

" An Act to provide for the Incorporation of **Religious Societies**" was passed April 6, 1784.[2]

" An Act authorizing the Incorporation of **Rural Cemetery Associations**" was passed April 27, 1847.

" An Act to provide for the **Incorporation of Villages**" was passed Dec. 7, 1847.[3]

Savings Banks, continued.

NAME.	Location.	Date of incorporation.	Amount due depositors.	Resources.
Emigrant Savings Bank of Buffalo	Buffalo	April 17, 1858	$ 5,490	$ 4,218
Erie County Savings Bank	Buffalo	April 10, 1854	542,641	549,722
Fishkill Savings Institute	Fishkill	Feb. 25, 1857	21,497	21,705
Greenwich Savings Bank	New York	April 24, 1833	3,528,851	3,678,180
Hudson City Savings Institution	Hudson	April 4, 1850	44,610	45,206
Institution for the Savings of Merchants' Clerks	New York	April 12, 1848	1,509,889	1,529,810
Irving Savings Institution	New York	July 1, 1851	719,498	736,323
Manhattan Savings Institution	New York	April 10, 1850	1,782,067	1,839,785
Manufacturers' Savings Bank of Troy	Troy	April 15, 1857	51,988	51,988
Mariners' Savings Institution	New York	April 16, 1852	419,689	430,141
Mechanics & Farmers' Savings Bank of Albany	Albany	April 12, 1855	179,049	179,049
Mechanics & Traders' Savings Institution	New York	April 16, 1852	361,612	372,417
Monroe County Savings Institution	Rochester	April 8, 1850	256,679	259,341
Mutual Savings Bank of Troy	Troy	April 15, 1857	23,637	23,637
Newburgh Savings Bank	Newburgh	April 13, 1852	91,188	92,993
Niagara County Savings Bank	Lockport	April 10, 1851	1,569	1,636
Onondaga County Savings Bank	Syracuse	April 10, 1855	129,601	130,262
Poughkeepsie Savings Bank	Poughkeepsie	April 16, 1836	247,505	263,619
Rochester Savings Bank	Rochester	April 21, 1831	1,371,911	1,476,425
Rome Savings Bank	Rome	June 30, 1851	33,621	36,289
Rose Hill Savings Bank	New York	April 17, 1854	71,854	72,285
Savings Bank of Utica	Utica	April 26, 1839	334,262	368,499
Schenectady Savings Bank	Schenectady	April 29, 1834	211,886	227,559
Seamen's Bank for Savings	New York	Jan. 31, 1829	7,349,474	7,825,443
Sing Sing Savings Bank	Sing Sing	March 9, 1854	35,410	35,711
Sixpenny Savings Bank of Albany	Albany	April 17, 1854	10,601	10,601
Sixpenny Savings Bank of the City of New York	New York	June 4, 1853	112,361	113,548
South Brooklyn Savings Institute	Brooklyn	April 10, 1850	522,350	538,664
Southold Savings Bank	Southold	April 7, 1858	6,970	7,001
State Savings Bank of Troy	Troy	April 18, 1856	47,479	47,479
Syracuse Savings Bank	Syracuse	March 30, 1849	237,580	238,619
Troy Savings Bank	Troy	April 23, 1823	634,904	671,716
Ulster County Savings Institution	Kingston	April 18, 1851	62,435	63,622
Union Savings Bank of Albany	Albany	April 13, 1854	15,187	15,187
Westchester County Savings Bank	Tarrytown	July 21, 1853	103,734	108,729
Western Savings Bank	Buffalo	July 9, 1851	77,048	77,048
Williamsburgh Savings Bank	Brooklyn	April 9, 1851	1,086,882	1,119,001
Yonkers Savings Bank	Yonkers	April 3, 1854	47,405	48,069

1 The first savings bank in England was formed in 1804, and the first in New York in 1819, under the auspices of the " Society for Prevention of Pauperism." A public meeting was called and the plan discussed and approved Nov. 29, 1816. The first deposits were made July 3, 1819, and $2,807 were received the first evening from 80 depositors, in sums of from $2 to $300. Within 6 mo., $153,378.31 had been deposited, by 1,527 persons, and but $6,606 had been withdrawn. Up to 1857, $47,530,067.61 had been intrusted to the care of this institution.—*Common Council Manual*, 1858, *p.* 623.

The first savings bank in Albany was established in 1820; in Troy, in 1823; in Brooklyn, in 1827; and in Buffalo, in 1836. Most of these banks were originally required to report to the Legislature; but their returns were seldom published. Under the act of March 20, 1857, they are required to report to the Superintendent of the Banking Department. Sixteen savings banks have been incorp. that never organized. Only two of the whole number chartered have ever failed. The "Knickerbocker Savings Institution," of N. Y., incorp. April 8, 1851, failed and went into the hands of a receiver in 1854; and the "Sixpenny Savings Bank of Rochester," incorp. July 13, 1854, failed.

2 This act was amended, so far as it related to the Ref. Prot. D. Societies, March 7, 1788. Other amendments were made in 1801, 1813, and 1828. For statistics see p. 139.

3 Previous to this act, villages were incorp. by special acts of the Legislature, and the articles were filed in the State Department: but since, the filing of articles has become a mere local affair; and it is extremely difficult to obtain a complete list of the incorporated villages of the State.

AGRICULTURE.

THE climate of the State is adapted to the cultivation of most of the crops and fruits of the temperate zone. The improved lands comprise a little more than one-half of the entire area of the State, and of these 37 per cent. is devoted to pasturage and 25 per cent. is occupied by meadow lands. The principal crops, in the order of relative amount, are oats, corn, wheat, buckwheat, rye, and barley, together occupying 37 per cent. of the cultivated lands,—leaving 1 per cent. for the minor crops and gardens. The northern cos. of the State and the highland regions along the s. border and upon the Hudson are much better adapted to pasturage than tillage; and the people in these sections are almost exclusively engaged in stock and sheep raising and in dairying. Little more grain is raised than is strictly necessary for a proper rotation of crops; and the greater part of the grain for home consumption is imported from other sections of the country. The low lands that surround the great lakes and occupy the greater portion of the surface in the w. part of the State are best adapted to grain growing. Several sections of the State are found peculiarly adapted to particular products. The Mohawk Valley intervales have been long almost exclusively devoted to the cultivation of broom corn. The Chemung Valley, parts of Onondaga co. and several other sections are becoming known as tobacco raising districts. Hops are extensively cultivated in Madison, Oneida, Otsego, and Schoharie cos. The Hudson Valley below the Highlands, the N. shore of Long Island, and the s. extremity of several of the lake valleys in the central portion of the State are well adapted to the culture of grapes. Maple sugar is largely produced in the northern cos. and in the central highland districts. Upon Long Island and in Westchester large sections are devoted to the cultivation of vegetables for the New York market. The people of Orange, Rockland, Westchester, Putnam, and Dutchess cos. are largely engaged in furnishing the city of New York with milk.[1]

The New York State Agricultural Society was formed by a convention held at Albany in Feb. 1832; but for several years it received no support from the State and held no regular fairs. In 1841 the society was re-organized, and measures were adopted for raising funds and holding annual fairs. On May 5 of that year, an act was passed by the Legislature, appropriating $8,000 for the encouragement of agriculture, $700 of which was to go to the State Society, and the remainder was to be divided among the co. societies in the ratio of Assembly representation. This appropriation has been continued until the present time. The society is required annually to report to the Legislature a full account of its proceedings, and such facts concerning the agricultural condition of the State as may be of general interest. The volumes of Transactions are published by the State, and are widely distributed among the farming population. The annual fairs are held in different parts of the State, and are largely attended.[2] They usually succeed in

[1] Hay is most largely produced in St. Lawrence, Oneida, Chenango, Otsego, Chautauqua, Delaware, and Orange counties; wheat, in Livingston, Monroe, Genesee, Niagara, Ontario, and Jefferson counties; oats, in Onondaga, Montgomery, Oneida, Cayuga, and Otsego; rye, in Columbia, Rensselaer, Ulster, Orange, Albany, Saratoga, and Washington; barley, in Jefferson, Onondaga, Ontario, Cayuga, and Wayne; buckwheat, in Schoharie, Montgomery, Otsego, Saratoga, and Tioga; corn, in Onondaga, Cayuga, Monroe, Wayne, Oneida, and Ontario; and potatoes, in Washington, Monroe, Oneida, St. Lawrence, Rensselaer, and Franklin. The counties having the greatest number of cows are St. Lawrence, Jefferson, Oneida, Orange, Chenango, Herkimer, and Chautauqua; and the greatest number of sheep, Ontario, Livingston, Steuben, Cayuga, Washington, Wyoming, Monroe, and Genesee. The counties that produce the greatest quantity of butter are St. Lawrence, Delaware, Chenango, Jefferson, Chautauqua, Orange, and Otsego; and the greatest amount of cheese, Herkimer, Oneida, Jefferson, Madison, Erie, Cattaraugus, St. Lawrence, and Otsego.

[2] The earliest agricultural exhibition on record within the present limits of the State was a cattle fair, held at New Amsterdam, Oct. 15, 1641. An act passed Nov. 11, 1692, entitled "An act for settling fairs and markets in each respective city and co. throughout this province," remained in force until repealed by the State Legislature, March 12, 1788. A special act was passed for the fairs of Albany, Cumberland, and Tryon cos., March 8, 1773, but scarcely took effect before the Revolution. Acts applying to particular towns were passed by the earlier State Legislatures; but the custom of holding fairs soon fell into disuse. These fairs were more properly market days; no premiums were offered, and no inducements to competition existed beyond the ordinary stimulus of trade. The products of farm culture being placed side by side, their comparative excellence was left to the decision of the purchaser, which doubtless contributed to excite emulation among the producers. These fairs were generally held semi-annually, upon fixed days, under the direction of "Governors and Rulers," appointed in colonial times by the Governor, and afterward by the judges of the co. courts. The expenses were defrayed by tolls, usually 1 per cent., upon the commodities sold, half of which was paid by the buyer and half by the seller.

The Society for the Promotion of Agriculture, Arts, and Manufactures was instituted Feb. 26, 1791, and incorp. March 12, 1793. For more efficient action, it in 1801 divided the State into as many agricultural districts as there were cos., in each of which a secretary was appointed, to convene the members of the society within his district, inquire into the state of agriculture and manufactures, receive communications and arrange and transmit them to the President of the society. The transactions of this body were printed by the State, and the society numbered among its members nearly every person of eminence throughout the State. Its charter expired in 1804; and its corporate powers were revived and continued April 2 of that year, under the name of the Society for the Promotion of the Useful Arts. The affairs of the new body were managed by a council of 9 members, and State patronage was continued in the printing of its Transactions. In 1808–12 liberal premiums were offered for the best cloths of household manufacture, a part of which were awarded by the co. judge and a part by this society. The samples, upon which $10,000 were thus paid, are still preserved in the library of the Albany Institute. After being once extended, the Society for Promoting Agricultural Arts was superseded, in part, by a Board of Agriculture, but continued as a local institution of Albany until merged, with the "Albany Lyceum of Natural History," in the "Albany Institute," in 1829. The latter has most of the books, papers, and effects of its predecessors; and tracing back through its change it is the oldest scientific society in the State. "An act to improve the agriculture of this State,"

awakening a great local interest in agricultural matters. The office of the society is kept at the Agricultural Rooms, corner of State and Lodge Sts., Albany, where it has a museum and library.

County and Town Societies.—The act of 1853 allows county agricultural societies to purchase and hold real estate to an amount not exceeding $25,000 and personal property not exceeding $1,000, for the purposes set forth in their articles of incorporation, and for no other purposes. Town and other societies may hold real estate to the amount of $10,000 and personal property to the amount of $3,000. Each county or union society must have at least one director or manager for each town; and each town, village, or city society must have not less than 10 directors, who are elected annually by ballot. Upon application of two-thirds of their members to the Supreme Court of the district in which they are located, these societies may obtain an order for the sale of a part or the whole of their property. An amendment to the act was passed April 13, 1855, by the provisions of which the number of directors was changed to 6, 2 of whom are elected each year for a term of three years. Any person may become a life member by the payment of a sum not exceeding $10; and the officers are jointly and severally liable for all debts due from the society contracted while they are in office, if suit be commenced within one year

passed April 7, 1819, created a board of agriculture and appropriated $10,000 annually for 2 years, to be distributed for the promotion of agriculture and family domestic manufactures in the several cos., on condition that a similar sum should be subscribed by the co. societies formed under this act. A board, formed of the president, or a delegate chosen from each co. society, met annually at Albany, elected officers, examined reports, and selected for publication such returns as they deemed proper. These were published by the State. Three volumes of Memoirs were issued, and the board continued in existence but little longer than the appropriation was continued. County societies, on the plan of the Berkshire Co. Agricultural Society, began to be formed in 1817; and, by the exertions of De Witt Clinton, Elkanah Watson, and other friends of the measure, they were extended to most of the cos. These societies, after a brief period, fell into disuse; and that of Jefferson co. is the only one of this class that can trace an unbroken descent from that period.

The first officers of the present State Agricultural Society, formed in 1832, were Le Ray de Chaumont, *President;* E. P. Livingston, Jacob Morris, and Robert L. Rose, *Vice Presidents;* P. S. Van Rensselaer, *Recording Secretary;* Jesse Buel, *Corresponding Secretary;* Charles R. Webster, *Treasurer;* and H. W. Delavan, John Townsend, and H. Hickox, *Executive Committee.* County societies were again instituted in many of the cos. under the influence of this society; but most of them were short lived. The "Cultivator" was begun in March, 1834, by Jesse Buel, under the guarantee of Stephen Van Rensselaer and James Wadsworth, as the organ of the society and medium of communication between the friends of agriculture; and it has been continued ever since, under private auspices, but entirely devoted to the interests of agriculture. It has for many years been published by Luther Tucker, of Albany.

Any person a citizen of the State may become a member of the State Society upon payment of $1 annually, or a life member by payment of $10 at one time. Presidents of co. societies and one delegate from each are *ex officio* members. The officers of the society are elected annually in Feb., and consist of a

President, one Vice President from each of the Judicial Districts, a Recording and a Corresponding Secretary, a Treasurer, and an Executive Committee, consisting of the above and 5 others chosen for the purpose.

Premiums are awarded in money, plate, medals, books, and diplomas; and the society embraces within the field of its patronage not only stock, farm, and garden products and implements of husbandry, but a wide range of useful and ornamental manufactures, particularly those which are the products of home industry. The places and times of holding the State fairs, names of Presidents, and total receipts of the State society have been as follows:—

YEARS.	Place of holding fair.	Time of holding fair.	Presidents.	Receipts.
1841	Syracuse........	Sept. 29, 30	Joel B. Nott........	(Free.)
1842	Albany...........	Sept. 27, 29	Jas. S. Wadsworth	$1,296.10
1843	Rochester.......	Sept. 20, 22	Jas. S. Wadsworth	3,000.00
1844	Poughkeepsie..	Sept. 18, 19	J. B. Beekman	3,650.00
1845	Utica.............	Sept. 17, 19	B. P. Johnston.....	4,370.18
1846	Auburn..........	Sept. 15, 17	J. M. Sherwood....	4,333.17
1847	Saratoga Sp'gs	Sept. 14, 16	George Vail.........	4,034.22
1848	Buffalo	Sept. 5, 7	Lewis F. Allen.....	6,272.86
1849	Syracuse	Sept. 11, 13	John A. King	8,114.55
1850	Albany...........	Sept. 3, 6	Ezra P. Prentice...	10,465.61
1851	Rochester.......	Sept. 16, 19	John Delafield.....	11,956.25
1852	Utica.............	Sept. 7, 10	Henry Wager......	8,125.41
1853	Saratoga Sp'gs	Sept. 20, 23	Lewis G. Morris...	6,009.90
1854	New York.......	Oct. 3, 6	William Kelly	9,248.70
1855	Elmira...........	Oct. 2, 5	Samuel Cheever...	11,527.25
1856	Watertown......	{ Sept. 30, } { Oct. 3 }	Theod're S. Faxton	8,010.00
1857	Buffalo	Oct. 6, 9	Alonzo S. Upham.	15,073.89
1858	Syracuse	Oct. 5, 8	Wm. T. McCoun...	10,815.81
1859	Albany...........	Oct. 4, 7	A. B. Cruger.......	

Town and Union Agricultural Societies.

(For County Societies see p. 103.)

NAME.	Date of organization.	NAME.	Date of organization.
Bainbridge Agricultural Society..............	Jan. 3, 1857	Jefferson Agricultural Society, Schoharie Co...	Feb. 23, 1858
Brookfield Agricultural Society................	March 5, 1856	Lebanon Agricultural Society.....................	Aug. 19, 1856
Canaseraga Agricultural & Mechanical Society,		Leon Agricultural Society.........................	Sept. 15, 1856
Dansville.................................	March 10, 1858	Lodi Agricultural Society, of	Aug. 22, 1857
Chautauqua Farmers' & Mechanics' Union at		Nelson Farmers & Mechanics'Association........	June 5, 1858
Fredonia.................................	March 14, 1859	Oswego City Agricultural Society.................	March 19, 1859
Connewango Agricultural, Horticultural, & Mechanical Society.....................	May 13, 1856	Otselic, Pitcher, Pharsalia, & Lincklaen Agricultural Society..................................	June 27, 1857
Connewango Union Agricultural & Horticultural Society.................................	Sept. 4, 1858	Rushville Union Agricultural Society.............	Feb. 9, 1855
Constantia Town Agricultural Society	Oct. 19, 1857	St. Lawrence International Agricultural & Mechanical Society, Ogdensburgh..............	June 21, 1856
Coventry Agricultural Society.....................	March 23, 1857	Sandy Creek, Richland, Orwell, & Boylston Agricultural Society.................................	March 20, 1859
Dryden Agricultural Society......................	Aug. 16, 1856	Sangerfield & Marshall Town Agricultural Society.................................	Nov. 10, 1857
Ellisburgh, Adams, & Henderson Agricultural Society..................................	Dec. 28, 1855	Somerset Agricultural Society.....................	Jan. 27, 1857
Farmers' Club, of Little Falls....................	Jan. 8, 1858	Susquehanna Valley Agricultural & Horticultural Society.................................	April 4, 1857
Farmers' & Mechanics' Association of Cazenovia	Jan. 12, 1859	Union Agricultural Society, (Broome and Delaware cos.).................................	March 29, 1859
Farmers' & Mechanics' Association of Fenner...	Jan. 3, 1857	Union Agricultural Society, of Palmyra...........	June 26, 1856
Galen Agricultural Society.......................	Jan. 3, 1857	Virgil Agricultural Society.........................	Feb. 26, 1857
Gorham Agricultural Society.....................	Jan. 13, 1857	Wilson Agricultural Society........................	June 10, 1859
Gouverneur Agricultural & Mechanical Society	Feb. 9, 1859	Winfield Union Agricultural Society.............	April 18, 1859
Hamilton Agricultural & Horticultural Association of	Aug. 22, 1857	Wiskoy Agricultural Society, Genesee Falls, Pike, & Eagle.................................	Dec. 6, 1855
Harpersfield Union Agricultural Society.........	April 5, 1859		
Hartland Agricultural Society....................	Feb. 2, 1856		
Hornellsville Agricultural Society................	March 31, 1856		

of the time when due. Each society formed under these acts is obliged to report annually to the State Society.[1]

An examination of the returns of the census of 1855 shows that *Cattaraugus* excels all other counties in the production of millet; *Columbia* in pears, rye, garden seeds, and onions; *Dutchess* in plums and quinces, and in number of swine; *Herkimer* in cheese; *Jefferson* in spring wheat and barley; *Livingston* in fallow lands, in winter wheat, and in wool; *Monroe* in value of farms and nurseries; *Montgomery* in lint; *Oneida* in value of stock and amount of apples and honey; *Onondaga* in acres plowed and quantity of oats, corn, tobacco, and cider; *Ontario* in sheep; *Orange* in milk; *Orleans* in beans; *Otsego* in hops and in domestic linen; *Queens* in garden seeds and strawberries; *Rensselaer* in flaxseed; *St. Lawrence* in pasture and meadow lands, quantity of peas, sugar and butter, number of horses and cows, and yards of fulled cloth, flannel and other

[1] *Summary of County Agricultural Societies.*
(For Town and Union Societies see p. 102.)

COUNTIES.	Date of present organization.	First President.	First Secretary.	Present place of holding annual fair.	Total receipts from the beginning.	Date of purchase or lease.	Extent in acres.	Cost of grounds.	Cost with fixtures.
Albany a	Aug. 9, 1853	James W. Jolly	Joseph Warren	Albany.					
Allegany.									
Broome	April 27, 1858								
Cattaraugus	Jan. 28, 1855	P. Ten Broeck	D. R. Wheeler	Little Valley	$5,500	1856	10	Leased.	
Cayuga	June 21, 1856	H. Howland	Wm. Richardson.	Auburn		1856	19	$2,850	$5,850
Chautauqua	1836	T. B. Campbell		Migratory	{ 2,000 per ann.				
Chemung	1851	Simeon L. Rood	A. J. Wynkoop	Horseheads	1,836				
Chenango	1845	Abram Perlee	A. Sanford	Norwich	13,000		5	Leased.	1,000
Clinton.									
Columbia	March 8, 1856	E. Livingston	Jas. M. Gifford	{ Chatham 4 Corners }	11,625	1856	15¼	2,600	6,400
Cortland	Oct. 1838	W. Bewry			10,000	1858	15		6,500
Delaware	July, 1841	Samuel A. Law	D. McFarland	b	6,215				
Dutchess	Oct. 16, 1841	Henry Staats	Geo. Kneeland	Wash. Hollow	10,800		7	Leased.	2,100
Erie	June 2, 1856	Lewis F. Allen	Warren Bryant	Buffalo	7,050		52	Leased.	1,400
Essex	Dec. 1850	W. C. Watson	R. S. Hale	Elizabethtown.					
Franklin	July 30, 1856	S. Lawrence	Harry S. House	Malone		1856	10	1,000	
Fult. & Ham.	Oct. 18, 1838	Elias Prindle	T. S. Persse	Johnstown	2,368				
Genesee	May 26, 1857	T. C Peters	C. P. Turner	Batavia.					
Greene	Oct. 11, 1856	Lewis Sherrill	H. L. Day		10,113				
Herkimer	Sept. 4, 1841	A. Loomis	Aaron Petrie	Ilion			5	Leased.	1,000
Jefferson	Dec. 7, 1854	J. D. Le Ray	E. Ten Eyck	Watertown	30,000	1851	14	1,600	
Lewis	1841	E. Merriam		{ Turin and Lowville.					
Livingston	June 30, 1855	Aaron Barber	Jos. Kershner	Geneseo	12,000		15	Leased.	4,000
Madison	Feb. 8, 1856	J. D. Ledyard	A. S. Sloan	Morrisville		1853	6	3,500	
Monroe	March 19, 1856	Willard Hodges	D. D. T. Moore.	Brighton			25	4,000	15,926,95
Montgomery	Oct. 13, 1841	T. J. Van Deville.	John Frey	Fonda.					
Niagara	Dec. 2, 1858								
Oneida	April, 1841	Pomeroy Jones	B. P. Johnston	Utica and Rome.					
Onondaga	Jan. 25, 1856			Syracuse.					
Ontario	May 18, 1854	Wm. Hildreth	J. S. Bates	Canandaigua	20,836	1854–5		2,461	13,160
Orange	1841								
Orleans	Oct. 17, 1856	T. C. Bailey	Hiram Goff	Albion	6,500	1857	12	1,600	3,350
Oswego	Dec. 27, 1855								
Otsego	Jan. 22, 1856	D. H. Little	Chas. McLean	Cooperstown	8,635		8		
Putnam	1851	T. B. Arden	Hugh C. Wilson.	c					
Queens	Nov. 30, 1857	E. Lawrence	A. G. Corll	d	9,590				
Rensselaer	Jan. 7, 1855	Jos. Hastings	Luther D. Eddy	Lansingburgh	30,385				
Richmond.									
Rockland	June 29, 1844	Abrams Stevens	N. C. Blauvelt	New City.					
St. Lawrence	June 21, 1856	H. Van Rensselaer	Henry G. Foote	Canton.					
Saratoga	June 24, 1841	H. Gardner	John A. Corey	Mechanicsville.					
Schenectady.									
Schoharie	Oct. 26, 1841	Wm. C. Bouck	Ralph Brewster.						
Schuyler	March 14, 1855								
Seneca	Jan. 24, 1856								
Steuben	June 22, 1853	G. Denniston	George S. Ellas	Bath.				Leased.	
Suffolk.									
Sullivan	Nov. 9, 1847	Lotan Smith	J. O. Dunning	Monticello.					
Tioga	Aug. 11, 1855	Henry Corgell	Wm. Smythe	Owego.			8		
Tompkins	Jan. 8, 1858								
Ulster	Jan. 7, 1858	Peter Crispell		b					
Warren	March 5, 1857	B. C. Butler	C. H. Skillman	Luzerne.					
Washington	Aug. 4, 1841	Henry Holmes	Asa Fitch, Jr	b	6,120	1857	8	2,500	
Wayne	May 5, 1855	{ De Witt C. Van Slyck. }	P. P. Bradish	Lyons	4,239		17		
Westchester.									
Wyoming	July 20, 1856	Jas. C. Ferris	L. W. Thayer	Warsaw	4,356		10		
Yates	Jan. 13, 1855	John Hatmaker	Darius A. Ogden.	Penn Yan	6,520	1854	3¼		

a Societies in italics were organized under acts of 1853 and 1855. Most of them had been in existence many years under a previous organization.
b Fairs in the town that will give most to pay expenses.

c Fairs held alternately in different parts of the county, and generally at the place that contributes most toward expenses.
d Fair held alternately at Jamaica, Flushing, and Hempstead. Receipts the first 10 years, $3,532.

domestic cloths; *Schenectady* in broom corn; *Schoharie* in buckwheat, and about equal with Montgomery in clover; *Washington* in potatoes; and *Wayne* in peaches and dried fruits.

In connection with the table of agricultural products, it should be remembered that these

Agricultural Products of the several Counties in the State

COUNTIES.	*Bushels Winter Wheat.*	*Bushels Spring Wheat.*	*Tons of Hay.*	*Bushels of Oats.*	*Bushels of Rye.*	*Bushels of Barley.*	*Bushels of Buckwheat.*	*Bushels of Corn.*
Albany	7,424	6,927¼	54,579¼	495,177½	186,567	9,126½	84,812¾	193,691½
Allegany	82,929	56,422½	54,637¾	665,490	2,834	28,454½	39,298½	189,588½
Broome	11,927½	8,121½	53,685	466,870½	20,546	2,337	73,214¼	214,998
Cattaraugus	21,721	57,278½	62,546¾	697,670½	2,373½	14,095	26,183	309,762
Cayuga	193,729½	27,327	57,732	956,636	6,331¾	308,303½	54,076½	868,543
Chautauqua	66,249½	78,636¼	105,672	539,765	2,808	19,656¼	9,664¾	558,507½
Chemung	63,754	18,624	24,941	473,469	3,558	23,862	69,046½	239,285½
Chenango	4,560½	20,283½	117,370¾	564,242	14,329	22,229	50,304½	354,480
Clinton	2,138½	57,172¾	48,241	276,080¼	13,073	6,877	30,651⅝	92,567¾
Columbia	7,972½	587½	65,103	543,034	445,036	3,801	54,334½	383,339½
Cortland	4,696¼	24,361	56,769¼	382,786	4,172	45,665½	28,115½	240,703½
Delaware	955½	8,538¾	103,896¼	416,659½	56,527½	2,219	86,330	119,383
Dutchess	54,470½	250	83,878½	626,347	239,063	2,818	43,124¼	558,308
Erie	238,812¾	46,913	98,011½	724,747½	24,979½	57,256½	24,558½	483,228
Essex	2,484	44,009¼	39,139¾	234,946	13,357½	1,118½	13,701¾	105,369
Franklin	1,353¾	69,559½	37,594½	144,617	20,191½	6,188¾	13,625¼	83,615
Fulton	3,644½	7,500¼	33,903	355,855	22,383½	14,704	69,759	155,733
Genesee	760,461	11,154	41,398¾	299,809	1,149	59,819	14,913½	437,052½
Greene	7,346	3,175½	58,524¼	160,907½	72,232	1,787½	33,913½	99,204
Hamilton	6	245	4,274	16,701	277	42	2,913¾	7,151
Herkimer	5,904½	38,149	78,254¾	724,585	17,550	51,439½	42,875¾	283,748
Jefferson	70,509½	428,672⅜	98,575	456,230¾	99,391½	392,684½	5,909¾	321,779
Kings	18,086	....	6,183	11,679	4,860	....	235	54,179
Lewis	3,845¼	59,940	51,802	295,445½	11,383½	37,513½	10,443¼	92,398¼
Livingston	1,094,779	18,025	39,187¾	261,990	4,118	123,255½	13,836¼	431,464½
Madison	29,320½	52,777	68,263½	571,637	1,477	197,231	13,853½	449,583
Monroe	810,363	2,620	58,738¾	792,370	9,166½	179,755	22,623¾	805,811
Montgomery	23,904½	18,978½	44,532¼	997,605	39,112½	39,252½	141,677½	247,516½
New York	30	....	157	435	25	....	....	1,180
Niagara	589,911	5,386	41,117½	353,398	1,014	79,593	29,151½	509,505
Oneida	20,439¾	41,883¼	124,933½	975,800¼	24,121	137,430	54,767⅝	732,294½
Onondaga	97,058¾	85,148	63,246⅜	1,015,227½	5,340½	371,785½	32,453¾	907,453
Ontario	528,488	27,659	42,448⅜	525,937½	16,002	320,375	18,325¾	617,485¼
Orange	43,363½	32	103,211¼	291,111	202,301	179	23,023¾	357,490½
Orleans	376,949	2,206	34,620¼	229,731	2,777	36,071	12,903	436,975
Oswego	12,596	44,300⅞	58,138	535,432½	45,557½	28,054	31,605¾	503,812
Otsego	5,678	53,446¼	108,069¾	903,647	34,218¼	43,889	112,732¾	340,170½
Putnam	3,550¾	....	27,756¾	66,922	22,890½	....	10,718¼	119,919½
Queens	402,169¼	48	51,395	199,518	71,019	2,769	21,224½	337,685
Rensselaer	2,658	13,383½	58,557¾	558,377	299,864	12,807	52,821	393,413½
Richmond	11,335¾	575	7,032	15,991½	3,131½	627	1,325	43,037½
Rockland	2,945¾	6	14,828	28,168	31,600½	14	8,722¼	51,873
St. Lawrence	24,780½	295,464	139,400	437,041	25,725	28,187	12,912½	220,593
Saratoga	14,826¼	8,074	52,743¾	744,220	132,774¾	9,524	108,882½	479,449
Schenectady	5,165½	6,377½	16,185½	293,768	44,752½	5,569½	41,858	92,279
Schoharie	18,645	23,074¾	48,774¾	490,063½	87,592½	44,136	169,078	161,153½
Schuyler	80,431½	33,139¾	17,996¼	357,247	6,168	60,507	67,523	160,780½
Seneca	151,721	11,379	20,879¾	556,238	7,862	104,856	21,436½	387,998½
Steuben	219,590	82,014	58,749¼	711,307	10,212	78,873	89,990½	292,689½
Suffolk	151,520½	129¼	41,505¾	262,067½	52,212½	10,974	18,856½	504,767
Sullivan	1,472½	98	40,716¼	109,883	75,153	1,053½	65,571½	102,594
Tioga	19,355	11,938¼	38,401¾	452.978	25,884½	5,925	91,402½	260,074
Tompkins	84,395½	32,642¾	38,143¾	812,983	17,521	65,295	74,305	372,202
Ulster	19,370¾	815	64,795	278,105	235,993½	130	70,676	242,229½
Warren	1,212	4,285	22,088¾	120,347	10,952½	39	19,214¾	123,817
Washington	8,387	23.854	69,881	798,321	121,967	12,944½	40,658½	589,678½
Wayne	282,474¾	2,687	45,271½	875.624½	7,259½	229,495	39,766¼	756,677¼
Westchester	33,751½	1,497	90,496⅞	204,759	51,404	545	20,890¾	402,238½
Wyoming	382,498½	37,497½	58,421¼	496,837	2,777½	68.267	20,277¾	234,006
Yates	168,969½	18,063	15,850¼	160,457¾	24,517	152,134	24,007¼	174,181
Total	7,054,049¼	2,033,353	3,256,948⅞	27,015,296	3,039,438	3,563,540	2,481,079¼	19,290,691½

Items not included in the above Tables.

Cash value of farms	$799,355,367	Gallons of wine made	18,181
" " stock	$103,776,053	Pounds of cocoons	267½
" " tools and implements	$26,927,502	Value of other textile fabrics	$8,824
Acres plowed the year previous	3,377,471	Bushels of beets	29,332½
Acres in fallow the year previous	506,030⅛	Value of cabbages	$18,668
Acres in pasture the year previous	4,984,114½	Bushels of carrots	478,277
Bushels of turnips harvested	985,522½	Bushels of cherries	3,787¾
Pounds of tobacco harvested	946,502½	Bushels of cranberries	87
Value products market gardens	$1,138,682	Value of cucumbers	$9,619
Pounds of maple sugar made	4,935,815¾	Bushels of currants	506½
Gallons of maple molasses made	85,091½	Bushels of fruits (not specified)	43,074

numbers refer to the yield of 1854, which was distinguished by a severe and prevalent drought. From 20 to 50 per cent. should be added to obtain the proximate results of years of ordinary production.

of New York, as reported by the State Census of 1855.

Bushels of Potatoes.	*Bushels of Peas.*	*Bushels of Beans.*	FLAX. *Pounds of Lint.*	FLAX. *Bushels of Seed.*	*Pounds of Hops.*	*Pounds of Tobacco.*	*Bushels of Apples.*	*Barrels of Cider.*
375,654½	15,989½	2,306	2,675	210¼	7,440	....	234,251	6,038
206,258	22,844½	3,174¾	879	205¼	2,768	128½	214,136	2,983
160,420½	932½	949⅞	478	35½	21,808	23,650	224,463	4,747½
300,245¾	14,492¼	4,496½	2,738	58⅜	488	1,770	177,173½	1,257
251,718⅛	6,565	5,638½	18,385	1,166	2,640	3,300	522,751	10,362¼
282,451	7,693	4,038	4,584	302¼	2,416	1,390	368,115	4,524½
131,291	1,360½	1,859¼	130	66¼	102	33,597	107,364	2,961
270,542	4,018½	2,763¼	16,636	203½	163,332	550	553,554	7,559½
385,492	14,545	6,993¼	7,700	236½	1,014	20	76,936½	852½
259,419½	1,336¾	739	1,128	54¾	....	418	210,342	9,480
155,389	9,527	1,726¼	58,269	2,173¾	2,037	40	351,975	3,738
209,567¼	2,229½	2,128¼	1,477	25¾	69,028½	....	259,160	5,918¼
205,498	670	788¼	557	15	3,104	18,507	216,593	8,247¾
445,350½	15,321½	6,124	5,026	276½	2,862	50	266,195	6,084¾
318,021	11,625¾	2,818	195	6½	9	....	64,200½	909½
484,425	12,074½	1,839¼	704	6½	231,217	153	26,273	377¼
182,964	14,202	761¼	223,005	1,215½	....	....	100,142	2,670½
167,274	8,797½	8,569½	118,500	595½	12,007	4,130	296,121	5,767
116,871	1,532½	693½	10,620	14½	26	75	192,814½	3,954½
25,257	140	154½	6,000	....	....	....	3,459	18
257,875	27,864	1,616	308,050	4,241	510,033	115	333,901	6,446
289,031	63,338	4,281¼	12,066	760¾	28,995	3,691	215,431	3,459½
368,243	16,930	7,042	....	....	....	....	54	
243,841	12,978½	1,030½	65,782	1,566	8,870	....	72,198	1,451
132,256½	6,398½	1,003¼	90	13½	14,255	10	242,200	5,928½
224,278½	20,973½	4,836½	102,581	735½	1,312,308	13,680	531,677	7,417½
654,551	16,028½	14,342¾	1,000	56½	44,010	86,520	491,491	10,312
145,154	22,855½	3,941	1,016,929	7,746¾	241,603	249	155,861	5,608½
1,808	250	645	....	....	....	....	....	
275,448	15,981	9,256½	380	322	....	13,010	255,997	4,461½
624,648	12,912½	7,770¾	6,635	1,233½	616,054	39,220	634,262	12,735
380,141½	34,915½	8,984	57,287	2,644¾	13,427	554,987	624,545½	13,725¼
188,900	15,297½	2,404¾	2,070	199½	32,751	9,180	397,098	8,044
123,551½	230	348¼	30	....	39	800	80,180½	3,188½
171,867	5,471	40,185¾	19,030	285	16	22,871	281,781½	4,534
391,912¼	11,116½	4,326	37,109	749	29,206	15	425,915	8,105½
412,703½	29,935⅞	2,811½	98,504⅝	1,424¼	3,122,258½	543	601,196	8,880
64,504	48	210½	....	....	20	....	27,158	814½
291,135	33,444	22,282½	300	1	25	....	3,346	29
596,559	1,574	5,979	672,780	19,266½	1,615	....	131,241	4,364
21,739	410	166¾	....	....	....	....	28	
47,223½	49	63	....	....	3	....	3,253	47
604,023	69,016	5,131	1,206½	4	197,875	....	90,497	719
487,672	6,466	972⅞	15,125	515¾	18,364	200	289,478	11,386½
105,132	5,551¼	714½	206,200	2,346	2,600	150	105,551	2,848½
190,432½	33,482½	1,656½	13,916	526¾	440,754	15	222,182	3,689½
81,106	1,710¼	1,931	8,058	420½	730	30	143,229	3,212
72,544	640¼	573¼	529.811	7,035	....	16,500	175,278	4,629
255,938	25,006½	2,686½	1,777	306	8,649	16,950	297,289	4,580
304,063	142	1,382¼	....	....	304	1,000	27,799	427½
103,188¾	168½	698¼	92	2⅝	176	52	73,298	1,699¼
150,518½	3,992½	2,495¼	712	140½	1,200	160	169,183	4,359
111,106	4,659½	2,100½	79,932	1,706	1,138	27,090	417,757	6,172
134,539½	296¼	534	2,017	78	2,735	2,524	397,754	5,606½
173,328	2,270½	915¾	....	....	7	20	58,772¾	1,002
767,285	14,210½	5,075¼	839,420	23,003	62	2,390	189,103	5,809½
261,403	8,455½	5,866¾	23,260	527½	737	38,432	509,626	8,893½
286,249	230	278½	....	....	5	2,202	60,137½	2,325¼
203,932	13,326½	8,232½	6,630	518¼	17,526	115	323,290	4,517½
57,912½	1,444	745¾	245,000	1,850	1,605	6,003	143,773	3,760½
15,191,852⅛	705,967⅝	244,079	4,907,556⅛	87,093½	7,192,254	946,502½	13,668,830¾	273,639

Value of garden seeds	$40,889
Bushels of grapes	1,610¾
Value of melons	$4,682
Bushels of millet	6.453½
Bushels of onions	15.026½
Value of osier willow	$251
Bushels of quinces	2,035¼
Value of root crops (miscellaneous)	$16,703
Bushels of ruta baga	3,111
Pounds of saffron	1,798
Bushels of strawberries	371
Value of fruit and ornamental trees	$142,328
Miscellaneous	$611,397
Neat cattle under one year old	311,474
Neat cattle over one year, exclusive of working oxen and cows	577,887
Number of cattle killed for beef	225,338
Gallons of milk sold	20,965,861
Pounds of wool	9,231,959¼
Value of poultry sold	$1,076,598
Value of eggs sold	$1,360,673
Yards of fulled cloth made	198,203
Yards of flannel made	379.922½
Yards of linen made	105,086
Yards of cotton and mixed cloths	245,464
Yards of carpeting	213,617¼

The State appropriations for the promotion of agriculture, in 1819, through the Board of Agriculture, and, since 1841, through the State and County Agricultural Societies, have been as shown in the table commencing at the foot of this page.

Agricultural Products of the several

COUNTIES.	*Pounds of Honey.*	*Pounds of Wax.*	*Total No. of Neat Cattle.*	*No. of Working Oxen.*	*No. of Cows.*	*Pounds of Butter.*
Albany	53,650	3,436½	23,247	1,813	13,332	1,173,527
Allegany	68,998	3,321½	47,332	3,392	19,009	1,700,775
Broome	47,380	2,113½	37,544	3,531	17,116	1,753,417
Cattaraugus	62,486	3,378	58,489	4,137	23,633	1,957,183
Cayuga	83,553½	4,165½	46,178	2,506	19,822	2,082,022
Chautauqua	53,465	4,142	76,890	4,515	36,046	3,389,837
Chemung	39,191	1,670½	20,899	1,510	9,690	924,645
Chenango	48,702	3,451	68,391	3,887	36,939	3,990,564
Clinton	51,459	2,238½	25,555	1,484	11,284	891,431½
Columbia	31,618	1,466	27,676	3,701	14,500	1,347,428
Cortland	56,148	3,619½	37,671	1,709	21,668	2,379,257
Delaware	101,571	5,285¼	65,181	4,780	34,484	4,026,575
Dutchess	38,503	1,830	44,126	6,263	24,584	1,681,595
Erie	59,659	3.220	55,439	3,794	29,831	1,866,132
Essex	27,342	1,419	23,567	2,081	8,749	625,542
Franklin	19,622	919	23,677	1,859	10,919	1,050,040
Fulton	23,761	1,300	19,922	1,173	10,268	840,397
Genesee	32,359	1,568	24,785	1,417	10,541	919,130
Greene	32,940	2,202½	25,239	2,349	12,592	1,191,930
Hamilton	5,610	401½	2,456	360	852	83,282
Herkimer	38,347	2,927½	49,820	785	36,653	1,305,377
Jefferson	18,444	1,290½	79,249	2,522	49,472	3,949,608
Kings	....	....	3,204	41	2,834	17,425
Lewis	11,912	831	29,748	2,423	19,151	1,575,515
Livingston	26,693	1,950½	29,383	1,751	10.980	1,045,591
Madison	55,615	3,366¾	44,924	1,874	24,067	1,840,298
Monroe	46,038	1,842¾	39,545	1,944	17,564	1,643,515
Montgomery	58,571	3,544	30,502	1,046	16,801	1,211,385
New York	....	....	3,323	......	719	....
Niagara	27,205	1,460	28,238	2,058	11,708	1,038,307
Oneida	138,475	3,455½	77,832	3,476	47,794	2,912,176
Onondaga	81,575	3,857¾	50,228	2,454	24,801	2,294,287
Ontario	53,135	2,458¾	33,962	2,113	14,202	1,223.097
Orange	25,111	2,128½	57,602	3,489	40,187	3,285,587¾
Orleans	23,113	1,151½	23,412	1,164	8,921	912,013
Oswego	47,700	2,142½	42,172	3,093	21,983	2,036,174
Otsego	93,020	4,665¾	63,798	2,942	34,713	3,075,206
Putnam	13,237½	459	15,507	3,200	7,851	493,696
Queens	5,989	276	14,326	1,926	9,240	441,983½
Rensselaer	33,684½	1,840½	29,601	2,704	16,864	1,291,738
Richmond	475	22	2,250	400	1,189	24,365
Rockland	8,667	174½	7,198	573	4,708	266,006
St. Lawrence	51,614	2,814½	96,408	5,576	52,161	4,268,809
Saratoga	45,202½	2,499	34,769	2,625	16,778	1,468,136½
Schenectady	12,688	782½	8,614	597	5,768	515,662
Schoharie	89,676	4,496½	38,771	2,440	18,213	1,832,257
Schuyler	52,167	2,076	19,004	1,128	7,676	798,953
Seneca	37,549	1,609½	16,996	577	7,136	705,574
Steuben	113,653	5,429½	52,483	4,351	20,284	1,976,129
Suffolk	6,087	414	24,215	2,006	10,833	634,405
Sullivan	40,946	2,398½	27,346	4,265	10,775	931,927
Tioga	38,378	1,612¼	29,664	2,323	12,954	1,365,783
Tompkins	83,627	4,075¾	30,847	1,666	14,572	1,645,947
Ulster	49,898	3,125	34,140	4,671	17,332	1,669,631
Warren	20,062	1,061½	14,282	1,423	6,161	482,786
Washington	30,000	1,945	40,410	2,100	18,689	1,625,138
Wayne	58,204	2,820½	38,464	1,762	16,769	1,446,080
Westchester	17,592	6,370¼	33,132	5,427	20,078	1,116,589
Wyoming	36,248	2,000	39,048	2,674	16,737	1,333,948
Yates	29,260	1,510½	16,784	747	7,250	717,259¼
Total	2,557,876	138,033½	2,105,465	144,597	1,068,427	90,293,073½

Appropriations for the Promotion of Agriculture.

COUNTIES.	1819. 2 *years*.	1841.	COUNTIES.	1819. 2 *years*.	1841.	COUNTIES.	1819. 2 *years*.	1841.	COUNTIES.	1819. 2 *years*.	1841.
Albany	$350	$205	Chenango	$200	$122	Essex	$125	$71	Kings	$75	$143
Allegany	75	123	Clinton	125	84	Franklin	100	50	Lewis	100	53
Broome	100	67	Columbia	300	133	Fult. & Ham	......	60	Livingston	......	117
Cattaraugus	......	86	Cortland	125	75	Genesee	250	179	Madison	250	120
Cayuga	250	151	Delaware	200	106	Greene	200	91	Monroe	......	194
Chautauqua	50	143	Dutchess	400	157	Herkimer	200	112	Montgomery	400	107
Chemung	......	62	Erie	......	186	Jefferson	200	183	New York	650	950

By an act of April 11, 1842, Genesee receives $92 and Wyoming $87 annually; and by another of April 13, 1855, the co. of Schuyler was allowed to receive a proportional share from the moneys previously belonging to Chemung, Steuben, and Tompkins cos.

Counties in the State of New York, continued.

Pounds of Cheese.	*No. of Horses.*	*No. of Mules.*	*No. of Sheep.*	*No. of Swine.*	*Tons of Broom Corn.*	*Bushels of Peaches.*	*Bushels of Pears.*	*Bushels of Plums.*
36,520	10,954	31	37,054	24,035	127	834½	334½	359
1,044,978	11,223	36	104,799	13,148	.....	147	52	1,592½
40,896	5,998	7	40,894	12,251	13½	137½	11	14
1,717,484	9,497	11	59,725	13,834	2½	647½	39	146
199,333	15,405	4	103,631	29,081	.....	5,041	395	15
1,198,361	13,047	15	90,154	21,105	62	4,742	149	135½
7,861	4,856	6	21,364	9,853	¼	924	27	190
1,212,544	10,971	10	85,923	18,092	.....	....	55	
105,906	8,444	36	38,351	7,868	.....	....	.....	25
67,167	9,103	211	87,549	32,568	4½	1,999	759	313
708,679	7,410	27	41,321	12,302	1	55	43	11
61,185	9,140	5	71,315	15,870	.....	38½	11	5
54,119	10,829	29	73,687	42,986	.....	1,072	278	1,780
2,038,392	16,983	10	65,085	24,791	.....	2,616	139	207
93,594	6,149	43	47,654	6,504	.....	....	.....	23
143,916	6,029	3	23,958	7,535				
579,079	5,829	1	16,969	10,514	1⅛	....	6	
105,873	11,395	13	100,391	10,273	.....	3,506	267	
21,317	6,203	23	19,382	14,074	⅛	140	232	
2,670	338	.....	1,481	510	.....	....	.....	
9,068,519	9,098	10	17,706	18,227	25⅛	....	48	10
2,819,459	17,059	20	63,401	23,327	.....	....	.....	121
....	6,314	122	2	3,964	.....	15	115	
1,896,741	5,097	9	10,086	8,353	.....	....	1	1½
79,346½	12,502	47	112,562	19,275	70½	618	38	24
2,087,594	11,753	32	66,547	16.794	5	....	485	21
131,253	18,913	16	116,817	34,727	.....	22,134	240	4
1,538,654	8,836	3	29,661	18,834	256½	....	77	125
....	14,099	256	....	1,249				
71,443	14,334	5	78,359	21,765	4¾	12,378	47	87
3,311,114	17,398	34	50,841	31,228	14¾	....	468½	27
860,644	17,330	8	94,202	31,539	.....	1,165	376	201
205,921	13,660	159	132,725	26,419	.....	3,073	599	265
80,660	9,986	74	21,377	40,684	.....	2,705	69	146
110,298	9,640	2	91,285	15,692	.....	4,031	136	100
975,461	12,398	23	36,088	21,836	.....	2,244	450	129½
1,638,493	14,652	17	109,937	22,368	.....	8½	62½	82
3,475	1,938	1	5,804	6,997	⅛			
765	7,954	178	9,714	14,228	.....	111	60	
538,462	10,184	10	64,609	25,007	48	392	341	341
....	845	26	57	1,726				
2,500	3,715	170	926	3,185	.....	8	.....	5
1,672,999	20,261	20	86,454	24,286	.....	....	.....	5
152,901¾	11,293	2	46,018	26,003	.....	....	94	
72,019	4,219	4	10,759	7,727	727	....	.....	312
71,016	9,682	2	45,596	18,804	134⅝	28	8	
32,168	5,700	4	48,918	9,451	.....	3,195	.....	630
13,812	7,497	6	47,534	17,532	¼	5,777	378	
203,329	13,899	40	111,353	24,154	.....	1,148	4	397
1,580	7,111	163	28,016	19,727	1	1,330	91	8
4,598	3,092	87	12,591	8,231	¼	568	134	
50,357	5,678	13	36,152	11,248	.....	586	31	22
60,128	9,443	3	61,036	14,358	.....	1,919	127	4
520	9,893	58	29,841	34,025	.....	1,721	111	3
64,634	3,341	6	16,472	5,703	.....	....	.....	144
634,491	11,707	11	118,533	30,305	2½	....	.....	75
163,763½	14,928	5	104,845	29,799	7½	25,394	156	5
2,180	7,332	73	11,321	20,861	.....	895		
823,105	10,358	6	93,365	11,674	.....	397	70	212
59,972	6,773	8	64,827	12,586	.....	1,689	15	281
38,944,249¾	579,715	2,254	3,217,024	1,069,792	1,509⅞	115,410½	7,629½	8,604

Appropriations for the Promotion of Agriculture, continued.

Counties.	1819. 2 *years.*	1841.	Counties.	1819. 2 *years.*	1841.	Counties.	1819. 2 *years.*	1841.	Counties.	1819. 2 *years.*	1841.
Niagara	.....	$93	Putnam	$100	$38	Schoharie	$200	$97	Ulster	$250	$137
Oneida	$400	255	Queens	200	91	Seneca	150	74	Warren	100	40
Onondaga	300	204	Rensselaer	350	180	Steuben	150	138	Washington	350	123
Ontario	500	130	Richmond	75	34	Suffolk	200	97	Wayne	.....	126
Orange	300	152	Rockland	100	36	Sullivan	100	47	Westchester	250	146
Orleans	.....	75	St. Lawrence	100	170	Tioga	150	61	Yates	.....	61
Oswego	.....	131	Saratoga	300	121	Tompkins	150	114	State Ag. Soc.	.....	700
Otsego	400	148	Schenectady	100	51						

County societies usually require the payment of $1 annually from each member, or $10 for life membership without further payment. It is customary to restrict competition for premiums to members of the society, and to collect of all others an entrance fee to the exhibition grounds.

Dwellings, Area, and Products.

Counties.	Number of Dwellings.					No. of Farms.	Number of Acres.	
	Stone.	*Brick.*	*Frame.*	*Log.*	*Total.*[1]		*Improved.*	*Total.*
Albany	88	3,769	9,385	19	13,591	3,539	242,735	313,512¼
Allegany	13	29	6,287	966	8,192	5,392	280,863	635,132¼
Broome	4	82	5,529	560	6,436	3,925	198,839⅝	404,048⅜
Cattaraugus	5	9	4,942	1,252	7,515	5,441	266,435¾	699,056⅜
Cayuga	73	325	9,620	475	10,916	4,299	315,795⅜	503,032⅞
Chautauque	14	113	8,314	639	9,988	6,547	360,110	654,255½
Chemung	1	47	3,264	516	4,837	1,948	120,219¾	230,605
Chenango	20	21	7,226	240	7,602	5,203	347,828⅜	530,764⅜
Clinton	163	460	3,959	1,988	6,994	3,551	168,932⅜	570,018⅞
Columbia	52	388	6,665	29	7,287	3,242	304,277⅜	373,532⅜
Cortland	9	45	4,276	295	4,727	3,388	194,736⅞	308,399¾
Delaware	44	8	6,040	888	7,238	5,458	364,400¼	802,852½
Dutchess	177	434	8,947	58	9,705	3,797	366,359⅜	464,464⅛
Erie	111	2,427	12,834	1,638	21,674	7,257	340,307¼	593,651⅞
Essex	30	168	4,176	663	5,227	2,715	185,443⅜	959,638⅝
Franklin	88	71	2,545	1,353	4,444	3,247	144,627¼	979,692
Fulton	2	53	3,817	238	4,179	2,288	133,415¾	280,486½
Genesee	60	107	4,976	408	5,753	3,063	219,012¼	294,744½
Greene	100	163	4,964	145	5,419	3,145	212,223⅞	362,828⅜
Hamilton	2	....	273	147	461	404	16,675¾	783,654¼
Herkimer	62	165	6,332	191	6,898	3,447	267,414½	773,072
Jefferson	429	208	9,534	1,369	11,975	6,992	465,222	716,513
Kings	515	8,061	14,901	....	23,970	398	15,871¼	21,466
Lewis	34	18	3,195	1,094	4,707	3,945	184,540½	681,686¼
Livingston	57	113	5,787	608	6,990	3,375	262,462½	358,840¾
Madison	50	95	7,688	173	8,221	4,680	277,393⅜	388,898¾
Monroe	301	1,760	13,713	650	16,916	4,879	216,840¼	295,022¼
Montgomery	59	147	4,700	23	4,960	2,852	194,457⅝	241,178⅜
New York	1,617	29,977	10,595	....	42,668	48	1,150¾	1,974¼
Niagara	348	299	5,361	1,525	8,698	3,968	207,043⅞	308,153⅞
Oneida	59	623	16,062	496	17,782	8,315	435,800⅜	722,394⅝
Onondaga	60	762	13,175	498	15,215	6,336	344,528	459,229½
Ontario	120	516	6,591	513	7,828	3,943	290,639¾	387,748½
Orange	232	474	8,162	405	9,582	3,982	308,599⅜	498,214⅜
Orleans	182	133	4,119	346	5,299	2,454	181,948¾	244,275⅜
Oswego	67	131	10,516	821	12,649	6,720	244,126	572,173⅝
Otsego	84	50	8,837	287	9,324	6,109	428,932⅝	608,491⅞
Putnam	1	47	2,270	63	2,405	1,368	94,205⅞	138,653⅝
Queens	21	70	7,071	....	7,896	3,113	119,549	176,753
Rensselaer	16	1,559	9,719	203	11,683	3,869	292,212⅞	393,215⅜
Richmond	74	122	3,018	....	3,220	876	15,072⅜	22,674½
Rockland	251	106	2,775	40	3,188	1,221	46,481¾	97,334¼
St. Lawrence	312	176	8,427	3,443	13,191	8,946	499,554	1,385,085
Saratoga	32	343	7,944	163	8,631	4,208	315,728¼	455,577½
Schenectady	15	605	2,449	14	3,105	1,328	93,448½	125,131¾
Schoharie	13	31	5,333	435	5,846	4,011	227,904⅜	359,950⅝
Schuyler	2	13	2,634	405	3,582	2,446	134,336¼	197,335½
Seneca	41	267	3,924	254	4,669	2,238	151,949¾	197,886⅛
Steuben	12	57	8,042	1,938	11,351	7,042	361,450	799,700½
Suffolk	9	56	7,089	7	7,241	4,338	163,818⅞	424,389¾
Sullivan	15	....	4,230	757	5,403	3,683	125,489¼	620,318½
Tioga	5	35	4,351	483	5,049	3,088	154,894⅛	293,317⅜
Tompkins	9	77	4,871	287	6,051	3,623	205,616⅝	290,580⅝
Ulster	903	329	9,028	582	11,068	4,851	240,641	618,843¾
Warren	6	90	2,524	461	3,614	2,145	111,202⅝	442,543⅝
Washington	23	321	7,243	124	7,875	4,192	333,030¼	476,585
Wayne	250	323	6,889	859	8,708	4,767	254,451⅜	356,513⅝
Westchester	158	470	12,044	3	12,758	3,722	209,146¾	291,094¼
Wyoming	11	50	5,181	603	6,041	4,131	241,654¼	364,418¾
Yates	25	52	3,275	452	3,873	2,242	155,542½	206,676½
Total	7,536	57,450	397,638	33,092	522,325	231,740	13,657,490¾	26,758,183⅜

[1] This column includes the four preceding ones, and also a miscellaneous class reported as "Planks," "Boards," "Shanties," &c. Of 4,196 dwellings, the material and value were not given. The value, so far as reported, was as follows:—

	Number.	*Total Value.*	*Average Value.*
Stone	7,172	$49,184,819	$6,857.89
Brick	56,752	312,151,135	5,500.26
Frame	378,967	297,453,492	784.90
Log	28,831	1,330,168	46.13
Total	487,904	664,899,967	1,362.76

MANUFACTURES.

THE manufactures of the State are very extensive, embracing an almost endless variety of articles. In many sections the manufacturing interests surpass those of agriculture or commerce. The lines of internal communication through the State have greatly facilitated the spread of manufactures; and now flourishing establishments are found in nearly every part of the State.[1] The most im-

[1] *Manufacturing Establishments in the several Counties, as reported by the State Census of 1855.*

COUNTIES.	Bakeries.	Blacksmith shops.	Boot and shoe shops.	Breweries.	Brick manufactories.	Cabinet making shops.	Carding and cloth dressing establishments.	Carpenter shops.	Chandlers' and soap factories.	Coach and wagon manufactories.	Cooper shops.	Furnaces.	Gristmills.	Harness, saddle, and trunk manufactories.	Hat and cap manufactories.	Lime manufactories.	Machine shops.	Marble manufactories.
Albany	15	27	27	9	11	8	3	9	5	29	12	25	23	7	8	3	2	8
Allegany	1	37	23	...	1	13	2	2	...	24	3	4	23	13	2	...	2	2
Broome	...	23	16	1	1	5	4	...	1	15	7	2	27	6	1	1	5	2
Cattaraugus	2	32	16	1	1	15	3	1	...	18	8	4	20	10	...	1	1	...
Cayuga	...	59	36	...	2	11	3	7	3	32	9	10	30	13	1	2	3	2
Chautauqua	2	43	37	4	3	13	3	3	1	31	22	7	31	11	...	...	5	2
Chemung	...	19	15	2	1	6	...	4	2	9	7	7	17	3	3	2	...	2
Chenango	1	41	28	...	1	7	8	...	...	21	16	15	28	10	...	2	1	
Clinton	1	22	15	...	9	6	3	1	...	20	4	6	19	9	...	4	2	2
Columbia	1	47	29	1	2	5	1	7	2	34	1	4	43	6	4	...	2	2
Cortland	1	26	26	...	2	7	...	1	1	15	10	1	23	8	1	3	1	2
Delaware	1	31	26	...	...	9	5	...	...	25	10	3	26	10	...	...	2	1
Dutchess	6	44	35	1	13	9	1	3	3	40	7	9	39	9	3	...	3	3
Erie	16	29	31	18	11	19	2	3	9	26	15	9	43	14	...	3	3	2
Essex	...	28	8	...	...	5	1	...	...	15	4	2	16	4	...	1	1	...
Franklin	2	15	7	...	1	5	1	...	1	8	3	1	11	3	...	...	1	1
Fulton	...	12	7	...	1	2	...	7	...	6	10	...	9	5	...	5	...	...
Genesee	2	33	36	1	2	6	2	...	...	25	16	4	22	15	...	2	1	3
Greene	...	19	6	1	22	5	1	3	1	8	4	4	27	3	5	4	2	...
Hamilton	...	...	...	...	...	1	...	...	...	1	...	...	1	...	...	...	...	...
Herkimer	3	36	34	1	1	10	2	5	1	27	11	4	18	10	...	2	5	3
Jefferson	4	52	42	1	4	17	7	3	1	33	10	10	48	17	2	2	6	5
Kings	9	11	10	12	...	16	...	10	2	14	6	15	5	5	2	3	11	7
Lewis	1	9	7	...	1	5	1	1	...	12	1	1	10	6	...	2	...	...
Livingston	2	35	30	4	1	11	1	10	2	26	13	13	29	11	3	...	1	3
Madison	1	27	30	1	...	12	1	...	6	21	9	9	22	16	1	2	4	3
Monroe	8	69	34	16	3	15	3	11	3	48	52	12	54	27	2	5	11	4
Montgomery	2	44	20	...	2	9	3	...	...	21	5	3	24	9	...	...	...	2
New York	54	53	71	19	...	98	...	76	31	59	59	37	8	32	51	4	36	32
Niagara	...	32	24	1	5	6	...	1	...	24	10	4	17	10	1	5	4	2
Oneida	9	65	72	8	5	21	4	1	6	61	19	21	42	26	5	5	7	2
Onondaga	1	53	53	5	9	15	2	12	2	45	38	11	36	26	4	8	9	2
Ontario	...	40	29	1	3	8	1	1	1	19	13	8	40	10	1	2	3	1
Orange	1	37	20	2	14	9	1	2	5	33	8	4	38	15	1	1	3	...
Orleans	2	38	26	...	...	8	2	1	...	21	10	5	26	7	...	...	2	2
Oswego	3	26	29	...	9	13	4	1	...	21	48	9	42	12	2	...	4	1
Otsego	...	66	54	1	2	15	4	11	...	55	17	9	39	20	1	...	5	2
Putnam	...	6	12	...	2	2	...	1	...	2	...	1	7	1	2	...	...	...
Queens	5	14	8	...	2	4	...	2	1	26	...	1	24	7	1	...	...	2
Rensselaer	9	43	25	8	7	10	1	...	4	20	12	7	34	8	1	1	7	3
Richmond	2	6	5	1	1	1	...	3	1	2	...	...	2	...	1	...	...	...
Rockland	1	7	5	1	33	...	...	1	...	7	1	3	13	1	...	1	4	...
St. Lawrence	1	47	37	1	6	12	5	...	...	26	8	8	36	14	3	4	4	2
Saratoga	4	47	29	...	4	7	...	...	2	29	11	3	33	12	...	2	3	3
Schenectady	...	8	9	...	1	5	...	...	1	7	...	3	5	8	...	1	3	...
Schoharie	...	34	21	...	...	5	5	...	...	27	14	4	27	7	...	1	2	1
Schuyler	...	23	16	...	...	4	1	...	...	15	7	2	15	6	...	...	1	...
Seneca	1	23	13	1	4	5	1	...	3	19	7	5	15	8	...	2	1	...
Steuben	2	49	28	...	3	16	3	...	1	36	12	9	42	15	2	1	...	2
Suffolk	1	22	18	...	7	5	3	...	1	16	2	1	29	6	1	...	...	2
Sullivan	...	29	10	1	...	7	2	...	...	13	1	1	16	5	...	...	...	...
Tioga	3	20	17	...	1	5	1	...	...	16	10	2	17	8	...	...	1	1
Tompkins	4	45	34	...	1	16	3	3	...	26	15	9	28	14	2	2	1	2
Ulster	3	37	9	...	11	8	2	2	1	29	29	5	42	8	1	3	1	1
Warren	...	14	7	...	1	2	2	1	1	6	...	...	5	3	...	2	1	...
Washington	...	40	24	1	2	9	2	...	...	25	8	5	15	13	...	1	4	1
Wayne	1	49	22	1	2	8	2	10	1	29	17	10	25	15	2	4	2	2
Westchester	6	27	52	2	38	7	1	12	1	28	1	5	29	7	2	1	2	7
Wyoming	...	37	34	...	...	17	...	...	2	30	6	6	30	9	1	...	2	4
Yates	2	14	15	...	...	6	1	...	...	15	8	6	15	5	1	1	1	...
Total	196	1,921	1,467	128	269	616	114	232	111	1,397	666	388	1,476	595	124	101	187	138

portant and extensive manufactories are those of iron and machinery, leather, articles of wood, and cotton and woolen goods. Such articles as relate to the professions and fine arts, to books, maps, and engravings, and to the heavy machinery used in ocean steamships, are principally manufactured in New York City and its suburbs. Immense quantities of brick are manufactured on the Hudson for the New York and Southern markets. Lime, waterlime, and gypsum are largely manufactured on the Hudson and through the center of the State; and iron ware is produced in large quantities in the iron districts of Essex, Clinton, Dutchess, Orange, and Oneida counties. Details of the principal manufacturing establishments are given in the statistics of the cities or towns in which they are located.[1]

[1] *Manufacturing Establishments in the several Counties, continued.*

COUNTIES.	Millinery shops.	Paper mills.	Plaster mills.	Printing offices.	Salt manufactories.	Sash and blind manufactories.	Sawmills.	Shingle factories.	Stair building establishments.	Silver ware manufactories.	Tailor shops.	Tanneries.	Tin and sheet iron manufactories.	Tobacco and cigar manufactories.	Turning shops.	Woolen cloth and yarn factories.	Other manufactories.
Albany	3	3	3	3	...	10	43	29	3	6	25	10	5	8	1	1	131
Allegany	1	1	2	...	...	...	183	...	4	1	2	17	8	...	...	2	315
Broome	2	1	2	...	...	...	159	...	4	...	...	20	8	...	1	...	22
Cattaraugus	1	...	...	1	1	1	169	15	3	...	6	15	6	...	1	1	25
Cayuga	7	1	4	7	...	4	79	...	3	3	6	18	8	4	...	6	54
Chautauqua	3	3	...	3	...	1	184	10	7	1	8	25	11	1	7	3	40
Chemung	1	...	2	3	...	...	99	4	2	...	7	11	10	1	4	2	20
Chenango	3	1	5	...	...	3	110	...	5	...	2	17	7	...	5	4	30
Clinton	...	...	1	...	...	1	110	2	1	...	...	13	5	...	...	1	73
Columbia	...	15	6	...	...	4	21	2	2	2	13	8	12	1	...	6	49
Cortland	...	1	...	...	...	...	68	...	2	1	5	13	6	...	3	2	29
Delaware	2	1	...	1	...	...	224	2	2	...	5	24	5	...	1	4	8
Dutchess	7	1	7	4	...	2	12	1	6	5	23	8	18	13	2	6	72
Erie	3	...	1	1	...	10	151	11	7	2	7	134	13	5	6	9	164
Essex	...	1	1	...	...	1	73	5	2	...	2	10	3	...	...	5	62
Franklin	1	...	1	...	...	2	85	4	3	...	4	6	5	...	...	2	34
Fulton	2	3	1	...	...	1	90	5	...	...	1	25	1	1	5	2	81
Genesee	5	...	7	...	...	4	46	3	3	...	8	9	5	...	1	3	38
Greene	2	4	4	...	...	4	62	...	1	...	1	9	4	1	8	5	36
Hamilton	...	...	...	...	...	...	23	...	...	...	...	3	...	...	...	1	...
Herkimer	3	5	6	1	...	2	94	...	4	...	14	21	8	...	6	3	80
Jefferson	5	2	1	1	...	2	101	12	4	1	17	25	19	1	...	3	119
Kings	...	1	1	...	...	...	2	1	11	2	...	4	5	9	1	...	221
Lewis	...	1	...	...	...	2	95	2	1	...	2	15	4	...	2	3	29
Livingston	4	3	...	...	...	...	35	...	2	...	8	7	6	1	2	1	34
Madison	2	2	4	2	...	4	75	1	4	...	7	22	10	...	2	6	54
Monroe	...	1	6	...	...	4	55	2	11	2	8	15	12	4	2	3	158
Montgomery	...	...	5	1	...	1	43	2	2	...	3	15	7	1	4	3	38
New York	12	...	5	53	1	...	13	...	21	83	126	14	54	36	8	...	1248
Niagara	2	1	1	...	...	6	41	9	3	...	8	4	5	1	...	2	30
Oneida	15	3	6	6	...	58	238	17	5	4	28	38	21	6	2	13	185
Onondaga	1	6	12	5	190	4	81	...	6	3	10	19	17	5	4	6	121
Ontario	...	2	7	...	...	...	54	1	1	...	14	5	13	...	1	4	46
Orange	6	3	4	...	...	2	21	...	4	4	9	12	9	6	...	8	51
Orleans	4	1	1	...	...	6	33	3	2	...	2	10	6	...	...	...	13
Oswego	6	2	1	...	...	...	218	22	3	...	10	38	10	2	2	6	48
Otsego	5	2	...	...	...	...	142	2	8	2	17	24	10	...	6	6	59
Putnam	1	1	...	...	...	1	2	...	...	...	2	2	...	...	...	...	7
Queens	2	6	...	2	...	...	7	...	3	2	4	2	9	...	1	3	40
Rensselaer	1	8	5	...	...	6	91	...	...	2	15	13	13	3	6	4	76
Richmond	...	...	...	...	...	...	....	...	1	...	...	2	1	...	...	...	26
Rockland	...	...	...	...	...	...	7	...	...	1	1	2	1	3	...	2	24
St. Lawrence	1	2	3	2	...	2	138	36	12	2	12	25	14	1	...	7	70
Saratoga	...	7	4	1	1	1	80	5	7	...	4	9	6	1	5	4	53
Schenectady	4	1	...	...	...	1	13	...	...	...	9	1	2	...	1	2	29
Schoharie	...	3	...	...	...	1	118	1	1	...	4	17	5	...	7	...	23
Schuyler	2	...	2	...	...	...	84	10	3	...	6	13	...	...	...	2	10
Seneca	...	...	2	...	...	4	15	...	3	1	6	5	5	...	1	6	34
Steuben	4	...	3	2	...	1	238	15	4	3	9	19	7	2	2	...	28
Suffolk	3	...	...	...	...	...	11	...	5	1	3	4	5	2	1	2	77
Sullivan	2	...	...	...	...	...	145	...	1	...	...	39	3	2	12	1	18
Tioga	1	...	2	...	...	...	146	7	...	3	27	12	3	2	...	1	16
Tompkins	6	2	4	...	...	...	97	7	2	3	15	14	2	6	1	3	31
Ulster	2	3	3	1	...	40	95	...	3	...	9	30	5	3	5	4	40
Warren	2	...	...	...	...	...	68	...	...	...	1	14	2	...	1	1	13
Washington	1	3	3	...	...	3	49	2	3	...	3	13	4	1	...	8	36
Wayne	5	...	1	...	...	...	85	...	1	2	11	14	11	...	1	1	42
Westchester	...	2	3	...	...	1	31	1	7	1	2	9	10	4	1	3	94
Wyoming	1	...	...	...	...	...	77	10	3	...	5	16	8	1	2	3	29
Yates	5	...	4	2	...	...	19	1	1	...	7	5	5	...	...	2	17
Total	151	109	144	151	193	200	4,948	262	212	143	560	863	480	139	136	184	4,458

The returns of manufacturing establishments from many counties are quite unsatisfactory, as an examination of the table will show. It is to be hoped that the next census will be more complete in this particular.

COMMERCE.

THE position of New York in the confederacy of States gives it peculiar facilities for maritime affairs, and through its various ports a large proportion of the foreign and internal commerce of the nation is carried on. This commerce extends to every accessible port in the world, and in amount and variety excels that of all the other States of the Union. It is regulated by acts of Congress; and the revenues arising from duties upon articles imported are collected by officers appointed by the President and Senate, or subordinate to those thus appointed. These officers are accountable to the U. S. Treasury Department.

Collection Districts.—The Federal Government has established 11 Collection Districts within this State for the collection of these revenues. Each of these has one port of entry, in charge of a collector, and several ports of delivery, at which one or more deputy collectors, inspectors, or other officers reside.[1] The number of officers employed in collecting these revenues in New York City and its dependencies is nearly 800. Duties on foreign importations form much the largest item of revenue for the support of the General Government, and those collected at the port of New York form the largest part of the whole amount. The absolute and relative amounts of moneys collected from this source in the United States and State of New York have been steadily increasing, except as influenced by pecuniary embarrassments; and now the former amount to about $60,000,000 annually.[2]

---

[1] *Collection Districts in New York.*

DISTRICT.	Date of Establishment.	Principal Office.	Subordinate Offices.
Sag Harbor.........	July 31, 1789	Sag Harbor.........	Greenport.
New York City...	July 31, 1789	New York.........	Albany, Troy, Cold Spring Harbor, Port Jefferson.
Champlain	Mar. 2, 1793	Plattsburgh	Whitehall, Rouses Point, Champlain, Perrysville, Mooers, Centerville, Chateaugay, Burke, Trout River, Westville, Fort Covington, Hogansburgh, Malone.
Oswegatchie.......	Mar. 2, 1811	Ogdensburgh......	Hammond, Morristown, Lisbon, Waddington, Louisville, Massena.
Cape Vincent...	April 18, 1818	Cape Vincent......	Alexandria Bay, Millens Bay, Clayton, Chaumont, Three Mile Bay, Point Peninsula.
Sackets Harbor...	Mar. 3, 1803	Sackets Harbor..	Dexter, Henderson, Sandy Creek.
Oswego.............	Mar. 2, 1799	Oswego.............	Big Sodus, Little Sodus, Texas, Port Ontario.
Genesee.............	Mar. 3, 1805	Rochester.........	Carthage Landing, Kelsey Landing, Pultneyville, Charlotte.
Niagara.............	Mar. 2, 1799	Lewiston............	Niagara Falls, Niagara Bridge, Youngstown, Wilson, Eighteen Mile Creek, Oak Orchard.
Buffalo Creek......	Mar. 3, 1805	Buffalo.............	Black Rock, Black Rock Dam, Tonawanda, Schlosser.
Dunkirk	July 27, 1854	Dunkirk............	Barcelona, Irving, Cattaraugus Creek, Silver Creek.

Albany was made a port of delivery in N. Y. Dist. July 31, 1789.

Cape Vincent was made a port of delivery in Sackets Harbor Dist. Mar. 2, 1811.

Hudson was made a port of delivery in N. Y. Dist. July 31, 1789, and a district and port of entry Feb. 26, 1795. Annexed to N. Y. Dist. May 7, 1822.

Catskill and *Kinderhook* were made ports of delivery from Feb. 26, 1795, to May 27, 1796.

New Windsor, Newburgh, Poughkeepsie, and *Esopus* were made ports of delivery July 31, 1789.

Niagara.—Office removed from Ft. Niagara to Lewiston Mar. 2, 1811.

[1] The following table exhibits the receipts for customs for the ports of the U.S. and N. Y. for a series of years:—

Receipts into United States Treasury.

YEARS.	Total from all sources.	FROM CUSTOMS. United States.	FROM CUSTOMS. New York.
1795	$9,419,802.79	$5,588,461.26	$2,717,361
1800	12,451,184.14	9,080,932.73	3,611,588
1805	13,689,508.14	12,936,487.04	6,958,008
1810	12,144,206.53	8,583,309.31	5,223,696
1815	50,961,237.60	7,282,942.22	14,646,816
1820	20,881,493.68	15,005,612.15	5,506,516
1825	26,840,858.02	20,098,713.45	15,762,142
1830	24,844,116.51	21,922,391.39	15,031,003
1835	35,430,087.10	19,391,310.59	14,568,660
1840	25,032,193.59	13,499,502.17	7,557,441
1845	29,941,853.90	27,588,112.70	21,318,408
1850	47,649,388.88	39,668,686.42	24,487,610
1855	65,351,374.68	53,025,794.21	
1857	68,969,212.57	63,875,905.05	42,510,753.79
1858	70,273,869.59	41,789,620.96	

The amount of revenue from duties varies with the amount of tariff, and the sum thus collected becomes a very uncertain measure of the amount of commerce. The present tariff was adopted March 3, 1857, and admits a large class of goods free of duty. The system of bonding, introduced in 1846, permits goods to be stored in Government warehouses until re-exported or sold, before the payment of duties is required. The State Government took early measures for establishing custom houses and regulating duties upon foreign importations. By an act of Nov. 18, 1784, Sag Harbor and New York were made ports of entry and delivery, and officers were appointed by the Governor and Council of Appointment at each. The reluctance of New York to part with these revenues led to much delay in her ratifying the Constitution of the U.S., by which her revenues were surrendered to the General Government.

Registered and enrolled tonnage of the port of New York and of the United States at different periods.

YEARS.	REGISTERED TONNAGE. United States.	REGISTERED TONNAGE. New York.	ENROLLED TONNAGE. United States.	ENROLLED TONNAGE. New York.	TOTAL TONNAGE. United States.	TOTAL TONNAGE. New York.
1825	700,788	136,384	800.213	144,210	1,423,112	280,594
1830	576,475	92,361	615,301	167,922	1,191,776	260,283
1835	885,821	162,874	939,119	196,483	1,824,940	359,357
1840	899,765	184,542	1,280,999	244,774	2,180,764	429,316
1845	1,095,172	217,089	1,321,830	288,187	2,417,002	505,276
1850	1,585,711	388,438	1,949,743	391,380	3,535,454	779,818
1855	2,535,136	737,509	2,676,865	538,162	5,212,001	1,275,671
1858	2,577,769	841,686	3,201,430	580,488	5,049,808	1,422,174

The Foreign Trade of New York from 1700, although fluctuating considerably, has exhibited a general progressive increase. The commerce of the country was suspended during the Revolution; and no statistics of its amount have been preserved during the period in which the States formed each an independent sovereignty under the Confederation. The amount of imports has been reported separately by States only since 1821.[1]

Amount of American as compared with Foreign Tonnage at different periods in the District of New York.

YEARS.	TONNAGE ENTERED.		
	U. S.	*Foreign.*	*Total.*
1825	259,524½	20,655¼	280,179¾
1830	280,918	33,797¾	314,715¾
1835	373,465	90,999	464,464
1840	409,458	118,136	527,594
1845	472,491¾	140,858¼	613,350
1850	807,580½	441,756	1,249,337
1854	1,442,278½	477,034¾	1,919,313¼
1858	2,411,087	1,124,020	3,535,107

YEARS.	TONNAGE CLEARED.		
	U. S.	*Foreign.*	*Total.*
1825	245,512	17,914¾	263,430¾
1830	209,598½	33,686½	273,285
1835	289,551¾	80,038¼	369,590
1840	275,393¼	117,204	392,597¼
1845	377,163¼	140,222¼	517,385½
1850	705,162	407,054	1,112,216
1855	1,082,799¾	445,305	1,528,104¾
1858	2,152,835	1,132,568	3,285,403

Amount of Registered, Enrolled, and Licensed Tonnage in the several Collection Districts, June 30, 1858.

DISTRICTS.	*Registered.*	*Enrolled and Licensed.*
Sag Harbor	7,408.72	7,057.94
New York	841,685.35	593,599.73
Champlain	....	888.02
Oswegatchie	....	11,866.60
Cape Vincent	....	6,129.88
Sackets Harbor	....	1,321.22
Oswego	....	46,420.19
Genesee	....	3,704.31
Niagara	....	1,272.31
Buffalo Creek	....	73,478.80
Dunkirk	....	5,382.50

Amount of Registered and Enrolled Tonnage of the United States and District of New York at different periods.

YEARS.	REGISTERED.		ENROLLED AND LICENSED.	
	U. States.	*N. York.*	*U. States.*	*N. York.*
1827	747,170	133,403	873,438	165,542
1832	686,990	116,395	752,460	162,419
1837	810,447	169,050	1,086,237	216,351
1842	975,359	193,911	1,117,035	247,023
1847	1,241,313	254,541	1,597,733	337,381
1852	1,899,448	496,507	2,238,992	445,674
1858	2,499,550	841,685⅓	2,550,742	593,600

Number of Entries of Merchandise at the Port of New York for 10 years, ending June 30, 1856.

1847	40,418	1852	68,967
1848	53,949	1853	83,470
1849	54,506	1854	93,282
1850	61,752	1855	76,448
1851	71,068	1856	89,377

General Statistics for 1858.

	American Vessels.	*Foreign Vessels.*
Exports of American produce	$ 65,037,159	$24,002,631
" foreign "	12,430,450	6,870,684
Imports	123,928,283	54,547,453
Number of vessels cleared	4,471	4,486
Crews " "	67,240	55.757
Number of vessels entered	4,976	4,510
Crews " "	73,866	55,903

[1] *Trade of New York from* 1700 *to* 1776.

YEARS.	TOTAL VALUE.		YEARS.	TOTAL VALUE.	
	Imports.	*Exports.*		*Imports.*	*Exports.*
1700	$247,050	$ 87,835	1739	$ 580,350	$ 92,295
1701	159,550	92,735	1740	593,885	107,490
1702	149,955	39,825	1741	602,150	105,710
1703	87,810	37,355	1742	837,955	67,680
1704	111,470	52,700	1743	672,435	75,335
1705	139,510	36,965	1744	599,600	72,635
1706	157,940	14,245	1745	274,785	70,415
1707	149,275	71,415	1746	433,560	44,205
1708	134,495	54,235	1747	689,940	74,960
1709	172,885	61,295	1748	716,555	61,790
1710	157,375	91,015	1749	1,328,865	117,065
1711	144,280	60,965	1750	1,335,650	178,160
1712	92,620	62,330	1751	1,244,705	211,815
1713	232,350	72,140	1752	970,150	203,290
1714	223,215	149,050	1753	1,389,320	202,765
1715	273,195	106,580	1754	637,485	133,315
1716	260,865	109,855	1755	755,355	145,275
1717	220,700	122,670	1756	1,252,125	120,365
1718	314,830	135,655	1757	1,766,555	95,840
1719	281,785	97,980	1758	1,782,775	71,300
1720	181,985	84,180	1759	3,153,925	108,420
1721	253,770	78,405	1760	2,400,530	105,625
1722	287,390	100,590	1761	1,447,850	243,240
1723	265,065	139,960	1762	1,440,230	294,410
1724	315,100	105,955	1763	1,192,800	264,990
1725	353,250	124,880	1764	2,577,080	268,485
1726	424,330	191,535	1765	1,911,745	274,795
1727	337,260	158,085	1766	1,854,145	335,100
1728	408,170	105,710	1767	2,089,785	307,110
1729	323,800	79,165	1768	2,414,650	435,575
1730	321,780	43,700	1769	374,590	367,430
1731	330,580	103,780	1770	2,379,955	349,410
1732	327,700	47,055	1771	3,268,105	479,375
1733	327,085	58,130	1772	1,719,850	413,535
1734	408,790	76,535	1773	1,446,070	381,230
1735	402,025	70,775	1774	2,189,685	400,040
1736	430,000	89,720	1775	6,140	935,090
1737	629,165	84,165	1776	....	11,590
1738	667,190	81,140			

Trade of New York since the adoption of Federal Constitution.

YEARS.	*Imports.*	*Exports.*	YEARS.	*Imports.*	*Exports.*
1791	....	$ 2,505,465	1825	$49,639,174	$35,259,261
1792	....	2,535,790	1826	38,115,630	21,947,791
1793	....	2,932,370	1827	38,719,644	23,834,137
1794	....	5,442,183	1828	41,927,792	22,777,649
1795	....	10,304,581	1829	34,743,307	20,119,011
1796	....	12,208,027	1830	35,624,070	19,697,983
1797	....	13,308,064	1831	57,077,417	25,535,144
1798	....	14,300,892	1832	53,214,402	26,000,945
1799	....	18,719,527	1833	55,918,449	25,395,117
1800	....	14,045,079	1834	73,188,594	13,849,469
1801	....	19,851,136	1835	88,191,305	30,345,264
1802	....	13,792,276	1836	118,253,416	28,920,638
1803	....	10,818,387	1837	79,301,722	27,338,419
1804	....	16,081,281	1838	68,453,206	23,008,471
1805	....	23,482,943	1839	99,882,438	33,268,099
1806	....	21,762,845	1840	60,440,750	34,264,080
1807	....	26,357,963	1841	75,713,426	33,139,833
1808	....	5,606,058	1842	57,875,604	27,576,778
1809	....	12,581,562	1843*	31,356,540	16,762,664
1810	....	17,242,330	1844	65,079,516	32,861,540
1811	....	12,266,215	1845	70,909,085	36,175,298
1812	....	8,961,922	1846	74,254.283	36,935,413
1813	....	8,185,494	1847	84,167,352	49,844,368
1814	....	209,670	1848	94,525,141	53,351,157
1815	....	10,675,373	1849	92,567,369	45,963,100
1816	....	19,690,031	1850	111,123,524	52,712,789
1817	....	18,707,433	1851	141,546,538	86,007,019
1818	....	17,872,261	1852	132,329,306	87,484,456
1819	....	13,587,378	1853	178,270,999	78,206,290
1820	....	13,163,244	1854	195,427,933	122,534,646
1821	$23,629,246	13,162,918	1855	164,776,511	113,731,238
1822	35,445,628	17,100,482	1856	210,160,454	119,111,500
1823	23,421,349	19,038,990	1857	236,493,485	134,803,298
1824	36,113,723	22,897,134	1888	178,475,736	108,340,924

* From Oct. 1, 1842, to June 30, 1843. The fiscal year was changed at this time, and now begins July 1.

The reports of commerce and navigation do not specify the amount imported and exported in each collection district. The relative amount of the port as compared with the State of New York has been as follows at different periods:—

YEARS.	IMPORTS.		EXPORTS.		Importation of Dry Goods.			
	Port of N.Y.	State of N.Y.	Port of N.Y.	State of N.Y.	ENTERED FOR CONSUMPTION.	1856.	1857.	1858.
1840	$56,845,924	$60,440,750	$30,186,470	$34,264,080	Manufactures of wool.	$22,671,010	$20,261,826	$17,035,032
1845	68,932,207	70,909,085	34,196,184	36,175,298	" cotton.	13,225,234	15,813,299	9,012,911
1848	89,315,968	94,525,141	45,863,916	53,351,157	" silk.	27,738,090	25,192,465	17,581,099
1855	152,539,783	164,776,511	62,918,442	113,731,238	" flax.	7,760,145	6,857,433	3,701,555
1858	171,473,336	178,475,736	100,667,890	108,350,924	Miscell. dry goods....	6,575,816	6,709,004	3,761,788

Trade of New York for the Three Years ending June 30, 1858.

| | | | | Total............... | $77,970,295 | $74,833,527 | $51,092,385 |

IMPORTS.	1856.	1857.	1858.	WITHDRAWN FROM WAREHOUSE.	1856.	1857.	1858.
Ent. for consumption	$150,088,112	$141,430,109	$94,019,659	Manufactures of wool.	$2,025,697	$2,929,179	$6,369,118
" warehousing	29,568,397	62,275,673	44,463,806	" cotton.	1,888,578	2,492,516	4,018,693
Free goods.............	17,432,112	16,036,530	23,665,487	" silk.	2,241,785	2,004,190	5,394,970
Specie and bullion....	1,126,097	6,441,855	9,324,384	" flax.	1,131,408	1,100,183	2,215,472
				Miscell. dry goods....	507,675	601,035	1,385,173
Total...............	$198,214,718	$226,184,167	$171,473,336	Total...............	$7,890,143	$9,127,103	$19,383,381
Withdrawn from warehouse...........	21,934,130	27,950,212	49,376,593				
Dry goods.............	85,898,690	92,699,088	67,317,736	ENTERED FOR WAREHOUSE.	1856.	1857.	1858.
General merchandise.	112,316,028	133,485,079	104,155,600	Manufactures of wool.	$2,184,687	$6,081,505	$5,028,533

EXPORTS.	1856.	1857.	1858.				
				" cotton.	2,006,493	3,780,715	4,048,530
Domestic produce......	$75,026,244	$75,928,942	$55,931,987	" silk.	2,225,515	4,497,447	3,667,521
Foreign mdse. free ...	1,268,914	2,396,903	3,104,160	" flax.	861,657	2,228,768	1,964,891
" " dutiable	3,691,600	3,932,370	7,309,672	Miscell. dry goods....	650,113	1,247,126	1,515,876
Specie and bullion....	22,280,991	44,348,468	34,322,071				
Total	$102,267,749	$126,606,683	$100,667,890	Total...............	$7,929,495	$17,835,561	$16,225,351

Commerce of New York with Foreign Countries for the year ending June 30, 1858.

	ENTERED.						CLEARED.					
FOREIGN COUNTRIES.	AMERICAN.			FOREIGN.			AMERICAN.			FOREIGN.		
	Vessels.	Tons.	Crews.	Vessels.	Tons.	Crews.	Vessels.	Tons.	Crews.	Vessels.	Tons.	Crews.
England...............	390	441,043	11,313	80	130,016	5,959	276	333,165	8,732	116	146,347	6,435
Cuba...................	634	227,453	7,626	40	11,288	445	442	179,940	6,647	11	6,040	227
France.................	131	136,408	4,542	11	3,926	163	58	74,938	2,784	9	2,743	122
Bremen................	14	21,965	809	86	58,564	1,993	15	21,856	998	51	39,759	1,542
Hamburg..............	8	5,122	125	56	52,797	2,057	...	....	......	42	47,257	1,878
British North America............	44	7,315	284	279	43,869	1,746	99	41,830	1,139	400	80,215	2,806
New Grenada.........	80	48,990	2,704	3	819	27	86	54,765	2,727	3	852	84
British West Indies...	153	32,335	1,206	118	17,321	748	142	28,919	1,091	99	15,549	744
Porto Rico.............	162	35,596	1,338	30	5,715	227	73	14,492	562	9	1,557	67
Scotland..............	15	9,289	226	24	31,231	1,469	43	23,360	629	23	31,492	1,250
Brazil.................	101	29,997	1,064	28	7,811	284	58	15,585	590	4	1,079	51
China..................	37	33,554	923	6	3,464	109	19	18,127	528	1	369	14
Peru...................	24	28,910	696	1	503	16	3	9,449	76			
Belgium................	25	23,140	592	3	4,195	193	21	10,429	459	3	4,195	192
British East Indies ...	29	23,912	646	5	2,867	87	18	14,041	386	12	6,406	198
Hayti..................	111	20,849	849	8	1,717	70	53	8,926	392	5	1,167	50
Two Sicilies...........	37	13,258	412	22	6,016	216	5	1,347	45	6	2,077	77
Spain..................	50	13,870	480	26	5,741	231	70	20,054	655	24	6,962	256
Venezuela.............	58	13,956	511	14	2,935	120	31	6,810	278	2	413	19
Holland................	14	8,721	229	11	7,657	214	11	6,565	165	22	11,525	353
Mexico................	38	14,522	441	...	....	......	24	8,932	291	4	1,068	49
Tuscany...............	17	10,743	277	4	1,315	47						
Philippine Islands.....	10	9,416	242	1	200	8	2	755	24			
Russia.................	10	6,333	170	5	2,235	65	5	3,188	85	1	1,715	72
Buenos Byres.........	22	7,436	237	1	261	10	26	10,272	333	2	636	23
Central Republic......	14	5,383	155	4	740	30	7	2,301	80	2	425	25
Dutch West Indies....	24	5,133	193	1	181	8	37	7,897	314	1	116	9
British Guiana........	17	4,881	171	...	....	......	23	6,180	218			
Danish West Indies...	20	4,226	152	2	315	13	36	8,452	326	1	247	9
Africa (except Egypt and British Possessions)....	19	4,176	168	1	167	7	13	3,022	121			
British Honduras......	15	3,829	141	1	130	5	12	3,353	119			
Sardinia...............	2	859	25	8	2,383	86	3	982	35	1	360	10
British Possessions, Africa.	14	2,833	110	2	331	14	16	6,079	204	3	987	32
Austria................	2	794	26	6	2,065	70	2	821	25	4	1,369	48
Portugal...............	4	1,590	44	5	1,313	49	13	5,148	154	4	1,137	44
St. Domingo...........	14	2,227	94	4	560	26	13	1,619	76	5	1,021	18
Sweden and Norway..	2	1,073	31	4	1,644	56	....	....	......	2	467	17
Turkey in Asia........	5	2,035	68	1	335	10						
Egypt..................	...	....	......	6	2,317	80	1	405	13			
Uruguay...............	7	1,767	63	1	350	12	13	4,694	149	1	382	15
Ireland................	...	....	......	5	2,116	64	5	2,525	72	17	3,868	138
French West Indies ...	2	1,987	43	...	....	......	25	4,629	193	6	905	45
British Australia......	3	1,557	45	1	250	7	35	27,975	717	6	4,762	133
Canary Islands........	7	1,542	51	...	....	......	1	257	8	7	2,051	83
Swedish West Indies..	8	1,293	54	...	....	......	2	263	12			
Chili..................	1	756	19	1	380	12	15	11,224	282	1	346	12
French North American Possessions.	...	....	......	8	1,005	68	1	120	6	5	813	46

Statistics of American and Foreign Trade.

Year ending Sept. 30	EXPORTS		TONNAGE CLEARED	
	American Produce.	Foreign Produce.	American Vessels.	Foreign Vessels.
1821	$ 7,896,605	$ 5,264,313	$ 158,174	$ 10,720
1825	20,651,558	14,607,703	255,878	19,851
1830	13,618,278	6,079,705	229,341	36,574
1835	21,707,867	8,637,397	589,855	343,078
1840	22,676,609	11,587,471	518,202	343,114
1845	25,929,904	10,245,394	926,280	414,688
1850	41,502,800	11,209,989	1,411,557	737,539
1855	96,414,808	17,316,430	1,861,682	1,140,197
1858	89,039,790	19,301,134	2,152,835	1,132,568

Value of Articles Imported for the year ending June 30, 1858.

ARTICLES.	VALUES.	
	New York.	U. States.
Duty free.		
Articles from B. A., duty free......	$ 624,060	$14,754,255
Produce U. S. brought back........	1,024,992	1,244,692
Bullion, gold............................	269,833	2,286,099
" silver...........................	271,027	408,879
Coffee....................................	6,730,168	18,341,081
Tea.......................................	6,414,700	6,777,295
Coin, gold..............................	8,096,651	9,279,969
" silver............................	689,533	7,299,549
Dye stuffs..............................	559,635	887,486
Linseed.................................	940,077	3,243,174
Ground madder	477,087	643,642
Guano...................................	242,648	525,376
Painting and statuary...............	389,519	504,634
Rags, cotton and linen..............	696,399	971,126
Seeds, trees, and plants.............	276,030	392,440
Silks, raw or reeled..................	1,293,921	1,300,065
Tin, blocks.............................	463,067	470,023
" pigs................................	327,207	594,258
Wool.....................................	1,173,075	3,843,320
Total duty free........................	$33,072,626	$80,319,255
Paying duty ad valorem.		
Coal......................................	521,774	772,925
Cotton, piece goods, plain..........	430,948	741,077
" hosiery..........................	1,625,833	2,120,868
" thread, twist, and yarn...	751,429	1,080,671
" manufactured, not specified.........................	399,425	966,017
" bleached or dyed...........	8,383,552	12,391,713
Feathers and flowers................	549,894	654,452
Linens, bleached or unbleached..	4,308,238	5,598,571
" manufactured, not specified...........................	511,276	953,436
Currants................................	272,469	342,869
Raisins..................................	762,568	1,441,471
Furs, undressed.......................	247,510	321,935
" hatters'..........................	870,336	876,156
Glass, plate............................	388,241	397,310
" window.........................	454,344	626,744
Gems, not set..........................	332,503	329,241
Jewelry, real or imitation..........	332,097	385,945
Goat's hair, Angora, and other piece goods..........................	488,741	515,641
Hats and bonnets, straw............	1,128,651	1,182,837
Hemp, manufact'd, not specified..	332,821	520,029
India rubber, not manufactured	567,061	666,583
Indigo...................................	467,379	467,379
Iron, bar	1,610,970	3,318,913
Cutlery.................................	1,155,761	1,489,054
Fire arms..............................	281,963	382,610
Iron, pig...............................	329,785	739,949
" rail road.........................	1,556,538	2,987,576
" rod................................	324,897	426,499
" sheet..............................	677,659	945,073
Steel, shear, cast, and German....	702,595	1,147,773
" other............................	546,596	725,338
Iron and steel, other manufactures..................................	817,687	970,133
Jute and sisal grass..................	970,723	2,298,709
Laces, embroidery....................	2,274,033	2,845,029
" cotton...........................	285,183	405,439
Lead.....................................	1,638,087	1,972,243
Gloves..................................	1,362,096	1,449,672
Skins, dressed........................	437,268	806,412
Leather, sole and upper.............	1,205,714	1,259,711
" other manufactured......	248,815	278,946
Liquorice paste.......................	452,723	477,995
Molasses................................	1,414,168	4,116,759
Musical instruments.................	247,233	378,928
Opium...................................	309,415	447,534
Paper, writing.........................	238,402	256,322
Printed books, English..............	354,973	456,450

Value of Articles Imported, continued.

ARTICLES.	VALUES.	
	New York.	U. States.
Raw hides and skins..................	5,629,029	9,884,358
Salt......................................	282,644	1,124,920
Silk, hosiery	341,528	417,168
" piece goods.....................	15,304,255	16,121,395
" and worsted piece goods......	1,183,788	1,249,385
" raw................................	240,501	242,130
" manufactured, not specified..	2,032,614	3,207,043
Soda, ash...............................	515,700	1,211,305
" carb..............................	267,097	373,599
Spices, cassia..........................	323,041	356,614
" nutmegs	235,168	378,257
" black pepper	269,486	631,723
Spirits, brandy........................	1,410,426	2,232,452
" from grain......................	706,945	1,158,517
Sugars, brown.........................	13,514,098	23,317,435
Tea and coffee from places not free by treaty.........................	442,910	484,520
Tin plates..............................	3,042,152	3,842,968
Tobacco, cigars........................	2,040,898	4,123,208
" unmanufactured	1,078,666	1,255,831
Porcelain, earthen, and stone ware......................................	1,755,011	3,215,236
Wine, sherry and St. Lucien........	286,954	343,100
" white, not enumerated......	237,710	285,125
" champagne......................	679,421	860,942
Wool, blankets........................	976,018	1,574,716
" carpeting.........................	1,195,004	1,542,600
" hosiery...........................	1,378,660	1,837,561
" piece goods......................	6,719,713	7,626,830
" worsted...........................	9,192,641	10,780,379
" shawls............................	1,742,396	2,002,653
" manufact'd, not specified ..	494,915	663,373
Unenumerated articles.		
At 4 per cent...........................	908,789	1,367,425
At 15 per cent..........................	1,046,668	2,314,065
At 24 per cent..........................	836,423	1,465,074
Total ad valorem......................	$137,208,207	$202,293,875
Total imports..........................	$170,280,887	$282,613,150

Value of U. S. products exported during the year ending June 30, 1858.

ARTICLES.	VALUES.	
	N. Y.	U. S.
Ashes, pot and pearl..................	$ 527,867	$ 554,744
Beef......................................	1,312,957	2,081,856
Boards, planks, and scantling.......	751,334	3,428,520
Butter...................................	236,928	541,863
Carriages and rail road cars, &c ...	526,831	777,921
Cheese	561,451	731,910
Cloverseed	232,764	332,250
Copper and brass manufactures.....	1,705,426	1,985,223
Cotton...................................	8,368,500	131,386,661
Drugs and medicines.................	452,929	681,278
Gold and silver coin..................	14,917,585	19,474,040
" " " bullion..........	12,456,256	22,933,206
Hams and bacon.......................	1,485,958	1,957,423
Hides....................................	393,158	875,753
Household furniture..................	331,281	932,499
Indian corn............................	1,331,570	3,259,039
Indian meal............................	234,945	877,692
Iron castings...........................	314,936	464,415
" manufactures	1,922,734	4,059,528
Lard.....................................	1,172,950	3,809,501
Leather	303,579	605,589
Manufactured tobacco...............	1,113,428	2,400,115
" cotton (white)...........	473,838	1,598,136
" other	1,358,779	1,800,285
" wood	413,806	2,234,678
Oil, spermaceti........................	1,046,453	1,097,503
" whale..............................	412,999	597,107
Whalebone..............................	1,105,223	1,105,223
Pork......................................	1,169,707	2,852,942
Rice......................................	664,969	1,870,578
Rosin and turpentine	1,219,553	1,464,210
Skins and furs.........................	822,986	1,002,378
Spirits from grain	243,118	476,722
" molasses........................	387,084	1,267,691
" of turpentine...................	904,242	1,089,282
Staves and heading...................	960,390	1,975,852
Sugars (brown)........................	231,879	375,062
Tallow	258,226	824,970
Tobacco (leaf)..........................	1,482,970	17,009,767
Wheat...................................	5,451,491	9,061,504
" flour..............................	7,017,790	19,328,884
Total of exports......................	$83,403,564	$293,758,279

Tonnage.—The size of registered American vessels engaged in foreign trade has been steadily increasing, and has more than doubled within twenty years. Steam vessels were first enrolled in 1823 and first registered in 1830. They now form 12 to 15 per cent. of the total amount of tonnage.[1]

Steamboats applying for registry, enrolment, or license must be inspected under the direction of a Board of Supervising Inspectors. The United States is divided into 9 Supervising Districts, the 2d of which includes the seaboard and the 9th the lakes of New York. Steamboats are required to be well guarded against fire, to have suitable pumps worked by hand and by steam, at least two boats, and large steamers more, in proportion to their tonnage, (except upon rivers,) one life preserver to every passenger, and a certain number of floats, and fire buckets and axes. Their boilers, engines, and hull must be examined and approved by inspectors appointed by the Collector, the Supervising Inspector for the district, and the Judge of the U. S. District Court; and every requirement of the law must be found complied with. Pilots and engineers on steamers must be examined and licensed by the Inspectors. The present steamboat law was passed Aug. 30, 1852.[2]

The Coasting Trade of the United States is entirely restricted to American vessels, and the share belonging to New York is very great; but from the want of official returns it cannot be definitely ascertained. Unless carrying distilled spirits or foreign goods, these vessels are not required to report their entrance and clearance; and, as they oftener leave than arrive with these articles, the number of clearances reported is disproportionately high.[3]

[1] Average tonnage of vessels at different periods arriving at New York.

Yrs.	American.	Foreign.	Yrs.	American.	Foreign.
1835	245	193	1850	427	338
1840	280	253	1855	527	223
1845	319	267	1858	530	452

Vessels built in New York for 1858.

Districts.	Ships and barques.	Brigs.	Schooners.	Sloops and canal boats.	Steamers.	Total number of vessels.	Tonnage.
Sag Harbor	...	...	2	2	...	4	536.58
New York	7	2	22	84	26	141	6,093.75
Oswegatchie	...	...	...	1	...	1	26.74
Cape Vincent	...	...	...	...	3	3	468.78
Oswego	...	...	6	2	2	10	1,990.79
Niagara	...	...	3	...	...	3	601.05
Buffalo Creek	...	1	10	4	14	39	7,215.77
Dunkirk	...	...	1	1	...	2	252.26

Amount of registered and enrolled steam tonnage of U. S. at different periods.

Years.	Registered.	Enrolled.	Total.
1825	....	23,061	23,061
1830	1,419	63,053	64,472
1835	340	122,474	122,814
1840	4,155	319,527	202,339
1845	6,492	481,005	525,947
1850	44,942	655,240	770,947
1855	115,045	651,363	970,890
1858	78,027		

Vessels built in the U. S. at different periods.

Years.	Ships and barques.	Brigs.	Schooners.	Sloops and canal boats.	Steamers.	Number of vessels.	Tonnage.
1815	136	226	681	274	.....	1,315	154,624.39
1820	21	60	301	152	.....	524	47,784.01
1825	56	197	538	168	35	994	114,997.25
1830	25	56	403	116	37	637	58,094.24
1835	25	50	301	100	30	507	46,238.52
1840	97	109	378	224	64	872	118,309.23
1845	124	87	322	342	163	1,038	146,018.02
1850	247	117	547	290	159	1,360	272,218.54
1855	381	126	605	669	253	2,034	583,450.04
1858	122	46	431	400	226	1,225	242,286.69

[2] Statistics of Steamers for 1858.

	Second Dist. N. Y.	Ninth District.			Total. U. S.
		Buffalo.	Oswego.	Burlington.	
No. of steamers inspected and approved	124	47	8	8	839
Tonnage of steamers inspected	79,065	38,314	5,465	3,565	325,262
Pilots originally licensed within the year	21	40	......	......	364
Pilots whose licenses were renewed	104	87	21	13	1,540
Engineers and assistants originally licensed within the year	90	35	......	......	435
Engineers and assistants whose licenses were renewed	302	87	18	13	1,809
Lives lost from accidents during the year	2	26	......	5	126

[3] Statistics of the Coasting Trade of the Port of New York.

Years.	Entered.		Cleared.	
	Vessels.	Tons.	Vessels.	Tons.
1849	1,855	424,976	3,994	895,589
1850	1,928	489,395¼	4,719	1,020,070
1851	1,768	455,542	4,803	1,214,942
1852	1,766	497,840	4,680	1,173,762
1853	1,733	507,531	4,789	1,310,697
1854	1,880	543,452	4,779	1,499,969
1855	1,966	614,045	4,563	1,378,888
1856	1,669	539,461	4,696	1,482,310

Tonnage of Vessels engaged in the Coasting Trade, June 30, 1858.

District.	Tonnage.
Sag Harbor	7,057.94
New York	580,487.32
Champlain	888.02
Oswegatchie	11,866.60
Cape Vincent	1,312.16
Sackets Harbor	1,321.22
Oswego	46,420.19
Genesee	3,704.31
Niagara	1,272.31
Buffalo Creek	73,478.80
Dunkirk	5,383.50
Total in N. Y.	733,192.62
Total in U. S.	2,361,595.72

The affairs of commerce relating to police, sanitary, and municipal regulations are governed by the laws of the State, and their care is intrusted to officers appointed under its authority. These officers are divided into several classes, each of which has charge of a particular department.

1. **The Board of Commissioners of Pilots** consists of 5 persons,—3 elected for 2 years by the Chamber of Commerce, and 2 for a like term by the presidents and vice-presidents of the marine insurance companies of N. Y., composing or representing the Board of Underwriters in that city. This Board appoints a secretary, has an office, meets once a month or oftener, and licenses, for such term as it may think proper, as many pilots as may be deemed necessary for the port of New York.[1]

2. **The Board of Health of New York** is composed of the Mayor and Common Council of the city.[2]

3. **The Commissioners of Health** are composed of the President of the Board of Aldermen, the Health Officer, the Resident Physician, the Health Commissioner, and the City Inspector.

4. **The Health Officer,** appointed by the Governor and Senate, is required to board every vessel subject to quarantine or visitation, upon its arrival, to ascertain whether infectious diseases are present, and to obtain, in such case, the facts necessary to determine the period that such vessel must be detained.[3]

5. **The Resident Physician** for the city and county of New York is appointed by the Governor and Senate. He is required to visit all sick persons reported to the Board of Health, or to the Mayor and Commissioners of Health, and to perform such other professional duties as the Board may require.

6. **The Health Commissioner,** appointed in like manner, is required to assist the Resident Physician.[4]

7. **The Quarantine Hospital** is located in the town of Castleton, in Richmond co.; and vessels detained on account of infectious diseases are anchored in the adjacent waters, or, in sickly seasons, in the lower bay.[5]

8. **Harbor Masters** are appointed by the Governor and Senate, for the purpose of assigning piers and other stations for landing and receiving cargoes.[6]

9. **The Port Wardens of the Port of New York** are appointed by the Governor and Senate, for the purpose of inspecting vessels and the stowage of cargoes and of estimating all damages to the same. They consist of a Board of 9 members, one of whom must reside in Brook-

---

Enrolled Tonnage of the U. S. engaged in the Coasting Trade for different periods.

Years.	Tonnage.	Years.	Tonnage.	Years.	Tonnage.
1815	435,066.87	1835	792,301.20	1850	1,730,410.84
1820	539,080.46	1840	1,176,694.46	1855	2,491,108.00
1825	587,273.07	1845	1,190,898.27	1858	2,361,595.72
1830	516,978.18				

In June, 1858, there were, of small vessels under 20 tons licensed for the coasting trade, 189.21 tons at Sag Harbor and 71.25 tons at Greenport.

[1] The licenses thus granted may express different degrees of qualification, appropriate to different branches of duty, and may be revoked at pleasure. Candidates must sustain a satisfactory examination and be found of good character and temperate habits. They must also give bonds for the faithful discharge of their duties. The board has power to regulate pilotage; and the fees of pilots are fixed by law. The masters of vessels of under 300 tons, owned by a citizen of the U. S. and licensed in the coasting trade, need not employ a pilot unless they prefer. If the master of a vessel of from 150 to 300 tons, owned and licensed as above, be desirous of piloting his own vessel, he may obtain a license from the Commissioners of Pilots for such purpose. All masters of foreign vessels and vessels from a foreign port, and all vessels sailing under register by way of Sandy Hook, are required to take a licensed pilot, or, if they refuse, they must pay the pilotage to the pilot first offering his services. Pilots licensed by other States have no privileges in this. Candidates for recommendation as Hellgate pilots must have served an apprenticeship of 3 years, and until they attain the age of 21 years, must have served 2 years after as deputy pilots and sustained repeated examinations before the Board of Wardens in the presence of at least 2 Hellgate pilots.

The first act regulating the pilotage of New York was passed in 1731; and since that period this service has been conducted under rules and penalties established by the Colony or State of New York. All special laws concerning pilotage by the way of Sandy Hook were repealed in 1845. The present law was enacted in 1853 and amended in 1854-57. The pilots belonging

upon steamboats are licensed by inspectors appointed under the Treasury Department of the U. S. Those employed in conducting vessels by way of Sandy Hook are licensed by the Board of Commissioners of Pilots; and those by way of Hellgate, by the Governor and Senate, upon recommendation of the Board of Wardens.

[2] Boards of Health are by law created in every city, incorporated village, and town, under an act of 1850; but the greater number of these have never acted officially. In towns the Supervisor and Justices of the Peace are a Board of Health, and may appoint a physician as health officer.—*Revised Statutes, 5th Edition,* II, p. 53.

[3] The Health Officer resides at quarantine, has general direction of the location of vessels detained, their purification, and the discharge of their cargoes, and other duties connected with the health of vessels in quarantine. He is paid by fees, and reports to the Mayor or Commissioners of Health.

[4] This officer receives all moneys applied to the Marine Hospital, and pays all demands against the same that shall have been approved by a majority of the Commissioners of Health. He reports his accounts monthly to the Board of Health, gives a bond of $20,000 for the faithful discharge of his duties, and receives a salary of $3,500, to be paid by the Commissioners of Emigration. The Board of Health may from time to time appoint as many visiting, hospital, and consulting physicians as may be deemed proper, and may also fix their duties and compensation.

[5] The Hospital buildings, destroyed Sept. 1-2, 1858, (see page 565,) have been temporarily rebuilt.

The removal of quarantine to some place less dangerous to the public health has been fully shown to be *necessary*; but the final disposition of the important question as to whither, is not settled. The only available place for the construction of buildings seem to be upon some of the shoals in the lower bay. Old Orchard Shoal, on which the water is from 1 to 3 fathoms deep at mean low tide, has been proposed for this purpose. The East Bank and Dry Romer Shoals have about the same depth, but are more exposed to the open sea.

[6] There are 9 Harbor Masters in New York, 2 in Brooklyn, and 1 in Albany. They enforce the regulations of the city authorities relative to clearing docks and preventing nuisances or obstructions. They are paid by fees and report the amount thereof annually to the Governor.

lyn, and 3 must be nautical men. They choose one of their number President, appoint a Secretary, use a seal, and keep an office. They are exclusive surveyors of vessels damaged or wrecked, or arriving in distress, and, when called upon, judge of the fitness of vessels to depart upon voyages. They are also, upon application, required to estimate the value or measurement of vessels when the same is in dispute or libeled; and they may examine goods in warehouses that have been damaged on shipboard. The Board, or some member thereof, must attend all sales of vessels or their cargoes condemned and in a damaged state; and such sales by auction must be made under the direction and by order of the Wardens, and are exempt from auction duties.[1]

The Commissioners of Health are authorized to collect of the masters of every vessel entering the port of New York a certain tax, for the benefit of the Health Office.[2]

The Board of Commissioners of Emigration, consisting of the Mayors of New York and Brooklyn, the Presidents of the German Society and Irish Emigrant Society, and 6 Commissioners appointed by the Governor and Senate, have charge of the interests of immigrants when they first arrive at New York.[3]

The Marine Court of the City of New York has jurisdiction in civil cases arising between persons engaged in maritime affairs, where the sum in dispute does not exceed $500.[4]

Canadian Trade.—The revenues collected on the Canada frontier, in some periods, have fallen short of the cost of collecting them. The Reciprocity Treaty of 1854 admits the greater part of articles the produce of the U. S. and B. A. into each country respectively free of duty.[5]

[1] The Wardens are paid by fees and percentages upon sales. Special Wardens are appointed to reside at quarantine. They report to the Board of Wardens of N. Y., and have jurisdiction as wardens over vessels detained in quarantine. The Board of Port Wardens reports annually to the Comptroller a statement of its receipts and expenses, with an affidavit of each member and of the Secretary that they have not received directly or indirectly any moneys except their legal fees.

[2] Under an act passed in March, 1801, the amount of this tax was fixed at $1.50 for every cabin and 75 cts. for every steerage passenger, mate, and mariner. In 1813 the tax was fixed at $1.50 for every captain and cabin passenger; $1.00 for every steerage passenger and mariner of foreign vessels; and 25 cts. for master, mate, and sailor of every coasting vessel. The moneys thus paid, after supporting the Marine Hospital at Quarantine and contingencies and yielding $8,000 annually to the Society for the Reform of Juvenile Delinquents, was invested by the Comptroller as the "Marine Fund." In 1831 the Board of Trustees of the Seamen's Fund and Retreat was created, under whose direction the present establishment known as the "Seamen's Retreat," on Staten Island, more particularly described on page 566, has since been managed. Of the 44,932 admitted up to Jan. 1, 1859, 80 per cent. were discharged cured, 8¼ per cent. were relieved, 3 per cent. were discharged by request, and 4¾ per cent. died.

[3] The master of every vessel bringing passengers from foreign countries must give a bond of $300, conditioned that such persons shall not become chargeable for support within 5 years. They may commute this bond by paying $2 upon each passenger, of which sum ¼ is set apart for the counties other than N. Y. toward the support of emigrants in the several counties. For every lunatic, idiot, deaf and dumb, blind, maimed, or infirm person, and every widow with children, or person over 60 years of age, and liable to become a public charge, a bond of $500 is required.

The Commissioners of Emigration have a large establishment on Wards Island for the support of the sick, infirm, and destitute, and have leased Castle Garden as a general landing place. Emigrants may here purchase tickets for any part of the Union, and procure such articles as they may stand in need of, without encountering the horde of faithless agents and mercenary runners that formerly proved the scourge of immigration and the disgrace of the city. The Marine Hospital at

Quarantine was placed under these Commissioners in 1847. See pages 116, 427, 565.

[4] These actions may be for compensation for the performance, or damages for the violation, of a contract for services on board a vessel during a voyage performed in whole or in part, or intended to be performed, by the vessel; or for assault and battery, false imprisonment, or other injury committed on board a vessel upon the high seas, and not coming within the jurisdiction of the U. S. District Courts. The Marine Court is held daily, except on Sundays and holidays; and its Justices, three in number, are elected for a term of 4 years, and enter upon their duties on the second Tuesday of May after their election. Their Clerk is appointed by the Supervisors, and their salary is fixed by the Common Council and cannot be increased during their term of office.

The State Government, before the adoption of the Federal Constitution, had instituted a court of Admiralty; but in 1789 it surrendered these powers to the General Government, and they have since been exercised by the District Court of the U. S. Suits for salvage, and other questions arising in the sale of wrecked property, are decided in this court.

The Governor appoints 15 Wreck Masters in Suffolk, 12 in Queens, 3 in Kings, 2 in Richmond, and 2 in Westchester cos. These officers have, with coroners and sheriffs, the custody of wrecks and property cast ashore by the sea. Such property belongs to the owners, and may be recovered by paying reasonable salvage and in due course of law.

[5] Imports from Canada duty free for the year ending June 30, 1858.

District.	Value.
Champlain	$1,499,819
Oswegatchie	934,708
Cape Vincent	1,210,351
Sackets Harbor	2,892
Oswego	1,859,798
Genesee	263,574
Niagara	786,070
Buffalo Creek	1,336,820
New York	624,060
Total in New York	7,918,092
Total in United States	14,752,255

Statistics of the several Collection Districts upon the Canada Frontier for different periods.

COLLECTION DISTRICT.	1830 to 1848, (19 years.)		1848 to 1851, (3 years.)		1851 to 1854, (3 years.)	
	Gross Revenue.	Expenses of Collection.	Gross Revenue.	Expenses of Collection.	Gross Revenue.	Expenses of Collection.
Champlain	$192,877.80	$130,938.86	$133,326.68	$22,965.22	$297,601.76	$32,267.44
Oswegatchie	63,201.74	116,874.47	42,842.41	16,002.22	98,754.11	21,446.80
Cape Vincent	21,649.98	78,437.26	22,410.78	14,222.58	84,577.74	22,935.52
Sackets Harbor	13,983.04	106,492.84	16,603.54	27,000.95	21,204.23	22,164.23
Oswego	206,759.84	157,519.67	273,173.92	38,210.43	389,711.03	48,211.98
Genesee	133,019.97	80,954.47	45,324.66	13,368.47	29,430.52	21,860.28
Niagara	53,527.07	117,943.82	44,076.44	21,277.69	74,641.59	25,618.04
Buffalo	150,437.60	197,653.80	148,740.03	49,601.19	263,222.58	49,473.89

As the only avenue to the sea which Canada possesses is closed by ice during about five months in the year, the foreign trade of that country in winter must seek other avenues; and, from the acknowledged superiority of New York as a commercial point, a large part of the trade is through that port. Over half the vessels that arrive in Quebec come in ballast; while none leave port without cargoes of timber or other commodities of the country. This renders the outward freights disproportionately high; and, although vessels may load in the upper lakes and pass without transhipment down the St. Lawrence, the difference of ocean freights makes it cheaper to send by the canals to New York.

The number of vessels and amount of tonnage employed upon the great lakes have been rapidly increasing for the last 10 years. In the several collection districts of this State, the ratio of increase has been much greater in ports where railroads terminate.[1]

[1] *Arrivals and Tonnage of the several Districts bordering upon Canada during a series of nine years.*

DISTRICT.	1850. Vessels.	1850. Tons.	1851. Vessels.	1851. Tons.	1852. Vessels.	1852. Tons.	1853. Vessels.	1853. Tons.	1854. Vessels.	1854. Tons.
Champlain	689	107,957	630	89,842	340	22,538	563	31,836	585	57,721
Oswegatchie	380	196,915	536	250,492	798	341,188	1,001	701,560	482	273,272
Cape Vincent	281	156,351	318	208,186	197	95,548	959	451,587	1,034	471,577
Sackets Harbor	279	153,169	230	166,748	218	145,169	139	87,758	77	54,670
Oswego	1,657	195,793	1,599	216,444	1,731	234,625	2,243	274,307	593	65,213
Genesee	215	40,077	232	46,924	264	38,903	295	53,660	285	51,571
Niagara	981	173,286	624	220,528	691	213,613	696	219,241	584	236,051
Buffalo Creek	722	108,337	654	96,290	759	106,464	1,037	149,356	792	137,088
Dunkirk	......	....	....	....	....	....	......	....	......	....

DISTRICT.	1855. Vessels.	1855. Tons.	1856. Vessels.	1856. Tons.	1857. Vessels.	1857. Tons.	1858. Vessels.	1858. Tons.
Champlain	397	25,129	852	54,367	1,053	74,710	1,100	78,256
Oswegatchie	500	249,909	636	320,834	644	320,505	398	170,667
Cape Vincent	1,278	557,840	1,240	749,787	1,128	661,025	1,018	555,408
Sackets Harbor	209	125,496	193	135,442	174	128,685	110	80,417
Oswego	1,517	166,641	1,866	314,657	1,815	263,007	1,543	193,691
Genesee	286	85,063	338	109,881	363	116,411	208	57,330
Niagara	536	209,646	563	166,893	671	238,019	616	254,195
Buffalo Creek	816	152,540	1,002	166,020	837	118,377	1,153	448,786
Dunkirk	2	476	......	....	3	300	6	1,180

Commerce of Canada with the United States since 1850, as shown by the Canadian Official Reports.

YEARS.	Value of Exports from Canada.	Value of Imports into Canada.
In 1850	$4,951,159.58	$6,594,860.49
" 1851	4,071,544.65	8,365,765.25
" 1852	6,284,521.75	8,457,693.27
" 1853	10,725,455.15	11,782,147.40
" 1854	10,418,880.69	15,533,097.94
" 1855	20,002,290.95	20,825,432.44
" 1856	20,218,652.66	22,704,509.05
" 1857	13,206,436.10	20,224,650.97

Commerce of United States with Canada for a series of years, as shown by the U. S. Official Reports.

YEARS.	EXPORTS. Foreign.	EXPORTS. Domestic.	EXPORTS. Total.	IMPORTS.
1852	$3,853,919	$6,655,097	$10,509,016	$6,110,299
1853	5,736,555	7,404,087	13,140,642	7,550,718
1854	9,362,716	15,204,144	24,566,860	8,927.560
1855	11,999,378	15,806,642	27,806,020	15,136.734
1856	6,314,652	22,714,697	29,029,349	21,310.421
1857	4,326,369	19,936,113	24,262,482	22,124,296
1858	4,012,768	19,638,959	23,651,727	15,806,519

Arrivals and Clearances for the several Collection Districts for 1858.

DISTRICT.	NUMBER OF VESSELS. ENTERED. American.	NUMBER OF VESSELS. ENTERED. Foreign.	NUMBER OF VESSELS. CLEARED. American.	NUMBER OF VESSELS. CLEARED. Foreign.	TONNAGE. ENTERED. American.	TONNAGE. ENTERED. Foreign.	TONNAGE. CLEARED. American.	TONNAGE. CLEARED. Foreign.
Champlain	623	477	623	477	44,590	33,666	44,590	33,666
Oswegatchie	150	248	153	248	119,649	51,018	131,727	51,018
Cape Vincent	439	579	434	579	356,972	198,436	354,943	198,436
Sackets Harbor	110	......	106	......	80,417	....	75,191	
Oswego	410	1,133	382	1,129	60,367	133,324	60,999	132,055
Genesee	31	177	39	175	3,207	54,123	3,602	52,826
Niagara	128	488	104	488	101,817	152,378	77,440	152,318
Buffalo Creek	680	473	721	450	369,433	79,353	375,432	77,449
Dunkirk	1	5	2	3	80	1,100	117	1,000

The above indicates but a part of the commerce of these districts. It is probable that the amount of coasting trade which is not entered upon the custom house books is much larger in each district than that here given.

The canals and rail roads of Canada terminating upon our frontiers are intimately connected with the commercial prosperity of this State; and a notice of their extent and capacity is necessary to a full understanding of our commercial possibilities.[1]

Custom Houses have been erected by the General Government at New York, Plattsburgh, Oswego, and Buffalo; and a site has been purchased at Ogdensburgh. These edifices are built of stone, fireproof, and are generally fine specimens of architecture. Efforts have been made to secure the erection of similar buildings at Rochester, Sackets Harbor, Albany, Brooklyn, and Sag Harbor, but so far without success.[2]

---

1. *The Welland Canal* extends from Port Colborne, on Lake Erie, to Port Dalhousie, on Lake Ontario. It has a feeder branch to Dunnsville, on Grand River, and another from the feeder to Port Maitland. It passes sloops, schooners, and propellers of a capacity of 400 tons. In 1856 its tolls amounted to $261,568.13; in 1857 to $232,437.38; and in 1858 to $207,771.52.

The Rideau Canal was built as a military work by the Home Government and transferred some years since to the Province. It extends from Kingston to Ottawa, most of the way along the channel of rivers. Its total length is 126 miles. It rises from Kingston to the summit 165 feet by 13 locks, and descends to the Ottawa 292 feet by 34 locks. Its total cost was $3,860,000. *The Galoppe, Point Iroquois, Rapid Plat, Farrans Point, Cornwall, Beauharnois,* and *Lachine Canals* extend around the rapids on the St. Lawrence. Steamers usually pass down the rapids, but must return by the canals and pay toll both ways. Sail vessels pass both up and down by canal. These canals afford navigation down to Montreal, to which point ships come up from the sea. The total fall by river without locks is 204¾ feet to Montreal and 13¾ feet thence to tide water at Three Rivers. The rapids of the St. Lawrence have been surveyed with the design of deepening them to afford a channel 200 feet wide and 10 feet deep, but nothing further has been done. These surveys make Lake Erie 534¾ feet above tide.

Chambly Canal extends from the foot of navigation on Lake Champlain to Chambly Basin, and with a lock at St. Ours, upon Richlieu River, completes the line of navigation from the lake to the St. Lawrence. A ship canal has recently been proposed between these important navigable waters.

The amount of tonnage on these canals, in which this State is interested, is very large; and in the Welland Canal more than half the duties are paid by American vessels.

Statistics of the Business of the Canadian Canals for two years.

	Welland Canal.		St. Lawrence Canal.		Chambly Canal.	
	1856.	1857.	1856.	1857.	1856.	1857.
Total tons passing up	276,919	245,256	131,430	134,382	107,878	112,634
" " " down	699,637	655,816	503,106	459,270	21,788	21,053
Canadian to American ports, up	31,334	67,476	5,274	4,493	96,868	107,925
" " " down	52,100	29,128	33,888	30,366		
American to Canadian ports, up	34,716	137,574	6,380	9,328		
" " " down	116,582	163,217	15,612	3,765		
American to American ports, up	200,373	280,546	213	17	16,741	18,272
" " " down	341,225	245,256	306	30	725	156
	£ s. d.	£ s. d.	£ s. d.	£ s. d.	£ s. d.	£ s. d.
Revenues from tolls on property	59,408 10 7	52,239 16 5	16,813 13 5	13,741 10 3	2,467 9 9	2,577 6 8
" " vessels	6,108 3 11	5,919 9 7	1,978 6 5	1,898 8 11	432 16 1	443 19 10
" " passengers	88 7 6	82 3 2	638 16 4	579 10 4	6 18 4	10 11 0
" " fines	440 1 3	155 0 0	910 7 10	203 10 4	....	60 10 4
" " rents	1,967 4 4	1,504 5 7	1,042 10 0	1,503 19 10	....	28 5 0

Statistics of the Canadian Canals.

	Canals.	Miles in length.	No. of locks.	Lockages in feet.	Size of Locks. Length between gates.	Size of Locks. Width of Channels.	Size of Locks. Depth on miter sill.	Width of Canal. At bottom.	Width of Canal. At surface.
	Welland	28	24	330	150	26½	8½	45	81
			3		200	45	9		71
	Feeder	21	1	8	150	26½	8½	35	85
	Broad Creek Branch	1½	1	8	200	45	9	45	75
	Rideau	126¼	47	457	134	33	5	......	90
St. Lawrence Can's.	Galoppe	2	2	8	200	45	9	50	90
	Point Iroquois	3	1	6	200	45	9	50	90
	Rapid Plat	4	2	11½	200	45	9	50	90
	Farrans Point	¾	1	4	200	45	9	50	90
	Cornwall	11½	7	48	200	45	9	100	150
	Beauharnois	11¼	9	82½	200	45	9	80	120
	Lachine	8½	5	44¾	200	45	9	80	120
	Chambly	11½	9	74	120	24	6	36	60
	St. Ours (lock)	......	1	5	200	45	6		

It has been proposed to build a ship canal from Lake Huron to Lake Ontario at Toronto, by way of Lake Simcoe, 80 mi. A cutting to allow Lake Simcoe to pass southward would not exceed 175 ft. in depth; and in the 8 mi. surveyed the principal obstacles would not average over 40 ft. It has been estimated that the cost for a canal 120 ft. wide at bottom, and 136 ft. at surface, 12 ft. deep, with 64 double locks 50 ft. wide, and 250 ft. long, would be $20,051,000, and that it could be constructed in 5 years.

Great Western Railway of Canada, from Suspension Bridge to Windsor, 229 mi., and thence by ferry to Detroit, was opened Jan. 27, 1854. Branches extend from Hamilton to Toronto, 38 mi.; from Harrisburgh to Guelph, 23¾ mi.; from Preston to Berlin, 10½ mi.; and from Kamoka, near London, to Port Sarnia, 60 mi.

Buffalo & Lake Huron Railway extends from Fort Erie, opposite Buffalo, to Goderich Harbor, on Lake Huron, 165 mi.

Erie & Ontario Railway extends from Chippewa to Niagara, 17 miles.

Welland Railway, from Fort Dalhousie to Port Colborne, 27 mi., is on the eve of completion.

Grand Trunk Railway of Canada extends from Portland, Me., and Quebec to Richmond, and thence to Montreal, Toronto, and Port Sarnia, at the foot of Lake Huron. More than 700 mi. of this road are finished. A branch extends from Belleville to Peterborough, 50 mi., and others are proposed.

Ontario, Simcoe & Huron Railway extends from Toronto to Collingwood, on Georgian Bay, 95 mi.

Coburg & Peterborough Railway is 28½ mi. long, with privilege of extending to Marmora Iron Works.

Ottawa & Prescott Railway extends from Prescott to Ottawa City, 54 mi.

Montreal & New York R. R. extends from Montreal to Lachine, 8 mi., and thence by ferry, 2 mi., always open, to Caughnawaga, the terminus of a road leading to Plattsburgh, 52 mi. This line is now united with the *Champlain & St. Lawrence R. R.*, from St. Lambert, opposite Montreal, to Rouses Point, 44 mi.; and the consolidated company is known as the *Montreal & Champlain Rail Road Co.*

2 *Custom Houses of New York.*

Place.	Total appropriation.	Cost: Of site.	Cost: Total.
New York	$1,068,743	$270,000	$1,105,313.57
Plattsburgh	99,900	5,000	86,443.73
Ogdensburgh	118,000	8,000	....
Oswego	131,100	12,000	121,092.89
Buffalo	290 000	40,000	191,680.08
Total New York	$1,707,743	$335,000	$1,504,530.27
Total U. States	$24,104,799	$3,388,827	$10,529,951.72

Marine Hospitals.—Since 1778, every American seaman has been taxed 20 cents per month for a Hospital Fund; and in return he is entitled in case of sickness to assistance and support from the revenues thus collected. This fund is in charge of the U. S. Government, and is entirely independent of the various State and private hospital funds of New York City.[1]

Light Houses.—The United States Government has erected 62 light houses, lighted beacons, and floating lights within the State of New York, for the benefit of navigation. Of these, 3 are upon the seacoast, 15 upon Long Island Sound, 4 within the Harbor of New York, 16 upon Hudson River, 3 upon Lake Champlain, 14 upon Lake Ontario and St. Lawrence River, and 7 upon Lake Erie. The Government has also erected buoys, spindles, beacons, and other signals to indicate channels or to point out dangerous localities.[2]

The site for the New York Custom House was purchased Jan. 9, 1833, the building was completed Feb. 22, 1842: it is used for a custom house only. The site for the Plattsburgh Custom House was purchased Nov. 22, 1856, the building was completed May 19, 1858: it is used for a custom house, post office, and courthouse. The site for the Ogdensburgh Custom House was purchased Jan. 20, 1857, the building has not been commenced: it is designed to be used for a custom house, post office, and courthouse. The site for the Oswego Custom House was purchased Dec. 15, 1854, the building was completed Sept. 1, 1858: it is used for a custom house and post office. The site for the Buffalo Custom House was purchased Jan. 26, 1855, the building was completed July 12, 1858: it is used for a custom house, post office, and courthouse.

The Custom House in New York occupied before the present one was finished was erected in 1816, at a cost of $928,312.96. In 1850 the only custom house building in the State belonging to the United States was at New York City. On the 19th of Feb. 1857, the Federal Government purchased a site for stores at Atlantic docks, Brooklyn, for $100,000; but as yet no use has been made of it.

[1] The Federal Government has built 34 marine hospitals, none of which are in this State. Those entitled to aid are supported in this State in private families or local hospitals. The number of seamen relieved and supported in the several collection districts in the year ending June 30, 1858, was as follows:—

COLLECTION DISTRICT.	Admitted.	Discharged.	Died.	Total expenditures.	Hospital money collected.
Sag Harbor	.....	.....	...	$ 19.19	$ 289.63
New York.......	824	924	...	22,485.94	42,576.78
Champlain......	.....	.....	...	403.81	412.60
Oswegatchie....	.....	.....	...	15.15	544.93
Cape Vincent...	.....	.....	...	.....	253.50
Sackets Harbor	10	12	...	142.15	60.70
Oswego	86	98	2	3,632.21	975.42
Genesee	.....	.....	...	.....	98.00
Niagara	4	3	1	183.86	92.19
Buffalo Creek...	76	86	...	3,770.92	2,320.50
Dunkirk..........	.....	.....	...	.....	269.88
Total New York	1,000	1,123	3	$30,653.23	$47,894.13
Total U. States..	10,703	9,444	381	$358,020.53	$161,161.82

[2] *Light Houses.*

NAME.	Location.	Distance visible in nautical miles.	Fixed or revolving, &c.	Color of tower.	Height of tower from base, in feet.	Height of light above water.	When built.	When refitted.	Order of lens.	Remarks.
Montauk	E. point of S. Branch, L. I.	20	Flashing ...	White	85	160	1795	1857	1	Fresnel lens; flash 2 min.
North Dumpling	Fishers Island Sound...	12	Fixed	Red	25	70	1848	1855	6	
Little Gulls Island....	S. side main entrance Sound......	13	"	"	56	74	1806	1857	3	Fog bell. Machine.
Gardners Island	N. point Island............	6	"	Brown	27	29	1855	......	6	
Plum Island	w. end Plum Island.....	12	Revolving	White	34	63	1827	1856	4	Flash 30 sec.
Cedar Island..........	Entrance Sag Harbor...	10	Fixed	"	31	34	1839	1855	6	Light on keeper's house.
Hortons Point..........	N. side of Southold......	18	"	Red	30	110	1857	......	3	
Stratford Pt. Vessel...	Middle ground of Stratford Shoals..	10	2 "	Straw col..	32	40	1837	1855	...	2 reflector lights. Fog bell.
Oldfield Point..........	Brookhaven	13	"	White	34	67	1823	1855	4	
Eatons Neck..........	E. of Huntington Bay...	17	"	"	56	138	1798	1857	4	
Lloyds Harbor..........	Entrance of harbor......	10	"	"	34	48	1857	......	5	
Great Captains Island	Near Greenwich Point..	12	"	"	34	62	1829	1858	4	Fog bell. Machine.
Execution Rocks	Off Sands Point	12	"	"	42	54	1848	1856	4	Flash 30 sec.
Sands Point.............	E. of Cow Bay............	15	Revolving	"	41	53	1809	1856	4	
Throggs Neck..........	N.E. side of Fort Schuyler	10	Fixed	"	61	66	1826	1855	6	Fog Bell. Machine 7 per min.
Great West Bay........	Ponquogue Point N. of Shinnecock Bay.....................	20	"	Brick........	150	160	1857	......	1	
Fire Island..............	E. of Fire Island Inlet...	15	Revolving	Yellow......	150	166	1858	......	1	First light house built in 1826.
Swash Channel Beacon.	Staten Island, near Elm Tree Station.	14	2 Fixed....	White, red.	.....	59 189	1856	......	3 2	
Princess Bay...........	s. of Staten Island........	16	Flashing ...	White	33	106	1828	1857	3	
Fort Tompkins.........	w. of Narrows	15	Fixed	"	46	89	1828	1855	4	
Robbins Reef...........	Off Tompkinsville........	13	"	"	51	66	1839	1855	4	Fog bell.
Stony Point.............	w. side entrance Narrows............	20	"	"	150	22	1826	1855	5	
West Point.............	Gees Point, w. side......	10	"	"	32	38	1853	......	6	
Esopus Meadows......	Opposite Esopus, w. side	10	"	"	32	38	1839	1854	6	On keeper's house.
Rondout	Mud flat. s. of N. entrance creek w. of river............	10	"	"	32	38	1838	1854	6	" " "
Saugerties	w. of river, N. of Saugerties ....)	10	"	"	37	42	1835	1854	6	" " "

Lifeboat Stations have also been established by the General Government upon the sea-coast and great lakes. On the shores of Long Island and the adjacent islands are 30 lifeboat stations, the first of which were established about 1850. Each of these consists of a house, containing a lifeboat, boat wagon, life cars, mortar for throwing lines, and every fixture that could be used in affording aid to vessels in distress. The houses are furnished with stoves for warming them when necessary, and with fuel and matches for kindling a fire on short notice. They are each intrusted to a local agent, and are under the general care of a superintendent appointed by the Secretary of the Treasury. Their location is indicated on the map.

Coast Survey.—A survey of the coast, with soundings of its adjacent waters, was ordered by the General Government about 50 years since; but many years were necessarily employed in making preliminary arrangements. Active surveys were begun about 1832, and during the last 15 years they have been prosecuted with great effect. The triangulations of this survey are conducted with great precision, and extend up all rivers navigable from the sea as far as tide flows.

Light Houses, continued.

NAME.	Location.	Distance visible in nautical miles.	Fixed or revolving, &c.	Color of tower.	Height of tower from base.	Height of light above water.	When built.	When refitted.	Order of lens.	Remarks.
Catskill Reach	Half way Athens and Catskill, E. of river	10	Fixed	White	32	38	1854	......	6	
Prymes Hook	2 mi. N. Hudson, E. side	10	"	"	32	38	1851	1854	6	
Four Mile Point	w. side. Half way Athens and Coxsackie	10	"	"	20	35	1854	......	6	
Coxsackie	w. side. N. end of Cow Island	10	"	"	32	38	1829	1854	6	On keeper's house.
Stuyvesant	E. side	10	"	"	32	38	1829	1854	6	
New Baltimore	E. side on island	...	"	"	20	21	1854	......	6	
Five Hook Island	Calvers Plat Island	...	"	"	......	25	1857	......	6	
Coeymans Bar	N. end Poplar Island	...	"	"	......	25	1857	......	6	
Schodack Channel	w. side Mulls Plat	...	"	"	......	25	1857	......	6	
Cow Island	E. side near Castleton	...	"	"	20	21	1854	......	6	
Van Wies Point	E. of dike below Albany. w. side	...	"	"	15	15	1854	......	6	
Split Rock	Near Essex	15	"	"	32	100	1838	1856	4	
Cumberland Head	Near Plattsburgh	12	"	"	36	55	1837	1855	5	
Point au Roche	w. of Lake Champlain	...	"		......	......	1857	......	4	Building. (1858.)
Ogdensburgh	Mouth of Oswegatchie	12	"	White	27	30	1834	1855	4	Light on keeper's house.
Cross Over Island	Above Oak Point	12	"	"	25	37	1847	1855	4	Light on keeper's house.
Sunken Rock	In front of Alexandria Bay	9	"	"	28	31	1847	1855	6	
Rock Island	Near Mullet Creek	9	"	"	27	39	1847	1855	6	Light on keeper's house.
Tibbetts Point	Entrance of St. Lawrence	14	"	"	47	67	1827	......	4	Rebuilt 1854.
Galloo Island	w. side island	14	"	"	51	59	1820	1857	4	Shoal N. W. 1 mi.
Horse Island	Near Sackets Harbor	11	"	"	34	42	1831	1857	5	Light on keeper's dwelling.
Stony Point	On Stony Point	11	Revolving.	"	34	39	1837	1857	6	Light on keeper's dwelling.
Salmon River	N. side entrance harbor	9	Fixed	"	46	49	1838	1855	6	Light on keeper's dwelling.
Oswego	w. pier harbor	14	"	"	45	59	1837	1855	4	
Big Sodus Bay	w. of Sodus Harbor	13	Revolving	"	50	64	1825	1858	4	Lake coast light.
Genesee	w. of entrance to river	14	Fixed	"	37	81	1822	1855	4	Lake coast and harbor light.
Genesee Beacon	End of w. pier	6	"	"	22	28	1822	1855	6	Frame. Harbor light.
Niagara Fort	Outlet of Niagara River.	14	"	"	44	78	1813	1857	4	On mess house. Fort Niagara.
Black Rock Beacon	Near head Niagara River	10	"	"	13	25	1853	......	5	
Horse Shoe Reef	Entrance Niagara River	14	Flashing	"	50	50	1856	......	4	Lake coast light.
Buffalo	s. pier. Harbor	16	Fixed	"	51	65	1828	1857	3	
Cattaraugus	w. pier. Cattaraugus Creek	9	"	"	35	44	1847	......	6	Rebuilt 1857.
Dunkirk	Harbor	16	Flashing	"	50	87	1837	1857	3	Lake coast light.
Dunkirk Beacon	Pier w. side harbor	9	Fixed	"	25	40	1837	1854	6	Harbor light on pier.
Barcelona	Portland or Barcelona	14	"	"	40	80	1829	1857	4	Lighted with natural gas. No harbor at this place.

Besides the above, there are nine State lights established in 1856 in the marshy "Narrows" at the head of Lake Champlain. Big Sodus Beacon was destroyed in a gale in 1857.
A flashing light has been authorized at Crown Point.

There are lifeboats on Lake Ontario at Tibbetts Point, Sandy Creek, Salmon River, Oswego, Sodus, Genesee River, and Niagara River, which were supplied by the U. S. Government in the summer of 1854. Several have also been placed on Lake Erie. None of those on the lakes have been provided with houses, except such as have been erected by the persons having them in charge.

Immigration into the U. S. for many years past has been very great; but the proportion landing in New York has been less than the relative amount of trade. Other routes in some respects afford superior facilities for immigration. The large number of ships arriving in Canada without cargoes favors immigration to a great extent; and hundreds of thousands of immigrants have crossed into this State from Canada without their names ever appearing on the U. S. Government records. These immigrants have consisted chiefly of Irish and Germans; though there has also been a large number of English, Scotch, and Norwegians. The greater part of the immigrants either locate in the cities or immediately pass on to the wild lands of the West. The English and Scotch usually prefer to settle in Canada.[1]

Assay Office.—By an act of 1853, the Secretary of the Treasury was directed to establish an assay office at New York, for the special accommodation of the business of the city. At this place the owners of gold or silver bullion, or of foreign coin, may deposit the same, have its value ascertained, and certificates issued payable in coin of the same metal as that deposited, either at the office of the assistant treasurer in New York, or at the Mint in Philadelphia. The metal assayed may, at the option of the owner, be cast into bars, ingots, or discs, of pure metal, or of standard fineness, and stamped with a device designating its weight and fineness. This office is under the general direction of the Director of the Mint, in subordination to the Secretary of the Treasury. The Assay Office is located on Wall St., adjacent to the Custom House, and is fitted up with every appliance for carrying on its operations upon a very extensive scale. Its lofty chimney, emitting dense, orange colored fumes of nitric acid, forms a conspicuous object in the district. About 50 men are employed upon the premises. Its officers are a superintendent, treasurer, assayer, melter, and refiner, with their assistants and clerks. The site of the Assay Office was bought Aug. 19, 1853, for $553,000, and the premises were fitted up and completed Oct. 9, 1854, at a total cost of $761,493.62.[2]

The Mail Service of the State of New York forms about 5 per cent. of the whole U. S. in miles, and 7 per cent. in cost, while the receipts from postage in this State amount to 22 per cent.

---

[1] *Passengers arriving by Sea at New York since 1820.*

Years.	No. of passengers.	Years.	No. of passengers.	Years.	No. of passengers.	Years.	No. of passengers.
1820	3,834	1830	13,748	1840	60,609	1849	213,736
1821	4,038	1831	10,737	1841	55,885	1850	184,882
1822	4,116	1832	28,914	1842	74,014	1851	294,445
1823	4,247	1833	39,440	1843	38,930	1852	303,153
1824	4,889	1834	46,053	1844	59,762	1853	294,818
1825	7,662	1835	32,715	1845	76,514	1854	327,976
1826	6,908	1836	58,617	1846	98,863	1855	161,490
1827	12,602	1837	51,676	1847	145,830	1856	162,108
1828	19,860	1838	24,935	1848	160,994	1857	203,500
1829	14,814	1839	47,688				

Until 1850 these returns were made up to Sept. 30; but since 1851 they began upon Jan. 1 each year. The number between Sept. 30 and Dec. 31, 1850, not included in the above, was 38,831.

The total number of passengers who arrived in the U. S. from 1820 to 1858 was 4,482,837, of which number 3,028,225 arrived in New York.

[2] The establishment of a mint at New York has been repeatedly urged, and the addition of coining machinery to the existing Assay Office could be made at a moderate expense.

Amounts Assayed at the U. S. Assay Office in New York.

Years.	Fine Gold bars.	Value.	Fine Silver bars.	Value.
1854	822	$2,888,059.18		
1855	6,182	20,441,813.63		
1856	4,727	19,396,046.89	52	$6,792.00
1857	2,230	9,335,414.00	550	123,317.00
1858 to June 30	7,052	21,798,691.04	894	171,961.79
Total	21,013	$73,860,024.74	1,496	$302,071.79

	Total Pieces.	Total Value.
1854	822	$2,888,059.18
1855	6,182	20,441,813.63
1856	4,799	19,402,839.52
1857	2,780	9,458,721.00
1858 to June 30	7,946	21,970,652.83
Total	22,509	$74,162,096.16

Amounts Deposited.

	Gold.	Silver.
From Oct. 10 to Dec. 31, 1854	$9,260,893.69	$76,307.00
From Jan. 1 to Dec. 31, 1855	26,687,701.24	350,150.08
From Jan. 1 to Dec. 31, 1856	17,803,692.40	474,161.38
From Jan. 1 to Dec. 31, 1857	18,997,365.40	1,397,702.99
Total	$72,749,652.73	$2,298,331.45
		72,749,652.73

Total gold and silver $75,047,974.18

Proportion of the above payable in fine bars $47,817,597.00
"   "   "   coin 27,230,377.18

Total.. $75,047,974.18

Amounts transmitted to the Mint for Coining.

	Gold.	Silver.
From Oct. 10 to Dec. 31, 1854	$5,142,262.60	$41,417.89
From Jan. 1 to Dec. 31, 1855	7,722,476.47	71,587.34
From Jan. 1 to Dec. 31, 1856	5,797,652.33	412,416.06
From Jan. 1 to Dec. 31, 1857	9,307,928.89	1,842,768.71
Total	$27,970,260.29	$2,368,190.00

Cost of transportation from the Assay Office to the Mint and return:—

On gold, $1 per $1,000.................................. $27,834.17
On silver, $3 per $1,000 .... 7,101.98

Total.. $34,936.15

of the whole sum collected, and exceed by over $300,000 per annum the expenses of the establishment within its borders. The total expenses in the U. S. overrun the receipts by about $3,500,000 annually.[1]

There were four Distributing Post Offices in New York, Jan. 1, 1859, located respectively at New York, Albany, Troy, and Buffalo. The Troy post office was discontinued as a distributing office July 1, 1859.

[1] *Post Office Summary for the year ending June* 30, 1858.

	New York State.	*United States.*
Length of routes in miles	13.078	260,603
Transportation in coaches, miles	4,961	53,700
" " cost	$109,490	$1,909,844
" in steamboats, miles	168	17,043
" " cost	$7,298	$1,233,916
" by railroad, miles	2,894	24,431
" " cost	$333,163	$2,828,301
" mode not specified, miles	5,055	165,429
" " " cost	$68,100	$1,823,357
Total cost of transportation	$518,060	$7,795,418
Total number of miles by coaches	2,430,792	19.555,734
" " steamboats	108,944	4.569,610
" " railroads	3,961,795	25,763,452
" " modes not specified	1,468,312	28,876,695
" " every method.	7,969,843	78,765,491
Number of mail routes	828	8,296
" contractors	702	7,044
" route agents	55	440
" express agents	11	28
" local agents	2	43
" mail messengers	315	1,464

Exchange Offices under the postal arrangement with Canada.

In the United States.	In Canada.
Black Rock	Waterloo.
Buffalo	Toronto, Hamilton, London, and Queenston, (by through bags,) Fort Erie, and Ports Denver, Simcoe, Rowan, Burwell, Vienna, and Stanley, Montreal.
Cape Vincent	Kingston.
Fort Covington	Dundee.
Lewiston	Queenston.
Mooers	Hemingford.
Morristown	Brockville.
Ogdensburgh	Prescott.
Oswego	Kingston. By steamer in summer.
Plattsburgh	Montreal, St. Johns.
Rochester	Coburg. By steamer in summer.
Rouses Point	St. Johns.
Sackets Harbor	Kingston. By steamer in summer.
Suspension Bridge	Suspension Bridge and Canada; Route agents.
Troy	Montreal; by through bag.
Whitehall	St. Johns.
Youngstown	Niagara.

From New York City to every port and country with which the U. S. has postal arrangements.

Mail Routes in New York by Railroad and Steamboat.

Termini.	*Distances.*	*No. of trips per week.*	*Annual pay.*	*Total annual cost.*	*Number of Route.*
By Railroad. (June 30, 1858.)					
New York to Dunkirk	460	19	$92,000	$117,378	1,026
New York to Albany	144	19	32,400	44,612	1,002
New York to Chatham Four Corners	130½	6	5,593	8,865	1,003
Brooklyn to Greenport	98	18	8,225	11,147	1,007
Sufferns to Piermont	18	6	772	870	1,026
Newburgh to Chester	19	6	814	891	1,032
Hudson to West Stockbridge, Mass	35	6	1,750	1,770	1,064
Albany to Buffalo	298	25	51,600	62,442	1,073
Albany to Troy	7	13	1,050	1,050	1,074
Albany to Eagle Bridge	33	12	2,829	3,946	1,075
Troy to North Bennington, Vt	32½	12	3,250	4,329	1,082
Troy to Schenectady	22	12	1,650	1,725	1,083
Troy to Saratoga Springs	32.81	12	3,281	3,942	1,084
Eagle Bridge to Rutland, Vt	62½	12	6,250	7,244	1,091
Saratoga Springs to Castleton, Vt	54	12	5,400	6,567	1,099
Plattsburgh to Canada Line	23	6	986	1,163	1,122
Rouses Point to Ogdensburgh	119	12	9,700	11,252	1,123
Watertown to North Potsdam	76	6	3,800	5,505	1,146
Sackets Harbor to Pierrepont Manor	18½	6	792	1,117	1,153
Schenectady to Ballston	16	6	800	950	1,164
Utica to Boonville	35	12	2,625	2,886	1,200
Rome to Cape Vincent	97	18	8,329	10,975	1,210
Syracuse to Rochester	104	12	20,800	23,099	1,228
Syracuse to Oswego	35½	12	3,043	3,463	1,229
Syracuse to Binghamton	80	6	3,429	4,952	1,230
Canandaigua to Elmira	68½	12	5,137½	6,524	1,269
Canandaigua to Niagara Falls	97	18	6,100	8,094	1,270
Rochester to Niagara Falls	75	12	11,400	14,230	1,275
Rochester to Avon	18	6	772	1,030	1,278
Batavia to Attica	11	6	550	650	1,300
Buffalo to Lockport	22	12	1,100	1,100	1,312
Buffalo to Lewiston	29	12	1,450	1,560	1,313
Buffalo to Hornellsville	91	12	6.825	7,657	1,314
Buffalo to State Line	69	19	13,800	17,741	1,315
Corning to Batavia	100	6	4,286	7.533	1,369
Owego to Ithaca	33	12	1,415	2,313	1,375
By Steamboat. (Sept. 30, 1858.)					
New York to Manhasset	18	6	300	....	1,004
Albany to New Baltimore	15	6	485	....	1,076
Whitehall to Plattsburgh	95	11 (for 7 months)	4,800	....	1,108
Ithaca to Cayuga	40	6	1,713	....	1,375

The Fisheries in New York, although considerable in amount, are quite subordinate to other branches of industry. The whale fisheries, formerly of great importance, are now chiefly limited to Sag Harbor, Greenport, and Cold Spring Harbor.[1] The shores and bays of Long Island support great numbers of fishermen, and the product of their labor chiefly finds a market in New York City.[2] The Hudson yields shad, sturgeon, and other fish in great quantities;[3] and there are extensive fisheries upon the great lakes, especially near the E. end of Lake Ontario and in the waters of Chaumont Bay.[4] The waters of Lake Champlain and the St. Lawrence formerly abounded in salmon; but, from the building of dams and mills, or other causes, the tributaries of these waters now afford but very small supplies. Trout and other fish highly prized for food abound in the clear mountain streams of Northern New York. Hundreds of millions of "bony fish" are taken annually around Long Island for manure; and the manufacture of oil from sharks, porpoises, and other fish has been at various times carried on with encouraging success. Numerous special laws have been passed for the preservation of fish in certain waters and at particular seasons; but this is now made one of the subjects within the legislative jurisdiction of Boards of Supervisors.

United States Ocean Mail Lines connecting with New York, Sept. 30, 1858.

ROUTES.	Distance in miles.	Trips per an.	Annual Pay.	REMARKS.
N. Y. via Southampton, England, to Bremenhaven, Germany.........	3,700	13	$60,000	Act of June 14, 1858.
N. Y. to Aspinwall, New Grenada, direct......................................	2,000	24	} 290,000	{ Contract under Acts of 1847
N. Y. via Havana to New Orleans..	2,000	24		{ and 1851.
N. Y. to Liverpool, England.............................	3,100	20	385,000	Contract Act 1847. Now under
				Act of June 14, 1858.
N. Y. via Cowes, England, to Havre, France................................	3,270	13	Postages	Act of June 14, 1858.

Comparative Receipts and Expenses of the Post Office in New York and all the Offices in the United States for the year ending July 30, 1858.

	New York.	United States.		New York.	United States.
Letter postage..............................	$285,207.46	$882,122.95	Pay of Post Masters....................	$316,267.39	$2,349,260.49
Newspaper postage........................	90,244.30	593,407.19	Incidental expenses....................	311,893.98	1,104,183.53
Registered letters..........................	2,874.65	28,146.95	Total of above...........................	628,161.37	3,453,444.02
Stamps sold.................................	1,080,384.98	5,692,366.63	Transportation...........................	525,950.00	7,344,619.44
Total receipts..............................	1,458,711.39	7,196,043.72	Total expenses...........................	1,154,111.37	10,798,063.46

[1] The right to drift whales was often made a subject of special reservation or sale by the Indians of Long Island; and the capture of whales in open boats from the shore has continued from the first settlement to the present time. Scarcely a year passes without one or more being taken along the shore of the island. The whale fisheries from Hudson, Poughkeepsie, and Newburgh, once large, have ceased altogether. On the 30th of June, 1858, 5,927.92 tons were employed in the whale fisheries at Sag Harbor, 1,942.12 tons at Greenport, and 2,136.27 tons at Cold Spring Harbor. The total of whaling vessels in the U.S. at the same time was 198,593.51 tons.

[2] The wholesale fish mart of N. Y., on the East River, at the foot of Fulton St., occupies an entire block. The rarer kinds are oftener sold in the Washington Market. A record kept in 1856 enumerated 79 species, in 56 genera and 20 families, as found in these markets, the majority of them being marine fish from the waters adjoining Long Island and the New England coast. A few came from the South, and many from the interior lakes and rivers.

[3] It is estimated that $100,000 worth of shad are taken annually below the Highlands. They are caught in seines nearly as far up as Albany. About $20,000 worth of sturgeon are sold annually at the Albany market.

[4] As many as 10,000 bbls. have been taken at Chaumont Bay in one season, although sometimes no more are taken than enough to supply the local want. The fish are chiefly lake herring and whitefish. The amount of tonnage invested in this State in the cod fisheries is quite unimportant, and amounted in June, 1858, to 131.32 tons at Greenport, and 159.34 tons at New York, consisting of licensed vessels under 20 tons.

COLLEGES AND ACADEMIES.

IN 1754 King's College was incorporated in N. Y. City by patent, and liberally endowed by a lottery and grants of land. At the commencement of the Revolution it was the only incorporated educational institution in the colony. In 1784 its name was changed to Columbia College; and in connection with it an extensive scheme of education was devised, in which the college was to be the center of the system, and subordinate branches were to be established in different parts of the State,—the whole to be under the control of a board denominated "Regents of the University." This board was to consist of the principal State officers, two persons from each co., and one chosen by each religious denomination. The number of the Regents was afterward increased by adding 33 others, 20 of whom resided in N. Y. City. This whole scheme was found to be impracticable; and by act of April 13, 1787, it was superseded by a system which has continued without essential change to the present time.[1] By this act the Governor, Lieut.-Governor, and 19 persons therein named were constituted

Regents of the University, and required to visit and inspect all colleges and academies, and report their condition, annually. They might appoint presidents of colleges and principals of academies for one year, in case of vacancy, and incorporate new colleges and academies, providing the revenue of the latter should not exceed the value of 4,000 bushels of wheat annually. In 1842 the Secretary of State, and in 1854 the Superintendent of Public Instruction, were made *ex officio* members of the Board of Regents. Vacancies are filled by the Legislature in the same manner that U. S. Senators are appointed; and Regents hold their office during life, unless they resign or forfeit their place by removal from the State, by accepting the office of trustee in an incorporated college or academy, or by accepting a civil office the duties of which are incompatible with their duties as Regents:[2] but the members may be removed by concurrent resolution of the Senate and Assembly.[3] They receive no pay. Under a special act of 1791, the Regents appoint the faculty of the College of Physicians and Surgeons of the City of N. Y. and confer degrees upon its graduates.[4] They confer the honorary degree of M.D. upon four persons annually, upon recommendation of the State Medical Society, and may grant any honorary degree. They have exercised this right by conferring the degree of LL.D. upon 12 persons since their first organization.[5] In 1821 they were authorized to incorporate Lancasterian and select schools.[6] In 1844 the Regents were made trustees of the State Library, and, with the Superintendent of Schools, were charged with the supervision of the State Normal School. In 1845 they were made trustees of the State Cabinet of Natural History, and in 1856 were intrusted with what remained of the publication of the colonial history. Their secretary and the Secretary of State are commissioners to superintend the completion of the publication of the natural history of the State.

The Regents annually apportion $40,000 of the income of the Literature Fund[7] among academies, in proportion to the number of students pursuing the classics or the higher English branches;

[1] The authorship of this system has been generally ascribed to Alexander Hamilton, then in the Assembly. The original drafts of the act, still preserved, and the legislative journals of that period, show that Ezra l'Hommedieu, then in the Senate, was prominently concerned in its passage, if not the original mover. The bill was introduced in the Senate upon a petition from Clinton Academy, in Suffolk co.

[2] What these offices are does not appear to have been settled. On several occasions an appointment to the bench of the Supreme Court has created a vacancy. Non-attendance at the meetings of the Board during one year has also been construed to vacate the seat of a Regent.

[3] This power has never been exercised by the Legislature.

[4] A similar power existed with regard to the Western College of Physicians and Surgeons at Fairfield, during its existence.

[5] The honorary degree of M. D. had been conferred upon 120 persons previous to 1859. Resolutions were passed, Oct. 14, 1851, for conferring the degrees of Doctor of Philosophy and Doctor of Literature; but none have been granted.

[6] This right has been exercised four times, viz.:—
Select School at Henrietta, Monroe co., July 2, 1827.
Lewiston High School Academy, Niagara co., April 16, 1828.
Fabius Select School, Onondaga co., Feb. 27, 1841.
Hunter Classical School, Greene co., June 23, 1851.
Lancasterian schools were incorporated by special acts, as follows:—
Albany, Lancaster School Soc., May 26, 1812.

Catskill, Lancaster School Soc., March 14, 1817. Repealed April 20, 1830.
Hudson, Lancaster Soc., April 15, 1817.
Schenectady, Lancaster School Soc., Nov. 12, 1816.
Poughkeepsie, Lancaster School Soc.

[7] This fund originated with certain tracts of land reserved for literature, and was largely increased by four lotteries, granted April 3, 1801, by which $100,000 were to be raised for the joint benefit of academies and common schools, but chiefly for the latter. In 1816, the avails of the Crumhorn Mountain Tract, amounting to $10,416, were given from the general fund to academies and common schools; and in 1819 the arrears of quitrents, amounting to $53,380, were also thus equally divided. In 1827, $150,000 were given to this fund by the Legislature; and on the 17th of April, 1838, the sum of $28,000 was set apart annually from the income of the U. S. Deposit Fund, for distribution among academies. The sum previously applied for this purpose was $12,000 annually; and since 1834 a small part of the income, aside from this, has been applied, from time to time, to the purchase of apparatus.

This fund was managed by the Regents until, by act of Jan. 25, 1832, it was transferred to the Comptroller for investment,—the Legislature appropriating the proceeds annually, and the Regents designating the scale of apportionment.

The principal of the fund amounted, Sept. 30, 1858, to $269,952.12, aside from the U. S. Deposit Fund, and was invested chiefly in stocks and Comptroller's bonds.

designate such academies as shall receive aid in establishing classes for instructing teachers of common schools; conduct exchanges of books and documents with other States and countries; maintain a system of meteorological observations at certain academies; and make full reports annually to the Legislature upon the condition of the colleges and academies of the State, the State Library, and the Cabinet of Natural History.

The officers of the Regents are, a chancellor, vice-chancellor, and secretary. They appoint a librarian and assistants to the State Library, and a curator to the State Cabinet. Six members form a quorum for the transaction of business. Their annual meeting is held on the first Thursday of January, in the Senate chamber, and is adjourned for short periods during the session of the Legislature. Most colleges report annually to the Regents, but are not uniformly subject to visitation, nor do they share in the income of the Literature Fund. They have generally been assisted by grants of land or money from the State.

Colleges and Academies are entrusted to boards of trustees, who possess the usual powers of corporations, and usually fill all vacancies occurring in their number.[1] They appoint professors and instructors, and remove them at pleasure, unless employed by special agreement. All degrees in colleges, whether honorary or in due course of study, are conferred by the trustees.

By an act passed April 12, 1853, the Regents were required to establish general rules under which colleges, universities, and academies might claim incorporation, subject to such limitations and restrictions as might be prescribed by law, or which, by the Regents, might be deemed proper; and institutions thus formed should possess, in addition to the powers thus vested in them, the general powers of a corporation, under the Revised Statutes of this State. The trustees of academies

[1] Genesee College, N. Y. Agricultural College, People's College, University of Buffalo, and University of the City of N. Y., are owned by shareholders, who elect trustees, or officers analogous, for stated terms. The principal State officers are *ex officio* trustees of Union College; and the Mayor and Recorder of cities are, in some cases, trustees of medical colleges. The principal facts concerning colleges and professional schools may be classed as follows:—

Literary and Medical Colleges.

NAME.	Location.	Date of Charter.	How Incorporated.	Remarks.
Alfred University............	Alfred	Mar. 28, 1857	Law	Seventh-day Bap., 33 trustees.
Columbia College..............	New York	Oct. 31, 1754	Patent	Prot. E., 24 trustees. Formerly King's College.
Elmira Female College......	Elmira	April 13, 1855	Law	Changed from Elmira Collegiate Institute.
Genesee College................	Lima	Feb. 27, 1849	Law	Meth. E., 28 to 30 trustees, elected for 5 years by classes.
Hamilton College.............	Clinton	May 26, 1812	Regents	N. S. Presb., 24 trustees. Changed from Hamilton Oneida Academy.
Hobart Free College..........	Geneva	April 5, 1824	Regents	Prot. E., 24 trustees. Originally Medical Dep. connected. Changed from Geneva College, April 10, 1852.
Ingham University..........	Le Roy	April 3, 1857	Law	N. S. Presb., 24 trustees. Changed from Ingham Collegiate Institute.
Madison University...........	Hamilton	Mar. 26, 1846	Law	Bap., 27 trustees. Theological Depart. connected.
N. Y. Central College Assoc.	McGrawville	April 17, 1851	Law	Located on a farm. Students not excluded on account of sex or color.
N. Y. State Agric'l College	Ovid	April 15, 1853	Law	10 trustees. In course of erection. See *Ovid*.
People's College*..............	Havana	April 12, 1853	Law	24 trustees. In course of erection. Capital, $250,000.
St. John's College.............	Fordham	April 10, 1840	Law	R. C., 7 trustees. Theological Depart. connected.
St. Lawrence University...	Canton	April 3, 1856	Law	Universalist, 25 trustees. Theological Department connected. In course of organization.
Troy University................	Troy	April 12, 1855	Regents	Methodist E., 64 trustees. Charter conditioned to $100,000, which is obtained. Organized.
Union College................	Schenectady	Feb. 25, 1795	Regents	15 trustees, besides those *ex officio*. Changed from Schenectady Academy.
University of Albany.........	Albany	April 17, 1851	Law	Law Department only organized.
Univ. of the City of N. Y....	New York	April 18, 1831	Law	32 trustees. Medical Department connected.
University of Rochester.....	Rochester	May 8, 1846	Law	Bap., 20 trustees. Theological Depart. connected.
University of Buffalo.........	Buffalo	May 11, 1846	Law	Medical Department only organized.
Albany Medical College[b] ...	Albany	Feb. 16, 1839	Law	
College of Pharmacy of City of New York................	New York	April 25, 1831	Law	For education of druggists. Does not report.
College of Physicians and Surgeons of N. Y...........	New York	Mar. 10, 1807	Regents.	
Medical Inst. of Geneva Coll.	Geneva	April 8, 1835	Trusts. of G. Coll.	
Metropolitan Medical Coll.,[c]	New York	Mar. 27, 1857	Law.	
New York Medical College,	New York	1850	Law	Mayor and Recorder *ex officio* trustees.
Univ. of Buffalo, Med. Dep.,[d]	Buffalo	May 11, 1846	Law	Medical Dep. only one organized. Full univ. charter.
University of the City of New York, Med. Dep.[e]....	New York	Feb. 1, 1837	Law.	

[a] Trustees elected for 6 years. Students and teachers expected to labor from 10 to 20 hours each week. Located on a farm of 200 acres.
[b] Mayor and Recorder of Albany *ex officio* trustees. Building erected for Lancasterian school, and leased by the city at a nominal rent.
[c] A college of similar name, incorp. March 28, 1827, did not organize. See *Regents' Report*, 1858, p. 168.

[d] Capital limited to $100,000. Proprietors elect council of 16 for 4 years, besides which each department elects one to the council to hold at their pleasure.
[e] The council of the University of the City of New York consists of 32 shareholders elected for 4 years, besides the Mayor of New York and 4 of the Common Council designated for the purpose.

possessing a capital stock may be elected by the proprietors for such terms as shall be fixed. The capital stock of an academy may not exceed $50,000, and that of a medical college formed under the general law cannot be less than $50,000, nor more than $200,000. All such charters, excepting those containing provisional conditions, are perpetual.

Theological Seminaries in the State of New York.[a]

NAME.	Location.	Denomination.	Date of Establishment.	Number of Professors.	Students.	Number Educated.	Volumes in Library.
General Theological Seminary of P. E. Church..............	New York	P. E.	1817	5	58	430	11,963
Hartwick Seminary (Theological Department)..............	Hartwick	Lutheran	1816	2	5	52	1,250
Martin Luther College (Theological Department)............	Buffalo	Lutheran					
Rochester Theological Seminary.................................	Rochester	Baptist	Nov. 4, 1850	3	36	50	5,500
St. Joseph's Theological Seminary.............................	Fordham	R. C.	1846				
St. Lawrence University (Theological Dep.)..................	Canton	Universalist	1858	1			
Theological Department Madison University................	Hamilton	Baptist	1820	3	24	262	7,500
Theological Seminary of Auburn................................	Auburn	N. S. Presb.	April 14, 1820	4	30	580	6,000
Theological Seminary of Associate Reformed Church......	Newburgh	A. R. Presb.	1836	1	11	143	3,200
Union Theological Seminary.....................................	New York	N. S. Presb.	1836	5	106	211	18,000

[a] Mostly upon authority of the American Almanac of 1859. Several of these possess liberal endowments, and defray the personal expenses of the students attending them. Tuition fees are, it is believed, in no cases required from those receiving instruction. All the above are now in operation.

The following institutions have been projected, but have not been established, or have ceased to exist:—

NAME.	Date of Incorp.	Remarks.
Albany College..	....	Applications were made for a college in 1795, but refused.
Auburn University...................................	Feb. 26, 1826	Provisions of charter not complied with.
Auburn Female University.........................	Jan. 29, 1852	Never organized.
Brockport College...................................	March 4, 1830	Never organized.
Cayuga College......................................	....	Applications made Feb. 15, 1802. Refused.
Central Medical College and Syracuse Medical College...	1849	After a few courses of lectures, these institutions were abandoned.
Clinton College, Fairfield..........................	Mar. 25, 1816	Conditions not complied with.
College of Physicians and Surgeons of Western District, Fairfield............................	June 12, 1812	Courses of lectures were held until 1840, the Regents conferring the degrees.
Flushing College....................................	....	Applications refused Feb. 20, 1845.
Ithaca College.......................................	April 10, 1822	Conditions not complied with.
Kingston College....................................	....	Applications refused in 1779, 1804, and 1811.
Medical Department of Columbia College......	1793	Discontinued in 1814.
N. Y. College of Dental Surgery, Syracuse......	April 13, 1852	Discontinued in a short time.
Richmond College, Richmond co..................	April 18, 1838	Never organized.
St. Paul's College, College Point, Flushing, L. I.	May 9, 1840	Closed in a short time.
Troy Medical College...............................	....	Application refused, Feb. 16, 1824.
University of Western N. Y., Buffalo..............	April 8, 1836	Never organized.
Washington College, Richmond co................	Jan. 27, 1827	Conditions not complied with.
Westminster College, Buffalo.....................	April 17, 1851	Never organized.

Besides these, several institutions bearing the name of colleges have been established, but of which no general statistics have been obtained. Among them are the "Martin Luther College," at Buffalo, the "College of St. Francis Xavier," (R. C.,) in New York; "Franciscan College and Convent," inaugurated Oct. 4, 1858, at Allegany, Cattaraugus co.; the "De Veaux College for Orphan and Destitute Children," incorporated April 15, 1853, and located at Suspension Bridge, Niagara co.; and the "St. Peter's College," (R. C.,) in course of organization, at Troy. Most of these are unincorporated, none of them possess the right of granting degrees, and they generally partake more of the character of academies than of colleges.

Tabular Summary of Colleges as reported Jan. 1859, for the year previous.

NAME.	No. of Professors and Tutors.	No. of Students during the year.	No. of Graduates during the year.	Value of college buildings and grounds.	Tuition and room rent received.	Salaries of Professors and Tutors.	Matriculation fees received.	Graduation fees received.	Volumes in Library.
Albany Medical College............................	9	121	56	$	$	$	$605	$1,120	
College of Physicians and Surgeons, N. Y........	9	173	50	90,000	......	....	635	1,325	
Columbia College..................................	12	153	25	114,336	6,515	44,150			
Genesee College....................................	6	96	15	24,500	......	5,250			
Hamilton College..................................	9	134	27	125,000	1,464	8,019			
Hobart Free College...............................	7	92	20	35,000	Free.	4,595			
Madison University................................	9	119	23	18,700	2,402	7,285			
Medical Institute Geneva College................	7	31	8	16,049	....	....	199	160	
Medical Department of University of N. Y........	7	347	128	70,000	....	....	1,735	3,840	
Medical Department of University of Buffalo.....	9	38	9	14,000					
Metropolitan Medical College.....................	6	18	10	....	....	....	84	132	
New York Central College.........................	9	16	4	30,000	1,497				
New York Medical College........................	12	99	37	50,000	....	....	335	1,110	
St. John's College..................................	27	49	6	74,200	....	4,000			
Troy University....................................	4	53		100,000					
Union College......................................	16	297	89	70,993	10,177	12,151			
University of City of New York...................	16	125	16	200,000	12,207	11,150			
University of Rochester...........................	8	149	22	38,201	5,360	10,835			

Statistics of Academies from the Regents' Report of 1859.

NAMES.	No. of Teachers.	Whole No. of Students in attendance during the year.	The No. that pursued classical studies.	Amount appropriated from the Literature Fund.	TOTAL VALUES. Value of Lot and Buildings.	Value of Library.	Value of Apparatus.	Total Revenues.	Total Expenditures.	No. of Volumes in Library.
Academy at Little Falls...............	3	131	92	$178.52	$10,200	$361	$584	$1,295	$1,195	444
Academy of Dutchess Co..............	4	181	110	213.44	11,000	310	681	3,116	2,928	339
Albany Academy.......................	10	242	116	225.58	90,000	1,631	2,917	5,717	10,062	946
Albany Female Academy.............	13	200	136	263.89	33,347	1,028	2,415	6,662	7,508	1,082
Albion Academy.........................	3	224	133	258.57	7,100	606	350	2,139	2,138	439
Alfred Academy.........................	13	476	355	688.84	17,266	680	1,375	12,124	10,989	737
Amenia Seminary......................	7	168	125	234.79	18,500	1,596	1,267	10,302	10,301	1,711
Ames Academy..........................	2	80	67	130.21	2,440	275	200	742	712	305
Amsterdam Female Seminary........	4	45	35	64.03	9,000	400	405	674	760	381
Argyle Academy.........................	5	99	71	137.77	3,100	242	150	1,330	1,319	173
Auburn Academy.......................	3	135	95	170.75	8,214	332	500	1,478	1,477	249
Augusta Academy......................	1	41	18	34.93	2,487	368	289	260	260	181
Aurora Academy........................	2	226	101	195.98	2,900	610	400	1,501	1,412	653
Ball Seminary..........................	2	113	33	62.09	3,810	197	485	507	514	178
Binghamton Academy.................	3	182	101	194.54	6,500	400	438	1,612	1,611	409
Brockport Collegiate Institute......	7	351	148	287.68	30,000	1,022	377	3,204	3,244	474
Brookfield Academy....................	2	95	71	131.94	3,000	170	155	700	700	126
Brooklyn College & Polytech. Inst..	19	507	240	461.81	69,754	367	1,875	30,453	30,313	335
Buffalo Female Academy.............	10	159	82	159.11	55,000	360	1,742	5,970	6,078	195
Cambridge Washington Academy...	3	172	69	133.89	4,250	650	566	1,700	1,695	391
Canajoharie Academy.................	4	186	98	190.18	5,580	260	244	1,284	1,406	192
Canandaigua Academy................	6	145	87	168.81	12,500	690	1,345	3,139	3,189	813
Canton Academy........................	2	129	59	114.48	3,500	440	327	1,094	1,094	293
Cary Collegiate Seminary............	5	210	106	203.74	15,140	546	600	4,078	4,078	612
Cayuga Academy.......................	6	107	87	168.81	10,000	3,027	879	1,622	1,665	2,345
Champlain Academy...................	3	148	76	147.47	5,504	342	552	1,440	1,440	263
Cherry Valley Academy..............	9	210	64	124.18	13,000	223	762	4,768	4,768	144
Chester Academy.......................	3	90	29	56.26	2,950	370	284	1,180	1,196	250
Cincinnatus Academy.................	3	133	98	184.34	3,183	174	206	1,232	1,066	155
Clarence Academy.....................	2	111	47	91.20	5,000	182	151	836	776	213
Claverack Academy & H. R. Inst...	14	433	367	712.12	35,330	173	846	13,214	11,385	281
Clinton Grammar School..............	4	127	70	133.89	2,600	200	175	6,059	6,165	175
Clinton Liberal Institute.............	7	67	22	42.69	30,300	1,775	475	1,553	1,553	1,257
Cortland Academy.....................	6	394	344	667.40	5,000	1,000	1,000	3,973	4,208	1,129
Cortlandville Academy................	4	234	161	312.40	2,800	711	500	1,752	1,819	668
Dansville Seminary....................	3	....	....	....	3,043	164	170	574	720	67
Deaf and Dumb Institution..........	...	....	306	593.76						
Delaware Academy....................	10	225	186	360.91	26,000	1,183	630	2,286	8,250	838
Delaware Literary Institute.........	9	261	205	397.78	21,000	1,053	395	4,144	3,975	1,032
De Ruyter Institute...................	3	139	64	124.18	8,800	426	542	1,101	991	280
Dundee Academy.......................	4	230	106	205.69	2,350	267	178	2,308	2,440	201
East Bloomfield Academy............	3	60	53	100.96	5,000	558	478	713	713	596
Ellington Academy....................	3	210	113	219.26	3,650	228	160	971	964	188
Erasmus Hall Academy..............	3	103	52	97.02	9,500	2,604	497	2,196	1,858	2,435
Fairfield Academy.....................	10	389	308	597.64	20,200	1,044	1,280	14,307	13,024	953
Falley Seminary.......................	11	383	191	370.62	17,800	655	1,062	4,632	4,632	436
Farmers' Hall Academy..............	1	56	41	79.56	3,350	581	223	649	641	739
Fort Covington Academy.............	3	168	105	203.74	2,150	205	262	1,049	1,017	112
Fort Plain Seminary and Female Collegiate Institute..................	7	264	167	324.54	24,600	152	456	3,159	4,359	208
Franklin (Malone) Academy........	3	287	145	281.36	8,000	338	415	1,767	1,819	285
Franklin (Prattsburgh) Academy..	4	170	148	287.18	10,000	1,251	457	2,280	2,645	1,196
Fredonia Academy.....................	4	281	171	331.81	4,500	2,111	752	2,177	2,459	1,744
Friendship Academy...................	3	166	91	176.58	3,125	214	168	1,198	1,198	189
Galway Academy......	9	103	99	192.10	....	....	.....	3,417	3,339	98
Genesee Conference Seminary......	4	235	146	283.30	8,800	210	152	1,393	1,475	216
Genesee Wesleyan Seminary.......	11	587	495	960.49	27,500	2,366	2,319	4,603	4,644	2,044
Genesee and Wyoming Seminary...	7	210	104	201.80	8,581	864	702	1,905	1,885	520
Geneseo Academy......................	5	218	168	325.98	11,200	708	500	3,699	3,923	
Geneva Union School..................	13	921	43	83.44	10,000	1,000	516	5,434	4,440	1,200
Gilbertsville Academy & Coll. Inst.	2	103	46	89.26	4,500	558	455	1,101	702	389
Glens Falls Academy..................	4	233	127	238.67	4,500	240	385	1,215	1,215	228
Gloversville Union Seminary........	7	265	60	116.42	17,497	160	168	2,631	2,631	101
Gouverneur Wesleyan Seminary...	6	340	156	302.70	6,800	432	939	2,449	2,134	433
Grammar School Columbia College	7	90	71	137.77	....	550	222	5,990	4,157	1,148
Grammar School Madison Univ......	1	43	23	36.86	....	....	......	611	600	
Grammar School N. Y. Cent. Coll..	6	135	106	201.80	....	250	250	1,403	1,404	
Granville Academy....................	...	77	48	93.14	2,900	233	45	443	473	199
Greenville Academy...................	1	86	26	50.44	2,500	251	160	816	758	355
Groton Academy........................	3	193	93	180.46	5,850	441	625	1,502	1,330	392
Hamilton Academy.....................	3	130	67	130.00	3,775	823	473	774	1,341	831
Hamilton Female Seminary..........	6	158	117	213.44	8,513	410	368	4,905	4,852	427
Hartwick Seminary....................	2	88	88	170.75	7,800	1,579	202	1,813	1,734	1,050
Holley Academy........................	4	264	100	194.04	2,900	243	228	1,751	1,751	221
Hudson Academy.......................	2	100	52	100.90	3,200	177	200	702	705	164
Ithaca Academy........................	6	345	216	419.12	12,500	437	900	3,328	3,181	447
Jamestown Academy..................	3	185	120	238.85	4,400	283	740	1,317	1,317	308
Jefferson County Institute...........	4	165	126	244.49	11,050	1,445	1,566	2,136	2,135	1,637
Johnstown Academy...................	3	205	119	230.90	3,000	240	282	1,530	1,529	193
Jonesville Academy...................	8	216	153	296.88	9,652	441	366	5,447	5,447	405
Jordan Academy.......................	2	158	125	242.52	3,800	209	350	1,583	1,584	191

Statistics of Academies from the Regents' Report of 1859, continued.

NAMES.	No. of Teachers.	Whole No. of Students in attendance during the year.	The No. that pursued classical studies.	Amount appropriated from the Literature Fund.	TOTAL VALUES. Value of Lot and Buildings.	Value of Library.	Value of Apparatus.	Total Revenues.	Total Expenditures.	No. of Volumes in Library.
Keeseville Academy	4	378	246	$461.81	$3,600	$227	$200	$2,328	$2,328	231
Kinderhook Academy	4	106	67	130.00	4,000	600	524	1,294	1,294	580
Kingsboro' Academy	3	66	....	....	3,700	417	555	570	567	285
Kingston Academy	5	209	114	219.26	15,000	567	400	3,176	3,058	520
Liberty Normal Institute	2	115	9	17.46	1,250	185	164	701	683	189
Lockport Union School	9	491	181	351.21	13,000	259	500	4,459	4,522	144
Lowville Academy	4	267	176	279.42	7,500	860	627	2,170	2,046	1,119
Lyons Union School	4	128	68	131.94	15,000	745	403	1,757	1,807	986
Macedon Academy	4	240	179	347.33	5,055	207	736	2,482	2,471	177
Manlius Academy	2	99	25	48.51	3,000	410	200	978	812	417
Marion Collegiate Institute	5	158	74	141.65	11,500	248	592	1,546	2,503	196
Mayville Academy	2	78	49	95.08	3,750	194	205	889	910	186
Medina Academy	5	171	164	318.22	6,200	350	235	1,839	1,967	349
Mexico Academy	4	223	159	308.52	14,000	630	326	2,001	2,083	527
Middlebury Academy	5	229	142	275.54	5,500	930	499	2,015	1,976	852
Monroe Academy	4	152	75	145.53	5,465	158	150	1,369	1,368	141
Montgomery Academy	2	77	28	50.45	6,000	200	300	811	806	480
Monticello Academy	7	153	60	116.42	4,350	251	170	2,359	2,443	216
Moravia Institute	2	122	53	102.84	2,200	362	361	830	830	366
Mount Morris Union Free School	4	98	70	135.83	....	222	193	710	710	315
Mount Pleasant Academy	7	82	59	114.48	17,000	1,467	300	7,033	6,650	1,376
Munro Collegiate Institute	3	134	95	182.40	21,500	869	719	1,639	1,256	.722
New Paltz Academy	2	61	33	62.09	7,900	486	553	981	980	447
New York Conference Seminary	11	460	226	438.53	20,000	350	250	19,939	20,473	350
New York Free Academy	25	613	567	1,100.70	117,324	9,296	8,988	59,783	50,671	6,528
North Granville Female Seminary	13	114	132	256.14	19,000	228	375	13,372	10,034	358
North Hebron Institute	...	.....	....	....	2,400	40	137	110	110	112
North Salem Academy	1	60	32	32.98	3,000	536	250	487	440	262
Norwich Academy	5	311	222	430.77	8,400	400	899	2,123	2,114	500
Nunda Literary Institute	5	309	241	467.64	2,900	174	184	1,902	1,703	171
Ogdensburgh Academy	3	161	116	225.58	11,000	501	579	4,686	4,449	1,248
Oneida Conference Seminary	8	351	258	500.62	26,000	2,327	2,694	4,321	4,502	1,946
Onondaga Academy	3	.....	.....	....	12,700	516	306	....	....	635
Ontario Female Seminary	13	128	110	211.50	20,000	931	924	4,855	4,854	895
Oswego High School	3	121	80	155.23	11,000	2,500	500			
Ovid Academy	8	273	196	350.91	15,500	350	600	3,784	3,625	470
Owego Academy	4	249	109	211.50	5,000	601	180	2,373	2,344	402
Oxford Academy	6	300	165	318.22	9,350	953	790	2,131	2,149	1,285
Packer Collegiate Institute	24	673	375	727.75	121,765	1,338	1,595	30,574	24,474	1,128
Palmyra Classical Union School	5	282	134	225.58	12,000	574	250	2,438	2,385	1,094
Peekskill Academy	3	101	50	97.02	17,000	645	446	2,387	2,185	609
Perry Academy	5	127	49	85.38	16,750	567	210	1,225	1,735	347
Peterboro' Academy	1	42	14	27.17	4,528	207	174	334	319	184
Phelps Union Classical School	5	408	91	176.58	5,200	315	201	1,996	2,053	504
Phipps Union Seminary	10	217	176	310.46	10,200	471	212	3,674	3,673	405
Plattsburgh Academy	4	215	160	310.46	5,500	229	474	1,948	1,948	146
Pompey Academy	2	43	39	75.67	5,400	351	150	502	513	366
Poughkeepsie Female Academy	8	119	98	190.18	15,963	578	760	4,497	4,597	634
Prospect Academy	1	87	24	38.81	2,900	312	325	294	317	376
Pulaski Academy	3	170	61	118.36	9,028	301	175	2,557	2,514	293
Randolph Academy	4	184	87	168.81	6,420	388	278	1,263	1,263	320
Red Creek Union Academy	5	250	158	291.56	9,650	175	175	1,560	1,559	200
Rensselaerville Academy	2	91	30	58.21	2,610	203	155	375	435	223
Richburgh Academy	3	86	51	93.14	3,200	172	185	927	855	132
Rochester Female Academy	4	122	62	120.30	6,000	186	170	2,224	2,224	171
Rogersville Union Seminary	4	96	76	147.47	7,850	160	174	939	939	120
Rome Academy	3	233	110	213.44	10,500	420	350	2,060	2,131	506
Rural Seminary	3	122	77	149.41	4,100	647	237	1,081	1,081	678
Rushford Academy	2	201	141	273.60	5,963	283	837	1,531	1,531	162
Rutgers Female Institute	18	278	156	302.70	27,500	2,314	3,138	10,397	12,272	3,032
Sag Harbor Institute	2	320	61	118.36	2,400	210	187	1,546	1,521	206
St. Lawrence Academy	5	293	125	236.73	10,000	784	493	2,484	1,925	936
Saugerties Academy	3	179	50	97.02	5,000	152	185	1,117	1,347	180
Sauquoit Academy	3	115	87	168.81	2,500	192	186	712	743	92
Schenectady Union School	5	206	143	260.51	41,000	4,000	200	19,278	19,532	2,904
Schoharie Academy	3	112	91	176.58	4,000	351	161	1,305	1,337	331
Schuylerville Academy	3	169	123	238.67	2,850	211	400	1,073	1,094	215
Seneca Falls Academy	4	193	98	168.81	3,000	496	600	1,879	1,863	293
Sodus Academy	4	129	72	131.94	3,300	184	283	919	1,106	133
Spencertown Academy	5	78	62	102.84	2,750	192	210	993	971	240
Springville Academy	2	166	86	166.87	3,500	200	410	1,002	951	160
S. S. Seward Institute	6	157	101	195.98	10,000	262	150	4,045	2,108	129
Starkey Seminary	5	161	112	217.32	10,350	853	558	1,220	1,483	1,268
Susquehanna Seminary	7	232	192	364.79	37,000	158	457	2,376	2,479	138
Troy Academy	5	45	28	54.32	7,575	240	275	2,486	2,409	244
Troy Female Seminary	21	319	212	411.36	12,100	1,374	903	8,743	8,270	1,065
Trumansburgh Academy	2	158	34	65.97	4,300	163	150	756	1,051	200
Unadilla Academy	2	80	21	40.75	3,550	256	151	630	629	266
Union Hall Academy	9	220	143	277.48	15,400	634	369	3,686	3,532	667
Union Literary Society	6	209	173	335.69	10,500	731	481	2,778	2,414	604
Union Village Academy	4	215	140	271.66	4,581	305	187	1,938	1,941	373

Statistics of Academies from the Regents' Report of 1859, *continued.*

NAMES.	No. of Teachers.	Whole No. of Students in attendance during the year.	The No. that pursued classical studies.	Amount appropriated from the Literature Fund.	Value of Lot and Buildings.	Value of Library.	Value of Apparatus.	Total Revenues.	Total Expenditures.	No of Volumes in Library.
Utica Academy............................	7	188	159	$308.52	$7,000	$313	$760	$3,947	$3,944	169
Utica Female Academy.................	11	179	69	133.89	23,000	189	257	3,861	3,728	127
Vernon Academy........................	5	162	96	186.28	4,000	464	583	891	890	530
Wallkill Academy........................	3	198	110	213.44	6,510	340	190	2,811	2,811	423
Walton Academy.........................	6	131	73	141.65	3,429	409	473	1,899	1,685	222
Walworth Academy......................	3	84	35	67.91	8,440	200	789	998	855	130
Warsaw Union School.................	3	150	137	265.83	4,800	279	461	1,396	1,396	231
Warwick Institute......................	3	112	62	91.20	5,300	150	150	1,382	1,320	104
Washington Academy..................	4	124	63	122.24	5,000	271	700	1,109	1,103	366
Washington Co. Seminary & C. I...	16	777	512	993.98	14,100	646	947	9,192	9,191	549
Waterloo Union School.................	9	608	27	52.39	6,500	435	475	3,090	3,372	789
Waverly Institute......................	5	176	43	83.44	7,354	165	178	1,391	1,580	166
Webster Academy.......................	3	92	47	91.20	4,300	166	168	743	738	112
Westfield Academy.....................	3	250	113	219.26	4,300	540	300	1,216	1,161	510
West Winfield Academy...............	9	357	165	293.50	10,000	778	925	3,142	3,142	600
Whitehall Academy.....................	3	187	77	149.31	3,560	260	503	1,058	1,040	220
Whitestown Seminary..................	9	400	286	554.95	12,500	1,305	1,236	3,635	3,612	1,193
Wilson Collegiate Institute...........	4	232	138	267.77	2,685	785	546	1,210	1,209	790
Windsor Academy.......................	2	59	36	69.85	3,780	488	190	506	578	589
Yates Academy..........................	2	157	43	83.44	2,750	480	519	795	840	332
Yates Polytechnic Institute..........	7	251	109	211.50	10,000	242	358	3,182	3,182	296
Total...............................	949	35,009	20,812	$39.911.66	$2,009 076	$111,438	$101,693	$595,125	$582,135	93,959

Academies incorporated since the organization of a State Government in 1777.

NAME.	Location.	Incorp. by Legislature.	Incorp. by Regents.	Remarks.
Academy of the Sacred Heart..	Rochester, Monroe co...............	April 11, 1849		
Academic Department of Union School.................................	Warsaw, Wyoming co..............	....	Jan. 11, 1855	
Adams Collegiate Institute......	Adams, Jefferson co...............	....	April 22, 1855	
Addison Academy..................	Addison, Steuben co...............	....	Feb. 8, 1849	Extinct.
Albany Academy....................	Albany, Albany co..................	....	Mar. 4, 1813	
Albany Female Academy..........	Albany, Albany co..................	Feb. 16, 1821	Jan. 29, 1828	
Albany Female Seminary........	Albany, Albany co..................	April 9, 1828	April 16, 1828	
Albany Pearl Street Academy.	Albany, Albany co..................	April 23, 1836	....	Extinct.
Albion Academy....................	Albion, Orleans co..................	May 1, 1837	Feb. 27, 1841	
Alexander Classical School......	Alexander, Genesee co............	May 6, 1834	Feb. 5, 1839	Extinct.
Alfred Academy....................	Alfred, Allegany co.................		Jan. 31, 1843	
Amenia Seminary..................	Amenia, Dutchess co..............	....	Mar. 29, 1836	Sold, fall of 1858.
Ames Academy......................	Ames, Montgomery co.............	April 22, 1837	Feb. 5, 1839	
Amsterdam Female Seminary..	Amsterdam, Montgomery co......	Mar. 29, 1839	Feb. 16, 1841	
Angelica Academy..................	Angelica, Allegany co..............	May 12, 1836		Not organized.
Antwerp Liberal Lit. Inst.......	Antwerp, Jefferson co.............	....	Feb. 1, 1856	
Argyle Academy....................	Argyle, Washington co............	....	May 4, 1841	
Astoria Institute..................	Astoria, Queens co.................	....	Feb. 13, 1844	Extinct.
Auburn Academy...................	Auburn, Cayuga co.................	....	Feb. 14, 1815	
Auburn Female Seminary*.	Auburn, Cayuga co.................	April 18, 1838	Feb. 11, 1840	
Augusta Academy..................	Augusta, Oneida co.................	....	Feb. 28, 1842	
Aurora Academy*..................	Aurora, Erie co......................	April 30, 1833	Jan. 29, 1839	
Avon Academy......................	Avon, Livingston co................	April 30, 1836	Feb. 27, 1841	Extinct.
Ball Seminary*.....................	Hoosick Falls, Rensselaer co.....	....	April 11, 1843	
Ballston Academy..................	Ballston, Saratoga co..............	....	Mar. 21, 1808	Extinct.
Batavia Female Academy........	Batavia, Genesee co................	Mar. 5, 1838	Feb. 5, 1839	Extinct.
Bedford Academy...................	Bedford, Westchester co..........	April 8, 1826		
Bernville Acad. & Fem. Sem...	Bern, Albany co.....................	Mar. 8, 1833	....	Extinct.
Bethany Academy..................	Bethany, Genesee co...............	Mar. 29, 1841	Feb. 28, 1842	
Binghamton Academy.............	Binghamton, Broome co...........	....	Aug. 23, 1842	
Blooming Grove Academy	Blooming Grove, Oneida co.......	....	April 1, 1811	
Bridgewater Academy............	Bridgewater, Oneida co...........	April 8, 1826	April 16, 1828	
Brockport Collegiate Institute.	Brockport, Monroe co..............	....	Feb. 15, 1842	
Brookfield Academy...............	Brookfield, Madison co............	....	April 17, 1847	
Brooklyn Coll. & Polytech. Ins.	Brooklyn, Kings co..................	....	April 7, 1854	
Brooklyn Coll. Inst. for Young Ladies.................................	Brooklyn, Kings co..................	April 23, 1829		
Brooklyn Female Academy.....	Brooklyn, Kings co..................	May 8, 1845	Jan. 14, 1847	Merged in Packer Inst.
Broome Academy...................	Union, Broome co...................	April 30, 1839		Not organized.
Brownville Female Seminary...	Brownville, Jefferson co...........	....	Jan. 10, 1850	Extinct.
Buffalo Female Academy........	Buffalo, Erie co......................	....	Oct. 14, 1851	
Buffalo Female Seminary.......	Buffalo, Erie co......................	April 23, 1831	....	Extinct.
Buffalo Literary & Sci. Acad*..	Buffalo, Erie co......................	April 17, 1827		Diss. by act Apr. 21, 1846.

a Jan. 29, 1852 and July 21, 1853. The Institution had become extinct under its first charter.
   b Incorp. as the "Aurora Manual Labor Seminary." Name changed April 16, 1838.

c Named from L. Chandler Ball, principal founder of the Institution.
   d Incorp. as the "Buffalo High School Association." Name changed.

Academies incorporated since 1777, continued.

NAME.	Location.	Incorp. by Legislature.	Incorp. by Regents.	Remarks.
Cambridge Washington Acad...	Cambridge, Washington co........	....	Mar. 30, 1815	
Canajoharie Academy............	Canajoharie, Montgomery co......	April 13, 1826	Feb. 26, 1828	
Canandaigua Academy...........	Canandaigua, Ontario co...........	....	Mar. 4, 1795	
Canton Academy...................	Canton, St. Lawrence co...........	April 24, 1837	Jan. 23, 1840	
Carlisle Seminary.................	Carlisle, Schoharie co.............	....	Oct. 20, 1853	
Cary Collegiate Seminary.......	Caryville, Genesee co.............	....	May 16, 1845	
Catskill Academy.................	Catskill, Greene co...............	....	Mar. 12, 1804	Extinct.
Catskill Female Seminary......	Catskill, Greene co...............	Mar. 24, 1820		Not organized.
Cayuga Academy..................	Aurora, Cayuga co................	....	Mar. 23, 1801	
Champlain Academy..............	Champlain, Clinton co............	....	Aug. 23, 1842	
Charlotteville Seminary........	Charlotteville, Schoharie co......	....	Jan. 15, 1857	
Chautauqua Coll. Inst...........	Stockton, Chautauqua co.........	....	July 9, 1857	Provisional charter.
Cherry Valley Academy.........	Cherry Valley, Otsego co.........	....	Feb. 8, 1796	
Chester Academy	Chester, Orange co..............	....	Feb. 27, 1844	
Cincinnatus Academy...........	Cincinnatus, Cortland co.........	....	April 21, 1857	
Clarence Academy	Clarence, Erie co................	....	Oct. 12, 1854	
Clarkson Academy...............	Clarkson, Monroe co.............	....	Mar. 17, 1835	
Claverack Academy.............	Claverack, Columbia co..........	April 25, 1831	Feb. 5, 1839	
Claverack Acad. & Hud. R. Ins.	Claverack, Columbia co..........	....	June 14, 1854	
Clermont Academy...............	Clermont, Columbia co...........	April 26, 1834	Feb. 26, 1839	Extinct.
Clinton Academy.................	East Hampton, Suffolk co.........	....	Nov. 17, 1787	
Clinton Grammar School........	Clinton, Oneida co...............	Mar. 28, 1817	Feb. 27, 1826	
Clinton Liberal Institute........	Clinton, Oneida co...............	April 29, 1834	Mar. 29, 1836	
Clinton Seminary................	Clinton, Oneida co...............	....	Feb. 15, 1842	Extinct.
Clover Street Seminary..........	Brighton, Monroe co.............	April 7, 1848	Feb. 23, 1849	
Collegiate Inst. City of N. Y...	New York City..................	July 10, 1851		Not organized.
Collinsville Institute............	West Turin, Lewis co............	May 2, 1837	....	Extinct.
Columbia Academy...............	Kinderhook, Columbia co.........	....	Mar. 13, 1797	Extinct.
Cooperstown Female Academy	Cooperstown, Otsego co..........	April 15, 1822		
Cooperstown Seminary and Female Coll. Institute...........	Cooperstown, Otsego co..........	....	June 14, 1854	Provisional charter.
Cortland Academy	Homer, Cortland co..............	....	Feb. 2, 1819	
Cortland Female Seminary......	Cortland, Cortland co...........	April 18, 1828	....	Extinct.
Cortlandville Academy..........	Cortlandville, Cortland co........	....	Jan. 31, 1843	
Coxsackie Academy.............	Coxsackie, Greene co............	May 5, 1837	Feb. 5, 1839	
Dansville Seminary..............	Dansville, Livingston co.........	....	Jan. 14, 1858	
De Lancey Institute.............	Hampton, Oneida co.............	....	April 13, 1842	Extinct.
Delaware Academy..............	Delhi, Delaware co..............	....	Feb. 2, 1820	
Delaware Literary Institute.....	Franklin, Delaware co...........	April 23, 1835	Jan. 29, 1839	
De Ruyter Institute.............	De Ruyter, Madison co...........	Mar. 30, 1836	Jan. 30, 1838	Extinct.
De Ruyter Institute	De Ruyter, Madison co...........	....	Dec. 3, 1847	
Dover Academy...................	Dover, Dutchess co..............	May 9, 1835		
Dundee Academy.................	Dundee, [Starkey] Yates co......	....	Mar. 22, 1855	
Dunkirk Academy...............	Dunkirk, Chautauqua co.........	May 1, 1837		
Dutchess County Academy......	Poughkeepsie, Dutchess co......	....	Feb. 1, 1792	
East Bloomfield Academy.......	East Bloomfield, Ontario co......	April 9, 1838	Jan. 23, 1840	
Eastern Coll. Inst. City of N.Y.	New York City..................	May 7, 1844	....	Extinct.
Ellington Academy..............	Ellington, Chautauqua co........	....	Feb. 11, 1853	
Elmira Academy.................	Elmira, Chemung co.............	....	Mar. 31, 1840	
Elmira Collegiate Seminary....	Elmira, Chemung co.............	....	Oct. 20, 1853	Provisional Charter.
Erasmus Hall....................	Flatbush, Kings co..............	....	Nov. 17, 1787	
Essex County Academy..........	Westport, Essex co..............	May 1, 1834	Mar. 6, 1838	
Fairfield Academy...............	Fairfield, Herkimer co...........	....	Mar. 15, 1803	
Falley Seminary[a]...............	Fulton, Oswego co..............	May 24, 1836	Feb. 5, 1839	
Farmer's Hall....................	Goshen, Orange co..............	....	Jan. 21, 1791	
Fayetteville Academy...........	Fayetteville, Onondaga co.......	May 4, 1837	Feb. 5, 1839	
Fayetteville Seminary...........	Fayetteville, Onondaga co.......	....	April 21, 1857	Provisional Charter.
Fem. Acad. of the Sacred Heart	New York City..................	July 9, 1851		
Fishkill Education Society......	Fishkill, Dutchess co...........	May 11, 1835		
Flushing Institute................	Flushing, Queens co.............	April 16, 1827		
Fonda Academy..................	Fonda, Montgomery co...........	May 13, 1845	Oct. 11, 1845	
Fort Covington Academy........	Fort Covington, Franklin co......	April 21, 1831		
Fort Plain Seminary and Female Collegiate Institute.....	Fort Plain, Montgomery co.......	....	Oct. 20, 1853	
Franklin Academy[b].............	Malone, Franklin co.............	....	April 28, 1831	
Franklin Academy...............	Prattsburgh, Steuben co..........	....	Feb. 23, 1824	
Fredonia Academy	Fredonia, Chautauqua co........	Nov. 25, 1824	Feb. 23, 1830	
Friendship Academy.............	Friendship, Allegany co..........	....	Feb. 8, 1849	
Gaines Academy	Gaines, Orleans co..............	April 14, 1827	Jan. 26, 1830	Extinct.
Galway Academy	Galway, Saratoga co.............	May 26, 1836	Jan. 29, 1839	Extinct.
Galway Academy...	Galway, Saratoga co.............	....	Oct. 11, 1845	
Genesee Conference Seminary...	Pike, Wyoming co...............	....	Feb. 1, 1856	
Genesee Manual Labor Sem[c]...	Bethany, Genesee co............	April 13, 1832		
Genesee Seminary...............	Batavia, Genesee co.............	May 11, 1835		
Genesee Valley Seminary.......		....	Jan. 8, 1857	Provisional Charter.
Genesee Wesleyan Seminary[d]..	Lima, Livingston co.............	April 30, 1833	Mar. 9, 1836	Merged in Genesee Coll.
Genesee & Wyoming Seminary	Alexander, Genesee co...........	....	Mar. 27, 1845	
Geneseo Academy[e].............	Geneseo, Livingston co..........	Mar. 10, 1827	Feb. 7, 1829	
Geneva Academy.................	Geneva, Ontario co..............	....	Mar. 29, 1813	Merged in Geneva Coll.
Geneva Union School............	Geneva, Ontario co..............	April 15, 1853		
Genoa Academy..................	Genoa, Cayuga co...............	....	Feb. 4, 1847	
Gilbertsville Acad. & Coll. Inst.	Gilbertsville, Otsego co..........	....	May 4, 1841	
Glens Falls Academy............	Glens Falls, Warren co...........	....	Jan. 12, 1842	
Gloversville Union Seminary...	Gloversville, Fulton co...........	....	Jan. 11, 1855	
Gouverneur Wesleyan Sem[f]...	Gouverneur, St. Lawrence co......	April 5, 1828	Feb. 19, 1829	

[a] Incorp. as "Fulton Female Seminary;" name changed to "Fulton Academy," April 11, 1842; to the "Falley Seminary of the Black River Conference," April 11, 1849; and to the name given above, March 5, 1857.
[b] Charter made perpetual June 23, 1851.

[c] See act of March 27, 1834.
[d] See act of March, 1836.
[e] Incorp. as the "Livingston County High School." Name changed May 13, 1846.
[f] Incorp. as the "Gouverneur High School." Name changed April 24, 1840.

Academies incorporated since 1777, continued.

NAME.	Location.	Incorp. by Legislature.	Incorp. by Regents.	Remarks.
Grammar School Colum. Coll.ᵃ	New York City		April 17, 1838	
Grammar School Madison Uni.	Hamilton, Madison co		June 17, 1853	
Grammar School University of City of New Yorkᵃ	New York City		April 17, 1838	
Gram. School of N. Y. Cen. Coll.	McGrawville, Cortland co.			
Granville Academy	Granville, Washington co	Mar. 31, 1828	April 16, 1830	
Greenbush & Schodack Acad.	East Greenbush, Rensselaer co	April 25, 1831	Feb. 27, 1841	Extinct.
Greenville Academy	Greenville, Greene co		Feb. 27, 1816	
Groton Academy	Groton, Tompkins co	May 6, 1837	Jan. 29, 1839	
Half Moon Academy	Half Moon, Saratoga co		Feb. 14, 1851	Sold in 1859.
Hamilton Academy	Hamilton, Madison co		Feb. 23, 1824	
Hamilton Female Seminary	Hamilton, Madison co		Jan. 17, 1856	
Hamilton Oneida Academy	Kirkland, Oneida co		Jan. 29, 1793	Merg. in Ham. Coll., 1812.
Harlem Lit. & Sci. Academy	Harlem, New York City	Jan. 24, 1829		Extinct.
Hartwick Seminary	Hartwick, Otsego co		Aug. 13, 1816	
Hedding Literary Institute	Ashland, Greene co		Oct. 12, 1854	Now a private institution.
Hempstead Institute	Hempstead, Queens co		Jan. 14, 1858	Provisional charter.
Hempstead Seminary	Hempstead, Queens co	May 2, 1836	Jan. 29, 1839	Extinct.
Herkimer County Academy	Herkimer, Herkimer co		Feb. 11, 1840	Extinct.
Highland Grove Gymnasium	Fishkill, Dutchess co	April 11, 1831		
Hobart Hall Institute	Holland Patent, Oneida co	Mar. 16, 1839	Jan, 23, 1840	
Holland Patent Academy	Trenton, Oneida co	April 24, 1834		
Holley Academy	Holley, Orleans co		Mar. 28, 1850	
Hubbardsville Academy	Hubbards Corners, Madison co		Feb. 14, 1850	Extinct.
Hudson Academy	Hudson, Columbia co		Mar. 3, 1807	
Hudson River Agricult. Sem.	Stockport, Columbia co	May 6, 1837		Extinct.
Ingham Collegiate Instituteᵇ	Le Roy, Genesee co	April 6, 1852	Jan. 28, 1853	Merged in Ingham Univ.
Ithaca Academyᶜ	Ithaca, Tompkins co	Mar. 24, 1823		
Jamestown Academy	Jamestown, Chautauqua co	April 16, 1836	Feb. 5, 1839	
Jefferson Academy	Jefferson, Schoharie co	Nov. 27, 1824	Jan. 22, 1833	Extinct.
Jefferson County Instituteᵈ	Watertown, Jefferson co	May 25, 1836	Jan. 30, 1838	
Johnstown Academy	Johnstown, Montgomery co		Jan. 27, 1794	
Jonesville Academy	Clifton Park, Saratoga co	April 1, 1850	Oct. 26, 1850	
Jordan Academy	Jordan, Onondaga co		Jan. 12, 1842	
Keeseville Academy	Keeseville, Clinton co	May 4, 1835	Feb. 5, 1839	
Kinderhook Academy	Kinderhook, Columbia co	April 3, 1824	Feb. 19, 1828	
Kingsborough Academy	Kingsborough, Fulton co		Feb. 5, 1839	
Kingston Academy	Kingston, Ulster co		Feb. 3, 1795	
Knoxville Academy	Knox, Albany co	May 9, 1837	Feb. 15, 1842	
La Fayette High School	La Fayette, Onondaga co	April 23, 1836		
Lancaster Academy	Lancaster, Erie co		Jan. 22, 1846	Extinct.
Lansingburgh Academy	Lansingburgh, Rensselaer co		Feb. 8, 1796	Merged in Public Schools.
Laurel Bank Seminary	Deposit, Delaware co		Mar. 17, 1854	Now a private institution.
Le Roy Female Seminary	Le Roy, Genesee co		Feb. 16, 1841	Merged in Ing. Coll. Inst.
Lewiston High School Acad.	Lewiston, Niagara co		April 16, 1828	Extinct.
Liberty Normal Institute	Liberty, Sullivan co	April 10, 1849	Sept. 20, 1849	
Literary & Sci. Inst. of York	York, Livingston co	Mar. 27, 1839		Extinct.
Little Falls, The Academy at	Little Falls, Herkimer co		Oct. 17, 1844	
Lockport Academy	Lockport, Niagara co	May 26, 1841		Extinct.
Lockport Union School	Lockport, Niagara co	Mar. 18, 1850	Oct. 26, 1850	
Lowville Academy	Lowville, Lewis co		Mar. 21, 1808	
Lyons Academyᶜ	Lyons, Wayne co	Mar. 29, 1837		Extinct.
Lyons Union School	Lyons, Wayne co			
Macedon Academy	Macedon, Wayne co	April 11, 1842	Jan. 30, 1845	
Manlius Academy	Manlius, Onondaga co	April 13, 1835	Jan. 29, 1839	
Mansion Square Female Sem.	Poughkeepsie, Dutchess co	Mar. 15, 1849		Private School.
Marion Academy	Marion, Wayne co	Mar. 27, 1839		Extinct.
Marion Collegiate Institute	Marion. Wayne co.			
Mayville Academy	Mayville, Chautauqua co	April 24, 1834	Feb. 5, 1839	
Medina Academy	Medina, Orleans co	April 10, 1850	April 25, 1851	
Mendon Academy	Mendon, Monroe co	April 20, 1836	Feb. 5, 1839	
Mexico Academyᶠ	Mexico, Oswego co	April 13, 1826	Feb. 26, 1828	
Middlebury Academy	Middlebury, Wyoming co		Jan. 26, 1819	
Millville Academy	Millville, Orleans co	April 25, 1840	Feb. 16, 1841	Extinct.
Montgomery Academy	Montgomery, Orange co		Jan. 21, 1791	
Monticello Academy	Monticello, Sullivan co		April 1, 1852	Provisional charter.
Moravia Institute	Moravia, Cayuga co		Jan. 23, 1840	
Moriah Academy	Moriah, Essex co		Feb. 16, 1841	Extinct.
Mount Pleasant Academy	Mount Pleasant, Westchester co.	Mar. 24, 1820		Extinct.
Mount Pleasant Academy	Mount Pleasant, Westchester co.		April 3, 1827	
Mount Pleasant Female Sem.	Sing Sing, Westchester		May 10, 1836	Extinct.
Monroe Academy	Henrietta, Monroe co		July 2, 1827	Extinct.
Monroe Academy	Henrietta, Monroe co		Feb. 7, 1843	
Munro Academy	Elbridge, Onondaga co		April 23, 1839	Changed to Munro Coll. Inst.
Nassau Academy	Nassau, Rensselaer co	May 11, 1835		
New Berlin Academy	New Berlin, Chenango co		Feb. 13, 1844	
Newburgh Academy	Newburgh, Orange co		Mar. 3, 1806	Extinct.
New Paltz Academy	New Paltz, Ulster co	April 12, 1833.	April 29, 1836.	Extinct.
New Paltz Academy	New Paltz, Ulster co		Oct. 11, 1845.	
New Rochelle Academy	New Rochelle, Westchester	April 13, 1826		Extinct.
Newtown Female Academy	Newtown, Queens co	Mar. 15, 1822		Extinct.
New Woodstock Academy	Cazenovia, Madison co	May 2, 1834		Extinct.
New York Conference Sem.	Charlotteville, Schoharie co		Oct. 26, 1850	Extinct.
New York Free Academy	New York City	May 7, 1847	Oct. 31, 1849	

ᵃ See act of above date.

ᵇ Changed to the Ingham University, April 3, 1857.

ᶜ Entitled to share in Literature Fund, by act of April 17, 1826.

ᵈ Incorporated as the "Black River Literary and Theological Institute." Name changed May 12, 1846.

ᵉ Again incorp. by statute May 7, 1840.

ᶠ Incorp. as the "Rensselaer Oswego Academy." Name changed May 14, 1845.

Academies incorporated since 1777, continued.

NAME.	Location.	Incorp. by Legislature.	Incorp. by Regents.	Remarks.
New York Inst. Deaf & Dumb⁂	New York City....................	April 15, 1817	....	
North Granville Female Sem...	Granville, Washington co..........	....	Feb. 10, 1854	
North Hebron Institute	Hebron, Washington co...........	....	Mar. 17, 1854	
North Salem Academy...........	North Salem, Westchester co......	....	Feb. 19, 1790	
Norwich Academy................	Norwich, Chenango co,...........	....	Feb. 14, 1843	
Norwich Union Seminary........	Norwich, Chenango co...........	Mar. 16, 1837	....	Extinct.
Nunda Literary Institute.......	Nunda, Livingston co.............	....	Jan. 30, 1845	
Ogdensburgh Academy⁶........	Ogdensburg, St. Lawrence co......	April 20, 1835	Feb. 5, 1839	Merged in Public Schools.
Olean Academy...................	Olean, Cattaraugus co...........	....	April 11, 1853	
Oneida Conference Seminaryᶜ..	Cazenovia, Madison co............	April 6, 1825	Jan. 29, 1828	
Oneida Inst. of Sci. & Industry	Whitesboro', Oneida co...........	....	Mar. 24, 1829	Extinct.
Oneida Seminary.................	Oneida, Madison co..............	....	July 9, 1857	Provisional Charter.
Onondaga Academy..............	Onondaga, Onondaga co..........	....	April 10, 1813	
Ontario Female Seminary.......	Canandaigua, Ontario co.........	April 14, 1825	Jan. 29, 1828	
Ontario High School............	Victor, Ontario co...............	April 6, 1830	....	
Orleans Academy	Orleans, Jefferson co............	....	Feb. 5, 1851	Extinct.
Oswegatchie Academy...........	Ogdensburgh, St. Lawrence co...	April 26, 1833	....	Extinct.
Oswego Academy	West Oswego, Oswego co........	April 25, 1833	....	
Otsego Academy..................	Cherry Valley, Otsego co........	....	Feb. 8, 1796	
Ovid Academy....................	Ovid, Seneca co.................	April 13, 1826	Jan. 26, 1830	
Owego Academy	Owego, Tioga co.................	....	April 16, 1828	
Oxford Academy.................	Oxford, Chenango co............	....	Jan. 27, 1794	
Oyster Bay Academy............	Oyster Bay, Queens co..........	....	Mar. 15, 1803	Extinct.
Packer Collegiate Institute.....	Brooklyn, Kings co..............	Mar. 19, 1853	Jan. 11, 1855	
Palmyra Academy	Palmyra, Wayne co..............	April 11, 1842	....	
Palmyra High School............	Palmyra, Wayne co..............	Mar. 28, 1829	July 2, 1833	Extinct.
Palmyra Classical Union School	Palmyra, Wayne co..............	April 7, 1857	....	
Peekskill Academy	Peekskill, Westchester co........	April 16, 1838	Feb. 5, 1839	
Pembroke & Darien Class. Sch.	Pembroke, Darien, Genesee co.....	April 6, 1838	....	
Penfield Seminary................	Penfield, Monroe co.............	....	Oct. 8, 1857	Provisional Charter.
Perry Academy	Perry, Wyoming co..............	....	April 7, 1854	
Perry Center Institute...........	Perry Center, Wyoming co.......	....	Jan. 31, 1843	Extinct.
Peterboro Academy..............	Peterboro, Madison co...........	....	Jan. 23, 1853	
Phipps Union Seminary	Albion, Orleans co..............	....	Feb. 11, 1840	
Piermont Academy...............	Piermont, Rockland co...........	....	Mar. 15, 1842	Extinct.
Plattsburgh Academy...........	Plattsburgh, Clinton co..........	April 21, 1828	Mar. 4, 1829	
Pompey Academy.................	Pompey, Onondaga co...........	....	Mar. 11, 1811	
Poughkeepsie Collegiate School	Poughkeepsie, Dutchess co.......	May 26, 1836	Feb. 9, 1839	
Poughkeepsie Female Academy	Poughkeepsie, Dutchess co.......	May 10, 1836	Feb. 28, 1837	
Poughkeepsie Female Seminary	Poughkeepsie, Dutchess co.......	Mar. 19, 1834	....	
Prattsville Academy..............	Prattsville, Greene co............	....	Jan. 31, 1850	Extinct.
Preble High School..............	Preble, Cortland co..............	April 24, 1834	....	Not organized.
Princetown Academy	Princetown, Schenectady co......	....	Oct. 20, 1853	Extinct.
Prospect Academy................	Prospect, Oneida co.............	....	Jan. 24, 1851	
Pulaski Academy.................	Pulaski, Oswego co.............	June 4, 1853	....	
Randolph Acad. Association.....	Randolph, Cattaraugus co........	....	Jan. 24, 1851	
Red Creek Academy.............	Red Creek, Wayne co...........	Mar. 27, 1839	Feb. 5, 1846	
Redhook Academy...............	Redhook, Dutchess co...........	April 23, 1823	Feb. 23, 1829	Extinct.
Rensselaer Polytechnic Inst....	Troy, Rensselaer co.............	May 8, 1837	Feb. 5, 1846	
Rensselaerville Academy........	Rensselaerville. Albany co.......	....	Jan. 30, 1845	
Rhinebeck Academy.............	Rhinebeck, Dutchess co.........	....	Feb. 23, 1841	Became private inst. 1855.
Richburgh Academy.............	Richburgh, Allegany co..........	....	April 12, 1850	
Richmondville Union Seminary & Female Collegiate Inst....	Richmondville, Schoharie co......	....	Feb. 10, 1854	Extinct.
Ridgebury Academy.............	Minisink, Orange co.............	April 30, 1839	Feb. 11, 1840	
Riga Academy...................	Riga, Monroe co................	....	May 11, 1846	
Rochester Collegiate Institute..	Rochester, Monroe co...........	....	Feb. 26, 1839	Extinct.
Rochester Female Academy.....	Rochester, Monroe co...........	April 21, 1837	Feb. 5, 1839	
Rochester High School..........	Rochester, Monroe co...........	Mar. 15, 1827	April 19, 1831	Merged in Rochester Collegiate Institute.
Rochester Inst. General Educ..	Rochester, Monroe co...........	April 19, 1828	....	Extinct.
Rochester Inst. Practical Educ.	Rochester, Monroe co...........	April 14, 1832	....	Extinct.
Rockland County Female Inst.	Orangetown, Rockland co.........	....	Oct. 12, 1855	Provisional charter.
Rogersville Union Seminary....	Rogersville, Steuben co..........	....	Jan. 28, 1853	
Rome Academy..................	Rome, Oneida co................	April 28, 1835	....	
Rome Academy..................	Rome, Oneida co................	Jan. 28, 1848	Mar. 15, 1849	Extinct.
Royalton Center Academy......	Royalton, Niagara co............	April 9, 1839	....	
Rural Academy..................	Montgomery, Orange co	....	April 1, 1852	Not organized.
Rushford Academy.	Rushford, Allegany co...........	....	Mar. 4, 1852	
Rutger's Female Instituteᵈ.....	New York City	April 10, 1838	Jan. 23, 1840	
Rye Academy....................	Rye, Westchester co.............	April 13, 1826	....	
Sag Harbor Institute............	Sag Harbor, Suffolk co..........	....	Jan. 20, 1848	
St. Lawrence Academy..........	Potsdam, St. Lawrence co........	....	Mar. 25, 1816	
St. Paul's College, The Proprietors of...	Flushing, Queens co.............	May 9, 1840	....	Extinct.
Sand Lake Academy.............	Sand Lake, Rensselaer co........	....	Feb. 19, 1846	Extinct.
Saratoga Acad. & Sci. Inst......	Saratoga Springs...............	April 28, 1835	....	
Saugerties Academy.............	Saugerties, Ulster co............	....	April 7, 1854	
Sauquoit Academy...............	Sauquoit, Oneida co.............	....	April 6, 1849	
Schaghticoke Seminary..........	Schaghticoke, Rensselaer co......	May 4, 1836	....	Extinct.
Schenectady Academyᶜ.........	Schenectady, Schenectady co.....	....	Jan. 29, 1793	Merged in Union Coll. 1795
Schenectady Lyceum & Acadᶠ..	Schenectady, Schenectady co.....	Mar. 21, 1837	Feb. 5, 1839	Extinct.
Schenectady Young Ladies' Sem	Schenectady, Schenectady co.....	Mar. 22, 1837	Feb. 5, 1839	
Schoharie Academy..............	Schoharie, Schoharie co.........	April 28, 1837	Feb. 5, 1839	

ᵃ Entitled to a share of the Literature Fund by act of April 15, 1830.
ᵇ Merged in the Public School System of Ogdensburgh by act of April 13, 1857.
ᶜ Incorp. as the "Seminary of the Genesee Conference;" name changed to "Seminary of Genesee and Oneida Conference" March 24, 1829, and to the present name May 8, 1835.
ᵈ Charter amended March 16, 1858.
ᵉ Revived by act of April 17, 1818. See also act of April 25, 1831.
ᶠ Allowed to educate females by act of March 28, 1839.

Academies incorporated since 1777, continued.

NAME.	Location.	Incorp. by Legislature.	Incorp. by Regents.	Remarks.
Schuylerville Academy	Schuylerville, Saratoga co.........	....	Jan. 23, 1840	
Scientific & Military Academy of Western District............	Whitesboro', Oneida co..............	April 17, 1826	Jan. 9, 1829	Extinct.
Seneca Falls Academy............	Seneca Falls, Seneca co.	April 27, 1837	Feb. 5, 1839	
Seward Female Seminary of Rochester	Rochester, Monroe co................	April 5, 1839	Feb. 11, 1840	Extinct.
Sherburne Academy................	Sherburne, Chenango co...........	....	Jan. 23, 1840	Merged in Public Schools.
Skaneateles Academy.............	Skaneateles, Onondaga co..........	April 14, 1829		
Sodus Academy.....................	Sodus, Wayne co....................	....	Jan. 11, 1855	
Southold Academy.................	Southold, Suffolk co.................	April 21, 1837		
Spencertown Academy...........	Spencertown, Columbia co.........	May 13, 1845	Dec. 3, 1847	
Springville Academy.............	Springville, Erie co.................	Mar. 19, 1827	Jan. 26, 1830	
S. S. Seward Institute...........	Florida, Orange co..................	May 7, 1847	Feb. 4, 1848	
Starkey Seminary.................	Starkey, Yates co...................	....	Feb. 25, 1848	
Steuben Academy.................	Steuben, Oneida co.................	April 17, 1826	Jan. 29, 1828	Extinct.
Stillwater Academy...............	Stillwater, Saratoga co.............	....	Jan. 29, 1839	Extinct.
Stillwater Seminary..............	Stillwater, Saratoga co.............	....	Feb. 25, 1848	Extinct.
Sullivan County Academy.....	Bloomingburgh, Sullivan co.......	April 5, 1828	Mar. 31, 1831	Extinct.
Susquehanna Seminary..........	Binghamton, Broome co............	....	April 7, 1854	
Syracuse Academy.................	Syracuse, Onondaga co............	April 28, 1835	Feb. 5, 1858	Extinct.
Ticonderoga Academy............	Ticonderoga, Essex co..............	....	April 8, 1858	
Troy Academy......................	Troy, Rensselaer co.................	May 5, 1834	Feb. 5, 1839	
Troy Episcopal Institute.........	Troy, Rensselaer co.................	April 13, 1839		
Troy Female Seminary..........	Troy, Rensselaer co.................	May 6, 1837	Jan. 30, 1838	
Trumansburgh Academy........	Ulysses, Tompkins co...............	....	July 6, 1854	
Turin Academy....................	Turin, Lewis co.....................	April 30, 1839	....	Extinct.
Unadilla Academy.................	Unadilla, Otsego co.................	....	April 1, 1852	
Union Academy....................	Stone Arabia, Montgomery co.....	....	Mar. 31, 1795	Extinct.
Union Academy....................	Granger, Allegany co...............	....	Jan. 11, 1855	Provisional charter.
Union Hall	Jamaica, Queens co.................	....	Feb. 29, 1792	
Union Literary Society..........	Belleville, Jefferson co.............	April 13, 1826	Jan. 5, 1830	
Union Village Academy.........	Union Village, Washington co.....	....	Jan. 23, 1840	
Utica Academy....................	Utica, Oneida co....................	....	Mar. 14, 1814	Merged in Public Schools.
Utica Academy....................	Utica, Oneida co....................	May 26, 1853		
Utica Female Academy..........	Utica, Oneida co....................	April 28, 1837	Feb. 5, 1839	
Vernon Academy.................	Vernon, Oneida co..................	April 18, 1838	Feb. 5, 1839	
Victory Academy.................	Victory, Cayuga co.................	May 21, 1836		
Wallabout Select Gram. School of the 7th Ward in the City of Brooklyn......................	Brooklyn, Kings co..................	May 4, 1839	....	Extinct.
Wallkill Academy.................	Wallkill, Ulster co.................	May 26, 1841	Feb. 13, 1842	
Walton Academy..................	Walton, Delaware co................	....	Feb. 10, 1854	
Walworth Academy..............	Walworth, Wayne co................	May 12, 1841	April 19, 1843	
Warnerville Union Seminary & Female Institute............	Warnerville, Schoharie co.	....	Jan. 27, 1854	Not organized.
Warsaw Union School...........	Warsaw, Wyoming co...............	....	Jan. 11, 1855	
Warwick Institute................	Warwick, Orange co................	....	Mar. 17, 1854	
Washington Academy...........	Salem, Washington co..............	....	Feb. 15, 1791	
Washington Academy...........	Warwick, Orange co................	....	Mar. 25, 1811	Extinct.
Washington County Seminary & Collegiate Institute	Fort Edward, Washington co......	....	July 6, 1854	
Waterford Academy..............	Waterford, Saratoga co.............	April 28, 1834	Feb. 5, 1839	Extinct.
Waterford Female Academy....	Waterford, Saratoga co.............	....	Mar. 19, 1819	Extinct.
Waterloo Academy	Waterloo, Seneca co................	April 11, 1842	Aug. 23, 1842	Merged in Union School.
Waterloo Union School.........	Waterloo, Seneca co................	....	Oct. 11, 1855	
Watertown Academy[a]...........	Watertown, Jefferson co...........	May 2, 1835		
Waverly Institute.................	Waverly, Tioga co..................	....	Jan. 21, 1858	
Weedsport Academy..............	Weedsport, Cayuga co..............	April 18, 1838		
Westfield Academy...............	Westfield, Chautauqua co.........	May 5, 1837	Feb. 5, 1839	
West Hebron Classical School.	Hebron, Washington co............	....	Mar. 22, 1855	
Westtown Academy...............	Westtown, Orange co...............	April 18, 1839	Jan. 30, 1840	Extinct.
West Winfield Academy........	West Winfield, Herkimer co.......	....	Feb. 14, 1851	
Whitehall Academy..............	Whitehall, Washington co..........	April 20, 1839		Extinct.
Whitehall Academy..............	Whitehall, Washington co..........	....	Oct. 27, 1848	
White Plains Academy..........	White Plains, Westchester co......	April 19, 1828	Jan. 26, 1830	Extinct.
Whitesboro' Academy............	Whitesboro', Oneida co.............	....	Mar. 13, 1813	Extinct.
Whitestown Seminary...........	Whitesboro', Oneida co.............	....	Mar. 27, 1845	
Wilson Collegiate Institute.....	Wilson, Niagara co.................	....	Feb. 19, 1846	
Windsor Academy.................	Windsor, Broome co................	May 16, 1837	....	Extinct.
Windsor Academy.................	Windsor, Broome co................	....	Mar. 15, 1849	
Yates Academy....................	Yates Center, Orleans co...........	....	Aug. 23, 1842	
Yates County Academy & Female Seminary	Penn Yan, Yates co.................	April 17, 1828	Jan. 25, 1830	Extinct.
Yates Polytechnic Institute.....	Chittenango, Madison co...........	....	April 11, 1853	

[a] Charter repealed Feb. 19, 1841. Merged in Black River Literary and Religious Institute.

PUBLIC SCHOOLS.

AMPLE provisions have been made by the State for the establishment and support of public schools throughout its borders. To this end the whole inhabited portions of the State have been divided into convenient districts, in each of which a school is taught some portion of the year and is open to all and within the reach of all. These schools are supported in part by money derived from the State, in part by a rate bill collected from parents of children attending school, and in part by a tax upon the property of the district.[1]

School Districts are formed and altered by school commissioners. These districts are so formed as to best accommodate all the inhabitants of the various localities and at the same time secure efficiency in school organizations. Each district has a schoolhouse and a library. Its monetary affairs are arranged, and its officers elected, at annual meetings of all the taxable inhabitants. Its officers are trustees, a clerk, a collector, and a librarian.[2]

School Commissioners are elected in each of the Assembly districts of the State outside of the cities, and have the general supervision of schools. They examine and license teachers, visit the schools, and in every possible way endeavor to advance the general interests of education. They report annually to the State department of education.

The State Superintendent of Public Instruction is the administrative officer of the school department. He has an office in the State Hall at Albany, and has a deputy and the necessary number of clerks. He hears and decides appeals from the school officers and Commissioners, and has the general supervision of the common schools, Indian schools, the Institution for the Deaf and Dumb, and all similar institutions in the State. He is *ex officio* a member of the Board of Regents of the University, is chairman of the Executive Committee of the Normal School, and a trustee of the State Asylum for Idiots. He also apportions the school fund among the several counties and districts as the law directs.

The school fund of the State, derived from a variety of sources, in 1859 yielded a revenue of $264,500.[3] This sum, and the amount derived from the ¾ mill tax, is divided among the schools as follows:—One-third is divided among the districts in proportion to the number of teachers employed, and the remaining two-thirds are distributed to the several counties in proportion to their population, and thence distributed to the districts in proportion to the number of children between the ages of 4 and 21.

District Libraries were established in 1838; and from that period to 1851, with few intermissions, the sum of $55,000 was annually appropriated for the purchase of books.[4] These

---

[1] In 1859 the amount divided by the State among the several districts was $1,316,607.18. Of this sum $1,052,107.18 was derived from the ¾ mill State tax, and $264,500 from the interest of the common school fund.

A record is kept of the attendance of each pupil, and the amount due for teachers' wages above that received from the State is assessed in proportion to this attendance. Cost of fuel, repairs, and the amount of rate bills abated to indigent parents are met by a tax upon the property of the district.

[2] *District Meetings* decide upon questions of building and repairing schoolhouses, furnishing them, providing fuel and facilities for teaching, within the limits of the law. The annual meetings for the election of officers are held on the second Tuesday of Oct. throughout the State. *The Board of Trustees*, consisting of 1 or 3 at the option of the district, constitute the executive officers of the district. *The Trustees* engage teachers, properly furnish the schoolhouse, provide fuel, and execute the wishes of the district as expressed in the district meetings. They have also the care of the district library. *The Clerk* preserves the records of the district and calls district meetings.

[3] The school fund was chiefly derived from the following sources:—

1799, Seven-eighths of four lotteries of $100,000, aggregate .... $ 87,500
1801, One-half of lotteries of $100,000, aggregate 50,000
1805, Proceeds of 500,000 acres of land sold.
" Stock subscribed in Merchants' Bank, and increased in 1807 and '08.
1816, One-half of the proceeds of the Crumhorn Mountain Tract of 6,944¼ acres, amounting to 5,208

1819, One-half of the arrears of quitrents...................... $26,690
" An exchange of securities between general and common school fund, by which the school fund gained.. 161,641
" Proceeds of escheated lands in Military Tract given.
1822, By the Constitution, all public lands, amounting to 991,659 acres, were given to the school fund.
1827, Balance of loan of 1786, amounting to................ 33,616
" Bank stock owned by the State........................ 100,000
" Canal "   "   "   " 150,000
1838, From the revenue of the United States deposit fund, annually... 110,000
An additional sum from the same fund for libraries 55,000

The sum of $25,000 from the revenue of the United States deposit fund is annually added to the capital of the common school fund; and the capital of this fund is declared by the Constitution to be inviolate.

In directing the sale of the public lands, the State reserved certain lots in the 10 Towns of St. Lawrence co. and in the Chenango 20 Townships, for gospel and school purposes. The proceeds from the sales of these lands have formed a local fund for the benefit of the towns in which they lie. Many other towns have small funds, derived from fines and penalties, applicable to schools. See p. 47.

[4] The following directions are given in the selection of books:—
"1. No works written professedly to uphold or attack any sect or creed in our country claiming to be a religious one shall be tolerated in the school libraries.
"2. Standard works on other topics shall not be excluded

135

libraries, free to every person in the district, generally comprise books on scientific and literary subjects and affording means of information which would otherwise be unattainable.

The State Normal School was established in 1844, for the instruction and practice of teachers of common schools in the science of education and the art of teaching. It is supported by an annual appropriation from the literature fund, and is under the immediate charge of an executive committee appointed by the Regents of the University. Each county in the State is entitled to send twice as many pupils to the school as it sends members to the Assembly. The pupils receive tuition and the use of textbooks free, and also receive a small amount of mileage. The school is located at the corner of Howard and Lodge Streets, Albany.[1]

The law makes provision for the establishment of **Union Free Schools** wherever the inhabitants may desire it, and for the formation of **Colored Schools** in districts where the presence of colored children is offensive to a majority of the people of the district.[2]

Previous to the Revolution no general system of education was established. All the schools that had been founded were of a private character or the result of special legislation. The necessity and importance of common schools had not been recognized, and education was principally confined to the wealthier classes. At the first meeting of the State Legislature, in 1787, Gov. Clinton called the attention of that body to the subject of education, and a law was passed providing for the appointment of the Regents of the University. In 1789 an act was passed appropriating certain portions of the public lands for gospel and school purposes. In 1793 the Regents in their report recommended the establishment of a general system of common schools; and in 1795 Gov. Clinton in his message to the Legislature strongly urged the same.[3] On the 9th of April of that year a law was passed "for the purpose of encouraging and maintaining schools in the several cities and towns in this State, in which the children of the inhabitants of the State shall be instructed in the English language, or be taught English grammar, arithmetic, mathematics, and such other branches of knowledge as are most useful and necessary to complete a good English education." By this act the sum of £20,000, or $50,000, was annually appropriated for 5 years for the support of these schools.[4]

The beneficial result of this system, imperfect as it was, became at once apparent; and from time to time measures were taken to increase the funds and to improve the system.[5] The successive Governors nearly all strongly recommended the passage of new laws for the encouragement and support of schools;[6] but nothing definite was accomplished until 1811, when 5 commissioners were

because they incidentally and indirectly betray the religious opinions of their authors.

"3. Works, avowedly on other topics, which abound in direct and unreserved attacks on, or defense of, the character of any religious sect, or those which hold up any religious body to contempt or execration by singling out or bringing together only the darker parts of its history or character, shall be excluded from the school libraries. In the selection of books for a district library, information, and not mere amusement, is to be regarded as the primary object. Suitable provision should, however, be made for the intellectual wants of the young, by furnishing them with books which, without being merely juvenile in their character, may be level to their comprehension and sufficiently entertaining to excite and gratify a taste for reading. It is useless to buy books which are not read."—*Code of Public Inst.*, 1856, p. 326.

[1] Males are admitted at 18 and females at 16 years of age; and upon entering each one is required to sign a pledge that he intends to become a teacher. The number of graduates up to the close of the thirteenth year, 1856-57, was 999, and the number of pupils at that time was 223. The school for several years occupied the building near the head of State Street, now known as "Van Vechten Hall." In 1848 the present building was erected, at a cost of $25,000. The experimental school taught by the graduating class numbers somewhat over 100 pupils. These pay tuition, and are elected or appointed by the Executive Committee.

[2] Under the Union Free School law a large number of schools have been established in different parts of the State. These schools are supported by a direct tax upon the property of the district, and the rate bill system is discarded. Free schools are established in all the cities and in most of the larger villages in the State by special laws. In most cases the free schools are graded, and comprise 3 or 4 distinct departments, furnishing instruction from the primary to a full academic course. Being entirely free and within the reach of all, they afford to every child, regardless of his position in life, an opportunity to secure a thorough English education. These free schools rank among the best public schools in the country; and they have thus far proved superior to those in which the rate bill system is retained.

[3] Governor Clinton uses the following language.—"While it is evident that the general establishment and liberal endowment of academies are highly to be commended and are attended with the most beneficial consequences,

yet it cannot be denied that they are principally confined to the children of the opulent, and that a great portion of the community is excluded from their immediate advantages. The establishment of common schools throughout the State is happily calculated to remedy this inconvenience, and will therefore engage your early and decided consideration."

[4] The principal features of the system inaugurated by this act were as follows:—

1. The public money was to be appropriated to the several counties in the proportion of their representation in the Legislature, and to the towns in proportion to the number of taxable inhabitants in each.

2. The Boards of Supervisors were required to raise by tax one-half as much as they received from the State.

3. Each town was to elect not less than 3 nor more than 7 commissioners, to take general charge of the schools, to examine teachers, and to apportion the public moneys in the several districts.

4. The people in each district were authorized to elect 2 or more trustees, to employ teachers, and to attend to the special interests of the school.

5. The public money was to be divided among the various districts in proportion to the number of days' instruction given in each.

6. Annual reports were to be made from the districts, towns, and counties.

The returns of 1798 show a total of 1,352 schools organized and 59,660 children taught.

[5] An act was passed in 1799 authorizing the raising of $100,000 by 4 lotteries, $87,500 of which was appropriated for the support of common schools. In 1801 $100,000 more was raised by lottery for school purposes, of which sum $50,000 was devoted to common schools. In 1800 a bill appropriating $50,000 to the support of common schools passed the Assembly, but was defeated in the Senate.

[6] Gov. Jay, in 1800, Gov. Geo. Clinton, in 1802, Gov. Lewis, in 1804 and '05, and Gov. Tompkins, in several successive years, urged upon the Legislature the necessity of revising the school laws and of making more liberal appropriations for the support of schools. Several bills were introduced into the Legislature; but they were all defeated in either the Senate or Assembly. In the mean time the school moneys gradually increased, and were funded by the Comptroller, laying the foundation of the present large school fund.

appointed to report a complete system for the organization and establishment of common schools. The commissioners made a report, accompanied by a draft of a bill, Feb. 14, 1812. The report was accepted by the Legislature, and the bill became a law.[1] Under this act, Gideon Hawley was appointed Superintendent, and continued in office from 1813 to 1821. The great success which this system met with, and the firm hold which it speedily attained, is mainly due to the administrative abilities and indefatigable exertions of Mr. Hawley. Several important changes were made in the law during his administration, all of which tended greatly to improve the schools. In 1821 the office of State Superintendent was abolished, and the superintendence of schools was made an appendage to the department of Secretary of State. Every successive year the Governor and Secretary of State urged upon the Legislature the necessity of systematizing the schools and of correcting obvious defects in the existing laws.[2] In 1835 a law was passed providing for the establishment of teachers' departments in 8 academies, 1 in each of the Senatorial Districts of the State.[3] In 1838 the District Library system was established by law;[4] and in 1841 the office of Deputy Superintendent was created.[5] In 1843 the Board of Town Inspectors and School Commissioners was abolished and the office of Town Superintendent was substituted. May 7, 1844, an act was passed for the establishment of a State Normal School; and the school was opened at Albany on the 18th of Dec. following.[6]

On the 13th of Nov. 1847, the Legislature abolished the office of County Superintendent,—although the act was strongly resisted by many of the best friends of education in the State.[7] During the same session Teachers' Institutes, which had existed for several years as voluntary associations, were legally established.[8]

On the 26th of March, 1849, an act was passed establishing free schools throughout the State. By the conditions of this act the rate bill system was abolished, and the whole expense of the schools beyond the State appropriation was made a tax upon the property of the district. This act was submitted to a vote of the people and was sustained by a majority of 3 to 1. In consequence of the inequality of the laws in regard to taxes, it was found that the Free School system did not work well in practice. Remonstrances poured in upon the next Legislature from all parts of the

---

[1] These commissioners, appointed by Gov. Tompkins, were Jedediah Peck, John Murray, jr., Samuel Russel, Roger Skinner, and Samuel Macomb. The principal features of this bill were,—

1. $50,000 was annually to be divided among the counties of the State.
2. The Boards of Supervisors were obliged to raise an equal sum, to be distributed among the towns and districts.
3. Three commissioners were to be appointed in each town to superintend the schools and examine teachers.
4. Three trustees were to be elected in each district to engage teachers and otherwise provide for the local necessities of the school.
5. The whole system was to be placed under the charge of a State Superintendent.

[2] In 1812 the office of School Commissioner was created, and from 3 to 6 school inspectors were annually elected in each town, with the same powers and duties as school commissioners. Bills were introduced from time to time to place the whole system again under the charge of a distinctive officer, to provide for more efficient supervision of schools, to secure more competent teachers, and to establish a seminary for the instruction of teachers; but they all failed of receiving the necessary support. In 1828 the number of inspectors was reduced to 3. The laws that were passed corrected the most obvious abuses; but no great step was taken in advance until 1838.

[3] Erasmus Hall Academy in Kings co., Montgomery Academy, Orange co., Kinderhook, St. Lawrence, Fairfield, Oxford, Canandaigua, and Middlebury Academies, were the institutions in which this department was established.

[4] On the 13th of April of this year, the foundations of the District School Library were laid by "an act authorizing the taxable inhabitants of the several school districts to impose a tax not exceeding $20 for the first year and $10 for each succeeding year, for the purchase of a district library, consisting of such books as they shall in their district meeting direct." This bill was ably advocated in the Senate by Col. Young, of Saratoga, and the Hon. Levi Beardsley, of Otsego; and its friends were indebted for its success to the untiring exertions and extensive influence of James Wadsworth, of Geneseo. By act of July 9, 1851, the law was modified, giving to supervisors of towns a discretionary power of levying a tax for library purposes.

In 1838 an act was passed requiring $55,000 of the school moneys to be distributed among the school districts and expended by the trustees in the purchase of suitable books for district libraries, and the residue for the payment of the wages of duly qualified teachers. An equal amount was also required to be raised by taxation on the several counties and towns and applied to the same purposes.

The first definite proposition to establish district libraries was made by A. C. Flagg, in his report of 1830.

[5] In 1839, John C. Spencer, Superintendent of Schools, recommended a plan of county supervision, which "was urged upon the department and the Legislature; and under the strong recommendation of the Superintendent, backed by the exertions of several of the most eminent friends of popular education,—among whom may be enumerated the Hon. Jabez D. Hammond, who as early as 1835 had given to the public the details of a plan essentially similar; the Rev. Dr. Whitehouse, of Rochester; Francis Dwight, Esq., editor of the District School Journal, then of Geneva; Professor Potter, of Union College; and James Wadsworth, Esq., of Geneseo,—this project became, in 1841, by the nearly unanimous action of the Legislature, incorporated with our system of common schools."—Randall's Common School System, p. 44.

[6] The establishment of a Normal School for the professional education of teachers was strongly advocated by several Superintendents, and had been a favorite measure of many distinguished friends of the cause for many years. The bill for the establishment of the Normal School was introduced March 22, 1844, by Hon. Calvin T. Hurlburd, of St. Lawrence. The bill, as passed, appropriated $9,600 for the first year, and $10,000 per year for five years, for the support of the school, under the direction of the State Superintendent and Regents of the University. The Superintendent of Schools, (Samuel Young,) Rev. Alonzo Potter, Rev. W. H. Campbell, Hon. Gideon Hawley, and Francis Dwight, Esq., were appointed an executive committee to attend to the interests of the school. The committee proceeded to organize the school by the appointment of David P. Page, Principal; Frederick I. Ilsley, Teacher of Music; and J. B. Howard, Teacher of Drawing. Only 29 pupils were in attendance the first day; but the number speedily increased to 100, and since that time the school has been an uninterrupted success.

[7] This office had become very unpopular in some sections of the State, in consequence of appointments having been frequently made by the Board of Supervisors upon political considerations merely, without the least regard to the qualifications of the appointees. Under the supervision of the County Superintendents the schools had progressed more rapidly than ever before, in the same period; and after the abolishment of that office they steadily retrograded for several years.

[8] The first Teachers' Institute in the State was held at Ithaca, Tompkins co., April 4, 1843, under the direction of James S. Denman, County Superintendent. Immediately afterward, institutes were held in other counties; and in a few years they became a fixed institution. In 1847 they were recognized by the Legislature, and appropriations were made for their support.

State; and in 1850 the law was again submitted to a vote of the people and again sustained,—though by a decreased majority. In April, 1851, the Free School Act was repealed and the rate bill system was reinstated.[1]

During the session of 1853 a law was passed allowing Union Free Schools to be established under certain conditions.[2] On the 30th of March, 1854, the office of Superintendent of Public Instruction was created,—thus substantially restoring the original system of general supervision.[3] On the 13th of April, 1855, a law was passed allowing the Regents of the University to designate certain academies in the several counties in which a teachers' class might be taught free, the State allowing $10 for each pupil so taught, to a number not exceeding 20 in each academy.

[1] At the time of the repeal of the Free School act a provision was made for raising $800,000 annually by a State tax, which in many of the rural districts practically made free schools. This tax was afterward made a ¼ mill tax upon all the property of the State, producing a sum somewhat larger in the aggregate, and one increasing with the wealth and wants of the State.

[2] The law for the creation of Union Free Schools was a recognition of the free school principle and an important step in the progress of education.

[3] While the School Department was a subordinate branch of the Department of State, it was impossible to give to it that character and efficiency necessary to the best interests and welfare of the schools. Since the change, every department of education has felt a new impulse and has been constantly improving. The administration of the schools has been much more perfect, the reports have been more regular and reliable, and the standard of teaching has materially advanced.

School Statistics from the Report of the Superintendent of Public Instruction for 1859.[a]

	No. of school houses.	No. of districts.	No. of teachers employed.	No. of children between 4 and 21.	No. of volumes in district library.	Apportionment of State moneys for 1859.	Total receipts.	Total expenses.
Albany	170	169	243	39,559	27,018	$34,755.46	$122,068.91	$124,673.71
Allegany	252	259	262	16,411	20,196	18,443.07	28,818.51	32,258.36
Broome	211	214	221	13,510	17,314	15,680.38	24,123.23	27,529.65
Cattaraugus	253	255	255	16,121	20,859	17,569.93	27,601.80	33,362.17
Cayuga	248	247	278	19,438	45,109	21,647.28	48,535.41	59,294.50
Chautauqua	305	307	318	19,935	33,260	22,937.75	40,785.66	45,440.26
Chemung	114	116	127	10,641	11,571	10,727.63	19,119.92	20,558.93
Chenango	274	277	286	14,747	31,941	18,622.61	29,341.34	32,506.47
Clinton	182	182	189	18,327	18,203	16,448.91	23,529.05	26,198.33
Columbia	187	188	199	16,503	21,719	17,196.20	34,767.79	36,898.14
Cortland	182	182	183	9,254	18,588	11,586.07	17,255.54	20,937.05
Delaware	332	337	337	15,696	28,075	19,703.21	28,757.16	33,603.46
Dutchess	213	217	247	21,446	33,915	22,672.83	46,222.93	61,889.61
Erie	326	327	497	50,773	45,445	49,449.52	138,417.98	197,465.83
Essex	180	187	182	11,400	17,393	12,252.48	19,337.32	21,271.35
Franklin	156	157	156	11,299	11,868	11,126.18	15,637.73	20,802.87
Fulton	110	111	113	10,551	12,308	9,236.79	14,102.19	18,713.68
Genesee	146	151	151	10,644	17,842	12,312.75	23,487.48	28,726.57
Greene	163	164	172	11,689	21,051	12,793.84	22,016.69	27,027.94
Hamilton	28	33	29	1,046	1,454	1,515.11	2,105.87	2,364.82
Herkimer	193	199	203	14,136	24,676	15,765.92	27,365.25	33,533.20
Jefferson	373	375	398	25,757	41,536	28,164.96	49,185.46	58,063.32
Kings	47	47	355	50,772	37,529	68,798.02	246,461.75	230,877.31
Lewis	176	178	179	10,358	15,628	11,580.04	17,348.67	19,408.54
Livingston	193	196	207	14,055	28,040	15,664.48	26,652.77	34,072.68
Madison	238	239	254	15,654	30,445	18,430.01	31,594.17	34,847.48
Monroe	244	244	336	34,370	36,518	34,972.62	112,104.41	107,480.57
Montgomery	120	126	129	12,033	18,048	11,649.24	23,430.67	23,430.67
New York	95	95	1,350	200,000	4,000	207,332.95	951,178.40	951,178.40
Niagara	171	163	197	18,051	23,764	18,105.71	37,950.86	37,950.86
Oneida	397	408	458	38,455	54,588	41,891.72	72,376.15	72,376.15
Onondaga	297	296	369	32,478	44,978	33,261.15	80,114.54	80,114.54
Ontario	207	204	224	15,375	27,248	17,391.78	36,443.60	36,443.60
Orange	184	179	201	21,651	32,929	21,434.10	53,077.70	53,077.70
Orleans	134	132	143	10,514	16,082	11,302.71	19,239.56	19,239.56
Oswego	298	297	344	27,248	31,341	28,152.08	72,476.06	72,476.06
Otsego	319	320	320	18,027	35,009	21,994.48	32,171.15	32,171.15
Putnam	65	65	68	5,489	9,064	5,319.28	9,103.17	9,103.17
Queens	75	76	111	17,058	23,023	15,251.77	42,506.25	42,506.25
Rensselaer	199	210	273	28,372	30,382	28,962.54	14,029.12	14,029.12
Richmond	24	24	38	8,133	7,025	6,617.81	16,871.53	16,871.53
Rockland	39	41	43	6,939	9,365	6,311.17	12,295.09	12,295.09
St. Lawrence	464	464	482	31,219	42,898	33,173.93	58,331.45	58,331.45
Saratoga	257	230	245	18,145	31,228	19,624.40	34,626.32	34,626.32
Schenectady	63	68	83	7,281	9,537	7,394.20	17,979.08	17,979.08
Schoharie	203	203	204	12,024	22,578	14,505.51	21,844.73	21,844.73
Schuyler	112	112	112	7,108	13,092	7,912.37	13,528.71	13,528.71
Seneca	104	102	117	10,164	16,347	9,968.53	24,109.69	24,109.69
Steuben	350	355	354	25,717	32,010	26,672.33	42,912.11	42,912.11
Suffolk	148	150	161	15,192	23,999	15,123.09	38,755.50	38,755.50
Sullivan	159	163	163	12,280	12,519	12,004.20	19,238.58	19,238.58
Tioga	159	159	166	10,874	17,872	11,737.21	19,627.49	19,627.49
Tompkins	165	165	183	11,993	21,088	13,272.59	24,285.06	24,285.06
Ulster	219	223	231	25,758	32,632	24,249.37	43,763.04	43,763.04
Warren	130	132	123	7,812	9,896	8,832.63	12,953.77	14,063.80
Washington	238	241	247	16,296	30,743	18,526.88	31,963.60	36,966.24
Wayne	219	219	252	17,052	26,240	19,301.57	37,833.48	45,994.11
Westchester	159	148	211	27,738	31,803	26,908.02	84,648.40	95,156.04
Wyoming	191	189	197	12,072	25,114	13,924.49	21,756.20	27,744.76
Yates	106	106	110	7,536	12,170	8,263.32	19,089.09	16,417.96
Total	11,566	11,617	14,286	1,240,176	1,448,113	$1,316,607.18	$3,277,255.14	$3,792,948.79

[a] The above Table embraces returns from Jan. 1 to Oct. 1, 1858, except the last column, which is for the year 1857.

The office of School Commissioner was created by law April 12, 1856, and by the same act the office of Town Superintendent was abolished. This substantially reinstated the office of County Superintendent, the abolishment of which in 1847 was so disastrous to the interests of education.[1] On the 15th of March, 1856, an act was passed directing that the school laws should be digested and codified.[2] By act of April 12, 1858, the school year was changed so as to commence Oct. 1, and the annual district school meetings were directed to be held on the second Tuesday of October.

Mercantile Colleges, especially adapted to instruction in opening, conducting, and closing business accounts of every kind, and an elucidation of the laws and customs that have been established concerning them, have within a few years been opened in most of our cities. They depend entirely upon individual enterprise for support, and instruction is usually given by oral illustrations, lectures, and examples.[3]

CHURCHES.

The various church organizations in the State are independent of each other and are supported entirely by private contributions. The aggregate amount of church property in the State, and the amount annually raised for religious purposes, is immense. The following is a list of the different denominations, arranged in alphabetical order:—

The African Methodist Episcopal (Zion) Church was formed in 1820. The State of New York forms one conference, having in 1852 1,928 members.

The American Swedenborgian Association was formed in 1857, and has its office in New York City. A Printing and Publishing Society of this denomination, formed in 1850, collected in the year ending in 1858 $3,108.25. It owns the stereotype plates of all the theological writings of Swedenborg.

The Anti Mission or Old School Baptist, in 1855, had in the State 18 churches and 1,101 members.

The Associate Presbyterian Church, in 1855, had 26 churches and 3,926 members, and **The Associate Reformed Presbyterian Church** 38 churches and 5,634 members. These two denominations united in May, 1858, under the name of **The United Presbyterians.**

The Baptist Church has in the United States 565 associations, 11,600 churches, 7,141 ordained ministers, 1,025 licentiates, and 923,198 members. Of these 43 associations, 812 churches, 738 ordained ministers, 90 licentiates, and 84,266 members are in New York. Its general Benevolent Associations are the "American Baptist Missionary Union," "American Baptist Publication Society," "American Baptist Historical Society," "American Baptist Home Mission Society," "American and Foreign Bible Society," "American Baptist Foreign Mission Society," "Southern Baptist Convention," 1845, and "Southern Baptist Publication Society," 1847. It has in this State 2 colleges and 2 theological seminaries, and has 5 periodicals devoted to its interests.[4]

---

[1] The School Commissioners have generally succeeded in awakening a new interest in their respective districts by personally visiting the schools and teachers, by encouraging the formation of teachers' associations and institutes, and by requiring a higher standard of qualification on the part of teachers. The schools under their supervision are steadily improving.

[2] The expense of this codification of the school laws was defrayed from the library fund.

[3] These institutions are almost indispensable in every mercantile community. They afford instruction upon every department of business accounts, and incidentally upon methods of conducting business generally. Courses of lectures are usually given, in which are unfolded the laws relating to all business matters, and a vast amount of information is given relating to all departments of commercial transactions. The most extensive of these colleges are those of Bryant & Stratton, 7 in number, of which 3 are in this State,—1 at Buffalo, 1 at Albany, and 1 at New York,—Eastman's Colleges, at Rochester and Oswego, and Bassett's College, at Syracuse. There are various other institutions of the kind in the State, of good local repute, and of great value to the villages and towns in which they are established.

[4] *The Missionary Union* was formed in 1814; its receipts for 1857–58 were $97,808.77. It has 19 missions, 80 missionaries, and over 300 churches. The headquarters of the Society are at Boston. *The Baptist Publication Society* was formed in 1824, and has its depository at Philadelphia. It supports 53 colporteurs, and its receipts for 1857–58 were $60,585.12. *The American Baptist Home Missionary Society* was formed in 1832, and has its office in New York. It employs 99 missionaries and supplies about 250 stations. Its receipts for 1857–58 were $52,093.33. *The American and Foreign Bible Society*, formed in 1838, has its office at New York. Its receipts for 1857–58 were $57,049.98. Madison University, at Hamilton, and the University of Rochester are Baptist institutions; and attached to each is a theological seminary. The papers published by this denomination are,—The New York Examiner, New York Chronicle, American Baptist, (newspapers,) and the Home Mission Record, and Mothers' Journal, (magazines,) all published in New York City.

The Christian Connexion[1] divide the State into the New York Eastern, New York Central, New York Western, Northern, Black River, and Tioga Christian Conferences, each having distinct boundaries. They have in the U. S. and Canada over 1,500 ministers and 335 communicants. The census reports 85 churches in this State and 9,825 persons usually attending them.

The Congregational Churches of the Union number about 2,900, with 2,400 ministers and 240,000 members. Of these, 425 churches, 400 ministers, and 25,000 members are claimed within the State of New York.[2]

The Congregational Methodists[3] were first composed of seceders from the Methodist Episcopal Church, in 1820. They have 3 churches in the State.

The Disciples of Christ have in the Union over 1,700 churches, 1,100 ministers, and 130,000 members.[4] In New York they reported, in 1855, 28 churches and 2,015 members. The New York State Convention embraces, besides the State, parts of Connecticut and Vermont.

The Evangelical Lutheran Church embraces 35 synods in the U. S., of which 25 are connected with a general synod. It numbers 1,083 ministers and 1,920 congregations,[5] and has of general societies the Parent Educational, Home Missionary, Foreign Missionary, Church Extension, Lutheran Historical, and Lutheran Publication, for the purposes indicated by their respective titles. It has within this State a Theological Seminary and Academy at Hartwick, Otsego county, and Martin Luther College, with a theological department, at Buffalo.

The Free Will Baptist Church in the U. S. has 28 yearly and 129 quarterly meetings, 1189 churches, 957 ordained and 164 licensed preachers, and 55,209 communicants.[6] This State comprises 5 whole yearly meetings and parts of 2 others. As no attention is paid to State lines

The Fifty-First Annual Report of the Baptist Missionary Convention of the State of New York (Oct. 1858) gives the following statistics of this denomination in New York. The dates of organization are from the Baptist Almanac:—

ASSOCIATIONS.	Organized.	Churches.	Ordained Ministers.	Members.
Black River	1808	32	35	2.958
Broome & Tioga	1823	25	19	2,755
Buffalo	1815	21	21	2,512
Canisteo River	1835	10	9	381
Cattaraugus	1835	23	18	1,534
Cayuga	1800	19	17	2,106
Chemung River	1842	20	17	1,856
Chenango	1832	29	21	2,571
Cortland	1827	19	18	2,188
Deposit	1854	15	11	992
Dutchess	1834	20	19	1,738
Erie	1847	19	13	1,344
Essex & Champlain	1834	14	7	1,079
Franklin	1811	17	12	1,702
Genesee	1811	17	16	1,908
Genesee River	1828	15	13	1,435
Harmony	1838	20	16	1,868
Hudson River North	1851	29	21	4,985
Hudson River South	1851	41	57	9,013
Lake George	1809	11	10	646
Livingston	1812	10	8	693
Madison	1808	19	18	2,290
Mohawk River	1837	10	9	731
Monroe	1827	24	19	3,056
New York	1791	35	33	5,532
Niagara	1824	14	12	1,563
Oneida	1820	23	28	2,549
Onondaga	1822	21	17	1,866
Ontario	1814	19	19	1,544
Orleans	1843	11	9	1,061
Oswego	1832	16	13	1,670
Otsego	1795	17	16	1,398
Rensselaerville	1799	12	11	1,372
Saratoga	1805	23	25	3,258
Seneca	1821	15	13	1,797
Stephentown	1832	12	10	1,139
Steuben	1817	19	21	2,149
St. Lawrence	1813	23	20	2,168
Union	1810	15	15	2,282
Washington Union	1834	23	18	3,691
Wayne	1834	16	13	1,728
Worcester	1830	17	12	1,286
Yates	1842	8	6	804

[1] Otherwise named "Unitarian Baptists." They originated between 1793 and 1801, in secessions from Baptists, Methodists, and Presbyterians. Each church is independent in government; and full statistics are not accessible.

[2] The General Association of New York includes the Oneida, Black River, Essex, St. Lawrence, Western New York, Long Island, New York & Brooklyn, Ontario, Susquehanna, Albany, and Puritan of Wyoming & Allegany Associations. The American Congregational Union has for one of its objects the aid of feeble churches. In the year ending in 1858 it expended $6,154.05 for this purpose.

[3] Otherwise known as "Stilwellites."

[4] Sometimes known as "Campbellites," from Rev. Alexander Campbell, the founder.—Fox & Hoyt's Quad. Reg., 1852, p. 253.

[5] From the Lutheran Almanac, 1859. The synods embraced in New York are as follows:—

SYNODS.	When formed.	Ministers.	Congregations.
New York Ministerian	1785	59	55
Hartwick Synod	1830	25	33
Franckean Synod	1838	24	30
Synod of Buffalo	1839	16	16

Of these the last two are not connected with the General Synod.

These synods have no definite boundaries, but overlap each other, and in some instances extend into neighboring States.

The Kirchliches Informatorium and Historische Zeitblatt, of Buffalo, and Der Lutherische Herold, of New York, are the official organs of this denomination.

[6] The Free Will Baptist Register for 1859 gives the following statistics. To those extending partly into neighboring States a star is prefixed; and those entirely out of the State are in Italics.

ANNUAL MEETINGS.	QUARTERLY MEETINGS.	Churches.	Ordained Preachers.	Licensed Preachers.	Communicants.
Holland Purchase	Cattaraugus, Cattaraugus Center, Chautauqua, Erie, *French Creek, and Genesee.	43	43	7	2,170
Genesee	Rochester, Monroe, Union, Wayne, Freedom.	38	30	3	1,666
*Susquehanna	*Owego, Gibson, Spafford, *Walton.	37	29	8	1,262
*New York and Penn.	Yates and Steuben, *Potter Co.,Bradford and Tioga, *Tuscarora.	34	22	10	246
St. Lawrence	Lawrence, Jefferson.	16	7	3	488
Union	McDonough, Chenango, Otselic.	17	13	3	826
Central N. Y.	Whitestown, Oswego, Rensselaer, *Otsego, Lake George.	40	36	2	2,163

in these divisions, the exact numbers in the State cannot be determined from the reports. Its general institutions are 3 mission societies, an anti-slavery society, a biblical school and institution at New Hampton, N. H., and a seminary in this State.

The Friends or Quakers have, since 1827, been divided into 2 distinct branches, known as "Hicksite" and "Orthodox." The Hicksites have a general meeting for the United States and Canada, which is divided into 6 yearly, 33 quarterly, and 138 monthly meetings in the U. S., and 2 half-yearly and 6 monthly meetings in Canada. This State is embraced within the New York and the Genesee yearly meetings, the former of which extends into New Jersey and the latter into Canada. There are of the New York yearly meeting in this State 7 quarterly and 31 monthly meetings; of the Genesee yearly meeting 2 quarterly and 8 monthly meetings.

The Orthodox Friends divide the United States and Canada into 8 yearly, 1 half-yearly, 65 quarterly, and 222 monthly meetings. The New York yearly meeting comprises 1 half-yearly, 15 quarterly, and 43 monthly meetings, of which 9 entire and a part of 1 other quarterly and 28 monthly meetings are within the State, the remainder being in adjoining States and Canada.[1]

The German Methodists[2] originated in the year 1800, and number about 20,000. They have in New York about 15 churches and 3,000 members.

The Mennonites have in the Union 300 churches and 36,280 members: of these, 6 churches and 442 members were reported in Western N. Y. in 1855.

The Methodist Episcopal Church in the United States was divided in 1844 into the Church North and the Church South, forming two independent organizations, differing only upon the question of slavery. The Church North embraces 49 annual conferences, 5,365 traveling, 769 superannuated, and 7,169 local preachers, and 820,514 members and probationers. The total number of preachers in both divisions is 20,644, and of members 1,476,291. This State embraces 5 entire and parts of 4 other conferences, which are subdivided into districts and circuits, each with definite boundaries. The Sunday School Union of the M. E. Church North reports 11,229 schools, 120,421 officers and teachers, 639,120 scholars, and 2,054,253 volumes in S. S. libraries. Its Tract Society has auxiliaries in each conference, and distributes large quantities of tracts and a small paper called "The Good News." Its Missionary Society supports 44 foreign missionaries and 76 helpers, and 302 missionaries and 214 helpers among the Indians and foreign populations. Its "Book Concern" carries on an amount of publication equaled by that of few private firms in the country, including books, papers, and magazines. This denomination has within the State 1 college and 10 seminaries, in connection with annual conferences.[3]

The Methodist Protestant Church was formed Nov. 1830. It divides the Union into conferences, stations, and circuits. The census reports as belonging to this denomination in this State, in 1855, 46 churches and 1,605 members.

The Presbyterian Church existed as one body until 1837, when it was divided into "Old School" and "New School," which form two distinct organizations, with similar professions of faith but different views of discipline. The Old School General Assembly of the U. S. report 33 synods, 159 presbyteries, 2,468 ministers, 3,324 churches, and 259,335 communicants. During

---

The missionary societies under the charge of this society are the Free Will Baptist Foreign Mission Society, which supports 3 missionaries and their families at Arissa, India, the Free Will Baptist Home Mission Society, and the Free Will Baptist Female Missionary Society. The Whitestown Seminary, occupying the premises erected for the Oneida Institute, formerly a manual labor school, is under the auspices of this denomination.

[1] The names of quarterly meetings within the State, with the number of monthly meetings in each, according to *Foulke's Friends' Almanac* for 1858, are, in the New York yearly meeting, Westbury, 6, Purchase, 3, Nine Partners, 3, Stanford, 4, Easton, 5, Saratoga, 5, Duanesburgh, 5; in the Genesee yearly meeting, Farmington, 5, Scipio, 3.

The quarterly meetings within the yearly meeting, according to *Wood's Book of Meetings*, 1858, are as follows, with the date of establishment and number of monthly meetings in each:—Westbury, (1676,) 2; Purchase, (prior to 1746,) 3; Nine Partners, (1783,) 3; Stanford, (1800,) 3; Ferrisburgh, (partly in Vermont, 1809,) 1; in New York, 2; in Vermont, Farmington, (1810,) 5; Butternuts, (1812, under the name of Duanesburgh, changed in 1838,) 3; Saratoga, (1793, in 1795 changed to Easton, in 1815 divided into Saratoga and Easton, and in 1835 the latter was discontinued,) 3; Scipio, (1825,) 2; Le Ray, (1830,) 3. The first meeting within New York was established at Oyster Bay, by Richard Smith and others who were banished from Boston in 1656. The persecutions of that colony drove others to Rhode Island and Long Island, and meetings were established at Oyster Bay, Gravesend, Jamaica, Hempstead, Flushing, and other places, at an early period.

[2] Correctly known as Evangelical Association, or Albrights.

[3] The following is a summary of the Conferences in New York. Those marked with a star are partly in other States.

CONFERENCE.	Conference first held.	PREACHERS.			MEMBERS IN SOCIETY.			Benevolent contributions, in dollars.
		Traveling.	Superannuated.	Local.	Members.	Probationers.	Total.	
New York..........	......	207	38	161	26,666	4,477	31,143	15,245
Genesee..........	1810	110	14	102	9,511	1,133	10,644	3,883
Oneida..............	1829	147	34	142	16,380	2,134	18,514	108
*Troy..............	1833	165	50	177	22,990	3,382	26,372	11,532
Black River......	1836	168	30	159	16,972	3,128	20,100	3,542
*Erie..............	1836	167	26	206	20,306	2,607	22,913	6,445
East Genesee.....	1848	150	33	139	16,861	2,257	19,118	4,693
*New York East	1849	142	45	176	22,236	3,029	25,265	27,289
*Wyoming.......	1852	93	11	134	11,652	2,485	14,137	3,225

The districts within the State of New York forming the above Conferences are:—

New York—Poughkeepsie, Rhinebeck, Prattsville, Monticello, N. Y. German Mission, Rochester, and German Mission.

the year ending May, 1858, $2,544,692 was raised for various religious and benevolent objects. Its general objects of promotion and extension are conducted by Boards; and it has various funds for special objects. The State of New York embraces the greater part of 3 synods.[1]

The New School Presbyterian General Assembly of the United States reports 26 synods, 120 presbyteries, 1,612 ministers, 1,687 churches, and 143,510 communicants. During the year ending May, 1858, $273,965.90 was raised for domestic and foreign missions, education, and publication. It has several committees for the promotion of its general objects, and has in this State 2 theological seminaries and several periodicals.[2]

The Primitive Methodists have 2 churches and about 500 members in this State. They have in the Union over 1,200 members.

The Protestant Episcopal Church embraces in the Union 31 dioceses and 4 missions, 1,995 parishes, 39 bishops, 1,979 clergymen, and 127,953 communicants. Total contributions for missionary and charitable purposes, $1,265,642.96. Its general institutions are the "General Theological Seminary," New York, the "Domestic and Foreign Missionary Society," the "General Protestant Episcopal Sunday School Union and Church Book Society," the "Protestant Episcopal Historical Society," the "Western Church Extension Society," and the "Prot. E. Society for the Promotion of Evangelical Knowledge."

The Diocese of New York[3] embraces all E. of the E. lines of Broome, Chenango, Madison, Oneida, Lewis, and Jefferson cos., and comprises 275 parishes, 321 clergymen, and 22,411 communicants.

Genesee—Buffalo, Niagara, Genesee, Wyoming, and Olean.
Oneida—Oneida, Chenango, Cortland, Auburn, and Cazenovia.
Troy—Troy, Albany, Saratoga, Plattsburgh, and 3 in Vt.
Black River—Rome, Syracuse, Oswego, Adams, Watertown, Ogdensburgh, and Potsdam.
Erie—Fredonia. The remainder in Ohio and Penn.
East Genesee—Geneva, Rochester, West Rochester, Bath, Corning, Elmira, and Lima.
New York East—New York, (E. district,) Long Island, and 2 in Conn.
Wyoming—Binghamton and Owego, in part; the remainder in Penn.
The offices of the several Missionary Societies and of the Book Concern are at 200 Mulberry St., N. Y. The periodicals issued from that establishment are the Christian Advocate and Journal, a weekly newspaper; the Quarterly Review, the National Magazine, and the Ladies' Repository, octavo magazines; and the Sunday School Advocate, The Good News, and the Missionary Advocate, small newspapers. The Northern Christian Advocate, at Auburn, is also an official publication of this denomination. Under the auspices of this Church are the Genesee College, at Lima, Livingston co.; the Amenia Seminary, Dutchess co.; Ashland Collegiate Institute, Greene co.; Charlotte Boarding Academy, Schoharie co.; Falley Seminary, Fulton, Oswego co.; Genesee Wesleyan Seminary, Lima, Livingston co.; Gouverneur Wesleyan Seminary, St. Lawrence co.; Jonesville Academy, Saratoga co.; New York Conference Seminary, Charlotteville, Schoharie co.; Oneida Conference Seminary, Cazenovia, Madison co.; and the Susquehanna Seminary, Binghamton, Broome co. Besides these, a large number of institutions, including several of the incorporated academies, are owned and patronized mainly by members of this denomination.
[1] The names of presbyteries and statistics of churches of this branch in the State are reported in the Old School Presbyterian Almanac for 1859 as follows:—

SYNODS.	Organized.	Presbyteries.	Ministers.	Churches.	Communicants.
Albany	1803	Londonderry, Troy, Albany, Mohawk	99	64	7,756
Buffalo	1843	Ogdensburgh, Genesee R., Buffalo City, Michigan, Rochester City	60	62	5,028
New York	1788	Hudson, North River, Bedford, Long Island, New York, New York 2d, Canton, Ningpo, Connecticut, Nassau, Western Africa	169	130	17,495

The Board of Domestic Missions has 610 missionaries and 990 churches and missionary stations. Receipts for the year ending March 1, 1858, $105,277.52. Its offices are located in Philadelphia and Louisville.
The Board of Education is divided into ministerial education and education in schools, academies, colleges, and parochial

schools. Under the auspices of this denomination are 22 colleges, 60 academies, and 100 parochial schools. The receipts for 1857 were $56,492.06. Its office is at Philadelphia.
The Board of Foreign Missions has 69 ministers, 30 male and 90 female assistant missionaries, and 23 native teachers. The receipts for 1857 were $223,977.79. Its office is at the corner of Center and Reade Sts., N. Y.
The Board of Publication issues tracts, books, newspapers, and other periodicals in great numbers. Its receipts for 1857 were $126,960.28. Its office is at Philadelphia.
[2] The following summary of the New School Presbyterian Church in New York is from the American Presbyterian Almanac for 1859, and other authentic sources:—

SYNODS.	Organized.	Presbyteries.	Ministers.	Churches.	Communicants.
Albany	1803	Champlain, Troy, Albany, Columbia, Catskill	84	70	8,257
Utica	1829	St. Lawrence, Watertown, Oswego, Utica	65	72	7,106
Geneva	1812		109	93	9,725
Onondaga	1855	Onondaga	80	70	7,769
Susqueh'nna	1853	Otsego, Chenango, Delaware	42	51	3,989
Genesee	1821	Genesee, Ontario, Rochester, Niagara, Buffalo, Angelica	125	108	12,371
N. Y. & N. J.	1788	Hudson, North River, Long Island, New York 3d, New York 4th, Brooklyn, and 4 others not in the State	226	155	24,905

The various societies under the care of this denomination are in charge of the Presbyterian Publication Committee, Foreign Mission Committee, Permanent Committee on Education, and Church Extension Committee. Young men preparing for the ministry are educated at the Union Theological Seminary, of New York City, and Auburn Theological Seminary, of Cayuga co. The newspapers of the denomination are the Evangelist, of New York, and the Genesee Evangelist, of Rochester.
[3] Its institutions are the "Society for the Promotion of Religion and Learning," the "Corporation for the Relief of Widows and Children of Clergymen," the "Prot. E. Tract Society," the "New York Bible and Common Prayer Book Society," the "New York Prot. E. City Mission Society," the "Prot. E. Christian Mission Society for Seamen in the City and Port of New York," the "Prot. E. Brotherhood of New York," the "Northern Missionary Convocation," the "Bible and Common Prayer Book Society of Albany and its Vicinity," the "Brotherhood of St. Barnabas," (Troy,) "Columbia College," "Trinity School," (N. Y.,) "St. Luke's Hospital," (N. Y.,) "St. Luke's Home for Indigent Christian Females," the "Church Charity Foundation," (Brooklyn,) and the "Pastoral Aid Society."

The Diocese of Western New York[1] embraces the remainder of the State, comprising 149 parishes, 129 clergymen, and 10,551 communicants.

The Reformed Methodists originated in 1814, in Vt. Their church government is Congregational. They report in the State 8 churches and about 500 members.

The Reformed Presbyterians, or Covenanters, is derived from the church of the same name in Scotland. In 1855 it numbered in the State 15 churches and 2,274 members.

The Reformed Protestant Dutch Church of the State belongs to the General Synod of the Ref. Prot. Dutch of N. A. It is subdivided into the particular Synods of New York and Albany, the former embracing 16 and the latter 14 classes, of which 29 are entirely within the State and 1 partly in New Jersey. In 1855 it reported 364 churches, 348 ministers, 130,120 persons attending congregations, and 38,927 communicants. Of these, 260 churches, 259 ministers, 21,027 families, 97,553 total of congregations, and 31,208 communicants, were in this State.

The Roman Catholic Church divides the Union into 7 Provinces, 43 Dioceses, and 3 Vicarates Apostolic. The Province of New York comprises the New England States, New York and New Jersey, and the dioceses of New York, Portland, Burlington, Boston, Hartford, Brooklyn, Albany, Buffalo, and Newark. Four of these are within this State. There are 3 theological seminaries, 1 preparatory seminary, 2 colleges, and a large number of benevolent and educational institutions belonging to this denomination within the State, and 9 periodicals devoted to its interests.[2]

The Seventh Day Baptists have in the United States 67 churches, 70 ordained ministers, and 7,250 members. Of these 36 churches are in New York. In 1835 the denomination was divided into associations, of which the Eastern, Central, and Western are embraced wholly or in part in this State. De Ruyter Institute and the Alfred Academy are under the patronage of this denomination.

Shakers, or the "United Society of Believers," otherwise called the "Millennial Church," numbers in the Union 18 communities and about 6,000 members. They live in "families," and in New York they are principally located at New Lebanon, Watervliet, and Groveland.

The Unitarians number in the Union 293 clergyman and 250 societies, mostly in Massachusetts. They have within this State 10 societies. Their only periodical within the State is the "Christian Inquirer," a weekly newspaper in New York City, published under the auspices of the "Unitarian Association of the State of New York."[3]

The Universalists United States Convention is composed of clerical and lay delegates from each State and Territorial Convention, and meets on the third Tuesday of Sept. annually.[4] The denomination has a Historical Society, composed of all preachers and laymen in good standing who sign the constitution. It also has a General Reform Association, that meets in Boston on the

---

[1] Its institutions are Hobart Free College, at Geneva; and De Veaux College, at Suspension Bridge. There are besides several incorporated and private academies supported by members of this denomination.—*Church Almanac for 1859, pp.* 32, 47.

[2] The following statistics are upon the authority of the Catholic Almanacs of 1859.

General Statistics for 1858.

	Diocese of New York.	Diocese of Brooklyn.	Diocese of Albany.	Diocese of Buffalo.
Churches........................	69	34	113	102
Chapels..........................	9	...	5	....
Stations	30	7	50	30
Clergymen on missions	89		84	98
" otherwise employed	35	}31{	84	114
Ecclesiastical institutions.....	....	...	13	2
Seminaries.....................	1	...	...	....
Clerical students	49	18	13	14
Literary institutions for young men...................	4	...	2	2
Literary institutions for young ladies...................	12	...	1	9
Charitable institutions........	....	...	10	14
Hospitals and infirmaries ...	1	...	...	
Houses of protection.........	1	...	...	
House of the Good Shepherd	1	...	...	
Orphan asylum.................	2	2	...	
Parochial and other schools	27	...	9	
Religious communities........	....	7	...	
Religious institutions.........	....	...	...	26
Catholic population............	380,940	...	...	100,000

The Diocese of New York, formed in 1808, comprises Delaware, Dutchess, New York, Orange, Putnam, Richmond, Rockland, Sullivan, Ulster, and Westchester counties. *The Diocese of Brooklyn,* formed in 1853, comprises Kings, Queens, and Suffolk counties. *The Diocese of Albany,* formed in 1847, comprises the remainder of the State E. of the west lines of Cayuga, Tompkins, and Tioga counties. *The Diocese of Buffalo,* formed in 1847, comprises the counties W. of the west lines of Cayuga, Tompkins, and Tioga.

The distinctive schools under the patronage of this denomination are the St. John's College, at Fordham, Westchester co.; College of St. Francis Xavier, New York City; St. Joseph's Theological Seminary, Fordham; Ecclesiastical Seminary, Buffalo; Franciscan Convent, Allegany; and Preparatory Seminary of Our Lady of the Angels, Niagara.

The Catholic papers in the State are The New York Freeman's Journal and Catholic Register, The New York Tablet, The Pilot, (N. Y. and Boston,) Katholische Kirchen Zeitung, weekly, of N. Y.; The Buffalo Sentinel, weekly; Catholic Institute Magazine, Newburgh; Brownson's Quarterly Review, N. Y.; American Catholic Almanac and Clergy List; and the Six Cent Catholic Almanac and Laity's Directory, of N. Y.

[3] *Year Book of the Unitarian Cong. Churches,* 1857.

[4] *The New York State Convention* embraces the Central, Niagara, Cayuga, Buffalo, Mohawk River, Ontario, Genesee, Black River, St. Lawrence, Otsego, Allegany, Steuben, Chautauqua, Chenango, Hudson River, and New York Associations, and contains 220 societies, 194 church edifices, and employs 107 preachers. It has a State Educational Society, with $40,000 subscribed, and $25,000 invested for the Theological School in Canton; and has in charge the Clinton Liberal Institute. The Universalist Paper and Book Establishment has assets amounting to $13,796, and unredeemed stock to the amount of $4,169. The profits of the concern are applied to the purchase of the shares, which will thus become the property of the State Convention. It has a relief fund for aged and disabled preachers. The Young Men's Christian Union, formed Jan. 1856, and the

last Tuesday in May. This denomination has organizations in 32 States and Territories, in 19 of which State Conventions are held. It has 4 educational, 9 missionary, 1 tract, and 4 Sunday school associations, 1 relief fund, and 1 book and newspaper establishment,—all of which are of a State character. It has 85 associations, 1,334 churches or societies, 913 church edifices, 655 preachers, 18 periodicals, and 9 institutions of learning.

The Wesleyan Methodists.[1] This denomination in the United States was formed by seceders from the M. E. Church, May, 1843.

Besides these, there are churches in the State known as *Bethels, Evangelical, German Evangelical Reformed, Jewish, Calvinistic Methodists, German Methodists, Moravians, French Evangelical Presbyterian, Protestant Community of Inspiration, Second Advent, True Dutch, Free,* and *Union,* numbering in the aggregate a large number of church edifices and communicants.[2]

RELIGIOUS, LITERARY, AND BENEVOLENT SOCIETIES.

SOCIETIES of a religious, humane, and benevolent character began to be formed in considerable numbers about 1822–25. The objects of these societies enlisted the co-operation of members of the different religious denominations and of other philanthropic persons, and annual meetings were held in New York for the several objects.

The time of meeting has been usually in the second week in May, and the appointments were so made that the same persons could attend several of them in succession. These societies have become numerous, and "Anniversary week" thus becomes a season of interest to thousands. The assembling of so large a number of persons from distant sections of the Union has led reformers of every degree to appoint the anniversary meetings of their societies at the same time and place; and there is scarcely a society for the promotion of religion, morality, charity, or civil and social reform that is not thus annually brought to public notice, its operations exhibited, and its claims urged.

The societies exclusively under the control of a single denomination are noticed under the religious sects.

The principal societies of a general character are as follows:—

The American Bible Society, formed by a convention of 60 persons, mostly clergymen, May 8, 1809, has for its object the publication and distribution of the Bible and parts

N. Y. City Missionary Society are connected with this denomination. Its periodicals are the Christian Ambassador, at Auburn and New York, and a monthly periodical by the female department of the Clinton Liberal Institute.
[1] The M. E. Church in England and Canada is thus known.

The church of this name in the U. S. differs from the others in rejecting the classification of the ministry as bishops, elders, and deacons. Their official organ is the True Wesleyan.
[2] The following table shows the general statistics of churches in the several counties:—

Church Statistics.

COUNTIES.	Number of churches.	Value of church property.	COUNTIES.	Number of churches.	Value of church property.	COUNTIES.	Number of churches.	Value of church property.	COUNTIES.	Number of churches.	Value of church property.
Albany.........	129	$1,272,025	Fulton..........	39	$ 96,350	Ontario........	84	$283,730	Seneca..........	48	$144,333
Allegany......	75	122,360	Genesee........	61	164,300	Orange.........	112	443,855	Steuben........	105	161,438
Broome........	63	207,564	Greene..........	74	168,325	Orleans........	51	228,600	Suffolk........	112	278,260
Cattaraugus..	61	112,370	Hamilton	5	1,400	Oswego........	84	234,715	Sullivan.......	46	60,000
Cayuga........	100	311,620	Herkimer....	85	173,500	Otsego.........	117	231,952	Tioga..........	45	106,700
Chautauqua.	105	225,250	Jefferson....	127	346,785	Putnam.......	30	85,000	Tompkins.....	66	183,690
Chemung.....	33	150,750	Kings..........	149	2,840,700	Queens.........	73	492,135	Ulster..........	100	409,350
Chenango.....	111	232,030	Lewis..........	54	65,845	Rensselaer....	114	746,640	Warren	33	57,250
Clinton........	45	137,975	Livingston...	86	263,260	Richmond....	29	285,100	Washington..	95	287,120
Columbia.....	85	276,650	Madison......	94	202,580	Rockland.....	41	136,300	Wayne.........	80	272,000
Cortland	51	118,000	Monroe........	141	804,230	St. Lawrence.	117	263,485	Westchester..	148	868,250
Delaware......	92	183,555	Montgomery.	52	141,300	Saratoga	103	313,975	Wyoming.....	74	169,365
Dutchess......	132	693,650	New York....	252	12,092,750	Schenectady.	26	173,710	Yates..........	48	133,650
Erie............	155	1,176,285	Niagara........	74	229,205	Schoharie....	85	129,830			
Essex..........	51	121,600	Oneida........	201	635,960	Schuyler.......	50	99,125	Total	5,077	31,480,144
Franklin......	35	66,195	Onondaga.....	142	563,610						

thereof without note or comment.[1] Auxiliary to the American Bible Society are numerous county and local societies, through which the greater part of the funds are raised.[2]

The American Tract Society was instituted in 1825, by the several evangelical denominations, for the purpose of disseminating tracts and books upon moral and religious subjects.[3] Several of the religious denominations have tract societies of their own.

The American Board of Commissioners for Foreign Missions was formed in 1809, for the purpose of supporting missions in foreign lands. Its central office is in Boston; but it has auxiliary societies throughout this State. It is chiefly supported by the Congregational and New School Presbyterian societies.[4]

[1] The first society within the State for the gratuitous distribution of the Scriptures was the N. Y. Bible and Common Prayer Book Society, formed in 1809. A large number of co. societies was formed within the next five years. The present society, formed in 1816, has gradually increased in wealth and influence, until its operations have extended to almost every section of the globe. It has a Bible house in New York,—one of the most extensive publishing houses in the world. Its books are gratuitously distributed, or sold at cost; and the total number of volumes issued up to May, 1858, was 12.804,014. These are produced in great varieties of style and in upward of forty different languages. The society has also published the Bible in English with raised characters for the blind.

The Baptist and Protestant Episcopal denominations have separate societies for publishing the Scriptures, although many members belonging to both of these co-operate with the American Bible Society.

[2] The following table gives the names of these societies, the date of their organization, and the amount of their donations and remittances up to May, 1858:—

NAME.	Date.	Donations.	Remittances for Bibles.
Albany Co	May, 1816	$19,621.00	$16,385.20
Allegany Co	April, 1825	1,526.49	3,326.92
Amity Female	Sept. 1816	329.15	130.85
Ausable Valley	Dec. 1845	370.04	804.05
Brooklyn City	Feb. 1849	5,683.76	10,054.75
Broome Co	Feb. 1817	1,960.01	5,171.46
Buffalo City	Nov. 1847	2,339.91	5,329.05
Caledonia	April, 1818	3,366.72	111.28
Caledonia Female	May, 1817	1,673.97	232.50
Carlton	Jan. 1855	....	91.53
Cattaraugus Co	Aug. 1829	127.06	1,879.62
Cayuga Co	June, 1817	3,738.99	7,807.61
Chautauqua Co	April, 1820	1,397.13	7,547.60
Chemung Co	July, 1828	2,949.35	3,404.26
Chenango Co	Nov. 1826	5,538.99	6,634.34
Clinton Co	April, 1821	718.56	4,291.26
Cold Spring	Aug. 1838	101.01	324.39
Columbia Co	Oct. 1817	10,835.30	6,131.77
Cortland Co	Aug. 1816	4,320.90	5,830.78
Delaware Co	July, 1816	1,450.75	5,341.42
Dutchess Co. Female	Oct. 1817	4,754.87	3,985.20
Dutchess Co	Oct. 1839	15,930.45	5,355.39
Erie Co	April, 1848	698.06	4,163.76
Essex Co	Jan. 1817	909.14	4,244.35
Floyd and Western Welsh	April, 1854	50.30	81.70
Franklin Co	June, 1821	381.95	3,385.60
Fulton & Hamilton Co	Dec. 1816	21,182.49	11,237.37
Geneva	April, 1846	1,117.86	2,280.75
Genesee Co	July, 1818	3,169.47	6,950.40
Genoa	April, 1825	972.15	1,072.20
Greene Co	Sept. 1816	6,477.23	5,746.56
Greene	Mar. 1855	25.00	175.00
Herkimer Co	May, 1817	3,268.27	4,699.15
Hudson Female	Oct. 1816	1,970.50	805.32
Jasper	Aug. 1855	....	87.00
Jefferson Co	Jan. 1817	3,936.37	12,274.47
Lewis Co	April, 1828	544.51	2,997.44
Lewis Co. Welsh	May, 1850	341.66	147.65
Livingston Co	May, 1824	6,542.59	5,482.53
Long Island	Sept. 1817	20,786.70	30,785.72
Madison Co	Oct. 1816	5,701.51	6,814.87
Montgomery Co	Dec. 1816	390.00	1,345.11
Monroe Co	Oct. 1821	22,828.47	19,282.30
Newburgh	Sept. 1818	3,784.74	3,768.00
New York Female	June, 1816	102,926.12	17,369.47
New York Calvinistic Welsh	Sept. 1844	546.23	72.86
New York Marine	Feb. 1817	....	6,043.89
New York	Mar. 1829	42,091.43	264,911.73
Niagara Co	May, 1830	2,457.41	5,401.51
North Brooklyn	May, 1816	1,726.16	1,726.20
North Seneca	July, 1852	582.19	767.73
Nyack Ref. D. Ch. Female	May, 1842	74.80	7.20
Oneida Co	Jan. 1817	15,226.06	20,521.48
Onondaga Co	April, 1832	7,594.00	12.805.50

NAME.	Date.	Donations.	Remittances for Bibles.
Ontario Co	Mar. 1817	$ 8,405.15	$ 4,870.93
Orange Co	June, 1816	24,141 22	6,426.71
Orleans Co	July, 1830	3.230.82	4,058.68
Oswego Co	Mar. 1826	2,488.15	7,286.94
Otsego Co	June, 1816	3,116.79	7,573.77
Peekskill Female	Feb. 1817	713.59	166.76
Poughkeepsie Fem. Union	Sept. 1850	1,080.81	
Putnam Co	May, 1828	120.00	316.16
Remsen Steuben Welsh and Vicinity	Jan. 1817	3,893.68	2,141.06
Rensselaer Co	June, 1816	35,452.61	22,289.21
Rockland Co	July, 1816	1,985.72	2,289.64
Sandy Hill and Fort Edward	Nov. 1848	164.64	243.93
Saratoga Co	July, 1816	12,779.61	7,277.96
Schenectady Co	May, 1823	2,741.56	4,454.40
Schoharie Co	Jan. 1817	3,934.40	3,982.19
Schuyler Co	Feb. 1856	358.50	513.23
Seneca Associate Ref	May, 1846	319.71	16.08
South Seneca	Feb. 1846	1,735.67	1,077.02
South Steuben	June, 1848	1,267.85	1,264.36
Steuben Co	Feb. 1817	2,085.38	5,201.34
St. Lawrence Co	April, 1820	2,115.40	14,193.70
Sullivan Co	Aug. 1826	2,388.90	3,156.15
Tioga Co	June, 1823	4,272.81	5,373.82
Tompkins Co	May, 1828	4,044.04	6,249.34
Ulster Co	Nov. 1816	11,145.91	2,191.24
Utica Welsh and Vic	Jan. 1817	4,479.71	2,450.12
Warren Co	Sept. 1821	194.44	2,300.38
Washington Co	Mar. 1817	19,002.11	7,458.51
Watervliet	Jan. 1849	3,720.58	2,117.34
Wayne County	April, 1847	3,731.48	4,775.31
Welsh B. S. of Nelson	Sept. 1856	12.00	53.35
Welsh B. S. of Rome	Mar. 1855	228.08	132.73
Welsh B. S. of Holland Patent	May, 1855	184.48	77.40
Westchester Co	Aug. 1827	19,614.17	6,977.71
Wyoming Co	Feb. 1850	2,310.82	4,634.73
Yates Co	Dec. 1827	4,372.10	3,468.60

[3] This society has a large property vested in a publishing house and grounds, corner of Nassau and Spruce Streets, New York, and in the stock, machinery, and materials used in the manufacture of books and tracts. Its fiscal affairs are managed by a finance committee. It has 31 auxiliaries in the State of New York. The receipts up to May, 1858, were $5,856,711.05,—about three-fifths of which were derived from sales, and the remainder from donations. Previous to May, 1858, this society had circulated 13,098,013 volumes, 188,971,408 publications, 4,753,741,573 pages; including 149,761 volumes (9,831 sets) of the Evangelical Family Library, 94,026 volumes (2,089 sets) of the Christian Library, 48,638 volumes (1,990 sets) of the Religious or Pastor's Library, 319,323 volumes (4,557 sets) of the Youth's Library, and 160,921 volumes (20,044 sets) of the Youth's Scripture Biography. The society publishes an Almanac, the American Messenger, (in English and German,) and Child's Paper, in large editions; and issues books and tracts in the English, German, French, Spanish, Portuguese, Italian, Welsh, Dutch, Danish, Swedish, and Hungarian languages. It operates through branch and auxiliary societies, general agents and superintendents, and paid and volunteer colporteurs. The American Tract Society of Boston, which formerly co-operated with this, is now a distinct organization.

Societies of kindred character were formed in the State previous to this,—the more important of which was the New York Religious Tract Society, formed in 1812, with auxiliaries in various parts of the country.

[4] This society has established 27 missions, 121 stations, and 101 out stations in Africa, Greece, Western and Southern Asia, China, Sandwich Islands, Micronesia, and among the North American Indian Tribes. It employs 373 missionaries and assistants, and 524 native pastors and assistants, has 8 printing presses, and up to 1858 had issued 1,080,481,083 pages of tracts and religious books. These missions numbered 318 churches, and 27,740 members; and the educational department embraced

The American Home Missionary Society was formed May 12, 1826, for the purpose of supporting the ministry in feeble and destitute Presb. and Cong. churches in the U. S.[1]

The American Sunday School Union was formed in 1824, for the purpose of encouraging the establishment of Sunday schools and of supplying them with books. Its central office is at Philadelphia. The New York Sunday School Union, auxiliary to this, was established in 1816, and has numerous local subordinate societies in different parts of the State.[2]

The American Seamen's Friend Society was formed in 1828, and endeavors to carry out the intentions expressed in its title by distributing Bibles and tracts, supporting the ministry, and otherwise promoting the moral welfare of seamen.[3]

The American Bethel Society was instituted in 1836, for the purpose of opening chapels for boatmen and mariners, distributing tracts, and extending other means for their moral improvement. It established a magazine named the "Bethel Flag;" and has auxiliaries in many places on the lakes, rivers, and canals.

The American and Foreign Christian Union was formed in 1849, for the special object of counteracting the influence of the Romish and other churches opposed to the class usually denominated "evangelical."[4]

The Central American Education Society was formed for the purpose of assisting young men preparing for the ministry. In 1858 the society aided 111 students.

The American Colonization Society was formed at Washington, Jan. 1817, for the colonization of free colored persons in Africa. **The New York State Colonization Society** was formed at Albany, April 9, 1829, and has had numerous auxiliaries in the State.[5]

The National Compensating Emancipation Society, formed in 1857, has for its object the purchasing of slaves for the purpose of giving them freedom.

The American Anti Slavery Society was organized Dec. 4, 1833.[6]

The American Missionary Association was formed Sept. 1846, as a Home and Foreign Missionary Society. Business office in N. Y. City. Receipts for first 12 years of its existence, $421,001.98. Present and monthly income, $3,000 to $5,000. It has a slaves' Bible Fund, and labors for the extinction of slavery. The association publish The American Missionary (paper) and American Missionary Magazine, both monthly.

Young Men's Christian Associations have been formed in most of the cities and

---

6 seminaries, 17 other boarding schools, 619 free schools, (of which 312 were supported by the Hawaiian Government,) and 17,020 pupils. The receipts in the year ending July 31, 1858, were $334,018.48, the principal part of which was derived from donations.—*Forty-Ninth Report A. B. C. F. M.*, 1858.

1 This society was formed by the union of two societies previously formed by the Presbyterian and Reformed Protestant Dutch Churches. It is supported by the Congregationalists and New School Presbyterians, and to some extent by the Reformed Protestant Dutch, Lutheran, and German Reformed Churches. In 1858, 1,012 persons were connected with this society or its agencies and auxiliaries, of which 133 are within this State. The number of congregations and stations fully or statedly supplied is 2,034; Sabbath school scholars, 65,500; contributions to benevolent objects, $24,272.28. The receipts in 12 months were $175,971.37; the payments in the same time were $190,735.70. Total receipts in 32 years, $3,456,082; total years of labor, 18,871; total additions to churches, 150,275.

There is a central and a western agency in this State,—the office of the former of which is at Utica and of the latter at Geneva. The number of missionaries aided within the year was 133. Total contributions, $39,347.96.

2 This movement was supported by most of the evangelical denominations; but several of them have since established Sunday school organizations among themselves. The American Sunday School Union had, in 1858, expended about $2,500,000 in books, and $1,000,000 more in organizing Sunday schools. Its receipts for the last year were $65,076.14; and it had formed 1,524 new schools, with 57,787 pupils and 9,694 teachers. The New York Sunday School Union had, in 1858, 210 schools, reporting 60,000 pupils, 4,825 teachers, 82,294 books in libraries, and $13,089 raised by contributions. Sunday schools in some form are supported by nearly every religious denomination, and are chiefly for Biblical instruction. A State Sunday School Teachers' Convention, formed in 1855, meets annually. Its third report, made Oct. 1858, gave a total in the State of 1,895 schools, 22,263 officers and teachers, and 212,312 pupils.

3 This society has 15 stations in various parts of the world, and grants aid to various Bethel operations not connected with it. The receipts for the year ending in 1858 were $25,236.20; and the total expenses in the seamen's cause about $100,000; 2,257 mariners had been received at the Sailors' Home in New York, and the whole number received into that institution from its establishment was 52,353.

4 The association has 61 home laborers; and its receipts in the year ending in 1858 were $76,603.22. Its expenses in the same time were $79,604.33. It has agents, and supports chapels in several foreign countries.

5 The slave trade was abolished in 1807, and after Jan. 1, 1808, the cargoes of captured slaves were to be sold for the benefit of the State where they might land. By an act of March 3, 1819, the General Government appropriated $100,000 for the restoration of a large number of Africans to their native country. By the co-operation of the Government with this Society a purchase was made in Dec. 1821, in the neighborhood of Cape Montserado, on the w. coast of Africa, from which has grown the present Republic of Liberia, under the special patronage of this society. Formal possession was taken April 28, 1822.

Several of the subordinate State societies have been merged in anti-slavery and other more radical societies for the termination of slavery. In the year ending in 1858 the receipts of the New York Colonization Society were $15,624.62.

6 The expenses of the society for the year ending in 1858 were $17,052, including those of the Anti Slavery Standard, its principal organ. Receipts, $15,200 from the paper and donations, and $17,355 by auxiliaries.

A New York State Anti Slavery Society, with numerous auxiliaries, was formed about 1834-36, and its friends soon organized themselves into a political party. The highest State vote of this party was in 1844, when it amounted, on the Governor's ticket, to 15,136. Slavery existed under the Dutch, and was continued through the English period of our colonial history. An act was passed March 31, 1817, declaring that every child born of a slave in this State after July 4, 1799, should be free at the age of 28 if a male, or at 25 if a female. Every child born after the passage of the act was to become free at the age of 21, and measures were ordered for the education of children held in service. The importation of slaves was prohibited. The first emancipation under this law, therefore, took effect July 5, 1827, as the law fixed the period as *after* instead of *upon* the 4th of July, as was perhaps intended. The 5th of July has sometimes been celebrated as their anniversary of independence; and hence arises the slang expression of "Fourth of July one day *arter*." Those born before the above date remained slaves till their death, and the census of 1855 reported one such as living in the State. The number of slaves in New York at different periods has been as follows:—

1790......21,324 | 1810......15,017 | 1820......10,046 | 1840.......... 4
1800......20,613 | 1814......11,480 | 1830......   75 | 1850..........—

large villages in the United States and British Provinces. They form a general confederation, the State of New York forming the fourth district. These associations embrace within their objects a library, reading room, lectures and prayer meetings.[1]

The Young Men's Christian Union of New York is supported by the Unitarian and Universalist denominations principally.

Young Men's Associations for mutual improvement have been formed in various parts of the State and under various names. The plan of organization is essentially alike; and it usually includes a library, reading room, cabinet, lecture course, and debating club. Most of these associations have been organized by special acts, and their affairs are managed by executive committees chosen annually by the members. They can hold a limited amount of property for the special objects of their organization.[2]

In most of the large villages, associations have been formed for the support of lectures at stated intervals in the winter months. They are generally of a temporary character, are re-organized every season or are attached to academies or other existing institutions.

The New York State Temperance Society was formed April 2, 1829. Its objects were to suppress intemperance and limit the traffic in intoxicating liquors. It received the support of a large number of the best and most philanthropic citizens, and its influence spread rapidly throughout the State.[3] Since the formation of the first society, efforts to suppress intemperance have been made upon an extended scale, and the strong arm of the law has been invoked to prohibit the traffic in alcoholic liquors.

Fraternity of Free and Accepted Masons. "The Ancient and Honorable Fraternity of Free and Accepted Masons" of the State of New York is under the government of a Grand Lodge, composed of its Grand Officers and the representatives (the Master and Wardens) of every lodge in the jurisdiction. As at present constituted, the Grand Lodge dates from 1785, when Chancellor Robert R. Livingston was elected Grand Master, and continued in office till 1801.[4] In 1859 there are 430 chartered lodges in the State, (numbered to 474,) with about 33,000 members, numbering among them a very respectable class in all the walks of life. There is at least one lodge in every county in the State, (except Hamilton;) 93 of the lodges are in the city of New York; and a lodge is located in every considerable town and village. The annual receipts of the

[1] In July, 1858, associations of this kind were in active operation in Albany, *Albion*, Black Rock, *Brooklyn*, Buffalo, Catskill, Flushing, Hudson, Jamestown, New York, *Oswego*, Poughkeepsie, Rondout, Saratoga Springs, *Stapleton*, Troy, Utica, and Waterford. Those in italics belonged to the confederation.

[2] The first organization of this kind in the State was the Albany Young Men's Association, formed Dec. 13, 1833, and incorp. March 12, 1835. The following is a list of these associations in the State formed under special acts:—

NAME AND LOCATION.	Date of incorporation.	Remarks.
Albany, Albany co.......	March 12, 1835	Fully organized. Library 7,000 vols.
Buffalo, Erie co............	March 3, 1843	Library in 1855, 7,500 vols.
" " (German)	May 12, 1846	Library in 1855, 1,800 vols.
Elmira, Chemung co....	April 11, 1842	
Fulton, Oswego co........	May 13, 1846	
Geneva, Ontario co.......	April 17, 1839	
Port Byron, Cayuga co.	April 10, 1844	
Sackets Harbor, Jefferson co........	March 2, 1843	Closed.
Saratoga Springs, Saratoga co..................	May 14, 1840	
Franklin Institute, Syracuse, Onondaga co	Dec. 1849	{ Library in 1859, { about 3,000 vols.
Schenectady, Schenectady co....................	March 9, 1839	
Troy, Rensselaer co......	April 10, 1835	Fully organized.
Utica, Oneida co..........	March 25, 1837	Closed.
Watertown.Jefferson co.	April 17, 1841	Burned out in 1849.

[3] The fourth report of the State Society, in 1838, gave 1,538 societies and 231,074 members. Its principal organ, the Temperance Recorder, was begun March 6, 1832, at Albany, and issued many years. It also published almanacs, tracts, and circulars to a large extent. The American Society for the Promotion of Temperance, formed in 1827, was in 1836 succeeded by the "American Temperance Union." The latter, in the year ending in 1858, received $1,987.20. Its principal organ is the Journal of the American Temperance Union, at New York. Both this

and the State Society are still in operation. About 1841-45 the "Washingtonian" temperance movement, originating among reformed inebriates, spread over the State, and several thousand independent societies were formed under it,—most of which, however, died out with the enthusiasm under which they were created. The secret orders of "Rechabites" and "Sons of Temperance" originated in New York, about 1842, and subsequently those of "Cadets of Temperance," "Daughters of Temperance," "Good Samaritans," "Daughters of Samaria," "Knights Templar," "Social Circles," and other associations of a similar class were formed for the avowed purpose of promoting temperance reform. Numerous lodges or encampments were formed, and these societies at one time embraced large numbers of members. Several of them have been given up entirely; and it is believed none of them are increasing. They required a form of initiation and pledge of secrecy, had fixed dues payable at regular intervals, provided money to assist the sick and bury the dead, and gave certificates of membership, which, with passwords and other tokens of recognition, might enable a person to claim assistance among strangers belonging to the order.

The License question was submitted to the popular vote May 5, 1846, with the result of 111,884 *for*, and 177,683 *against*, license. The operation of the law was deemed by many to be unequal; and its effect upon the temperance cause was unquestionably adverse. In 1847 the majorities *for* license were large in most of the towns. The "Maine Law," or prohibition movement, began in 1851, and was urged by its friends with great force during several sessions of the Legislature. A prohibitory law was passed, but was declared unconstitutional by the Court of Appeals. The present law regulating the sale of intoxicating liquors, passed April 16, 1857, provides a Board of Excise Commissioners in each county for granting licenses and prosecuting violations of the law.

[4] At the close of his term there were 94 lodges in the State, of which the oldest was St. John's, No. 1, (yet in active existence,) established in the city of New York in 1757. Gen. Jacob Morton was Grand Master from 1801 to 1806, De Witt Clinton from 1806 to 1820, and Daniel D. Tompkins from 1820 to 1822, when the Grand Lodge became divided. In 1826, at the commencement of the Anti-Masonic excitement, (see Genesee co.,) there were about 360 lodges in the State, (numbered to 507,) with about 22,000 members. In 1836 the number of lodges had been reduced below 75, with a corresponding membership,—say 4,000.

Grand Lodge are about $16,000; and during the year ending in June, 1859, the amount expended for charitable relief by the Grand Lodge and its immediate agents was about $3,000; and probably three times more than that sum was expended for the same purposes by lodges and individual Masons. There is in the Hall and Asylum Fund, raised for charitable and educational purposes, about $25,000, controlled by trustees chosen by the Grand Lodge, (it not being incorporated;) and this sum is constantly being increased from various sources,—a portion of it arising from the stated revenues of the Grand Lodge. The fraternity are now all united in one body, under the jurisdiction of the Grand Lodge and its subordinates, and are in a sound and flourishing condition. The office of the Grand Secretary and place of business of the fraternity is in Odd Fellows Hall, corner of Grand and Center Sts., New York. The Grand Lodge is in correspondence and direct communication with all the Grand Lodges and Masonic fraternity throughout the world.[1]

Independent Order of Odd Fellows. This order was introduced into the United States from Manchester, England; and the first regular lodge was opened at Baltimore, in 1819. The Grand Lodge of the U. S. includes 42 subordinate Grand Lodges in the States and Territories, Canada, and the Sandwich Islands. There are 2 Grand Lodges and 623 subordinate lodges in this State.[2]

Sons of Malta. This order embraced in this State, on the 1st of July, 1859, the Grand Lodge of the State and 8 subordinate lodges, with an aggregate membership of 12,680.

MEDICAL SOCIETIES.

THE formation of County Medical Societies was authorized by an act passed April 4, 1806. They were empowered to grant licenses to practice medicine in the State and to collect of the members a sum not exceeding $3 annually. Delegates sent from each co. society, in number equal to the representation of the co. in Assembly, were to constitute a State Medical Society, which had the power of granting diplomas to practice medicine and to decide upon cases appealed from the co. societies. Although local societies were formed under this act in most of the counties then existing, several of them have ceased to exist; and there are at present but about 40 county societies that are represented by delegates. The State Society was formed Feb. 5, 1807, and is

[1] The stated festivals of the fraternity are on the 24th of June and 27th of December, usually styled St. John's days. The officers of the Grand Lodge and of the subordinates are elected annually; and the time and place for the "Annual Communication" of the Grand Lodge is on the first Tuesday of June, in the city of New York. The elective Grand Officers of the Fraternity are Grand Master, Deputy Grand Master, Senior Grand Warden, Junior Grand Warden, Grand Treasurer, Grand Secretary, and 5 Grand Chaplains.

[2] *Statistics of the Odd Fellows for the year ending Jan. 30, 1858.*

	LODGES.				ENCAMPMENTS.			
	Total number U. S. Grand Lodge.	Grand Lodge Northern New York.	Grand Lodge Southern New York.	Total, New York.	Subordinate Encampments, United States.	Subordinates, Northern New York.	Subordinates, Southern New York.	Total, New York.
Lodges, or Subordinate encampments	3,390	493	130	623	651	71	13	84
Number of initiations	16,549	690	448	1,138	2,755	56	60	116
" " rejections	1,713	51	27	78	79	2	....	2
" " died	1,739	82	118	200	220	8	4	12
" " members	176,700	11,783	8,475	20,258	22,319	979	487	1,466
" " " relieved	23,151	715	1,345	2,060	902	22	32	54
No. of widows and families relieved	2,705	113	393	506	93	....	1	1
Amount paid for relief of members	$294,992.91	$11,263.80	$29,663.62	$40,927.42	$28,171.10	$211.00	$363.00	$574.00
Amount paid for relief of widowed families	66,614.55	3,185.18	6,545.17	9,730.35	3,111.60	....	3.00	3.00
Amount paid for education of orphans	11,284.06	207.29	388.69	595.98	10.00	10.00	....	10.00
Amount paid for burying the dead	67,364.70	2,250.00	5,091.17	7,341.17	5,377.24	40.84	90.00	90.84
Amount of annual receipts	1,223,685.03	44,756.78	69,981.18	114,737.96	110,156.54	2,019.92	2,426.75	4,446.67

now composed of delegates from co. societies, 1 delegate from each medical college, 5 from the New York Academy of Medicine, honorary members by virtue of office or by election, and permanent members elected after 4 years' service as delegates. The annual meetings of the society are held on the first Tuesday of February. The State Society has maintained a regular organization from the beginning; and since 1848 its proceedings have been reported annually to the Legislature and published with their documents.[1]

Homeopathic Medical Societies may be organized in the several counties under an act of April 13, 1857; and such have been formed in Kings, Livingston, New York, Oneida, and perhaps other counties.[2]

County Medical Societies.

COUNTY.	Date of Organization.	First President.	First Secretary.	First No. of Members.	Present No. of Members.
Albany	July 29, 1806	Wm. McClelland	Charles D. Townsend	9	45
Allegany					
Broome	Nov. 6, 1823	Chester Lusk	Ammi Doubleday	7	20
Cattaraugus					
Cayuga					
Chautauqua					
Chemung	1836	Lemuel Hudson	Asa R. Howell	17	15
Chenango	Aug. 5, 1806	Tracy Robinson	Geo. Mowrey	6	40
Clinton					
Columbia	June, 1806	Wm. Wilson	Wm. Bay	11	27
Cortland	Aug. 10, 1808	Lewis S. Owen	Geo. W. Bradford	8	22
Delaware	1806	Joshua H. Brett	Adam J. Doll	20	40
Dutchess	1806	Samuel Bard	—— Van Kleek	10	35
Erie	1815	Josiah Trowbridge		8	95
Essex					
Franklin	Oct. 1809	Records lost.			
Fulton and Hamilton					
Genesee					
Greene					
Herkimer	Aug. 5, 1806	Westel Willoughby, jr.	Andrew Farrell	9	
Jefferson	Dec. 17, 1806	John Durkee	Hugh Henderson	13	
Kings	March 2, 1822	Cornelius Low	Andrew Vanderze	9	65
Lewis		Records burned.	Organization abandoned.		
Livingston	May 29, 1821	Charles Little	Cyrus Wells	9	32
Madison	July 27, 1806	Israel Farrell	Elijah Pratt	20	46
Monroe	May 9, 1821	Alexander Kelsey	Frederick F. Backus	20	94
Montgomery	July 3, 1806	Alexander Sheldon	Stephen Reynolds	8	20
New York	July 1, 1806	Nicholas Romayne	Edward Miller	106	450
Niagara					
Oneida	1806	Amos G. Hull	David Hasbrouck	29	90
Onondaga	July 1, 1806	John H. Frisbie	Walter Colton	11	62
Ontario					
Orange	July 1, 1806	Jonathan Sweezey	Nathaniel Elmer	22	50
Orleans					
Oswego	July 17, 1821	Benjamin Coe	Luther Cowen	7	36
Otsego	July 1, 1806	Joseph White	Caleb Richardson	14	37
Putnam					
Queens					
Rensselaer	July 18, 1806	Benjamin Woodward	Ira M. Wells	20	
Richmond					
Rockland	May 18, 1850	John Demarest	Charles Whipple	11	11
St. Lawrence	Oct. 14, 1807	Joseph W. Smith	W. Noble	5	
Saratoga					
Schenectady					
Schoharie	Oct. 1857	S. B. Wells	C. C. Van Dyck	10	14
Schuyler	Dec. 29, 1857	Nelson Winton	Thomas Shannon	7	7
Seneca					
Steuben					
Suffolk	July 22, 1806	David Conklin	D. Moses Blachely		
Sullivan					
Tioga					
Tompkins					
Ulster					
Warren					
Washington	July 1, 1806	Andrew Proudfit	Wm. Livingston	23	28
Wayne					
Westchester	May 8, 1797	Archibald Macdonald	Watson Smith	...	41
Wyoming					
Yates	March 4, 1823	Joshua Lee	John Hatmaker	12	25

[1] The first act regulating the practice of physic and surgery in New York was passed June 10, 1760. It was amended in 1792 and 1797, and under the latter the judges of State courts and courts of Common Pleas and Masters in Chancery were, upon proof of two years' study of medicine, authorized to license persons to practice as physicians. By the act of 1806, medical societies might be formed in each co. by securing five or more members; and where there were less than five physicians in a co. they might unite with the society of a neighboring co. The restrictions upon practice without a diploma were finally abolished in 1844; and the law now makes no distinction between the different classes of practitioners. Those assuming to act as physicians become responsible for their practice, and, if not licensed by a county or the State Society or regularly graduated at a medical school, can collect pay according to the time employed, but they cannot collect the specific fees, implying professional skill, which are recognized by the established usages of the profession.

[2] The number of homeopathic practitioners in the State is about 600, of whom 150 are in New York and Brooklyn. The Central, Bond St., and Northern Homeopathic Dispensaries in New York, the Homeopathic Dispensary of Brooklyn, the Hahnemann Academy of Medicine of New York, and the Homeopathic Medical Society of Northern N. Y., are sustained by this class of physicians, and the North American Homeopathic Journal, (quarterly.) the Homeopathic Review, (mo.,) and the Homeopathic, (semi-mo.,) all published at New York, are devoted to their interests.

Population, Classified by Color, Political Relation, Nativity, &c., according to the State Census of 1855.

COUNTIES.	Total Population.	COLOR. White.	COLOR. Black and Mulatto.	POLITICAL RELATIONS. Voters.	POLITICAL RELATIONS. Aliens.	NATIVITIES. New York State.	NATIVITIES. United States.	NATIVITIES. Foreign Countries.	Over 21 who cannot Read or Write.	Deaf and Dumb.	Blind.	Insane.	Idiotic.
Albany.........	103,681	102,842	839	18,616	20,282	64,705	70,407	33,247	3,231	18	25	46	46
Allegany......	42,910	42,729	181	9,884	2,032	32,826	39,150	3,153	536	18	11	20	46
Broome........	36,650	36,135	515	8,282	2,056	27,874	32,921	3,225	611	18	5	32	35
Cattaraugus..	39,530	39,401	129	8,637	2,645	28,918	34,629	4,066	496	21	16	31	26
Cayuga........	53,571	53,171	390	11,526	4,863	40,720	46,033	6,854	890	17	14	39	45
Chautauque...	53,580	53,271	109	11,912	4,795	37,965	46,444	6,797	749	14	11	21	38
Chemung......	27,288	26,825	463	5,859	1,191	19,983	24,075	2,876	675	8	5	11	11
Chenango.....	39,915	39,701	214	9,700	977	32,402	37,728	1,747	273	17	19	34	46
Clinton........	42,482	42,351	131	6,374	8,404	25,222	29,279	13,021	4,449	20	18	18	28
Columbia.....	44,341	43,137	1,254	9,412	3,800	36,500	39,141	5,107	1,069	20	11	34	28
Cortland	24,575	24,547	28	5,902	704	19,989	23,139	1,380	245	7	13	25	34
Delaware	39,749	39,555	194	9,065	1,532	33,575	36,072	3,564	283	18	6	29	25
Dutchess	60,635	58,806	1,829	12,498	6,861	48,073	50,724	9,707	1,567	19	15	43	17
Erie............	132,331	131,473	858	21,743	37,274	66,945	77,620	54,257	2,315	35	32	66	43
Essex..........	28,539	28,403	136	5,652	2,994	19,057	23,799	4,684	1,154	7	10	15	21
Franklin......	25,897	25,460	17	4,462	3,739	14,583	19,258	6,622	1,323	15	15	17	20
Fulton	23,284	23,124	160	5,066	1,559	19,632	20,811	2,448	531	12	10	20	20
Genesee........	31,532	30,948	86	6,477	4,107	20,339	24,920	6,427	436	16	9	30	35
Greene	31,137	30,325	812	6,952	1,522	27,338	28,755	2,261	516	11	8	27	27
Hamilton	2,543	2,539	4	599	168	1,998	2,225	310	53	—	—	1	4
Herkimer......	38,566	38,394	172	8,578	3,955	30,283	32,607	5,803	608	21	26	37	36
Jefferson......	65,420	65,223	197	14,206	5,377	50,103	56,471	8,630	991	41	28	62	66
Kings..........	216,355	211,875	4,480	32,627	65,536	94,122	115,245	100,206	8,924	45	44	16	27
Lewis...........	25,229	25,186	43	5,284	2,751	17,583	19,669	5,470	722	8	7	21	36
Livingston	37,943	37,734	209	8,136	4,329	26,141	31,185	6,549	376	13	9	14	13
Madison.......	43,687	43,362	325	9,974	3,232	34,060	39,336	4,351	848	27	18	43	41
Monroe........	96,324	95,835	489	17,272	22,837	53,939	63,048	33,276	2,105	27	30	56	30
Montgomery..	30,808	30,407	401	6,786	2,688	25,762	26,714	3,880	625	26	14	14	21
New York....	629,810	618,064	11,840	88,877	232,678	262,156	303,721	322,469	25,858	411	316	655	52
Niagara.......	48,282	47,880	402	8,257	10,327	27,753	33,205	14,717	976	11	14	25	24
Oneida.........	107,749	107,134	615	20,946	18,472	68,302	76,868	30,354	3,062	48	42	517	56
Onondaga.....	86,575	86,073	502	16,933	73,549	57,589	65,126	20,949	2,150	24	28	22	40
Ontario........	42,672	42,088	584	9,147	4,757	30,666	35,639	6,803	570	21	10	26	32
Orange........	60,868	58,720	2,148	11,301	7,955	45,339	49,718	10,761	1,241	18	14	42	36
Orleans	28,435	28,325	110	5,704	3,813	19,841	23,363	4.966	736	13	4	10	11
Oswego........	69,398	69,030	368	14,609	7,372	50,731	56,895	12,024	1,778	33	24	41	62
Otsego........	49,735	49,518	217	12,177	1,640	42,205	46,674	2,770	569	24	18	54	60
Putnam........	13,934	13,805	129	3,037	1,215	11,628	12,228	1,694	425	5	2	5	13
Queens........	46,266	43,216	3,050	8,187	8,618	33,092	34,800	11,135	1,588	21	9	46	8
Rensselaer	79,234	78,340	894	14,933	14,921	51,667	57,447	21,445	3,080	19	13	42	32
Richmond.....	21,389	20,799	590	3,795	5,078	14,094	15,441	5,882	245	3	12	12	2
Rockland......	19,511	19,014	497	3,580	3,457	13,512	15,030	4,436	980	7	2	7	16
St. Lawrence .	74,977	74,875	102	13,984	9,915	47,991	59,667	15,016	2,272	26	23	39	51
Saratoga......	49,379	48,737	642	10,377	5,748	37,423	41,305	7,927	1,271	18	13	35	43
Schenectady..	19,572	19,261	311	3,790	2,943	14,596	15,217	4,303	269	7	8	8	16
Schoharie.....	33,519	33,063	456	7,376	874	31,195	32,117	1,294	601	9	9	7	19
Schuyler......	18,777	18,701	76	4,377	587	15,379	17,648	966	219	4	4	10	24
Seneca........	25,358	25,190	168	5,395	2,153	19,253	22,498	2,763	365	5	8	19	18
Steuben	59,099	62,557	408	14,151	3,605	48,737	56,489	2,196	870	21	7	28	29
Suffolk	41,066	39,018	1,888	7,939	3,083	34,983	36,807	4,211	681	12	6	26	13
Sullivan.......	29,487	29,377	110	5,727	3,606	21,508	23,185	6,128	655	8	7	11	20
Tioga..........	26,962	26,732	230	6,181	979	20,760	25,208	1,597	436	11	13	16	13
Tompkins.....	31,516	31,267	249	7,456	1,160	25,587	29,538	1,849	271	6	5	28	43
Ulster.........	67,936	66,510	1,426	13,197	9,487	53,156	54,753	13,162	2,997	26	21	23	28
Warren........	19,669	19,589	70	4,165	1,643	14,632	17,122	2,479	348	9	1	10	12
Washington...	44,405	44,185	220	9,355	4,822	32,297	37,482	6,791	1,030	22	12	44	44
Wayne........	46,760	46,515	245	10,205	4,767	35,077	39,380	7,103	668	21	15	22	36
Westchester..	80,678	78,750	1,928	14,245	16,741	52,035	57,401	23,132	3,130	14	20	56	41
Wyoming	32,148	32,119	29	7,064	2,827	22,438	26,978	5,060	266	17	11	21	30
Yates..........	19,812	19,715	97	4,474	942	16,082	18,277	1,408	281	9	16	19	23
Total.........	3,466,212	3,420,926	45,286	652,322	632,746	2,222,321	2,528,444	917,708	96,489	1,422	1,136	2,742	1,812

Percentages of the Several Classes to the Total Population.

White males.................... 49.23	Aliens................................. 18.54	Aged 20 and under 30, males......... 9.43
" females 49.47	Owners of land...................... 10.41	" " females 10.44
Colored males 0.61	Over 21 years who cannot read and	Aged 30 and under 40, males......... 7.28
" females 0.69	write ,.............................. 2.78	" " females 6.78
Total males..................... 49.84	Ages under 5, males.................. 6.85	Aged 40 and under 50, males......... 4.79
" females 50.16	" females.................. 6.74	" " females 4.39
Single 60.08	Aged 5 and under 10, males......... 5.73	Aged 50 and under 60, males......... 2.91
Married 36.15	" females....... 5.64	" " females 2.76
Widowers........................ 1.02	Aged 10 and under 15, males....... 5.46	Aged 60 and under 70, mules......... 1.55
Widows 2.75	" females....... 5.35	" " females 1.56
Native voters 14.90	Aged 15 and under 20, males....... 4.91	Aged over 70, males 0.84
Naturalized voters 3.91	" females....... 5.45	" females 0.85

Summary of Population at different periods in the several Counties, as now organized.

COUNTIES.	1790.	1800.	1810.	1814.	1820.	1825.	1830.	1835.	1840.	1845.	1850.	1855.
Albany.........	13,717	25,155	34,661	33.885	38,116	42,821	53,520	59,762	68,593	77,268	93,279	103,681
Allegany	......	......	1,443	2.207	6,520	13,184	20,238	27,295	30.254	31,402	37,808	42,910
Broome.........	45	2,730	6,481	7,423	11,100	13,893	17,579	20,199	22,338	25.808	30.660	36,650
Cattaraugus..	......	......	458	537	4,090	6,643	16,724	24,986	28,872	30,169	38,250	39,530
Cayuga.........	......	10,817	29,843	33,609	38,897	42,743	47,948	49,202	50,338	49,663	55,458	53,571
Chautauqua...	......	......	2,381	4,259	12,568	20,639	34,671	44,869	47,976	46,548	50.493	53,380
Chemung......	2,931	1,848	2,852	3,115	4,272	8,011	11,562	14,439	15,483	17,742	21,737	27.288
Chenango......	......	6,500	21,704	24,221	31,215	34,215	37,238	40,762	40,785	39,900	40,311	39,915
Clinton.........	1,036	3,916	8.802	7,764	12,070	14,486	19,344	20,742	28.157	31,278	40,047	42,482
Columbia......	27,732	35,322	32,390	33,979	38,330	37,970	39,907	40,746	43,252	41,976	43,073	44,341
Cortland.......	......	982	8,879	10,893	16,507	20,271	23,791	24.168	24,607	25,081	25,140	21.575
Delaware......	2,745	10,228	20,303	21,290	26.587	29,565	33,024	34,192	35,396	36,990	39.834	39,749
Dutchess......	36,334	37,909	41,190	43,707	46,615	46,698	50,926	50,704	52,398	55,124	58,992	60,635
Erie............	......	......	4,667	6,201	10,834	24,316	35,719	57,594	62,465	78,635	100,993	132,331
Essex.........	578	4,157	9,477	9,949	13,811	15,993	19,287	20,699	23,634	25,102	31,148	28,539
Franklin......	......	443	2,719	2,568	4.439	7,978	11,312	12.501	16,518	18,692	25,102	25.897
Fulton.........	......	6,931	15,048	14,491	15,723	17,006	20,451	21,597	18,049	18,579	20,171	23.284
Genesee.......	......	......	3,660	9,435	18,578	20.708	26,008	29,145	28,705	28,845	28,488	31,532
Greene.........	7,028	12,584	19,536	20,210	22,996	26,229	29,525	30,173	30,446	31,957	33,126	31,137
Hamilton.....	......	......	465	556	1,251	1,296	1,325	1,654	1,907	1,882	2,188	2,543
Herkimer.....	2,827	16,332	24,742	23,725	31,017	33,040	35,870	36,201	37.477	37,424	38,244	38,566
Jefferson......	......	262	15,140	18,564	32,952	41,650	48,493	53,088	60,984	64,999	68,153	65,420
Kings...........	4,495	5,740	8,303	7,655	11,187	14,679	20,535	32,057	47,613	78.691	138,882	216,355
Lewis.........	......	1,362	6,433	6,848	9,227	11,669	15,239	16,093	17,830	20,218	24,564	25,229
Livingston....	......	2,448	10,526	13,181	21,006	26,731	27,729	35,683	42.498	38,389	40,875	37,943
Madison......	......	8,036	25,141	26,276	32,208	35,646	39,038	41,741	40,008	40.987	43,072	43,687
Monroe........	......	1,192	4,683	11.178	27,288	39,108	49,855	58,085	64,902	70,899	87,650	96,324
Montgomery..	18,261	13,015	23,007	22,705	21,846	22,660	23,264	25,108	35.818	24,643	31,992	30,808
New York.....	33,131	60,489	96,373	95,519	123,706	166,086	197,112	268,089	312,710	371,223	515,547	629,810
Niagara........	......	......	1,465	1,276	7,322	14,069	18,482	26,490	31,132	34,550	42,276	48,282
Oneida.........	1,891	20,839	30,634	45,627	50,997	57,847	71,326	77,518	85,310	84,776	99,566	107,749
Onondaga.....	......	6,434	25,495	30,020	41,467	48,435	58,973	60,908	67,911	70,175	85,890	86,575
Ontario........	1,075	8,466	22,088	22,812	35,292	37,422	40,288	40,870	43,501	42.592	43,929	42,672
Orange........	22,809	29,368	34,347	34,908	41,213	41.732	45,366	45,096	50.739	52,227	57,145	60,868
Orleans........	......	......	1,164	1,524	5,349	14,460	17,732	22,893	25.127	25,845	28,501	28,435
Oswego........	......	348	3,889	5,382	12,364	17,875	27,119	38,245	43,619	48,441	62,198	69,398
Otsego.........	1,702	21,636	38,802	41,587	44,856	47,898	51,372	50,428	49,628	50,509	48,638	49,735
Putnam........	8,932	9,836	10,293	9,353	11.268	11,866	12,628	11,550	12.825	13,258	14,138	13,934
Queens........	16,014	16,893	19,336	19,269	21,519	20,331	22,460	25,130	30,324	31,849	36,833	46,266
Rensselaer....	22,428	30,442	36,309	36,833	40,153	44,065	49,424	55,515	60,259	62,338	73,363	79,234
Richmond....	3,835	4,563	5,347	5,502	6,135	5,932	7,082	7,691	10,965	13,673	15,061	21,389
Rockland.....	6,001	6,353	7,758	7,817	8,837	8,016	9,388	9,696	9,696	11,975	13,741	16,962	19,511
St. Lawrence.	......	454	7,885	8,252	16,037	27,595	36,354	42,047	56,706	62,354	68,617	74,977
Saratoga......	17,077	24,483	33,147	31,139	36,052	36,295	38,679	38,012	40.553	41,477	45,646	49,379
Schenectady..	5,698	8,888	10.205	11,203	13,081	12,876	12,347	16,230	17,387	16,630	20,054	19,572
Schoharie.....	2,073	9,808	18,945	19,323	23,154	25,926	27,902	28,508	32,358	32,488	33,548	33.519
Schuyler......	......	266	3,609	5,552	10,411	13,773	13,754	15,163	16,388	17,327	18,519	18,777
Seneca.........	......	4,057	11,306	13,935	17,773	20,169	21,041	22,627	24,874	24,972	25,441	25,358
Steuben.......	......	1,788	6,036	8,983	18,068	20,282	28,012	34,961	40,651	46,203	58,388	59,099
Suffolk........	16,440	19,464	21,113	21,368	24,272	23,695	26,780	28,274	32,469	34,579	36,922	41,066
Sullivan.......	1,763	3,222	6,108	6,233	8,900	10,373	12,364	13,751	15,629	18,727	25.088	29,487
Tioga..........	......	2,034	5,860	5,188	7,966	9,988	13,425	16,534	20,527	22,456	24,880	26,962
Tompkins......	......	927	5,153	9,816	22,167	27,951	31,333	32,345	32,296	32,264	32,694	31,516
Ulster..........	16,297	21,633	26,576	26,428	30,934	32,015	36,550	39,960	45,822	48,907	59,384	67,936
Warren........	1,080	4,825	7,565	7,838	9,453	10,906	11,796	12,034	13,422	14,908	17,199	19,669
Washington...	20,497	30,982	36,724	36,359	38,831	39,280	42,635	39,326	41,080	40,554	44,750	44,405
Wayne.........	......	1,410	6,575	11,220	20,309	26,761	33,643	37,788	42,057	42,515	44,953	46,760
Westchester...	24,003	27,347	30,272	26,367	32,638	33,131	36,456	38,789	48,686	47,394	58,263	80,678
Wyoming.....	......	......	2,736	5,411	16,149	22,307	29,047	32,771	34,245	30,691	31,981	32,148
Yates..........	......	1,702	4,867	5,434	18,025	15,313	19,009	19,796	20,444	20,777	20,590	19,812
Total.......	340,120	588,603	961,888	1,035,910	1,372,812	1,614,458	1,913,131	2,174,517	2,428,921	2,604,495	3,097,394	3,466,212

Abstract from the Census of the Indians residing on Reservations in 1855.

RESERVATIONS.	Where located.	Males.	Females.	Families.	Schools.	Children bet. 5 & 16.	Children at school.	Churches.	Christians.	Acres of improved land.	Cattle.	Oxen and Cows.	Horses.	Sheep.	Swine.
Allegany	Cattaraugus co..................	376	378	138	5	242	100	2	117	1,714	389	203	96	9	526
Cattaraugus a..	Cattaraugus, Erie, & Chautauqua cos...............	575	604	228	6	200	200	2	56	3,032½	729	389	197	91	1,054
Oneida b.......	Madison and Oneida cos......	88	73	21	2	52	80	1	31	354½	43	20	18	...	36
Onondaga b.....	Onondaga co.....................	173	176	57	1	73	50	1	38	2,063½	141	49	42	44	142
St. Regis c......	Franklin co.....................	206	207	87	2	132	34	1	...	1,425½	161	95	108	...	142
Shinnecock......	Suffolk co.....................	89	71	32	1	54	...	1	...	......	16	14	6	...	32
Tonawanda.....	Genesee, Erie, and Niagara cos.....................	290	312	106	2	153	...	1	40	2,515	261	144	97	...	409
Tuscarora........	Niagara co.....................	150	166	66	2	91	...	1	63	3,092	349	180	109	92	464
Total d........		1,947	1,987	735	21	997	464	10	350	13,867½	2,089	1,094	673	236	2,805

a The total number reported was. from neglect of the marshal, too small. In May, 1855, 1,388 were returned as entitled to share in annuities.
b The returns of civil condition are too indefinite to be relied on.
c The larger part of this village is in Canada.

d In the returns of the last State census 235 Indians (102 males and 133 females) not residing on reservations were enumerated and reported with the population of the towns in which they live. These, added to the numbers in the above table, make 2,049 males and 2,120 females, or a total of 4,169 Indians residing in the State in 1855.

Persons engaged in the various Professions, Trades, and Occupations

Counties.	Blacksmiths.	Boot and Shoe Makers.	Cabinet Makers and Dealers.	Carpenters and Joiners.	Clerks, Copyists, and Accountants.	Clergymen.	Coach and Wagon Makers and Wheel-wrights.	Coopers.	Dress Makers, Sewers, and Seamstresses.	Farmers.	Grocers.	Hotel and Inn Keepers.	Laborers.
Albany	561	869	214	1,202	1,148	87	244	204	767	5,728	498	122	4,216
Allegany	242	218	59	465	107	80	105	52	24	7,364	49	66	892
Broome	196	177	33	422	137	67	70	87	92	5,851	34	25	477
Cattaraugus	160	163	44	326	79	64	57	52	28	6,855	36	39	643
Cayuga	289	335	107	647	238	89	137	148	186	8,223	98	49	1,362
Chautauqua	290	298	115	691	202	104	166	121	176	9,249	50	85	1,200
Chemung	156	126	44	413	140	38	69	50	108	2,848	57	26	652
Chenango	206	200	52	353	62	86	104	103	51	7,457	32	48	442
Clinton	185	182	30	206	127	47	71	30	58	3,925	30	32	2,005
Columbia	221	252	49	490	204	67	113	33	158	5,260	49	60	2,021
Cortland	135	159	27	272	77	56	60	46	48	4,835	12	26	250
Delaware	183	183	38	377	64	72	67	48	58	7,448	16	39	571
Dutchess	292	351	147	703	209	88	155	90	252	5,591	30	52	2,608
Erie	764	1,050	227	2,023	1,085	167	289	311	385	10,182	370	108	5,367
Essex	159	105	19	223	72	31	54	32	28	3,782	17	21	918
Franklin	109	97	26	212	60	37	42	27	30	4,410	4	15	254
Fulton	111	117	24	297	61	24	44	43	36	2,899	11	21	1,156
Genesee	195	150	37	382	98	61	144	53	64	5,507	18	35	1,057
Greene	132	153	43	234	82	58	63	36	66	4,190	26	34	587
Hamilton	10	3	1	14	2	1	1	...	2	511	...	...	49
Herkimer	240	249	41	404	156	52	78	53	86	6,321	51	33	855
Jefferson	356	379	95	763	213	116	144	144	134	7,000	53	89	1,045
Kings	735	1,816	466	2,935	4,708	313	265	533	1,734	476	1,199	226	7,044
Lewis	84	102	29	218	54	35	46	59	44	4,975	5	27	564
Livingston	224	236	76	427	145	76	106	102	119	4,774	46	55	2,167
Madison	243	259	73	484	136	86	129	101	144	7,019	9	51	1,338
Monroe	618	878	183	1,381	668	141	277	519	418	7,957	265	93	4,901
Montgomery	165	168	27	352	103	37	67	34	111	3,131	106	50	1,722
New York	2,611	6,745	2,606	7,204	13,897	393	757	1,018	7,436	193	4,079	709	19,748
Niagara	230	235	50	441	272	61	77	125	87	5,505	104	63	2,592
Oneida	570	726	221	1,487	683	174	258	184	483	11,880	190	131	4,487
Onondaga	451	560	107	1,132	551	133	216	394	265	9,079	139	102	3,168
Ontario	268	243	48	410	163	103	112	101	82	6,333	53	34	1,259
Orange	340	299	69	667	298	102	198	78	298	5,455	78	85	2,695
Orleans	153	157	23	269	111	54	75	83	118	4,067	41	19	1,618
Oswego	303	338	97	768	308	112	101	698	147	8,667	110	53	1,976
Otsego	332	281	66	580	129	93	154	88	167	9,985	16	78	642
Putnam	92	133	9	230	37	25	18	19	36	1,957	7	4	539
Queens	189	285	37	679	198	53	104	21	132	3,598	67	46	2,316
Rensselaer	404	555	112	947	624	98	151	126	480	5,824	208	86	3,477
Richmond	80	86	34	386	134	31	19	16	8	574	54	68	728
Rockland	133	178	20	269	59	32	41	20	41	1,323	12	15	423
St. Lawrence	319	329	62	700	267	110	109	157	98	11,427	56	56	1,349
Saratoga	208	183	39	508	185	79	86	69	87	5,960	53	56	1,293
Schenectady	132	149	37	212	137	26	42	8	94	2,234	41	31	2,912
Schoharie	160	161	39	379	60	42	79	81	41	5,372	8	42	1,613
Schuyler	113	89	16	218	37	33	41	36	27	3,409	22	17	174
Seneca	125	133	26	289	89	42	74	114	72	3,033	47	31	608
Steuben	335	264	66	632	155	104	147	68	64	9,696	37	43	629
Suffolk	149	231	27	602	117	80	82	48	213	3,942	4	26	1,179
Sullivan	164	127	24	305	49	35	45	14	32	3,616	10	43	1,455
Tioga	139	146	25	318	91	43	62	60	35	4,145	27	20	692
Tompkins	172	169	53	387	97	52	107	62	82	5,038	22	35	502
Ulster	352	270	31	698	267	68	171	283	164	5,703	92	96	3,451
Warren	79	63	16	168	27	39	26	54	14	2,088	10	18	520
Washington	237	269	45	455	171	87	121	61	119	7,204	50	32	1,258
Wayne	226	265	65	561	192	83	126	156	146	7,494	66	43	1,172
Westchester	342	1,555	182	1,389	369	138	204	78	322	4,239	142	97	4,151
Wyoming	162	181	45	324	75	64	93	39	60	6,328	22	32	320
Yates	117	124	33	212	73	41	72	69	82	2,794	15	14	491
Total	16,948	24,804	6,656	40,731	30,359	4,810	7,135	7,539	16,939	321,930	9,056	3,755	115,800

Nativities of the Population of New York.

The following Table shows the nativities of the population of the State, as reported by the census of 1855:—

Where born.	Number.	Per cent.	Where born.	Number.	Per cent.
New York	2,222,321	64.077	Ohio	5,256	.151
Connecticut	63,691	1.863	Michigan	3,413	.098
Massachusetts	57,086	1.648	Illinois	1,255	.036
Vermont	54,266	1.565	Wisconsin	1,163	.033
New Hampshire	14,941	.431	Indiana	606	.017
Rhode Island	11,737	.339	Southern States	13,124	.378
Maine	5,818	.168	Other States	183	.005
New Jersey	40,391	1.164	Foreign Countries	922,019	26.585
Pennsylvania	31,472	.907	At sea and unknown	17,749	.512

in the several Counties, as reported by the State Census of 1855.

Lawyers.	Machinists.	Masons, Plasterers, and Bricklayers.	Merchants.	Millers.	Milliners.	Painters, Glaziers, and Varnishers.	Physicians.	Printers.	Railroad Employees.	Saddle, Harness, and Trunk Makers.	Stone and Marble Cutters.	Tailors.	Tanners and Curriers.	Teachers.	Teamsters.	Tinsmiths.	Weavers.
212	338	468	634	88	183	399	174	178	103	137	136	1,070	64	354	162	92	490
52	28	82	184	59	64	39	85	23	46	45	11	156	74	171	43	20	24
46	28	133	200	56	50	65	68	26	134	45	22	185	110	136	31	32	9
33	22	54	137	34	37	27	74	11	59	29	4	112	55	99	27	17	14
73	151	192	176	96	99	132	114	73	77	73	17	428	45	158	31	39	98
67	90	108	226	62	111	88	125	41	145	55	12	309	72	239	36	50	50
46	52	128	93	45	68	71	52	22	66	36	8	203	44	100	14	23	20
54	19	68	164	40	63	46	77	17	...	43	2	156	53	124	4	23	24
36	71	86	170	34	32	28	44	18	57	39	7	105	35	86	115	16	11
65	80	105	216	71	77	98	83	43	65	39	15	271	24	155	47	35	148
20	8	57	99	51	42	36	49	8	12	33	4	117	34	116	9	21	8
41	6	61	200	37	67	26	70	14	3	30	2	118	97	205	20	12	17
76	171	205	385	124	67	166	103	42	104	53	8	288	54	201	72	59	185
196	176	687	714	141	131	438	218	210	118	146	180	1,063	187	313	100	157	58
44	17	56	112	33	31	24	34	10	1	22	3	48	34	76	99	14	3
12	7	35	88	22	19	20	29	8	28	16	3	57	14	72	1	14	26
25	2	75	112	22	36	49	32	3	...	22	4	99	193	71	44	15	11
33	13	128	149	74	27	73	75	19	45	55	22	124	31	108	5	14	8
29	19	54	156	53	62	36	47	6	3	26	46	141	60	115	36	15	55
...	3	...	6	1	...	...	1	...	...	1	1	3	43	10	13	1	
33	52	99	123	53	61	52	62	20	23	51	32	152	111	125	23	26	47
68	84	173	329	139	153	104	125	28	56	86	27	414	109	210	40	50	39
354	556	1,628	2,649	37	411	1,150	336	676	102	163	543	2,481	122	290	147	340	69
11	3	54	74	25	32	37	42	...	...	28	11	88	8	89	9	12	5
64	56	97	137	86	44	67	73	15	16	60	13	150	18	128	20	16	10
43	61	105	175	60	84	97	88	22	13	67	15	301	41	189	38	32	79
140	401	565	394	234	183	358	197	109	248	109	70	858	88	281	149	100	43
44	15	78	162	60	44	42	47	14	23	35	61	139	24	99	39	14	28
1,112	1,714	3,634	6,001	130	1,585	3,400	1,252	1,901	523	884	1,755	12,609	228	1,268	160	897	589
41	41	250	165	75	58	99	75	17	32	50	67	207	20	113	27	39	12
147	225	412	480	116	190	290	200	115	136	117	97	988	146	334	118	103	121
118	122	365	342	142	123	275	131	68	146	126	92	488	42	250	76	53	53
49	56	137	164	101	51	95	102	23	67	55	6	183	5	108	40	32	11
59	87	239	308	92	99	109	89	37	225	64	42	357	47	191	118	61	77
32	9	76	99	66	59	61	60	21	12	32	12	104	20	94	9	19	5
74	92	231	241	171	84	125	113	38	14	65	25	281	75	246	87	33	24
52	32	94	197	68	100	82	89	26	1	78	7	263	38	172	23	23	17
13	84	34	68	26	18	25	12	1	12	9	18	54	2	44	21	12	
36	76	174	187	45	25	105	49	17	12	40	16	157	2	125	2	78	86
99	301	330	529	77	108	226	121	46	424	90	55	512	98	232	210	70	18
35	7	137	217	12	3	81	17	35	2	9	18	79	11	36	8	20	2
12	72	62	67	14	18	40	23	7	87	25	9	88	5	36	...	25	11
86	40	120	245	79	91	82	61	23	87	67	10	216	54	243	17	39	19
54	105	89	218	45	68	90	101	37	62	30	19	150	29	141	28	21	74
30	189	63	120	8	52	51	37	11	96	15	4	216	12	56	16	7	12
39	13	81	138	61	53	33	68	10	2	32	2	147	28	159	9	18	12
18	12	48	69	42	39	33	46	10	2	26	...	107	32	95	21	3	12
33	97	67	107	58	54	55	49	6	14	26	18	124	16	77	17	19	47
51	80	154	230	79	65	74	75	27	97	55	11	152	58	117	32	28	9
24	5	95	268	41	51	75	48	23	28	24	8	234	7	133	8	27	17
15	1	55	102	24	33	15	36	7	13	17	4	91	120	82	42	13	3
16	25	60	88	40	28	31	49	10	64	23	5	106	33	94	4	19	2
23	46	78	128	81	57	85	61	15	43	38	8	148	26	124	17	7	17
56	27	186	315	102	73	95	76	30	3	47	96	326	163	154	133	35	24
12	6	33	59	15	16	20	32	4	29	15	10	52	90	52	11	5	
62	36	97	202	49	99	86	76	16	30	61	34	214	36	148	62	31	23
43	44	161	186	67	103	83	116	14	39	85	21	257	45	203	17	49	7
127	113	525	631	54	102	304	114	62	121	58	314	437	30	303	108	87	241
36	14	72	147	55	42	53	69	13	28	56	9	127	34	114	4	20	8
21	9	41	82	45	37	35	39	13	8	32	5	126	20	95	6	8	9
4,542	6,309	13,781	20,664	3,917	5,862	10,081	6,010	4,339	4,006	3,895	4,076	29,236	3,416	9,959	2,825	3,160	3,141

The total number of persons reported in 1855 as engaged in pursuits other than the foregoing was as follows:—

Actors.................... 325	Barkeepers................. 987	Booksellers and Stationers 544	Calico Printers............. 28
Agents.................... 2,340	Basket Makers............. 783	Bottlers...................... 14	Calkers.................... 659
Agri. Implement Makers 386	Bell Founders............. 8	Box Makers................. 379	Card Makers............... 47
Apothecaries and Druggists 1,438	Bellhangers and Locksmiths...................... 659	Brass Workers............. 756	Carpet Makers and Dealers...................... 330
Apprentices 1,421	Bellows Makers............ 24	Brewers and Distillers.... 1,176	Carters and Draymen.... 7,350
Architects 261	Billiard Makers.......... 5	Brickmakers................ 1,627	Carvers and Gilders..... 1,125
Artificial Flower Makers 237	Bill Posters.............. 7	Bridge and Dock Builders 142	Case Makers............... 32
Artists and Designers..... 751	Bird Cage Makers........ 7	Britannia Ware Makers.. 13	Cattle Dealers............. 13
Auctioneers................. 220	Blacking Makers.......... 32	Brokers................... 1,233	Cement Makers............. 264
Authors..................... 58	Block Makers............. 391	Broom Makers............. 183	Chandlers and Soap Makers.................... 622
Ax Makers................. 283	Boarding House Keepers 1,680	Brushmakers................ 622	Charcoal Burners and Dealers.................... 556
Bakers..................... 5,136	Boat Builders............. 693	Builders................... 1,081	Chemists.................... 183
Bankers................. 432	Boatmen and Watermen. 9,136	Butchers................. 6,308	Chimney Sweeps.......... 12
Bank Officers.............. 539	Boiler Makers............ 708	Button Makers............ 61	
Barbers..................... 2,142	Bookbinders................ 2,121	Cadets 201	

Professions and Occupations, concluded:—

Chronometer Makers.....	4	Grindstone and Millstone Makers..............	23
Civil Engineers...........	249	Gunsmiths...............	496
Civil Officers..............	1,427	Gutta Percha Manufacturers............	3
Clock Makers and Repairers................	164	Hair Cloth Makers........	17
Clothiers..................	1,084	Hair Workers.............	89
Cloth Manufacturers not specified................	123	Hame Makers.............	69
Coal Dealers..............	138	Hardware Dealers........	426
Coffee, Spice, and Mustard Makers.........	25	Hat and Cap Makers.....	2,928
Collectors.................	222	Hemp Dressers...........	11
Comb Makers..............	229	Horse Dealers............	102
Confectioners..............	1,088	Hose Makers.............	6
Contractors................	699	Hosiers..................	28
Cooks.....................	1,424	Hunters..................	59
Coopers...................	7,539	Ice Dealers..............	152
Coppersmiths.............	409	Importers................	409
Cork Cutters..............	45	India Rubber Manufacturers............	73
Cotton Manufacturers....	75	Ink Makers...............	61
Custom House Officers....	346	Inspectors................	295
Cutlers...................	249	Instrument Makers.......	172
Dairymen and Milk Dealers.................	1,050	Insurance Officers........	319
Dealers not otherwise specified..............	1,668	Intelligence Officers.....	3
Dentists..................	761	Inventors and Patentees..	30
Dock Keepers.............	54	Iron Mongers............	44
Drivers, Coachmen, &c...	3,253	Iron Workers.............	990
Drovers...................	362	Ivory Black Makers......	17
Dyers and Bleachers.....	470	Ivory Workers............	5
Editors...................	384	Japanners................	73
Electrotypists............	11	Jewelers..................	2,055
Embroiderers.............	218	Junkshop Keepers........	321
Enamelers.................	3	Keepers and Wardens of Prisons, &c..........	284
Engineers.................	3,180	Lace Makers.............	61
Engravers.................	761	Lampblack Makers........	6
Envelope Makers.........	29	Lamplighters.............	18
Expressmen...............	422	Lamp Makers............	51
Factory Operatives........	2,477	Lapidaries...............	17
Farriers..................	150	Last Makers.............	98
Feather Dressers..........	8	Lath Makers.............	11
Ferrymen.................	6	Laundresses..............	3,557
File Cutters..............	358	Lecturers................	35
Fire Engine Makers......	6	Librarians................	5
Firemen..................	416	Lighthouse Keepers......	30
Fish Dealers..............	165	Lime Burners............	129
Fishermen................	965	Linguists................	10
Fishing Tackle Makers...	14	Lithographers............	176
Flax Dressers and Workers....................	66	Livery Stable Keepers....	741
Fortune Tellers and Astrologists................	4	Looking Glass Makers....	53
Forwarders...............	274	Lumbermen and Dealers.	2,933
Frame Makers............	164	Mail Agents and Carriers.	231
Fringe, Tassel, and Gimp Makers.................	155	Manufacturers (not specified)................	1,448
Fruit Dealers.............	322	Map Makers..............	11
Furnacemen..............	1,807	Marble Dealers...........	66
Furriers..................	227	Market Men and Women..	295
Gamblers.................	7	Mat and Rug Makers.....	83
Gardeners and Florists...	3,269	Match Makers............	223
Gas Fitters and Fixture Makers.................	527	Matrons of Asylums, &c .	37
Gas Makers...............	132	Mechanics (not otherwise specified)..........	3,837
Gas Meter Makers........	8	Midwives................	47
Gatekeepers..............	499	Military Equipment Makers...................	5
Geologists and Mineralogists...................	5	Millwrights..............	1,262
Glass Cutters.............	80	Mineral Water Makers...	117
Glass Makers.............	466	Miners...................	415
Glass Stainers............	52	Model Makers............	8
Glovers..................	106	Modelers................	1
Glue Makers..............	37	Morocco Dressers.........	250
Goldbeaters..............	134	Moulders................	3,114
Gold and Silver Smiths..	820	Mould Makers...........	42
Grate Makers and Setters.....................	98	Musical Instr. Manufac..	130
		Music Dealers............	37
		Musicians...............	1,177
		Music Teachers..........	621
		Nail Makers..............	433

Naturalists...............	10	Sandpaper Makers........	3
Needle Makers...........	1	Sash and Blind Makers..	1,004
Newsboys................	197	Saw Filers...............	45
Nurserymen..............	240	Saw Makers..............	228
Nurses...................	968	Sawyers.................	3,724
Oculists..................	17	Scale Makers............	69
Oilcloth Makers..........	133	Scavengers..............	41
Oil Makers...............	124	Screw Makers...........	8
Opticians................	63	Sculptors................	86
Organ Builders...........	81	Sealing Wax Makers.....	1
Ostlers..................	948	Servants.................	58,441
Overseers and Superintendents...............	475	Sextons..................	147
Oyster Men and Dealers..	458	Shingle Makers..........	217
Packers..................	112	Ship Carpenters, Mast and Spar Makers......	3,632
Paint and Color Makers..	21	Shirt and Collar Makers	434
Paper Dealers............	20	Shoe Peg Makers.........	7
Paper Hangers...........	196	Shot Makers.............	9
Paper Makers............	914	Showmen................	15
Paper Stainers..........	87	Silk Workers.............	81
Patent Leather Makers...	10	Soldiers and Military Officers.................	709
Patent Medicine Makers..	59	Speculators..............	487
Pattern Makers..........	427	Spinners................	463
Pavers...................	341	Spring Makers...........	26
Pawnbrokers.............	20	Stage Proprietors........	174
Pearl Workers...........	4	Starch Makers...........	40
Peddlers.................	4,131	Stave Makers............	20
Pen Makers..............	61	Steel Makers.............	9
Pencil Makers............	49	Stereotypers.............	47
Perfumers...............	35	Stevedores...............	280
Photographers and Daguerreotypists.........	389	Stewards.................	281
Piano Makers............	1,076	Storekeepers.............	1,120
Pickle and Preserve Makers...................	11	Stove Makers............	160
Pilots...................	387	Straw Workers..........	131
Pin Makers..............	5	Students.................	4,184
Pipe Makers.............	26	Sugar Refiners..........	144
Plaster Figure Makers...	41	Surgeons................	48
Plate Printers...........	31	Surgical Instr. Makers...	38
Platers..................	269	Surveyors................	382
Plumbers................	958	Telegraph Operators.....	258
Pocket Book Makers......	212	Tobacconists.............	3,744
Policemen................	1,513	Tool Makers.............	404
Polishers and Burnishers	578	Toy and Fancy Dealers and Makers............	164
Porcelain Makers.........	12	Traders..................	115
Porters..................	3,916	Trimmers................	308
Portfolio Makers.........	6	Turners..................	909
Portrait Painters.........	37	Turpentine Makers.......	5
Postmasters..............	184	Type Cutters............	21
Pot and Pearl Ash Makers...................	36	Type Founders..........	155
Potters..................	287	Umbrella Makers.........	374
Powder Makers...........	27	Undertakers..............	213
Produce Dealers..........	526	Upholsterers.............	1,106
Professors................	188	Varnish Makers..........	267
Publishers...............	160	Victualers...............	57
Pump Makers............	40	Vinegar Makers..........	25
Pursers..................	10	Watchmakers and Repairers.................	813
Pyrotechnists............	22	Watchmen...............	412
Quarrymen..............	1,031	Wax Bleachers..........	2
Ragpickers...............	250	Whalebone Workers......	122
Razor Strop Makers......	5	Whip Makers............	51
Reed Makers.............	16	White Lead Makers......	46
Refiners and Assayers...	91	Whitewashers...........	262
Reporters................	59	Window Shade Makers...	31
Restaurant Keepers......	288	Wine and Liquor Dealers	749
Riggers..................	469	Wire Drawers...........	15
Roofers and Slaters......	175	Wire Workers...........	91
Rope and Cord Makers...	663	Wood Cutters...........	240
Runners.................	150	Wood Dealers...........	75
Safe Makers.............	88	Wooden Ware Makers...	41
Sailmakers...............	563	Wool Carders and Combers...................	282
Sailors and Mariners....	9,720	Wool Dealers............	49
Saleratus Makers........	15	Woolen and Worsted Workers................	147
Salesmen................	723		
Saloon Keepers..........	871		
Salt Makers..............	602		

ALBANY COUNTY.

THIS was an original county; formed Nov. 1, 1683, and confirmed Oct. 1, 1691.[1]

Tryon and Charlotte (now Montgomery and Washington) counties were taken off in 1772, Columbia in 1786, Rensselaer and Saratoga in 1791, a part of Schoharie in 1795, a part of Greene in 1800, and Schenectady in 1809. The Manor of Rensselaerwyck was erected into a district March 24, 1772, and subdivided into east and west districts soon after the Revolution. The county lies on the west bank of Hudson River, about 150 miles from its mouth, and contains an area of 544 square miles. Its surface is undulating and hilly, and it has a general inclination toward the southeast. A narrow intervale extends along the course of the river, bounded by a series of steep bluffs from 100 to 180 feet high, from the summits of which an undulating and slightly ascending plateau stretches westward to the foot of the Helderbergh[2] Hills, where it reaches an elevation of about 400 feet above tide. This range of hills rises from 400 to 800 feet above the plateau, and 800 to 1200 feet above tide. Their declivities are very steep, and sometimes precipitous, on the east, but more gradually sloping upon the west. Several other ranges of hills, inferior to them in height, extend in a general northerly and southerly direction through portions of the county. The highest point is the summit of the Helderberghs, in the northeast corner of the town of Bern, and is 1200 feet above tide. All these ranges of highlands may be considered as outlying spurs of the Catskills, which, in turn, are but a northerly continuation of the Allegany Mountains, and a part of the great Appalachian system.

The geological formations of this county belong to the Upper Silurian system, and comprise nearly all the rocks of the "New York System," from the Utica slate to the corniferous limestone. Above the rocks, in the eastern part of the county, are thick deposits of drift, consisting of sand, gravel, and clay; and along the river intervales are rich alluvial deposits. The lowest rock, cropping out on the Hudson, Normans Kil, and Mohawk, is the Utica slate. Next above is the graywacke and shales of the Hudson River group, appearing in the valleys of all the streams that flow into the Hudson, and apparently underlying the entire eastern part of the county. This stone is quarried for building stone and flagging.[3] The red rocks that form the base of the Helderberghs evidently belong to the Medina sandstone series, though they have sometimes been confounded with the red shales of the Onondaga salt group. Next above, forming the first terrace of the mountains, is the water-lime group, from 50 to 200 feet in thickness, furnishing both water and quick-lime. Next in order is the pentamerus limestone, 50 feet in thickness, consisting of impure gray and black limestone mixed with slate and shale. Overlying this is the Catskill limestone, from 50 to 180 feet in thickness, consisting of thick, compact masses of limestone alternating with thin layers of shale. It is used for building stone and lime. The Oriskany sandstone is next developed, in a strata only 2 feet in thickness, followed by the cauda-galli grit, from 50 to 60 feet in thickness. This last has a fine grit, and resembles black or gray slates, but is easily disintegrated, and crumbles upon exposure to the air. Next in order come the Onondaga and corniferous limestones, the latter crowning the summits of the mountains. These rocks furnish both a superior quality of lime and an excellent building stone. The surface of the eastern part of the county is covered with immense beds of clay, gravel, and sand. The highlands west of Albany City are covered 40 feet deep with sand, which rests upon a bed of clay estimated to be 100 feet deep. In this drift are found small beds of bog ore and numerous chalybeate and sulphuretted springs. In the limestone regions are numerous caves, sink holes, and subterranean water courses, forming a peculiar and interesting feature of the county.

The principal streams are,—the Hudson River, which forms the eastern boundary; the Mohawk, which forms a part of the northern boundary; the Patroon Creek, Normans Kil, Vlomans, Coey-

---

[1] The county by these acts embraced "the Manor of Rensselaerwyck, Schenectady, and all the villages, neighborhoods, and Christian plantations on the east side of Hudson's River, from Roeloffe Jansen's Creek; and on the west side, from Sawyer's Creek to the outermost end of Saraghtoga." The Manor of Livingston was annexed to Dutchess co. May 27, 1717, and by subsequent statutes the county of Albany was also made to comprise every thing within the colony of New York north and west of present limits, and at one time the whole of Vermont.

[2] Signifying "Clear Mountain," from the fine prospect from their summit.

[3] Several of the intermediate series of rocks, including the gray sandstone, Clinton, Niagara Falls, and Onondaga salt groups, are not found in the county.

mans, Haanakrois, and Catskill Creeks, and their branches. Nearly all the streams that flow into the Hudson have worn deep gulleys in the sand and clay. Many of these gorges are 100 feet deep, and extend from one-fourth of a mile to one mile from the river. The streams farther west generally flow through narrow, rocky ravines bordered by steep banks. These streams are mostly very rapid, and subject to extremes of flood and drouth. There are several small lakes among the hills, but none of special importance.

The soil upon the intervales is a deep, rich alluvial loam. In Watervliet, Albany, and the eastern parts of Guilderland and Bethlehem, it consists of almost pure sand, with strips of clay along the banks of the streams. A belt of land lying between the sandy region and the foot of the Helderberghs is principally a clayey and gravelly loam, and very productive. Upon the Helderberghs the soil consists of alternate layers of clay, slate, and gravel, generally with a subsoil of tenacious clay called "hard-pan." Patches in this region are also stony, and much of it is wet and cold, and only moderately productive. Pitch pine, oak, and chestnut are the principal kinds of timber that grow upon the sandy region. In the most barren parts these trees are mere dwarfs, and the region has much the appearance of a desert. In the southeast corner of the county is a limited amount of red cedar. West of the sandy tract are found the usual trees of this northern climate, including both the deciduous and evergreen.[1]

In the farming districts the people are principally engaged in raising spring grains, dairying, the raising of stock, and in gardening for the markets of Troy and Albany. The people of Albany, West Troy, and Cohoes are principally engaged in manufactures and commerce.

The city of Albany is the county seat and State capital. The county buildings are commodious, and the county institutions are well organized. The City Hall[2] at Albany, erected at the joint expense of the city and county, contains the principal city and county offices. The Albany County Penitentiary[3] is a fine building in the western part of the city. Persons convicted of certain crimes, and sentenced to short terms of imprisonment, are confined here; and prisoners are received from Dutchess, Columbia, Rensselaer, Washington, Saratoga, and Schenectady counties. The county has no poor-house, but contracts with the city for the support of its paupers.

Albany is 145 miles above New York, upon the Hudson. The tide rises about one foot in the river.[4] In low water, navigation is obstructed, except for vessels of light draught, by the "overslaugh," or bar, near Castleton, and at other points; and considerable sums have been expended in attempting to deepen the channel, by dredging, and building a long stone dike below Albany.[5] The most important works of internal improvement in the county are,—the Erie Canal,[6] the New York Central, and the Albany, Vermont, and Canada Railroads, all terminating in the city of Albany. Connected with these lines, and terminating at Greenbush, directly opposite Albany, are the Hudson River, Albany and West Stockbridge,[7] Harlem, and Troy and Greenbush Railroads. A company has been chartered to build a R. R. from Albany in a s. w. direction to Binghamton, and the work upon it is now in progress. A pier has been built in the river in front of Albany, for the benefit of navigation.[8]

Hendrick Hudson is supposed to have ascended the river as far as Albany in 1609. During the next three or four years, several Dutch traders commenced a traffic with the Indians, and small trading houses were built at Manhattan and Albany. In after years these stations were fortified, the one to protect from invasion by sea, and the other against incursions from the French settlements in Canada. The principal military work at Albany (built in 1623) was known as Fort Orange. The station at Albany remained a mere trading post until 1630, when agricultural improvements began. The Dutch West India Co. was formed in 1621, for promoting settlement in "New Netherlands," as the Dutch possessions in America were then called. In 1629, this company granted to Killian Van Rensselaer, one of the commissioners, (a pearl merchant of Amsterdam,) a charter conferring upon him privileges similar to those enjoyed by the feudal barons of Europe. His

---

[1] A geological and agricultural survey of Albany co. was made, in 1820, by Dr. T. Romeyn Beck, for the Co. Ag. Soc., and was the first enterprise of the kind in the state.—*Mem. Bd. Ag.*, i. 367.

[2] See page 160.

[3] This penitentiary was built in 1845–46, and opened for prisoners in April, 1846. It was organized under the direction of Amos Pilsbury, in 1848, and has since continued under his direction and that of his son, Louis D. Pilsbury. It has 300 cells, and the average number in confinement has been 220. The convicts are principally employed in the manufacture of cane-seat chairs and saddlery hardware. During the first 8 years the total receipts were $115,082, and the total expenditures $104,680.

[4] The tide rises here 6 h. 34 m. behind time of the moon's southing.

[5] *Senate Doc.* 40, 1857, *p.* 171.

[6] The Erie Canal terminates in a basin at Albany, and communicates with the Hudson at West Troy. It crosses the Mohawk River, above Cohoes Falls, upon a stone aqueduct. A company has been incorp. for building a ship-canal from Albany to New Baltimore, a point below the bars which obstruct navigation.

[7] Leased by the Western (Mass.) R. R. Co.

[8] The pier is built across a curve in the west shore, and opens into the river at both ends. It is divided for the accommodation of the railroad ferries, and is 1¼ miles long. It was formerly closed by locks. The basin inclosed within the pier affords a secure harbor, during winter, for river vessels and canal boats, which otherwise would be exposed to destruction from ice. The pier is owned by an incorporated company.

agents[1] made large purchases of land lying on both sides of the Hudson, near Albany,[2] in 1630–37, at which last date the manor embraced a territory 24 mi. N. and S. and 48 mi. E. and W., including nearly all of the present counties of Albany and Rensselaer.[3] By the terms of the grant the charter would be forfeited unless the lands were settled in 7 years by at least 50 persons over 15 years of age. A ship load of emigrants was forwarded in 1630, and others in each of several succeeding years. The emigrants were furnished with stock, seeds, and farming implements, and the land was leased at an annual rent, payable in grain, beeves, and wampum, or a share of the products.[4] The proprietor received the title of Patroon, and in him was vested authority in civil and military affairs subordinate only to the West India Co. and the States General. He had his forts, soldiers, cannon, and courts of justice; and, although the laws allowed an appeal from the decisions of the local courts, he required every person who settled within his jurisdiction to pledge himself never to exercise this right. Altercations soon arose between the agents of the patroon and the officers of the garrison at Fort Orange, in regard to the land immediately around the fort; and the controversy was not settled until after the English conquest.[5] The settlement formed under Van Rensselaer gradually acquired importance as a trading post, and a considerable hamlet was built under the guns of Fort Orange.[6] Mills were built on several of the streams, and a church was erected. By the surrender of the colony to the English, in 1664, the personal rights of the colonists were secured, and a new charter was granted to the patroon, restricting his civil power, but confirming the relations existing between landlord and tenant.[7] The feudal tenure was finally abolished in 1787.[8]

The leasehold tenures, from an early period, excited discontent among the tenants.[9] The late patroon, by his indulgence, had secured their regard; and when he died, in 1839, the course that would be pursued by his successor became a matter of solicitude. A committee of respectable men, appointed by the tenants to wait upon him and confer upon subjects of mutual interest, were treated with marked coldness and disdain, which quickly led to the organization of armed resistance to the enforcement of civil processes in the collection of rent. In Dec. 1839, the excitement was so great in the W. part of the county, that the Governor issued a proclamation, and sent an armed force to assist the civil officers. The people finally dispersed, and no collision ensued. For many years the anti-rent question greatly excited the public mind in all sections of the State where the leasehold tenure prevailed.[10] Within a few years, much of the land has been conveyed in fee to the lessees; and probably in a few years the whole question will be amicably arranged in this manner.[11] There are 17 newspapers and periodicals now published in the county.[12]

---

[1] Janson Krol and Derick Cornelissen Duyster, commissary and under commissary at Fort Orange.

[2] The tract first purchased, W. of the Hudson, extended from Beeren (Bear) Island—called by the Indians "Passapenock"—up to Sneackx Island, and "of a breadth of two days' journey."

[3] On the 1st of Oct. 1630, a copartnership was formed between Van Rensselaer on the one part, and Saml. Godyn, Johannes de Laet, Saml. Bloemmaert, Adam Bissels, and Toussaint Moussart on the other, by which the latter were constituted co-directors of Rensselaerwyck, and were bound to do homage and fealty to the lord of the manor.

[4] The patroon reserved the right to trade with the Indians. For several years this trade was carried on by the settlers, who received goods from the patroon's store, and sent the peltries which they received to be sold by him in Holland. This business afterwards fell into the hands of local traders.

[5] So active did this controversy become, that at one time Gov. Stuyvesant sent an armed force to Albany to support the rights of the company against the proprietor.

[6] This place soon became the seat for holding all great councils with the Indian tribes. Among the curious things mentioned in the annals of the "old colonie" is the fact that, during an almost unprecedented freshet in the spring of 1646, a whale 40 feet long came up the river and stranded on an island near the mouth of the Mohawk. Four others stranded the same season, 40 Dutch mi. above New Amsterdam.

[7] For a concise view of the changes made by this charter, see *Barnard's Hist. Sketch of Rensselaerwyck*, p. 107.

[8] The manorial title has descended as follows:—

KILLIAN VAN RENSSELAER, first Patroon, died in 1647, at Amsterdam, leaving the property with his two sons.

JOHANNES and JEREMIAH. Each of these had a son named KILLIAN, the former of whom died without issue in 1687, leaving the title with

KILLIAN, son of JEREMIAH. Dongan's patent was confirmed to the two cousins Nov. 5, 1685, and all other claimants released to the survivor in 1695; to whom also Queen Anne's patent of confirmation was granted May 20, 1704. He willed the property to his son,

JEREMIAH, and to the male heirs of his body; but, dying without issue, the title passed to his younger brother,

STEPHEN, who had a son (sole heir under the will above mentioned,) named

STEPHEN, who died in 1769, leaving the title with

STEPHEN, the late patroon, who was born in 1764, and died in 1839. The entail ended with this person, who, in his will, gave the W. part of the manor to his son, STEPHEN, the present proprietor, and the E. part to his son, WILLIAM P., of New York.

[9] The "Quarter Sales," as they were technically called, in which the landlord claimed a part of the purchase money at each transfer of a lease, was particularly obnoxious. In 1850 the Quarter Sales were declared unconstitutional by the Supreme Court.

[10] This movement led to the adoption of Art. 1, Sec. 14, in the constitution of 1846, prohibiting the lease of agricultural lands for a longer period than 12 years.

[11] The relative amount of the land held by lease and in fee in the county is now nearly as follows:—In Watervliet, nearly all held in fee; in Guilderland, three-fourths; in Bethlehem, Coeymans, and New Scotland, two-thirds; in Knox, Rensselaerville, and Westerlo, half; and in Bern, one-third,—the remainder being held by lease.

[12] The following list is imperfect, but is supposed to include all the more important newspapers ever published in the Co. We are indebted to Joel Munsell, printer, for assistance, and the use of his immense collection of specimen numbers, in the preparation of this class of statistics.

The Albany Gazette was first issued in Nov. 1771, by Alex. and James Robertson, who joined the loyalists in N. Y. in 1776.

The New York Gazetteer or Northern Intelligencer, in 1782, by Solomon Balantine and Charles R. Webster. In 1784 the name was changed to

The Albany Gazette, and in 1788 a semi-weekly edition was issued. In March, 1817, united with the Albany Daily Advertiser, and took the name of

The Albany Gazette and Daily Advertiser, continued until 1845.

The Albany Journal, or Montgomery, Washington, and Columbia Intelligencer, semi-w. in winter and w. in summer was started in Jan. 1788, by Chas. R. & Geo. Webster, and published in connection with the Gazette.

The Albany Daily Advertiser, Sept. 1815, by Theodore Dwight.

In 1817 W. L. Stone united it with the Albany Gazette.

The *Albany Register* was published by John Barber from 1788 till 1808, and by S. Southwick till 1817.

The *Federal Herald*, by Claxton & Babcock, brought from Lansingb'gh in Feb. 1788, and again returned :hither.

The *Albany Centinel*, semi-w., 1796. In Nov. 1806 changed to

The *Republican Crisis*. Backus & Whiting and Isaac Mitchell were successively publishers.

The *Albany Chronicle* was commenced in 1797 by John McDonald. Joseph Foy and Henry C. Southwick were afterward its editors. It was discontinued in 1799.

The *Guardian*, 1807. Van Benthuysen & Wood, 2 years.

The *Balance*, and *New York State Journal*, semi-w., 1808–11, Croswell & Frary; removed from Hudson.

The *Albany Republican* was started in April, 1812, by Samuel R. Brown.—Romaine succeeded the next year, and after several years it was merged in the Saratoga Patriot.

The *Stranger*, 1813–14, 8vo. John Cook, pub.

The *Albany Argus* was established as a semi-w., tri-w., and w., Jan. 1, 1813, by Jesse Buel; and d., semi-w., and w. editions were issued in Oct. 1825. Edwin Croswell was many years its publisher. Feb. 15, 1856, merged in

The *Atlas and Argus*, da., semi-w., and w. Comstock & Cassidy, pub.

The *Albany Atlas*, da., semi-w., and w., was started in 1841 by Vance & Wendell; in 1856 it was united with the Argus.

The *Christian Visitant*, 4to, was begun June 3, 1815, by S. Southwick, and continued 2 years.

The *Friend*, 8vo, mo., was begun in 1815 by D. & S. A. Abbey. 1 vol. published.

The *Statesman*, pub. by — Carter; removed to N.Y. in 1818.

The *Plough Boy* was started 1819, by Solomon Southwick, under the *nom de plume* of Henry Homespun.

The *Albany Microscope*, 1820, by Chas. Galpin, continued till 1842.

The *National Democrat*, published at Albany and N.Y., was started in 1823 by Wm. McDonald, and continued 1 year.

The *Religious Monitor*, mo., was commenced in May, 1824, by Chauncey Webster. It is now published in Philadelphia.

The *Escritoire, or Masonic and Miscellaneous Album*, was started in 1826 by E. B. Child. Its name was changed to

The *American Masonic Record*, and was pub. by E. B. Child for 4 or 5 yrs.

The *American Masonic Register* was pub. 5 y. by L. G. Hoffman.

The *National Observer*, w. and semi-w., was started in 1826 by Geo. Galpin, and continued 4 years: S. Southwick, ed.

The *Albany Telegraph and Christian Register* was started in 1826, and in 1827

The *Albany Christian Register*, L. G. Hoffman, pub., and J. R. Boyd, ed., May 19, 1827.

The *Albany Daily Chronicle* was started April 22, 1826, and published a short time by Galpin & Cole.

The *Comet* was begun Aug. 4, 1827. D. McGlashan, ed.

The *Standard* was published in 1827 by Matthew Cole.

Signs of the Times was started Oct. 13, 1827, and discontinued Nov. 8, 1828. D. McGlashan, pub., S. De W. Bloodgood, ed.

The *Antidote* was pub. in 1827. Webster & Wood, pub., S. Southwick, ed.

The *Morning Chronicle*, da., and *The Albany Chronicle*, semi-w., were published in 1828 by Beach, Denio, & Richard.

The *Age* was published in 1828 by Galpin & Sturtevant.

The *Albany Times and Literary Writer* was started Dec. 27, 1828, by Jas. McGlashan; Bloodgood & Van Schaick, eds.

The *Albanian*, semi-mo., was started Jan. 30, 1828, by Arthur N. Sherman.

The *Albany Minerva* was published in 1828 by J. Munsell.

The Albany Evening Journal was commenced March, 1830. It was published by B. D. Packard & Co., Thurlow Weed, ed. A w. and a semi-w. journal are now issued from this office by Weed, Dawson & Co.

The *Farmers, Mechanics, and Working Men's Advocate*, da., was started in 1830 by McPherson & McKercher. The following year it appeared as

The *Daily Freeman's Advocate, and Farmers, Mechanics, and Working Men's Champion*, and was pub. 1 or 2 yrs.

The *Albany Bee*, da., was started in April, 1830, by J. Duffey, W. S. McCulloch, and Charles Angus.

The *Temperance Recorder*, mo., was published in 1831 by the State Temperance Society.

The *Albany Quarterly*, 8vo. Commenced in 1832 by the Alb. Hist. Soc. Jas. R. and Sam'l. M. Wilson, eds. 1 vol. pub.

The *Daily Craftsman* was removed from Rochester in 1831. E. J. Roberts & Henry James, publishers.

American Temperance Intelligencer, mo., was started in Jan. 1834.

The *Silkworm*, 8vo, mo., begun May, 1835. The 3d vol. was changed to

The *Silk Worm and Sugar Manual*, devoted in part to sugar beet culture. It was discontinued in 1838.

The *American Quarterly Hemp Magazine* was commenced Feb. 1833. 2 vols. published.

The *Albany Transcript*, da., the first penny paper in Albany, was started Oct. 12, 1835.

The *Albany Bouquet and Literary Spectator*, mo., was published in 1835 by Geo. Trumbull.

The *Albany Whig* was commenced in 1834, by J. B. Van Schaick & Co., as the weekly of *The Daily Advertiser*. It was soon merged in *The Albany Gazette*, a semi-w. paper issued from the same office.

The *Common School Assistant*, mo., was published in 1836 by J. Orville Taylor.

The *Associate Presbyterian Magazine*, 8vo, mo., Rev. P. Bullions, ed. Pub. from 1838 to 1842.

Southwick's Family Newspaper was published in 1838.

The *Jeffersonian* was published by Horace Greeley during the campaign of 1838.

The Cultivator, mo., was commenced in March, 1839, by Jesse Buel. It was afterward published by W. Gaylord and L. Tucker, and now by L. Tucker & Son.

The *Tomahawk and Scalping Knife* was published a short time.

The *Albany Patriot* was started in 1840 by Jas. C. Jackson, and continued 4 years.

The *Unionist*, da., was published by J. Munsell, and

The *Rough Hewer* by Theo. M. Burt, during the campaign of 1840.

The *District School Journal*, mo., was established at Geneva in 1840, Francis Dwight, ed. Removed to Albany in 1841, and continued by the State School Dep. until 1852.

The *Examiner* was published in 1841 by G. Galpin.

The *American Magazine*, 8vo, mo., started in 1841 by J. S. & B. Wood. 3 vols. pub.

The *Irishman* was published seven weeks in 1842 by H. O'Kane, J. Munsell, printer.

The *New York State Mechanic* was started in 1842 by J. Munsell, and continued eighteen months.

The *Northern Star and Freeman's Advocate* was started in 1842 by J. G. Stewart and Charles S. Morton.

The *Sunday Tickler* was published in 1842 by C. W. Taylor.

The *Albany Switch* was commenced in 1842 by H. J. Hastings. In 1855 Edward Leslie became its editor.

The *Youth's Temperance Enterprise*, mo., started Nov. 13, 1842, by J. Stanley Smith, ed. and pub., and continued 3 years.

The *American Citizen*, da. and w., was started in 1843 by Stone & Henley, and ed. by J. S. Smith.

The Albany Knickerbocker, da. and w., was commenced in 1843 by H. J. Hastings, and is still continued.

The *Albany Daily Patriot* was published in 1843 by C. T. Torry

The *Subterranean* was started Mar. 23, 1843, by Jas. Duffey.

The *Albanian*, da., was published in 1844.

The *Albany Religious Spectator* was started in 1844 by J. Munsell and E. H. Pease. The next year it passed into the hands of B. F. Romaine, who continued it until 1857.

The *Birney Advocate*, semi-mo., was pub. during the campaign of 1844 by E. W. Goodwin.

The *Anti-Renter* was started by Thos. A. Devyr Aug. 16, 1845.

The *Albany Freeholder* was started April 9, 1845, by Thos. A. Devyr, and continued until 1854.

The *American Quarterly Journal of Agriculture and Science*, 8vo, was commenced Jan. 1845, by E. Emmons and A. T. Prime. Jan. 1846 it was pub. monthly by E. Emmons and A. Osborne. It was sold to Ch. Bement in 1848, and discontinued in Dec. of the same year.

The *Gavel*, mo., published in 1845 from Munsell's press.

The *Scourge* was published in 1845 by Woodward & Packard.

The *Vesper Bell*, da., a few numbers pub. by Abbott & Crosby.

The *Albany Herald*, da. and tri-w., was commenced in 1846 by A. B. Van Olinda, and in Dec. it took the name of

The *Morning Telegraph*, and in March, 1847, of

The *Statesman*, edited by W. M. Watson.

The *Balance* was published in 1846.

The *Mechanics' Advocate*, 1846, J. Tanner, pub., continued 1 yr.

The *Mechanics' Journal*, 1846, Munsell & McFarlan, pub., was issued 1 year.

The *Horticulturist, and Journal of Rural Art and Rural Taste*, was commenced in July, 1846. A. J. Downing, ed., L. Tucker, pub. The 8th vol. was removed to Rochester. In 1855 it was pub. at Philadelphia by R. P. Smith; John J. Smith, ed. In Jan. 1858 removed to N.Y.; Saxton, pub., J. J. Smith, ed.

The *Mechanics' Mirror*, 8vo, was published in 1846 from Munsell's press.

The *Son of Temperance and Rechabite*, 8vo, mo., was pub. in Aug. 1846 by J. Stanley Smith & Co.

The *Albany Castigator* was issued in 1847 by M. J. Smith.

The *American Literary Magazine*, mo., started July, 1847, T. Dwight Sprague, pub.; removed to Hartford, June, 1848.

The *Christian Palladium*, J. Hazen, ed., was brought from Fulton co. in 1847 or '48, and removed to Irvington, N.J., Oct. 1855.

The *Busy Bee*, E. Andrews, ed., was pub. from 1848 to 1850.

The *Odd Fellows' Literary Magazine* was pub. in 1848. W. K. Cole, ed.

The *Telegraph and Temperance Journal*, mo., was commenced in 1848 by S. Myers, and continued 4 years.

The *Daily Artizan* was pub. a short time in 1849 by Tanner & Stow.

The *Albany Daily Messenger* was pub. 1849 by B. F. Romaine.

The *American Christian Messenger* was commenced by Jasper Hazen Jan. 17, 1841.

Transactions of N.Y. State Institute of Civil Engineers, 4to, with plates, was pub. Feb. 1849. Two nos. issued.

The *Christian Herald and Messenger* was issued Feb. 10, 1849, by J. Hazen, and afterward removed to Irvington, N.J. It was in part successor to the Ch. Messenger, pub. at Newburyport, Mass., many years, and is the oldest religious newspaper in the country.

The Courier and Journal was started Feb. 10, 1849, and is now published by J. T. Hazen.

The *Albany Dutchman* and *The Albany Sunday Dutchman*

ALBANY CITY[1]—was incorporated by patent July 22, 1686,[2] having previously enjoyed divers rights and privileges, under the names of "*Beverwick*," "*William Stadt*," and Albany. The Dutch styled it "*New Orange.*" The part of the city north of Patroon and Quackenboss Streets, known as the "*Colonie*," was incorp. March 31, 1791; and again, March 30, 1801. It was made a village April 9, 1804; and was erected as a town April 11, 1808. The town was divided, and merged in Albany and Watervliet, Feb. 25, 1815. The city lies upon the w. bank of the Hudson River, a little N. of the center of the county; and embraces a strip of land about one mile wide, extending 13½ miles in a N. w. direction to the N. boundary of the county. A narrow intervale of low land lies along the course of the river, bounded by steep banks from 150 to 250 feet high, where a barren region commences, rising toward the w., and broken by numerous sand hills and ridges. The banks which form the declivities of this tract are separated into several distinct ridges by the deep gulleys worn in the clay by the streams which flow through them. The soil, except near the river, is a light sand, not adapted to cultivation without the aid of costly artificial means. A mineral spring was obtained on Ferry St. in 1827, while boring for water.[3] Albany is situated near the head of navigation upon the Hudson, and at the eastern terminus of the Erie Canal.[4] The several railroads before mentioned render it a place of considerable commercial importance.[5] It is the largest barley market in the U.S., and immense

<hr />

were started in 1849 by Griffin & Farnsworth, and subsequently removed to N.Y.

The Temperance Courier was commenced Feb. 10, 1849, by J. T. Hazen, and subsequently pub. by J. Hazen & Son.

The Washingtonian and Rechabite was issued in 1849 by J. T. Hazen, and in 1855 united with *The Courier.*

Florence Oneida Telegraph was printed at Albany in 1849.

The Albany Morning Express was started in 1850 by Stone & Henley. In 1854 it passed into the hands of Munsell & Co., and in 1856 its title was changed to

The Daily Statesman, now published by J.B. Swain & Co.

The Albany State Register, da., semi-w., and w., was started in 1850 by Fuller & Seward. S. H. Hammond and C. D. Brigham were afterward eds., and in 1856 it was removed to N.Y.

The Albany Daily Times commenced Feb. 16, 1850. Five nos. were issued.

The New York Reformer, John Abbott, ed., Munsell, pr., was pub. 10 mos.

The State Military Gazette, C. G. Stone, pub., was commenced in 1858, and was soon after removed to N.Y.

The Half-Dollar Monthly was pub. in 1850 by B. F. Romaine.

The Journal of the N. Y. State Agricultural Society, mo., was started in May, 1850.

The Daily Albany Eagle was started Sept. 1, 1851, by John Sharts, and continued 4 months.

The American Mechanic was started Jan. 4, 1851, by J. M. Patterson.

The Carson League, published by J. T. Hazen & T. L. Carson, was removed from Syracuse in March, 1851.

The Albany Mirror and Literary Cabinet was published in 1851 by J. H. Canoll and W. M. Colburn.

The Cithern was started Oct. 11, 1851, Warner & Rooker, pub.

The Northern Light, mo., conducted by Dix, Hawley, Dean, Beck, Olcott, and Delavan, and subsequently by A. B. Street, was started in 1851, and continued about 3 yrs.

Deutsche Freie Blaetter, tri-w., was started in 1852. Henry Bender and Augustus Miggael, present pub.

The Family Intelligencer was commenced by Jasper Hazen. Sept. 11, 1852, now pub. by J. T. Hazen.

The New York Teacher, mo., the organ of the N. Y. State Teachers' Association, was started in 1852, and is now conducted by James Cruikshank.

The Evening Transcript, da. and w., commenced Jan. 31, 1853, by Cuyler & Henry, was last published by Snyder & Ells.

The Country Gentleman, started by J. J. Thomas and L. & L. H. Tucker in 1853, is now pub. by L. Tucker & Son.

The Prohibitionist, mo., ed. by A. McCoy, the organ of the N.Y. State Temperance Society, was started in 1854, and in 1857 united with the *Jour.* of the Am. Temp. Union.

The Family Dental Journal, mo., was pub. in 1854 by D. C. Estes.

The State Police Tribune was started July 21, 1855, by S. H. H. Parsons and R. M. Griffin. Removed to New York.

The Albany Morning Times was started in 1856, and is published by Barnes & Godfrey.

The Albany Evening Union, edited by J. McFarlan, and subsequently by John New, begun 1856, and ended 1857.

The Albany Volksblatt was published in 1856 by Geo. Herb.

The Albany Morning Express was started in 1856 by Stone & Henley, and edited by J. C. Cuyler.

The Albanian, semi-mo., boys' paper, commenced June, 1857.

The Hour and the Man, da. and w., Geo. W. Clarke, pub., John Thomas, ed., commenced Aug. 1858.

The Mercantile Horn, w., was pub. gratis Oct. 1858.

The Voice of the People. Republican campaign of 1858.

The Albany Evening Standard, da., was begun Dec. 1858. R. M. Griffin & Co., pub.

The Independent Press, da., started Dec. 1858, was pub. a few mo.

Astronomical Notices was started at Ann Arbor, Mich., in 1858. Since the 7th no. it has been pub. at Albany. Prof. Brunow, ed.

The American Magazine, mo., by J. S. & B. Wood, was pub. 1¼ yr.

The Gavel, mo., was published by John Tanner 2 years.

The Albany Literary Gazette was published by John B. Germain.

The Rural Folio was started at Rensselaerville in Jan. 1828, by C. G. & A. Palmer, and continued 2 years. An Anti-Rent paper has also been published.

The Zodiac, mo., was published about 1836 by Gen. De Coudrey Holstein.

The West Troy Advocate was commenced at West Troy in Oct. 1837, by Wm. Hollands, and is now published by his widow and son.

Watervliet Daily Democrat was started at West Troy Jan. 20, 1859. Allen Corey, ed.

The Cohoes Advertiser was started at Cohoes in 1845 by Winants & Agnes. In 1849 its name was changed to

The Cohoes Cataract. J. H. Masten, publisher.

[1] The name Albany was derived from the Scotch title of the Duke of York, to whom the province was granted.

[2] The charter conveyed municipal jurisdiction over the territory bounded E. by the low water mark on the Hudson; S. by a line drawn from the southernmost end of the pasture at the N. end of Martin Gerritsen's island, and running back due N. w. 16 miles into the woods to a certain creek called Sandkil; N. by a line parallel to the former, about 1 mile distant; and w. by a straight line drawn from the western extremities of the N. and s. lines. This charter embraced the right of certain public buildings and fields, the ferry, all waste land within their boundaries, the right of fishing in the Hudson within the county, and of purchasing of the Indians 500 acres of meadow land at "Schaatcogue" on the N., and 1,000 acres at "Tionnonderoge" (Fort Hunter) on the w., in the Mohawk country, on which to plant colonies as barriers against hostile incursions. The quit-rent was fixed at one beaver skin, payable at Albany on the 25th of March annually forever.

[3] This boring was commenced to obtain water for a brewery. At a depth of 480 feet, sparkling water, of a saline taste and impregnated with carburetted hydrogen gas, was obtained. The boring was continued to a depth of 617 feet without any change in the character of the products. A few rods distant a second well was bored, with similar results. One of the wells was ruined by placing a pump in the other. [4] See page 156.

[5] Besides the river, canal, and railroads, there are 5 plank roads and 2 turnpikes terminating in the city.

quantities of this grain are here manufactured into malt and beer.[1] Albany, Troy, and West Troy are the largest lumber markets in the State. "The Lumber District" in Albany is along the canal, above the little basin, where extensive wharves and slips have been built for transferring lumber from canal boats to vessels and barges upon the river.[2] The manufactures of the city are varied and extensive.[3] Among those that may be considered specially important are the stove-founderies and breweries. The city is amply supplied with water from works erected at public expense.[4] The water is obtained from several creeks w. and n. of the city. The main reservoir (Rensselaer Lake,) is 5 miles w. of the City Hall, and is elevated 262 feet above the river. It covers 39 acres, and its capacity is 180,000,000 gallons. A brick conduit conveys the water to Bleeker Reservoir, on Patroon St., whence it is distributed through the portion of the city w. of Pearl St. This reservoir has a capacity of 30,000,000 gallons. The lower portion of the city is supplied from Tivoli Reservoir, on Patroon Creek, covering 20 acres, and has a capacity of 30,000,000 gallons. These works are under a Board of Water Commissioners, and the rents are charged to property owners and collected with the taxes.[5] Pop. 57,333.

The State buildings at Albany, including the Capitol, State Hall, State Library, Geological and Agricultural Hall, Normal School, and State Arsenal and Armory, have already been described under the head of State Institutions.[6] Besides these, there are several buildings and institutions worthy of a particular notice.

The *City Hall* is situated on Eagle St., fronting the e. end of Washington Avenue. It is an elegant structure, faced with Sing-Sing marble, and surmounted by a gilded dome,—the only one in the U. S. It was built at the joint expense of the city and county, and it contains most of the city and county offices.[7] The jail is in Maiden Lane, near the City Hall.

The *Albany Exchange*, a massive granite building, is situated on Broadway, at the foot of State St. It was erected in 1839 by a joint-stock company, and contains the post-office, the general offices of the New York Central R. R. Co., and a variety of other offices.

The *Public Schools*[8] have hardly kept pace with the progress of other institutions of the city, or with the public schools of other cities in the State. Until within the last few years, the whole public school interest was under the charge of a Board of Commissioners, appointed by the Regents of the University. The people, having no power over school matters, took but little interest in them, and the schools languished in every department. There was a great deficiency in schoolhouses, in the number of teachers employed, and in the general supervision of schools. This system has been changed of late, and a series of improvements have commenced which bid fair to soon place the schools of Albany on a par with those of her sister cities. In 1857, there were 13 school districts, employing 53 teachers, 16 males and 37 females. The number of children between 4 and 21 was 18,359, of whom 6729, or 37 per cent., were in attendance some portion of the year.[9] There are 70 private schools, reporting 3827 pupils.

The *Albany Academy*, (for boys,) fronting on Eagle St., opposite the State Hall, is a flourishing institution. It was chartered by the regents, March 4, 1813: the corner-stone of the present building was laid July 29, 1815, and it was opened for students Sept. 1, 1817. Dr. T. Romeyn Beck was its principal for 31 years; and under him the school obtained a deservedly high reputation. The building is an imposing structure, of red Nyack freestone, in the Italian style, fronting on a park of 3 acres.[10]

---

[1] In 1856, the receipts of barley at tide water exceeded 2,000,000 bushels.

[2] In 1858 there was received at Albany by canal, principally from the N., 267,406,411 feet of boards and scantling, 11,949,700 feet of timber. 31,823 M. of shingles, and 67,505 tons of staves.

[3] The directory of 1858 gives the following aggregate of the manufacturing establishments in the city: 4 ag. implement facs.; 8 boiler and steam-engine shops; 9 bookbinderies; 10 breweries; 9 brick yards; 17 carriage and car fac.; 1 car wheel fac.; 5 distilleries; 4 drain tile fac.; 9 flour mills; 13 harness shops; 8 hat fac.; 13 iron founderies; 11 machine shops; 14 malt houses; 15 printing offices; 3 safe fac.; 5 sawing and planing mills; 2 type and stereotype founderies; 13 stove manufac.; and 4 piano factories. There are about 50 commission merchants; 60 dealers in flour and grain; and 50 lumber dealers.

[4] In 1796 the corporation was empowered to construct water works, but nothing was done. Afterward the enterprise was completed by a private company, who obtained their supply of water from Maezlandt Kil, N. of the city. This supply not being sufficient, and an act was passed in 1850 for the construction of public water works. The vote in the city stood, "For water," 4405; "No water," 6; "Brandy and water, strong," 1. The property of the old company were purchased and the present works built.

[5] The original cost of construction was $850,000; and the total cost up to Jan. 1, 1858, $1,018,495. The main pipes measure 42 78-100 miles. The receipts for the year ending Oct. 31, 1857, were $75,550. The revenues are sufficient to pay the interest on the debt for construction and the cost of maintenance, and leave a considerable balance to form a sinking fund for the final liquidation of the debt.

[6] See pages 27, 44, 136.

[7] This building is 109 feet front by 80 feet deep. In front it has a recessed porch, supported by 6 Ionic columns. In the center of the hall, in the second story, is a statue of Hamilton, by Hewes; and in the common council room are portraits of the first 13 Governors of the State.

[8] A Lancasterian School Society was incorp. May 26, 1812, a school having been maintained for some time previous. The members of the common council were ex-officio members of the society, and those giving $25 were entitled to a scholarship. In 1817, the society erected the building now occupied by the Albany Medical College, for the use of the school, which continued to be occupied until 1834, when the school was superseded by the public school system of the State. Wm. Tweed Dale was principal of the school for 23 years.

[9] The total expenses of the schools for 1857 were $44,310 10. Total receipts, the same. No. of volumes in Dist. Libraries, 9285.

[10] The late Henry W. Delavan bequeathed $2000 to this institution, the income of which is devoted to the education of indigent youth.

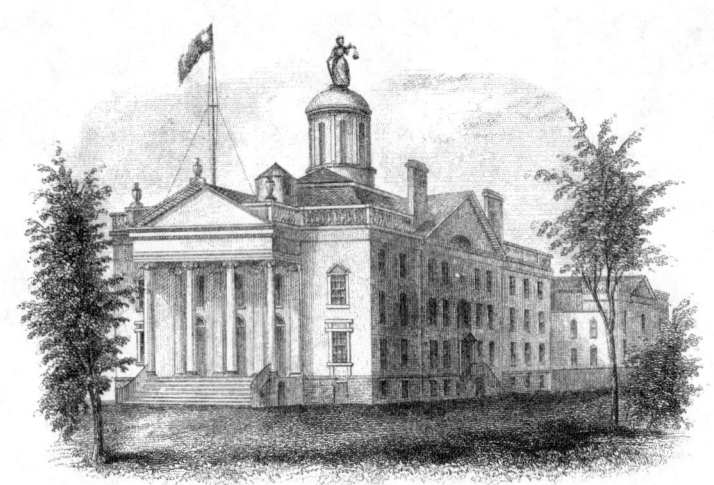

NEW YORK STATE CAPITOL;
ALBANY.

The *Albany Female Academy*, on N. Pearl St., was established in 1814, and incorp. in 1821, and the present building was completed May 12, 1834. The institution has uniformly borne a high reputation. The building is in Grecian style, with an Ionic portico.[1]

The *Albany Female Seminary*, situated on Division St., was incorp. April 9, 1828. It is under the charge of the Meth. denomination.

The *Albany Institute*, a society for the promotion of science and art, was incorp. Feb. 27, 1829 by the union of Society of Arts and the Albany Lyceum of Natural History.[2] It has three departments, devoted to—1st, Physical Sciences and the Arts; 2d, Natural History; and 3d, History and Gen. Literature. During the winter months it holds semi-monthly meetings. It has a valuable library, and an extensive cabinet of minerals and of specimens of natural history.[3]

The *Young Men's Association* was formed in 1833, and incorp. March 12, 1835. It supports a lecture course during the winter, and has a library of above 7000 vols., and a reading room supplied with 70 papers and 15 other periodicals. It is the oldest institution of the kind in the U. S., and has about 1000 members.

A *Catholic Young Men's Association* has sustained a course of lectures for several winters.

The *Albany Industrial School*, erected by the city in 1857, for vagrant children, is not completed. It is located in the rear of the Penitentiary, and, with those buildings, presents a fine architectural appearance.

The *Dudley Observatory*, on an eminence in the N. border of the city, was founded through the munificence of Mrs. Blandina Dudley and other liberal patrons of science. It was incorp. April 2, 1852, and its management intrusted to 15 trustees. The building is admirably arranged, and furnished with instruments, several of which are the largest and most delicate ever constructed. It was dedicated Aug. 28, 1856, and placed under the charge of a scientific council, to be employed by the coast survey in the determination of longitudes, and other purposes connected with that great national enterprise. It has a special library of about 1000 volumes.[4]

The *Albany Medical College*, located upon Eagle St., was incorp. Feb. 16, 1839. Two courses of lectures are held annually; and the institution has secured a deservedly high reputation in the medical profession. It has an extensive medical museum, and a choice library of 5000 vols.

The *Law School of the University of Albany* was instituted under the university charter of April 17, 1851. Two courses of lectures are annually held in rooms attached to the medical college building. This school has obtained an excellent reputation.

The *Albany Almshouse*, consisting of a poor house,[5] insane asylum,[6] and a fever hospital,[7] is located upon a farm of 116 acres, 1½ miles S. W. of the city, and is entirely owned and managed by the city authorities. These departments are supplied with commodious and appropriate buildings. The Industrial School building is located upon the same farm.

The *Albany City Hospital*, located on Eagle St., was incorp. April 11, 1849. It was founded by private subscription, and the present building[8] was opened for the reception of patients Aug. 8, 1854.[9]

The *Albany Orphan Asylum*, on Washington St., at the junction of the Western Turnpike, was incorp. March 30, 1831, at which time it had been in practical operation for nearly two years. It was commenced as a private enterprise, and the present building was erected by subscription and the product of several ladies' fairs. It is now supported by funds received from the State, the interest on its endowment, and the proceeds of an annual fair.

The *St. Vincent Orphan Asylum* was incorp. in 1849. The female department, situated on N. Pearl St., is under the charge of the Sisters of Mercy. The male department, 2 mi. w. of the capitol, is under the care of the Christian Brothers.

The first church (Ref. Prot. D.) was formed in 1640. Rev. Johannes Megapolenses was settled as pastor in 1642, under the patronage of the patroon. A regularly organized Lutheran church existed in 1680, but the date of its formation is unknown. It was reorganized Aug. 26, 1784.

---

[1] The Albany Library, kept in this building, was incorp. Feb. 14, 1792. It contains about 5,000 vols.

[2] Prof. Henry, of the Smithsonian Institution, read his first scientific papers before this association, and performed his first original experiments while a pupil at the Albany Academy. The Society for the Promotion of Agriculture, Arts, and Manufactures, was established in 1791, incorp. 1793, and expired in 1804, by limitation of charter. Revived as the Society for the Promotion of Useful Arts: incorp. 1804. These were State Institutions, and became local on the establishment of the Board of Agriculture, in 1819, and continued a city institution until its union with the Albany Lyceum of Natural History in 1829.

[3] The library and cabinet are kept in the Albany Acad. building.

[4] The building is in the form of a cross, 86 by 70 feet. Among the instruments is a calculating engine, made by C. Scheutz, a Swede, and purchased by John F. Rathbone. It is the only one in existence. A large class of calculations is performed by its use, and the results are impressed upon leaden plates, ready to electrotype and print. This institution has been involved in an unhappy controversy between the trustees and council, which has embarrassed its plans; but it is now in active operation under cheering auspices.

[5] The city contracts to support county paupers at $1.25 per week each. A school connected with this institution is kept throughout the year.

[6] Built at an expense of $12,000, and with accommodations for 80 inmates.

[7] Cost $5000.

[8] This building was erected by the city for a jail.

[9] The whole cost of the institution has been about $50,000.

11

The first Prot. E. Church (St. Peter's) was erected in 1715, on a site granted by the governor of the colony. It stood in the center of State St., opposite Barrack (now Chapel) St., and was demolished in 1802, and the present edifice built by Philip Hooker. The communion plate of this church was presented to the Onondagas by Queen Anne. The most imposing and costly church edifices in the city are the Catholic Cathedral of the Immaculate Conception, corner of Eagle and Lydius Sts., and St. Joseph's (R. C.) Church. There are now (1858) 48 churches in the city.[1]

At an early period Albany acquired much importance from being the principal center of the Indian trade, and afterward the place where the great military expeditions against Canada were fitted out.[2] Its importance as a military station led to its being fortified at an early period; and, although it was often threatened with invasion, no hostile army ever reached it.[3] It became the permanent seat of the State government in 1797. For 30 years after the Revolution, Albany was the seat of the entire trade of the western part of the State, the produce being brought in by sleighs in winter. The first great impulse to its commercial prosperity was given by the successful trip of the Clermont,[4] the first steamboat of Fulton, in 1807, and the improvements in steam navigation which immediately followed. The steamboats now upon the Hudson River are among the very largest that navigate any inland waters.[5] The completion of the Erie Canal, in 1825, and of the various lines of railroads since that time, have each essentially added to the growth and prosperity of the city.[6] Business is principally centered upon Broadway, State, S. Pearl, and Washington Sts. The Dutch language and customs, which continued until long after the English conquest, have almost entirely disappeared. Very few families retain any characteristics of their origin, although many occupy the same lots that were conveyed to their ancestors two centuries ago. The peculiar Dutch architecture has now nearly disappeared, and within the limits of the city there are not more than a dozen houses with the sharp gables fronting even with the street, the tile roof, and antiquated appearance, so common but a few years ago. The city has been visited by several disastrous fires,[7] and the lower part has often been inundated by water.[8]

BERN[9]—was formed from Rensselaerville, March 17, 1795. Knox was taken off in 1822. It lies near the center of the western border of the county. The Helderbergh Mts., 1200 feet above tide, form the eastern border. Grippy and Irish Hills, two broad mountains, with steep declivities and rolling summits, 900 to 1000 feet above tide, occupy the center. The s. and w. parts are hilly, and the N. rolling. The principal streams are the Foxen Kil and the Switz Kil. These streams flow N. W. through narrow valleys bordered by steep hill sides. Werners and Thompsons Lakes, in the N. E., are small sheets of water. In the lime rock, in the N. E. part, are numerous small caves and sink holes.[10] There are several sulphur springs in town. The soil is a sandy and gravelly loam interspersed with clay. **Bernville** (Bern p. o.) contains 50 houses;[11] **E. Bern**[12] (p. v.) 15; **S. Bern** (p. v.) 15; and **Reidsville** (p. v.) 12. **Peoria** is a small village on the line of Knox. Settlement was begun about 1750 by a few German families. In 1777, a company of 85 militia were raised in this town, of which the captain and 63 men joined the British, and the remainder the Americans at Saratoga. Bernville, then called "*Beaver Dam*," was fortified during the war, and sentinels were posted at night to prevent surprise by the Indians.[13] The place at one

[1] Of these there are 8 Meth. E., 7 Bap., 5 Prot. E., 5 Presb., 5 R. C., 3 Ref. Prot. D., 3 Jewish Syn., 3 Evang. Luth., 2 Wes. Meth., Cong., Evang. Ger. Asso., Evang. Prot. Ger., Asso. Presb., Friends, Unita., and Univ.

[2] On the 19th of June, 1754, the first Congress of the colonies assembled at Albany, to devise a general plan of union and measures of defense, in view of the French and Indian hostilities, then just commencing. This Congress consisted of delegates from N. H., Mass., R. I., Conn., N. Y., Penn., and Md. The "plan of union" drawn up by Dr. Franklin was adopted, but it was afterward rejected by the British government as being too democratic, and by the colonies as giving too much power to the king.

[3] The first fort was built by the Dutch, in 1614, on the island below the city, which is hence called Castle Island. In 1617 a fort was built at the mouth of the Normans Kil; and in 1628 another was erected near the present steamboat landing, in the s. part of the city, and named Fort Orange, in honor of the reigning prince of Holland. A quadrangular fort, called "Fort Frederick," drawn up by afterward built on the high ground, now State St., between St. Peter's Church and the Geological Hall, with lines of palisades extending down Steuben and Hudson Sts. to the river. These fortifications were demolished soon after the Revolution, and the only evidence of their existence now remaining is the curved outlines which they have given to the streets in the older parts of the city.

[4] The Clermont was 100 feet long, 12 feet wide, and 7 feet deep. The first voyage to Albany was accomplished in 28 hours and 45 minutes. This boat was afterwards enlarged, and her name changed to the "North River."

[5] As a contrast to the "Clermont," it may be stated that the "Isaac Newton," of the People's Line of Steamers, is 404 feet long. 75 wide, and 47 deep, and has sleeping accommodations for more than 700 passengers.

[6] The sloop "Experiment," of 80 tons, Capt. Stewart Dean, sailed in the fall of 1785 from Albany to China. She was the second vessel from the U.S. to Canton. She was absent 18 months, and returned with a cargo of teas, nankeens, damask silks, and 13 sets of China ware, to order, for family gifts.

[7] A fire in 1797 burned 96 dwellings, and rendered 150 families houseless. Aug. 17, 1848, a most destructive fire broke out, which destroyed a considerable portion of the commercial part of the city bordering upon the river, and also many boats in the basin.

[8] Upon the breaking up of the ice in the river, Feb. 9, 1857, the water completely submerged the lower part of the city, and came up so high that it covered Broadway in front of the Exchange. The damage to property was immense.

[9] Named from the native place of Jacob Weidman, first settler and mill owner.

[10] In one of these caves, during the war, a notorious tory and spy named Salisbury was concealed for some time, but was at last arrested. The place is still known as "Tory's Hole."—*Simms's Schoharie*, p. 525.

[11] Formerly an extensive ax factory was erected here; but it was soon after removed to Cohoes.

[12] Formerly called "Philadelphia," and still locally known as "Philla."

[13] The family of Johannes Deitz, consisting of 8 persons, were murdered by the Indians.—*Simms's Schoharie*, p. 499.

time became a rendezvous for tories.[1] The Ref. Prot. D. Church of Beaver Dam was formed in Jan. 1763. The first settled pastor was Johannes Schuyler, in 1767.[2]

BETHLEHEM—was formed from Watervliet, March 12, 1793. New Scotland was taken off in 1832. It lies on the bank of the Hudson, E. of the center of the county, and includes the islands w. of the main channel of the river. Its surface consists of a rolling upland, ending upon the river in steep bluffs 100 to 150 feet high. Near the center of the town are a few sand ridges and rocky knolls. The principal streams are Coeymans Creek, Vlamans Kil and Normans Kil. The declivities of the upland are broken by numerous deep gulleys worn by streams flowing into the Hudson. There are two small caves, several sulphur springs, and quarries of coarse brown sandstone, in town. The soil is sand and clay.[3] **Groesbeck** is a suburb of Albany. Pop. 1,232. **Kenwood,** a small village near the mouth of Normans Kil, contains an extensive mill, and a manufactory of silver and Britannia ware. **Upper Hollow, Adamsville, Normanskill,** (p. o.,) **Bethlehem Center,** (p. o.,) **Beckers Corners, Cedar Hill,** (p. o.,) and **S. Bethlehem** are hamlets. **Callanans Corners,** in the N. W. corner, is a p. o. On the hills overlooking the Hudson below Albany are several fine country seats. The first settlement was made upon Castle Island,[4] in 1614, and a fort erected the same year. As this island was liable to overflow, in 1617 another fort was built at the mouth of Normans Kil.[5] Agricultural improvements commenced in 1630, by tenants under Van Rensselaer. Mills were built on the Normans Kil and Beaver Kil at a very early period. A part of the house known as "Whitehall," near the Delaware Road, was built by Gen. Bradstreet, and during the Revolution is said to have been a secret rendezvous for tories. Cherry Hill, just out of Albany, on the river road, was the residence of Gen. Solomon Van Rensselaer. A Ref. Prot. D. church was formed in colonial times, and in 1794 S. Van Rensselaer gave the society 100 acres of land, known as the parsonage farm.[6]

COEYMANS—(Quee'mans) was formed from Watervliet, March 18, 1791. A part of Westerlo was taken off in 1815. It was named from the patentee. It is the S. E. corner town in the county, and includes the adjacent islands in the Hudson. Its surface consists of an upland, 200 to 400 feet above the river, broken by ridges and hills rising 100 to 400 feet higher. The principal streams are the Coeymans[7] and Haanakrois Creeks. In the former, at Coeymans village, are two falls at which the stream descends, in the aggregate, 75 feet. Lawsons Lake is a small sheet of water in the N. W. part of the town. A stratum of marble or limestone extends through the town 3 or 4 mi. from the river. In the N. E. part are two caves, the largest extending 40 rods into a perpendicular ledge. Feuri-Spruyt Kil, a small stream in the N. part, disappears, and flows for half a mi. in a subterranean passage, coming to the surface again in New Scotland. At the place where the stream disappears it falls perpendicularly into a deep cavity, forming a considerable water power. Another brook, in the w. part, flows in a similar manner under ground for 40 or 50 rods. There are several mineral springs in town, impregnated with sulphate of magnesia. In the E. the soil is sand mixed with clay, and in the w. it is gravel and clay. The fossil remains of an elephant were found on the farm of Mr. Shears, 4 mi. w. of the river. Large quantities of hay are sent annually from this town to the New York market. **Coeymans Landing,** (Coeymans p.o.,) on the Hudson, is a village of considerable trade. Pop. 650. **Coeymans Hollow,** (p.o.,) **Stephensville,** and **Indian Fields** (p.o.) are small villages in the valley of the Haanakrois. **Keefers Corners** is a p.o. Barent Peterse Coeymans, an emigrant from Utrecht in 1636, settled under the patroon as miller, and leased the mills upon the Patroon Creek and Normans Kil. In 1673 he bought the territory included in this town of the Catskill Indians, and a patent was granted him April 17, 1673, by Gov. Lovelace. Van Rensselaer had previously bought the same lands of the Mohawks; and a conflict of titles ensued. The matter was finally settled in 1706, by Coeymans agreeing to receive title under the patroon and pay a small annual quit rent.[8] Settlement commenced early in the last century.[9] The first mills were erected by the patentee at Coeymans

---

[1] Cornelius Schermerhorn kept a tory rendezvous, and at one time an absconding paymaster from Burgoyne's army is said to have been murdered at his house.

[2] A parsonage farm was given to this church by S. Van Rensselaer, midway between Bernville and Peoria, and a church was erected upon it. In 1835 the society was divided, and a new edifice was erected at each of the villages, the farm being held in common by both societies. The census reports 13 churches in town; 4 M. E., 3 Christian, 3 Ref. Prot. D., and one, each, Bap., Evang. Luth., and Friends.

[3] The proximity of this town to Albany has afforded an excellent market for produce, and much of the land has been devoted to the production of milk, butter, and culinary vegetables.

[4] In 1668 Martin Gerritsen Van Bergen had a lease of this island, and on some old maps, it is called Martin Gerritsen's Island.

[5] A map dated 1630 gives the name of "Godyns Kil" to this stream. The Indian name was Ta-wal-sou-tha. The present name is derived from Albert Andriessen Bradt de Noorman, the lessee of the falls at an early period, and one of the first settlers.

[6] The census reports 5 churches; 2 R. P. D., 2 M. E., 1 Presb.

[7] The Indian name of this creek is said to have been O-nis-ke-thau, and the flats at Coeymans Hollow Ach-que-tuck.

[8] This arrangement was confirmed by patent from Queen Anne, Aug. 6, 1714.

[9] Andreas and Lendert Whitbeck were early settlers near Ach-que-tuck; Daniel Traver and Balthus Keefer near Keefers Corners; and John and Thos. Witbeck near Indian Fields.

Falls. The first church (Ref. Prot. D.) was built in 1797, 1 mi. west of Coeymans Landing. This church was organized March 5, 1793, Rev. Jacob Sickles first pastor.[1]

GUILDERLAND—was formed from Watervliet, Feb. 26, 1803. It lies near the center of the northern border of the county. Its surface is greatly diversified. In the w. rises the precipitous wall of the Helderberghs to a height of 800 feet above the general level of the valleys. The central part is undulating, and the eastern is occupied by numerous sand ridges. The Normans Kil with its branches, the Bozen Kil,[2] Black Creek, Wildehause Kil, and Hunger Kil, are the principal streams. The lower course of the Normans Kil in this town is through a narrow ravine, with steep clayey banks. The soil is light and sandy in the E., and gravelly loam mixed with clay in the w. A mineral spring is found upon the farm of Wm. McGowan. **Hamiltonville,** (Guilderland p.o.,) formerly known as the "Glass House,"[3] is situated on the old turnpike, 8 mi. w. of Albany. **Guilderland Center,** (p.v.,) locally known as "Bangall," contains 18 houses. **Dunnsville,**[4] (p.o.,) **Knowersville,**[5] (p.o.,) and **Frenchs Mills,**[6] on the Normans Kil, are small villages. During the Revolution, a portion of the inhabitants sided with the British; and the feuds which grew up between families and neighborhoods have not yet entirely subsided.[7] The Ev. Luth. church (St. John's) was organized Oct. 13, 1787. Heinrich Moeller was the first pastor.[8]

KNOX—named from John Knox, the Reformer—was formed from Bern, Feb. 28, 1822. It is the N.W. corner town of the county. Its surface consists of a high plateau region broken by a few small hills. Its eastern part constitutes a portion of the Helderbergh region; but the declivities are so gradual that they only serve to give to the town a moderate inclination towards the N. and w. The Bozen Kil, forming a part of the E. boundary, with its tributaries, and the Beaver Dam Creek, are the principal streams. There are two caves, supposed to be of considerable extent, about 1¼ mi. N. of Knoxville. The soil is principally gravel and clay, with hard pan underneath. **Knoxville**[9] (Knox p.o.) contains 23 houses. **W. Township,** (p.o.,) **E. Township,** and **Peoria,** on the line of Bern, are small villages. This town was settled by Germans before the Revolution. During the war the people became divided in politics, and after the defeat of Burgoyne many of the tory families went to Canada.[10] Saml. Abbot and Andrew Brown, from Conn., settled in town in 1789; and soon after 20 to 30 families came in from the same State. The first church was a Ref. Prot. D.[11]

NEW SCOTLAND—was formed from Bethlehem, April 25, 1832. It is the central town of the county. The eastern and central parts are high and rolling, with occasional isolated hills and ridges; and the western border is occupied by the Helderbergh Mountains. The principal streams are Normans Kil, Vlamans Creek, and Coeymans Creek, (or Oniskethau Kil,) and several of their tributaries. Upon the side of Bennett Hill, in the s.w. part, is a strong sulphur spring. Near Clarksville are two caves, extending respectively ⅓ and ½ mi. under ground. Streams flow through each of them. The outlet of Lawsons Lake, in the s.w. part, about 1 mi. from the lake, falls into a deep cavity and flows ½ mi. in a subterranean passage, and in its course it receives a considerable tributary.[12] At the northern foot of Copeland Hill, near the same locality, are remarkable sink holes, 5 to 8 feet in diameter, and extending down through the soil and lime rock to a depth of 10 to 20 feet. A subterranean stream connects the bottoms of these cavities.[13] The soil is a gravelly loam mixed with clay. **Clarksville** (p. v.) is situated at the foot of the Helderberghs, on Coeymans Creek, and contains 211 inhabitants. **New Salem** (p. v.) contains 27 houses; and **New Scotland** (p. v.) 15. **Unionville,** (Union Church p. o.,) **Feuribush,**

Since the Revolution, a small number of Indians belonging to the Oneida tribe lived in this town. They removed, but returned for a short time in 1812. An acct. of £10 was audited in 1792, for building stocks and a whipping post.

[1] The census reports 6 churches in town; 3 M. E., R. P.D., R. C., and Union.

[2] From "Boos," angry, because of its rapid descent and severe freshets.

[3] A glass factory was erected here in 1792; and in 1793 the State loaned the proprietors £3000 for 8 years,—3 years without interest and 5 at 5 per cent. In 1796 the project was conceived of establishing here a manufacturing town, and the ground was laid out into streets and lots, under the name of Hamilton. To encourage the project, the company and workmen were exempted from taxation for 5 years. The works were discontinued in 1815 for want of fuel.—*Munsell's Annals,* vol. III. p. 157.

[4] Named from Christopher Dunn, original owner; locally known as "Hardscrabble."

[5] An inn was kept here during the Revolution by Jacob Aker. It was the seat of a factory in 1800.

[6] Named from Abel French, who built a factory here in 1800. A clothing works was erected here in 1795, by Peter K. Broeck.

[7] The news of Burgoyne's surrender was celebrated by the whigs by burning a hollow chestnut tree on a hill. A barrel of tar had previously been turned down the hollow trunk and branches.

[8] A R. P. D. church was formed Dec. 14, 1793. The census reports, besides those already mentioned, 3 churches; 2 Presb. and 1 M. E.

[9] Knoxville was formerly known as "Union Street," and is still locally called "The Street."

[10] Capt. Jacob Van Aernden was an active leader of the whigs of this section during the war.

[11] The census reports 6 churches; 3 M. E., R. P. D., Luth., and Bap.

[12] This cavity has been explored, and in it are found beautiful stalactites, and thousands of bats clinging to the roof.

[13] This passage has been explored, and is found to contain several rooms of considerable size. Some years ago a notorious thief used this cavity as a depository for stolen goods, and for a

and **Oniskethau** (locally known as "Tarrytown") are hamlets. Teunis Slingerland, from Holland, was the first settler on the Oniskethau flats. He purchased 9874 acres, and built a dwelling near the center of the tract, and erected the first mills.[1] The first church (Ref. Prot. D.) was organized at New Salem about 1786.[2]

RENSSELAERVILLE—named from the Van Rensselaer family—was formed from Watervliet, March 8, 1790. Bern was taken off in 1795, and a part of Westerlo in 1815. It is the s. w. corner town of the county. Its surface is mostly upland, broken by parallel ridges extending N. and s. and rising 400 to 600 feet above the valleys. The principal streams are Catskill Creek and its tributaries, Scrub, Fox, Ten Mile, and Eight Mile Creeks, and Willow Brook. The valleys of these streams are narrow, and are bordered by steep hill sides, and the streams are rapid, and subject to sudden and destructive freshets. Upon Ten Mile Creek, near Rensselaerville, is a fall of 100 feet; and upon Willow Brook is another of 40 feet. Bog iron has been found in the E. part. There is a sulphur spring 2½ miles N. E. of Preston Hollow. The soil is clay and gravel, underlaid by hard pan. **Rensselaerville**[3] (p. v.) contains an academy.[4] Pop. 561. **Williamsburgh,** on the w. border of the town, contains 18 houses; **Preston Hollow**[5] (p. v.) 40; and **Medusa**[6] (p. v.) 30; **Potters Hollow**[7] and **Cooksburg**[8] are post-offices.[9] The town was mostly settled by emigrants from New England soon after the Revolution. Michael Brandt, a German from Schoharie, lived in town during the war.[10] Daniel Shay, the leader of the revolt known as Shay's Rebellion, moved to this town in 1795. Maj. John Edmonds, a Revolutionary officer, was also a settler in this town. The first church (Presb.) was formed in Nov. 1793, and the edifice erected in 1796.[11] Rev. Samuel Fuller was the first pastor.

WATERVLIET—was formed March 7, 1788, and included the w. district of the manor of Rensselaerwyck.[12] Rensselaerville was taken off in 1790, Coeymans in 1791, Bethlehem in 1792, Guilderland in 1803, and Niskayuna in 1809.[13] It lies at the junction of the Hudson and Mohawk, in the N. E. corner of the county. Its surface is mostly an upland, 200 to 300 feet above the river. The declivities of this upland are broken by numerous gulleys worn by the small streams. A fine intervale, nearly half a mile in width, extends along the Hudson. At Cohoes, on the Mohawk, the river flows over a rocky declivity 78 feet in height, of which 40 feet is perpendicular.[14] The banks, both above and below the falls, are high and precipitous. The Erie Canal rises, by a series of 18 locks, from the Hudson, through the village of Cohoes, to the most northerly angle of the town 3 mi. above, and 188 feet above tide. At this point it crosses the river into Saratoga co., in a stone aqueduct, 1137½ feet long, 26 feet high, and resting upon 26 piers. The soil is a deep, rich alluvial upon the river intervale, and a light, sandy loam upon the upland. Sulphur and chalybeate springs, and bog iron ore, are found in town. The quarries of graywacke furnish an excellent flagging and building stone. This is the most populous town in the State. **West Troy,** (p.v.,) incorp. April 30, 1836, is a commercial and manufacturing village opposite the city of Troy. Pop. 8306. It is especially noted for the extent of its lumber trade, and for being the seat[15]

---

long time eluded the vigilance of those who were searching for him. At length he was tracked to his hiding place, and the existence of the cavity was made known.

[1] Among the other first settlers were Daniel Pangburn and Wm. Van Walter, at Stoney Hill; Ebenezer Wands, John Watt, Geo. Swan, and Wm. Kirkland, Scotch emigrants, near New Scotland; and Geo. Reed, John Patterson, Saml. Ramsey and sons, James McMullin, David Allen, Wm. McCulloch, and —— Brandt in other parts of the town.

[2] There are in town 8 churches; 4 Ref. Prot. D., 3 M. E., Presb. The Friends organized a meeting in 1812.

[3] Samuel Jenkins, the first settler, located here February 22, 1788. [4] Opened Jan. 17, 1847.

[5] Named from the family of first settlers, who came in soon after the Revolution.

[6] Formerly called "Halls Mills," or "Halls Hollow."

[7] Named from Saml. Potter, who, with his sons and brothers, were first settlers.

[8] Named from Thomas B. Cook, who purchased land here in anticipation of business from the Catskill and Canajoharie R. R., which was completed to this place from the Hudson. The road was run two years, when the rails were taken up.

[9] Upon the farm of Ezra Lester, in a place known as Willow Glen, formerly stood a village, known as "Peckham Hollow," consisting of 2 stores, 2 smith's shops, and 14 houses. For a time it was a rival of Rensselaerville; but now not a vestige of it remains.

[10] At the time of the Indian incursion into Bern, Mr. B. had gone to Catskill Landing, leaving his family alone. On their return, the savages passed close by with their scalps, prisoners, and plunder, but offered no molestation.

[11] A Bap. church was formed at Rensselaerville in 1797; Rev.

Truman Beman was the first pastor. A Bap. church was formed at Preston Hollow in 1800; a Friends meeting at Potters Hollow in 1808; and Trinity Church (P. E.) was organized in 1816. There are besides, in town, 2 M. E. churches.

[12] The manor was divided into the East and West Districts, March 5, 1779, the river being the separating bounds. This district, as defined by act of March 24, 1772, embraced all that part of the manor north of an E. and w. line from Beeren Island north to Cumberland co., except the city of Albany.

[13] It includes the former village of "Gibbonsville," (incorp. April 23, 1823,) and places known as "Washington" and "Port Schuyler."

[14] The cascade is in full view from the R. R. bridge, a few rods below Cohoes. The Champlain Canal crosses the Mohawk a short distance below, in a pond formed by a dam 1650 feet long and 7 feet high, and unites with the Erie Canal 2 mi. s. of this point.

[15] The arsenal grounds occupy about 100 acres, located between the Troy and Albany turnpike and the Erie Canal, the latter furnishing water-power for the machinery of the arsenal. The grounds are inclosed by a high wall, excepting the part between the river and the turnpike. This is the principal government manufactory of gun carriages, machines, equipments, ammunition, and military supplies for the troops and forts of the United States. The building of this establishment was begun in 1814, under Col. Geo. Bomford, of the Ordnance department, and it was for many years under the charge of Maj. Jas. Dalliba. The Watervliet Arsenal now consists of more than thirty buildings, of brick and stone, mostly large shops and storehouses,—the former of which will accommodate, in case of need, more than 500 workmen. The stores deposited here exceed $1,500,000 in value. A company of soldiers of the

of an extensive U. S. arsenal. It has a bank, printing office, 8 churches,[1] and extensive manu-factures of woolen goods, bells, butts and hinges, castings, carriages, and malt. The annual aggregate value of manufactured products is about $1,000,000.[2] **Green Island** (p. v.) was incorp. Oct. 14, 1853. Pop. 1,324. It contains 2 churches,[3] a car factory, brass, malleable iron, and 2 iron founderies and R. R. machine shops. It is also the seat of considerable lumber trade.[4] **Cohoes,** (p. v.,) incorp. under general act, is a manufacturing village upon the Mohawk.[5] Pop. 6106. A dam is here erected across the Mohawk,[6] and the water is con-ducted by canals to convenient places for factories.[6] The whole fall is 103 feet, and the water is used 5 times from canals of different levels. The annual aggregate of manufactured products is nearly $2,000,000.[7] The village contains a savings bank, 6 churches,[8] and a large number of stores, shops, &c. **Boght**[9] (p.v.) contains 15 houses. The Ref. Prot. D. church of this place was organized April 14, 1784, by Rev. E. Westerlo. **Lishas Kil, Newtonville,**[10] and **Ireland Corners**[11] are hamlets and p. offices. **Loudonville** is a hamlet, 2½ miles from Albany. **Tivoli Hollow,** on Patroon Creek, adjoining Albany, has extensive manufactures of ag. implements, bolts, and hollowware. **North Albany** lies on the river, north of the city, and contains 40 houses. It includes a portion of the "Lumber District" and several manu-factories. **Spencerville,** or **West Albany,** is the name applied to the recent establishments of the N. Y. C. R. R., 3¼ mi. N. W. of the city, including the cattle and wood yards and car and engine houses of the company. The **Shaker Settlement,**[12] in the W. part of the town, consists of about 300 persons, living in 4 distinct families, in a manner peculiar to that people. **Town House Corners** is a populous neighborhood near the center of the town, where town business has usually been transacted. **Watervliet Center** (p. o.) is a hamlet. The Albany Rural Cemetery[13] was incorp. April 20, 1841, and the site selected April 20, 1844. The premises were dedicated and consecrated Oct. 7 of the same year. Haver (Dutch for "Oat") and Van Schaicks Islands, in the Hudson above Green Island, are separated from each other and the mainland by the "Sprouts" of the Mohawk. Upon the approach of Burgoyne, in the summer of 1777, Gen. Schuyler retired to these islands and threw up fortifications to check the advance of the enemy expected from both the N. and W. Upon the retreat of St. Leger from the siege of Fort Stanwix, no further trouble was apprehended from the direction of the Mohawk Valley; and Gen. Gates, upon assuming the command of the northern army, advanced into Saratoga County. The traces of the fortifica-tions are still visible.

WESTERLO[14]—was formed from Coeymans and Rensselaerville, March 16, 1815. It lies upon the center of the southern border of the county. Its surface is broken and hilly, with a general southerly inclination. The highest point in the northerly part of the town is 800 feet above tide. The hills are very steep and irregular, and the valleys are mere narrow ravines. The streams are Haanakrois, Basie, Wolf, Fly, and Eight Mile Creeks and their branches. These are all rapid streams, and are liable to severe freshets. The soil is a sandy and gravelly loam, inter-

---

Ordnance department forms the guard of the arsenal, and the men are also employed in the shops. Most of the employees are citizen mechanics. A large number of trophy cannon are de-posited upon the premises.
1 Bap. org. 1827; Ref. Prot. D., 1844; P. E., (Trinity,) 1835: 2 R. C., (St. Patrick's, 1839, and St. Bridget's, 1851,) and 2 M. E.
2 The village is built on land formerly held by the Bleeker family. It was purchased by a company of Troy capitalists and laid out as a village, and has mostly grown up since the com-pletion of the canals.   3 Presb. and M. E.
4 It is situated upon an island in the Hudson directly op-posite the city of Troy, of which it forms a suburb.
5 The Cohoes Co. was incorp. March 28, 1826, with a capital of $250,000, afterward increased to $500,000. This co. built the dam, and constructed the canals, for the purpose of leasing the water power.
6 This dam is half a mile long, and the canal 2 miles long.
7 The following manufactories were reported here in the census of 1855:

6 knitting mills, value of product	$647,100
2 cotton factories	618,000
1 ax and edge tool factory	210,000
2 bedstead factories	45,000
1 veneering factory	42,000
2 mills	28,000
1 machine shop and foundery	34,200
1 tobacco factory	21,450
1 shoddy mill	21,840
1 wheel factory	9,000
1 straw paper factory	9,000
1 bobbin shop	6,000

There are now a considerable number of manufactories not in-cluded in the above list.

8 M. E., Ref. Prot. D., Presb., P. E., (St. John's,) Bap., and R. C., (St. Bernard.)
9 The Dutch for "bend," in reference to the bend in the Mo-hawk; sometimes called "Groesbeck Corners," from Wm. G. Groesbeck. One of the earliest settlements in the county was made in this neighborhood.
10 Named from J. M. Newton.
11 Named from E. H. Ireland, innkeeper.
12 This community was formed in 1776, by Ann Lee and her followers, by whom she is regarded as the spiritual mother of mankind. It is the oldest of the kind in the U. S., and now owns 2540 acres, including about 300 acres of alluvial land on the Mohawk at the mouth of the Schoharie Creek and on Shaker Island, which are annually fertilized by the floods of the Mohawk, and chiefly devoted to the raising of broom corn. The whole number of buildings in the settlement is about 150, several of which are of stone or brick. They have a commodious church, (built in 1848,) 3 offices, 1 schoolhouse, 8 dwellings, (suitable for 50 to 100 persons each,) 2 grist mills, 3 saw mills, 3 machine shops, for turning, sawing, &c., and numerous other shops and storehouses. Their pursuits are agriculture, horti-culture, the manufacture of brooms and medicines, and such mechanical trades as their own wants require. The females are employed in household work, dressmaking, spinning, weaving, braiding whiplashes and bonnets, and in making small salable articles. They keep 40 to 50 horses, 80 cows, 16 yoke of oxen, 500 sheep, and young stock in proportion. "Mother Ann" (as their founder is affectionately named) was buried in the cemetery near the church family.
13 This cemetery is located upon the hills west of the Troy and Albany Road, 4 miles from the city. The grounds are taste-fully laid out, and contain many elegant monuments.
14 Named in honor of Rev. Eilardus Westerlo, of Albany.

spersed with clay and underlaid by hardpan. There are several fine quarries of flagging stone in town. **Chesterville**[1] (Westerlo p. o.) contains 196 inhabitants. **Dormansville,**[2] (p. o.,) **South Westerlo,** (p. o.,) **Lambs Corners,** and **Van Leuvens Corners,**[3] are hamlets. Settlement commenced before the Revolution.[4] A Bap. church was organized, about 1800, at Chesterville; Roswell Beckwith was the first pastor.[5]

Acres of Land, Valuation, Population, Dwellings, Families, Freeholders, Schools, Live Stock, Agricultural Products, and Domestic Manufactures of Albany County.

Names of Towns.	Acres of Land.		Valuation of 1858.			Population.					Schools.	
	Improved.	Unimproved.	Real Estate.	Personal Property.	Total.	Males.	Females.	No. of Dwellings.	No. of Families.	Freeholders.	No. of Districts.	Children taught.
Albany	2,958	1,530½	19,486,071	6,477,850	25,963,922	27,661	29,672	6,386	8,536	2,767	13	21,500
Bern	31,171	8,115½	385,387	86,575	471,962	1,578	1,628	575	574	475	21	1,300
Bethlehem	26,804¾	6,616½	1,842,115	186,650	2,028,765	2,646	2,505	795	981	476	15	1,806
Coeymans	22,563	10,066	1,017,475	202,273	1,219,748	1,486	1,477	560	554	343	15	1,134
Guilderland	32,590	9,701½	719,950	79,039	798,989	1,587	1,601	492	564	411	12	1,288
Knox	21,136	5,115½	255,250	67,885	323,135	939	949	352	344	312	12	730
New Scotland	19,012	8,114	1,083,215	110,400	1,193,615	1,680	1,647	612	613	263	15	1,337
Rensselaerville	31,501¾	6,603	627,750	170,825	798,575	1,507	1,581	584	582	466	18	1,126
Watervliet	25,897½	8,193¾	4,921,325	831,100	5,752,425	10,246	10,643	2,734	2,736	1,525	29	8,407
Westerlo	29,101	6,721	592,966	97,544	690,510	1,327	1,321	501	499	440	19	931
Total	242,735	70,777¼	30,931,504	8,310,141	39,241,646	50,657	53,024	13,591	15,983	7,478	169	39,559

Names of Towns.	Live Stock.					Agricultural Products.							Domestic Manufactures in Yards.
						Bush. of Grain.					Dairy Products.		
	Horses.	Working Oxen and Calves.	Cows.	Sheep.	Swine.	Winter.	Spring.	Tons of Hay.	Bushels of Potatoes.	Bushels of Apples.	Pounds of Butter.	Pounds of Cheese.	
Albany	1,224	297	540	144	860	3,714	9,484	425½	15,235	786	7,125		
Bern	1,172	1,518	1,772	6,686	2,002	5,870½	99,842½	5,311¼	18,875	22,016	152,166	4,699	2,706½
Bethlehem	1,155	927	1,629	1,722	3,593	39,910	123,045	8,927½	94,585	16,239	124,210	100	1,555
Coeymans	790	931	699	1,767	1,943	25,836	42,583½	6,016½	9,104	19,977	93,252	410	1,106
Guilderland	1,416	1,180	1,691	2,824	3,835	50,273½	150,411	7,952½	46,929	38,004	165,555	1,285	2,951½
Knox	790	959	1,032	5,245	1,189	5,620	83,686¾	3,036½	10,530½	18,092	90,530	2,666	2,925½
New Scotland	749	682	966	1,914	2,563	30,577	60,387½	5,738½	13,768	20,256	100,050	472	2,479
Rensselaerville	962	1,463	1,632	12,003	2,502	5,539	71,780¾	4,421	13,448	37,176	171,440	11,535	874¾
Watervliet	1,724	884	1,912	1,034	3,306	16,059	101,313	5,228	143,023	17,273	124,751	6,563	1,618
Westerlo	972	1,074	1,459	3,715	2,242	10,592	65,497	7,522	10,157	44,432	144,448	8,790	1,744
Total	10,954	9,915	13,332	37,054	24,035	193,991	808,031	54,579¼	375,654½	234,251	1,173,527	36,520	17,960¼

1 Named in honor of Rev. John Chester, former pastor of 2d Presb. Ch. of Albany.

2 Named from Daniel Dorman, former inn and store keeper.

3 Named from Isaac Van Leuven. First called "*Sackets Corners*," from Jas. Sacket, and afterward "*Prestons Corners*," from an innkeeper named Preston.

4 Among the early settlers were Nicholas Stoddard, Philip Meyer, and Lodowyck Haynes. Apollus Moore, afterward first judge of the county, taught school in 1788. Robt. O. K. Bemet taught a school in 1790. Grant & Eadie kept a store and made potash at Chesterville in 1798. Lobdell & Baker built the first mill, about 1795.

5 The Ref. Prot. D. Ch. was formed about the same time. Emanuel Church, (P. E.,) at S. Westerlo, was formed in 1854. There are also 1 Christian and 2 M. E. churches, and a society of Friends, in town.

ALLEGANY COUNTY.

This county was formed from Genesee, April 7, 1806. A portion of Steuben co. was annexed March 11, 1808. Portions were set off to Genesee in 1811, and to Wyoming and Livingston in 1846. It lies upon the s. line of the State, w. of the center; is centrally distant 220 mi. from Albany, and contains 1,033 sq. mi. The surface is mostly an upland, separated into ridges and broken by the deep valleys of the streams. A large portion of the co. is rough and mountainous. The highest summits, in the s. part, are 500 to 800 feet above the valleys and 2,000 to 2,500 feet above tide. The declivities are usually too steep for profitable cultivation. Toward the N. the co. gradually loses its mountainous character and spreads out into a hilly region. The Genesee River flows in a N. E. direction through near the center of the co., forming a deep valley bordered by abrupt hillsides. The main ridges —parallel to the river and about 10 mi. distant from it—form watersheds, dividing the waters flowing N. from those flowing s. The streams E. of the E. ridge are tributaries of the Susquehanna, and those w. of the w. ridge of the Allegany. Narrow valleys break the continuity of these ridges, and in numerous instances streams flowing in opposite directions take their rise within a few rods of each other. The principal tributaries of the Genesee are Wigwam, Angelica, Philips, Vandemark, Dike, Chenunda, and Cryders Creeks on the E., and Fords, Knight, Van Campens, White, Black, Caneadea, and Six Town Creeks on the w. The streams flowing E. from the E. border of the co. are Canaseraga and Sugar Creeks, Canisteo River, Karr Valley, McHenry Valley, and Whitney Valley Creeks; and the streams flowing w. from the w. border are Oil, Wolf, Dodges, Deer, and Little Genesee Creeks.

The rocks of the co. belong to the shales and sandstones of the Portage and Chemung groups,— the former appearing in the deep valleys in the N. part, and the latter covering the tops of the s. hills. At various localities the sandstone furnishes an excellent building material; and in Rushford it is quarried for grindstones. The shales in the s. w. part are highly charged with bituminous matter; and many of the springs have a strong bituminous taste and smell. From a spring in Cuba petroleum, or rock oil, issues in considerable quantities. Iron pyrites are found to some extent associated with the shale. Drift deposits are found in some portions of the co., though not in large quantities. The soil upon the uplands is generally a heavy clay, derived from the disintegration of the shales, and in most sections largely mixed with undecomposed fragments of the rocks. In the valleys the soil is mostly a gravelly loam and alluvium. From the nature of its surface and geological formation, the co. is best adapted to grazing; and, although wheat and the spring grains are successfully produced, stock and wool growing and dairying form the principal branches of agricultural pursuit. The manufacture of lumber has formed the leading interest for a long series of years, and facilitated the occupation and cultivation of the lands; but as the primitive pine forests have disappeared the pursuits of the people have become more and more exclusively agricultural. A considerable portion of the s. part of the co. is yet covered with forests, and lumbering is still pursued to some extent.

The county seat is located at the village of Angelica.[1] The courthouse is an old, dilapidated brick building, built in 1819, and now entirely inadequate to the comfortable accommodations of the courts. The jail is a wood structure, erected in 1849. It has no facilities for the proper classification of prisoners, and no means of ventilation.[2] The clerk's office is in a separate building, contiguous to the courthouse. The poorhouse is located upon a farm of 180 acres in Angelica, 2 mi. E. of the courthouse. It is a stone building, affording ample accommodations for

---

1 By the act erecting the county in 1806, courts were directed to be held at Angelica on the 2d of June, 1807. By an act of March 11, 1808, the county seat was permanently located at Angelica, and a courthouse and jail were authorized to be erected, under the direction of Moses Carpenter, John Gibson, and Wm Higgins. The jail was built soon after; but the courts continued to be held in private rooms until 1819, when the present courthouse was erected. The old jail continued to be occupied until 1849, when it was superseded by the present structure. An act was passed, April 2, 1858, providing for the immediate removal of the county seat s. to the line of the N. Y. & Erie R. R.; but the execution of the law has been arrested and restrained by legal proceedings now pending in the State courts. The first co. officers were Philip Church, *First Judge*; Jacob S. Holt, *County Clerk*; John Gibson, *Sheriff*; and Luke Godspead, *Surrogate.*

2 The jail has an average number of 6 inmates, supported at a weekly cost of $2.75 each.

the inmates, but is destitute of means of ventilation.   The average number of inmates is 57, supported at a weekly cost of $1.03 each.   The farm yields a revenue of $1,000.[1]

The Genesee Valley Canal extends s. from the N. boundary of the co. along Genesee River to Belfast, thence up the valley of Black Creek to New Hudson, and thence across to the valley of Oil Creek, and down the valley of that stream to the w. bounds of the co.   The N. Y. & Erie R. R. extends from Steuben co. up Whitney Valley Creek; thence across to Dyke Creek, and down the valley of that stream to Genesee River; thence down the Genesee to Belvidere; thence up Van Campens Creek to Friendship Village; thence across to the valley of Oil Creek, and down that stream to the w. bounds of the co.   It passes through Almond, Alfred, Andover, Wellsville, Scio, Amity, Friendship, and Cuba.   The Buffalo & N. Y. City R. R. extends through Burns and Grove, in the N. E. corner of the co.

Four weekly newspapers are now published in the co.[2]

The two western tiers of towns in this co. were included in the Holland Land Purchase, and the remaining part belonged to the Morris Reserve.   John B. Church became the owner of 100,000 acres of this tract.   His son, Judge Philip Church, subsequently became the proprietor of one-half, or 50,000 acres, and the pioneer settler of the tract at Angelica, in 1804.   A few settlers had previously located at different points in the valley of the Genesee; and the settlement of the co. may be said to have commenced with the century.   The roughness of the surface, and the superior richness of the lands further N., had a tendency to retard the development of this co.; and for many years comparatively little progress was made.   The construction of the Genesee Valley Canal and of the Erie R. R. gave an impulse to improvement and afforded an opportunity to convey the rich products of the extensive pine forests to a profitable market.   Agricultural improvements have slowly followed the retreat of the forests; and now nearly one-half of the co. is under improvement to some extent.

ALFRED—was formed from Angelica, March 11, 1808.   A part of Angelica was annexed in 1816.   Almond and Independence were taken off in 1821, a part of West Almond in 1833, and a part of Ward in 1856.   It lies upon the E. border of the co., a little s. of the center.   The surface consists of deep, irregular hills separated by narrow valleys.   The highest summits are 500 to 800 feet above the streams.   Whitney Valley Creek flows to the N. E., and Dyke Creek to the s.   The soil upon the hills is a clayey or shaly loam, and in the valleys a gravelly loam.   **Alfred Center** (p. v.) contains a church, the Alfred Academy and University,[3] and 177 inhabitants; **Bakers Bridge,** (Alfred p. o.,) in the N. E. corner, contains a church, flouring mill, and 134 inhabitants.   It is a station upon the Erie Rail Road.   **Tip Top Summit** is also a rail road station.   The first settlement was made near Alfred Center, in May,

---

[1] In the report of the Senate committee of 1857, this institution is reported as poorly kept. Lunatics were confined for weeks together without attendance and without having their cells cleaned; and it was a custom of the keeper to flog the inmates with a raw hide.

[2] *The Angelica Republican* was started in Oct. 1820, by Franklin Cowdery, and was continued 2 years. In 1827 it was revived as

The Allegany Republican, published by Samuel P. Hull. In 1832 it was changed to

The Angelica Republican and Farmers and Mechanics' Press, issued by B. F. Smead. During the same year it was again changed to

The Allegany Republican and Internal Improvement Advocate, and published by Peter Cherry. In 1836 it was passed into the hands of Wm. Pitt Angell, who changed it to

The Angelica Reporter and Allegany Republican. It soon after passed into the hands of Samuel C. Wilson, and was issued for several years as

The Angelica Reporter. In 1841 it was published by Horace E. Purdy and Chas. Horton; and in 1844 Mr. Horton became sole proprietor. In 1856 he purchased The Advocate and Whig, and published the combined paper as

The Angelica Reporter and Angelica Advocate and Whig, under which name it is still issued.

The Republican Ægis and Allegany Democrat was published at Angelica in 1830.

The Allegany Gazette was issued at Angelica in 1840.

The Allegany Co. Advocate was started at Angelica in Jan. 1842, by Erastus S. Palmer. It was successively issued by Ellroy & Churchill, Peter S. Norris, and Wm. H. & C. M. Beecher. In 1852 it was united with The Cuba Whig and issued as

The Advocate and Whig. In 1856 the Beechers sold to Charles Horton, who united the paper with The Reporter.

The Republican Era was started at Angelica in 1844 and issued a short time.

The Republican Era was started at the village of Oramel in 1846 by Horace E. Purdy. Its publication was continued by different persons until 1857.

The Cuba Advocate was commenced at Cuba, Oct. 29, 1838, by Isaac C. Sheldon, and was continued several years.

The Political Investigator (mo.) was published at Angelica a short time in 1848.

The American Banner was commenced at Cuba in Feb. 1855, by Hatch & Pratt. In July, 1857, the name of the paper was changed to

The Southern Tier, and its publication continued by C. Pratt, M. B. Champlin, editor.

The Almond Herald was commenced at Almond in 1853 by R. Denton, who published it 1 year, when it was suspended. In about 6 months it was resuscitated by Melvin Hyde and Isaac Busby, and appeared under the name of

The Allegany Sentinel. Subsequently it passed into the hands of Pruner & Spencer, by whom the paper was published until 1856.

The Genesee Valley Free Press was commenced at Belfast in Jan. 1853, by A. N. Cole. In March following, the paper was removed to Wellsville, where the publication is continued by Mr. Cole.

The Rural Budget was commenced at Wellsville in Oct. 1856, by Richard O. Shant, by whom the publication is continued.

[3] The academic part of this institution was incorp. in 1842, and the university in 1857. The erection of the university building has been commenced. It is under the charge of the Seventh Day Baptists. The building occupied by the female department was burned Feb. 14, 1858.

1807, by Clark Crandall, from Rensselaer co.[1] The first church (Seventh Day Bap.) was formed in 1816. There are now 2 churches in town; both Seventh Day Bap.

ALLEN—was formed from Angelica, Jan. 31, 1823. A part of Birdsall was taken off in 1829. It is an interior town, situated north of the center of the co. Its surface is a hilly upland, divided into ridges by the valleys of the streams. The highest summits are 500 to 700 feet above the valleys. The principal streams are Wignam, Plum, and Baker Creeks. The soil upon the uplands is clay underlaid by hardpan, and in the valleys a gravelly loam and alluvium. **Allen,** (p. o.,) in the E. part, and **Allen Center** (p. o.) are hamlets. There are no stores, taverns, doctors, or lawyers in the town. A few small settlements were made about the commencement of the century, but the principal settlements were made subsequent to 1820.[2] The first religious services were conducted by Rev. Robert Hunter, (Presb.,) in 1821; and the first church (Presb.) was formed in 1830.[3]

ALMA—was formed from Willing, Nov. 23, 1854. It is the central town on the s. border of the co. The surface is broken and mountainous. Honeoye Creek and its branches, flowing in deep, narrow ravines, form the drainage. The greater part of the surface is yet covered with forests. The soil upon the uplands is a clayey and sandy loam, and in the valleys a gravelly loam and alluvium. Lumbering is the principal pursuit; and large quantities of pine lumber are annually manufactured. **Alma,** (p. v.,) in the w. part of the town, contains a steam sawmill and 15 houses. The first settlement was made in 1833, by Warren Huff, from Quebec, Canada.[4] The first religious services were performed by Rev. Reuben Kent, in 1838; and the first and only religious association (M. E.) in town was formed in 1850. There is no church edifice in town.

ALMOND—was formed from Alfred, March 16, 1821. A part of Birdsall was taken off in 1829, and a part of West Almond in 1833. It lies upon the E. border of the co., a little N. of the center. Its surface is mostly an upland, separated into several distinct ridges by the deep valleys of Canisteo River and the Karr Valley, McHenry Valley, and Whitney Valley Creeks. The highest summits are 500 to 800 ft. above the valleys. The soil is a gravelly and clay loam. Quarries of good building stone, and sulphur springs, are found in various localities. **Almond,** (p. v.,) near the E. line, contains 2 churches, 2 flouring mills, several manufactories, and about 1,000 inhabitants. **Center Almond,** in Karr Valley, and **North Almond** are p. offices. The first settlement was made at Karr Valley, by Rev. Andrew Gray, Wm. Gray, Jos. Rathbun, and —— Vandemark, all from Penn., in the spring of 1796.[5] The first religious meeting was held at Karr Valley, by Rev. Andrew Gray, (Presb.,) in his own house, May 1, 1797; and the first church was formed, the same year, by Mr. Gray.[6]

AMITY—was formed from Angelica and Scio, Feb. 22, 1830. A part of Ward was taken off in 1856. It is an interior town, lying a little s. of the center of the co. The surface is hilly and broken, the summits rising 500 to 800 feet above the valleys. Genesee River flows N. w. through the w. part and receives as tributaries Van Campens and Philips Creeks. The valleys of these streams are narrow and are bordered by steep hillsides. The soil is principally a clayey and sandy loam. **Philipsville,** (p. v.,) on the Genesee, was incorp. Feb. 21, 1853. It contains 3 churches, 2 sawmills, a flouring mill, and about 1,000 inhabitants. It is a station upon the rail road. **Belvidere,** (p. v.,) on the Genesee, at the mouth of Van Campens Creek, in the N. w. corner of the town, contains 3 sawmills and 181 inhabitants. It is also a rail road station. The first settlement was made in 1804, near Belvidere, by John T. Hyde.[7] The first religious

1 Nathan Green, from Madison co., settled at Bakers Bridge in 1807. The first child born was Rebecca Stillman, in 1808; the first marriage, that of Luke Maxson and Susan Green; and the first death, that of Chas. H. Clark, who accidentally shot himself. Nancy Teater taught the first school, in 1815; John Teater kept the first inn, in 1818; and E. S. Davis built the first sawmill, in 1821, and the first gristmill, in 1824.

2 The first school was taught near the s. line, in 1820. The first inn was kept by Mrs. Armstrong, near the s. line, in 1827. The first sawmill was erected by Asher Miner, on Wigwam Creek, in 1825.

3 The census reports 3 churches; Cong., Bap., and M. E.

4 The first child born was Emeline, daughter of Azor Hurlbut, Sept. 1, 1836; and the first death, that of John Bagley, in 1838. The first school was taught by Clarinda Kent, in 1839. Azor Hurlbut kept the first inn, in 1837, Sam'l J. Peet the first store, in 1844; and John W. Post erected the first sawmill, in 1843.

5 Maj. Moses Van Campen, Capt. Henry McHenry, Walter, Jos., and Sam'l Karr, Silas Ferry, Stephen Major, Benj. Van Campen,

Matthew McHenry, Jos. Coleman, and Geo. Lockhart, all from Luzerne co., Penn., settled in the town in 1797. The first child born was Wm. McHenry, in 1799; the first marriage, that of Peter Putnam and Polly Waters, in 1804; and the first death, that of Matthew McHenry, in 1801. The first school was taught at Karr Valley, by Jos. A. Rathbun, in Dec. 1802. Benj. Van Campen kept the first inn, at Karr Valley, in 1805; and Phineas Stevens built the first sawmill, in 1806, at Almond Village, and Asa Clark the first gristmill, in 1818.

6 The census reports 3 churches; Presb., Bap., and Wes. Meth.

7 Harry Davis, from Hampshire co., Mass., settled near Philipsville in 1805. The first child born was Hannah Hyde, Nov. 4, 1804; the first marriage, that of Loammi Asthley and Rachel Baker, in 1807; and the first death, that of Harvey Manning, in 1806. Polly Baker taught the first school, in 1810; Ebenezer Hyde kept the first inn, at Belvidere, in 1809; Alvin E. Parker the first store, at Philipsville, in 1830; and Philip Church built the first sawmill, on Genesee River, in 1806, and the first gristmill, in 1808.

meeting was held at the house of Samuel Van Campen, by Rev. Robert Hubbard, (Presb.,) in 1814; and the first church (Bap.) was formed by Rev. Jonathan Post, in 1816.[1]

ANDOVER—was formed from Independence, Jan. 28, 1824. A part of Independence was taken off in 1824, and a part of Wellsville in 1855. It lies upon the E. border of the co., s. of the center. The surface is very hilly and still retains some of the original pine forests. Dyke Creek flows s. w., receiving several small tributaries. The soil is chiefly a heavy loam resting on hard-pan. The primitive forests had a large proportion of pine; and the manufacture of pine lumber —for many years a leading pursuit—is still carried on to some extent. **Andover,** (p. v.,) near the center of the town, contains 4 churches, a grist and saw mill, and 374 inhabitants. It is a R. R. station. **Shoemakers Corners** (Elm Valley p. o.) is a hamlet on the w. line of the town. The first settlement was made in the spring of 1795, by Nathaniel Dyke, from Tioga Point, Penn.,—originally from Conn.[2] The first religious meeting was held at the house of Mr. Dyke, by Rev. Silas Hubbard, in 1808; and the first church (Cong.) was formed by Rev. Robert Hubbard, July 4, 1824.[3]

ANGELICA[4]—was formed from Leicester, (Livingston co.,) Feb. 25, 1805. Alfred and Cane-adea were taken off in 1808, Allen and Scio in 1823, a part of Amity in 1830, and a part of West Almond in 1833; and a part was annexed to Alfred in 1816. It lies a little N. of the center of the co. Its surface is a hilly upland, broken by the deep ravines of the streams. Genesee River flows across the s. w. corner, and its tributary, Knights Creek, through the center. The soil is a clayey loam upon the uplands, and a gravelly loam in the valleys. **Angelica,** (p. v.,) on Knights Creek, a little N. of the center of the town, was incorp. May 2, 1835. Besides the co. buildings, it contains the Angelica Academy, 5 churches, 1 bank, 2 newspaper offices, and several mills and manufactories. Pop. 846. The first settlement was made on the site of the village, in 1802, by Philip Church.[5] The first church (Presb.) was formed by Rev. Robt. Hubbard, in 1811.[6]

BELFAST—was formed from Caneadea, March 24, 1824, as *"Orrinsburgh."* Its name was changed April 21, 1825. A part of Caneadea was annexed in 1831. It lies a little N. w. of the center of the co. Its surface is a hilly upland, separated into distinct ridges. Genesee River flows across the N. E. corner. Black and White Creeks, the other principal streams, flow through narrow, irregular valleys bordered by abrupt hillsides. The highest summits are 600 to 800 feet above the streams. The soil is a clayey loam upon the hills, and a gravelly loam in the valleys. **Belfast,** (p. v.,) on the Genesee, near the mouth of Black Creek, contains 3 churches, the Genesee Valley Seminary,[7] and several mills. Pop. 801. At this place considerable commerce is carried on by means of the Genesee Valley Canal. **Rockville,**[8] (p. o.,) in the w. part, and **Transit Bridge,** (p. o.,) in the E., are hamlets. The first settlement was made on Genesee River, in 1803, by Benjamin, Elisha, Calvin, and David Chamberlin, brothers, from Penn.[9] Rev. Ephraim Sanford (Bap.) held the first religious meeting, at the house of Nath'l Reynolds, in 1806, and formed the first church, in 1807–08.[10]

BIRDSALL[11]—was formed from Allen and Almond, May 4, 1829. It is an interior town, lying N. E. of the center of the co. Its surface is principally a hilly upland, separated into several distinct ridges. The declivities are usually very abrupt, and the highest summits are 500 to 800 feet above the valleys. Black Creek and its branches form the principal drainage. The soil is

---

[1] The census reports 4 churches; Bap., Cong., M. E., and Univ.

[2] Mr. Dyke was educated at Yale College, served as an officer during the Revolutionary War, was attached to the staff of Gen. Warren at Boston, and subsequently to that of Gen. Washington. Stephen Cole settled on lot adjoining Dyke, in 1796, and Benj. Brookings and John T. Hyde, from Vt., near the same place, soon after. The first child born was Daniel Cole, Feb. 18, 1797; the first marriage, that of Isaac Dyke and Pamelia Gibson, in 1802; and the first death, that of Zeriah, daughter of James Dyke, Jan. 21, 1798. Robert Reed taught the first school, in 1820; Luther Strong built the first saw and grist mill, in 1819, and kept the first inn, in 1820; and Asa S. Allen kept the first store, in 1823.

[3] The census reports 4 churches; Bap., Cong., M. E., and R. C.

[4] Named from Angelica, wife of John B. Church and eldest daughter of Gen. Philip Schuyler.

[5] Mr. Church was son of John B. Church and grandson of Gen. Schuyler. Evert Van Wickle, John Gibson, and John Lewis settled in the town in 1802, and John Ayers in 1803. The first child born was Catharine S. Mullender; the first marriage, that of Sylvanus Russel and Esther Van Wickle, in 1805; and the first death, that of Ira Stephens, Sept. 20, 1803. Widow S. Smith taught the first school, in 1804–05; Philip Church built the first saw and grist mill, in 1802–03, and kept the first store, in 1803; and Jos.

Taylor kept the first inn, in 1804. Hyde de Neuville—an exile during the Government of the Empire, and minister to the U. S. upon the restoration of the French monarchy from 1816 to 1822 —resided at Angelica in 1807–08. Victor Dupont, also a distinguished French exile, was an early settler at Angelica.

[6] The census reports 6 churches; Presb., Prot. E., Bap., M. E., Ref. Prot. D., and R. C.

[7] This institution was chartered in 1856 and opened Dec. 2, 1857. It will accommodate 300 students, and is under the charge of the M. E. Church.

[8] Named from a grindstone quarry in the vicinity. This quarry is not now worked.

[9] Jedediah Nobles, from Elmira, settled on the river. and Benj. Littleton, from the same place, on Wigwam Creek, in 1805. The first child born was Moses V. Chamberlin; and the first marriage, that of John Sanford and Mary Collar, in 1806. Elijah Reynolds taught the first school, in 1807; Jos. S. Raymond kept the first inn, near the village, in 1821, and Sam'l King the first store, in 1824. David Sanford erected the first saw and grist mill, on the river, near the village, in 1809.

[10] There are 5 churches in town; Bap., Cong., M. E., Univ., and R. C.

[11] Named from Judge John Birdsall, Circuit Judge of the Eighth Judicial District in 1828–29.

a clay loam underlaid by hardpan. **Birdsall,** (p. o.,) in the N. w. part, and **Birdsall Center,** (p. o.,) are hamlets. The first settlement was made by Josiah Whitman, on Lot 24, in 1816. The first religious meeting was held at the house of Wm. Day, in 1823,[1] by Rev. Robert Hubbard; and the first church (M. E.) was formed by Rev. Eleazur Day, in 1825.[2]

BOLIVAR—was formed from Friendship, Feb. 15, 1825 ; and a part of Wirt was taken off in 1838. It lies upon the s. border of the co., w. of the center. Its surface is a broken, mountainous upland, in some parts too steep for profitable cultivation. The streams are Little Genesee, Honeoye, and Horse Creeks. The soil upon the hills is a reddish clay loam, and in the valleys a gravelly loam. **Bolivar,** (p. v.,) N. of the center, contains a church, flouring mill, and 157 inhabitants. **Honeoye Corners** (S. Bolivar p. o.) is a hamlet near the s. border.   Timothy Cowles, from Otsego co., settled in the w. part of the town in 1819.[3] The first religious services were held by Austin Cowles, (M. E.,) in 1820 ; and the first church (M. E.) was organized in 1828.[4]

BURNS—was formed from Ossian, (Livingston co.,) March 17, 1826. It lies upon the E. border of the co., N. of the center. Its surface is very hilly and broken, the highest summits being 400 to 700 feet above the valleys. The principal streams are Canaseraga, South Valley, and Slader Creeks. **Canaseraga,**[5] (p. v.,) in the N. part, contains 2 churches, the Canaseraga Academy,[6] several mills, and about 200 inhabitants. It is a station on the B. & N. Y. City R. R. **Burns,** (p. v.,) on the E. line of the town, contains 1 church and 20 dwellings. It is also a R. R. station. **Whitneys Crossing** is a p. o. in the w. part.   The first settlement was made at Whitney Valley, in 1805, by Moses and Jeremiah Gregory, John Gaddis, and Samuel Rodman.[7] The first religious meeting (M. E.) was held at the house of Moses Gregory, by Robert Parker, in 1806 ; and the first church (Bap.) was formed at Whitney Valley, by Rev. Jesse Braman, in 1817.[8]

CANEADEA—was formed from Angelica, March 11, 1808. Friendship was taken off in 1815, Rushford in 1816, "*Orrinsburgh*" (now Belfast) in 1824, and a part of Belfast in 1831. It is an interior town, lying N. w. of the center of the co. Its surface is divided into two ridges by Genesee River, which flows in a northerly direction through the center. The soil upon the highlands is a gravelly and clayey loam, and in the valleys a gravelly loam and alluvium. Upon Caneadea Creek is a valuable stone quarry. **Oramel,** (p. v.,) upon the Genesee, in the s. part, was incorp. June 9, 1856. It is an important canal village, and contains 2 churches, several mills, and 733 inhabitants. **Caneadea,** (p. v.,) at the mouth of Caneadea Creek, contains 1 church, 3 mills, and about 400 inhabitants. **Houghton Creek** is a p. o. in the N. part.   The first settlement was made about the commencement of the century, by a Mr. Schoonover, from Penn.[9] The first religious meeting (Bap.) was held by Elder Ephraim Sanford, in his own house, at Oramel Village, in 1804.[10]

CENTERVILLE—was formed from Pike, (Wyoming co.,) Jan. 15, 1819. It is the N. w. corner town of the co. Its surface is a moderately hilly upland. Six Town Creek and its branches form the principal drainage. The soil is a heavy clay loam. **Centerville** (p. v.) contains 2 churches and about 150 inhabitants. The first settlements were made by Jos. Maxson, of R. I., in April, 1808, and by James Ward, in the fall of the same year.[11] The first religious meeting

---

[1] James Mathews, from N. J., settled on Section 21, near the center, in 1818. Previous to this, —— Vance, Wm. P. Schaanck, from N. J., Jeremiah Van Wormer, and Wm. Day, from Cayuga co., had located in town. The first child born was James E. Mathews, March 7, 1820; and the first marriage, that of Sam'l Van Wickle and Harriet Freeman, in 1821. Hannah Scott taught the first school, in 1822. Josiah Whitman kept the first inn, in 1820, and Joseph B. Welch the first store, in 1828. The first sawmill was erected on Black Creek, by Elias Hull and David Peterson, in 1823.

[2] There are 3 churches in town; M. E., F. W. Bap., and R. C.

[3] Christopher Tyler settled in 1819, Austin and Asa Cowles in 1820, in the w. part of the town,—all from Otsego co. The first birth was that of Almond W. Cowles, in 1820; the first marriage, that of Daniel Kellogg and Sophia Hitchcock, in 1825; and the first death, that of a child of Luther Austin, in 1823. The first school was taught by Austin Cowles, in 1820–21. Hollis B. Newton kept the first inn, in 1831, and Newton & Cowles the first store, in 1825. The first sawmill was built by Asa and Austin Cowles, near the village, on Genesee Creek, in 1822, and the first gristmill by Asa Cowles, at the village, in 1824.

[4] The census reports 3 churches; 2 M. E. and Bap.

[5] Formerly called "*Whitney Valley*."

[6] This institution was formed in 1856, and is in charge of the Bap. denomination.

[7] Wm. Carroll and Wm. Hopkins settled at South Valley, Elijah and Daniel Abbott, Elias Van Scoter, and Thos. Quick, all from

Penn., at De Witts Valley, and Sam'l Boylan, at Whitney Valley, in 1806. The first child born was Lewis W. Carroll, Aug. 1, 1807 ; the first marriage, that of John Gregory and Betsey Doty; and the first deaths, those of Jeremiah Gregory, who was killed by the fall of a tree, April 4, 1812, and his twin-brother, killed in the same manner, Sept. 17 of the same year. The first school was taught at Canaseraga, by Wm. Crooks, in 1810. S. De Witt Brown kept the first inn, at "*De Witts Valley,*" (now Burns Village,) in 1826, and Isaac N. Town the first store, at Canaseraga, in 1828. Daniel Schull erected the first gristmill, in 1810, and David McCardy the first sawmill, in 1813.

[8] There are 5 churches in town; Bap., F. W. Bap., Presb., Prot. E., and M. E.

[9] Ephraim Sanford, jr., Zephaniah Huff, David Sanford, and Nehemiah Sears settled in 1803, and Ezra Sanford and others soon after. The first children born were Moses V. Chamberlain and Betsey Sanford, both in 1806. The first school was taught, near the center, by Asa Harris, in 1811. The first inn was kept by Widow Bradley, from Penn., in 1810; and the first store, at the same place, by —— Hunt, in 1812. John Hoyt erected the first sawmill, at the mouth of Caneadea Creek, in 1816, and David Hitchcock put the first carding machine in operation, in 1810, on Caneadea Creek.

[10] The census reports 2 churches; Cong. and M. E.

[11] Calvin P. Perry, from Berkshire co., Mass., settled near Mr. Maxson in 1809. Abraham and David Jolatt, brothers, were the next settlers in the order of time; and next were Zaccheus, Thos.,

(Bap.) was held by Rev. John Griffith. The first church (Presb.) was formed in July, 1824, by Rev. Silas Hubbard.[1]

CLARKSVILLE—was formed from Cuba, May 11, 1835. It lies upon the w. border of the co., s. of the center. Its surface is a mountainous upland, divided into several steep ridges by the narrow valleys of the streams. The highest summits are 700 to 1,000 ft. above the canal at Cuba. Dodges Creek and its branches form the principal drainage. The soil is principally a heavy clay loam. Considerable pine lumber is still made in town. **Clarksville Corners,** (West Clarksville p. o.,) near the center, contains a church, sawmill, and 12 dwellings. The first settlement was made a little s. of the center, in 1822, by John and Horatio Slayton, from Warsaw, Wyoming co.[2] The first religious meeting (M. E.) was held at the house of Nelson Hoyt, in 1828, by Rev. Mr. Cole, from Friendship; and the first church (Bap.) was organized by Rev. Holden E. Prosser, in 1842, and is still the only church in town.

CUBA—was formed from Friendship, Feb. 4, 1822. Genesee was taken off in 1830, and Clarksville in 1835. It lies upon the w. border of the co., s. of the center. Its surface is a broken and mountainous upland, divided into irregular ridges by steep and narrow valleys. Oil Creek and its branches form the principal drainage. The canal and R. R. both extend through the narrow valleys of this town.[3] The highest summits are 600 to 800 ft. above the level of the canal. The soil is a clayey and gravelly loam.[4] **Cuba,** (p. v.,) on Oil Creek, incorp. Nov. 11, 1850, contains 5 churches, a newspaper office, and several mills and manufactories. Pop. 816. **North Cuba,** (Seymour p. o.,) in the N. part; contains 20 houses. **Cuba Summit** is a R. R. station. Settlement was commenced in 1817, by Salmon Abbott, — Freer, and — Hall, from Conn.[5] The first religious meeting was held by Rev. Robt. Hubbard, in 1818; and the first church (Bap.) was formed in 1824.[6]

FRIENDSHIP—was formed from Caneadea, March 24, 1815. Cuba was taken off in 1822, Bolivar in 1825, and a part of Wirt in 1838. It is an interior town, lying a little s. w. of the center of the co. Its surface is broken by high, mountainous ridges, the summits of which are 600 to 800 feet above the valleys. It is drained by Van Campens Creek and its branches. The soil is a clay and gravelly loam. **Friendship,** (p. v.,) near the Center, contains 4 churches, the Friendship Academy, 2 flouring mills, 25 sawmills, and about 800 inhabitants; **Nile,** (p. v.,) in the s. part of the town, contains a church, 3 mills, and 40 dwellings. The first settlement was made in Nov. 1806, by Richard Frair, from Kingston, Ulster co.[7] The first religious service was held in a barn, by Samuel Vary, in July, 1810; and the first church (Presb.) was formed by Rev. Robert Hubbard, in the spring of 1813.[8]

GENESEE—was formed from Cuba, April 16, 1830. It is the s. w. corner town in the co. Its surface is very broken and mountainous; and the highest summits are 1,000 to 1,400 feet above the valleys.[9] The streams are Little Genesee, Dodges, Deer, Windfall, and Oswaya Creeks,—all flowing through narrow, mountainous ravines. The soil is a sandy and clayey loam. A considerable portion of the surface is still covered with pine, and lumbering is extensively carried on. **Little Genesee,** (p. v.,) in the s. E. part of the town, contains a church, sawmill, and 30

---

and Strong Warner, Perkins B. Woodward, from Ashford, Conn., settled a little N. of the center, Sargent Morrell, from Vt., in the s. part of the town, in 1810, and Benj. Blanchard, from Vt., on Lot 25, in 1811. The first birth and the first death in town was that of a child of Calvin P. Perry, in June, 1809; and the first marriage, that of Wm. Foy and Ruth Morrill, in 1811. Perkins B. Woodward taught the first school, in the winter of 1813–14; Benj. and Mark Blanchard and Eber Hotchkiss erected the first sawmill, on Six Mile Creek, in 1813, and Russell Higgins and Packard Bruce the first gristmill, in 1817, on the same stream. —— Thatcher kept the first inn, at the center, in 1810, and Sparrow Smith the first store, at the same place, in 1820.

[1] The census reports 4 churches; 2 Presb., Cong., and M. E.

[2] James McDougal, from Steuben co., settled a little E. of the center, and Jabez Survey near the same place, in 1827. The first child born was Jos. P. Slayton, in 1826; the first marriage, that of Van Rensselaer Delivan and Harriet Palmer, in 1827; and the first death, that of Mrs. Sally Olds, in 1831. The first school was taught by Maria McDougal, E. of the center, in 1827. Daniel S. Carpenter kept the first inn, near the center, in 1828; and Samuel King erected the first sawmill, on Dodge Creek, in 1832.

[3] The R. R. crosses the Genesee Valley Canal in this town, near the reservoir built to feed the summit level of the canal. The reservoir—built, at a cost of $150,000, by the erection of a dam across Oil Creek—is 60 ft. high. It raises a pond that covers an area of 500 acres, and finds an outlet near its head, so that no water runs over the dam. Its capacity when full is estimated to be equal to 200 mi. of canal.

[4] The celebrated Oil Spring, in the w. part of this town, is

situated upon the Indian Oil Spring Reservation. It is a dirty pool, 20 ft. in diameter, and has no outlet. The water is mixed with bitumen, which collects upon the surface. There are several quarries of good building stone in town.

[5] John Bennett, Andrew Hawley, and Stephen Cole came about the same time. The first death was that of Andrew Hull. The first school was taught by David Row, in 1822. Stephen Cole kept the first inn, near the center, in 1814, and King & Graves the first store, in 1821 or '22. The first sawmill was built by Wm. Dovner, on Oil Creek, in 1815; and the first gristmill, by Cady & Baldwin, on the same stream, in 1822.

[6] The census reports 5 churches; Bap., Presb., Prot. E., M. E., and R. C.

[7] John Harrison and Simon and Zebulon Gates settled in June, 1807. The first birth was that of Sherman Haskins, in a sugar camp, in March, 1808; the first marriage, that of Jas. Sanford and Sally Harrison, in Dec. 1809; and the first death, that of Hattie Frair, in Dec. 1806. The first school was taught by Pelatiah Morgan, in the winter of 1810–11. Simon Gates opened the first inn, in May, 1808, and Stephen Smith the first store, in the spring of 1818. Sylvanus Meriman and Aaron Axtell built the first gristmill, in 1810; and Ebenezer Steenrod the first sawmill, in 1815, and a mill for wool carding and cloth dressing, in 1816.

[8] The census reports 5 churches; Bap., Seventh Day Bap., Cong., M. E., and Univ.

[9] Upon a high summit near the center is a locality known as "Rock City." It consists of a tract of 40 acres covered with conglomerate, composed of milkwhite pebbles broken into regular layers, forming alleys and streets.

dwellings; and **Ceres,** (p. v.,) on the s. line, a church and 12 dwellings. The first settlement was made on Genesee Creek, on Lot 3, in the E. part of the town, in 1823, by Jabez Burdick, from Rensselaer co.[1] The first religious services (Seventh Day Bap.) were held by Rev. John Green, in 1826; and the first church (Seventh Day Bap.) was organized, in 1827, by Rev. Henry P. Green.[2]

GRANGER—was formed from Grove, as "*West Grove,*" April 18, 1838. Its name was changed March 6, 1839. It is the central town upon the N. border of the co. It is a hilly upland, divided into several distinct ridges. Genesee River, forming a portion of the w. boundary, is bordered by abrupt hillsides 600 to 800 feet high. The soil is a clayey loam upon the hills, and a gravelly loam in the valleys. **Short Tract** is a p. o. in the s. part of the town, **Granger** a p. o. in the N., and **Grove** a p. o. in the E. The first settlement was made near Short Tract, in Feb. 1816, by Reuben Wilcox, Isaac Smith, and Rufus Trumbull, from Vt., and Elias Smith, from Otsego co.[3] The first religious meeting was held at the house of Elias Smith, in 1818, by Rev. Mr. Hill, (M. E.;) and the first church (M. E.) was organized about 1830.[4]

GROVE—was formed from Nunda, (Livingston co.,) March 8, 1827, as "*Church Tract.*" Its name was changed in 1828, and Granger was taken off in 1838. It lies upon the N. border of the co., near the N. E. corner. Its surface is a hilly upland, divided into several distinct ridges. A valley in the E. part is known as Chautauqua Valley. Branches of Black and Canaseraga Creeks form the drainage. The soil upon the hills is a clay loam underlaid by hardpan, and in the valleys a gravelly loam. **Swainsville** is a p. o. on the R. R., in the E. part of the town, and **Chautauqua Valley** a. p. o. on the R. R., in the N. E. part. **Grove Center** is a hamlet. John White, from Herkimer co., made the first settlement, in May, 1818, in the N. w. part.[5] The first religious meeting (M. E.) was held at the house of Mr. White, by Rev. Cyrus Story, in 1820; and the first church (M. E.) was formed in the White Settlement, in 1821.[6]

HUME—was formed from Pike, (Wyoming co.,) Feb. 20, 1822. It lies upon the N. border of the co., w. of the center. Its surface is a hilly upland. Genesee River flows through the s. E. corner and forms a portion of the E. boundary. It is bordered by abrupt hills rising to a height of 400 to 700 feet. The other principal streams are Six Town and Cold Creeks. The soil is a gravelly and clayey loam. **Cold Creek,** (Hume p. o.,) near the center of the town, contains 2 churches, a saw and grist mill, and about 300 inhabitants; **Fillmore,** (p.v.,) a canal village at the mouth of Cold Creek, contains a church, a saw and grist mill, and 372 inhabitants. **Wiscoy,** on Wiscoy Creek, and **Mill's Mills,** in the N. part, are p. offices. **Mixville,** at the mouth of Wiscoy Creek, contains a church, saw and grist mill, and 200 inhabitants. An immense water-power at this place is but little used. The first settlement was made at Mill's Mills, in 1807, by Roger Mills, from Montgomery co.[7] The census reports 5 churches in town.[8]

INDEPENDENCE—was formed from Alfred, March 16, 1821. Andover was taken off in 1824, and a part of Willing in 1851. It is the s. E. corner town in the co. The surface is a mountainous upland, broken by deep, narrow valleys. The highest summits are 800 to 1,200 ft. above the valleys. The streams are Cryder and Chenunda Creeks. The soil is principally a gravelly loam with sections of sand. **Whitesville,** (p.v.,) s.E. of the center, contains 2 churches and several mills and manufacturing establishments. Pop. 220. **Spring Mills,** (p. v.,) in the s. E. corner, contains several mills and 14 dwellings; **Greens Corners,** (Independence p. o.,) in the N. part, contains a church and 16 dwellings. The first settlement was made in 1798, by John Cryder, who built a house, a sawmill, and made other improvements, and soon after abandoned them and left the country. The first permanent settlement was made by Samuel S. White, from Madison co.,

---

[1] Roswell Streeter, from Rensselaer co., settled in 1825, and Ezekiel Crandell and Joseph Wells, from R. I., in 1826, on Windfall and Genesee Creeks. Joseph Maxson, from R. I., and John Cook, settled in the w. part in 1827. The first child born was Edward W. Burdick, in 1826; the first marriage, that of Joseph Allen and Phebe Maxson, in the same year; and the first death, that of Arvilla Burdick, in 1824. The first school was taught by Henry P. Green, near the mouth of Windfall Creek, in the winter of 1826-27. Lewis P. Coon kept the first inn, in 1842, at Genesee Valley, and Albert Langworthy the first store, in 1831. The first sawmill was built on Genesee Creek, by Newman Crabtree, in 1820. No liquor license has ever been granted in the town; and it is claimed that no inhabitant has ever been sent to a prison or a poorhouse.

[2] The census reports 3 churches; all Seventh Day Bap.

[3] The first birth was that of a child of Elias Smith, in March, 1817; and the first death, that of Olive Linee, in 1817. The first school was taught in the Smith Settlement, by Miss Williams, in

1819. Elias Smith kept the first inn, in 1819, and the first store, in 1820. Isaac Van Nostrand erected the first gristmill, in 1831, and the first sawmill, in 1823.

[4] The census reports 2 churches; M. E. and Wes. Meth.

[5] In the same year Alex. Bailey, from Vt., settled near Mr. White. The first child born was Laura Bailey, Dec. 25, 1820; and the first marriage, that of Elijah White and Lucy Dana, in 1822. The first school was taught by Emily Page, in 1826. Henry Andrews kept the first inn, in 1828, in the N. w. corner, and Thayer & Smith the first store, at or near the same place, in 1825. John S. Culver erected the first sawmill, in the N. part.

[6] There are 4 churches in town; 3 M. E. and Bap.

[7] The first school was taught in the barn of Roger Mills, jr., in the summer of 1812, by Caroline Russell, from Montgomery co. Geo. Mills kept the first inn, at Mills Mills, in 1815, and Elisha Mills the first store, at the same place, in 1809. Roger Mills erected the first sawmill, in 1807, and the first gristmill, in 1808.

[8] Cong., Bap., F. W. Bap., M. E., and Wes. Meth.

in the spring of 1819, at Whitesville.[1] The first religious meeting was held at the house of Sam'l S. White, by Rev. Daniel Babcock, (Seventh Day Bap.,) Jan. 1, 1820.[2]

NEW HUDSON—was formed from Rushford, April 10, 1825, as *"Haight."* Its name was changed April 4, 1837. It lies upon the w. border of the co., a little N. of the center. The surface is a hilly upland, broken by valleys extending N. E. and S. W. The principal streams are Black, Oil and Rush Creeks. The soil is a gravelly or clayey loam. **McGrawville,** (New Hudson p. o.,) on the N. line, contains a church, 2 sawmills, and 20 dwellings; **New Hudson Corners,** (Black Creek p. o.,) in the s. part, contains 2 churches and 30 dwellings. **North Valley** is a hamlet near McGrawville. The first settlement was made on Lot 49, in the s. part, by Spencer Lyon, from Waterbury, Vt., in 1820.[3] The first religious meeting was held by Rev. James Eastwood, (M. E.,) at his own house, in 1821. The first church (Presb.) was formed with 6 members, by Rev. Robert Hubbard, June 4, 1822.[4]

RUSHFORD—was formed from Caneadea, March 8, 1816. New Hudson was taken off in 1825. It lies upon the w. border of the co., N. of the center. Its surface is a hilly upland, divided into two distinct districts by Caneadea Creek, which flows E. through near the center. The valleys of several smaller streams, tributaries of the Caneadea, divide the highlands into narrow ridges. The soil is a shaly loam underlaid by hardpan. Quarries of building stone, several sulphur springs, and a brown mineral paint resembling ocher are found in town. A woolen factory upon Caneadea Creek manufactures about 12,000 yds. of cloth annually; and a pineapple cheese factory turns out 70,000 lbs. of cheese annually. **Rushford,** (p. v.,) at the center of the town, contains 4 churches, the Rushford Academy, and several manufacturing establishments. Pop. 654. **East Rushford** (p. v.) contains several mills and 40 dwellings. The first settlement was made on Lot 30, in 1808, by Enos Gary, from Vt.[5] The first religious meeting was held by Rev. Mr. Sanford, (Bap.,) in 1813; and the first church (Bap.) was formed in 1815, by Rev. Nathan Peck, a missionary from Boston.[6]

SCIO—was formed from Angelica, Jan. 31, 1823. A part of Amity was taken off in 1830, a part of Willing in 1851, and a part of Wellsville in 1855. It is an interior town, lying S. E. of the center of the county. Its surface is a mountainous upland, the highest summits being 700 to 1,000 ft. above the valleys. The streams are Genesee River and Knights and Vandemarks Creeks. The soil is principally a sandy loam. **Scio,** (p. v.,) on Genesee River, contains a church, several mills, and 496 inhabitants. The first settlement was made at the mouth of Knights Creek, in 1805, by Joseph Knight and his son Silas, from Oneida co.[7] The census reports 5 churches.[8]

WARD—was formed from Alfred and Amity, Nov. 21, 1856. It is an interior town, lying S. E. of the center of the co. The surface is a hilly upland, the highest summits being 500 to 800 feet above the valleys. The streams are Philips and Vandemarks Creeks. The soil is a clayey loam upon the hills, and a gravelly loam in the valleys. **Philips Creek,** (p. v.,) in the N. part, contains 2 churches and 16 dwellings. The first settlement was made in 1817, by Abraham Waldruff, from Ontario co.[9] The first church (M. E.) was organized at an early period. There are now 2 churches; M. E. and Univ.

WELLSVILLE—was formed from Scio, Andover, and Willing, Nov. 22, 1855. It is an

---

[1] In the spring of the same year John Teater, from Dutchess co., David Wilson and Stephen Boyce, from Mass., settled in or near Whitesville. The first child born was Dugald C. White, Oct. 23, 1819; the first marriage, that of Daniel Remington and Eliza Eaton, Jan. 1, 1824; and the first death, that of Sam'l W. Goodridge, Jan. 27, 1822. The first school was taught at Whitesville, by Deborah Covel, in the summer of 1822. Sam'l S. White kept the first inn, in 1827, at Whitesville, and Josiah W. Green the first store, at Greens Corners, in 1822. Nath'l Covel erected a sawmill on Cryders Creek, in 1822; and Jas. Maxwell the first gristmill, at Spring Mills, in 1820.

[2] The census reports 5 churches; Bap., Seventh Day Bap., Presb., M. E., and Univ.

[3] James Eastwood, John C. McKeen, and Jas. Davidson, from N. H., settled in the s. part in 1821. The first birth was that of Mary McKeen, in June, 1821; the first marriage, that of Earl Gould and Catharine Eastwood, in June, 1822. The first school was taught by Mrs. Graham McKeen, in the summer of 1821. Wm. Andrews kept the first inn, near Black Creek Corners, in 1826, and Nelson McCall the first store, near the same place, in 1830. The first sawmill was erected by James Davidson, on Black Creek, in 1829.

[4] The census reports 4 churches; 2 Cong. and 2 M. E.

[5] Chas. Sniff, Abel Belknap, Amos Rose, and Joshua Wilson,

from New England, were settlers in the town in 1809–10; Levi Benjamin, from Windsor, Vt., settled on Lot 30, near Rushford Village, in 1813. Bethiah Belknap, born in the spring of 1810, and Sam'l Gordon, June 12, 1810, were the first births in town; Wm. Rawson and Lawrence Swift were the first married, in 1811. Plina Bannister taught the first school, near the center, in the winter of 1813–14. Levi Benjamin kept the first inn, a little N. of Rushford Village, in 1813, and Jas. McCall the first store, at the same place, in 1814. The first sawmill was built by Matthew P. Cady, on Caneadea Creek, in 1815; and the first gristmill, by Jas. McCall, on the same stream, in 1818.

[6] The census reports 4 churches; Bap., Cong., M. E., and Univ.

[7] Silas Bellamy and Silas Palmer settled in 1809,—the former at Scio Village and the latter in the N. part of the town. Polly, daughter of Silas Knight, was the first child born, in 1806, and the first one that died, in 1808; the first marriage was that of Silas Bellamy and Betsey Knight, in 1809. The first school was taught by Lucy Moore, near the village, in 1816. Alfred Johnson kept the first inn, in 1822, and the first gristmill in 1823, by Benj. Palmer.

[8] 2 R. C., Cong., Bap., and M. E.

[9] Daniel Hart and Hezekiah Ward settled in the N. part, in 1817–18. Geo. Waldruff kept the first inn, at Philips Creek Village, and Waldruff & Cartwright the first store.

interior town, lying s. e. of the center of the co. Its surface is very broken and mountainous, the highest summits being 800 to 1,200 feet above the valleys. The declivities are too steep for profitable cultivation. The streams are Genesee River and Dyke and Chenunda Creeks, all flowing in narrow and deep valleys winding among the almost precipitous mountains. The soil is mostly a sandy loam. Considerable pine lumber is still manufactured in town. **Wellsville,** (p. v.,) on Genesee River, was incorp. Oct. 12, 1857; it contains 4 churches, 2 weekly newspaper offices, 2 flouring and 3 saw mills. Pop. 1,286. The first settlements were made in the valley of the Genesee, about the commencement of the century.[1] There are 4 churches in town.[2]

WEST ALMOND—was formed from Angelica, Almond, and Alfred, April 15, 1833. It is an interior town, lying a little n. e. of the center of the co. Its surface is a broken and elevated upland. The streams are Angelica, Black, Philips, and Karr Valley Creeks,—all flowing in narrow ravines bordered by steep hillsides. The soil is principally a clay loam underlaid by hardpan. **West Almond** (p. v.) contains a church and 15 houses. The first settlement was made at the center, in 1816, by Daniel Atherton.[3] The first religious meeting was held by Rev. Robert Hubbard, (Presb.,) at the house of Daniel Dean, in 1823; and the first and only church (Bap.) was formed in 1824.

WILLING—was formed from Independence and Scio, Nov. 19, 1851. Alma was taken off in 1854, and a part of Wellsville in 1855. It lies upon the s. border of the co., e. of the center. Its surface is a broken and mountainous region, the highest summits being 800 to 1,200 ft. above the valleys. The streams are Genesee River, Cryder, Chenunda, and Fords Creeks, all flowing in narrow valleys bordered by steep mountain declivities. The soil is a clay and sandy loam. A considerable part of the surface is still covered with forests, and lumbering is extensively carried on. **Beanville,** (Shongo p. o.,) on Genesee River, in the s. part of the town, contains a church and 61 inhabitants; and **Halls Port,** (p. v.,) in the n. e. corner, a sawmill and 64 inhabitants. Elijah Robinson, from Brookfield, Madison co., settled on the Genesee, adjoining the State line, in 1825. He built a sawmill, made other improvements for four or five years, when he became deranged, and left the town.[4] The first religious meeting (Prot. Meth.) was held at the house of Daniel Baker, by Rev. Seneca Fish, in 1834.[5]

WIRT—was formed from Bolivar and Friendship, April 12, 1838. It is an interior town, lying s. w. of the center of the co. Its surface is a wild, mountainous upland, divided into three general ridges extending n. and s. The streams are headwaters of Van Campens, Little Genesee, and Dodges Creeks. **Richburgh,** (p. v.,) in the s. w. part of the town, contains 2 churches, the Richburgh Academy,[6] 2 steam gristmills, 2 sawmills, and 50 dwellings. **Wirt** is a p. o., near the center of the town. The first settlement was made in the n. part of the town, in 1812, by Benj. Crabtree and Levi Abbott, from Amsterdam, Montgomery co.[7] The first religious meeting (Bap.) was held at the house of Benj. Crabtree, in 1816, by Rev. Jonathan Post. The first church (Bap.) was organized in 1826.[8]

---

[1] The first child born was Rachel Dyke, in 1805; and the first death, that of Thos. Brink, in 1807. The first school was taught, near the e. line, by Ithamer Brookings, in 1814. Nath'l Dyke built the first grist and saw mill, in 1803, on Dyke Creek, near the e. line.

[2] Cong., M. E., Bap., and R. C.

[3] Jason Bixby, Isaac Pray, and Daniel Hooker settled on the road leading from Almond to Angelica, and John Alfred, from N. J., near the n. line, all previous to 1818. The first child born was Jerusha, daughter of Daniel Atherton, in the fall of 1817; and the first death, that of Jason Bixby, in the spring of 1818. The first school was taught, in the e. part, by Jasper White, in 1818. Daniel Atherton kept the first inn, in 1817, at the center, and Samuel M. Eddy the first store, at the same place, in 1832. The first sawmill was erected by Enoch Hawks, on Angelica Creek, in 1833.

[4] The first death was that of a child of Austin Butler, in 1837. The first school was taught near Beanville, in 1836, by Betsey Lovell. Allen Gifford kept the first inn, in 1838, at Beanville, and Jas. R. Wood the first store, at the same place, in 1839. Elijah Robinson erected the first sawmill, near the Penn. line, on the Genesee.

[5] There are 2 churches in town; M. E. and Univ.

[6] This institution has lately been incorp. with the common school system.

[7] Azel Buckley, from Unadilla, Otsego co., settled in 1814, and Daniel Willard, from Mass., in 1815. Mr. W. is the oldest settler now living in town. The first child born was Benj. Crabtree, jr., in 1813; and the first marriage, that of Hyra Axdell and Lucy Crabtree, in 1814. The first school was taught, in the n. part of the town, by Sophia Hitchcock, in 1820. Alvan Richardson erected the first sawmill, in 1824, and the first gristmill, in 1825, on Genesee Creek, near Richburgh. Mr. Richardson also kept the first inn, in 1824, and Francis L. Leroy the first store, in the same year.

[8] There are 4 churches in town; Bap., F. W. Bap., Seventh Day Bap., and M. E.

Acres of Land, Valuation, Population, Dwellings, Families, Freeholders, Schools, Live Stock, Agricultural Products, and Domestic Manufactures, of Allegany County.

Names of Towns.	Acres of Land.		Valuation of 1858.			Population.		No. of Dwellings.	No. of Families.	Freeholders.	Schools.	
	Improved.	Unimproved.	Real Estate.	Personal Property.	Total.	Males.	Females.				No. of Districts.	Children taught.
Alfred	17,733	11,000	327,639	75,899	403,538	859	848	343	372	328	9	527
Allen	11,125½	11,514½	221,612	9,648	231,260	518	508	191	203	173	8	417
Alma	925½	22,174	102,584	1,000	103,584	243	169	73	74	37	3	212
Almond	25,249	8,051	400,866	70,283	471,149	993	959	348	384	323	11	729
Amity	11,210½	23,032	364,341	10,700	375,041	1,339	1,316	506	522	384	8	840
Andover	10,443½	13,045	308,243	10,100	318,343	907	868	339	340	285	7	630
Angelica	9,417½	18,036½	377,891	46,730	424,621	929	903	307	330	254	8	662
Belfast	9,425¾	13,250¾	369,660	19,000	388,660	1,077	1,053	414	414	266	10	754
Birdsall	7,324	16,754	160,307	5,037	165,344	452	386	155	156	126	6	329
Bolivar	4,203¾	17,736	179,210	14,100	193,310	503	482	189	195	155	6	364
Burns	8,760¼	7,526½	274,883	44,817	319,700	566	521	201	211	165	7	412
Caneadea	6,415	11,784½	339,626	10,150	349,776	1,237	1,163	474	493	272	14	991
Centerville	14,488	7,583	316,350	29,180	345,530	674	675	255	254	242	12	506
Clarksville	4,836	17,454	174,725		174,725	421	360	158	164	140	6	266
Cuba	13,302½	8,911	594,310	110,895	705,205	1,120	996	388	421	330	13	886
Friendship	11,167	9,958	420,245	78,050	498,295	900	938	357	386	331	10	695
Genesee	3,733¼	15,842	168,730	9,975	178,705	449	446	169	175	154	7	391
Granger	8,685	7,380	215,011	12,655	227,666	630	588	250	265	196	7	502
Grove	6,431¾	11,069	223,750	850	224,600	595	523	212	285	185	9	441
Hume	12,956½	10,388½	354,906	29,200	384,106	1,070	1,024	425	428	295	15	755
Independence	11,912½	9,252	223,046	76,605	299,651	585	551	224	227	218	7	475
New Hudson	11,282	9,003½	269,290	9,250	278,540	751	700	275	274	246	14	628
Rushford	13,943½	8,278	433,850	86,400	520,250	1,005	990	391	404	372	8	410
Scio	7,223	24,189½	304,658	3,850	308,508	1,657	1,527	620	639	415	13	699
Ward[1]			163,370	3,875	167,245						7	619
Wellsville[a]			272,835	24,000	296,835						8	361
West Almond	11,404	10,572	289,577	24,848	314,425	508	464	185	194	94	7	446
Willing	3,910¾	7,767	135,331	750	136,081	587	540	218	225	203	11	657
Wirt	12,526½	9,937	280,750	10,925	291,675	797	727	291	299	285	8	807
Total	270,035	341,549¼	8,267,596	828,872	9,096,468	21,372	20,225	7,958	8,334	6,483	259	16,381

Names of Towns.	Live Stock.					Agricultural Products.							Domestic Cloths, in Yards.
						Bush. of Grain.					Dairy Products		
	Horses.	Working Oxen and Calves.	Cows.	Sheep.	Swine.	Winter.	Spring.	Tons of Hay.	Bushels of Potatoes.	Bushels of Apples.	Pounds of Butter.	Pounds of Cheese.	
Alfred	574	1,388	1,131	11,183	598	790	47,934¾	3,552	10,302½	23,694	81,224	176,260	2,633
Allen	436	1,152	630	7,716	387	1,147	42,226	3,024	7,352	5,691	63,540	10,170	710
Alma	63	248		165	141	184	4,979½	190½	2,049	175	7,960	340	100
Almond	695	1,947	997	8,236	919	9,293	55,003	3,088½	7,299½	22,144	106,930	4,699	1,033
Amity	406	1,179	698	3,697	516	3,547	47,486	2,439	7,825	11,609	57,895	15,750	1,698½
Andover	355	1,268	777	3,190	483	57	45,448¾	1,623½	12,063	3,751	81,430	13,570	1,654
Angelica	365	996	612	4,219	427	2,833	27,281	2,025	6,350	3,780	43,510	1,835	1,146
Belfast	484	1,006	716	3,220	517	3,587½	25,656¼	1,943½	5,271½	6,837	58,565	14,964	1,081
Birdsall	281	943	435	1,581	320	851	34,526½	1,919	5,648	2,527	48,168	1,270	214
Bolivar	167	488	287	1,499	216	114	27,947½	1,032	6,611	1,452	35,484	1,237	1,139¾
Burns	400	883	478	3,077	423	8,522	29,123¼	1,295	3,953	4,643	44,420	20,125	518¾
Caneadea	312	925	544	1,484	450	7,737	32,998¾	1,458½	5,833	7,260	50,901		468
Centerville	563	1,273	1,449	4,392	485	741	43,735	3,797½	12,005	14,683	103,337	221,075	1,653
Clarksville	163	664	335	2,518	226	1,275	24,037	1,123	4,354	1,480	29,466	850	1,036
Cuba	546	1,290	941	7,001	625	750	58,545½	2,851¼	8,481	11,833	105,360	42,840	2,062
Friendship	490	1,033	734	3,547	562	3,323	43,417	1,937	6,320	9,009	77,200	10,825	2,342
Genesee	183	501	293	2,207	241	387	16,685	1,006½	6,065	1,342	33,715	3,950	647
Granger	391	934	536	3,716	432	3,427	44,889	1,823	6,755	4,761	50,001	4,410	599
Grove	287	723	449	2,067	466	1,213	31,233½	1,256	4,201	2,253	49,325	2,525	762½
Hume	765	1,416	934	5,414	730	13,352	48,660¾	2,580¾	11,540	15,721	86,334	12,265	655
Independence	432	1,384	705	3,047	457	201	28,403¾	925¼	11,917½	7,315	63,505	52,070	1,051½
New Hudson	509	1,233	1,043	3,417	610	481	38,522½	2,573¼	7,791	7,150	81,530	93,305	1,245
Rushford	641	1,191	1,667	2,685	565	504	31,261½	3,426¾	12,269	16,866	96,435	317,955	594
Scio	345	696	541	2,213	384	672	28,761	1,439¾	8,165	4,684	38,400	2,650	643
Ward[1]													
Wellsville[a]													
West Almond	395	1,222	661	3,177	414	1,962	47,768½	2,421½	8,134	4,480	65,350	11,368	1,180
Willing	153	488	267	828	251	358½	9,099¾	496¾	3,450	816	29,301	410	957
Wirt	457	1,181	709	6,657	604	2,470	64,582	2,290	10,226	15,315	72,799	6,885	2,885½
Total	10,858	27,652	18,569	102,153	12,449	69,799	990,213	53,538¾	202,231	211,271	1,662,085	1,043,603	30,708¾

[a] Formed since 1855.

BROOME COUNTY.

This county was formed from Tioga, March 28, 1806.[1] Owego and Berkshire were annexed to Tioga co. March 21, 1822. It is situated near the center of the s. border of the State, centrally distant 110 mi. from Albany, and contains 706 sq. mi. Its surface is greatly diversified, consisting of rolling and hilly uplands, broad river intervales, and the narrow valleys of small streams. The hills extend from the Penn. line northerly through the co. They are divided into 3 general ranges by the valleys of the Susquehanna and Chenango Rivers. The first range lying E. of the Susquehanna forms the E. border of the co. Its highest summits are 400 to 700 feet above the Delaware and 1,400 to 1,700 feet above tide. The declivities of the hills are usually steep, and the summits spread out into a broad and hilly upland. This ridge is divided by the deep ravines of a large number of small streams; and in several places it rises into peaks. The second ridge lies in the great bend of the Susquehanna, and is bounded by the valleys of that river and the Chenango. The highest summits are 300 to 500 feet above the Susquehanna and 1,200 to 1,400 feet above tide. The hills are generally bounded by gradual slopes, and the summits are broad, rolling uplands. The southern portion of this ridge is high above the valleys; but toward the N. the hilly character subsides into that of a fine rolling region. The third ridge lies w. of Chenango and Susquehanna Rivers. Its summits are a little less in elevation than those of the second ridge; and the general characteristics of the two regions are nearly the same. The wide valley of the Susquehanna divides it into two distinct parts, the southern of which is more hilly than the northern. The hills in the central and western parts of the co. are rounded and arable to their summits. The narrow valleys that break the continuity of the ridges are usually bordered by gradually sloping hillsides.

The rocks of this co. all belong to the Chemung and Catskill groups. The former—consisting of slaty sandstone and shales—occupy all the N. and w. portions of the co.; and the latter—consisting of gray and red sandstone, red shale, and slate—crown all the summits in the s. and w. portions. Drift—consisting of sand, gravel, clay, and hardpan—covers a large share of the more level parts of the co., the rocks only cropping out upon the declivities and summits of the hills. The valleys throughout the co. appear to have been excavated by the action of water, showing that a force immensely greater than any now in existence must once have swept over this portion of country. Weak brine springs were early found, extending for several mi. along the valley of Halfway Brook, in the N. part of this co.[2] Several excavations have been made for coal, but without success, as all the coal measures are above the highest strata of rocks found in the co.

The principal rivers are the Susquehanna,[3] Delaware, Chenango, Tioughnioga,[4] and Otselic. The Susquehanna enters the co. from the N., and flows in almost a due s. direction through Colesville and Windsor to the Great Bend in the State of Penn., whence, turning N., it again enters the co. in Conklin, flows through that town in a N. w. direction, and thence westerly to the w. border of the co. In the upper course of this river the valley is narrow and bordered by high and steep declivities; but further w. it expands into broad intervales bordered by gradually sloping hillsides. The whole valley is celebrated for its beauty. The majestic river, with its strong current of clear, sparkling water, the deep, rich intervales, and the beautiful slopes crowned with forests, all together form a landscape rarely equalled for beauty and quiet repose. The Delaware forms a small portion of the E. boundary. It flows through a deep, rocky valley bordered by steep and often

---

1 Named from John Broome, of N. Y., then Lieut. Gov. of the State. For the compliment Lt. Gov. Broome presented the co. with a handsomely executed silver seal, appropriately designed by himself, emblematical of the name.

2 A few years since, a boring was commenced in Lisle, on the site of an old deer lick, and was continued to a depth of more than 400 feet, without any practical result. The theory of the operators was, that the salt came from the same source as the

Onondaga brine, and that, to obtain water of the same amount of saltness, all that was necessary would be to bore to the geographical level of those wells. Sulphur springs have been observed in Nanticoke, 14 mi. from Binghamton, and at Bellona.

3 Called by the Indians Ga-wa-no-wa-na-neh, at the Great Island.

4 Indian name, O-nan′no-gi-is′ka, Shagbark hickory.

precipitous hills. Chenango River enters the co. from the N. and flows in a general southerly direction until it enters the Susquehanna at Binghamton. A broad intervale extends along the lower part of this river, but farther N. the high ridges shut close in on either side, confining the valley to very narrow limits. The Tioughnioga enters the co. from Cortland and flows S. E. until it unites with the Chenango at Chenango Forks. The valley of this river is very narrow, and is bordered by high and steep hillsides. Otselic River, also from the N., flows through a similar narrow valley and unites with the Tioughnioga at Whitneys Point. The other principal streams are Oquaga Creek, a tributary of the Delaware, Okkanum, Little Snake, Little and Big Choconut, and Nanticoke Creeks, tributaries of the Susquehanna, and Castle Creek, tributary of the Chenango.

The soil along the river intervales is generally very fertile, consisting of deep, sandy and gravelly loam mixed with disintegrated slate and vegetable mold. The narrow valleys of the smaller streams are also fertile. The soil upon the N. and W. hills consists principally of gravelly loam intermixed with clay and disintegrated shale, and is well adapted to grazing. The declivities of the S. and E. hills are similar to the last in character, but their summits are generally covered with clay and hardpan. The large proportion of upland and the unevenness of the surface render this co. best adapted to pasturage. While all branches of agriculture are pursued, fruit raising, and stock and wool growing, in connection with the products of the dairy, form the leading interests. A limited amount of manufacturing is carried on at Binghamton and several other places.

The co. seat is located at Binghamton, at the junction of the Chenango and Susquehanna Rivers.[1] The courthouse, situated at the head of Chenango St., fronting Court St., is a fine stone and brick edifice, with a Grecian portico in the Ionic style. It contains the usual co. offices, and in many respects is a model building.[2] The jail is on Hawley St., at a little distance from the courthouse.[3] A fireproof co. clerk's office is situated adjacent to the courthouse. The co. poorhouse is located upon a farm of 130 acres 3 mi. N. of Binghamton. The average number of inmates is 45, kept at a weekly cost of $1 08 each, exclusive of the products of the farm, which are estimated at $800 per annum. The children are sent to the district school, and when of proper age are bound out. No religious instruction is afforded. The sexes are kept in separate buildings, and the general arrangement of the institution is such as to secure the health and comfort of the inmates.

The principal works of internal improvement are the Chenango Canal, connecting the Susquehanna River at Binghamton with the Erie Canal at Utica; the N. Y. & Erie R. R., and the Syracuse, Binghamton, & N. Y. R. R.[4] These various routes furnish all necessary facilities for traveling and commercial purposes, and bring the agricultural lands of the co. into close proximity to the great Eastern markets.[5] Several plank roads have been built; but they are now mostly abandoned.

There are 6 newspapers published in the co.[6]

---

[1] Binghamton (then *"Chenango Point"*) was a half-shire of Tioga co. previous to the erection of Broome co. The co. was divided into 2 jury districts in 1801, and a courthouse was built in 1802. Previously the courts had been held a part of the time at the house of J. Whitney, in Binghamton. A courthouse was built in 1826, which was superseded by a new and elegant brick edifice in 1857. The first co. officers were John Patterson, *First Judge;* James Stoddard, Amos Patterson, Daniel Hudson, Geo. Harper, and Mason Wattles, *Associate Judges;* Ashbel Wells, *Co. Clerk;* and Wm. Woodruff, *Sheriff.* The first court was held on the 2d Tuesday of May, 1806.

[2] This building was erected in 1857, at a cost of $32,000. It is 96 feet long by 58 wide. The front is ornamented by a portico supported by 4 Ionic pillars 6 feet in diameter and 36 feet high. The basement is built of stone and the upper stories of brick. The rooms are all large, convenient, and well ventilated.

[3] The portion of the jail containing the cells was built in 1858, at a cost of $15,000. In its construction due provisions were made for the safety, health, and classification of prisoners.

[4] The Albany & Susquehanna R. R., now in process of construction, extends from Binghamton N. E. through the co. to Albany. This road will probably be completed in a few years.

[5] The Delaware, Lackawanna, & Western R. R. connects with the N. Y. and Erie R. R. at Great Bend Station, just s. of the line of this co., thus forming a direct communication with the coal mines of E. Penn. Large quantities of this coal are sent over the Erie and the S. B. & N. Y. R. R., supplying the salt works at Syracuse and the markets in the w. part of the State; and a considerable amount is shipped on the canal at Binghamton.

[6] *The American Constellation* was pub. at Union Village (then in Tioga co.) in 1800.

The Broome Co. Patriot was commenced at Binghamton in 1812, by Chauncey Morgan. In 1815 it was changed to

The Phœnix, and was published by Morgan & Robinson. In 1819 it was discontinued.

The Republican Herald was commenced in 1818, and successively published by Morgan & Howard, Abraham Burrell, and Dorephus Abbey, until 1822.

The Broome Republican was established at Binghamton in 1822, by Maj. Augustus Morgan. It was published by Morgan until 1824, by Morgan & Canoll until 1828, by Evans & Canoll until 1835, by Canoll & Cooke until 1839, when it passed into the hands of Davis & Cooke. It was continued by T. Cooke until 1848, and by E. R. Colston until 1849. It subsequently became the property of Wm. Stuart, and is now published daily and weekly.

The Evening Express, d., was issued from the Republican office in 1848.

The Daily Iris was started in 1849, by Wm. Stuart and E. T. Evans. It was soon after changed to

The Binghamton Daily Republican, and is still published by Wm. Stuart.

The Broome Co. Courier was started in 1831, by J. R. Orton, and was continued by him until 1837. It then successively passed into the hands of Sheldon & Marble; I. C. Sheldon; E. P. Marble; E. P. & J. W. Marble; and Marble & Johnson. In 1843 it was changed to

The Binghamton Courier and Broome Co. Democrat, and was published by J. & C. Orton. In 1846 it passed into the hands of N. S. Davis. In 1849 it passed into the hands of J. K. Dickinson and was changed to

The Binghamton Democrat. It is now published by Adams & Lawyer.

The Iris, semi-mo., was started in July, 1839, by C. P. Cooke. In July, 1841, it was purchased by Edwin T. Evans, and by him it was enlarged, and published weekly until 1853, when it was merged in the Binghamton Republican.

The Binghamton Standard was started in Nov. 1853, by J. Van Valkenburg, and is still published.

The Binghamton Mercury, semi-mo., was issued a short time by Chester Dehart.

The Susquehanna Journal, started in Oct. 1853, by W. H. Pearne, was merged in the Broome Republican in 1855.

The Broome Co. American was started in May, 1855, by Ransom Bostwick.

The Union News was established at Union in 1851, by

By a treaty held at Fort Herkimer, June 28, 1785, between the Governor and Commissioners of Indian Affairs in behalf of the State, and the Oneidas and Tuscaroras, the latter for $11,500 ceded all their lands, bounded N. by an E. and w. line from the Chenango to the Unadilla, 10 mi. above the mouth of the latter, E. by the Line of Property,[1] s. by Penn., and w. by the Chenango and Susquehanna. At the Hartford Convention, in 1786, a tract of 230,400 acres, between the Chenango and Tioughnioga on the E. and Owego River on the w., was ceded to Massachusetts.[2] This tract was afterward known as the "Boston Ten Towns," and was sold by Mass. (Nov. 7, 1787) to 60 persons for £1500.[3] It is embraced in Broome, Tioga, and Cortland cos. The Indian title to this tract was extinguished in 1787, and the remaining Indian titles within the co. were extinguished by the treaty of Fort Stanwix in 1788. The s. and E. parts of the co. were granted to Hooper, Wilson, Bingham, Cox, and others, several of whom resided in Philadelphia.[4]

The first settlements in the co. were made in the valleys of the Susquehanna and Chenango, in 1785. The settlers were people who had traversed the region in the Revolution; and they located while the country was still threatened with Indian hostilities, and before Phelps and Gorham had opened the fertile lands of Western N. Y. to immigration. The early settlement was retarded by a remarkable ice freshet in 1787–88, which destroyed most of the property of the settlers upon the river intervales. Scarcely less calamitous to life and property was the scarcity that followed in 1789. Oquaga, on the E. branch of the Susquehanna, was a noted rendezvous of tories and Indians during the Revolution.[5] Most of the invasions into the Schoharie and Mohawk settlements, as well as those upon the frontiers of Ulster and Orange cos., were by way of the Tioga and Susquehanna Rivers from Niagara; and this war path, with its sufferings and cruelties, has been often described in the narratives of returned captives.

BINGHAMTON—was formed from Chenango, Dec. 3, 1855. It lies at the junction of the Susquehanna and Chenango Rivers, and extends s. to the s. line of the co. The surface is hilly in the s., but the N. part embraces the wide and beautiful intervales extending along the two rivers at and near their junction. The hills are 300 to 400 feet above the river, and are generally arable to their summits. The soil in the valleys is a deep, rich, alluvial and gravelly loam, and upon the hills it is a fine quality of slaty loam. **Binghamton**[6] (p. v.) was incorp. April 2, 1813. By a subsequent charter, passed May 3, 1834, its limits were enlarged and its territory was divided into 5 wards. It is beautifully situated on the N. bank of the Susquehanna at its junction with the Chenango. It contains the State Inebriate Asylum,[7] the Binghamton Academy, and the Susquehanna Seminary,[8] 3 female seminaries,[9] a commercial college,[10] 2 water cures,[11] 9 churches,[12] 5 newspaper offices, ~~and~~ several manufactories. The village is an important station upon the Erie R. R., and is connected with Syracuse by the S. B. & N. Y. R. R. It is also the s. w. terminus of the Chenango Canal and of the Albany & Susquehanna R. R. It is the center of a large trade,

A. F. Quinlan. It was subsequently sold to Cephas Benedict and Ebenezer M. Betts, and is still published. **The Broome County Gazette** was commenced at Whitneys Point, in July, 1858, by G. A. Dodge, its present publisher.

[1] This line was agreed upon at Fort Stanwix in 1768, and was surveyed by Simon Metcalf the next year. It forms the E. boundary of this co.

[2] The s. bounds of this tract were to be the N. line of the tract granted to Daniel Cox and Robert Lettice Hooper, and it was to extend as far N. as was necessary to include the above quantity of land. Upon survey it was found to overlap the Military Tract by 17,264 acres, which was allowed, and an equivalent was granted to the claimants under the latter in Junius, Seneca co.—*Balloting Book, pp.* 20, 23.

[3] The partition of a part of this tract by lot was legalized March 3, 1789, in an act reciting the names of the 60 associates. —*Laws of N. Y., Fol. Ed., 12th Sess., p.* 76, *Map No.* 148, *State Engineer and Surveyor's Office.*

[4] A tract of 1000 acres on both sides of the Susquehanna was sold to Jacob and John Springstead, Josiah, David, and Daniel Stow, David Hotchkiss, and Joseph Beebee. Other tracts were sold to Wm. Allison, James Clinton, Isaac Melcher, Abijah Hammond, and others. The islands in the Susquehanna were bought by Jas. Clinton, at 4 shillings per acre.

[5] This place is sometimes found written Oh-oh-ogh-wa-ge and Ogh-qua-ga. There is here a hill or mountain on both sides of the river, gently sloping from a beautiful vale of 3 or 4 mi. in length and a mi. to a mi. and a half wide. When first settled, it bore evidence of having long been occupied by the Indians. Apple trees of great age were found growing, and traces of fortifications existed, supposed to have been erected by Gen. Clinton. Missionary labors were directed to this locality about the middle of the last century, and in 1753 the Rev. Gideon Hawley was sent hither

from Mass.—*Doc. Hist.*, III.1031; *Wilkinson's Binghamton, p.*142.

[6] Binghamton was originally called "*Chenango Point.*" Its present name was given in honor of William Bingham, the original purchaser of a large tract of land lying on both sides of the Susquehanna, and including the site of the village. He made liberal donations of land to the village.

[7] The New York State Inebriate Asylum was incorp. in 1854 for the term of 50 years. It is designed for the medical treatment and restraint of inebriates. It owes its origin mainly to the persevering efforts of Dr. J. Edward Turner. Every person donating $10 is deemed a subscriber and stockholder. The building is located E. of the village, on a beautiful site, 240 feet above the water. It is 365 feet long by 82 feet broad, built of stone and brick in the Tudor castellated style of architecture. The citizens donated a farm of 250 acres, upon which the buildings are erected.

[8] This institution is under the charge of the M. E. denomination, and is designed for a large boarding school. The building is a 4 story brick edifice, pleasantly located N. w. of the village upon an eminence overlooking the valley.

[9] River Side Seminary, established in 1848 by Miss R. S. Ingalls; Miss Barton's Seminary, established in 1857; and Harmony Retreat Seminary, established in 1857 by Misses March.

[10] Lowell & Warner's Commercial College.

[11] Binghamton Water Cure, established in 1855 by O. V. Thayer; and the Mt. Prospect Water Cure, under the supervision of J. U. North.

[12] 2 M. E., and 1, each, Bap., Presb., Cong., Prot. E., Univ., R. C., and Af. Meth.

[13] There was transhipped from the Del., Lackawanna & Western R. R. cars to the Chenango canal boats, in 1857, 51,700 gross tons of coal, and from these boats to the cars 25,895 tons of Clinton (Oneida co.) iron ore.

and is an important point for the transhipment of coal.[13] Pop. 8,818. **Hawleyton** (p. o.) is a hamlet in the s. part, near the Penn. line. The first settlement was made in 1787, by emigrants mostly from New England.[1] The first religious services were conducted by Rev. Mr. Howe, (Bap.,) in 1788. Hon. Daniel S. Dickinson is a resident of this town.

BARKER[2]—was formed from Lisle, April 18, 1831. A part of Greene was annexed April 28, 1840. It lies upon Tioughnioga River, N. w. of the center of the co. The surface consists of a high, broken plateau divided into two distinct parts by the valley of the river. The declivities of the hills are in some places very steep; but their summits spread out into a broken region generally covered with timber and adapted to pasturage. The highest point, in the N. w. part of the town, is about 1400 feet above tide. The river valley is very narrow, but the limited amount of intervale is excellent land. Halfway Brook flows through a narrow valley in the E. part of the town. In this valley brine springs have been found; and here also the unsuccessful boring for salt was made.[3] The soil in the valley is a rich alluvium and gravelly loam, and that upon the hills is a clayey loam mixed with disintegrated slate and shale. **Chenango Forks** (p. v.) is situated mostly in this town, at the fork of Chenango and Tioughnioga Rivers. It is a station on the S. B. & N. Y. R. R. Pop. 506,—in Barker 287, in Chenango 127, and in Greene (Chenango co) 92. **Barker** is a p. o. in the central part of the town. The first settlement was made in 1791, by John Barker, from Branford, Conn.[4] There are 3 churches in town.[5]

CHENANGO—was formed Feb. 16, 1791. Windsor was taken off in 1807, Conklin in 1824, and Binghamton and Port Crane in 1855. A part of Union was annexed Feb. 26, 1808, and a part of Maine, Nov. 27, 1856. It lies upon the w. bank of Chenango River, a little w. of the center of the co. Its surface consists of the river intervale and several high ridges extending in a N. and s. direction and separated by the narrow valleys of small streams. The declivities of the hills are steep, and their summits are 300 to 600 feet above the valleys. Castle and Kattel Creeks, tributaries of Chenango River, are the principal streams. The former was named from the location of an Indian castle near its mouth, and the latter from a family of early settlers. The soil upon the N. hills is a gravelly loam mixed with disintegrated slate and underlaid by hard-pan, but farther s. it becomes a deeper and richer gravelly loam. It is productive, but, from its moist character, it is largely devoted to grazing. Stock growing and dairying form the leading branches of agricultural interest. **Castle Creek** (p. v.) is on the creek of the same name, in the w. part of the town. Pop. 185. **Glen Castle,** (p. o.,) on a branch of the same stream, is in the central part. **Chenango,** (p. o.,) on Chenango River, is a station on the S. B. & N. Y. R. R. **Kattelville** is a hamlet on Kattel Creek. The first settlement was made in 1787, by Thos. Gallop.[6] There are 4 churches in town.[7]

COLESVILLE[8]—was formed from Windsor, April 2, 1821. It lies upon the Susquehanna, E. of the center of the co. Its surface consists principally of a high and broken upland divided into 2 parts by the deep valley of the river. The summits of these uplands are 400 to 700 feet above the valley, and considerable portions are still covered with forests. The soil upon the river bottoms is a deep, fertile, gravelly loam, and upon the summits of the hills it consists of clay and slate. It is generally much better adapted to pasturage than tillage. **Harpersville,** (p. v.,) on Susquehanna River, contains 3 churches and has a pop. of 230. **Center Village,**[9] (p. v.,) on the Susquehanna, has a pop. of 147. **New Ohio,** (p. o.,) in the N. part of the town, **Osborne Hollow,** (p. o.,) in the w. part, **West Colesville,** (p. o.,) in the s. w. part, **Colesville,** (p. o.,) s. of the center, **Ouquaga,** (p. o.,) and **Nineveh,** (p. o.,) on the Susquehanna, are hamlets. **Valonia Springs** and **Unitaria** are p. offices. The first settlement[10]

---

[1] Among the early settlers were Capt. Joseph Leonard, Col. Wm. Rose, the two brothers Whitney, —— Lyon, Jesse Thayer, Peter and Thos. Ingersoll, Saml. Harding, Capt. John Sawtell, —— Butler, and Solomon Moore. The first birth was that of Amasa Leonard, Sept. 23, 1788; the first marriage, that of Ezekiel Crocker and Polly Benton; and the first death, that of Mrs. Blunt, in 1787. Lewis Keeler opened the first inn, and Delano & Monroe the first store. Ezekiel Crocker erected the first grist-mill, in 1794. The first school was taught by Col. Wm. Rose, in 1794. For details of early history see *Wilkinson's Annals of Binghamton.*
[2] Named from John Barker, the first settler.
[3] See p. 178.
[4] Simeon Rogers, John Allen, Asa Beach, and Sol. Rose, from Conn., settled in town in 1792. The first marriage was

that of Simeon Rogers and a daughter of John Barker, in 1792; the first birth, that of Chauncey, a son of Simeon Rogers, in 1793; and the first death, that of Thos. Gallop, the same year. Simeon Rogers opened the first inn, in 1795, kept the first store, and built the first mill. The first school was taught by Thos. Cartwright, in 1795.
[5] 2 M. E. and Cong.
[6] Stephen Palmer and Jared Page were among the earliest settlers. The first birth was that of Sally Smith, in 1791.
[7] 3 M. E. and 1 Bap.
[8] Named from Nathaniel Cole, one of the first settlers.
[9] At this place is a tannery, which turns out 50,000 sides of leather per annum.
[10] Lemuel and Nath'l Badger and Casper Spring settled in the town in 1786; Nathaniel and Vena Cole, Daniel Picket, Jed.

was made in 1785, by John Lamphere, from Watertown, Conn. The first religious services were conducted by Rev. Joseph Badger, in 1793. There are 10 churches in town.[1]

CONKLIN[2]—was formed from Chenango, March 29, 1824. A part of Windsor was taken off in 1831, and a part was annexed from Windsor in 1851. It lies upon the Susquehanna, s. of the center of the co. Its surface consists of the fine broad intervale of the river and high, broken uplands which rise upon each side. The summits of the hills are 400 to 600 feet above the valley. The declivities upon the w. side of the river are very steep, but upon the e. they are generally more gradual. Little Snake Creek flows in an easterly direction through the s. w. part. Its valley is narrow and is bordered by steep hills. The soil upon the summits of the hills is a hard clayey and gravelly loam largely intermixed with fragments of slate. In the valley the soil is a deep, rich alluvium and gravelly loam. **Kirkwood** (p. v.) is situated on the e. bank of the Susquehanna, in the s. part of the town. It is a station on the Erie R. R., and contains 25 houses. **Conklin Center** and **Corbettsville** are p. offices, and **Millburn** and **Conklin** are hamlets. At Millburn are extensive pyroligneous acid works. The settlement of the town was commenced in 1788, at the mouth of Snake Creek, by Jonathan Bennett, Ralph Lathrop, and Waples Hance.[3] The first religious services were conducted by Revs. David Dunham and John Leach, Methodist missionaries. There are 4 churches in town; M. E., Presb., Bap., and Christian.

LISLE[4]—was formed from Union, April 7, 1801. Nanticoke, Barker, and Triangle were taken off in 1831. The line of Berkshire was altered in 1812, and a part was annexed to Union in 1827. It is the n. w. corner town of the co. The surface is mostly a hilly and broken upland, divided by the valley of Tioughnioga River into 2 unequal parts. The summits of the hills are 400 to 700 feet above the river, and their declivities are generally steep. Dudley or Yorkshire Creek flows easterly through near the center of the town, its narrow valley breaking the continuity of the w. ridge. The soil along the valley is a rich, gravelly loam, but upon the hills it consists of clay and a slaty gravel underlaid by hardpan. The declivities of the hills are usually too steep for easy cultivation, and the soil upon the summits is a moist clay loam, better adapted to grazing than grain growing. **Lisle** (p. v.) is situated on the w. bank of the Tioughnioga. It is a station on the S. B. & N. Y. R. R., and contains about 30 houses. The old Catskill & Ithaca Turnpike, built in 1796, crossed the river at this point. **Yorkshire,** (Center Lisle p. o.,) near the center of the town, contains about 30 houses. **Killawog,** (p. o.,) in the n. part, on the Tioughnioga, is a station on the S. B. & N. Y. R. R. The first settlement was made in 1791, by emigrants from N. E.[5] The first religious services were conducted in 1795, by Rev. Seth Williston. There are 5 churches in town.[6]

MAINE—was formed from Union, March 27, 1848. A part of Chenango was taken off in 1856. It is the central town upon the w. border of the co. Its surface consists of ranges of hills divided by numerous narrow valleys, the principal of which extends in a n. and s. direction. These hills are 400 to 600 feet above the valley of Chenango River. The principal streams are Nanticoke, Bradley, and Crocker Creeks. The soil is a gravelly loam largely intermixed with the underlying slate. **Maine,** (p. v.,) situated on Nanticoke Creek, w. of the center, contains 3 churches. Pop. 220. **East Maine** is a p. o. The first settlement was made in May, 1797, by Daniel Howard, Alfred and Russell Gates, and Winthrop Roe.[7] There are 4 churches in town; 2 M. E., Bap., and Cong.

NANTICOKE[8]—was formed from Lisle, April 18, 1831. It lies upon the w. border of he co., n. of the center. Its surface consists of an upland broken by a few narrow ravines.

Merchant, Bateman S. Dickinson, —— Wilmot, Daniel Crofoot, and Titus Humiston, in 1795; John Ruggles and Isaac Tyrell, in 1796; and Eli Osborne and Peter Warn, in 1800. The first birth was that of Louisa Badger, May 28, 1788; the first death, that of John Lamphere, the same year; and the first marriage, that of Benj. Bird and Mrs. John Lamphere, in 1794. Benj. Bird kept the first inn, in 1794, and Bateman S. Dickinson the first store, in 1805. The first school was taught by Job Bunnel.

1 4 M. E., 2 Bap., 2 Union, Prot. E., Presb.

2 Named from Judge John Conklin, one of the early settlers.

3 Among the early settlers were Gerret Snedaker, David Bound, Daniel Chapman, Peter Wentz, Asa Rood, Nathaniel Tagot, Asa Squires, John Bell, Silas Bowker, Joel Lamoreaux, Abraham Sneden, David and Joseph Compton, Abraham Miller, Ebenezer Park, Noel Carr, and Thos. Cooper. The first birth was that of William Wentz, Feb. 18, 1795; the first marriage, that of Noel Carr and Sally Tousler, in 1803; and the first death, that of Silas Bowker. The first gristmill was built at " Fitchs

Creek," in 1790. The first school was taught by George Lane, in 1801.

4 Named from Lisle, in France.

5 The first settlers were Josiah Patterson, Ebenezer Tracy, Edward Edwards, David Manning, Eliphalet Parsons, and Whittlesey Gleason. The first birth was that of Henry Patterson, in 1793; the first marriage, that of Solomon Owen and Sylvia Cook; and the first death, that of Wright Dudley. The first gristmill was built in 1800, by Jacob Hill. The first store was kept by Moses Adams, and the first tavern by O. Wheaton, in 1799.

6 2 Bap., Cong., Presb., and M. E.

7 Benjamin Norton settled in the town in 1798. The first birth was that of Cynthia, daughter of Winthrop Roe, in July, 1797. The first school was taught by Betsey Ward, in 1802. Daniel Howard built the first gristmill, in 1810; Jared Ketchum kept the first store, in 1825, and Oliver Whitcomb the first tavern, in 1829.

8 This name is derived from the Indian name of Nanticoke Creek.

The summits of the highest hills are 100 to 300 feet above the river and 1,200 to 1,400 feet above tide. The town is drained principally by the two branches of Nanticoke Creek, which flow s. through the central portions of the town. The soil upon the hills is a slaty loam underlaid by hardpan. The settlements are principally confined to the valleys. **Lambs Corners,** in the central part of the town, contains about 12 houses. **Nanticoke Springs,** in the s. part, and **Glen Aubrey,** are p. offices. The first settlement was made on Nanticoke Creek, in 1793, by Philip Counselman and John Beachtle, from Luzerne co., Penn.,[1] and —— Stoddard, from Conn. There are 2 churches in town; Bap. and M. E.

PORT CRANE[2]—was formed from Chenango, Dec. 3, 1855. It lies upon the E. bank of Chenango River, extending from the central portions of the co. N. to the borders of Chenango. Its surface consists principally of a high and rolling upland region. The valley of the Chenango is very narrow, and the hills rise steeply to an elevation of 500 to 700 feet above the river. Page Brook flows in a southerly direction through the center of the town, dividing the uplands into 2 distinct ridges. The soil upon the hills is a clay and slaty loam underlaid by hardpan, and in the valleys it consists of a fine, rich gravelly loam and alluvium. **Port Crane,** (p. v.,) on the Chenango Canal, in the s. part of the town, has a pop. of 193. **Doraville,** (p. o.,) in the N. part, is a hamlet. Settlement was commenced in 1788, by Elisha Pease.[3] The first religious services were conducted by Rev. John Camp, in 1798. There is a M. E. church in town.

SANFORD—was formed from Windsor, April 2, 1821. It is the s. E. town of the co., bordering upon Delaware River. Its surface is principally occupied by the high, mountainous range that extends between Delaware and Susquehanna Rivers. The summits of the hills are 600 to 900 feet above the valley, and the declivities are usually very steep.[4] The deep, narrow valley of Oquaga Creek, flowing s. through the center of the town, separates the highlands into 2 parts. This valley and that of Delaware River are both bounded by nearly precipitous mountain declivities. In its course the creek has numerous falls, furnishing an abundance of water power. The soil in the valleys is a fertile, gravelly loam, but upon the hills it is a cold, clayey loam underlaid by hardpan. Considerable portions of the central and s. parts of the town are still unsettled. Lumber and leather are largely manufactured. **Deposit** (p. v.) is situated partly in this town and partly in Tompkins, (Delaware co.) The depôt, several hotels, and about half of the dwellings are in this town. Pop. 1249,—656 in Sandford, 593 in Tompkins.[5] **Sanford,** in the central part of the town, **N. Sanford,** in the N. part, and **Gulf Summit,** in the s., are p. offices. Settlement commenced in 1787, by Wm. McClure, from N. H., —— Whitaker, and Capt. Nathan Dean.[6] There are 3 churches in town; Bap., M. E., and R. C.

TRIANGLE[7]—was formed from Lisle, April 18, 1831. It is situated in the extreme N. part of the co., bordering upon both Cortland and Chenango. Its surface consists of a hilly and rolling upland divided into ridges by the valleys of Otselic River and Halfway Brook. The summits of the hills are 300 to 500 feet above the valleys. The soil is generally a gravelly loam, better adapted to grazing than to tillage. **Whitneys Point,**[8] (p. v.,) situated at the junction of Otselic and Tioughnioga Rivers, contains 3 churches and has a pop. of 205. **Upper Lisle,** (p. v.,) on the Otselic, in the N. part of the town, contains 2 churches and 35 houses; and **Triangle,** (p. v.,) on Halfway Brook, in the s. E. part, 3 churches and 175 inhabitants. The first settlement was made at Whitneys Point, in 1791, by Gen. John Patterson, from Berkshire co., Mass.[9] The first religious services were conducted by Deacon Josiah Lee, in 1792; and the first sermon was preached by Rev. Seth Williston, in 1795. There are 9 churches in town.[10]

---

[1] The first birth was that of Betsey Stoddard, in 1794, and the first death, that of Miss Bird, sister of Mrs. Stoddard.

[2] Named from Jason Crane, one of the engineers on the Chenango Canal.

[3] Jared Page and —— Vining were among the first settlers. The first birth was that of Chester Pease, in 1793; the first marriage, that of Gardner Wilson and Polly Rugg, in 1800; and the first death, that of Mrs. Pease, in 1789. Elisha Pease erected the first sawmill, in 1797, and Thomas Cooper kept the first store, in 1813. The first school was taught by Ozias Masch, in 1800.

[4] The highest point between the two rivers, by the State Road Survey, is 1688 feet above tide.

[5] See page 265.

[6] Among the first settlers were Daniel Race, Noah Carpenter, Nathan Austin, Simeon Alexander, Russel Farnham, S. P. Green, Anthony West, Joseph Page, John Pinney, J. P. Appleton, Silas Seward, Capt. Parker, Isaac Denton, and Dexter May. The first marriage was that of Conrad Edict and Elizabeth Whitaker, in

April, 1787; the first birth, that of Phebe Edict, in 1788; and the first death, that of Stephen Whitaker, Oct. 23, 1793. Capt. Dean built the first sawmill, in 1791, the first gristmill, in 1792, opened the first store, in 1794, and kept the first inn. The first school was taught by Hugh Compton, in 1793.

[7] This name was applied to the tract s. of the Military Tract and "Twenty Towns" and between the Chenango and Tioughnioga Rivers. It was bought by Col. Wm. Smith, at 3 shillings 3 pence per acre. The Chenango Triangle embraces Smithville and part of Greene in Chenango co., and Triangle and part of Barker in Broome.

[8] Named from Thos. Whitney.

[9] In 1792, David Seymour and family settled at Whitneys Point; and between 1794 and 1797, Timothy Shepherd, Asa Rodgers, Benj. and Hendrick J. Smith, and John Landers, settled at Upper Lisle. The first death was that of Mrs. Hannah Lee, in 1791. The first school was taught by Martha Seymour, in 1793.

[10] 4 Bap., 2 M. E., 2 Cong., and 1 Univ.

UNION—was formed Feb. 16, 1791. A part of Norwich and Oxford (Chenango co.) were taken off in 1793, a part of Greene (Chenango co.) in 1798, Tioga (Tioga co.) in 1800, Lisle in 1801, a part of Chenango in 1808, Vestal in 1823, and Maine in 1848. A part was annexed from Tioga, (Tioga co.,) April 2, 1810, and a part from Lisle, April 11, 1827. It lies upon the N. shore of the Susquehanna, s. w. of the center of the co. The surface consists of the Susquehanna intervale and the hilly region N. of it. The highlands are nearly centrally divided by the deep valley of Nanticoke Creek. The soil in the valley consists of a mixed clayey, sandy, and gravelly loam and alluvium, and is very productive. The hills have a rich soil of slaty and gravelly loam, and are cultivated to their summits. **Union**, (p. v.,) situated near the Susquehanna, in the s. part of the town, is a station on the N. Y. & E. R. R. The Union News is published at this place. Pop. 520. **Union Center**, (p. v.,) on Nanticoke Creek, partly in this town and partly in Maine, contains 2 churches and about 40 houses. **Hooper**, (p. o.,) in the s. part of the town, is a station on the Erie R. R. The first settlement was made in 1785, by Joseph Draper, Nehemiah Crawford, Bryant Stoddard, Nathan Howard, Jabesh Winchop, Caleb Merriman, and Winthrop Roe.[1] The first church (Ref. Prot. D.) was organized in 1789, at Union Village, and Rev. John Manley was the first settled preacher. There are 4 churches in town.[2]

VESTAL—was formed from Union, Jan. 22, 1823. It lies upon the s. bank of the Susquehanna, and is the s. w. corner town of the co. The surface consists of the river intervale and the hilly region immediately s. of it. The soil upon the hills is a fine quality of slaty loam, and in the valley it is a deep, rich, gravelly loam and alluvium. It is adapted to both grain raising and grazing. **Vestal**, (p. v.,) near the mouth of Big Choconut Creek, contains 1 church and about 45 dwellings, **Vestal Center**, (p. v.,) on the same stream, 1 church and about 20 houses, and **Tracy Creek**, (p. o.,) in the w. part, 1 church and about 10 houses. Settlement was commenced in 1785, by emigrants from New England.[3] The M. E. church at Vestal was the first religious organization in town.[4]

WINDSOR[5]—was formed from Chenango, March 27, 1807. Colesville and Sanford were taken off in 1821, and a part of Conklin in 1851. A part of Conklin was annexed April 18, 1831. It lies upon the s. border of the co., s. E. of the center. Its surface is principally occupied by 2 high ridges separated by the valley of the Susquehanna. Upon the E. side of the valley the hills attain an elevation of 400 to 800 feet above the river, and culminate in several sharp ridges ; on the w. the hills are less elevated, though the highest summits attain an elevation of 400 to 800 feet above the valley.[6] The declivities of these hills are generally quite abrupt. Oquaga Hill, in the N. E. part of the town, is one of the highest peaks, and it has some historical notoriety. (See p. 180.) The valley of the river is generally narrow. The soil is a deep, rich, gravelly loam in the valleys, and a slaty loam underlaid by clay and hardpan upon the hills. Considerable portions of the E. and s. parts of the town are yet uncultivated. **Windsor**, (p. v.,) situated on the Susquehanna, near the center of the town, contains 3 churches and Windsor Academy. Pop. 339. **Stillson Hollow** (West Windsor p. o.) contains about 20 houses. **Randolph Center**[7] (p. o.) is a hamlet. The first settlement was made on the Susquehanna, at the mouth of Doolittle Creek, in 1786, by John Doolittle, from Conn.[8] The first church (Cong.) was organized Aug. 15, 1793, by Rev. Mr. Judd. There are 5 churches in town.[9]

---

[1] Among the early settlers were Joshua and John Mersereau, Gen. O. Stoddard, Nehemiah Spaulding, Walter Sabin, Capt. Wm. Brink, Moses Chambers, Ezekiel and Oliver Crocker, Jeremiah and Benj. Brown, Amos Patterson, Abner Rockwell, and Medad and Elisha B. Bradley. The first death was that of Mary J. Fisk, June 13, 1789. James Ross and Jabesh Winchop built the first gristmill, in 1791, and the latter opened the first tavern, the same year. The first school was taught by Flavel Sabin, in 1787. The first birth was that of Joseph Chambers, July 4, 1790.
[2] 2 Presb. and 2 M. E.
[3] Samuel and Daniel Seymour, David Barney, Daniel Price, Wm. Coe, Ruggles Winchel, and Asa Camp, were the first settlers. Saml. Coe kept the first inn, in 1791, and R. Winchel built the first grist mill, in 1786. The first school was taught by John Routch, in 1793.

[4] The census reports 3 churches; Bap., M. E., and Ref. Meth.
[5] Named from Windsor, Conn.
[6] The surface of the Susquehanna in this town is about 910 feet above tide.
[7] So called from its being the center of Randolph's Patent.
[8] David Amaphad and Cyrus Hotchkiss, John Gurnsey and —— Swift, settled in town in 1787. The first birth was that of David Doolittle, Dec. 27, 1786; the first marriage, that of Capt. Andrew English and Miss Rachel Moore; and the first death, that of Mrs. Ashley, the interpreter at the Oquaga Mission, in Aug. 1787. Josiah Stow opened the first inn and store, in 1788, and Nathan Lane built the first gristmill, in 1797. The first school was taught by Stephen Seymour, in 1789.
[9] 2 M. E., and 1 each F. W. Bap., Bap., and Presb.

Acres of Land, Valuation, Population, Dwellings, Families, Freeholders, Schools, Live Stock, Agricultural Products, and Domestic Manufactures, of Broome County.

Names of Towns.	Acres of Land.		Valuation of 1858.			Population.		No. of Dwellings.	No. of Families.	Freeholders.	Schools.	
	Improved.	Unimproved.	Real Estate.	Personal Property.	Total.	Males.	Females.				No. of Districts.	Children taught.
Barker	13,155	9,299	305,712	13,410	319,122	639	685	256	257	234	14	2,876
Binghamton[a]			1,829,290	605,609	2,434,899							
Chenango	29,486	21,040½	326,075	20,100	346,175	6,626	6,502	1,943	2,305	1,352	12	470
Colesville	27,023¼	20,102	536,559	30,806	567,365	1,613	1,522	705	644	550	27	1,234
Conklin	16,041¾	19,513	508,901	22,150	531,051	1,340	1,199	465	483	403	17	1,032
Lisle	13,493	10,963	373,229	18,260	391,489	925	890	253	376	382	13	744
Maine	13,879½	17,001½	317,916	22,620	340,536	1,008	971	393	406	355	13	784
Nanticoke	6,020	8,424	119,895	1,750	121,645	426	393	152	160	129	7	277
Port Crane[a]			198,867	1,600	200,467						20	1,160
Sanford	14,350¼	40,509¾	478,626	3,640	482,266	1,604	1,456	555	559	434	9	362
Triangle	16,830	8,575	342,724	30,150	372,874	912	872	340	374	283	12	696
Union	14,167	6,061	534,699	33,386	568,085	1,259	1,204	477	498	383	17	1,046
Vestal	12,026	13,919	345,156	14,151	359,307	997	970	378	370	363	19	872
Windsor	22,367⅞	29,801	492,960	30,085	523,045	1,337	1,300	519	530	480	22	930
[a] Total	198,839⅝	205,208¾	6,710,609	847,717	7,558,326	18,686	17,964	6,436	6,962	5,348	212	12,483

Names of Towns.	Live Stock.					Agricultural Products.							Domestic Manufactures, in Yards.
						Bush. of Grain.					Dairy Products.		
	Horses.	Working Oxen and Calves.	Cows.	Sheep.	Swine.	Winter.	Spring.	Tons of Hay.	Bushels of Potatoes.	Bushels of Apples.	Pounds of Butter.	Pounds of Cheese.	
Barker	284	1,379	1,326	2,910	741	1,553½	39,504	3,874	9,822	19,154	47,727	5,076	1,390
Binghamton[a]													
Chenango	1,230	2,659	2,705	7,116	2,192	6,084½	133,403⅝	7,844	25,207	28,023	212,788	1,220	5,232
Colesville	740	2,738	2,207	6,185	1,342	3,138	39,549¾	7,730½	20,225½	28,248	201,059	7,105	4,435½
Conklin	524	1,722	1,233	4,526	1,194	5,182	78,212	5,205	11,293	17,474	153,514	1,105	1,422
Lisle	460	1,442	1,212	3,148	588	704	54,705	4,162	10,763	21,640	119,700	5,575	1,947
Maine	396	1,521	1,131	3,091	742	969	52,616½	3,774½	14,557	9,926	111,265	2,100	1,584
Nanticoke	173	642	570	629	286	927	18,202½	1,713	4,433	4,955	66,000	2,470	495
Port Crane[a]													
Sanford	344	1,630	1,067	2,366	673	2,424	36,299	4,937½	11,998	7,765	238,350	1,216	3,189¼
Triangle	503	1,868	1,745	1,858	922	543	36,800½		10,552	22,286	208,177	5,207	1,084¼
Union	448	1,264	1,260	2,240	1,322	4,540	77,248½	3,871½	18,568	23,029	145,251	2,985	551
Vestal	369	953	644	1,700	908	2,344½	41,806	2,632	10,197	9,899	57,562	810	3,056
Windsor	527	2,610	2,016	5,125	1,241	4,064¾	159,116¼	7,941	12,805	32,064	192,024	6,027	2,865
Total	5,998	20,428	17,116	40,894	12,151	32,473½	767,463⅝	53,685	160,420½	224,463	1,753,417	40,896	27,251

[a] Formed since 1855.

CATTARAUGUS COUNTY.

This county was formed from Genesee, March 11, 1808. It lies upon the Penn. line, near the s.w. corner of the State. It is 260 mi. from Albany, and contains 1,334 sq. mi. The surface is a hilly upland, forming the N. spurs of the Alleghany Mts. The upland is separated by deep valleys into distinct ridges, having a general N. and s. direction. The valleys deepen toward the s., and the hills rise abruptly to a height of 800 to 1,300 feet above them and 2,500 to 3,000 feet above tide. Nearly the whole co. is very broken; and many of the hills, though arable to their summits, are too steep for profitable cultivation. Toward the N. border the extreme mountainous character is somewhat modified, and the summits of the hills spread out into high, rolling uplands. Allegany River enters the s.e. corner of the co. from Penn., flows in a N.w. direction to near the center, thence s.w. to the s. border. It receives Four Mile, Trout, Tunegawant, Red House, Tunessassa, and Split Rock Creeks from the s., and Oswaya, Dodges, Haskill, Ischua, Five Mile, Mill, Wrights, Little Valley, Cold Spring, and Bone Run Creeks from the N. Cattaraugus Creek, forming the N. boundary, receives Buttermilk and South Middle Branch Creeks. Connewango Creek, draining the w. border, flows into Chautauqua co. Upon all these streams are numerous falls, furnishing an abundance of water-power.

The rocks of this co. mostly belong to the shales and sandstones of the Portage and Chemung groups. The former are exposed along Cattaraugus Creek, and the latter in the valleys in the central and s. parts of the co. The summits of the southern hills are covered with Catskill conglomerate. These rocks afford a good building stone in a few localities, but generally they are too easily acted upon by the elements to be very valuable. Drift deposits are found to some extent, scattered over the co.; and beds of clay, alluvium, and muck are found in limited quantities in the valleys.[1] The only lime in the co. is derived from small, isolated beds of marl and tufa. Springs of sulphur, weak brine, petroleum, and carburetted hydrogen are found in different localities. The "Oil Spring" of Freedom, yielding petroleum, is a place of considerable note. A very small amount of bog iron ore has been discovered in the swamps, but not in sufficient quantities to be profitably worked. The soil in the valleys is a yellowish loam, composed chiefly of disintegrated sandstone and shale; upon the uplands it is clay alternating with sand and gravel and underlaid by hardpan. The whole region is best adapted to grazing. For many years lumbering has been extensively carried on, and it still is a leading branch of business in the s. part of the co. The pine lands now remaining are exceedingly valuable; and the revenue derived from them forms no inconsiderable portion of the wealth of the co. Stock and wool growing and dairying form the leading pursuits in the other parts of the co.

The county seat is located at Ellicottville.[2] The courthouse is a brick edifice, situated near the center of the village, upon ample grounds donated by the Holland Land Company. The clerk's office is a fireproof brick building, adjacent to the courthouse. The jail is a stone building, amply provided for the accommodation and classification of prisoners. The poorhouse is located upon a farm of 200 acres in Machias, 16 mi. N.E. of Ellicottville. The average number of inmates is 35, supported at a weekly cost of $1.40 each. The farm yields a revenue of about $1,000.[3]

The N.Y. & Erie R.R. enters the co. from the E., and extends along Oil Spring and Ischua Creeks to Olean, thence along Allegany River to the mouth of Little Valley Creek, thence up the valley of that creek about 9 mi., and thence in a N.w. direction to the w. border of the co. It passes through the towns of Hinsdale, Olean, Allegany, Carrolton, Great Valley, Bucktooth, Little ___, New Albion, Persia, Dayton, and Perrysburgh.[4] The Genesee Valley Canal

---

[1] The superficial deposits and alluvium of the N. and S. portions of the co. are essentially different. The hillsides and valleys of the N. are covered with hemlock, and those of the S. with pine.

[2] Upon the organization of the co., in 1808, Jonas Williams, Isaac Sutherland, and Asa Ransom were appointed commissioners to locate the county seat. They fixed upon the site of Ellicottville, then a wilderness, and erected a large iron-wood post to indicate the spot. Up to 1817 the co. was merged in Niagara. The first co. courts were held at Olean, July 3, 1817. The first co. officers were Timothy H. Porter, *First Judge*; James Brooks,

Ashbel Freeman, and Francis Green, *County Judges*; Sands Boughton, *County Clerk*; Israel Curtiss, *Sheriff*; and Jeremy Wooster, *Surrogate*. The first courthouse and jail was erected at Ellicottville, in 1817–18. It was burned in 1829, and the present buildings were soon after erected.

[3] This establishment is represented by the Senate Committee of 1857 as being in bad repair and indifferently kept. The food supplied was plain and wholesome; but the house was old and dilapidated, and little attention was paid to cleanliness.

[4] Several railroads have been surveyed through the co., and upon

extends through Hinsdale and Olean, uniting with Allegany River at the latter place. An extension of this canal 7 mi. up the Allegany to the Penn. line is in process of construction.

Five weekly newspapers are now published in the co.[1]

This co. was included in the territory ceded by the Six Nations to the Holland Land Co. in 1797. Three reservations made within the limits of the co. are held by the Indians at the present day. The Oil Spring Reservation, containing 1 sq. mi., is partly in Ischua, Cattaraugus co., and partly in Cuba, Allegany co. The Allegany Reservation, containing 42 sq. mi., extends from the Penn. line 25 mi. N. E. along Allegany River. The tract is, on an average, about 2 mi. wide, and embraces nearly all of the river intervale,—the finest agricultural region in the co. It embraces portions of Allegany, Carrolton, Great Valley, Bucktooth, Cold Spring, and South Valley. A small portion of the Cattaraugus Reservation lies in the N. part of Perrysburgh.[2] The Philadelphia Quakers established a mission on the Allegany Reservation, in what is now South Valley, as early as 1798. The first permanent settlement was made at Olean, by Maj. Adam Hoops and his brother Robert, from Albany, in 1804. For many years a large share of Western emigration was by way of the Allegany River and Pittsburgh; and, being at the head of boat navigation upon the river, Olean speedily became a place of importance. Upon the completion of the Erie Canal travel was diverted from this route and improvements advanced very slowly. The completion of the N. Y. & Erie R. R. gave a new impulse to enterprise and industry; and the co. is now rapidly progressing in all the elements of wealth and civilization.

ALLEGANY—was formed from Great Valley, as "*Burton*," April 18, 1831. Its name was changed March 28, 1851. Humphrey was taken off in 1836. It lies upon the s. border of the co., E. of the center. The surface is a hilly upland, broken by the deep valley of Allegany River, which extends E. and w. through the center. The declivities of the hills are steep, and their highest summits are 700 to 900 feet above the valleys. The streams are Four Mile, Five Mile, and Mill Creeks, tributaries of the Allegany. About nine-tenths of the town is still covered with forests. The soil is a shaly and sandy loam on the hills, and a clayey and gravelly loam in the valleys.

---

some of them considerable labor has been expended. The Erie & N. Y. City R. R. extends w. from the N. Y. & Erie R. R. at Bucktooth to Erie, Penn. A large portion of this road is graded. The Buffalo & Pittsburgh and the Attica & Allegany Railroads, both to terminate at Olean, have been surveyed; but work upon them has been indefinitely postponed.

[1] *The Allegany Mercury,* the first paper in the co., was started at "*Hamilton*," now Olean, in 1818, by Benj. F. Smead. In 1819 Franklin Cowdery became interested in its publication, and the name was changed to

The Hamilton Recorder. It was continued but a few years.

The Western Courier was started at Ellicottville in 1826 by *The Cattaraugus Gazette,* and was continued about 2 years.

The Lodi Pioneer was started at "*Lodi*," now Gowanda, in 1827 by Lewis E. Edwards. At the end of 3 years it was changed to

The Lodi Freeman and Messenger, and issued by G. N. Starr. In 1833 it passed into the hands of Eliakim Hough, and was changed to

The Cattaraugus Freeman, under which name it was continued until 1844, when it was changed to

The People's Advocate and Lodi Banner. In Oct. 1850, it passed into the hands of Henry M. Morgan, and its name was changed to

The Cattaraugus Chronicle. It was soon after changed to

The Independent Chronicle, under which name it was published 4 years. In 1854 John M. Henry became interested in its publication, and it was changed to

The Gowanda Chronicle, and was continued until the office was burned, April 30, 1856.

The Ellicottville Republican was commenced in May, 1833, by Delos E. Sill. In 1834 it passed into the hands of R. H. Shankland, and was changed to

The Cattaraugus Republican. In 1855 it became the property of Fred. A. Stanton, by whom it is still published.

The Allegany Mercury was started at Olean in 1835 by G. W. Cutler. In 1836 it was changed to

The Olean Advocate, and was issued by Rufus W. Griswold for about 1 year. In 1837 Carlos Woodcock had charge of it; and in 1838 it passed into the hands of Dudley Bryan and was changed to

The Olean Times. It was afterward published by A. M. Badger until 1841.

The Hinsdale Democrat was started at the village of Hinsdale in 1836 by Joseph T. Lyman. It soon passed into the hands of Edward Hughs & Co., and was continued 2 years.

The People's Gazette was started at Hinsdale in 1840 by Geo. C. Smith. In 1842 it was removed to Geneseo, Livingston co.

The Cattaraugus Whig was started at Ellicottville in July, 1840, by Delos E. Sill. It was continued by him until 1854, when its name was changed to

The Cattaraugus Freeman, under which title it is still issued by Sill & Beecher.

The Randolph Herald was started at Randolph in March, 1842. It was successively issued by Wm. Mason, Lorenzo and Julius Marsh, and Fletcher & Russell until 1845, when it passed into the hands of J. J. Strong, who continued it 2 years. Strong then joined the Mormons, and removed the establishment to Nauvoo, Ill.

The Freeman and Messenger was started at Hinsdale in 1843 by L. E. Smith. Its name was soon changed to

The Expositor, and it was issued by Edwin and Allen C. Fuller until 1846.

The Gowanda Whig was started at Gowanda in Nov. 1850, by James T. Henry. In the following Feb. it was removed to Ellicottville, and its name changed to

The Whig and Union; soon after it appeared as

The Union, under which title it is now published by R. H. Shankland.

The Gowanda Phœnix rose from the ashes of the great fire of April, 1856, and was issued 1 year by Louis S. Morgan, when it was removed to Bradford, Penn.

The Cattaraugus Sachem was started at Randolph in June, 1851, and was continued about 1 year, when the press was removed to Olean.

The Randolph Whig was started at Randolph in July, 1852, by C. K. Judson and Benj. F. Morris. In 1857 its name was changed to

The Randolph Reporter, and it was issued by Morris until July 5, 1858, when it was removed to Gowanda and changed to

The Gowanda Reporter. It is now published by N. W. Henry and Frank Stebbins.

The Olean Journal was started at Olean in 1853 by Chas. Aldrich. In June, 1856, it passed into the hands of James T. Henry, who changed its name to

The Olean Advertiser, under which title he still issues it.

The Neosophic Gem, mo., was started at Randolph in 1848 by A. M. Shattuck, and was continued 4 years.

[2] The Indian titles to these lands have been questioned; but both the State and U. S. courts have decided them to be original, absolute, and exclusive. By an act of Feb. 19, 1857, the Legislature formally renounced all right upon the part of the State to tax these lands. The Indians are mostly engaged in agricultural pursuits, in which they have made considerable progress

Lumbering is extensively pursued. **Allegany,** (p.v.,) upon Allegany River, E. of the center, contains a tannery, door and blind factory, 3 churches, and 70 houses. It is a station on the N. Y. & E. R. R. The Franciscan College is located near the village.[1] **Five Mile Run** is a p. o. The first settler was Ebenezer Reed, from Conn., who located near the mouth of Nine Mile Creek in 1820.[2] The first religious services (Bap.) were held at the house of James Strong, by Elder Benj. Cole, in 1823. The first church (M. E.) was formed in 1829.[3]

ASHFORD—was formed from Ellicottville, Feb. 16, 1824. It is centrally located on the N. border of the co. The surface is hilly, with ridges extending generally in a N. and S. direction. The highest points in the S. part are 300 feet above the valleys. Cattaraugus Creek, forming the N. boundary, and Buttermilk Creek, are the principal streams. The soil is a slaty loam intermixed with gravel and clay. Maple sugar is largely manufactured. **Ashford,** (p.v.,) in the S.w. part of the town, contains a grist and saw mill, 2 churches, and 36 dwellings; **East Ashford** (p.o.) contains 2 churches and 11 dwellings. The first settlers were Henry Frank and his two sons Andrew and Jacob H., from Herkimer co., who located on Lot 56, in 1816.[4] The first church (F. W. Bap.) was organized in 1821, by Elder Richard M. Cary. There are now 6 churches in town.[5]

BUCKTOOTH—was formed from Little Valley, Nov. 19, 1854. It lies upon the S. border of the co., w. of the center. Its surface is mostly a broken and mountainous upland, the highest summits being 800 to 1,000 feet above the valleys. Allegany River flows w. and S.w. through the N. part. The other principal streams are Red House, Little Valley, and Bucktooth Creeks, and Sawmill Run. The soil is a clay and sandy loam. A large share of the town is yet covered with forests; and lumbering forms the leading pursuit.[6] **Bucktooth** is a p.o. in the N. part. A few settlements were made previous to 1812; but they were abandoned during the war. The first permanent settler was James Rosenbury, who located in town in 1816.[7] The only church (M. E.) was formed about 1830.

CARROLTON[8]—was formed from Great Valley, March 9, 1842. Part of Allegany Reservation was annexed in 1847. It is the central town upon the S. border of the co. Ball Hill, in the S. E. part, is 800 feet above the valley. The Allegany flows N. w. through the N. part, receiving as tributaries Tunegawant and Windfall Creeks. The soil is a clay and shaly loam upon the uplands, and a gravelly loam in the valleys. Lumbering is the leading pursuit. **Limestone,**[9] (p. o.,) in the S. part, and **Tuna,** (p. o.,) in the N., are hamlets. Charles Foster, Horace Howe, and Marcus Leonard located upon Lots 28 and 29 in 1814.[10] The first religious meeting (Bap.) was held by Rev. Aaron Kellogg, at his own house, in 1831; and the first church (M. E.) was organized in 1843. The census reports 2 churches; M. E. and R. C.

COLD SPRING—was formed from Napoli, March 20, 1837. Parts of South Valley were taken off in 1847 and '48. It is an interior town, near the S. w. corner of the co. The surface is a hilly and broken upland, the highest summits being 400 to 500 feet above the valleys. The Allegany flows S. w. through the N. E. corner, and receives from the N. Cold Spring Creek, which flows through the center. The soil is a clay and slaty loam upon the uplands, and a sandy and gravelly loam in the valleys. A sulphur spring is found in the N. E. part. There is no village, p. o., or church edifice in town. Lumbering is extensively carried on. The first settlements were made by Chas. Crook, with his 3 sons Chas., jr., Ira, and Nathan, from Vt., on Lot 32, and Joshua Basson,

---

1 This institution is under the control of the Franciscan (R. C.) Association. The buildings are now in process of erection. Nicholas Devereux donated to the association, for the institute, 200 acres of land and $5,000.

2 Among the other early settlers were Andrew L. Allen, Hiram Wood, James Strong, Isaac Eggleston, Amos B. and David Orton, who located on Five Mile Creek in 1821. The first child born was Nathan Reed, Oct. 2, 1820; the first marriage, that of Wm. B. Fox and Sally Strong, in 1825; and the first persons who died were children of Isaac Eggleston, in 1823. Leonard Cronkhite taught the first school, in a house of James Strong's, in the winter of 1825–26; Ebenezer Reed kept the first inn, in 1820; Aaron Wheeler, the first store, in 1833; and Reuben Lamberton erected the first sawmill, on Five Mile Creek, in 1826.

3 The census reports 4 churches; Bap., Cong., M. E., and R. C.

4 Among the other early settlers were John Goodemote, Saml. Flagg, Griffin and David Wyley, Amos, David, Thomas, and Maley Sampson, David Oyer, Augustus Van Slyke, Calvin Woodruff, Marcena Brooks, Jacob and Michael Houghstader, John Quackenbush and his son Peter, all from Herkimer and Montgomery cos., and all of whom located in town in 1818. The first birth was that of Elizabeth, daughter of Jacob H. Frank, in the fall of 1817; and the first death, that of Phœbe, a child of Andrew Frank, Aug. 30, 1818. Danl. Thomas and Norman B. Carter taught the first schools, in 1822–23.

5 2 Bap., F. W. Bap., Cong., M. E., and Wes. Meth.

6 This town contains an area of 47,620 acres, of which less than 1,000 acres were under cultivation in 1855.

7 Among the other early settlers were James Green, Adam Johnson, and John Boutell. The first birth was that of a child of David Hathaway, in 1834; and the first marriage, that of Andrew Mills and Sally Hadly. Leister Granger taught the first school, in 1834; Adam Johnson kept the first inn, in 1832, and John Boardman the first store, in 1834. The first sawmill was built by the Indians, in 1813, on Sawmill Run.

8 Named from G. Carrolton, one of the original proprietors.

9 Upon the flats near Limestone are the remains of an ancient fortification. It is in the shape of a figure 8, the remains of the ditch and earthworks being plainly visible.

10 John and Wm. Moore, Elias Stone, Peter Zeluff, —— Hecock, Isaac Farr, Aaron Kellogg, and Wm. Smith settled on Tuna Creek in 1828. The first birth was that of Merit Zeluff, in June, 1829; the first marriage, that of —— Brown and Emeline Fuller, in 1828; and the first death, that of Enoch Fuller, in 1828. The first school was taught by Milton Northrop, at Limestone, in the winter of 1830–31. Elias Stone kept the first inn, near the mouth of Tuna Creek, in 1828, and Chas. Lewis the first store, in 1832. The first sawmill was built by Marcus Leonard, in 1826.

from Mass., on Lot 22, in 1820.[1] The first religious meeting (Cong.) was held in 1823, by Rev. Wm. J. Wilcox.

CONNEWANGO—was formed from Little Valley, Jan. 20, 1823. Randolph was taken off in 1826, and Leon in 1832. It lies upon the w. border of the co., s. of the center. The surface in the s. w. and w. parts is level and swampy, the Connewango Swamp being 30 to 50 feet below the bed of Allegany River at its nearest point. The remaining parts are hilly. It is drained s. by Connewango, Little Connewango, and Clear Creeks, and other small streams. The soil on the uplands is clay and gravel, and on the flats a gravelly loam. **Rudledge,** (Connewango p. o.,) in the N. w. part, on Connewango Creek, contains a church and 17 dwellings. **Clear Creek** (p. v.) is on the line of Chautauqua co. **Axville** is a hamlet. Settlement was commenced in 1816, by Eliph. Follet, near Rutledge.[2] The first church (Presb.) was organized at Rutledge, in 1816.[3]

DAYTON—was formed from Perrysburgh, Feb. 7, 1835. It lies upon the w. border of the co., N. of the center. Its surface is generally a rolling and hilly upland. The highest elevations in the N. part are about 300 feet above the R. R. at Dayton Station. It is drained s. by two branches of Connewango Creek and other small streams. The soil is a clayey and gravelly loam. Lumbering is an important branch of industry. **Dayton,** (p. v.,) on the N. Y. & E. R. R., in the N. E. corner of the town, contains 13 dwellings; and **West Dayton,** (Cottage p. o.,) in the N. w. corner, a church, 2 sawmills, and 14 dwellings. **Sociality** is a hamlet, in the s. E. part. The first settlement was made by Silas Nash and Simeon Bunce, from Otsego co., in 1810.[4] The first religious meeting (Bap.) was held at the house of Joshua Webb, in 1816, by Rev. Elnathan Finch; and the first church (Bap.) was organized in March, 1818, at the house of Mr. Webb.[5]

EAST OTTO—was formed from Otto, Nov. 30, 1854. It lies upon the N. border of the co., w. of the center. The surface is hilly and broken; Mt. Tug, the highest summit, being 300 feet above the valleys. Cattaraugus Creek forms the N. boundary; and South Middle Branch flows w. through the town, s. of the center. The soil is a clay and gravelly loam, favorable for both grain and grass. **Otto Corners,** (East Otto p. o.,) a little s. w. from the center, contains 3 churches and 17 dwellings. The first settlements were made by Joseph Bates, on Lot 20, and Horace Wells, near Otto Corners, about 1816.[6] The first religious meetings were held at the house of Tyler M. Beach, in 1821. The first preaching (M. E.) was at the same house, by Rev. Ira Brownson, in 1822.[7]

ELLICOTTVILLE[8]—was formed from "*Ischua,*" now Franklinville, April 13, 1820. Ashford was taken off in 1824. It is an interior town, lying a little N. E. of the center of the co. The surface is a hilly upland, broken by the deep and narrow ravines of the streams. The principal stream is Great Valley Creek, flowing s. through near the center. The soil upon the hills is a clay loam, and in the valleys a gravelly loam. **Ellicottville,** (p. v.,) on the creek, in the s. w. part of the town, was incorp. April 1, 1837. Besides the co. buildings, it contains 4 churches, 3 newspaper offices, and an iron foundery. Pop. 695. **Plato** and **Ash Park** are p. offices. The first settlements were made in 1815, by David Waldo, from Oneida co., and Orin Pitcher, from Mass.[9] The first religious meeting was held at the house of Wm. Vinton, by Rev. John Spencer, in 1818. The first church (Presb.) was formed Sept. 10, 1822.[10]

---

[1] Eastman Prescott and his father settled in the s. part, and Isaac Morrill in the N. w. part, in 1821. The first birth was that of Martha, daughter of Charles Crook, jr., in the spring of 1824; and the first death, that of Miss Jones, in the fall of 1821. Miss E. Sanford taught the first school, in the summer of 1822. Philenus Hall kept the first inn and the first store, in 1821. Chas. Crook and Joshua Basson erected the first sawmill, in 1820, on Cold Spring Creek.

[2] Sampson Crooker, from Cairo, Greene co., settled near Rutledge in 1818; and Calvin Treat, H. Camp, Wm. Holbrook, and John Darling about the same time. The first school was taught by Olive Cheeney, in the summer of 1819. Eliphalet Follet kept the first inn, in 1817, near Rutledge, and H. Camp and Wm. Holbrook the first store, in 1822, at Olds Corners. The first sawmill was erected by Sampson Crooker, on Mill Creek, in 1819, and the first gristmill by Calvin Treat, near the center of the town, in 1821. Mrs. Crooker, wife of Sampson Crooker, killed a wildcat at her hen roost with a pair of tongs, in the winter of 1819.

[3] The census reports 3 churches; Presb., Bap., and M. E.

[4] Joshua Webb, from Madison co., settled on Lot 56, Leman H. Pitcher, on Lot 58, in the s. w. part; Ralph Johnson, Heman and Anson Merrill, and Timothy M. Shaw in the N. E. part,—all in 1815. The first child born was Amos Nash, in June, 1811; the first marriage, that of Benj. Parsell and Mary Redfield, in March, 1818; and the first death, that of De Witt, son of Silas Nash, in Feb. 1812. Caleb Webb kept the first inn, in 1827, at West

Dayton, and Wm. H. Leland, the first store in 1833, in the s. E. part of the town. Silas Nash erected the first sawmill, in 1817, at West Dayton.

[5] The census reports 3 churches; Bap., F. W. Bap., and M. E.

[6] Soon after, Moses T. and Tyler M. Beach, Justice Bartholomew, Abraham Gibbs, and Saml. Tuttle settled in the town. The first children born were Arzan and Brittaina,—twins,—son and daughter of Justice Bartholomew; the first marriage was that of Moses N. Leland and Brittaina Wells, in 1823; and the first death of an adult, that of Mrs. John Darling, in Dec. 1824. Hezekiah Scovel kept the first inn, near Otto Corners, in 1823, and Vine Plumb the first store, near the same place, in 1824. Moses T. Beach built the first sawmill, in 1823, and the first gristmill, in 1824, on South Middle Branch, in the E. part of the town.

[7] The census reports 3 churches; M. E., Cong., and Bap.

[8] Named from Joseph Ellicott, agent of the Holland Land Co.

[9] Grove Hurlbut built the first house, in 1815, on Lot 57, and settled in March, 1816. Rickartson Burlinghame and Ephraim Fitch settled in 1816. The first child born was Orlando F. Pitcher, in June, 1816. The first school was taught by Eunice Carpenter, at the house of Orin Pitcher, in the summer of 1817. Baker Leonard kept the first inn, in 1817, and the first store, in 1818. Orin Pitcher erected the first sawmill, in 1821, on Great Valley Creek.

[10] The census reports 4 churches; Presb., Prot. E., M. E., and R. C.

FARMERSVILLE—was formed from "*Ischua*," now Franklinville, March 29, 1821. It lies on the E. border of the co., N. of the center. The surface is a hilly upland, forming the watershed between the streams flowing N.W. into Lake Erie and those flowing E. into Genesee River and S. into Allegany River. The highest point, near the center, is 800 to 900 feet above the R. R. at Olean. Mud Lake, in the N. part, covering an area of about 30 acres, discharges its waters N.; and Ischua Creek flows S. through the W. part. On the uplands the soil is chiefly a vegetable mold resting on clay, shale, and slate; in the valleys, a gravelly loam. **Farmersville,** (p. v.,) near the center, contains 2 churches and 17 dwellings. **Fairview** is a p. o. The first settlement was made by Peter and Cornelius Ten Broeck and Richard Tozer,—all from Otsego co.,—on Lots 4 and 36, in 1817.[1] The first religious meeting was held by Rev. Eliab Going, (Bap.,) at the barn of Levi Peet, in 1821. The census reports 2 churches; Bap. and M. E.

FRANKLINVILLE—was formed from Olean, June 16, 1812, as "*Hebe.*" Its name was changed to "*Ischua*," April 17, 1816; and to Franklinville, March 3, 1824. A part of Perrysburgh was taken off in 1814, Ellicottville, Freedom, and Yorkshire in 1820, Farmersville in 1821, and Lyndon in 1829. It is an interior town, lying N. E. of the center of the co. Its surface is undulating and hilly. It is drained S. by Ischua and Great Valley Creeks and several other small streams. The soil is clay and gravelly loam. **Franklinville,** (p. v.,) on Ischua Creek, in the N. E. corner of the town, contains 2 churches, 2 sawmills, and 370 inhabitants; **Cadiz** (p. v.) a church and several mills. Pop. 165. The first settlement was made at the village of Franklinville, by Joseph McClure, originally from Vt., in March, 1806.[2] The first church (Bap.) was formed in 1823. There are 3 churches in town; Bap., Presb., and M. E.

FREEDOM—was formed from "*Ischua*," now Franklinville, April 13, 1820. A part of Yorkshire was taken off in 1844. It is the N. E. corner town of the co. The surface is a rolling or moderately hilly upland. Clear Creek and the S. branch of Cattaraugus Creek are the principal streams. Beaver Lake, in the S. part, Fish Lake, in the E., and Scum and Laws Lakes, in the center, are small ponds. The soil is a clay and gravelly loam. Several quarries of good building stone are found in different parts of the town. **Sandusky,** (p. v.,) on Clear Creek, in the N. part, contains 2 churches, a gristmill, and 2 sawmills. Pop. 175. **Elton,** (p. v.,) near the s. w. corner, contains a church and 14 dwellings. **Freedom** is a p. o. The first settlements were made in 1811, by Warren Stanley, Ezekiel Reynolds, from N. H., and Earl Lawyer, Rufus Metcalf, and Enoch Howlett, from Vt.[3] The first religious meeting was held at the house of Rufus Metcalf, in April, 1813, by Elder P. Root. The first church (M. E.) was formed in 1820.[4]

GREAT VALLEY—was formed from Olean, April 15, 1818. "*Burton*," now Allegany, was taken off in 1831, and Carrolton in 1842. Part of Allegany Reservation was taken off in 1847. It is an interior town, lying a little S. of the center of the co. Its surface is a mountainous and hilly upland. The highest summit, near the s. w. corner, is 1,300 feet above the river. The declivities are generally very abrupt, and many of them are too steep for cultivation. Allegany River flows through the s. w. corner, and receives as tributary Great Valley Creek. The soil upon the highlands is a hard clay mixed with disintegrated slate and shale; and in the valleys a gravelly loam. Lumbering is the leading pursuit, five-sixths of the surface being still covered with forests.[5] **Great Valley Station,** (Killbuck p. o.,) at the mouth of Great Valley Creek, in the s. part, contains 18 dwellings; and **Peth** (Great Valley p. o.) 11. Settlement was commenced at the

---

[1] Levi Peet and Peleg Robins, from Otsego co., settled on Lots 36 and 3, in 1817. The first child born was Addison, son of Richard Tozer, in 1817; the first marriage, that of Peter Ten Broeck and Polly Tremain; and the first death, that of Mrs. Magdalene Adams, Nov. 7, 1820. The first inn was kept in 1817, by Richard Tozer, and the first store by Jacob Comstock, in 1828. James Worden erected the first sawmill, in 1824, on the outlet of Mud Lake.

[2] Mr. McClure was an agent and surveyor of the Holland Land Co., and located his lot in 1805. He was a leading man in the town for many years, filled the principal town offices, served with the rank of captain on the Niagara frontier in the War of 1812, and represented the co. in the Assembly of 1814–15. His brother David settled in the town in 1806, Thos. Morris and Henry Conrad in 1807, and Timothy Butler, Jeremiah Burroughs, and Danl. Cortwright, soon after,—all in the valley of Ischua Creek. The first child born in the town and co. was Hiram W., son of David McClure, April 30, 1806. John McClure taught the first school, in 1809; Joseph McClure kept the first inn, in 1806, and Thos. Morris the first store, in 1816, at or near Franklinville Village. Henry Conrad built the first gristmill, in 1808, and sawmill, in 1809, at Cadiz.

[3] These settlers made improvements and put up log houses in 1811, and moved in with their families in the spring of 1812. The first child born was Rufus Metcalf, jr., Dec. 24, 1812; and the first death of an adult was that of Peter Davis, Dec. 17, 1816. Elihu Daggart and Sally McKee, and Sylvester Davis and Miss Daggart, were all married at the same time, in 1817. The first school was taught in 1816, by Jemima Clark. Enoch Howlett kept the first inn and the first store, in 1824. He also erected the first sawmill, in 1821, on Clear Creek. Dr. Elihu Cruttenden erected the first gristmill, on the same stream, in 1822.

[4] The census reports 5 churches; 2 Bap., F. W. Bap., Calv. Meth., and Univ.

[5] On Lot 19, about 1 mi. E. of the center of the town, is a place known as the "Breathing Well." About 1850, Nicholas Flint attempted to dig a well; but, after reaching a depth of 25 feet and obtaining no water, he abandoned the undertaking, but stoned up the well, hoping that water might come. Noticing a current of air proceeding from the well, he inserted a pump log in it, and covered it up, except the end of the log. A current of air is continually blowing either into or out of the well; and a whistle placed at the end of the log has been heard half a mi. The current is sometimes steady in one direction for a whole day, and sometimes it changes every hour.

mouth of Great Valley Creek, by Judge James Green, in 1812.[1] The first religious meeting was held at the house of Orin Pitcher, by Rev. John Spencer, in 1815. The first religious association (Cong.) was formed, with 8 members, in 1817. There is now no church edifice in town, and but 1 church, (M. E.)

HINSDALE—was formed from Olean, April 14, 1820. Ischua was taken off in 1846. It lies on the E. border of the co., s. of the center. The surface is a hilly and broken upland. The hills are 500 to 600 feet above the valleys and are bordered by abrupt declivities. The highest points, on Lots 23 and 24, are 500 feet above the R. R. at Hinsdale Village. Reservoir Lake is a small sheet of water near the s. E. corner. Ischua and Oil Creeks—the former from the N. E. and the latter from the N. W.—form a junction near the center, and thence the united stream takes the name of Olean Creek, flowing s. through the town. The soil upon the uplands is chiefly clay, and in the valleys a gravelly loam. **Hinsdale,** (p. v.,) at the junction of Ischua and Oil Creeks, contains 2 churches and several mills and manufacturing establishments. Pop. 255. It is a canal village and a station upon the N. Y. & Erie R. R. **Scotts Corners,** in the N. part, contains a church and 13 houses. **Haskel Flat** is a p. o. The first settlers were Horace Noble, Chas. Foot, and Thos. Lusk, who located near the present site of the village in 1806.[2] The first religious meeting was held at the log barn of Zachariah Noble, in June, 1807. The first regular preacher was Rev. Reuben Aylesworth, (M. E.,) in 1820, who organized the first religious association in 1821.[3]

HUMPHREY[4]—was formed from "*Burton,*" now Allegany, May 12, 1836. It is an interior town, lying a little s. E. of the center of the co. The surface is a broken and hilly upland, the highest summits being 600 feet above the R. R. at Olean. Its streams are Great Valley, Five Mile, Wrights, and Sugar Town Creeks. The soil upon the hills is mostly clay, occasionally intermixed with sand, and in the valleys it is a gravelly loam. **Humphrey Center** is a hamlet. **Humphrey** and **Sugar Town** are p. offices. The first settlement was made in the N. W. corner, on Lot 56, by Russel Chappell, in 1815.[5] The first religious association (M. E.) was formed in 1834.[6]

ISCHUA—was formed from Hinsdale, Feb. 7, 1846, as "*Rice.*" Its name was changed March 27, 1855. It lies upon the E. border of the co., a little s. of the center. Its surface is a broken and hilly upland, the highest summits being 600 feet above the valleys. Ischua Creek flows s. through the town and receives several tributaries. The soil is chiefly clay, with a thin surface mold and some gravelly loam. Quarries of good building stone are found in the town. **Ischua,** (p. v.,) formerly called "*Rice,*" on Ischua Creek, in the N. part, contains a gristmill and 19 dwellings. The first settlement was made on Lot 45, on the creek, by Abraham M. Farwell, from Mass., in 1812.[7] The first religious meeting was held at the house of Mr. Farwell, by Rev. John Spencer, in 1815; and the first church (M. E.) was formed in 1827.

LEON—was formed from Connewango, April 24, 1832. It lies on the w. border of the co., a little N. of the center. Its surface in the w. and N. w. is level and marshy, and in the remaining parts moderately hilly. It is drained s. by Connewango Creek and its tributaries. The soil is a clay, sandy, and gravelly loam. **Leon,** (p. v.,) near the center, contains 2 churches and 18 dwellings. **East Leon** is a p. o. **Thompsonville** is a hamlet in the s. E. part. Settlements were made on Mud Creek, in 1819, by Jas. Franklin and his son James, from Riga, Monroe co., and Abner Wise and his son Abner W., Thos. W. Cheney, and Ed. Dudley, from Otsego co.[8]

---

[1] Among the other early settlers were Danl. McKay, Judge Benj. Chamberlin, and ——Hibbard, who located in 1813; Lewis Worcester and Laurin Norton, in 1814. The first child born was Ira Green, in 1813; and the first death, that of Mrs. Hibbard, the same year. The first school was taught at the house of James Green, by Joel Fairbanks, in the winter of 1817–18. James Green kept the first inn, in 1813, at the mouth of Great Valley Creek, and Lewis Worcester the first store, in 1815, at Peth. The first sawmill was erected by James Green, in 1812.

[2] Zachariah and Seymour Noble also settled in 1806. All the settlers at this time were from Ontario co. and originally from Mass. The first child born was Clarissa, daughter of Horace Noble, in the fall of 1808; and the first death, that of Bibbin Follet, in 1809. Rachael Turner taught the first school, at Scotts Corners, in 1818. Elihu Murray kept the first inn, near Hinsdale Village, in 1810, and Emery Wood the first store, in 1825. The first sawmill was erected by Lewis Wood, in 1815; and the first gristmill, by Henry Conrad, in 1825.

[3] The census reports 2 churches; Bap., and M. E.

[4] Named from Charles Humphrey, of Tompkins co., Speaker of the Assembly at the time of the formation of the town.

[5] Among the other early settlers were Alonzo Berry, Abijah

Rowley, Nathan Howe, Thomas Scott, and Stephen S. Cole. The first school was taught by John Howe, at Sugar Town, in 1820. Mr. Howe has since been a member of Congress from Penn. Russel Chappell kept the first inn, in 1824, and Averill Lawyer the first store, at Humphrey Center, in 1848. The first sawmill was erected by Foster B. Salisbury, on Wright Creek.

[6] There are 4 churches in town; Bap., F. W. Bap., M. E., and R. C.

[7] Seymour Boughton, from Westchester co., settled at the village in 1815, and William Kimball, Amos Pitcher, and Jonathan Davis about the same time. The first child born was C. Adaline, daughter of A. M. Farwell, in 1816; and the first death, that of Henry Boughton, by the fall of a tree, in 1811. The first school was taught on the premises of Mr. Farwell, by Caroline Putnam, in the summer of 1821. Mr. Farwell erected the first sawmill, on Lot 45, in 1814, and Cook & Tyler the first gristmill, in 1826, both on Ischua Creek. The first store was opened by Albert Lawrence and Henry Stephens, in 1832, and the first inn by Seymour Boughton, in 1816.

[8] Robert Durfee, from R. I., settled on Lots 50 and 57, in 1819, where he still resides; and John Fairbanks and John Battles, in 1819–20. The first birth was that of Edward Dudley, July 26,

The first religious meeting was held at the house of Abner Wise, in 1820, by Elder Hadley; and the first church (Ref. Meth.) was formed by Rev. Ezra Amadon, in 1822.[1]

LITTLE VALLEY—was formed from "*Perry*," now Perrysburgh, April 10, 1818. Conne-wango and Napoli were taken off in 1823, Mansfield and New Albion in 1830, and Bucktooth in 1854. It is an interior town, lying a little s. w. of the center of the co. The surface is mostly a hilly upland, divided into two principal ridges by the deep valley of Little Valley Creek. The highest summits are 500 to 600 feet above the creek. Upon Lot 77, in the s. E. part of the town, is a peculiar rock formation, known as "Rock City."[2] The soil is a hard, clay loam upon the hills, and a gravelly loam in the valleys.[3] **Little Valley,** (p. v.,) in the N. w. corner, contains a church and 36 dwellings. It is an important station upon the N. Y. & Erie R. R. **Little Valley Creek,** near the center, contains a church and 11 dwellings. The first settlements were made in the valley, in 1807, by John Green, Judge Benj. Chamberlin, and several other families, who left during the War of 1812.[4] The first church (F. W. Bap.) was formed by Elder Richard M. Cary, Oct. 8, 1826.[5]

LYNDON—was formed from Franklinville, Jan. 24, 1829. Its name was changed to "*Elgin*" April 7, 1857, and back to Lyndon April 16, 1858. It lies on the E. border of the co., N. of the center. Its surface is hilly, the highest ridges, near the center, being about 500 feet above the R. R. at Olean. It is drained by Oil Creek and branches of Ischua Creek. The soil is chiefly clay covered with a light vegetable mold upon the hills, and a gravelly loam in the valleys. **Elgin,** (p. o.,) near the center, and **Rawson,** (p. o.,) in the E. part, are hamlets. The first settlement was made by Solomon and Wm. Rawson, who located upon Lots 6 and 7 in 1808.[6] The first religious services (F. W. Bap.) were conducted by Seth Markham, at his own house, in 1810. The first church (F. W. Bap.) was organized in the E. part of the town, in 1816, by Elders Jeremiah and Abraham Folsom.[7]

MACHIAS—was formed from Yorkshire, April 16, 1827. A part of Yorkshire was annexed in 1847. It is an interior town, lying N. E. of the center of the co. The surface forms a portion of the elevated table land dividing the waters of Allegany River from those of Cattaraugus Creek. Lime Lake, in the N. E. part, 1,100 feet above Lake Erie, discharges its waters N. into Cattaraugus Creek. Ischua Creek flows s. into the Allegany. The soil is a clay and gravelly loam, mostly of good quality. Maple sugar is largely produced. **Machias,** (p. v.,) in the N. E. part, contains 2 churches, a gristmill, sawmill, and 30 dwellings. **Lime Lake** is a hamlet at the head of the lake of the same name. Timothy Butler and Jeremiah Ballard, from Me., located on Lots 13 and 14, on the creek, below the village, in 1813.[8] The first religious services were performed by Rev. John Spencer, a missionary from Conn.; and the first church (M. E.) was organized in 1822.[9]

MANSFIELD—was formed from Little Valley, Feb. 23, 1830. It is an interior town, a little

---

1820; the first marriage, that of Abner W. Wise and Laura Davison, in 1823; and the first death, that of Laura. daughter of Capt. John Fairbanks, in 1821. Richard Outhout taught the first school, in the winter of 1822-23. Asa Franklin kept the first inn, in 1823, and Johnson Noyes the first store, in 1828. Ebenezer Collar erected the first sawmill, in 1824, on Mud Creek; and Jabez Thompson, the first gristmill, on the same stream, in 1832.

[1] There are now 3 churches in town; Bap., M. E., and United Brethren.

[2] Rock City is situated upon the nearly level summit of a hill 400 feet above the valley and 2,000 feet above tide, and covers an area of about 100 acres. The rock, consisting of Catskill conglomerate, is arranged in regular blocks, with sharp angles and perpendicular sides, presenting the appearance of courtyards or squares in the midst of numerous streets and alleys. In a more minute description of the place, Prof. Hall, in his "*Geology of New York*," says, "The large trees which stand upon the top of the immense blocks have often sent their roots down the sides, where they are sustained by the deep soil, supporting the huge growth above upon an almost barren rock. The rectangular blocks, composed of pure white pebbles conglutinated, are from 30 to 35 feet in thickness, and, standing regularly arranged along the line of outcrop, present an imposing appearance."

[3] A successful experiment in domesticating the American elk has been made in this town by Mr. Lorenzo Stratton. This gentleman purchased a pair in 1853, and subsequently 3 more, from the head branches of the Missouri, and placed them in a pasture of 125 acres of well fenced woodland. By frequent attention and feeding, the animals have become so domesticated that they are driven to the annual co. fairs without trouble. His original number of 5 have increased to 15, including a pair of 5 year olds sold for $1,000 for shipment to England, in 1857, and a 3 year old buck slaughtered July 4, 1858.

[4] Among the first settlers before the war were Luther Stewart, Wm. Gillmore, David Powers, and Alpheus Bascom. After the war, Stephen Crosby, from Madison co., located on Lot 30, in Feb. 1816; and Noah Culver, Enoch, David, and Alvin Chase, and John Stratton, from New England, soon after. David Powers built the first saw and grist mill, in 1809, on Little Valley Creek.

[5] The census reports 3 churches; F. W. Bap., Cong., and Prot. Meth.

[6] Among the other early settlers were J. Simons, David, Seth, and Jephtha Markham, from Penn., who settled on Lot 7 in 1809. The Markhams were originally from Conn. The first child born was Nattella, daughter of Solomon Rawson, in Aug. 1809; the first marriage, that of Wm. Markham and Rachel Phillips, March 1, 1815; and the first death, that of James Markham, the father of the 3 Markhams among the first settlers, in 1811. Sally Osborne taught the first school, in the summer of 1815, in the E. part of the town. The first inn was kept by Wm. Rawson, in the E. part, in 1825, and the first store by Charles Gillmore, at the center, in 1827. The first sawmill was built by Jason Sherman, in 1843.

[7] The census reports 4 churches; F. W. Bap., Wes. Meth., Asso. Presb., and Asso. Ref. Presb.

[8] Joseph Kinney settled in 1815; Obadiah Vaughn in 1818; E. T. Ashcraft, Chas. Button, Chas. H. Briggs, and Wiggen M. Farrer soon after. The first marriage was that of Brigham Brown and Polly Mason, in April, 1823; and the first death, that of Esther Ashcraft, in Dec. 1819. Nathl. Bowen taught the first school, in 1819, on Lot 25. Andrew McBuzzell erected the first sawmill, in 1822, and Danl. Potter the first gristmill, in 1823,—both on the outlet of Lime Lake. The first store was kept at the same place, by Howard Peck and Alva Jeffersen; and the first inn, on Ischua Creek, by Widow Freeman, in 1820.

[9] The census reports 2 churches; M. E. and Christian.

N, w. of the center of the co. The surface is hilly, the highest elevations, in the s. E., being about 300 feet above the N. Y. & E. R. R. where it crosses the s. w. corner of the town. The s. branch of Cattaraugus Creek flows w. through the N. part, and several small streams s. into the Allegany. The soil is a hard, clay loam on the uplands, and a gravelly loam in the valleys. **Eddyville,** (p. o.,) in the N. part, contains 2 churches, a sawmill, and 11 dwellings. The first settler was Amos Morgan, who located in the s. part in 1817.[1] The first church, (Bap.,) formed in 1828, has since broken up.[2]

NAPOLI—was formed from Little Valley, Jan. 20, 1823, as "*Cold Spring.*" Its name was changed April 15, 1828; and the present town of Cold Spring was taken off in 1837. Its surface is a hilly upland, the highest summits being 600 feet above the valley. The principal stream is Cold Spring Creek. The soil is a clay and gravelly loam. **Napoli,** (p. v.,) s. of the center, contains a church and about a dozen houses. The first settlement was made on Lot 27, by Major Timothy Butler, in 1818.[3] The first religious meeting was held by Rev. John Spencer, in 1820. The first church (Cong.) was organized in 1820.[4]

NEW ALBION—was formed from Little Valley, Feb. 23, 1830. It is an interior town, N. w. of the center of the co. The surface is a hilly upland. It is drained by streams flowing into Cattaraugus Creek on the N. and into the Allegany in the s. The soil is a clay loam on the hills, and a gravelly loam in the valleys. **New Albion,** (p. v.,) a little s. of the center, contains 20 dwellings; **Cattaraugus,**[5] (p. v.,) in the N. part, contains a steam flouring mill and 50 dwellings. It is an important station upon the N. Y. & E. R. R., and has grown up since this road was completed. The first settlement was made on the s. w. corner of Lot 57, by Matthew Dimmick, in 1818.[6] The first religious association (M. E.) was organized in 1830. There are 3 churches in town, but no church edifice.[7]

OLEAN—was formed March 11, 1808, and at first included the whole territory of Cattaraugus co. "*Ischua,*" now Franklinville, was taken off in 1812, a part of Perrysburgh in 1814, Great Valley in 1818, Hinsdale in 1820, and Portville in 1837. It lies upon the s. line of the co., near the s. E. corner. The surface is a hilly upland, separated into two distinct parts by the valley of the Allegany. The highest points are 500 to 600 feet above the valley. Lumbering is the leading occupation. **Olean,** (p. v.,) on the Allegany, at the mouth of Olean Creek, was incorp. in 1854. It contains 6 churches, the Olean Academy,[8] a newspaper office, a flouring mill, foundery, tannery, and 3 sawmills. Pop. 994. It is a station upon the N. Y. & E. R. R., and an important commercial point upon the river; and it was for some years the southern terminus of the Genesee Valley Canal.[9] The first settlement was made prior to 1805. In that year Robert Hoops, agent of Adam Hoops, and David Heusten were residents near the river on small improvements, and must have settled as early as 1804.[10] The first church (M. E.) was formed in 1820.[11]

OTTO[12]—was formed from Perrysburgh, Jan. 29, 1823. East Otto was taken off in 1854, a

---

[1] Among the other early settlers were Nathaniel Fish, Sewell Gunn, and —— Bennett, who located in the s. part in 1817; and Samuel L. Hollister, from Great Valley, who located in the N. E. part in 1822. The first child born was Mahala Fish, Dec. 9, 1820; and the first marriage, that of Prince W. Fish and Lois Grover, Jan. 1, 1824. The first school was taught by Lefo Chase, in 1821. Nathaniel Fish kept the first inn, on the old Johnson Road, in the s. E. part, in 1818, and Thos. H. McKay the first store, in 1848, at Eddyville. The first sawmill was erected by George and Munson Clark, in 1837, on the s. branch of Cattaraugus Creek.

[2] The census reports 3 churches; M. E., F. W. Bap., and Univ.

[3] In 1819, Geo. Hill located on Lot 29, Harvey Parmalee and Harlow Butler on Lot 51, Sargent Morrill on Lot 50, and Timothy Boardman on Lot 43. The first child born was Joseph Foy, in June, 1820; the first marriage, that of Dr. Noble and Statira Canfield, in 1821; and the first death, that of a child of Timothy Butler, in 1820. The first school was taught by Fanny Boardman, in the summer of 1819. Moses Cook kept the first store, in 1826, and Eastman Prescott the first inn, in 1831. James Wait erected the first sawmill, in 1829, on a branch of Cold Spring Creek.

[4] There are 4 churches in town; Cong., Bap., F. W. Bap., and M. E.

[5] Joseph Plumb, the owner of the lands on which the village is built, deeded the lots with the condition on penalty of forfeiture that no intoxicating liquors should be sold on the premises. It is, of course, a temperance village.

[6] David Hammond, jr. located on Lot 33, and Jonathan Kinnecutt on Lot 10, in 1818; A. Smith Waterman on Lot 25, and James Godard on Lot 9. about the same time; Benj. Chamberlin on Lot 1, and David Hill and John A. Kinnecutt on Lot 18, in Dec. 1820; Robert and Timothy P. Gay subsequently located on

Lot 33. The first birth was in the family of Matthew Dimmick, in Dec. 1818. Capt. Rosecrantz, an Indian trader, froze to death in this town in the winter of 1810, while on his way from the mouth of Cattaraugus Creek to Olean. The first inn was kept by Jas. Godard, on Lot 9, in 1819, and the first store by Erastus Hooth, in 1833, at the center. Matthew Nealy built the first sawmill, on a s. branch of Cattaraugus Creek, and Charles Sibley the first gristmill, on Lot 49, in 1836.

[7] M. E., Wes. Meth., and Prot. Meth.

[8] The academic buildings were burned April 1, 1856. The new buildings are nearly ready for the reception of students.

[9] An act was passed in 1856 authorizing the extension of this canal 7 mi. to the Penn. line. The work is now in progress; and, when completed, it will, in connection with slackwater navigation upon the river, open a direct communication with the coal mines of Penn.

[10] John Brooks, James Green, Cornelius Brooks, Wm. Shepard, and Willis Thrall located in 1806. Jas. G. Johnson was the first settler in the village, in 1808. The first lumber was rafted down the Allegany in 1807, by Bibbins Follet, Jedediah Strong, and Dr. Bradley. The first birth in town was that of Olean, daughter of Wm. Shepard, May 22, 1807; and the first death, that of Wm. B. Shepard, Sept. 21, 1809. Sylvanus Russell kept the first inn, in 1808, at Olean Point, and Levi Gregory the first store, in 1811, at Olean Village. Wm. Shepard and Willis Thrall erected the first sawmill, in 1807, on Olean Creek; and Adam Hoops, the first gristmill, in 1809, at the mouth of the Creek. Mr. Hoops was a proprietor of lands and a pioneer settler. He had served with distinction in the Continental army,—at one period as aid to Gen. Washington.

[11] There are now 7 churches in town; 2 Evan. Luth., M. E., Prot. E., Presb., Bap., and R. C.

[12] Named from Jacob S. Otto, agent of the Holland Land Co.

13

part of Perrysburgh in 1823, and a part of Ashford in 1835. It lies on the N. line of the co., w. of the center. The surface is a hilly and broken upland. It is drained w. by Cattaraugus Creek, which forms its N. boundary, and several tributaries, the principal of which is the South Branch, forming the w. boundary. The soil is chiefly a hard, clay loam, with occasional spots of gravelly loam. **Waverly,** (Otto p. o.,) in the s. part, contains a church, woolen factory, and gristmill. Pop. 277. The first settlement was made on Cattaraugus Creek, in 1816, by Joseph Adams and his son Bina, and Joseph Bartlet.[1] The first church (Christian) was formed about 1826.[2]

PERRYSBURGH[3]—was formed from Olean and "*Ischua,*" now Franklinville, April 13, 1814, as "*Perry.*" Its name was changed April 10, 1818. Little Valley was taken off in 1818, Otto in 1823, and Dayton and Persia in 1835. Part of Otto was annexed in 1823. It is the N. w. corner town in the co. Its surface is a hilly and broken upland. Cattaraugus Creek forms the N. boundary. The streams are small branches of Cattaraugus and Silver Creeks. The soil is a clay and gravelly loam. **Perrysburgh,** (p. v.,) s. of the center, contains a church and 23 dwellings. It is a station on the N. Y. & E. R. R. **Versailles,** (p. v.,) on Cattaraugus Creek, in the N. E. part, contains a church, 2 flouring mills, and a tannery. Pop. 274. The rapid descent in the creek at this point affords an extensive water-power. The first settlement was made in 1815, by John Clark.[4] Religious meetings (M. E.) were held in 1820; but the first church (Bap.) which drew the lands granted by the Holland Land Co. was formed in 1821.[5]

PERSIA—was formed from Perrysburgh, Feb. 7, 1835. It lies on the N. line of the co., w. of the center. The surface is a hilly upland, with a general inclination toward the N. The highest points are about 650 feet above Lake Erie. The principal streams are Cattaraugus Creek, forming the N. boundary, and South Branch. The soil is a clay and gravelly loam. **Gowanda,**[6] (p. v.,) on Cattaraugus Creek, in the N. w. corner, was incorp. Dec. 7, 1847. It contains 2 churches, a newspaper office, a large flouring mill, 2 sawmills, and various other manufacturing establishments. Pop. 908, of which 520 are in Persia and 388 are in Collins, (Erie co.) The first settlement was made a little above Gowanda Village, in 1811, by John Russell, from Vt. Upon the breaking out of the War of 1812, he left with his family and never returned. In 1814, Ahaz Allen, from Vt., settled permanently on the lot left by Russell.[7] The first religious meetings were held by Elder Elnathan Finch, (F. W. Bap.,) in 1815–16. The first church (Presb.) was formed in 1826, at Gowanda.

PORTVILLE—was formed from Olean, April 27, 1837. It is the s. E. corner town of the co. The surface is mostly a hilly upland, the highest summits being 500 to 600 feet above the valleys. The Allegany River enters the town upon the s. border, flows N. to near the center, and thence N. w. to the w. border. It receives as tributaries Oswaya, Dodges, and Haskill Creeks. The soil is a sandy loam; and the flats were originally covered with a magnificent growth of white pine. Lumbering is the leading pursuit. **Portville,** (p. v.,) on the Allegany, contains 2 churches, 2 sawmills, and a gristmill. Pop. 287. **Mill Grove,** s. of Portville, on the Allegany, contains 2 sawmills, a gristmill, and 18 dwellings. The first settlement was made in 1805, by James Green, on Haskill Creek, in the N. part of the town.[9] The first church (M. E.) was formed in 1824. The census reports 2 churches; M. E., and Presb.

RANDOLPH—was formed from Connewango, Feb. 1, 1826, and named from Randolph, Vt. A part of South Valley was taken off in 1847. It lies upon the w. border of the co., s. of the center. Its surface is an undulating and hilly upland, the highest summits being about 400 feet above the valleys. Little Connewango Creek is the principal stream. The soil is mostly a clay

---

1 Stephen, Isaac, and Benj. Ballard, from Vt., and Ephraim Brown, settled in 1818, in different parts of the town. David S. Elliott kept the first inn, and Vine Plumb the first store, in 1828, at Waverly. The first sawmill was erected by Isaac W. Sherman, in 1822; and the first gristmill, by Stephen Rogers, in 1828, at Waverly.

2 There are now 3 churches in town; Christian, M. E., and Presb.

3 Named from Commodore O. H. Perry.

4 Among the other early settlers were Edward Russell, Phineas Spencer, Hugh Campbell, Ralph Griswold, Wm. Cooper, John Sprague, and Simon Waterman, who came in about 1816; and Elisha Ward, Stephen Crocker, and Freeman Edwards, who located near Perrysburgh Village in 1817. The first school was taught by Olive Barto, in the summer of 1819. Benj. Waterman kept the first inn, in 1816, and Cobb, Cook & Pelton the first store, at the village, in 1827. The first sawmill was erected on the branch of Silver Creek, by Isaac Balcomb; and the first gristmill, at Versailles, about 1820.

5 The census reports 4 churches; 3 M. E., and Bap.

6 Formerly called "*Lodi.*"

7 Thomas Farnsworth located in 1814, and Merrill Aldrich and Daniel Wheeler in 1815. The first child born was Anice Farnsworth, in the summer of 1815. The first school was taught by Polly Redfield, in 1817. Ahaz Allen erected the first sawmill, in 1814; the first clothing works, in 1821; and first gristmill, in 1823, on Cattaraugus Creek. Phineas Spencer kept the first store, about 1825, at Gowanda. "Point Peter" is the name given to a locality 1¼ mi. above Gowanda that marks the site of an ancient fortification.

8 There are 2 churches in town; Presb. and M. E.

9 The first child born was Hannah Green, daughter of Jas. Green, April 28, 1807; the first marriage was that of Jonathan Dodge and Eunice Atherton, in 1809; and the first death, that of David Heusten, killed by the spring of a tree while getting out spars, in the spring of 1807. Anna Carpenter taught the first school, near Portville Village, in the summer of 1822. Luman Rice kept the first inn, in 1822, and Allen Rice the first store, in 1823. The first sawmill was erected by James Green and Alpheus Dodge, on Haskill Creek, in 1807; and the first gristmill, by Samuel King, on Dodges Creek, in 1830.

and gravelly loam. A sulphur spring is found ½ mi. N. of East Randolph. **Randolph,** (p. v.,) on Little Connewango Creek, in the N. part, contains a sawmill, 3 churches, and about 600 inhabitants; **East Randolph,** (p. v.,) in the N. E. corner contains 2 churches, a grist and saw mill, a furnace, machine shop, tannery, and about 700 inhabitants. Randolph Academy is situated upon an eminence about midway between the villages. The first settlement in town was made at Randolph Village, by Edmund Fuller, from Oneida co., in 1820.[1] The first church (M. E.) was organized in 1823.[2]

SOUTH VALLEY—was formed from Randolph and Cold Spring, April 2, 1847. A part of Cold Spring was annexed in 1848. It is the s. w. corner town of the co. The surface is mountainous and broken. Allegany River flows s. w. through the town and receives as tributaries Split Rock, Hotchkiss, Tunessassa, Pierce, Sawmill, and Bone Run Creeks. The soil is a clay loam on the hills, and a rich, gravelly loam in the valleys. Lumbering is the principal occupation of the people.[3] **Onoville** is a p. o. The first settlement was made, under the auspices of the Friend's Mission, upon the Allegany Indian Reservation. The Mission was established in 1798, by the Yearly Meeting of Philadelphia Friends; and Joel Swayne, Holliday Jackson, and Chester Simmons, from Chester co., Penn., settled upon the Reservation, in the N. part of the town.[4] It does not appear that any other religious association has ever been formed in the town. The Presb. missions on the Reservation, however, have an extensive range in the valley of the Allegany.

YORKSHIRE—was formed from Franklinville, April 13, 1820. Machias was taken off in 1827. A part of Freedom was annexed in 1844, and a part of Machias was taken off in 1847. It lies upon the N. border of the co., E. of the center. Its surface is a rolling and hilly upland. Cattaraugus Creek forms the N. boundary. South Branch flows through near the center and receives several tributaries. The soil is a clay and gravelly loam. A large amount of maple sugar is annually produced. **Yorkshire Corners,** (Yorkshire p. o.,) on Cattaraugus Creek, contains 38 dwellings. **Yorkshire Center,** (p. v.,) a little E. of the center, contains 2 churches, 2 sawmills, a gristmill, and 42 dwellings. **West Yorkshire,** (p. v.,) on the N. line, at the junction of the South Branch with Cattaraugus Creek, contains a gristmill, sawmill, carding machine, and 14 dwellings. The first settlement was made in 1810, on Lot 1, in the N. E. corner, by Abner Bomp, from Vt.[5] The first church (M. E.) was formed about 1814.[6]

---

[1] The first child born was James Fuller. in June, 1822; and the first death was that of Zalmon C. Smith, June 17. 1824, while at work on mills of Chauncey C. Helms. The double marriage of David Salisbury and Clement Russell with daughters of Thos. Harvey, at the same time, were the first in town. The first school was taught by Sally Morton, at Randolph Village. in the summer of 1822. Benj. Clark kept the first inn, in 1823, and Robert Helms the first store, in 1837. Thos. Harvey erected the first sawmill, in 1823; Chauncey C. Helms, the first gristmill, in 1826; and Jonathan Wood, the first carding and cloth dressing mill, in 1827.

[2] There are 5 churches in town; M. E., Bap., F. W. Bap., Cong., and R. C.

[3] The extensive pine forests which grew in town are nearly exhausted; and the lumbering is now mostly confined to the coarser kinds of lumber. The town has an area of 37,749 acres, of which only about 2,000 acres are under improvement.

[4] Soon after the first settlement the Yearly Meeting at Phila-delphia purchased 300 acres of land of the Holland Land Company and built a saw and grist mill. The mills did work for white settlers on the usual terms, and furnished lumber and ground corn for the Indians free. The Indians were also instructed in agriculture and the arts of civilized life. The mills were built by Jacob Taylor and Jonathan Thomas. Robert Clendenon, from Chester co., Penn., occupied the Mission Station in 1812. It is said that descendants of Sir Wm. Johnson are now residing on the Allegany Reservation.

[5] Benj. and Wm. Felch, Edward Bomp, Thos. Dow, and Luther Thompson were among the first settlers. Saml. G. Sutton and Robert Steel, from N. H., settled in 1818, and are now the oldest residents in town. The first store was kept by Henry L. Baker, in 1823. and the first inn by Prescott Williams, in 1826,—both at Yorkshire Corners. Isaac Williams erected the first grist and saw mill, in 1814. on Cattaraugus Creek.

[6] There are now 3 churches in town; M. E., Bap., and Univ.

Acres of Land, Valuation, Population, Dwellings, Families, Freeholders, Schools, Live Stock, Agricultural Products, and Domestic Manufactures, of Cattaraugus County.

Names of Towns.	Acres of Land.		Valuation of 1858.			Population.		No. of Dwellings.	No. of Families.	Freeholders.	Schools.	
	Improved.	Unimproved.	Real Estate.	Personal Property.	Total.	Males.	Females.				No. of Districts.	Children taught.
Allegany	4,098½	40,677	$198,096	$750	$198,846	820	763	297	303	228	9	689
Ashford	12,138¾	16,423	280,728	1,270	281,998	966	947	359	389	337	13	724
Bucktooth	794	4,617	90,065	9,400	99,465	244	209	84	69	38	4	244
Carrolton	1,096¾	22,809⅜	81,500	600	82,100	256	255	81	89	59	3	192
Cold Spring	2,319½	15,497	94,495	250	94,745	351	313	110	119	80	4	266
Connewango	10,954½	9,512½	175,719	13,000	188,719	674	671	267	275	228	11	491
Dayton	10,108¾	12,587¼	212,510	17,600	230,110	581	558	217	226	157	8	513
East Otto	10,753½	11,619	202,064	13,480	215,544	604	624	227	242	227	6	400
Ellicottville	9,384⅞	17.722⅜	251,493	67,700	319,193	921	917	350	343	152	9	760
Farmersville	19,575¼	13,456¼	264,458	36,250	300,708	761	682	265	267	244	11	565
Franklinville	13,972	17,401	270,898	36,450	307,348	845	841	316	334	348	11	725
Freedom	15,874¼	9,398	364,350	10,500	374,850	743	700	285	300	261	12	514
Great Valley	4,586¾	26,285	133,284	6,200	139,484	608	590	224	236	183	7	543
Hinsdale	7,762½	15,232	188,342	13,650	201,992	1,099	1,030	409	434	229	8	592
Humphrey	10,378¼	6,348	183,080	4,000	187,080	395	364	147	151	130	7	382
Ischua	7,394	12,566¼	155,987	1,300	157,287	585	518	204	204	167	8	355
Leon	11,740	9,225⅝	258,499	14,457	272,956	682	648	261	264	283	11	516
Little Valley	5,073⅝	13,213½	115,015	5,050	120,065	417	384	158	160	142	6	354
Lyndon	10,289¼	9,627	166,190	6,550	172,740	593	530	225	220	220	9	424
Machias	10,683	9,604½	202,767	17,070	219,837	669	697	256	226	210	12	605
Mansfield	11,301½	11,267½	197,341	8,200	205,541	576	549	213	257	185	12	534
Napoli	10,332	11,361¼	240,771	11,800	252,571	589	633	229	243	231	8	456
New Albion	11,270¾	10,272¾	219,823	16,952	236,775	799	763	305	310	241	8	649
Olean	2,518	9,219	302,129	33,550	335,679	839	772	337	310	223	4	720
Otto	11,049½	8,487¾	335,216	29,119	364,335	563	531	211	213	189	7	399
Perrysburgh	12,332⅞	5,551½	269,261	37,500	306,761	727	729	276	288	248	9	566
Persia	5,483⅞	6,165½	223,441	34,200	257,641	620	584	240	185	240	5	528
Portville	3,189	18,823¾	185,637	14,700	200,337	610	554	204	213	173	7	564
Randolph	7,206⅛	13,214½	284,530	18,500	303,030	842	881	318	327	226	8	814
South Valley	1,714¾	33,074½	128,650	5,000	133,650	322	264	92	111	72	7	332
Yorkshire	11,059	11,361	232,619	14,275	246,894	910	818	348	338	312	11	706
Total	266,435⅜	432,620⅝	6,508,958	499,323	7,008,281	20,211	19,319	7,515	7,646	6,263	255	16,122

Names of Towns.	Live Stock.					Agricultural Products.							Domestic Cloths, in Yards.
						Bush. of Grain.					Dairy Products.		
	Horses.	Working Oxen and Calves.	Cows.	Sheep.	Swine.	Winter.	Spring.	Tons of Hay.	Bushels of Potatoes.	Bushels of Apples.	Pounds of Butter.	Pounds of Cheese.	
Allegany	121	489	296	882	183	510	20,403½	1,187½	9,327	1,586½	31,175	1,045	518
Ashford	475	1,804	1,304	2,880	724	1,021	57,371	2,824½	14,679	9,358	113,313	144,876	2,620
Bucktooth	35	186	94	136	49	40	3,655	224½	2,540	220	9,805	520	145
Carrolton	36	236	137	94	194	10	4,699	283	2,866	90	8,995	500	75
Cold Spring	104	286	170	573	162	15	10,107	551½	3,980	1,829	12,813	375	458
Connewango	434	2,282	1,019	1.922	732	314	49,097½	3,086½	10,085	9,650	107,988	14,245	879
Dayton	344	1,241	1,007	1,415	455	866	36,522	2,365½	8,591	11,641	61,016	113,814	1,708
East Otto	331	1,203	1,510	1,381	358	323	38,908	2,556	8,453	7,657	86,099	265,000	1 427
Ellicottville	251	1,083	591	2,040	440	209	38,311½	1,569½	14,485¼	2,518	44,845	22,195	417
Farmersville	621	2,665	1,774	4,360	695	686	66,400	4,758	18,700	11,244	161,745	151,539	2,050
Franklinville	477	2,103	999	4,303	667	1,761	66,434½	3,567	18,021	6,235	77,870	78,710	693
Freedom	535	1,749	1,604	3,272	645		55,672¼	3,857½	13,219	7,356	152,942	37,890	2,186
Great Valley	220	630	395	1,259	347	206	20,562	1,138½	10,015	1,730	34,957	240	631
Hinsdale	366	1,045	624	2,828	576	857	57,502½	2,041	10,393	5,665	58,200	10,640	426
Humphrey	203	888	422	1,822	268	216	30,189	1,387½	8,635	1,800	35,464	9,900	797
Ischua	306	1,277	542	2,603	486	1,724½	45,342	1,903	8,078	5,488	44,640	5,870	1,334
Leon	369	1,450	1,021	2,314	695	1,346	42,750½	3,140½	10,961	16,060	69,314	114,475	2,349¼
Little Valley	166	668	238	698	215	205	11,546¼	1,030	6,421	2,387	38,635	9,310	263
Lyndon	356	1,350	826	4,063	501	909	40,480½	2,502	13,055	3,647	77,700	46,370	949
Machias	380	1,325	840	3,446	531	641	55,932	1,749	12,351	3,183	75,694	10,644	1,685
Mansfield	312	1,190	954	2,560	421	290	47,514½	2,009½	11,013	6,269	72,703	199,500	1,217
Napoli	402	1,225	790	2,155	488	135	55,350½	2,486	12,068	11,377	91,775	5,550	1,232½
New Albion	383	1,557	1,079	2,588	606	561	48,555¼	2,643	11,840	4,743	90,458	77,166	1,954
Olean	155	249	286	228	326	364	12,690	634	3,905	1,426	5,310	560	128
Otto	335	1,167	1,229	1,410	452	890½	41,776	2,540	6,686½	9,186	77,823	208,476	1,945
Perrysburgh	425	1,465	1,215	2,437	713	4,279	39,334	3,430½	10,334	9,718	91,875	128,994	2,047
Persia	240	825	658	760	324	3,777	25,679	1,460½	7,202	5,260	42,666	38,666	747½
Portville	193	336	323	854	354	178½	16,561	789	9,474	3,069	27,983	2,895	586½
Randolph	434	1,139	647	1,253	576	318	28,129	1,961½	7,479	6,200	49,090	4,615	1,332
South Valley	88	314	171	486	136	354	4,859	613½	2,370	800	15,365		239
Yorkshire	400	1,329	868	2,703	515	1,088	46,645½	2,193¾	13,019	9,781	88,925	12,904	2,034
Total	9,497	34,756	23,633	59,725	13,834	24,094½	1,118,979¾	62,546¾	300,245¾	177,173½	1,957,183	1,717,484	35,072¾

CAYUGA COUNTY.

THIS county was formed from Onondaga, March 8, 1799. Seneca was taken off in 1804, and a part of Tompkins in 1817. It is a long, narrow co., lying w. of the center of the State, and extending from Lake Ontario s. to near the head of Cayuga Lake. It is centrally distant 146 mi. from Albany, and contains 756 square mi.[1] It has a general northerly inclination, and is divided geographically into two nearly equal parts by a line extending eastward from the foot of Cayuga Lake. The N. half is level, or gently undulating, and contains numerous marshes. Some portions of its surface are covered with small, isolated drift-hills 50 to 75 ft. high. The surface of the s. half is rolling, and gradually rises until it attains an elevation of 500 to 800 ft. above the level lands of the N. These highlands are divided into two general ridges, the first lying between Skaneateles and Owasco Lakes, and the second between Owasco and Cayuga Lakes. The summits of both ridges are rolling, and have an elevation of 1000 to 1200 ft. above tide. Their E. declivities are often precipitous, forming high, bold bluffs upon the shores of the lakes, but their w. declivities are more gradual, generally sloping gently down to the very edge of the waters. The s. part of the w. ridge is divided near its center by the valley of Salmon Creek, which is bordered by steep banks 50 to 200 ft. high. Among the most peculiar of the natural features of the co. are the three long, narrow lakes which extend from the level regions of the N. between the parallel ridges far into the highlands of the s. Skaneateles Lake, upon the E. line, is 840 ft. above tide, and is bordered by bluff shores within the limits of the co. Owasco Lake, near the center, is 770 ft. above tide, and its shores are generally bold, and in some places precipitous. Cayuga Lake, on the western border, is 387 ft. above tide, and along nearly its whole extent in the co. the land slopes beautifully and evenly upward from its surface to the summits of the ridges. The water of these lakes is clear and transparent, and may be taken as the very type of purity. This lake region, with its beautifully rolling surface and rich and productive soil, with its green lawns apparently stretching upward from the very bosom of the water, and with its highly cultivated farms, presents one of the finest landscapes in the country. Seneca River flows eastward through near the center of the lowlands which form the N. half of the co. It receives Cayuga and Owasco Outlets from the s. and numerous smaller streams from both the N. and s. A swampy region, known as the Montezuma Marshes, extends along the whole course of the river.[2] The streams that drain the central ridges are small creeks and brooks. Upon the level land in the N. part of the co. are a series of small, shallow lakes and ponds, the principal of which is Cross Lake.

The rocks in this co. generally lie in nearly horizontal layers, but in some places they are disrupted and broken. Their edges appear one above the other, forming the declivities of the hills that rise toward the s. The lowest formation is the Medina sandstone, which outcrops upon the shore of Lake Ontario and covers the N. half of Sterling. Above this successively appear the Oneida, conglomerate, and Clinton groups in the s. part of Sterling; the Lockport group in Victory; the red shale of the Onondaga salt group in Cato, Brutus, Conquest, and Mentz; the gypsum of the same group in Auburn, Aurelius, and Springport, and for a distance of 10 miles along Cayuga Lake; the waterlime and Oriskany sandstone in Owasco, Auburn, Fleming, and Springport; and, successively above the Onondaga and corniferous limestone, the Marcellus and Hamilton shales, Tully limestone, Genesee slate, and the Portage and Ithaca groups, the last occupying the summits of the southern hills. Weak springs of brine are found in the Medina sandstone upon the borders of Lake Ontario, and also in the red shale of the salt group along the course of Seneca River. In the central part of the co., and along the shores of Cayuga Lake, are numerous quarries, which furnish a good quality of waterlime, quicklime, and gypsum. The red sandstone and the Onondaga and corniferous limestone are quarried extensively for building stone. Thin layers of corniferous limestone and of sandstone are extensively quarried along Cayuga Lake, and make an excellent quality of flagging.

The soil in the N. half of the co. is generally a fine quality of sandy or gravelly loam, inter-

---

[1] Exclusive of 160 sq. mi. in Lake Ontario.
[2] Several efforts have been made by the State to drain these marshes, and large sums have been expended. A portion only, however, has yet been redeemed.

mixed with clay, muck, and alluvium; and in the s. it is a gravelly and clay loam and very productive. The whole co. is well adapted to either grain raising or pasturage. Until within a few years wheat has been the staple production; but it has been nearly superseded by rye, oats, barley, and corn. Wool growing and dairying are also extensively pursued. The cultivation of fruit, for which the climate and soil are admirably adapted, is beginning to receive considerable attention. The manufactúres of the co., mostly confined to Auburn, are extensive, though comparatively less than in 1810.[1]

The county seat is located at the city of Auburn.[2] An elegant and substantial courthouse was built in 1807–09.[3] It is located upon a commanding site in the s. w. part of the city, and contains rooms for the usual co. offices. A fireproof clerk's office is situated adjacent to the courthouse. A substantial stone jail was erected in 1833, in the rear of the courthouse.[4] The county poorhouse is located upon a farm of 90 acres in Sennett, 3 mi. N. E. of Auburn. It is a poor, old, dilapidated building, containing about 30 rooms. The average number of inmates is about 100, supported at a weekly cost of 70 cts. each. A school is kept during a portion of the year.[5] The Cayuga Orphan Asylum, located in the city of Auburn, was incorp. in April, 1852. It receives orphans and destitute children and has an average attendance of 30. The institution is well managed, and the children receive good care and instruction. The Erie Canal extends through Brutus, Mentz, and Montezuma. Cayuga Lake and Outlet are navigable, and form a connection with the canal at Montezuma. The direct branch of the N. Y. Central R. R. from Syracuse to Rochester extends through Brutus, Mentz, and Montezuma, and the Auburn branch through Sennett, Auburn, and Aurelius.[6]

Two daily, 7 weekly, and 3 monthly papers are published in the co.[7]

---

[1] "The number of looms in the co. were 1,360, producing 340,870 yds. of cloth annually; there are 19 tanneries, 47 distilleries, 48 asheries, 11 carding machines, 11 cloth dressing-mills, 3 oil mills, an air furnace, triphammer, several nail factories, 6 earthen ware factories, and several hatters' shops. About 2,500 skeins of silk and 60,000 bushs. of salt are made annually. The inhabitants clothe themselves principally in the products of their own families, and were it not for the exorbitant number of their distilleries, I should add, are very temperate and industrious,—the character given them by correspondents."—*Spafford's Gazetteer*, ed. 1813.

[2] When organized in 1799, Cayuga included Seneca co., the territory lying between the Cayuga and Seneca Lakes; and, as central to the thin population, the first courthouse was located at Aurora, on the E. shore of Cayuga Lake. It was built of poles and covered with brush. In 1803 a circuit court and court of Oyer and Terminer was held at this place by Daniel D. Tompkins, at which an Indian by the name of John was tried and convicted of the murder of Ezekiel Crane, jr., and sentenced to be hung. He urgently requested that he might be shot,—a privilege, of course, not granted by our laws. A log building at Cayuga Village was authorized to be used as a jail March 25, 1800. In 1804 an act was passed, authorizing John Tillotson, Augustus Chidsey, and John Grover, jr., commissioners to build a courthouse on the S. E. corner of Lot 46 of Scipio, (now Auburn.) This act was afterward repealed. On the 6th of March, 1805, Edward Savage, of Montgomery co., Jas. Burt, of Orange, and Jas. Hildreth, of Montgomery, were appointed commissioners to locate the site of a courthouse. The commissioners neglected to fix the site; and, April 6, 1808, John Glover, Stephen Close, and Noah Olmstead were appointed to superintend the finishing of the courthouse at Auburn.

[3] The first co. officers were Seth Phelps, *First Judge;* William Stuart, *District Attorney;* Benjamin Ledyard, *County Clerk;* Joseph Annin, *Sheriff;* Glen Cuyler, *Surrogate.*

[4] This building is 45 by 65 feet, 2 stories high, with 2 double and 26 single cells, arranged in the center of the building, with a hall on three sides, open to the prisoners in daytime.

[5] No means are provided for ventilating the rooms or for classifying the inmates. The insane are sometimes confined in dark cells not provided with means of warmth; and the whole establishment and its management are by no means creditable to the intelligence and humanity of the citizens of the co.

[6] The Ontario, Auburn & N. Y. R. R., extending from Little Sodus Bay s. to Ithaca, has been surveyed through the co. and partially graded; but work upon it has been suspended.

[7] The *Levana Gazette, or Onondaga Advertiser,* the first paper published in Cayuga co., was established July 20, 1798, at Levana, in the town of Scipio, (then Onondaga co.,) by R. Delano.

The *Western Luminary* was published at Watkins' Settlement, in Scipio, in 1799.

The *Aurora Gazette* was established in 1799 by H. & J. Pace, and continued until 1805, when it was removed to Auburn and changed to

The *Western Federalist.* It was published as

The *Auburn Gazette* by Skinner and Crosby in 1816.

The *Cayuga Tocsin* was commenced at Union Springs in 1812 by R. T. Chamberlain. It was soon after removed to

Auburn, and continued by different persons until 1847, when it was united with the Cayuga Patriot.

The *Cayuga Patriot* was started at Auburn by Samuel R. Brown in 1814. Isaac S. Allen, Ulysses F. Doubleday, and others, were afterward interested in its publication. In June, 1847, it was united with the Tocsin, the joint papers taking the name of

The *Cayuga New Era.* It was successively published by Merrill, Stone & Co., Stone, Hawes & Co., Finn & Hallett, and William L. Finn, and was discontinued in 1857.

The *Advocate of the People* was commenced at Auburn in Sept. 1816, by Henry C. Southwick.

The *Cayuga Republican* was commenced in 1819 by A. Buckinham, and was afterward published by Thomas M. Skinner. In 1833 it was united with the Free Press and issued as

The *Auburn Journal and Advertiser* by Oliphant & Skinner. Skinner subsequently withdrew, and the paper was continued by Oliphant. In 1846 it was issued as

The Auburn Journal; and the same year

The Auburn Daily Advertiser, the first daily paper published in the co., was established in connection with it. In the fall of the same year, Oliphant sold out to Henry Montgomery, by whom the papers were continued until 1850, when Knapp & Peck, the present publishers, became proprietors.

The *Auburn Free Press* was commenced by Richard Oliphant in 1824 and published by him until 1829. It was then sold to Henry Oliphant, and in 1833 it was united with the Cayuga Republican.

The *Gospel Messenger* (Prot. E.) was established at Auburn by Rev. Dr. Rudd in 1827. It was removed to Utica a few years after.

The *Diamond* was published in 1830.

The *Gospel Advocate* was published in 1830.

The *Cayuga Democrat* was published by Fred. Prince in 1833.

The *People's Friend* was published in 1836 by Oliphant & Skinner.

The *Western Banner* was published in 1836 by Francis S. Wiggins.

The *Peoples Library,* mo., was published in 1836 by F. S. Wiggins.

The *Primitive Christian* was published in 1836 by Silas E. Shepard.

The *Conference Record* was published in 1837 by Rev. J. S. Chamberlain.

The *Northern Christian Advocate* (M.E.) was commenced in April, 1841, by Rev. John E. Robie. It was edited by Rev. F. G. Hibbard and Rev. Wm. Hosmer until May, 1844, when it was purchased by the Meth. Genl. Conference and changed to

The Northern Advocate. It was edited successively by Rev. Nelson Rounds and Wm. Hosmer, and is now under the editorial charge of Rev. F. G. Hibbard.

The *Star of Temperance* was published in 1845 by L. H. Davey.

Auburn's Favorite was published in 1849 by Newton Calkins.

The *Cayuga Chief* was commenced at Auburn in January, 1849, by Thurlow W. Brown, and continued until 1857.

The *Auburn Daily Bulletin* was published in 1849 by Stone, Hawes & Co.

The *Masonic Union,* mo., was published in 1850.

This co. formed a portion of the Military Tract, and included the original townships of Cato, Brutus, Aurelius, Scipio, Sempronius, and parts of Milton and Locke. Sterling was included in the lands granted as a compensation for portions of the original grants, which upon survey were found to belong to the Boston Ten Towns. Before the advent of the whites it formed the chief hunting grounds of the Cayuga Nation. The people of this nation were more migratory in their habits than those of the Onondaga and Seneca nations, and they had fewer towns and villages. The principal town or place of council of the tribe was upon the shore of Cayuga Lake, near the present village of Aurora. The first white settlers were soldiers, who had served during the Revolution and who drew lots upon the Military Tract, or those who had purchased soldiers' warrants. The first immigration was by the way of Oneida Lake and River, and from the s. by way of Cayuga Lake; but in 1796 a State road, extending from Whitestown to Geneva by way of Auburn, was cut through; and in 1800 the celebrated Cayuga Bridge[1] was built, the new route speedily becoming the great highway of Western emigration. The population steadily and rapidly increased from 1790, a great impulse being given to it by the completion of the Erie Canal in 1825. The first inhabitants were principally from New England and the eastern cos. of New York.

AUBURN CITY—was formed as a town from Aurelius, March 28, 1823. It was incorp. as a village April 18, 1815, and as a city March 21, 1848. It lies upon Owasco Outlet, near the center of the co. Its surface is rolling, with an inclination toward the N. Owasco Outlet, flowing N. w. through near the center, descends 120 ft., and furnishes an abundance of water-power, which is mostly improved. Along its course are valuable quarries of waterlime, Oriskany sandstone, and Onondaga and corniferous limestone. The city is finely laid out upon both sides of the creek, most of the streets having a gentle inclination. It is situated in the midst of a rich farming country, and it has a large share of internal trade. Its manufactures are extensive and important, consisting principally of woolen goods,[2] paper, agricultural implements, books, flour, and machinery. Besides the co. buildings, it contains 12 churches,[3] 3 banks, and many other fine public and private buildings. Seven weekly, 2 daily, and 2 monthly papers are published in the city. Pop. 9,476.

The *Public Schools* are under a Board of Education, consisting of 4 members, elected annually. The schools, 5 in number, employ 23 teachers,—5 males and 18 females. In 1858 the number of children between the ages of 4 and 21 was 3001, of whom 2187, or 72 per cent., attended school during some portion of the year. The total expenses of the schools for 1858 were $13,231.19. The number of volumes in the district libraries is 3986.

The Christian Ambassador (Univ.) was commenced in Jan. 1851, and is now edited by John M. Austin.
The Spiritual and Moral Instructor was published in 1851 by Peleg S. Collrell & Co.
The Auburn American, d. and w., was established in Feb. 1855, by Wm. J. Moses. In 1859 the name of the daily was changed to
The Daily Union, Moses & Vail publishers.
The Journal of Specific Homeopathy, mo., was started in March, 1855, and is pub. by F. Humphreys.
The Spiritual Clarion, commenced Nov. 15, 1856, is published weekly by Uriah Clark.
The Northern Independent was estab. in Aug. 1856, by a pub. com. of the M. E. Ch.; Rev. Wm. Hosmer, ed.
The Orphans' Friend, mo., commenced in Feb. 1857, is pub. by the managers of the Cayuga Orphan Asylum.
The Cayuga Farmer and Mechanic was commenced in Sept. 1856, by P. J. Becker. In Dec. 1857 its name was changed to
The Teachers' Educational Journal; it is still issued by its original proprietor.
The Auburn Democrat was established in Aug. 1857, by Stone and Hawes, by whom it is still published.
The Weedsport Advertiser was published in 1827.
The Northern Phœnix was published at Weedsport in 1830 by Frederick Prince.
The Genoa Spy was published in 1840 by Gelim Hine.
The Port Byron Herald was first published at Port Byron in Oct. 1844. by Frederick Prince.
The Port Byron Gazette was started in 1851 by Oliver T. Baird, and continued until 185-

The Cayuga Telegraph was published at Union Springs in 1850.
The Meridian Sun was started in 1854 by Arthur White. It was afterward published as
The Meridian Advertiser by W. H. Thomas.
The Family Scrap Book, mo., was published at Victory Center in 1855-56.

[1] The Cayuga Bridge was finished Sept. 4, 1800, by the Manhattan Company. It was 1 mi. and 8 rods long, 22 ft. wide and 22 ft. between trestles. It was built in 18 months, and cost $150,000. The Cayuga Bridge Company, consisting of John Harris, Thos. Morris, Wilhelmus Mynderse, Charles Williamson, and Jos. Annin, was incorp. in 1797. The bridge was destroyed in 1808, but afterward rebuilt. For a great number of years the Cayuga bridge was considered one of the greatest public improvements in the State, and it was taken as the dividing line between the E. and w. The bridge was abandoned in 1857; and the lake is now crossed by a ferry.
[2] The Auburn Woolen Mills give employment to 175 hands and manufactures 250,000 yds. of cloth per annum. The Auburn Paper Mills employ 50 hands and manufacture $80,000 worth of paper annually. The founderies and machine shops give employment to a large number of men, and turn out work to the amount of $100,000 annually. The N. Y. C. R. R. Repair Shops employ 52 hands exclusively in repairing passenger cars. For a number of years books were very extensively manufactured; but of late much of this branch of business has been removed to other cities. Besides these, there are in the city a card factory, belting factory, carpet factory, distillery, rolling mill, and 2 grist mills.
[3] 2 Presb., 2 M. E., 2 R. C., Prot. E., Af. Meth., Bap., Second Advent, Univ., and Disciples.

The *Auburn Academy* is a fine stone edifice on Academy St. It was first erected in 1811, but was burned in 1816, and the present building was soon after erected.

The *Auburn Female Seminary*, a private institution, is in the building erected for a city hall, at the junction of Market, Franklin, and North Sts.

The *Auburn Theological Seminary*, a Presb. institution, was established by the Synod of Genesee in 1819. It was incorp. in 1820 and opened in 1821. The building is located upon a commanding site, fronting Seminary St., in the N. E. part of the city.

The *Cayuga Orphan Asylum*, an institution for the care of orphan and destitute children, is supported by State and co. appropriations and private contributions.

The *Auburn State Prison* is situated on the N. bank of Owasco Outlet, N. of the center of the city. The site, containing 10 acres, is surrounded by high walls, and within this enclosure are the prison proper[1] and the various workshops in which the convicts are employed. The main building, fronting upon State Street, is 3 stories high and 276 feet long, and is flanked by two wings 42 feet wide and 242 feet deep.

The *Asylum for Lunatic Convicts*, situated upon a lot of 10 acres, formerly the prison garden, in the rear of the prison, is a fine brick building, faced with cut stone. It contains 64 cells, and rooms for physicians, attendants, &c.[2]

Fort Hill is a beautiful rural cemetery, located upon the site of an ancient fortification and Indian village. It contains a monument to the memory of Logan, the celebrated Cayuga chief.[3]

The first settlement at Auburn was made in 1793, by Col. John Hardenburgh, from Ulster co.[4] Hon. Wm. H. Seward resides in this city.

AURELIUS—was formed Jan. 27, 1789. Brutus, Cato, Owasco, and *"Jefferson"* (now Mentz) were taken off March 30, 1802, Auburn and Fleming in 1823, a part of Springport in 1833, and a part of Throop in 1859. It lies upon Cayuga Lake, near the center of the w. border of the co. Its surface is undulating, with a slight inclination toward the N. and w. Owasco Outlet flows through the N. E. corner; and upon its course are several fine mill privileges. Cayuga Brook, Crane Creek, and several other small streams take their rise in the town. The soil is mostly a heavy clay and gravelly loam. **Cayuga,** (p. v.,) upon Cayuga Lake, 2 mi. s. of the outlet, was incorp. in 1858. It is an important station upon the Central R. R., and is connected with Ithaca by a daily line of steamers. It contains 2 churches and 400 inhabitants. **Fosterville,** (p. v.,) in the N. part, contains a church and 12 dwellings; and **Aurelius,** (p. v.,) in the s. E. part, a church and 12 dwellings. **Clarksville,** on the E. line, is a manufacturing village, and forms a suburb of Auburn. It contains a paper mill,[5] gristmill, hoe factory, woolen factory, and 300 inhabitants. The first settlement was made at Cayuga in 1788, by John Harris, from Harrisburgh, Penn.[6] The first church was formed in 1804, by Rev. David Higgins.[7]

BRUTUS—was formed from Aurelius, March 30, 1802. Sennett was taken off in 1827. It lies on the E. border of the co., N. of the center. In the N. and w. its surface is level, with an

---

[1] The cells of the prison are built in a block 5 stories high, separated from the exterior walls by an open space and surrounded by galleries. Each cell is 7 feet long by 3¼ wide and 7¼ high, closed by an iron grate. Breakfast and dinner are eaten at narrow tables, so arranged that the convicts cannot exchange looks or signs. Supper is eaten in the cells. The workshops form a range of near 1000 feet, built against the outer wall and lighted from the .roof and inner sides. Water-power is afforded by the Owasco. These prison buildings were commenced in 1816 and completed in 1819, by the State, at a cost of $300,000, exclusive of the labor of convicts upon them. The general control is vested in a Board of Inspectors; 54 officials, including a guard of 20 men, a chaplain, a physician, and 2 teachers, are employed in the management and government of the establishment. The average number of convicts is about 700. Their earnings in 1857 were $70,000, and the current expenses of the establishment about $72,000.

[2] This building was erected by the State in 1858, at a cost of $60,000.

[3] This ancient fortification was evidently the work of a people who occupied the country prior to the advent of the Indians. The monuments left by this people, the remains of the language still existing, and the traditions of the Indians, all show that they belonged to the same general stock as the aborigines of Mexico. They are known as the "Mound Builders," and in history are generally called the "Alleghans." The fort at this place was probably built prior to the discovery of America by Columbus, and was occupied by them for several hundred years; but they were finally driven out by the Cayugas. It was named by them Osco or Was Kough, and became the principal village of the nation until the advent of the whites. The celebrated Indian chief, Logan, was born here about the commencement of

the last century. He afterward emigrated to Penn., and finally to Ohio. He was always known as a peacemaker and friend to the whites until his wife and children were murdered by Col. Cresap, after which he took up the hatchet and became one of the most noted of the Indian warriors. His address to the Peace Commissioners at the close of the war has scarcely its parallel in history for true eloquence and pathos. This ancient work is particularly described in the *Smithsonian Contributions,* Vol. II, Art. VI, p. 35.

[4] Among the other early settlers were Col. Brinkerhoff, Dr. Hackcliat Burt, Wm. Bostwick, Barnabas Caswell, and Lyman Paine, who came about 1795. John Hardenburgh built the first gristmill, in 1794; and Wm. Bostwick took the first inn, in 1796. The place was called "*Hardenburgh Corners*" until 1805, when its name was changed to Auburn.

[5] The Auburn Paper Mill was incorp. here Feb. 17, 1848, with a capital of $50,000. It gives employment to 40 hands, and manufactures paper to the amount of $150,000 annually.

[6] Mr. Harris established the first ferry across Cayuga Lake. Wm. Harris and John Richardson came in the same year. The first marriage was that of John Harris and Mary Richardson, in 1789; the first birth, that of John Harris, jr., in 1790; and the first death, that of —— Depuy, in 1797. Hugh Buckley taught the first school, in 1797; John Harris kept the first inn, in 1790, and the first store, in 1789. The celebrated Cayuga Bridge, 1 mi. 8 rods in length, was built in 1797, by Swartwood & Deman, of New York City, and Joseph Annin and others, of Cayuga. It fell in 1804, but was rebuilt in 1812–13, and was abandoned in 1857. After it was built, the road across it was the great highway of emigration until the canal was finished. The county seat was located here at the first organization of the co.

[7] There are 4 churches in town; 2 Presb. and 2 M. E.

average elevation of not more than 10 feet above Seneca River, which forms its N. boundary. The portions immediately bordering upon the river are generally swampy. In the S. E. the surface is rolling and broken by isolated drift hills 50 to 75 feet above the general level. The principal streams are Bread Creek and Cold Spring Brook, both flowing into Seneca River. The former is a canal feeder, and along its banks are outcrops of limestone and plaster, which are quarried to some extent. The soil is a fine quality of sandy and gravelly loam intermixed with clay and alluvium. **Weedsport**[1] (p. v.,) was incorp. April 26, 1831. It is situated upon the Erie Canal, and is a station on the N. Y. Central R. R. It contains a bank, insurance office, union school, 4 churches, a foundery, a large distillery, and several mills. Pop. 1,226. The first settlement was begun in 1800, by Wm. Stevens, from Mass, on Lot 76.[2] The first church (M. E.) was formed in 1816.[3]

CATO—was formed from Aurelius, March 30, 1802. Sterling was taken off in 1812, and Conquest, Ira, and Victory in 1821. A part of Ira was annexed in 1834. It lies upon the E. border of the co., N. of the center. Its surface is level in the s. and gently rolling in the N. The ridges extend N. and s., and their summits are about 50 feet above the valleys and 150 to 200 feet above Lake Ontario. Seneca River forms the s. boundary. Cross Lake, upon the E. border, is a shallow body of water about 5 mi. long, through which flows Seneca River. Otter Lake and Parkers Pond, in the N. part, discharge their waters through Otter Creek into Seneca River. The soil is a sandy and gravelly loam mixed with clay and disintegrated red shale. **Meridian,**[4] (p. v.,) in the N. part of the town, was incorp. Oct. 17, 1854. Pop. 360. **Cato,** (p. v.,) on the line of Ira, in the N. W. corner, contains 3 churches and 53 dwellings. **Seneca River** is a p. o. The first settlement was begun in 1800, by Samson Lawrence, on Lot 32.[5] The first church (Bap.) was formed Oct. 26, 1810; Rev. Daniel Palmer was the first pastor.[6]

CONQUEST[7]—was formed from Cato, March 16, 1821. It lies on the w. border of the co., N. of the center. The surface is gently rolling, the ridges extending N. and s. The s. part along the course of Seneca River is marshy, and a swamp about one-fourth of a mi. wide extends N. and s. through the town along the course of the small stream which flows through Mud Pond. Duck Pond, in the N. W., is about 1 mi. in diameter. Howlands Island, in Seneca River, contains 2,700 acres, one-third of which is swampy, and overflowed during high water. The soil is a sandy loam interspersed with clay and underlaid by red shale. **Conquest Center** (Conquest p. o.) contains 2 churches and 26 houses; **Pineville,** in the w. part, contains 15 houses. The first settlers were George Snyder, from Schoharie co., who located on Lot 37, and Israel Wolverton, from Tompkins co., on Lot 4, in 1800.[8] The first church (Prot. Meth.) was formed at Conquest Center, in 1803; Rev. Joshua Beebe was the first settled preacher.[9]

FLEMING[10]—was formed from Aurelius, March 28, 1823. It lies w. of the foot of Owasco Lake, a little s. of the center of the co. Its surface is rolling, with an inclination toward the N. and E. The banks of the lake slope upward for about three-fourths of a mi. The highest portions are 150 to 250 feet above the lake, and 800 to 1,000 feet above tide. Wheeler and Crane Creeks are the principal streams. The soil is principally a gravelly loam, with an occasional intermixture of clay and sand. **Fleming,** (p. v.,) near the center, contains 2 churches and 25 dwellings.

1 Named from Elisha and Edward Weed, first settlers at the village.

2 Among the other early settlers were Caleb, Nathan, and Jonah Rood, and —— Powers, from Saratoga co., who located at and near Weedsport; John Hamilton, from Washington co., on Lot 64, in March, 1802; Edward Horton, Peter Douglass, and Samuel Moore, from N. J., on Lot 86; Adam Helmer, from Herkimer co., on Lot 67, in 1804; and —— Van Dyck and Daniel Miller, from N. J., on Lot 76, in 1805. The first child born was Burnett Stevens, Nov. 13, 1801; the first marriage, that of Peter Douglass and Polly Hamilton, Jan. 12, 1804; and the first death, that of an infant child of Sunderland Sweet, in 1800. Harriet Phelps taught the first school, in 1806; Walter and Elisha Weed kept the first store; and Lewis Putnam built the first sawmill and gristmill, on Bread Creek.

3 The census reports 4 churches; Presb., Bap., M. E., and R. C.

4 Formerly "Cato Four Corners."

5 Among the other early settlers were Solomon Knapp, on Lot 100, L. Sheldon, on Lot 84, Jacob Labertaux, from Penn., on Lot 57, in May, 1803; Jesse Elwell and Abner Hollister, at Meridian, in 1805. The first child born was Alvira Stockwell, May 4, 1805; the first marriage, that of Andrew Stockwell and Sybil Root, June 4, 1804; and the first death, that of Stephen Olcott, in 1805. Solomon Knapp kept the first inn at Cato, in 1803; and Jesse Elwell, the first at Meridian, in 1805. Daniel M. Bristol kept the first store, in 1806; and Samuel Woodford erected the first gristmill, on the outlet of Otter Lake, in 1811.

6 The census reports 4 churches; Presb., M. E., Bap., and Ref. Prot. D.

7 Name given to commemorate the conquest achieved by those who favored the division of the old town of Cato over those who opposed it.

8 Among the other early settlers were James Perkins, from Onondaga co., on Lot 3, Ephraim Witherill, from Tompkins co., on Lot 4, Theophilus Emerson, on Lot 27, and Clement B. Emerson, on Lot 15, in 1802; Dijar Wilcox, from Saratoga co., on Lot 74, Wm. McCollom and John Crowell, from Newburgh, on Lot 76, in 1805; and William Crowell, on Lot 77, in 1807. The first child born was Amos Wolverton, in 1803; the first marriage, that of Gilbert Perkins and Betsey Snyder; and the first death, that of a traveler and stranger, at Musquito Point. John Perkins taught the first school, at Conquest Center, in 1807; Ephraim Witherill kept the first inn, in 1803; Jonathan Davis, the first store, at Conquest Center, in 1827; —— Twitchell erected the first sawmill, in 1808, and Abram Cherry the first gristmill, in 1810. This mill was long known as the "Pepper Mill," from the fact that a store was at first kept in it. The first settlers joined in making a canoe which would hold 60 bush. of grain; and in this they carried the grists of the whole neighborhood to Springport, by the way of Seneca River, to be ground. The journey usually took 4 days. In 1813 John Filkins took a load of wheat to Albany, but was obliged to sell the wheat and one horse to defray the expenses of the journey. In 1804 Jas. Perkins built the first framed house, sawing out the whole lumber with a whip-saw. The building still stands (1858) a monument of persevering industry.

9 The census reports 3 churches; 2 Prot. Meth. and M. E.

10 Named from Gen. George Fleming, an old resident.

Owasco Lake is a p.o. The first settlements were made in 1790–91.[1] The first religious services were held by Elder Daniel Irish (Bap.) about 1794.[2]

GENOA—was formed as "*Milton*," Jan. 27, 1789; and its name was changed April 6, 1808. Locke was taken off in 1802. It is the s. w. corner town of the co., lying upon the E. bank of Cayuga Lake. The surface is a rolling region, gradually rising from the lake to a height of about 600 ft. and divided into ridges by the valleys of Big and Little Salmon Creek, which extend through near the center.[3] The declivities that border upon the streams in some places are steep and 50 to 150 ft. high. The soil consists of a strip of clay along the banks of the lake, and a deep, rich, gravelly loam in the other parts of the town. **Genoa,** (p.v.,) on Big Salmon Creek, contains 2 churches, 2 flouring mills, a tannery, and a furnace and machine shop. Pop. 300. **Northville** (Kings Ferry p. o.) is situated in the N. w. part of the town. Pop. 200. **Five Corners** (p.v.) contains 35 dwellings. **East Genoa** (p.o.) is a hamlet. The first settlements were made anterior to the organization of the co. Jabez Bradley was the first settler, at Northville. The census reports 6 churches in town.[4]

IRA—was formed from Cato, March 16, 1821, and a part was annexed to Cato in 1824. It lies upon the E. border of the co., N. of the center. Its surface is rolling, the summits of the ridges being 50 to 75 ft. above the valleys and 225 to 275 feet above Lake Ontario. The streams are small brooks and creeks. The soil is a sandy loam underlaid by red sandstone, and is very productive. **Ira Center,** (p.v.,) the only village, contains 2 churches and 145 inhabitants. The first settlements were made by David, Eleazur, and Andrew Stockwell, 3 brothers from White-hall, on Lot 58, Wm. Patterson, on Lot 32, and Henry Conrad, (a German,) on the same lot, all in 1800.[5] The first church (Cong.) was formed at Ira Corners, July 7, 1807, by Rev. Francis Pomeroy; Rev. Silas Barnes was the first preacher.[6]

LEDYARD[7]—was formed from Scipio, Jan. 30, 1823. It lies upon the E. bank of Cayuga Lake, s. w. of the center of the co. Its surface inclines toward the w., its extreme E. border being elevated 500 to 600 ft. above the surface of the lake. The slopes of the hills are generally gradual, but are steep in a few places. Its streams are small, rapid brooks, the principal of which is Paines Creek, flowing through a narrow ravine in the s. part. The soil is a sandy and clayey loam, very fertile. **Aurora,** (p.v.,) incorp. May 5, 1837, is beautifully located on the E. bank of Cayuga Lake. Its fine situation and the comparative mildness of its climate have made it a place of considerable resort; and it contains some of the finest residences to be found in the interior of the State. It is the seat of the Cayuga Academy.[8] Pop. 459. **Talcotts Corners,** (Ledyard p. o.,) near the s. E. corner, contains 2 churches and 12 dwellings. **Levana** (p. v.) is a steamboat landing, 2 mi. N. of Aurora. Pop. 106. Roswell Franklin, from Wyoming, settled at Aurora in 1789, and was the first settler in Cayuga co. Benj. Avery was the first settler at Talcotts Corners.[9] Rev. Seth Williston (Presb.) conducted the first religious services; and Rev. H. Woodruff was the first settled minister.[10]

LOCKE—was formed from "*Milton*," (now Genoa,) Feb. 20, 1802. Summer Hill was taken off in 1831. It lies upon the high ridges which border upon Owasco Inlet, in the s. part of the co. The inlet flows through near the center in a deep, narrow valley bordered by steep hills rising 200 to 400 ft. above it. The summits of the hills spread out into a beautifully undulating

---

[1] Among the early settlers were Benj. Irish, Joseph Grover, Edward Wheeler, Ichabod and Abel Wilkinson, and James Herrington. The first child born was Aurelius Wheeler, in 1791; and the first death, that of Mrs. West, in 1792. John Herring taught the first school, in 1794; Abel Wilkinson kept the first inn, in 1792; and Joseph Grover the first store, in 1797.

[2] There are 3 churches in town; Ref. Prot. D., Bap., and M. E.

[3] The s. part of the town was settled by emigrants mostly from Penn. and N. J., and the N. part by emigrants from New England. In 1800 the town had a pop. of 3,553; in 1810 it rose to 5,425; in 1820, after its territory was reduced to its present limits, the pop. was 2,585; and in 1855, 2,352.

[4] Two Presb., 2 M. E., Cong., and Univ.

[5] Among the other early settlers were Daniel Parker, on Lot 69, John C. Barnes and Rev. Silas Barnes, on Lot 70, and Zadock Barnes, on Lot 83, all from Marcellus, and Edward Wood, from Sennett, on Lot 89, in 1802; Archibald and Chas. Green, on Lot 70, in 1803; Eli Mattison and Abraham Willey, from Conn., on Lot 34, Henry Ferris and his son, Augustus, from Saratoga co., on Lot 71, in 1804; and Thos. Barnes, from Washington co., at Ira Corners, in 1805. Dr. Squire, the first physician, taught the first school, in 1805; David Stockwell kept the first inn, in 1800; Sam'l and Israel Phelps, the first store, at Ira Corners, in 1813; and John Hooker erected the first gristmill, in 1818. The first child born was Polly, daughter of David Stockwell, in April, 1802; the first marriage was that of Eleazur Stockwell and Mar-

garet Noble, March 7, 1802; and the first death, that of the wife of Rev. Silas Barnes, in 1802.

[6] The census reports 5 churches; 2 M. E., and 1 each Bap., Presb., and Disciples.

[7] Named from Benjamin Ledyard, agent and clerk for the disposal of the lands belonging to the Military Tract. The trace of an ancient fortification is found within this town. It stood upon a hill between two ravines, and enclosed about 20 acres.—*Smithsonian Contributions, Vol. II, Part VI, p. 63.*

[8] The Academy building stands upon an eminence commanding a fine view of the bay and lake. The institution has a well selected library, competent teachers, and is in a prosperous condition. The Gospel and School Lot No. 36 of this town having been given to Union College, Lot 89 was taken for school purposes, and assigned to this academy.

[9] Elisha Durkee, and Atwell and Edward Paine, settled at Aurora in 1790. The first settler, Mr. Franklin, was in the battle of Wyoming, at which his wife was killed and his youngest child taken prisoner by the Indians. He died at Aurora in 1791, under the weight of his misfortunes. Betsey Durkee (now Mrs. Sweetland) was the first child born in town. The first inn was kept by Joshua Patrick, at Aurora, in 1793, in a house still standing. Abiathar Hull kept the first store, and T. Wheeler erected the first mill, a little N. of Aurora.

[10] The census reports 6 churches; 2 Friends, 2 M. E., Presb., and Prot. E.

region with a mean elevation of about 1,000 ft. above tide. The soil is a gravelly loam inter-spersed with clay. **Milan,** (Locke p. o.,) situated on the s. branch of Owasco Lake Inlet, con-tains 2 churches, 2 woolen factories, 2 gristmills, and several mechanics' shops. Pop. 180. **Cen-terville** contains 18 houses. The first settlement was made by Ezra Carpenter, Jas. Cook, Jas. Durell, and Solomon Love, in 1790.[1] The first church (M. E.) was formed in 1819.[2]

MENTZ—was formed from Aurelius, as "*Jefferson,*" March 30, 1802. Its name was changed April 6, 1808. Montezuma and a portion of Throop were taken off in 1859. It lies upon Seneca River, N. w. of the center of the co. Its surface is generally flat, with a few low sand ridges near the s. border. A swampy region extends along Seneca River. Owasco Outlet, flowing through the center, is the principal stream. Limestone, gypsum, and red shale are the underlying rocks. The soil is a clayey, sandy, and gravelly loam. **Port Byron,** (p. v.,) incorp. March 2, 1837, is situated upon the Owasco Outlet and Erie Canal, near the center of the town. The N. Y. C. R. R. station is 1 mi. N. of the village. It contains 3 churches, a woolen factory, cabinet ware manufactory, and a flouring mill with 10 run of stones. Pop. 1,669. **Centerport,** a canal village on the E. line, contains 22 houses. The first settlement was made in 1797.[3] There are 3 churches in town; Bap., M. E., and Presb.

MONTEZUMA—was formed from Mentz, April 8, 1859. It lies in the N. w. angle formed by the great easterly bend in Seneca River, on the w. border of the co. Its surface is mostly low and flat. An extensive swamp, known as the Montezuma Marshes, extends along the river. The only considerable stream is Cayuga Brook. The soil is generally a clayey loam. Brine springs are found along Seneca River. **Montezuma** (p. v.) is located upon Seneca River, in the w. part of the town. The Seneca and Cayuga Canals here unite with the Erie Canal. Salt and some other articles are manufactured.[4] Pop. 650. The first settlement was made in 1798.[5] The first church (Bap.) was formed in 1803, by Rev. John Jeffries. There are 3 churches in town; 2 M. E. and Bap.

MORAVIA—was formed from Sempronius, March 20, 1833. It lies upon Owasco Lake and Inlet, in the E. part of the co. The greater part of its surface is a rolling upland, broken by the deep and narrow valleys of Owasco Inlet and its branches.[6] These valleys are 300 to 400 ft. below the summits of the hills, and are bordered by steep and in many places nearly perpen-dicular sides. Upon the streams in their course through the ravines are several beautiful cas-cades, furnishing an abundance of water-power. Mill Brook, just below its junction with Trout Brook, flows over a precipice of 80 ft. Upon the E. tributary of the outlet, near the s. border, is a cascade known as Dry Falls, from the fact that in summer the stream ceases to flow. A little below this cascade is a circular recess in the face of the perpendicular precipice, 42 ft. deep, and sur-mounted by a limestone arch 55 ft. high and 125 ft. long. Upon this arch rises a lofty hill covered with primitive forest trees. A large spring of carburetted hydrogen gas, highly inflammable, is situated upon the lowlands near the lake. The soil among the hills is a gravelly loam mixed with clay, and in the valleys it consists of a deep, rich loam formed of gravel and disintegrated limestone and slate. **Moravia** (p. v.) is situated on Mill Brook, in the valley 3 mi. s. E. of the head of Owasco Lake. The rapids and cascades in the stream at this point furnish an abundance of water-power. The village is incorp., and contains 130 dwellings, the Moravia Institute, and several mills and other manufacturing establishments. **Montville,**[7] a small village 1 mi. E. of Moravia, contains 15 houses. The first settlement was made at Moravia Village, by John Stoyell, in 1791.[8] The first church (Cong.) was formed March 12, 1806.[9]

---

[1] A daughter of Jas. Durell was the first child born; Aaron Kellogg kept the first store, at Milan; James Cook, the first inn; Lyman Brown erected the first factory, at Milan, in 1810, and Mr. Durell the first gristmill. The traces of an Indian burying ground, half a mi. w. of Milan, between 2 deep gulfs, covering about 2 acres, are still visible. The graves are ranged in rows E. and w.

[2] The census reports 3 churches; 2 M. E. and Bap.

[3] Among the early settlers were Philip King, Seth Higby, from Saratoga co., on Lot 72, Josiah Patridge, from Mass., on Lot 73, in 1797; Charles Annes, Aholiab and Elijah Buck, from Chemung co., on Lot 73, (now Port Byron,) in 1798; Dan'l Love-land, from Vt., on Lot 49, in 1799; Peter Rausier and Moses Lent, from Owego, on Lot 62, in 1800; James Dixon and Joseph Hamilton, from Washington co., Caleb Hopkins, from N. J., and Ira Hopkins, from Washington co., on Lot 85, from 1800 to 1804.

[4] Salt was first manufactured in Montezuma about 1798; but the business was abandoned about 1840, in consequence of the brine becoming too weak to successfully compete with the salt springs of Syracuse and Salina. Strong brine springs have

lately been discovered, and the manufacture of salt has been suc-cessfully resumed. These salt springs, like those of Onondaga, belong to the State.

[5] Among the early settlers were Peter Clark, from New York City, Comfort Tyler, and Abram Morgan, at Montezuma, in 1798, who located there to manufacture salt.

[6] The Owasco Flats were in part cultivated by the Indians anterior to the settlement by the whites, and still bear traces of the ancient occupation.

[7] Ex-President Fillmore read law at this place with Judge Wood.

[8] Among the other early settlers were Winslow Perry, Amos Stoyell, and Jabez L. Bottom, in 1793; Gursham Morse, in 1794; and Cotton Skinner, in 1795. The first child born was Seth Perry, in 1794; the first marriage, that of Jonathan Eldridge and Sally Perry, in 1795; and the first death, that of Cynthia Wright, in 1796. Levi Goodrich taught the first school, in 1797; Zadock Cady kept the first inn, in 1801, David Wright the first store, and John Stoyell built the first mill.

[9] The census reports 3 churches in town; Cong., Prot. E., and M. E.

NILES—was formed from Sempronius, March 20, 1833. It lies between Owasco and Skaneateles Lakes, s. e. of the center of the co. Its surface is principally a rolling and hilly upland. The highest summits are 700 ft. above Owasco Lake. The declivities are gradual toward Owasco but more abrupt toward Skaneateles Lake. Dutch Hollow Brook, flowing N. through near the center, is bordered by high, steep banks.[1] The soil is a gravelly and clayey loam. **Kelloggsville**, (p. v.,) in the extreme s. part, contains 2 churches and 30 dwellings; **New Hope**, in the s. e. part, contains a church, gristmill, sawmill, and 12 dwellings; **Niles**, (p. o.,) in the N. part, **West Niles, Twelve Corners**, and **Nine Corners**, are hamlets. The first settlements were made in 1793.[2] There are 4 churches in town; 2 M. E., Bap., and Univ.

OWASCO—was formed from Aurelius, March 30, 1802. It lies e. of the foot of Owasco Lake, s. e. of the center of the co. Its surface is rolling and inclined to the N. w. From the lake it slopes gradually upward, and the highest summits attain an elevation of 500 ft. Owasco Creek, flowing w. across the s. part, and Millers Brook, in the N. part, are the only streams. The soil is a clayey loam. **Owasco**, (p. v.,) in the s. e. corner, contains 3 churches and 45 dwellings. The first settlements were made in 1792.[3] The first church was formed in 1798, by Rev. Abram Brokaw.[4] Ex-Gov. Throop is a resident of this town.

SCIPIO—was formed March 5, 1794. Sempronius was taken off in 1799, a part of Marcellus (Onondaga co.) in 1804, Ledyard, Venice, and a part of Springport in 1823. It lies on the w. shore of Owasco Lake, s. of the center of the co. Its surface is rolling, the highest summits being 500 ft. above the lake. A steep bluff, 20 to 50 ft. high, extends along the lake, and from the summit the surface slopes gradually upward for about one mi. The streams are mere brooks. The soil is a clayey loam. **Scipio Center** (Scipio p. o.) contains 2 churches and 80 inhabitants; **Scipioville**, (p. v.,) near the w. line, 80 inhabitants; **Sherwood**, (p. v.,) near the s. w. corner, 80 inhabitants. **The Square** is a p. o. in the N. w. part, and **Bolts Corners** a hamlet in the s. The first settlements were made in 1790.[5] The first religious services were held by Elder David Irish, in 1794; and the first church (Bap.) was formed the same year.[6]

SEMPRONIUS—was formed March 9, 1799. A part was annexed to Marcellus (Onondaga co.) March 24, 1804, and Moravia and Niles March 20, 1833. It lies upon Skaneateles Lake, in the s. e. part of the co. From the valley of the lake and inlet the hills rise abruptly to a height of 800, to 1,000 feet, and from their summits the surface spreads out into a rolling and hilly upland. The highest points are about 1,700 ft. above tide. Mill Brook, flowing w., Bear Swamp Brook, N., and Fall Brook, s., all have excavated deep valleys in the drift deposits and shales. The soil is a good quality of clayey, sandy and gravelly loam, mixed with disintegrated slate and limestone. **Dresserville**, (p. v.,) located on Mill Brook, in the s. part of the town, contains 30 dwellings; **Vansville**, (Sempronius p. o.,) 15; **Glen Haven** (p. o.) is a noted water cure establishment near the head of Skaneateles Lake. Its situation is extremely beautiful, and it is supplied with pure, soft spring water. The first settlement was made in 1794, by Ezekiel Sales,[7] Jotham Bassett, and Seth Burgess. The first church (Bap.) was formed Feb. 29, 1798; Rev. John Lasure was the first preacher. The census reports 1 church (Bap.) in town.

SENNETT—was formed from Brutus, March 19, 1827; it was named from Judge Daniel Sennett, a pioneer settler. A portion of Throop was taken off in 1859. It lies upon the e. border of the co., N. of the center. Its surface is level or gently undulating, the ridges rising in long, gradual slopes 50 to 100 ft. above the valleys. The streams are all small brooks. The soil is a deep, fertile, clayey and sandy loam, and is under a high state of cultivation. **Sennett**, (p. v.,) a station on the Auburn branch of the N. Y. Central R. R., contains 2 churches and 30 dwellings. The first settlement was made in 1794, by Ebenezer Healy, Jos. Atwell, Thos. Morley, and Thos.

---

[1] On the highest point of land, 3 mi. e. of Owasco Lake, is a quarry of fine flagging stone.

[2] Among the early settlers were Garret Conover and his sons John and Aaron, Isaac Selover, James Brinkerhoff, and William Bowen. The first child born was Sally Amerman, in 1798.

[3] Among the early settlers were Samuel and Benj. De Puy, Moses Cartwright, and Jacob and Roeliff Brinkerhoff. Cornelius Delamater kept the first inn, in 1800; James Burrows, the first store, in 1807; and David Bovier built the first gristmill, in 1798.

[4] There are 3 churches in town; M. E., Ref. Prot. D., and True D. Reformed.

[5] Among the early settlers were Elisha Durkee, Henry Wat-

kins, Gilbert and Alanson Tracy, Sam'l Branch, Ebenezer Witter, and Gideon Allen. The first child born was Betsey Durkee, Dec. 5, 1790; and the first marriage, that of Wm. Allen and Betsey Watkins, June 25, 1793. Wm. Daniels taught the first school, in 1798, and Dr. Strong kept the first store, in 1808.

[6] There are 4 churches in town; Bap., Presb., M. E., and Univ.

[7] The first child born was Benj. Sales, in 1794; the first marriage, that of Sam'l Rice and Matilda Summerston; and the first death, that of Sam'l Rice. Cyrus Powers taught the first school, in 1800; John Husted kept the first inn and store, and Artimus Dresser erected the first mill.

Morley, jr., from Conn., on Lot 21.[1] The first church (Bap.) was organized Sept. 12, 1799, by Rev. Manasseh French, who was the first preacher. There are now 2 churches in town; Presb. and Bap.

SPRINGPORT—was formed from Scipio and Aurelius, Jan. 30, 1823. It lies upon the E. shore of Cayuga Lake, s. w. of the center of the co. Its surface rises in gradual slopes from the water to the E. border, where it attains an elevation of 400 to 500 ft. Waterlime, plaster, and limestone used for flagging, are quarried along the shore of the lake and in the adjoining ravines. Two immense springs flow from the ground near the village, furnishing a valuable water-power.[2] The soil is a superior quality of sandy and gravelly loam, in some places mixed with clay. The lake is so deep that it rarely freezes, and the warmth of the water essentially moderates the intensity of the frosts of winter.[3] **Union Springs** (p. v.) is beautifully situated upon Cayuga Lake, s. of the center of the w. border of the town. It contains several manufactories, a private academy, and many fine residences. Pop. 1,118. The first settlement was made in 1800, by Frederick Gearheart, Thos. Thompson, and Jas. Carr.[4] The first church (Cong.) was formed by Rev. Joshua Lane, the first preacher.[5]

STERLING—named from William Alexander, Lord Sterling, of the Revolution—was formed from Cato, June 19, 1812. It lies upon Lake Ontario, in the extreme N. part of the co. Its surface is rolling and has a slight inclination toward the N. The summits of the ridges in the s. are 200 to 300 ft. above the lake; and Big Bluff, upon the lake shore, has about the same elevation. The streams are Little Sodus Creek and its branches, flowing into Little Sodus Bay, and Cortright Brook, flowing into Blind Sodus Bay.[6] Little Sodus Bay is about 2 mi. long by 1 mi. wide, and is one of the best harbors upon the s. shore of the lake. An extensive swamp, covering several hundred acres, extends along the lake shore, E. of the bay, and another lies on the s. border of the town. The soil is a sandy and gravelly loam; some portions of the surface are very stony and hard of cultivation. Outcrops of Medina sandstone[7] and Oneida conglomerate are quarried in this town for building stone. **Sterling Center** (Sterling p. o.) contains 40 dwellings; **Fairhaven,** (p. v.,) on Little Sodus Bay, 40; **Martville,** (p. o.,) near the s. E. corner, 25; and **Sterling Valley** 20. **North Sterling** (p. o.) is a hamlet. The first settler was Peter Dumas, who located upon Lot 19 in 1805.[8] The first church (Asso. Ref. Presb.) was formed in 1818.[9]

SUMMER HILL—was formed from Locke, as "*Plato,*" April 26, 1831; its name was changed March 16, 1832. It is the s. E. corner town of the co. Its surface is a rolling upland, 1000 to 1100 ft. above tide. Fall Brook, the principal stream, flows s. through the E. part. Its valley is 300 to 400 ft. below the summits of the hills, and forms the only considerable break in the general level of the surface. Summer Hill Lake is a small pond in the N. E. part, discharging its waters into Fall Brook. The soil is a clayey and gravelly loam, the clay predominating. **Summer Hill,** (p. v.,) in the s. part of the town, contains 115 inhabitants. The first settle-

---

[1] In 1795 Judge Dan'l Sennett, Amos Bennett, and Jacob, Rufus, and Dan'l Sheldon, from Conn., settled on Lot 99. In 1797 Jacob Hicks, a Revolutionary soldier, who drew Lot 99, settled on it; Benj. Miller, also a Revolutionary soldier, on Lot 17; and Jabez Remmington and Hezekiah Freeman, from Vt., on Lots 21 and 10. The first child born was Sally Smith, in 1795; the first marriage, that of Nehemiah Smith and Mindevill Morley, in 1794; and the first death, that of Thos. Morley, in 1795. Betsey Morley taught the first school, in 1795; Joseph Atwell kept the first inn, the same year; and Sheldon & Lathrop the first store.

[2] These springs are about 10 rods apart. From the larger flows a stream of sufficient size to furnish water-power for running a flouring mill with 6 run of stones, a plaster mill, sawmill, and several other kinds of machinery. The stream from the smaller spring drives the machinery of a planing mill, sawmill, and tannery. From the springs the town and village both derive their names.

[3] Fruit growing, for which the climate and soil are admirably adapted, begins to attract attention. The vine is successfully cultivated; and a single vineyard of 10 acres, devoted to grapes, produces fine crops.

[4] Amos Comely taught the first school, near Union Springs; Thomas Collins kept the first inn; Laban Haskins and Walter Low, the first store; Philip Winegar erected the first woolen factory.

[5] The census reports 9 churches; 2 Friends, 2 M. E., and 1 each Cong., Presb., Bap., Christian, and R. C.

[6] Since work commenced on the Ontario, Auburn & N. Y. R. R.

an effort has been made to change the name of this bay to On tario Bay.

[7] This stone is much used for the underpinnings of houses and farm buildings. It has been observed that hogs are very fond of licking the stone whenever they have access to it; and in consequence they foam at the mouth, and can only be fatted with great difficulty.

[8] Mr. Dumas was a Frenchman, who came to this country with La Fayette and served during the Revolution. For his services he received a lot in the Military Tract, and drew Lot 19, in Sterling. Capt. Andrew Rassmusen settled the same year on Lot No. 1. He was killed on board of an American vessel, on Lake Ontario, during the War of 1812. Francis Decamp located near Martville, in 1806; Wm. Divine, Nathan Wilmot, and Jehial Peck, on Lot 11, in 1807; Jacob Wilsey, from Saratoga co., on Lot 14, in 1808; John Cooper, on Lot 12, John Duzenbury, on Lot 44, Curtis Stoddard, on Lot 19, John McFarland and Jos. from Washington co., on Lot 27, John and Matthew Harsha, from Washington co., at Martville, in 1810; Wm. Cooper, Jos. Bunnell, and John Turner, from Long Island, in 1811; and Geo. Cooper, from Saratoga co., in 1812. The first child born was Isaac Hoppins, March 16, 1807; the first marriage, that of Matthew Harsha and Charity Turner; and the first death, that of Ezra, son of Peter Dumas, July 21, 1806. The first school was taught by Benj. Clark, in 1812; Wm. Cooper kept the first inn, in 1810; John Cooper erected the first sawmill, in 1810, and the first gristmill, in 1815.

[9] The census reports 6 churches; 2 M. E., and 1 each Asso. Ref., Presb., Bap., Ref. Prot. D., and Ref. Presb.

ment was made in 1797, by Hezekiah Mix, from Genoa, on Lot 37, near the village.[1] The first church (Bap.) was formed in 1807; Elder Whipple was the first pastor.[2]

THROOP[3]—was formed from Aurelius, Mentz, and Sennett, April 8, 1859. It is an interior town, lying a little N. W. of the center of the co. Its surface is generally level, broken in a few places by sand and gravel ridges 100 to 150 ft. high. Its principal streams are Owasco Outlet and Cayuga Brook. The soil is a sandy and gravelly loam. **Throopsville,** (p. v.,) on Owasco Inlet, S. E. of the center, contains 3 churches, a grist and saw mill, and woolen factory. Pop. 160. The first settlement was made on Lot 2, in 1790, by Ezekiel Crane and his son Shadrach, from N. J.[4] There are 3 churches in town; Bap., M. E., and Disciple.

VENICE—was formed from Scipio, Jan. 30, 1823. It is an interior town, lying S. of the center of the co. Its surface is a rolling upland, the highest summits being 300 to 400 ft. above Owasco Lake. Salmon and Little Salmon Creeks flow S. in deep valleys dividing the surface into distinct ridges. Owasco Lake borders upon the N. E. corner. The declivities bordering upon the lake and upon the w. bank of Salmon Creek are steep, but generally the hillsides are long, gradual slopes. The soil is a fine quality of clayey and gravelly loam. **Venice,** (p. v.,) in the N. E. part of the town, contains 1 church and 20 dwellings; and **Poplar Ridge,** upon the highest summit in the N. W., contains a foundery and machine shop and 20 dwellings. **East Venice** (p. o.) and **Venice Center** (p. o.) are hamlets. The first settlement was made in 1800.[5] The first church (Bap.) was formed at Stuarts Corners, in 1800, by Elder Irish, the first preacher.[6] Upon the ridge E. of Salmon Creek, near the s. border of the town, are the remains of an ancient fortification. Upon the creek, near the center of the town, were extensive cleared and cultivated fields at the first advent of the whites. Near these fields was an Indian burial ground.

VICTORY—was formed from Cato, March 16, 1821. It lies upon the w. border of the co., N. W. of the center. Its surface is gently undulating, the highest points being scarcely 50 ft. above the general level. Little Sodus and Red Creeks are the principal streams. The underlying rocks are red shale and blue limestone, covered deep with drift. The soil is a gravelly and sandy loam. A swamp in the s. w. part covers several hundred acres. **Victory,** (p. v.,) near the center of the town, contains 25 houses; and **Westbury,** (p. v.,) on the line of Wayne co., 50. The settlement of the town was commenced in 1800, by John McNeal, from Montgomery co., and John and Samuel Martin, from Ireland, on Lot 65.[7] The first church (M. E.) was formed in 1813, by Rev. Zenas Jones, the first preacher.[8]

---

[1] Among the early settlers were Nath'l Fillmore, (father of Millard Fillmore, Ex-Pres. U. S., who was born in this town,) Martin Barber, Wm. Webster, Jos. Cone, Wm. Honeywell, Jas. Savage, Harvey Hough, and Josiah Walker. . The first school was taught by Nath'l Fillmore, in 1804. The first child born was Millard Fillmore or Anson Cone; the first marriage, that of Ebenezer Crowl and Rosanna Mix, in 1803; and the first death, that of Amos Mix, killed by the falling of a tree in 1798. Jos. Cone kept the first inn, in 1803; Chas. Crane, the first store; and Ebenezer Bennett erected the first mill, in 1816.

[2] The census reports 3 churches; Bap., Cong., and M. E.

[3] Named from Hon. Enos T. Throop, Ex-Gov. of the State.

[4] Among the other early settlers were Isaac Barnum, Othniel Palmer, and his son, from Conn., Israel Clapp, from Mass., on Lot 16; Jas. Leonard and Wm. Durell, from N. J., on Lots 2 and 4, Manonah Clark, from Oneida co., on Lot 4, Jonas Ward and his son Caleb, from N. J., on Lot 92, in 1796; Christopher and Rev. John Jeffries, from Saratoga Springs, on Lot 16, Ephraim Wethy, from Dutchess co., on Lot 4, in 1799; Amos and David Codner, on Lot 14, in 1801. The first marriage was that of Shadrach Crane and Hannah Palmer; and the first birth, that of Ezekiel Crane. Edward Carpenter taught the first school. in 1800; Israel Clapp kept the first inn, in 1800; Luther Harden

the first store, in 1804; and Prentice Palmer erected the first saw and grist mill, in 1798.

[5] Among the early settlers were Henry Hewit, Ezekiel Landon, Samuel Robinson, and Zadock Bateman, at Stewarts Corners, Samuel Childsey, and Amos Rathbun, at Poplar Ridge, Luke Taylor, and Thomas Carman, all of whom came in between 1790 and 1800. The first child born was Lemon Cole; and the first death, that of —— Herrick, one of the pioneer settlers: he was killed by the fall of a tree. The first inn was kept by Samuel Robinson. The first mill was erected at Venice Village, in 1835.

[6] The census reports 3 churches; 2 Friends and 1 Bap.

[7] Patrick Murphy, from Ireland, settled on Lot 54, in Feb. 1806; Matthias Vanderhuyden, from Albany co., on Lot 62, and Asahel Carter, from Vt., on Lot 66, in 1810; John Ramsey, and Wm. and Dan'l Griswold, from Herkimer co., on Lot 25, in 1811; Jacob W. and Martin De Forrest, from Washington co., Conrad Phrozine, from Newburgh, on Lot 43, Manasseh French, from Scipio, Judge C. Smith, from Saratoga co., on Lot 40, Philander Phinney, from Saratoga co., Silas Kellogg, from Brutus, on Lot 39, and Ebenezer Bird, from Onondaga co., on Lot 29, all in 1812. Mrs. Jane Wood was the first child born in town, in 1804; and the first death, that of John McNeal, in 1800.

[8] The census reports 5 churches; 2 M. E., Presb., Bap., and Christian.

Acres of Land, Valuation, Population, Dwellings, Families, Freeholders, Schools, Live Stock, Agricultural Products, and Domestic Manufactures, of Cayuga County.

Names of Towns.	Acres of Land.		Valuation of 1858.			Population.		No. of Dwellings.	No. of Families.	Freeholders.	Schools.	
	Improved.	Unimproved.	Real Estate.	Personal Property.	Total.	Males.	Females.				No. of Districts.	Children taught.
Auburn	4,427¾	172	$2,105,674	$1,630,869	$3,736,543	4,819	4,657	1,514	1,644	1,122	5	3,001
Aurelius	18,003¾	3,298	1,031,666	115,300	1,146,966	1,367	1,207	484	511	360	12	923
Brutus	9,395	3,301	627,910	186,950	814,860	1,466	1,341	543	409	335	7	926
Cato	15,210¾	5,159	645,665	41,950	687,615	1,164	1,088	429	455	323	13	796
Conquest	13,919¾	7,702	533,317	24,425	557,742	968	904	360	314	280	13	821
Fleming	10,287½	1,866	449,145	41,700	490,845	604	560	223	226	216	6	342
Genoa	19,951½	6,710	1,032,390	196,735	1,229,125	1,150	1,202	472	489	363	13	824
Ira	15,845	5,639	619,001	83,050	702,051	1,064	1,069	400	432	342	13	893
Ledyard	17,770¼	4,161½	955,020	290,110	1,245,130	994	982	369	393	266	11	702
Locke	11,466	3,216	368,865	39,500	408,365	636	657	261	265	208	9	487
Mentz	21,331	6,197	1,252,833	73,750	1,326,583	2,637	2,421	918	794	694	17	1,949
Montezuma[a]												
Moravia	11,994¾	4,830¼	432,926	115,028	547,954	906	913	344	361	250	12	785
Niles	18,220½	6,035	571,990	92,468	664,458	973	939	385	319	279	13	690
Owasco	9,578	2,522	429,340	74,340	503,680	636	667	239	258	275	8	504
Scipio	18,975¼	3,698	917,253	203,275	1,120,528	965	930	369	370	258	15	711
Sempronius	11,278	6,486	291,191	34,640	325,831	614	655	244	258	258	9	471
Sennett	17,453	3,684	828,836	40,830	869,666	1,054	1,028	386	389	298	12	741
Springport	11,313⅛	82,477½	797,264	108,480	905,744	1,167	1,004	392	399	282	9	777
Sterling	14,134	12,020½	364,804	24,617	389,421	1,541	1,483	567	579	492	14	1,241
Summer Hill	10,941½	5,678¼	261,200	32,300	293,500	606	578	254	256	127	9	419
Throop[b]												
Venice	19,843½	5,457	869,290	184,940	1,054,230	1,007	932	377	389	306	13	589
Victory	14,455½	6,927½	435,648	54,235	489,883	1,025	901	386	413	327	14	771
Total	315,795⅜	187,237½	$15,821,228	$3,689,492	$19,510,720	27,363	26,208	10,916	9,923	7,661	247	8,282

Names of Towns.	Live Stock.					Agricultural Products.							Domestic Cloths, in yards.
						Bush. of Grain.		Tons of Hay.	Bushels of Potatoes.	Bushels of Apples.	Dairy Products.		
	Horses.	Working Oxen and Calves.	Cows.	Sheep.	Swine.	Winter.	Spring.				Pounds Butter.	Pounds Cheese.	
Auburn	377	128	123	471	384	831	11,148	393	2,175	1,617	13,550	200	148
Aurelius	806	1,094	977	5,923	1,578	20,376	131,187	3,117½	6,260	8,880	93,290	7,694	311
Brutus	527	1,110	656	2,350	1,412	10,116	80,753½	2,073	13,886	22,624	61,088	12,085	156
Cato	854	1,672	1,004	3,311	1,379	21,268½	147,509½	2,618¾	17,393	26,368	93,410	4,411	633
Conquest	791	1,498	998	5,374	1,713	17,751	133,569½	2,457	15,082	21,137	92,992	4,851	1,943
Fleming	404	481	441	3,483	965	3,787	87,263½	1,485	5,848	14,758	41,690	4,535	234
Genoa	892	1,371	1,245	7,748	1,462	11,769	162,313	3,462¾	10,698	48,284	151,586	9,851	572
Ira	957	1,785	1,227	4,518	2,024	12,993	129,055½	2,900½	16,877	44,502	128,399	19,783	1,316
Ledyard	680	930	684	9,696	1,132	10,264	105,957½	2,155	5,516	10,212	49,210	8,629	20
Locke	527	1,212	943	1,901	728	1,405	62,395	3,035	5,249	26,190	105,008	3,976	1,140
Mentz	1,153	2,330	1,629	5,348	2,760	27,171	151,294	5,513¾	20,905	23,568	131,564	16,997	313
Montezuma[a]													
Moravia	544	1,062	968	4,824	935	1,566	62,153	2,960½	6,627	41,524	124,237	9,519	724½
Niles	833	1,393	1,196	4,369	1,424	2,958	104,470	2,808½	8,293⅛	31,147	145,517	16,273	1,990½
Owasco	449	649	582	3,957	975	2,073¼	57,399½	1,861¾	10,828	18,159	62,637	10,470	651½
Scipio	812	1,131	854	7,953	1,261	10,865	127,173	1,970½	8,590	28,968	72,969	7,139	524
Sempronius	518	922	1,056	1,517	784	72	52,844	3,286	10,518	29,080	140,702	5,064	1,227
Sennett	751	1,583	1,164	5,286	1,530	6,105½	116,123½	3,340½	21,838	27,430	84,439	29,645	338
Springport	566	703	2	4,720	1,378	10,770	85,992	1,383	4,251	9,134	48,630	3,775	
Sterling	849	1,490	1,179	4,192	1,768	9,622	105,626½	2,630	27,027	20,086	112,872	4,917	1,180½
Summer Hill	492	912	912	2,752	634	113	48,359	2,732	6,942	20,333	124,670	5,643	1,074
Throop[b]													
Venice	773	1,523	975	10,257	1,239	6,722	137,404	3,105	10,077	25,488	101,575	10,640	569
Victory	850	1,377	1,007	3,681	1,616	11,462	127,099	2,443	16,838	23,262	101,987	3,236	1,524½
Total	15,405	26,356	19,822	103,631	29,081	200,061¼	2,227,089½	57,732	251,718⅛	522,751	2,082,022	199,333	16,589½

[a] Montezuma was formed in 1859, and its statistics are embraced in the town of Mentz.

[b] Throop was formed in 1859, and its statistics are included in Mentz, Sennett, and Aurelius.

CHAUTAUQUA COUNTY.

This county was formed from Genesee, March 11, 1808. It lies upon the shore of Lake Erie, and is the s. w. corner co. of the State. It is centrally distant 288 mi. from Albany, and contains 1,099 sq. mi. The surface is mostly a hilly and rolling upland. A bluff, with a mean elevation of 20 ft., extends along the lake; and from its summit the land spreads out into an undulating region, gradually rising for a distance of 3 or 4 mi. This comparatively level tract is bordered by the declivities of a hilly upland, which occupies the center and s. part of the co. The highest summits are 1,000 to 1,200 feet above Lake Erie and 1,800 to 2,000 ft. above tide. The uplands are broken by several deep valleys, the principal of which are those of Chautauqua Lake and Connewango Creek. The summits of the hills, 4 to 6 mi. s. of the lake shore, form the watershed which divides the waters of Lake Erie from those of Alleghany River. The declivities bordering upon the valleys are in many places too steep for profitable cultivation.

Connewango Creek, flowing along the e. border and receiving Cassadaga Creek and Chautauqua Outlet, is the largest stream in the co. The other principal streams are Cattaraugus, Silver, Walnut, Canadaway, Little Cattaraugus, and Twenty Mile Creeks, flowing into Lake Erie; French and Little Brocken Straw Creeks, tributaries of Alleghany River; and Prendergast Creek, flowing into Chautauqua Lake. Besides these and their tributaries are numerous smaller streams flowing directly into Lake Erie. Chautauqua Lake is a beautiful sheet of water, 18 mi. long and 1 to 3 mi. wide, occupying a deep valley in the highland region about 10 mi. s. e. of Lake Erie.[1] It is 726 feet above Lake Erie and 1,291 ft. above tide. The hills that surround it are 600 to 800 ft. above its surface. Its outlet forms a branch of Connewango Creek, which latter stream is a tributary of Alleghany River. Several other small lakes are located among the highlands, the principal of which are Bear, Cassadaga, Mud, and Finleys Lakes, all 700 to 900 ft. above Lake Erie.

The rocks of this co. belong to the Portage and Chemung groups,—the former occupying the n. half of the co. and the latter the s. half. The summits of the highest hills in the s. are crowned with conglomerate, belonging to the Catskill group and affording the only good building stone in the s. part of the co. The sandstones of the Portage group are quarried to some extent in the n. part. Lime is obtained in limited quantities from limestone boulders and marl beds. One of the most peculiar geological features of the co. is the numerous springs of carburetted hydrogen gas found in various localities and especially along the shore of Lake Erie. It comes from the shales of the Portage group, and at various places is turned to profitable account.

The soil upon the uplands is principally clay mixed with disintegrated shale, generally known as *flat gravel;* and in the valleys it is a fine quality of sandy and gravelly loam mixed with alluvium. Along the lake shore is a strip of productive clay loam. The uplands are arable to their summits, but are generally much better adapted to pasturage than tillage. The various branches of agriculture form the leading pursuits of the people. Stock and wool growing, and dairying, are largely and successfully carried on. Spring grains and fruits are also largely produced.

Manufactures are few and unimportant and are chiefly confined to the local wants of the people. Commerce—an important item in the business and wealth of the co.—is chiefly concentrated at Dunkirk, which is at once an excellent harbor upon the lake and the w. terminus of the Erie R. R.

The county seat is located at Mayville, in the town of Chautauqua, at the head of Chautauqua Lake.[2] The courthouse is a fine brick edifice, erected in 1834, at a cost of $11,000. The jail is a brick building, with stone cells, on the opposite side of the street from the courthouse. The clerk's office is a fireproof brick building contiguous to the courthouse.[3]

The poorhouse is located upon a farm of 160 acres, near De Wittville, 3½ mi. s. e. from Mayville.

---

[1] Near the middle this lake is contracted to the width of a few rods, giving it the appearance of two lakes connected by a narrow strait.

[2] This co. was united with Niagara from the date of its organization in 1808 until 1811. The first court was held June 25, 1811. The commissioners to locate the co. buildings were Jonas

Williams, Isaac Sutherland, and Asa Ransom. The first co. officers were Zattu Cushing, *First Judge;* Matthew Prendergast, Philo Orton, Jonathan Thompson, and Wm. Alexander, *Associate Judges;* David Eason, *Sheriff;* and John F. Marshall, *Co. Clerk.*

[3] In 1858 the supervisors authorized the erection of a new clerk's office at a cost of $2,500.

The average number of inmates is 130, supported at a weekly cost of 44 cts. each. A school is taught 6 to 8 months in the year. The buildings are poor and dilapidated and are destitute of proper accommodations and means of ventilation.

The N. Y. & Erie R. R. extends through Hanover and Sheridan and terminates at Dunkirk. This road opens a direct communication with New York, and, taken in connection with the connecting railroads and vessels upon the lake, is one of the most important of the great thoroughfares between the Atlantic seaboard and the Valley of the Mississippi. The amount of freight carried over the road is immense; and the business connected with it gives employment to thousands of men. The Buffalo & Erie R. R. extends along the lake through Hanover, Sheridan, Pomfret, Portland, Westfield, and Ripley. This forms another link in the great chain of Western travel, and connects with the Erie R. R. at Dunkirk and with the N. Y. Central at Buffalo. The proposed Erie & New York City R. R. extends through the s. part of the co., connecting Erie, Penn., with the N. Y. & Erie R. R. at Great Valley.[1]

Nine weekly newspapers are now published in the co.[2]

In 1782 a party of British and Indians, with a train of artillery and other munitions of war, spent the months of June and July around Chautauqua Lake in constructing canoes and making other preparations to navigate Alleghany River in a contemplated attack upon "Fort Pitt," near

[1] The surveys of this R. R. have been made, and considerable work has been done in grading.

[2] The *Chautauque Gazette,* the first paper published in the co., was started at Fredonia in Jan. 1817, by Jas. Percival. It was afterward issued by Carpenter & Hull, and by Jas. Hull, until 1822, when it was suspended. In 1823 it was revived by Jas. Hull, and continued until 1826, when it was united with the People's Gazette and its name was changed to

The *Fredonia Gazette.* It was issued a short time by Hull & Snow, when it was removed to Dunkirk by Mr. Hull and changed to

The *Dunkirk Gazette.* In a few months it was removed to Westfield and united with The Chautauque Phœnix.

The *People's Gazette* was started at Forestville in 1824 by Wm. S. Snow. In 1826 it was removed to Fredonia and united with The Chautauque Gazette.

The *Chautauque Eagle* was commenced at Mayville in May, 1819, by Robt. J. Curtis, and was continued about 1 year.

The Fredonia Censor was commenced in 1821 by Henry C. Frisbee, who continued its publication for 17 years. In 1838 it passed into the hands of E. Winchester, and was published by him 2 years and by R. Cunnington 1 year. In 1841 it was bought by Wm. McKinstry, and it is now published by W. McKinstry & Co.

The *Western Star* was started at Westfield in June, 1826, by Harvey Newcomb, and was discontinued after 2 years. It was soon after revived, as

The *Chautauque Phœnix,* by Hull & Newcomb. In 1831 its name was changed to

The *American Eagle,* and it was issued by G. W. Newcomb. In 1838 it was changed to

The *Westfield Courier,* and was issued a short time by G.W. Bliss.

The Jamestown Journal was commenced in June, 1826, by Adolphus Fletcher, and was continued by him until 1846. It was then issued by John W. Fletcher, a son of the original proprietor, for 2 years, when it passed into the hands of F. W. Palmer, who continued at the head of the establishment until 1858, having had in the mean time associated with him as partners Francis P. Bailey, Ebenezer P. Upham, and C. D. Sackett. It is now issued by Sackett & Bishop.

The *Chautauque Republican* was started at Jamestown in 1828 by Morgan Bates. Richard K. Kellogg, Lewis C. Todd, Chas. McLean, Alfred Smith, and Wm. H. Cutler were successively interested in its publication until 1833, when it passed into the hands of S. S. C. Hamilton and its name was changed to

The *Republican Banner.* It was soon after removed to Mayville, and in a few months was discontinued.

The *Genius of Liberty* was started at Jamestown in 1829 by Lewis C. Todd, and was continued about 2 years.

The *Western Intelligencer* was published at Forestville a short time in 1833.

The Mayville Sentinel was started in 1834 by Timothy Kilby; and the next year it passed into the hands of Beman Brockway, who continued it 10 years. In 1845 it was sold to John F. Phelps, by whom it is still issued.

The *Chautauque Whig* was started at Dunkirk in Aug. 1834, by Thompson & Carpenter. About 1844 its name was changed to

The *Dunkirk Beacon,* and it was discontinued a short time afterward.

The *Westfield Lyceum,* started in 1835, was issued a short time by Sheldon & Palmer.

The *Western Democrat and Literary Inquirer* was started at Fredonia in 1835 by Wm. Verrinder. It was successively issued by Randall, Crosby & Co. and Arba K. Maynard,

and by the latter it was removed to Van Buren Harbor in 1837 and issued as

The *Van Buren Times.* It soon after passed into the hands of W. H. Cutler, and was continued about 2 years.

The *Western Farmer* was started at Westfield in 1835 by Bliss & Knight, and was continued about 2 years.

The *Settler* was issued a short time in 1840 from the Fredonia Censor office by E. Winchester.

The *Westfield Advocate* was commenced in May, 1841, and was discontinued in a few months.

The *Westfield Messenger* was started in Aug. 1841, by C. J. J. & T. Ingersoll. In 1851 it passed into the hands of Edgar W. Dennison and was changed to

The *Westfield Transcript.* In 1856 Buck & Wilson became its proprietors, and continued it about 1 year.

The *Panama Herald* was started at Panama in Aug. 1846, by Dean & Hurlbut. Stewart & Pray afterward became proprietors, and continued it until 1848.

The *Frontier Express* was started in June, 1846, by Cutler, Cottle & Perham. In 1849 it was changed to

The *Fredonia Express,* and was published by J. P. Cobb & Co., and afterward by T. A. Osborn & Co. In 1850 it was changed to

The *Chautauque Union,* and was published a short time by E. F. Foster.

The *Liberty Star* was started at Jamestown in 1847 by Harvey A. Smith. In 1849 it passed into the hands of Adolphus Fletcher and was changed to

The *Northern Citizen.* In 1853 John W. Fletcher became proprietor; and in 1855 it was changed to

The Chautauqua Democrat, under which name it is now issued by Adolphus Fletcher and Jas. Parker.

The *Silver Creek Mail* was started at Silver Creek in 1848 by John C. Van Duzen. In 1852 it was changed to

The *Home Register,* and was published by Jas. Long. In 1854 Samuel Wilson became proprietor, and changed it to

The *Silver Creek Gazette,* and continued it until 1856, when it was discontinued. In Aug. of that year it was revived, as

The Lake Shore Mirror, by H. M. Morgan, by whom it is still published.

The *Tocsin,* a temperance paper, was published at Mayville by Lloyd Mills a short time about 1845.

The *Chautauque Journal* was started at Dunkirk in May, 1850, by W. L. Carpenter. In a short time its name was changed to

The Dunkirk Journal, and it is still issued by the original proprietor.

The Fredonia Advertiser was started July 4, 1851, by Tyler & Shepard. It is now published by Levi S. Pratt & J. C. Frisbee.

The *Undercurrent* was published at Jamestown a short time in 1851–52 by Harvey A. Smith.

The *Jamestown Herald* was started in Aug. 1852, by Dr. Asaph Rhodes. In 1853 Joseph B. Nessel became proprietor, removed it to Ellington Center, and changed its name to

The *Ellington Luminary.* It was discontinued in 1856.

The *Philomathian Exponent* was issued at Ellington by the students of the academy in 1852.

The Westfield Republican was commenced April 25, 1855, by M. C. Rice & Co., by whom it is still continued.

The *Botanic Medical Journal* was published a short time at Fredonia.

The *Pantheon* was published at Fredonia a short time.

The *Western Argus* was started at Westfield in 1857 by John F. Young. In about 1 year it was removed to Dunkirk, and changed to

The Dunkirk Press and Argus, and is now issued by Howard & Young.

14

Pittsburgh. Their plan was to build a dam across the outlet of the lake and descend the river upon the flood so created. The party finally returned without attempting the project.

The first settlement in the co. was made at the mouth of Cattaraugus Creek in 1797, by Amos Sottle.[1] Soon after making the first improvements, Sottle left, and returned in 1801, with Mr. Sidney and Capt. Rosecrantz. At the time of the first exploration of the co. the only Indian settlement was on Connewango Creek, within the limits of the present town of Carroll. In 1802, Gen. Paine, agent for the State of Connecticut, opened a wagon road from Buffalo to Chautauqua Creek, to enable emigrants to reach the Conn. Reserve lands in Ohio. This road was soon after finished to the Penn. line. In 1804 the town of Chautauqua was formed, and embraced the entire territory now included within the limits of the co. In April of the succeeding year the first town meeting was held, at which John McMahan was elected supervisor, and John McMahan, David Eason, and Perry G. Ellsworth were appointed the first justices of the peace.[2] In 1806 the first mail route was established between Buffalo and Erie, Penn.[3] The lands in the co. were included in the Holland Purchase. A tract of 60,000 acres in the s. e. part was sold to Levi Beardsley, James O. Morse, and Alvan Stewart. In 1835 the Holland Land Company sold their outstanding contracts and unsold lands to Trumbull Cary & Co., of Batavia; and the new proprietors imposed such conditions upon the extension of contracts that the settlers rose *en masse* and demolished the land office at Mayville and burned the records in the public highway.[4] In 1838 the interests of the co. were transferred to Duer, Morrison, & Seward, and the troubles were satisfactorily settled.

ARKWRIGHT—was formed from Pomfret and Villenova, April 30, 1829. A part of Pomfret was annexed in 1830. It is an interior town, lying N. E. of the center of the co. Its surface is an elevated upland, broken and hilly in the s. w., and rolling in the N. E. The highest summit—near the center, said to be the highest land in the co.—is 1,000 to 1,200 ft. above Lake Erie. The principal streams are Canadaway and Walnut Creeks. Mud Lake, on the E. border, covers about 10 acres. The soil is a clay and gravelly loam. Upon Canadaway Creek, in the s. w. part, is a fine cascade with 22 ft. perpendicular fall. **Arkwright Summit** is a p. o. in the E. part of the town. **Arkwright** (p. o.) is a hamlet in the N. part. The first settlement was made in the N. w. corner, by Byron T. Orton, Benj. Perry, and Augustus Burnham, from the eastern part of the State, in 1807.[5] The first religious meeting was held at the house of Aaron Wilcox, in 1810, by Rev. John Spencer. The first church (Bap.) was organized by Elder Thos. Grennel, in 1820.[6]

BUSTI[7]—was formed from Ellicott and Harmony, April 16, 1823. A part was annexed to Ellicott in 1845. It lies upon the s. border of the co., E. of the center. Its surface is hilly and broken. It is drained by several small streams flowing into Chautauqua Lake, which lies along the N. border, and by others flowing E. into Connewango Creek. The soil is a clay and gravelly loam. **Busti Corners** (Busti p. o.) contains a church, gristmill, and sawmill. Pop. 201. The first settlement was made on Lot 61, in 1810, by John L. Frank, from Herkimer co.[8] The first church (Cong.) was formed Aug. 30, 1819; Rev. Lemuel Smith was the first minister.[9]

---

[1] Elial T. Foote, (now of New Haven, Conn.,) for 20 years First Judge of Chautauqua co., says that the first settlement in the co. was made in 1794, by several persons from Erie, Penn.; and among them were the brothers Lowry. These persons had been induced to locate in Penn. by fraudulent representations, and were afterward obliged to leave their improvements and commence anew in the wilderness. They settled within the limits of Chautauqua co.; but the precise place is unknown.

[2] Previous to 1804 the whole of the present co. formed a part of the town of Batavia, in Genesee co. The elections were held at Batavia, nearly 100 mi. distant, to which place the electors were compelled to go if they voted. In 1812 the Board of Supervisors consisted of 2 members, representing the towns of Chautauqua and Pomfret. The county seat had been located at Mayville, much against the wishes of the people of Pomfret; and, in consequence, the supervisor of Pomfret voted against the appropriation of $1,500 to build the courthouse and jail. After repeated attempts to effect the object, the question was temporarily laid aside. When the accounts of the town officers of Pomfret were presented, the Chautauqua member voted in the negative, and affairs came to a dead lock, but were finally settled by a compromise, which allowed both the appropriation and the account to go through.

[3] The first mail was carried by a man named Metcalf, who went on foot and carried the mail matter in a handkerchief.

[4] The company demanded compound interest on all sums due, and an increase of one-third upon all extensions of contracts.

[5] Aaron Wilcox settled in 1809, Nathan Eaton in 1810, Uriah L. Johnson, Jonathan and Benj. Sprague, from Otsego co., near the center, in 1811, and Simeon Clinton, from Otsego co., at the center, in 1813. The first child born was Horatio Nelson Johnson, May 11, 1811; the first marriage, that of Asahel Burnham and Luania Eaton, May 11, 1815; and the first death, that of Augustus Burnham, in 1813. The first school was taught by Lucy Dewey, near the center, in the summer of 1813. Simeon Clinton kept the first inn, in 1817; and Benj. Orton built the first sawmill, in 1818, on the E. branch of Canadaway Creek.

[6] The census reports 3 churches; 2 M. E. and Christian.

[7] Named from Paul Busti, of the Holland Land Company.

[8] Lawrence Frank settled on Lot 62 in 1810, Heman Bush and John Frank, from Herkimer co., and Theron Plumb, from Mass., on Lot 60, in 1811. The first marriage was that of Zebrick Root and Polly Parmiter, in 1813; and the first death, that of Lawrence Frank, in 1811. Eve Frank, a young lady, was carried off by the Indians in 1811, and was gone 3 years, when she re-off by the Indians in 1811, and detained about the same length of turned home and was married. Soon after, her husband was taken by the Indians and detained about the same length of time. These incidents are noted upon a tombstone in the graveyard at Busti. The first school was taught by Olive March, on Lot 61, in 1813. Capt. Heman Bush kept the first inn and store, and erected the first mill, on Stillwater Creek, in 1815.

[9] The census reports 5 churches; Cong., Bap., M. E., Univ., and Christian.

CARROLL[1]—was formed from Ellicott, March 25, 1825. Kiantone was taken off in 1853. It is the s. e. corner town in the co. Its surface is broken and hilly in the n. e. and e., and rolling in the s. and s. w. The highest summits are 900 ft. above Lake Erie. The principal stream is Connewango Creek, forming part of the w. boundary. The soil is a clay loam in the n. and e., and a gravelly loam in the s. and w. **Frewsburgh,** (p. v.,) in the n. w. part, contains 2 churches, a gristmill and sawmill. Pop. 400. **Fentonville** is a p. o. near the s. w. corner. Joseph Akins, from Rensselaer co., the first settler in town, located on Lot 29 in Jan. 1807.[2] There are 2 churches in town; Bap. and M. E.

CHARLOTTE—was formed from Gerry, April 18, 1829. It is an interior town, lying n. e. of the center of the co. The surface is moderately hilly and divided into several ridges by the valleys of the streams. North Hill and Lake Hill, the highest points, are about 1,000 feet above Lake Erie. It is drained by Mill Creek and several tributaries. The soil is chiefly a clay loam. **Charlotte Center** (p. v.) contains 2 churches, a good water-power with some manufactories, and 10 dwellings; **Sinclearville,**[3] (Gerry p. o.,) near the s. line, contains 4 churches, 2 gristmills, and 2 sawmills. Pop. 450. The first settlement was made near the center, in 1809, by Robt. W. Seaver and Wm. Divine, from Oneida co.[4] The first religious meeting (Presb.) was held at Sinclearville, in 1811; and the first church (M. E.) was formed in 1816. There are now 6 churches in town.[5]

CHAUTAUQUA—was formed from Batavia, (Genesee co.,) April 11, 1804, and embraced all the territory now included within the limits of Chautauqua co. Pomfret was taken off in 1808, Portland in 1813, Harmony in 1816, and Clymer, Ellery, and Stockton in 1821. It is an interior town, lying a little w. of the center of the co. The surface is elevated and moderately hilly, occupying the watershed between the waters of Chautauqua Lake and those of Lake Erie. Chautauqua Lake is on the e. border, and chiefly within the limits of the town. The soil is a clay loam of good quality. **Mayville,** (p. v.,) pleasantly located near the head of Chautauqua Lake, was incorp. April 30, 1830; it contains the co. buildings, 3 churches, the Mayville Academy, a newspaper office, and a flouring mill. Pop. 501. **De Wittville,** (p. v.,) in the e. part, contains a church, the co. poorhouse, and 133 inhabitants; **Hartfield,** (p. v.,) on the lake inlet, contains a church, gristmill, sawmill, and furnace. Pop. 123. **Magnolia** is a p. o. on the lake, near the s. line. The first settlement was made at Mayville, in 1804, by Dr. Alexander McIntyre.[6] The first church (Bap.) was formed at Mayville, in 1820, by Elder Wilson.[7]

CHERRY CREEK—was formed from Ellington, May 4, 1829. It lies on the e. border of the co., a little n. of the center. The surface is hilly in the n. w., and rolling in the s. e. Along the s. border are several small swamps. It is drained by Connewango Creek and several tributaries, flowing s. The soil is clay and a gravelly loam. **Cherry Creek,** (p. v.,) in the s. e. part, contains 3 churches, 2 sawmills, and a gristmill. Pop. 240. The first settlement was made on Lot 15, in 1812, by Joshua Bentley, from Rensselaer co.[8] The first religious services were held at the house of Ward King, in 1817; the Rev. Mr. Hadley (Bap.) was the first preacher.[9]

CLYMER[10]—was formed from Chautauqua, Feb. 9, 1821. Mina was taken off in 1824, and French Creek in 1829. It lies upon the s. border of the co., w. of the center. The surface is a hilly upland, broken by the valleys of Brocken Straw Creek and its tributaries. The soil is a gravelly loam. Considerable lumber is still manufactured. **Clymer,** (p. v.,) near the s. w. corner, con-

---

1 Named in honor of Charles Carroll, of Carrollton.
2 Laban Case settled on Lot 31, Wm. Akins on Lot 21, in 1807, Jas. Akins on Lot 13, in 1818; James Hall on Lot 11, in 1810; and Wm. Sears on Lot 11, in 1811. The first child born was Hamilton Tyler, in 1810; the first marriage, that of Wm. Bowles and Jerusha Walton, in 1811; and the first death, that of —— Woodcock, killed by the fall of a tree in 1810. Stephen Rogers taught the first school, in 1813, on Lot 51. The first sawmill was built by John Fren and Thos. Russell, on Lot 61, in 1811, and the first gristmill by John Fren, on the same lot, in 1817. William Sears kept the first store, on Lot 11, in 1814, and James Hall the first store, on the same lot, in 1824.
3 The village derives its name from its first settler, Maj. Sam'l Sinclear, who came in from Madison co. in 1810.
4 John Picket, John Cleveland, Chas. Waterman, and Harvey O. Austin, from Eastern N. Y., settled in the w. part in 1809. The first school was taught at Sinclearville, in the winter of 1811–12, by Wm. Gilmore. Maj. Sinclear kept the first inn, in 1811, and Plumb, Edson & Winsor the first store, in 1817, at Sinclearville. Maj. Sinclear erected the first sawmill in 1810, and the first gristmill, in 1811, on Mill Creek.
5 2 M. E., 2 Univ., Cong., and Bap.

6 Jonathan Smith settled about the same time, near the w. shore of the lake, and Peter Barnhart, from Penn., on the e. shore; Martin Prendergast and Messrs. Griffith and Bemus, also on the e. shore, in 1806. Judge Peacock was also an early settler. John Scott kept the first inn, at Mayville, in 1808, and J. & M. Prendergast the first store, in 1811.
7 The census reports 7 churches; 2 Bap., 2 M. E., Cong., Prot. E., and F. W. Bap.
8 Jos. Kent settled on Lot 9, in 1815, and Willard Cheney on Lot 10, Wm. Weaver on Lot 16, Anson Hendrick on Lot 16, and Cogsdill Brown on Lot 15, in 1816. Reuben Cheney taught the first school, in 1818; Geo. H. Frost kept the first inn, in 1823, and Seth Grover the first store, in 1831, at the village. Wm. Kilbourn built the first sawmill, in 1824, on Cherry Creek, near the village. The first death was that of Lydia Page; she was buried in the woods near the village. Joshua Bentley lost a daughter, 2 years old, in 1817,—supposed to have been carried off by the Indians.
9 The census reports 3 churches; 2 Bap. and F. W. Bap.
10 Named in honor of Geo. Clymer, one of the signers of the Declaration of Independence.

tains 2 churches and 110 inhabitants. **Clymer Center** is a p. o. John Cleveland settled on Lot 58 in 1820.[1] The first religious meeting (Bap.) was held at the house of Mr. Cleveland, in 1820, by Elder Powers. The first church (Bap.) was formed in 1830.[2]

ELLERY[3]—was formed from Chautauqua, Feb. 29, 1821. A part of Stockton was taken off in 1850. It is the central town in the co. The surface is hilly, the highest summits being about 400 ft. above the valleys and 1,000 ft. above Lake Erie. Chautauqua Lake forms the s. w. boundary, and into it flow several small streams, which form the principal drainage. The soil is a clay loam upon the uplands, and a gravelly loam in the valleys. **Ellery Center** (p. v.) contains a church and 16 dwellings. **Ellery** is a p. o. near the shore of the lake. The first settlements were made on the lake by Wm. Bemus and Jeremiah Griffith, from Rensselaer co., in 1806; the former located at Bemus Point, and the latter farther s.[4] The first church (Bap.) was formed in 1809, by Elder Asa Turner, the first minister.[5]

ELLICOTT[6]—was formed from Pomfret, June 1, 1812. A part of Busti was taken off in 1823, Carroll in 1825, and Poland in 1832. A part of Busti was annexed in 1845. It is an interior town, lying s. e. of the center of the co. Its surface is a hilly upland, with a gentle inclination toward the s. w. The foot of Chautauqua Lake extends into the s. w. corner; and the outlet flows e. through the s. part of the town, receiving Cassadaga Creek as a tributary The soil is a sandy and gravelly loam. **Jamestown,** (p. v.,) located on the outlet of Chautauqua Lake, in the s. part of the town, was incorp. March 6, 1827. It contains 7 churches, the Jamestown Academy, 2 newspaper offices, 2 banks, the office of the Farmers' Insurance Company, 2 woolen factories, 2 furnaces, 2 flouring mills, and various other manufacturing establishments, and an ample water-power. Pop. 1,625. **Fluvanna,** (p. v.,) at the foot of the lake, near the w. line, contains a church and 14 dwellings. **Levant** is a p. o., on the e. border, at the junction of Cassadaga Creek with the lake outlet. **Dexterville** is a hamlet. The first settlement was made on the outlet of Chautauqua Lake, in 1806, by Wm. Wilson.[7] The first church (Cong.) was formed July 6, 1816, by Rev. John Spencer, a missionary preacher from Conn. There are 12 churches in town.[8]

ELLINGTON—was formed from Gerry, April 1, 1824. Cherry Creek was taken off in 1829. It lies upon the e. border of the co., a little s. of the center. Its surface is an undulating and hilly upland. Clear Creek flows through near the center, and, with its tributaries, forms the principal drainage. Connewango Creek flows through the n. e. corner. The soil is a sandy and gravelly loam. **Ellington,** (p. v.,) near the center, contains 4 churches, the Ellington Academy, and 2 gristmills. Pop. 487. **Clear Creek** is a p. o. Jos. Bentley made the first settlement, on Lot 7, in 1814.[9] The first religious services were held at the house of James Bates, in 1817, by Rev. Daniel Hadley. The F. W. Bap. denomination organized the first church.[10]

FRENCH CREEK—was formed from Clymer, April 23, 1829. It is the s. w. corner town of the co. The surface is hilly and broken by the deep valley of French Creek. The soil is chiefly a heavy clay loam. **French Creek** is a p. o. in the n. part, and **Marvin** a p. o. in the s. Andy Nobles, from Oswego co., made the first settlement, on Lot 44, in 1812.[11] The first religious meeting was held on Lot 46, in 1818, by Elder Ashford; and the first church (Bap.) was formed in 1821. There is no church edifice in town.

---

[1] Wm. Rice, from Washington co., settled on Lot 59, in 1821, Horace and Anson Starkweather, from Vt., on Lot 43, in 1822. The first birth was that of Patience Russell, in 1823; the first marriage, that of Walter Freeman and Rowencia Brown, in 1823. Alvin Williams kept the first inn, in 1826, at the village, John Stow the first store, in 1823; and Peter Jacquins built the first mill, in 1825.

[2] The census reports 5 churches; 2 M. E., Bap., Germ. Evang. Ref., and Ref. Prot. D.

[3] Named in honor of Wm. Ellery, a signer of the Declaration of Independence.

[4] Isaac Young, from Genesee co., settled on Lot 3, near the lake, in 1806. About the same time, or soon after, Dan'l Cheney, Alanson Weed, Abijah Bennett, John Putnam, and Nahum Aldrich settled in town. Clark Parker, from Washington co., located near the center, in 1810. The first school was taught by Dr. Cary, in the n. w. part, in 1808. Wm. Bemus kept the first inn, in 1811, erected the first sawmill, in 1808, and the first gristmill, in 1811, on Bemus Creek. David Bellamy kept the first store, at the center, in 1830.

[5] The census reports 3 churches; Bap., M. E., and Univ.

[6] Named from Joseph Ellicott, agent of the Holland Land Company.

[7] Thomas R. Kennedy and Edward Works located upon the Outlet, in 1807, and Wilson Ellicott, Jas. Culbertson, and Geo. W. Fenton, in 1808. Edward Works built the first sawmill, in

1808, and the first gristmill, in 1809,—this being the first improvement of the water-power of the Outlet. The first school was taught in the house of John Bloover, in 1815, by Rev. Amasa West.

[8] 2 M. E., Cong., Presb., Prot. E., Bap., F. W. Bap., Christian, Wes. Meth., Luth., Univ., and R. C.

[9] Among the other early settlers were Jas. Bates, from Mass., Sam'l McConnel, from Cayuga co., and Joshua Bentley, jr., from Rensselaer co., in 1816; Simon Lawrence, from Vt., Abner Bates and Ward King, from Mass., in 1817. The first child born was Simon Lawrence, jr., in 1817; the first marriage, that of Rufus Hitchcock and Ranah Hadley, in 1817; and the first death, that of Mr. Hitchcock, who fell from a building and was killed six weeks after his marriage. Jas. Bates kept the first inn, at Ellington Village, in 1814, and Lewis Holbrook the first store, in 1821. Ward King built the first gristmill, near the village, in 1821.

[10] The census reports 5 churches; Bap., Christian, Presb., M. E., and F. W. Bap.

[11] John Cleveland settled on Lot 31, in 1812; Roswell Coe on Lot 39, and Nath'l Thompson on Lot 9, in 1813; and Paul Colbourn, from Oneida co., on Lot 44, in 1814. The first death was that of a son of Nath'l Thompson, drowned in French Creek. The first school was taught by —— Chitsey, in 1818. William Graves kept the first inn, and built the first gristmill, in 1822; and John Dodge opened the first store, in one end of the gristmill.

GERRY[1]—was formed from Pomfret, June 1, 1812. Ellington was taken off in 1824, and Charlotte in 1829. It is an interior town, lying a little E. of the center of the co. The surface is a hilly upland, the highest summits, in the N. E. corner, being 900 ft. above Lake Erie. It is drained by Cassadaga Creek and its tributaries, Mill Creek, and several smaller streams. The soil is a clay loam upon the uplands, and a sandy loam in the valleys. There are several sulphur springs in town. Upon Lot 44, s. w. of the center of the town, a gas spring has been found; and the owner, James H. Mix, uses the gas for lighting his house. **Bucklins Corners,** (Vermont p. o.,) in the s. part, contains 23 dwellings. The first settlement was made in 1811, by John Love, jr. and Stephen Jones, in the N. W. part.[2] The first religious meeting was held in the spring of 1818, by Elder Jonathan Wilson. The first religious association (M. E.) was formed in 1819, and drew the lot appropriated by the Holland Land Company for religious purposes. They erected a church a little w. from the center, the only one now in town.

HANOVER—was formed from Pomfret, June 1, 1812. Villenova was taken off in 1823, and a part of Sheridan in 1827. It lies upon Lake Erie, in the N. E. corner of the co. A part of Cattaraugus Indian Reservation lies in the N. E. part of the town. The surface along the lake is level or undulating, and in the center and s. it is hilly, with an inclination toward the N. Cattaraugus Creek forms a portion of the N. boundary. Silver Creek flows in a N. W. direction through the town into Lake Erie, receiving Walnut Creek at its mouth,[3] and several other tributaries. The soil is clay and gravelly loam. **Silver Creek,** (p. v.,) upon the lake shore, at the mouth of Silver Creek, was incorp. June 8, 1848; it contains 2 churches, a bank, a weekly newspaper office, 2 mills, 2 tanneries, and various other manufacturing establishments. Pop. 652. Lake vessels were formerly built at this place,[4]—the first by Ira Fairchild, in 1816. **Irving,** (p. v.,) on Cattaraugus Creek, near its entrance into the lake, contains 2 churches, a gristmill, and 2 sawmills. Pop. 404. At the mouth of the creek is a harbor admitting of the entrance of vessels. **Smith Mills,** (p. v.,) a little s. from the center, contains a flouring mill, a distillery, and 22 dwellings. **Forestville,** (p. v.,) in the s. w. part, was incorp. April 4, 1849. It contains 2 churches, 2 gristmills, and 2 sawmills. Pop. 540. It is a station on the N. Y. & Erie R. R. **Nashville,** (p. v.,) in the s. E. part, contains 2 churches and 26 dwellings. **Hanover** is a hamlet. Amos Cottle settled at the mouth of Cattaraugus Creek in 1797.[5] The first religious meetings (Bap.) were held by Rev. Joy Handy, in 1811; and the first church (M. E.) was organized in 1816, at Forestville.[6]

HARMONY—was taken from Chautauqua, Feb. 14, 1816. A part of Busti was taken off in 1823. It lies upon the s. border of the co., a little w. of the center. The surface is a moderately hilly upland, the highest summits being about 900 ft. above Lake Erie. Chautauqua Lake forms the N. E. boundary. It is drained by Goose Creek and several smaller streams, flowing N. into the lake, and by Little Brocken Straw Creek, flowing s. to Penn. The soil is clay, yellow and gravelly loam. Quarries of a fine quality of sandstone for building purposes are found in several localities. **Ashville,** (Harmony p. o.,) on Goose Creek, near Chautauqua Lake, contains 3 churches, a gristmill and sawmill. Pop. 247. **Panama,** (p. v.,) upon Little Brocken Straw Creek, near the center, contains 4 churches and 500 inhabitants. **Blockville** (p. v.) contains 20 dwellings. **Stedman** is a p. o. in the N. part of the town. The first settlement was made on Lot 43, in 1806, by Reuben Slayton, from Otsego co.[7] The first religious meeting (Bap.) was held in a schoolhouse at Blockville, by Rev. Simon Bowers.[8]

---

[1] Named from Elbridge Gerry, a signer of the Declaration of Independence.

[2] Jesse Dexter, David Cobb, and Hugh B. Patterson were among the early settlers. The town settled slowly until after the close of the war in 1815, when the settlements progressed rapidly. The first death was that of Alva Eaton, who was killed by the fall of a tree in the spring of 1818. Jas. Bucklin kept the first inn, in 1820, and Howard B. Blodget the first store, in 1826, at Bucklins Corners. John Hines and Wm. Newton erected the first sawmill, on Cassadaga Creek, in the s. w. part, in 1819, and the first gristmill, in 1822.

[3] Named from a gigantic walnut tree that grew near its mouth. This tree was 9 ft. in diameter and 27 ft. in circumference. It was cut into sections and sold as curiosities.

[4] The steamboat W. F. B. Taylor was built here in 1836.

[5] Among the first settlers were Wm. Sidney and Capt. Rosecrantz, in 1801; Sylvanus Maybee, Benj. Kinyon, and Amos Avery, at the mouth of Cattaraugus Creek, Nathan Cass, from Boston, Jehial More and Jonas Green, at Forestville, in 1805; Abel Cleveland and David Dickerson, in 1802; John E. Howard, in 1806; and Artemus R. Clothier, in 1809,—all at Silver Creek. The first child born was Caroline Sidney, in 1804; the first marriage, that of

Richard Smith and Sally Mack, in 1807; and the first death, that of Wm. Sidney, in Jan. 1807. John Mack kept the first inn, in 1807, at the mouth of Cattaraugus Creek, and Parker Brownell the first store, in 1811. Abel Cleveland and David Dickerson built the first sawmill, in 1804, and the first gristmill, in 1806, at Silver Creek. In 1805 Mr. Dickerson erected a saw mill at Silver Creek, to which he attached a mortar and pestle, for the purpose of pounding corn for food. —— Moore erected a gristmill at Forestville about the same period.

[6] There are 8 churches in town; 4 M. E., 3 Bap., and Presb.

[7] Daniel B. Carpenter, from Washington co., settled on Lot 64, in 1806; Jonathan Cheney on Lot 52, in 1807; Theron Bly, from Otsego co., on Lot 44, and Wm. Mattison on Lot 52, in 1811; and Jas. Carpenter on Lot 56, in 1811. The first child born was Thos. Slayton, in Nov. 1807; the first marriage, that of Reuben Slayton and Clarissa Slayton, in 1808; and the first death, that of Thomas Slayton, Nov. 26, 1807. Eben Pratt taught the first school, in 1817; Jas. McCallen kept the first inn, in 1816, on Lot 43; and Tibbets & Kellogg the first store, on the same lot, in 1818. Reuben Slayton built the first sawmill, on Lot 43, in 1818.

[8] The census reports 9 churches; 5 M. E., 3 Bap., and Presb.

KIANTONE—was formed from Carroll, Nov. 16, 1853. It lies upon the s. border of the co., E. of the center. The surface is undulating in the E., and hilly in the w. The highest summits are about 100 ft. above Chautauqua Lake. Connewango Creek forms the greater part of the E. boundary. Kiantone and Stillwater Creeks are the other principal streams. The soil is a clay loam intermixed with gravel. **Kiantone** (p. v.) contains about 20 dwellings. The first settlement was made on Lot 1, in 1807, by Robt. Russel.[1] The first religious meeting was held at the house of Joseph Akins, in 1814, by Rev. Mr. Smith; and the first church (Cong.) was formed in 1815. There are 3 churches in town; Cong., M. E., and Univ.

MINA—was taken from Clymer, March 23, 1824. Sherman was taken off in 1832. It is the central town upon the w. border of the co. Its surface is rolling and hilly. The principal streams are French and several smaller creeks, flowing s. and w. Findleys Lake is a fine sheet of water in the s. w. part. The soil is a clay and gravelly loam. **Mina Corners,** (Mina p. o.,) a little E. of the center, contains 15 dwellings; and **Findleys Lake,** (p. v.,) near the outlet of the lake, 20 dwellings. **Friends** is a p.o. in the s. w. part. The first settlement was made on Lot 52, in 1816, by Alex. Finley, from Penn., originally from Ireland.[2] The first religious services (Ref. Prot. D.) were held in the barn of Benj. Hazen, by Rev. Mr. Bradley, in 1826. The first and only church (Ref. Prot. D.) was formed in 1853, and the church edifice was erected in 1857.

POLAND—was formed from Ellicott, April 9, 1832. It lies on the E. border of the co., s. of the center. Its surface is a hilly upland, divided into several distinct ridges. The principal streams are Connewango and Cassadaga Creeks, which form a junction near the s. line. The soil is a clay and sandy loam. Considerable lumber is still manufactured. **Falconer,**[3] (p. v.,) on Connewango Creek, contains a church, gristmill, sawmill, and 23 dwellings. **Poland Center** is a p. o. The first settlement was made at Falconer, on the Connewango, in 1805, by Dr. Thos. R. Kennedy, from Meadville, Penn.[4] A church (Union)—the only one in town—is located at Falconer.

POMFRET—was formed from Chautauqua, March 11, 1808. Ellicott, Gerry, and Hanover were taken off in 1812, a part of Sheridan in 1827, and parts of Arkwright in 1829 and '30. It lies upon Lake Erie, a little E. of the center of the co. A strip of comparatively level land extends along the lake, and the remaining part of the surface is a rolling upland, the higher summits being 700 to 800 ft. above the lake. It is principally drained by Canadaway Creek and several smaller streams flowing into the lake. Several small branches of Cassadaga Creek take their rise in the s. part. The soil is a clay and gravelly loam. Quarries of excellent building stone are found along the lake shore. **Dunkirk,**[5] (p. v.,) on Lake Erie, was incorp. May 15, 1837. It is a commercial port upon the lake, and the w. terminus of the N. Y. & Erie R. R. It has a fine harbor, and commodious wharves and warehouses for the accommodation of the large amount of commerce that centers here during the season of navigation.[6] The R. R. company have also extensive warehouses, work and repair shops, and accommodations for an immense freighting business. The port is the most important one on the lake between Buffalo and Cleveland; and regular lines of steam propellers run in connection with the R. R. The village contains a bank, 4 churches, 2 newspaper offices, a union school, several machine shops and furnaces, and a brewery and distillery. Pop. 4,754. **Fredonia,** (p. v.,) upon Canadaway Creek,[7] 3 mi. s. of Dunkirk, was incorp. May 2, 1829. It contains 4 churches, the Fredonia Academy, 2 banks, 2 weekly newspapers, 3 flouring mills, 2 furnaces, and various other manufacturing establishments. The celebrated "Fredonia Garden Seeds" are raised and put up at this place.[8] Pop. 2,004.

---

[1] James Hall settled on Lot 28, in 1810. The first school was taught by Stephen Rogers, in 1814. Jas. Hall kept the first store, on Lot 28, and Wm. Sears the first inn, on Lot 11. Robert Russel built the first sawmill, on Kiantone Creek.

[2] Aaron Whitney, from Dunnville, Canada, settled on Lot 59, Zina Reckford on Lot 28, and Roger Haskill on Lot 50, in 1821; James Ottaway, from Kent Co., England, on Lot 14, in 1823. The first birth was that of a daughter of Nathaniel Throop, in 1823; the first marriage, that of Isaac Stedman and Nancy Wilcox, in April, 1826; and the first death, that of the mother of Nathaniel Throop, in 1825. The first school was taught by Elisha More, near Finleys Mills, in 1826. Cullin Barnes kept the first inn, on Lot 20, in 1827, and Horace Brockway the first store, in 1824, on Lot 52. Alex. Finley built the first mill, in 1824, on the outlet of Finleys Lake.

[3] Formerly known as "Kennedyville."

[4] Edward Shillitto settled about the same time at the mills on the Connewango; Amasa Ives, Isaac Young, —— Owens, —— Miles, Jos. and Daniel Wheeler, Nicholas Dolloff, and Joshua

Woodard were also early settlers. Dr. T. R. Kennedy erected the first sawmill, in 1805, and the first gristmill, in 1806, on the Connewango. The first lumber rafted down the Alleghany was made at Dr. Kennedy's mill.

[5] Formerly called "Chadwicks Bay," from the first settler.

[6] At this port were received, in 1857, 242,957 bbls. flour, 38,532 bbls. whiskey, 20,153 bbls. beef, pork, and bacon, 93,448 bush. wheat, 114,652 bush. corn, 2,152,800 lbs. wool, 1,208,400 lbs. butter, 9,236 head of cattle, 10,782 sheep, and 10,865 hogs.

[7] Upon the banks of the creek—just below the bridge, in the village—is a spring of carburetted hydrogen gas, yielding about 10,000 cubic ft. of gas every 24 hours. This gas is collected in a gasometer and distributed in pipes, affording sufficient light for about one-half of the village. About one mi. E. of the village the gas oozes from the shale rocks on the banks of the creek over the space of an acre. The amount of gas escaping here is supposed to be much greater than at the spring in the village, and a company has been formed to collect it for use.

[8] Over 600 acres of land are devoted to this business.

Laona, (p. v.,) on Saw Creek, near the E. border, contains 2 churches, a paper mill, saw and grist mill, and 406 inhabitants. **Brigham,** in the S. part, is a p. o. **Shumla** is a hamlet, near the S. E. corner. David Eason and Thomas McClintock, from Penn., settled at Fredonia, in 1804.[1] The first church (Bap.) was organized Oct. 20, 1808, at the house of Judge Cushing.[2]

PORTLAND—was formed from Chautauqua, April 9, 1813. Ripley was taken off in 1817, and a part of Westfield in 1829. It lies upon Lake Erie, a little W. of the center of the co. Its surface is level along the lake shore, but broken and hilly in the center and W. Its streams are small creeks and brooks flowing into Lake Erie. The soil is a clay and gravelly loam. **Centerville,** (Portland p. o.,) near the center, contains 2 churches and 233 inhabitants; **Salem,** (Brockton p. o.,) in the N. E. part, contains 2 churches and 258 inhabitants. The first settlement was made a little W. of the center, by Capt. Jas. Dunn, in 1805.[3] The first religious meeting was held at the house of Capt. Dunn, in 1810, by Rev. John Spencer, who afterward organized the first church (Cong.) in 1817.[4]

RIPLEY[5]—was formed from Portland, March 1, 1817. A part of Westfield was taken off in 1829. It lies upon Lake Erie, in the N. W. corner of the co. Its surface is level along the lake shore, and broken and hilly in the S. E. The highest summits are 800 ft. above the lake. It is drained by Twenty Mile Creek and its tributaries and a large number of small streams flowing into the lake. The soil is a clay and gravelly loam. Along the lake shore are several valuable stone quarries. **Quincy,** (Ripley p. o.,) about 1 mi. E. of the lake, contains 2 churches and 289 inhabitants. **State Line** is a station on the B. & E. R. R. Josiah Farnsworth, from the E. part of the State, settled at Quincy in 1804. The first religious services (Bap.) were held at the house of Nathan Wisner, by Rev. Samuel Wisner, in 1806; the first church (Presb.) was formed in 1820.[6]

SHERIDAN—was formed from Pomfret and Hanover, April 16, 1827. It lies upon the shore of Lake Erie, E. of the center of the co. The surface is level in the N. W., and hilly in the S. E., with a gradual inclination toward the lake. A nearly perpendicular bluff, 50 to 200 ft. high, extends along the lake shore. It is drained by Scotts Creek, and several smaller streams, flowing into Lake Erie. The soil is a clay loam, mixed in some parts with gravel. **Sheridan Center** (p. v.) contains 2 churches and 20 dwellings. The first settlements were made on Lot 17, at the center, by Francis Webber, from Mass., in 1804.[7] The first religious meeting (Presb.) was held at the house of Orsamus Holmes, by Rev. John Spencer, in 1807; and the first church (Presb.) was organized by Mr. Spencer, in 1816.[8]

SHERMAN[9]—was formed from Mina, April 17, 1832. It is an interior town, lying s. w. of the center of the co. The surface is rolling and hilly, broken by the deep ravines of the streams. It is drained by French Creek and its tributaries. The soil is clay and sandy loam. Considerable lumber is manufactured in the town. **Sherman,** (p. v.,) in the N., contains 4 churches, a grist-mill, sawmill, and several manufacturing establishments. Pop. 401. **Center Sherman** is a p. o. **Pleasant Valley** and **Waits Corners** are hamlets. In 1824,[10] Alanson Weed set-

---

[1] Low Minegar, Benj. Barrett, Zattu Cushing, —— Barnes, —— Cole, and —— Geer settled, in 1804 and '05, at and near Fredonia. Timothy Goulding settled 1 mi. w. of the harbor, in 1808. Solomon Chadwick located at Dunkirk in 1809, and —— Gaylord, Daniel Pier, and Luther Goulding soon after. Samuel Perry brought the first vessel into the harbor, in 1810. The first death was that of a daughter of Oliver Woodcock, 12 years of age, killed by the fall of a tree in 1808. The first school was taught by Samuel Perry, at Fredonia, in the winter of 1808–09. Thos. McClintock kept the first inn, in 1809, and E. Risley the first store, in 1808, at Fredonia. Baker, Berry & Co. built the first sawmill and gristmill, in 1807, on Canadaway Creek.

[2] The census reports 11 churches; 3 Bap., 2 Prot. E., 2 Presb., 2 M. E., Christian, and R. C.

[3] In 1806, Nathan, Elisha, and Nath'l Fay settled on Lot 25, Peter Kane on Lot 38, John Price on Lot 34, David Eason on Lot 37, and Benj. Hutchins in the same vicinity. The first birth was that of George W. Dunn, Jan. 18, 1807; the first marriage, that of Absalom Harris and Polly Kane, in 1810; and the first death, that of Mrs. Nathan Fay, in 1807. The first school was taught by Anna Eaton, on the premises of Capt. Dunn, in the summer of 1810. The first inn was kept near Centerville, by Capt. Dunn, in 1806, and the first store by Thos. Clump, in 1817, in the w. part of the town. Moses Sage and Wm. Dunham built the first sawmills, near the lake shore. The first gristmill was built at Salem.

[4] The census reports 6 churches; 2 Bap., 2 M. E., Prot. Meth., and Cong.

[5] Named in honor of Gen. Eleazur W. Ripley. Among the other early settlers were Perry G. Ellsworth, on Lot 12, near Quincy, Samuel Truesdail, near the Penn. line, Alexander Cochrane, on

Lot 10, and Wm. Alexander, all of whom came in 1804; Silas Baird settled on Lot 6, and Ira Loomis in town, in 1806; Chas. Forsyth in 1808. The first school was taught by Ann Riddle, a little w. of Quincy, in 1810. The first inn was kept near the State line, by Sam'l Truesdail, in 1805.

[6] The census reports 5 churches; 2 Presb., M. E., Bap., and Union.

[7] Jerrard Griswold, John Walker, Orsamus and Alanson Holmes, and Uriah Lee, from Eastern New York, settled near the center in 1804–05; Wm. Griswold, from Conn., on Lot 35, in 1805; and Rev. John Spencer, from Conn., at the center, in 1807. The first birth was that of Jos. Ellicott, son of Alanson Holmes, in the spring of 1805; the first marriage, that of Benj. Parrows and Betsey Stebbins, in 1807–08; and the first death, that of Alanson Holmes, in the fall of 1805. The first school was taught by Wm. Griswold, in the winter of 1808–09, at his own house. Orsamus Holmes kept the first inn, w. of the center, in 1808, and Elisha Gray the first store, the same year. Haven Brigham built the first gristmill, in 1807, on Brighams Creek.

[8] The census reports 3 churches; Presb., Bap., and Wes. Meth.

[9] Named in honor of Roger Sherman, one of the signers of the Declaration of Independence.

[10] In the same year, Harvey W. Goff settled on Lot 30, Lester R. Dewey on Lot 31, Otis Skinner on Lot 32, and Hiram N Gleason on Lot 24. The first child born was Amasa Dormas, in 1824; the first marriage, that of Lester R. Dewey and Fanny Patterson. in 1825; and the first death, that of —— Arnold, in 1826. Otis Skinner taught the first school, in his own house, in 1828. Josiah Keeler kept the first store and inn, on Lot 27, in 1827. Alanson Weed erected the first mill, on Lot 30 in 1825.

tled on Lot 31. The first religious meeting (Bap.) was held at the house of Jonathan Reynolds, by Elder Spencer; and the first church (Cong.) was formed in 1826.[1]

STOCKTON[2]—was formed from Chautauqua, Feb. 9, 1821. A part of Ellery was annexed in 1850. It is an interior town, lying a little N. of the center of the co. Its surface is a rolling and hilly upland. Cassadaga and Bear Lakes, two small bodies of water near the N. border, give rise to Cassadaga and Bear Creeks. These streams unite in the s. part of the town. The soil upon the upland is a clay loam, and in the valleys a sandy loam. **Delanti,** (Stockton p. o.,) near the center, contains 3 churches, a grist and saw-mill, and 180 inhabitants. **Cassadaga,** (p. v.,) upon Cassadaga Lake, in the N. E. corner, contains a church, a sawmill, and 151 inhabitants. **South Stockton,** in the s. E. part, and **Oregon,** in the s., are p. offices. The first settlement was made in the s. part of the town, in 1810, by Shadrack Scofield, David Waterbury, and Henry Walker, from Saratoga co.[3] The first church (Bap.) was organized in the s. part, in 1815,[4]

VILLENOVA—was taken from Hanover, Jan. 24, 1823. A part of Arkwright was taken off in 1829. It lies upon the E. border of the co., N. of the center. Its surface is rolling in the s. E., and broken and hilly in the center and N. The highest summit is 900 ft. above Lake Erie. Two small lakes—one on the N. and the other on the w. border—form the sources of the two branches of Connewango Creek, which unite in the s. E. corner. The soil is a clay and gravelly loam. **Omar,** (Hamlet p. o.,) a little s. w. of the center, contains 2 churches, a grist and saw mill, and 181 inhabitants. **Villenova** is a p. o. at Connewango Forks, in the s. E. part. The first settlement was made in 1810, on Lot 3, by Daniel Whipple, from Herkimer co., originally from Mass.[5] The first religious meeting was held by Rev. Mr. Dunham; and the first church (M. E.) was formed in 1812. There are 3 churches in town; M. E., Wes. Meth., and F. W. Bap.

WESTFIELD—was formed from Portland and Ripley, March 19, 1829. It lies upon Lake Erie, w. of the center of the co. The surface is level or rolling along the lake, and hilly in the center and s. It is drained by Chautauqua and Little Chautauqua Creeks and several smaller streams flowing into the lake. The soil is a clay and gravelly loam. **Westfield,**[6] (p. v.,) upon Chautauqua Creek, about 2 mi. from the lake, was incorp. April 19, 1833. It contains 4 churches, 2 banks, a weekly newspaper, the Westfield Academy, an agricultural implement factory, a hardware factory, woolen factory, cotton mill, and 3 flouring mills. Pop. 1,433. **Barcelona,** (p. v.,) a port of entry upon the lake, contains 169 inhabitants. **Volusia** is a p. o. in the s. part of the town. The first settlement was made in 1801, by Edward McHenry, from Penn.[7] The first church (Presb.) was organized in 1807, by Rev. John Linsley.[8]

---

[1] The census reports 5 churches; Cong., Bap., F. W. Bap., M. E., and Univ.

[2] Named in honor of Richard Stockton, a signer of the Declaration of Independence.

[3] The first child born was Wm. Walker, Aug. 25, 1811. Abigail Durfey taught the first school, in the s. part, in the summer of 1815. The first inn was kept by Ichabod Fisher, at Cassadaga, in 1811, and the first store by James Haywood, at Delanti, in 1817. Hines, Lazell & Nelson built the first gristmill, at Delanti, on Bear Creek, in 1819.

[4] The census reports 6 churches; 3 Bap., Cong., Christian, and Univ.

[5] Among the other early settlers were Daniel Wright, from Herkimer co., on Lot 19, Villeroy Balcomb, John Kent, and Eli Arnold. The first child born was Electa Whipple, May 5, 1812; the first marriage, that of Jas. Maffit and Mary Dighton; and the first death, that of John Arnold, in 1811. Mrs. Battles taught the first school, in her own house, near Wrights Corners, in 1815. Norris & Grover kept the first store, and Villeroy Balcomb the first inn, at Wrights Corners, in 1829. John Kent

erected the first sawmill, in 1815, on the Connewango, below the Forks; and a gristmill was attached in 1818.

[6] The business of this place was ruined by the finishing of the N. Y. & Erie R. R. to Dunkirk. A lighthouse here is lighted by gas obtained from a gas spring, on the bank of the creek, about a mile distant.

[7] Among the other early settlers were Arthur Bell and James Montgomery, from Penn., who located a little w. of Westfield Village, Abraham Fredrick, from Penn., on Lot 71, and Dan'l Kinkaid, on Lot 14, all in 1802; and Gen. John and Jas. McMahan, on the present site of the village, in 1803. The first child born was John McHenry, in 1802; the first marriage, that of James Montgomery and Sarah Taylor, June 30, 1805; and the first death, that of Edward McHenry, drowned by the upsetting of a small boat on Lake Erie, in 1803. John McMahan erected the first sawmill and gristmill, in 1804, on and near the mouth of Chautauqua Creek. Edward McHenry kept the first inn, in 1802, and Jas. Atkins the first store, in 1808, at Westfield Village. The first school was taught by Wm. Murray, in 1803.

[8] The census reports 7 churches; 2 M. E., Presb., Prot. E., Wes. Meth., Bap., and Univ.

Acres of Land, Valuation, Population, Dwellings, Families, Freeholders, Schools, Live Stock, Agricultural Products, and Domestic Manufactures, of Chautauqua County.

Names of Towns.	Acres of Land.		Valuation of 1858.			Population.		No. of Dwellings.	No. of Families.	Freeholders.	Schools.	
	Improved.	Unimproved.	Real Estate.	Personal Property.	Total.	Males.	Females.				No. of Districts.	Children taught.
Arkwright	12,256	9,199	$287,734	$18,300	$306,034	561	549	202	205	187	10	463
Busti	18,399	11,342	562,565	20,650	583,215	940	980	354	375	339	13	675
Carrol	6,712	12,755	271,874	31,175	303,049	698	710	267	278	274	9	551
Charlotte	12,696	8,658	386,336	73,655	459,991	845	827	329	337	327	12	677
Chautauqua	25,318	19,617	784,050	139,230	923,280	1,324	1,267	520	521	418	18	1,092
Cherry Creek	11,090	14,477	247,170	9,450	256,620	632	594	246	258	234	9	437
Clymer	9,260	13,965	229,812	10,800	240,612	607	557	234	216	211	8	462
Ellery	19,598½	10,800	546,627	31,950	578,577	972	893	348	355	327	12	549
Ellicott	9,951¼	9,298½	750,119	333,276	1,083,395	1,971	1,964	715	757	409	19	1,554
Ellington	14,171	8,675	340,556	64,250	404,806	972	958	374	407	364	11	941
French Creek	6,668½	16,448½	190,516	4,025	194,541	400	366	153	153	146	7	316
Gerry	11,917	9,837	285,065	21,010	306,075	635	623	242	253	211	8	489
Hanover	21,011	11,736¾	952,119	137,450	1,089,569	2.057	2,044	798	815	641	17	1,590
Harmony	28,728	25,805	821,779	117,580	939,359	1,742	1,701	713	707	621	26	1,405
Kiantone	6,040	4,234	208,446	85,075	293,521	257	233	96	96	91	5	205
Mina	10,103½	12,786	245,841	9,475	255,316	522	514	199	200	192	11	500
Poland	8,534½	13,386	252,535	11,100	263,635	702	623	251	245	206	10	548
Pomfret	21,588½	10,941¼	1,631,057	320,540	1,951,597	4,754	4,403	1,627	1,841	1046	20	3,063
Portland	15,330½	5,504	507,222	45,489	552,711	978	958	136	373	303	11	652
Ripley	16,696	12,630	646,470	82,600	729,070	852	851	319	331	281	12	699
Sheridan	15,559½	6,719	630,235	54,300	684,535	763	828	318	335	295	9	582
Sherman	11,499	12,638	305,409	33,600	339,009	652	662	268	274	240	9	441
Stockton	16,028	12,900½	439,836	33,950	473,786	869	819	343	350	319	12	621
Villenova	12,759¾	9,521	323,081	36,150	359,231	721	692	290	315	264	12	493
Westfield	18,194½	10,272	1,082,696	164,860	1,247,556	1,675	1,663	646	569	582	17	1,126
Total	360,110	294,145½	12,929,150	1,889,940	14,819,090	27,101	26,279	9,988	10,566	8,528	307	20,091

Names of Towns.	Live Stock.					Agricultural Products.							Domestic Cloths, in Yards.
						Bush. of Grain.		Tons of Hay.	Bushels of Potatoes.	Bushels of Apples.	Dairy Products.		
	Horses.	Working Oxen and Calves.	Cows.	Sheep.	Swine.	Winter.	Spring.				Pounds of Butter.	Pounds of Cheese.	
Arkwright	391	1,376	1,348	2,174	647	545	37,129½	2,906	10,188	11,252	99,029	120,515	1,784
Busti	639	2,040	1,925	5,748	863	735	75,708	5,810	15,196	20,589	195,463	51,780	1,427
Carrol	266	1,039	534	1,675	380	1,480	26,429	2,542	7,957	7,219	50,460	4,700	1,765
Charlotte	349	1,517	1,429	1,001	652	90	46,740	3,339	10,685	10,154	139,761	70,280	781
Chautauqua	861	2,391	2,799	4,601	1,539	1,456	71,190	8,250	13,703	26,196	279,574	115,272	726
Cherry Creek	375	1,367	981	2,077	571	587½	40,243½	2,736	9,088	12,448	10,782	20,580	2,612
Clymer	303	1,230	1,012	1,624	483	885½	28,579¼	2,512	12,272	3,915	95,669	16,741	1,931¾
Ellery	784	1,962	2,033	3,813	1,743	5,625	86,337¾	4,985	13,091	32,104	173,569	119,439	1,855
Ellicott	413	954	725	3,832	462	1,625½	41,907½	2,697	11,274	12,454	64,694	12,884	649½
Ellington	578	1,648	1,168	4,895	782	289	73,293½	3,553	13,574	22,387	144,717	15,155	1,693
French Creek	246	788	551	4,614	292	327	18,505½	1,745	6,038	2,226	58,050	2,218	1,002
Gerry	430	1,381	1,155	3,323	568	282	42,158½	3,147	8,475	15,567	103,685	61,220	827
Hanover	898	2,599	2,365	4,659	1,664	8,235	66.542¼	6,541½	17,706	30,058	229,772	58,300	2,201
Harmony	1,076	3,710	3,312	5,845	1,741	2,978	96,779¼	8,586	27,642	28,352	332,495	83,172	3,941
Kiantone	168	657	613	1,560	235	387	20,478	1,914	3,532	5,742	56,530	21,400	136
Mina	331	1,548	1,002	2,101	456	38	28,206½	3,246	9,916	6,007	111,065	10,610	988
Poland	296	1,196	727	1,941	493	674	32,801	2,921	11,029	7,098	71,910	6,375	1,008
Pomfret	1,139	2,073	2,748	3,785	1,896	6,936	64,938	6,759½	12,870	19,037	175,368	91,509	848
Portland	510	1,427	1,117	5,204	883	6,872½	49,098	4,742½	7,411	12,671	131,836	8,425	995
Ripley	605	2,069	1,257	8,740	976	10,058	55,968½	5,371	7,443	9,016	122,800	17,425	1,221
Sheridan	481	1,690	1,035	4,331	863	10,010	42,258¼	4,332	8,288	22,202	105,786	54,706	1,619
Sherman	409	1,218	1,260	2,135	509	280	32,277	3,614½	11,554	3,243	143,745	14,100	1,497
Stockton	457	1,398	2 299	1,097	790	435	47,402	4,418½	11,243	24,300	212,926	179,472	1,245
Villenova	457	1.368	1,451	3,285	919	325½	44,113	3,492	14,772	14,529	168,087	36,509	2,990¾
Westfield	585	2,198	1,200	6,094	698	7,901	48,875	5,511½	7,504	9,349	112,064	5,214	515
Total	13,047	40,844	36,046	90,154	21,105	69,157½	1,217,958¾	105,672	282,451	368,115	3,389,837	1,198,361	35,258

CHEMUNG COUNTY.

This county was formed from Tioga, March 29, 1836.[1] A portion of Schuyler was taken off in 1854. It lies upon the s. border of the State, is centrally distant 158 mi. from Albany, and contains 406 sq. mi. Its surface is principally a hilly upland broken by the deep ravines of the streams. The highest points are 400 to 600 ft. above the valleys and 1300 to 1500 ft. above tide. The ridges extend in a general N. and S. direction, and have steep declivities and broad and rolling summits. A deep valley, extending s. from Seneca Lake, divides the highlands into two general systems, and forms an easy communication between the Susquehanna Valley and the central portions of the State. Chemung River flows s. E. through the s. part of the co. and cuts the ridges diagonally. Wide alluvial flats, bordered by steep hillsides, extend along nearly its whole course. Catharine Creek flows N. through the central valley and discharges its waters into Seneca Lake. The other principal streams, all tributaries of the Chemung, are Post, Sing Sing,[2] Newtown, Goldsmith, Wynkoops,[3] and Cayuta Creeks from the N., and Hendy and Seely Creeks from the s. The valleys of these streams are generally narrow, and are bordered by steep hills. The valleys of the smaller streams are mere ravines and gulleys.

The principal rocks in the co. belong to the shales and sandstones of the Chemung group. In the N. part the rocks of the Portage group are exposed in the ravines. The sandstone is quarried in several places, and furnishes a good quality of stone for building and flagging. Bog iron ore and marl are found to a limited extent. The soil is a gravelly and sandy loam, intermixed in some places with clay. The valleys are covered with a deep, rich alluvium. The highlands are best adapted to pasturage. The people are principally engaged in agriculture. Until within a few years, lumbering has formed a leading pursuit;[4] but since the disappearance of the fine forests this business has been mostly superseded by stock and wool growing and dairying. Since the completion of the railroads and canals, commerce and manufactures have received considerable attention, although they are still subordinate to the agricultural interests of the co.

The county seat is located at Elmira, upon Chemung River.[5] The courthouse and jail are located near the center of the village, E. of the canal. The jail is poorly arranged, and in construction it meets neither the requirements of humanity nor the law. The average number of inmates is 12, kept at a cost of $2 50 per week each. The poorhouse is located upon a farm of 180 acres in the town of Horseheads, on the line of Erin. The average number of inmates is 70, supported at a cost of $ .80 each per week. The farm yields a revenue of $1000.[6] The Chemung Canal extends s. from Seneca Lake through the central valley to Chemung River at Elmira, forming a direct connection with the great chain of internal water navigation of the State. A navigable feeder from Corning, Steuben co., forms a junction with the canal on the summit level at Horseheads Village. Junction Canal extends several mi. along the Chemung, affording navigation at points where the river is obstructed by rapids and narrows. The New York & Erie R. R. extends along Chemung River through Chemung, Southport, Elmira, and Big Flats. The Chemung R. R. extends N. from Elmira through Horseheads and Veteran. The Williamsport & Elmira R. R. extends s. from Elmira through Southport into Penn., forming a direct line to Philadelphia.

One daily and 2 weekly newspapers are published in this co.[7]

---

[1] Name derived from the principal river, signifies "Big horn," or "Horn in the water." It is called by the Delawares Con-on-gue, a word of the same signification. These names were applied to the stream in consequence of numbers of immense deers' horns having from time to time been discovered in the water. In his "Views of Elmira," Solomon Southwick says that the Indian name of the Chemung was Con-e-wa-wa, signifying "a head on a pole."

[2] Named from John Sing Sing, a friendly Indian.

[3] Named from Wm. Wynkoop, an early settler.

[4] For many years 10,000,000 ft. of pine lumber were floated down the Chemung and Susquehanna from Elmira annually.

[5] Upon the erection of Tioga co. Elmira, then "Newtown," was made half-shire; and upon the erection of Chemung co. in 1836 it was designated as the county seat, and the old co. buildings were taken for the use of the new co. The first co. officers were

Joseph L. Darling, First Judge; Andrew K. Gregg, District Attorney; Isaac Baldwin, County Clerk; Albert A. Beckwith, Sheriff; and Lyman Covill, Surrogate.

[6] The poorhouse is entirely inadequate for the comfort or health of the inmates. Many insane persons are confined, without proper care or medical attendance. No school is kept, but at proper age the children are bound out.

[7] The Telegraph, the first paper published in the co., was established at "Newtown" (now Elmira,) by Prindle & Murphy at an early period. In 1816 it was issued as
The Vidette by Prindle & Murphy, and subsequently by Wm. Murphy.
The Investigator was commenced at Elmira, in 1820, by Job Smith. In 1822 its name was changed to
The Tioga Register, and in 1828 to
The Elmira Gazette, and its publication was continued

218

In 1779, Gen. Sullivan and his army entered the co. from the s. by the way of Chemung River. Below "*Newtown Point*" (now Elmira) he encamped and threw up a breastwork, which was afterward called Fort Sullivan. At this point he first encountered the Indians and tories in force, and on the 29th of Aug. a battle ensued. The Indians were commanded by Brant, and the tories were led by Cols. Butler and Johnson. After an obstinate engagement of two hours, the enemy gave way at all points and fled, and no more resistance was offered to the advance of the American army. The first settlements were made from 1787 to 1790, by immigrants from Penn., who had accompanied Sullivan in his expedition. They located principally in the valley of the Chemung, at Elmira, Southport, and Big Flats. Soon after, settlements were made at Catlin and Veteran, by immigrants from Conn.; at Erin, by Dutch and Scotch from N. J. and Del.; and at Chemung, by immigrants from Lancaster co., Penn.[1] The portion of the co. lying s. of the Chemung River was included in a royal grant made previous to 1775. The remaining parts of the co. were included in the Watkins and Flint purchase.

BALDWIN[2]—was formed from Chemung, April 7, 1856. It lies s. e. of the center of the co., and a narrow strip extends to the e. border. Its surface is a hilly upland, broken by the deep valleys of Baldwin and Wynkoops Creeks. The soil upon the hills is a clayey and shaly loam underlaid by hardpan, and in the valleys a gravelly loam. **Hammonds Corners** (North Chemung p. o.) contains a church, tannery, and 18 houses. Henry Sice made the first settlement, a little n. of the village, in 1813, and Warren and Charles Granger settled at the village in 1814.[3] The only church in town (Union) was formed in 1852, by Dr. Murdock, the first preacher.

BIG FLATS—was formed from Elmira, April 16, 1822. It lies upon the w. border of the co., s. of the center. Its surface consists of a broken upland in the n. and s., separated by a wide intervale or flat, which extends n. e. from the Chemung through the center and gives name to the town. Chemung River receives several small tributaries from the n., the principal of which is Sing Sing Creek. The soil is a slaty loam upon the hills, and a productive gravelly loam in the valleys. Tobacco is raised in considerable quantities upon the flats.[4] **Big Flats,** (p. v.,) situated in the valley near the w. border of the town, is a station upon the N. Y. & Erie R. R. Pop. 180. The first settlement was made by Christian Miner, from Penn., in 1787.[5] The first church (Bap.) was formed in 1807. Rev. Roswell Goff was the first preacher.[6]

CATLIN—was formed from Catharine, Schuyler co., April 16, 1823. It is the n. w. corner town of the co. The surface is a hilly upland, the highest summits being 200 to 400 feet above the valleys. The principal streams are Post and Sing Sing Creeks and Hubbards Run. The soil is chiefly a gravelly loam, and is best adapted to grazing. There is no village or church in town.

---

by Mr. Smith until 1831. It was successively issued by Brinton Paine, Cyrus Pratt, Pratt & Beardsley, Mason & Rhodes, Geo. W. Mason, and Wm. C. Mason, until 1857, when it passed into the hands of S. C. Taber, by whom it is still published.

The Elmira Republican was commenced in 1820, and in 1828 it was changed to

The Elmira Whig, and published by James Durham. In 1829 it was changed again to

The Elmira Republican, and issued by C. Morgan. It was soon after called

The Elmira Republican and Canal Advertiser. In 1831 it passed into the hands of John Duffy, and its name was changed back to

The Elmira Republican. It was successively issued by Birdsall & Huntley, Ransom & Birdsall, Polly & Carter, Polly & Cook, Polly & Huntley, S. B. & G. C. Fairman, G. C. Fairman, Fairman & Baldwin, Baldwin & Dumas, and ——— Calhoun, until 1857, when it was discontinued.

The Elmira Daily Republican was issued a short time in 1846.

The Daily Republican was issued from the Republican office from the fall of 1851 to 1855.

The Elmira Advertiser was commenced in 1853 by Fairman Brothers. In 1856 F. A. De Voe became interested in the publication, and the paper is still issued by Fairman & De Voe.

The Elmira Daily Advertiser was commenced simultaneously with the weekly, and is still issued, by the same publishers.

The Elmira Daily Democrat was issued a short time in 1851 by J. Taylor & S. C. Taber.

The Chemung Patriot was published in 1837 at Horseheads by J. T. Bradt.

The Philosopher was commenced at Horseheads, April 7, 1855, by Sam'l C. Taber, and was continued until 1857, when it was merged in *The Elmira Gazette.*

The Daily Press was commenced in 1859, by Dumas, Van Gelder & Paine, its present publishers.

The Temperance Gem (mo.) was published at Elmira about 1850.

[1] Louis Philippe, the Duke de Nemours, and the Duke de Berri, visited Elmira in 1797, having traveled on foot to that place from Canandaigua, a distance of 70 mi. They went down the river to Harrisburgh upon an ark.

[2] Named from Baldwin Creek, which received its name from Isaac, Walter, and Thomas Baldwin, brothers, who settled at an early period at the mouth of the creek. It was formerly called Butlers Creek. They were attached to Gen. Sullivan's expedition against the Indians in 1778–79, and Walter was wounded at the battle of Newtown.

[3] The first child born was Simeon Hammond, and the first death was that of Thos. Wheeler, killed by the fall of a tree. The first school was taught by Polly Blandin, a little n. of the village. D. R. Harris kept the first inn, and Miles Covel the first store, n. of the village.

[4] In 1850, Sanford Elmore, from Conn., commenced the cultivation of tobacco in this town, and it has since become a staple product. In 1858 nearly 1000 acres were devoted to it, and 250 tons of the Conn. seed leaf were produced.

[5] Caleb Gardner and Henry Starell, from Penn., settled on the river below Miner in the same or the next year. Geo. Gardner settled at the village in 1788, Clark Winans on the river in 1789, and John Winters, Jesse and Joel Rowley, and Geo. Gardner, jr., all from Penn., in 1790. The first birth was that of Christian Miner, jr., in 1790; the first marriage, that of Wm. Applegate and Catharine Miner; and the first death, that of T. Dolson. Cornelius McGinnis taught the first school, near the village; John Hay kept the first store, and Capt. Geo. Gardner the first inn at the village. The first gristmill was erected by Robt. Miller, e. of the village.

[6] The census reports 4 churches; Bap., F. W. Bap., Presb., and M. E.

Catlin Center and **Post Creek** are p. offices. The first settlers were John Martin, from Tompkins co., and Aaron Davenport, from N. J., who located in the s. w. corner of the town.[1]

CHEMUNG—was formed Feb. 28, 1789. Elmira was taken off in 1792, Erin in 1822, and Baldwin in 1856. It is the s. E. corner town of the co. Its surface is a hilly upland broken by deep and narrow valleys. Chemung River flows s. E. through the s. part. Wynkoops Creek flows s. through near the center, in a deep valley bordered by steep hillsides. The soil on the uplands is a gravelly loam, and in the valleys gravel mixed with alluvium. Broomcorn and tobacco are largely cultivated. **Breckville**, (Chemung p. o.,) on Chemung River, contains a church and 57 dwellings. It is a station on the N. Y. & Erie R. R. **Chemung Center** and **Baldwin** are p. offices. The first settlement was made at Breckville, in 1788, by Elijah Breck, Capt. Daniel McDowell, and William Wynkoop,—the first two from Penn.[2] The first church (Bap.) was formed in 1790, by Rev. Roswell Goff.[3]

ELMIRA—was formed from Chemung, as "*Newtown*," April 10, 1792, and its name was changed April 6, 1808. Catharine, Schuyler co., was taken off in 1798, Big Flats and Southport in 1822, and Horseheads in 1854. It is situated s. of the center of the co. Ranges of hills occupy the E. and w. borders, and a wide valley extends through the center. The declivities of the hills are generally steep, and their summits are 400 to 600 ft. above the valleys. The principal streams are Chemung River, forming the s. boundary, and Newtown and Goldsmiths Creeks. The soil upon the uplands is a gravelly loam, and in the valleys a productive, sandy loam. **Elmira** (p. v.) is situated upon the Chemung, near the center of the s. border of the town. Upon an eminence 2½ mi. E. of Elmira Village is the remains of an ancient fortification. It is protected on one side by the river, and on the other by a deep ravine. An embankment 200 feet long, 14 feet wide, and 3½ feet high still extends along the rear of the fortification, and upon it large trees grew when the whites first occupied the country. It was incorp. as "*Newtown*" March 3, 1815, and its name was changed April 21, 1828. The people are largely engaged in manufacturing[4] and in commercial pursuits,[5] for which the location of the place is admirably adapted. Besides the co. buildings, the village contains 3 banks, 1 daily and 2 weekly newspaper offices, 8 churches, and a large number of fine and commodious commercial buildings. It is also the seat of the Elmira Female College,[6] the Elmira Seminary,[7] the Elmira Academy,[8] and a large water-cure establishment.[9] The public schools are graded and are in a flourishing condition. Pop. 8,308, of which 7,173 are within the limits of the town, and 1,135 in the town of Southport. The first settlement was made by Col. John Hendy and Christian Loop, who located on the present site of the village in 1788.[10] Col. Hendy

---

[1] Among the other early settlers were N. Swick, Homer Tupper, Edward Beebe, Jacob Bucher, Alanson Owen, John Woolsey, and J. M. Barker, who located in the s. part. Jacob Bucher kept the first inn on Post Creek, and —— Ostrander erected the first saw and gristmills on the same stream. Reuben Beebe died in the town in 1854, at the age of 105. His widow, Hannah Beebe, was living, 1858, at the age of 105. Mr. Beebe served as a soldier in the Revolutionary army.

[2] The first marriage was that of Guy Maxwell and Nellie Wynkoop, and the first death, that of Wm. Bosworth. The first inn was kept by Wm. Wynkoop, on Wynkoops Creek, and the first store by Elijah Breck, at Breckville. Epinetus Owen erected the first gristmill, on Wynkoops Creek. Wm. Wynkoop was from Ulster co., and settled at the mouth of the creek bearing his name. Samuel Wallace, the first school teacher, was killed by the Indians.

[3] The census reports 4 churches; 2 Union, Bap., and Cong.

[4] The principal of the manufacturing establishments are as follows:—The Elmira Woolen Manufactory, employing 64 hands, and turning out 230,000 yds. of cloth annually; the Phœnix Furnace Iron Works gives employment to 40 men; the Elmira Ax Factory to 25 men; and a barrel manufactory to 50 men. Besides these, there are several flouring mills, a planing mill, and other establishments.

[5] An immense lumber trade is still carried on by means of the Chemung River and Canal. The W. & E. R. R. opens a direct communication with the coal mines of Penn., and a large coal-trade is rapidly springing up. The village is also the center of an extensive trade.

[6] This institution was chartered in 1855, with all the powers and privileges granted to the other colleges in the State. It extends to woman, opportunities for the highest culture. It is beautifully situated upon an eminence a little N. w. of the village. The building is 230 feet long, with an octagonal center 70 feet in diameter and 4 stories high, flanked by 2 wings, each 80 by 50 feet, and 3 stories high, all erected at a cost of $80,000. The catalogue of 1858 reports 188 pupils in attendance.

[7] The Elmira Seminary for young ladies, a private institution, has been in successful operation for 11 years, under the management of Miss C. Thurston. The catalogue of 1857 reports 205 pupils.

[8] The Elmira Academy, once incorp., is now a private institution. It has an endowment of $10,000. New buildings for the school are in process of erection. In 1858, 262 pupils were reported.

[9] The Elmira Water-Cure is situated on the hill 1 mi. E. of the village, commanding an extensive view of the valley and surrounding country. It contains accommodations for 110 patients.

[10] Among the early settlers were John Konkle, James Cameron, Wm. Seeley, Nathaniel Seeley, John Muller, Caleb Baker, —— Marks, Thomas Hendy, and John J. AcMody. Cornelius Low kept the first inn, in 1791, at *Newtown Point*, and Cyrus Hallenbeck the first store, at about the same time and place. The first gristmill was built by Wm. Dunn and Brinton Parne, at the village in 1791, and the first sawmill, wool carding and cloth dressing mill by Gen. Matthew Carpenter, on the site of the present woolen factory. The following account of the first birth in town was given in the N. Y. Commercial Advertiser:—"One Saturday afternoon, about 4 o'clock, in the summer of 1788, while Col. John Hendy was working on his log house, a man and woman, both on horseback, emerged from the Indian pathway and crossed the Newtown Creek to his land. The man rode before, with a basket on each side of his horse, and a child in each basket, while the woman brought up the rear, having on her nag the goods and chattels of the family; for they were man and wife. The husband rode up to Col. H., inquiring with much anxiety if there was a doctor to be found in the vicinity. 'What is the matter?' said the veteran. 'My wife has got hurt by the stumbling of her horse, and wants a doctor as soon as possible,' was the reply. 'That is very unfortunate,' said the Col., 'for there is no doctor in this wilderness.' He had no shelter nor resting place to offer them, save the ground, the pine trees, and the canopy of heaven. They rode on a few rods, and stopped—for they were obliged to stop—under the best shelter they could find. On Sunday morning Col. Hendy met the man in the woods, near the spot where they had conversed before, and, inquiring how his wife was, was answered, 'She is as well as could be expected.' The Col. did not think again of the traveler till Monday, when he sent his son to look after them. The boy returned with the intelligence that they were getting ready to start. 'But how is the woman, my boy?' said he. 'The

was the pioneer in the valley of the Chemung, and one of the most prominent of the early settlers. The first preacher (Presb.) was Rev. Nathan Culver.[1]

ERIN—was formed from Chemung, March 29, 1822. A part of Van Etten was taken off in 1854. It extends from near the center of the co. to the N. border. Its surface is a hilly upland broken by the deep and narrow valleys of the streams. The principal streams are Wynkoops, Bakers, Baldwins, and Newtown Creeks. Upon Bakers Creek, in the s. part of the town, is a fine sulphur spring. The soil is a medium quality of gravelly loam, and is best adapted to grazing. Considerable lumber is still manufactured, little more than one-third of the surface being under improvement. **Erin, South Erin,** and **State Road** are p. offices. The first settlement was made in 1817, by Robert Park and John Bonfield.[2] There are 2 churches in town; Presb. and M. E.

HORSEHEADS[3]—was formed from Elmira, Feb. 17, 1854. It is an interior town, lying near the center of the co. The surface is rolling and level in the w. and hilly in the E. The summit level of the Chemung Canal at Horseheads Village is 443 ft. above Seneca Lake, and the summits of the hills are 200 to 400 feet higher. Its principal streams are Newtown Creek and its branches. The soil is generally a good quality of gravelly loam. Considerable attention is paid to raising tobacco, and, in 1857, 1000 acres were devoted to this crop. **Horseheads** (p. v.) was incorp. May 15, 1837, as "*Fairport*," and its name was changed April 18, 1845. It contains 2 steam flouring mills, a plaster mill, a gang sawmill, and 3 churches. Pop. 1000. The Chemung navigable feeder from Corning intersects the canal at this place. **Breesport** (p. v.) contains 2 churches and 18 dwellings. The first settlement was made at Horseheads in 1788, by Nathan Huntington.[4] The first church (Presb.) was formed by Rev. Daniel Thatcher; the first settled minister was Rev. Ethan Pratt.[5]

SOUTHPORT—was formed from Elmira, April 16, 1822. It is the s. w. corner town of the co. Its surface is mostly a hilly upland broken by the deep valleys of the streams. Chemung River, forming most of the N. boundary, is bordered by wide, fertile alluvial flats. Seely Creek, the principal stream, receives as tributaries South, Bird, and Mud Lick Creeks; Hendy Creek flows along the N. border. The soil upon the hills is a slaty loam, and in the valleys a fine quality of gravelly loam. **Wellsburgh,** (p. v.,) on the Chemung, in the s. E. corner of the town, contains 2 churches and several mills and manufacturing establishments. It is a station on the N.Y. & E. R. R. Pop. 365. **Southport** (p. v.) contains 2 churches, 2 mills, a woolen factory, and 44 houses. **Webbs Mills** (p. o.) is a hamlet, and **Seely Creek** is a p. o. The 3d ward of **Elmira,** containing a pop. of 1135, is on the s. bank of the Chemung in this town. The first settlement at Wellsburgh was made by Green Bentley in 1788 and Abner and Henry Wells in 1789. Abraham Miller located at Southport in 1789.[6] The first church (Bap.) was formed at Wellsburgh, in 1790; Rev. Roswell Goff was the first preacher.[7] On an eminence known as Fort Hill, near the Chemung, in the w. part, are the remains of an ancient fortification, supposed to have been French.

VAN ETTEN—named from James B. Van Etten—was formed from Erin and Cayuta, April 17, 1854. It is the N. E. corner town of the co. Its surface is a hilly upland. Cayuta Creek flows

---

woman, eh? oh, the woman has got a baby; and I guess she wants another basket to put it in.'" The child whose birth is told above was Clark Winans, jr. The place was surveyed, in 1788, by Jas. Clinton, Gen. John Hathom, and John Cantine Conis; and the first lands were sold at 18 pence per acre. In 1790, a council with the Indians was held under a tree on Lake St., just E. of the present site of the courthouse. About 1200 Indians were present. Nathaniel Seely, the first patentee, of Elmira Village, sold to Moses De Witt, who sold to —— White; and in 1794 White sold to Guy Maxwell and Saml. Hepburn.

[1] The census reports 8 churches; 2 M. E., Bap., Cong., Presb., Af. M. E., Prot. E., and R. C.

[2] Among the other early settlers were Jesse L. White, Isaac Shoemaker, Alexander and John McKay, Thomas Baker, Wm. and Robert Stewart, John and James Hallenbeck, B. Sperry, Thomas Van Houton, Philip Thomas, J. Boyn, Robert McDowell and his son Barnum, and Andrew Austin, Joseph, Daniel, and Samuel Vaughn. The first death was that of Mrs. Thomas Baker. The first school was kept on Newtown Creek, and the first sawmill was erected at the same place by J. and J. McMillen.

[3] This name was derived from the following incident. While Gen. Sullivan's army was encamped at this place, some 30 or 40 worn-out horses were shot. The Indians afterward gathered the heads and arranged them on the sides of the path, and the locality became known as the Horseheads.

[4] John Breese (from N. J.) settled at the same place in 1789, and Jonathan S. Concklin, Nathaniel Huntington, Asa Guildersleve, and a family named Gilbert, in 1791. Soon after, a company from Orange co., among whom were James, Ebenezer, and John Sayre, purchased a tract of 1400 acres, covering the site of the village, and settled on it. The first child born was Susanna Concklin, in 1792; the first marriage, that of Wm. Dunn and Mary Sayre; and the first death, that of Susanna Concklin. Amelia Parkhurst taught the first school at the village. Vincent Concklin kept the first inn, in 1822, and Westlick & Dunn the first store. The first gristmill was erected by Lewis Breese, E. of the village.

[5] The census reports 5 churches; 2 M. E., 2 Bap., and 1 Presb.

[6] Col. Abraham Miller was from Penn. He served with distinction as a captain in the army of the Revolution, and was appointed *First Judge* of Tioga co. by Gov. Geo. Clinton, in 1791. The first birth was that of Eunice Kelsey, and the first death, that of Stephen Kent. The first school was taught by Caleb Baker; the first inn was kept by Wm. Baldwin, and the first store by Wm. and Henry Wells, on the river at Wellsburgh. The first sawmill was erected by Col. Abraham Miller, on a branch of Seely Creek; the first gristmills were erected by David Griswold and Solomon Bovier, and the first factory by Charles Evans, at Southport.

[7] The census reports 5 churches; 2 Bap., 2 M. E., and Presb.

S. E. through near the center, and receives as tributaries Jackson and Langfords Creeks from the N. and Baker Creek from the S. The soil on the hills is a clay loam, and in the valleys a gravelly loam. **Van Ettenville** (p. v.) contains 3 churches and 20 dwellings; **Cayuta** is a p. o. The first settlements[1] were made along the valley of Cayuta Creek in 1795, by Alexander and Benjamin Ennis, Peter, Jacob, Emanuel, and Isaac Swartwood, from N. J. The first church (Bap.) was formed by Rev. Ebenezer Jayne, the first settled preacher.[2]

VETERAN—was formed from Catharine, April 16, 1823. It lies on the N. line of the co., W. of the center. The surface is principally a hilly upland. Catharine Creek flows N. along the W. border, affording an abundance of waterpower.[3] The other streams are Newtown and Beardsley Creeks. The soil is a clay and gravelly loam of good quality. **Millport** (p. v.) contains 2 churches, flouring and saw mills, and various manufacturing establishments. Pop. 706. **Sullivanville,** (p. v.,) in the S. part of the town, contains a church and 155 inhabitants. **Veteran** and **Pine Valley** are p. offices. The first settlements were made at about the commencement of the century,—in the N. part of the town by immigrants from Conn., and in the S. part by immigrants from Penn.[4] The first church (M. E.) was formed in 1817.[5]

Acres of Land, Valuation, Population, Dwellings, Families, Freeholders, Schools, Live Stock, Agricultural Products, and Domestic Manufactures, of Chemung County.

Names of Towns.	Acres of Land.		Valuation of 1858.			Population.		No. of Dwellings.	No. of Families.	Freeholders.	Schools.	
	Improved.	Unimproved.	Real Estate.	Personal Property.	Total.	Males.	Females.				No. of Districts.	Children taught.
Baldwin*											7	427
Big Flats	12,616½	11,125	641,430	54,576	696,006	929	924	342	353	203	8	655
Catlin	11,670	9,316	276,084	6,064	282,148	759	759	295	300	245	13	651
Chemung	19,864	20,364	561,100	54,600	615,700	1,437	1,348	493	498	386	14	929
Elmira	10,094¾	6,425	2,130,801	869,850	3,000,651	4,137	4,349	1,463	1,589	1,023	11	2,865
Erin	9,638	18,169	141,873	3,227	145,100	604	586	229	231	232	10	524
Horseheads	12,490	7,840	707,870	81,850	789,720	1,356	1,292	430	467	314	9	1,037
Southport	15,831½	16,990¼	903,544	34,950	938,494	2,285	2,194	814	869	578	18	1,833
Van Etten	12,689	12,083	102,448	2,650	105,098	781	741	277	281	268	12	659
Veteran	15,326	8,073	482,471	24,600	507,071	1,423	1,384	574	568	416	14	1,061
Total	120,219¾	110,385¼	5,947,621	1,132,367	7,079,988	13,711	13,577	4,857	5,156	3,665	116	10,621

Names of Towns.	Live Stock.					Agricultural Products.							Domestic Manufactures, in Yards.
						Bush. of Grain.		Tons of Hay.	Bushels of Potatoes.	Bushels of Apples.	Dairy Products.		
	Horses.	Working Oxen and Calves.	Cows.	Sheep.	Swine.	Winter.	Spring.				Pounds of Butter.	Pounds of Cheese.	
Baldwin*													
Big Flats	549	1,422	959	3,009	1,215	13,867½	132,203	2,654	12,101	16,771	86,702	570	252
Catlin	503	1,002	694	3,530	809	4,863	83,270	2,031	9,225	5,503	65,720		1,333
Chemung	674	1,961	2,183	2,482	1,785	8,583	117,986½	4,856	15,189	19,511	209,735	560	1,128
Elmira	627	767	938	368	1,019	6,778	75,813½	2,461	34,842	6,870	79,767	350	280
Erin	289	1,025	845	1,632	676	2,697	51,960	1,898	8,947	8,322	72,140		1,587
Horseheads	570	1,165	995	2,496	1,232	10,873½	120,262½	2,825½	13,741	13,916	108,260	2,770	213
Southport	729	1,473	1,220	1,408	1,542	9,813	95,526½	3,391	15,625	9,513	118,899		192
Van Etten	348	1,076	684	2,065	589	2,708	41,055	1,868	6,936	8,964	57,870		1,370
Veteran	567	1,318	1,172	4,374	986	7,129	109,430	2,956½	14,685	17,994	125,552	3,611	658
Total	4,856	11,209	9,690	21,364	9,853	67,312	827,507	24,941	131,291	107,364	924,645	7,861	7,013

* Formed since 1855.

---

1 James Van Etten, John and David Hill, Isaac and Levi Decker, Sam'l, James, Daniel, and Joshua Westbrook, John Lattimore, —— Johnson, and —— Crammer, all from Delaware River, settled on the Cayuta Flats, at and near Van Ettenville, from 1795 to 1800. Harmon White, (from Litchfield, Conn.,) David Jayne and Gabriel Ogden, (from N. J.,) settled, in 1802, on a branch of Cayuta Creek. Most of these persons served as soldiers during the Revolution. James Van Etten and Isaac Decker were wounded by musket balls, which they carried to their graves. Flanders & Skaats kept the first store, at Van Ettenville; Isaac Swartwood erected the first gristmill, in 1803; Jacob Swartwood opened the first inn, in 1801. His old sign (still hanging) reads as follows:—

"You jolly topers, as you pass by,
Call in and drink; for I know you are dry!
And if you have but half a crown,
You are welcome to my jug, sit down!
Entertainment
by
J. Swartwood."

2 The census reports 3 churches; Bap., F. W. Bap., and M. E.

3 In the summer of 1857 a sudden and destructive flood occurred upon this stream, which swept away every dam upon it, and every lock on the canal from Horseheads to Seneca Lake. The whole valley was flooded; and at Millport and other places the people were obliged to flee for their lives.

4 Among the early settlers were E. Mallary and son, Eli and David Banks, and families named Meeker, Baldwin, and Parsons, from Conn.; Theodore Valleau, D. Shaffer, N. Botsford, and B. Lockesby, from Penn. Daniel Parsons kept the first inn, on the middle road, and E. Crandell the first store, at Millport. The first sawmill was erected by G. Bennett, on Catharine Creek, below Millport.

5 The census reports 3 churches; 2 M. E. and Presb.

CHENANGO COUNTY.

This county was formed from Herkimer and Tioga, March 15, 1798. Sangerfield (Oneida co.) was taken off in 1804, and Madison co. in 1806. It is an interior co., lying s. e. of the center of the State; is centrally distant 94 mi. from Albany, and contains 898 sq. mi. Its surface is a hilly upland, broken by the deep ravines of the streams. The highlands consist of two principal ridges, extending n. and s.,—the first lying between Unadilla and Chenango Rivers, and the second between the Chenango and Otselic. These ridges are subdivided by numerous parallel and lateral valleys, and their declivities are often too steep for profitable cultivation. The summits are broad and rolling, and of nearly uniform elevation throughout the co.; and the highest points are 600 to 800 feet above the principal valleys.

Susquehanna River flows s. w. through the s. e. corner, receiving from the n. the Unadilla, which forms the greater part of the e. boundary of the co. The principal branches of the Unadilla and Susquehanna are Beaver Creek, Shawler, Great, Kent, and Kelsey Brooks. Chenango River flows in a generally southerly direction from the n. border of the co. to near the center, and thence s. w. to the s. w. corner. It receives from the e. Handsome Eddy, Padgets, and Pages Brooks, and from the w. Canasawacta, Fly-Meadow, Ludlow, and Genegantslet Creeks, and Pleasant, Fly, Cold, and Mill Brooks. Otselic River flows s. w through the n. w. corner, receiving from the e. Middletown Brook and Brackel Creek, and from the w. Manns, Buck, and Ashbel Brooks and Mud Creek. In basins among the hills, far above the valleys, are numerous small ponds. The valleys of the Susquehanna and Chenango are among the finest in the State. They consist generally of a fertile and highly cultivated intervales of an average width of about 1 mi., usually bordered by steep and finely wooded hillsides. All the valleys of the co. seem to have been formed by the action of great currents of water, which have plowed deep furrows in the gently rolling region which probably once formed the general face of the country.

The lowest rocks in the co., appearing upon the n. border, belong to the Hamilton group. Successively above these toward the s. appear the Tully limestone, Genesee slate, the Portage, Chemung, and Catskill groups. The sandstone of the Portage group furnishes a good material for building and flagging. Several quarries have been opened along the Chenango Valley between Greene and Oxford. A quarry of the same stone a little below Oxford furnishes grindstones and whetstones. The rock which crowns the summits of the s. hills is the red sandstone of the Chemung group. The soils are almost entirely derived from the disintegration of the rocks. In a few localities is found a very limited amount of drift. Upon the hills the soil is principally a shaly loam, and in the valleys a fine quality of productive alluvium.

The co. is almost exclusively agricultural. Dairying is the leading pursuit, and is gradually gaining upon all the other branches of agriculture. Stock and wool growing are carried on to some extent. Grain is produced, though not in sufficient quantities for the wants of the people. Hops are cultivated to some extent along the river valleys.

The co. seat is located at Norwich.[1] The courthouse is a fine stone building, situated near the center of the village, fronting the public park.[2] It is built in the Grecian style of architecture, with a colonnade in front, supported by Corinthian columns. The jail is a stone building, contiguous to the courthouse. The clerk's office is a fireproof brick building, upon the courthouse lot. The poorhouse is situated upon a farm of 170 acres in Preston, 6 mi. w. of the courthouse. The average number of inmates is 90, supported at a weekly cost of 56 cts. each. The farm yields a revenue of $800. The house is poor and dilapidated, and the accommodations for the inmates are extremely poor. A school is taught 6 months in the year.

---

[1] The co. at first had half-shires, the courts being held alternately at Hamilton (now in Madison county) and Oxford. From the organization of Madison co., in 1806, until 1809, the courts were held alternately at Oxford and North Norwich. By act of March 6, 1807, the co. seat was located at Norwich. The new courthouse was built and first occupied in 1809. The first courthouse was a wooden building, erected at a cost of $6,500. The present courthouse was built in 1837, at a cost of $16,000,

under the direction of Wm. Randall, Wm. Knowlton, and Erastus Lathrop, commissioners. The present jail was erected in 1830, at a cost of $2,000. It is a two story building, containing 10 cells and a house for the jailer.

[2] The first co. officers were Isaac Foot, *First Judge;* Joab Enos, and Joshua Leland, *Judges;* Oliver Norton and Elisha Payne, *Assistant Justices;* Uri Tracy, *Sheriff;* Sidney S. Breese, *Clerk;* and John L. Mercereau, *Surrogate.*

The Chenango Canal extends along Chenango River through the co. It crosses the river below Earlville, below Sherburne, and below Greene, upon wood aqueducts, supported by stone piers. The Albany & Susquehanna R. R., now in process of construction, extends along the Susquehanna through Bainbridge.

Five weekly newspapers are now published in the co.[1]

This co. included 11 of the "Twenty Towns" or "Governor's Purchase," the "Gore" lying between them and the Military Tract, the Harper Patent of 16,000 acres, Vermont Sufferers' Tract of 40,960 acres,[2] Livingston Tract of 16,000 acres, the French Tract of nearly the same extent, a portion of the Chenango Triangle Tract, and several smaller tracts. The territory included within the Twenty Townships was ceded to the State by the Indians, in a treaty held with Gov. George Clinton, at Fort Schuyler, Sept. 22, 1788.[3] This tract is sometimes called "Clinton's Purchase," and sometimes "The Governor's Purchase."

The early settlers were principally from Vt., Conn., and the eastern part of the State. The settlers in the N. part of the co. came in by way of Rome, and those in the central and s. parts by way of Chenango and Susquehanna Rivers. Many of the early settlers almost perished from want of food, at times, during the first few years. A colony of French settled at Greene in 1792, but,

[1] *The Western Oracle*, the first paper published in the co., was commenced by A. Romeyn, previous to 1804, at Sherburne Four Corners. It was discontinued in 1808 or '09.

The Olive Branch was started at Sherburne in May, 1806, by Phinney & Fairchild. In 1808 John F. Fairchild became sole proprietor. —— Miller, Lot Clark, and John B. Johnson were successively interested in its publication. In 1812 or '13 Johnson changed its name to

The Volunteer. In 1816 the press was purchased by John F. Hubbard, who commenced

The Norwich Journal. In 1844 it passed into the hands of La Fayette Leal and J. H. Sinclair, who merged it with The Oxford Republican in 1847 and changed the name to

The Chenango Union. Harvey Hubbard purchased Leal's interest Oct. 20, 1847, and the paper is now published by Hubbard & Sinclair.

The Chenango Patriot was commenced at Oxford in 1807 by John B. Johnson, and its publication continued for 3 or 4 yrs.

The President was published at Oxford in 1808 by Theophilus Eaton.

The Republican Messenger was commenced at Sherburn in 1810 by Petit & Percival.

The Oxford Gazette was started in 1814 by Chauncey Morgan, who published it some years, when it was sold to Geo. Hunt, and afterward to Hunt & Noyes. Mr. Morgan again became proprietor in 1826, and after a few years the paper was discontinued.

The Republican Agriculturalist was commenced Dec. 10, 1818, by Thurlow Weed. It soon passed into the hands of —— Curtiss, who continued it for a short time, when it was discontinued.

The People's Advocate was commenced at Norwich in 1824 by H. P. W. Brainard. It passed into the hands of Wm. G. Hyer, and was discontinued in a short time.

The Chenango Republican was commenced at Oxford in 1826 by Benj. Cory. In 1828 it was purchased by Mack & Chapman. March 3, 1831, Wm. E. Chapman and T. T. Flagler commenced a new series, and soon after changed its name to

The Oxford Republican. In 1838 Mr. Chapman became sole proprietor. It was successively published by J. Taylor Bradt, Benj. Welch, jr., R. A. Leal, C. E. Chamberlin, and La Fayette Leal. In 1847 it was merged with The Oxford Journal and published as The Chenango Union.

The Anti Masonic Telegraph was commenced at Norwich in Nov. 1829, by E. P. Pellet. In 1831 B. T. Cook became associated in its publication. Its name was subsequently changed to

The Chenango Telegraph. In 1840, on the death of E. P. Pellet, it passed into the hands of his brother, Nelson Pellet; and upon his death, in 1851, it was conducted for the estate by E. Max Leal and F. P. Fisher. In Sept. 1855, it was purchased by Rice & Martin, by whom it is now published.

The Chenango Patriot was commenced at Greene in 1830 by Nathan Randall. It afterward passed into the hands of Joseph M. Farr, who changed its name to

The Chenango Democrat, and in a short time it was discontinued.

The New Berlin Herald was commenced in 1831 by Samuel L. Hatch. In 1834 it was published by Randall & Hatch. It soon after passed into the hands of Isaac C. Sheldon; and afterward into the hands of Hiram Ostrander, who changed its name to

The New Berlin Sentinel. It was discontinued about 1840.

The Chenango Whig was published at Oxford a short time in 1835.

The Miniature, a small mo., was issued from the same office.

The Sherburne —— was commenced in 1836 by J. Worden Marble. In 1839 it was removed to Binghampton.

The Oxford Times was commenced in 1836 by a joint stock company. It was for some time conducted by H. H. Cook. In 1841 it passed into the hands of E. H. Purdy and C. D. Brigham. In 1844 it was published by Waldo M. Potter; in 1845, by Potter & Galpin; and in 1848 J. B. Galpin became sole proprietor, and still continues its publication.

The Bainbridge Eagle was commenced in 1843 by J. Hunt, jr. In 1846 its name was changed to

The Bainbridge Freeman; and in 1849 it was merged in

The Chenango Free Democrat, commenced at Norwich Jan. 1, 1849, by Alfred G. Lawyer; and J. D. Lawyer soon after became associated in its publication. It was then early removed to Cobleskill, Schoharie co.

The New Berlin Gazette was commenced in 1849 by Jos. K. Fox and M. E. Dunham, and was published about 1 year.

The Chenango News was commenced in 1850 by A. T. Boynton. J. M. Haight soon after became associated in its publication, and subsequently became sole proprietor. He removed the press to Norwich, and, in connection with A. P. Nixon, commenced the publication of

The Temperance Advocate in 1855, and published it 1 year, when it was discontinued.

The Saturday Visitor was commenced in 1852 by Joseph K. Fox. Its name was soon after changed to

The Social Visitor, after which it was published about 5 years.

The Spirit of the Age was commenced at Berlin in 1852 by J. K. Fox, J. D. Lawyer, editor. It was continued but a short time.

The Oxford Transcript was commenced in 1853 by G. N. Carhart, and was published about 6 months.

The Sherburne Transcript was commenced in 1855 by James M. Scarritt, and was published about 2 years.

The Chenango American was commenced at Greene, Sept. 20, 1855, by Denison & Fisher, its present publishers.

The Daily Reporter was commenced at Norwich in 1857 by J. H. Smith. In 1858 it was purchased by Rice & Martin, and was soon after discontinued.

The Literary Independent was commenced at Norwich in the fall of 1858 by a company of young gentlemen connected with the academy. It was published about 4 months.

The New Berlin Pioneer was commenced Feb. 19, 1859, by Squires & Fox, its present publishers.

[2] This tract was granted to relieve those persons who had purchased lands of the State of N. Y. within the present limits of Vt. These lands were claimed by both N. H. and N. Y., and, after an angry and protracted controversy, extending through several years, New York surrendered her claim to Vermont.

[3] These towns were designated originally by their numbers only, and are now in the counties of Madison, Chenango, and Oneida, as follows:—

Nos.	Present Towns.	Nos.	Present Towns.
1	Nelson, Madison co.	11	Plymouth, Chenango co.
2	Eaton, "	12	Pharsalia, "
3	Madison, "	13	McDonough, "
4	Hamilton, "	14	Preston, "
5	Lebanon, "	15	Norwich, "
6	Georgetown, "	16	New Berlin, "
7	Otselic, Chenango co.	17	Columbus, "
8	Smyrna, "	18	} Brookfield, "
9	Sherburne, "	19	
10	Norwich and } New Berlin, } "	20	Sangerfield and } Bridgewater, } Oneida co.

from defect in title, most of them left. The greater part of the later immigration was also from New England. In consequence of the gradual change which has been going on for the last 20 years in the business of the co., and the substitution of dairying for all other branches of farming, the population of the co. has gradually decreased, and is now no greater than it was 40 years ago.

AFTON—was formed from Bainbridge, Nov. 18, 1857. It is the s. e. corner town of the co. Its surface consists principally of a rolling upland, separated into two nearly equal parts by the broad valley of the Susquehanna. The summits of the hills are 300 to 500 feet above the valleys, and their declivities are generally gradual slopes. The Susquehanna flows s. w. through near the center, in a broad and beautiful valley. It receives from the n. Kelseys and Harpers Brooks. Round Pond, one mi. n. e. of the village, covers an area of about 40 acres. It is 25 feet above the surface of the river, and without any visible outlet. The soil upon the hills is a shaly loam, and in the valleys a clayey loam and alluvium. **Afton,** (p. v.,) upon the Susquehanna, near the center of the town, contains 4 churches and 270 inhabitants. **Ayreshire,** (p. o.,) upon Kelsey Brook, in the n. part, is a hamlet. The first settlement was made upon the Susquehanna, below Afton, in 1786, by immigrants from Conn. and Vt.[1] There are 5 churches in town.[2]

BAINBRIDGE—was formed as part of Tioga co., by the name of *"Jericho,"* Feb. 16, 1791. Its name was changed April 15, 1814. Parts of Norwich and Oxford were taken off in 1793, of Greene in 1798 and '99, and Afton in 1857. It lies upon the e. border of the co., s. of the center. Its surface is a rolling upland, divided into two parts by the Susquehanna, which flows s. w. through the center. The valley of the river is about one mi. wide, and is bordered by moderately steep hillsides. The highest summits are 400 to 600 feet above the valleys. The soil upon the hills is a gravelly and shaly loam, and in the valleys a clay loam and alluvium. **Bainbridge,** (p. v.,) upon the Susquehanna, was incorp. April 21, 1829. It contains 3 churches and 350 inhabitants. **Bennettsville,** (p. v.,) upon Bennetts Creek, in the s. e. part, contains 2 churches, a gristmill, sawmill, and about 20 houses. **West Bainbridge** is a p. o. in the n. w. corner, and **East Bainbridge** is a hamlet in the n. e. corner. The lands in this town were first claimed by Robert Harper under a grant from the Indians; but the title was repudiated by the State, and a portion of the lands was granted to settlers from Vt. who had suffered from failure of title to lands in that State granted to them by N. Y. The first settlements were made in 1785, by immigrants from Vt. and Conn.[3] The first church (Presb.) was formed about 1790, by Rev. William Stone.[4]

COLUMBUS—was formed from Brookfield, (Madison co.,) Feb. 11, 1805. A part of Norwich was annexed in 1807. It is the n. e. corner town in the co., and occupies a portion of the high ridge between Unadilla and Chenango Rivers. The highest summits are 400 to 600 feet above the valleys. Unadilla River forms its e. boundary, receiving as tributaries Beaver Creek, Shawlei Brook, and several other small streams. The soil is a gravelly and shaly loam.[5] **Columbus Center,** (Columbus p. o.,) upon a branch of Shawler Brook, contains 3 churches, a tannery, and 25 houses. The first settlement was made upon Lot 44, in 1791, by Col. Converse.[6] The first religious meeting was the funeral of Mrs. Dorcas Howard, conducted by Elder Campbell, (Bap.,) in 1797.[7]

COVENTRY—was formed from Greene, Feb. 7, 1806. Parts of Oxford and Greene were annexed in 1843. It is situated centrally on the s. line of the co. The highest elevations, midway between the Susquehanna and Chenango Rivers, are about 800 feet above the valleys. The hills are arable to their summits, and their slopes are generally long and gradual. Harpers and Kelseys Creeks, flowing into the Susquehanna, are the principal streams. The soil is a gravelly and sandy

---

[1] Among the early settlers were Seth Stone, Nath'l Benton, Isaac Miner, and Japhet Bush and sons, from Conn., and Hezekiah Stowell and sons, Orlando Bridgman and sons, and Ebenezer Church and sons, from Vt. The three last named families were "Vermont Sufferers." The first child born was Wm. Bush, in 1786; and the first death was that of —— Polly. Nath'l Church taught the first school, in 1790; Asa Stowell kept the first inn, in 1788, Peter Betts the first store, in 1805; and David Cooper and Isaac Miner built the first sawmill, on Kelseys Brook.

[2] Two M. E., Cong., Bap., and Univ.

[3] Among the early settlers were Wm. Gutherie, Abraham Fuller, Reuben Kirby, and Gould Bacon, from Conn.; Stephen and John Stiles, Heath Kelsey, Chas. Bush, Eben and Jos. Landers, and Jas. Graham. Sam'l Bixby settled on Lot 75, in 1788, and Maj. Henry Evans on Lot 80, in 1789. The first birth was that of K. Landers, daughter of Jos. Landers, in March, 1791; the first marriage, that of Charles Bush and Joan Harrington, in 1794; and the first death, that of Mrs. Reuben Kirbey, in 1792. William Gutherie kept the first inn, in 1793, on Lot 85. Phineas

and Reuben Bennett erected a gristmill on Bennetts Creek, in 1789.

[4] There are 7 churches in town; 2 M. E., 2 Bap., F. W. Bap., Presb., and Prot. E.

[5] The people are almost solely engaged in dairying. For 30 years the population has been continually decreasing and the dairies increasing.

[6] Among the other early settlers were Henry, Daniel, and Jas. Williams, from R. I., who located upon Lot 90, in 1792; Thos. Howard, from R. I., on Lot 89, Israel Greenleaf, from N. H., on Lot 62, Gilbert Strong, on Lot 61, and Josiah Rathbone, on Lot 54, in 1794. The first child born was Sally Williams; the first marriage, that of Joseph Medbery and Hannah Brown, in 1794; and the first death, that of Mrs. Dorcas Howard, in 1797. Nicholas Page taught the first school; Col. Converse kept the first inn, in 1793; Amos C. Palmer, the first store, in 1797; and Job Vail built the first sawmill, in 1794, and the first gristmill, in 1795.

[7] The census reports 5 churches in town; Bap., F. W. Bap., Cong., M. E., and Union.

loam, with occasional spots of a red, slaty loam, better adapted to grazing than tillage. **Coventry,** (p. v.,) a little N. w. of the center, contains 2 churches and 40 dwellings; and **Coventryville,** (p. v.,) 2 mi. E. of Coventry, a church, mill, and 25 dwellings. **Church Hollow** is a p. o. on the s. line. The first settlement was made near the center, by Simon Jones, in 1785.[1] The first church (Cong.) was formed Nov. 19, 1807. Rev. David Harmon was the first preacher.[2]

GERMAN[3]—was formed from De Ruyter, (Madison co.,) March 21, 1806. Otselic was taken off in 1817, Lincklaen in 1823, and a part of Pitcher in 1827. It is located centrally upon the w. line of the co. The surface is hilly, and watered by several brooks, forming what is called Five Streams, which flow through the town in a s. direction. The soil is a sandy and gravelly loam, well adapted to grazing. **Livermores Corners,** (German p. o.,) near the w. line, is a hamlet; and **East German** is a p. o. The first settlement was made in 1795, by Benjamin Cleveland, from Oneida co.[4] The first church (Presb.) was formed at an early period, and a M. E. association was formed in 1815, at the house of Walter Oyshlenbank.[5]

GREENE[6]—was formed from Union (Broome co.) and *"Jericho,"* (now Bainbridge,) March 15, 1798. A part of *"Jericho"* was annexed in 1799. Coventry was taken off in 1806, and Smithville in 1808. A part of Barker (Broome co.) was taken off in 1840, and a part of Coventry in 1843. It is the s. w. corner town of the co. Its surface is a rolling and hilly upland. The hills rise 500 to 700 feet above the river, and are broken by the ravines of the streams. Chenango River flows s. w. through the center of the town, in a broad valley about 1 mile in width. The Chenango Canal passes through the valley. Genegantslet Creek flows s. through the w. part in a wide valley, and joins the Chenango a few miles below the village of Greene. Pages Brook flows through the s. E. corner; and several small streams are tributary to the Chenango. The soil is a gravelly and shaly loam on the hills, and alluvium in the valleys. **Greene,** (p. v.,) near the center, was incorp. April 12, 1842. It contains 4 churches, a flouring mill, furnace, and 814 inhabitants. **East Greene** (p. v.) contains a church and 158 inhabitants. **Genegantslet** (p. v.) contains 1 church and 12 houses. **Chenango Forks** (p. v.) is partly in this town. S. Ketchum settled in 1792.[7] The first church (Bap.) was organized in 1795,[8] by Elder Nath. Kellogg.

---

[1] —— Goodell and —— Clark settled near Mr. Jones in 1786, and Benj. Jones at the same place in 1788. Ozias Yale and Wm. Starks located a little N. of Coventry in 1792, Elijah Warren on Lot 2, in 1804, and Moses Allis, Roger Egerton, and Z. Hutchinson soon after. The first birth was that of Wm., son of Moses Allis, in 1794; the first marriage, that of Simeon Parker and Polly Sprague; and the first death, that of a son of Roger Egerton, in 1790. Sherman Page taught the first school; Benj. Jones kept the first inn, in 1788, and Jotham Parker the first store, in 1799. The first gristmill was erected by Capt. Parker, in 1795, and the first carding and cloth dressing mill by A. and Wm. H. Rogers, about the same time.

[2] The census reports 5 churches; 2 Cong., 2 M. E., and Bap.

[3] Named from Gen. Obadiah German, the original owner of the township. It was first named *"Brakel Township."*

[4] Abraham Livermore settled at Livermores Corners, in 1796, with his wife and children, Abraham, jr., Becka, Daniel, Polly, Abel, Cyrus, Hepsey, Sally, and Martin Livermore. From their isolated position in the wilderness—remote from any settlement —the Cleveland and Livermore families suffered great privations and hardships during the first years of their settlement. In June, 1776, Mr. Cleveland set out for *"Fort Stanwix"* for provisions, his family being entirely destitute. He intended to return in 3 or 4 days, but was detained for some time. On the fourth day of his absence, his wife and children, who had eaten nothing for 3 days except a few roots found in the woods, set out for their nearest neighbors, in Cincinnatus, on Otselic River, 4½ mi. distant. When about a mile from home, they encountered a bear, and were frightened back. The next morning the mother was too weak to walk, and the two elder children again set out for Mr. Raymond's, on the Otselic. Upon learning the suffering condition of the family, Mrs. Raymond made them a pudding of bran,—the only food she had in the house. This and a bottle of milk kept the family from starvation until relief came. At another time, when the family were reduced to the last extremity, two unmilked cows came to their house one night, and went away in the morning, furnishing them with milk for several days. It was never known where the cows came from or where they went to. Other families in the vicinity suffered in a similar manner. The first birth was that of Polly Cleveland, in 1796; the first marriage, that of Jonathan Head and Hepsey Livermore; and the first death, that of —— Hartshorn. Abraham Livermore kept the first inn; Jonathan Chandler kept the first store, and erected the first mill and factory, on the E. branch of Otselic River.

[5] The census reports 3 churches; Presb., M. E., and F. W. Bap.

[6] Named in honor of Gen. Nath'l Greene. That part of the original township of Greene lying E. of Chenango River was included in a purchase made by the State from the Oneida and Tuscarora Indians in 1785. These lands were subsequently sold by the State to individual patentees.

[7] Mr. Ketchum located within the bounds of the present village of Greene. In the fall of 1792 a settlement was made by a company of French refugees. One of their number, Chas. Felix De Bulogne, had preceded the main body, and made a purchase of 15,000 acres lying on the E. side of Chenango River. The first party that came consisted of M. Bulogne, M. Shamont, M. Le Fevre, M. Bravo, M. Du Vernet, and M. Obre. A portion of them had families; and several young ladies were among the party. In Otsego co. Simon Barnet joined the party, and subsequently M. Dutremont, with his family, settled with them. Before the dispersion of the colony they were joined by Jos. Juliand, who was the only French emigrant that became a permanent resident. M. Bulogne, on his way to Philadelphia in the spring of 1795, was drowned while fording a creek much swollen by the floods. The untimely death of the leader of this adventurous band proved fatal to the future success of the settlement. The failure of the company to pay the balance of the purchase money due on the tract caused the title to revert to the original patentees. After all the hardships and privations they had endured, the failure to secure a title to their land proved a signal for dispersion. The majority of them left in the year 1796. In 1794, Talleyrand, the celebrated French diplomatist, visited his fellow-countrymen in Greene. Among the early permanent settlers were Nath'l Kellogg, Zopher Betts, Benajah Loomis, Cornelius Hill, and Daniel Tremaine, who located at East Greene in 1793. The first road that was cut through the town was called *"The Chenango Road."* It runs from the present village of Bainbridge to the mouth of Page Creek, on the Chenango,—a distance of about 25 mi. The first settlers upon this road within the then limits of the town, commencing at the w., were Nathan Bennett, Joshua Root, Eleazur Skinner, Thomas Elliott, Joab Elliott, Roswell Fitch, Aden Elliott, Philo Clemmons, Capt. Mandeville, Simeon and Benj. Jones, Hardin Bennett, Record Wilber, and Deacon Richards, who came in from 1792 to '95. The settlers who located in the s. part, w. of the river, were Jas. and Herman Terwilliger, Elisha and Noah Gilbert, Stephen Palmer, and Jos. and Cornish Messenger, as early as 1796. The first birth was that of Johnston Rundall, son of Jos. Rundall,—for which honor the mother subsequently received a deed of 50 acres of land from the Hornby Estate. —— Cartwright taught the first school, in 1794; Conrad Sharp kept the first inn, in 1794; Elisha Smith the first store, in 1801 Conrad Sharp built the first sawmill, in 1795, and Abraham Storm and Henry Vorse the first gristmill, in 1794.

[8] The census reports 9 churches; 5 Bap., 2 M. E., Presb., and Prot. E.

and was the first church of that denomination in the co. Elder Kellogg continued its pastor about 30 years.

GUILFORD—was formed from Oxford, April 3, 1813, as "*Eastern.*" Its name was changed March 21, 1817. It lies on the E. border of the co., s. of the center. The surface is hilly and broken, consisting of the elevated lands between Chenango and Unadilla Rivers, the hills rising 200 to 700 feet above the valleys. It is drained by the Unadilla, which forms the entire E. boundary, Guilford Pond Creek,[1] and several other smaller streams. The soil is a gravelly and slaty loam, occasionally intermixed with clay. **Guilford**, (p. v.,) located in the valley of Guilford Pond Creek, contains 3 churches, an iron foundery and machine shop, and several mills; pop. 263. **Guilford Center** (p. v.) contains 2 churches and 20 dwellings. **East Guilford,** (p. v.,) in the s. E. corner of the town, contains a church, a mill, and 15 dwellings. **Mount Upton,** (p. v.,) upon the w. bank of the Unadilla, contains 4 churches, several mills, and other manufacturing establishments; pop. 190. **Rockdale**, (p. v.,) on the river, 4 miles below Mount Upton, contains 2 churches, a grist and saw mill, and 25 dwellings. The first settlement was made in 1787, by Ezekiel Wheeler, a little N. of Mount Upton, on the farm now occupied by his grandson, Silas Wheeler, 2d.[2] The first church (Bap.) was formed by Elder Orange Spencer, in 1803.[3]

LINCKLAEN[4]—was formed from German, April 12, 1823. Parts of Pitcher were taken off in 1827 and '33. It is the N. w. corner town of the co. Its surface is a hilly, broken upland, divided into ridges by narrow ravines extending N. and s. The declivities of the hills are usually steep, and the summits are 400 to 600 feet above the valleys. Mud Creek, a branch of the Otselic, flows s. through the w. part of the town. Ashbel Creek and several other small streams take their rise in the s. and E. parts. The soil is a shaly and clayey loam. **Lincklaen**, (p. v.,) on Mud Creek, contains a church and 15 dwellings. **Burdick Settlement,** in the N. part, contains a church and 12 dwellings. **North Lincklaen** is a p. o. in the N. E. part. The first settlements were made about 1796. The first religious services were held by Rev. Seth Williston, in 1798. The census reports 4 churches in town.[5]

MACDONOUGH[6]—was formed from Preston, April 17, 1816. It is an interior town, lying w. of the center of the co. The surface is hilly, and in some places broken by deep ravines and sharp ridges extending N. and s. It is drained s. by Bowmans and Genegantslet Creeks and several other streams. Genegantslet Lake lies near the w. border. The soil is a clay loam, better adapted to grazing than tillage. **Macdonough**, (p. v.,) on Genegantslet Creek, contains 2 churches, several mills, and 168 inhabitants. **East Macdonough** (p. v.) contains 2 churches and 14 dwellings. The first settlements were made in 1795, by Nathaniel Locke, Loring and Emery Willard, Henry Ludlow, and others.[7] The first religious association (M. E.) was formed in 1798. The first church edifice (F. W. Bap.) was erected in 1831; Elder Steer was the first pastor.[8]

NEW BERLIN—was formed from Norwich, April 3, 1807, changed to "*Lancaster*" May 9, 1821, and original name restored March 22, 1822. A part of Sherburne was taken off in 1852. It lies upon the E. border of the co., N. of the center. Its surface is a rolling and hilly upland, the ridges extending N. and s. Unadilla River forms its E. boundary; and Great Brook flows s.

---

[1] This stream has a fall of 140 feet in passing through Guilford Village, affording a fine and very valuable water-power.

[2] Joshua Mercereau and his brother (Frenchmen) settled at the mouth of Guilford Creek, and erected the first mill in town, in 1789. James Phelps and —— Button settled near Rockdale in 1790; Robert McLeod, on Lot 1, and Isaac Fuller, from Guilford, Conn., in 1791; Dan'l Savage, John Nash, and Nelson Robbins, from Ballston Spa, in 1792, at and near the old Four Corners; John Secor, from Haverstraw, on Lot 2; Gurdon and Wyatt Chamberlin, at Mount Upton; Wm. and Nathaniel Hyer, —all in 1793. Major Richmond and his sons Joseph and Seth, Asa Haven, father of Hon. Solomon G. Haven, of Buffalo, Dan'l T. Dickinson, father of Hon. Daniel S. Dickinson, of Binghamton, Caleb Burdick, Sam'l Smith, and Paris Windsor were also among the pioneer settlers of the town. The first child born was Prudence Fuller, in April, 1791; the first marriage, that of —— Powell and the widow of Isaac Fuller, in 1793; and the first death, that of Isaac Fuller, in 1793. Ezekiel Wheeler kept the first inn, in 1796; and Sullivan Reynolds kept the first store and erected the first mill on the Unadilla, in 1790. The first school was taught by Nathan Bennett, in 1794.

[3] The census reports 12 churches; 5 M. E., 2 Bap., 2 Cong., Presb., Prot. E., and Union.

[4] Named from John Lincklaen, former proprietor of the township and several adjacent tracts. Among the early settlers were

Guerdon Wells, Abel Fairchild, Elisha Catlin, Joseph Pulford, —— Backus, Nathaniel Gray, Wolcott Bennett, Joseph Darling, Jesse Catlin, Aaron Peet, John Wilson, Elisha Blount, Christopher Shipman, and —— Walters. The first child born was Matilda Wells, about 1800; and the first death, that of a child of Christopher Shipman. Wm. Bly taught the first school; Elisha Catlin kept the first inn; Fairchild Brothers, the first store; Catlin & Shipman built the first sawmill, and J. Pulford the first gristmill.

[5] Bap., Seventh Day Bap., Cong., and M. E.

[6] Named in honor of Commodore Macdonough.

[7] Edward Colburn, Benj. Ketchum, Benj. Kenyon, Ephraim Fish, John Anderson, Nehemiah Dunbar, Jonah and Sylvanus Moore, Joseph and Ransom Cook, Wm. Mead, Wm. Norton, Danl. Wainwright, Adam Oyshlenbank, and M. Turner settled in town from 1795 to 1808. The first marriage was that of Sylvanus Moore and wife; and the first death, that of Mrs. Benj. Ketchum. The first school was taught by Capt. Joshua A. Burke. Sylvanus Moore kept the first inn, in 1799, and Henry Ludlow the first store, in 1802. Gates Wilcox erected the first gristmill, in 1808; John Nevins, the first paper mill, in 1828, at Macdonough Village. Henry Ludlow built the first sawmill, on the outlet of Genegantslet Lake, in 1798.

[8] The census reports 4 churches; Bap., M. E., Presb., and Union.

through near the center. Mathewson Pond is near the w. border. The soil is a shaly loam, occasionally intermixed with clay. **New Berlin,** (p. v.,) upon the Unadilla, in the N. E. part of the town, was incorp. April 17, 1816. It contains 4 churches, the New Berlin Academy, a newspaper office, paper mill, cotton factory, tannery, and several minor manufactories. Pop. 740. **South New Berlin,** (p. v.,) upon the Unadilla, in the s. E. part, contains 2 churches, a large tannery, and 285 inhabitants. A portion of the village is in Otsego co. **Holmesville,** in the extreme s. E. corner, contains a tannery, gristmill, and about 20 houses. **New Berlin Center** is a p. o. **Ambler Settlement** is a hamlet in the s. part. Daniel Scribner settled upon the Unadilla in 1790.[1] The census reports 8 churches.[2] Hon. Henry Bennett, who has been elected to Congress five successive terms from this district, resides at New Berlin Village.

NORTH NORWICH—was formed from Norwich, April 7, 1849. It is an interior town, lying N. E. of the center of the co. Its surface consists of the valley of Chenango River and the high rolling uplands which rise upon either side. The summits of the hills are 200 to 600 feet above the valley. It is drained by Chenango River, Cold and Fly Brooks, and several other small streams. The soil is a gravelly and slaty loam, in some places mixed with clay. **North Norwich,** (p.v.,) upon the Chenango, contains 2 churches, several mills, and about 150 inhabitants. It is an important village upon the Chenango Canal. **Kings Settlement** is a p. o. in the E. part; and **Plasterville,** a hamlet in the s. w. Jos. Lothrop and A. Mead located on Lot 1, in 1794.[3] The first church (Bap.) was formed in 1796; Elder Eleany Holmes was the first preacher.[4]

NORWICH—was formed from Union (Broome co.) and "*Jericho*," (now Bainbridge,) Jan. 19, 1793. Pharsalia, Plymouth, and Preston were taken off in 1806, New Berlin, and a part of Columbus, in 1807, and North Norwich in 1849. A part of Preston was annexed in 1808, and a part taken off in 1820. It is the central town upon the E. border of the co. Its surface consists of two high, rolling ridges, separated by the valley of the Chenango. The highest summits are about 500 ft. above the valleys. Chenango River flows s. through the w. part. It receives the Canasawacta and several other streams as tributaries. Unadilla River forms the E. boundary. The soil upon the uplands is a shaly and gravelly loam, and in the valleys a gravelly loam and alluvium. **Norwich,** (p.v.,) upon Chenango River, in the N. part, was incorp. April 16, 1816. It contains the co. buildings, 4 churches, the Norwich Academy, 2 banks, 2 newspaper offices, a piano forte factory, 3 carriage factories, 2 tanneries, 2 blast furnaces, a hammer factory, planing mill, foundery and machine shop, sash and door factory, and plaster mill. Pop. 2,430. **White Store,** (p. o.,) on the Unadilla, contains a church, gristmill, and 10 houses. The first settlement was made in 1788, by Avery Power.[5] The first religious services were held by Rev. Manasseh French, in 1793 or '94.[6]

OTSELIC[7]—was formed from German, March 28, 1817. It lies on the N. border of the co., w. of the center. Its surface is hilly, consisting of high ridges 500 to 800 ft. above the valley of Otselic Creek, which are broken by the ravines of the streams. Otselic Creek is the principal stream, and flows s. w. through the center of the town. Several small streams are tributaries of the Otselic. The soil on the hills is a shaly loam, and in the valleys alluvium. **Otselic,** (p. v.,) in the N. part, contains 100 inhabitants; **South Otselic,** (p. v.,) in the s. w. corner, 1 church and 225 inhabitants. Settlement was commenced about 1800, by Ebenezer Hill.[8] The first preacher was Stephen C. Nicholas. There are 4 churches in town; 2 Bap., F. W. Bap., and Christian.

OXFORD—was formed from Union (Broome co.) and "*Jericho*," (now Bainbridge,) Jan. 19,

---

[1] Among the other early settlers who came about the same time were Nathl. and Joseph Medbery, who located upon Great Brook; Saml. Anderson, Silas Burlingame, Jeremy Goodrich, Levi Blakeslee, Charles Knapp, and Joseph Moss, who located upon the present site of the village. The first child born was Louisa Bancroft, in 1797; and the first marriage, that of Danl. Williams and Phila Packer, in 1794. Josiah Burlingame taught the first school; Danl. Scribner kept the first inn; Levi Blakeslee the first store; and Job Vail built the first mill.

[2] 2 Bap., 2 Cong., 2 M. E., F. W. Bap., and Prot. E.

[3] Among the other early settlers were Judge Joel Thompson, Jeremiah and Abner Purdy, and Benj. Ferris, from Dutchess co., in 1795; and Jesse Rundell, Jacob Grow, Gen. Obadiah German, Ebenezer Hartwell, and James Purdy, in 1796,—all of whom settled at the village and along the valley of the Chenango. The first child born was Amos Mead, jr., Sept. 12, 1794; the first marriage, that of Ebenezer Hartwell and Rachel Mead, in 1795; and the first death, that of Mrs. Abner Purdy, in 1796. Thomas Brooks taught the first school; Amos Mead kept the first inn, in 1803, and Gen. Obadiah German the first store. Benj. Hartwell built the first gristmill, in 1803.

[4] The census reports 4 churches; 2 M. E., Bap., and Univ.

[5] Among the other early settlers were David Fairchild, Silas Cole, Wm. Smiley, Nicholas Pickett, Maj. Thomas Brooks, Israel, Charles, and Matt. Graves, Josiah Brown, John Wait, Wm. Ransford and sons Hascall and William, jr., John Harris, Manasseh French, Joab Enos, Josiah Brown, Elisha Smith, Wm. and Chauncey Gibson, Mark, Wm., and Stephen Steere, Stephen Collins, Jas. Gilmore, Moses Snow, John Randall, John McNitt, and David and John Shattuck. The first child born was Lucy Power; the first male child, Marcus Cole; the first marriage in the town and co. was that of Hascall Ransford and Fanny Graves, July 12, 1792. Benj. Edmunds kept the first inn; Jonathan Johnson was the first physician; and Elisha Smith built the first saw and grist mill.

[6] There are 6 churches in town; Bap., M. E., Cong., Prot. E., Union, and R. C.

[7] An Indian name, signifying Plum Creek.

[8] Among the early settlers were Reuben Buckingham, David Steadman, Wm. Fish, Jonah Wolcott, Wm. Cross, Wm. Hurlbut, and Wm. Smith, in the N. part; Elias Benjamin, Buell Warner and his sons Oliver, Abner, and Buell, jr., Benoni Parce, Lewis Cook, Æneas Thompson, John and James Warner, Abraham Fairchild, and Wm. Greene, in the s. part. Hannah Warner taught the first school. Ebenezer Hill kept the first inn, in 1810, and built the first gristmill, in 1820. Geo. Coles kept the first store, in 1812. Jas. Rush built the first sawmill.

1793. Guilford was taken off in 1813, and a part of Coventry in 1843. It is an interior town, lying a little s. of the center of the co. Its surface is divided into two parts by the valley of the Chenango. The hills bordering upon the river are 500 to 800 feet above the valleys. Chenango River flows s. w. through the w. part in a valley having an average width of about 1 mi. It receives Eddy Brook from the E., and Fly-Meadow, Mill, and Ludlow Brooks from the w. The soil is a shaly loam upon the hills, and a gravelly loam and alluvium in the valleys. **Oxford,** (p. v.,) upon the Chenango, in the N. part of the town, incorporated April 6, 1806, contains 6 churches, the Oxford Academy,[1] a hoe factory, sash and blind factory, carriage shop, grist and saw mill, and plaster mill. Pop. 1,218. **South Oxford** is a p. o. in the s. w. corner; and **Cheshireville** a p. o. near the s. line. The first settlements were made in 1790, by Benjamin Hovey.[2] The first preacher was Rev. Uri Tracy, (Presb.,) in 1792.[3]

PHARSALIA—was formed from Norwich, as "*Stonington,*" April 7, 1806. Its name was changed April 6, 1808. It is an interior town, lying N. w. of the center of the co. Its surface is a rolling and hilly upland, occupying a portion of the watershed between Chenango and Otselic Rivers. The latter flows through the extreme N. w. corner. Canasawacta, Genegantslet, and Brackel Creeks take their rise near the center. The soil is a shaly loam. **Pharsalia,** (p. v.,) in the w. part, contains 12 houses; **East Pharsalia,** (p. v.,) in the s., 1 church, 2 gristmills, a sawmill, and 15 houses. **North Pharsalia** is a p. o. The first settlement was commenced in 1797, by John Randall, on Lot 48.[4] John Peck was the first settled minister. There are three churches in town; Bap., F. W. Bap., and Presb.

PITCHER[5]—was formed from German and Lincklaen, Feb. 13, 1827. A part of Lincklaen was annexed in 1833. It lies upon the w. border of the co., N. of the center. Its surface consists principally of two high ridges 500 to 800 ft. above the valleys. Otselic River flows s. E. through the center. Brackel Creek flows s. E. through the s. part. The ravines of the streams are narrow and are bordered by steep hillsides. The soil is a shaly and gravelly loam. **Pitcher,** (p. v.,) upon the Otselic, s. w. of the center, contains 3 churches, a woolen factory, and 25 dwellings. **North Pitcher,** (p. v.,) upon the Otselic, N. E. of the center, contains 2 churches, 2 sawmills, a hame factory, fork factory, and about 20 dwellings. **Pitcher Springs** (p. o.) is a hamlet E. of the center.[6] **South Pitcher** is a p. o. John Wilson and —— Schuyler settled in 1794 or '95.[7] The first religious services were held by Rev. Seth Williston, in 1797.[8]

PLYMOUTH—was formed from Norwich, April 7, 1806. It is an interior town, lying N. of the center of the co. Its surface is a hilly upland, broken by deep ravines. Canasawacta Creek, and its E. and w. branches, flow s. E. through deep and narrow valleys and form a junction near the center of the town. Southwest of the center are 2 small ponds, covering an area of 100 to 150 acres each. The soil is a gravelly and clayey loam. **Plymouth,**[9] (p. v.,) N. of the center, contains 2 churches and 150 inhabitants; **South Plymouth,** (p. o.,) in the s. E., a gristmill and 10 houses. The first settlement was commenced about 1794, by some French families.[10] The first church (M. E.) was organized about 1806; and the Rev. —— White was the first preacher.[11]

PRESTON—was formed from Norwich, April 2, 1806. Macdonough was taken off in 1816. A part of Norwich was taken off in 1808, and a part of the same town was annexed in 1820.

---

[1] This institution for many years bore the highest reputation of any academy w. of the Hudson. Many distinguished citizens of the central portions of the State received their academic education at this place.

[2] Among the other early settlers were Elijah Blackman, Eben Enos, John Bartle and 6 sons, Peter Burgot, John Church, Theodore Burr, Benj. Loomis, Samuel Farnham, Chas. Hurst, and John Holmes. The first child born was Ellis Loomis, in May, 1792; the first marriage was that of Peter Bartle and Tabitha Loomis, in May, 1795; and the first death was that of a child of Peter Burgot, and the first death of an adult, that of Andrew Loomis, in 1793. Mrs. Philip Bartle taught the first school, in 1793. Philip Bartle built the first schoolhouse, individually, on "*Panther Hill,*" in 1793; John Bartle kept the first inn, on Bowmans Creek; Samuel Farnham kept the first store, and Peter Burgot built the first mill, on Mill Brook.

[3] The census reports 7 churches in town; Bap., F. W. Bap., M. E., Presb., Prot. E., R. C., and Univ.

[4] Among the other early settlers were Joseph Brud, on Lot 49, Sanford Morgan, on Lot 36, John Weaver, on Lot 28, Daniel Denison, on Lot 70, Lodowick Weaver, on Lot 32, Joshua Weaver and David Davis, on Lot 69,—all from Conn. The first birth was that of Denison R. Weaver; the first marriage, that of Jabish Brown and Ketura Brown; and the first death, that of Mrs. Nehemiah Lewis. Aruna Wait taught the first school. The first tavern and store were kept by Sanford Morgan, on Lot 36; the first mill was built by Asa Weaver, on Lot 27, on Canasawacta Creek.

[5] Named from Nathaniel Pitcher, Lieutenant Governor of the State.

[6] Pitcher Springs, formerly quite a watering place, was named from the sulphur springs located there. It is now almost deserted.

[7] Among the other early settlers were Ebenezer Wakely, Benj. Fairchild, Jonathan Chandler, George Taylor, Silas Beebe, Jonas Hinman, Abijah Rhines, Simon Peet, —— Millard, and Elijah Fenton. The first child born was a son of Silas Beebe, in Nov. 1796; and the first marriage, that of John Wilson and Polly Hinman, May 16, 1799. Ebenezer Wakely taught the first school; Benj. Fairchild kept the first inn, Reuben Root the first store, and John Lincklaen built the first mills.

[8] The census reports 6 churches in town; 2 Cong., 2 M. E., Bap., and Union.

[9] Formerly called "*Frankville.*"

[10] Among the early settlers were John Raynor and G. D. Jeffrey, (Frenchmen;) James Bumford, Nathan Wales, John Miller, Col. Wm. Munroe, Silas Holmes, Dan'l Prentiss. Jas. Purdy, Judah Bement, and R. D. Dillaye. The first death was that of —— Blowers; Elizabeth Bowdish died about the same time. Clarissa Brooks taught the first school, in 1800 or '01; Charles Babcock kept the first inn, and John Raynor the first store. Nathaniel Prentiss built the first mill, and John Thorp the first woolen factory, at an early day.

[11] There are 4 churches in town; M. E., Bap., F. W. Bap., and Cong.

It is the central town of the co.   Its surface is a high, rolling upland, divided into two distinct ridges.   The summits of the hills are 200 to 800 feet above the Chenango Valley at Norwich.   The principal streams are Fly-Meadow Creek and Mill Brook, flowing s. into the Chenango.   The soil is a gravelly and slaty loam,—in many places stony and hard to cultivate.   It is generally well adapted to grazing.   **Preston Corners,** (Preston p. o.,) in the N. part, contains 2 churches and 105 inhabitants.   The first settlement was made on Fly-Meadow Creek, in 1787, by James Glover, who erected the first gristmill, in 1788–89.[1]   The first church (Bap.) was formed in 1806, by Elder Haskall, the first preacher.[2]

SHERBURNE—was formed from Paris, (Oneida co.,) March 5, 1795.   Smyrna was taken off in 1808, and a part of New Berlin was annexed in 1852.   It lies on the N. border of the co., E. of the center.   The highest summits are 200 to 500 feet above the valleys of the streams. Chenango River enters the co. from Madison and flows in a s. E. direction through the town, receiving Handsome and Mad Brooks and several other tributaries.   The soil is chiefly a gravelly and slaty loam, but some portions of the valley lands are a sandy loam.   The Chenango Canal passes through the valley parallel to the river.   On the bottom lands of the river hops are extensively grown.   **Sherburne,** (p. v.,) on the Chenango, s. of the center, was incorp. April 16, 1830.   It contains 6 churches, the Sherburne Academy, and several manufactories.   Pop. about 1200.   **Earlville,** (p. v.,) on the line of Madison co., contains 441 inhabitants, of whom 208 are in this town.   Joseph Gutherie settled in the valley of the Chenango, near Sherburne Village, in 1792.   Major Brooks, one of the "Shay's men," is supposed to have been there a year or two earlier.[3]   The first religious services were held by a number of families from New England, who purchased the s. w. quarter of the 9th township, (Sherburne,) and settled on it in March, 1793.[4]

SMITHVILLE—was formed from Greene, April 1, 1808.   It lies on the w. line of the co., s. of the center.   The surface consists of high ranges of hills, with narrow valleys extending N. and s.   It is drained s. by Genegantslet and Ludlow Creeks and their tributaries, and several other streams flowing into the Chenango.   The soil is a gravelly and clay loam in the valleys, and a clay and slaty loam on the hills.   **Smithville Flats,** (p. v.,) on Genegantslet Creek, in the s. w. corner, contains 4 churches, 3 sawmills, a gristmill, and 315 inhabitants.   **East Smithville,** on Ludlow Creek, near the E. line, contains 2 churches and 18 dwellings.   The first settlement was made in the valley of the Genegantslet, in 1797, by Robert Lytle, from Ireland.[5]   The first church (Bap.) was formed in 1805, by Elder Gray, the first preacher.[6]

SMYRNA—was taken from Sherburne, March 25, 1808, as "*Stafford.*"   Its name was changed April 6 of the same year.   It is the central town upon the N. border of the co.   Its surface is a broken and hilly upland, the highest summits being 500 to 800 feet above the valleys. The principal stream is Pleasant Brook, flowing s. E. through near the center.   Cold Brook and several other small streams flow through portions of the town.   These streams mostly flow through narrow valleys bordered by hillsides, a considerable portion of which are too steep for cultivation. The soil is a gravelly and shaly loam.   **Smyrna,** (p. v.,) upon Pleasant Brook, near the E. line, was incorp. April 20, 1829.   It contains 3 churches, a gristmill, a tannery, and 320 inhabitants. The first settlement was made by Joseph Porter, in 1792.[7]   The first religious society (Friends) was formed at an early period.[8]

---

1 David Fairchild and his sons John and Amos settled at Preston Corners in 1795; Randall Billings and Silas Champlain, from Conn., at Preston Center, in 1796; Jonas Marsh, from Mass., Col. Gurdon, and Dudley Hewitt, in 1799. Among the other early settlers were Sam'l and Clark Lewis, Rev. Hazard Burdick, David Eccleston, Jonas Marsh, —— Champlain, Wm. Packer, Abraham Avery, and Wm. Walsworth. The first child born was Fanny Billings, July 16, 1796; the first marriage, that of Capt. Lyon and Widow Crandall, in 1798; and the first death, that of an infant child of Geo. Crary. The first school was taught by Wm. McAlpine, who surveyed the Livingston Patent in 1798 and subsequently the Morris Tract. Jonas Marsh kept the first inn, in 1800; Jas. Glover kept the first store and erected the first mill.

2 The census reports 5 churches; Bap., F. W. Bap., Seventh Day Bap., Presb., and Univ.

3 A company from New England, consisting of Nath'l Gray, Joel Hatch, Abraham, James, and Newcomb Raymond, Joseph, John, and Eleazur Lothrop, Cornelius Clark, and Joel Northrop, with their families, settled in 1793. The deed of their purchase is dated in June of that year.

4 During the first week after their arrival they erected a log meetinghouse, and on the succeeding Sabbath met in it, after the example of the Pilgrim Fathers, to make public and united acknowledgments for the protection and guidance of an over-ruling Power while on a perilous and tedious journey through the wilderness to their new homes. The census reports 9 churches; 2 Bap., 2 M. E., F. W. Bap., Cong., Prot. E., Univ., and Union.

5 Jos. Agard and Eppaphes Sheldon, from Litchfield, Conn., bought out the log house and improvement of Mr. Lytle in Feb. 1798, moved in their families, and became the sole residents of the town. They were joined in 1798–99 by Edward Loomis, who settled on Ludlow Creek, Simeon Neal, Robt. Williams, Asa Straight, Dan'l Phillips, Capt. Samuel A. Skeel, John Young, and John Palmer. The first child born was Jane Loomis, May 2, 1800; the first marriage, that of Jason Smith and Hannah Rorapaugh, in 1807; and the first death, that of a son of George Shaddock, in 1799. Capt. John Palmer kept the first inn and store and erected the first distillery. Timothy Scoville built the first sawmill, in 1805, and Nicholas Powell the first gristmill, in 1809.

6 The census reports 4 churches; 2 M. E., Bap., and Univ.

7 Among the other early settlers were Jos. Collins, Jos. Billings, Joshua Talcott, David Wilbur, and John Parker. The first gristmill and clothing works were erected by Collins & Billings, in 1795.

8 The census reports 5 churches in town; Bap., F. W. Bap., Cong., M. E., and Friends.

Acres of Land, Valuation, Population, Dwellings, Families, Freeholders, Schools, Live Stock, Agricultural Products, and Domestic Manufactures, of Chenango County.

| NAMES OF TOWNS. | ACRES OF LAND. | | VALUATION OF 1858. | | | POPULATION. | | No. of Dwellings. | No. of Families. | Freeholders. | SCHOOLS. | |
	Improved.	Unimproved.	Real Estate.	Personal Property.	Total.	Males.	Females.				No. of Districts.	Children taught.
Afton[1]			$383,045	$22,300	$405,345						13	571
Bainbridge	27,680¼	20,092	385,550	23,700	409,250	1,688	1,689	618	643	555	14	668
Columbus	14,319	7,393	382,312	54,343	436,655	670	661	253	292	238	9	446
Coventry	21,447	10,605	454,715	43,450	498,165	842	842	333	357	214	12	640
German	10,663¼	6,035½	157,990	3,675	161,665	406	400	146	146	133	8	360
Greene	28,175¾	14,082½	1,031,905	332,565	1,364,470	1,880	1,837	697	743	528	22	1,283
Guilford	23,533	10,953	640,220	82,900	723,120	1,272	1,280	492	524	443	19	892
Lincklaen	10,544½	6,201½	149,740	8,700	158,440	549	582	214	219	194	9	445
Macdonough	13,181¼	8,619	232,900	19,340	252,240	701	716	279	282	252	9	521
New Berlin	19,942	10,046	1,223,675	510,436	1,734,111	1,224	1,283	479	524	354	20	890
North Norwich	10,106½	6,591	362,341	27,850	390,191	585	541	210	235	194	8	444
Norwich	19,528¼	6,477¼	546,761	56,945	603,706	2,005	2,104	761	822	583	19	1,401
Otselic	14,352	9,871	292,760	15,250	308,010	887	834	339	360	277	13	729
Oxford	19,159	12,101	627,600	162,725	790,325	1,519	1,597	629	636	521	19	1,219
Pharsalia	12,794	12,248	234,380	13,000	247,380	594	558	210	218	209	10	462
Pitcher	13,354½	4,395¾	241,090	22,740	263,830	652	629	250	315	260	11	486
Plymouth	15,166	9,671	376,645	39,300	415,945	769	772	299	577	503	15	620
Preston	15,935½	5,361	277,010	26,040	303,050	512	532	180	483	279	8	362
Sherburne	20,702	5,544½	776,686	115,100	891,786	1,367	1,409	532	392	297	17	1,029
Smithville	20,341	9,366½	400,565	29,100	429,665	837	824	311	198	175	10	581
Smyrna	16,903½	7,281½	442,428	68,364	510,792	920	946	370	270	236	14	698
Total	347,828¾	182,936	9,620,318	1,677,823	11,298,141	19,879	20,036	7,602	8,236	6,435	289	14,747

| NAMES OF TOWNS. | LIVE STOCK. | | | | | AGRICULTURAL PRODUCTS. | | | | | | | |
| | Horses. | Working Oxen and Calves. | Cows. | Sheep. | Swine. | BUSH. OF GRAIN. | | Tons of Hay. | Bushels of Potatoes. | Bushels of Apples. | DAIRY PRODUCTS. | | Domestic Cloths in yards. |
						Winter.	Spring.				Pounds Butter.	Pounds Cheese.	
Afton[1]													
Bainbridge	753	3,146	2,226	6,438	1,351	3,185½	98,411½	8,771½	30,609	40,714	225,645	14,000	6,109
Columbus	464	1,106	1,807	2,835	898	135	48,605	5,418	13,531	25,738	107,410	283,019	1,360
Coventry	534	1,771	2,140	2,750	1,021	936	56,962	5,706	15,795	31,330	250,270	6,510	1,343
German	290	826	1,160	964	361	286	16,934	3,176	5,827	11,616	123,600	700	2,358
Greene	848	2,822	3,603	4,090	1,640	3,272½	88,283½	9,865½	22,634	41,268	451,433	17,758	5,530½
Guilford	697	2,206	2,721	3,756	1,296	2,384	58,908½	8,615	15,931	34,093	344,045	29,226	1,109
Lincklaen	376	802	981	2,297	486	54	30,134¾	3,315½	6,160	13,358	95,785	19,680	1,582½
Macdonough	374	1,009	1,535	2,143	535	177	18,274	4,448½	8,545½	16,153	164,985	1,805	3,448½
New Berlin	645	1,363	2,439	2,697	1,047	675½	55,390	6,908	12,976	30,227	196,839	248,173	1,298
North Norwich	372	985	1,061	3,335	727	1,454	45,291½	3,243½	13,314	18,162	136,381	99,260	347
Norwich	632	1,933	2,220	7,287	1,003	492	46,446	8,523	14,291	31,889	198,380	107,328	1,188¾
Otselic	526	1,278	1,433	2,562	676	21	48,310½	4,713½	13,612	11,116	141,505	57,300	1,772
Oxford	735	2,216	1,714	5,835	1,450	1,750	59,623	7,766	17,028	43,924	289,502	17,100	2,297
Pharsalia	330	812	1,318	1,925	506	165	26,674	4,090	9,186	11,714	114,648	51,450	2,399
Pitcher	445	1,122	1,259	4,487	585	128	29,816½	3,795½	8,369	21,582	144,200	13,797	1,412½
Plymouth	553	1,386	1,531	4,413	643	579	47,884	5,246	13,291	27,997	155,663	76,504	1,052
Preston	349	1,287	1,497	6,793	625	82	24,797¾	4,623	9,094½	35,255	176,953	23,380	1,475½
Sherburne	841	1,856	2,179	11,726	1,189	1,601	111,742½	6,815	15,118	47,115	208,415	92,708	694
Smithville	496	1,882	2,620	2,290	1,135	584	41,791½	7,131	11,399	32,689	319,695	13,660	3,387½
Smyrna	711	1,744	1,495	7,300	1,018	1,128	63,942	5,200	13,831	27,614	145,210	39,186	2,488½
Total	10,971	31,452	36,939	85,923	18,092	19,089¼	1,018,320¼	117,370¾	270,542	553,554	3,990,564¼	1,212,544	42,652

[1] Formed since 1855.

CLINTON COUNTY.

This county was formed from Washington, March 7, 1788.[1] Essex was taken off in 1799. St. Lawrence was provisionally annexed in 1801, and taken off in 1802; and Franklin was taken off in 1808. It lies upon Lake Champlain, and is the N. E. corner co. in the State. It is centrally distant 143 mi. from Albany, and contains 1,092 sq. mi. The surface is generally hilly and broken, and in some parts mountainous. The Au Sable Range enters the s. w. corner from Essex co. and extends in spurs and broken ranges through more than one-half of the w. part of the co. The highest peaks along the w. border are 3,000 to 4,000 feet above tide. These mountains have the same general characteristics as those further s. They are wild and broken, and their declivities and summits are so covered with ragged ledges of rocks that they can produce but a scanty crop of timber and are almost inaccessible. The uplands decline toward the N.; and along the N. line of the co. is a wide tract nearly level. Along the lake shore the surface is level or moderately uneven; and from this tract it rises gradually but unevenly to the summits of the ridges in the interior. A large share of the central and w. portions of the co. is covered by the original forests, and is too rough to ever admit of profitable cultivation. The mountainous region in the s. w., comprising about one-third of the co., is underlaid by gneiss, granite, and other primary rocks. A belt of Potsdam sandstone extends in a great curve around the primary region and occupies more than one-half of the remaining part of the co. On the N. it extends nearly to Canada, but toward the s. it gradually diminishes, and on the s. line it is but a few miles wide. Surrounding this, and lying next above it, is a narrow belt of calciferous sand rock, outcropping on the surface, along the lake shore, between Au Sable and Salmon Rivers. The limestones next appear, occupying the N. E. corner of the co. and outcropping along the lake from Salmon River to Rouses Point. Tertiary clay is found in a few places along the lake; and drift deposits are abundant in the N. and E. parts. Peat bogs are numerous in the N. E. part. The primitive region is exceedingly rich in minerals. Magnetic iron ore is found in inexhaustible quantities, and of a quality equal to the best in the world.[2]

Au Sable River forms most of the s. boundary. North of this are Little Sable, Salmon, Saranac, Little Chazy, and Great Chazy or Champlain Rivers, all flowing into Lake Champlain. English River flows N. into Canada. Upon all these streams are numerous falls, furnishing an immense amount of water-power. In the western wilderness are numerous small lakes, the principal of which are Chateaugay and Chazy Lakes, and Sampson, Taylor, and Slush Ponds. The soil along the lake is clayey, and in the interior and w. a sandy loam, best adapted to pasturage.

The people are principally engaged in stock raising, dairying, lumbering,[3] mining, and in the manufacture of iron[4] and starch. A large business is carried on in peltries, the wilderness still furnishing numerous valuable fur-bearing animals.[5] Fish are abundant in the mountain streams and lakes, although the salmon, once so abundant, have now nearly disappeared.[6] The Northern (Ogdensburgh) R. R. extends w. from Rouses Point, on Lake Champlain, through Champlain, Mooers, Altona, Ellenburgh, and Clinton. The Plattsburgh & Montreal R. R. extends N. through Plattsburgh, Beekmantown, Chazy, and Mooers.

The co. seat is located at the village of Plattsburgh, on Lake Champlain.[7] The courthouse is a

[1] Named from Geo. Clinton, then Governor. When organized, it embraced all the land on both sides of Lake Champlain, as claimed by the State of New York. The claim E. of the lake was abandoned upon the recognition of Vermont as an independent State, in 1791.

[2] Clinton and Essex are the two most important mining cos. in the State. The veins of iron, in extent and richness, surpass those of any other part of the world. Ore was first discovered in the "Winter" ore bed, in Au Sable, by Geo. Shaffer, in 1800, —although travelers had previously frequently noticed the immense quantities of iron sand upon the lake shore. The principal veins now opened are the Arnold, Rutgers, Finch, Winter, Indian, Cook, Battie, Mace, Jackson, and McIntyre Mines, in Au Sable; the Palmer and Rutgers Mines, in Black Brook; and the Skinner and Averill Mines, in Dannemora. Veins of greater or less richness are found in all the towns underlaid by the primary rocks.

[3] Au Sable and Saranac Rivers flow through valuable lumber districts, and upon them are numerous sawmills. Immense quantities of logs are annually floated down these streams and worked up at the mills below. Several important plank roads have been constructed in the wilderness for the special accommodation of the lumber and iron business.

[4] The iron manufactured is principally in the form of blooms.

[5] Hunting is pursued as a business to some extent; and during the summer large numbers of amateur hunters from the cities flock to the wilderness for recreation and amusement.

[6] So abundant were salmon that 30 years ago 100 bbls. were annually taken in the co.; and from its importance to the early settlers this fish was taken as a device for the first co. seal.

[7] The first court was held Oct. 28, 1788. A blockhouse erected at the time of the alarm occasioned by the defeat of St. Clair by the Indians was used for the first jail. A courthouse and jail of wood was erected in 1802–03, and burned in 1814 by the invading British army. A new one erected soon after was burned in 1836, and the present one was erected on its site. The first

232

substantial brick building, with a stone basement, fronting the public square and river. The jail, a stone building in rear of the courthouse, affords no accommodations for the classification of prisoners, and is destitute of means of ventilation. The clerk's office is a fireproof brick building on an adjacent lot. The poorhouse is located in Beekmantown, 4 mi. N. of Plattsburgh. It has an average of 65 inmates, supported at a weekly cost of $1.00 each. The farm—90 acres—yields a revenue of $800.[1]

Four weekly newspapers are published in the co.[2]

The first white man that ever visited this co. was Samuel Champlain, in 1609, under the auspices of the French. From that time until the final surrender of Canada in 1760, the French claimed and held this region of country, and the lands were mostly occupied by parties holding title under French grants.[3]

At the close of the war in 1760, settlement rapidly spread down the lake shore. By the terms of the treaty between England and France, the French settlers were to be secured in their rights; but the Government of New York made conflicting grants, which gave rise to controversies and quarrels and seriously retarded the progress of settlement. A few families were scattered along the shore previous to the Revolution; but the expedition of Burgoyne in 1777 broke up every settlement in the co. An important naval engagement took place Sept. 11, 1776, in the strait between Valcour Island and the w. shore, between the British and American forces, without any decisive results. The conflict was renewed on the 13th, and the American vessels were nearly all run ashore on the Vt. side and burned.[4]

Settlements were made at all the principal places bordering upon the lake within 10 years after the close of the Revolution. Point Au Fer was occupied by the British until 1796, when, in common with several other posts along the N. frontier, it was surrendered to the Americans.[5] During the same year the St. Regis Indians ceded their claims to the State. The embargo of 1808 was openly violated, and many severe encounters took place between the revenue officers and organized bands of smugglers.[6] Several attempts were made by lawless bands to seize the collectors and revenue officers, but without success. During the last war with Great Britain this co. was the seat of important military transactions, and along its frontiers and upon the adjacent waters of the lake many skirmishes and engagements took place.[7]

---

co. officers were Chas. Platt, *First Judge;* Josiah Throop and Chas. Hay, *Judges;* Robt. Cochran, Peter Sailly, Wm. McAuley, and Pliny Moore, *Assistant Justices;* Theodorus Platt, *Surrogate;* Benj. Mooers, *Sheriff;* and Melancthon Lloyd Woolsey, *Clerk.*

[1] The Senate Committee of 1857 report that "this house is a very poor one, indifferently kept, and a disgrace to the co." The rooms were filthy and not at all ventilated; and the water supplied to the establishment is furnished from springs into which drains from the barnyard and privies empty. No school is taught; and the children are not admitted to the public schools. The Supervisors have authorized a loan of $4,000 for rebuilding this establishment.

[2] *The American Monitor* was established at Plattsburgh in 1807 by W. Nichols and Sam'l Lowell, and continued a short time.

The Plattsburgh Republican was begun in July, 1811, by —— Reynolds. In 1813 Azariah C. Flagg became publisher, and continued it until 1826. It was subsequently under the charge of H. C. Miller and Wm. Laud. In Aug. 1833, it passed into the hands of Roby G. Stone, by whom it is still continued.

The Northern Herald was begun April 10, 1813, by Fred. C. Powell. In 1815 it was changed to
The Plattsburgh Herald, and soon after it was discontinued.
The Northern Intelligencer was begun at Plattsburgh in May, 1821, by Fred. R. Allen. In 1832 it was united with
The Aurora Borealis, which was established in 1828, the combined papers taking the name of
Plattsburgh Aurora. It was continued but a short time.
The Democratic Press was published at Plattsburgh in 1834 by J. K. Averill.
The Whig was started at Plattsburgh in 1835 by G. W. Platt. In 1838 it was changed to
Clinton County Whig. After several changes of ownership, in Oct. 1855, it was changed to
The Plattsburgh Express, published by Albert G. Carver, and is still continued by him.
The Berean Guide was published a short time at Beekmantown in 1837 by Rev. Mr. Bailey.
The Free Democrat was published in 1848 by Oliver Hart.
The Northern Lancet, mo., was begun in 1849 by Dr. Horace Nelson. It was soon changed to
The Lancet, and was continued till 1856.
The Champlain Beacon was commenced in 1850 by Ketchum & Averill. In 1852 it was sold to D. Turner, of Keeseville, who changed it to
The Rouses Point Advertiser, under which name it is still published.
The Cottage Gazette was published in 1851 by Arthur C. Nelson.
The American Sentinel was started Jan. 10, 1855, by Warren Dow. It was soon changed to

The Plattsburgh Sentinel, and is still published.

[3] The Governor General and Intendant, on the 10th, 11th, and 12th days of April, 1733, granted 3 seigniories within the present limits of Champlain and Chazy, each 3 leagues in depth and fronting upon Lake Champlain. The first, granted to Hugues Jacques Péan, Sieur de Liviandière, captain in the marines, extended from Chazy River 2¼ leagues northward; the second was granted to Sieur Migeon de la Gauchitère, also a captain in the marines, and the third to Sieur de St. Vincent, jr., an ensign in the marines; each grant being 2 leagues in front. These grants were ensigned forever, in fief and seigniory, with the right of superior, mean, and inferior jurisdiction, (*haute, moyenne,* et *basse justice,*) with the right of hunting, fishing, and Indian trade, subject to the performance of fealty and homage at the Castle of St. Louis, in Quebec, agreeable to the custom of Paris followed in Canada. They were conditioned to the preservation by tenants of the oak-timber fit for the royal navy, the reservation of mines and highways to the crown, and the use of the beaches to fishermen unless actually occupied by the seignior. The patentees might grant concessions to tenants, subject to the customary *cens et rentes* and dues, for each arpent of land in front by 40 arpents in depth. If used for military purposes, materials for the erection of fortifications and firewood for the use of garrisons were to be given without charge, and the grant was to be submitted for the royal approbation within one year. The grantees having failed to make improvements on the 10th of May, 1741, all these grants were declared to have reverted to his majesty's domain. On the 1st of Nov., 1752, a seigniory of 2½ leagues in front by 3 in depth, and including Chazy River, was granted to the Sieur Bedou, councellor in the Superior Council of Quebec, under conditions like those of Péan.—*Titles and Docs. relating to the Seignorial Tenure.*

[4] This engagement was one of the most gallant fought during the war, and, although resulting disastrously, it reflected no dishonor on the American arms. The American forces, commanded by Benedict Arnold, consisted of 1 sloop, 2 schooners, 4 galleys, and 8 gondolas, with 84 guns and 144 swivels; and the British force, commanded by Capt. Thos. Pringles, of 1 ship, 2 schooners, 1 razee, 1 gondola, 20 gunboats, and 28 long boats, with 89 guns and 697 men. The American loss was 80 to 90, and the British about the same. The Americans saved themselves by running their vessels aground and swimming ashore.

[5] Judge Pliny Moore, who settled in Champlain in 1785, was visited on the 1st of every month by a British corporal and file of men, from Point Au Fer, to notify him that his claim under the State would not be recognized; but no attention was paid to these repeated warnings.—*Palmer's Hist. Lake Champlain, p.* 152.

[6] In 1808 two Government officers were killed in attempting to seize a smuggling vessel called the Black Snake.

[7] The following is a brief chronological list of the most important events of the war connected with this co.

In the summer of 1814, Sir Geo. Provost, Gov. of Canada, made extensive preparations for an invasion of the country along Lake Champlain. Toward the last of Aug. a land force of 14,000 men assembled on the frontier and commenced their march, supported by a formidable fleet under Commodore Downie. Gen. Macomb, who commanded the Americans, had a force of less than 3,000; but, as the invading army drew nigh, he was continually re-inforced by volunteers and militia.[1] The American fleet, under the command of Commodore MacDonough, took position in Cumberland Bay, awaiting the attack of the British. On Sunday morning, Sept. 11, a simultaneous attack was made by the British land and naval forces, and a bloody and desperate battle ensued. At the end of 2 hours Commodore Downie's flag struck, and nearly the whole British fleet fell into the hands of the Americans.[2] The cannonade was continued upon the shore until night, when the British slowly and sullenly retreated and in a few days returned to Canada.[3] These engagements were justly considered among the most brilliant that occurred during the war,

1812,   Sept. 1.—Gen. Bloomfield, with 8,000 troops, prepared to attack Canada.
  "   Sept. 16.—Troops consisting of 3,000 regulars and 2,000 militia, under Gen. Dearborn, encamped within a half mile of the Canada line.
  "   Sept. 20.—Guardhouse at La Cole surprised; but, as plans of attack were frustrated, the troops retired to Plattsburgh for winter quarters.
1813,   Feb.—Two brigades marched to Sackets Harbor, leaving the w. side of the lake entirely unprotected till Sept.
  "   June 2.—Naval engagement near Ash Island, Canada, between an American force, under Lieut. Sidney Smith, and several British gunboats, resulting in the loss of the American sloops Growler and Eagle and 112 men. The vessels were subsequently re-captured.
  "   July 31.—A British force of 1,400 men, under Col. Murray, made a descent upon Plattsburgh and destroyed a large amount of public and private property.
  "   Sept. 19.—A body of 3,000 American troops, under Gen. Hampton, concentrated at Cumberland Head and started on an expedition against Canada.
  "   Sept. 21.—After remaining one day in Canada, the Gen. changed his plan, and, ostensibly on his way to Montreal, he marched to Chateaugay, and there remained idle 26 days.
  "   Oct. 1.—A small party of American militia surprised a picket guard at Odeltown, Canada.
  "   Oct. 11.—Col. Isaac Clark, with 110 men, crossed the lake from Champlain, attacked a party of British at Missisco Bay, killed 9, wounded 14, and took 101 prisoners.
  "   Nov.—A party of Vt. militia crossed the lake and placed themselves under General Hampton. The Gov. of Vt. ordered them to return; but they refused to obey.
  "   Dec. 1.—A British naval force, consisting of 6 armed galleys, under Capt. Pring, entered the lake and burned an empty storehouse near Rouses Point. In the report of Sir George Provost, this building was converted into a large magazine of stores at Plattsburgh.
1814,   Jan. 18.—A detachment of infantry from Plattsburgh arrived upon the frontier, soon followed by another body of troops, under Gen. Wilkinson.
  "   March 30.—Under the direction of Gen. Wilkinson, Maj. Forsyth attacked a gristmill at La Cole, but was repulsed with a loss of 104 in killed and wounded. The British loss was 56.
  "   May 9.—A British naval force, consisting of 5 sloops and 13 row-galleys, under Capt. Pring, were repulsed in an attack upon Otter Creek, in Vt. On their retreat they entered Baquet River, but were attacked by a body of militia, and nearly all the men in the rear galley were killed or wounded.
  "   June 24.—Lieut. Col. Forsyth, with 70 riflemen, entered Canada, and was attacked by a British force of 200 men. He effected his retreat with little loss, but a few days after was killed in another skirmish.
  "   Aug. 29.—Gen. Izard, with the greater part of the American force, left Champlain, leaving the immense amount of military stores at Plattsburgh in charge of Gen. Macomb, at the head of 3,400 men, 1,400 of whom was sick.
  "   Aug. 30.—Gen. Brisbane, with the advance guard of the British army, took possession of Champlain.
  "   Sept. 3.—Sir Geo. Provost, Gov. of Canada, at the head of 14,000 men, advanced s. from Champlain, arriving within 8 mi. of Plattsburgh on the evening of the 5th.
  "   Sept. 6.—Skirmish at Culvers Hill, and the first attack on Plattsburgh, in which the British lost 200 men and the Americans 45.

1814,   Sept. 11.—Naval engagement in Cumberland Bay, resulting in the complete victory of the Americans; and an attack upon the American landworks, which was repulsed. The British army retreated during the following night.
  "   Sept. 24.—Last division of the British army retired to Canada.
  [1] Gov. Chittenden of Vt. issued a proclamation calling upon the militia to rally and repel the invasion; and large numbers promptly responded to the call and repaired to the camp. The call upon Washington and Warren cos. was answered by 350 more men than had ever mustered at an inspection or review.
  [2] The comparative strength and loss of the two parties on the lake were as follows:—

AMERICAN.

Vessels.	Men.	Guns.	Killed.	Wounded.
Flagship *Saratoga*, Com. Macdonough...	212	26	28	29
Brig *Eagle*, Capt. Henlyn......................	150	20	13	20
Schooner *Ticonderoga*, Lieut. Cassin......	110	17	6	6
Sloop *Preble*, Lieut. Chas. Budd............	30	7	2	
Galleys *Allen, Burrows, Borer, Nettle, Viper,* and *Centipede* (each 1 long 24 and 1 Columbian).....................	210	12		
Galleys *Ludlow, Wilmer, Alwin,* and *Ballard* (each 1 12 pound)...............	140	4		
Total........................	852	86	49	55

BRITISH.

Vessels.	Men.	Guns.	Killed.	Wounded.
Frigate *Confiance*, Capt. Downie........	300	39	41	83
Brig *Linnet*, Capt. Pring..................	120	16	10	14
Sloop *Chub*, Lieut. McGhee..............	45	11	6	10
" *Finch*, " Hicks..............	45	11		2
Galleys *Sir Jas. Yeo, Sir Geo. Provost, Sir Sidney Beckwith, Broke,* and *Murray* (each 2 guns)..................	225	10		
Galleys *Wellington, Tecumseh, Drummond, Simcoe,* and 4 names unknown (each 1 gun)....................	360	8		
Total........................	1,095	95	57	109

The action lasted 2¼ hours. The British galleys lowered their colors; but, not being pursued, they escaped, as did also a storeship which lay near the point of Cumberland Head during the engagement. The loss upon the enemy's galleys was not ascertained, but was large; and the total British loss was one-fifth of their whole number. In their retreat the British left behind them a vast quantity of provisions, tents, camp equipage, and ammunition, together with their sick and wounded. The British and American officers were buried separately near the center of the village cemetery; and the sailors and marines of both fleets side by side in one common grave, on Crab Island. Some time after, the sister-in-law of Com. Geo. Downie placed a tablet over his grave; and on the anniversary of the battle, in 1843, the citizens of Plattsburgh and the Clinton Co. Military Association erected plain marble monuments at the unmarked graves of Lieut. G. W. Runk, Lieut. Peter Gamble, Lieut. John Stansbury, Sailing Master Rogers Carter, Midshipman J. M. Baldwin, and Pilot Joseph Barrow of the American navy; and Col. Willington, Ensign J. Chapman, Lieut. R. Kingsbury, Boatswain Chas. Jackson, Capt. Purchase, Capt. Alex. Anderson, (marines,) Acting Capt. Wm. Paul, and Midshipman V. M. Gunn, of the British army and navy.
  [3] Sir Geo. Provost, in his official report, says, "This unlooked for event deprived me of the co-operation of the fleet, without which the further prosecution of the service was become impracticable. I did not hesitate to arrest the course of the troops advancing to the attack, because the most complete success would have been unavailing, and the possession of the enemy's works offered no advantage to compensate for the loss we must have sustained in acquiring possession of them."

and they served to partially obliterate the disgrace that attached to most of the movements that were planned and executed along the N. frontier. The immense sums of money expended within the co. during the war greatly stimulated its industry; and although Plattsburgh was twice in the hands of the enemy and partly burned, still business prospered. At the close of the war the excitement subsided, and a commercial re-action followed that entirely prostrated business. Upon the completion of the Champlain Canal in 1823, business again revived; and a new impulse has again been given to it by the railroads and plank roads since constructed. In 1838–40 the co. shared the intense excitement attending the "Patriot Wars," and several encounters between the insurgents and the military authorities took place in the neighboring parts of Canada.

The lands in this co. were mostly granted in comparatively small patents. The w. portion embraces 4 townships of the Old Military Tract. A tract of 231,540 acres in the N. E. and central parts of the co. was included in the lands granted by the Legislature of New York to the refugees from Canada and Nova Scotia at the close of the Revolution.[1] These lands were divided into 80 and 420 acre lots, except 5,000 acres, which was divided into 15 equal parts, which were granted to the officers and privates among these refugees. Considerable land lying along the lake was granted in small tracts to English officers who served during the French War. Among the principal remaining patents were Platt's, Livingston's, Beekman's, Duerville, Dean's, and Graves.

ALTONA—was formed from Chazy, Dec. 2, 1857. It is an interior town, lying N. of the center of the co. Its surface is a rolling upland, with a slight inclination toward the N. E. The w. half is underlaid by Potsdam sandstone, and hundreds of acres are covered with the naked rock. Great Chazy River is the principal stream. The soil is light and sandy, and a large share of it is unfit for cultivation. A few settlements are scattered through the town, and the people are mostly engaged in lumbering. There is no village or p. o. in town. **Chazy**, in the N. part, is a station on the N. R. R. **Ellenburgh Depot** lies on the w. line. The first settler was Simeon Wood, who located in town in 1800.[2] The town embraces parts of the Refugee Tract and Duerville Patent. The first church (French Bap.) was formed Jan. 1, 1856.

AU SABLE[3]—was formed from Peru, March 29, 1839. It is the s. E. corner town in the co. Its surface is nearly level in the E., rolling in the center, and hilly in the w. The highest summits are 500 to 600 ft. above the lake. Au Sable River forms the s. boundary, and the Little Au Sable flows N. E. through the w. part. The soil is generally a light, sandy loam, moderately fertile in the E. and center and nearly unfit for cultivation in the w. Upon the Au Sable where it breaks through the Potsdam sandstone is a beautiful cascade known as Birmingham Falls.[4] Iron ore of an excellent quality is found in abundance.[5] **Keeseville**,[6] (p. v.,) upon the Au Sable, 5 mi. from the lake, contains 7 churches, the Keeseville Academy, 2 extensive rolling mills, 3 nail factories, a machine shop, an ax and edge tool factory, a cupola furnace, an axletree factory, a horseshoe factory, a planing mill, 2 gristmills, and a nail keg factory.[7] Pop. 2,569,—of whom 1,999 are in Au Sable and 570 are in Essex co. **Clintonville**, (p. v.,) upon the Au Sable, in the w. part of the town, was incorp. April 11, 1825. It contains 2 churches and an extensive iron manufactory.[8] Pop. 855. **New Sweden**, (p. v.,) upon the Au Sable, in the s. w. corner of the town, contains 2 forges and 150 inhabitants. **Birmingham Falls,** at the head of the rapids upon the Au

1 The act making this grant bears date of May 11, 1782. The names of Canadian refugees were reported by Brig. Gen. Moses Hazen and Col. Jeremiah Throop, and those of the Nova Scotia refugees by Col. James Livingston. The small lots were laid out in narrow strips fronting upon the lake, and the remainder in the rear. These lands were distributed among 252 persons, who drew the lots by ballot. The greater part of the tract was not occupied in the time specified by the act, and reverted to the State.

2 Among the early settlers were Lyman Clothier, Eliphalet Hascall, Daniel and Robert Baker, Thos. Cudworth, Simon Goodspeed, and Daniel Robinson. The first birth was that of Matilda K. Wood, May 30, 1802. Sarah Stockwell taught the first school, in 1804; and Lyman Clothier kept the first inn.

3 Pronounced Au Saw'ble, a French name signifying river of sand. The name is said to have been derived from a sandy bar at the mouth of the river.

4 This cascade is located about 2 mi. below Keeseville. From the face of the cliff the river has worn back a ragged and irregular channel in the solid sandstone for a distance of nearly 2 mi. and to the depth of 100 to 130 feet. The rocks that border it are perpendicular, and in some places overhanging, so that the water can scarcely be seen from the banks above. At several points this ravine is compressed to a width of less than 30 feet. The river plunges into the chasm in a perpendicular descent of 70 feet, and struggles through the tortuous channel, foaming, whirling, and eddying over its rocky bed.

5 The Arnold ore bed, 2¼ mi. N. W. of Clintonville, was first opened in 1809. The shaft is 350 feet deep, and the ore is raised by steam. For many years the average annual yield has been 1,000 tons; and for 5 years before 1856 it was 1,500 tons. There are 5 veins, with a total width of 25 feet, yielding ores of different qualities. This mine has supplied the forges of Jay, Wilmington, and Chesterfield, in Essex co., and of Peru, Au Sable, and Black Brook, in Clinton co. Other ore beds are found, of which the Finch vein, a continuation of the Arnold, is the only one now worked. It has supplied the forge in Jay. The ore from this bed is a peroxid, and may be worked without washing or other separation.

6 Named from Richard and Oliver Keese, sons of John Keese, one of the original proprietors. The two parts of the village are connected by 3 bridges,—one of stone, one of wood, and one an iron suspension foot bridge. The stone bridge is a single arch of 110 feet.

7 About 3,500 tons of nails and 1,500 tons of merchant iron and 70,000 nail kegs are manufactured here annually. The first rolling mill in the State was established here, in 1816.

8 The Peru Iron Co. was incorp. Nov. 11, 1824, with a capital of $200,000. The iron works built by them at Clintonville subsequently passed into the hands of Francis Salters, and are now owned by him and his sons. In one building are 20 forge fires, and the blooms made are entirely worked up into merchant iron, of which 7,500 tons are produced annually.

Sable, contains 20 houses. **The Union** is a hamlet, on the line of Peru, and contains two Quaker meetinghouses. Edward Everett located upon the site of The Union in 1786.[1] The first religious society (Friends) was organized in 1799.[2]

BEEKMANTOWN[3]—was formed from Plattsburgh, Feb. 25, 1820. Dannemora was taken off in 1854. It lies upon Lake Champlain, near the center of the E. border of the co. The surface is level in the E. and moderately hilly in the w. Its streams are small creeks and brooks. St. Armands Bay extends into the s. E. corner. Point au Roche and Rams Head are capes upon the lake. The soil is a clay loam in the center and E., and a light sand in the w. A spring emitting sulphuretted hydrogen and carbonic acid gases is found in town. **Beekmantown** (p. o.) and **East Beekmantown** (p. o.) are hamlets. The first settlers were Maj. Benj. Mooers and 7 associates, who located at Point au Roche Aug. 10, 1783.[4] The British passed through the town in 1814, and on the 6th of Sept. a slight skirmish took place, in which several were killed.[5] The census reports 4 churches; 3 M. E. and 1 Presb.

BLACK BROOK[6]—was formed from Peru, March 29, 1839. It is the s. w. corner town in the co. Its surface is a rocky and mountainous upland, the highest summits being 1,500 to 2,500 ft. above the lake. Among the mountains are several nearly level table lands 200 to 300 ft. above the general level. Ledges, crags, and boulders cover a large share of the surface. The forest trees are thinly scattered, and nearly the whole town is too rough and poor for cultivation. Saranac River flows across the N. w. corner, and the Au Sable forms a portion of the s. boundary. Great Black Brook and Little Black Brook, tributaries of the Au Sable, drain the central parts of the town. In the mountainous region are several small lakes or ponds, the principal of which are Mud, Sampson, Taylors, Slush, and Military Ponds. The soil is cold, wet, and unproductive. Extensive beds of iron ore are scattered through the town.[7] The people are principally engaged in the manufacture of iron[8] and charcoal, and in lumbering.[9] **Au Sable Forks,** (p. v.,) on the Au Sable, in the s. E. part of the town, is mostly on the s. bank of the river, in Essex co. **Black Brook,** (p. v.,) near the s. border, contains extensive iron works, several sawmills, and about 85 houses. **Clayburgh,** on the Saranac, in the N. part, lies partly in the town of Saranac. It contains iron works and 30 houses.[10] **Union Falls** (p. o.) and **Garlick Falls,** (p. o.,) both on the Saranac, are hamlets and lumber stations. The first settler was Zephaniah Palmer, who located at Au Sable Forks about 1825.[11] The census reports one church (R. C.)

CHAMPLAIN—was formed March 7, 1788. Chateaugay (Franklin co.) was taken off in 1799, and Mooers and Chazy in 1804. It lies upon Lake Champlain, in the N. E. corner of the co. Its surface is generally level, with a gentle slope toward the lake. The crest of a swell of land between Champlain Village and Rouses Point is about 200 feet above the lake. Great Chazy or Champlain River flows in a tortuous course through the town and discharges its waters into

---

1 Among the other early settlers were John Keese and his sons Richard, John, Oliver, Stephen, and William, Caleb Green and his sons Henry, Rodman, John, and James, Peter Halleck, Danl. Jackson, Gilbert and Gerrit Thew, John Haff, Elisha Arnold, and John Stanton, about 1795. The first child born was in the family of John Stanton, about 1795. The mother of this child was a servant girl in the family. The wife, not being exactly reconciled to the circumstance, insisted upon being immediately taken to her friends in Dutchess co. It being winter, the husband took her upon a hand sled and drew her upon the lake to "*Skenesborough*," thence to Fort Edward, and down the Hudson to her father's, after which he returned to Au Sable, having been 5 weeks in performing the journey. Upon his return he married the mother of the child, and lived with her many years. The first school was taught in 1791, by —— Thompson; the first inn was kept by Joel Buck, in 1800; and the first forge was erected by Geo. Griswold, in 1812.

2 The census reports 8 churches in town; 2 Cong., 2 M. E., 2 Friends, Presb., and R. C.

3 Named from Wm. Beekman, to whom, with 29 others, the town was granted March 27, 1769. It embraced 22,475 acres.

4 Mooers was appointed to survey the Refugee Tract. After several years he removed to Cumberland Head, and afterward to Plattsburgh. Thos. Treadwell, Ezekiel Hubbard, Henry Deming, Jonathan Scribner, Abner Pomeroy, Simon Newcomb, jr., Capt. John Jersey, and Joseph Main settled near Beekmantown Corners; Philip Roberts, Henry Barnes, Ephraim and Amos Moores and John Deming were also among the early settlers. The first birth was that of Silas Pomeroy; the first marriage, that of Eli Howe and Miss Hubbard, in 1794; and the first death, that of a child of Simon Newcomb.

5 Among the killed were Lieut. Col. Willington and Ensign Chapman, of the enemy, and several of the American militia.—*Palmer's Hist. Lake Champlain, p. 152.*

6 Named from its principal stream. The town comprises portions of the Old Military Tract and of Livingston's Patent. The military lands were finally conveyed to Benj. Birdsall and his associates by act of Feb. 4, 1793, to satisfy claims growing out of the suppression of the lease of all of the Indian lands in the State for 999 years.—*Folio Laws, XVI. Sess., p. 24. Clark's Hist. Onon., vol. I, p. 368.*

7 The *Palmer Mine*, 2 mi. N. of Au Sable Forks, was discovered by Z. Palmer in 1825. It is situated on a hill 400 to 500 feet above the river. The ore is raised by steam, and the yield is 16,000 to 20,000 tons per year. The *Myers Mine*, at Clayburgh, has been worked since 1846. It yields annually 1,500 tons of ore, principally used in the manufacture of wire, tacks, and small nails. The *Trombois Mine* was discovered in 1845, and about 10,000 tons of ore have been raised. The iron made from it is soft and tough, and is principally used in the manufacture of boiler plates, horse nails, and car axles.

8 The Sable Iron Company have extensive works at Au Sable Forks and at Black Brook, and they manufacture 2,600 tons of blooms, 900 tons of merchant iron, 50,000 to 55,000 kegs of nails, and 1,600,000 bush. of charcoal per annum. 2,500 tons of blooms are manufactured at their establishment at Black Brook alone. The Co. was incorp. in Sept. 1834, and the stock is now owned by J. & J. Rogers.

9 There are 8 to 10 large sawmills in town.

10 The products of the Myers Mine are principally manufactured at this place. A water-power near the mine is improved, and a forge of 5 fires is in active operation. A steam forge and steam hammer for the manufacture of R. R. axles was in operation here about 4 years.

11 Several plank roads have been built in this town to facilitate the iron and lumber business. —— Curtis kept the first inn, near the center, in 1828. Halsey Rogers and John McIntyrs located in town in 1830. The Sable Iron Co. erected the first forge the same year.

Kings Bay. It is navigable to near Champlain Village. Corbeau Creek, its tributary, is the other principal stream. Point au Fer[1] and Stony Point are two capes projecting into the lake. The soil is a clay or clayey loam. Peat is found in numerous localities. **Champlain,** (p. v.,) upon the Chazy, near the N. line of the town, contains the Champlain Academy, 3 churches, 2 founderies, a linen factory, planing mill, and carriage factory.[2] Pop. 1,473. **Perrys Mills**[3] (p. o.) is a lumber station upon the Chazy, in the N. W. corner of the town. **Rouses Point,**[4] (p. v.,) upon the lake, in the N. E. corner of the town, contains 3 churches, a brewery, newspaper office, and extensive depôts and repair shops belonging to the Northern R. R. Co. It is divided into the Upper and Lower Villages, the latter being about twice as large as the former. Pop. 1,769. **Coopersville,**[5] or **Corbeau,** is a village upon Chazy River, opposite the mouth of Corbeau Creek. It contains 1 church and 40 houses. The first settlers were Canadian and Nova Scotia refugees, who located in town soon after the Revolution. The first English settler was Pliny Moore, who came in to reside in 1789.[6] The census reports 4 churches in town.[7]

CHAZY[8]—was formed from Champlain, March 20, 1804. Altona was taken off in 1857. It lies upon Lake Champlain, N. of the center of the co. Its surface is rolling and has a gentle inclination toward the E. The principal stream is the Little Chazy, flowing N. E. through near the center. Corbeau Creek flows through the N. border. Potsdam sandstone underlies the W. part, and Chazy and Trenton limestone the E. Tertiary clay extends along the lake shore. The soil is clayey and productive in the central and E. parts, but sandy in the W. **Chazy,** (p. v.,) upon Little Chazy River, contains 2 churches and a saw and grist mill. Pop. 326. **West Chazy,** (p. v.,) upon Little Chazy River, in the S. W. part of the town, contains 2 churches, a saw and grist mill, and starch factory. Pop. 280. It is a station on the P. & M. R. R. **Sciota** (p. v.) is a station on the P. & M. R. R., in the N. W. corner of the town. **Chazy Landing** is a hamlet on the lake shore. **Ingraham** is a p. o. in the S. E. corner. The first settler was John La Trombois,[9] who came in town in 1763. After the Revolution the first settlers were refugees from Canada and Nova Scotia. Of these, Lieutenant Murdock McPherson was the first one that could speak English.[10] The census reports 5 churches in town.[11]

CLINTON—was formed from Ellenburgh, May 14, 1845. It is the N. W. corner town in the co. Its surface is generally level, with a gentle inclination toward the N. W. The highest points along its S. border are about 1,050 feet above Lake Champlain. A portion of the surface is undulating. It is nearly all underlaid by Potsdam sandstone, which here is remarkably white. The streams are small brooks. More than three-fourths of the town is yet a wilderness. The soil is a light, sandy loam, capable of supporting but a thin growth of forest trees. A large part of the land is owned by capitalists and speculators. **Cherubusco,** (p. o.,) the summit station upon the O. R. R., **The Frontiers,** (Frontier p. o.,) and **Wrightsville,** upon the W. border, are hamlets. This town lies within No. 6 of the Old Military Tract. The first settlers located upon the Old Military Road and near The Frontiers.[12] A M. E. church has lately been organized.

DANNEMORA[13]—was formed from Beekmantown, Dec. 14, 1854. It is the central town upon the W. border of the co. Its surface is mostly a wild, mountainous upland, covered with a sandy soil and light growth of forest trees. Chazy Lake, near the center, 3½ miles long by 1¼

---

[1] Called Point au Fer (Fire Point) upon a map bearing date of 1748. During the Revolution, the Moira, a vessel of war, anchored off this point, and barracks were built upon the land for the winter quarters of the marines. The place was occupied by the British until 1796. It was reserved by the State in 1787 for military purposes, but was not used.

[2] This place contains a fine water-power, and a large amount of manufacturing is carried on. The greater part of the lumber brought down by the Ogdensburgh R. R. is shipped here.

[3] Named from Geo. Perry, former proprietor.

[4] Named from Jacques Rouse, a Canadian, who settled here in 1783. This village has grown to importance since the completion of the R. R. The passenger and freight depôts are both among the largest R. R. structures in the State. A bridge a mi. long here crosses the lake. A floating draw of 300 feet, opened and shut by steam, admits the passage of vessels. About one mi. N. of the village, upon the banks of the lake, Fort Montgomery is situated. This fort commands the entrance to the lake. It was begun soon after the War of 1812; but in 1818 it was found to be within the limits of Canada, and the work was abandoned. It became known as "Fort Blunder;" but by the Webster Treaty of 1842 it was ceded again to the U. S. Work upon it has been resumed; and it is estimated that the completed works will cost $600,000, of which sum $275,000 has already been expended.

[5] Named from Ebenezer Cooper, who erected mills there.

[6] Moore came in to survey the tract granted to Smith, Graves, and others, in 1785. He erected the first saw and grist mills, in 1789. Among the other early settlers were Elnathan Rogers, Wm. Beaumont, Chas. L. Sailly, Samuel Ashman, Joseph Corbin, Silas Hubbell, Elias Dewey, Charles Bedlow, David Savage, and Benj. Tyler.

[7] M. E., Prot. E., Presb., and R. C. Since 1855, 3 churches have been organized at Rouses Point; R. C., M. E., and Prot. E.

[8] Pronounced Shá-zee. It included the patent granted to Elkanah Dean and 29 others, July 11, 1769.

[9] He was accompanied by two men, named Gonde and Swarte. He was driven off in 1776, but returned after the war, and died there in 1810.—Palmer's Hist. Lake Champlain, p. 80.

[10] Among the early settlers were Levi Hazen, Septa Fillmore, John Bronson, Elisha Ransom, George Root, and John Douglas. Miss M. Bingham taught the first school, in 1802.

[11] 2 M. E., Bap., Cong., and Wes. Meth.

[12] Among these early settlers were Junio Howard, Calvin Johnson, C. A. Smith, Ebenezer Gates, George Peters, and Stephen Martin, mostly from Vt. The first child born was Rhoda S. Howard, Feb. 7, 1819; the first marriage, that of Cornelius Austin and Fanny Hall, in 1822; and the first death, that of a child of William Hunter, in 1820. Mary Emmonds taught the first school, in 1821; Benjamin Roberts kept the first inn; Charles D. Bachus the first store, in 1835; and John McCoy erected the first sawmill.

[13] Named by Gen. Skinner, from a celebrated iron locality in Sweden.

wide, discharges its waters E. into Chazy River. Upper Chateaugay Lake, on the w. border, 5 mi. long by 1½ broad, discharges its waters w. into Chateaugay River. The few settlements in town are confined to the S. E. corner. **Dannemora** (p. v.) is a small village grown up around the Clinton Prison. This prison was located here in 1845, for the purpose of employing convicts in the mining and manufacture of iron, so that their labor would not come so directly in competition with the other mechanical trades.[1] The first permanent settler was Thomas Hooker, who came to reside in 1838. The census reports 1 religious society (Presb.) in town.

ELLENBURGH[2]—was formed from Mooers, April 17, 1830. Clinton was taken off in 1845. It lies upon the w. border of the co., N. of the center. Its surface is an upland, mountainous in the s. and rolling in the N., with an inclination toward the N. E. English River flows E. across the N. border. The soil is generally sandy; but in many places the sand is covered with a rich vegetable mold. The settlements are principally confined to the valley. Potatoes are raised in large quantities. Lumbering is extensively carried on. **Ellenburgh** (p. v.) contains 3 churches, a sawmill, tannery, and 125 inhabitants. **Ellenburgh Center** (p. v.) contains a church, saw and grist mill, 2 starch factories, a machine shop, and 15 dwellings. **Ellenburgh Depot** is a hamlet on the line of Altona. James Hanchett came to this town in 1796, but left soon after. The first permanent settler was Abner Pomeroy, from Vt., about 1800.[3] There are 4 churches in town.[4]

MOOERS[5]—was formed from Champlain, March 20, 1804. Ellenburgh was taken off in 1830. Its surface is generally level, with a gentle inclination to the N. E. The principal streams are Great Chazy and English Rivers. The surface is entirely underlaid by Potsdam sandstone, and is covered with a light, sandy soil. Along the N. border are several small swamps. Upon the Canada line, in the N. w. corner, is a remarkable chasm in the rocks, called The Gulf.[6] **Centerville,** (Mooers Forks p. o.,) upon the Chazy, contains 2 churches, a sawmill, stave factory, and 30 houses. It is a station on the N. R. R. **Mooers,** (p. v.,) upon the Chazy, in the E. part, contains 2 churches and 40 houses. It is near the junction of the O. and P. & M. R. R's. **Angellville,** upon Corbeau Creek, in the s. E. corner, is a hamlet. The first settler was Joshua C. Bosworth, who located in town in 1796.[7] The first preacher was Rev. Andrew Blackman, in 1800; and the first settled minister was Rev. Martin Powell, in 1807.[8]

PERU[9]—was formed from Plattsburgh and Willsborough, (Essex co.,) Dec. 28, 1792. A part was annexed to Willsborough in 1799, and Au Sable and Black Brook were taken off in 1839. It lies upon the lake, s. of the center of the co. The surface in the center and E. is rolling and slightly inclined toward the lake, and in the w. broken and mountainous. The Au Sable flows across the s. E. corner, and along its course are extensive swamps. Little Sable drains the greater part of the remaining portions of the town. The principal body of water is Military Pond, on the w. line. A strip of land 2 mi. wide, extending along the lake, has a soil composed of clay and clay loam. West of this is a plain 4 mi. wide, covered with sand and interspersed with swamps. In the w. the soil is a light, sandy loam. **Peru,** (p. v.,) on the Little Sable, near the center of the town, contains 2 churches, a gristmill, starch factory, and tannery. Pop. 504. **Laphams Mills,** 2 mi. below Peru, contains a large flouring mill, a plaster mill, forge, and 15 dwellings; **Peasleville,** on Salmon River, in the N. w. corner, a forge and 25 dwellings. **Port Jackson,** (Valcour p. o.,) on the lake, opposite Valcour Island, is a hamlet containing a church. **Peru**

1 The prison was erected under the superintendence of Ransom Cook, under an act passed May 1, 1844. The prison grounds, comprising 25 acres, are located upon the slope of a hill, and are surrounded by pickets 20 feet high. The main buildings, constructed of dressed stone, are in the form of a T, and are respectively 364 by 56 feet, and 160 by 46 feet. The cells are constructed in a block 3 stories high in the center of the building, a wide corridor extending completely around between them and the outer walls. The main buildings have slate roofs and are completely fireproof. Within the grounds are a steam forge, with 10 fires, a rolling mill, foundery, steam separator capable of washing 600 tons of ore per month, 7 coal kilns, a steam sawmill, machine shop, and the ruins of a blast furnace, burned June 26, 1856. A large share of the labor of constructing these works has been done by convicts. The prison works were first supplied with ore from the Skinner Mine, owned by the State; but more recently from the Averill Mine. A new mine has lately been discovered upon the State grounds. Besides the manufacture of iron, stave making, coopering, and shoemaking are carried on. The total earnings in 4 years, ending in 1857, were $120,537.56; and the total expenses, $212,901.22.

2 Named in compliment to Ellen, daughter of John R. Murray, of N. Y., the principal proprietor of Township No. 5 of the Military Tract.

3 Among the early settlers were Aaron Broadwell and Lewis

Ransom, in 1822; and Benjamin Hine, W. Jennings, jr., Joseph Serey, Pardon Daily, Joseph Lawrence, and Samuel Hazleton, soon after. The first child born was Lloyd Rogers Hine. He was named after Lloyd Rogers, and received a farm of 50 acres for the name. The first marriage was that of Smith Delamater and Phœbe Eastabrook. John R. Murray built the first saw and grist mill.

4 M. E., Prot. E., Presb., and Union. The Union Church was built by J. R. Murray.

5 Named from Maj. Gen. Benj. Mooers, an early settler and prominent citizen of the co.

6 This gulf is 16 rods wide and 300 feet deep. At its bottom is a pond of water said to be 150 feet deep. The walls are of sandstone, and perpendicular. No existing agencies could have produced the chasm.—N. Y. Geol., 2d Dist., p. 309.

7 Among the early settlers were Ichabod Bosworth, Geo. and Daniel Perry, Andrew Blackman and sons, Daniel Southwick, John, Joseph, and Samuel Churchill, John Sheldon, and Robert Tripp. The first child born was Wm. Hallenbeck, in 1801; the first marriage, that of David Anderson and Rhoda Perry, Dec. 5, 1805; and the first death of an adult, that of Mrs. J. C. Bosworth Sept. 26, 1802.

8 The census reports 4 churches in town; Cong., M. E., Prot. E., and Presb.

9 Name applied from its mountainous character.

Landing is a hamlet, N. of the mouth of the Little Sable. The first settler was Wm. Hay, a Scotchman, who located upon Stewart's Patent in 1772.[1] The census reports 4 churches in town.[2]

PLATTSBURGH—was first recognized as a town April 4, 1785. A part of Peru was taken off in 1792, Beekmantown in 1820, Saranac in 1824, and Schuyler Falls in 1848. It lies upon Lake Champlain, a little S. of the E. border of the co., and includes Valcour[3] and Crab[4] Islands in the lake. The surface is level in the E. and broken and hilly in the W. It is slightly inclined toward the E., its W. border being elevated about 500 feet above the lake. It is principally drained by Saranac River and its branches. In the E. part the soil is a clayey loam, underlaid by Trenton limestone; in the center, a sandy loam, underlaid by calciferous sandstone; and in the W. a light sand, underlaid by Potsdam sandstone. Cumberland Head is a peninsula extending into the lake and forming Cumberland Bay.[5] **Plattsburgh,** (p. v.,) upon Cumberland Bay, at the mouth of Saranac River, was incorp. March 3, 1815. It has a safe and commodious harbor, and an excellent water-power, giving it facilities for a large amount of both commerce and manufactures. Besides the co. buildings, it contains a town hall,[6] customhouse,[7] the Plattsburgh Academy, 6 churches, a foundery, planing mill, sawmill, gristmill, and 2 tanneries. Pop. 2,926. Upon a sandy plain, 1 mi. S. of the village and 90 feet above the lake, are situated extensive barracks belonging to the U. S. Government.[8] **Cadyville,** (p. v.,) upon the Saranac, 10 mi. above Plattsburgh, contains a church, sawmill, and 25 houses. **Elsinore,** 1 mi. above Cadyville, contains a forge and a half dozen houses. **Salmon River,** (South Plattsburgh p. o.,) in the S. part, contains a church, sawmill, and 25 houses. **West Plattsburgh** is a p. o. The first settlement was made before the Revolution, by Chas. de Fredenburgh and several associates, under royal grants. During the war the settlers were driven off and the improvements were destroyed. In 1785 a tract 7 mi. square was granted to Zephaniah Platt and 32 associates, who had bought up military land warrants to that amount.[9] The first 3 families who settled under this grant were those of Charles Platt, Chas. McCreedy, and Kinner Newcomb. Nathaniel Platt was the first surveyor and agent for the proprietors. A farm of 80 acres was offered to each of the first 10 settlers in town.[10] Rev. Benj. Vaughan preached the first sermon, in 1787; and Rev. Frederick Halsey was the first settled minister, in 1795.[11] There are 9 churches in town.[12]

SARANAC—was formed from Plattsburgh, March 29, 1824. It lies upon the W. border of the co., S. of the center. Its surface is a broken and mountainous upland. The highest summits, along the W. border, are 4,000 feet above tide. Saranac River, flowing through the S. E. part, is the principal stream. Upon its course are several falls, affording an immense amount of water-power.[13] The E. part, sloping toward the river, is covered with a light, sandy soil, and the river intervale with a sandy loam and alluvium. The soil among the mountains is sandy; but the whole

[1] Hay lived opposite Valcour Island, and witnessed the naval engagement of Arnold. He soon after removed to Canada, but returned in 1785. Among the other early settlers were John Cochrane, John Howe, Isaac Finch, Abijah Ketchum, Lott and John Elmore, Ezekiel Lockwood, Samuel Jackson, Cyrenus Newcomb, Geo. Hayworth, Benj. Sherman, and Silas and Robert Cochrane. The first child born was Ira, son of John Howe, in 1784; the first marriage, that of Lott Elmore and Mary Hay, Dec. 17, 1788; and the first death, that of Wm. Hay, Feb. 28, 1779. M. Finch taught the first school, in 1790–91; John Cochrane built the first grist and saw mill; —— Weed built the first forge, and Geo. Hayworth and John Hockstrass built the first factory. A large stone woolen factory built in 1836, by Richard Hayworth, was changed in 1851 to a starch factory.

[2] 2 M. E., Cong., and R. C.

[3] This island is memorable for the naval engagement which took place near it during the Revolution. The remains of the schooner Royal Savage, sunk at that time, may still be seen.

[4] The sailors and marines killed in the naval battle of Sept. 11, 1814, were buried upon this island.

[5] Extensive military works were begun here in 1814, but were abandoned upon the approach of the enemy. The State of Vt. presented Com. MacDonough with a farm on this point, which is still owned by his descendants.

[6] Built in 1856, at a cost of $3,000. It is a fireproof brick building, and contains a town hall, armory, and fire engine room.

[7] This is a fine fireproof brick building, built at a cost of $80,000, and contains rooms for the customhouse, postoffice, and U.S. Court.

[8] These buildings were commenced in 1838, and were originally designed to inclose a space of 600 feet square. Only a part of the design has been carried out. Troops were stationed here until 1846, when they were sent to join the army in Mexico. The buildings are now used by the Clinton Co. Agricultural Society for its annual fairs.

[9] This grant was made in accordance with the provisions of an act passed in 1781, which provided that when 61 rights, or 30,500

acres, should be jointly located, a tract 7 mi. square should be granted, including 860 acres for gospel and schools.

[10] Among the settlers who received lots under this offer were Kinner Newcomb, Jacob Ferris, Thos. Allen, John B. Hartwick, Derrick Webb, Jabez Pettit, Moses Soper, Lucius Reynolds, and Henry Ostrander. Among the other early settlers were Ichabod Truesdale, Peter Roberts, Wm. Campbell, Benj. Ketchum, and Benj. Graves, who settled at the village; Melancthon L. Woolsey, —— Adams, Frederick Durant, Wm. Coe, Russell Ransom, Benj. Mooers, Wm. P. and Theodorus Platt, who settled on Cumberland Head; Lambert Hoppin, John Stevenson, Gideon Ruger, Joshua Hillyard, and Abm. Webb, who located on South St.; Benj. Reynolds, Sam'l Norcross, John Roberts, and Benj. Hammond, on Center St.; Nath'l Platt, Sam'l Benson, Eliphalet Haskins, Jos. Ormsby, Benj. Vaughn, and John Wait, on North St.; and Melancthon Smith, Zephaniah Platt, Thos. Treadwell, Peter Sailly, and Wm. Bailey, in other parts of the town.

[11] The first child born was Ida Ostrander, Sept. 7, 1785; the first male child, Platt Newcomb, Nov. 1, 1785; the first marriage was that of Peter Sailly and Marianne 'Adelaide Greille, June 8, 1789; and the first death, that of Mrs. Sailly, first wife of Peter Sailly, Dec. 23, 1786. Twelve of the original proprietors met at the house of Judge Platt, at Poughkeepsie, Dec. 30, 1784, and took measures for the immediate erection of a grist and saw mill and forge. These buildings were the first in town.

[12] 3 R. C., Bap., M. E., Wes. Meth., Presb., Prot. E., and Union.

[13] At the Saranac Falls the river flows through a narrow, tortuous channel, bounded by nearly perpendicular rocks, for the space of a mi. In its course its descent is very rapid, and at several places it is precipitated down precipices of 20 or 30 ft., and at last it plunges into a basin in a perpendicular fall of 60 feet. The ragged rocks upon the bottom and sides, and the abrupt angles in the channel, cause the water to boil and seethe and struggle in the wildest commotion. In high water, thousands of saw logs float down the river, and in their passage down the falls they are pitched and tossed upon the surges, or thrown bodily into the air like playthings.

w. region is too rough for cultivation. **Saranac,** (p. v.,) upon Saranac River, contains a church, sawmill, forge, and 50 houses. **Redford,** (p. v.,) on the Saranac, near the s. border, contains 3 churches, several sawmills, and 60 houses.[1] **Russia,** 2 mi. above Saranac, contains 2 forges and 20 houses. The first settlement was begun in 1802, by Russell Case and Ezekiel Pearce.[2] The first preacher was Rev. Lambert Hopper, in 1805.[3]

SCHUYLER FALLS[4]—was formed from Plattsburgh, April 4, 1848. It is an interior town, lying a little s. e. of the center of the co. Its surface is rolling in the e. and hilly in the w., with an inclination toward the e. The Saranac forms its n. boundary, and Salmon River flows along its s. border. The soil is a light, sandy loam. **Schuyler Falls,** (p. v.,) on Salmon River, near the s. line of the town, contains a church, gristmill, starch factory, and 50 dwellings. **Morrisonville,** (p. v.,) on the Saranac, lies partly in Plattsburgh. It contains 3 churches, a gristmill, sawmill, starch factory, foundery, machine shop, and 35 houses. **Norrisville,** upon Salmon River, 3 mi. w. of Schuyler Falls, contains a starch factory, 2 forges, and 15 dwellings. The first settler was Ezra Turner, who located upon Salmon River in 1797.[5] The census reports 2 M. E. churches in town.[6]

Acres of Land, Valuation, Population, Dwellings, Families, Freeholders, Schools, Live Stock, Agricultural Products, and Domestic Manufactures, of Clinton County.

Names of Towns.	Acres of Land.		Valuation of 1858.			Population.		No. of Dwellings.	No. of Families.	Freeholders.	Schools.	
	Improved.	Unimproved.	Real Estate.	Personal Property.	Total.	Males.	Females.				No. of Districts.	Children taught.
Altona[a]			$202,375	$2,575	$204,950						10	749
Au Sable	11,067½	10,634	506,712	64,327	571,039	1,854	1,949	616	655	257	12	1,614
Beekmantown	24,103	13,286½	531,385	15,300	546,685	1,480	1,453	483	482	425	15	1,135
Black Brook	5,983¾	69,550¾	155,634	3,100	158,734	1,557	1,468	499	541	192	14	1,395
Champlain	18,208	9,035	763,383	52,230	815,613	3,080	3,117	996	1,052	373	14	2,205
Chazy	23,526	56,053	523,655	50,880	574,535	2,233	2,229	780	809	575	17	1,619
Clinton	4,213	24,760	117,592		117,592	709	662	245	248	157	7	785
Dannemora		54,919	113,806		113,806	501	222	84	84	62	1	222
Ellenburgh	7,423¾	56,608½	177,937	1,450	179,387	907	844	321	348	231	9	684
Mooers	12,012½	25,308	405,003	6,800	411,803	1,819	1,803	608	630	492	22	1,837
Peru	25,050⅛	19,346½	616,294	102,700	718,994	1,788	1,732	606	635	441	21	1,536
Plattsburgh	14,764½	12,094	1,069,290	348,400	1,417,690	2,998	3,082	896	984	642	17	2,602
Saranac	11,058¾	39,507¾	201,352	2,200	203,552	1,656	1 402	523	533	362	13	1,119
Schuyler Falls	11,521½	9,984	246,694	29,600	276,294	974	963	337	344	272	10	849
Total	168,932⅜	401,086½	5,631,112	679,562	6,310,674	21,556	20,926	6,994	7,345	4,481	182	18,351

Names of Towns.	Live Stock.					Agricultural Products.							Domestic Cloths, in yards.
						Bush. of Grain.		Tons of Hay.	Bushels of Potatoes.	Bushels of Apples.	Dairy Products.		
	Horses.	Working Oxen and Calves.	Cows.	Sheep.	Swine.	Winter.	Spring.				Pounds Butter.	Pounds Cheese.	
Altona[a]													
Au Sable	633	814	716	2,139	555	954½	27,311½	3,126	25,185	944	38,245	6,475	230
Beekmantown	1,085	2,265	1,821	6,491	1,117	1,195	82,263½	7,232	52,827	15,545	172,695	17,823	2,951
Black Brook	371	553	554	486	370	668	9,227½	1,262	18,875	20	30,091½	600	
Champlain	919	1,427	1,096	4,037	708	83	75,919¾	6,571	20,106	8,762	84,210	10,690	
Chazy	1,233	2,199	1,666	8,776	1,173	1,686	81,195½	7,645¾	36,552	16,704	101,239	14,500	955½
Clinton	192	355	371	562	272	72½	6,723	1,007½	12,865	415	23,560	4,000	1,214
Dannemora													
Ellenburgh	350	439	447	959	277	291	13 028½	1,990¾	32,019	210	39,505	755	
Mooers	602	1,257	818	1,581	469	695½	16,091⅛	4,084½	14,668	2,345	81,681	7,505	1,373¼
Peru	1,049	1,942	1,395	5,528	1,089	3,551	84,142¼	6,117¾	58,058	11,918½	111,404	15,696	1,702½
Plattsburgh	1,005	1,259	1,016	3,794	856	2,002	40,123½	4,247¾	35,224	11,967	76,350	12,357	509½
Saranac	511	822	660	1,067	450	1,367	19,225	2,331½	28,271	1,442	57,661	710	259
Schuyler Falls	494	939	724	2,931	532	2,646	29,636½	2,624½	50,842	6,664	74,790	14,795	1,385
Total	8,444	14,271	11,284	38,351	7,868	15,211½	484,887⅝	48,241	385,492	76,936½	891,431½	105,906	10,579¾

[a] Formed since 1855.

[1] In 1831, John S. Foster, agent of a company, came to this place and erected a saw and grist mill, and, during the next season, a large manufactory of crown glass. The manufacture of glass was carried on with varying success until 1852, when it was finally abandoned. Mr. Foster went to Jefferson co. in 1832, and there commenced the manufacture of glass, (see page ——;) Gershom Cook, Elias W. Corning, and Matthew Lane, of Troy, were proprietors of the establishment.

[2] Among the early settlers were Sylvanus Smith, Wright Spaulding, Lyman Manly, Nath'l Lyon, John Gregory and son Czar, Lewis Ferris and sons, Isaiah and John Lambert, John M. Hopper and John Chamberlain. Samuel Stone, first agent for Township No. 4 of the Old Military Tract, with another man, attempting to go to Malone, was caught in a snow storm, and his companion frozen to death, Oct. 8, 1802. He was himself so injured that he died in 3 weeks. John D. Fiske, the second agent, was killed by a falling tree, June 21, 1805. The first birth was that of Isaac Smith, May 9, 1804; the first marriage, that of Cornelius Hopper and Sophia Case, in 1810; and the first death of a settler, that of John D. Fiske, June 8, 1805. Royal Spaulding taught the first school, in 1805; and Isaiah Ferris built the first saw and grist mill, in 1806.

[3] There are 4 churches in town; 2 M. E., Presb., and R. C.

[4] Named from the proprietor of the present village site.

[5] Among the early settlers were Daniel and Roswell Jones, John P. Roberts, David Hare, Daniel Hillson, Henry Purdy, Jonathan Wickham, and Jas. Brand, all of whom located upon Salmon River.

[6] 2 churches (Bap. and Union) at Morrisonville are located n. of the river, in Plattsburgh.

COLUMBIA COUNTY.

THIS county was formed from Albany, April 4, 1786.[1] It lies upon the E. bank of the Hudson, between Rensselaer and Dutchess cos., and extends E. to the Massachusetts line. It contains an area of 688 sq. mi., and is centrally distant 29 mi. from Albany. The Taghkanick Mts. extend along the E. border, and the adjoining parts of the co. are broken by numerous irregular ranges of hills which constitute the outlying spurs of those mountains. The w. part of the co. consists of an undulating plateau terminating in bluffs on the Hudson River. The principal streams are Roeliff Jansens Kil[2] and Claverack and Kinderhook Creeks. Upon these streams and their tributaries are numerous valuable mill sites. In the E. and N. parts of the co. are several picturesque lakes, the principal of which are Kinderhook, Copake, and Charlotte Lakes, and Whitings, Robinsons, Snyder, and Rhoda Ponds. The prevailing rocks are the Hudson River shales. The slate rocks in this co. crop out toward the w., usually at an angle of 45°, but sometimes almost vertically. Limestone crops out in different parts of the co. Brown hematitic iron ore is found in numerous localities in the E. part of Ancram and Copake.[3] Lead has been mined in Ancram,[4] and manganese, peat, and marl are found in different localities. In New Lebanon are the celebrated thermal springs; in Stockport are other mineral springs, and in Chatham is a small sulphur spring.

The various branches of agriculture form the leading industrial pursuits of the people. Hay, (of which large quantities are pressed and sent to market,) rye, oats, corn, potatoes, and buckwheat, are the staple productions. Stock raising and dairying receive considerable attention. The manufacture of paper, cotton fabrics, vegetable extracts, and iron, is largely carried on.[5] A greater quantity of paper is made in this co. than in any other in the State, and the co. also takes precedence of all others in the amount of tinctures and extracts prepared from medicinal plants.

The city of Hudson is the county seat.[6] The courthouse and jail is a fine building, fronting on Washington Square. It has a marble front, with an Ionic portico, and contains the court and jury rooms, and the co. clerk's, sheriff's, and district attorney's offices.[7] The poorhouse is a spacious brick building located upon a farm of 200 acres in Ghent.[8]

The most important works of internal improvement are the Hudson River R. R., extending through the w. part of the co., the Albany & West Stockbridge R. R., through the N. part, the Hudson & Boston R. R., terminating at Hudson, and the New York & Harlem R. R., terminating at Chatham Four Corners. Four newspapers are published in the co.[9]

[1] By this act the N. boundary was defined as the N. line of "Kinderhook District," and the s. boundary as the s. line of "Kings District." The latter line was more accurately defined, April 1, 1799.

[2] Named from Roeliff Jansen, Overseer of the Orphan Chamber (an office similar to that of surrogate) under the Dutch Government. The Indian name was "Sauk-hen-ak."—Doc. Hist., III. 612.

[3] Large quantities of ore have been taken from these localities. It is obtained near the surface, and its depth is not known.

[4] This ore is found near the junction of the slate and limestone strata, and occurs in strings and bunches.—Geol. Rep., 1838, p. 59.

[5] There are 15 paper mills and 8 cotton factories in the co. The first paper mill was erected at Stuyvesant Falls, in 1802, by Geo. Chittenden; and the first cotton factory, in 1813, by Nath'l Wilde.

[6] The co. seat was formerly located at Claverack. The first meeting of the board of supervisors was held at the house of Gabriel Esselstyne, in Claverack. An appropriation of £2000 was made for a courthouse, and Wm. B. Whiting, Abraham J. Van Alstyne, John Livingston, Henry I. Van Rensselaer, Matthew Scott, Seth Jenkins, and Wm. H. Ludlow were appointed commissioners to superintend its erection. In 1788, an additional appropriation of £1200 was made, and in 1798 another of £400. The first co. officers were Peter Van Ness, First Judge; Peter Sylvester, Peter R. Livingston, Henry I. Van Rensselaer, and Wm. B. Whiting, Judges; Killian K. Van Rensselaer, Surrogate; Lawrence Hogeboom, Sheriff; Robert Van Rensselaer, Clerk; and Walter Vrooman Wemple, Treasurer. By the act of Feb. 25, 1805, the co. seat was removed to Hudson on condition that the city appropriate for the use of the co. the city hall, a lot of land, (upon which to erect co. buildings,) and the sum of $2000. A committee, consisting of Wm. Wilson, Jacob Ford, Thos. Jenkins, Benj. Birdsall, and Nathaniel Green, was appointed to superintend repairs and the erection of a jail.

[7] The courthouse was erected in 1835, at a cost of $3500.

[8] This building was erected in 1857, at a cost of $22,000, and, together with the surrounding buildings, has accommodations for 500 persons. The farm is mostly worked by the inmates of the institution.

[9] The Hudson Gazette, the first paper published in the co., was established April 7, 1785, by Ashbel Stoddard and Chas. R. Webster. Webster soon after withdrew, and the paper was continued by Stoddard until 1803–04.

The Bee was removed from New London, Conn., to Hudson, Aug. 17, 1802, and was published by Chas. Holt until 1810. It then passed into the hands of Saml. W. Clark, and afterward into those of John W. Dutcher. It was changed, about 1820, to

The Columbia Centinel, and two years afterward it was united with the Columbia Republican.

The Balance and Columbia Repository was started in 1802, by Ezra Sampson, George Chittenden, and Harry Croswell. It was removed to Albany in 1808, and discontinued in 1811.

The Wasp was edited a short time by "Robt. Rusticoat," in the early part of the present century.

The Hudson Newspaper and Balance Advertiser was commenced in Oct. 1806, by Harry Croswell.

The Republican Fountain, established in Dec. 1806, was published about 1 year, by Sylvester Roberts.

The Northern Whig was begun in 1808, by W. B. Stebbins. Wm. L. Stone became the publisher in 2 or 3 years,

The first settlements were made in the N. part of the co., under the Dutch Government. The E. border was settled chiefly by squatters from New England. Livingston Manor[1] was patented July 22, 1686, and first settled by tenants about the beginning of the last century. The most important settlement was made by German Palatinates, in 1710, upon a tract of 6000 acres—now constituting the principal part of Germantown—which had been sold back to the Government by Robert Livingston. The territory of Mass., under its charter, extended westward to the Pacific Ocean, and grants were made by that colony.[2] Conflicting claims gave rise to bitter contentions and riotous outbreaks. Arrests made under Mass. warrants led to riots and bloodshed.[3] Combinations were formed to dispossess the proprietor of the Livingston Manor, which resulted in tumults and murders.[4] These difficulties continued until after the Revolution. During the Revolutionary War, and for several years after, this section of the country was much infested by robbers, and acts of violence were of frequent occurrence.[5] The anti-rent movement of 1840–50 extended to the Livingston Manor, the John J. Van Rensselaer Tract, and other districts held by leasehold. In Dec. 1844, the Governor ordered out 7 companies of militia to assist the sheriff of this co. in the discharge of his duties. Most of the leases which had then been issued were for 1, 2, or 3 lives; but the anti-rent difficulties have led to the policy of conveying the title in fee as rapidly as circumstances will admit.[6]

ANCRAM—was formed from Livingston, March 19, 1803,[7] as "*Gallatin.*" Its name was changed March 25, 1814, and Gallatin was taken off in 1830. It is the S. E. corner town of the co.

Richard L. Cross in 1816, and W. R. Stebbins in 1821. It was discontinued in 1824.

The Columbia Magazine was published at Hudson at an early date, by Rev. John Chester.

The Spirit of the Forum and Hudson Remarker was published in 1817, by a literary association.

The Columbia Republican was started in Aug. 1818, by Solomon Wilbur. In 1820 it passed into the hands of Ambrose L. and Allen Jordan, and is now published by Wm. Bryan. For a year or two, about 1835–36, it was issued as

The Columbia Republican and Hudson City Advertiser.

The Hudson Gazette was established in 1824, by Peleg G. Sturtevant, and is now published by Williams & Brother, John W. Edmonds, Ed.

The Messenger of Peace was started in 1824, at Hudson, by Richard Carrique, and continued 1 year.

The Rural Repository, semi-mo., was commenced, June 12, 1824, by Wm. B. Stoddard, and continued until 1851.

Columbia and Greene Co. Envoy was started at Hudson, in 1831, by Edwin G. Lindsley, and continued 2 years.

The Diamond, semi-mo., was published at Hudson, in 1833, by G. F. Stone.

The Magnolia, semi-mo., was published at Hudson, in 1834, by P. D. Carrique.

The Hudson Flail was published by J. R. S. Van Vliet, during the campaign of 1840.

The Columbia Washingtonian was started at Hudson in 1842, by J. R. S. Van Vliet. The paper changed hands several times, and was changed to

The Daily Evening Star, Dec. 28, 1847, by Alex. N. Webb. It is now published as

The Hudson Star, da. and w.

The Columbia Democrat was commenced at Chatham Four Corners, in 1847, by ——

The Temperance Palladium was published at Hudson in 1851, by J. W. Dutcher.

The Hudson Daily News was published in 1855, by Richard Van Antwerp.

The Kinderhook Sentinel was established at Kinderhook in June, 1825, by Peter Van Schaack, and in Jan. 1832, was changed to

Columbia's Sentinel. In 1834 it passed into the hands of John V. A. Hoes, but about 18 months afterward it reverted to Van Schaack. It has since been changed to the

Rough Notes, and since 1854 it has been published at Kinderhook, by P. H. Van Vleck.

The Valatie Weekly Times was published in 1853, by H. N. Hopkins.

The Equal Rights Advocate was started at Chatham Four Corners, by an anti-rent association. In 1848 it was removed to Hudson and changed to

The Democratic Freeman. It was discontinued in 1855–56.

The Columbia Co. Journal was published at Chatham Four Corners in 1850, by Philip H. Ostrander.

The Journal of Materia Medica was commenced at New Lebanon in 1857; H. A. Tilden, pub., Joseph Bates, M. D., ed.

[1] The patent of this manor conferred upon Robert Livingston, the patentee, feudal privileges, and imposed an annual quitrent of 28 shillings. The manor contained 160,240 acres, and included nearly all the present towns of Clermont, Germantown, Livingston, Gallatin, Taghkanick, Ancram, and Copake. It consisted of 2 purchases: the Livingston purchase, obtained of

the Mohegan Indians in July, 1683, and the Taghkanick purchase, obtained Aug. 10, 1685. They were confirmed by Gov. Dongan, the former, Nov. 4, 1684, and the latter, Aug. 12, 1685. In 1701 there were but 4 or 5 houses on the manor. From and after 1716 the manor was represented by a member in General Assembly. Before his death—which took place in 1728—Robert Livingston bequeathed to his son Robert that part of the manor now included in the town of Clermont, and the residue to his eldest son, Philip. The latter was succeeded by Robert Livingston, Jr.; and in 1792 the land E. of the post road was divided between Walter, Robert C., John, and Henry Livingston, the devisees of Robert Livingston, Jr., according to the provisions of his will.—*Sutherland's Deduction of the Title of the Manor of Livingston; Doc. Hist. III, Colonial Hist.*

In the patent and upon the maps of the manor, several places are designated by their Indian names, viz.,—

Ahashawaghkick, a hill in N. W. corner, on Mass. line. *Acawanuk,* a flat or rock in N. part of North East, (Dutchess co.) *Kachwawyick,* a place w. of a certain mountain. *Kickua,* or *Kickpa,* one of 3 plains near Roeliff Jansens Creek. *Mananosick,* hill in w. part, on or near Mass. line. *Mawanaguasick,* stone heaps on N. line, "where Indians have laid several heaps of stones together, by an ancient custom amongst them." *Mahaskakook,* a "cripple bush" on S. line of patent. *Mawichnak,* a flat on both sides of a creek where it joins R. Jansens Creek. *Minmisichtanock,* a piece of land N. of Roeliff Jansens Creek. *Nowanagquasick,* on N. line of manor, (Sauthier's map.) *Nachawawachkano,* creek tributary to Twastawekak. *Nichankooke,* one of 3 plains near Roeliff Jansens Creek. *Pottkook,* patented to K. Van Rensselaer, s. of Kinderhook. *Quisichkook,* a small creek N. of Roeliff Jansens Creek. *Saaskahampka,* or *Swaskahamaka,* a place opposite Saugerties, Ulster co. *Sacahka,* on N. line of the town of North East. *Sankhenak,* Roeliff Jansens Kil. *Skaankook,* a creek. *Towastawekak,* or *Twastawekak,* a creek. *Wachanekaisck,* a small stream opposite Catskill Creek. *Wahankasick,* near Roeliff Jansens Creek, (Sauthier's map.) *Wawyachtonock,* a place. *Whichquopuhbau,* s. w. corner of Mass.

[2] With the view of settling their claims upon the Hudson, the Boston Government, in March, 1672, sent John Paine to New York to solicit permission to pass and repass by water. The application was received with cold civility, and the subject referred home for the decision of his Majesty. Gov. Lovelace improved the occasion to remind the Mass. people of the distrust with which they had received the commissioners sent over in 1664, and intimated that their application under other circumstances might have been differently received.—*General Entries,* IV. 177, 178. *Sec. Office.*

[3] *Doc. Hist.* III., 754.

[4] In 1791 the sheriff of the co. was murdered by an armed mob while in the discharge of his official duty.

[5] A party of rangers was organized to suppress these; and under the act of May 11, 1780, £1500 was raised to defray the expenses thus incurred.

[6] *Assem. Doc.* 156; 1846, p. 2.

[7] This town was included in the Livingston Manor. The line bordering upon Taghkanick was altered March 25, 1814. A narrow triangular tract of about 1000 acres, in the extreme E. part of the town, known as "Boston Corner," formerly belonged to the town of Mt. Washington, Berkshire co., Mass. The Taghkanick Mts. extend along the E. border of the tract, and form an almost impassable barrier between this and the remaining parts of that town. Thus entirely isolated from the

The surface is broken and hilly. In the E. part the hills range in a N. and S. direction, but elsewhere they are irregular. Roeliff Jansens Kil[1] crosses the town in a s. w. direction. A narrow intervale, bordered by steep, irregular hills, extends along its course. The soil is a gravelly loam intermixed with clay. Iron ore has been obtained at different places from the hills upon the E. border of the town,[2] and lead ore is mined at Hot Ground.[3] **Ancram,**[4] (p.v.,) situated on Roeliff Jansens Kil, in the w. part of the town, contains 2 churches, a paper mill, a sawmill, and about 30 houses. **Hot Ground** (Ancram Leadmines p. o.) and **Boston Corner,** (p. o.,) a station on the Harlem R. R., are hamlets. The town was first settled by the Dutch, in the neighborhood of Ancram Village. There are 3 churches in town.[5]

AUSTERLITZ—was formed from Canaan, Chatham, and Hillsdale, March 28, 1818. It lies on the E. border of the co., N. of the center. The E. and central parts are broken by irregular ranges of hills, and the w. part is undulating. The principal streams are Green River in the E. and Punsit Creek in the w. The soil is a gravelly loam intermixed in some parts with slate and clay. The hills are mostly arable to their summits. **Spencertown,** (p.v.,) on Punsit Creek, in the w. part of the town, contains 2 churches, an academy,[6] and 2 gristmills. Pop. 225. **Austerlitz,** (p.v.,) in the valley of Green River, contains 2 churches and 150 inhabitants. **Upper Green River** is a hamlet in the s. E. part of the town. The first settlements were made about 1745 to 1750, by squatters from Conn.[7] Disputes concerning the ownership of lands thus appropriated arose; and on the 31st of May, 1757, the settlers appointed a committee to adjust the difficulties. About 1774, Nathaniel Culver and Jas. Savage were sent to England to secure a grant of these lands to the settlers; but, owing to the trouble existing between the mother country and the colonies, they were unsuccessful. The land titles were finally settled by the act of March 22, 1791. The first church (Cong.) was organized in 1750, and Rev. Jesse Clark was the first pastor.[8]

CANAAN—was formed as "*Kings District*," March 24, 1772, and its name was changed March 7, 1788. A part of Chatham was taken off in 1795, and New Lebanon and a part of Austerlitz in 1818. It is situated on the E. border of the co., between Austerlitz and New Lebanon. A range of mountains or hills separates it from Massachusetts. The surface is broken and hilly. Whitings Pond, in the E. part of the town, is about 2 mi. in circumference. Its outlet is tributary to Kinderhook Creek and affords several valuable mill sites. The soil is a gravelly or slaty loam and clay. The hills are mostly arable to their summits. Near the center of the town is a slate quarry.[9] **Canaan Four Corners,** (p.v.,) a station on the A. & W. S. R. R., contains 1 church and 32 dwellings; **Flat Brook,** (p.v.,) a station on the same R. R., contains 1 church and 15 dwellings. **Canaan** (p.o.) and **Canaan Center** (p.o.) are hamlets. **Queechy,** on the outlet of Whitings Pond, contains 1 church, 2 paper mills, a sawmill, a gristmill, and 21 dwellings; and **Red Rock,**[10] in the s. w. corner of the town, contains 3 churches, a sawmill, a gristmill, and 30 dwellings. Two families of Shakers, consisting of about 75 persons, reside in the N. E. part of the town. They are chiefly engaged in farming, and their estate consists of over 1400 acres. They raise garden seeds to a limited extent, and manufacture brooms, mop sticks, and other similar articles. The settlement of the town was commenced about 1756.[11] At a meeting of the citizens of "*Kings District*," (June 24, 1776,) held for the purpose of choosing delegates to the Provincial

---

seat of civil authority, it became the resort of fugitives from justice, prize fighters, and others of like character, who bade defiance to the laws and practiced their unlawful acts with impunity. In Dec. 1848, the inhabitants petitioned to be annexed to N. Y. The State of Mass. consented in May, 1853. The cession was accepted by New York, July 21 of the same year, confirmed by Congress, Jan. 3, 1855, and the Corner was annexed to this town, April 13, 1857.—*N. Y. Assem. Docs.,* 54 & 194, 1849.

[1] Called "Ancram Creek" in this town.

[2] These mines have been worked many years. Considerable quantities of ore are obtained on the land of A. McArthur and sent to Millerstown (Dutchess co.) on the Harlem R. R. An ore bed N. of this, owned by the Empire Co., is connected with the R. R. by a track 1¼ mi. long.

[3] This mine was discovered on land leased by the keeper of the Livingston Manor. Robt. R. Livingston purchased the lease, and sold it to a N. Y. Co., by whom the mine was worked until within a few years. A shaft has been sunk 100 feet, and galleries opened in different directions. The mine is on land now owned by H. McIntyre.

[4] This place was formerly celebrated for its iron works. These were erected as early as 1756. The ore was obtained from Salisbury, Conn., and from mines in the E. part of this town, and pig and bar iron of a superior quality was made.

[5] Evang. Luth., M. E., and Presb.

[6] The Spencertown Academy was established mainly through the exertions of Rev. Dr. T. Woodbridge.

[7] Among the early settlers were John Dean, John Williams, Seth and Truman Powell, Jas. Sexton, Ephraim Kidder, and families by the names of Osborne, Lawrence, Spencer, and Whitmore.

[8] The census reports 4 churches in town; Christian, Cong., M. E., and Presb.

[9] This quarry is on the land of L. D. Ford. The slate is of a dark blue color, and plates of any required size or thickness may be obtained.

[10] So named from a large rock by the roadside, painted red, and surmounted by a wooden column about 10 feet high, bearing the date "Jan. 1825."

[11] Among the early settlers were families named Douglass, Warner, Whiting, Alesworth, Baldwin, and Hawley. The first mill was built by Wm. B. Whiting, about 1775. This mill, stored with grain belonging to the government, was burned by tories during the war. In the first book of records is a memorandum, without date or signature, stating that "the town records were kept on loose paper previous to 1772, but not probably but a few years. The deed from the Indians of 6 mi. sq. was executed in 1758. The compensation was £250, that being paid for the 6 mi. sq." The record is continuous since May 5, 1772.

Congress, it was voted to recommend to that body the passage of a declaration of independence.[1] There are 7 churches in town.[2]

CHATHAM—was formed from Canaan and Kinderhook, March 17, 1795, and parts of Austerlitz and Ghent were taken off in 1818. It lies near the center of the N. border of the co. The surface is moderately hilly, the ranges generally extending N. and S. The principal stream is Kinderhook Creek, upon which are numerous mill sites. The soil in the valleys is a gravelly loam intermixed with clay, and upon the hills it is slaty. The valleys are broad and fertile, and the hills arable to their summits. Near New Concord is a sulphur spring. **Chatham Four Corners** (p. v.) is situated partly in this town and partly in Ghent. It is an important station on the A. & W. S. R. R. and the H & B. R. R., and is the terminus of the Harlem R. R. The depôts of these roads are in Ghent. The village contains 3 churches, a machine shop, and 3 foundries. Pop. 697. **East Chatham,** (p. v.,) a station on the A. & W. S. R. R., near the line of Canaan, contains 2 churches, a gristmill, sawmill, and candle factory. Pop. 245. **New Concord** contains 1 church and 109 inhabitants; **Chatham,** (p. v.,) 1 church, a furnace and plow factory, gristmill, and sawmill, and a pop. of 214; **Rayville** a Friends meeting house and 13 houses; **Chatham Center,** (p. v.,) 1 church and 127 inhabitants; **Malden Bridge,** (p. v.,) 1 church, a paper mill, sawmill, and tannery, and a pop. of 193; and **Riders Mills,** a gristmill, sawmill, and 12 houses. **North Chatham,** (p. v.,) contains 2 churches, a sawmill, gristmill, and plaster mill. Pop. 179. The settlement of this town commenced about 1725. The settlers were from Kinderhook, but originally from Holland. A company from Connecticut settled at New Concord in 1758.[3] The census reports 11 churches in town.[4]

CLAVERACK[5] (Claw′ve-rack)—was formed as a district, March 24, 1772. Hillsdale was taken off in 1782, and Hudson in 1785. It was recognized as a town, March 7, 1788. A part of Ghent was taken off in 1818. It lies near the center of the co. The surface in the w. part is undulating, and in the E. hilly. Claverack Creek, upon the w. border of the town, and its tributaries, are the principal streams. The soil is a rich loam in the w., and a gravelly loam intermixed with slate in the E. **Claverack,** (p. v.,) in the w. part of the town, a station on the H. & B. R. R., contains 2 churches and the Claverack Academy and Hudson River Institute;[6] pop. 496; **Mellenville,** (p. v.,) a station on the H. & B. R. R., contains 2 churches, a gristmill, and 30 dwellings; and **Philmont,** (p. v.,) a station on the Harlem R. R., contains several manufacturing establishments[7] and 35 dwellings. **South Bend Mills, Martindale Depot,** (p. o.) and **Humphreysville** (p. o.) are hamlets. **Smoky Hollow** (p. v.) contains several manufactories[8] and 25 dwellings, and **Churchtown** (p. v.) 1 church and 14 dwellings. The Ref. Prot. D. church, Claverack, was organized in 1716, and the present edifice was erected in 1765. There are 6 churches in town.[9]

CLERMONT—was formed from the Livingston Manor, March 12, 1787.[10] It lies upon the Hudson, in the s. w. corner of the co. The surface is undulating. Roeliff Jansens Kil forms the E. boundary. The soil is a fertile loam, and in some places sandy. **Clermont,** (p. v.,) near the E. part of the town, has a pop. of 155. The first settlement was made at an early day by Germans, who occupied the lands as tenants. A school was established, in 1791, by a special act of the legislature, before any general school system had been adopted in the State.[11] Robert R. Livingston, a prominent statesman of the Revolution and the first chancellor of the State, was a resident of this town. A German Lutheran church, about 3 mi. w. of the village of Clermont, is the only church in town.

COPAKE—was formed from Taghkanick, March 26, 1824. It lies on the E. border of the co., between Hillsdale and Ancram. Its surface is broken by ranges of hills separated by broad

1 William B. Whiting, Asa Waterman, Philip Frisbie, Martin Beebe, Elisha Pratt, Capt. Baldwin, Daniel Buck, Elijah Bostwick, Gideon King, Jarvis Mudge, Saml. Johnson, Saml. Gillett, L. A. Herrick, Joseph Wood, John Woodworth, and Saml. Baily were appointed a committee to prepare a memorial making such recommendation to Congress.

2 2 Bap., 2 M. E., Christian, Cong., and Presb.

3 Among these were John Beebe, and others named Cady, Hurlburt, Palmer, and Davis. A little w. of Chatham Center was a stone house, used as a defense against the Indians during the Revolution. A man named Vosburgh, who lived near this house, was killed and scalped; but his family escaped.

4 6 M. E., 2 Bap., Christian, Cong., and Ref. Prot. D.

5 This town formerly extended to the Hudson, and the bluffs on the bank were named the "Klauvers," (clovers,) whence "Claver-reach," or "Claverack."—*Benson's Memoir,* p. 44.

6 This institution is located upon a beautiful eminence in the N. part of the village, and commands an extensive view of the surrounding country and of the distant Catskills. It is one of the most flourishing institutions in the State. It has accommodations for 500 to 600 pupils.

7 Three paper mills, a carpet factory, woolen factory, sash and blind factory, furnace and machine shop.

8 Among these are a woolen factory, cradle factory, gristmill, and sawmill.

9 2 Ref. Prot. D., Bap., Evang. Luth., M. E., and Prot. E.

10 By an act of legislature passed March 2, 1858, a triangular tract, now constituting the N. part of Germantown, was taken off from Clermont.

11 An academy was incorp. April 26, 1834, and received under the regents Feb. 26, 1837, but it was never successfully organized.

and fertile valleys. A high and nearly unbroken range extends along the E. border. In the town are several small lakes, the principal of which are Copake Lake in the W., and Robinsons, Snyder, and Rhoda Ponds in the S. The soil is a gravelly and clayey loam. Near Copake Station are several iron mines.[1] **Copake Station,** (Copake Iron Works p. o.,) on the Harlem R. R., contains 1 church, a blast furnace, and 26 houses; **Copake Flats** (Copake p. o.) contains 1 church and 20 houses; and **Baines Station,** (North Copake p. o.,) a station on the Harlem R. R., 15 houses. The settlement of this town commenced about the middle of the last century.[2] A Ref. Prot. D. church was the first church organized, and Rev. Jeremiah Romeyn was the first pastor.[3]

GALLATIN[4]—was formed from Ancram, March 27, 1830. It lies near the center of the S. border of the co. The surface is broken by several ranges of hills, which extend in a N. and S. direction. The highest point is Mattashuk Hill, S. of Lake Charlotte. Roeliff Jansens Kil is the principal stream: its banks are steep and in some places rocky. Charlotte Lake, in the N. part of the town, is a fine sheet of water, surrounded by gentle slopes cultivated to the water's edge. The soil is a slaty and gravelly loam, and moderately fertile. **Gallatinville,** (p. v.,) on Roeliff Jansens Kil, contains a gristmill and 11 houses; **Weaver Hollow, Jacksons Corners,** (on the line of and p. o. in Dutchess co.,) and **Union Corners,** (partly in Livingston,) are hamlets. The town was settled at a very early day by emigrants from Holland and Germany.[5] A Ref. Prot. D. church was organized in 1748, and the Rev. Mr. Freymoot was the first pastor.[6]

GHENT[7]—was formed from Chatham, Claverack, and Kinderhook, April 3, 1818; and a part of Stockport was taken off in 1833. It is an interior town, N. of the center of the co. Its surface is hilly in the E. and undulating in the W. The town is watered by several small streams tributary to Kinderhook and Claverack Creeks. The soil is mostly a gravelly loam, but in some parts it is clayey. **Ghent,**[8] (p. v.,) in the E. part of the town, is a station on the H. & B. and Harlem R. Rs. It contains 2 churches and 18 houses. **West Ghent** (p. v.) contains 1 church and 16 houses. **Pulvers Station** is on the H. & B. R. R. The first settlement was made about 1735, by emigrants from Holland and Germany.[9] There are 4 churches in town.[10]

GREENPORT—was formed from Hudson City, May 13, 1837. It lies upon the Hudson, near the center of the W. border of the co. Its surface is broken and hilly. Beacrofts Mt., in the E. part of the town, is nearly precipitous upon its W. side. Merino Point,[11] near the Hudson, has an elevation of 250 feet above the river. Claverack Creek forms the E. boundary of the town, and a small tributary of this stream and Kahseway Creek are the principal watercourses. The intervale of the latter is broad and fertile. The soil is clayey along the river and a sandy and gravelly loam in the interior. Limestone is extensively quarried on the E. side of Beacrofts Mt. **Oak Hill** (p. o.) is a station on the Hudson R. R. R. in the S. W. part of the town. A steam ferry connects this place with Catskill Point on the opposite side of the Hudson. Settlement commenced in this town about the middle of the last century.[12] There is but one church (Ref. Prot. D.) in town.

GERMANTOWN[13]—was formed as a district April 1, 1775, and recognized as a town March 7, 1788. A part of Clermont was annexed, March 2, 1858.[14] It lies upon the Hudson, in the S. part of the co. The surface is undulating. Roeliff Jansens Kil forms the N. boundary. The soil is a rich, fertile loam, sandy in a few places. **Germantown** (p. v.) contains 1 church and 19 houses, and **East Camp** 17 houses. The first settlement was made in 1710, by German Palatinates, under the patronage of Queen Anne. The first arrival was in 1710; and on the 1st of May, 1711, there were 1178 settlers in town, and the four villages "*Hunterstown*," "*Queensbury*," "*Annsberg*," and "*Haysburgh*" had sprung into existence.[15] A school was estab-

---

[1] The ores obtained from these mines are hematites. A new ore bed, that promises an abundant supply of an excellent quality, has recently been opened to the depth of 13 feet.
[2] Families by the names of Snyder, Briese, and Lampman were among the early settlers.
[3] The census reports 3 churches; M. E., Presb., and Prot. E.
[4] Named in honor of Hon. Albert Gallatin.
[5] The Knickenbackers and the Snyders were among the first settlers. An Englishman, named Ross, was one of the first settlers in the neighborhood of Gallatinville.
[6] There are 2 churches in town; Ref. Prot. D. and M. E.
[7] Named from Ghent, in Holland.
[8] The Indian name of this locality was "*Scom-pa-muck.*"
[9] Among the first settlers were John, Cornelius, Andrew, and Lawrence Sharp, and Abraham Hogeboom, who located near Ghent Village. A man named Cox had settled near the same place a short time before.
[10] 2 Ref. Prot. D., Evang., Meth., and Friends.
[11] This point was formerly called "*Rorabuck.*" Its present

name was derived from the fact that a large sheep farm was established here many years ago.
[12] Jacob Johannes Van Hoesen and Erneric Plaice settled in the town as early as 1763.
[13] Named "*East Camp*" and "*German Camp*" in some early records.
[14] That part annexed was almost isolated from the rest of Clermont, and lay N. of this town.
[15] A tract of 6000 acres, forming the present town of Germantown, was purchased, on the 9th of Sept. 1710, of Robt. Livingston by Gov. Hunter, for the use of these people. It was designed to employ them in raising hemp and making tar, pitch, and rosin for the royal navy, and they were furnished with provisions and tools. The management of their affairs was intrusted to a board of commissioners, consisting of Robt. Livingston, Richard Sacket, John Cast, Godfrey Walsen, Andrew Bagger, and Herman Schureman. John Peter Knieskem was appointed "master" in Hunterstown, John Conrad Weiser in Queensbury, Hartman Windecker in Annsberg, and John Chris-

lished in 1711. The Ref. Prot. D. church was formed in 1728, and Johannes Van Driesen was the first pastor.[1]

HILLSDALE—was formed from Claverack, as a district, March 26, 1782, recognized as a town March 7, 1788, and a part of Austerlitz was taken off in 1818. The surface is broken by ranges of high hills extending in a N. and S. direction and separated by narrow valleys. Green River crosses the N. E. corner; and several small streams, which form the headwaters of Roeliff Jansens and Claverack Creeks, take their rise in the town. The soil is a gravelly loam and clay. **Hillsdale,** (p. v.,) a station on the Harlem R. R., in the S. part of the town, contains 2 churches and has a pop. of 225; **Harlemville** (p. v.) contains 1 church and 225 inhabitants, and **Green River** (p. v.) 1 church and about 12 houses. The town was settled at a very early day,—the S. part by immigrants from Mass. and the N. by Dutch settlers.[2] The first church (Bap.) was organized June 23, 1787, and Rev. Stephen Gano, D.D., was the first pastor. There are 6 churches in town.[3]

HUDSON CITY—was formed from Claverack, and incorp. as a city, April 22, 1785.[4] A part of Stockport was taken off in 1833, and Greenport in 1837. It lies upon the E. bank of the Hudson, at the head of ship navigation, near the center of the W. border of the co. The surface is a rolling upland. A slate bluff rises abruptly from the river to the height of 60 ft., and from its summit a beautifully rolling ridge extends eastward and slopes gradually upward for a distance of one and a half mi., terminating in Prospect Hill, a high, rounded eminence 300 ft. above the surrounding lands and 500 ft. above the river. This ridge is from 6 to 50 rods in width, and is bounded on the N. and S. by gradual and uniform slopes. North and South Bays (two shallow bodies of water) extend about 1000 ft. inland from the river, converting the W. extremity of the ridge into a promontory.[5] A public square, containing an area of about an acre and a half, has been laid out upon the summit of the bluff overlooking the river, and furnishing one of the most beautiful public promenades in the country. From the summit of Prospect Hill an extensive view is obtained of the windings of the Hudson, with the distant Catskills on one side, and the Green Hills of Mass. on the other.

In the river, opposite the city, is an extensive mud flat, through which a canal has been cut for the Hudson and Athens Ferry. This canal has recently been abandoned.

This city is the western terminus of the Hudson & Boston R. R., and an important station on the Hudson R. R. R. The manufactures are extensive, consisting principally of iron and clothing.[6] A considerable amount of commerce is carried on by means of the Hudson.[7]

The *City Hall* is a brick building, situated on Warren St. near the center of the city. The lower story is used for mercantile purposes.

The *Public Schools* are in a flourishing condition. In 1857 the city was divided into 4 districts, and gave employment to 21 teachers,—5 males and 16 females. The number of children between the ages of 4 and 21 was 2562, of which 1095 (or 42¾ per cent.) were in attendance some portion of the year. The total expenses of the schools for that year was $4448 38; total receipts, the same; number of volumes in district libraries, 700. A Lancasterian School Society was incorp. April 15, 1817, and it maintained a school many years.[8]

The *Hudson Academy* building, a plain, 3 story brick edifice near Prospect Hill, was erected in 1805.

---

tian Tucks in Haysburgh. The enterprise was unsuccessful, and many of the settlers removed to the Mohawk and Schoharie Valleys. In the summer of 1711 a company of 25 men from "*Hunterstown*" volunteered in the expedition against Canada. In 1725 the tract was granted by letters patent to the inhabitants of "*East Camp*," to be divided equally in fee after reserving 40 acres for church and school purposes.

[1] The census reports 3 churches in town; Evang. Luth., M. E., and Ref. Prot. D.

[2] Among the early Dutch settlers were families named Showerman, Blackman, Kinyon, Fregers, Evarts, and Shurts. ——Foster was one of the first settlers near Hillsdale Village. The State surrendered its claims to the lands actually occupied, March 12, 1793.

[3] 3 M. E., Bap., Christian, and Presb.

[4] The express object of this incorporation was to facilitate commercial operations. The charter included all the territory N. of Livingston Manor, W. of Claverack Creek, and S. of Major Abrahams Creek, extending 180 feet into the Hudson.

[5] Warren St., the principal street of the city, extends along the crest of this ridge from the foot of Prospect Hill to the promenade grounds on the bluff. Few streets in any city have a finer location than this.

[6] The Hudson Iron Co. have a double blast furnace, driven by an engine of 300 horse power: 80 to 90 men are employed, and 40 to 50 tons of pig iron turned out per day. At the Columbia Iron Works about 40 men are employed, and 20 to 25 tons of pig iron made daily. The ore used in these furnaces is obtained from Weston, Mass., and from Dutchess, Orange, and Essex cos. Clark's Clothing Manufactory employs about 400 hands. In 1858, sales were made to the amount of $130,000, mostly for the Southern market. Beside these, there are in the city 2 machine shops, 2 iron foundries, a stove foundry, gunshop, cutlery manufactory, bookbindery, flouring mill, brewery, and brickyard.

[7] An immense quantity of pressed hay, annually sent to the New York market, forms the principal export of the co.

[8] By act of May 11, 1835, this society was allowed to raise $400 annually.

The *Hudson Female Academy* was organized in 1851, and occupies a substantial stone edifice formerly used as a private lunatic asylum.

The *Orphan Asylum* was established in Oct. 1843, and is in charge of a board of lady managers. Forty to 60 children are provided for. It is supported by private donations, assisted by an annual stipend of $1000 from the co.

The city contains 11 private schools, 2 public libraries, 3 banks, and 3 newspaper offices. Pop. 6,720.

A lunatic asylum was established here in 1832, but it was given up upon the opening of the State Asylum at Utica.[1] The first religious organization (a society of Friends) was formed in 1784, and a meeting house was built in 1785. There are now 11 churches in the city.[2]

Hudson was formerly known as "*Claverack Landing.*"[3] The foundation of its future prosperity as a city was laid by Seth and Thos. Jenkins and their associates, in 1783.[4] It grew with great rapidity, and soon became the center of a very extensive commercial business. In 1775 it became a port of entry,[5] and at an early period its commerce extended to the West Indies and Europe.[6] Shad and herring, from the river and coast fisheries, ship timber, and country produce were exported, and numbers of ships were employed in the whale fisheries. The embargo, and the war which followed, destroyed this trade. The whaling business was afterward resumed, and for some time prosecuted with success; but it has since been entirely abandoned. A daily line of steamers plies between this city and Albany, and the day line between Albany and New York touches here.

KINDERHOOK[7]—was formed as a district, March 22, 1772, and reorganized as a town March 7, 1788. A part of Chatham was taken off in 1795, a part of Ghent in 1818, and Stuyvesant in 1823. It occupies the central part of the N. border of the co. The surface is level or undulating. Kinderhook Lake, in the N. E. part, is about 4 mi. in circumference. The principal streams are Kinderhook Creek and the outlet of Kinderhook Lake. The soil is a fertile, sandy, and gravelly loam. **Kinderhook,** (p. v.,) situated on the creek of the same name, was incorp. April 18, 1838. It contains 4 churches, the Kinderhook Academy, a newspaper office, 2 banks, and several manufacturing establishments.[8] Pop. 1078. **Lindenwald,** the residence of Ex Pres. Martin Van Buren, is about 2 mi. s. of this village. **Valatie,**[9] (vol'a-che, p. v.,) situated at the junction of Kinderhook Creek and the outlet of Kinderhook Lake, was incorp. June 30, 1856. It contains 4 churches, 5 cotton factories,[10] and several other manufactories.[11] **Niverville,** (p. v.,) on the outlet of Kinderhook Lake, is a station on the A. & W. S. R. R. It contains a wadding factory, batting factory, gristmill, and 21 houses. Settlements commenced under the Dutch Government.[12] The rights of certain settlers were confirmed by the act of March 12, 1793. A controversy concerning the patent of John Hendrick De Bruyn, granted in 1686, was settled by commissioners June 8, 1812. A Ref. Prot. D. church was organized in 1712. Rev. Johannes Lydius, of Albany, conducted the first religious services, and Rev. J. Van Driesen was the first settled pastor. There are 8 churches in town.[13]

LIVINGSTON—was granted as a manor,[14] July 22, 1686, formed as a district, March 24, 1772, and organized as a town, March 7, 1788. Clermont was taken off in 1787, and Ancram and Taghkanick in 1803. It is situated in the s. w. part of the co., bordering on the Hudson. The surface is generally undulating. Claverack Creek crosses the N. E. corner, Kleina Kil[15] flows through near the center, and Roeliff Jansens Kil forms the s. w. boundary. In most of its course

---

[1] Established by Dr. S. White. It was continued 6¼ years, and during that time 297 patients were admitted.

[2] Bap., M. E., Presb., Prot. E., Ref. Prot. D., R. C., Univ., Wes. Meth., Af. Meth., and 2 Friends meeting houses.

[3] In 1783, Peter Hogeboom, Peter Van Hoesen, Caspar Huyck, John Van Allen, and John, Jacob, Jonathan, and Leonard Hendricks lived at this place. Van Allen kept a store, and Conrad Flock kept a canoe ferry to Loonenburgh.

[4] Seth and Thomas Jenkins, and 28 others, that year formed themselves into an association for commercial purposes, and selected "*Claverack Landing*" as the seat of their operations. A city plot was at once surveyed, docks were built, and shipbuilding commenced. The following year the Hudson, a ship of 300 tons, was launched by Jenkins & Gelston. Cotton Gelston opened a store the same year, and in 1785 Thomas Jenkins and Josiah Alcott built a ropewalk, 600 feet long. Josiah Barnard built a wind gristmill on Prospect Hill, in 1787; and Thos. and Seth Jenkins and Stephen Paddock, a hemp ducking factory, in 1789.

[5] Henry Malcomb, the first collector, was appointed June 12, 1795.

[6] It is said that at one time a greater amount of shipping was owned at this port than at New York.

[7] A Dutch name, signifying "Childrens Point." There are several versions of the origin of this name: one is, that it was

given by Hudson from the number of Indian children congregated to see his vessel at a point above Stuyvesant Landing; and another, that it was derived from the number of children belonging to a family residing at the forks of an Indian trail, where the village of Kinderhook now is.

[8] A steam cotton factory, gristmill, sawmill, 2 hat factories, and a candle factory.

[9] A Dutch word, signifying "Little Falls." There is a fall here of about 15 feet; and hence the name.

[10] There are about 400 looms in these factories, and 400 to 500 persons employed: warp and wicking exclusively are made at one of them.

[11] A paper mill, furnace, machine shop, plaster mill, and sawmill. Pop. estimated at about 1500.

[12] A record belonging to the Ref. Prot. D. church, dated 1729, and signed by Johannes Van Driesen, gives the names of 100 families then residing in town. Among these are the names Van Alsteyn, Van Allen, Van Schaack, Van Burjren, Van Der Pool, Conyn, Huijk, Vosburg, Schermerhorn, Klauw, Gardenier, Van Valkenburgh, Van Sleijk, Wieber, and Mulder.

[13] 2 M. E., Bap., Evang. Luth., Presb., Prot. E., Ref. Prot. D., and R. C.

[14] The manor, of which this town is a part, was granted to Robert Livingston.

[15] Little Creek.

this last stream flows through a broad and fertile valley, but near the Hudson its banks are steep and rocky. The soil is a fertile, sandy loam. **Johnstown,** (Livingston p. o.,) situated near the center of the town, contains 1 church, a parochial school, and 28 houses. **Glencoe Mills,** (p. v.,) on Claverack Creek, contains a free chapel, 2 sawmills, and 16 houses. **Bakers Mills,** (p. o.,) on Roeliff Jansens Kil, contains a woolen factory, 2 paper mills, a gristmill, and 10 dwellings. **Elizaville,** (p. o.,) **Blue Store,** and **Linlithgo** are hamlets. Settlement commenced soon after the patent was granted.[1] There are 4 churches in town.[2]

NEW LEBANON—was formed from Canaan, April 21, 1818. It is the N. E. corner town of the co. The surface consists of steep hills separated by broad, irregular valleys. The Taghkanick Mts., upon the E., separate this town from Mass. The Wyomanock or Lebanon Creek is the principal stream. The soil is a gravelly and slaty loam intermixed with clay. The valleys are generally narrow and the hills arable to their summits. **Lebanon Springs,** (New Lebanon Springs p. o.,) in the E. part of the town, is celebrated for its thermal springs.[3] It contains 2 churches, 4 hotels, a female seminary, and a gristmill. Pop. 278. **Tildens** (New Lebanon p. o.) contains 1 church, a barometer and thermometer manufactory, a laboratory for the preparation of medicinal extracts,[4] and 35 houses. **New Lebanon Center** (p. v.) contains a gristmill, sawmill, tannery, and 22 houses; **Moffatts Store,** (p. v.,) 1 church and 23 houses; and **New Britain,** (p. o.,) 1 church and 6 houses. In the E. part of the town, about 2 mi. s. of Lebanon Springs, is a large Shaker community.[5] The first settlement was made about 1760, by immigrants mostly from Mass. and Conn.[6] There are 8 churches in town.[7]

STOCKPORT—was formed from Hudson, Ghent, and Stuyvesant, April 30, 1833. It lies upon the Hudson, N. of the center of the co. The surface consists of a high table land, rising from the river in bluffs and descending with a moderate slope toward the E. Kinderhook and Claverack Creeks unite near the center of the town. The valleys of these streams are narrow and their banks often steep and rocky. Near Stottsville are 4 mineral springs, known as the Columbia Springs.[8] **Stockport,** (p. v.,) situated at the junction of Kinderhook and Claverack Creeks, contains 3 churches, several manufactories,[9] and 44 dwellings. **Chittendens Falls** contains 1 church, 2 paper mills, and 14 dwellings, and **Stottsville** 2 woolen factories and 21 dwellings. **Columbiaville**[10] (Stockport station on the Hudson R. R. R.) is situated on the Hudson. This town was settled at an early period by the Dutch. There are 4 churches in town.[11]

STUYVESANT[12]—was formed from Kinderhook, April 21, 1823, and a part of Stockport was taken off in 1833. It is the N. W. corner town of the co., is situated on the bank of the Hudson, and includes the adjacent islands E. of the middle of the river. The surface is generally level, except along the river bank, where it is broken by ravines and low hills. Kinderhook Creek crosses the s. part of the town. The soil is generally clayey, but in some places it is a light, sandy loam. **Stuyvesant Falls,** (p. v.,) on Kinderhook Creek, contains 1 church, several manufactories,[13] and 35 houses. **Stuyvesant Landing,** (Stuyvesant p. o.,) on the Hudson, contains 1 church, a flouring mill, a foundry, 2 coal yards, a lumber yard, and 34 houses. It is a steamboat

---

1 On Beatty's map of 1714, the manorhouse and mill are located within this town, near the Hudson, and the residences of families named Witbeck, Claas, and Brusie near Claverack Creek.

2 2 Ref. Prot. D., Evang. Luth., M. E.

3 The spring is 10 feet in diameter and 4 feet deep, and discharges 16 barrels of water per minute. The water is wholly tasteless, and has a temperature of 73° at all seasons. According to an analysis made by Dr. Meade, 1 pint of water contains 1.25 grs. solid matter, as follows:—0.25 grs. chloride of calcium, 0.44 grs. chloride of sodium, 0.19 grs. carbonate of lime, and 0.37 grs. sulphate of lime. Bubbles of gas constantly rise from the bottom of the spring, giving it the appearance of boiling. This gas is composed of 89.4 parts nitrogen and 10.6 parts oxygen, and is given out in the proportion of 5 cubic inches from a pint of the water. So great is the volume of water discharged that it not only supplies several baths, but 2 or 3 mills are kept running by it both summer and winter.—*L. C. Beck's Report,* 1848, p. 48, and *Geology 1st Dist.,* p. 105. The medicinal properties of these waters were first brought to the notice of the public by Jas. Hitchcock. There are several similar springs of less volume in the vicinity.

4 Tilden & Co. have under cultivation 40 acres of medicinal plants,—chiefly dandelion, hyoscyamus, lettuce, belladonna, stramonium, yellow dock, burdock, poppies, digitalis, aconite, horehound, wormwood, and valerian. They also use large quantities of conium, gathered from the surrounding country, as well as imported medicinal herbs and roots. Sixty persons are employed in the preparation of their extracts.

5 There are 500 to 600 persons in this community. They own

about 2000 acres of land in this State, besides a considerable tract in Mass. They have a large meeting house, a laboratory furnished with steam power, a gristmill, 4 sawmills, 2 machine shops, 8 dwellings, and several other buildings. They are principally engaged in farming, and in preparing extracts, roots, herbs, botanic medicines, and garden seeds. They also manufacture brooms, sieves, and fancy baskets. About 200,000 lbs. of medicinal articles and garden seeds are put up annually. The neatness of their grounds and premises is proverbial.

6 Among the first settlers were families named Gilbert, Cornell, King, Skinner, Mudge, Gurnsey, Jones, Waddams, Sanford, and Patchin. An inn was kept at Lebanon Springs for several years before the close of the Revolutionary War. The house is still standing, and is supposed to be nearly a century old.

7 3 M. E., Bap., Christian, Presb., R. C., and a Shaker meeting house.

8 The waters of these springs have never been analyzed. A hotel and bathing houses have recently been erected near them, and they are now much frequented.

9 2 cotton factories, a matrass factory, machine shop, and sash and blind factory.

10 Columbiaville was incorp. Feb. 21, 1812, but the act of incorporation was repealed April 20, 1833. It was formerly a manufacturing place of considerable importance. In 1813 it had a cotton factory of 1500 spindles, 2 paper mills, 4 cording mills, 2 fulling mills, together with grist, saw, and plaster mills.

11 M. E., Presb., Prot. E., and Univ.

12 Named in honor of Gov. Peter Stuyvesant.

13 3 cotton factories, a woolen factory, a gristmill, sawmill, machine shop, and an agricultural implement factory.

landing[1] and a station on the Hudson R. R. R. **Coxsackie Station,** on the Hudson R. R. R., has half a dozen houses. At this place is a ferry to Coxsackie, (Greene co.,) on the opposite side of the river. The first settlement was made by the Dutch about the period of the English conquest.[2] There are 3 churches in town.[3]

TAGHKANICK[4]—was formed from Livingston as "*Granger,*" March 19, 1803. Its name was changed March 25, 1814, and Copake was taken off in 1824. It is an interior town, lying s. of the center of the co. The surface is hilly. Taghkanick Creek is the principal stream. Its banks are low and rocky, and upon it are numerous mill sites. The soil is a gravelly and slaty loam. The hills are generally arable to their summits, although some are wooded and rocky. **West Taghkanick** (p. v.) contains 1 church, a gristmill, and 14 houses. **Taghkanick** (p. o.) and **New Forge** are hamlets. The first settlements were made by German and Dutch settlers, among whom were families named Brises, Shurts, and Shoefelts. A tract of about 600 acres, called Taghkanick, included in this town, was purchased by Robert Livingston in 1685. The first church (M. E.) was organized in 1843. There are now 2 churches in town; Evang. Luth., and M. E.

Acres of Land, Valuation, Population, Dwellings, Families, Freeholders, Schools, Live Stock, Agricultural Products, and Domestic Manufactures, of Columbia County.

Names of Towns.	Acres of Land.		Valuation of 1858.			Population.		No. of Dwellings.	No. of Families.	Freeholders.	Schools.	
	Improved.	Unimproved.	Real Estate.	Personal Property.	Total.	Males.	Females.				No. of Districts.	Children taught.
Ancram	21,135	5,784	$625,300	$49,900	$675,200	929	872	284	323	171	11	757
Austerlitz	22,805	4,987	401,800	68,450	470,250	796	822	323	354	228	15	574
Canaan	16,501	5,218	447,810	66,100	513,910	989	957	359	426	235	10	634
Chatham	26,856	4,381	1,094,968	271,730	1,366,698	2,030	1,993	724	821	460	20	1,497
Claverack	25,055	4,916	927,201	138,353	1,065,554	1,654	1,709	569	519	444	14	1,179
Clermont	10,231⅜	2,047	279,057	151,331	430,388	538	520	183	183	136	6	383
Copake	18,344	4,524	433,820	100,250	534,070	838	782	271	269	180	9	542
Gallatin	17,588	6,151	288,924	126,069	414,993	778	739	260	272	166	7	672
Germantown	5,768	573	220,407	100,305	320,712	573	558	175	193	132	5	446
Ghent	22,506	5,420	881,504	92,103	973,607	1,272	1,265	412	471	237	10	700
Greenport	9,866	1,549	357,280	222,600	579,880	685	698	215	242	146	4	445
Hillsdale	21,058	5,641	462,830	132,050	594,880	1,101	1,093	394	366	273	18	979
Hudson	373	77	1,000,500	1,350,042	2,350,542	3,120	3,600	895	1,365	500	4	2,390
Kinderhook	15,865	2,811	721,857	994,240	1,716,097	1,800	2,064	671	743	161	10	1,528
Livingston	20,648	2,055	592,072	254,500	846,572	1,025	1,039	328	370	204	12	932
New Lebanon	16,218	3,804	286,090	104,000	390,090	1,151	1,178	352	370	291	15	821
Stockport	5,650	901	233,818	64,250	298,068	776	845	282	304	125	4	519
Stuyvesant	10,820	2,448	450,752	203,000	653,752	974	963	316	354	287	6	849
Taghkanick	16,991	5,968	283,980	63,106	347,086	828	837	274	291	178	8	656
Total	304,277⅜	69,255	$9,989,970	$4,552,379	$14,542,349	21,857	22,534	7,287	8,236	4,554	188	16,503

Names of Towns.	Live Stock.					Agricultural Products.							Domestic Manufactures, in Yards.
						Bush. of Grain.		Tons of Hay.	Bushels of Potatoes.	Bushels of Apples.	Dairy Products.		
	Horses.	Working Oxen and Calves.	Cows.	Sheep.	Swine.	Winter.	Spring.				Pounds Butter.	Pounds Cheese.	
Ancram	510	1,268	852	11,381	3,835	22,298½	101,274	3,383	21,006	14,580	91,035	300	230
Austerlitz	514	800	827	8,485	1,193	12,821	47,564	3,698	17,066	12,526	98,665	8,300	151
Canaan	454	690	678	8,711	1,013	12,325	60,779	3,078	18,790	14,702	75,080	12,385	1,017
Chatham	897	1,338	1,452	6,579	2,924	40,844	110,398	4,283	17,706	17,532	130,875	10,284	321
Claverack	841	964	1,113	4,573	2,888	49,049	68,701½	6,050	23,680	18,581	107,575	1,168	522
Clermont	378	289	595	2,539	1,355	14,867	22,806½	3,242	6,499	6,508	42,045		487
Copake	436	981	804	7,211	2,837	40,774	71,454	3,011	20,075	11,671	72,295	1,220	305
Gallatin	520	1,035	837	5,135	2,530	28,431	55,373	2,848	13,084	7,662	69,075	750	1,208
Germantown	220	189	435	243	723	5,736	7,920	2,229	2,517	3,959	33,068		
Ghent	806	962	981	4,469	2,272	50,172	71,132	4,815	13,428	7,914	104,023	100	105
Greenport	346	366	498	740	925	12,324	19,915½	3,926	6,177	9,493	45,088	250	68
Hillsdale	538	866	893	5,900	2,186	26,367	73,928	4,258	19,353	26,585	98,767	5,061	236
Hudson	248	7	118		512	160	936	178	232½	270	1,700		
Kinderhook	542	642	639	3,865	1,639	33,911	99,730	2,802	20,050	7,876	64,640	626	13
Livingston	611	597	995	3,954	1,859	49,238	49,446¾	4,997	9,519	9,440	90,246	144	139
New Lebanon	448	833	925	9,230	972	8,809	51,295	4,783	15,868	22,436	84,022	25,794	3,016
Stockport	133	203	327	87	250	2,784	9,786	1,894	4,114	5,170	26,173		
Stuyvesant	180	347	650	1,442	532	10,552	27,619	2,934	21,236	5,689	45,468	255	59
Taghkanick	481	799	881	3,005	2,123	31,546	37,114	2,694	9,019	7,748	67,588	530	698
Total	9,103	13,176	14,500	87,549	32,568	453,008½	987,172¼	65,103	259,419½	210,342	1,347,428	67,167	8,575

[1] 2 propellers, owned by parties here, ply on the Hudson and run from this place.

[2] Among the early settlers were families by the names of Van Alstyne, Van Allen, Van Ness, Van Slyke, Van Dyke, Van Valkenburgh, Vosburgh, and Schermerhorn.

[3] Evang. Luth., Ref. Prot. D., and M. E.

[4] Pronounced Toh-kon/nick, and supposed to signify "Water Enough." Upon this side of Mt. Tom, in Copake, was formerly a spring which was a favorite resort of the Indians; and hence the name "Taghkanick" for the locality.

CORTLAND COUNTY.

This county was formed from Onondaga, April 8, 1808, and embraces the original townships of Virgil, Cincinnatus, Homer, Solon, and the south half of Tully and Fabius[1] in the s. e. corner of the Military Tract. It was named in honor of Pierre Van Cortlandt, first Lieut. Gov. of the State of N. Y.[2] It lies near the center of the State, upon the northern spurs of the Allegany Mts., and just s. of the watershed between the Susquehanna and Lake Ontario. It contains an area of 485 square miles, and is centrally distant 120 miles from Albany. Its surface is hilly and occasionally broken, consisting mostly of arable ridges with narrowish valleys between them. The highlands are divided into three general ridges extending through the county in a northerly and southerly direction. The first of these occupies the extreme eastern edge of the county, and is bounded on the w. by the valley of the Otselic River; the second lies between the Otselic and Tioughnioga Rivers; and the third embraces all the highlands lying w. of the Tioughnioga. These highlands are all divided laterally by the valleys of small streams, and in some places they are but little more than a collection of sharp ridges separated by narrow ravines. The northern portion of the county spreads out into a high plateau, broken by hills. This level has an average elevation of 1,100 to 1,200 feet above tide, and the ridges rise from 200 to 500 feet higher. A broad plain, into which nearly all the valleys of the tributaries of the Tioughnioga converge, occupies the center of the western part of the county; and here the county seat is located. South of this the valleys contract until they become ravines. The highest points in the county are Mount Toppin, in Preble, the Truxton Hills, and the Owego Hills, in Virgil and Harford, which attain an elevation of 1,600 to 2,100 feet above tide.

The drainage is nearly all through the Tioughnioga River, which flows through near the center of the county. In its upper course, it consists of two principal branches, the eastern entering the town of Cuyler from Madison county, and the western taking its rise in the small lakes in the northern part of Preble and the southern part of Onondaga county. The principal branches of the Tioughnioga are the Otselic,—which flows through a deep valley in the eastern part of the county from Chenango county,—Trout, Cheningo, and Labrador Creeks, and Cold and Factory Brooks. The Skaneateles Outlet drains the northwestern, the branches of Fall Creek the extreme western, and Owego Creek the southwestern, parts of the county. The only considerable bodies of water in the county are the Skaneateles Lake, which borders upon the n. w. corner, and several small lakes in the northern part of the Tioughnioga Valley.

The Hamilton group of rocks—consisting of calcareous shale, with limestone and slate intermixed—enters the northern portions of the county; and successively above this, toward the south, appear the Genesee slate, and the Portage and Chemung groups. Quarries of sandstone and limestone, affording excellent building material, are worked in Scott, Homer, Cortlandville, and several other parts of the county. A little s. e. of Cortlandville are several small lakes, containing deposits of marl, from which an excellent quality of lime is manufactured. The soil upon the hills is principally a sandy or gravelly loam; and that of the valleys is of the same character, with a large mixture of disintegrated slate, shale, and limestone.

From its considerable elevation above tide, the climate of this co. is colder than the lower regions n. and w. The winters are longer, and snow falls to a greater depth. The people are almost exclusively engaged in the different branches of agriculture. Spring grains are largely produced in the valleys, but the whole county is better adapted to pasturage than tillage. Dairying and stock raising are extensively pursued. The production of wool also receives considerable attention. The more hardy fruits generally flourish, but are liable to injury from early and late frosts.

---

[1] The following lots in these towns were set apart for the support of the gospel and schools:—In Tully, 69, 76, 81; Fabius, 55, 58; Homer, 4, 34, 70, 85, 93, 98; Solon, 22, 25, 30, 41, 64, 98; Virgil, 20, 36, 51, 86, 91, 99; Cincinnatus, 1, 16, 37, 49, 53, 62. The territory of the "Boston Ten Towns," lying immediately south of this, was found to overlap or extend over a portion of this tract, and to embrace nearly all of the two southern tiers of lots in Virgil, and 4 lots in the s. w. corner of Cincinnatus. Two additional townships (Junius, Cayuga co., and Galen. Wayne co.) were set apart by the Land Commissioners, July 31, 1790, to supply the deficiency thus occasioned in the Military Tract.

[2] Gen. Van Cortlandt was an extensive owner of lands upon the Military Tract in this and adjoining counties.

Manufactures are of limited extent. The completion of the Syracuse, Binghamton, and New York R. R. through this county has given an additional impulse to every branch of business, and has greatly enhanced the value of the farms by furnishing an easy and direct avenue to market.[1]

Cortland Village, the county seat, is situated upon the Tioughnioga, near the center of the town of Cortlandville. The county clerk's office and the court house are finely situated in the center of the village.[2] The jail is located in the basement of the court house, the floors of the cells being 4 or 5 feet below the surface of the ground. The average number of prisoners is 2. The poor house is situated upon a farm of 118 acres, 3 mi. N. E. of Cortland Village. The average number of inmates is about 50. The farm yields a revenue of $600.

There are four papers published in the county.[3]

Few events of general interest have occurred in this county. Settlement began in Homer in 1791, in Virgil and Cortlandville in 1794, and in several other towns before the commencement of the present century. Being remote from the great routes of travel, its settlement advanced but slowly for many years, and the fertile but more distant valley of the Genesee had been mostly taken up by immigrants before civilization spread over the hills and along the valleys of Cortland county. The fear of Indian massacre then had not entirely subsided, and at times occasioned distress almost as real as if hostilities actually existed. The wild beasts often claimed a share of the little flocks and herds of the pioneers; and long, weary forest roads to distant mills and markets, for many years, proved a heavy burden to the early settlers in this and many other sections of the State not favored with navigable streams.

CINCINNATUS—was formed from Solon, April 3, 1804. It embraced the township of Cincinnatus, or No. 25 of the military tract, a name applied by the Land Commissioners upon its first survey. The present town is one-fourth of its original size,—having been reduced by the erection of Freetown, Willett, and Marathon, in 1818. It lies upon the eastern border of the county, s. of the center. Its surface consists of the narrow valley of the Otselic River and of the high ridges which rise upon each side. Deep ravines, forming the valleys of small tributaries to the river, extend laterally far into the highlands, dividing nearly the whole surface of the town into steep ridges of hills. The soil is generally a gravelly loam, and best adapted to grazing. **Cincinnatus** (p. v.) contains about 290 inhabitants, and **Lower Cincinnatus** 150. The former contains 3 churches[4] and an academy.[5] The first settlers were Ezra and Thos. Rockwell, from Lenox, Mass., who located upon lot 19; and Dr. John McWhorter, from Salem, N.Y., on lot 29, in 1795.[6] The first church (Presb.) was formed by a union of the people of Cincinnatus, Solon, Taylor, and Pitcher, Chenango co.

[1] This road is built along the Tioughnioga Valley, connecting with the N. Y. C. R. R. at Syracuse, and with the N. Y. & E. R. R. at Binghamton. It has stations at Preble, Little York, Homer, Cortlandville, Blodgets Mills, State Bridge, and Marathon.

[2] The county courts were first directed to be held at the schoolhouse on lot 45, in Homer. By an act of April 5, 1810, Joseph L. Richardson, of Auburn, Nathan Smith, of Herkimer, and Nathaniel Locke, of Chenango, were appointed commissioners to select the site for a court house, and $2000 was appropriated for the erection of the building. The first county officers were John Keep, *First Judge;* Wm. Mallory, *Sheriff;* and John McWhorter, *Surrogate.*

[3] *The Cortland Courier* was established at Homer in 1810 by Jas. & Saml. Percival. In 1812 H. R. Bender & R. Washburne became the proprietors, and changed its name to
The Farmers Journal. They sold it to Jesse Searl in 1813, by whom it was issued as
The Cortland Repository, and continued until 1825. Then Milton A. Kinney became proprietor, and changed its title to
The Cortland Observer. It passed into the hands of S. S. Bradford in 1833, and in 1836 into those of —— Holmes, by whom its title was changed to
The Homer Eagle. In 1837 it was united with the *Cortland Republican,* and issued by R. A. Reid as
The Republican and Eagle, and continued until 1852. C. B. Gould then became proprietor, and changed it to
The Cortland County Whig. In 1856 it was sold to J. R. Dixon, and by him it is now published as
The Cortland County Republican.
The Protestant Sentinel was started at Homer in 1831 by John Maxson, and continued until 1833.
The Cortland Republican was commenced in 1815, at Cortland Village, by James Percival, and was continued by him, by Osborn & Campbell, and by the Campbell Bros., until 1821.
The Western Courier was founded at Homer in 1821 by Roberts & Hull, and was soon after removed to Cortland Village. In 1824 it appeared as

The Cortland Journal, and in 1832 as
The Cortland Advocate. It was published successively by C W. Gill, H. S. Randall, and David Fairchild, and in 1845 it was styled
The Cortland Democrat. Seth Haight & H. G. Crouch have been interested in its management; and it is now published by A. P. Cole, as
The Cortland Gazette, which name it received in 1857.
The Cortland Chronicle was started in 1828 by Reed & Osborn. It was sold to R. A. Reed in 1832, and by him called
The Anti-Masonic Republican. In 1833 it was styled
The Cortland Republican, and in 1837 it was united with
The Homer Eagle.
The Liberty Herald, semi-mo., was published at Cortland Village in 1844 and '45 by E. F. Graham.
The True American and Religious Examiner was started in 1845, at Cortland Village, by C. B. Gould. The following year it passed into the hands of S. R. Ward, was issued by him as
The True American, and continued until 1848.
The Republican Banner was started in 1858 by E. D Van Slyck & P. H. Bateson.
The South Cortland Luminary was published in 1840, at South Cortland, by M. Reynolds.
The Morning Star was published at McGrawville in 1850, and *The Central Reformer* in 1858.
[4] Cong., Bap., Meth.
[5] Cincinnatus Academy was chartered by the regents, April 21, 1857.
[6] Eb'r Crittenden, from Barrington, Mass., removed to the present town of Willett in 1793, and to the present limits of this town in 1797. The first child born was Sally Rockwell, the first marriage that of Dr. McWhorter to Katy Young, and the first death that of Daniel Hartshorn.—all in 1796. Mrs. H. Beebe taught the first school, in 1797; Col. John Kingman, the first inn; Elijah Bliss, the first store; and Eph'm Fish built the first mill, in 1814.

CORTLANDVILLE—was formed from Homer, April 11, 1829, and embraces the southern half of the original township of Homer, and a small portion of the N. E. corner of Virgil. The name was applied to the town from its being the county seat of Cortland county. It is situated at the junction of the eastern and western branches of the Tioughnioga River, and extends from the central portion of the county to the extreme western border. The surface of much of the town is level; but the eastern and southern parts are hilly. From an eminence just w. of Cortland Village can be seen 7 distinct valleys, separated by ranges of hills radiating in different directions. The ridges are 200 to 400 feet above the valleys; and the southern part of the town is a broken upland region, the hills being arable to their summits. The tributaries of the Tioughnioga in this town are Trout Brook from the E. and Dry and Otter Brooks from the w. A small part of the western portion of the town is drained by streams flowing westward into Cayuga Lake. In the S. W. part of the town are three small ponds, fed by springs, and furnishing an almost unlimited supply of marl, from which an excellent quality of lime is manufactured.[1] The soil is generally a sandy or gravelly loam. **Cortland Village**[2] (p.v.) is finely situated upon the Tioughnioga, near the center of the town. It contains an academy,[3] 5 churches, 3 hotels, and a population of 1,576. **McGrawville** (p. v.) is situated upon Trout Brook, 4¼ mi. E. of Cortland Village. It contains 3 churches and several manufacturing establishments, and is the seat of the N.Y. Central College.[4] Pop. 558. **South Cortland,** (p.v.,) in the s.w. part of the town, contains 161 inhabitants. **Blodgets Mills** is a p.o. The first settlers of this town were Jonathan Hubbard and Col. Moses Hopkins,—the former upon the lot where Cortland Village now stands, and the latter upon lot 94.[5] The census reports 9 churches in town.[6]

FREETOWN—was formed from Cincinnatus, April 21, 1818, and embraces the N. w. quarter of that township. Lot 20 of Virgil was annexed in 1850. It is situated upon the ridge between the Otselic and Tioughnioga Rivers, s. E. of the center of the county. It is high and hilly, and its surface is much broken by the narrow ravines of the watercourses which flow N. and s. A considerable part of the more hilly portions is yet covered with the original forests. Its soil is a sandy and gravelly loam, and is best adapted to pasturage. **Freetown Corners** (p. v.) has 2 churches and about 100 inhabitants. Robert Smith, a soldier of the Revolution, drew lot 2, and, accompanied by his son-in-law, Ensign Rice, took possession of it in 1795.[7] The first church (Bap.) was organized in 1810, by Elder Caleb Shepard, of Lisle, who was the first preacher.[8]

HARFORD—was formed from Virgil,[9] May 2, 1845, and it embraces the s. w. quarter of that township. It is the s. w. corner town in the county. Its surface consists of a high, broken upland, 500 to 700 feet above the valleys and 1500 to 1700 feet above tide. The Owego Hills, in the southern part, are the most elevated portions. The declivities are usually steep, and often rocky, and the summits are crowned with forests. One half of the town is yet a wilderness. The streams are mere brooks. The soil is a moderately productive sandy and gravelly loam, best adapted to pasturage. **Harford** (p. v.) contains 30 houses, and **South Harford** 20. The first settler was Dorastus De Wolf, in 1803.[10] Religious meetings were held as early as 1804; but the first church (Bap.) was not organized till 1815.[11]

HOMER—was formed March 5, 1794. Solon was taken off in 1798, Virgil in 1804, and Cortlandville in 1829. It lies upon the w. border of the county, N. of the center. Its surface

---

1 Crandalls Pond covers an area of 15 acres; Swains, 6, and Chatterdons, 4. The marl is generally of an ash color when first taken out, but the vegetable matter which it contains whitens upon exposure to the air. When partially dried, it is moulded into the form of bricks, and these are thoroughly dried and burned. The greatest known thickness of these deposits of marl is about 20 feet.—*Geol. Third Dist.,* p. 291.

2 The Cortlandville Academy, incorp. Jan. 13, 1843.

3 This institution was incorp. in 1850. It was originally started as a manual labor school, and is open to all, without distinction of color or sex.

4 In 1795, Thos. Wilcox, from Whitestown, located upon lot 94; Reuben Doud, from New Haven, Jas. and John Morse, and Joseph Lee, upon lot 75. In 1796–97, Aaron Knapp located near Cortland Village, —— Hotchkiss upon lot 73, and Saml. Inglis and son on lot 75. In 1800, Wilmot Sperry (from Woodbridge, Conn) settled on lot 73; and a few settlers came yearly until 1810, when the growth became more rapid. The first school-house stood on the present site of the Eagle Hotel. The first inn was kept by Saml. Inglis, in 1810.

5 2 Bap., 2 M. E., 2 Presb., Christian, Ref. Presb., and Univ.

6 About 10 years after, Smith and Rice sold their improvements to Saml. G. Hathaway and Saml. Jennings; and about the same time Caleb Shepard and David H. Munro, from Wash-

ington co., settled on lot 22. In 1806, Remembrance Curtiss settled on lot 12; and Curtis and Chas. Richardson, from Saratoga co., on lot 32. Henry Gardner, Wm. Tuthill, Jacob Hicks, Gideon Chapin, Simeon Doty, John Backus, and Amos Eaton, were among the other early settlers. The first marriage was that of Robert Smith, jr., with Amity Smith. The first school teacher was Don A. Robertson. The first store was kept by Peter McVean, at "The Corners." The first permanent merchant was Walton Sweetland, still a resident of the town.

8 The census reports 3 churches; 1 Bap., 2 M. E.

9 The p.o. of "Worthington" was established in this part of Virgil in 1825 or '26. Its name was changed to Harford about 10 years after. From this the town derives its name.

10 Among the other first settlers were Thos. Nichols, in 1804, John Green, in 1805, Eben Burgess, —— Barns, Gordon Burlingame, Nathan Heaton, Theodore E. Hart, and Lewis Moore. Theodore E. Hart kept the first store, in 1824. The first birth was that of Dr. Chas. Barns; the first marriage, that of Obed Graves and Alice Munroe; and the first death, that of Dorastus De Wolf. Betsey Carver taught the first school, in 1806; Lewis Moore kept the first inn; and Nathan Heaton built the first grist mill, in 1814.

11 The census reports 3 churches; Christian, Cong., and Union.

is quite uneven, consisting of the valleys of the two branches of the Tioughnioga River and the ridges which border upon them. The valley of the western branch is over a mile wide, and elevated 1,096 feet above tide. The eastern valley is narrower. A ridge of hills. 200 to 500 feet above the river, separates the two valleys; and a similar ridge occupies the s. e. corner of the town. The western part is a hilly upland, 1500 to 1600 feet above tide. The principal branches of the Tioughnioga are Cold and Factory Brooks, from the w. The valleys of these streams open northward into corresponding valleys, through which flow streams emptying into Otisco and Skaneateles Lakes. The soil upon the river intervales is a deep, rich alluvial and dark loam, well adapted to tillage; among the hills, it is a sandy or gravelly loam, better for pasturage. **Homer**[1] (p. v.) is finely situated on the Tioughnioga, 3 mi. n. of Cortland Village. It contains 6 churches, a printing office, and several manufacturing establishments, including the only cotton factory in the county. It is the seat of Cortland Academy,[2] an old and very flourishing institution. Pop. 1625. **East Homer** (p. v.) contains 25 houses, and **Little York** (p. v.) 15. Spencer Beebe and his brother-in-law, Amos Todd, were the first settlers of this town, and of Cortland county, in 1791.[3] The first religious meetings were held in 1793, when there were but 6 families in town; and all attended. The first church (Cong.) was founded in 1801, chiefly through the influence of Mrs. Hobart, wife of Lieut. Hobart.[4]

LAPEER—was formed from Virgil, May 2, 1845, and embraces the s. e. quarter of that township. It lies upon the high ridges w. of the Tioughnioga River, on the s. border of the county, w. of the center. The declivities of the hills bordering upon the river are precipitous. "Luce Hill," in the north western part of the town, is the highest point, and is 1,600 to 1,700 feet above tide. The streams are all small brooks. Upon Fall Creek, near the s. border of the town, is a wild and beautiful cascade, 71 feet high, known as Hunts Falls. The soil is a sandy and gravelly loam. Nearly one half of the town is still unsettled. **Hunts Corners** contains 10 houses. **Lapeer** (p.o.) is near the center of the town. There is no church edifice in town.[5] The first settler was Phineas Grant, a colored man.[6]

MARATHON—was formed from Cincinnatus, April 21, 1818, as "*Harrison,*" embracing the s. w. quarter of the military township. Its name was changed in 1827. It lies upon the southern border of the county, e. of the center. Its surface is rugged and hilly, the ridges rising 500 to 700 feet above the valleys. The Tioughnioga flows through its western part, in a deep, narrow valley with precipitous sides. Hunt Creek in the n. w. and Merrill Creek in the e. part of the town also flow through deep and narrow valleys. The arable land lies principally along these valleys, the uplands being broken and only fit for pasturage. The soil is a sandy and gravelly loam **Marathon**[7] (p. v.) contains 3 churches, the oldest of which is the Presb., organized Feb. 11, 1814.[8] Pop. 500. **Texas Valley** is a p. o. in the n. e. corner. Dr. Japheth Hunt, a surgeon of the army, who served in both the French and Revolutionary Wars, settled on Lot 93, in 1794.[9]

---

[1] Incorp. May 11, 1835.

[2] Incorp. February 2, 1819. This institution, from its commencement, has uniformly borne a high reputation. Samuel B. Woolworth, LL.D., present Secretary of the Regents of the University, was at the head of this institution for nearly 22 years. At a jubilee celebration, held July 7 and 8, 1846, it was stated that 4000 students had been connected with the academy. The whole number up to 1859 was over 8,000.

[3] They came in the fall, and erected a temporary dwelling, a little n. of Homer Village, near the bridge, and returned in the winter for their goods, leaving Mrs. Beebe the sole occupant of the house, and the only representative of civilization within a circuit of 30 miles. They were prevented from returning for 6 weeks by the deep snows; and during the whole of that period the lone woman remained in anxious doubt as to the fate of her husband and brother. Mr. Todd located on lot 42, "West Hill." Among the other early settlers were John House, John Miller, Jas. Matthews, Jas. Moore, Silas and Danl. Miller, (from Binghamton,) in 1792; Darius Kinney, (from Brimfield, Mass.,) in 1793; Roderick Owen, (from Lebanon, N.Y.,) Jonathan Hubbard, and Moses Hopkins, in 1794; Thos. Wilcox, (from Whitestown,) Zebulon Keene, and John Stone, (from Brimfield,) John Keep, Solomon and John Hubbard, and Asa White, in 1795. The first male child born was Homer Moore, and the first female Betsey House; the first death, that of Mrs. Gould Alvord. The first marriage was that of Zadoc Strongand Wid. Russell, who were obliged to go through the forests to Ludlowville, Tompkins co., on horseback, to have the ceremony performed. The first school-house was built a little n. of Homer Village in 1798. The first teacher was Joshua Ballard. Enos Stimson kept the first inn, and A. M. Coats the first store. The first permanent and successful merchant was Jedediah Barber. John Keep, Solomon Hubbard, and Asa White built the first grist mill in 1798, on the

present site of that of Cogswell & Wilcox. The old mill for some time was used as church. public hall, and ball room.

[4] The first sermon was preached by Rev. Mr. Hillard, of N.J. He was assisting at a raising; and, when it became known that a minister was present, a sermon was clamorously called for and was delivered on the spot. The census reports 6 churches in town; Cong. Bap., M. E., Prot. E., and Univ. at Homer, and M. E. at East Homer.

[5] Free Bap., Meth., and Christian denominations hold meetings in schoolhouses. The Free W. Bap. Society was formed by Elder Lake in 1820.

[6] Among the other first settlers were Peter Gray, (on lot 70,) Robt. K. Wheeler, and Thomas Kingsley, who came in 1802; Seth Jennings and Timothy Roberts, in 1805; Zac'h Lynes, John R. Smith, Urial Sessions, Simeon Luce, Avery Hartshorn, and H. J. Richards. The first marriage was that of Simeon Luce and Rebecca Ayres, Oct. 9, 1805; and the first death, that of Simeon Luce, in 1808. Ebenezer Luce taught the first school, in 1814; and Harvey Jennings built the first mill, in 1813.

[7] About one mile s. of the village, on the e. bank of the river, is the site of an old Indian village and burial ground. Tradition says that this was once the seat of a powerful tribe of Indians.

[8] The census reports 4 churches; 2 Presb., Bap., and M. E.

[9] Among the other pioneer settlers were John Hunt, in 1796; Abram Brink, (first innkeeper,) Barnabas Wood and Son, and Zachariah Squires, in 1802. The first child born was S. M. Hunt, a grandson of the first settler; the first marriage, that of Nicholas Brink and Polly Alfred; and the first death, that of the first settler, in March, 1808, aged 97 years. Wm. Cowdrey taught the first school, in 1803; John Hunt built the first saw mill; and Weed & Waldo, James Burgess, and David Munroe were the early merchants. The first successful mercantile firm was that of Peck, Archer & Dickson, now of New York City.

2

PREBLE—named in honor of Commodore Edward Preble, was formed from Tully upon the organization of Cortland co., April 8, 1808, and embraced the southern half of the latter town. Scott was taken off in 1815. It lies upon the northern border of the county, w. of the center. Its surface consists of the valley of the western branch of the Tioughnioga River, which is here nearly 2 miles wide, and the ridges which rise on the E. and w. Mount Toppin, s. w. of the village, is 1,700 feet above tide; Truxton Hills are the highest land in the county. The declivities of the hills are steep, and some of their summits sharp ridges. North of Mount Toppin a valley extends northward and opens into the valley of the Otisco Inlet. In the northern part of the town are several beautiful little lakes; and upon the southern borders are others of a similar character, known as the Little York Lakes. The soil is a fine quality of gravelly loam. **Preble Corners** (Preble p.o.) contains 200 inhabitants, and **Baltimore** 75. The first settlers were James and Robert Cravarth, John Gillett, and Elijah Mason, who came in 1798.[1] The first church (Cong.) was formed through the efforts of Revs. Theodore Hinsdale and Joel Hall, missionaries from Conn.[2] Rev. Matt. Harrison was the first pastor.

SCOTT—was formed from Preble, April 14, 1815, and named in honor of Gen. Winfield Scott. It is the N. w. corner town of the county. Its surface is mostly upland, broken by two deep and narrow valleys which extend N. and s. through the town. The declivities of the hills are very steep, and in many places precipitous. Cold Brook flows through the eastern valley, and Factory Brook and Skaneateles Inlet through the western. Skaneateles Lake borders upon the N. w. corner. The soil is a sandy and gravelly loam, and is best adapted to grazing. **Scott Center** (Scott p.o.) contains about 300 inhabitants. **Scott Corners** (East Scott p. o.) is a hamlet. Peleg and Solomon Babcock and Asa Howard (from Mass.) and George Dennison (from Vt.) located on lot 82 in 1799.[3] The first church was a Seventh Day Baptist, organized in 1820, Wm. B. Maxson first pastor.[4]

SOLON—was formed from Homer, March 9, 1798, and embraced the townships of Solon and Cincinnatus. A portion was annexed to Truxton, April 4, 1811. Cincinnatus was taken off in 1804, and Taylor in 1849. It is an interior town, lying near the center of the county. The surface is mostly upland, broken by numerous narrow valleys of small brooks and creeks. The hills on the eastern border are 1400 to 1500 feet above tide. Many of the highest summits are too rough for cultivation, and are crowned with forests. Trout Brook flows in a westerly direction through near the center, forming a narrow but fertile valley. The soil is a gravelly loam, well adapted to grazing. **Solon** (p.v.) contains about 100 inhabitants. The first settlers were Johnson Bingham and Eddy Wildman, from Canterbury, Conn., who located, the former on lot 62, and the latter on lot 51, in 1796.[5] The first church was formed in 1804, Rev. Josiah Butler the first preacher.[6]

TAYLOR—was formed from Solon, Dec. 5, 1849, and named in honor of Gen. Zachary Taylor. It lies near the center of the eastern border of the county. Its surface is mostly upland and is very broken and hilly. The declivities are generally precipitous, rising 600 to 800 feet above the valleys. Mount Rhoderick, lying partly in this town and partly in Solon, is the highest point. The streams are mere brooks, generally flowing in a southerly direction and discharging their waters into the Otselic. Solon Pond is a small sheet of water near the center of the town. The soil is a sandy and gravelly loam. **Taylorville,** (Taylor p. o.,) or "Bangall," contains 25 houses, and **Union Valley** (p. v.) 20.[7] The first settlers were Zerah Beebe, a Revolutionary soldier, Latus Beebe, his son, and John Tinker, his son-in-law, from Waterbury, Conn., in 1794.[8]

---

[1] Among the other first settlers were Amos Skeel, Seth and Samuel Trowbridge, Richard Egbertson, Samuel Orvis, Jabez B. Phelps, Ed. Cummings, and Francis, Albert, and Garret Van Hoesen. The first child born was Nancy Gill; the first marriage, that of Amos Ball and Sally Mason; and the first death, that of John Patterson, a Revolutionary patriot, in 1799. Ruth Thorp taught the first school, in 1801; Davis & Taylor kept the first store, and Moses Nash the second; Samuel Trowbridge kept the first inn.

[2] The census reports 2 churches; 1 Presb., 1 M. E.

[3] Among the other first settlers were Cornish Messenger and Daniel Jakeway, (from De Ruyter,) Maxon Babcock, (from Mass.,) Gershom Richardson, Jared and John Babcock, Elisha Sabins, Henry and Jesse Burdick, Timothy Brown, and Nathl. Morgan. The first child born was Harriet Babcock; the first marriage, that of Solomon Babcock and Amy Morgan, and the first death, that of an infant daughter of Peleg Babcock. Amy Morgan taught the first school, in 1804; James Babcock kept the first inn, and Nathan Babcock the first store.

[4] Besides this, there are in town 3 societies; Bap., M. E., and Presb.

[5] Among the other first settlers were Benj. Beebe, Lewis Beebe, (first innkeeper,) Daniel Porter, Zerah Tinker, Jas. H. Wheeler, Elisha Johnson, Saml. G. Hathaway, Stephen N. Peck, and Noah Greeley, (first mill owner.) The first child born was a daughter of Johnson Bingham; the first marriage, that of Robt. Smith and Amy Smith, and the first death, a daughter of Johnson Bingham. Roxana Beebe and Lydianna Stewart taught the first school, in 1804; and B. Tubbs kept the first store.

[6] The census reports 2 churches; 1 Bap. and 1 R. C.

[7] The census reports 5 churches; Bap., Cong., Wes. Meth., 2 M. E.

[8] The first child born was Kezia Beebe, the first marriage, that of Asaph Butler and Lucy Beebe; and the first death, that of Zerah Beebe, in 1800. ——— Beers taught the first school, in 1810; Orlando Beebe kept the first inn, Hurlbut & Gilbert the first store, and Ezra and Thos. Rockwell built the first saw mill, in 1816.

TRUXTON[1]—named in honor of Commodore Thomas Truxton, was formed from Fabius, April 8, 1808, and embraced the s. half of the latter town. The N. 4 tiers of lots of Solon were annexed April 4, 1811. Cuyler was taken off in 1858. It is the N. E. corner town of the co. The surface consists of a broken upland divided into ridges, which have a general northerly and southerly direction. The east branch of the Tioughnioga River flows in a s. w. direction through the center of the town, cutting the ranges of hills diagonally. The Truxton Hills are the highest in the co. North of the river, nearly the whole surface is divided into sharp ridges with steep declivities, their summits being technically termed "hog backs." Muncey Hill, in the s. E. part, the highest land in town, is a wild, broken region, poorly adapted to cultivation. On the N. border is a small lake known as Labrador Pond, noted for its wild and picturesque scenery. Upon a small brook, which flows into the outlet of this pond from the E., is a beautiful cascade, called Tinkers Falls. The soil is generally a sandy and gravelly loam. In amount of dairy products this town is one of the first in the State. **Truxton** (p. v.) contains 257 inhabitants, and **Cuyler** (p. v.) 112. **Keeney Settlement** is a hamlet on the N. line. There are in town a woolen, a sash and blind, and butter tub factory, and an extensive carriage shop. The first settlers were Saml. Benedict, Chris. Whitney, and Jonas Stiles, in 1795, who located on Lots 12, 93, and 2, respectively.[2] The first church (Bap.) was formed in 1806, under Eld. Rufus Freeman.[3]

VIRGIL—was formed from Homer, April 3, 1804. Harford and Lapeer were taken off in 1845. A small portion of its E. part has been annexed to Cortlandville and Freetown. It lies upon the w. border of the county, s. of the center. Its surface is a broken and hilly upland. The Owego Hills, in the s. w. part, are about 600 feet above the valleys and 1600 to 1700 feet above tide. The valleys are narrow, bordered by the steep declivities of the hills. Virgil Creek, flowing E., and Gridley Creek, flowing w., are the principal streams. The soil is a sandy and gravelly loam, and is best adapted to grazing. **Virgil** (p. v.) contains 206 inhabitants, and **East Virgil** (p. v.) about 60. **State Bridge** (Messengerville p. o.) is a R. R. station. **Franks Corners** is a hamlet in the s. w. part. The first settler was Joseph Chaplin, in 1792.[4] The first religious meeting was held in 1802; and the first church (Cong.) was formed, Feb. 5, 1805, by Rev. Seth Williston.[5]

WILLET—was formed from Cincinnatus, April 21, 1818, and was named in honor of Col. Marinus Willett, of Revolutionary memory. It lies in the s. E. corner of the county. Its surface consists of the narrow valley of the Otselic River and of the high ridges which rise on either side. The uplands are broken by the narrow ravines through which the small streams flow. Nearly one-third of the town is yet unsettled, the surface being too rough for profitable cultivation. In the N. w. part of the town is a small lake, known as Bloody Pond,—its sanguinary name having been bestowed in consequence of the vagaries of *delirium tremens*. The soil is a sandy and gravelly

1 In Nov. 1858, this town was divided into 2 nearly equal parts by a line extending N. and S.; and the E. half now forms the town of CUYLER.

2 Among the other first settlers were Robt. Knight, (from Monmouth, N. J.,) Hugh Stewart, (from Colerain, Mass.,) John Jeffrey and Enos Phelps, (from N. J.,) Billy Trowbridge and Dr. John Miller, (from Dutchess co.) The last named was the first physician, and is still living, (1858,) aged 82. The first child born was a son of Samuel Benedict; and the first death was a child in the same family. A. W. Baker taught the first school, in 1799; Bowen Brewster kept the first inn, in 1801, and Stephen Hedges the first store.

3 The census returns 4 churches; 2 M. E., Bap., Presb.

4 Mr. Chaplin was engaged to open a road from Oxford to Cayuga Lake, which he commenced in 1792 and finished in two years. This road was 60 mi. in length, and it became the thoroughfare for emigrants. Mr. Chaplin brought in his family from Oxford in the winter of 1794–95. Among the other first settlers were John M. Frank, John Gee, John E. Roe, James Wright, Jas. Knapp, Jas. and John Glenny, Joseph Bailey, and Enos Bouton. The first flock of sheep, brought in by Mr. Frank, were all destroyed by the wild animals. Mr. Roe and Capt. Knapp killed 15 wolves in one year. The first child born was a son of Joseph Chaplin; the first marriage was that of Buluff Whitney, of Dryden, and Susan Glenny, in 1800; and the first death was that of a stranger, named Charles Hoffman, who was found dead in the woods in April, 1798. Chas. Joyce was the first teacher; Peter Vanderlyn and Nathl. Knapp built the first grist mill, in 1805; Daniel Edward built the first saw mill in 1801, and Danl. Sheldon kept the first store, in 1807. As early as 1828, in a series of articles in the "Cortland Observer," Nathaniel Bouton, a farmer in this town, strongly advocated the construction of a R. R. through the southern tier of counties. From the proceedings of a "Festive Gathering" of the early settlers and inhabitants of the town of Virgil we make the following extracts:— "The patents issued to the purchasers of the military lots contained the whole mile square; yet the State reserved to itself the right to retain 100 acres in the s. E. corner of each lot and give an equal amount of land in Ohio. This reserved lot was known as 'The States Hundred.' By giving notice that he wished to retain his land together, and paying $8.00 for the survey, the patentee could retain the whole lot. In default of the payment, the State retained 50 acres of the *Mile Square*, called the 'Survey of Fifty Acres.'" As an illustration of the hardships to which the pioneers of this town and co. were subjected, we extract the following:—"In the spring of 1797, John E. Roe came on from Ulster co. and made a beginning on his lot,—the same occupied till recently by himself and family,—boarding with Mr. Frank. He cleared a spot, put up the body of a log house, split plank and laid a floor, peeled bark for a roof, and agreed with a man in Homer to put it on. He also cut and cured some of the wild grass growing in the swamp, for hay, and returned. Preparations were then made for moving on; which was done in the winter following. He and his wife came in a sleigh, with a young cow following them. When they came to the river, opposite Mr. Chaplin's, they found the water high, and the canoe that had been used in crossing carried away. Mr. Chaplin's hog trough was procured, and Mrs. Roe was safely carried over in it. She then stood upon the bank to await the crossing of what remained. The horses, being urged in, swam across with the sleigh, the cow following, and came near being carried away with the current, but, after a hard struggle, made the shore in safety. They put up for the night, the horses being fastened to the sleigh, (as no accommodations could be procured,) and they ate out the flag bottoms of the chairs to allay the keen demands of appetite. The snow was two feet deep, with no track, and the whole day was consumed in coming from the river to their new home. When they arrived, they were surprised to find their house without covering, consequently the snow as deep in it as out of it. Persons of less perseverance would have been disheartened. But no time was to be lost. The snow was cleared away from a portion of the floor, a fire built against the logs, some blankets drawn across the beams for a covering, the horses tied in one corner, with some of that coarse hay before them; and thus their first and several successive nights were passed."

5 The census reports 5 churches; Bap., F. W. Bap., Cong., M. E., Union.

loam. **Dyersville** (Willet p. o.) contains 20 houses. The first settler was Ebenezer Crittenden, from Barrington, Mass., in 1793.[1] The first church (M. E.) was formed in 1816. There is also a Cong. church in town.

CUYLER—was formed from Truxton, Nov. 18, 1858. The statistics of this town are embraced in the town of Truxton, page 255.

Acres of Land, Valuation, Population, Dwellings, Families, Freeholders, Schools, Live Stock, Agricultural Products, and Domestic Manufactures, of Cortland County.

Names of Towns.	Acres of Land.		Valuation of 1858.			Population.					Schools.	
	Improved.	Unimproved.	Real Estate.	Personal Property.	Total.	Males.	Females.	No. of Dwellings.	No. of Families.	Freeholders.	No. of Districts.	Children taught.
Cincinnatus	10,368	6,015	$253,635	$8,500	$262,135	551	568	220	247	179	9	500
Cortlandville	24,150	8,399½	1,161,940	210,400	1,372,340	2,127	2,202	827	879	749	24	1,590
Cuyler[2]												
Freetown	10,848½	5,159	229,930	11,550	241,480	484	471	188	137	164	8	387
Harford	7,054½	7,812	138,174	4,750	142,924	477	449	180	190	168	7	356
Homer	21,575	11,167⅜	1,039,950	146,200	1,186,150	1,807	1,978	732	477	573	21	1,274
Lapeer	9,371	5,654½	129,545	11,440	140,985	383	367	142	149	133	10	371
Marathon	9,530¾	5,462	276,931	15,700	292,631	686	655	249	275	214	7	519
Preble	10,713½	5,920	274,545	15,390	289,935	614	605	240	268	212	11	428
Scott	8,772½	5,081	221,020	33,505	254,525	670	623	247	259	225	9	517
Solon	10,548¼	7,563	255,325	12,000	267,325	549	508	206	206	188	10	455
Taylor	10,244	7,787	171,025	3,450	174,475	615	586	226	232	221	10	376
Truxton	32,707⅛	21,054¼	672,757	41,040	713,797	1,736	1,708	646	765	601	29	1,306
Virgil	20,756¼	8,789¾	308,225	15,200	323,425	1,094	1,137	446	456	410	19	827
Willet	8,097½	7,798½	145,140	14,860	160,000	464	461	178	182	175	8	318
Total	194,736⅞	113,662⅞	5,278,182	543,985	5,821,127	12,257	12,318	4,727	4,722	4,212	182	9,224

Names of Towns.	Live Stock.					Agricultural Products.							Domestic Manufactures in Yards.
						Bush. of Grain.					Dairy Products.		
	Horses.	Working Oxen and Calves.	Cows.	Sheep.	Swine.	Winter.	Spring.	Tons of Hay.	Bushels of Potatoes.	Bushels of Apples.	Pounds of Butter.	Pounds of Cheese.	
Cincinnatus	369	978	1,154	2,221	487	568	29,020	3,521	6,560	14,015	118,760	3,070	859
Cortlandville	1,078	1,648	2,833	4,918	1,975	2,397¾	117,772½	5,964	21,375	54,928	319,229	28,021	1,347¼
Cuyler[2]													
Freetown	363	880	1,233	2,052	526	226	34,936	3,289	8,414	13,850	108,690	71,580	971
Harford	227	519	628	1,961	380	1,306	32,646	1,503½	5,260	10,295	72,305	16,220	1,000½
Homer	930	1,924	2,390	3,438	1,851	554	90,381¼	5,653½	21,500	55,052	279,625	28,622	903
Lapeer	340	884	802	1,696	450	253	29,411¼	2,544	5,676	8,671	76,970	10,520	1,664
Marathon	338	862	1,068	3,260	573	406	27,774	2,887	5,937	17,627	135,009	8,101	2,785
Preble	478	920	1,032	2,301	966	784	80,709½	2,078	11,411	24,840	141,030	4,540	329
Scott	390	775	755	2,058	514	206	44,317	2,080	9,841	18,020	91,825	7,604	1,227
Solon	446	816	1,170	1,826	637	23	30,507	3,545	8,537	21,788	140,975	300	1,130
Taylor	328	1,053	1,133	2,225	502	169½	29,640	3,643	7,805	13,517	151,885	5,835	1,804½
Truxton	1,044	2,406	4,724	5,002	1,955		77,561	12,712¾	25,177	60,686	416,246	517,281	2,147½
Virgil	813	1,449	1,909	6,800	1,049	1,575½	90,052½	4,721	12,485	30,474	243,423	4,390	3,749¾
Willet	266	889	837	1,563	437	399½	18,156½	2,627½	5,411	8,212	83,285	2,595	1,883
Total	7,410	16,003	21,668	41,321	12,302	8,868¼	732,884¾	56,769¼	155,389	351,975	2,379,257	708,679	21,800½

[1] Mr. Crittenden embarked, with his wife, child, and goods, upon a rude boat, at Chenango Forks, and with a paddle and setting-pole worked his way up the rapid current of the Tioughnioga and Otselic Rivers to his place of settlement. For 9 years he was the sole inhabitant of the town. Among the other first settlers were Jabez Johnson, (from Vt.,) Benj. Wilson, (from Westchester co.,) John Fisher, Thos. Gayley, Thos. Leach, Phineas Sargent, and John Covert. The first birth was that of a child of Eb'r Crittenden. The wives of Solomon Smith, Danl. Roberts, and Edward Nickerson all died in 1812; and these were the first deaths in town. The first school was taught in 1814. Benj. Wilson kept the first inn and built the first mill, and John E. Dyer kept the first store.

[2] Formed since 1855.

DELAWARE COUNTY.

THIS county was formed from Ulster and Otsego, March 10, 1797.[1] It lies upon the headwaters of Delaware River, from which it derives its name. It contains an area of 1,580 sq. mi., and is centrally distant 70 mi. from Albany. Its surface is a hilly and mountainous upland, divided into 3 general ridges by the valleys of the 2 principal branches of Delaware River. This upland region is a connecting link between the Blue Ridge upon the s. and the Catskill and Helderbergh Mts. on the N. In the s. part of the co. these ridges form a mountainous region, with lofty, rocky peaks and precipitous declivities broken by wild and narrow ravines. In the N. the highlands are less wild and precipitous, and the whole region assumes the character of a rugged, hilly upland.[2] The main or w. branch of the Delaware[3] River takes its rise in Utsyanthia Lake,[4] a small sheet of water upon the N. E. line of the co. It flows 60 mi. in a s.w. direction to the w. border of the co., thence turns abruptly to the s. and forms the s. E. boundary of Tompkins and Hancock. In its course in the co. it descends about 1000 feet. Pepachton River,[5] the E. branch of the Delaware, rises in Roxbury and flows 60 mi. s.w., uniting with the Delaware at Hancock. The Susquehanna forms a portion of the N. boundary of the co. Charlotte River and Ouleout Creek are tributaries of the Susquehanna. The other streams are creeks and brooks, principally tributaries to the 2 branches of the Delaware. The valleys of these streams are usually narrow, and bordered by steep hills which often rise into mountains. The rocks of the co. mostly belong to the old red sandstones of the Catskill division.

The mineral wealth of the co. is limited to stone useful for building and flagging, of which large quantities of a fine quality are found. Vague traditions of silver and lead mines have here, as in other counties, haunted the brains of dreaming adventurers. A brine spring is reported 4 mi. N. W. of Delhi Village, and 1384 feet above tide, another 3½ mi. from Colchester, and several chalybeate springs in various parts of the co.; but none of them are important.[6] The soil is generally of a dark reddish color, composed of the disintegrated sandstone and shale. In the valleys are occasionally narrow strips of fertile alluvium. Dairying is at present the leading occupation of the people. The numerous fresh springs of water issuing from its hillsides,[7] the fresh herbage, and bracing mountain air, seem peculiarly adapted to this business.[8] Lumber was formerly rafted in large quantities to Philadelphia; but, although still extensively exported by R. R., the quantity is diminishing.[9] Since the completion of the R. R., tanneries have sprung up in favored localities, and will continue until the supply of bark is exhausted. The other manufactures are chiefly limited to the local wants of the inhabitants. The immense amount of water power in the co. will greatly facilitate the establishment of manufactories whenever the exigencies of the co. may demand them.

---

[1] The w. branch of the Delaware was formerly the boundary line between Otsego and Ulster cos. The line between this co. and Broome was run according to the treaty of Fort Stanwix of Nov. 5, 1768, and was known for a long period as the "*Line of Property.*"

[2] The following is a list of elevations above tide, principally derived from the State Road Survey in 1825, and various R. R. surveys of more recent date:—

Delaware River, E. border (estimated)	830 feet.
Junction of the two branches of Delaware	922 "
Hancock Station	943 "
Delaware River at Hales Eddy	950 "
Dickinsons Station	953 "
Deposit (State Road Survey)	1004 "
Sidney Village	1010 "
Mouth of Beaver Kil	1018 "
Franklin Village	1240 "
Arkville, near Margaretville	1345 "
Courthouse Square	1453 "
West Meredith (John Stittson)	1726 "
Perch Pond	1765 "
Stamford Village (Newburgh & Syracuse R. R. Survey)	1765 "

Fish Lake, near Delhi	1770 feet.
Elk Creek Summit (3 or 4 mi. from Delhi)	1859 "
Warner Pass (3 mi. w. of Stamford Village)	1887 "
Head of Delaware, Stamford	1888 "
Davenport Center	1898 "
Lowest summit between Ouleout Creek and Delhi	2143 "
Mt. Pisgah, Andes (estimated)	3400 "

[3] Otherwise called the "Mohawk Branch of the Delaware," and by the Indians "*Cookquago*" or "*Cacquago*."

[4] This lake is often mentioned in early documents. In colonial times it was at one of the angles of Albany co.

[5] Sometimes written Popacton, Papotunk. In the Government returns the p. o. named from the river is written Pepacton.

[6] *Beck's Mineralogy N. Y.*, p. 160.

[7] The first court held in the co. adopted as its seal the device of a "stream of water issuing from a high mountain."

[8] In amount of butter this co. ranks second only to St. Lawrence.

[9] In number of sawmills this co. is now surpassed by none but Steuben and Oneida.

The co. seat is located at Delhi.[1] The present courthouse was erected in 1820.[2] The co. clerk's office and jail[3] are in separate buildings, adjacent to the courthouse. The poorhouse is an old, two story wood building, situated upon a farm of 175 acres about 2 mi. s. of Delhi Village. The average number of inmates is 65, supported at a cost of $1.00 per week each. The farm yields an income of $250. The N. Y. & Erie R. R. extends along the Delaware, and the Albany & Susquehanna R. R. through the N. W. corner. Soon after the completion of the N. Y. & E. R. R., in 1849, plank roads were built, extending from several of the stations into the interior of the co.[4]

The co. has 7 weekly newspapers.[5]

The great Hardenburgh Patent,[6] embracing that part of the co. s. and E. of the w. branch of the Delaware, was granted April 10, 1708, to Johannes Hardenburgh, of Kingston, Ulster co., and associates, who had previously purchased the lands of the Indians. A tract of 250,000 acres, between the w. branch of the Delaware and a line a mi. E. from the Susquehanna, was bought from the Indians at "*Johnson Hall*," Montgomery co., June 14, 1768, by John Harper, Sen., and Gen. Wm., Joseph, and Alex. Harper and others. On the s. E. side it extended from Utsyanthia Lake down the Delaware to the mouth of a small stream called Camskutty. Within this tract 5 towns, with full privileges of townships, were created by patent in 1770; but in none of them was an organization ever effected under this authority.[7]

Most of the lands in this co. were settled upon leases;[8] and this region shared largely in the excitement and mob violence which distinguished the anti-rent movement. Combinations to resist the execution of civil processes were formed in 1844, and open resistance began to be made in March, 1845, by armed bands in the disguise of Indians, and led by "chiefs" named after the Indian fashion. They were pledged to secrecy and mutual aid; and whenever the sheriff or his deputies appeared, to levy upon property for rent, they assembled in overpowering numbers and prevented the execution of the writs. An act was passed, Jan. 25, 1845, forbidding persons from

---

1 The courthouse was located by the judges, justices, and supervisors; and the sum of $1200 was granted April 4, 1798, for the erection of the co. buildings, on a lot given by Levi Baxter and George Fish. Under an act of March 28, 1806, the sheriff's mileage was reckoned from the courthouse; and under an act of June 18, 1812, a tavern was allowed to be kept in the courthouse. The courthouse and jail was burned April 17, 1820, and a prisoner confined for some trifling offence perished in the flames. An act passed April 11, 1820, authorized a loan of $8000 for rebuilding, and the present edifice was erected in the summer of that year. About a dozen prisoners, on "the limits" at the time the jail was burned, were released upon bail; and it happened that while the co. was without a jail there was no occasion for its use; but within a few hours after a prison room was so far completed as to hold a prisoner, it was needed and occupied.

2 Supervisors' meetings and courts were held at the house of Gideon Frisbie until the courthouse was completed. The first co. officers were Joshua H. Brett, *First Judge;* Patrick Lamb, Wm. Horton, and Gabriel North, *Judges;* Isaac Hardenburgh and Alex. Leal, *Asst. Justices;* Ebenezer Foote, *Clerk;* Elias Butler, *Sheriff;* and Anthony Marvin, *Surrogate.*

3 The jail is of wood, warmed by furnaces. It contains 4 rooms, and generally has 1 or 2 inmates.

4 During the first 10 years of this century several turnpikes were built through this co., and these tended greatly to promote settlement, by opening routes to market.

5 **The Delaware Gazette** was established at Delhi, Nov. 18, 1819, by John Jas. Lappan. In 1833 it was sold to A. M. Paine, by whom it is now published.

The *Delaware Republican* was started at Delhi, July 4, 1822, by Elijah J. Roberts, and was continued about 2 years.

The *Delaware Journal* was started at Delhi in 1834, by Geo. Marvine, and was continued 1 year. It was revived by Boune & McDonald, but was again discontinued.

The Delaware Express was started at Delhi, in Jan. 1839, by Norwood Bowne, the present publisher.

Voice of the People, an anti-rent paper established at Delhi in 1845, and continued about 4 years.

The *Deposit Courier* was started in March, 1849, by C. E. Wright, and was continued till May, 1853. From the same office, in Sept. 1853, Sylvester D. Hulse issued

The Deposit Union Democrat, and still continues to publish it.

The Bloomville Mirror was begun May 28, 1851, by S. B. Champion. The first number contained but 101 words, and till July no price was fixed. The "office," located in the corner of a mill, consisted of 10 lbs. of type without a press; and the paper was "printed" by striking with a mallet on a block laid over the type. It has grown into respectable size, and has an unusually large patronage for a country newspaper. It is now printed on a power press.

The Hobart Free Press was started Jan. 1855, by E. B. Fenn.

The *Weekly Visitor* was commenced April 14, 1855, at Franklin, by Geo. W. Reynolds. It has been changed to

The Franklin Visitor, and is still published.

The Walton Journal, commenced in 1856 by E. P. Berray, was continued 2 years.

The Village Record was established at Hobart in 1856, by G. W. Albright.

The Walton Blade was commenced in 1856 by E. P. Berray, but was soon after discontinued.

6 Most of the Hardenburgh Patent was surveyed by Ebenezer Wooster, in 1749; and in that year the proprietors released to each other certain lots, bounded by monuments on the Delaware and Papakunk Rivers. After the Revolution it was found that the monuments were lost, and an act, passed March 29, 1790, appointed Charles Tappen and Jas. Cockburn commissioners to make a survey of certain lines, to be properly marked by stone heaps every 2 mi. along the division lines. The tract was divided into great tracts, numbered from 1 to 42. Of these, 35 to 42 lay between the branches of the Delaware, and parts of 2 to 8 s. of the E. branch.

7 These towns were as follows:

Names of Townships.	Date of Patent.	Acres.	Patentees.
Bedlington,	May 24, 1770,	27,000	John Lake and associates.
Franklin,	Feb. 26, 1770,	30,000	Thomas Wharton and Reese Meredith.
Goldsborough,	June 15, 1770,	6,000	Edward Tudor, Bernard Ratzer, and John Clark.
Strasburgh,	Dec. 4, 1770,	37,000	John Butler and associates.
Whiteborough,	March 10, 1770,	38,000	Henry White and associates.

The quitrents of these lands were fixed at 2 shillings sixpence per 100 acres, payable annually on the Feast of the Annunciation of B. V. M. There was generally in the patent 1 name to each 1000 acres of the grant, although the *bona fide* owners were usually few in numbers.

8 A select committee of the Assembly, in 1846, reported the following tracts under lease in this co.: *Kortright Patent,* 20,000 acres, mostly leased in fee, at sixpence sterling per acre. It was offered for sale at $2 per acre. *Desbrosses Tract,* (Hardenburgh Patent,) 60,000 acres, mostly leased in fee between 1790 and 1807, at 1 shilling per acre after the first 7 years. Farms from 100 to 200 acres. *Morgan Lewis Estate,* 20,000 acres, about 15,000 under perpetual lease, at 20 bush. of wheat per 100 acres after 15 years: for the first 5 of the 15 years it was rent free, 5 years for one-half rent, and 5 for three-quarters. *G. and S. Verplanck,* 3 tracts, originally 50,000 acres, of which less than 20,000 were under lease. *R. R. Livingston* and *Mrs. Montgomery,* 20,000 acres, under perpetual lease, on a rent of 20 bush. of wheat per 100 acres. *Gen. Armstrong,* 8,000 acres, under lease for 3 lives, at 20 bush. of wheat per 100 acres. *Hunter's and Overing's* large tracts in this co., Sullivan, and Greene, in fee, with a rent of 12½ to 15 or 18 cents per acre.

appearing disguised and armed, under a penalty of imprisonment in the co. jail for a term not exceeding 6 months. Persons thus armed and disguised might be prosecuted under the fictitious names they assumed, if their real names could not be discovered; and such persons assembling in public houses or other places to the number of three or more might, upon conviction, be imprisoned 1 year in the co. jail. If convicted upon an indictment for a conspiracy or riot or other misdemeanor, in which offense they were armed with deadly weapons, they were further liable to a fine not exceeding $250, with or without a year's imprisonment. To men inflamed by passion and intent upon the resistance to law in one form, its violation in other points was a matter of slight account; and the statute against the wearing of disguise was openly disregarded in the sections where the anti-rent spirit prevailed. An arrest under the above act was made in Roxbury, in Feb., and "Big Thunder," (Daniel W. Squires,) the culprit, was lodged in jail. The excitement which this arrest occasioned was so intense that the sheriff deemed it prudent to place a strong guard over the jail; and the decision with which the affair was conducted occasioned a temporary calm. On the 7th of Aug. 1845, Osman N. Steele, deputy sheriff, an active, fearless, and faithful officer, was shot in the town of Andes while in the performance of his duty, and died in a few hours.[1] The Governor immediately issued a proclamation declaring the co. to be in a state of insurrection, and placing it under martial law. A battalion of 300 militia, one-half of whom were mounted, were called out and placed at the disposal of the local officers.[2] They continued in service several months. The mounted men were actively employed the first 2 or 3 months in small detachments, aiding the civil authorities in making arrests, and in patrolling day and night such districts as the exigency of the service required. The residue was employed in guarding the jail, and as foot patrols in the vicinity of Delhi on the occasion. On two occasions detachments of troops attended the sheriff to State prison with prisoners.[3]

ANDES[4]—was formed from Middletown, April 13, 1819. It lies on the s. e. border of the co., e. of the center. Its surface is a broken and hilly upland, intersected by the deep, narrow ravines of the e. branch of the Delaware and its branches. The hills are high, rocky, and irregular, and are bordered by steep declivities.[5] The Delaware flows s. w. through near the center of the town. Trempers Kil, Little Bush Kil, and Shaw Brook are the other principal streams. The valleys of these streams are all narrow and tortuous and are bordered by rocky hillsides. A considerable portion of the town is still covered with forests. The soil is a clayey and shaly loam underlaid by hardpan upon the hills, and a gravelly loam of good quality in the valleys. **Andes**, (p. v.,) on Trempers Kil, in the n. part of the town, contains an academy,[6] 3 churches, a flouring mill, and 2 tanneries. Pop. 350. **Cabin Hill**, (p. o.,) in the n. w., is a hamlet. **Shavertown** and **Trempers Kil** are p. offices. Permanent settlement commenced in 1784. A few farms were taken up prior to the Revolution, but were abandoned. The w. part of the town began to be settled in 1794–96.[7] During the anti-rent excitement this town was the scene of much violence, and Deputy Sheriff Steele was murdered here by a mob, Aug. 7, 1845. Rev. Mr. House, of Colchester, held the first religious meetings, in 1797.[8]

BOVINA[9]—was formed from Delhi, Stamford, and Middletown, Feb. 25, 1820. It is an interior town, lying directly e. of the center of the co. Its surface is a hilly upland, broken by the deep valleys of small streams. The highest summits are 1500 to 2500 ft. above tide. The streams are Little Delaware River, flowing w. through the center of the town, Bush Creek, the outlet of Teunis Lake, and Coulter, Maynard, Mountain, and Grants Brooks. The valleys of these streams

---

[1] For full particulars see *Governor's Message in* 1846, and *Gould's Hist. Del. Co.*, Chap. xii. About 90 persons were indicted for the murder, of whom one-third were arrested. Two (O'Conner and Van Steenburgh) were convicted and sentenced to be executed, but their punishment was commuted to State prison for life by Gov. Wright, and they were fully pardoned by Gov. Young. The co. remained under martial law from Aug. 18 to Dec. 22, 1845. The murder of Steele led to the speedy abandonment of secret organizations and Indian costumes.

[2] A company of volunteers under Benj. T. Cook, and another under John R. Baldwin, were formed, and organized into a battalion under Thomas Marvine as major. A company of light infantry from Unadilla, under Capt. Bolles, was also called out, and reported themselves to Maj. Marvine.

[3] Adjutant General's Report; *Assem. Doc.* 6, 1846. The whole expense of this service was $63,683 20, which was charged to the co., but has never been repaid. Considerable tracts of land have since been conveyed in fee; and of others, the rent is now paid as formerly, and if in arrears, suits are instituted without difficulty.

[4] Named from the mountainous character of its surface.

[5] "Mt. Pisgah" is the highest point between the two branches of the Delaware. By a R. R. survey from Oneonta by way of Elk Creek, Delhi and Fish Lake, the Fish Lake summit is ascertained to be 1640 ft. above tide. By another route, up the Little Delaware and Coulters Brook, the highest point on the line was almost the same height. Mt. Pisgah measured 1800 ft. above this, or about 3400 feet above tide.

[6] Erected by Henry Down in 1847. It is not incorp.

[7] Among the first settlers were James Phœnix, —— Olmsted, Peter Burgher, Joseph Erskine, Silas Parish, E. Washburn, Eli Sears, Jacob, Adam, and Philip Shaver, and Philip Barnhart. The first birth was that of Philip, son of Adam Shaver, Oct. 9, 1786; the first marriage, that of Henry Myers and Catharine Shaver, June 17, 1789; and the first death, that of Mrs. June. Wm. Washburn taught the first school, in 1792–93; Edward Sands kept the first store, Russell Comstock the first inn, and Robt. More built the first mill on Trempers Kil in 1797.

[8] The census reports 8 churches; 2 Asso. Ref. Prot., and 1 each Bap., O. S. Bap., Cong., M. E., Presb., and Union.

[9] Name applied by Gen. Erastus Root, from the Latin, in allusion to its fitness for grazing.

are narrow and are bordered by steep, rocky hillsides. Teunis[1] and Landons Lakes are small bodies of water near the s. border. The surface is stony, and the soil is generally a clay loam, admirably adapted to grazing. **Brushland,**[2] (p. v.,) on the Little Delaware, contains a tannery, gristmill, and clothing works. Pop. 183. **Bovina,**[3] (p. v.,) at the junction of Maynard and Mountain Brooks, contains about a dozen houses. **Mountain Brook** is a hamlet. The first settlement was begun in 1792, by Elisha B. Maynard, and during the succeeding 3 years many families from Conn. and Scotland located in the valleys.[4] Rev. James Richie conducted the first religious services, in 1795. The first church (Asso. Presb.) was formed in 1809. The census reports 3 churches; M. E., Asso. Presb., and Ref. Presb.

COLCHESTER[5]—was formed from Middletown, April 10, 1792. A part was annexed to Walton in 1799; Hancock was taken off in 1806, and a part of Walton was annexed in 1827. It occupies a central position upon the s. e. border of the co. Its surface is a mountainous upland, broken by the narrow valleys of the streams. The e. branch of the Delaware flows westward through the n. part of the town, dividing the highlands into two distinct parts. From the n. it receives West Trout, Downs, and Coles Brooks, and from the s. Clearwater and several smaller brooks. Beaver Kil flows through the s. w. corner, receiving Spring Brook as a tributary. The valleys of these streams are all narrow, and many hundred feet below the summits of the hills which rise on either side. The soil is a reddish clay, and is often very stony. A considerable share of the surface is still covered with forests. Lumbering is extensively pursued. **Downsville,**[6] (p. v.,) on the Delaware, at the mouth of Downs Creek, contains 3 churches. Pop. 206. **Pepacton** and **Colchester** are p. offices. The first settlement was begun in May, 1774.[7] The first religious services (Bap.) were conducted by Elder Haynes, and the first church (Bap.) was formed in 1803. There are now 2 churches in town; M. E. and Presb.

DAVENPORT[8]—was formed from Kortright and Maryland, (Otsego co.,) March 31, 1817. It lies along the n. border of the co., e. of the center. Its surface is a broken upland, divided into two ridges by the valley of Charlotte River, which extends e. and w. through the center of the town. These ridges are subdivided by the narrow, lateral valleys of tributaries of Charlotte River. The soil is a chocolate colored clay loam mixed with slate. **Fergusonville,**[9] (p. v.,) on Charlotte River, on the e. border of the town, contains an academy,[10] a church, and several manufacturing establishments. Pop. 125. **Davenport,** (p. v.,) 3 mi. below, contains a population of 95. **Davenport Center** (p. v.) contains a cradle and rake factory and 5 sawmills. Pop. 125. **West Davenport**[11] (p. v.) contains a woolen factory, 3 sawmills, and 90 inhabitants. The first settlers were Daniel Farnsworth and —— Pross, who located upon the present site of Davenport Center in 1786.[12] At that time an Indian trail, of sufficient width to admit the passage of wagons, extended along Charlotte River. Elder Mudge (M. E.) conducted the first religious services, and commenced regular preaching in 1813.[13]

DELHI[14]—was formed from Middletown, Kortright, and Walton, March 23, 1798. A part of Bovina was taken off in 1820, and a part of Hamden in 1825. A part was annexed to Walton in

---

[1] This lake lies at the foot of Mt. Pisgah, and its shores are muddy, and covered with bushes and coarse grass. It was named from a friendly Indian who saved the early settlers of Middletown from massacre by giving them a timely warning. His hut was near the lake, and he remained several years after the war. Tradition attributes to this region rich lead mines known only to Indians.

[2] Named from Alex. Brush, first settler and proprietor.

[3] Locally known as "Butt End."

[4] Francis Coulter, Levi and Jacob Mabie, Jas. Kidzie, Andrew Chisholm, Jas. Ray, and Thos. Liddle were early settlers along the Little Delaware. The first birth was that of Elisha H., son of Elisha B. Maynard, Aug. 26, 1793; the first marriage, that of James Russell and Nancy Richie, in 1802; and the first death, that of Aaron, son of Abraham Nichols. Abel Adams taught the first school, in 1810; James Wetmore kept the first inn, at the "Hook;" James McClure the first store, at Brushland; Stephen Palmer built the first mill, in 1796, for Gov. Lewis; and John Jerome the first factory, in 1808.

[5] Name applied by Joseph Gee, from Colchester, Conn.

[6] Named from Abel Downs, who erected there extensive tanneries and mills.

[7] Timothy Russell, Thos. and John Gregory, (from Westchester co.,) Frederick Miller, (still living, 1859, aged 100 years,) Jas. and S. Shaver, Silas Bowker, Peter, Harry, and Nehemiah Avery, Jacob Bramhart, Daniel and Wm. Parish, and Wm. Rose, began settlement before the war, but were driven off by the Indians and tories. Before leaving they buried their iron implements, to preserve them. After the war several of the families returned, and were joined by Wm. Horton, Abraham Sprague, Thos. Cal-

breth, Nathan Elwood, Nathan Fuller, Joseph Gee, Caleb and Henry Sutton, Jas. Miller, and Dennis, Jared, and John Hitt. The first birth was that of Catharine, a daughter of Wm. Roe, Dec. 24, 1784; and the first death, that of Thomas Gregory. Adam J. Doll opened the first store, and built the first bridge across the river at the place now known as Brooks Bridge. Wm. Rose built a sawmill in 1790. On the farm of Wm. Early, near the mouth of Coles Brook, is the site of an Indian village, with many of the apple trees planted by the natives still standing.

[8] Named from John Davenport, an early settler and first supervisor.

[9] Named from Messrs. Ferguson, who were largely engaged in business here.

[10] Erected by the Fergusons about 1848.

[11] Called Ad-a-quigh-tin-ge, or Ad-i-qua-tan-gie, by the Indians.

[12] Among the other first settlers were Humphrey Denio, Geo. Webster, Daniel Olmstead, —— Van Valkenburgh, Harmon Moore, and Elisha Orr. Dr. Dan'l Fuller came in 1796, and was the first physician. The first marriages were those of Harmon Moore and Mary Orr, and Richard Moore and M. Banks, in 1791, the two marriages taking place at the same time; the first birth was that of a child of Harmon Moore, who died in infancy; this was the first death. The first death of an adult was that of Mrs. Harmon Moore, in 1796. Wid. Hannah Dodge taught the first school; Dan'l Prentice built the first grist and saw mill, in 1792-93, and it is believed he kept the first inn. Ezra Denio kept the first store, in 1800.

[13] The census reports 5 churches; 3 M. E., F.W. Bap., and Presb.

[14] Named through the influence of Judge Ebenezer Foote. The name of "Mapleton" was suggested by several prominent citizens.

1812. It occupies a nearly central position in the co. Its surface is a hilly upland, broken by the deep valleys of the streams. The w. branch of the Delaware flows s. w. through the center of the town, receiving from the n. w. Platners, Peeks, Steels, and Elk Creeks, and from the s. e. Little Delaware River. The valleys are generally narrow and bordered by steep hills. The soil is a clay loam, and the surface is very stony in places. **Delhi,** (p. v.,) the county seat, is finely situated on the n. bank of the w. branch of the Delaware. It was incorp. March 16, 1821. Besides the co. buildings, it contains the Delhi Academy,[1] 4 churches, a bank, 2 printing offices, a woolen factory, an iron foundry, a gristmill, and a sawmill. Pop. 919. The first settlement was commenced by Abel and John Kidder, in 1785.[2] The first religious meetings were conducted by Elder Kidder Beck, in 1786. The first church (Cong.) was formed in 1798.[3]

FRANKLIN[4]—was formed from Harpersfield, April 10, 1792. Walton was taken off in 1797, and a part was restored in 1801. A part of Meredith was taken off in 1800, Sidney in 1801, and a part of Otego, (Otsego co.,) as "*Huntsville,*" in 1822. It lies upon the n. border of the co., w. of the center. Its surface is a hilly upland, broken by deep and narrow valleys. The principal streams are Ouleout[5] Creek, flowing w. through the n. part of the town, and its two tributaries from the s., Croton Creek and Handsome Brook. The soil upon the hills is a shaly loam underlaid by hardpan, and in the valleys a gravelly loam and alluvium. **Franklin,** (p. v.,) on the Ouleout, in the n. w. part of the town, contains the Delaware Literary Institute,[6] printing office, and 3 churches. Pop. 490. **Croton** (p. v.) is situated upon Croton Creek, near the line of Meredith. Pop. 200. **North Franklin** is a p. o. Sluman Wattles, afterward judge, was the first white settler who built his cabin in the valley of the Ouleout. He came in 1785, and was accompanied by his brothers John and Roger and his sisters Sarah and Caroline. The town was surveyed under Judge Wattles, who acquired one of the 4 shares.[7] The first church (Bap.) was formed at the house of Gad Merrick by Elder Hamilton, in 1798.[8]

HAMDEN—was formed from Walton and Delhi as "*Hampden,*" April 4, 1825. Its name was corrected March 17, 1826. It is the central town of the co. Its surface is a mountainous upland, divided into two parts by the valley of the w. branch of the Delaware. The s. part is covered by lofty peaks and ridges scarcely susceptible of cultivation. Bagleys Brook, a tributary of the Delaware, and Clove Brook, in the s. e. part, are the other principal streams. The soil is generally a brownish clay loam underlaid by hardpan. **Hamden,** (p. v.,) upon the Delaware, near the center, contains mills, a woolen and satinet factory, and 2 churches. Pop. 191. **Lansingville,** 1½ mi. above, on the s. side of the river, contains 2 churches and 116 inhabitants. **North Hamden** is a p. o. The first settlers were Daniel Harrower and Benajah McCall, who came in some time previous to 1795.[9] The census reports 4 churches in town.[10]

HANCOCK[11]—was formed from Colchester, March 28, 1806. It lies upon Delaware River, in the s. w. corner of the co. Its surface is a mountainous upland, ending in high and nearly precipitous bluffs upon the Delaware, and divided into two parts by the e. branch of the Delaware, which flows w. through the n. part. Beaver Kil flows into the e. branch in the e. part of the town. Sands and Hawks Creeks and Rieds and Baxters Brooks are tributaries of the e. branch of the Delaware, from the n.; and Big Trout, Basket Pond, Giers, Sand Pond, Lords, and Holmes Pond

---

[1] The first academic building was erected in 1820, on the public square, near the courthouse. In 1856–57 a new site was procured, containing 20 acres, upon the w. bank of Steels Brook, and a new edifice, with two spacious boarding halls, was erected. The site is commanding, and affords a fine view of the village. The institution has been endowed by moneys derived from the sale of escheated lands in the co. to the value of $5114. Its total property amounts to $28,820.

[2] Among the first settlers were Judge Gideon Frisbee, Thos. Farrington, Bartholomew Yandes, Joseph Denio, Geo. Fisher, John, Francis, and Levi Baxter, —— Preston, and Gideon Rathbone and his sons John, David, and Gideon, jr. The first birth was that of Huldah, daughter of Gideon Frisbee, June 14, 1787; the first marriage, that of Philip Frisbee and Jerusha Harmon, in 1791; and the first death of an adult, that of Dr. Philip Frisbee, in 1797. Thos. Averill taught the first school. The first mills were built in 1788.

[3] The census reports 8 churches; 2 Christian, 2 Presb., and 1 each Prot. E., Bap., M. E., and Asso. Presb.

[4] The township of Franklin, embracing 30,000 acres, was patented Feb. 26, 1770, with the usual powers of a township, and a quitrent of two and sixpence for every 100 acres annually. The patentees were Thos. Wharton, Reese Meredith, and 28 others. It was named from Temple Franklin, a natural son of Dr. Benj. Franklin.

[5] In the great Indian purchase of 250,000 acres, June 14, 1768, this stream is named Au-ly-ou-let.

[6] The buildings consist of one large stone edifice, containing recitation rooms, &c., and two large boarding halls. The total property of the institution is valued at $20,000.

[7] Among the early settlers were Nath'l Edgerton, Jas. Follett, Alex. Smith, Daniel and Chauncey, sons of Enos Parker. Gen. Aaron Chamberlain, Moses Clark, Asa Turner, Gad Merrick, Hugh Thompson, Eph'm McCall, —— Case, Turner and Daniel Clarke, Sol. Green, John Dewey and sons, Maj. Joel Gillett, —— Mix, —— Sharp, and —— Fitch. The first child born was Thos. Edgerton; the first marriage was that of Judah Bartlett and Caroline Wattles; and the first death, that of Mrs. Alexander Smith, in 1795. Shuman Bartlett taught the first school, and Asa Turner kept the first inn and store.

[8] The census reports 8 churches; 3 M. E., 2 Bap., 2 Cong., and 1 Union.

[9] Among the first settlers were Joseph Fisk, Henry Van Waggoner, Jas. Mason, Reuben Ward, Henry Edwards, Henry and John Howard, Sam'l Robinson, Wm. Cornell, and John and Silas Grimes. Jas. Howard kept the first inn, in 1796, and Matthias Sweney built the first gristmill, in 1797. Gen. Elias Butler was the first merchant near the Walton line.

[10] Asso. Presb., Christian, Cong., and Presb.

[11] Named in honor of John Hancock, President of Continental Congress.

Brooks, are tributaries of the Delaware. These streams all flow through narrow ravines bordered by steep, rocky hills nearly perpendicular. The valley at the junction of the two branches is 922 feet above tide, and at the mouth of Beaver Kil it is 1018 ft. above tide. The summits are 1000 to 1500 ft. above the valleys. A large portion of the surface is still covered with forests. The soil upon the uplands is a hard clayey loam, scarcely susceptible of cultivation. Lumber, leather, shingles, and staves are largely manufactured. **Hancock,**[1] (p. v.,) at the junction of the two branches of the Delaware, is an important trading and R. R. station. Pop. 502. **Stockport Station** and **Lordsville** are R. R. stations and p. offices. **East Branch,** (p. v.,) at the mouth of Beaver Kil, contains 2 churches and 20 houses; and **Harvard,** (p. v.,) 3 mi. above E. Branch, 15 houses; **Partridge Island,** on the E. branch, at the mouth of Rieds Brook, and **Cadosia Valley,** (p. o.,) on Hawks Brook, 3 mi. above Hancock, are hamlets. Before the Revolution two families settled in town; but they soon after left and never returned. The first permanent settlement was made soon after the close of the war by families from Dutchess co.[2] In 1784, Canope, a friendly Indian, was treacherously killed in this town by Ben Haines.[3] The first religious meetings (M. E.) were conducted by Rev. Titus Williams.[4]

HARPERSFIELD[5]—was formed March 7, 1788. Franklin was taken off in 1792, Kortright in 1793, and a part of Stamford in 1834. It is the N. E. corner town of the co. Its surface is a rolling upland, constituting a portion of the high plateau region stretching westward from the Catskill Mts. The principal streams are head branches of the w. branch of the Delaware, in the S.; of Middle Brook, in the center; and of Charlotte River, in the N. The valleys are usually narrow, and bordered by gradually sloping hills arable to their summits. The soil is a shaly and slaty loam of good quality. The quality of the soil, and the great abundance of pure soft water which issues from the hillsides, render this co. one of the finest grazing regions in the State. **Harpersfield,** (p. v.,) near the E. line, contains 20 houses. **North Harpersfield** (p. o.) is a hamlet. **Fergusonville** (p. v.) lies on the line of Davenport, **North Kortright** (p. v.) on the line of Kortright, and **Stamford** (p. v.) on the line of Stamford. This town formed part of a large purchase made from the Indians by the Harpers in 1768.[6] In 1771, Col. John Harper and David Hendry surveyed this town, and a small settlement was made soon after. One of the first settlers was Samuel Claxton, a tory. Several murders were committed by tories and Indians during the war, and the settlement was abandoned. In 1784, Col. John, Capt. Wm., Col. Alex., and Joseph Harper returned, and began the first permanent settlement.[7] Rev. John Lindsley conducted the first religious services, at an early period. There are now two churches in town, Bap. and Presb.

KORTRIGHT[8]—was formed from Harpersfield, March 12, 1793. A part of Delhi was taken off in 1798, a part of Meredith in 1800, a part of Davenport in 1817, and a part of Stamford in 1834. It is an interior town, lying N. E. of the center of the co. Its surface is a hilly upland, broken by narrow valleys and ravines. The mean elevation of the town is 1700 ft. above tide, and the highest summits attain an elevation of 2400 ft. The streams are the w. branch of the Delaware, forming its S. boundary, and its tributaries, and several small tributaries of Charlotte River, draining the N. half of the town. The hills are steep, but are generally susceptible of cultivation. The soil is a dark, shaly loam, well adapted to pasturage. **Bloemville** (p. v.) is in the S. w. part of the town. Pop. 184. **Kortright Center** (Kortright p. o.) contains a church and 25 houses. **North Kortright** (p. o.) and **South Kortright** (p. o.) are farming neighborhoods. Set-

1 Formerly "*Shohakin*," or "*Chehocton*," said to signify the union of streams. A plank road extends from this place to Walton, a distance of 21½ mi.

2 Among the first settlers were Dr. Elnathan Gregory and his son Samuel, John Barber, Daniel Bouker, Henry Ruff, Timothy Rine, Chris. Ruff, Dennis Hitt, —— Gilbert, —— Leonard, (from New England, who settled on Reeds Flat,) John Hitt, John and Richard Biddlecon, Ebr. Wheeler, Wm., Jos., John, and Sam'l Mallory, (near Partridge Island,) Josiah Parker, Geo. Hanks, and —— Jones, (at Hancock Village.) The first birth was that of Elisha, son of Dan'l Bouker, May 11, 1792; the first marriage, that of Abm. Sprague and Polly Parish, in 1791; and the first death, that of Lieut. Day. John Gregory taught the first school.

3 *Gould's Hist. Del. Co.,* p.184.

4 The census reports 6 churches; 3 M. E., and 1 each Bap., Cong., and R. C.

5 Named in honor of Col. John Harper, a proprietor and pioneer settler. The family consisted of John and his wife Abigail and nine children,—Wm., James, Mary, John, Joseph, Alexander, Abigail, and two others. The brothers were ardent patriots of the Revolution and active defenders of liberty. Their names are intimately associated with our State history.

6 On the 2d of April, 1780, a party of 14 persons, under Capt. Alex. Harper, was sent from Schoharie to Harpersfield for the purpose of making maple sugar and watching the disaffected in that quarter. On his return, Capt. H. was taken prisoner by a party of tories and 43 Indians. Of the party he had left, 3 were killed and the rest taken prisoners. The representation made by Capt. Harper concerning the strength of the Schoharie settlement saved it from destruction at that time.

7 Roswell Hotchkiss, and Levi and Jedediah Gaylord, settled with the Harpers near the center of the town. Josiah Seely, Matthew Lindsley, Sam'l and John Knapp, —— 2 Hamiltons, —— Washburn, Isaac Pierce, Stephen Judd, Sam'l, Eliab. and John Wilcox, Richard and John Bristol, Abijah Baird, Byron McIlvaine, David and John McCullough, Isaac Patchin, Wm. Lamb, Caleb Gibbs, and Wm. McFarland were among the early settlers. Rebecca Harper, born Jan. 8, 1783, was the first birth after the war. Rev. John Lindsley is believed to have taught the first school. A gristmill, erected about 1775 by Col. Harper, was burned by the enemy, and was rebuilt soon after the war.

8 Named from Lawrence Kortright, the patentee.

tlements commenced before the Revolution, but were broken up by the war.[1] The first permanent settlers after the war were from Conn., Dutchess co., N. Y., and Scotland.[2] The first church (Presb.) was formed in 1789: Rev. Wm. McAuley settled in town in Sept. 1794, and was installed pastor June 6, 1795. He filled that office until the time of his death, March 21, 1857, a period of 56 years.[3]

MASONVILLE[4]—was formed from Sidney, April 4, 1811. Its surface is a hilly upland, divided into 2 ridges by the valley of Bennetts Creek, which extends E. and W. through the N. part of the town. These ridges are subdivided by numerous lateral ravines, through which flow small brooks. The highest summits are 600 to 1000 feet above the valleys and 1800 to 2000 feet above tide. The surface is stony, and the soil a shaly loam, difficult of cultivation except in the valleys. **Masonville** (p. v.) is situated on Bennetts Creek, in the W. part of the town. Pop. 234. The first settlement was commenced in 1795, on "*Cockburns Gore*,"[5] upon the W. border of the town, by immigrants from Mass.[6] In 1797, the State Road from Cherry Valley to Jericho was opened through the town. The first religious services were conducted by Rev. Joel Chapin, in 1797. The first church (Bap.) was formed Dec. 7, 1820. There are now 2 churches in town; Presb. and M. E.

MEREDITH[7]—was formed from Franklin and Kortright, March 14, 1800. It is an interior town, lying N. E. of the center of the co. Its surface is a hilly upland, less broken than most of the towns in the co. The S. and E. parts of the town are occupied by the high ridges forming the watershed between Susquehanna and Delaware Rivers. The streams are small brooks and creeks. The soil is a reddish clay and shaly loam. **Ouleout** (p. v.) contains 25 houses. **Meredith Square** (Meredith p. o.) contains 2 churches and 20 houses. **West Meredith** (p. o.) is a hamlet. These last two places are on the old Catskill Turnpike. Settlement was begun in 1787, by Joseph Bramhall, whose family were sole inhabitants till 1793.[8] Elder Nathan Stilson (Bap.) held the first meetings. He was not a regular preacher, but a zealous promoter of education and religion.[9]

MIDDLETOWN—was formed from Rochester and Woodstock, (Ulster co.,) March 3, 1789. Colchester was taken off in 1792, a part of Delhi in 1798, Andes in 1819, and a part of Bovina in 1820. It is the S. E. corner town of the co. Its surface is a mountainous upland, bisected by the deep, narrow valley of the E. branch of the Delaware. The principal streams are Delaware River, Platte Kil, Batavia Kil, Red Kil, Bush Kil, and Mill Creek. The valleys of these streams are bordered by steep, rocky hillsides often rising into mountains. The soil is a shaly and gravelly loam. **Margaretville**,[10] (p. v.,) on the N. bank of the Delaware, near the center of the town, contains 40 houses. **Griffins Corners**,[11] (p. v.,) on the Bush Kil, in the S. E. part, contains 30 houses. **Clovesville**, (p. o.,) **Solitude**, and **Arkville** are hamlets on the Bush Kil, below Griffins Corners. **Dry Brook Settlement** is a lumber station on the S. branch of the Bush Kil. **Halcottsville**,[12] (p. o.,) on the Delaware, near the E. border of the town, is a hamlet of a dozen houses. **Spruceville** is a little settlement between Halcottsville and Margaretville. **New Kingston**[13] (p. o.) is a hamlet upon the Platte Kil, in the N. part of the town. **Clarks Factory**[14] (p. o.) is a little settlement on the Platte Kil, near its mouth. **Lumberville** (p. o.)

[1] Among these early settlers were Alex. Mills, agent for the proprietor, Alex. Leal, Daniel McGilivrae, and Hough Clark. The township was surveyed by Wm. Cockburn in 1770, and the first improvement began soon after.
[2] By an advertisement dated Jan. 1785, it appears that 30 families were then settled in town. The proprietor offered 150 farms, more or less improved, free of rent 5 years, and sixpence sterling per acre annually after forever. The first school was taught by Jane Blakeley, in 1795. Thos. McAuley, brother of the minister, and afterward Prof. in Union College, taught here in 1799. Judge Keeler was the next teacher. A Mr. Alexander built a mill before the war, and the irons concealed then have never been found. The first birth was that of Dan'l McGilivrae; the first marriage, that of Michael Sexsmith and Mary Ann Riggs; and the first death, that of a son of Isaac Randell. By an act of April 5, 1810, fairs were established in the village of "Health," in this town, for the sale of live stock, agricultural produce, and domestic manufactures. It was to be supported by a tax of 1 per cent. on all sales.
[3] The census reports 6 churches; 3 Asso. Ref. Presb., 2 M. E., and 1 Ref. Presb.
[4] Named for the Rev. John M. Mason, of N. Y., principal owner of the Evans Patent in this town.
[5] A narrow strip of land between Evans Patent and the "Line of Property."
[6] Among the early settlers were Wm. and Aden Wait, Danl. Scranton, Enos Goodman, Justin Nash, Peres Moody and son Moses, Asa, Terry, and Caleb Monson. The first birth was that of Sally, daughter of Daniel Wait. Aug. 10, 1797, and the first death was that of Wm. Wait, the same summer. Dr. Eli Em-

mons taught the first school; Simeon Wells kept the first inn; Fitch & Phelps the first store, in 1808; and Joseph Bicknell built the first saw and grist mill, in 1802.
[7] Named from Sam'l Meredith, of Philadelphia, who owned a part of Franklin Patent. Hon. Saml. A. Law came into this town in 1796, as agent and part owner of the Franklin Patent. Being a New England man he influenced a large immigration of New Englanders to this place, giving to it the peculiar characteristics of a Connecticut town.
[8] Among the early settlers who came in 1793 were Nathan Stitson, Caleb Strong, Nath'l Stewart, Oliver Dutton, Dan'l North, and Truman Stitson. Lucy Austin taught the first school; Jos. Bramhall kept the first inn, and the first birth and death occurred in his family. Rufus Bunnell kept the first store, at the Square, in 1799; David Spoor built the first gristmill, in 1802. The first marriage of settlers was that of Elijah Georgia and Keziah Stewart, who eloped and were married in the fall of 1796.
[9] The census reports 4 churches; 2 Bap., 1 F. W. Bap., and 1 Cong.
[10] The old Indian village of "*Pa-ka-tagh-kan*" was situated about 1 mi. E. of this village, at the mouth of the Bush Kil.
[11] Named from the Griffin family, early proprietors and residents.
[12] A woolen factory is located at this place.
[13] This village is situated in the center of a tract of land given by Wm. Livingston to 100 sufferers of the Kingston fire in 1777 Each family received 50 acres.
[14] Named from the Messrs. Clarks, who have an extensive tannery at this place.

is a lumber station at the mouth of Mill Creek, in the w. part of the town. A vague tradition exists of an early settlement of this town by French traders, but no positive proof. In 1762–63 a party from Hadley, Ulster co., commenced a settlement, which increased rapidly and in a few years spread over the Delaware bottom lands.[1] The settlers were driven out in 1778,[2] but returned soon after the war. The first church (Ref. Prot. D.) was formed in 1794. There are 3 churches in town; 2 M. E. and 1 Asso. Ref. Presb.

ROXBURY[3]—was formed from Stamford, March 23, 1799. It occupies the extreme E. portion of the co. Its surface is a mountainous upland, forming a portion of the great plateau extending w. from the Catskill Mts. The declivities of the hills are steep and rocky and are mostly unfit for cultivation. The highest points on the N. and w. borders of the town are estimated to be 2800 feet above tide. The principal streams are the E. branch of the Delaware, flowing s. w. through the center of the town, Bear Kil in the E., Batavia Kil and Red Kil in the s., and numerous smaller creeks. The soil is a reddish clay loam. **Roxbury** (p. v.) lies on the Delaware, near the center of the town. Pop. 232. **Moresville,**[4] (p. o.,) near the N. E. border, **Strattons Fall,**[5] (p. o.,) in the s., **Little Falls,** upon the E. border, and **Batavia Kil** are hamlets. The first settlement was made by John More, a Scotchman, on the site of Moresville, in 1786.[6] The first religious meetings were conducted by Rev. H. Myres.[7]

SIDNEY[8]—was formed from Franklin, April 7, 1801. Masonville was taken off in 1811. It lies upon Susquehanna River, in the N. w. corner of the co. Its surface is a hilly upland, ending in high bluffs upon the valley of the river. The highest summits are 800 to 1200 ft. above the valley. Ouleout and Carrs Creeks[9] flow w. through the town and empty into the Susquehanna. The valleys of these streams are deep and narrow, and are bordered by steep, rocky hills. The soil in the valleys is a fine fertile alluvium, and upon the hills a dark, shaly loam. **Sidney,** (p. v.,) on the s. bank of the Susquehanna opposite Unadilla, contains 2 churches and 25 houses, **Sidney Center,** (p. v.,) on Carrs Creek, 1 church and 20 houses, and **Sidney Plains,** (p. v.,) upon the Susquehanna, in the N. w. corner of the town, 2 churches and about 20 houses. In May, 1772, Rev. Wm. Johnston, with an Indian guide, explored this region of country, and finally selected the present site of Sidney Plains as a place of settlement.[10] Early in 1773 he moved in with his family, being the first settler in the Susquehanna Valley within the limits of the State. Several others soon followed. Just before the war, Gen. Herkimer held an interview with Brandt at this place; and the menacing attitude assumed by the Indians led Johnston and others who sympathized with the Continental cause to leave their new home for a less exposed situation. A few inhabitants remained during the war, and many returned immediately after its close.[11] By an act of April 6, 1790, £800 was granted for the construction of a road from "Olehoudt" Creek to Catskill on the Hudson.[12] The census reports 5 churches; 2 M. E., 2 Cong., and 1 Bap.

STAMFORD[13]—was formed April 10, 1792. Roxbury was taken off in 1799, and a part of Bovina in 1820. A part was annexed from Harpersfield and Kortright, April 22, 1834. It lies N. of Roxbury, on the N. E. border of the co. Its surface is a mountainous upland. Mt. Prospect, E. of Stamford Village, is estimated to be 1500 ft. higher than the valleys. From its summit Albany City is visible in a clear day. The streams are the w. branch of the Delaware, forming a portion of its N. boundary, and Town and Rose Brooks. The soil is principally a reddish clay

---

1 The first settlers were Harmanus and Peter Dumond, Johannes Van Waggoner, and —— Hendricks, who located near the old Indian village. Among those who came soon after were families named Kittle, Gaple, Brugher, Slyter, Hinebaugh, Green, and Bieurch.

2 Most of the settlers became tories, and in 1779 the Governor was empowered to cause the removal or destruction of grain in the back settlements of Ulster co., to prevent it from being serviceable to the enemy. Soon after the war, the settlers of "*Pakataghkan*" came before the legislature for redress; but no act was passed in their favor.—*Legislative Papers, St. Lib.*

3 Named from Roxbury, Conn., from which place many of the early settlers came.

4 Named from the first settler.

5 Named from an early settler. Strattons Brook falls about 40 feet at this place, furnishing a good water power.

6 John More, Israel Inman, Abm. Gould, Geo. Squiers, Josiah Patchin, Nehemiah Hayes, David Squiers, (most of them from Fairfield, Conn.,) settled along the valley near the present village of Roxbury, in 1789.—*Gould's Hist. Del. Co.*, 197–98–99. The first child born was Charlotte, daughter of Nath'l Tiffany, in March, 1792; and the first male child born was John Gould, in Oct. of the same year. David Smith taught the first school, in the winter of 1794–95; Isaac Hardenburgh owned the first store, John More kept the first inn, and John Pierson built the first gristmill.

7 The census reports 8 churches; 3 M. E., 2 O. S. Bap., 2 Ref. Prot. D., and 1 Christian.

8 Named from Sir Sidney Smith, the British Admiral. The name was first applied by John Mandeville, an English schoolmaster, then living on Sidney Plains.

9 Named in memory of John Carr, a tory, who built a sawmill upon this stream at an early period.

10 At this place was the site of an old Indian fort. Three acres of ground were enclosed by mounds of earth surrounded by a ditch. From early times the place has been called "*The Fort Grounds.*"

11 The first gristmill w. of Harpersfield was built, in 1778, by Abm. Fuller, on the Ouleout, near Wattles Ferry. An inn was opened at the ferry in 1785, by Nathaniel Wattles. The first raft was sent down to Harrisburgh in 1795, by Capt. David McMasters. In 1787 a great scarcity of provisions occasioned much distress in this valley, and the settlers were saved from starvation by a boat load of flour from Northumberland, Penn., got to them through the exertions of Gen. Daniel Bates.

12 The contract for building this road was awarded to Nathaniel Wattles and Medad Hunt; but, proving ruinous, the parties were relieved, in 1793, by a further grant of £120.

13 Originally named "*New Stamford,*" from Stamford in Conn. It is situated on Great Lot No. 42 of Hardensburghs Patent.

and shaly loam. **Stamford,** (p. v.,) upon the Delaware, in the N. E. part of the town, on the line of Harpersfield, contains a seminary,[1] 2 churches, and 2 woolen factories. Pop. 185. **Hobart** (p. v.) is situated on the Delaware, 4 mi. below Stamford. Pop. 391. The first settlement was made in 1773, by Dr. Stewart and John and Alex. More, from Scotland.[2] The first church (St. Peters Prot. E.) was formed at Hobart, Dec. 8, 1799. Rev. Philander Chase, afterward Bishop of Ohio and Ill., the first pastor, was installed Aug. 1799.[3]

TOMPKINS[4]—was formed from Walton, Feb. 28, 1806, as "*Pinefield*," and its name was changed March 11, 1808. It is the central town on the w. border of the co. Delaware River flows westward through near the center of the town to the w. border, where it turns s. and forms a portion of the w. boundary. The portion of the town s. of the river is composed of broken and rocky mountain masses too steep and rough for cultivation. The N. part is broken and hilly and but partially cultivated. The soil is a clay, slate, and gravelly loam. **Deposit**[5] (p. v.) is situated on Delaware River, at the mouth of Oquaga Creek, on the line of Sanford, Broome co. It was incorp· April 5, 1811.[6] It is the center of a large lumber business, and is an important trading station and wood depôt upon the N. Y. & Erie R. R. It contains a seminary,[7] printing office, sawmill, a large tannery, and 4 churches. Pop. 1249,—of which 593 are in Tompkins and 656 are in Sanford, Broome co.: the depôt and R. R. buildings are in the latter town. **Cannonsville,**[8] (p. v.) at the mouth of Trout Brook, on the Delaware, 7 mi. above Deposit, contains a sawmill, flouring mill, a large tannery, and 2 churches. Pop. 325. **Hales Eddy,**[9] (p. o.,) on the Delaware, 5 mi. below Deposit; **Barbourville,** (p. o.,) on Cold Spring Brook, near the N. border, and **Trout Creek,** (p. o.,) in the N. E., are hamlets. **Dickinsons Station** is near the s. line. The first settler was Squire Whittaker, from Wyoming,[10] Penn., who came in 1787 ; John Hulse,[11] from Neversink, (Sullivan co.,) came in April, 1789, and Philip Pine and Conrad Edict in 1791.[12] The first religious meetings were held at the house of John Hulse, by Rev. Hugh Compton, in 1794.[13]

WALTON[14]—was formed from Franklin, March 17, 1797. A part of Delhi was taken off in 1798, Tompkins in 1806, a part of Hamden in 1825, and a part of Colchester April 14, 1827. A part of Colchester was set off Feb. 1, 1799, a part of Franklin March 13, 1801, and a part of Delhi was annexed June 17, 1812. It is an interior town, lying w. of the center of the co. The deep valley of the Delaware divides the town into two nearly equal parts. The s. half is a broad, rocky, mountainous region with abrupt declivities and a surface too rough for cultivation; the N. half is broken and hilly, but generally well adapted to pasturage. The principal streams are East, West, and Hydes Brooks. The soil is a shaly loam upon the hills and a fertile alluvium in the valley. Tanning and lumbering are extensively carried on. **Walton,** (p. v.,) upon the N. bank of the Delaware, near the center of the town, contains the Walton Academy[15] and 3 churches. Pop. 430. **New Road** is a p. office in the extreme N. part. **West Brook** is a p. office. Dr. Platt Townsend,[16] of Dutchess co., purchased a tract of 5,000 acres in this town in 1784. He surveyed it the same year, and in 1785 he located upon the present site of Walton Village. He was accompanied by 5 families, of 20 persons, mostly from Long Island. A large number of immigrants

---

[1] The Stamford Collegiate Institute was established here in 1851.
[2] Jas. Stewart, Wm. Frazer and son Simon, from Scotland, came in 1775. During the war most of the settlers left, but returned in March, 1786. In 1789, a company consisting of 20 heads of families and 2 single men (principally from Fairfield co. Conn.) came into Delaware co. to examine the country and select locations. Several of them located in this town, and others soon followed. Dea. John Grant taught the first school, in the winter of 1788–89. Lieut. Paine kept the first inn and store, and —— Calden built the first mill, near Bloomville, before 1780. Andrew Beers, the almanac maker, resided in this town.
[3] The census reports 6 churches ; 2 M. E., 2 Asso. Ref. P., Prot. E., and Union.
[4] Named from Daniel D. Tompkins, soon afterward elected Governor.
[5] Named from having formerly been an important station, or place of "deposit," for lumber preparatory to rafting in "the spring freshets." It was called by the Indians "*Coke-ose*," (Owls Nest,) a name corrupted by the English into "Cookhouse," by which it is still designated by the old inhabitants.
[6] The original corporate limits of the village were entirely within the town of Tompkins. A part of Sanford, Broome co., was annexed in 1852. The charter was amended in 1858.
[7] Laurel Bank Seminary was opened Dec. 14, 1853. It is a fine building, situated s. of the river, on a commanding site overlooking the village and valley. It has accommodations for 200

boarding students. The recent death of the principal has caused a temporary suspension of the school.
[8] In 1786 Jesse Dickinson, of Philadelphia, made a purchase of an extensive tract of land in this vicinity, and made preparations for the building of a city, to be called "*Dickinsons City*." He built a gristmill upon Trout Creek, and a large hotel, which he called the "*City Hall*." The town meetings were held in this building for several years. Dickinson run the first raft that went from the w. branch of the Delaware. Upon his failure, Benjamin Cannon purchased the property, and from him the village derived its name.
[9] Named from the Hale family, who were early settlers.
[10] Mr. W. was one of the survivors of the massacre of Wyoming; and his sons John and Benjamin, then children, remember many incidents of that event and the subsequent escape. He stated that Brandt was at Cherry Valley at the time of the massacre, and, of course, was not a participant in its atrocities.
[11] The place where he settled is now (1859) occupied by his grandson, Martial R. Hulse.
[12] Mr. Edict was a soldier of the Revolution. The first birth was that of Polly Hulse, in 1789 or '90; and the first death, that of Dorcas, wife of Oliver Hale, about 1790.
[13] The census reports 7 churches; 3 Bap., 2 M. E., and 2 Presb.
[14] Named from Wm. Walton, a large land proprietor in this vicinity. Walton's Patent (20,000 acres) was granted in 1770. The academy building was erected in 1853. The institution has a good library and is in a flourishing condition.
[15] The academy building was erected in 1853. The institution has a good library and is in a flourishing condition.
[16] Dr. Townsend received 1700 acres for surveying, and paid $2.50 per acre for the remainder, receiving his deed in 1786.

from New Canaan, Conn., came in within a few years.[1] The first church (Cong.) was formed in 1793.[2]

Acres of Land, Valuation, Population, Dwellings, Families, Freeholders, Schools, Live Stock, Agricultural Products, and Domestic Manufactures, of Delaware County.

Names of Towns.	Acres of Land.		Valuation of 1858.			Population.		No. of Dwellings.	No. of Families.	Freeholders.	Schools.	
	Improved.	Unimproved.	Real Estate.	Personal Property.	Total.	Males.	Females.				No. of Districts.	Children taught.
Andes	22,853	21,629	$407,233	$51,348	$458,581	1,337	1,199	432	441	365	20	1,107
Bovina	16,682½	8,217	240,753	57,926	298,679	638	586	208	220	183	11	516
Colchester	14,189½	72,626	242,931	18,450	261,381	1,237	1,123	411	427	376	21	1,039
Davenport	19,220½	14,844	376,533	40,154	416,687	1,113	1,120	399	422	279	19	979
Delhi	22,020¼	16,273¾	668,490	237,467	905,957	1,335	1,376	465	489	409	18	1,022
Franklin	34,514	14,499	728,725	92,710	821,435	1,581	1,605	618	651	557	27	1,091
Hamden	17,310	13,783	349,910	28,044	377,954	957	924	339	360	307	16	818
Hancock	6,329	95,648	373,640	7,900	381,540	1,335	1,177	430	456	204	19	858
Harpersfield	16,002½	6,711	338,650	69,375	408,025	722	758	285	298	283	15	461
Kortright	24,307½	9,339½	435,515	73,252	508,767	958	1,055	380	389	330	20	666
Masonville	13,519¾	17,442¾	259,292	14,207	273,499	801	742	285	294	307	15	675
Meredith	21,194	10,840¼	339,470	45,900	385,370	738	765	303	316	273	16	597
Middlebury	26,213¾	24,381½	364,512	61,500	426,012	1,490	1,456	534	575	370	22	1,346
Roxbury	34,635¼	15,043½	548,503	102,554	651,057	1,276	1,257	460	473	277	18	1,003
Sidney	19,051	11,478	405,210	14,000	419,210	920	877	345	373	299	14	710
Stamford	19,055¼	9,522	378,488	119,313	497,801	780	817	295	322	249	13	622
Tompkins	18,721½	40,314½	500,629	127,100	627,729	1,671	1,619	592	653	539	33	1,405
Walton	18,581	35,859½	478,635	74,534	553,169	1,202	1,202	457	491	398	19	885
Total	364,400¼	438,452¼	$7,437,119	$1,235,734	$8,672,853	20,091	19,558	7,238	7,650	6,005	336	15,800

Names of Towns.	Live Stock.					Agricultural Products.							Domestic Cloths, in yards.
						Bush. of Grain.					Dairy Products.		
	Horses.	Working Oxen and Calves.	Cows.	Sheep.	Swine.	Winter.	Spring.	Tons of Hay.	Bushels of Potatoes.	Bushels of Apples.	Pounds Butter.	Pounds Cheese.	
Andes	598	1,895	2,175	6,710	933	4,001	44,776½	6,707	7,774	9,737	269,052	480	3,686
Bovina	414	1,144	1,774	3,673	706	4,029	24,324¼	4,924	6,109	6,966	223,490	2,998	2,413
Colchester	349	1,725	1,035	3,201	736	3,096½	24,519¾	4,805½	7,168¾	16,165	97,572	390	1,883
Davenport	563	1,382	1,749	3,445	973	4,088	43,109	4,452	13,926	9,984	192,860	1,955	2,613
Delhi	526	1,441	2,051	4,544	870	2,065	30,731½	6,002	7,847	9,676	216,202	1,080	1,235
Franklin	871	2,545	3,195	6,930	1,502	6,394	66,666	9,476¾	26,599	29,156	393,332	12,249	1,254
Hamden	440	1,809	1,682	5,926	693	3,432	26,691¼	4,898	7,146	7,526	170,785	1,146	1,825
Hancock	192	695	494	816	408	1,619	16,839	1,946	7,489	5,835	45,608		454
Harpersfield	439	1,583	1,775	2,614	764	1,987	31,715½	5,455½	13,180	20,635	240,010	3,364	2,464
Kortright	613	1,855	2,385	3,975	1,054	2,556½	36,572	6,629	9,561	20,645	326,740	1,310	2,569
Masonville	370	1,703	1,291	3,599	567	2,396	36,314¾	4,531¼	14,310½	13,700	124,252	6,171	2,625
Meredith	474	1,336	1,763	2,826	823	1,509	34,741	4,434½	13,063	11,722	221,217	3,777	666½
Middletown	752	2,610	2,441	4,138	1,118	4,259	39,965	7,069	14,506½	21,275	261,611	520	5,020
Roxbury	677	2,139	3,817	3,346	1,595	5,495	30,616½	9,078	9,786½	21,379	472,090	2,115	4,335
Sidney	502	1,622	1,756	4,449	907	2,888	54,517¾	5,342½	17,441	17,471	204,329	7,880	1,909
Stamford	434	1,205	1,867	3,809	791	1,997	23,596	5,103½	8,887	11,460	245,658	2,980	705½
Tompkins	490	2,017	1,616	3,583	736	1,588	45,041½	6,851	14,526	13,205	166,262	11,500	2,009
Walton	436	1,991	1,618	3,731	724	4,083	26,750¼	6,190¾	10,247	12,623	155,505	1,27	1,891¾
Total	9,140	30,697	34,484	71,315	15,870	57,483	637,488	103,896¼	209,567¼	259,160	4,026,575	61,185	39,557¾

[1] Among the early settlers were Gabriel and Robert North, Isaac and Wm., sons of Platt Townsend, Wm. Farnum, Joshua Pine and sons, Daniel and Joshua, Michael Goodrich, —— Beers, —— Cable, Thaddeus Hoyt, Chas. W. Stockton, Matthew Benedict, John Eells, Alan Mead, Lindal Fitch, Dan'l Weed, Nathan Kellogg, Cephas Bush, Eph'm Waring, Sam'l Hanford, jr., Seth Berray, David and Sellick St. John, and Seymour Fitch. The proprietor offered a lot of land to the first male child born in town who should be named Wm. Walton; and the prize was within reach of a son of Mrs. Robert North, the first woman who came into town, but she had set her heart upon the name of Samuel, and a lot of land could not induce her to change her mind. The first marriage was that of Boutram Olmstead and Savory Goodrich. Lewis Seymour and Judd Raymond kept the first store, in 1791; M. Goodrich built the first saw and grist mill, and Gabriel North the first framed house.—*Hist. of Walton. in Nos. 6 to 22, Vol. II. of "The Walton Jour."* Hon. Joel T. Headley, late Sec'y of State, was a native of this town.

[2] The census reports 4 churches; 2 Cong., and 1 each M. E. and Prot. E.

DUTCHESS COUNTY.

This county was formed Nov. 1, 1683.[1] It was provisionally annexed to Ulster co., and was first represented separately in the General Assembly in 1713. Livingston Manor was taken off, and annexed to Albany co., in 1717; and Putnam co. was taken off in 1812. It lies on the E. bank of the Hudson, about midway between New York and Albany, is centrally distant 60 mi. from Albany, and contains 810 sq. mi. Its surface is principally a rolling and hilly upland broken by the deep valleys of the streams. The Taghkanick Mts., extending along the E. border of the co., are 300 to 500 ft. above the valleys and 1000 to 1200 ft. above tide. Their declivities are generally steep, and in some places rocky. A wide valley skirts the w. foot of this range, bounded on the w. by the Matteawan or Fishkill Mts., a high, broad range which extends N. and S. and occupies the whole central part of the co. A spur from this range extends eastward along the S. border to the Hudson, forming the N. extremity of The Highlands. This range has an average elevation of about 1000 ft. above tide, the highest peaks along the S. border attaining an elevation of 1500 to 1700 ft.[2] In the S. part of the co. the declivities of these mountains are steep and in many places rocky, but toward the N. they become more gradual, and the country assumes a rolling character, broken by rounded hills. West of this range the surface is a rolling upland, occasionally broken by deep ravines and isolated hills, and terminating upon the Hudson River Valley in a series of bluffs 100 to 180 ft. high. The greater part of the streams that drain the co. are tributaries of the Hudson. They mostly flow in a S. W. direction, and have worn deep valleys through the bluffs that border upon the river. The principal of these streams, commencing upon the N., are the Sawkil, Landimans, Crum Elbow, Fall, Wappingers, and Fishkill Creeks. Sprout Creek is a considerable branch of the Fishkill. The wide valley extending N. and S. through the co., separating the Taghkanick Mts. from The Highlands farther w., is drained by several streams. Ten Mile River flows S. in this valley through Amenia to near the S. line of Dover, where it turns E. and discharges its waters into the Housatonic River, in Conn. It receives Swamp River from the S. Croton River takes its rise in the S. part of the valley. Roeliff Jansens Kil flows through a small portion of the extreme N. part of the co. Among the highlands in the central and E. parts are numerous beautiful little lakes, noted for the purity of their waters and the beauty of the scenery immediately about them. The principal rock formation in the co. is the Hudson River slate, which crops out upon the hills and along the courses of the streams. The rock has been quarried at Red Hook for flagging, and in various places for roofing slate.[3]

A low ridge of metamorphic limestone extends longitudinally through near the center of the valley, which lies at the base of the Taghkanick Mts. and along its course are numerous quarries, from which is obtained a fair quality of marble.[4] Hematitic iron ore is found in almost inexhaustible quantities along the E. and S. parts of the co., and it has been extensively mined in several places.[5] Thin veins of galena have also been found, but none have been worked since the Revolution.[6] Mineral springs are found in several parts of the co., but none of them have acquired notoriety.[7] Marl and peat beds are scattered over the whole co. The soil is generally a

---

[1] The act by which this co. was formed defines its original boundaries as follows:—"The Dutchess co. to be from the bounds of the co. of Westchester, on the S. side of the Highlands, along the E. side as far as Roeliff Jansens Creek, and E. into the woods 20 miles."

[2] Old Beacon, 2 mi. E. of Matteawan Village, is 1470 ft. above tide; and New Beacon, or Grand Sachem, a ¼ mi. S. of the same place, is 1680 ft. above tide.

[3] A company, styled the "N. Y. Slate Co.," was incorp. March 23, 1810, to continue 15 years; and another, styled the "Dutchess Co. Slate Co.," June 8, 1812, to continue 21 years. The operations of the latter co. were to be confined to Northeast.

[4] This marble is of the variety called dolomite, and yields upon analysis about 39½ per cent. of carbonate of magnesia; but the proportion is not uniform. The principal workings have been in Dover, where a portion of the marble is pure white, fine grained, and capable of receiving a good but not a high polish. Clouded varieties are found in Amenia and Northeast.—Geol., 1st Dist., p. 68.

[5] This ore is generally compact, but in some places it is fibrous. Its cavities are lined with a glossy black surface, and often contain stalactital and botryoidal concretions of the ore.

[6] Considerable excavations were made in Northeast in colonial times—it is said as early as 1740—by a company of Germans, who sent the ore to Bristol, Eng. The mines were re-opened during the Revolution, and a few tons of ore were obtained. Traces of lead ore have been also observed in Rhinebeck and Amenia.—Geol., 1st Dist., pp. 46, 47. Among the other useful minerals that have been observed in the co. are, graphite, formerly worked to some extent in the Fishkill Mts., oxyd of manganese, and the sulphurets of copper and iron, &c. Besides these are found calcite, asbestus, gibbsite, garnet, staurotide, epidote, feldspar, and tourmaline.

[7] Inflammable carburetted hydrogen gas is emitted from the bottom of a lake in Northeast, and from a locality ¼ of a mi. from Ameniaville on the road to Poughkeepsie. A sulphur spring is situated 1¼ mi. N. W. of Ameniaville.—Beck's Mineralogy N. Y., p. 160.

fine quality of sandy and gravelly loam.   Upon the hills in some places it is composed of disintegrated slate, and upon the Hudson River intervale it is a deep, rich alluvium.   Agriculture is the
leading pursuit, and few cos. in the State offer greater attractions to the farmer.   The richness and
variety of its soil, and its proximity to the New York market, insure a rich return for all agricultural labor.   Farming is of a mixed character, all branches being successfully pursued.   Sending
milk to New York and the raising of improved breeds of cattle have become important branches
of business.[1]

A considerable amount of manufacturing is carried on in the co., the principal establishments
being located at Poughkeepsie and Fishkill, and a large amount of commerce is carried on by
means of the Hudson.

The county seat is located at the city of Poughkeepsie.   The colonial courthouse and jail was
burned in 1785, and a new one was built soon after.   This was burned in 1808.[2]   The present
building was erected in 1809,[3] and contains the courtroom, jail,[4] clerk's office, and all the usual co.
offices except that of surrogate, which is in a small building adjacent.   The co. poorhouse is situated on a farm of 107 acres in the town of Poughkeepsie, 1 mi. E. of the courthouse.   The average
number of inmates is 220, supported at a weekly cost of 95 cents each.   The farm yields a revenue
of $1631.[5]   The Hudson River R. R. extends along the E. bank of the Hudson, through Fishkill,
Poughkeepsie, Hyde Park, Rhinebeck, and Redhook; and the New York & Harlem R. R. extends
along the E. border of the co., through Pawling, Dover, Amenia, and North East.   In summer,
regular lines of steamers ply between Poughkeepsie, New York, and Albany.

One daily and seven weekly papers are now published in the co.[6]

---

[1] In cultivated area Dutchess co. is excelled only by Jefferson, Oneida, Otsego, and St. Lawrence cos.; and in cash value of farms by Monroe and Westchester only.   Over 2,000,000 gallons of milk are sent annually to the N. Y. market.

[2] A courthouse and jail were first ordered to be built July 21, 1715; but they do not appear to have been completed until 30 years afterward.   In 1760, an act authorized the conversion of a jury room into a jail, and 4 years after money was raised to complete the arrangement.   The act of April 11, 1785, appropriated the sum of £1500 to re-construct the buildings, which had been destroyed by fire, and Cornelius Humfrey, Peter Tappen, and Gilbert Livingston were appointed a building committee.   A further tax of £2000 was ordered in 1786, and of £1300 in 1787.   In the mean time, prisoners were sent to the Ulster co. jail.   By act of March 19, 1778, the sheriff's mileage was to be reckoned from the house of Myndert Vielle, in Beekman's Precinct.

[3] The act for the re-construction of these buildings was passed March 24, 1809, and $12,000 was raised for that purpose.   Jas. Talmadge, John B. Van Wyck, and John Van Benthuysen were appointed building commissioners.   The next year, $13,000 additional was raised, and the building was completed soon after.   It is a stone edifice, 50 by 100 ft.   The first deed on record was entered Dec. 26, 1718, conveying property from Henry Van De Bogart to Capt. Barent Van Kleeck, and others.

[4] The condition of the jail was represented by the Senate Committee of 1856 as extremely unfit for its purpose and unhealthy to its inmates.

[5] The buildings are large, and can accommodate 350 inmates.   The sexes are kept separate, and an asylum is provided for lunatics.   A school is taught during the whole year, and religious worship is regularly conducted.

[6] The New York Journal, first established in the city of New York by John Holt in 1734, was removed to Poughkeepsie in 1776, in consequence of the British occupation.   In 1778 it became the first State paper under the new Government; and on the 11th of April, 1785, its name was changed to
The Poughkeepsie Journal, published by Nicholas Power.   In 1786 its name was changed to
The Country Journal and Poughkeepsie Advertiser; and in 1789 to
The Country Journal and Dutchess and Ulster Family Register.   In 1808 it was sold to Paraclete Potter, who changed it to
The Poughkeepsie Journal and Constitutional Republican.   In 1812 it was changed to
The Poughkeepsie Journal, and in 1834 Jackson & Schram became the proprietors.   In 1844 it was united with The Eagle, and was issued as
The Journal and Poughkeepsie Eagle.   In 1850 the name was changed to
The Poughkeepsie Eagle, under which title it is still published by Platt & Schram.
The New York Packet and American Advertiser, published by Sam'l Loudon, was removed from New York when the British took possession of the city, and was first issued at Fishkill Oct. 1, 1776.   It was removed to New York again after the close of the war.
The American Farmer and Dutchess County Advertiser was commenced in Aug. 1798, by John Woods, and was continued a short time.

The Barometer, commenced in May, 1802, by Isaac Mitchell, was changed to
The Political Barometer in 1806, and was published by Thomas Nelson.   Its name was changed to
The Northern Politician, and it was soon after discontinued.
The Farmer was published at Poughkeepsie in 1806-07.
The Republican Herald was started in Nov. 1811, by Derick B. Stockholm and Thos. Brownjohn.   It was continued until 1823 under the charge of Johnston Verplank & Wm. Orr.
The Dutchess Observer was first started May 10, 1815, by Chas. P. Barnum & Richard Nelson.   Nicholas Jaycocks, Nathan Myers, jr., and Orrin Osborne were successively interested in the publication until 1826, when the paper was united with The Telegraph, and issued as
The Poughkeepsie Telegraph and Observer.   It was successively under the charge of Chas. P. Barnum, Egbert B. Killey, Aaron Low, and Benson J. Lossing.   In 1841 it was changed to
The Telegraph, and was published by Killey & Lossing.   Albert S. Pease & E. K. Olmsted were afterward interested in its publication; and in 1852 it was united with The Democrat, and was issued as
The Poughkeepsie Telegraph and Dutchess Democrat, now published by Osborne & Killey.
The Republican Telegraph was first issued May 5, 1824, by Wm. Sands & Isaac Platt.   In 1826 it was united with
The Observer.
The Dutchess Intelligencer was first issued April 30, 1828, by Chas. F. Ames & Fred. T. Parsons.   It was afterward published by Platt & Parsons and Isaac Platt until 1833, when it was united with
The Republican, and was issued as
The Intelligencer and Republican, published by Platt & Ranney.   In 1834 the name was changed to
The Poughkeepsie Eagle; and in 1844 it was united with The Journal.
The Dutchess True American was published at Poughkeepsie in 1828, by Peter K. Allen.
The Dutchess Inquirer was started in Aug. 1829, by Pet. K. Allen.   In 1830 it was changed to
The Anti Mason.   It was under the charge of John M. Vethake and Stephen Butler until 1831, when it was discontinued.   It was soon after revived by Eliphaz Fay, and was issued a short time as The Independence.
The Dutchess Republican was started in Aug. 1831, by Thos. S. Ranney.   In April, 1833, it was united with The Intelligencer.
The Poughkeepsie Casket was published by Killey & Lossing in 1836.
The Branch was issued a short time in 1836 by Jos. H. Jackson.
The Youth's Guide (semi-mo.) was issued in 1837 by Isaac Harrington, jr.
The Thomsonian (medical) was issued at Poughkeepsie in 1840 by Thos. Lapham.
The Free Press was started at Fishkill in 1841 by Fred. W. Ritter.   In 1842 it was removed to Poughkeepsie· its name was changed to
The Dutchess Free Press, and was continued until 1844.
The Temperance Lifeguard was started at Poughkeepsie in 1843 by G. R. Lyman, and was continued 2 or 3 years.

The first settlements in the co. were made by the Dutch at Rhinebeck and Fishkill before 1690.[1] Other settlements were made along the river in 1700; but for some years the progress of growth was very slow. About 1720 a considerable number of settlers came in; and from that time the settlements increased rapidly until all the lands of the co. were taken up.[2] Among the early settlers were considerable numbers of French Huguenots, who had fled from the persecutions that followed the revocation of the Edict of Nantes. A portion of the co. was settled upon leaseholds, which here, as elsewhere, led to much difficulty.[3] The first civil divisions were established in 1737.[4]

This co. comprises the greater part of the Oblong,[5] Great and Little Nine Partners, Beekmans, Rumbouts, and Schuylers Patents.[6] In 1777, the co. for a short time was in possession of the British, and for a considerable time during the Revolution it was the seat of the colonial convention and legislature. By an act of April 11, 1808, semi-annual fairs of sale were directed to be held in this co. under the management of five commissioners to be appointed by the judges of Common Pleas.[7]

AMENIA[8]—was formed March 7, 1788. It lies on the E. border of the co., N. of the center. The Taghkanick Mts. extend along the E. border, and the highlands belonging to the Fishkill Range extend through the w. part. The wide valley separating these two ranges occupies the central portions. The declivities of the mts. are often steep, and their highest summits are 300 to 500 feet above the valleys. Amenia Station, on the Harlem R. R., is 540 feet above tide. The

---

The Anti Bank Democrat (mo.) was issued from the office of The Free Press in 1843.

The American was started in Nov. 1845, by Augustus T. Cowman. It was soon changed to

The Poughkeepsie American, and was published by Isaac Tompkins and Elias Pitts until 1853, when it was sold to E. B. Osborne, and changed to

The Dutchess Democrat. In 1856 it was united with The Telegraph.

The Safeguard (Temperance) was issued in 1845 by Wm. Patton.

The Daily City Press was commenced at Poughkeepsie, May 1, 1852, by Nichols, Bush, & Co. It was soon after changed to

The Daily Press, under which name it is still issued by its original proprietors.

The Independent Examiner was started in Feb. 1855, by Henry A. Gill, and was discontinued in 1858.

The American Banner was started at Poughkeepsie in 1856 by Chas. J. Ackert. In 1857 it was removed to Fishkill, and was changed to

The Dutchess Co. Times, under which name it is still published by J. Carpenter Mills.

The Fishkill Standard was started Aug. 2, 1842, at Fishkill Landing, by Wm. R. Addington, and is still issued by him.

The Fishkill Journal, started in 1853 by H. A. Guild, was discontinued in 1855.

The American Mechanic was started at Poughkeepsie in 1849 by Geo. W. Clark. In 1850 it was removed to Rhinebeck, and was united with The Gazette, under the name of

The American Mechanic and Rhinebeck Gazette. It was soon changed to

The Rhinebeck Gazette and Dutchess County Advertiser. It was successively issued by Edward M. Smith and L. R. Blanchard, and is now published by Wm. Luff.

The Rhinebeck Gazette was established in 1846 by Smith & Carpenter, and in 1850 was united with The Mechanic.

The Rhinebeck Advocate was published by Robert Marshall in 1840. It was subsequently changed to

The Dutchess County Advocate, and was discontinued about 1850.

The American Citizen was commenced June 12, 1858 at Rhinebeck, by Geo. W. Clark.

The True Balance, a campaign paper, was published at Rhinebeck by C. J. Ackert in 1858.

The Amenia Times was started at Ameniaville, April 7, 1852, under the charge of Joel Benson. It was subsequently issued by H. Livingston & Co., and Palmer, Vail & Co. It is now pub. by J. W. Dutcher.

The Redhook Daily Journal was commenced April 29, 1859, by L. Piester.

[1] The following copy of a letter, now in possession of T. Van Wyck Brinkerhoff, of East Fishkill, throws some light upon the early history of the co. "In the year 1823, I saw Isaac Upton, a coaster from Newport, who informed me that about 1760 he came up the North River to Poughkeepsie, and, in company with another person, went to Mabbitt's store, in Washington, on business. That, on their return, they took a circuitous route from Pleasant Valley, and passed a German by name of Hoffman, who was then 118 years old. He supposed himself to be the first white settler in Dutchess co.; and that, when young, he deserted from a Dutch ship of war in New York, squatted where he then lived, built him a shanty, and lived a number of

years a solitary life without being able to find a white woman for a wife; that afterward, finding a German family at Rhinebeck, he married, and had lived where he then was to that advanced age. I was informed that he died two years afterward, at 120 years. (Signed) PAUL UPTON."

[2] Smith, in his history, written in 1732, says of this co., "The only villages in it are Poughkeepsie and the Fishkill, though they scarce deserve the name. The inhabitants on the banks of the river are Dutch, but those more easterly, Englishmen, and for the most part immigrants from Conn. and Long Island. There is no Epis. church in it. The growth of this co. has been very sudden, and commenced but a few years ago. Within the memory of persons now living, it did not contain above 12 families; and according to the,late returns of the militia it will furnish at present above 2500 fighting-men."—*Hist. N.Y., Alb. Ed., p.* 304.

[3] In 1766, the district now embraced in Rensselaer, Columbia, and Dutchess cos. was involved in a domestic war, arising from the conflicting jurisdiction of adjacent colonies and resistance to the claims of proprietors. In June of that year, the sheriff of Albany Co., with 105 men, went to a house on the manor to disperse a band of rioters, 60 in number. Several shots were exchanged: Cornelius Ten Broeck, of Claverack, was killed, and 7 others of the militia were wounded. Three of the rioters were killed, and many wounded, among whom was Capt. Noble, one of their leaders. In July, the 28th Regiment was ordered into Dutchess co., to quell riots; and a small body of light infantry was soon after fired upon, and 3 were wounded. One Pendergrast, a leader, was taken, tried before Judge Horsmanden for high treason, and sentenced to be executed, but was afterward pardoned. Fifty to 60 others were fined, imprisoned, or pilloried. Soon after the sentence of Pendergrast, an advertisement was issued, offering a good reward to any one willing to assist as the executioner, and promising disguise against recognition and protection against insults.—*Dunlap's Hist. N.Y., II., Appen. CXCIII.*

[4] By an act of the General Assembly, passed Dec. 16, 1737, this co. was divided into 3 divisions. The s. division extended from below the Highlands to Wappingers Creek; the middle division from the latter, N. to Cline Sopas Island, (Little Esopus Island;) and the N. division from this point to the N. bounds of the co. Each of these divisions elected a supervisor. The subsequent formation of precincts is mentioned under the several towns.

[5] The Oblong, a tract 580 rods wide, extending across the E. border of this co. and Putnam, was mostly granted to Thos. Hawley and others, in 1731; South, Beekmans, Crum Elbow, and North Precincts were extended across to the Conn. line, Dec. 17, 1743. The patent was divided into lower, middle, and upper districts, March 9, 1774, to facilitate the collection of quitrents.

[6] Several of these patents were granted as follows: Rumbout, to Francis Rumbout and others, Oct. 17, 1685; Great or Lower Nine Partners, to Caleb Heathcote and others, May 27, 1697; Rhinebeck, to Henry Beekman, June 5, 1703; Little or Upper Nine Partners, to Sampson Boughton and others, April 10, 1706.

[7] These fairs were to be supported by a tax of 1 per cent. on all sales, one-half to be paid by the purchaser and one-half by the seller.

[8] According to Benson, this term was applied by Young, the American poet, in his "*Conquest of Quebec,*" in a description of the several provincial troops employed in that campaign. The precinct of this name was formed from Crum Elbow Precinct, March 20, 1762, and included a part of Amenia and North East, and the whole of Washington, Pleasant Valley, Stanford, Clinton, and Hyde Park.

principal streams are Ten Mile River, Wassaic Creek, and West Brook, and their branches. A low range of metamorphic limestone extends N. and S. through near the center of the valley.[1] Iron ore has been extensively mined in the highlands w. of the valley.[2] The soil is a clayey and sandy loam. **Ameniaville,** (Amenia p.o.,) N. of the center of the town, contains the Amenia Seminary,[3] 3 churches, and 30 houses. It is a station upon the Harlem R. R. **The City,** (City p.o.,) in the N. w. corner, contains a church and 17 houses; **Wassaic,** (p.v.,) a R. R. station, a furnace, sash and blind factory, and 18 houses; **Amenia Union,** (p.v.,) upon the Conn. line, 2 churches, a woolen factory, and 30 houses;[4] and **South Amenia** (p.v.) a church and 14 houses. **Leedsville** (p. o.) is a hamlet near the E. border. **Sharon Station,** on the line of Northeast, is a p. o. Richard Sackett purchased large tracts of the Indians in this town and in Sharon, Conn., and settled in 1711; he failed of getting his title recognized by the crown, and died in poverty in 1748 or '49.[5] During the Revolution a furnace and foundery for the manufacture of steel for the use of the army was established about 1 mi. s. of Wassaic. The site, known as "The Steel Works," is still covered by coal dust and cinders. There are 7 churches in town.[6]

BEEKMAN—was formed as a town, March 7, 1788.[7] A part of "*Freedom*" (now La Grange) was taken off in 1821, and a part of Union Vale in 1827. It lies in the S. E. part of the co.,—one corner extending to the s. border. Its surface is a hilly and broken upland. Pleasant Hill, on the N. border, is the highest summit. Limestone and slate crop out on the summits and declivities of nearly all the hills. The streams are small creeks and brooks tributaries of the Fishkill, and are bordered by wide, fertile intervales. Silver Lake is a fine body of water near the w. line.[8] Iron ore is found s. of this lake.[9] The soil is a productive, gravelly loam. **Green Haven,** (p.v.,) near the w. border, contains 1 church and 18 dwellings; **Beekmanville,** (Beekman p.o.,) near the center, 1 church and 12 dwellings; **Poughquag** (p.v.) 2 churches and 15 dwellings; and **Beekman Furnace,** on the N. line, an iron manufactory and 10 houses.[10] The first settlements are supposed to have been made about 1710; but the early records are lost. A. Delong located in 1716, and kept an inn at an early day. Rt. Rev. Alonzo Potter, Bishop of Penn., and his brother, Rt. Rev. Horatio Potter, Provisional Bishop of the Diocese of N. Y., were natives of this town. There are 4 churches in town.[11]

CLINTON[12]—was formed from "*Charlotte*" and Rhinebeck Precincts, March 13, 1786. Hyde Park and Pleasant Valley were taken off in 1821. It is an interior town, lying N. w. of the center of the co. Its surface is a rolling upland considerably broken by hills in the N. and w. Shultz Mts., on the N. border, and Sippe Barrack, in the w., are the highest points.[13] Salt Point Creek, the principal stream, flows s. through near the center. Crum Elbow Creek forms a portion of the w. boundary. Several small lakes, the principal of which is Long Pond, lie in the N. part. The soil in the N. is a sandy loam, and in the center and s. it is a productive, slaty loam. **Clinton Hollow,** (p.v.,) near the center, contains 25 houses, **Clinton Corners** (p.v.) 25 houses, **Schultzville** (p. o.) a gristmill and 10 houses, and **Pleasant Plains** (p. o.) a church and 8 houses. **Bulls Head, Clinton Point,** and **Hibernia** are p. offices. Derrick Van Vliet located in town about 1755. There are 3 churches in town; Friends, Presb., and Prot. E.

DOVER—was formed from Pawling, Feb. 20, 1807. It lies on the E. border of the co., s. of the center. The E. and w. borders are occupied by hills and mts., and the center by a deep, wide valley. The valley is about 400 feet above tide, and the summits of the hills are 300 to 500 feet higher. Ten Mile River flows s. from the N. line to near the s. boundary, thence turns E. and discharges its waters into the Housatonic. It receives from the s. Swamp River, a stream that is

---

1 This limestone is of a bluish color, hard and brittle; and where it crops out it is considerably disintegrated, covering the ground in the immediate vicinity with a white sand.

2 An ore bed ¼ mi. w. of Ameniaville has been extensively worked for 25 or 30 years, and the supply of ore seems inexhaustible. Another ore bed has been opened 2 mi. N. w. of Wassaic, and another near the N. line of the town.

3 This institution has been under the charge of the M. E. denomination.

4 1 church, the woolen factory, and about half of the buildings are in Conn.

5 Mr. Sackett was connected with the Livingstons in the settlement of the Palatinates at "*German Camp*," (now Germantown, Columbia co.) Ulric Winegar and his son, Capt. Garrett, were the next families. They removed from "*German Camp*" in 1724 and settled on the Oblong tract. The father died in 1754, aged 102 years. —— Delamater settled soon after the Winegars, N. w. of Amenia Union. Henry Nase, Stephen Hopkins, Joel Gillett, Hez. King, Abm. and Joshua Paine, J. Howe,

and Elisha Kinney settled previous to 1743. After this time the town rapidly filled up with settlers, mostly from New England. The first mill is supposed to have been built by John Delamater, at Leedsville, and the first inn to have been kept by Michael Hopkins, near the center of the town.

6 3 Presb., 2 M. E., and 1 each Bap. and Prot. E.

7 The town embraced the land granted to Col. Henry Beekman. Beekman Precinct was formed Dec. 16, 1737, and Pawling's Precinct was set off in 1768.

8 The Indian name for this lake is A-po-qua-gue, signifying round lake.

9 Ore from this bed is extensively mined and taken to Poughkeepsie and Fishkill Furnace.

10 The furnace at this place is supplied with ore from Unionvale: 700 tons of iron are annually produced.

11 Bap., M. E., Prot. E., and Union.

12 Named from Geo. Clinton, first Governor.

13 A slate quarry was formerly worked at the N. extremity of the Shultz Mts.; but it is now abandoned.

bordered by swamps upon the greater part of its course. The limestone ridge extends N. and S. through the center of the principal valley. Along its course several marble quarries have been opened.[1] Iron ore is found in abundance.[2] The soil is a fine quality of sandy, gravelly, and slaty loam. The small streams flowing from the W. hills have worn deep ravines, and in several places form beautiful cascades. The most noted of these is known as "Dover Stone Church."[3] **Dover Plains,** (Dover p. o.,) a R. R. station, in the N. part of the town, contains 3 churches, a gristmill, and plaster mill. Pop. 375. **South Dover,** (p. v.,) on Ten Mile River, contains 2 churches, a grist and saw mill, and 30 houses. **Chestnut Ridge** (p. o.) and **Wing Station** (p. o.) are hamlets. The first settlements are said to have been made by the Dutch from the river towns. Among the early settlers are found the names of Knickerbacker, Osterhout, Dutcher, and Van Duzen. The first settlers upon the Oblong tract were from Conn. The first church (Ref. Prot. D.) is said to have been formed about 1770.[4]

EAST FISHKILL—was formed from Fishkill, Nov. 29, 1849. It is the center town upon the S. border of the co. Its surface is mountainous in the S. and E. and hilly in the N. and w. The highest points of the Fishkill Mts., in the S., are 1000 to 1200 ft. above tide.[5] The principal streams are the Fishkill and its tributaries, Wortel Kil and Sprout Creek. Black Pond is a small sheet of water near the S. line. The intervales along the streams are generally wide, and bordered by steep hillsides in the S. and more gradual slopes in the N. The soil is a gravelly loam. Fatting cattle for the New York market is one of the leading pursuits. **East Fishkill,** (p. v.,) near the center, contains a grist and saw mill and 15 houses; **Johnsville,** (p. v.,) near the w. border, 1 church and 14 houses; **Stormville,** (p. v.,) in the E. part, 20 houses; **Fishkill Plains,** (p. v.,) in the N. w., 1 church and 15 houses; and **Shenandoah Corners,** in the S., a church and 15 houses. **Pecksville, Hopewell,** (Adriance p. o.,) and **Fishkill Furnace**[6] are hamlets. The first settlers were Genet, Geo. and Isaac Storm, about the year 1730; Cornelius Wiltsie and Isaac Adrience came in about 1740. There are 4 churches in town.[7]

FISHKILL—was formed as a town, March 7, 1788. A part of "*Freedom*" (now La Grange) was taken off in 1821, and East Fishkill in 1849. A part of Philipstown (Putnam co.) was annexed March 14, 1806. It lies upon the Hudson, in the S. w. corner of the co. Its surface is mountainous in the S. and hilly in the N. The Fishkill Mts., extending along the S. border, are high, rocky, and precipitous. Old Beacon and Grand Sachem, in the S. E. corner, the highest summits, are respectively 1471 and 1685 ft. above tide. A break in these mountains, in the E. part, opening toward the S., is known as the Wiccopee Pass.[8] The Fishkill flows S. w. through near the center of the town, skirting the foot of the mountains and separating them from the hilly region in the N. w. Wappingers Creek forms the w. boundary. A high rolling ridge lies between these two streams, and the highest point is Mt. Hope, 1000 ft. above tide, near the E. border.[9] Sprout Creek, a tributary of the Fishkill, forms a portion of the E. boundary. A series of bluffs, 150 to 200 ft. high, extends along the river, broken by the valleys of the streams. The soil is a clay and gravelly loam. **Fishkill Landing,** (p. v.,) on the Hudson, opposite Newburgh, contains a newspaper office, 2 machine shops, and 4 churches. Pop. 1100. It is a R. R. station and steamboat landing, and is connected with Newburgh by a steam ferry. **Matteawan,** (p. v.,) on Fishkill Creek, 2 mi. above the landing, is an important manufacturing village. It was formerly the seat of extensive cotton mills; but these have mostly been converted to other purposes.[10] It contains 4

---

[1] The principal quarries are between Dover Plains and South Dover.

[2] White's ore bed, 3 mi. N. w. of South Dover, has been extensively worked, and the ore produced is of good quality. The Dover Iron Works formerly did an extensive business: they closed about 2 years since. White's Furnace, halfway between South Dover and Dover Plains, is making 5 to 6 tons of iron per day.

[3] This ravine is about a ¼ mi. w. of Dover Plains. It is 20 to 25 feet wide at the bottom and 1 to 3 feet at the top, and the rocks that border it are 40 to 50 feet high. It extends into the hill 30 to 40 feet, and at its farther extremity the stream flows from the mountain above in a succession of rapids. The name was given in consequence of its resemblance to the Gothic arch. In another ravine, about ¼ mi. S. of Stone Church, are the "Wells." A small stream here flows down from the mountain in a succession of rapids 3 to 12 feet in height; and at the foot of each fall smooth, rounded holes, called the Wells, have been worn in the rocks to the depth of 3 to 8 feet. The holes occupy the whole width of the bottom of the ravine, and the rocks on each side are shelving and slippery, rendering a near approach difficult and dangerous. These two localities are frequently visited by the lovers of nature during the summer season.

[4] This is now a Union church. A Friends meeting house was built here about the same time.

[5] The highest point on the S. border is locally known as "*Wiccopee*," or "*Long Hill*," and the highest on the E. border as "*Looking Rock*."

[6] A furnace at this place manufactures pig iron from the ore. It employs 40 hands, and makes about 400 tons of iron per annum. The ore is obtained from the mine near Silver Lake, in Beekman. A mine on the E. line, after being worked 20 years, was exhausted.

[7] 2 Bap., M. E., and Ref. Prot. D. The last named has an endowment of $5000.

[8] This pass was carefully guarded during the Revolution. to prevent the British from turning the American works at West Point. A considerable American force was stationed at its upper extremity during the campaign of 1777.

[9] Mt. Hope is ½ mi. S. of Myers Corners. A beautiful and extended view is obtained from its summit. A beacon has been erected here by the Coast Survey. to serve as a point in the triangulation of the Hudson River Valley.

[10] Among the most important of these are the following:—"The Seamless Clothing Manuf'g Co.," incorp. with a capital of $50,000. It gives employment to 95 hands, and turns out $350,000 worth of goods annually. The Matteawan Machine Works, incorp. with a capital of $100,000, gives employment to 200 hands, and turns out annually goods to the amount of $500,000. J. Rothey's file factory employs 70 hands, and manufactures goods to the

churches. Pop. 1476. **Wappingers Falls,** (p. v.,) at the head of navigation on Wappingers Creek, 1½ mi. from the Hudson, lies partly in Poughkeepsie. It is largely engaged in manufacturing.[1] Wappingers Creek here falls 75 feet, furnishing an excellent water power. The village contains 4 churches. Pop. 1819, of which 1139 are in this town. **Hughsonville,** (p. v.,) 1½ mi. s. of Wappingers Falls, contains a church and a steam saw and grist mill. Pop. 245. **New Hackensack,** (p. v.,) in the N. part, contains 1 church and 15 dwellings; **Fishkill,** (p. v.,) near the center, contains the Fishkill Seminary, the Fishkill Collegiate Institute, 2 private schools, a newspaper office, a bank, savings' bank, 3 churches, and 130 dwellings. **Glenham,** (p. v.,) 2½ mi. below Fishkill, contains a woolen factory,[2] 3 churches, and 75 dwellings. **Carthage Landing,** (p. v.,) on the Hudson, 5 mi. above Fishkill Landing, contains 1 church and 30 dwellings. **Myers Corners, Swartoutville,** and **Brinkerhoffville** are hamlets. The first settlement is supposed to have been made before 1690. The earliest records, dated in 1697,[3] are papers relating to lands. The town lies within the tract granted to Francis Rumbout and others, Oct. 17, 1685.[4] In colonial times it formed a part of the Rumbout and Fishkill precincts. The first constitutional convention held a session in this town in the fall of 1776. There are 22 churches in town.[5]

HYDE PARK[6]—was formed from Clinton, Jan. 26, 1821. It lies upon the Hudson, a little N. of the W. border of the co. Its surface is principally a rolling and moderately hilly upland, terminating on the Hudson in a bluff 180 ft. high. Hog and Lloyds Hills, in the N. part, each about 500 ft. above the river, are the highest points in town. The principal streams are Crum Elbow Creek, and Fall Kil, tributaries of the Hudson. The soil is a sandy and gravelly loam underlaid by slate. **Hyde Park,** (p. v.,) finely situated upon an eminence half a mi. E. of the river, contains 4 churches, a gristmill, and 692 inhabitants. **Staatsburgh** (p. o.) is a R. R. station and hamlet in the N. part of the town; **Union Corners** and **Hyde Park Landing** are hamlets. Numerous elegant residences, occupying splendid sites, have been erected along the banks of the river. The first settler is supposed to have been Jacobus Stoughtenburgh, the owner of one of the nine "water lots;" he came to the town about 1720. Gov. Morgan Lewis formerly resided upon the place now occupied by Hon. J. K. Paulding. The census reports 7 churches in town.[7]

LA GRANGE[8]—was formed from Beekman and Fishkill, as "*Freedom,*" Feb. 9, 1821. Its name was changed in 1828. A part of Union Vale was taken off in 1827. It is an interior town, lying s. w. of the center of the co. Its surface is a rolling and moderately hilly upland. Sprout Creek, the principal stream, flows s. through near the center. Wappingers Creek forms the w. boundary. The valleys of these creeks are broad and very fertile. The soil is a gravelly loam. **La Grangeville,** (p. v.,) in the S. E. part, contains 2 gristmills and 14 houses; and **Freedom Plains,** (p. v.,) near the center, a church and 14 houses. **Sprout Creek** (p. o.) is a hamlet in the s. part. **Manchester Bridge,** (p. o.,) on the w. line, is mostly in Poughkeepsie. **Arthursburgh** (p. o.) is a hamlet in the s. corner. The first religious society (Friends) was formed before 1800. There are 2 churches in town; Friends and Presb.

MILAN[9]—was formed from Northeast, March 16, 1818. It lies on the N. border of the co., w. of the center. Its surface is a hilly upland broken by the deep valleys of the streams. The declivities are generally gradual slopes, and the hills are arable to their summits. Roeliff Jansens Kil crosses the N. E. corner. The other streams are small and are bordered by fertile intervales. The soil is a clayey, gravelly, and slaty loam. **Jacksons Corners,** (p. v.,) on Roeliff Jansens

---

amount of $45,000 annually. Wiccopee, ¼ mi. below Matteawan, was the seat of the Wiccopee Color Mills, since changed to the New York Rubber Co., engaged in the manufacture of rubber toys. This co. has a capital of $125,000, employs 125 men, and turns out $100,000 to $150,000 worth of goods per year.

[1] The Dutchess Printing Co., incorp. with a capital of $300,000, employs 300 hands, and produces $750,000 worth of prints per annum. The Franklin Dale Manuf'g Co., incorp. with a capital of $150,000, employs 250 hands, and turns out $150,000 worth of printing cloths per annum. There are, besides, a foundry, comb factory, and numerous machine shops. A large cotton factory was burnt here a few years since, and has not been rebuilt.

[2] The Glenham Woolen Co., incorp. with a capital of $75,000, employs 175 hands, and turns out $275,000 worth of goods annually. It was first started in 1811.

[3] The first mill was erected at the mouth of Fishkill, some time before 1709. A ferry to Newburgh was authorized in 1743.

[4] The house now occupied by Hon. Isaac Teller and his sisters at Matteawan—one of the first built in town—belonged to Roger Brett, a son-in-law of Rumbout. It was built about 1710. The house is one story, 87 by 36 ft., the sides and roof covered with cedar shingles. It was often filled with officers and soldiers

in the Revolution, and salt was stored in its cellar for the army.

[5] The first church (Ref. Prot. D.) was formed at Fishkill Village early in the last century; but the precise date cannot be ascertained. The earliest church records bear date of Sept. 30, 1727. Rev. Dr. De Witt supposed that the church was formed as early as 1716. The present edifice was built in 1786, in the place of one built in 1731. The old church was used for barracks by the American army during the Revolution. A parsonage lot, held in common by this church and the one at "*Hopewell*" and Hackensack, was sold Feb. 17, 1806. The present churches are as follows:—Presb., M. E., Ref. Prot. D., and Af. Meth. at Fishkill Landing; Presb., Prot. E., Prot. Meth., and R. C. at Matteawan; M. E., Ref. Prot. D., and Prot. E. at Glenham; M. E., Ref. Prot. D., and Prot. E. at Fishkill; M. E., Prot. E., and Bap. at Wappingers Falls; Presb. at Brinkerhoffville; M. E. at Carthage Landing; Presb. at Hughsonville; and Ref. Prot. D. at New Hackensack.

[6] Named by Dr. John Bard from Hyde Park, London.

[7] Prot. E., M. E., Bap., Presb., Ref. Prot. D., R. C., and Friends.

[8] Named from La Fayette's residence in France.

[9] This town is included in the tract known as the "Little Nine Partners."

VIEW FROM WEST POINT.

LOOKING UP THE HUDSON.

Kil, in the N. E. corner, contains 1 church and 25 houses; **Rock City**[1] (p. v.) a grist and saw mill and 20 houses; **Milanville** (Milan p. o.) 12 houses; and **La Fayetteville** (p. v.) 16 houses. **Shookville** and **Thornville** are hamlets. The first settlements were principally made by tenants under the original proprietors, about 1760,[2] and a large share of the land is still held by leasehold tenure. The first church (M. E.) was formed about 1790. The census reports 4 churches.[3]

NORTHEAST[4]—was formed as a town, March 7, 1788. Milan was taken off in 1818, and Pine Plains in 1823. It is the N. E. corner town of the co. A tongue of land 1½ mi. wide, upon the E. border, extends 4 mi. N. of the remaining part of the town. The surface is a hilly and broken upland. The Taghkanick Mts., extending along the E. border, are rocky and broken, and are 1000 to 1200 ft. above tide. The highest point in the valley w. of the mountains, forming the summit level of the N. Y. & H. R. R., is 771 feet above tide. Ten Mile River, the principal stream, flows s. through nearly the whole length of the town. Chekomiko Creek flows N. through the w. part. Indian Pond, on the E. line, Round Pond, on the s. line, and Ruds Pond are the principal bodies of water. The valleys have generally a gravelly and clayey soil, but the hills in many places are rocky and fit only for pasturage. An extensive bed of iron ore has been opened 1 mi. N. E. of Millerton, near the Conn. line.[5] **Northeast Center** (p. v.) contains 2 churches and 20 houses; **Millerton,** (Northeast Station p. o.,[6]) a R. R. station, 1 church and 27 houses; and **Spencers Corners** (Northeast p. o.) a church and 12 houses. **Coleman Station** is in the s. part. **Federal Store** and **Oblong** are p. offices. The pioneer settlers were mostly from Conn., and located here from 1725 to 1730.[7] The first religious services were held by Moravian missionaries, at an Indian mission house at the N. end of Indian Lake.[8] There are 4 churches in town.[9]

PAWLING[10]—was formed as a town, March 7, 1788. Dover was taken off in 1807. It is the s. E. corner town in the co. A high range of hills extends along the E. border, and another occupies the w. part. A fine, broad valley occupies the central portions and separates the two highland regions.[11] Swamp and Croton Rivers take their rise in the valley, the former flowing N. and the latter s. Whaleys and Little Ponds—the sources of the Fishkill—lie near the w. border, and Oblong Pond lies in the N. E. part. The ridge of limestone from which marble is quarried extends into the N. part from Dover. The soil is a slaty and gravelly loam. Large quantities of milk are daily sent to the New York market. **Pawling,** (p. v.,) a station on the H. & N. Y. R. R., contains a bank, 2 churches, and 25 houses. **Campbellville,** (p. v.,) in the N. part, contains 14 houses. **Quaker Hill** (p. o.) and **Farmers Hill** (p. o.) are hamlets. Settlements are supposed to have commenced at Quaker Hill between 1720 and 1730, by Friends from N. J., who organized the first religious society soon after their arrival.[12] There are 3 churches in town; M. E., Bap., and Friends.

PINE PLAINS[13]—was formed from Northeast, March 26, 1823. It lies on the N. border of the co., E. of the center. The surface is a hilly upland, the ridges being separated by broad valleys. The highest summit is Stissing Mt., in the w. part, 400 to 500 feet above the valleys. Its declivities are steep, and it is crowned with a mass of naked rock. Roeliff Jansens Kil crosses the N. w. corner, and the Shekomeko or Cheecomico flows N. through near the center. Thompsons, Stissing, and Mud Ponds lie at the E. foot of Stissing Mt., and Buttermilk Pond and several smaller ones are in the s. part. The soil is generally a productive, gravelly loam. Marl is found in several

---

[1] Named from the rock which crops out in the adjacent hills and along the streams.

[2] In 1760, Johannes Rowe bought of Robert Livingston 911 acres a little N. of La Fayetteville, and located upon it. Among the other early settlers we find the names of Clark, Stewart, Simons, and Herrick, a part of whom were from Conn.

[3] 2 M. E., and 1 each Christian and Union.

[4] Named from its geographical position in the co. Northeast Precinct was formed from the North Precinct, Dec. 16, 1746, and embraced the Little or Upper Nine Partners Tract. The North Precinct was extended across the Oblong Tract to the Conn. line, Dec. 17, 1743.

[5] The Dakin ore bed was opened in 1846 by the proprietor, who erected a furnace in the vicinity and run it until 1856. The mine is at the foot of the Taghkanick Mt., which it makes a bend into Conn., and about 1½ mi. above the Salisbury (Conn.) mines. From 8000 to 10,000 tons of ore are taken out annually, and are mostly sent by R. R. to Hudson. Benedict's Furnace, 1 mi. N. W. of Millerton, makes 5 tons of pig iron daily, principally from Salisbury ore. A cupola furnace has also been erected here, and the manufacture of car wheels commenced. A slate company was incorp. in this town in 1812.

[6] Large quantities of milk are daily sent to the N. Y. market.

[7] Baltus Lott and Adam Showerman first settled in the s. part of the town. Barzillai Rudd, Elder Dakin, and —— Spencer were also early settlers.

[8] The remains of this old mission house are still visible on the farm of Douglas Clark.

[9] 2 M. E., Bap., and Cong.

[10] Pawling Precinct was formed from Beekman Precinct, Dec. 31, 1768.

[11] Mt. Tom, a prominent peak ¼ mi. w. of Pawling Station, is about 300 feet above the valley.

[12] The Friends meeting house on Quaker Hill was used as a hospital during the Revolution, and a considerable number of soldiers were buried in the vicinity. A body of troops were stationed here for some time; and Gen. Washington spent a short time here in 1778.

[13] This town formed a portion of the "Little Nine Partners" tract. Many of the farms are still owned by the heirs of the original proprietors, and are leased to the occupants. All efforts to convert the leasehold tenure into a freehold have proved unsuccessful.

localities.[1] **Pine Plains,** (p. v.,) near the center of the town, contains a bank and 3 churches. Pop. 382. **Hammertown** contains an extensive scythe factory and a dozen houses.[2] **Pulvers Corner** (p. o.) and **Mount Ross** are hamlets. The first settlements were probably made about 1740.[3] A Moravian mission was established among the Indians at Shekomeko, 2 mi. s. of Pine Plains, in Sept. 1740.[4] There are 5 churches in town.[5]

PLEASANT VALLEY—was formed from Clinton, Jan. 26, 1821. It is an interior town, lying w. of the center of the co. Its surface is a rolling and hilly upland. Barnes and Dennis Hills, in the N. W., are the highest points. Wappingers Creek flows s. w. through near the center; Sprout Creek takes its rise in a pond in the s. w. part. Slate crops out along the hills, and a vein of marble has lately been discovered. The soil is a clayey and gravelly loam. **Pleasant Valley,** (p. v.,) in the s. w. part, was incorp. April 15, 1814; it contains a cotton factory[6] and 4 churches. Pop. 500.[7] **Salt Point,** (p. v.,) on Wappingers Creek, contains a grist and plaster mill and 17 houses. **Washington Hollow,** (p. v.,) on the line of Washington, contains a church, cotton factory,[8] and 16 houses. **Crum Elbow** is a p. o. The first church (Presb.) was formed in 1765; Rev. Wheeler Case, the first pastor, was installed Nov. 12 of the same year. There are 5 churches in town.[9]

POUGHKEEPSIE[10]—was formed as a town March 7, 1788. The city of Poughkeepsie was taken off March 28, 1854. It lies upon the Hudson, s. of the center of the co. Its surface is mostly a rolling upland. Wappingers Creek, forming the E. boundary, and Fall Kil, flowing s. through Poughkeepsie City, each furnish a considerable amount of water power. The soil is clayey in the w. and a sandy and gravelly loam in the remaining parts. **New Hamburgh,** (p. v.,) on the Hudson, in the extreme s. angle, contains 2 churches. It is a R. R. station, and is connected by a ferry with Marlborough, Orange co. Pop. 339. **Channingville,** opposite Wappingers Falls, contains a gristmill, 2 churches, and 50 houses. **Manchester,** (Manchester Bridge p. o.,) on the line of La Grange, contains about a dozen houses.[11] **Rochdale,** in the N. E. corner, contains 2 cotton factories and 15 houses. **Locust Glen** is a p. o. The first settlements were made by the Dutch, about 1700.[12] There are 4 churches in town; 2 M. E., Presb., and R. C.

POUGHKEEPSIE CITY—was formed from Poughkeepsie, and incorp. as a village March 27, 1799, and as a city March 28, 1854. It is situated upon the Hudson, a little s. of the center of the w. border of the co. The ground gradually rises from the river to a table land, 150 to 200 ft. high, upon which most of the city is built, and about 1 mi. back into a hill 500 ft. high.[13] Fall Kil, a small stream, flows in a tortuous channel through the city, affording a limited amount of water power. The city is finely laid out on the bluff overlooking the Hudson; and, besides the co. buildings, it contains 4 banks, 1 savings' bank, 18 churches, and many other fine public and private buildings. Its location gives to the city commercial advantages which are fully improved. During the summer daily lines of steamers run to New York and to

---

[1] Upon draining Hoag Pond, 1½ mi. s. E. of Pine Plains Village, a very deep bed of marl, covering 6 or 8 acres, was found. Marl is also found in Buttermilk Pond.

[2] Harris's Scythe Factory gives employment to 50 hands, and turns out about 2000 dozen scythes per annum.

[3] In 1740, John Rau, a German, lived on a hill N. E. from Shekomeko. John Tice Smith, Jas. Graham, C. W. Rautz, Ebr. Dibble, and —— Snyder were also early settlers.

[4] This mission was commenced in Sept. 1740, by Henry Rauch, and on the 22d of Feb. 1742, the first 3 Indian converts were baptized. Before the end of the year, 26 more were converted, and a place of worship was erected. This little community had not become fully settled before its quiet was disturbed by the intrusion of an armed force under the orders of the sheriff, at the instigation of intolerant and bigoted neighbors; and, although neither arms nor any thing else were found that could be construed into hostile designs against the Government, the missionaries were seized and brought before the Governor and Council at New York, under charge of being in the interests of the French and of endeavoring to seduce the Indians from their alliance with the English. Upon refusing to take the oath of allegiance, they were reprimanded and discharged. Their enemies, well knowing their conscientious scruples in regard to oaths, in 1744 obtained the passage of an act "for securing his majesty's government in New York," by which an oath of allegiance was made obligatory. Rather than do violence to their consciences, the missionaries removed to Bethlehem, Penn.,

followed by several of their Indian converts. The mission was visited by Count Zinzendorf and Bishop David Nitschman soon after its location in this town. During the last 2 years, 62 native converts were baptized and admitted to the church. Gottlieb Buettner, one of the missionaries, died in Feb. 1745, at this place.—*Heckewelder's Hist. Morav. Missions,* 20; *Doc. Hist. N.Y.,* III. 1014; *Davis's Shekomeko,* p. 29.

[5] Bap., M. E., Presb., Prot. E., and Friends.

[6] This factory was built in 1815, by John Gibbons. It contains 80 looms, and gives employment to 75 hands.

[7] The charter of this village is a dead letter, as no election has taken place in 10 years. The village records are lost.

[8] This factory gives employment to about 40 hands.

[9] 2 M. E., Friends, Prot. E., and Presb.

[10] Poughkeepsie Precinct was formed Dec. 16, 1737. In early documents the name is spelled in a variety of ways, as "*Picipsi*" and "*Pokipsi.*" The original name is said to have been Apokeep-sink, signifying "pleasant harbor."

[11] A cotton factory was formerly in operation here. In 1849 it was changed to a paper mill, which was run until 1857.

[12] Near the s. line of the city is a house built before the Revolution and formerly owned by Philip Livingston. It still bears the marks of balls fired by the British. The dwelling of Gov. Geo. Clinton, still standing, 6 mi. below the city, is now owned by Philip S. Van Rensselaer. Prof. S. F. B. Morse, the inventor of the electric telegraph, resides 2 mi. s. of the city.

[13] About 1 mi. N. of this hill is another of about the same ele-

Albany, and a considerable trade is carried on by barges and boats. The daily line of steamers between New York and Albany touches here. A steam ferry connects the city with New Paltz Landing. The manufactures are extensive and various. They consist chiefly of pig iron, carriages, carpets, pins, chairs, drugs, files, sewing silk, and ale.[1]

The *City Hall* is a plain brick building, situated on Main St., a little w. of the courthouse.

The *Public Schools* are under the charge of a board of education, consisting of 12 members, of whom 3 are elected annually. The schools are 6 in number, and employ 23 teachers,—3 males and 20 females. In 1857 the number of children between 4 and 21 was 4329, of whom 1900 (or 44 per cent.) were in attendance at school during some portion of the year. The total expenses of the schools were $8444 13. The number of volumes in the district libraries was 4683.

The *Dutchess Co. Academy* occupies a large 3 story brick building on Hamilton St.[2]

The *Poughkeepsie Female Seminary*, situated on Cannon St., was founded by a stock co., at a cost of $15,000.

The *Poughkeepsie Collegiate School* is situated on a hill ¾ of a mi. E. of the city. A lot of 80 acres is connected with the institution, and the building and grounds are valued at $75,000.[3]

The *Mansion Square Female Institute* is a private institution, corner of Mansion and Catharine Sts. It has 9 teachers and 80 pupils.

The *Poughkeepsie Female Collegiate Institute*, a private institution, is situated at the corner of Mill and Catharine Sts. It occupies a 3 story brick building, and has an average of 4 teachers and 100 pupils.

The *Cottage Hill Seminary*, a private institution for young ladies, is located on a beautiful site upon Garden St. It is under the charge of a principal, assisted by 12 teachers and lecturers. A library of 2000 volumes is connected with it, and the number of pupils is limited to 50.

The *Law School*, incorp. in 1851, and first located at Ballston Spa, was removed to this city in 1853, and its sessions are still held here. A *Young Men's Association* has been established, for the purpose of furnishing winter lectures.

The *Poughkeepsie Lyceum of Literature, Science, and Art* was incorp. April 6, 1838.

The *Poughkeepsie Orphan Asylum and Home of the Friendless*, having for its object the care of orphans and destitute children, was organized June 21, 1847. Besides these, there is a *Rural Cemetery Association*,[4] a well organized *Fire Department*, and an *Aqueduct Association*. Population of the city, 12,763.[5]

The first settlement was begun in 1690 and 1700. Baltus Van Kleeck built the first house within the present limits of the city, in 1702, on land now owned by Matthew Vassar, near the Cong. Church.[6] The first church (Ref. Prot. D.) was formed about 1700. Rev. Cornelius Van Schie was installed pastor of this church and the one at Fishkill in 1727.[7]

The *Van Kleeck House*, a substantial stone building, was used for purposes of defence, and just under the eaves the walls were pierced with loop-holes for musketry. This building was afterward the meeting place of the inhabitants to consult upon the public welfare when the Boston Port Bill and kindred measures awakened a spirit of resistance through the country. There the Committee of Correspondence of Dutchess held their meetings; and there the pledge to sustain the Continental Congress and the Provincial Assembly was signed by the inhabitants of Poughkeepsie in June and July, 1775.

---

vation. Many beautiful and costly dwellings are built upon these table lands about the city, affording a fine view of the city and valley. The eye here has an uninterrupted range of view over 2500 sq. mi. of country.

[1] The Poughkeepsie Iron Works were established in 1848, with a capital of $200,000; 75 hands are employed, and 10,000 to 11,000 tons of pig iron are manufactured per annum. The ores used are the hematite from Fishkill, and the magnetic ore from Essex co. The Poughkeepsie Carriage Manufactory, with a capital of $35,000, employs 60 hands, and turns out $90,000 to $100,000 worth of carriages per annum, which are chiefly sold in the Southern markets. Pelton's Carpet Factory, with a capital of $60,000, employs 60 to 70 hands, and produces 60,000 to 65,000 yds. of carpeting per year. A pin factory, in the same building, employs 15 hands. The Poughkeepsie Chair Manufactory employs 300 hands, and produces $60,000 worth of chairs per year, which are mostly sent to South America. An establishment for the preparation of dye stuffs and drugs employs 30 hands, and manufactures $200,000 worth of goods annually. A file factory, started in 1856, employs 12 men; and a sewing silk factory, started in 1858, employs 15 to 20 hands. M. Vassar & Co.'s Brewery and Malt Works, commenced in 1795, has a capital of $150,000, employs 50 men, and manufactures 30,000 bbls. of ale per year.

[2] This building was erected in 1836, at a cost of $14,000.

[3] The building of this institution is of wood, modeled after the Parthenon. It was organized under the charge of Chas. Bartlett, N. P. Tallmage, and —— Cunningham. See p. 750.

[4] The Poughkeepsie Rural Cemetery consists of 54 acres, situated in the town of Poughkeepsie, a short distance below the city, between the Highland Turnpike and the Hudson.

[5] The population of the town of Poughkeepsie (including the city recently organized) at different periods has been as follows:—

1790......2,529	1814......5,673	1830...... 7,222	1845......11,791
1800......3,246	1820......5,726	1835...... 8,529	1850......13,944
1810......4,669	1825......5,935	1840......10,006	1855......15,873

[6] Among the early settlers were Dutch families named Van De Bogart, Van Benschoten, Van De Bergh, Van Wagener, De Graff, Le Roy, Parmentier, Messier, Ostrom, Hogeboom, Filkins, Swartwout, Frear, Hegeman, and Livingston. The first house stood until 1835. It was built of stone, and was furnished with loopholes for the use of musketry. During the Revolution the colonial legislature held several sessions in it.

[7] In 1758, the controversy between the Cetus and Conferentie parties distracted this church, and led to its division in 1763. The former of these parties wished to sever their connection from the Classis at Amsterdam and become independent, and the latter wished to still preserve their connection with the mother church. The controversy divided nearly all the Ref. Prot. D. churches in America, and it was not entirely settled until about 1790, when a reconciliation took place. There are now 18 churches in the city; 4 M. E., 2 Ref. Prot. D., 2 Prot. E., (Christ's and St. John's.) 2 Bap., and Cong., Presb., Univ., Ger. Luth., Af. Meth., Friends, R. C., and Jewish.

As soon as the alarm occasioned by the invasion of Sir Henry Clinton (in 1777) had subsided, Gov. Clinton called a meeting of the Legislature at Poughkeepsie. It assembled at the Van Kleeck House early in Jan. 1778. Various acts to complete the organization of the State Government were passed; provisions were made for strengthening the civil and military powers of the State; and it was during that session that the State gave its assent to the Articles of Confederation, the organic law of the Federal Union until our present Constitution was formed and adopted.

The State Convention to consider the Federal Constitution assembled at the Van Kleeck House on June 17, 1788. There were 57 delegates present, and Gov. George Clinton was chosen President of the Convention. In that assembly were some of the most distinguished men of the Revolution, and the debates were of the most interesting character. In no State in the Union was hostility to the Federal Constitution more extensive and violent than in the State of New York. Forty-six of the 57 delegates, including the governor, were Anti-Federalists, or opposed to the Constitution. The principal advocates of the instrument were John Jay, Alexander Hamilton, and Robert Livingston. Mr. Hamilton had been a leading member of the National Convention that framed the Constitution, and also one of the principal writers of *The Federalist*. He felt the responsibility of his situation, and the Convention readily acknowledged the value of his judgment. He was perfectly familiar with every topic included in the wide range which the debates embraced, and he was nobly sustained by his colleagues Jay and Livingston. The hostile feelings of many of the Anti-Federalists gradually yielded, and on the 26th of July the final question of ratification was carried in the affirmative by a majority of 3 votes.

Huddlestone, the famous spy, who was captured upon Wild Boar Hill, near Yonkers, Westchester co., was tried, condemned, and hung in Poughkeepsie in April, 1780. The place of his execution was upon a verge of the plain on which the town stands known as Forbuses Hill. He was accompanied to the scaffold by the co. officers and a small guard of militia enrolled for the purpose.[1]

REDHOOK[2]—was formed from Rhinebeck, June 2, 1812. It lies upon the Hudson, in the N. W. corner of the co. Its surface is a rolling upland, terminating on the Hudson in a series of bluffs 100 to 150 ft. high. The E. part is hilly. Prospect Hill is a prominent peak a little s. of Upper Redhook Village. The streams are the Saw Kil and White Clay Kil. The valleys of the streams are broad and their banks low. Long Pond, in the E. part, forms the source of the Saw Kil. The soil along the river is a clay loam, and in the remaining parts a sandy, gravelly, or slaty loam. **Redhook,** (p. v.,) near the center, contains a cigar and tobacco manufactory, a female orphan asylum,[3] and 3 churches. Pop. 625. **Tivoli,**[4] (p. v.,) in the N. w. part, is a steamboat landing and a R. R. station. A large forwarding business is carried on here. It is adjacent to **Myersville,** the two places forming a continuous village. They contain 5 churches and about 600 inhabitants. **Barrytown** (p. v.) is a R. R. station, 6 mi. below Tivoli. It contains 1 church, and is a place of considerable trade. Pop. 250. **Upper Redhook,** (p. v.,) in the N. E. part, contains 1 church and 175 inhabitants. **Cedar Hill,** on the Saw Kil, contains 1 church, a carpet yarn manufactory, a flouring mill,[5] and 175 inhabitants. The first settlements were made between 1713 and 1727, by the Dutch. There are 11 churches in town.[6] Along the river are numerous elegant country seats. The old residence of Gen. John Armstrong is now owned by his son-in-law, William B. Astor. The former estate of Gen. Montgomery is now occupied by Mrs. Edward Livingston.[7]

RHINEBECK[8]—was formed as a town, March 7, 1788. Redhook was taken off in 1812. It lies upon the Hudson, N. w. of the center of the co. Its surface is a rolling and moderately hilly upland, terminating on the river in bluffs 100 to 150 ft. high. Landmans Creek, the principal stream, flows s. w. through near the center. Rhinebeck Kil is its tributary. Lake Sepasco is a small body of water in the N. E. corner. The soil is principally a fine quality of sandy loam.

---

[1] *Lossing's Field Book*, Vol. I, pp. 383, 384.
[2] By the Dutch called Roode Hoeck. Tradition ascribes the name of the town to a marsh near Tivoli, covered with ripe cranberries when first seen.
[3] Supported entirely by Mrs. William B. Astor.
[4] Pronounced Tiv'o-le. A ferry connects this place with Saugerties, Ulster co.   [5] Erected in 1856, at a cost of $30,000.
[6] 4 Prot. E., 3 M. E., Luth., Bap., Union, and Independent; the last is the Sylvanian Chapel at Barrytown, owned by Robert Donalson.
[7] Among the early settlers were families named Haeners, Shufoldt, Zippertie, Hagerdorn, Wiederwax, Trauvs, Staats, Mellhau, Bermar, Woldorf, Near, Proseus, and others, mostly from

Germany. They first settled near Barrytown and Tivoli. The first marriage on record is that of Adam Shaffer and Maria Schoett, July 31, 1746. The first baptism on the church record is that of Catherine Woldorf, April 23, 1734.
[8] Rhinebeck Precinct, as formed Dec. 16, 1737, included the lands purchased of the widow Paulding and her children by Dr. Sam'l Staats; all the land granted to Adrian, Roosa, and Cotbe; land patented by Col. Henry Beekman, June 5, 1703; and the land granted to Col. Peter Schuyler, called the Magdalen Island Purchase. The name is derived from the first settlers, who were from near the Rhine, in Germany, and Beekman, an original proprietor.

Rhinebeck, (p. v.,) near the center of the town, was incorp. April 23, 1834. It contains a bank, paper mill, 2 newspaper offices, a private academy,[1] and 5 churches. Pop. 1051. **Rhinebeck Station,** (p. v.,) on the Hudson, contains a paper mill and 18 houses. A steam ferry connects the place with Rondout, Ulster co. **Monterey,**[2] near the N. border, contains a church and 10 houses. The first settlement was made some time before 1700, but the precise date cannot be determined. The first family that came in was that of Wm. Beekman, the original proprietor.[3] His homestead (known as the Beekman House, built on a high point above Rhinebeck Station) is still standing.[4] The first religious services are said to have been held in this house. The first church (Ref. Prot. D.) was formed May 23, 1724, at the present village of Monterey.[5] The Lutheran church at Monterey was formed in 1730.[6] There are 6 churches in town.[7]

STANFORD[8]—was formed from Washington, March 12, 1793. It is an interior town, lying N. E. of the center of the co. Its surface is a broken and hilly upland. The hills are generally rounded, and admit of cultivation to their summits. Slate crops out in numerous places along their declivities, and bowlders and water-worn pebbles are thickly strewn over a considerable portion of the surface. The highest point is Carpenter Hill, in the N. E. corner. Wappingers Creek, flowing s. w. through near the center, is the principal stream. Hunns Lake,[9] in the N. E., and Uptons Pond, in the s. w., are the principal bodies of water. The soil is a good quality of gravelly and slaty loam. A considerable quantity of milk is sent daily to New York by the Harlem R. R. **Stanfordville,** (p. v.,) near the center of the town, contains a gristmill, carriage axle factory, paper mill, 3 churches, and 35 dwellings. **Bangall,** (p. v.,) on Wappingers Creek, contains 2 gristmills, 2 sawmills, a foundry, 2 churches, and 30 dwellings. **Attlebury,** (p. o.,) **Stissingville,** and **Old Attlebury**[10] are hamlets. Smith Thompson, U. S. Circuit Judge, was a native and resident of this town. There are 5 churches in town.[11]

UNION VALE[12]—was formed from Beekman and *"Freedom,"* (now La Grange,) March 1, 1827. It is an interior town, lying s. E. of the center of the co. Its surface is a hilly and broken upland divided into two parts by a broad valley which extends N. and s. through the center. Slate crops out upon the summits and the declivities of the hills. The Clove Kil, a tributary of Fishkill Creek, flows s. w. through near the center. The soil is a gravelly and slaty loam. An iron mine near Clove p. o. supplies the Beekman Furnace, 2 mi. farther s. **Verbank,** (p. v.,) in the N. W. corner, contains 2 gristmills, a paper mill, church, and a dozen dwellings. **Oswego Village,** (p. o.,) near the w. border, contains a church and 10 dwellings. **Clove,** (p. o.,) near the center, contains 2 churches and about a dozen dwellings. **Crouse Store,** in the s. part, **Mansfield,** in the N. E. corner, and **Pleasant Ridge,** in the s. E. corner, are p. offices. Henricus Beekman, the patentee, conveyed 1,000 acres to his son Henry in 1716, and settlement is supposed to have commenced soon after. There are 4 churches in town.[13]

WASHINGTON[14]—was formed March 7, 1788. Stanford was taken off in 1793. It is an interior town, lying near the center of the co. The surface is a rolling and hilly upland. Slate crops out on the hills, and water-worn pebbles are thickly strewn over a small portion of the surface. The principal elevations are Muckle Hill, near the center, Molly Mt., in the N. w. corner, Plymouth Hill, in the s. E. corner, and Canoe Hill, near the N. line. The streams are small creeks and brooks. Round and Shaw Ponds, in the N. part, form the sources of Wappingers Creek. A large quantity of milk is sent from the E. part to N. Y. by the Harlem R. R. The raising of blooded stock receives considerable attention.[15] **Harts Village,** (p. v.,) near the center, contains 2 gristmills, 2 sawmills, a spoke factory, and 28 dwellings.[16] **Mabbettsville,**[17] (p. o.,) 2 mi. E. of Harts

---

1 The Rhinebeck Academy was formerly incorp., but is now a private institution. It employs 2 teachers, and has an average of 100 pupils.

2 Named by Geo. Pink, who was appointed first postmaster in 1849. The p. o. has since been discontinued.

3 Wm. Beekman came from Germany with his son, Henricus, in May, 1647; and with them came a number of poor families, who afterward settled in this town. Among the first families were those named Sipperly, Kipp, Pink, Schmidt, Shoptown, Backman, and Elseffer.

4 This house was built of stone, and was used as a fortress in early times. The brick used in the chimneys were brought from Holland. It is now owned by A. J. Hermance, Esq.

5 About 1800 this church divided, by mutual consent of the members; one branch located at Rhinebeck and the other at Redhook. The first baptism on record is that of John Schmidt, April 5, 1730.

6 Fred. Henry Quitman—father of Gen. Quitman, of the Mexican War—was for several years pastor of this church. He was born in the Duchy of Cleves, Westphalia, in 1760, and died in 1832.

7 Ref. Prot. D., Luth., Prot. E., M. E., and Bap. at Rhinebeck, and Luth. at Monterey.

8 This town was included in the Great Nine Partners Tract.

9 Formerly Thompsons Pond.

10 An immense spring of pure cold water near this place has considerable local notoriety.

11 Orthodox Friends, Hicksite Friends, Christian, Bap., and M. E.

12 This town constitutes a portion of the Beekman Purchase.

13 2 M. E., Friends, and Christian.

14 This town is mostly comprised within the Great Nine Partners Tract.

15 Saml. Thorn, of Thorndale, 1 mi. w. of Four Corners, is extensively engaged in raising the short horn Durham cattle. His herd of 70 head, valued at $70,000, is the most valuable one in America.

16 A mill was built at this place about 1760, and is supposed to have been the first in town.

17 Named from Jas. Mabbett, a former proprietor.

Village, contains 12 dwellings, **Lithgow,** (p.o.,) near the E. line, 2 churches and 10 dwellings, **Mechanic,** (Washington p.o.,) 2 mi. S. of Harts Village, a boarding school,[1] 2 churches, and 15 dwellings, and **Little Rest,** (p.v.,) in the S.E. part, 2 gristmills and 15 dwellings. **Four Corners** is a hamlet. **Washington Hollow** (p.v.) is on the line of Pleasant Valley. There are 4 churches in town.[2]

Acres of Land, Valuation, Population, Dwellings, Families, Freeholders, Schools, Live Stock, Agricultural Products, and Domestic Manufactures, of Dutchess County.

Names of Towns.	Acres of Land.		Valuation of 1858.			Population.		No. of Dwellings.	No. of Families.	Freeholders.	Schools.	
	Improved.	Unimproved.	Real Estate.	Personal Property.	Total.	Males.	Females.				No. of Districts.	Children taught.
Amenia	17,709	6,859	$1,113,550	$274,750	$1,388,300	1,080	1,119	376	409	250	12	732
Beekman	13,003	4,227	544,432	177,550	721,982	678	701	242	269	169	5	402
Clinton	19,635	4,429	511,195	206,830	718,025	940	900	343	390	282	11	652
Dover	17,482	9,187	902,455	206,713	1,109,168	971	954	289	282	161	12	679
East Fishkill	22,511	7,455	876,426	367,307	1,243,733	1,289	1,330	462	495	239	11	881
Fishkill	25,672	4,210	2,164,463	1,265,057	3,429,520	4,244	4,520	1,205	1,602	568	13	3,201
Hyde Park	17,090	5.410	1,321,925	340,600	1,662,525	1,219	1,261	415	207	238	7	821
La Grange	22,528½	3,153	940,209	247,020	1,187,229	904	948	328	360	235	14	819
Milan	18,370½	5,049	472,307	128,576	600,883	812	818	203	330	231	10	663
Northeast	18,056¼	6,193½	770,020	126,400	896,420	875	882	291	336	193	14	763
Pawling	19,076⅜	9,773¾	602,993	271,950	874,943	895	897	324	361	280	10	650
Pine Plains	14,235	3,941	612,687	179,305	791,992	754	699	275	272	150	8	505
Pleasant Valley	17,454½	2,594	626,970	157,200	784,170	915	938	374	269	362	11	750
Poughkeepsie	15,810¾	5,118	1,179,940	333,350	1,513,290	1,549	1,561	502	495	256	9	959
Poughkeepsie City	1,176¾	85	2,177,940	1,925,282	4,103,222	5,936	6,827	1,706	2,436	933	11	4,337
Redhook	19,423	2,725	1,913,974	409,500	2,323,474	1,895	1,855	604	701	292	7	1,274
Rhinebeck	17,387¼	4,379	1,853,905	504,603	2,358,508	1,527	1,538	525	611	335	12	1,097
Stanford	26,067	5,514	1,013,721	237,479	1,251,200	1,107	1,094	403	446	301	15	795
Union Vale	12,000½	2,875½	436,572	70,530	507,102	727	736	255	300	204	9	579
Washington	31,671	4,977	1,134,555	271,500	1,406,055	1,321	1,419	483	510	305	13	887
Total	366,359⅜	98,104¾	21,170,239	7,701,502	28,871,741	29,638	30,997	9,705	10,081	5,984	214	21,446

Names of Towns.	Live Stock.					Agricultural Products.							Domestic cloths, in Yards.
						Bush. of Grain.		Tons of Hay.	Bushels of Potatoes.	Bushels of Apples.	Dairy Products.		
	Horses.	Working Oxen and Calves.	Cows.	Sheep.	Swine.	Winter.	Spring.				Pounds Butter.	Pounds Cheese.	
Amenia	429	1,111	1,592	4,547	1,666	4,619	63,812	5,109	14,716	15,435	85,055	9,866	105
Beekman	317	1,111	796	2,027	1,563	9,597	49,042	3,422	7,530	6,868	56,565	5,497	183
Clinton	658	905	1,359	2,985	3,103	24,747	73,791	3,324	9,715	6,184	122,844	636	328
Dover	283	1,283	1,285	1,480	1,276	2,050	36,077	4,464	9,632	4,431	55,951	3,840	140
East Fishkill	599	1,737	1,681	2,750	2,806	13,694	75,237	5,770	12,318	6,990	150,087	864	139
Fishkill	1,059	1,291	1,646	2,738	2,671	19,718	104,357	7,003	6,779	3,227	105,548	200	
Hyde Park	642	824	1,366	911	2,171	16,535	48,993½	3,867	5,703	11,147	93,550	720	48
La Grange	552	899	1,166	3,418	2,113	23,988	73,818½	4,242	6,129	6,156	89,460	100	155
Milan	506	853	873	4,916	2,300	24,405	48,244½	3,049	11,486	7,716	90,916	1,782	506½
Northeast	455	1,002	1,151	7,497	2,077	10,903	74,939	3,475	18,273	31,511	62,825	8,259	
Pawling	337	1,268	1,479	2,689	1,259	3,061½	30,146½	5,210	18,099	7,999	89,460	950	106
Pine Plains	407	711	678	5,723	2,117	14,914½	46,618¼	2,369	11,005	6,319	39,990	5,188	
Pleasant Valley	476	698	1,067	2,142	1,896	21,487	65,097	3,720½	6,942	5,938	106,785		
Poughkeepsie	660	607	1,819	1,242	2,329	11,183	59,730½	3,610	4,072	1,137	48,058		
Poughkeepsie City	439	48	264		504	592	4,672	354	1,335	330	1,350		
Redhook	654	906	962	3,151	2,204	25,302	53,721	5,729	10,742	14,837	67,900	600	149
Rhinebeck	652	880	1,157	2,141	2,155	17,155½	47,830¼	5,098½	9,699	13,257	75,065		787½
Stanford	661	1,308	1,680	12,116	4,152	25,614	109,180	4,256	14,503	24,898	126,019	8,116	183
Union Vale	326	602	693	3,177	1,192	7,538½	45,099¾	3,146½	6,481	11,392	57,614	1,757	241
Washington	717	1,698	1,870	8,037	3,432	16,430	121,898½	6,660	20,339	30,821	156,553	5,744	122
Total	10,829	19,542	24,584	73,687	42,986	293,534	1,232,305½	83,878½	205,498	216,593	1,681,595	54,119	3,193

[1] The Nine Partners Boarding School was founded at this place in 1796, by the Friends' Yearly Meeting. A farm of 100 acres is attached to it, and it has a cash endowment of $10,000. It is devoted to the education of the children of Friends in indigent circumstances, and for many years it has had an average attendance of 100 pupils.

[2] An Orthodox and a Hicksite Friends at Mechanic, and a M. E. and Prot. E. at Lithgow.

ERIE COUNTY.

This county was formed from Niagara, April 2, 1821. It lies upon Lake Erie and Niagara River, on the w. line of the State, is centrally distant 253 mi. from Albany, and contains 1,071 sq. mi. Its surface is level in the n., rolling in the center, and hilly in the s. A region perfectly flat, and much of it marshy, lies along Tonawanda Creek, and occupies the greater part of the n. tier of towns. This low region is bounded on the s. by a limestone terrace, 20 to 60 ft. high, extending from Black Rock e. through the s. part of Amherst, Clarence, and Newstead. A nearly level region, extending s. from the summit of this ridge, embraces the city of Buffalo and the towns of Chicktowaga, Lancaster, and Alden, and terminates in the rolling region which occupies the entire central part of the co. The ridges in the center and s. have a general n. and s. direction, and rise gradually toward the s., their highest summits attaining an elevation of 200 to 300 ft. above the valleys, 900 to 1,000 ft. above Lake Erie, and 1,400 to 1,600 ft. above tide.[1] The highlands are divided into several distinct ridges by the valleys of Cazenove and Eighteen Mile Creeks. The slopes of the hills are generally long and gradual; but in some places the banks immediately bordering upon the streams are very steep. The land along the lake in the n. is low and level, but in the s. it rises in steep banks to a height of 20 to 50 ft. Niagara River, the outlet of Lake Erie, forms a portion of the w. boundary of the co. Its current flows at the rate of 2½ miles per hour. Grand Island, commencing about 5 miles below Buffalo, divides the river into two nearly equal branches. Squaw, Strawberry, Rattlesnake, Tonawanda, Beaver, and Buckhorn Islands, also in Niagara River, are within the limits of this co. The river is navigable to the head of the rapids, about 2 mi. above Niagara Falls.

Tonawanda Creek[2] forms the n. boundary of the co. It flows in a tortuous course through a low, marshy region. A dam, 4½ ft. high at its mouth, furnishes slack water navigation for the Erie Canal for about 10 miles. Its principal branches are Murder and Ellicott—or Eleven Mile—Creeks. Buffalo Creek[3] enters the lake at Buffalo City, its estuary forming the harbor. Its principal tributaries are Cayuga Creek, from the n., and Cazenove Creek,[4] from the s. The other principal streams are Little Buffalo, Eighteen Mile,[5] Big Sister, and Cattaraugus Creeks, all flowing into the lake, and the last forming the s. boundary of the co.

The lowest rocks are those of the Onondaga salt group; and these are succeeded by the hydraulic, Onondaga, and corniferous limestones. The central part of the co. is occupied by the Marcellus and Hamilton shales, and the summits of the southern hills are covered by the rocks of the Portage group. The rocks of the salt group occupy nearly all the low land below the limestone terrace. They are covered so deep with drift and alluvium, however, that they have but little influence upon the surface, and can never be profitably quarried for commercial purposes. Hydraulic limestone of an excellent quality crops out along the n. base of the limestone terrace, and is extensively quarried. The terrace is composed of Onondaga and corniferous limestone; and along its whole extent are numerous quarries, furnishing an abundance of lime and building stone of excellent quality. Numerous sulphur springs are found near the n. base of the terrace. The shales of the central and southern parts of the co. are generally covered with a thick deposit of drift, and are only visible along the margin of the streams. These rocks furnish an inferior kind of building stone, but are not otherwise valuable.

The soil in the n. is generally a stiff, clay loam interspersed with beds of marl and muck; further s. it is a clay and gravelly loam resting upon limestone. The southern hills are covered with

---

[1] The following heights have been obtained from the surveys of the proposed Buffalo & Pittsburgh R. R.:—
South Wales, 507 ft. above Lake Erie.
Holland Village, 699 ft. " "
Sardinia (summit), 891 ft. " "
Concord ("), 920 ft. " "
The hills generally rise to about 200 feet above the grade of the R. R.

[2] Seneca, *Ta-no'wan-deh*, meaning, "at the rapids or ripples," or perhaps more nearly literally, " at his rapids."

[3] On a map made in 1804 by Joseph Ellicott, agent of the Holland Land Company, this stream is laid down as "*Tos-e-o-*

way" Creek. In an ancient Indian treaty it is called "*Te-ho-se ro-ron.*"

[4] Named from Theophilus Cazenove, agent for the Holland Land Company.

[5] The Seneca name is "*Gaah gwahge-gŭ-aah,*" literally, "it was the residence of the Gaah-gwah people." Leaving off the suffix for the past tense, the name is "Gaah-gwah-gĕh," literally, "Gaah-gwah" place or residence. The Gaah-gwah Indians, or Eries, who formerly resided in this region, are supposed to be the Neuter Nation spoken of by early French writers and sometimes called Cat Indians. The remnant of them now living beyond the Mississippi are called Quawpaws.

279

drift, consisting of clay and gravel. The soil of the valleys is generally a gravelly loam and alluvium.

The principal pursuits in the N. are grain raising, and in the S. stock and wool growing and dairying. The hilly regions are much better adapted to pasturage than tillage. The people of Buffalo and Tonawanda are mostly engaged in commerce and manufactures.[1]

Buffalo is the county seat.[2] The courthouse, situated on the corner of Clinton and Ellicott Sts , is a substantial brick building, containing the court and jury rooms, the office of the co. clerk, and most of the other co. offices.[3] The jail is a small stone building on the same lot. The Erie Co. Penitentiary is located on Fifth St., in Buffalo. The buildings are 5 in number,—the male and female prisons, the workhouse, the warehouse, and the superintendent's dwelling. Prisoners are received from Allegany, Chautauque, Cattaraugus, Wyoming, Genesee, Orleans, and Niagara cos. The average number in confinement is 130.[4] The Erie Co. Poorhouse is located on a farm of 153 acres in the N. E. part of Buffalo. There are 2 buildings,—one designed for use as the poorhouse proper, and the other for the accommodation of the insane. The average number of inmates is 300, supported at a weekly cost of $1.00 each.[5]

The principal works of internal improvement are the Erie Canal, the Rochester & Buffalo, and the Lockport, Niagara Falls and Buffalo branches of the New York Central Rail Road, the Buffalo, New York & Erie. and the Buffalo & Erie Rail Roads,[6] all terminating in the city of Buffalo, and the Canandaigua & Niagara Falls branch of the N. Y. C. R. R., extending through Newstead, Clarence, Amherst, and Tonawanda. A railroad from Buffalo to Pittsburgh is now in process of construction. A pier, lighthouse, and breakwater have been built at the mouth of Buffalo Creek.[7]

With the exception of the Indian Reservation and the Mile Strip, along Niagara River, this co. was all included within the Holland Purchase.[8] The Indian lands, containing 130 sq. mi. and lying upon both sides of Buffalo Creek, at its mouth, were purchased in parcels, at different times; and the whole territory is now thickly settled. ·The first settlements were made at Buffalo, about 1794–95, and in other places within a few years after. The generous outlays made by the Holland Company in the construction of roads, bridges, mills, &c. led to a rapid occupation of all the best lands in the co.[9] On the morning of the 30th of Dec., 1813, a British force of about 1,000 men crossed over from Canada and captured Black Rock and Buffalo. The American forces then stationed at these places were superior to the British in point of numbers; but the officers were not qualified for command, and a large share of the militia fled upon the commencement of the action. The village of Buffalo was burned in retaliation of the wanton destruction of Newark, in Canada, by the Americans under Gen. George McClure, (then of Steuben co.,) a short time before.[10] The finishing of the Erie Canal and of the N. Y. Central R. R. tended greatly to develop the resources of the co., and to convert Buffalo, its chief city, into the greatest commercial place on the upper lakes.

The first newspaper in the co. was established in 1811.[11]

---

[1] See pages 285.

[2] By the act of March 11, 1808, erecting the co. of Niagara, Buffalo was named the co. seat, on condition that the Holland Land Company deed to the county not less than half an acre of land for a site for the public buildings, and erect thereon a courthouse and jail. The company complied with these conditions, and erected, in 1810, a wooden courthouse and a stone jail. In the mean time the courts were held at the house of Joseph Landon. The courthouse was burned by the British in 1813. Soon after the close of the war, a new one was erected on Washington St., fronting La Fayette Park. The first officers of Erie co. were Sam'l Wilkeson, *First Judge;* John G. Camp, *Sheriff;* James L. Barton, *Co. Clerk;* and Roswell Chapin, *Surrogate.*

[3] The present courthouse was built in 1850, at a cost of $18,000. The commissioners under whose supervision it was erected were Albert H. Tracy, Ralph Plumb, and Timothy A. Hopkins.

[4] The penitentiary lot contains 5 acres, and is enclosed by a stone wall 14 ft. in height. The male prison is built of stone, and the other buildings of brick. Four-fifths of all the convicts are of foreign birth. They are maintained at an average weekly expense of 65 cts., and are employed principally in the manufacture of harness findings, upon contract,—the males at 20 cents per day, and the females at 15.

[5] The poorhouse was built in 1852, under the supervision of Silas Kingsley, at a cost of $30,000. It consists of an octagonal center, 75 ft. in diameter, with 2 wings, each 80 ft. long by 40 ft. wide; the whole 3 stories high and built of stone. Of the inmates in 1857, 71 were lunatics and 11 idiots.

[6] The main lines of the N. Y. Central and the Buffalo, N. Y. & Erie R. Roads extend through Alden, Lancaster, and Chicktowaga; the Lockport & N. F. branch of the N. Y. Central, through Tonawanda; and the B. & State Line R. R., through

West Seneca, Hamburgh, Evans, and Brandt. The Buffalo & Brantford (Canada) R. R. terminates opposite Buffalo.

[7] See page 284.

[8] See page 321.

[9] A large share of the later settlers of the co. have been Germans; and this class of people now constitute about one-fifth of the entire population of the co. The population of several of the towns in the immediate vicinity of Buffalo is almost exclusively German.

[10] The loss at Buffalo was reported at 66 frame, 1 stone, and 2 brick houses, 16 stores and offices, 35 barns, and 15 shops, valued together at $190,000; at Black Rock, 16 frame and 11 log houses, 8 barns, and 5 outhouses, valued at $19,000; and at other places 20 frame and 67 log houses, 5 stores, 29 barns, 16 shops, &c., worth $141,000. Total, 334 buildings, worth $350,000, not including the buildings of the Messrs. Porter.—*Albany Argus, April 22,* 1814.

[11] *The Buffalo Gazette,* the first paper in the county, was commenced Oct. 3, 1811, by S. H. & H. A. Salisbury. It was removed to Harris Hill in 1813, and back to Buffalo in the spring of 1814. In April, 1819, H. A Salisbury became sole proprietor, and changed the name to
The Niagara Patriot. On the erection of Erie co. in 1820 it was changed to
The Buffalo Patriot. It was successively under the editorial charge of Wm. A. Carpenter, Harvey Newcomb, and Guy H. Salisbury.
The Daily Commercial Advertiser was issued from the same office, Jan. 1, 1835. Soon after, Dr. T. M. Foote and B. A. Manchester became associated in the management of the two papers; and in Aug. 1838, the Aurora Standard was merged in them, and A. M. Clapp, its publisher, became one of the proprietors of the joint con-

ALDEN—was formed from Clarence, March 27, 1823, and a part of Marilla was taken off in 1853. It lies upon the E. border of the co., N. E. of the center. Its surface in the w. is level, and

cern. In May, 1839, they were united with the Buffalo Journal, and the weekly was published as **The Patriot and Journal**, and the daily as *The Commercial Advertiser and Journal*, by E. R. Jewett & Co. The following year the daily appeared as **The Buffalo Commercial Advertiser**, and under these titles the papers are still published, under the editorial charge of Dr. S. B. Hunt. Since 1856 a semi-weekly Commercial Advertiser has been issued.

The Niagara Journal was established in July, 1815, by David M. Day; and in 1820 its name was changed to *The Buffalo Journal*. In 1834 it passed into the hands of E. J. Roberts, and in 1835 it was suspended.

The Buffalo Whig was established in 1834 by D. M. Day; and in 1835 it was united with the Buffalo Journal, and appeared as *The Buffalo Whig and Journal*. Jan. 1, 1838, M. Cadwallader and Dr. H. R. Stagg were associated with Day, and in Feb. they issued *The Buffalo Daily Journal*. In 1838 the establishment passed into the hands of E. R. Jewett, by whom the papers were united the following year with the Buffalo Patriot and the Commercial Advertiser.

The Gospel Advocate (Univ.) was begun in 1822 by Rev. Thomas Gross. In 1823 Simeon Bunton, and in 1826 Revs. L. S. Everett, Theophilus Fisk, and M. Tuttle, became proprietors. In 1828 it was removed to Auburn.

The Black Rock Beacon was published by L. G. Hoffman from 1822 to 1824.

The Buffalo Emporium was issued in 1824 by J. A. Lazelle and Simeon Francis, and continued about 5 years.

The Black Rock Gazette was begun in 1824 by Bartemus Ferguson, who disposed of it to S. H. Salisbury in 1825. In 1827 it was removed to Buffalo, and its name changed to *The Buffalo and Black Rock Gazette*. It was discontinued in 1828.

The Black Rock Advocate was begun in Feb. 1826, and was published 1 year by Dan'l P. Adams.

The Western Advertiser, after an existence of 3 months, was merged in the Buffalo Patriot in the spring of 1828.

The Buffalo Republican was commenced in April, 1828, by W. P. M. Wood. It was successively under the charge of S. H. Salisbury & W. S. Snow, S. H. Salisbury, H. L. Ball, Chas. Faxon & Jas. Stryker, and Chas. Faxon. In 1835 the Buffalo Bulletin was merged in the Republican, and the Daily Star was bought by Faxon and continued under its old name. Horatio Gates and W. L. Crandall were successively editors. In Dec. 1838 the office was burned and the papers were suspended; but the weekly was resumed by Quartus Graves in 1839. Jan. 1, 1842, Henry Burwell, then proprietor, changed its name to *The Democratic Economist;* and in Oct. following Joseph Stringman succeeded, and changed it to *The Mercantile Courier and Democratic Economist*. In Feb. 1843, it appeared as *The Buffalo Courier and Economist;* and in March as *The Buffalo Courier*. July 1, 1846, it was united with The Pilot, and *The Courier and Pilot*, d., tri-w., and w., was published by Stringman, Manchester & Brayman. In Dec. it was changed to **The Buffalo Courier**, its present title. It has passed successively through the hands of Robt. D. Foy & Co., Seaver & Foy, Wm. A. Seaver, Seaver & Sandford, and to J. H. Sandford, its present publisher.

The Buffalo Bulletin was issued in 1830, and was published by Horace Steel 4 years, by James Faxon 1 year, and was united with The Republican in 1835.

The Daily Star was commenced in 1834 by Jas. Faxon, and in 1835 it was united with Tho Republican.

The National Pilot was started in Feb. 1845, by Manchester & Brayman, and was united with The Courier in July, 1846.

The Warning, semi-mo., was published in 1828 by Rev. J. B. Hyde.

The Buffalo Herald, (Presb.,) edited by Rev. Randolph Stone in 1831, only reached its second number.

The Gospel Banner was begun in 1832 by Benj. Clark, and continued 2 years.

The Philanthropist, mo., was started in 1832 by Nathaniel Potter, jr., and continued 1 year.

The Examiner, mo., (Unit.,) was published in 1833.

The Literary Enquirer, semi-mo., commenced Jan. 1, 1833, was published 2 years by Wm. Verrinder.

The Transcript, d. and w., commenced in Aug. 1835, by Henry Faxon, was continued only 6 months.

The Young Men's Temperance Herald was started in 1835 by A. P. Grosvenor & E. B. French, and continued 1 year.

The Daily Enquirer, *The Daily Whig*, and *The Loco Foco* were campaign papers issued in 1835.

The Buffalo Spectator (Presb.) was started in 1836 by J. & W. Butler, and continued 2 years.

The Bethel Magazine, mo., was commenced by the Bethel Society in 1836. It was afterward changed to

The Bethel Flag, and in 1846 united with the Sailors' Magazine, of New York.

The Buffalonian, w. at first and d. afterward, was published about a year; and in 1838 it was united with *The Mercury*. This paper was continued until 1840 by T. L. Nichols and R. Simpson successively.

Der Weltbuerger was started in 1837 by Geo. Zahm, and was published successively by him, by his administrators, and by Brunck & Domidion. In 1853 it was united with The Buffalo Democrat, and took the name of **The Buffalo Democrat and Weltbuerger**, d. and w., by which title it is now published by Brunck, Held & Co.

The Buffalo Democrat (German) was started in 1850 by Chas. de Haas; and in 1853 it was united with The Weltbuerger.

The Sun, d. and w., was issued in the winter of 1838, and was published 1 year by Abraham Densmore and E. H. Eastabrook successively.

The Moon, a penny daily, was issued during the summer of 1839.

Bristol's Gazette and Herald of Health, mo., was commenced in 1839 by C. C. Bristol. The next year it appeared as *Bristol's Gazette*, and was discontinued in 1842.

The Friend of Youth, mo., was started in 1839 by Rev. A. T. Hopkins, and was published 1 year.

The Buffalo Sentinel, d. and w., was published during the summer of 1839 by Thomas Newell.

The Morning Tattler, d., was started in 1840 by Langdon, Fouchette & Shaeffer. Its name was changed to *The Morning Times*, by J. S. Walker, and it was discontinued soon after.

Der Volks Schild was published by F. H. Singer during the summer of 1840.

The Phalanx, d. and w., was published 6 weeks in 1840 by C. D. Ferris.

The Buffalo Garland was published in 1840 by Geo. W. Bungay.

Honest Industry was published in 1840 by Dr. Daniel Lee.

The Volksfreund (German) was published in 1840 by Adolphus Meyer.

The Western Presbyterian was issued in March, 1841, by Rev. J. C. Lord, and continued 1 year.

The Western Literary Messenger, semi-mo., was started in July, 1841, by J. S. Chadbourne. C. D. Ferris, Jesse Clement, Chas. Faxon, and E. R. Jewett, at different times, were interested in its publication. From 1842 it was published weekly until 1857, when it was discontinued.

Bannister's Life in Buffalo was published a few weeks in 1841 by N. H. Bannister.

The Sublime Patriot, semi-mo., was published during the winter of 1841–42 by T. J. Southerland.

The Buffalo American was started in 1842 by T. Foster & C. F. Butler, and continued 1 year.

The Old School Jeffersonian and The Daily Gazette were published from 1842 to '43 by Charles Faxon.

The Temperance Standard was published in 1842 by H. H. Salisbury & A. M. Clapp.

The School Reader was published about 3 months in 1842 by A. W. Wilgus.

Prescott's Telegraph was published in 1842 by W. Prescott.

The Buffalo Gazette, d. and w., was started in 1843 by H. A. Salisbury, B. A. Manchester & J. O. Brayman, and continued 3 years.

The Freimüthige (German) was started Jan. 1843, by Alexander Krause & Adolphus Meyer, and continued 2 years.

The Telegraph, da. and w., (German), was started in Nov. 1845, by H. B. Miller. Louis Tickers, Adolphus Hilman, and C. Essellen have successively had the editorial charge. It is now published by P. H. Bender, and edited by C. Essellen.

The Buffalo Medical Journal and Monthly Review of Medical and Surgical Science was started in June, 1845, by Dr. Austin Flint. In 1853 Dr. S. B. Hunt became associated in its management, and in 1855 its sole proprietor. In 1858 it passed into the hands of Dr. Austin Flint, jr., its present proprietor.

The Western Cataract was started in 1845 by L. P. Judson. Jas. Dubois, W. B. Williams, and Chauncey Hulburt were successively editors. In Jan. 1847, it was changed to *The Western Temperance Standard*, and was discontinued the following year.

The Impetus was started in 1845 by E. W. Spaulding, and continued 6 months.

The Morning Express was started Jan. 14, 1846, by A. M. Clapp & Co. In 1855 The Daily Democracy was united with The Express, and it appeared as **The Buffalo Morning Express and Daily Democracy**, by which name it is now published. A weekly and tri-weekly edition are also issued.

The Democracy, d. and w., was started in May, 1854, by G. W. Haskins. The Rough Notes was merged in The Democracy soon after; and in Aug. 1855, The Democracy was united with The Express.

The Rough Notes, d., was started in March, 1852, by Geo. Reese

in the E. gently undulating. It is watered by the head waters of Cayuga and Eleven Mile Creeks. The soil is a deep, fertile, sandy, gravelly, and clayey loam. **Alden,** (p. v.,) a station on the B. & N. Y. R. R., contains 2 churches and has a pop. of 285; **Alden Center** (p. v.) contains 1 church and 20 houses; and **Mill Grove,** (p. v.,) in the N. W. corner, 18 houses. **Alden** (Crittenden p. o.) and **Wende** are stations on the N. Y. C. R. R. Settlement was commenced in the spring of 1810, by Moses Fenno.[1] Rev. John Spencer conducted the first religious services, in 1811. The first church (Presb.) was organized in 1813–14. There are now 6 churches in town.[2]

AMHERST[3]—was formed from Buffalo, April 10, 1818; and Chicktowaga was taken off in 1839. It lies upon the N. border of the co., between Clarence and Tonawanda. Its surface is level. Eleven Mile and Ransoms Creeks flow across the town in a N. E. direction; and Tona- wanda Creek forms its N. boundary. The soil is a sandy and clayey loam. Upon the land of John Foglesonger, in the S. part of the town, is a very copious sulphur spring. A gristmill with 3 run of stone has been built on the stream formed by it. A ledge of limestone extends across the S. part of the town, from which limestone is quarried in various places. Beneath this ledge is a layer of hydraulic limestone, which is extensively quarried at Williamsville and burned for waterlime. **Williamsville,**[4] (p. v.,) incorp. in 1850, is situated on Eleven Mile Creek, in the S. part of the town. It contains 4 churches, an academy,[5] and several manufactories.[6] Pop.

In 1854 Rann & Cowan became proprietors, and the same year it was united with The Democracy.

The Western Evangelist (Univ.) was started in June, 1846, by Rev. L. S. Everett, and continued 1 year.

The Ambassador, (Univ.,) started the same year, was removed to Auburn in 1847.

The Journal of Commerce, d., was started in 1847 by John W. Jones, and continued 6 months.

The Republic, d. and w., was started by Livingston, Albro & Co., Jan. 26, 1847. Quartus Graves, Maynard & Welsh, C. A. Kellogg, and C. C. Bristol were successively inter- rested in its management. In 1857 The Buffalo Daily Times was united with The Republic, and it was issued as **The Buffalo Republic and Times,** d., tri-w., and w. Guy. H. Salisbury is the present proprietor. A campaign paper was published in connection with this paper in 1856.

The Buffalo Daily Times was started in Aug. 1857, by the Times Association; and the next year it was united with The Republic.

Der Freie Demokrat was published in 1848.

The Wool Grower and Magazine of Agriculture and Horticulture, mo., was started in 1849 by T. C. Peters, and continued until 1852.

The Daily Queen City, a penny paper, was started in 1850 by G. J. Bryan. The title was changed in 1852 to **The Buffalo Evening Post,** under which name it is now published.

The Buffalo Christian Advocate was started in Jan. 1850, by John E. Robie. In 1857 it was changed to **The Advocate,** under which name it is now published.

Common Sense was published in 1850 by D. P. Stile.

Die Aurora, w. and semi-w., was started in 1850 by Chris- tian Wieckmann, its present publisher.

Das Kirchliche Informatorium, semi-mo., was started in July, 1851, by Conrad Bär; and in 1854 T. Andr. A. Grabau, its present editor, assumed its charge.

The Sunday Bulletin was started in 1851 by Wm. F. Rodgers, and continued 9 months.

The Youth's Casket, mo., was started in 1851 by Beadle & Vanderzee. It is now published by Robt. Adams.

The American Miller was published in 1851 by Wm. C. Hughes.

The Evangelical Christian was published in 1851 by Geo. Stanbro & Co.

The American Celt and Catholic Citizen was brought from Bos- ton, Mass., to Buffalo in June, 1852, and continued until May, 1853, when it was removed to New York.

Die Homœopath and Diœtetischer Hansfreund was started in 1852 by Conrad Bär, and continued 1 year.

Sonntags Blatt was started in 1852 by Brunck, Held & Co., and continued 1 year.

The Sunday Visitor was started in 1852 by Reed & Moore, and continued 1 year.

The United States Mail, mo., was published in 1852 by Jewett, Thomas & Co.

The Buffalo Daily Ledger was published a few months in 1852 by T. Richardson.

The Pathfinder was published in 1852 by Charles Faxon.

The Sunday Herald was published about 3 months in 1853 by Geo. W. Weeks.

The School and House Friend, semi-mo., (German,) was started in March, 1853, by Conrad Bär, and continued 1 year.

The Library and Garden was published in 1853 by D. S. Manly & Co.

The Buffalo Catholic Sentinel was started in June, 1853, by Michael Hagan, its present publisher.

Illustrirte Abend Schule, semi-mo., was published in 1854 by Rev. C. Dichlman.

The Atlantis, mo., (German,) brought from Cleveland, Ohio, to Buffalo in 1856, is edited by C. Essellen.

The American Rights was published from Sept. 1854, to July, 1855, by Geo. Reese & Co.

The Age of Progress, conducted by Stephen Albro, was com- menced in 1854 and discontinued in 1858.

The Zeitschrift was published about 4 months in 1854 by Conrad Bär.

Zeichen der Zeit, mo., was started in June, 1855, by —— Drexler. In 1858 T. Gottlieb Ade became its editor.

The Home has been published since Jan. 1856, by E. F. Beadle.

The Buffalo Allegemeine Zeitung, w. and semi- w., was started in May, 1856, by Frederick Reinecke, the present publisher.

The Buffalo Patriot, d., (German,) was published during the campaign of 1856 by Voght & Jung.

Das Historische Zeitblatt und Literarischer Anzeiger, mo., was started in May, 1857, by Conrad Bär, its present publisher.

The Home Monthly was started Jan. 1, 1859, under the editorial charge of Mrs. H. E. G. Arey and Mrs. —— Gildersleve.

The Inventor's Advertiser was published at Buffalo by Thos. P. How.

The Aurora Democrat was established at West Aurora in Oct 1835, by Deloss E. Sill, publisher, and continued about 1 year.

The Aurora Standard was started at East Aurora Aug. 1, 1835, by A. M. Clapp. In 1838 it was removed to Buffalo and merged in the Buffalo Commercial Advertiser.

The Springville Express was commenced in May, 1844, by Edwin. Hough, and continued until the fall of 1848.

The Springville Herald was established in May, 1850, by E. D. Webster; and in Dec. 1856, it passed into the hands of J. B. Saxe, its present publisher.

The American Citizen was started at Springville in Feb. 1856, by Lucius C. Sanders, and continued nearly a year.

The Tonawanda Commercial was started at Tonawanda in 1846 by Sylvester Hoyt, and continued about a year.

The Niagara River Pilot was commenced at Tonawanda in 1853 by Packard & Foxlonger. In Aug. 1856, it passed into the hands of S. O. Hayward, by whom, in Nov. 1857, it was changed to **The Niagara Frontier,** under which name it is still published.

The Mental Elevator was published a short time in the Seneca language.

[1] Among the first settlers were Joseph Freeman, John Easta- brook, Wm. Snow, and Arunah Hibbard, who came in 1810; Saml. Slade, James Crocker, Saml. Huntington, and Jonas Stick- ney, who came in 1811; and Wm. Dayton, who came in 1812. The first birth was that of a daughter of Arunah Hibbard; and the first death, that of Polly Cransaky, in 1812. John Rogers built the first sawmill, in 1813 or '14, and the first gristmill, in 1817. Amos Bliss kept the first inn, and Seth Eastabrook the first store, both in 1816. The first school was taught by Mehe- tabel Eastabrook, in 1815.

[2] Bap., Presb., Evang. Luth., M. E., and 2 R. C.

[3] Named in honor of Lord Amherst, commander of the English forces in America in 1759–60.

[4] Named from Jonas Williams, one of the early settlers.

[5] The Williamsville Classical Institute. The whole number of students for the year 1857 was 222.

[6] A gristmill, a sawmill, a tannery, a furnace, a broom factory, a chair factory, and a waterlime mill, the last producing 3,000 to 6,000 bbls. of hydraulic cement per year.

1,166. Eggertsville, Getzville, East Amherst, and **Westwood** are p. offices. The first settlement was made in 1804, by Timothy S. Hopkins and Elias Ransom, from Great Barrington, Mass.[1] There are 9 churches in town.[2]

AURORA—was formed from Batavia, as "*Willink*," April 11, 1804. Its name was changed April 15, 1818. Clarence was taken off in 1808, Buffalo in 1810, Concord, Hamburgh, and Eden in 1812, Holland and Wales in 1818, and a part of Elma in 1857. It occupies nearly a central position in the co. Its surface is rolling in the N. and hilly in the S. The declivities of the hills are generally gradual slopes, and their summits are 150 to 300 feet above the valleys. The principal streams are Cazenove Creek and its branches. The soil is gravelly loam in the valleys and clayey among the hills. **Willink,** (p. v.,) incorp. Dec. 29, 1849, is situated on the E. branch of Cazenove Creek, in the N. part of the town. It contains 2 churches and a woolen factory and has a pop. of 365. **East Aurora,** (p. v.,) about 1 mi. E. of Willink, contains 2 churches, an academy,[3] and several manufacturing establishments. Pop. 360. **West Falls,** (p. v.,) on the w. bank of Cazenove Creek, in the S. part of the town, contains 1 church, 2 sawmills, a gristmill, and about 30 houses; and **Griffins Mills,** (p. v.,) on the same stream, near the center of the town, contains 1 church, a sawmill, a gristmill, and 25 houses. The first settlement was made in the fall of 1803, by Jabez Warren, Henry Godfrey, and Nath'l Emerson.[4] The evidences of ancient Indian occupation were plainly visible upon the advent of the whites.[5] The first church (Bap.) was organized with 16 members, in 1810, by Elder Irish. There are 7 churches in town.[6] Ex-Pres. Millard Fillmore and Hon N. K. Hall, Judge of Supreme Court and Ex-P. M. Gen., were for some years residents of East Aurora.

BOSTON—was formed from Eden, April 5, 1817. It is an interior town, lying S. of the center of the co. Its surface is a hilly upland, broken by the valley of the N. branch of Eighteen Mile Creek, which flows N. w. through near the center of the town. The valley of this stream is about three-fourths of a mile wide. In this valley the soil is a fine, fertile loam, and upon the hills it is a gravelly and clayey loam. **Boston,** (p. v.,) on the N. branch of Eighteen Mile Creek, contains 3 churches, 2 gristmills, 2 sawmills, a tannery, a cow-bell factory, and 40 houses; **Boston Center,** (Patchin p. o.,) on the same stream, contains 2 churches, a sawmill, and 20 houses; and **North Boston,** (p. v.,) 1 church, a gristmill, a sawmill, and 20 houses. The first settlement was made by Didemus Kinney, in 1803.[7] The first religious services were conducted by Rev. John Spencer, in 1810. There are 7 churches in town.[8]

BRANDT[9]—was formed from Collins and Evans, March 25, 1839. It lies upon the shore of Lake Erie, in the S. w. corner of the co. The surface is generally level, with a gentle inclination toward the lake. Cattaraugus Creek forms a part of the S. boundary. The other principal streams are Big Sister, Delaware, and Muddy Creeks. The soil is generally a gravelly loam intermixed with clay. **Brandt** (p. v.) contains 20 houses. **Mill Branch** (Farnham p. o.) is the **Saw Mill Station** on the B. & E. R. R., and contains 30 houses. The first settlement was made in 1817, by Moses Tucker.[10] The first religious services were conducted by Benj. Olmsted, in 1820. A union church is the only one in town.

---

[1] Among the early settlers were Wm. Maltbury, Jonas Williams, James Harmon, Horatio Kelsey, Seth Canfield, Enos A. Armstrong, and Jas. Harris. The first sawmill was built in 1801, by —— Thomson; and the first gristmill, by Wm. Maltbury, in 1808. Elias Ransom kept the first inn, in 1805, and Juba Storrs & Co. the first store, in 1812.

[2] Bap., Disciples, M. E., and Germ. Cath. at Williamsville, and 2 Evang. Luth., Free, Mennonite, and R. C. in other parts of the town.

[3] The Aurora Manual Labor Seminary was chartered Oct. 18, 1833; and in 1838 its name was changed to the Aurora Academy. The manual labor department was long since abandoned.

[4] These were followed by Joel and John Adams, Tabor Earlle, and Humphrey Smith, in 1804, and Wm. Warren, Thos. Tracy, Christopher Stone, and Luther Hibbard, in 1805. The first birth was that of Orra Warren, in Dec. 1805; and the first death, that of a daughter of Humphrey Smith, in 1806. Phineas Stevens built the first sawmill, in 1806, and the first gristmill, in 1807. Gen. Wm. Warren kept the first inn, in 1806, and Adams & Hascall the first store, in 1808. The first school was taught by Mary Eddy, in 1806.

[5] Two hills, in the N. part of the town, were fortified by circular breastworks, in many places 6 to 8 ft. high. Human bones, of almost giant size, have been dug up near the fortifications; and pieces of pottery and iron axes have been found in the vicinity.—*Letter of Rev. Asher Wright.* In 1809 an ancient copper plate, 12 by 16 inches, covered with letters or hieroglyphics, was plowed up upon the land of Ephraim Woodruff,

in Aurora: the finders, not knowing its value as a specimen of antiquity, converted it into a dipper and skimmer.—*Turner's Hol. Pur.*, p. 668.

[6] 2 Presb., Bap., Cong., M. E., Univ., and R. C.

[7] Oliver and Charles Johnson settled in the town in 1805, and Richard Cary and Sam'l Eaton in 1807. The first birth was that of Phinney Johnson, in 1806; the first marriage, that of David Stannard and Esther Yaw, in 1810; and the first death, that of Joel Beebe, in 1809. Ethan Howard built the first mill, in 1810; Job Palmer kept the first inn, in 1811; and Aaron J. Tupper the first store, the same year. The first school was taught by Joel Eddy, in 1810.

[8] Bap., Free Will Bap., Evang. Luth., Friends, M. E., Meth. Prot., and Univ.

[9] Named from Col. Joseph Brant, the Mohawk chief. His Indian name was "*Tha-yan-da-nee-gah*," said to signify "wood partly burned," or "a brand;" and as the Indians are unable to distinguish d from t in their pronunciation, it became Brant.—*Asher Wright, Missionary at the Cattaraugus Reservation.*

[10] John, Robert, and Major Campbell, and John West, settled in the town in 1808, and Ansel Smith, Robt. and Wm. Grannis, and Benj. Olmsted, in 1819. The first birth was that of a son of John West, in 1818; the first marriage, that of Levi Grannis and Leah Hallida, in 1819; and the first death, that of Matthew West, in 1822. The first mill was built by Sam'l Butts, in 1822; the first inn was kept by Josephus Hubbard, in 1825; and the first store, by Milton Morse, in 1835. Julia Bradley taught the first school, in 1823.

BUFFALO CITY—was formed as a town from Clarence, Feb. 8, 1810.[1] Amherst was taken off in 1818, and Tonawanda in 1836. Buffalo Village was incorp. April 2, 1813, re-organized in 1815, and again in 1822, and incorp. as a city April 20, 1832, with its limits enlarged by the addition of that part of the Mile Strip Reservation[2] s. of York and North Sts. By the provisions of a new charter, granted April 13, 1853, the then town of "*Black Rock*" was included within the city limits. The city lies at the E. extremity of Lake Erie, extending nearly 10 mi. along the lake shore and the upper part of Niagara River, and occupies an area of about 40 sq. mi. The principal streams are Big Buffalo and Scajaquady[3] Creeks,—the former emptying into Lake Erie and the latter into Niagara River. The principal business part of the city is on the lake shore around the harbor. The land in this locality is low, and was once considered "an irreclaimable morass; but it is now densely covered with substantial warehouses and large stores, intermingled with factories, foundries, mechanics' shops, and dwellings."[4]

The site rises gradually, and attains in one or two places an elevation of about 100 ft.; but the greater portion of the area occupies an extended plain of an average height of 50 ft. above the lake. On the "*Buffalo Plains*," and along the river at North Buffalo, are extensive quarries of limestone, furnishing an excellent building material.[5] The city is regularly laid out, and the streets are broad and straight. The flagging and paving are done in the most substantial manner, and are kept in excellent repair.[6] The main part of the city is supplied with wholesome water from Niagara River by the Buffalo Water Works Company. The reservoir, situated on Niagara between Connecticut and Vermont Sts., is 88 ft. higher than the river, and has a capacity of 13,500,000 gallons. The water is elevated by two force pumps, each of a capacity of 235 gallons, and is distributed through 31 mi. of pipe.[7] Lower Black Rock is supplied by the Jubilee Water Works with water obtained from the Jubilee Springs. It is conducted through wooden pipes, of which there are more than two miles laid.[8] There are 5 post-offices in the city,—Buffalo, North Buffalo, Buffalo Plains, Red Jacket, and Black Rock.

The harbor of Buffalo is formed by Big Buffalo Creek, along which for more than a mile is a continuous line of wharves. A pier extends from the s. side of the harbor 1500 ft. into the lake, forming an effectual barrier against the encroaching sands, which everywhere on the lake have a tendency to accumulate on the w. side of piers. At its extremity is a lighthouse.[9] The Erie Canal enters the city along Niagara River, from which it is separated by a seawall, and extends southward to near the mouth of Buffalo Creek, and thence eastward to Hamburgh St. The Erie Basin, just N. of the mouth of Buffalo Creek, protected lakeward by a breakwater, and the Ohio Basin, about one and one-fourth mi. from the mouth of the creek, containing an area of 10 acres, are both connected with the harbor and canal and are sufficiently deep to float the largest lake vessels.[10] A ship canal more than a mi. in length extends along the w. side of Big Buffalo Creek parallel to the shore of the lake. This canal, the basins, the Erie Canal, and the harbor are all connected by numerous slips. Six railroads terminate in the city; and another—the Buffalo & Pittsburgh—is in process of construction.[11]

---

[1] The city of Buffalo was taken off in 1832, and Tonawanda in 1836. The village of "*Black Rock*," in this town, was incorp. April 24, 1837, and receives its name from the color of the rock which outcrops at the ferry landing. The remaining part of the town was organized as Black Rock, Feb. 14, 1839; and in 1853 it was annexed to the city.   [2] See p. 280.

[3] Named from an Indian of that name, and pronounced Ska-joc'quad-da.

[4] *Buffalo City Directory*, 1858.

[5] The pier, the breakwater, the arsenal, St. Joseph's Cathedral, and many of the most substantial buildings in the city, are in part or wholly built of this stone.

[6] There are 251 mi. of located streets within the city limits, 37½ mi. of paved streets, 205,000 lineal or feet of stone sidewalks, and 108 mi. of plank walks. There are 1,960 street lamps in the city, lighted by gas furnished by the Buffalo Gas Light Company. The present cost of the street improvements is estimated at $2,000,000; and the aggregate of taxes for local improvements in 1857 was $356.913.

[7] The Buffalo Water Works Company was incorp. March 15, 1849. The original cost of the works was $400,000; and $65,000 of the earnings have been expended in extending the works. Connected with them are 320 street hydrants, and 20 underground reservoirs, having an aggregate capacity of 407,850 gal.

[8] The Jubilee Water Works Company was organized in 1827, with a capital of $20,000. At one time the company had 16 mi.

of wooden pipe laid, fully supplying Black Rock and a part of Buffalo; but, while the increase of population created a greater demand for water, the supply from the springs diminished, and in 1845 the citizens of Lower Black Rock purchased the works and confined the supply to their own village.

[9] The lighthouse is built entirely of stone and iron. It is 44 ft. high, 26 ft. in diameter at its base, and 12 ft. at the top. The molehead upon which it stands is 160 ft. in diameter and has a depth of 15 ft. below the surface of the water. The pier and lighthouse were completed in 1833. It is furnished with a first class dioptric Fresnel apparatus.

[10] These basins were constructed by the State as parts of the great system of internal navigation; but their sites were furnished by the city. The Erie Basin cost $300,000, and the Ohio Basin $60,000. They were commenced in 1848 and finished in 1858. Vessels driven by storms and failing to gain an entrance to the harbor find a capacious and sheltered retreat in the harbor of Black Rock,—formed by a mole from Bird Island to Squaw Island, a distance of 2915 yards. This, with the islands, forms a harbor 4,565 yards long and from 88 to 220 yards wide, with an area of 136 acres. Besides affording an exceedingly convenient harbor, with an average depth of 15 feet, this work secures a water-power of about 4½ ft. A ship lock is constructed at its foot; and it is on the line of the Erie Canal.

[11] Besides these, 5 plank roads, a macadamized road, and a turnpike terminate in the city.

Buffalo is the second commercial city of the State, and the largest and most important upon the great lakes.[1] Its situation at the foot of navigation upon Lake Erie and at the western terminus of the Erie Canal makes it the principal port for the transhipment of the products of the great grain region of the Upper Mississippi Valley, and gives to it the command of the greater part of the commerce of the lakes.[2] The number of entries at this port during the year 1857 was 4,017, with an aggregate of 1,618,672 tons; and the number of clearances was 3,564, with an aggregate of 1,603,134 tons.[3] The exportation and importation by canal is also immense;[4] and it is estimated

[1] It is often called "The Queen City," and "The Queen City of the Lakes."

[2] The amount of grain received in 1857 was 15,443,778 bush., and of flour 925,411 bbls., of which 15,348,930 bush. of grain and 845,953 bbls. of flour were received by lake. The same year there were received by lake 29,799 head of cattle, 75,174 hogs, and 44,972 sheep. The following table shows the imports, by lake, of flour and grain for a series of years:—

Year.	Flour.	Wheat.	Corn.	Oats.	Barley.	Rye.
1836...	139,178	304,090	204,355	28,640	4,876	1,500
1837...	126,805	450,350	94,490	2,553		3,267
1838...	277,620	933,117	34,148	6,577		909
1839...	294,125	1,117,262				
1840...	597,742	1,004,561	71,327			
1841...	730,040	1,635,000	201,031	14,144		2,150
1842...	734,308	1,555,430	454,530		4,710	1,228
1843...	917,517	1,827,241	223,963	2,489		1,332
1844...	915,030	2,177,500	137,978	18,017	1,617	456
1845...	746,750	1,770,740	54,200	23,100		
1846...	1,374,529	4,744,184	1,455,258	218,300	47,530	28,250
1847...	1,857,000	6,489,100	2,862,300	446,000		70,787
1848...	1,249,000	4,520,117	2,298,100	560,000		17,809
1849...						
1850...	1,103,039	3,681,346	2,593,378	359,580	3,600	
1851...	1,258,224	4,167,121	5,988,775	1,140,340	142,773	10,652
1852...	1,299,513	5,549,778	5,136,746	2,596,231	497,913	112,271
1853...	975,557	5,424,043	3,665,793	1,480,655	401,098	107,152
1854...	739,756	3,510,792	10,109,973	4,441,739	313,885	177,066
1855...	936,761	8,022,126	9,711,230	2,693,222	62,304	299,591
1856...	1,126,048	8,465,671	9,632,477	1,733,382	46,327	245,810
1857...	845,953	8,334,179	5,713,611	1,214,760	37,844	48,536

The annual average receipts of flour during the first five years was about 360,000 bbls.; during the next five it was 820,000; during the next five, 1,474,000; and during the next five, 969,000. The whole amount of grain received in 1847 was 9,668,187 bush., and in 1855 20,788,475 bush.,—the greatest amount in any one year. This was a greater amount than was received that year in any other port in the world. The following table shows the receipts of leading articles during three seasons:—

	1855.	1856.	1857.
Ashes, casks...............	4,295	3,255	2,975
Beef, bbls.................	97,804	33,320	59,911
Broom Corn, bales......	9,725	7,366	5,086
Barley, bush.............	62,304	46,327	37,844
Butter, lbs...............	1,988,920	1,241,600	923,000
Bacon, lbs................	10,768,396	9,220,932	3,612,519
Cattle, No................	14,049	25,283	29,799
Cranberries, bbls.......	225	404	91
Coal, tons................	59,878	53,512	57,247
Copper Ore, lbs.........	560,000	1,870,488	2,587,000

	1855.	1856.	1857.
Cotton, bales............	239	681	317
Corn, bush...............	8,711,230	9,632,477	5,713,611
Eggs, bbls................	5,591	5,326	8,286
Feathers, sacks..........	379	820	242
Fish, bbls................	6,752	5,826	5,211
Furs, bdls................	1,112	890	635
Flax, bales...............	1,276	729	622
Flour, bbls...............	936,761	1,126,048	845,953
Hemp, bales..............	1,191	327	912
Hides, No.................	90,964	111,856	139,051
Horses, No...............	362	408	193
Hogs, No.................	59,944	72,713	75,174
Iron, pig, tons..........	3,994	2,077	1,323
Lard, lbs.................	10,357,136	5,335,500	643,000
Lead, pigs...............	67,309	30,677	22,247
Leather, rolls...........	2,265	2,326	2,513
Lumber, ft...............	72,026,651	60,584,541	68,283,319
Lath, No.................	245,000	920,000	1,602,000
Meal, corn, bbls.........	867	1,800	150
Nuts, bbls...............	346	805	113
Oil, bbls.................	4,700	2,870	1,789
Oats, bush...............	2,693,322	1,733,382	1,214,760
Pork, bbls...............	106,682	60,477	20,283
Pelts, bdls...............	4,311	3,368	1,595
Robes, Buffalo, bales...	480	287	1,150
Rye, bush................	299,591	245,810	48,536
Seeds, bbls...............	20,522	15,297	14,830
Skins, bbls...............	2,391	1,814	2,173
Staves, No...............	16,421,568	18,556,039	23,024,213
Shingles, No.............	1,764,000	398,000	1,669,000
Sheep, No................	26,508	41,467	44,972
Tobacco, hhds...........	489	623	270
Tobacco, cases...........	3,470	3,837	2,102
Tallow, lbs...............	1,234,100	634,900	445,750
Whisky, bbls.............	37,087	36,009	42,140
Wheat, bush.............	8,022,126	8,466,671	8,334,179
Wool, bales..............	47,168	41,592	35,613

The total value of the importations of these three years were, in 1855, $48,767,315; in 1856, $40,429,871; and in 1857, $34,846,592.

[3] Following is an exhibit of the number of entrances and clearances, their tonnage and crews, for six successive years:—

Year.	No.	Tonnage.	Men.
1852............	9,441	3,092,247	127,491
1853............	8,298	3,252,978	128,112
1854............	8,912	3,990,284	120,838
1855............	9,211	3,360,233	111,515
1856............	8,128	3,018,587	112,051
1857............	7,581	3,221,806	132,183

[4] The following tables show the receipts and shipments of leading articles for the year 1857:—The total value of the canal shipments that year was $16,956,740, and the tolls of the same received at the collector's office amounted to $569,537.44.

RECEIPTS.

Lumber, ft....................	1,853,693	Bran, &c. lbs...........	236,689	Foreign salt, lbs.........	193,839
Timber, 100 cubic ft.............	30,920	Beans and peas, bush..........	10,908	Sugar, lbs................	12,768,136
Staves, lbs....................		Potatoes, bush..........	3,342	Molasses, lbs...........	7,701,144
Wood, cords...................	25,835	Dried fruit, lbs.........	130,900	Coffee, lbs..............	4,900,077
Cheese, lbs...................	22,662	Hops, lbs................	621,852	Nails, spikes, &c. lbs...	2,856,471
Wool, lbs.....................	1,320	Domestic spirits, gals...	24,720	Iron and steel, lbs........	12,417,665
Hides, lbs....................	130,500	Leather, lbs.............	714,135	Railroad iron, lbs.......	32,187,521
Flour, bbls...................	28,621	Furniture, lbs...........	4,363,775	Crockery and glassware, lbs	5,606,277
Wheat, bush..................	19,966	Pig iron, lbs............	12,417,164	All other mdse., lbs.....	92,894,060
Rye, bush....................	7,778	Castings and ironware, lbs....	30,902,457	Stone, lime, and clay, lbs.	74,134,242
Corn, bush...................	1,131	Domestic cottons, lbs....	594,868	Gypsum, lbs.............	560,687
Barley, bush.................	37,434	Domestic salt, lbs.......	52,278,989	Coal, lbs................	115,193,297
				Sundries, lbs............	10,471,711

SHIPMENTS.

Lumber, ft....................	43,727,523	Rye, bush...............	6,341	Furniture, lbs...........	393,025
Timber, 100 cubic ft............	12,485	Corn, bush..............	5,001,263	Lead, lbs................	214,416
Staves, lbs...................	185,921,748	Barley, bush............	11,638	Pig iron, lbs............	1,240,408
Ashes, casks.................	1,829	Oats, bush..............	905,814	Bloom and bar iron, lbs........	87,736
Pork, bbls....................	9,195	Bran, &c. lbs...........	4,796,624	Castings and ironware, lbs.....	121,789
Beef, bbls....................	5,256	Dried fruits, lbs........		Domestic salt, lbs.......	32,100
Bacon, lbs....................	2,112,093	Cotton, lbs.............		Iron and steel, lbs.......	201,703
Cheese, lbs...................	65,469	Tobacco, lbs............	16,563	Railroad iron, lbs.......	
Butter, lbs...................	9,874	Hemp, lbs...............	49,690	Crockery and glassware, lbs.	122,594
Lard, tallow, and lard oil....	710,435	Seed, lbs...............	506,364	All other mdse. lbs......	674,242
Wool, lbs.....................	1,325,289	Flaxseed, lbs...........	1,077,228	Stone, lime, and clay, lbs.	4,989,599
Hides, lbs....................	780,885	Hops, lbs...............	1,529	Coal, lbs................	28,051,852
Flour, bbls...................	88,092	Domestic spirits, gals...	836,000	Copper ore, lbs..........	2,565,201
Wheat, bush..................	6,673,827	Leather, lbs............	56,786	Sundries, lbs............	12,771,000

that the value of merchandise and property transported by R. R. is greater than the entire amount of the lake commerce of this port.[1] About one-fourth of the shipping of the lake is owned by the citizens of Buffalo.[2] Shipbuilding is extensively carried on.[3] The manufactures of the city are extensive and various.[4]

The principal public buildings are the Custom House, Fort Porter, the State Arsenal, and the city markets. The *Custom House*, on the corner of Seneca and Washington Sts., is a handsome and well built structure, containing, beside the custom house office, accommodations for the post-office and the U. S. courts. It was constructed, at a cost of $140,000, from designs furnished by the U. S. Treasury Department.[5] *Fort Porter*, built in 1842–48, is a fortification on the bank of Niagara River at the point where it emerges from Lake Erie. The *State Arsenal*, erected in 1858, is a massive stone building fronting on Batavia St.[6] There are four large markets, conveniently located in different parts of the city.[7]

The *Public Schools* of the city have long enjoyed a deservedly high reputation. They are carefully nurtured through the operations of an enlightened public sentiment, and are so excellent in all their departments that scarcely any other elementary schools are supported or needed. They are thoroughly graded, consisting of three general departments. The third department is an advanced school for the whole city; and in it a complete academic course, excepting the classics, is taught. There were, in 1857, 32 school districts, employing 189 teachers,—24 males and 165 females. The number of children, between 4 and 21 years of age, was 28,000, of whom 15,593, or a small fraction more than 55½ per cent., were in attendance some portion of the year.[8]

The *Buffalo Female Academy*, a flourishing institution, situated on Delaware Avenue, was opened for students in July, 1852.[9]

---

[1] The amount of live stock received by R. R. in 1857 was 78,404 head of cattle, 232,375 hogs, and 72,496 sheep.

[2] The amount of shipping owned in Buffalo, as shown by the custom house books, is as follows:—

Vessels.	No.	Tonnage.
Steamers	10	9,067
Propellers	50	30,186
Tugs	20	2,629
Barks	7	3,537
Brigs	21	6,784
Schooners	129	35,460
Scows	5	473
Total	242	88,136

[3] The following table shows the shipping launched in 1857:—

Vessels.	Tonnage.	Value.
4 Steamers	4,086	$352,000
10 Propellers	5,070	349,000
13 Tugs	1,145	126,800
21 Schooners	7,955	353,400
1 Dredge		
25 Canal Boats		

In connection with one of the shipyards of the city is a dry dock of sufficient capacity to admit a steamer of over 2,500 tons; also a marine railway; and near by is a large derrick for hoisting boilers and heavy machinery.

[4] The following is a list of the manufacturing establishments in operation in 1857 :—

Agricultural Works	5	Earthenware Manufactories	2
Ax & Edge Tool M'factory	3	Fence (iron) "	4
Awl "	1	Fire Works "	2
Basket Manufactories	6	Flour Mills	10
Bellows "	2	Flour Mill Manufactories	3
Billiard Table "	3	Foundries	7
Blank Book & Bookbinding	8	Glove Manufactory	1
Boiler Manufactories	4	Glue "	1
Box "	5	Gold Beaters "	2
Brass "	3	Gunshops	3
Breweries	31	Harness, Saddle, &c. M'facts	13
Brickyards	9	Hat & Cap Manufactories	16
Britannia Ware	2	Iron Works	8
Boot & Shoe Manufactories	3	Japanned Ware	4
Brush "	2	Lantern Manufactories	2
Burr Millstone "	2	Last Manufactories	2
Cabinet Ware Manufactories	11	Leather "	11
Car and Car Wheels	2	Lithographing	3
Carriage Manuactories	9	Lock Manufactories	5
Chair "	2	Marble Works	6
Chromotype Printing	1	Machine Shops	10
Coach & Harness Hardware	2	Melodeon Manufactory	1
Comb Manufactory	1	Oakum "	1
Confectioneries	10	Oil "	4
Cooperages	14	Organ "	1
Distilleries	3	Pail and Tub "	1
Engraving	9	Paper Mill "	1
Engine (steam) M'factories	6	Patent Leather "	1
Philosophical Instruments	1	Shipyards	7
Piano Forte Manufactory	3	Silver Plating	4
Planing Mills	5	Soap & Candle M'factories	14
Plane Manufactory	1	Soda & Sarsaparilla "	4
Pocket Book "	1	Starch "	2
Pottery	1	Stave "	2
Printing Establishments	17	Steam Sawmills	3
Pump Manufactories	3	Stone Ware Manufactory	1
Regalia "	5	Tobacco	9
Rope "	4	Tanneries	2
Sail "	4	Type & Stereotype F'dries	3
Sash & Blind "	7	Upholsteries	10
Saw "	2	Vice Manufactory	1
Shingle "	2	White Lead "	2
Stove Manufactories	3	Whip "	1
Silk "	1		

The value of the articles manufactured in 1857 was about $10,000,000, of which the leading products are estimated as follows:—ships and boats, $1,800,000; leather, $1,500,000; flour, $1,000,000; stoves and other castings, $600,000; machines, $600,000; distilled stuffs, $400,000; piano fortes, $350,000; boots and shoes, $100,000.

For most of the statistics of the commerce and manufactures of Buffalo we are indebted to the *Annual Statement of the Trade and Commerce of Buffalo for* 1857, issued from the office of the *Commercial Advertiser.*

[5] The custom house building was commenced in 1855 and completed in 1858. It is 3 stories high, exclusive of basement, and has a front of 110 ft. on Seneca St. and 60 ft. on Washington St., with a total elevation of 70 ft. above the sidewalk. Its exterior is of light gray sandstone, obtained from Cleveland, Ohio; and the whole is fireproof throughout, the floors being of small, segmental brick arches, turned from wrought iron beams, resting on tubular girders. The girders rest upon the walls, and are supported in the middle by cast iron columns reaching to the foundation of the building.

[6] The arsenal is 165 ft. long by 65 ft. wide. Its front, 50 ft. wide, projecting 16 ft. from the main building, is flanked by octagonal towers 60 ft. high. The walls are 40 ft. high; and at each corner is a heavy, square turret. The cost of the building was $35,000.

[7] Elk Street Market is 30 ft. wide by 375 ft. long, having a veranda 24 ft. wide extending the whole length of each side. The Court Street Market consists of a main building, 51 ft. sq., with 4 wings, one on each side. The N. and S. wings are each 91½ ft. long by 36 ft. wide, and the E. and W. wings are each 61 ft. long by 36 ft. wide. The Clinton St. and Washington St. Markets are each 395 ft. long by 36 ft. wide, with a veranda 24 ft. wide extending the whole length of each side.

[8] The total expenses of the schools for 1857 were $160,019.86, and the total receipts the same; number of volumes in district libraries 8,216.

[9] This institution owes its existence in a great measure to the liberality of Jabez Goodell, who contributed over $10,000 toward its establishment. The academy occupies one of the most eligible and beautiful sites in the city. There are two academic buildings, Goodell Hall and Evergreen Cottage,—the former occupied for school purposes, and the latter as a dwelling by the family of the principal.

The *Buffalo Medical College,* on the corner of Main and Virginia Sts., was organized in Aug. 1846, under the charter of the *University of Buffalo.* A course of lectures is given each winter; and the students are admitted to the hospital of the Sisters of Charity, on stated days, during the visits of the medical and surgical officers.

The *Buffalo Mercantile College,* on the corner of Main and Seneca Sts., was established Oct. 10, 1854. Its object is to impart a theoretical and practical knowledge of business transactions.

The *Buffalo Commercial College,* on Main St., is an institution similar in character to the Mercantile College.

The *Buffalo Law Library Association,* incorp. April 2, 1833,—capital $10,000, in shares of $100 each,—was formed for the purpose of securing the benefits of a professional library beyond the reach of private means.

The *Young Men's Association* was established in the winter of 1835–36, and incorp. in March, 1843. It has a library of about 10,000 volumes, and a reading room, which is well supplied with papers from most of the principal cities of the Union. During the winter months lectures are maintained by the association.

The *German Young Men's Association* was organized in 1841 and chartered in 846. The library contains about 2000 volumes, mostly German works.

The *Young Men's Christian Union* was established in May, 1852, and incorp. March, 1853. It has for its object the moral and intellectual improvement of young men. Its library and reading rooms are in Kremlin Hall, at the junction of Niagara and Erie Sts.

The *Young Men's Catholic Association* and the *Buffalo Catholic Institute* are societies similar to the preceding.

The *Buffalo Medical Association* was formed in 1845 and incorp. in 1856. Its objects are purely scientific and professional, and its membership is confined to the medical profession of the county.

The *Mendelssohn Association,* organized Jan. 1858, has for its object the improvement and cultivation of vocal and instrumental music.

The *Deutsche Leidertafel* and the *Deutscher Saengerbund* are German societies of a similar character.

The *Buffalo Orphan Asylum,* located on Virginia St., was organized in 1835 and incorp. April 24, 1837. The site was donated by Louis S. Le Couteulx, and the present building was erected in 1850. The average number of inmates is about 80.

The *Buffalo Female Orphan Asylum,* on the corner of Batavia and Ellicott Sts., was established in 1848, under the care of the Sisters of Charity of St. Joseph. The present number of children is 98.

The *Buffalo Hospital of the Sisters of Charity,* on Virginia St., was incorp. July 5, 1848. The building contains 20 wards, and the average number of patients is 130.

The *Buffalo General Hospital* was incorp. Nov. 21, 1855, and went into operation in 1858. It was founded by individual donations, amounting to $20,000, and a State appropriation of $10,000.[1]

The *Lying-In Hospital,* on Edward St., is under the charge of the Sisters of Charity.

The *Buffalo City Dispensary,* a society of physicians, was organized to afford gratuitous medical services to the destitute.

The *Association for the Relief of the Poor* disburses among the needy each winter sums ranging from $1,500 to $8,000.

The *Firemen's Benevolent Association* was incorp. March 23, 1837, and has for its object the accumulation of a fund for the relief of indigent and disabled firemen and their families.

The *Buffalo Physicians' Charitable Fund Association* was organized in 1858, to provide means for the assistance and relief of the widows and orphans of medical men.

A M. E. church was founded in Buffalo, in 1809, by the Rev. Jas. Mitchell; but it had no permanent organization. The oldest church now in the city (1st Presb.) was organized Feb. 2, 1812, by the Rev. Thaddeus Osgood. The next established were a Prot. E., Bap., a M. E., and a Univ. There are now 57 churches in the city.[2] Most of the church edifices are large and commodious; and many of them are of a high order of architectural beauty. *St. Joseph's Cathedral* (R. C.) is

---

[1] This hospital is located on High St., and is a two story brick structure, 160 ft. long by 75 ft. wide. The w. wing only of the general plan is finished; but that is complete in itself, and has 4 wards, capable of accommodating 100 patients.

[2] 14 R. C., 8 Presb., 7 Prot. E., 7 M. E., 6 Bap., 4 Ger. Evang., 3 Luth., 2 Ref. Prot. D., and 1 each Asso. Presb., French Prot., Unit., Univ., Mission, and Bethel. The R. C. Church of St. Louis,

in this city, has been prominently before the public from the refusal of its trustees to convey their church property to the bishop, and the extraordinary but ineffectual efforts made by the Roman pontiff to induce obedience to this order. In 1853 Cardinal Bedini visited America, having this as a prominent object of his mission; but the trustees were inflexible, and still continue the owners of their property.

the largest and most costly in the city.[1] St. Paul's[2] and St. John's, (Prot. E.,) and the North and Central Presb. churches, are elegant and substantial structures.

The earliest notice of the site of the city of Buffalo is found in the travels of Baron La Hontan, who visited this locality in 1687.[3] No white settlers located here until after the American Revolution. A village of the Seneca Indians lay on Buffalo Creek, about 3 mi. from its mouth. In March, 1791, Col. Thos. Proctor, U. S. Commissioner, visited "Buffalo Creek,"—as this village was then called,—on an embassy to the Indians. The locality around the mouth of the creek was then called "Lake Erie," and Cornelius Winney, an Indian trader, resided there.[4] The place was visited in 1795 by La Rochefoucault Liancourt, a French nobleman, who says that "at the post on Lake Erie there was a small collection of four or five houses."[5] Buffalo was laid out by the agent of the Holland Land Company in 1801, and was called by them "New Amsterdam."[6] Settlement was commenced at Black Rock in 1807.[7] In 1808 "New Amsterdam" was made the county seat of Niagara co.; and its name was then changed to Buffalo. In 1812 it became a military post. In Dec. 1813, a party of British and Indians crossed over from Canada, defeated the American forces, and fired the villages of Black Rock and Buffalo. Only two dwelling houses were left standing.[8] The rebuilding of the village was not commenced until 1815. Buffalo had from the first a formidable rival in Black Rock. While the mouth of Buffalo Creek was obstructed by a bar, Black Rock possessed an excellent harbor and monopolized the infant commerce of the lake. The "Walk-in-the-Water," the first steamboat on Lake Erie, was built at Black Rock in 1818. The construction of Buffalo harbor was commenced in 1820, by the citizens;[9] and in 1827 the General Government assumed its completion and built the present pier and lighthouse. The Erie Canal was finished in 1825; and from that time to the present Buffalo has increased in wealth and population with the characteristic rapidity of the cities of the West.[10]

CHICTAWAUGA[11]—was formed from Amherst, March 22, 1839; and a part of West Seneca was taken off in 1851. It is an interior town, lying N. of the center of the co. The surface is level. The principal streams are Eleven Mile, Cayuga, and Slate Bottom Creeks The soil is a heavy, tough clay. Chictawauga and Four Mile Creek are p. offices. The first settlement was made by Apollos Hitchcock, in 1808.[12] There is but 1 church (R. C.) in town.

CLARENCE—was formed from "Willink," (now Aurora,) March 11, 1808. Buffalo was taken off in 1810, Alden in 1823, and Lancaster in 1833. It lies upon the N. border of the co., E. of the center. Its surface is level. A limestone terrace about 50 feet high, with a wall-like front facing the N., extends E. and W. through the center of the town. The streams are Tonawanda Creek, on the N. border, and Ransoms Creek, flowing N. w. through near the center of the town. The soil in the N. part is clayey, and in the S. a sandy and gravelly loam underlaid by

---

1 The cathedral is 236 ft. long, 86 ft. wide in the body, and 120 at the transept. The ceiling is 75 ft. high, the roof outside 90 feet, and the spire, when finished, will be 220 ft. high. The windows are all of beautiful stained glass, the larger ones in figures representing sacred scenes and characters. The tripartite window above the altar represents the birth, crucifixion, and ascension of Christ. This window was executed in Munich, at a cost of $5,000.

2 This church was erected at a cost of about $100,000. It has a chime of 10 bells, which cost $15,000.

3 La Hontan recommended to the French Government the erection of a fort at this place.

4 Winney's house—undoubtedly the first erected in Buffalo—stood near where the Washington St. Canal Bridge now is.

5 Besides Winney, Johnston, the British Indian interpreter, Martin Middaugh and his family, and his son-in-law, Ezekiel Lane, resided here at that time; and in 1796 Asa Ransom, Jesse Skinner, and "Black Joe" were also here. Skinner kept an inn, and Winney and "Black Joe" an Indian store.

6 The principal streets were named from members of the Holland Land Company. Main St. was called "Willinks Avenue," Niagara St. "Schimmelpennicks Avenue," Genesee St. "Busti Avenue," Erie St. "Vollenhovens Avenue," and Church St. "Stadnitzki Avenue." In 1826 these names were changed by the trustees of the village. The business of the Holland Land Company was transacted here for a short time previous to the opening of their office at "Ransoms Grove," now Clarence Hollow, in 1801.

7 The surveyor general was directed (April 11, 1804) to lay out the land about Black Rock—forming a part of the Mile Strip—into lots and report to the legislature. This was accordingly done; and in his report the surveyor general stated his belief that this was the best, if not the only, place at this end of the lake where a harbor of proper size could be constructed. From the earliest period the U. S. had designated this vicinity as the site of a fortification. The report closed with the following words:—"It will be observed that

streets are laid where it will either be impracticable or useless to open them soon. It may, notwithstanding, be useful now to contemplate, in the plans of towns, what will be necessary arrangements a century hence. Such plans on record, while for the present they can be productive of no harm, may prevent those aberrations from order that might hereafter be a cause of much inconvenience; and, without being governed by extravagant calculations, no doubt can be entertained that the future importance of this place will justify extensive views in the projection of its arrangements." The village, like Lewiston, Oswego, Salina, and Fort Covington, was patented in small parcels.

8 See p. 280. In 1825, Congress made an appropriation of $80,000 to compensate the inhabitants for the losses incurred by this disaster.

9 The sum of $1,861.25 was raised by subscription, and a loan of $12,000 was obtained from the State. A pier, extending 80 rods into the lake, was built, and a lighthouse erected upon the land. The Superior—the second steamboat launched upon Lake Erie—was built at Buffalo in 1822.

10 The population at different periods has been as follows:—

1810	1,508	1830	8,668	1845	29,773
1814	1,060	1835	19,715	1850	42,261
1820	2,095	1840	18,213	1855	74,214
1825	5,141				

The population of Black Rock (now about 12,000) is included in the returns of 1855 only.

11 This name was given at the suggestion of Alex. Hitchcock. It is a corruption of the Seneca word "Jiik-do-waah-geh," signifying "the place of the crab-apple tree," the Indian name of this locality.

12 Among the early settlers were Sam'l Lasure, Roswell Judson, Abraham Hatch, and Maj. Noble. The first birth was that of a child of Roswell Hatch, in 1810; and the first death, that of Franklin Hitchcock, in 1818. The first mill was built by Sam'l Lasure, in 1810; and the first inn was kept by Jesse Munson, in 1815.

BUFFALO HARBOR.

FROM THE LIGHT HOUSE

limestone. **Clarence Hollow,** (Clarence p. o.,) near the s. e. corner of the town, contains 3 churches, the Clarence Academy,[1] and a pop. of 400; **Clarence Center** (p. v.) contains 2 churches and about 40 houses. **Harris Hill** (p. o.) and **North Clarence** (p. o.) are hamlets. The first settlement was made at Clarence Hollow in 1799, by Asa Ransom.[2] The census reports 7 churches in town.[3]

COLDEN[4]—was formed from Holland, April 2, 1827. It is an interior town, lying s. of the center of the co. The surface is an elevated upland, rolling in the e. and hilly in the w. The w. branch of Cazenove Creek flows through the w. part of the town and is bordered by steep declivities 150 to 200 ft. high. The soil is a gravelly loam intermixed with clay. **Colden,** (p. v.,) on Cazenove Creek, contains a sawmill, a gristmill, and 34 houses; **Glenwood,** (p. v.,) on the same stream, contains 1 church, 3 sawmills, 2 lath mills, a tannery, and 30 houses. The first settlement was made in 1810, by Richard Buffum.[5] The Presbyterian, at Glenwood, is the only church in town.

COLLINS—was formed from Concord, March 16, 1821. A part of Brandt was taken off in 1839, and North Collins in 1852. It lies on the s. border of the co., w. of the center. The surface is a rolling upland, sloping gradually to the w. and descending abruptly to Cattaraugus Creek upon the s. The summits of the ridges are 150 to 300 ft. above the valleys. Cattaraugus Creek forms the s. boundary of the town; and the other streams are Clear Creek and its tributaries. The channels of these streams are narrow and deep. The soil is a clayey loam on the uplands and a gravelly loam along the streams. **Collins Center** (p. v.) contains 1 church and 36 houses. **Angola** is a p. o. near the n. w. corner of the town. **Gowanda** lies partly in this town.[6] The first settlement was made in 1806, by Jacob Taylor.[7] There are 5 churches in town.[8]

CONCORD—was formed from "*Willink,*" (now Aurora,) March 20, 1812; and Collins and Sardinia were taken off in 1821. A part of Sardinia was annexed in 1822. It lies upon the s. border of the co. The surface is a rolling upland, with steep declivities bordering upon Cattaraugus Creek. Townsend Hill, the highest point, is nearly 1500 ft. above tide. The principal streams are Cattaraugus Creek, upon the s. boundary of the town, and its tributaries. Several small brooks, forming the head waters of Eighteen Mile and Cazenove Creeks, take their rise in this town. The soil in the s. part is a gravelly loam, and in the n. a clayey loam underlaid by hardpan. **Springville,** (p. v.,) incorp. April 11, 1834, is situated in the s. part of the town, and contains 5 churches, the Springville Academy, a newspaper office, and several manufacturing establishments.[9] Pop. 953. **Mortons Corners,** (p. v.,) in the s. w. part, contains 1 church, 2 sawmills, a gristmill, and 20 houses. **Woodwards Hollow** (p. o.) is a hamlet. The first settlement was made in 1808, by Christopher Stone.[10] The first church was organized Nov. 2, 1816, by Rev. John Spencer. There are 7 churches in town.[11]

EAST HAMBURGH—was formed from Hamburgh, as "*Ellicott,*" Oct. 15, 1850. A part of West Seneca, as "*Seneca,*" was taken off in 1851. Its name was changed Feb. 20, 1852. It is an interior town, lying near the center of the co. The surface is a broken upland. Chestnut Ridge, the highest land in the town, has an elevation of about 500 ft. above Lake Erie. The declivities of the hills are generally gradual slopes, broken by narrow ravines formed by the streams. Smokes Creek and its branches are the most considerable streams. The soil is a loam, gravelly in the n. and clayey in the s. **East Hamburgh,** (p. v.,) n. of the center of the town,

---

[1] Established as the Clarence Classical School in 1841, by J. Hadley and R. Blennerhassett.

[2] Asa Ransom was a man of considerable influence with the Indians. They gave him the name of "*O-wis-ta-no-at-squo-nich,*" signifying "maker of silver," or "maker of silver money." Gen. Timothy Hopkins settled in the town in 1797; Asa Chapman, Timothy James, Wm. Updegraff, Christopher Saddler, Levi Felton, Abraham Shope, John Haines, and John Gardner, in 1801; Andrew Durnet, Geo. Shurman, Bera Ensign, and Jacob Shope, in 1803; and Daniel Bailey in 1804. The first birth was that of Harry B. Ransom, in 1801; and the first death, that of —— Keyes, in 1804. Asa Ransom opened the first public house, in 1801, built the first sawmill, in 1805, and the first gristmill, in 1806; Otis R. Hopkins kept the first store, in 1811. The first school was taught by Rebecca Hamlin, in 1805.

[3] 3 Mennonites, Bap., Seventh Day Bap., Presb., and Union.

[4] Named from Cadwallader D. Colden, then in the State Senate.

[5] Thos. Pope, Josiah Brown, and L. Owen settled in the town in 1810, and Jesse Southwick, Richard Sweet, Nath'l Bowen, and Silas Lewis in 1811. The first birth was that of a child of Thos. Pope, in 1811; the first marriage, that of Jas. Sweet and Charlotte Buffum, in 1810; and the first death, that of Nathaniel Bowen, in 1812. Richard Buffum built the first mill, in 1810.

[6] The first school was taught by Mary Eddy, in the winter of 1814.
See page 194.

[7] Joshua Palmerton, Stephen Peters, Turner Aldrich, and Stephen Lapham settled in the town in 1810, and Stephen Wilbur and Sylvanus Bates in 1811. The first birth was that of a son of Aaron Lindsley, in 1810; the first marriage, that of Stephen Peterson and Sarah Palmerton, in 1811; and the first death, that of —— Straight, in 1812 Jacob Taylor built the first mill, in 1812; John Hanford kept the first store, in 1813, and Nathan King the first inn, in 1816. The first school was taught by John King, in 1815.

[8] Christians, Friends, F. W. Bap., Presb., and Union.

[9] A woolen factory, 2 planing mills, a turning shop, a saw mill, 2 gristmills, a tannery, a stone sawing mill, and a furnace and machine shop.

[10] John Albro and John Russell settled in the town the same year, Sam'l Cochrane in 1809, and Rufus Eaton, Joseph Adams, Alva Plumb, and David Shultiez in 1810. The first birth was that of Lucius Stone, in 1809; the first marriage, that of Jas. Runnell and Anna Richmond, in 1813; and the first death, that of Mrs. John Albro, in 1808. Anna Richmond taught the first school, in 1811.

[11] Bap., F. W. Bap., M. E., Presb., R. C., Union, and Univ.

19

contains 2 churches, 2 sawmills, and 40 houses. **Ellicott** (p. o.) is a hamlet. The first settlement was made in 1803, by David Eddy, from Rutland, Vt.[1] There are 3 churches in town; Friends, M. E., and Union.

EDEN—was formed from "*Willink*," (now Aurora,) March 20, 1812. Boston was taken off in 1817, and Evans in 1821. It is an interior town, lying s. w. of the center of the co. Its surface is hilly and broken in the E. and level in the w. A ridge about 500 ft. above the lake extends along the E. border. The principal streams are Eighteen Mile Creek and its branches. The soil is a gravelly loam intermixed with clay. **Eden,** (p. v.,) situated near the center of the town, contains 3 churches, a sawmill, a stave and shingle mill, a tannery, and 63 houses; **Eden Valley,** (p. v.,) on Eighteen Mile Creek, contains a gristmill, a sawmill, and 20 houses. **Clarksburgh** (p. o.) and **East Eden** (p. o.) are hamlets. The first settlement was made in 1808, by Benj., Joseph, and Samuel Tubbs.[2] The first religious services were conducted by Rev. Wm. Hill, in 1812. There are 8 churches in town.[3]

ELMA—was formed from Lancaster and Aurora, Dec. 4, 1857. It is an interior town, lying N. E. of the center of the co. Its surface is gently rolling, the summits of the ridges being 50 to 100 ft. above the valleys. Big Buffalo and Cazenove Creeks flow through the town. The soil is a clayey loam in the N. and a gravelly loam in the s. **Spring Brook,** (p. v.,) on Cazenove Creek, contains 2 churches and several manufactories.[4] Pop. 300. **Elma**[5] (p. v.) has several manufacturing establishments[6] and 34 houses; and **Upper Ebenezer** 27 houses. The first settlement was made in 1827, by Taber Earlle.[7] There are 2 churches in town; Presb. and R. C.

EVANS[8]—was formed from Eden, March 23, 1821. A part of Hamburgh was annexed in 1826, and a part of Brandt was taken off in 1839. It lies upon the lake shore, in the s. part of the co. The land rises from the lake in a bluff 20 to 40 ft. high; and the highest part of the town, near the E. border, is 160 ft. above the lake. The streams are Big and Little Sister Creeks. The soil is a sandy and gravelly loam intermixed with clay. **Evans,** (p. v.,) situated on Big Sister Creek, contains 3 churches, a gristmill, a sawmill, a tannery, and about 45 houses; **Angola,** (p. v.,) on the same stream, is a station on the Erie R. R., and contains a gristmill, a sawmill, and about 45 houses; **North Evans,** (p. v.,) on Eighteen Mile Creek, in the N. E. part of the town, contains 3 churches, a gristmill, a sawmill, a tannery, and about 40 houses; **East Evans,** (p. v.,) in the N. part of the town, and **Pontiac,** (p. v.,) on Big Sister Creek, in the s. E. part, contain about 20 houses each. The first settlement was made in 1804, by Joel Harvey.[9] There are 7 churches in town.[10]

GRAND ISLAND—was formed from Tonawanda as a town, Oct. 19, 1852. It is the N. w. corner town in the co., and comprises Grand, Buckhorn, and Beaver Islands, in Niagara River. Its surface is nearly level, and a considerable portion of it is still covered with forests. The soil of the upper part is clayey, and of the lower part sandy. The people are principally engaged in grain raising and lumbering. **Grand Island** is a p. o. on the E. shore. There is no village on the island, although it is thickly settled along the shores. The first settlers were squatters, who located soon after the War of 1812 and before it was decided to which Government the island belonged.[11] In 1820, Mordecai M. Noah, of New York, conceived the project of forming a

---

[1] Ezekiel Cook and Zenas Smith settled in the town in 1803, and Amos Colvin and Ezekiel and Daniel Smith in 1804. The first marriage was that of Almon C. Laire and Lydia Sprague, in 1808; the first birth, that of a son of Daniel Smith, in 1805; and the first death, that of the same child, in 1806. Dan'l Smith built the first mill, in 1807; John Green kept the first inn, in 1807, and David Eddy the first store, in 1809. The first school was taught by Anna Eddy, in 1807.

[2] Among the first settlers were John Marsh, Silas Este, and Calvin Thompson, who came in 1809, and Daniel and Edward Webster, in 1810. The first birth was that of Hannah Tubbs, in 1809; the first marriage, that of David Doan and Anna Hill, in 1815; and the first death, that of Jas. Welch, in 1812. Elisha Welch built the first sawmill, in 1811, and the first gristmill, in 1812. Wm. Hill kept the first inn, in 1814, and Fillmore & Johnson the first store, in 1820. The first school was taught by Rowena Plack, in 1812.

[3] 3 Ref. Prot. D., Bap., Evang. Luth., M. E., Presb., and R. C.

[4] 2 sawmills, a shingle and turning mill, 2 gristmills, and a tannery.

[5] Named from a very large elm tree near Elma Village.

[6] 1 gristmill, 2 planing mills, and a chair factory.

[7] Timothy Treat, Isaac Williams, Willard and Jas. Fairbanks, and Amasa Adams settled in the town in 1830, and Zima A. Hemstreet, Abraham Taber, and Jacob Pettengill in 1831. The first birth was that of H. Scott Fairbanks, in 1831; the first marriage, that of Gould Hinman and Louisa Adams, in 1835; and the first death, that of the wife of Isaac Williams, in 1830. The first mill was built by —— Eastabrook, in 1824; and the

first inn was kept by Taber Earlle, in 1829. Emily Paine taught the first school, in 1831.

[8] Named from David E. Evans, agent of the Holland Land Company.

[9] —— Fisk and —— Worder settled in the town in 1808, Aaron Salisbury and Aaron Cash in 1809, and Andrew Tyler and Elijah Gates in 1810. The first birth was that of a daughter of David Cash, in Jan. 1811; the first marriage, that of Whiting Cash and Persis Taylor, June 28, 1815; and the first death, that of Jonathan Cash, in 1811. Henry Tuttle built the first mill, in 1817; Joel Harvey kept the first inn, in 1806; and John Harris the first store, in 1815. The first school was taught by —— Hibbard, in 1811.

During the War of 1812 a party of British sailors and mariners landed near Sturgeon Point, in the night, and commenced plundering the inhabitants. Judge Aaron Salisbury, then a young man, seized his musket and started off alone to get a shot at them. When he arrived they were retreating to their boats, and an exchange of shots produced no damage on either side. They started for the mouth of Eighteen Mile Creek, and he on foot endeavored to get there before them; but they had landed when he arrived. He immediately commenced firing; and they, not knowing how large a force was opposing them, retreated to their boats and speedily left. Here one man frightened away 100 and saved the inhabitants from plunder.

[10] 3 Bap., 3 Cong., 3 M. E., and R. C.

[11] The treaty of peace fixed the boundary between the two countries along the principal branch of Niagara River. A dispute in regard to which was the principal branch was settled in

colony of Jews upon Grand Island, as an Ararat, or resting place, for that scattered and broken people.[1]

HAMBURGH[2]—was formed from "*Willink,*" (now Aurora,) March 20, 1812. A part of Evans was taken off in 1826, East Hamburgh in 1850, and a part of West Seneca, as "*Seneca,*" in 1851. It lies on the shore of Lake Erie, near the center of the w. border of the co. Its surface in the e. is rolling; but in the w. it is nearly level, with a gentle inclination toward the lake. A bluff averaging 50 to 100 feet high borders the lake. The principal stream is Eighteen Mile Creek. The soil is mostly a clayey loam; in the s. e. corner it is gravelly. **Whites Corners,** (p. v.,) on the n. branch of Eighteen Mile Creek, in the s. e. part of the town, contains 5 churches, a gristmill, a sawmill, a tannery, and has a pop. of 609; **Water Valley,** (p. v.,) on the same stream, w. of Whites Corners, contains a woolen factory, a furnace, and 20 houses; **Abbotts Corners,** (Hamburgh p. o.,) on the line of East Hamburgh, contains 2 churches, a sawmill, a shingle mill, and 145 inhabitants. **Big Tree Corners** and **Hamburgh-on-the-Lake** are p. offices. The first settlement was made in 1804, by Nathaniel Titus and Dr. Rufus Belden.[3] There are 7 churches in town.[4]

HOLLAND—was formed from "*Willink,*" (now Aurora,) April 15, 1818; and Colden was taken off in 1827. It lies upon the e. border of the co., s. e. of the center. The surface is a high, broken upland, divided by the valley of Cazenove Creek. The summit of the highland is about 900 ft. above Lake Erie. The soil is a gravelly loam, intermixed in some places with slate and clay. The valley of Cazenove Creek is very fertile. **Holland,** (p. v.,) on Cazenove Creek, contains 1 church, several manufacturing establishments,[5] and 28 houses. The first settlement was made in 1807, by Jared Scott, Abner Currier, and Arthur Humphrey, from Vt.[6] There is but 1 church (Bap.) in town.

LANCASTER—was formed from Clarence, March 20, 1833. A part of West Seneca was taken off in 1851, and a part of Elma in 1857. It is an interior town, n. e. of the center of the co. The surface is level. Cayuga and Eleven Mile Creeks are the principal streams; upon them are several mill sites. The soil is a clayey and gravelly loam. **Lancaster,** (p. v.,) incorp. March 13, 1849, is a station on the N. Y. C. R. R., in the w. part of the town. It contains 6 churches, a bank, and several manufactories.[7] Pop. 1,259. **Bowmansville,** (p. v.,) in the n. w. corner of the town,

---

1818, by commissioners appointed respectively by the United States and British Governments. While the matter was still undecided, a large number of lawless persons—mostly refugees from justice from both sides of the river—squatted upon the island, locating principally along the shores. Remaining for some time unmolested, they began to commit extensive depredations upon the timber; and finally they set up an independent government and elected a full quota of municipal officers. In April, 1819, the legislature passed an act authorizing the removal of these intruders. During the succeeding summer the governor issued a proclamation commanding them to desist from depredations upon the property of the State, and at once to remove. A few obeyed the command; but, seeing no active demonstrations on the part of Government, they returned. In the fall of 1819, Gov. Clinton directed Col. Jas. Cronk, the sheriff of Niagara co., to call out a sufficient military force for the purpose and forcibly expel them. On the 9th of Dec. 1819, the sheriff, accompanied by Lieuts. Benj. Hodge and —— Osborne, 2 serjeants, 4 corporals, and 24 privates, went to the island in boats, manned by 20 boatmen, to carry into execution the orders of the governor. Every facility was given the people to remove with their effects; and the boatmen took them to either shore, as they might elect. The military were divided into 3 parties: a vanguard, to read the governor's orders and assist in clearing the houses; a second party, to forcibly remove all property left in the buildings; and a rear guard, to burn the buildings and complete the removal and destruction. Seventy houses were burned, and 150 people, consisting of men, women, and children, were turned out shelterless upon the U. S. and Canada shores. Two buildings, filled with grain, alone were saved. The removal and destruction occupied 5 days and cost the State $568.99. A few families returned immediately, but did not remain.

[1] In a memorial to the legislature in 1820 for the purchase of the island, Maj. Noah explained his object; recounted the persecution which his co-religionists in the Old World had suffered through many centuries; pointed out the benefits that had resulted to Spain, Portugal, France, and Germany from the commercial enterprise and the capital of the Jews when allowed the exercise of their rights; and painted in brilliant colors the benefits that would accrue to the U. S. if his people could exchange "the whips and scorns of Europe, Asia, and Africa for the light of liberty and civilization" which this country afforded. He estimated that there were 7,000,000 of Jews in the world, and predicted that, if the existence of an asylum of freedom were

made known, large numbers would be induced to emigrate. The sanction of law was asked to give confidence to those who might not otherwise be induced to remove. His attempt to gather the Jews, like those before it, ended in day dreams. The European rabbii refused to sanction the effort; and Maj. Noah soon gave up the attempt, leaving no trace of his "city" upon the island but a monument of brick and wood. It bore, on a marble tablet, the following inscriptions from Deuteronomy vi. 4:—

שְׁמַע יִשְׂרָאֵל אֲלֹהֵינוּ
דְּדְּהֹר

ARARAT,

A CITY OF REFUGE FOR THE JEWS,

Founded by MORDECAI M. NOAH, *in the month of* TIZRI 5,586, (September, 1825,) and in the 50th year of American Independence.

The monument has since tumbled down; and the schemes of Maj. Noah have now scarcely a place in memory or a trace in history.

A Boston company was formerly extensively engaged in the manufacture of ship timber upon the island.

[2] Named from Hamburgh, in Germany.

[3] Benj., Enos, and Joseph Sheldon settled in the town in 1805, and John Fox and Elisha and David Clark in 1806. The first marriage was that of Ezekiel Cook and Anna Smith, in 1807. Nath'l Titus kept the first inn, in 1804; and John Cummings built the first mill, in 1805.

[4] Bap., F. W. Bap., Evang. Luth., M. E., and R. C. at Whites Corners, and M. E. and Presb. at Abbotts Corners.

[5] 2 sawmills, a gristmill, and a tannery; the last named is a large establishment, employing about 20 men, and turning out about 30,000 sides of leather per annum.

[6] They were followed by Dan'l McKean and Ezekiel and Harvey Colby the same year, and by Increase Richardson, Samuel Miller, Theophilus Baldwin, and Sandford Porter in 1808. The first birth was that of Dan'l McKean, in 1808. Joshua Parsons kept the first inn, in 1817, and Leonard Cook the first store, the same year. The first school was taught by Abner Currier, in 1808.

[7] A glass factory, a bedstead factory, a tannery, a gristmill, and a sawmill.

contains 1 church and has a pop. of 196. **Town Line, Winspear,** and **Looneyville** are p. offices. The first settlement was made in 1803, by Jas. and Asa Woodward.[1] The first religious services were conducted by Rev. John Spencer, at the house of Benj. Clark, in 1809. There are 8 churches in town.[2]

MARILLA[3]—was formed from Alden and Wales, Dec. 2, 1853. It is situated near the center of the E. border of the co. The surface is rolling. Big Buffalo Creek crosses the s. w. corner; but the principal part of the town is drained by the head waters of Little Buffalo Creek. The soil in the N. E. and s. w. is a sandy and gravelly loam; but elsewhere it consists of clay and muck. **Marilla,** (p. v.,) situated near the center of the town, contains 3 churches, 2 sawmills, a shingle mill, and 235 inhabitants. The first settlement was made by Jerry and Joseph Carpenter, in 1829.[4] There are 3 churches in town; Disciples, M. E., and R. C.

NEWSTEAD—was formed from Batavia, (Genesee co.,) as "*Erie,*" April 11, 1804; its name was changed April 18, 1831. It is the N. E. corner town of the co. A limestone terrace extends through near the center of the town. North of this the surface is level, in many places marshy; and the soil is a clayey loam intermixed with marl and sand. To the s. the surface is level, or gently undulating, and the soil a sandy and clayey loam underlaid by limestone. The town is watered by several small streams, the principal of which is Murder Creek.[5] A layer of hydraulic limestone crops out along the terrace, and waterlime is extensively manufactured from it. **Akron,**[6] (p. v.,) incorp. Oct. 1850, is a station on the Canandaigua & N. F. branch of the N. Y. C. R. R., near the center of the town. It contains 4 churches and several manufacturing establishments.[7] Pop. 462. **Falkirk,** 1 mi. E. of Akron, is a hamlet. The first settlement was made in the early part of the present century.[8] The first religious society (M. E.) was organized in 1807, with 12 members, at the house of Charles Knight, by Rev. Peter Van Nest and Amos Jenks. There are 4 churches in town.[9]

NORTH COLLINS—was formed from Collins, Nov. 24, 1852, as "*Shirley;*" its name was changed June 24, 1853. It is an interior town, lying in the s. w. part of the co. Its surface is rolling, the summits of the ridges being 200 to 300 ft. above the valleys. The town is watered by the head branches of Eighteen Mile, Clear, and Big Sister Creeks. The streams generally flow through deep ravines bordered by steep declivities. The soil is a gravelly loam. **North Collins,** (Collins p. o.,) in the N. w. part of the town, contains 2 churches and 34 houses. **Shirley,** (p. v.) and **Langford,** (p. o.,) in the N. E. part, **New Oregon,** (p. o.,) in the E. part, and **Marshfield,** (p. o.,) in the s., are hamlets. The first settlers were Stephen Sisson, Abram Tucker, and Enos Southwick, from Warren co., who moved into the town in 1810.[10] There are 8 churches in town.[11]

SARDINIA—was formed from Concord, March 16, 1821. A part of Concord was taken off in 1822. It is the s. E. corner town of the co. The surface in the E. part is gently rolling, and in the w. hilly. Shepherd Hill, s. w. of the center, is 1,040 ft. above Lake Erie. Cattaraugus Creek forms the s. boundary. In the E. part the soil is a gravelly loam, and in the w. it is clay underlaid by hardpan. **Sardinia,** (p. v.,) in the s. E. part, contains 2 churches, a woolen factory, a gristmill, a tannery, and 40 houses. **Protection** is a p. o. The first settlement was made by George Richmond, from Vt.[12] The first religious services were conducted by the Rev. John Spencer, in Feb. 1815. There are 2 churches in town; Bap. and M. E.

[1] Among the early settlers were Alanson Eggleston and David Hamlin, who came in 1804, Joel Parmalee, in 1805, Warren Hamlin, in 1806, Wm. Blackman, Peter Pratt, —— Kerney, and Elisha Cox, in 1807, and Elias Bissell, Pardon Peckham, and Benj. Clark, in 1808. The first birth was that of a pair of twins, children of Zophar Beach, and the first death, that of a child of Wm. Blackman, both in 1808. —— Robinson built the first sawmill, in 1808; Ahaz Luce opened the first store, in 1810, and Jos. Carpenter the first inn, in 1812. The first school was taught by Freelove Johnson, in 1810.

[2] 2 Evang. Luth., 2 M. E., Disciples, Ger. Meth., Presb., and R. C.

[3] Named from Mrs. Marilla Rogers, of Alden.

[4] Rice Wilder, Cyrus Finney, and Rodman Day settled in the town in 1831. The first birth was that of Sarah Finney, in Oct. 1831. Jesse Barton built the first sawmill, in 1828, and the first gristmill, in 1832. Miles Carpenter kept the first store, in 1848, and the first inn, in 1850. The first school was taught by Sophia Day, in 1833.

[5] Called by the Indians "*See-un-gut,*" noise or roar of distant water. The creek was named from the fact that about the time of the first settlement a white man was murdered upon it, within the present village limits of Akron, by an Indian who was conducting him to Canada.

[6] Named from Akron, Ohio, and the latter from a Greek word signifying "summit."

[7] 2 gristmills, 2 sawmills, 1 waterlime mill, 1 furnace and machine shop, 1 planing mill, 1 stave and shingle mill, and a tannery.

[8] Among the early settlers were Otis Ingalls, David Cully, Peter Van de Venter, Sam'l Miles, John Felton, Charles Barney, Aaron Beard, Robt. Durham, Tobias Cole, and Sam'l, Silas, John, and Thomas Hill. Peter Van de Venter kept the first inn, in 1802, and Archibald Clark the first store, in 1809. The first school was taught by —— Keith, in 1807.

[9] Bap., Presb., M. E., and R. C.

[10] The first birth was that of Geo. Tucker, in Aug. 1810; the first marriage, that of Levi Woodward and Hannah Southwick, in 1812; and the first deaths, those of two girls, twin daughters of Stephen Sisson. Stephen Stancliff built the first mill, in 1818; Stephen Tucker kept the first inn, and Chester Rose the first store, both in 1813. The first school was taught by Phebe Southwick, in the summer of 1813.

[11] 2 Friends, 2 M. E., 2 R. C., Bap., and Cong.

[12] Among the early settlers were Ezra Nott, Henry Godfrey, and Josiah Sumner. Elisha Rice and Giles Briggs settled in the town in 1810. The first birth was that of Ray Briggs, in

TONAWANDA—was formed from Buffalo, April 16, 1836; and Grand Island was taken off in 1852. It lies in the N. W. part of the co., at the angle formed by the junction of Tonawanda Creek and Niagara River. Its surface is generally level. Eleven Mile Creek crosses the N. part of the town. The soil along Niagara River is clayey; in the interior it is sandy. **Tonawanda,** (p. v.,) incorp. Dec. 3, 1853, is situated on the Erie Canal, at the confluence of Niagara River and Tonawanda Creek. It has a good harbor,[1] and is an important station on the B. & N. F. R. R. It is the western terminus of the C. & N. F. branch of the N. Y. C. R. R. It contains 5 churches, a newspaper office, a bank, an elevator,[2] and several manufacturing establishments.[3] Pop. 1,257.[4] The first settlement was made in 1805.[5] There are 8 churches in town.[6]

WALES—was formed from Aurora, April 15, 1818; and a part of Marilla was taken off in 1853. It is situated near the center of the E. border of the co. Its surface is broken and hilly and inclined toward the N. The principal stream is Big Buffalo Creek. The soil in the N. is a gravelly loam, and in the S. clay underlaid by hardpan. **Wales Center,** (p. v.,) on Big Buffalo Creek, in the N. part of the town, contains 2 churches, a gristmill, a sawmill, and 40 dwellings; **Wales,** (p. v.,) on the same stream, contains 1 church, a gristmill, a sawmill, and 30 dwellings; and **South Wales** (p. v.) contains a gristmill, a sawmill, and 25 dwellings. The first settlement was made in 1805, by Oliver Pettengill.[7] There are 3 churches in town; 2 M. E. and a Free Will Bap.

WEST SENECA—was formed, as "*Seneca*," from Chicktowaga, Hamburgh and East Hamburgh, and Lancaster, Oct. 16, 1851; its name was changed March 25, 1852. It is situated on the shore of Lake Erie, near the center of the W. border of the co. Its surface is gently undulating in the E. and level in the W. The streams are Big Buffalo, Cazenove, and Smokes[8] Creeks. The soil is generally a sandy loam. The town is mainly settled by a society of German religionists, generally known as Ebenezers, but who style themselves the "Community of True Inspiration."[9] **Middle Ebenezer,** on Buffalo Creek, contains a church, calico printing factory, wooler factory, sawmill, oil mill, and 67 houses; **Lower Ebenezer,** on Cazenove Creek, contains a church, sawmill, gristmill, tannery, and 50 houses; and **New Ebenezer** contains a large manufactory of cotton and woolen goods, an extensive dyeing works, and 9 dwellings. **Reserve, West Seneca Center,** and **West Seneca** are p. offices. The first settlement was made by Reuben Sackett, in 1826.[10] There are 4 churches in town.[11]

1811; and the first death, that of a son of Henry Godfrey, in 1814. Sumner Warren built the first mill, in 1811; Geo. Richmond kept the first inn, in 1811; and Clark & Co. the first store, in 1816. The first school was taught by Melinda Abbey, in 1814.

[1] Large quantities of lumber are received at this port from Canada and the Western States. The quantity re-shipped by canal in 1857 was, of timber, 841,011 cubic feet; of sawed stuff, 4,815.441 ft.; and of wood, 16,007 cords.

[2] This elevator has a storage capacity of 250,000 bush., and facilities for elevating 2000 bush. per hour.

[3] 3 sawmills, 3 shingle mills, a planing mill, and a furnace and machine shop.

[4] This is the pop. of that part of the village in Erie co. A part of the village is across the creek, in Niagara co.; and the pop. of this is not known.

[5] Alex. Logan, John King, and John Hersey settled in the town in 1805; Emanuel Winter, Jos. Hayward, Oliver Standard, John Cunningham, Josiah Guthrie, Ebenezer Coon, Thos. Honnan, and Joseph Hersey, in 1806; Henry Anguish, in 1808; and Frederick Buck, in 1809. Henry Anguish kept the first inn, in 1811, and Judge Wilkinson the first store, in 1823. The first mill was built by —— Osborne, in 1819.

[6] Disciples, Evang. Luth., M. E., R. C., and Wes. Meth. at Tonawanda Village, and Evang. Luth., M. E., and R. C. in other parts of the town.

[7] Ethan and Wm. Allen and Jacob Turner settled in the town in 1806, and Chas. and Alex. McKay, Ebenezer Holmes, and Wm. Hoyt in 1807. The first birth was that of Wm. Pettengill, in June, 1806. Isaac and Eli Hall built the first mill, in 1811; Isaac Hall kept the first inn, in 1816; and Orsamus Warren the first store, in 1824. The first school was taught by Jas. Wood, in 1811. In 1813 an Indian hatchet was found imbedded in a tree at Wales Center, and in 1825 John Allen related the following circumstance concerning it. About the time of the first settlement of Buffalo an Indian came to that place and exhibited the skin of a white child, and boasted that he had murdered and skinned the child for the purpose of making a tobacco pouch. Truman Allen, (brother of the narrator,) hearing the boast, became so enraged that he followed the Indian to Wales and shot him. He buried the body and rifle in the sand, and stuck the tomahawk into a tree, where it was afterward found as above stated.

[8] Named from an Indian who resided near its mouth and who was an inveterate smoker.

[9] This community purchased 7,622 acres belonging to the Buffalo Indian Reservation in 1844, and commenced their settlements the same year. They are largely engaged in agriculture and manufactures; and their wares have obtained so excellent a reputation that they find a ready market at Buffalo and elsewhere. They have a community of property, reside in villages, and several families usually occupy the same house. They are governed by a board of trustees; and their business is done through an agent, who appears to have almost unlimited control of matters. They are honest, industrious, and frugal; and in the contented and peaceful tenor of their lives they present a model which might well be copied by some of the restless and ambitious Yankee race.

[10] Among the other early settlers were Artemus W. Baker, John G. Wells, Isaac Earlle, and Geo. Hopper, who located in 1828. The first child born was a daughter of Joel Decker, in Aug. 1828; and the first death, that of Peter Beal, in 1834. Geo. E. Elderkin taught the first school, in 1839; Reuben Sackett kept the first inn, in 1826; the Ebenezer Society, the first store, in 1845; and Ballou & Tubell built the first mill, in 1837.

[11] 2 Lutheran and 2 Community of True Inspiration.

Acres of Land, Valuation, Population, Dwellings, Families, Freeholders, Schools, Live Stock, Agricultural Products, and Domestic Manufactures, of Erie County.

Names of Towns.	Acres of Land.		Valuation of 1858.			Population.		No. of Dwellings.	No. of Families.	Freeholders.	Schools.	
	Improved.	Unimproved.	Real Estate.	Personal Property.	Total.	Males.	Females.				No. of Districts.	Children taught.
Alden	11,721	8,960	$643,985	$15,400	$659,385	1,230	1,174	469	469	395	13	987
Amherst	17,298½	12,003	1,274,820	86,500	1,361,320	2,565	2,553	951	1,016	727	17	2,270
Aurora	19,363¾	13,934¾	452,240	52,120	504,360	1,872	1,793	733	759	578	14	973
Boston	13,604¼	6,153	290,300	11,600	301,900	908	861	310	311	298	10	691
Brandt	7,666¾	1,513⅜	269,310	11,200	280,510	570	523	196	211	169	9	378
Buffalo City	10,612½	2,336¼	29,334,840	6,182,220	35,517,060	37,561	36,653	10,613	14,715	6,153	34	28,000
Chicktowaga	9,280½	6,405½	867,992	9,800	877,792	1,314	1,212	488	497	365	7	995
Clarence	17,770	14,637	1,032,130	96,675	1,128,805	1,695	1,558	587	630	459	14	1,116
Colden	9,716	12,702	221,250	3,575	224,825	709	672	289	283	286	10	549
Collins	18,174	11,692½	610,090	75,900	685,990	1,013	1,012	362	408	287	13	633
Concord	23,950¼	17,080	524,648	20,950	545,598	1,409	1,396	531	535	527	19	1,166
East Hamburgh.	15,184¼	8,170	560,470	49,160	609,630	1,012	934	394	388	330	13	825
Eden	15,261¼	7,814	490,430	23,125	513,555	1,241	1,185	470	470	414	13	961
Elma[a]			405,625	7,600	413,225						11	896
Evans	14,400¼	10,977	701,088	19,900	720,988	1,194	1,058	452	463	384	14	969
Grand Island	4,017	13,684	237,567		237,567	483	355	161	173	90	5	420
Hamburgh	14,468¾	8,183	734,685	114,375	849,060	1,617	1,420	550	564	385	13	1,020
Holland	12,035¼	9,369	222,403	6,500	228,903	691	630	265	255	260	12	586
Lancaster	14,660½	16,303½	890,275	73,400	963,675	2,854	2,635	1,065	1,080	794	11	1,649
Marilla	7,037½	652	300,175	16,600	316,775	704	673	292	294	257	9	546
Newstead	19,491	11,886	954,055	30,375	984,430	1,576	1,411	596	595	486	15	1,165
North Collins	18,691½	8,353½	498,076	60,080	558,156	964	895	358	367	340	12	748
Sardinia	16,032¼	13,994	337,500	15,475	352,975	888	877	360	369	328	15	682
Tonawanda	8,699½	3,772½	516,477	61,100	577,577	1,385	1,184	450	507	323	8	916
Wales	14,538¾	7,025	330,315	14,600	344,915	870	819	336	341	329	11	641
West Seneca	6,632	11,743¾	555,293	2,250	557,543	1,333	1,190	416	493	602	6	923
Total	340,307¼	253,344⅝	43,256,039	7,060,480	50,216,519	67,658	64,673	21,674	26,193	15,566	328	51.503

Names of Towns.	Live Stock.					Agricultural Products.							Domestic Cloths, in yards.
						Bush. of Grain.					Dairy Products.		
	Horses.	Working Oxen and Calves.	Cows.	Sheep.	Swine.	Winter.	Spring.	Tons of Hay.	Bushels of Potatoes.	Bushels of Apples.	Pounds Butter.	Pounds Cheese.	
Alden	555	765	1,011	2,306	728	10,556	46,890	3,547	16,412	5,853	55,424	4,000	410
Amherst	1,004	1.230	1,294	1,568	1,975	36,170½	82,616½	3,173	19,496	8,740	69,605	100	310½
Aurora	1,033	1,191	1,236	6,828	1,233	5,934	77,611¾	6,388½	31,068	17,985	111,094	15,095	1,186
Boston	453	1,016	1,165	2,431	603	2,185	48,763½	4,029½	16,107	10,997	56,135	115.545	769
Brandt	281	789	817	1,326	503	1,421	23,221½	2,020¾	12,860	5,391	55,737	82,282	1,403
Buffalo	2,116	332	1,609	56	2,503	7,616	42,716	4,184	22,519	2,970	15,400		
Chicktowaga	611	588	862	870	814	9,687	40,432¾	3,272½	17,271	5,743	64,139	4,950	681
Clarence	1,073	896	1,161	4,844	1,859	45,471	99,576	2,606	17,064	30,864	86,743	890	1,184
Colden	337	824	797	1,710	372	1,297	27,798½	2,697	11,710	3,819	54,205	42,000	1,562
Collins	618	1,559	2,764	1,628	776	5,045	40,530	5,905	10,691	16,866	78,736	586,384	1,541
Concord	709	1,757	2,461	3,329	886	1,949¾	93,043	5,724½	22,566	17,365½	98,115	460,881	2,004½
East Hamburgh.	664	688	1,368	4,150	852	3,799½	59,357¾	5,623½	31,256½	19,254½	110,120	38,500	1,432¾
Eden	617	1,149	1,271	2,587	914	6,515½	59,425½	4,312½	20,371	14,121	112,660	36,455	1,868
Elma[a]													975½
Evans	614	1,384	1,467	3,157	846	2,241½	50,281	5,333¾	13,922	11,138	94,069	27,625	
Grand Island	129	489	250	631	779	4,047	15,845	1,002	9,928	148	23,420	40	687½
Hamburgh	780	638	818	1,545	1,007	3,358½	55,645	6,208	21,119	11,170	102,800	23,380	2,137¾
Holland	485	1,187	780	3,604	558	9,057½	43,647¾	3,041	7,107	10,761	77,850	7,907	270
Lancaster	908	1,125	1,176	1,236	1,494	22,235	84,964	4,439	31,934	13,520	80,300	3,130	
Marilla	337	616	487	1,896	508	958½	22,974¼	1,821¾	7,779	1,118	43,394	2,904	702
Newstead	1,051	1,252	1,018	5,706	1,668	48,700	100,677½	3,322	20,553	20,726	107,777	4,190	397
North Collins	574	1,576	2,588	2,464	816	1,432	45,981	6,410	19,992	12,506	103,429	515,804	2,251
Sardinia	712	1,874	1,036	6,062	697	1,484	66,294	3,401	18,811	10,266	95,645	28,470	3,329
Tonawanda	465	534	629	346	888	19,818	43,499	2,415	8,991	2,179	26,920		175
Wales	575	1,546	1,258	4,784	688	5,119	55,540¾	4,336	15,431	12,229	112,155	37,860	1,347½
West Seneca	282	603	508	21	824	7,154	31,017	2,798	20,392	470	30,260		30
Total	16,983	25,608	29,831	65,085	24,791	263,792¼	1,358,349	98,011¼	445,350½	266,195	1,866,132	2,038,392	26,654

[a] Formed since 1855.

ESSEX COUNTY.

THIS county was formed from Clinton, March 1, 1799, and a corner was taken off in the erection of Franklin co. in 1808. It lies upon Lake Champlain, in the N. E. part of the State; is centrally distant 100 miles from Albany, and contains 1,926 square miles. It is by far the most broken and mountainous county in the State. With the exception of a narrow strip of level land along the shore of Lake Champlain, nearly the whole co. is of an Alpine character. High, rocky peaks, and immense mountain masses, abounding in wild, broken crags and stupendous precipices, and separated by narrow ravines and deep gorges, form the general characteristics of the landscape. With the exception of the Black Mountain, of North Carolina, and the White Mountain group, of New Hampshire, the mountains of this co. attain a higher elevation than any others belonging to the great Appalachian system; and, taking into consideration their great number of lofty peaks, they surpass in magnitude all other groups E. of the Mississippi. The mountains seem thrown together without regard to order or system; and from this fact, and the frequent misapplication of names, much confusion has arisen in attempting to describe them.

The 5 mountain ranges N. of the Mohawk valley extend through portions of this co., and terminate upon the shores of Lake Champlain. They all have a general N. E. and s. w. direction, rising successively higher toward the N. until they culminate in the most northerly range. The axes of these ranges are nearly parallel, and are respectively about 8 mi. apart. They are not always distinct and continuous, but in some places their lateral spurs interlock, and in others their continuity is broken by the intervention of valleys and brief intervals of lowland. They are not regularly serrated, but appear to consist of groups of sharp pointed peaks connected by immense ridges. The principal mountain masses appear to extend in a due N. and s. direction, and are thus placed obliquely in the range of which they form a part. Single mountains are often sufficiently large to occupy the whole intervening space between the ranges, thus destroying the continuity of the valleys and reducing them to narrow, isolated ravines. This arrangement of mountains, in regard to the ridges, affords the key to the peculiar plan of the construction of this whole mountain system. The most southerly of the 5 ranges barely enters the extreme s. E. corner of the co. It is known as the Palmertown or Luzerne Mts. It has also sometimes been called the Black Mountain Range and the Tongue Mts. It constitutes the highlands which rise upon both sides of Lake George and upon the narrow peninsula between the Lake George Outlet and Lake Champlain. Mt. Defiance, the extremity of the ridge, has an elevation of about 750 feet above the lake. The second range, known as the Kayaderosseras, extends through the s. E. part of Schroon and the center of Crown Point, ending in the high cliff which overlooks Bulwagga Bay, and is elevated about 1,150 feet above the surface of the lake. Along the course of this range, in Schroon, is a cluster of mountain peaks, the highest of which, Mt. Pharaoh, is 3,500 to 4,000 feet above tide. The third range occupies the w. and N. parts of Schroon, and extends through the N. part of Moriah and the center of Westport, ending in the high promontory of Split Rock, in the s. part of Essex.[1] Bald Mountain, in Westport, one of the most noted peaks of this range, attains an elevation of 2,065 feet above tide This range takes the name of the Schroon Mts. from the principal lake which lies at its foot.

The fourth range extends through the central parts of Minerva and N. Hudson, the s. E. corner of Keene and Lewis, the N. w. part of Elizabethtown, and the center of Willsborough, ending in the high bluffs which border upon Perou Bay. It might with propriety be called the Boquet Range, from the principal river which flows at its base. Dix Peak, in N. Hudson, the highest mountain in this range, attains an elevation of 5,200 feet above tide, and, next to Mt. Marcy, is the

---

[1] The name of Split Rock was applied to this promontory in consequence of about ⅓ acre of the extreme point being detached from the mainland by a chasm 10 feet wide, extending downward to near the water's edge. It was once supposed that this mass was split off from the mainland by some great convulsion of nature, and writers have gravely asserted that 500 feet soundings have been taken in the chasm; but it is probable that the fissure was formed by the disintegration of the rock, which at this point contains iron pyrites and is easily acted upon by the elements. The height of this dissevered mass above the lake is about 30 feet.

highest point in the co. Nipple Top has an elevation of 4,900 feet. Raven Hill, in Elizabethtown, and Mt. Discovery, in Lewis, each attain an elevation of over 2,000 feet. The fifth range extends through Newcomb, Keene, Jay, Lewis, and Chesterfield, ending in the rocky promontory of Trembleau Point. It has sometimes been called the Clinton Range, but it is more widely known as the Adirondack Range.[1] Mt. Marcy, the highest peak of this range, and the highest land in the State, has an elevation of 5467 feet above tide. Mounts McMartin, McIntyre, and San-da-no-na, belonging to this range, are each upward of 5000 feet high. A spur of this range extends northward on the borders of Jay and Chesterfield, in a high, unbroken ridge, with a mean elevation of about 2,000 feet above tide.

North of the Adirondack Range the mountains are not disposed in regular ranges, but are scattered in groups over a large space of country. These groups, however, lie in a line parallel to the other ranges, and for convenience of description they might be considered under the head of the "Au Sable Range." Mt. Seward, the highest peak, 5,100 feet above tide, is situated just beyond the limits of the co. Whiteface, in Wilmington, has an elevation of 4,855 feet.

The rocks of Essex co. are primary, consisting of granite, gneiss, and hypersthene. The mountains generally are composed of huge masses of naked rocks, more or less disintegrated by the action of the elements. Nearly the whole mountain region is composed of this primitive rock. Along the base of the mountains, on the E., appear the Trenton limestone and Utica slate; while upon the immediate borders of the lake are found the clayey masses of the tertiary formation. In the primary rocks, among the mountains, are immense beds of rich magnetic iron ore, some of which have been extensively.worked, though generally in a very rude and primitive manner. The iron produced from this ore has been subjected to the most severe tests, and has been pronounced equal to the best which is produced in the world.

The s.w. portion of the co. is drained by the Hudson and its principal branch, the Schroon River. These streams take their rise upon the highest peaks of the Adirondack and Schroon Ranges, and flow through the winding valleys that lie at their base. Upon the E. Putnams Creek drains the region between the Luzerne and Kayaderosseras Ranges; Mill Brook, between the Kayaderosseras and Schroon; and the Boquet[2] River, between the Schroon and Boquet Ranges. The Au Sable, flowing along the N. base of the Adirondack Range, drains the N. portion of the co. The valleys of these streams are generally narrow, and are bounded by steep banks, which are not unfrequently huge masses of precipitous or overhanging rocks.

Lakes Champlain and George lie partly in this co., and more than 100 small lakes lie wholly within its limits. The greater part of these are comprised in three groups, lying near the base of the principal mountain peaks. The first of these groups surrounds Mt. Marcy; the second, Mt. Pharaoh; and the third, Whiteface. Many others are found scattered along the whole course of the mountain ranges. These lakes are generally long and narrow; and Prof. Emmons says "that, instead of occupying shallow basins scooped out of the softer materials,—as earth and the ordinary slates and shales,—they lie in chasms formed by uplifts and fractures in the primary rock." Many of these lakes have precipitous banks, presenting a great variety of wild and picturesque scenery. The soil along Lake Champlain consists of a stiff, hard clay, alternating with a dark loam and gravel, and, in the narrow valleys, of disintegrated rocks. Upon the mountains the soil is thin and light, many of the peaks being masses of naked rocks, destitute of both soil and vegetation. The declivities of the hills are generally wooded, but not very heavily. Three-fourths of the entire surface of the co. is too rough and broken for cultivation.

Farming, iron mining, and the manufacture of iron from the ore, constitute the leading pursuits; and the immense mineral wealth of this section must for centuries continue to afford an object of profitable investment. In the infancy of the settlement, and until the supply became exhausted, the manufacture and exportation of lumber and staves to the Quebec market formed the leading, and, in some neighborhoods, almost the sole, objects of industry. Rafts of great size were formed in the coves and sheltered points along the lake shore, and were wafted by sails and oars to the Richlieu River, and down that stream and the St. Lawrence to Quebec, where they were transferred to ships for the British market. The completion of the Champlain Canal gave a new impulse to lumbering; but the timber suitable for exportation is now nearly exhausted, except on the extreme w. borders of the co. The logs of this latter region are floated down the Saranac,

---

[1] The name Adirondack is strictly applied only to the group of elevated peaks of which Mt. Marcy is the center, but by common usage it is now made to comprehend the whole system of mountains N. of the Mohawk.

[2] Pron. bo-kwét. Probably from the French "baquet," a trough. It is also said to have been named from Henry Boquet, an English officer; but the name appears on French maps previous to his residence in the country.

VIEW ON LAKE GEORGE.

ADIRONDACK OR INDIAN PASS

ESSEX COUNTY

Racket, Hudson, and other streams, to some convenient place for sawing; and large sums have been appropriated by the State for improving the channels of these rivers for this purpose.[1] Tanneries, within the last few years, have greatly increased in the woody sections of the State, and about a dozen of them are located in this co. The iron manufacturing business of this region was commenced at Willsborough Falls in 1801,[2] and now forms one of the leading pursuits of the people. Iron ore is exported from this co. in large quantities to Pittsburgh and other distant localities, to be mixed with other ores.[3] The manufacture of sash and blinds, tubs, pails, and other articles of pine and cedar, starch, paper, and black lead, receives considerable attention. Shipbuilding, to some extent, has been carried on in Essex and Willsborough.

The county seat is located at Elizabethtown,[4] situated upon the Boquet, about 8 mi. w. of the lake. It contains the courthouse, jail, and county clerk's office.[5] These buildings are plain and substantial. The poorhouse is located upon a farm of 100 acres, in Essex, 10½ mi. N. E. of Elizabethtown. The average number of inmates is 70, supported at a cost of 62 cts. per week each. The farm yields a revenue of about $1,200.[6]

There are 2 papers now published in the county.[7]

In 1609, Samuel Champlain, with two attendants, accompanied a party of Canadian Indians on an expedition against the Five Nations. On the 4th of July his party entered the lake which now bears his name, and on the 30th they met their enemies. A sanguinary battle ensued, the fate of which was decided by the firearms of the whites, then for the first time used within the limits of the State. This act of unprovoked hostility on the part of Champlain laid the foundation for the long and bloody wars between the Five Nations and the French, and rendered the former the willing and steadfast friends and allies of the English. The whole region bordering upon the lake was claimed, by constructive title, by both France and England; and during the wars that ensued it became the great battle ground for supremacy, and the principal highway for war parties in their mutual incursions upon the defenseless frontier settlements. Fort Frederick was erected by the French at Crown Point in 1731. This measure was met by remonstrance, but no open resistance, on the part of the English. Previous to the erection of the fort, French settlements had commenced in various places along both shores of the lake. These settlements had made considerable progress,

---

1 $6000 was appropriated in 1853, and $5000 in 1854, for improving the log navigation of the Au Sable River. A lighthouse has been erected at Split Rock by the General Government. The proposed Sacketts Harbor and Saratoga R. R. has been surveyed across the s. corner of the co., and another route has been projected from Plattsburgh to Whitehall; but there is little prospect of either of these lines being soon finished.

2 In that year George Throop and Levi Higby, in connection with Charles Kane, of Schenectady, began the manufacture of anchors at Willsborough Falls. For the first 10 years the ore was obtained in part from Canada, but principally from Vermont. A bed at Basin Harbor was the only one then known within the co. Mill and steamboat irons were afterward made, and the foundry was finally converted into a forge. Early in the present century W. D. Ross erected a rolling mill on the Boquet, for making nail plates for the factory at Fair Haven, Vt. About 1809, Archibald McIntyre and his associates erected works on a branch of the Au Sable, in the present town of N. Elba, designated as the "Elba Iron Works," which were at first supplied from the vicinity, and afterward from the Arnold mine, in Clinton co. The forge was abandoned in 1815, after several years of prosperous business. The iron interest rapidly extended after the completion of the Champlain Canal, and several large manufactories were erected in the valley of the Au Sable and the surrounding region. The forges, rolling mills, and nail factories of this section are among the most extensive of the kind in the country. Bar, pig, and bloom iron of superior quality are produced in large quantities. Within a few years, anthracite coal has nearly superseded the use of charcoal in the furnaces along the lake shore. These establishments afford a home market for a large part of the agricultural products of the co. Most of the above dates and facts are condensed from *Watson's Ag. Survey of Essex Co.*, 1852, *p.* 814.

3 The principal ores in this co. are magnetic, and they are separated from the stone by water and by magnetic machines. Hundreds of bbls. of iron sand are collected upon the shores of Lake Champlain and sold to the N. Y. stationers.

4 David Watson and John Savage, of Wash. co., were appointed commissioners to locate a site for the co. buildings, which were to be erected under the care of 3 commissioners appointed by the supervisors. The first co. officers were Daniel Ross, *First Judge*; Stephen Cuyler, *Clerk*; Thos. Stowers, *Sheriff*; and Wm. Gilliland, *Surrogate.*

5 When the co. was formed, the new blockhouse in Essex, then Willsborough, was used as a courthouse and jail. By an act passed April 7, 1807, Elizabethtown was selected as the co. seat, and to this place the courts and clerk's office were transferred upon the completion of the proper buildings, in 1814.

6 This establishment is old, and in some respects inconvenient; but it is spoken of as extremely well kept, and in this respect is one of the best in the State.

7 *The Reveille,* the first paper in the co., was started at Elizabethtown, about 1810, by Luther Marsh.
The Essex Patriot was published at the same place, in 1817–18, by L. and O. Person.
The Essex County Times was started at Elizabethtown, by R. W. Livingston, and in 1833 sold to —— Macomb, who continued it about 15 months. It was printed on an old "*Ramage*" press brought from Skaneateles, Onondaga co.
Another paper was commenced at Elizabethtown, in Jan. 1849, by D. Truair, and removed to Keeseville in about 4 months.
The Elizabethtown Post was established by Robert W. Livingston in 1851, and was subsequently united with the Northern Standard, of Keeseville.
The Keeseville Herald was commenced in 1825 by F. P. Allen, and soon after passed into the hands of A. H. Allen, by whom it was continued, with a few interruptions, until 1841.
The Keeseville Argus, edited by Adonijah Emmons, was begun about 1831, and continued 5 or 6 years.
The Essex County Republican was established at Keeseville in 1839, and is now published by J. B. Dickinson.
The Au Sable River Gazette was started at Keeseville about 1847, by D. Truair, and continued 5 or 6 years.
The Old Settler, mo., was commenced at Keeseville by A. H. Allen in 1849, and was afterward removed to; Saratoga Springs.
The Northern Gazette was started at Keeseville in 1851, and continued several years.
The Northern Standard was established at Keeseville in 1854 by A. W. Lansing, and is now published by A. W. Lansing & Son.
The Essex County Republican was started at Essex about 1822 by J. K. Averill, and was continued by him, and by Walton & Person, until 1833.
The Berean Guide was started in 1840, at Essex, by Rev. M. Bailey, and continued 1 year.
The Westport Patriot and Essex County Advertiser was commenced in 1845, at Westport, by D. Truair.
The Essex County Patriot was issued at Essex, about 1847, by A. H. Allen. It was changed to
The Westport Herald, and continued 6 or 7 years.
The Essex County Times was published at Westport in 1851.

and thriving villages had sprung up, before they were finally broken up by invading armies. Still more extended schemes of settlement were planned, and extensive grants of land were made upon the same condition as the French grants in Canada.[1] Soon after their first occupation, the French caused a survey of the lake and its shores to be made by Sieur Anger, surveyor to the King; and the work seems to have been carefully done. In 1755 the French advanced 12 mi. nearer to the English settlements, and commenced the fortification of Ticonderoga upon a point that entirely commanded the passage of the lake. The fort was named by them "*Carillon;*"[2] but it is now generally known by the Indian name of Ticonderoga. Upon it vast sums of money were afterward expended by both the French and English, and it became the most formidable fortress in America. The French here made a stand against the advances of the English; and when at length it was found to be no longer tenable, Crown Point and all the posts along the lake were at once abandoned.

The repeated incursions of the French and Indians into the English settlements, and the continual advancements of the French military posts, at length aroused the attention of the English Government and led to the conviction that the very existence of the frontier settlements depended upon the complete overthrow of the French power in America. One of the great expeditions of 1755 was directed against Crown Point. The English troops, under the command of Gen. Lyman, built Fort Lyman—afterward Fort Edward—on the Hudson, and, under Sir Wm. Johnson, who assumed the command, advanced to the head of Lake George. Here, learning that the French were fortifying Ticonderoga and that they had received large reinforcements, Sir William chose a commanding position and fortified his camp. In the mean time, Baron Dieskau, the French commander, at the head of a superior force, endeavored to cut off his communication with Fort Lyman. A body of provincial troops, under Col. Williams,[3] of Mass., and of Indians, under the famous Mohawk chief Hendrick, thrown out as an advance guard by Sir Wm., fell into an ambush, and the whole party were cut to pieces, and the two leaders killed. The French immediately attacked the English camp, but were repulsed with great loss, and the retreating fugitives were mostly killed or taken prisoners by a party of fresh English troops from Fort Lyman. Sir Wm. did not follow up his success, but spent the remainder of the season in constructing Fort Wm. Henry on the site of his camp, leaving the French to strengthen their works at Crown Point and Ticonderoga without molestation. No general expedition was projected during 1756, and the only active warfare was carried on by adventurous parties of rangers.[4]

From this time to the close of the war, and again during the Revolution, this co. was the theater of important military events. We have space only for a brief chronological recapitulation of the principal ones as they occurred. The partisan warfare, with varying success, continued through the winter and spring of 1756–57. In July, Montcalm, Gov. of Canada, assembled 9,000 men at Ticonderoga, and marched to the head of Lake George, for the purpose of reducing Fort Wm. Henry; which object he accomplished Aug. 3.[5] In the summer of 1758 an expedition was fitted out against Ticonderoga, and was intrusted to the command of Gen. Abercrombie. On the 5th of July he crossed Lake George with 17,000 men; and on the 6th the advanced guard of his army was surprised by the French, and many killed, among whom was Lord Howe,[6] second in command. On the 8th the English army endeavored to take the fort by storm, but were repulsed with a loss of 2,000 men. In 1759, Gen. Amherst, at the head of 12,000 men, proceeded to invest Ticonderoga. The French troops having been mostly withdrawn for the defense of Quebec, the whole fortress was dismantled, and abandoned on the 30th of July. Crown Point was soon after abandoned, and the whole region came into the undisputed possession of the

---

[1] A seigniory, extending 3 leagues along the lake shore and 2 leagues back, was granted, June 13, 1737, to Sieur Louis Joseph Robert, the king's storekeeper at Montreal. Its northern boundary was to be half a league below the "*Bacquet*" (Boquet) River, and its southern 2¼ leagues above. This territory embraced the present town of Essex and a large part of Willsborough. Another seigniory, extending 6 leagues along the lake and 5 back, was granted, Nov. 15, 1758, to Michael Chartier de Lotbinière. It was called "*D'Alainville,*" and embraced the present towns of Ticonderoga, Crown Point, and Schroon. Settlements which commenced upon this grant were broken up by the English armies. Most of the seigniory was granted to officers and soldiers of the English army, in accordance to his majesty's proclamation of Oct. 7, 1763. After the cession of Canada, the French proprietor presented his claims to the English Government, with no other effect than to create a considerable temporary alarm among the English settlers.

[2] See page 304.

[3] On his way to the frontiers, Col. Williams stopped at Albany

and made his will, leaving a sum of money to found a free school in Western Mass. This legacy founded and gave the name to Williams College. In 1851 the alumni of the college erected a monument to his memory on the spot where he was killed.

[4] The most enterprising of these rangers were Majs. Israel Putnam and Robert Rogers. The party commanded by the latter officer consisted of old hunters, accustomed to all kinds of hardships and privations. Among his officers was John Stark, afterward Gen. Stark of the Revolution. These parties hung upon the outskirts of the French forts, took off their sentinels, burned their villages, killed their cattle, destroyed their boats, and annoyed them in every possible manner.

[5] See page 668; *Lossing's Field Book of the Revolution; Bancroft's Hist. U. S.*

[6] Brother of Sir William Howe and Admiral Howe, English commanders during the Revolution. Lord Howe was a brave and enterprising officer, greatly beloved by the army, and his loss was deeply deplored.

English. The works at Ticonderoga and Crown Point were enlarged and strengthened, at a cost of $10,000,000.[1]

By the provisions of the Treaty of Paris, signed Feb. 10, 1763, in which the French ceded their possessions in North America to the English, the latter government was bound to respect the titles to land previously granted by the former. The proclamation of the King of Oct. 7, 1763, authorized the granting of the lands upon Lake Champlain to officers and soldiers who had served in the war. These incompatible acts led to much confusion. Overlapping claims and conflicting titles unavoidably followed; and the matter was not finally settled until after the Revolution. In the mean time, the controversy had the tendency to retard settlement, by destroying confidence in the titles by which the land could be held and conveyed.

Settlement was commenced upon the Boquet in 1765, under the auspices of Wm. Gilliland, a wealthy merchant of N. Y.[2] Through his agency, and that of other capitalists, several miles of the lake shore between the mouth of the Boquet and Crown Point were settled, mills and roads were built and schools established. Mr. G. held a justice's commission, and for many years was the only judicial authority.[3] The settlers whom he induced to locate upon his estate were mostly Irish.

After the cession of Canada the great fortresses on the lake were allowed to fall into partial decay, and were held by only small bodies of troops. Upon the receipt of the news of the commencement of hostilities at Lexington, a small body of troops, known as "Green Mountain Boys," under Col. Ethan Allen, surprised and took both Ticonderoga and Crown Point in May, 1775.[4] During the summer and autumn of the same year the expedition, under Schuyler and Montgomery, against Canada, passed down the lake, and returned the next spring, unsuccessful. During the summer of 1776, naval forces were organized upon the lake by both the British and Americans, the latter under the command of Benedict Arnold. In an engagement that ensued, the Americans were defeated, and their remaining vessels were obliged to take refuge under the guns of Fort Ticonderoga. Crown Point was dismantled, and the stores removed; and soon after it was taken possession of by the British. Mr. Gilliland and the colonists ardently embraced the American cause, and materially aided Montgomery's army in its advance on Canada, by furnishing provisions, and, on its return, by affording relief to the sick and wounded.[5] Mr. G.'s estate was wasted by both friends and foes, and finally the whole settlement was broken up by Burgoyne.[6]

Burgoyne landed on the banks of the Boquet, June 21, 1777, and spent several days in conferences with the Indian tribes; and on the 27th the invading army advanced to Crown Point. On the 30th they invested Ticonderoga; and on the night of July 4 they took possession of "Sugar Loaf Hill," (now Mt. Defiance,) and erected upon it a battery of heavy guns, completely commanding the fort. On the night of the 5th the Americans hastily embarked their stores and munitions of war upon bateaux, and sent them up to Skenesborough under convoy, and the main body of the army escaped into Vt.[7] Both parties were quickly pursued, and the tide of war slowly and sullenly rolled southward, beyond the limits of the co.

In Sept. Gen. Lincoln, at the head of a body of militia stationed at Manchester, Vt., made an attack upon these works, took Mts. Hope and Defiance, released 100 American prisoners, took 293 of the enemy, and captured an armed sloop, several gun boats, and more than 200 bateaux.[8] The fort was not taken. After the surrender of Burgoyne the place was dismantled, and the garrison retreated down the lake. The rear division of their boats, with 50 men and a large quantity of

[1] The fort and field works at Ticonderoga spread over an area of several miles, and the fortress at Crown Point embraced seven acres. The ruins of these works now visible still attest their extent and magnitude.

[2] Mr. Gilliland at first designed to lay the foundation of a vast baronial estate; and hence he sold no land, but leased it on the most favorable terms.

[3] A convention of the settlers was held March 17, 1775, (St. Patrick's Day,) and a local, independent government was adopted. The management of affairs was intrusted to a moderator, two supts. of roads and bridges, three appraisers of damages, and a town clerk. Just before the Revolution, a scheme was devised to form a separate colonial government, embracing all the territory north of Mass. and between the Connecticut and St. Lawrence Rivers. Philip Skene, the founder of "Skenesborough," (now Whitehall,) is believed to have been the leading spirit of this movement, and his appointment as gov. of the forts of Ticonderoga and Crown Point in June, 1775, seems to give color to this belief. See Journals of Congress, June 8, 1775; Watson's Ag. Survey, Tr. Ag. Soc., 1852, p. 694.

[4] The capture of these forts, and of the armed schooner upon the lake, was of immense importance to the Americans, as it supplied them with a great amount of cannon and other munitions of war.

[5] Gen. Carlton offered a reward of $500 for the delivery of Gilliland in Canada. Sheriff White, of Tryon co., and a party

of Tories and Indians, who attempted to capture him, were themselves captured and sent to Gen. Schuyler.

[6] Mr. G. assisted Arnold in the prosecution of his designs to the extent of his ability; and, in return for the kindness, Arnold, by an arbitrary stretch of power, destroyed his dwellings, mills, and stores, and nearly reduced him to poverty. In a memorial to Congress in 1777, Gilliland held the following truthful and prophetic language in regard to Arnold:—" It is not in mine, but it is in your power to bring him to justice. Bursting with pride, and intoxicated with power,—to which he ever ought to have been a stranger, but which he has had art enough to obtain from you,—he tyrannizes where he can. If temerity, if rashness, impudence, and error, can recommend him to you, he is allowed to be amply supplied with these qualities; and many people think they ought to recommend him in a peculiar manner to Lord North, who, in gratitude for his having done more injury to the American cause than all the ministerial troops have had the power of doing, ought to reward him with a generous pension."

[7] A heavy chain, 1000 feet long, and an immense boom, erected across the lake by the Americans at great labor and expense, were cut through in 2 hours.

[8] In this expedition the Continental standard left behind by St. Clair was recovered.

military stores, were captured by a party of "Green Mountain Boys" under Capt. Ebenezer Allen. In 1780, Gen. Haldeman, with a party of British soldiers, advanced to Ticonderoga and occupied it for some time. Maj. Carleton here made a diversion in favor of Sir John Johnson, by an attack upon Forts Anne and George. In 1781 the British fleet several times entered the lake, but retired without accomplishing any thing.[1] In 1784, Gilliland returned to his ruined settlement and endeavored to retrieve his waning fortunes. Relinquishing his ideas of manorial greatness, he offered his lands for sale; but adverse lawsuits and treacherous friends soon dissipated the remnant of his wealth and brought his existence to a miserable close.[2] The progress of settlement at first was not very rapid. In 1795 there were in Clinton co.—then embracing Essex—but 624 legal voters. From that time forward, however, settlement progressed with great rapidity, and several public roads were opened to facilitate it.[3] Soon after the war an arsenal was erected at Elizabethtown. During the patriot excitement it was robbed; and since, it has been sold.

CHESTERFIELD—was formed from Willsborough, Feb. 20, 1802. It lies in the N.E. corner of the co., upon the shore of Lake Champlain. Its surface is broken and mountainous. The Jay Mountains, a northern spur of the Adirondack Range, extend northward through the w. part. This range is a continuous, high, rocky ridge, without a single pass, forming an almost impassable barrier between Chesterfield and Jay. The main Adirondack Range extends through the center of the town from s. w. to N.E., ending at Trembleau Point, a high, rocky bluff 1200 to 1500 feet above the surface of the lake. Bosworth Mountain and Poke-a-Moonshine, each attaining an elevation of about 3000 feet, are the two principal peaks within the limits of the town. The s.E. part is hilly. The N. E. part is a rolling table land, with a light, sandy, and unproductive soil. There are several lakes in the interior, the principal of which are Augur and Butternut Ponds. Not more than one half of the surface is susceptible of cultivation. The principal valuable minerals that have been found are iron, graphite, and a beautiful light brown marble. Schuyler Island, in the lake, belongs to this town. The Au Sable River, upon the N. border, affords a large amount of hydraulic power, and some very attractive scenery. The falls at Birmingham have a descent of 90 feet, including the rapids above the main fall.[4] **Keeseville** (p. v.) is situated on both sides of the Au Sable River, its northern part being in Clinton co.[5] It is the seat of extensive iron works and other important manufactures. The iron from the ore is made into nails, horseshoes, merchant iron, edge tools, and machinery. The village has a bank, an academy, and 5 churches. Pop. according to last census, 2569, of which 1370 were in Chesterfield. **Port Kent,**[6] (p. v.,) on Lake Champlain, contains 25 houses; **Port Douglas** 5; **Port Kendall** 6; and **Birmingham Falls** 6. Matthew Adgate and sons came into town about 1792.[7] The first church was Cong.; and the first preacher was Rev. Cyrus Comstock.[8]

CROWN POINT—was formed March 23, 1786, and named from the old French fortress[9] situated on the lake. Elizabethtown was taken off in 1798, Schroon and Ticonderoga in 1804, and Moriah in 1808. It lies upon the shore of Lake Champlain, s. E. of the center of the co. A strip of nearly level land, about 4 mi. wide, extends along the lake shore. The central part of the town is broken, the hills gradually rising into the Kayaderosseras Mts. in the w. Putnams Creek, the principal stream, takes its rise in the ponds and lakes among the mountains, and upon its course are numerous falls, furnishing an abundance of water power. The soil upon the lake shore is a deep, rich, clayey loam; and in the interior it is of a light, sandy nature. Abundance

---

1 For a long time there was a great mystery connected with these movements, which was afterward explained by the publication of the negotiations which took place between the Gov. of Canada and the "Vt. Council of Safety."

2 For some time he was confined in N.Y. for debt; but, regaining his freedom, he returned to the scene of his former enterprise. Here meeting with new disappointments and treachery, and becoming partially deranged by his misfortunes, he wandered into the wilderness and perished of cold and exposure.

3 Among these public roads were one from Willsborough Falls to Peru; another, known as the "Old State Road," from Sandy Hill, along the Schroon Valley, to Canada Line; and another across the s. w. corner of the county from Canton to Chester. In 1790, Platt Rogers established a ferry across the lake, at Basin Harbor. He also built several roads, and a bridge over the Boquet at Willsborough Falls. For constructing these and other public works, Rogers and his associates received a grant of 73,000 acres of unappropriated land.

4 See page 235.

5 The first settler of Keeseville was Robert Hoyle, who built the first bridge and sawmill and kept the first store, in 1802. It was first called "Long Chute." About 1812 the property came into the hands of Richard and Oliver Keese and John W. Anderson, who erected a woolen factory and iron works in 1813. The name was first changed to "Andersons Falls," and afterwards to Keeseville. See Clinton co., town of Au Sable.

6 Both Port Kent and Keeseville are centers of extensive and important iron districts.

7 Alva Bosworth, Elihu Briggs, Edward Palmer, Levi Cooley, Dr. Clark, John and Benj. Macomber, John Page, and —— Norton, were among the first settlers. The first child born was Thos. Rangnam, and the first death that of Abel Handy.

8 The census reports 5 churches; F. W. Bap., M. E., Presb., Prot. E., and R. C.

9 The point which contains the ruins of this fortress is supposed to have been an important commercial mart previous to the French War; but now it contains only a single farm house.

of rich iron ore is found; and in connection with it are beds of natural phosphate of lime. Graphite and black clouded marble are also found in great abundance. On the shore of the lake is a mineral spring, containing sulphates of lime and magnesia. The manufacture of iron is carried on to a great extent; there are also establishments for the manufacture of lumber, shingles, pails, sash and blinds, and woolen goods. **Crown Point,** (p. v.,) in the E. part, on Putnams Creek, contains 2 churches and about 60 houses. **Hammonds Corners** contains 35 houses, and **Irondale** (late "*Penfield*") 20. The French made the first settlement, at a very early period. The country around Fort St. Frederick, upon the point, seems to have been once the seat of thriving villages, the remains of which are still visible.[1] All these settlements were obliterated during the French War of 1755–60. During the peace which followed, settlements were again made, and in 1777 were again destroyed.[2] Religious services were early held in the chapel of the fort, and were continued during its military occupation.[3]

ELIZABETHTOWN—was formed from Crown Point, Feb. 12, 1798, and was named in compliment to Elizabeth, wife of Wm. Gilliland. Parts of Moriah and Keene were taken off in 1808, and Westport in 1815. A part of Jay and Lewis were annexed Jan. 31, 1844, and a part of Lewis, Nov. 11, 1854. It is an interior town, lying a little N. of the center of the co. The Boquet Mts. occupy the N.W. and the Schroon Range the S.E. corner of the town. Raven Hill, an offshoot from the former range, in the N.E. corner, is 2,100 feet above tide; and the "Giant of the Valley," the highest peak of the latter range, has an elevation of 2,500 to 3,000 feet. A perpendicular precipice of 700 feet lies on the northern declivity of this mountain. The Boquet River flows in a N.E. direction through near the center of the town. Its valley, one-fourth of a mile to a mile in width, comprises the greater part of the arable land. Not more than one-fourth of the surface is susceptible of cultivation. Extensive beds of iron ore are found in various parts of the town. In the S.E. part, a hill, 200 feet high, covering 40 acres, is supposed to be nearly a solid mass of iron, except a slight covering of drift. An extensive bed of kaolin, or porcelain clay, is also found in town. The manufacture of iron is one of the leading pursuits: there are several forges in town. The soil is a sandy or gravelly loam. **Elizabethtown**[4] (p. v.) is pleasantly situated upon the Boquet River, near the foot of several high peaks. It is the co. seat, and a place of considerable trade. Pop. about 500. **New Russia** (p. v.) contains about 100 inhabitants. Among the first settlers were Jonah Hanchett, Sampson Smith, Herman and Joel Finney, Wareham Barber, Nathan Lewis, Hez. and Ira Phelps, Wm. Kellogg, and Gardner Simonds, who came in about 1792. The first school was taught by Dr. Kincade. The first church (Bap.) was organized in 1796 or '97.[5]

ESSEX—was formed from Willsborough, April 4, 1805. It lies upon the shore of Lake Champlain, N. of the center of the co. The surface is rolling in the E. and mountainous in the w. Boquet Mt., in the N.W. part, has an elevation of about 1,000 feet above the lake. Split Rock, the extremity of the Schroon Mountain Range in the S.E. corner of the town, has already been described.[6] The Black River limestone crops out in this town, and is used both for building purposes and for the manufacture of lime. The Boquet River flows northerly through near the center of the town. Upon it are several falls, affording abundance of water power. The soil is a clayey loam upon the lake, and a light sandy loam among the mountains. Manufactures, consisting of wrought iron, nails, spikes, lumber, and woolen goods, are carried on. **Essex**[7] (p. v.) has a population of about 700, **Whallonsburgh** (p. v.) 250, and **Boquet** 200. The town was first settled by Wm. Gilliland, in 1765.[8] Wm. McAuley, a relative and coadjutor of Mr. G., located upon the site of the present village of Essex.[9] This settlement was broken up during the Revolution.[10] The first church (Prot. E.) was organized in 1805.[11]

---

[1] The Swedish traveler Kalm mentions the existence of this early settlement; and the "Journal of Major Rogers" speaks of villages, well filled barns, herds of cattle, and fields of grain. Chimney Point, upon the eastern shore of the lake, derives its name from the remains of early habitations found there by the present race of settlers.

[2] Among the first settlers after the Revolution were George Trimble, James Morrow, Aaron Townsend, Dennis Meagher, Andrew Hardy, Saml. Foot, and Elisha Rhodes. The first mill was a windmill, a short distance s. of the fort. James Morrow erected the first mill and kept the first inn and store after the Revolution. Washington visited Crown Point in 1784.

[3] Benj. Wooster was the first preacher after the Revolution. The first church (Cong.) was organized in 1804. The census reports 4 churches; 2 Cong., M. E., Union.

[4] Elizabethtown was named "*Pleasant Valley*" by the first settlers, and is now locally known as "The Valley."

[5] The census reports 3 churches; Bap., Cong., M. E.

[6] See page 295.

[7] A blockhouse was built in this village in 1797, in consequence of the alarm occasioned by St. Clair's defeat; and in 1799, upon the organization of the co., it was used for a co. courthouse, and continued as such until the erection of the co. buildings at Elizabethtown, under the act of 1807.

[8] See pages 299, 305.

[9] Among the first settlers after the Revolution were Danl. Ross, (first merchant and mill owner,) Isaac and Benj. Sheldon, Benj. Stafford, Danl. Murray, Hen. Van Ormand, Dr. Colborn Clemens, (first physician,) David, Abram and Abner Reynolds, Nehemiah Payn, and James Eldrich. The first school was taught by Miss Towner. The first male teacher was Enoch P. Henry.

[10] In Oct. 1777, in this town, the retreating British garrison of Ticonderoga was attacked by a party of "Green Mountain Boys," under Capt. Ebenezer Allen, and 50 men and all the military stores were captured.

[11] The census reports 6 chs.; M. E., Wes. Meth., 2 Bap., 2 Presb.

JAY[1]—was formed from Willsborough, Jan. 16, 1798. A part of Keene was taken off, in 1808, of Wilmington (as "*Dansville*") in 1821, and a part of Elizabethtown in 1844. Parts of Peru (Clinton co.) and Chatauga (Franklin co.) were annexed, March 22, 1822. It lies upon the N. border of the co., w. of the center. The Au Sable Mts., extending through the w. part, gradually decline toward the N. Mts. Hamlin, Clark, and Bassitt, each 2000 feet above tide, are the highest peaks; the Jay Mts., a N. spur of the Adirondacks, lie along the E. border. The extreme s. angle of the town is occupied by some of the most lofty and rocky peaks of the Adirondacks. The E. branch of the Au Sable flows through near the center of the town. Veins of black lead have been found, but not worked. Iron ore is found in abundance. The soil is a light, sandy and gravelly loam. A mineral spring, near Upper Jay, contains iron and sulphur. The manufacture of bar iron, nails, and bloom iron is extensively carried on. **Au Sable Forks**, (p. v.,) an iron manufacturing village, contains 70 houses; **Jay** (p. v.) 50, and **Upper Jay** (p. v.) 20. Nathaniel Mallory was the first settler, about 1796.[2] The first church (Bap.) was formed in 1797; the first preacher was Solomon Brown.[3]

KEENE—was formed from Elizabethtown and Jay, March 19, 1808. North Elba was taken off in 1849. It extends from the center of the co. toward the N. and w. The Adirondack Mts. extend through the center of the town and occupy nearly its entire surface, leaving little or no arable land. The principal peaks are Mt. Marcy, 5467 feet above tide; Long Pond Mt., 3000 feet; and Pitch Off,[4] 2500 feet. The Au Sable, flowing N., forms the principal drainage. The valley is so narrow that there is scarcely room for a road between the mountain and stream; and freshets often occur that sweep every thing before them.[5] Lake Colden, in the s. w. part, is 2,851 ft. above tide. Iron is found in numerous veins along the course of the river, and is manufactured to some extent. **Keene** (p. v.) contains about 30 houses. The first settlement was made about 1797.[6] The M. E. church was organized in 1800, and the Cong. in 1815.

LEWIS—was formed from Willsborough, April 4, 1805, and named in honor of Morgan Lewis, then Governor of the State. Parts of Elizabethtown were taken off in 1844 and 1854. The Adirondack Mts. occupy the N. w. and the Boquet Mts. the s. E. part of the town. The latter range is not a continuous ridge through this town, but consists of several isolated peaks, the principal of which is Mt. Discovery, 2000 feet above tide. The remaining parts of the town consist of steep rocky hills and narrow valleys, and not more than one-third of the surface is susceptible of cultivation. Numerous beds of iron ore are found; but none have been extensively worked. The soil is a sandy and gravelly loam. In the N. w. part is a mineral spring of some repute. **Lewis** (p. v.) contains 130 inhabitants. Wm. Hinckley made the first purchase of land and the first settlement, in 1796.[7] The first church (Cong.) was formed in 1804; and the first preacher was Rev. Mr. Burbank.[8]

MINERVA—was formed from Schroon, March 7, 1817; a part of Newcomb was taken off in 1828. It is the s. E. corner town of the co. Its surface is a high, broken upland, bordered by mountain ranges. The Boquet Range traverses the N. w. border, and the Schroon Range the s. E. The intermediate portion is hilly, with a mean elevation of 1200 to 1500 feet above tide. Nearly the whole town is still covered with forests, the settlements being confined to the s. E. corner. The soil is cold and hard, and only moderately productive. On Orrin West's farm is a cave of considerable extent. Lumbering is the leading pursuit. **Olmsteadville**[9] (p. v.) contains 20 houses; **Minerva** is a p. o. The first settlers were Ebenezer West, and his sons Nathan, Ebenezer and John, in 1804.[10] The first church (Bap.) was formed in 1810, by Elder Fort.[11]

MORIAH—was formed from Crown Point and Elizabethtown, Feb. 12, 1808. A part of

1 Named from John Jay, then Governor of New York.
2 Among the other first settlers were J. W. Southmaid, Joseph Storrs, John Purmort, Robert Otis, Ezekiel Lockwood, Nathl. Ray, Josiah Way, and Joseph Fowler. Wm. Mallory built the first mill.
3 The census reports 6 churches; Bap., Cong., and 4 M. E.
4 A perpendicular cliff on the north side of this mountain, 300 to 500 feet high, gives to it its singular name.
5 A most destructive flood occurred from excessive rains, Sept. 30, 1856; and the damage which this occasioned was increased by the breaking away of the State dam across the s. branch of the Au Sable, in this town. The testimony relating to this accident (forming a vol. of 368 pp.) was printed by order of the Canal Board, in 1858.
6 Among the first settlers were Benj. Payne, Timothy Pangburn, Thos. Roberts, Zadock Hurd, Eli Hall, Thos. Taylor, Gen. Reynolds, and David Graves. The first child born was Betsey Payne; the first marriage, that of Thos. Dart and Cynthia Griswold; and the first death, that of Eli Bostwick. Asa A. Andreas taught the first school, and Zadock Hurd kept the first inn.

7 Among the other early settlers were Dea. Putnam, Samuel Bishop, Charles, Saml., and Noah Lee, Ishmael H. Holcomb, Hooker and Timothy Woodruff, Ziba Westcott, and Ziba Flagg. The first child born was Oliver Holcomb; the first marriage, that of Timothy Woodruff and Eunice Newell; and the first death of an adult, that of Mrs. John Smith. Levi Parsons taught the first school.
8 The census reports 1 M. E. church. A Meth. church was formed in 1808.
9 There is an extensive tannery at Olmsteadville, which makes the village.
10 Among the other first settlers were Wm. Hill, (first mill owner,) Thos. Leonard, Richard Miller, Abner Talman, James Cary, Philo Hawley, and A. P. and Asa Morse. The first settlements were chiefly made along the line of the Canton and Chester Road. The first child born was Francis West; the first marriage, that of Richard Miller and —— West; and the first death. that of Elizabeth West.
11 The census reports 3 churches; Bap., M. E., R. C.

Newcomb was taken off in 1828, North Hudson in 1848, and a part of Westport was annexed, April 9, 1849. It lies upon the shore of Lake Champlain, s. of the center of the co. A narrow strip of level land extends along the shore of the lake, from which the surface gradually rises to a height of about 500 feet, where it spreads out into a hilly plateau region, rising into mountains on the w. border. About one-half of the surface is susceptible of cultivation. The soil upon the lake is a clayey loam, and in the hilly regions a light, sandy loam. This town is very rich in minerals. Fourteen veins of iron ore have been opened, producing iron of a very superior quality:[1] the supply seems to be inexhaustible. Black lead, and a beautiful variety of *verd antique* serpentine, are also found. The manufacture of iron forms one of the leading pursuits. **Moriah** (p. v.) contains Moriah Academy and a pop. of 275, and **Port Henry**[2] (p. v.) contains a pop. of 503. The first settlers after the Revolution were Wm. McKenzie, Abel Butler, James McClane, Jabez Carpenter, G. H. and John Havens, and Joseph Curtis.[3] The first church formed was a Cong.[4]

NEWCOMB—was formed from Minerva and Moriah, March 15, 1828. It lies near the center of the w. border of the co. The Adirondack Range extends through the center of the town and occupies more than one-half of its entire surface. The principal peaks are Mts. Goodwin, Moore, Sandanona, and Henderson, each 3,000 to 5,000 feet above tide. The remaining part of the surface is a broken upland, with a hard, sour, unproductive soil. Among the gorges in the mountains are numerous small lakes. The Preston Ponds, Lakes Henderson, Harkness, Sanford, Harris, Dalia, Moose, and Ridge Pond, are within the limits of the town; and Lake Catlin and the Chain Lakes are on the line of Hamilton co. The Adirondack iron beds, near Lakes Sanford and Henderson, are among the most extensive in the world. One of them has been traced upon the surface for a mile in length, 700 feet in width, and has been penetrated to the depth of 40 feet without any signs of diminution in quantity or quality of ore. It forms a bar across the river, the water literally falling over an iron dam. This ore yields 75 per cent. of pure metal, is easily worked, and makes an admirable quality of iron. For the manufacture of steel it surpasses all other ores in America, and equals those of the most celebrated mines of Sweden and Russia. The mountainous character of this town, and its remoteness from the great routes of public improvement, have prevented the development of its immense mineral resources. There is very little tillable land in the town. **Adirondack** has about 15 houses. The first settlement was commenced in 1816, by Joseph Chandler.[5] A M. E. church was formed in 1843, and a Wes. Meth. in 1845.

NORTH ELBA—was formed from Keene, Dec. 13, 1849. It lies upon the w. border of the co., N. of the center. The Adirondack Range occupies the s. part, and a branch of the Au Sable traverses the N. E. part. At the foot of Whiteface Mt. lies Lake Placid, a beautiful sheet of water, 4½ mi. long by 1½ broad, and nearly divided in the center by 3 islands. The noted Adirondack or Indian Pass, partly in this town and partly in N. Elba, is a deep gorge between Mts. McIntyre and Wallface. The bottom of the pass is 2,800 feet above tide, and the mountains on each side are 1,000 to 1,500 feet higher. Wallface, forming the w. border of the pass, is bounded by a perpendicular precipice a mile in length and 800 to 1,000 feet in height. Mts. McIntyre, McMartin, and Sugar Loaf are each over 3,000 ft. high. Bennets, Connery, and Round Ponds are in the immediate vicinity. Avalanche Lake, on the E. line, is 2,901 ft. above tide. The central portion of the town is a hilly upland, and the N. w. part a rolling table land, known as "the Plains." The Au Sable and Saranac Rivers form the principal drainage. The soil is a thin, sandy and gravelly loam. The people are principally engaged in lumbering. **North Elba** and **Saranac Lake** are p. offices. Settlement was commenced about 1800, by Elijah Bennett.[6] The first church (Cong.) was formed in 1824; and the first preacher was the Rev. Cyrus Comstock.

[1] In 1852, 26,800 tons of ore were exported from Moriah to Penn., Vt., Va., Me., and Md. The quantity contracted for exportation from that town, in 1853, amounted to 107,500 tons, of which 16,000 were to Penn., 10,000 to Mass., 3500 to Va., 1500 to Ohio, 1500 to N. J., and 1000 to Me.—*Tr. N. Y. S. Ag. Soc.*, 1852, p. 827.

[2] The site and water power of Port Henry were granted to Benj. Porter in 1766. It is supposed that he erected a mill soon after, which was destroyed during the Revolution. After the war, he returned, and, in connection with Robt. Lewis, of Albany, rebuilt the mill, which has remained up to a recent date. One of the first furnaces in the co. was erected here in 1824, by Maj. James Dalliba. It was a cold blast furnace, and was used for the manufacture of pig iron, and the casting of hollow ware and agricultural implements. Several extensive anthracite coal furnaces have lately been put in operation.

[3] The first child born was Alex. McKenzie, in 1785; the first marriage, that of John Ferris and Deborah Wilcox; and the

first death, that of John Atwater, (by drowning.) Miss Abi Collins taught the first school. The first authorized ferry was granted to Robert Lewis, April 3, 1811. for 10 years.

[4] The census reports 5 churches; Bap., M. E., Presb., R. C., Union.

[5] James Chandler, Collins Hewitt, and Wm. Butler came in to reside in 1818. Among the other first settlers were Elijah Bissell, Abner Belden, David Pierce, Cromwell Catlin, and James Ramsey. The first child born was Nathl. P. Hewitt; the first marriage, that of Abner Belden and Bershelia Butler; and the first death, that of Eliza Butler. Harriet Chandler taught the first school.

[6] Among the other early settlers were Isaac Griswold Eb'r Mack, Jonathan Bliss and son, Iddo Osgood, Jerem. Kneeland, James Porter, and Daniel McArthur. The first marriage was that of Elijah McArthur and Electa Brooks; and the first death, that of Arunah Taylor, who perished by cold in the woods. Fanny Dart taught the first school.

NORTH HUDSON[1]—was formed from Moriah, April 12, 1848. It is an interior town, lying a little s. of the center of the co. The Boquet Mts. occupy the central and w. portions, the principal peaks of which are Dix Peak, 5200, and Nipple Top, 4900 feet high. The Schroon Mts. traverse the E. border of the town. There are numerous small lakes in town, the principal of which are Bull Pout, Mud, Boreas, and Clear Ponds. The soil is a light, sandy loam, and not more than one-eighth of the surface is arable. The Moriah iron district extends into the E. part, and the manufacture of iron forms a leading pursuit. **North Hudson** (p. v.) contains 15 houses; and **Dead Water Iron Works** (p. o.) 10. The first settler was Benj. Pond.[2] The first church (M. E.) was formed in 1838.

ST. ARMAND—was formed from Wilmington, April 23, 1844. It derived its name from the old French name of the Saranac River. It is the N.W. corner town of the co. Its surface is rolling and is inclined toward the N. W. The ridges extend in a N. E. and s. w. direction, and are 200 to 300 feet above the valleys. The average height of the town is 1500 to 1800 feet above tide. The Saranac, flowing in a N. E. direction, forms the principal drainage. Moose Creek, a tributary, flows through Moose Pond, a small lake covering an area of about 200 acres. The soil is a sandy and gravelly loam. The people are chiefly engaged in lumbering. **Bloomingdale,** (p. v.,) in the N. w. corner, the only village, contains about a dozen houses. Settlements are of recent date. Among the first settlers were Daniel Crouch, Thos. and Antrim Peck, Geo. Lowrie, of recent date. Among the first settlers were Daniel Crouch, Thos. and Antrim Peck, Geo. Lowrie, Wm. Stranahan, Aaron Brimhall, and Ellis and Milton Goodspeed.[3] The first church (Bap.) was formed in 1852.

SCHROON[4]—was formed from Crown Point, March 20, 1804. Minerva was taken off in 1817, and a part was reannexed to Crown Point, Feb. 26, 1840. It lies near the center of the s. border of the co. The w. and N. w. portions are occupied by the Schroon Range, and the S. E. portion by the Kayaderosseras Range. Mt. Pharaoh, the highest peak of the latter range, is 3000 to 3500 feet above tide. There are great numbers of other elevated mountain peaks, that have never been named. Not more than one-fourth of the town is susceptible of cultivation; and the greater part of the arable land is in the narrow valley of Schroon River. Schroon Lake is a fine body of water, 10 mi. long. Near the foot of Mt. Pharaoh lies a cluster of small lakes, the principal of which is Pharaoh Lake. Paradox Lake[5] is near the center. The soil is a thin, sandy loam. Iron is found in various parts, and black lead has also been found. **Schroon Lake** (p. v.) contains 192 inhabitants. **Schroon River** is a p. o. Settlement was commenced in 1797, by Samuel Scribner, Thos. Leland, Moses Pettee, Benj. Bowker, and Simeon Rawson, all from New England.[6] The first church (Bap.) was organized in 1830.[7] Jehial Fox was the first preacher.

TICONDEROGA[8]—was formed from Crown Point, March 20, 1804. It lies upon the shore of Lake Champlain, and is the S. E. corner town of the co. The portion between Lakes George and Champlain is the extremity of a mountain ridge ending in Mt. Defiance, 750 feet above the surface of the lake. North of this a strip of level land, about 4 mi. wide, extends along the lake shore, from which the surface gradually rises into the mountainous region which forms its w. border. About three-fourths of the town is susceptible of cultivation. The outlet of Lake George, the principal stream, in the course of a mile and a half descends 150 feet; and as the water never freezes, and its quantity does not materially change during the year, it furnishes one of the most valuable water-powers in the State. The soil is a stiff clay upon the lake, a clayey loam in the center, and a sandy loam in the w. part. The manufacture of lumber,[9] leather, and black lead[10] is extensively carried on. **Ticonderoga,** (p. v.,) or **Lower Falls,** contains 325 inhabitants. **Upper Falls** is a village of 40 houses, and **Ti Street** of 30. Settlements were begun in this town by the French, soon after the commencement of the fortress in 1755; but they were soon

---

[1] Named from its location upon the upper branches of the Hudson.

[2] Among the first settlers were Randall Farr, (first innkeeper,) Wm. Pond, Samuel Norton, Wm. Everett, Benj. Cummings, Russell Walker, Wm. Mallory, Timothy Chellis, Hez'h Keep, and Titus Walker. The first death was that of Mrs. Halloway. Janet Post taught the first school.

[3] The first child born was Silas Crouch; the first marriage, that of Adrian Storrs and Lovina Hough; and the first death, that of —— Goodspeed.

[4] This name is said to be a corruption of "Scharon," and to have been applied in honor of the Duchess of Scharon, favorite of Louis XIV. Some say Schroon is derived from an Adirondack word, signifying a child or daughter of the mountain.

[5] The surface of this lake is so near the level of the Schroon River, which forms its outlet, that in seasons of flood the water flows into instead of out of it; hence its not inappropriate name.

[6] Among the other early settlers were George Moore. Elijah Garfield, James Livingston, Geo. Whitney, Cornelius Travers, Abel Tupp, and John Bowker. The first child born was John T. Leland; the first marriage, that of John Scribner and Silence Leland; and the first death, that of Mrs. Benj. Bowker. Clark Ransom taught the first school.

[7] The census reports 4 churches; Bap., M. E., Presb., Union.

[8] The Indian name "Tsinondrosie," or "Cheonderoga," signifying "Brawling Water," and the French name "Carillon," signifying a "Chime of Bells," were both suggested by the noise of the rapids upon the outlet of Lake George.

[9] In 1852, 600,000 pieces of lumber were shipped from this point.

[10] Above 30 tons of black lead are manufactured per year; and the vein of graphite seems inexhaustible.

broken up. During the French War many skirmishes[1] and one general engagement[2] took place in the town. The subsequent history of the fortress belongs to the general history of the country. Permanent settlement commenced immediately after the Revolution.[4] The first church was St. Pauls, Prot. E.; and the first preacher, Rev. Mr. Harwood.[5]

WESTPORT—was formed from Elizabethtown, March 24, 1815. It lies upon the shore of Lake Champlain, near the center of the E. border of the co. The Schroon Mts. extend N. E. and S. W. through the town, occupying nearly all of the w. half. A wide valley extends w. from Northwest Bay, breaking the continuity of this range and completely separating the highlands at Split Rock from the southern continuation of the chain. The Boquet and its branches drain the N. part, and numerous small streams flowing into the lake drain the remainder. About one-half of the surface is susceptible of cultivation. The soil is clayey along the lake shore and sandy among the mountains. Iron, leather, and lumber are largely manufactured. **Westport,** (p. v.,) formerly "*Northwest Bay,*" contains the Essex Academy and 456 inhabitants. **Wadhams Mills** (p. v.) contains 25 houses. A small settlement was begun, and a mill built in the s. part of the town, before the Revolution. After that period, settlement was commenced by Charles Hatch, (first store and inn keeper,) Joseph Stacy, and Nathan Hammond.[6] The first church (M. E.) was formed in 1800, and the first preacher was Rev. Cyrus Comstock.[7]

WILLSBOROUGH—was formed from Crown Point, March 7, 1788, and named from Wm. Gilliland. A part of Peru was taken off in 1792, Jay in 1798, Chesterfield in 1802, and Essex and Lewis in 1805. A part of Peru was reannexed to this town upon the formation of Essex co. in 1799. It lies upon the shore of Lake Champlain, N. of the center of the co. The surface is rolling and in parts hilly. A range of highlands and isolated hills marks the course of the Boquet Mts., ending in the cliffs which overlook Perou Bay. The Boquet River flows through the s. E. corner. East of the river the soil is clayey, and w. a sandy loam. The falls upon the Boquet furnish an excellent water power. Iron is found in places; and the Black River limestone crops out, from which both quicklime and waterlime are obtained. Leather, lumber, and iron are largely manufactured. **Willsborough Falls** (Willsborough p. o.) contains 300 inhabitants. Settlement was commenced by Wm. Gilliland, a merchant of New York, in 1765.[8] Mr. G., in 1764, purchased a tract of 2000 acres, intending to convert it into a manor. He succeeded in laying the foundation of quite a flourishing settlement, which was broken up during the Revolution. In 1784, Mr. G. returned, and commenced selling his land to settlers. Joseph Sheldon and Abraham Aiken, from Dutchess co., became the first purchasers, and located in 1784.[9] The first church (Cong.) was organized before 1800.[10]

WILMINGTON—was formed from Jay, March 27, 1821, as "*Dansville.*" Its name was changed March 22, 1822, and St. Armand was taken off in 1844. It lies upon the N. border of the co., w. of the center. A branch of the Au Sable Mts. occupies the N. w. border of the town, and another branch of the same range lies between the Au Sable Forks in the E. part. The highest peaks, 2500 to 3000 feet high, lie in the s. part, and from them the surface declines toward the N. Wilmington Notch, in the s. w. corner, is a place worthy of note.[11] Copperas Pond, near the foot of Whiteface, covers about 100 acres.[12] Beds of iron ore are numerous. The soil is a sandy and

---

[1] Bodies of rangers from the vicinity of Fort Wm. Henry often carried their petty warfare up to the very walls of the fortress. Among the partisan officers distinguished in this warfare were Maj. Robert Rogers and Maj. Israel Putnam. The former named officer conducted no less than 25 parties to the invasion of this region. In 1758, at the head of a party of 180 men, he was attacked by a large party of French and Indians a short distance w. of the fort, and defeated, with the loss of 125 men. The remnant of the party escaped, but suffered great hardships before reaching a place of safety.

[2] See p. 298.

[3] When the fortress of Ticonderoga was surprised by Allen, in 1775, its garrison consisted of 48 men, commanded by Capt. Delaplace. The military stores captured consisted of 120 iron cannon, 50 swivels, 2 10 inch mortars, 1 howitzer, 1 cohorn, 10 tons of musket balls, 3 cart loads of flints, 30 new carriages, a large quantity of shells, a warehouse full of materials for boat building, 100 stand of small arms, 10 casks of poor powder, 2 brass cannon, 30 bbls. of flour, 18 bbls. of pork, and a large quantity of other provisions.

[4] Among the first settlers were Charles Hay, Isaac Kellogg, (first merchant,) Wm. Hurlbert, Wm. Wilson, (first innkeeper,) Nathl., Charles, Noah, and Manoah Miller, John Kirby, John and Robt. Hammond, Jedediah Ferris, Francis Arthur, Peter Deall, Elisha Belden, Gardner Shattuck, and Samuel Cook.

[5] There are 3 other churches; Bap., M. E., and R. C.

[6] Among the other first settlers were John Halsted, Jesse Brayman, John Stringham, John and Bouton Lobdell, Aaron Felt, Joseph Fisher, Abram Slaughter, Joseph Storrs, and Jacob Southwell. The first death was that of Mrs. Webster Felt.

[7] The census reports 3 churches; M. E., Cong., and Bap.

[8] See pages 299, 301.

[9] Among the first settlers were Aaron Fairchild, Jonathan Lynde, Martyn Pope, Melchor and John Hoffnagle, John and Wm. Morehouse, Hooker Low, Stephen Taylor, Elisha Higgins, Peter Payne, and Daniel Collins. The first school was taught by —— Scott, in 1787. The first death was that of Thos. Hyer, in 1786. Jonathan Lynde and Stephen Taylor kept the first inn, John Hoffman the first store, and Danl. Ross built the first mill.

[10] The census reports 3 churches; Cong., M. E., and Union.

[11] Here the Au Sable is compressed to a few feet in width, and breaks through the mountain barrier. Whiteface rises nearly perpendicularly, upon one side, to a height of 2000 feet; and another mountain, upon the opposite side, is but a little less in height. In the midst of its rapid and tortuous course through this passage, the stream leaps down a perpendicular precipice of 100 feet.

[12] Its waters are strongly impregnated with sulphate of iron: hence its name. Copperas is also found in the rocks in the vicinity, formed by the decomposition of iron pyrites; at some future time it will probably be manufactured for commercial purposes.

20

gravelly loam, and is moderately fertile. Whiteface,[1] belonging to the Adirondack Range, has an elevation of 4,855 feet above tide. **Wilmington** (p. v.) contains 20 houses. Settlement was commenced, near the close of the last century, by Thaddeus and Leonard Owen, and Paul Thayer.[2] The first church (M. E.) was formed in 1799.[3]

Acres of Land, Valuation, Population, Dwellings, Families, Freeholders, Schools, Live Stock, Agricultural Products, and Domestic Manufactures of Essex County.

Names of Towns.	Acres of Land.		Valuation of 1858.			Population.		No. of Dwellings.	No. of Families.	Freeholders.	Schools.	
	Improved.	Unimproved.	Real Estate.	Personal Property.	Total.	Males.	Females.				No. of Districts.	Children taught.
Chesterfield	15,309	21,897	$442,920	$148,950	$591,870	1,661	1,666	559	636	288	13	1,339
Crown Point	17,489⅛	9,961	361,535	23,800	385,335	1,167	1,049	394	435	297	20	998
Elizabethtown	9,487¼	34,094	138,905	24,050	162,955	734	668	232	252	175	9	595
Essex	14,857	4,405	338,236	132,800	471,036	1,042	1,073	359	358	195	12	730
Jay	13,687	28,859	209,264	46,250	255,514	1,458	1,392	452	501	292	12	1,070
Keene	7,537	79,165	71,316	500	71,816	386	388	143	155	128	7	380
Lewis	14,068	27,246	165,108	2,000	167,108	934	869	321	325	251	16	717
Minerva	5,329¼	143,215	97,459	5,951	103,410	403	364	144	148	133	7	309
Moriah	13,281	27,511	570,316	20,700	591,016	1,590	1,530	494	592	317	15	1,224
Newcomb	950	89,964	154,142	2,000	156,142	130	96	38	39	21	4	72
North Elba	2,008	88,912	73,795	800	74,595	175	126	53	60	61	4	117
North Hudson			51,897		51,897	275	244	80	79	41	4	161
St. Armand	1,107¼	31,433	41,060		41,060	155	134	57	58	42	2	98
Schroon	15,712¾	131,485¾	250,833	11,375	262,208	1,145	940	348	378	284	16	776
Ticonderoga	15,059	12,075	371,232	45,275	416,507	1,072	1,053	409	435	197	14	878
Westport	17,077½	16,052	375,537	16,250	391,787	1,044	997	396	408	207	12	814
Willsborough	14,316¼	7,746½	284,549	22.960	307,509	842	833	390	312	212	12	654
Wilmington	8,168	20,174	44,107	2,207	46,314	435	469	358	168	112	9	418
Total	185,443⅜	774,195¼	4,042,211	505,868	4,548,079	14,648	13,891	5,227	5,339	3,253	194	11,350

Names of Towns.	Live Stock.					Agricultural Products.							Domestic Manufactures, in Yards.
						Bush. of Grain.					Dairy Products.		
	Horses.	Working Oxen and Calves.	Cows.	Sheep.	Swine.	Winter.	Spring.	Tons of Hay.	Bushels of Potatoes.	Bushels of Apples.	Pounds of Butter.	Pounds of Cheese.	
Chesterfield	537	902	764	2,281	492	490	28,164	3,591	25,293	1,088½	46,929	4,594	43
Crown Point	702	1,900	842	7,589	778	3,716	52,227	3,991½	37,865	9,060	49,791	9,266	450
Elizabethtown	304	690	472	1,620	297	402	13,424½	1,690½	9,832	3,036	28,020	2,550	198
Essex	528	1,172	718	6,340	456	333	35,598½	3,969½	10,965	8,812	42,515	8,371	
Jay	401	1,396	735	2,325	557	1,430	39,648½	2,597	32,192	1,598	61,245	6,390	589
Keene	162	625	353	1,673	201	232½	10,816¾	1,315	11,663	884	21,257	2,290	1,117
Lewis	443	1,071	635	4,159	427	3,220½	22,673½	2,287⅓	19,892	3,599	50,985	7,920	1,012
Minerva	139	376	250	732	184	148	11,941½	1,134	10,855	2,171	17,666	240	471
Moriah	651	1,152	764	3,316	485	651	30,047½	3,253¾	26,211	4,092	53,685	8,000	407
Newcomb	26	76	53	73	30½	124	2,360	204	4,500		3,065		
North Elba	57	234	142	344	76	457	7,447	413	10,140		7,856	170	186
North Hudson	15	7	21		18								
St. Armand	42	102	79		152	200	4,901	322½	36,005		8,430	300	
Schroon	426	1,067	638	1,568	571	505½	29,528	3,121	23,378	3,385	55,980	6,508	792½
Ticonderoga	623	1,348	663	4,497	590	1,496	47,209	4,169	16,513	7,995	56,126	5,378	133
Westport	498	1,022	623	5,231	506	181	31,468	3,047½	12,999	6,815	45,713	8,377	285
Willsborough	448	1,087	654	4,941	556	1,633	37,656½	3,075	19,729	10,638	50,718	22,430	194
Wilmington	147	591	343	965	128	622	7,477	958	9,989	1,027	25,561	810	583
Total	6,149	14,818	8,749	47,654	6,504	15,841½	413,588¼	39,139¾	318,021	64,200½	625,542	93,594	6,460½

1 Whiteface derives its name from a landslide, which has laid bare the rocks upon its S. E. slope, giving it a whitish gray appearance. This mountain is nearly isolated; and from its summit is obtained one of the finest and most extensive views in Northern N. Y.

2 Among the other early settlers were Cyrus Wilson, Isaac Peck, Reuben and Daniel Hamblin, Danl. Ray, John Blanchard, Z. Gray, and Nathl. Warner. The first marriage was that of Danl. Hamblin and Keziah Ray; and the first death, that of John Blanchard. Esther Kellogg taught the first school; Reu ben Sanford kept the first inn, Elias Wilson the first store, and Leonard Owen built the first mill.

3 The census reports 2 churches; Cong., M. E.

FRANKLIN COUNTY.

This county was formed from Clinton, March 11, 1808, and named in honor of Benjamin Franklin. A small portion was annexed to Essex co. March 22, 1822. It contains an area of 1,718 sq. mi., and is centrally distant 130 mi. from Albany. It lies upon the northern frontier, between St. Lawrence and Clinton counties. Its surface is mostly level in the N., undulating and hilly in the center, and broken and mountainous in the s. The Au Sable Mts. occupy the s. E. portions; Mt. Seward, 5,100 feet above tide, is the highest peak. There are several other elevated peaks; but their heights have never been ascertained by actual measurement. The plateau of the central and the valleys of the s. part of the co. have an elevation of about 1,600 feet above tide.

The N. W. corner, including the townships of Bombay, Fort Covington, Westville, and portions of Constable and Moira, is underlaid by calciferous sandstone. The soil upon this rock is generally a heavy clay. Next s. of this region is a belt about 8 mi. wide, extending N. E. and s. W., underlaid by Potsdam sandstone. A strip next to the calciferous sandstone, about 4 mi. wide, has a sandy soil, and the remainder a fine fertile loam, mixed with clay. The underlying rock in the central and s. portions of the co. is gneiss; and the soil is of a light, sandy nature, nearly unfit for cultivation. Upon approaching the mountainous region toward the s. the soil becomes more and more sterile, and large tracts are valuable only for their timber and iron ore. Bog iron ore is found in considerable quantities along the line of junction of the calciferous and Potsdam sandstones, and in times past it has been quite extensively used in the manufacture of bar iron.

The co. is mostly drained by tributaries of the St. Lawrence, the principal of which are the Chateaugay, Salmon, Little Salmon, Deer, St. Regis, and Racket Rivers. The Saranac River flows through the s. E. corner. In the southern wilderness are immense numbers of lakes, some of which are several miles in extent. Their general elevation is about 1,600 feet above tide, and they are so located that slight improvements only are needed to connect them, and to form a communication between the head waters of streams flowing in opposite directions. In the N. part the people are engaged in the various branches of agriculture, the soil yielding a good return in spring grain, and in potatoes. The whole region, however, is best adapted to pasturage, and dairying forms the leading pursuit. In the central and s. parts the people are mostly engaged in lumbering. The manufacture of starch has become an important business within the last few years.[1]

The principal work of internal improvement in the co. is the Ogdensburgh R. R., (formerly Northern R. R.,) extending through Moira, Bangor, Malone, Burke, and Chateaugay. This road was completed in 1850, and has been of immense value to the co., though a total loss to the stockholders. Steamboats from the St. Lawrence land regularly at Fort Covington, and occasionally at Hogansburgh, during the summer. The Salmon River has been improved for log navigation, and a portion of the Au Sable improvement is within the limits of the co.

The co. seat is located in Malone Village.[2] A courthouse and jail, in one building, was erected on the w. bank of Salmon River in 1811–13, and a new stone jail in 1852.[3] The co. poorhouse is located upon a farm of 110 acres, 2 mi. s. w. of the village. It was built in 1826, at a cost of $1,200 and has since been burnt and rebuilt. There are two newspapers in the co., both published at Malone.[4]

---

[1] Within 10 years, 40 factories for the manufacture of starch from potatoes have been erected in the co. When potatoes are less than 30 cts. per bushel, the business is considered profitable; but since the completion of the R. R. they have at times been worth much more to transport to the city markets.

[2] The first co. officers were Ebenezer Brownson, *First Judge;* Wm. Bailey, Joshua Nichols, and Asa Wheeler, *Judges;* Jas. S. Allen, *Clerk;* John Wood, *Sheriff;* Joshua Nichols, *Surrogate;* and Ezekiel Payne and Oliver Brewster, *Coroners.*

[3] Before the court house was completed, courts were held in the academy.

[4] *The Franklin Telegraph* was the first paper published in the co. It was first issued at Malone, in 1821, by Francis Burnap, and in 1829 it was removed to Potsdam.

The Northern Spectator was published at Malone from 1830 to 1835, successively by John G. Clayton, Geo. P. Allen, and F. P. Allen.

The Palladium was begun in March, 1835, at Malone, by F. P. Allen. It is now published as

The Frontier Palladium, by F. T. Heath and J. K. Seaver.

The Franklin Republican was begun in 1827, at Fort Covington, by J. K. Averill, and continued under several owners till 1833.

The Franklin Gazette was begun in 1827, at Fort Covington, by F. D. Flanders. In 1847 it was removed to Malone, where it is still published by the original owner.

The Salmon River Messenger was begun in 1850, at Fort Coving-

A tract 10 mi. by 40, on the E. side of this co., formed a part of the old Military Tract;[1] a portion in the N. W. corner, of 24,000 acres, was reserved by the St. Regis Indians,[2] and the remainder of the co. was included in Great Tract No. I. of the Macomb Purchase.[3] Wm. Constable, agent and part owner of the last mentioned tract, and the executors of his estate, sold the northern part, and actively assisted in promoting settlement.[4]

The earliest settlement in the co. was made at St. Regis, by a colony of Indians from Caughnawaga, on Lake St. Louis,[5] and from Oswegatchie, under Father Anthony Gordon, a Jesuit, about 1760. They are now known as the St. Regis Indians, and number about 1,000, of whom 420 reside in this co., and the remainder on the N. side of the national boundary, which passes through the village.[6] During the Revolution a portion of the Indians joined the Americans; and Louis Cook, one of their number, received a colonel's commission from Gen. Washington. In the war of 1812 a part of the tribe joined the British and a part the Americans; and they are thus historically divided into British and American parties.[7] This tribe is gradually increasing in numbers, although, from their filthy habits, they are frequent sufferers from virulent epidemic diseases. They are mostly Catholics,—a Catholic mission being supported among them. A few profess to be Methodists.[8] Two schools are sustained by the State, though they are thinly attended, and apparently of little benefit. The first white settlements were made in Chateaugay in 1796, and in other towns in the two northern ranges in 1800–02, by emigrants from Vermont. At the commencement of the war of 1812 the population of the co. numbered about 2,500. In 1813–14 it became the seat of important military events, in the abortive attempt to invade Canada. Upon the withdrawal of the troops from French Mills in Feb. 1814, the co. was overrun by the enemy, who visited Chateaugay, Malone, and Hopkinton, and seized a considerable amount of military stores.[9] In 1832, the cholera appeared at St. Regis, spreading a panic throughout the whole region. Since the completion of the R. R., systematic efforts have been successfully made to bring into market the valuable timber in the central and southern parts of the co.

BANGOR[10]—was formed from Dickinson, June 15, 1812. Brandon was taken off in 1828. It is an interior town, lying N. W. of the center of the co. Its surface is gently undulating, with a general northerly inclination. The principal streams are the Little Salmon and Deer Rivers. The underlying rock is Potsdam sandstone, appearing only in the valleys of the streams. The soil is sandy in the N. and a clay and loam in the s. **South Bangor,** (Bangor p. o.,) **North Bangor,** (p. o.,) and **West Bangor,** (p. o.,) are small villages. The first settlement was made in 1806, and the town was rapidly settled along the Central Road and St.

---

ton, by Jas. Fisk. During the year it passed into the hands of J. S. Sargent, and was published as *The Messenger* for a few months.

The Jeffersonian was begun in 1853, at Malone, by J. R. Flanders, and was issued about 2 years.

[1] Embracing the present towns of Chateaugay, Burke, Bellmont, and Franklin. Township 7 was patented to Jas. Caldwell; No. 8, to Col. McGregor; Nos. 9 and 10, to different parties in later times.—*Hough's Hist. of St. Lawrence and Franklin Cos.*

[2] From 1816 to 1825 the Indians ceded 10,000 acres of this reservation to the State. The remainder of the lands are held in common, and are managed by trustees elected annually.

[3] Among those who became directly proprietors under this title were John McVickar, Hezekiah B. Pierrepont, (executor of Wm. Constable,) Wm. S. Smith, Abijah Hammond, Richard Harrison, Theodosius Fowler, Jonathan Dayton, Robert Gilchrist, and James D. Le Ray.

[4] These townships were named and numbered as follows by the original proprietors:—

1. Macomb.	10. Williamsville.	19. Cheltenham.
2. Cormachus.	11. Westerly.	20. Margate.
3. Constable.	12. Ewerettaville.	21. Harrietstown.
4. Moira.	13. Dayton.	22. Loughneagh.
5. Bangor.	14. Ennis.	23. Killarney.
6. Malone.	15. Fowler.	24. Barrymore.
7. Annastown.	16. Johnsmanor.	25. Mt. Morris.
8. St. Patrick.	17. Gilchrist.	26. Covehill.
9. Shelah.	18. Brighton.	27. Tipperary.

[5] An expansion of the St. Lawrence above the Lachine Rapids, in Canada.

[6] This line was surveyed after the treaty of 1795, and intended to be run on the 45th degree of N. latitude; but a new survey in 1818 showed that the line was run too far N. By the treaty of 1842, the old line was restored, and permanent monuments were placed at the crossing of roads, and navigable streams, and at intervals of one mile through the forests.

[7] This distinction is hereditary from mother to son, and the annuities of each government are bestowed accordingly, without reference to the locality on either side of the line.

[8] The Black River Conference has supported a mission at Hogansburgh since 1847.

[9] There is good reason to believe that some of the inhabitants were traitors to their country, and supplied the enemy with cattle and provisions and kept them informed in regard to public movements. Extensive frauds were perpetrated upon the National Treasury, soon after the war, in the way of claims for alleged damages and losses in Wilkinson's campaign; but the plot was detected, and some of the guilty ones were lodged in the State prison. A most remarkable scheme to defraud the State and non-resident landholders was devised about 1818, and continued until effectually ended by law in 1822. This consisted in the voting of excessive bounties for the destruction of wolves and other noxious animals, to be paid by the towns and co. As the law then existed, the State allowed as much bounty as the co.; and the result of the scheme was to throw almost the entire burden of the tax upon non-residents and landholders; but, to render the home burden endurable, large sums were remitted by the claimants toward paying the *residents' taxes.* The bounties amounted on grown wolves to $60 per head, and led to shameless frauds, and the issue of great numbers of certificates upon the heads of dogs and other animals, and upon the same head several times over. In one instance a deer's head was passed for that of a wolf. These certificates were bought by co. officials, and passed the co. audit. A commission was appointed by law to visit the locality and search into the fraud; and, although no convictions were obtained, a large sum was saved to the State. The commissioners stated that they found these certificates, to some extent, the "currency of the co." The total number of bounties issued and sums allowed, in 1820–21–22, were as follows:—Wolves, 929, $51,685; panthers, 25, $1075: foxes, 587, $1852.50; bears, 93, $243; besides small sums for minor animals, amounting, in all, to $55,521.50, or nearly $12.25 to every man, woman, and child in the co. Those who had been concerned in this affair quickly sunk into merited obscurity, and have since remained objects of public contempt.

[10] This town embraces township No. 5 of Great Tract No. II. of the Macomb Purchase.

Lawrence Turnpike.[1] Religious meetings were first held by Alexander Proudfit, in 1808. A Cong. society was formed at N. Bangor at a very early period.[2]

BELLMONT[3]—was formed from Chateaugay, March 25, 1833. Franklin was taken off in 1836. It occupies a wild, rocky region on the E. border of the co., N. of the center, and has a general inclination toward the N. The Owls Head is a prominent elevation upon its W. border. Its streams are Chateaugay, Trout, and Little Trout Rivers, and the E. branch of Salmon River. Among the hills are several beautiful lakes, the principal of which are Lower Chateaugay and Ragged Lakes, and Ingraham and Round Ponds. A considerable portion of the town is unfit for agricultural purposes, and valuable only for its timber. The settlements are chiefly confined to the vicinity of an E. and W. road extending through the N. part.[4] **Chateaugay Lake** is a p. o. in the N. E. part. There is a Presb. society in town, formed from the church at Malone.

BOMBAY[5]—was formed from Fort Covington, March 30, 1833. It lies in the N.W. corner of the co., and one corner borders upon the St. Lawrence. The surface is generally level, and the soil is sandy in the S. and a deep, fertile, clayey loam in the N. The principal streams are the Racket, St. Regis, and Little Salmon Rivers, and Pike Creek. The St. Regis is navigable to Hogansburgh, at which place is a good water power.[6] **Hogansburgh**[7] (p. v.) lies at the head of navigation on the St. Regis River, 2 mi. from its mouth. Pop. 250. **St. Regis** is an Indian village, in the Indian Reservation,[8] lying mostly in Canada. Pop. in this co. 200. **Bombay Corners** (Bombay p. o.) and **South Bombay** are hamlets. The first improvement was made in 1811, by Michael Hogan, who had acquired the title to Township No. 1 of Macomb's Purchase.[9] In 1818, Hogansburgh was laid out as a village and considerable improvements were made. In the same year a road was laid out across the Indian Reservation to Fort Covington. The title to the township passed from Hogan to Robert Oliver, of Baltimore. In 1822, settlers began to arrive quite rapidly, and in two or three years most of the land not covered by the Reservation was taken up. There are 3 churches in town; 2 M. E. and R. C. A Prot. E. church was also commenced · some years since, but is not yet finished.

BRANDON[10]—was formed from Bangor, Jan. 23, 1828. It lies W. of the center of the co., and embraces a territory 6 to 8 mi. wide and 47 mi. long, extending to the S. border of the co. The N. part is moderately hilly, and has a general inclination toward the N.; the S. part is broken and mountainous, and mostly unfit for cultivation. The principal streams are the Little Salmon, Deer, E. Branch of the St. Regis, and Racket Rivers, all flowing across the town in a N. W. direction. A great number of lakes and ponds lie among the mountains in the central and southern parts. The waters of the Saranac Lake and Stony Creek Pond are separated only by a narrow strip of land, forming the only portage for canoes between Lake Champlain and the Racket River. The soil is generally light and sandy and poorly adapted to cultivation. Along the river courses and borders of the lakes the soil may be cultivated at some future period. The settlements are confined to the extreme N. border. Within the past few years the lumber trade has received considerable attention here, and large numbers of pine logs have been floated down the Racket River. The first settlement was made in 1820.[11] There is no village, p. o., or church in town.

BURKE[12]—was formed from Chateaugay, April 26, 1844. It lies on the N. border of the co., E. of the center. Its surface is undulating and has a general inclination toward the N. It is watered by Trout and Little Trout Rivers. A swamp extends along the N. border. The soil is clay, sand, and loam. **Burke** (p. o.) is a hamlet on Little Trout River. **Burke Hollow**, (Andrusville p. o.) is a small village on the O. R. R. **North Burke** is a p. o. The first

---

[1] Among the first settlers were Benj. Seeley, Joseph Plumbs, Jehial and James Barnum, Chester Tuller, Robert Wilson, Joel Griffin, G. Dickinson, H. Conger, J. Bowen, and L. Sylvester. At this time Daniel McCormack owned the N. half of the town, Wm. Cooper the S. E. quarter, and Asahel Baker the S. w. quarter. Samuel Russell taught the first school, in 1808.

[2] Two buildings, erected by the town in 1834–35, are used for religious meetings. A Christian church was formed in 1818.

[3] Named in honor of Wm. Bell, an early proprietor. It includes township 8, and parts of 7 and 9, of the old Military Tract.

[4] Recently settlement has commenced upon No. 9, in the S. part.

[5] Named by Hogan, whose wife had resided at Bombay, in India. It embraces "Macomb," or No. 1 of Great Tract No. I. of Macomb Purchase, and the St. Regis Indian Reservation.

[6] A controversy in regard to title has prevented the full improvement of this power.

[7] Formerly "*Gray's Mills.*" It was the residence of the late Rev. Eleazar Williams, the reputed Bourbon Louis XVII.

[8] The lands of this reservation are partly leased to whites; but the cultivation of all is extremely slovenly and improvident.

[9] Previous to the settlement, most of the valuable timber had been stolen by parties from Canada.

[10] Named from Brandon, Vt., from which place the first settlers emigrated. It embraces the townships of " St. Patrick," "Westerly," "Ennis," "Gilchrist," "Margate," "Killarney," and "Cove Hill," or Nos. 8, 11, 14, 17, 20, 23, and 26, of Great Tract No. I.

[11] Josiah Hastings, Aaron Conger, Wilson Spooner, Luther Taylor, and John Thomas, settled in town in 1820; and Andrew and Henry Stevens, Levi Conger, G. W. Taylor, Clark Adams, Daniel K. Davis, Jonathan H. Farr, and Orrin Wellington, in 1821.

[12] Named in honor of Edmund Burke, the British statesman.

settlement was made in 1796–98, by Jehial Barnum, Noah Lee, and others. There are 3 churches in town.[1]

CHATEAUGAY[2]—was formed from Champlain, March 15, 1799. *"Harrison"* (now Malone) was taken off in 1805, Bellmont in 1833, and Burke in 1844. A part was annexed to Jay, (Essex co.,) in 1822. The surface is rolling, with a northerly inclination. The principal streams are the Chateaugay River and its branches. The river has worn a deep channel through the drift deposits and Potsdam sandstone, forming a wild and peculiar feature in the landscape.[3] Half a mi. E. of the village of Chateaugay is an intermitting spring, rising from the sand, sometimes flowing in sufficient quantities to carry a mill, and at others perfectly dry. It has no regular periods of intermission, sometimes flowing steadily one or two years, and again only a few weeks. Bubbles of nitrogen gas are emitted with the water. There is a constant gas spring 1 mi. N. E. of this. The soil is a clayey loam interspersed with clay. **Chateaugay**[4] (p. v.) lies on the plain, a little E. of the deep, narrow valley of the Chateaugay River.[5] Pop. 360. The first settlement was commenced in 1796, at the village, and was the first in the co.[6] Within the next five years many families came in from Vermont. In 1812 a blockhouse was built for protection against invasions by the enemy. In the fall of 1813, Gen. Hampton was encamped here for several weeks, with a force designed to co-operate with Gen. Wilkinson in the invasion of Canada; but late in Nov., he returned to Plattsburgh without accomplishing his object. In the spring of 1814 the enemy invaded the place, pressed teams, and took away a considerable amount of provisions left by the American army. There are 4 churches in town.[7]

CONSTABLE[8]—was formed from *"Harrison,"* (now Malone,) March 13, 1807. Fort Covington was taken off in 1817, and Westville in 1829. The surface is rolling, with a northerly inclination. The streams are Trout River and its tributary Little Trout River. The soil is principally a light, sandy loam. A strip of sand lies along the s. border, and of swamp along the N. **Constable** (W. Constable p. o.) is a small village upon Trout River. **Trout River** (p. o.) is a hamlet near the N. line, and **East Constable** is a p. o. The first settlement was commenced near the s. line, in 1800.[9] The first church (Presb., organized as Cong.) was formed in 1817.[10]

DICKINSON[11]—was formed from *"Harrison,"* (now Malone,) April 4, 1808. Bangor was taken off in 1812, and Moira in 1828. It lies on the w. border of the co., and is 47 mi. in length. The N. part is rolling and hilly, and has a soil of sandy loam of good quality; the central and s. parts are mostly sterile and rocky mountain regions. It is watered by the same streams as Brandon, and among the hills are great numbers of small lakes. **Dickinson** (p. o.) is on the St. Lawrence Turnpike. **East Dickinson** and **Dickinson Center** are p. offices. **Thomasville** is a small settlement on Deer River, founded by John Thomas in 1839. The principal settlements are in the N. part.[12] There are in town 2 churches; M. E. and F. W. Bap.

DUANE[13]—was formed from Malone, Jan. 24, 1828. Harrietstown was taken off in 1841. Brighton was taken off in 1858. It is an interior town, lying s. E. of the center of the co. Its surface is broken and mountainous, and the soil is light and sandy. Much the greater part of the town is unfit for cultivation. The principal streams are the Deer River and the E. branch of St. Regis River. Magnetic iron ore has been found in considerable quantities. There is no village in town. **Duane** is a p. o. Jas. Duane, of Schenectady, son-in-law of Wm. Constable, acquired by marriage the title to this town, and began settlement here in 1823–24. A forge was built in 1828, and a high furnace in 1838, both of which were run a few years and supplied with ore found

---

1 Bap., Presb., and M. E.
2 Pronounced Shat-a-ghé; probably of French origin.
3 About a mile above the village this ravine is 200 feet deep, and in it is a waterfall of 50 feet.
4 On the 30th of June, 1856, a destructive tornado passed over the village, more or less injuring every building in it. In the course of 6 mi. 185 buildings were destroyed, unroofed, or moved from their foundations; and several lives were lost.
5 The R. R. crosses this valley on an embankment 160 feet above the river, and 800 feet long.
6 The first settlers were Benj. Roberts, Saml. and Nathan Beeman, Levi Trumbull, Joshua and Kincade Chamberlain, Ethan A. Roberts, and Jared Munson. Nathan Beeman in his youth resided near Ticonderoga, and acted as guide to Ethan Allen when he surprised that place in May, 1775. He died in this town in 1850. David Mallory built the first grist mill in the co., on Marble River, 1¼ mi. N. E. of the village. In 1803–04 a forge was built by Wm. Bailey, 3 mi. above the village, and run a short time, being supplied with bog ore.
7 Bap., M. E., Presb., and R. C.

8 Named from Wm. Constable, agent and part proprietor. It embraces the E. part of township No. 3 of Great Tract No. I.
9 Among the first settlers were Jona. Hapgood, (1800,) Chris. Austin, (1800,) Wm. Cooper, Solomon Cook, Eli Titus, Saul Clark, and James Welch. A. Mead taught the first school, in the summer of 1806. Dr. Solomon Wyman was the first physician. The first sawmill was built by James Welch, in 1803, and the first grist mill, soon after the war, by Joseph Colburn.
10 There are in town 3 churches; Presb., Bap., and M. E.
11 This town embraces the townships of "Annastown," "Williamsville," "Dayton," "Johnsmanor," "Cheltenham," "Loughneagh," and Mount Morris, "or Nos. 7, 10, 13, 16, 19, 22, and 25," of Great Tract No. I.
12 The first settlers were William Thomas, Jonathan and Jesse D. Rice, and Reuben Cady.
13 Named from James Duane, proprietor and first settler. It embraces the townships of "Ewerettaville," "Fowler," and "Brighton," or Nos. 12, 15, and 18 of Great Tract No. I.

in the town.[1] After making about 600 tons of iron, the works were abandoned, with the loss of the entire capital invested in them. There is but one church (M. E.) in town.

FORT COVINGTON[2]—was formed from Constable, Feb. 28, 1817. Bombay was taken off in 1833. It lies on the N. border of the co., w. of the center. Its surface is level, or gently undulating. Salmon River, the principal stream, is navigable to Fort Covington Village. The soil in the N. is a rich, clayey loam, and in the s. a light, sandy loam. **Fort Covington**[3] (p. v.) is situated in the N. w. part of the town, upon Salmon River. Pop. 894. The first settlements were made by French families, about 1796, around *"French Mills."* Settlers from Vt. began to arrive about 1800.[4] Much of the timber near Salmon River was stolen before this, and sold in the Montreal market. Soon after the battle of Cryslers Field the American army passed up Salmon River and took up winter quarters at *"French Mills."*[5] In Feb. the place was evacuated,[6] and immediately taken possession of by the enemy.[7] The Fort Covington Academy, incorp. April 21, 1831, has been changed to a district school. The census reports 4 churches.[8]

FRANKLIN[9]—was formed from Bellmont, May 20, 1836. It lies on the E. border of the co., s. of the center. Its surface is broken and mountainous, and it has an elevation of 1200 to 2000 feet above tide. The principal streams are the Saranac, which flows across the s. E. corner, and the head branches of the Salmon River. Among the mountains are numerous ponds and lakes. The soil is sandy, and scarcely fit for agricultural purposes, except along the streams. Iron ore abounds, and has been worked to some extent. The settlements are mostly confined to the s. E. corner, and the people are chiefly engaged in lumbering. The old Port Kent and Hopkinton Road passes diagonally through the town, and a plank road extends from Franklin Falls to Keeseville. **Franklin Falls**[10] (p. v.) contains 12 houses, and **Vermontville** 20. **Alder Brook** and **Merrillsville** are p. offices. The first settlement was made at Franklin Falls, in 1827, at which time a forge and sawmill were erected.[11] In town are 5 large gang sawmills, and several small manufactories of buckskin leather, mittens and gloves. There are 2 churches in town,—M. E. and R. C.

HARRIETSTOWN[12]—was formed from Duane, March 19, 1841. It is the s. E. corner town of the co. Its surface is very rocky and mountainous, and its soil a light, sandy loam, generally unfit for cultivation. Mt. Seward lies along the s. border.[13] It is the least populous and wealthy town in the co. It is principally drained by the Saranac. Among the mountains are a great number of small lakes, the principal of which are the Lower Saranac, Big Clear, and St. Regis. There are no villages or churches in town. **Saranac Lake,** on the line of Essex co., is a p. o. The first settlers located on the North West Bay Road, about 1812.[14]

MALONE[15]—was formed from Chateaugay, March 2, 1805, as *"Harrison."* The name was changed to *"Ezraville,"* April 8, 1808, and to Malone, June 10, 1812. Constable was taken off in 1807, Dickinson in 1808, and Duane in 1828. It is an interior town, lying N. of the geo-

---

[1] By an act of May 20, 1841, a company was chartered by the name of "The Franklin Native Steel Manufacturing Co.;" but it was never organized. The making of steel directly from the ores of this region has proved to be practically a failure. A few years since, silver was said to be discovered; but it has never been successfully worked.

[2] Named from Brig. Gen. Leonard Covington, who was mortally wounded at Cryslers Field and buried here. It embraces the w. part of the township of "Cormachas," or No. 2 of Great Tract No. I., and a part of the original St. Regis Reservation, since ceded to the State.

[3] Formerly called *"French Mills."* It is situated on a mile square reserved by the Indians in 1796. This tract was leased by the Indians to Wm. Gray, in 1793, and assigned to Jas. Robertson, of Montreal, in 1798. These Indian leases occasioned much difficulty concerning title, which was finally settled by commissioners, after the purchase of the E. part of the reservation, in 1816-18.—*Hough's Hist. of St. Law. and Frank. Co's.*

[4] Mills were built at a very early period, and were swept away by a flood in 1804.

[5] Here a fearful mortality occurred among the troops, on account of exposure to the rigors of a northern winter in tents and slight board shanties. The medicines and hospital stores had been lost or destroyed on the passage down the St. Lawrence, nor could fresh supplies be obtained nearer than Albany. The surrounding country was mostly a wilderness; and the army of Gen. Hampton the fall previous had exhausted the resources of the inhabitants, and, consequently, provisions were of a bad quality and were procured with difficulty.

[6] As an appropriate finale to an imbecile enterprise, the retreating army destroyed the boats on the river, sunk 60 tons of biscuit, and destroyed all the public property too heavy for

transportation. The enemy soon completed the work of destruction.

[7] A few years after the war, an extensive series of frauds upon government was perpetrated at this place. They consisted of fictitious claims for damages, in which the documents were forged, and the parties, witnesses, and magistrates were perjured.

[8] Asso. Ref. Presb., (Scotch,) Wes. M., Bap., and R. C., (St. Mary's.)

[9] This town includes No. 10, and a part of No. 9, of the old Military Tract.

[10] Formerly called "McClenathans Falls," from the proprietor. On the 29th of May, 1852, the entire village, consisting of 23 houses, store, tavern, extensive lumber mills, and a large amount of lumber, was destroyed by running fires. Loss, $30,000.

[11] Among the first settlers were Wm. McClenathan, Jas. Mallory, Horace Gould, John Griffin, Harry Wood, Richmond and Davis Spaulding, Simeon French, and John Hough. The first birth was that of Sanford Hough; and the first death of an adult, that of Mrs. H. Wood. McClenathan kept the first inn and store and built the first mill and forge.

[12] Named from Harriet, daughter of Wm. Constable and wife of Jas. Duane. It embraces the townships of "Harrietstown," "Barrymore," and "Tipperary," or Nos. 21, 24, and 27 of Great Tract No. I.

[13] Mt. Seward, named from Wm. H. Seward, was called by the Indians *"On-no-wan-lah,"* the big eye.

[14] Among the first settlers were Isaac Livingston, Isaiah C. Flanders, Pliny Miller, Wm. Kelly, and Nehemiah White.

[15] Named *"Harrison"* from Richard Harrison, proprietor; *"Ezraville"* from Ezra L'Hommedieu, of Suffolk co.; and Malone from a family related to Harrison. It embraces the townships of "Malone" and "Shelah," or Nos. 6 and 9 of Great Tract No. I.

graphical center of the co. and s. of the center of population. Its surface is level in the N. and broken and hilly in the s. The principal stream is the Salmon River, which flows northerly through the town in a deep valley worn by its waters, and nearly its whole course in town is a succession of rapids and cascades. Along the N. border are extensive pine plains. The soil in the N., where not covered by light drift deposits, is fertile and well improved, but in the s. it is sandy and unproductive. An iron ore, from which a paint resembling sienna is manufactured, has been discovered in the s. part. Potsdam sandstone, of an excellent quality for building, has been extensively quarried near the village. **Malone,**[1] (p. v.,) the co. seat, and the only incorp. village in the co., is pleasantly situated on Salmon River. Pop. 1993. It is the seat of the Franklin Academy,[2] and is the most important intermediate station upon the Ogdensburgh R. R.[3] The village is supplied with spring water by an incorp. company.[4] **Titusville** (p. o.) is a small village at the Great Falls, on Salmon River in the s. part of the town.[5] The first settlements were made near Malone Village, about the beginning of the present century, by emigrants from Vt.[6] An arsenal was built at the village in 1812, and sold in 1850.[7] In 1813–14 the place was visited and plundered by the British. The first church (Cong.) was formed in 1806–07, by Ebenezer Hibbard and Amos Pettengill. Rev. Ashbel Parmelee was the first pastor, and the first settled minister in the co.[8]

MOIRA[9]—was formed from Dickinson, April 15, 1828. It lies on the w. border of the co., N. of the center. The surface is generally level, with a slight inclination toward the N. The principal streams are Little Salmon River and Lawrence Brook. The soil is a sandy loam, generally fertile. **Moira Corners** (Moira p. o.) is a small village near the center. **Brushs Mills,**[10] (p. v.,) on Little Salmon River, is an important wooding station on the R. R. This town fell to the share of Gilchrist and Fowler, upon apportionment, and was first settled by Appleton Foote, as agent, in 1803.[11] Luther Bradish,[12] Robert Watts, and Peter Kean afterward became the owners respectively of the N., middle, and s. thirds of the town. There are 3 churches in town.[13]

WESTVILLE[14]—was formed from Constable, April 25, 1829. It lies near the center of the N. border of the co. The surface is nearly level, with a slight inclination toward the N. It is drained by Salmon River, upon which are several falls, affording a good supply of water power. The soil is a fertile, clayey loam. Bog iron ore, found on the s. border, has been used to some extent in forges in the town. A sulphur spring, of some local notoriety, lies near the center of the N. border. **Westville** (W. Constable p. o.) is a small village on Salmon River. This town was held by the Constable family; and for many years Wm. Bailey, of Chateaugay, and Albon Mann, were agents. In 1822 the unsold portions were sold to Edward Ellice, of London. The first settlements commenced about 1800, by emigrants from Vt.[15] There are 4 churches in town.[16]

---

1 Incorp. 1853.

2 The academy building is finely located in the w. part of the village.

3 The machine and repair shops of the R. R., located here, are on a magnificent scale, and are fitted up in a superior style. The repairs of the Potsdam and Watertown R. R. rolling stock are also done here.

4 The Malone Water Works Co., incorp. March 23, 1857. Capital, $15,000.

5 Henry B. Titus commenced improvements in this part of the town, by building mills and a scythe factory, in 1831. After several years' suspension, improvements and settlements have been renewed under James H. Titus, of N. Y.

6 Among the first settlers were Enos, Nathan and John Wood, Nowell Conger, Luther Winslow, Jehial Berry, Noah Moody, Roswell Wilcox, and David and Lyman Sperry. The first child born was Malone, daughter of L. Winslow. The first sawmill was built in 1804, by N. and J. Wood.

7 The proceeds of this sale were applied to the improvement of the arsenal green and parade ground; and a further sum of $500 was appropriated for the same purpose in 1858.

8 The census reports 6 churches; Cong., Prot. E., Union, M. E.,

Bap., and R. C. In Nov. 1857, Rev. Barnard McCabe, Catholic priest, was accidentally burned to death.

9 Named from the Earl of Moira. Embraces " Moira," or No. 4 of Great Tract No. I. The name was applied to the township long before the incorporation of the town.

10 Named from Henry N. Brush, an extensive proprietor of lands in this vicinity and resident of the village.

11 Among the first settlers were Benj. Seeley, Jonathan Lawrence, Joseph Plumb, and David Bates. Schools were established in 1807.

12 Mr. Bradish resided here for several years. He represented the co. in the Assembly in 1828–29–30–36–37–38, and was a resident here when elected Lieut. Gov. in 1838.

13 Cong., R. C., and Union, (the last belonging to the M. E. and Christian denominations.)

14 Named from the village, so called from its location in the old town of Constable.

15 Among the first settlers were Amos Welch, —— Haskins, Elisha Sabins, Saml. Fletcher, John Reed, Alex. McMillen, Silas Cushman, John Livingston, Jas. and Thos. Wright, and Alric and Albon Mann. The first sawmill was built by Amos Welch. The first school was taught by Samuel Russell, in 1806

16 Presb., M. E., Univ. and Union.

BRIGHTON—was formed from Duane, Nov. —, 1858. It embraces Township 18 and the s. half of Township 15 of Great Township No. 1 of Macomb's Purchase. The settlements are chiefly in the E. part. The inhabitants are mostly engaged in lumbering. There is no village or p. o. in town. (This town was formed after the remainder of the letter-press of this co. was stereotyped; and hence it is inserted in this place.)

Acres of Land, Valuation, Population, Dwellings, Families, Freeholders, Schools, Live Stock, Agricultural Products, and Domestic Manufactures, of Franklin County.

NAMES OF TOWNS.	ACRES OF LAND.		VALUATION OF 1858.			POPULATION.		No. of Dwellings.	No. of Families.	Freeholders.	SCHOOLS.	
	Improved.	Unimproved.	Real Estate.	Personal Property.	Total.	Males.	Females.				No. of Districts.	Children taught.
Bangor	13,931	15,609	$352,656	$49,645	$402,301	1,101	1,053	395	421	335	11	942
Bellmont	5,345	82,708½	131,913	2,875	134,788	463	410	160	62	135	8	437
Bombay	13,177¾	9,889	224,924	20,500	245,424	1,168	1,144	376	377	229	11	981
Brandon	4,957	177,890	144,576	2,450	147,026	361	367	135	141	228	8	339
Burke	9,175	9,115	264,662	5,400	270,062	957	943	339	339	278	14	875
Chateaugay	13,840	12,682	346,484		346,484	1,344	1,332	466	440	283	16	1,201
Constable	9,473¾	11,005	172,028	5,507	177,535	746	697	254	259	198	9	586
Dickinson	8,651	181,017	211,504	4,750	216,254	654	601	230	241	230	10	695
Duane	2,015	89,790	60,848		60,848	171	154	44	44	43	4	98
Fort Covington	14,290	5,759¾	388,275	27,405	415,680	1,252	1,307	430	448	312	12	1,033
Franklin	4,170	97,088	128,255	1,000	129,255	503	444	165	169	136	9	391
Harrietstown	842½	83,613	68,207		68,207	158	148	58	66	56	2	96
Malone	25,563	33,546	985,456	259,950	1,245,406	2,598	2,588	871	943	653	24	2,399
Moira	11,031¼	16,452½	297,188	13,500	310,688	747	712	274	295	203	11	585
Westville	8,165	8,800	175,576	5,976	181,552	704	650	247	247	223	8	702
Total	144,627¼	834,964¾	3,952,552	398,958	4,351,510	12,927	12,550	4,444	4,492	3,542	157	11,360

NAMES OF TOWNS.	LIVE STOCK.					AGRICULTURAL PRODUCTS.							Domestic Manufactures, in Yards.
						BUSH. OF GRAIN.		Tons of Hay.	Bushels of Potatoes.	Bushels of Apples.	DAIRY PRODUCTS.		
	Horses.	Working Oxen and Calves.	Cows.	Sheep.	Swine.	Winter.	Spring.				Pounds Butter.	Pounds Cheese.	
Bangor	558	1,249	1,002	2,040	578	853¾	33,483¾	3,156	65,963	2,822	80,438	8,685	1,740
Bellmont	195	428	335	692	243	124	9,662½	1,334	12,631	165	29,550	2,160	1,222
Bombay	591	1,461	1,158	2,551	702	1,056½	35,196¼	3,612	21,349	1,054	258,671	10,715	2,482
Brandon	123	312	253	706	169	430	7,281	771	33,962	66	17,883	1,750	663
Burke	511	987	866	1,886	534	1,287	19,002	2,938½	30,221	2,626	61,065	13,620	2,283½
Chateaugay	670	989	990	2,194	755	1,293	22,760	3,385	58,716	2,349	66,145	4,752	2,136
Constable	382	620	538	1,368	471	2,784½	14,018	3,481½	28,356	4,048	46,885	4,861	1,404
Dickinson	314	703	652	1,666	389	2,473	20,258	1,755	29,950	440	57,400	12,344	2,292
Duane	66	159	91	191	85	193	7,505½	304	6,233		7,448		92
Fort Covington	634	1,424	1,422	2,250	1,111	607	41,889	4,768	18,843	4,042	123,055	2,849	1,946½
Franklin	114	329	251	179	218	2,391½	11,067¼	890	20,559		17,966	440	165½
Harrietstown	24	92	75	139	59	35	5,111½	285	6,365		5,010		58
Malone	1,084	1,879	1,842	4,452	1,342	4,695	57,822	6,224	94,772	7,619	135,952	57,190	2,025
Moira	391	1,183	872	1,548	420	1,183	21,531½	2,911½	33,581	635	77,876	22,430	2,604
Westville	372	944	572	2,096	459	2,139	24,931	1,779	22,924	407	64.696	2,120	2,101
Total	6,029	12,759	10,919	23,958	7,535	21,545¼	331,519¼	37,594½	484,425	26,273	1,050,040	143,916	23,214½

FULTON COUNTY.

This county was formed from Montgomery, April 18, 1838.[1] It lies N. of the Mohawk, E. of the center of the State. It is centrally distant 45 miles from Albany, and contains 544 sq. mi. Its surface is a rolling and hilly upland, rising into a mountainous region on the N. border. The highland region is divided into three general ridges, extending N. E. and S. W. The most eastern of these ridges, occupying the S. E. corner, consists of rounded drift hills of moderate elevation, bounded by gradual slopes, the highest summits being about 400 ft. above the Mohawk. The second ridge extends through near the center of the co. and occupies a wide space along the N. border. The declivities in the N. are usually steep and rocky; and the highest summits are 800 to 1,000 ft. above the Mohawk. The third ridge, similar in character to the second, extends through the w. part of the co. Its highest summits are 1,200 ft. above the Mohawk.

Sacondaga[2] River flows S. E. through the N. E. corner of the co. It receives from the w. Mayfield Creek, which has for its tributaries Fondas Creek and Cranberry Creek. The Chuctenunda flows through the S. E. corner. The Cayadutta flows S. W. through near the center, its valley separating the central from the eastern ranges of hills. Garoga Creek flows S., a little w. of the center, its valley separating the western and central ranges of hills. Stony Creek, a tributary of the Sacondaga, flows N. E. in the northerly continuation of the Garoga Valley, and breaks through the central ranges of hills. East Canada Creek forms the greater part of the w. boundary, receiving as tributaries North, Fish, and Little Sprite Creeks. The other streams are branches of the foregoing or of the Mohawk. They are mostly rapid streams, frequently interrupted by falls, and affording an ample supply of water-power.

Among the hills in the N. part of the co. are many of the small lakes forming a characteristic feature of the wilderness region of Northern N. Y. Along the Sacondaga, near the mouth of Mayfield Creek, and occupying portions of Northampton, Broadalbin, and Mayfield, is an extensive swamp or vlaie, said to contain an area of 13,000 acres.[3]

The greater part of the surface of the co. is covered with drift deposits. The southern part of the central and w. ridges are principally composed of calciferous sand rock; and farther N. Potsdam sandstone and gneiss appear and cover a considerable portion of the surface. Black River limestone, Trenton limestone, and Utica slate are also found in different localities. Quarries of gneiss and of birdseye limestone have been opened in Johnstown and Mayfield. An excellent building stone is found in all the N. part of the co.

The soil in the s. part and along the valleys is mostly a gravelly and clayey loam, derived from the drift deposits. It is well adapted to pasturage, and in the most favorable localities produces good crops of grain. A large portion of the N. part is too rough and broken for profitable cultivation.[4] The manufactures consist principally of leather, lumber, and buckskin gloves and mittens.[5]

The co. seat is located at Johnstown.[6] The courthouse is a brick building in the N. part of the village, erected in 1772, by Sir Wm. Johnson, for the courthouse of " Tryon" co.[7] The jail, a stone building, situated in the s. E. part of the village, contains the usual jail accommodations, and the residence of the jailer. The clerk's office is a fireproof brick building, in the vicinity of the courthouse. The poorhouse is situated upon a farm of 94 acres at West Bush, 6 mi. N. of the

---

[1] A dissatisfaction arising from the removal of the county seat of Montgomery co. from Johnstown to Fonda was the immediate cause of the division of that co.

[2] This name is said to signify "Drowned Lands," from the great marsh which lies along its course.

[3] This vlaie was apparently a lake at no remote period. It is now covered with a small growth of evergreens around its border, and a wet prairie in the center, where hundreds of tons of coarse grass of poor quality are cut annually.

[4] The mountainous portion in the N. part of this co. forms the s. extremity of the Great Northern wilderness of N. Y. The settlements are very sparse, and are confined to the narrow valleys of the streams. The hills are covered with a light growth of forest trees; and when once cleared, the soil is too light and thin to produce any thing else.

[5] More buckskin gloves and mittens are manufactured in this

co. than in all other parts of the U. S. The center of the manufacture is at Gloversville, though it is largely carried on at Johnstown and other villages. Work is given out to families through a large section of country, forming the most productive branch of labor in the co.

[6] The first officers of "Tryon co." were Guy Johnson, First Judge; John Butler and Peter Congue, Judges; and Sir John Johnson, Kt., Daniel Claus, John Wells, and Jellis Fonda, Assistant Judges. The first co. court was organized Sept. 8, 1772. Upon the organization of Fulton co., the first co. officers were Donald McIntyre, First Judge; John W. Cady, Dist. Attorney; T. A. Stoutenburgh, Clerk; David J. McMartin, Sheriff; and Archibald McFarland, Surrogate.

[7] The Johnson family retained a lien upon the building until annulled by the forfeiture of their estates.

314

courthouse. The average number of inmates is 50, supported at an average cost of $1.25 per week each. The children attend the public school. The farm yields a revenue of $200.

Four weekly newspapers are now published in the co.[1]

The history of this co. is intimately connected with that of Sir William Johnson and his family. At the age of 21, Johnson came to America as agent of his uncle, Sir Peter Warren, and located in the Mohawk Valley. He soon became identified with the interests of that section of the colony, and a zealous promoter of its prosperity. He was appointed Indian Agent, learned the language of the natives, adopted with facility their habits when it suited his interests, and gradually ac-quired an ascendency over these people which his official relations served to strengthen. His suc-cessful management in the expedition to Lake George in 1755 gave him a high position in the esteem of the home Government, and secured him, as an especial favor, the grant of a large tract of land N. of the Mohawk, as a direct gift from the king. He was also honored with knighthood. His first residence was fixed at what is still known as Fort Johnson, on the Mohawk, in the town of Amsterdam; but about 1761 he removed to a new mansion, near the village of Johnstown, still standing, and known as Johnson Hall. At this time he possessed an estate that had few rivals in extent and value in the country; his tenants were numerous and attached to his interests, and the prospects of future greatness to his family were most flattering. On the approach of the Revolu-tion he is supposed to have been liberally inclined; but his duty to the Government, whose offices he held, forbade him from favoring the cause of the colonies, while his attachment to his neighbors and the inhabitants of the colony rendered the thought of any measures tending to their ruin extremely painful to his feelings. It was apparent that a struggle between the mother country and the colonies must ensue; but, with the prescience that foreshadowed the significant purpose of his mind, he intimated to his friends that he should never live to see it, and he besought the British Government to appoint his son to his office,—that of Indian Agent. He died suddenly at Johnson Hall, on the afternoon of June 24, 1774, at the age of nearly sixty years.[2]

[1] *The Johnstown Gazette* was published in 1796.
The Montgomery Advertiser was published at Johnstown in 1796 by Jacob Doxtader. It soon passed into the hands of Jas. Smith, and subsequently into the hands of Alvin Romeyn and —— Clark. It was afterward continued several years by David Holden.
The Montgomery Republican was commenced at Johnstown in Aug. 1806, by Wm. Child. His brother, Asa Child, soon after became editor. In 1823 Wm. Holland became owner, and published it 2 years. Peter Mix continued it until 1834, when the office was burned. The paper was revived by him; and in Nov. 1836, the office was again burned, and the publication of the paper was discontinued.
The Montgomery Intelligencer was commenced in 1806, and dis-continued in 1807.
The Montgomery Monitor was commenced at Johnstown in 1808 by Robbins & Andrews. It soon passed into the hands of Russell Prentice, who sold it in 1824 to Duncan and Daniel McDonald. In 1828 they removed it to Fonda, thence to Canajoharie, and finally to Schoharie.
The Johnstown Herald was removed from Amsterdam in 1824 by Philip Reynolds. It had been published there as the "Mohawk Herald." In 1837 it was removed to Fonda and published as the "Fonda Herald."
The Montgomery Freeman was published at Johnstown by Yates & Co.
The Northern Banner was commenced at Union Mills, Broad-albin, by John Clark. It was removed in a few months to Johnstown and published as
The Northern Banner and Montgomery Democrat. In 1837 its name was changed to
The Montgomery Republican. It was soon afterward sold to Wm. S. Hawley, who changed its name in 1838 to
The Fulton County Democrat. In 18— it passed into the hands of A. T. Norton; and in 1842 it was pur-chased by Walter N. Clark, its present publisher.
The Christian Palladium, semi-mo., was published in 1836 by Joseph Badger. It was removed to Albany in 1846 or '47.
The Fulton County Republican was commenced at Johnstown in 1838 by Darius Wells. In 1840 Alexander U. Wells became proprietor; and in 1842 he sold it to George Henry, its present publisher.
The Garland, semi-mo., was published at Union Mills by Wm. Clark. It was afterward issued a short time at Johns-town.
The Literary Journal was published at Kingsboro' in 1843 by S. R. Sweet.
The Johnstown American was commenced in Jan. 1856, by N. J. Johnson. In Feb. 1857, it was sold to J. D. Houghtaling. In April, 1858, its name was changed to
The Johnstown Independent, under which title it is now published.

The Gloversville Standard was commenced in Sept. 1856, by W. H. Case, and is still published.
[2] It has been the general belief that Sir William ended his own life; and there is not much doubt but that he hung him-self in his garden. His gardener, who found him and took him down, intimated, in his old age, facts which confirm this belief; and his will—dated Jan. 27, 1774—indicates that the near approach of death was a familiar thought, as his burial was an event for which he gave the most minute directions. In this instrument—after commending his soul to God, who gave it —he directs his body to be buried in the place he had selected by the side of his wife, Catharine. He directs mourning for his housekeeper, Mary Brant, and her children, and for young Brant and William, half-breed Mohawks, and for his servants and slaves. The sachems of both Mohawk villages are to be invited to his funeral, and to receive each a black stroud blanket, crape, and gloves, which they were to receive and wear as mourners next after his family. The bearers are to have white scarf, crape, and gloves; and the whole cost of the funeral is not to exceed £300. The funeral debt is to be first paid by Sir John, out of his 3 per cent. consolidated annuities, within 6 months. He bequeathed to Peter £300, and to the other children of Mary Brant (7 in number) £100 each,—the interest to be expended on their education. To young Brant, alias Kaghneghago, and William, alias Tagawirunta, two Mohawk lads, £100 York currency each; to Sir John, his son, one-half of the rest of his money; and to Daniel Claus and Guy Johnson, his sons-in-law, each one-half of the remainder. He then gives his library and plate, slaves, stock, and personal estate, (certain portions excepted,) to Sir John; and his landed estate is divided between his children and friends, specifically naming to each the lots they are to receive, and especially enjoining upon his children never to sell or alienate any portion of the Royal Grant, as he had received it as a free gift from the king. The legatees of his lands were Sir John and Col. Guy Johnson, Daniel Claus, each of the children of Mary Brant, and her brothers, Joseph and William, Mary McGrah, John and Warren Johnson, his brothers, and Dease, Sterling, Plunket, and Fitzimons, brothers-in-law, and John Dease, his nephew. To Robert Adams, Joseph Chew, and Wm. Byrne, old friends, and Patrick Daly, a servant, he gave the free use for life of certain lands. And he provided for the further division of his estate in case Sir John died without issue. He appointed his executors, his son, two sons-in-law, two brothers, and Dan'l Campbell, of Schenectady, John Butler, Jellis Fonda, Capt. Jas. Stevenson, of Albany, Dr. John Dease, Henry Frey, and Jos. Chew. The guardians of the children of Mary Brant were John Butler, Jellis Fonda, John Dease, James Stevenson, Henry Frey, and Joseph Chew. Each executor and guardian was to receive a ring, as a memento from their once sincere friend. Sir William was buried in a vault under the Episcopal church in Johnstown. About 1793 the vault was filled up; and Nov. 26, 1836, the church, with its bell and organ, (the presents of Sir William,) were burned. The spot of his burial is just outside of the present church edifice.

The active interest in the royal cause taken by Sir John Johnson and all whom he could influence, is well known. He fortified Johnson Hall late in 1775, armed the Scotch Highlanders on the Kingsborough Patent, and spread discontent among the Indian tribes under his control. His conduct could not be tolerated; and in Jan. 1776, Gen. Schuyler was sent with an army of 700 militia to disarm the tenants and to secure a strict neutrality on the part of Sir John and his friends. After several days' negotiation, a feigned acquiescence was received, and on the 19th the Scotch surrendered their arms, and Sir John gave his word of honor to abstain from further hostile measures. His intrigues continued notwithstanding; and in May, 1776, a patriot force, under Col. Dayton, was sent to apprehend him. Upon their approach, he left his family papers, money, and plate to be buried by a faithful slave, and, attended by large numbers of his dependents, he fled through the woods northward to Canada.[1] In May, 1780, Sir John made his appearance with 500 troops from the Northern wilderness, to recover his buried treasure and take vengeance upon his old neighbors. The settlements were surprised, and the Mohawk Valley, from Tribes Hill upward to The Noses, was ravaged. Many houses were burned, 11 persons were slain, and several others were left as dead but finally recovered. An ineffectual rally was made for pursuit; but the invaders returned without molestation. In the fall of the same year, Sir John, with 800 men, invaded the Schoharie and Mohawk Valleys with fire and sword, while an army advanced by way of Lake Champlain to create a diversion on the northern frontier. In returning, he was pursued by a body of troops under Gen. Robert Van Rensselaer, and would have been overtaken and captured had not the cowardice or treachery of that officer prevented.[2] The battle of Stone Arabia was fought upon this occasion. In Aug. 1781, Major Ross and Walter N. Butler, with a band of tories and savages, appeared by way of Sacondaga with 607 men,[3] and encamped a little N. of Johnson Hall. Col. Willett moved from Fort Plain on the 22d, with 300 men, to attack the enemy, and, upon approaching, detached 100 men, under Col. Harper, to make a circuit and attack the rear of the camp. A short distance above the Hall, Willett's forces met those of Ross, and the former retreated; but at the village they rallied, and were joined by 200 militia. The enemy were finally driven from the ground, with a loss of 17, while the Americans lost 13. Ross retreated all night, and was followed. At West Canada Creek the infamous Butler was killed.[4]

The estates of the Johnsons were forfeited, and a race of New Englanders succeeded the Scotch Highlanders in this co. No further event of especial interest has since disturbed the even current of events.

BLEECKER[5]—was formed from Johnstown, April 4, 1831. A part was re-annexed to that town in 1841, and a part of Caroga was taken off in 1842. It is the central town upon the N. border of the co. Its surface is a hilly and mountainous upland, the highest summits upon the N. border being 2,000 ft. above tide. The streams are head branches of West Stony[6] and Garoga Creeks. In the valleys are several small lakes, the principal of which are Chases Lake, in the N., and Woodworth Lake, on the S. border. The soil is thin and light, and the surface is very stony. Lumbering and tanning[7] are the leading pursuits. **Bleecker,** (p. v.,) near the S. border, contains a church, a sawmill, a large tannery, and 20 dwellings. The first settlements were commenced about 1800.[8] The census reports 3 churches; M. E., Germ. Meth., and R. C.

BROADALBIN[9]—was formed from "*Caughnawaga,*" (now Broadalbin, Johnstown, and Mayfield,) March 12, 1793. Northampton was taken off in 1799, and a part of Perth in 1842. It is the central town on the E. border of the co. Its surface is rolling and mostly susceptible of cultivation. Chuctenunda Creek flows through the S. E. corner. Fondas Creek flows W. through near the center; Frenchmans Creek through the N. part; and Mayfield Creek through the N. W. corner. The soil is mostly of the drift formation, inclining to sand. The N. part extends into the great Sacondaga Vlaie, which is annually overflowed, and in which the soil is alluvial. **Fondas Bush,** (Broadalbin p. o.,) on Fondas Creek, near the W. line, was incorp. April 17, 1815, as

"Rawsonville." It contains 3 churches, 3 buckskin dressing mills, a saw and grist mill, and 3 mitten factories. Pop. 651. **Mills Corners,** (p. o.,) in the E. part, is a hamlet. **Union Mills** (p. o.) contains a sawmill, paper mill, a peg factory, and 10 houses. **North Broadalbin,** (p. o.,) in the N. E. part, contains a church, saw and grist mill, and 10 houses. The first settlement was commenced before the Revolution.[1] The census reports 5 churches in town.[2]

CAROGA[3]—was formed from Stratford, Bleecker, and Johnstown, April 11, 1842. It lies on the N. border of the co., w. of the center. Its surface is rolling in the s. and broken in the N. by small, sharp mountains. A large hill lies w. of Garoga Creek; and a swell of land rises about 300 ft. between the principal branches. Numerous clusters of lakes lie in the center and N. part of the town, the principal of which are E. and W. Eish Lakes, Garoga Lake, the Stink Lakes, Bellows, Prairie, Green, and Pine Lakes. Garoga Creek flows s. from Garoga Lake. A small portion of the area only is susceptible of cultivation. Lumbering is the principal business. **Newkirks Mills** (p. v.) contains a church, (Ref. Prot. D.,) a large tannery, and 30 houses. The first settlement commenced about 1790.[4]

EPHRATAH—was formed from Palatine, (Montgomery co.,) March 27, 1827. A part was re-annexed to that town on the division of the co. in 1838. It lies on the s. border of the co., w. of the center. Its surface is mostly a hilly upland, 400 to 1,500 ft. above the Mohawk. Garoga Creek flows s. w. through the town, in a deep valley, the hills on either side rising about 800 feet above the creek. The soil is sandy, and in the s. E. a clayey loam. **Ephratah,** (p. v.,) in the s. part, contains a church, gristmill, a large tannery, and 359 inhabitants. **Garoga,** (p. v.,) in the N. part, contains a saw and grist mill and 12 houses. **Rockwood,** (p. v.,) in the N. E. corner, contains 2 churches, 2 sawmills, a gristmill, 2 tanneries, a buckskin dressing mill, and 196 inhabitants. **Lassellsville,** (p. v.,) in the w. part, contains 2 churches and 20 houses. The first settlement commenced under the auspices of Sir Wm. Johnson, in 1765.[5] The census reports 6 churches in town.[6]

JOHNSTOWN[7]—was formed from *"Caughnawaga,"* (now Broadalbin, Johnstown, and Mayfield,) March 12, 1793. Lake Pleasant was taken off in 1812, Bleecker in 1831, Mohawk in 1837, and a part of Caroga in 1842. A part of Bleecker was re-annexed in 1841. It lies on the s. border of the co., near the center. A series of hills occupy the N. part. A high ridge extends through the w.; and the remaining parts of the town are rolling. Cayadutta Creek flows s. w. through the E. part; Garoga Creek flows through the N. w. corner; and Garoga Creek through the w. part. The soil is a clayey and sandy loam. The manufacture of buckskin gloves and mittens forms an important item in the business of the town. **Johnstown** (p. v.) was incorp. April 1, 1808. It is situated on the Cayadutta, s. E. of the center; and it contains the co. buildings, 7 churches, the Johnstown Academy,[8] 3 printing offices, a bank, 2 gristmills, a sawmill, planing mill, and gas works. Pop. 1,661. **Gloversville,** (p. v.,) on the Cayadutta, 4 mi. N. of Johnstown, is noted for its manufacture of gloves and mittens.[9] It was incorp. in April, 1853, and contains 3 churches, the Gloversville Union Seminary, a printing office, a bank, a paper box factory, machine shop, and gristmill. Pop. 1,965. **Kingsborough,** (p. v.,) in the E. part, contains a church, an academy, 10 mitten factories, and 300 inhabitants. **Sammonsville,** (p. v.,) in the s. w., contains a paper mill, gristmill, and 15 houses. **West Bush,** (p. o.,) in the N. part, **Kecks Center,** (p. o.,) in the w. part, and **McEwens Corners** are hamlets. The first

---

[1] Henry Stoner, Joseph Scott, Benj. Deline, Philip Helmer, Andrew Bowman, Herman Salisbury, John Putnam, Joseph Desilver, John Homan, Elias Cady, settled near Fondas Bush before the Revolution.—*Simms's Trappers of N.Y.*, p. 21. James McIntyre, Alexander Murray, Alexander Oliver, Daniel McIntyre, and Nathan Brockway, from Scotland, Peter Demarest and Derrick Banta, from N. J., Abram Manchester, Reuben Burr, and Enoch Cromwell, from New Eng., settled soon after the Revolution. Rev. —— Romeyn held the first religious services, after the war, in 1790–92.

[2] Presb., M. E., Bap., Christian, and Union.

[3] Named from the principal stream. Custom has applied the name "Garoga" to the latter, and "Caroga" to the town.

[4] David, Robert, and Solomon Jeffers settled in 1798; Samuel Gage, Reuben Brookins, Wm. Jefferson, Abram Carley, Anthony Stewart, Nathan Lovelace, Isaac Peckham, Elijah Gardner, Ira Beach, John Mead, Jas. McLellan, Titus Foster, Lemuel Lewis, and Daniel Goff, were also early settlers. The first marriage was that of Francis Vandercook and Lucy Jeffers, in 1800. The first death was that of Mrs. Amy Mead, in 1804.

[5] Frederick Getman, Jacob Empie, and Jacob Schell settled near the village. Nicholas Rector, Jacob Fry, Henry Herring, Philip Kreitzer, Wm. Cool, —— Deutzler, Johannes Winkle,

Wm. Smith, Henry Hart, Zachariah Tripp, John Cassleman, Peter Schutt, and Jacob Eplie, from Germany, came in from Schoharie, mostly before the Revolution. The first German school was taught by —— Moot, and the first English school by —— McLean. A gristmill was built by Sir Wm. Johnson soon after the first settlement. It was afterward burned by the tories. Johannes Winkle built the first mill after the Revolution.

[6] 2 M. E., 2 Union, Bap., and Ref. Prot. D.

[7] Named from Sir William Johnson. The town embraces the Kingsborough Patent, granted June 23, 1753, a part of Stone Arabia, Butler's, and the Sacondaga Patents.

[8] This academy was built in 1798–99, by Wm. Van Vort. Sir Wm. Johnson set apart a portion of the Kingsborough Patent for the benefit of a free school. This reservation was respected by the courts of forfeiture, and trustees were appointed to take charge of the trust. The proceeds were appropriated to the use of this academy.

[9] There are in this town over 100 establishments for the manufacture of gloves and mittens, and 10 mills for dressing the skins. This business was first commenced by Ezekiel Case, in 1803, and has grown from a small beginning, until now it is said that over $500,000 capital is invested in it.

settlement was commenced under the auspices of Sir Wm. Johnson, in 1760. He removed to "John-son Hall," about ¾ of a mi. N. W. of Johnson Village, in 1761 or '62. There were then about a dozen houses in the village, and 100 tenants on farms adjacent. The lands were leased by him with the evident intention of establishing a baronial estate for his family.[1] The census reports 11 churches in town.[2]

MAYFIELD[3]—was formed from "*Caughnawaga*," (now Broadalbin, Johnstown, and May-field,) March 12, 1793. Wells was taken off in 1805, and another portion of Mayfield was annexed to that town in 1812. A part was annexed to Perth in 1842. It lies on the N. border of the co., E. of the center, and extends nearly to the S. line. Its surface in the N. part is broken by mountains rising 1,500 to 2,000 ft. above tide. These elevations are of primary formation, with rounded summits, the higher peaks having steep declivities. The central and S. parts are rolling and generally susceptible of cultivation. Stony Creek flows through the N. W. corner; Mayfield Creek through near the center; Fondas Creek[4] through the S. E. part; and Cranberry Creek in the E. part. The soil is sandy and gravelly, in some places strewn with boulders. The valleys are alluvial, with some clayey loam. **Mayfield** (p. v.) contains 2 churches, a saw and grist mill, and 600 inhabitants. **Vails Mills,** (p. v.,) in the S. E. part, contains a sawmill, a gristmill, a tannery, and 20 houses. **Jackson Summit** is a p. o. The first settlement was commenced about 1760 or '61, under Sir Wm. Johnson, on the old road from Tribes Hill to the Sacondaga, and was then called "*Philadelphia Bush*."[5] There are 2 churches in town; M. E. and Presb.

NORTHAMPTON[6]—was formed from Broadalbin, Feb. 1, 1799. It is the N. E. corner town of the co. Its surface is hilly in the N., the hills rising about 1,000 ft. above the valley. In the S. part the Sacondaga[7] Vlaie occupies several thousand acres, which cannot easily be drained. Sacondaga River flows S. E. through the center of the town, in a valley ¼ to 1¼ mi. wide. Mayfield Creek flows E. near the S. border. The soil in the valley is a rich alluvium, and on the upland a sandy loam. In places it is stony and rocky. Shell marl abounds in the bed of the Vlaie. **Northville,** (p. v.,) in the N. part, contains 3 churches, 4 mitten factories, and 450 inhabitants. **Northamp-ton,**[8] (p. v.,) in the S. E. corner, contains 2 churches, a large tannery, and 210 inhabitants; and **Osborns Bridge** (p. o.) a church and 10 houses. **Cranberry Creek** is a p. o. The first settlement commenced under Sir Wm. Johnson, about 1770.[9] The census reports 5 churches in town.[10]

OPPENHEIM—was formed from Palatine, (Montgomery co.,) March 18, 1808. St. Johns-ville (Montgomery co.) was taken off in 1838. It is the S. W. corner town of the co. Its surface is a hilly upland, inclining gradually to the S. W. In the N. E. part the hills rise 1,200 to 1,500 ft. above the Mohawk. East Canada Creek flows S. along the W. border. Fish Creek flows through the N. W. corner. Little Sprite, Crum, Zimmerman, and Fox Creeks all flow S. W. The soil in the S. W. is clay, in the S. E. a clayey loam, and in the center and N. a light, sandy and gravelly loam. Boulders are scattered over the surface in profusion; and primary rock appears in the N. Limestone has been extensively quarried in the S. W. part, for the Erie Canal and for private use. **Oppenheim,** (p. v.,) near the center, contains a church, a sawmill, and 59 inhabitants. **Brockets Bridge,** (p. o.,) in the W. part, on the line of Herkimer co., **Lottville,** (p. o.,) in the

---

[1] Among the tenants were Dr. Wm. Adams; Gilbert Tice, inn-keeper; Peter Young, miller; William Phillips, wagon maker; Jas. Davis, hatter; Peter Yost, tanner; Adrian Van Sickle, Maj. John Little, and Zephaniah Bachelor. The first school was taught by —— Ralworth, and the second by G. B. Throop. The tenants were imbued with the political sentiments of the John-son family, and shared its fortunes. The estates were confiscated during the Revolution; and many from New England settled there after the war.

[2] The first clergyman, according to the records, was Rev. —— Moseley, in 1770. The churches are 2 M. E., 2 Presb., Bap., Cong., Evan. Luth., Asso. Presb., Prot. E., and Ref. Prot. D., and R. C.

[3] Named from the Mayfield Patent, granted June 27, 1770. The town comprises parts of this and Bleecker, Kingsborough, Sacon-daga, Kayaderosseras, Glen, Dan'l Claus's, and Norman McLeod's Patents.

[4] Called by the Indians Ken-ne-at-too.

[5] Nathaniel Conners, Michael Croman, two families of Wal-ters, Peter Whitman, —— Schutt, —— Circaman, Michael Haynes, George Cough, Simon Christie, and John Anderson, settled before the Revolution. William and Robert Jackson, David Knapp, Alvin McDougal, Peter and John McKinley, Duncan Anderson, Isaac Bemas, Captain and Major Van Beuren, Douw and Jellis Fonda, Samuel Lefferts, William Vail,

David and Luke Woodworth, and Jonah Bartlett were also early settlers. The first birth was that of Mary Cough, in 1766. Christian Furtenback taught a German school in 1771. Mills were built for Sir Wm. Johnson in 1773.

[6] Named from the patent granted to Jacob Mase, John R. Bleecker, and others, Oct. 17, 1741.

[7] Local pronunciation, Sock-na-daw-gar.

[8] Locally known as "Fishhouse."

[9] Godfrey Shew was the first settler; John Eikler, Lent and Nicholas Lewis, Robert Martin, Zebulon Alger, families of Ketchums and Chadwicks, Asahel Parker, John Trumbull, John Rosevelt, Alexander St. John, and John Fay, were among the other early settlers. Soon after the Revolution, Zadoc Sher-wood and Samuel Olmsted settled at Northville. They were followed by Thos. Foster, Daniel and Timothy Ressequie, John McNeil, Calvin Young, Adam Olmsted, Cornelius Richardson, Elihu Coleman, Sylvanus Sweet, Robert Palmer, John Randall, Eli Sprague, Green Wells, Cornelius Harving, Felix Porter, and John Denison,—mostly from New England. The first birth was that of Godfrey Shew, about 2 years before the Revolution; the first marriage was that of Alexander St. John and Martha Scribner, about 1798; and the first recorded death, that of Gideon Olmsted.

[10] 2 Presb., 2 M. E., and Bap.

N., and **Crum Creek,** (p. o.,) in the s. part, are hamlets. The first settlement was commenced by Germans, before the Revolution.[1] Rev. Jacob Frisband held the first religious services, about 1800.[2]

PERTH[3]—was formed from Amsterdam, (Montgomery co.,) April 18, 1831. Parts of Mayfield and Broadalbin were annexed Feb. 17, 1842. It is the S. E. corner town of the co. Its surface is gently rolling. Chuctenunda Creek flows through the extreme E. part of the town. The soil is mostly a clay loam. Limestone crops out in several places; but the prevailing rock is slate. **West Galway,** (p. v.,) in the N. E. corner, on the line of Saratoga co., contains a church and 20 houses. **Perth,** (p. o.,) in the N. part, contains a church and 8 houses. **West Perth** (p. o.) is a hamlet. The first settlement commenced on the road from Tribes Hill to Sacondaga, about 1760.[4] The census reports 2 churches in town; Presb. and Asso. Ref. Presb.

STRATFORD[5]—was formed from Palatine, (Montgomery co.,) April 10, 1805. A part of Caroga was taken off in 1842. It is the N. W. corner town of the co. Its surface is a high, rolling, and hilly upland, 800 to 1,200 ft. above the Mohawk, and in the extreme N. 1,800 to 2,000 ft. above tide, with a general inclination to the S. W. East Canada Creek flows through the N. W. corner and forms a part of the W. boundary. North, Ayers, and Fish Creeks are the principal streams. In the N. part are several small lakes, the principal of which are Dexter, Spectacle, North Pleasant, and Ayers Lakes. The soil in the S. W. and in the valley of East Canada Creek is a clayey loam; and in other parts it is light, sandy, and gravelly. **Nicholsville,** (Stratford p. o.,) on the W. border, partly in Herkimer co., at the junction of Ayers and East Canada Creeks, contains 2 churches, 4 sawmills, a gristmill and tannery, and 32 houses. **Whitesburgh** (p. o.) is a hamlet, in the S. W. corner. The first settlement was commenced by Samuel Bennett, in 1800.[6]

Acres of Land, Valuation, Population, Dwellings, Families, Freeholders, Schools, Live Stock, Agricultural Products, and Domestic Manufactures, of Fulton County.

Names of Towns.	Acres of Land.		Valuation of 1858.			Population.					Schools.	
	Improved.	Unimproved.	Real Estate.	Personal Property.	Total.	Males.	Females.	No. of Dwellings.	No. of Families.	Freeholders.	No. of Districts.	Children taught.
Bleecker	2,638¾	35,138	$71,292	$1,745	$73,037	479	425	173	182	150	6	401
Broadalbin	17,413	6,972	339,765	44,545	384,310	1,248	1,398	506	559	397	12	982
Caroga	2,306	12,343	67,556	5,874	73,430	378	336	125	142	83	4	248
Ephratah	12,389½	8,896	300,098	27,940	328,038	1,117	1,066	375	393	288	10	1,130
Johnstown	29,590	10,751½	1,584,374	440,092	2,024,466	3,829	4,083	1,287	1,500	748	23	3,210
Mayfield	18,100½	16,546¼	365,594	26,975	392,569	1,170	1,223	471	503	358	16	1,086
Northampton	12,932½	5,308	162,983	14,875	177,858	983	960	406	406	286	11	753
Oppenheim	20,289¾	11,760	438,199	14,525	452,724	1,250	1,162	436	450	369	16	1,109
Perth	12,505½	3,993	286,836	32,517	319,353	569	562	206	214	169	6	449
Stratford	5,250¼	35,363	127,827	4,510	132,337	550	496	194	211	148	7	393
Total	133,415¾	147,070¾	3,744,524	613,598	4,358,122	11,573	11,711	4,179	4,560	2,996	111	9,761

Names of Towns.	Live Stock.					Agricultural Products.							Domestic Cloths, in yards.
						Bush. of Grain.					Dairy Products.		
	Horses.	Working Oxen and Calves.	Cows.	Sherp.	Swine.	Winter.	Spring.	Tons of Hay.	Bushels of Potatoes.	Bushels of Apples.	Pounds Butter.	Pounds Cheese.	
Bleecker	95	136	177	98	113	255	2,326¼	490	5,968	1,110	12,670		164
Broadalbin	644	1,335	1,121	2,487	1,220	952	73,389	4,063½	29,938	11,512	99,405	10,015	980
Caroga	115	139	177	149	186	50	4,871	506	4,487	490	13,325	87	221
Ephratah	606	956	1,011	1,374	1,135	7,619	53,804	3,085	16,998	4,400	83,525	52,900	487
Johnstown	1,231	1,936	2,250	4,703	3,356	10,363½	183,495	7,713	38,673	27,844	242,117	10,114	1,463
Mayfield	1,389	1,370	1,287	2,601	1,232	3,768½	80,963	4,131½	24,016	18,136	102,631	27,306	197
Northampton	357	972	509	1,764	507	268	36,195	2,825	17,193	6,441	53,198	6,045	825
Oppenheim	731	1,452	2,345	1,501	1,373	694	67,899	7,116½	22,199	15,435	127,741	433,971	2,165½
Perth	491	975	892	1,965	1,119	2,026	100,324	2,607	15,601	11,902	80,575	9,816	474
Stratford	170	383	499	327	273	42	15,248½	1,365½	7,891	2,872	25,210	28,825	500½
Total	5,829	9,654	10,268	16,969	10,514	26,028	618,514¾	33,903	182,964	100,142	840,397	579,079	7,477

1 Rudolph Yonker was the first settler; John Shaver, Jacob Youron, Moses Johnson, Daniel Dickman, Wm. Alterburgh, Henry Burkdorf, Frederick Bellenger, and Simeon Schuyler settled in the s. part; Benjamin Berry, Peter Clive, Jacob Ladue, James Johnson, Wm. Bean, Richard Hewett, and Daniel Guile, from New England, settled in the central part in 1797. William Alterburgh kept the first inn; Andrew Zabriskie the first store; and John Beardsley built the first mill. Mr. B. was the pioneer millwright in Central New York, and took an active part in the first improvements of this class.

2 There are 4 churches in town; 2 Univ., M. E., and Ref. Prot. D.

3 Named from Perth, in Scotland, by Archibald McFarlane. This town contains parts of the Kayaderosseras and Sacondaga Patents.

4 Charles Mereness, Richard Bowen, Marcus Reese, —— Davis, Michael Swobe, and Francis Frey settled before 1770. Lawrence E. Van Allen, Henry Van Valkenburgh, Ira Benedict, Conrad and Francis Winne, Derby Newman, James and Wm. Robb, and Peter Vosburgh, settled soon after the Revolution.

5 This town comprises parts of Glen, Bleecker & Co.'s Patent, one tier of lots of Lott & Low's Patent, and a part of the Jerseyfield Patent, granted to Henry Glen and others, April 12, 1770.

6 John Wells, Amos Kinney, Eli Winchell, Nathan Gurney, Eleazer, Levi, and Samuel Bliss, Abial Kibbe, and Daniel Shottekirk settled on the Johnstown road, and Stephen and John Wilcox, Amasa Chappell, and Abiathar Moshur in other parts of the town. The first birth was that of Lansing Wells, in 1800; the first marriage, that of Samuel Ellis and Polly Gurney; and the first death, that of Jesse Wilson, killed by the fall of a tree, Dec. 25, 1802 or '03. S. Bennett kept the first inn; Sanders Lansing, son of one of the patentees, built the first gristmill, on Fish Creek, in 1810; and Daniel Cross built the first tannery, in 1812.

GENESEE COUNTY.

THIS county was formed from Ontario, March 30, 1802. It originally comprised all that part of the State lying w. of Genesee River, and a line extending due s. from the point of junction of the Genesee and Canaseraga Creek to the s. line of the State. Allegany was taken off in 1806, Cattaraugus, Chautauqua, and Niagara in 1808, parts of Livingston and Monroe in 1821, Orleans in 1824, and Wyoming in 1841. A part of Covington was annexed to Livingston co. in 1823, and Shelby was added to Orleans in 1825. It is one of the western cos. in the State, separated by Orleans from Lake Ontario and by Erie from Niagara River. It is centrally distant 229 mi. from Albany, and contains 507 sq. mi. The surface is mostly level or gently undulating. The s. border is occupied by ranges of hills which extend N. from Wyoming co. and attain an elevation of 200 to 300 feet above the valleys and about 1000 feet above tide. A limestone terrace, bordered in many places by nearly perpendicular ledges, extends E. and w. through the co., N. of the center. At each extremity in the co. this terrace ranges in height from 50 to 100 feet, but it declines toward the center to a height of 20 to 40 feet. Tonawanda Creek[1] enters Alexander from the s., and flows in a N.E. direction to the village of Batavia, thence turns and flows in a general N. w. direction to the w. border of the co. Its course is very tortuous, and its current generally sluggish.[2] Its principal tributaries are Little Tonawanda and Bowens Creeks. Oak Orchard Creek takes its rise near the center of the co. and pursues a winding course to the N. E. corner of Elba, thence turns w. and flows through the great Tonawanda Swamp, which occupies the N. part of Elba, Oakfield, and Alabama. Black Creek[3] flows N. through near the center of Bethany, Stafford, and Byron, thence easterly through Bergen into Monroe co. Its tributaries are Bigelow and Spring Creeks. Oatka Creek flows across the s. E. corner of the co., and Murder[4] and Eleven Mile[5] Creeks across the s. w. corner. Tonawanda, Black, and Oatka Creeks form a series of fine cascades in their passage down the limestone terrace near the center of the co. The lowest rocks in the co. belong to the Onondaga salt group, extending along the N. border. Gypsum is quarried in Le Roy, Stafford, and Byron. This is succeeded by the hydraulic, Onondaga, and corniferous limestones, which form the limestone terrace extending through the co. Lime and building stone are extensively obtained from the outcrop of these rocks.

Succeeding the limestone in order are the Marcellus and Hamilton shales, occupying the whole s. part of the co. The surface generally is covered thick with drift deposits, and the underlying rocks only appear in the ravines of the streams. Nearly all the swamps contain thick deposits of muck and marl, furnishing in abundance the elements of future fertility to the soil. Many of the springs and streams are constantly depositing lime in the form of marl. Along the N. border are numerous wells yielding water strongly impregnated with sulphuric acid, and known as "Sour Springs." The soil is generally a very deep and fertile sandy or gravelly loam intermixed with clay and mostly underlaid by clay or limestone. This co. embraces a portion of the "Genesee Country," which from the first settlement has been famed for its fertility. The people are almost exclusively engaged in agriculture. For many years wheat formed the staple product; but of late the ravages of the midge have led to the more general raising of the coarser grains, and have turned the attention of farmers to the cultivation of fruit, wool growing, cattle raising, and dairying.

The co. seat is located at the village of Batavia.[6] The courthouse is a fine stone edifice, 3 stories high, containing the co. clerk's office and the other co. offices.[7] The jail is a new brick building, a few rods w. of the courthouse.[8] The poorhouse is situated on a farm of 133 acres in Bethany, near

---

[1] Signifying "swift running water," from the rapid current for 10 mi. below Batavia.

[2] Between Attica (Wyoming co.) and Batavia this stream flows between two parallel roads about 1 mi. apart. The distance by the highway is 11 mi., and by the stream 43 mi.

[3] Indian name "Checkanango."

[4] So named because the body of a man supposed to have been murdered was found in it by Joseph Peters, Esq., of Darien.

[5] So named from crossing the old Buffalo Road 11 mi. from Buffalo.

[6] By the act of organization, the Holland Land Co. were required to donate 1 acre of land for co. purposes and erect the necessary co. buildings. Joseph Ellicott, agent of the company, complied with the requirement of the law, and erected the buildings in 1802. The first officers of the co. were Joseph Ellicott, *First Judge*; Daniel D. Brown, *District Attorney*; James W. Stevens, *Co. Clerk*; Richard M. Stoddard, *Sheriff*; Jeremiah R. Munson, *Surrogate*.

[7] The new courthouse was erected in 1841–42, at a cost of $17,000.

[8] The new jail was erected in 1851. The average number of inmates is 5.

the s. line, and 9 mi. s. e. of Batavia. The average number of inmates is 90, supported at a weekly cost of $ .72 each, in addition to the income of the farm, which is about $1300. A school is maintained 7 months in the year, and at suitable age the children are bound out. The general management is creditable to the co., and is far better than that of a large majority of similar establishments in the State.[1]

The N. Y. Central R. R. extends in a s. w. direction through Bergen, Byron, Stafford, Batavia, Pembroke, and the n. w. corner of Darien. A branch of this road extends s. from Batavia through Alexander to Attica. The Canandaigua and Niagara Falls Branch extends w. through Le Roy, Stafford, Batavia, and Pembroke, crossing the main line at Batavia. The Buffalo, New York & E. R. R. extends through Le Roy, Stafford, Batavia, and Alexander.[2] Several plank roads have been built in the co.; but most of them have been abandoned. An important canal feeder extends from Tonawanda Creek through the n. w. corner of Alabama. There are 5 newspapers published in the co.[3]

This co. embraced within its original limits all that portion of the State included in the purchase of Robert Morris. Phelps and Gorham, the original purchasers of the whole of Western N. Y., failed to meet the obligations to the State of Mass., and a large share of their tract reverted, and was purchased by Samuel Ogden for Robert Morris, May 12, 1791.[4] Morris sold the w. portion of the tract, constituting about seven-eighths of the whole, to the Holland Land Company, July 20, 1793,[5] reserving to himself a strip of an average width of 12 mi., lying between the Phelps and Gorham and the Holland Purchases, and known as the Morris Reserve.[6] The Holland Land Company, an association of capitalists in Holland, made this purchase through agents who were citizens

---

[1] The poorhouse is a brick edifice, with a stone wing for the accommodation of the insane.

[2] A few years since, a route for a R. R. was surveyed from Batavia to the mouth of Oak Orchard Creek, on Lake Ontario.

[3] The *Genesee Intelligencer* was commenced in the spring of 1807, at Batavia, by Elias Williams, and was the first paper published w. of Genesee River. It was suspended in Oct. of the same year. In the spring of 1808 Benj. Blodgett and Samuel Peck commenced
The Cornucopia, and continued it until 1811.
The Republican Advocate was commenced in 1811, by Benj. Blodgett and David C. Miller. It soon passed into the hands of Mr. Miller, and was published by him until 1828. It was then successively in the hands of Charles Sentell, Chas. W. Miller, Edwin Hough, Andrew W. Young, Lewis & Brown, C. C. Allen, Waite & Cooley, and Daniel D. Waite. In 1854 it was merged in the Genesee Co. Whig, and was issued by Kimberly & Goodrich as the
Republican Advocate and Genesee Co. Whig. In 1855 Mr. Goodrich withdrew, and the name was changed to
The Republican Advocate, and was continued by J. H. Kimberly until 1857, when the office passed to D. D. Waite, one of its former proprietors, by whom the paper is still published.
The Daily Advocate was commenced in May, 1859, by D. D. Waite.
The Spirit of the Times was commenced at Batavia, Feb. 3, 1819, by Oran Follett. In May, 1825, it was sold to his brother, Frederick Follett, who continued the publication until Aug. 1836. It was successively published by Nelson D. Wood, Fred. Follett, Lucas Seaver, Wm. Seaver & Son, and Charles Hurley, until 1856.
The People's Press was commenced at Batavia in 1825, by an association, Benj. Blodgett, editor. It was afterward issued by Martin, Adams & Thorp. Adams & Thorp, and Adams & McCleary, and was subsequently merged in the Spirit of the Times, and for some years was published as
The Spirit of the Times and The People's Press.
The Morgan Investigator was published at the office of the Republican Advocate during the Morgan excitement in 1827, and continued about a year.
The Masonic Intelligencer, instigated by the same excitement, was published for about the same period from the office of the People's Press.
The Farmers and Mechanics Journal was commenced at Alexander, Nov. 4, 1837, by Peter Lawrence. In June, 1840, it was moved to Batavia and issued as
The Batavia Times and Farmers and Mechanics Journal, by Frederick Follett and Peter Lawrence. Soon after, Fred. Follett became the sole proprietor, and published it until Sept. 1843, when it was sold to Lucas Seaver and was merged in the Spirit of the Times.
The Temperance Herald, mo., was issued from the office of the Spirit of the Times, by Lucas Seaver, for one year from March, 1842.
The Le Roy Gazette was commenced in 1826, by J. O. Balch. It was successively issued by Starr & Hotchkin, Henry D. Ward, Richard Hollister, Rufus Robertson, F.

Goodrich, Seth M. Gates, Martin O. Coe, and Cyrus Thompson, until 1840, when it passed into the hands of C. B. Thompson, its present publisher.
The Genesee Republican and Herald of Reform was commenced at Le Roy in 1829, and was published for 1 or 2 years by Freeman & Son,—Orestes A. Brownson, editor.
The Genesee Courier was commenced at Le Roy in the spring of 1844, by Edw. Bliss, and was published about a year. Mr. B. resuscitated it in 1853, and published it a short time.
The Genesee Herald was commenced at Le Roy in 1854, by Wm. C. Grummond. In Jan. 1857, it was removed to Batavia, where it is now published by A. J. McWain.
The Genesee Daily Herald was issued from the same office in 1858, and is still published.
The Le Roy Democrat was commenced in Dec. 1852, by Henry Todd. In Nov. 1853, it was removed to Batavia and its name changed to
The Batavia Democrat. In Dec. 1856, it passed into the hands of John Bergen, by whom it was changed to
The Genesee Weekly Democrat, still published.
The Genesee Co. Whig was commenced at Batavia in 1852, by Kimberly & Tyrell, and was published by them until 1854, when it was merged in the Republican Advocate.
The Le Roy Advertiser was commenced April 1, 1857, by Thos. B. Tufts. It was discontinued in July, 1858.

[4] The e. line of the Morris Purchase commenced upon the Penn. line, 44 78-100 mi. w. of the pre-emption line, and ran due n. to an elm tree at the forks of the Genesee River and Canascraga Creek, thence northerly along that river to a point 2 mi. n. of the Canawagus Village, thence due w. 12 mi., thence n. 24° e. to Lake Ontario.

[5] The line forming the division between the Holland Purchase and the Morris Reserve commenced upon the Penn. line, 12 mi. w. of the w. line of the Phelps and Gorham Purchase, and from thence ran due n. to near the center of Stafford, Genesee co., thence due w. 2.07875 mi., and thence due n. to Lake Ontario. This line is known as the Transit Line, from its being run by a transit instrument, then first used in surveys. The offset was made in this line to prevent the Holland lands from overlapping the Conn. Tract. The names of the members of the Holland company were Wilhelm Willink, Jan Willink, Nicholas Van Stophorst, Jacob Van Stophorst, Nicholas Hubbard, Pieter Van Eeghen, Christian Van Eeghen, Isaac Ten Cate, Hendrick Vollenhoven, Christina Coster, (widow,) Jan Stadnitski, and Rutger J. Schimmelpennick.

[6] This Reserve was sold out in several large tracts to different purchasers. A tract containing 87,000 acres, lying immediately w. of Phelps and Gorham's "Mill Yard," was sold to Le Roy Bayard and M. Evers, and is known as the Triangular Tract The Connecticut Tract lies immediately w. of the Triangle, and contains 100,000 acres. It was purchased by the State of Conn. and Sir Wm. Pultney and was divided between them. The Cragie Tract, containing 50,000 acres, joins the Conn. Tract on the s., and immediately e. is the 40,000 Acre Tract. South of these are successively the Ogden Tract, of 50,000 acres, the Cottinger Tract, of 50,000 acres, the Sterritt Tract, of 150,000 acres, and the Church Tract, of 100,000 acres. A small tract joining the 40,000 Acre Tract on the s. is known as Morris's Honorary Creditors' Tract.

of this country, as at that time aliens could not hold real estate. Immediately after the passing of title, measures were taken to extinguish the Indian titles and to survey the tract. A council of the Senecas was held at "*Big Tree*," now Geneseo, in Sept. 1797, at which time the Indians ceded most of their lands to the whites.[1]

The general office of the Holland Land Co. was located at Philadelphia. Theophilus Cazenove, the first general agent, took charge of all the business relating to the company from the first purchase of the lands until 1799. He was succeeded by Paul Busti, who took the chief management of affairs until 1824,—a period of 25 years. His successor was John J. Vander Kemp, who continued to manage the affairs of the company until their final settlement. In July, 1797, Joseph Ellicott was engaged as principal surveyor of the Holland Land Co.[2] In 1798, Mr. Ellicott and his assistants ran the E. line of the territory—since known as the Transit Line—from Penn. to Lake Ontario, forming the basis for the future surveys and divisions of the territory. The surveys were continued until the whole territory was divided into ranges and townships. The former numbered from E. to w. and the latter from s. to N.

In 1798 the first State roads were laid out from Conewagas, on Genesee River, to the mouth of Buffalo Creek, and to Lewiston, on Niagara River. A few settlers located in various places in 1798–99, but the settlements did not progress with great rapidity until after the opening of the Land Office in Oct. 1800. The first place of business opened was the "*Transit Store House*," located on the present site of Stafford Village, in 1798, to furnish supplies to the surveyors engaged in running the Transit Line. The land office was first established at "*Pine Grove*," the residence of Asa Ransom, on the present site of Clarence Hollow, Erie co. Upon the organization of Genesee co., in 1802, the office was transferred to Batavia, where it continued until the final closing up of the affairs of the company. In 1821, Mr. Ellicott resigned his agency, and was succeeded by Jacob S. Otto, who held the office until his death, in 1827. His successor was David E. Evans, who continued in charge of affairs until 1837, when the business of the company was closed.[3] In 1811, Ebenezer Mix entered the service of the company as clerk, and for 27 years he had control of the entire sales and subdivisions of lands,—a post for which his mathematical abilities, a tenacious memory, and habits of order admirably qualified him. In 1835 the Holland Company sold all their remaining lands and all their interests to a new company, principally of Batavians, and a new order of things was established. Difficulties at once arose between the new company and the settlers in various parts of the purchase; and, finally, mobs collected to destroy the land offices.[4] The opening of this new region to settlement, under the auspices of a liberal and wealthy company, instituted a new order of things in the general history of the co., and was of incalculable benefit to the settlers. Mills were erected, costly roads opened, and every thing done to facilitate settlement and to remove difficulties in the path of settlers. The lands were sold at fair prices and on the most liberal terms. The affairs of the company, both at their general and local offices, were conducted by gentlemen of liberal culture, enlarged views, and humane hearts. In consequence of the richness of the lands and the liberal terms offered by the company, the whole region rapidly filled up with an industrious, intelligent, and enterprising population. Many of the early settlers afterward occupied high official positions and became known throughout the State for their ability and integrity.

---

[1] The tracts reserved by the Indians were the Cannawagus Reservation, of 2 sq. mi., on the Genesee, w. of Avon; Little Beards and Big Tree Reservation, of 4 sq. mi., on the Genesee, opposite Geneseo; Squakie Hill Reservation, of 2 sq. mi., on the Genesee, N. of Mt. Morris; Gardeau Reservation, of 28 sq. mi., on both sides of the Genesee, in Castile and Mt. Morris; the Caneadea Reservation of 16 sq. mi., on both sides of the Genesee, in Allegany co.; the Oil Spring Reservation, of 1 sq. mi., on the line between Cattaraugus and Allegany; the Allegany Reservation, of 42 sq. mi., on both sides of the Allegany River, extending N. from the Penn. line; the Cattaraugus Reservation, of 42 sq. mi., on both sides of the mouth of Cattaraugus Creek; the Buffalo Reservation, of 130 sq. mi., on both sides of Buffalo Creek; the Tonawanda Reservation, of 70 sq. mi., on both sides of Tonawanda Creek, mostly in Genesee co.; and the Tuscarora Reservation, of 1 sq. mi., 3 mi. E. of Lewiston, Niagara co. The titles to all these reservations, except the Tonawanda, Buffalo, Cattaraugus, Tuscarora, and Allegany, have since been extinguished.

[2] Mr. Ellicott took entire charge of the surveys of these lands, and completed them in 10 or 12 years. In 1800 he received the appointment of local agent, and for a period of more than 20 years he had almost exclusive control of the company's local business. Under his management an immense tract of wilderness was converted into one of the finest agricultural regions in the world. From his first advent into Western N. Y., he took a high position as an enterprising citizen, independent of his connection with the land office. He conducted the large and complicated business committed to his charge with marked ability, and he left a name highly honored throughout the extensive domain over which he exerted so commanding an influence.

[3] In 1850 an act was passed directing the original field notes and maps to be deposited in the secretary's office for preservation and as legal proofs. In closing the affairs of the company, it was found necessary to obtain evidence of the death of certain original proprietors; and an act, passed May 13, 1846, directed the appointment of a special commissioner to visit Europe. Julius Rhoades was intrusted with this duty.

[4] One of the principal causes of disturbance was a rumor that the new company intended to exact a certain sum for the renewal or extension of every contract. This rule became very obnoxious; the extra payment received the name of the "Genesee Tariff," and opposition to it was extensively resolved upon. The office at Mayville, Chautauque co., was broken open Feb. 6, 1836, and the books and papers were seized and burned in the public highway. On the 13th of May, a report reached Batavia that 700 armed men were on their way to burn the land office at that place. Mr. Evans, the agent, at once fortified the office, and collected a force of 50 men, well armed, to protect it. The militia were also called out. The mob soon came into town; but, learning the preparations made to give them a warm reception, and well knowing the resolute character of Mr. Evans, they concluded that "discretion was the better part of valor," and went away without offering any violence. Between 50 and 60 of the ringleaders were arrested; but the difficulties were afterward amicably adjusted, and the prosecutions were dropped.

The location of the principal land office of the company at Batavia converted it at once into a place of business and consequence; and the subsequent selection of the village as the co. seat of Genesee co. made it for many years one of the most important places in Western N. Y. Several other land offices were afterward established, but they were all subordinate to the one at Batavia.

In the summer of 1826, William Morgan, of Batavia, a mason, commenced the preparation of a work disclosing the secrets of free masonry, to be published by David C. Miller, a printer of the same place. When this fact became known, members of the masonic order became excited, and took measures at once to suppress the book. A stranger was introduced to the printer, who, under the pretense of friendship, labored to gain an interest in the publication, and thus get possession of the MS. Morgan was arrested on a civil suit, and gave bail; but in Aug. 1826, his bail surrendered him to the sheriff, and he was imprisoned over the Sabbath, while his lodgings were searched, and it is said some of his papers were seized. An attempt was also made to burn the office where the book was to be printed. On Sunday, Sept. 10, a warrant was obtained at Canandaigua, by Nicholas G. Chesebro, for the arrest of Morgan at Batavia, 50 mi. distant, on a charge of stealing a shirt and cravat, which he had borrowed of one E. C. Kingsley. The next day he was arrested and taken in a stage coach to Canandaigua, but was discharged by the justice who had issued the warrant. He was immediately re-arrested, at the instance of Chesebro, on a claim of $2 for a tavern bill assigned to him by one Ackley; and, although he took off his coat that the officer might levy upon it for payment, he was lodged in jail. On the evening of the 12th, while the jailer was absent, his wife, acting under the advice of Chesebro, released the prisoner, as the claim upon which he was held had been paid by Loton Lauson, a pretended friend. As Morgan passed out of the jail, he was seized by Lauson and a man called Foster, gagged, thrust into a carriage, and driven toward Rochester. This was the last that was seen of him except by masons; and whatever else is known was ascertained by judicial inquiry. Various theories were advanced as to his fate, the most prevalent one being that he was drowned in Niagara River.

The disappearance of Morgan excited suspicion, and led to an investigation. Citizens of Batavia, Le Roy, and other places along the route of the abduction, held meetings, appointed committees which brought to light the facts above stated, and an intense excitement followed. Several persons were tried for participating in the abduction. Some plead guilty, and were imprisoned, and others escaped conviction. The delays finally barred new prosecution, by the statute of limitation, except for murder. The excitement following the investigation, at first directed against the immediate participants in the outrage, was soon turned against the masonic fraternity. The belief that a powerful organization, bound by secret oaths, with their members occupying high official positions, would perpetrate a crime of this magnitude, excited alarm, and led at once to the formation of anti-masonic organizations as a political party. The excitement spread through the State and country, members of the fraternity seceded in large numbers, and a systematic effort was made to crush the order. The intense feeling continued, and the mutual recriminations of the two parties entered into all the political, religious, and social relations of society until about 1832, when other political questions arose, and the excitement gradually died away, and now it is understood that members of the masonic order generally condemn the deed as heartily as others.[1]

Immediately after the abduction of Morgan, an attempt was made to obtain the MS. of Morgan's "Revelations," then in the hands of Miller the printer, but without success.[2]

---

[1] In 1828, a law was passed authorizing the Governor to appoint a commissioner to make a full investigation of the Morgan affair. Daniel Moseley, of Onondaga co., was appointed to this office; but upon receiving the appointment of Circuit Judge, in 1829, he resigned, and was succeeded by John C. Spencer, who made a report to the Legislature in 1830, containing all the information upon the subject then known.

The personal characters of the two men who were made the victims of these outrages would have ruined their schemes had they been made publicly known. Morgan was a bricklayer and stonemason of damaged reputation, and Miller a refugee debtor from N.H., and finally left Batavia under circumstances extremely inconsistent with honor. For details, see *Hammond's Political Hist. N.Y.*, chap. xxxviii; *Assembly Jour.*, 1828, p. 961; do. 1829, p. 469, and *Appendix F; Assem. Docs.* 1830, *No.* 67–186; *Anti-Masonic Almanacs*, 1828–32; *Brown's Narrative of Anti-Masonic Excitement, &c.*

[2] In Sept. 1827, Jesse French, Roswell Wilcox, and James Hurlburt were tried and convicted for assault and battery upon David C. Miller, and for false imprisonment and riot. In the evidence before the court it appeared that, on the 12th day of Sept. 1826, French, then holding the office of constable, came into the printing office of Miller, and arrested him upon a writ issued by Justice Bartow, of Le Roy. Miller was taken into a carriage and driven off, attended by a large party armed with clubs,

conspicuous among whom were Wilcox and Hurlburt. At Stafford he was taken into a masonic lodge room, where efforts were made to frighten him, and he was threatened with the fate of Morgan. When taken out of the lodge room, a large number of his friends had collected, and he was there first permitted to see counsel, and to know the nature of the suit against him, which was a civil action for debt. Bail was refused, and repeated demands to be taken immediately before the magistrate were unheeded. From Stafford to Le Roy he was closely guarded by a large number of armed men and attended by an equally large number of his friends. Upon his arrival at Le Roy he resolutely insisted upon going before the magistrate, and, assisted by his crowd of friends, he was enabled to do so, taking the unwilling constable along with him. After a short delay he was discharged. On his way back to Batavia, under escort of a number of his friends, who had followed him to Le Roy, efforts were made to re-arrest him, which his friends prevented. It is said that a portion of the MS. was preserved by the wives of some of the masons who were most prominent in their efforts to destroy it. French was sentenced to one year's imprisonment in the co. jail, Wilcox to 6 months, and Hurlburt to 3 mos. James Granson was tried and acquitted.

Great excitement followed these events, and a civil war was anticipated. At the celebration of Saint John's Day following

ALABAMA[1]—was formed from Shelby (Orleans co.) and Pembroke, as "*Gerrysville*,"[2] April 17, 1826. Its name was changed April 21, 1828. A part of Wales was annexed in 1832. It is the N. W. corner town of the co. The surface is level or gently undulating. The N. and w. portions are covered by marshes, forming a part of the Tonawanda Swamp. Oak Orchard Creek flows across the N. E. corner, and Tonawanda Creek across the s. w. corner. A limestone terrace, 50 to 75 ft. high, extends across the s. part of the town. Tonawanda Creek flows down this declivity in a perpendicular cascade known as Tonawanda Falls, furnishing a fine water power. Near the center of the N. part of the town, a few rods from the banks of Oak Orchard Creek, are the "Oak Orchard Acid Springs."[3] The soil is a gravelly and sandy loam with a clay sub-soil. **Alabama Center** (Alabama p. o.) contains 2 churches and several mills. Pop. 166. **Wheatville** (p. v.) lies in the N. E. part of the town. Pop. 93. **Smithville** (South Alabama p. o.) lies near the E. line. Pop. 147. The first settlement was made in 1806, by James Walsworth.[4] The first church (F. W. Bap.) was formed in the E. part of the town, in 1824, by Elder Samuel Whitcomb, the first preacher.[5] The Tonawanda Indian Reservation occupies a section of land 2 mi. wide, lying on Tonawanda Creek and comprising about one-fourth of the area of the town.

ALEXANDER[6]—was formed from Batavia, June 8, 1812. It lies on the s. border of the co., w. of the center. Its surface is hilly in the center and s. and rolling in the N. The summits in the s. w. are 200 to 250 ft. above the valleys. The streams are Tonawanda Creek, flowing N. through the center of the town, Little Tonawanda, Huron, and Bowens Creeks, and several smaller streams. The soil upon the hills is a gravelly loam with a clay sub-soil, and in the valleys it is a rich alluvium. **Alexander,** (p. v.,) incorp. April 24, 1834, is situated upon Tonawanda Creek, near the center of the town. It contains a flouring mill, seminary,[7] and 3 churches. It is a station upon the Attica branch of the Central R. R., and also upon the B., N. Y. & E. R. R. Pop. 345. **Brookville** (p. o.) is a hamlet. The first settlement was made by Alexander Rea, in 1802.[8] The first church (M. E.) was formed in 1835.[9]

BATAVIA—was formed March 30, 1802. Alexander, Bergen, Bethany, and Pembroke were taken off in 1812, and Elba and a part of Stafford in 1820. It is the central town of the co. Its surface is level or gently undulating. A limestone ridge, forming a terrace 20 to 50 ft. high, extends E. and w. through the N. part of the town. Tonawanda Creek flows northward from the line of Alexander to Batavia Village, where it turns westward and flows centrally through the town to the w. border. Bowens Creek is the only other considerable stream. The soil is a deep, fertile, sandy and gravelly loam with a clay sub-soil. **Batavia,** (p. v.,) the co. seat, was incorp. April 23, 1823. Besides the co. buildings, it contains a female seminary,[10] union school,[11] bank, 3

---

the abduction, an incident occurred which showed the excited state of feeling that pervaded the community. During the day, Frederick Follett, late Canal Commissioner, a mason, while attending to his duties as marshal of the day, suddenly found himself surrounded by an infuriated crowd of armed men, evidently determined to kill him. He drew his sword, put spurs to his horse, and succeeded in throwing off the grasp of two men upon the bridle, and escaped from the crowd.

[1] Named from the State of Alabama, and said to signify "Here we rest."

[2] Intended to be named in honor of David Gary, one of the early settlers; but through a cheat it was called "*Gerrysville*," from Elbridge Gerry, Ex Vice-President.

[3] These springs are 9 in number, and are all found within a circle of 50 rods. They issue from mounds, evidently formed by the action of the water, 2½ to 4 ft. above the surrounding surface. No two of these springs are alike; and in one instance three springs issue from a single mound within 10 ft. of each other, and the waters are essentially dissimilar. The following is an analysis of the waters of the three principal springs:—

No. 1, by Profs. Silliman and Norton.		No. 2, by Prof. E. Emmons.	
		Sulphate lime............	1.552
Sulphuric acid............	134.732	" iron..............	4.904
Proto-sulphate iron.....	28.623	" magnesia......	0.623
Sulphate alumina.......	21.690	Free sulphuric acid......	16.132
" lime......	74.891	" organic matter......	1.360
" magnesia......	35.596	" silica..............	0.230
" potash.........	5.519		
" soda.........	6.343	Total No. of grs. in 1 pt.	24.801
Chloride sodium.........	2.434	*No. 3.*	
" silica............	4.592	Free sulphuric acid......	12.414
		Sulphate lime............	0.736
Grains............	314.420	" iron.............	3.920
		" magnesia......	1.236
		Organic matter..........	0.100
		Silica, a trace.............	0.000
		Total No. of grs. in 1 pt.	18.406

Large quantities of this water are annually bottled and sold for medicinal purposes.

[4] Among the other early settlers were Robt. Harper, Jesse Lund, Dr. Smith, (from Vt.,) and Peter, Joseph, and James Holmes, (from Delaware co.) The first births were those of twin children of James Walsworth, in 1806; the first death was that of an unknown traveler, at the house of Mr. Walsworth, in 1808. He was buried without a coffin or religious services. The first school was taught by Henry Howard, in 1817; the first inn was kept by James Walsworth, in 1808; the first store, by Nahum Loring, in 1828; and the first sawmill was erected in 1824, by Sam'l Whitcomb, at Wheatville.

[5] The census reports 4 churches; 3 Bap. and 1 M. E.

[6] Named from Alexander Rea, the first settler, and for several years a State Senator.

[7] The Genesee and Wyoming Seminary was founded in 1834, through the efforts and liberality of Samuel Benedict and Henry Hawkins. In 1845, Mr. Hawkins bequeathed to the institution $4000, his private library, and a geological cabinet. It has now a respectable library and cabinet of natural history; and its main building, erected of stone in 1837, has the capacity of accommodating 300 students.

[8] John Oney, Lewis Disbrow, Geo. Darrow, and Mr. Blackman settled in the town in 1802–03. The first death was that of Wm. Whitney, in 1803, by the fall of a tree. The first school was taught by Mr. Jones, in the winter of 1805–06, at Alexander Village. Harvey Hawkins kept the first inn, in 1809, and the first store, in 1807. Alexander Rea and Joseph Fellows built the first sawmill, in 1804; and Wm. Adams the first gristmill, in 1807.

[9] The census reports 3 churches in town; Presb., M. E., and Univ.

[10] Mrs. Bryan's Female Seminary, a boarding school for young ladies. The school building is the former mansion of David E. Evans.

[11] The Batavia Union Schoolhouse was erected in 1847, at a cost of $7000. It includes a higher English and classical department.

newspaper offices, 5 churches, an arsenal,[1] and a number of manufacturing establishments.[2] Pop. 2868. **Bushville** is a hamlet. In 1800, Joseph Ellicott fixed upon the site of Batavia Village as the most eligible place for the location of the office of the Holland Land Co., and in the spring of 1802 the office was removed to this place. The land office building is still standing. The old courthouse and jail is now occupied as a public hall. In March, 1801, Abel Rowe came to the place and erected the first building, and immediately opened it as an inn.[3] The first church (Cong.) was formed by Rev. Royal Phelps, in 1809. Rev. Ephraim Chapin was the first preacher.[4] Batavia was the focus of the great anti-masonic excitement which followed the abduction of William Morgan in 1826.[5]

BERGEN—was formed from Batavia, June 8, 1812. Byron was taken off in 1820. Its surface is gently undulating, and has a slight inclination toward the N. Black Creek flows E. through the town a little N. of the center. The soil is a gravelly and clay loam. **Bergen Corners,** (Bergen p. o.,) on the E. border of the town, contains 3 churches and 30 dwellings. **Wardville,** formerly called "*Cork,*" on the Central R. R., ½ mi. N. of Bergen Corners, contains 443 inhabitants. **Stone Church** (p. o.) is a hamlet on the line of Le Roy. **North Bergen** (p. o.) and **West Bergen** (p. o.) are hamlets. **East Bergen** is a p. o. The first settlement was made at Bergen Village, by Samuel Lincoln, from Conn. about 1805.[6] The first religious meeting was held at South Bergen, in Sept. 1807; Rev. Calvin Ingals (Presb.) was the first settled minister.[7]

BETHANY—was formed from Batavia, June 8, 1812. It lies on the S. border of the co., E. of the center. Its surface is hilly in the S. and rolling in the N. Black Creek flows N. through near the center of the town, and Little Tonawanda Creek through the S. W. and N. W. corners. The soil in the E. is a dark, gravelly loam, and in the W. a heavy, clay loam. Weak brine springs have been found; but all attempts to procure salt water by boring have proved unsuccessful. **Bethany Center** (Bethany p. o.) contains 2 churches and 35 dwellings, **East Bethany** (p. v.) a church and about 20 dwellings, and **Linden,** (p. v.,) a station on the B. & N. Y. City R. R., a flouring and saw mill, a furnace, and 40 dwellings. **West Bethany Mills** is a p. o. **Canada** (formerly "*Bennetts Settlement*") is a hamlet. The first settlement was made in the N. E. part of the town in 1803, by John Torrey, from Cayuga co.[8] The census reports 5 churches in town.[9]

BYRON—named from Lord Byron—was formed from Bergen, April 4, 1820. It lies on the N. border of the co., E. of the center. Its surface is gently undulating, with a slight inclination to the N. Black Creek flows N. to near the center of the town, receiving the waters of Bigelow and Spring Creeks, then turns N. E. and flows into Bergen. The soil is a fine quality of gravelly and sandy loam. A sulphur spring, from which issues carburetted hydrogen gas, is found on Black Creek a little N. of Byron. An acid spring, known as the "Sour Spring," is found in the S. W. part of the town.[10] **Byron,** (p. v.,) located near the center of the town, contains 2 churches and about 150 inhabitants. **South Byron**[11] (p. v.) is a station on the Central R. R. Pop. about 200. **Pumpkin Hill**[12] is a hamlet. Benham Preston, from Batavia, was the first settler, on lot 197,

---

[1] This arsenal was erected by the State, at Batavia, under an act of 1808 for the protection of the northern and western frontiers. It continues in use as a depository of arms and military equipage.

[2] This village is one of the most important R. R. stations in Western N.Y. From it three branches of the N. Y. Central R. R. extend W. and S. W.,—one to Niagara Falls, one to Buffalo, and one to Attica; and two toward the E.,—one to Rochester and one to Canandaigua. The Buffalo, N. Y. & Erie R. Road also passes through the place.

[3] The village was named by Mr. Ellicott in 1802, the locality having previously been known as "*The Bend.*" The first road was opened through the village in Feb. 1802. Among the early settlers were Stephen Russell, Isaac Sutherland, Gen. Worthy L. Churchill, Col. Wm. Rumsey, John Thomson, John Lamberton, David E. Evans, James Brisbane, James W. Stevens, Richard Abbey, Jedediah Crosby, Gideon Elliott, Cotton Leach, Samuel F. Geer, Benajah Worden, and —— Munger. The first marriage was that of Wm. Leston and Lavinia How; and the first death, that of —— Harris, in 1807. Hannah Austin taught the first school, in 1806; Stephen Russell opened an inn, in 1801; James Brisbane kept the first store, in 1802; and Jos. Ellicott erected the first sawmill, in 1801; and the first gristmill, in 1804, on the Tonawanda Creek, for the Holland Land Co.

[4] The census reports 6 churches; 2 Presb., Prot. E., Bap., M. E., and R. C.

[5] See page 323.

[6] Among the early settlers were Jedediah Crosby, David Potter, Wm. White, Jas. Landen, and David Franklin, (from Conn.,) who came in 1805–06; and Simon Pierson, (also from Conn.,) in 1808. The first child born was Luther Crosby, in 1806; the first inn was kept at Bergen Corners by Samuel Butler, in 1810; the first store by Levi Ward, in 1808. Jared Merrill erected the first sawmill, in the N. W. part of the town, in 1811; and Titus Wilcox (from Conn.) taught the first school, in the winter of 1807–08, at Bergen Corners.

[7] The census reports 5 churches; 2 Cong., and 1 each Presb., M. E., and R. C.

[8] In the same year Capt. Geo. Lathrop, from Conn., settled on lot 40, in the N. part of the town, and Orsemus Kellogg, from Sheffield, Mass., in the E. part. Lyman D. Prindle, from Hoosick, settled at East Bethany in 1805; Joseph Adgate, from Ulster co., and Mather Peck, from Lyme, Conn., near East Bethany in 1803; and the first birth was that of a child of Orsemus Kellogg, in 1806. Matilda Wedge, from New England, taught the first school, in 1808. Sylvester Lincoln kept the first inn; Elisha Hurlburt, from Vt., the first store, in 1808; and Judge Wilson built the first gristmill, in 1811.

[9] 2 Presb., and 1 each M. E., Bap., and F. W. Bap.

[10] The acid spring issues from a hillock about 230 feet long and 100 broad, elevated 4 or 5 feet above the plain. The strength of the acid is increased by drouth, and in some places it is quite concentrated and nearly dry in its combination with the charred vegetable coat which everywhere covers the hillock to a depth of from 5 to 40 inches.—*Beck's Mineralogy N. Y.*, p. 149.

[11] Locally known as "*Brusselville.*"

[12] Named from the fact that an early tavern sign at that place was painted yellow and resembled a pumpkin.

in 1807.[1] The first religious services were held by Rev. Royal Phelps, (Presb.,) from Cayuga co., in 1809. The first church (Bap.) was formed in 1810, by Elder Benjamin M. Parks.[2]

DARIEN—was formed from Pembroke, Feb. 10, 1832. It is the s. w. corner town of the co. The surface is hilly in the s. and rolling in the N. The streams are the Eleven Mile, Crooked, and Murder Creeks. The soil in the N. is a sandy and gravelly loam, and in the s. a clayey loam underlaid by limestone. **Darien Center,** (p. v.,) formerly *"Kings Corners,"* contains a church, seminary,[3] and 20 dwellings. **Darien City,** (Darien p. o.,) in the E. part of the town, contains a church and 50 dwellings. The first settlement was made near Darien City, by Orange Carter, from Vt., in 1803.[4] The census reports 4 churches in town.[5]

ELBA—was formed from Batavia, March 14, 1820. Oakfield was taken off in 1842. It is the central town on the N. border of the co. The surface is level or undulating. Oak Orchard Creek flows N. E. through the center of the town to the N. E. corner, and thence turns w. and flows through the N. part into Oakfield. The Tonawanda swamp extends along its course in the N. part of the town. The soil is a fertile, sandy, gravelly and clayey loam. **Pine Hill** (Elba p. v.) lies near the center of the town. Pop. 400. **Transit,**[6] on the line of Byron, is a hamlet. **Langtons Corners, Mills Corners,** (East Elba p. o.,) and **Daws Corners** are farming neighborhoods. The first settlement was made at Daws Corners in 1801, by Samuel and Amos Ranger, from Vt.[7] The first religious meetings were held by Rev. Mr. Mitchell, (M. E.,) in 1807. The first church (Bap.) was formed by Elder John Miner, in 1821.[8]

LE ROY[9]—was formed from Caledonia (Livingston co.) as *"Bellona,"* June 8, 1812. Its name was changed April 6, 1813. A part of Stafford was taken off in 1820, and a part of Pavilion in 1842. It is the central town on the E. border of the co. Its surface is level or gently undulating. A limestone ridge, 40 to 100 feet high, extends through the N. part of the town. Oatka Creek, the principal stream, flows from the s. w. corner of the town N. E. to a point a little N. of the center, thence turns and pursues a s. E. course to the E. border. Buttermilk Falls, 90 feet high, marks its descent over the limestone terrace.[10] The soil is generally a sandy or gravelly loam. Gypsum and Onondaga limestone, for building purposes, are obtained in this town. In the E. part, s. of Oatka Creek, is an extensive tract of oak openings, covered thickly with stone and hard of cultivation. **Le Roy** (p. v.) was incorp. May 5, 1834. It is finely located on Oatka Creek, and contains a bank, 1 newspaper office, a female seminary,[11] 6 churches, and several manufacturing establish-

1 Among the other first settlers were —— Hoskins, in 1808; Elisha Taylor, from Otsego co., (on lot 186;) Thester T. Holbrook, from Cayuga co.; Wheaton Carpenter, from R. I.; and Elisha Miller, from Penn., on lot 2, in 1809; Nathan Holt, from Otsego co., in 1810; and Asa Merrills, from Oneida co., in 1811. The first child born was a son of Elisha Taylor, in 1809; the first marriage, that of Saml. Montgomery and Polly Parks, in 1811; and the first death, that of a son of Mr. Hoskins. Thester T. Holbrook taught the first school, in 1810–11; Ira Newbury kept the first inn, in 1815; Amos Hewett, the first store, in 1813; Wm. Shepard erected the first sawmill, in 1813; and Asa Williams the first gristmill, in 1814.

2 The census reports 4 churches in town; 2 M. E., and 1 each Presb and F. W. Bap.

3 The Darien Seminary was established in 1850, by Robert Blennerhassett.

4 Isaac Chaddock, from Vt., settled near Darien City in 1804. The first child born was Harriet Carter, in 1805. Stephen Parker kept the first inn, in 1808, at Darien City; and Stephen King the first store, in 1815, at Darien Center. The first sawmill was erected by Amos Humphrey, in 1809, on Eleven Mile Creek.

5 Cong., Bap., F. W. Bap., and M. E.

6 Named from its location on the E. transit meridian of the Holland Land Company's survey.

7 Sam'l Clark, from Mass., and his son Sam'l, settled in 1802, and Samuel Hall, from Seneca co., and John Young, came soon after. The first birth was that of Betsey White, in 1802; the first death, that of David Kingsley, in 1804. Mason Turner taught the first school, near the center, in 1811; Stephen Harmon kept the first inn, in 1815; and Sam'l Lane the first store, in 1819, at Pine Hill. Horace Gibbs erected the first sawmill, on a branch of Spring Creek, in the E. part of the town, in 1810; and Comfort Smith the first gristmill, on the same stream, in 1815. The widow of John Young gives the following account of some of the trials of pioneer life:—"My husband having the year before been out and purchased his land upon the Holland Purchase, in the fall of 1804 we started from our home in Virginia, on horseback, for our new location. We came through Maryland, crossing the Susquehanna at Milton, thence via Tioga Point and the then usual route. In crossing the Alleghany Mts. night came upon us: the horses became frightened by wild beasts, and refused to proceed. We wrapped ourselves in our

cloaks and horse blankets, and attempted to get some rest, but had a disturbed night of it. Panthers came near us, often giving terrific screams. The frightened horses snorted and stamped upon the rocks. Taking an early start in the morning, we soon came to a settler's house, and were informed that we had stopped in a common resort of the panther. My husband built a shanty, which was about 10 feet square, flat roofed, covered with split ash shingles; the floor was made of the halves of split basswood; no chimney. A blanket answered the purpose of a door for a while, until my husband got time to make a door of split plank. We needed no window; the light came in where the smoke went out. For chairs we had benches, made by splitting logs and setting the sections upon legs. A bedstead was made by boring holes in the side of the shanty, inserting pieces of timber which rested upon two upright posts in front, a side piece completing the structure, peeled basswood bark answering the place of a cord. We of course had brought no bed with us on horseback; so one had to be procured. We bought a cotton bag of Mr. Brisbane, and, stuffing it with cat-tail, it was far better than no bed. The second year we were in, I had an attack of the fever and ague, which confined me for nearly a year. That year my husband cleared four acres, besides taking care of me and doing the cooking. It was not uncommon thing, in the first years of settlement, for women in childbirth to be deprived of the aid of a physician; and often the attendance of their own sex had to be dispensed with. Mr. Young died in 1836." *Turner's Pion. Hist.*

8 The census reports 5 churches in town; 1 each Bap., Cong., M. E., Prot. M., and Friends.

9 Named in honor of Herman Le Roy, one of the original purchasers of the *"Triangle Tract."*

10 When the water is low, it disappears in the bed of the stream about 2 miles above the falls, and finds its way to the lower channel through a subterranean passage.

11 The Ingham University, late Ingham Collegiate Institute, was incorp. 1857. The institution was first established at Attica, in 1835, by Miss Marietta Ingham, and a younger sister, Emily E. Ingham, (now Mrs. Phineas Stanton,) from Mass. In 1837 it was removed to Le Roy, and was established as the "Le Roy Female Seminary" by the founders, aided and supported by Messrs. Saml. Comstock, Jonathan P. Darling, Seth M. Gates, Albert Brewster, A. S. Upham, Enos Bachelder, A. P. Hascall, Lee Comstock, Israel Rathbone, Richard Hollister, and Wm. S. Bradley. It was chartered in 1841; and in 1855 the whole

ments. Pop. 2081. **Fort Hill**[1] is a hamlet. The first settlement was made in 1797, by Charles Wilbur, near Le Roy Village.[2] The first religious services (Prot. E.) were held at the village by the Rev. Davenport Phelps, in 1802.[3]

OAKFIELD[4]—was formed from Elba, April 11, 1842. It lies on the N. border of the co., w. of the center. The surface is level or gently undulating. Oak Orchard Creek, the principal stream, flows w. through the N. part of the town. A marsh, forming a portion of the Tonawanda swamp, extends along its course. The soil is a sandy and gravelly loam underlaid by clay. Brine springs, from which salt was formerly manufactured, are found near the center of the town. **Caryville**[5] (Oakfield p. o.) was incorp. in July, 1858. It contains an academy[6] and 2 churches. Pop. 500. **Oakfield** and **Mechanicsville** are hamlets. Most of the town was an Indian Reservation, and the lands were not sold to the whites until subsequent to 1832. The first settlers were Erastus Walcott, Gideon Dunham, and Christopher Kenyon, who came in 1801.[7] One mi. w. of Caryville are the remains of an àncient fortification known as the "*Old Fort*," consisting of a ditch and breastworks, including about 10 acres of ground. There are 2 churches in town ; Presb. and M. E.

PAVILION—was formed from Covington, (Wyoming co.,) May 19, 1841. Portions were annexed from Le Roy and Stafford, March 22, 1842. It is the S. E. corner town of the co. The surface is hilly in the s. and undulating in the N. Oatka Creek, the principal stream, flows N. a little w. of the center of the town. The soil is a fertile, gravelly loam underlaid by clay. Fruits are extensively cultivated. **Pavilion** (p. v.) is situated on Oatka Creek, near the s. border of the town. Pop. 216. **Pavilion Center**, (p. v.,) formerly "*South Le Roy*," contains a church and 20 houses. **Union Corners** is a hamlet. The first settlement was made in 1809, by Peter Crosman.[8] The first church edifice (Univ.) was erected at the village of Pavilion, in 1832.[9]

PEMBROKE—was formed from Batavia, June 8, 1812. A part of Alabama was taken off in 1826, and Darien in 1832. It is the central town upon the w. border of the co. Its surface is level or gently undulating. Tonawanda Creek flows through the N. E. corner, and Murder Creek through the s. and s. w. parts. The soil is a sandy and gravelly loam intermixed with clay. The Tonawanda Indian Reservation occupies a portion of the N. part of the town. **East Pembroke**, (p.v.,) on the line of Batavia, contains an academy,[10] 2 churches, and 35 dwellings, **Richville**,[11] (Pembroke p. o.,) 1 church and 40 dwellings, **Longs Corners**, (*Corfu* p. o.,) in the s. part of the town, 2 churches and 45 dwellings, and **Mogadore**, (North Pembroke p. o.,) 20 dwellings. **Prospect Hill** is a hamlet. The first settlement was made in the town in 1804, by David Goss, from Mass.[12] The first church (Cong.) was formed by Rev. Joshua Spencer, first minister, in 1810, at Longs Corners.[13]

STAFFORD—was formed from Batavia and Le Roy, March 24, 1820. A part of Pavilion was taken off in 1842. It is an interior town, lying E. of the center of the co. Its surface is undulating, with a general slight slope to the N. Black Creek flows N. through the center of the town, and Bigelow Creek rises in the w. and flows in the same direction. The soil is a productive, sandy

establishment, costing over $20,000, was donated by its founders to the Synod of Genesee, upon the conditions that a full collegiate course should be established, and a permanent fund raised for its support. The gift was accepted by the Synod, and the present name bestowed.
1 On the brow of the hill at this place are the ruins of an old fort.—*Smithsonian Contributions, vol. II., art. 6, p.* 48.
2 Capt. John Ganson, and his 2 sons John and James, settled near Le Roy Village in 1798, and Gideon Fordham, Alexander McPherson, and Hines Chamberlin in 1800–01. The first child born was Neoma Wilbur, in 1799; and the first after the town was named Le Roy was Wm. Le Roy Annin, in 1814. Geo. A. Tiffany kept the first store, in 1806; and the Holland Land Co. built the first mill, in 1804.
3 The census reports 6 churches in town; 1 each Prot. E., Presb., Cong., Bap., M. E., and R. C.
4 Named from the fact that the lands of the town were mostly "*Oak Openings*."
5 Named from Col. Alfred Cary, an early settler and prominent citizen.
6 The Cary Collegiate Institute was founded in 1840, mainly by the influence and means of Col. Alfred Cary, who died in this town Sept. 17, 1858, aged 79. The building (which is of stone) and apparatus cost $15,000. The institution has accommodations for 200 students. Besides large contributions to its establishment, Col. Cary has endowed the institution with $20,000. It is now under charge of the Prot. E. Church.
7 The first store was kept in 1833, by Col. Cary, at Caryville; and the first inn by Gideon Dunham, at Dunhams Corners, in

1805. The first saw and grist mill were erected by Christopher Kenyon, in 1811.
8 Among the other first settlers were James McWithey, Solomon Terrill, Reuben Burnham, and Joshua Shumway, in 1810; Sylvanus Young, Elijah Phelps, Amasa Allen, and several brothers of the name of Burgess, in 1811; and Isaac Storm, in 1812, most of whom located in the E. part of the town. The first death was that of a child of Reuben Burnham, in 1812. Laura Terrill (from Vt.) taught the first school, in 1813; Seth Smith kept the first inn, in 1815; and Horace Bates the first store, in 1817, at the village of Pavilion. The first mill was erected by Bial Lathrop, on Oatka Creek, in 1816.
9 The census reports 7 churches in town; 3 M. E., and 1 each Presb., Bap., Union, and Univ.
10 The Rural Academy was incorp. by the regents in 1856 Average number of students about 100.
11 Named from Charles B. Rich, a prominent man in town.
12 John Long, Dr. David Long, (from Washington co.,) and Samuel Carr settled in the town in 1808, and Joseph Lester (from Conn.) in 1809. The first child born was Jonathan Hastings, jr., in 1810; and the first marriage, that of Ansell Hastings and Polly Long, in 1812. Anna Horton taught the first school, at Corfu in 1811; Samuel Carr kept the first inn, at W. Pembroke, in 1809; John Ball the first store, at the same place, in 1812; and Samuel Carr erected the first gristmill and sawmill, in 1808–09.
13 The census reports 6 churches in town; 2 Bap., and 1 each Presb., M. E., Prot. M., and Christian.

loam intermixed with clay. **Stafford** (p. v.) lies on Black Creek, near the center of the town. It is a station on the C. & N. F. branch of the N. Y. C. R. R., and contains 3 churches, a private seminary, and a pop. of 350. **Morganville**[1] (p. v.) contains 2 churches, 2 sawmills, a flouring mill, a brown earthen ware factory, and 200 inhabitants. A fall in Black Creek at this place is 30 ft. perpendicular and 30 ft. in rapids, affording a fine water power.[2] **Roanoke,**[3] (p. v.,) formerly "*Orangeburgh*," contains a church, several mills, and 20 dwellings. The settlement was commenced in 1801, by Col. Wm. Rumsey and Gen. Worthy Lovel Churchill, (from Vt.,) who located on the Buffalo Road, w. of Stafford.[4] The first religious services were held at the house of Col. Rumsey, by Rev. Mr. Green. The first church (Bap.) was formed by Rev. Amos Lampson, in 1815.[5]

Acres of Land, Valuation, Population, Dwellings, Families, Freeholders, Schools, Live Stock, Agricultural Products, and Domestic Manufactures, of Genesee County.

Names of Towns.	Acres of Land.		Valuation of 1858.			Population.		No. of Dwellings.	No. of Families.	Freeholders.	Schools.	
	Improved.	Unimproved.	Real Estate.	Personal Property.	Total.	Males.	Females.				No. of Districts.	Children taught.
Alabama	18,345½	10,194¼	805,535	43,350	848,885	1,159	1,035	416	436	315	14	903
Alexander	17,234	4,539	769,370	66,650	836,020	911	887	351	378	268	14	585
Batavia	20,803¾	5,320½	2,371,128	723,600	3,094,728	2,653	2,651	924	990	723	16	1,705
Bergen	12,504	4,126	684,266	40,410	724,676	905	895	366	363	303	9	638
Bethany	18,118	4,882½	517,316	48,338	565,654	925	954	356	382	327	11	604
Byron	15,409	4,162	775,776	151,835	927,611	843	798	313	329	272	9	562
Darien	23,527	6,907	696,870	71,282	768,152	1,112	1,064	418	435	362	16	822
Elba	15,614	6,535	678,131	112,130	790,261	959	910	375	384	251	9	616
Le Roy	20,427	5,872	1,266,937	392,770	1,659,707	2,117	2,098	716	532	511	13	1,363
Oakfield	9,208½	3,476¼	398,916	36,600	435,516	817	693	286	279	178	8	589
Pavilion	16,986¼	4,322¼	606,308	81,400	687,708	915	843	323	333	280	10	536
Pembroke	15,187¼	12,297¼	814,001	38,600	852,601	1,432	1,412	549	566	452	14	977
Stafford	15,648	3,098	773,125	151,099	924,224	1,073	982	360	385	186	9	744
Total	219,012¼	75,732	11,157,679	1,958,064	13,115,743	15,821	15,222	5,753	5,792	4,428	152	10,644

Names of Towns.	Live Stock.					Agricultural Products.							Domestic Cloths in yards.
						Bush. of Grain.		Tons of Hay.	Bushels of Potatoes.	Bushels of Apples.	Dairy Products.		
	Horses.	Working Oxen and Calves.	Cows.	Sheep.	Swine.	Winter.	Spring.				Pounds Butter.	Pounds Cheese.	
Alabama	1,049	1,288	927	8,844	2,209	76,574	91,094	1,821	12,892	10,355	74,517	12,248	992
Alexander	700	1,279	781	11,530	991	39,795	65,907	4,859	11,351	33,644	74,925	12,385	511
Batavia	1,229	1,340	1,240	7,802	2,198	85,868	87,350	3,684¾	18,350	18,436	88,348	4,825	223
Bergen	683	832	589	4,667	1,312	43,805	49,366	2,106	7,052	15,872	59,907	4,686	295½
Bethany	803	1,122	832	9,304	1,277	48,063	54,201½	4,406	12,991	41,912	77,271	16,179	20
Byron	970	1,314	746	5,429	1,752	57,538	66,597	2,309	8,440	12,366	62,820	7,345	307
Darien	978	1,306	1,095	14,729	1,016	21,052	70,398¼	6,411½	17,604	34,858	88,117	11,528	700
Elba	988	979	739	4,618	1,789	63,564	76,616	2,690	11,567	29,041	71,340	1,325	332
Le Roy	1,246	1,155	970	7,714	1,972	112,421	66,258¼	3,266½	13,142	26,180	89,247	6,980	159
Oakfield	461	545	329	3,007	982	35,175	47,643	1,355	4,834	9,818	18,574	1,293	73
Pavilion	805	1,205	842	11,221	1,113	55,096	57,782½	3,668	10,448	32,896	80,087	15,140	598½
Pembroke	781	1,024	888	6,594	1,175	33,073	62,103	3,423	25,634	17,585	93,497	8,438	401½
Stafford	702	855	563	4,932	1,487	89,566	44,848½	1,399	12,969	13,158	40,480	3,501	33
Total	11,395	14,244	10,541	100,391	19,273	761,590	840,165	41,398¾	167,274	296,121	919,130	105,873	4,645½

[1] Named from the wife of Wm. Morgan, of masonic notoriety.

[2] Two caves are found in the W. bank of the creek a few rods below the falls.

[3] Named from the residence of John Randolph by Major Jas. Ganson.

[4] Peter Stage (from Onondaga co.) settled in 1802. Benj. Ganson and John Annis were the first settlers in the E. part of the town. Gen. W. L. Churchill served with credit in the War of 1812, and subsequently as sheriff of Genesee co. from 1820 to 1825. The first birth was that of a child of W. L. Churchill, March 9, 1803; and the first death, that of the wife of W. L. Churchill, at about the same time. The first school was taught by Esther Sprout, in 1806. Frederick Walthers kept the first inn, at Stafford Village, in 1799; and this was one of the first three taverns kept on the Holland Purchase. The village was then known as the "*Transit Store House*," from its being the principal supply station for the surveying company while running the "*Transit Line*." The first sawmill was built on Bigelow Creek, in 1810, by Amos Stow; and the first gristmill, on the same stream, in 1811, by Seymour Ensign.

[5] The census reports 7 churches in town; 2 M. E., and 1 each Prot. E., Cong., Bap., Christian, and Univ.

GREENE COUNTY.

This county was formed from Albany and Ulster, March 25, 1800, and named in honor of Gen. Nathaniel Greene, of the Revolution. Parts were annexed to Ulster co. May 26, 1812. It lies upon the w. bank of Hudson River, centrally distant 32 mi. from Albany, and contains 686 sq. mi. Its surface is very broken and mountainous. The main range of the Catskill Mts. commences 8 to 10 mi. w. of the Hudson and extends along the s. border of the co. to Delaware co. These mountains are 3000 to 3800 feet above tide.[1] Their summits are broad, wild, and rocky, and their declivities steep and often precipitous. A branch from the main ridge extends in a n. w. direction through the co., separating the towns of Durham and Cairo from Windham and Hunter and dividing the co. into two nearly equal parts. This ridge is 2500 to 3000 feet above tide. It has a steep and wall-like front on the e., and on the w. it sends off numerous spurs, which extend to the valley of Schoharie Creek. The whole intermediate territory consists of high, rocky ridges separated by narrow valleys. The declivities are generally steep on the n., but more gradual on the s.[2] Another branch from the main ridge extends northward through the extreme w. part of the co., between the towns of Halcott and Lexington, and forms the series of highlands that rise upon the w. bank of Schoharie Creek. This range forms the watershed between Schoharie Creek and Delaware River. The e. half of the co. is hilly and broken. An irregular line of bluffs extends along the Hudson, with an average elevation of about 100 ft. Parallel to these bluffs, and 2 to 4 mi. further w., is a range of hills 500 to 700 ft. above the river. These highlands are known as the Potick Hills in the town of Athens. Between this ridge and the e. foot of the Catskills the surface is moderately hilly, gradually sloping toward Catskill Creek.

The principal streams of the co. are Hudson River, forming its e. border, Schoharie Creek and its tributaries, draining the w. slope of the mountains, and Catskill Creek[3] and its principal tributary the Kaaterskil, draining the e. slope. Small branches of these streams flow through narrow, rocky ravines, which break entirely through the mountains and form passes locally known as "cloves." The principal of these cloves are the Kaaters Kil, opening westward from the Hudson into the valley of Schoharie Creek, and the Bushkil Clove, Stoney Clove, Mink Hollow, and Plattekil Hollow, opening southward from Schoharie Creek into the valleys of Ulster co. In many places these ravines are bordered by naked cliffs, nearly perpendicular, and 1000 to 1700 ft. above the streams. The small streams that drain the w. slope of the range in Halcott form branches of the Delaware. Schoharie Creek rises in the town of Hunter, within 12 mi. of the Hudson, flows w. and n., and forms a branch of the Mohawk. The streams are mostly rapid, and are subject to sudden and violent freshets. The e. slope of the mountain and the outcropping strata of the Catskill and Kaaterskil Creeks present to the geologist one of the most interesting and comprehensive fields of investigation to be found on the continent. Within the distance of 12 mi. from the village of Catskill to the Mountain House may be seen nearly all the strata composing the New York system. The gray grits and conglomerates forming the floor of the coal measures are found 110 ft. deep at the summit of the Pine Orchard. The depth of the whole series, within the 12 mi. referred to, is scarcely less than 4000 feet. Few or no metallic veins or valuable minerals, except building and flagging stone, are found in the co.

The soil on the w. slopes of the Catskill is chiefly a reddish, gravelly or shaly loam extensively underlaid by hardpan. The surface is stony, except upon the river bottoms, where the soil is fertile and productive. North and e. of the mountains the soil is greatly diversified by sections of gravelly, shaly, clayey, and sandy loams; but a stiff clay predominates. Where properly cultivated, it is moderately productive. The whole region is best adapted to grazing; and the principal agricultural exports are butter, cheese, and pressed hay. Oats, barley, and potatoes are extensively cultivated, but, like most of the other eastern course, the grain grown is insufficient for the consump-

---

[1] High Peak has an elevation of 3804 feet above tide, Round Top 3718 feet, and Pine Orchard 3000 feet. The Catskill Mountain House is situated upon the last named mountain.

[2] The n. sides of these spurs are generally rocky and bare, and the s. sides covered with vast deposits of drift, indicating that a great current of water from the n. once swept over them. Nearly all the valuable land in this section lies upon the n. side of the valley.

[3] Named by the Dutch from wild cats found in this vicinity. Kaaters Kil has a similar signification, but is limited to the male animals.

tion of the population. The principal manufactured products are brick, leather, and paper. Brick are extensively made on the banks of the Hudson, in Catskill, Athens, and Coxsackie, for the New York market. The co. has a considerable interest in the commerce of the Hudson, but less, perhaps, than it had many years ago. No co. has been more seriously damaged in its commercial and manufacturing prospects by the public works of the State than Greene. Before the Erie Canal was completed, Catskill, the co. seat, commanded the trade of the adjacent cos. w., and of the s. tier through to Lake Erie, and some portions of Northern Penn. It was a large wheat market; and at the falls of Catskill Creek, 3 mi. w. of the village, were the most extensive flouring mills in the State.[1] The canals and railroads have limited the commercial transactions of the co. strictly to home trade. A change scarcely less marked and important has taken place in the industrial pursuits of the mountain towns. About 1817, upon the discovery of improved methods of tanning leather, tanners rushed into the Catskill Mts., purchased large tracts of mountain lands covered with hemlock timber, and erected extensive tanneries. The valleys of Schoharie Creek, Batavia, and West Kils soon teemed with a numerous, active laboring population, and the solitude of the deep mountain glens was made vocal by the hum of industry, the buzz of the waterwheel, and the rattling of machinery. Villages of considerable magnitude, with churches, schools, stores, and taverns, rose up in the wilderness as if by magic. Thirty years ago Greene co. made more leather than all the State beside. The supply of bark in this region was soon exhausted, and the proprietors gradually abandoned their establishments and followed the mountain chain s., erecting new factories in Ulster and Sullivan cos.; and their successors are now pursuing the hemlock into the heart of the Alleganies. The result of all this was to facilitate the occupation of the lands in the mountain towns, and in many cases to carry cultivation to the summits of the most lofty ranges, thereby opening one of the finest dairy and wool growing regions in the State.

The county seat is located at Catskill, on the Hudson.[2] The first courthouse was a wood building, erected under act of May 26, 1812.[3] Some years since, this building was burned, and a new brick edifice was soon after erected in its place. It contains the court and jury rooms, and district attorney and co. clerk's offices. A stone jail was erected in 1804, and a fireproof clerk's office in 1812. The co. poorhouse is located on a farm of 130 acres in Cairo, 10 mi. w. of Catskill. The farm yields a revenue of $900. It has on an average 130 inmates, supported at a weekly expense of $ .75 each. A school is taught in the house most of the year. The condition and adaptation of the building, and the management of the inmates, are not thought creditable to the co. authorities.

Six weekly newspapers are published in the co.[4]

More than two centuries have elapsed since the settlements in the valley of the Hudson commenced at various points between New York and Albany. It was 150 years later when a few,

---

1 Of this place Spafford's Gazetteer (ed. of 1813) says, "Catskill has considerable trade already, and must probably experience a rapid growth as the market town of an extensive back country. At some place in this vicinity, and on the w. bank of the river, future ages will probably find the third, if not the second, city on the Hudson, in wealth, population, and commercial importance."

2 Ira Day, Isaac Dubois, Orin Day, Joseph Klein, Ezra Hawley, and Lyman Hall, having executed to the supervisors a bond, under a penalty of $16,000, to procure a lot and build a courthouse, an act was passed May 26, 1812, allowing the judges to accept the premises when completed. Courts were previously held at the academy, and the prisoners confined in Albany co. jail.

3 The first co. officers were Leonard Bronk, First Judge; Ebenezer Foot, District Attorney; James Bill, Co. Clerk; George Hale, Sheriff; John H. Cuyler, Surrogate.

4 The Catskill Packet, the first paper in the co., was published prior to 1800.

The Catskill Recorder was started in 1801 by Mackey Croswell. In 1817 Edwin Croswell assumed its control, and continued it until 1822. In 1827 it was published by Field & Faxton, and in 1828 it was issued as

The Catskill Recorder and Greene Co. Republican, by Faxton, Elliott & Gates. In 1849 it was united with The Democrat, and issued as

The Catskill Recorder and Democrat, under which name it is still published by Joseph Josebury.

The American Eagle was published at Catskill in 1810 by N. Elliott & Co.

The Catskill Emendator was commenced in 1813, and continued a short time.

The Greene and Delaware Washingtonian was commenced at Catskill in 1814, by Michael J. Kappel. In 1816 it was changed to

The Middle District Gazette, and published by Wm. L. Stone.

The Greene Co. Republican was established at Catskill in Nov. 1826, by —— Hyer. In 1827 it was sold to Ralph Johnson; in 1828, to C. Hull; and in 1829 it was merged in

The Catskill Recorder.

The Catskill Messenger was started in 1830, by Ira Dubois. It was subsequently issued by Wm. Bryan, C. H. Cleveland, and Trowbridge & Gunn. In 1849 it was changed to

The Greene Co. Whig; and in 1857 to

The Catskill Examiner, by which name it is now published.

The Catskill Democrat was started in 1843 by Joseph Josebury, and in 1849 it was united with The Recorder.

The American Eagle was started at Prattsville in 1854 by E. & H. Baker, who removed it to Catskill the same year. In 1855 its name was changed to

The Banner of Industry, and published by Jas. H. Van Gorden. In 1857 it was sold to Henry Baker, by whom it is now published as

The Catskill Democratic Herald.

The Greene Co. Advertiser was started at Coxsackie in 1832, and published for a time by Henry Van Dyck. In 1836 it was changed to

The Standard, and published by Thomas B. Carroll. It was subsequently issued a short time as

The Coxsackie Standard.

The Coxsackie Union was established in 1851 by Fred. W. Hoffman. In Jan. 1857 it passed into the hands of D. M. & B. S. Slater, by whom it is still published.

The Prattsville Bee was started in 1852.

The Baptist Library was started at Prattsville in 1843 by L. L. & R. H. Hill. In 1845 it was removed to Lexington.

The Prattsville Advocate was established by John L. Hackstaff in 1846, and was discontinued in 1858.

The Mountaineer was published at Prattsville in 1853 by Chas. H. Cleveland.

The Windham Journal was started at Windham Center, March 21, 1857, by W. B. Steele.

The Athens Visitor was commenced in 1858 by R. Denton.

small, isolated settlements were made in the valleys of the streams in the interior of Greene co. The great Hardenburgh Patent, granted by Queen Anne, covered nearly all of that portion of the co. lying w. of the mountains. The N. line of this grant commenced at the headwaters of the Kaaters Kil, being the head of the upper lake at Pine Orchard, and ran a N. w. course to the headwaters of the w. branch of the Delaware, in Stamford, Delaware co. This line was run at three different periods, near the close of the last century, by three different surveyors, no two of them agreeing by the width of whole farms. This disagreement has proved a prolific source of litigation in the courts of the State for 50 years. The patent included all that part of Delaware co. lying E. of the w. branch of Delaware River, and nearly all of Ulster and Sullivan cos. When the settlements commenced, the tract was owned by a great number of individuals, who had purchased by townships. At an early period, Stephen Day (from Conn.) purchased a large tract in Greene co., embracing a considerable portion of the old town of Windham, now forming the towns of Windham, Ashland, Jewett, and a portion of Lexington and Hunter. This tract was principally settled by immigrants from Connecticut.

ASHLAND—named from the home of Henry Clay—was formed from Windham and Prattsville, March 23, 1848. It lies in the N. w. part of the co. Its N. and s. borders are occupied by two parallel spurs of the Catskill Mts., 800 to 1000 ft. above the valley. Batavia Kil flows westward through the town at the foot of the s. range. This stream is bordered upon the N. by steep bluffs 150 to 200 ft. high; and from their summits the surface gradually slopes upward to the s. foot of the N. ridge near the N. border of the town. Lewis Creek and several smaller streams are tributaries of Batavia Kil. About two-thirds of the land in the town is improved. **Ashland,** (p. v.,) on Batavia Kil, in the s. part of the town, contains 2 churches and a collegiate institute.[1] Pop. 400. **East Ashland** is a hamlet. The first settlement was made in the valley of Batavia Kil, previous to the Revolutionary War, by a few Dutch families from Schoharie co. During the war, being harassed by the Indians and tories, the settlers returned to Schoharie co. The first permanent settlement was made in 1788, by Elisha Strong and several brothers named Stimpson.[2] There are 6 churches in town.[3]

ATHENS—was formed from Catskill and Coxsackie, Feb. 25, 1815. It is situated on the Hudson, near the center of the E. border of the co. Its surface is broken by several rocky hills and ridges lying parallel with the Hudson, with uneven or undulating intervales between. A range of high clay bluffs borders upon the river; and a high rocky ridge, known as Potick Hill, extends through the w. part of the town. Several small streams flow southerly through the town, and Potick Creek forms its w. line. In the w. part of the town are 3 small lakes. In their vicinity, 4 or 5 mi. w. of the Hudson, are extensive beds of the Helderbergh limestone, large quantities of which are quarried for building purposes and for the manufacture of lime. Near the river the soil is a tough clay, bordered by sand; elsewhere it is a sandy and gravelly loam of a good quality. Brick and lime are the principal articles manufactured, and these, with hay, form the exports of the town. **Athens,**[4] (p. v.,) incorp. April 2, 1805, is situated on the Hudson, opposite the city of Hudson. Pop. 1747. The E. part of the town was settled at a very early period by immigrants from Holland.[5] There are 5 churches in town.[6]

CAIRO—was formed from Catskill, Coxsackie, and "*Freehold,*" (now Durham,) March 26, 1803, as "*Canton,*" and its name was changed April 6, 1808. It is situated at the E. foot of the Catskill Mts., the crest of the mountain forming its w. boundary. Its central and E. parts are broken by several high, rocky ridges. Round Top, also called the Dome Mountain, is a rocky, isolated hill 500 ft. high. The Catskill Creek flows s. E. through the town, and receives from the N. John Debackers Creek and Platte Kil, and from the s. Shingle and Hagel Kils. The soil is a clayey, gravelly, and shaly loam, fertile in the valleys and of medium quality among the hills. **Cairo,** (p. v.,) situated near the center of the town, on the Old Susquehanna Turnpike, contains 4 churches and several manufacturing establishments. Pop. 353. **Acra,** (p. o.,) in the w., **S. Cairo,** (p. o.) and **Cairo Forge,** about 1 mi. s. of Cairo, are hamlets. Settlements were made on the Shingle Kil previous to the Revolution.[7] A Presb. church was organized May 22, and a Bap. May 25, 1799. There are 7 churches in town.[8]

---

[1] The Ashland Collegiate Institute was founded in 1854, under the care of the M. E. denomination. The present number of boarding pupils (1858) is 100.

[2] Among the early settlers were Agabus White, John Tuttle, Jairus Strong, Solomon Ormsbee, Dr. Thomas Benham, and Medad Hunt, most of whom were from Connecticut. The first birth was that of Deborah Stone, in 1789. Sandford Hunt kept the first store, and Medad Hunt the first inn, in 1795. Ex Gov. Washington Hunt, son of Sandford Hunt, was born in this town.

[3] 3 M. E., Prot. E., Presb., and R. C.

[4] Formerly called "*Loonenburgh*" and "*Esperanza.*" The steamer Swallow, on her way to New York with a large number of passengers, was wrecked in the river opposite this place on the evening of April 7, 1845, and about 20 persons were lost.—*Senate Doc., No.* 102, 1845.

[5] A tannery was erected in 1750 by Nicholas Perry.

[6] Bap., Friends, Luth., Prot. E., and Ref. Prot. D.

[7] A family by the name of Strobe, living on the Shingle Kil, were murdered by the Indians during the war.

[8] 3 M. E., Bap., Presb., Prot. E., and Union.

CATSKILL[1]—was formed March 7, 1788, as part of Albany co. It was annexed to Ulster co. April 5, 1798. A part of Woodstock (Ulster co.) was annexed March 25, 1800; a part of Cairo was taken off in 1803 and a part of Athens in 1815. It lies upon the Hudson, in the s. e. corner of the co. The surface is broken by several rocky ridges parallel to the Hudson: these ridges are principally composed of shales and gray grit. In the latter formation are extensive quarries, from which a fine quality of flagging stone is obtained and largely exported. A swamp, covering an area of several hundred acres, extends along the Hudson below Catskill Village. The Catskill Creek flows s. e. through the n. e. corner to the Hudson, and receives the Kaaters Kil after the latter has pursued an irregular course through the center and s. w. part of the town. The other streams are Kiskatom Creek, and Jan Vosent Kil. The soil is principally tenacious clay, with sections of gravelly and shaly loam. Hay is the principal agricultural export. Large quantities of brick are manufactured and exported. Catskill Village being the chief entrepôt for the co., commerce forms one of the leading pursuits of the people. **Catskill,** (p. v.,) the co. seat, was incorp. March 14, 1806. It is situated on the Hudson, at the mouth of Catskill Creek. It contains 5 churches, 3 newspaper offices, 2 banks, and a large number of mercantile and manufacturing establishments. Pop. 2520. **Leeds,** (p. v.,) situated at the falls on Catskill Creek, contains 2 churches and several manufactories. Pop. 450. **Palensville,** (p. v.,) on the Kaaters Kil, in the w. part of the town, contains 2 tanneries, a woolen factory, and 18 dwellings. **Kiskatom** is a p. o. Settlements were made upon the banks of the Hudson, at a very early period, by immigrants from Germany. The flats in the valley of Catskill Creek w. of Leeds were first settled by Martin G. Van Bergen and Sylvester Salisbury, who in 1677 purchased the Indian title to an extensive tract. There are 9 churches in town.[2] The Catskill Mountain House is on the line of Hunter. See page 333.

COXSACKIE[3]—was formed, as a district, March 24, 1772, and as a town, March 7, 1788. Durham was taken off in 1790, a part of Cairo and Greenville in 1803, New Baltimore in 1811, and a part of Athens in 1815. It lies upon the Hudson, n. e. of the center of the co. A range of clay bluffs about 100 ft. high extends along the course of the river, and a range of hills 500 ft. high through the center of the town. The surface is level or undulating in the e. and is hilly and broken in the w. The principal streams are the Coxsackie, Potick, and Jan Vosent Creeks. The soil in the e. is clayey and sandy, and in the w. it is a gravelly, shaly, and clayey loam. Brickmaking is extensively pursued. **Coxsackie,** (p. v.,) situated near the Hudson, contains 6 churches, an academy, a newspaper office, a bank, and several manufactories.[4] Pop. 1,800. **Coxsackie Landing** is 1 mi. e. of the village. **Jacksonville,** in the w. part, is a hamlet. The Dutch settled in town about 1652, on a tract about 6 mi. sq. purchased of the Indians. There are 8 churches in town.[5]

DURHAM—was formed from Coxsackie as "*Freehold*," March 8, 1790, and its name was changed March 28, 1805. Parts of Cairo and Greenville were taken off in 1803. It lies near the center of the n. border of the co. Its surface is hilly and broken, the n. e. corner being occupied by the s. slopes of the Helderbergh Mts., and the w. border by the Catskills. The principal streams are Catskill Creek, flowing s. e. through the e. part, and its tributaries Fall, Bowery, Posts, and Brink Street Creeks. The soil is generally a heavy clay, with occasional sections of gravel. There are several mills and tanneries on Catskill Creek, which stream affords a fair amount of water power. **Oak Hill,** (p. v.,) on Catskill Creek, has a pop. of 320. **Durham,** (p. v.,) 1 mi. w. of Oak Hill, contains 2 churches and 30 houses, **East Durham** (p. v.) 17 houses, **Cornwall-ville,** (p. v.,) in the central part of the town, 15 houses, and **South Durham** (p. o.) 10 houses. **Centerville** is a hamlet. The settlement of the town was commenced in 1776. Capt. Asahel Jones and Rozel Post, from Conn., settled in 1788.[6] There are 7 churches in town.[7]

GREENVILLE—was formed from Coxsackie and "*Freehold*," (now Durham,) March 26, 1803, as "*Greenfield*." Its name was changed to "*Freehold*" in 1808, and to Greenville, March 17, 1809. It lies on the n. border of the co., e. of the center. Its surface is hilly,—the southern extremity of the Helderbergh Mts. occupying the central and w. parts of the town. The principal streams are Potick, John Debackers, and Basic Creeks. The soil is chiefly a heavy, clay loam, well adapted to grazing; but much of it has been exhausted by too frequent croppings with hay. About 1 mi. w. of Greenville Center is a sulphur spring. **Greenville,** (p. v.,) n. of the center

---

1 Great Imbocht District, including this town, was formed March 24, 1772.
2 3 M. E., 2 Ref. Prot. D., Pap., Presb., Prot. E., and Union.
3 Pron. Cook-sock'ey. Derived from an Indian word signifying "Owl-hoot."
4 Shipbuilding was formerly carried on at the lower landing,

near this place; and several of the early Hudson River steamboats were built here.
5 2 Ref. Prot. D., 2 M. E., Prot. E., R. C., Union, and Af. M. E.
6 Mr. De Witt built the first gristmill, in 1788, and Jared Smith the first sawmill, about the same time.
7 2 Cong., 2 M. E., Bap., Presb., and Prot. E.

of the town, contains 3 churches, the Greenville Academy, and 35 houses; **Freehold,** (p.v.,) in the s. w. part, 1 church and 24 houses; **Norton Hill,** (p. v.,) in the n. w. part, 16 houses; **Greenville Center** 15; and **East Greenville** 1 church and 10 houses. **Gay Head** is a p. office. In 1768 the British Government granted 2 patents—one for 2000 and one for 5000 acres, located together in the w. part of the town—to Major Augustine Prevost, of the 6th British infantry, who served in this country during the Old French War.[1] Stephen Lantiman, Godfrey Brandow, and Hans Overpaugh, who settled in the town in 1774, were among the earliest settlers.[2] There are 7 churches in town.[3]

HALCOTT—was formed from Lexington, Nov. 19, 1851, and named from George W. Halcott, then sheriff of Greene co. It is situated in the s. w. corner of the co., and is separated from the other towns of the co. by a mountain ridge 1000 feet high. This ridge is crossed by difficult and unfrequented roads. A considerable portion of the territory is covered with forests. The surface is mountainous, comprising four valleys, in which rise the sources of the e. branch of the Delaware. The soil is chiefly a gravelly loam of medium quality, and stony, but is well adapted to grazing. From its isolated position among the mountains,[4] the chief avenue of communication with the outside world is on the s., by way of Middletown, Delaware co. **West Lexington** (p. o.) is in the central part of the town. The first settlement was made on the Bush Kil, in 1790, by Reuben Crysler, —— Thurston, Joseph Brooks, and Timothy Tyler.[5] There are 2 churches in town; O. S. Bap. and M. E.

HUNTER[6]—was formed from Windham as "*Greenland*," Jan. 27, 1813. Its name was changed April 15, 1814, a part of Saugerties was taken off in 1814, and a part of Jewett in 1849. The surface is rocky and mountainous, not more than one-fourth being susceptible of cultivation. Several of the highest peaks of the Catskills—among which are High Peak, Round Top, and Pine Orchard—lie within the limits of this town.[7] Two narrow valleys extend quite through the mountains and cross each other at nearly right angles near the center of the town. The first of these is the valley of Schonarie Creek and its southerly continuation, that of the Platte Kil; and the second, that of the Kaaters Kil and Stony Clove. The soil is generally a heavy, clayey and shaly loam, very stony, and poorly adapted to agriculture. **Hunter,** (p.v.,) situated on Schoharie Creek, in the n. w. part of the town, contains 2 churches and several manufacturing establishments. Pop. 393. **Tannersville,** near the center, is a p. office. Settlements were made during the Revolution, by "*cowboys*" from Putnam co. Their property was confiscated by the Whigs.[8] Col. Wm. W. Edwards and his son Wm. W., from Northampton, Mass., moved into town in July, 1817, and erected the first extensive tannery in the State in which the then new method of tanning was adopted. Within a few years after, other tanneries were built, and a very large amount of leather was made in the town annually for a long series of years, until the hemlock bark was exhausted. Most of the establishments are now abandoned. There are 3 churches in town; Presb., M. E., and R. C.

JEWETT—was formed from Lexington and Hunter, Nov. 14, 1849. It lies near the center of the w. half of the co. Its surface is principally occupied by high and rocky spurs extending w. from the principal n. branch of the Catskills. A high and almost precipitous ridge extends along the s. w. border of the town. Schoharie Creek and its tributary East Kil are the principal streams. The soil is a heavy, reddish, gravelly loam of medium quality, often stony and rocky, and largely underlaid by a tough hardpan. **Jewett,**[9] (p.v.,) in the n. w. part of the town, contains 2 churches and 14 houses. **Jewett Center,** at the junction of East Kil and Schoharie Creek,

---

[1] Major Prevost erected a fine mansion on one of these tracts, a little w. of the village of Greenville, in which he resided until his death.

[2] Abraham Post, Eleazar Knowles, Bethuel Hinman, Peter Curtis, and Edward Lake, from Conn., settled in the town in 1783. David Hickock and Davis Denning erected the first gristmill, in 1785.

[3] 2 Bap., 2 M. E., Prot. E., Presb., and Christian.

[4] Wild game is still found in the mountains, and the pure, limpid streams abound in trout.

[5] Ralph Coe and Henry Hosford built the first sawmill, in 1820. Ralph Coe kept the first inn, and Henry Hamican the first store. There is now no tavern, lawyer, nor doctor in town.

[6] Named from John Hunter, an early proprietor of a part of the Hardenburgh Patent.

[7] The Catskill Mountain House, upon Pine Orchard, is situated upon a precipice overlooking the Hudson, and is 2212 ft. above tide. It was built by the Catskill Mountain Asso'n, at a cost of $22,000, for the accommodation of visitors. Among the hills, ½ mi. w. of the house, are 2 small lakes, each 1½ mi. in circumference,—their outlet forming the Kaaters Kil. Upon this stream, a little

below the lakes, are the Kaaters Kil Falls, where the stream plunges down a perpendicular descent of 175 ft., and, in a few rods, another of 85 ft., falling into a deep, rocky ravine or clove, and finally finding its way into Catskill Creek. The views from the Mountain House, and the scenery among the mountains, are among the finest in the country, and the place is visited annually by thousands of tourists.

[8] Samuel, Elisha, and John Haines, and Gershon Griffin, entered the mountains by way of Kingston and Mink Hollow, and settled on Schoharie Kil. Their location was discovered a year or two after by some Dutchmen from the e. side of the mountain, while hunting bears. They were followed, in 1786, by a number of Shay's followers, from Mass., who, on the suppression of his rebellion, fled to the mountains. James and Jacob Carl settled in the town in 1785; Saml. Merritt, and Saml. and Wm. Hayes, in 1791. Roger Bronson was the first settler at the village of Hunter. The first birth was that of John Haines. Mr. Olmsted built the first gristmill, in 1794, and subsequently the first tannery, and kept the first store and inn.

[9] Formerly called "*Lexington Heights*."

and **East Jewett,** are p. offices.   The first settlement was made near Schoharie Creek in 1783–84, by Wm. Gass, a Scotchman.[1]   There are 4 churches in town; 3 M. E. and Presb.

LEXINGTON—was formed from Windham as "*New Goshen,*" Jan. 27, 1813, and its name was changed March 19, 1813.   A part of Jewett was taken off in 1849, but reannexed in 1858, and a part of Halcott was taken off in 1851.   It lies on the s. border of the co., w. of the center.   More than one-half of the surface is occupied by the lofty peaks and ridges of the Catskills.   Schoharie Creek, flowing through the N. E. corner of the town, is bordered by high and steep rocky ridges. West Kil, its principal tributary, drains a valley 9 mi. in length, everywhere bordered by lofty mountains except on the w.   Bush Kil Clove is a natural pass in the mountains, extending from the Schoharie Valley s. into Ulster co.   The soil is a slaty and gravelly loam.   Only about two-fifths of the surface is susceptible of cultivation.   **Lexington,** (p. v.,) on Schoharie Creek, N. of the center of the town, contains 2 churches and 27 dwellings, and **West Kill** (p. v.) 1 church and 31 dwellings.   **Bushnellsville** is a p. o. on the line of Ulster co.   The first settlement was made in 1788, on the flats of Schoharie Kil.[2]   There are 3 churches in town; 2 Bap. and M. E.

NEW BALTIMORE—was formed from Coxsackie, March 15, 1811.   Scutters, Little, and Willow Islands were annexed from Kinderhook April 23, 1823.   It lies upon the Hudson, in the N. E. corner of the co.   The general surface is hilly and broken.   A line of high, rugged clay and slate bluffs rises from the river to a height of 100 to 200 feet, and a range of high, broad hills extends s. through the center of the town.   The w. part is comparatively level.   The principal streams are Haanakrois Creek in the N. W. corner, Deep Clove Kil, Cabin Run, and the E. branch of Potick Creek.   Nearly all these streams flow through narrow and rocky ravines.   The soil is chiefly a heavy, clay loam, with limited patches of sand and gravel.   **New Baltimore,** (p. v.,) on the Hudson, in the N. part of the town, contains 2 churches, and has a pop. of 709.   **Medway** is a p. office.   Settlement was commenced upon the Coxsackie flats at an early period.   The Broncks, Houghtalings, and Conyns were among the first settlers.   There are 9 churches in town.[3]

PRATTSVILLE—was formed from Windham, March 8, 1833, and named from Col. Zadock Pratt.   A part of Ashland was taken off in 1848.   It is the N. W. corner town of the co.   Its surface is principally occupied by broad mountain uplands bordered by steep and rocky slopes. Schoharie Creek and Batavia Kil flow through wild and narrow mountain gorges.   The soil is a heavy, reddish, gravelly and clayey loam, moderately fertile and profitable only for grazing. **Prattsville,** (p. v.,) on Schoharie Kil w. of the center of the town, contains 3 churches and several manufactories.[4]   Pop. 617.   **Red Falls,** (p. v.,) on Batavia Kil, contains a cotton factory, a paper mill, and several other manufacturing establishments.   Pop. 231.   Settlements were made on the flats at Prattsville by Dutch immigrants from Schoharie co., during the period between the close of the Old French War in 1763 and the breaking out of the Revolution in 1776.[5]   During the latter war the settlement was attacked by a body of Indians and tories led by a British officer. The inhabitants rallied, and a battle took place upon the bank of Schoharie Kil, a little below the Windham Turnpike Bridge, N. of the village, in which the Indians and their allies were routed. Rev. Cornelius D. Schermerhorn was the first settled preacher.   There are 3 churches in town; Ref. Prot. D., Prot. E., and M. E.

WINDHAM—was formed from Woodstock, (Ulster co.,) as part of Ulster co., March 23, 1798. "*Greenland*" (now Hunter) and Lexington were taken off in 1813, Prattsville in 1833, and a part of Ashland in 1848.   A part of "*Freehold*" (now Durham) was annexed March 26, 1803.   It lies upon the w. declivities of the Catskills, N. w. of the center of the co.   Its surface is very broken and hilly. A high range of mountains extends along the s. border, at the N. foot of which flows Batavia Kil,[6] in a deep, rocky valley.   The central and N. parts are occupied by mountain spurs divided by narrow ravines.   The soil is a heavy, gravelly and clayey loam, of which disintegrated shale forms a large

---

1 Zephaniah Chase, from Marthas Vineyard, (Mass.,) settled in the town in 1787; and Chester Hull, from Wallingford, Conn., a soldier of the Revolution, in 1789.   Among those who settled soon after were Zadock Pratt, Theop. and Sam. Peck, Eb'r David, and Stephen Johnson, Laban, Ichabod, Abraham, and Amherst Andrews, Benajah, John, and Jared Rice, Henry Goslee, Justus Squires, Daniel Miles, Adnah Beach, Isaac and Munson Buel, Gideon, Reuben, and Joel Hosford, and Samuel and Daniel Mervin.   The first birth was that of Henry Coslee, Jr.   Wm. Gass kept the first inn, in 1790, Elisha Thompson the first store, in 1795, and Laban Andrews built the first gristmill the same year.

2 Among the early settlers were Amos Bronson, Saml. Amos, Richard Peck, David and Benj. Bailey, and Benj. Crispell.   John T. Bray built the first tannery, in 1791 or '92; Thaddeus Bron-

son the first gristmill, in 1792; and Richard Peck opened the first inn, in 1795.

3 3 Friends, 2 M.E., Bap., Christian, Ref. Prot.D., and Prot. Meth.

4 At this place, at the extensive tannery of the Hon. Zadock Pratt, 60,000 sides of sole leather were tanned and 6,000 cords of bark consumed annually for 25 years.

5 Among the first settlers were John Laraway and his sons John, Jonas, Derick, and Martinus, Isaac Van Alstyne, —— Vrooman, John and Peter Van Loan, John Becker, and a family by the name of Schoonmaker.   The first school was taught by Mr. Banks, in 1790.   Martinus Laraway kept the first inn, soon after the Revolution, and, with his brother John, erected the first gristmill.

6 The Indian name of this stream was Chough-tig-hig-nick.

part. **Windham Center,** (p. v.,) on Batavia Kil, in the w. part of the town, contains 3 churches, and has a pop. of 350. **Hensonville,** (p. v.,) on the same stream, s. of the center of the town, contains 124 inhabitants, and **Big Hollow,** (p. v.,) in the s. part, 2 churches and 12 houses. **East Windham** and **Union Society** are p. offices. The first settlement was made in 1790, by Geo. Stimpson, Abijah Stone, and Increase Claflin.[1] Rev. Henry Stimpson was one of the earliest settled ministers. There are 5 churches in town.[2]

Acres of Land, Valuation, Population, Dwellings, Families, Freeholders, Schools, Live Stock, Agricultural Products, and Domestic Manufactures, of Greene County.

Names of Towns.	Acres of Land.		Valuation of 1858.			Population.		No. of Dwellings.	No. of Families.	Freeholders.	Schools.	
	Improved.	Unimproved.	Real Estate.	Personal Property.	Total.	Males.	Females.				No. of Districts.	Children taught.
Ashland	9,846½	4,198	$135,080	$9,500	$144,580	555	584	217	235	140	7	503
Athens	10,351½	4,502½	499,308	54,050	553,358	1,470	1,400	438	551	343	7	1,046
Cairo	22,541	10,982	555,377	88,175	643,552	1,290	1,267	448	478	341	15	827
Catskill	19,146½	17,613	1,437,035	532,312	1,969,347	2,812	2,898	930	1,094	544	19	2,020
Coxsackie	17,698¼	4,516	782,710	165,334	948,044	1,891	1,791	592	603	432	13	1,354
Durham	23,166¼	5,855	394,145	68,300	462,445	1,239	1,301	482	491	393	15	935
Greenville	20,273¾	5,535½	580,315	70,632	650,947	1,088	1,085	415	450	342	16	909
Halcott	7,137	4,007	84,775	9,900	94,675	246	228	86	89	79	4	207
Hunter	10,264⅞	40,456½	135,395	10,642	146,037	833	761	258	276	207	12	735
Jewett	15,167	10,468¾	136,200	25,620	161,820	578	551	205	220	176	10	491
Lexington	14,727¾	21,600	227,539	41,150	268,689	788	807	319	217	235	11	601
New Baltimore	18,279¼	6,124¼	804,599	103,820	908,429	1,248	1,154	425	455	306	15	865
Prattsville	8,784	4,854	111,200	29,250	140,450	746	842	267	290	225	8	665
Windham	14,840¼	9,892	244,283	41,100	285,383	807	877	327	258	188	12	531
Total	212,223⅞	150,604½	$6,127,961	$1,249,795	$7,377,756	15,591	15,546	5,409	5,707	3,951	161	11,869

Names of Towns.	Live Stock.					Agricultural Products.							Domestic Cloths in yards.
						Bush. of Grain.					Dairy Products.		
	Horses.	Working Oxen and Calves.	Cows.	Sheep.	Swine.	Winter.	Spring.	Tons of Hay.	Bushels of Potatoes.	Bushels of Apples.	Pounds Butter.	Pounds Cheese.	
Ashland	251	897	727	962	487	1,935½	12,252	2,344½	7,524	11,366	69,815	1,025	283
Athens	393	349	509	164	886	4,280½	23,373	4,493½	5,099	10,935	42,776	300	262½
Cairo	714	998	1,040	1,069	1,663	13,804½	27,991	4,350	8,254	22,771	96,675	937	1,114
Catskill	713	910	1,076	1,615	1,723	12,538½	39,337½	7,592	9,245	15,153	90,720		617
Coxsackie	635	523	791	397	1,565	8,705½	36,091¼	6,699	17,009	18,318	83,735		590
Durham	745	1,299	1,352	3,507	2,244	7,064	35,087¼	3,998	5,821½	25,805	121,917	6,876	711½
Greenville	698	741	1,051	1,779	1,443	7,665½	37,193	6,067	5,679	25,703	109,906	2,079	1,011
Halcott	152	496	526	1,390	200	830	11,917	1,907	1,348	2,490	60,916	50	1,164
Hunter	192	1,019	605	1,205	286	870	3,610	2,495¾	8,264	2,540½	52,311	130	584
Jewett	236	1,401	1,163	1,869	467	1,869	8,978	3,391	5,864½	13,611	113,520	4,928	146
Lexington	354	1,657	1,144	2,013	591	2,449	13,176¾	4,468	6,902	13,128	105,290	1,285	779
New Baltimore	610	517	991	1,248	1,569	13,471½	35,093½	5,498½	21,789	19,361	90,589		720½
Prattsville	239	680	750	608	384	2,075	5,461½	1,834	3,536	3,380	73,780	50	385
Windham	271	1,160	867	1,556	566	2,019½	11,651½	3,386	10,536	8,253	79,980	3,657	244
Total	6,203	12,647	12,592	19,382	14,074	79,578	301,213¼	58,524¼	116,871	192,814½	1,191,930	21,317	8,611½

[1] Perez Steel and his son Perez, from Tolland, Conn., settled in town in 1795, and Joshua Jones, Wm. Henderson, and Lemuel Hitchcock (from New Haven co., Conn.) in 1796. The first marriage was that of Daniel Perry and Mamva Hitchcock; and the first death was that of Mrs. Lemuel Hitchcock, in 1804. Nathan Blanchard taught the first school, in 1809; Tobias Van Dusen built the first gristmill, in 1793; —— Van Orden kept the first inn, in 1796; and Bennett Osborn built the first tannery, in 1822.

[2] 2 Presb., 2 M. E., and Prot. E.

HAMILTON COUNTY.

THIS county was formed from Montgomery, Feb. 12, 1816; but its independent organization has never been fully completed.[1] It occupies the central portions of the great wilderness region in the N. E. part of the State; is centrally distant 80 miles from Albany, and contains 1,745 sq. mi. Its surface is a rocky, mountainous, and hilly upland and is still mostly covered with the original forests. The highlands are divided into several ranges, generally distinct, but in many places sending out spurs that interlock with each other, and all extending N. E. and s. w. The Schroon Range—called in Fulton co. the Mayfield Mts.—crosses the s. E. corner of Hope. This range ends upon Lake Champlain at Crown Point, the highest point being Mt. Crane, in Warren co. The Baquet Range, parallel to the first, extends through the co. between Wells and Lake Pleasant. This range terminates upon Lake Champlain at Split Rock, the highest peak being Dix Peak, in Essex co. The Adirondack Range, next N., extends from the Mohawk, at Little Falls, N. E. through Morehouse, Arietta, Long Lake, Gilman, and Wells, ending at Trembleau Point, on Lake Champlain, Mt. Marcy being the highest peak, and the highest point in the State. Its course is in a wave or undulating line occupying a space of 4 to 6 mi. in width. Next N. is the Au Sable Range, extending N. of the Fulton chain of lakes and Long and Racket Lakes. The highest points are Mt. Emmons, in this co., and Mt. Seward, in Franklin co. Spurs from this range occupy the entire N. part of the co. and extend into St. Lawrence and Herkimer cos.[2]

Within the valleys between these mountain ranges are several remarkable chains of lakes, many of them connected by considerable streams and all affording a large amount of boat navigation. These lakes are generally long and narrow, are bordered by steep banks and high mountain peaks. Their waters are clear and cold, and they form the most interesting features of the landscape. Although flowing in different directions, separated by high mountains, and extending over an area of more than 60 mi., they have a nearly uniform elevation.[3] The first chain on the s., commencing in Stratford, Fulton co., includes several small ponds in the s. E. corner of Hope, several ponds in Johnsburgh, Warren co., and Schroon and Paradox Lakes in Essex co. The second chain embraces Jerseyfield Lake and several others in Herkimer co., flowing s., Piseco, Round, Spy, and Ox Bow Lakes, Lake Pleasant, and a great number of smaller ones, all flowing into Sacondaga River. The third chain, lying between the two highest ranges of mountains, is composed of lakes less in extent than either of the other chains. It comprises Woodhull Reservoir and about 20 small lakes, principally in Herkimer co., flowing into Black River; a large number of small ponds in the immediate vicinity, flowing into West Canada Creek; Indian, Square, Beaver, Wilmurt, and a dozen smaller ones, in Hamilton co., flowing into Black and Indian Rivers; and the Indian Lakes, flowing into the Hudson. In Essex co. this chain embraces Lakes Rich, Sanford, and Henderson, and numerous others, lying near the foot of Mt. Marcy. The fourth or N. chain is the most extensive of all. It comprises Brantingham and other Lakes in Lewis co., flowing into Moose and Black Rivers; the Fulton chain and about 20 other lakes in the N. part of Herkimer, respectively flowing into Beaver and Moose Rivers; Cranberry Lake and many others in the s. part of St. Lawrence, flowing into Oswegatchie and Grasse Rivers; Tuppers, Racket, Forked, and Long Lakes, and 50 others, in Hamilton co., and a large number in Franklin, flowing into Racket River; St. Regis Lake, Osgoods Pond, and numerous others, into St. Regis River; Ragged Lake, Round and Ingraham Ponds, into Salmon River; Lake Placid, into the Au Sable; the Chateaugay Lakes, into Chateaugay River; and the Chazy Lakes, into Chazy River. All these last named lakes are in Hamilton, Franklin,

---

[1] Named in honor of Alexander Hamilton. The territory was included in Herkimer co. Feb. 16, 1791, but was re-annexed to Montgomery March 31, 1797. It can complete its organization when it has a sufficient population to entitle it to a member of Assembly. It remained appended to Montgomery until 1838, when it was annexed to Fulton on the erection of the latter co. Courts were established in 1837.

[2] This region was called by the natives Coughsarage, "the dismal wilderness." The following entry on a map published about the period of the Revolution, or soon after, gives the prevailing opinion of that day concerning these lands:—"Through

this tract of land runs a chain of mountains, which, from Lake Champlain on one side and the river St. Lawrence on the other side, show their tops always white with snow; but altho' this one unfavorable circumstance has hitherto secured it from the claws of the harpy land jobbers, yet no doubt it is as fertile as the land on the east side of the lake, and will in future furnish a comfortable retreat for many industrious families."

[3] The eighth lake in the N. chain, flowing W., is 1,678 feet above tide; Racket Lake, 2 mi. N., flowing E., 1,745 feet; the Upper Saranac, flowing E., 1,567 feet; and Lake Sanford, flowing s., 1,826 feet.

Essex, and Clinton cos., in close proximity to each other. The streams, forming the outlets of the lakes, are mostly small. The whole region being a mountainous plateau higher than the surrounding country, the streams that rise here flow in all directions and form tributaries of the St. Lawrence, Lake Champlain, the Hudson, Mohawk, and Black Rivers. Several of the rivers have the same name as the lakes which respectively form their headwaters; as the Racket, Chazy, and Chateaugay.[1]

This whole region is primitive, the rock being principally gneiss. Calciferous sandstone and Trenton limestone are found upon Sacondaga River. White limestone is also found in several localities. Peat is found in great abundance in the vlaies, or natural meadows, which extend along the valleys. Iron ore and graphite are both found,—though no surveys have been made to ascertain their extent. A large amount of labor has been expended in mining for silver; with what success is unknown. The soil is a light, sandy loam, and, except in the valleys, is not susceptible of profitable cultivation. The mountain sides are covered with a thin growth of forest trees, and when cleared seem incapable of supporting vegetation. The valleys at first are productive, but, being deficient in lime, as soon as the vegetable mold is exhausted they become barren.

The county seat is located at Sageville, in the town of Lake Pleasant.[2] The co. buildings, consisting of a courthouse, jail, and clerk's office, were erected in 1840. Each town supports its own poor, and the co. poor are provided for by the Superintendent at the most convenient place. There has never been a paper printed within the co.[3] The public works are entirely prospective.[4] Most of the territory of the co. is included in the Totten and Crossfield Purchase of 1773.[5] Grants within the limits of the co. were made in colonial times to Sir Jeffrey Amherst, Henry Balfour, and Thomas Palmer. Arthursboro, in Morehouse, was granted to Arthur Noble. The first settlement was made about 1790.

ARIETTA[6]—was formed from Lake Pleasant, May 13, 1836. A part of Long Lake was taken off in 1837. It extends from the s. w. border northward nearly across the co., a little w. of the center. Its surface is much broken, and it contains a great number of wild, picturesque lakes. Of these, Racket and Forked Lakes, in the N. part, and Piseco,[7] in the s., are the most important. The principal streams are the w. and s. branches of Sacondaga River. A considerable amount of lumbering is carried on.[8] **Piseco,** formerly a p. o., and once a busy village of some 250 inhabitants, is now nearly deserted, and contains but 4 families.[9] There is no p. o. in town. The first settler was Shadrack Dunning, at the E. end of Piseco Lake, in 1827, and David Woolworth, in the s. part, about the same time. Rensselaer Van Rensselaer, of Albany, settled in 1834.[10]

GILMAN[11]—was formed from Wells, April 23, 1839. A part was annexed to Wells in 1858. It is an interior town, extending in a long, narrow strip near the E. border of the co. Its surface is much broken by mountains and diversified by small lakes. Several of the highest peaks in the co. are in this town; but their elevations have never been ascertained. It is the least populous town in the State. **Gilman** (p. o.) is in the s. border. Most of the settlers are in the s. part, a few only living on the extreme N. border, quite isolated from their fellow townsmen. Philip Rhinelander, a wealthy merchant of New York, began the first settlement.[12]

---

[1] If this system of naming lakes could be extended, it would greatly assist those who wish to understand the geography of this region. To make it complete, the eighth lake in the Fulton chain should be named Moose Lake; Cranberry Pond, Oswegatchie Lake; Messewepie Pond, Grasse Lake; Ragged Lake, Salmon; Colden Lake, Hudson; and Piseco Lake, Sacondaga; and then the direction of the flow of the waters would be at once apparent from the names of the lakes.

[2] The first co. officers were Richard Peck, *First Judge;* Saml. Call, *County Clerk;* James Harris, *Sheriff;* G. R. Parburt, *District Attorney;* and Thos. H. Kline, *Surrogate.*

[3] **The Hamilton County Sentinel,** printed at Johnstown and edited at Sageville, was started in 1845 by Clark & Thayer. It was subsequently in the hands of Clark & Holmes, and is now issued by Clark & Fish.

[4] The route of the Ontario & Hudson R. R., from Saratoga to Sackets Harbor, extends through the N. part of the co. The route is located; but no grading has been done within the co. Several surveys have been made to test the practicability of connecting Piseco Lake with Lake Pleasant, the Fulton chain with Racket Lake, and Racket River with the Upper Saranac Lake, for the purpose of forming a slackwater navigation through the co. These schemes have been pronounced feasible. Considerable sums have been expended upon some of the streams so that logs might be floated down.

[5] A large share of this tract has reverted to the State by escheat, confiscation, and tax sales. It was purchased, at the request and expense of Joseph Totten, Stephen Crossfield, and others, from the Mohawk and Canajoharie Indians, at Johnsons

Hall, in July, 1773. It was estimated to contain 800,000 acres. —*Council Minutes, XXXI, p.* 31.

It was surveyed by Ebenezer Jessup and associates.

[6] Named by Rensselaer Van Rensselaer, in honor of his mother.

[7] Named by Joshua Brown, a surveyor, from an Indian chief of his acquaintance. It is about 5 mi. long and 1 to 1¼ wide. It is one of the most picturesque sheets of water in the co. The mountains around it are over 500 feet above its surface.

[8] Henry Devereaux, some years since, began lumbering on a large scale in the s. part, and built a tram R. R. some 8 or 10 mi. long. He also spent many thousand dollars in buildings and machinery; but the enterprise proved a failure.

[9] In 1838 Andrew K. Morehouse, an extensive landholder, built at this place a gristmill, sawmill, machine shop, a large hotel and boarding house, and some half dozen dwellings. Strong inducements were offered to settlers; but they became dissatisfied with the title, and one by one dropped off. In 1843 he again tried to retrieve his fortunes by the formation of a joint stock Co. and induced some 200 settlers to come in. Some returned the same day; others remained a week or a month.

[10] Eli Rood, of Saratoga, settled on the beech flats S. E. of Piseco Lake; R. Dibble and Seth Whitman near the foot of the lake; and Zadock Ross, from Clifton Park, s. of the lake. The first birth was that of Miss M. M. Dunning, Aug. 28, 1829; the first marriage, that of Amos Dunning and Ann Eliza Plummer; and the first death, that of Seth Whitman. A school was taught by Ann E. Plummer, in 1833.

[11] Named from John M. Gilman, an early settler, from N. H.

[12] Mr. Rhinelander cleared 300 acres for a stock farm, and built

HOPE[1]—was formed from Wells, April 15, 1818. A part of Lake Pleasant was annexed May 10, 1847. It lies upon Sacondaga River, in the s. e. corner of the co. Its surface is broken and mountainous. It is the most populous town in the co., and the settlements are chiefly in the e. part. The w. portion is still a wilderness, known only to hunters. The mountains are very irregular; but in general they extend upon both sides of the river, and, as usual in this region, have their longest slope to the s. w. The principal tributary of the Sacondaga is East Stony Creek; and the main range of mountains lies between this stream and the river.[2] Lumbering and tanning are extensively carried on. **Hope Center, Benson,** and **Benson Center** are p. offices. **Hope Falls** (p. o.) is a hamlet. Settlement was begun in 1790, in the s. border of the town.[3]

INDIAN LAKE—was formed from Gilman, Long Lake, and Wells, Nov. 13, 1858. It lies upon the e. border of the co., n. of the center.[4]

LAKE PLEASANT—was formed from Johnstown, Fulton co., May 26, 1812. Parts of Stafford, Johnstown, and Salisbury were annexed at the time of the formation of Hamilton co. Morehouse was taken off in 1835, Arietta in 1836, and a part of Long Lake in 1837. A part was annexed to Hope in 1847, and a part to Wells in 1858. It is the central town of the co., and includes a long tract extending from n. to s. to within a few mi. of each extremity of the co. Its surface is broken and mountainous, and most of it is still a wilderness. Lake Pleasant, from which it derives its name, is about 4 mi. long by 1 wide. Round Lake, ½ mi. from this, is very irregular in form, and about 1½ mi. across in the widest part.[5] The Eckford chain of lakes, in the n. part, are in the midst of wild mountain solitudes. The upper of these is named Janet Lake.[6] The principal streams in the s. are the n. and w. branches of the Sacondaga, and in the n. the Racket and its tributaries. A mine of graphite has been opened 4 mi. n. of Sageville. Limestone mixed with silex and mica, from which quicklime is obtained, is found s. of Lake Pleasant. Lumbering and shingle making are carried on to a considerable extent. **Lake Pleasant,** (p. o.,) at the foot of the lake, contains a hotel and 2 dwellings. **Sageville**[7] (p. v.) is situated on a beautiful elevation 50 feet above Lake Pleasant[8] and Round Lake, about one-fourth of a mi. distant from each. It contains the co. buildings, a large hotel, a church, and several dwellings. Settlement was commenced about 1795, by Joseph Spier, of Columbia co.[9] Meetings were first held by Rev. Elisha Yale; and the first settled minister was Rev. Ryan Bristol.

LONG LAKE—was formed from Arietta, Lake Pleasant, Morehouse, and Wells, May 4, 1837. It extends across the n. end of the co., and is named from the principal lake within its borders. Its surface is very broken, and numerous small lakes are scattered through its forests. Settlement was begun in Township 21, a few years before the date of its organization.[10] There is no p. o. in town.

MOREHOUSE[11]—was formed from Lake Pleasant, April 13, 1835. A part of Long Lake was taken off in 1837. It extends along the w. border of the co., from the s. extremity to Long Lake.

---

a costly mansion on Elm Lake, in Township 9, several mi. distant from neighbors. He remained here until the death of his wife, in 1818 or '19, and soon after, being struck with paralysis, was obliged to return to New York. The property, after repeated sales, is now owned by Dr. Elliott, an oculist of New York City. Gilman and his sons were the next settlers. John Carter, Andrew Morrison, Samuel Johnson, jr., Wm. B. Peck, Wm. Orcutt, and others were early settlers. Mrs. Rhinelander was the first person that died. Susan Gilman taught the first school, in 1823. No inn has ever been licensed in town.

[1] There are 2 large tanneries in town, and several sawmills.

[2] These mountains are entirely primitive, and incline to the hypersthene and feldspathic varieties.

[3] Gideon and Jeremiah Olmstead, from Mass., were the first settlers. Issachar Robinson, Peter Wager, Asa Deville, Jacob Houck, John Graff, and Elisha Wright settled about 1791–92, a little N. of the center of the town. Zadock Bass, —— Conklin, Elkanah, Amos, and Isaac Mason came into the E. part in 1805. The first birth was that of Lucinda Olmstead; and the first death, that of Mrs. Conklin, about 1800. —— Wilson, a Scotchman. kept the first school.

[4] This town has been formed since the statistics were collected; and its description and history are included in those of the towns from which it was formed.

[5] The summit level between Round Lake and Little Long Lake is but a few feet above the water. In wet seasons water runs both ways, and 25 mi. of slackwater navigation might be made at comparatively small expense. Round Lake flows into the N. branch of the Sacondaga, and Little Long Lake into the w. branch,—so that, after running 25 and 35 mi. respectively, their waters again unite.

[6] Named from Mrs. James E. De Kay, by Dr. Emmons, while making the geological survey of the 2d district. She was the daughter of Henry Eckford, the celebrated shipbuilder, from whom the chain of lakes was named.

[7] Known for several years as "*Lake Pleasant*," until changed through the agency of Hezekiah Sage, of Chittenango, who built a large hotel and attempted to establish an extensive business there. Efforts have been made to procure a change of the present name, but without success.

[8] A few years since, Abraham R. Lawrence, of New York City, built a large hotel for summer resort at the head of Lake Pleasant. As a speculation it proved a failure.

[9] Benj. Macomber, John Barnes, Joseph Davis, Joshua and Jonathan Rich, Jesse Callop, Caleb Nichols, Geo. Wright, Ephraim Page, Daniel Fish, Henry Burton, Lemuel Holmes, and B. Saterlee settled in town before 1806. The first birth was that of Olivia Spier, in 1806; and the second, that of Eleanor Macomber, who died a missionary in Burmah. Geo. Wright kept the first inn, in 1806, and Wm. B. Peck the first store, in 1817. A sawmill was built by —— Foster, in 1795; and a gristmill, by Joseph Spier, in 1797.

[10] David Keller, James Sargent, Owen Skinner, Zenas Parker Joel Plumley, and John Cunningham were first settlers. The first death occurred in 1838. A school was first taught in 1840 by Lucina Bissell. There are now 3 schools in town. A Cong church was formed in 1842, by Rev. John Todd, of Pittsfield, Mass., and placed under the charge of Rev. M. Parker. This is the most secluded town in the State. It is usually reached from Essex co., to which the settlers resort for their mails and trade. **Schroon River** p. o., Essex co., is the nearest and most convenient office for receiving mails.

[11] Named from the first settler.

Its surface is hilly and mountainous. In the several valleys which extend across the town are numerous lakes. Jerseyfield Lake, upon the s. border, is the principal lake in the s. part. The 5th, 6th, 7th, and 8th lakes of the Fulton chain, in the n. part, discharge their waters into Moose River. Jones, Deer, Goose, and several other lakes flow into West Canada Creek. **Morehouseville,** in the s. part, is a p.o. The Arthurboro Patent was mostly within the limits of this town. The tract of 50,000 acres purchased by Jonathan Lawrence was also partly in this town.[1] The first settlement was commenced, under the agency of Andrew K. Morehouse, in 1833.[2]

WELLS[3]—was formed from Mayfield and Northampton, Fulton co., May 28, 1805. Hope was taken off in 1818, a part of Long Lake in 1837, and Gilman in 1839. A part of Mayfield was annexed June 19, 1812; parts of Mayfield and Northampton in 1816; and parts of Gilman and Lake Pleasant in 1858. It lies along the e. border of the co. and forms a part of the hunting grounds of Northern N.Y. Its s. part is inhabited by a few families on Indian Lake. It is intersected by mountain ranges separated by deep, narrow valleys. The highest peaks are 2,000 to 2,500 feet high and are covered by masses of naked rock. The three branches of the Sacondaga unite in the s. part, forming a large stream. Jessup and Cedar Rivers, in the n., are large streams. Indian Lake is a sheet of water about 6 mi. long; and further n. is a cluster of small lakes flowing into the Hudson. There are numerous other small lakes in other parts, known only to hunters. The soil is light and sandy. Calciferous sandstone appears *in situ* above Wells Village. **Wells** (p.v.) contains a large tannery, gristmill, sawmill, and 15 dwellings; **Pickleville,** one-half mi. above, contains 2 churches and 15 dwellings. Settlement began in 1798.[4]

Acres of Land, Valuation, Population, Dwellings, Families, Freeholders, Schools, Live Stock, Agricultural Products, and Domestic Manufactures, of Hamilton County.

Names of Towns.	Acres of Land.		Valuation of 1858.			Population.		No. of Dwellings.	No. of Families.	Freeholders.	Schools.	
	Improved.	Unimproved.	Real Estate.	Personal Property.	Total.	Males.	Females.				No. of Districts.	Children taught.
Arietta	674	197,760	$75,015	$380	$75,395	77	72	32	32	18	6	31
Gilman	803	90,902	46,559		46,559	52	38	21	21	19	1	21
Hope	6,729	56,168	65,231	1,028	66,259	451	371	135	148	116	8	351
Indian Lake												
Lake Pleasant	2,737	150,418	99,046	550	99,596	162	138	52	53	33	5	147
Long Lake	744	150,835	49,937		49,937	71	68	28	29	22	3	60
Morehouse	1,186¼	6,796½	39,276		39,276	147	128	56	59	51	2	89
Wells	3,802½	114,099	96,313	1,420	97,733	430	338	137	146	93	7	318
Total	16,675¾	766,978½	471,377	3,378	474,755	1,390	1,153	461	488	352	32	1,017

Names of Towns.	Live Stock.					Agricultural Products.							Domestic Cloths in yards.
						Bush. of Grain.					Dairy Products.		
	Horses.	Working Oxen and Calves.	Cows.	Sheep.	Swine.	Winter.	Spring.	Tons of Hay.	Bushels of Potatoes.	Bushels of Apples.	Pounds Butter.	Pounds Cheese.	
Arietta	16	92	52	7	27	6	871	444	1,450		3,770		20
Gilman	17	109	16		16		652	229	1,247	45	2,900		
Hope	164	585	306	861	205	24	12,475½	1,751½	9,916	2,326	28,803	1,300	
Indian Lake													
Lake Pleasant	35	193	123	155	89	31	3,348¼	586	2,641	128	16,935	570	374
Long Lake	7	59	36	38	39	152	1,509	141	2,226		3,622		70
Morehouse	16	175	98	116	25		1,976½	456½	3,188	7	8,202		317
Wells	83	391	221	304	109	70	6,515	666	4,589	953	19,050	800	682
Total	338	1,604	852	1,481	510	283	27,347¼	4,274	25,257	3,459	83,282	2,670	1,463

[1] The Arthurboro Patent included 3 townships, one 10 and the others each 8 mi. square. It was granted to Arthur Noble, Feb. 15, 1787, for 1 shilling per acre. He endeavored to effect the settlement of 100 families, but failed. The tract to Mr. Lawrence was granted for 3¼ shillings per acre.

[2] Mr. Morehouse bought a tract of land, built a sawmill, store, and dwelling, and came in with his family early in Aug. 1834. He began a small village 1 mi. w. of Morehouseville, called "*Bethuneville;*" but the project failed. Dennis and Henry Tucker, Theodore Marnche, Ezra Combs, Jonathan Tift, Christian Weaver, Elias Rickard, J. B. Reily, and B. Bennett were early settlers. The first birth was that of a son of Wm. Baker; the first marriage, that of David Bushnell and Miss Squires; and the first death, that of a son of Christian Weaver, by a falling tree. A gristmill was first built in 1843, by John Cummings; and the first tannery, in 1854, by Henry and Theodore Larken.

[3] Named from Joshua Wells, the first settler.

[4] Joshua Wells, a native of Long Island, who came on as agent for the proprietors of Palmer's Purchase, in 1798, built the first mills. Isaac and Joshua Brown came with Wells, and kept "bachelors' hall" several summers before any families came in. Amasa Gage, Giles Vanderhoof, Nicholas Bradt, John Francisco, Elnathan Lacy, Michael Overacken, Isaiah Whitman, —— Rose, and others, were early settlers. —— Van Zandt kept the first store; and Platt Whitman built the first tannery, in 1825.

HERKIMER COUNTY.

This county was formed from Montgomery, Feb. 16, 1791.[1] Onondaga was taken off in 1794, Oneida and a part of Chenango in 1798; the present territory of Hamilton co. was taken off and annexed to Montgomery in 1797; parts of Montgomery co. were annexed April 7, 1817; and parts of Richfield and Plainfield, Otsego co., were annexed in forming Winfield in 1816. It is centrally distant 80 mi. from Albany, and contains 1,745 sq. mi. Its surface is a hilly upland, with a series of ridges extending in a general N. and s. direction. Mohawk River flows E. through the co. in a deep valley which cuts the ridges at right angles and separates the highland into two distinct parts. A broad ridge extends from the s. border to the Mohawk, and thence N. of that river along the w. bank of East Canada Creek to the N. line of the co. The Hasenclever Mts., another broad ridge, lie along the w. border of the co., N. of the Mohawk. From the Mohawk the highlands rise toward the s. in a series of hills, the declivities of which are steep and their summits 500 to 1,000 ft. high. North of the river the surface gradually rises to a height of 1,000 to 1,500 ft., where it spreads out into a rocky and broken plateau region, the highest summits being 2,500 to 3,000 ft. above tide.

Mohawk River breaks through a mountain ridge at Little Falls, the valley forming a natural channel of communication between Lake Ontario and Hudson River. At this place the mountains on each side of the river are masses of naked rock rising nearly perpendicular to a height of 500 to 600 ft. An intervale, with an average width of 2 mi., extends along the river w. of the pass, and from it the land rises on each side in gradual slopes. East of this point the Mohawk flows for some distance through a valley bordered by steep and nearly perpendicular hills. The river receives from the N., Sterling, West Canada, Cathatachua, and East Canada Creeks; and from the s. Furnace, Browns Hollow, and Nowadaga Creeks. East Canada Creek[2] forms a portion of the E. boundary of the co., and receives as tributaries Trammel, Spruce, and several other small creeks. West Canada Creek flows s. w. through Wilmurt, Ohio, and Russia, thence s. E. along the w. border of Russia, thence s. through Newport, Fairport, and Herkimer, to the Mohawk. It receives from the E. Black, White, and North Creeks, and from the w. several small brooks. Several small streams take their rise in the s. part of the co. and form branches of the Unadilla. The N. part of the co. is yet an unbroken wilderness. It is a wild, mountainous region, with very little land susceptible of cultivation. The streams, usually flowing in deep, rocky ravines, form headwaters of Black, Moose, Beaver, and Oswegatchie Rivers.

The portion of the co. lying N. of a line extending w. of Brocketts Bridge, on East Canada Creek, is covered with primary rocks.[3] This same formation also outcrops at Little Falls on the Mohawk. Rising successively above the primary are the Trenton limestone, appearing in Norway and Russia; the Utica slate, appearing upon the summits of all the hills immediately N. of the Mohawk; the Frankfort slate, appearing immediately s. of the river; the Oneida conglomerate and Clinton group, extending in a belt through near the center of the s. half of the co.; the Onondaga salt group, waterlime, Onondaga and corniferous limestones, appearing in thin layers next s.; and the Marcellus shales and limestones of the Helderbergh Range, covering the summits of the s. hills. These rocks yield an abundance of lime, waterlime, and building material in nearly every part of the co.; and for these purposes they are extensively quarried. Drift is found in deep deposits in many parts of the co. The useful minerals are few in number.[4]

Agriculture forms the leading pursuit. The hilly character of the surface particularly adapts this co. to pasturage; and dairying has long been the leading branch of industry.[5] Hops are

---

[1] This name was originally "*Erghemar;*" and it has been variously written, as Herchkeimer, Hareniger, Harkemeir, Herchamer, Harchamer, Harkemar, and Herkimer.—*Benton's Herkimer, p.* 150.

[2] West Canada Creek was called by the Indians Teugh-taghra-row, and the East Creek Ci-o-ha-na.

[3] The rocks peculiar to this region are granite, gneiss, feldspar and hornblende. Calciferous sandrock is found associated with gneiss at Little Falls.

[4] Gypsum is found in small quantities; and this co. is said to

be the most easterly point in the State where it can be obtained. The discovery of small particles of anthracite, found associated with sandstone near Little Falls, has led to the erroneous supposition that coal might be obtained in the vicinity. Among the other minerals found are crystals of quartz, adapted to optical instruments, iron sand, iron and copper pyrites, lead ore, heavy spar, graphite, alum, and alum slate.

[5] The amount of cheese produced in this co. is three times as great as in any other co. in the State.

largely produced. At Little Falls, and a few other localities, considerable manufacturing is carried on.

The county seat is located at the village of Herkimer.[1] The courthouse is a fine brick building fronting Main St., near the center of the village. The jail is a stone building, on the opposite side of the st. from the courthouse. The clerk's office is a fireproof brick building, upon the courthouse lot, fronting Court St. The poorhouse is located upon a farm of 65 acres 6½ mi. N. of the courthouse. The average number of inmates is 130, supported at a weekly cost of $1.30 each. The farm yields a revenue of about $700. A school is taught about 6 months in the year. The institution is in good condition and seems to be well managed.[2] The works of internal improvement within the co. are the Erie Canal and the N. Y. Central R. R., both extending along the valley of the Mohawk.

Four weekly newspapers are now published in the co.[3]

The lands of this co. adjacent to the river were granted mostly in the first half of the last century, and the greater portion now settled was conveyed before the Revolution. The N. portion and small tracts in other sections remained in possession of the State Government until conveyed to Macomb and others.[4]

[1] The first courthouse of the co. was located at Whitesboro, now Oneida co. The first courthouse and jail at Herkimer was burned Jan. 25, 1834. The first co. officers were Henry Staring, *First Judge;* Michael Myers, Hugh White, and Abraham Hardenburgh, *Judges;* Jonas Platt, *Clerk;* Wm. Colbreath, *Sheriff;* and Moses De Witt, *Surrogate.*

[2] The two main buildings of this institution are of stone, and are each 30 by 46 feet.

[3] *The Telescope* was commenced at Herkimer about 1802 by Benj. Corey. It was purchased by David Holt and J. B. Robbins, and discontinued in Jan. 1805.

The Farmers' Monitor was commenced in the same office in 1805 by Holt & Robbins. It was discontinued in 1807.

The Herkimer Pelican was commenced in 1807 or '08 by Benj. Corey, and was discontinued about 1810.

The Herkimer American was commenced in 1810 by J. H. & H. Prentiss. Wm. L. Stone afterward became the publisher. In 1813 or '14 he sold it to Edward P. Seymour, who continued its publication until 1831, when it was discontinued.

Bunker Hill was commenced at Herkimer in 1810 by G. G. Phinney. Its name was changed in 1812 to

The Honest American, under which title it was published a few years.

The People's Friend was commenced at Little Falls in Sept. 1821, by Edward M. Griffin. It was successively published by Joseph A. Noonan, Horatio N. Johnson, and E. G. Palmer & H. N. Johnson. In 1830 it was published as

The People's Friend and Little Falls Gazette. In July, 1834, it passed into the hands of N. S. Benton & Co., who changed its name to

The Mohawk Courier, under which title it is now published by A. W. Eaton.

The Herkimer Herald was commenced in 1828 by John Carpenter. It was removed in a few years to Oswego.

The Republican Farmers' Free Press was commenced at Herkimer in 1830 by —— Holt; B. B. Hotchkin, editor. In 1834 it was removed to Little Falls and its name changed to

The Herkimer County Whig, under which title it was published about 2 years by Larned W. Smith.

The Inquirer was published a short time at Little Falls by Larned W. Smith.

The Herkimer County Journal was commenced in Dec. 1837, by a company; J. C. Underwood, editor, E. P. Seymour, printer. In 1838 it passed into the hands of O. A. Bowe, and in 1849 to Orlando Squires, who removed it to Little Falls. He was succeeded by Daniel Ayer, by whom the paper is now published.

Key of David,
Eclectic Bulletin, } Small papers. A few numbers were issued in 1853 or '54 by O. Squires. The latter paper was designed as a daily, but was issued only tri-weekly.

The Watchman was issued by Squires about 6 months in 18—.

The Democratic Vindicator was issued by Squires about 2 weeks in 18—.

The Enterprise was issued at Little Falls in 1839 by E. M. Griffin. In 1841 it was succeeded by

The Mohawk Mirror, semi-mo. This paper was discontinued in 1844.

*The Tribune and Spirit of '98 was published at Little Falls a short time in 18— by H. V. Johnson.

The Herkimer Freeman was commenced at Little Falls in July, 1844, by O. A. Bowe. In 1850 he removed it to Mohawk and changed the name to

The Mohawk Times. It was soon after discontinued.

The Frankfort Democrat was commenced in 1842 by J. M. Lyon & W. B. Holmes. In 1844 it was removed to Herkimer and its name changed to

The Herkimer County Democrat. In 1848 Mr. Lyon was succeeded by Robert Earl. In 1850 C. C. Witherstine became interested in its publication, and in March, 1854, he became sole proprietor. In Sept. 1854, J. L. Hayse was associated with Mr. Witherstine, and in Dec. 1855, the name of the paper was changed to

The Herkimer American. In May, 1856, Mr. Hayse withdrew; and in July following the paper passed into the hands of R. W. Crain & J. T. Stevens, who changed its name to

The Herkimer County Democrat. —— Witherstine soon after became proprietor; and in June, 1859, the paper passed into the hands of H. G. Crouch, its present publisher.

The Ilion Independent was commenced in Jan. 1855; G. W. Bungay, editor, Wm. L. Fish & H. W. Lyman, publishers. In Jan. 1858, it was removed to Utica.

The Mohawk Valley Sentinel was commenced at Mohawk in Jan. 1855, by L. W. Peters & G. W. Gould. In May following Mr. Peters became sole proprietor, and is its present publisher.

[4] *List of Patents, Tracts, and Grants of Land in Herkimer County.*

Tracts.	Patentees.	Date.	Acres.
Adgate's Patent*	Mathew Adgate	1798	43,907
Brown's Tract*	Part of Macomb's Purchase	1792	210,000
Burnetsfield Patent*	John Joost Petrie and 93 others	1725	9,400
Colden, C., Patent	Cadwallader Colden and C. Rightmeyer	1738	3,000
Colden, N., Patent	Alexander Colden and 3 others	1761	4,000
Cosby's Manor*	Joseph Worrell, Wm. Cosby, and 9 others	1734	22,000
Fall Hill Patent	John Joost and Hendrick Herkimer	1752	2,324
Free Mason's Patent*	Wm. and Robert Bayard and 53 others	1771	50,000
Glen's Purchase	Jacob Glen and others	1736, '39, '60	25,477
Hasenclever's Patent*	Peter Hasenclever and 17 others	1769	18,000
Henderson's Patent*	Jas. Henderson and 2 others	1739	6,000
Jerseyfield Patent*	Henry Glen and 93 others	1770	94,000
Johnson's, Guy, Patent	Guy Johnson (forfeited)	1765	2,000
Kast's Patent	Johan Jurgh Kast and others,—his children	1724	1,100
Lansing's Patent*	Jacob Lansing and 2 others	1753	6,000
L'Hommedieu's Patent	Ezra L'Hommedieu and N. Platt	1786	4,000
Lindsay's Patent	John Lindsay and Philip Livingston	1730	3,000
Lispenard's Patent*	Leonard Lispenard, sen. and jr., and 13 others	1770	9,200
Livingston's Patent*	Philip Livingston and 19 others	1762	20,000
Machin's Patent*	Thomas Machin	1786	1,600

The first settlements were made upon the river intervales above Little Falls, about 1722, by a colony of Palatinates. Accessions were made to their number from time to time, and up to the close of the Revolution they constituted almost the sole inhabitants of the co. During the French War of 1756, this colony was twice invaded, and numbers of the people were killed or carried away prisoners.[1] During the Revolution also it was repeatedly invaded: the buildings and crops were destroyed; and at last the inhabitants were obliged to abandon their homes and seek protection in the lower part of the valley. The German Flats were invaded by a body of 300 tories and 152 Indians, under Brant, in Sept. 1778. This party burned 63 dwellings, 57 barns, 3 gristmills, 2 sawmills, and killed or took off 235 horses, 229 horned cattle, 269 sheep, and 93 oxen. Only 2 persons lost their lives; and the forts were not attacked. A party of militia pursued them on their retreat, but without effecting any thing. Andrustown, in Warren, was burned in July of the same year. A stockade fort was built at the German Flats, and another at Danube, a short time previous to the commencement of the French War. In 1776 another fort was built at Herkimer, N. of the Mohawk; and strong blockhouses were erected in several other parts of the co.[2]

This co. shared in the loss of men at the battle of Oriskany. Gen. Arnold came as far as German Flats in the summer of 1777, on his way to relieve Fort Schuyler; and from this place was sent the tory Han Yost Schuyler, to spread alarm among the savages in St. Leger's camp and hasten the abandonment of the siege.

After the war the settlements rapidly spread, and within 15 years over 10,000 persons from New England and the eastern cos. of the State located in the central and s. portions of the co. From that time its progress has been gradual and continually prosperous.

COLUMBIA[3]—was formed from Warren, June 8, 1812. It lies on the s. border of the co., w. of the center. Its surface is rolling and moderately hilly, with an average elevation of 500 to 600 ft. above the Mohawk. The streams are small brooks, a portion of them flowing N. to the Mohawk and the remainder flowing s. to the Unadilla. The soil is a clayey loam and generally fertile. **Columbia Center** (Columbia p. o.) contains 98 inhabitants; **Cedarville,** (p. v.,) on the line of Litchfield, 2 churches, a tannery, and 145 inhabitants. **South Columbia,** in the s. E. part, is a p. o. The first settlement was commenced before the Revolution, by families from the Mohawk;[4] but their improvements were abandoned during the war. The first religious services (Ref. Prot. D.) were held at an early period. Abram Rosegrantz was the first preacher.[5]

DANUBE[6]—was formed from Minden, (Montgomery co.,) April 7, 1817. Stark was taken

Tracts.	Patentees.	Date.	Acres.
McNeil's Patent*	John McNeil and 3 others	1761	4,000
Moose River Tract*	Anson Blake	1847	13,080
Nobleborough Patent*	Arthur Noble	1787	40,960
Petrie's Purchase	Philip Livingston and 2 others	1747	6,000
Remsenburgh Patent*	Henry Remsen and 3 others	1787	48,000
Royal Grant	Sir Wm. Johnson, (after 1755)		43,000
Schuyler's Patent	Abraham Lynsen and 21 others	1755	43,000
Snell & Zimmerman's Patent	Jacob Zimmerman and J. J. Schnell	1755	3,600
Staley's Patent, 1st and 2d Tract	Rudolph Staley and 17 others	1755	34,000
" " 3d Tract	Coenradt and Fred. Frank and 4 others	1765	5,000
Totten & Crossfield's Purchase*	Zephaniah Platt	1786	25,200
Van Driessen, John's, Patent	John Van Driessen	1786	428
Van Driessen, Petrus', Patent	Petrus Van Driessen	1737	1,000
Van Horne's Patent*	Abraham Van Horne and 3 others	1731	8,000
Vaughan's Potent	John Vaughan and 7 others	1770	8,000
Vrooman's Patents* (3)	Isaac Vrooman	1786, '90	14,193
Walton's Patent	Wm. Walton, jr., and 11 others	1768	12,000
Watson's East Tract*	Part of Macomb's Purchase	1792	
Young's Patent*	Theobald Young and 10 others	1752	14,000

Those marked with a star extend into neighboring cos. Some tracts reverted to the State by attainder, or conviction for adhering to the enemy in the Revolution; and subsequent grants may thus overlap. For a full statement of titles, see *Benton's Herkimer*, pp. 200, 475.

[1] See page 344.
[2] Fort Herkimer was built in the French War, and Fort Dayton just before the Revolution. The former stood around the present stone church and other buildings in German Flats, and the latter a few rods from the site of the present courthouse, in Herkimer Village. At the time of the Revolution there were but about 70 dwellings near these forts, but there was a large population for the number of dwellings in the country around.
[3] This town embraces Staley's Second Tract,—except 1¼ tiers of lots on the w.,—a small triangular piece from the N. w. corner of Henderson's Patent, and all of the patent to Coenradt Frank and others, except 7 lots on the E.

[4] Among the early settlers were Conrad Orendorf, Conrad Frank, Conrad Fulmer, Frederick Christian, Timothy Frank, Nicholas Lighthall, Joseph Moyer, and Henry Frank. The settlement was named "*Coonrodston*" at an early day.—*Benton's Herkimer*, p. 390.
Philip Ausman taught the first school, (German,) in 1795, and Joel Phelps an English school, in 1796. The first store was kept by David W. Golden and Benj. Mix, in 1796. The first gristmill was built in 1791-92, by Andrew Miller and Geo. Bell, at Millers Mills.
[5] There are 2 churches in town; Ref. Prot. D. and F. W Bap.
[6] Named from the river Danube.

off in 1828. It lies on the E. border of the co., s. of the center. Its surface is hilly in the center, rising 400 to 800 ft. above the Mohawk; and it is broken by ravines on each side of the valley of the creek. Fine flats extend along the Mohawk on the N. border. The principal stream is Nowadaga[1] Creek, which flows N. E. through the town near the center. The soil is gravelly in the N. and a sandy loam in the s. In the N. part are two sulphur springs. **Newville** (p. v.) contains 1 church and 20 houses, and **Indian Castle**[2] (Danube p. o., a hamlet) 1 church. Settlements are supposed to have commenced as early as 1730; but no records have been preserved. During the Revolution the settlements were broken up, and did not commence again until about 1780.[3] The first patents are dated 1730–31.[4] A mission church was established here by Sir William Johnson in 1768. This church had a bell, which the Indians attempted to carry off in the war, and for that purpose secreted it. Search was made in vain. After sufficient time had elapsed the thieves, on returning by night to bear away the coveted treasure, had their presence and business betrayed by the unruly member which they neglected to muffle. As it was borne along on a pole, its ringing brought the Germans to its rescue with such weapons as they in their haste could snatch, and the bell was recovered. The present church occupying the site of the old Mission Church is known as the "Indian Castle Church." There are 2 union churches in town. This town was the residence of King Hendrick[5] and Joseph Brant,[6] the celebrated Mohawk chiefs, and of Gen. Nicholas Herkimer.[7] King Hendrick sustained a high character for sagacity and integrity, was warmly attached to the English, and especially to Sir Wm. Johnson, whom he accompanied to Lake George in the summer of 1755, where he was killed. He was recognized as a chief as early as 1697.

FAIRFIELD[8]—was formed from Norway, Feb. 19, 1796. A part of Newport was taken off in 1806, and a part of Little Falls in 1829. It lies in the interior of the co., near the center. Its surface is a hilly upland, the center rising into a ridge 800 to 1,000 ft. above West Canada Creek.[9] The streams are small. West Canada Creek flows s. on the w. border. The soil on the uplands is mostly clay, and in the valleys it is gravelly, with local drift deposits of sand. Several fine quarries of limestone are found in different parts.[10] **Fairfield,** (p. v.,) near the center, contains 3 churches, an academy,[11] a cheese box factory, and 60 houses; **Middleville,** (p. v.,) on the line of Newport, 1 church, a woolen factory, tannery,[12] chair factory, grist and saw mill. Pop. 295. Settlements were first made in 1770, by 3 German families named Maltanner, Goodbrodt, and Shaffer, who located upon the Royal Grant.[13] The first preacher was Rev. —— Fields, (Presb.,) in 1791.[14]

1 Called by the Indians In-cha-nan-do.

2 Named from the upper Indian castle, or fort, built in 1710 on the flat just below the mouth of Nowadaga Creek. It was built as one of the chain of defenses that guarded the approach to Canada, and was armed with small cannon. The Indians lived in clusters of huts around it.

3 An inn was kept by Cornelius C. Van Alstyne, in 1795, and a store by Peter Smith, at the same time. Andrew Nellis built the first gristmill, near the mouth of Nowadaga, in 1800.

4 Small portions of Fall Hill, Vaughan's, and L'Hommedieu's Patents, the whole of Lindsey's, and parts of J. Vrooman's, C. Colden's, Van Horne's, and Lansing's Patents are in this town.

5 The dwelling of King Hendrick stood upon the high ground near the site of the present Indian Castle Church. On one occasion he remarked to Sir William Johnson that he had dreamed a dream. On being questioned, he related that the English agent had in his slumber appeared to present him a suit of new clothes. Johnson fulfilled the dream, and not long after had in turn a dream to relate to the chief, in which he thought the latter had presented to him a large tract of land. The Indian was caught in his own trap. He, however, gave the necessary title, but hinted, as he conveyed the lands described, that they would have no more dreaming. This tract was afterward known as the Royal Grant.

6 Brant lived in the same place that had been occupied by Hendrick. Fort Hendrick stood on land now owned by Abram Owens, w. of the Nowadaga, on a small eminence overlooking the flat. The fort was built in the French War.

7 General Herkimer's house is still standing, 3 mi. below Little Falls, s. of the canal. It is of imported brick, and was built in 1763, at a cost of $7,500 to $8,000. Some of the rooms were finished in panel work and were plastered on the brick walls; and in its day the house was surpassed by none in this section. It is now owned by Daniel Conner. Efforts were made to burn it in the Revolution by throwing combustibles upon the roof; but further attempts of this kind were prevented by covering it with a layer of clay. Gen. Herkimer's grave is 25 rods s. E. from the house, on a knoll, and is marked by a plain white tombstone inscribed as follows:—

"Gen.
NICHOLAS HERKIMER.
Died
Aug. 17, 1777,
Ten days after the battle of Oriskany, in which engagement he received wounds which caused his death."

Attempts have been repeatedly made to obtain the means to erect a suitable monument; but, notwithstanding the resolution of Congress on the 4th of October, 1777, "that the Governor and Council of New York be desired to erect a monument, at Continental expense, of the value of $500, to the memory of the late Brigadier Harkemer, who commanded the militia of Tryon co., in the State of N. Y., and who was killed fighting gallantly in defense of the liberty of these States," this order has been neglected, and the citizen chief lies forgotten by the country for whose cause he gave his life. He was chairman of the Tryon co. committee of safety. At the time of his death he was about 50 years of age.

8 This town included nearly all of the Glen Purchase and the first allotment of the Royal Grant.

9 The s. w. corner of the old college building is 1,276.8 ft. above tidewater at Troy. The chapel threshold is 727 feet above low water at W. Canada Creek at Middleville, and Barts Hill is 1,177 feet above the same.

10 Near Middleville are found beautiful crystals of quartz. Most of them are perfectly transparent; and sometimes they inclose a few drops of water or small pieces of anthracite coal.

11 Fairfield Academy was established in 1803. A medical department, incorp. as the College of Physicians and Surgeons, was founded in 1809, and continued until 1840. A conditional college charter was granted to the academy in 1812, under the name of "Clinton College;" but the conditions were not complied with.

12 This establishment manufactures $40,000 worth of calfskins and upper leather annually.

13 These settlers, though Royalists, were attacked by the Indians in 1779. Two members of the families were killed, and the others were carried into captivity. Families named Keller, Windecker, and Pickert settled near the Manheim line, and others settled on the Glen Purchase, before the war. Cornelius Chatfield settled in March, and Abijah Mann in May, 1785. Josiah, David, and Lester Johnson, John Bucklin, Benj. Bowen, John Eaton, Nath'l and Wm. Brown, Sam'l Low, David Benseley, Elisha Wyman, Comfort Eaton, Jeremiah Ballard, Wm. Bucklin, —— Arnold, Daniel Venner, Nathan Smith, Nahum Daniels, Amos and Jas. Haile, —— Neely, and Peter and Bela Ward, all from New England, settled soon after. The first store was kept by Smith & Daniels, in 1792–93. The first gristmill was built by —— Empie, and the first sawmill by Samuel & Paul Green. A school was taught in 1795, by Wm. D. Gray; but others had been previously taught in the N. part of the town.

14 There are now 6 churches in town; 2 M. E., Bap., Prot. E., Presb., and Cong.

FRANKFORT[1]—was formed from German Flats, Feb. 5, 1796. It was divided in the formation of Oneida co. in 1798, and a part annexed to Deerfield. It lies on the w. border of the co., s. of the Mohawk. Its surface is a broad intervale, rising into hills of moderate elevation on the s. w. border, the highest points being about 500 ft. above the river. The Mohawk flows s. e. on the N. border. The streams are small brooks and creeks. The soil on the uplands is a clayey and slaty loam, and on the flats an alluvial loam. Limestone ledges are found in the s. w. The most important of these is called Horsebone Ledge. The stone is whitish and makes excellent lime. Slate and calciferous sandstone are also found in some places. **Frankfort,** (p. v.,) in the N. E., near the Mohawk, contains 4 churches, 1 bank, a grist and saw mill, woolen factory, and distillery. Pop. 1,150. **New Graefenberg** (p. o.) is the seat of a water cure, 4½ mi. from Utica. **Howards Bush** (Frankfort Hill p. o.) is w. of the center. Jacob Folts made the first settlement, on Lot 3, Burnetsfield Patent, before the Revolution.[2] The census reports 7 churches in town.[3]

GERMAN FLATS[4]—was formed, as a district of *"Tryon co.,"* March 24, 1772. Its name was exchanged with the Kingsland District, March 8, 1773. It was recognized as a town March 7, 1788. Frankfort, Litchfield, and Warren were taken off in 1796, and a part of Little Falls in 1829. It lies upon the s. bank of the Mohawk, s. of the center of the co. A fine intervale extends along the river, and from it the surface gradually rises to a height of 300 to 400 ft. and spreads out into an undulating upland. The valley of Fulmer Creek divides this upland into two nearly equal parts. The other streams are small brooks. The soil is a clay and slaty loam upon the hills, and a gravelly loam and alluvium in the valleys. **Mohawk,** (p. v.,) a canal village, in the N. w. part of the town, was incorp. April 16, 1844. It contains 3 churches, a bank, and newspaper office. Pop. 1,355. **Ilion** (p. v.) is a canal village, 1½ mi. w. of Mohawk. It contains 2 churches, a bank, and Remmington's rifle factory. Pop. 813. **Fort Herkimer,** upon the Mohawk, in the E. part, contains 2 churches and 20 houses. **Dennisons Corners** (Dennison p. o.) and **Pains Hollow** are hamlets. The first settlements were made in 1722, by a colony of Palatinates who had previously located upon the Hudson.[5] The population rapidly increased until 1756, when the whole settlement was laid waste by a party of Canadians, French, and Indians.[6] A council was held with the Indians at this place, June 28, 1775, at which the Oneidas and Tuscaroras agreed to remain neutral.[7] During the Revolution the Indians committed many murders in town; and in July, 1782, they destroyed nearly the whole settlement.[8] The German inhabitants early espoused the Patriot cause; and the first liberty-pole in the Mohawk Valley, erected here, was cut down by Sheriff White and a body of militia, who came up from Johnstown for the purpose, in the spring of 1775. At the close of the war the settlements progressed with great rapidity. A treaty was held with the Indians at Fort Herkimer, June 28, 1785, at which time the Oneidas and Tuscaroras ceded to the State the territory lying between Unadilla and Chenango Rivers. The first church was built of logs, in 1725; it was superseded by one built of stone, in 1767. The building is still standing, and is the most ancient structure in the co. It was commenced under a permit granted in 1746, but from apprehension of Indian troubles it was delayed, and a new permit was granted Oct. 6, 1751. It was not fully completed for use until 1767. On the 24th of Sept. 1730, Nicholas Wolever deeded Lot 30 of Burnetsfield Patent for church and school purposes. A society was formed soon after, and the conveyance was perfected April 26, 1733. Lots 45, 46, and 47 in German Flats were conveyed Sept. 18, 1755, by Hans Dedrick Stelly, and others, to Peter Remsen, for the support of the Ref. Prot. D. church at this place. The first preacher was Rev. A. Rosegrantz.[9]

---

[1] Named from Lawrence Frank, an early settler. A large part of Cosby's Manor, 1½ tiers of great lots of Bayard's Patent, 4 lots in Burnetsfield Patent, ⅓ of 1 lot in Frank's, 4½ lots in Staley's, and a part of Colden's Patent, are in this town.—*Benton's Herkimer,* p. 400.

[2] Among the other early settlers were Conrad Folts, Andrew Piper, David Dederick, Aaron James, —— Morgan, Evan Evans, Joseph Harris, John Morris, John Myers, and Adam Weber. Several Welsh families settled about 1800. The first inn was kept by John Myers, in 1795; the first sawmill was built by John Hollister, in 1794; and the first gristmill by Adam J. Campbell, in 1808.

[3] [4] M. E., Bap., Ref. Prot. D., and Univ.

[4] Named from the German settlers who located on the Mohawk Flats at this place.

[5] Among the early settlers were families named Erghemar, Herkimer, Fox, Editch, Bellinger, Starring, Wolever, and Herter, —names still common in the co.

[6] This attack was made Nov. 11, 1776. The settlers were totally unprepared, and the greater part were murdered or captured without resistance. The French account states that a mill, 60 houses, and a large number of barns, were destroyed,

40 persons were killed, and 150 taken prisoners. These numbers were doubtless much exaggerated. A small stockaded fort, called Fort Kouari, was garrisoned at this time, and afforded shelter for a portion of the inhabitants. On the 30th of April, 1758, the French and Indians made another attack upon the settlers, and killed 30, losing 15 of their own number.

[7] On the 15th and 16th of Aug. 1775, another council was held here by Turbot Francis and Valkert P. Doun, on the part of the Commissioners for the Northern Department, to induce the Indians to go to Albany to hold a great council. They attended at Albany soon after; but sufficient inducements could not be offered to detach them from the royal cause.

[8] In July, 1782, a party of 600 Indians and tories entered the settlement, and were discovered by Peter Wolever, who, with Augustinus Hess, lived about 50 rods from the fort. Both families escaped to the fort, except Hess, who was killed at the picket gate. Valentine Starring was tortured within hearing of the fort, which was too feeble to attempt a rescue.—*Benton's Herkimer,* p. 406.

[9] There are now 7 churches in town; 2 Ref. Prot. D., Bap., Ev. Luth., F. W. Bap., Univ., and Union.

HERKIMER[1]—was formed from Kingsland District, March 7, 1788. A part of Palatine (Montgomery co.) was annexed in 1791. Norway and Schuyler were taken off in 1792, a part of Newport in 1806, and a part of Little Falls in 1829. A part was annexed to Schuyler in 1808, and restored in 1811. It lies on the N. bank of the Mohawk, near the center of the settled portions of the co. A wide intervale extends along the river, and from it the surface gradually rises to the N. line of the town. West Canada Creek flows s. through near the center, dividing the uplands into two distinct ridges. The Hasenclever Mts., w. of the creek, are 600 to 800 ft. above the Mohawk. The soil upon the hills is a gravelly loam, and in the valleys a deep, fertile alluvium. **Herkimer,**[2] (p. v.,) upon the Mohawk, w. of the mouth of West Canada Creek, was incorp. April 6, 1807. It contains the co. buildings, 3 churches, a bank, newspaper office, paper mill,[3] and gristmill. Pop. 1,371. It is a station upon the N. Y. C. R. R. **Eatonville** (p. o.) is a hamlet, in the N. E. corner, on the line of Fairfield and Little Falls. The early history of the town is blended with that of German Flats, of which it formed a part until its organization as a town. The first settlements were made by Palatinates, under the patronage of Gov. Hunter, in 1722.[4] It had its share of suffering during the Revolution; and all the patriot families that remained during the war were those sheltered by Fort Dayton. This fortress stood upon a point of the stone ridge about 30 rods above the present site of the courthouse. After the destruction of Fort Schuyler by flood and fire, in May, 1781, Forts Dayton and Herkimer became the frontier defenses of the Mohawk Valley.[5] After the war, many of the Indians and tories who had been actively engaged in hostilities returned to the settlements; but they were received by the settlers in a way little calculated to inspire sentiments of friendship, and the greater part emigrated to more congenial places.[6] The first church (Ref. Prot. D.) was formed at an early period, by Rev. A. Rosegrantz; but the precise date has been lost.[7]

LITCHFIELD[8]—was formed from German Flats, Feb. 5, 1796. A part of Winfield was taken off in 1816. It lies on the w. border of the co., s. of the Mohawk. Its surface is elevated and moderately hilly, its mean elevation being about 500 feet above the river. A series of ridges in the w. and s. are known as the "Dry Lots,"[9] no water being found upon them. The streams are small; some flow s. into the Unadilla and others N. into the Mohawk. In the E. part is a sulphur spring.[10] **Litchfield** (p. v.) contains 1 church and about 15 houses; **Cedar Lake** (p. o.) 1 church and 9 houses; **Jerusalem,** a hamlet near the center, 2 churches and 7 houses. The first settlement was commenced about 1789, by Jabez Snow, on Snow Hill.[11] The first religious services were held in 1794; Rev. —— Spaulding was the first preacher.[12]

LITTLE FALLS—was formed from Fairfield, Herkimer, and German Flats, Feb. 16, 1829. It lies in the interior of the co., s. of the center. Its surface is a broken upland, divided by the

---

[1] Named in honor of Gen. Nicholas Herkimer. It was intended to apply the name to the territory including the old residence of the General, but by mistake it was given to this town. The Kingsland District was one of the divisions of Tryon co. formed March 24, 1772. Its name was exchanged with that of German Flats District, March 8, 1773. It included all that portion of the co. lying w. of Palatine District and N. of the Mohawk. This town embraces the whole of Winner's and a part of Burnetsfield, Hasenclever's, Colden's, and Willet's Patents, and small portions of the Royal Grant and Glen's Purchase.

[2] Originally called "*Stone Ridge.*"

[3] This paper mill was established in 1849; it gives employment to 120 hands.

[4] Among the early settlers were Johan Joost Petrie, Frederick and A. M. Pell, Jury Docksteder, Nicholas Feeter, Melgert Fols, Henry Heger, —— Lendert, Frederick Johan, Adam and Philip Helmer, and families named Schmidt, Weaver, and Bellinger. The first schools were German. —— Robinson taught the first English school, at the village.

[5] Lieut. Solomon Woodworth was stationed at Fort Dayton with a small force of Continental troops. He rendered great service to the settlers in this part of the valley. In the summer of 1781, with 40 men, he went out to reconnoiter; but about 3 mi. N. of Herkimer the party fell into an Indian ambuscade, and only 15 escaped. The commander and 20 men were killed. A Mrs. Smith, scalped by the Indians during the war, recovered and lived to a good old age. On the 6th of August, 1781, a party of tories and Indians, under Donald McDonald, a Scotch refugee, from Johnstown, made an attack upon the settlement at Shells Bush. The inhabitants mostly fled to Fort Dayton; but John Christian Shell and his family, consisting of his wife and 6 sons, took refuge in their own house, which was a strong blockhouse. His two little sons, twins, 8 years of age, were taken prisoners; but the remainder of the family escaped within and secured the entrance. In trying to force the door, McDonald was wounded, and made prisoner. The attack continued until dark, when the tories fled, with a loss of 11 killed and 6 wounded. McDonald

died of his wounds the next day. The two little boys were returned after the war.—*Benton's Herkimer.*

[6] John Adam Hartman, an active and successful ranger, was engaged in perilous service through the war. Soon after the peace, an Indian came into an inn, in the w. part of this town, where Hartman was present, and, getting intoxicated, began to boast of his exploits, and showed a tobacco pouch made from the skin of a white child's arm and hand, with the nails still on. When the Indian left, Hartman found business on the same road. They both passed into a swamp; and the Indian never came out. In reply to questions put to him, Hartman said that he last saw the Indian, some distance ahead, standing on a log; and that he fell as if hurt. Hartman was tried for murder, but was acquitted. He lived in town till his death, in the spring of 1836.—*Benton's Herkimer, p. 409.*

[7] There are 3 churches in town; 2 M. E., Ref. Prot. D.

[8] Named from Litchfield, Conn., whence many of the early settlers came.

[9] These hills have limestone ledges belonging to the Heldbergh series. These lots, 2 in number, contain about 1,600 acres each. Water is obtained by wells at great expense.

[10] The Columbian Springs, in Browns Hollow, have been brought to public notice, but have yet gained only a local reputation.

[11] Among the other early settlers were John Everett, Nathaniel Ball, and Ebenezer Drury, from N. H.; and Ezekiel Goodell and S. Sherry, from Conn. Selah Holcomb settled 2 mi. E. of Jerusalem. Wm. and Thos. Jones, Oliver Rider, Joseph Crosby, and others, were also early settlers. The first birth was that of Luke Andrews, in 1790; the first marriage, that of Joseph Day and ——, in the same year. Jeremiah Everett taught the first school; Joseph Shepard kept the first inn; David Davis kept the first store; —— Talcott built the first sawmill, and John Littlejohn the first gristmill, in 1806–07.

[12] The census reports 8 churches in town; 2 Presb., 2 M. E., 2 Univ., Bap., and Wes. Meth.

deep, narrow gorge of the Mohawk. A range of hills extend N. and S. from the village. They are rocky and precipitous near the river, but less rugged on the N. and S. borders.[1] The Mohawk flows N. E. through near the center of the town in a series of cascades and rapids. Its banks are rocky and in places precipitous. The soil is a sandy, gravelly loam. **Little Falls,** (p. v.,) in the E. part, on the line of Manheim and Danube, was incorp. March 30, 1811. Its name was changed to "*Rockton*," April 16, 1850, and again changed to Little Falls, April 16, 1852. It is an important station on the N. Y. C. R. R. It contains 9 churches, a bank, 2 printing offices, the Little Falls Academy, a union school, and a large number of manufactories.[2] Pop. 3,984. **Jackson-burgh,** in the W., on the canal, has 206 inhabitants; and **Bethel,** in the S., 1 church and 15 houses. **Paines Hollow** is a p. o. Lots 12 and 13 of Burnetsfield Patent, embracing all the water-power N. of the river, were owned before the Revolution by —— Petrie. This town also embraces portions of several other patents issued at an early period.[3] The first settlements were made by a colony of Palatinates, in 1722.[4] The settlers suffered much during the war, and most of them were driven off.[5] The first settler at the village after the war was John Proteus, in 1790.[6] A great impulse was given to the business and population of the place by the construction of the locks of the Western Navigation Co. in 1796.[7] The first church was built about 1815. It was octagonal, with a steep roof, and surmounted by a cupola. The census reports 10 churches in town.[8]

MANHEIM[9]—was formed from Palatine, (Montgomery co.,) April 7, 1817. It lies on the N. bank of the Mohawk, upon the E. border of the co. Its surface gradually rises from the intervales along the Mohawk to the N. border, where it attains an elevation of 500 ft. above the river. East Canada Creek forms its E. boundary.[10] Cathatachua Creek flows S. through near the center, and Bennett Brook flows S. E. through the N. E. corner. Upon East Canada Creek, 1 mi. above its mouth, is a series of cascades, where the water descends 180 ft. in three-fourths of a mi. The soil is a gravelly loam upon the upland, and a fine, fertile alluvium in the valleys. **Brocketts Bridge,** (p. v.,) upon East Canada Creek, in the N. part, contains 2 churches, a large tannery,[11] gristmill, and 50 houses; and **Inghams Mills,** upon East Canada Creek, 3 mi. below Brock-etts Bridge, a church and 25 houses. **East Creek** (p. o.) is a hamlet and station upon the N. Y. C. R. R., near the mouth of East Canada Creek. **Manheim Center** is a p. o. The first settlements were made by Germans, probably in about the year 1736.[12] During the Revolution they were frequently attacked by the Indians and were mostly destroyed. On the 30th of April, 1780, a party of 60 tories and Indians fell upon the settlements at Rheimen Snyder's Bush, burned a grist-mill, and carried 19 persons away into captivity.[13] The first church, built in 1774 or '75, was burned during the war, and was rebuilt soon after. The census reports 5 churches; 2 M.E., 2 Union, and Ref. Prot. D.

---

[1] The rocks at Little Falls are chiefly hypersthene and gneiss, overlaid by calciferous sandstone on the S. side of the river. Falls Hill, S. of the village, is 518 feet above the canal, and Roll Way Bluff, N. of the village, is little less in height. In the im-mediate vicinity of the village are quarries of limestone, from which is obtained lime and a good building material. Small caves and pot holes are numerous among the rocks near the river. The largest of the latter is 28 feet in diameter and 37 feet deep. The break through the mountains at this place was one of the most formidable barriers in the construction of the Erie Canal. The N. part of the town is covered with Utica slate, and the S. part by the Hudson River and Clinton groups.

[2] Among these manufactories are 4 paper mills, turning out $150,000 worth of paper annually; 2 woolen factories, producing about $250,000 worth of goods annually; a stocking yarn mill, producing goods to the amount of $30,000, and a starch factory, using $30,000 worth of corn, annually. Besides these are 2 flouring mills, a cotton factory, 3 large shoe manufactories, and an extensive carriage shop.

[3] This town includes a portion of the Glen Purchase of 1739; Guy Johnson's Tract, granted in 1765; Vaughan's Patent, granted in 1770; Fall Hill Patent, granted in 1752; 6 lots of Butterfield's Patent, granted in 1725, and small portions of several other patents.

[4] Among these early settlers were John Jost Temouth, Mary Beerman, Nicholas Kesler, Johannes Pouradt, and Christian Fox. John Petrie kept the first inn, before the Revolution. A gristmill built on Casler Creek, in the N. part of the town, was stockaded during the war.

[5] In June, 1782, a party of tories and Indians invaded the town, burned a gristmill on Furnace Creek, killed Daniel Petrie, and carried away several prisoners.

[6] Among the first settlers after the war were Wm. Alexander, Richard Phillips, Thos. Smith, Joel Lankton, Richard Winsor,

Wm. Carr, Wm. Moralee, Washington Britton, Alpheus Park-hurst, John Drummond, Eben Britton, and Josiah Skinner,—all of whom came in town between 1790 and 1800.

[7] These locks were planned by Roswell Weston, an English engineer, and built under the direction of Philip Schuyler. The first locks, built of wood, were replaced by stone in 1804.

[8] Bap., Ev. Luth., M. E., Af. Meth., Meth. Prot., Presb., Prot. Episc., R. C., Univ., and Union.

[9] Named from Manheim, in Baden, the native place of the early settlers. The town embraces 6 lots of Glen's Purchase, a part of the fourth allotment of the Royal Grant, the Patents of John Van Driessen and of Snell and Zimmerman, a part of the patents of Peter Van Driessen and of Vrooman, and several minor tracts granted since the Revolution.

[10] This stream was called by the Indians Ci-o-ha-na and Sag-o-ha-ra.

[11] This is the largest tannery in the co. It has a capital of $250,000, consumes 5,000 cords of bark per annum, and manu-factures sole leather exclusively.

[12] Among the early settlers were families named Snell, Zim-merman, and Van Driessen. Snell was the patentee of a large tract. Seven of the name, including several of his sons, were killed at the battle of Oriskany. John Beardsley built the first mill, in 1793. The first school (German) was taught by —— Kaufman.

[13] A blockhouse stood at this place, and many of the inhabit-ants took refuge in it. Twelve of the prisoners were taken at one house by half the number of Indians, without resistance. The captives all returned after the war, except one who died in Canada, and one that escaped. John G. Snell, while searching for cattle in the woods, was surprised by the Indians and shot through the body. He recovered, however, and lived to an advanced age. The town was deserted after this by all but tories.

NEWPORT[1]—was formed from Herkimer, Fairfield, Norway, and Schuyler, April 7, 1806. It lies on the w. border of the co., near the center. Its surface is broken by ridges of highlands, which rise 400 to 500 ft. each side of the narrow intervale of West Canada Creek. This stream flows s. e. through the town, near the center. White Creek flows s. through the e. part. The soil is a clayey loam, with some gravel on the hills. It is chiefly underlaid by limestone, which is quarried in some localities. **Newport,** (p. v.,) near the center, incorp. March 20, 1857, contains 3 churches, 1 bank, a gristmill, cotton factory,[2] and 671 inhabitants. Settlement was commenced in 1791, by Christopher Hawkins, from R. I.;[3] Rev. David Haskell (Bap.) held the first meetings, in 1796.[4]

NORWAY[5]—was formed from Herkimer, April 10, 1792. Fairfield was taken off in 1796, Russia, as "*Union,*" and a part of Newport, in 1806, and Ohio in 1823. It lies in the interior of the co., n. of the Mohawk. Its surface is elevated and rolling. It is drained by several small streams, tributaries of West Canada Creek. The soil is sandy in the n. w., and loam and gravelly in the e. and s. Limestone is quarried in several places; and fossils have been found near White Creek. There is a sulphur spring 1 mi. n. of the village. **Norway,** (p. v.,) near the center, contains 3 churches, a cheese box factory, tannery, and 30 houses; **Graysville,**[6] (p. v.,) on the line of Ohio, contains an extensive tannery and 30 houses.[7] The first settlement was made by —— Whipple and Christopher Hawkins, from R. I., in 1786; but it was soon abandoned.[8] The first religious meetings were held by Rev. —— Robertson, in 1792.[9]

OHIO[10]—was formed from Norway, as "*West Brunswick,*" April 11, 1823. Its name was changed May 3, 1836. A part of Wilmurt was taken off in 1836. It lies in the interior, on the n. border of the settlements. Its surface is moderately hilly, with an elevation of 700 to 900 ft. above the Mohawk. A range of high, steep hills extends through the n. part. It is drained by West Canada and Black Creeks and their tributaries. The soil is a sandy loam, with some clay. A large portion of the town is still a wilderness. **Graysville,** (p. v.,) on the line of Norway, contains 1 church, a tannery, and 30 houses. **Ohio City,** (Ohio p. o.,) in the w. part, contains 10 houses. A few scattering settlements were begun before the Revolution, but were broken up during the war.[11] Religious services were first held at Ohio City, in 1808.[12]

RUSSIA[13]—was formed from Norway, as "*Union,*" April 7, 1806. Its name was changed April 6, 1808. A part of Wilmurt was taken off in 1836. It lies on the w. border of the co., n. of the Mohawk, its n. part extending into the border of the great northern wilderness. Its surface is rolling and moderately hilly, and on the w. descends abruptly to the valley of West Canada Creek. The hills are 800 to 1,000 ft. above the Mohawk. West Canada and Black Creeks flow w. through the n. w. part, the former forming a part of the w. boundary. On it are some extensive lumber works.[14] Trenton Falls, upon West Canada Creek, is on the w. border. The soil is sandy

---

1 Named from Newport, R. I., the former residence of many of the early settlers.

2 A cotton factory was built in 1808, by Benj. Bowen. The Herkimer Manufacturing Co. was formed in 1814, with a capital of $40,000. In 1844 V. S. Kinyon became proprietor by purchase, and at present gives employment to 80 persons, and turns out $45,000 to $50,000 worth of sheetings annually.

3 Among the other early settlers were Benj. Bowen, John C. Green, Israel Wakely, and Geo. Fencer, all from R. I.; Dr. Westel Willoughby, and Sherman Wooster, from Conn. Joseph Benseley, A. M. Daniels, Geo. Cook, and Wm. Whipple were also early settlers. The first death was that of Silas Hawkins, in 1793. Abby Justine taught the first school, in 1795. Wm. Wakely kept the first inn, in 1793, and Geo. Cook the first store, the same year. Benj. Bowen built the first sawmill, in 1793, and the first gristmill, in 1794. The first settlers derived title from parties who had purchased from the courts of forfeiture.

4 The census reports 7 churches in town; Bap., M. E., Calv. Meth., Presb., Union, Univ., and R. C.

5 Named from Norway, in Europe. This town is included in the second and third allotments of the Royal Grant.

6 Named from Lathan Gray, a resident of the place.

7 La Dew's tannery, established in 1853, with a capital of $150,000, employs 75 men, and produces $150,000 worth of sole leather annually. The works are driven by a steam engine of 50 horse power.

8 Jeremiah Potter and his son, Fisher Potter, came in with their families from R. I. in 1788. Their whole store of provisions to carry them through the first winter was a crop of potatoes and some salt. For meat they depended upon hunting. Thos. Manly settled in 1789. John, Andrew, and Simeon Coe; Capt. Hinman, from Conn.; John and David Corp, N. Fanning, David Underhill, 5 families of Braytons, Angell, Lemuel, and Philip Potter, Edward Henderson, Uri H. Cook, Henri Tillinghart, Abijah Tombling, and Westel Willoughby, were early settlers.

The first birth was that of a child of Gideon Brayton; and the first death, that of the wife of E. Hinman. The first school was taught by Jeanette Henderson, in 1793. Amos Coe kept the first inn; Thaddeus Scribner & Bro., the first store, in 1793; Capt. Hinman built the first sawmill, in 1793; and Carpenter Cole the first gristmill, the same year. Vale & Eddy built a fulling mill, in 1793.—*Benton's Herkimer*, p. 450.

9 The census reports 5 churches; Bap., F. W. Bap., M. E., Presb., and Prot. E.

10 Named from the State of Ohio. This town includes the Jerseyfield and a small part of the Remsenburgh Patents.

11 —— Mount settled on Lot 50 of the Jerseyfield Patent some years before the Revolution. During the war, Mr. Mount was attacked by Indians; his two sons were killed, and himself, wife, and daughter fled to Little Falls, a distance of 20 miles. He did not see his wife and daughter after leaving his house until they met at Little Falls.—*Benton's Herkimer*, p. 455. John Miller settled in 1789-90. —— Warner, David Thorp, Aaron Thorp, Harmanus Van Epps, and others, were early settlers. David Thorp kept the first inn, Ephraim Ash the first store, in 1820. —— Mount built the first mills after the war. They were burned at the time, or soon after, he was driven off. The infamous Walter N. Butler was killed about 2 miles above the junction of Black and West Canada Creeks, on or near the line between this town and Russia, Dec. 30, 1781.

12 The census reports 3 churches in town; Evan. Luth., German Meth., and R. C.

13 This town contains a part of the third allotment of the Royal Grant, portions of Jerseyfield, Remsenburgh, and Machin's, and the whole of Lush's, Marvin's, and Jacob's Patents.

14 Hinckley & Ballou have an extensive sawmill, planing mill, blacksmith shop, trip hammer, and edge tool manufactory, employ 100 men, and turn out work to the amount of $80,000 annually.

loam and clay. **Russia,** (p. v.,) in the s. part, contains 2 churches and 140 inhabitants; **Gravesville,** (p. v.,) in the s. w., a church and 20 houses; **Poland,** (p. v.,) near the s. line, a church and 179 inhabitants; **Cold Brook,** (p. v.,) in the s. e., a saw set factory, cheese box factory, gristmill, and 218 inhabitants; **Booth,** (p. o.,) on Black Creek, a church, grist and saw mill, tannery, and 10 houses. **Prospect** is a hamlet, and contains — sawmills. The first settlement was commenced in 1792, by Stodard Squires, from Conn.[1] The first religious meetings (F. W. Bap.) were held by Rev. Benajah Corp.[2]

SALISBURY[3]—was formed from Palatine, (Montgomery co.,) March 3, 1797, and annexed from Montgomery co., April 7, 1817. It lies on the e. border of the co., and extends n. into the great wilderness. Only about one-fourth of its surface is cultivated. It is a broken and mountainous upland in the n. and hilly in the s. The principal streams are East Canada Creek, which forms a part of the e. boundary, and Spruce Creek, which flows through the s. w. and s. parts. The soil is a sandy and clayey loam. A bed of iron ore has been worked to some extent on Lot 105, fourth allotment of the Royal Grant. **Salisbury Center,** (p. v.,) in the s. part, contains 2 churches, a tannery, and 319 inhabitants; **Salisbury Corners,** (Salisbury p. o.,) in the s. w., 2 churches and 30 houses; **Diamond Hill,** 25 houses; **Devereaux,** 15 houses. **Whitesburgh,** (p. o.,) on the line of Fulton co., is a hamlet. Settlement was begun before the Revolution, by tenants of Sir Wm. Johnson, who followed his lead during the war, and shared his fate at the hands of the Commissioners of Forfeiture.[4] The census reports 4 churches in town[5]

SCHUYLER[6]—was formed from Herkimer, April 10, 1792. Trenton was taken off in 1797, Deerfield (Oneida co.) in 1798, and a part of Newport in 1806. A part was annexed from Herkimer in 1808, and re-annexed to Herkimer in 1811. It lies on the w. border of the co., n. of the Mohawk. Its surface is hilly. The Hasenclever Mts. extend through the center, attaining in this town an elevation of 1,000 to 1,200 ft. above tide. A wide intervale extends along the Mohawk, which forms the s. boundary. Its streams are tributaries of the Mohawk and generally flow through narrow ravines. The flats bordering the river are annually overflowed. The soil upon the hills is slaty and gravelly. **East Schuyler,** (p. v.,) in the s. e., contains 25 houses; and **West Schuyler,** (p. v.,) in the s. w., a church and 25 houses. Settlement was commenced previous to 1775, by several German families.[7] There was a good carriage road in 1757, on the bank of the river, from the crossing, where Utica now stands,[8] to the Palatine village, German Flats. There are 2 churches in town; M. E. and Meth. Prot.

STARK[9]—was formed from Danube, March 18, 1828. It is the s. e. corner town of the co. Its surface is hilly and broken, with a mean elevation of 500 feet above the Mohawk. The principal streams are Otsquago and Nowadaga Creeks. Otsquago Creek flows through a narrow valley, bordered by steep banks 150 to 200 ft. high. The soil is generally a sandy loam in the valleys, and sandy and gravelly on the hills. **Starkville,** (p. v.,) in the n. e. part, contains 2 churches, a gristmill, and 190 inhabitants; **Van Hornesville,** (p. v.,) in the s. part, 1 church, a cotton factory, (not in operation,) a grist and saw mill, and 228 inhabitants. **Smiths Corners** is a

---

[1] Jonathan Millington, from Vt., —— Smith, Farley Fuller, Geo. Taylor, Roscum Slocum, —— Austin & Son, Wm. Buck, Jeremiah Smith, Jotham Carpenter, —— Coon, and others, settled soon after; and, in 1794, many others came in. The first marriage was that of Farley Fuller and Minerva Smith, in 1794; the first death, that of a son of —— Allen, and the second, that of Waite Robinson. The first school was taught by —— Morehouse, at Graves Hollow, and another, about the same time, by —— Steuned. The first inn was kept by Jotham Carpenter, the first store by —— Swintburn, at Graves Hollow, in 1797. The first sawmill was built in 1797, and the first gristmill by Benj. Hinman, the same year. A cotton factory was built at Poland some years since.

[2] The census reports 4 churches in town; M. E., Presb., Union, and Univ.

[3] Named from Salisbury, Conn., whence many of the early settlers came. This town includes part of the Jerseyfield Patent, and parts of the first, second, and fourth allotments of the Royal Grant. Several of the Indian children of Sir Wm. Johnson had tracts of land assigned to them in this part of the Royal Grant,—viz.: William, 1,000 acres; Brant, 1,000; Anne, 3,000; Susan, 3,000; Mary, 2,000; George, 3,000; Margaret, 2,000; Magdalen, ——, and Elizabeth, ——. Of these children, the last three were convicted of adhering to the enemy; but, no record of conviction existing against the others, acts were passed by the Legislature, Feb. 26, 1796, and March 30, 1798, authorizing John Robinson, George Pearson, and James Coch-

ran, purchasers under the Commissioners of Forfeiture, to receive from the treasury the part of the purchase money which they had paid and convey back the lands.

[4] John Faville and Cornelius Lamberson settled about 1778, near Burrills Corners; Asa Sheldon and Abijah Ford about 1793. Abial Pratt, Stephen Todd, Jabez Ayers, Jonathan Cole, —— Bidwell, Ira Bartholomew, Atwater Cook, Amos Ives, Moses De Witt, —— Low, Jonathan Hallet, and others, were early settlers. John Ford was the first child born; Elizabeth Rice taught the first school; Aaron Hackley kept the first inn and store, at Burrill's Corners.

[5] 2 M. E., Bap., and Union.

[6] This town contains the whole of Kast's Patent and parts of Cosby's Manor and Hasenclever's and Walton's Patents.

[7] Among the early settlers were families named Kasts, Starrings, Widvig, Rymour, Lintz, and Bridenbecker. Judge Henri Starring (who is said to have granted the celebrated Yankee pass) formerly resided in this town. A store was kept on Cosby's Manor in 1766.

[8] In 1757, M. De Bellette, with a body of French and Indians, traversed this road, and burned every house upon it within the town.—*Benton's Herkimer,* p. 461.

[9] Named in honor of Gen. Stark, of the Revolution. Parts of Henderson's, L'Hommedieu's, Vaughan's, McNeil's, J. Vrooman's, C. Colden's, Livingston's, and Lansing's Patents are in this town.—*Benton's Herkimer, p.* 453.

hamlet. Small settlements were commenced before 1775, but were broken up during the Revolution.[1] The census reports 4 churches in town.[2]

WARREN[3]—was formed from German Flats, Feb. 5, 1796. Columbia was taken off in 1812. It lies centrally on the s. border of the co. Its surface is hilly, the highest points being 500 to 800 feet above the Mohawk. The principal stream is Fish Creek, which flows s., and is bordered by steep banks 100 to 200 ft. high. Mud Lake, in the E., and Weavers and Youngs Lakes, in the s., are small bodies of water. The soil is a sandy and clay loam. There are 2 small sulphur springs in town. **Jordanville** (p. v.) contains 2 churches and 125 inhabitants; **Pages Corners** (p. v.) a gristmill, sawmill, and 82 inhabitants; **Little Lakes**,[4] (Warren p. o.,) in the s. part, 1 church and 117 inhabitants. **Crains Corners** is a hamlet. Some settlements were commenced before the Revolution, by Germans from the Upper Valley.[5] Elder Phineas Holcomb was the first settled minister in town, about 1793.[6]

WILMURT[7]—was formed from Russia and *"West Brunswick,"* (now Ohio,) May 3, 1836. This is the largest town in the State, and is one of the least populous. It includes the whole N. part of the co., extending nearly 50 mi. in length, by about 16 mi. in breadth, entirely within the wild primeval forests of Northern New York. Its surface is rocky and mountainous, and the greater part is unfit for cultivation. In the deep valleys among the mountains are numerous beautiful, picturesque lakes, forming one of the finest features of the landscape.[8] The soil is a sandy loam. The hills are usually covered with a thin growth of forest trees; but in the valleys only is found soil fit for profitable pasturage. The settlements are confined to the s. part. There is no p. o., village, store, church, or gristmill in town. The lumber cut in this region is mostly floated down West Canada Creek, and manufactured at Prospect in the town of Russia. An attempt was made to settle the town in 1790, by Arthur Noble, the patentee, and a sawmill was built at that time; but the project failed. It was again tried in 1793, with no better success. Toward the close of the last century, John Brown, a wealthy capitalist of Providence, R. I., who owned a large tract in this town, made an attempt at settlement; but his project failed. In 1812 his son-in-law, Chas. T. Harrisoff, made another attempt to settle upon this tract. He built a forge and sawmill, and cleared 2,000 acres; but, the outlay bringing no return, and his supply of money from the E. being cut off, the project was abandoned, and the colonists returned to their respective homes.[9]

WINFIELD[10]—was formed from Litchfield, Richfield, (Otsego co.,) and Plainfield, (Otsego co.,) April 17, 1816. The bounds of the co. were enlarged upon the formation of this town. It is the s. w. corner town of the co. Its surface is moderately hilly, and forms the dividing upland between the Mohawk and Unadilla Valleys, the general elevation being about 500 feet above the Mohawk. A range of hills in the s. E. rises about 200 ft. higher. The E. branch of the Unadilla flows s. through a deep valley in the w. part. Browns Hollow Creek, a branch of the Mohawk, rises on the N. border. Near East Winfield is a sulphur spring; and several limestone quarries are found in different parts of the town. **East Winfield** (Winfield p. o.) contains 30 houses; **West Winfield** (p. v.) 2 churches, the West Winfield Academy, a bank, 2 gristmills, 2 saw-

[1] One of these settlements was on Otsquago Creek, and consisted of the families of John Shull, John Bronner, —— Tetherly, and others. Another settlement was commenced at The Kyle, so called.—*Benton's Herkimer*, p. 463. The families of Walwrath, Adam Young, and others, were early settlers. Abraham Van Horne, from N.J., settled in town in 1791, at what is now Van Hornesville. The first German school was taught by —— Garner, and the first English school by —— Haight. Abraham Van Horne built the first mills, soon after his settlement, and his sons kept the first store.

[2] Bap., Bap. and Luth., M. E., and Union.

[3] Named from Gen. Joseph Warren, of the Revolution. This town embraces the principal part of Henderson and Theobald Young's Patents.

[4] Called by the Indians Wa-i-on-tha.

[5] Andrewstown, in the N. part,—then containing 7 families,—was plundered and burned by Brant in July, 1778. A part of the inhabitants were killed, and the remainder carried away captive. Young's settlement at the Lakes was spared by the Indians on account of the tory principles of the proprietor; but the Americans soon after plundered and burned this place in retaliation. In March, 1792, Samuel Cleland, from Mass., and his sons Norman, Salmon, Jonas, Martin, and Moses, settled in town. Danforth Abbott, Hugh Panell, Amos Allen, Elder Phineas Holcomb, Richard Schooley Hull, Thomas, James, and Garret Abeel, and —— Thayer were early settlers. Stephen Luddington kept the first inn, Outhout & Vrooman the first store, and Isaac Freeman built the first gristmill, in 1795.

[6] The census reports 6 churches; 4 M. E., Bap., and Ref. Prot. D.

[7] This immense town embraces parts of the Remsenburgh and Vrooman's Patents, Adgate's, Brown's, Nobleborough, Moose River, and Watson's Tracts, and Totten and Crossfield's Purchase. Brown's tract, owned by L. R. Lyon and others, embraces 210,000 acres, and extends across the co. into Hamilton and Lewis cos.

[8] Nos. 1 to 4 of the Fulton chain of lakes are sources of Moose River; Transparent, Woodhull, Bisby, and Chub Lakes flow into Black River. Several of these lakes are used as reservoirs for the canal. Upon the shores are large quantities of iron sand, derived from the abrasion of the rocks containing iron ore.

[9] Harrisoff continued upon the land until Dec. 19, 1819, when, disappointed at his immense losses and the utter ruin before him, he committed suicide. It is said that the day before his death he made preparations for going to Providence, and gave particular orders for his men to go out the next morning after he left and fill up a large hole that had been dug for ore. They went out to perform their labor; but one of them went down to see if any tools had been left, and at the bottom he found Harrisoff, who had secreted himself there, intending to be buried. The next day he accomplished his object by a pistol shot.

[10] Named from Gen. Winfield Scott. This town comprised within its limits parts of Bayard's, Lispenard's, and Schuyler's Patents.

mills, a clover mill, and tannery. Pop. 381. **North Winfield** is a p. o. The first settlement was commenced in 1792.[1] The census reports 3 churches.[2]

Acres of Land, Valuation, Population, Dwellings, Families, Freeholders, Schools, Live Stock, Agricultural Products, and Domestic Manufactures, of Herkimer County.

Names of Towns.	Acres of Land.		Valuation of 1858.			Population.		No. of Dwellings.	No. of Families.	Freeholders.	Schools.	
	Improved.	Unimproved.	Real Estate.	Personal Property.	Total.	Males.	Females.				No. of Districts.	Children taught.
Columbia	15,668	5,134½	$303,103	$59,390	362,493	742	889	352	397	304	11	657
Danube	13,719	3,333	402,033	74,567	476,600	987	804	295	296	188	9	671
Fairfield	18,443½	5,402	584,358	157,523	741,881	746	747	266	265	440	13	470
Frankfort	15,511½	5,058	492,357	96,850	589,207	1,639	1,578	658	648	407	14	1,249
German Flats	14,406¼	5,429	488,203	324,940	813,143	1,983	1,872	725	783	506	11	1,340
Herkimer	13,371	4,945½	538,960	151,527	690,487	1,447	1,419	447	487	303	12	968
Litchfield	13,329	4,118	1,115,564	385,338	1,500,902	829	753	298	319	207	10	611
Little Falls	12,359	3,686	257,106	44,761	301,867	2,424	2,506	726	922	413	10	1,958
Manheim	14,657	2,741	694,744	78,555	773,299	858	814	304	315	207	8	536
Newport	15,233	4,289½	365,130	105,550	470,680	995	1,020	369	407	283	9	652
Norway	14,604¼	5,477¾	245,470	66,530	312,000	535	524	182	207	150	10	410
Ohio	6,351¼	14,201	128,225	4,089	132,314	582	505	194	191	185	7	483
Russia	20,360	14,869	369,052	78,754	447,806	1,175	1,113	424	448	374	17	817
Salisbury	17,218¼	47,598	541,594	72,000	613,594	1,204	1,102	448	466	336	14	834
Schuyler	17,507	4,871	565,741	32,005	597,746	842	848	295	317	196	11	658
Stark	14,187	3,903	286,753	64,697	351,450	744	734	272	303	224	9	483
Warren	17,119½	5,954¼	433,404	194,218	627,622	890	851	335	297	281	11	588
Wilmurt	705	361,859	273,708	165,410	439,118	180	88	38	42	29	2	73
Winfield	12,665	2,788	74,624		74,624	691	706	270	286	186	9	629
Total	267,414½	505,657½	8,160,129	2,156,704	10,316,833	19,693	18,873	6,898	7,396	5,219	187	13,887

Names of Towns.	Live Stock.					Agricultural Products.							Domestic cloths, in Yards.
						Bush. of Grain.					Dairy Products.		
	Horses.	Working Oxen and Calves.	Cows.	Sheep.	Swine.	Winter.	Spring.	Tons of Hay.	Bushels of Potatoes.	Bushels of Apples.	Pounds Butter.	Pounds Cheese.	
Columbia	706	802	1,801	2,134	893	516	81,013½	4,500	18,572	27,029	79,985	353,309	1,237
Danube	539	840	1,937	1,224	1,208	3,101	76,929	3,931½	10,794	14,416	62,090	343,125	1,045
Fairfield	429	723	3,753	621	1,485	94	44,811	6,982	8,609	37,772	76,523	1,238,820	545½
Frankfort	679	893	1,359	1,576	1,247	1,303	94,536½	4,610	21,008	21,828	111,708	78,365	1,002¾
German Flats	667	1,095	1,524	1,105	1,004	5,381	63,435	3,649	12,053	17,687	54,377	285,500	759
Herkimer	614	703	2,266	862	1,387	3,803	65,234	4,201	10,338	20.626	93,541	379,200	1,366
Litchfield	436	832	1,676	952	930	60	67,191	3,880	18,623	36,411	73,825	395,679	340
Little Falls	469	711	2,176	449	1,271	1,596	47,542½	4,939	10,412	17,515	59,270	587,500	204
Manheim	451	713	3,320	363	1,390	573	44,428	7,234	11,344	15,174	87,533	1,087,200	605
Newport	374	517	2,688	340	1,263	505	49,227¼	3,786	12,598	21,256	70,530	829,989	620
Norway	257	389	2,137	154	652	280	27,596¾	3,294½	11,751	8,635	38,145	549,823	530
Ohio	219	392	500	331	201	92	19,143½	1,149½	11,101	33	30,550	58,220	758
Russia	525	729	2,326	1,062	821	1,417	73,679	3,978	24,386	17,175	94,651	561,425	1,483
Salisbury	453	842	1,827	491	734	187	48,823¾	5,283¼	16,298	9,310	65,219	694,500	1,001
Schuyler	644	717	2,296	1,009	1,461	2,900	145,510	4,181	18,370	14,224	76,000	585,450	755½
Stark	603	742	1,540	1,321	919	1,241½	90,309½	2,841½	7,563	16,586	90,140	140,205	660
Warren	673	872	1,917	2,904	835	109	76,403	5,306	17,009	19,782	83,135	374,299	1,158½
Wilmurt	29	34	46	39	19	50	2,349	87½	1,021		3,350	700	40
Winfield	331	621	1,564	769	507	246	55,115	4,421	16,025	18,442	54,805	525,210	
Total	9,098	13,167	36,653	17,706	18,227	23,454½	1,170,277¼	78,254¾	257,875	333,901	1,305,377	9,068,519	14,110¼

[1] Among the early settlers were Jos. Walker, Timothy Walker, Capt. Nathan Brown, Oliver Harwood, Oliver Corbit, Benj. Cole, and Dea. Gile, from Mass. Abel Brace came in from Conn. in 1793. Josiah Harwood taught the first school, in 1794; Charles Brace kept the first inn, in 1794; John Dillingham the first store, in 1796. Joseph Walker built the first saw and grist mill, soon after his settlement; Benj. Harrington built the first clothing works, at West Winfield, about 1800.

[2] M. E., Cong., and Bap.

JEFFERSON COUNTY.

This county was formed from Oneida, March 28, 1805, and named in honor of Thomas Jefferson. Its bounds have been changed by setting off a portion of Rodman to Lewis co. in 1809, and by annexing a portion of Lewis co. to Wilna in 1813. It lies in the angle formed by the St. Lawrence River and Lake Ontario, is distant 145 mi. from Albany, and contains 1868 sq. mi. The s. w. part is marshy, but at a short distance from the lake the land rises in gentle undulations, and, farther inland, by abrupt terraces, to the highest point, in the town of Worth. A plateau, about 1000 feet above the lake, spreads out from the summit, and extends into Oswego and Lewis cos. An ancient lake beach, 390 feet above the present level of the lake, may be traced through Ellisburgh, Adams, Watertown, and Rutland. North of the Black River the surface is generally flat or slightly undulating: in the extreme N. E. corner it is broken by low ridges parallel to the St. Lawrence. With the exception of a few isolated hills, no part of this region is as high as the ancient lake ridge mentioned above.[1]

The rocks of the co. belong to the primary formation and the lower strata of the N. Y. system. Gneiss is the underlying rock of the E. border in Wilna and Antwerp, of the Thousand Islands and the shore at Alexandria Bay, and of two strips of land extending from the E. border, one toward Theresa Falls, and the other toward Evans Mills. Next above this is a thick deposit of Potsdam sandstone, extending through Wilna, Antwerp, Philadelphia, Theresa, Alexandria, Orleans, and Clayton, the margin of which may be traced along its entire extent by a low mural precipice. The soil upon this rock is thin, and principally derived from drift deposits. The rock itself is almost indestructible, and preserves diluvial scratches and marks with great distinctness. Above this is a thin deposit of calciferous sandstone, extending through parts of Cape Vincent, Lyme, Clayton, Orleans, and Le Ray. The soil upon this rock is deeper than that upon the Potsdam sandstone, and is derived principally from disintegration. The Black River limestone overlies this, and forms the surface rock in most of the remaining parts of the co. N. of the river, and in a part of Champion and Rutland, s. Above this is the Trenton limestone, appearing on the lake shore at Cape Vincent and extending in a s. E. direction through Lyme, Brownsville, Watertown, Rutland, and Champion. This rock is of great thickness, and it forms the principal declivities of the plateau in the s. part of the co. About midway in this strata is found the ancient lake ridge before noticed. The caves near Watertown are in the lower strata of this rock. Next above come the Utica slate and Lorraine shales, forming the summit of the irregular table land which covers the s. "peak" of Champion, the s. border of Rutland, the greater part of Rodman, a corner of Adams, the E. part of Ellisburgh, and the whole of Lorraine and Worth. These shales are easily decomposed, and produce a deep, rich soil. Along the streams that flow from this formation the water has worn deep and often highly picturesque ravines, sometimes miles in length, and almost through the soft and yielding strata. The rounded outline of the slate hills, the abrupt terraces of the limestone, and the sharp, wall like margins of the sandstone, afford characteristic features to the country underlaid by these several formations. Alluvial deposits uniformly occur where the streams from the slate flow out upon the limestone; and drift deposits are scattered promiscuously over the whole co. The most remarkable of these is the "Pine Plains," a sand barren several miles in extent in Wilna and Le Ray. The lake shore in Ellisburgh consists of drifting sand, behind which are marshes. From Stony Point to Cape Vincent the shore is bordered by the level edges of the Trenton limestone; but farther down the river it presents that alternation of rounded ridges of rocks, intervales, and marshes peculiar to the primary formation. The highest point in Worth is about 1200 feet above the lake. The streams are Black,[2] Indian, and Perch Rivers, the two Sandy Creeks,[3] Stony, Catfish, Kent, French, Pleasant, and Black Creeks, and their tributaries. Hungry Bay[4] (including Henderson,

---

[1] An isolated hill in Pamelia formerly bore a crop of red cedar; and, as this timber is now only found upon the islands in the lake, it is supposed that the hill was an island at a time when at least three fourths of the county was covered by water.

[2] Indian name Ka-hu-ah'-go, great or wide river.
[3] Called by the Indians Te-ka'-da-o-ga'-he, sloping banks.
[4] Called by the French "La Famine."

Black River, and Chaumont Bays) has a coast line of great length; and the Thousand Islands present many attractions from their romantic scenery and historical associations. Several small lakes, filling deep gorges, in Antwerp, Theresa and Alexandria,—one in Rutland, two in Henderson, Perch Lake in Pamelia and Orleans, and Pleasant Lake in Champion, constitute the other waters of the co. Iron ore abounds in Antwerp. Traces of lead and copper are found in the primary region; limestone, capable of a great variety of uses, water limestone and barytes are also abundant. The Black River enters the co. at Carthage, where commence a series of cascades and rapids which continue almost to the lake, with a total fall of 480 feet. Indian River affords water power at half a dozen places, and most of the streams s. of Black River are available for the same purpose.

The flat country along the St. Lawrence at times is affected by drouth, which is never felt on the uplands; while the latter are somewhat noted for the great depth of their snows. The mirage has been frequently seen on the lake, bringing into view places beyond the horizon. One form of this refraction, in which a line of clear sky appears along the shore, is almost a constant attendant upon clear, pleasant days in summer. Waterspouts, attended with dark clouds and a roaring noise, have been seen upon the lake and its bays. In the primary regions the intervales are remarkably fertile, while the ridges are often naked rock. The soil over a part of the sandstone is too thin for cultivation, but the barren region is comparatively limited. The limestone and slate districts are exceedingly fertile, and particularly adapted to dairying and the raising of spring grains. Of these, barley, within a few years, has become the most important. Winter wheat is raised less than formerly; oats, corn, rye, and peas are staple products. For many years manufactures have received much attention and employed a large amount of capital. They consist of iron from the ore, castings, machinery, cotton and woolen fabrics, paper, leather, and flour, and have been chiefly carried on along the line of the Black River, and in Antwerp, Theresa, Philadelphia, Adams, and Ellisburgh. Rafting, shipbuilding, and lake commerce form prominent pursuits at several points along the St. Lawrence.

Upon the erection of the co., in 1805, Watertown was selected for the co. seat.[1] A combined courthouse and jail was erected in 1807 and burned in 1821. Soon after, separate buildings, of stone, were erected, which are still in use. In 1816 a fireproof clerk's office was built, and occupied until 1831, when the present one was erected. The jail having become unfit for use, and having been officially complained of, a writ was issued, Dec. 1, 1848, by the Supreme Court, ordering its immediate improvement.[2] This led to the erection of an additional building, with excellent arrangements for both the security and convenience of prisoners. The first poorhouse was erected on the Dudley Farm, in Le Ray, about 5 mi. N. of Watertown, in 1825; and it was used until 1833, when the present spacious buildings were erected in Pamelia, 1 mi. below Watertown. In 1852 a special act was passed for the supervision of the poor in this co.

The first newspaper in the co., called the "American Eagle," was established at Watertown, in 1814, by Henry Coffeen. Its name was soon after changed to the "American Advocate."[3]

---

[1] The commissioners appointed for the selection of the co. seat by the Gov. and Council were Matthew Dorr, David Rodgers, and John Van Benthuysen. The first court and the first board of supervisors met at a schoolhouse on the site of the present Univ. Church. The first co. officers were Augustus Sacket, *First Judge;* Joshua Bealls and Perley Keyes, *Judges;* Thomas White, Lyman Ellis, Wm. Hunter, and Ethni Evans, *Assistant Justices;* Henry Coffeen, *Clerk;* Abel Sherman, *Sheriff;* Benj. Skinner, *Surrogate and Treasurer;* and Hart Massy, Ambrose Pease, and Fairchild Hubbard, *Coroners.* At the time of its erection most of the taxes of the co. were paid by non-residents.

[2] In 1807 the jail liberties were first established, which were so extraordinary as to demand a passing notice. "They covered a small space around the courthouse and part of the public square, and included most of the houses of the village; while between these localities, along the sides of the roads, and sometimes in the center, were *paths,* from 4 to 8 feet wide, with occasional crossings; so that, by carefully observing his route, turning right angles, and keeping himself in the strict ranges which the court had established, a prisoner might visit nearly every building in the village; but if the route was, by any accident, obstructed, by a pile of lumber, a pool of mud, or a loaded wagon, he must pass over, through, or under, or else expose himself to the peril of losing this precarious freedom, by close imprisonment, and subjecting his bail to prosecution for the violation of his trust."—*Hough's Hist. of Jeff. Co.,* p. 31.

[3] The *Jefferson and Lewis Gazette* was started at Watertown in 1817 by D. Abbey & J. H. Lord, Jr., and continued until 1819.

The *Independent Republican,* commenced in 1819 by S. A. Abbey, was continued until 1825.

The *Herald of Salvation,* semi-mo., (Univ.) was commenced in 1822 by Rev. Pitt Morse, and continued 2 years.

The *Watertown Freeman* was established in 1824, and continued until 1833, and was then changed to The *Democratic Standard.* In July, 1835, it was united with the Watertown Eagle, and became The *Eagle and Standard.*

Thursday's Post was commenced in 1826 by Theron Parsons & Co., and in 1828 sold to Henry L. Harvey, who changed it to The *Register.* It was afterward united with the *Genius of Philanthropy,* and in 1830 it became the *Watertown Register and General Advertiser.* In 1831 it passed into the hands of B. Cory, and in 1835 it was changed to the *North American.* It was published by J. Huxton a short time, and afterward by H. S. Noble, by whom in 1839 it was issued as The *Watertown Register.* In 1843 Joel Green became proprietor, and changed it to The *Black River Journal,* and continued it until 1846. The *Genius of Philanthropy* was started in 1828 by Henry L. Harvey, and was afterward united with *The Register.* The *Censor* was started at Adams in 1828, by Theron Parsons, and was soon after removed to Watertown. In 1830, Enoch E. Camp became its proprietor, and changed it to The *Anti-Masonic Sun.* Shortly after, Dr. R. Goodale, becoming proprietor, changed it to The *Constellation,* and continued it until 1832, when it passed into the hands of Abner Morton, who published it as The *Jefferson Reporter* until 1834. It was then discontinued.

This co. is all embraced in the Macomb purchase[1] of 1791, except the islands in the lake and river, a small reservation at Tibbetts Point near Cape Vincent, and a tract 10 mi. square, with one corner extending to the St. Lawrence at French Creek, reserved by the Oneida Indians in the treaty of 1788 for Peter Penet, and called "Penets Square." That part N. of a line running E. from Chaumont Bay, in the line of the S. bounds of Diana, was known as Great Tract No. IV., and was sold to the "Antwerp Company," of Holland. Gouverneur Morris became the first agent, and afterward Jas. D. Le Ray de Chaumont became extensively interested in the title, and under him much of it was settled. The land between No. IV. and Black River (210,000 acres) was purchased by Peter Chassanis, of Paris, for a company of capitalists; a romantic scheme of colonization was formed, and settlement begun at its southern point, near the High Falls, in Lewis co. A few years after, the emigrants returned to France. Ellisburgh was mostly purchased by Marvel Ellis, of Troy, in March, 1797, but it afterward reverted to Constable. A tract known as the "Eleven Towns" was purchased in 1795 by Nicholas Low, Wm. Henderson, Richard Harrison, and Josiah Ogden Hoffman: it was divided by them and sold by their agents. Penets Square was mostly settled by squatters, with whom the owners afterward had much difficulty. With the exception of Carlton Island, the first settlement in the co. was made in Ellisburgh, in 1797, and within 10 years nearly the whole of this town and of the "Eleven Towns" was taken up by actual settlers. Settlement commenced under Le Ray in Wilna, Antwerp, Le Ray, and Philadelphia, about 1806, and in the N. part of the co., along the St. Lawrence, after the war of 1812–15. But a small part is now owned by the original purchasers or their heirs, much the greater portion having long been owned in fee by actual settlers.[2]

The embargo and non-intercourse laws were quite unpopular along the N. frontier, and met with open hostility or secret evasion in many cases. The declaration of war filled the co. with alarm, and some families hastily prepared to leave. Ft. Carlton,[3] within the American boundary, had been held until this time by the British, and was immediately captured by a small volunteer party and the buildings burned. A regiment of drafted militia, under Col. C. P. Bellinger, was stationed at Sackets Harbor in May. A fleet of 5 sail of the enemy was repulsed from that place July 19, with loss. On the 30th Capt. Forsyth was stationed there with a fine company

The Independent Republican and Anti Masonic Recorder was published at Watertown, from 1828 until 1830.

The Voice of Jefferson was published during the summer and fall of 1828.

The Watertown Eagle was commenced in Sept. 1832, by J. Calhoun. In 1833 Alvin Hunt became associate editor; and in 1835 it was united with the *Democratic Standard,* and issued as

The Eagle and Standard. In 1837 it was changed to

The Jeffersonian, and afterward to

The Watertown Jeffersonian, and continued until 1855, when it was united with the *Democratic Union,* and appeared as

The Jefferson County Union. By this title it is now published by E. J. Clark & Co.

The Veto was published during the campaign of 1832.

The Spirit of Seventy Six was published a few months in 1834.

The Patriot and Democrat was published during the campaign of 1838.

The Aurora was published by Alvin Hunt during the campaign of 1840.

The Daily Journal was started in 1843, by Joel Greene. It was soon after changed to

The Watertown Journal, tri-w., and continued until 1846.

The Democratic Union was started in 1846, by T. Andrews, and continued until 1855, when it was united with *The Jeffersonian.*

The Northern State Journal was started in August, 1846, by Ambrose W. Clark. It was afterward changed to

The Northern New York Journal, and is now published by A. W. Clark.

The Watertown Spectator was established in Jan. 1847, by Joel Greene, and continued until 1849.

The New York Reformer was commenced in Aug. 1850, by Ingals, Burdick & Co., and is now published by Ingals & Haddock. They also publish

The Daily News, commenced in March, 1859.

The Daily Jeffersonian was published about 6 mo. in 1851.

The Monitor and *The Student* were issued a short time. All of the above were published at Watertown.

The Sackets Harbor Gazette and Advertiser, the first paper published at Sackets Harbor, was commenced in March, 1817, by Geo. Camp. In Feb. 1821, it was changed to

The Jefferson Republican, and was continued about a year.

The Farmers Advocate was started in 1824, by Truman W. Hascall, and continued until 1828.

The Courier, afterward called

The Sackets Harbor Courier, was published by J. Howe.

The Jefferson County Whig was published in 1837, by E. H. Purdy.

The Sackets Harbor Journal was established in Oct. 1838, by E. M. Luff, and continued until 1851.

The Harrisonian was published by E. M. Luff during the campaign of 1840.

The Sackets Harbor Observer was founded in March, 1848, by O. H. Harris. In 1852 it was changed to

The Jefferson Farmer, and continued 2 or 3 years.

The Carthaginian was started at Carthage in Dec. 1839, and in 1843 it was changed to

The Black River Times. It was discontinued soon after.

The People's Press was commenced in 1847 by M. F. Wilson.

The Carthage Standard has been published since Jan. 1858, by W. R. Merrill.

The Jefferson County Democrat was established at Adams in June, 1844, by E. C. Hatch. In 1847 it passed into the hands of E. J. Clark. It is now published, as

The Jefferson County News, by J. Eddy.

The Theresa Chronicle was started Jan. 14, 1848, by E. C. Burt, at Theresa, and continued about 6 months.

Le Phare des Lacs (the Beacon of the Lakes) was commenced at Watertown, in May, 1859, by Petit & Grandpre.

The Cape Vincent Gazette was commenced in 1858 by P. A. Leach.

[1] Alexander Macomb, Daniel McCormick, and Wm. Constable, of New York, were the parties owning this purchase. The first two failed, and Constable became chief agent and party to the sales that were subsequently made.—*Hough's Hist. St. Law. Co.*

[2] The present names of these towns are in most cases different from those applied by the landholders. Their names, numbers, and owners under the allotment of 1796 are as follows. Harrison and Hoffman held their interests in common several years later.

No.	Original Names.	Present Names.	Owners
1.	Hesiod.	Hounsfield.	Har. & Hoff.
2.	Leghorn.	Watertown.	Low.
3.	Milan.	Rutland.	Henderson.
4.	Howard.	Champion.	Har. & Hoff.
5.	Mantua.	Denmark.	Har. & Hoff.
6.	Henderson.	Henderson.	Henderson.
7.	Aleppo.	Adams.	Low.
8.	Orpheus.	Rodman.	Har. & Hoff.
9.	Handel.	Pinckney.	Henderson.
10.	Platina.	Harrisburgh.	Har. & Hoff.
11.	Lowville.	Lowville.	Low.

The several tracts were appraised by Benj. Wright, of Rome, the surveyor, and their value equalized from a part of Worth.

[3] On Carlton or Buck Island. It was built by the French, and during the Revolution was an important rendezvous for scalping parties of tories and Indians.

of riflemen, and, Sept. 20, made a descent upon Gananoqui, Canada, and destroyed a large quantity of provisions. The details of the operations upon the N.· frontier belong to general history. Sackets Harbor became the principal seat of military and naval preparations, and from this post were fitted out the armaments that captured Little York and Ft. George, and the disgraceful expedition, under Gen. Wilkinson, that descended the St. Lawrence late in the fall of 1813.[1] Large bodies of troops were stationed here during most of the war; and a fleet of frigates of the largest class was fitted out at this point, to cope with one, equally formidable, built at Kingston. The enemy were repulsed in an attack upon Sackets Harbor, May 29, 1813, and were subsequently defeated at Cranberry Creek and Sandy Creek and in several minor engagements. After the war the costly navy was left to rot, or was sold for commercial purposes; and, in accordance with the provisions of the convention of April, 1817, but one armed vessel was left afloat upon the lake. Extensive barracks were built in 1816-19 at Sackets Harbor. A considerable body of regular troops was stationed here until withdrawn for service in the Indian wars of the Northwest and of Florida. In the abortive scheme known as the "Patriot War," in 1837-40, this co. became the scene of intense excitement, and the seat of many grave as well as ludicrous events. "Hunter Lodges" were formed in every village to promote the Patriot cause, and large sums raised for the same purpose found their way into the pockets of the leaders, most of whom evinced a cowardice as little creditable to their honor as was their financial management to their honesty.

The earliest market of this co. was down the St. Lawrence, which has ever been the route of the lumber trade. Several State roads were built through the co. before the war, and a military road was laid out and partly worked from Sackets Harbor to Plattsburgh. Soon after the introduction of canals and railroads many projects of internal improvement were formed, and surveys were made in this co., without result. The Watertown and Rome R. R. extends from Cape Vincent s. through Lyme, Brownville, Pamelia, Watertown, Adams, and Ellisburgh, connecting with the N. Y. Central at Rome. The Sackets Harbor and Ellisburgh R. R., a branch of the preceding, extends from Sackets Harbor through Henderson to Pierrepont Manor. The Potsdam and Watertown R. R. extends N. E. from Watertown through Pamelia, Le Ray, Philadelphia, and Antwerp, forming a connection with the Ogdensburgh R. R. in Potsdam. In 1848-51 about 170 mi. of plank road were built within the co., by over 20 companies; but most of the lines have been surrendered to the towns in which the roads were laid. Steam navigation commenced upon Lake Ontario in 1816, and commodious lines have since been run, touching at Sackets Harbor, Cape Vincent, Clayton, and Alexandria Bay, within this co.

---

[1] The following is a chronological list of the principal events which took place at Sackets Harbor and vicinity during the war:—

1812, May.—The *Lord Nelson*, a British schooner, was taken, and condemned, for violating the revenue laws. Her name was changed to "Scourge."

" Col. C. P. Bellinger was stationed here with a regiment of militia.

" June 14, Schooner *Ontario* taken, and discharged.

" July 19, Village attacked by 5 vessels of the enemy. No injury done to the Americans, and the British retired with loss.

" July 30, Capt. Benj. Forsyth arrived with the first regular troops.

" July 31, Schooner *Julia* sailed for Ogdensburgh, and encountered 2 hostile vessels at Morristown.

" Aug. 20, Col. Bellinger's regiment were disbanded before they were paid.

" Sept. 20, Capt. Forsyth started upon an expedition against Gananoqui.

" Sept. 21, Gen. Dodge arrived, and ordered Gen. Brown to proceed to Ogdensburgh.

" Oct.· Commodore Chauncey and Gov. Tompkins arrived, the former having been appointed commander of the naval forces on the lake.

" Oct. 12, Capt. Forsyth's company and others were sent to Ogdensburgh.

" Nov.8-14, Com. Chauncey cruised upon the lake before Kingston, and took several vessels.

" Nov. 26, Ship *Madison* was launched 45 days after commencement. Fort Tompkins and barracks were completed about the same time.

1813, March.—Gen. Dearborn arrived and took command.

" April 7, Brig *Jefferson* launched.

" " 10, Brig *Jones* launched.

" " 19, The *Growler* sailed to reconnoiter.

" " 22, Gen. Pike's forces embarked for Little York.

" " 25, Expedition sailed.

" May 13, Expedition returned laden with spoils.

" " 22, Com. Chauncey sailed with the fleet for Niagara.

" " 29, Sackets Harbor attacked by the enemy, who were repulsed with the loss of 150 men. The Americans lost a large quantity of military

stores, including the spoils of Little York, from the accidental burning of the storehouse.

1813, June 1, Com. Chauncey returned with the fleet.

" " 12, Ship *Pike* launched.

" " 14, Lieut. Wolcott Chauncey went on a cruise, and took a schooner laden with stores and arms.

" July 2,—Maj. Gen. Morgan Lewis arrived and took command.

" " 3, A secret expedition to burn the *Pike* was defeated.

" " 14, The *Neptune* and *Fox* sailed on a privateering expedition down the St. Lawrence. (See p 355.)

" " 20, Com. Chauncey, with the *Pike*, sailed for Niagara. The *Sylph* (built in 33 days) accompanied him.

" Aug. 26, Gen. Wilkinson held a council to decide upon offensive measures.

" Sept. 5, Gen. Armstrong, Sec. of War, arrived.

" Oct. 26, Gen. Wilkinson sailed on an expedition down the St. Lawrence, with disastrous results.

" Nov. 2, The *Pike* and other armed vessels sailed on a cruise among the Thousand Islands.

Dec. and Jan. The remaining part of the fall and winter was spent in ship building and in strengthening fortifications.

1814, May 1.—Frigate *Superior*, of 66 guns, was launched in 80 days from the commencement of building.

" June 15, The crew of the ship *Congress* began to arrive from Portsmouth.

" " " An expedition under Lieut. Gregory sailed, and a few days after captured the gunboat *Black Snake* in the St. Lawrence, for which act Congress awarded $3000 in 1834.

" " 26, Another expedition, under the same, sailed, and in a few days burned a vessel on the stocks and a quantity of stores near Prescott.

" July 31, The American fleet sailed for Niagara.

" Sept. 14, Gen. Izard arrived from Lake Champlain.

" " 30, A gig belonging to the *Superior* captured several boats laden with goods for Kingston.

" Oct. Great alarm was felt for the safety of the harbor, which led to the assembling of large bodies of militia.

ADAMS[1]—was formed from Mexico, April 1, 1802, and named in honor of John Adams, Ex-President. Rodman was taken off in 1804. It is an interior town, lying s. w. of the center of the co. Its surface is rolling, and generally inclined toward the lake, and, with the exception of its s. e. border, is underlaid by Trenton limestone. Several remarkable upheavals of this formation occur along its n. and w. borders, and a bold terrace extends into Watertown and Rutland. It is well watered by the N. Sandy and Stony Creeks. The soil is a clayey loam, with occasional sand and gravel, especially along the ancient lake ridge, which may be traced through this town. It is very productive, and equally adapted to dairying and the cultivation of grains. Manufactures are carried on to some extent. **Adams,** (p. v.,) situated on North Sandy Creek and the W. & R. R. R., contains 4 churches, a bank, a seminary, printing office, and several small manufactories. Pop. 1,268.[2] **Adams Center** (p. v.) and **Smithville** (p. v.) have each about 250 inhabitants. **Appling**[3] and **North Adams** (p. o.) are hamlets. The town was mostly settled under Isaac W. Bostwick, agent of Nicholas Low, the proprietor.[4] The first sermon was preached in 1802, by Rev. Mr. Woodward, a missionary.[5] A private academy—now called the Philharmonic Institute—has been taught at Adams Village for many years. The remains of several ancient fortifications are found in town.

ALEXANDRIA—was formed from Brownville and Le Ray, April 3, 1821, and named from Alexander Le Ray, a son of the proprietor. Theresa was taken off in 1841. It lies on the St. Lawrence, in the n. extremity of the co., and embraces the e. part of Wells Island and a considerable portion of the Thousand Islands. The surface underlaid by gneiss is rough and rocky, but that portion underlaid by sandstone is level, with a thin, clayey and sandy soil. A vein of lead has been discovered near Redwood, and examined to the depth of 40 feet. **Alexandria Bay**[6] (Alexandria p. o.) contains 24 houses, **Plessis**[7] (p. v.) 32, and **Redwood**[8] (p. v.) 429 inhabitants. Settlement commenced in 1811, under Le Ray. An engagement took place within the limits of this town during the war of 1812.[9] An elegant Ref. Prot. D. church was erected at Alexandria Bay in 1848–51.[10]

ANTWERP—was formed from Le Ray, April 5, 1810, and named from the Antwerp Company.[11] It is the extreme e. town in the co. The n. and e. portions are broken by low rocky ridges parallel to the river. The s. w. part is more level. The soil in the valleys is a clayey loam, and is very fertile.[12] The ridges are made up of masses of gneiss,[13] white crystalline limestone,[14] and sandstone.[15] Between the gneiss and sandstone in this town are several of the richest iron mines in the State. The "Sterling Mine"[16] lies about 3 mi. N. of Antwerp Village; another, of less extent, 1 mi. N.; a third, known as the "Keene Mine,"[17] on the borders of St. Lawrence co.; and a fourth, known as the "Parish Mine,"[18] immediately adjacent. In this same range are found the mines of Rossie and Gouverneur, which have furnished most of the ore used at the furnaces in this region. Bog iron ore is found near Ox Bow.[19] One or two sulphur springs are found in town. **Antwerp,** (p. v.,) on the P. and W. R. R., was incorp. July, 1853. It contains

---

[1] Aleppo, or No. 7 of the Eleven Towns.

[2] This village was first settled by David Smith, about 1800, and for many years it was known as "*Smiths Mills*." Incorp. Nov. 11, 1851.

[3] Named from Maj. Daniel Appling, the hero of the battle of Sandy Creek.

[4] The first settlers came on for permanent residence in 1800; among them were Nicholas and Alexander Salisbury, Solomon Smith, Daniel Comstock, Daniel Smith, Abram Ripley, Jonathan Cable, Stephen Shippey, and Enon D'Estaing. The first inn was kept by Abel Hart, and the first store by Jesse Hale. Daniel Smith erected the first grist and saw mills in 1801–02, the former superseding the stump mortars of the first season. The first birth was that of Edmund Salisbury; the first marriage, that of Daniel Ellis to Mrs. A. Salisbury, widow of Alexander Salisbury, in 1802; and the first death, that of Alexander Salisbury, drowned in 1801. Schools were first taught in 1803.

[5] Rev. Chas. G. Finney, Pres. of Oberlin College, was a law student in this town. The census reports 9 churches; 3 Bap., 2 Seventh Day Bap., 2 Cong., M. E., and Prot. E.

[6] This place was surveyed and laid out as a village for Le Ray in 1818. A custom house was established here in 1828. Sunken Rock Lighthouse was built in 1847. It is an important wooding station for steamers, and within a few years has become a favorite resort for fishing and excursion parties among the Thousand Islands.

[7] Named from a town in France. Formerly called "*Flat Rock*," from the naked sandstone in the vicinity. A grist mill was built here in 1817 for Le Ray. Wm. Merrill, the first innkeeper, was murdered in 1826.

[8] A glass factory was established at this place in 1833, by John S. Foster. It is devoted to the manufacture of cylinder glass, and is now carried on by a joint stock company known

as the Redwood Manufac. Co. A stream a few rods in length, flowing from Mud to Butterfield Lake, has here a fall of 94 feet, and furnishes water power to a grist and saw mill.

[9] The "Neptune" and "Fox," two small American armed vessels, captured a brigade of bateaux belonging to the enemy, July 20, 1813, and took their prizes into Cranberry Creek, in this town. They were pursued, and a sharp skirmish ensued, resulting in the retreat of the British with considerable loss.

[10] This church was built through the agency of Rev. G. W. Bethune, of Brooklyn, and is called "The Church of the Thousand Isles." A parsonage was built in 1852. The sites for both edifices were given by Francis Depau. The census reports 6 churches; 2 Prot. E., Bap., M. E., Presb., and R. C.

[11] This land company, formed in Holland, bought Great Tract No. IV., within which this town is situated. For particulars see *Hough's Hist. Jeff. Co., p. 58–61.*

[12] According to the last census, this town produces more butter than any other town in the co.; and, with one exception, it has the greatest number of cows of any town in the State.

[13] From 1805 to 1828 about 100 pairs of millstones were manufactured from this rock in this town.

[14] This limestone is especially valuable for lime and as a flux for iron ore.

[15] This sandstone furnishes an excellent building material, and is used for the lining of furnaces.

[16] Discovered by Hopestill Foster; owned and worked by Jas. Sterling.

[17] On the farm of Hiram B. Keene, and owned by a company.

[18] Owned by Geo. Parish, of Ogdensburgh.

[19] This ore is of the red specular variety. The region in which it is found is one of the richest in the country for specimens of rare minerals.

The Antwerp Liberal Institute[1] and 3 churches. Pop. 621. **Ox Bow**[2] (p. v.) is situated on the Oswegatchee River. Pop. 240. **Sterlingburgh,**[3] 1 mi. above Antwerp, and **Spragues Corners,** on the line of St. Lawrence co., are hamlets. The first improvements were made in 1803, at the Ox Bow, under the direction of Lewis R. Morris, the original proprietor.[4] In 1808, Morris sold 29,033 acres to George and David Parish, under whose agents the greater part of the settlements were made. A party of militia was stationed here in 1808, to enforce the embargo, and a blockhouse was built at the village in 1812. The first church was built, in 1816, by Parish.[5]

BROWNVILLE—was formed from Leyden, April 1, 1802, and was named from Gen. Jacob Brown, its founder. Le Ray was taken off in 1806; Lyme, in 1818; Pamelia, in 1819; and Orleans, and a part of Alexandria, in 1821. It is situated on the N. side of Black River and Black River Bay. Its surface is level or gently undulating. The soil is a sandy and clayey loam. Sulphate of barytes is found on Pillar Point, and the vein has been worked to some extent for lithic paint. Upon the w. bank of Perch River, a few rods below Limerick, is a cave extending 150 yards into the bank and 30 feet below the surface. Manufactures receive considerable attention. **Brownville,** (p. v.,) on Black River, 4 mi. below Watertown, was incorp. April 5, 1828. It has a valuable water power, and contains 3 churches, a cotton factory, and several foundries and machine shops. Pop. 621. **Dexter**[6] (p. v.) is situated at the head of navigation on Black River. It is the seat of an extensive woolen factory built in 1836.[7] Pop. 429. **Limerick** (p. o.) and **Moffatville,** (Perch River p. o.) contain a dozen houses each. **Pillar Point** (p. o.) is situated across the bay from Sackets Harbor. Pop. 50. Gen. Jacob Brown began the settlement of the town in 1799, as proprietor and agent.[8] During the war Brownville village became the seat of a hospital; and on different occasions large bodies of troops were posted in the vicinity. For several years it was the residence and headquarters of Maj. Gen. Brown, commander in chief of the N. department, and afterward of Col. Edward Kirby,[9] his son-in-law. There are 10 churches in town.[10]

CAPE VINCENT—was formed from Lyme, April 10, 1849, and named from Vincent Le Ray, son of the proprietor. It is the N. w. corner town of the co., and embraces Carlton, Grenadier, and Fox Islands in the St. Lawrence. The surface is level, or slightly undulating, and the soil is a clayey loam. Kent Creek is the principal stream. There are 2 or 3 sulphur springs in town. Considerable attention is paid to ship building. **Cape Vincent,**[11] (p. v.,) the terminus of the W. and R. R. R., near the head of the St. Lawrence River, is a thriving commercial village. Pop. 1026. **Saint Lawrence** and **Millens Bay** are p. offices and hamlets. The first settlement in the town and co. was made upon Carlton Island,[12] at about the time of the Revolution. A regular fortification, known as "Fort Carlton,"[13] was erected upon the island, and a tract of 30 acres was cleared and cultivated, and long known as the "*Kings Garden.*" The first settlement upon the mainland was commenced in 1801 at Port Putnam, 2 mi. below Cape Vincent, by Capt. Abijah Putnam.[14] Count Real, Chief of Police under Napoleon, and other French families of note, resided in this town for some time. A custom house was established in 1819. Upon the shores of Grenadier Island,[15]

---

1 This institution is not yet fully organized.

2 This name is derived from a remarkable bend in the Oswegatchie River, upon which the village is situated. The village was settled by Scotch emigrants.

3 Sterlingburgh, 1 mi. above Antwerp Village, is the seat of an iron furnace built by Jas. Sterling in 1846. A forge was built here for David Parish in 1817.

4 The first settler was Wm. Lee. Mills were built at Antwerp Village in 1806-07, for Morris, by John Jennison. The first school was taught in the Foster Settlement, by Benj. Cook.

5 This church was the second in the co., and for many years was used by all the denominations in town. It is now in possession of the R. C. There are in town 8 churches; 2 Bap., M. E., Wes. Meth., Presb., Asso. Ref. Presb., R. C., Union.

6 Named from S. Newton Dexter, of Whitesboro', one of the proprietors. It was formerly known as "*Fish Island.*" During the war the mills at this place furnished lumber for the public works at Sackets Harbor. The steamer "Brownville," built in 1827, and designed to run between this place and the lake ports, was burned upon her first trip. The Black River Nav. Co., incorp. in 1810, built locks here, which were little used. Piers for the improvement of navigation were built at the mouth of the river by the Gen. Government; but they have resulted in injury.

7 This factory is of stone, and cost $140,000. It is fitted for 10 sets of machinery, and employs 75 hands.

8 In 1800, Gen. Brown built a sawmill, and in 1801 a small grist mill, at the mouth of Philomel Creek. A bridge was built in 1802, and a dam across the river in 1806. In 1828, Henry

Evans was hung near Watertown for murder committed in this town,—the only execution by civil authority that ever took place in the co.

9 Col. Kirby held the office of paymaster in the army from 1824 till his death, April 18, 1846.

10 2 M. E., 2 Prot. E., 2 Univ., 2 Presb., 1 Bap., 1 Union.

11 Called "*Gravelly Point*" by many of the old inhabitants. It was first settled in 1809, laid out as a village in 1817, and incorp. in 1853. A lighthouse was built at Tibbets Point, 2 mi. distant, in 1826. The R. R. company have built here a wharf 3000 feet long, 2 immense freight houses, a grain elevator, &c. The Ontario Line of Steamers touch at this point, and ferry boats run regularly to Kingston. A few years since, a canal was dug across Wolf or Grand Island, to afford a more direct route for this ferry. This place received several visits from the enemy during the war.

12 This island contains 1274 acres. A military class right (see page 46) of 500 acres was located here in 1786. For several years after 1822 it was a thriving lumber station, where rafts were made up for the Quebec market.

13 This fort commanded the s. channel of the river, and was an important post during the Revolution. It was mostly excavated in the rock, and the materials taken out were used in the construction of the rampart and escarpment.

14 Mr. Putnam established a ferry from this place to Wolf Island. In 1803 a State road was opened to this place, and in 1804 a village plot was laid out, but soon after abandoned.

15 This island was the rendezvous of Gen. Wilkinson's army on their way down the river in 1813. At the eastern extremity is a

and of the mainland opposite, are valuable seine fisheries. A town ag. soc. was formed in 1850.[1] There are 3 churches in town.[2]

CHAMPION[3]—was formed from Mexico, March 14, 1800. A part of Harrisburgh was taken off in 1803. It is the central town on the s. e. border of the co. The surface is broken and hilly. The most elevated portions are the slate hills in the s. angle, (known as the "peak,") which are about 1700 feet above tide. From their summits the land descends in a series of broken and irregular terraces to the river. The n. part is more level. The soil is generally a clay loam, but near the river in some places it is sandy. **Champion** (p. v.) contains 20 houses, **Great Bend** (p. v.) and **West Carthage**[4] about 30 each. **Champion South Roads** is a p. o. The first settlement was begun in 1798, by Noadiah Hubbard, as agent for Storrs. The first settlers came by water down the river as far as the Long Falls, and the town was settled with great rapidity.[5] The first church (Cong.) was formed in 1805.[6]

CLAYTON—was formed from Orleans and Lyme, April 27, 1833, and named in honor of John M. Clayton, U. S. Senator from Del. It is centrally situated on the n. w. border of the co. It embraces two-fifths of Penets Square, a gore w. and another n. of that tract, and Grindstone and several smaller islands in the St. Lawrence. The surface is level, or slightly rolling. Water lime has been manufactured in considerable quantities. **Clayton,**[7] (p. v.), situated at the mouth of French Creek,[8] is largely engaged in the lumber trade and in ship building.[9] Pop. 896. **Depauville**[10] (p. v.) is situated at the head of navigation on Chaumont (Sha-mo) River, (or Catfish Creek;) 6 mi. from the bay. Pop. 386. **Clayton Center** is a p. o. Settlement commenced in 1803, but progressed slowly until after the war. For many years the titles to the portions included in Penets Square and the islands became the subject of much controversy and litigation. In early times the shores of the St. Lawrence in this and adjoining towns became the scene of many lawless adventures in the prosecution of smuggling.[11] In 1813, the enemy attacked the advanced guard of Wilkinson's expedition, commanded by Gen. Brown, at Bartlets Point, but were repulsed. The census reports 7 churches in town.[12]

ELLISBURGH[13]—was formed from Mexico, Feb. 22, 1803. Henderson was set off in 1806. It is situated in the s. w. corner of the co., upon the shore of Lake Ontario. The surface is rolling and inclined toward the lake. A range of low sand hills extend along the shore, and these are succeeded by a wide marshy region, producing wild grasses that in dry seasons may be mown. North and South Sandy Creeks are the principal streams. The soil is sandy on the w., clayey through the center, and a slaty loam in the e. There is a sulphur spring in town. This is the wealthiest agricultural town in the co., and is surpassed by but few in the State. **Ellis Village,**[14] (Ellisburgh p. o.,) situated on S. Sandy Creek, 4 mi. from its mouth, has a limited amount of manufactures. Pop. 230. **Belleville,**[15] (p. v.,) is situated on N. Sandy Creek, 3 mi. from Ellis Village, and on the S. H. & E. R. R. Pop. 363. The Union Literary Society (academy) is located here. **Pierrepont Manor,**[16] (p. v.,) at the junction of the W. & R. and S. H. & E. R. R., contains 255 inhabitants. **Woodville,**[17] (p. v.,) is situated on N. Sandy Creek. Pop. 180. **Mannsville,**[18] (p. v.,) on Skinners Creek and the W. & R. R. R., has a population

capacious bay, known as "Basin Harbor," which affords a shelter for boats. The whole island is now a single dairy farm.

[1] This society is open to the citizens of Lyme, Clayton, and Wolf Island.   [2] Presb., Prot. E., and R. C.

[3] No. 4, or "Howard," of the "Eleven Towns." It fell to the share of Harrison and Hoffman, and by them was sold to Gen. Henry Champion, of Colchester, Conn., and Lemuel Storrs. It was settled under Judge Noadiah Hubbard and Alfred Lathrop, agents of the last named proprietor. The name was given in honor of Gen. Champion, who presented the town with a bell for the compliment.

[4] Considerable amounts of lumber, oil, flour, and cloth are manufactured in this village.

[5] Among the first settlers, who came in in 1798–99, were John, Thos. and Salmon Ward, David and Saml. Starr, Joel Mix, Ephm. Chamberlain, Jonathan Mitchell, Bela Hubbard, and David Miller. The first school was taught by E. Chamberlain, in 1800. The first sawmill was built in 1802, by John Eggleson and Wm. Hadsall. The first grist mill was built at West Carthage, by David Coffeen, in 1806. A furnace was built at the same place in 1834, and about 1000 tons of iron produced. Several prominent lawyers, among whom were Moss Kent, brother of the chancellor, Egbert Ten Eyck, and Henry R. Storrs, settled in Champion, in expectation of its becoming the co. seat of the new co. to be erected from Oneida.

[6] Rev. Nathl. Dutton was the first regular settled pastor in the town and co. There are 6 churches in town; 2 Cong., 2 M. E., Bap., and Union.

[7] Formerly called "Cornelia," and still frequently called

"French Creek." A party of Patriots made this place their rendezvous in preparing to invade Canada. The same party took possession of Hickory Island; but upon the approach of the British they fled, leaving their armament behind.

[8] This stream is called by the Indians Wet-er-ingh-ra-gu-en-te-re, or "Fallen Fort," from a fort taken by the Oneidas from another tribe long before the advent of the whites.

[9] The timber is brought in vessels from the upper lakes, and here made up into rafts. Most of the steamers belonging to the American line have been built at this port and at Wolf Island.

[10] De-po-ville. Named from Francis Depau, an early proprietor. The place was formerly known as "Catfish Falls." Stephen Johnson built the first mill and opened the first store at this place, in 1824.

[11] During the embargo of 1808 a road was cut through the woods, and immense quantities of potash were taken to Canada without restraint.

[12] 4 M. E., and one each Bap., R. C., and Union.

[13] "Minos," of the "Eleven Towns." Named from Marvel Ellis, an early proprietor, and Lyman Ellis, the first settler.

[14] The oldest settlement in the co.

[15] Named from Belleville, in Canada.

[16] It is the residence of Hon. Wm. C. Pierrepont, from whom the village derives its name.

[17] Named from Ebenezer, Ephraim, and Jacob Wood, the first settlers.

[18] Named from Col. H. B. Mann, who erected a factory at this place, but which was afterward burned.

of 315. **Rural Hill**[1] (p. o.) and **Wardwell** (p. o.) are hamlets. Lyman Ellis and a large number of others made the first settlement, in 1797.[2] A tract of 3000 acres in the s. w. corner of the town was sold by Wm. Constable, in 1796, to Brown and Eddy, and was settled by squatters. Upon the advent of the first settlers, near Ellis Village, on Sandy Creek, were found numerous traces of an early occupation by civilized races.[3] During the war an engagement took place near the mouth of S. Sandy Creek, between a party of 150 American regulars and a few militia and Indians, under Maj. Appling, and a party of 200 British, who were pursuing a flotilla of boats, commanded by Lieut. Woolsey, laden with stores for Sackets Harbor. The British were defeated, and nearly the whole party were killed or taken prisoners.[4] The census reports 11 churches in town.[5]

HENDERSON[6]—was formed from Ellisburgh, Feb. 17, 1806. It lies on Lake Ontario, s. w. of the center of the co. The surface is rolling; and it is deeply indented with Henderson Bay, formed by a long rocky point known as Six-Town Point.[7] There are in town two small lakes and several marshes. Stony and Little Stony Creeks are the principal streams. The soil is clay and loam. **Henderson**[8] (p. v.) is situated near the center, on Stony Creek. Pop. 404. **Henderson Harbor**[9] contains 12 houses; and **Smithville**[10] (p. o.) 40. **Roberts Corners** (p. o.) is a hamlet. Settlement was begun in 1802, under Asher Miller, agent for the proprietor.[11] At the head of Henderson Bay is a curved embankment or bar of stone, 100 rods long, and a little above the water, known as "Indian Wharf;" and from this point to Stony Creek there was an Indian trail or portage. The census reports 5 churches in town.[12]

HOUNSFIELD[13]—was formed from Watertown, Feb. 17, 1806. It is situated on Black River Bay, on the w. border of the co. Its surface is very level, and the soil is a clayey and sandy loam. Ship building and manufactures have received considerable attention. **Sackets Harbor**[14] (p. v.) is the principal village. Pop. 994. This was the principal military and naval station on the northern frontier during the last war with Great Britain, and millions of dollars were spent in fortifications and in building vessels. **East Hounsfield** (p. o.) and **Stowells Corners** (p. o.) are hamlets. Amasa Fox was the first settler. In 1802 there were 30 families in town.[15] In 1805 several English families came in.[16] During the war this town was the center of important military events. Several expeditions were here fitted out against Canada; and, in turn, the town was invaded on several occasions.[17] Large bodies of troops were frequently quartered here, and the citizens became familiar with the lights and shades of military life.[18] After the war most of the troops were withdrawn, leaving only enough to keep the

---

[1] Formerly called "Buck Hill."

[2] Among the first settlers were Caleb Ellis, Robert Fulton, Elijah Richardson, Hez. Pierce, Chauncey Smith, Wm. Root, Vial Salisbury, Isaac Waddle, and Abram Wilcox. The early settlers suffered much from sickness. The first child born was Ontario Pierce, and the first death, that of Caleb Ellis. Lyman Ellis built the first sawmill, in 1797, and the first grist mill, in 1803.

[3] It is probable that the French expedition, under De La Barre, against the Onondagas in 1684, met with their terrible disasters from famine and sickness within the limits of this town.

[4] The stores were taken by land from this point to the "Harbor." Among them was a cable weighing 9600 lbs., which was too heavy for loading upon any wagon that could be obtained. It was accordingly placed on the shoulders of 250 men and carried to its place of destination. As the bearers approached the Harbor, the sailors met them with loud cheers, relieved them of their burden, and marched triumphantly into the village.

[5] 3 Bap., 2 Cong., 2 M. E., Presb., Prot. E., Univ., Union.

[6] No. 6 of the "Eleven Towns."

[7] Upon this point are the remains of a small 4 sided fortification, evidently built during the French or Revolutionary War.

[8] Formerly called "Salisbury Mills," from Lodowyck Salisbury, an early merchant and mill owner.

[9] The bay upon which this place is situated was called the "Bay of Naples" by Henderson, the proprietor.

[10] Named from Jesse Smith, who, from a common laborer, became one of the most extensive lumber dealers in the county, and a man of influence.

[11] Among the first settlers were Anthony Sprague, Levi Scofield, Jedediah McComber, Samuel Hubbard, Moses Barrett, Wm. Petty, and Daniel Spencer. Willis Fellows kept the first inn and built the first saw and grist mills. The first child born was Betsy Scofield, and the first death, that of a child of Hosea Heath. Elisha Skinner taught the first school. A small woolen factory was erected in 1814. A Scotch settlement was made in 1803–07, on the bay. A lighthouse was erected on Stony Point in 1837.

[12] 2 M. E., Ev. Luth., Univ., and Union.

[13] The town embraces No. 1, or "Hesiod," of the "Eleven Towns," and was named from Ezra Hounsfield, one of the early proprietors. In the division it fell to the share of Harrison and Hoffman; and by them the w. half was sold to Champion and Storrs, and the remainder to Peter Kemble and E. Hounsfield. It was called "Newport" in early documents. Gull, Snake, Great and Little Galloo, and Stony Islands belong to this town. Upon Galloo Island a lighthouse was erected in 1820.

[14] Named from Augustus Sacket, the first settler. Called by the Indians Ga-hú-a-go-je-twa-da-â-lote, fort at the mouth of Great River. Incorp. April 15, 1814. A collection district was formed in 1805. Madison Barracks, built in 1816–19 at a cost of $85,000, are the principal military works. Upon a point in the harbor is the hull of the frigate New Orleans, sheltered by a house built over it. It was commenced during the war, but has never been finished. It measured 3200 tons, and was pierced for 110 guns. The frigate Chippewa, of like dimensions, built farther up the bay, has been taken down.

[15] Among these were John and Wm. Evans, Squire Reed, Amasa Hollibut, and Charles Baird.

[16] Among these were Saml. Luff, his sons Edmund, Saml., Jr., Joseph, and Jesse, David Merritt, William Ashby, John Roots, Henry Metcalf. and Geo. Slowman. Dr. Wm. Baker, who settled in 1803, was the first physician; Ambrose Pease and Step. Simmons were early innkeepers, and Loren Buss and Hezekiah Doolittle, early merchants. In 1808 Samuel F. Hooker brought in a stock of goods worth $20,000. Meetings were first held by Edmund Luff, who built a church, and preached many years without fee or reward. Elisha Camp settled in 1804, as a lawyer and agent, and has since been more prominently concerned in the affairs of the town than any other person. Samuel Luff built the first grist mill, Augustus Sacket, the first sawmill, and Solon Stone, the first cotton factory, on Mill Creek. The first child born in town was Wealthy Rowlison. At an early period, John Jacob Astor and other capitalists invested large sums here in the manufacture of potash, that article commanding $200 to $350 per ton in the Montreal market.   [17] See page 354.

[18] About a dozen military executions took place here during the war. A duel was fought with muskets, June 13, 1818, between two soldiers, one of whom was killed. During the command of Col. Brady at this station, the remains of Gens. Zebulon M. Pike and Leonard Covington, Col. John Tuttle, Lieut.

works in repair. In 1832 a canal, for hydraulic purposes, was completed from Huntington's Mills, above Watertown, to Sackets Harbor; but in about 10 years it was abandoned.[1] Dr. Samuel Guthrie, one of the discoverers of chloroform, and inventor of the percussion compound for firearms, which has superseded flints, resided at Sackets Harbor. A Union school was established in the village in 1840. There are 5 churches in town.[2]

LE RAY[3]—was formed from Brownville, Feb. 17, 1806. Antwerp was taken off in 1810, a part of Wilna in 1813, and a part of Philadelphia and Alexandria in 1821. It is an interior town E. of the center of the co. The surface is level, or gently rolling, and the soil is principally a clayey loam. A strip of barren sand, once covered with pine, but now almost a desert, extends along Black River. The streams are Black and Indian Rivers, Pleasant Creek, and several small brooks. **Le Raysville**[4] (p. v.) contains 22 houses. **Evans Mills**[5] (p. v.) is situated on Pleasant Creek and the P. & W. R. R. Pop. 410. **Sandfords Corners,** (p. v.,) on the P. & W. R. R., contains a dozen houses. **Black River,**[6] a village of 50 houses, is partly in this town. The first settlement was made in 1802, by a party under Benj. Brown, agent for Le Ray.[7] Le Ray removed to this place in 1808, and began a liberal system of settlement, by opening roads and building bridges and mills. The census reports 6 churches.[8]

LORRAINE[9]—was formed from Mexico, March 24, 1804, as *"Malta."* Its name was changed April 6, 1808. Worth was taken off in 1848. It is the central town on the s. border of the co. The town is elevated, and is underlaid by slate and traversed by immense gulfs. The surface is rolling, and the soil is a clay and loam. It is mostly drained by Sandy and Skinners Creeks. **Lorraine,** (p. v.,) the only village, contains about 30 houses. Settlement was begun in 1802, by James McKee and Elijah Fox.[10] The State Road from Rome to Sackets Harbor was laid through this town in 1804. A sulphur spring is found on the farm of —— Totman. The town has 2 churches, Bap. and M. E.

LYME[11]—was formed from Brownville, March 6, 1818. A part of Clayton was taken off in 1833, and Cape Vincent in 1849. It lies upon Chaumont Bay, in the w. part of the co. The surface is very level. The w. border is deeply indented by Chaumont Bay[12] and its branches. The soil is principally clay. There are several sulphur springs in town. Near Chaumont are extensive and valuable limestone quarries.[13] **Chaumont** (p. v.) is situated upon the bay at the mouth of Chaumont River. Pop. 306. **Three Mile Bay**[14] (p. v.) lies upon a bay of the same name. Pop. 295. **Point Peninsula** (p. o.) is a scattered settlement containing 25 houses. The first settlement was begun under Jonas Smith and Henry A. Delamater, agents for Le Ray, in 1801.[15] The first location was 2½ mi. above Chaumont; but in 1805 the settlers removed to the site of the present village. During several years much sickness prevailed; but this gradually disappeared as the co. became more settled. In 1812 the inhabitants, numbering about a dozen families, built a blockhouse, which was taken and destroyed by the enemy. The first church (Bap.) was organized in 1816.[16]

ORLEANS—was formed from Brownville, April 3, 1821. A portion was annexed to Pamelia, April 1, 1829. Clayton was taken off in 1833. The boundary between it and Alexandria has twice been changed. It lies on the N. border of the co., and embraces the w. part of Wells and

Cols. Electus Backus, Timothy Dix, Jr., and John Mills, Maj. John Johnson, Capts. Ambrose Spencer, Jr., and Joseph Nicholson, and Lieut. Michael P. Vanderventer, officers who had been killed or had died of sickness during the war, were collected, and buried in one grave. A monument of *painted pine boards* was erected to their memory by a grateful country; but it soon rotted down, and there is now a strong probability that the place of their interment will be forgotten.

1 This canal was 20 feet wide at the top, 12 at the bottom, and 4 feet deep.

2 M. E., Prot. E., Presb., Christian, and Seventh Day Bap.

3 Named for James Le Ray de Chaumont, the proprietor.

4 The land office for much of the land in the co. N. and E. of the river was located here until 1835, when it was removed to Carthage. P. S. Stewart has been the agent many years.

5 Named from Ethni Evans, who built the first mill in 1805–06.

6 This village is locally known as "Lockport." A trace of an ancient Indian fort was found near it; another 1 mi. N.; and another near Sandfords Corners.

7 Among these first settlers were David Coffeen, Dyer Rhodes, Gershom and John Matoon, Joseph Child and sons, Thomas Ward, William Cooper, and Benj. Kirkbride. The first child born was Abi Brown; the first marriage, that of Jonas Allen and Sarah Dyke; and the first death, that of Chester Ballou. Margaret Comstock taught the first school.

8 Bap., Friends, M. E., Presb., R. C., and Union.

9 This town embraces "Atticus," or No. 1, of the Boylston Tract.

10 In the following year, Comfort Stancliff, Benjamin Gates, Seth Cutler, John Alger, and others, came in. McKee and Fox kept the first inn. Mr. Frost built the first sawmill, and Mr. Cutler the first grist mill, in 1804. The first death was that of A. M. Child, killed by a falling tree.

11 Name selected by Eben. Kelsey, a native of Lyme, Conn.

12 Name derived from Le Ray de Chaumont. Upon old maps this bay is named "*Niahoure,*" "*Niaoure,*" and "*Nivernois.*" The last name is probably derived from that of the Duc de Nivernois, a French nobleman.

13 The limestone quarries of this place have furnished large quantities of stone for the piers at Oswego, locks on the canal, and for other public works.

14 Name given from its being 3 miles w. of Chaumont. This bay is celebrated for its fisheries. In 1856, $90,000 worth of fish were taken, consisting principally of "ciscoes" (lake herring) and whitefish. It has been the seat of considerable ship building.

15 Among the first settlers were Richard M. Esselstyn, T. Wheeler, Peter Pratt, and Jonas, David, and Timothy Soper. James Horton was the first settler on Point Salubrious, in 1806.

16 The census reports 6 churches; 2 M. E., 2 Bap., Presb., and Free W. Bap.

several smaller islands in the St. Lawrence. The surface is level, or slightly rolling. The principal streams are Perch River, Catfish and Mullet Creeks. Perch Lake lies upon the s. boundary. The soil is clay and loam. **La Fargeville,**[1] (p. v.,) on Chaumont River, near the center of the town, is the seat of Orleans Academy. Pop. 295. **Omar,**[2] (p. o.,) on Mullet Creek, and **Stone Mills,**[3] (p. o.,) are small villages. **Orleans 4 Corners,** (p. o.,) **Port Orleans,** and **Collins Landing** are hamlets. Penets Square, which embraced most of this town, was settled by squatters.[4] The first settlements commenced about 1806.[5] In 1824, John La Farge, a large owner in these lands, came into town to assert his claim. After a great deal of difficulty and some resistance, he succeeded in establishing his title. In 1838 the mansion and farm of La Farge, 1 mi. s. of the village, was purchased by Bishop Dubois as the site for a Catholic seminary. This institution, named *"St. Vincent de Paul,"* combining a theological seminary and classical boarding school, was soon after opened; but in two or three years it was removed to Fordham, Westchester co., and was afterward incorp. as St. Johns College. Rock Island Lighthouse was built in 1853. The British steamer Sir Robert Peel was plundered and burned on the night of May 29, 1838, while taking in wood at Wells Island, in this town, by a party of 22 self-styled patriots, led by Bill Johnston.[6] The census reports 8 churches.[7]

PAMELIA[8]—was formed from Brownville, April 12, 1819. In 1824 its name was changed to *"Leander;"* but soon after the former name was restored. A portion of Orleans was annexed April 1, 1829. It is the central town of the co. The surface is level, or gently undulating, and the soil is clay and sand. Near the cascade opposite Watertown are several caves in the limestone rock.[9] In the vicinity of Perch Lake have been found several barrows, or sepulchral mounds. **Pamelia Village** and **Juhelville**[10]—the former opposite the lower part and the latter the upper part of Watertown Village—are places of considerable manufactures,[11] and have each 200 to 300 inhabitants. **Pamelia Four Corners** (p. v.) contains about 30 houses. The first settlement began in 1799.[12] The census reports 2 churches.[13]

PHILADELPHIA—was formed from Le Ray, April 3, 1821. It is an interior town, E. of the center of the co. Its surface is level in the E., but rocky and broken in the w. The soil is generally a clayey loam. Indian River and Black Creek are the principal streams. Iron ore is found in considerable quantities. The principal bed that is worked is known as the Shurtliff mine. In Sterlingville is a large chalybeate spring. **Philadelphia,**[14] (p. v.,) upon Indian River, has 55 houses, and **Sterlingville,**[15] (p. v.,) upon Black Creek, 40. At the latter place are a large blast furnace[16] and a forge.[17] The first settlement was commenced in 1804, by Friends from Penn. and N. J.[18] In 1810 the Friends erected a building which for 17 years was used for a school and meeting house.[19]

---

[1] Named from John La Farge, the proprietor; formerly known as *"Log Mills."*

[2] Named from a character in one of Johnson's allegories, found in the English Reader: formerly called *"Mudges Mills."*

[3] Formerly called *"Collins Mills,"* from John B. Collins, owner.

[4] The improvident waste of timber and the slovenly clearings made by this lawless set promised little in the way of civilization; and their appearance, as they emerged from the swamps with an ox harnessed to a crotched piece of wood, laden with a trough full of "black salts," or, as they returned in like manner, with a sack of meal and a jug of whiskey, was little calculated to inspire hope of speedy improvement. They had a kind of law among themselves in relation to land, and were accustomed to run "possession lines" by lopping down bushes. "Claims" were often sold and secured by quit claim deeds.

[5] Among the first settlers were Roderic C. Frazier, Peter Pratt, Dr. Reuben Andrus, Samuel and Daniel Ellis, and others. Alvah Goodman kept the first inn; Lemuel George, the first store; Collins & Platt erected the first grist mill, and Dr. Andrus, the first sawmill, in 1819.

[6] After driving the passengers ashore and plundering the boat, the brigands cast her off from the shore and set her on fire. Large rewards were offered for their apprehension, and several persons were arrested, but none convicted. In 1853, Johnston was appointed keeper of the Rock Island Light, which shines on the spot where the Peel was burned.

[7] Two Evang. Luth., Bap., Cong., M. E., R. C., Wes. Meth., and Union.

[8] Named from the wife of Gen. Jacob Brown. Her maiden name was Pamelia Williams.

[9] These caverns have been traced nearly 500 feet. Just below and partly under the village of Juhelville, the open mouths of several caves appear on the river bank, opening at both ends on the cliff. The passages are lined with calcareous deposits, in the form of agaric mineral, stalactites, and tufa. These caves

are evidently all formed by currents of water flowing through the natural seams in the rock and gradually wearing away the soluble and yielding limestone. In the rear of the principal cavern a large area of land has sunk to a considerable depth, as though a portion had fallen in.

[10] Named from Madame Juhel, a relative of the Le Ray family.

[11] These manufactures consist of lumber, spirits, leather, cotton yarn, and portable steam engines.

[12] The first settlers were Wm. Cooper and Wm. Watkins. Anson Sigourney taught the first school; Samuel Mack kept the first inn, Jabez Foster, the first store; and Tuttle and Bailey built the first mill.

[13] M. E. and Union.

[14] Often called "Quaker Settlement" by the old inhabitants.

[15] Named from James Sterling, the owner of the iron works. Formerly called *"De Launey's Mill,"* from the builder of the first mill, in 1807.

[16] Built in 1837, by James Sterling. The ore is principally obtained from the Sterling mine of Antwerp, and the Shurtliff mine of this town, near the line of Theresa, the ore from the latter being used principally as a flux.

[17] Built by Caleb Essington, in 1839.

[18] These settlers purchased 16 lots of 440 acres each, lying in the corners of a square containing 25 lots, of which the central range each way was reserved by Le Ray. The center lot, (No. 611,) embracing the site of the present village, was conveyed to trustees "for the promotion of religion and learning" under the care of the Quakers. This trust afterward occasioned much contention, and led to a miniature anti-rent war. The matter was finally settled in 1844. Cadwallader Child, Mordecai Taylor, and Samuel Evans came in the first year. Robert Comfort kept the first inn, Saml. Case, the first store, and Thos. and John Townsend built the first mill. Anna Comstock kept the first school. The first child born was John Townsend, and the first death was a daughter of Robt. Comfort, in 1807.

[19] The census reports 5 churches; 2 M. E., Bap., Friends, Univ.

RODMAN[1]—was formed from Adams, March 24, 1804, under the name of *"Harrison."* Its name was changed April 6, 1808. A part of Pinckney (Lewis co.) was taken off in 1808. It lies upon the borders of Lewis, in the s. part of the co. The surface is hilly, and broken by the deep ravines of Sandy Creek and its branches. The soil is generally a fertile, gravelly loam. There are 3 sulphur springs in town. **Rodman** (p. v.) has 45 houses, **Zoar** and **Whitesville**[2] (E. Rodman p. o.) each about 20. Settlement began in 1801, and from 1803 to 1806 it progressed with great rapidity.[3] In 1813 an epidemic prevailed, causing 60 deaths in 3 months. The census reports 3 churches.[4]

RUTLAND[5]—was formed from Watertown, April 1, 1802. It lies upon the s. bank of Black River, E. of the center of the co. Its surface consists of the narrow river valley on the N., a terraced plateau in the center, and a hilly region in the s. The central plateau, embracing the greater part of the town, is 300 to 400 feet above the flat country farther N., and it descends by a succession of steep declivities to the level of the river. It is underlaid by Trenton limestone. Upon the s. the surface gradually rises to the summits of the slate hills which occupy the s. part of the co. A remarkable valley, known as "Rutland Hollow," extends through the town upon the lower terrace of the plateau, parallel to the river. It is deeply excavated in the limestone, and appears like the bed of an ancient river. Another smaller and deeper valley extends in the same direction across the summit of the plateau, and forms the bed of a deep, narrow lake. Pleasant Lake, in Champion, is situated in the continuation of this latter valley. These valleys and terraces seem the result of abrasion rather than of upheaval. Upon the edge of the terrace, 100 feet below the summit, may be seen the ancient lake ridge before described. There are 2 or 3 sulphur springs in town. The soil is a very fertile loam upon the plateau, and a sandy loam upon the river. **Felts Mills**,[6] (p. v.,) on Black River, contains 50 houses; **Black River**,[7] (p. v.,) on the river, partly in this town and partly in Le Ray, 40; **Tylerville**,[8] (South Rutland p. o.,) in the narrow valley of Sandy Creek, 30; and **Rutland Center**,[9] (Rutland p. o.,) 10. This town fell to the share of Wm. Henderson, and settlement was begun in 1799, under Asher Miller, his agent. The greater part of the land was sold[10] to New England farmers, who came in within 3 years after the first settlement.[11] An old Indian fort is to be seen on the farm of Geo. Wilson; and a bone pit was found near the line of Watertown. The census reports 5 churches.[12]

THERESA—was formed from Alexandria, April 15, 1841, and named from a daughter of Le Ray. It is the central town upon the N. w. border of the co. The surface along Indian River is broken, and traversed by ridges of gneiss rock, with fertile intervales. A part of the town, underlaid by sandstone, is level or undulating. In the primary regions are a number of romantic lakes; and some of these have highly interesting mineral localities upon their shores and islands.[13] **Theresa**, (p. v.,) upon the High Falls[14] of the Indian River, was early selected by Le Ray as a favorable point for settlement, and about 1810 he caused several "jobs" to be cleared and a sawmill to be built.[15] **West Theresa** is a p. o. A furnace, built near Millseat Lake in 1847, was in part supplied with ores from the vicinity. A private academy has been taught several years. The census reports 3 churches.[16]

---

[1] It embraces No. 8, or "Orpheus," of the "Eleven Towns." Its former name was from Richard Harrison, of N. Y., a proprietor; and its present one, from Daniel Rodman, of Hudson, Clerk of the Assembly in 1808–09.

[2] Named from Thos. White, sub-agent and early settler.

[3] Among the settlers who came in this year were Anson and Ebenezer Moody, Noah, Jonathan, and Aaron Davis, Benj. Thomas, Wm. Rice, and Simeon Hunt. Miss M. Nobles taught the first school, in Anson Moody's barn, in 1803. Willard Sykes kept the first store; and Wm. Rice built the first sawmill, in 1804, and gristmill, in 1806. The first child born was Walter Harrison Moody; and the first death, that of the same child, 3 years after. His father received 50 acres of land from Mr. Harrison for the name. Timothy Greenly moved into the s. w. corner of the town in 1803.

[4] 2 M. E., Cong.

[5] No. 3, or "Milan," of the "Eleven Towns." Named from Rutland, Vt., the former home of an early settler.

[6] Named from John Felt, who purchased the site in 1813, and still resides here. Formerly the seat of an extensive lumber manufactory; now changed to a tannery.

[7] Locally known as "Lockport." See p. 359.

[8] Named from Josiah and Frederick Tyler, early settlers.

[9] On some maps called "Brooksville," from Curtis G. Brooks, a former citizen. It is never known by this name in town.

[10] 17,549 acres were sold, in farms within 3 years, for $50,738.

[11] Among the settlers who came in during the first and second years were Levi Miller, Perley and Wm. Keyes, David and Goldsmith Coffeen, Amos Stebbins, Raphael Porter, Israel Wright, Jonathan and Clark Ross, Jas. Kilham, Chas. Kelsey, Jephtha King, John Dale, C. Cummings, Gardner Cleveland, Warren Foster, and John Cotes. Miss A. Porter taught the first school, in 1803. Levi Butterfield kept the first inn, and Jacob Williams the first store. David Coffeen built the first gristmill in the co., near the mouth of Mill Creek, in the present village of Felts Mills, in 1801, and a sawmill in 1802. The first child born was in the family of Chas. Kelsey, and the first death, that of Mrs. Francis Towne. [12] 2 M. E., 2 Union, and Cong.

[13] Fluorspar, sulphate of barytes, sulphurets of iron and copper, phosphate of lime, zircon, feldspar, tourmalines, hyalite, pyroxene, Rensselaerite, idocrase, calcite, phlogopite, and other minerals, are found in this locality, and some of them are beautifully crystallized. Iron ore has been found in considerable quantity.

[14] The river here descends 85 feet within a quarter of a mile. From this place to Rossie its banks are low, and large tracts are often overflowed, causing much sickness. A small steamer has run upon this part of the river.

[15] Among the first settlers were James Shurtliff, Anson and Jeremiah Cheeseman, M. B. Ashley, Sylvester Bodman, Azariah Walton, Col. S. Ball, Abram Morrow, Joseph Miller, Archibald Fisher, Jas. Lake, Ebenezer and N. W. Lull, and J. D. Davidson. Mr. Lull built the first store, in 1820. Dr. Jas. Brooks, the first physician, settled in 1822, and died the next year. The first school was taught by Lindley Gibbs, at Hyde Lake. The first child born was Fanny A. Cole, May 26, 1819. The first marriage was that of Ebenezer Lull and Elmira Barnes. The first death was that of Mr. Casselman, who was drowned. A gristmill and inn were erected in 1819 for the proprietor.

[16] Presb., M. E., and Prot. E.

WATERTOWN[1]—was formed from Mexico, March 14, 1800. Rutland was taken off in 1802, and Hounsfield in 1806. It lies upon Black River, s. w. of the center of the co. The surface in the s. e. part is broken by the irregular terraces of the Trenton limestone, and in the n. it is level or rolling. The river bank is rocky throughout its whole extent; and in the village, about 3 mi. below, are several extensive caves. It is an important agricultural town; but it is chiefly distinguished for the extent of its trade and manufactures. In amount of business it is unsurpassed by any town in Northern N.Y. **Watertown,**[2] (p. v.,) the co. seat, pleasantly situated upon the s. bank of Black River, was incorp. April 5, 1816. Pop. 5873. It contains an academy,[3] 3 newspaper offices, 5 banks, and 9 churches. Black River here flows, for the space of a mile, in a succession of rapids over the limestone terraces, affording an abundance of water power, which is largely improved, making the village one of the most important manufacturing places in the State.[4] Three road and 2 r. r. bridges cross the river within the limits of the village: one of the former is a wire suspension bridge. An ice cave, near Whittleseys Point,[5] extends under a part of the village. By an act passed March 22, 1853, a board of water commissioners was created, with power to borrow $50,000 for the construction of water works for the village. The work was finished during the following summer. The water is taken from the river, near the upper part of the village, and thrown by water power into a reservoir 200 feet above the village, and about 1 mi. distant; and from the reservoir it is distributed through the streets. A beautiful fountain is constructed in the center of the principal square.[6] At an early day, two rectangular pieces of land were given by the owners of the adjacent lots for public use;[7] and these now constitute beautiful public squares.[8] **Burrs Mills**[9] (p. o.) is a hamlet, on Sandy Creek, in the e. part of the town. **Watertown Center** and **Fields Settlement** are hamlets. Henry Coffeen and Zachariah Butterfield were the pioneer settlers, in 1800; they located upon the present site of the village.[10] An arsenal was built at Watertown in 1809, and a building for an academy in 1811; the latter was used as a hospital during the war. The census reports 10 churches.[11]

WILNA[12]—was formed from Le Ray, and Leyden (Lewis co.) April 2, 1813. It lies upon Black River, in the extreme e. part of the co. Its surface is somewhat broken. It is chiefly underlaid by the primary rock, which rises into low, naked ridges, and by calciferous sandstone. Black River forms its w. boundary; and upon it are a series of rapids, forming an abundance of water power.[13] The Indian River, in the n. part, also affords water power at several places. At Natural Bridge this stream flows beneath the surface through passages worn in the coarse white limestone which here forms the surface rock. Several interesting minerals are found at this place.

---

1 Its present limits embrace No. 2, or "Leghorn," of the "Eleven Towns." It first contained Nos. 1, 2, and 3.

2 First settled in 1800; and became the co. seat in 1805. In 1849 the business portion was almost destroyed by fire, but it recovered from the disaster in 2 years.

3 The Watertown Acad. was incorp. May 2, 1835, and a large academic building was erected in a grove in the s. e. part of the village. It was soon after merged in the Black River Literary and Religious Institute, founded under the joint auspices of the Watertown Presbytery and B. R. (Cong.) Assoc. in 1836. In May, 1846, its name was changed to the Jefferson County Institute.

4 During the war a factory was built, at a cost of $75,000, for the manufacture of cotton and woolen cloths. In 1827, Levi Beebe purchased Cowans Island and erected upon it an immense stone cotton factory. It had just been put in operation when, July 7, 1833, it was burned, under suspicious circumstances. The loss was $200,000; and the site has since remained a ruin. The manufactures of cotton and woolen goods, flour, paper, iron castings, machinery, leather, agricultural implements, lead pipe, sash and blinds, and furniture, are extensively carried on.

5 Named from the wife of Samuel Whittlesey, who in 1815 threw herself from this point into the river, and was drowned. Her husband, a lawyer, and paymaster to the drafted militia, had received in N.Y. the sum of $30,000, in bills, and while returning to Watertown was secretly robbed of $8700 by his wife. He was greatly alarmed, but was persuaded by her to keep quiet, as it would be difficult to convince the public that a thief would have left so large a portion, and, as they must themselves be suspected of having taken a *part*, they might as well keep the *whole*. Her logic succeeded upon the weak-minded old man, and before reaching home she had matured plans for concealment and evasion. He started with his portmanteau for Oneida co., leaving appointments along the road for paying on his return; but on arriving at Trenton he found he had been robbed. The news of the robbery spread quickly over the country; but the most active inquiry and very liberal rewards failed to bring the thief to justice. On his return home he met his family frantic with grief; but there was an inconsistency in his story, and upon a searching conversation, held separately, with his two bondsmen, Perley Keyes and Jason Fairbanks, the latter were convinced that there was fraud. By an ingenious course of inquiry and eavesdropping, they were not only confirmed in the belief, but assured that the family soon intended to remove, and that summary means must be employed to recover the money. They accordingly invited W. to take a walk, which led as if by accident to a lonely spot near the village, previously prepared, where they suddenly charged him with the robbery and threatened instant drowning unless he disclosed. He was twice submerged and life nearly extinguished, when he confessed and was liberated. The money was found sewed into a pair of drawers fitted to be worn by either husband or wife. Mrs. W. immediately after slipped away from the crowd unobserved, rushed down to the river, and was drowned.—*Hough's Hist. Jeff. Co., p. 263.*

6 An Artesian well was bored 127 feet deep upon Factory Square in 1829, and a copious supply of water was obtained, slightly impregnated with sulphur and iron.

7 These lots are respectively 12 by 28 and 9 by 32 rods.

8 The principal business of the village is located around the Square and upon Court St.

9 Named from John Burr & Sons, who settled here in 1804. Hart Massey built a saw and grist mill here, in 1801, for Low, the proprietor.

10 Oliver Bartholomew came in the same year, (1801,) and in 1802, about 80 families arrived. Jonathan Cowan built the first grist mill, in 1802, and Dr. Isaiah Massey opened the first inn the same year. In 1803, a bridge was built near the present courthouse. In 1805, Wm. Smith and John Paddock opened the first store; and a dam was built across Black River the same year. The first birth was in the family of Moses Bacon; and the first death, that of —— Thornton, who was killed by a falling tree.

11 Two Presb., 2 M. E., Bap., Wes. Meth., Prot. E., R. C., Union, and Univ.

12 Named from Wilna, in Russia, then fresh in memory from its battle.

13 After affording 42 mi. of navigation, the river here commences to descend by a series of rapids, extending to the lake, falling, in all, 480 feet. The "Long Falls" here descend 55 feet in a distance of 5090; and in the rapids are about 50 small islands. The State Dam, built at this place, is 900 feet long, and the State Bridge 500.

The soil is sandy and moderately fertile. **Carthage**[1] (p. v.) is finely situated upon Black River, at the lower terminus of the B. R. Canal improvement. It contains 5 churches, a private academy,[2] and is the seat of important manufactures.[3] Pop. about 1,500. **Natural Bridge,**[4] (p. v.,) on Indian River, contains 40 houses. **Wilna** and **North Wilna** are p. offices; and **Wood Settlement** is a hamlet. Settlement was commenced in 1798, at Carthage, by Henry Boutin, one of the French Company.[5] The village and town were chiefly settled under Le Ray.[6] The census reports 7 churches.[7]

WORTH[8]—was formed from Lorraine, April 12, 1848. It lies upon the high, slaty, and shaly ridges in the s. part of the co. It is 1200 to 1500 feet above tide, and is the most elevated land in the co. It is subject to deep snows and early frosts. Wherever the surface is exposed to the action of running water, deep gulfs have been worn in the soft and yielding rock. There are several sulphur springs in town. The soil is principally derived from the disintegration of the underlying rocks, and is well adapted to grazing. About one half of the town is settled. **Worthville** is a hamlet, and is the only p. o. The first settlement was made in 1802, by an association from Litchfield, Herkimer co., who bought the n. w. quarter, balloted for the lots, built rude mills, and began small improvements.[9] A part of the settlers left during the war, and during the succeeding cold seasons of 1816–17 the whole settlement was abandoned. Settlement was not recommenced until several years after. The census reports 1 church, (M. E.)

---

[1] Formerly called "*Long Falls.*" Incorp. May 26, 1841. A bridge was erected here in 1813, by Ezra Church, for Russell Atwater and David Parish.
[2] Erected by Harrison Miller in 1842; now owned and taught by B. F. Bush.
[3] Consisting of iron, leather, lumber, staves, heading, &c.
[4] Joseph Bonaparte, having purchased a large tract of land in this town and Diana, made this village his residence for two summers. It was laid out in 1818.
[5] Jean B. Bossout, familiarly known as "Battice," kept the first inn and ferry.
[6] The land office of Le Ray was removed from Le Raysville to Carthage in 1835, by Hon. P. Somerville Stewart.
[7] 2 Presb., 2 Prot. Meth., Bap., M. E., and R. C.
[8] Named in honor of Gen. Wm. J. Worth. It comprises No. 2, or "Fenelon," of the Boylston Tract. The e. part was divided among several proprietors, to equalize the division of the "Eleven Towns."
[9] Among the first settlers were Amos and Abijah Gillett, Nathan Matoon, W. Flower, Lodowyck Edwards, John Griswold, Asa Sweet, Abner Rising, and Phineas Rose. The first school was taught in a log barn in 1806. The first death was that of Elisha Sweet. L. B. Gillett kept the first inn and store.

Acres of Land, Valuation, Population, Dwellings, Families, Freeholders, Schools, Live Stock, Agricultural Products, and Domestic Manufactures, of Jefferson County.

Names of Towns.	Acres of Land.		Valuation of 1858.			Population.		No. of Dwellings.	No. of Families.	Freeholders.	Schools.	
	Improved.	Unimproved.	Real Estate.	Personal Property.	Total.	Males.	Females.				No. of Districts.	Children taught.
Adams	19,399½	6,745½	$774,418	$252,460	$1,026,878	1,502	1,603	598	653	524	15	1,161
Alexandria	19,168	18,263	309,591	41,490	351,081	1,724	1,629	602	623	369	21	1,553
Antwerp	41,099	30,424	617,678	69,780	687,458	1,962	1,801	639	675	574	25	1,404
Brownville	26,636	8,216	682,600	75,300	757,900	1,773	1,816	675	697	360	21	1,529
Cape Vincent	20,631	10,561¾	465,816	34,996	500,812	1,712	1,663	592	639	463	14	1,393
Champion	18,716½	7,275	534,599	85,623	620,222	977	969	384	402	315	17	761
Clayton	29,257½	19,986½	523.965	56,859	580,824	2,142	2,090	797	772	581	25	1,817
Ellisburgh	36,327¾	12,242½	1,325,762	111,510	1,437,272	2,677	2,662	1,018	1,034	831	30	1,958
Henderson	16,885	6,616	463,295	70.500	533,795	1,091	1,048	393	419	322	13	810
Hounsfield	21,622	6,168¾	455.213	83,750	538,963	1,641	1,580	620	646	443	17	1,221
Le Ray	38,264¼	14,592	667,208	129,173	796,381	1,666	1,537	603	635	516	19	1,247
Lorraine	13,192½	6,678	225,003	23,640	248,643	787	683	295	297	230	13	681
Lyme	20,803	8,109	380.453	38,734	419,187	1,294	1,269	455	554	325	17	987
Orleans	13,765½	15,157	506.788	41,445	548,233	1,438	1,368	472	537	436	20	1,208
Pamelia	19,810	3,836	524,551	79,675	604,226	1,284	1,227	420	442	223	12	884
Philadelphia	16,093	5,747	389,394	66,700	456,094	898	845	315	335	267	10	611
Rodman	15,749	6,848	522.530	138,950	661,480	882	870	338	363	319	13	584
Rutland	20,768½	6,470	501,695	59,649	561,344	961	1,016	391	400	383	12	731
Theresa	15,667	9,937	357,934	89,380	447,314	1,148	1,130	397	418	390	17	1,053
Watertown	20,013½	5,186½	2,423,000	1,519,960	3,942,960	3,639	3,918	1,299	1,387	687	21	2,648
Wilna	17,372½	20,396	329,489	72,268	401,757	1,556	1,468	577	598	416	17	1,339
Worth	3,981	21,835½	66.690	3,350	70,040	238	236	95	103	90	6	177
Total	465,222	251,291	13.047,672	3.145.192	16,192,864	32,992	32,428	11,975	12,629	9,063	375	25,757

Names of Towns.	Live Stock.					Agricultural Products.							Domestic Manufactures in Yards.
						Bush. of Grain.					Dairy Products.		
	Horses.	Working Oxen and Calves.	Cows.	Sheep.	Swine.	Winter.	Spring.	Tons of Hay.	Bushels of Potatoes.	Bushels of Apples.	Pounds of Butter.	Pounds of Cheese.	
Adams	822	1,457	1,827	2,452	1,068	12,496½	82,304½	3,492½	15,707	17,302	99,756	369,109	1,789
Alexandria	770	1,761	2,200	2,689	1,022	7,838	51,926¾	5,055½	7,518	932	183,209	48,366	3,903½
Antwerp	1,085	1,753	4,293	2,260	1,446	1,844	86,271½	7,798	12,246	1,492	379,109	186,215	958½
Brownville	1,090	1,493	2,752	3,582	1,366	14,178	121,802½	5,096	9,663	10,490	267,182	118,655	2,382
Cape Vincent	899	1,593	2,054	2,050	1,280	7,892	88,427½	4,736½	13,107	9,419	159,146	24,800	2,877½
Champion	649	1,032	1,941	1,082	736	4,670	48,511½	2,949	23,440	10,262	160,596	148,718	1,126
Clayton	978	1,997	3,011	2,801	1,782	15,018	91,930½	7,503	13,816	2,770	206,851	179,475	2,796
Ellisburgh	1,472	3,312	3,761	4,260	2,445	23,170¼	214,699¼	6,386½	34,662	50,656	261,311	342,465	4,154
Henderson	776	1,621	1,368	3,975	838	7,350	71,899	3,219½	12,016	24,532	136,048	36,937	1,561
Hounsfield	908	1,227	1,842	4,021	959	17,686½	84,472½	3,982	12,588	10,147	148,966	60,118	1,877¾
Le Ray	998	1,528	3,258	17,787	1,530	11,999	87,962¾	6,242	16,759	7,322	249,898	257,182	4,312
Lorraine	395	843	1,601	1,279	592	587	57,375½	3,437	13,381	9,489	94,323	211,822	1,368
Lyme	857	1,370	1,716	2,379	982	5,306	120,380½	4,731	6,870	4,475	120,497	91,716	2,289
Orleans	909	1,806	2,662	2,269	1,262	12,874	100,261½	5,488	7,531	1,681	212,975	8,320	3,047
Pamelia	584	1,006	1,990	1,687	891	8,885	61,079	4,729	7,780	1,529	151,117	192,427	1,626
Philadelphia	564	848	1,729	1,181	534	218½	50,541	2,994	5,762	83	152,784	90,790	691
Rodman	540	1,200	2,149	2,830	896	2,018	68,289	3,972	11,964	12,716	181,235	121,325	2,179
Rutland	568	926	2,643	966	928	3,623	42,036⅝	4,206	16,832	13,943	234,065	247,331	1,815
Theresa	486	1,065	1,808	861	859	2,427	40,000	4,177½	5,057	640	163,775	93,780	2,324
Watertown	955	963	2,808	1,499	1,078	8,022½	55,329	4,305½	11,766	25,122	222,247	111,240	817
Wilna	645	731	1,654	1,322	713	1,797½	35,604¾	3,058½	24,983	318	142,220	47,850	1,476½
Worth	109	245	405	169	120		11,790½	1,016	5,583	111	22,298	30,818	586
Total	17,059	29,777	49,472	63,401	23,327	169,901	1,672,895⅝	98,575	289,031	215,431	3,949,608	2,819,459	45,955¾

KINGS COUNTY.

THIS county was organized with its present limits, Nov. 1, 1683.[1] It lies upon the w. end of Long Island, adjacent to New York Harbor, and embraces several small islands adjacent to the coast. It is centrally distant 140 mi. from Albany, and contains 72 sq. mi. The surface is generally level or gently undulating. A broad range of drift hills, 50 to 300 feet above tide, extends from the shore of the bay in the s. w. corner in a N. E. direction through the co. From their summits the surface gradually declines both to the N. and s., and terminates upon the shores in extensive salt meadows. The portion lying N. of the hills is moderately uneven, being occasionally broken by low, isolated drift hills. The shores are deeply indented by bays, which for the most part are shallow, and very irregular in outline. The principal of these are Hallets Cove, Newtown Creek,[2] Wallabout, Gowanus, and Gravesend Bays on the w., and Sheeps Head Bay on the s. Jamaica Bay, a large, shallow, landlocked bay upon the s. shore, is partially in this co. It incloses a large number of low, marshy islands separated by narrow and irregular tidal currents. Wide salt marshes extend along the shores of the bays, and far inland along the courses of the small creeks.[3] The soil is mostly a light, sandy loam. A strip immediately surrounding the marshes and embracing a large share of the w. extremity is fertile, and capable of producing almost any crop adapted to the climate. Its close proximity to New York, the great commercial center of the country, renders it favorably situated for the development of manufactures and commerce; and both of these pursuits are largely carried on at the centers of population. The agriculture of the co. is mostly confined to gardening for the N. Y. market. All of the business of the co.—manufacturing, commercial, and agricultural—are so intimately connected with the interests of New York that the co. may be considered as a suburb of the great city.[4]

The county seat is located at the city of Brooklyn.[5] The courts are accommodated at the City Hall, which belongs exclusively to the city. The jail, located upon Raymond St., is closely surrounded by other buildings, and its ventilation is very imperfect. The average number of inmates is 80, supported at a weekly cost of $2.10 each.[6] The Kings Co. Penitentiary is located upon a farm of 38 acres near the s. line of Brooklyn. The buildings, now nearly completed, are of stone, and sufficiently spacious for the accommodation and care of all the prisoners of the co. The main building is 490 feet long by 86 feet broad, with two wings of 50 feet each. The total cost up to January 1, 1857 was $190,414.35. The institution is designed to be self supporting. The county clerk's office is kept at the City Hall.[7] The Kings County Almshouse is located upon a farm of 70 acres in Flatbush, about three miles s. of the City Hall of Brooklyn. This institution consists of four large brick buildings,—the almshouse proper, hospital, nursery, and lunatic asylum. These buildings are spacious and well arranged, but poorly ventilated. A school is maintained through the year, and religious instruction is given upon the Sabbath.

[1] From 1665 to 1683 this co. formed a part of the "West Riding of Yorkshire," England. See p. 544.

[2] This creek is a tidal current, receiving several small fresh water streams, and is properly a narrow bay.

[3] Upon the beach the General Government has established 2 lifeboat stations. In Jan. 1821, the bay and the Narrows between the w. extremity of Long Island and Staten Island was frozen so that persons crossed on the ice.

[4] For more minute description of the business of the co., see town descriptions.

[5] The courts were originally held at Gravesend; but, by an act of the General Assembly, passed Nov. 7, 1685, they were removed to Flatbush, and a courthouse was built there the succeeding year. This building was used until 1758, when a new combined courthouse and jail was erected. By an act passed April 6, 1784, a tax of £200 was authorized to be raised to repair the injuries which had been done to the courthouse and jail by the British. The repairs were expended under the direction of Philip Nagel and Jeremyas Vanderbilt. By an act of March 10, 1791, the courthouse and jail were directed to be rebuilt under the direction of Johannes E. Lott, John Vanderbilt, and Chas. Doughty, and £1,200 was appropriated for that purpose. During the next year £300 additional was raised to finish the buildings. These buildings were burned Nov. 3, 1832; and by act of Feb. 27, 1834, the co. seat was removed to Brooklyn. The first co. officers after the Revolution were Nicholas Covenhoven, *First Judge*; Jacob Sharp, jr., *Clerk*; Wm. Boerum, *Sheriff*; and Johannes E. Lott, *Surrogate*.

[6] Up to June 1, 1858, 39,910 prisoners had been confined in this jail.

[7] By an act of May 1, 1828, a fireproof co. clerk's office was directed to be built in Brooklyn. A more spacious one was built in 1837, which was used until the office was removed to its present location in the City Hall. By an act passed in 1852, an office of Register was created; and by a later act, discretionary powers have been granted to a Board of Commissioners for the better preservation of the public records.

Children are bound out at the age of 12 years. The average number of inmates is 1,800, supported at a weekly cost of about $2.00 each. The farm yields a revenue of $3,500.

The Brooklyn & Jamaica R. R. extends from the s. ferry of Brooklyn eastward through near the center of the co. The Flushing R. R. extends from Hunters Point, (Queens co.,) N. of Brooklyn, to the village of Flushing, a distance of 8 mi. In the city of Brooklyn are several local rail roads; and from the city lines of stages extend to every village in the co.

The Long Island Intelligencer, the first newspaper in the co., was published some time before 1807.

Four newspapers—three daily and one weekly—are now published in the co.[1]

The first settlements of this co. were made mostly by the Dutch, about 1625. In 1640, a colony of Mass. Quakers, in quest of religious freedom, settled at Gravesend under the protection of the Dutch Government. Long previous to the English conquest of 1664, settlements had been made, mills erected, and churches and schools established in every town in the co. The settlers were so exclusively Dutch that the Dutch language and customs prevailed until within a comparatively recent period. Bushwick, Brooklyn, Flatbush, Flatlands, and New Utrecht were known under the English Government as the "*Five Dutch Towns;*" and they were associated, for certain purposes, until 1690.[2] The Five Towns also formed an ecclesiastical society, and joined in the support of their minister until the final separation of the American church from the Classis of Holland, in 1772.

Few events of interest occurred within the limits of this co. during the colonial period. Its Revolutionary annals belong to the general history of the country. During its occupation by the British, from 1776 to 1782, the people were subjected to a series of disgraceful and oppressive acts.[3] Many of the inhabitants left the co. from fear of hostile visits during the War of 1812–15; and at times much alarm was felt,—although no hostile visit actually took place. It has shared in the growth of New York City, and is closely identified with it in business. This co. is included in the "Metropolitan Police District" created by act of April 15, 1857, and in the Board of Police Commissioners it is represented by the Mayor of Brooklyn and one other member. Vast schemes of speculation have from time to time arisen, most of which have resulted in loss, and several of them, devised upon a magnificent scale, have seriously retarded the progress of needful improvement.

From 1850 to 1853 about 40 building associations were organized in this co., ostensibly to enable those of humble means to acquire *a home*, but practically to form contributions to a fund which was loaned to those members who would allow the highest premium. The rates submitted to were often extremely ruinous, and the speculation had but a brief existence.

[1] *The Courier and New York and Long Island Advertiser,* the first paper published on Long Island, was commenced June 26, 1799.

The Long Island Intelligencer was commenced at Brooklyn May 26, 1806.

The Brooklyn Daily Evening Star, begun by Alden B. Spooner & Sons, Jan. 4, 1841, is still issued by Edwin B. Spooner. A semi-weekly edition was issued in 1824.

The Long Island Patriot was started at Brooklyn March 7, 1821, by Geo. L. Birch. In 1833 it was changed to *The Brooklyn Advocate,* and was issued by James A. Bennett. In 1835–36 it was changed to *The Brooklyn Advocate and Nassau Gazette.*

The Williamsburgh Gazette was started in 1835 by Francis G. Fish. It was afterward changed to *The Williamsburgh Daily Gazette,* and was issued a short time.

The American Native Citizen and Brooklyn Evening Advertiser, da., was published in 1836 by F. G. Fish.

The Mechanics' Advocate was issued a short time in 1840 at East New York.

The Real Estate Gazette, also started at East New York, had an ephemeral existence.

The Williamsburgh Democrat was commenced June 3, 1840, by Thomas A. Devyr.

The Brooklyn Daily Eagle was commenced in 1841 by Isaac Van Anden, and is still published. From the same office was issued *The Brooklyn Weekly Eagle,* which was changed in 1855 to *The Saturday Evening Miscellany.*

The Brooklyn Daily News was started in 1841 by Worthall & Watts, and was continued until Nov. 1843.

The Brooklyn News and Times was issued in 1843 by J. S. Noble.

The Age was started at Williamsburgh in Dec. 1844, and was continued a short time.

The Democratic Advocate was published at Williamsburgh in 1844 by J. G. Wallace.

The Brooklyn Daily Advertiser was started in 1844 by H. A. Lees and W. Foulkes, and was continued about 8 years.

The American Champion was published at Brooklyn a short time in 1844.

The Daily Long Islander was started at Williamsburgh in 1845 by Bishop & Kelley.

The Williamsburgh Morning Post was published in 1847 by Devyr & Taylor.

The Saturday Evening Bee was issued a short time in 1848 at Brooklyn.

The Orbit was issued at South Brooklyn in 1848.

The Kings County Patriot was started at Williamsburgh in 1848 by Geo. Thompson and S. R. Hasbrook.

The Williamsburgh Times was started in 1848 by Bennet Smith & Co. Soon after the consolidation of Williamsburgh and Brooklyn its name was changed to **The Brooklyn Daily Times,** under which title it is now published.

The Excelsior was commenced in 1848 at South Brooklyn, and was issued a short time.

The Brooklyn Daily Freeman was published in 1849.

The Daily Independent Press was commenced July 16, 1850, at Williamsburgh, by W. G. Bishop and J. A. F. Kelley, and was continued until 1855.

The Brooklyn Morning Journal was established in 1851 by Hogan & Heighway.

The Union Ark, a temperance mo., was published at Brooklyn in 18—— by J. Schuebly.

The Long Island Anzeiger (German) was started at Brooklyn, Sept. 2, 1854, by Edward Rohr.

The Triangle (German semi-mo.) was started at Brooklyn, April 7, 1855, by Edward Rohr.

The Kings Co. Advertiser and Village Guardian (semi-mo.) was started at East New York in May, 1857, by C. Warren Hamilton.

The Green Point Advertiser was published a short time in 1847 by L. Masquerier.

[2] A Secretary or Register was especially commissioned by the Governor to take the proof of wills, of marriage settlements, the acknowledgment of "transcripts" or other conveyance, and such important contracts and agreements as required to be recorded.

[3] By an act of March 6, 1784, Kings co. was taxed $13,000 to repay Revolutionary expenses.—*Onderdonk's Rev. Inc.*

BROOKLYN[1]—was incorp. by patent, with the usual privileges of townships, under Gov. Lovelace, Oct. 18, 1667, and its rights were confirmed by Gov. Dongan, May 13, 1686. It was recognized as a town under the State Government March 7, 1788. The village of Brooklyn was incorp. as a fire district April 2, 1801, and as a village April 12, 1816, and both town and village were incorp. as a city April 8, 1834. The city of Williamsburgh and town of Bushwick were annexed April 17, 1854.[2] The city extends along New York Bay and East River to Newtown Creek, occupying the N. part of the co. Its exterior line is 22 mi., and it contains an area of 16,000 acres. The s. and E. borders are occupied by a broad range of low hills, which extend E. into Queens co. Along the shore opposite the lower point of New York is an irregular bluff known as "Brooklyn Heights." A considerable portion of the s. part of the city is low and level. Newtown Creek, forming the N. boundary, is an irregular arm of the sea, receiving several small fresh water streams. Wallabout Bay is a deep indentation lying between the old cities of Williamsburgh and Brooklyn. Gowanus Bay extends into the s. part of the city.[3] The land that borders upon these bays is flat and marshy.

Within the limits of Brooklyn are several districts known by the names which they bore when they were distinct localities, before the city was incorporated. These will eventually all be lost in the growth and consolidation of the business of the city. **Brooklyn** (p. o.) includes the old settled parts of the city s. of Wallabout Bay. Upon East River, in this district, are several large manufactories. The water front is entirely occupied by wharves and warehouses. **Williamsburgh** (p. o.) includes the thickly settled portions N. of Wallabout Bay. It contains a large number of manufacturing establishments, and its entire water front is devoted to commercial purposes. **Green Point,** (p. o.,) comprising the 17th ward, lies between Bushwick and Newtown Creeks, and occupies the extreme N. w. part of the city. It contains extensive shipyards, and manufactories of porcelain, coal oil, lifeboats, and many other articles. **Wallabout** (sometimes called East Brooklyn) lies E. of Wallabout Bay. **Bedford** and **New Brooklyn** are localities on the R. R., in the E. part of the city. **Bushwick Cross Roads** and **Bushwick Green** are villages E. of Williamsburgh. **Gowanus** is a village near the head of Gowanus Bay. **South Brooklyn** comprises the portion of the city lying s. of Atlantic St. It has an extensive water front; and along the shore immense works have been constructed to facilitate commerce.[4] It contains extensive wood, coal, stone, and lumber yards, and numerous planing mills, distilleries, breweries, plaster mills, founderies, and machine shops. The city is connected with New York by 11 steam ferries, all supplied with excellent boats, which perform regular and frequent trips.[5] From the Atlantic St. Ferry the Brooklyn & Jamaica R. R. extends E. to the E. bounds of the co.[6]

From the principal ferries lines of city railroads extend through the principal avenues and radiate to nearly every part of the city, affording easy, rapid, and cheap means of communication.[7] The commerce of Brooklyn is extensive, though it scarce has an independent existence, from its intimate relations with that of New York. The docks and piers at South Brooklyn are among the most extensive and commodious in the country. Ship and boat building and repairing are extensively carried on at Williamsburgh and Green Point. The whole water front of the city is occupied by ferries, piers, slips, and boat and ship yards; and the aggregate amount of business

---

[1] The name is derived from the Dutch "*Breuck-landt*," (broken land.) The patent for the township was issued to Jan Everts, Jan Daman, Albert Corneliser, Paules Verbeeck, Michael Eneyle, Thos. Lamberts, Teunis Gisbertse, Bogart and Jovis Jacobsen. The annual quitrent under this patent was 20 bush. of wheat.

[2] Bushwick—signifying wood-town—was invested with certain powers of government March 14, 1661. Another patent was granted Oct. 25, 1667; but it remained associated with other towns until Aug. 12, 1708. Williamsburgh Village, in this town, was incorp. April 14, 1827, and the town of Williamsburgh was formed March 16, 1840. The village and town were united and incorp. as the City of Williamsburgh April 7, 1851, and the city and town of Bushwick were annexed to Brooklyn April 17, 1854. Bushwick now constitutes the 17th and 18th wards, and Williamsburgh the 13th, 14th, 15th, 16th, and a part of the 19th wards.

[3] Acts have been passed authorizing a canal, with basins, wharves, and slips, to be constructed along the creek that flows

into this bay. The mouth of the creek has been improved for a short distance.

[4] The Atlantic Dock contains an area of 40 acres, and has sufficient depth of water for any vessel. An outside pier is 3,000 feet long. The warehouses upon the piers are of granite. The Erie Basin and other extensive docks along the bay have been projected, and work upon them has commenced. These docks afford perfect security to vessels while loading and unloading, and security to goods against theft. It is estimated that $1,000,000 worth of goods are annually stolen from the wharves and ships at New York and Brooklyn.

[5] These several ferries are all chartered by the Corporation of N. Y. City. The boats average 400 tons, and are noted for the regularity with which they perform their trips. See page 428.

[6] This road is leased to the Long Island R. R. during the term of its charter. A tunnel 2,750 feet long, extending under a portion of Atlantic St., commences near the ferry. It was finished in Dec. 1844, at a cost of $96,000.

[7] In 1855 the city authorized the granting of charters for these

transacted there forms an important item in the commerce of the State. In the extent and variety of its manufactures Brooklyn ranks among the first cities in the country. Located near the great commercial center, it has become the seat of an immense manufacturing interest.[1]

The U. S. Navy Yard is located upon Wallabout Bay.[2] The premises connected with it occupy an area of 45 acres, and are inclosed on the land side by a high wall. Within the inclosure are various mechanic shops necessary in building and repairing vessels, a large and costly dry dock,[3] two large buildings to cover ships of war while in process of building, extensive lumber warehouses, several marine railways, and a large amount of balls, cannon, and other munitions of war. The Naval Lyceum is filled with curiosities sent home by naval officers. Upon a gentle rise, a little E. of the Navy Yard, is a U. S. Marine Hospital[4] for the care of sick and infirm seamen belonging to the navy. Near it is an extensive laboratory for the manufacture of medicines for the navy.[5] The grounds belonging to these establishments occupy an area of 35 acres. A little s. of the Navy Yard, upon Park Avenue, are extensive Marine Barracks.

The city is well supplied with pure, soft water, derived from Hempstead Hook, Valley, and Spring-

city railroads to the parties who should offer to carry passengers at the lowest price. The Brooklyn City R. R. Co., formed Dec. 17, 1853, received the grants; and the fare upon the several lines, without regard to distance, is 5 cents. The following is a list of these several railroads :—

LINES OF RAILROADS.	Routes.	Length in Miles.	When Opened.
Fulton Ferry to Washington Av...............................	Fulton Av.	2.31	July, 1854.
Washington Av. to Brooklyn Av...............................	....	1.12	Sept. "
Fulton St. to Nostrand Av...............................	Myrtle Av.	2.04	July, "
Nostrand Av. to Division Av...............................	....	.87	Nov. "
Flushing St. to Throop Av...............................	Flushing St.	2.57	July, "
Throop Av. to Division Av...............................	....	.14	April, 1855.
Kent Av. to Bushwick Av...............................	....	2.08	Oct. 1854.
Bushwick Creek to Kent St...............................	....	.49	Oct. 1855.
Kent St. to Freeman St...............................	....	.26	Dec. "
Fulton St. to Gowanus Creek...............................	Greenwood.	1.56	Aug. 1854.
Gowanus Creek to Thirty-Sixth St...............................	....	1.88	Nov. "
Thirty-Sixth St. to City Line...............................	....	1.17	July, 1855.
City Line to Yellow Hook Lane...............................	....	.56	July, 1856.
Court St. to Ferry...............................	Hamilton Av.	.93	May, 1855.

[1] The following table, derived from the State Census of 1855, shows the amount and kinds of manufactures.

NAMES OF MANUFACTORIES.	No.	Amount of Manufactures.	Men.	NAMES OF MANUFACTORIES.	No.	Amount of Manufactures.	Men.
Agricultural Implements..............	1	$28,000	22	Lamp and Lanterns....................	2	55,000	36
Ax and Edge Tools.....................	1	55,000	6	Liquorice............................	1	49,340	35
Bakers................................	9	92,535	49	Machine Shops........................	11	276,000	260
Block................................	2	70,000	58	Malt.................................	1	90,000	12
Breweries............................	12	157,255	52	Marble...............................	6	88,500	100
Cabinet..............................	16	251,324	149	Oil Cloth............................	5	170,250	94
Camphene.............................	3	1,670,000	85	Oil Mills............................	2	286,000	36
Chandlery and Soap...................	2	229,100	64	Paint and Color......................	2	50,000	16
Chemical Laboratories................	6	320,000	42	Patent Leather.......................	2	140,000	47
Coach and Wagon......................	11	70,550	86	Planing Mills........................	6	476,600	153
Coffee, Spice, and Mustard...........	4	58,640	25	Porcelain............................	2	90,000	128
Cotton Batting.......................	2	70,000	67	Rope.................................	10	2,205,153	677
Dentists' Gold.......................	1	100,000	2	Rosin Oil............................	5	161,300	46
Distilleries.........................	7	2,499,000	215	Safes................................	2	115,000	60
Fish and Whale Oil...................	2	173,000	19	Sash and Blind.......................	11	102,178	60
Flax Dressing........................	3	590,000	98	Ship.................................	6	945,000	540
Fur Dressing.........................	3	114,700	30	Silver Ware..........................	2	54,000	12
Furnaces.............................	15	900,000	600	Steamboat Finishing..................	1	150,000	64
Gas..................................	3	278,000	278	Steam Pump...........................	1	60,000	76
Glass................................	2	322,000	282	Stone Cutting........................	14	256,300	334
Glue.................................	1	150,000	7	Tin and Sheet Iron...................	4	150,000	95
Gold and Silver Refining.............	1	225,000	7	Tobacco and Cigar....................	9	205,620	139
Gold Pen.............................	1	112,000	41	White Lead...........................	1	800,000	195
Gristmills...........................	3	635,000	48	Whiting..............................	1	60,000	17
Hat and Cap..........................	2	986,000	666	Window Shades........................	1	50,000	19
House Building.......................	11	254,000	151	Minor Manufactories..................	89	700,446	865
Ivory Black and Bone Manure.........	4	106,960	49				
Japanned Cloth.......................	1	189,600	64	Total...................	296	$18,494,351	7,368

[2] The land occupied by the Navy Yard was ceded to the General Government by the State in 1807.

[3] The site for the dry dock was fixed by Col. Baldwin, in 1826; but efficient work was not commenced until 1841. It was subsequently prosecuted under the charge of several engineers, as follows:—

Prof. Edward H. Courtenay; Aug. 1, 1841, to Aug. 1, 1842.	$35,264.25
Gen. William Gibbs McNeil; Oct. 10, 1844, to April 1, 1845.	114,671.83
W. P. S. Sanger; April 1,1845, to June 23, 1846.	115,951.81
Wm. J. McAlpine; June 23, 1846, to Oct. 1, 1849.	1,114,311.09
Gen. Chas. B. Stuart; Oct. 1,1849, to Aug. 30, 1851	732,974.63
Total cost..................	$2,113,173.61

The work was suspended from Aug. 1842, till Oct. 1844. The main chamber is 286 feet long by 35 feet wide at the bottom, and 307 feet long by 98 feet wide at the top. Depth, 36 feet. The masonry foundations are 400 by 120 feet, upon piles driven 40 feet into the earth. It is emptied by steam pumps in 4½ hours.—*Stuart's Naval Dry Docks of the U. S.*

[4] This building is faced with white marble and presents a fine architectural appearance. The average number of inmates is about 50.

[5] This laboratory has been gradually formed within the last 10 years, and is said to be the only institution of the kind owned by any Government. The chemical and mechanical arrangements are extremely well adapted to their use.

field Creeks. It is brought 7¾ mi. in an open canal and 4¾ mi. in a brick conduit, thence pumped into a reservoir on Cypress Hill, 170 ft. above tide, and thence distributed in iron pipes throughout the city. The conduit has a capacity of 40,000,000 gallons per day, and the pumps can raise 10,000,000 gal. per day. The reservoir is 20 feet deep, and has a capacity of 167,000,000 gals. The whole cost of the work is estimated at $4,200,000.[1] The Fire Departments of the Eastern and Western Districts are separately organized under special acts.[2] The city is supplied with gas by 3 companies.

The *City Park*, between Park and Flushing Avenues and Navy and Park Sts., contains 7 acres: *Washington Park*, between Myrtle and De Kalb Avenues and Cumberland and Canton Sts., contains 33 acres. It occupies the site of Fort Green of the Revolution. In the newly surveyed sections several sites for parks have been reserved by the city.

The *City Armory*, at the corner of Henry and Cranberry Sts., was erected in 1858, at a cost of $14,000. A *State Arsenal*, on Clinton St., was built in 1856, at a cost of $40,000.

The *City Hall*, situated at the junction of Fulton and Court Sts., is a fine building, faced with white marble.[3] Besides these, there are in the city 9 banks of discount, 5 savings' banks, and 10 stock fire insurance companies.

The *Public Schools* are under the charge of a board of education, consisting of 45 members. The city contains 32 school districts; and in 1857 there were employed 320 teachers,—27 males and 293 females. The whole number of children between 4 and 21 years of age is 46,000, of whom 35,817, or 78 per cent., attended school during some portion of the year. The total expenses of the schools for 1857 was $231,474.61. A normal school for the professional instruction of teachers has been established.

The *Packer Collegiate Institute*, for girls, occupies an elegant building upon Jorolimon St., w. of the City Hall. It was incorp. May 8, 1845, as the *"Brooklyn Female Academy."* Its name was changed March 19, 1853, in honor of Mrs. Wm. S. Packer, who endowed the institution with $65,000. An astronomical observatory is connected with it.[4]

The *Brooklyn Collegiate and Polytechnic Institute*, for boys, on Livingston St., was incorp. April 7, 1854. It was established by a stock company, with a capital of $75,000, and has accommodations for 150 pupils. Besides these, there are in the city 100 private schools and seminaries, several of which are large institutions, with corps of professors and with permanent investments. The aggregate number of pupils in attendance at the schools is 2,600.

The *Brooklyn Institute* was incorp. Nov. 20, 1824. It occupies a commodious building on Washington St., the gift of Augustus Graham. It has a free library, provides free lectures and lessons in drawing and painting for apprentices, and its rooms are depositories for books, maps, models, and drawing apparatus.

The *Brooklyn Athenæum and Reading Room*, on the corner of Atlantic and Clinton Sts., was incorp. Jan. 28, 1852. It occupies a large three story edifice, erected at a cost of $60,000. The first story is used for mercantile purposes, the second for a library and reading room, and the third for public lectures.

The *Law Library* in Brooklyn, incorp. Jan. 8, 1850, is located at 341 Fulton St.

The *Naval Lyceum*, within the Navy Yard, was established in 1833 by officers of the navy. It has a fine library and museum.

The *Kings County Lodge Library Association*, at Williamsburgh, was incorp. Feb. 7, 1847.

Among the societies for intellectual improvement are the *Hamilton Library Association*, founded in 1830; the *Franklin Debating Association*, in 1852; the *Young Men's Association*, in 1853; the *St. Charles Institute*, in 1854; the *Eccleston Literary Association*, in 1854; and the *Columbia Literary Association*, in 1855. The *Great Northwestern Zephyr Association*, designed to encourage native talent in music, painting, and sculpture, was organized in 1838. The *Philharmonic Society*

---

[1] This great work is just completed. Until a very recent date the city has depended upon wells and cisterns for its supply of water. There were 122 public cisterns in the city; but all the supplies were entirely inadequate to the demand for water. The first agitation for a better supply of water commenced in 1835; but nothing was accomplished until 1847, when a report was made recommending the building of reservoirs to be supplied from wells. In 1849, W. J. McAlpine submitted a plan for obtaining a supply from the streams flowing into Jamaica Bay. The question of prosecuting this work at public expense was repeatedly voted down. Several private companies caused surveys to be made, and one of them acquired titles to the streams in question; and June 4, 1856, the Common Council subscribed $1,300,000 to the stock of the Nassau Water Company. The work was commenced July 31, 1856, under the charge of James

P. Kirkwood, Chief Engineer. Feb. 11, 1857, the rights of the Nassau Company were vested in the city. The works were completed in May, 1859. It is contemplated erecting another reservoir upon Prospect Hill.

[2] The Fire Department of the Western District, under the care of 5 commissioners, has 7 fire districts, 22 engines, 4 hook and ladder companies, 7 hose companies, and 10 alarm bells. The Fire Department of the Eastern District has 6 fire districts, 13 engines, 3 hook and ladder companies, 4 hose companies, and 2 alarm bells.

[3] This building contains the city and most of the co. offices. It was commenced in 1836; but work was suspended in 1837 and was not resumed until 1846. It was completed in 1848, in a style much less costly than that of the original design.

[4] See pp. 747, 748.

of Brooklyn, for the encouragement of music, was incorp. May 6, 1857. The *Brooklyn Horticultural Society* was incorp. April 9, 1854, and holds annual fairs. The *Hunt Horticultural and Botanical Garden* was incorporated April 9, 1855, with a capital of $150,000. It has a garden of 16 acres.

The *Brooklyn City Hospital*, on Raymond St. near De Kalb Avenue, was incorp. May 8, 1845. Its present buildings were opened April 28, 1852. It is supported by voluntary contributions and legislative appropriations. The *Brooklyn City Dispensary*, located at 109 Pineapple St., was incorp. March 5, 1850. It is supported in the same manner as the hospital. The *Brooklyn Dispensary*, (Homeopathic,) 83 Court St., was incorp. Dec. 3, 1852. It is supported by private subscriptions. The *Williamsburg Dispensary*, on the corner of 5th and South Sts., was incorp. March 4, 1851; 2,221 persons received medical treatment at the institution in 1857. It is supported by private contributions. The *Brooklyn Central Dispensary*, 473 Fulton St., was incorp. Dec. 11, 1855. The *Brooklyn German General Dispensary* is located at 145 Court St. The *Brooklyn Eye and Ear Infirmary*, 109 Pineapple St., was incorp. March 27, 1851.

The *Orphan Asylum Society* was incorp. May 6, 1834. The institution is situated upon a fine site on Cumberland St. near Myrtle Avenue.

The *Roman Catholic Orphan Asylum* of Brooklyn was incorp. May 6, 1834. The asylum for boys is located at the corner of Clinton and Congress Sts., and the asylum for girls upon Congress St. near Clinton. The former has 120 inmates, and the latter 250. The girls are under the charge of the Sisters of Charity. The support of these institutions is principally derived from the income of a large property bequeathed by Cornelius Heeney and under the charge of the Brooklyn Benevolent Society.[1]

The *Brooklyn Association for Improving the Condition of the Poor* was formed March 26, 1844. It numbers about 180 visitors, whose duty it is to investigate the condition of the poor in every part of the city, afford such temporary relief in the way of food and clothing as the cases may warrant, and to refer the needy to the appropriate sources for permanent relief. This association distributes $6,000 to $7,000 per year. The *Brooklyn Benevolent Society*, founded upon a bequest of Cornelius Heeney, was incorp. in May, 1845. It is managed by 11 trustees, of whom the Archbishop of N. Y. and the Mayor of Brooklyn are *ex officio* members. Its funds are principally devoted to the support of various Catholic charities. The *Brooklyn Society for the Relief of Respectable and Indigent Females*, incorp. in 1851, was founded by John B. Graham, who erected a fine edifice, corner of Washington and De Kalb Sts., as a home for the unfortunates named in the title. It derives its support from private subscriptions. The *Children's Aid Society* was organized in Feb. 1854, as an industrial school. The *Brooklyn Industrial School Association*, under the management of ladies of the several churches, was incorp. April 4, 1854. It has established schools in different parts of the city for girls who do not attend the public schools, and who are entirely deprived of moral training. The *Brooklyn Female Employment Society*, an association of ladies to furnish employment to respectable females who may be reduced to want, was incorp. April 19, 1854. Its office and salesroom is at 65 Court St. The *Church Charity Association* for the relief of the aged, sick, and indigent was incorp. in March, 1851. It is under the patronage of the Prot. E. Church.

The churches of Brooklyn are justly celebrated for their general elegance and beauty of architectural design. Large numbers of people doing business in New York reside in Brooklyn; and this has led to the erection of so great a number of churches that the city has been denominated the "city of churches." In 1858 there were 139 churches in the city.[2] Connected with these churches are various religious and charitable societies.[3] The Freemasons, Odd Fellows, and Sons of Tem-

---

[1] The other benevolent Catholic societies in the city are as follows:—*St. James's School*, Jay St., with 500 pupils under the Brothers of Christian Schools, and 450 pupils under the Sisters of Mercy; *St. Paul's Female School*, with 400 pupils, under the Sisters of Charity; *St. Peter's and Paul's School*, with 300 girls, under the Sisters of St. Joseph; *St. Mary Star of the Sea*, with 300 girls, under the Sisters of Charity; *Convent and Female School* attached to the Church of the Holy Trinity; *Convent and Boarding Academy of the Sisters of St. Joseph*; *Convent and Academy of the Visitation*; *St. Francis of Assisi's Convent of Sisters of Mercy and Nuns of the Order of St. Dominic*. The *R. C. Beneficial Society of St. Peter's and St. Paul's Church* was incorp. June 15, 1858, to sustain a Sunday school and library, and support the sick and bury the dead. *Free schools* are connected with all the churches except that of St. Charles.

[2] 25 Prot. E., 22 M. E., 17 Presb., 15 Ref. Prot. D., 15 R. C., 15 Bap., 10 Cong., and 20 consisting of Covenanters, Asso. Presb., Asso. Ref. Presb., Unita., Univ., Ger. Evang., Moravian, Friends, Ind. Cong., Ind. Meth., and Jew.

[3] The following is a list of the principal of these societies, with the dates of their formation:—

The Brooklyn City Tract Society	1830
The Brooklyn Bible Society	1841
The Prot. Benevolent and Library Association	1844
The Williamsburgh Bible Society	1845
The Navy Mission S. S. Association	June 16, 1849
The Brooklyn Female Bible Society	1850
The Benev. Asso. of the Ch. of the Holy Trinity	May 10, 1850
The Warren Street Mission	Feb. 3, 1853
The Williamsburgh City Mission Society	March, 1853
The Brooklyn Y. M. Chris. Association	Dec. —, 1853
The Mount Prospect Mission Society	Jan. 23, 1854
The Hope Mission School	Mar. 16, 1854
The Brooklyn Sunday-School Union	Sept. 12, 1854
The Brotherhood of the Prot. E. Churches	Sept. 21, 1854
The Howard Benev. Society (Unita.)	Dec. —, 1854
The Convocation for Church Extension (Prot. E.)	June 25, 1854
The Vanderbilt Av. Mission S. S.	Mar. 16, 1858

perance all have lodges in the city; and besides these are numerous societies for mutual relief and protection.[1]

Greenwood Cemetery, upon the s. line, is mostly within the limits of the city. It is owned by a joint stock company, incorp. April 18, 1838. It comprises an area of 400 acres, beautifully located upon the elevated and broken ground E. of Gowanus Bay. The grounds were purchased, and opened for burial in 1842; and up to Aug. 1858, 64,000 burials had been made. It is one of the oldest and most beautiful of the rural cemeteries connected with the great cities in this country. The grounds are laid out with taste; and many of the sculptured monuments are costly and beautiful specimens of art.

The *Cemetery of the Evergreens*, upon the E. line, is partly in Queens co. It is beautifully located upon a bluff, affording fine views of New York, the bay, the ocean, and the surrounding country. It was opened for interment in 1849.

The *Friends' Cemetery* lies near the city line, N. of Greenwood. It has a fine location; but, in accordance with the principles of the sect, no ornamental monuments are allowed to be erected in it.

The *Citizens' Union Cemetery*, incorp. in 1851, contains an area of 29 acres. The trustees allow the burial of persons of color and of the poor for no charge except that of opening and closing the ground.

The first settlements were made under the Dutch Government, in 1625, by several families of French Protestants from near the river Waal, in Netherlands, who located near Wallabout Bay. They named their settlement "*Walloons*," and the bay "*Walloons Boght*," from which is derived its present name Wallabout.[2] Little progress was made in settlement for many years; and no governmental organization was effected under the Dutch. Up to the commencement of the present century the population was principally confined to several little hamlets scattered over the territory now embraced in the city. Since 1840 the increase of population and the growth of the city have been very rapid, scarcely paralleled by the magical growth of the cities of the West.[3] Although possessing a separate municipal government, in all its business and interests it forms an integral part of the city of New York. In the summer of 1776, New York and vicinity became the theater of stirring military events. After the British had evacuated Boston, Washington marched immediately to New York, believing that the enemy would make this the next point of attack. Every effort was made to construct and strengthen the military defenses of the place. Strong works were erected in Brooklyn and other points upon Long Island, and large bodies of troops were posted there to defend them. The British arrived, and landed their troops upon Staten Island July 8; and on the 22d of Aug. they passed over to Long Island, to the number of 10,000 strong. They landed in New Utrecht, whence three roads led over the hills to where the Americans were encamped. One of these roads passed near the Narrows, the next led from Flatbush, and the third far to the right by the route of Flatlands. It was the design of Gen. Putnam, who commanded the American forces, to arrest the enemy upon the heights; and the appearance of columns of troops early on the morning of the 27th on the middle road led to the belief that the main attack was to be made at that point. While intent upon this movement, it was found that the main army of the enemy were approaching from the direction of Bedford, and that there was imminent danger of being surrounded by them. Attacked in front and rear, the Americans fought with bravery; but a part only succeeded in gaining their entrenchments. The loss of the Americans was more than 3,000 in killed, wounded, and prisoners; and of the enemy, less than 400. Gens. Sullivan, Stirling, and Woodhull were taken prisoners,—the last named of whom died from wounds inflicted after his surrender. The Americans withdrew to New York early on the 30th, under the personal direction of Gen. Washington.[4] The American prisoners taken at this battle, and those taken afterward during the war, were confined in the hulks of old ships anchored in Wallabout Bay,

---

[1] The following is a list of these societies:—

The Erin Fraternal Benev. Society	Formed 1835
The Emerald Benev. Society	1839
The Emmet Benev. Society	May 8, 1848
The Shamrock Benev. Society	May 5, 1848
The Laborers' Union Benev. Soc. of Williamsburgh	April 17, 1850
The Laborers' Union Benev. Society	Jan. 30, 1851
Williamsburgh Mut. Ben. Soc. of Operative Masons	June 14. 1853
" Laborers' Union Benev. Society	May 13, 1853
Operative Plasterers' Benev. Society	Dec. 27, 1854
Society for Visiting the Sick and Burying the Dead	Oct. 13, 1855
Ancient Order of Hibernians	July 18, 1856
United Brethren	Aug. 8, 1856
Washington Sick Supporting Association	Feb. 17, 1858

[2] Among these settlers were families named De Rapalje, Le Escuyer, Duryee, Le Sillier Cershou, Conseiller, and Murserol.—*Benson's Memoir, p.* 18. Sarah Rapelje—born here on the 9th of June, 1625—was the first white child born on the island. She received 20 morgens of land from Peter Minuet, the Dutch Governor. A tide mill was built at the head of Wallabout Bay at an early period.

[3] The following table shows the increase of population of the whole territory included within the city since 1790:—

1790	2,143	1830	17,014
1800	3,034	1835	27,854
1810	5,200	1840	42,622
1815	4,564	1845	72,769
1820	8,105	1850	130,757
1825	11,749	1855	205,250

[4] A heavy fog—very unusual for the time of year—completely enshrouded the island, and under its protection the Americans silently passed over to the N. Y. side. The British did not discover the movement until the rearguard of the Americans were beyond the reach of pursuit.—*Onderdonk's Rev. Inc.*

where they perished by hundreds and thousands from violence, cold, foul air, and stinted food.[1] During the War of 1812 a considerable amount of voluntary labor was expended in erecting a line of fortifications around the city, and bodies of troops were stationed there to protect the people.

FLATBUSH[2]—was chartered by Gov. Stuyvesant in 1652, and its rights were confirmed by Gov. Nicoll, Oct. 11, 1667, and by Gov. Dongan, Nov. 20, 1685.[3] It was recognized by the State Government March 7, 1788. New Lots was taken off in 1852. It is the central town in the co.. lying immediately s. of Brooklyn. A low, broad range of hills extends along the n. border, occupying nearly one-fourth of its surface. The remainder of the town is level. The soil is light and sandy, but productive. **Flatbush** (p. v.) is a long, scattered village, extending through the center of the town. It contains 4 churches,[4] the Erasmus Hall Academy,[5] and many elegant dwellings. **Greenfield** is a thinly settled village plat in the s. w. corner of the town. A part of Greenwood Cemetery lies in the n. w. corner. Galilee Cemetery lies e. of the village. The first settlement was made by the Dutch at an early period.

FLATLANDS[6]—was incorp. by patent under Gov. Nicoll, Oct. 4, 1667, confirmed by Gov. Dongan, March 11, 1685,[7] and recognized by the State Government March 7, 1788. It is the s. e. town in the co. The surface is very flat, as indicated by the name; and a considerable portion consists of salt marshes bordering upon Jamaica Bay.[8] Several small, marshy islands belong to the town.[9] **Flatlands** (p. o.) is a farming settlement. **Canarsie**[10] (p. o.) is a hamlet, upon the road leading to the bay. The first settlement was made by the Dutch, in 1636. Ex-Gov. Wouter Van Twiller had a tobacco farm in this town while it was under Dutch rule. There are 3 churches in town; 2 M. E. and Ref. Prot. D.

GRAVESEND[11]—was granted to English settlers, by patent under Gov. Keift, Dec. 19, 1645, and confirmed by Gov. Nicoll, Aug. 13, 1667, and by Gov. Dongan, Sept. 10, 1686.[12] It was recognized as a town March 7, 1788. It is the most southerly town in the co. The surface is generally very level. A beach and ridge of sand hills extend along the coast, and in the rear of these are extensive salt meadows. Coney Island is separated from the mainland by a narrow tidal current flowing through the marshes.[13] **Gravesend,** (p. v.,) near the center, is compactly built, and was formerly fortified with palisades. It was the county seat prior to 1686.[14] **Union-ville** is a small settlement on the bay, near the w. line. **The Cove** is a settlement on Sheeps Head Bay. This town was settled before 1640, by English Quakers, from Mass. Lady Deborah Moody—a woman of rank, education, and wealth—was a prominent person in this enterprise. The liberal terms of their first grant were not fully regarded by the Dutch; but the prudence and firmness of Lady Moody eventually secured a good degree of respect and a more indulgent policy toward them. In 1655 the settlement was saved from destruction by North River Indians by a guard from the city. In 1656 the people petitioned for and obtained 3 big guns for their protection. In 1659 the town agreed to give Henry Brazier 500 gilders for building a mill, and

---

[1] The first prison ship was the Whitby; but this and another were burned, and, in April, 1778, the Jersey became the receiving ship for prisoners. The Hope and the Falmouth, anchored near by, were the hospital ships; and upon these most of the deaths occurred. It is reported that 11,500 prisoners died upon these ships during the war. The persistent barbarity and cold-hearted inhumanity practiced by the British toward these prisoners finds no parallel in the history of civilized nations; and the horrible sufferings of the prisoners in their foul dungeons, reeking with filth, disease, and the air of the charnel house carried through months and years, completely cast into the shade the lesser horrors of the Middle Passage, or of the Black Hole of Calcutta. The graves of these martyrs of freedom were uncovered while grading for the Navy Yard, in 1808. Twenty hogsheads of bones were collected, deposited in 13 coffins,—representing the 13 original States,—and, May 26, 1808, they were buried upon Hudson Avenue, near the Navy Yard, under the auspices of the Tammany Society. The land upon which they were interred was given for that purpose by John Jackson. Several years since, Benj. Romaine inclosed the remains in a vault; and, April 11, 1851, an association was incorp. for collecting funds to build a monument.

[2] Named "*Midwout*" (Mid wood) by the Dutch.

[3] In the first patent, Jan Snedecor, Arent Van Hatten, Johannes Megapolensis, and others, were named as grantees; and in the second, Rev. J. Megapolensis, Cornelius Van Ruyven, J. P. Adrien Hegeman, Jan Snedecor, Jan Stryker. Frans Barents, (pastor,) Jacob Stryker, and Cornelius Janse Bougart were patentees.—*Patents*, IV, 48, 51.

[4] Ref. Prot. D., (formed in 1654,) M. E., Prot. E., and R. C.

[5] This institution, incorp. Nov. 17, 1787, was the first one chartered by the regents.

[6] Called "*New Amesfort*" by the Dutch, from a place in Holland.

[7] The patentees named in the first instrument were Elbert Elberts, Govert Lockermans, Roeliffe Martens, Pieter Claes, Wm. Garrits, Thos. Hillebrants, Stephen Coertsen, and Coert Stevens; and those in the second were E. Elberts, R. Martens, Pieter Classen, Wm. Garretsen, Coert Stevens, Lucas Stevensen, and John Teunissen. The annual quitrent was 14 bushels of wheat.

[8] These marshes and flat lands produce large quantities of hay.

[9] The principal of these are Bergen Island, on the bay, and Barren Island, upon the coast. Upon the latter island is a large bone boiling establishment, to which place are removed all the dead animals from New York. The business is very extensive, and large quantities of hides, fat, bones, hair, and manure are annually produced.

[10] Named from a tribe of Indians that formerly occupied this region.

[11] Named from the English town of this name, or from the deep sounds on the shore.—*Thompson's Hist.*, II, 169.

[12] The grantees named in the first patent were Lady Deborah Moody, Sir Henry Moody, Bart., Ensign Geo. Baxter, and Sergt. James Hubbard; those in the second were Thos. Delavall, Jas. Hubbard, Wm. Bound, sr., Wm. Goulding, and John Tilton; and those in the third were James Hubbard, John Tilton, jr., Wm. Goulder, Nicholas Stillwell, and Jocham Guilock. The quitrent was 6 bushels of wheat.

[13] "*Conysis Island*," from a family of that name. It is a favorite summer resort. A fine shell road and bridge connect it with the mainland. It embraces 60 acres of arable land, and about half a dozen families winter there.

[14] The village plat embraced 10 acres, subdivided into 39 lots for houses and gardens. A street surrounded this plat. The land around was laid out in lots diverging from the central nucleus.

every man a day's work, with a team, or 2 days without, in building a dam. The first church (Ref. Prot. D.) was formed in 1655. Besides this, there are in town 2 M. E. churches.

NEW LOTS[1]—was formed from Flatbush, Feb. 12, 1852. It lies in the extreme E. part of the co. Its surface is generally level, the S. half being occupied by extensive salt meadows. **East New York** (p. v.) is a prospective city of "magnificent distances" near the N. line.[2] It contains a newspaper office, 4 churches, a manufacture of dyestuffs and colors, several shoe manufactories, and 1,000 inhabitants. **Cypress Hills** is a newly surveyed village near the N. E. corner. The Cypress Hills Cemetery, Cemetery of the Evergreens, and Cemetery of the Congregation of Emanuel (Jewish) are partly in this town. The first settlement was made by about 20 families from Holland and a few Palatinates, in 1654. In 1660 the portions of lands previously held in common were divided into lots and assigned to individuals. During the same year a horse-mill was erected. For many years the deacons of the church were chosen overseers of the poor, and from 1799 to 1812 the schools were under the direction of church officers. A detachment of 1,200 militia was stationed here in the War of 1812, in anticipation of an attack from the British. There are 5 churches in town.[3]

NEW UTRECHT—was incorp. by Gov. Stuyvesant in 1662, by Gov. Nicoll, Aug. 15, 1668, and by Gov. Dongan, May 13, 1686.[4] It was recognized as a town March 7, 1788. It lies upon the Narrows, in the W. part of the co. A range of low hills extends across the N. border, and the remaining part of the surface is level. The soil is a light, sandy loam, but for the most part is highly cultivated. **New Utrecht,** (p. v.,) in the S. part, is a small, compact village. In ancient times it was inclosed by a palisade as a defense against Indians and pirates. **Fort Hamilton,** (p. v.,) near the U. S. grounds, is a fine village, chiefly inhabited by persons doing business in New York. **Bath** is a place of summer resort on Gravesend Bay. **Bay Ridge** is a suburban village adjoining Brooklyn. Fort Hamilton is a U. S. fortification upon the bluff commanding the passage of the Narrows.[5] Fort La Fayette is a strong water battery built upon Hendricks Reef, 200 yards from the shore.[6] There are 6 churches in town.[7]

Acres of Land, Valuation, Population, Dwellings, Families, Freeholders, Schools, Live Stock, Agricultural Products, and Domestic Manufactures, of Kings County.

Names of Towns.	Acres of Land.		Valuation of 1858.			Population.					Schools.	
	Improved.	Unimproved.	Real Estate.	Personal Property.	Total.	Males.	Females.	No. of Dwellings.	No. of Families.	Freeholders.	No. of Districts.	Children taught.
Brooklyn	1,652¼	1,196¼	$88,136,781	$10,338,494	$98,475,275	97,129	108,121	22,573	41,438	10,887	80	47,500
Flatbush	2,616	179	1,124,142	510,000	1,634,142	1,559	1,721	266	308	162	2	578
Flatlands	3,235½	1,950	563,351	150,525	713,876	879	699	232	258	172	3	673
Gravesend	2,506	695	544,241	124,850	669,091	664	592	200	226	127	2	388
New Lots	1,862	983½	746,915	182,800	929,715	1,181	1,080	335	444	285	3	817
New Utrecht	3,999½	591	1,573,067	301,400	1,874,467	1,435	1,295	364	459	239	4	816
Total	15,871¼	5,594¾	92,688,497	11,608,069	104,296,566	102,847	113,508	23,970	43,133	11,872	94	50,772

Names of Towns.	Live Stock.					Agricultural Products.							Domestic Cloths, in yards.
						Bush. of Grain.					Dairy Products.		
	Horses.	Working Oxen and Calves.	Cows.	Sheep.	Swine.	Winter.	Spring.	Tons of Hay.	Bushels of Potatoes.	Bushels of Apples.	Pounds Butter.	Pounds Cheese.	
Brooklyn	4,750	14	1,731		1,808	1,828	31,324	400	28,565	50			
Flatbush	361	24	218		356	2,560	13,462	1,097	84,822				
Flatlands	320	52	258		577	4,979	11,380	1,789	103,750				
Gravesend	300	126	223		378	4,182	9,137	683	70,595		11,030		
New Lots	268	84	188		316	4,486	10,647	871	30,186		6,395		
New Utrecht	315	70	216	2	529	4,911	14,115	1,343	50,325	4			
Total	6,314	370	2,834	2	3,964	22,946	90,065	6,183	368,243	54	17,425	—	—

[1] This part of Flatbush was called by the Dutch "*Oswout,*" East Woods. A patent was granted to 40 of the principal inhabitants, March 25, 1677, by Gov. Andross.

[2] This city was laid out during the speculative days of 1835–36 as a rival of New York. A ship canal, extending to Jamaica Bay, was to make the place a port of entry.

[3] Ref. Prot. D., Prot. E., Ger. Evang. Luth., M. E., and R. C.

[4] The grantees in the patent of Gov. Nicoll were Nicasius de Sille, Jacques Cortilleau, Francis Browne, Robt. Jacobsen, and Jacob Swart,—*Patents*, IV, 52; and those in the patent of Gov. Dongan were Jacques Corteljour, Ruth Goosten, John Verkerke, Hendrick Mathyse, John Kiersen, John Van Dyck, Guisbert Thyson, Carel Van Dyck, Jan Van Cleef, Cryn Jansen, Meyndert Coerten, John Hansen, Barent Joosten, Teunis Van Pelt, Hendrick Van Pelt, Lawrence Janse, Gerrit Cornelissen, Dirk Van Sutphen, Thomas Tierkson, Gerrit Stoffelsen, Peter Thysen, Anthony Van Pelt, Anthony Duchaine, Jan Vanderventer, and Cornelis Wynhart. The annual acknowledgment was 6 bush. of good winter wheat, payable, at the city of New York, March 25.—*Patents*, V, 407.

[5] This fortress was commenced in 1824 and completed in 1832. The total cost of the structure in 1858 was $552,000. It mounts 60 heavy guns, of which 48 bear upon the channel.

[6] Formerly called "*Fort Diamond.*" It was commenced in 1812, and in 1851 it had cost $341,941. It mounts 73 heavy guns. These forts were located and planned by Gen. Bernard, a French engineer.

[7] 2 Prot. E., 2 Ref. Prot. D., M. E., and R. C.

LEWIS COUNTY.

THIS county was formed from Oneida, March 28, 1805, and named in honor of Gov. Morgan Lewis. Slight changes were made in the boundary on the erection of Pinckney, in 1808, and of Wilna, in 1813. It lies mostly within the valley of Black River, N. of the center of the State. It is centrally distant 116 mi. from Albany, and contains 1,288 sq. mi. Its surface consists of the broad inter-vales which extend along the course of Black River, and uplands which rise upon the E. and W. The eastern half rises gradually to the E. border of the co., where it attains an elevation of about 1400 feet above tide. This part of the co. forms a portion of the great wilderness of Northern N. Y. The surface in many places is broken by low ridges or isolated masses of naked gneiss. The streams generally flow over rocky beds, and in places through wild ravines. The soil is a light, yellow, sandy loam and unprofitable for cultivation. In the eastern forests are great numbers of picturesque lakes, many of which are scarcely known except to hunters and fishermen. The streams flowing from the plateau are generally rapid, furnishing an abundance of water power.[1] Magnetic iron ore has been found interstratified with gneiss and red specular ore on the N. E. border of the co., and along the margins of the streams is an abundance of iron sand. At the junction of the gneiss and white limestone in Diana are a great number of interesting minerals.[2]

The W. side rises from the valley of Black River by a series of terraces to near the center of the W. half of the co., whence it spreads out toward Lake Ontario. These terraces are occasionally broken by oblique valleys from the N. W. The summit is 1500 to 1700 feet above tide. The inter-vale along the river, and the banks which immediately border upon it, are underlaid by Black River limestone. Next above this, in an irregular terrace, rises the Trenton limestone, 300 feet thick in the N. part of the co. and gradually diminishing toward the S. This limestone is very compact and strongly resists the action of the elements. In many places it presents the face of steep declivities approaching the perpendicular, and the streams from the W. plateau generally flow over this formation in a single perpendicular fall. This rock underlies an extremely fertile and nearly level tract of 1 to 3 mi. wide. Above it, on the W., the strata of the Utica slate and Lorraine shales rise about 500 feet higher, and from the summit the surface spreads out into a nearly level region, with its waters flowing both toward the E. and W.[3] This range in Lewis co. is known as Tug Hill. The soil in the limestone region is sometimes thin, but is everywhere productive. Near the foot of Tug Hill is a strip of stiff clay a few rods wide, extending the whole length of the co., and marked by a line of springs and swamps. The soil upon the slate is deep and well adapted to grazing, but, from its great elevation, it is liable to late and early frosts. Upon the summit of the slate table lands are extensive swamps, which give rise to streams flowing into Black River, Lake Ontario, Oneida Lake, and the Mohawk. Drift deposits are scattered promiscuously, and sometimes lie at a great depth, more particularly upon the northerly sides of the oblique valleys before mentioned.

The streams which rise on the summit of Tug Hill in many places flow through ancient beaver meadows, and upon the brow of the hill they have invariably worn deep ravines into the slates and shales, in some instances 3 or 4 mi. in length and 100 to 300 feet deep. Chimney Point and Whetstone Gulf, in Martinsburgh, are localities of this kind. There are but few ravines in the lime-stone terraces, though the Deer River Falls, near Copenhagen, are in a gorge worn in this rock. A thin layer of Potsdam sandstone rests immediately upon the gneiss in Martinsburgh. Waterlime of excellent quality has been made from the lower strata of Black River limestone, and veins of lead ore have been worked in the upper part of the Trenton limestone in Martinsburgh and Lowville.[4] The outline of the hills readily indicates the character of the underlying rocks.[5]

---

[1] The water of these streams is discolored by organic matter, manganese, and iron, and imparts to Black River the color which has given it its name.

[2] Zircon, sphene, tabular spar, pyroxene, nuttallite, blue cal-cite, bright crystallized iron pyrites, Rensselaerite, and coccolite are found near the Natural Bridge.

[3] The highest part of this range is said to be on Lot 50, in High Market, and is 1700 feet above tide. On a clear day the hills of Madison co. can be seen from this place.

[4] About the year 1828 a silver mine was announced as dis-covered near Lowville; and in 1837 a lead mine was somewhat extensively wrought 1 mi. N. W. of Martinsburgh Village, and several tons of lead were made at a great loss. More recently a company of speculators have bought the premises; but work has not been resumed, and probably will not be. Black oxyd of manganese has been found in swamps upon the summit of Tug Hill, in the S. W. part of Martinsburgh.

[5] In the primary region the upheavals retain their original

The s. w. part of the co. is drained by Fish Creek and its branches, and the headwaters of the Mohawk. Salmon River rises upon the w. border, and the Oswegatchie and Indian[1] Rivers take their rise in the N. E. The principal tributaries of Black River are Moose[2] and Beaver Rivers,[3] Otter,[4] Independence, and Fish Creeks, and Fall Brook, on the E.; and Sugar River, Mill, Houses, and Whetstone Creeks, Roaring Brook, Lowville Creek, and Deer River[5] upon the w. Several mineral springs are found within the co.[6] Spring grains are readily cultivated; but this co. is particularly adapted to pasturage, dairying forming the principal pursuit of the people. Droughts seldom occur; but the uplands are noted for their deep snows. Within a few years, several extensive establishments have been erected upon Black, Moose, Beaver, and Deer Rivers, for the manufacture of leather, paper, lumber, and articles of wood. Two furnaces for the manufacture of iron from the ore are located near the N. border.

The county seat is located at Martinsburgh. A wooden courthouse and jail were built here in 1810–11, upon a site given by Gen. Martin.[7] The present clerk's office was erected by citizens of Martinsburgh in 1847. Active efforts were made at an early day, and renewed in 1852, to obtain the removal of the co. seat to Lowville, and a fine edifice was built at that place for the courts, in the hope of securing their removal. The co. poorhouse is located upon a farm of 59 acres 1 mi. w. of Lowville. The average number of inmates is about 90. The institution is well managed in regard to economy, neatness, and the health of the inmates. The only internal improvement in the co. is the Black River Canal, connecting Black River below Lyons Falls with the Erie Canal at Rome.[8] From Lyons Falls the river is navigated to Carthage, a distance of 42½ mi., by small steamers. Three newspapers are now published in the co.[9]

This co. is entirely within Macomb's Purchase, and includes a part of Great Tract No. IV.,[10] most of the Chassanis Purchase,[11] Watson's West Tract,[12] the Brantingham Tract,[13] and a small part of John Brown's Tract,[14] on the E. side of the river: and 4 of the "Eleven Towns,"[15] 5 of the Thirteen Towns of the Boylston Tract,[16] Constable's Five Towns,[17] and Inman's Triangle[18] on the w.

The first settlers came from New England and settled at Leyden in 1794. The fame of the

---

forms without change; the limestone terraces rise by steep slopes to their level summit; and the slate and shale hills exhibit the yielding character of the rocks which compose them, by their rounded outline and the gorges which every spring torrent has worn upon their sides.

[1] Called by the Indians O-je'quack, Nut River.

[2] Indian name Te-ka'hun-di-an'do, clearing an opening.

[3] Indian name Ne-ha-sa'ne, crossing on a stick of timber.

[4] Indian name Da-ween-net, the otter.

[5] Indian name Ga-ne'ga-to'do, corn pounder.

[6] The largest of these arises from the limestone in Lowville, near the line of Harrisburgh. Others rise from the slate upon Tug Hill. All of them emit sulphuretted hydrogen gas, and some have been used for medicinal purposes.

[7] The co. seat was located by the same commissioners that were appointed for Jefferson co. Benj. Van Vleeck, Daniel Kelly, and Jonathan Collins, by act of 1811, were appointed to superintend the completion of these buildings. The first co. officers were Daniel Kelly, *First Judge;* Jonathan Collins, Judah Barnes, and Solomon King, *Judges;* Lewis Graves and Asa Brayton, *Asst. Justices;* Asa Lord, *Coroner;* Chillus Doty, *Sheriff;* Richard Coxe, *Clerk;* and Isaac W. Bostwick, *Surrogate.*

The Black River & Utica R. R., now finished to Boonville, will probably be extended through the Black River Valley.

[9] *The Black River Gazette* was established at Martinsburgh, March 10, 1807, by James B. Robbins, and was removed to Watertown the following year. This was the first paper published in the State N. of Utica.

The Lewis Co. Sentinel was started at Martinsburgh, Oct. 12, 1824, by Charles Nichols, and continued 1 year.

The Martinsburgh Sentinel was commenced in 1828 by —— Pearson, and continued until March, 1830.

The Lewis County Republican was established at Martinsburgh, in 1831 or '32, by James Wheeler, who sold it to Daniel S. Bailey. its present publisher, in 1837. It was removed to Lowville in 1844, but has since been returned to Martinsburgh.

The Lewis Co. Gazette was started at Lowville, in the spring of 1821, by Lewis G. Hoffman, and continued 2 years.

The Black River Gazette was issued at Lowville, Oct. 19. 1825, by Wm. L. Easton. It was sold in 1830 to J. M. Farr, by whom it was continued a year or more.

The Lewis Democrat was started at Lowville. March 25, 1834, by Le Grand Byington, and continued 1 year.

The Northern Journal was commenced at Lowville, Feb. 14, 1838. by A. W. Clark. It has frequently changed owners, and is now published by Henry A. Phillips.

The Lewis County Banner was started at Lowville. Sept. 3, 1856, by N. B. Sylvester, and is now published by Henry Algœver.

The Lewis Co. Democrat was commenced Sept. 22, 1846, at Turin,

by H. R. Lahe. It was removed to Martinsburgh in 1849 and discontinued a few weeks after.

The Dollar Weekly Northern Blade was started at Constableville in 1854. It was changed to

The News Register in April, 1857, by Merrill & Cook, its publishers, and was afterward removed to Carthage.

[10] This tract was bought by the Antwerp Company, and embraced an area of 450,950 acres. See p. 353.

[11] This tract was purchased by Pierre Chassanis in 1792, and was supposed to contain 600,000 acres. Upon a survey being made, it was found that the tract fell far short of this; and a new agreement was made, April 2, 1793, for 210,000 acres. A narrow strip of this tract extended along the E. side of the river to High Falls. The settlers of this tract were principally refugees of the French Revolution. Many of them were wealthy, titled, and highly educated, and, in consequence, were poorly fitted for the hardships of pioneer life. Large sums of money were expended to render the settlement successful, but the settlers soon after returned to France and the enterprise was abandoned. Rodolph Tillier was the first agent; and in 1800 he was superseded by Gouverneur Morris, who appointed Richard Coxe his agent. The first buildings were erected near the present residence of Francis Seger.

[12] James Watson purchased 61,433 acres, in 2 tracts, connected by a narrow isthmus. The eastern tract is mostly in Herkimer co.

[13] So called from Thomas H. Brantingham, of the city of Philadelphia, who at one time held the title. It is mostly in Greig, and contains 74,400 acres.

[14] This tract, which is popularly regarded as the whole northern wilderness of New York, included 210,000 acres sold by Constable to John Julius Angerstein, and afterward conveyed to John Brown, of Providence, R. I. It was divided into 8 townships, as follows :—

1. Industry.
2. Enterprise.
3. Perseverance.
4. Unanimity.
5. Frugality.
6. Sobriety.
7. Economy.
8. Regularity

It has been said that all these social virtues are needed for the settlement of this region. The first 4 townships are partly in Lewis co.

[15] Numbers 5, 9, 10, and 11,—now Denmark, Pinckney, Harrisburgh, and Lowville.

[16] Named from Thos. Boylston, of Boston. who held the title a few days. Nos. 3, 4, 8, 9, and 13. now Montague, Osceola, and parts of Martinsburgh and High Market, are in Lewis co. The whole tract included 817,155 acres.

[17] These towns were Xenophon. Flora, Lucretia, Pomona, and Porcia, and now form parts of Lewis. High Market, and Martinsburgh and the whole of Turin and West Turin.

[18] Leyden as it existed before Lewis was erected. It included 26,250 acres, forming a perfect triangle.

"Black River country" spread through Mass. and Conn., and within the next ten years the country between Tug Hill and the river rapidly filled up with a laborious, intelligent, and enterprising population. A romantic project of settlement formed by refugees of the French Revolution, in which Arcadian dreams of rural felicity were to be realized, was abandoned after a short experience of the real hardships of pioneer life. Except an expensive but ineffectual attempt by Brown to settle his tract, toward the close of the last century, little improvement was made E. of the river until about 1820; and this section has at present less than one-fourth of the population, and a still less proportion of the wealth, of the co. A systematic effort at settlement of the extreme w. part was first made in 1840–46, under Seymour Green and Diadate Pease, agents of the Pierrepont estate. Much of this region is still a wilderness.

CROGHAN[1]—was formed from Watson and Diana, April 5, 1841, and a part of New Bremen was taken off in 1848. It lies E. of Black River, in the N. part of the co. The surface has an inclination toward the w. and N., and in the central and E. parts it is broken and hilly. Oswegatchie and Indian Rivers rise in the town and flow northerly into Diana; and Beaver River forms a portion of its s. boundary. In the E. part of the town are several lakes. The soil is light and sandy, and along the river intervales it is moderately fertile. The town is thinly settled along Black and Beaver Rivers, but in the N. and E. it is still a wilderness. **Croghan,** (p. o.,) on Beaver River, and **Naumburg,**[2] (p. o.,) in the w. part of the town, are small villages. **Indian River,** (p. o.,) N. of the center of the town, and **Belfort,** on Beaver River, are hamlets. Settlement commenced before 1830, under P. S. Stewart, agent for Le Ray. Many of the settlers are French and Germans. There are 5 churches in town.[3]

DENMARK[4]—was formed from Harrisburgh, April 3, 1807. It lies w. of Black River, on the N. border of the co. Its surface descends to Black River on the E. by a succession of irregular terraces. Deer River flows through the town, and upon its course are several falls, affording an abundant water power. The High Falls, one mi. below Copenhagen, descend 160 feet, at an angle of about 80°, and are celebrated for their picturesque beauty. Kings Fall, 2 mi. below, has a descent of about 40 feet. The E. part of the town is covered with deep deposits of drift. Near the mouth of Deer River are extensive flats; and Black River is bordered by a cedar swamp. The soil is very fertile. **Copenhagen,**[5] (p. v.,) on Deer River, in the w. part, contains 3 churches and several manufactories.[6] Pop. 505. **Denmark,** (p. v.,) in the E. part, contains about 50 houses; and **Deer River,** (p. v.,) on the river of the same name, 2 mi. from its mouth, 35.[7] The first settlement was made in 1800, by Jesse Blodget.[8] The census reports 6 churches in town.[9]

DIANA—was formed from Watson, April 16, 1830, and a part of Croghan was taken off in 1841. This is the extreme N. E. town in the co. Its surface is level, or gently rolling. In the N. part are 2 isolated hills, 300 to 500 feet above the surrounding surface. The principal streams are Oswegatchie and Indian Rivers and their branches. Bonaparte[10] and Indian Lakes, in the N. part, and Cranberry, Legiers, and Sweets Lakes, in the E., are the principal bodies of water. The greater part of this town is yet a wilderness. The soil is light and sandy. Iron ore is found in the N. and E. parts, and coarse, crystalline marble, of a sky-blue tint, on the banks of Indian River, near Natural Bridge. **Sterlingbush,**[11] (p. v.,) in the w. part, contains 15 houses; and **Harrisville** 12. **Blanchards Settlement** (Diana Center p. o.) is in the s. part. **Diana** is a p. o., and **Alpina**[12] is a hamlet. There are 2 churches in town, (Bap. and M. E.,) but no church edifice.

GREIG[13]—was formed from Watson, April 5, 1828, as "*Brantingham.*" Its name was changed Feb. 20, 1832. It is the s. E. corner town of the co. Its surface is rolling in the w., but it is broken, rocky, and in some places hilly, in the E. The principal streams, all tributaries of Black River, are Moose River, Otter, Stony, and Fish Creeks, and Cole and Fall Brooks. The scenery

---

1 Named in honor of Col. Geo. Croghan. It is locally pronounced " Cro'gan;" its proper pronunciation is " Crawn."
2 Locally known as the "*Prussian Settlement.*"
3 Evan. Asso. or Germ. Meth., Ref. Prot. D., M. E., and 2 R. C.
4 This town embraces Township No. 5, or Mantua, of the Eleven Towns.
5 Originally called " *Mungers Mills,*" from Nathan Munger, one of the early settlers.
6 About 1830 the manufacture of cordage was commenced here on an extensive scale; but it has recently been abandoned.
7 Abel French was the first settler at this place, and it was originally known as " *Frenchs Mills.*"
8 Among the early settlers were Freedom Wright, Major J.

Crary, Robert Howe, Asa Pierce, Ichabod Parsons, Lewis Graves, Jonathan Barker, J. Rich, and Andrew Mills.
9 Bap., organized in 1810, Cong., M. E., Univ., and 2 Union.
10 Bonaparte Lake was so called in honor of Joseph Bonaparte, who built a log house upon its banks, for the accommodation of himself and friends while upon hunting and fishing excursions, during his stay at his summer residence at Natural Bridge.
11 Formerly called " *Louisburg.*" It owes its origin to an iron furnace built here in 1833.
12 An iron furnace was built here in 1847 by Suchard & Farvager, Swiss capitalists, and the place has grown up around it.
13 Named from the late John Greig, of Canandaigua, who owned large tracts of land in the town.

along Moose River is celebrated for its wildness and beauty. The greater part of the town is yet a wilderness. In the E. part are several small lakes, which constitute some of the favorite resorts of fishermen. The soil is principally a light, sandy loam. Iron ore and ocher are found, and near Brantingham Lake is a sulphur spring. Lumber, leather, and paper are made, and on Otter Creek is an extensive match box factory. **Lyonsdale,**[1] on Moose River, 3 mi. from its mouth, and **Greig** and **Brantingham,** near Black River, are p. offices. In 1792 the French, under Rodolph Tillier, settled on the Chassanis Tract, near Black River, below the High Falls.[2] The only church in town (Presb.) was formed in 1807.

HARRISBURGH[3]—was formed from Lowville, Champion, (Jefferson co.,) and Mexico, (Oswego co.,) Feb. 22, 1803. Denmark was taken off in 1807, and a part of Pinckney in 1808. It lies upon the slate hills and limestone terraces N. w. of the center of the co. Its general inclination is toward the N. E., its s. w. corner being 300 to 500 feet above Black River. Its surface is generally rolling, but in the s. w. it is moderately hilly. Deer River and its tributaries are the principal streams. The soil is generally a rich loam largely intermixed with disintegrated limestone and slate. **Harrisburgh,** in the N. E. part, and **South Harrisburgh,** in the s., are p. offices. Settlement commenced a short time previous to the War of 1812.[4] The first religious services were conducted by Elder Amasa Dodge, a Free Will Baptist minister. There are 4 churches in town.[5]

HIGH MARKET[6]—was formed from West Turin, Nov. 11, 1852. It lies upon the elevated slate region w. of Black River, a little s. of the center of the co. Its general inclination is toward the s. E. Its surface is rolling in the s., but broken and moderately hilly in the N. and w. Its streams are Fish Creek and its branches, the principal of which are Big and Little Alder Creeks. The soil is a loam mixed with disintegrated slate, and is best adapted to pasturage. **High Market** (p. o.) is in the s. E. part of the town. Most of the town is still unsettled. Among the first settlers were Alfred Hovey, L. Fairchild, John Felshaw, Sol. Wells, and Benj. Martin.[7] A large proportion of the people are of Irish nativity.[8] There are no churches in town.

LEWIS[9]—was formed from West Turin and Leyden, Nov. 11, 1852. It lies upon the elevated plateau in the s. angle of the co. Its surface is generally rolling, but in the w. part it is broken and hilly. Its entire surface is 700 to 1200 feet above the valley of Black River. The principal streams are Fish Creek, the w. branch of the Mohawk, and the w. branch of Salmon River. Most of the town is yet an uninhabited wilderness. The soil is generally a sandy loam, moderately fertile and best adapted to grazing. Owing to the elevation of the town, spring is late, autumn early, and snows deep. **West Leyden,** (p. v.,) situated on the headwaters of the Mohawk, in the E. part of the town, contains about 20 houses. Settlement was commenced about 1800; but the present inhabitants of the town are mostly new comers, of German nativity.[10] The first church (Presb.) was organized in 1826. There are now 4 churches in town.[11]

LEYDEN[12]—was formed from Steuben, (Oneida co.,) March 10, 1797. Brownville (Jefferson co.) was taken off in 1802, Boonville (Oneida co.) in 1805, a part of Wilna (Jefferson co.) in 1819, Watson in 1821, and a part of Lewis in 1852. It lies on the w. bank of Black River, upon the s border of the co. Its inclination is toward the E., the w. border being about 500 feet above the river. Its surface is undulating. Its principal streams are Sugar River and Moose Creek.[13] The soil is a fertile loam mixed with disintegrated slate and limestone. **Port Leyden,** (p. v.,) on Black River, has a population of 192; **Talcottville,** (Leyden p. o.,) in the center of the town, of 50; and **Leyden Hill,** in the N. part, of 40. Settlement began in 1794,[14] under the owners

1 The first settlement was made in this place by Caleb Lyon, in 1819. He died in 1835, the year before his long cherished project of a State canal to the Black River was authorized by law. His son, Caleb Lyon of Lyonsdale, has at this place a Gothic villa, located in the midst of picturesque scenery and adorned with elegant collections of art.

2 See page 375.

3 Named from Richard Harrison, of N. Y., one of the early proprietors. The town embraces No. 10, or Platina, of the Eleven Towns. See page 353.

4 Among the early settlers were John and Silas Bush, Amos Buck, Geo. Stoddard, and Thomas and Gilbert Merrills.

5 Bap., Free Will Bap., M. E., and R. C.

6 This town embraces Township No. 9, or Penelope, of the Boylston Tract, and parts of Nos. 2 and 3, or Flora and Lucretia, of Constable's Towns.

7 S. C. Thompson kept the first store and inn and built the first gristmill; and James McVickar erected the first sawmill. The first school was taught by Ada Higby.

8 They settled in town soon after the suspension of the public works in 1842.

9 Named from the co.

10 Among the earliest settlers were John Barnes, Medad Dewey, Joel Jenks, Matthew Potter, C. and J. Putnam, and Augustus Kent.

11 Presb., Bap., M. E., and R. C.

12 This town, with that part of Lewis which was set off from it, forms the tract known as "Inman's Triangle."

13 Upon Sugar River is a beautiful cascade of about 60 feet fall in the space of 200 feet; and upon Black River, a little below Port Leyden, are a series of rapids, known as "The Narrows," where the banks are so contracted that a person can jump across the stream during the dry season.

14 Among the first settlers were Wm. Topping,——Butterfield, Brainard and David Miller, Hezekiah Talcott, Asa Lord, Wm. Bingham. Theo. Olmstead, —— Adams, Allen Auger, J. Hinman, L. Hart, and Benj. Starr. The first birth was that of Jonathan Topping, in 1794; and the first death, that of Calvin Miller, March 22, 1797. The second mill in the co. was built at Port Leyden, about 1800, by Ebenezer Kelsey and Peter W. Aldrich.

of the Triangle. A Cong. church was formed at a very early period, by Rev. —— Ely, and a Bap. church in 1798. There are now 6 churches in town.[1]

LOWVILLE[2]—was formed from Mexico, (Oswego co.,) March 14, 1800, and a part of Harrisburgh was taken off in 1803. It lies upon the w. bank of Black River, a little N. of the center of the co. Its w. border is about 400 feet above the river. Its surface is gently rolling. A wide intervale, the N. part of which is swampy, extends along the course of the river. The soil is a deep, fertile loam intermixed with disintegrated limestone.[3] A mineral spring is found near the N. border of the town. **Lowville,** (p. v.,) incorp. under the act of 1847,[4] is situated near the s. border of the town. It contains 5 churches, an academy,[5] 2 printing offices, and a bank. Pop. 908. **West Lowville,** (p. o.,) in the w. part of the town, **Stows Square,** about 3 mi. N. of Lowville, and **Smiths Landing,** on Black River, are hamlets. Settlement was commenced about 1797, under Silas Stow, agent for N. Low, and the town was rapidly filled with immigrants from New England.[6] The first church (M. E.) was founded in 1804. There are now 6 churches in town.[7]

MARTINSBURGH[8]—was formed from Turin, Feb. 22, 1803, and a part of Turin was annexed in 1823. It lies upon the w. bank of Black River, near the center of the co. It has an easterly inclination, its w. border being nearly 1000 feet above the river valley. Its surface is rolling, with a wide, level intervale bordering upon the river. The principal streams are Martins and Whetstone Creeks.[9] The soil is a deep, fertile loam, except along the river, where it is sandy. Near the head of Whetstone Gulf is a sulphur spring. **Martinsburgh** (p. v.) is situated on Martins Creek, near the center of the town. It contains the co. buildings, 3 churches, and a newspaper office. Pop. 210. **West Martinsburgh,** (p. v.,) in the N. part of the town, has a pop. of 164. **Glensdale,** (p. o.,) in the s. E. part, is a hamlet of about 12 dwellings. Settlement was begun by Gen. Walter Martin, at Martinsburgh, in 1801.[10] The first church (Presb.) was organized in 1804, by Rev. —— Norton. There are 7 churches in town.[11]

MONTAGUE[12] (Mon-ta-gu')—was formed from West Turin, Nov. 14, 1850. It lies near the center of the w. border of the co. Its inclination is toward the N. w., and its elevation is 1200 to 1600 ft. above tide. Its surface is generally rolling, but in some places it is broken and hilly. It is watered by numerous small streams, flowing into Deer River. The N. branch of Salmon River flows through the s. w. corner. Upon lot 22, in the N. w. part, is a sulphur spring. The soil is a moderately fertile, sandy and gravelly loam. **Gardners Corners** (Montague p. o.) is in the N. part of the town. Settlement commenced in 1846, under the agency of Diadate Pease, agent of the Pierrepont estate. There are 2 churches in town; M. E. and Bap.

NEW BREMEN—was formed from Watson and Croghan, March 31, 1848. It lies upon the E. bank of Black River, N. of the center of the co. Its surface is level in the w., but rolling, broken, and rocky in the E. It is watered by several tributaries of Black River, the largest of which is Beaver River, on the N. boundary. The E. part is sparsely settled. The soil is a light, sandy loam. **Dayansville**[13] (New Bremen p. o.) is in the w. part of the town. Pop. 200. Settlement was commenced in 1798, by Samuel Illingsworth and some French families.[14] In the w. part is a settlement of Germans, and in the N. one of French. There are 4 churches in town.[15]

OSCEOLA[16]—was formed from West Turin, Feb. 28, 1844. It lies upon the high region in

1 2 Cong., Bap., M. E., Calv. Meth., Univ.

2 This town embraces No. 11 of the Eleven Towns. It was named from Nicholas Low, of N. Y., the early proprietor.

3 In the Trenton limestone are veins of the sulphurets of lead and iron, intermixed with calcite and fluor spar.

4 The charter was confirmed Feb. 27, 1858. In 1852–53 active efforts were made to secure the location of the co. seat in this village; and a fine brick building, now used as a town hall, was erected in anticipation of its removal.

5 The Lowville Academy has from the first maintained a high rank. Its 50th anniversary was celebrated July 22, 1858.

6 Among the early settlers were Jonathan Rogers, Ehud Stephens, Moses Waters, A. Wilcox, B. Hillman, Daniel Kelley, Isaac Perry, J. H. and S. Leonard, John Schull, Wm. Darrow, Jas. Bailey, John Bush, A. F. and J. Snell, David and Benj. Rice, and Ebenezer Hills. The first birth was that of Harriet Stephens. The first inn was kept by Capt. Rogers, and the first store by Fortunatus Eager. The first mill was built by D. Kelley.

7 2 Bap., Cong., Friends, M. E., and Prot. E.

8 This town embraces Township No. 4, or Cornelia, of the Boylston Tract, and Porcia and a part of Lucretia, of Constable's Towns.

9 Martins Creek was formerly called "*Roaring Brook*." At Chimney Point, near the center of the town, this stream has worn a channel through the shale and Utica slate, for 2 mi., to the

depth of 200 to 250 feet. This remarkable chasm above the "*Chimney*" is tortuous, with precipitous sides, and in many places is so narrow that the stream occupies the entire space between the ledges. Whetstone Gulf, upon Whetstone Creek, in the s. part of the town, is a similar ravine.

10 Among the first settlers were Elijah Baldwin, Mrs. Richard Arthur and sons, Reuben Pitcher and sons, N. Cheney, Eli Rogers, Ehud Stephens, Gaius Alexander, Stephen Searls, Joseph Sheldon, Chillus Doty, A. Conkey, D. Ashley, S. Gowdy, C. and D. Shumway, and Orrin Moore. W. Martin built the first mills, and in 1807 a paper mill.

11 2 M. E., 2 Union, Bap., Presb., and Second Advent.

12 This town embraces Township No. 3, or Shakspeare, of the Boylston Tract. It was named from the daughter of H. B. Pierrepont, the proprietor.

13 This place was laid out in 1826, by Charles Dayan.

14 Several of the French company located at the head of Beaver River, where they designed to build a city. A sawmill was built, a half dozen houses were erected, and the place received the name of "*Cartonville*." Jacob Obesier and Rodolph Tillier were engaged in this project.

15 Bap., M. E., Evan. Luth., and R. C.

16 This town embraces Townships 13 and 8, or Rurabella and Hybla, of the Boylston Tract. It was named from the celebrated Seminole chief.

the s. w. corner of the co. Its general inclination is toward the s. w. Its surface is undulating, and the highest points are 1500 to 1600 ft. above tide. The streams are branches of Fish Creek and Salmon River. The soil is a moderately fertile, sandy loam. Nearly all the town is yet a wilderness. **Osceola** is a p. o. in the s. part. Settlement was commenced about 1838, by Seymour Green, agent for Pierrepont. There are 2 churches in town, M. E. and Ind.

PINCKNEY[1]—was formed from Harrisburgh and "*Harrison*," (now Rodman, Jefferson co.,) Feb. 12, 1808. It lies upon the highlands in the N. w. corner of the co., and has an average elevation of 1300 ft. above tide. It forms the watershed between Deer River and Sandy Creek, the head branches of which constitute the principal streams. A series of swamps extend along the E. border. In the town are several mineral springs, one of which has acquired considerable local notoriety for its medicinal qualities. The soil is a light, slaty loam upon the hills, and a deep, black loam in the valleys. **Pinckney, New Boston, Barnes Corners,** and **Cronks Corners** are p. offices. Settlement was commenced in 1804, under Abel French, agent of Mr. Henderson.[2] The first church (Bap.) was formed in 1810. There are now 4 churches in town.[3]

TURIN—was formed from Mexico, (Oswego co.,) March 14, 1800. Martinsburgh was taken off in 1803, another portion was annexed to Martinsburgh in 1823, and West Turin was taken off in 1830. It lies upon the w. bank of Black River, s. of the center of the co. Its w. boundary is 800 to 1000 ft. above the river, giving to the town an easterly inclination. The surface is level, except near the w. border, where it ascends to the slate hills, and in the E., where it descends to the river intervale. The soil is generally a deep, fertile loam mixed with disintegrated slate and limestone. **Turin,** (p. v.,) situated in the s. part, contains 3 churches and several manufactories.[4] Pop. 438. **Houseville,**[5] (p. v.,) in the N part, has a pop. of 90. The first settlement was made about 1798, by Nathaniel Shaler, of Middletown, agent of Wm. Constable and part owner, and the town was rapidly settled by immigrants from New England.[6] The first church (Presb.) was organized Sept. 19, 1802, by Rev. John Taylor. There are 6 churches in town.

WATSON[8]—was formed from Leyden, March 30, 1821. "*Brantingham*" (now Greig) was taken off in 1828, Diana in 1830, a part of Croghan in 1841, and a part of New Bremen in 1848. It lies upon the E. bank of Black River, and extends from near the center of the co. to its E. border. Its surface is level or gently rolling in the w. part, but in the central and E. parts it is more hilly and broken. It is watered by Beaver River, Independence Creek, and several smaller branches of Black River. The central and E. parts are yet covered with unbroken forests; and a large tract upon the extreme E. border, constitutes a portion of the far famed "John Brown's Tract." In the recesses of these forests are numerous beautiful lakes that are scarcely known except to hunters. Chases Lake, on the s. border, is noted for its beautiful scenery and is much visited by tourists. The soil is light and sandy. **Watson,**[9] (p. o.,) situated on Black River, in the w. part of the town, is a hamlet. The early settlers located along the river, and settlements were not made in the interior until about 1815.[10] The first church (M. E.) was organized in 1820. There are 3 churches and 1 church edifice (M. E.) in town.[11]

WEST TURIN—was formed from Turin, March 25, 1830. Osceola was taken off in 1844, Montague in 1850, and High Market and a part of Lewis in 1852. It lies upon the w. bank of Black River, s. of the center of the co. Its inclination is toward the E., its surface rising by successive terraces from the intervale of Black River to the hills 800 feet above. Its streams are Sugar River, which flows easterly through near the center of the town, and numerous smaller creeks and brooks. Lyons Falls, upon Black River, plunge over a ledge of gneiss rock 63 feet in height, at an angle of about 60°.[12] These falls form an excellent water power but little used.

---

1 By the act organizing this town, Township No. 9, or Handel, of the Eleven Towns, was annexed to Lewis co. The town was named in honor of Charles C. Pinckney, a statesman of S. C.

2 Among the early settlers were J. Penington, Phineas Woolworth, N. E. Moody, Stephen and James Hart, and Stephen Armstrong. French was succeeded in 1805 by Jesse Hopkins, and he by J. W. Bostwick, a few years after. Owing to its great elevation, the town is liable to deep snows, and, in consequence, its settlement was retarded until a recent date. Since the introduction of dairying, it has become an important town for the production of the staple products of the county,—butter and cheese.

3 Bap., M. E., Univ., and R. C. The only church edifice belongs to the M. E. society.

4 There are 3 gristmills upon Mill Creek, near Turin, and a woolen factory 1 mi. below the village.

5 Named from its founder, Eleazar House.

6 Among the early settlers were Enoch Johnson, Zaccheus and John Higby, Levi, Elijah, Justus, and Reuben Woolworth, Thos. Kilham, Ezra Clapp, C. Williston, Eleazar House, Z. Bush, and W. and J. Shepherd. The first birth was that of Cynthia Clapp; and the first marriage, that of Levi Collins and Mary Bush.

7 3 M. E., 2 Presb., and O. S. Bap.

8 Named from James Watson, of N. Y., former proprietor.

9 Among the first settlers were Eliphalet Edmonds, Isaac and Jabez Puffer, Jonathan Bishop, David Durfy, Ozem Bush, J. Beach, and R. Stone.

10 A bridge was built across the river near this place in 1828. It has recently been rebuilt at the joint expense of the State and town.

11 Bap., Seventh Day Bap., and M. E.

12 Formerly called "*High Falls.*" The rock has been but slightly worn; but the iron which enters into its composition

The soil is a deep, fertile loam upon the river valley, and a slaty loam upon the w. hills. **Constableville**[1] (p. v.) is situated upon Sugar River, at the foot of the Slate Hills, near the center of the town. Pop. 472. **Collinsville,**[2] (p. v.,) in the E. part of the town, contains 2 churches and a population of about 200. **Lyons Falls,**[3] (p. o.,) on Black River, is a hamlet. The first settlement was made at Constableville, in 1796, by Nathaniel Shaler.[4] There are 9 churches in town.[5]

Acres of Land, Valuation, Population, Dwellings, Families, Freeholders, Schools, Live Stock, Agricultural Products, and Domestic Manufactures, of Lewis County.

Names of Towns.	Acres of Land.		Valuation of 1858.			Population.		No. of Dwellings.	No. of Families.	Freeholders.	Schools.	
	Improved.	Unimproved.	Real Estate.	Personal Property.	Total.	Males.	Females.				No. of Districts.	Children taught.
Croghan	5.524	100,361	$145,905	$53,589	$199,494	829	702	354	300	296	11	734
Denmark	21,951½	9,697½	483,101	93,018	576,119	1,162	1,219	490	489	430	12	899
Diana	5,747½	84,953½	86,457	2,068	88,525	530	647	222	227	190	9	461
Greig	4,854½	81,481¼	154,688	3,560	158,248	660	543	241	245	192	8	468
Harrisburgh	12,410¾	10,264	198,993	22,500	221,493	661	579	239	243	113	11	511
High Market	7,718½	28,966	66,822	500	67,322	593	532	181	182	189	7	600
Lewis	4,099½	14,538	77,629	4,900	82,529	600	557	212	225	219	8	578
Leyden	13,670¼	5,937	351,466	52,600	404,066	926	930	369	399	277	14	707
Lowville	16,230½	6,724	471,957	150,625	622,582	1,048	1,096	358	421	342	12	682
Martinsburgh	22,024	20,716	451,758	49,700	501,458	1,164	1,325	452	429	393	23	1,053
Montague	15,559	9,999	28,387	200	28,587	312	259	116	118	120	7	228
New Bremen	8,030	25,585½	140,504	35,270	175,774	864	783	305	313	300	10	693
Osceola	1,629	61,992½	68,087	200	68,287	261	252	104	110	107	6	255
Pinckney	11,265½	13,150½	170,113	10,100	180,213	546	493	123	232	207	10	550
Turin	13,720	5,642	252,598	30,450	283,048	841	907	344	349	287	12	760
Watson	4,705½	8,545	113,013	14,035	127,048	508	422	173	183	185	9	381
West Turin	15,400½	8,593	315,695	74,500	390.195	1,295	1,183	424	462	251	10	798
Total	184,540½	497,145¾	3,577,173	597.815	4,174,988	12,800	12,429	4,707	4,927	4,098	179	10,358

Names of Towns.	Live Stock.					Agricultural Products.							Domestic Cloths, in Yards.
						Bush. of Grain.					Dairy Products.		
	Horses.	Working Oxen and Calves.	Cows.	Sheep.	Swine.	Winter.	Spring.	Tons of Hay.	Bushels of Potatoes.	Bushels of Apples.	Pounds of Butter.	Pounds of Cheese.	
Croghan	120	580	256	170	354	3,575	12,006	1,460	14,353	40	33,212		259
Denmark	648	1,034	2,160	1,791	727	1,257¼	44,573	5,487	16,940	8,571	183,849	237,796	980
Diana	179	401	387	317	227	148	14,642½	836	9,538	78	36,900	524	839
Greig	223	319	425	188	280	1,022	20,424	1,147½	10,985	235	41,240	60,600	380
Harrisburgh	365	631	1,320	684	484		28,148¼	4,084	11,029	3,337	130,111	147,798	881¼
High Market	153	608	763	458	277	141½	19,124¼	2,353½	17,850	35	54,761	24,200	1,796½
Lewis	117	340	505	88	182	43	11,724	1,926	8,011	210	34,824	53,400	104
Leyden	446	790	2,164	944	875		52,135½	5,565	23,130	7,600	178,566	204,600	750½
Lowville	494	664	2,377	630	807	2,209	38,518	4,555	13,047	18,939	123,103	497,514	759
Martinsburgh	712	1,167	2,427	1,365	978	978½	72,123	6,047½	25,896	16,088	164,956	332,327	1,438
Montague	55	177	169	17	61	31	8,092	486½	7,599		8,305		437
New Bremen	177	625	642	403	491	3,486½	18,450	1,385	17,271	112	68,437	7,200	643
Osceola	60	282	167	160	131	40	7,349	730	4,829	183	16,090		163
Pinckney	323	610	1,148	884	465	269	38,218	4,117½	13,636	1,202	109,480	67,180	1,055½
Turin	412	843	1,784	557	803	487	45,373	4,403	11,694	11,013	158,731	124,845	190
Watson	164	382	402	392	280	1,503	17,130	1,035½	8,974	164	43,030	25,600	718
West Turin	449	1,144	2,055	1,038	931	38	58,719	6,183	29,059	4,391	189,920	113,157	1,408
Total	5,097	10,597	19,151	10,086	8,353	15,228¾	506,749½	51,802	243,841	72,198	1,575,515	1,896,741	12,801¾

has gradually dissolved, and the precipitous banks at and below the falls are so colored by it that they seem to have been painted by art; hence they are called the "Pictured Rocks."

[1] Named from William Constable, son of the original proprietor.

[2] Named from Homer Collins.

[3] Named from Caleb R. Lyon, first resident agent and proprietor of the Brantingham Tract.

[4] Among the early settlers were John Ives, Levi Hough, H. Scranton, Willard Allen, Horatio G. Hough, —— Rockwell, and Jonathan Collins. Ex Bishop L. S. Ives is a son of Levi Ives, formerly of this town.

[5] 3 Union, 3 R. C., 2 M. E., Prot. E.

LIVINGSTON COUNTY.

This county was formed from Genesee and Ontario, Feb. 23, 1821. A portion of Allegany was annexed in 1846, and another portion in 1856. It occupies a nearly central position in the w. half of the State. It is centrally distant 205 mi. from Albany, and contains 655 sq. mi. Its surface is an upland, rolling in the N. and hilly in the s. The hills upon the s. border are 1,000 to 1,200 ft. above the valleys and 2,000 to 2,200 ft. above tide. From their summits the surface declines toward the N., the extreme N. border being 500 to to 800 ft. above tide. The slopes are usually smooth and gradual, except along the banks of the streams; and nearly every acre of land in the co. is arable.

The streams generally flow in deep ravines. They are usually bordered by steep, and sometimes precipitous, hillsides. The principal stream is Genesee River, flowing N. E. through the w. part of the co. In the s. its course is between steep and often precipitous banks, but further N. it is bordered by broad and beautiful intervales.[1] Its tributaries are Conesus Creek, Fall Brook, and Canaseraga Creek, from the E., and Beards, White, and several other small creeks, from the w. Coshaqua Creek is a tributary of the Canaseraga. Hemlock and Honeoye Outlets flow along the E. border, and a few tributaries of the Susquehanna take their rise in the s. part. Conesus Lake, near the center, and Hemlock Lake, along the E. border, occupying long, narrow valleys, are the only considerable bodies of water.

The underlying rocks, commencing upon the N. border, are the waterlime of the Onondaga salt group, the Onondaga and corniferous limestones, Marcellus and Hamilton shales, Genesee slate, and Portage shales and sandstones. The limestones of the N. are extensively quarried for lime and building stone; and the sandstones of the Portage group furnish excellent building stone and flagging. The soil, derived from the disintegration of these rocks, in all the elements of fertility has no superior in the State. Until the commencement of the ravages of the midge, wheat was the staple production; but it has been principally superseded by the spring grains. Broomcorn is largely cultivated along the Genesee Flats; and considerable attention is paid to cattle and sheep growing and dairying in the s. part.

The county seat is located at the village of Geneseo. The courthouse is beautifully situated upon a fine lot in the N. part of the village.[2] The jail, in the rear of the courthouse, is an old building, without means of ventilation, and it is impossible properly to classify the prisoners. The clerk's office is a small fireproof building upon the courthouse lot. The co. poorhouse is located upon a farm of 118 acres about 1 mi. E. of Geneseo. Its average number of inmates is 107, supported at a weekly expense of 75 cts. each. The farm yields a revenue of $2,000. A school is taught 9 or 10 months in the year. The house is well constructed and is very well kept.

The Genesee Valley Canal extends along the valley of the Genesee from the N. bounds of the co. to Mt. Morris; thence it turns s. E. to Coshaqua Creek and up the valley of that stream to Nunda, and thence s. w. to the Genesee at Portage, where it crosses the river upon a wood aqueduct supported by stone piers. The Dansville Branch Canal extends from Mt. Morris s. E. to Dansville.[3] The Canandaigua & Niagara Bridge Branch of the N. Y. Central R. R. extends through Caledonia. The Buffalo & N. Y. City R. R. extends s. E. through Portage and Nunda. The Buffalo, New York & Erie R. R. extends s. E. through Caledonia, Avon, Livonia, Conesus, and Springwater. The Genesee Valley R. R. extends s. through Avon, Geneseo, and Groveland to Mt. Morris.

Five newspapers—one daily, three weekly, and one monthly—are now published in the co.[4]

---

[1] The Genesee is subject to an annual overflow, the water often covering the entire flats which border upon it. This frequently causes destruction of property; but it is a source of constant fertility to the soil.

[2] The first co. officers were Moses Hayden, *First Judge;* James Ganson, *County Clerk;* Gideon T. Jenkins, *Sheriff;* and James Roseburgh, *Surrogate.*

[3] The highest level of the Genesee Valley Canal within this co. is 622 feet above the Erie Canal at Rochester and 1,132 feet above tide.

[4] *The Moscow Advertiser and Genesee Farmer,* the first paper published in the co., was commenced at Moscow in 1817 by Hezekiah Ripley. About 1821 it passed into the hands of James Percival, who removed it to Geneseo and changed the name to

The Livingston Register. In 1829 Anson M. Weed and Allen Warner became proprietors; and it was successively published by Warner, Percival, Elias Clark, Wm. H. Kelsey, and Richard M. Miel. In 1835 Miel became sole proprietor. He was soon after succeeded by D. S. Curtis. In 1837 its publication was suspended. It was soon after revived, and published for a short time by Hugh Harding. He was succeeded by John Kempshall, who published it until 1840, when it was discontinued.

The Livingston Journal was commenced at Geneseo in 1822 by Chauncey Morse. Asahel Harvey was subsequently

381

Before the advent of the whites, this co. was the seat of several of the principal villages of the Seneca Nation. Considerable advances had been made in the arts of civilization, and a large quantity of land had been cleared and was cultivated. Corn, apples, and peaches were extensively produced. The orchards were destroyed, and the whole region was laid waste, by Gen. Sullivan, in 1779. The co. was included in the Phelps and Gorham Purchase, and in the Morris Reserve.[1] The latter tract was subdivided into several tracts, generally distinguished as separate patents.

In Sept. 1797, a treaty was held with the Indians at Geneseo, at which they ceded all their lands in this co. to the whites, except several small reservations.[2] The first settlements were made about 1790, previous to the extinguishment of the Indian title. The most prominent of the early settlers were James and Wm. Wadsworth, from Durham, Conn., who located at Geneseo, June 10, 1790. They were large landowners, and by a wise and liberal policy they greatly facilitated the settlement of the surrounding region. The greater part of the early settlers were immigrants from New England. York and Caledonia were settled principally by a colony of Scotch.

AVON—was formed, as "*Hartford*," in Jan. 1789. Its name was changed in 1808. Rush was taken off in 1818. It is the center town upon the N. border of the co. Its surface is a rolling and moderately hilly upland, terminating in flats on Genesee River. Deming Hill, on Lot 192, is the highest point in town. The principal stream is Conesus Creek, or Outlet, a tributary of Genesee River. The soil upon the uplands is a sandy and gravelly loam intermixed with clay, and on the flats, a deep, rich alluvium. **Avon,** (p. v.,) in the w. part, a station on the G. V., and B., N. Y. & E. R. R's., celebrated for its medicinal springs,[3] was incorp. June 13, 1853. It contains 3 churches, 5 large hotels, and 879 inhabitants. **East Avon,** (p. v.,) near the center, contains 2 churches and about 35 houses. **South Avon,** (p. o.,) in the s. part, contains 9 houses. **Littleville,** 1½ mi. s. of Avon, contains a church, gristmill, furnace, and 23 houses. The first

associated with him. In 1829 Levi Hovey became proprietor; and it was successively published by Benj. Dennison, H. F. Evans, Evans & Woodruff, and Wm. J. Ticknor. Its publication was suspended in 1834 or '35. In the fall of 1835 the establishment was purchased by David Mitchell and W. H. Kelsey, who revived the paper under the name of *The Livingston Democrat.* It was continued until 1837, when its publication was suspended. In the fall of that year S. P. Allen became proprietor of the press, and revived the paper under the name of **The Livingston Republican.** In Sept. 1846, it passed into the hands of John M. Campbell; and was successively published by Joseph Kershner and Chas. E. Bronson. In 1849 James T. Norton became proprietor, and is its present publisher.
The Dansville Chronicle was commenced in 1830 by David Mitchell and Benj. Dennison. Dennison soon retired, and its name was changed to *The Village Record;* it was soon after discontinued.
The Western New Yorker was published at Dansville a short time in 18— by A. Stevens & Son. It was succeeded by *The Dansville Whig,* published by Geo. W. Stevens. Chas. W. Dibble was the publisher about 1 year, when it again passed into the hands of Stevens, who in 1848 changed the name to *The Dansville Courier.* In 1849 or '50 it passed into the hands of H. D. Smead, who changed it to *The Dansville Democrat.* It subsequently passed into the hands of Geo. A. Sanders, who removed it to Geneseo and changed the name to *The Geneseo Democrat.* In Oct. 1857, it was returned to Dansville and published as **The Livingston Sentinel** by H. C. Page, the present publisher.
The Livingston Courier was commenced at Geneseo in 1831 by C. Dennison. In 1832 it passed into the hands of Henry F. Evans, and was discontinued in 1833 or '34.
The Livingston Courier was published at Geneseo in 1832 by A. Bennett.
The Mount Morris Spectator was commenced in 1834 by Hugh Harding. In 1848 he united it with The Livingston County Whig and changed its name to **The Livingston Union,** under which title it is still published by Hugh Harding.
The Dansville Times was published in 1835 by D. C. Mitchell.
The Nunda Gazette was started in 1841 by Ira G. Wisner. It was continued about 1 year, when it was removed to Mount Morris and its name changed to *The Genesee Valley Recorder.* It was discontinued about 1843.
The Dansville Republican was published in 1842 by David Fairchild.
The Livingston County Whig was started at Mount Morris in 1843 by Geo. B. Phelps. It subsequently passed into the hands of James T. Norton, and in 1848 was sold to Hugh Harding, who united it with The Mount Morris Spectator.
The Geneseo Democrat was started at Geneseo in 1843 by Gilbert

F. Shankland. It was removed to Nunda in 1847, and in 1848 to Ellicottville, Cattaraugus co.
The Livingston Express, semi-mo., was published at Mount Morris in 1843 by J. G. Wisner.
The Mount Morris Daily Whig was issued from the office of The Livingston County Whig in June, 1846, and discontinued in August following.
The Cuylerville Telegraph was started at Cuylerville in 1847 by Franklin Cowdery. In 1848 it passed into the hands of Peter Lawrence, who soon after removed it.
The Dansville Chronicle was started in June, 1848, by Richardson & Co., and was discontinued in 1851.
The Nunda Democrat was started at Nunda in 1848 by Milo D. Chamberlain. It was soon discontinued.
The Fountain, mo., was started at Dansville in 1849 by J. R. Trembly, and continued about 2 years.
The Dansville Herald was published in 1849 by H. L. & L. H. Rann. In 1857 it was merged in The Livingston Sentinel.
The Nunda Telegraph was started in 1850 by Chas. Atwood. It was continued about 1 year.
The Nunda Times was started in Jan. 1852, by N. T. Hackstaff. In July following the office was burned and the paper discontinued.
The Lima Weekly Visitor was started at Lima in 1853 by A. H. Tilton and M. C. Miller. It was subsequently published by Raymond & Graham and by S. M. Raymond, who changed its name to *The Genesee Valley Gazette.* It was discontinued about 1856.
The New Era was commenced at Hunts Hollow in 1854 by David B. and Merritt Galley, boys, respectively 15 and 17 years of age. In 1855 it was removed to Nunda and its name changed to *The Young America.* It was discontinued in about 1 year.
The Letter Box, mo., started at Glen Haven, Cayuga co., in 1857, by J. M. Jackson and Miss H. N. Austin, was removed to Dansville in 1858, and is now published by M. W. Simons.
The Dansville Daily Times was commenced in May, 1859, by W. J. Larue, publisher. In June of the same year its title was changed to **The Dansville Daily Register;** and it is still published by Larue; H. C. Page, editor.

[1] The w. boundary of the Phelps and Gorham Purchase was a line extending due N. from the Penn. line to the junction of Genesee River and Canaseraga Creek, and thence northerly along Genesee River to the N. bounds of the co.
[2] The Indian Reservations within the limits of the co. were: Cannawagus, containing 2 sq. mi. on the w. bank of Genesee River, w. of Avon; Little Beards Town and Big Tree, containing 4 sq. mi. on the w. bank of the Genesee, opposite Geneseo; Squakie Hill, containing 2 sq. mi. on the w. bank of the Genesee, N. of Mt. Morris; and the Gardeau Reservation, of 28 sq. mi., lying one half in this co., s. of Mt. Morris. See p. 711. The Indian titles to these lands have all since been extinguished.
[3] These springs—two in number, and about one-fourth of a mile apart—are located about 1 mi. s. w. of the village. The lower spring discharges about 54 gallons of water per minute.

settlement was made in 1785.[1] The first church (Presb.) was organized in 1795; Rev. Daniel Thatcher was the first preacher. There are 6 churches in town.[2]

CALEDONIA—was formed, as "*Southampton*," March 30, 1802. Its name was changed April 4, 1806. A part of York was taken off in 1819. It is the N. W. corner town of the co. The surface is level or gently undulating, and a considerable portion of it is stony. Genesee River forms the E. boundary. Caledonia Spring, in the N. part, covers an area of about 2 acres; and the outlet forms a good water-power, a few rods N. of the spring. The soil is a clay loam, underlaid by limestone.[3] In the s. part is a valuable quarry of limestone, yielding excellent lime and a fine quality of building stone. **Caledonia,** (p. v.,) in the N. part, a station on the B., N. Y. & E. R. R. and C. & N. B. Branch of the N.Y.C. R. R., contains 3 churches, a grist and saw mill, a brewery, and 623 inhabitants. The first settlement was made about 1797, by —— Peterson, a Dane, and —— Brooks, an Englishman.[4] The first church (Presb.) was organized in 1805; and the first settled preacher, Rev. Alexander Denoon, was installed Aug. 17, 1808.[5]

CONESUS—was formed from Livonia and Groveland, as "*Freeport*," April 12, 1819. Its name was changed to "*Browersville*," March 26, 1825, and to Conesus, April 15, 1825. It is the central town upon the E. border of the co. Hemlock Lake forms the E. and Conesus Lake a part of the w. boundary. Its surface is hilly. The Marrowback Hills in the E. part, w. of Hemlock Lake, rise to about 1,200 feet above it. A deep valley extends s. E. from near the center into Springwater, through which the B., N. Y., & E. R. R. passes. The principal stream is Mill Creek. The soil is generally a clay loam. **Conesus Center** (p. v.) contains 2 churches, a grist and saw mill, and about 40 houses. **Conesus** (p. o.) is a R. R. station. **Foots Corners** and **Union Corners** are hamlets. Settlement was commenced at the head of Conesus Lake, in 1794 or '95, by James Henderson, from Penn.[6] The first church (Meth.) was organized in 1814.[7]

GENESEO—was formed in Jan. 1789. It is an interior town, lying N. of the center of the co. Its surface is undulating, with an abrupt declivity of 200 to 300 feet toward the river, on the w. Genesee River, forming its w. boundary, is bordered by fertile flats of an average width of about half a mi. The other principal streams are Fall Creek, and several small brooks that flow w. into the river and E. into Conesus Lake. On Fall Creek, s. of the village, is a perpendicular fall of 70 feet. The soil is clay and clay loam. **Geneseo,**[8] (p. v.,) a station on the G. V. R. R., was incorp. April 21, 1832; it contains the co. buildings, 5 churches, the Geneseo Academy,[9] 2 banks, a library, gristmill, furnace, and machine shop, and about 2,000 inhabitants. Settlement was commenced by Lem'l B. Jenkins and Capt. Noble, about 1788 or '89, near the village.[10] The first church organization is supposed to have been in 1795, in the N. E. part of the town, near Lakeville.[11]

GROVELAND—was formed Jan. 27, 1789. A part of Conesus was taken off in 1819, and a part of Sparta in 1856. It lies near the center of the co. Its surface is moderately hilly. In the w.

The quantity of water from both springs continues about the same during the year. Several large hotels have been erected for the accommodation of visitors, large numbers of whom visit the springs annually. The following is the analysis of a wine gallon of water from each of the springs:—

Lower Spring.

	Grains.
Carbonate of lime	29.33
Chloride of calcium	8.41
Sulphate of lime	57.44
Sulphate of magnesia	49.61
Sulphate of soda	13.73
Amount of solid contents	158.52

	Cubic inches.
Sulphuretted hydrogen	10.02
Nitrogen	5.42
Oxygen	.56

Upper, or New Bath Spring.

	Grains.
Carbonate of lime	26.96
Chloride of sodium	5.68
Sulphate of lime	3.52
Sulphate of magnesia	8.08
Sulphate of soda	38.72
Amount of solid contents	82.96
Sulphuretted hydrogen	31.28

[1] Among the early settlers were Gilbert R. Berry, at the river, w. of Avon Village, and Timothy Hosmer, at Littleville, Capt. Thompson, and —— Rice, in 1789. Gilbert R. Berry kept the first inn, and established the first ferry across Genesee River, in 1789. The first sawmill was built by Timothy Hosmer, at Littleville, in 1790, and the first gristmill by the Wadsworths, in 1792. The first school was kept by Pedie Joiner, at Avon, in 1792.

[2] 2 M. E., Prot. E., Bap., Presb., and R. C.
[3] Before the ravages of the wheat midge commenced, this was one of the best wheat growing towns in the State.
[4] David Fuller settled near the Spring, in 1798; and in that year and 1799 John McLaren, Peter Campbell, Alex. McDonald, John Cameron, and John and Donald McVean, from Scotland, settled in town. Hines Chamberlain was an early settler. The first death was that of John McLaren, in 1800; and the first marriage, that of Hines Chamberlain and Widow McLaren. The first inn was kept by —— Peterson; David Fuller kept an inn in 1798. The first store was kept by Alex. McDonald, in 1799. The first mill was built by the Pulteney Land Company, at the Spring, in 1801-02; and the first woolen factory, by Donald McKenzie, in 1822. The first school was taught near the Spring, by Jeannette McDonald, in 1804.
[5] The census reports 3 churches; M. E., Presb., and Ref. Presb.
[6] Hector McKay settled in 1798, Harvey May in 1806, Davenport Alger in 1808, Jas. Steel and Wait Arnold in 1810, Thomas Young in 1811, and Andrew Arnold in 1816. The first store was kept by A. & G. Arnold, at the center, in 1818. The first sawmill was built in 1803 or '04, on Mill Creek, near the center; and the first woolen factory in 1819, by Hosea Gilbert.
[7] There are 2 churches in town; M. E. and Univ.
[8] Originally called "*Big Tree*," from an immense elm tree that stood on the banks of the river near the village.
[9] This institution is located on Temple Hill, in the E. part of the village. The buildings were erected in 1826. James Wadsworth was principally instrumental in starting the school. It is under the control of the Buffalo Synod.
[10] Wm. and James Wadsworth settled in town in 1790. They came from Durham, Conn., with a small party, and located on the present site of the village. Richard Steele kept the first inn, in 1793, and Hall & Miner the first store, in 1794.
[11] The census reports 5 churches; 2 Presb., M. E., Prot. E., and R. C.

part are extensive flats, occupying about one-fourth of the area of the town. The principal streams are Canaseraga and Coshaqua Creeks, which empty into Genesee River near the N. W. corner of the town. The soil upon the upland is clay loam, and upon the flats a rich alluvium. **Groveland Corners,** (Groveland p. o.,) E. of the center, contains 1 church and 14 houses. **Hunts Corners,** (East Groveland p. o.,) in the N. part, contains 1 church and 9 houses. **Groveland Center** is a p. o. in the N. W. part. The first settlement was made by Charles Williamson, agent for the Pulteney Estate, in 1792.[1] In that year he built several houses in the N. W. corner of the town, and there located a small colony of Germans, and called the settlement "*Williamsburgh.*" This colony soon after left, and the entire village disappeared. In the S. W. part, at the junction of the Dansville Branch with the G. V. Canal, is a Shaker settlement, numbering 120 persons. They own a tract of 2,000 acres. There are 2 churches in town; M. E. and Presb.

LEICESTER[2]—was formed, as "*Leister,*" March 30, 1802. Its name was changed Feb. 9, 1805. Mount Morris was taken off in 1813, and a part of York in 1819. It is the center town on the W. border of the co. The surface is undulating, with extensive flats in the E. It is drained by Genesee River, which forms its E. and S. boundaries, and by Beards Creek[3] and its tributaries. The soil is a sandy and clayey loam on the upland, and a rich alluvium on the flats. Squakie Hill and Big Tree Reservations were within the limits of this town. **Moscow,** (p. v.,) near the center, incorp. about 1850, contains 3 churches and 320 inhabitants. **Cuylerville,** (p. v.,) in the E. part, incorp. in 1848, contains a church, a distillery, and 354 inhabitants; **Gibsonville,** (p. v.,) in the S. W. part, a paper mill, sawmill, and 16 houses. Ebenezer Allen was the first settler, soon after the close of the Revolution, but left soon after. The first permanent settlement was commenced by Horatio and John H. Jones, in 1789.[4] The census reports 4 churches in town.[5]

LIMA—was formed, as "*Charleston,*" Jan. 27, 1789. Its name was changed April 6, 1808. It is the N. E. corner town of the co. Its surface is undulating and hilly. It is drained chiefly by Honeoye Creek, which forms the E. boundary. The soil in the S. E. is clay and clay loam, and in the N. W. sandy and gravelly loam. **Lima,** (p. v.,) near the center, was incorp. ——, ——. It contains 4 churches, the Genesee Wesleyan Seminary, Genesee College,[6] and about 1,200 inhabitants. **South Lima,** (p. v.,)—Hamiltons Station, on the B. N. Y. & E. R. R.,—in the S. W. corner, contains 13 houses. Settlement was commenced by Paul Davidson and Jonathan Gould, from Penn., in 1788.[7] The first religious society (Presb.) was organized Oct. 1, 1795, by Rev. Daniel Thatcher.[8]

LIVONIA—was formed from "*Pittstown,*" (now Richmond, Ontario co.,) Feb. 12, 1808. A part of Conesus was taken off in 1819. It lies on the E. border of the co., N. of the center. The surface in the S. part is moderately hilly, and in the N. undulating. Conesus and Hemlock Lakes lie partly within the town. Their outlets, and that of Canadice Lake, are the principal streams. The soil in the valleys is a clay loam, and on the uplands a sandy and gravelly loam. **Livonia Center,** (Livonia p. o.,) a R. R. station, contains 2 churches and 408 inhabitants; **Livonia Station,** (p.v.,) 1½ mi. W., on the B., N. Y. & E. R. R., a manufactory of agricultural implements, and 31 houses; **South Livonia** (p. v.) 1 church and 13 houses; **Hemlock Lake,** (p. v.,) in the S. E., 2 churches, 2 gristmills, 2 sawmills, and 319 inhabitants; and **Lakeville,** (p. v.,) at the foot of Conesus Lake, 4 churches, a gristmill, sawmill, and 28 houses. The first settlement was

---

[1] Among the early settlers were Wm. Ewens, Wm. Lemon, John Ewart, and W. Harris. The first school was taught at "*Williamsburgh,*" by Sam'l Murphy, about 1793. The first mill was built by Chas. Scholl, for Chas. Williamson, on Lot 58, in 1797; the first inn was kept in "*Williamsburgh,*" by Wm. Lemon, in 1795; and the first store, in the same place, by Alexander McDonald, in 1795 or '96.

[2] Named from Leicester Phelps, son of Judge Oliver Phelps.

[3] Named from Little Beard, an Indian chief, whose principal village, Little Beards Town, was situated on the present site of Cuylerville. Little Beard was one of the worst specimens of his race. He was chiefly instrumental in the horrid torture of Lieut. Boyd in 1799. In a drunken row, in which both Indians and whites were engaged, at Stimson's tavern, in Leicester, he was pushed out of the door, and, falling from the steps, received a fatal injury.

[4] Among the other early settlers were Elijah Hunt, Alexander Ewing, and Maj. Wm. Lemon. Jellis, Thomas, and Wm. Clute, from Schenectady, were also early settlers. The first child born was James Jones, May 5, 1791; and the first death, that of Mrs. Horatio Jones, in June, 1792. The first inn was kept by Leonard Stimson, in 1797. He also opened the first store, soon after. The first sawmill was built by Ebenezer Allen, at Gibsonville, in 1792; and the first gristmill, by Oliver L. Phelps, near Moscow, in 1799.

[5] Presb., M. E., Bap., Ref. Presb.

‹ These institutions are located on a beautiful eminence in the

N. W. part of the village. The seminary was founded in 1830 by the Genesee Conference of the M. E. Church. It was opened for pupils in 1832. The first building, erected at a cost of $20,000, was destroyed by fire in May, 1842. The present building was immediately erected of brick, at a cost of about $24,000. It has a main S. front of 136 feet, with an E. and W. front, by wings extending back each 96 feet. Between these wings is a paved court. A farm of 70 acres is attached to the institution. This seminary has sent out more students than any other institution in Western New York. The college was founded in 1849, has — professorships, and is under the general supervision of the Genesee and East Genesee Conferences of the M. E. Church.

[7] Abner Miles, from Mass., settled in 1789; John Miner and Asahel Burchard in 1790; Steven Tinker and Solomon Hovey, from Mass., in 1791; and Col. Thomas Lee, Willard and Amasa Humphrey, Reuben and Gideon Thayer, Col. David Morgan, and Zebulon, Moses, Asahel, William, and Daniel H. Warner, from Mass., previous to 1795. The first marriage was that of Simeon Gray and Patty Alger, in 1793; the first death, that of Mrs. Abbott, mother of Mrs. Paul Davidson, in 1791. John Sabin taught the first school, in 1792 and '93. Reuben Thayer kept the first inn, in 1793, and Tryon & Adams the first store, in 1794. The first sawmill was built by Reuben Thayer, in 1796; and Zebulon Norton built the first gristmill, in 1794.

[8] The census reports 6 churches in town; M. E., Presb., Bap., Univ., Christian, and R. C.

made by Solomon Woodruff, from Conn., on Lot 32, in 1792.[1] There are 10 churches in town.[2]

MOUNT MORRIS[3]—was formed from Leicester, April 17, 1818. It lies on the w. border of the co., s. of the center. Its surface is rolling and moderately hilly. It is drained by Genesee River, which forms its N. and w. boundaries, Coshaqua Creek, which flows through the s. E. corner, and several small streams, its tributaries. The soil is a clay loam. A part of the Gardeau Reservation was in the s. w. part of this town. **Mount Morris,**[4] (p. v.,) in the N. part, was incorp. May 2, 1835. It is on the G. V. Canal, and is the southern terminus of the G. V. R. R. It contains 5 churches, 2 furnaces, a printing office, bank, machine shop, 3 flouring mills, a sawmill, paper mill, and 1,851 inhabitants. **Tuscarora,** (p. v.,) in the s. E. part, contains 2 churches, a gristmill, and 192 inhabitants; **Brooks Grove,**[5] (p. v.,) in the s. part, a church and 16 houses; **Ridge** (p. v.) a church and 13 houses. **River Road** (River Road Forks p. o.) is a hamlet. Ebenezer Allen commenced settlement, in 1784 or '85.[6] The census reports 9 churches in town.[7]

NORTH DANSVILLE[8]—was formed from Sparta, Feb. 27, 1846. A part of Sparta was annexed in 1849. It lies on the s. border of the co., E. of the center. Its surface is hilly, the highest summits being 600 to 800 feet above the valleys. The hills are generally arable. Canaseraga[9] Creek flows through the N. w. part, and Mill Creek through the s. The soil upon the hills is a clayey and gravelly loam, and in the valleys a sandy loam. In town are valuable quarries of building and flagging stone. **Dansville,** (p. v.,) w. of the center, was incorp. May 7, 1845. It is the terminus of the Dansville Branch of the G. V. Canal. It contains 9 churches, the Dansville Seminary,[10] 2 printing offices, a bank, a water cure, 5 flouring mills, 3 paper mills, 2 furnaces, a plaster mill, machine shop, pail factory, sash and blind factory, distillery, 2 tanneries, and 5 breweries. Pop. 2,879. **Commonsville,** in the N. w. part, contains a sawmill, furnace, and about 25 houses. Settlement was commenced at Dansville Village, by Amariah Hammond and Cornelius McCoy, from Penn., in 1795. David and Jas. McCurdy, step-sons of McCoy, came at the same time.[11] The first religious services were held by Rev. Andrew Grey, in 1798. The first church (Presb.) was formed in 1800.[12]

NUNDA—was formed from Angelica, (Allegany co.,) March 11, 1808. Portage was taken off in 1827. It lies on the s. border of the co., w. of the center. Its surface is hilly, the highest summit, near the center, being about 1,200 feet above the canal at Nunda Village. The principal stream is Coshaqua Creek, which flows through the N. w. part. The soil is a sandy loam, intermixed with gravel and clay. On Lot 53, stone is quarried for building purposes. A small spring on the same lot emits gas. **Nunda,** (p. v.,) in the w. part, on the G. V. Canal, was incorp. April 26, 1839. It contains 6 churches, the Nunda Literary Institute,[13] a gristmill, sawmill, furnace, machine shop, and tannery. Pop. 1,125. **Nunda Station,** (p. v.,) on the B. & N. Y. C. R. R., in the s. w. part, contains about 20 houses; **Coopersville,** in the N. part, a gristmill and about 20 houses. **East Hill,** in the s. E. part, is a p. o. The first settlement was commenced near the village, by Phineas Bates and Beela Elderkin, in 1806.[14] The first church (Bap.) was formed in 1819; Elder Samuel Messenger was the first preacher[15].

---

[1] Among the other early settlers were —— Higby and Peter Briggs, in 1794, Philip Short, in 1796, David Benton, in 1798, and Geo. Smith, Jesse Blake, Nathan Woodruff, Smith Henry, and Thomas Grant, mostly from Conn., and all of whom came in previous to 1800. The first child born was Philip Woodruff, Feb. 19, 1794; the first death, that of a child of —— Higby, in 1797. Dorias Peck taught the first school, in 1798 and '99; Solomon Woodruff kept the first inn, in 1794; Isaac Bishop the first store, in 1803 or '04. The first sawmill was built by —— Higby, in 1795; and the first gristmill, by Thomas Van Fossen, in 1799.

[2] 3 Bap., 2 M. E., 2 Presb., Christian, Univ., and R. C.

[3] Named from Robert Morris.

[4] Formerly called "*Allens Hill,*" from Ebenezer Allen, the first settler. Col. John Trumbull, of Revolutionary memory, at one time contemplated making it his place of residence. He planted an orchard, selected a site, and made some preparations for building. He changed the name to "*Richmond Hill.*" When he abandoned the idea of settling here, the place received its present name.

[5] Named from General Micah Brooks, one of the purchasers of the Gardeau Reservation, and who settled at this place.

[6] Among the early settlers were Benj. W. Rogers, Isaac Bronson, Gen. Mills, and Jesse Stanley, from Conn. The first store was kept by Ebenezer Allen, about 1790. He brought in a lot of goods from Philadelphia, for the purpose of trading with the Indians. The first mill was built about 1820, by William Shull.

[7] 2 Presb., 2 M.E., Meth.Prot., Bap., Prot.E.,Ref.Prot.D., and R.C.

[8] Named from Daniel P. Faulkner, a prominent pioneer settler familiarly known as Capt. *Dan* Faulkner; hence the name "Dansville." In area this is the smallest town in the co., and one of the smallest in the State.

[9] Can-a-se-ra-ga, an Indian name signifying "among the slippery elms."

[10] This institution was started in the spring of 1858. The building and grounds cost $12,000 to $15,000. It is under the supervision of the M. E. denomination.

[11] Among the other early settlers were Daniel P., Samuel, and James Faulkner, Nathaniel and William Porter, from Penn., in 1796; Jacob Welsh, Jacob Martz, and his son Conrad, George Shirey, and Frederick Barnhart, from Penn., in 1798. William Phenix, Jas. Logan, David Scholl, and John Vandeventer, were also early settlers. The first marriage was that of William McCartney and Mary McCurdy. Thos. McLain taught the first school, in 1798 or '99; Samuel Faulkner kept the first inn, in 1796; Daniel P. Faulkner, the first store, in 1797 and '98; David Scholl erected the first sawmill, in 1795, and the first gristmill, in 1796. Mr. Scholl was Charles Williamson's millwright, and built the mills for the Pulteney Estate.

[12] There are 9 churches in town; 2 Presb., 2 R. C., Prot. E., M. E., Bap., Evang. Luth., and Germ. Evang. Ref.

[13] Opened in 1844. The building was burned in June, 1859.

[14] Among the other early settlers were David Corey and brother, Peleg and Reuben Sweet, Abner Tuttle, Gideon Powell, Wm. P. Wilcox, John H. Townser, and James Paine. The first inn was kept at the village, by Alanson Hubbell, in 1820, and the first store by Wm. P. Wilcox, near the center. Willoughby Lovell built the first sawmill, in 1818, and Samuel Swain and Lindsey Joslyn the first gristmill, in 1828.

[15] There are 7 churches in town; Bap., F. W. Bap., Presb., M. E., Prot. E., Univ., and R. C.

OSSIAN—was formed from Angelica, (Allegany co.,) March 11, 1808. It was set off from Allegany co. in 1856. It is the center town on the s. border of the co. Its surface is broken and hilly, the highest summits being 600 to 800 feet above the valleys. Sugar Creek flows s. e. through near the center. The soil in the valleys is a gravelly loam, and on the hills a sandy loam, with some clay in the e. part. In the n. w. part is a small gas spring. **Ossian Center** (Ossian p. o.) contains 2 churches and about 18 houses; and **West View** (p. v.) a sawmill and about 12 houses. The first settlement was made at the center, by Judge Richard W. Porter, and his brother, James Porter, from N. J., in 1804.[1] The first church (Presb.) was formed Sept. 29, 1818.[2]

PORTAGE[3]—was formed from Nunda, March 8, 1827. It is the s. w. corner town of the co. Its surface is hilly, the highest point, near Portageville, being about 200 feet higher than the r. r. Genesee River forms the w. boundary of the town. Its banks are steep and rocky, 100 to 200 ft. high and in many places perpendicular. Coshaqua Creek flows through the e. part. The soil in the e. part is a clay loam, and in the w. a sandy loam. **Oakland,** (p. v.) in the n. e. part, contains 2 churches, a grist and saw mill, woolen factory, tannery, furnace, and 35 houses; **Hunts Hollow** (p. v.) 2 churches, a tannery, and 31 houses. **Portage Station,** on the B. & N. Y. C. R. R., is on the line of Wyoming co. Settlement was commenced by Jacob Shaver, on Lot 150, in 1810.[4] The first church (Presb.) was formed at Hunts Hollow, about 1820.[5]

SPARTA—was formed in Jan. 1789. A part of Springwater was taken off in 1816, West Sparta in 1846, and parts of North Dansville in 1846 and '49. A part of Dansville (Steuben co.) was annexed in 1822, and a part of Groveland in 1856. It lies s. e. of the center of the co. Its surface is hilly, the highest summits being 800 to 1,000 ft. high. Canaseraga Creek flows on the w. border. The soil on the hills is a gravelly loam, and in the valleys a sandy, clayey, and gravelly loam. Several small sulphur and gas springs are found near Scottsburgh. **Scottsburgh,**[6] (p. v.,) in the n. part, contains 2 churches, a steam saw and grist mill, a furnace, and 34 houses. **North Sparta,** (p. o.,) in the n. w. corner, **Sparta,** (p. o.,) in the w., and **Reeds Corners,** in the s. part, are hamlets. Settlement was commenced near Scottsburgh, by Jesse Collar, from Penn., about 1794.[7] The census reports 6 churches.[8]

SPRINGWATER—was formed from Sparta and Naples, (Ontario co.,) April 17, 1816. It is the s. e. corner town of the co. Its surface is very hilly, the highest summits being 600 to 1,000 ft. above the valleys. The principal stream is the inlet of Hemlock Lake, which flows n. through the town, w. of the center. Conhocton River rises in the s. e. part and flows s. into Steuben co. The soil is a sandy and gravelly loam. **Springwater,** (p. v.,) a r. r. station, n. w. of the center, contains 2 churches, a sash and blind factory, a sawmill, and 62 houses. **East Springwater,** (p. o.,) in the n. e., is a hamlet. The first settlement was made by Seth Knowles, from Conn., on Lot 18, about 1807.[9] The first church (Bap.) was formed in 1816.[10]

WEST SPARTA—was formed from Sparta, Feb. 27, 1846. It is an interior town, s. of the center. Its surface is hilly, the summits being 500 to 700 ft. above the valleys. In the n. e. is an extensive marsh, known as the Canaseraga Swamp. Canaseraga Creek flows n. along the e. border. The soil is a clay loam in the n. and a sandy loam in the s. About one-half mi. n. of Byersville, in a small stream called Butter Brook, is a perpendicular fall of about 60 ft. **Kysorville,** (p. v.,) in the n. part, on the G. V. Canal, contains 79 inhabitants; **Union Corners,** (p. v.,) locally known as "Brushville," on the line of Mt. Morris, 2 churches and 17 houses; **Byersville,**

---

1 Among the other early settlers were Richard N. Porter, Jas. Haynes, and James Croghan, about 1806, Jacob Clendenin, in 1807, Orrison Cleveland, Wm. and John Gould, and Heman Orton, about 1810. Luther Bisbee was an early settler in the n. w. corner of the town. The first child born was Abraham Porter, in 1805; the first marriage was that of John Gelson and Betsey Shay, in 1816; and the first death, that of John Turner, killed by the fall of a tree, in 1807. —— Weston taught the first school, in 1813 and '14; Oliver Stacy kept the first inn, in 1817; and Daniel Canfield the first store, in 1824. The first sawmill was built by Nathaniel Porter, in 1808 or '09; and the first gristmill, by John Smith, in 1826.

2 There are 2 churches in town; Presb. and M. E.

3 Name derived from the portage or carrying place around the falls of Genesee River. For description of Portage Falls and R. R. Bridge, see pp. 710.

4 Ephraim Kingsley and Seth Sherwood settled on Lot 169 in 1811; Joseph Dixon, above Portageville. Col. Geo. Williams, Russel Messenger, and Sanford Hunt all settled about 1814. Horace Miller taught the first school, in 1817. The first inn was kept by Prosper Adams, in 1817; and the first store, at Hunts Hollow, by Sanford Hunt, in 1818. Russel Messenger built the first sawmill, in 1816, and the first gristmill, in 1817.

5 There are 4 churches in town; Presb., Meth. Prot., Prot. E., and Bap.

6 Named from Matthew and William Scott, early settlers at this place.

7 Darling Havens settled at North Sparta; John Niblack, on Lot 28; John Smith, Asa Simmons, Robert Wilson, and Thomas Hovey, previous to 1798; and Peter Roberts, on Lot 27, in 1799. Samuel and James Rodman were early settlers. Most of these were from Penn. The first school was taught by Thos. Bohanan, in 1800–01. The first inn was kept by Darling Havens, at North Sparta, about 1800; and the first gristmill was built by Wm. D. McNair, in 1810. 8 2 M. E., 2 Presb., Bap., and Evang. Ref.

9 Among the other early settlers were Eber Watkins, Joshua Herrick, Peter Welch, Adam Miller, and Samuel Hines, in 1808; Reuben and Phineas Gilbert, from Mass., in 1810; Hugh Wilson, Henry Cole, Samuel Sparks, James Blake, Benj. Livermore, and David Frazer. Jacob Cannon settled on the e. hill in 1812. The first death was that of Mrs. Benjamin Farnham, in 1813. James Blake taught the first school, in 1813–14. Oliver Jennings kept the first inn, about 1815. Hosea H. Grover kept the first store, in 1815. The first sawmill was built by Samuel Hines in 1809; and the first gristmill, by Hugh Wilson, in 1813.

10 There are 4 churches in town; Presb., Bap., M. E., Christian.

(p. v.,) in the s. part, 61 inhabitants. **Woodville,** in the s. e. corner, is a hamlet. Settlement was commenced in the s. part, by Jeremiah Gregory, in 1795.[1] The first church organization was Bap.[2]

YORK—was formed from Caledonia and Leicester, March 26, 1819. A part of Covington was annexed in 1823. It lies on the w. border of the co., n. of the center. Its surface is undulating, with a general inclination to the e. Brown and Calder Creeks flow e. through the central and n. parts. The soil in the center and s. is a clay loam, and in the n. e. part a sandy and gravelly loam. **York Center** (York p. o.) contains 4 churches and 321 inhabitants; **Fowlerville,**[3] (Inverness p. o.,) in the n. e. part, 2 churches, a machine shop,[4] and 369 inhabitants; **Greigsville,** (p. v.,) in the s. part, a church and 22 houses; **Piffardinia,**[5] (Piffard p. o.,) in the s. e. part, on the G. V. Canal, a church and 23 houses. Settlement was commenced in the n. e. part, by several Scotch families, about the year 1800.[6] The first church (Scotch Ref. Presb.) was formed in 1816.[7]

Acres of Land, Valuation, Population, Dwellings, Families, Freeholders, Schools, Live Stock, Agricultural Products, and Domestic Manufactures, of Livingston County.

Names of Towns.	Acres of Land.		Valuation of 1858.			Population.		No. of Dwellings.	No. of Families.	Freeholders.	Schools.	
	Improved.	Unimproved.	Real Estate.	Personal Property.	Total.	Males.	Females.				No. of Districts.	Children taught.
Avon	20,743	5,084	991,606	64,700	1,056,306	1,352	1,342	467	483	344	13	994
Caledonia	20,602	5,276	1,022,484	151,067	1,173,551	1,063	928	453	346	242	9	607
Conesus	13,455½	6,889½	445,061	77,831	522,892	718	695	270	300	184	9	537
Geneseo	22,306¼	6,979	1,152,820	637,725	1,790,545	1,471	1,412	479	505	338	11	1,002
Groveland	16,479	8,058½	701,563	61,632	763,195	800	810	280	272	177	9	.636
Leicester	17,309¾	3,418	671,277	58,509	729,786	1,026	1,050	357	330	239	13	765
Lima	14,410¼	3,342	868,639	341,595	1.210,234	1,324	1,346	641	227	381	10	934
Livonia	19,444¼	3,882½	792,626	207,525	1,000,151	1,301	1,334	481	498	455	12	770
Mount Morris	22,469	5,679	1,293,812	187,507	1,481,319	2,045	1,997	563	790	506	15	1,495
North Dansville	3,384	1,532	492,448	314,932	817,380	1,658	1,823	695	711	457	6	1,284
Nunda	12,788¾	5,902½	553,173	69,600	622,773	1,425	1,462	552	403	430	16	1,076
Ossian	10,828	12,720	296,443	6,450	302,893	711	602	234	250	179	11	525
Portage	10,361	5,625½	352,961	25,755	378,716	787	782	302	313	430	10	623
Sparta	12,225⅜	8,217	447,358	24,150	471,508	626	607	232	141	217	8	447
Springwater	18,787¼	13,313½	484.436	163,844	648,280	1,296	1,185	450	482	355	17	964
West Sparta	12,973⅞	7,085¾	456,118	39,551	495,669	774	722	286	283	192	12	656
York	24,723¼	6,093½	1,166,549	112,960	1,279,509	1,434	1,348	482	587	381	13	940
Total	273,290½	109,098¼	12,189,374	2,545,333	14,734,707	19,811	19,445	7,224	6,921	5,507	197	14,255

Names of Towns.	Live Stock.					Agricultural Products.							Domestic Cloths, in Yards.
						Bush. of Grain.					Dairy Products.		
	Horses.	Working Oxen and Calves.	Cows.	Sheep.	Swine.	Winter.	Spring.	Tons of Hay.	Bushels of Potatoes.	Bushels of Apples.	Pounds of Butter.	Pounds of Cheese.	
Avon	838	1,359	676	12,745	1,507	109,079	88,064½	3,094	10,389	21,010	56,170	4,670	144
Caledonia	1,101	2,582	772	10,552	1,809	134,445	53,807½	3,056	10,646	9,350	72,831	3,879	684
Conesus	618	971	508	8,733	778	39,504	34.225	2,263	4,502	8,120	52,043	1,196	93
Geneseo	616	1,277	610	8,015	1,271	88,643	64,736½	3.207½	6,714	25,141	43,392	5,297½	70
Groveland	892	1,422	837	5,634	1,035	70,331	42,636½	2.205½	5,180	21,302	72,385	1,364	863½
Leicester	820	1,365	700	4,487	1,079	105,624	79,436	2,128	8,604	10,899	63,711	3,500	434
Lima	793	856	606	8,361	1,309	75,540	77,442	2,469	8,057	16,654	58,805	10,025	
Livonia	1,034	1,303	586	11,771	1,745	87,779	68,316	3,377	8,092	29,422	90,122	15,529	587
Mount Morris	1,058	1,546	1,081	6,934	1,756	85,327	72,615½	2,504½	9,122	11,431	95,250	2,085	899½
North Dansville	212	143	221	1,498	338	13,821	9,580	424	1,787	3,345	16,275		35
Nunda	754	994	794	3,516	1,028	33,149	33,698½	1,828¾	9,723	10,918	82,736	2,085	1.352
Ossian	365	671	440	2,646	699	15,984	18,060	1,099	4,027	2,865	38,690	1,375	254
Portage	474	658	486	4,155	751	39,288	36,478¼	1,409½	12,026	14,549	54,964	3,590	614½
Sparta	613	967	646	2,173	1,084	37,578	32,869¾	1,799½	5,948	17,435	57,749	1,351	573
Springwater	903	1,159	831	6,298	1,169	18,530	55,475	2,539½	13,711½	11,910	85,862	6,173	871½
West Sparta	570	941	665	3,992	1,099	31,708	29,991	1,550¼	5,226	6,845	59,590	8,741	822
York	1,206	1,860	961	13,698	1,517	128,551	76,600½	5,331¾	12,529	23,869	83,706	9,861	962
Total	12,867	19,074	11,420	115,208	19,974	1,114,881	874,033	40,286¾	136.283½	245,065	1,084,281	80,721½	9,259

1 Among the other early settlers were William Stevens, in 1796, Abel Willsey, in 1797, Benjamin Wilcox, in 1798, and Samuel McNair, in 1804. The first inn was kept at Kysorville, by Ebenezer McMaster, about 1820; the first store, at Union Corners, by Jonathan Russel, in 1823. The first wool-carding and cloth dressing mill was built by Benjamin Hungerford, in 1814; and the first gristmill, by Samuel Stoner, in 1823.

2 There are 4 churches in town; Presb., M. E., Bap., and Christian.

3 Named from Wells Fowler, the first settler at the village.

4 Manufactures all kinds of agricultural implements, and turns out $70,000 to $80,000 worth of goods per year.

5 Named from David Piffard, a prominent settler at this place.

6 Among the early settlers were Donald and John McKenzie, Angus McBean, John and Alexander Frazer, Archibald Gillis, and John McCall. David Martz was an early settler. John Russ, from Vt., settled at the center, in 1807; Ralph Brown, in 1808; and John Darling, from Vt., in 1809; and James Calder in the n. part of the town. The first birth was that of Angus McKenzie. The first inn was kept by Nathan Russ, in 1817; the first store, by Chandler Piersons, in 1816. Ralph Brown built the first gristmill, in 1818.

7 The census reports 9 churches in town; 2 Presb., 2 M. E., Bap., Cong., Asso. Presb., Asso. Ref. Presb., and Ref. Presb.

MADISON COUNTY.

THIS county was formed from Chenango, March 21, 1806, and named in honor of President Madison. That part of Stockbridge E. of Oneida Creek was annexed from Oneida in 1836. It is situated in the central part of the State, is centrally distant 98 mi. from Albany, and contains an area of 670 sq. mi. The extreme N. part is low, level, and swampy; but the central and S. parts are hilly, and constitute a portion of the general system of highlands which occupy Central New York. The hills generally have rounded outlines and steep declivities, their highest summits being 500 to 800 ft. above the valleys and 900 to 1,200 ft. above tide. The highlands are divided into separate ridges by a series of valleys extending N. and S., and they form the watershed between Susquehanna River and Oneida Lake. The principal streams upon the N. slope are Chittenango[1] Creek, forming a part of the W. boundary of the co., Oneida Creek, forming a part of the E. boundary, and the Canaseraga,[2] Canastota,[3] and Cowaselon Creeks: and the principal flowing S. are Unadilla River, upon the E. border, Beaver Creek, Chenango River and its branches, Otselic[4] Creek, and Tioughnioga River. The principal bodies of water are Oneida Lake, forming the N. boundary, and Owahgena or Cazenovia Lake, near the center of the W. border. The latter, a beautiful sheet of water, 4 mi. long, is 900 ft. above tide, and is completely surrounded by gradually sloping hillsides. The lowest rocks of the co., outcropping along Oneida Lake, belong to the Clinton group. The red iron ore peculiar to this group is found to a limited extent, but not in sufficient quantities to render mining profitable. Next above this successively appear the Niagara and Onondaga groups, underlying the whole swampy region.[5] The red shales form the surface rock S. of the swamp, and beds of gypsum extend along the base of the hills. These beds are extensively quarried in some sections, and furnish an excellent quality of plaster. Upon the N. declivities of the hills successively appear the water limestone, Pentameros limestone, Oriskany sandstone, and Onondaga limestone. From these groups are obtained an abundance of waterlime, quicklime, and building stone, all of excellent quality. Next above appear the Marcellus and Hamilton shales, covering more than one-half of the entire surface of the co. The Tully limestone, Genesee slate, and Ithaca groups are found to a limited extent covering the tops of the southern hills. A large share of the co. is covered deep with drift deposits. The soil upon the flat lands of the N. is generally a red clay, with great quantities of muck and marl in the swampy regions. Upon the northern declivities of the hills the soil is a gravelly loam intermixed with lime and plaster, and is very productive. Farther S. the soil upon the hills is a clayey, gravelly, and shaly loam, best adapted to pasturage, and in the valleys a gravelly loam and alluvium. The people are principally engaged in stock raising and dairying. Hops are largely cultivated. Manufactures are principally confined to two or three villages.

The co. seat is located at Morrisville. The courthouse is a two story wooden building, pleasantly situated on a small park, fronting on a main street. It was built in 1849, and contains the court[6] and jury rooms.[7] The clerk's office is a small, brick, fire-proof building adjoining the courthouse. The jail was burned in the winter of 1858. The poorhouse is located upon a farm of 135 acres near Eaton village, 5 mi. S. E. of Morrisville. The average number of inmates is 130, supported at a cost of 56 cts. per week each. A school is taught during the whole year. The farm yields a revenue of $1,500.[8] The principal public works in the co. are the Erie Canal and the N. Y. Central

---

[1] Meaning "waters divide and run N." Seaver, in "The Life of Mary Jemison," says it is a corruption of the Oneida word "Chu-de-nääny," signifying "where the sun shines out."

[2] Meaning "Big Elkshorn." Seaver gives it as "Ka-na-so-wa-ga," signifying "several strings of beads with a string lying across."

[3] "Ka-ne-to-ta," signifying "pine tree standing alone."

[4] Meaning "Capfull."

[5] In the marsh near Canastota a brine spring is found. A boring of 190 ft. was made here; but the water obtained was not sufficiently strong to warrant the further prosecution of the work.

[6] The first courts were held alternately at "the schoolhouse, near David Barnard's, in Sullivan, [now Lenox,] and at the schoolhouse in the village of Hamilton." The first officers were Peter Smith, First Judge; Sylvanus Smalley, Edward Green, Elisha Payne, and David Cook, Associate Judges; Asa B. Sizer, Co. Clerk; Jeremiah Whipple, Sheriff; and Thos. H. Hubbard, Surrogate. In 1810, Cazenovia was selected as the site of the co. buildings, and Col. John Lincklaen and Capt. Jackson were appointed to superintend the building of a courthouse. A brick building was erected, and the first court was held in it in Jan. 1812. In 1817 the co. seat was removed to Morrisville, and the first court was held there Oct. 7, 1817.

[7] Ellis Moss, Sam'l White, and Oliver Pool were appointed to superintend the erection of the courthouse.

[8] This institution consists of three two story stone buildings; the poorhouse proper, a lunatic asylum, and a hospital.

R. R., extending through Lenox and Sullivan. Among the hills are several large artificial reservoirs, used as feeders for the canal. Cazenovia Lake is used for the same purpose.

There are seven weekly newspapers published in the co.[1]

Nearly all the s. half of this co. belonged to the tract known as the "Chenango Twenty Towns."[2] A strip lying between this tract and the Military Tract, including De Ruyter and the greater part of Cazenovia, was embraced in the Lincklaen Purchase. The Oneida Indian Reservation, originally embracing all the N. part of the co., was subsequently divided into several large tracts. The "New Petersburgh Tract," or purchase of Peter Smith, includes nearly all of Smithfield and Fenner, the N. part of Cazenovia, and a strip a mile wide across the s. part of Stockbridge. The remainder of Stockbridge was included in the reservation of the Stockbridge Indians. Lenox and Sullivan constituted the N. w. portion of the Oneida Indian Reservation. The first settlements were made by squatters upon the Oneida Reservation, in 1790.[3] The permanent settlements were commenced about 1795, and the co. rapidly filled up with immigrants, principally from New England.

[1] The Madison Freeholder was commenced at Peterboro, before or in the early part of 1808, by Jonathan Bunce & Co. It soon after appeared as
The Freeholder, and was continued until 1813. It was then changed to
The Madison County Herald, and was continued several years.
The Christian and Citizen was published at Peterboro, in 1854, by Pruyn & Walker.
The Pilot was established at Cazenovia, in Aug. 1808, by Oran E. Baker, and continued until Aug. 1823.
The Republican Monitor was started at Cazenovia, in Sept. 1823, by L. L. Rice. It was published by John F. Fairchild from April, 1825, until Jan. 1832, by J. F. Fairchild & Son until July, 1840, and by J. F. Fairchild until March 4, 1841, when it was discontinued.
The Students Miscellany, semi-mo., was published at Cazenovia, in 1831, by A. Owen and L. Kidder.
The Union Herald was commenced in May, 1835, by L. Myrick and E. W. Clark. In 1836 Clark withdrew; and in 1840 the paper was discontinued.
The Cazenovia Democrat was started in Sept. 1836, by J. W. Chubbuck & Co.; it was edited by J. W. Dwinelle. In Feb. 1837, it was discontinued.
The Madison County Eagle was commenced at Cazenovia, in Feb. 1840, by Cyrus O. Pool. In 1841 it was published by Thos. S. Myrick and W. H. Phillips. In June, 1842, Myrick withdrew; and in May, 1845, its name was changed to
The Madison County Whig. In Aug. 1848, Phillips was succeeded by H. A. Cooledge, by whom the paper was changed to
The Madison County News, in Oct. 1853. In May, 1854, it was again changed to
The Madison County Whig; and in Jan. 1857, it was discontinued.
The Abolitionist was started at Cazenovia, in 1841, by Luther Myrick, and continued 2 years.
The Madison and Onondaga Abolitionist was published in 1843, by Luther Myrick.
The Madison Republic was commenced at Cazenovia, in Jan. 1850, by W. H. Phillips, and continued about 3 months.
The Cazenovia Gazette was published by Baker & Debnam, from Oct. 1851, until May, 1852.
The Progressive Christian was established in April, 1853, by A. Pryne, and was continued 2 years.
The Cazenovia Republican was commenced May 1, 1854, by Seneca Lake, its present publisher.
The Gazette and Madison County Advertiser was established at Peterboro in May, 1817, by John B. Johnson and son. It was removed to Morrisville in 1819, and discontinued in 1822.
The Madison Observer was commenced at Cazenovia, in Jan. 1821, by Rice & Hale. It was removed to Morrisville in 1822; and in 1824 Bennett Bicknell became its publisher. In 1829 it was united with The Hamilton Recorder, and was issued as
The Observer and Recorder. In 1832 it passed into the hands of H. C. Bicknell and Jas. Norton, and in 1834 into those of Jas. Norton. In 1835 it was changed to
The Madison Observer. In 1839 J. and E. Norton became its publishers, and in 1856 Edward Norton, by whom it is still published.
The Hamilton Recorder was started in 1817, by John G. Stower and P. B. Havens. In 1819 it passed into the hands of Stower & Williams, and afterward into those of John P. Van Sice. In 1829 it was removed to Morrisville and united with The Observer.
The Madison Farmer was published at Hamilton, in 1828, by Nathaniel King.
The Civilian was started July 27, 1830, by Lauren Dewey. In Feb. 1831, it passed into the hands of Lewison Fairchild, and in Nov. 1831, it was discontinued.
The Hamilton Courier was commenced by G. R. Waldron, in Feb. 1834, and the following year it appeared as
The Hamilton Courier and Madison Co. Advertiser. It was continued until 1838.

The Hamilton Palladium was started in 1838, by John Atwood, and continued 6 years, a part of the time by J. & D. Atwood.
The Hamilton Eagle was published in 1839, by G. R. Waldron.
The Literary Visitor was published at Hamilton about 3 months, in 1842, by Dennis Redman.
The Democratic Reflector was started at Hamilton by G. R. Waldron, in 1842, and was published by Waldron & Baker from 1843 until 1854, and 2 years by Waldron alone, when it was united with The Madison Co. Journal, and appeared as
The Democratic Republican. It is now published by Waldron & James.
The Madison County Journal was commenced in Sept. 1849, by E. F. & C. B. Gould. W. W. Chubbuck, F. B. Fisher, and T. L. James were afterward interested in its publication; and in 1856 it was united with The Democratic Reflector.
The Mill Boy } were published during the campaign of 1844, and } the former at the Palladium and the latter at The Polker } the Reflector office.
The Land Mark was published as a campaign paper in 1850.
The New York State Radii was removed from Fort Plain, Montgomery co., in 1854, by L. S. Backus, and continued about 18 months, when it was returned to Fort Plain.
The Democratic Union was commenced at Hamilton, in 1856, by Levi S. Backus; and in 1857 it passed into the hands of W. H. Baker, its present publisher.
The Canastota Register was published in 1830, by Silas Judd and H. B. Mattison, and in 1831 by H. S. Merritt.
The Canastota Times was commenced in 1857, by Geo. H. Merriam, and was discontinued the following year.
The Canastota Eagle was started Nov. 4, 1858, by J. E. N. Backus, its present publisher.
The Chittenango Herald was established in 1832, by Isaac Lyon, and was published successively as
The Chittenango Republican,
The Phœnix, and
The Democratic Gazette, until 1856, when it was discontinued.
The De Ruyter Herald was published in 1835, by C. W. Mason.
The Protestant Sentinel was brought from Schenectady to De Ruyter in Nov. 1836, and was published by J. & C. H. Maxon until the fall of 1837. It then passed into the hands of Wm. D. Cochran, by whom it was issued as
The Protestant Sentinel and Seventh Day Baptist Journal. In Feb. 1840, Joel Greene became its publisher, and changed it to
The Seventh Day Baptist Register. In 1841 it passed into the hands of James Bailey, by whom it was continued until 1845.
The National Banner was commenced at De Ruyter in Oct. 1847, by A. C. Hill, and continued 2 years.
The Central New Yorker was published at De Ruyter, by E. F. & C. B. Gould, from Sept. 1848, until May, 1851.
The Banner of the Times was started at De Ruyter, by Walker & Hill, and continued until 1855.
The Oneida Telegraph was commenced at Oneida, in Sept. 1851, by D. H. Frost. In June, 1854, it passed into the hands of John Crawford, and was changed to
The Oneida Sachem, under which name it is still published.
The Circular was established in 1852, and is published weekly at the Oneida Community.
[2] The following is a list of these townships within the limits of this co.:

Nelson.............	No. 1.	Lebanon............	No. 5.
Eaton...................	" 2.	Georgetown......	" 6.
Madison...............	" 3.	Brookfield.........	" 19 & 20.
Hamilton............	" 4.		

The Canastota Tract in this co. was granted in lieu of the school lots reserved in the "Twenty Towns;" but by some oversight was sold with those lands.
[3] See page 461.

BROOKFIELD—was formed from Paris, (Oneida co.,) March 5, 1795; and Columbus (Chenango co.) was taken off in 1805. It is the S. E. corner town of the co. Its surface is a hilly upland, broken by the valleys of Unadilla River and Beaver Creek. Unadilla River forms the E. boundary. Beaver Creek flows through near the center, and the E. branch of the Chenango through the N. W. part. Several smaller streams take their rise in the town. The soil is a gravelly loam. **Clarkville,**[1] (Brookfield p.o.,) incorp. April 5, 1834, contains 2 churches, the Brookfield Academy, a hoe and fork manufactory, gristmill, and tannery. Pop. 578. **Leonardsville** (p. v.) contains 1 church, a bank, and several manufactories.[2] Pop. 366. **North Brookfield** (p. v.) has 275 inhabitants. **South Brookfield** (p. o.) is a hamlet, and **De Lancy**[3] a p. o. The first settlement was made by Daniel Brown, in 1791.[4] The census reports 6 churches in town.[5]

CAZENOVIA[6]—was formed from Paris and Whitestown, (Oneida co.,) March 5, 1795. De Ruyter was taken off in 1798, Sullivan in 1803, Smithfield and Nelson in 1807, and a part of Fenner in 1823. It is the central town upon the w. border of the co. Its surface is a rolling upland, broken by the valleys of Chittenango and Limestone Creeks. The summits of the hills are 300 to 500 feet above the valleys. Owahgena or Cazenovia Lake, in the N. part of the town, is a beautiful sheet of water about 4 mi. long. Its outlet—Chittenango Creek—forms a part of the boundary between this town and Fenner. In its course it has a fall of several hundred feet, affording a great number of valuable mill sites. At the Chittenango Fall the water plunges in a beautiful cascade perpendicularly over a ledge of limestone rock 136 feet in height. Limestone Creek flows across the s. part of the town. Hydraulic and common limestone are quarried near Chittenango Falls. The soil in the N. and central parts is a gravelly loam, and in the s. a clayey loam underlaid by hardpan. **Cazenovia,** (p. v.,) incorp. Feb. 7, 1810, is beautifully situated on Chittenango Creek, at the foot of Cazenovia Lake. It contains 7 churches, an academy,[7] a bank, and several manufactories.[8] Pop. 1177. **New Woodstock** (p. v.) contains 2 churches and 273 inhabitants. **Chittenango Falls** is a p. o. Settlement was commenced in 1793, by John Lincklaen, from Amsterdam, Holland.[9] The first church (Presb.) was organized May 17, 1799, with 5 members; and the Rev. Joshua Leonard was the first pastor. The census reports 9 churches in town.[10]

DE RUYTER[11]—was formed from Cazenovia, March 15, 1798. Georgetown was taken off in 1815, and German (Chenango co.) in 1806. It is the s. w. corner town of the co. Its surface consists of hilly upland, broken by the valley of Tioughnioga River. The summits of the hills are 400 to 500 ft. above the valleys. The principal streams are Tioughnioga River and its tributaries. The soil is a gravelly and sandy loam on the hills and alluvium in the valleys. **De Ruyter,** (p. v.,) incorp. April 15, 1833, contains 3 churches, an academy,[12] and several manufactories.[13] Pop. 727. **Sheds Corners** is a p. o. The first settlers were Elijah and Elias Benjamin and Eli Colgrove, in 1793.[14] The first church (Bap.) was formed by Elder Joel Butler, Nov. 5, 1799.[15]

EATON[16]—was formed from Hamilton, Feb. 6, 1807. It is an interior town, situated near the center of the co. The surface is a rolling upland, broken by the valley of Chenango River into two ridges, whose summits are 400 to 600 ft. in height. The Chenango flows s. through the center. The outlet of the Eaton Reservoir flows through a deep, narrow ravine, and affords a large number of valuable mill sites. Hatchs Lake and Bradley Brook Reservoir, and several smaller reservoirs, are in this town. The soil is a gravelly loam, intermixed with clay in the valleys. **Morrisville,**[17] (p. v.,) situated on Chenango River, was incorp. April 13, 1819. It contains 3

---

1 Named from Joseph Clark, formerly State Senator.
2 A fork manufactory, gristmill, sawmill, and tannery.
3 Named from John De Lancy.
4 John and Elias Button, Lawton Palmer, Saml. H. Burdick, Saml. Billings, David Maine, Stephen Collins, Thos. and James Rogers, and Paul and Perry Maxon settled in the town in 1792. Stephen Hoxie, Simeon, Nathaniel, and Eleazer Brown, Henry Clark, Robert Randall, Asa Frink, Ethan, Oliver, and Phineas Babcock, Ira and Nathan Burdick, and Youman York were also early settlers. John Button built the first gristmill, in 1792; and Reuben Leonard opened the first store, in 1801. The first school was taught by Asa Carrier, in the winter of 1796–97.
5 2 Seventh Day Bap., 2 M. E., Bap., Univ.
6 Named from Theophilus Cazenove, the first general agent of the Holland Land Company.
7 The Oneida Conference Seminary is a large and flourishing institution, under the care of the Methodist denomination.
8 In and near Cazenovia, on Chittenango Creek, are a woolen factory, paper mill, oil mill, town clock factory, furnace, machine shop, 2 gristmills, and a sawmill.
9 Archibald Bates, Wm. Gillett, Wm. Miles, Benj. Pierson, Noah Taylor, Saml. S. Forman, Ira Peck, Nathan Webb, Shubael Brooks, and others named Tyler and Auger settled in the town

in 1793; and Joseph Simms, Isaac Moss, Gideon Freeman, and David Fay soon after. The first birth was that of a child of Noah Taylor, in 1794. John Lincklaen built the first saw and grist mills, in 1794.
10 2 Bap., 2 M. E., Cong., Presb., Prot. E., Union, and Univ.
11 Named from Admiral De Ruyter, of the Dutch Navy.
12 The De Ruyter Institute is under the care of the Seventh Day Baptist denomination.
13 2 tanneries, 2 sawmills, a gristmill, oil mill, furnace, and cabinetware manufactory.
14 Joseph Messenger and Sam'l Thomson settled in the town in 1795. Darius Benjamin, Justus, Jeremiah, and Ebenezer Gage, and Daniel Page were also early settlers. The first birth was that of Frederick Benjamin, about 1798: Joseph Messenger opened the first inn, in 1796; Samuel Bowen kept the first store; Joseph Rich built the first sawmill, in 1807, and the first gristmill, in 1809. The first school was taught by Eli Gage, in the winter of 1799.
15 There are 6 churches in town; 2 Friends, and 1 each Bap., Seventh Day Bap., M. E., and Presb.
16 Named from Gen. Wm. Eaton, commander of the U. S. military forces in the expedition to Tripoli.
17 Named from a family of early settlers in town.

churches, a newspaper office, and several manufactories.[1] Pop. 715. **Eaton,** (p. v.,) commonly called "*Log City,*" contains 3 churches and several manufactories.[2] Pop. 510. **West Eaton,** (p. v.,) commonly called "*Leeville,*" contains 2 churches, a woolen factory, sawmill, and about 40 houses; and **Pratts Hollow**[3] (p. v.) 1 church and about 20 houses. **Pine Woods** is a p. o. Settled in 1792, by John and James Salisbury, from Vt.; but the first permanent settler was Joshua Leland, from Sherburne, Mass., in 1793.[4] The first church (Presb.) was formed in 1805.[5]

FENNER[6]—was formed from Cazenovia and Smithfield, April 22, 1823. It is an interior town, lying N. w. of the center of the co. Its surface is a rolling upland. Oneida, Canaseraga, and Chittenango Creeks have their sources in this town. The latter forms a part of its w. boundary. Extensive marl beds are found; and on the bank of Chittenango Creek calcareous tufa is quarried and burned into lime. The soil is a gravelly and clayey loam. **Perryville,** (p. v.,) partly in this town, contains 2 churches and 25 houses. **Fenner** (p. o.) is a hamlet. The first settlement was made about the year 1793.[7] The first church (Bap.) was organized Aug. 23, 1801.[8]

GEORGETOWN—was formed from De Ruyter, April 7, 1815. It lies upon the s. border of the co., w. of the center. The surface is a hilly upland, broken by the valley of Otselic Creek into two ridges. The summits of the hills are 500 to 600 ft. above the valleys. The principal streams are Otselic Creek and its branches. The soil upon the hills is yellow loam, and in the valleys a gravelly alluvium. **Georgetown** (p. v.) contains 3 churches, and has a population of 280. The first settlement was made by Ezra Sexton, in 1804.[9] Lewis Anathe Muller, a French refugee, settled in this town about 1810, and remained until the restoration of Louis Philippe.[10] The first religious services were conducted by Ezra Sexton, at the house of Bethel Hurd, in 1805.[11]

HAMILTON—was formed from Paris, (Oneida co.,) March 5, 1795, and was named from Alexander Hamilton. Eaton, Lebanon, and Madison were taken off in 1807. It lies upon the s. border of the co., between Lebanon and Brookfield. Its surface is a rolling upland, broken by the valleys of Chenango River and its east branch. The soil is a gravelly loam in the valleys and a clayey loam upon the hills. **Hamilton,**[12] (p. v.,) incorp. April 12, 1812, is situated on the Chenango Canal. It contains 4 churches, the Hamilton Academy, the Hamilton Female Seminary, 2 newspaper offices, and a bank. Pop. 1448. The Madison University, located at this place, under the care of the Baptist denomination, was incorp. March 26, 1846. It consists of a grammar school, a collegiate and a theological department. Nine professors are employed, and in 1857 31 theological students, 123 under-graduates, and 71 grammar school students were in attendance. The libraries connected with the university contain about 8,900 volumes.[13] **Earlville,**[14] (p. v.,) on the line of Sherburne, (Chenango co.,) contains 2 churches, and has a pop. of 441, of which 233 are in this town. **Poolville** (p. v.) contains 2 churches and about 40 houses, and

---

[1] A silk factory, distillery, tannery, iron foundry, machine shop, gristmill, and sawmill. There were formerly several woolen factories in and near Morrisville, but they have been abandoned.

[2] A woolen factory, a tool factory and trip hammer, distillery, tannery, gristmill, and sawmill.

[3] Named from John and Matthew Pratt, early settlers.

[4] John H. and Benj. Morris settled in the town in 1794; Benj. Morse, Daniel Abbey, Simeon Gillett, Levi Barney, and Elijah Hayden, in 1795; Joseph Moss, Wm. Mills, Lewis Wilson, Sam'l Sinclair, Humphrey Palmer, and —— McCrellis, in 1796; and Rawson Harmon, in 1797. Thos. Morris, Windsor and Ziba Coman, Constandt, Robert, and Cyrus Avery, Joseph French, and Abiathar Gates were also early settlers. The first birth was that of Col. Uriah Leland, Nov. 1, 1793; the first marriage, that of Lewis Wilson and Dorcas Gillett, in 1796; and the first death, that of Simeon Gillett, in 1796. Joshua Leland opened the first inn, in 1794, and erected the first saw and grist mills, in 1795. David Gaston kept the first store, in 1804. The first school was taught by Dr. James Pratt, in the winter of 1797-98,—the first month at the house of Joseph Moss, the second near Morrisville, the third near Log City, and the fourth near the residence of Joshua Leland.

[5] The census reports 8 churches in town; 3 Bap., 3 M. E., and 2 Cong.

[6] Named from Gov. Fenner, of Rhode Island.

[7] Among the early settlers were Alpheus Twist and James Munger, from Conn., who located a mi. s. of the center, Jonathan Munger and —— Page in the N. part, and Elisha Freeman, Ithuriel Flower, Ames Webster and Amanda Munger in the s. part. The first birth was that of a child of Alpheus Twist; and the first death, that of the wife of Alpheus Twist. Elder Nathan Baker was the first preacher.

[8] The census reports 5 churches; 3 M. E., Bap., and Prot. E.

[9] Matthew Hallenbeck, Joab Bishop, John C. Paine, and Bailey Carter settled in the town in 1804, and Mitchell Atwood, Wm. Paine, Bethel Hurd, Joseph P. Harrison, and Josiah Purdy in 1805. Ebenezer Hull, Apollos Drake, Elijah and Alfred Brown,

Jesse Jerrold, Zadock Hawks, John Gibson, —— Hunt, David Parker, Philetus Stewart, Calvin Cross, Dr. Smith, Benj. Bonner, Capt. White, and —— Alvord, were also early settlers. The first birth was that of Weston Paine. in 1805; and the first death, that of Mrs. Ezra Sexton, in 1807. Mitchell Atwood built the first sawmill, in 1806, and Bishop & Hunt the first gristmill, in 1807. J. C. Paine was an early innkeeper.

[10] Muller settled on the hill, about 3 mi. w. of Georgetown, erected a large and spacious dwelling, laid out extensive grounds, excavated an artificial pond, and planted great numbers of fruit trees. He attempted the establishment of a village, by erecting 2 storehouses, several dwellings, a blacksmith shop, and a gristmill. It is supposed that he brought with him to town not less than $150,000, and that he carried away not to exceed $1500. When Bonaparte abdicated, Muller returned to France, leaving his wife and children in New York. He afterward returned to dispose of his property here. When he reached Georgetown, his house was stripped of its furniture; his stock and every movable article had disappeared; weeds covered the gardens, the walks, the roads, and fields; his village was forsaken, and the mill deserted. The agent in whose charge he had left his property had sold every movable article and deserted the place. Muller sold the property and returned to France; and to this day no one knows who or what he was.

[11] There are 3 churches in town; Bap., Presb., and Union.

[12] Formerly called "*Paynesville.*"

[13] The "*Hamilton Theological Seminary*" was established in 1820, under the auspices of the Baptist Education Society of the State of New York. In 1834 a collegiate course was instituted, and the seminary assumed the name of the "*Hamilton Literary and Theological Seminary;*" and in 1846 the institution was incorp. as the Madison University. The theological department is still under the control of the Baptist Educational Society. The aggregate number of graduates of the theological department is 302, and of the collegiate department 462.

[14] Named from Jonas Earl, Canal Commissioner.

Hubbardsville[1] (p. v.) 20 houses. **East Hamilton** (p. o.) is a hamlet, and **South Hamilton** a p. o.   The first settlers were John Wells and Abner Nash, from Mass., and Patrick Shields and John Muir, from Scotland, but late from Oneida co.   They located upon Chenango, near Earlville, in 1792.[2]   The first church (Bap.) was formed in 1796.[3]

LEBANON—was formed from Hamilton, Feb. 6, 1807. It is the central town upon the s. border of the co.   Its surface is a hilly upland, lying between the Chenango and Otselic Rivers. The summits in the w. part are 500 to 800 ft. above the valleys.   The valley of Chenango River, extending through the·e. part, is about 1 mi. wide and is bordered by steep hillsides.   The other streams are small brooks.   The soil is a yellow loam underlaid by hardpan upon the hills and alluvium in the valleys. **Lebanon** (p. v.) contains 1 church, a sawmill, tannery, and 25 houses. **Smiths Valley**[4] and **Middleport** are hamlets. The first settlement was made in 1792, by Enoch Stowell and Jonathan Bates, from Vt.[5]   There are 4 churches in town.[6]

LENOX—was formed from Sullivan, March 3, 1809, and a part of Stockbridge was taken off in 1836. It is the n. e. corner town of the co.   Its surface is level in the n. and moderately hilly in the s.   Canastota and Cowaselon Creeks flow through the town.   Oneida Creek forms its e. boundary, and Oneida Lake a part of its n. boundary.   The Cowaselon Swamp occupies a portion of the n. part.   The soil in the n. is alluvium and in the s. a gravelly and clayey loam. In the town are beds of gypsum and of red fossiliferous iron ore.   Near Cowaselon Creek is a small sulphur spring; and in the marsh near Canastota is a salt spring.[7] **Oneida** (p. v.) is the principal station between Syracuse and Rome, on the N. Y. Central R. R.   It is situated on Oneida Creek, and was incorp. June 20, 1848.   It contains 5 churches, the Oneida Seminary,[8] a newspaper office, and a bank.   Pop. 1713. **Canastota,** (p. v.,) incorp. April 28, 1835, is a canal village and a station on the N. Y. Central R. R.   It contains 3 churches, a newspaper office, a bank, and a manufactory of astronomical and optical instruments.[9]   Pop. 1081. **Wampsville,** (p. v.,) a station on the N. Y. Central R. R., contains 1 church and 25 houses. **Pine Bush,** (Bennetts Corners p. o.,) **Merrelsville,** (Cowaselon p. o.,) and **Lenox Furnace** are hamlets. **Clockville,**[10] (p. v.,) contains 2 churches, a woolen factory, 2 flouring mills, and a sawmill.   Pop. 279. **Quality Hill** (Lenox p. o.) is a thickly settled country street near Canastota. **Oneida Lake** (p. o.) and **South Bay** are hamlets. **Oneida Valley** (p. v.) contains 1 church and about 30 houses. **Durhamville** (p. v.) contains 1034 inhabitants, of whom 234 are in this town;[11] the p. office is in Oneida co.   The "Oneida Community," of about 200 persons, organized upon a peculiar religious and social basis, are located upon a farm of 390 acres on Oneida Creek, 3 mi. s. of Oneida.[12]   The first settlement was made in 1792, by Conrad Klok and his sons Joseph, John, and Conrad.[13]   The census reports 14 churches in town.[14]

MADISON—was formed from Hamilton, Feb. 6, 1807. It lies on the e. border of the co., s. of the center.   Its surface is a rolling upland.   The principal stream is Oriskany Creek.   The Madison Reservoir and several smaller ponds of water are in this town.   The soil consists of a gravelly loam in the valleys and a clayey loam upon the hills. **Madison,** (p. v.,) incorp. April 17, 1816, contains 4 churches, and has a population of 315. **Bouckville**[15] (p. v.) contains 1 church and 35 houses, and **Solsville** (p. v.) 17 houses.   The first settlement was made in 1793.[16]

---

1 Named from Calvin Hubbard.

2 Among the other early settlers were Sam'l and Elisha Payne, who located upon the present site of Hamilton Village in 1794. Theophilus and Benj. Pierce, Jonathan Olmsted, Daniel Smith, and Nathan Foster settled in the town in 1795, and Thomas Greenly in 1796.

3 The census reports 10 churches in town; 4 M. E., 2 Bap., 2 Cong., Prot. E., and Univ.

4 Named from Justus Smith, a former resident.

5 Among the early settlers were John, Charles, James, and Isaac Campbell, Thos. Hueston, Lent Bradley, Solomon Jones, Abram Webster, Dan'l Stowell, David Hartson,———— Rider, Josh. Smith, Dea. Finney, David Shapley, Malchiah Hatch, Dr. Merrick, Elihu Bosworth, Benj. Hewes, and Capt. Moore.   Elisha Wheeler built the first sawmill, and Daniel Wheeler the first gristmill; Israel Thayer kept the first store.   The first school was taught by Widow Nancy Campbell, a lady about 70 years of age.

6 Bap., Cong., M. E., and Univ.

7 At this spring a boring was once made 196 ft. deep.   At that depth the auger broke, and the work was abandoned.   The strength of the water at the surface was 24° by the instrument used, and it was increased to 9°.—*Geol. N. Y., III.* p.273.

8 The school was opened Sept. 29, 1858, with about 200 pupils and 5 male and 4 female teachers.

9 Established by Chas. A. Spencer. The microscopes and other instruments made here have acquired merited celebrity.   The equatorial telescope at Hamilton College was made here.

10 Named from Conrad Klok, who settled near this place.

11 See page 470.

12 This community was organized in 1847, under John H. Noyes, with whom their peculiar religious and social tenets mostly originated.   They form a general community, holding a common interest in all things.   The relation of the sexes is placed, not, like that of civilized society, on the basis of law and constraint, neither on the opposite one of mere freedom, but on that of "*inspiration.*"   They are principally engaged in gardening, the nursery business, milling, and the manufacture of steel traps, sewing silk, traveling bags, cravats, and palmleaf hats. *The Circular*, a weekly paper, is published by the Communists.

13 The Forbeses, Buyas, and Snyders were the early settlers.

14 5 M. E., 5 Presb., 2 Bap., Cong., and R. C.

15 Named from Gov. Bouck; formerly called "*Johnsville*."

16 Samuel and Francis Clemens, Stephen F. Blackstone, John Niles, Seth Snow and his son Seth, Wm. and David Blair, James Collister, Daniel Perkins, Henry W. and Israel Bond, Elijah Blodget, Amos and Jesse Maynard, and Joel Crawford, settled in the town in 1793; Gen. Erastus Cleveland, Thos. Mellen, Abial Hatch, Jas. McClenathan, Geo., Chas., and Job Peckhand, Benj. Simmonds, Sylvester Woodward, Elijah Thompson, Sam'l Jones, Jas. and Alex. White, Luther, Abial, and Ephraim Clough, and Jonathan Sloan, were also early settlers.   The first births in town were those of Marcena Collister and Stephen Blackstone, both in 1794.   Gen. Cleveland built the first gristmill and kept the first store.   Henry W. Bond built the first sawmill, in 1793. Sam'l Clemens was an early innkeeper.

The first church (Cong.) was organized in 1795, and the Rev. Ezra Woodworth was the first pastor.[1]

NELSON—was formed from Cazenovia, March 13, 1807. It is an interior town, lying s. w. of the center of the co. Its surface consists of a rolling upland. The principal stream is Chittenango Creek. The Erieville and Eaton reservoirs are in this town. The soil is generally a gravelly loam. **Erieville** (p. v.) contains 3 churches and 191 inhabitants, and **Nelson Flats** (Nelson p. o.) 2 churches and 146 inhabitants. The first settlement was made in 1794, by Asa and Jedediah Jackson.[2] The census reports 5 churches in town.[3]

SMITHFIELD—was formed from Cazenovia, March 13, 1807. Fenner was taken off in 1823, and a part of Stockbridge in 1836. It is an interior town, lying N. of the center of the co. Its surface is a hilly and rolling upland. The principal streams are Cowaselon and Oneida Creeks. The soil is a sandy and gravelly loam. Limestone and gypsum are obtained in the N. E. corner. Near Siloam is a small sulphur spring. **Peterboro,**[4] (p. v.,) on Oneida Creek, near the center, contains 3 churches and the Peterboro Academy. Pop. 350. **Siloam** (p. o.) is a hamlet. The first settler was Jasper Alesworth, in 1795.[5] Judge Greene C. Bronson resided in this town for several years; and Hon. Gerrit Smith now resides in Peterboro. In 1858, Wm. Evans, of Boston, donated to this town the sum of $10,000, to be invested, and the proceeds devoted to the relief and support of the destitute and needy.[6] There are 3 churches in town.[7]

STOCKBRIDGE—named from the Stockbridge Indians—was formed from Vernon and Augusta (Oneida co.) and Smithfield and Lenox, May 20, 1836. It lies upon the E. border of the co., N. of the center. Its surface is a rolling upland, broken by the deep valley of Oneida Creek, which extends in a N. and s. direction through near the center of the town. The summits of the hills are 500 to 800 ft. above the valley. The falls of Oneida Creek consist of a succession of rapids and low falls, affording numerous valuable mill sites.[8] Oriskany Creek takes its rise in the s. part. The soil is a clayey and gravelly loam. Limestone is extensively quarried from the ledges that crop out upon the hillsides. Hydraulic limestone is also quarried near the falls of Oneida Creek. Gypsum is obtained near Cooks Corners. In this town are an ancient burial place and the ruins of an old fortification.[9] **Munnsville,**[10] (p. v.,) on Oneida Creek, contains 1 church and several manufactories.[11] Pop. 287. **Knoxville**[12] (Stockbridge p. o.) contains 3 churches, and has a population of 138. **Cooks Corners** (p. v.) contains 1 church, a plaster mill, and about 15 houses. The first settlement was made in 1791.[13] A mission church was erected on the Indian Reservation, near Cooks Corners, about 1800.[14]

SULLIVAN[15]—was formed from Cazenovia, Feb. 22, 1803, and Lenox was taken off in 1809. It is the N. w. corner town of the co. Its surface is level in the N. and rolling in the s. The Cowaselon Swamp extends across the town from Chittenango Creek to the line of Lenox. South of this swamp is the Vlaie, or natural meadow.[16] Chittenango Creek flows through the town and

---

[1] There are 6 churches in town; 2 M. E., Bap., Cong., Friends, and Univ.

[2] Joseph Yaw, Ebenezer Lyon, Sam'l and Chas. Swift, Jonathan Buell, Samuel Kinney, and —— Mitchell settled in the town in 1794; Oliver Stone and James Hinman, in 1795; Joshua Wells, David Wellington, Israel Patterson, Rich. Karley, Dan'l Adams, Horatio Simms, Abner Camp, and Lemuel and Eldad Richardson, in 1796. The first birth was that of Palmer Wells, in 1796; and the first death, that of Mrs. Bishop, about 1800. Jedediah Jackson kept the first inn, in 1794; Jeremiah Clark built the first sawmill, about 1800, and Oliver Pool the first gristmill. Daniel Russell was the first storekeeper. Dea. Dunham was one of the earliest schoolteachers.

[3] 2 M. E., Bap., Cong., and Univ. [4] Named from Peter Smith.

[5] Oliver Trumbull settled in the town the same year. Peter Smith was the proprietor of the soil, and settled at Peterboro at an early day. Among the early settlers were families named Cleveland, Coon, Babcock, Taylor, Messenger, Stone, Rich, Loveland, Loomis, Merrill, Spencer, Bump, Northrup, Lathrop, Soper, Shipman, Howard, Chaffer, Lyons, Moody, Spring, Myers, Brown, Austin, and Wright. Peter Smith built the first saw and grist mill, Jas. Livingston kept the first store, and Lewis Cook kept the first inn. Tabitha Havens taught the first school, in 1801.

[6] The provisions of the benefaction are, that the amount shall be loaned in sums of not over $1000 each, upon good bond and mortgage security; and that as soon after 1862 as the accumulated interest amounts to a sufficient sum, a farm, of not less than 50 acres, shall be bought, and suitable buildings erected thereon, to be used as a home for the destitute.

[7] Bap., Presb., and Free.

[8] About ¼ mi. E. of Munnsville, near the center of the town, are several caves, in limestone, which have been explored but partially on account of noxious gases. In the rock that forms

the bed of the stream are depressions resembling the footprints of men, cattle, and horses.

[9] The burial place is on the side hill, about 1 mi. s. E. of Munnsville. A small bone image of a woman, iron and steel axes, gun barrels and fragments of gun locks, brass kettles, and tobacco pipes have been found. The axes were hatchet shaped, and were marked under the eye with three stars. The ruins of the fortification are in the s. w. part of the town.

[10] Named from Asa Munn, the first storekeeper in the town.

[11] A woolen factory, a furnace, tilt hammer and edge-tool factory, a sawmill, planing mill, and sash factory, and a gristmill.

[12] Named from Herman Knox, an early resident.

[13] Among the early settlers were Oliver Steward, Nathan, Calvin, Barney, John, and Alfred Edson, Wm., Elijah, and Joseph Devine, Wm. Sloan, Benajah House, Annos Bridge, Jas. Tafft, Aaron, Jairus, and Matthew Rankin, Jonathan Snow, Isaac Chadwick, Talcott Divan, Watrous Graves, and Daniel Thurston. These settlers all located in the s. E. part of the town. The first marriage was that of John Devine and Polly Edson, in 1793; and the first death, that of Widow Anna Hall, in 1795. The first saw and grist mills were built by the Stockbridge Indians, on their reservation, about 1794. The first school was taught by Edward Foster, in 1797.

[14] The census reports 5 churches; 2 Cong., Bap., M. E., and Univ.

[15] Named from Gen. John Sullivan.

[16] The Vlaie is covered to the depth of several feet with muck or peat underlaid by marl. It is destitute of timber, and supports a rank growth of ferns and weeds. "A ditch cut by the side of the road shows vertical stumps 3 feet below the surface, and then a small growth near the surface; so that it would appear that two forests have existed there." This land was originally covered with water; but it is now partially drained by a ditch dug by the State.

forms a part of its w. boundary. The Canastota and Cowaselon Creeks unite in the swamp and flow in an artificial channel to the lake. These streams afford numerous valuable mill privileges. On the Canaseraga, near Perryville, is a waterfall 130 feet in height. Black Creek is a tributary of the Chittenango. Gypsum is found in numerous localities and is extensively quarried.[1] Waterlime is also obtained in the s. part.[2] Marl and peat abound in the swampy regions. There are several mineral springs in town, the principal of which are the "White Sulphur Spring" and the "Yates Spring." The former—known as Chittenango Springs—is fitted up for the reception of visitors; and the waters of both are celebrated for their medicinal properties.[3] The soil in the N. is a clayey loam alternating with muck and marl, and in the s. it is a gravelly loam. **Chittenango,** (p.v.,) on Chittenango Creek, was incorp. March 15, 1842. It contains 3 churches, the Yates Polytechnic Institute, a bank, a woolen factory, gristmill, and tannery. Pop. 916. **Perryville**[4] (p.v.) is partly in this town. **Canaseraga** (Sullivan p.o.) contains 1 church and 25 houses, and **Bridgeport** (p.v.) 1 church and about 35 houses. **Lakeport** is a p.o. The first settlement was made in 1790, by squatters from the Mohawk Valley.[5] The census reports 9 churches.[6]

Acres of Land, Valuation, Population, Dwellings, Families, Freeholders, Schools, Live Stock, Agricultural Products, and Domestic Manufactures, of Montgomery County.

Names of Towns.	Acres of Land.		Valuation of 1858.			Population.		No. of Dwellings.	No. of Families.	Freeholders.	Schools.	
	Improved.	Unimproved.	Real Estate.	Personal Property.	Total.	Males.	Females.				No. of Districts.	Children taught.
Brookfield	30,640⅜	13,564¾	$599,120	$183,630	$782,750	1,891	1,879	692	788	631	27	1,330
Cazenovia	23,256½	6,870	999,550	475,950	1,475,500	2,162	2,333	890	975	746	18	1,474
De Ruyter	12,959	6,859	338,085	29,675	367,760	973	948	334	379	309	11	727
Eaton	20,828⅝	8,616½	775,285	149,800	925,085	2,014	2,047	727	799	557	19	1,227
Fenner	15,021	3,561	387,606	23,350	410,956	791	831	311	327	291	14	670
Georgetown	11,336½	10,275	225,170	34,870	260,040	728	714	310	333	264	12	564
Hamilton	19,080¾	5,369½	721,330	227,010	948,340	1,847	1,890	700	795	575	16	1,235
Lebanon	19,964⅛	6,171	518,640	73,120	591,760	840	821	309	344	256	13	616
Lenox	32,206⅛	16,496½	1,690,330	434,550	2,124,880	4,021	3,779	1,422	1,512	858	30	2,935
Madison	17,468	4,812	640,250	123,400	763,650	1,222	1,261	524	541	355	13	783
Nelson	20,931	6,130⅛	455,450	65,250	520,700	967	909	362	194	351	14	624
Smithfield	11,820	3,426	327,100	48,700	375,800	758	756	290	314	184	11	569
Stockbridge	15,512	3,647	321,910	41,850	363,760	1,037	1,015	381	217	298	15	856
Sullivan	26,369⅜	15,707	1,433,000	343,000	1,776,000	2,764	2,489	969	1,026	674	26	2,051
Total	277,393⅜	111,505⅜	$9,432,786	$2,254,155	$11,686,941	22,015	21,672	8,221	8,544	6,349	239	15,661

Names of Towns.	Live Stock.					Agricultural Products.							Domestic Cloths, in Yards.
						Bush. of Grain.					Dairy Products.		
	Horses.	Working Oxen and Calves.	Cows.	Sheep.	Swine.	Winter.	Spring.	Tons of Hay.	Bushels of Potatoes.	Bushels of Apples.	Pounds of Butter.	Pounds of Cheese.	
Brookfield	1,055	2,029	2,435	8,728	1,710	148	99,221½	9,053½	30,179	53,627	173,670	250,146	3,124½
Cazenovia	1,052	1,540	2,157	4,713	1,578	1,851½	126,940½	5,127	20,669	49,753	186,705	186,356	638
De Ruyter	448	638	1,131	4,943	577		44,108	3,756	8,398	28,337	76,975	106,550	627
Eaton	892	2,112	2,147	4,606	1,209	308	80,565¾	6,284	16,788½	45,402	159,410	290,775	702½
Fenner	631	1,069	974	4,388	875	642	82,585	2,520	9,342	45,740	84,740	62,705	642
Georgetown	311	634	812	2,867	399		35,368	3,476½	7,800	9,509	70,906	69,586	731
Hamilton	1,092	1,679	2,022	3,700	1,208	382	72,020	5,159	15,650	39,152	118,423	186,750	886
Lebanon	690	1,748	2,096	6,423	1,068		72,376½	6,108	11,453	31,845	137,488	161,492	844
Lenox	1,588	2,556	2,765	6,547	2,677	11,880½	236,579	6,201	25,627	48,418	219,062	75,965	1,251¾
Madison	585	1,227	1,346	4,752	828	1,313	67,761	4,582	16,856	40,860	113,045	113,490	758½
Nelson	630	1,325	1,793	4,586	1,083	47	58,648¼	5,594	17,367	60,864	160,978	209,207	3,008
Smithfield	670	856	1,243	2,149	801	778	71,973	2,423	9,590	17,850	96,414	122,078	215
Stockbridge	681	1,327	1,430	2,501	853	5,956½	89,969	2,742	11,976	26,166	94,895	187,656	1,758
Sullivan	1,428	2,117	1,716	5,644	1,928	7,491	162,776	5,237½	22,583	34,154	147,587	64,838	1,978
Total	11,753	20,857	24,067	66,547	16,794	30,797½	1,300,891½	68,263½	224,278½	531,677	1,840,298	2,087,594	17,164¼

1 Gypsum is said to have been quarried here in 1800.

2 In this town is a bed of waterlime,—the first discovered in the State. The material was first quarried and burned for quicklime to be used on the canal; but it was found that it would not slack. Experiments were then made, and the material was discovered to be hydraulic lime.

3 Following is a statement of an analysis of a pint of water from each of these springs.

	White Sulphur Spring.	Yates Spring.
Carbonate of lime	1.33	0.88
Sulphate " "	8.22	} 12.75
Sulphate of magnesia	3.11	
" " soda		1.66
Chloride of calcium	trace.	0.14
Organic matter	trace.	trace.

4 See page 291.

5 These squatters were James and Joseph Pickard, Jacob, David, and Hon-Yost Schuyler, Jacob Seeber, Garrett and Geo. Van Slycke, John Polsley, and John Freemyer. They settled on the Indian Reservation near Canaseraga. The Indians complained to the Governor of their intrusion, and they were ordered to remove. They neglected to do so; and in 1791, Col. Colbraith, the sheriff of Montgomery co., was sent with a posse of 60 men to dislodge them. They still refused; and their movables were taken from their dwellings and their houses burned. They then removed to the neighborhood of Chittenango and settled on lands that the State had lately acquired of the Indians. John G. Moyer, John Walroth, Capt. Timothy Brown, Solomon, Joseph, and David Beebe, Col. Zebulon Douglas, John Mathews, Philip Daharsh, Nicholas Pickard, Ovid Weldon, Peter Dygart, John Keller, John Sower, Wm. Miles, David Burton, Timothy Freeman, and Peter Ehle settled in the town shortly after. The first birth was that of Peggy Schuyler, in 1791; and the first death, that of a child of David Freemyer. John G. Moyer built the first saw and gristmill, and Jacob Schuyler kept the first inn.

6 3 Bap. 2 M. E., Cong., Wes. Meth., Ref. Prot. D., and Union.

MONROE COUNTY.

THIS county was formed from Ontario and Genesee, Feb. 23, 1821. It lies on Lake Ontario, N. W. of the center of the State. It is centrally distant 202 mi. from Albany, and contains 682 sq. mi. The surface is generally level or slightly undulating, with a moderate inclination toward the lake. The shore of the lake rises in bluffs 10 to 30 ft. in height; and from its summit the surface gradually slopes upward to the lake ridge, a distance of 5 to 8 mi. from the lake. The summit of this ridge is 160 ft. above the lake; and from it the surface declines a few feet to the S., and then rises to the summit of the Mountain Ridge, a distance of 1 to 3 mi., and 310 ft. above the lake. South of this point the surface is gently rolling, the ridges extending N. and S. The summits of the ridges along the S. border are about 400 ft. above the lake and 600 to 650 ft. above tide. The principal stream is Genesee River, which flows a little E. of N. through the center of the co. Its valley is ½ mi. to 2 mi. wide, bordered by ridges 30 to 60 ft. high. At Rochester the river flows over the solid limestone which forms the Mountain Ridge a distance of 96 ft., forming the Upper Genesee Falls, and 2½ mi. below it again descends 105 ft., to near the level of the lake, forming the Lower Genesee Falls.

The principal tributaries of the Genesee are Oatka and Black Creeks from the W., and Honeoye Creek from the E. The other principal streams of the co. are Sandy, Little Salmon, Salmon, Buttonwood, and Long Pond Creeks, W. of the Genesee, and Irondequoit and Four Mile Creeks, E. of that river, all flowing into Lake Ontario or some of its bays. In their passage from the central part of the co. to the lake, these streams nearly all flow over the limestone ridge in a succession of falls, forming an abundance of water-power. The principal bodies of water are Lake Ontario, which forms its N. boundary, Irondequoit and Braddocks Bays, and Buck, Long, and Cranberry Ponds, all indentations from Lake Ontario and connected with it by narrow and shallow straits.[1]

The lowest rock in the co. is the Medina sandstone, extending in a broad belt along the lake shore. Next above this is a thin stratum of the Clinton group, almost disappearing upon the W. border of the co.; and next above is the Niagara group, forming the abrupt terrace of the Mountain Ridge. This rock forms an excellent building material, and is extensively quarried. It also yields weak brine springs in several localities. The underlying rocks in the S. part of the co. belong to the Onondaga salt group. Lime is extensively manufactured from the Niagara limestone; and the rocks in the S. part yield gypsum and waterlime. A large part of the co. is covered with drift deposits, which mostly assume the character of ridges and rounded hills, many of them rising 50 to 100 ft. above the general surface. Tufa and marl are found in several localities, forming elements of fertility to the soil almost invaluable. A small quantity of iron is found associated with the Clinton group.

The soil is generally very fertile. Along the lake shore it consists of a red, argillaceous loam, principally derived from the disintegration of the Medina sandstone. This is succeeded by a clay derived from the disintegration of the Clinton and Niagara shales. The soil in the S. part is impregnated with lime and gypsum,—two of the most important elements of wheat lands. Agriculture forms the leading pursuit. Until within a few years past, wheat has been the great staple; but since the commencement of the ravages of the wheat midge, barley, corn, and oats have become the staple productions. Most parts of the co. are well adapted to the culture of fruit, and apples and peaches are largely produced. Wool growing is extensively carried on, and stock growing and dairying are beginning to receive considerable attention. The manufactures are extensive, though mostly confined to Rochester and vicinity. They consist chiefly of flour, machinery, edge tools, cars, and almost every variety of articles of iron. Rochester is the business center of the co.; and from it a large trade is carried on with the surrounding rich agricultural regions. The canals and railroads centering at this place give it facilities for an extensive inland trade and commerce. A limited amount of commerce is carried on upon Lake Ontario.

---

[1] The Irondequoit Bay is a narrow, deep body of water, extending inland about 6 mi. from the lake shore. From its s. extremity a deep valley extends several mi. further s., forming the deepest ravine along the N. border of the State. Some geologists have supposed that Genesee River formerly flowed through this valley.

The co. seat is located at the city of Rochester.[1] The courthouse, situated upon Buffalo St., near the center of the city, is a commodious brick edifice, with an Ionic portico supported by four massive pillars. The building is surmounted by a dome, the summit of which is 150 ft. high. It contains the usual offices and rooms for the court and co. officers, the co. clerk's office, and rooms for the city officers.[2] The jail is an old stone building, situated upon the bank of the Genesee, in the s. part of the city. The poorhouse establishment is located upon a farm of 134 acres in Brighton, just s. of the city line of Rochester. It consists of three large buildings, one of which is used for an insane asylum. The average number of inmates is 360, supported at a weekly cost of 68 cts. each. A school is taught throughout the year. The farm yields a revenue of $3,500.

Four daily, 2 tri-weekly, 8 weekly, 1 semi-monthly, and 3 monthly papers are published in the co.[3]

---

[1] The first co. officers were Elisha B. Strong, *First Judge;* Timothy Barnard, *Judge;* Joseph Spencer, *Assistant Justice;* James Seymour, *Sheriff;* Nathaniel Rochester, *Clerk;* and Elisha Ely, *Surrogate.*

[2] The first courthouse was built in 1821, soon after the organization of the co. It was removed to give place to the present structure in 1852. The present courthouse was built at a cost of $50,000, at the joint expense of the city and co.

[3] *The Rochester Gazette,* the first paper published in Monroe co., was commenced in 1816 by Augustine G. Danby. John Sheldon and Oran Follett were subsequently associated with him; and in 1821 the paper passed into the hands of Levi W. Sibley, publisher, with Derick Sibley as editor, and its name was changed to *The Monroe Republican.* In 1825 Whittlesey & Mumford became proprietors. In July, 1827, it was purchased by Luther Tucker & Co., who changed its name to **The Rochester Republican,** and continued its publication in connection with the Rochester Daily Advertiser until 1839, when the establishment passed into the hands of Thomas H. Hyatt. After passing through various hands, it is now published by Curtis, Butts & Co.; Isaac Butts, editor.

The Rochester Telegraph was commenced July 7, 1818, by Everard, Peck & Co. In 1824 Thurlow Weed became its editor, and in 1825 he and Robert Martin purchased the establishment. In 1827 they commenced *The Semi-Weekly Telegraph,* which in a short time was changed to *The Rochester Daily Telegraph.* In 1828 Weed retired, and the papers, daily and weekly, were continued by Martin. On the 1st of Jan. 1829, the daily was united with the Rochester Daily Advertiser, and in 1830 the weekly was merged in the Rochester Daily Republican.

The True Genesee Farmer, mo., was published a short time about 1824 by Wm. A. Welles; N. Goodsell, editor.

The Rochester Album was commenced in Oct. 1825, by Marshall, Spaulding & Hunt. In 1827 it was united with the Telegraph.

The Rochester Daily Advertiser, the first daily paper w. of Albany, was commenced Oct. 25, 1826, by Luther Tucker and Henry C. Sleight, under the firm of Luther Tucker & Co. In 1828 the partnership was dissolved, and the publication was continued by Tucker. On the 1st of Jan. 1829, the paper was united with the Rochester Daily Telegraph and issued as *The Rochester Daily Advertiser and Telegraph,* by Tucker & Martin. In 1829 Martin retired, and in 1830 Tucker dropped the sub-title of Telegraph. Henry O'Reilly, H. L. Stevens, Thomas W. Flagg, and Hiram Humphrey were successively interested with Tucker in its publication as associate editors, until May 1839, when the establishment was transferred to Thomas H. Hyatt, who became editor and proprietor. After passing through several hands, the paper was united with the Rochester Daily Union, Sept. 1, 1856, and is now published as **The Rochester Daily Union and Advertiser.** Isaac Butts, editor; Curtis, Butts & Co., proprietors.

The Rochester Mercury was commenced in Jan. 1827, by Luther Tucker & Co. It was issued weekly in connection with the Daily Advertiser, and was merged in the Rochester Republican when that paper passed into the hands of the Daily Advertiser.

The Rochester Observer was commenced in 1827. Luther Tucker & Co., printers; Rev. G. G. Sill, editor; Josiah Bissell, jr., proprietor. After several successive changes of editors and publishers, it was united with the New York Evangelist in 1832.

The Rochester Balance was commenced in Jan. 1828, by D. D. Stephenson. It soon passed into the hands of Thurlow Weed and Samuel Heron, who changed its name to *The Anti-Masonic Inquirer.* D. N. Sprague succeeded Heron, and Weed retired in 1830. In 1831 Erastus Shepard united the Western Spectator of Palmyra with it. In 1832, Alva Strong became connected with Shepard in the publication, and in 1834 the paper was merged in the National Republican.

The Craftsman (Masonic) was commenced at Rochester in 1828 by E. J. Roberts. It was published about a year and a half and then removed to Albany.

The Western Wanderer was commenced at Rochester in 1828 by Peter Cherry. It soon passed into the hands of Edwin Scranton, who changed its name to *The Rochester Gem.* It subsequently passed into the hands of Strong & Dawson, and was discontinued in 1843.

The Spirit of the Age, semi-mo., was published in Rochester in 1830 by Ames & Barnum.

The Rochester Morning Courier was published in 1830 by E. J. Roberts.

The Genesee Farmer was commenced in Rochester in Jan. 1831, by Tucker & Stevens, with N. Goodsell as nominal editor. It was continued by Tucker until the close of 1839, when it was united with the Cultivator, at Albany.

The National Republican was commenced at Rochester in the spring of 1831 by Sidney Smith. In 1833 a daily edition, entitled *The Morning Advertiser,* was issued from the same office. It was soon after changed to *The Evening Advertiser,* and in 1834 Smith sold the establishment to Shepard & Strong, who united the Republican with the Inquirer and changed the name to *The Monroe Democrat,* and the name of the daily to *The Rochester Daily Democrat.* In 1836, George Dawson became interested in the establishment, and acted as editor until 1839. In 1846, Alva Strong, Samuel P. Allen, and Henry Cook were editors and proprietors. In Dec. 1857, the papers were united with the Daily and Weekly American, and the daily is now issued as **The Daily Democrat and American,** and the weekly as **The Monroe Democrat,** by Strong, Allen & Huntington, proprietors, and S. P. Allen, editor. **The Tri-Weekly Democrat** is issued from the same office.

The Rochester Mirror was published in 1832 by Scranton & Holstein.

The Age was published at Rochester in 1833.

The American Revivalist and Rochester Observer was published in 1833 by N. C. Saxton.

Goodsell's Genesee Farmer was commenced at Rochester in 1833 by Nahum Goodsell, and continued a short time.

The Rights of Man was published at Rochester in 1834 by the Anti-Slavery Society.

The Family Journal and Christian Philanthropist was published at Rochester in 1834 by W. B. Van Brunt.

The Monthly Genesee Farmer was commenced in 1836 by Luther Tucker. It was made up from the Weekly Genesee Farmer, and, with that paper, was united with the Cultivator in 1839.

The Watchman was published at Rochester in 1838 by Delazon Smith.

McKenzie's Gazette was published at Rochester in 1838 and '39 by Alexander McKenzie.

The New Genesee Farmer, mo., was commenced in 1840. M. B. Bateman, editor. Its name was afterward changed to **The Genesee Farmer.** It was successively edited by Henry Coleman, Daniel Lee, D. D. T. Moore, and James Vick, and is now edited and published by Joseph Harris.

The Working Man's Advocate, daily, was commenced in Rochester, Oct. 19, 1839, by the Typographical Association. Henry C. Frink, editor. They also issued a weekly edition. In April, 1840, it was purchased by James Vick and George P. Frost, who changed its name to *The Evening Advocate.* In 1841 it passed into the hands of John J. Reilly & Co., who changed its name to *The Evening Post,* and published in it connection with a weekly paper called *The Western New Yorker.* On the 1st of April, 1843, Erastus Shepard became proprietor, and in November following the two papers were discontinued.

The Rochester Daily Whig, a campaign paper, was published in 1840 by Wm. A. Welles.

The Erie Canal extends E. and W. through the co. It crosses the Irondequoit Valley upon the highest embankment upon the whole canal line. At Rochester it crosses Genesee River upon an aqueduct built of solid blocks of Onondaga limestone. The Genesee Valley Canal intersects the Erie Canal at Rochester, affording water communication S. to near the Penn. line, and opening into Allegany River at Olean. The New York Central R. R. extends through the co., several of its branches radiating from Rochester. The direct branch E. extends along the line of the Erie Canal, through Brighton, Pittsford, and Perinton, to Syracuse. The Auburn Branch extends S. E. through Brighton and Pittsford to Auburn and Syracuse. The Buffalo Branch extends S. W. through Gates, Chili, and Riga; and the Niagara Falls Branch extends W. through Gates, Greece, Ogden, and Sweden. The Genesee Valley R. R. extends S. from Rochester through Brighton, Henrietta, and Rush; the Canandaigua & Niagara Bridge Branch of the N. Y. C. R. R. extends through Rush and Mendon; and the Rochester & Charlotte Branch of the N. Y. C. R. R. extends from Rochester N. to the lake shore.

The territory now forming Monroe co. formerly constituted a portion of the hunting grounds of the Seneca Nation, although it contained none of their principal villages. The region was frequently visited by the French; but no permanent settlement was made till after the Revolution.

The Daily Sun was published in Rochester a few months in 1840 by Alfred Oakley.

The American Citizen was published at Rochester and Perry (Wyoming co.) in 1841 by W. L. Chaplin.

The Jeffersonian, daily, was published in Rochester a short time about 1842 by Thomas L. Nichols.

The Christian Guardian was published a short time in 1842 by Rev. J. Whitney.

The Mechanics' Advocate was published a short time in 1843.

The Rochester Daily American was commenced Dec. 23, 1844, by Leonard Jerome & J. M. Patterson; Alexander Mann, editor. A tri-weekly and a weekly edition were also issued. In July, 1845, Lawrence R. Jerome became a partner, and in 1846 the establishment passed into the hands of Leonard & Lawrence R. Jerome. In 1846 Dr. Daniel Lee was associated as assistant editor; and in 1847 Reuben D. Jones was assistant. Dec. 1, 1857, the paper was united with the Rochester Daily Democrat and issued as the Democrat and American.

The Rochester Herald, daily, was published in 1844 by E. S. Watson.

The Voice of Truth and Glad Tidings of the Kingdom at Hand, (Second Advent,) was commenced at Rochester in 1844 by Elder Joseph Marsh. In 1848 it was changed to *The Advent Harbinger*, and in 1849 to *The Advent Harbinger and Bible Advocate*. It was subsequently changed to **The Prophetic Expositor and Bible Advocate**, under which title it is still issued by the original proprietor.

The Rochester Temperance Journal was commenced in 1846, and continued a short time.

The Genesee Evangelist was commenced at Rochester in 1846 by Rev. John E. Roby. It is at present issued semi-monthly by R. W. Hill.

The Christian Offering was published at Rochester a short time in 1847 by S. B. Shaw.

The Penny Preacher was published a short time by Erastus Shepard.

The Genesee Olio, semi-mo., was published in Rochester in 1847 by Franklin Cowdery.

The North Star was published at Rochester in 1847 and '48.

Algemeen Handeelsblad was published at Rochester in 1848.

Frederick Douglass's Paper was commenced at Rochester in 1848 by Frederick Douglass, editor and proprietor, and is still published by him.

The Washingtonian was published at Rochester in 1848 by C. H. Sedgwick.

The Rochester Germania was published in 1849.

The Groninge Courant was commenced in 1849, and continued a few months.

The Christian Sentinel was commenced in 1849, and continued a short time.

Brewster's Insurance Reporter was published in 1849 by H. A. Brewster.

The Rochester Daily Magnet was published in 1849 by Lawrence & Winants,—C. H. McDonald & Co., proprietors. It was discontinued in 1850.

The Wool Grower and Stock Register, mo., was commenced in July, 1849. While in the hands of T. C. Peters, as editor, and D. D. T. Moore, it was merged in the Rural New Yorker.

The Investigator was published a short time in 1850.

The Medical Truth Teller was published a few months in 18— by Dr. J. Gates.

The Annunciator was published in 1850.

The Cygnet was published in 1850 by the Young Men's Temperance Association.

The Flag of Freedom was published in 1850 by Calvin H. Chase.

The Advent Review and Sabbath Herald, semi-mo., was commenced in Nov. 1850, by James White. In connection with it was published *The Youth's Instructor*.

Moore's Rural New Yorker was commenced in 1850 by D. D. T. Moore, its present publisher.

The Western Luminary was commenced at Rochester by Rev. G. M. Cook. It was afterward removed to Buffalo.

The Rochester Daily Herald was commenced in 1850; L. K. Falkner, editor. In a few months it passed into the hands of Geo. G. Cooper, who changed its name to *The Rochester Daily Times*, C. Hughson, editor. It was discontinued in 1851.

Anzeiger des Nordens, w. and tri-w., was commenced in 1852 by Kraneer & Felix,—Louis Hurtz, editor,—and is still published.

The Youth's Temperance Banner, mo., was published a short time in 18— by a committee of the Temperance Society.

The Evening News was issued about 3 months in 1852 by R. Chamberlain & Co.

The National Reformer was published a short time about 1852.

Beobachter am Genesee was commenced in 1852 by Adolphe Nolte, its present editor and proprietor.

The Rochester Daily Union was commenced Aug. 16, 1852, by Curtis & Butts; O. Turner, editor. In Dec. following, Isaac Butts became editor. In Sept. 1858, it was united with the Rochester Daily Advertiser. A weekly and a tri-weekly edition were issued from the same office.

The Rochester Daily Tribune was issued in 1855–56, by Snow & Ingersoll.

The Rochester Daily Free Press, a campaign paper, was issued in 1856 by John N. Ingersoll.

The Mercantile Journal was issued for 6 months in 1856 by C. H. McDonnell.

The Evening American, a campaign paper, was issued in 1858, A. H. St. Germaine, editor.

The Rochester Daily Times was commenced Jan. 24, 1859, by Charles W. Hebard, editor and proprietor. It was discontinued in April following, and revived in June as **The Daily Express**, by C. W. Hebard & Co., by whom it is still published.

The Journal of the Home, mo., connected with the Home for the Friendless, is published in Rochester. Mrs. N. S. Barnes, editress.

The Brockport Recorder was commenced in 1828 by Abiather M. Harris: it was published about 2 years.

The Brockport Free Press was published in 1831 by Harris & Hyatt, and in 1832 by Thos. H. Hyatt.

The Western Star was published at Brockport in 1832 by Justin Carpenter.

The Monroe Chronicle and Brockport Advertiser was published in 1833.

The Atlas was published at Brockport in 1835 by D. D. Wait.

The Brockport Watchman was published in 1844 by E. F. Bridges.

The Brockport Weekly Journal was commenced in Sept. 1852, by Wm. Gardiner & Co. It was published about 1 year.

The Brockport Gazette was commenced Oct. 1, 1855, by Wm. Haskell, and continued about 3 months.

The Daily Advertiser was commenced in Oct. 1856, by Wm. H. Smith. It is circulated gratuitously, deriving its support from advertisements.

The Brockport Republican was commenced in Jan. 1857,—H. W. Beach, editor,—and is still published.

The Jeffersonian was published in Clarkson in 1830 by —— Balch.

The Honeoye Standard was published at Honeoye Falls in 1839 by Garry A. Hough, and afterward by Morris & Vedder.

The School Visitor, mo., is published at Spencerport.

The first settler was Ebenezer Allen, a tory, who located upon the Genesee, near the present site of Rochester, in 1788. He soon after removed to Canada. The first permanent settlements were made in 1789, in Wheatland and near the head of Irondequoit Bay. During the next five years settlements sprung up in various parts of the co., though the general growth was greatly retarded by the difficulty of access, the dense forests, and the unhealthiness of the climate when the lands were first cleared. The unsettled condition of Indian affairs also had the effect to retard settlement; and the War of 1812 almost put an end to improvement. At the close of the war, settlers came in more rapidly, and a great business began to develop itself at Rochester. The construction of the Erie Canal gave an impetus to business, and speedily pushed settlements into every portion of the co. From that time the progress of the co. has been rapid and continuous. The co. was contained in the Phelps and Gorham Purchase. The three western towns belonged to the Triangle Tract, and the remainder of the co. w. of the Genesee constitutes a portion of the celebrated "Mill Yard Tract."[1]

BRIGHTON[2]—was formed from "*Smallwood*,"[3] March 25, 1814. A part of Rochester was taken off in 1834, and Irondequoit in 1839. It is an interior town, lying upon the E. bank of the Genesee, a little S. E. of the center of the co. Its surface is gently rolling, with a slight inclination toward the N. The deep valley of Irondequoit Bay is on the E. border. Its streams are small brooks, tributaries of the Genesee and Irondequoit. The soil is a sandy loam in the E. and a clay loam upon the river. Near the center are gypsum beds, formerly extensively worked. The people are largely engaged in raising vegetables for the Rochester market. There are several extensive nurseries in town. **Brighton,** (p. v.,) in the N. E. part, contains a church and about 30 dwellings. It is a canal village and a station upon the N. Y. C. R. R., where the two branches from the E. unite. A large brick and tile manufactory is located about 2 mi. s. of the village; and the Genesee Model School[4] is situated upon a beautiful site 2 mi. s. E. **West Brighton,** (p. v.,) near the Genesee, s. of the line of Rochester, contains about 15 dwellings. In its immediate vicinity are the co. workhouse, poorhouse, and insane hospital, the Mount Hope Rural Cemetery, the Monroe co. almshouses, an extensive glue factory, and several other manufactories. The first settlement was made in 1790, by John Lusk and Oran Stone, who located about 4 mi. E. of the river.[5] Rev. Solomon Allen, from Northampton, Mass., preached the first sermon and w s the first settled minister. There is but one church (Cong.) in town.

CHILI—was formed from Riga, Feb. 22, 1822. It is an interior town, lying s. w. of the center of the co. Its surface is level or gently rolling, with a slight inclination to the E. Genesee River forms the E. boundary; and Black Creek, a sluggish stream, flows E. through near the center. The soil is a clay loam, mixed with sand. South of Black Creek are several peculiar gravelly knolls, the principal of which is Dumpling Hill, near the river. **Chili,** (p. v.,) in the N. part, contains a church and 15 houses; **North Chili,** (p. v.,) a R. R. station in the N. W. corner, contains a church and 25 houses; **Clifton,** (p. v.,) in the s. w. part, contains 1 church, a saw and grist mill, plaster mill, furnace, and 201 inhabitants; **South Chili** is a hamlet. The first settlement was made in the E. part, by Joseph Morgan, in 1792.[6] There are 5 churches in town.[7]

CLARKSON[8]—was formed from Murray, (Orleans co.,) April 2, 1819. Union was taken off in 1852. It lies on the w. border of the co., N. of the center. Its surface is level, with slight un-

<hr>

1 In his treaty with the Indians, Mr. Phelps wished to obtain a tract w. of the Genesee; but the Indians were only willing to cede the lands E. of that river. A compromise was finally effected, by which a tract 24 mi. long by 12 mi. wide was granted to Phelps and Gorham for a mill yard. It is said that the Indians were much astonished when they came to see the mill and know how much land was really required for a yard. The Mill Yard Tract was bounded E. by the Genesee, w. by a line parallel to and 12 mi. w. of it, and it extended 24 mi. s. from Lake Ontario.

2 This town embraces Township 3 of Range 7 of the Phelps and Gorham Purchase. It was originally purchased by Gen. Hyde, Prosper Polly, Enos Stone, Col. Gilbert, and Joseph Chaplin, from Lenox, Mass.

3 The original name, "*Boyle*," was organized April 6, 1806, and embraced the six N. towns E. of the river. Penfield was taken off in 1810, and Perinton in 1812. Some time in 1812 or '13 the name was changed to "*Smallwood*;" and March 25, 1814, it was divided into two parts, one taking the name of Brighton and the other of Pittsford.

4 This institution was widely known as the "Clover Street Seminary," under the care of Mrs. Brewster, the author of Bloss's Ancient History.

5 John Lusk owned 1,500 acres at the head of Irondequoit Bay. Among the other early settlers were Joel Scudder, Chaun-

cey and Calvin Hyde, Samuel Shaffer, Enos Blossom, Timothy Allyn, and Oliver Culver,—the last named from Orwell, Vt. In 1800, most of the business upon the lake was done at Irondequoit Landing. In 1798, Judge John Tryon laid out a village 3 mi. above the head of the bay, and built a large warehouse. The place was called "*Tryons Town*." Asa Dayton kept an inn at this place, in 1801. A tannery and distillery were afterward built, and the place became quite a lively little village; but it is now entirely deserted. —— Turner taught the first school; Ira West kept the first store; and Solomon Hatch and Oliver Culver built the first mill, on Allyns Creek, in 1806.

6 Among the early settlers were Andrew Wortman, in 1794; Stephen Peabody, Col. Josiah Fish and his son Libbeus, from Vt., who located at the mouth of Black Creek, in 1795. —— Widener and his sons Jacob, Abraham, William, and Peter;—Sottle and family, Joseph Cary, Lemuel and Joseph Wood, Samuel Scott, Joshua Howell, Benj. Bowen, John Kimball, —— Dillingham, —— Franklin and family, all settled previous to 1800. The first birth was that of a child of Joseph Wood, in 1799. The first death occurred in the family of Joseph Morgan. James Chapman kept the first store, in 1807; and Joseph Cary built the first mill.

7 2 M. E., 2 Bap., and Presb.

8 Named from Gen. —— Clarkson, an extensive landholder, who gave 100 acres to the town.

dulations in the s. It is drained to the N. E. by the head branches of Salmon and Little Salmon Creeks. The soil is a sandy loam, mixed with clay. **Clarkson,** (p. v.,) in the s. part, contains 2 churches, a brewery, and 325 inhabitants. It is the residence of Ex-Lieut. Gov. Henry R. Selden. Salt was manufactured to a limited extent by the early settlers. **East Clarkson,** (p. v.,) in the s. E. corner, contains a church and 20 houses; **West Clarkson,** in the w. part, 30 houses. The first settlement commenced in 1809, by James Sayres, Moody Truman, and Elijah Blodgett[1]. There are 3 churches in town; 2 M. E. and Cong.

GATES[2]—was formed March 30, 1802, as "*Northampton.*" Its name was changed June 10, 1812. Parma and Riga were taken off in 1808, and Greece in 1822. It is near the geographical center of the co. Its surface is undulating, with a gentle inclination toward the N. Genesee River forms a small portion of the E. boundary on the s. E. corner. It is drained by small streams. The soil is a fine quality of calcareous loam, intermixed with clay. The people are largely engaged in raising vegetables for the Rochester market. **Gates** (p. o.) is 1 mi. N. of Gates Center. **Gates Center** and **West Gates** are hamlets; and **Coldwater** is a station upon the Buffalo Branch of the N. Y. C. R. R. The first settlement was made in 1809, by Isaac Dean, from Vt.[3] The census reports 2 churches in town; M. E. and Presb.

GREECE—was formed from Gates, March 22, 1822. It lies near the center, on the N. border of the co. Genesee River and Lake Ontario form its E. and N. boundaries. Its surface is rolling, with a general inclination toward the lake. It is drained by several streams that flow into the small bays that indent the lake shore. These bays, six in number, beginning at the w., are respectively Braddocks Bay and Cranberry, Long, Buck, Round, and Little Ponds. The shifting sand bars at their mouths destroy their commercial utility. The soil is a clay loam, with large tracts of drift sand along the lake shore. **Charlotte,**[4] (p. v.,) in the N. E. corner, near the mouth of Genesee River, is a U. S. port of entry in the Genesee District, and the lake port for Rochester, 7 mi. above. It contains 2 churches, a lighthouse, 3 shipyards, a steam sawmill, 2 grain elevators, planing mill, and lumber yard. Pop. 400. Six schooners are owned in the place; and the lake steamers touch here daily during navigation. **West Greece,** (p. v.,) on the line of Parma, contains 2 churches and 30 houses; **North Greece** (p. v.) a church and 20 houses; **South Greece,** (p. v.,) in the s. w. corner, 25 houses; and **Greece** (p. v.) a church and 20 houses. **Hanfords Landing,** (p. v.,) in the s. E. corner, at the head of navigation on Genesee River from the lake, contains 20 houses. **Greece Center** and **Reads Corners** are hamlets. The first settlement was made at the mouth of the Genesee, in 1792,[5] by Wm. Hencher and family. The census reports 7 churches in town.[6]

HENRIETTA[7]—was formed from Pittsford, March 27, 1818. It is an interior town, lying s. of the center of the co. Its surface is rolling, Genesee River forming its w. boundary. The streams are small, and usually dry in summer. The soil is a fertile, argillaceous loam. **East Henrietta,** (Henrietta p. o.,) E. of the center, contains 2 churches, the Monroe Academy, and 181 inhabitants. **West Henrietta,** (p. v.,) s. w. of the center, contains a church, a steam mill, furnace, extensive carriage shops, and 40 houses. The first settlement was commenced by Jesse Pangburn, in 1806.[8] The first church (Bap.) was organized in 1811.[9]

---

[1] The first settlement was made at Clarkson; and among the early settlers at that point were David Forsyth and Dea. Joel Palmer, from Conn. Eldridge, John, and Isaac Farwell came in 1810, and located w. of Clarkson Village. Dr. Abiel Baldwin, from Saratoga, came in 1811. The first male child born was a son of Mrs. Clarkson; the first female birth was that of Betsey Palmer, in 1812. Charlotte Cummings taught the first school, in 1812. Henry McCall kept the first store, about 1810.

[2] Named in honor of Gen. Horatio Gates.

[3] Among the early settlers who arrived in 1809 were John Sickles and Augustus B. Shaw. In 1811, Ezra Mason,—Hartford, and Richard, Paul, Philip, Lisle, and Lowell Thomas, located in town. William Williams came in 1819. The first child born was a daughter of Ezra Mason, in 1818. Ira West kept the first store, and Isaac Dean built the first mill.

[4] In June, 1813, the British fleet, under Sir James Yeo, landed at Charlotte and seized a quantity of provisions and whiskey. In Sept. of the same year the fleet again made its appearance at the mouth of the Genesee, and commenced a heavy fire upon the place; but the American fleet made its appearance, relieved the place, and the British escaped with considerable difficulty. In May, 1814, the British came once more, and, under cover of a flag of truce, a demand was made to deliver up the public stores at Rochester. The few militiamen who were present passed into and out of the woods in sight of the British, giving the appearance of a great number;

and the enemy, suspecting an ambuscade, retired, after having furiously bombarded the woods for an hour.

[5] Among the other early settlers were John Love, in 1793, at the mouth of the river; Zadoc Granger and Gideon King, at the Lower Genesee Falls, now Hanfords Landing, in 1796; and, in the winter of 1796 and '97, Eli Granger, Thomas King, Simon King, Elijah Kent, Frederic Bushnell, and Samuel Latta located in town. Eli Granger and Abner Migells built a schooner at Hanfords (then Kings) Landing, in 1799. This was the first merchant vessel built by Americans on Lake Ontario. The first marriage was that of Thomas Lee and a daughter of Wm. Hencher. Frederic Hanford kept the first store, in 1810; and Nathaniel Jones built the first sawmill.

[6] 2 M. E., Presb., Bap., Cong., Union, and R. C.

[7] Named from Henrietta Laura, Countess of Bath, daughter of Sir Wm. Pulteney.

[8] Maj. Isaac Scott received for military services 900 acres in the s. w. part of the town, and attempted a settlement in 1790, but abandoned it in 1792. In 1806, Charles Rice, Wm. Thompson, Thomas Sparks, Moses Goodall, Geo. Dickinson, Selah Reed, and Gideon Griswold settled in the w. part. In 1807, Ira Hatch, Jonathan Russell, Benjamin Hale, and the Baldwin family settled on what was called the Wadsworth Road. In 1809, the Spring family settled near the center. Sarah Leggett taught the first school, in 1809; James Smith kept the first store; and Jonathan Smith built the first sawmill.

[9] The census reports 5 churches; 2 M. E., 2 Bap., and Cong.

IRONDEQUOIT[1]—was formed from Brighton, March 27, 1839. It lies on the N. border of the co., E. of the center. Lake Ontario forms the N., Irondequoit Bay the E., and Genesee River the W. boundary. Its surface is rolling, with an inclination in the N. part toward the lake and the deep valley of Irondequoit Bay on the E. The streams are small and flow N. and E. into the lake and bay. The soil in the N. part is sandy, and in the s. clay loam. **Irondequoit,** (p. v.,) near the center, contains 15 houses. A suburb of Rochester, in the s. w. corner, contains 50 houses. The first settlement was made by Wm. Walker, in 1791.[2] There is no church in town.

MENDON—was formed from Bloomfield, (Ontario co.,) May 26, 1812. It lies on the s. border of the co., E. of the center. Its surface in the N. and E. is rolling, and in the s. w. moderately hilly. Honeoye Creek flows through the s. w. corner, and the headwaters of Irondequoit Creek through near the center. There are three small ponds in the N. w. part. The soil is a clayey, calcareous loam. **Honeoye Falls,**[3] (p. v.,) near the s. w. corner, incorp. April 12, 1833, contains 4 churches, 3 flouring mills, 1 gristmill, a sawmill, 2 woolen factories, a plaster mill, a manufactory of agricultural implements, and a stone quarry. It is a station on the Canandaigua & Niagara Falls Branch of the N. Y. C. R. R. Pop. about 1,100. **Mendon,** (p. v.,) in the E. part, contains 2 churches, a steam flouring mill, a steam sawmill, a foundery, and 20 houses; and **Mendon Center** (p. v.) a grist and saw mill and 15 houses. **Sibleyville,** in the s. w., is a hamlet. The first settlement was made at Honeoye Falls, by Zebulon Norton, from Vt., in 1790.[4] The first church (Bap.) was organized in 1809;[5] Rev. Jesse Brayman was the first settled minister.

OGDEN[6]—was formed from Parma, Jan. 27, 1817. It is an interior town, lying w. of the center of the co. The surface is level or gently undulating, with a slight inclination toward the N. The streams are small brooks forming head branches of Sandy, Salmon, and Little Black Creeks. The soil is a fine quality of calcareous and clayey loam. It is one of the best wheat growing towns in the co. **Spencerport,**[7] (p. v.,) a canal village and R. R. station, in the N. E. part of the town, contains 4 churches, a furnace, tannery, gristmill, and sawmill. Pop. 578. **Adams Basin,** (p. v.,) is a canal village and R. R. station of 30 houses, in the N. w. part of the town. **Ogden Center** contains a church and 35 houses. **Ogden** is a p. o. Settlement was commenced in 1802, by George W. Willey, from East Haddam, Conn.[8] The first preacher was Rev. Daniel Brown, in 1807; and the first church (Presb.) was formed in 1811.[9]

PARMA[10]—was formed from *"Northampton,"* now Gates, April 8, 1808. Ogden was taken off in 1817. It lies upon Lake Ontario, w. of the center of the co. The surface is level in the N., and gently rolling in the s., with a slight inclination toward the N. Its streams are Salmon, Little Salmon, Buttonwood, and Long Pond Creeks. The soil is principally a gravelly loam, intermixed in places with sand and clay. Weak brine springs are found s. of Unionville. **Parma Corners,** (Parma p. o.,) upon the ridge, in the s. part, contains a church, the Parma Institute, a pump factory, and 116 inhabitants. **Parma Center** (p. v.) contains 2 churches, a machine shop, and 109 inhabitants. **Unionville,** N. of the center, contains 2 churches, a furnace, machine shop, and 145 inhabitants. **North Parma** is a p. o. The first settlement was made in the N. E. part, in 1794, by Rozaleet Atchinson and his sons Stephen and John, from Tolland, Conn.[11] The first church (Bap.) was formed May 27, 1809.[12]

---

1 Named from the bay. Called by the Indians Neo-da-on-da-quat, signifying a bay.

2 Walker was a ranger. He settled at the mouth of Genesee River, but shortly after removed to the w. side of the river, into the present town of Greece. Among the other early settlers were —— Dunbar, Elisha Scudder, Dr. Hosmer, Emmer Reynolds, Jesse Case, and Adonijah Green, from Vt. The first death was that of Elijah Brown, in 1806.

3 Long known as "Nortons Mills," from the first mills, erected by Zebulon Norton.

4 Capt. Ball and Peter Sines, from Conn, came in with Mr. Norton. Among the other early settlers were Daniel Williams, Capt. Treat, Rufus Parks, Ebenezer Rathbun, Benj. Parks, Wm. Hickox, Lorin Wait, and Reuben Hill, from Mass., in 1793. These all settled in the E. part of the town. —— Sterling, Jason Cross, —— Moore, and Calvin Perrine settled at Honeoye Falls, in 1794; John Parks, Jonas Allen, and Joseph Bryan, in 1795; Charles Foot and Samuel Lane, in 1797. The first birth was that of Wm. E. Sterling, in 1795; the first marriage, that of Jason Cross and Mary Moon, in 1796; and the first death, that of John Moon, in 1801. Welcome Garfield taught the first school; Abram Parrish kept the first inn; and James Dickinson the first store.

5 The census reports 9 churches in town; 2 Presb., 2 Union, Prot. E., M. E., Bap., Cong., and Christian.

6 Named from Wm. Ogden, son-in-law of John Murray, original proprietor. The town embraces a portion of "Mill Yard Tract."

7 Named from Wm. H. Spencer, the pioneer settler.

8 Among the other early settlers were Ephraim, Abraham, Timothy, and Isaac Colby, and Wm. H. Spencer, in 1803; Josiah Mather, Jonathan Brown, Henry Hahn, Daniel Wandle, Benajah Willey, John Webster, Benj. Freeman, and Daniel Spencer, in 1804; Judge William B. Brown and Daniel Arnold, in 1805; and Austin Spencer, in 1808. These early settlers were all from Conn. The first child born was John Colby, in 1805; and the first death was that of Mrs. G. W. Willey, in 1803. Miss —— Willey taught the first school, in 1807. George Huntley kept the first inn; Charles Church the first store; and Wm. H. Spencer built the first sawmill.

9 The census reports 7 churches in town; Bap., Cong., M. E., Meth. Prot., Presb., R. C., and Union.

10 This town embraces the N. w. portion of the Mill Yard Tract.

11 Among the other early settlers were Michael Beach, Silas Leonard, Geo. Goodhue, and Timothy Madden, in 1802; Jonathan Underwood, Gibbon Jewell, Geo. Huntley, Abner Brockway, jr., Jas. Egbert, and Jonathan Ogden, in 1805; Hope and Elisha Downs in 1809; Augustus Mather, Lendell Curtiss, Sam'l Castle, and Kinnicone Roberts, in 1810; and Joshua Whitney, in 1811. The first marriage was that of Capt. Jonathan Leonard and a daughter of Wm. Hincher. Alpheus Madden taught the first school, in 1804; J. Thompson kept the first store: Hope and Elisha Downs the first inn; and Jonathan Whitney built the first saw and grist mill.

12 The census reports 9 churches in town; 2 Bap., 2 M. E., 2 Presb., F. W. Bap., Christian, and Cong.

GENESEE FALLS AT ROCHESTER

PENFIELD[1]—was formed from *"Boyle,"* March 30, 1810. Webster was taken off in 1840 It lies on the E. border of the co., N. of the center. Its surface is rolling, and in the w. it is much broken. Irondequoit Bay enters the N. w. corner. Irondequoit Creek flows through the s. w. corner and forms a part of the w. boundary. It falls about 90 ft. in the village of Penfield. The other streams are small brooks. The soil is drift sand over argillaceous loam. **Penfield,** (p. v.,) in the s. w. part, on Irondequoit Creek, contains 3 churches, 2 gristmills, 2 sawmills, a woolen factory, a foundery, and a manufactory of agricultural implements. Pop. 560. **Lovetts Corners** (East Penfield p. o.) contains 20 houses; **Penfield Center** contains 15 houses. The first permanent settlement was made by Lebbeus Ross and Calvin Clark, in 1801.[2] There are 4 churches in town.[3]

PERINTON[4]—was formed from *"Boyle,"* May 26, 1812. It is the s. town on the E. line of the co. Its surface is uneven, a ridge from the s. E. terminating near the center. Turk Hill, in the s. part, is the highest point in the co. The town is drained by the headwaters of Irondequoit Creek and its branches. The soil is a sandy loam. **Fairport,** (p. v.,) N. w. of the center, a canal and R. R. station, contains 5 churches, 3 flouring mills, 2 sawmills, a plaster mill, 2 planing mills, a saleratus factory, machine shops, and carriage shops. Pop. 685. **Bushnells Basin,** (p. v.,) in the w. part, on the canal, contains a church and 252 inhabitants; and **Egypt,** (p. v.,) s. E. of the center, a church and 30 houses. **Fullams Basin** is a hamlet, on the canal. The first settlement commenced in 1790, but was mostly abandoned soon after. Glover Perrin was the first permanent settler, in 1793.[5] Rev. —— Crane preached the first sermon. There are 8 churches in town.[6]

PITTSFORD—was formed from *"Smallwood,"* March 25, 1814. Henrietta was taken off in 1818. It is an interior town, lying E. of the center of the co. Its surface is undulating, with a gentle inclination toward the N. Irondequoit Creek flows through the N. E. part, and Allyns Creek through the w. part. The soil is sandy in the N., and clayey and gravelly in the s. **Pittsford,** (p. v.,) near the center, a canal and R. R. station, was incorp. April 7, 1827. It contains 4 churches, a union school, and a flouring mill. Pop. 702. **Cartersville,** in the E. part, on the canal, contains a distillery and 12 houses. The first settlement was commenced in 1789, by Israel and Simon Stone.[7] The first church (Cong.) was organized in 1809.[8]

RIGA—was formed from *"Northampton,"* now Gates, April 8, 1808. Chili was taken off in 1822. It lies on the w. border of the co., near the s. w. corner. Its surface is level or gently undulating. Black Creek, a dull, sluggish stream, flows E. in a tortuous course through near the center. The soil is a clayey loam. **Churchville,**[9] (p. v.,) N. w. of the center, on Black Creek, is a R. R. station, and contains 4 churches, a saw and flouring mill, foundery, and machine shop. Pop. 450. **Riga Center,** (Riga p. o.,) near the center, contains a church, the Riga Academy, and 25 houses. The first settlement was commenced in 1805, under the auspices of James Wadsworth.[10] The first church (Cong.) was formed in the fall of 1806;[11] Rev. Allen Hollister was the first pastor.

---

[1] Named from Daniel Penfield, an extensive landholder during the early settlement.

[2] Asa Carpenter had previously settled, but did not remain. Gen. Jonathan Fassett, of Vt., Caleb Hopkins, —— Maybee, and four others, made a settlement, but soon after abandoned it on account of sickness. Hopkins and Maybee remained. As early as 1804, Josiah J. Kellogg, Dan'l Stilwell, Benj. Minor, Jonathan and David Baker, Isaac Beatty, and Henry Paddock, moved in. Daniel Penfield came in 1810. The first birth was that of a child of Mrs. Fiske; and the first death was that of Benj. Stilwell, in 1804. Jos. Hatch taught the first school; Daniel Stilwell kept the first inn, in 1806; and Wm. McKinster the first store. The first mills were built by Daniel Penfield.

[3] Bap., F. W. Bap., M. E., and Presb.

[4] Named from Glover Perrin, the first permanent settler.

[5] Among the early settlers were Jesse Perrin, in 1794, Abner Wright, in 1795, Caleb Walker, in 1799, and Asa and Edward Perrin, Levi Treadwell, Maj. Norton, John Scott, John Peters, and Gideon Ramsdell, soon after. The first inn was that of Asa Wright, in 1797. Glover Perrin kept the first inn; Gregory & Dean the first store; and Richard Lincoln built the first gristmill.

[6] 2 Wes. Meth., M. E., Cong., Bap., F. W. Bap., Univ., and Union.

[7] Silas Nye, Joseph Farr, Alex. Dunn, and David Davis, from Washington co., settled near the center about the same time;

Thos. Clelland, Ezra Patterson, and Josiah Girninson soon after. In 1790 and '91, the Stone family, of 7 persons, Caleb Hopkins, Wm. Acker, Israel Canfield, and Benj. Miller, came in. The first marriage was that of N. Armstrong and Miss E. Cole. The first school was taught in 1794. John Mann built the first mill, in 1805, on Irondequoit Creek, in the E. part of the town.

[8] There are 4 churches in town; Presb., Prot. E., M. E., and Bap.

[9] Named from Samuel Church, the pioneer settler at the village in 1808.

[10] The first settlers were mostly from Mass. Elihu Church settled near the center, in March, 1806. Soon after, Samuel Shepard settled in the s. w. part; Henry Brewster, Sam'l Baldwin, William Parker, Ezekiel Barnes, Nehemiah Frost, Samuel Church, Jas. Knowles, Thos. Bingham, Jos. Tucker, Enos Morse, and Geo. Richmond, in 1807; and Jos. Emerson and Eber and Chester Orcutt, in 1808. The first birth was that of a daughter of Sam'l Church; the first male child born was Hiram Shepard, in 1806; the first death was that of Richard Church, in 1807. Jos. Thompson kept the first inn; Thompson & Tuttle the first store, in 1808. Samuel Church built the first sawmill, in 1808, and the first gristmill, in 1811, both at Churchville.

[11] The census reports 6 churches in town; 2 Cong., M. E., Presb., Bap., and Univ.

26

ROCHESTER[1]—was taken from Brighton and Gates, and incorp. as a village, by the name of "*Rochesterville*," March 21, 1817. Its name was changed April 12, 1822, and it was enlarged and incorporated as a city April 28, 1834.[2] It is located N. of the center of the co., upon Genesee River, 7 mi. from its mouth; and it contains an area of about 8 sq. mi. The surface is level or gently undulating. The N. Y. C. R. R. track is 280 ft. above Lake Ontario; and Mt. Hope Ridge, the highest point upon the s. border, is 160 ft. higher. The city has a solid foundation of Niagara limestone, cropping out along the course of the river, but in other parts of the city usually covered with drift deposits. The Genesee flows N., dividing the city into two nearly equal parts. Its course through the city is mostly a succession of rapids and falls, affording an extensive and valuable water-power, which is fully improved for manufacturing purposes.[3]

The city is quite regularly laid out, most of the streets crossing each other at right angles. The N. and s. streets are parallel to the river, and upon the principal E. and w. streets bridges are built across the river.[4] The streets are usually well paved and bordered by commodious sidewalks. The city is divided into 12 wards.

The immense water-power furnished by Genesee River gives to the city great advantages for manufacturing.[5] Mills were erected at an early period; and gradually other machinery was added, until the present great amount and variety have been attained. The staple manufacture of the city is flour. There are now in operation 24 mills and an aggregate of 125 runs of stone. The mills have a capacity for grinding 800,000 bbls. of flour per annum; and the aggregate capital invested is $700,000. Since the failure of the wheat crop in Western New York, a considerable portion of the water-power has been directed to other manufacturing purposes.[6]

The culture of fruit and ornamental trees has for many years formed an important business of the city; and now the nurseries are among the most extensive in the country.[7]

The commerce of the city is large, though of much less importance than the manufactures. It

---

[1] Named from Col. Nath'l Rochester, one of the original proprietors.

[2] At the first village meeting, held May 13, 1828, under charter, Francis Brown was elected President, and Wm. Cobb, Everard Peck, Dan. Mack, and Jehiel Barnard, Trustees. The village corporation embraced 750 acres. The first city officers—elected in June, 1834—were Jonathan Child, *Mayor;* Louis Brooks, Thos. Kempshall, Elijah F. Smith, Fred'k F. Backus, and A.W. Ripley, *Aldermen;* John C. Nash, *Clerk;* and E. F. Marshall, *Treasurer.*

[3] The whole fall of Genesee River within the co. is 280 ft., of which 265 are below the s. line of the city. The falls evidently all once formed a single cascade; but the different degrees of hardness of the several rocks over which the river flows have caused an unequal retrograde movement of the falls, until they have assumed their present position. The surface shales have worn away gradually to a uniform slope, over which the water flows in a series of rapids. At the Upper Falls the stream falls a distance of 96 feet over the perpendicular edge of the Niagara limestone underlaid by shale. Below the Upper Falls the river flows 1½ mi., through a deep ravine bounded by nearly perpendicular sides, to the Middle Falls, where it has a descent of 25 ft. One hundred rods below, it descends 84 ft. over a ledge of Medina sandstone to the level of Lake Ontario. Several sulphur springs flow out of the rocks below the Middle Falls.

[4] The river is crossed by 4 bridges, respectively at Buffalo, Court, Andrew, and Clarissa Sts. The Court and Andrew St. Bridges are of iron, and the others of wood. The first bridge was built upon the site of the present Buffalo St. Bridge, in 1810–12, under a special act. The cost—$12,000—was raised by tax, in Ontario and Genesee cos. The Court St. Bridge was first built in 1826, by individuals. It was replaced by the present structure in 1858, at the city expense. The Central R. R. Bridge crosses the river a few rods above the Upper Falls. The canal is crossed by 5 substantial iron bridges, built by the State. Other bridges are built across the canal feeder and the various mill-races extending through the city.

[5] The situation of this water-power is very favorable for the growth of manufactures. Vessels from Lake Ontario can come up the river to the foot of the Lower Falls, 2 mi. below the center of the city; and above the rapids the river is navigable to Mount Morris, a distance of 53 mi. The first mill was built by Ebenezer Allen, in 1788–89. He soon after sold out to Col. Fish and removed to Canada. This mill and one other were the only ones at this place until 1814, when Elisha and Henry Ely and Josiah Bissell built another at the Upper Falls. During this year a few hundred bbls. of flour were sent to the Niagara frontier,—the first flour ever exported from Rochester. The Phœnix Mills were built in 1818; since that time the number has largely increased, until now Rochester is one of the largest flour manufacturing places in the country. It is called the "Flour City."

[6] *Flour Barrels* form an important item in the manufacturing interests of the city. There are now engaged in this business 41 firms, producing in the aggregate 250,000 bbls. annually, and giving employment to 400 men.

Axes and Edge Tools are manufactured by 3 firms, with an aggregate capital of $180,000, and employing 200 men.

Machine Shops, 9 in number, have an aggregate capital of $300,000, turn out goods to the amount of $600,000 per annum, and employ 750 men.

Furnaces, 8 in number, employ 150 men, and have a capital of $320,000.

The Duryee and Forsyth Safe and Scale Manufacturing Co. was incorp. in Dec. 1854, with a capital of $100,000. It gives employment to 250 men, and produces goods to the amount of $250,000 per annum.

Cotton Factories, 2 in number, give employment to 26 men, and produce $230,000 worth of goods annually.

Breweries, 17 in number, have an aggregate capital of $130,000, and produce $250,000 worth of ale and lager beer annually.

Boat Yards, 15 in number, have a capital of $70,000, and manufacture $375,000 worth of boats annually.

Coach and Carriage factories, 8 in number, turn out $150,000 worth of carriages annually.

Boot and Shoe factories, 5 in number, give employment to 900 hands, and turn out goods annually to the amount of $500,000.

Cabinet Shops, 8 in number, employ 625 men, and turn out work to the amount of $500,000 annually.

Chair Factories, 2 in number, employ 300 men, and turn out chairs to the amount of $200,000 per annum.

Among the other articles annually manufactured are woolen cloths to the amount of $50,000, soap and candles to the amount of $60,000, carpets. paper, linseed oil, alcohol, paint, fire engines, rifles, &c. A carpet manufactory was started in 1832; and in 1838 there were 2 in successful operation,—one at the Lower and one at the Middle Falls. The first paper mill was built at the Upper Falls, in 1819. A large paper mill below the Lower Falls now produces paper to the amount of $150,000 annually. It is chiefly engaged in the manufacture of printing paper. There are several sawmills, planing mills, and tanneries in the city. Besides these, there are many minor manufactories, in the aggregate giving employment to a large number of men and making use of a great amount of capital. The city ranks among the first manufacturing towns in the State.

[7] Ellwanger & Barry's Mount Hope Nursery, occupying 500 acres, is probably the most extensive nursery in the world. Samuel Moulson's Old Rochester Nursery occupies 350 acres; Alonzo Frost & Co's. Genesee Valley Nursery, about 250; and Hooker & Bissell's East Avenue Nursery, about 200. J. O. Bloss & Co., Chas. Moulson, —— Burtis, Mattison & Co., Wm. King, and Wm. Bryan & Co.'s nurseries occupy 50 to 100 acres each.

is carried on by means of the canals, railroads, and Lake Ontario.[1] The exports consist of the products of the Genesee Valley and of the manufactured goods of the city. Pop. 43,877.

Besides the co. buildings, the city contains several fine public edifices.

The City Hall, combined with the co. courthouse, has already been described.

Corinthian Hall contains the reading room and library of the Atheneum and Mechanics' Association, and is one of the finest public halls in the country.

The Arcade, fronting Buffalo St., is a commodious building, containing the p. o., telegraph offices, and a variety of other offices, stores, &c. It has a broad promenade extending through the center, from which the various rooms open on either side. The roof is built mostly of glass, and the public walk is open to the roof. The rooms of the upper stories open upon galleries, which extend the entire length of the building on either side above the main walk or promenade.

The Central R. R. Depot is one of the finest buildings of the kind in the State. It contains ample accommodations for the various R. R. offices, passenger rooms, and for the cars which arrive on the various roads that center there. Its roof is supported by iron; and the whole structure presents a fine and imposing appearance. Several of the mercantile blocks, the banks, and private residences, are beautiful structures and worthy of becoming architectural models.

The Public Schools of the city are under the control of a Board of Education, consisting of 2 members from each ward and a Superintendent. The schools are graded, and the course of instruction embraces all studies, from the primary through the higher branches taught in academies. The school buildings are 16 in number. The number of teachers employed is 104; 13 are males and 91 females. The number of children between the ages of 4 and 21 is 16,108, of whom 6,320, or 38 per cent., attend school during some portion of the year. The total expenses for 1857 were $58,945.55. Number of volumes in school libraries, 7000.

The University of the City of Rochester was incorp. in Jan. 1850, and is under the patronage of the Baptist denomination. This school has an optional classical and scientific course. The present number of pupils is 140.[2]

The Baptist Theological Seminary,[3] connected with the University, was established Nov. 4, 1850. Its present number of students is 31.

The Rochester Collegiate Institute, corner of Atwater and Oregon Sts., was established in 1854, and is at present a flourishing institution.

The Rochester Female Academy, on Fitzhugh St., was incorp. in 1837.

The Allen Female Seminary and *The Tracy Female Institute* are flourishing private seminaries. There are 8 parish schools connected with the R. C. churches of the city.

The Rochester Atheneum and Mechanics' Association was founded in 1849. It has an extensive reading room and a library of 8,000 volumes. It sustains an annual course of lectures.

The Female Charitable Society was organized in 1826, to furnish clothing and other articles of necessity to the destitute.

The Home for the Friendless was organized April 11, 1849, to provide work for the needy who cannot obtain employment.

The House for Idle and Vagrant Children was opened June 2, 1854. It is connected with the school department of the city; and to it are sent all vagrant children that are wandering about the streets.

The Rochester Orphan Asylum was established in 1836 and incorp. in 1838. It is a fine brick edifice, situated in the s. w. part of the city, upon a lot donated by the Hon. John Greig. Its average number of inmates is 84, supported by State and county appropriations and private subscription.

The Roman Catholic Orphan Asylum was opened in July, 1842. It is under the charge of the Sisters of Charity. It is situated in the rear of St. Patrick's Church.

The Cartmen's Mutual Benevolent Society was incorp. in July, 1849.

The St. Andrew's Benevolent Society for extending aid to indigent Scotchmen was formed in 1850.

The St. George's Society was formed in March, 1849, by the English residents of the city.

The other societies in the city are the *Monroe Co. Bible Society,* organized in 1821; *The Rochester*

[1] The principal landing for the port of Rochester is at Charlotte, at the mouth of Genesee River, 7 mi. below the city. The amount of imports at this port for the year 1858 was $338,252; exports, $126,197. The principal imports are wheat, flour, fish, lumber, horses, hides and skins, peas, and wool; and exports, castings, fruit, fruit-trees, furniture, cheese, potatoes, and machinery. The lighthouse is 57 ft. high, surmounted by a lantern 11 ft. diameter and 8 ft. high, with a 4th order of lens. It was erected in 1822, at a cost of $5,000. The pier is ⅜ of a mi. in length, built of wood and stone; and on the end is a beacon lighthouse.

[2] This institution at present occupies temporary buildings upon Buffalo St., in the midst of the city. It owns a site of 12 acres just E. of the city limits, upon which suitable buildings are in process of erection. Connected with the institution is a valuable library and a fine mineralogical cabinet.

[3] This institution has an endowment of $75,000. It has a German Theological Department. Its library contains 5,500 vols., 4,600 of which belonged to Dr. Augustus Neander, the German ecclesiastical historian.

City Tract Society; the *Industrial School Association;* the *Christian Doctrine Society; Society of St. Alphonsus,* (German;) *St. Joseph's Convent of Redemption;* the *Academies of St. Patrick, The Sacred Heart,* and *Our Lady of Mercy.* The *St. Mary's Hospital* has an average of about 70 patients.

The Western House of Refuge for Juvenile Delinquents, a State institution, established in 1844. is located upon a farm of 42 acres 1½ mi. N. of the courthouse. The buildings consist of a large and imposing main edifice, with wings containing offices, cells, a chapel, &c. and a variety of workshops. They occupy a site of 4½ acres, surrounded by a high wall. The average number of inmates is nearly 400.[1]

The first religious services held in the co. were connected with the French missions in the 17th century. The first church at Rochester (Presb.) was formed in 1815, and the church edifice was erected in 1817 ; Rev. Comfort Williams was the first settled minister, in 1816. Several of the city churches are among the finest church edifices in the State. There are now 46 churches in the city.[2]

Mount Hope Cemetery is located in Brighton, near the s. line of the city. It embraces a lot of 70 acres located upon Mount Hope, the highest point of land in the vicinity, and one completely overlooking the city. It is laid out in excellent taste, and is one of the finest rural cemeteries in the country. *St. Patrick's Cemetery* contains 15 acres, and *St. Joseph's Cemetery* (German) 9 acres.

The territory about the mouth of the Genesee first became known to the whites in the early exploring expeditions of the French. A map of the region, prepared by Baron La Hontan, was published at London in 1703. Views of the Upper and Lower Genesee Falls had been published as early as 1768.[3] Many other adventurers visited the place and gave descriptions of it long previous to the Revolution. The country remained in the peaceable possession of the Indians until after the war, when immigration began to set in toward Western N. Y. The first settler who located at the falls was Ebenezer Allen, the notorious tory.[4] He built a mill in 1788 or '90, but soon after sold out his improvements to the Pulteney Estate. The mill went to decay ; and there were no other white settlers for several years.[5] Among the earliest settlers were Jeremiah Olmstead, who located a short distance s. of the present site of the House of Refuge, in 1798–99 ; Wm. Cole, who established a ferry, in 1805 ; and Enos Stone, who built a mill, in 1808. In 1802, Nath'l Rochester, Wm. Fitzhugh, and Charles H. Carroll, from Md., purchased a tract of 300 acres at the Upper Falls ; and in 1812 they caused their land to be laid out for settlement. In the same year Francis and Matthew Brown, from Mass., and Thomas Mumford, laid out a tract of 200 acres adjoining the former, and commenced the erection of mills, &c.[6]

The war with Great Britain broke out at the time when the first efforts were made to build up Rochester, and seriously retarded the progress of settlement. The fear of Indian hostilities and of hostile invasion from Canada caused many of the pioneer settlers to abandon their new homes and emigrate to the more populous sections of the country. At the close of the war, settlements commenced throughout Western N. Y. with increased rapidity ; and Rochester immediately felt the new impulse. A large number of settlers came in, mills were built, and the place immediately became the commercial and manufacturing center of the fertile Genesee country. The finishing of the Erie Canal gave a new impetus to the business of the place and served to greatly extend its manufacturing interests. Since that time the city has steadily and rapidly increased both in population[7] and business, until it has arrived at a front rank among the inland cities of the State.

RUSH—was formed from Avon, (Livingston co.,) March 13, 1818. It lies near the center of the s. border of the co. Its surface is rolling, with a w. inclination. Genesee River forms its w. boundary; and Honeoye Creek flows w. through the town and enters the river near the center of the w. border. In the w. part, along the river, are extensive flats. The soil is a sandy, calcareous

---

[1] The central building is 86 by 60 ft., and 3 stories high. The wings are each 148 by 32 ft.,—making the entire length of the building 382 feet. Juvenile delinquents are sentenced to this institution from the central, northern, and western parts of the State,—those from the eastern part being sent to a similar institution on Wards Island, New York City. The inmates spend a portion of each day in study and a portion in laboring at some useful employment. The principal business carried on is the manufacture of shoes and brushes. A library of 9,000 volumes is connected with the institution. The yearly cost is about $31,000, and the earnings of the inmates $12,000. See p. 42.

[2] 10 Presb., 8 M. E., 7 R. C., 4 Prot. E., 4 Bap., 2 Friends, and 1 each Cong., Univ., Unit., Ref. Prot. D., Germ. Evan., Germ. Ref., Second Advent, Society of Christians, Brothers in Christ, Evang. Association, and Jewish.

[3] Those early maps the Genesee was called "Casconchiagon," or Little Senecas River. The water-power was not immediately improved, because every creek in the vicinity afforded sufficient power for the wants of the people.

[4] Aaron Burr visited the place in 1795 and made a minute and critical survey of the Falls. In 1797 Louis Philippe and his

two brothers, then in exile, accompanied by Robert Morris, visited the place.

[5] See p. 398.

[6] Charles Harford built a small mill in 1807,—the first one after that of Ebenezer Allen. The Browns built a race in 1812, and started a store. The same year Samuel J. Andrews and Moses Atwater laid out a tract of land for settlement. Among the settlers who came in about this time were Rev. Abelard Reynolds, Dr. Jonah Brown, (the first physician,) Abraham Starks, John Matlick, (the first lawyer,) Henry Skinner, Israel Scranton, Luscum Knapp, Hezekiah Noble, Joseph Hughes, Ebenezer Kelly, Ira West, Elisha and Henry Ely, Porter P. Peck, Josiah Bissell, jr., Michael Cully, Harvey Montgomery, Charles D. Farman, and Geo. G. Sill. The first child born was a son of Enos Stone, May 4, 1810. Hamlet Scranton built the first framed dwelling, in 1812, on the present site of the Eagle Tavern.

[7] The following table shows the progress of population since 1830 :—

1830	9,207	1845	26,965
1835	14,414	1850	36,403
1840	20,191	1855	43,877

loam on the uplands, and a rich alluvium on the flats. **East Rush** (Rush p. o.) contains a church, a saw and grist mill, a carriage factory, and about 250 inhabitants; **West Rush,** (p. v.,) in the w. part, a station on the C. & N. F. Branch of the N. Y. C. R. R., contains a saw and grist mill and 30 houses; **North Rush,** (p. v.,) in the N. w. part, about 1 mi. E. of Scottsville station, contains a church and 16 houses. **Genesee Valley R. R. Junction** is 1 mi. w. of West Rush. The first settlement was commenced in 1799, by Maj. Wm. Markham and Ransom Smith, from N. H.[1] The first settled minister was Elder Goff, (Bap.)[2]

SWEDEN—was formed from Murray, (Orleans co.,) April 2, 1813. It lies on the w. border of the co., near the center. Its surface is level and gently rolling. A high ridge passes E. and w. through the town, N. of the center. Salmon Creek rises in the s. w. part and flows in an E. and N. E. course through the town. The soil is clay and clay loam. **Brockport,**[3] (p. v.,) in the N. part, a canal village and R. R. station, was incorp. April 26, 1829, contains 6 churches, the Brockport Collegiate Institute,[4] a bank, 2 newspaper offices, 4 founderies, a planing mill, a manufactory of mowers and reapers, an extensive carriage manufactory, and a rotary pump manufactory. Pop. 2,143. **Sweden Center,** (Sweden p. o.,) near the center, contains 2 churches and 20 houses; and **West Sweden,** near the s. w. corner, 2 churches and 15 houses. The first settlement was commenced in 1807,[5] by Nathaniel Poole and Walter Palmer. There are 10 churches in town.[6]

UNION—was formed from Clarkson, Oct. 11, 1852. It is the N. w. corner town of the co. Lake Ontario forms its N. boundary. Its surface is slightly rolling and inclines toward the lake. It is drained by a number of small streams, the principal of which is Sandy Creek. The soil is a sandy, clayey, and gravelly loam. Salt was manufactured to a limited extent by the early settlers. **Clarkson Center,** (p. v.,) in the s. part, contains 35 houses; **North Clarkson,** (p. o.,) in the E. part, 8 houses; **Kendalls Mills,** near the s. w. corner, partly in Kendall, (Orleans co.,) is a hamlet. The first settlement was commenced in 1810, by Aretus Haskell.[7] There are 5 churches in town.[8] A Fourierite community was organized and located at the mouth of Sandy Creek, in 1843, under Dr. Theller, of Canadian Patriot War notoriety. The bubble soon burst.

WEBSTER—was formed from Penfield, Feb. 6, 1840. It lies on Lake Ontario, in the N. E. corner of the co. Irondequoit Bay forms its w. boundary. Its surface from the ridge in the s. part has a gentle inclination to the lake. The shore rises in places 50 ft., and in the w., on Irondequoit Bay, 80 to 100 ft. The streams are small and flow N. into the lake. The soil is a sandy loam N. of the ridge, and clay and clay loam.in the s. Salt was manufactured to some extent by the early settlers. **Webster,** (p. v.,) in the s. part, on the ridge, contains 4 churches, the Webster Academy, and 310 inhabitants; **West Webster,** (p. v.,) in the s. w. part, contains 40 houses. The first settlement was commenced in 1805, under the agency of Caleb Lyon.[9] The first church (M. E.) was formed in 1812, by Rev. Solomon Pierce.[10]

WHEATLAND—was formed from Caledonia, (Livingston co.,) as *"Inverness,"* Feb. 23, 1821. Its name was changed April 3, 1821. It lies upon the s. border, in the s. w. part of the co. Genesee River flows s. on the E. border. Its surface is rolling. Oatka (or Allens) Creek flows E. through near the center of the town. It is joined at Mumford by the Outlet of Caledonia Springs, forming an excellent water-power. The soil is loam, mixed with clay in the interior, and with sand and gravel in some localities, the whole underlaid by limestone. Gypsum is found in large quantities. **Scottsville,**[11] (p. v.,) in the E. part, contains 4 churches, a union school, extensive flouring mills,

---

1 Among the early settlers were Joseph Morgan, from the w. side of the river, and —— Spraker, from the Mohawk. Philip Brice, Chrystal Thomas, Jacob Stall, and John Bell, came in 1801, from Md.; Joseph Sibley and Elisha Sibley, from Rensselaer co., in 1804; Elnathan Perry and Thomas Daily, in 1806. The first birth was that of Joseph Morgan, in 1789. The first deaths were Mr. and Mrs. Markham, in 1791. John Webster kept the first inn; Benj. Campbell the first store; and John Webster built the first gristmill.

2 The census reports 5 churches in town; 2 M. E., Evan. Luth., Bap., and Christian.

3 Named from Hiel Brockway, a prominent early settler in the village.

4 This institution is under the supervision of the Baptist denomination, and is in a flourishing condition.

5 Samuel Bishop, —— Hopkins, Isaiah White, and Stephen Johnson came in 1807; John Reed, Timothy Tyler, and Edward Parks, in 1808. Reuben Moon, with his sons James, Amos, and Isaac, settled in 1809 and '10, in the E. part. James Scott (colored) was the first settler in the s. part, in 1809. John Phelps, Rufus Hammond, and —— Knight were the original purchasers of the site of Brockport. James Seymour, George Allen, Thomas R. Roby, Ralph W. Goold, Luke Webster, and Charles Richardson were early settlers. Samuel Bishop kept

the first inn, in 1809; Charles Richardson the first store; and Brockway & Blodgett built the first mill.

6 3 M. E., 2 Bap., F. W. Bap., Cong., Presb., Prot. E., and R. C.

7 Josiah and Samuel Randall, from Maine, settled in 1810; Stephen Baxter and John Nowlan, in 1811; —— Strunk settled at the mouth of Sandy Creek, in 1811; —— Billings and Alanson Thomas, soon after. But few settlers came in until after 1817. The first death was that of —— Strunk, in 1812. A. D. Raymond kept the first inn; Daniel Pease the first store; and Alanson Thomas built the first mill, for Le Roy & Bayard.

8 M. E., Meth. Prot., Bap., F. W. Bap., and Union.

9 John Shoecraft, from Ulster Co., Isaac Straight, Daniel Harvey, Abram Foster, Paul Hammond, William Mann, William Harris, John Letts, Samuel Pierce, Samuel Goodenough, and Benjamin Burnett, mostly from N. H. and Vt., settled about 1806. The first birth was in the family of Caleb Lyon; and the first death, that of a child of N. Caines. Wm. Harris taught the first school, in 1810. John Letts kept the first inn; F. B. Corning the first store, in 1825; and Caleb Lyon built the first saw and grist mill, in 1806.

10 There are 4 churches in town; Bap., M. E., Presb., and Univ.

11 Named from Isaac Scott, the first settler and owner of the present site of the village.

plaster mills, a woolen factory, furnace, brewery and distillery, and a steam planing mill. Pop. 925. **Mumford,** (p. v.,) in the s. w. part, contains 3 churches, a saw and grist mill, machine shop, a thrashing machine manufactory, and plaster mill. Pop. 535. **Garbuttsville** contains extensive quarries of plaster, flour and plaster mills, and 20 houses; **Wheatland Center,** (Wheatland p. o.,) near the center, contains 15 houses. The first settlement was made in 1789,[1] by Peter Shaeffer, from Penn. The first church (Bap.) was formed in 1811. The first pastor was Rev. Solomon Brown. The census reports 11 churches in town.[2]

Acres of Land, Valuation, Population, Dwellings, Families, Freeholders, Schools, Live Stock, Agricultural Products, and Domestic Manufactures, of Monroe County.

Names of Towns.	Acres of Land.		Valuation of 1858.			Population.		No. of Dwellings.	No. of Families.	Freeholders.	Schools.	
	Improved.	Unimproved.	Real Estate.	Personal Property.	Total.	Males.	Females.				No. of Districts.	Children taught.
Brighton	12,079¾	1,672	$1,032,786	$36,453	$1,069,239	1,777	1,546	499	532	291	9	1,005
Chili	19,855½	5,172½	816,200	35,454	851,654	1,131	1,072	390	400	318	11	697
Clarkson	15,473	4,626	568,235	112,035	680,270	1,107	1,070	392	415	291	10	790
Gates	10,601	1,935	720,860	116,700	837,560	1,221	1,126	423	459	296	10	1,044
Greece	24,289	5,770½	1,320,638	120,953	1,441,591	2,323	2,164	805	852	589	18	1,527
Henrietta	18,527½	3,991	883,332	207,250	1,090,582	1,105	1,039	416	357	300	10	706
Irondequoit	9,968	3,083½	587,840	48,234	636,074	1,660	1,574	582	614	460	6	1,291
Mendon	18,931¼	4,412	950,965	102,186	1,053,151	1,525	1,490	549	594	444	18	913
Ogden	18,042	3,631	787,045	79,700	866,745	1,604	1,476	553	585	464	14	911
Parma	20,020¾	6,012½	705,965	85,121	791,086	1,404	1,379	532	556	453	16	1,164
Penfield	17,954½	4,962	707,297	43,600	750,897	1,544	1,487	607	612	434	12	1,111
Perington	17,295	5,094	838,533	54,000	892,533	1,661	1,514	570	647	433	11	985
Pittsfield	12,648	2,080½	580.380	92,100	672,480	1,123	1,010	375	412	315	10	747
Riga	17,091½	4,000	736,992	78,452	815,444	1,050	975	384	385	202	13	835
Rochester	641¾	61½	9,362,408	2,582,565	11,944,973	21,682	22,195	7,408	8,557	5,584	18	15,863
Rush	14,837	3,556	860,920	83,910	944,830	889	861	301	318	215	10	646
Sweden	17,602¼	4,145½	1,033,086	275,229	1,308,315	1,982	1,985	712	523	523	13	1,293
Union	19,969½	5,706½	576,966	28,400	605,366	1,253	1,116	442	444	323	15	896
Webster	15,454	4,703	552,277	94,871	647,148	1,228	1,160	496	518	333	11	931
Wheatland	15,559	3,567	736,440	137,149	873,589	1,439	1,377	480	503	283	10	967
Total	316,840¼	78,182	24,359,165	4,414,362	28,773,527	48,708	47,616	16,916	18,283	12,551	245	32,916

Names of Towns.	Live Stock.					Agricultural Products.							Domestic Cloths, in Yards.
						Bush. of Grain.					Dairy Products.		
	Horses.	Working Oxen and Calves.	Cows.	Sheep.	Swine.	Winter.	Spring.	Tons of Hay.	Bushels of Potatoes.	Bushels of Apples.	Pounds of Butter.	Pounds of Cheese.	
Brighton	594	633	561	2,110	1,036	19,304	80,077½	3,388½	34,815	20,187	50,828	1,480	152
Chili	956	1,479	966	8,745	2,142	49,074	96,288¼	4,239	25,206	26,819	117,665	4,360	282
Clarkson	824	1,151	728	7,736	1,669	17,398	88,855	3,327	13,542	27,154	69,411	11,630	263
Gates	500	546	616	1,165	827	17,226	69,955	2,594	22,952	17,430	41,285	850	20
Greece	1,365	1,667	1,449	9,174	3,009	38,556	135,684¾	5,289½	98,293	61,656	159,985	4,745	1,379
Henrietta	867	1,061	822	6,055	1,966	54,710	115,292	3,939½	16,520	25,061	72,319	7,873	372
Irondequoit	513	630	654	1,167	932	24,809	43,881	2,074	87,633	12,031	45,512	1,160	53
Mendon	1,155	1,222	1,067	8,658	1,303	83,321	117,683½	2,444	18,453	10,670	96,020	13,035	338
Ogden	1,009	1,343	956	5,690	1,793	52,183	107,706½	3,666½	32,509	40,526	110,217	9,163	289
Parma	1,180	1,655	1,235	9,626	2,905	27,602½	128,811½	3,969½	31,631	42,509	150,751	9,593	731
Penfield	1,044	1,027	1,040	4,999	2,053	35,316	131,003	2,193½	57,044	38,714	94,318	10,495	680¾
Perington	1,000	1,606	918	5,008	1,676	44.943½	101,503	3,062¼	62,150	25,729	81,868	10,626	144
Pittsfield	831	838	593	3,669	1,207	32,343	68,965½	1,586	30,668	7,818	40,633	670	
Riga	894	1,146	745	7,154	1,782	74,831	84,054½	2,431	9,697	23,707	68,930	10,425	218
Rochester	1,544	25	844		323	200	2,179	94	2,130	1,715	376		
Rush	702	861	686	6,734	2,102	47,013	71,728	1,981	10,890	16,790	78,910	4,400	180
Sweden	986	1,432	1,002	5,816	1,895	62,059	82,999	3,057	10,553	30,210	86,909	12,600	685
Union	1,043	1,629	968	10,617	2,398	10,765½	151,385	3,670½	27,899	20,820	108,101	7,011	486
Webster	891	1,025	921	5,825	1,731	19,876	94,973	3,227	42,586	33,477	126,350	3,335	671
Wheatland	1,015	1,005	793	6,869	1,978	107,999	60,526	2,505	19,380	8,468	43,127	7,802	404
Total	18,913	21,981	17,564	116,817	34,727	819,529½	1,833.551	58,738¾	654,551	491,491	1,643,515	131,253	7,347¾

[1] Mr. Shaeffer and his sons Peter and Jacob came in Dec. 1789. They found a settlement commenced by Ebenezer Allen and his brother-in-law, Christopher Dugan, near the mouth of Allens Creek, a short distance below Scottsville. Allen had a comfortable log house and about 60 acres of improvement. The Shaeffers became the purchasers of his farm, paying $2.50 per acre. After the sale, Allen left with his family for Mount Morris. The valley of the river below Shaeffer's was slow in settling; Joseph Morgan came in 1792, Andrew Wortman in 1794 or '95. Caleb Aspinwall, Peter Conkle, Frederick and Nicholas Hetztiller were early settlers in the Shaeffer neighborhood. Reuben Heath came from Vt. in 1799. The s. w. part was early settled, under the auspices of Charles Williamson, by Scotch, among whom were John McNaughton and family, near Mumford. Isaac Scott settled at Scottsville about 1790, and Donald McVean soon after. Zachariah Garbutt and family settled at what is now Garbuttsville, in 1803; and Powell Carpenter, near Scottsville, in 1804. The first marriage was that of Peter Shaeffer, jr., and a daughter of Jacob Schoonover, in 1790. (Ebenezer Allen had previously added another inmate to his harem by a pretended marriage with Lucy Chapman. See p. 711.) The first death was that of Peter Shaeffer, sen. Jacob Scott kept the first inn, Philip Garbutt and Abram Hanford the first store; and Peter Shaeffer, jr., built the first sawmill, in 1810, and the first gristmill, in 1811. John and Robert McKay built the first gristmill, at Mumford, in 1808; and Donald McKenzie erected the first cloth dyeing works w. of Genesee River.

[2] 2 Presb., 2 Bap., 2 Friends, 2 R. C., Prot. E., M. E., and Asso. Ref. Presb.

MONTGOMERY COUNTY.

THIS county was formed from Albany, March 12, 1772, under the name of *"Tryon Co."*[1] Its name was changed April 2, 1784. Ontario was taken off in 1789, Herkimer, Otsego, and Tioga in 1791, Hamilton in 1816,[2] and Fulton in 1838. It lies on both sides of the Mohawk, centrally distant 39 miles from Albany, and contains 436 sq. mi. The general system of highlands which forms the connecting link between the northern spurs of the Alleghany Mts. on the S. and the Adirondacks on the N. extends through this co. in a N. E. and S. W. direction. Mohawk River cuts through the upland, and forms a valley 1 to 2 mi. wide, and 200 to 500 ft. below the summits of the hills. The valleys of several of the tributaries of the Mohawk extend several miles into the highland district at nearly right angles to the river valley. The hills bordering upon the river generally rise in gradual slopes, and from their summits the country spreads out into an undulating upland, with a general inclination toward the river, into which every part of the surface of the co. is drained. The principal tributaries of the Mohawk are the East Canada, Garoga, Cayadutta, Chuctenunda Creeks, and Evas Kil, on the N., and Cowilliga, Chuctenunda, Schoharie, Auries, Flat, Canajoharie, and Otsquaga Creeks, on the S. The highest point in the co. is Bean Hill, in Florida, and is estimated to be 700 ft. above tide, and the lowest point is the bed of the Mohawk, on the E. line of the co., 260 ft. above tide.

Gneiss, the only primary rock in the co., is found in patches, the principal locality being at *"The Noses,"* on the Mohawk.[3] Resting directly upon this are heavy masses of calciferous sandstone, appearing mostly on the N. bank of the river and extending into Fulton co.[4] Next above this are the Black River and Trenton limestone, not important as surface rocks, but furnishing valuable quarries of building stone. The slates and shales of the Hudson River group extend along the S. border of the co. and are found in a few places N. of the river. Drift and boulders abound in various places. The soil along the river consists of alluvial deposits and a deep, rich, vegetable mold, and upon the uplands it is mostly a highly productive sandy and gravelly loam. The productions are principally grass and spring grains. The uplands are finely adapted to pasturage, and dairying forms the leading pursuit. Upon the Mohawk Flats immense quantities of broomcorn are raised. There are several important manufactories in the co., consisting chiefly of woolen goods, carpets, paper, agricultural implements, sash and blinds, and castings. Quarrying is extensively carried on.[5]

The principal public works are the Erie Canal, extending along the S. side of the Mohawk, and the N. Y. Central R. R.,[6] on the N. bank. A wire suspension bridge crosses the Mohawk at Fort Hunter, and wooden bridges at Amsterdam, Fonda, Canajoharie, Fort Plain, and St. Johnsville. An iron bridge was built at Fort Plain, in 1858.

The county seat is located at Fonda, a pleasant village on the Mohawk, built on the site of the ancient Dutch settlement of *"Caughnawaga."*[7] The courthouse is a fine brick edifice, containing the usual co. offices.[8] The jail is a stone building, adjacent to the courthouse.[9] The co. poorhouse is located upon a farm of 150 acres situated in Glen, about 3 mi. E. of Fonda. The building is old and poor, and has few arrangements for the health, comfort, or convenience of its inmates. The average number of inmates is 125. The farm yields a revenue of $1,000.

The first newspaper in the co. was established at Fort Plain, in 1827.[10]

---

[1] Named from Wm. Tryon, Colonial Governor. Present name given in honor of Gen. Richard Montgomery, of the Revolution. As first formed, this co. embraced all of the State W. of Delaware River and a line extending N. through Schoharie, and along the E. lines of the present cos. of Montgomery, Fulton, and Hamilton, and continuing in a straight line to Canada.

[2] Taken off with Herkimer in 1791, and restored to Montgomery March 31, 1797.

[3] This rock here contains pink colored garnets.

[4] This rock often contains in its cavities quartz and nodules of anthracite coal, which has led to foolish expenditures of large sums in mining for coal. Near Sprakers Basin traces of lead have been found.

[5] Stone from these quarries were used in the construction of canal locks and other public works.

[6] Formerly *"Schenectady & Utica R. R."* The Catskill & Canajoharie R. R., incorp. in 1830, was opened to Cooksburgh

from Catskill at a cost of $400,000. In 1842 it was abandoned, the track sold for $11,000 and taken up.

[7] *"Caughnawaga"* was one-half mi. E. of the courthouse, but is now included within the incorporation of the village of Fonda. The co. seat was removed from Johnstown in 1836. The conditions of the removal were that a subscription of $4500 should be raised, and a site of not less than 3 acres donated to the co. This removal occasioned great dissatisfaction, and led to the division of the co. in 1838.

[8] By an act passed March 19, 1778, the sheriff's mileage in Tryon co. was directed to be reckoned from *"The Noses,"* which practice appears to have been continued for some time.

[9] The jail is so constructed as not to answer the requirements of the law in the classification of prisoners. The courthouse and jail were erected at a cost of $30,500.

[10] *The Watch Tower* was begun at Fort Plain in 1827 by S. M.

The early history of this co. is full of incident and interest. At the time of the first advent of the whites it was the principal seat of the Mohawks, one of the most powerful tribes of the Five Nations. The policy adopted by the early Dutch settlers of the colony, and continued by their English successors, strongly attached a majority of these savages to their interests; and the unprovoked attack of Champlain, in 1609, made them hate the French in Canada with intense bitterness. In the wars that ensued, the Five Nations proved faithful allies to the English, and on many occasions shielded them from hostile attacks. In 1665–66 a French expedition, consisting of 600 men, under De Courcelles and De Tracy, was sent against the Indians, and proceeded as far as Schenectady; but, after much suffering and the loss of many men, the army returned to Canada without affecting any thing. Within the next few years several French expeditions were sent against the western tribes of the Five Nations, and in return the Indians made a descent upon Montreal in 1689, laid waste whole plantations, and destroyed many lives.[1] In retaliation, Count Frontenac sent several expeditions against the Indians and English, one of which destroyed Schenectady in 1690.[2] In the winter of 1692–93 the French again invaded the Mohawk country, surprised and destroyed two of their three castles,[3] and took about 300 prisoners. In the engagement at the third castle they lost 30 of their number; and in their retreat they were pursued by Maj. Peter Schuyler at the head of 200 regulars and militia, who succeeded in killing 33 and wounding 26 of their number and in rescuing 50 prisoners. Favored by the severe cold, the remainder escaped and fled to Canada through the great northern wilderness. Their sufferings on this journey were intense. As early as 1642–43, a French Jesuit visited the Mohawk settlements; and between that date and 1678, 10 missionaries of this order labored to bring over the Indians of this region to the French interests and the Catholic religion. Though attended with great hardships, and in one or two instances with death, these labors were in some measure successful, and in 1671 a large number of Indians removed from Caughnawaga to Canada.[4]

A military post, known as Fort Hunter, was established near the mouth of Schoharie Creek in 1711. About the same time a large number of German Palatinates, sent over by Queen Anne, settled upon the Hudson, and shortly after removed to Schoharie and the Mohawk Valley and settled upon lands given them by Government. At about the same period a considerable number of Holland Dutch, from Schenectady and vicinity, found their way into the co. and extended their improvements up the valley. In 1730 the first mill N. of the Mohawk was built on the site of "Cranes" Village by two or three brothers named Groat; and this for a time served the settlements at German Flats, 50 mi. beyond.[5]

The land grants in this co. were made in comparatively small tracts. The first were issued as early as 1703. On the 19th of Oct. 1723, a patent of 12,000 acres, called "*Stone Arabia*," N. of the

S. Gant, who was succeeded by John Calhoun & —— Platt. In 1830 it was published as
The Fort Plain Sentinel.
The Fort Plain Gazette was begun in 1833 by H. L. Gros.
The Fort Plain Republican was begun in 1835 by E. W. Gill. It was succeeded by
The Tocsin in 1836, H. Link, publisher.
The Fort Plain Journal was commenced in 1838 by W. L. Fish. It changed owners several times, and was finally merged in
The Lutheran Herald, which continued a short time.
The Students Gleaner, by students of the Fort Plain High School, was issued from *The Journal* office.
The Montgomery Phœnix was begun at Fort Plain Feb. 3, 1841, by L. F. Backus, publisher, and D. F. Young, editor. In Feb. 1854 it was changed to
The Mohawk Valley Register, under which name it is now published by Webster & Wendell.
The Mohawk Farmer was published at Caughnawaga at an early period.
The Canajoharie Telegraph was published by Henry Hooghkirk in 1825–26.
The Canajoharie Sentinel was published in 1827; Samuel Caldwell, editor.
The Canajoharie Republican was published in 1827–28; Henry Bloomer, editor, and afterward John McVean & D. F. Sacia.
The Montgomery Argus was published by J. McVean in 1831–32, and continued by S. M. S. Grant till 1836.
The Canajoharie Investigator was published from 1833 to '36 by Andrew H. Calhoun.
The Radii was begun in 1837 by Levi S. Backus, a deaf mute; in Nov. 1840, it was burned out, and removed to Fort Plain; in 1854 it was removed to Madison co., but has since returned to Fort Plain. For several years the State made appropriations for sending this paper to deaf mutes throughout the State.
The Mohawk Valley Gazette was published at Canajoharie by W. H. Riggs from 1847 to '49.

The Montgomery Union was published at Canajoharie by W. S. Hawley, 1850–53. Four numbers of another paper were published at the same place in 1854 by S. M. S. Gant.
The Mohawk Advertiser, published at Amsterdam by Darius Wells, was changed to
The Intelligencer and Mohawk Advertiser in 1834. In 1835 it was published by John J. Davis, L. H. Nicholds, editor. In 1836 it was published by S. B. Marsh, and, after several changes, it was changed in 1854 to
The Amsterdam Recorder, which is now issued by H. Hayward, editor and publisher.
The Mohawk Gazette was published at Amsterdam by Josiah A. Nooman in 1833–34.
The Fonda Herald was issued by J. Reynolds, Jr., in 1837.
The Fonda Sentinel was begun in 1845; it is now published by Clark & Thayer.
The American Star, commenced at Canajoharie April 5, 1855, by Wm. S. Hawley, was removed to Fonda May 17, 1855. In 1857 it was changed to
The Mohawk Valley American, and published by C. B. Freeman. In 1858 this title was changed to
The American Star, which is now published by Wm. S. Hawley, original proprietor.
The Montgomery Whig was begun at Fultonville in 1840 by B. F. Pinkham. It passed into the hands of Thos. Horton, and in 1855 its name was changed to
The Montgomery Republican, and is now published by P. R. Horton.
We are indebted to Prof. O. W. Morris, of New York, and to the files of The Phœnix, for the above list. Many changes of ownership are not stated.

[1] Colden's *Five Nations; Smith's Hist. N. Y.*
[2] See p. 598.
[3] The "Lower Castle" was situated at the mouth of Schoharie Creek, the "Middle Castle" at the mouth of the Otsquago, and the "Upper Castle" at the mouth of the Now-a-da-ga or Indian Castle Creek, in Danube, Herkimer co.
[4] An Indian village named Caughnawaga, 9 mi. above Montreal, is the result of this emigration.   [5] *Simms's "Hist. Schoharie."*

Mohawk, was granted to John Christian Garlock and others for the benefit of the Palatinates. The principal grants were made between 1730 and 1740; and in 1762 there remained little, if any, unpatented land in the co.

About the year 1735, the British Admiral, Sir Peter Warren, acquired the title to a large tract of land known as "*Warrensbush*," mostly in the present town of Florida, and sent out his nephew, Wm. Johnson, then but 21 years of age, as his agent. Johnson first located at the mouth of Schoharie Creek: afterward he removed to 3 mi. above Amsterdam, and finally to Johnstown. Through the influence of his uncle he received the appointment of Agent of Indian Affairs, which gave him great facilities for intercourse and traffic with the natives. Applying himself industriously to the study of the character and language of the Indians, and adopting their habits and dress whenever it suited his convenience, he gained an ascendency and influence over them never before enjoyed by any white person. His easy and obliging manners made him equally a favorite with the white settlers; and until his death, which took place on the 24th of June, 1774, the events of his life are intimately interwoven with the history of the co.[1] His title and estates descended to his son, Sir John Johnson; but his commanding personal influence could not be inherited. Guy Johnson, son-in-law of Sir William,[2] Col. Daniel Claus, and Col. John Butler, were attached to the interests of the Johnson family, possessed large estates, and lived in what were then considered sumptuous residences in the Mohawk Valley. They had considerable influence with both whites and Indians. In the controversy between the colonists and the mother country which resulted in the Revolution, the Johnsons and their adherents strongly espoused the cause of the King, from whom they had received so many favors.

As a class, the German Palatinates sided with the colonies, and a majority of the other settlers entertained similar sentiments; but for a long time they were overawed, and their efforts at organization were thwarted by the zeal and activity of the tory leaders. In the spring of 1775, while the court was in session at Johnstown, through the influence of the tories the signatures of most of the grand jurors and magistrates were procured to a document opposing the measures of the Continental Congress.[3] This proceeding, coupled with others of a more aggressive and personal character, tended greatly to organize the opposition forces, to separate the friends and enemies of freedom, and to kindle feelings of bitter and vindictive hatred, which naturally led to all the horrors of civil war.

"*Tryon co*" was divided into 6 districts;[4] and, for the purpose of a more thorough organization, delegates were appointed in each by the Patriots to form a committee of public safety. Upon a meeting of these delegates a significant remonstrance was addressed to Col. Guy Johnson, Indian Agent, for his aggressive and partisan acts; he withdrew in June, 1775, to Cosbys Manor, above German Flats, under pretense of holding a council with the Indians in the w. part of the co.; and in a short time he fled to Montreal, by the way of Oswego, accompanied by a large number of dependents and followers. He continued to act as Indian Agent during the war, and by liberal rewards and still more liberal promises he greatly stimulated the natural ferocity of the Indians, and incited them to more active hostility. He was joined in Canada by Joseph Brant, a distinguished and educated Mohawk chief, and John and Walter N. Butler, 2 tories who afterward gained an infamous notoriety. At the head of marauding parties of tories and Indians, they afterward returned and committed the most inhuman atrocities upon their old friends and neighbors. Sir John Johnson remained at "Johnson Hall," but continued active in his intrigues, and kept up a correspondence with Col. Guy Johnson in Canada. His preparations to fortify "Johnson Hall" excited alarm; and in Jan. 1776, a committee, consisting of Gen. Philip Schuyler, Gen. Ten Broeck, and Col. Varick, was despatched from Albany to consult with the local committee of safety and satisfactorily arrange matters. Gen. Herkimer called out the militia; and the affair was finally settled by the surrender of Sir John as prisoner, and an agreement that his Scotch tenants should be disarmed. He was sent to Fishkill, but, being released on parole, he soon returned to Johnstown and resumed his intrigues. In May, Col. Dayton was sent with a regiment to again arrest him; but, being warned of their approach, Sir John and his followers fled to the woods, and finally reached Canada by the way of Sacondaga and Racket Rivers, after 19 days of fasting and suffering.[5] Sir John received a commission as colonel in the British service, raised a regiment of tories known

---

[1] For his services while in command of the expedition which resulted in the defeat of the French under Dieskau, at the head of Lake George, he received the title of Baronet and a gift of £5000 from Parliament. From this time until his death he lived in ease and opulence, devoting his time to the management of public affairs and the improvement of his estate.

[2] Succeeded Sir William as Indian Agent.

[3] *Annals of Tryon co.*, p. 46.

[4] These districts were "*Mohawk*," adjoining Albany, "*Canajoharie*," on the s. side of the Mohawk, and "*Palatine*," on the N.,

extending up the river to Little Falls, "*German Flats*," and "*Kingsland*," still farther up the river, and "*Old England District*," w. of the Susquehanna. The first 5 of these districts were formed March 24, 1772. On the 8th of March, 1773, the original name—"*Stone Arabia*"—was changed to "*Palatine*," "*German Flats*" to "*Kingsland*," and "*Kingsland*" to "*German Flats*." Old England Dist. was formed April 3, 1775.

[5] The Indians at St. Regis still preserve a tradition of this event, and state that the party were reduced to the utmost extremity before they reached the inhabited region.

as "Johnson's Greens," and was active and bitter in his hostility throughout the war.[1] Through the influence of the Johnsons, all of the Five Nations, with the exception of a portion of the Oneidas and Tuscaroras,[2] were attached to the British interests, and were liberally aided by arms and provisions in their frequent incursions into the frontier settlements under the Butlers and Brant.[3]

In the summer and fall of 1777, this co., in common with the whole northern and western frontier, was the scene of great alarm and of stirring military events, produced by the expedition of Burgoyne. Gen. St. Leger, at the head of a large body of tories and Indians, was dispatched by the way of Oswego to reduce the rebel posts and settlements on the Mohawk and join the main army at Albany. On the 3d of Aug. they laid siege to Fort Schuyler, upon the site of the present village of Rome. The militia of Montgomery co. were called out, and, under Gen. Herkimer, marched to the relief of the fort. On the way the bloody battle of Oriskany was fought, in which 200 of the brave patriots of the co. were killed and as many more carried into Indian captivity.[4] In the latter part of the same month, Gens. Arnold and Learned, at the head of 900 troops, marched up the river, and St. Leger hastily abandoned the siege and fled.[5] The destruction of the valley was thus averted, and for several months the inhabitants were allowed to remain undisturbed, save by small scalping parties, that hung round the unprotected frontiers and cut off the defenseless inhabitants.

In the spring of 1778, Gen. La Fayette, accompanied by Gen. Schuyler and Col. Duane, went to Johnstown and held a conference with a body of Indians, which resulted in a treaty of considerable subsequent benefit to the settlers. In the following summer the horrible butcheries at Wyoming, Harpersfield, German Flats, and Cherry Valley were perpetrated; and in the summer of 1779 the army of Gen. Clinton marched from this co. to join Gen. Sullivan's expedition against the chief villages and farming grounds of the Onondagas, Cayugas, and Senecas. On the 21st of May, 1780, Sir John Johnson, at the head of 500 Indians and tories, suddenly made his appearance at Johnson Hall. He arrived about sunset on Sunday, and, dividing his force into two parties, at daylight the next morning he made a simultaneous attack upon Tribes Hill and Caughnawaga. Several persons were killed and others taken prisoners, and every building upon the route, except those belonging to tories, was burned. The militia began to collect in considerable numbers, and toward night Sir John hastily retreated, and safely reached Canada by the way of the wilderness w. of the Adirondack Mts.[6] Near the last of the July succeeding, the militia of the co. were employed to convey a provision train sent to the relief of Fort Schuyler; and on the 2d of Aug., while they were absent, Brant, at the head of 500 Indians and tories, made an attack upon the settlements in the neighborhood of Fort Plain. Fifty-three dwellings were burned, 16 persons slain, and 60 women and children carried into captivity. Upon the approach of the militia from Johnstown and Schenectady, the party retreated. On the 15th of the following Oct. a large party of tories, Indians, and Canadians, under Sir John Johnson, Brant, and Cornplanter, made their appearance in the Mohawk Valley, at the mouth of Schoharie Creek, after having laid waste the Schoharie settlements above. From this point they marched up the valley, burning the houses, destroying the property, and murdering or taking prisoners all that they met. The militia under Gen. Robert Van Rensselaer hastily came together and marched to attack the invaders. On the 18th of Oct., Col. Brown, who commanded a small stockade fort at Stone Arabia, acting under the order of Van Rensselaer, marched out with 150 men to attack the enemy; but, receiving no support from the main army, the little detachment was soon routed, with the loss of the commander and 30 to 40 men killed. Sir John halted at Fox's Mills, about 8 mi. above Fort Hunter, in the town of St. Johnsville, and erected a temporary breastwork. At a late hour in the day he was attacked by a detachment under Col. Dubois, and the Indians under his command were defeated.[7] The Americans, under Van Rensselaer, fell back 3 mi. and encamped; and the next morning, upon marching forward to renew the attack, they found that the enemy had fled.[8] Sir John finally succeeded in making his escape,

---

[1] *Annals of Tryon Co.*; *Simms's Hist. Schoharie Co.*; *Hough's Hist. St. Law. Co.*; *Dunlap's Hist. of N. Y.*; *Benton's Hist. Herk. Co.*

[2] About 150 Oneidas and 200 Tuscaroras joined the British.—*Annals of Tryon Co.*

[3] The Americans made several efforts to attach the Six Nations to their interests, or at least to induce them to remain neutral. In the winter of 1776–77, Col. Harper was sent to ascertain the object of the assembling of a large body of Indians at Oquago, on the Susquehanna. In the succeeding June, Brant, with a party of Indians, made a levy upon the settlers of the Unadilla; and many fled to a place of safety. Gen. Herkimer, at the head of 380 militia, made a levy to meet him; and on the 27th of June, 1777, a conference was held between the general and the chief, but without producing any definite results. All efforts to propitiate the Six Nations were then abandoned, and all conferences ceased

until the close of the war, when the Indians were called upon, as vanquished enemies, to confirm the surrender of most of their lands as an atonement for their hostility.

[4] There was scarcely a hamlet in the valley that did not lose one or more of its inhabitants.

[5] For further particulars concerning these transactions, see page 316.

[6] The principal object of this incursion was to obtain the silver plate which had been buried by Sir John on his first hasty flight from Johnson Hall. The plate was recovered and carried to Canada in the knapsacks of 60 men.

[7] This engagement is known as the battle of "*Klock's Field.*"

[8] Du Bois had nearly gained the victory, when Van Rensselaer came up and gave orders not to renew the battle until the signal should be given from headquarters. The forces of the former were under arms all night, momentarily expecting the promised

though his force was greatly reduced by hunger, fatigue, and the continual, harassing attacks of the militia, which hung upon their rear.

The prospects of the Mohawk Valley were now gloomy in the extreme. Nearly every settlement had been desolated, and nearly every family had lost some of its members.[1] In the spring of 1781, Col. Willett assumed the command of the American forces on the Mohawk, and, by his military skill, daring, and knowledge of Indian warfare, he not only successfully repelled all attacks made upon the Mohawk settlements, but carried the war into the enemy's own country.

On the 9th of July, 1781, 300 Indians, under a tory named Doxtader, made a sudden attack upon the settlement of Currytown, (in the town of Root.) After burning the buildings and collecting a large amount of booty, they retreated. Col. Willett, at the head of 150 militia, immediately pursued and overtook them at "*Durlah*," (Dorlach,) a few mi. over the line of Schoharie co. A severe skirmish ensued, when the Indians fled, leaving 40 of their number dead on the field.[2] The final incursion into the Mohawk Valley was made Oct. 24, 1781, by a party of 600 British and Indians, under Maj. Ross and Walter N. Butler, and made their first appearance in the neighborhood of Warrensbush. They marched to the vicinity of Johnson Hall and commenced the usual work of plunder and murder, but were arrested by a sudden attack by forces under Cols. Willett, Rowley, and Harper. A severe engagement ensued, resulting in the retreat of the enemy. Col. Willett pursued, and, coming up with the rear guard at West Canada Creek, another skirmish took place, in which the infamous Walter N. Butler was killed.[3] The shattered remnant of the British forces escaped by way of Oswego. This affair practically ended the war in Tryon co., and the remaining citizens, stripped of almost every thing except the soil, were allowed to resume in peace their accustomed employments.[4] In a few years the ravages of the war were completely obliterated, and the fertile regions of Central and Western N.Y., which had become known through the military expeditions that had traversed them, soon began to fill up with a New England population. The splendid domains of the Johnsons and other royalists were confiscated, and the feudal tenants of the colonial period were replaced by enterprising freeholders under the new government.[5]

AMSTERDAM[6]—was formed from "*Caughnawaga*,"[7] March 12, 1793. Perth (Fulton co.) was taken off in 1838. It lies on the N. bank of the Mohawk, in the N.E. corner of the co. Its surface consists of the intervale along the river, and a rolling upland gradually rising for the space of 2 mi. and attaining an elevation of 300 to 500 feet. The principal streams are the Kayaderosseras, 3 mi. W. of Amsterdam Village, Chuctenunda,[8] at the village, and Evas Kil,[9] near the E. border. The soil in the valley is a deep, rich alluvium, and upon the hills it is a fertile, gravelly loam. Near Tribes Hill are extensive stone quarries. A considerable amount of manufactures is carried on in town, consisting of mill machinery, agricultural implements, carriages, car springs, and carpets, at Amsterdam Village, and of woolen goods at Hagemans Mills. **Amsterdam**,[10] (p. v.,) incorp. April 20, 1830, contains 4 churches, the Amsterdam Female Seminary, a bank, printing

signal; and they had the inexpressible mortification and chagrin to see the beaten foe slipping through the net in which they had been caught, without the possibility of preventing their escape. Had it not been for the indecision or cowardice of Gen. Van Rensselaer, the whole party might have been taken. At the time, he was openly charged with cowardice or treachery by the Oneida chief, and he entirely lost public confidence.

[1] Some idea of the extent of these ravages may be formed from a statement prepared by the supervisors of "*Tryon co.*," dated Dec. 20, 1780, and addressed to the legislature. They therein stated that 700 buildings had been burned within the co.; that 354 families had abandoned their habitations and removed; 613 persons had deserted to the enemy; 197 had been killed, 121 taken prisoners; and 1200 farms lay uncultivated by reason of the enemy. This statement did not include Cherry Valley, Newtown-Martin, Middlefield, Springfield, Harpersfield, and Old England District, which had been totally deserted and abandoned. The population of the co. at the beginning of the war was about 10,000. While the sufferings of the colonists were thus great, the Indian loss was much greater. Their whole country had been ravaged, their homes and crops destroyed, and a large portion of their number had died in battle or by starvation. At the close of the war the miserable remnant of the once powerful nations humbly sued for peace, and were content to accept terms that deprived them of almost their entire country.

[2] By stratagem Col. Willett succeeded in drawing the Indians into an ambuscade. They fled so hastily that all their baggage and plunder was captured. On their retreat they murdered a number of prisoners to prevent their escape.

[3] Walter N. Butler was one of the most inhuman wretches that ever disgraced humanity. Ferocious, bloodthirsty, and cruel, he seemed to revel in perfect delight at the spectacle of

human suffering. He surpassed the savages in barbarity; and many a victim was saved from his clutches by the interposition of the Indian chief Brant.

[4] Special acts were passed in 1780, '81, and '83, directing the commissioners of sequestration to relieve certain distressed families. Rev. Daniel Gros, of Canajoharie, acted as almoner of the commissioners; and his acts are preserved among the public papers of the State.

[5] For several years after the war, ghosts were reported as frequently seen stalking about the old residences of the royalists. The appearances which gave rise to these reports were doubtless the tories themselves, returned in disguise to obtain valuables which had been secreted upon their previous hasty flight. The settlers, who had suffered so much, were slow in forgetting the injuries they had received; and for many years after, few, either Indians or tories, who had been engaged in the war, could show themselves in the settlement with safety.

[6] Named by Emanuel E. De Graff, a Hollander and early settler.

[7] On the 9th of March, 1780, the portion of Mohawk district N. of the river was set off and named "*Caughnawaga.*" The first town meeting was held at the house of John B. Wimples. "*Caughnawaga*" was formed as a town, March 7, 1788. It embraced all that part of Montgomery co. lying N. of the Mohawk and E. of a line extending from The Noses N. to Canada. This town was divided in 1793 into Amsterdam, Mayfield, Broadalbin, and Johnstown.

[8] Signifying "Twin Sisters," and applied to the streams flowing into the Mohawk on opposite sides; in some documents spelled Chuct-to-na-ne-da.

[9] Pronounced E-vaws-kil; named from Mrs. Eva Van Alstyne, who was wounded and scalped by the Indians in 1755, while crossing this stream.

[10] Formerly called "*Veedersburgh.*"

office, and several manufactories. Pop. 2044. **Hagamans Mills** (p. v.) has 124 inhabitants, **Cranesville**[1] (p. v.) 92, and **Mannys Corners** 8 houses. **Tribes Hill**,[2] (p. o.,) on the line of Mohawk, is a hamlet. A wire suspension bridge here crosses the Mohawk to Florida.[3] The first settlement was commenced about 1710, by Dutch and Palatinates. About 1740, Sir Wm. Johnson built a large stone mansion upon the w. side of the Kayaderosseras, 3 mi. w. of Amsterdam Village.[4] This building was fortified and named "Fort Johnson." Col. Daniel Claus and Guy Johnson, sons-in-law to Sir William, occupied fine mansions respectively 1 and 2 mi. below Fort Johnson,[5] previous to the Revolution. The first settlers at Amsterdam Village were Albert Veeder, E. E. De Graff, Nicholas Wilcox, and Wm. Kline. The first church (Ref. Prot. D.) was formed in 1792.[6] The first settled minister was Rev. Conrad Ten Eyck, in 1799. There had been preaching in town at a much earlier period.

CANAJOHARIE[7]—was formed as a district March 24, 1772, and as a town March 7, 1788. Minden was taken off in 1798, a part of Root in 1823, and a part of Minden in 1849. It lies on the s. border of the co., w. of the center. The surface consists of the intervale of Canajoharie or Bowmans Creek,[8] and undulating uplands 200 to 600 feet above the valley. The soil is a gravelly loam, derived from the disintegration of the underlying slate, in some places intermixed with clay. The cultivation of hops receives some attention. A small woolen factory is located on Bowmans Creek. **Canajoharie,** (p. v.,) incorp. April 30, 1829, contains 5 churches, the Canajoharie Academy, and a bank; pop. 1500. A bridge crosses the Mohawk at this place, connecting it with the village of R. R. station of Palatine Bridge. **Ames,**[9] (p. v.,) in the s. part of the town, contains an academy and 204 inhabitants, and **Buel,**[10] (p. v.,) in the s. w. part, 25 houses. **Sprout Brook,** (p. o.,) **Mapleton,** and **Marshville** are hamlets. The first settlement in town was commenced in early colonial times; but the precise date is not known.[11] During the Revolution the people warmly espoused the American cause, and were afterward among the greatest sufferers in the Mohawk Valley.[12] Gov. Clinton, while marching to join Sullivan in 1779, made this place his headquarters for some weeks.[13] In Aug. 1780, Brant made an incursion into the valley and destroyed nearly the whole settlement.[14] During the war several other incursions were made; and the people were often driven to the utmost extremity. Several small forts were built in the town, which afforded some protection to the people.[15] In 1795, Archibald and James Kane established themselves as merchants at this place, and commenced a business which soon grew to be one of the largest in the interior of the State.[16] In 1823, the "Central Asylum for the Instruction of the Deaf and Dumb" was located near Buel, in this town; but in 1836 it was united with the one previously established in New York City.[17] The first church (Free Will Bap.) was organized at Ames, in 1796–97, by Rev. George Elliott.[18]

CHARLESTON—was formed from Mohawk, March 12, 1793.[19] Glen and a part of Root were taken off in 1823. It is the most southerly town in the co., and the only one not bordering upon the Mohawk. It lies upon the high plateau region immediately w. of Schoharie Creek; and the

---

[1] Named from David Crane, who settled here in 1804.

[2] So named because the Indian tribes were wont to assemble here.

[3] A Remington suspension bridge built here some years since fell of its own weight before it was finished.

[4] This edifice was richly ornamented with carvings of oak and mahogany; and at the time of its erection it was one of the finest mansions in the colony. It is still standing, and is the property of Algneyson Young, Esq. Sir William lived here for many years, surrounded by numerous dependents, and was frequently visited by great numbers of Indians, by whom he was highly esteemed. He built a mill upon the Kayaderosseras, near his mansion.

[5] The former of these was burned, and its site is now occupied by the hotel of Chas. Chase. The latter, known as "Guy Park," is still standing, between the R. R. and river, 1 mi. w. of Amsterdam. It is now owned by Jas. Stewart. A tract 1 mi. square was originally attached to each of these residences, but the whole was confiscated and sold with the estates of the tories.

[6] This church became Presb. in 1803. There are now 8 churches in town; 2 Presb., 2 M. E., Bap., Ref. Prot. D., Prot. E., and Evang. Luth.

[7] "Canajoxharie" in the act of incorporation. Indian name, Ga-na-jo-hi-e, said to signify a "a kettle-shaped hole in the rock," or "the pot that washes itself," and refers to a deep hole worn in the rock at the falls on the creek 1 mi. from its mouth.

[8] It is said that the Indian name of this stream is " Te-ko-ha-ra-wa." The falls on this creek, about 1 mi. from its mouth, are interesting to scientific men for the different geological formations there exposed and the holes of various sizes worn in the rocks.

[9] Named in honor of Fisher Ames.

[10] Named in honor of Jesse Buel, of Albany.

[11] An Indian school was taught at Canajoharie, in 1764, by Philip Jonathan.

[12] At the battle of Oriskany many of the prominent citizens of this place were killed. Among them were Col. Cox, Lieut. Col. Hunt, Maj. Van Slyck, Capt. Henry Devendorf, Robert Crouse, Jacob Bowman, Andrew Dillenback, Capt. Jacob Leeber, Charles Fox, and Lieut. Wm. Leeber.

[13] While Gov. Clinton was at this place, Henry Hare and Wm. Newbury, two notorious tories, were arrested and executed as spies. They had formerly been citizens of the town. A deserter named Titus was also shot here.

[14] See page 410.

[15] A fort was built here at an early period as one of the chain of fortifications to Oswego. It was 100 feet square, 15 ft. high, with bastions at the angles, and was armed with several small cannon. In 1781 the house of Philip Van Alstyne was palisaded, and named Fort Van Rensselaer. It is still standing. Fort Ehle stood 1 mi. E. of Canajoharie. An Indian burial ground occupied the hillside just w. of the village, and several skeletons have been found, in a sitting posture, facing the E.

[16] In 1799 their purchases of potash and wheat amounted to $120,000.

[17] This asylum was established mainly through the instrumentality of Robt. Bowman, of this town, and its course of instruction was modeled after that at Hartford, Conn. Prof. O. W. Morris, now of the New York Asylum, was its last principal.

[18] The census reports 11 churches; 3 M. E., 2 Ref. Prot. D., 2 Evang. Luth., Presb., F. W. Bap., True Dutch, and Union.

[19] By an act bearing this date, the old town of Mohawk was abolished, and its territory was erected into Florida and Charleston. The present town of Mohawk is of much more recent origin.

greater part of the surface is an undulating upland. On the E. it descends in steep declivities to the valley of the creek, which is here a narrow ravine. Its streams are small. The soil is generally loam intermixed with clay, and is particularly adapted to spring grains and dairying. The town has a limited amount of manufactures, consisting principally of sash and blinds, woolen goods, and flour. **Burtonsville,**[1] (p. v.,) on Schoharie Creek, in the S. E. corner of the town, contains 32 houses; **Charleston Four Corners,** (p. v.,) in the S. w. corner, 30; and **Charleston,** (p. v.,) near the N. border, 20. **Carytown** and **Oak Ridge** are hamlets. A portion of this town was included in the patent of 24,500 acres granted to Wm. Corry in 1637; and others were portions of the "*Stone Heap Patent,*" granted to John Bowen and others in 1770, and Thomas Machin's Patent of 1787. The first settlements were probably made previous to the Revolution.[2] The census reports 5 churches in town.[3]

FLORIDA—was formed from Mohawk, March 12, 1793. It embraces that part of the co. lying S. of the Mohawk, and E. of Schoharie Creek. The greater part of the surface is a rolling upland, 600 ft. above the valley. Bean Hill, in the S. w. part, is the highest land in the co. The declivities bordering upon the streams are usually steep. The two principal streams within its borders are Chuctenunda and Cowilliga[4] Creeks. The soil and productions are similar to those of neighboring towns. Several sulphur springs are found in town, the most noted of which is near Scotch Bush. The Erie Canal crosses the Schoharie Creek between this town and Glen, on a costly aqueduct. Broomcorn is one of the principal agricultural products, and brooms are extensively manufactured. **Port Jackson** (p. v.) is a canal village on the Mohawk, opposite Amsterdam. Pop. 369. **Minaville,** (p. v.,) on Chuctenunda Creek, near the center, contains 95 inhabitants. **Fort Hunter,**[5] (p. o.,) at the mouth of Schoharie Creek, and **Scotch Bush,** (p. o.,) near the S. border, are hamlets. One of the 3 Mohawk castles was situated at the mouth of Schoharie Creek at the first advent of the whites. The first white settlement in this co. is supposed to have been made in this town. Fort Hunter[6] was built here by the whites in 1711. Queen Anne's Chapel was soon after erected, and was furnished with a valuable set of communion plate by Queen Anne.[7] The fort was garrisoned until after the French War, when it was abandoned. During the Revolution the chapel was enclosed with palisades, and converted into a strong fortress defended by cannon. In Oct. 1780, several houses were burned on the opposite side of the creek by the forces under Sir John Johnson, but the fort was not molested. Before the close of the war several newly arrived German emigrants settled in town, and they were followed soon after by Scotch and Irish families.[8] The first preacher after the war was Rev. Thos. Romeyn, (Ref. Prot. D.,) in 1784. The census reports 5 churches in town.[9]

GLEN[10]—was formed from Charleston, April 10, 1823. It lies in the S. w. angle formed by the junction of Schoharie Creek and the Mohawk. Its surface consists principally of uplands about 600 feet high, descending by abrupt declivities to the narrow intervales along the streams. The principal streams are Auries[11] Creek, a tributary of the Mohawk, and Irish Creek, a branch of the Schoharie.[12] The soil is generally a clayey loam. One mi. E. of Voorheesville is a chalybeate spring.[13] **Fultonville**[14] (p. v.) is situated on the Mohawk and the Erie Canal. Pop. 850. **Voorheesville,** (Glen p. v.,) near the center of the town, contains 40 houses, and **Auriesville,** (p. v.,) a canal village near the mouth of Auries Creek, 170 inhabitants. The land bordering upon the river was granted in 10 patents to different persons in 1722 to 1726, and the greater part of the remainder to James De Lancey in 1737. Peter Quackenboss settled on Scott's Patent, near Auries Creek.

---

1 Buckwheat flour for the New York market is extensively manufactured at this place.

2 Robt. Winchell, Nathan Tracy, Aden Brownley, and Joseph Burnhap settled near Kimballs Corners, Abia Beaman near Charleston P. O., Henry Mapes, Abner Throop, and David and Nathan Kimball at Charleston. Thomas Machin, Capt. John Stanton, John Eddy, and Ezekiel Tracy were also early settlers.

3 Bap., M. E., Ref. Prot. D., Christian, and Union.

4 Said to signify "*Willow.*"

5 The Indian name for this place was I-can-de-ro-ga, or Te-on-da-lo-ga, "two streams coming together." The first Indian castle, which stood near this place, was called "*Os-sev-ne-non,*" or "*On-e-on-gon-re.*"—*N. Y. Colonial Hist.*

6 The contracts to build this fort, and one at Oswego, were taken Oct. 11, 1711, by Garret Symouce, Barent and Hendrick Vroman, John Wemp, and Arent Van Patten, of Schenectady. The walls of the first were 150 feet square and 12 feet high, and were formed of logs pinned together. It was afterward enlarged and strengthened.

7 This chapel was for a long time under the charge of the "Society for Propagating the Gospel in Foreign Parts," and a missionary and Indian school were supported here. The chapel was demolished in 1820 to make room for the canal. The parsonage, still standing, is probably the oldest building w. of Schenectady. It was sold a few years since for $1500, and the proceeds were divided between the Prot. E. churches at Port Jackson and Johnstown.

8 Wm. Bent kept the first store at Port Jackson. The first bridge of any importance over Schoharie Creek was built in 1796, by Maj. Isaiah De Puy. The route S. of the Mohawk was the one principally traveled for a great number of years. An Indian school was taught at Fort Hunter in 1769.

9 2 Ref. Prot. D., M. E., Asso. Presb., and R. C.

10 Named from Jacob S. Glen, a prominent citizen of the town.

11 Auries Creek is the Dutch for "Aarons Creek." It was named from an Indian in the vicinity. The Indian name was Ogh-rack-ie.

12 Upon Schoharie Creek, about 2 mi. above its mouth, is a high bank formed by a landslide, and called by the Indians Co-daugh-ri-ty, signifying "steep bank," or "perpendicular wall."—*Simms's Hist. Schoharie.*

13 In early days fruitless attempts were here made to obtain iron.

14 Named in honor of Robert Fulton. The village site was known as "*Van Epps Swamp*" during the Revolution.—*Simms's Hist. Schoharie.*

soon after it was secured, and was probably the first white inhabitant of the town. About 1740, 16 Irish families, under the patronage of Sir Wm. Johnson, settled on Corry's Patent, a few mi. s.w. of Fort Hunter. After making considerable improvements, they abandoned their location and returned to Ireland in consequence of threatened Indian disturbances.[1] The first church (Ref. Prot. D.) was formed at Glen; Rev. Henry V. Wyckoff was the first pastor.[2] This town was the scene of many interesting incidents connected with the war. It furnished its full proportion of victims at the battle of Oriskany, and sustained an equal share in the losses and sufferings from Indian incursions.[3] The last council within the co. previous to the Revolution was held between the Indians and Americans Oct. 13, 1775, on the farm now owned by John S. Quackenboss, on the Mohawk Flats, 2 mi. E. of Fultonville.

MINDEN—was formed from Canajoharie, March 2, 1798. Danube (Herkimer co) was taken off in 1817. It lies upon the s. bank of the Mohawk, in the extreme w. part of the co. Its surface is principally an undulating upland, with steep declivities bordering upon the streams. The principal streams are the Otsquaga[4] and its tributary the Otsquene. Prospect Hill, called by the Indians "*Ta-ra-jo-rhies*,"[5] lies upon the Otsquaga opposite Fort Plain. The soil is a fine quality of gravelly and clayey loam, and is particularly adapted to grazing.[6] **Fort Plain**, (p. v.,) incorp. April 5, 1832, is situated upon the Mohawk, in the E. part of the town. It contains an academy,[7] bank, printing office, and 4 churches. Pop. 1502. **Mindenville**, (p. v.,) on the Mohawk, in the w. part of the town, contains 30 houses, and **Fordsborough**, (Minden p.o.,) on the w. border, 25. **Hallsville**,[8] (p. o.,) **Freysbush**,[9] (p. o.,) and **Hessville**, are hamlets. In this town are found the remains of one of those ancient fortifications which are so common in Central and Western New York and throughout the Western States, showing that the co. was inhabited long prior to the advent of the Indians.[10] During the French War, Fort Plain was erected on the summit of the hill, half a mi. N. w. of the village.[11] During the Revolution, several other forts were built to protect the people from the sudden attacks of the Indians.[12] The first settlements in this town were among the first in the co. The early settlers were Germans, among whom were the Devendorf, Waggoner, and Gros families, Andrew Keller, and Henry H. Smith.[13] John Abeel, an Indian trader, settled here in 1748.[14] In common with the other valley towns, these settlements were ravaged by Brant and Johnson in 1780. At the time of Brant's incursion the men were mostly absent, and the women were shut up in the forts for safety. Upon the

---

[1] A son of the first settler married Annie, daughter of Capt. John Scott, the patentee, and settled on the site of the present co. poorhouse. Their son John, born about 1725, was the first white child born on the s. side of the Mohawk, between Fort Hunter and German Flats. Cornelius Putnam settled at Cadaughrity, Richard Hoff 1 mi. w. of Glen, Nicholas Gardiner and John Van Eps on the Mohawk, and Charles Van Eps at Fultonville. Near the house of the Van Eps a small blockhouse was erected toward the close of the Revolution. ——Hazard taught the first school, at the house of J. S. Quackenboss; Wm. Quackenboss kept the first inn at Auriesville, in 1797, and Myndert Starin one still earlier at the present village of Fultonville. John Smith opened the first store in Glen, in 1797. Isaac Quackenboss kept a store on the Mohawk, E. of Fultonville. Peter and Simon Mabie built the first sawmill and carding machine, in 1797, and Peter Quackenboss a gristmill, on Auries Creek, soon after.

[2] The census reports 4 churches in town; 2 Ref. Prot. D., M. E., True Dutch.

[3] In the fall of 1779 George Cuck, a noted tory, who had often led scalping parties of Indians to the homes of his old neighbors, was seen lurking about, and at one time was fired upon and narrowly escaped. It was supposed that he had returned to Canada; but toward spring it became known that he was concealed at the house of John Van Zuyler, a kinsman and brother tory. A party surrounded the house, dragged Cuck from his hiding place and shot him, and arrested Van Zuyler and sent him prisoner to Albany. In the fall of 1780 the whole settlement was ravaged, and many of the people were murdered. One day Isaac Quackenboss, while out hunting, discovered three hostile Indians sitting upon a log. He fired, and killed two, and mortally wounded the third.

[4] Mohawk, Osquago, signifying "under the bridge."

[5] Said to signify "Hill of Health," or "Fort on a hill."

[6] The dairy products of this town are greater than those of any other in the co. Hops are also largely cultivated.

[7] The "Fort Plain Seminary and Female Collegiate Institute" is chiefly under the patronage of the M. E. denomination. The academic building is a fine structure, situated upon a commanding eminence overlooking the village and valley.

[8] Named from Capt. Robert Hall.

[9] Named from John Frey, a lawyer and leading patriot who resided here during the Revolution.

[10] These mounds and ruins are the most easterly of any of the kind yet discovered. They are situated 4 mi. s. of Fort Plain, on a tongue of land formed by the valleys of Otsquaga Creek and one of its tributaries. This tongue is 100 ft. above the streams, and the declivities are almost precipitous. Across the tongue, at its narrowest part, is a curved line of breastworks 240 ft. in length, inclosing an area of about 7 acres. A gigantic pine, 6 ft. in diameter, stands upon one end of the embankment, showing that the work must have been of great antiquity.—*Smithsonian Contributions, Vol. II. Art. 6.*

[11] This fort was built by a French engineer for the Government, and was the finest fortification in the valley. It was octagonal, 3 stories high, each story projecting beyond the one below. In the lower story was a cannon, which was fired in cases of alarm to notify the people of danger.

[12] Fort Plank was situated about 2 mi. N. w. of Fort Plain, on the farm now occupied by C. House. Fort Clyde was situated 2 mi. s. w. of Fort Plain, near the residence of Peter Devendorf, at Freysbush. Fort Willett was w. of Fort Plank.

[13] Henry Hayse, a German, taught the first school; Isaac Countryman built the first gristmill, soon after the war, and Isaac Paris kept the first store, about the same time. A large stone dwelling was erected here for the sons of Gov. Clark in 1738, but was soon abandoned. It obtained the reputation of being haunted, and was given away, 50 years ago, on condition that it should be demolished.

[14] In his previous intercourse with the Indians, Abeel had married the daughter of a Seneca chief, after the Indian fashion. A child of this marriage was the famous chief Cornplanter. Abeel subsequently married a white woman, and at the commencement of the war was living upon his farm. During the incursion of Oct. 1780, Abeel was taken prisoner by a party of Indians, and, while momentarily expecting death, Cornplanter addressed him as father and assured him of his safety. He was given his choice either to accompany the Indians under the protection of his son, or to return to his white family. He chose the latter; and after the war Cornplanter visited him, and was received by his Fort Plain relatives with the civilities due his rank and manly bearing. The chief died at his residence in Penn., March 7, 1836. Stone, in his Life of Brant, says that Cornplanter was more than 100 years old at the time of his death. Mr. Webster, of Fort Plain, a descendent of John Abeel, states that Abeel did not make his appearance in the Indian country until 1748, and that Cornplanter was born about 1750. This would make his age about 30 when he accompanied the expedition that took his father prisoner, and but 86 when he died.

approach of the enemy the women showed themselves dressed in men's clothes, and the Indians thereupon kept at a respectful distance. The first church (Ref. Prot. D.) was organized at Fort Plàin, long before the war. The census reports 9 churches in town.[1]

MOHAWK—was formed from Johnstown, April 4, 1837.[2] It lies upon the N. bank of Mohawk River and near the center of the N. border of the co. The surface is uneven, and gradually rises from the river to the N. line, where it attains an elevation of about 400 ft. above the valley. Its principal streams are Cayadutta and Da-de-nos-ca-ra[3] Creeks. The soil is generally a good quality of gravelly loam. **Fonda,**[4] (p.v.,) pleasantly situated upon the Mohawk, is the co. seat. Besides the co. buildings, it contains 2 churches, a bank, printing offices, and several manufactories. Pop. 687. **Tribes Hill,** (p.v.,) on the border of Amsterdam, contains 327 inhabitants. The site of the present village of Fonda was called "*Caughnawaga*"[5] by the Indians, and was one of the favorite resorts of the Mohawks. It was the scene of some of the earliest labors of the French Jesuits among the Five Nations, two of whom lost their lives here in 1646. The names of the first actual white settlers are not known. Nicholas Hausen[6] settled at Tribes Hill before 1725, and others, by the names of Fonda, Vanderworker, Doxtader, and Fisher, at an early day.[7] Among the other residents of the town before the Revolution were Col. John Butler and his son Walter N., who afterward attained an infamous notoriety for their inhuman atrocities and for the vindictive hate which they seemed to cherish against their old whig neighbors.[8] The principal weight of the incursion of Sir John in May, 1780, fell upon the two settlements of Tribes Hill and Caughnawaga.[9] In the autumn of the same year the second incursion of Sir John swept over the town, destroying the greater part of the property that escaped the first. A stone church (Ref. Prot. D.) erected in 1763 is still standing.[10] Rev. Thos. Romeyn was the first pastor. In 1795 he was succeeded by Rev. Abraham Van Horne.[11] The census reports 3 churches in town; Ref. Prot. D., True D., M. E.

---

[1] 3 Evan. Luth., 3 M. E., Ref. Prot. D., 2 Univ.

[2] Care should be taken not to confound this town with one of the same name s. of the river, abolished in 1793. See Note 1 to Charleston.

[3] Signifying "trees having excrescences."

[4] Named from Douw Fonda, who removed from Schenectady and settled here in 1751. At the time of the Revolution he was living on the flats, between the present turnpike and the river, a few rods E. of the road leading to the bridge, at which place he was murdered by the Indians under Sir John, May 22, 1780. At the time of his death he was 84 years old. In former years he had greatly befriended the Johnson family; but the ruthless savages led by Sir John spared neither friend nor foe. His three sons, John, Jellis, and Adam, were stanch whigs, residing in the neighborhood. Indian name, Ga-na-wa-da, "on the rapids."

[5] Meaning "stone in the water," or "at the rapids."

[6] Patents of 1000 acres each, on the Mohawk, were granted to Nicholas Hausen and his brother Hendrick July 12, 1713.

[7] The first birth N. of the river, of which there is any record, was that of Henry Hausen. —— Collins taught a school in 1774. Jellis (Giles) Fonda is said to have been the first merchant w. of Schenectady. He carried on an extensive trade with the native tribes, and with the whites at Forts Schuyler and Stanwix and the forts at Oswego, Niagara, and Schlosser. His sales consisted chiefly of blankets, trinkets, ammunition, and rum, and his purchases of peltries, ginseng, and potash. At one time before the Revolution his ledger showed an indebtedness of over $10,000 in the Indian country. John Chaley was an early settler at Tribes Hill. He was in the war, and found his own brother arrayed against him.

[8] Alexander White, Colonial Sheriff of Tryon co., resided on the present site of the courthouse. He was a zealous tory, and was obliged to flee to Canada. He was succeeded by John Frey, appointed by the Provincial Congress.

[9] The detachment against Tribes Hill was led by Henry and Wm. Bowen, who had lived in the vicinity. Passing the tory settlement of Albany Bush (in Johnstown) without molestation, they proceeded to the home of Gerret Putnam, a stanch whig at Tribes Hill, and there by mistake murdered two tories, who had hired the place a short time before. From this place they went up the river, plundering the houses and murdering their old friends and neighbors. Every building was burned except the church and parsonage, and several slaves and white male prisoners were carried to Canada. The women were not particularly molested on this occasion. At the house of Col. Fred. Fisher they were warmly received by the Col.'s family, consisting of himself, his mother, and his two brothers John and Harmon. The Col.'s wife and children had been sent to Schenectady for safety; and his two sisters and an old negro, on the first alarm, fled to the woods and escaped. The Indians made a desperate attack upon the house, and a constant firing was kept up by the inmates until their ammunition was exhausted. They then all retreated to the chamber except John, who stood in the stairway and defended it with a hatchet until he had killed 7 Indians. He then retreated above, and, slipping upon some peas which lay upon the floor, he fell, and was dispatched with a tomahawk. Harmon jumped out of the window

to put out the fire that had been applied to the roof, and while standing on the fence he was shot, and fell across the fence dead. The mother was knocked down with the breech of a gun and left for dead. The Col. was also knocked down by a tomahawk, dragged down stairs by his hair, and thrown upon the ground, when an Indian jumped upon his back, drew a knife across his throat, as was supposed, cutting it from ear to ear, then, cutting round the scalp, seized it by his teeth and tore it from his head, and finally gave him a blow in the shoulder with his hatchet and fled. The Col. had not lost his senses through all this mangling, and his throat, being protected by a leather belt worn inside of his cravat, was only slightly wounded. As soon as the Indians disappeared, he arose, went up stairs and brought down his mother, placed her in a chair and leaned her up against the fence; returned, and brought down the body of his brother John and laid it on the grass; then, becoming exhausted from loss of blood and the effect of the scalping, he lay down upon an old rug that lay out of doors,—as he supposed, to die. The old negro and girls soon returned, and found the house burned down and the dead and wounded as described. By signs the Col. made known to the negro that he wanted water, who immediately brought it from the creek near by and gave it to him to drink, and also bathed his head, which restored his speech. A tory named Clement passing by, the negro asked what he should do: the reply, given in German, was, "Let the d——d rebel die." According to the directions of the Col., the negro caught the colts, which had never been broken, harnessed them to the wagon, and took him to the house of Putnam, at Tribes Hill. From there he, together with his mother, sisters, and the bodies of his brothers, was conveyed across the river to Wemples, and thence in a canoe to Schenectady, where they arrived about sundown, and he had his wounds dressed for the first time. After five years' suffering, he nearly recovered from the effects of his wounds. He built a new house on the site of the old one, and lived 29 years after he was wounded,—for several years holding the office of First Judge of the co. His mother also recovered from her wounds, and lived with him. After the war the Indian who scalped him returned to the settlements, and stopped at a tavern kept by a tory at Tribes Hill. The wife of the landlord, who was a whig, sent word immediately to the house of Col. Fisher that the Indian was there and would soon call at his house. The family, knowing that the Col. had sworn revenge, and wishing to prevent any more bloodshed, kept the news from him. As they were all in the front room, about the time the Indian was expected they oversat a pot of lye upon the hearth, and persuaded the Col. to go into the back room and lie down until they cleaned it up. While the Col. was gone, the Indian came to the door, where he was met by the old lady, who addressed him in the Indian tongue, told him her son's intentions, and pointed to a gun which was always kept loaded in readiness for him. The Indian listened, gave a grunt, and ran away with all speed.

[10] In 1845 it was fitted up as an academy; but the school was soon after discontinued.

[11] He died in 1840, at an advanced age. During his ministry he married 1500 couples.—*Simms's Schoharie.*

PALATINE—was formed as a district, by the name of "*Stone Arabia*," March 24, 1772, and its name was changed March 8, 1773. It was formed as a town March 7, 1788, embracing all the territory between "Little Falls and The Noses," and extending from the Mohawk to Canada. Salisbury (Herkimer co.) was taken off in 1797, Stratford (Fulton co.) in 1805, Oppenheim (Fulton co.) in 1808, and Ephrata (Fulton co.) in 1827. It lies along the N. bank of the Mohawk, w. of the center of the co. Its surface is mostly an upland, 200 to 500 ft. above the valley, much broken by deep, narrow ravines, and descending irregularly toward the river. The principal streams are the Kau-a-da-rauk,[1] in the E. part of the town, and the Garoga, in the w. The soil is fertile, and well adapted to grazing.[2] **Stone Arabia,** (p. v.,) near the center of the town, contains about 50 houses, and **Palatine Bridge,** (p. v.,) on the Mohawk opposite Canajoharie, 40. **Palatine Church,** (Palatine p. o.,) on the w. border, is a hamlet. The first settlement was made in town in 1713, by German Palatinates, who came over in 1710. The larger part of the Stone Arabia Patent was within the limits of this town.[3] Wm. Fox settled near Palatine Church, and Peter Waggoner a little below, on the Mohawk, in 1715. The early records of the settlement are lost.[4] A stockade called Fort Paris, the ruins of which are still visible, was built at Stone Arabia, and another, called Fort Keyser, 1 mi. N. The disastrous engagement resulting in the death of Col. Brown was fought within this town, between Stone Arabia and the river.[5] The Ref. Prot. D. church at Stone Arabia is one of the oldest in the valley.[6] The stone church (Luth.) at Palatine Church was built in 1770.[7] The census reports 3 churches in town; 2 Ev. Luth., Ref. Prot. D.

ROOT[8]—was formed from Canajoharie and Charleston, Jan. 27, 1823. It lies upon the s. bank of the Mohawk, near the center of the co. The hills which border upon the river rise abruptly to a height of 630 feet,[9] and from their summits the country spreads out into an undulating upland. The high hills just below Sprakers, on opposite banks of the river, are called "The Noses." The high ridge near the E. border is known as "Stone Ridge." The principal streams are Platte Kil, and Lashers and Flat Creeks. Mitchells Cave,[10] in the vicinity of The Noses, consists of several apartments, with the roof hung with stalactites. The soil is a fine, gravelly loam. **Leatherville** (Root p. o.) contains 15 houses, and **Currytown,**[11] **Sprakers Basin,** (p. o.,) **Flat Creek,** (p. o.,) and **Browns Hollow,** about a dozen each. **Yatesville** is a hamlet on the canal. The first settlers were Jacob Devendorf, at Currytown, Rudolph Keller, David and Fred. Luce, and Jacob Lainner.[12] The first church (Ref. Prot. D.) was formed at Currytown. Rev. Peter Van Buren became its pastor in 1806.[13] The principal incursions into this town during the war were those made in the summer and fall of 1781. The weight of the first of these, led by the tory Doxtader, July 9, 1781, fell upon the settlements in and near Currytown.[14] In Oct. of the same year Ross and Butler passed through the town, but committed no depredations, except capturing part of a funeral procession, and taking a few prisoners at Stone Ridge.

ST. JOHNSVILLE[15]—was formed from Oppenheim, (Fulton co.,) April 18, 1838. It lies upon the N. bank of the Mohawk, in the w. part of the co. Its surface consists of a broad river intervale and a broken upland gradually rising N. of it. Its streams are East Canada, Crum, Fox, Zimmermans, Caldwell, and Mother Creeks. Upon East Canada Creek, 1½ mi. from its mouth, are a succession of falls and rapids descending 75 feet in a distance of 80 rods. The soil is a fine quality of gravelly loam. **St. Johnsville,** (p. v.,) on the Mohawk, was incorp. in 1857. It contains a woolen and pitchfork factory, and is an important station on the Central R. R. Pop. 648. The first settlement at the village was made by Jacob Zimmerman, in 1776.[16] During the Revolution

---

1 Said to signify "broad."

2 More cheese is made in this town than in any other in the co. The aggregate is more than 500,000 lbs.

3 This purchase extended along East Canada Creek, in the rear of Hausen's and Van Slyke's patents.

4 The German was the language taught in the first schools. —— Robinson taught an English school in 1782, and Alexander Ewing in 1783. Chris. Fox built a gristmill in 1750, which was burned in 1780. 5 See page 410.

6 The records of this church commence in 1739, when it had but 10 members. The present edifice was erected in 1785, and the church was reorganized in 1790. A Luth. church built at Stone Arabia in 1770 was burned in 1780.

7 The subscriptions for this church were mostly furnished by the Nellis families, who became tories; and in consequence the church was not burned. Several shots were fired into it by the party under Sir John Johnson, one of the shot holes being still visible.

8 Named in honor of Erastus Root, of Delaware co.

9 As surveyed by Capt. Thomas Machin.

10 Named from the former owner of the farm on which the cave is situated.

11 Named from Wm. Curry, the patentee.

12 The first schools were German. —— Glaycher taught an English school at The Noses, in 1784. Albert Vanderworker kept the first inn, at an early day.

13 The census reports 3 churches in town; Christian, M. E., Ref. Prot. D.

14 Upon the alarm being given, the settlers hastened to a picketed blockhouse near the dwelling of Henry Lewis, closely pursued by the enemy. Every house in the village except one was set on fire; but the flames were extinguished by the vanguard of Col. Willett's forces, under Capt. Robert Kean. Frederick, son of Jacob Devendorf, was scalped, but he recovered. Jacob, jr., another son, was taken prisoner, and was scalped on the retreat of the Indians. He also recovered, and lived to the age of 85 years. He died in 1854, one of the wealthiest farmers in the valley. Mary Miller, a little girl, was scalped and found alive, but died soon after. Several other prisoners were murdered. Most of the cattle driven away were abandoned, and found their way back to the settlement.

15 Named from St. John's Church, built in the village at an early day.

16 The first settlers of the town came in long prior to this.

the house of Christian Klock, three-fourths of a mi. w. of Palatine Church, was stockaded and named "Fort House."[1] The house of Jacob Zimmerman was also stockaded. These forts were both attacked, but never taken. Fort Hill, situated on an eminence E. of East Creek, was erected during the French War. It was repaired and used during the Revolution. The battle between the forces of Sir John and the advanced guard of Van Rensselaer's army, under Col. Dubois, was fought at "*Klocks Field,*" near "*Fort House,*" Oct. 18, 1780. The enemy forded the river, and retreated up the valley during the night following. The Indians, in small parties, continued to prowl about the settlement during the war, and shot and captured several of the inhabitants.[2] A church was built by Christian Klock in 1756: the Rev. Mr. Rosekrantz was the first preacher, and John Henry Disland the second. The census reports 2 churches; Ref. Prot. D. and Union.

Acres of Land, Valuation, Population, Dwellings, Families, Freeholders, Schools, Live Stock, Agricultural Products, and Domestic Manufactures, of Montgomery County.

Names of Towns.	Acres of Land.		Valuation of 1858.			Population.		No. of Dwellings.	No. of Families.	Freeholders.	Schools.	
	Improved.	Unimproved.	Real Estate.	Personal Property.	Total.	Males.	Females.				No. of Districts.	Children taught.
Amsterdam	16,065½	3,989	779,698	75,900	855,958	1,969	2,043	749	500	188	13	1,482
Canajoharie	20,596¾	3,701½	849,073	113,200	962,273	2,054	1,968	612	673	391	15	1,566
Charleston	21,716⅞	4,923	311,517	23,100	334,617	952	947	359	385	249	11	828
Florida	26,053	5,886½	588,024	93,400	681,424	1,632	1,522	544	512	395	13	1,196
Glen	18,731½	4,442¼	501,470	43,150	544,620	1,542	1,414	483	556	304	10	1,137
Minden	24,156	5,794½	938,762	98,280	1,037,042	2,401	2,270	754	850	565	18	1,765
Mohawk	16,517	3,705½	602,022	56,350	658,372	1,567	1,510	487	560	348	12	1,270
Palatine	19,512½	4,329½	607,813	68,073	675,886	1,291	1,234	231	428	349	11	1,095
Root	23,043½	7,372	657,033	50,975	708,008	1,476	1,272	464	519	309	14	1,012
St. Johnsville	8,065	2,577	279,479	41,651	321,130	903	841	277	327	208	4	677
Total	194,457⅝	46,720¾	6,114,891	664,079	6,778,970	15,787	15,021	4,960	5,310	3,306	121	12,028

Names of Towns.	Live Stock.					Agricultural Products.							Domestic Cloths, in Yards.
						Bush. of Grain.					Dairy Products.		
	Horses.	Working Oxen and Calves.	Cows.	Sheep.	Swine.	Winter.	Spring.	Tons of Hay.	Bushels of Potatoes.	Bushels of Apples.	Pounds of Butter.	Pounds of Cheese.	
Amsterdam	689	960	1,059	2,402	1,399	3,894½	121,000½	3,497	14,207	16,532	91,993	1,320	154
Canajoharie	901	1,779	1,967	2,641	2,007	4,313	155,944	4,208½	14,367	11,187	140,765	184,512	463¾
Charleston	850	1,411	1,204	4,855	1,188	1,783	127,914½	2,905½	6,509	18,237	114,398	16,050	3,344
Florida	1,212	1,694	1,356	2,887	2,050	10,240	213,334	4,937½	13,676	23,776	125,140	4,836	306
Glen	986	1,199	1,132	3,824	2,033	10,469	181,592½	3,962	14,749	15,983	105,410	13,290	1,097
Minden	1,074	1,691	3,120	2,197	2,641	5,658	192,221½	6,461¾	24,923	15,756	187,345	465,417	1,451
Mohawk	857	1,381	1,558	3,818	2,620	10,648	171,619	5,490	23,194	21,024	173,952	13,490	1,309
Palatine	865	1,525	2,676	1,692	2,457	10,070	134,371	6,405½	14,824	10,746	117,548	494,923	1,829
Root	1,036	1,549	1,582	4,885	1,628	3,294½	146,218½	3,434½	11,449	18,070	120,124	79,016	1,992
St. Johnsville	366	512	1,147	460	811	2,647	27,611	3,230	7,256	4,550	34,710	265,800	341
Total	8,836	13,701	16,801	29,661	18,834	63,017	1,471,826½	44,532¼	145,154	155,861	1,211,385	1,538,654	12,286¾

but the precise date is unknown. They were Germans, and among them were families named Hellebralt, Waters, Getman, Van Riepen, Walrath, and Klock. A German school was taught by Henry Hayes at an early day. The first English school was taught by Lot Ryan, an Irishman, in 1792. Chris. Nellis kept an inn in 1783, and a store in 1801. Jacob Zimmerman built the first gristmill, during the Revolution, and Geo. Klock the second, in 1801.

1 Named in compliment to Christian House, the builder.

2 In the spring of 1780 Philip Helmer deserted to the enemy. He had previously been paying his addresses to a daughter of Philip Bellinger, and upon a plan being formed to take the family of the latter prisoners, he forewarned them in time to rally a party to their assistance. An ambuscade was formed, and the Indians would have been killed or captured, had it not been for the indiscretion of one of the party, who, upon their approach, yelled out, at the top of his voice, "Lord God Almighty, friends, here they are!" The Indians fled with the loss of only one.

NEW YORK COUNTY.

The city of New York[1] was incorp. by Gov. Stuyvesant in 1652, and its municipal powers were confirmed and enlarged by Gov. Dongan, April 22, 1686, and by Gov. Montgomerie, April 19, 1708. An act was passed Oct. 14, 1732, confirming its rights; and subsequent enactments were embodied in one act in the revised laws of 1813 and in the revised statutes of 1828. Numerous changes in the details of the municipal government have been made from time to time.[2]

The co., from the beginning, has embraced Manhattan, Governors, Bedloes, Ellis's, Blackwells, Wards, and Randalls Islands, and the lands under water to low water mark on the shores opposite, in Westchester, Queens, and Kings cos., and in New Jersey.[3] Manhattan Island is 13½ mi. long, by 2½ mi. wide at the broadest part. It is centrally distant 130 mi. from Albany, and contains an area of 22,000 acres.[4] It is separated from Westchester co. by a strait known as Spuyten Duyvil Creek,[5] and Harlem River. The surface of the island was originally quite broken by ridges of gneiss and hornblendic slate, especially in the N. part; and immense masses of rock and earth have been removed in grading.[6] A deep valley extended across the island on the line of Canal St.;[7] another near Carmansville;[8] a third at Manhattanville; and a fourth at Tubby Hook, near the N. extremity. The s. part of the island was covered with drift and boulders, presenting conical hills, some of which were 80 ft. above the present grade of the streets. Fresh water was readily obtained by wells sunk to the surface of the rock; and the porous nature of the soil has greatly favored the construction of deep foundations and vaults without annoyance from water.[9]

Along the E. shore, from 94th St. northward, and around Harlem, the surface is very level, and to some extent covered with salt marshes. On the w. side, toward the N., the valleys are often deep and the hills precipitous. The highest point, at Fort Washington, is 238 ft. above tide.

Both sides of the island afford ample facilities for commerce; and the noble harbor embraced within the shores of New Jersey, Staten Island, Long Island, and the city has scarcely an equal for extent, safety, and facility of access, and for the amount of its commercial transactions.[10]

The preservation of this harbor from injurious encroachments has been a subject of solicitude; and investigations which these have occasioned have developed many interesting facts connected with its interests.[11]

---

[1] Named from the Duke of York, afterward James II. By the Dutch named "*New Amsterdam*," and by the Indians "*Manhattan*."

[2] Important acts were passed in 1830, 1849, 1851, 1853, and 1857, the last mentioned embracing all the essential features of the city government.

[3] The question of jurisdiction upon the river was long a subject of dispute with New Jersey. A summary of the controversy is given in our account of the Boundaries of the State, pp. 17, 18

[4] The widest part of the island is at 88th St., where it is 12,500 feet across.

[5] The creek flows from Hudson to Harlem River, at Kingsbridge.

[6] White limestone of coarse quality appeared at the surface on the E. side, between 13th and 16th Sts., and on the w. from 29th to 31st Sts. The strata of gneiss are nearly vertical, often bent and contorted, and in places they contain interesting minerals.

[7] A body of water known as the Collect Pond, (from Kolk, a pit,) bordered by a marsh, extended from near Pearl to Franklin St. and from Elm to Orange St. It was 50 feet deep, and was connected with the Hudson by a narrow inlet nearly on the present line of Canal St. It was a favorite resort for skating in winter; and upon it experiments in steam navigation were made by John Stevens in 1796–97 and '98, and by John Fitch in 1796 and '97. The Halls of Justice, known as the Tombs, and the "Five Points" district, now occupy the site of the ancient pond; and a large sewer under Canal St. represents the position of the outlet.

[8] Known as the Clendening Valley. The Croton Aqueduct crosses this on a magnificent series of arches and piers of solid masonry.

[9] Until 1842 the city was entirely dependent upon wells for its supply of fresh water. See p. 424.

[10] The strait known as Harlem River and Spuyten Duyvil Creek is too shallow and crooked to be available for commerce. Various plans have been proposed to improve it; but none have been carried into effect. Harlem River is about 800 to 1,000 ft. wide, and mostly bordered by narrow, marshy flats, behind which the banks rise into hills. At Kingsbridge the bank is 180 ft. high and nearly perpendicular. The Hudson River R. R. and the Harlem R. R. cross these waters, and also the High Bridge, (used only for the Croton Aqueduct and foot passengers,) and the Harlem Bridge, at the head of 3d Avenue. The latter was a toll bridge until the expiration of the charter in the spring of 1858. Macomb's Bridge, formerly at the head of 7th Avenue, was much used; but it is now down. A dam was constructed at this place for using tide water; but, being found to impede navigation, it was removed. In 1827 a company formed to build a canal across the upper end of the island, and in 1836 a similar plan was proposed, and a canal was partly built, traces of which may be seen on the E. side of the island, at 106th St. One of the objects of this canal was to gain access to a marble quarry; but the stone was found to be of inferior quality, and the project was abandoned. The capacity of the harbor of New York is limited only by the depth of water on the bars at its entrance near Sandy Hook. Vessels of about 23 ft. draft can pass at high tide. The approaches by way of Long Island Sound have no practical limitation of this kind; and vessels of 60 ft. draft could approach the upper part of the island and land on the Westchester shores adjacent without difficulty.

[11] The Colony and State have at sundry times granted to the city lands under water adjacent to its shores, the riparian owners being usually secured in the right of pre-emption. The principal of these grants have been as follows:—
1686.—All vacant lands on Manhattan Island to low water mark, with rivulets, coves, and ponds, were secured by the charter granted by Gov. Dongan.

Although the city forms but a single organization, it has localities known by distinct names as villages or neighborhoods; but the number of these is gradually becoming obliterated as population increases; and most of them will soon be known only to the student of history.[1]

Of the several islands, other than Manhattan, comprised in New York City and co., those in the harbor are owned by the General Government and occupied as military posts, and those in the East River are chiefly owned by the city and devoted to charitable and penal institutions.[2]

1708.—All vacant lands on Long Island shore, between high and low water marks, between the Navy Yard and Red Hook, were granted.

1730.—Land under water, 400 ft. wide, between junction of Charlton and Washington Sts. and Marketfield St. on the Hudson, and from Whitehall to Houston St. on the East River, was secured. These grants, with the previous ones, comprise 209¼ acres.

1807.—Land under water, 400 ft. wide, extending northward from previous grant 4 mi. on the Hudson and 2 mi. on the East River, was granted.

1826.—The same was extended to Spuyten Duyvil Creek on the w. and Harlem R. on the E.

1821.—Land 600 ft. wide in front of the Battery was added.

1837.—Land under water on the w. to 13th Avenue line was secured.

1852.—Land under Harlem R. from such exterior line as the corporation might fix, to the shore, was granted. Other extensions were authorized in 1828, 1830, 1835, 1846. *Assem. Doc.* 8, 1856.

In 1811 the exterior line was fixed by the commissioners for laying out the city into streets; but changes of their plan and the extension of streets led to encroachments upon the channel, requiring remedial measures. An act was accordingly passed, March 30, 1855, appointing 5 commissioners in pursuance of advice of a Senate committee of the year previous, and these persons, associating with themselves several officers of the General Government, proceeded to examine the subject. The harbor and shores were surveyed and sounded, the effects of tides and currents examined, maps constructed, and lines for the limitation of piers and bulkheads recommended, and mostly confirmed by law, April 7, 1857. These surveys were performed by 10 parties of about 200 persons from the U. S. Coast Survey, at a cost of $85,000. The reports of the commission embrace a large amount of statistical and historical information.—*Assem. Doc.* 8, 1856; *Sen. Doc.* 40, 126, 1857.

The first dock was built from Broad to Dock St., on the East River. There are now 66 piers on the w. and 78 on the E. side of the city. A part of these are built and owned by the corporation, others by individuals or companies, and others jointly by the city and individuals. Of the last class the city pays one-third the cost of building and receives one-half of the revenues. The city owns 39 piers and 7 half-piers on the Hudson, and 31 piers and 20 half-piers on the East River,—the former valued at $1,428,500, and the latter at $1,829,000. They are under the care of the Street Department.

The wants of commerce led to the erection of a lighthouse on Sandy Hook, at the expense of the colony of New York, in 1762, which was supported by special duties upon commerce until ceded to the U. S. Feb. 3, 1790. The commissioners for its erection were John Cruger, Philip Livingston, Leonard Lispenard, and Wm. Bayard. It was burned in 1776. Within the Hook are lights at Princes Bay, Fort Tompkins, Robins Reef, and Whitehall Landing, and numerous buoys to mark the channels.

The tide enters at Sandy Hook at 7h. 29m. past the moon's southing, and rises at Governors Island from 2.2 to 6.1 ft., the mean rise being 4.3 ft. The harbor was frozen over in 1780, and again in 1820. On the former occasion persons passed on the ice to Staten Island. It sometimes happens that the Hudson and East Rivers will be closed for a few hours in intensely cold seasons, and people have on these occasions rashly attempted to cross; but the occurrence is not common.

[1] The following is a list of the principal of these localities:—

Bloomingdale, on Broadway, between 100th and 110th Sts., 7 mi. from the City Hall, presents a very neat appearance, and consists mostly of suburban dwellings. It is the seat of an orphan and a lunatic asylum, the latter forming a branch of the N. Y. Hospital. It was called by the Dutch "*Bloemend Dal,*"—Flowery Valley.

Carmansville, on 10th Av. above 155th St., named from families named Carman, former owners of the adjoining lands, is chiefly made up of country seats.

Corlaers Hook, at the angle in the East River near Grand St., named from Arent Van Corlaer, was called by the Indians "Nechtank."

Dominies Hook lies on the Hudson, between Duane and Canal Sts., embracing 62 acres. It was acquired by ground brief from Stuyvesant July 4, 1654, and was afterward granted to the English Church.

Fort Washington, (Washington Heights p. o.,) a short distance above Carmansville, is an elevated site, once fortified, and now occupied by fine dwellings. The Deaf and Dumb Asylum is located near this place.

Greenwich, now merged in the city, was 3 mi. above the City Hall, on the Hudson. It was named by Capt., afterward Sir Peter, Warren, who owned it. The Indian name was

"Sapokanigan." The N. Y. State Prison was formerly located here.

Harlem (p. o.) lies between 8th Avenue and East River, about 106th St. The principal business is on 3d Avenue. It has several churches, important manufactories of India rubber, chemicals, candles, ale, beer, carriages, and row boats, and several private schools.

Kings Garden, west of Broadway, between Fulton and Reade Sts., is now partly held by Trinity Church and leased.

Lispenards Meadows was an irregular tract on both sides of West Broadway from Reade to near Spring St., and along Canal St. from the Hudson to Orange St.

Manhattanville, (p. o.,) on the Hudson, between 125th and 132d Sts., w. of 9th Avenue, contains a convent, Catholic college, and manufactories of iron, paint, and refined sugar.

Strykers Bay, on the Hudson, at 96th St., is a R. R. station.

Tubby Hook lies on the Hudson, one-half mi. s. of Spuyten Duyvil Creek.

Turtle Bay is on the East River, 2 mi. N. of Corlaer Hook. Its name is a corruption of the Dutch "Deutel Bay," or Wedge Bay.

Yorkville, on the east side of Central Park, extends to the East River, from 79th to 90th Sts.

[2] **Governors Island** was formerly called "*Nutten' Island,*" and by the Indians "Pag-ganck." It lies 1,066 yards s. E. from the Battery, and contains 72 acres. It is separated from Long Island by Buttermilk Channel, formerly shallow, but now of sufficient depth for the largest ships. This island was bought by Gov. Van Twiller, and has always been reserved for public defense. Quarantine was located here from 1794 to 1797. In the settlement of accounts with the U. S., New York undertook to erect fortifications here as payment for her proportion of the expenses of the Revolution. Jurisdiction was ceded to the U. S. Feb. 15, 1800, with Fort Jay, then partially erected. By the authority of an act passed March 26, 1794, £30,000 were expended by the State in fortifications, under the supervision of Geo. Clinton, Matthew Clarkson, James Watson, Richard Varick, Nicholas Fish, Ebenezer Stevens, and Abijah Hammond. A further sum of £20,000 was granted April 6, 1795, to complete the works on this and "*Oyster*" (now Ellis) Islands. Castle William (named from Gen. Williams of the N. Y. Militia) is a round tower on the w. shore of the island, 600 feet in circumference and 60 feet high, mounting 80 casemate and 40 barbette guns. The land side is open, and a covered way leads to the works in the center of the island. Fort Columbus is a star-shaped work of 5 points on the summit of the island, mounting 105 guns; and South Battery, fronting Buttermilk Channel, has 13 guns. These works from 1830 to 1853 cost $285,897; and they are adapted to a garrison of 800 men. The island is used as a receiving station for newly enlisted troops, and a school for instructing boys in music. About 60 lads of 14 years and upward are usually under instruction upon the drum, bugle, and other instruments.

Bedloes Island, 2,950 yards s. w. from the Battery, was named from Isaac Bedloe, the patentee under Gov. Nicoll. It was known for some years as "*Kennedys Island.*" It was ceded to the U. S. in 1800, having been previously used for quarantine purposes. It is now occupied by Fort Wood, erected in 1841 at a cost of $213,000, on the site of a fort built about the beginning of the century. It mounts 77 guns, and accommodates a garrison of 350 men. During several months in 1849 it was used by the Commissioners of Emigration as a hospital.

Ellis Island, formerly known as "*Oyster,*" "*Bucking,*" and "*Gibbet*" Island, lies 2,050 yards s. w. of the Battery, and is occupied by Fort Gibson, a work built in 1841-44, at a cost of $5,096, mounting 15 guns and requiring a garrison of 80 men. The pirate Gibbs and 3 associates were hung here April 22, 1831.

Blackwells Island is a long, narrow island in the East River, extending from 51st to 88th Sts., and containing 120 acres. It was named from the Blackwell family, who owned it for a hundred years or more. It is now owned by the city corporation, and is the seat of various penal and charitable institutions. This island was formerly called "*Manning Island,*" from Capt. John Manning; and by the Indians it was named "Minnahanock." It was patented to Gov. Van Twiller, and continued private property until 1828, when it was sold by James Blackwell to the city for $30,000. In 1843 the city paid $20.000 more to perfect the title.

Wards Island, named from Jasper and Bartholomew Ward, former proprietors, extends along the East River, opposite New York, from 101st St. to 115th St., and contains 200 acres. It was formerly called "*Great Barcut*" or "*Great Barn*" Island, and by the Indians was named "Ten-ken-as." It was

The city is divided into 22 Wards, which are again subdivided into 149 Election Districts, and such other civil divisions as the election of State, city and co. officers, the administration of justice, and the regulation of municipal ordinances require.[1]

The Board of Supervisors in New York co. is composed of 12 persons, who are so classified that 2 are elected or appointed annually. A ballot can have but one name; and it is the duty of the canvassers to declare that the two persons having the highest number of votes are elected.[2] Their general powers and duties—which chiefly concern taxes and assessment—are the same as those of Supervisors in other cos.

The Legislative Power of the city government is vested in the Common Council, consisting of 2 co-ordinate branches,—a board of 17 Aldermen and a board of 24 Councilmen.[3] The former are elected by single districts for 2 years, and the latter are elected annually, 6 to each Senatorial district.[4] Ordinances must be passed by both bodies the same year, and receive the assent of the Mayor, to become valid.

The regular sessions of the Board of Councilmen commence at 5 o'clock P. M. on the first Monday in each month, and continue on each Monday and Tuesday until the business of the month is concluded. Each house elects a presiding officer, clerk, and other officers; and the journals of each are published.

The Executive Power is vested in a Mayor,[5] elected for 2 years, and in 7 Executive Departments, viz., those of Police, Finance, Streets, Croton Aqueduct, Almshouse, Law, and City Inspector,—most of which are subdivided into bureaus, each having specific duties to perform. The Mayor is charged with the general administration of the city, nominates for the approval of the Aldermen certain officers, and may suspend or remove officers within limits fixed by statute. He communicates annually and from time to time to the Common Council such messages as he deems proper.

The Police Department has general charge of police regulation in New York City, Kings, Richmond, and Westchester cos. By act of April 15, 1857, it was placed under the Commissioners of the Metropolitan Police District,[6] of whom the Mayors of New York and Brooklyn are *ex officio* members.

bought by Van Twiller in 1637, confiscated in 1664, and granted to Thos. Delavel. The Wards bought it in 1806; and in Dec. 1847, a part was leased by the Commissioners of Emigration for an Emigrant Refuge and Hospital. The Commissioners have since purchased 106 acres; and a portion of the remainder is used as a Potter's Field. The cost of buildings and improvements up to 1858 was $260,000. The structures erected before 1850 were slight barracks and shanties; but those built since are chiefly of brick. The island is supplied with Croton water; and a ferry connects it with 106th St.

Randalls Island, named from Jonathan Randall, who purchased it in 1784 and resided here nearly 50 years, lies N. of Wards Island, near the Westchester shore. It was formerly known as "*Little Barn*" Island. It was patented under the Dutch Government, but was confiscated in 1664 and granted to Thos. Delavel. It was subsequently named "*Belleisle*," "*Talbots Island*," and "*Montressors Island*." The city purchased it in 1835 for $50,000. It is now occupied by nursery schools and by the establishment of the Society for the Reformation of Juvenile Delinquents. A ferry connects it with 122d St.

Sunken Meadow Island lies adjacent to Randalls Island.

[1] The city was divided Dec. 8, 1683, into 6 wards, known as South, East, North, West, Dock, and Out Wards. They were designated by *numbers*, and a new ward was created by act of Feb. 23, 1791, to take effect Sept. 28, 1792. Those subsequently erected have been as follows:—

8th, 1803.	16th, 1836, from 12th.
9th, 1803.	17th, 1837, " 11th.
10th, 1808, from 7th.	18th, 1846, " 16th.
11th, 1825.	19th, 1850, " 12th.
12th, 1825.	20th, 1851, " 16th.
13th, 1827, " 10th.	21st, 1853, " 18th.
14th, 1827, " 6th and 8th.	22d, 1853, " 19th.
15th, 1832, " 9th.	

[2] This arrangement is made so as to place the Board of Supervisors above the reach of party politics.

[3] The Aldermanic Districts, identical with the Assembly Districts, are as follows:—

1. South of Chambers, Duane, Frankfort, Pearl, and Dover Sts.
2. S. by 1st, within Broadway, from Chambers, through Frankfort, Baxter, Bayard, Bowery, Center, and Catharine Sts. to East River.
3. S. by 1st, within Broadway, from Chambers, through Spring St. to Hudson River.
4. S. by 2d, within Broadway, from Franklin, through Grand and Clinton Sts. to East River.
5. S. by 3d, within Broadway, from Spring, through 4th and Christopher Sts. to Hudson River.
6. Within Broadway, Houston, Clinton, and Grand Sts.
7. S. by 5th, within Broadway, from 4th, through 14th St. to Hudson River.
8. S. and E. by East River; w. and N. by Clinton and Houston Sts. to East River.
9. S. by 7th, within 6th Avenue, from 14th St., through 26th St. to Hudson River.
10. Within Broadway and 14th St., Avenue A, and Houston St.
11. S. by 9th, within 6th Avenue, from 26th St., through 40th to Hudson River.
12. Within Houston St., Avenue A, 14th St. and East River, 22d Ward.
13. 22d Ward.
14. Within 14th St., from East River, 6th Avenue, 26th St. and East River.
15. S. by 14th, within 6th Avenue, from 26th St., through 40th St. to East River.
16. 19th Ward.
17. 12th Ward.

[4] The election of city officers takes place annually on the first Tuesday of Dec., and that of co. officers on the day of the general State election, which is on the Tuesday after the first Monday of Nov. The officers of the co. are the Recorder, City Judge, and other Judges of the city courts, District Attorney and his assistants, Sheriff and his Deputies, Constables, Coroners, County Clerk, Register, Treasurer, Assessors, Tax Commissioners, Receiver of Taxes, Commissioner of Juries, Commissioners of Deeds, and Supervisors.

The Recorder is presiding judge of the criminal courts and a magistrate. Several of the co. officers are *ex officio* charged with duties more properly belonging to the city government; and the line of distinction between the two sets of officers is not well defined.

[5] The Mayor was originally appointed by the Governor and Council, and from 1777 to 1822 by the Council of Appointment. Since 1822 the Mayor has been elected.

[6] This District includes New York, Kings, Richmond, and Westchester cos. The Governor and Senate appoint 3 commissioners from the city of N. Y., 1 from Kings, and 1 from Westchester or Richmond co. The city is divided into 11 Surgical Districts, each with 1 Surgeon; and into 25 Police Precincts, under a General and Deputy Superintendent. According to the Council Manual for 1858, the number of employees in the police was 1,004, of whom 11 were surgeons, 7 were attached to the office of the Commissioners, 5 were employed in the office of the General Department, 24 in that of the Deputy Superintendent, 21 as Detectives, 79 in attendance at public offices and courts, 26 as harbor police, and 841 on police stations. The number is at times largely increased, and is annually becoming permanently greater.

The Department of Finance is under a Comptroller, elected by separate ticket for a term of 4 years. This officer has charge of the fiscal concerns of the city, and reports the condition of its finances annually to the Common Council. The Department is divided into the Auditing Bureau, a Bureau of Arrears, a Bureau of Taxes, a Bureau of City Revenue, and a Bureau of Deposits and Disbursements, the officers of which are appointed by the Comptroller.[1]

Number of cases annually before the Court of Sessions, for a term of years.

YEARS.	PETIT LARCENY. Convictions.	Acquittals.	ASSAULT AND BATTERY. Convictions.	Acquittals.	Discharges.	MISDEMEANORS. Convictions.	Acquittals.	TOTAL.	Trials in special sessions.	Sentenced to county prisons.	Sentenced to house of refuge.
1838	261	73	125	26	429	...	...	914	434	296	27
1839	349	93	163	33	581	...	...	1,219	614	241	25
1840	526	97	226	32	488	...	...	1,369	839	508	28
1841	666	78	296	30	396	...	...	1,466	1,001	682	67
1842	744	138	287	33	375	...	...	1,577	1,119	737	63
1843	907	142	395	54	537	...	...	2,035	1,311	987	55
1844	896	148	551	86	838	...	...	2,519	1,495	1,058	56
1845	991	193	615	90	1,158	...	...	3,047	1,741	1,128	66
1846	977	220	509	87	1,109	...	...	2,902	1,651	1,075	56
1847	.....	173	334	48	697	...	...	1,252	1,399	981	51
1848	1,064	258	436	52	672	...	...	2,548	1,635	1,003	52
1849	1,180	261	558	59	938	...	...	2,996	1,837	1,120	71
1850	1,419	219	837	76	1,382	...	...	3,933	2,218	1,402	112
1851	1,453	187	662	43	1,194	...	...	3,539	2,079	1,179	94
1852	1,475	214	978	51	1,167	...	...	3,885	2,405	1,254	97
1853	1,415	179	1,230	67	1,120	...	...	4,011	2,570	1,242	119
1854	1,411	108	1,152	66	1,184	...	...	3,921	1,528	1,159	77
1855	2,047	196	929	84	1,064	28	6	4,354	1,942	1,528	69
1856	1,788	208	986	84	1,454	25	4	4,549	2,803	1,426	41
1857	2,041	273	1,589	284	1,627	101	40	5,955	3,752	1,824	195
1858	1,919	317	1,697	344	1,784	139	60	6,260	4,576	2,061	134

Cases tried in the courts of Oyer and Terminer and of General Sessions, for a period of eighteen years.

OFFENSES.	1841.	1842.	1843.	1844.	1845.	1846.	1847.	1848.	1849.	1850.	1851.	1852.	1853.	1854.	1855.	1856.	1857.	1858.
Murder	1	2	...	...	2	1	1	1	...	...	8	4	3	1	1	...	3	1
Arson, 1st degree	...	...	...	1	...	...	...	...	1	...	...	...	...	...	...	...	...	1
Manslaughter, various degrees	8	...	3	7	2	2	1	3	6	4	8	6	17	15	9	12	15	28
Assault and battery with intent to kill or maim	2	3	4	8	4	6	4	3	6	5	9	7	10	11	12	19	12	21
Assault and battery with intent to rob	...	...	1	...	...	...	...	...	2	2	...	...	1	1	5	10	6	18
Rape, and intent to commit rape	4	...	1	1	5	4	5	1	4	2	1	1	4	4	...	...	4	3
Abandoning child in highway	1	...	...	...	...	...	1	...	...	...	...	...	...	...	...	...	...	...
Robbery, 1st degree	4	5	...	3	2	3	11	6	4	10	3	15	10	7	5	6	22	10
Kidnapping	...	...	...	...	...	...	...	...	...	...	...	...	...	...	...	...	...	2
Riot with assault	26	6	8	17	7	2	...	4	13	49	6	17	45	32	...	...	...	1
Assault and battery	10	73	86	81	52	39	40	47	19	50	41	37	71	63	47	55	79	121
Procuring abortion	2	...	...	5	...	2	1	...	...	...	...	4	...	2	1	5	5	12
Bigamy	2	1	2	...	3	2	5	3	1	3	1	...	...	...	...	...	...	...
Incest	...	...	...	...	...	...	...	...	...	1	1	...	...	...	...	...	...	...
Sodomy	...	...	...	...	...	...	1	...	1	...	...	...	...	...	...	...	...	...
Perjury and subornation of perjury	...	2	2	2	2	...	...	2	...	...	2	...	...	2	1	...	...	...
Arson, not 1st degree	1	1	...	...	...	...	...	...	...	...	1	...	...	1	...	...	8	3
Burglary, various degrees	28	55	68	55	43	24	32	31	18	51	47	54	64	52	67	76	89	85
Attempt to commit felonies	7	2	5	6	4	6	10	6	10	10	9	14	9	19	48	64	101	137
Embezzlement	...	1	...	1	...	...	1	1	1	...	...	...	3	...	2	4	1	1
Grand larceny, &c., 2d offense	90	71	84	58	73	76	61	91	87	86	105	119	155	112	62	94	89	110
Petit larceny, and attempt to commit	57	48	40	42	40	88	66	54	95	101	76	51	75	91	130	109	116	109
Petit larceny, 2d offense	4	...	...	3	1	3	...	...	...	...	6	8	2	...	...	...	...	...
Conspiracy	...	1	2	4	...	...	2	5	...	2	3	...	...	...	3	...	...	2
Carrying slung shot (felony)	...	...	...	...	...	...	...	...	3	3	1	1	4	4	...	...	...	...
Receiving stolen goods	10	8	3	10	6	5	7	8	13	8	4	9	6	6	10	15	5	15
Accessory to felony	...	...	...	1	...	1	...	...	...	...	1	...	...	...	...	...	...	...
Forgery, various degrees	4	27	22	8	11	9	7	7	12	13	17	15	15	25	19	30	49	54
Receiving challenge to fight a duel	...	1	...	...	...	...	...	...	...	...	...	...	...	...	...	...	...	...
Breaking jail	...	...	...	...	1	...	...	...	...	...	...	...	...	...	...	...	...	...
Aiding prisoners to escape	...	...	...	1	...	1	...	...	...	...	...	...	...	...	...	...	...	...
Keeping gambling and disorderly house	12	16	12	24	7	36	18	...	16	16	15	16	14	38	7	9	3	5
Nuisance	13	2	2	1	4	5	...	3	1	...	...	...	2	...	...	...	...	...
Selling, insuring, and advertising lottery tickets	10	4	2	3	...	2	2	4	...	1	1	...	6	10	2	...	...	...
Libel	2	10	13	2	2	4	...	...	1	...	1	...	6	4	2	...	...	3
Cruelty to animals	...	...	...	...	...	...	...	...	...	...	...	...	...	...	...	...	...	...
Selling liquor without license	1	...	...	4	3	1	1	...	...	1	...	14	307	10	1	...	...	...

During 29 years ending with 1858, 38 persons have been sentenced for capital crimes, of whom 17 have been executed, 14 had their sentences commuted to imprisonment for life, 1 was pardoned, 1 committed suicide, and to 4 a new trial was granted, of whom 3 were convicted of manslaughter and 1 discharged.

One was under sentence of death at the beginning of 1859.— *Common Council Manual*, 1859, *p. 75.*

1 The Comptroller reports quarterly a list of accounts audited; and all drafts upon the city treasury must be upon his warrant, accompanied by vouchers. The following aggregates show the

The Street Department is under the charge of the Street Commissioner, who is appointed for 2 years by the Mayor with the advice and consent of the Board of Aldermen. He has the general direction of opening, altering, regulating, grading, guttering, and lighting streets, roads, places, and avenues, of building, repairing, and lighting wharves and piers, and of the construction and repair of public roads and the filling up of sunken lots, under the ordinances of the Common Council. The paving of streets is not under his charge. The department has a Bureau of Street Improvements, of Repairs and Supplies, of Lands and Places, of the Chief Engineer of Fire Department, of Collection of Assessments, of Wharves, of Roads, and of Lamps and Gas. Of each of these bureaus there is a superintendent, or chief, and several clerks, numbering in the several offices of the Department nearly sixty persons.[1]

condition of the city finances at the beginning of 1859 and the operations of the preceding year:—

Appropriations in 1858 for city government	$ 5,950,967.94
Expenditures	4,959,355.19
Expenditures in 1858 on trust and special accounts	10,549,621.54
Receipts in 1858	17,152,471.19
Permanent city debts redeemable from Sinking Funds, Jan. 1, 1859	14,399,998.00
Funded debt redeemable from taxation, same date	1,224,000.00
Funded debt redeemable from Central Park assessments	1,600,000.00
Estimated value of public parks	14,761,526.00
" " bulkheads, wharves, and piers	3,257,500.00
" " real estate occupied by markets	1,114,000.00
" " Croton Aqueduct Department	15,475,000.00
" " property used for Common Schools	1,200,000.00
" " property used for ferry purposes	1,200,000.00
" " property used by Fire Department	315,813,00
" " property used by Governors of Almshouse	1,250,000.00
" " real estate of all kinds	41,625,639.00
Assessed value of real estate within city in 1858	368,346,296.00
" " personal estate within city resident	150,813,462.00
" " personal estate within city non resident	12,034,532.00
" " personal estate within city, total	162,847,994.00
" " real and personal estate	531,194,290.00

The valuation, tax, and rate, for a series of years, at intervals of 5 years, from 1805 to 1825, was as follows:—

YEARS.	Valuation.	City and County Tax.	State Tax.	Total Tax.	Cts. Dolls.
1805	$25,645,867	$127,094.87			50 per 1
1810	25,486,370	129,727.15			51 " "
1815	81,636,042	197,613.38	$163,372.08	$361,285.46	41¼ " "
1820	69,530,753	270,361.19	69,530.75	339,891.94	49 " "
1825	101,160,046	336,868.82	50,580.03	387,448.85	38¼ " "

The property, both real and personal, in New York, is of immense value, and is increasing at a very rapid ratio. The taxes are uniformly heavy, and much higher than the average taxes of the other portions of the State. The following tables show a summary of the

Valuation and Taxes for a series of years.

YEARS.	Value of Real Estate.	Value of Personal Estate.	Total Value.	Amount raised by Tax.
1826	$64,804,050	$42,434,981	$107,238,931	$383,759.89
1830	87,603,580	37,684,938	125,288,518	509,178.44
1835	143,742,425	74,991,278	218,723,703	965,602.94
1840	187,221,714	65,011,801	252,233,515	1,354,835.29
1845	177,207,299	62,787,527	239,995,517	2,096,191.18
1850	207,142,576	78,919,240	286,061,816	3,230,085.02
1855	336,975,866	150,022,312	486,998,278	5,843,822.89
1858	368,346,296	162,847,994	531,194,290	8,621,091.31

Comparative Valuation and Taxes of the City and State for a series of years.

YEARS.	TOTAL VALUATION.		TOTAL TAX.		RATE OF TAX IN MILLS, ON $1.	
	City.	State.	City.	State.	City.	State.
1835	$218,723,703	$532,418,407	$518,494.00	$2,299,290.57	4.5	5.0
1840	252,135,515	641,359,819	1,354,797.29	3,089,920.94	5.4	4.9
1845	239,995,517	605,646,095	2,096,191.18	4,170,527.95	8.7	6.9
1850	286,061,816	727,494,583	3,230,085.02	6,312,789.23	11 3	8.6
1855	487,060,838	1,402,849,304	5,844,772.42	11,679,015.69	12.0	8.3
1858	531,222,642	1,404,907,679	8,621,091.31	15,426,593.20	16.2	10.98

1 Most of the streets in the lower part of the city are winding and crooked; but above the old settled Dutch portion they are very regular. An act passed April 3, 1807, appointed Simeon De Witt, Gouverneur Morris, and John Rutherford to lay out and survey the whole island N. of Fitzroy Road, (Gansevoort St.,) Greenwich Lane, (Greenwich Avenue,) and Art Street, (Waverly Place,) to the Bowery Road; and down the same to North St., (Houston St.,) and thence to the East River. The powers of these commissioners were amply specified in an act passed March 24, 1809; and Canal St. was by this act to be made a covered passage for the waste waters of its vicinity. The labors of the commission ended within the time specified, and their maps were filed in the secretary's office March 11, 1811. The surveys under this plan were executed by John Randall, jr., with great accuracy, and finally completed in 1821. To the commendable forethought of these gentlemen is the city indebted for the admirable arrangement of its up town streets and avenues.

The Streets of the portion covered in this survey generally extend from the Hudson to the East River direct, and are known by their numbers, the highest being at the time of first survey 154, but since extended to 228. Above 14th St. these are known only by their numbers, and the lots upon them are numbered E. and W. from Fifth Avenue. They are each 60 feet wide, except 14th, 23d, 34th, 42d, 57th, 72d, 79th, 86th, 96th, 106th, 116th, 125th, 135th, 145th, and 155th, each of which is 100 feet wide.

The blocks between them vary from 184 to 212 feet, being generally about 200 feet, or about 20 blocks to the mile.

The Avenues run nearly N. and S., and are numbered from E. to W., beginning upon the East River. Several short avenues on the E. side of the city are designated by letters, as Avenue A, beginning at the one next E. of First Avenue. These avenues are each 100 feet wide, except S. of 23d St., where Avenues A and C are 80 feet and Avenue B 60 feet. North of 33d St. Fourth Avenue is 125 feet wide. The blocks between the avenues are 610 to 920 feet, being generally 800 feet.

The Lands and Places belonging to the city date their title from Dongan's charter, by which all waste and unappropriated lands on Manhattan Island to low water mark, and all rivers, bays, and waters adjoining, were confirmed to the city. The real estate now belonging to the Corporation, amounting to $41,453,039, is mostly in use for Waterworks, Police, Fire, Almshouse, School, or Market purposes, or as parks, piers, bulkheads, and wharves, ferries, and public buildings for municipal purposes. The city owns, besides these,

Uncommuted quitrents reserved on property when sold, and water grants yet to be issued	$900,000
Lots under lease without covenants of renewal	325,000
" " " with "	500,000
Common lands	500,000
Sundry lots and gores of land	250,000
Real estate in Brooklyn	50,000

The city contains 20 public and several private parks, most of which are inclosed with iron railing and handsomely laid out.[1]

The Fire Department in some form has existed since 1653, when the city enjoyed the privilege of collecting a beaver for each house and a guilder yearly for each chimney to support a fire apparatus. The Fire Department in its present form was incorp. April 16, 1831; and its powers have been modified by acts of March 25, 1851, and April 3, 1855.[2]

[1] *The Central Park,* for the purpose of construction, is in charge of a special Board of Commissioners, consisting of 10 members, who serve without pay, and report annually to the Common Council. The history of this park is briefly as follows:—

On the 5th of April, 1851, Mayor Kingsland, in a special message to the Common Council, called attention to the importance of a public park sufficiently ample to meet the growing wants of the city population. The message was referred to a select committee, who reported in favor of purchasing the tract of 150 acres between 66th and 75th Sts. and 3d Avenue and the East River, known as Jones's Wood. An act was passed July 11, 1851, allowing this to be taken; but, from some errors in the act, the Supreme Court refused to appoint Commissioners, and the law was repealed April 11, 1854. On the 5th of August, 1851, a committee was appointed to examine whether another more suitable site for a park could not be found; and the result of the inquiry was the selection of the site now known as the "Central Park," between 5th and 8th Avenues, originally extending from 49th to 106th Sts., and in 1859 extended to 110th St. The act for creating this park passed July 23, 1853, and an act for its regulation and government April 17, 1857. The grounds are 2½ miles long by ⅖ mile wide, embracing 840 acres, of which 136 are occupied by Croton reservoirs. It will be crossed by 4 thoroughfares, sunk below the general surface and passing under the carriage ways and other avenues of the park, so as not to obstruct the movement of visitors. Access to the grounds cannot be had from these transverse roads. This park is now under construction, and will embrace a parade ground 50 acres in extent, for the maneuver of large bodies of infantry, cavalry, and artillery; a botanical garden, cricket grounds, playgrounds, ponds for skating in winter, and every variety of scenery which a surface naturally rugged and broken can be made to present. The plan embraces carriage drives and bridle paths, winding ways for pedestrians, and broad, noble avenues for promenade; fountains, lawns, terraces, and every variety of woodland scenery. Ground is reserved for a public hall intended for concerts; for a large conservatory, and exotic terraces; for a geometrical flower garden, with wall fountains; for an architectural terrace, with a large jet and tazza fountain; for public houses of refreshment; for residences of the Superintendent and head gardener; for a police station, a zoological garden, and for an astronomical observatory, chartered in 1859. The grounds now include the building erected and still used for a State Arsenal, but sold to the corporation, and the Mount St. Vincent Academy of the Sisters of Charity. There will be over 25 miles of walks, 5 miles of bridle paths, and 8 miles of carriage road. The main entrance will be at the corner of 5th Avenue and 59th St.; but other entrances will be provided at convenient points on 7th Avenue on both ends, and along 5th and 8th Avenues.

The Battery comprises a tract of about 20 acres at the s. point of the island, planted with trees and fronting upon the harbor. It was formerly a place of fashionable resort; but, in the extension of commerce, it has lost most of its prestige. It is still attractive on account of its cool breezes and refreshing shade. The point, formerly called "*Schreyers Hook,*" showed a number of rocks above water, upon which a platform was built in 1693 for a battery. This shallow spot was afterward filled in; and in 1853–56 it was further extended so as to embrace its present limits. It is valued at $3,000,000.

The Bowling Green is a triangular park between Broadway and Whitehall St. and Battery Place. It is supplied with a fountain, but is not open to the public. This Park or Green formerly fronted the fort upon the Battery. Prior to the Revolution, a leaden equestrian statue of Geo. III. was placed in it, which at the commencement of the war was thrown down and melted into bullets. The Green is valued at $135,000.

The Park is a triangular space of 10½ acres between Broadway, Chatham, and Chamber Sts., near the present center of commercial business in the city. The City Hall, Hall of Records, Rotunda, and New City Hall, used for courts and public offices, are located upon it. It has a large fountain, which is seldom used. This tract, formerly called "*The Fields,*" or "*The Common,*" from the beginning has been owned by the city and used for public purposes. While distant from the settled portion, it was used as a place of execution; and the victims of the negro plot proscription were here burned. In the early part of the Revolution the Sons of Liberty here rallied to assert their rights; and at a later period it became the scene of cruelty as the prison and execution ground of American patriots. The s. gateway was formerly of marble, beautifully finished, and surmounted by two marble balls, gifts from the Turkish Government to Commodore Perry, and by him presented to the city. They had been made for cannon balls. The foundation of this gateway was laid with great pomp, the Mayor presiding and depositing in it various coins, papers, and memorials. The Park is now

partly surrounded by an iron fence, and its sides are open for some distance to allow the easy passage of pedestrians. Its central location renders it a favorite place for popular gatherings, and, from the throng constantly passing, an audience can be swelled to thousands in a brief space of time. This Park is valued at $3,000,000.

Washington Square, containing 9¼ acres, formerly the "*Potter's Field,*" lies between Waverly Place, McDougal, Fourth, and Wooster Sts. It is handsomely laid out, and is surrounded with residences of a superior class. It has a fountain, and is a favorite resort for promenade. It is estimated that 100,000 persons were buried here before the ground was taken for a park. It is valued at $816,000.

Union Park is an oval area, with a fine fountain, on Broadway, bounded by University Place, 4th Avenue, 14th and 17th Sts. It is much frequented in summer by nurses and children. It is valued at $504,000. Adjoining the park, but not within its paling, is the equestrian statue of Washington, in bronze, by H. K. Browne, erected in 1856 at a cost of over $30,000. It is 14 feet high, and stands on a granite pedestal of about the same height.

Tompkins Square, formerly a parade ground, is bounded by Avenues A and B and by 6th and 10th Sts. It is still new; but it is well laid out and will become an ornament to the eastern side of the city. A fountain is under construction, and other improvements are in progress.

Madison Square, comprising 10 acres, between 5th and Madison Avenues and 23d and 26th Sts., is beautifully laid out and planted with trees. The adjoining streets are built up with first class dwellings, and it is one of the most fashionable places of promenade in the city. It is valued at $520,000. Adjoining this square on the west is a monument to the memory of General Worth.

Stuyvesant Square lies between 15th and 17th Sts. and 1st and 3d Avenues, the 2d Avenue passing through it. It has a fountain on each side of 2d Avenue, and is tastefully laid out and planted with trees and shrubs. It was presented to the corporation by the late Peter G. Stuyvesant, and is valued at $196,000.

Reservoir Square, adjoining the distributing reservoir, between 40th and 42d Sts., on 6th Avenue, from 1851 to 1858 was occupied by the Crystal Palace. It is valued at $150,000, and is at present unimproved as a park.

Manhattan Square, between 8th and 9th Avenues and 77th and 81st Sts., is a rough, unimproved piece of land, valued at $88,000.

Hamilton Square, at Yorkville, between 3d and 5th Avenues and 68th and 69th Sts., has a rolling surface, mostly above the level of adjoining streets, and is uninclosed and unimproved. The corner stone of a monument to Washington was laid with pompous ceremonies on this park Oct. 4, 1847; but the patriotism that instigated the enterprise was expended in the effort, and the work was abandoned without further action. The park is valued at $97,000.

Mount Morris Square, between 120th and 124th Sts., on both sides of 5th Avenue, not yet laid out, is valued at $40,000.

A square of 17 acres was reserved for a park at Bloomingdale, between 8th and 9th Avenues and 53d and 57th Sts.; but the location of the Central Park has led to its abandonment. In various parts of the city are several small triangular plats at the intersection of streets, valued at $10,000 to $15,000 each. The city also contains several parks not belonging to the city, which are laid out with great care and are truly ornamental.

St. John's Park, or *Hudson Square,* fronting St. John's Church and bounded by Hudson, Varick, Beach, and Laight Sts., belongs to Trinity Church, and is valued at $400,000. It is kept for the exclusive use of the inhabitants living near it, who purchase keys of the keeper at $10 per annum. It contains a beautiful fountain.

Grammercy Park, between 20th and 21st Sts. and 3d and 4th Avenues, is owned by those living around it, having been ceded to them by Samuel B. Ruggles. It is inclosed with an iron railing and a thick hedge of sweet prim, and is planted with ornamental trees and shrubs. It has a fountain in the center.

[2] This department has a *Board of Fire Wardens,* consisting of 14 members, a *Chief Engineer* and 13 assistants, and 3,700 men, of whom 1,922 are members of engine companies, 1,262 of hose companies, and 50? of hook and ladder companies. This body of men constitutes a distinct and powerful combination, whose services, although gratuitous, are prompt and in every respect praiseworthy, and whose interests the city authorities find it their policy to protect. The city is divided into 8 fire districts, furnished with 11 district fire alarm bells, all connected by telegraphic signals. There are 47 engine companies, 57 hose companies, 15 hook and ladder companies, and 4 hydrant companies. The first class engines have companies of

The Bureau of Lamps and Gas has in charge the lighting of the streets.[1]

The Croton Aqueduct Department is under a board styled the Croton Aqueduct Board, consisting of a President, Commissioner, Chief Engineer, and Assistant, appointed by the Mayor and Aldermen for five years. It has charge of all structures and property connected with the supply of Croton water and the collection of water rents, of the underground drainage of the city, of public sewers, of permits for street vaults, of paving and repairing streets, and of digging and constructing wells. It has a Bureau of Water Rents, and one of Pipes, Sewers, and Pavements. The department was organized in July, 1849, under an act passed April 11 of that year. Previous to this the Water Commissioners were appointed by the Governor and Senate.[2]

70 men, the second of 60, and the third of 50. The hook and ladder companies have each 50 men, and the hose companies each 30. The number of fires in the year, ending Feb. 17, 1859, was 261, and of alarms, 160. The loss by fire on buildings was $593,647, and on stock $514,999,—of which the Crystal Palace, burned in Oct. 1858, formed a large item. During the last year two large steam fire engines have been obtained; but, except in extraordinary cases, they are not used. The city owns about 80,000 feet of hose. The Department elects one Fire Commissioner annually for a term of 5 years from among exempt firemen. These commissioners form a Board to decide upon the formation of new volunteer companies, to investigate applications for admission to companies, to examine into charges against members, and for cause to suspend or remove them. The Fire Department possesses a fund derived from special trusts, donations, festivals, concerts, fines for violation of fire laws, and other sources, the income of which is applied in aid of the families of deceased and disabled firemen. The report of 1857 showed an expenditure of $30,567.91 by the trustees of this fund. Among the items of this expense were 1,978 pairs of shoes and 500 tons of coal. The invested fund amounts to $95,250. Two scholarships for educating the sons of firemen in the University of New York have been endowed by Myndert Van Schaick.

[1] The city gas lights are furnished by three general companies, as follows:—

The New York Gas Light Company was incorp. March 26, 1823, with a capital of $1,000,000. It has works on 21st and 22d Sts., from 1st Avenue to East River, and has 6 large gas holders at that station and 7 others at different parts of the city. It supplies the lamps s. of Grand St., and has about 130 miles of mains under the streets.

Manhattan Gas Light Company was incorp. Feb. 26, 1830, with a capital of $4,000,000. It has 2 manufactories of gas,—one on the Hudson, at the foot of 18th St., capable of making daily 2,000,000 ft., and one on East River, at the foot of 14th St., making 400,000 ft., and when completed will be capable of making 3,000,000 ft. daily. It supplies the city N. of Grand St., and has about 200 miles of street mains. It lights 8,000 street lamps and supplies 22,000 stores and dwellings. In 1857 it made 600,000,000 feet of gas.

Harlem Gas Light Company was incorp. Feb. 8, 1855, with a capital of $250,000. Its works are situated upon Harlem River, at the N. extremity of 1st Avenue. There are also several minor gas works for furnishing light to hotels and private establishments.

[2] The Croton Aqueduct is the most extensive and costly work in America for supplying a city with water; and its magnitude justifies a somewhat minute account of its origin and subsequent history.

In 1741 the General Assembly passed a law (which was continued by repeated enactments) for mending and keeping in repair the public wells and pumps of the city. In 1774 Christopher Colles contracted to erect a reservoir on Broadway, between Pearl and White Sts.; and the plan was partially carried into effect before the Revolution. In 1785 schemes were again agitated, which led to surveys and examinations; and in 1799 the Manhattan Company was formed, ostensibly to supply the city with water, but really as a banking institution, with a perpetual charter and large privileges. Its principal well was at the corner of Duane and Cross Sts., whence the water was raised by steam and distributed in pipes; but the supply was limited in amount and was of very impure quality. During the next thirty years various schemes were proposed for constructing common and artesian wells, and open canals from the Bronx and other streams in Westchester and Conn., and several companies were formed; but no practical steps were taken to secure the result. An act was passed May 2, 1834, which authorized the city to supply itself with "pure and wholesome water" and to issue its stock to defray the cost. The Governor and Senate appointed Stephen Allen, R. M. Brown, Charles Dusenberry, Saul Alley, T. T. Woodruff, and William W. Fox Commissioners, under whom accurate surveys were made and various plans and estimates considered, which resulted in recommending that the water of the Croton be taken near its mouth and brought in an aqueduct to a reservoir on Murray Hill, 114 ft. above tide. This plan was approved, March 11, by the Mayor, and in April, 1835, by the people, by a vote of 11,367 to 5,963. David B. Douglass was appointed Chief Engineer; but in Oct. 1836, he was succeeded by John B. Jervis. The work was begun in the spring of 1837, and so far completed as to allow the admission of water into the distributing reservoir, July 4, 1842.

Its completion was commemorated by a grand civic celebration Oct. 14 of the same year.

This aqueduct is a covered canal, of solid stone and brick masonry, arched above and below, 8 ft. 5½ in. high, 7 ft. 5 in. wide at the widest part, and 40¼ mi. in length from the dam to the distributing reservoir. It has a descent of 47.9 ft., or 13 in. to a mi., and a capacity of supplying 60,000,000 gallons of water per day. At intervals of 1 mi. are openings through small towers for ventilation. The flow of water is generally 2 to 3 ft. in depth, or 27,000,000 gallons a day. It is covered below the reach of frosts; and the surface works are carefully guarded by fences from injury by cattle. It passes through 16 tunnels in rock, varying from 160 to 1,263 ft., with a total of 6,841 ft. In Westchester co. it crosses 25 streams 12 to 70 ft. below the line of grade, besides numerous small brooks furnished with culverts. Harlem River is crossed upon High Bridge in two 48 inch mains, 12 ft. below the level of the grade of the aqueduct, and furnished with gate chambers at each end. This bridge is of granite, 1,450 ft. long, 21 ft. wide between the parapets, 100 ft. above the surface of high tide to the crown of the arch, and 114 ft. to the top of the parapets. It rests upon 15 arches, 8 of which are of 80 ft. span and 7 of 50 ft. Upon one of the piers is inscribed the following record of the construction of the bridge:—

AQUEDUCT BRIDGE.		
BEGUN 1839; FINISHED 1848.	JOHN B. JERVIS, *Chief*	ENGI-
STEPHEN ALLEN,	H. ALLEN, *Princ. Assist.*	NEERS
SAUL ALLEY,	P. HASTIE, *Resident*	
C. DUSENBERRY, WATER COM-	E. H. TRACY, *Assistant*	
W. W. FOX, MISSIONERS.	GEORGE LAW,	CONTRACT-
T. T. WOODRUFF,	SAMUEL ROBERTS,	ORS.
	ARNOLD MASON,	

The aqueduct of masonry is continued from the bridge 2 mi. to the Manhattan Valley, a depression which is 4,171 ft. wide and 102 ft. deep. This is crossed by an inverted siphon of iron pipes 4,180 ft. in length, with a gate chamber at each end. The masonry is then resumed, and the aqueduct is carried $2\frac{173}{1000}$ mi. to the receiving reservoir in the Central Park, crossing in this distance the Clendening Valley, 1,900 ft. across and 50 ft. deep, on an aqueduct, with archways for three streets, each of which has 30 ft. span for carriage way and 10 ft. span on each side for foot passengers.

The receiving reservoir in the Central Park is 1,826 ft. long, 836 ft. wide, covers an area of 3,505 acres, and has a capacity of 150,000,000 gallons. The banks are of earth, 18 ft. wide at top, and rise 9 ft. above the level of the water. The pipes pass through brick vaults. A new reservoir is now under construction adjacent to the former ones, and also upon Central Park. It will cover an area of 106 acres, and will be surrounded by an earth bank of irregular outline, which will constitute a broad promenade. The distributing reservoir at Murray Hill, between 40th and 42d Sts. and 5th and 6th Avenues, is a stone structure in 2 divisions, designed to contain 36 ft. or 20,000,000 gallons. Its surface is 115 ft. above mean tide.

The cost of the work was $8,575,000, including water rights and land, besides $1,800,000 for distributing pipes. The expense came within 5 per cent. of the estimate of Mr. Jervis, the Engineer. The annual interest, amounting to $665,000, is paid by direct water taxes and by some indirect taxes; and a sinking fund is provided for the final liquidation of the debt. The construction of this work has lowered the annual rates of fire insurance about 40 cts. on every $100 insured. Sing Sing Prison is supplied from the aqueduct as it passes near that place.

The amount of pipe laid in different years has been as follows, up to 1859:—

Previous to 1849,	1,024,051 feet.	Previous to 1854,	30,575 feet.
July to Dec. 1849,	20,236 "	1855,	36,921 "
In 1850,	41,328 "	1856,	29,983 "
1851,	65,199 "	1857,	23,320 "
1852,	63,535 "	1858,	19,550 "
1853,	33,782 "		
		Total	1,388,380 ft.

or 262 mi. 5,020 ft.

The amount of pipe of different sizes (internal diameter) laid up to 1859 has been—

4 inch pipe	9,472 feet.	20 inch pipe	41,324 feet.
6 " "	930,816 "	24 " "	5,400 "
10 " "	5,875 "	30 " "	44,862 "
12 " "	279,804 "	36 " "	60,878 "
16 " "	14,978 "	48 " "	4,087 "

A survey of the Croton Valley was begun in 1857, with the

The Almshouse Department is under the charge of a Board of Ten Governors of the Almshouse, generally known as the "Ten Governors."[1] The department was organized under an act of April 6, 1849, and was modified the succeeding year. This board has charge of the Almshouse, of the Relief and Support of the Poor, of the County Lunatic Asylum, of the Nurseries for Poor and Destitute Children, the Penitentiary, and all the city prisons and houses of detention, except the sheriff's jail in Elbridge Street and the House of Refuge. All ordinary appropriations for this department must be submitted to a board consisting of the Presidents of the Boards of Aldermen and Councilmen, the Mayor and Comptroller.[2] If this board approves, it reports to the

---

view of ascertaining its topography minutely, the better to decide upon future reservoirs or other structures as they may be found necessary. The ridge line or watershed inclosing the valley above the dam is 101 mi. in length. The stream is 39 mi. in length, and its tributaries 136 mi. The total area of the valley is 352 square mi.; and within it are 31 natural lakes and ponds, many of which are available as reservoirs, and 16 of which have been minutely surveyed and estimated.

The revenues from water rents from Oct. 5, 1842, to Dec. 31, 1858, have amounted to $6,725,947.98; and the amount has increased from year to year,—except in 1851 and 1856, when it fell off.

The public sewers connected with this department, since Feb. 6, 1846, have cost an expenditure of $163,527.13; and the amount of $248,572.00 has been collected from permits to connect premises with the public sewers. The length of sewers constructed by this department since its organization in 1849 has been 92 mi. 1,340 ft.

[1] The Governors of the Almshouse are elected by single ballot, one being voted for and two elected. This places the board above the control of party politics.

[2] Public measures for the relief of the poor are among the first necessities of a civilized government; and one of the earliest statutes of the General Assembly in 1683 was for this object. In 1699 a law was passed for the relief of the poor at their homes; and about 1714 the first almshouse was built, on the present site of the City Hall. In 1795 a lottery of £10,000 was granted for a new almshouse, and the large brick building on the Park near Chambers St. (burned in 1854) was erected. In 1811 a tract on the East River, at the foot of 26th St., was bought; and the first stone was laid Aug. 1, 1811. The present main edifice at Bellevue Hospital was opened April 22, 1816, as a hospital, penitentiary, and almshouse, at a cost of $421,109. The management was for many years intrusted to five commissioners appointed by the Common Council. In 1822 the average number of paupers was 1,547; and the cost of the establishment for several years was as follows:—

In 1817	$90,886	In 1820	$84,420
" 1818	107,600	" 1821	85,000
" 1819	105,509	" 1822	82,200

The law then required paupers to be returned to the town where they had gained residence; but this was often difficult, and vessels then, as since, often landed paupers in or near the city from distant places. In 1822 two vessels put about 100 paupers on shore a few miles from the city, and brought on their baggage. Efforts were made to remedy these abuses; but it was found difficult in a large population to distinguish those coming into the city liable to public charge, until they applied for relief in the early winter months.—*Sen. Doc. No. 86, 1824.*

Meanwhile the affairs of the institutions at Bellevue became very corrupt and mercenary; but a malignant fever, which broke out in 1825 and committed frightful ravages in the filthy wards and loathsome cells, forced the question of reform upon the public. In 1845 the Almshouse was placed under the care of a single commissioner, and in 1849 the present system of supervision went into operation.

Blackwells Island was bought in 1828, and Randalls Island in 1835. In 1848 the Almshouse was completed on the former; and the whole of both islands is now devoted to objects of charity and reform, Randalls Island being in part under the care of the Governors of the Almshouse and in part under the Trustees of the House of Refuge.

Upon Blackwells Island, commencing at the S. end, are located respectively the Small Pox Hospital, the Penitentiary, Island Hospital, female and male Almshouses, Workhouse, and Lunatic Asylum. Upon Wards Island is the Potters' Field, under the charge of the Ten Governors; and upon Randalls Island are the extensive nurseries and hospitals for poor children. Bellevue Hospital, the largest in the city, remains under the charge of the Governors as a fever, surgical, and general hospital. The Colored Orphan Asylum, Colored Home, four city prisons, and the out-door poor, are also under the care of this department. A short sketch of these several charges is essential to a full knowledge of the city.

Bellevue Hospital is 350 ft. long, the center portion 5 stories high and the wings 4 stories. Upon each story are verandas and outside stairways of iron. Its arrangements throughout are ample and judicious, and it can accommodate 1,350 patients. It has a clinical theater fitted up for the accommodation of large classes of students. In 1858 the number of prescriptions was 145,503; and the number of births is about 350 annually.

The results of its operation during 10 years have been as follows:—

YEARS.	Admitted.	Discharged.	Remaining.	Died.
1849	3,114	2,716	512	483
1850	3,728	3,224	571	445
1851	5,401	5,304	609	550
1852	5,020	4,449	547	633
1853	4,836	4,210	594	579
1854	6,213	5,634	674	725
1855	5,743	5,476	582	629
1856	5,484	5,186	602	604
1857	7,074	6,166	853	667
1858	7,925	7,512	843	812

The Small Pox Hospital, Blackwells Island, was commenced April 1, 1854, and was finished in the same year. It is built, in the English gothic style, of stone quarried upon the island. It is 104 ft. by 44, 3 stories high, and cost $38,000. It is not designed for the treatment of paupers only, but is fitted up with express reference to receiving persons able and willing to pay for their treatment, and where, secluded from friends to whom they might impart their disease, they may receive every attention that science and the most attentive nursing can bestow. It is the only hospital of the kind in or near the city, and takes the place of some old wooden buildings previously erected on the island.

Its statistics have been as follows:—

YEARS.	Admitted.	Discharged.	Remaining.	Died.
1849	263	241	13	29
1850	208	132	48	41
1851	296	276	10	58
1852	149	122	12	25
1853	156	104	25	39
1854	185	165	5	46
1855	56	48	3	10
1856	134	99	11	27
1857	197	148	27	33
1858	216	198	5	40

The Penitentiary, opposite 55th St., is built of hewn stone and rubble masonry. It consists of a middle building, 65 by 70 ft., and two wings, each 50 by 200 ft., making the whole length of the building 465 ft. A new wing was finished in 1859; and another is needed for the accommodation of the inmates. The total number of cells is 1,736. The convicts are employed as occasion requires in quarrying and dressing stone for buildings upon the island, and as blacksmiths, shoemakers, carpenters, weavers, coopers, painters, wheelwrights, &c. This establishment was finished in 1848,—since which time there have been admitted and discharged the following numbers:—

YEARS.	Admitted.	Discharged.	Remaining.	YEARS.	Admitted.	Discharged.	Remaining.
1849	2,109	2,066	809	1854	5,983	6,286	873
1850	3,575	3,581	803	1855	5,197	5,503	511
1851	3,450	3,374	879	1856	4,011	1,549	533
1852	4,444	4,150	1,173	1857	3,058	1,640	743
1853	5,236	5,233	1,176	1858	2,974	2,075	773

Much the largest number of convicts are received from the police courts; over a third are females, and a very large proportion are foreigners. Over half are committed for petit larceny; and the next largest number for assault and battery. The term of sentence is usually 1, 2, 3, 4, or 6 months; and but very few are sentenced to 1 year and upward. The longest term of years reported in 1858 was 10, and this in only a single instance.

The Island Hospital, Blackwells Island, was first erected in 1848, under the name of the "*Penitentiary Hospital.*" Its name was changed Dec. 15, 1857. The building was found to be constructed "in a most reckless and careless manner, and as a public building was a reproach to any city." It continued in use, however, until destroyed by fire, Feb. 13, 1858. At the

Supervisors; and if it disapproves, it returns to the Ten Governors with objections. If the latter still adheres by a vote of two-thirds, the subject must be reported to the Supervisors.

time of the fire it contained 600 inmates; but they were all removed without loss of life. In Feb. 1858, a most humane regulation was adopted, by which the suffering poor are relieved without being committed as vagrants. The building now in the process of erection to supply the place of the former is 3½ stories high, includes 14 wards and accommodations for 744 patients. As on other buildings on the island, convict and workhouse labor is largely employed in the erection. The statistics of the hospital have been as follows:—

YEARS.	Admitted.	Discharged.	Remaining.	Died.
1849	2,148	1,919	192	292
1850	2,009	1,923	198	80
1851	2,343	2,177	267	97
1852	2,767	2,651	272	111
1853	3,136	2,864	314	109
1854	3,744	3,415	499	144
1855	2,158	2,241	350	66
1856	1,733	1,697	348	38
1857	2,810	2,549	535	74
1858	4,140	4,175	388	113

Almshouses.—Of these there are two separate and similar structures, 650 ft. apart, entirely distinct in their arrangements, and each devoted to one sex only. They are each composed of a central building 50 ft. square, 57 ft. high to the roof, and 87 ft. to the top of the cupola, and two wings, each 60 by 90 ft. and 40 ft. to the roof. They are devoted to the care of the aged and infirm, and present the following result of operations:—

YEARS.	Admitted.	Discharged.	Remaining.	Died.
1849	1,672	1,115	1,197	95
1850	2,355	1,995	1,304	169
1851	2,783	2,535	1,349	203
1852	2,624	2,510	1,282	181
1853	2,198	2,186	1,143	151
1854	2,981	2,434	1,402	288
1855	3,096	2,730	1,511	257
1856	3,359	3,137	1,458	255
1857	4,204	3,782	1,561	319
1858	3,890	3,369	1,696	393

Less than one-fourth of the whole number thus thrown upon the charities of the city are of native birth; and more than one-half are females. The present almshouses have been in use since 1848.

Workhouse.—This establishment was authorized by act of April 11, 1849, and grew out of a recommendation of the Prison Association of New York, in which the Society for Improving the Condition of the Poor concurred. A plan for buildings was adopted the succeeding season, and work was begun Oct. 3, 1849. The N. wing, 3 stories high, has 150 rooms, opening upon galleries around a common central hall, and capable of lodging 600 persons. At the N. end is a cross arm 4 stories high, containing workshops. A central building contains the residence of the Superintendent, the kitchen, storerooms, offices, chapels; and a S. wing, for females, is constructed upon the plan and of the size of the N. wing. This establishment was designed for those able to work and who, not finding means of support, were willing to be committed, as well as such paupers, vagrants, and others as might be deemed fit subjects for employment. The males are usually kept employed as circumstances permit, in quarrying and grading, and as carpenters, coopers, wheelwrights, painters, boat builders, blacksmiths, tinsmiths, shoemakers, and tailors. The females are employed in knitting, sewing, and other light occupations. This institution has scarcely resulted in the benefits anticipated, and of all the charities under the care of the Governors is perhaps the only one that might possibly be dispensed with. It is found impracticable to keep all hands profitably employed; and the name of "workhouse" loses its terrors when coupled with the idea of leisure hours, comfortable quarters, and sufficient food.

Its statistics have been as follows:—

YEARS.	Admitted.	Discharged.	Remaining.	Died.
1850	757	504	328	28
1851	637	501	286	8
1852	515	89	210	11
1853	1,458	921	529	15
1854	3,894	3,237	1,186	110
1855	4,447	4,482	956	41
1856	4,034	3,890	1,022	63
1857	4,347	3,669	1,701	
1858	4,164	4,585 ·	1,240	40

The number discharged does not include those escaped or sent to other institutions.

The Lunatic Asylum, near the N. end of Blackwells Island, consists of an octagonal building 80 ft. in diameter and 50 ft. high, with a cupola and two wings at right angles to each other, each 245 ft. long. One wing is devoted to either sex; and the arrangement of the wards admits of classification. Apart from this, on the E. side of the island, is a building of stone, 59 by 90 ft. and 43 ft. high, with a veranda on each side, which is exclusively devoted to the noisy and violent class, where they cannot disturb the more quiet. This structure is named "The Lodge," and, for obvious reasons, is not usually open to visitors. The Lunatic Asylum proper was begun in the spring of 1835, and, after some months of suspension, the work was resumed in 1837, and the W. wing was finished June 10, 1839. The S. wing was built in 1847; and this, with "The Lodge," was finished in 1848. The statistics during 10 years have been as follows:—

YEARS.	Admitted.	Discharged.	Remaining.	Died.
1849	459	283	401	212
1850	391	251	464	77
1851	441	308	517	80
1852	495	357	527	130
1853	487	357	542	115
1854	486	283	555	190
1855	371	253	573	100
1856	366	276	597	66
1857	326	296	627	75
1858	355	235	655	92

This institution is admirably managed; but the proportion of recoveries is necessarily less than in those asylums in which only recent cases are admitted and the patients discharged when there is no longer a hope of recovery. This is, in one sense, an asylum of the incurable.

The Potters' Field, on Randalls Island, was placed under the charge of the Governors of the Almshouse June 19, 1850; but its location and quality of soil were made a subject of complaint, and it was repeatedly presented by grand juries. A tract of 69 acres was purchased on Wards Island, and brought into use in June, 1852, since which time the former field has not been used. About 2,500 interments are made annually at the public charge.

The Nurseries and *Nursery Hospitals* on Randalls Island consist of about a dozen detached buildings, not arranged on any systematic plan. The grounds are inclosed and of ample extent; and a farm is connected with the institution, which goes far toward furnishing it with culinary vegetables. The institution is provided with ample schools and playgrounds. The numbers remaining here at the beginning of 1859 were 88 men, 96 women, 833 boys, and 303 girls. The children are indentured, given for adoption, or returned to friends, as circumstances warrant.

The Colored Orphan Asylum was begun in the fall of 1836, and was incorp. April 16, 1838. It is situated on 5th Avenue, between 43d and 44th Sts., and is under the immediate charge of lady managers, who report to and receive funds from the Governors of the Almshouse Department. The numbers remaining at the close of the several years since, under this arrangement, have been as follows:—

1849	156		1854	237
1850	176		1855	233
1851	201		1856	234
1852	207		1857	225
1853	219		1858	219

In 22 years it has received in the aggregate 970 colored orphans. This institution is partially supported by benevolent contributions and partially by occasional appropriations from the State.

The Colored Home, on 1st Avenue, between 64th and 65th Sts., has 44 lots of ground, on which substantial buildings are erected. It was originally intended as a House of Industry. In Oct. 1858, the foundations of a new building were laid, 90 ft. by 40, with a corridor from 6 to 12 ft. wide on the S. side, extending from each wing of the present building nearly 120 ft., so that access may be had from all parts of the house without exposure to the weather. It contains departments for male and female hospitals, home for the aged and infirm, schools, and lying-in and nursery accommodations. This is also under the immediate care of lady managers, and is sustained by contributions, legacies, and grants from the State. In point of order and neatness it equals any hospital in the city. The male hospital usually has about 30 inmates, the female hospital 75, the lying-in department 40, and the home of the aged 150. The average number of births is about 90 annually.

The City Prisons—four in number, under charge of the Governors—are situated as follows:—

The Halls of Justice, or "Tombs," is situated on Center St. between Leonard and Franklin. A portion is occupied by courtrooms and prisons for persons awaiting sentence. The house

The Commissioners of Emigration were incorp. by an act of May 7, 1847, and consist of 6 commissioners appointed by the Governor of the State, and of the Mayors of New York and Brooklyn, and the Presidents of the German Society and the Irish Emigrant Society. They have charge of the Marine Hospital at Quarantine, the Emigrant Depot at Castle Garden, and numerous buildings on Wards Island for the accommodation of the sick.[1]

The Law Department is under a chief officer called the "Counsel to the Corporation," elected for three years. He has charge of all the law business in which the city is interested, when so ordered by the corporation, and institutes all legal proceedings necessary for the opening and widening of streets. He draws all leases, deeds, and other papers connected with the finances of the city. This department has a Bureau of Corporation Attorney, and another of Public Administrator.

The City Inspector's Department is under a chief officer styled the City Inspector, who has cognizance of all matters affecting the public health, pursuant to the ordinances of the Common Council and the lawful requirements of the Commissioners of Health and of the Board of Health. It has a Bureau of Sanitary Inspection and Street Cleaning, of Records and Statistics, and of Superintendent of Markets. Coroners report to this department all inquests made by them. The Inspector is required to report all births, marriages, and deaths within the city. He also appoints 2 Inspectors and Sealers of Weights and Measures, who hold office upon the same terms as Chiefs of Bureaus. One Street Inspector is appointed to each of the 22 wards, 1 clerk to each of the 11 markets,[2] and a keeper and assistant to each of the corporation yards.

The Judiciary Department comprises the First Judicial District of the Supreme Court

---

of detention adjacent is an isolated building, containing 148 cells.

The Jefferson Market Prison, at the corner of Greenwich St. and 6th Avenue, was enlarged in 1856, and 36 new cells were built.

The Essex Market Prison, at the corner of Grand and Ludlow Sts., was completed in 1857.

The Prison at Yorkville was abolished in March, 1856; but it has since been revived.

The commitments during the year 1858 were as follows:—

		1st Dist.	2d Dist.	3d Dist.	4th Dist.
WHITE.	Males..........	13,955	3,091	2,876	589
	Females......	11,477	1,334	693	191
BLACK.	Males..........	478	64	33	11
	Females......	301	45	31	3
	Total..................	26,211	4,534	3,633	794
	General Total...35,172				

The Outdoor Poor receive aid upon application at the office of the Governors, in the Rotunda, on the Park. These poor are under the care of a superintendent and visitors; and some of the principal items for a series of years have been as follows:—

YEARS.	Donations.	Children's Nursing.	Trans'n of Paupers and Children.	Total of every kind.
1850...	$25,793.18	$5,934.41	$ 978.30	$ 60,507.05
1851...	27,808.13	7,925.06	1,521.57	59,336.54
1852...	31,119.86	9,560.37	980.05	91,189.88
1853...	27,449.75	10,158.50	1,005.94	82,136.74
1854...	26,516.76	9,284.00	1,687.41	83,704.09
1855...	29,217.88	9,900.25	1,647.78	121,861.14
1856...	41,334.13	12,803.73	2,448.15	95,522.60
1857...	24,700.25	10,585.47	2,479.21	108,756.75
1858...	19,171.31	10,774.75	1,283.37	140,924.71

Large items are included in the last column for coal and wood, transportation of coal, and wages. The total expenditures of the department for all the charities and other institutions connected with them have been as follows:—

1850 .... $406,652.60	1853 .... $541,280.66	1856 ..... $839,172.58
1851 .... 481,967.36	1854 .... 653,874.46	1857 ..... 896,204.45
1852 .... 501,896.18	1855 .... 816,672.00	1858 ..... 835,228.52

[1] Castle Garden, (formerly "Castle Clinton,") at the lower point of the Battery, on the Hudson, was granted by the corporation of the city to the United States, in May, 1807, for the purpose of erecting a fortification. The present structure was built soon after; but the foundations were found not sufficiently strong for heavy ordnance, and the site was re-conveyed to the corporation under an act of Congress passed March 30, 1822. The building was subsequently used for the public reception of distinguished strangers, and for concerts, operas, public meetings, the annual fairs of the American Institute, and similar

purposes, until leased in 1855 to the Commissioners of Emigration as a landing place for emigrants.

The Emigrant Refuge and Hospital, upon Wards Island, consists of several large buildings for hospitals, nurseries, and other purposes, located upon a farm of 106 acres. The total number of emigrants who have arrived in the port of New York since 1846 has been 2,486,463, distributed as follows:—

1847........ 129,061	1851........ 289,515	1855........ 136,233
1848........ 189,176	1852........ 300,992	1856........ 142,342
1849........ 220,603	1853........ 284,945.	1857........ 183,773
1850........ 212,796	1854........ 318,438.	1858........ 78,589

The greater number of these proceed to their destination without expense to the Commissioners.

The Marine Hospital is noticed under Richmond County. See page 566.

[2] **The Markets** of New York are owned by the city, and leased in small portions to occupants. They are as follows:—

Catharine—Catharine St., East River.
Center—Grand and Center Sts.
Clinton—Washington and Canal Sts.
Essex—Grand and Ludlow Sts.
Franklin—Old Slip, East River.
Fulton—Fulton St., East River.
Gouverneur—Water, corner of Gouverneur St.
Jefferson—Sixth Avenue, corner of Greenwich Avenue.
Tompkins—Third Avenue and Sixth St. (now building of iron.)
Union—Second and Houston Sts.
Washington—Fulton St., Hudson River.

The principal market for wholesale is the Washington Market; and thither most of the teams from the surrounding country resort for the sale of produce. The principal fish market is adjacent to Fulton Market, where facilities are provided for unloading fishing vessels. The immense supply of animal food required by the population of New York has led to enormous investments of capital for the production, and corresponding arrangements for the bringing forward of this class of provisions. Cattle are now seldom driven to market on foot. Illinois is the greatest beef producing State in the Union, and its market cattle are brought by R. R., stopping on the way only 3 or 4 times to rest and feed. About $12,000,000 are annually expended by New York and its suburbs for beef alone. The measures for supplying the city with fish, oysters, and game are correspondingly great, and have each in their several departments led to organized systems for furnishing their proportion with great regularity and in quantities proportioned to the demand.

The markets for live stock in New York are provided entirely by individual enterprise; and the principal ones are now on 44th St. and 5th Avenue. The great market days are Tuesdays and Wednesdays; and, since supplies can reach the city at all seasons with equal facility, the amount is distributed throughout the year in a proportion nearly uniform. This market occupies 14 acres, and has 150 yards, and, with its stalls, can accommodate 5,000 bullocks, and an equal number of sheep and calves. The largest hog markets are at the w. end of 40th St., and on the Hudson, at the foot of 37th St. There are 2 other market places,—one on 6th St. E. of 3d Avenue, and one in Robinson St., where nearly 450,000 sheep have been sold, besides cows and calves. There are also extensive markets at Bergen Hill.

of the State, with 5 justices, the Superior Court, with a chief justice and 5 justices, the Court of Common Pleas, with 3 justices, the Marine Court, with 3 justices, and the Surrogate's Court. The criminal courts consist of a Court of Oyer and Terminer, held by a justice of the Supreme Court, a Court of General Sessions, held by the Recorder or city judge, Courts of Special Sessions, held by the police justices, 4 Police Courts, and 6 Justices' or District Courts.

The Burials from the city are regulated by law; and none can take place without a certificate from the Inspector's Department, and a record of the time, cause, and circumstances of the death, as far as can be ascertained.[1]

The Board of Health consists of the Mayor and Common Council. The Mayor is President. The Mayor, the Presidents of the two branches of the Common Council, the Health Officer, the Resident Physician, the Health Commissioner, and the City Inspectors, are constituted a Board of Commissioners, who render advice to the Board of Health. The Health Officer is appointed by the Governor and Senate. The Mayor, with the advice of the Board of Aldermen, appoints an Inspector of Vessels. It is the duty of the Board of Health to watch over the health of the city and port, and conduct and attend to the business of the Quarantine establishment.[2]

Ferries are established from New York to Brooklyn, Jersey City, the islands, and to numerous points around the harbor. Up to 1810 the ferry boats were propelled by horse and man power; but during that year steam was introduced, and now it is exclusively used on all important routes. A few of the islands are reached only by row boats.[3]

The facilities for passing from one point to another in the city are numerous, cheap, and con-

---

The number of animals sold during 5 years at the New York live stock markets has been as follows:—

YEARS.	Beeves on sale market days.	Total No. of beeves sold in the city.	No. of cows.	No. of veals.	No. of sheep.	No. of swine.	Total No. of slaughtered animals.
1854	115,846	169,864	13,131	68,584	555,474	252,328	1,058,690
1855	97,654	185,574	12,110	47,969	588,741	318,107	1,147,509
1856	125,505	187,057	12,857	43,081	462,739	345,911	1,051,655
1857	116,546	162,243	12,840	34,218	444,036	288,984	940,819
1858	144,749	191,374	10,128	37,675	447,445	551,479	1,238,101

The number of bullocks from the several States sending to this market, in 1858, was as follows:—

	No.	Weekly Average.		No.	Weekly Average.
New York	30,980	595	Virginia	895	17
Pennsylvania	1,664	45	Connecticut	590	11
Ohio	4,389	84	Texas	1,214	23
Indiana	11,130	214	New Jersey	603	11
Illinois	52,818	1,015	Iowa	2,724	52
Kentucky	9,409	181	Michigan	1,682	32

The mode of reaching market was as follows:—

Bullocks, by Harlem R. R. 10,558
" Hudson River R. R. 50,916
" New York & Erie R. R. 93,820
" on foot 2,863
Swine, by New York & Erie R. R. 301,671

The above statistics do not include barreled beef and pork, and animals slaughtered elsewhere and sent thither for sale. In some seasons over 3,000 sheep are slaughtered per week, at Albany, for the New York market; and the amount from other places is very large.

[1] *The Burial Places* of New York were originally around the churches; and in 1822 there were 22 places of interment s. of the City Hall. The practice was found to be offensive to the senses and prejudicial to the public health, and was accordingly prohibited in the older parts of the city. The plan of marble cemeteries within the city was proposed, and two were constructed between 2d and 3d Sts. and the Bowery and 2d Av. These contained 234 and 156 vaults respectively, were built entirely of stone, and intended to receive each a large number of bodies. The plan was found unsuccessful, and soon after was superseded by that of rural cemeteries. This appropriate custom, introduced at Greenwood in 1842, has led to the laying out of many similar grounds, each rivaling the other in beauty of location and in plans for the adornment of the resting places of the dead. The principal of these are Greenwood, Cypress Hills, Evergreens, Mount Olivet, Calvary, Citizens' Union, Friends, Shearith Israel, and Washington, on Long Island; Trinity, on New York Island; Beechwood, at New Rochelle; Dale, at Sing Sing; Oak Hill, at Nyack; and Machpelah, in Westchester co.; and New York Bay and others, in New Jersey. The Potters' Field belonging to the city is on Wards Island. By an ordinance of Feb. 3, 1851, no burials are allowed s. of 86th St.; and Trinity Church Cemetery, embracing $23\frac{94}{100}$ acres between the Hudson and 10th Av. and 153d and 155th Sts., is the

principal one now in use on the island. It was purchased in 1842.

[2] Pestilence has on several occasions committed frightful ravages among the population of the city. Among these visitations the following are worthy of record:—

1702.—A pestilence, probably yellow fever, was brought from St. Thomas, of which 500 died up to Sept., and 70 more during the first week of that month, out of a population of 6,000 to 7,000.

1732.—In autumn an infectious fever prevailed, of which 70 died in a few weeks.

1743.—A "bilious plague" broke out, of which 217 died in one season. It was confined to swampy ground. This is the first official report on mortality to the Mayor.

1745.—Malignant yellow fever prevailed.

1747.—The bilious plague re-appeared.

1791.—The yellow fever prevailed, of which 200 died.

1794.—Yellow fever again appeared, occasioning much alarm,—though only 20 to 30 died.

1795.—The yellow fever prevailed, carrying off 730, of whom 500 were foreigners recently arrived.

1796.—A malignant fever prevailed, from filling in of docks, of which 70 died.

1797.—The yellow fever occasioned 45 deaths.

1798.—Memorable for its pestilence,—probably yellow fever,—which appeared in New York in the first week in August, and proved fatal to 2,086 persons, of whom 1,110 were men, 589 women, and 885 children.

1799.—Yellow fever again prevailed, but much less aggravated.

1801.—About 160 died of yellow fever.

1803.—From 600 to 700 died in New York of yellow fever. Since this year regular statistics of mortality for the city are preserved for each year, from which it appears that yellow fever in 1805 destroyed 270, and in 1822, 166; and that cholera destroyed 3,513 in 1832; 971 in 1834; 5,071 in 1849; and 374 in 1852. The mortuary tables show during the 50 years ending with 1853 a total of 364,698 deaths.

[3] The ferries running to and from New York are under the exclusive jurisdiction of the corporation, and derive their authority by lease, usually for a term of years. The following is a summary of those now running:—

Staten Island Ferry, from Whitehall St. to Quarantine, Clifton, and Stapleton. Also extends to New Brighton, Factory Village, and Port Richmond. It is leased to the Staten Island & New York Ferry Co. until 1865, at an annual rent of $5,100.

Hamilton Avenue Ferry, from Whitehall St. to Hamilton Av., Brooklyn, 1,765 yards in length, is leased to the Union Ferry Co. until 1861.

South Ferry, from Whitehall St. to Atlantic St., and Long Island Rail Road, Brooklyn, 1,476 yards in length, is leased to the Union Ferry Co.

Wall Street Ferry, from Wall St. to Montague Place, Brooklyn, 1,150 yards in length, belongs to the Union Ferry Co., and is leased until 1862, at an annual rent of $5,000.

Fulton Street Ferry, from Fulton St. to Fulton St., Brooklyn, 730 yards, belongs to the Fulton & Union Ferry Co., and, including the South and Hamilton Avenue Ferries, rents for $35,000. It is leased until 1861.

Peck Slip Ferry, from Peck Slip, foot of Ferry Street, to South 8th Street, Williamsburgh, 2,800 yds., is leased to J. V. Merserole & Co. until 1869, at an annual rent of $21,000.

venient, and the establishment of all of them is so recent as to be within the memory of every adult citizen. They consist of 5 city rail roads and 29 lines of omnibuses.[1] Since the introduction of rail roads and the multiplication of steam ferries and steamboat routes, a large number of persons transacting business in the city have been enabled to provide residences in the country adjacent, where they can enjoy the comforts and luxuries of a rural home without a sacrifice of business interests. A large proportion of the inhabitants of Brooklyn, and great numbers residing within 30 mi. of the city, on Long Island and Staten Island and in the adjacent parts of Westchester county and New Jersey, are in this manner closely identified with the business of the city, and might in one sense be included in its population. New York and its immediate suburbs are thus so united in interests that they virtually constitute one great metropolis, and would probably at this time number, within a radius of 10 mi. from the City Hall, about a million and a quarter of inhabitants.[2]

The institutions of New York designed to meet the intellectual and social wants of the people in extent and variety have no equals in America; and many of them surpass all similar institutions in the world. These institutions, noticed under special heads, are devoted to education, both general and special, to benevolent objects in various forms, to religion and morality, to intellectual culture, and to the promotion of the useful and fine arts. They do not strictly all belong to the city, nor do they adequately represent the wants of the city population. Many of the schools and other institutions, from their peculiarities and excellence, attract great numbers from abroad; and, on the other hand, a great number of educational institutions in the adjoining counties depend for support almost entirely upon city patronage. A reciprocity of interests between city and country is thus kept up in intellectual as well as in business affairs.

The Public School System of New York now constitutes one of the most important interests of the city, both in regard to its effect upon the social position of the people and in the amount of its annual expenditures. There were reported, at the close of 1858, a free academy[3] for the complete collegiate educations of boys, 4 normal schools for the instruction of teachers, 57 ward schools, including 51 grammar schools for boys, 48 grammar schools for girls, and 55 primary departments for both sexes; 35 primary schools, 42 evening schools, of which 23 are for males and

---

Roosevelt Street Ferry, from Roosevelt Street to Bridge Street, Brooklyn, 1,450 yds., is leased to the Union Ferry Co. until 1867, at $3,000 per annum.
James Street Ferry is established from James Slip to South 7th Street, Williamsburgh.
Catharine Street Ferry, from Catharine Street to Main Street, Brooklyn, 736 yds., is leased to the Union Ferry Co. until 1863, at $16,000 per annum.
Division Avenue Ferry extends from Grand Street to South 7th Street, Williamsburgh.
Grand Street Ferry, from Grand Street to Grand Street, Williamsburgh, is 900 yds. in length.
Houston Street Ferry, from Houston Street to Grand Street, Williamsburgh, 700 yds., is leased to the Houston Street Ferry Co. until 1863, at $6,500 per annum.
Tenth Street Ferry, from 10th Street to Green Point, is leased until 1865, at $250 per annum.
Twenty-Third Street Ferry, from 23d Street to Green Point, is leased until 1863, at $100 per annum.
Hunters Point Ferry, from 34th Street to Hunters Point, Queens co., is leased to A. W. Winants until 1867, at $100 per annum.
Blackwells Island Ferry extends from 61st Street to Blackwells Island.
Hellgate Ferry, from 86th Street to Astoria, Queens co., is leased to S. A. Halsey until 1867, at $50 per annum.
Wards Island Ferry extends from 106th Street to Wards Island.
Randalls Island Ferries extend from 122d Street to the Institutions under the charge of the Ten Governors, and from 117th Street to the House of Refuge.
Jersey City Ferry, from Cortland Street to Jersey City, 1 mile, is leased to the Jersey City Ferry Co. until 1866, at $5,000 per annum.
Barclay Street Ferry, from Barclay Street to Hoboken, N. J., is leased to J. C. & R. L. Stevens until 1865, at $100 per annum.
Canal Street Ferry, from Canal Street to Hoboken, N. J., is leased to J. C. & R. L. Stevens until 1860, at $600 per annum.
Christopher Street Ferry, from Christopher Street to Hoboken, N. J., is leased to J. C. & R. L. Stevens until 1862, at $350 per annum.
Weehawken Ferry extends from 42d Street to Weehawken, N. J.
Elysian Fields Ferry extends from 19th Street to Elysian Fields, N. J.
The Union Ferry Co. owned on the 1st of Nov. 1858, eighteen boats, valued at $489,800.
[1] Some of the principal facts concerning the city rail roads are as follows:—

Cars run at frequent intervals and use horse-power. Fare, uniformly 5 cts.
Second Avenue extends from Peck Slip, through Pearl, Chatham, Bowery, Grand, and Chrystie Streets and 2d Avenue, to 23d Street; thence to 42d Street. Returns through 2d Avenue, 23d Street, 1st Avenue, Allen and Grand Streets, Bowery, Chatham, Oliver, and South Streets.
Third Avenue extends through Park Row, Chatham, Bowery, and 3d Avenue, to 61st Street, Yorkville.
New York & Harlem R. R. extends through Park Row, Centre, Broome, and Bowery Streets, to 4th Avenue, and up to 42d Street, where locomotive trains stop.
Sixth Avenue extends through Vesey, Church, Chambers, W. Broadway, Canal, Varick, and Carmine Streets, and 6th Avenue, to 44th Street.
Eighth Avenue extends through Vesey, Church, Chambers, W. Broadway, Canal, and Hudson Streets and 8th Avenue to W. 59th Street.
Ninth Avenue, track laid but not used.
The Hudson River R. R. and New Haven R. R. run no city cars.
The omnibuses all have the names of their routes painted upon the outside. The rates of fare are 4, 5, or 6 cts., which is paid without regard to distance traveled upon or within them. Licenses are granted annually; and in 1858 439 stage licenses were taken at $20, and 5 out-of-town lines, at $5 per stage, amounting in the aggregate to $10,355. All other conveyances for public hire are also licensed, the number in 1858 being, hacks, 402, and special hacks, 320.
[2] Most of the suburban districts of New York within this State are particularly noticed in this work in the counties and towns in which they are located. Jersey City, which has grown up within a few years, had, in 1855, 21,715 inhabitants. It is the terminus of the New Jersey R. R., connecting with lines s. and w., and the Union R. R., connecting with the New York & Erie and the Northern New Jersey R. R. It is the landing place of the Cunard steamers, the seat of important manufactures, and the residence of multitudes doing business in New York City. Hoboken City is also a place of considerable importance from its proximity to the city. It had, in 1855, 6,727 inhabitants. Hudson City, in the rear of these, had 3,322 inhabitants; and numerous other places along the Hudson in N. J. are receiving attention as desirable places for homes.
[3] *The Free Academy* was established by an act of May 7, 1857, subject to a popular vote, which gave 19,404 for and 3,409 against the measure. An edifice in the gothic style of the townhalls of the Netherlands, 80 by 100 ft., was erected on Lexington Avenue, corner of 23d Street, in 1848, with accommodations for

19 for females, and 11 corporate schools.[1] In the same year there were employed 1,729 teachers, —of whom 440 were males and 1,289 were females.

The Public Schools are managed by a Board of Education, consisting of two commissioners from each ward. The local affairs of each ward are managed by local Boards of Trustees. The present system was organized under an act of 1812; but it has been modified by various acts since. In 1853 the Public School Society was dissolved and the schools under its control were merged in the ward schools of the city. The Board of Education distributes its duties among committees, and appoints a City Superintendent to exercise a general supervision over the schools.[2]

Academies and Colleges. There are in the city 3 academic institutions, 2 colleges, 4 medical colleges, 2 theological schools, and a great number of schools for perfecting students in special branches of education.[3] In addition to the schools sharing in the distribution of the school fund, there are a great number of mission, charity, parish, denominational, and private schools, of

1,000 pupils. The cost of the grounds, buildings, furniture, apparatus, and library was $100,801.48; and the cost of maintenance to Jan. 1, 1859, was $33,238.17. The students and the graduates in each year have been as follows:—

	1849.	1850.	1851.	1852.	1853.
Students......	201	285	383	498	536
Graduates....	.....	.....	.....	.....	17

	1854.	1855.	1856.	1857.	1858.
Students......	537	688	875	805	885
Graduates....	20	32	20	21	25

Applicants for admission to this school must reside in the city, be 14 years of age, and must have been students in the common schools 12 months, and must sustain an examination in the ordinary English studies. The school has a 5 years' course of study, and its graduates receive the degree of A.B. Several medals and money prizes have been endowed, and societies of students and alumni have been formed.

[1] The number of pupils in 1858 was as follows:—

Free Academy.............	885	Normal schools............	850
Boys' grammar school..	29,309	Corporate schools......	10,697
Girls' " " ..	26,991		
Primary department....	59,276	General aggregate......	171,768
Primary schools.........	23,760	Average attendance.....	51,430
Evening schools, about.	20,000		

[2] The "Free School Society," afterward the "Public School Society," was founded in June, 1805, and its first school was opened May 17, 1806. During its long career this honored society disbursed millions of dollars of public money, afforded education to 600,000 children, and fitted 1,200 teachers at its normal schools. It twice tendered its property to the city authorities to satisfy a popular objection that so much property should not be managed by a corporation; but in both instances the tender was declined. After the society was dissolved, its books and papers were deposited with the New York Historical Society. Its real estate used for school purposes consisted of 15 public schoolhouses, a trustees' hall on Grand Street, and a workshop on Crosby Street.—*Dissolution of Pub. School Soc. and Rep. of Com., p. 7.*

The 11 corporate schools share in the public money, but are in no sense under the care of the Board. The expenses of the public schools in 1858 were as follows:—

Salaries of teachers and janitors.........................	$ 556,445.93
New schoolhouses, repairs, purchase of new sites..	228,810.13
Fuel..	25,217.08
Books, stationery, and apparatus.........................	105,328.31
Salaries of superintendents, clerks, and officers of the board...	23,398.51
Support of Free Academy, including repairs.........	45,834.73
Evening schools...	64,515.03
Normal schools..	11,290.22
Contingent expenses......................................	45,427.05

Total expenses of public schools.................... $1,106,266.99

[3] The academies subject to the visitation of the Regents are— The Deaf and Dumb Institution, incorp. April 15, 1830. Grammar School of Columbia College, incorp. April 7, 1838. New York Free Academy, incorp. Oct. 31, 1849. Rutgers Female Institute, incorp. Jan. 23, 1840. Columbia College was chartered as "King's College" Oct. 31, 1754, and under the Colonial Government was aided by a lottery, grants of lands, and liberal private donations from England. A plot of ground between Murray, Barclay, Church, and Chapel Streets was given by Trinity Church for the college site, and the corner stone was laid July 23, 1756. The building was finished in 1760, and during the Revolution it was used for a hospital. In 1792 the trustees established a medical school, and sustained it until 1813. The college remained in its first location until the premises were greatly enhanced in value by the growth

of the city and the spread of commercial establishments around and beyond it. An act was passed March 19, 1857, authorizing the purchase of another site for college purposes, in accordance with which the grounds at the foot of Park Place were sold for $596,650, the college still retaining many lots on Barclay Street, Park Place, Murray Street, and College Place, which are rented for long periods, and whose prospective value it is impossible to estimate. The premises lately owned by the Trustees of the Deaf and Dumb Asylum on 49th Street, near 4th Avenue, were purchased, with 4 other lots, for $75,366.10, and fitted up at a total cost of $114,336.01. This change is understood to be only a temporary one, the ultimate intention being to locate on the premises of the Botanical Garden, between 47th and 51st Streets, on 5th Avenue. This garden, originally embracing about 20 acres, was laid out by Dr. David Hosack, early in the present century, for the introduction of exotic plants, experiments in agriculture and horticulture, and the promotion of science. The Governor, in his message of 1806, commended the object as worthy of public aid. In 1810 a memorial from the corporation of New York, the County and State Medical Society, and the Governors of the New York Hospital was addressed to the Legislature, in pursuance of which the Garden was purchased for $73,000, upon the appraisal of 3 commissioners, and placed in charge of the Regents of the University. The latter placed it in the hands of the Trustees of the College of Physicians and Surgeons, April 1, 1811. In 1814 it was granted by the Legislature to Columbia College, upon the condition that within 12 years the College should be removed thither; but in 1819 this condition was rescinded, and $10,000 was given to the College to aid in extending the premises upon the original location. These grounds have also increased greatly in value, and the College is at this moment perhaps the wealthiest in the Union, with this important feature: that its wealth is not coupled with irksome conditions and provisions, but left free to the discretion of its trustees. A grammar school has been many years connected with the College.

The University of the City of New York, located on the E. side of Washington Square, occupies a fine marble building in the English collegiate style of architecture. It is 100 by 200 ft. on the ground; and besides the portion occupied by the College, it contains rooms leased to societies, artists, and professional persons. This College grew out of a university with regard to a University on a more extended plan than any in the Union. A convention of literary and scientific gentlemen was held in the fall of 1830, and in that year a subscription was opened to raise $100,000 for the establishment of a University. An unhappy controversy arising directly upon the appointment of a chancelor, the institution did not attain the pre-eminence to which it aspired. Its course of study is essentially the same as that of other American colleges.

The College of Physicians and Surgeons is located on 23d St. and 4th Avenue. The site and grounds are leased with privilege of purchase, and funds derived from the proceeds of the sale of the building on Crosby St., formerly owned by it, have been raised to effect the purchase. The edifice now used is 75 by 100 ft., and is valued at $90,000. The first story is leased for stores. The College was incorp. by the Regents in 1807, by virtue of an act passed March 21, 1791. Lectures were first held in 1807–08. The Medical Department of Columbia College was merged in this Nov. 1, 1813. The College has 2 courses of lectures annually, and a library of 1,200 volumes.

The University Medical College, formed under an act of [Feb. 11, 1837, as a branch of the University of New York, is located on 14th St. between Irving Place and 3d Avenue. The building is 80 by 103 ft., 4 stories in front and 5 in rear, and is valued at $50,000. Its charter provides that 5 students of the Free Academy shall be admitted free of charge except the matriculation fee. Its library numbers 5,000 volumes, and its museum?is valued at $25,000. Two courses of lectures are delivered annually.

The New York Medical College, located on E. 13th St., was incorp. in 1850. The college building is 60 by 120 ft., and is valued at $70,000. It has a 5 months' course of lectures annually. Ten students are admitted upon payment of $20 and matriculation fee.

The Metropolitan Medical College, located at 68 E. Broadway,

which no reports are made collectively to the public. Many of these have special courses of study, or are limited to objects not embraced in a general plan of education. Several of these are numerously attended; and in some the extent of the course of study is equal to that in our colleges.[1]

About 250 periodicals, embracing daily, tri-weekly, semi-weekly, weekly, semi-monthly, monthly, and quarterly, are issued in the city of New York, counting under one title the several editions issued from the same press, unless bearing different names.[2]

---

was incorp. March 28, 1857. It has 2 courses of lectures annually.

The New York Preparatory School of Medicine, incorp. April 13, 1859, has not been fully organized. Its charter allows it to confer the degree of Bachelor of Medicine upon persons of not less than 19 years of age, after sustaining an examination in the studies embraced in its course, and places it under the visitation of the Regents.

The College of Pharmacy, chartered April 25, 1831, has rooms in the New York Medical College, at which lectures are delivered 4 months annually, on Chemistry, Materia Medica, and Botany, and diplomas are given. By an act of March 11, 1839, a diploma from this college is necessary for a person not otherwise duly qualified, to act as an apothecary in the city.

The New York County Medical Society was formed July 12, 1806, and now numbers 450 members.

The Pathological Society for improvement in medical practice meets semi-monthly.

The Academy of Medicine was formed in 1847 and incorp. in 1851. It meets monthly at the University, and sends 5 representatives to the State Medical Society. There are several other medical and surgical societies in various parts of the city.

The General Theological Seminary of the Prot. E. Church of the U. S. was established at New Haven in 1819 and removed to this city in 1822. It was incorp. April 5, 1822, and is well endowed. Its library numbers over 12,000 volumes. It occupies 2 handsome stone buildings, each 50 by 110 ft. on 20th St., between 9th and 10th Avenues. Its trustees consist of the Bishops of the U. S. and others appointed in proportion to moneys granted to the seminary.

The Union Theological Seminary (Presb.) was founded in 1836, and incorp. March 27, 1839. It is located in Waverly Place, on 8th St., and near Washington Square. It has a library of 16,000 volumes. Its Board of Directors are clergymen and laymen, an equal number of each, elected for 4 years.

Commercial colleges, writing schools, and studios for instruction in the fine arts, are numerous in the city. The *School of Design* at the Cooper Union is eminent among these for the extent of its facilities and the numbers that avail themselves of them. Music, drawing, and painting are carefully taught in many of the city schools; and the facilities at the Free Academy for these studies are superior to those in most other institutions.

[1] *The Protestant Episcopal Public School* was founded in 1710, and has continued until the present time. At some future time it will be largely aided by a bequest made Sept. 20, 1796, by Dr. John Baker, who, having no heirs, devised his country seat near 80th St., on the East River, embracing 46 acres, for a charity school. With a prudent forecast, the testator preserved the property from sale until after the death of 9 persons then living; and the dense part of the city has already approached the premises. An act passed April 16, 1859, authorized the sale of portions, but no benefit has hitherto been received. In April, 1859, 3 of the 9 lives were existing.

The following are the principal of the Roman Catholic schools :—

The College of St. Francis Xavier, 39 W. 15th St., is an institution under the care of 10 Jesuit priests.

Convent of the Most Holy Redeemer, in 3d St., is under the care of 7 priests of the Order of Redemptorists.

St. Vincent's Academy, 44 2d St., is under the care of the Brothers of the Christian Schools.

Academy of the Holy Infancy, in Manhattanville, and the *Convent and Academy of the Sacred Heart*, in Manhattanville, are under the charge of the Ladies of the Sacred Heart; the latter has 180 pupils. An institution of the same name at 49 W. 17th St., under similar direction, has 86 pupils.

Mother House and Academy of Mount St. Vincent, on 105th St., upon the premises of the Central Park, has 180 pupils.

St. Mary's School, at 229 East Broadway, is under the charge of Sisters of Charity, and has 108 pupils.

St. Peter's School, at 16 Barclay St., is under the charge of Sisters of Charity, and has 80 pupils.

St. Joseph's School, on 6th Avenue, is under the charge of Sisters of Charity.

St. Lawrence School, Yorkville, is under the charge of Sisters of Charity, and has 40 pupils.

St. Stephen's School.

St. Vincent's School has 80 boys and 50 girls; and 65 girls in the preparatory department.

Free Catholic Schools.—There are 25 schools of this class reported in the city; at which 4,920 boys and 5,530 girls are taught. Most of the schools have male and female departments; and of these 7 are taught by Brothers of the Christian Schools, 9 by Sisters of Charity, 2 by Ladies of the Sacred Heart, 2 by Sisters of Notre Dame, 1 by Sisters of Mercy, and 1 by lay teachers. Of several the teachers are not specified. These schools are named St. Patrick's, St. Mary's, St. Joseph's, St. James's, St.

Francis Xavier's, Manhattanville, St. Bridget's, Transfiguration, Mount St. Vincent, St. Lawrence, Sacred Heart Free School, St. Catharine's, Most Holy Redeemer's, St. Alphonso's, St. Vincent de Paul's, Nativity, St. Columba, Holy Cross, St. Stephen's, St. John the Evangelist's, St. Paul's, Immaculate Conception, St. Nicholas, St. Francis's, and St. Johns's.

[2] *New York Gazette*, the first paper published in the Colony of New York, was commenced in 1725 by William Bradford. It was the fifth then in existence in the American Colonies. Bradford continued its publisher about 17 years. In 1742 its name was changed to the

New York Gazette and Weekly Post Boy, and it was published by James Parker and a succession of owners until 1773, when it was discontinued.

New York Weekly Journal, the second paper in the Colony, was commenced in New York in 1733 by John Peter Zenger. He died in 1746, and the paper was conducted by his widow, and afterward by his son, until 1752, when it was discontinued. This paper opposed the administration of Governor Crosby and supported the interest of Rip Van Dam, who had previously conducted the administration. The ballads, serious charges, and, above all, the home truths in his democratic journal irritated Crosby and his Council to madness. Zenger was confined several months by order of the Governor and Council for printing and publishing seditious libels, treated with unwarrantable severity, deprived of pen, ink, and paper, and denied the visits of his friends. The popular feeling, however, was strongly against these proceedings. The Assembly, notwithstanding the application of the Governor, refused to concur with him and his Council. The Mayor and the magistrates also refused to obey the mandate of the Governor and Council, and to attend the burning of the libelous papers "by the common hangman and whipper, near the pillory." The grand jury manifested equal contumacy, and ignored the presentment against Zenger. The attorney general was then directed to file *an information*. The judges refused to hear and allow the exceptions taken by Zenger's counsel, and excluded them from the bar; but he was ably defended by other counsel, and especially by Andrew Hamilton, then a barrister of Philadelphia. Zenger pleaded not guilty. His counsel admitted the printing and publishing of the papers, and offered to give their truth in evidence. The counsel for the prosecution then said, "The jury must find a verdict for the king;" and gave the usual definition of a libel, asserting that "whether the person defamed was a private man or a magistrate, whether living or dead, whether the libel was true or false, or whether the party against whom it was made was of good or evil fame, it was nevertheless a libel." He then quoted from the Acts of the Apostles and from one of the Epistles of Peter, to show that it was a very great offense to speak evil of dignities, and insisted upon the criminality by the laws of God and man of reviling those in authority, and consequently that Mr. Zenger had offended in a most notorious and gross manner in scandalizing his Excellency our Governor, "who," said the counsel, "is the king's immediate representative, and supreme magistrate of this province." Mr. Hamilton remarked in his reply, that we are charged with printing a certain *false*, malicious, seditious, and scandalous libel. The word *false* must have some meaning; or else how came it there? and he put the case, whether if the information had been for printing a certain *true* libel, would that be the same thing. "And to show the court that I am in good earnest," said he, "I will agree that if he can prove the facts charged upon us to be *false*, I will own them to be scandalous, seditious, and a libel." He then further offered that, to save the prosecution the trouble of proving the papers to be false, the defendant would prove them to be true. To this Chief Justice De Lancey objected, "You cannot be admitted to give the truth of a libel in evidence: the law is clear that you cannot justify a libel." Mr. Hamilton maintained that leaving the court to determine whether the words were libelous or not rendered juries useless, or worse. "It was true," he said, "in times past it was a crime to speak truth, and in that terrible court of Star Chamber many worthy and brave men suffered for so doing; and yet even in that court and in those bad times a great and good man durst say, what I hope will not be taken amiss in me to say in this place, to wit :—'The practice of information for libels is a sword in the hands of a wicked king and an arrant coward to cut down and destroy the innocent.'

The Benevolent Institutions of New York are numerous, and comprehend measures for the relief of nearly every variety of human suffering. Those under the direct charge of the city have already been noticed. The greater part of other institutions of like character are under the management of companies incorporated for limited and special objects. Prominent among these are the hospitals and dispensaries, affording relief to every class of the sick and distressed. Up to 1857, at these various institutions, 179,377 persons had been vaccinated; 1,666,559 patients had been treated; and $297,761.60 had been expended. The Legislature usually appropriates money to several of these institutions.[1] Several of the more important of the benevolent institutions are supported wholly, or in part, by the State, among which are the Deaf and Dumb Asylum,[2] the Institution for the Blind, and the Society for the Reformation of Juvenile Delinquents.

the one cannot, because of his high station, and the other dare not, because of his want of courage, defend himself in another manner.'" The jury, after a short consultation, returned a verdict of not guilty, to the great mortification of the court and of Zenger's persecutors, but with great satisfaction to the people. Such was the struggle which the press had to maintain only one hundred years ago, and only forty years before the Revolution gave to its freedom the sanction of Government and the impress of authority.—*Introduction to the Nat. History of the State by Wm. H. Seward.*

The New York Evening Post was commenced in 1746, but was soon discontinued.

The New York Mercury was commenced by Hugh Gaine, and continued by him 31 years. It was discontinued at the close of the Revolutionary War.

The New York Gazette was commenced in 1759 by Wm. Wyman. It continued irregularly until 1767, when it was discontinued.

The American Chronicle was commenced by S. Farley in 1761, and was discontinued the next year.

The New York Packet was commenced in 1763. It had only a brief existence.

The New York Journal and General Advertiser was commenced in 1766 by John Holt.

The New York Chronicle was commenced in 1768 by Alexander and James Robinson, and continued until 1772.

Rivington's New York Gazetteer; or, The Connecticut, New Jersey, Hudson's River, and Quebec Weekly Advertiser, was commenced in 1773 by James Rivington. This paper appeared during the Revolution as

The Royal Gazette, semi-w., published by "James Rivington, printer to the king's most excellent majesty."

New York Packet and American Advertiser was commenced in 1776 by Samuel Loudon. No other papers appeared in New York until the close of the war.

For list of papers since the Revolution, see p. 442.

[1] *The New York Hospital,* founded in 1770, was incorp. June 13, 1771, and is under the care of 26 governors. It has two very extensive establishments,—the hospital proper, upon Broadway, between Worth and Duane Sts., and the Bloomingdale Lunatic Asylum, on 117th St. near 10th Avenue. The first hospital, built in 1773–75, was burned. A new one was soon after begun, and while still unfinished was occupied by British and Hessian troops for barracks, and it was not finally opened for patients until Jan. 3, 1791. On the 14th of March, 1806, the Legislature enacted that $12,500 should be given to the hospital annually for 50 years, on condition that apartments for various forms and degrees of insanity should be prepared, and that an annual report be made to the Legislature. The sum thus appropriated was to be chargeable upon duties on auction sales. In 1801 a lying-in ward was opened, and continued 20 years. In 1806 the lunatic department was organized, and one of the buildings of the present hospital was erected; but in 1816 a change of site was authorized. A library was founded in 1796, and a pathological cabinet in 1840; but a suitable building was not provided for the latter until 1856. In 1853 a new and spacious building, s. of the main hospital, was erected, upon a plan the most perfect that experience could devise. It was finished in 1855, at a cost of $140,103.92. Clinical instruction, both medical and surgical, has long been given; and two operating theatres have been provided for this purpose. The hospital on Broadway is now limited to the receiving of cases of sudden injuries from accident, and non-contagious diseases in which there is prospect of improvement; and it is not intended for the support of the incurable, or to supply in any sense the place of a poorhouse. Those received are either supported gratuitously, or pay at a rate barely sufficient to defray cost of support. The former constitute about 40 per cent. of the entire number treated. Seamen are received and their expenses are paid wholly or in part from the hospital money paid by the U. S. Government. From Feb. 1, 1792, to 1856, 106,111 patients had been received, of whom 77,390 had been cured and 4,768 relieved. Of the 10,893 who died, many were brought in from the street in a dying condition. Nearly 4,000 now receive the benefits of the hospital yearly.

The Lunatic Asylum, in 1818, was located at Bloomingdale. A building was commenced May 7, 1818, and was opened to patients in June, 1821. The plan comprehends a center building 211 by 60 feet, with 2 detached wings. A wing for the violent insane male patients was built in 1830, and another for the

like class of females in 1837, making the whole cost, up to 1839, $200,000. In 1854 two spacious 2 story brick buildings were erected, at a cost of $52,000. From May, 1821, to Jan. 1856, 4,182 patients were received here, of whom 1,911 were cured, 851 improved, and 471 died. The grounds have an extent of about 40 acres, and are finely adapted to outdoor exercise in fine weather. The annual expense of both institutions is about $146,000.

St. Vincent's Hospital, at 102 and 104 E. 13th St., was established by, and is under the care of, Sisters of Charity.

St. Luke's Hospital is located at the corner of 5th Avenue and 54th St. The building was erected in 1854, and is designed to accommodate 230 patients.

Jews' Hospital is on W. 28th St., between 7th and 8th Avenues. The society was formed and a building erected in 1854. The hospital has received a bequest of $20,000 from the late Mr. Touro, of New Orleans.

Woman's Hospital, on Madison Avenue, was established in Feb. 1855, by Dr. J. Marion Sims, and incorp. April 18, 1857, under 27 governors.

New York Eye and Ear Infirmary, at the corner of 2d Avenue and 13th St., was incorp. March 29, 1822. The present building was completed in 1856, at a cost of $41,252.39, including the lot. It has usually received appropriations from the city and State. Previous to 1856, 51,580 persons had received treatment in the institution.

New York Ophthalmic Hospital, on Stuyvesant St., was incorp. April 21, 1852, and opened May 25 following. A course of lectures upon diseases of the eye is delivered annually.

The Children's Hospital, on E. 51st St., near Lexington Avenue, was established for the cure of poor children otherwise destitute of aid. It is under the care of an association of ladies.

New Asylum for Lying-in Women, at 85 Marion St., is under the care of lady managers.

The New York Dispensary, on White, corner of Center St., was established in 1790, and incorp. April 8, 1795. It supplies the district s. of a line passing through Spring, Broadway, 14th, 1st Avenue, Allen, and Pike Sts.

The Eastern Dispensary, at 74 Ludlow St., was incorp. April 25, 1832. It supplies the district e. of the latter and s. of 14th St.

The Northern Dispensary, on Christopher, corner of 6th St., was incorp. Nov. 28, 1828, and opened in 1829. Its district lies w. of Broadway, between Spring and 23d Sts.

The Demilt Dispensary, on the corner of 23d St. and 2d Avenue, was incorp. May 7, 1851. It was founded upon the bequest of Miss Demilt, and cost about $30,000. Its district is e. of 5th Avenue, between 14th and 40th Sts.

North Western Dispensary, at 511 8th Avenue, was incorp. May 29, 1852. Its district is w. of 5th Avenue, between 23d and 60th Sts.

The German Dispensary, at 132 New Canal St., was organized in Jan. 1857. Professors of the College of Physicians serv gratuitously, and have distributed the labor into divisions.

The Homeopathic Dispensary, at 59 Bond St., was established in 1855 by Dr. Otto Fullgraff, and is supported entirely by private subscription.

[2] *The New York Institution for the Deaf and Dumb* was incorp. April 15, 1817, and opened May 12, 1818. It was located in the "New City Hall" until 1839, when it was removed to E. 50th St., corner of 4th Avenue,—the premises now occupied by Columbia College. It there remained until the wants of the institution required more ample accommodations and the growth of the city suggested a retreat from the approaching pressure of business. A fine tract of nearly 40 acres at Fanwood, on the Hudson, on 164th St., was accordingly purchased, and the erection of buildings was commenced in 1853. They are in the aggregate 650 feet in length, and cover 2 acres. The institution has accommodations for 450 pupils. The work was sufficiently advanced to justify removal toward the close of 1856. The cost greatly exceeded the estimate; and under an act of April, 1857, the institution was assumed by the State, with all the property connected therewith. Pupils are received from every co. of the State, and to a limited extent from New Jersey. It is strictly an educational institution, and is designed to impart a useful amount of literary instruction, and the knowledge of some mechanical operation by which to gain support. Dr. Harvey P. Peet has been for many years President of the Institution.

The New York Institution for the Blind, incorp. April 21, 1831, was opened March 15, 1832, principally through the influence of Dr. Samuel Akerly, Samuel Wood, and Dr. John D. Russ. A

The city of New York has a large number of charitable corporations chiefly dependent upon private subscriptions for support; and their management is highly creditable to those who have bestowed their time and money for the relief of the suffering and friendless. Several of these have received aid from the State and the city in their organization and support.[1]

school with 6 pupils was opened May 19, 1832, at 47 Mercer St., under Dr. Russ. By the aid of fairs and donations from individuals and the city, a piece of ground and buildings on 8th Avenue were obtained of James Boorman at a nominal rent, with a covenant to sell. An instructor in the mechanic arts was procured, and Dec. 2, 1833, the first public exhibition was held at the City Hall. The success in teaching from raised letters and characters, the proficiency of the 16 pupils in reading, geography, arithmetic, and especially in music, and the skill of their workmanship in mats, mattresses, and baskets, excited great interest. The present site, between 8th and 9th Avenues and 33d and 34th Sts., was purchased of Mr. Boorman at a reduction of more than $10,000 below what it could have been sold for; and on the 30th of April, 1836, $12,000 was given by the State, conditioned to the raising of $8,000 more by the managers. In 1839 $15,000 was given to erect buildings. Annual reports are made to the State Legislature. State pupils have been received since 1834; and for many years the institution has received pupils from New Jersey. The site, originally beyond the improved portion of the city, is now in the midst of a densely settled quarter, and the square which it occupies is valued at $400,000. The managers are endeavoring to obtain leave to sell and erect new buildings on the upper part of the island. The proceeds of the sale would, it is believed, procure new and superior premises without other aid. The institution now has 200 pupils, and employs 11 blind instructors and assistants. The manual trades taught are broom, mat, bandbox, and mattress making and needle work. Musical instruction is received with great facility by the blind; and with those that evince decided talent it often becomes a means of support. Those of proper age are instructed in the common and higher branches of English education; and the number of books with raised characters now prepared for the blind is quite extensive, including the entire Bible, and volumes upon almost every branch of useful learning.

The New York Juvenile Asylum is intended to secure the maintenance and promote the welfare of children under 14 years of age who may be in destitute circumstances. This asylum was incorp. June 30, 1851. Its office is located at 23 W. 13th St., and its temporary asylum is at the foot of E. 50th St. A permanent asylum, erected on 175th St., near High Bridge, was opened April 2, 1856. This society takes children between 7 and 14 intrusted to it by parents, guardians, or other competent authority, and affords them the means of a moral and industrial education. A fund originally of $50,000, and afterward of $20,000 in addition, was raised by subscription; and to this $40,000 was added by the city. The total number sent to the house of reception up to Jan. 1859, was 4,893. Several companies of children are sent annually to the Western States, to be indentured to farmers and others, under the direction of a judicious person. Children are also bound out in the city and vicinity as occasion offers. An act of March 25, 1856, directed a sum not exceeding $75 per annum to be levied by tax and paid to this asylum for each child committed by the city and supported by the society, and gave $20,000 toward the erection of a new house of reception on 13th St. The edifice is now nearly completed.

The Society for the Prevention of Pauperism, formed Dec. 16, 1817, after promoting the establishment of the first Savings Bank and other institutions of public utility, resolved itself into *The Society for the Reformation of Juvenile Delinquents*, Dec. 19, 1823, and measures were taken to carry the purpose implied by the name into effect. An act of incorporation was obtained March 29, 1824; and, having in that year raised $17,000 and obtained possession of the U. S. Arsenal near Madison Square, the establishment was opened Jan 1, 1825, with 9 inmates. This place was burned in 1839, and the location changed to a building on the East River at the foot of 23d St., erected for a fever hospital. In 1851 the society exchanged a parcel of land it possessed on Wards Island for about 36 acres on the s. end of Randalls Island, where the corner stone of a new building was laid Nov. 24, 1852, by the Mayor. The buildings were opened Nov. 24, 1854. The male department will consist of a central building and 4 wings, of which 2 are parallel to the front of the center building, and form together with it a front of 590 ft. upon the river. The other two wings are to radiate from the center of the rear at angles of 60°; they have not yet been erected. The arrangement admits of the necessary classification and embraces every modern improvement. A workshop 3 stories high and 30 by 100 ft. is erected in the rear of each of the front wings. The female department, when completed, will be on a plan similar to the other, of 250 ft. front, and otherwise proportionally smaller. With the refuse stone obtained in excavation and grading, a sea wall was built out to low water mark; and some seven acres were thus added to the grounds. The entire cost, including the buildings, up to Nov. 1854, was $310,441.15, of which $14,199.39 had been for the Female Department. The whole number of inmates from its first opening to 1859 was 7,650; and at the beginning of that year it contained 463 boys and 77 girls. A female department is now in course of building,

and when complete will afford to the whole a capacity for 1,000 inmates. Juvenile offenders from the several counties have been as follows :—

	1851.	1852.	1853.	1854.	1855.	1856.	1857.	1868.
N. Y. Police	126	125	102	142	96	61	93	83
" Sessions	90	75	123	70	73	44	203	139
Gov. of Almshouse	4	7	6	11	8	7	5	1
Rensselaer Co	17	25	27	37	40	48	52	18
Kings Co	26	27	46	44	70	55	57	23
Albany Co	30	27	27	24	47	23	23	32
Other Cos	7	7	8	14	8	8	19	17

Of the cos. not enumerated, Westchester has sent 15, Ulster 11, Queens 10, Dutchess 9, Orange and Columbia each 8, Suffolk 7, Greene 6, Schoharie, Saratoga, and Oneida each 4, Monroe and Sullivan each 3, Onondaga, Putnam, and Rockland each 2, and Erie and Richmond each 1. Of 2,641 received in 8 years, 2,039 were white boys, 439 white girls, 138 black boys, and 25 black girls; as to nativity, 1,548 were Irish, 445 American, 218 German, 150 English, 53 Scotch, 30 French, 10 Italian, 4 Swedes,and 1 each Spanish, Polish, Russian, Prussian, Dane, Dutch, Welsh, and Belgian.

The Prison Association of New York, incorp. in 1846, for the relief and encouragement of discharged convicts, is elsewhere more fully noticed. It has a female department, organized in 1844, to provide employment for discharged female prisoners.

[1] *The Orphan Asylum Society of New York* was incorp. April 7, 1807. It was located on the banks of the Hudson, near 80th St., in 1840. It has 9 acres of grounds and a building 120 by 60 ft., pleasantly situated. About 200 orphans are supported in the institution.

The Society for the Relief of Half-Orphans and Destitute Children was established Dec. 16, 1835, and incorp. April 18, 1837. It is located at No. 7 10th St., and is usually known as the "Protestant Half-Orphan Asylum." It has received donations of $20,000 from John Hosburgh and of $5,000 each from James Boorman, John Jacob Astor, Peter G. Stuyvesant, and the daughters of John Mason. The whole number of inmates received up to 1859 was 1,884, and the number then remaining was 136 boys and 101 girls.—*Common Council Manual*, 1859, *p*. 580.

The Roman Catholic Orphan Asylum, on Prince St., was incorp. April 29, 1836. It is under the charge of Sisters of Charity, and has 300 inmates,—all females.

St. Patrick's Orphan Asylum has a male and female department. The male department, on 51st St., has 400 inmates, and the female department, on Prince St., corner of Mott St., 300. They are both under the same trustees, and are managed by Sisters of Charity.

The Orphans' Home of the Protestant Episcopal Church, at 74 Hammond St., was incorp. April 16, 1838.

Leake and Watts Orphan House is located at Manhattanville, between 9th and 10th Avenues and 111th and 112th Sts. This noble charity was founded by the bequest of J. A. Leake, and enhanced by the liberality of Mr. Watts, who waived a claim he had upon the legacy. It is incorp. under the general law.

St. Luke's Home for Indigent Christian Females is at 453 Hudson St.

House and School of Industry, at 100 W. 16th St., is for the gratuitous instruction of poor females in needle work.

Association for the Relief of Respectable Aged and Indigent Females is located at 20th St., between 2d and 3d Avenues.

Nursery for the Children of Poor Women, at 223 6th Avenue, is under lady managers.

Magdalen Female Benevolent Asylum, between 88th and 89th Sts. and 4th and 5th Avenues, is under the care of lady managers, has 40 inmates, and is designed to encourage reform in abandoned females.

American Female Guardian Society and Home for the Friendless, on E. 30th St., between 4th and Madison Avenues, was formed in 1834. It received by donations in 1857 and '58 $49,719.79. The home school had 108 girls and 112 boys, industrial school No. 1 340 girls, and No. 2 165 girls. It is managed and chiefly supported by ladies.

St. Catharine's Convent and House of Protection, on Houston St., corner of Murray St., is under the charge of Sisters of Charity.

New York Ladies' Home Missionary Society of the Methodist Episcopal Church, on the site of the "Old Brewery," 61 Park St., was incorp. March 20, 1856.

St. Joseph's Asylum was incorp. April 15, 1859. It is designed to support and educate in some useful employment poor orphan, half-orphan, homeless, and neglected children, especially of German origin. It has 16 managers.

Five Points House of Industry is located on North St., Nos. 155, 157, 159.

Numerous institutions of beneficence are established upon the principle of mutual support, all of which derive their means from fixed contributions of members. The number of these is very great, including many which are limited to particular nationalities and to certain mechanical or other occupations.[1] The city has a large number of religious associations and societies for the promotion of morality,—some national or cosmopolitan in their field of operation, and others local in their range. While some of these oppose vice and wrong in their widest sense, others restrict their efforts to narrower limits of labor and concentrate upon a single object the united efforts of their members. There are at present about 290 churches in the city of New York.[2]

Children's Aid Society, office No. 11 Clinton Hall, Astor Place, was formed in 1853. It has for its object to provide homes and employment for destitute children, and, to a limited extent, for adults of both sexes. Up to 1858 it had provided homes for 3,576. In 1857 it sent 468 boys, 200 girls, 28 men, and 37 women to other States. It had opened 6 industrial schools, with a total of 968 pupils, maintained a lodginghouse for newsboys and peddlers, at a low charge, and another one for girls, and had under its direction several boys' meetings and libraries. Its annual expenses are about $15,000, not including a large amount of gratuitous services.

New York Association for Improving the Condition of the Poor was formed in 1843, and incorp. Dec. 6, 1848. Its object is to afford temporary relief to such as do not come within the sphere of other existing charities, and to elevate the physical and moral condition of the indigent. To discountenance indiscriminate almsgiving and street begging, it inquires through its visitors into the merits of applications, and for this end has a supervisory council of 5 to each ward, and as many visitors as may be needed. It is supported by annual donations and collections, and in the year ending Oct. 14, 1857, expended $41,480.88.

The American Bible Society, formed May, 1816, as a national institution, claims notice in this place from the spacious and elegant edifice which it has erected. This structure occupies three-fourths of an acre, and is nearly triangular, extending 198 ft. on 4th Avenue, 202 ft. on 8th St., 96 ft. on 3d Avenue, and 232 ft. on 9th St., with a court within. It cost nearly $300,000, and contains the offices of numerous religious and denominational societies. Its manufactory of Bibles and Testaments, when in full operation, employs 600 persons. A City Bible Society was formed several years before the one above noticed; and numerous kindred associations have been formed at different periods.

[1] Of this class are Masonic, Odd Fellows, and other secret societies who possess funds for the relief of the sick, the support of widows and orphans, and the burial of the dead. Others, limited to particular occupations, some of which have been discontinued, have been chiefly as follows:—

The Marine Society of New York was created by patent April 12, 1770. It has for its principal object to collect moneys, by admission fees and yearly dues of members, for the relief of the widows and orphans of seamen. Up to 1826 it had distributed $88,100 for these objects. Its meetings are held at the United States Hotel, corner of Pearl and Fulton Sts.; and its chief importance now arises from the circumstance that its president is one of the trustees of the Sailors' Snug Harbor, on Staten Island. The importance of that noble trust will serve to perpetuate this society.

The New York Nautical Society was established in 1820, for charitable purposes and the promotion of useful improvements. Its members were those who had been shipmasters or commanders of vessels.

The New York Waterman's Society was formed in 1825, for benevolent purposes and the promotion of useful improvements in navigation. It is supposed to have been discontinued.

The Pilot's Charitable Society was formed in 1817, for benevolent and charitable purposes.

The Humane Society was formed in 1787.

The Association for the Relief of Disabled Firemen is a charity devoted to the objects expressed in its title.

General Society of Mechanics and Tradesmen was incorp. March 14, 1792.

The Mutual Benefit Society and the *Mutual Aid Society of the City of New York* are now extinct. *The House Carpenters' Society*; the *New York Society of Journeymen Shipwrights*; the *Provident Society*; and the *Benevolent Society* are charitable associations, from which we have no returns.

Manhattan Provident Society of the City of New York was formed Nov. 17, 1708.

Friendly Society of the Town of Harlem was formed Feb. 10, 1809.

New York Masons' Society was formed Feb. 20, 1807.

Saint David's Benevolent Society (Welsh) was formed in 1800. It was soon discontinued.

Albion Benevolent Society was formed about 1800. It was soon discontinued.

Ancient Britons' Benefit Society was formed about 1805, from the two latter, and incorp. Feb. 27, 1807. It continued until 1835, when the *Saint David's Benefit & Benevolent Society* was formed. It divided 3 years after; and in Jan. 1841, *Saint David's Benefit Society* and

The Welsh Society were formed. These were merged in the *Saint David's Benefit Society*, which is still continued.

Saint Patrick's Society and the *Hibernia Provident Society of the City of New York* were formed in April, 1807.

Saint Andrew's Society (Scotch) was formed in 1756. Its anniversary is Nov. 30.

Caledonia Society of the City of New York was formed April 6, 1807.

Saint George's Society is a society of English.

Saint Nicholas Society (Dutch) is chiefly composed of the descendants of the old Dutch colonists.

New England Society holds its anniversary Dec. 22.

Besides these, there are and have been a great number of societies and unions, particularly among the German, Irish, Italian, and other foreign classes, and among the Jews and other denominations, concerning which it is difficult to procure full statistics, or even the names. The "George Clinton Society," "Washington Benevolent Society," "Tammany Society," or "Columbian Order," (the latter founded in 1805, and still existing,) are among those memorable for their political influence; the "Society of Cincinnati," for its Revolutionary associations, and the "Wilberforce Philanthropic Society," "Manumission Society" of 1785, "Society for the Relief of Imprisoned Debtors," and a great variety of others, for their labors in the field of charities, but which have disappeared with the abuses they combated, and their elements re-organized under other names, for new labors which the misfortunes, vices, and crimes of mankind are constantly providing.

[2] The following table contains some of the principal statistics of the churches in the city. The dates of first churches in the several denominations are given upon the authority of Greenleaf's *History of the Churches of New York*. The lists given by that author include several societies not owning church edifices, on which account the numbers are larger than those of the census:—

DENOMINATIONS.	Date of first church.	No. in 1845. (Greenleaf.)	No. in 1850. (Greenleaf.)	No. in 1855. (Census.)	No. in 1859. (Directory.)	No. extinct up to 1850. (Greenleaf.)
African Methodist	1801	7	7	6	5	
Associate Presbyterian	......	...	...	6		
Associate Reformed Presbyterian	......	...	...	4	2	
Baptist	1724	31*a*	38*a*	29	32*a*	15
Calvinistic Methodist and other	......	3	3	5	1	
Christian	1829	2	2	1	1	
Congregational	1804	7	8	9	5	10*b*
Congregational Methodist	......	...	...	1	1	
Disciples	......	...	...	1	1	
Evangelical Lutheran	1663	5	8	...	7	1
Free Will Baptist	......	...	...	1		
Friends	1703	4	4	4	3	1
Jews	1706	9	10	10	17	
Methodist Episcopal	1766	25	31	33	32	
Moravian	1748	1	1	1	2	
Presbyterian	1716	38	44	33	43	21
Primitive Methodist	1829	1	1	1		
Protestant Episcopal	1664	41	49	43	51	10
Protestant Methodist	......	2	2	...	1	
Reformed Covenanters	......	...	...	4	1	
Reformed Protestant Dutch	1626	16	17	22	21	3
Roman Catholic *c*	1783	16	19	24	29	
Second Advent	......	...	...	2	1	
Seventh Day Baptist	......	...	...	1	1	
Swedenborgian or New Jerusalem	1808	2	2	..	2	
Unitarian	1819	2	2	2	2	
Universalist	1796	4	4	4	4	2
United Covenanters	......	...	...	4		
Wesleyan Methodist	1841	2	2	3	4	
Other churches	......	...	...	...	11	
Total		218	254	249	288	63

a These numbers may include churches other than those termed common or "Close Communion" Baptists.

b Several of these became Presbyterian.

c Father Jogues, a Jesuit, was the first Roman Catholic priest

The Literary and Library Societies of the city exert an important influence upon the intellectual condition of the people. Many of the libraries are extensive and are provided with ample accommodations for the preservation and care of the books and for the convenience of students.[1]

The population of New York has increased with great rapidity since the commencement of the

in New York. He suffered martyrdom at Caughnawaga, Sept. 27, 1642, at the hands of the Iroquois. The first religious services of this Church were held by Father Farmer, of Philadelphia, about 1781–82. The first church was built in 1786, and named St. Peter. Its chief benefactor was Charles III., King of Spain, who gave $10,000.

The first church edifice was erected near the Fort, in 1633, and in 1642 was superseded by one built of stone within the Fort. The Reformed Dutch Church retained the ascendency until 1664, when the chapel in the Fort was devoted to the English service. Trinity, formed in 1697, received grants of property from the Government, which by the subsequent growth of the city have become enhanced in value beyond parallel in America, if not in the world. Its revenues are usually considered adequate not only for the support of its several chapels and other edifices of worship, but for aiding liberally the poorer churches of this denomination throughout the country. Its income, already very large, will in a few years be greatly increased as leases at a low rate for long periods expire and the property is again offered for lease. The property of the Collegiate Dutch Church is also of great value, and surpassed only by that of Trinity Church. During the Revolution the Presbyterian and Dutch Churches were used by the British as riding schools, prisons, and for other military purposes. Within a few years most of the church buildings in the lower part of the city have been sold, their sites occupied for commercial purposes, and costly edifices of great architectural beauty have been erected "up town."

[1] *The New York Library Society* was first started in 1700, when Rev. John Sharp, chaplain of Lord Bellemont, gave a collection of books to be styled the "Public Library of New York." The society was incorp. in 1752, and was organized under its present name in 1754. The library was mostly scattered during the Revolution; but its charter was revived Feb. 18, 1789, and the books as far as possible were recollected. It was at first kept in the City Hall. In 1793 it was removed to a building in Nassau St., afterward to Chambers St., and in 1840 to a new building corner of Broadway and Leonard Sts. It was afterward moved to the Bible House, and in 1857 to its present quarters, University Place, between 12th and 13th Sts. The library building is a fine edifice, and the library now contains 40,000 vols.

The New York Historical Society was organized Dec. 10, 1804, and incorp. Feb. 10, 1809. After occupying rooms many years in the New York University Buildings, it was removed in 1857 to a new, fireproof building on 2d Avenue, corner of 11th St., which was dedicated Nov. 17 of that year. This society possesses a library of 30,000 volumes, particularly rich in historical works and manuscripts, a choice gallery of paintings and collection of antiquities, coins, medals, and charts. Among its collections are a series of large tablets of Assyrian sculpture, the gift of James Lenox, Esq. Under a special act of April 12, 1856, the premises were made exempt from sale on execution, and the law is so framed that the society's property cannot be encumbered by mortgage. Regular meetings of the society are held on the first Tuesday of each month.

The Mercantile Library Association, at Clinton Hall, Astor Place, was organized in 1820, and has a library, reading room, lecture room, and cabinet. It was originally intended for the use of merchants' clerks, but is now accessible to all. Its library, especially full in periodicals, numbers 55,000 volumes; and the association has about 4,500 members. It formerly occupied the premises of Old Clinton Hall, on Beekman St., near the Park.

New York Law Institute, founded through the exertions of the late Chancellor Kent, was formed in 1828 and incorp. Feb. 22, 1830. It contains about 6,500 volumes, forming one of the most valuable and perfect collections of the kind in the United States. It is located at 45 Chambers St., to which place it was removed in 1855. Membership is confined to counsellors, solicitors, and attorneys. Judges of the Federal and State Courts, and strangers generally, are allowed to visit and use the library.

The Mechanics' Institute, located at No. 20 4th Avenue, was incorp. April 24, 1833. Its objects are to diffuse knowledge among the mechanical classes, to found lectures on natural, mechanical, and chemical philosophy, and scientific subjects, to open schools, and hold annual fairs. It has established classes in modeling, machinery, architecture, and ornamental drawing, a winter course of lectures, a reading room, and a library of 6,000 volumes, all of which are free to mechanics, workingmen, and apprentices of the city.

The Astor Library was founded upon a bequest of $400,000 made by John Jacob Astor in his will, Aug. 22, 1839. Its trustees organized in May, 1848, and employed Dr. Joseph G. Cogswell to visit Europe for the purchase of books. On the 10th of Dec. 1849, they adopted a plan for an edifice, 120 by 65 ft., which was opened to the public Feb. 1, 1854. On the 31st of Oct. 1855, Wm. B. Astor presented to the trustees a lot, 80 by

100 ft., adjoining the library, upon which has been erected a building similar to the first, the two forming the most spacious library rooms in America. The buildings will contain 200,000 volumes, and half that number are already in the library. This noble institution is situated on La Fayette Place, in a quiet quarter of the city, and is open to all without charge. Books are not allowed to be taken from the rooms. The trustees are required to report annually to the Legislature.

The Printers' Free Library, located at No. 3 Chambers St., was founded in 1823 by the New York Typographical Society, for the benefit of those employed in printing and binding books. It has 3,500 volumes.

The Apprentices' Library, at Mechanics' Hall, 472 Broadway near Grand St., is free to apprentices, and open to journeymen upon payment of $1 annually. It numbers 16,000 volumes.

The Libraries of the City Corporation, of Columbia College, of the Free Academy, of the several hospitals, of the medical colleges, of the theological seminaries, of the Bible Societies, and of several other institutions, are extensive, and some of them are very valuable in their several departments.

The Cooper Institute, a fine edifice of brownstone, covers an entire block between 3d and 4th Avenues and 7th and 8th Streets. It was erected by Peter Cooper, Esq., at a cost of $300,000, to promote the advancement of science and a knowledge of the useful arts. The first and second stories are to be rented and the avails devoted to the expenses of the establishment. In the basement is a lecture room, 125 ft. by 82 ft., and 21 ft. high. The three upper stories are arranged for purposes of instruction, and contain a very large hall, with a gallery designed ultimately as a free public exchange. A school of design is in operation in these rooms, and is attended by some 50 young ladies under instruction in engraving, lithographic drawing, and painting. The design of this institution is eminently creditable to the enlightened views of its munificent projector, and will associate his name with those who have done much for the useful arts and deserved well of mankind. The building is known as "The Union," and, in accordance with an act of February 17, 1857, it has been placed in charge of trustees.

The American Institute was incorp. May 29, 1829, for the purpose of encouraging and promoting domestic industry in this State and the United States, in agriculture, commerce, manufactures, and the arts. It aims to promote these objects by an annual exhibition of machines and manufactures, the awarding of premiums, and the formation of a repository of models and a library of books relating to the useful arts; and for this purpose it may hold property producing an income of $30,000 per annum. It has connected with its organization a farmers' club, which holds monthly meetings, and occasional cattle shows, plowing, and spading matches, as its officers may direct. The annual fairs of the Institute were formerly held at Castle Garden, but in 1857 were transferred to the Crystal Palace, where its 30th fair was prematurely ended by the burning of the Palace Oct. 5, 1858. The amount awarded for premiums from 1835 to 1857, both inclusive, has been distributed as follows:—

1835,	$779.00	1841, $1,183.03	1847, $2,592.78	1852, $4,917.43
1836,	1,039.50	1842, 1,155.96	1848, 3,089.83	1853, 3,366.77
1837,	1,093.50	1843, 1,191.55	1849, 2,482.61	1855, 3,269.97
1838,	1,259.50	1844, 1,192.44	1850, 4,303.72	1856, 5,593.49
1839,	1,155.44	1845, 1,848.17	1851, 4,091.76	1857, 3,160.34
1840,	820.50	1846, 3,225.10		

This society has successively occupied premises on Liberty St. near Broadway, at 41 Cortland St., 187 Broadway, the City Hall, Broadway, corner of Anthony St., and 351 Broadway. The last named premises it now owns. In 1859 it removed to the Cooper Institute building. In 1835 it commenced the publication of a monthly journal that continued through several volumes. The annual reports of the Institute to the Legislature since 1841 are voluminous and valuable.

The Lyceum of Natural History, located on 14th St., was incorp. in 1818. It has a large library relating to the natural sciences, and a cabinet. It was first opened in the rear of the City Hall; thence it was removed to Stuyvesant Institute, and finally to its present locality.

The American Geographical and Statistical Society was incorp. under the general law April 30, 1852, and, after several years' sojourn in the University Building, has recently been removed to Clinton Hall, Astor Place. It holds monthly meetings at the rooms of the Historical Society, and is forming an extensive and valuable statistical library. The objects of the society are expressed in its name. It publishes a monthly journal, chiefly of original papers.

The New York Academy of Music, corner of Irving Place and 14th St., was incorp. April 10, 1852. The building is 121 ft. by 114 ft., and will seat 4,000 persons. It is richly decorated, and is constructed with express reference to fine acoustic effect. The cost is estimated at $350,000.

The city has about 15 theaters and a great number of

present century.[1] The completion of the Erie Canal gave an impetus to its growth and greatly increased its business transactions. The commerce of the city, without a parallel on the Western continent, has already been noticed in the general article upon the commerce of the State. The financial institutions are of a number and magnitude commensurate with its wants as the great center of commercial wealth in the nation.[2]

The manufactures of the city form one of the most important branches of the industry of the inhabitants. They embrace nearly every variety of article produced in the civilized world, and the aggregate capital employed is very great. The last State census reported 2,424 manufacturing establishments. In single instances the capital invested exceeds a million of dollars, and the number of persons dependent upon these large establishments for employment extends to several hundred. The above estimate does not profess to include the minor trades, in which little is invested beyond an industrial education and a small stock of implements and materials, but which in the aggregate amount to considerable sums. A large number of manufacturing establishments legitimately belonging to the city are located in the several suburban places for economy of rent and for room ; and if these were added to those located in the city the aggregate would probably be nearly equal to that of the most noted manufacturing cities of Europe.

The Public Buildings of New York are many of them elegant and substantial structures, combining strength and durability with architectural beauty. Among the most noted of these is the U. S. Custom House, the Merchants' Exchange, and the City Hall.[3]

---

minor places of amusement, generally of a special character and devoted to exhibitions of art, curiosities, and other objects of attraction. The first theater in New York was opened in Nassau St. Sept. 17, 1753, and the first play acted was "The Conscious Lovers."

[1] *Population at various periods.*

1698	4,937	1756	13,046	1825	166,086
1703	4,375	1771	21,862	1830	197,112
1723	7,248	1790	33,131	1835	268,089
1731	8,622	1800	60,489	1840	312,710
1737	10,664	1810	96,373	1845	371,223
1746	11,717	1814	95,519	1850	515,547
1749	13,294	1820	123,706	1855	629,810

[2] There are now 5 incorporated and 49 free banks in New York City, which together presented the following total aggregate of resources in their quarterly returns of March 12, 1859 :—

Capital	$68,324,657
Notes in circulation	7,845,947
Profits	6,640,888
Due banks	27,251,889
Due individuals and corp. other than banks	531,061
Due Treasurer of State of New York	119,822
Due depositors on demand	80,679,650
Other sums due	471,666
Total liabilities	191,865,843
Loans and discounts	123,983,075
Over-drafts	59,467
Due from banks	5,357,188
Due from directors	4,119,438
Due from brokers	3,281,632
Real estate	5,967,164
Specie	25,068,132
Cash items	17,481,781
Stocks and promissory notes	12,020,306
Bonds and mortgages	523,869
Bills of solvent banks	1,023,402
Loss and expense account	372,920
Total resources	191,865,643

There are 16 savings banks in the city, with an aggregate amount of $36,804,419 on deposit, and with $38,757,860 in resources.—*Report of Supt. Bank Department* 1859 ; *Assem. Doc., No. 87.*

The first movement toward a savings bank was made Nov. 29, 1816, when at a public meeting the plan was discussed and approved. The first deposits were made July 3, 1819, and within six months $153,378.31 had been deposited by 1,527 persons, and of this sum $6,606 had been withdrawn. Up to 1857, $47,530,067.61 had been deposited in these institutions. They owe their origin to the Society for the Prevention of Pauperism.—*Common Council Manual, 1858, p. 624.*

The *Clearing House Association* was formed Oct. 1, 1853, for the purpose of facilitating the settlements of banks with each other. Its office is on Wall, corner of William St. The arrangements are so perfected that the entire daily settlements of all the banks in their immense transactions with each other are made in six minutes. The whole amount of bank funds which passed through this institution up to Aug. 31, 1858, was $30,675,933,556.56; and during that period so perfect has been the system of balances that the error of one cent has never been made.

Fire Insurance Companies, to the number of 75, with an aggregate capital of $17,654,000, are located in the city. Besides these, a large number of agencies for companies in other States and in foreign countries are established in the city. The amount of capital invested in marine, life, and other insurance companies is not known, as no general reports are published. A list of these companies is elsewhere given. There are also several trust companies, with large capital, and a very great number of companies, associations, and individuals engaged in the business of banking and exchange, of which no statistics are attainable.

The *Chamber of Commerce* was instituted in 1768, and incorp. by patent March 13, 1770. It probably owes its origin to the necessity felt toward the close of the colonial period, of concerted action to protect the interests of trade against the usurpations of the British Government. Its rights were confirmed April 13, 1784, and it has since continued in operation without material interruption. Its objects are to adjust disputes and establish equitable rules concerning trade, and to operate upon public sentiment in the procuring of such acts and regulations as the commercial interests require. Within a short time it has commenced the formation of a library of statistical and commercial works, and opened rooms sufficiently ample and convenient for the wants of the association. Its first report was published in 1859.

[3] The *Custom House*, located on Wall St., on the site of the old Federal Hall, is a marble structure, in the Greek order of architecture, with a Doric portico at each end. It has a marble roof, and is fireproof throughout. It was commenced in May, 1834, and finished in May, 1841, at a cost of $950,000.

The *Merchants' Exchange*, on Wall St., built of Quincy granite, is 171 by 144 ft., and 77 feet high. A portico in front is supported by 18 Ionic columns, 38 feet high, each formed of a single stone weighing 45 tons. The rotunda is 80 ft. in diameter and 80 ft. high. The building is owned by an incorporated company, and cost over $1,000,000.

The *City Hall*, on the Park, is 216 by 105 ft., with two stories and a high basement. It is built in the Italian style, and is faced with marble except on the north side. It was begun Sept. 26, 1803, and finished in 1812, at a cost of over half a million of dollars. The upper story and cupola were burned Aug. 17, 1858, and have not been rebuilt. It is occupied by the Common Council, County Clerk, and various city and county offices. The first City Hall, built in 1698, stood on the present site of the Custom House, at the head of Broad St.

The *Hall of Records*, on the Park, is chiefly interesting from its historical associations. It was formerly the debtors' prison, and in the Revolution it was the prison into which American prisoners were crowded, and from which great numbers were taken to execution. In 1832 it was a cholera hospital. The pillars upon the ends are of modern origin.

The *Rotunda*, on the Park, was built by John Vanderlyn in 1818, for the exhibition of panoramic views, and is now an office of the Almshouse. It reverted to the city at the expiration of a ten years' lease.

The *Halls of Justice*, or "The Tombs," on Center St., is a structure built of Maine granite, in the Egyptian style of architecture. It is a hollow square, 252 by 200 ft., with a large central building. It was erected in 1838. Executions take place in the open courts within its walls.

The *New Armory*, or *Down-Town Arsenal*, corner of White and Elm Sts., is 131 by 84 ft. and 2 stories high. It is built of blue stone, and is supplied with narrow windows for easy defense against mobs. It is used as a receptacle for a part of the artillery of the 1st Division N. Y. State Militia, and as a drill room.

An arsenal was built by the State a few years since, on ground

The Commercial Buildings and Private Residences of New York are many of them on a scale of great magnificence. The first of these are built of marble or a beautiful kind of brownstone; and in the upper part of the city are numerous streets which for miles present unbroken lines of palatial residences. Within the past few years a great improvement has taken place in the character of the commercial buildings erected, and many of them now in size and elegance have no superiors in the world.[1]

The Bay of New York was first discovered by Henry Hudson, then in the employ of the Dutch East India Co., Sept. 12, 1609. A settlement was made upon Manhattan Island by a company of Dutch traders, under the auspices of the West India Co., in 1612; but no permanent agricultural occupation began until 1623. During this year 30 families of Walloons from the Flemish frontiers, and a number of domestic animals, were sent over to form the nucleus for the permanent occupation of the country. Sarah Rapelje, a child of one of these families, born soon after their arrival, was the first white child born in New York. In 1626, Peter Minuet, the first Dutch Governor of the colony, purchased Manhattan Island of the natives for $24, and during the same year he caused a fort surrounded by cedar palisades to be erected. A new fort was begun in 1633 and was finished 2 years after.[2] The Colony of New Netherlands increased slowly; but in 1652 a feud arose between the company and settlers, which continued during the entire period of the Dutch occupation. The interest of the company was solely to make money by their operations; and they pursued their object by the exercise of an arbitrary power and without any regard to the prosperity of the settlers. This controversy tended greatly to develop democratic sentiments in the hearts of the people, and prepared them for the events which subsequently happened. In 1664 the colony fell into the hands of the English, and a new immigration took place, which materially changed the character of the population. A city charter, granted in 1652 and confirmed in 1686, secured many of the privileges since uninterruptedly enjoyed by the people, and formed the basis of all subsequent enactments. From the English conquest to the Revolution the history of the city is merged in that of the State and has no features of special interest.

Trade and commerce have been from the first the leading elements of the industry and wealth of the city, and in colonial times every measure of Government tending to embarrass trade occa-

now within the Central Park, and which has recently been sold to the Commissioners of the Park for $275,000. It was constructed very poorly, and was hardly finished before it began to tumble down. From a part of the proceeds of this property a new arsenal was built, in 1858, corner of 7th Avenue and 35th St.; but, before it was finished, the roof, constructed on a novel plan, fell in by its own weight on the morning of Nov. 19, 1858.

The Post Office occupies the old stone edifice of the Middle Dutch Church, on Nassau, Pine, and Liberty Sts. It is small and inconvenient, and poorly adapted for the purposes of a post office. In the Revolution the pews of the church were broken up for fuel, and the building was used as a prison, and at one time as a riding school. The project of a building for a post office on or near the Park has been agitated; but there is at present no arrangement tending to that result.

The Assay Office occupies an unassuming marble building adjacent to the Custom House, formerly one of the branches of the United States Bank. Its operations are elsewhere noticed. See p. 122.

[1] Under the first race of colonists the style of architecture was an exact copy of that prevailing in Holland; and for many years New York was noted for buildings with peaked gables, tiled roofs, and high, wooden stoops. After the English conquest, a greater variety in style was introduced. Of late years the march of improvement has completely obliterated the old style of houses, and scarcely a vestige of the olden time remains. One of the most interesting relics of the infancy of New York now remaining is a venerable pear tree at the corner of 13th St. and 3d Avenue, formerly on the farm of Governor Peter Stuyvesant. It is widely known as "The Stuyvesant Pear Tree."

[2] The first fort was built in the rear of Trinity Church, near the river, and portions were found in 1751 by some workmen in digging through a bank. The next fort stood on what is now the Bowling Green, then a high mound of earth overlooking the bay and adjacent country. A threatened invasion by the forces of Cromwell, in 1653, led to the construction of an embankment and ditch across the then N. line of the city. This fortification extended along the present line of Wall St.; and from it that street derives its name. In 1692 a war with France occasioned a further attention to the defenses of the city, and led to the erection of a battery on the rocky point at the s. end of the island. A stone fort, with 4 bastions, afterward built at the same place, included most of the Government offices, and bore the name of the reigning sovereign for the time being. It remained until finally taken down in 1788. In the summer of 1776, while an attack was expected from the British army, the city was strongly fortified. On the s. point was the Grand Battery, of 23 guns, with Fort George Battery, of 2 guns, just above it and near the Bowling Green. McDougall's Battery, of

4 guns, was built on a little hill near the North River, a little w. of Trinity Church. The Grenadiers' or Circular Battery, of 5 guns, was above, and the Jersey Battery, of 5 guns, on the left of the latter. On the E. of the town were Coenties Battery, of 5 guns, on Ten Eyck's wharf; Waterbury's Battery, of 7 guns, at the shipyards; Badlam's Battery, of 8 guns, on Rutgers Hill, near the Jews' burial ground; Thompson's Battery, of 9 guns, at Hoorners Hook, and the Independence Battery, on Bayards Mount, corner of Grand and Center Streets. Breastworks were erected in several places in the city, and fortifications were erected on Governors Island, Paulus Hook, (Jersey City,) Brooklyn Heights, and Red Hook. During the War of 1812-15 great apprehension prevailed at several times, and during the first year bodies of militia were stationed in New Utrecht and on Staten Island to repel any attempt on the part of the enemy to land. Subsequently, fortifications were begun at Harlem, and in Brooklyn volunteer companies were formed, and the citizens generally became familiar with the discipline of the camp and the duties of the soldier. In Aug. 1814, for the purpose of constructing a line of fortifications to prevent the expected approach of the enemy, it was arranged that 3 military companies of Brooklyn should turn out to work on Monday, 3 military companies and 1 fire company on Tuesday, the people of Bushwick on Wednesday, of Flatbush on Thursday, of Flatlands on Friday, of Gravesend on Saturday, of New Utrecht on Monday, and the Mechanics' Society of Brooklyn, the military exempts, and 2 fire companies, on Tuesday. The patriotic diggers crossed the ferries every morning with banners and music, and large parties worked in the night by moonlight. The citizens of New York were not behind their neighbors in patriotism, and numerous volunteer associations pressed their services upon the Committee of Defense, without regard to party or station in life, and the rich and the poor wrought together with the most patriotic emulation. Many gave money freely to the work, and these zealous labors continued so long as there appeared reason to anticipate danger. During the same month the General Government made a requisition for 20,000 militia from New York and New Jersey to repel an attack which was reported to be in preparation. The funds to meet the expenses were raised by the city, but were repaid by the General Government the next year. Four hundred heavy cannon were mounted on the various forts, and large quantities of ammunition were collected. The fleet in charge of Commodore Decatur was also prepared for the emergency; and it is probable that these prompt preparations saved the city from an attack. Toward winter the hostile fleet bore off to the south. and the enemy closed their operations before New Orleans. On "Evacuation Day" in 1814 the Governor reviewed 25,000 troops in New York,—a larger number than ever before or since mustered in one body in America.

sioned great uneasiness. This city was among the first to feel the effects of the arbitrary measures of Great Britain, and was among the earliest to resist their tendencies.[1] The aristocratic element was probably stronger in this city than in any other part of America; and this was arrayed in favor of the British measures and against the "Sons of Liberty." Many prominent citizens, who had warmly sympathized with the popular movement in the hope of gaining redress of grievances, at length yielded their opposition when there appeared no alternative but war, and continued active or quiet friends of the Royal Government while it lasted. Several members of the first Provincial and Continental Congress afterward became friends of the king. The British forces took possession of the city immediately after the battle upon Long Island, Aug. 26, 1776, and remained until Nov. 25, 1783. The anniversary of this last event, known as "Evacuation Day," is still held in grateful remembrance, and is usually celebrated by military parade or other ceremonies.

In 1785 the first Congress of the United States after the war met in this city and held its sessions in the City Hall, corner of Wall and Nassau Streets. In the gallery of this building, facing Broad St., Gen. Washington was inaugurated first President, April 30, 1789. The New York Legislature returned to this city in 1784 and continued its sessions with intervals until finally removed to Albany with the State offices in 1797. The Port of New York was made a port of entry soon after the peace. Its revenues were collected under the State Government till 1789, but have since formed a most important source of income to the Federal Government. The receipts from customs at this port considerably exceed those of all the other commercial cities of the Union together, and defray nearly one-half the expenses of the General Government. In the midst of its general prosperity the city has had seasons of adversity.[2] At different times destructive fires have occurred, which have for a time seriously retarded business.

---

[1] The principal events which occurred in the city during the troubles leading to the Revolution are briefly as follows:—

1765,   "Sons of Liberty" were organized to oppose the Stamp Act.

1765, Oct. 31.—A committee of correspondence with other colonies was appointed.

1765, Nov. 1.—The Stamp Act took effect, and popular excitement became extreme. The Lieut. Governor was burned in effigy before the fort.

1765, Dec. 26.—The ship Minerva was boarded by the Sons of Liberty in search of stamp paper. The paper was traced to a brig soon after, and ten packages were seized and burned.

1766, June 29.—The Assembly petitioned for a bronze statue of Pitt to be erected.

1766, Oct. 18-22.—The liberty pole on the Common (Park) was repeatedly destroyed, and there was imminent danger of a collision between the populace and the troops.

1770, Jan. 13.—New attempts were made to destroy the liberty pole, and the soldiers became riotous.

"   Jan. 17.—At a meeting of 3,000 citizens, resolutions were passed not to submit to the acts of oppression.

"   Jan. 18.—A collision took place between the soldiers and citizens at Golden Hill.

"   Jan. 30.—The Corporation forbade the erection of a new liberty pole, and the people soon after planted one on their own land, inscribed "Liberty and Property."

"   March 29.—Another attack was made upon the pole, which excited great indignation, and led to its being nightly guarded, until May 3.

"   May.—A committee of 100 was formed to resist the importation of goods under the obnoxious laws; but they receded from their purpose July 9, and agreed to import everything but tea.

"   Aug. 21.—A leaden equestrian statue of George III. was erected in Bowling Green. This statue was thrown down by the populace on the receipt of the Declaration of Independence, July 10, 1776. It was subsequently melted up into bullets in the family of Gov. Wolcott, of Connecticut. It is said that 42,000 bullets were made from the metal, and these did service against 400 British soldiers afterward sent into Conn. by Gov. Tryon.

"   Sept. 7.—A marble statue of Pitt was placed in Wall Street, in gratitude for his services in the repeal of the Stamp Act. In consequence of the course of Pitt after he became Lord Chatham, this statue was mutilated by a mob May 21, 1772, and, having become an unsightly, headless trunk, it was removed, under an act of

March 7, 1788. It is now preserved in the Fifth Ward Hotel, West Broadway.

1773, Nov. 5.—The Committee of Vigilance denounced the importation of tea and agreed to resist its landing.

1774, April 21.—A vessel laden with tea arrived at Sandy Hook, but was not permitted to land; and in a few days it was sent back to London. About the same time 18 chests of tea privately brought into port were destroyed.

"   May 19.—A great meeting was held in the "Fields," at which strong revolutionary resolutions were passed. A committee of 51 were appointed; but the next day a majority of them receded from their position, and the Whigs requested their names to be struck off.

1775, April 3.—The Colonial General Assembly finally adjourned.

"   July 25.—Delegates were elected to the Continental Congress.

"   Aug. 23.—Capt. Lamb was ordered by Provincial Congress to remove the cannon from the battery in the city for the forts in the Highlands. Resistance was offered from the Asia man-of-war, stationed off the battery; but 21 pieces—all that were mounted—were safely carried away.

[2] Two dreadful fires occurred while the city was in possession of the enemy. On the 21st of Sept. 1776, a fire spread from Whitehall Slip w. of Broadway, s. of Barclay Street, burning 492 houses, or one-eighth of the entire city. Another broke out on Cruger's Wharf, Aug. 7, 1778, which burned 300 houses in Great and Little Dock and the adjacent streets. Commissioners were appointed May 4, 1784, to settle claims to the soil and lay out streets in these burned districts. Destructive fires have since occurred, as follows:—

1811, May 19.—Upon Chatham Street 80 to 100 buildings were burned.

1828, $600,000 worth of property was burned.

1835, Dec. 16.—A fire broke out in the lower part of the city, which was not arrested until 40 acres, mostly covered by large stores, were burned over, and $18,000,000 worth of property was destroyed. It was the most disastrous fire that ever occurred in the city.

1845, July 19.—A fire broke out near Wall Street, and extended to Stone Street, ravaging the entire district between Broadway and the E. side of Broad Street. Five to eight million dollars' worth of property was destroyed.

1858, Oct. 5.—The Crystal Palace was burned.

Theaters in New York have been burned as follows:—Park, 1820, 1848; Bowery, 1828, 1836, 1838, 1845; Mount Pitt Circus, 1828; La Fayette, 1829; National, 1839, 1841; Niblo's, 1846; and Franklin, 1849.

Papers and Periodicals now published in the City.

NAME.	Original Publishers.	When first published	Remarks.
American Agriculturist..........................	A. B. & R. L. Allen........................	1842	w. Orange Judd, present publisher.
American Baptist & Home Missionary Record..	C. C. P. Crosby.......................	1835	w.
American Craftsman	G. F. Tisdall............................	......	s. mo.
American Druggists' Circular........................	H. Bridgeman.		
American Farmers' Magazine.........................	J. A. Nash.		
American Foreign & Christian Union...............	Edward Vernon	1849	mo.
American Free Mason...............................	J. F. Brennan.		
American Home Missionary Journal................		1829	mo.
American Homeopathic Review.....................	Henry M. Smith	......	mo.
American Journal of Education & College Review..	Absalom Peters & S. S. Randall........	1856	mo.
American Medical Gazette...........................	C. Meredith Reese, ed.; A. J. Dix, pub.	......	mo.
American Medical Monthly..........................	E. H. Parker, ed.; E. P. Allen, pub.	1854	E. H. Parker & S. H. Douglass, present publishers
American Merchant	Bryant & Stratton..........................	1858	mo.
American Mining Chronicle........................	W. B. Monck & Co.....................	......	w.
American Missionary................................	George Whipple	1846	mo.
American National Preacher.......................	Wm. H. Bidwell, ed...................	1826	
American Phrenological Journal....................	Fowler & Wells........................	1839	mo.
American Publishers' Circular....................	Charles R. Rode........................	......	w.
American Rail Road Guide.........................	Dinsmore & Co...........................	......	mo.
American Rail Road Journal.......................	D. K. Miner & G. C. Shaffer..........	1831	w. Now published by Schultz & Co.; H. V. Poor, ed.
American Railway Review............................	Alexander Mann, ed....................	1859	American Railway Bureau, pub.
American Temperance Union & New York Prohibitionist	Rev. Dr. Marsh........................	1837	Begun at Philadelphia as Journal of the American Temperance Union; united with Prohibitionist, at Albany, in 1851, and removed to New York.
American Turf Register..........................	W. T. Porter	1840	mo. John Richards, present pub.
Americanischer Agriculturist........................	Orange Judd.............................	......	mo.
Americanischer Botschafter........................	American Tract Society..............	......	mo.
Appleton's Railway & Steam Navigation Guide..	D. Appleton & Co...................	......	mo.
Architectural Advertiser & Builders' Register...	W. H. Randall & Co.................	1859	mo.
Argus & United States Military & Naval Chronicle..	J. Crawley.............................	1845	w.
Atlantische Blätter..........................	F. Rauchfuss.		
Bankers' Magazine & Statistical Register........	J. Smith Homans, jr., ed............	1853	mo. Com. in Baltimore in 1846.
Bank Note List...................................	L. S. Lawrence & Co................	......	w.
Bank Note List & Reporter........................	A. Nichols & Co......................	......	w.
Bank Note Register & Detector of Counterfeits..	Gwyne & Day..........................	......	w.
Bible Advocate...................................	American & Foreign Bible Society ...	......	mo.
Bible Society Record................................	American Bible Society..............	1850	mo.
Bible Union Quarterly, Bible Union Reporter	American Bible Union.		
Billiard Cue...................................	O'Conner & Collender.		
Booksellers' Medium & Publishers' Advertiser..	O. A. Roorback.........................	1858	s. mo.
Boys' & Girls' Own Magazine.....................	William L. Jones.....................	1859	mo.
Brother Jonathan..................................	Wilson & Co............................	1840	Benj. H. Day, present publisher.
Carrington's Commissionaire.......................	J. S. Penn, ed.; J. W. Carrington, pub.	1855	
Chess Monthly....................................	P. Miller & Sons.		
Christian Ambassador..............................	Hallock & Lyon	1848	Henry Lyon, present publisher.
Christian Advocate & Journal & Zion's Herald..	Waugh & Mason.......................	1830	Carlton & Porter, present publishers.
Christian Inquirer................................	Unitarian Association................	1847	
Christian Intelligencer...........................	Charles Van Wyck.....................	1830	
Church Journal...................................	Rev. John Henry Hopkins, jr..........	1853	
Churchman's Monthly Magazine..................	Rev. B. T. Onderdonk.................	......	E. P. Allen, present publisher.
Coach Makers' Monthly............................	E. M. Stratton.		
Corn Exchange Reporter...........................	William H. Trafton...................	......	w.
Corner Stone...................................	Dr. S. Jacobs.		
Cosmopolitan Art Journal...........................	Quarterly Association................	1856	
Courrier des États-Unis............................	Charles Lasalle.......................	1828	d. & w.
Y Cymbro Americanidd...........................	John M. Welch.........................	1855	Cambro-American, Eng. & Welsh.
Democratic Age....................................	C. Edwards Lester, ed................	1858	mo.
Democratic Review & United States Magazine..		1838	mo. Conrad Swackhamer, pres. pub.
Dental Monitor...................................	J. G. Ambler..........................	1857	mo.
Dinsmore's Railway Guide........................	Dinsmore & Co.........................	1850	mo.
Disturnell's Rail Road Guide......................	J. Disturnell.........................	......	mo.
Dollar Weekly Express.............................	J. & E. Brooks........................	......	A s. w. edition was some time issued, as the New York Express and Advertiser.
Eclectic Magazine of Foreign Literature..........	J. H. Ayremand & W. H. Bidwell.....	1844	mo. W. H. Bidwell, present pub.
Educational Herald................................	Smith, Woodman & Co................	1857	mo.
Educational News	Ivison & Phinney......................	1858	Quarterly.
Engineer....................................	John Hillyer..........................	......	w.
Examiner....................................	Edward Bright.........................	......	w.
Excelsior....................................	Albert Palmer.........................	......	w.
Familienblätter	Dilthey & Gambs......................	......	w.
Fleur de Lis	H. H. Lloyd & Co.		
Foreign Missionary................................	Board of Missions of Presb. Church..	1842	
Frank Leslie's Budget of Fun.....................	Frank Leslie..........................	......	mo.
Frank Leslie's Illustrated Newspaper...........	Frank Leslie..........................	1854	w.
Frank Leslie's Illustrated Zeitung...............	Frank Leslie..........................	......	w.
Frank Leslie's New Family Magazine.............	Frank Leslie..........................	......	mo.
German Bank Note Reporter......................	Frederick Gerhard....................	......	w.
Golden Prize....................................	Merrick B. Dean.......................	......	w.
Good News....................................	Carlton & Porter......................	......	mo. Child's Paper, Meth. Epis.

Papers and Periodicals now published, continued.

NAME.	Original Publishers.	When first published.	Remarks.
Great Republic Monthly....................	Oaksmith & Co........................	1859	Changed from Emerson's Putnam's Magazine.
Hall's Journal of Health....................	W. W. Hall	1854	mo.
Handel's Zeitung...............................	W. Meyer.................................	......	d. & w.
Harper's New Monthly Magazine...........	Harper & Brothers.....................	1850	mo.
Harper's Weekly Journal of Civilization........	Harper & Brothers.....................	1857	
Herald of Light	New Church Publication Society.		
Historical Magazine & Notes and Queries........	C. Benj. Richardson..................	1857	mo. Begun at Boston; removed to New York.
Home..	Beadle & Adams.		
Home & Foreign Record of Presbyterian Church			
Home Journal................................	George P. Morris & N. P. Willis.......	1846	w.
Home Magazine..............................	James G. Reed....	......	mo.
Home Missionary............................	American Home Mission Society......	1854	mo.
Home Mission Record........................	American Baptist Home Miss. Soc...	1849	mo.
Homeopathic Review.........................		......	mo.
Horticulturist	A. D. Downing, ed.; L. Tucker, pub.	1846	Begun at Albany. Removed to Rochester; P. Barry, ed. Removed to Philadelphia in 1855; J. J. Smith, ed.; R. P. Smith, publisher. Removed to New York in 1858; A. O. Moore, present publisher.
Humorist....................................	Max Conheim & Otto Brethauer.		
Humphrey's Journal of the Daguerreotype & Photographic Arts.................	S. D. Humphrey.......................	......	mo.
Hunt's Merchants' Magazine................	Francis Hunt	1839	G. W. & A. G. Wood, present pubs.
Insurance Monitor & Commercial Reporter.....	T. Jones, Jr...........................	1853	mo.
Irish American.............................	Lynch & Cole............................	1849	w.
Irish News.................................	Tho. Fr. Meagher.....................	1854	J. R. Taylor, present publisher.
Irish Vindicator..........................	E. D. Connery & Co...................	......	w.
Jewish Messenger.........................	Rev. S. M. Isaacs & Son..............	......	w.
Journal of the American Geographical & Statistical Society.................	John T. Schultz & Co.................	1859	mo.
Journal of Commerce, Jr....................	Hallock, Hale & Hallock.............	......	d. Issued from the office of The New York Journal of Commerce.
Journal of Finance & Bank Reporter..........	S. T. Hodge	1854	w.
Journal of Industry & Monthly Price Current of Labor.................	Association.............................	1859	
Journal of Medical Reform.................	J. D. Friend............................	1855	
Journal of Medicine & Collateral Science........	Purple & Smith, eds.; H. Billiere.		
Journal of Missions & Youth's Day Spring......	A. Mervin...............................	......	mo.
Journal of Specific Homeopathy.............	Humphrey & Palmer...................	......	mo.
Knickerbocker, or New York Monthly Magazine	Peabody & Co...........................	1833	mo. John A. Gray, present publisher; L. G. Clarke, ed.
La Cronica.................................	M. De La Pena.........................	......	s. w.
Ladies' Newspaper..........................	John Hillyer.		
Ladies' Repository.........................	Carlton & Porter......................	......	mo.
Ladies' Visitor............................	Laura J. Curtis........................	......	mo.
Ladies' Wreath............................	John F. Scovill........................	1847	mo.
Leader.....................................	John Clancy............................	......	w.
Le Bon Ton.................................	S. T. Taylor............................	......	mo. magazine.
L'Écho Français...........................	Alex. Trey..............................	......	s. w.
L'Eco d'Italia.............................	G. F. Secchi de Casale..............	......	d.
Life Boat..................................	American Seaman's Friend Society..	......	mo.
Life Illustrated...........................	Fowler & Wells........................	1854	w.
Little Guide...............................	H. H. Lloyd & Co.		
Little's Living Age........................	Stanford & Delisser.		
Livingston's Monthly Law Magazine..........	John L. Livingston....................	1853	
Lutherischer Herold........................	Henry Ludwig..........................	......	s. mo.
Masonic Messenger.........................	M. J. Drummond......................	1856	mo.
Mercantile News & Manufacturers' Reporter.....	W. Gutman & Co.......................	1858	w.
Merchants' & Manufacturers' Journal.........	Thos. K. Kettel, ed.; A. Palmer, prop.	1852	mo.
Mercury....................................	Krauth & Caldwell.....................	1839	Caldwell, Southworth & Whitney, present publishers.
Merry's Museum & School Fellow.............	S. G. Goodrich.........................	1841	J. N. Stearns & Co., present pubs.
Message....................................	W. C. Conant.		
Methodist Quarterly Review.................	J. McClintock..........................	1828	Carlton & Porter, present publishers.
Metropolitan Record........................	E. Dunnigan & Bro....................	1859	w.
Military Gazette...........................	C. G. Stone.............................	......	mo. Removed from Albany.
Mining and Statistical Magazine............	Geo. M. Newton	1853	Changed from Mining Magazine; Thos. McElrath, present ed.
Missionary Advocate........................	J. P. Durbin............................	1845	Carlton & Porter, present publishers.
Missionary Herald	Presb. Board Miss.; A. Merwin, ed...	1843	
Monthly Record of the Five Points House of Industry	L. M. Pease.		
Morning Courier & New York Enquirer..........	James Watson Webb..................	1828	The w. ed. formerly Weekly Courier & New York Enquirer.
Mother's Magazine & Family Monitor..........	Rev. S. Whittlesey....................	1833	H. H. Lloyd, present publisher.
Musical Pioneer............................	J. P. Woodbury.......................	1855	F. J. Huntington, present publisher.
Musical Review & Record of Musical Science, Literature, and Intelligence.............	Mason Brothers........................	1858	
Musical World & New York Musical Times......	Richard Storrs Willis................	1849	
National Anti Slavery Standard.............	American Anti Slavery Society.......	1840	w.
National Humorist.........................	Stearns & Co...........................	1856	mo.
National Magazine.........................	Abel Stevens and......................	1852	mo. Carlton & Porter, present pubs.
National Police Gazette...................	Robert A. Seymour....................	1845	w. Geo. W. Matsell & Co., present publishers.
New Jerusalem Messenger...................	John L. Jewett.........................	1855	w.
New Yorker.................................	Cornelius Mathews....................	......	w.
New Yorker Abendzeitung....................	Rudolph Leow.		

Papers and Periodicals now published, continued.

NAME.	Original Publisher.	When first published.	Remarks.
New Yorker Beobachter	F. Schwedler		w.
New Yorker Demokrat	F. Schwedler		d. & w.
New Yorker Humorist	Cohnheim & Brethauer		w.
New York Daily News	{ Gideon J. Tucker, ed.; McIntyre & Parsons, pubs. }	1855	W. D. Parsons, present pub. Weekly ed. issued as the New York National Democrat.
New York Day Book	R. W. Stimson		d. & w. Vanevrie, Horton & Co. pubs.
New York Dispatch	A. J. Williams	1846	
New York Clipper	Frank Queen	1843	w.
New York Colonization Journal	J. B. Pinney	1832	mo.
New York Commercial Advertiser	Francis Hall & Co	1826	d. semi. w. issued as New York Spectator.
New York Commercial Times	Adams, Upham & Co.	1858	w.
New York Evangelist	Field & Craighead	1830	Issued part of the time as the New York Evangelist and New York Presbyterian.
New York Evening Post	Wm. Coleman	1802	d., s. w., & w. Wm. C. Bryant & Co., present publishers.
New York Express	Townsend & Brooks	1836	d. & s. w. James & Erastus Brooks, present publishers. The Dollar Weekly Express issued from the same office.
New York Family Courier	Jas. Watson Webb		d., s. w., & w. Changed from the Weekly Courier & Enquirer.
New York Freeman's Journal	J. A. McMasters	1853	(R. C.)
New York Herald	James Gordon Bennett	1835	d., s. w., & w. The d. begun in 1837.
New York Ledger	D. Anson Pratt	1847	Robert Bonner present publisher.
New York Observer	Sydney E. Morse & Co	1848	
New York Municipal Gazette	E. Merrian, ed	1848	Published occasionally.
New York Spectator	Noah Webster	1797	s. w. Begun as The Herald. Name changed the same year. Now published by Francis Hall & Co.
New York Times	Henry J. Raymond	1851	d., s. w., & w. ; also California and European editions. Raymond, Wesley & Co., present publishers.
New York Tribune	Greeley & McElrath	1841	d., s. w., & w. ; also California and European editions. H. Greeley & Co., present publishers.
New York Weekly	A. J. Williamson.		
New York Weekly Chronicle	Holman & Gray	1850	Pharcellus, Church & Co., present publishers.
Nick Nax	Leison & Haney	1857	
North American Homeopathic Journal	Wm. Radde	1855	
Our Musical Friend		1858	w. (Sheet music.)
Parish Visitor	H. Dyer; Rev. C. W. Adams, pub.	1852	mo.
Path Finder	John F. Whitney	1847	w.
Periodical Paper of the Am. & For. Bible Soc.		1845	
Photographic & Fine Art Journal	Henry H. Snelling.		
Picayune	Gunn & Co.		
Polylingual Journal	Hiram C. Sparks.		
Porter's Spirit of the Times	Wm. T. Porter	1831	Geo. W. Wilkes & Co., present pubs.
Principle	John B. Conklin		mo.
Programme	C. M. McLachlin & Co		d.
Protestant Churchman	{ H. Anthon, S. H. Tyng, & E. H. Canfield. }	1843	
Protestant Episcopal Quarterly Review.			
Racing Calendar & Trotting Record	Geo. W. Wilkes & Co.		
Radical Abolitionist	Wm. Goodell	1857	
Rail Road & Financial Advertiser	John Hillyer		w.
Real Estate Advertiser & Reporter	J. W. Wheeler		mo.
Republican	John Hillyer		
Sabbath Recorder		1845	Seventh Day Bap. Publication Society.
Sabbath School Visitor	W. B. Maxon	1850	Seventh Day Baptist.
Sailor's Magazine		1832	American Seaman's Friend Society.
Scalpel	H. G. Lawrence	1848	mo.
Scientific American	Mann & Co	1845	
Scottish American Journal	Jas. W. Finlay		w.
Scott's Report of Fashions	G. C. Scott	1825	s. an.
Seventh Day Baptist Memorial	W. B. Maxon.		
Shipping & Commercial List & N. Y. Price Current	Antrus & Bourne		s. w.
Shoe & Leather Reporter	D. J. Field		w.
Shoemaker	D. J. Field & Co		w.
Sociale Republic	Gustave Struve		w.
Sower & Missionary Recorder			mo. Board of Publication Reformed Protestant Dutch Church.
Spectator	Orville A. Roorback		mo.
Spirit of Missions	Daniel Dana, Jr		Removed from Burlington, N. J.
Spirit of the Times	John Richards	1836	
Spiritual Telegraph	C. Patridge		w.
Staats-Zeitung	Anna Uhl.	1854	
Standard Bearer			
Student & School Mate	N. A. Calkins.		
Sunday Advocate	James L. Smith	1848	
Sunday School Advocate	Carlton & Porter.		s. mo.
Sunday School Banner	American S. S. Union	1858	
Sunday School Gazette	" " "	1858	
Sunday School Times	" " "	1858	w.
Swedenborgian	Rev. Benj. F. Barrett.		

Papers and Periodicals now published, concluded.

NAME.	Original publisher.	When first published.	Remarks.
Tablet..........	D. & J. Sadlier & Co....................		w.
The Advocate of Moral Reform & Family Guardian...........	J. R. McDowell...........	1835	Formerly McDowell's Journal.
The Albion...........	W. Young & Co	1822	Devoted to British news.
The Atlas...........	Herrick & Seaman...........	1839	
The Carrier Dove........	Daniel Dana, Jr...........		Missions.
The Century...........	Thos. McElrath...........	1858	
The Children's Magazine...........	F. D. Haniman...........	1852	mo. P. E. S. S. Union.
The Child's Paper...........			mo. American Tract Society.
The Churchman...........	John Hecker...........	1831	
The Constellation	Park Benjamin, ed...........	1859	Geo. Roberts, publisher.
The Crayon	W. J. Stillman & J. Durand, eds......	1855	W. Hollingsworth, publisher.
The Homeopathist			s. mo.
The Independent...........	B. W. Benedict...........	1848	Joseph H. Richards, present pub.
The Inventor	Low, Hascall & Co...........	1857	
The Israelite Indeed...........	G. R. Lederer...........	1857	
The New York Journal of Commerce	Association...........	1827	d., s. w., & w. Hallock, Hale & Hallock, present publishers.
The Press...........	Daniel Adee.		
The Printer	Henry & Huntington...........	1858	d. & w. M. S. Beach, present pub.
The Sun	Moses Y. Beach	1833	Franklin Knight, present publisher.
Theological & Literary Journal...........	Daniel N. Lord, ed...........	1848	
Thompson's Bank Note Reporter...........	J. F. Thompson...........	1840	w. P. Adams, publisher.
Tiffany's Monthly	Joel Tiffany.		
Truth Teller	Wm. Durman...........	1830	w. Michael Madder, present pub.
United States Economist & Dry Goods Reporter.	Joseph Mackey...........		s. w.
United States Hotel Directory...........	Ropes, Williams & Co...........	1858	w.
United States Insurance Gazette...........	G. E. Currie...........		mo.
United States Journal	Albert Palmer...........	1851	mo. J. M. Emerson & Co., present publishers.
United States Mining Journal...........	John Hillyer...........		w.
United States Railroad and Mining Register.....	Geo. M. Newton.		
Wall Street Broker...........	John S. Dye		w.
Water Cure Journal	Fowler & Wells...........	1843	mo.
Working Farmer...........	Fred. McCready...........		mo.
Yankee Notions	J. W. Strong...........	1852	
Young Christian	Thos. Lyon...........	1855	mo.
Young Men's Magazine...........	N. A. Calkins. Rich. McCormick, ed..	1851	
Youth's Temperance Advocate	John Marsh...........	1840	
Y Drych a'r Gwyliedydd		1854	w. (Mirror & Watchman.)
Y Traethodydd...........	Wm. Roberts.		

Papers and Periodicals discontinued since the Revolution.

Since the Revolution, the following papers have appeared and been discontinued. The list is very imperfect; as, among the constant changes that are going on, it is impossible to ascertain precise data. It is possible that a few in this list may be still issued, and very probable that others may continue to exist under a different name:

NAMES OF PAPERS.	Publishers.	When commenced.	When discontinued.
Abbott's Religious Magazine.mo.	John Wiley...........	1834	
Academician, The....................	A. & J. W. Picket, eds..................	1818	1820
Account, Weekly...........	Bacon & Stimson....	1848	
Advertiser, Daily...........	Childs & Swaine...	1785	
Advertiser, New York Daily......	Dwight, Townsend & Co...........	1830	
Advocate & Journal, New York, d. & w.	Redwood & Fisher.	1830	
Advocate, New York American, changed from Journal...........	Redwood & Fisher.	1833	
Age, The	Jacob Acker...........	1831	
Age, The	Grattan & Meighan	1844	
Age, The ....d.	Kendrick & Co...........	1856	
Age of Reason...........		1846	1850
Agricultor, New York...........	Allen & Co...........	1852	
Alexandrian		1835	
Alliance, New York...........	C. C. Leigh, C. J. Warren & E. Wilkes...........	1852	1855
Alligator, The	Stephen H. Branch	1858	1859
Almighty Dollar, The...........	C. C. Champlin	1851	
Amaranth, The...........mo.	John Henry...........	1848	
Amateur, The...........mo.		1832	
Ambassador, The ....mo.		1842	
American Advocate for Equal Rights to Man ....w.		1844	
American Architect	C. M. Saxton...........	1847	
American Artisan...........	S. Fleet	1847	
American Biblical Repos.......qr.	J. H. Agnew...........	1843	
American Celt...........	McGee & Mitchell..	1855	
American Chronopress ....mo.	Alba Honeywell....	1850	
American Citizen	James Cheetham...	1806	1810
American Citizen ....d.	John R. De Puy.....	1843	
American Citizen & Watch Tower		1806	
American Eclectic...........	Absalom Peters & S. B. West...........	1841	
American Eclectic...........bi-mo.	J. H. Agnew...........	1843	
American Ensign ....w.	Burns & Gammons	1844	
American Ensign ....d.	Association. Burns & Gammons...........	1845	
American Family Journal....mo.	Rev. D. Newell & J. R. Wisner...........	1847	
American Farmer & Mechanic..	E. B. Carter...........	1843	
American Flora...........mo.	A. B. Strong, ed.....	1849	
American Foreign Anti Slavery Reporter...........mo.		1844	
American Journal of Education.	Joseph McKean.....	1847	
American Journal of Photography...........	C. A. Steele...........	1845	
American Jubilee...........	Wm. Goodell...........	1856	
American Keystone...........	Callicot & Webster	1851	
American Laborer ....mo.	Greeley & McElrath	1842	1843
American Lancet...........mo.		1831	
American Magazine...........	Samuel Loudon....	1787	1788
American Mail...........	Park Benjamin....	1847	
American Mechanic...........	J. M. Van Osdel & S. T. Porter........	1840	
American Mechanics' Magazine.	D. K. Minor...........	1832	
American Metropolis...........	H. G. Dayler...........	1845	
American Mineralogical Journal	Archibald Bruce....	1819	1844
American Minerva...........d.	Geo. Bruce & Co....	1793	
American Missionary Register, mo.	U. F. M. Soc. Z. Lewis & others...	1820	1826
American Monthly Magazine....	W. Hallet & A. D. Patterson	1833	1845

Papers and Periodicals discontinued since the Revolution, continued.

NAMES OF PAPERS.	Publishers.	When commenced.	When discontinued.	NAMES OF PAPERS.	Publishers.	When commenced.	When discontinued.
American Monthly Magazine & Critical Review.	J. H. Bigelow & O. L. Holley	1817	1819	Calumet ....bi-mo.	L. D. Dewey	1835	
American Moral & Sentimental Magazine	Thomas Kirk	1797	1799	Calumet of Peace		1832	
				Campaign, The	O'Sullivan & Tilden	1844	
American Musical Journal...mo.	Jas. Dunn	1835		Campaign of Freedom		1848	
American Patriot	Association	1841		Canfield's American Argus	P. Canfield	1830	
American Patriot		1843		Catholic Expositor & Literary Magazine		1841	
American Patriot & Public Advertiser	Samuel O. Brower	1806	1812	Catholic Expositor & Literary Magazine..............mo.		1843	
American Penny Magazine	Theod. Dwight, jr.	1845		Catholic Magazine		1839	
American Phonographer	John W. Leonard	1851		Catholic Register	John Dillon Smith & P. Gallagher	1840	
American Plow Boy	D. K. Minor	1833					
American Protestant	C. R. Moore, agent.	1845		Child's Magazine ....mo.		1827	
American Repertory of Arts, Science, & Manufacture	J. J. Mapes, ed	1840	1844	Childrens' Magazine ....mo.	Rev. A Ten Broeck	1835	
American Repository...........mo.	W. A. Cox, Mechanic Institute.	1840		Choral Advocate & Singing Class Journal	Mason & Law	1850	
American Review & Literary Journal	C. B. Brown, ed	1801		Christian Diadem.................mo.	Z. Patten Hatch	1848	
				Christian Family Magazine..mo.	Rev. D. Newell	1843	
American Review & Whig Journal	Wiley & Putnam	1845		Christian Inquirer	B. Bates	1825	
American Spectator	B. F. Romaine	1841		Christian Journal & Christian Register	T. & J. Swords	1817	1824
American Sporting Magazine, mo.	C. R. Colden	1832		Christian Magazine...............mo.	Hopkins& Seymour	1806	1811
American Temperance Intelligencer		1834		Christian Parlor Magazine...mo.	Rev. D. Mead	1845	
American Temperance Magazine	S. F. Carey	1851		Christian Review..............quar.	James Woolsey	1835	
American Temperance Magazine & Sons of Temperance Offering		1851	1852	Christian Spiritualist		1854	
American Temperance Recorder, mo.	Oliver & Bro	1848		Chronicle Express		1802	
				Chronicle of the Times	F. S. Wiggins	1828	
American Whig Review, changed from American Review & Whig Journal.				Churchmen's Monthly Magazine	T. Swords	1804	1811
				Citizen, The	John McClanahan	1854	
America's Own	E. B. Childs, ed	1849		Citizen of the World	G. Vail	1834	
America's Own & Weekly Fireman's Journal		1851		City Chronicle		1847	
Anglo American	H. D. Patterson, ed	1842		City Guide	Solon Horn	1850	
Anglo Saxon ....mo.		1847		City Hall Reporter & New York General Law Magazine	John Lomas	1833	1833
Annalist, The	R. & G. S. Wood	1849	1850	City Journal and Ladies' Daily Gazette		1842	
Anti Masonic Review & Monthly Magazine	Henry Dana Ward	1829		City Recorder	Daniel Rogers	1816	1821
Anti Slavery Reporter	Am. Anti Sla. Soc.	1834		Cobbett's Political Register		1816	
Appleton's Mechanics' Magazine..................mo.	J. M. Adams, ed	1851	1854	Code Reporter.....................mo.		1848	
Arcturus	Matthews & Duyckinck	1841		Colored American	Sam. E. Cornish, ed.	1837	
				Columbian ....d. & s. w.	Charles Holt	1810	
Argus, or Greenleaf's New Daily Advertiser	J. Greenleaf	1795		Columbian for the Country		1819	1821
Argus & United States Gazette..	Capt. N. Cook	1841		Columbian Ladies and Gentlemen's Magazine	John Juman, ed	1844	
Aristidean	Lane & Co	1845		Columbian Magazine...........mo.	Israel Post	1845	
Arthur's Home ....mo.	DeWitt & Davenport	1857		Comet, The	H. D. Duhecquet	1834	
Artist, The ....mo.	F. Guarre	1843		Commercial Advertiser & Spectator		1807	
Asmonean	Robert Lyon	1849	1858	Commercial Register...........mo.	Franklin Woods & Co	1855	
Atlantic Magazine..............mo.	E. Bliss & E. White	1824	1825	Constellation	Green, Clark & Bartlett	1830	1834
Atlas, The	J. D. Porter & E. Prescott	1830		Constellation	John Henry	1845	
Atlas Magazine................s. mo.	Swinburne, Rogers & Co.	1834		Corrector, or Independent American..................mo.		1815	
Atom, The	Robert G. Hatfield.	1847		Corsair, The	N. P. Willis	1839	
Badger's Weekly Messenger	B. Badger, ed	1831		Cosmopolite ......a semi-mo. mag.	Prentiss, Clark & Co	1849	
Banner of the Constitution	Condy Raquet	1831			—— Burton.		
Baptist Advocate	Robert Sears	1840		Cosmorama		1845	
Baptist Memorial...............mo.	Rev. Enoch Hutchinson, ed.			Cricket, The		1845	
Baptist Repository	Jas. Van Valkenburgh	1829		Criterion, The	Chas. R. Rode	1855	
				Critic, The	Wm. Leggett	1828	
Barnburner, The	W. J. Tenney	1848		Crystal Fount	Burnett & Allen	1843	
Beacon, The	G. Vail	1843		Cuban	J. Mesa	1855	
Belle Lettres Repository......mo.	A. T. Goodrich & Co.	1819	1823	Cyclopedia Indianensis	Platt & Peters	1843	
Better Times	U. Hagedorn	1840		Daily Court Calendar		1845	
Bible Examiner................s. mo.	George Storrs	1844		Daily Evening State Register	J. A. Scovill	1856	
Biblical Inquirer	J. E. Jones	1850		Daily Gazette		1843	
Biblical Journal	Israel Post	1842		Daily Globe	L. D. Shaumm	1845	
Bibliotheca Sacra & Theological Review.	B. B. Edwards & E. A. Park	1844	1849	Daily Plebeian	Childs & Co	1842	
				Daily Statesman	Abijah Ingraham.	1848	
Bisbee's New Monthly Magazine		1839		Day's New York Bank Note List	Mahlon Day	1819	
Booksellers' Advertiser	West & Trour	1834		Democratic Chronicle ....d.	Wm. D. Hait	1834	1835
Book Trade, The..............mo.	H. Wilson	1850		Democratic Republican	W. Hagadorn	1831	
Bowery Boy, The	P. F. Harris	1856		Dental Recorder	Chas. W. Ballard.	1855	
British Chronicle	P. Brown, ed	1842		Dewitt & Davenport's Monthly Literary Gazette.		1851	
British News & Old Countryman	Vinter & Moody	1849		Diary, or Loudon's Register...	Samuel Loudon...	1791	1795
Broadway Journal	John Biscoe	1845		Dime, The	De Land & Clay	1854	
Bunker Hill, The	S. B. Dean & Co	1844		Dispatch & Tattler	Jas. G. Wilson & Co.	1840	
Business Reporter & Merchants and Mechanics' Advertiser	H. L. Barnum	1834		Dollar Weekly	Herrick & Roper	1843	
				Downfall of Babylon		1835	
				Dry Goods Reporter & Merchants' Gazette		1845	
Cabinet, The	Henry P. Piercy	1830	1831	Dye's Bank Bulletin............d.	John S. Dye	1855	
				Dye's Bank Mirror..........s. mo.	John S. Dye.		

Papers and Periodicals discontinued since the Revolution, continued.

Names of Papers.	Publishers.	When commenced.	When discontinued.	Names of Papers.	Publishers.	When commenced.	When discontinued.
Dye's Wall St. Broker	John S. Dye	1847		Gazette of the Union, Golden Rule, & Odd Fellows' Companion	Crampton & Clark.	1838	1852
Echo & Literary Military Chronicle	Crawley, Milne & Co	1846		Gazette of the United States...d.	Lany & Turner	1789	
Eclectic Museum	John H. Agnew	1843	1844	Genius of Temperance	Wm. Goodell & S. P. Hines		1832
Edmund, Charles & Co.'s Bank Note List		1840		Geographical & Commercial Gazette...mo.	J. Disturnell	1855	1855
Emancipator	Joshua Leavit, ed	1834		Gleaner, The	Charles King	1840	
Emerald & Political Literary & Commercial Recorder	Hugh H. Byrne	1824		Globe & Democratic Union ....d.	Caspar C. Childs	1848	
Emerson's Putnam's Monthly			1859	Globe & Emerald, or Saturday Journal of Literature, Politics, & Arts	T. W. Clerke & Co.	1825	
Emigrant, The	John S. Bartlett	1832	1836	Golden Rule		1845	
Emigrant & Old Countryman	John S. Bartlett	1836		Good Samaritan Messenger		1850	
Emigrants' Magazine...mo.	John Wiley	1834		Gospel Herald	F. Fisk	1830	
Empire Magazine...mo.	M. R. Andrews	1848		Gospel Luminary	Millard & Clough	1830	
Empire State		1840		Gospel Sun		1850	
Empire State Democrat	Hiram Cummings	1842		Gospel Witness		1838	
Enterpriad, The...s. mo.	G. W. Bleecker	1831		Green's National Guardian			
Epicurean Gondola	Isaac D. Geiger	1853		Halcyon Luminary & Theological Repository	Association	1812	1819
Era, The	W. T. Adams & Co.	1850		Harbinger, The	American Union of Associationists	1848	
Eureka, or National Journal of Inventions, Patents,& Sciences	J. L. Kingsley & J. P. Pierson	1846	1848	Hart's Path Finder		1847	
European, The	John W. Moore	1836		Herald of Christian Love & Working Man's Friend		1850	
European, The		1856		Herald & Gazette for the Country	Geo. Bunce & Co	1795	
European American	G. F. S. de Casale	1849		Herald of the Union	C. Edwards Lester.	1851	
European News	Kimber & Fine	1847		Hewitt's Excelsior	H. W. Hewitt	1846	
Evangelical Guardian & Review	Asso. of Clergymen	1817	1818	Holden's Dollar Magazine...mo.		1850	
Evening City Gazette		1828		Home Circle...mo.	Garret & Co	1855	
Evening Gazette	K. G. Evans	1845		Home Companion	S. M. Giddings &Co.	1857	
Evening Herald...d.	Kingsley, Barton & Co	1843		Home Missionary	Absalom Peters	1828	
Evening Mirror...d.	Morris & Willis	1827		Honest Wrath	M. Doheney, ed	1856	
Evening Signal	Jonas Winchester	1840		Horne's Rail Road Gazette	C. Horne	1849	
Evening Star...d. & s. w.	Noah & Gill	1834		Hudson's Exchange Shipping List...tri-w.	Wm. H. Hudson	1836	
Evening Star	W. Burns	1845		Human Rights	Amer. Anti Slavery Society	1836	
Evening Tattler	Dillon & Hooper	1840		Illustrated American News		1852	
Evergreen...mo.		1841		Illustrated News		1843	1843
Evergreen, The...mo.	J. Winchester	1840		Illustrated News	P. T. Barnum & H. D. Beach.	1853	1855
Evergreen, or Monthly Church Offering		1844		Illustrated New York News		1851	1852
Every Youth's Gazette	J. Winchester	1843		Independent Journal	Webster & McLean	1783	
Examiner, The...mo.	B Gardnier, ed	1812	1817	Independent Reflector		1752	
Examiner, The	J. Stevenson	1833		Independent Republican		1806	1807
Excelsior	W. H. McDonald & Co	1849		Industrial Agent	Wm. Newell & Co..	1848	
Expositor & Banking Circular		1849		Infant Drummer	J. Hillyer	1851	
Express Messenger	A. L. Stimson	1855		International Monthly Magazine	Stringer & Townsend	1850	1852
Family Companion...mo.	P. Childs & Co	1846		Investigator, The	Jarvis F. Hauks....	1830	
Family Keepsake...mo.	Burdick & Scovill	1857		Inveterate, The	Denman & Horn	1849	
Family Magazine...mo.	Redfield & Lindsley	1834	1840	Irish Democrat	John McLaughlin.	1832	
Family Minstrel...s. mo.	Chas. Dingley	1835		Irish Evangelist	John Hurley	1851	
Family Record	Ridgeway & Co.	1851		Irish Volunteer	M. O'Connor	1843	
Family Visitor & Silk Culturist	Theodore Dwight & others	1839		Iron Platform	Wm. Oland Bourne	1857	
Farmers' Guide to Science & Practical Agriculture	L. Scott & Co.			Island City		1846	
Farmers' Library & Monthly Journal of Agriculture		1846	1848	Israel's Herald		1849	
Farmers, Mechanics, Manufacturers, & Sporting Man's Magazine...mo.	Geo. Houston	1826		Janus	R. Henisen	1852	
Fathers' Magazine...mo.	John Wiley	1834		Jeffersonian, The	Childs, Devoe & Hill	1835	
Female Advocate...s. mo.	W. Goodell & S. P. Hines	1832		Jewish Chronicle...mo.	E. R. McGregor.....	1843	1856
Fireman's Gazette	Robert Sears	1835		Journal, The	B. Brandreth	1837	
Fisher's National Magazine & Historical Record	Rev. Wood Fisher.	1845	1848	Journal of Christian Education.	Rev. Benj. O. Pier & B. J. Height....	1843	
Flag of the Free	Williams Brothers.	1848		Journal des Dames...mo.			
Flag of Our Union	S. French	1848		Journal of the Fine Arts	Wm. B. Taylor	1845	
For. & Domestic Chronicle...mo.		1843		Journal of the Fine Arts & Musical World	W. T. Brockelbank & Co	1851	
Forcep, The...quar.	Tooth Manufac. Co	1855		Journal of the People...tri-w.		1847	
Forrester's Boy's & Girl's Magazine	W. C. Locke	1845		Journal of Progress	Harmonical Asso.	1853	
Frank Leslie's Gazette of Fashion	Frank Leslie	1853		Journal of Public Morals	Goodell, Hines & Niles	1832	
Frank Leslie's New York Journal...mo.	Frank Leslie	1855		Journal of Useful Knowledge & Monthly Record of New Publications		1850	
Franklin Daily Advertiser		1832		Journal of Women		1834	
Freedom's Journal	Cornish & Ruswarn	1827		Juvenile Wesleyan	Worthy L. Lee.	1839	
Free Enquirer	Frances Wright & R. D. Owen	1830	1834	Knickerbocker Gazette	L. Neely	1844	
Freeman's Journal & Catholic Register	Jas. M. White	1843		Ladies' Casket...mo.	J. C. Burdick	1848	
Free Press	Wm. Hagadorn	1834		Ladies' Companion...mo.	Wm. Snowdon ,	1835	
Free State Advocate	Jas. B. Swain	1856		Ladies' Diadem...mo.	J. C. Burdick	1848	
Gazette of Education & Sunday School Journal...s. mo.		1843		Ladies' Keepsake & Home Library...mo.	Burdick & Scovill	1855	
Gazette Extraordinary		1843		Ladies' Weekly Miscellany		1807	
Gazette of the Union		1847					

Papers and Periodicals discontinued since the Revolution, continued.

Names of Papers.	Publishers.	When commenced.	When discontinued.
Lady's Own	E. B. Childs, ed	1849	
Lancet, The	J. G. Bennett	1843	
Lantern, The	Jackson & Co	1852	
Last Section Visitor	W. O. Bourne	1846	
Leonori's Bank Note List	L. J. Leonori	1850	
Liberia Advocate, New York & St. Thomas		1848	
Life Insurance Examiner	John C. Johnston	1849	
Life in New York		1850	
Light Ship		1845	
Light Ship & Sunday School Monitor	Myron Finch		
Literary American	G. P. Quackenboss, ed	1848	
Literary Gazette	Swinburne & Patterson	1835	
Literary Journal	R. F. Tuckerman & Co	1852	
Literary Miscellany	J. Trow & Co	1849	
Literary & Scientific Repository & Critical Review	Wiley & Halsted	1820	1824
Literary & Theological Review mo.	Leon. Wood, jr., ed.	1834	
Literary World	C. F. Hoffman	1847	
Livingston & Wilmer's Express		1843	
Lyceum Reporter & Critical Miscellany mo.	Mortimer J. Smith	1843	
Magazine for the Million		1844	
Magazine of Horticulture		1840	
Magazine of Useful & Entertaining Knowledge			
Magnet	Le Roy Sunderland	1843	
Mason & Tuttle's Advertiser		1844	
Masonic Register & Union mo.	J. F. Adams	1854	
McKenzie's Gazette	Alex. McKenzie	1838	
Mearson's U. S. Bank Note Reporter		1848	
Mechanics & Farmers' Magazine of Useful Knowledge		1830	1831
Mechanics' Magazine	Miner & Shaeffer	1837	
Medical & Phil. Journal & Review	J. & T. Swords	1810	
Medical Repository & Review of Medicine & Surgery	J. & T. Swords	1810	
Mentor & Fireside Review		1839	
Mercantile Advertiser	Butler & Munford in 1830	1807	
Mercantile Advertiser & New York Advocate	Amos Butler & Co.	1834	
Mercantile Guide & Family Journal	Wm. E. Blakeney	1852	
Merchant's Day Book d.	N. R. Stimson & G. Foster	1849	
Merchant's Intelligencer	Eustis, Prescott & Co	1832	
Merchant's Ledger d.	Pratt & Requa	1846	
Message Bird	T. Brockelbank & Co	1842	
Methodist Protestant	A. T. Piercy	1836	
Metropolitan		1852	1852
Metropolitan Courier of the Union	Geo. Mearson	1847	
Metropolitan Magazine	Joseph Mason	1835	
Mid-Day Courier with the Morning Mails		1814	
Midnight Cry	Joshua V. Hines	1839	
Military Monitor & American Register	Joseph Desnones	1812	
Minerva, The	E. Bliss & E. White	1822	
Minerva, or Literary, Entertaining, & Scientific Journal	J. Houston & J. G. Brooks	1824	1825
Ming's New York Price Current		1809	
Mining Journal & American Rail Road Gazette	John E. Grant	1847	
Mirror of Fashion	Genio C. Scott	1839	
Mirror of the Times	W. W. Wallace	1848	
Monitor, The		1850	
Monitor & Messenger	J. E. Jones & C. B. Turner	1851	
Monthly Bulletin		1840	
Monthly Cosmopolite	Prentiss, Clark & Co	1848	
Monthly Diadem		1850	
Monthly Distribution		1835	
Monthly Family Circle & Parlor Annual	Geo. P. Metcalf	1841	
Monthly Journal of Agriculture	John S. Skinner	1845	1848
Monthly Lecturer of the National Society of Literature & Science	Theodorus Foster	1841	
Monthly Magazine & American Monthly Review	C. B. Brown, ed.; T. & J. Swords	1799	1801
Monthly Military Repository	Chas. Smith	1796	1797
Monthly Recorder		1813	1813
Monthly Recorder of Five Points House of Industry	L. M. Pease		
Monthly Record of Prison Association	Prison Asso. of New York	1857	
Monthly Register, Magazine, & Review of U. S	John Bristed	1855	
Monthly Repository & Library of Entertaining Knowledge	F. S. Wiggins	1830	1834
Monthly Trade Gazette	G. S. Wells	1855	
Moral & Daily Advertiser	Goodell & Hines	1832	
Moral Lyceum	C. C. P. Crosby	1833	
Mormon, The	John Taylor	1855	
Morning Chronicle d.	Lazarus Beach	1803	
Morning Chronicle d.	Lewis Jones & Co	1802	
Morning Chronicle d.	John W. Moore	1842	
Morning Chronicle & Tippecanoe Advertiser		1840	
Morning Post	Joseph Osborne	1810	
Morning Post & Family Gazette. d	Story & Hildreth	1832	
Morning Star	Williams Bro	1848	
Morning Telegraph	S. De Witt Bloodgood	1845	
Morning Times & Commercial Intelligencer	N. J. Eldridge	1840	
Morning Watch	J. V. Hines & others	1838	1846
Morris's National Press Journal for Home		1846	
Musical Magazine		1835	
Mustang Bulletin mo.		1853	
National Advocate s. w	Geo. White & Co	1812	
National Advocate for the Country	M. M. Noah	1825	
National Democrat	A. Ingraham, ed.; C. C. Childs, pub.	1851	
National Trades Union	D. Darling & E. J. Van Cleve	1835	
National Union		1824	
Naval Magazine bi-mo.	Rev. C. S. Stewart	1836	
Ned Buntline's Own	Edward Z. C. Judson	1848	
New Charitable Monthly	W. C. Conant	1855	
New Church Messenger quar.		1851	
New Church Repository mo.		1850	
New Era & American Courier. d. & w	J. W. Bell	1836	
New Industrial World	John White	1851	
New Mirror	Geo. P. Morris	1843	
New Monthly Messenger	B. Badger	1842	
News Boys' Pictorial	—— Dexter	1856	
New World	Park Benjamin, ed.; J. Winchester, pub	1839	
New York American	Johnson Verplanck	1820	
New York American for the Country	D. K. Miner	1834	
New York American Republic	J. F. Trow	1843	
New York American Sentinel		1846	
New York Amulet & Ladies' Literary & Religious Chronicle	F. Fisk, ed	1830	
New York Aurora	Thos. Dunn English	1841	
New York Bulletin		1840	
New York Business Chart	W. H. Starr	1847	
New York Cabinet	J. N. Moffatt	1830	1833
New York Cadet		1850	
New York Cadet & Daughter of Temperance	Daniel Cady	1847	
New York Christian Messenger	P. Price	1832	
New York Chronicle	Judd & Maclay	1851	
New York City Budget	J. F. Trow & Co	1843	
New York Columbian s. w	R. F. Mather	1851	
New York Commercial Transcript	Alden Spooner; Kellogg & Taylor	1842	
New York Crusader	G. F. Secchi de Casale	1853	
New York Cynosure		1843	
New York Daily Bee	John L. Knapp	1834	
New York Daily Gazette	Archibald McLean	1788	1817
New York Daily News		1843	
New York Daily Sentinel	Evans & Stanley	1830	

Papers and Periodicals discontinued since the Revolution, continued.

NAMES OF PAPERS.	Publishers.	When commenced.	When discontinued.
New York Daily Times	E. Philip Williams.	1849	
New York Democrat		1842	
New York Directory & Business Bulletin		1849	
New York Dissector....quar.	Dr. H. H. Sherwood	1845	
New York Dutchman	E. Weston & Co......	1848	
New York Ecclesiologist......mo.	H. M. Onderdonk, ed.	1848	1853
New York Evening Journal	Bush, Cook & Thompson	1830	
New York Evening Ledger	Greene & Co........	1846	
New York Examiner	R. Tyrrell..........	1824	
New York Examiner	M. M. Noah..........	1826	
New York Examiner	Wm. L. McKenzie.	1843	
New York Expositor.........mo.		1847	
New York Family Herald	Jas. Warnock......	1855	
New York Farmers & American Gardeners' Magazine	D. K. Miner.........	1843	
New York Farmers' & Historical Repository		1830	
New York Farmer & Mechanic...	W. H. Stewart & J. M. Stearns......	1845	1857
New York Fireman's Journal....	John W. Fowler...	1858	1858
New York Galaxy		1826	
New York Gazette & General Advertiser	Long, Turner & Co.	1831	1840
New York Herald		1802	
New York Jeffersonian	E. Charles..........	1845	
New York Journal.............s. w.		1810	
New York Journal of Education	J. McKean, S. S. Randall & J. S. Denman	1846	
New York Journal & Patriotic Register	Thos. Greenleaf.....	1757	
New York Journal, or Weekly Register	Eleazer Osgood......	1786	
New York Legal Observer	S. Owen.........	1843	
New York Literary Gazette & Φ B K Repository	Jas. G. Brooks...	1826	1827
New York Literary Journal & Belle Lettre Repository		1819	1821
New York Literary Magazine & American Atheneum	Jas. S. Brooks	1825	
New York Luminary & Weekly Messenger		1843	
New York Machinist............mo.	S. C. Hill............	1850	
New York Magazine & Literary Repository		1790	
New York Mechanic	R. Roster & Co.....	1843	
New York Medical Gazette...mo.	D. M. Reese, ed......	1850	
New York Medical Inquirer..mo.	Association of Physicians & Surgeons	1830	
New York Medical Magazine.mo.		1810	1811
New York Medical & Philosophical Journal.	Anonymous	1809	1811
New York Medical & Philosophical Journal............quar.	John W. Francis, Jacob Dyckman, & John Beck	1810	1814
New York Medical & Philosophical Register	Drs. Hosack & Francis	1822	
New York Medical Times.....mo.	H. D. Bulkley	1851	
New York Medical Repository	S. L. Mitchell, E. Miller, & E. H. Smith	1797	
New York Mentor.......semi. mo.	S. Wild..............	1831	
New York Mercantile Journal tri-w.	Lyon & Hillyer......	1854	
New York Messenger & Traveller	A. L. Stimson	1839	
New York Mirror	D. Fanshaw	1843	
New York Mirror & Ladies' Literary Gazette	S. Woodworth & G. P. Morris ...	1823	1842
New York Miscellany		1850	
New York Missionary Magazine. mo.	T. Swords	1800	1804
New York Monthly Chronicle....	Association of Physicians	1824	
New York Morning Herald	A. Nash & Co.......	1830	
New York Morning News	J. L. O'Sullivan & S. J. Tilden....	1844	
New York Morning Post	Morton & Horner..	1781	
New York Morning Post & Daily Advertiser	Wm. Morton.........	1788	
New York Musical Gazette & Literary Lyceum	Chas. Dingley........	1840	
New York Musical Review & Gazette............s. mo.	Mason Bros...........	1855	
New York National Reformer ...	Thos. Ainge Devyn	1844	
New York Patriot & Morning Advertiser	J. J. Negrin..........	1808	
New York People's Organ	Jas. McKean	1841	1856
New York Picayune	Woodard & Co	1850	
New York Pilot	S. Skinner.........	1831	
New York Planet	Kellogg & Co........	1840	
New York Quarterly	C. B. Norton........	1852	
New York Quarterly	Jas. G. Reed........	1855	
New York Recorder	Colley & Ballard.....	1845	
New York Recorder & Baptist Register	E. Wright, jr., & L. S. Cutting	1848	
New York Register & Anti Masonic Review...........semi.	Henry Dana Ward	1831	
New York Register & Gazette.mo.	W. Green..............	1844	
New York Register of Medicine & Pharmacy..............mo.	C. B. Norton.........	1850	
New York Religious Chronicle...	Gray & Bunce.......	1823	
New York Review		1837	1843
New York Review & Atheneum Magazine..............mo.	E. Bliss & E. White.	1825	1827
New York Saturday Post	Henry Clapp & T. B. Aldrich.		
New York Scorpion	Geo. Mearson & Co.	1848	
New York Sentinel.............s. w.		1830	
New York Shamrock	Michael Tookey.....	1822	
New York Shanghai		1855	
New York Spectator.........s. w.	Francis Hall & Co..	1830	
New York Sporting Magazine.mo.	C. R. Colden........	1835	
New York Spy		1807	
New York Spy		1820	
New York Standard...........s. mo.	Henry House.		
New York Standard & Statesman	John G. Mumford.	1831	
New York Statesman...........s. w.	A. Nash & Co.......	1822	
New York Telegraph	Rev. A. Dickinson..	1845	
New York Telescope	Wooster Beach	1830	
New York Times	Holland, Sanford & Davies............	1835	
New York Transcript.............d.	Haywood, Stanley & Co............	1833	
New York Traveler	Simon Hunt........	1832	
New York Visitor ....mo.	J. W. Harrison.....	1843	
New York Visitor & Parlor Companion	D. Joseph...........	1838	
New York Washingtonian.........	J. Burns.............	1842	
New York Washington Reformer & Literary Journal		1843	
New York Watchman		1836	
New York Waverley and Literary Home Circle	B. Baker & Co......	1858	
New York Weekly Critic	Cleaveland & McElrath	1855	
New York Weekly Globe	Geo. R. Hazewell...	1846	
New York Weekly Leader	Cleaveland & McElrath	1853	
New York Weekly Magazine & Miscellaneous Repository	John Bull............	1795	
New York Weekly Messenger		1831	
New York Weekly Messenger	P. Donaldson........	1840	
New York Weekly Messenger & Young Men's Advocate	Burnett & Smith...	1832	
New York Weekly Mirror	Morris & Willis.....	1827	
New York Weekly Museum	M. Harrison........	1810	
New York Weekly News		1845	
New York Weekly Record	Gavin, Rodgers & Co..................	1832	
New York Weekly Register & Catholic Diary	Association..........	1834	
New York Weekly Whig	J. S. Wilson........	1833	
New York Weekly Whig.d. & w.	O. L. Holley & H. D. Ward........	1833	
Nichols' Monthly	Thos. L. Nichols...	1855	
Nineteenth Century		1848	
Nisbitt's American Times	G. F. Nisbitt & Co..	1849	
Norton's Literary Advertiser...	Chas. B. Norton...	1851	
Norton's Literary Gazette & Publishers' Circular...	Chas. B. Norton...	1854	
Odd Fellows' Literary Magazine..		1848	
Old Countryman		1829	
Olio, The...	S. Marks...........	1813	
Olive Plant		1841	
Olive Plant & Ladies' Temperance Advocate	Pierce & Reed.......	1841	
L'Oracle, L'Echo du Jour, & Daily Advertiser	J. J. Negrin........	1808	
Organ of the Washington Soc. & Auxiliaries		1843	
Parker's Journal & Weekly Gaz.	Wm. B. Parker.....	1850	

Papers and Periodicals discontinued since the Revolution, continued.

Names of Papers.	Publishers.	When commenced.	When discontinued.
Parley's Magazine.............mo.	C. S. Francis & Co..	1843	
Parlor Annual...........mo.	Rev. D. Newell......	1845	
Parlor Magazine.............	John W. Moore......	1835	
Passion Flower..............	Miss A. Reed........	1836	
Path Finder.................	Park Godwin	1843	
Paul Pry...................	A. Noonan & Co....	1840	
Peabody's Parlor Journal..	Peabody & Co......	1834	
Pekin Tea Company's Gazette...		1847	
People's Democratic Guide...	James Webster.....	1841	
People's Friend and Daily Advertiser.....	J. Frank...........	1806	
Penny Dispatch.............	Pooler & Co........	1850	
Penny Gazette..............	Dr. J. M. Lovell.....	1854	
Petit Courrier des Dames, or Monthly Journal of Fashion....		1836	
Photographic Art Journal....mo.		1851	
Picture Gallery............		1844	
Plain Dealer...............	Wm. Leggett........	1830	
Pooler & Co.'s Weekly Dispatch..	(Formerly Wilson's Dispatch)........	1851	
Popular Educator........mo.	A. Montgomery....	1853	
Price Current..............	Alex. Miny........	1807	
Progressive Democrat........	E. Stranahan......	1849	
Propagandist............mo.	John F. Trow......	1850	
Protestant Episcopal Pulpit.mo.	H. Dyer	1831	
Protestant Magazine........	L. D. Dewey.......	1834	
Protestant Vindicator............	Bowne, Wisner & Co............	1835	
Public Advertiser............	J. Frank & Co......	1807	
Public Ledger..............		1842	
Publishers' Journal & Teachers & Parents' Companion..........	O. Hutchinson......	1847	
Pulpit Reporter............	Holbrook, Buckingham & Co....	1850	
Putnam's Monthly Magazine.....	Geo. P. Putnam....	1853	1856
Quarterly Anti Slavery Magazine	Elizur Wright, jr...	1836	
Quarterly Paper of Foreign Evangelical Society........	John S. Taylor	1843	
Rail Road Advocate...........	Z. Colborn..........	1857	
Rambler's Magazine & Historical Register............mo.		1809	
Real Estate Gazette............	Joseph Barlow......	1855	
Rechabite and Temperance Bugle............mo.	M. & T. J. Strong..	1845	
Reformed Dutch Magazine........	R. P. D. Clergymen.....	1834	
Register and Spirit of the Press..	V. B. Palmer........	1849	
Register of the Times.........	J. Crooker..........	1797	
Religious Magazine........mo.	O. Batcheler, ed.....	1835	
Reporter & Banking Circular....		1831	
Reports of Practice Cases in New York Courts.........mo.	Abbott Bros......		
Republic, A Monthly Magazine of Am. Lit. Pol. & Arts........	Thos. R. Whitney...	1851	1855
Republican Watch Tower ...s. w.	Jas. Chatham......	1801	
Reviser...................mo.	Rev. Silas E. Shepherd..........	1854	
Revue Française des Familles et des Personnages.......		1844	
Richardson's Journal........		1857	
Rough & Ready...............		1847	
Rush Light.................	Wm. Cobbett......	1799	1799
Sabbath Magazine........mo.		1835	
Sabbath Monitor............	Myron Finch......	1845	
Sabbath School Monitor....s. mo.	Myron Finch & Chas. Parker......	1841	
Sachem....................	Thos. Picton........	1853	
Sacred Circle..............	Judge Edmonds, Dr. Dexter, & O. G. Warren........	1852	
Sargent's New Monthly...........	Epes Sargent......	1843	
Saturday Emporium.........	Edmund B. Green..	1844	
Saturday Evening Gazette........	T. W. Clarke & S. Paine........	1827	
Saxoni's Musical Times.......mo.		1849	
Sears' Family Visitor.......mo.		1851	
Sears' New Monthly Magazine..	Robert Sears......	1846	
Self Instructor...........mo.	Josiah Holbrook....	1843	
School Fellow............	J. S. Dickerson......	1855	
School and Home Journal........	Marcius Willson....	1857	1858
School Mate...............	Rev. A. R.Phippen..	1850	
Scientific Correspondent............	A. C. Morey........	1846	
Scientific Mechanic.........	Rufus Porter......	1847	
Scottish Journal............	J. G. Cummings....	1840	
Scottish Patriot............		1840	
Scovill's Family Gazetteer........		1850	
Scrutinizer..............s. w.	Chas. Y. Baldwin...	1827	
Shamrock, or Hibernian Chron..	Edward Gillespie...	1830	

Names of Papers.	Publishers.	When commenced.	When discontinued.
Shekinah................	Partridge & Britton...............	1853	
Shilling Gazette ....mo.	Moore & Jackson...	1845	
Sober Second Thought.............	Daniel E. Sickles...	1844	
Spectator.................	Geo. F. Hopkins....	1798	
Spirit of the Age		1845	
Spirit of the Age	Scovill & Hyatt.....	1847	
Spirit of the Age	Fowler & Wells.....	1849	
Spirit of Seventy-Six................	J. G. Brooks & E. V. Sparhawk.....	1835	
Sporting Chronicle................	Wm. T. Porter......	1852	
Standard Bearer..................mo.	Rev. H. Dyer........	1847	
Starns & Co.'s Monthly Bulletin...		1847	
Stars and Stripes..............	Fay & Carr..........	1843	
Star Spangled Banner..........	Dexter & Bro......	1857	
Star in the West, or Marion Chronicle..............	T. W. Cummings...	1812	
Statesman...................	C. C. Tunison.......		
Stimmet's & Pettigrew's American Report of Fashions........		1851	
Student & Young Tutor............	J. S. Denman......	1848	
Sunday Era.................		1850	
Sunday Herald.............	Geo. Glentworth....	1851	
Sunday Leader.............	Ingraham & Sweet	1855	
Sunday Mail................		1831	
Sunday Morning News............	Sam. Jenks Smith.	1836	
Sunday Morning News............	J. Leavitt...........	1840	
Sunday News...............		1847	
Sunday Reporter............	S. Vail...............	1832	
Sunday School Journal....s. mo.	Amer. S. S. Union..	1829	
Sunday School Visitor.........	P. E. S. S. Union...	1835	
Sunday Times & Noah's Weekly Messenger.........			
Sylvester's New Reporter	Sylvester & Co	1840	
Sylvester's Reporter, Counterfeit Detector, and New York Price Current............	S. J. Sylvester.....	1832	
Tailor's Eclectic Repository..mo.	D. S. & G. Williams	1845	
Teachers' Advocate & Journal of Education..............	J. M. McKean & E. P. Allen..........	1846	
Temperance Advocate..............	Goodell & Hines....	1831	
Temperance Budget......s. mo.	W. Goodell & S. P. Hines	1832	
Thalia, or the Gentleman's Company.			
The German Correspondent......	Herman..............	1820	
The Great City..............		1845	
The Log Cabin..............	H. Greeley........	1840	1840
The Man..................	Geo. H. Evans......	1834	
The Nation................		1849	
The New Yorker...........	H. Greeley & Co....	1835	
The New Yorker...........	Stuart & Webster..	1850	
The Old Countryman	J. T. Pickering, ed.	1842	
The Parthenon.............	S. Woodworth......	1827	
The Parthenon.............		1851	
The People................	J. Devin Riley & W. E. Robinson..	1849	
The People's Press...........	R. & T. Hamilton...	1841	1856
The People's Rights..........	Windt & Evans	1844	
The People's Weekly Journal....	R. Walsh	1850	
The Pick..................	Joseph E. Scovill..	1836	
The Plain Dealer.............	Wm. Van Norden..	1836	
The Plow..................mo.	C. M. Saxton......	1852	
The Plow, the Loom, & the Anvil	J. S. Skinner & Sons	1848	1851
The Prophet...............	S. Brannon..........	1845	
The Protestant, or Exposer of Popery..............	Rev. Geo. Eourne & Dr. Brownlee.....	1830	
The Rainbow..............		1841	
The Ramshorn.............	Van Rensselaer & Rogers.............	1847	
The Recruit................	Gallagher& Morrell	1848	
The Republic..............	Jonas Winchester..	1843	
The Rights of All..........	S. E. Cornish......	1830	
The Rising Sun............		1850	
The Rover	Labra & Dean.......	1844	
The Sun..................	Day & Wisner......	1834	1837
The Transcript.............	Haywood, Lynd & Stanley	1835	
The Town.................	Andrews, Beaumont & Co.........	1845	
The Uncle Sam............	Dexter & Bro......	1847	
The Union................d.	J. Phillips & Co.....	1843	
The Union................d.	M. M. Noah.........	1842	
The Unit.................		1850	
The War.................	S. Woodworth & Co.	1812	
The Way of Life..........	Edgar & Herries....	1858	
The Whig.................		1850	
The Whip.................	Geo. B. Wooldridge	1843	

Papers and Periodicals discontinued since the Revolution, concluded.

Names of Papers.	Publishers.	When commenced.	When discontinued.	Names of Papers.	Publishers.	When commenced.	When discontinued.
The World	J. M. Church	1837		Weekly Inspector	Thos. G. Fessenden	1806	1807
The Yankee	Williams Bro	1848		Weekly Journal	N. R. Stimson	1850	
Time Piece	Philip Freneau	1797	1800	Weekly Memorial & New York City Record	Pickering, Beaumont & Oakes	1812	
Transactions of American Ethnological Society	Society	1845		Weekly Museum		1807	
Traveller, Times, & Journal	Hunt & Adams	1831		Weekly New Yorker	Wm. Fairman & C. D. Stuart	1851	
True American	Wm. E. Blakeney	1852					
True Flag	Dexter & Bro	1857		Weekly Review	VanWinkle& Riqua	1845	
True Sun, Daily	Assoc'n of Printers	1843	1845	Weekly Tattler	Dillon & Hooper	1842	
True Sun	Gallagher & Kettell	1849		Weekly Times	N. T. Eldredge	1849	
True Wesleyan	O. Scott	1845		Weekly Universe	Williamson&Burns	1845	
Two Worlds	John W. Moore	1843		Weekly Visitor	Daniel Cady	1832	
United States Advertising Circular		1851		Weekly Western World	J. F. Bridge	1837	
United States Economist	J. P. Kettell	1852		Welcome Guest	Winchester& Hackstaff	1851	
United States Farmer & Journal of American Institute...mo.	S. Fleet	1843		West's Sunday News	Frederick West	1846	
United States Law Journal..mo.	George F. Hopkins	1825		Whig Union	S. De Witt Bloodgood, ed	1848	
United States Magazine	J. M. Emerson& Co.	1854		White Man's Newspaper		1851	
United States Military and Naval Argus	John Crawley, ed.	1838		Whittlery's (Mrs.) Magazine	A. G. Whittlery, ed.	1849	
United States Nautical Magazine & Naval Journal	Griffiths & Bates	1855		Wide Awake	R. Bonner	1854	
United States Review "Democracy" .....mo.	Lloyd & Campbell	1853		Wilson & Co.'s Dispatch.....mo.			
United States Service Journal	S. W. W. Tompkins	1825		Woman's Temperance Paper	MaryC.Vaughan,ed	1854	
Univercœlum & Spiritual Philosopher		1847		Wood's Quarterly Retrospect of American & Foreign Practice of Medicine & Surgery	R. & G. S. Wood	1847	1848
Universal Traveller	Daniel Hewitt	1843		Woodworth's Youth's Cabinet	F. C. Woodworth	1839	
Universalist Union	P. Price	1836		Workers' Journal		1849	
Vial of Wrath; Junk Bottle of Destruction	(Satire upon Millerites)	1843		Working Farmer.....mo.	Kingman, Cross & Co. J. J. Mapes, ed.		
Visitor & Ladies' Parlor Magazine		1840		Working Men's Advocate	Geo. H. Evans	1830	
Voice of the People	W. S. Hawley	1846		Yankee Doodle	W. H. Graham	1847	
Wall Street Journal	Fred. Robinson	1851		Y Cyfail (The Friend)	W. Rowland.		
Wall Street Reporter		1842		Young America	Geo. H. Evans	1844	
Washingtonian	Herrick & Ropes	1843		Young America		1856	
Washingtonian Daily News	L. Starr & Co.	1843		Youth's Cabinet.....s. m.	N. Southard	1838	
Washingtonian Organ	James Burns	1843		Youth's Companion & Weekly Family Visitor	Burnett & Smith	1832	
Washington Republican		1810		Youth's Friend.....mo.		1843	
Water Cure Visitor & Health Journal	Joel Shew.			Youth's Penny Gazette	Amer. S. S. Union.	1851	1858
Weekly Chronicle	Hudson & Co	1840		Youth's Temperance Lecturer mo.	Goodell, Hines & Niles	1832	
				Zion's Watchman	Le Roy Sunderland	1836	

NIAGARA FALLS:

FROM THE AMERICAN SHORE.

NIAGARA COUNTY.

This county was formed from Genesee, March 11, 1808. Erie was taken off April 2, 1821. It lies upon the w. border of the State, in the angle formed by the junction of Niagara River and Lake Ontario. It is centrally distant 255 mi. from Albany, and contains 558 sq. mi. The surface is generally level or gently undulating. It is divided into 2 distinct parts or terraces by a ridge extending E. and W. The lake shore is a bluff 10 to 30 feet high, and from its summit the lower terrace slopes gradually upward to the foot of an elevation known as the mountain ridge, where it attains an elevation of 100 to 150 feet above the lake. This ridge extends E. and W. through the N. part of Royalton and Lockport, and near the center of Cambria and Lewiston, and forms the N. declivity of the s. terrace. At its w. extremity it has an elevation of 250 feet above the lower terrace, and is nearly perpendicular. This height gradually declines toward the E., and upon the E. line of the co. it has an elevation of 80 to 100 feet. Through the central part of the co. the ridge is divided into two declivities, separated by a plateau from a few rods to a half mi. in width. The upper ridge is limestone, and for many mi. presents the face of a perpendicular cliff. Throughout the co. the ridge is too steep for cultivation. The s. half of the co., extending s. from the summit of this ridge, is very level. It has a slight inclination toward the s., and terminates in the Tonawanda Swamp. The whole inclination of the slope within the limits of the co., however, does not exceed 30 feet. The lake ridge—supposed to have been the ancient shore of the lake—extends w. from Orleans co. through Hartland and Newfane, thence turns s. w., and appears to terminate near Lockport Village. It appears again farther w., and at Cambria it is divided into two parts, the N. extending N. w. about 3 mi. and gradually declining to a level of the general surface, and the s. extending s. w. and uniting with the mountain ridge 4 mi. E. of Lewiston.[1] This ridge is composed of sand and gravel and the usual debris thrown up by a large body of water, and in character is essentially different from the surrounding surface. It varies from 5 to 25 feet in height, and is 20 to 150 feet in width. The N. descent is generally slightly longer and steeper than the s. The lowest rock in the co. is the Medina sandstone, which crops out in the ravines along the shore of the lake. It is the underlying rock of the w. half of the co., and extends to the foot of the mountain ridge. This ridge is composed of the sandstones and limestones belonging to the Niagara and Clinton groups, the heavy masses of compact limestone appearing at the top. The Onondaga salt group occupies a narrow strip along the s. border of the co. Nearly the entire surface is covered with deep deposits of drift, the rocks only appearing on the declivities of the mountain ridge and in the ravines of the streams.

Springs of weak brine are found in the ravines throughout the N. half of the co. They exude from the Medina sandstone; but none of them are sufficiently strong to be profitably worked. The Medina sandstone which lies at the foot of the mountain ridge has been quarried at several places for paving and flagging. Above the sandstone is a layer of impure limestone, about 4 feet thick, from which water cement is manufactured. The Niagara limestone furnishes an excellent building material and a good quality of lime. The principal quarries are situated in the vicinity of Lockport, and from them were obtained the stone for the construction of the canal locks at that place.[2] A vein of this stone filled with fossils admits of a high polish, and is used for ornamental purposes, presenting a beautiful variegated appearance.

Niagara River forms the w. and a part of the s. boundary of the co. It flows almost due w. from the E. extremity of Grand Island to the Falls, and thence nearly due N. to Lake Ontario. It contains several small islands belonging to this co., the principal of which are Tonawanda, Cayuga, Buckhorn, and Goat Islands. In its passage from Lake Erie to Lake Ontario, a distance of about

---

[1] This deflection in the course of the lake ridge must have been caused by a large bay that extended s. toward Lockport; and the N. branch of the ridge which terminates so abruptly in Cambria was undoubtedly a bar extending into the lake. Two large streams probably discharged their waters into this bay,— one through the ravine in which the Erie Canal is located, and one through a deep ravine about 2 mi. w. of Lockport. At the

head of the latter ravine is a nearly perpendicular precipice, at which point must have been a waterfall.

[2] This stone is found along the whole course of the mountain ridge, and can be quarried in every town. The deep cut in the canal w. of Lockport is through this strata, and the perpendicular ledges of rock on each side present the most favorable location in the co. for quarrying.

30 mi., the river descends 334 feet, the difference of level between the two lakes. Above Schlosser and below Lewiston the current of the river is not very rapid, and the descent is trifling, so that nearly the whole fall is condensed into a space of about 8 mi. The plateau in which the basin of Lake Erie is situated extends to the mountain ridge at Lewiston, the summit of the ridge being 34 feet higher than Lake Erie. The river originally must have flowed over the face of this precipice, at which time Niagara Falls were 7 mi. below their present position. By the wearing away of the rocks the falls have gradually receded, becoming lower at each period of their progress, and leaving a deep, rocky channel, with ragged and precipitous banks 200 feet high, to mark their course and attest their power.[1] At the present time the falls are at the abrupt angle where the river changes from a w. to a n. course, and the water is precipitated in part over the front or extremity of the chasm and in part over the side, the two parts of the fall being at nearly right angles to each other. Goat Island, having an area of about 70 acres, lies between the two falls, its w. edge being a continuation of the precipice over which the water flows.[2] The principal fall at the head of the chasm on the w. side is known as the Canadian or Horse Shoe Fall,[3] and the fall e. of Goat Island as the American Fall. The Canadian Fall is 2000 feet wide and 154 feet high, and the American Fall 900 feet wide and 163 feet high; and it is estimated that 100 million tons of water flow over the two falls every hour. A mi. above the edge of the falls a series of rapids commences, the water descending 60 feet before taking the final plunge.[4] From the foot of the cataract the river flows about 2 mi. in a comparatively still current, but from that point to Lewiston it is compressed within narrow banks, and flows through the tortuous, rocky channel in a perfectly tumultuous and resistless torrent. The immense body of water in Niagara gives to the falls, and to the rapids both above and below, a grandeur scarcely equaled by any other of nature's works. Here one of the largest rivers in the world, forming the outlet of the great internal fresh water seas of North America, plunges down the shelving rapids and leaps into the profound chasm below, and then whirls and struggles with an apparently almost irresistible force in its rocky channel for 7 mi., and at last emerges from its mountain barrier and spreads out into the calm and peaceful waters of Ontario. Scenes of surpassing sublimity and grandeur open upon the view at every point, and pilgrims from every part of the world flock hither to offer their devotions at one of the great shrines of universal nature.

Tonawanda Creek forms the greater part of the s. boundary of the co. Along its course are a series of extensive marshes known as the Tonawanda Swamp.[5] The other principal streams are

[1] The precipice over which the water flows is composed of solid, compact limestone, with shale above and below. The wearing away of the shale above has formed the rapids, and the disintegration of that below has left the limestone in overhanging masses until they break off with their own weight. The dip of the rock is toward the s.; and as the falls recede the surface of the limestone will come nearer and nearer the present bottom of the fall, until, at a distance of 4 mi. farther back, it will entirely disappear, and, the soft shales wearing away irregularly, the river will at some distant period of the future fall in a series of rapids.

[2] Luna Island lies upon the precipice n. of Goat Island, and is separated from it by a stream 65 feet wide, which forms a distinct fall. Beneath the shelving rock over which this small cataract flows is a recess of 30 feet, known as the Cave of the Winds. Three small islands lying near the head of Goat Island are called the Three Sisters. Bath Island lies between Goat Island and the American shore, about 50 rods above the falls. A bridge extends from the American shore to Bath Island, and another thence to Goat Island. The first bridge was built in 1817; but the next spring it was swept away by the ice. The one built in 1818, and rebuilt in 1839, was replaced by the present iron bridge in 1857. The cribs were sunk in the rapids from the end of a long platform projecting from the shore and heavily loaded with stone to keep it firm. As one crib was sunk and filled with stone, the platform was pushed forward and another sunk at its extremity; and so on to the island. Before the bridge was built, access to the island was attended with great peril, and very few persons had attempted it. It was done by shooting down in boats from above, a strong rope being fastened to the shore, by which the boat in returning was swung back. It is related that the first white person who visited the island was Israel Putnam, in 1755, while on a campaign against Fort Niagara.—*Dwight's Travels, IV.* 88. The Indians appear to have crossed occasionally, and traces of their graves are still seen. On the 23d of Feb. 1811, Augustus Porter applied for the purchase of the island, upon which to keep sheep, and alleged in his petition that the wolves that infested the settlement rendered this business next to impossible without some asylum like this for their preservation. It was afterward bought by the Porters.

[3] This name was given from the semicircular shape of the edge of the cliff over which the water flowed. The shape now is nearly that of a right angle.

[4] Numerous improvements have been made to afford facilities to visitors. A staircase constructed at the n. extremity of the American Fall, some years since, was burnt and rebuilt in 1858; another, upon Goat Island, was built in 1829, and called the Biddle Staircase; and another near Table Rock, upon the Canada shore, by which visitors can descend to the bottom of the precipice. A row boat ferry crosses the river from the foot of the American Staircase, and a carriage road extends up the bank on the Canadian side. A little w. of Goat Island, in the midst of the rapids near the edge of the precipice, a stone tower 45 ft. high was constructed, in 1833, to afford a more extensive view of the falls. The *"Maid of the Mist,"* a small steamer, makes trips upon the river from her dock, a little above Suspension Bridge, into the foam and mist just below the Canadian Fall. The awful majesty of this cataract is seen to great advantage in the winter season, when the spray settling upon all objects in the vicinity covers them with a glittering crust of ice. The rocks below become loaded with immense masses; and in extremely cold winters the river below gets blocked in so as to form a natural bridge, over which people venture to cross to the Canada shore and even up to the island. In the winter of 1841-42 the river was passable for several months, and a small house was built near the center for the sale of refreshments. The ice was estimated to be 100 ft. thick. A year seldom passes without several fatal accidents happening at these falls, and an enumeration of those who have been drawn into the rapids, or who have slipped from the precipice and been mangled upon the rocks below, would form a long and mournful catalogue. In 1827 the Michigan, a condemned schooner, was sent over the falls, with several animals on board, in the presence of 15,000 spectators. She mostly went to pieces in the rapids. In 1829 the schooner Superior, and in 1841 the ship Detroit, were towed into the rapids, but the former lodged several days, and the latter was permanently grounded upon the rocks in the rapids.

[5] This swamp could be drained if the State dam at the mouth of Tonawanda Creek was removed; and this only is needed to convert the tract into the most productive region in the co. As the land is cleared, it becomes sufficiently dry for agricultural purposes. The muck and marl which abound in the swamp, and the limestone and gypsum which underlie it, are all sources of great agricultural wealth.

Four Mile, Six Mile, Twelve Mile, and Eighteen Mile Creeks,—named from their respective distances from the mouth of Niagara River,—Fish and Golden Hill Creeks, all emptying into Lake Ontario; Mud Creek and East Branch, tributaries of Tonawanda Creek, and Cayuga and Gill Creeks, tributaries of Niagara River. The streams that flow N. have all worn deep ravines in the drift deposits; and they are frequently interrupted by falls, furnishing abundance of water-power.

A strip of land extending from the summit of the mountain ridge about 2 mi. s. is covered with a sandy loam, and the remainder of the upper terrace is clayey, largely intermixed with muck along the s. border. The soil between the mountain and lake ridges is a clayey loam, and along the lake ridge and N. of it it is a sandy and gravelly loam. The people are principally engaged in grain raising, for which the co. is most admirably adapted; barley, oats, corn, and potatoes are the staple agricultural products.[1] The manufacture of flour and other articles is largely carried on at Lockport, and the manufacturing interests at Niagara Falls are on the increase. The vast water power that can be made available at the falls will continually attract the attention of practical men, until eventually an immense manufacturing interest will be built up.

The co. seat is located at the village of Lockport.[2] The courthouse is a stone building erected upon a fine lot in the w. part of the village.[3] The jail, situated upon the same lot, is a well constructed stone building, but destitute of means of ventilation. The average number of inmates is 27. The co. clerk's office is a stone fireproof building contiguous to the courthouse.[4] The poorhouse is located upon a farm of 130 acres 3 mi. N. w. of the courthouse. The average number of inmates is 95, supported at a weekly cost of 50 cts. each. The farm yields a revenue of $1000. A teacher is constantly employed to teach the children and to exercise a constant supervision over them. The insane are properly provided for, and are uniformly treated kindly.[5]

The Erie Canal enters the co. near the N. line of Royalton, and extends s. w. to Lockport, thence nearly due s. to Tonawanda Creek, and thence along that creek to its mouth. The heaviest and most extensive work upon the canal is at Lockport, where the passage of the mountain ridge is effected. A series of combined double locks, 5 in number, overcomes an elevation of 56 ft., and from the summit a deep cut through the solid limestone extends several miles westward.[6] The Rochester, Lockport, & Niagara Falls Division of the N. Y. Central R. R. extends through Royalton, Lockport, Cambria, and Niagara, and a corner of Lewiston and Wheatfield, terminating at Suspension Bridge upon Niagara River. The Buffalo & Lockport Branch R. R. extends s. w. from Lockport through Cambria, Pendleton, and Wheatfield. The Buffalo & Niagara Falls R. R. extends along Niagara River through Niagara and Wheatfield, and a N. branch is extended to Lewiston. The Canandaigua & Niagara Falls Branch R. R. unites with the B. & N. F. R. R. at Tonawanda.[7]

Three daily and five weekly newspapers are published in the co.[8]

---

[1] Wheat formed the great staple of the co. until about 1850, when the midge commenced its ravages.

[2] When the co. was first erected, the co. seat was fixed at Buffalo. The buildings were given up to Erie co. upon the erection of the latter county.

[3] This building was erected in 1824. The first co. officers were, Augustus Porter, First Judge; Louis S. Le Couteulx, Co. Clerk; Asa Ransom, Sheriff; and Archibald S. Clarke, Surrogate.

[4] Built in 1856, at a cost of $13,000.

[5] The Senate Committee in 1856 concluded the report upon this institution as follows:—"The house is well kept, and by the result proves that, as a question of economy merely, it is less expensive to maintain a good poorhouse than it is a poor one."

[6] The project of building a ship canal around Niagara Falls has from time to time excited much attention, and several surveys have been made, but thus far without result. The earliest incorporation for this object was in 1798.

[7] In 1838 a horse-car R. R. was built from Lewiston, 3 mi., to connect with the Lockport & Niagara Falls R. R.; but the track has been transferred to the Central R. R. Co. The Niagara & Lake Ontario R. R., extending from Niagara Falls to Youngstown, has been built, but it is not yet in operation.

[8] The Niagara Democrat, the first paper published in the co., was started at Lewiston in 1821 by Benjamin Furguson. In the following year it was removed to Lockport, and soon after changed to

The Lockport Observatory. In Aug. 1822, it passed into the hands of Orsamus Turner, and in 1828 it was united with the Niagara Sentinel and issued as

The Sentinel and Observatory. In 1828, Peter Besançon, jr., became the proprietor, and changed it to

The Lockport Journal. In 1829 it was purchased by Asa Story and changed to

The Lockport Balance. In 1834 it was united with The Gazette, under the name of

The Balance and Gazette. It was soon afterward changed again to

The Lockport Balance. It was successively published by Isaac C. Colton and T. H. Hyatt until 1837, when it was sold to Turner & Lyon and merged in The Niagara Democrat.

The Lewiston Sentinel was commenced at Lewiston in 1823 by James O. Daily. It soon after passed into the hands of Oliver Grace, who removed it to Lockport and issued it as

The Niagara Sentinel. In 1828 it was united with The Lockport Observatory.

The Gazette was started at Lockport in 1833 by P. Baker. In 1834 it was united with The Balance.

The Niagara Democrat was started at Lockport in 1835 by Turner & Lyon. In 1837 it was united with The Balance and issued as

The Niagara Democrat and Lockport Balance. The latter part of the title was soon dropped. In 1839 it passed into the hands of T. P. Scoville; and in 1846, into those of Turner & McCollum. It was continued by different publishers until 1858, when it was united with The Lockport Advertiser. The weekly edition is now issued as

The Niagara Democrat, by John Campbell.

The Lockport Daily Advertiser was commenced in Feb. 1854, by A. S. Prentiss. June 1, 1858, it was united with The Democrat as

The Lockport Daily Advertiser and Democrat, under which title it is still issued.

The Niagara Courier was started at Lockport, May 1, 1827, by M. Cadwallader. It was successively issued by Geo. Reese, T. C. Flagler, Crandall & Bingham, C. L. Skeels, and S. S. Pomroy.

The Lockport Daily Courier was commenced by Pomroy & Fox in 1847, and continued until 1859, when both the daily and weekly were united with The Journal; the daily as

The Journal and Courier, and the weekly by the name of

This co. was a portion of the domain of the Seneca Nation, though none of its principal villages were located within its limits. The first European visitant of whom there is any record was La Salle, a French adventurer, who, accompanied by Tonti and Father Hennepin, conducted an expedition up the lakes for the double purpose of traffic with the Indians and of extending the French influence among the native tribes. In the fall of 1678 he established a trading post on the present site of Fort Niagara, at the mouth of Niagara River, and soon after laid the keel of a small vessel of 60 tons, at the mouth of Cayuga Creek, above the falls. This vessel was launched in the commencement of the following summer, and christened the Griffin; and on the 7th of Aug. the party set sail upon Lake Erie.[1] The first work at Fort Niagara was a simple palisade; but in 1687 De Nonville, the French commander, constructed there a fort with four bastions. This was soon after besieged by the Senecas; and, a fatal sickness having destroyed most of the garrison, it was soon after abandoned. Joncaire, another French adventurer, built a house on the present site of Lewiston in 1721; and about 4 years after another defensive work was erected on the old site of the palisade of La Salle. This fortress was afterward enlarged, and became one of the most important French posts w. of Montreal. In the summer of 1759, Gen. Prideaux, at the head of a large force of regulars and provincial troops, was sent to reduce the place. The fort was besieged about the 1st of July; and on the 25th it was surrendered to Sir Wm. Johnson, upon whom the command of the expedition had devolved upon the death of Gen. Prideaux.[2]

The fortress was repaired and garrisoned by the English; and during the Revolution it became the headquarters of the marauding parties of tories and Indians that desolated the frontier settlements along the Mohawk, Susquehanna, and Delaware.[3] Fort Niagara continued in possession of the British until 1796.[4] The portion of the Tuscarora Indians who were allies of the English during the Revolution removed to the neighborhood of Fort Niagara after the destructive campaign of Sullivan, in 1779, to obtain means of preventing absolute starvation. The Senecas donated them a square mi. of land, and subsequently the Holland Land Co. 2 sq. mi. In 1804 they purchased an additional tract of 4329 acres, for $13,722. On the 19th of Dec. 1813, Fort Niagara, then in possession of an American garrison, was surprised and taken by the British; and it continued in their possession until the close of the war. The villages at Lewiston and Niagara Falls were burnt about the same time. In 1826, Fort Niagara was the scene of Morgan's imprisonment previous to his final disappearance.[5] The land in this co. was all included in the Holland Purchase, except the small reservations of the Tonawanda and Tuscarora Indians, and a strip of a mile in width along Niagara River, reserved by the State for the purposes of a portage road around Niagara Falls. The first settlements were commenced about the beginning of the present century, and the growth of the co., in common with the whole territory of the Holland Purchase, was rapid. The great impetus to growth, however, was given by the completion of the Erie Canal in 1825 and the subsequent construction of railroads. In 1837 the co. became the seat of great excitement connected with the so-called Patriot War. Most of the Patriot forces that rendezvoused upon Navy Island—within British territory; and just above the rapids of the falls—were transported from Schlosser, upon the

---

The Intelligencer, both of which are now issued by Richardson & Freeman.

Priestcraft Exposed was published from 1828 to 1830 at Lockport by L. A. Spaulding.

The Lockport Journal was started in July, 1851, by M. C. Richardson; and in 1852

The Lockport Daily Journal was commenced, and both editions were continued until 1859, when they were united with the daily and weekly Courier, as already noticed.

The Frontier Sentinel was published at Lockport in 1837, during the "Patriot War" excitement, by T. P. Scoville.

The Lockport Chronicle was started at Lockport April 9, 1859, by S. S. Pomroy & Co.

The Lewiston Telegraph was started at Lewiston in 1836 by John A. Harrison & Co., and was continued about 3 years.

The Niagara Falls Journal was published a short time in 1837 by Francis & Ward.

The Niagara Chronicle was published at Niagara Falls in 1838 by J. Simpson.

The Niagara Cataract was started in 1846 at Niagara Falls by Stephens & Humphreys, and continued a short time.

The Iris was commenced at Niagara Falls in 1846 by George H. Hackstaff, and was continued until 1854.

The Niagara Times was published at Niagara Falls from Oct. 1855 to Oct. 1857, by W. E. Tunis.

The Niagara Falls Gazette was started May 17, 1854, by Pool & Sleeper, by whom it is still issued.

The Niagara City Herald was started at Suspension Bridge in Oct. 1855, by G. H. Hackstaff; and in the following year it passed into the hands of N. T. Hackstaff, by whom it is now published.

[1] The vessel sailed through Lakes Erie and Huron to Green Bay, where it cast anchor and remained some time. After being freighted with a rich cargo of furs, it started on its return voyage; but from that time no tidings ever came of the vessel or crew. La Salle and Father Hennepin left the vessel on its upward voyage at Detroit, and afterward penetrated the western wilderness to the Mississippi River.

[2] While Sir Wm. Johnson remained at this place he made a contract with Wm. Stedman to construct a road for a portage from Lewiston to Schlosser above the Falls. This road was finished in 1763; and on the 20th of June of that year the contractor started with 25 loaded wagons from Lewiston, under the convoy of 50 soldiers. As the party were passing a deep gulf upon the very edge of the cliff known as the Devil's Hole, they were assailed by a large force of Senecas who were lying in wait for them, and the whole party except one were driven off the precipice, which here has a perpendicular height of 180 ft. Wm. Stedman escaped by forcing his horse through the ranks of the Indians; and one soldier—a drummer—was saved by his belt catching in the top of a tree below and so breaking the force of his fall.

[3] The prisoners taken upon the war-paths were generally conducted to this place, where they were often obliged to submit to the terrible ordeal of the gauntlet. A premium was also here given for scalps, stimulating the Indians to murder. The tories who rendezvoused here were usually more inhuman than the Indians.

[4] Col. Smith, who commanded this post at the time of its surrender, was the commanding officer of the British at the battle of Lexington. As Niagara was one of the very last posts surrendered, Col. Smith may with propriety be said to have participated in both the opening and closing acts of the American Revolution.   [5] See page 323.

American shore; and great excitement prevailed in consequence. The steamer Caroline, engaged in furnishing re-inforcements and supplies to the insurgents, was cut from her moorings, on the night of Dec. 29, by a British force, set on fire, and sent over the falls. This event was the occasion of a long diplomatic controversy between the Governments of the United States and Great Britain, and at one time war seemed almost inevitable. Since that time no event has occurred to disturb the peaceful progress of improvement.

CAMBRIA—was formed from "*Willink*," (now Aurora, Erie co.,) March 11, 1808. Hartland, Niagara, and Porter were taken off in 1812, Lewiston in 1818, and a part of Lockport in 1824. It is an interior town, w. of the center of the co. The mountain ridge[1] crosses through the center of the town and divides it into two nearly equal portions. In the N. and s. the surface is level or undulating. The lake ridge crosses the N. part of the town. The principal stream is Twelve Mile Creek. The soil consists of alternations of sandy and clayey loam. **Pekin** (p. v.) lies partly in Lewiston, but principally in this town. It contains 2 churches and about 60 dwellings. **North Ridge** and **Cambria,** in the N. part of the town, are p. offices. The first settlement was made in 1800, by Philip Beach, from Le Roy.[2] There are 2 churches in town, Cong. and M. E.

HARTLAND[3]—was formed from Cambria, June 1, 1812. Royalton was taken off in 1817, Somerset in 1823, and a part of Newfane in 1824. It is the central town upon the E. border of the co. The surface is level or gently undulating, the greatest inequality being along the lake ridge, which crosses the s. part of the town. The principal streams are Eighteen Mile and Johnsons Creeks. The soil s. of the ridge is a clayey loam, and N. it is a sandy and gravelly loam. **Johnsons Creek,** (p. v.,) located on the creek of the same name where it crosses the lake ridge, contains 1 church and has a population of 114. **Hartland Corners,** (Hartland p. o.,) on the ridge in the w. part of the town, contains about 18 dwellings. **Middleport**[4] is partly in this town. The first settlement was made in 1803, by John and David Morrison.[5] The first church (Bap.) was organized at Johnsons Creek in 1817. There are 5 churches in town.[6]

LEWISTON[7]—was formed from Cambria, Feb. 27, 1818. It is the central town upon the w. border of the co. The mountain ridge extends through the town, dividing it into two nearly equal portions. Along the base of this ridge the surface is broken or rolling, but elsewhere it is level. Gill and Six Mile Creeks, and several smaller streams, take their rise in this town, and Niagara River forms its w. boundary. The soil is a sandy loam. The Devil's Hole—a dark chasm, 150 ft. deep, upon the high bank of the Niagara, in the extreme s. part of the town—was the scene of a sanguinary battle during the Old French War.[8] Five mi. above Ft. Niagara, bordering upon the river, is a flat of several acres, about 65 ft. lower than the surrounding country. It is called Five Mile Meadow: it was here that the British forces landed the night before the capture of Fort Niagara, in Dec. 1814.[9] **Lewiston,**[10] (p. v.,) incorp. April 17, 1822, was reserved by the State and patented by single lots. It is situated on Niagara River, at the base of the mountain ridge. It is the terminus of the Lewiston & N. F. R. R., and the head of navigation from Lake Ontario. It contains 4 churches, and has a pop. of 1,014. The Lewistown Suspension Bridge across the Niagara River was erected in 1850 and '51.[11] **Dickersonville** (p. o.) is a hamlet. **South Pekin** is a p. o. in the s. E. part. **Pekin** lies partly in this town. Fort Gray, a temporary fortification erected during the War of 1812, occupied the verge of the mountain ridge just above the village of Lewiston. The Seminary of our Lady of Angels, a Catholic institution, is situated on

---

[1] Upon the verge of this ridge, in the E. part of the town, are an ancient fortification and burial places, occupying about 6 acres. Rude iron implements, pieces of copper, fragments of earthenware, charred wood, and corncobs have been plowed up within the area. Nearly in the center, overlaid by sandstone slabs, was a deep pit filled with human bones, many of which apparently belonged to men of almost giant size.—*Turner's Hist. Holland Purchase.*

[2] John Forsyth and Walter Neal settled in the town in 1804, and Chapman Hawley, Daniel Howell, Joseph Hewett, James Prentice, and Amariah Stoughton soon afterward. The first birth was that of Philip Beach, jr., in 1803; and the first death, that of Nehemiah Street, a traveler, who was murdered in 1790. Philip Beach opened the first inn, in 1800, and Joshua Sheppard the first store, in 1815. Joseph Hewett built the first sawmill, in 1806, and Christian Howder the first gristmill, in 1815. The first school was taught by Mrs. Neal, in 1808.

[3] Named from Hartland, Vt.

[4] See page 456.

[5] Zebulon Barnum, Jedediah Riggs, Isaac Southwell, and Dan'l

Brown moved into town the same year, and Abel Barnum and Oliver Castle in 1805. The first death was that of Isaac South well, in 1806; the first inn was opened by Jephtha Dunn, in 1809, and the first store, by Dan'l Van Horn, in 1816. The first school was taught by Nancy Judson, in the summer of 1813.

[6] Bap., Friends, M. E., Prot. M., and R. C.

[7] Named from Gov. Morgan Lewis, at the suggestion of Judge Silas Hopkins.

[8] See p. 452.

[9] See p. 280.

[10] An academy was established at this place in 1828. Besides participating in the general fund, it was endowed by the Legislature with the proceeds of the ferry license, which some years yielded $800 to $900. When the Lewiston Suspension Bridge was finished, the ferry was abandoned and the academy discontinued.

[11] This bridge was built by two joint stock companies,—one incorp. by the Legislature of N. York and the other by the Canadian Parliament. The roadway is 849 ft. long, 20 ft. wide, and 60 ft. above the water. Cost of the structure, $58,000.

the river bank in the s. w. part of the town.[1] The site of the village of Lewiston was occupied by the French at different times previous to and during the Old French War; but the first permanent settlements were made about the year 1800.[2] The first church is said to have been founded by Brant, at the Mohawk settlement, a little E. of Lewiston.[3] There are now 8 churches in town.[4]

LOCKPORT—was taken from Cambria and Royalton, Feb. 2, 1824. It extends from the central part to the southern bounds of the co. The surface in the northern part of the town, through which the mountain ridge extends, is broken and hilly; in the central and southern parts it is level. Eighteen Mile and Mud Creeks are the principal streams. The soil is a clayey loam intermixed with marl, and in the N. it is stony. The Niagara limestone crops out along the mountain ridge, and extensive quarries have been opened in and near the village of Lockport.[5] Underlying this is a stratum of hydraulic limestone, from which waterlime is made; and sandstone belonging to the Medina formation is also quarried N. of the ridge.[6] The manufactures of the town are extensive, and consist principally of flour, lumber, leather, and machinery. **Lockport**,[7] (p. v.,) the co. seat, was incorp. March 26, 1829. It is situated on the Erie Canal and the declivities of the mountain ridge. It is an important station on the Niagara Falls R. R., and is the terminus of the branch road to Buffalo. The water-power created by the canal locks at this place has given rise to numerous and extensive manufacturing establishments.[8] The village contains 15 churches, a high school,[9] 3 newspaper offices, 3 banks of issue, and 1 savings' bank. Pop. 8,939. **Wrights Corners,** (p. o.,) in the N. part of the town, and **Rapids,** (p. o.,) in the s. part, are hamlets. **Hickory Corners,** in the w., is a p. o. The first settlement was made at Cold Spring, about 1 mi. E. of Lockport Village, by Charles Wilbur, in 1805.[10] There are 21 churches in town.[11] Ex-Gov. Washington Hunt is a resident of this town.

NEWFANE—was formed from Hartland, Somerset, and Wilson, March 20, 1824. It extends from near the center of the co. to the lake shore. The surface is level. Eighteen Mile Creek crosses the town, dividing it into two unequal portions. The soil is generally a sandy loam; but in some parts it is clayey. **Olcott,** (p. v.,) on the lake shore, at the mouth of Eighteen Mile Creek, contains 3 churches and about 30 dwellings. **Charlotte,** (Newfane p. o.,) on Eighteen Mile Creek, near the center of the town, contains 2 churches and about 25 dwellings. **Hess Road,** in the E., and **Coomer,** in the w. part, are p. offices. The first settlement was made in 1807, by Wm. Chambers[12] and John Brewer, from Canada.[13] The first religious services were conducted in 1811, by a colored Methodist minister from Canada. There are 5 churches in town.[14]

NIAGARA—was formed from Cambria, June 1, 1812, as "*Schlosser;*" its name was changed Feb. 14, 1816. Pendleton was taken off in 1827, and Wheatfield in 1836. It is the s. w. corner town of the co., occupying the angle made by the abrupt northerly bend of Niagara River. Its

---

[1] This Seminary is under the charge of the "*Priests of the Congregation of the Mission of St. Vincent du Paul Institution,*" and is designed to educate boys and young men for the priesthood. It was incorp. in 1858. The buildings are not yet completed.

[2] Among the settlers who were in the town in 1800 were Jos. and John Howell, —— Middaugh, Henry Hough, Henry Mills, —— McBride, Thos. Hustler, Wm. Gambol, and Fred'k Woodman. Geo. Howell was the first child born in the town and in the co., in 1799. Middaugh kept tavern in 1788, and McBride built a tannery about 1799. The first sawmill was built by Jos. Howell, in 1808, and the first gristmill by John Gray, in 1815. The Tuscarora Reservation is in this town.

[3] This was probably some time during the Revolutionary War. Brant was an Episcopalian; and the services were usually conducted by some one attached to the British garrison at Ft. Niagara. The church was built of logs and had no belfry. The bell was hung upon a cross-bar resting in the crotch of a tree near by.

[4] Presb., Prot. E., Univ., and R. C. at Lewiston, Cong. and M. E. at Pekin, M. E. at Dickersonville, and Indian church on the Reservation.

[5] The principal of these quarries are along the canal, in the s. part of Lockport Village. There are also quarries about a mile E. of the village, and others a little further w. This limestone is a very excellent building material, and large quantities are shipped to distant places. The locks at this place, and numerous culverts on the canal, are built of it. A cave of small extent exists under the village of Lockport.

[6] The principal quarries from which sandstone is obtained are at Rattlesnake Hill, N. w. of the village. This stone is used principally for flagging and paving.

[7] So named from there being a greater number of locks here than at any other place on the canal; and to these the village owes its origin.

[8] Five flouring-mills, with an aggregate of 30 run of stone, 7 sawmills, 5 stave and shingle factories, 1 sash, door, and blind factory, 1 planing mill, 2 tanneries, a woolen factory, 2 machine shops and foundries, a plow factory, a distillery, and a plaster-mill. A hydraulic canal three-fourths of a mi. long has been constructed upon the declivity of the ridge, from which the water is distributed to various manufactories. The water is taken from the upper level of the canal and returned to the lower. A considerable proportion of the water-power is obtained from the water taken from the lower level.

[9] The "*Lockport Union School*" was incorp. March 31, 1847. Connected with it is an academic department, under the supervision of the regents. The number of pupils in attendance in 1856 was 742.

[10] Jedediah Darling settled in the town in 1808, —— Gregory in 1809, Thomas Miles, Silliman Wakeman, David Carlton, and Geo. Miller in 1810, and Alex. Freeman and John Dye in 1811. The first inn was opened by Chas. Wilbur, in 1800; the first sawmill was built by Alex. Freeman, in 1811, and the first gristmill by Otis Hathaway, on Eighteen Mile Creek. This was a small mill, which was built in 20 days. L. A. Spaulding was then building, and soon after finished, a stone mill of 7 stories in height. Simeon Ford erected a woolen factory in 1828. The first school was taught by Olinda Moore, in the summer of 1816.

[11] Bap., Cong., Friends, Luth., 2 M. E., 2 Presb., 2 Prot. E., 2 R. C., Univ., and 2 Af. Meth. at Lockport Village, and Dutch Evang., Dutch Ref., Luth., 2 M. E., and Wes. Meth. in other parts of the town.

[12] Chambers removed to Grand Island; and about the year 1825, attempting to cross Niagara River above the cataract in a skiff, he was drawn into the rapids and carried over the falls.

[13] —— Cotton settled in the town the same year, Burgoyne, Kemp, and Peter Hopkins in 1808, and Wm. and James Wisner in 1810. Levi Ellis built the first saw and grist mill, in 1811, for James Van Horn. Asa Douglas opened a store at Olcott, in 1812. The first school was taught by Bezaleal Smith, in 1815.

[14] 2 M. E., Bap., Univ., and Wes. Meth.

surface is level. Cayuga and Gill Creeks are the principal streams. The soil is a heavy clay. Goat Island and the American part of Niagara Falls belong to this town. At Suspension Bridge, on the river bank, is a sulphur spring, which has been fitted up for the accommodation of visitors. **Niagara Falls,** (p. v.,) incorp. July 7, 1848, is situated on Niagara River, at the cataract. It is the terminus of the Rochester & N. F. R. R., of the N. F. & Lewiston R. R., of the Buffalo & N. F. R. R., and of the Canandaigua & N. F. R. R. It contains 5 churches, 1 newspaper office, 11 hotels, and several manufacturing establishments.[1] Pop. 2,976. The village owes its existence to its proximity to the great cataract. Thousands of visitors, from every part of the U. S. and from almost every country in the world, annually visit this, one of nature's greatest wonders. Nearly all the business of the community is connected with this periodical visitation, and consists of hotel keeping, livery business, and matters of a kindred nature. A large and by no means unimportant business has grown out of the sale of spar ornaments and fancy articles made by the Indians. **Niagara City,** (*Suspension* Bridge p. o.,) incorp. June 8, 1854, is situated on Niagara River, 2 mi. below the falls. The Rochester & N. F. R. R. connects at this place with the Lewiston & N. F. R. R., and with the Great Western Railway across the Suspension Bridge.[2] The village contains 6 churches, a newspaper office, 15 hotels, and a charitable institution known as the De Veaux College for Destitute Orphans and Children.[3] Pop. 1,365. This place participates with Niagara Falls in the business made by the annual influx of visitors to the cataract. No place of equal size on the Continent has a greater amount of hotel accommodations than these. **La Salle** is a p. o. at the mouth of Cayuga Creek. In the fall of 1678 the French *voyageurs* La Salle, Tonti, and Father Hennepin, with their companions, established themselves at the mouth of Cayuga Creek and remained until the "*Griffin*" was launched the following season.[4] Other places along the river were temporarily occupied by the French at different times; but the first permanent settlement was made at Schlosser in 1759, by John Stedman, accompanied by his brothers Wm. and Philip.[5] The first religious services were conducted by Father Hennepin, at the time of the French sojourn at Cayuga Creek.[6] There are now 12 churches in town.[7]

PENDLETON[8]—was formed from Niagara, April 16, 1827. It is the central town on the s. border of the co. The surface is level or gently undulating. Tonawanda Creek forms the s. bounds of the town, and Sawyers Creek crosses the w. part. The soil is generally a clayey loam. **Pendleton,** (p. o.,) on Tonawanda Creek, contains 1 church and 16 dwellings. **Pendleton Center, Beach Ridge,** and **Mapleton** are p. offices. The first settlement was made in 1805, by Jacob Christman.[9] There are 5 churches in town.[10]

PORTER[11]—was formed from Cambria, June 1, 1812. Wilson was taken off in 1818. It is the most westerly town on the lake shore. Its surface is level. Four Mile and Six Mile Creeks, and the w. branch of Twelve Mile Creek, cross the town in a northerly direction, and Niagara River forms its w. boundary. The soil along the lake shore is composed principally of a marly clay; in the central and southern parts it is a sandy and gravelly loam. Besides the crops which

[1] A hydraulic canal has recently been constructed from a point on Niagara River about ¼ mi. above the rapids, diagonally across the point of land upon which the village is situated, to near the river bank ¼ mi. below the falls. Along the bank is a long basin, in which the canal terminates, and from which the water is discharged through a great number of races into the river below. This canal is ¾ of a mi. long, 70 ft. wide, and 10 ft. deep, and will maintain a running stream equal in quantity to 2436 cubic ft. per second. The company by whom the canal has been built was organized March 22, 1853, with a capital of $500,000. One of the largest paper mills in the U. S., on Bath Island, was burned during the past year, (1858.)

[2] The Niagara Suspension Bridge, which crosses the river at this place, was commenced in 1852 and finished in 1855. It is 821 ft. in length from center to center of the towers, and 247 ft. above the water. It has 2 floors,—the lower for a carriage way, and the upper for a rail way, upon which 4 rails are so laid as to make tracks of 3 different gauges. The cost of the structure was about $400,000, and the stock of the company $500,000. The first line was got across the river at this place by the aid of a kite. With this a larger cord was drawn over; and finally a rope, upon which pulleys could be run, bearing the wires of which the bridge is composed. The chief engineer was John A. Roebling.

[3] The De Veaux College was established according to the provisions of the will of Samuel De Veaux, who bequeathed for that purpose personal property to the amount of $154,432 and real estate valued at $36,213, besides 330 acres of inalienable land. The building was erected in 1855–56. It is built of stone, has 2 stories and an attic above the ground story, and a front of 100 ft., with a depth of 54 ft. The members of the school are supplied by the institution with food, clothing, and books. By the pro-

visions of the will of Mr. De Veaux, the president of the college must always be a clergyman of the Prot. E. Church, and the institute itself under the control of the Diocese of Western New York. Members of the school are appointed by the board of trustees, the children of parents belonging to the Prot. E. Church having the preference. When once received, the children are under the sole charge of the trustees until they attain their majority. See *Senate Doc.* 1858, No. 118. The college reports annually to the Legislature.

[4] See page 452.

[5] During the period of English occupancy a small settlement grew up at Schlosser. There were, besides the Stedman house, (which was a large and spacious 2¼ story building,) about 15 other dwellings. The Stedmans moved away in 1795 and left Jesse Ware in possession. Judge Augustus Porter settled at Schlosser in 1806. The first sawmill was built by John Stedman. The first school was taught by Ezekiel Hill, in 1807.

[6] In his account of their sojourn Father Hennepin says, "I had one hut especially designed for observing prayers in holydays and Sundays."

[7] Bap., Presb., Prot. E., M. E., and R. C. at Niagara Falls, Cong., D. Ref. D., Evang., Prot.E., Presb., and M. E. at Niagara City, and M. E. at Cayuga Creek.

[8] Named from Sylvester Pendleton Clark, Ex-Gov. of Grand Island.

[9] Among the first settlers were Martin Van Slyke and John and Adam Fulmer. The first death was that of Martin Van Slyke, in 1814. S. P. Clark kept the first inn, in 1822, and Jerry Jenks the first store, the same year. The first school was taught by —— Dawson, in the winter of 1816.

[10] 2 M. E., Presb., Luth., and R. C.

[11] Named from Judge Augustus Porter.

are common to all parts of this co., considerable quantities of apples, peaches, and other fruits are raised. **Youngstown,**[1] (p. v.,) incorp. Aug. 22, 1854, is situated on Niagara River, about one mi. from its mouth. It contains 3 churches and has a pop. of 768. **Ransomville,**[2] (p. v.,) in the s. E. part of the town, contains 2 churches. Pop. 195. **East Porter** is a p. o. **Fort Niagara**[3] is situated on the lake shore, at the mouth of Niagara River. Transient settlements were made at very early periods by the French at Ft. Niagara; but no permanent settlement was made until the early part of the present century.[4] There are 7 churches in town.[5]

ROYALTON[6]—was formed from Hartland, April 5, 1817, and a part of Lockport was taken off in 1824. It is the s. E. corner town of the co. The surface is generally level or undulating, except in the N. part, where the mountain ridge crosses the town. Johnsons, Eighteen Mile, and Mud Creeks take their rise in this town, and the Tonawanda forms its s. boundary. The soil is a clayey loam. **Middleport**[7] (p. v.) incorporated in 1858, lies partly in Hartland, but principally in the N. E. part of this town. It is situated upon the Erie Canal, and is a station on the R. & N. F. R. R. It contains 5 churches and has a pop. of 689, (586 in Royalton, 103 in Hartland.) **Gasport,**[8] (p. v.,) situated on the canal near Eighteen Mile Creek, is a station on the R. & N. F. R. R. It contains 1 church and an academy.[9] Pop. 273. **Orangeport,** (p. v.,) on the canal, in the N. w. part of the town, has a pop. of 224; **Royalton,** (p. v.,) in the central part, of 168; and **Reynales Basin,** (p. v.,) on the canal, of 132. **Locust Tree** and **South Royalton** are p. offices. **McNalls Corners** is a hamlet in the w. part. The first settlement was made in 1803, by Thos. Slayton and Gad Warner.[10] The first religious services were held in 1806; the first religious society (Christian) was organized in 1817, and the first church edifice was built the same year.[11] There are 12 churches in town.[12]

SOMERSET—was formed from Hartland, Feb. 8, 1823, and a part of Newfane was taken off in 1824. It is the most eastern town upon the lake shore. The surface is level. Golden Hill and Fish Creeks cross the town in a N. E. direction. The soil is generally a sandy loam; but in some places it is clayey. Near the mouth of Fish Creek is a small salt spring, from which salt was formerly made. **Somerset,** (p. v.,) N. of the center of the town, contains 3 churches and about 30 dwellings. **County Line,** on the line of Orleans co., and **Lake Road** and **West Somerset,** are p. offices. The first settlement was made in 1810, by Jacob Fitts and Zacharias Patterson.[13] The first religious services were conducted by Daniel Shepardson, in 1816, and the first church (Bap.) was organized in 1820. There are 5 churches in town.[14]

WHEATFIELD—was formed from Niagara, May 12, 1836. It is the most southerly town in the co., and lies partly on Niagara River and partly on Tonawanda Creek. The surface is level or gently undulating. Cayuga and Sawyers Creeks cross the town, the former in the western part and the latter in the eastern. The soil is generally a hard, clayey loam, difficult to cultivate. About a mi. E. of Tonawanda is a sour spring, and about 2 mi. N. a sulphur spring. A considerable part of the town is yet unimproved. The greater proportion of the population consists of immigrants from Prussia and other parts of Germany.[15] **Bergholtz,**[16] (p. v.,) near the center of the town, contains 1 church and about 80 houses; **Martinsville,** (p. v.,) in the s. E. part, 1 church

---

[1] Named from John Young, the first merchant at the place.
[2] Named from Clark Ransom, one of the early settlers.
[3] See pages, 45, 452.
[4] John Lloyd, who was a soldier stationed at Fort Niagara in 1799, settled in town in 1801, 3 mi. from the fort. Silas Hopkins settled in 1802, Thos. Brown, Elijah Doty, John Clement, and John Waterhouse, in 1803, and John Brown in 1805. Robert Gurnsett kept the first inn, and John Young the first store, in 1808. John Clapsaddle built the first sawmill, in 1816, and the first gristmill, in 1817. The first school was taught by Wm. Cogswell, in the winter of 1806.
[5] 3 M. E., Bap., Presb., Wes. Meth., and R. C.
[6] Named from Royalton, Vt.
[7] So named from its being midway on the canal between "*Newport*" (now Albion) and Lockport.
[8] So called from the fact that gas escapes from the earth here. This gas is inflammable; and at one time it was conveyed through iron pipes from the spring to a store, which was lighted by it.
[9] Founded in 1854.
[10] Joshua Slayton, —— Elsworth, Louden Andrews, and Alex. Haskins settled in town in 1804, Stephen Bugby, Stephen Hoyt, and Sam'l Capon, in 1805, and Barnum Treadwell in 1806. The first birth was that of Dan'l Vaughn; the first marriage, that of Henry Elsworth and Polly Cornish, in the spring of 1810; and the first death, that of —— Elsworth, in 1804. Gad Warner built the first sawmill, in 1817. The first tavern was opened in 1809, by —— Fisk.
[11] This was one of the first churches upon the Holland Pur-

chase. It was painted red, and was called "*The Red Meeting House.*"
[12] 3 M. E., Bap., Christian, Cong., F.W. Bap., Luth., Presb., R.C., Univ., and Wes. Meth.
[13] Archibald Whitton, Philip Fitts, and Truman and David Mudgett settled in the town the same year. The first birth was that of Delilah Fitts, in 1811; the first marriage, that of John Sherwood and Rebecca Mead, in 1817; and the first death, that of Philip Fitts, in 1814. Josiah S. Bailey opened the first inn, in 1817, and Jos. M. Carpenter the first store, in 1823. The first sawmill was built by John Randolph, in 1822, and the first gristmill by Archibald McDowell, in 1826. The first school was taught by Marston Sherwood, in the winter of 1817.
[14] 2 Bap., Friends, Presb., and M. E.
[15] They nearly all cultivate the soil; but their farms are usually very small, consisting generally of not more than 5 to 10 acres. They retain in a great measure their own manners, customs, and nationality. They have their own churches and schools; their pastors and schoolmasters came from Germany with them, and German is the language of the pulpit and the schoolroom. Their houses are nearly all one story, rough framed buildings, unclapboarded, and filled in with unburned bricks. Several of them are built of hewn logs, the crevices filled with clay; and some are clapboarded on the gable ends down as far as the level of the eaves.
[16] These villages were named from places of the same names in Germany.

and about 60 houses; **Johnsburg,** in the central part, 1 church and about 50 houses; and **Walmore,**[1] (p. v.,) in the N. W. corner of the town, 2 churches and 12 houses. These are straggling German villages. **Shawnee,** (p. v.,) in the N. E. corner of the town, contains 1 church and 15 houses. **Tonawanda,** (p. v.,) on the line of Erie co., lies partly within this town. The first settlement was made by Geo. Van Slyke, in 1802, at the mouth of Tonawanda Creek.[2] There are 7 churches in town.[3]

WILSON[4]—was formed from Porter, April 10, 1818, and a part of Newfane was taken off in 1824. It is situated on the lake shore, N. W. of the center of the co. The surface is level. The E. branch of Twelve Mile Creek[5] crosses the town near the center, and the W. branch in the N. W. part. The soil is a sandy and clayey loam. **Wilson,** (p. v.,) incorp. June 25, 1858, is situated on the E. side of Twelve Mile Creek, near its mouth. It contains 3 churches and the Wilson Collegiate Institute. Pop. 666. **East Wilson, South Wilson,** and **North Wilson** are p. offices. The first settlement was made in 1810, by Stephen Sheldon, Reuben Wilson, —— Goodman, John Eastman, and Gilbert Purdy.[6] The first church (Presb.) was organized Jan. 18, 1819. There are now 3 churches in town; Bap., Presb., and M. E.

Acres of Land, Valuation, Population, Dwellings, Families, Freeholders, Schools, Live Stock, Agricultural Products, and Domestic Manufactures, of Niagara County.

NAMES OF TOWNS.	ACRES OF LAND.		VALUATION OF 1858.			POPULATION.		No. of Dwellings.	No. of Families.	Freeholders.	SCHOOLS.	
	Improved.	Unimproved.	Real Estate.	Personal Property.	Total.	Males.	Females.				No. of Districts.	Children taught.
Cambria	17,214	5,767	$760,557	$47,890	$808,447	1,125	1,091	392	407	287	12	727
Hartland	20,836¾	9,600	839,722	41,300	881,022	1,527	1,506	608	642	523	18	1,160
Lewiston	15,812	6,519¾	724,371	67,732	792,103	1,665	1,595	530	581	280	13	1,214
Lockport	21,813¼	13,584½	2,689,229	474.400	3,163,629	6,675	6,711	2,364	2,286	1,613	18	5,011
Newfane	22,268½	10,173	818,182	32,065	850,247	1,641	1,523	618	619	340	16	1,217
Niagara	6,754¼	6,088	1,448,126	284.700	1,732,826	2,913	2,544	808	967	439	7	1,986
Pendleton	9,843¾	6,169¼	420,049	27,100	447,149	972	854	374	359	272	8	772
Porter	14,014	5,721	597,597	21,550	619,147	1,362	1,281	484	484	336	11	979
Royalton	27,748½	12,968	1,253,211	102,791	1,356,002	2,598	2,332	905	931	600	24	1,561
Somerset	18,202	5,313	555,161	38,950	594,111	952	971	379	378	275	14	780
Wheatfield	10,768⅞	10,937	866,310	833,800	1,700,110	1,641	1,511	616	675	522	7	1,070
Wilson	21,768	8,269½	802,867	27,104	829,971	1,739	1,553	650	622	492	17	1,258
Total	207,043⅞	101,110	11,775,382	1,999,382	13,774,764	24,810	23,472	8,698	8,951	5,979	165	17,725

NAMES OF TOWNS.	LIVE STOCK.					AGRICULTURAL PRODUCTS.							Domestic Cloths, in yards.
						BUSH. OF GRAIN.					DAIRY PRODUCTS.		
	Horses.	Working Oxen and Calves.	Cows.	Sheep.	Swine.	Winter.	Spring.	Tons of Hay.	Bushels of Potatoes.	Bushels of Apples.	Pounds Butter.	Pounds Cheese.	
Cambria	946	1,768	1,018	5,316	1,369	67,773	89,816	3,499	22,343	35,352	98,077	12,280	211
Hartland	1,301	1,696	1,196	9,090	2,221	20,201	88,124	3,801¼	33,865	22,514	110,450	12,353	2,182
Lewiston	2,798	1,151	746	5,034	1,418	68,238	63,962	3,436	18,884	26,900	76,322	405	775
Lockport	1,634	1,555	1,540	6,834	3,207	59,320½	120,453½	5,400	29,513	30,191	124,265	4,170	707
Newfane	1,177	1,837	1,082	8,243	2,031	56,661	94,506½	3,342½	29,714	15,441	91,246	3,460	1,218
Niagara	562	535	485	800	848	21,637	37,176½	1,675½	6,905	5,934	22,386		132
Pendleton	592	813	588	2,111	932	28,540	62,968½	1,627	8,526	6,939	46,434	1,351	469
Porter	824	1,054	720	5,327	1,389	69,291	47,797½	2,893½	18,724	19,868	66,779	3,697	12
Royalton	1,635	1,900	1,479	12,450	2,701	41,480½	171,280	6,337¾	30,874½	49,217	154,271	17,813	2,498
Somerset	966	1,376	816	9,929	1,514	38,021	54,593½	2,453½	21,927½	18,065	70,063	6,711	1,214½
Wheatfield	606	992	887	2,028	1,566	35,090	68,305	2,595½	19,475	4,629	50,515	820	574
Wilson	1,293	1,853	1,151	11,197	2,569	84,672	103,288	4,056	34,697	20,947	127,499	8,383	1,506½
Total	14,334	16,530	11,708	78,359	21,765	590,925	1,002,271	41,117½	275,448	255,997	1,038,307	71,443	11,499

[1] See note 16, p. 456.

[2] John Harvey and —— Walton settled in the town in 1807, and Geo. Burgher, Jacob Stoner, and Wm. Scott, in 1809. James Field kept the first inn, in 1808, and Judge Wilkinson the first store, in 1822. The first sawmill was built by Col. John Sweeney, in 1825.

[3] 4 Evang. Luth., Bap., M. E., and Mennonite.

[4] Named from Reuben Wilson, one of the earliest settlers, and the first supervisor.

[5] In 1811, about 4 mi. from the mouth of this creek, in the lake, a few rods from the shore, Mr. Goodman found a 4 lb. French swivel, loaded with a ball and 3 grape shot. A large pile of bullets and considerable quantities of ballast iron were subsequently found on the shore near by.

[6] The first birth was that of Warren Wilson, in 1811. Joshua Williams and Daniel Sheldon built the first sawmill, in 1815, and Reuben and Luther Wilson the first gristmill, in 1824. Benj. Douglas opened the first store, in 1817, and T. T. Upton the first inn, in 1818. The first school was an evening school for adults, taught by Luther Wilson during Jan. and Feb. 1817.

ONEIDA COUNTY.

This county was formed from Herkimer, March 15, 1798. Lewis and Jefferson were taken off in 1805, and a part of Oswego in 1816. Portions were annexed to Clinton in 1801 and to Madison in 1836. A portion of Chenango was annexed in 1804.[1] It lies near the center of the State, 100 mi. from Albany, and contains 1,215 sq. mi. A broad valley, nearly level, extends E. and W. through the center of the co., and from it, both N. and S., the surface rises into a broken and hilly region. The highlands which occupy the s. part are arranged in ridges extending N. and S., the highest summits, on the s. border, being 600 to 1,000 ft. above the valley of the Mohawk. North of the central valley the surface rises abruptly to a height of 800 to 1,200 ft., and spreads out into a nearly level plateau, broken by the ravines of the streams. The E. part of the central valley is drained by the Mohawk, flowing E., and the w. part by Wood Creek, flowing W. This valley affords a natural road from the Hudson to the great lakes, and is the lowest pass through the Appalachian Mt. system. The Mohawk rises upon the N. border of the co.; and flows in a southerly direction to Rome, and thence s. E. to the E. border of the co. Its principal tributaries from the N. are Nine Mile Creek and Lansing Kil, and from the s. Sauquoit and Oriskany Creeks. Black River flows across the N. E. corner of the co. East Canada Creek forms a portion of the E. boundary; the head branches of the Unadilla and Chenango drain the s. border, and Oneida, Wood, and Fish Creeks drain the w. part. Oneida Lake, extending several mi. along the w. border, is the only large body of water in the co. In the extreme N. E. corner are several small lakes and ponds.

The rocks of this co. include nearly the whole series lying between the gneiss, which covers the N. E. part, and the Hamilton group, which outcrops on the s. hills. The Trenton limestone, Utica slate, Oneida conglomerate, and Clinton group have received their names from being so distinctly developed in this co. Of useful minerals the co. has the lenticular clay iron ore of the Clinton group, bog ore in the swamps near Oneida Lake, and, probably, magnetic ore in the N. E. part. Marl and peat have been found in some places. Waterlime and gypsum quarries have been wrought to some extent. Building stone in great variety and of superior quality has been extensively quarried. Mineral springs are found in several places. The soil in the N. E., derived from the disintegration of the primitive rocks, is light and sandy, and is capable of producing only a scanty vegetation. This region is sparsely settled, and is not capable of supporting many inhabitants. The central valley is one of the most fertile portions of the State. The soil is a fine quality of sandy and gravelly loam and alluvium, finely tempered with lime and gypsum. The highland region s. of the river has a soil composed of clay and sandy and gravelly loam, and is best adapted to pasturage. The richness and diversity of the soil make this co. one of the best agricultural regions of the State. The people are chiefly engaged in agriculture, the principal branches of which are grain raising in the valleys and dairying and stock raising upon the hills. Hops are largely cultivated in the s. towns. The manufactures of the co. are extensive, though principally confined to Utica and the villages along Oriskany and Sauquoit Creeks.

The county is a half-shire, the co. buildings being respectively located at Utica and Rome.[2] The courthouses and jails at both places are well built and conveniently arranged. The clerk's

---

[1] Montgomery, Herkimer, and Oneida counties originally extended in long, narrow strips to the St. Lawrence. In 1801, Lisbon—then an immense town upon the N. border—was annexed to Clinton co. It is not certain whether Tracts 1, 2, and 3 of Macomb's Purchase were intended by this arrangement to belong to Clinton; but in 1802 they were annexed to St. Lawrence co. Oneida co. was named from the Oneida Indians, who inhabited and owned this and some adjoining counties. The word Oneida signifies "the people of the stone." The Indians had a strange tradition concerning a certain stone, which followed them in their wanderings and finally rested on the summit of one of the highest hills in the co., from which their beacon fires could be seen to a great distance, and upon which they assembled to hold council or prepare for war. A boulder of gneiss, which tradition identified as this palladium of the Oneidas, a few years since was taken from the farm of James H. Gregg, in the town of Stockbridge, and placed in a prominent position near the entrance of the Utica Cemetery,

on the Bridgewater Plank Road, about a mi. s. of Utica.— Jones's Oneida, p. 840; Rules and Regulations of the Utica Cemetery Asso. 1849, p. 33; Senate Doc. 1846, No. 24, p. 46; Schoolcraft's Hist. Condition and Prospects of Indian Tribes, I, p. 176.

[2] The co. seat of Herkimer co. was originally located at Whitestown; and upon the division of the co. the records were retained by Oneida. The act erecting Oneida co. directed the first courts to be held at the schoolhouse near Fort Schuyler, (Rome,) and required the courthouse to be built within 1 mi. of the fort. By an act of April 6, 1801, Thomas Jenkins and Hez. L. Hosmer, of Hudson, John Thompson, of Stillwater, and Dirck Lane, of Troy, were appointed to locate the courthouse and jail of Oneida co. These buildings were completed several years afterward, and the courts were held here and at Whitesboro' during many years. The courthouse and jail at Rome were burned about 1848, and rebuilt within 3 years after. The clerk's office was removed to Utica in 1816, and the academy at

458

office is a fireproof building, located at Utica. The poorhouse is situated upon a farm of 195 acres about 2 mi. s. w. of Rome. It has an average of 222 inmates, supported at a cost of $1.00 per week each. Separate buildings have been provided for lunatics and for a pesthouse.[1]

The Erie Canal extends through Utica, Whitestown, Rome, and Verona. The Chenango Canal extends s. from Utica, up the valley of Oriskany Creek, through New Hartford, Kirkland, Marshall, and a corner of Augusta, connecting with the Susquehanna River at Binghamton. The Black River Canal extends N. from Rome along the valleys of the Mohawk and Lansing Kil through Western and Boonville, connecting with Black River above Lyons Falls, in Lewis co. The Oneida Lake Canal extends w. from Rome to Wood Creek and along that stream to its mouth The N. Y. Central R. R. extends through Utica, Whitestown, Rome, and Verona. The Black River & Utica R. R. extends from Utica N. through Marcy, Trenton, Remsen, and Steuben to Boonville.[2] The Watertown & Rome R. R. extends from Rome N. w. through Annsville and Camden. A large number of plank roads have been built in the co.; but they are mostly abandoned.

Four daily, 9 weekly, 1 semi-monthly, 1 quarterly, and 4 newspapers are now published in the co.[3]

At an early period of the English occupation of New York the colonists became acquainted with

that place was used for holding courts for many years. A new courthouse was built at Utica in 1851–53. The first co. officers were Jedediah Sanger, *First Judge;* Geo. Huntington and David Ostrom, *Judges;* Jonas Platt, *Clerk;* Wm. Colbrath, *Sheriff;* and Arthur Breese, *Surrogate.*
[1] An act was passed in 1859 for the sale of the poorhouse premises and the purchase of a new site.
[2] This road has been partially built along Black River through Lewis co.; but work upon it is now suspended. It was the original design to extend the road to Clayton and Ogdensburgh.
[3] *The Western Centinel* was commenced at Whitesboro' in Jan. 1794, by Oliver P. Eaton. He was succeeded by —— Lewis, and afterward by Lewis & Webb. The paper was continued about 6 years.
The Whitestown Gazette was commenced in June, 1796, by Wm. McLean. In 1798 it was removed to Utica and continued as
The Whitestown Gazette and Cato's Patrol. In 1803 it was purchased by John H. Lathrop, and was soon after merged in
The Utica Patriot, commenced by Asahel Seward and Ira Merrill, Mr. Lathrop continuing as editor. In 1811 it passed into the hands of Wm. H. Maynard; and in 1816 it was united with
The Patrol, commenced in Jan. 1815, by Seward & Williams, and the combined paper was published as
The Patriot and Patrol, W. H. Maynard, editor, and Seward & Williams, publishers. In 1821 its name was changed to
The Utica Sentinel. In 1825 it was united with the Columbian Gazette and published as
The Sentinel and Gazette. In 1828 S. D. Dakin became proprietor, and in 1829 he sold to Rufus Northway and D. S. Porter. In 1831 Mr. Porter withdrew. In 1834 Mr. Northway united the Elucidator with it and changed its name to
The Oneida Whig. In 1848 it was merged in the Oneida Weekly Herald. In 1842 Mr. Northway commenced
The Utica Daily Gazette, Wm. Allen and R. U. Sherman, editors. Erastus Clark, Wm. H. Underhill, Ezekiel Barron, Alex. Seward, H. C. Potter, J. M. Lyon, John Arthur, N. D. Jewell, and Ellis & Roberts were successively interested in its publication. In Jan. 1857, it was united with The
Utica Morning Herald and Gazette, and is still published.
The Columbian Patriotic Gazette was commenced at Rome by Thos. Walker and Ebenezer Eaton in Aug. 1799. In 1800 Mr. Eaton retired, and in 1803 it was removed to Utica and published as
The Columbian Gazette; and in 1825 it was united with the Utica Sentinel by Wm. J. Bacon and S. D. Dakin.
The Elucidator was commenced in 1829 by B. B. Hotchkin, editor, and W. Williams, publisher. It was united with the Oneida Whig in 1834.
The Oneida Morning Herald was commenced by R. W. Roberts, R. U. Sherman, and Geo. R. Colston, in Nov. 1847. A weekly edition was also published, called
The Oneida Weekly Herald. In 1848 Mr. Colston withdrew, and in 1857 the papers were united with the Utica Daily Gazette.
Utica Christian Magazine was commenced by the Oneida Association and Presbytery in 1813, and was published about 3 years.
The Club was published at Utica by Henry Goodfellow & Co. about 3 months in 1814.
The Civil and Religious Intelligencer was started in 1815 at Utica by Jos. Tenney. In 1825 it was changed to
The Sangerfield Intelligencer, and in 1835 it was removed to "*Franklin Village,*" now Fabius, Onondaga Co.
The Utica Observer was commenced by E. Dorchester in 1816.

In 1818 it was removed to Rome and its name changed to
The Oneida Observer. In 1819 it was returned to Utica and its original name was resumed. A. G. Danby, E. A. Maynard, Eli Maynard, C. C. Griffith, John P. Bush, John F. Kittle, and A. M. Beardsley were successively interested in the publication. In 1848 a daily edition was issued, called
The Utica Daily Observer. In 1853 the papers united with the Utica Democrat, and are now published by D. C. Grove, the weekly edition as the
Observer and Democrat.
The Utica Democrat was commenced by John G. Floyd in 1836. It was successively published by Edward Morris, Jarvis M. Hatch, and Benjamin Welch. In 1853 D. C. Grove became owner, and united it with the Observer.
The Utica Christian Repository, mo., was commenced by Merrill & Hastings in 1822, Wm. Williams, publisher. About 1825 its name was changed to
The Western Recorder, a weekly religious paper, G. Tracy, publisher. It was continued several years.
The Baptist Register was commenced by Elders, Galusha & Wiley. In 1825 it was published under the auspices of the Baptist denomination, Alex. Beebe, editor, and Cephas Bennett, publisher. In 1830 it was leased to Bennett & Bright for 5 years; and in 1835 the lease was renewed for 7 years. In 1840 Mr. Bright withdrew. It was successively published by Bennett, Backus & Hawley, Dolphus Bennett, A. M. Beebe, and D. Bennett, and in 1854 it was sold and united with the New York Recorder, of the city of New York.
The Baptist Sunday-School Journal, mo., was commenced in 1828 by C. Bennett.
The Universalist, mo., was commenced at Utica by Rev. J. S. Thompson, L. R. Smith, & G. B. Lislier in 1825. It was removed to Philadelphia in about 1 year.
The Western Sunday School Visitant and Christian Miscellany was commenced at Utica by G. S. Wilson in 1826.
The Utica Intelligencer was commenced by E. S. Ely in 1826. In 1830 Joseph H. Buckingham became editor and Joseph Colwell publisher, and in 1831 the paper was united with
The Mechanics' Press, commenced by J. M. Ladd & W. Schram in 1829. The united papers were published a short time as
The Utica Intelligencer and Mechanics' Press, by Joseph Colwell, proprietor.
The Utica Magazine was commenced in 1827. It soon passed into the hands of Rev. Dolphus Skinner, who issued it semi-monthly as
The Evangelical Magazine. In 1830 he united it with the Gospel Advocate of Auburn, and published it weekly as
Evangelical Magazine and Gospel Advocate. In 1851 it was merged in the Christian Ambassador, since published simultaneously in New York and Auburn.
The Gospel Messenger was commenced at Auburn by Rev. John C. Rudd in 1827, and was removed to Utica about 1835 and published as
The Gospel Messenger and Church Record. After the death of Mr. Rudd, Rev. Wm. A. Matson became editor. The paper is still published as
The Gospel Messenger.
The American Citizen was published at Utica by Geo. S. Wilson —Bennett & Bright, printers—in 1830.
The Christian Journal was published at Utica in 1830 by E. S. Barrows.
The Co-Operator, semi-mo., was published at Utica in 1832 by Quartus Graves, M. K. Bartlett, editor.
The Lever was published at Utica by Wm. S. Spear in 1832.
The Oneida Democrat was commenced at Utica in 1833, and continued about 2 years.

the wonderful natural channel of navigation that extended through this co., and which, with a short and easy portage, connected the Mohawk with the great lakes and the fertile regions of the West. About the commencement of the last century, plans were proposed for improving this route and for fortifying the most important points upon it. The portage at Rome, from the Mohawk to Wood Creek, became a point of the first importance, and it was occupied as early as 1725; and a fortification known as Fort Bull was built upon Wood Creek soon after. On the 27th of March, 1756, this fort was surprised by a party of French and Indians, under M. De Lery, who had penetrated through an interior route from La Presentation, on the St. Lawrence, by an exhausting march of 15 days. The garrison were unprepared; yet they made a spirited but ineffectual, resistance, and nearly every person perished. Alarm was carried to Fort Williams, on the Mohawk, 4 mi. distant, and a force was hastily sent to relieve Fort Bull, but arrived to late too render assistance. The enemy, after wasting the stores and provisions, retired with their prisoners and plunder

The Oneida Standard was commenced at Waterville in 1833. It was subsequently removed to Utica, and after the discontinuance of the Democrat it assumed the name of *The Standard and Democrat*, Quartus Graves, publisher. In 1835 it became obnoxious to its enemies from its abolitionism, and on the evening of Oct. 21 the office was entered by a mob and a part of the type and furniture were thrown into the street.

The Friend of Man was commenced at Utica by the N. Y. State Anti-Slavery Society in 1836, Wm. Goodell, editor. In 1841 Stanley P. Hough became editor, and in 1842 Wesley Bailey became proprietor, and united with it the Abolitionist, of Cazenovia, and changed the name to *The Liberty Press*. It was discontinued in 1849.

The Utica Teetotaler was commenced by Wesley Bailey in 1849. In 1856 A. K. Bailey became proprietor. In 1858 it was united with the Ilion Independent, the new paper taking the name of **The Central Independent,** under which title it is now published by G. W. Bungay & A. K. Bailey, editors.

Youth's Miscellany was published at Utica by Bennett & Bright in 1834.

The Christian Visitant, mo., was published at Utica by A. B. Groosh in 1835.

The Talisman was published at Utica by Bennett & Bright in 1835.

Mothers' Monthly Journal was published at Utica by Kingsford, Bennett & Bright in 1836.

The Examiner was published at Utica in 1836, and *The Freeman* at Utica in 1837, both by E. Dorchester.

Y Cenhadwr Americanidd, mo., (Welsh, American Messenger,) was commenced at Utica in 1832. In 1834 it was removed to Steuben, and is now published by Rev. Robert Everett.

Anti-Slavery Lecturer was published at Utica a short time by Wm. Goodell in 1839.

Y Cyfaill (Welsh, The Friend) was removed from New York by Rev. W. Rowland in 1841. In 1844 it was returned to New York. In 1854 it was removed to Rome, and in 1857 to Utica. It is now published by Thos. Jenkins.

Central New York Washingtonian was published at Utica and Rome in 1842.

The Wesleyan Methodist was commenced at Utica by David Plumb in 1841. A paper, known successively as the Cortland Luminary and Ref. Meth. Intelligencer and the Fayetteville Luminary, was united with it, and the name changed to *Methodist Reformer*. In 1842 it was removed to Cazenovia, and soon after to Utica, W. Bailey, publisher. In 1843 it was merged in the True Wesleyan, of New York City.

The Utica Daily News, the first daily paper in Utica, was commenced by Joseph M. Lyon, John Arthur, C. Edwards Lester, and Jarvis M. Hatch, in Jan. 1842. It was continued about 7 months.

The Uticanian was published a short time by Squires & Soliss in 1842.

The American Journal of Insanity (quarterly) was commenced by Dr. A. Brigham in 1843, and was edited for a time by Dr. T. R. Beck.

The Washingtonian was published at Utica by J. C. Donaldson in 1843.

Cysell Hen Wladyn Americanidd (Welsh) was published at Utica by E. E. Roberts in 1843.

Young Ladies' Miscellany was published at Utica by Bennett, Backus & Hawley in 1843.

Seren Arllewinol, (Welsh, Western Star,) mo., was commenced at Utica in June, 1844. In 1846 it was removed to Penn.

Washingtonian News was published at Utica by Matteson Baker in 1845.

The Clinton Signal was commenced by Paine & McDonald in 1846. In 1848 its name was changed to *The Radiator*; and in 1849 the original name was resumed. In 1850 it was published as the *Oneida Chief*, by Ira D. Brown. In 1855 it passed into the hands of Francis E. Merritt, and in 1857 into the hands of John H. Osborn, who changed its name to the

Clinton Courier, and still continues its publication.

The Central News was published at Utica by M. Baker in 1846. *Haul Gomer*, (Welsh, Gomerian Sun,) semi-mo., was commenced in 1847 and issued 1 year.

The Central City Cadet was started at Utica in 1849 by James & Howard. In 1850 it was changed to *The Cadet's Banner*, and was soon after discontinued.

The Equalizer, a campaign paper, was published at Utica in 1850.

The Opal, mo., was commenced in 1851. It is edited and printed by patients of the Lunatic Asylum.

The American Free Missionary was removed from McGrawville to Utica in 1850 or '51.

The American Baptist was commenced by the Free Mission Soc., W. Walker, editor, in 1850. In 1856 it was removed to New York City.

The Diamond, mo., a boys' paper, was published at Utica 2 months in 1850 by A. K. Bailey, E. Wetmore, and C. W. Butler.

The Northern Farmer, mo., was commenced at Utica in Jan. 1852. It is now edited by T. B. Miner.

The Rural American was commenced at Utica in Jan. 1856, as a semi-mo. In Jan. 1859, its publication was commenced weekly. It is now edited by T. B. Miner.

Mechanics' National Reporter was published at Utica a short time in 1851.

The Utica Evening Telegraph was commenced by Thos. R. McQuade, J. F. McQuade, editor, in May, 1852. In Feb. 1858, the office was burned. The publication was resumed in May, and is still continued.

The Scientific Daguerrean, mo., was commenced at Utica by D. T. Davie and Guerdon Evans in Jan. 1853.

Y Gwyliedydd (Welsh, The Watchman,) was commenced at Utica by a company, Morgan Ellis, editor, in 1854. In 1856 it was removed to New York City and united with Y Dryck.

The Oneida Demokrat, semi-w., was published at Utica in 1854 by Paul Keiser & Co.

Young Folk's Advocate, mo., was commenced at Utica in July, 1858. It is now edited and published by T. B. Miner.

The Civil and Religious Intelligencer was published at Sangerfield in 1818.

The Rome Republican was commenced by Lorin Dewey in Feb. 1825. In May following, Chauncey Beach succeeded as publisher; and in 1830 the paper was united with the *Oneida Republican*, commenced in June, 1828, by J. P. Van Sice. The united papers were continued by Van Sice, under the title of *The Republican*. In 1831, E. Moon purchased and enlarged the paper, and changed its name to the *Rome Telegraph*. Jas. N. Harris, John Boydon, H. A. Foster, and others were successively interested in its publication. In 1838 it passed into the hands of R. Waldley, who changed its name to the *Democratic Sentinel*, Calvert Comstock, editor. In 1840 L. D. Dana became editor; and in 1845 H. T. Utley and S. W. Morton purchased it and changed its name to the **Rome Sentinel.** In Sept. 1846, Morton sold to A. J. Rowley; and in 1847 Utley sold to A. J. Rowley & Co., E. Comstock, editor. In 1850 Rowley became sole proprietor; and in Jan. 1852, he sold to Elan Comstock.

Rome Daily Sentinel was commenced by C. & E. Comstock, in connection with the Rome Sentinel, in July, 1852. In Oct. 1854, E. Wager and D. D. Rowley, the present publishers, bought one-half, and in April, 1856, the remainder, of the establishment.

The Vernon Courier was commenced in July, 1835. In 1840 it was removed to Rome, and its name changed to **The Roman Citizen,** C. B. Gay, and H. N. Bill, proprietor. J. K. Kenyon, J. P. Fitch, Alfred Sanford, Geo. Scott, G. H. Lynch, A. D. Griswold, and A. C. Sanford were successively interested in its publication. In Oct. 1854, A. Sanford became sole proprietor. In 1855 the office was burned. The publication of the paper was soon after resumed by Mr. Sanford, and is still continued by him.

toward Black River. Oswego was besieged by the French during the summer, and was surrendered on the 14th of Aug. Alarmed at the success of the French, and greatly in fear for his personal safety, Col. Webb, then commanding on the Mohawk, destroyed Forts Williams and Craven, and hastily retreated down the valley to Albany, leaving the frontiers to the mercy of the savages; and the sequel is written in blood in the annals of the Upper Mohawk Valley.

Fort Stanwix was erected in the summer of 1758, on the site of the present village of Rome. It was heavily armed; but the war ended without furnishing occasion for its use, and upon the peace it was allowed to fall into ruin. In June, 1776, Col. Dayton was sent by the Continental authorities to rebuild this fort, which was from this time named Fort Schuyler. Col. Peter Gansevoort was ordered hither in April, 1777, with the 3d Regiment, and while still unfinished the fort was besieged by the tories and Indians under St. Leger. This movement formed part of a plan of operations against the colonies which contemplated the reduction of this fort and the ultimate meeting at Albany of the three British armies from Lake Champlain, the Mohawk, and New York. To relieve this post, Gen. Herkimer was sent with a detachment of troops chiefly raised in "*Tryon*" co. This army fell into an ambuscade at Oriskany, where the memorable battle, elsewhere noticed, was fought on the 5th of Aug. 1777. While most of the savages were absent from their camp, a well conducted sortie from Fort Schuyler, by a party under Colonel Willett, attacked the camp of the enemy and took a large quantity of baggage and stores, 5 British standards, and the papers of most of the officers. The discontent which this incident occasioned among the Indians was increased to insubordination by the mysterious reports brought in by the emissaries of the Americans; and on the 22d of Aug. the siege was raised, and the enemy retreated by the way of Oswego to Montreal. Portions of these troops subsequently joined Gen. Burgoyne and shared the fortunes of that officer. The fort was destroyed by fire and flood in May, 1781. Through the influence of Rev. S. Kirkland and others, the Oneidas were induced to remain neutral or join the American cause, and were rewarded by liberal concessions at subsequent treaties.[1]

Settlement had extended into the borders of the co. before the Revolution; but every vestige of improvement was swept away during the war. Civilization re-appeared with peace; and before the beginning of the present century the hardy pioneers of New England had pressed into nearly every town. The completion of the Western Inland Navigation Co.'s improvement in 1796, and of the Seneca turnpike and other early thoroughfares for emigration, and the construction of the Erie Canal and the 3 lateral canals which here join it, and of the railroads which cross it, have formed marked eras in the improvement and prosperity of the co. In wealth, population, and enterprise it now ranks among the first cos. in the State.

ANNSVILLE[2]— was formed from Lee, Florence, Camden, and Vienna, April 12, 1823. It lies on the N. border of the co., W. of the center. Its surface is broken with ridges or swells, running E. and W., gradually increasing in height toward the N. There appear to have been at some period three small lakes in the town, two of which have broken through their barriers and left fine, fertile valleys. The E. branch of Fish Creek[3] forms a part of the E. boundary, and flows through the S. E. part; and the W. branch of the same stream forms a part of the S. boundary. Several small streams are tributaries of the E. branch, the principal of which are Furnace and Fall Creeks. On the latter near its mouth, are three falls, of 14, 20, and 60 ft. respectively. The soil is clayey in the S., and sandy, gravelly, and stony in the other parts. **Glenmore,** (p. v.,) near the center, contains 2 sawmills, 1 gristmill, and 15 houses. **Taberg,**[4] (p. v.,) in the S. part, contains 2 churches, 3

The Compass was published at Verona in 1840.

The Parlor Journal and Literary News Letter of Central New York, mo., was published at Rome by Graham & Co. in 1843.

The Primitive Christian, semi-mo., was published at Rome by R. Mattison in 1845.

The Camden Gazette was published at Camden by Munger & Stewart in 1842.

The Spiritual Magazine, mo., was published at the Oneida Reserve in 1848.

The Oneida Mirror was published at Camden by Edward Packard in 1849.

The Central State Journal was commenced in 1850 by L. W. Paine, S. S. Norton, editor. Its name was soon after changed to *The Central New York Journal,* and in Jan. 1853, to

The Vernon Transcript, J. R. Howlett, proprietor. In Oct. 1855, Niles Jewell became a partner; and in 1856 the paper was discontinued.

The Boonville Ledger was commenced by James H. Norton in March, 1852. It afterward passed into the hands of Ela Kent. In March, 1855, Mr. Kent sold to L. L. Childs & Co., who changed its name to the

Black River Herald, under which title it is now published by L. L. Childs.

The Waterville Advertiser was commenced by R. W. Hathway in 1851.

The Empire State Health Journal was commenced at Rome in 1851.

The Waterville Journal was commenced in Jan. 1855, by A. P Fuller & Co., C. B. Wilkinson, editor. It was discontinued in March, 1856.

The Waterville Times was commenced in Jan. 1857, by McKibbin & Wilkinson, and is still published.

Y Arweinydd, semi-mo., (Welsh, The Leader,) was commenced at Rome in Jan. 1858, by R. R. Meredith, editor, and Thos. T. Evans, assistant editor.

[1] The Oneidas reserved a large tract of land in the treaty of 1788, but ceded portions in 1795, 1798, 1802, 1805, 1807, 1809, 1810, 1811, 1815, 1817, 1824, 1826, 1827, and 1840, when they finally ceded the last of their lands held in common and received individual portions. Most of them have emigrated to Wisconsin; and but about 60 now live in this co.—*Census of 1855, pp.* 500, 503, 513.

[2] Named from the wife of J. W. Bloomfield, the first settler.

[3] Called by the Indians Te-ge-ro-ken, "between the mouths." A branch of the creek was called A-on-ta-gillon, "Creek at point of rocks." In the neighborhood of Fall Creek are several ravines with very picturesque scenery.

[4] Named from an iron-mining town in Sweden. The Oneida

sawmills, 1 gristmill, a furnace, tannery, several small manufactories, and 40 houses. **Bloss-vale** is a p. o. in the s. part. The first settlement was commenced in 1793,[1] by John W. Bloom-field, from N. J. The census reports 4 churches in town.[2]

AUGUSTA[3]—was formed from Whitestown, March 15, 1798. A part of Vernon was taken off in 1802, and a part of Stockbridge (Madison co.) in 1836. It lies on the w. border of the co., s. of the center. Its surface is a rolling upland. Two ranges of hills extend N. and S. through the town on opposite sides of Skanandoa Creek, affording limestone of excellent quality for lime and building purposes. Oriskany Creek flows through the extreme S. E. corner, and Skanandoa Creek flows N. through near the center. The soil is a fertile, clayey and sandy loam. **Augusta,** (p. v.,) near the center, contains 2 churches and 100 inhabitants. **Knox Corners,** (p. v.,) N. W. of the center, contains a church and 200 inhabitants. **Oriskany Falls,** (p. v.,) in the S. E. corner, contains a church, a saw and grist mill, machine shop, distillery, and 711 inhabitants. The first settlement was made by —— Gunn, in 1793.[4] The first religious services were held at the house of —— Fairbanks, in 1794.[5]

AVA[6]—was formed from Boonville, May 12, 1846. It is the central town on the N. border of the co. Its surface is a moderately uneven upland, 700 to 1,000 ft. above the Rome level. It is drained by Fish Creek, the E. and W. branches of the Mohawk, Point Rock, and Blue Brooks. Several small sulphur springs have been found in town. The soil is a gravelly loam. **Ava Corners,** (Ava p. o.,) w. of the center, contains 20 houses. The first settlement was commenced by Ebenezer Harper, in 1798.[7] A Friends meeting house is the only place of worship in town.

BOONVILLE[8]—was formed from Leyden, (Lewis co.,) March 28, 1805. Ava was taken off in 1846. It lies on the N. border of the co., E. of the center. Its surface is a hilly, broken up-land, 800 to 1,000 ft. above the canal at Rome. Black River flows through the N. E. part, and Lansing Kil rises near the center and flows s. to the Mohawk. Its soil is clayey loam, in many places thickly covered with boulders and often inclining to sand. Near the village are immense deposits of drift. Its E. border extends into the great forest, and presents the meager, sandy soil and naked rocks peculiar to that region. There is a gas spring 1½ mi. w. of the village, and a sulphur spring 1½ mi. s. The latter has acquired some local celebrity. **Boonville,** (p. v.,) in the N. W. part, was incorp. in 1855. It contains 3 churches, a printing office, several manu-factories, and 1,000 inhabitants. It is the present N. terminus of the Black River & Utica R. R. It is on the summit level of the Black River Canal, and has a large trade with the country N., W., and E. **Alder Creek,** (p. v.,) in the S. E. part, contains a church and 20 houses. **Forest Port,** (p. v.,) near the S. E. corner, on the line of Remsen, contains 20 houses. **Hawkinsville,** (p. v.,) N. W. of the center, contains a saw and grist mill, chair factory, carding mill, and 339 in-habitants. **Hurlbutville** is a p. o. The first settlement commenced in 1795.[9] The first church was formed in 1805.[10]

BRIDGEWATER[11]—was formed from Sangerfield, March 24, 1797. It is the s. E. corner town of the co. Its surface is uneven. The valley of the w. branch of the Unadilla and its tribu-taries, locally known as "Bridgewater Flats," in the N., is about a mi. wide, but decreases to about

---

Glass and Iron Manufacturing Co. began operations here in 1809. In 1811 a blast furnace was erected. Formerly hollow ware was extensively made; but at present pig iron is the chief product.

[1] The first settlement was made at Taberg. Among the early settlers were Elias Brewster, Adam P. Campbell, Nicholas Arm-strong, and Squire Fairservice.

[2] Presb., M. E., Bap., and R. C.

[3] This town is included in the s. part of the tract leased from the Oneidas in 1794 to Peter Smith. The lease is said to have been for 999 years. The tract was divided into 4 allotments, the first of which lies wholly within this town. The lease was assumed by the State in 1795–97, and patents were granted to settlers, Smith retaining 6 lots in the town as part payment for his lease. The first settlers took their lands as tenants under Smith. Part of the Oneida Reservation, purchased in 1795 and sold at auction in 1797, is included in the N. part of the town.

[4] Among the early settlers were Benjamin Warren, David Morton, John Alden, Ichabod Stafford, Joseph and Abraham Forbes, Isaac and Benjamin Allen, Amos Parker, Thos. Cassaty, Ozias and Lemuel Hart. James Reynolds, Abel Prior, Thomas Spafford, Ezen Saxton, Abiel Lindsey, and Francis O'Toole. The first birth was that of Peter Smith Gunn; the first marriage, that of Daniel Hart and Catharine Putnam; and the first death, that of Eleazer Putnam, in 1795. T. Cassaty built the first sawmill, in 1795, at Oriskany Falls. A gristmill was built the next year.

[5] The census reports 5 churches in town; 2 Cong., M. E., Bap., and Union.   [6] Named from a city in Burmah.

[7] Zephaniah and Abner Wood settled in town about 1800. Messrs. Barnard, Fanning, Adams, Mitchell, Beck, and Tiffany were early settlers. Salmon Bates kept the first inn, in 1800. Benj. Jones built the first sawmill, in 1801,—at which time there were only 9 other inhabitants in town. The road cut through from Fort Stanwix to the French settlement on Black River, toward the close of the last century, led through this town; and traces of it may still be seen. Several tributaries of Black River take their rise in swamps in the N. E. part of the town.

[8] Named from Gerrit Boon, agent of the Holland Land Co., who made the first settlement. In early times it was called "Boon's Upper Settlement."

[9] Andrew Edmunds came on in 1795 as an agent of the Hol land Land Co., with several men, built a sawmill, and com-menced a gristmill, which was finished the next year. Luke Fisher and son, Phineas, Martin, and Silas Southwell, Asahel and Ezekiel Porter, Aaron Willard, Jacob Springer, Jephtha King, and Hezekiah Jones came in 1796. Lemuel Hough and Daniel Pitcher were early settlers. The first birth was that of a daughter of Jacob Springer; and the first marriage, that of Henry Evans and Elizabeth Edmunds. The first store and inn were opened by the agents of the company.

[10] Rev. Daniel Smith was the first minister. There are now 5 churches in town; Presb., M. E., Bap., Union, and R. C.

[11] The "Line of Property," run in accordance with a treaty of 1718, passed through this town.—Jones's Annals, p. 123.

half that width in the s.[1] The hills rise, on the E. and W. borders, 300 to 500 ft. above the valley, their declivities being often steep. The W. branch of the Unadilla[2] flows S. through the town. The soil in the E. is a gravelly loam, and in the W. clay. Stone is quarried in the N. E. part. **Bridgewater,** (p. v.,) in the S. part, contains 3 churches, the Bridgewater Academy, and 306 inhabitants. **North Bridgewater** (p. v.) contains 15 houses. **Babcock Hill** (p. o.) is a hamlet. The first settlement was commenced in 1788,[3] by Joseph Farwell. There are 3 churches in town; Cong., Bap., and Univ.

CAMDEN—was formed from Mexico, (Oswego co.,) March 15, 1799. Florence was taken off in 1805, Vienna in 1807, and a part of Annsville in 1823. It lies upon the W. border of the co., near the N. W. corner. Its surface is rolling, gradually rising toward the N., where it is broken by hills whose summits are several hundred feet above Oneida Lake. The W. branch of Fish Creek flows diagonally through the town toward the S. E. Mad River from the N. unites with it near Camden Village; and Little River, a tributary, forms part of the S. boundary. The soil is a sandy loam, in some places gravelly and stony, but generally well adapted to grazing. **Camden,** (p. v.,) in the E. part, was incorp. in 1834. It contains 3 churches, saw and grist mills, a sash and blind manufactory, pump factory, 2 tanneries, a cloth manufactory, and 862 inhabitants. **West Camden,** (p. v.,) near the N. W. corner, contains 20 houses. **Hillsborough,** (p. o.,) in the S. part, is a hamlet. The first settlement commenced near the close of the last century.[4] The first religious society was formed Feb. 19, 1798, by Rev. Eliphalet Steele.[5] The church received from the heirs of John Murray an endowment in lands yielding a revenue of $112.

DEERFIELD—was formed from Schuyler, (Herkimer co.,) March 15, 1798. Marcy was taken off in 1832. It lies near the center of the E. border of the co. Its surface is mostly a high plateau, 600 to 1,000 ft. above the Mohawk, forming the N. continuation of the Hassenclever Mts. of Herkimer co. A broad intervale, partly overflowed in high water, extends along the Mohawk opposite Utica; and on the N. E. the surface descends abruptly to the creek. The Mohawk flows along the S. W. border of the town, and West Canada Creek along the N. E. border. The soil on the flats is a deep, rich, alluvial loam, and on the hills a slaty and gravelly loam. **Deerfield Corners,** (Deerfield p. o.,) in the S. part, contains 2 churches, 3 carriage shops, and 50 houses. A thickly settled suburb of Utica extends toward the village. **North Gage,** (p. o.,) in the N. part, is a hamlet. The first settlement was commenced in 1773.[6] The first religious services were held in 1798, by Rev. —— Eddy. There are 4 churches in town.[7]

FLORENCE[8]—was formed from Camden, Feb. 16, 1805. A part of Annsville was taken off in 1823. It is the N. W. corner town of the co. Its surface is rolling, and 250 to 300 ft. above the Rome level. Mad River flows S. E. through the town. The soil is stony and light, and is underlaid by the Hudson River shales. A portion of the town is still covered by forests, which extend N. to near Jefferson co. **Florence,** (p. v.,) N. of the center, contains 3 churches, 3 sawmills, a grist-mill, tannery, and 40 houses. **Empeyville,** in the E. part, contains a church and 20 houses. **East Florence** (p. o.) and **Florence Hill** are hamlets. The first settlement commenced in 1801,[9] by Amos Woodworth. The first religious society (Cong.) was formed Dec. 16, 1816;[10] Rev. Samuel Sweezey was the first settled minister.

FLOYD[11]—was formed from Steuben, March 4, 1796. It lies in the interior, E. of the center of the co. Its surface is rolling, gradually rising to the N. border, where it attains an elevation of 200 to 300 ft. above the valley of the Mohawk. Nine Mile Creek[12] flows through a small portion

---

[1] The excavation which forms the valley has been filled to an immense depth with drift; and rock cannot be found within a great distance below the surface. Cedar swamps extend along several of the streams.

[2] Called also the Ti-a-na-da-ra.—*Jones's Annals*, p. 122.

[3] Among the early settlers were Ezra Parker, Ephraim and Nathan Waldo, —— Lyman, and Jesse, Joel, and Abner Ives. Ezra Parker kept the first inn; Major Farwell built the first sawmill; and —— Thomas the first gristmill. This is the smallest and least populous town in the co.

[4] Henry Williams was the first permanent settler, in 1796-97. Jesse Curtis had previously built a sawmill; but he did not settle in town until some time after. Levi Matthews, Daniel Parker, Seth and Joel Dunbar, Aaron Matthews, Samuel Wood, Thos. Comstock, Elihu Curtis, Samuel Royce, Noah and Andrew Tuttle, Benjamin Barnes, sr. and jr., Philip Barnes, Israel Stoddard, and —— Carrier were early settlers. The first birth was that of Noah P. Tuttle; the first marriage, that of Elihu Curtis and Anna Northrop; and the first deaths were those of Mrs. Bacon and a child, who were drowned in crossing Mad River in a canoe. Elihu Curtis kept the first inn, in 1799; and Timothy W. Wood the first store, about the same time.

[5] There are now 5 churches in town; M. E., Wes. Meth., Prot. E., Cong., and R. C.

[6] George G. Weaver, Capt. Mark Damoth, and Christian Real settled at the Corners in 1773. In 1776, hearing that a band of tories and Indians were planning a descent upon the settlement, they retreated to Little Stone Arabia. In 1784 they returned, and about the same time Peter, Nicholas, and George Weaver, Geo. Damoth, Nicholas and Philip Harter, came in. During the first 15 or 20 years the settlements did not extend to the N. part of the town. The Cox and Coffin families were the first in that part.   [7] Bap., Calv. Meth., Union, and R. C.

[8] Named from the city of Florence, in Italy.

[9] The first settlement commenced under the auspices of Wm. Henderson, owner of Township 4 of Scriba's Patent. He gave Amos Woodworth, John Spinning, and —— Turner 50 acres each, to commence a settlement. Azariah Orton, —— Crawford and his son Clark, Norman Waugh, Benoni and Ebenezer Barlow, Ambrose Curtis, Ephraim Wright, Joseph Olcott, and Benj Young came soon after. Several of the latter settled at Florence Hill. Nathan Thompson kept the first inn.

[10] There are 5 churches in town; 2 M. E., 2 Union, and Bap.

[11] Named from Gen. Wm. Floyd, one of the signers of the Declaration of Independence, who purchased a part of Fonda's Patent and removed to this co. in 1803.—*Jones's Annals of Oneida Co.*, pp. 155, 705.

[12] Called by the Indians Te-ya-nun-soke, "a beech tree standing."

of the s. e. part. The soil is of good quality and well adapted to grain and grass. **Floyd Corners** (Floyd p. o.) contains a church and 20 houses. The first settlement commenced about 1790, by Capt. Benjamin Pike.[1] There are 4 churches in town; Cong., Welsh Meth., Union,[2] and R. C.

KIRKLAND[3]—was formed from Paris, April 13, 1827. Marshall was taken off in 1829, a part was annexed to New Hartford in 1834, and a part of Paris was annexed in 1839. It lies in the interior, s. of the center of the co. Its surface is a hilly upland, divided into two general ridges by the valley of Oriskany Creek. The hills are 200 to 500 ft. high, and the declivities are generally steep. Oriskany Creek flows n. e. through near the center. The soil is a rich, calcareous loam. Near Clinton Village are quarries of good building stone. Iron ore is found; and several thousand tons are annually shipped by the Chenango Canal, to Constantia, Taberg, and Penn. Great attention is paid to fruit growing, and this town excels every other town in the co. in the amount of fruit raised. The town derives its greatest interest from its extensive educational institutions, which entitle it to the appellation of the Literary Emporium of Oneida co. **Clinton** (p. v.) was incorp. April 12, 1843. Hamilton College[4] is located upon a hill overlooking the Oriskany Valley. Its buildings consist of Dexter Hall, or North College; Kirkland Hall, or Middle College; Hamilton Hall, or South College; a chapel, laboratory, and an observatory. The course of study embraces a collegiate and a law department. A grammar school, under a separate board of trustees, is connected as a preparatory department. The college libraries contain about 10,000 volumes, and the cabinet of natural history contains about as many specimens. The village also contains 5 churches, 2 newspaper offices, the Clinton Liberal Institute,[5] a grammar, a boarding, and a high school, and a few manufactories. Pop. 1,174. **Manchester,** (Kirkland p. o.,) a manufacturing village,[6] in the n. part, contains 30 houses. **Franklin,** near the center, contains the Franklin Iron Works[7] and 35 houses. **Clarks Mills,**[8] in the n. corner, is a manufacturing village, and contains a cotton factory, grist and saw mill, and 40 houses. The first settlement commenced in 1787, by 8 families.[9] Religious services were first held in the cabin of Capt. Foot.[10]

1 Among the early settlers were Stephen Moulton, Wm. and Nathaniel Allen, James Chase, Elisha Lake, —— Howard, Hope Smith, David Bryan, Samuel Denison, James Bartlett, —— Putney, Jarvis Pike, Capt. Nathan Townsend, and Thomas Bacon—mostly from Conn. The first death was that of —— Foster; the second, that of Nathan Thompson, who was killed by a falling tree.

2 The plan of ownership of the union church is peculiar. The seats are owned and transferred by purchase, and the owners meet on the first Monday in each year and vote what denomination shall occupy the house the ensuing year.

3 Named from the Rev. Samuel Kirkland, an early missionary among the Oneida Indians, who settled in the county in 1792. He was the principal founder of an academy since merged in Hamilton College. He died in 1808; and a monument was erected to his memory by the Northern Missionary Society.

4 Hamilton Oneida Academy was incorp. by the Regents, Jan. 31, 1793, mainly through the exertions of the Rev. Samuel Kirkland. In 1794 a commodious building was erected, the corner stone of which was laid with much ceremony by Baron Steuben. The school was opened the same year under the Rev. John Niles, whose successors were Rev. Robert Porter, Seth Norton, and Rev. James Robbins. The success of this academy was highly gratifying to its friends; and the rapid development of Central New York suggested the necessity of more ample facilities for instruction and an extension of its course of study. Clinton and Fairfield became active competitors for the honors of a college, and charters of similar character and conditions were granted to each, under the names of Hamilton and Clinton Colleges respectively. By a compromise between the friends of the rival locations, the latter institution was never organized. Clinton went on with its literary college, and employed the most active person in the Fairfield enterprise as its agent; while Fairfield organized a medical college. Hamilton College was chartered May 26, 1812, and went into operation soon after, under the presidency of the Rev. Azel Backus. His successors have been Henry Davis, in 1817; Sereno E. Dwight, in 1833; Joseph Penny, in 1835; Simeon North, in 1839; and Samuel Ware Fisher, in 1858. The college is chiefly under the influence of the New School Presbyterian and Congregational Churches. From 1819 to 1832, dissensions between the Trustees and President seriously retarded the prosperity of the institution; and during the same period insubordination among the students was of frequent occurrence. From 1838 to 1846 the college received $3,000 annually from the State; but the present Constitution cut it off from the receipt of a balance previously appropriated, and the grant has not been since continued. The Trustees many years since adopted the custom of admitting students unable to pay tuition fees; and, from incautious extension, this usage became an abuse that showed itself upon the treasurer's books. The receipts from tuition became only a quarter as great as previously, while the catalogue indicated by its numbers an increasing prosperity. It was found more difficult to abandon this practice than it had been to adopt it; and it is still continued to as great an extent as the means of the institution will justify.

These causes have embarrassed the finances of the college; but efforts are about being made to relieve it from debt. The sum of $50,000 was granted by the State, June 19, 1812, to aid in founding the college. Wm. H. Maynard, of Utica, in 1832 gave $20,000 to endow a professorship of law: and S. Newton Dexter, of Whitesboro, in 1836 gave his personal obligations for $15,000 to endow a professorship of the Greek and Latin languages. The observatory was built in 1854, at a cost of $5,000 besides the instruments, which have cost more than twice that sum.

5 The Clinton Liberal Institute was founded in 1832; it is under the patronage of the Universalist denomination, and has a male and a female department. The building for the former is of stone, 96 by 52 feet, 4 stories above the basement, and has accommodations for 100 students. The female department is an elegant structure, 144 by 60 ft., 2 stories high above the basement, and has an average attendance of 50 pupils. A small monthly paper, named the "Leaf Bud," "Summer Leaves," "Autumn Leaves," or "Wintergreen," according to the season, is published at this institution. Home Cottage Seminary is a private institution, established in 1854 as a ladies' seminary, by Miss L. M. Barker. The edifice is 60 by 112 ft., and cost—including 8 acres of land—$20,000. It has been united with another ladies' school under Miss A. Chipman, and is very prosperous. An issue styled the "Home Cottage Quarterly" is published by the pupils. This seminary forms the female department of the grammar school. The Clinton High School, for males only, was established May, 1858, by Rev. B. W. Dwight and D. A. Holbrook. It is located ½ mi. from the village, cost $18,000, and has accommodations for 80 students.

6 The Manchester Manufacturing Co., incorp. in 1815, gave employment to 100 hands, and manufactured cotton cloths to the amount of $100,000 per year until Aug. 19, 1855, when it was burned.

7 The Franklin Iron Works manufacture 4,000 tons of pig iron annually, from ore obtained in the immediate vicinity. It gives employment to 100 men, and turns out work to the amount of $100,000 annually.

8 Clark's Mills manufacture brown sheeting, and are furnished with 128 looms. The proprietors also have a manufactory of cotton cord, rope, and batting, and a gristmill and sawmill.

9 Moses Foot, his three sons Bronson, Luther, and Ira, and his son-in-law, Barnabas Pond, were of this number. Levi Shearman, Solomon Hovey, Ludin Blodget, Timothy Tuttle, Samuel Hubbard, Randall Lewis, Cordial Storrs, John Bullen, and Capt. Cassey were early settlers. Mrs. S. Hovey was the first white woman who moved into town. The first child born was Clinton Foot; the first marriage was that of Roger Leveret and Elizabeth Cheseborough; and the first death was that of Mrs. Merah Tuttle. Skenandoah, an Oneida chief, died in this town, March 11, 1816, aged 110 years. Capt. Cassey built the first gristmill, in 1787, and a sawmill the next year. The village was early named from Gov. Clinton; and the vicinity was known by the Indians as Ka-de-wis-day.

10 There are 5 churches in town; 2 Cong., Bap., R. C., and Union,

LEE[1]—was formed from Western, April 3, 1811. A part of Annsville was taken off in 1823. It lies in the interior, N. of the center of the co. Its surface is rolling or moderately hilly, gradually rising from the lowlands in the S. to an elevation of 500 to 800 ft. above the canal at Rome. The W. branch of the Mohawk flows through the N. E. corner, and Fish Creek forms a part of the W. boundary. The soil is a clayey, sandy, and gravelly loam, and in some localities very stony. **Lee Center** (p. v.) contains a church, saw and grist mill, tannery, and 40 houses. **Lee,** (p. v.,) in the S. W. corner, contains a church and 20 houses. **Delta,** (p. v.,) in the S. E. corner, on the line of Western, contains a foundery, tannery, and 228 inhabitants. **West Branch,** (p. v.,) in the N. E. corner, contains a saw and grist mill and 20 houses. **Stokes**[2] (p. o.) is a hamlet. The first settlement commenced in 1790, at Delta, by Stephen and Reuben Sheldon.[3] The first religious society (Cong.) was formed in 1797, under Rev. James Southworth.[4]

MARCY[5]—was formed from Deerfield, March 30, 1832. It lies on the N. bank of the Mohawk, E. of the center of the co. Its surface is rolling; a wide intervale borders upon the river, from which rises an irregular table-land 300 to 500 ft. above the valley. Nine Mile Creek flows through the W. corner. The soil on the upland is a rich, sandy and gravelly loam, and on the flats an alluvial deposit, which is annually increased by the spring floods. **Stittsville,** (p. v.,) on the line of Trenton, contains a church, saw and grist mill, cotton factory, and 40 houses. **Marcy** is a p. o. The first settlement commenced in 1793,[6] by John Wilson. The census reports 6 churches in town.[7]

MARSHALL—was formed from Kirkland, Feb. 21, 1829. It lies in the S. part of the co., the S. W. corner bordering on Madison co. The surface is a hilly upland, the hills rising 200 to 300 ft. above the valleys. Oriskany Creek flows N. E. through the W. part. The soil is a fertile, sandy loam. **Deansville,**[8] (p. v.,) on the N. border, contains 2 churches, an academy, and 185 inhabitants. **Hanover,** (Marshall p. o.,) near the center, contains a church and 15 houses. **Forge Hollow** contains a church, a forge, and 35 houses. The first white settlement was commenced in 1793,[9] by David Barton. The first church (Cong.) was formed in 1797.[10]

NEW HARTFORD—was formed from Whitestown, April 12, 1827. A part of Kirkland was annexed in 1834. It lies upon the E. border of the co., S. of the center. Its surface is level or gently undulating, except in the extreme E. part, where is a low range of hills. Sauquoit Creek flows N. through near the center. The soil is a rich, calcareous loam. **New Hartford** (p. v.) contains 4 churches, 2 cotton factories, a batting factory,[11] a flouring mill, tannery, and 892 inhabitants. **Washington Mills** (p. v.) contains the Washington Steam Mills, Oneida Woolen Mills, and 50 houses. **New York Upper Mills,** (New York Mills p. o.,) on the N. border, contains a church, a cotton factory, dye house, steam mills, and 40 houses. **Willow Vale,** in the S. part, contains a factory for making cotton machinery,[12] a foundery, and 40 houses. The first settlement was commenced by Jedediah Sanger, in 1788.[13] The first church (Presb.) was formed in 1791, by Rev. Jonathan Edwards; and the first settled minister was Rev. Danl. Bradley. The census reports 6 churches in town.[14]

PARIS[15]—was formed from Whitestown, April 10, 1792. Brookfield, Hamilton, and a part of

1 Named from Lee, Mass., whence some of the early settlers came.

2 Sometimes called "Nisbets Corners," and "Lee corners."

3 Among the early settlers were David Smith, John and Benj. Spinning, Stephen and Nicholas Salisbury, Nathan Barlow, Wm. Taft, Dan. and Seth Miller, Frederic Sprague, —— Hall, Jas. Young, Chas. Gifford, Elisha Parke, and —— Potter. The first birth was that of Fenner Sheldon, in 1791; the first marriage, that of Dan. Miller and Amy Taft; the first death, that of Job Kaird, in 1798. David Smith built the first sawmill, at Delta, and Gen. Floyd the first gristmill, in 1796.

4 There are 4 churches in town; 2 M. E., Friends, and Union.

5 Named from William L. Marcy, since Governor of the State.

6 James, Thos., Isaac, and Jacob Wilson and —— Tull were early settlers. The first death was that of John Wilson, in the fall of 1793. —— Camp kept the first inn, about 1810; and John F. Allen built the first mill, about 1825.

7 2 Cong.. 2 Bap., M. E., and Calv. Meth.

8 Named from Thos. Dean, long an agent of the Brothertown Indians.

9 The Brothertown Indians were settled previous to the Revolution on a reservation in this town and Kirkland given them by the Oneidas. They were remnants of New England, Hudson River, and Long Island Indians, who were collected toward the close of the Colonial period, and numbered, when first removed hither, about 400 souls. Coming from many different stocks, they adopted the English language and some of the arts of civilized life. They were mostly scattered during the war, but afterward returned, and many of them became thrifty farmers; but the greater part acquired the vices of the whites, and a part of them sold out and went to Green Bay. In 1850 the last of the tribe bade adieu to their homes and moved West. Among the early white settlers were Warren Williams, Hezekiah Eastman, Capt. Simeon Hubbard, and Levi Baker. The first birth was that of Col. Lester Baker.

10 It was called the Hanover Society; and their edifice, after standing 40 years, was rebuilt in 1841. There are now 4 churches in town; 2 Cong., M. E., and Univ.

11 The "Utica Cotton Mills" have a capital of $100,000, run 8,000 spindles and 150 looms and employ 190 hands, and turn out 1,800,000 yds. of cloth annually. They have a dry house, machine shop, and gas works.

12 This establishment has a capital invested of $40,000, and employs 80 hands.

13 Among the early settlers were Asahel Beach, Amos Ives, Solomon Blodget, Salmon Butler, Joel Blair, Agift Hill, —— Wyman, Stephen Bushnell, Oliver Collins, Joseph Jennings, Joseph Higles, Nathan Seward, John French, —— Kellogg, —— Risley, —— Olmstead, —— Seymour, —— Butler, —— Hurlbut, —— Kilborn, and —— Montague. Jedediah Sanger built the first mill.

14 Presb., M. E., Prot. E., Bap., Union, and Friends.

15 Named by the inhabitants in acknowledgment of the kindness of Isaac Paris, a merchant of Fort Plain, who, in the year

Cazenovia, (Madison co.,) Sherburne, (Chenango co.,) and Sangerfield, were taken off in 1795, and Kirkland in 1827. A part of Kirkland was annexed in 1839. It lies on the E. border, near the S. E. corner of the co. Its surface is a hilly upland, broken by the valley of Sauquoit Creek. The hills bordering the valley are 200 to 400 ft. high, and their declivities are generally steep. Sauquoit Creek flows N. through the town, E. of the center. The soil is a sandy, calcareous loam. **East Sauquoit** and **West Sauquoit**, (Sauquoit p. o.,) contiguous villages on opposite sides of Sauquoit Creek, contain 2 churches, extensive cotton factories,[1] 2 paper mills in the immediate vicinity,[2] 2 sawmills, a gristmill, a tannery, and 690 inhabitants. **Clayville**, (p. v.,) near the center, contains a church, 2 furnaces, an agricultural implement manufactory,[3] extensive woolen mills,[4] and 817 inhabitants. **Cassville**, (p. v.,) near the S. border, contains a church, gristmill, tub factory, and 40 houses; **Paris Hill**, (Paris p. o.,) in the W. part, a church and 30 houses; **Holman City,** in the E. part, a furnace, a whiffletree iron manufactory, and 12 houses. The first settlement commenced in 1789.[5] The first church (Cong.) was formed in 1791, by Rev. Jonathan Edwards; Rev. Eliphalet Steele was the first pastor. There are now 8 churches in town.[6]

REMSEN[7]—was formed from Norway, (Herkimer co.,) March 15, 1798. A part of Steuben was annexed in 1809. It is the N. E. corner town of the co. Its surface is an elevated upland, broken by hills and ridges and with a mean elevation of 1,200 to 2,000 ft. above tide. Black River and its tributaries drain the central and N. parts; and West Canada Creek forms a small part of the S. E. boundary. Otter, Long, and White Lakes are in the N. part. The soil is generally a light, sandy loam. A large part of the town is still covered by the primitive forests forming a portion of the great Northern Wilderness. **Remsen,** (p. v.,) a station on the B. R. & U. R. R., in the S. W. corner, contains a church, furnace, steam mill, and 510 inhabitants. **Forest Port,** (p. v.,) on the line of Boonville, contains 20 houses. **Port Woodhull** is a hamlet. The first settlement commenced in 1792, by Barnabas Mitchell.[8] There are 12 churches in town.[9]

ROME—was formed from Steuben, March 4, 1796. It lies upon the Mohawk, a little W. of the center of the co. Its surface is level, and some portion of the W. part is low and marshy. The Mohawk flows S. E. through the E. part, and Wood Creek flows W. through the N. W. part.[10] Fish Creek forms the N. W. boundary. The soil is generally a highly productive, gravelly loam. **Rome,** (p. v.,) upon the Mohawk, S. E. of the center of the town, was incorp. March 26, 1819. It is a half-shire of the co., and it contains the co. buildings, 12 churches, 4 banks, 2 newspaper offices, the Rome Academy, and several manufactories.[11] It is the S. terminus of the W. R. & C. V. R. R. and of the Black River Canal, and is an important station upon the Central R. R. and the Erie Canal. Pop. 7,083. **West Rome** is a thickly settled suburb just W. of the limits of Rome. **Stanwix,** (p. v.,) a canal village, contains about 15 houses. **Greens Corners** is a station on the Central R. R., near the S. W. corner. **Ridge Mills,** near the center, contains 15 dwellings; and **North Rome** is a hamlet. The first settlement was made at the "Carrying Place," before the [12]French

---

of scarcity, 1789, supplied them with Virginia corn on a liberal credit, and finally accepted payment in such produce as they were enabled to supply.

[1] The "Quaker Woolen Factory," established in 1812. In 1827 it commenced the manufacture of cotton, and now employs 100 hands, runs 110 looms, and can make 3,000 yards per day. The same Co. have another mill, that employs 50 hands and runs 60 looms.

[2] These mills employ 30 hands, and make about 1¼ tons of printing paper daily.

[3] The manufacture of scythes was commenced in 1834. The business has since been largely increased; and at present about $200,000 is invested in the works. Scythes, hoes, forks, and other farming tools are extensively manufactured.

[4] The woolen mills were started in 1843. They manufacture broadcloths and blankets, and employ 80 hands.

[5] The first settlement was made by Capt. Rice. Among the early settlers were Benj'n Barnes and his son Benjamin, John Humarton, Stephen Barnet, Aaron Adams, Abiel Simmons, Phineas Kellogg, John and Sylvester Butler, Asa Shepard, Kirkland Griffin, and Benjamin Merrill. The first death was that of Wm. Swan, in 1790. Abner Bacon kept the first inn, and James Orton the first store, in 1802.

[6] 2 M. E., 2 Prot. E., 2 Cong., Bap., and Presb.

[7] Named from Henry Remsen, Patentee of Remsenburgh. The town embraces most of Remsenburgh Patent, and portions of Easton's Woodhull's, Service's, and other tracts.

[8] Among the early settlers were John Bomer, Nath'l Rockwood, Bettis Le Clerc, Perez Farr, and Jonah Dayton, in 1793. In 1808, David Mound, John Gas, Griffith I. Jones, John Owens, and Hugh Hughes, Welsh immigrants, settled, and were soon followed by a large immigration of their countrymen. This town contains more natives of Wales than any other town in

the State; and, including their children of American birth, the Welsh number more than half the population. The first birth was that of Polly Mitchell; and the first death, that of Capt. Peck. Broughton White kept the first store, in 1803.

[9] 5 Calv. Meth., 3 Cong., 2 M. E., and 2 Bap.

[10] Between the Mohawk and Wood Creek was a portage of about 1 mi. in length over level ground. Early in the last century propositions were made to build a road across this point; and in 1796 the Western Inland Navigation Co. constructed a canal between the two streams, and the route speedily became the great thoroughfare of travel. This canal was most of the way on the line of the present Erie Canal, through the village. The Indians called the place De-o-wain-sta, "a carrying place for canoes." Wood Creek was called Ka-ne-go-dick. The old canal was constructed under the superintendence of Peter Colt.

[11] The principal manufactories are a plow factory, foundery, planing mill, several sawmills, and the repair shops of the W. R. & C. V. R. R.

[12] The first settlers came in at an early period, but their names are unknown. John Roof and —— Brodock were engaged in the carrying trade at this place in 1760. The former was first store and inn keeper. Jedediah Phelps, John Barnard, George and Henry Huntington, Joshua Hathaway, Dr. Stephen White, Roswell Fellows, Matthew Brown, sen. and jun., Seth Ranney, David Brown, Ebenezer, Daniel W., and Thomas Wright, Thomas Selden, Solomon and John Williams, Peter Colt, Wm. Colbrath, Abijah and Clark Putnam, Caleb Reynolds, Rufus Easton, Thos. Gilbert, Moses Fish, Stephen Lampman, Jeremiah Steves, and John Niles were early settlers.—*Jones's Annals*, p. 372. The first birth was in the family of John Roof, Aug. 28, 1769. The first sawmill was erected in 1758, and the first gristmill in 1795. A State Arsenal was erected here in 1808, on the present site of St. Peter's Church. The U. S. erected an arsenal and workshop a

War of 1755. The subsequent history of the place is full of incidents of general interest.[1] The first church (Cong.) was formed Sept. 5, 1800.[2]

SANGERFIELD[3]—was formed from Paris, March 5, 1795. Bridgewater was taken off in 1797. It was transferred from Chenango to Oneida co. April 4, 1804. It is the w. town on the s. line of the co. Its surface is a moderately hilly upland, 700 to 800 ft. above the Mohawk at Utica. The streams are small, and flow N. to the Mohawk and s. to Chenango River. The soil in the valleys is a rich alluvium, and on the hills a gravelly loam. **Waterville,**[4] (p. v.,) near the N. border, contains 4 churches, a bank, an academy, a newspaper office, a saw and grist mill, distillery, and 1,109 inhabitants. **Sangerfield Center** (Sangerfield p. o.) contains a church and 30 houses; and **Stockwell Settlement,** in the s. part, about 20 houses. The first settlement was commenced by Zerah Phelps, from Mass., in 1791.[5] There are now 7 churches in town.[6]

STEUBEN[7] was formed from Whitestown, April 10, 1792. A part of Mexico (Oswego co.) was annexed, and Floyd and Rome were taken off, in 1796; and Leyden (Lewis co.) and Western in 1797. Parts of Steuben's Tract in Western and Remsen were annexed in 1803; and a part was annexed to Remsen in 1809. It lies in the interior, N. E. of the center of the co. Its surface is a hilly, broken upland, rising 800 to 1,200 feet above the Mohawk.[8] The streams are small. Cincinnati Creek rises in the interior, and forms part of the E. boundary. The soil is a gravelly loam; and boulders are numerous. Quarries are worked, from which a good quality of building stone is obtained. **Steuben Corners**·(Steuben p. o.) is a hamlet, in the s. part. **Steuben Station,** on the B. R. & U. R. R., is on the line of Boonville. The first settlement was commenced in 1789,[9] under Baron Steuben. The census reports 7 churches in town.[10]

TRENTON—was formed from Schuyler, (Herkimer co.,) March 24, 1797. It lies upon the w. bank of West Canada Creek, near the center of the E. border of the co. The surface rises from the creek to the height of 400 to 600 feet; and from the summits it spreads out into an upland broken by ridges of drift. Cincinnati Creek flows through the N. part, and Nine Mile Creek through the s. part. The soil is a sandy and clayey loam, best adapted to grazing. The celebrated Trenton Falls, upon West Canada Creek, are within the limits of this town.[11] **Trenton,**[12] (p. v.,) upon Cincinnati Creek, at the mouth of Steuben Creek, contains 3 churches and 50 houses. **Trenton Falls,** (p. v.,) a short distance below the Falls, contains a church, gristmill, sawmill, and 20 houses. **South Trenton,** (p. v.,) upon the old Utica turnpike, contains 2 churches and 30 houses. **Holland Patent,**[13] (p. v.,) in the w. part of the town, is a station upon the B. R. &

---

little w. of the village, in 1813, under the direction of Major James Dalliba. It is still owned by the General Government, but is not in use. In 1784, Gen. Washington came thus far on a tour of business and pleasure. He, in company with Geo. Clinton, owned a tract of land in this co. of about 2,000 acres, comprising a part of Coxborough and Carolina Townships, in the town of Westmoreland.

[1] Fort Williams, on the Mohawk, and Fort Bull, on Wood Creek, were built on the line between Albany and Oswego about 1725. Fort Bull was surprised by M. De Lery and a party of French and Indians, numbering 362 men, March 27, 1756. The English lost the fort and all the stores which it contained, and 90 men. Forts Williams and Craven, located on the Mohawk, just below Rome, were destroyed by Gen. Webb in 1756, after the reduction of Oswego by the French. Fort Stanwix was begun July 23, 1758, by Brigadier Gen. John Stanwix, of the royal army. It was a square work, with bastions at the corners, and stood a few rods s. of the present park in the village. It was of earth and timber, surrounded by a ditch and mounted with heavy cannon. In June, 1776, Col. Dayton took possession of it and named it Fort Schuyler. It was besieged in 1777 by St. Leger. Within the last few years the ground upon which the fort stood has been leveled; and not a vestige of it now remains. Fort Newport was a small square fort on Wood Creek, built in the French War. An octagonal blockhouse was built about 1795, during the alarm from Western Indian wars.

[2] The census reports 17 churches; 5 Calv. Meth., 2 Bap., 2 M. E., 2 Presb., 2 R. C., Ev. Luth., Germ. Meth., Prot. E., and Univ.

[3] Named from Jedediah Sanger the pioneer of New Hartford, who gave 50 acres of land to the first church. This town is No. 20 of the Chenango 20 Townships, and, together with No. 18 and part of 19, was purchased in 1790–91 by Michael Myers, J. Sanger, and John J. Morgan, for 3 shillings and 3 shillings 3 pence per acre. Much of it was settled under perpetual leases.

[4] Called by the Indians Ska-na-wis, "Large Swamp."

[5] —— Hale and wife, and Nathan Gurney, came in 1792; and Benj. White, Phineas Owen, Sylvanus Dyer, Asahel Bellows, Nathaniel Ford, Henry Knowlton, Jonathan Stratton, ——Clark, Col. David Norton, and about 30 others, in 1794. The first birth was that of a daughter of Z. Phelps, in 1792; the first marriage, that of Sylvanus Dyer and Hannah Norton; and the first death, that of Sybil Knowlton. Polly Dyer taught the first school; and Justus and Ebenezer Hale kept the first inn and store. The first store in Waterville was kept by Sylvanus Dyer, in 1799.

[6] 2 Cong., M. E., Prot. E., Presb., Bap., and R. C.

[7] Named from Baron Steuben. In May, 1786, the Legislature granted him 16,000 acres in this town. He settled soon after, built a log house, and collected a colony of tenants, but did not live to see his contemplated improvements carried out. He was struck by paralysis Nov. 25, 1799, and died 3 days after. He was wrapped in his cloak and laid in the earth with his star of knighthood upon his breast. Shortly before La Fayette's visit in 1826, his remains were taken up and re-interred under a tablet upon raised masonry. His property was mostly bequeathed to Wm. North and Benj. Walker, his aids. His library was given to a young man named Mulligan. Col. Walker gave a Welsh Bap. Society a lease of 50 acres of land, 5 of which was woodland, around the grave, with no other rent than the obligation to keep this woodland fenced and the range of animals prevented therein. This condition is carefully observed.

[8] Starrs Hill is the highest point in the co. On a clear day, Lake Ontario, parts of 7 counties, and the buildings of Hamilton College can be seen from its summit.

[9] Samuel Sizer, Capt. Simeon Fuller, and David Starr were early settlers. The first birth was that of Stephen Brooks, jr.; and the first marriage, that of William Case and —— Platt. The town was extensively settled by Welsh immigrants. A religious magazine, (Welsh,) "Y Cenhadwr Americanidd," is published in town.

[10] 2 M. E., 2 Cong., 2 Bap., and Calv. Meth.

[11] This favorite place of resort was first brought to public notice by John Sherman, proprietor of the first public hotel for visitors, erected in 1822. The falls are less interesting from the volume of water and height of fall than for the peculiar wildness of the surrounding scenery. The ravine through which the stream flows is worn through the Trenton limestone to the depth of 70 to 200 ft. The sides are nearly perpendicular; and the water descends by 5 distinct cascades a total depth of 200 ft. in the space of half a mile. The Indian names Ka-na-ta, "dark brown water," and Kuy-a-ho-ra, "slanting water," have been applied to this place. Trenton Village was called One-ti-a-dah-que, "in the bone."

[12] Incorp. April 19, 1819, as "Oldenbarnevelt," and changed April 26, 1833, to its present name. Its first name was given by Boon, in memory of a Dutch patriot and statesman who perished on the scaffold in 1619, aged 82.—Jones's Oneida, p. 449.

[13] Named from Henry, Lord Holland, patentee of 20,000 acres, principally in this town. He sold to Seth and Horace Johnson and Andrew Cragie.

U. R. R. It contains 6 churches, the Holland Patent Academy, and 353 inhabitants. **Prospect**, (p. v.,) on West Canada Creek, above the Falls, contains 2 churches, Prospect Academy, an extensive sawmill, a tannery, and 60 houses. **Stittsville**, (p. v.,) on the line of Marcy, in the s. w. corner of the town, contains a church, cotton factory, sawmill, tannery, and about 40 houses. It is a station upon the B. R. & U. R. R. Settlement was commenced in 1793, by Gerrit Boon, from Holland.[1] The first church (Presb.) was formed soon after; Rev. —— Fish was the first pastor.[2]

UTICA[3]—was incorp. as a village April 3, 1798. It was formed as a town, from Whitestown, April 7, 1817, and was incorp. as a city Feb. 13, 1832. It lies upon the s. bank of the Mohawk, on the e. border of the co. A wide intervale extends along the river; and from it the surface rises in gradual slopes toward the s. w. It lies upon the Erie Canal, and is the n. terminus of the Chenango Canal. It is an important station upon the N. Y. C. R. R., and the s. terminus of the B. R. & U. R. R. It is the center of one of the best agricultural sections of the State; and its trade is extensive. It is largely engaged in manufactures, among which are cotton and woolen goods, millstones, screws, musical instruments, telegraphic apparatus, and a great variety of other articles.[4]

The City Hall is a fine, large, brick building on Genesee St., s. of the canal. It contains a large public hall, common council room, and rooms for the several city officers.

The Public Schools are under the charge of a Superintendent and Board of Education. They are graded, and include all departments from the primary to a thorough academic course. They employ 45 teachers,—6 males and 39 females. The whole number of children between the ages of 4 and 21 is 8,000, of which 3,226, or 40 per cent., attend school during some portion of the year. The total expenses of the schools for 1858 were $15,546.82. The number of volumes in the district libraries is 3,018.

The Utica Academy, long an independent school, now constitutes the High School of the public school system of the city.

The Utica Female Academy is a flourishing institution, situated between Washington St. and Broadway, near Genesee St. It was founded in 1837, and its property is valued at $25,000.

The Academy of the Assumption is under the care of the Brothers of the Christian Schools.

The State Lunatic Asylum is located upon a large lot on an eminence near the w. line of the city. It receives insane persons subject to co. charge, where there is a reasonable prospect of relief, and such others as its accommodations will admit. Until recently it has received insane convicts; but this class will hereafter be sent to the asylum built for that purpose at Auburn. The average number of inmates during the last 16 years has been 381 annually.[5]

---

[1] Boon was an enterprising pioneer and agent of the Holland Land Company, the same that purchased in Western New York. Alone, or with Le Roy, Bayard, McEvers, and Busti, he purchased in trust for that company 46,057 acres of Outhoudt's Patent, 6,026 of Steuben's Patent, 1,200 of Machin's Patent, and 23,609 of Servis's Patent. The last named, lying mostly in this town, was granted in 1768 to Peter Servis and 24 others for the benefit of Sir Wm. Johnson. This tract was conveyed by the trustees above named to the Holland Company in 1801. Among the other early settlers were Col. Adam G. Mappa, Dr. Fr. A. Vanderkemp, Judge John Storrs, Col. Robert Hicks, Peter Schuyler, John P. Little, Cheney and John Garrett, Wm. Rollo, Col. Thos. Hicks, Edward Hughes, and Hugh Thomas. Boon returned to Holland, where he died many years after. The first child born was Adam Parker, in 1796; the first marriage, that of Jacob Joyce and Widow Peck; and the first death, that of —— Nelson, in 1795.

[2] The census reports 15 churches; 4 M. E., 3 Bap., 2 Presb., (O. S.,) Bap., Cong., Calv. Meth., Prot. E., Union, and Unita.

[3] The Indians called the locality Ya-nun-da-da-sis, or U-nun-da-ga-ges, "around the hill." After an old stockade, built in early times, was razed, it was called Teva-dah-ah-to-da-gue, "ruin of fort."

[4] *The Eagle Mills* give employment to 120 hands, and produce 1,500,000 yards of cotton cloth annually.
The Utica Steam Cotton Mills employ 330 hands, and produce 1,100 yds. of cotton cloth daily.
The Utica Woolen Mills employ 180 hands, and use 350,000 lbs. of wool in the manufacture of cassimeres annually.
The Utica Steam Woolen Co. gives employment to 250 hands, and uses 1,800 lbs. of wool per day.
The Utica Screw Manufacturing Co. employs 50 hands, and turns out goods to the amount of $60,000 annually.

The Utica Millstone Manufactory and Plaster Mills give employment to 50 men, and turn out $60,000 worth of products annually.
The city also contains extensive manufactories of starch, flour, clothing, organs, pianos, castings, machinery, stone ware, fire brick, carpets, oilcloths, leather, lumber, beer, and cigars.

[5] An asylum of this kind was recommended by the Governor in 1830, and was annually urged by its friends, until an act was passed, March 10, 1836, appointing 3 commissioners to purchase a site not exceeding $10,000 in value, and to contract for building. N. Dayton, C. McVean, and R. Withers were appointed; and in 1837 a farm of 130 acres was bought at the joint expense of the State and the citizens of Utica, ($6,300 of $16,300,) and in that year Wm. Clarke, Francis E. Spinner, and Elam Lynds were appointed commissioners to erect buildings. The first plan (prepared by Clarke) embraced 4 buildings, each 550 feet long, facing outward, connected by open verandas, and inclosing a court of about 13 acres. The main building was erected and the foundations were laid, when the plan was reduced and attention given to finishing the main building. By act of April 7, 1842, the asylum was put in charge of 9 managers, appointed for a term of 3 years each by the Gov. and Senate, a majority of whom must reside within 5 mi. of the asylum. Dr. Amariah Brigham was chosen Superintendent, and upon his death (Sept. 8, 1849) Dr. Nathan D. Benedict succeeded. The present Superintendent is Dr. John P. Gray, who was appointed in 1853.
The building was partially destroyed by a fire set by one of the inmates July 14, 1857. The walls remained standing, and the premises have been refitted without interruption of operations, and with improvements far exceeding in safety and convenience those that were destroyed. The sum of $68,742 was granted in 1858 to rebuild the premises; and the labor is now

Besides the foregoing institutions, there are in the city 10 private schools, 5 banks, and 24 churches.[1]

The site of the city is included in the colonial grant of 1734, styled Cosby's Manor. Settlement began soon after the Revolution; and in 1787 there were 3 log huts at this place.[2] The construction of the Seneca Turnpike and of a bridge gave the first impulse to its growth; and the Erie Canal in a few years doubled its business and population. Although the city has experienced disasters, its general growth in wealth and numbers has been steadily forward, and its geographical position, lines of communication, and natural advantages are guarantees of its future increase.[3]

VERNON—was formed from Westmoreland and Augusta, Feb. 17, 1802. A part of Stockbridge (Madison co.) was taken off in 1836. It lies on the w. border of the co., s. of the center.[4] Its surface is rolling, the mean elevation being about 200 ft. above the Mohawk. The principal streams are Oneida Creek, forming the w. boundary, and Skanandoa Creek,[5] flowing through the E. part. The soil is a fine quality of gravelly and clay loam, underlaid by limestone, waterlime, and gypsum. Very few towns in the State surpass this in all the elements of fertility. A mineral spring is found a mi. N. W. of Vernon Center. **Vernon**, (p. v.,) upon Skanandoa Creek, N. of the center, was incorp. April 6, 1827. It contains 2 churches, the Vernon Academy, a private seminary, bank, newspaper office, and tannery. Pop. 330. **Vernon Center** (p. v.) contains 2 churches and 30 dwellings. **Oneida Castle**, (p. v.,) on the w. line, contains a church, academy, and 337 inhabitants, of whom 275 are in this town. **Turkey Street** is a

---

nearly completed. The buildings are well supplied with water and gas, and have ample fixtures for the extinguishment of fires in future, including steam force pumps, ample reservoirs of water, and pipes for filling the attic and upper rooms with steam. The asylum has shops and gardens for the employment of such as prefer it, and various amusements,—fairs, festivals, musical and theatrical entertainments, books, pictures, innocent games, and such other modes of occupation as are found to exert a salutary influence upon the "mind diseased." The Opal, a monthly magazine, is edited and printed at the asylum by its inmates; and the American Journal of Insanity, a quarterly journal, is conducted by its officers. The aggregate statistics of the asylum from Jan. 16, 1843, to Dec. 1, 1858, have been as follows:—

YRS.	Average Number.	Admitted.	Recovered.	Died.	Whole No. treated.	PERCENTAGE OF RECOV'S.		PERCENTAGE OF DEATHS.	
						On average Number.	On No. received.	On whole No. treated.	On average Number.
1843	109	276	53	7	267	48.62	19.20	2.53	6.44
1844	236	275	132	16	471	55.93	48.80	3.39	6.78
1845	265	293	135	21	553	50.94	46.07	3.79	7.92
1846	283	237	133	22	622	46.99	39.46	3.53	7.77
1847	415	428	187	48	802	45.06	43.69	5.98	11.56
1848	474	405	174	86	877	36.70	42.96	9.80	18.14
1849	454	362	203	69	857	44.71	56.07	8.05	15.19
1850	433	367	171	51	816	39.49	46.59	6.25	11.77
1851	440	366	112	48	795	23.45	30.60	6.03	10.91
1852	441	390	156	39	825	35.37	40.00	4.72	8.84
1853	423	424	169	39	849	39.95	39.85	4.59	9.22
1854	444	390	164	65	836	37.16	42.05	7.75	14.63
1855	467	275	128	32	725	27.40	46.54	4.41	6.85
1856	454	242	100	30	697	22.24	41.73	4.30	6.61
1857	463	235	95	32	696	20.52	40.42	4.59	6.88
1858	489	333	114	31	787	23.31	34.23	3.95	6.33

Of the 5,516 patients received up to Dec. 1, 1858, 4,896 were discharged, of whom 2,226 recovered, 801 were improved, and 1,194 were unimproved; 636 had died, and 39 were not insane. Great success attends the treatment in most cases when received at an early stage; but when the disease has continued a year or more the chances of recovery rapidly diminish, and in a few years cease altogether. The asylum is not designed as a hospital for incurables; and when the prospects of recovery or improvement cease, it is the general custom to return patients to their friends or to local institutions of support.

Of those admitted in the year ending Nov. 30, 1858, 172 were males and 161 females; 23 were between 10 and 20; 91 between 20 and 30; 108 between 30 and 40; 62 between 40 and 50; 36 between 50 and 60; and 11 between 60 and 70. 98 males and 87 females were married; 76 males and 64 females were single; 6 were widowers and 10 widows; 17 had received academic and 239 a common school education; 43 could only read and write; 12 could read but not write; and 11 were entirely without education. 296 had laborious, and 25 professional and literary, em-

ployments; 8 were in trade, and 4 had no occupation. 210 were natives of New York; 44 of Ireland; 19 of Eng.; 16 of Germany; 6 of Conn.; 4 each of Canada, Scotland, France, Penn., Vt., and Mass.; 3 each of N. H. and Wales; 2 each of Maine and Switzerland; and 1 each of R. I., Ohio, Ill., and Sweden. The principal causes were, so far as ascertained, ill health, 48; hereditary, 28; predisposed, 22; intemperance and vice, 20; religious excitement, 19; excessive labor and anxiety, 17; vicious indulgences and domestic trouble, each 15; business perplexities, 12; menstrual irregularities, 11; and puerperal fever, and excessive labor and exposure, each 10.

[1] 4 Bap., 3 M. E., 3 Prot. E., 3 R. C., 2 Presb., Evang., Ev. Luth., Jewish, Calv. Meth., Ref. Prot. D., Germ. Meth., Wes. Meth., O. S. Bap., and Univ.

[2] Fort Schuyler at this place was built in 1758, and named from Col. Peter, an uncle of Gen. Philip Schuyler. It was a stockaded work, and stood between Main and Mohawk Streets below Second Street. A blockhouse was built before the close of the Revolution on the site of the present depot. Among the early settlers were Uriah Alverson, Philip Morey, Francis Foster, Stephen Potter, Joseph Ballou, Jason Parker, John Cunningham, Jacob Chrestman, and Matthew Hubbell. The first store and inn were kept by John Post, in 1790, on the N. corner of Genesee and Whitesboro' Streets. Post had been a dealer among the Indians, and purchased large quantities of ginseng. Some years after, he ran 3 "stage boats" for passengers to Schenectady. In 1804, Parker & Stephens received a grant of the sole right of running a stage to Canandaigua twice every week between May and October. Mails were extended from Canajoharie to this place in 1793, the inhabitants along the route paying the expense. Bryan Johnson, in 1797, commenced purchasing produce for cash, and began a business that have been mostly monopolized by the Kanes of Canajoharie. The latter soon removed to Utica; and the spirited rivalry of these men, and others who soon joined in it, gave a wide reputation to the place as a market town. John C. Devereux, Watts Shearman, John Bissell, and Daniel Thomas were also early merchants. Nathan Williams, Erastus Clark, Francis A. Bloodgood, and Joseph Kirkland were early lawyers.

[3] The population of the town and city of Utica has been as follows:—

1813	1,700	1840	12,782
1820	2,972	1845	12,190
1825	5,040	1850	17,565
1830	8,323	1855	22,169
1835	10,183		

[4] The territory of this town was included in the original Oneida Reservation. Among the patents granted in town were Bleecker's South Patent, Bas Chard's Patent of 4,911 acres, Abraham Van Eps and Rev. John Sargent's Patent. The principal Oneida village was called Kan-on-wall-o-hu-le. A small remnant of this once powerful nation of Indians still live in the s. w. part of the town.

[5] Named from the celebrated Oneida chief, and signifying Hemlock, or stream of hemlocks. Alluding to this interpretation of his name, this chief once made this striking remark: —"I am an aged hemlock. An hundred winters have whistled through my branches. I am dead at the top!"

thickly populated farming neighborhood. The first settlements were made in 1794–97.[1] The first religious services were held in 1801.[2]

VERONA—was formed from Westmoreland, Feb. 17, 1802. It lies on the w. border of the co., near the center. Its surface is generally level, slightly rolling in the E., and marshy in the w. Oneida Lake and Creek form the w. boundary, and Wood Creek[3] the N. boundary. Several small streams in the town are tributaries to these. The soil is a deep, rich, alluvial loam. There is a mineral spring in the E. part of the town.[4] **Verona** (p. v.) contains 2 churches, a tannery, and 30 houses. **Durhamville,** (p. v.,) on the w. border, partly in Madison co., contains 2 churches, a glass factory, foundery, tannery, and 1,034 inhabitants. **Verona Depot,** (p. o.,) a station on the N. Y. C. R. R., contains 10 houses. **State Bridge** (p. v.) contains 20 houses; **Higginsville** (p. v.) 25 houses; **New London,** (p. v.,) in the N. part, 30 houses; **Sconon-doa,** (p. v.,) in the S. part, on the line of Vernon, 20 houses; **Verona Mills** (p. v.) 20 houses; **Dunbarton** a glass factory and 20 houses; and **Staceys Basin** 10 houses. Settlement was commenced in 1792, by Geo. A. Smith;[5] Rev. Joseph Avery preached the first sermon. There are now 10 churches in town.[6]

VIENNA[7]—was formed from Camden, April 3, 1807, as "*Orange.*" Its name was changed to "*Bengal,*" April 6, 1808, and to Vienna, April 12, 1816. A part of Annsville was taken off in 1823. It lies on the w. border of the co., N. of the center. Its surface, rising from Oneida Lake on the S. border to an elevation of about 100 ft., spreads out into a rolling plateau. The N. w. part is hilly. Wood Creek and Oneida Lake form the S. boundary. Fish Creek forms most of the E. boundary, and unites with Wood Creek before it enters Oneida Lake. The w. branch of Fish Creek forms a part of the N. boundary. The soil is a light, sandy loam, underlaid by clay; in the S. w., along Fish Creek, it is alluvium. Good building stone is quarried in the E. part, and large quantities of bog ore have been raised from the marshes near the lake. **Vienna,** (p. v.,) in the E. part, contains a church and 110 inhabitants. **North Bay,** (p. v.,) in the S. part, near the lake, contains 2 churches, 3 sawmills, a shingle mill, and 25 houses. **McConnellsville,** (p. v.,) in the N. part, on the line of Annsville, contains 20 houses; **Elpis,** a church and 8 houses. **Fish Creek Landing** contains 20 houses; **West Vienna,** (p. v.,) on the lake, 20 houses. **Pine** is a hamlet, in the E. part. The first settlement was commenced near the close of the last century.[8] There are now 6 churches in town[9].

WESTERN—was formed from Steuben, March 10, 1797. Lee was taken off in 1811. It lies in the interior, N. of the center of the co. Its surface is a hilly upland, broken by numerous gulleys worn in the slate by the streams. Mohawk River and Lansing Kill Creek meet near the center and flow S. and S. w. into Rome. The soil in the valleys is alluvium. Stone quarries are worked which have furnished large quantities of stone for the Black River Canal. **Western-ville** (p. v.) contains a church, a tannery, and 287 inhabitants. **North Western** (p. v.) con-

---

[1] The first settler was Josiah Bushnell, in 1794. Upon the relinquishment of the Indian title in 1797, a large number of families from Mass. and Conn. came in; and within 2 years every farm in town was taken up. Among the early settlers were families named Hills, Bronson, Wetmore, Holmes, Stone, Gridley, Smith, Bissell, Foot, Goodwin, Frisbie, De Votie, Austin, Stannard, Griswold, Alvord, Thrall, Wilcox, Church, Spencer, Carter, Marshall, Tuttle, Bush, McEwen, Wilcoxson, and Webber, on Bas Chard's location, around Vernon Center; Rev. John Sargent, and families named Codner, Marvin, and McEwen, on Sargent's Patent; Skinner, Lawrence, Shedd, Gratton, Deland, Spaulding, Grant, Kellogg, Tryon, Carter, Moore, Simons, Doane, May, Mahan, Page, Ingraham, Crocker, Graves, Soper, Norton, Dix, Vaughan, Wright, Cody, Kelsey, Raymond, Alling, Haseltine, Carpenter, Hungerford, Burley, and Darling, on the "Reservation;" Griffin, Webster, Stone, Hotchkiss, Warren, Youngs, Willard, Langdon, and Neller, in the S. w. part; Brockway, Upham, Cole, Davis, Blount, Brookins, Day, Frink, Neys, Campbell, Huntington, and Cook, in the N.; and Van Eps, Hubbell, Warner, Pierson, Patten, and Root on the Van Eps Patent. The first death was that of a daughter of Josiah Bushnell, in 1795. —— Sessions taught the first school, in 1798; A. Van Eps kept the first store, in 1798; and Asahel Gridley built the first gristmill.

[2] There are now 8 churches in town; 3 Presb., 2 M. E., Bap., Cong., and Unita.

[3] A royal blockhouse was built at the mouth of this creek about 1722. It was about 8 rods square, on a slight elevation, and surrounded by a ditch.

[4] A hotel and water-cure has been erected for the accommodation of visitors and patients. The water is nearly saturated

with sulphuretted hydrogen gas, and yielded to Prof. Noyes's analysis the following ingredients to the gallon:—

Muriate of soda...........................720 gr.
Lime, with a little magnesia....................68 "
Sulphate of lime..............................60 "

The water resembles in many respects that of the Harrowgate Springs in England.

[5] Smith was 8 days working his way through snow, swamps, and thickets from Westmoreland. Among the early settlers were Asahel Jackson, in 1796, near the blockhouse; La Whitten de Wardenou, at Oak Orchard, on Wood Creek, in 1796 or '97. Among the early settlers in the S. part in 1798 were Brooks, Langdon, Avery, Eames, Bosworth, Pomeroy, Day, Ellis, Fisher, Phelps, Benedict, Loomis, Warren, Tilden, Todd, Skinner, Billington, Wheelan, Robbins, Clark, Bishop, and Brown. The first birth was that of Eva Smith, in 1795; and the first death was that of a child of Wardenou, in 1797, who was buried in its cradle for want of a coffin.—*Jones's Oneida Co., p. 671.* Asahel Jackson kept the first inn, in 1796. The first saw and grist mills were built for the Indians.

[6] 3 M. E., 2 S. D. Bap., Presb., Bap., Friends, Union, and R. C.

[7] Gen. A. Hamilton, John Lawrence, and John B. Church, under proceedings in chancery, became owners of this town.

[8] Timothy Halsted, —— Fisher, —— Jarvis, Peter Gibbons, Isaac Babcock, Alex. and Jonathan Graves, Eliakim Stoddard, Allen Nichols, and David Stone were early settlers. The first birth was that of Polly Blakesley, in 1803; and the first death, that of Alex. Graves, by an accident in a sawmill, in 1801. Lyman Mathers taught the first school; Wm. Smith kept the first inn, in 1801. Ambrose Jones built the first sawmill, in 1801; and Wm. Smith the first gristmill, about 1804.

[9] 3 M. E., Cong., O. S. Bap., Bap.

tains a church and 15 houses. **Hillside** (p. o.) contains 8 houses. **Big Brook** (p. o.) is a hamlet, near the E. line. **Delta** (p. v.) is in the S. W. corner, mostly in the town of Lee. The first settlement commenced in 1789, by Asa Beckwith and his sons Asa, Reuben, Wolcott, and Lemuel, and Henry Wager.[1] The first church (Bap.) was formed in 1798; Rev. Stephen Parsons preached occasionally. There are now 6 churches in town.[2]

WESTMORELAND—was formed from Whitestown, April 10, 1792. A part of Whitestown was annexed March 15, 1798. Verona and part of Vernon were taken off in 1802. It is an interior town, lying s. of the center of the co. Its surface is a rolling upland, with a mean elevation of 150 to 250 ft. above the Mohawk. The streams are mostly small brooks. Iron ore has been obtained in large quantities for the Westmoreland, Lenox, Onondaga, and Paris furnaces. Several quarries of fine building stone have been wrought; and from some of these grindstones were formerly manufactured. The soil is principally a gravelly and clayey loam, adapted to grain raising and pasturage. **Hampton,** (Westmoreland p. o.,) in the E. part of the town, contains 3 churches, several manufactories,[3] and 400 inhabitants. **Lowell,** (p. v.,) in the N. W. part, contains a church and 25 houses. **Hecla Works,** (p. v.,) s. w. of the center, contains a large furnace[4] and 16 houses. **Lairdsville,**[5] (p. v.,) in the s. part, contains a church and 15 houses. **Spencer Settlement,** on the N. line, and **Eureka,** 2 mi. s., each contains about 15 houses. The first settlement was made by James Dean, upon a patent granted to him under an act of May 5, 1786.[6] The first church (Cong.) was formed Sept. 20, 1792.[7]

WHITESTOWN[8]—was formed March 7, 1788, and originally included an indefinite amount of territory extending westward, at the present time forming several counties. Steuben, Mexico, Paris, and Westmoreland were taken off in 1792; Augusta in 1798; Utica in 1817; and New Hartford in 1827. It lies upon the s. bank of the Mohawk, a little S. E. of the center of the co. A broad, flat intervale extends along the Mohawk; and from it the surface rises in gentle slopes about 100 ft. and from the summits spreads out into a rolling upland. Oriskany Creek[9] flows N. E. through near the center, and Sauquoit Creek through the E. part. The soil is mostly a fine quality of gravelly loam and alluvium, well adapted to grain raising. **Whitesboro',**[10] (Whitestown p. o.,) in the Mohawk Valley, in the S. E. part of the town, was incorp. March 26, 1813. It contains 4 churches, the Whitestown Seminary, a bank, and several small manufactories. It is a canal and R. R. station. Pop. 953. **Oriskany,** (p. v.,) near the mouth of Oriskany Creek, is a canal village and R. R. station. It contains 5 churches and several extensive manufactories.[11] Pop. 711. **Yorkville** and **New York Mills,** in the s. part, are manufacturing villages, upon Sauquoit Creek, the former containing about 50 houses and the latter 3 churches and 60 houses.[12] **Walesville,** (p. o.,) **Colemans Mills,** and **Pleasant Valley** are hamlets or thickly settled farming neighborhoods. The first settlement was made by Judge Hugh White and his 5 sons, Daniel C., Joseph, Hugh, jr., Ansel, and Philo, in May, 1784.[13] This was the first settlement in the co., and became the nucleus of civilization for Central N. Y. The first church (Presb.) was formed Aug. 20, 1794; the first settled pastor was Rev. Bethuel Dodd.[14]

---

[1] These settlers, with one exception, continued to reside on their first locations until their deaths. Gen. Wm. Floyd, one of the signers of the Declaration of Independence, settled here in 1803, and continued a resident until his death in 1821. The leasehold tenure long retarded settlement, and is still a source of dissatisfaction.

[2] 3 M. E., Calv. Meth., Presb., and Friends.

[3] The Malleable Iron Works of Smith, Parker, Hallack & Co., at this place, employ 40 hands, and have a capital of $20,000. Buell's Hardware Manufactory has a capital of $30,000, and gives employment to 50 hands.

[4] These works, engaged in the manufacture of shelf hardware, have a capital of $40,000, and employ 40 hands. A blast furnace established here near the commencement of the century was run 30 years.

[5] Named from Samuel Laird, an early settler.

[6] This patent names Dean's Creek as Kanaghtarageara, and a small branch of Oriskany Creek, Kan-you-stot-ta. Among the other early settlers were Jonathan Dean, Silas Phelps, Ephraim Blackmer, Nehemiah Jones, Joseph Jones, Joseph Blackmer, jr., and Samuel Laird,—all of whom located on Dean's Patent. In 1789, settlements spread rapidly, and John and Nathaniel Townsend, Benjamin Blackmer, John Vaughan, Josiah Stillman, Nathan Loomis, Joshua Green, Joseph Blackmer, sen., Amos Smith, John Morse, Daniel Seely, Elijah Smith, Samuel Starr, Alexander Parkman, and Stephen Brigham located in town. Mr. Dean was an Indian trader, acquired the language of the natives, and exercised much influence over them. He received this grant through a stipulation made by the Indians as a reward for services rendered to their nation. Although greatly attached to him, these savages upon one occasion came near

taking his life to atone for the death of one of their number who was accidentally killed by a Dutchman on the Mohawk. He died Sept. 10, 1823, aged 76 years.—*Jones's Oneida,* p. 749. A MSS. account of Indian mythology, written by him, is in the State Library.

[7] The census reports 6 churches in town; 3 M. E., Bap., O. S. Bap., and Friends.

[8] Named from Hugh White, the pioneer settler.

[9] Signifying "river of nettles."

[10] The first courthouse of Herkimer co. was erected here in 1793. A clerk's office of the Supreme Court of the State was established at this place April 4, 1807.

[11] Oriskany Manufacturing Co., incorp. Feb. 16, 1811, for the manufacture of woolen cloths, was the oldest co. of the kind in the State. It had 8 sets of machinery, and employed 130 hands. The Dexter Manufacturing Co. has 12 sets of machinery, and employed 130 hands. These factories are not now in operation.

[12] The New York Mills, an extensive manufactory of cotton, has branches at Yorkville, New York Mills, and Upper New York Mills,—the last named in New Hartford. It has a capital of $200,000.

[13] Among the other early settlers were Amos Wetmore, Jonas Platt, Geo. Doolittle, Thomas R. Gold, Reuben Wilcox, Arthur Breese, Enoch Story, Elizur Moseley, Caleb Douglass, Wm. G. Tracy, Gerret Y. Lansing, and Henry R. Storrs. The first child born was Esther White; and the first death, that of Mrs. Blacksley, soon after the first settlement. The first gristmill in the town and co. was built in 1788, by Judge White, Amos Wetmore, and John Beardsley.

[14] There are now 13 churches in town; 3 Presb., 3 M. E., 2 Bap., 2 Prot. E., Cong., Calv. Meth., and Union.

Acres of Land, Valuation, Population, Dwellings, Families, Freeholders, Schools, Live Stock, Agricultural Products, and Domestic Manufactures, of Oneida County.

Names of Towns.	Acres of Land.		Valuation of 1858.			Population.		No. of Dwellings.	No. of Families.	Freeholders.	Schools.	
	Improved.	Unimproved.	Real Estate.	Personal Property.	Total.	Males.	Females.				No. of Districts.	Children taught.
Annsville	14,188½	18,843	$256,260	$6,950	$263,210	1,380	1,335	469	521	415	17	1,172
Augusta	14,247½	3,321½	315,190	53,200	368,390	1,183	1,200	428	480	378	12	983
Ava	9,192	13,295	96,262	4,800	101,062	670	572	219	229	207	9	501
Boonville	18,290⅞	21,810⅛	412,895	12,400	425,295	2,355	2,069	748	823	560	23	1,550
Bridgewater	11,575½	3,105½	231,240	31,370	262,610	615	588	246	257	191	8	485
Camden	13,421¼	17,683	294,849	9,300	304,149	1,431	1,469	564	606	522	14	1,159
Deerfield	16,990	4,516	298,999	4,300	303,299	1,149	1,108	387	421	292	11	769
Florence	13,131	17,145	137,985	2,650	140,635	1,451	1,361	490	539	417	17	1,204
Floyd	15,715¾	5,889	253,760	22,615	276,375	725	718	273	285	195	11	519
Kirkland	15,303¼	3,706	588,750	104,700	693,450	1,865	1,944	635	728	522	17	1,258
Lee	18,059	9,957	287,430	28,550	315,980	1,533	1,487	555	595	481	17	1,190
Marcy	16,151	3,356	279,410	8,400	287,810	916	851	342	355	281	12	682
Marshall	16,374	3,621½	347,166	28,750	375,916	1,095	1,052	391	431	325	10	535
New Hartford	15,365¾	2,630½	654,030	34,900	688,930	2,132	2,385	707	827	418	18	1,536
Paris	15,769	3,609½	546,729	81,450	628,179	1,825	1,870	679	768	481	15	1,251
Remsen	14,056¼	57,687	217,085	13,400	230,485	1,423	1,261	478	505	365	14	1,028
Rome	22,942	19,326½	1,795,690	620,931	2,416,621	5,449	5,271	1,660	2,032	848	21	3,531
Sangerfield	14.810⅛	3,803	332,510	180,550	513,060	1,216	1,208	449	491	340	11	927
Steuben	17,884½	8,041½	158,103	5,180	163,283	827	765	299	307	246	13	530
Trenton	21,800¼	6,843½	348,160	56,760	404,920	2,078	1,909	626	734	527	14	1,183
Utica	2,323	292	3,126,920	1,347,511	4,474,431	10,548	11,621	3,193	4,339	2,173	19	8,000
Vernon	19,564¾	4,282½	675,410	24,170	699,580	1,524	1,481	538	619	329	12	1,090
Verona	26,325¼	15,341½	193,350	17,700	211,050	3,712	3,211	1,205	1,350	882	27	2,327
Vienna	13,595	22,139	278,900	27,952	306,852	1,685	1,563	623	662	453	19	1,363
Western	21,762⅝	9,292½	278,900	27,952	306,852	1,286	1,260	462	490	325	21	1,027
Westmoreland	22,425¾	4,242¾	422,500	33,000	455,500	1,615	1,664	389	675	503	17	1,166
Whitestown	14,536½	2,813⅞	729,650	231,218	960,868	2,289	2,549	727	1,106	340	13	1,649
Total	435,800⅜	286,594¼	13,558,133	3,020,659	16.578,792	53,977	53,772	17,782	21,175	13,016	412	38,615

Names of Towns.	Live Stock.					Agricultural Products.							Domestic Cloths, in Yards.
						Bush. of Grain.					Dairy Products.		
	Horses.	Working Oxen and Calves.	Cows.	Sheep.	Swine.	Winter.	Spring.	Tons of Hay.	Bushels of Potatoes.	Bushels of Apples.	Pounds of Butter.	Pounds of Cheese.	
Annsville	537	1,473	1,256	1,360	1,075	1,537	73,370¾	3,709½	20,004	8,341	195,966	3,585	1,995½
Augusta	628	1,050	1,061	2,178	1,857	2,337½	74,592	2,401	11,349	38,135	107,980	34,330	803
Ava	287	642	1,217	922	470	92	28,945	3,615	13.182	1,942	81,020	110,200	1,124
Boonville	607	1,064	2,612	800	1,059	323	59,051¾	6,585¼	32,052	3,775	223,525	5,300	973½
Bridgewater	459	809	1,131	2,039	853	727	58,789	3,540	15,844	22,150	66,705	146,670	249
Camden	520	1,150	1,106	1,878	881	1,470	39.484¾	3,233	15,600	23,508	108,645	15,925	1,694
Deerfield	506	866	2,378	874	1,258	606	82,205	4,199	30,211	17,330	120,170	482,900	1,319
Florence	299	749	1,006	807	810	1,919	36,940½	4,001	15.982	11,770	124,550	53,350	46
Floyd	636	872	2,062	1,641	1,086	1,508	73,807¼	4,426	19,888	18,201	120,310	186,400	1,135
Kirkland	697	1,131	1,255	2,041	985	1,754½	91,642	3,991	25,820	49.296	131,368	37,508	413
Lee	751	1,287	2,215	2,155	1,095	3,153	87,065	5,561½	21,675	22,812	205,859	112,687	2,215
Marcy	585	994	1,889	2,068	1,134	1,716	70,814	4.282½	38,846	19,355	160,319	24,907	742
Marshall	635	1,652	1,280	1,903	768	3,455½	98.374	3,869¾	20,380	37,309	103,260	31,372	657
New Hartford	746	935	1,471	1,352	1,261	785	66,768	4,988	27,076	52,328	109,263	67,425	1,273
Paris	746	1,129	1,734	2,219	1,129	1,281¾	106,944¼	4,300	34,185	39,342	148,775	150,155	650
Remsen	464	639	1,786	852	715	986½	37,538	4,153½	22,022	1.466	184,969	116,000	1,250
Rome	1,090	1,339	2,526	2,353	2,369	9,008	133,412	5,495	43,757	22,534	174,296	127,629	1,141
Sangerfield	527	1,008	876	5,974	722	887	56,894	4,006	19,681	22,536	71,609	15,080	385
Steuben	526	1,020	2,764	1,267	981	30	38,774½	6,116½	17,739	11,057	260,800	131,473	2,427
Trenton	778	1,245	3,163	1,148	1,210	465	86,566½	7,453	28,175	28.819	157,958	539,529	859
Utica	493	106	497	84	831		10,347	1,155	5,715	1,242	7,712	400	
Vernon	835	1,218	2,051	1,910	1,164	2,634	104,170¼	4,197	17,561	28,069	136,465	357,375	536
Verona	1,051	2,482	2,663	3,094	2,091	1,509	127,368½	8,931	31,306	37,952	244,277	176,565	1,552½
Vienna	578	1,403	1,100	2,253	1,161	2,082	61,257⅝	3,229	16,876	19.440	82,715	25,210	2,065½
Western	774	1.289	2,989	2,647	1,365	3,047	85,288	6,995½	23,781	22,713	263,090	247,900	1,736½
Westmoreland	852	1,528	2,411	3,636	1,559	623	103,397¼	5,792¼	28.336	46,596	225,012	99,474	432
Whitestown	791	958	1,295	1,386	1,339	624	69,051½	4,707¼	27,605	26,244	95,558	11,765	316
Total	17,398	30,038	47,794	50,841	31,228	44,560¾	1,962,859⅛	124,933½	624,648	634,262	3,912,176	3,311,114	27,989½

ONONDAGA COUNTY.

This county was formed from Herkimer, March 5, 1794, and included the original Military Tract. Cayuga was taken off March 8, 1799; Cortland, April 8, 1808; and a part of Oswego, March 1, 1816. It was named from the Onondaga tribe of Indians, whose principal residence was within its border. It lies near the center of the State, centrally distant 127 mi. from Albany, and contains 812 sq. mi.

Its surface is naturally divided into two nearly equal parts by an E. and W. line, the N. half being nearly level, and the S. broken by ridges of hills and gradually sloping upward to a height of about 1,000 feet on the S. border. These highlands constitute a portion of the most northerly spurs of the Central Allegany Mountains, where they sink down to a level with the lowlands which surround Lake Ontario. They are divided into five distinct ridges, all having a general N. and S. direction and separated by narrow and deep valleys. The most eastern of these ridges enters the town of Manlius from the E., and extends northward to the immediate vicinity of the Erie Canal, the valley of Limestone Creek forming its w. boundary. Its highest point is 600 to 800 ft. above the valley. The second ridge lies between the valleys of Limestone and Butternut Creeks and embraces the highlands of Fabius and Pompey, the w. part of Manlius, and the E. part of La Fayette and De Witt. In Pompey this range attains an elevation of 1,743 ft. above tide. The lower or N. part of this ridge is subdivided by the deep valley of the w. branch of Limestone Creek. The third range, between the valleys of Butternut and Onondaga Creeks, comprises the highlands of the central part of La Fayette, the w. part of De Witt, and the E. portions of Tully, Onondaga, and Syracuse. Its highest point, in La Fayette, is several hundred ft. lower than the hills of Pompey. The fourth range, between Onondaga and Nine Mile Creeks, comprises the highlands of Otisco, the w. portions of Tully, La Fayette, Onondaga, and Geddes, and the E. portions of Marcellus and Camillus. The highest point of this range, in Otisco, is but a few ft. lower than the highest point of Pompey. The fifth range, lying between Nine Mile Creek and Skaneateles Lake and Outlet, comprises the highlands of Spafford, the w. parts of Marcellus and Camillus, and the E. parts of Skaneateles and Elbridge. Its highest point, Ripley Hill, in Spafford, is 1,981 ft. above tide. The axis of this whole system of highlands, extending through Pompey, Fabius, and Tully, forms a part of the watershed between Susquehanna River and Lake Ontario. The declivities of these hills are generally steep; but their summits are rolling and crowned with forests or cultivated fields.

The geological formation of the co. consists of alternate strata of shale and limestone, overlying each other in nearly horizontal layers. The lowest of these, cropping out on the s. shore of Oneida Lake, is the Clinton group of shale, and successively above these, toward the s., the Niagara limestone, the red and green shales and gypsum belonging to the Onondaga salt group, the waterlime group, Oriskany sandstone, Onondaga limestone, corniferous limestone, Seneca limestone, Marcellus shales, Hamilton shales, Tully limestone, Genesee slate, and Ithaca shales. The last four mentioned are found upon the summits of the southern hills. The salt group occupies the very base of the hills; and the limestones crop out along their declivities in an E. and w. line extending through the center of the co. The celebrated Onondaga Salt Springs are in the deep valley in which Onondaga Lake is situated, and the salt water is found above or within the strata of red shale. The salt wells are 200 to 400 feet deep. The green shales, embracing the hopper-formed strata, the magnesian or vermicular lime, and large quantities of gypsum in isolated masses, lie immediately above the red shales, and form the first declivities of the ranges of hills. The gypsum is extensively quarried, and is one of the most important minerals in the State.[1] Next above these shales is the waterlime stone,—another important and valuable mineral.[2] The Onondaga limestone

---

[1] Throughout the gypsum regions are found numerous tunnel-shaped cavities at the surface of the ground, 5 to 30 ft. deep and about the same in circumference. These are supposed to be caused by the underlying rocks being slowly dissolved by the rains, and the earth above falling into the cavity so formed. From year to year new cavities are continually forming.

[2] This stone is burned and ground, and used for cement. It readily hardens under water, and may be used in all places exposed to continual dampness. It was used in constructing the locks on the Erie Canal, and is used on rail road work throughout the Western States and Canada. It forms one of the most valuable exports of the co.

furnishes a beautiful and valuable building stone; and nearly all of the limestone strata furnish quicklime of a superior quality.

In variety, strength, and fertility, and in all the elements of perpetual productiveness, the soil of this co. is not surpassed by that of any other co. in the State. It is extensively derived from the decomposition of the underlying rocks.[1] But the northern towns are nearly all covered with drift, and their soil is generally a light, sandy loam, alternating with heavy clay. The vast deposits of lime upon the hills go far toward enriching the soil of the valleys.[2] In the central and N. portions the marshes are covered many feet thick with peat and muck formation, formed by the decaying vegetation of centuries, and furnishing the elements of almost boundless future fertility.[3] More than one-half the entire tobacco crop of the State is raised in this co.

The streams of the co. nearly all flow in a northerly direction and discharge their waters through Oswego River into Lake Ontario. In their course from the highlands they often flow over perpendicular ledges and through narrow ravines, forming a great number of beautiful cascades, the principal of which will be more particularly noticed in the description of the different towns. Oswego River, which forms a part of the E. boundary of Lysander, is formed by the junction of Seneca and Oneida Rivers. Seneca River[4] enters the N. part of the co. from the w. and pursues a winding course until it unites with Oneida River. It is a broad, deep stream, and has upon it one series of rapids, which has been converted into a valuable water-power. In the lower part of its course it contains a broad sweep or bend from a s. E. to a N. w. direction; and at its extreme s. point it receives the Onondaga Outlet from the s. Oneida River, the outlet of Oneida Lake, is a deep, sluggish, crooked stream, 18 mi. in length, and forms a link in the chain of internal navigable waters of the State. Limestone and Butternut Creeks, after flowing through narrow and deep parallel valleys among the hills, unite in the N. part of the town of Manlius, and flow into Chittenango Creek a few mi. above its entrance into Oneida Lake. Onondaga and Nine Mile Creeks— the latter being the outlet of Otisco Lake—both flow into Onondaga Lake. Otisco Inlet, a small stream entering the co. from the s., may be considered the head branch of Nine Mile Creek. Skaneateles Outlet discharges its waters into Seneca River just beyond the w. border of the co. Several small streams take their rise in the s. part of the co., and, flowing s., form the head branches of Tioughnioga River. The principal lakes in the co. are Oneida, Onondaga, and Cross Lakes, upon the level land of the N., and Skaneateles and Otisco Lakes, in deep valleys among the hills of the s. Oneida Lake, extending along the N. E. border of the co., is about 30 mi. in length; and it forms a portion of the chain of the internal navigable waters of the State.[5] Onondaga Lake, celebrated for the salt springs which are found in its immediate vicinity, is about 5 mi. long.[6] Cross Lake, upon the N. w. border of the co., is a shallow body of water, about 5 mi. long, and may be considered as simply an enlargement of Seneca River. Skaneateles Lake, 16 mi. long, occupies a deep and narrow valley among the hills, and is considered one of the finest sheets of water in the State. The banks along its s. part rise precipitously to a height of several hundred ft., and the scenery is singularly wild and rugged. Toward the N. the summits decline in height, and the land gradually and smoothly slopes down to the very edge of the water, forming a rich and exceedingly beautiful landscape. Otisco Lake is about 4 mi. long, and is nearly surrounded by steep hills, 400 to 800 ft. above its surface. In the region occupied by the waterlime and Onondaga limestone formations are many deep rents and fissures, from 50 to 200 ft. below the surface, some of which contain little sheets of water. These remarkable depressions are evidently the result of

1 "These systems of rocks constitute the basis of our soils; their particles, separated by the action of the elements, have been decomposed and in process of time rendered fruitful. Besides these rocks, we have beds of gravel and rounded stones, that have been brought to us from the far North by water; and we often see large boulders of granitic rocks that were brought here on islands of ice that once drifted about in the sea that, in a period far back in the world's history, submerged all this part of the continent. The springs that flow from the lime rocks deposit tufa,—in many instances in sufficient quantities to make farm fences and to burn lime. So highly are many of these springs charged with carbonate of lime that as soon as the water meets the air it parts with a part of the lime and incrusts leaves and twigs and whatsoever may be encountered. These substances, perhaps, then decay, leaving perfect forms upon the solid rock."—Ag. Address of Hon. George Geddes.

2 "There are large deposits of marl in this co.; one just E. of Syracuse is finely shown by the rail road cutting through it. The great Cicero Swamp is rich in this valuable fertilizer. Lake Sodom, in Manlius, is constantly depositing this mineral; the trees that fall into the lake are whitened with it. Onondaga Lake is surrounded by a marl bed. The lakes of Tully are also marl lakes."—Ag. Address of Hon. Geo. Geddes.

3 "As we go south, the ragged front of the limestone gives us a

hard soil to work,—being mixed with stones,—but of a most fruitful character. On still farther s. a grazing district takes the place of a wheat growing one. This change, however, may not be due entirely to changes in the composition of the formations. The country has become decidedly hilly. We now find steep slopes, inclined surfaces, deep ravines, rounded hills,—in fine, all the characteristics of good fields and walks for sheep and cows, for sweet grass and pure streams of water."— Emmons.

4 This stream forms the drainage of nearly all of the small lakes in Central N. Y. Large sums of money have been expended in deepening its channel at Jacks Reefs, upon the w. border of the co., for the purpose of draining the extensive marshes near the outlet of Cayuga Lake. The enterprise has been partially successful, and a large amount of valuable land has been reclaimed.

5 The outlet of this lake is navigable; and a canal 7 mi. in length connects Wood Creek, one of its tributaries, with the Erie Canal at Higginsville.

6 A low, semi-marshy piece of ground, about 2 mi. in length and 1 in width, extends southward from the head of this lake, and is bordered by steep bluffs 15 to 25 ft. high,—probably the ancient border of the lake. In and around this marsh the salt springs are found.

subsidence, as the faces of the cliffs are nearly perpendicular, and the surface of the rocks above is much cracked and broken.[1]

The co. seat is located at the city of Syracuse. The courthouse, a beautiful structure, built of Onondaga limestone and elaborately finished, is situated on W. Genesee St., near the center of the city.[2] It is one of the finest buildings of the kind in the State.[3] The Onondaga Penitentiary, a city and co. prison and workhouse, is a commodious brick edifice, situated upon an eminence a mi. N. E. of the courthouse. It contains apartments for a jail, and is also used for the imprisonment of criminals sentenced for short terms. Prisoners are received from Oswego and Madison cos. The clerk's office is a fireproof brick building, situated at the corner of Church and North Salina Sts. It contains rooms for the Surrogate and Supervisors. The poorhouse is located upon a farm of 34 acres on Onondaga Hill, 4 mi. s.w. of Syracuse. The average number of inmates is 200, supported at a weekly cost of $1.26 each. The building is commodious, but poorly ventilated. Little attention is paid to the improvement of the inmates; and in accommodations, cleanliness, and attention to the sick and insane, the institution is not above the average of similar institutions in the State.

The Erie Canal extends E. and W. through near the center of the co. The Oswego Canal extends from the Erie at Syracuse, N. through Salina and Clay, to Lake Ontario at Oswego. The N. Y. Central R. R. extends through Manlius, De Witt, Syracuse, Geddes, Camillus, Van Buren, and Elbridge. From Syracuse two divisions of this R. R. extend westward to Rochester, one via Clyde and Lyons, called the New Road, and the other via Auburn and Geneva, called the Old Road. The Oswego & Syracuse R. R. extends from Syracuse N. through Geddes, Van Buren, and Lysander; and the Syracuse, Binghamton & New York R. R. extends from Syracuse s. through Onondaga, De Witt, La Fayette, Fabius, and Tully, uniting with the N. Y. & Erie R. R. at Binghamton. The Union R. R. is a short road extending from the N. terminus of the Binghamton road to the Erie Canal, in Geddes.

Fifteen newspapers are published in the co.; 3 daily, 10 weekly, 1 semi-monthly, and 1 monthly.[4]

---

[1] These lakes are sometimes called "crater lakes," from their peculiar form, and sometimes "green lakes," from the color of their waters.

[2] The first courts were held in barns and private residences at Onondaga, Levana, on the shore of Cayuga Lake, Cayuga co., and Ovid, Seneca co. The first courthouse was erected at Onondaga Hill, in 1805-06. The commissioners appointed to select the site for the courthouse were Asa Danforth, George Ballard, and Roswell Tousley. In 1829 an act was passed to remove the co. seat to the village of Syracuse, and John Smith, Oren Hutchinson, and Samuel Forman were commissioners to select the site. The courthouse was finally built on a lot about midway between the then rival villages of Syracuse and Salina. It was destroyed by fire in 1856, and the present structure was erected soon after. The first co. officers were Seth Phelps, First Judge; Benj. Ledyard, Clerk; John Harris, Sheriff; and Moses De Witt, Surrogate.

[3] The library of the Court of Appeals is kept in the courthouse.

[4] The Derne Gazette, established at Manlius in 1806 by Abraham Romeyn, was the first paper published in the co. At that time an effort was made to change the name of the village from "Manlius" to "Derne." The paper was continued about 1 year.
The Herald of the Times was started at Manlius in 1808 by Leonard Kellogg. In 1813 its name was changed to
The Manlius Times, and it was successively issued by James Beardsley, Seneca Hale, and Daniel Clark. October 28, 1818, Mr. Clark changed its name to
The Onondaga Herald; soon after it was changed to
The Times, and continued about 3 years. June 27, 1821, Thurlow Weed became editor, and the name was changed to
The Onondaga County Republican. October 27, 1824, it passed into the hands of Laurin Dewey, who changed it to
The Onondaga Republican. Soon after Luman A. Miller became proprietor, and the name was changed to
The Manlius Repository. It afterward passed into the hands of L. Stilson, and was continued about 5 years.
The Onondaga Flag was published at Manlius a short time in 1831 by —— Fonda.
The Lynx was started at Onondaga Hollow in 1811 by Thomas C. Fay, and was continued about 2 years. Thurlow Weed commenced his apprenticeship in this office.
The Onondaga Register was established at Onondaga Hollow in 1814 by Lewis H. Redfield, and was continued until 1829, when it was removed to Syracuse and united with the Gazette, under the name of
The Onondaga Register and Syracuse Gazette. In 1832 it passed into the hands of Sherman & Clark, who changed it to
The Syracuse Argus, and continued it about 2 years.
The Onondaga Gazette was established at Onondaga Hill in 1816 by Evander Morse. Wm. Ray, author of "The Horrors

of Slavery," was editor at one time. In 1821 it passed into the hands of Cephas S. McConnell, and was changed to
The Onondaga Journal. In 1827 Vivus W. Smith became proprietor, and in 1829 he removed it to Syracuse and united it with the Syracuse Advertiser,—the combined paper taking the name of
The Onondaga Standard, Sept. 10, 1829, published by Wyman & Smith. S. F., T. A., and A. L. Smith, W. L. Crandal, and Marcellus Farmer were subsequently interested in its publication at different times till 1848, when it passed into the hands of Agan & Summers. In 1856 Agan sold his interest to Wm. Summers; and the paper is now published by Summers & Brother.
The Syracuse Daily Standard was started in June, 1846, by Smith & Agan, and was continued 3 months. It was revived January 1, 1850, and is now published by Summers & Brother.
The Onondaga Gazette was established at Syracuse in April, 1823, by John Durnford, and was the first paper started at Syracuse. In about a year it was changed to
The Syracuse Gazette and General Advertiser, and continued until 1829, when it was united with the Onondaga Register.
The Syracuse Advertiser was started in 1825 by John F. Wyman & Thos. B. Barnum; Norman Rawson was afterward connected with it, but John F. Wyman soon assumed the entire control, and continued it till 1829, when it was united with the Journal and its name changed to the Standard.
The Salina Sentinel was started in October, 1826, in what is now the First Ward of Syracuse, by Reuben St. John. In 1827 it was changed to
The Salina Herald, and it was issued a short time by Josiah Bunce.
The Courier was published at Jordan a short time in 1831 by Fred. Prince. In 1832 it was removed to Salina and changed to
The Salina Courier and Enquirer, but was discontinued after a few numbers.
The Onondaga Republican was started at Syracuse in 1830 by W. S. Campbell. In 1834 it passed into the hands of J. B. Clark & Co., and its name was changed to
The Constitutionalist. In 1835 L. A. Miller became its proprietor, and changed it to
The Onondaga Chief. In 1837 it was sold to J. M. Patterson and published as
The Syracuse Whig. In 1838 J. K. Barlow became proprietor, and continued it about 1 year.
The Syracuse American was started at Syracuse in 1835 by John Adams, and was continued about 1 year.
The American Patriot was started at Franklin Village (now

This co. was the chief seat of the Onondaga Nation of Indians, the central of the Five Nations. Their name is said to signify "sons of the hills," or "men of the mountains." To this nation was intrusted the care of the sacred council fire; and upon their territory were held the great councils of the Iroquois, to decide upon peace, war, and matters of general policy. The Onondagas were regarded as particularly a sacred nation; and their chiefs were more influential than those of any other nation. The most authentic accounts of these Indians seem to indicate that they were originally a subordinate tribe, living upon the St. Lawrence near Montreal, and were held in subjection by the Adirondacks, then the most powerful nation of the North. Several hundred years before the discovery of America, they rose upon their oppressors, but were defeated. They then fled, and,

Fabius) in 1836 by J. Tenney, and was continued for 3 years.

The Western State Journal was started March 20, 1839, by V. W. & S. F. Smith. In 1844 its name was changed to

The Syracuse Weekly Journal. In 1847 it was published by Barnes, Smith & Cooper; and in 1849 it passed into the hands of V. W. Smith. In 1850 Seth Haight became proprietor, and George Terwilliger editor. In 1853 Danforth Merrick became proprietor, and in 1854 it passed into the hands of T. S. Truair, Andrew Shuman editor. In 1855 J. G. K. Truair, bought the establishment; and Sept. 1, 1856, Anson G. Chester assumed the editorial charge. It is now published by J. G. K. Truair & Co., Rodney L. Adams, editor.

The Syracuse Daily Journal was established July 4, 1844, by S. F. Smith. It is now issued by J. G. K. Truair & Co., and edited by R. L. Adams and T. S. Truair.

The Empire State Democrat and United States Review was started in 1840 by Hiram Cummings, and continued about 3 years.

The Onondaga Messenger was started in 1841 by Joseph Barber. In 1842 it was changed to

The Syracusean, and was continued about 1 year.

The Morning Sentinel (first daily paper in Syracuse) was started in Jan. 1843, by N. M. D. Lathrop, and was continued about 1 year, when it was changed to

The Onondaga Sentinel, and issued weekly, with a few intervals, until 1850.

The Democratic Freeman was started in 1844 by J. N. T. Tucker, continued a short time thereafter by James Kinney as publisher and J. N. T. Tucker as editor, when it was changed to

The Syracuse Star. In 1846 it was published by Kinney, Marsh & Barnes; in 1847–48 by Kinney & Marsh; in 1849–50–51 by Kinney & Masters. It soon after passed into the hands of Geo. F. Comstock, publisher, and Winslow M. Watson, editor. In 1852 S. Corning Judd became editor and proprietor. In October, 1853, it passed into the hands of Edward Hoogland, who changed it to

The Syracuse Republican and continued it about 1 year.

The Syracuse Daily Star was established in 1846, and issued with the *Weekly Star* until 1853, when it was changed to

The Syracuse Daily Republican, and discontinued in about 1 year.

The Bugle Blast, a campaign paper, was published 3 months in 1844 by S. F. Smith.

Young Hickory, another campaign paper, was issued about the same time by Smith & Farmer.

The Religious Recorder (Presb.) was started in May, 1844, by Terry & Platt. In 1847 it passed into the hands of Avery & Hulin, who continued it until 1853.

The Liberty Intelligencer was started in 1845 by Silas Hawley, and was continued about 1 year.

The Young Ladies' Miscellany was started Nov. 7, 1845, by a committee of young ladies belonging to the Syracuse Female Seminary, and was continued 12 weeks.

The Teachers' Advocate was commenced in 1846 by L. W. Hall, publisher, and Edward Cooper editor. In 1847 it passed into the hands of Barnes, Smith & Cooper, and was continued about 1 year, when it was sold to Joseph McKean and removed to New York.

The Onondaga Democrat was started in the spring of 1846 by Clark & West; Wm. L. Crandal, editor. In 1847 it was sold to John Abbott, who changed it to

The Syracuse Democrat. At the end of 1 year it was sold to Wm. W. Green, and in 1847 to Agan & Summers and merged in the Onondaga Standard.

The District School Journal, organ of the State School Department, was removed to Syracuse from Albany in 1847, and published 2 years by L. W. Hall, and 1 year by Barnes, Smith & Cooper, when it went back to Albany.

The Syracuse Reveille, daily, was started in 1848 by Wm. L. Palmer & W. Summers, and was continued until Jan. 1, 1850.

The Free Soil Campaigner, a campaign paper, was published 3 months in 1848 by Agan & Summers.

The Clay Banner, a campaign paper, was published about the same time from the Journal office.

The Impartial Citizen, semi-mo., was started in 1848 by Samuel R. Ward, and was continued about 1 year.

The Crystal Fountain was started in 1848 by A. B. F. Ormsby, and continued 3 months.

The Adventist was published 3 months in 1849 by L. Delos Mansfield.

The Literary Union was commenced April 7, 1849, by W. W. Newman, J. M. Winchell, and James Johonnot, and was continued about 1¼ years.

The Free School Clarion was published a few months in the fall of 1849 by Wm. L. Crandal.

The Liberty Party Paper was started July 4, 1849, by John Thomas, and was continued 2 years.

The Central City, daily, was published a short time in 1849 by Henry Barnes.

The Syracusean, mo., was established in 1850 by Wm. H. Moseley. In 1851 it was changed to

The Syracusean and United States Review, and in 1856 to

The Syracusean and Onondaga County Review. It is still issued occasionally.

The Syracuse Independent was published about 3 months in 1850.

The Evening Transcript was started in 1850 by Washington Van Zandt, and continued about 2 months.

The Archimedian was commenced in 1850; B. F. Sleeper, publisher, and John Abbott, editor. It was discontinued in 1851.

The Central New Yorker was begun in 1850 by L. P. Rising, and was continued but a short time.

The Family Companion, mo., was published a short time in 1850.

The Temperance Protector, semi-mo., was commenced in 1850 by Wm. H. Burleigh, and was continued about 2 years.

The Carson League was started in 1851; Thomas L. Carson, publisher, and John Thomas, editor. It was continued about 2 years, when it was removed to Albany.

The American Medical and Surgical Journal, mo., was started Jan. 1, 1851, by Potter & Russell, and was continued until 1856.

The Journal of Health was issued about 6 months by S. H. Potter in 1851.

The Onondaga Demokrat (German) was started in September, 1852, by George Saul. In October, 1856, it was changed to

The Syracuse Democrat, and is still continued by the original proprietor.

The Deutsche Republican (German) was issued a short time in 1852.

The Free Democrat was started in 1852 by J. E. Masters, publisher, and R. R. Raymond, editor. In February, 1853, it was changed to

The Syracuse Chronicle. The paper was owned by a joint stock company, and edited by R. R. Raymond about 1 year, when George Barnes became proprietor. In June, 1855, Samuel H. Clark bought the concern, and S. W. Arnold assumed the editorship of the paper. In February, 1856, the office was burned, and the paper was merged in the Journal.

The Evening Chronicle, daily, was issued from the Chronicle office during the continuation of the weekly paper.

The Seraph's Advocate, mo., was started in the fall of 1852 by Miss Keziah E. Prescott, and was continued 1 year.

La Ruche, a French paper, was started in 1852 by A. L. Walliot. A few numbers only were issued.

The Wesleyan was removed to Syracuse from New York, Jan. 1, 1858, by Rev. L. E. Matlack. In October, 1856, Cyrus Prindle became editor; and the paper is still issued by him.

The Juvenile Instructor, semi-mo., is issued from the Wesleyan office, and is under the same management.

The Reformer was published a short time in 1854 by A. Pryne.

The Unionist, mo., and

The Union Herald, mo., were issued from the Reformer office.

The Evangelical Pulpit was started in January, 1854, by Rev. Luther Lee, and was continued about 2 years.

The Home Circle was published by L. W. Hall about 1 year in 1855.

The American Organ, mo., was commenced in 1855 by Way & Minier. It soon passed into the hands of H. P. Winsor and continued about a year.

The Onondaga Hard Shell was started October 26, 1855, and was

embarking in canoes, went up the St. Lawrence to Lake Ontario, coasted along the lake to the mouth of Oswego River, and went up that river and settled upon the Seneca, near Three River Point. The nation finally divided into five tribes, and the central or Onondaga tribe went up the valley and settled near Onondaga Lake. Upon first entering the co. they found it inhabited by the Alleghans, or "Mound Builders," a tribe supposed to be akin to the Aztec tribes of Mexico, and one considerably acquainted with agriculture. The Iroquois gradually drove them off and took possession of their lands. The celebrated League of the Five Nations is said to have been made about 100 years before the first Dutch colony was planted at Manhattan,—though there are many reasons for believing it was of a much older date. The principal villages of the Onondagas were along the shore of Onondaga Lake and Creek. The first visit ever made by a white person to the Onondaga country of which any record has been preserved was that of Samuel Champlain in 1615.[1] In the summer of that year Champlain, with 10 Frenchmen, accompanied a party of Hurons in an attack upon the Iroquois. A battle was fought before the principal fort of the Onondagas; but the invaders were repulsed with loss and were obliged to retreat.[2] The French at an early period saw the necessity of obtaining the friendship of the Five Nations, the most powerful of all the Indian tribes. To this end, Jesuit missions were established at an early period, and one of the principal stations was at the seat of the Onondagas. The first missionary that ever visited the Onondaga country was Father Isaac Jogues, in 1642. He was afterward murdered by the Mohawks at Caughnawaga, Montgomery co. In the course of the next hundred years more than 60 missionaries were sent to this region, and at different times many of them were murdered.[3] In 1655 a colony of 50 Frenchmen under the guidance of the priests, and with the consent of the Onondagas, made a settlement on the N. shore of Onondaga Lake, near the principal Indian village. For some time the colony flourished, and large numbers of the Indians were converted and baptized; but at length the Indians became jealous of their neighbors, and in March, 1658, they determined to exterminate them. A friendly Indian having exposed the plan, the whites managed to escape.[4]

---

discontinued after the publication of the second number. Supposed to have been edited by J. J. Peck and John A. Green, jr.

The Syracuse Daily News was started in 1856 by C. B. Gould, but was discontinued in a short time.

The Syracuse Zeitung (German) was started August 15, 1855, by Otto Reventlow, and was continued a short time.

The Syracuse Weekly Courier was started October 1, 1856, by F. L. Hagadorn. In November, 1858, it passed into the hands of Halsted & Co. and was changed to **The Onondaga Courier,** under which title it is still issued.

The Syracuse Daily Courier—started at the same time as the Weekly—was changed by Halsted & Co. to **The Central City Daily Courier,** and is still published; H. S. McCollum, editor.

The Syracuse Central Democrat (German) was started July 2, 1858, by Joseph A. Hofman, and is still continued.

The State League was started in Aug. 1858 by Thomas L. Carson, and is still continued.

The Skaneateles Telegraph was started in 1829 by William H. Child, and was continued several years.

The Columbian was commenced in 1831 by John Greves. The paper afterward passed into the hands of Milton A. and George M. Kinney, and was continued until 1853.

The Friendly Visitant, a child's paper, was commenced in 1833 by Joseph Talcott, a member of the Society of Friends. In 1837 it was changed to *The Child's Companion,* and was continued several months.

The Acorn was established by Mr. Talcott in 1841, and was continued 2 or 3 years.

The Skaneateles Democrat was commenced in 1840 by William M. Beauchamp. It was subsequently issued by W. H. Jewett, Philo Rust, and Jonathan Keeney. About 1851 it passed into the hands of Harrison B. Dodge, by whom it is still issued.

The Naval Bulletin was issued from the Democrat office a short time in 1843.

The Minerva was issued a short time in 1844 by W. H. Beauchamp, and was finally merged in the Democrat.

The Juvenile Repository was published at Skaneateles in 1838 by Luther Pratt. In 1840 it was removed to New York, and soon after discontinued.

The Citizens' Press was published six months at Onondaga Hollow in 1832 by Russell Webb and James S. Castle.

The Fayetteville Times was published at Fayetteville in 1836 by Henry W. De Puy.

The Communatist was started at Mottville Nov. 27, 1844, by John A. Collins, as the organ of the Skaneateles community. It was continued about 1 year.

The Baldwinsville Republican was started in 1844 by Samuel B. West. In October, 1846, it passed into the hands of C. M. Hosmer and was changed to

The Onondaga Gazette. In 1848 it was issued by Sheppard & Hosmer, and is now published by S. Van Allen.

The Jordan Tribune was established in 1849 by P. J. Becker. In 1853 it was changed to **The Jordan Transcript,** and is now issued by Nathan Burrell, jr.

The Daily Record was established in February, 1858, under the auspices of the Franklin Institute, Syracuse. It is published daily during the session of the Mechanics' Fair of the Franklin Institute; Anson G. Chester, editor.

[1] It is possible that some of the French or Spanish adventurers who flocked to this country about the commencement of the sixteenth century may have penetrated into the wilds of Central N. Y. In 1820 a farmer in Pompey found a stone, mostly buried in the earth, upon which was drawn the rude form of a tree with a serpent twined about it, and the inscription, Leo De Lon, VI, 1520. It is supposed that it was placed to mark the grave of some early adventurer.

[2] It is supposed that Champlain and his party came in by way of Oswego, and across the country to where Brewerton now stands. At this place they captured a party of Onondagas engaged in fishing. They then proceeded to the Onondaga fort, supposed to have been situated on Green Point, about 1 mi. N. W. of the principal salt springs. The fort was assaulted; but it was so bravely defended that the Hurons despaired of taking it, and retreated. They were pursued by the Onondagas until they embarked in their canoes upon Lake Ontario.

[3] The principal of these missionaries who have left records concerning the Onondaga country are Fathers Le Mercier, Dablon, Cholonec, Le Moyne, Quien, Le Jeune, Ragueneau, and Lallemant. Father Lallemant is the first one who mentions the salt springs, in his journal bearing date of 1645–46. At times these missionaries seemed to meet with considerable success; but the intrigues of the rival French and English Governments, who were striving to secure the friendship of the Indians, continually thwarted their work, and rendered their lives at all times insecure.

[4] Through the influence of the Mohawks, the Onondagas agreed to murder the French, and the day was fixed for the perpetration of the deed. A young Frenchman, who had obtained considerable influence with the chief, persuaded him to have a general feast a few days previous to the proposed massacre, and, while the Indians were sleeping off the effects of the debauch, the French launched upon the lake several light boats, which they had secretly constructed in the granary or storeroom of the Jesuits' house, and set off as rapidly as possible. The next day the Indians were surprised that the French did not leave their houses, but waited until near night before they broke in. They were completely astonished to find that the French had disappeared, and—entirely ignorant of the construction of the boats —they ascribed the escape to supernatural means.

It is reported, upon the authority of the missionaries, that the principal chief of the Onondagas invited the French to establish another colony among them, for the purpose of instructing the Indians in the arts of civilization. Accordingly, in 1665, a number of French families, under the guidance of the missionaries, came into the country and located near the Indian fort and village which stood in the vicinity of the present village of Jamesville. After living in peace for about 3 years, they were visited by a party of Spaniards who came in from the s., and the Indians became jealous of both and murdered them all.[1] It is supposed that several other attempts were made by the French to colonize the country, as numerous remains of French works are found in several places.[2] In the wars that ensued between the English and French the Onondagas bore their part, and were generally allies of the English. In 1695, Count Frontenac, the French Governor of Canada, invaded the Onondaga country; but he retired after burning a few villages and murdering one old man. During the Revolution the Onondagas espoused the English cause, and many of their warriors, under the leadership of Brant, were engaged in the various attacks upon the frontier settlements. On the 19th of April, 1779, Col. Van Schaick, at the head of 150 men, invaded the Onondaga country by the way of Oneida Lake. A skirmish was fought near the s. w. limits of the present city of Syracuse, in which the Indians were defeated.[3] In the fall of the same year, Col. Gansevoort, at the head of 100 men, was detached from Gen. Sullivan's army, at Geneva, and sent through the country of the Cayugas and Onondagas to complete the work of destruction which had been commenced. The villages of the Onondagas were burned, their corn was destroyed, and their sacred council fire was put out. In revenge, small bands of the Indians attacked the defenseless frontier settlements upon the Mohawk and committed the most horrible atrocities.

In 1788 a treaty was made with the Onondagas, in which they ceded to the State all their lands except the Onondaga Reservation.[4] The land thus obtained, and another tract lying w. of it, were set apart for bounty lands to Revolutionary soldiers, and became known as the Military Tract.[5] It included all the lands lying within the original limits of Onondaga co., and now constituting Onondaga, Cayuga, Cortland, and Seneca, and parts of Tompkins, Oswego, and Wayne cos.

[1] It is reported that 23 Spaniards came up the Mississippi, Ohio, and Allegany Rivers to Olean, and thence across the country to Onondaga, under the guidance of an Iroquois. They had been informed by the Indians that in the N. there was a lake the banks of which were covered with something shining and white, which they understood to be silver. Their disappointment was great when they found that the Indians meant salt instead. A quarrel arose between the French and Spaniards, which resulted in the murder of both by the Indians.

[2] In many of the old fortifications have been found the remains of French arms and merchandise, and a variety of remains evidently of much older date. The French doubtless found the fortifications partly built, and took possession of them. In Pompey were found several of these, and a considerable amount of land cleared; and it is supposed that quite a flourishing French settlement was here utterly destroyed at a period not long anterior to the Revolution.

[3] The official report makes the Indian loss 12 killed and 34 prisoners.

[4] The original Onondaga Reservation was a tract of land bounded on the E. by the military townships of Manlius and Pompey, S. by the townships of Pompey and Marcellus, w. by the townships of Marcellus and Camillus, N. by the townships of Camillus and Manlius and the public Reservation bordering upon Onondaga Lake. The N. E. corner was originally at the former N. E. corner of Syracuse. The Reservation was about 11¾ mi. long N. and S. by 9₂₀⁹ mi. wide E. and w., and included parts of the present towns of La Fayette, Camillus, Geddes, De Witt, and the city of Syracuse, and all of Onondaga. In 1793 it was purchased of the Indians, reserving a tract in the S. E. corner 4½ mi. N. and S. by nearly 4 E. and w., and subdivided into 221 lots, mostly of 250 acres each, exclusive of the sq. mi. originally granted to Webster by the Indians in 1788. The Lots 8 to 19, 25 to 33, 39 to 47, and 53 to 65, inclusive, were made no account of, having been converted into a public Salt Reservation. The remainder were sold in 1796. The second purchase was that of Feb. 25, 1817, being a strip 1½ mi. wide from the E. side of the tract reserved in the first purchase, and was subdivided into 27 square lots of 160 acres each. The third purchase was that of Feb. 11, 1822, being a strip ¼ mi. wide from the s. end of that remaining after the purchase of 1817. It was subdivided into 7 lots. The present reservation is 4 mi. N. and S. by a little less than 2½ E. and w., containing—exclusive of 300 acres in the N.W. portion, granted by the Indians to Ephraim Webster in 1823—about 6,100 acres. It is situated one-half in Onondaga and one-half in La Fayette. The number of Indians remaining of the once powerful Onondaga Nation, as reported by the last census, is 349. An Indian school is taught; but it has had little success. The condition of the tribe has visibly improved within the last few years, and they appear to be slowly learning the arts of civilization. The Onondaga Salt

Springs Reservation was subdivided in 1821-24, by John Randall, jr.

[5] The Military Tract was laid out into 25 townships, each intended to contain, as nearly as possible, 60,000 acres; and each township was subdivided into 100 lots. Three more townships were afterward added, making 28 in all. The following is a complete list of them:—

T'p No.	Township.	Present Towns.	County.
1	Lysander.....	Lysander .... and s. part of Granby ...	Onondaga. Oswego.
2	Hannibal.....	Town and w. part of city of Oswego, Hannibal, and N. part of Granby	Oswego.
3	Cato...........	Victory and Ira, and N. parts of Conquest & Cato.	Cayuga.
4	Brutus	Mentz and Brutus, and parts of Conquest, Cato, Montezuma, Throop, and Sennet	Cayuga.
5	Camillus.....	Van Buren and Elbridge, and part of Camillus.....	Onondaga.
6	Cicero.........	Clay and Cicero...............	Onondaga.
7	Manlius	Dewitt and Manlius, and part of Salina...............	Onondaga.
8	Aurelius	Fleming, Auburn City, and Owasco, most of Throop and Sennett, part of Aurelius, and 1 lot in Montezuma...................	Cayuga.
9	Marcellus...	Skaneateles and Marcellus, parts of Spafford and Otisco	Onondaga.
10	Pompey	Pompey, most of La Fayette, 3 lots in Otisco....	Onondaga.
11	Romulus	Romulus, w. parts of Fayette and Varick, 4 lots in Seneca Falls..............	Seneca.
12	Scipio	Scipio and Venice, s. part of Ledyard, 5 lots in Niles, and small point (N. W. cor.) of Moravia...	Cayuga.
13	Sempronius	Moravia, Sempronius, and most of Niles............... and part of Spafford......	Cayuga. Onondaga.
14	Tully..........	Tully, s. part Spafford, and Otisco........................... Scott and Preble..............	Onondaga. Cortland.

The first white person that took up his residence within the limits of the co. after the Revolution was Ephraim Webster, an Indian trader, who located his trading house on the banks of Onondaga Creek, near its mouth, in 1786. The next year he was accompanied by another trader named Neukerck, who died in the spring of 1787 and was buried near the trading house. In 1788, Asa Danforth and his son Asa, and Comfort Tyler, from Mass., came in, and located on the present site of Onondaga Valley. The salt springs soon became generally known and attracted many immigrants to this region. The State reserved for salt purposes the territory surrounding the lake and known as the Onondaga Salt Springs Reservation, embracing the greater part of the old town of Salina, now the towns of Salina and Geddes, and the city of Syracuse, all of which, except the land needed for the manufacturing establishments alone, has since been sold. In the treaty with the Indians, the salt springs were to be jointly used by the whites and Indians forever. The salt business immediately became important, and has since kept pace with the growth of the country. It is now one of the most important branches of business carried on in the State, and is constantly increasing.[1]

Townships of the Military Tract, continued.

Tp No.	Township.	Present Town.	County.
15	Fabius	Fabius .... and N. parts of Truxton and Cuyler	Onondaga. Cortland.
16	Ovid............	Ovid, Lodi, and Covert	Seneca.
17	Milton..........	Genoa........................... and Lansing..................	Cayuga. Tompkins.
18	Locke	Locke and Summer Hill ... and Groton..................	Cayuga. Tompkins.
19	Homer........	Homer and most of Cortlandville..................	Cortland.
20	Solon	Solon, Taylor, and S. part Truxton and Cuyler......	Cortland.
21	Hector.........	Hector	Schuyler.
22	Ulysses	Ulysses, Enfield, & Ithaca,	Tompkins.
23	Dryden	nearly the whole of Dryden.............................	Tompkins.
24	Virgil	Virgil, most of Harford and Lapeer, and 2¼ lots in Cortlandville, and 1 lot (20) in Freetown......	Cortland.
25	Cincinnatus.	Freetown, Cincinnatus, & most of Marathon.........	Seneca.
26	Junius........	Junius, Tyre, Waterloo, N. part of Seneca Falls......	Wayne.
27	Galen	Galen and Savannah........	Wayne.
28	Sterling.......	E. part Wolcott and Butler, and Sterling..................	Cayuga.

Junius was added to compensate those who drew lots afterward found to belong to the "Boston Ten Towns;" Galen, to supply those who belonged to the Hospital Department, and who at first were not provided for; and Sterling, to satisfy all the remaining claims. The U. S. granted 100 acres to each of the soldiers in Ohio; and it was left optional with them to surrender this claim and receive the whole 600 acres in this State, or to retain the claim and secure but 500 acres. The 100 acres reserved was taken from the S. E. corner of each lot, and became known as the *State's Hundred.* A charge of 48 shillings was made upon each for the survey; and in default of payment a reserve of 50 acres, known as the *Survey Fifty,* was made.

[1] The first mention in history of the Salt Springs of Onondaga is found in the journal of Father Lallemant, who visited this region in 1645–46. He speaks of a salt spring, and of a fine spring of fresh water, coming out of the same bank, within 80 or 100 paces of each other, on the margin of the lake. Father Le Moyne, who visited the country in 1654, speaks of a spring which the Indians told him was fouled by an evil spirit. He made a personal examination of it, and made some salt from the water, which he carried to Quebec. Other missionaries of an early period make frequent mention of the salt springs; and before the English occupied the country the Indians had learned how to manufacture salt.

At the time of the first settlement the salt spring was located upon the marsh, immediately in the rear of the site of the present Salina pumphouse, and the salt water came up from the bottom. The Indians had excavated a hole, which was constantly filled with water to the surface of the ground. In 1789, Asa Danforth and Comfort Tyler came down from Onondaga, and brought with them a kettle, which they suspended from a pole supported by 2 crotched sticks; and in this they made the first salt ever manufactured by the present race of settlers. In about 12 hours they made 13 bushels of salt; and, secreting their kettle in the bushes, they went home with the product of their day's labor,—feeling richer than they would had they discovered a mine of gold. For several years it was customary for the settlers from all the surrounding region to bring kettles with

them and manufacture sufficient salt for their own use. The first settlers of Salina came in 1790, and principally located upon the summit of the bluff above the salt springs. Most of them came with the intention of entering into the manufacture of salt. At first kettles suspended from poles were used exclusively; but in a short time it was found more convenient to rest the kettles upon a pile of stones. The "works" were afterward covered to protect the manufacturer from the weather. The first caldron kettle, set in an arch, was used by James Van Vleck, in 1793; and in a short time caldrons were exclusively used. Two kettles were afterward used, and additions have been made from time to time, until 20 to 104 kettles are now put in a single block. The first salt made under a permanent building was manufactured by Elisha Alvord, as agent of the Federal Company, organized in 1798, and consisting of Asa Danforth, Jedediah Sanger, Daniel Keeler, Thomas Hart, Ebenezer Butler, and Hezekiah Alcott. A new well, about 30 feet deep, was dug a little N. w. of the original one; and a building was erected large enough to contain 32 kettles, set in 8 arches of 4 kettles each. From this time the works increased rapidly in size and number. The manufacture of salt was commenced at Geddes, in 1793, by James Geddes, and in Liverpool about the same time, by John Danforth. The first wells at the old village of Syracuse were opened in 1830. By continuous pumping, the water in the wells becomes less and less salt,—the shallow wells failing first. This renders the constant opening of new wells a matter of necessity. The first solar works were constructed in 1821, by a company formed for that purpose. The introduction of the solar vats produced so much opposition that the Legislature was obliged to pass special laws for their protection.

The salt water was at first dipped up by pails and carried to the places for boiling. In 1790 this method was superseded by a pump placed upon a platform above the spring, with open troughs leading to each block. At first each manufacturer pumped water enough for his own use; but in a few years thereafter men were employed to pump for all. As the works increased and were located at a distance from the springs, lines of pump logs were laid from the springs to the various works, and a pump was used for each block, or group of blocks. A horse-power for elevating salt water was used by Asa Danforth, jr., in 1805; and a water-power was obtained from several springs in the vicinity by him soon after. In 1807 or '08, a water-power—obtained by conducting Yellow Brook from the vicinity of the present county clerk's office, in a race, to Salina—was used by John Richardson. All the works in which machinery was used elevated the water by means of a wheel, to which buckets were attached. An experiment was made at an early period to raise salt water by means of steam. An immense tub, placed over the spring and connected with it by tubes, was filled with steam, which was suddenly condensed by the admission of cold water, a vacuum was produced, and the water would rush up with great violence and fill the tub. This experiment was found too costly for general application. In 1821–22 the Coarse Salt Company erected a large pump, worked by machinery driven by the waste water from the canal, for the purpose of supplying themselves with salt water. They also made arrangements to supply others, at certain prices. Up to this time, the greater part of the water had continued to be raised by handpumps. In 1826 the State bought out the pump works of the Coarse Salt Company and enlarged them sufficiently to supply all the manufacturers with brine.

The Salina pumphouse is a fine stone building, completed in 1841, at a cost of about $30,000. The Syracuse pumphouse, also of stone, was erected in 1858, at a cost of $30,000. A large ground reservoir has lately been constructed near the Syracuse pumphouse, of sufficient capacity to contain water enough to manufacture 600,000 bushels of salt. The State designs to double its capacity immediately.

The first great improvement made in the manufacture of salt was the introduction of bittern pans, which took place within a few years after the commencement of the business. A great number of experiments have since been made; but the

CAMILLUS—was formed from Marcellus, March 8, 1799. A part of Onondaga was annexed in 1834. It is an interior town, lying a little N. W. of the center of the co. The surface is generally rolling, the ridges extending in a N. and S. direction. Nine Mile Creek flows N. E. through near the center, and along the S. line it is bordered by steep banks 100 to 200 feet high. In the N. W. corner is a swamp covering an area of several hundred acres. The soil is a rich, clayey and

process of manufacture remains essentially the same as at first. Many experiments have been made to completely separate the impurities from the water before boiling,—but so far without complete success. The addition of alum to the water is found to harden the salt and to render the process of crystallization more perfect. The immense consumption of fuel at the boiling works has almost stripped the surrounding country of wood, rendering that article scarce and high. Late experiments in the use of coal have been completely successful; and by the construction of the Binghamton R. R. an avenue is opened directly to the Pennsylvania coal mines.

In 1797 the Surveyor-General laid out a tract of 15,000 acres, surrounding the lake, known as the Onondaga Salt Springs Reservation, which was set apart for the location of salt works. It was supposed that this tract was more extensive than would ever be needed; and, pursuant to acts of the Legislature, all, except about 550 acres, was sold in 1822 and 1827. Since that time, however, the State has re-purchased several tracts, and large numbers of solar works have been erected upon private property. The amount of land at present owned by the State is about 700 acres.

The salt wells are all located in the low lands that surround the lake. Their existence is doubtless owing to the nature and position of the rocks forming the basin of the lake. The Niagara limestone—a solid and almost seamless rock, about 100 ft. thick—crops out 8 miles N. of the springs. In common with all the rocks in the vicinity, it has a dip to the S. of about 26 ft. to the mile. This would make it extend under the lake, forming a floor to the whole valley completely impervious to water. Above this formation are the red shales of the Onondaga salt group, nearly 500 feet in thickness. Observation and experiment have shown that these shales have been removed, by some great force of nature, from the whole valley which extends from the N. extremity of the lake several miles up the valley of Onondaga Creek; and the excavation has been filled with drift deposits, consisting chiefly of alternate strata of sand, clay, and gravel. The salt water is found permeated through this drift in all parts of the valley, the strongest being found where the old valley is the deepest. The salt water is probably derived from the dissolving of particles of salt distributed through the whole mass of the green shales and plaster beds, which lie next above the red shales and which extend perhaps many miles

under the hills. In evidence of the truth of this theory, it is shown that the green shales which have been exposed are full of small hopper-shaped cavities,—the precise shape assumed by crystals of salt when left to form by themselves, and one which no other crystal ever assumes. The water collects in this great basin, and is prevented from overflowing by the impervious floor of Niagara limestone. The waters of the lake are probably prevented from mingling with the salt water by strata of impervious clay and marl. About 50 different wells have been sunk for obtaining salt water, and a great number of experiments have been tried. The depth of the borings has been from 50 to 600 ft.; and in every case where the tubing has been sunk into the strata below the drift no brine has been obtained. Up to 1825 the water was obtained from square holes sunk in the marsh to the depth of about 30 ft. The first wells that were bored were 50 to 80 ft. deep. Subsequent experiment showed that by boring farther out on the marsh the wells could be deeper and a better quality of water could be obtained. A tube sunk to the depth of 414 ft. penetrated a clay bed or the Niagara limestone, and destroyed the well, although at a depth of 392 to 397 ft. a bountiful supply of excellent water was obtained. A boring undertaken through the limestone and entered the Clinton group below. This last boring was made with the hope of finding rock salt; but not a single salt crystal has ever yet been found here in a natural state.

Wells have been sunk at 4 points, giving to the salt manufacture 4 distinct centers. These are situated respectively at Salina, (now First Ward of Syracuse,) Syracuse, Liverpool, and Geddes. The number of wells now in use upon the Salt Springs Reservation is 15, of which 6—from 150 to 310 ft. deep—are at Salina, 6—from 255 to 340 ft. deep—are at Syracuse, and 3—from 80 to 100 ft. deep—are at Liverpool. The Geddes wells have been abandoned, as the water was not sufficiently strong to make the manufacture profitable. The Geddes works are now supplied from the wells at Syracuse.

The strength of the water is tested by an instrument called a salometer, graduated so as to mark pure water 0° and water saturated with salt 100°. The water from the wells as now drawn ranges from 60° to 76°, averaging about 70°. An analysis of the various springs was made in 1837, by Dr. Beck, with the following result:—

LOCALITIES.	Total amount of solid matter in 1,000 grains of brine.	Carbonic Acid.	Oxid of Iron and Silica.	Carbonate of Lime.	Sulphate of Lime.	Chloride of Magnesium.	Chloride of Calcium.	Chloride of Sodium, or Pure Common Salt.	Water with a trace of Organic Matter.	Total.
Geddes	138.55	0.06	0.10	0.04	4.93	0.79	2.03	130.66	861.39	
Syracuse	139.53	0.07	0.14	0.02	5.69	0.46	0.83	132.39	860.40	1,000
Salina	146.50	0.09	0.17	0.04	4.72	0.51	1.04	140.02	853.41	
Liverpool	149.54	0.07	0.13	0.03	4.04	0.77	1.72	142.85	850.39	

An analysis from a well yielding stronger water was afterward made, with the following result:—

Common salt	173.50
Sulphate of lime, &c.	8.50
Water	818.00
Total	1,000.00

The water at the present time does not essentially differ from that last given, a hundred pounds of brine yielding about 17¼ lbs. of pure salt. A bushel of salt, weighing 56 lbs., is made from 35 gallons of water. The temperature of the water as it rises from the ground ranges from 50° to 52° Fahrenheit. An analysis of the manufactured salt shows that 96 to 99 per cent. is pure salt, and the remainder is principally sulphate of lime and water. About four-fifths of the salt is made by boiling, and the remainder by solar evaporation. The water in the wells rises to the surface of the ground; thence it is raised by combined suction and force pumps into high reservoirs, from which it is distributed by pump logs to the various works. The machinery for pumping is propelled by water from the canals. The boiling works consist of two parallel arches, generally set with 25 to 30 kettles each. They are covered with a roof, partially open, to allow the egress of steam; and under the same covers are accommodations for storing and packing the salt. Each of these works is technically called a "block." A "cistern" is connected with each block, and from it a line of logs conducts the water along the top of the arch, between the rows of kettles, with a spout to each kettle. The greater part of the impurities are precipitated and fall to the bottom of the kettle before the water begins to boil. A shallow pan, called a

bittern pan, is placed in each kettle when first filled, to receive these bitterns as they settle. The pan is removed before the water boils, and the salt is left nearly pure. The kettles usually have a capacity of about 100 gallons, and average in weight about 900 lbs. each. The fuel is applied at one end of the arch, the chimney being situated at the other. Within the past few years several chimneys, ranging from 75 to 150 ft. in height, have been erected, for the purpose of using coal. The blocks are all situated along the canals, or side cuts from them, for convenience in obtaining fuel and in shipping the salt. The number of blocks upon the Reservation reported in 1859 was 312, distributed as follows:—

	No. of Blocks.	No. of Kettles.
Syracuse	52	2,998
Salina	152	8,042
Liverpool	62	3,304
Geddes	46	2,586
Total	312	16,930

The solar works consist of shallow vats, constructed of wood, and placed upon posts 2 to 3½ ft. above the ground. Each vat is 16 ft. square, or 16 by 18, and 9 inches deep. Movable roofs are so constructed that the vats can easily be covered in wet weather and exposed in dry. An acre of ground contains about 60 vats and covers, and an evaporating surface of more

SALT MANUFACTURE AT SYRACUSE

1. Solar Evaporation or Salt Fields.   3. Interior of Salt Blocks or Boiling Works.

2. Exterior of Salt Blocks.   4. State Pump House and Reservior.

gravelly loam. Limestone and gypsum are both found in abundance.[1] A large sulphur spring is found in the N. w. corner. **Camillus,** (p. v.,) on Nine Mile Creek, near the center of the town, was incorp. in 1852; it contains 3 churches, 2 flouring mills, and 552 inhabitants. **Amboy,** in the N. E. part, contains a church and 170 inhabitants. **Belle Isle,** (p. v.,) on the canal, 1 mi. E. of Amboy, contains 1 church and 140 inhabitants. **Fairmount** is a p. o. near the E. border. The first settler was Capt. Isaac Lindsay, who located upon Lot 80 in 1790.[2] The first church (Presb.) was formed in 1817. There are 6 churches in town.[3]

CICERO—was formed from Lysander, Feb. 20, 1807. Clay was taken off in 1827. It lies upon Oneida Lake, in the N. E. corner of the co. Its surface is level or very slightly undulating. An extensive swamp in the S. E part occupies one-third of the entire surface,[4] and another considerable swamp extends along the lake shore w. of South Bay. The soil is a clayey and sandy loam. **Cicero Corners,** (Cicero p. o.,) near the center of the w. line, contains 2 churches and 242 inhabitants. **Brewerton,** (p. v.,) on the outlet of Oneida Lake, contains 2 churches and 621 inhabitants, of whom 421 are in this town. South Bay and Frenchmans Island are places of resort for pleasure seekers.[5] Fort Brewerton,[6] one of the line of English fortifications between Oswego and the Mohawk Valley, was situated in Oswego co., on the shore of Oneida Outlet, opposite the present village of Brewerton. The first settlement was made by —— Dexter, a blacksmith, who located on the river, opposite the fort, in 1790.[7] The first church (Presb.) was formed at Cicero Corners, in 1819; Rev. James Shepard was the first preacher. The census reports 6 churches in town.[8]

CLAY—was formed from Cicero, April 16, 1827. It is the central town upon the N. border of the co. Its surface is very flat, and but little elevated above the level of Oneida Lake. Seneca River forms the w. and Oneida River the N. boundary. These streams are sluggish; and along the latter is an extensive swampy region. The soil is in part clayey, and in part a light sandy loam. Fruit and onions are largely produced. **Belgium,** (Clay p. o.,) upon Seneca River, contains a church and 190 inhabitants; **Euclid** (p. v.) 2 churches and 140 inhabitants; **Centerville,**[9] (Plank Road p. o.,) on the line of Cicero, 2 churches and 111 inhabitants. **Three River Point** (p. v.) lies at the junction of Oneida and Seneca Rivers, in the N. w. corner.[10] Pop. 90. The first settler was Patrick McGee, who located at Three River Point, in 1793.[11] The first church (Evang. Luth.) was located in the N. E. part of the town. The census reports 4 churches.[12]

DEWITT[13]—was formed from Manlius, April 12, 1835. A portion of Syracuse was annexed in 1858. It is an interior town, lying N. E. of the center of the co. The N. half is level, and the s. broken and hilly. The declivities of the hills are usually steep, and their summits are 500 to 700 ft. above the valleys. Butternut Creek, flowing N., divides the highlands into two nearly equal ridges. Upon this stream are several fine mill sites. In the s. w. corner, about 1 mi. N. w. of

---

than 15,000 sq. ft. The vats are usually arranged in three different grades, the water being drawn down at different times, and the salt being allowed to crystallize only in the lowest one. In this process the impurities nearly all crystallize before the brine is drawn into the last series of vats, leaving pure salt. It is found that, on an average, the covers can be taken off only 70 days in a season. More than 500 acres are now covered by solar works; and the aggregate number of covers is 30,786, and the amount of evaporating surface 8,403,840 sq. ft. The solar salt is much coarser than that produced by boiling. Large quantities of both kinds are ground for dairy and table purposes. The aggregate amount of bushels of salt manufactured in 1858 was as follows:—

	Solar.	Boiled.	Total.
Syracuse	573.236	943,037	1,516,273
Salina	469,483	2,764.383	3,233,866
Liverpool	35,128	956,807	991,935
Geddes	436,707	854,438	1,291,145
Total	1,514,554	5,518,665	7,033,219

The State levies a duty of one cent per bushel on all salt manufactured; and from the revenue so derived the State works are kept up. The salt is usually packed in bbls., each containing 280 lbs., or 5 bushels. The ground salt, for table and dairy use, is packed in sacks, containing 14, 20, or 28 lbs., and is small boxes. The barrels are principally manufactured in the towns lying N. of the city.

[1] It is said that the first gypsum in the U. S. was found in this town in 1792, by Wm. Lindsay. De Witt Clinton, Samuel Young, and other distinguished individuals visited the locality

in 1809; and about the same time quarrying was commenced by a joint stock company, and a successful business was carried on for many years.
[2] James, Wm., and Elijah Lindsay, brothers of the first settler, came soon after. Among the other early settlers were Nicholas Lamberson, Moses Carpenter, Judge Wm. Stevens, Dr. J. H. Frisbie, Wm. Reed, Selden Leonard, and David Hinsdale. Daniel Veal taught the first school, in 1808; Isaac Lindsay kept the first inn, in 1793; John Tomlinson the first store, in 1808; David Munro, Wm. Wheeler, and Samuel Powers built the first saw and grist mills, in 1806.
[3] 2 M. E., 2 Presb., 1 Bap., and R. C.
[4] The Indian name of this swamp is Ka-nugh-wa-ka, "where the rabbits run."
[5] See p. 521.
[6] The Indian name of this locality is Oh-saha-u-ny-tah-se-ugh-kah, "where the water runs out of Oneida Lake."
[7] Among the other early settlers were Oliver Stevens, Ryal Bingham, Elnathan Botchford, John Leach, and Patrick McGee. The first child born was John L. Stevens, in 1802. Geo. Ramsay taught the first school, in 1792; Patrick McGee kept the first inn, in 1791; Isaac Cody the first store, in 1818; and Moses and Freeman Hotchkiss built the first sawmill, in 1823.
[8] 2 M. E., 2 Disciples, Presb., and Union.
[9] Locally known as "Podunk."
[10] The junction of these two rivers forms the Oswego River, and from this is derived the name of the village.
[11] Among the other early settlers were Adam Coon, in 1798; Simeon Baker, in 1799; John Lynn, in 1800; and Joshua Kinne and Elijah Patchney, in 1807. —— Hall taught the first school, in 1808; A. L. Soule kept the first store; and Abraham Young built the first sawmill.
[12] 2 M. E., Bap., and Evang. Luth.
[13] Named from Moses De Witt, an early settler and prominent citizen.

31

Jamesville, is a small lake, occupying a deep chasm in the rocks. It is nearly circular in form, about 80 rods in diameter, and is almost surrounded by perpendicular banks 150 to 200 ft. high.[1] Another lake, of a similar character, lies 2 mi. N. E. of Jamesville.[2] Messina Spring, a strong sulphur spring, N. W. of the center of the town, has considerable local notoriety for medicinal qualities. Gypsum and waterlime are both extensively quarried along the banks of Butternut Creek. The soil is a sand and clay loam in the N., and a sandy and gravelly loam in the s. **Jamesville,**[3] in the s. part of the town, contains 3 churches and several manufactories.[4] Pop. 270. **Orville** (De Witt p. o.) contains 2 churches and 158 inhabitants. **Collamer,**[5] (p. o.,) in the N. part, is a hamlet. **Messina Springs** is near the w. line. The first settler was Benj. Morehouse, from Dutchess co., who came in April 26, 1789.[6] The census reports 7 churches in town.[7]

ELBRIDGE[8]—was formed from Camillus, March 26, 1829. It is the central town upon the w. border of the co. Its surface is level in the N. and rolling in the s. Seneca River and Cross Lake form a portion of the N. boundary. Skaneateles Outlet flows N. w. through the w. part. Upon the banks of the Outlet, near the center, are found the peculiar tunnel-shaped cavities in the earth, characteristic of regions abounding in gypsum. Several weak brine springs are found along Seneca River.[9] The soil is a rich, sandy and gravelly loam. **Elbridge,** (p. v.,) on Skaneateles Outlet, in the s. w. part of the town, was incorp. April 1, 1848; it contains the Munro Collegiate Institute,[10] 3 churches, a pail factory, and several mills. About 1 mi. down the stream is a mill for the manufacture of pearl barley. Pop. 630. **Jordan,** (p. v.,) upon the Outlet, 2 mi. below Elbridge, was incorp. May 2, 1835. It contains the Jordan Academy, 5 churches, 2 flouring mills, and a wheelbarrow factory. It is a station upon the direct branch of the N. Y. Central R. R., and an important canal village. A feeder from the Outlet connects with the canal at this place. Pop. 1,331. **Peru** (Jacks Reefs p. o.) is a hamlet, on the canal, near the N. E. corner. **Junction** (Hart Lot p. o.) is a R. R. station on the Auburn Branch of the N. Y. C. R. R. **Half Way** is a station on the same R. R. **California** is a hamlet, on the canal, 2 mi. E. of Jordan. The first settler was Josiah Buck,[11] who located on Lot 82, in 1793. The first church (Bap.) was formed Dec. 30, 1816; Elder Craw was the first preacher.[12]

FABIUS[13]—was formed from Pompey, March 9, 1798. Tully was taken off in 1803, and a part of Truxton (Cortland co.) in 1808. It is the s. E. corner town in the co. It has a general elevation of 1,000 to 1,200 ft. above the Erie Canal at Syracuse. The surface of the s. half is broken by a series of ridges extending in a N. and s. direction and separated by narrow valleys. Their declivities are generally steep, and the summits are 300 to 500 ft. above the valleys. South Hill, in the s. w. corner, is the principal elevation. The central and northern parts are level or moderately hilly. The streams from the center flow s. into the Tioughnioga, and those upon the

---

1 Called by the Indians Kai-yah-Kooh, signifying "satisfied with tobacco." Tradition says that an Indian woman once lost her child here in a marvelous manner, and that she was informed by a spirit that the child would be safe if she would annually cast a quantity of tobacco upon this pond. The custom continued until the advent of the whites; and hence the name. The water of the lake is pure upon the surface, but strongly impregnated with sulphur below. The water is about 60 ft. deep.—*Clark's Onondaga.*

2 In the vicinity of this latter lake two caves have been discovered and explored for several rods under ground. The caves and sinks in which the lakes are situated are evidently formed by the dissolving of the underlying rocks by the action of water.

3 Named from James De Witt, who started a forge here at an early day.

4 The principal manufactures are waterlime and plaster. The Orville (navigable) feeder of the Erie Canal and the S. B. & N. Y. R. R. afford ample facilities for transportation.

5 Locally known as "Britton Settlement."

6 Among other early settlers were Daniel Keeler, Dr. Holbrook, Jeremiah Jackson, Stephen Angel, Stephen Hungerford, John Young, Jeremiah and James Gould, William Bends, Roger Merrill, Caleb Northrup, and Benjamin Sanford,—all of whom located in the town between 1790 and 1800. The first child born was Sarah Morehouse, Feb. 16, 1790; and the first death was that of Egbert De Witt, May 30, 1793. Polly Hibbard taught the first school, in 1795; Benjamin Morehouse kept the first inn, in 1790; and Asa Danforth built the first sawmill, in 1792, and the first gristmill, in 1793.

7 3 M. E., 2 Presb., Prot. E., and Cong.

8 In the w. part of the town, at the time of the first settlement, were found the remains of three distinct fortifications: one was square, one quadrangular, and one circular. When first discovered, the embankments were 3 feet high; and upon

one of them stood an oak tree 4 ft. in diameter. These works were each situated near a living spring of water. The remains of various articles found here seem to indicate that these fortifications were known to the French.

9 The channel of this river at Jacks Reefs has been deepened by the State, for the purpose of draining the Cayuga marshes. The work was commenced in 1854 and finished in 1857, under the superintendence of Hon. George Geddes. More than 200,000 yards of rock cutting were removed, and the marshes were drained as far west as Musquito Point. The cost was $156,000. (— years previous to this work a deep channel was excavated for a distance of — mi., near Oswego River, at an expense of about $100,000.)

10 Founded in 1839. by Nathan Munro, who left it an endowment of $20,000. The building—among the finest in the State —is of brick, faced with brownstone, and has accommodations for 300 pupils. The school is well sustained.

11 The old elm tree under which Mr. Buck and family took shelter before their house was built is still standing, a little w. of the house of Col. John Munro. Among the other early settlers were Robert Fulton, James Strong, Col. Chandler, Dr. Pickard, —— Potter, Jas. Wiesner, Wm. Stevens, Dr. John Frisbie, Zenas and Aaron Wright, Martin Tickner, Reynolds Corey, Isaac Smith, Jonathan Rowley, Jonathan Babcock, Moses Carpenter, Squire Munro, Ezra and John Brackett, and Joseph and Aaron Colman. John Healy taught the first school, in 1801; Josiah Buck kept the first inn, in 1793; Wm. Stevens kept the first store and built the first sawmill, in 1797; and Isaac Strong the first gristmill, in 1798.

12 The census reports 8 churches in town; 3 M. E., 2 Bap., Cong., Presb., and Prot. E.

13 The town at first embraced the military townships of Fabius and Tully, each 10 mi. square. The s. half of the township of Fabius was erected into the town of Truxton, and now constitutes the N. part of Truxton and Cuyler.

E. and w. borders flow N. into Limestone and Butternut Creeks. A small lake, known as "Labrador Pond," lies at the w. foot of South Hill. The soil is generally a fine quality of gravelly loam, intermixed in places with clay and sand. Along the stream w. of Fabius Village is considerable swamp land. From its elevation, and the broken character of its surface, this town is best adapted to pasturage. Dairying is the principal occupation of the people; and in the amount of dairy products it is the first town in the co. and among the first in the State.[1] **Fabius**[2] (p. v.) is situated on a small stream, N. E. of the center of the town. Pop. 472. **Apulia** (p. v.) is a station of the S. B. & N. Y. R. R., in the w. part of the town. Pop. 140. **Gooseville** is a hamlet, in the N. E. corner. The first settlers were Josiah Moore and Timothy Jerome, from Stockbridge, Mass., who came in 1794.[3] The first church (Presb.) was formed at Apulia, in 1804; and the first pastor was Rev. Mr. Osborne. The first church edifice erected was a Bap., at Fabius Village, in 1806.[4]

GEDDES[5]—was formed from Salina, March 18, 1848 It lies upon the w. bank of Onondaga Lake, a little N. of the center of the co. Its surface is level in the N. and rolling in the s. In the s. E. part are several isolated, rounded drift hills, or knolls. Seneca River forms the N. boundary, and Onondaga Creek a part of the E. Nine Mile Creek flows E. through near the center. The soil is a clayey and sandy loam. Near the s. w. extremity of the lake are several salt wells.[6] The New York State Asylum for Idiots is in the E. part, near the line of Syracuse; and the S. B. & N. Y. R. R. coal depot is on the canal. In the s. E. part are extensive stone quarries. **Geddes,** (p. v.,) in the s. E. part, was incorp. April 20, 1832. It contains 2 churches, a brewery and distillery, and a large number of salt works. Pop. 950. The first settlement was commenced by James Geddes, in 1794.[7] The census reports 2 churches; Prot. E. and M. E.

LA FAYETTE—was formed from Pompey and Onondaga, April 15, 1825. It is an interior town, lying s. E. of the center of the co. Its surface is hilly and broken. Butternut Creek flows N. through the E. part, and Onondaga Creek through the w. The high ridge between the valleys of these streams has steep declivities, and its summit is 300 to 600 ft. high. Conklings Brook, in the s. E. part, flows from the E., and within the space of 1 mile it descends 500 ft. The soil is generally a sandy and gravelly loam; and a portion is thickly covered with large, water-worn pebbles. About one-half of the Onondaga Indian Reservation lies in the N. w. corner of this town. **La Fayette,** (p. v.,) on the ridge near the center of the town, contains 1 church and 35 houses; and **Cardiff,** (p. v.,) on Onondaga Creek, a church and 25 houses. **Linn** is a p. o., in the s. E. part. The first settler was John Wilcox, who located upon Lot 14 in 1791.[8] The first church (Cong.) was formed in Oct. 1809; Rev. Benj. Bell was the first preacher. There are 2 churches in town; Cong. and M. E.

LYSANDER—was formed March 5, 1794. Hannibal (Oswego co.) was taken off in 1806, and Cicero in 1807. It is the N. w. corner town in the co. Its surface is level and somewhat swampy in the E., and gently rolling in the w. Seneca River forms its s. and E. boundaries. This stream takes the name of Oswego River, below the mouth of the outlet of Oneida Lake. In the s. w. part is a slight fall in the river, known as Jacks Rifts. At Baldwinsville is a fall of 7 ft., affording a valuable water-power. Mud Lake, a large pond s. w. of the center, covers an area of about 300 acres. The soil is a sandy and gravelly loam, with occasional patches of clay, formed by the disintegration of the red shales. **Baldwinsville,** (p. v.,) on Seneca River, was incorp. in 1848. It contains a union school, a scythe factory, ax factory, tannery, several extensive

---

[1] The number of dairies in town of 50 to 125 cows each is about 35, and the aggregate number of cows about 3,500.

[2] Formerly called "*Franklinville.*"

[3] Among the other early settlers were Capt. Ebenezer Belden, Col. Elijah St. John, Thomas Miles, Jonathan Stanley, Abel Webster, James Harris, John Wallace, Thos. and Simeon Keeney, Jacob Penoyer, and Abel Pixley. The first child born was Charles Moore, in 1798; the first marriages, those of Abel Webster and Lydia Keeney, and of Luther St. John and Polly Joy, in 1804; and the first death, that of Josiah Moore, in 1802. A colored man belonging to Simeon Keeney died about the same time from drinking too much maple syrup. The first school was taught by Miss Jerome, (afterward wife of Judge James Geddes,) in the E. part of the town; Eunice Fowler taught the first school near Apulia, in 1802–03. The first inns were kept by Josiah Tubbs, near Tully, in 1797, and by Capt. St. John, at Apulia, in 1802; David Caldwell kept the first store, in 1804; Thos Miles built the first sawmill, in 1800; and John Meeker the first grist mill, in 1808.

[4] There are 6 churches in town; M. E. and Cong. at Apulia, and Bap., M. E., F. W. Bap., and Univ. at Fabius.

[5] Named from Hon. James Geddes, first settler.

[6] The first salt well was dug by James Geddes, in 1796. The Indians claimed the springs w. of the lake; but they adopted Mr. Geddes into their tribe. and allowed him to go on with his works. There are now in town 46 fine salt works, and 7,442 coarse salt covers. See page 479.

[7] Among the other early settlers were Freeman Hughs and James Lamb. Nancy Root taught the first school, in 1803; James Lamb kept the first inn, in 1803; and Noah Smith built the first sawmill, in 1825.

[8] Comfort Rounds and Wm. Haskens located in town in 1792; Solomon Owen and James Sherman, in 1793; John Houghtaling, Amaziah Branch, James Pearce, Samuel Hyatt, Amasa Wright, and Reuben Bryan, in 1794; and Isaac and Elias Conklin, Zenas and Ozias Northway, and Isaac Hull, soon after. The first child born was Amy Wilcox, in 1791; the first marriage, that of Solomon Owen and Lois Rounds, in 1793; and the first death, that of Moses De Witt, in 1794. Rev. Amaziah Branch was the first teacher; —— Cheney kept the first inn; Stoughton Morse the first store; and James Sherman built the first sawmill, in 1795.

flouring and saw mills, a newspaper office, furnace, machine shop, and a large distillery. Pop. 1,675,—of which 1,115 are in this town and 560 in Van Buren. **Betts Corners** (Lysander p. o.) contains 3 churches and 35 houses; **Little Utica,** 1 church and 30 houses; **Plainville** (p. v.) a church and 218 inhabitants; and **Jacksonville** (Polkville p. o.) a church and 25 houses. **Lamsons** (p. o) is a R. R. station. The first settler within the present limits of the town was Jonathan Palmer, a Revolutionary soldier, who drew Lot 36, and located upon it in 1793.[1] The first church (Presb.) was formed in 1813.[2]

MANLIUS—was formed March 5, 1794. A part of Onondaga was taken off in 1798, a part of Salina in 1809, and De Witt in 1835. It lies on the E. border of the co., N. of the center. The surface of the N. half is level, and that of the s. half rolling and hilly. Limestone Creek flows N. through near the center of the town, and at the northern extremity it receives Butternut Creek from the w., and the two united streams flow into Chittenango Creek, which latter stream forms the N. E. boundary of the town. A few rods s. of the canal, near the center, are two small lakes, similar in character to those already described in De Witt, but somewhat larger. They are known as the "Green Lakes." In the s. w. corner of the town is another small pond of the same kind.[3] The E. branch of Limestone Creek, near the s. border of the town, falls down a limestone precipice 100 ft., forming a beautiful cascade. Several sulphur and other mineral springs are found in town, but none of any considerable note.[4] In the w. part are extensive quarries, from which are obtained immense quantities of waterlime, quicklime and gypsum. The soil is a deep, fertile alluvium in the N., and a sandy and clayey loam in the s. **Manlius,** (p. v.,) on Limestone Creek, near the s. line of the town, was incorp. March 12, 1813. It contains the Manlius Academy, a union school, 4 churches, 2 carriage factories, 2 flouring mills, an ax factory, 2 founderies, and a paper mill. Pop. 934. **Fayetteville,** (p. v.,) on Limestone Creek, 2 mi. N. W. from Manlius, and 1 mi. from the Erie Canal, with which it is connected by a navigable feeder, was incorp. May 6, 1844. It is finely situated on a gentle elevation, and has a number of valuable water-privileges.[5] It contains 4 churches, a union school, a bank, 2 large flouring mills, 3 sawmills, 1 pearl barley mill, 1 paper mill, 1 sash blind and door factory, 3 lime and plaster mills, 1 tannery, 1 foundery and machine shop, 1 wheelbarrow factory and 1 cradle factory, 5 carriage factories, and several large establishments for the manufacture of lime, plaster, and waterlime.[6] Pop. in 1859, 1,376. **Manlius Center** (p. v.) is a canal village, containing 40 houses. **Manlius Station** (p. v.) and **Kirkville** (p. v.) are small villages and stations upon the Central R. R. **High Bridge,** in the s. w. part, contains a church, 2 plaster and lime mills, a sawmill, gristmill, and 20 houses.[7] **Matthews Mills,** (North Manlius p. o.,) **Eagle Village,** and **Hartsville** are hamlets. The first settlers were David Tripp, who located 1 mi. N. w. of the present site of Manlius Village, and James Foster, who located on the present site of Eagle Village, in 1790.[8] The first church (Prot. E.) was formed in 1798; Rev. Mr. Nash was the first preacher.[9]

MARCELLUS—was formed March 5, 1794. A part of Onondaga was taken off in 1798; Camillus in 1799; a part of Otisco in 1806; and Skaneateles in 1830. A part of Sempronius

---

[1] Among the other settlers were Benj. De Puy, Reuben Smith, Adam Emerick, Elijah and Solomon Toll, Thomas Farrington, Elijah Mann, John McHarrie, Wm. Lindsay, Ebenezer Wells, James Cowan, Abner and Manly Vickery, Job Lomis, and Dr. Jonas C. Baldwin. Dr. Baldwin was the early proprietor and founder of Baldwinsville. He built the first saw and grist mills, in 1807 ; and opened the first store, during the same year. By his energy, the place soon became an important manufacturing village. Daniel Ayers kept the first inn. The first child born was John Toll.

[2] The census reports 9 churches in town; 4 M. E., 2 Presb., Bap., Ref. Prot. D., and Christian.

[3] Among the hills are several other deep chasms; but they do not contain water. Some of them are filled with ice during the winter, and thus become natural icehouses during the greater part of the summer. The nature and origin of these remarkable depressions have given rise to many speculations and theories on the part of geologists and other men of science.

[4] Deep Spring, called by the Indians Te-ungh-sat-a-yugh, is a spring 60 ft. in diameter, on the E. line of the town, near the old Seneca Turnpike.

[5] These are formed by the Ledyard Canal—which was built by the citizens at a cost of $35,000—and Bishop Brook. The Ledyard Canal is formed by diverting the waters of Limestone Creek, 2 mi. s. of the village; and that, in connection with Bishop Brook, which runs parallel to it through the village, make 12 water-powers, with an average fall of 20 ft. each.

[6] During the year ending Jan. 1, 1859, 1,394 tons of limestone for the manufacture of quicklime, 903 tons of building stone, 10,298 tons of stone plaster, 3,216 tons of ground plaster, 85,459

barrels of waterlime, and 50,410 bushels of quicklime were sold in the village of Fayetteville.

[7] An extensive water-power is formed at this place by the construction of a hydraulic canal from Limestone Creek and another from a brook flowing from the E. This power is used in all the manufactories in the village, and but a small portion of it is occupied.

[8] Among the other early settlers were Joshua Knowlton and Origen Eaton, on the site of Fayetteville, in 1791 ; Conrad Lour, Cyrus Kinnie, and John A Shaeffer, in 1792; and Caleb Pratt, Capt. Joseph Williams, Wm. Ward, Col. Elijah Phillips, Charles Mulholland, Charles Moseley, Dr. Sturtevant, Alvan Marsh, and Dr. Ward, all of whom came previous to 1800. The first child born was Baron Steuben Shaeffer, in 1794. It is related that on the night of his birth Baron Steuben and a party of friends put up at Mr. Shaeffer's, who then kept an inn on the present site of Manlius. The baron was much disturbed during the night, and in the morning severely reprimanded Mr. S. for allowing his guests to be so annoyed that they could not sleep. Upon seeing the infant, he apologized for his ebullition of temper, bestowed his own name upon the child, and gave him a deed of 250 acres of land. The first marriage was that of Nicholas Phillips and Katy Garlock, Jan. 14, 1793; and the first death, that of the father of David Tripp, in 1792; Samuel Edwards taught the first school, in James Foster's barn; James Foster kept the first inn, in 1790; Charles Moseley the first store, in 1793; Elijah Phillips and three others built the first sawmill, in 1792–93; and Wm. Ward the first gristmill, in 1794.

[9] The census reports 13 churches in town; 3 M. E., 2 Bap., 2 Prot. E., 2 Presb., Meth. Prot., Wes. Meth., R. C., and Union.

(Cayuga co.) was annexed in 1804, and a part of Spafford in 1840. It is an interior town, lying s. w. of the center of the co. Its surface is a rolling upland, broken by the deep valley of Nine Mile Creek, which extends N. and s. through the center. The declivities which border upon the creek are steep, and 200 to 500 ft. high. Upon the creek are several falls, furnishing a large amount of water-power. Lime and plaster both abound. The soil is generally a deep, black loam, formed by the decomposition of the Marcellus shales, intermixed to some extent with clay. Manufacturing is carried on to a limited extent along Nine Mile Creek. **Marcellus,** (p. v.,) on the creek, near the center of the town, was incorp. April 29, 1853; it contains 4 churches, a woolen factory, and grist mill. Pop. 380. **Marcellus Falls** (p. v.) contains a gristmill, saw-mill, and 2 paper mills. Pop. 200. **Marietta,** (p. v.,) upon Nine Mile Creek, in the s. part, contains 30 houses. **Clintonville** is a hamlet. **Thorn Hill** (p. o.) is a hamlet in the s. w. part. The first settler was Wm. Cobb, who located on the E. hill in 1794.[1] The first church edifice (Union) was built in 1803; Rev. —— Atwater was the first preacher.[2]

ONONDAGA—was formed from Marcellus, Pompey, and Manlius, March 9, 1798. A part of Salina was taken off in 1809, and a part of Camillus in 1834. The surface is mostly a rolling and hilly upland, separated into two ridges by the valley of Onondaga Creek. The E. ridge is rocky and broken, and the w. is generally smooth and rolling. A fine, wide intervale extends along the creek, and is bordered by steep hillsides, the summits of which are 200 to 400 ft. high. A valley, forming a natural pass between Onondaga and Nine Mile Creeks, extends s. w. through the town. Along the N. line the highlands w. of the valley descend abruptly to the N., presenting in some places the face of a nearly perpendicular precipice 100 to 150 ft. high. This declivity is known as Split Rock. Upon these cliffs is an outcrop of Onondaga limestone, which is extensively quarried for building purposes.[3] The Split Rock stone quarry is near the N. w. corner. The soil in the valley is a sandy and gravelly loam, and on the uplands is gravelly and clayey loam. Lime and waterlime are both largely manufactured. About one-half of the Onondaga Indian Reservation lies in the s. E. part of this town. **Onondaga Hill,**[4] (Onondaga p. o.,) on the hill w. of the creek, contains a church and 53 dwellings. **Onondaga Valley** (p. v.) contains 2 churches and the Onondaga Academy. Pop. 385. **South Onondaga** (p. v.) contains 2 churches, several mills, and a population of 290. **Navarino,** (p. v.,) in the s. w. corner, near the line of Marcellus, contains a church and 115 inhabitants. **Onondaga Castle** is a p. o. near the Indian Reservation. **Howlet Hill** is a p. o. in the N. w. corner; and **West Onondaga** a p. o. near the w. line. The first white man who lived in this town and vicinity was Ephraim Webster,[5] an Indian trader. The first permanent settlers were Asa Danforth,[6] his son Asa, from Mass., and Comfort Tyler, a young man who accompanied him,—all of whom located upon a lot a little s. of Onondaga Hollow. This was the first settlement made in the co.[7] Rev. Samuel Kirkland, a

---

[1] Among the other early settlers were Cyrus Holcomb, —— Bowen, —— Cady, Samuel Tyler, Dan Bradley, Samuel Rice, Nathan Kelsey, Thomas Miller, Bigelow Lawrence, Martin Cossitt, and Samuel Wheadon,—all of whom located previous to 1800. The town rapidly filled up with settlers, principally from Mass. The first child born was a daughter of Wm. Cobb. Miss Asenith Lawrence taught the first school, in the summer of 1796; Dea. Samuel Rice kept the first inn, in 1796; Elnathan Beach the first store, in 1796; Dan Bradley and Samuel Rice built the first sawmill, in 1795–96; and May & Sayles the first gristmill, in 1800.

[2] The census reports 5 churches; 2 Presb., Bap., M. E., and Prot. E.

[3] In this ledge is an irregular crack or chasm, which is said to extend downward to the depth of 100 ft. Ice remains in it during the greater part of summer. The stone was obtained from these quarries for building the locks upon the canal and the aqueduct across Genesee River; and it is justly esteemed a building stone of superior quality.

[4] For many years after the organization of Onondaga co. the co. seat was located at this village. It was a place of considerable business, and the most important village upon the Seneca Turnpike w. of Whitestown. For a long time its only business rivals were Salina, or "*Salt Point*," and Onondaga Hollow; but, on account of the healthfulness of its situation, the Hill maintained its superiority until the completion of the Erie Canal, in 1825. It is now a mere hamlet.

[5] Mr. Webster was a native of N. H., and served 3 years in the army during the Revolution. After the war he became an Indian trader; and, in consequence of his thorough knowledge of the Indian language, he was employed as an interpreter in several of the councils between the whites and Indians. In 1786 he erected a trading house on the banks of Onondaga Creek, near its mouth, and continued his traffic there for several years. He married an Indian woman; and, becoming a great favorite, the tribe made him a present of a square mile of land upon

Onondaga Creek, a little s. of the present village of Onondaga Valley. The Indians also granted him 300 acres near the N. w. corner of the present reservation. He afterward married a white woman, by whom he had a large family of children. He was employed by the Government as a spy, interpreter, and counselor during the Indian wars that followed the Revolution; and he was in active service during the last war with Great Britain. For many years he was an Indian Agent, and probably had more influence with the Onondaga tribe than any other white man. He died in 1825. One of his Indian children—Harry Webster—is now chief of the Onondaga Nation.

[6] Mr. Danforth was the pioneer, and one of the most energetic and prominent of the early settlers of the co. He erected the first sawmill and gristmill in the co., on Butternut Creek, near Jamesville; and during the many years of privation which followed the first settlement, his cabin was always the welcome home of the distressed and suffering settlers. He held at different times the offices of Judge of Common Pleas, Superintendent of the Salt Springs, and Major General in the State Militia. He died in 1818.

[7] Among the other settlers who came soon after Mr. Danforth were Abijah Earll, Levi Hiscock, and Roderick Adams, in 1788 or '89; Nicholas Mickles, John C. Brown, Arthur Patterson, Job Tyler, Peter Tenbroeck, —— Lewis, Cornelius Longstreet, Peter Young, Joseph Forman, John Adams, Geo. Kibbe, Wm. and Gordon Needham, Wm. H. Sabine, Jasper Hopper, Aaron Bellows. George Hall, Joseph Swan, Thaddeus M. Wood, Jonas C. Baldwin, and Daniel and Nehemiah H. Earll. The first marriage was that of Ephraim Webster and an Indian woman, in 1789. The wife soon after died, and Mr. Webster took another Indian wife, agreeing to live with her as long as she kept sober. He lived with her nearly 20 years. As the settlement began to advance, he was desirous of obtaining a white wife, and to this end endeavored to make his wife drunk. For a long time she resisted every attempt; but at last, with the aid of milk punch, he succeeded. The next morning she left without speaking a

missionary from Mass., was the first preacher. The first church (Presbyterian) was formed at an early day, at the Hill.[1]

OTISCO—was formed from Pompey, Marcellus, and Tully, March 21, 1806. It is an interior town, lying s. w. of the center of the co. Its surface is principally occupied by the high ridge between the valleys of Onondaga Creek and Otisco Lake. The declivities of the hills are generally steep and the summits rolling, and elevated 800 to 1,000 ft. above the valleys and 1,600 to 1,700 above tide. Otisco Lake is 772 ft. above tide. It lies upon the w. border of the town, in a valley 1,000 ft. below the summits of the hills. Bear Mountain,[2] in the N. w. part, overhanging the valley of Onondaga Creek, is one of the principal elevations. The soil is generally a sandy or gravelly loam, mixed with clay, and well adapted to grazing. **Otisco,** (p. v.,) situated upon the high ridge near the center of the town, contains 30 houses ; and **Amber,** (p. v.,) at the foot of Otisco Lake, 25. **Maple Grove** is a p. o. in the N. E. corner. The first settler was Chauncey Rust, from Northampton, Mass., who moved his family from La Fayette in April, 1801. During this year and the following, a large number of settlers arrived, principally from Mass. and Conn. and the whole town filled up rapidly.[3] The first religious service was a prayer meeting, held in Sept. 1801, at the house of —— Rust. The first church (Cong.) was formed May 9, 1803, by Rev. Hugh Wallace. There are now two churches in town ; Cong. and M. E. This town is noted for being the birthplace and residence of several persons of distinguished literary reputation.[4]

POMPEY[5]—was formed in Jan. 1789. Fabius and a part of Onondaga were taken off in 1798 ; and La Fayette in 1825. It lies upon the E. border of the co., s. of the center. Its surface is principally occupied by the high, rolling ridge which lies between the E. branch of Limestone Creek and Butternut Creek. The highest summit is 906 ft. above the surface of Butternut Creek, near the La Fayette R. R. station, 1,343 ft. above the canal at Syracuse and 1,743 ft. above tide. The general ridge is subdivided into 3 ridges by the valleys of the 2 w. branches of Limestone Creek. These valleys are 200 to 300 ft. below the summits and are bordered by steep hillsides. The streams that drain the s. part of the town flow in a southerly direction. Pratts Falls, upon the w. branch of Limestone Creek, are 137 ft. high ; and within a few rods of them are several other fine cascades. Near the N. line, upon the same creek, is a cascade of 70 ft. Just E. of the co. line, near Delphi, on the E. branch of the same stream, are 2 other fine cascades. Carpenters Pond, in the s. E. part, covers an area of about 30 acres. The soil is a strong, clayey loam. **Pompey Hill,** (Pompey p. o.,) on the summit of the ridge,[6] contains 5 churches and the Pompey Academy. Pop. 270. **Delphi,** (p. v.,) upon Limestone Creek, in the s. E. corner, contains 3 churches and 219 inhabitants. **Watervale,** (p. v.,) upon Limestone Creek, N. of the center, contains a grist and saw mill and 20 houses. **Oran,** (p. v.,) in the N. E. corner, contains a church and 82 inhabitants. **Pompey Center**[7] (p. o.) is a hamlet. In the s. E. corner, above Delphi, are an edge tool factory, and a woolen mill not in operation. The first settler was Ebenezer Butler, who located on Lot 65 in 1792.[8] The first church (Presb.) was formed in 1794 ; the first preacher

word, and in a short time died of grief. The first child born was Amanda Danforth, daughter of Asa Danforth, jr., Oct. 14, 1789. Dr. Gordon Needham taught the first school, in 1795 ; Comfort Tyler kept the first inn ; George Kibbe the first store ; Gen. Danforth built the first gristmill, in 1794 ; and Turner Fenner the first sawmill, in 1793.

[1] The census reports 11 churches ; 5 M. E., 2 Presb., Cong., Bap., Wes. Meth., and Union.

[2] Named from the great number of bears that infested it when the country was first settled.

[3] Among the first settlers were Jonathan B. Nichols, Charles and Benoni Merriman, Solomon Judd, and Lemon Gaylord, in 1801 ; Otis Baker, Noah Parsons, Nathaniel Loomis, Amos and Isaac Cowles, in 1802 ; and Benjamin Cowles, Josiah Clark, Daniel Bennett, Elias and Jared Thayer, Henry Elethrop, Samuel, Ebenezer, and Luther French, Jared and Noah Parsons, and Rufus Clapp, soon after. Lucy Cowles (afterward wife of Rev. Geo. Colton) taught the first school, in 1802. The first child born was Timothy Rust, March 22, 1802 ; and the first death, that of Nathaniel Dady, jr., killed by the fall of a tree, July 19, 1802. Dan'l Bennett kept the first inn, in 1802 ; and Michael Johnson the first store, in 1808. Charles Merriman built the first gristmill, in 1806.

[4] Willis Gaylord, widely known as the editor of the Genesee Farmer and Albany Cultivator, and as a refined and graceful contributor to the light literature of the day, came into town with his father, from Bristol, Conn., in 1801. He was then 9 years of age ; and he resided here until a few years before his death, which occurred in 1844. Willis and Lewis Gaylord Clark, twin brothers, were born in this town in April, 1808. The former is known as a poet, the author of "Ollipodiana," and as the editor of the Philadelphia Gazette ; and the latter has obtained a national reputation as the editor of the Knickerbocker Maga-

zine, a position which he has held for the last 25 years. Willis died in 1841. Their father was Eliakim Clark, an officer in the Revolution, and their mother was sister to Willis Gaylord. Rev. Geo. Colton, father of Owen Colton, author of a series of Greek text books, and of Geo. H. Colton, founder and editor of the American Review, was many years a resident of the town.

[5] Named by the Indians Ote-ge-ga-ja-ke, "a place of much grass, openings or prairies." Another name given to this locality, not often repeated, and about which there is much superstitious reserve, is Ote-queh-sah-he-eh, "the field of blood, or bloody ground,—a place where many have been slain." It has been said that no Indian ever visits this neighborhood. They certainly dislike to converse much about it.—*Clark's Onondaga, Vol. II, p.* 325.

[6] Water from one side of the roof of the hotel at this place finds its way into the St. Lawrence, and from the other into Chesapeake Bay.

[7] Locally known as "Greens Corners."

[8] Moses Blower and Moses Savage came in the same year. Among the early settlers upon the hills were Artemus Bishop, Josiah Holbrook, Timothy Sweet, John and Samuel Jerome, Joseph Smith, Jesse Butler, Dr. Deodatus Clarke, Jacob Hoar, Jas. Olcott, Trueworthy Cook, Selah Cook, Noadiah and Epiphas Olcott, Dr. Samuel Beach, and families named Hinsdale, Hibbard, Messenger, Western, and Daniel Allen. The early settlers in the E. hollow were Samuel Draper, James McClure, Wm. Cook, Ozias Burr, Elihu Barber, John Lamb, Daniel Thomas, —— Savage, Daniel Hubbard, Wm. Shankland, and David Sweet. The first child born was Sally Hoar, about 1794 ; the first male child born was Orange Butler ; the first marriage was that of Zachariah Kinne and Diadama Barnes ; and the first death, that of Mrs. Jas. Cravath. Samuel Clement taught the first school in the town and co., on Lot 28, in 1794. Ebenezer Butler kept the first inn, in 1792 ; Henry Seymour the first store ;

was Rev. Mr. Robbins, a missionary from Conn.[1] Several eminent personages, distinguished in the fields of politics, literature, and art, were natives of this town, prominent among whom are Sara J. Clarke, (now Mrs. Sara J. Lippincott, better known as "Grace Greenwood,") Ex-Gov. Horatio Seymour, Charles Mason, late Commissioner of Patents, and Erastus D. Palmer, the sculptor,

SALINA—was formed from Manlius and Onondaga, March 27, 1809. Syracuse and Geddes were taken off March 18, 1848. It lies upon the E. bank of Onondaga Lake, N. of the center of the co. Its surface is level or gently undulating. Mud Creek, in the S. E. part, and its tributary, Bear Trap Creek, are the only streams. Along their course is a considerable amount of swamp land. The soil is principally a sandy loam, with occasional intervals of tough clay. The people are largely engaged in the manufacture of salt. Tobacco is cultivated to some extent. **Liverpool,** (p. v.,) upon the E. bank of Onondaga Lake, on the w. line of the town, was incorp. April 20, 1830. It contains 4 churches, a union school, a steam saw and stave mill, and a large number of salt works. Pop. 1,305. The first settlement was made at Liverpool, in 1795, by John Danforth and 3 sons, from Worcester co., Mass.[2] There are 4 churches in town.[3]

SKANEATELES[4]—was formed from Marcellus, Feb. 26, 1830. A part of Spafford was annexed in 1840. It is the S. town on the w. line of the co. The surface is rolling or moderately hilly. Skaneateles Lake divides the S. half of the town into two nearly equal parts. From the lake the land slopes beautifully upward to a height of 200 to 500 ft. The highlands upon both borders overlooking the lake furnish a great number of sites for country residences, which, in beauty of situation, have no superiors in the State. Many of these are occupied by fine cottages and villas. Skaneateles Outlet, flowing N., is the principal stream. Upon it are numerous falls, furnishing an abundance of water-power.[5] The soil is principally a clay loam. **Skaneateles,**[6] (p. v.,) beautifully located at the foot of the lake, was incorp. April 19, 1833. It contains 6 churches, a union school, and 3 carriage manufactories. Pop. 1,200. **Mottville,** (p. v.,) on Skaneateles Outlet, contains 1 church, 2 machine shops, a foundery, chair factory, fork factory, and gristmill. Pop. 250. **Mandana,** (p. v.,) on the w. bank of the lake, in the S. part of the town, contains 15 dwellings. **Kelloggs Mills,** a hamlet 1½ mi. N. of Skaneateles, contains a woolen factory which employs 125 hands. The first settler was John Thompson, a Scotchman, who located upon Lot 18 in 1793.[7] The first church edifice (Cong.) was erected in 1807; Rev. Aaron Bascom was the first pastor.[8]

SPAFFORD[9]—was formed from Tully, April 8, 1811. Parts of Marcellus and Skaneateles were taken off in 1840. It lies upon the E. bank of Skaneateles Lake, and is the w. town on the S. line of the co. Its surface consists principally of a high ridge between Skaneateles and Otisco Lakes, abruptly descending to the valleys on each side and gradually declining toward the N. The highest summit, Ripley Hill, is 1,122 ft. above Skaneateles Lake and 1,982 ft. above tide. Otisco Inlet is a small stream flowing through the valley which extends S. from Otisco Lake. The soil is a sandy and gravelly loam. **Borodino,** (p. v.,) in the N. part of the town, contains a population of 202. **Spafford,** (p. v.,) near the center, contains 2 churches and 30 houses. **Spafford Hollow** is a p. o. The first settlers were Gilbert Palmer and his son John, who located on Lot 76 in 1794.[10] The first church (M. E.)was formed at an early day; Elder Harmon was the first preacher.[11]

Pratt & Smith built the first sawmill, in 1796, and the first gristmill, in 1798; Dr. Hezekiah Clarke was the first settled physician. He served 2 years as a surgeon in the Revolutionary Army, and was at the massacre of Fort Griswold.
[1] The census reports 12 churches; 4 M. E., 3 Bap., Cong., Presb., Prot. E., Univ., and Disciples.
[2] Abel Hawley, John Eager, and Patrick Riley came in about the same time. The first marriage was that of Abram Shoemaker and Betsey Danforth, in 1809. The first school was taught by Capt. Conner, about 1797, in a salt block, which at that time contained 4 kettles; and the school was taught while the block was in operation. John Danforth kept the first inn, in 1796.
[3] 2 M. E., Evan. Luth., and Presb.
[4] Indian name: by some said to signify "very long lake," and by others, "the beautiful squaw." The outlet is called "Hanauttoo," or "Hanauto," meaning "water running through thick hemlocks."
[5] A recent survey makes Skaneateles Lake 860.25 feet above tide. Between Skaneateles and Mottville are two large distilleries, and below Mottville a woolen factory, a grist and saw mill, a paper mill, and a distillery.
[6] The beautiful location of this village upon one of the finest lakes in the State renders it a favorite summer resort of people from the cities and from the South.
[7] Among the other early settlers were —— Robinson, James Watson, Lovel Gibbs, Jonathan Hall, and Winston Day, who came in 1796; Warren Hecox, James and Samuel Porter, Dr.

Munger, Elnathan Andrews, John Legg, Moses Loss, John Briggs, Nathan Kelsey, Wm. J. Vredenburgh, Isaac Sherwood, Dr. Benedict, and families by the names of Kellogg and Earll, who came in soon after. Elisha Cole, now living, (1859,) came in with his father in 1793. Capt. Wm. Thomas came in 1796; Hezekiah Earll and Samuel Greenman in 1797. The first child born was Richard P. Watson, June 1, 1796; and the first death, that of Nehemiah Earll, in 1808. James Porter kept the first inn, and Winston Day the first store, in 1797; and Judge Jedediah Sanger built the first saw and grist mill, in 1796.
[8] The census reports 8 churches; 2 M. E., 2 Friends, Bap., Presb., Prot. E., and Univ.
[9] Named from Horatio Gates Spafford, author of the first Gazetteer of New York.
[10] Among the other early settlers were Jonathan Berry, Archibald Farr, Warren Kneeland, M. Harvey, Isaac Hall, Elisha Sabins, John Babcock, Peter Knapp, Samuel Smith, Otis and Moses Legg, Jethro Bailey, Elias Davis, Abel Amadon, Job Lewis, Daniel Tinkham, John Hullibut, Levi Foster, Benj. Horner, James and Cornelius Williamson, Benjamin Stanton, John Woodward, James Bacon, and Asahel Roundy. The first child born was Alvah Palmer; the first marriage, that of Elisha Freeman and Phœbe Smith; and the first death, that of Benj. Chaffee, in Aug. 1801. Sally Packard taught the first school, in 1803; Jared Babcock kept the first store, in 1809; Archibald Farr kept the first inn and built the first gristmill, in 1808; and Josiah Walker built the first sawmill, in 1810.
[11] The census reports 5 churches; 3 M. E., Presb., and Union.

SYRACUSE[1]—was incorp. as a village in the town of Salina, April 13, 1825, and as a city, Dec. 14, 1847. A portion was annexed to De Witt in 1858. It lies in a basin extending s. of the head of Onondaga Lake, and upon the ridges immediately E. A low portion, partly marshy, containing more than a square mi., lies upon the lake,[2] and is bordered by an abrupt declivity 10 to 30 ft. high. From the summit of this declivity the surface spreads out into an almost perfect flat, on which is built the greater part of the more thickly settled portions of the city. A ridge 100 to 200 ft. high extends through the E. part.[3] Upon the highlands that surround the city are some of the most beautiful sites for country residences to be found in the State. The city is located in the midst of a rich agricultural region, and near the center of the State.[4] The several canals and railroads that terminate at or pass through this city give to it important commercial advantages. Its local trade is very large. It is also largely engaged in manufactures, the principal of which are salt,[5] machinery, beer, and barrels.[6] A large trade is carried on with the surrounding country to supply the salt works with wood and barrels, and with Penn. to furnish them with coal. The city is supplied with water by the Syracuse Water Company, from springs and brooks which have their sources in the hills s. w. of the city.

The *City Hall* is a commodious edifice, on the s. side of the canal, fronting Washington St., and containing rooms for the officers of the city government.

The *Public Schools*, 13 in number, are under the charge of a Board of Education, consisting of 8 members, of whom 4 are elected annually. In 1858, 61 teachers were employed,—7 males and 54 females. The whole number of children, between the ages of 4 and 21, was 9,418, of whom 5,258, or 55 per cent., attended school during some portion of the year. The total expenses were $34,057.69. The number of volumes in the district libraries was 5,131.[7] The schools are graded, and have a classical department or High School. Few places have bestowed more attention upon common school education; and the schools now rank among the best in the State and country.

The *Onondaga County Orphan Asylum*, a city and county institution for the care of orphan and destitute children, is situated upon Fayette St., in the E. part of the city. It was incorp. April 10, 1845, and is supported by public appropriations and private donations. The children are well treated, and are amply provided with all the necessaries of life. A school is taught throughout the year. At a proper age the children are bound out in respectable families.

The *Syracuse Home Association*, incorp. in 1853, is an association of ladies for the purpose of systematically visiting the poor, and of furnishing a home for indigent and friendless females. It occupies a fine building upon E. Fayette St., and is in a flourishing condition.

The *New York State Asylum for Idiots* is located upon a beautiful site in Geddes, s. w. of the city, just outside of the city corporation. Its grounds contain 18 acres, lying upon an eminence overlooking the whole city. The building is a beautiful brick structure, in the Italian style of architecture, and is one of the best arranged and most convenient buildings of the kind ever constructed. It is under the superintendence of Dr. Hervey B. Wilbur. The average number of inmates is more than 100.[8]

---

[1] This city was known from 1806 to 1809 as "*Bogardus Corners*;" from 1809 to 1812, as "*Milan*;" from 1812 to 1814, as "*South Salina*;" from 1814 to 1817, as "*Cossitts Corners*;" from 1817 to 1820, as "*Corinth*;" and from that time it has been known as Syracuse,—the name given it by John Wilkinson, the first postmaster. "*Salina*," now constituting the N. part of the city, was incorp. as a village March 12, 1824, and continued as an independent corporation until 1847, when it was merged in Syracuse. It was long familiarly known as "*Salt Point*." The eastern part of the city was formerly known as "*Lodi*."

[2] The salt springs are situated upon this marsh and its borders. Near the lake, upon the Liverpool road, is a very strong sulphur spring.

[3] This ridge is divided into two parts by the valley through which the canal extends. Upon it, a short distance E. of the head of the lake, are large cavities in the ground, generally termed "salt holes." These holes are continually forming; and it not unfrequently happens that a tract of 20 ft. in diameter will suddenly fall to a depth of 10 to 30 ft. See p. 481.

[4] From its central location, the city is a favorite place for holding conventions, political, religious, civil, and miscellaneous. From this, it is often called "The City of Conventions," and sometimes "The City of isms." It is also called "The Central City," and "The City of Salt."

[5] See pages 480, 481.

[6] Several founderies and machine shops give employment to about 200 hands. Greenway's Brewery manufactures annually 50,000 bbls. of beer, worth $350,000. There are 8 other breweries in the city, producing 500 to 5,000 bbls. each. Barrels for the salt trade are also manufactured in the city, giving employment to a large number of hands. The Central R. R. repair shops employ 150 hands, and about 150 more are engaged as engineers, brakemen, and track hands, belonging to this station. The city also contains large manufactories of agricultural implements, boots and shoes, furniture, saddlery hardware, silver ware, cigars, and a variety of other articles.

[7] The Central Library, kept in the City Hall, is a consolidated library for the use of the central schools of the city. It was founded in 1858, and contains 4,000 volumes.

[8] The building for this institution was erected in 1853-54, at a cost of about $70,000. The site and grounds were donated by inhabitants of Syracuse. The enterprise has been highly successful, and has fully demonstrated the utility and necessity of schools of this description. The institution has attained a wide reputation, and it now undoubtedly ranks among the first of the kind in the world. The school was first established at Albany, in 1848, by its present supt., as a private institution. It was adopted by the State, and was continued several years at Albany, but was removed to this place on completion of the buildings, in 1854.

The *Franklin Institute*, a literary association, was incorp. under the general law, Dec. 1849. It has a fine library and reading room in Wieting Block, S. Salina St., and it supports an annual course of lectures during the winter. The number of volumes in the library is about 3,000.

Syracuse Post Office is situated near the center of the old village of Syracuse, s. of the Erie Canal. *Salina Post Office* is situated in the old village of Salina, near the Oswego Canal.

The *Library of the Court of Appeals* was formed by act of Legislature, April 9, 1849. It occupies rooms in the courthouse, and contains 4,500 volumes.

The *Office of the Superintendent of the Salt Springs*, on N. Salina St., is a fine building of cut stone.

The *State Armory* is a fine building, in Regimental Park, near Onondaga Creek. It was built in 1858, from a design by H. N. White.

The city also contains a Commercial College, 2 private seminaries, a classical school, a boarding school for boys, a large number of Masonic, Odd Fellows, and Sons of Malta lodges, a City Tract Society, a Bible Society, a Fugitive Aid Society, a Musical Institute, a German Turnverein, 11 banks of issue, 2 savings banks, 28 churches,[1] and a large number of beautiful and costly private residences. Its hotels and public halls rank among the best in the State.

The first settlement in the city and co. was made by Ephraim Webster, an Indian trader, who located near the mouth of Onondaga Creek in 1787. In 1788 or 1789 John Danforth, who came into the co. soon after his brother Asa, located at *"Salt Point"* and commenced the manufacture of salt.[2] The settlement at this place increased with great rapidity, in consequence of the prospective value of the salt springs. It took the name of *"Salina,"* and speedily became the most important place in the co.,—a superiority which it maintained for many years. The first settlers within the limits of the old village of Syracuse, after Webster, the Indian trader, were —— Hopkins, in 1797, and —— Butler, in 1799. Calvin Jackson settled in 1800, and several others before 1805.[3] The ground being low and marshy, the settlement did not progress rapidly for many years. The first great impulse to its growth was given by the location of the canal in 1817 and its completion in 1825. In 1829, when the courthouse was removed from Onondaga Hill, Salina and Syracuse were nearly equal in population, and the courthouse was placed about midway between the two villages. Since that time, however, the growth of Syracuse has been rapid and nearly uniform. In 1847 it completely absorbed its old rival, Salina, the two villages and Lodi at that time being incorp. and forming the city of Syracuse. The business prosperity of the place has been based principally upon the salt interests and its commercial advantages. The most notable incidents of the later history of the city are the great gunpowder explosion of Aug. 20, 1841;[4] and the rescue of the slave Jerry from the custody of the U. S. Marshal, Oct. 1, 1851.[5]

TULLY—was formed *from Fabius, April 4, 1803. A part of Otisco was taken off in 1806, and Spafford in 1811. It is the center town upon the s. line of the co. Its surface is an upland, level in the center, but hilly on the E. and W. borders. In the s. part of the central valley are several small lakes, known as the Tully Lakes. Two of these lakes lie but a few rods apart. The smaller, just 800 ft. above the canal at Syracuse, gives rise to Onondaga Creek, flowing N.; and the larger, 4 ft. lower, gives rise to Tioughnioga River, flowing S. In the immediate vicinity of these lakes is considerable swamp land. The soil is a sandy and clayey loam. **Tully,** (p. v.,) in the S. E. part of the town, contains 2 churches and 216 inhabitants; and **Vesper,** (p. v.,) on the line of Otisco, 2 churches and 25 houses. **Tully Valley** is a p. o. The first settler was David

---

[1] 4 R. C., 3 Prot. E., 3 M. E., 3 Presb., 2 Cong. 2 Bap., 2 Ger. Evan. Asso., 2 Jewish Synagogues, Ref. Prot. D., Unit., Ger. Luth., Ger. Prot., Af. Meth., Wes. Meth., and Swedenborgian.

[2] In Aug. 1790, Col. Jeremiah Gould and family, consisting of a wife, three sons, and a daughter, came to *"Salt Point,"* and found there Deacon and Nathaniel Loomis, Hezekiah Olcott, John Danforth, Asa Danforth, jr., and Thomas Gaston. In 1791 two families named Woodworth and Sturges came in, and March 2, 1792, Isaac Van Vleck and family. Among the other early settlers were Thomas Osmon, Simon Phares, Patrick Riley, Wm. Gilchrist, James Peat, Aaron Bellows, Elisha Alvord, Richard Sawyer, and Dioclesian Alvord. The first child born was Abraham Van Vleck, in 1792; the first marriage was that of Thomas Osmon and Katharine Van Derwricher, in 1795; and the first death, that of an infant child of —— Thompson, in 1794. Dr. Burnet, the first physician, died the same year. The provisions for the first settlers were brought from Tioga, by way of Cayuga Lake, and from Herkimer, by way of Oneida Lake. In 1793, 30 of the 33 inhabitants of the village were sick,—the 3 well ones, with the help of the Indians, taking care of the sick for 2 months. In 1794, out of a population of 63 persons 23 died. The first regular innkeeper was Wm. Gilchrist, about 1795; though Isaac Van Vleck had for several

[3] years previous entertained travelers. Elisha Alvord kept the first store, in 1795. In 1793 Mr. Van Vleck brought from Albany a large coffee mill, which was used for grinding corn.

[3] Among the other early settlers were Wm. Lee, Aaron Cole, Amos Stanton, Henry Bogardus, and Jonathan Fay. The first child born was Albion Jackson, Dec. 28, 1800. A tract of 250 acres, lying near the center of the city, and including a mill privilege upon Onondaga Creek, was sold by the State to Abraham Walton and became known as the "Walton Tract." It afterward passed into the hands of the "Syracuse Company." Mr. Bogardus erected a log house for an inn, on the site of the present Voorhees Block, in 1805; and Mr. Walton erected his "Old Red Mill" the same year. The first steamboat ever used upon the canal was built a mi. s. of Oran, and launched at "Buellville," in Pompey, in 1823, by Wm. Avery.

[4] Twenty-seven kegs of powder, secretly stored in a carpenter shop, exploded, and 25 men—principally firemen—were killed, and more than 60 others were wounded.

[5] Jerry was arrested as a fugitive slave and confined in the police office; but in the evening a large number of citizens assembled and forcibly took him from the custody of the officers. Several men were arrested and tried for participating in the rescue, but no convictions were ever procured.

Owen, who came into town in 1795.[1] The first church (Bap.) was formed in 1818;[2] Rev. Mr. Hurd was the first preacher.

VAN BUREN—was formed from Camillus, March 26, 1829. It is an interior town, lying N. W. of the center of the co. Its surface is level or gently undulating. Seneca River forms its N. boundary; along its course is considerable swamp land. The soil is a clayey, sandy, and gravelly loam. **Canton,** (Canal p. o.,) on the Erie Canal, in the S. W. corner of the town, contains a church and 188 inhabitants; **Van Buren Center,** (p. v.; Warners Station on the N. Y. C. R. R.,) near the S. line, a church and 16 dwellings. **Van Buren** (p. o.) and **Ionia** are hamlets. **Baldwinsville,** (p. v.,) on Seneca River, is on the line of Lysander. The first settler was Joseph Wilson, who located in town in 1792.[3] The first church (Presb.) was formed in 1803; Rev. S. B. Barns was the first preacher.[4]

Acres of Land, Valuation, Population, Dwellings, Families, Freeholders, Schools, Live Stock, Agricultural Products, and Domestic Manufactures, of Onondaga County.

Names of Towns.	Acres of Land.		Valuation of 1858.			Population.		No. of Dwellings.	No. of Families.	Freeholders.	Schools.	
	Improved.	Unimproved.	Real Estate.	Personal Property.	Total.	Males.	Females.				No. of Districts.	Children taught.
Camillus	16,411	3,574¼	$1,087,490	$125,850	$1,213,340	1,401	1,339	489	535	328	10	1,023
Cicero	14,376⅜	14,912⅞	628,523	42,200	670,723	1,780	1,608	642	689	529	15	1,305
Clay	19,535¼	10,681¾	964,205	37,850	1,002,055	1,762	1,564	638	576	511	21	1,536
De Witt	15,643⅞	6,294	786,362	41,100	827,462	1,562	1,423	575	599	422	14	1,089
Elbridge	16,792¼	4,638	1,035,328	163,300	1,198,628	2,273	2,288	803	884	445	16	1,625
Fabius	19,784¼	6,994½	531,310	52,900	584,210	1,128	1,128	442	438	375	18	872
Geddes	4,786	1,472¾	1,147,950	17,000	1,164,950	1,116	950	366	384	157	3	638
La Fayette	18,004	5,982	516.045	59,925	575,970	1,214	1,126	481	473	365	12	783
Lysander	27,069½	10,329	1,353,700	172,820	1,526,520	2,642	2,418	953	997	654	22	1,838
Manlius	21,640¼	7,546⅝	1,779,115	256,500	2,035,615	3,116	3,112	1,148	1,404	764	20	2,283
Marcellus	15,558¼	3,319¼	800,160	99,600	899,760	1,258	1,289	488	517	394	13	1,858
Onondaga	33,001¾	7,846½	1,796,890	223,050	2,019,940	2,793	2,607	978	901	856	28	1,990
Otisco	14,803¼	3,803	466,265	56,555	522,820	830	895	362	361	298	12	641
Pompey	32,420¼	8,286	1,171,650	100,500	1,272,150	1,867	1,903	729	584	538	25	1,463
Salina	6,559¾	2,219	802,575	32,900	835,475	1,377	1,203	417	497	274		
Skaneateles	20,935½	3,979	1,354,400	224,400	1,578,800	2,005	1,971	735	745	445	17	1,484
Spafford	15,643½	4,429½	406,200	75,350	481,550	894	922	335	369	271	9	659
Syracuse	1,992½	293½	6,381.356	1,765,463	8,146,819	12,611	12,496	3,691	4,881	2,716	16	9,334
Tully	12,269½	3,996	366,355	98,400	464,755	806	813	352	352	289	7	633
Van Buren	17,301	4,104	974,086	104,400	1,078,486	1,598	1,467	591	612	426	16	1,174
Total	344,528	114,701½	24,349,965	3,750,063	28,100,028	44,033	42,542	12,215	16,798	11,057	294	31,428

Names of Towns.	Live Stock.					Agricultural Products.							Domestic cloths, in Yards.
						Bush. of Grain.		Tons of Hay.	Bushels of Potatoes.	Bushels of Apples.	Dairy Products.		
	Horses.	Working Oxen and Calves.	Cows.	Sheep.	Swine.	Winter.	Spring.				Pounds of Butter.	Pounds of Cheese.	
Camillus	879	1,165	1,047	5,649	1,933	10,006½	152,062½	2,566	19,857	30,343	110,209	12,470	103
Cicero	901	1,274	1,324	2,253	1,552	1,919½	113,649	3,391	24,842	20,131	129,140	28,035	2,904½
Clay	1,177	1,683	1,363	4,292	1,992	4,908½	150,909	4,671½	34,011	27,578	120,907	11,535	3,317½
De Witt	831	1,168	1,170	3,686	1,532	3,547	104,537½	3,344	14,321	12,564	97,235	13,360	140
Elbridge	879	1,559	1,215	5,325	2,093	11,774	138,119¾	3,209	17,670	26,816	120,304	17,730	374
Fabius	735	1,273	2,637	2,972	924	1,239	72,940½	5,205	11,162	40,056	143,500	527,770	695
Geddes	629	201	904	863	1,116	1,358	38,099¼	969¼	10,834½	4,067	40,945	5,150	41
La Fayette	811	994	1,088	3,359	1,382	4,862	133,968	2,528¼	15,291	36,368	114,382	6,915	606
Lysander	1,430	2,750	1,949	7,494	3,312	14,769½	217,045⅓	5,573½	38,268	48,181	207,813	40,738	2,470½
Manlius	1,109	1,548	1,365	4,160	2,041	5,473¼	148,686½	3,423¾	17,975	25,176	130,077	9,890	584
Marcellus	780	1,117	990	7,079	1,214	4,907½	103,133½	2,736½	18,220	35,395	95,150	13,073	246
Onondaga	1,621	2,051	2,034	11,660	3,277	13,290¾	259,385½	5,677½	40.518	73,302½	223,343	23,139	1,363½
Otisco	648	998	899	5,064	1,122	2.271	84,675¾	1,855½	15,620	48,715	83,387	22.613	700
Pompey	1,427	2,041	1,894	9,338	2,029	2,976	223,288	5,238	25,457	39,417	194,815	43,680	464
Salina	333	394	427	1,557	674	1,062	44,288	1,559	15,550	4,021	44,732	400	94
Skaneateles	886	1,528	1,081	8,937	1,391	4,264	130,483	3,756	13,076	45,658	90,223	23,286	335½
Spafford	703	1,214	906	4,430	1,019	1,362½	100,371½	2,159¼	12,800	41,900	99,575	8,320	710
Syracuse	87	109	144	756	137	737	14,176	756	3,663	1,251	6,471		25
Tully	562	863	1,102	2,176	763	1,424¾	66,626	1,797	8,059	24,[illegible]5	108,654	30,900	323
Van Buren	902	1,497	1,262	3,152	2,036	10,246	159,522½	2,830⅜	22,947	39,141	133,425	21,640	83
Total	17,330	25,427	24,801	94,202	31,539	102,398¾	2,455,967¼	63,246⅜	380,141½	624,545½	2,294,287	860,644	15,579½

[1] Among the other early settlers were James Cravath, Wm. Trowbridge, Phineas Howell, Phineas Henderson, and Michael Christian. The first child born was Peter Henderson, in 1796; the first marriage was that of Timothy Walker and Esther Trowbridge; and the first death, that of Timothy Walker. Ruth Thorp taught the first school, in 1801; Nicholas Lewis kept the first inn, in 1802; Moses Nash the first store; and Peter Van Camp built the first grist and saw mill, in 1810.

[2] The census reports 5 churches; 2 Bap., 2 M.E., and Disciples.

[3] Among the other early settlers were Gabriel Tappan, David Haynes, John McHarrie, Reuben Smith, James Wells, Amos and Seth Warner, Eleazur Dunham, Benj. Bolton, Ira and Phineas Barnes, Jonathan Skinner, Isaac Earll, Wm. Lakin, and Charles F. Hall. The first child born was Elizabeth Haynes; the first marriage was that of James Wilson and Roby Tabor; and the first death, that of Mrs. Jonathan Tabor. Augustus Robinson taught the first school; Charles Tull kept the first inn and store; James Paddock built the first gristmill; and Nathan Skeels and Solomon Paddock built the first sawmill.

[4] The census reports 5 churches; 2 Bap., M. E., Christian, and R. C.

ONTARIO COUNTY.

This county was formed from Montgomery, Jan. 27, 1789. It was named from Lake Ontario, which originally formed its N. boundary. Steuben co. was taken off in 1796, Genesee in 1802, parts of Monroe and Livingston in 1821, and Yates and a part of Wayne in 1823. A strip was annexed from Montgomery co., w. of Seneca Lake, Feb. 16, 1791, and a small tract in the fork of Crooked Lake, from Steuben, Feb. 25, 1814. It is centrally distant 180. mi. from Albany, and contains an area of 640. sq. mi. It lies upon the extreme N. declivities of the central Alleghany Mt. Range, and has a northerly inclination, the summits of the s. hills being elevated about 1000 feet above the general level of the N. portions of the co. The s. portion, lying w. of Canandaigua Lake, is a hilly and broken region, divided into ridges with steep declivities and summits 1,500 to 1,700 feet above tide. The ridges all have a general N. and S. direction, declining toward the N., and terminating in a beautifully rolling region, which embraces all of the co. E. of Canandaigua Lake, and that portion lying w. of the lake and N. of the line of Bristol. The ridges in this section gradually rise to a height of 20 to 250 feet above the valleys, and give to the land sufficient inclination for thorough drainage. A terrace with declivities 100 to 250 feet high, descending toward the N., extends through the N. portions of East and West Bloomfield and the s. part of Victor, at right angles to the general range of the ridges. The extreme N. parts of the co. are occupied by drift ridges similar to those in Wayne and Seneca cos.

The geological formation of this co. is nearly the same as that of the cos. lying E. of it in the same latitude. The lowest rocks, occupying the N. parts of Phelps, Manchester, Farmington, and Victor, belong to the Onondaga salt group. The gypsum of this group crops out along the banks of the streams, and is extensively quarried along the Canandaigua Outlet, in Phelps and Manchester, and upon Mud Creek, in Victor. The water limestone, next above, crops out in Phelps, Manchester, and Victor, and is quarried for waterlime and building stone. The Onondaga and corniferous limestones next appear, and are quarried for building stone in Phelps. The Marcellus and Hamilton shales occupy all the central portions of the co. s. of the foot of Canandaigua Lake; and next above them successively appear the Tully limestone, Genesee slate, and the Portage group, the last occupying South Bristol, Canadice, and Naples. This last group furnishes a sandstone used for flagging and building. Except in the extreme s. parts of the co., the underlying rocks have little influence upon the soil, as nearly the whole surface is covered deeply with drift deposits, consisting of sand, clay, and gravel, intermixed with the disintegrated limestone and gypsum evidently deposited by some great torrent that once swept across the co. in a s. direction. The rocks are seen at some points along the banks of the lakes and the courses of the streams. In Bristol are several springs of carburetted hydrogen gas emanating from the strata of Genesee slate.[1]

The co. is drained by the Honeoye Outlet, a tributary of the Genesee River, and by the Canandaigua Outlet and Mud Creek, tributaries of the Clyde River. Honeoye Outlet receives as tributaries Egypt Brook and the outlets of Hemlock and Canadice Lakes;[2] Mud Creek receives Beaver, Fish, and Hog Hollow Creeks; and Canandaigua Outlet receives Fall and Flint Creeks. Besides these, Irondequoit Creek flows through the N. w. corner of the co. Keshong Creek and Burralls and Castle Brooks flow into Seneca Lake. Several of the beautiful lakes which form the most peculiar and interesting feature of the landscape for which Central New York is celebrated lie partly or wholly in this co. Seneca, forming a portion of the E. boundary, is described under Seneca co.[3] Canandaigua Lake lies almost wholly within the limits of the co. The shores are beautifully sloping down to the very edge of the water, except near the head of the lake, where they rise in steep bluffs to a height of 300 to 800 feet. Its surface is 668 feet above tide.

---

[1] The principal of these gas springs are in Bristol Hollow, on both banks of Canandaigua Lake, within 3 mi. of the village, and in East Bloomfield and Richmond. A sulphur spring is found on the outlet of the lake, but the principal one is at Clifton.

[2] Hemlock Outlet, called by the Indians O-neh′da, signifying hemlock.

[3] See p. 613.

Honeoye,[1] Canadice,[2] and Hemlock Lakes are smaller bodies of water, and are each surrounded by bluffs and hills rising to a height of 500 to 700 feet above them.

The soil for the most part consists of clayey, sandy, and gravelly loam, formed from the drift deposits. In the valleys and the rolling region which extends through the central and N. parts of the co. the loam is very deep and rich, forming one of the finest agricultural regions in the State. Upon the hills in the S. part of the co. the soil is made up principally of disintegrated shale and slate, forming a fine, fertile grazing region. Upon the drift hills in the W. are some small sections covered with a deep, light sand, moderately productive.

The geographical and geological features of this co. render it eminently adapted to the various branches of agriculture; and few cos. in the State excel this in the progress of scientific improvement as applied to agricultural operations. Wheat was for many years the staple crop; but of late more attention has been given to the production of the coarser grains, to stock growing, and the cultivation of fruits. Wool growing has also received considerable attention, and the fine Merino sheep were introduced at an early period. The manufactures are mainly of a domestic character, such as pertain to agricultural districts.

The county seat is located at Canandaigua, at the foot of Canandaigua Lake. A courthouse, jail, and co. clerk's office were erected here in 1793, soon after the organization of the co.[3] In 1825 a new courthouse was built; and in 1858 a splendid edifice was erected at the joint expense of the co. and of the U. S. Government, containing a U. S. and co. courtroom, jury and supervisors' rooms, U. S. district clerk's and co. clerk's offices, surrogate's office, and p. office. The building is of brick, with iron and tile floors, and is entirely fireproof. The poorhouse is located upon a farm of 212 acres in Hopewell, 4 mi. E. of Canandaigua. It is built of brick, and contains ample accommodations. The average number of inmates is 136, supported at a weekly cost of 57 cts. each. The farm yields a revenue of $4,000. A school is taught during the whole year.[4] The general management and sanitary arrangements of this establishment are creditable to the co.

The principal works of internal improvement in the co. are the Erie Canal, which enters the extreme N. E. corner of Manchester, the N. Y. C. R. R., extending through the N. and central portions of the co., the Canandaigua & Niagara Bridge R. R., a branch of the Central, extending W from Canandaigua to Tonawanda, and the Elmira, Jefferson & Canandaigua R. R., extending S. E. and connecting with the N. Y. & E. R. R. at Elmira. Besides these, there are several lines of plank road in the co.; but most of them have been abandoned.

Seven newspapers were published in the co. in 1855.[5]

---

[1] Indian name Ha'ne-a-yeh, lying like a finger.

[2] Indian name Ska'ne-a-dice, long lake.

[3] The first Circuit Court was held at the inn of Mr. Patterson, in Geneva, in June, 1793; and the first court of Common Pleas, at the house of Nathaniel Sanborn, in Canandaigua, in Nov. 1794. The first co. officers were Oliver Phelps, *First Judge;* Nathl. Gorham, *Co. Clerk;* John Cooper, *Surrogate;* and Judah Coit, *Sheriff.* The first justices of peace appointed in Western N. Y. were Asa Ransom and Wm. Rumsey, for Ontario co., in Dec. 1801. By an act passed April 3, 1798, deeds were required to be recorded in the clerk's office. This was many years before the general act for recording in clerks' offices.

[4] This school is supported by the interest of a fund given by a private individual for this purpose. The schoolhouse is situated in a fine yard and is surrounded by trees.

[5] *The Ontario Gazette and Genesee Advertiser,* the first paper in the present co. of Ontario, was started at Geneva, April, 1797, by Lucius Carey, and removed to Canandaigua in 1799.

The Impartial American, or Seneca Museum, was published at Geneva in 1800, by Ebenezer Eaton.

The Expositor was started at Geneva, Nov. 19, 1806, by James Bogert, who in 1809 changed it to

The Geneva Gazette, and continued it until Dec. 4, 1833. In 1827 it bore the title of *The Gazette and General Advertiser.* It was published by John Greves and J. C. Merrill until 1837; by J. Taylor Bradt until 1839; and by Stone & Frazer a short time longer, when it was discontinued. It was revived in Jan. 1845 by Ira and S. H. Parker. Geo. M. Horton was at one time interested in its publication, and it is now published by S. H. Parker.

The Geneva Palladium was commenced in 1816 by Young & Crosby, and was published successively by S. P. Hull, John T. Wilson, and —— Connely, until 1828, when it was discontinued.

The Geneva Chronicle was started in 1828 by —— Jackson, and continued 2 years.

The Independent American was published by T. C. Strong in 1831.

The Geneva American was published by Franklin Cowdery in 1830.

The Geneva Courier was established by John C. Merrill in 1830, and continued until 1833. Its publication was continued by Snow & Williams, Ira Merrill, Howlett & Van Valkenburgh, Cleveland & Hook, and Winthrop Atwell, successively, until Oct. 1854, when it passed into the hands of William Johnson, its present publisher. A daily paper was issued from this office about 6 months in 1845–46.

The Herald of Truth (Univ.) was started in 1834, at Geneva, by Prescott & Chase, and continued until 1837, when it was removed to Rochester.

The Geneva Democrat was published during the campaign of 1840, by Stone & Frazer.

The District School Journal, mo., was started at Geneva in 1840 by Francis Dwight, and removed to Albany in 1841.

The Geneva Advertiser and Mechanics' Advocate was started in 1841 by S. Merrill & Co., semi-w., and continued 1 year.

The Geneva Budget was commenced in 1852, by Sproul & Tanner, and continued 2 years.

The New York State Intelligencer was published in 1848.

The Ontario Whig, semi-w., was started at Geneva by Wm. C. Busted in 1850, and continued until 1852.

The Geneva Independent and Freeman's Gazette was established in 1851, by W. K. Fowle, and continued by him until 1855, and by H. G. Moore until June, 1857. Since then it has been published by W. K. Fowle as

The Geneva Ledger.

The Geneva Daily Union has been published since May 10, 1858, by W. K. Fowle.

The Ontario Gazette and Genesee Advertiser was brought from Geneva to Canandaigua in 1799, and published by Lucius Carey until 1802. John Keep Gould, who then became the publisher, changed its name to

The Western Repository and Genesee Advertiser; and in 1803 it was again changed to

The Western Repository, James D. Bemis became interested in its publication in 1804, and in 1808 he issued it as

The Ontario Repository, and continued it until 1828. It was published by Morse & Ward, Morse & Wilson, and Morse & Harvey, until 1835, and until 1840 by Chauncey Morse. The last named was succeeded by Geo. L. Whitney, who in Jan. 1856, sold it to H. G. Moore. The fol-

The territory lying within the limits of this co. was the chief seat of the Senecas, the most numerous and powerful tribe of the "Six Nations." Their chief village was at Kanadesaga, upon and just w. of the present site of Geneva, at the foot of Seneca Lake. In all the wars of the Iroquois League the Senecas bore a conspicuous part; and especially did they incur the bitter enmity of the French occupants of Canada. In 1687, De Nonville, Governor of *"New France,"* at the head of 1,600 French soldiers and 400 Indian allies, invaded the Seneca country by way of the St. Lawrence and Lake Ontario. At a defile near the site of the present village of Victor an engagement ensued, resulting in the defeat of the Indians, though with great loss to the French. De Nonville marched forward, burned the village of Gannagaro and several others, and returned.[1] In the succeeding year the Senecas and their allies in turn invaded the French settlements in Canada and took bloody revenge.[2]

In the progress of the wars that ensued, the Six Nations were sometimes neutral and sometimes allies of the English; but the country of the Senecas was never afterward invaded by the French. During the Revolution the Senecas espoused the English cause; and in 1779 Gen. Sullivan invaded their country from the s., burned their villages, destroyed their corn and orchards, and left the most beautiful region in the Indian domains a desolate waste. At the conclusion of peace, the force and spirit of the Indians were annihilated, and they quietly yielded to the gradual encroachments of the whites, until the last acre of their hunting grounds within the limits of this co., and the very graves of their fathers, passed out of their possession.[3]

---

lowing month the office was burned and the paper suspended. In May following it was revived as

The National New Yorker and Ontario Repository, by H. G. Moore and Dr. B. F. Tifft; and in May, 1857, it passed into the hands of Geo. L. Whitney & Son, by whom it is now published.

The Ontario Freeman was established at Canandaigua by Isaac Tiffany in 1803. In 1806 it passed into the hands of John A. Stevens, who changed its name to

The Ontario Messenger. It was successively published by Day & Morse, L. L. Morse, B. W. Jones, and T. B. Hohn. The latter was succeeded in Nov. 1845, by Jacob J. Mattison, the present publisher.

The Republican was started at Canandaigua by A. N. Phelps in 1824, and was afterward published a short time by T. M. Barnum.

The Ontario Phœnix was issued at Canandaigua in 1827 by W. W. Phelps. R. Royce became its publisher soon after, and changed its name to

The Freeman. In 1836 it was united with The Repository.

The Clay Club, a campaign paper, was published at Canandaigua in 1844.

The Seminarian, a literary mo., was published at Canandaigua in 1851.

The Ontario Co. Times was established Jan. 1, 1852, by N. J. Milliken, and in 1855 sold to Wilson Miller, who changed it to

The Ontario Times. In Feb. 1856, the establishment was burned and the paper suspended. It was re-established in May following by Mr. Milliken, and is still published by him as

The Ontario Republican Times.

The Vienna Republican was started at *"Vienna"* (now Phelps) in Jan. 1831, by C. H. Lowre and A. Kilmer. In 1832 it was published by J. O. Balch and in 1834 changed to *The Phelps Journal,* E. N. Phelps, publisher, and soon after to *The Phelps Journal and Vienna Advertiser;* in 1838 to *The Phelps Democrat;* and again in 1845 to *The Western Atlas.* From 1845 until 1856 it was published by Washington Shaw, Dillon & Phelps, and W. W. Redfield; and since then it has been continued as

The Ontario Free Press.

The Naples Free Press was established at Naples in 1832 by Waterman & Coleman, and continued 2 years.

The Neapolitan was started in 1840 by David Fairchild. In 1845 it was sold to ——— Phelps, who changed its title to *The Naples Visitor.* It was discontinued soon after.

The Naples Record was published at Naples in 1842.

The Village Record was published at Naples in 1842.

The Naples Journal was published in 1851 by R. Denton.

The Phelps New Democratic Star was started Sept. 3, 1858, by E. N. Phelps.

[1] The commander of the expedition claimed that he desolated the whole Seneca country; but one of his officers, (Le Honton,) in giving the history of the expedition, lays no claim to a complete victory; and the Indian traditions state that only a small detachment of the Senecas were engaged in the battle, and that the French retreated before the warriors could rally from the different villages.

[2] In this expedition 1000 French were killed and 26 prisoners taken, who were afterward burned at the stake.

[3] Numerous traces of ancient occupation—perhaps by a people that preceded the late Indian race—are found in this co. Trench enclosures have been noticed in Canandaigua, Seneca, and other towns.—*Squier's Aboriginal Monuments of N. Y.,* 4to ed., pp. 39, 61, 62. 63.

Seaver, in his *Life of Mary Jemison,* gives the following:—

"The tradition of the Seneca Indians in regard to their origin is that they broke out of the earth from a large mountain at the head of Canandaigua Lake; and that mountain they still venerate as the place of their birth. Thence they derive their name, 'Ge-nun-de-wah,' or 'Great Hill,' and are called 'The Great Hill People,' which is the true definition of the word Seneca. The great hill at the head of Canandaigua Lake, from whence they sprung, is called Genundewah, and has for a long time past been the place where the Indians of that nation have met in council, to hold great talks and to offer up prayers to the Great Spirit, on account of its having been their birthplace; and also in consequence of the destruction of a serpent at that place, in ancient time, in a most miraculous manner, which threatened the destruction of the whole of the Senecas and barely spared enough to commence replenishing the earth. The Indians say that the fort on the big hill, or Genundewah, near the head of Canandaigua Lake, was surrounded by a monstrous serpent, whose head and tail came together at the gate. A long time it lay there, confounding the people with its breath. At length they attempted to make their escape,—some with their hominy blocks, and others with different implements of household furniture,—and in marching out of the fort walked down the throat of the serpent. Two orphan children, who had escaped this general destruction by being left on this side of the fort, were informed by an oracle of the means by which they could get rid of their formidable enemy,—which was to take a small bow, and a poisoned arrow made of a kind of willow, and with that shoot the serpent under its scales. This they did, and the arrow proved effectual; for, on its penetrating the skin, the serpent became sick, and, extending itself, rolled down the hill, destroying all the timber that was in its way, disgorging itself and breaking wind greatly as it went. At every motion a human head was discharged and rolled down the hill into the lake, where they lie at this day in a petrified state, having the hardness and appearance of stones; and the pagan Indians of the Senecas believe that all the little snakes were made of the blood of the great serpent after it rolled into the lake. To this day the Indians visit that sacred place, to mourn the loss of their friends and to celebrate some rites that are peculiar to themselves. To the knowledge of white people, there has been no timber on the great hill since it was first discovered by them, though it lay apparently in a state of nature for a great number of years, without cultivation. Stones in the shape of Indians' heads may be seen lying in the lake in great plenty, which are said to be the same that were deposited there at the death of the serpent. The Senecas have a tradition that previous to and for some time after their origin at Genundewah the country, especially about the lakes, was thickly inhabited by a race of civil, enterprising, and industrious people, who were totally destroyed by the great serpent that afterward surrounded the great hill fort, with the assistance of others of the same species; and that they (the Senecas) went into possession of the improvements that were left. In those days the Indians throughout the whole country—as the Senecas say—spoke one language; but, having become considerably numerous, the before mentioned great serpent, by an unknown influence, confounded their language, so that they could not understand each other, which was the cause of their division into nations,—as the Mohawks, Oneidas, &c. At that time, however, the Senecas retained the original language, and continued to occupy their mother hill, on which they fortified themselves against their enemies and lived peaceably, until, having offended the serpent, they were cut off, as I have before remarked."

By the terms of the charter of the colony of Mass., the region between its N. and S. boundaries, from the Atlantic to the Pacific, was embraced; and the title to this territory was claimed by Mass. after the Revolution. The subsequent charter of the State of New York intervened and conflicted with this claim,—from which difficulties arose, which were finally settled by commissioners at Hartford, Conn., on the 16th of December, 1786. It was there agreed that Mass. should cede to N. Y. the sovereignty of all the territory claimed by the former lying within the limits of the latter, and that N. Y. should cede to Mass. the property of the soil, or the right of the pre-emption of the soil from the Indians. This agreement covered all that part of the State lying w. of a line running N. from the "82d milestone," on the line between N. Y. and Penn., through Seneca Lake to Sodus Bay. This line is known as the "Old Pre-emption Line."[1] In 1787 Mass. sold the whole of this tract, containing 6,000,000 of acres, to Oliver Phelps and Nathaniel Gorham, for one million dollars. In the following spring Mr. Phelps left his home in Granville, Mass., with men and means to explore the country thus acquired. He collected the sachems, chiefs, and warriors of the Six Nations at Kanadesaga, and in July, 1788, concluded with them a treaty of purchase of a tract containing 2,250,000 acres, bounded E. by the pre-emption line, w. by a line 12 mi. w. of, and running parallel with, the Genesee River, s. by the Penn. line, and N. by Lake Ontario.[2]

The portion of the tract to which the Indian title had not been extinguished, constituting about two-thirds of the original purchase, was abandoned by Messrs. Phelps and Gorham and reverted to Mass. It was re-sold by that State to Robert Morris, in 1796, and subsequently formed what is known as the Holland Land Purchase. In 1789, Mr. Phelps, at Canandaigua, opened the first regular land office for the sale of land to settlers ever established in America. The system he adopted for the survey of his lands by townships and ranges, with slight modifications, was adopted by the Government for the survey of all the new lands in the U. S. When organized in 1789, Ontario was the first co. set off from Montgomery, and embraced all that part of the State lying w. of the E. line of Phelps and Gorhams Purchase, including what was called "The Genesee Country."

The first settlement was made on the site of the Indian village of Kanadesaga, (now Geneva,) in 1787. Soon after the land office at Canandaigua was opened, and several settlements were commenced in different parts of the co. From this period the progress of settlement was rapid, immigrants being attracted by the beautifully rolling character of the surface and the unsurpassed fertility of the soil. Few incidents of general interest have occurred to interrupt the steady and continued progress of peaceful industry. The most notable of its later historical events is its being the scene of the birth of Mormonism. Joe Smith resided for many years in Manchester; and his pretended discovery of the golden plates of the Book of Mormon was made on the 22d of September,

<hr/>

[1] The history of this Pre-emption Line is interesting. Of course, it was mere conjecture where the line would fall as far N. as Seneca Lake, and parties were interested to have the line fall w. of Geneva, leaving that space and a considerable tract of land between the Military Tract and the Mass. lands. Seth Reed and Peter Ryckman, both of whom had been Indian traders, applied to the State of New York for a remuneration for services rendered in some previous negotiations with the eastern portion of the Six Nations, and proposed to take a patent for a tract the boundaries of which should begin at a tree on the bank of the Seneca Lake and run along the bank of the lake to the S. until they should have 16,000 acres between the lake and the E. bounds of the land ceded to Massachusetts. Their request was acceded to and a patent issued. Thus situated, they proposed to Messrs. Phelps and Gorham to join them in running the Pre-emption Line, each party furnishing a surveyor. The line was run which is known as the "Old Pre-emption Line." Messrs. Phelps and Gorham were much disappointed in the result,—suspected error or fraud, but made no movement for a re-survey before they had sold to the English Association. Their suspicions had at first been excited by an offer from a prominent member of the Lessee Company for "all the lands they owned east of the line that had been run." They were so well assured of the fact that in their deed to Mr. Morris they specified a tract in a gore between the line then run and the w. bounds of the counties of Montgomery and Tioga, those counties then embracing all of the Military Tract. Being fully convinced of the inaccuracy of the first survey, Morris, in his sale to the English Company, agreed to run it anew. The new survey was performed under the superintendence of Maj. Hoops, who employed Andrew Ellicott and Augustus Porter to perform the labor. A corps of ax-men were employed, and a vista 30 feet wide opened before the transit instrument until the line had reached the head of Seneca Lake, when night signals were employed to run down and over the lake. So much pains were taken to insure correctness that the survey was never disputed; and thus the "New Pre-emption Line" was established as the true division line between the lands of the State of New York and those that had been ceded to Massachusetts. In examining the old survey,

Major Hoops had discovered the precise points of deviation to the westward. It had commenced soon after leaving the Pennsylvania line, gradually bearing off until it crossed the outlet of the Crooked Lake, where an abrupt offset was made, and then an inclination for a few miles almost in a N. W. course; then, as if fearful that it was running w. farther than was necessary to secure a given object, the line was made to incline to the E. until it passed the foot of Seneca Lake, when it was run nearly N. and S. to Lake Ontario. All this will be observed upon any of the old maps. It will at once be perceived that the site of Geneva—the 16,000 acres of Reed and Ryckman—had caused more than a usual variation of the surveyor's compass. Judge Porter's explanation is as follows:—"Geneva was then a small settlement, beautifully situated on the Seneca Lake, rendered quite attractive by its lying beside an old Indian settlement in which there was an orchard."

The Old Pre-emption Line terminated on Lake Ontario, 3 mi. w. of Sodus Bay, and the new line very nearly the center of the head of the bay. With the exception of the abrupt variations that have been noticed, the old line. parting from the true meridian about 5 mi. S. of the Chemung River, bears off gradually until it reaches the shore of Lake Ontario. The strip of land between the two lines was called "The Gore." In addition to the patent granted to Reed and Ryckman, the State had presumed the original survey to be correct, and made other grants, and allowed the location of military land warrants upon what had been made disputed territory. As an equivalent to the purchasers of this tract, compensation lands were granted by the State in the present towns of Wolcott and Galen, Wayne co.

[2] The w. boundary of this tract was a line "beginning in the northern line of Penn., due south of the corner or point of land made by the confluence of the Genesee River and the Canaseraga Creek; thence north on said meridian line to the corner or point, at the confluence aforesaid; thence northwardly along the waters of the Genesee River to a point two miles north of Canawagus Village; thence running due west twelve miles; thence running northwardly, so as to be twelve miles distant from the western bounds of said river, to the shore of Lake Ontario."—*Turner's Phelps and Gorham Purchase.*

1827. Brigham Young was also a long time a resident of Canandaigua; and the first Mormon society was formed at Fayette, in the adjoining co. of Seneca, in 1830.

BRISTOL[1]—was formed in Jan. 1789. South Bristol was taken off in 1838, and a part was annexed to Richmond, March 23, 1848, and restored Feb. 25, 1852. It is an interior town, lying s. w. of the center of the co. Its surface consists of a series of ridges, gradually declining to the N. The highest points are about 500 feet above the valleys. These ridges are divided by the deep valleys of Mud Creek and Egypt Brook. The declivities that border upon these streams in the s. part are usually very steep. The soil is a rich alluvial upon the intervales and disintegrated slate and shale among the hills. **Bristol Center** (p. v.) contains 30 houses; **Baptist Hill**[2] (Bristol p. o.) 25; and **Muttonville**[3] 15. **Egypt** is a hamlet in the s. E. part. Gamaliel Wilder and Joseph Gilbert settled in 1788, at what was called the "*Old Indian Orchard.*"[4] The first religious services were performed by Rev. Zadock Hunn, in 1793. There are now 4 churches in town.[5]

CANADICE[6]—was formed from Richmond, April 15, 1829, and a part was annexed to Richmond in 1836. It is the s. w. corner town of the co. Its surface consists of a high, broken upland separated into two ridges by Canadice Lake. The w. ridge, known as Bald Hill, is bordered by steep declivities, and the E. by more gradual slopes. The highest summits are about 700 feet above Honeoye Lake. The principal streams are the Canadice Inlet and Outlet and the Honeoye Inlet. The soil in the valleys is a clayey loam; upon the declivities of the hills it is mostly disintegrated shale and slate, and upon the summits in the s. part it consists of gravelly loam and black muck. **Canadice Corners** (p.o.) is a hamlet, forming the business center of the town. The first settlement was made by —— Kimball, in 1807.[7] There are now 3 churches in town.[8]

CANANDAIGUA[9]—was formed Jan. 27, 1789, and a part annexed to Gorham, March 16, 1824. It is the central town of the co., lying upon the w. and N. shores of Canandaigua Lake. The surface is hilly in the s., but level or gently rolling in the N. The highest summits are about 600 feet above the lake. Canandaigua Outlet, Beaver Creek, and Stevens Brook are the principal streams. The soil is a clayey loam in the N. and a deep, gravelly loam in the s., and in fertility this town ranks among the first in the State. **Canandaigua**, (p. v.,) situated at the outlet of Canandaigua Lake, is an important station on the N. Y. C. R. R., and a terminus of the N. F. & C. Branch and of the E. J. & C. R. R. A daily steamer connects it with Naples, at the head of the lake. It contains the co. buildings,[10] a State Arsenal,[11] 5 churches, an academy,[12] a female seminary,[13] a private lunatic asylum,[14] 3 newspaper offices, and a bank. It was incorp. April 18, 1815, and has a pop. of 4,154.[15] **Cheshire,** (p.v.,) in the s. part, contains 20 dwellings. **Centerfield** (p.o.) is a hamlet, and **Academy,** near the s. line, is a p.o. Wm. Morgan, of masonic notoriety, was imprisoned at Canandaigua previous to his disappearance.[16] Settlement was commenced in 1788, by Phelps and Gorham and their associates, and considerable accessions were made in 1789 and '90.[17] The first religious service at Canandaigua, was held in 1789, by

---

1 Named from Bristol co., Mass., from which the first settlers came.

2 So named because a Baptist church was erected there at an early date.

3 Derives its name from the establishment of a tallow chandlery there some years since. 30,000 sheep have been slaughtered there in a year.

4 William Gooding and George Codding settled in 1789, James, Elnathan, and George Gooding in 1790, and Alden Sears and John, George, Farmer, Burt, and William Codding in 1792. The first store and tavern were opened by Stephen Sisson, in 1793; Gamal. Wilder built the first gristmill, in 1790. Thomas Hunn taught the first school, in 1790. Cornelius McCrum was the first child born.

5 Bap., Cong., M. E., and Univ.

6 This name is a corruption of the Indian name of Canadice Lake.

7 Soon after, John Wilson settled at the head of Canadice Lake, and John Richardson, John Wheeler, Samuel Spencer, and And. Ward near Canadice Corners. The first tavern was kept by Llewelyn Davis; and Severance & Ford opened the first store. The first sawmill was built at the head of Canadice Lake, by John Algur.

8 M. E., Meth. Prot., and Wes. Meth.

9 This name was derived from Gan-a-dar-que, a village built by the Seneca Indians on the present site of the village of Canandaigua. It signifies a chosen spot.

10 In one of the courtrooms is a collection of portraits of the prominent first settlers and residents of the co.: viz., of Oliver Phelps, Gen. Peter B. Porter, Augustus Porter, Philip Church, Wm. Wadsworth, James Wadsworth, Abner Barlow, Moses Atwater, Micah Brooks, Vincent Mathews, Walter Hubbell, John C. Spencer, John Greig, Nathl. Rochester, Jos. Parish, Red Jacket, Judge Fitzhugh, Ambrose Spencer, Wm. Williams, M.D., N. W. Howell, Wm. Wood, Stephen A. Douglas, Danl. Barnard, and H. Welles. Among other distinguished residents of Canandaigua were Hon. Gideon Granger, P. M. Gen. under Jefferson's administration, his son, Francis Granger, P. M. Gen. under Harrison's administration, the late Hon. M. H. Sibley, and Hon. J. R. Giddings.

11 This arsenal was authorized before the war, and 1,000 stand of arms were ordered to be deposited there, Feb. 12, 1808.

12 This academy was founded in 1795, by Gorham and Phelps. It is in a prosperous condition.

13 The Ontario Female Seminary was founded in 1825. Its buildings are commodious, and pleasantly situated upon grounds containing 7 acres. The number of students in 1857 was 311.

14 Brigham Hall, incorp. in 1859, is about 1 mi. s. w. of the courthouse. The grounds consist of 70 acres, and the buildings, with accommodations for 80 patients, are located in a beautiful grove of 16 acres.

15 The co. Agricultural Society has a lot containing 10 acres within the village limits, with suitable buildings. 16 See p. 323.

17 Among the settlers in 1789 were Joseph Smith, Israel Chapin, Nathaniel Gorham, jr., Frederick Saxton, Benjamin Gardner, Daniel Gates, Daniel Brainard, Martin Dudley, and James D. Fish. The first birth was that of Oliver Phelps Rice; and the first death, that of Caleb Walker, both in 1790. Samuel Gardner opened the first store; and the first school was taught

Rev. John Smith. The first church (St. Matthew's, Epis., now St. John's) was organized Feb. 4, 1799; the Cong. church was formed Feb. 25, 1799. The census reports 10 churches in town.[1]

EAST BLOOMFIELD—was formed Jan. 27, 1789, as "*Bloomfield*." Mendon and Victor were taken off in 1812; its name was changed and West Bloomfield was taken off in 1833. It is an interior town, lying N. w. of the center of the co. Its surface is rolling, with a gentle inclination toward the N. The ridges are 50 to 600 feet above the valleys. The principal streams are the Mud, Fish, and Hog Hollow Creeks. The soil is a deep, fertile, gravelly loam, in places mixed with clay. **Griffiths Mills** in the E. and **Brag Village** in the S. E. part are hamlets. **East Bloomfield**, (p. v.,) ¾ of a mi. from East Bloomfield Station, on the N. Y. Central R. R., contains 3 churches, an academy,[2] manufactories of agricultural implements and carriages. Pop. 590. This township having been purchased of Phelps and Gorham by a company from Berkshire co., Mass., its settlement was commenced in the spring of 1789.[3] There are 4 churches in town;[4] the first (Cong.) was formed Sept. 8, and organized Nov. 15, 1795, by Rev. Zadock Hunn. The first church edifice in all Western N. Y. was erected in this town in 1801.

FARMINGTON[5]—was formed Jan. 27, 1789. It lies on the N. border of the co., w. of the center. Its surface is nearly level in the S., but in the N. it is broken by the drift ridges peculiar to this section of country, rising to a height of 50 to 100 feet above the general surface. The declivities of these ridges toward the N., E., and w. are generally steep, but toward the S. they become gradual slopes. The streams are Mud and Beaver Creeks and Black Brook. A strip of land across the S. part, embracing about 3 tiers of lots, has a clay soil. North of this is a marshy region; and farther N. the soil is a gravelly loam and very productive, with good proportions of arable, meadow, and grazing lands throughout the town. **New Salem**, (Farmington p. o.,) a village in the N. part, contains 206 inhabitants. **Brownville** (Nortons Mills p. o.) is a hamlet. **East Farmington** and **West Farmington** are p. offices. The settlement was commenced in 1789, by Friends from Berkshire, Mass., among whom were Nathan Comstock, his sons Otis and Darius, and Robert Hathaway.[6] The first house of worship was erected by the Friends, in 1804. There are now 2 churches in town; Friends and Wes. Meth.

GORHAM[7]—was formed Jan. 27, 1789, as "*Easton*." Its name was changed to "*Lincoln*," April 17, 1806, and to Gorham, April 6, 1807. Hopewell was taken off in 1822. A part of Canandaigua was annexed in 1824. It lies upon the E. shore of Canandaigua Lake, S. E. of the center of the co. Its surface is rolling, the ridges rising in gradual slopes to a height of 25 to 200 feet above the valleys. Flint Creek is the principal stream. The soil in the E. part is principally a gravelly loam, and in the w. it consists of clay, and is generally fertile and productive. **Gorham**,[8] (p. v.,) 3 mi. from the Gorham Station, on the C. & E. R. R., contains 3 churches and 310 inhabitants. **Reeds Corners** (p. v.) contains 3 churches and about 20 houses. The first settlement was made at Reeds Corners, in 1789, by James Wood.[9] There are now 6 churches in town.[10]

HOPEWELL—was formed from Gorham, March 29, 1822. It is an interior town, lying E. of the center of the co. The surface is level or gently undulating, with a northerly inclination. Canandaigua Outlet, Fall Creek, and Fall Brook are its principal streams. The soil is a sandy and gravelly loam in the w., and the same mixed with clay in the center and E. It is very fertile and highly cultivated. **Chapinville**, (p. v.,) a station on the N. Y. C. R. R., contains a church and about 30 dwellings; **Hopewell Center** (p. v.) contains 1 church and 16 dwellings.

---

by Major Wallis, in 1792. There were in that year 30 families in town. The Legislature granted, March 31, 1804, to Levi Stephens and Jason Parker the sole right of running stages from Utica to this place for a term of 7 years. The trip was to be performed twice a week, from June to October, within 48 hours, and at the rate of 4 cts. a mi. if with 6 or more passengers. A similar monopoly was granted, April 6, 1807, for 7 years, to John Metcalf, between this place and Buffalo.

[1] The census reports 2 Bap., 2 Prot. E., 2 M. E., Cong., Free Will Bap., Christian, and R. C.

[2] Incorp. April 9, 1838. The average number of students is 100.

[3] Deacon John Adams and his sons, John, William, Abner, Jonathan, and Joseph, his sons-in-law, Ephraim Rue and Loren Hull, and Elijah Rose, Moses Gunn, Lot Rue, John Barnes, Roger Sprague, and Asa Hickox moved in with their families in 1789. The first death was that of Lot Rue, in 1793; the first marriage—and the first upon the Phelps and Gorham Purchase—was that of Benj. Goss and a daughter of George Codding. The first sawmill was erected on Mud Creek, in 1790, by Gen. Fellows; and the first store was opened in 1806, by Norton & Beach. Laura Adams taught the first school, in 1794.

[4] Cong., M. E., Prot. E., and R. C.

[5] Named from Farmington, Conn. It was formed by the Court of General Sessions.

[6] Early in 1790, Nathan Aldrich, Isaac Hathaway, Nathan Herendun, Welcome Herendun, John McCumber, and Joshua Herington, from the same place, joined the infant settlement, and were followed by 18 others the same year. Jacob and Joseph Smith built a gristmill in 1793, and the first sawmill in 1795. The first birth was that of Welcome Herendun, in 1790; the first marriage, that of Otis Comstock and Huldah Freeman, in 1792; and the first death, that of Elijah Smith, in 1793.

[7] Named in honor of Nathaniel Gorham.

[8] Formerly called "*Bethel*."

[9] Parley Gates, from Mass., settled on Lot 49 in 1796; and soon after, Oliver Howard and Henry Greene, from Oneida co., N. Y., and Samuel and Silas Reed, Elijah Hurd, and others, came in. The first tavern was kept by William Sherwood, at Reeds Corners, in 1800; the first gristmill was built by Levi Benton; and the first sawmill, by Buckley & Craft, in 1807. Timothy Moore taught the first school, in 1802.

[10] 2 Bap., Cong., Prot. E., Presb., and M. E.

Ontario Female Seminary, Canandaigua, N.Y.

B. RICHARDS A.M PRINCIPAL.

Organized 1825. Course of Study Collegiate.—Religious, Intellectual, Physical, Social and Ornamental.

Hopewell is a p. o. Settlements were made in 1789–90.[1] There are 5 churches in town;[2] the first church (Presb.) was formed in 1808.

MANCHESTER—was formed from Farmington, March 31, 1821, as "*Burt,*" and its name was changed April 16, 1822. It lies upon the N. border of the co., E. of the center. Its surface is nearly level in the s., but is occupied by irregular sand and gravel ridges of the drift formation in the N. Canandaigua Outlet, Fall Creek, and Black Brook are the principal streams. The soil is a gravelly loam and is very productive. Hydraulic limestone is quarried on "the Outlet." There are 3 flouring mills in town. **Clifton Springs,** (p. v.,) incorporated in 1859, a station on the N. Y. C. R. R., is situated in the E. part of the town. Pop. 340. At this place are the celebrated Clifton Mineral Springs and an extensive water cure establishment.[3] **Manchester** (p. v.) contains 374 inhabitants; **Shortsville** (p. v.) contains 35 dwellings and a large distillery; and **Port Gibson,** (p. v.,) on the Erie Canal, 50 dwellings; **Manchester Center** (p. v.) contains 18 dwellings. **Plainsville** (Gypsum p. o.) contains 12 houses. **Coonsville** contains a flouring mill, plaster mill, and 12 houses. The first settlement was made in 1793, by Stephen Jared, Joel Phelps, and Joab Gillett.[4] Rev. David Irish preached in Manchester in Jan. 1797, and in Feb. following a Bap. society was organized. There are now 8 churches in town.[5] Joe Smith, the Mormon prophet, resided in this town with his father; and Mormon Hill, the place where the gold Bible was found, is situated a little N. w. of the center of the town.[6]

NAPLES[7]—was formed Jan. 27, 1789, as "*Middletown.*" The name was changed April 6, 1808. Italy was taken off in 1815, and a part of Springwater in 1816. It is the extreme s. town of the co. The surface consists of a hilly and elevated upland, broken by the narrow and deep valleys of Canandaigua and Honeoye Inlets and Grindstone Creek. The summits of the hills are 600 to 1000 feet above the surface of the lake and 1300 to 1700 feet above tide. Their declivities bordering on the streams are generally very steep. High Point and Hatch Hill are the highest summits. The soil upon the hills consists of clay and gravel mixed with disintegrated slate and shale; and in the valleys it is a rich, gravelly loam mixed with alluvium. Fruit growing is receiving much attention. Peaches are produced in great abundance; and an experiment is being made in the cultivation of grapes, which promises to be successful. Over 30 acres are now devoted to this object, and very satisfactory results have been realized. **Naples,** (p. v.,) on the Canandaigua Inlet, 4 mi. from the lake, contains 5 churches and 3 flouring mills. Pop. 700. The first settlement was commenced in 1790, by a company from Berkshire co., Mass., by whom the town was purchased from Phelps and Gorham.[8] The first sermon was preached by Rev. Zadock Hunn, in June, 1792.[9]

PHELPS[10]—was formed in 1796, under the act of Jan. 27, 1789. A part was annexed to Lyons, (Wayne co.,) April 11, 1823. It is the N. E. corner town of the co. Its surface is rolling, the ridges rising in gentle slopes 20 to 100 feet above the valleys. The highest point is 300 feet above Canandaigua Lake. The soil in the E. is a sandy loam with a clay subsoil, in the N. a mixed sandy and clayey loam, and in the w. a sandy and coarse gravelly loam, all highly productive. Canandaigua Outlet, the principal stream, flows E. and N. through the center. Along its course are extensive quarries of gypsum and water limestone. In the town are quarries of Onon-

---

[1] Among the first settlers were Daniel Gates, Daniel Warner, —— Sweet, Ezra Platt, Samuel Day, George and Israel Chapin, jr., Frederick Follett, Benj. Wells, and Thomas Sawyer, mostly from Mass., and William Wyckoff, from Penn. The first child—Benj. Wells, jr.—was born Feb. 4, 1791. Calvin Bacon taught the first school, in 1792. The first tavern was kept by Ezra Platt; and the first mill was built by Oliver Phelps and Israel Chapin, in 1789.

[2] 3 M. E., Wes. Meth., and Presb.

[3] A hotel was erected in 1806, as a dispensary; and the water cure was established in 1850, by a company organized for that purpose, with a capital of $45,000. It has accommodations for 150 patients, and is largely patronized. The water of the spring was analyzed in 1852, by Dr. Chilton, of N. Y., with the following result in grains to 1 quart:—

	grs.
Sulphate of lime	17.30
" " magnesia	4.12
" " soda	1.94
Carbonate of lime	2.42
" " magnesia	3.28
Chloride of sodium	2.32
" " calcium	1.02
" " magnesia	1.02
Organic matter	trace.
Total	33.42

Hydrosulphuric and carbonic acids are also found in small quantities.

[4] Nathan Pierce and John McLouth, from Berkshire, Mass., settled in the town in 1795; and John Van Fleet, Jedediah Dewey, Benjamin Barney, William Mitchell, and Peleg Redfield soon after. Sharon Boothe and a daughter of Joab Gillett were married in 1793. Theophilus Short erected the first mill, at Shortsville, in 1804; and the first store was opened by Nathan Burton. Elam Crane taught the first school, in 1800.

[5] 2 Bap., 3 M. E., 2 Prot. Meth., and a Univ.

[6] See p. 494.

[7] Originally called "*Watkinstown,*" from Wm. Watkins, of Berkshire, Mass., one of the purchasers under Phelps and Gorham, and called by the Indians Nun'da-wa-o, great hill.

[8] In Feb. 1790, Samuel, Reuben, and Levi Parish, with their families, came in; and in April following, Nathan and Wm. Watkins, John Johnson, Jonathan Lee, and William Clark, with their families, 30 persons in all. The first birth was that of Phineas P. Lee; and the first marriage, that of Benj. Clark and Thankful Watkins, in 1795. The first sawmill was erected in 1792, by Benj. Clark and Jabez Metcalf. Susannah Parish taught the first school, in 1792. Myron H. Clark, late Governor of the State, was born in this town, Oct. 23, 1806.

[9] There are 5 churches in town; Bap., M. E., Presb., Wes. Meth., and Christian.

[10] Named from Oliver Phelps, one of the original proprietors of the town.

daga and corniferous limestone. **Phelps**,[1] (p. v.,) on Flint Creek, near its junction with the Canandaigua Outlet, was incorp. Jan. 2, 1855. It contains a union school, newspaper office, and 6 churches. Pop. 1,278. **Orleans** (p. v.) is situated on Flint Creek. Pop. 218. **Oaks Corners** (p. o.) contains 15 houses.[2] J. D. Robinson, from Claverack, Columbia co., settled at Phelps in 1789.[3] Rev. S. Goodale was the first resident preacher; he held services in schoolhouses and dwellings before any church edifice was erected. The first church (Presb.) was built in 1804.[4]

RICHMOND—was formed in 1796, under the act of Jan. 27, 1789, as "*Pittstown*." Its name was changed to "*Honeoye*" April 6, 1808, and to Richmond April 11, 1815. A part of Canadice was annexed April 30, 1836, and parts of Bristol and South Bristol in 1848; but the latter were restored in 1852. It lies upon the w. border of the co., s. of the center. It consists of a nearly square portion of land lying near the foot of Honeoye Lake, and a narrow strip extending along the E. shore of that lake and its inlet to the s. border of the co.[5] A wide valley occupies the center, opening toward the N., and surrounded by hills from 50 to 200 feet high on the 3 remaining sides. The southern strip is very hilly, the summits rising 500 feet above the surface of the lake. Honeoye and Hemlock Outlets and Egypt Brook are the principal streams. The soil upon the lowlands is clay, upon the hills a sandy loam mixed with clay. Much attention is given to improving the breeds of cattle and sheep; and it is the largest wool growing town in the co., and second in the State. **Honeoye**, (p. v.,) at the foot of Honeoye Lake, is the business center of the town. Pop. 244. **Richmond Mills** (p. o.) and **Allens Hill**[6] (p. o.) are hamlets. This town was purchased of Phelps and Gorham by a company; and the first settlement was made by Capt. Peter Pitts and his sons William and Gideon, in 1789.[7] There are 5 churches in town.[8]

SENECA—was formed in 1793, under the act of Jan. 27, 1789. It is the s. E. corner town of the co., lying upon the w. shore of Seneca Lake. The surface is beautifully rolling, the ridges rising 20 to 200 feet above the valleys. The shores of the lake are bluffs about 100 feet above the surface of the water. The streams are Flint and Keshong Creeks and Burralls and Castle Brooks. The soil is a deep, rich loam, consisting of sand, gravel, and clay mixed together, the gravel predominating upon the ridges. The soil is admirably adapted to the production of fruit trees, and the business of the nursery has become one of the leading pursuits in the town. Two large nursery establishments are located within the limits of the village of Geneva. Commerce and manufactures receive considerable attention. **Geneva**,[9] (p. v.,) incorp. April 4, 1806, is beautifully situated at the foot of Seneca Lake. It contains a flourishing union school,[10] a large private boarding school,[11] 3 newspaper offices, and 9 churches. It is also the seat of Hobart Free College.[12] The Geneva Water Cure and Hygienic Institute is finely situated near the center of the village. A daily line of steamers connects this place with the upper ports upon Seneca Lake. Pop. 5,057. **Castleton**, (Seneca Castle p. o.,) on Flint Creek, in the N. w. part, contains 2 churches and 35 dwellings. **Flint Creek**, (p. o.,) **Halls Corners**, (p. o.,) and **Stanleys**

---

[1] Formerly called "*Vienna*."

[2] The culture of raspberries has recently been introduced in this vicinity, and promises to be successful.

[3] N. Sanborn, —— Gould, —— Pierce, Philetus Swift, and lihu Granger, from Conn., settled in town in 1789; Thaddeus Oaks, Seth Dean, Oliver and Charles Humphrey, John Salisbury, Nicholas Pullen, Walter Chase, and Elias Dickinson in 1791; John Patten and David Boyd in 1792; Jonathan Melvin in 1793; and John Sherman, Joseph and Lodowick Vandemark, and John and Patrick Burnett in 1794. Henry H. Robinson was the first child born in town; and the first marriage was that of Philetus Swift and Sally Dean, in 1793. Thaddeus Oaks opened the first tavern, in 1793; and the first saw and grist mills were built by Seth Dean.

[4] There are 10 churches in town; 4 Bap., 3 Presb., 2 M. E., and a Prot. Epis.

[5] This strip was added to the town in consequence of its position, high mountain ridges separating it from the business centers of both Canadice and South Bristol.

[6] Named in honor of Nathaniel Allen. Mr. Allen was among the first settlers, and established the first blacksmith's shop at Allens Hill. Subsequently he was sheriff of Ontario co.; in 1812 he was a member of the Assembly; during the War of 1812 he was army paymaster; and in 1819 he was elected member of Congress from the 21st district.

[7] In 1795, Lemuel and Cyrus Chipman, Philip Reed, Levi Blackmer, Nathaniel Harmon, Pierce Chamberlain, Asa Denison, and Isaac Adams, from Vermont, settled in town. Capt. Pitts opened the first tavern; and the first saw and grist mills were built by Thomas Morris, in 1795. Upon the division of the lands, Capt. Pitts secured 3,000 acres at the foot of Honeoye Lake, embracing the flats and a cleared field which had been the site of an Indian village destroyed by Sullivan's army. Louis Philippe, during his travels in this country, spent a night in the log house of Capt. Pitts; and subsequently the

Duke de Liancourt and suite went from Canandaigua to make him a visit.

[8] 2 Cong., Prot. Epis., Prot. Meth., and Wes. Meth.

[9] This village is justly celebrated for the beauty of its situation; and perhaps no village in the co. in this respect has been so generally and enthusiastically praised by tourists. For many years it was one of the leading business places in Central N. Y ; but the completion of the R. R. lines has turned a large share of the business into other channels.

[10] This union school was one of the first established in the State, and for a long time was taken as a model in establishing others. It early contained an academic department that enjoyed an excellent reputation. The schools of the village are now graded, and embrace a complete common school and academic course.

[11] The Walnut Hill Seminary, for boys, is a flourishing institution of its kind. For particulars see p. 741.

[12] Formerly Geneva College. It was incorp. in 1825, and was established mainly through the influence of Bishop Hobart, whose name it bears. A medical department was organized in 1836. The trustees and members of the College Faculty are generally members of the Prot. Epis. church. From the beginning, however, the college has been equally open to all; and it is now *free to all*, no charge being made for tuition and room rent. It has now two large buildings for the use of students— one for libraries and lecture rooms, one for a chapel—and a spacious building for the use of the medical department. The college has a president, 4 professors, an assistant professor, and a resident fellow, who takes part in the business of instruction; and the medical department has a Faculty of 6 professors. In 1859 the number of students in the free classes was 85. The aggregate value of the college property is about $160,000. The college buildings are beautifully situated in the s. part of the village, on a bluff which overlooks Seneca Lake. The college grounds contain above 12 acres. In 1858 the whole number of graduates in arts was 246 and in medicine 520.

Corners[1] (p. o.) are hamlets. The first settlement was commenced in 1787, upon the site of the Indian village of Kanadesaga, by immigrants from New England.[2] This village was situated at the foot of Seneca Lake, where Geneva now is; and for several years after Geneva had become a place of considerable importance it was called "*Kanadesaga.*" An ancient fortification, known as Fort Hill, is located on lot 58. It was covered with large forest trees upon the first settlement of the town. Another beautiful ground, called the "Old Castle," is about 1½ mi. N. w. of Geneva. It is covered by an Indian orchard, and the ground has never been plowed, because of a stipulation to that effect made with the Indians in the treaty of purchase.[3] It contains an Indian burial ground; and in one corner may be traced a trench of an ancient stockaded fortification. Here was the largest Indian settlement in Western New York, and it is still a place of much interest to the few remaining descendants of the once powerful Five Nations. Many relics—as stone hatchets, arrow heads, pipes, &c.—are found in the vicinity of "Old Castle." As early as 1765, the Rev. Samuel Kirkland came on a mission to the Indians at Kanadesaga.[4] The first church (Presb.) was organized in 1798; and the first settled minister was Rev. Jedediah Chapman.[5]

SOUTH BRISTOL—was formed from Bristol, March 8, 1838. It lies upon the w. shore of Canandaigua Lake, s. w. of the center of the co. The surface consists of an elevated upland, divided into 4 ranges by the valleys of Grindstone and Mud Creeks and Egypt Brook. The summits of the ridges are about 1000 feet above the lake, and the declivities are very steep. The bluffs upon the lake shore are 300 to 400 feet high. The soil is a mixture of clay and disintegrated slate. Although the soil is rich and productive, the hilly character of the town has tended to retard its settlement. **Cold Spring** (South Bristol p. o.) is a hamlet about a mi. from Canandaigua Lake. **Frost Hill** is a hamlet in the w. part. Gamaliel Wilder, from Mass., purchased this township from Phelps and Gorham, and settled at Wilburs Point, on Canandaigua Lake, in 1789.[6] An Indian orchard on the lake shore at this point induced him to settle here. Rev. Mr. Rolph was the first settled minister. There is now but 1 church (Presb.) in town.

VICTOR—was formed from Bloomfield, May 26, 1812. It is the N. w. corner town of the co. The N. part is occupied by the drift ridges, which rise 50 to 150 feet above the general surface. A ridge of 100 to 280 feet in height extends across the s. part in a general E. and w. direction. The principal streams are Irondequoit, Mud, Hog Hollow, and Fish Creeks, and Trout Brook. The soil in the center and N. is a light, sandy and gravelly loam, but in the s. E. it is principally clay. It is particularly adapted to the cultivation of potatoes and root crops. **Victor**,[7] (p. v.,) near the center, contains about 75 dwellings. The Indian village of Gannagaro, which was destroyed by the Marquis de Nonville, was situated near this place.[8] **Fishers** (p. o.) is a station on the N. Y. C. R. R., in the w. part; and **East Victor** is a hamlet, on Mud Creek The first settlement was commenced in 1789, by immigrants from Stockbridge, Mass. Among the first were Enos and Jared Boughton, and Jacob Lobdell.[9] Rev. Reuben Parmelee, from Goshen, the first settled minister, came to the town in 1798.[10]

WEST BLOOMFIELD—was formed from Bloomfield, Feb. 11, 1833. It lies upon the w. border of the co., N. of the center. A ridge 200 to 300 feet high, forming the declivity of a southern terrace, extends across the N. part. The surface is gently undulating. The soil is a deep, rich, gravelly loam mixed with clay. In the s. part there is a spring of inflammable or carburetted hydrogen gas. Tile and earthenware are manufactured to some extent in town. **West Bloomfield** (p. v.) is a village of 350 inhabitants,[11] situated 1½ mi. s. of the W. Bloomfield Station, on

[1] Gorham Station on the E. J. & C. R. R.
[2] Among the first settlers were Horatio Jones, Asa Ransom, Lark Jennings, Dr. Benton, Peter Ryckman, Peter Bortte, Col. Seth Reed, and Dominick Debartzch, an Indian trader. Jonathan Whitney, Jonathan Oaks, Benjamin Tuttle, Phineas Stone, and John Reed settled in 1788 and '89; Solomon and William Gates, Thomas Densmore, Solomon Weaver, and Oliver Whitmore in 1790, and Adam, Christian, Christopher, and George Fisher in 1791. Lark Jennings kept the first tavern, in 1788; the first gristmill was erected by Cornelius Roberts; and the first sawmill, by P. B. Wisner, in 1798. The first marriage was that of Dr. Joel Prescott and Miss Phila Reed; and the first school was taught by Samuel Wheaton, in 1792.
[3] For many years after this purchase the Indians came regularly at plowing time and watched this orchard, to see that the stipulation was not broken.
[4] Subsequently Mr. Kirkland was commissioned by the State of Mass. to treat with the Indians; and he conducted the treaty of purchase between them and Phelps and Gorham, in 1788; and afterward he acted as Indian agent for 30 years at Canandaigua.

[5] There are 12 churches in town; 2 Prot. E., 3 Presb., 2 Asso. Ref. Presb., 2 M. E., Bap., Ref. Prot. D., Univ., and R. C.
[6] Among the other early settlers who came in soon after Mr. Wilder, between 1789 and 1796, were Theophilus and Matthew Allen, Joseph Gilbert, Jared Tuttle, Peter Ganiard, Levi Austin, Nathaniel Hatch, and their families. Mr. Wilder built the first sawmill, the first gristmill, and distillery, at Wilburs Point, in 1795. He also erected the first public house, in 1808, which he conducted for 9 years. Dr. Hewitt and George Wilder opened the first store, in 1828. The first school was taught by Joanna Forbes. Eli Allen was the first child born, in 1793.
[7] Called by the Indians Ga-o/sa-ga-o, in the basswood country.
[8] See page 493.
[9] Levi Boughton and Rufus Dryer settled at Boughton Hill, in 1790. The first birth was that of Frederick Boughton, in June, 1791; and the first marriage, that of Zebulon Norton and Miss Boughton. The first tavern was opened at Boughton Hill, by Hezekiah Boughton, in 1792; and the first sawmill was built the same year, by Enos and Jared Boughton.
[10] There are 3 churches in town; Cong., M. E., and Univ.
[11] Called by the Indians Ga-nun/da-ak, village on a hilltop.

the N. Y. C. R. R. **North Bloomfield,** (p. v.,) on the Honeoye Outlet, and **Millers Corners,** (Taylorsville p. o.,) in the E. part, are R. R. stations. The territory forming this town was purchased by Amos Hall,[1] Robert Taft, Nathan Marvin, and Ebenezer Curtis; and the first settlement was made by them in 1789.[2] The first religious services were held in 1793.[3]

Acres of Land, Valuation, Population, Dwellings, Families, Freeholders, Schools, Live Stock, Agricultural Products, and Domestic Manufactures, of Ontario County.

Names of Towns.	Acres of Land. Improved.	Acres of Land. Unimproved.	Valuation of 1858. Real Estate.	Valuation of 1858. Personal Property.	Valuation of 1858. Total.	Population. Males.	Population. Females.	No. of Dwellings.	No. of Families.	Freeholders.	Schools. No. of Districts.	Schools. Children taught.
Bristol	17,023	5,945½	$452,676	$72,249	$524,925	862	853	334	397	316	12	571
Canadice	10,799	4,959½	195,699	35,101	230,800	491	486	185	185	163	9	449
Canandaigua	34,846½	8,433	2,422,920	678,074	3,100,994	3,166	3,314	1,108	1,184	767	20	2,213
East Bloomfield	13,277	2,906	717,501	121,050	838,551	1,117	1,051	397	406	339	11	701
Farmington	19,676½	5,419	761,849	151,805	913,654	998	952	354	368	309	15	669
Gorham	22,294¼	7,621¾	955,794	121,670	1,077,464	1,185	1,195	496	455	388	16	932
Hopewell	16,685	4,043	767,927	71,490	839,417	910	873	305	321	237	13	634
Manchester	18,085	3,175½	930,704	111,679	1,042,383	1,541	1,468	533	569	349	15	1,232
Naples	13,958	10,117	257,589	56,814	314,403	1,088	1,030	408	409	346	17	911
Phelps	33,409½	6,675	1,650,475	182,125	1,832,600	2,694	2,599	1,005	1,014	761	19	1,905
Richmond	18,827	6,979	656,152	240,600	896,752	767	728	285	291	206	11	543
Seneca	32,802	10,324	3,087,504	1,354,265	4,441,769	4,033	4,265	1,480	1,589	909	19	2,822
South Bristol	10,180	13,595	207,851	12,948	220,799	614	565	225	241	202	12	477
Victor	16,051	3,969	787,083	105,430	892,513	1,153	1,055	415	426	295	11	782
West Bloomfield	12,726	2,946½	486,966	82,435	569,401	820	801	298	325	258	9	594
Total	290,639¾	97,108¾	14,338,690	3,397,735	17,736,425	21,439	21,235	7,828	8,180	5,845	209	15,435

Names of Towns.	Live Stock. Horses.	Live Stock. Working Oxen and Calves.	Live Stock. Cows.	Live Stock. Sheep.	Live Stock. Swine.	Agricultural Products. Bush. of Grain. Winter.	Agricultural Products. Bush. of Grain. Spring.	Agricultural Products. Tons of Hay.	Agricultural Products. Bushels of Potatoes.	Agricultural Products. Bushels of Apples.	Agricultural Products. Dairy Products. Pounds Butter.	Agricultural Products. Dairy Products. Pounds Cheese.	Domestic Cloths, in yards.
Bristol	736	925	683	6,949	1,427	28,440	68,949	2,795¾	6,454	47,339	60,225	22,724	551½
Canadice	459	670	424	2,770	603	17,264	20,344¼	1,263½	3,119	6,543	36,625	4,262	130
Canandaigua	1,506	2,381	1,615	15,988	3,618	60,744	169,425	5,344½	10,836	34,331	146,897	22,901	670½
East Bloomfield	666	873	692	7,956	1,183	41,446	91,109	2,057½	9,511	19,052	53,939	8,838	10
Farmington	823	1,600	1,130	10,264	1,748	31,322	110,355½	2,875	11,696	30,848	93,258	27,407	325
Gorham	1,318	1,433	892	10,279	1,649	27,604½	97,796	2,972½	6,034	22,318	90,059	10,053	170
Hopewell	737	1,072	734	5,625	1,503	21,401	96,619	2,394	9,201	31,881	66,170	12,522	247
Manchester	882	1,315	965	7,419	1,773	29,827½	121,048	2,464½	14,838	22,729	79,571	15,293	189
Naples	643	1,089	708	6,602	1,121	16,867	27,348½	1,821	5,472	17,173	75,160	7,210	1,076
Phelps	1,710	2,200	2,043	13,141	3,575	66,184	257,571	5,085½	48,284	43,154	174,832	33,096	357
Richmond	719	1,485	658		1,413	38,050	64,936	3,224	4,172	19,773	54,236	12,715	51
Seneca	1,556	1,969	1,795	884	2,892	32,044	206,446	4,863	12,514	47,753	149,581	11,805	573
South Bristol	400	691	464	557	787	10,775	11,663	1,297	1,904	6,232	55,548	3,040	430
Victor	902	1,212	820	392	1,775	84,823	102,950	2,224	33,892	29,950	72,049	5,370	105
West Bloomfield	603	845	579	1,038	1,252	37,698	70,924	1,767	10,973	18,022	14,947	8,685	
Total	13,660	19,760	14,202	10,086	26,419	544,490	1,527,484¾	42,448¾	188,900	397,098	1,223,097	205,921	4,885

[1] Mr. Hall was from Guilford, Conn. He took the first census of Ontario co., in 1790; represented the co. in Assembly, in 1798; and was Major General of militia in the War of 1812.

[2] John P. Sears, Peregrine Gardner, Clark Peck, Jasper Marvin, Samuel Miller, John Algur, and S. Thayer settled in the town in 1789–90. Benjamin Gardner, with his sons John and Peregrine, are supposed to have been the first settlers. The first birth was that of Lucinda Gardner, in Sept. 1791. Jasper P. Sears kept the first inn, and Royal Hendee the first store. The first sawmill was built by Ebenezer Curtis; and the first gristmill, by Reuben Thayer.

[3] There are now 3 churches in town; Cong., M. E., and Chris.

ORANGE COUNTY.

THIS county was formed Nov. 1, 1683. Rockland was taken off in 1798, and a portion was annexed from Ulster the same year. It lies upon the w. bank of the Hudson, s. e. of the center of the State. It is centrally distant 90 miles from Albany, and contains 838 sq. mi. The surface is mountainous upon the s. e. and n. w. borders, and a rolling upland through the center. The Matteawan or South Mts. extend in several parallel ranges from the N. J. line n. e. to the Hudson, ending in the rocky and precipitous bluffs known as "The Highlands." The highest summits attain an elevation of 1,000 to 1,500 ft. above tide. The ranges and peaks of these mountains are known by several distinct names.[1] The whole region included between these ranges consists of steep and precipitous rocky peaks and narrow winding ravines, a small portion only being susceptible of cultivation. The Shawangunk Mt. Range extends from Delaware River n. e. through the n. w. corner of the co. It is a high, unbroken range, precipitous upon the w., but with more gradual slopes upon the e. The highest summits are 1,500 to 1,900 ft. above tide. The extreme n. w. corner of the co. is occupied by the series of highlands extending from the Delaware into Sullivan co. The central portion of the co., lying between the two mountain systems, is a rolling upland, broken in many places by abrupt and isolated hills and the deep valleys of streams. This whole region, comprising more than one-half of the entire surface of the co., is susceptible of cultivation, and forms a fine agricultural district.

Along the s. w. border, extending through several towns and into N. J., is a low, flat region, lying upon the streams, and known as the "Drowned Lands." This tract, consisting of about 17,000 acres, was originally covered with water and a dense growth of cedars; but a large portion of it has been drained and reclaimed; and it now forms one of the finest agricultural portions of the co.

Neversink River flows s. along the w. foot of the Shawangunk Mts. and forms a tributary of the Delaware. Shawangunk River flows n. along the e. foot of the same mountains and forms a tributary of the Hudson. Wall Kil flows n. through near the center of the co. and unites with the Shawangunk in Ulster co. Murderers Kil,[2] and its principal tributary, Otter Creek, flow e. through near the center of the co. and discharge their waters into the Hudson. Wawayanda Creek flows s. into N. J. and, re-entering the State as Potuck Creek, unites with the Wall Kil. Ramapo River rises in the s. part of the co. and flows s. into Rockland. In the s. are several small lakes, the principal of which are Greenwood Lake and Thompsons and Mambasha Ponds. The rocks of the southern highlands are principally granite, gneiss, and sienite, with occasional injected veins of trap. The rocks which compose the Shawangunk Mts. are the shales and sandstones of the Chemung group. The central portions of the co. are occupied by parallel strata of the Hamilton shales, Helderbergh limestones and grit, Medina sandstone, and the gray sandstones, all extending n. e. and s. w., respectively, from the e. foot of the Shawangunk Mts. An abundance of iron, consisting of magnetic ores and red and brown hematite, is found among the southern mountains; and several veins have been extensively worked.[3] The soil is as various as the surface. Among the primitive mountains it is light, sandy, and unproductive. In the n. w part it is a tough clay, generally underlaid by hardpan. Through the center it is a clay, sandy, and gravelly loam upon the hills, and a fine quality of gravelly loam and alluvium in the valleys, —all very productive. The Drowned Lands are covered with alluvium and vegetable mold, and are among the most fertile lands in the State. The various branches of agriculture form the leading pursuit of the people. The most important interest is the sending of milk to the N. Y. market. Butter, spring grains, and fruits are also largely produced. Market gardening is a large and increasing source of public wealth. The manufacturing interests of the co. are considerable, though they are mostly confined to a few places. The manufacture of iron has formed an exten-

---

[1] Among the principal ridges are the Warwick, Bellvale. Rough, and Sterling Ranges. near the s. border of the co., and the Schunemunk Range, between the towns of Monroe and Blooming Grove.

[2] Named from the murder of a family of whites who lived upon its banks, by the Indians, in early times.

[3] The skeletons of several mastodons have been found in this co.,—mostly in Montgomery and vicinity. One of these was exhibited many years in Peale's Museum, Philadelphia. One found in 1844 by Nathaniel Brewster, 20 ft. below the surface, was 33 ft. long The whole number of bones was 220, and the aggregate weight nearly 1,995 pounds.

sive business from an early period until within a few years; but at the present time only two furnaces are in operation in the co. The proximity to New York renders the lands of the co. exceedingly valuable; and, with proper care, almost any crop adapted to the climate can be successfully and profitably cultivated. Considerable commerce is carried on by means of the Hudson, the principal export being lumber brought from the West upon the R. R. and trans-shipped at Newburgh.

The county is a half-shire, the courts being held respectively at Goshen and Newburgh.[1] The courthouse at Goshen is a brick building, situated upon a fine lot in the E. part of the village. The jail is a stone building, in rear of the courthouse. The co. clerk's office is a fireproof brick building, upon the street opposite the courthouse. The courthouse at Newburgh is located upon the high land in the w. part of the village. It is a fine brick building, fronting s. upon Second St. The jail at Newburgh is connected with the police establishment of the village. The poorhouse is located upon a farm of 267 acres in Goshen, 3½ mi. s. w. of the village. The average number of inmates is 200, supported at a weekly cost of $1.04 each. The building is of stone, and has accommodations for 300. A school is taught during the entire year. The accommodations are reported by the Senate Committee of 1857 as good, and the general management of the institution as much above the average. The income from the farm is about $2,000. The N. Y. & Erie R. R. extends through Monroe, Blooming Grove, Chester, Goshen, Wawayanda, Walkill, Mount Hope, and Deerpark. The Newburgh branch of this road extends s. w. from Newburgh, through New Windsor and Blooming Grove, to Chester.[2] The Delaware & Hudson Canal extends from the Delaware River N. along the valley of the Neversink, through Deerpark.[3] In the central part of the co. a wide ditch has been dug, for the purpose of draining the Drowned Lands, which has been of immense value to the county.

Thirteen newspapers—1 daily, 9 weekly, 2 semi-monthly, and 1 monthly—are published in this co.[4]

[1] The first courts were held at Tappantown, in the present town of Orangetown, Rockland co., March 8, 1702. Courts were first held at Goshen in 1727. The first co. officers under State authority were John Haring, *First Judge*; Thos. Moffat, *Co. Clerk*; Isaac Nicoll, *Sheriff*; and James Everett, *Surrogate*. Jesse Woodhull was appointed sheriff May 8, 1777, a few months previous to Nicoll, but was not commissioned. A courthouse was built at Goshen in 1773, by James Webster, a Scotch Highlander, who served under Wolfe at the battle before Quebec in 1759. This building was afterward converted into a jail, and a portion of it is now used as a public house.

[2] The immense quantities of lumber brought from the pine forests of Allegany, Cattaraugus, and Steuben, over the N. Y. & E. R. R., are principally carried to Newburgh and trans-shipped. Milk trains run daily upon this road for the purpose of carrying the immense quantities of milk produced here to the N. Y. market. The milk business is the most important of all the local business of the R. R.

[3] This canal extends through the valley lying at the w. foot of the Shawangunk Mts. to Port Jervis, and thence up the valley of the Delaware to the w. bounds of the co.

[4] *The Goshen Repository*, the first paper published in Orange co., was commenced at Goshen in 1788 by David Mandeville. A few years after, it was issued by Mandeville & Westcott; and in 1800 it was sold to G. Hurton and Gabriel Denton, who changed the name to

The Orange County Patriot. In 1801 or '02 it passed into the hands of Wm. A. Carpenter, who changed it to

The Friend of Truth. In 1804 Ward M. Gazeley became proprietor, and changed its name to

The Orange Eagle; and soon after the office was burned and the paper discontinued.

The Newburgh Packet was started at Newburgh in 1795 by Lucius Carey, and was continued a few years.

The Mirror was commenced at Newburgh Sept 22, 1796, by Philip Van Horne. In 1803 it was merged in

The Recorder of the Times, published by Dennis Coles. In 1806 Ward M. Gazeley became proprietor, and the name was changed to

The Political Index. In 1829 Charles M. Cushman became publisher, and the name was changed to

The Orange Telegraph. Within a few years it was changed again to

The Newburgh Telegraph, and has since been issued respectively by H. H. Van Dyck, Elias Pitts, and E. M. Ruttenber, until 1857, when it passed into the hands of Joseph Lawson, by whom it is now published.

The New Windsor Gazette was commenced at New Windsor in 1797 by Jacob Schultz. In 1799 it was removed to Newburgh, and its name was changed to

The Orange County Gazette. John W. Barber and David Denniston afterward became interested in its publication. About 1803 it was changed to

The Citizen, and soon after it was merged in

The Rights of Man, which was commenced at Newburgh in 1799 by Elias Winfield, and was continued until 1809 or '10.

The Orange County Gazette was commenced at Goshen in 1805 by John G. Hurton and Gabriel Denton. It was successively issued by Gabriel Denton, Elliott Hopkins, F. T. & A. O. Houghton, until 1813, when Luther Pratt became the proprietor, and changed it to the

Independent Republican, and removed it to Montgomery, where it was published some years. It afterward passed into the hands of James A. Cheever, who removed it back to Goshen. In 1831 H. H. Van Dyck became proprietor. It was subsequently issued by V. M. Drake, Moses Sweezey, Clark and Montanye, James McNally, and Montanye & Green. It is now published by J. V. Montanye & Co.

The Orange County Republican was published at Wards Bridge in 1806.

The Orange County Patriot and Spirit of '76 was commenced at Goshen in 1808 by Gabriel Denton. In 1818 it was changed to

The Orange County Patriot, and was issued by Timothy B. Crowell. R. C. S. Hendries afterward became proprietor, and continued it until 1832, when it came into the hands of F. T. Parsons, who changed it to

The Goshen Democrat. It was soon after published by Mead & Webb; and in 1845 it was united with the True Whig, as

The Goshen Democrat and Whig. In a few years the name Whig, was dropped, and the paper again appeared as

The Goshen Democrat, under which title it is now published by Charles Mead.

The Newburgh Gazette was commenced in 1822 by J. D. Spaulding. It was successively issued by Spaulding & Parmenter, Spaulding & Risevels, Risevels & Leslie, Wallace & Street, S. T. Callahan, and Wm. L. Allison, until 1856, when it passed into the hands of E. W. Gray, its present publisher.

The Evangelical Witness, mo., was published a short time at Newburgh in 1824 by Rev. Jas. R. Wilson.

The Orange County Farmer was commenced in 1826 at Goshen by Samuel Williams. It afterward passed into the hands of Luther Pratt, who removed it to Montgomery, where it was continued but a short time.

The Beacon was published a short time at Newburgh in 1828 by —— Beebe.

Journal of the American Association, mo., was published at West Point in 1830. It was the organ of an association of cadets for the promotion of science, literature, and the arts.

The Orange Herald was published at Slate Hill, in Wawayanda, by John G. Wallace in 1831.

The Republican Banner was commenced at Walden, in Montgomery, in June, 1831, and was continued several years

The first settlements in the co. are supposed to have been made by the Dutch, soon after the first occupation of Manhattan Island. Traces of an early occupation were found upon the first advent of the progenitors of the present race, among which was a road known as the "Old Mine Road," extending from the s. line of the co. along the valley of the Shawangunk to Esopus, on the Hudson. These settlements were broken up; and no record is left of them. The next race of settlers came in about the commencement of the 18th century and located in various parts of the co. They were Dutch, French Huguenots, and English, nearly all seeking liberty in the wilderness. The first patent issued was the Minisink Patent, in 1697, embracing the greater part of the co. lying upon the Shawangunk Mts., and a considerable portion of Sullivan co. The remaining portions of the co. were embraced in Chesecock's Patent,[1] issued in 1702, embracing the s. e. part; the Wawayanda Patent,[2] issued in 1703, embracing the w. and n. parts; and the John Evans Patent,[3] the precise date of which is not known. The boundaries of these various patents were so vague that it was found impossible to locate them without conflicting with others; and serious difficulties arose between the different claimants.[4]

The policy of granting large patents was soon abandoned, and the remaining parts of the co. were patented in small tracts to actual settlers, from about 1718 to 1750. The settlements progressed but slowly, in consequence of the fear of Indian hostilities. During the French War of 1755 the frontier settlements were often attacked by small parties of hostile Indians and the defenseless inhabitants were murdered and carried into captivity. The principal weight of these attacks fell upon the settlements in the Neversink Valley. During the Revolution the frontiers were again constantly in a state of alarm. In July, 1778, Brant, at the head of a large Indian force, laid waste the whole Minisink settlement; and on his retreat the disastrous battle of Minisink was fought, in which nearly the whole force of the Americans was destroyed.[5]

The eastern part of the co. was also the scene of stirring military events. The importance of the passes through the Highlands was early appreciated by Washington, and strong fortifications were thrown up at various points to protect them. Fort Montgomery was erected on the river, at the s. line of the co., and Fort Clinton on the opposite side of a small creek in Rockland co. Several

The Signs of the Times, semi-mo., was commenced at New Vernon, in Mount Hope, in 1832, by Gilbert Beebe. In 1847 it was removed to Middletown, where it is now published by G. J. Beebe.

The Tablets of Rural Economy was published at Newburgh in 1832 by J. W. Risevels.

The Sentinel was published at Minisink, now Wawayanda, in 1833, by Peter K. Allen.

The Newburgh Journal was commenced in 1833 by J. D. Spaulding. Its name was afterward changed to

The Highland Courier. It was issued in 1855 by Wm. E. Laidey, and in 1858 passed into the hands of Edward Mixen, the present publisher.

The Reformed Presbyterian was commenced at Newburgh in 1836 by Rev. Moses Roney. In a short time it was removed to Pittsburgh, Penn.

The Family Visitor was published a short time at Newburgh in 1839 by D. L. Proudfit.

The Middletown Courier was started in April, 1840, by A. A. Bensel. In 1846 it was removed to Kingston and changed to the Ulster Democrat.

The True Whig was started at Goshen Aug. 5, 1842, by R. C. S. Hendries. In 1845 it was merged in the Goshen Democrat.

The Democratic Standard was commenced at Goshen in the fall of 1843 by Vait & Donovan. In 1844 it was changed to The Goshen Clarion, and it was continued until 1849.

The Christian Instructor was started at Newburgh in 1845 by D. L. Proudfit, and in a short time it was removed to Philadelphia.

The Orange County News was started at Goshen in July, 1846, by John L. Brown, and was discontinued in 1849.

The Banner of Liberty was commenced at Middletown in Aug. 1848, by Gilbert A. Beebe, as a monthly. In 1849 it was issued semi-monthly; and it is now published as a weekly.

Freedom's Guard was published at Middletown in Aug. 1849, by W. L. Beebe.

The Newburgh Excelsior was started in 1849 by Thomas George. In 1851 it was purchased by E. M. Ruttenber and merged in the Newburgh Telegraph.

Tri States Union was commenced at Port Jervis, Nov. 7, 1851, by John J. Minford. In 1854 L. F. Barnes became proprietor; and in 1855 it passed into the hands of James H. Norton, by whom it is still published.

The Mirror of Temperance was started at Port Jervis in 1851 by J. L. Barlow. In 1852 John Dow assumed the publication, and continued it until 1855.

The Whig Press was commenced at Middletown, Nov. 26, 1851, by John W. Hasbrouck, by whom it is still published.

The Separate American, a quarterly publication printed for the colored people of the Separate American Methodist Church, was commenced at Middletown in 1852 or '53, Rev. David James, editor. It was discontinued in 1856.

The Sentinel was commenced at Port Jervis in Jan. 1855, by John Williams. In June of the same year it was removed to Susquehanna, Penn.

The Literary Scrap Book, mo., was published at Newburgh in 1855 by R. Denton.

The Hardware Man's Newspaper, mo., was commenced Aug. 1855, at Middletown, by John Williams, by whom it is still published. It is issued from the office of the Whig Press.

The Newburgh American was commenced at Newburgh in 1855 by R. P. L. Shafer & Co., and was continued a short time.

The Newburgh Times was commenced at Newburgh in 1856 by R. B. Hancock. It soon passed into the hands of R. H. Bloomer, its present publisher.

The Daily News was commenced at Newburgh in 1856 by E. W. Gray. It was subsequently discontinued, and its publication resumed in 1857 by E. M. Ruttenber & E. W. Gray. It is now published by E. W. Gray & Joseph Lawson.

The Catholic Literary Magazine was published at Newburgh in 1856.

The Sybil, semi-mo., was commenced at Middletown in July, 1856, by Mrs. Dr. Lydia Sayer Hasbrouck. It is issued from the office of the Whig Press.

[1] Chesecocks.—March 25, 1797, to Anna Bridges and 6 others, a tract of upland and meadow called Chesecocks, bounded n. by Capt. J. Evans and Dr. Bridges & Co., w. by Bridges & Co. and w. side of Highlands, s. by patent Daniel Honan and Michael Handon, and e. by the Christian patented lands of Haverstraw and Hudson R. (Act March 17, 1783.)

[2] Wawayanda.—Queen Anne, on 29th of April, 1703, granted to Dr. John Bridges and 11 others certain tracts known as Wawayanda and other tracts, bounded e. by the High Hills of the Highlands and patent of Capt. John Evans, n. by line of O. and U. cos., and w. by Minisink Hills, and s. by N. J. (Act March 17, 1783.)

[3] This patent was afterward set aside, as it was described in so vague and unsatisfactory a manner that it was impossible to locate it. The others were but little better.

[4] A portion of the territory was claimed by N. J., and several collisions occurred between the settlers and the officers of the State, and numerous outrages were perpetrated under the color of law. The controversy was finally settled about 1767.

[5] See page 642.

other forts were built both above and below these, and chains were stretched across the river and various impediments were sunk in the channel, to prevent the passage of vessels. Gen. Putnam was left in command of these positions in 1777, when Gen. Howe marched to attack Philadelphia, but with an entirely inadequate force. About the 1st of October, Sir Henry Clinton, in command at New York, sent a force up the river to aid Gen. Burgoyne, who was then hard pressed by the American army. This force first landed at Verplancks Point on the 5th, but in the night following re-embarked, landed on the opposite shore, and on the 6th surprised and captured both Forts Montgomery and Clinton.

The official reports make the loss of the British and Americans about equal; but, as the former were fully exposed to a galling fire while approaching the works, and the latter mostly escaped, it is supposed that the British loss was much greater. The other American works were abandoned, and Gen. Putnam retreated to Fishkill. The British spent some time in removing the various obstructions from the river, and advanced slowly northward, plundering and destroying on their way. They reached Esopus on the 15th, and at the same time Gen. Putnam, whose force had been augmented to 6,000 men by Conn., N. Y. and N. J. militia, sent a detachment of 2,000 to take possession of Peekskill. The British, afraid to go farther N. with such a force in their rear, remained at Esopus until they received news of the surrender of Burgoyne; and then they returned to New York.

The result of this expedition demonstrated the necessity of stronger fortifications among the Highlands, and during the following winter the site of West Point was fixed upon, as the strongest and most eligible on the river. Earthworks were thrown up early in the spring, and from time to time more formidable works were added, until, at the close of the war, it was the most strongly fortified of any place in the country.[1]

It was afterward the center of the American operations in the North. In the spring of 1780, Gen. Arnold, who had not entirely recovered from the effects of a wound received at Saratoga, solicited and received the command of this post. The instruction which gave him this command was dated Aug. 3, 1780. Arnold had been in correspondence with the British for more than a year; and he soon negotiated with Sir Henry Clinton to deliver up West Point, for the sum of £10,000 in gold and a commission of Maj. Gen. in the British army. The final consummation of the compact on the part of the British was intrusted to Maj. Andre, who crossed the American lines in disguise and held an interview with Arnold on the 22d of Sept. Upon his attempting to return to New York, he was arrested as a spy, and the whole scheme was discovered. Arnold escaped to New York, and Andre was subsequently executed.[2]

The headquarters of the American army of the North was for a long time at Newburgh; and it was at this place that Washington finally took leave of his army,[3] Aug. 18, 1783.

BLOOMING GROVE—was formed from Cornwall, March 23, 1799. A part of Hamptonburgh was taken off in 1830, and a part of Chester in 1845. It lies a little E. of the center of the co. Its surface is mountainous in the S. and E., and rolling and moderately hilly in the N. and W. Schunemunk Mts., upon the line of Monroe, are 1,300 to 1,500 ft. above tide. The other principal elevations are Lazy Hill, on the line of Chester, Toms Rocks, Peddlers, Rainer, Round, Musquito, and Woodcock Hills, and Red Ridge. These hills are generally too steep and rocky to be ever susceptible of cultivation. The hills in the N. have more gradual slopes, and are arable to their summits. Otter Kil flows E. through the N. part, and receives as tributaries Cromlin,[4] Slatterleys, and several smaller creeks. The extensive bog meadows along Cromlin Creek, in the S. part, have been drained, and are now the most valuable agricultural lands in the town. The soil is a sandy and clayey loam. **Washingtonville,** (Blooming Grove p. o.,) upon Otter Kil, in the N. part, contains 3 churches and 369 inhabitants; **Salisbury Mills,** (p. v.,) upon the line of Monroe, a church, paper mill, gristmill, and 241 inhabitants; and **Craigsville,** (p. v.,) in the W. part, a church, cotton factory, and 20 dwellings.[5] These places are all stations upon the Newburgh Branch of the N. Y. & E. R. R. **Blooming Grove,** near the center, contains 1

---

[1] The erection of these works was intrusted to Kosciusko, the Polish patriot, then serving as a volunteer in the American army in the capacity of a military engineer. The works consisted of a formidable battery upon the bluff immediately upon the shore, named Fort Clinton, a strong fort upon Mt. Independence, in the rear, named Fort Putnam, and several redoubts and outposts.

[2] Andre was executed at Tappantown, Rockland co., Oct. 2, 1780.

[3] In the spring of 1782, while the army was stationed at Newburgh, a feeling of discontent arose among the officers and men, in consequence of the arrearages in their pay and the hardships they were called upon to endure. This was promptly checked by Washington, and a formidable conspiracy was broken up.

[4] This creek is called Gray Court Creek in Chester.

[5] During the Revolution a forge and powder mill were in operation at Craigsville. In 1790 James Craig erected a paper mill,—the first in the co.

church and 18 dwellings; **Oxford Depot** (p. o.) is a hamlet and station upon the Erie R. R. The first settlements are supposed to have been made about 1735.[1] The first church was erected at Blooming Grove, in 1759; Rev. Enos Ayres was the first pastor.[2]

CHESTER—was formed from Goshen, Warwick, Blooming Grove, and Monroe, March 22, 1845. It is an interior town, lying a little s. w. of the center of the co. The surface is rolling in the N. W., hilly in the center, and mountainous in the s. w. The principal elevations are Goose Pond Mt., Lazy Hill, Snake Hill, and Sugar Loaf Mt.,—all steep, rocky peaks, unfit for cultivation. The highest summits are 500 to 600 ft. above the valleys. The principal streams are Gray Court, Black Meadow, and Ditch Creeks. Along Gray Court Creek, near the N. boundary, are extensive peat meadows, thoroughly drained, and forming the most productive tract in town. The soil is a light, yellow loam, underlaid by clay. Limestone and slate are both found in town. **East Chester,** (Chester p. o.,) **Chester,** and **West Chester** are three villages, situated at the three angles of an equilateral triangle, 1 mi. apart. They contain the Chester Academy, a bank, 2 churches, and about 1,500 inhabitants. **Sugar Loaf,** (p. v.,) in the s. w. part, contains a church and 36 dwellings. The first settlement was made in 1716, at Gray Court, in the N. E. corner of the town, by Daniel Cromline, from Long Island.[3] There are 3 churches in town; 2 M. E. and Presb.

CORNWALL—was formed March 7, 1788, as "*New Cornwall.*" Its name was changed March 3, 1797. "*Chesecocks,*" now Monroe, was taken off in 1799. It lies upon the Hudson, in the E. part of the co. The surface is principally occupied by rocky peaks and ridges of "The Highlands." Their declivities are usually very steep, and their summits are masses of rocks, in some cases covered with a scanty growth of dwarfed forest trees. The highest peaks are Butter Hill, Crows Nest, and Bear Mountain,—respectively 1,529, 1,418, and 1,350 ft. above the river.[4] The valleys among the mountains are deep, narrow, and rocky. A small portion of the N. W. part of the town is rolling or moderately hilly. The principal streams are Murderers Creek and its principal tributary, Otter Kil, flowing through broad, beautiful valleys in the N. part, and Bog Meadow Creek, emptying into the Hudson below West Point. Upon the latter, near its mouth, is a series of cascades, known as Buttermilk Falls. Cranberry, Long, Sutherlands, and Bog Meadow Ponds are small bodies of water among the mountains. The soil in the valleys is a sandy, clayey, and gravelly loam. The hills are too steep and rocky for cultivation. **Canterbury,** (Cornwall p. o.,) in the N. E. part of the town, contains 4 churches, a woolen yarn factory, and tannery. Pop. 428. **Cornwall Landing,** on the Hudson, in the N. E. part, is the center of extensive brick manufactories. Pop. 615. **West Point,** (p. o.,) on the Hudson, is the seat of the U. S. Military Academy. It contains extensive barracks for the cadets and soldiers, 20 officers' quarters, a philosophical building, containing the library, apparatus, and observatory, a laboratory for ordnance and ammunition, a chapel, hospital, riding hall, stable, equipment shed, Catholic church, and 150 dwellings for employees.[5] **Buttermilk Falls,** (p. v.,) 2 mi. below West Point, contains 3 churches and 307 inhabitants. **Fort Montgomery,** (p. v.,) in the s. E. part, contains 1 church and 16 dwellings; **Bethlehem,** in the N. W., a church and 12 dwellings. **Ketchamtown,** in the w., and **Townsville,** in the N., are hamlets. The first settlements are supposed to have been made about 1720.[6] The first church (Presb.) was formed in 1730, at Bethlehem; Rev. Mr. Chalker was the first pastor, and Rev. Enos Ayres the second.[7] Fort Putnam, of the Revolution, was situated immediately in the rear of West Point, and Fort Montgomery on the s. E. border of the town.[8] Idlewild, the residence of N. P. Willis, is near the Hudson, in the N. E. part of the town.

---

[1] Among the early settlers were the families of Strong, Brewster, Howell, Dubois, Coleman, Moffatt, Seely, Gilbert, Woodhull, Tuthill, Goldsmith, Brooks, and Mathews.

[2] There are 8 churches in town; 4 M. E., 2 Cong., Presb., and Friends.

[3] In company with others, Mr. Cromline purchased the Wawayanda Patent of Philip Rockby and Hendrick Ten Eyck. He was accompanied by Wm. Bull, an Englishman, whom he had hired from an emigrant ship. During the first year of settlement he erected a house long afterward kept as a tavern and known as the "Cromline House." Its sign was the king's coat of arms; and as the colors became gray with age it was called the "Gray Coat," and in after years, a court being held in the house, its name was changed to the "Gray Court." The name of the stream, meadows, and hamlet was derived from this.

[4] The other principal elevations are Black Rock and Deer Hills, near the center; Ant Hill, Lawyers Hill, and Mount Rascal, in the s. w.; and Peat, Pine, Cold, and Round Hills, in the N. part.

[5] In the yard at West Point is a large number of cannon taken during the several wars of the U. S.; and among them are 89 brass pieces captured in the several battles of the Mexican War, each marked when, where, and by whom captured.

[6] The first settlement was made at and near the village of Canterbury. The tradition is that the first settlement was made there by Germans, who made some clearings and planted an orchard, but, becoming dissatisfied, sold out and left. The next settlers were English, some of whom had first settled in Conn. and Mass. Among the early settlers were the Sutherlands, Sacketts, Sherods, Brewsters, Woods, Clarks, Smiths, Townsends, Van Duzens, Mandevilles, Bartons, Sands, and Thorns. The first town meeting upon record in the precinct of Cornwall was held in April, 1765.

[7] There are 11 churches in town; 2 Presb., 2 Prot. E., 2 Friends, 2 M. E., Bap., R. C., and Free.

[8] A chain was stretched across the river from Fort Montgomery, but the fort was taken by the British and the chain broken in Oct. 1777. A chain was afterward put across the river at West Point, and remained there during the war.

CRAWFORD—was formed from Montgomery, March 4, 1823. It lies in the extreme N. angle of the co. Its surface is a hilly upland, broken by several high ridges extending N. E. and S. W. Collaberg and Comfort Hills, along the E. border, are 300 to 400 ft. above the valleys. The principal streams are the Shawangunk, forming the N. W. boundary, Dwaars Kil, Paughcaughnaughsink and Little Paughcaughnaughsink Creeks. These streams all flow in a general N. E. direction. Upon the Shawangunk is a large amount of water-power. The soil is a slaty and clayey loam upon the hills and a sandy and gravelly loam in the valleys. **Pine Bush**,[1] (p. v.,) on the Shawangunk, in the N. part, contains a sawmill, gristmill, and 120 inhabitants; **Searsville**, (p. v.,) on Dwaars Kil, near the center, a gristmill, 2 sawmills, and 16 dwellings; and **Bullville**, (p. v.,) in the S. part, 12 dwellings. **Hopewell** is a hamlet, in the S. W. **Collaburgh** is a p. o., 2 mi. E. of Bullville. The first church (Presb.) was formed at Hopewell, in 1779. The census reports 2 churches; Presb. and Asso. Ref. Presb.[2]

DEERPARK[3]—was formed from Mamakating, (Sullivan co.,) March 16, 1798. A part of Mount Hope was taken off in 1825. It lies in the extreme W. angle of the co. Its surface is a mountainous highland, broken by the valley of Neversink River and numerous deep, rocky ravines of small streams. The Shawangunk Mts. extend along the E. border, and form a high, rocky ridge 1,800 ft. above the valleys, with steep declivities on the W. The Neversink[4] River flows in a deep valley at the W. foot of the mountains. The central and W. parts are covered with a rocky and mountainous upland, ending in abrupt declivities on Delaware River in the S. The other principal streams are Mongaup River, forming the W. boundary, Bashes[5] Kil, Old Dam Fall Creek,[6] Shingle, and Grassy Swamp[7] Brooks. Big and Little Ponds are two small lakes in the interior. **Port Jervis**,[8] (p. v.,) upon the Delaware, near the mouth of the Neversink, was incorp. May 11, 1853. It is an important station upon the Erie R. R. and Delaware & Hudson Canal. It contains 5 churches, a saw factory, foundery, machine shop, planing mill, newspaper office, and bank. Pop. 3,023. **Honesville**, (Sparrow Bush p. o.,) upon the Delaware, 2 mi. W. of Port Jervis, contains a large tannery and 26 dwellings; **Huguenot**, (p. v.,) upon the canal, 4 mi. N. E. of Port Jervis, 25 dwellings; and **Cuddebackville**, (p. v.,) upon the canal, in the N. E. part, 1 church and 12 dwellings. **Carpenters Point** is a hamlet, at the mouth of the Neversink. The first settlements were made about 1690.[9] There are 7 churches in town.[10] De Witt Clinton was born at Fort De Witt, in this town, March 2, 1769, while his parents were on a visit at the residence of his mother's brother. Lead ore has recently been found in this town.

GOSHEN—was formed March 7, 1788. A part of Hamptonburgh was taken off in 1830, and a part of Chester in 1845. It is an interior town, lying a little S. E. of the center of the co. Its surface is rolling or moderately hilly. The hills are bordered by long and gradual slopes, and are arable to their summits. The S. W. corner is occupied by a portion of the "Drowned Lands," most of which have been reclaimed.[11] The principal streams are Wall Kil, forming the W., and Quaker Creek, the S. boundary, and Otter Kil, in the E. part. The soil is a sandy loam, underlaid by clay, slate, and limestone. **Goshen**, (p. v.,) N. E. of the center, was incorp. March 28, 1809. Besides the co. buildings, it contains 4 churches, a female seminary,[12] several classical schools, 2 newspaper offices, 2 banks, and about 1,800 inhabitants. It is the W. terminus of the Newburgh Branch of the N. Y. & E. R. R., and is an important freight and milk station upon the Erie R. R. The first settlements were made from 1703 to 1714. The first deeds of village lots in Goshen bear the date of 1714. The original Wawayanda Patent,[13] covering the greater part of this town, was granted by Queen

---

1 Formerly called "*Crawford*."

2 Nothing definite could be obtained in regard to the early history of this town.

3 A man named McDonald, in early time, inclosed a large tract by a brush fence, and the inclosure became known as McDonald's "Deer Park." This name was afterward given to the town.

4 Called by the Indians Ma-hack-e-meck.

5 Named from Bashe, an Indian woman who lived upon its banks.

6 This stream falls 600 ft. in 1 mi., and hence its name.

7 Named from a series of low natural meadows through which the stream flows.

8 Named from J. B. Jervis, the engineer who built the Delaware & Hudson Canal.

9 Peter Gummaer, Jacob Cuddeback, Thomas and Gerardus Swartout, John Tys, and David Jemison located in town in 1690. The first two were Huguenot exiles. The first general surveys were made in 1713. Jacob Cuddeback built the first mill. Among the other early settlers were —— Cuykendall, John Decker, Wm. Cole, and Solomon Davis.

10 2 Ref. Prot. D., Bap., Presb., M. E., Prot. E., and R. C.

11 Some 25 years ago a ditch of small size was dug about 3 mi. in length across a bend in Wall Kil, through the Drowned Lands, for the purpose of draining them. The action of the water upon the light soil through which it was dug has so enlarged it that in many places it is wider than Wall Kil, and much difficulty is experienced in maintaining bridges over the ditch.

12 The Goshen Female Seminary is a flourishing institution. Several small family classical schools are located in the village.

13 Christopher Denn, one of the proprietors of the Wawayanda Patent, located N. E. of Goshen Village in 1712. After visiting the place and deciding upon a location, he returned to his residence on Staten Island, and sent a company of carpenters, his household goods, and his adopted daughter, Mary Wells, then 16 years of age, to his new home, under the guidance of 3 friendly Indians. The carpenters erected a cabin, and Denn and his wife came on the next day after the cabin was built. Mr. Bull, a young Englishman just arrived in an emigrant ship, came in soon after. Among the other early settlers who came previous to 1721 were John Everett, John Carpenter, John Gale, William Ludlum, James Jackson, Isaac Finch, Michael Dunning, Solomon Carpenter, William Jackson, Samuel Seely, Samuel Webb, John Yelverton, Samuel Clowes, John Bradner, and John

Anne, March 5, 1703. The first church (Presb.) was formed in 1721; Rev. John Bradner was the first pastor.[1]

GREENVILLE—was formed from Minisink, Dec. 2, 1853. It lies on the s. w. border of the co., w. of the center. Its surface is a hilly and broken upland. The Shawangunk Mts., extending along the w. border, are 400 to 600 ft. above the valleys and 1,400 to 1,600 ft. above tide. The E. slopes of the mountains are generally gradual, and the hills are arable to their summits. The principal stream is Shawangunk River, which takes its rise near the center and flows N. E. Benin Water Pond is a small body of water in the N. part. The soil is a sandy, gravelly, and clayey loam. **Greenville**, (Minisink p. o.,) in the w. part, contains 2 churches and 12 houses; and **Smiths Corners**, N. of Greenville, contains 15 houses. **Center Point**, 1½ mi. s. E. of Greenville, is a p. o. **Woodsville** is a hamlet in the E. part. The first settlements were probably made from 1720 to 1730.[2] There are 2 churches in town; Bap. and M. E.

HAMPTONBURGH[3]—was formed from Goshen, Blooming Grove, Montgomery, New Windsor, and Walkill, April 5, 1830. It is an interior town, lying a little N. of the center of the co. Its surface is rolling and moderately hilly. The principal streams are Wall Kil, forming the N. w. boundary, and Otter Kil, flowing N. E. through near the center. The soil is a gravelly and slaty loam. **Otterville**, (p. o.,) on Otter Kil, near the E. boundary, is a hamlet. **Otterkill**, s. of Otterville, contains 12 dwellings. **Campbell Hall**, near the center, and **Hamptonburgh**, 1 mi. s., are hamlets. The first settlement was made by Wm. Bull, in 1719 or '20. In 1727 he erected a stone house, which is still standing. There are 2 churches in town; Presb. and Asso. Reformed.

MINISINK[4]—was formed March 7, 1788. A part of "*Calhoun*" (now Mount Hope) was taken off in 1825, Wawayanda in 1849, and Greenville in 1853. It lies upon the N. J. line, s. w. of the center of the co. Its surface is rolling and hilly. The slopes are generally gradual, and the hills are arable to their summits. The principal streams are Wall Kil and Rutgers Creek, each of which forms some portion of the N. and E. boundary. The Drowned Lands occupy a small portion of the E. angle. The soil is principally a gravelly loam. **Unionville**, (p. v.,) in the s. part, contains 2 churches and 25 dwellings; and **West Town**, (p. v.,) 3 mi. N. of Unionville, 2 churches and 15 dwellings. **Waterloo Mills** (p. o.) is a hamlet, containing 1 church and 6 dwellings. No records of the early settlement have been preserved. There are 5 churches in town.[5]

MONROE[6]—was formed from Cornwall, March 23, 1799, as "*Chesecocks.*" Its name was changed to "*Southfield*," April 3, 1801, and to Monroe, April 6, 1808. A part of Chester was taken off in 1845. It is the s. E. corner town in the co. It lies mostly among the Highlands; and its surface is a hilly and mountainous upland. The principal ranges are Schunemunk Mts., in the N., Black and Bear Mts., in the E., and the Southfield Mts., near the center,—all extending N. E. and s. w.[7] Their declivities are steep and in many places precipitous, and their summits are rough, rocky, and broken. A large share of the whole town is unfit for cultivation. In the N. w. part are several valleys containing arable land. The principal streams are Ramapo River, flowing s., and Murderers Creek, flowing N. The Forest-of-Dean Creek drains the E. part and discharges its waters into the Hudson. Among the mountains are a great number of fine, small lakes and ponds.[8] The soil in the valleys is a sandy and gravelly loam. The mountains are too rough for cultivation. **Monroe**, (p. v.,) in the N. w. part of the town, contains 2 churches and 266 inhabitants. It is a station upon the Erie R. R. **Turners**,[9] (p. v.,) a station upon the R. R., near the center, contains 18 dwellings. **Greenwood Works** (p. v.) is a station upon the R. R., 3 mi. s. of Turners

---

Denton, many of whose descendants still reside in the town. The first marriage was that of Wm. Bull and Sarah Wells, in 1718. The first inn was kept by Birdsye Yarrington. Noah Webster, author of Webster's Dictionaries, taught the first academic school, in the village of Goshen, in 1782. De Witt Clinton was a pupil at the academy at one time. William H. Seward studied law at the office of Judge Duer, in this village.

[1] There are now 4 churches in town; M. E., Prot. E., Presb., and R. C.

[2] Facts relating to the early history of this town could not be accurately ascertained.

[3] Named from Wolverhampton, the birthplace of Wm. Bull, the first settler.

[4] Tradition says that long ago, before the Delaware River broke through the mountain at the Water Gap, the lands for 30 or 40 mi. bordering upon it were covered by a lake, but became drained by the breaking down of that part of the dam which confined it, and that a part of a tribe of Indians from New Jersey

settled upon these lands from which the waters had retired. The lands were called "Minsies," signifying "lands from which the waters had gone," and the name was afterward applied to the Indians living upon it. From this name the term "Minisink" is derived.—*Eager's Hist. Orange Co., p. 408.*

[5] 3 Presb., Bap., and Christian.

[6] Named in honor of James Monroe, afterward President of the U. S.

[7] Among the principal mountain peaks are Black Top, Black Cup, and Long Hills, in the N.; Torn Mt. and Cape Hill, in the E.; Tom Jones Mt. and Hemlock Hill, in the s. E.; Pine and Prickly Ash Hills, in the s.; and Hogback, Hall, Tiger, Cedar, Burned, Rocky, and Macannon Hills, in the center.

[8] Among the principal ponds are Hazard Pond, in the N., Slaughters, Two Pond, Bull, Poplopens, and Cedar Ponds, in the E.; Little, Long, and Duck Cedar Ponds, in the s.; and Little Long, Round, and Mambasha Ponds, in the w.

[9] Formerly called "*Centerville.*"

Station. A blast furnace is situated near the R. R., and another about 1 mi. E. There are about 15 houses in the vicinity. **Monroe Works,** (p. o.,) 3 mi. s. of Greenwood Works, was the seat of extensive iron works, which have been abandoned. It is Southfield Station on the N. Y. & E. R. R. **Highland Mills,** (p. v.,) in the N. part, contains 2 churches and 15 dwellings. **Lower Smith Clove,** 1 mi. s., and **Woodbury Clove,** 1 mi. N., of Highland Mills, are hamlets. The first settlements were probably made about 1742.[1] The Chesecocks Patent, granted in 1702, embraced a portion of the Ramapo Valley in this town. There are 5 churches in town.[2]

MONTGOMERY[3]—was formed March 7, 1788. Crawford was taken off in 1823, and a part of Hamptonburgh in 1830. It lies upon the N. border of the co., E. of the center. Its surface is generally a hilly upland. The Comfort Hills,[4] 600 to 800 ft. above tide, extend along the w. border Wall Kil flows N. E. through near the center; and its principal tributary, Tin Brook,[5] flows through the E. part. Upon Wall Kil, in the N. part, is a fall of 40 ft., affording an excellent water-power. Along the same stream, in the s. part, is considerable swamp land. The soil is a fine quality of gravelly loam. **Montgomery,** (p. v.,) upon Wall Kil, s. of the center, was incorp. Feb. 17, 1810. It contains 2 churches, the Montgomery Academy, 3 gristmills, and a sawmill. Pop. 760. **Walden,** (p. v.,) on Wall Kil, 3½ mi. N. of Montgomery, was incorp. April 9, 1855. It contains 3 churches, a shawl factory, satinet factory, and a manufactory of cutlery. Pop. 641. **St. Andrews,** (p. o.,) in the N. E. part, contains 10 dwellings. **Coldenham,**[6] near the E. line, is a hamlet. The earliest patent comprising land in this town was granted in 1709, to Henry Hileman. It was located at the mouth of Tin Brook, below Walden. It was settled by the proprietor and divided into lots in 1712. Lieut. Gov. Cadwallader Colden, the owner of a patent in this town, located at Coldenham in 1728.[7] The first church (Ref. Prot. D.) was formed at Montgomery Village in 1732.[8]

MOUNT HOPE—was formed from Walkill, Minisink, and Deerpark, as "*Calhoun,*" Feb. 15, 1825. Its name was changed March 14, 1833. It lies upon the N. border of the co., N. w. of the center. Its surface is a hilly and broken upland. The Shawangunk Mts. extend through the w. part; the highest summits are 1,400 to 1,800 ft. above tide. Shawangunk River flows N. E. through the center, and the Little Shawangunk along the E. border. The soil is a sandy and gravelly loam. **Otisville,** (p. v.,) near the w. border, contains 2 churches and 309 inhabitants. It is a station upon the Erie R. R. **Mount Hope,** (p. v.,) 2 mi. s. E. of Otisville, contains 2 churches and 120 inhabitants; **New Vernon,** in the N. part, a church and 20 dwellings. **Finchville** is a hamlet, in the s. w. part. The precise date of the settlement of this town is unknown. James Finch settled some time previous to the Revolution.[9] There are 6 churches in town.[10]

NEWBURGH[11]—was formed March 7, 1788. It lies upon the Hudson, and is the N. E. corner town in the co. Its surface is a hilly and broken upland, the highest summits being 600 to 900 ft.

---

[1] A family of Smiths settled very early in the town, and from them the town was called "*Smiths Clove.*" Among the early settlers were families of Millers, Galloways, Carpenters, Bulls, Dobbins, Wygants, Wards, Coltons, Nobles, Cunninghams, Slaughters, and Lamoreaux,—mostly English families from the Eastern States. The first iron works was that of Ward & Colton, erected in 1751 for the manufacture of anchors. It was situated in Warwick, just over the line from Monroe. In 1752 Abel Noble, from Penn., erected a forge in this town, near the Ward & Colton furnace. Here the first anchor was made, in 1753. Steel was made in 1776; and during the Revolution one of the chains thrown across the Hudson was manufactured here. It weighed 186 tons. During the Revolution, Claudius Smith, a noted tory, resided in this town. He was hung at Goshen, Jan. 22, 1779.

[2] 3 M. E., Presb., and Friends.

[3] Named in honor of Gen. Richard Montgomery. In 1767 the town was called the "*Walkill Precinct,*" and in 1772 it was known as the "*Hanover Precinct.*" In 1782 its name was changed to the Montgomery Precinct.

[4] Named from a family of Comforts who were early settlers in that region.

[5] Name derived from Tinn and Broc, meaning small river.

[6] Named from the family of Cadwallader Colden, who was an early proprietor.

[7] Johannes Miller settled on Wall Kil, 2 mi. s. of Montgomery, in 1727. Among the other early settlers were John Neely, Charles Booth, Wm. Eager, Fred. Sinsabaugh, and Johannes Youngblood,—all of whom settled between 1730 and 1741. The E. part of the town was originally settled by Irish, and the valley of Wall Kil by Hollanders. The first store was kept by Alexander Colden, in 1742; and the first gristmill was built at Walden, by James Kidd. In the fall of 1775 the people of Bos-

ton, by reason of the great scarcity of supplies and provisions, applied to this State for aid; and accordingly a public meeting was called, which convened in the town of "*Hanover,*" (now Montgomery.) In the mean time the friends of the mother country, always on the alert, had procured the services of a talented orator for the purpose of defeating the objects of the meeting. As no one could be found among the adherents of the cause of liberty who was able to speak in public, recourse was had to the Rev. Mr. Annan, of Neelytown, who at first declined, but at length consented. A multitude were assembled on the occasion to hear a discussion upon a subject which was then the absorbing topic of the day. The discussion was continued for some time with fairness and ability on either side, until at length, to check a strife of angry words and to test the disposition of the assembly, Mr. Annan suddenly said, "As many as are in favor of assisting the people of Boston and the cause of Liberty, follow me." The effect was electric. Immediately upon his leaving the house he beheld, to his utter astonishment, the whole multitude at his heels.—*Eager's Hist. Orange Co.,* p. 636.

[8] There are 7 churches in town; 2 Ref. Prot. D., 2 M. E., Prot. E., Presb., and Covenanter. The Ref. Prot. D. church, near Montgomery, has connected with it a farm of 75 acres, valued at $7,000, and a parsonage.

[9] Mr. Finch was a soldier in the French War, and a minute-man during the Revolution.

[10] 2 Presb., 2 M. E., Cong., and Bap.

[11] Until 1763, the present towns of Newburgh and New Windsor were included in the "*Precinct of the Highlands.*" During that year this precinct was divided into the precincts of Newburgh and New Windsor, and continued as such until they were organized as TOWLS in 1788.

above the river. A series of bluffs 100 to 300 ft. in height extends along the river. The greater part of the hilly region is arable. The principal stream is Quassaic Creek,[1] forming a part of the boundary of New Windsor. It receives from the N. Fostertown and Gidneys Creeks and Orange Lake Outlet. Orange Lake,[2] in the w. part, covers an area of about 400 acres. Along its inlet is considerable marshy land. The soil is principally a clay and sandy loam. **Newburgh,** (p. v.,) on the Hudson, near the s. e. corner of the town, was incorp. March 25, 1800. It lies upon a steep slope which rises from the river to the height of about 150 ft. and thence spreads out into a rolling region. Besides the co. buildings, it contains 14 churches,[3] 5 banks, and several private schools and academies.[4] It is largely engaged in the manufacture of printed cotton cloths, castings, beer, and a variety of other articles.[5] The commercial interests of the place are also large and important.[6] The village is supplied with water brought from Little Pond, 3 mi. s. w., by the Newburgh Waterworks Co. These works were erected in 1853, at a cost of $96,000. In the lower part of the village the water has a head of 230 ft. A steam ferry connects this place with Fishkill Landing. Pop. 9,256. Overlooking the Hudson, in the s. part of the village, stands an old stone mansion known as "Washington's Head Quarters." It is surrounded by a fine lawn of several acres; and the whole premises are owned and kept in order by the State.[7] **Savil** is a p. o., about 5 mi. N. w. of Newburgh. **Middle Hope,** (p. v.,) in the N. E. part of the town, contains 1 church and 12 houses; **Fostertown,** 4 mi. N. w. of Newburgh, a church and 10 houses; and **Gardnertown,** E. of Orange Lake, a church and 14 houses. **Coldenham** is a p. o., in the w. part. **Balmville,** 2 mi. N. of Newburgh, is a hamlet. The first settlement was made on the present site of the village of Newburgh, by Palatinates, in 1708.[8] The first church (St. George's Prot. E.) was formed about 1728; and the first minister was Rev. Mr. Charlton, sent out by the "London Society for the Propagation of the Gospel."[9] An almshouse, for the support of the town poor, is situated upon a farm of 75 acres on the s. w. line of the village corporation of Newburgh. The buildings are of brick; and the cost of the whole establishment was about $30,000.[10]

NEW WINDSOR[11]—was formed March 7, 1788. A part of Hamptonburgh was taken off in 1830. It lies upon the Hudson, N. of the center of the co. Its surface is a rolling and hilly upland. The slopes and the summits of the hills are usually smooth and arable. Snake Hill is a rough, rocky eminence in the N. E. part, 500 to 600 ft. above tide. The principal stream is Murderers Creek, flowing through the s. E. corner. Tin Brook flows N. along the w. border. Little Pond, in the N. E. part, supplies the Newburgh Waterworks. It is 230 ft. above tide. The soil is a gravelly and slaty loam. **New Windsor,** upon the Hudson, 2 mi. s. of Newburgh, contains 2 churches and about 75 dwellings. It is a steamboat landing, and the center of a large brick

---

[1] Named from a tribe of Indians who formerly lived in this vicinity. Sometimes called "Chambers Creek."

[2] Formerly called "*Moose Pond.*" It was afterward called "*Machins Pond,*" from Capt. Machin, who erected upon its outlet a manufactory of copper coin.

[3] 4 Presb., 3 M. E., 2 Bap., 2 Asso. Ref., Ref. Prot. D., Prot. E., and R. C.

[4] The Highland Academy, a private boarding school, was commenced Sept. 1, 1858. (See p. 751.) The Newburgh Collegiate Institute was commenced May 1, 1857. There are several other select schools in the village.

[5] Among the manufacturing establishments are 3 founderies, giving employment to 117 men, and turning out work to the amount of $118,000 annually; the Newburgh Steam Printing Cloth Manufactory, employing 325 hands, and producing $200,000 worth of goods per annum; a brewery, employing 35 men, and producing 35,000 bbls. of beer; and an agricultural implement factory, a car factory, a car wheel factory, a piano forte factory, a soap factory, a machine shop, boiler works, and a barrel manufactory,—in the aggregate giving employment to 200 hands, and producing annually goods to the amount of $240,000.

[6] Shipping to the amount of about 4,000 tons burden is owned at this place. The receipts of lumber brought by the R. R. to this place in 1858 amounted to about 21,000,000 ft., and 20,000 bunches of shingles.

[7] The main body of this house was erected by Jonathan Hasbrouck in 1750, and from this circumstance it was formerly known as "The Old Hasbrouck House." The kitchen on the N. was added in 1760, making it a long, narrow building. In 1770 an addition was made upon the whole length of the w. side, and a new roof was thrown over the whole. There are 8 rooms on the first floor, and from the principal room 8 doors open leading to every part of the house, including the chambers and cellar. This building was used by Washington for his headquarters while the American army occupied this position upon the Hudson. It was purchased by the State in 1850, and is kept as nearly as possible in its original condition. The rooms and the grounds are filled with relics of the Revolution and

mementos of the War of 1812 and the Mexican War. The walls of the bedroom occupied by Washington are covered by original letters of Washington, La Fayette, and other distinguished men of the Revolution, framed and glazed. Among the curiosities are the tables used by Washington and La Fayette, links from the chain which was stretched across the Hudson, and a great variety of warlike implements. Near the N. E. corner of the house is the grave of Uzal Knapp, the last of Washington's Life Guards; he died in Jan. 1856.

[8] The "Newburgh Patent" was granted to George Lackstead, Michael Wiegard, Heman Shoreman, Christian Henreich, —— Cockertal, Burgher Myndus, Jacob Webber, Johannes Fisher, and Andreas Valch,—all from Palatine, on the Rhine. They made a settlement, designated a site for a village, and called it Newburgh. How long they remained is not known; but previous to 1752 they sold out their grant, as at that date the patent was renewed by Gov. Clinton to Alexander Colden, Richard Albertson, Edmund Conklin, jr., William Ward, Thomas Ward, Nathan Truman, Jacob Wandell, Johannes Wandell, Daniel Thurston, James Denton, Cahless Leveridge, Michael Demott, Wm. Smith, Henry Smith, Duncan Alexander, and William Mitchell. It is supposed that those last named were from England. Some of the early settlers were of Dutch descent; and a few were Huguenots originally from France. Of this last class were the Hasbroucks, Demotts, Slutts, Devines, Devolls, Degroves, Duboises, Hardenburghs, Snyders, Terwilligers, and Benscotens. The Hasbroucks came as early as 1750. The old Glebe School House was erected in 1752. Jonathan Hasbrouck erected the first mill, in 1753. A tract of 500 acres, called the "Glebe," near the N. line of Newburgh Village, was originally granted for the support of the gospel and schools.

[9] Outside of Newburgh Village there are 3 churches in town; all M. E.

[10] This building will accommodate 200 inmates. It is amply supplied with bath rooms and water, and is one of the best furnished and managed institutions of its kind in the country. A school is maintained throughout the year.

[11] The Precinct of New Windsor was formed from the "*Precinct of the Highlands,*" in 1763.

manufacture. **Moodna**[1] (p. o.) contains a cotton factory, paper mill, and 10 dwellings. **Mortonville,** (p. o.,) in the s. e. part contains 1 church, a gristmill, and 6 dwellings. **Little Britain,** near the center, is a p. o. The first settlements were made in 1731, by several emigrants from Ireland, prominent among whom was Col. Charles Clinton, grandfather of De Witt Clinton.[2] The first church (Asso. Ref.) was formed at Little Britain, in 1760; Rev. Robert Annan was the first pastor.[3]

WALKILL—was formed March 7, 1788. A part of *"Calhoun,"* now Mount Hope, was taken off in 1825, and a part of Hamptonburgh in 1830. It lies upon the n. w. border of the co., n. e. of the center. Its surface is a hilly and broken upland. The principal streams are Shawangunk River, forming the n. w. boundary, and Wall Kil, forming a part of the s. e. boundary. Monhagan Creek and several other streams are tributaries of these two. The soil is a clayey and gravelly loam. **Middletown,** (p. v.,) in the s. part, was incorp. Feb. 10, 1848. Next to Newburgh, it is the largest village in the co. It contains 7 churches, the Walkill Academy, several private seminaries, 2 banks, 2 newspaper offices, and several manufacturing establishments.[4] It is an important freight and milk station upon the Erie R. R.[5] Pop. 1,873. **Circleville,** (p. v.,) 5 mi. n. of Middletown, contains 2 churches and 16 dwellings. **Scotch Town,** (p. v.,) 4 mi. n. e. of Middletown, contains 1 church and 20 dwellings. **Howells Depot,** (p. v.,) a station upon the r. r., 4 mi. n. w. of Middletown, contains a church and 15 dwellings. **Mechanic Town,** 2 mi. e. of Middletown, contains a woolen factory and 20 dwellings. **Philipsburgh** and **Rockville** are hamlets. The first settlement was made by Wm. and Thomas Bull, sons of Wm. Bull, of Goshen, who located upon Wall Kil in 1767.[6] There are 12 churches in town.[7]

WARWICK—was formed March 7, 1788. A part of Chester was taken off in 1845. It lies upon the line of N. J., in the extreme s. angle of the co. Its surface is mountainous in the s. and e. and broken and hilly in the n. and w. The principal mountain ranges are the Sterling, Rough, and Warwick Mts. in the s. e., and the Bellvale Mts. in the e.[8] They are high, steep, and rocky, and have all the characteristics peculiar to a wild, mountain region. In the extreme w. part is a nearly level region, occupied by the Drowned Lands.[9] Several eminences in the midst of these lands are denominated islands.[10] The principal streams are Wall Kil, forming the w. boundary, Quaker Creek, forming the n. w. boundary, and the Wawayanda, or Warwick, and Pochuck Creeks. Greenwood Lake, upon the s. line, extends about 4 mi. into this town. The other principal bodies of water are Sterling, Wickhams, and Thompsons Ponds, near the e. border. The soil is light and unproductive upon the hills, and a gravelly and sandy loam in the valleys. **Warwick,** (p. v.,) on Wawayanda Creek, near the center of the town, contains 3 churches, the Warwick Institute, and 358 inhabitants. **Florida,** (p. v.,) in the n. part, contains 3 churches, the S. S. Seward Seminary,[11] and 45 dwellings; **Amity,** (p. v.,) in the w. part, 1 church and 30 dwellings; **Edenville,** (p. v.,) 2 mi. n. e. of Amity, a church and 24 dwellings; **New Milford,** (p. v.,) in the s. part, a church and 26 dwellings; **Bellvale,** (p. v.,) in the e., a church and 192 inhabitants; and **Dutch Hollow,** 2 mi. s. e. of Bellvale, a church and 15 dwellings. **Sterling Works,** in the extreme s. part, is a hamlet.[12] The precise date of the first settlement is unknown. Daniel Burt, from Conn., came into town in 1746.[13] The first church (Presb.) was formed in 1764, and the second (Bap.) in 1766.[14] Hon. Wm. H. Seward was born at the village of Florida.

---

[1] Name derived from Murderers Creek, and bestowed by N. P. Willis. Formerly known as Orangeville.

[2] In 1732 or '33, families named Alsop, Ellison, Chambers, and Lawrence settled upon the present site of New Windsor Village. The headquarters of the American army were at this place at one time during the Revolution.

[3] There are 6 churches in town; 3 M. E., Presb., Prot. E., and Asso. Ref.

[4] The principal establishments are a carpet bag factory, file factory, grain cradle factory, hat factory, 2 sash and blind factories, and a foundery and machine shop. In the aggregate these factories employ about 300 hands, and manufacture goods to the amount of $450,000 annually.

[5] 2,500 gall. of milk are sent daily to N. Y. from the r. r. stations in this town.

[6] Among the other early settlers were families named McCord, McNeal, Borland, Rogers, Butterfield, Wisner, Murray, McCarter, McVey, McWhorter, McDennis, McLaughlin, Campbell, Watkins, and Faulkner, the most of whom were Scotch emigrants.

[7] 4 Presb., 3 Bap., 2 Cong., 2 M. E., and R. C.

[8] The principal elevations in town are Hogback, Decker, One Pine, and Hulls Hills, in the e.; Bill and Coxcomb Hills, in the center; Long, Cedar, Pond, and Bill Whites Hills, in the s. e.;

Round, Rocky, and Chucks Hills, in the s.; Ponchuck Mt. and Green and Adneys Hills, in the w.; and Mts. Adam and Eve, and Round Hill, in the n. w.

[9] These lands have mostly been drained and converted into the most valuable meadows.

[10] Among these eminences are Pine, Merritt, Gardners, Black Walnut, Cranberry, and Fox Islands.

[11] This seminary was founded about 1845, by Judge S. S. Seward, father of Wm. H. Seward, who endowed it with a fund of $20,000.

[12] Sterling Works receives its name from the iron works located upon the outlet of Sterling Pond. The manufacture of iron has been carried on at this place for 100 years or more. Gen. Wm. Alexander, Lord Sterling, is said to have been interested in them at one time; and hence their name. Anchors and steel were manufactured here during the Revolution. 12 to 15 tons of pig iron are now made here per day.

[13] Among the other early settlers were Thos. Willing, Daniel Whitney, Benj. Burt, John Vance, and David McCauley. The first mill was built by David Burt, at Bellvale, in 1760. Many of the early settlers were Dutch, and others English, from Mass. and Conn.

[14] There are 11 churches in town; 6 M.E., 3 Presb., Bap., and Ref. Prot. D.

WAWAYANDA[1]—was formed from Minisink, Nov. 15, 1849. It is an interior town, lying s. w. of the center of the co. Its surface is rolling and hilly. The highest summit is Joe Gee Hill,[2] in the N. W. part. The Drowned Lands occupy a portion of the s. E. corner. The principal streams are Wall Kil, forming the s. E. boundary, Rutgers Creek, forming the s. w. boundary, Wawayanda Creek, in the w. part, and Monhagan Creek, in the N. E. corner. The soil is chiefly a clay and sandy loam, and is best adapted to pasturage.[3] **New Hampton,** (p. v.,) on Wall Kil, in the N. E. corner, contains a gristmill, sawmill, and 25 dwellings ; **Denton,** 1 mi. s. w. of New Hampton, 1 church and 25 dwellings ; **Ridgebury,** (p. v.,) near the center, 2 churches and 30 dwellings ; **Slate Hill,** (p. v.,) 1 mi. w. of Ridgebury, 1 church and 25 dwellings ; **Centerville,** in the w. part, 1 church and 15 dwellings ; **Millsburgh,** (Wells Corner p. o.,) 1 mi. s. of Centerville, on the line of Minisink, a grist and saw mill and 15 dwellings ; and **Gardnersville,** in the s. part, on the line of Minisink, a gristmill, sawmill, and 15 dwellings. The first settlements are supposed to have been made previous to 1700.[4] There are 5 churches in town ; 3 Presb., M. E., and Bap.

Acres of Land, Valuation, Population, Dwellings, Families, Freeholders, Schools, Live Stock, Agricultural Products, and Domestic Manufactures, of Orange County.

NAMES OF TOWNS.	ACRES OF LAND. Improved.	Unimproved.	VALUATION OF 1858. Real Estate.	Personal Property.	Total.	POPULATION. Males.	Females.	No. of Dwellings.	No. of Families.	Freeholders.	SCHOOLS. No. of Districts.	Children taught.
Blooming Grove........	15,491	5,549¼	$989,921	$320,109	$1,310,030	1,094	1,090	364	389	211	11	781
Chester..............	12,521½	2,968	689,132	311,850	1,000,982	841	855	277	310	189	5	403
Cornwall.............	10,874¼	15,594	656,729	107,650	764,379	2,420	2,158	648	808	401	9	1,348
Crawford.............	19,575	4,688	692,445	125,975	818,420	959	1,041	338	356	221	10	701
Deerpark.............	8,998¼	22,473	1,342,945	210,690	1,553,635	2,946	2,558	851	972	449	9	1,637
Goshen..............	20,853¼	3,676¼	1,288,175	438,450	1,726,625	1,566	1,647	482	529	226	10	1,040
Greenville...........	12,675	4,736	414,703	41,100	455,803	606	612	217	233	140	7	514
Hamptonburgh........	14,519½	2,184	693,287	131,607	824,894	662	641	212	223	141	6	434
Minisink.............	11,590	2,497	521,863	97,450	619,313	635	660	231	242	161	8	656
Monroe	19,959¼	77,666¼	1,034,800	149,662	1,184,462	2,380	2,171	737	812	290	16	1,703
Montgomery..........	23,186¼	5,703	1,434,841	460,135	1,894,976	1,820	1,972	642	715	380	15	1,376
Mount Hope..........	12,070¼	3,890	560,195	57,650	617,845	857	878	318	363	220	4	493
Newburgh............	23,244¼	4,078¼	3,939,875	2,383,716	6,323,591	6,122	6,651	1,729	2,443	630	13	5,047
New Windsor..........	17,500	3,371	977,825	301,687	1,279,512	1,278	1,277	386	444	216	9	817
Walkill..............	32,391½	7,358½	1,816,860	569,800	2,386,660	2,636	2,779	915	1,040	622	18	2,114
Warwick	36,003¼	20,326½	1,704,901	268,475	1,973,376	2,488	2,499	875	930	477	24	1,868
Wawayanda	17,145	2,855	724,934	139,894	864,828	1,007	1,062	360	377	172	10	643
Total................	308,599¾	189,615	19,483,431	6,115,900	25,599,331	30,317	30,551	9,582	11,136	5,146	184	21,575

NAMES OF TOWNS.	LIVE STOCK. Horses.	Working Oxen and Calves.	Cows.	Sheep.	Swine.	AGRICULTURAL PRODUCTS. BUSH. OF GRAIN. Winter.	Spring.	Tons of Hay.	Bushels of Potatoes.	Bushels of Apples.	DAIRY PRODUCTS. Pounds of Butter.	Pounds of Cheese.	Domestic cloths, in Yards.
Blooming Grove........	386	838	2,358	2,467	1,644	10,054	26,538½	5,815¼	4,363	2,004	95,060		
Chester..............	379	499	1,920	354	726	8,045½	24,719¼	5,099	14,582	347	21,175		
Cornwall.............	473	735	1,274	846	1,445	6,361	13,820½	3,251	2,649¼	3,179	77,844		
Crawford.............	570	798	2,395	1,000	3,500	13,826¼	44,723	5,481	6,617	11,836	252,020		747
Deerpark.............	378	738	726	270	779	10,548	21,818	2,149	12,304	5,505	46,194		142
Goshen..............	670	1,127	3,213	2,474	2,028	10,625¼	49,835	8,194	10,188	921	129,918		
Greenville...........	374	922	1,918	499	1,505	6,908	21,576	4,076	2,705	2,470	249,248	60	300
Hamptonburgh........	437	662	1,979	2,403	2,200	11,819	31,781	5,332	1,965	2,862	177,820		
Minisink.............	382	894	1,837	331	1,774	7,063¼	28,839¼	3,913	2,828	3,182	243,749		138
Monroe	541	1,340	2,409	810	1,572	10,708	33,673¼	6,650	8,162	2,173	98,270	600	130
Montgomery..........	782	1,025	2,859	2,856	5,097	34,928½	70,537¼	7,481	13,252	11,671	312,466		179
Mount Hope..........	377	539	1,681	415	986	7,513¼	19,217¼	3,344¼	3,379¼	1,066	141,146		171
Newburgh............	1,183	1,113	2,456	973	3,691	32,521	71,011¼	6,792½	10,758½	5,601	218,963¼		249
New Windsor..........	574	951	2,169	1,199	3,000	17,046	45,607¼	6,053	6,467	5,333	218,832		
Walkill..............	921	1,475	3,085	1,580	3,778	20,553¼	65,616	11,723¼	10,369	17,510	365,843		461½
Warwick	1,125	2,936	5,119	2,447	5,180	30,475	73,525¼	12,007½	8,932	3,886¼	416,494	80,000	345½
Wawayanda..........	434	823	2,789	453	1,779	6,668	29,575	5,849	4,030	634	220,545		85
Total................	9,986	17,415	40,187	21,377	40,684	245,664¼	672,414½	103,211¼	123,551½	80,180¼	3,285,587¼	80,660¼	2,948¼

[1] The name is said by some to be an Indian corruption of the English phrase "away over yonder."—*Eager's Hist. Orange Co., pp.* 432, 433.
[2] Named from the last Indian who had his cabin on the hill.

[3] 1,500 gallons of milk are sent daily from this town to the N. Y. market.
[4] Among the early settlers were John Denton, Richard Carpenter, Isaac Dolson, and Daniel and David Cooley. Isaac Dolson built a blockhouse as a protection against the Indians, in 1756.

ORLEANS COUNTY.

This county was formed from Genesee, Nov. 11, 1824; Shelby was annexed from Genesee April 5, 1825. It lies on Lake Ontario, between Monroe and Niagara cos., centrally distant 232 mi. from Albany, and contains 405 sq. mi. Its surface is level or undulating, and, except in the extreme s. part, it has a gradual inclination toward the lake. It is divided into three distinct plateaus by the lake and mountain ridges,[1] which extend E. and W. through the co. nearly parallel to the lake shore. The lower plateau slopes slightly and uniformly upward from the lake shore to the lake ridge, a distance of 6 to 8 mi., where it attains an elevation of about 165 feet. This ridge is composed of sand and gravel, and its seaward side is covered with coarse gravel and water-worn pebbles, resembling the present lake beach.[2] It is elevated 20 to 30 feet above the lower plateau, to which it descends with a gentle inclination uniform in its whole extent. There is generally a similar slope upon its inland side; but in many places the level of the country is nearly and sometimes quite as high as that of the ridge. The ridge is 100 to 300 feet wide at the top, and nearly level. From the earliest settlement of the co. its summit has been used for a road. The second plateau is gently undulating, and 4 to 6 mi. wide, attaining an altitude of about 300 feet at the base of the mountain ridge. This ridge, entering from Niagara co., runs nearly E. through the towns of Shelby and Barre, and s. and E. through Clarendon. It preserves the character of a steep declivity in Clarendon and Shelby, but in Barre its ascent is gradual. The upper plateau is undulating, and from the mountain ridge southerly it gently rises for about 2 mi. to the culminating ridge, which is the highest land in the co. and nearly 450 feet above the lake. For about 2 mi. further the surface is quite level; and thence it gradually descends to the Tonawanda Swamp, on the s. border of the co. The principal streams are Oak Orchard,[3] Johnsons,[4] and Sandy Creeks, which take their rise in or near the Tonawanda Swamp and flow N. and E. to the lake. Their channels are deeply excavated; and upon them are numerous waterfalls and rapids.

The underlying rock of the N. part is the Medina sandstone; while the upper plateau rests upon a base of Niagara limestone. Along the ridge in Clarendon and on the banks of Oak Orchard Creek in Shelby are outcrops of this limestone. Hydraulic limestone has been obtained from both these localities, and quicklime is burned at various places along the ridge. The upper layers of the Medina sandstone afford an excellent material for building and flagging purposes, and several quarries have been opened at Medina and other places on the line of the canal. Elsewhere in the co. this rock is friable, and readily disintegrates upon exposure to the atmosphere. It separates at first into small, angular fragments, and then decomposes into a dark red, loamy clay. Numerous salt springs originate in this formation, from which salt was manufactured until, by the completion of the Erie Canal, they were brought into competition with the salines of Onondaga.[5] The soil in the N. part of the co. is generally sandy; but it is everywhere modified by the underlying formation; and near the lake are several tracts in which clay predominates. In the s. it is a mixture of clay, sand, and lime, and the whole is well adapted to grain raising. The various branches of agriculture form the leading pursuits. Barley, oats, corn, beans, and potatoes are the principal crops,[6] and considerable quantities of apples and other fruits are raised. A limited amount of manufactures is carried on within the co.

The county seat is located at Albion,[7] on the Erie Canal, in the central part of the co. The

---

[1] The lake ridge has been at some time the lake shore; the mountain ridge is a continuation of the mountain ridge of Niagara co., and is formed by the outcropping of the Niagara limestone.

[2] The primitive character of this slope has become somewhat obliterated by cultivation.

[3] So named from a fine grove of oaks formerly at its mouth.

[4] Named after Sir Wm. Johnson, who, with his forces, encamped at its mouth one night when on his way to Fort Niagara in 1759.

[5] Salt works were erected at a spring near Oak Orchard Creek, about 1½ mi. N. of Medina, at Holley, and at Oak Orchard; and salt was made by the early settlers in nearly every town N. of the canal. A boring of 140 feet at Oak Orchard resulted in slightly increasing the strength of the brine, but not its quantity; and at other places, by blasting and boring, the springs were destroyed.

[6] Wheat was formerly the principal crop of this co.; but of late the ravages of the midge have been so extensive that its cultivation has been nearly abandoned.

[7] Previous to the erection of the co. buildings at Albion, the courts were held at the house of Selah Bronson, in the village of Gaines. The commissioners appointed by the Legislature to locate the county seat were Philetus Swift, of Phelps, Ontario co., Victory Birdseye, of Onondaga co., and J. Hathaway, of Cortland co. The site of the co. buildings was deeded to the supervisors by Nehemiah Ingersoll; and the courthouse was built in 1827. Gilbert Howell, of Ridgeway, Elihu Mather, of Gaines, and Calvin Smith, of Barre, were the commissioners

512

courthouse is a fine building, situated in the midst of a park, near the center of the village. It is built of brick, and is surmounted by a dome 110 feet above the ground. It contains the court, jury, supervisors', and surrogate's rooms.[1] The jail, situated just E. of the courthouse, is a commodious edifice, built of Medina sandstone. The county clerk's office is a small, one story brick building, adjoining the courthouse. The poorhouse is located upon a farm of 107 acres in the town of Barre, 3 mi. s. of Albion. Its average number of inmates is 56, supported at a weekly cost of 80 cts. each. The farm yields a revenue of about $700.

The works of internal improvement in the co. are the Erie Canal, extending through near the center; the Tonawanda Swamp Feeder, conducting the waters of the swamp into Oak Orchard Creek and the canal; and the Rochester & Niagara Falls R. R., a branch of the N. Y. Central.[2] Three weekly newspapers are now published in the co.[3]

Long before the advent of the whites this co. was the hunting ground and probable residence of the Iroquois; and there are traces of an occupation long anterior to them and by an entirely distinct race.[4] The 3 eastern towns of the co. belonged to the Conn. Tract and the Pulteney Estate, and the remaining part of the co. to the Holland Purchase. There is a tradition that a Canadian, with his family, settled at the mouth of Oak Orchard Creek as early as 1792–93; but his stay was of short duration, and by some he is now regarded as a myth. The first permanent settlers were James and Wm. Walsworth, two brothers, who came from Canada by the way of the lake, and who located respectively at the mouths of Oak Orchard and Johnsons Creeks, in the present town of Carlton. A few settlers came in each year until 1809, when the great natural thoroughfare, the ridge road, was opened, inducing a much more rapid influx of settlers. Immigrants continued to pour in rapidly and settle near the ridge road, until settlement was checked by the War of 1812. Upon the capture of Fort Niagara by the British, in 1813, many of the people fled from their homes, but soon returned.[5] After the return of peace, the tide of immigration again set in toward this region, and continued to flow steadily and uninterruptedly for several years. The settlers generally chose locations in the immediate vicinity of the ridge road, and continued to do so until the completion of the Erie Canal, when the regions further s. began rapidly to fill up. Since that time steady progress has been made in every element of material prosperity, until the co. has taken front rank among the best agricultural regions of the State.

BARRE[6]—was formed from Gaines, March 6, 1818. It is the most southerly of the middle tier of towns, and is the largest town in the co. Its surface is undulating, and its soil a rich loam underlaid by the Niagara limestone. The Tonawanda Swamp occupies the s. part. **Albion,**[7]

appointed to superintend its erection. The first officers of the co. were Elijah Foot, *First Judge;* S. M. Moody, Cyrus Harwood, Eldridge Farwell, and William Penniman, *Judges;* William Lewis, *Sheriff;* and Orson Nicholson, *Co. Clerk.*

[1] The courthouse was erected in 1857–58, at a cost of $20,000. The courtroom is a large and spacious apartment, 56 feet long by 55 feet wide, and 26 feet high.

[2] The Medina & Darien R. R. Co. was organized in 1835, and the road was opened as far as Akron. Stages drawn by horses were put upon the road; but the whole was abandoned in 2 or 3 years.

[3] *The Gazette,* the first paper published in the co., was started at Gaines in 1822 by Seymour Tracy, and was continued 4 years.

The Newport Patriot was started at "*Newport,*" now Albion, Feb. 9, 1824, by Franklin Cowdrey. In Feb. 1825, Timothy C. Strong became proprietor, and changed it to

The Orleans Advocate. In Feb. 1828, in the midst of the excitement following the abduction of Morgan, Mr. Strong changed it to

The Orleans Advocate and Anti Masonic Telegraph; and in Feb. 1829, it took the name of

The Orleans Anti Masonic Telegraph. In June of the same year it was changed to

The Orleans Telegraph; and soon after to

The American Standard. It was issued 2 years by J. Kempshall, when it passed back into the hands of Mr. Strong, who changed it to

The Orleans American. In April, 1844, it passed into the hands of J. & J. H. Denio, and was continued by them until 1853, when it was bought by S. A. Andrews, by whom it is now published.

The Orleans Republican was commenced at Albion in Oct. 1829, by C. S. McConnell. It was published by him until 1841; by H. W. Dupuy a few months; by an association until 1845; by H. E. Purdy until 1846; and by C. S. McConnell until 1848, when it was sold to Wilson & Beach, its present publishers.

The Albion Times was established Oct. 23, 1853, by J. O. Nickerson. Jan. 11, 1855, it was changed to

The Spirit of Seventy-Six, and continued until May 27, 1858.

The Orleans Whig was commenced at Gaines in July, 1827, by John Fisk, and continued several years.

The Medina Herald was issued in 1832 by Daniel P. Adams, and continued 2 or 3 years.

The Medina Sentinel was started in Aug. 1837, by J. & J. H. Denio. The following year it was changed to

The Orleans Sentinel, and continued until May, 1842.

The Bucktail was commenced in 1840 by S. M. Burroughs. It was subsequently changed to

The Medina Democrat, and continued 2 or 3 years.

The Medina Citizen was started in 1850 by H. A. Smith. In 1852 it was changed to

The Medina Tribune, and is still issued by Mr. Smith.

The People's Journal was published at Medina a short time in 1858 by J. W. Swan.

[4] About 1½ mi. w. of Shelby Center are the remains of an ancient fortification, nearly circular in form, enclosing an area of about 3 acres. A broad ditch encircled the whole. Flint arrow heads, stone axes, several piles of small stones, and pieces of earthenware have been found within the enclosure. Trees of 400 years' growth stand upon the embankment. Large numbers of human skeletons, many of them of giant size, have been exhumed near the fort. Many of these seem to have been thrown promiscuously into one common grave; and it is generally supposed that this has been the scene of a great battle.

[5] As soon as the news of the capture of Fort Niagara reached the village of Gaines, Capt. Eleazur McCourty, with a company of volunteers, started for the Niagara frontier. On their way they surprised and captured, after a short conflict, a body of marauding British and Indians at Mulenoux's tavern, in the town of Cambria, Niagara co. They subsequently captured another party near Youngstown, and compelled them to carry back their booty to "Hardscrable," (Dickersonville.) They remained upon the lines about 20 days, until the arrival of the militia drafted from Cayuga and the adjoining cos.

[6] Named from Barre, Mass.

[7] Originally called "*Newport,*" but changed at the time of its incorporation.

(p. v.,) the county seat, was incorp. April 21, 1828. It is situated on the Erie Canal, in the N. part of the town, and is the principal station upon the N. Y. C. R. R. between Rochester and Lockport. It contains 5 churches, the Phipps Union Female Seminary,[1] the Albion Academy, a bank, 2 newspaper offices, and several manufactories.[2] Pop. 3,776. **Barre Center,** (p. o.,) 4 mi. s. of Albion, contains 30 dwellings. **Eagle Harbor** lies partly in this town. **South Barre** (p. o.) and **Jacksons Corners** (West Barre p. o.) are hamlets. **Rich's Corners** is in the N. E. part. Settlement was commenced by Wm. McAllister, in 1811.[3] The first church (Cong.) was organized Nov. 5, 1816, by Revs. Eleazur Fairbanks and Comfort Williams.[4]

CARLTON—was formed from Gaines and Ridgeway, April 13, 1822, as "*Oak Orchard.*" Its name was changed in 1825. It lies on the lake shore, between Kendall and Yates, and is crossed in a N. E. direction by Oak Orchard and Johnsons Creeks. The surface is level, and the soil generally sandy. Salt water has been discovered near West Carlton.[5] **Carlton,**[6] (p. o.,) **East Carlton,** (p. o.,) **West Carlton,** (p. o.,) **Waterport,** (p. o.,) **Kenyonville, Carlton Center,** and **Manilla** are hamlets. Settlement was commenced in 1803, by two brothers, James and William Walsworth,—the former at the mouth of Oak Orchard Creek, the latter on Johnsons Creek. Matthew Dunham and his sons Matthew, James, and Charles, from N. Y. City, settled near Johnsons Creek in the fall of 1803.[7] The first church (M. E.) was organized at West Carlton, about 1816.[8]

CLARENDON—was formed from Sweden, Monroe co., Feb. 23, 1821. It is the S. E. corner town of the co. The E. branch of Sandy Creek rises in the Tonawanda Swamp and flows N. Upon this stream are two waterfalls,—one at the village of Clarendon and the other in the N. part of the town. Along the line of the mountain ridge the surface is broken, and elsewhere it is gently rolling or level. The soil is a sandy loam; in the N. stony. Limestone for building purposes and hydraulic limestone have been obtained at Clarendon. **Clarendon**[9] (p. v.) contains 2 churches, a limited number of manufactors,[10] and about 30 dwellings. The first settlement was made in 1811, at the village of Clarendon, by Eldridge Farwell.[11] There are now 3 churches in town.[12]

GAINES[13]—was formed from Ridgeway, Feb. 14, 1816. Barre was taken off in 1818, and a part of Carlton in 1822. It is the central town in the co. It is crossed by Otter and Marsh Creeks, branches of the Oak Orchard, and by the W. branch of Sandy Creek. The lake ridge extends E. and W. through the center. The surface is level and the soil sandy. **Eagle Harbor,** (p. v.,) on the Erie Canal, contains 2 churches, 2 flouring mills, and a large stave factory and cooperage. Pop. 639,—509 in Gaines and 130 in Barre. **Gaines**[14] (p. v.) contains 2 churches and 342 inhabitants. **East Gaines** and **West Gaines** are p. offices; and **Fairhaven** and **Gaines Basin,** on the canal, are hamlets. The first settlement was made prior to 1809, by —— Gilbert. Noah Burgess, Samuel Crippen, —— Elliott, and Elijah Downer came in 1809.[15] The first church (Bap.) was organized in 1816.[16]

---

[1] The Phipps Union Female Seminary was established in 1833. The main building was erected in 1836, and additions have been since made, until the whole outlays have reached $20,000. The average number of pupils is about 250.

[2] Flouring mills, furnaces, a woolen factory, a tannery, a cabinet ware manufactory, and a planing mill.

[3] McAllister settled on the present site of the Phipps Female Seminary, near the courthouse. Among the earliest settlers were Joseph Stoddart, Reuben Clark, Joseph Hart, and Elijah Darrow, who located in the N. part of the town in 1812. The first death, that of Mrs. McAllister, occurred in Sept. 1811. The first sawmill was built by Wm. White in 1816, on Sandy Creek, a little E. of Albion; the first gristmill, in 1819, by Wm. Bradner, near the same place; and the first tavern was kept by Abraham Mattison, in 1815, at Bentons Corners, about 2 mi. s. of Albion. The first school was taught by Mrs. Cyrus Benton.

[4] There are 7 churches in town; Presb., Bap., Prot. E., M. E., and R. C. at Albion, Cong. at Barre Center, and M. E. at Jacksons Corners.

[5] Lyman Fuller, in digging a well, bored through a stratum of rock, and obtained salt water of such strength that 2 galls. yielded a pint of salt. The hole through the rock was plugged up, and fresh water came in from above.

[6] Locally known as "Two Bridges."

[7] In 1804, Elijah Hunt, Henry Lovell, Moses Root, Elijah Brown, and Job Shipman settled in this town. The first death in town, unless it was that of a member of the Canadian family n.entioned on page ——, was that of a deserter from Fort Niagara, who was drowned in attempting to cross Johnsons Creek, about 1800. The first death of an actual settler was that of Elijah Brown, May 7, 1805. The first births were those of a pair of twins, children of James Walsworth, in 1806; and the first marriage, that of Wm. Carter and Amy Hunt, in 1804. The first gristmill was built on Johnsons Creek, by Matthew Dunham, in 1806; and the first store was opened in 1816, at West Carlton,

by Geo. Kuck. The first school was taught by Peleg Helms, in the winter of 1810–11.

[8] There are now 5 churches in town; Bap. and Presb. at Carlton, M. E. at West Carlton, Bap. at East Carlton, and M. E. at Kenyonville. The first religious services in town were conducted by "Old Mr. Steele," a M. E. preacher from Canada, some time prior to 1810.

[9] Formerly known as "*Farwells Mills.*"

[10] 2 sawmills, a gristmill, and a furnace.

[11] Benj. Thomas, Benajah Worden, Elisha Huntly, John Cone, John Stephens, David Church, and Chauncey Robinson were among the earliest settlers. Eldridge Farwell built the first sawmill, on Sandy Creek, in 1811, and the first gristmill, in 1813. The first store was kept by Hiram Frisbee, in 1821; and the first school was taught by Mrs. Amanda Bills.

[12] M. E. and Univ. at Clarendon, and a Christian church about 1¼ mi. w. of Clarendon.

[13] Named in honor of Gen. E. P. Gaines, through the instrumentality of Wm. J. Babbitt.

[14] Incorp. by the Legislature in 1832, but never organized under the act.

[15] Among the early settlers were Reuben Rowley, Harry Wilcox, Joseph and Aaron Adams, Robert and Cotton Leach, Newbury Chafey, Dyer Sprague, Samuel Rosier, Wm. Burlingame, Walter Fairfield, Lansing Bailey, John Proctor, and James Mather. The first death was that of —— Gilbert, who died in or before 1809. His wife and niece, Amy Scott, remained, and wintered a yoke of oxen and several cows upon browse cut by themselves. The first birth was that of Samuel Crippen, jr., in 1810; and the first marriage, that of Cyrus Daniels and Elizabeth Freeman, July 4, 1812. The first inn was kept by Wm. Sibley, in 1811; and the first store, by Wm. Perry, in 1815. Orin Gleason taught the first school, in the winter of 1813–14. Henry Drake built the first sawmill, in 1813; and the first gristmill was built by Jonathan Gates, in 1822.

[16] There are 6 churches in town; M. E. and Wes. Meth. at

KENDALL[1]—was taken from Murray, April 7, 1837. It lies on the lake shore,[2] in the E. part of the co., and is crossed by Bald Eagle Creek near the center, and Sandy Creek in the s. part. Its surface is level; and the soil, with the exception of a belt of clay across the s. part, is a sandy loam. There are several small salt springs in the town. **Kendall** (p.v.) contains 4 churches and about 25 dwellings. **West Kendall** (p.o.) and **Kendall Mills** (p.o.) are hamlets. The first settlement was made in 1812, by Samuel Bates, from Chittenden co., Vt.[3] The first religious service, conducted by Elder Stephen Randall, was held in the spring of 1816.[4]

MURRAY—was formed from "*Northampton*," (now Gates, Monroe co.,) April 8, 1808. Sweden was taken off in 1813, Clarkson in 1819, and Kendall in 1837. It lies on the E. border of the co., between Clarendon and Kendall, and is crossed by Sandy Creek, the two branches of which unite at Murray, in the N. part of the town. This stream has worn a deep channel; at Holley it is about 75 feet below the level of the land. The embankment over which the N. Y. C. R. R. crosses the gulf is one of the largest on the line of that road. The surface is generally level, except in the s. w. part, where it is rolling. The soil is mostly a sandy loam; in some parts, however, it is clayey. Near Holley are two sulphur and several salt springs, at the latter of which salt was manufactured previous to the opening of the canal. The Medina sandstone approaches near the surface; and quarries have been opened in the neighborhood of Hulberton.[5] **Holley,**[6] (p.v.,) incorp. Sept. 3, 1850, a station on the N. Y. C. R. R., is situated in the s. part of the town, on the Erie Canal. It contains 2 churches, the Holley Academy, and several manufacturing establishments.[7] Pop. 614. **Hulberton** (p.v.) contains 278 inhabitants; and **Hindsburgh** (p.v.) 167. **Murray**[8] (p.o.) and **Brockville** are hamlets. **Murray Depot** is a R. R. station. The first settlement was made by Epaphras Mattison, prior to 1809.[9] The first church (Cong.) was formed Jan. 5, 1819, by Rev. John F. Bliss.[10]

RIDGEWAY[11]—was formed from Batavia, (Genesee co.,) June 8, 1812. Gaines was taken off in 1816, Shelby in 1818, and Yates and a part of Carlton in 1822. It lies on the w. border of the co., between Shelby and Yates, and is crossed by Johnsons and Oak Orchard Creeks. Upon the latter, at Medina, is a waterfall about 30 feet high; and at Jeddo and Oak Orchard, where the streams cross the lake ridge, are low waterfalls. The surface is generally level, and the soil a sandy loam. Some of the most important of the salt springs of this co. are in this town.[12] Within and near the village of Medina are extensive quarries; and large quantities of building, flagging, and paving stone are sent to Rochester, Buffalo, and other places on the canal.[13] **Medina,** (p.v.,) incorp. March 30, 1832, lies on the Erie Canal, mostly within this town. It is an important station on the N. Y. C. R. R., and is connected with Ridgeway on the N. and Shelby Center on the s. by the Medina & Alabama Plank Road. It contains 5 churches, an academy,[14] a newspaper office, and several manufactories.[15] Pop. in 1855, 2,104,—in Ridgeway 1,915, in Shelby 189. **Knowlesville,**[16] (p.v.,) a station on the N. Y. C. R. R., situated in the E. part of the town, on the Erie Canal, contains 3 churches and several manufactories.[17] Pop. 490. **Oak Orchard**[18] (p.v.) has a pop. of 136; **Jeddo** (p.v.) of 124; and **Ridgeway** (p.v.) of 64. **North Ridgeway** is a p.o. The first settlement was made by Ezra D. Barnes, from De Ruyter,

Eagle Harbor, Cong. and Presb. at Gaines, Univ. at Fairhaven, and Free Will Bap. at East Gaines.

[1] Named in honor of Amos Kendall, P. M. Gen.

[2] Near the mouth of Bald Eagle Creek the lake makes rapid encroachments upon the land, and whole fields have been swept away.

[3] Among the early settlers were Amos Randall, David Jones, Benj. Morse, and Nathaniel Brown, who came in 1815. The first birth was that of Bartlett Morse, in 1816; the first marriage, that of James Aiken and Esther A. Bates, March 2, 1817; and the first death, that of a son of Geo. Balcom, in 1816. The first store was kept by Hiram Thompson, in 1823; the first inn, by Lyman Spicer, in 1823; and the first sawmill was built by Ammon Auger & Ebenezer Boyden, in 1819. The first school was taught by Gerdon Balcom, in 1819.

[4] There are 5 churches in town; Univ., Bap., Presb., and M. E. at Kendall, and M. E. at West Kendall.

[5] St. Paul's Church in Buffalo is built of material obtained at one of these quarries.

[6] Named in honor of Myron Holley, one of the first canal commissioners.

[7] A gristmill, a tannery, a furnace and plow factory, and a cabinet ware manufactory.

[8] Locally known as "Sandy Creek."

[9] Among the early settlers were Daniel Wait, Joshua Rockwood, and Peleg Sisson. The first birth in town was that of Betsey Mattison, in 1811; the first marriage, that of Zimri Perrigo and Lucetta Spafford, Jan. 17, 1815; and the first death, that of Mrs. Daniel Reed, in 1814. The first inn was kept by Epaphras Mattison, in 1809; the first store, by Isaac Leach, in

1815; and the first gristmill was built by Perry & Luce, in 1816. Fanny Furguson taught the first school, in the summer of 1814.

[10] There are 4 churches in town; Bap. and Presb. at Holley, M. E. at Hulberton, and Bap. in w. part of town.

[11] So named from the ridge way or road formed by the lake ridge running E. and w. through the town.

[12] Salt works were erected at a spring N. of Medina by the Holland Land Co. as early as 1805, and thrown open for the use of the settlers. Two roads opened by the Co. at the same time—one from the works s. to the "Old Buffalo Road," and the other E. to the "Oak Orchard Road"—were widely known as the "*Salt Works Roads.*"

[13] The principal quarries are owned by Isaac Hathaway and John Ryan. The upper layers cleave off in smooth slabs from 2 to 5 inches thick. The succeeding layers are thicker,—some of the lower ones several feet. Besides what has been sent to the larger places for building, flagging, and paving, large quantities have been quarried for building bridge abutments and canal walls.

[14] The Medina Academy was incorp. in 1849, and is both an academy and a common school, participating in both the literature and common school funds. The average number of pupils is 400.

[15] 5 flouring and grist mills, with an aggregate of 22 run of stone, 2 oil mills, 2 iron foundries, 2 sash and blind factories, a tannery, and a machine shop.

[16] Named after Dea. —— Knowles, one of the earliest settlers

[17] A steam sawmill, steam gristmill, tannery, and plaster mill

[18] At Oak Orchard is a distillery.

Madison co., N. Y., in 1809.[1] The first church (Presb.) was formed at Oak Orchard in 1817, by Rev. Jedediah Fairbanks.[2]

SHELBY[3]—was formed from Ridgeway, March 6, 1818. It is the s. w. corner town of the co. Johnsons Creek and a branch of the Oak Orchard take their rise in this town, and the Oak Orchard crosses it through the center. Upon the latter stream, at Shelby Center, is a fall, affording a valuable water-power. The surface is undulating; and the soil a mixture of sand, clay, and lime. The Tonawanda Swamp occupies the s. part. **Shelby**[4] (Shelby Center p. o.) contains 1 church and several manufactories;[5] **Millville** (p. v.) contains 3 churches, the Millville Academy, and about 45 dwellings. **East Shelby** (p. o.) and **Shelby Basin** (p. o.) are hamlets; and **West Shelby** is a p. office. **Medina** is partly in this town. The remains of Indian fortifications have been discovered in this town. The first settlement was made by Alex. Coon, from Rensselaer co., in 1810.[6] The first church (Bap.) was formed July 25, 1818.[7]

YATES[8]—was formed from Ridgeway, April 17, 1822, as "*Northton;*" its name was changed the following year. It is the most westerly town upon the lake shore. It is crossed by Johnsons Creek and two smaller streams. Marsh Creek and Four Mile Creek have their whole course in the town. The surface is level, except along Johnsons Creek, where it is undulating; the soil in the s. is a sandy loam, and along the lake clayey. **Lyndonville** (p. v.) contains 3 churches and several manufactories. Pop. 242. **Yates Center** (Yates p. o.) contains 1 church and the Yates Academy. Pop. 191. **County Line** (p. o.) is on the w. line of the town. George Houseman, from Adams, Jefferson co., settled in this town in 1809, and John Eaton, from Penn., in 1810.[9] There are now 6 churches in town.[10]

Acres of Land, Valuation, Population, Dwellings, Families, Freeholders, Schools, Live Stock, Agricultural Products, and Domestic Manufactures, of Orleans County.

Names of Towns.	Acres of Land.		Valuation of 1858.			Population.		No. of Dwellings.	No. of Families.	Freeholders.	Schools.	
	Improved.	Unimproved.	Real Estate.	Personal Property.	Total.	Males.	Females.				No. of Districts.	Children taught.
Barre	34,760¼	13,893	$2,417,118	$310,693	$2,727,811	3,428	3,369	1,223	1,142	888	25	2,372
Carlton	21,330	5,623½	888,673	27,720	916,393	1,233	1,096	460	466	364	17	1,039
Clarendon	15,080¾	11,350	711,951	97,569	809,520	918	831	336	350	258	10	713
Gaines	14,082	3,845	741,834	77,300	819,134	1,339	1,193	461	493	322	12	860
Kendall	16,297	4,940	551,947	70,287	622,234	975	909	375	381	306	10	693
Murray	16,387	4,786½	740,509	189,791	930,300	1,470	1,406	519	552	391	12	1,017
Ridgeway	24,386	6,798⅝	1,641,397	201,540	1,842,937	2,793	2,433	933	977	779	18	2,013
Shelby	20,573¾	6,913	1,043,007	71,900	1,114,907	1,593	1,453	593	205	395	15	999
Yates	19,052	4,177	729,387	79,600	808,987	1,023	973	399	427	322	13	808
Total	181,948¾	62,326⅝	9,465,823	1,126,400	10,592,223	14,772	13,663	5,299	4,993	4,025	132	10,514

Names of Towns.	Live Stock.					Agricultural Products.							Domestic Cloths in yards.
						Bush. of Grain.		Tons of Hay.	Bushels of Potatoes.	Bushels of Apples.	Dairy Products.		
	Horses.	Working Oxen and Calves.	Cows.	Sheep.	Swine.	Winter.	Spring.				Pounds Butter.	Pounds Cheese.	
Barre	1,937	2,655	1,845	16,579	3,615	90,573	164,055¼	6,696¾	37,415	66,000	184,996	31,116	1,142½
Carlton	1,063	1,673	907	12,452	1,450	44,954	76,578¼	3,532½	14,532	31,092	93,261	8,730	1,107½
Clarendon	870	1,172	872	4,805	1,278	36,782	58,037½	2,926	10,822	25,966	85,251	10,687	383
Gaines	639	1,119	638	6,842	972	21,817½	56,244¼	3,270½	12,295	29,372	90,317	6,555	79
Kendall	798	1,633	871	10,577	1,459	8,868	95,234½	3,391	19,597	16,216	77,035	5,375	886
Murray	807	1,318	731	5,703	1,079	26,863	56,145	3,176½	9,587	19,697	66,851	8,942	786
Ridgeway	1,538	1,923	1,246	11,402	2,144	53,822	93,784	4,879	28,181	32,417	115,124	17,719	270½
Shelby	1,058	1,483	967	10,648	2,092	59,296½	106,871	3,798½	23,955	40,824½	112,570	11,404	823½
Yates	930	1,515	844	12,277	1,603	34,750	56,590	2,949½	15,483	20,197	86,608	9,770	846
Total	9,640	14,491	8,921	91,285	15,692	379,726	763,542¾	34,620¼	171,867	281,781½	912,013	110,298	6,324

1 Eli More, Israel Douglas, Dyer Sprague, Otis Turner, Dr. Wm. White, David Hooker, and S. B. Murdock were among the first settlers. The first sawmill was built by the Holland Land Co., as early as 1805, to encourage settlement. The first gristmill was built by Otis Turner and Dr. White, in 1812; and the first tavern was opened in 1810, by Eli More. Lucy Judson taught the first school.

2 There are now 9 churches in town; Prot. E., Bap., M. E., Presb., and R. C. at Medina, Presb., M. E., and Bap. at Knowlesville, and Univ. at Ridgeway. 3 Named in honor of Gov. Shelby.

4 Generally known as "Shelby Center," and at an early day called "*Barnegat.*"

5 2 flouring and grist mills, 1 paper mill, 1 tannery, 1 carding mill, and 2 sawmills.

6 Eleazur Frary, Henry and Robert Garter, David Demara, Joseph Ellicott, and Wm. Bennett were among the earliest settlers. The first birth was that of Asa Coon, Feb. 14, 1811; and the first death, that of Wm. Bennett, Oct. 4, 1812. The first sawmill was built by Joseph Ellicott, on Oak Orchard Creek, in 1812, and the first gristmill, in 1813. The first inn was kept by David Timmerman, in 1816; and the first store, by Christian Groff, in 1818. Cornelius Ashton taught the first school, in the winter of 1815–16.

7 There are 9 churches in town; 4 M. E., 1 Presb., 1 Quaker, 1 Christian, 1 Bap., and 1 F. W. Bap.

8 Named in honor of Gov. Yates.

9 The first marriage in town was that of Geo. Houseman, jr. and Sally Covert, in 1817; and the first death, that of Mrs. Geo. Houseman, sr., in Dec. 1813. The first inn was kept by Samuel Tappen, at Yates Center, in 1825; and the first store, by Moore & Hough, in 1824. The first school was taught by Josiah Perry, in 1819.

10 Presb., M. E., and Christian at Lyndonville, Bap. at Yates Center, Wes. Meth. on E. town line, and M. E. on co. line.

OSWEGO COUNTY.

THIS county was formed from Oneida and Onondaga, March 1, 1816.[1] It is situated upon the S.E. extremity of Lake Ontario, centrally distant 135 mi. from Albany, and contains an area of 1,038 sq. mi. Its surface is generally level or gently undulating. A series of bluffs 20 to 40 feet high border immediately upon the lake; and from their tops the land stretches out in long and gradual slopes, occasionally broken by the valleys of the river courses. The general inclination is northerly, as indicated by the drainage, though the summits of the ridges within half a mi. of the lake have about the same altitude as those upon the s. border of the co. A low ridge extending in an easterly and westerly direction, from 3 to 5 mi. N. of Oneida Lake, forms the watershed between Lakes Ontario and Oneida. In the E. part of the co. this ridge turns northward and unites with the system of highlands which separates Lake Ontario and the valley of Black River. The highest point of this range, in the town of Redfield, is 1,200 to 1,500 feet above tide.

The rocks of this co. consist of the Lorraine shales, in the extreme N. part, on the lake; the gray sandstone,[2] extending from the N.E. corner to near the center, its southern limits being marked by a line drawn due E. from Oswego River about 1 mi. from its mouth; the Medina or red sandstone, bordering on the last, and comprising more than one-third of the area of the co.; and the Clinton group of shales, slate, and sandstone, occupying the extreme s. border. These rocks are exposed only in the N. E. part and along the river courses, being generally covered with a thick mass of drift and alluvial deposits, consisting of sand, gravel, and clay. The gray sandstone is hard and compact, and is little affected by the action of the elements; hence the disintegration is slight, and the soil upon it is thin and poor. The Lorraine shales are easily disintegrated, and form the basis of the strongest and richest soils in the co. The red sandstone crops out on the banks of all the streams which flow through the region which it occupies. It is extensively quarried for building stone, though it is more easily acted upon by the elements than the gray sandstone. Weak brine springs are found associated with this red sandstone throughout the co. The Clinton group, occupying the entire s. border, consists of parallel layers or beds of shale and red and gray sandstone. This is the same geological formation in which is found the principal iron ore beds of Penn. and Oneida co.; and throughout the formation in this co. iron ore is found.

The drainage of the w. and s. parts of the co. is principally through Oswego River, and of the N. and E. portions through Salmon River and a great number of smaller streams that flow directly into the lake. Oswego River is formed by the junction of Seneca and Oneida Rivers at Three River Point. It is 23 mi. in length, and falls 128 feet in its course, in several distinct falls, each of which furnishes an excellent water-power. Oneida River, forming the outlet of Oneida Lake, is 18 mi. in length, and falls about 12½ feet in its course. Salmon River and other streams flowing into the E. extremity of the lake all have successions of rapids and cascades, which furnish to that portion of the co. an abundance of water-power. The principal bodies of water are Lakes Ontario and Oneida. The former, constituting the N.W. boundary, presents an almost unbroken coast line for a distance of 40 mi. within the limits of the co. Little Sandy Pond, in the town of Sandy Creek, is the only considerable indentation. The mouth of Oswego River furnishes a valuable harbor, the only one of importance in the co. Oneida Lake, constituting a portion of the s. boundary, is 141½ feet above Lake Ontario.[3] It is one link in the chain of the internal water communication of the State. A considerable portion of the land in its immediate vicinity is marshy. Iron ore beds and a fine quartz sand, used in the manufacture of glass, are found upon its N. shores. The soil found in the shale and sandstone region has already been noticed. The drift and alluvial deposits which cover the greater portion of the co. furnish a great variety of soil. The sandy portions are light and weak, while the clayey portions are hard, tough, and unyielding in many places. Where these are mixed, a rich, deep soil is the result. Along the E. border of the co. are great quantities of limestone boulders, which essen-

---

[1] Its name was derived from the Indian On-ti-ah-an-taque. The early French explorers called it "*Chonaquen*." The portion lying E. of Oswego River was taken from Oneida, and that lying w. from Onondaga. The Onondaga portion embraced the township of Hannibal and 33 lots of Lysander, belonging to the Military Tract.

[2] This gray sandstone has been used for grindstones.
[3] This height is that given by the State Geologists. Joseph E. Bloomfield, Civil Engineer of Oswego co., who has made several surveys through this region, makes the height of Oneida Lake 124 feet above Lake Ontario.

tially modify the soil of that region.   The marshes are generally composed of beds of black muck and other vegetable matter, and form the richest kind of natural meadow when drained and cultivated. Agriculture, manufactures, and commerce about equally engage the attention of the people. Stock raising and dairying are the principal branches of agriculture; spring grains and wool are also extensively produced.[1]   The commerce is mostly concentrated at Oswego City, and is carried on by means of the lake, the Oswego Canal, and the R. R.   The manufactures consist of flour, lumber, barrels,[2] starch, and a variety of other articles.   The amount of flour annually manufactured is greater than in any other co. in the State.   The principal mills are at Oswego City, Fulton, and vicinity.

The Oswego Canal, connecting Lake Ontario with the Erie Canal at Syracuse, is 38 mi. long, and for most of the distance is formed by the slackwater navigation of Oswego River.   Oneida Lake and River also form a part of the internal navigable waters of the State, connecting with the Oswego Canal at Three River Point and with the Erie Canal at Higginsville.   The Oswego & Syracuse R. R. connects with the New York Central R. R. at Syracuse.   The Watertown & Rome R. R. enters the co. in the N. E. corner, and passes through Williamstown, Albion, Richland, and Sandy Creek.

This co. is divided into two jury districts,[3] the courts being held respectively at Pulaski Village and Oswego City.[4]   At the former place a brick building, including a courthouse and jail, was erected in 1820, and at the latter a wood courthouse about the same time.[5]   A stone jail was erected in the city in 1850, and a fireproof co. clerk's office in 1851.[6]   The co. poorhouse is located upon a farm of 60 acres in the town of Mexico.   It is an old building, and is poorly adapted to its purpose.   The average number of inmates is about 50.   An asylum for insane paupers is in process of erection adjacent to the poorhouse.   The Oswego Orphan Asylum, located at Oswego City, is in part a co. institution.   All the children of the inmates of the poorhouse between the ages of 4 and 6 years are supported at the Orphan Asylum at the co. expense.[7]

Two daily and 6 weekly papers are published in the co.[8]

---

[1] The first settlers of the co. were principally engaged in the manufacture of lumber and potash. Wheat was once a staple production; but since the commencement of the ravages of the midge it has given place to the coarser grains.

[2] Barrels to the amount of 1,500,000 are annually manufactured for the Oswego flour mills and the Syracuse salt works.

[3] The eastern district comprises the towns of Albion, Amboy, Constantia, Hastings, Mexico, New Haven, Orwell, Parish, Redfield, Richland, Sandy Creek, West Monroe, and Williamstown; and the western, the towns of Granby, Hannibal, Oswego, Palermo, Schroeppel, Scriba, Volney, and the city of Oswego.

[4] Parley Keyes and Ethel Bronson, of Jefferson co., and Stephen Bates, of Ontario, were appointed commissioners to locate the county seats and select the sites for the county buildings. The first co. officers, appointed by the Governor and council, were Barnet Mooney, First Judge; Henry Williams, Smith Dunlap, Peter D. Hugunin, David Easton, and Daniel Hawks, jr., Judges and Justices; Edmund Hawks, Judge; Elias Brewster, Surrogate; James Adams, Co. Clerk; and John S. Davis, Sheriff. The first courts were held in schoolhouses from the first organization of the co., in 1816, to the completion of the courthouses, in 1820-21.

[5] The city soon outgrew the first courthouse, and the courts for many years were held in the city hall. They are now held in Mead's Hall, on E. Bridge St. The old courthouse for several years was used as a schoolhouse; but recently it has been removed, and converted into a Sunday school chapel for the Church of the Evangelists, where 500 children receive religious instruction. At their last annual meeting the Board of Supervisors authorized the raising and appropriated $30,000 for the erection of a new courthouse in the city, on the E. public square; and the building is now being constructed of Onondaga limestone.

[6] Previous to this time the clerk's office was kept alternately in private houses at each of the shire towns for periods of 3 years, the books being carried back and forth at the end of each period.   [7] See page 524.

[8] The American Farmer, the first newspaper of the co., was issued at Oswego some time before 1807.

The Oswego Gazette was started at Oswego in 1817 by A. Buckinham, and continued 2 years.

The Oswego Palladium was commenced by John H. Lord and Dorephus Abbey in 1819. It subsequently passed into the hands of Mr. Lord, and was continued by him until 1830. John Carpenter then became the proprietor, and changed its name to

The Oswego Palladium and Republican Chronicle, and continued it until 1845, when it was sold to B. Brockway, who again changed it to

The Oswego Palladium. In 1851 he transferred it to a company, by whom it was sold in 1853 to Dudley Farling, the present editor, who sold his interest, in July, 1854, to T. P. Ottoway, the present publisher.

The Oswego Daily Palladium has been issued in connection with the weekly since 1850.

The Oswego Republican was established March 22, 1825, by Wm. W. Abbey. In 1827 it passed into the hands of Samuel Osgood, and was issued a short time as

The Oswego Gazette and Advertiser. In 1828 it was sold to Wm. C. Shope, who published it as

The Oswego Advertiser until 1829. It then passed into the hands of the late Dr. Burdell, of Cunningham notoriety, who changed its name to

The Freeman's Herald, and continued it 1 year. It was then suspended for 2 years, and revived in 1832 by John Q. Adams, by whom it was published as

The National Republican 1 year, and was then discontinued.

The Oswego Democratic Gazette was published a short time in 1830 by James Cochran.

The Oswego Free Press was published by Richard Oliphant from 1830 until 1834, and by Geo. G. Foster as

The Oswego Democrat until 1835, when it was discontinued.

The Oswego Observer was started in Feb 1835, by Bailey & Hawks, and continued until the latter part of 1836.

The Commercial Herald was published at Oswego by Hull & Henry from 1837 to 1843.

The Oswego Patriot was published at Oswego during the Patriot War of 1838-39 by John Bunner and John Cochran, member of the 35th and 36th Congress from the 6th district. (City of New York.)

The Oswego County Whig was founded in 1838 by Richard Oliphant, and sold to Daniel Ayer in 1844. In 1847 C. D. Brigham became proprietor, and changed its name to

The Oswego Commercial Times. In Nov. 1848, James N. Brown became the publisher; and in Feb. 1854. he was succeeded by Winchester & Fergerson, by whom the Oswego Journal was purchased and united with it, and the combined paper was issued as

The Weekly Times and Journal. In 1857 it was changed to

The Oswego Times, under which name it is still published by J. Tarbell.

The Oswego Daily Advertiser, the first daily in the co., was issued in 1845 in connection with The Whig, and was continued until 1847, when its name was changed to

The Oswego Daily Commercial Times. It was published in connection with The Commercial Times until 1854, when it was changed to

The Oswego Times and Journal. In 1857 it was changed again to

The Oswego Daily Times, and is still issued by J. Tarbell.

The People's Journal was started at Oswego in March, 1849, by O'Leary & Dean, and the next year it was sold to L. A. Winchester. In 1851 it passed into the hands of Sumner & Poucher, who started

The Oswego Daily News in connection with it. The following year L. A. Winchester again became proprietor, and changed the name of the daily to

The Oswego Daily Journal. In 1854 the two papers were united with the Daily and Weekly Times.

The Pulaski Banner was commenced in April. 1830, at Pulaski, and published by Nathan Randall until 1832; by A. A. Mathewson and G. G. Foster until 1833; and by James Gedd until 1834, when it was suspended. In 1836 it again appeared, as

The portion of the co. of Oswego lying near the mouth of the river was discovered in 1654 by French Jesuits, who established missions here for the conversion of the Iroquois.[1] The French had previously explored the St. Lawrence; and in 1615 Champlain, in an expedition against the Onondagas, passed through the E. part of the co. In 1700 the English explored the country occupied by the Five Nations as far w. as Oswego; and in 1722 a trading house was built here under the direction of the N. Y. colonial government. From that period considerable trade was carried on by the English between Oswego and Albany through Oswego River, Oneida River and Lake, Wood Creek, and the Mohawk.[2] In 1727 the English built a fort on the w. bank of the river, near its mouth.[3] The French, claiming this whole territory, remonstrated against the action of the English, and several times planned expeditions to destroy the fortifications, but did not carry them into effect. Upon the commencement of the "Old French War" of 1753, Fort Ontario was erected on the E. bank of the river; and another fort was built upon the summit of the w. ridge in 1755. In the summer of 1756, 5,000 French under Montcalm, with a heavy train of artillery, consisting of 30 guns of large caliber, crossed the lake from Fort Frontenac (now Kingston) and appeared before this place. The forts were invested Aug. 11, and, after 3 days' hard fighting, they were surrendered on the 14th.[5] The victors demolished the forts, burned the English vessels, and retired. In 1758, Col. Bradstreet, with 3,350 men, crossed the lake from this place and reduced Fort Frontenac. After destroying the fortifications and securing the military stores and vessels, he returned to Oswego and rebuilt the forts there. Fort Ontario was greatly enlarged, and built in the most substantial manner. In the summer of 1760, the powerful army of Lord Amherst embarked here on an expedition down the St. Lawrence. From this time Oswego became the most important military station upon the western frontier. During the Revolution it was strongly garrisoned, and formed the headquarters of many of the marauding parties that desolated the frontier settlements. It continued in possession of the British until 1796, when it was surrendered under the provisions of Jay's treaty.

In 1790, George Scriba, a merchant of N. Y. City, and a German by birth, purchased 500,000 acres of land lying between Lakes Oneida and Ontario, for the sum of $80,000.[6] This purchase, known as "Scriba's Patent," was bounded on the E. by Fish Creek and on the w. by Oswego River, and embraced 14 towns in Oswego co. and 4 in Oneida. In 1794, Mr. Scriba caused a settlement to be made and a sawmill built on the shore of Oneida Lake, to which he gave the name of "*Rotterdam*,"—now Constantia. In 1795 he built a gristmill—the first in the co.—and several other buildings at the same place. During the same year his patent was surveyed and divided into townships and subdivided into lots.[7] About the same time he commenced a settlement at the mouth of Little Salmon Creek, on the shore of Lake Ontario, 12 mi. N. E. of Oswego, which he called

The Pulaski Advocate, and was published by Daniel Ayer until 1838. It was then sold to —— Dickinson and united with the Port Ontario Aurora, the united papers taking the name of

The Advocate and Aurora. The name, Aurora, was dropped in 1840, when the Advocate again passed into the hands of Daniel Ayer, and was discontinued in 1842.

The Pulaski Courier was started in 1843 by W. Winans. In 1847 it passed into the hands of A. A. Mathewson, and was changed to

The Richland Courier. In 1850 it was sold to Joseph Hatch, who changed its title to

The Pulaski Democrat. In 1856 it passed into the hands of —— Miller, its present publisher.

The Fulton Chronicle was started in Nov. 1837, by Thomas Johnson. In 1840 it was sold to Isaac S. Clark and Edwin Thompson, who gave it the name of the

Ben Franklin. It was discontinued the following year, and succeeded by

The Weekly Despatch, published by E. C. Hatten about 1 year.

The Fulton Sun was started in 1841 by N. B. Northrop. In 1842 it was united with the Mirror.

The Fulton Mirror was established Aug. 20, 1842, by Daniel Ayer. It was soon after united with the Sun and issued as

The Fulton Sun and Mirror. In Sept. 1844, it was sold to Spencer Munroe, and soon after discontinued. It was succeeded by

The Fulton Patriot. M. C. Hough, John A. Place, and T. S. Brigham were successively interested in its publication. The latter was succeeded by R. K. Sandford, its present publisher.

The Oswego County Gazette, commenced at Fulton in 1853 by Geo. E. Williams, was merged in The Fulton Patriot in 1858.

The Port Ontario Aurora was published by —— Van Cleve and subsequently by —— Dickinson from 1837 to 1839, when it was united with The Pulaski Advocate.

The Oswego County Democrat was started at Mexico in 1838 by Thomas Messenger. It was afterward styled *The Messenger*, and was discontinued in 1839.

The Phœnix Gazette, started at Phœnix in 1851, was published by Jerome Duke, and afterward by Geo. E. Williams until 1853, when it was removed to Fulton.

The Phœnix Democrat was established in 1852 by an association. In 1854 it was sold to James H. Field, and the next year he gave it the name of

The Phœnix Banner. In 1855 it was published a short time as

The American Banner and Oswego County Times. It was suspended in 1855, and in 1856 it was revived by Mary Frances Tucker, and called

The American Banner and Literary Gem. Eight months afterward it was sold to Levi Murrill, by whom it was published as

The American Banner until 1857. After being suspended two months, it was revived, under the title of

The Phœnix Reporter, by Joshua Williams, by whom it is still published.

[1] There is a tradition that the French established a military post here at a very early period; but research among the papers of that period does not corroborate the statement.

[2] There were several portages on this route,—around the falls in the streams, and across from Wood Creek to the Mohawk.

[3] Not a single trace of this fortification now remains.

[4] This fort stood at the junction of West 6th and Van Buren Sts.

[5] The French landed 50 mi. E. of Oswego, and marched along the lake shore under cover of their naval force. The English garrison numbered 2,000 strong. Col. Mercer, the English commander, was killed by a cannon shot on the 2d day of the siege

[6] In this grant the State made reservations of the territory at the mouth of the river, within the limits of the city of Oswego, and also at the falls in the village of Fulton. Most of these reservations were disposed of at public sale in 1827. At an earlier date, considerable tracts in Scriba's Patent, on Oswego River, were jointly purchased by Gen. Alexander Hamilton, John Laurence, and John B. Church. Several other grants were also made along the river. Other tracts of considerable magnitude were purchased by Schroeppel, Rosevelt, and others.

[7] This survey and subdivision was made by Benjamin Wright, who in 1793-94 ran the base line from Rome to Fort Ontario, on which the towns of Scriba's Patent were laid out. The town-

"*Vera Cruz,*"[1] (now Texas.) He here built a saw and grist mill, store, and other buildings, and commenced an active trade on the lake; and for some years the place bid fair to become a formidable rival of Oswego, and the most important commercial station upon the lake. A few other settlements were made at other points in the co., principally under the auspices of Mr. Scriba, previous to 1800; but immigration did not begin to flow in rapidly until a few years later. The lands of Mr. Scriba were divided and sold to a great number of different parties; and while his exertions and expenditures were of great service to the first settlers, they proved extremely unprofitable to himself.[2] In common with all the frontier settlements, the growth of this region was seriously retarded by the War of 1812. Oswego Village became the theater of stirring military events; and on the 5th of May, 1814, it was taken by the British.[3] At the return of peace, immigration again flowed in, and the subsequent history has been one of steady and continuous progress. The opening of the Erie and Oswego Canals, in this State, and of the Welland Canal, in Canada, greatly increased the commercial importance of the city and stimulated the manufacturing interests throughout the co.

ALBION—was taken from Richland, March 24, 1825. It is an interior town, lying E. of the center of the co. Its surface is level or gently undulating. The summits of the ridges are 50 to 100 feet above the valleys, and the highest point in town is 392 feet above Lake Ontario. The lowlands are wet and in some places marshy. Salmon River flows through the N. part.[4] In the N.E. part are 2 or 3 small ponds. The soil consists of deposits of sand and gravel, and is of medium quality. Drift deposits cover the whole surface, except along the river courses, where the underlying rocks crop out. Much of the s. part of the town is yet unsettled. Considerable manufacturing is carried on.[5] **Sand Bank,** (p.v.,) on Salmon River, is a station on the Watertown & Rome R. R., midway between the two places. It contains 1 church, a hotel, 4 stores, 2 tanneries, 5 sawmills, and a flouring mill. Pop. 313. **Pineville,** (Salmon River p.o.,) a station on the W. & R. R. R., situated on Salmon River, contains 1 church, an inn, a store, a sawmill, and a large tannery. Pop. 144. **New Centerville,** (p.o.,) a station on the W. & R. R. R., **Dug Way,** (p.o.,) and **South Albion** (p.o.) are hamlets. Settlement was commenced in 1812, by Cary Burdic, of Williamstown, on Lot 29, and Peter Henderson, at Sand Bank.[6] There are 4 churches in town.[7]

AMBOY—was formed from Williamstown, March 25, 1830. It lies upon the E. border of the co., s. of the center. The surface is rolling and has a general southerly inclination. Its highest point is about 450 feet above Lake Ontario. It is drained principally by Fish Creek and other small tributaries of Oneida Lake. In the s. and w. parts are numerous small lakes and ponds, the principal of which are Painter Lake, North and South Ponds. The N. half of the town is in the region of the gray sandstone, and the s. half in that of the red or Medina sandstone. The soil is principally a sandy or gravelly loam. **Amboy Center** (p.v.) contains 13 houses; **West**

---

ships of Scriba's Patent, like those of Macomb's Purchase, received names from the proprietors that are known only in deeds; viz.,—

  1. Fulda....................Ava, Lee, and Annsville.
  2. Munden..................Lee and Rome.
  3. Solingen................Annsville.
  4. Florence................Florence.
  5. Franklin................Williamstown.
  6. Middleburgh.............Amboy.
  7. Linley..................Camden.
  8. Bloomfield..............Lee and Annsville.
  9. Embden..................Vienna.
 10. Edam....................Vienna.
 11. Rotterdam...............Constantia.
 12. Delft...................West Monroe.
 13. Breda...................Hastings.
 14. Brugen..................Palermo.
 15. Mentz...................Volney.
 16. Georgia.................Schroeppel.
 17. Fredericksburgh.........Scriba and Oswego City.
 18. Oswego..................Scriba and Oswego.
 19. Vera Cruz...............New Haven.
 20. Mexico..................Mexico.
 21. Richland................Richland.
 22. Alkmaer.................Albion.
 23. Strasburgh..............Parish.
 24. Erlang..................Schroeppel.
The townships of the Boylston Tract in this co. are,—
  6. Campania...............Boylston.
  7. Arcadia................Redfield, (once Greenboro'.)
 10. Richland...............Sandy Creek and Richland.
 11. Longinius..............Orwell.
 12. Redfield...............Redfield.
Richland appears to be uncertain, or this name has been applied to two surveys.

[1] Vera Cruz was laid out into city lots by Mr. Wright, who was an agent of Scriba, and considerable improvements were made. A 4 rod highway was cut from Rotterdam to Vera Cruz, a distance of 20 mi., from lake to lake. In 1798 a schooner was built there by Mr. Scriba's agent, which was engaged in the trade between Vera Cruz and the Canadian port of Kingston. It is said that in 1804 more merchandise was sold there than at Oswego or Utica; and in the imagination of many persons Vera Cruz was destined to command the trade of Canada and the West. But, by a series of disasters on the lake, a large portion of the male residents were lost to the infant settlement; and the restrictive policy of Mr. Jefferson's administration, followed by the War of 1812, extinguished the flattering prospects of Vera Cruz. The events and the action of half a century have nearly obliterated all traces of the once promising city.

[2] At the time of the purchase Mr. Scriba's fortune was estimated at $1,500,000; but the whole of it became swallowed up in his efforts to promote the interests of the infant settlements; and he died Aug. 14, 1836, at the age of 84, a poor man.

[3] See page 525.

[4] Before the dams were built upon this river, great numbers of salmon were annually taken.

[5] Large quantities of lumber, leather, and barrels are manufactured, the latter for the Onondaga salt and Oswego flour markets. There are 38 sawmills, 3 tanneries, and 2 gristmills in town.

[6] In 1813 David, Luther, and Benj. Lilly and Allen McClarn settled in the town. The first birth was that of a son of Luther Lilly, in 1813; the first marriage, that of Henry Baker and Lucy Burdic, in 1819; and the first death, that of a son of Luther Lilly, in 1813. The first inn was kept by Dr. Brace, at Sand Bank, in 1814; and the first store, by Ammi Hinkley, in 1828. The Lilly brothers built the first sawmill, in 1813, and Ezekiel Smith the first gristmill, in 1818. The first school was taught by Sylvia Breed, in the summer of 1817. [7] 2 Union, Bap., M. E.

Amboy (p. v.) 20; and **Carterville** (p. v.) 12. Joseph Perkins, from Conn., was the first settler, in 1805.[1] There are 2 churches in town; M. E. and Bap., both located at Amboy Center.

BOYLSTON[2]—was formed from Orwell, Feb. 7, 1828. It lies upon the N. border of the co., E. of the center. Its surface is rolling in the center and E., and moderately hilly in the w. It has a westerly inclination, and its highest points are 700 to 800 feet above tide. The soil in the N. and w. parts is a productive, gravelly loam, the underlying rock being the Lorraine shale. The s. E. corner of the town extends into the gray limestone region, and the soil is light and thin. **Boylston** (p. o.) is in the N. w. part. The first settlement was made in 1810, on Lots 2 and 3, by John Wort and Michael Sweetman, both from Canajoharie.[3] Meetings for religious worship are held in the town by the Episcopal Methodists and the Wesleyan Methodists.

CONSTANTIA[4]—was formed from Mexico, April 8, 1808. Hastings was taken off in 1825, and West Monroe in 1839. It lies upon the N. shore of Oneida Lake, in the s. E. corner of the co. The surface is nearly level, and is slightly inclined toward the s. The principal streams are Scriba and Black Creeks, flowing into Oneida Lake. Iron ore is found in the Clinton group of rocks, which extend through the s. part. The soil consists of clay, gravel, sand, and vegetable mold, and in general is fertile. Most of the interior is yet unsettled. Frenchmans Island, in Oneida Lake, about 4 mi. from Constantia, belongs to this town; it contains about 28 acres.[5] Lumber, leather, glass, and iron are extensively manufactured.[6] **Cleveland,**[7] (p. v.,) incorp. April 15, 1857, is located on Oneida Lake, in the E. part of the town. It contains 2 churches, 2 glass factories, and several other manufactories. Pop. 1,005. **Constantia,** (p. v.,) in the w. part, on Oneida Lake, contains 2 churches and has a pop. of 600. **Bernhards Bay,** (p. v.,) on the lake, contains 2 churches, a glass factory, and 360 inhabitants. **Constantia Center** is a p. o. Soon after the purchase of Scriba's Patent, in 1790, Mr. Scriba commenced the first settlement of his lands at Constantia, and established agents and laborers there in 1793.[8] There are 7 churches in town.[9]

GRANBY—was formed from Hannibal, April 20, 1818. A part of Oswego was taken off in 1836. It lies on the w. bank of Oswego River, in the s. w. part of the co. The surface is gently rolling, with a slight inclination to the N. E. Oswego River flows through a valley from 30 to 60 feet below the general level of the town; within this town it has a fall of 40 feet. Lake Nea-tah-wan-ta, near the center of the E. part, is about 1 mi. in diameter. It lies about 25 feet above the river at the head of the falls. The streams are Ox Creek, Six Mile Creek, and the outlet of Nea-tah-wan-ta Lake. The soil is generally a sandy or gravelly loam. Bradstreets[10] or Battle Island is in Oswego River, about 4 mi. below the Oswego Falls. Starch, leather, lumber, and the products of wood are extensively manufactured.[11] **Oswego Falls,** (p. v.,) incorp. Oct. 12, 1853, a station on the S. & O. R. R., is situated on Oswego River, opposite the village of Fulton. Pop. 703. **Granby Center** and **South Granby** are p. offices. The first settlement was made at the falls in 1792, by Laurence Van Valkin, from Rensselaer co., N. Y.[12] There are now 2 churches in town.[13]

---

[1] Among the early settlers were David Smith, in 1815; Wm. and Isaac Claxton and John Drought, in 1818; and Sage Park, in 1821. The first inn was kept by Joseph Perkins, in 1805; the first sawmill was built by Joseph Murphy, in 1822, and the first gristmill by Sage Park, in 1828. The first school was taught by Cynthia Stoddard, in the summer of 1823.

[2] Named from Thos. Boylston, who held, for a few hours, the title of a tract since known as the Boylston Purchase. He never owned the tract; the conveyance was simply a trust, and quickly passed into other hands.

[3] Among the first settlers were David Webb, in 1810; R. Streeter, in 1814; and Peter and Samuel Wells, in 1815. The first birth was that of Phebe Ann Wood; the first marriage, that of Samuel Wells and Elizabeth Gordon; and the first death, that of an infant child of Mr. Ward. Reuben Snyder built the first sawmill, in 1822. The first school was taught by Polly Allport, in 1817. [4] Named by the proprietor, Geo. Scriba.

[5] "During the French Revolution of 1793, when the French nobility were compelled to seek safety in flight, and the trains of exiles to this country were crowded with dukes and princes of the blood, the Count St. Hilary, a young Frenchman, and his beautiful and accomplished wife, a daughter of the noble house of Clermont, landed upon our shores. Following the trail of emigration westward, they reached Oneida Lake, then on the great thoroughfare of travel; and, attracted by the beautiful island and its primitive forests, they landed upon it, and concluded to make it their future home. Here, in the deep solitude of nature, they enjoyed for many months perfect peace and quietude. Their place of residence was at length discovered by Chancellor Livingston, who had formerly enjoyed the elegant hospitalities of the lady's family at Paris. He visited them in their rural home, and, after spending some time with them, he prevailed upon them to return with him to his mansion upon the Hudson. There they continued to reside until Bonaparte

had put an end to the reign of terror and restored much of the confiscated property to the exiles of the Revolution, when they returned to France. Several years after, as Livingston stood upon the bank of the Seine, amidst a crowd of distinguished Parisians, to witness the first experiment of Robert Fulton in steam navigation, he was recognized by the Count, who at once took him to his residence, and treated him during his stay at Paris as a generous benefactor and an honored guest. Livingston's mansion upon the Hudson and the first steamboat of Fulton and Livingston were both named, in honor of the lady's family, 'Clermont.'"

[6] There are 34 sawmills, 3 flouring mills, 3 glass factories, 2 tanneries, an iron foundery, and other manufacturing establishments in town.

[7] Named from James Cleveland, who settled here in 1828.

[8] Solomon Waring, Joshua Lynch, and Dr. Vandercamp settled in town in 1793; and John Bernhard in 1795. The first birth was that of George Waring, April 11, 1796. The first store was opened in 1793, by Mr. Scriba, and the first inn the same year, by Major Solomon Waring. In 1794-95, Mr. Scriba erected in this town the first sawmill and gristmill built in the co. The first school was opened in 1797, at Constantia.

[9] Presb., Prot. E., M.E., Asso. Presb., Friends, Ref. Prot. D., R.C.

[10] So named from the circumstance of a battle having been fought upon it between the English, under Col. Bradstreet, and the French, with their Indian allies, in 1756.

[11] There are 15 sawmills, 1 gristmill, 2 tanneries, and a starch factory in town.

[12] Henry Bush settled in town in 1793; —— Penoyer in 1794; Peter Hugunin in 1803; Barnet Morrey in 1804; and John Hutchinson in 1808. The first store was opened in 1792, by an Indian trader by the name of Fowler; and the first inn was kept by John J. Walrad, in 1807. The first sawmill was built by Schenck & Wilson, in 1814, and the first gristmill in 1822. Benj. Robinson taught the first school, in 1812. [13] Prot. Episc. and M. E.

HANNIBAL—was formed from Lysander, as a part of Onondaga co., Feb. 28, 1806, and embraced all that part of Oswego co. lying w. of the river. Oswego and Granby were taken off in 1818. It is the N. W. corner town of the co. Its surface is gently undulating, the ridges being 30 to 50 feet above the valleys. In the E. part are several swamps, one of which covers 500 acres. The soil is a rich, sandy and gravelly loam. A salt spring, from which salt has been manufactured, is found in the N. W. corner. Springs of brine, characteristic of the Medina sandstone strata, have been discovered in several other localities, but none of sufficient strength to render their working profitable. The principal manufacturing establishments are those of leather, lumber, and the products of wood.[1] **Hannibal,** (p. v.,) on Nine Mile Creek, a little w. of the center of the town, contains 3 churches and about 60 houses; **Hannibal Center** (p. v.) contains 20 houses; and **Hulls Corners** (South Hannibal p. o.) 18. **Wheelers Corners** is a hamlet in the N. part, and **Kinneys Four Corners** is a p. o. Settlement was commenced in 1802, by Thomas Sprague and his sons, from Milton, Saratoga co.[2] The first church (Bap.) was organized in 1815.[3]

HASTINGS—was formed from Constantia, April 20, 1825. It lies upon the N. shore of Oneida River, in the s. part of the co. Its surface is level or gently undulating, its northern boundary being about 75 feet above Oneida Lake. The soil is clay, sand, and gravelly loam. In some parts of the town it is difficult to find fresh water by digging. Brine springs are found in several parts in the red Medina sandstone formation. In the N. E. part is a tamarack swamp, of about 5 acres, in the center of which is an immense spring 10 feet in diameter. This spring is on a level with the surrounding summit; and it is surrounded by a deep, loose muck which extends downward to an unknown depth. There are 18 sawmills, several gristmills, and 2 tanneries in town. **Central Square** (p. v.) contains about 50 houses; **Hastings,** (p. v.,) in the N. part, 30; **Caughdenoy,** (Coc-e-noy,) (p. v.,) on Oneida River, in the s. w. part, 30; and **Hastings Center** (p. v.) 15. **Smiths Mills** and **Fort Brewerton** are villages of about 20 houses each. The latter is situated at the foot of Oneida Lake, on the site of old Fort Brewerton.[4] The first settlement was made at Fort Brewerton, by Oliver Stevens, in 1789.[5] There are 4 churches in town.

MEXICO—was formed from Whitestown, April 10, 1792, as part of Herkimer co. Parts of Richland and New Haven were annexed May 9, 1836. It included the northerly towns of Oneida co., nearly all of Lewis and Jefferson cos. w. of Black River, and all of Oswego co. E. of Oswego River. Camden was taken off in 1799, Champion, Redfield, Turin, Watertown, and Lowville in 1800, Adams in 1802, Lorraine and Williamstown in 1804, Volney in 1806, Constantia in 1808, New Haven in 1813, and Parish in 1828. Its surface is gently rolling. It is well watered by numerous small streams, the principal of which are Little Salmon and Sage Creeks. There is scarcely a foot of waste or broken land in the town. The underlying rock is gray sandstone, covered deep with alluvial deposits. The soil consists of clay, sand, and gravelly loam, and is very productive. Considerable attention is given to stock raising and dairying; the manufacture of lumber, barrels, and leather is carried on to some extent.[6] **Mexico,** (p. v.,) near the center, was incorp. Jan. 15, 1851, and contains 3 churches, an academy,[7] 12 stores, 2 banks, 3 hotels, 3 flouring and grist mills, a sawmill, a furnace and machine shop, 3 coach factories, 4 carriage shops, and 3 cabinet shops. Pop. 948. **Colosse,** (p. v.,) in the s. E. part, contains 1 church, 2 inns, a store, 2 sawmills, and 2 gristmills. Pop. 119. **Texas,**[8] (p. v.,) located near the mouth of Little Salmon Creek, contains 30 houses; **Union Square,** (p. o.) in the E., is a hamlet. The names of the earliest settlers within the present limits of this town are lost. There were about 25 who had already located in 1798; Jonathan Parkhurst and Nathaniel Rood, from Oneida co., came that year.[9] By the upsetting of a boat upon the lake, in 1799, Capt. Geerman and 6 others were lost, and in 1804, by a similar disaster, 9 others,

---

[1] There are 18 sawmills, a stave factory, 2 gristmills, and 2 tanneries in town.

[2] Watson Earl, Samuel Baron, Joseph Weed, Sterling Moore, David Wilson, and Israel Messenger settled at Hannibal Center in 1805. The first birth was that of Carr Sprague, in 1805; the first marriage, that of Daniel Thomas and Prudence Sprague, in 1803; and the first death, that of a daughter of Thomas Sprague, in 1806. The first gristmill was built by Earl & Colton, in 1805; and the first sawmill, by Silas Crandell, in 1811. The first inn was kept by Henry Jennings, in 1808; the first store, by Benj. Phelps, in 1815; and the first school was taught in 1810.

[3] The census reports 4 churches; 2 Bap., Cong., and M. E.

[4] A little E. of the fort ground is a sandbank, in which bones are found belonging to men over 7 feet high. A mound at the E. extremity of the bank is full of human bones, indicating the place of sepulture for thousands.—*Clark's Onondaga, vol. 2, p. 182.*

[5] Among the early settlers were Timothy Vickery, Chester Loomis, Solomon Allen, and Jacob Rice. The first birth was that of John L. Stevens, in 1802; the first marriage, that of Silas

Bellows and Betsey Vickery, in 1808; and the first death, that of Horatio Stevens, in 1792. Chester Loomis kept the first inn, in 1815; and Hastings Curtis, the first store, in 1820. The first school was taught by Patrick Vickery, at Caughdenoy.

[6] There are 19 sawmills, 5 gristmills, a fulling and cloth dressing mill, a woolen factory, and 3 tanneries.

[7] The Mexico Academy was organized in 1826, as the "*Rensselaer Oswego Academy.*" Its name was changed May 19, 1845.

[8] Formerly called "*Vera Cruz.*" See p. 520.

[9] Phineas Davis and Calvin Tiffany, from Conn., settled in 1799; John Morton and Asa Davis in 1801; Peleg Brown, Daniel Eames, and Leonard Ames in 1804; and Solomon Peck in 1805. The first birth was that of Truman Rood, Aug. 10, 1799; and the first marriage, that of Richard Gafford and Mrs. Rood, widow of N. Rood. The first grist and saw mill were built by Mr. Scriba's agent; and the first store was kept by Benj. Wright. The first school was taught by Sanford Douglass, at Colosse, in 1806.

leaving but 1 male adult inhabitant in the settlement.[1] There are 10 religious societies and 9 church edifices in town.[2]

NEW HAVEN—was formed from Mexico, April 2, 1813. A part was annexed to Mexico May 9, 1836. It lies upon the shore of Lake Ontario, w. of the center of the co. The surface is rolling and generally smooth. It is watered by Spring Brook, Catfish and Butterfly Creeks, 3 small streams flowing into Lake Ontario. There is quite an extensive marsh near the mouth of Butterfly Creek, in the N. E. part of the town, and another in the s. w. part. The underlying rock is gray sandstone, and the soil is principally a sandy and gravelly loam. Stock raising receives more attention in this than in the other towns of the co., and a limited amount of manufacturing is done.[3] **New Haven,** (p. v.,) situated near the center of the town, on Catfish Creek, contains 2 churches, 2 inns, a store, a sawmill, a gristmill, and about 50 houses. **Butterfly** is a p. o. near the E. line of the town. The first settlement was made by —— Rood and —— Doolittle, at New Haven, in 1798.[4] The first church (Cong.) was organized at New Haven Village, in 1817; and Rev. William Williams was the first minister. There are now 2 churches in town; Cong. and M. E.

ORWELL—was formed from Richland, Feb. 28, 1817, and Boylston was taken off in 1828. A part of Richland was annexed March 27, 1844. It is an interior town, lying N. E. of the center of the co. The surface has a s. w. inclination, its E. border being elevated 300 to 500 feet above its w. and 700 to 1,000 feet above Lake Ontario. It is moderately hilly, and is considerably broken in places by the deep ravines of the streams. Upon Salmon River is a fall worthy of note. The stream flows over a rocky bed in a series of rapids for 2 mi. and then falls over a precipice 110 feet perpendicular. The banks of the stream below the fall are 200 feet high. The soil is generally a gravelly loam. The E. half of the town is yet uncultivated. Lumber and other products of wood form the leading articles manufactured; and considerable attention is given to stock raising and dairying.[5] **Orwell Corners,** (Orwell p. o.,) in the w. part, contains 1 church, 3 stores, an inn, a sawmill, a gristmill, a tannery, a steam cabinet factory, and about 40 houses. **Maline** is a hamlet in the s. part. The first settlers were Nathaniel Bennett and his son Nathaniel, from Rensselaer co., N. Y., on Lots 82 and 83, and Capt. Noyes, on Lot 29, in 1806.[6] There are 3 religious societies in town.[7]

OSWEGO CITY—formed from Oswego and Scriba, was incorp. as a village March 14, 1828, and was enlarged and organized as a city March 24, 1848.[8] It is situated on Lake Ontario, at the mouth of Oswego River,[9] that stream dividing the city into two nearly equal parts. The river is bordered upon each side by a ridge, which rises in gradual slopes to a height of about 100 feet, and ends in bluffs on the lake shore 40 to 60 feet high. The summits of these ridges are about 1 mi. apart, and descend from the river in the same gradual slopes as toward it. One mi. w. is a valley opening through the ridge into the river above the falls, through which the Oswego must have once flowed into the lake. The s. border of the city is skirted by a bluff or escarpment about 160 feet above the lake, indicating an ancient lake or sea beach. Here commences the deep ravine excavated by the river through strata of red sandstone of the Medina group and underlying shale. From this the geological induction is made that, at the last great physical change which elevated the country from the bed of an ancient ocean and brought the river into existence, it fell directly into Lake Ontario, at the escarpment, by a fall of moderate

[1] Capt. Geerman, Nathaniel Rood, —— Spencer and son, —— Wheaton, —— Clark, and —— Doolittle were those who were lost by the first accident. Benj. Winch was the male survivor.
[2] 2 Bap., 2 M. E., Cong., Presb., Free and Union Bethels, R. C., Prot. Fren., and Union. The Union Society holds its meetings in the Town Hall at Mexico.
[3] There are 9 sawmills, 2 gristmills, and other manufacturing establishments in town.
[4] Mr. Wright settled in the town in 1798; Solomon Smith in 1800; C. Drake and Capt. Gardner in 1804; David Enos, Joseph Bailey, and James Jerret in 1805; and Warner Drake in 1808. The first birth was that of John D. Smith, in Feb. 1805. The first sawmill was erected by Ira Foot, in 1805, and the first gristmill by Waldo Brayton, in 1809. Harriet Eason taught the first school, in the summer of 1806.
[5] There are 16 sawmills, 16 shingle mills, a gristmill, and a tannery in town.
[6] Among the early settlers were Benj. Reynolds, Joshua Hollis, Alden, Gilbert, and Timothy Balch. The first marriage was that of Robert Wooley and a daughter of Nathaniel Bennett,

sen., in 1807; and the first death, that of the mother of Timothy Balch, in 1810. The first school was taught by Jesse Aiken, in 1810. Joseph Watson built the first sawmill, in 1810, and Jonah Tompson the first gristmill, in 1816.
[7] M. E., Presb., and Bap. A Union church at Orwell Corners is occupied by the Presb. and Bap. societies.
[8] At the first village meeting, held May 13, 1828, Hon. Alvin Bronson was elected President, and Daniel Hugunin, jr., George Fisher, Nathaniel Vilas, jr., David P. Brewster, Theophilus S. Morgan, Joseph Turner, and Orlo Steele, Trustees. The first city officers, elected in April, 1848, were as follows: *Mayor*, James Platt; *Aldermen*, Hunter Crane, Gilbert Mollison, Stephen H. Lathrop, Robert Oliver, Geo. S. Alvord, John Boigeol, Samuel S. Taylor, and William S. Malcolm. The council appointed J. M. Casey *City Clerk*.
[9] By the river and canal it is 38 mi., by R. R. 35 mi., N. N. W. of Syracuse; by the Oswego and Erie Canals 208 mi., by the Oswego and Central line of R. R. 183 mi., and by the surveyed route of the Oswego & Troy R. R. 170 mi., W. N. W. of Albany.

height, the upward movement being gradual and intermittent.   The pauses by which it was interrupted are marked by ancient beach lines, ridges, and terraces found at different heights above the
lakes.   The Oswego Falls are now 11 feet high; and, as they have receded s. 12 mi., to the village
of Fulton, with an ascending average grade of about 9 feet per mi. in the excavated bed of the river,
they must have diminished in height and grandeur from age to age during the whole period of re-
cession.   This hypothesis is sustained by geographical and geological analogy with the Falls of the
Genesee and the Niagara.   The aggregate fall of the river within the 12 mi. is 110 feet, of which
34 feet are within the limits of the city; and the whole fall is so distributed by 6 successive dams,
built by the State for canal and slackwater navigation, that the water of the river may be used by
raceways nearly the whole distance, affording one of the finest water-powers in the world.   The
river forms the outlet to the 11 lakes which cluster in the basin of Central New York, and drains
a wide extent of territory.   These lakes form natural reservoirs which prevent floods or undue ex-
haustion, the extreme elevation and depression of the river not exceeding 3 feet, so that destructive
freshets, so common to great water-power rivers, never occur.   The mouth of the river admits vessels
of the largest class navigating the lakes; and the erection of piers and a lighthouse by the U. S.
Government renders it one of the safest and most accessible harbors on the lakes, susceptible of indefinite enlargement, and combining canal and R. R. transportation with the advantages of position
as the nearest lake port to tidewater.   A hydraulic canal extending along both sides of the river is
studded with mills, elevating warehouses, and other manufacturing establishments.

The city is handsomely laid out, with streets 100 feet wide, intersecting each other at right angles.
The E. and W. banks of the river are connected by two bridges, built by the city,—the lower one,
an iron bridge with a draw for the passage of vessels, on Bridge St., the upper on Utica St., at the
terminus of the Oswego & Syracuse R. R.   The principal public buildings are an edifice recently
erected by the U. S. Government, containing a custom house, post-office, and U. S. courtroom,[1] a
city hall,[2] jail, orphan asylum, city hospital, city library, and 12 churches.[3]

The *Orphan Asylum* is situated upon the elevated ground in the southern part of the city, commanding a fine view of the city, harbor, and lake.   It was founded in 1853, mainly through the
influence of the ladies of Oswego, and continues to be principally supported by them.   Orphans
and children of destitute parents, from earliest infancy to 8 years of age, are admitted and cared
for and afterward placed out in respectable families.   A primary and Sabbath school are connected
with the institution.   The number of inmates ranges from 50 to 100.

The *City Library* was founded by a donation of $25,000 from Hon. Gerrett Smith.   The edifice is
finely located upon the E. side of the river; and the library at present contains 9,000 volumes.[4]

The *Public Schools* are graded and free; they are under the care of a Board of Education and
Superintendent.   The system embraces the primary, junior, senior, and high school departments; and
pupils can receive instruction from the primary branches to an extended academic course.   In 1857
there were in the city 23 school districts, in which were employed 47 teachers,—8 males and 39
females.   The number of children between 4 and 21 was 5,516, of which 4,175, or 75 per cent.,
attended school during some portion of the year.   The total receipts and expenses during the year
was $26,341 14; the number of volumes in the district libraries, about 3,000.

The commerce of Oswego is very extensive, and is increasing much more rapidly than the population.[5]   Being situated near the foot of lake navigation, and nearer to N. Y. than any other lake port,
it has commercial facilities superior to those of most of the Western cities.   A considerable share of
the produce of the West flows through this port on its way to the seaboard markets; and it is the
principal entrepôt of the agricultural products of Canada West.   The salt of Onondaga is mostly
distributed through the Great West from this place; and vast quantities of the manufactured goods
of the East are sent through the same channel.   The official report of the value of the lake and
canal trade, derived from the Custom House and Canal Collector's Office, for 1845, was $7,951,409,
and for 1856 was $50,612,603, showing an annual average increase of nearly 20 per cent.   The
amount of registered tonnage in 1846 was 15,513 tons, and in 1856 it was 46,467 tons.[6]

The manufacturing interests of the city have attained to considerable magnitude, although the
vast water-power of Oswego River is occupied but to a limited extent.   Flour made from the wheat

---

[1] This edifice is constructed of Cleveland sandstone and iron,
and is entirely fireproof. Its cost was about $120,000.

[2] This building contains the rooms of the Common Council
and Board of Education, and the offices of the City Clerk, Recorder, and other city officers.

[3] 2 Prot. E., 2 Presb., 2 Bap., 2 M. E., 2 R. C., Univ., and
Af. Meth.

[4] This edifice, erected in 1856, is built of brick, and is 92 by
52 feet, with a vestibule 15 by 16 feet, a basement 9 feet high,

with 2 stories above, having an aggregate height of wall of 36
feet above the basement.

[5] Pop. in 1855, 15,816.   Estimated in 1858, 18,000.

[6] The operation of the late Reciprocity Treaty with England
has proved, as was anticipated, most favorable to Oswego. The
importation of grain at the port in 1856 was 13,504,074 bushels;
and the peculiar manufacturing and commercial advantages of
the place have made it the great flour and grain market of Central New York and Northern New England.

of Canada and the Western States forms the leading article manufactured. The Oswego mills, 18 in number, with an aggregate of 100 run of stone, are capable of grinding and packing 10,000 barrels of flour per day,—a greater amount than is manufactured at any other place on the continent.[1]

Shipyards and 2 marine railways rank among the important manufacturing establishments of the city, and give large employment to labor. The Oswego Starch Factory, erected in 1848, upon the hydraulic canal, on the w. bank of the river, is one of the most prosperous and extensive establishments of the kind in the world.[2] Lumber is extensively dressed in the city for the Western markets, from Canadian sawed lumber entered free under the Reciprocity Treaty. The Oswego Cotton Mills is a well managed and productive establishment, operating 83 looms, 2,664 spindles, and giving employment to 65 operators. A little above, on the same canal, is an extensive tannery. The Ontario Foundery, Steam Engine and Machine Works, is one of the most extensive and prosperous establishments of the kind in the State. Many other branches of manufactures are carried on in the city.

The early history of Oswego has already been noticed in the general history of the co.[3] Its distinctive and modern history dates from its surrender by the British in 1796. The withdrawal of the British garrison took away from the place all that had ever been established of civilized society, and left it as new as though man had never resided there. During the year following the evacuation, Neil McMullin, a merchant of Kingston, moved thither, bringing with him a house framed at Kingston.[4] In 1802 but 2 or 3 vessels were owned on the American side of the lake, trade being principally carried on by vessels belonging to the Northwest Fur Company. During this year Benajah Boyington built a warehouse on the w. side of the river, and Arch. Fairfield became a forwarding merchant. Salt from the Onondaga Springs was at that time the most important item in the commerce of Oswego. In 1803, Matthew McNair engaged in the forwarding business and purchased a schooner. In 1804 he built another, and, in connection with other gentlemen, purchased a number of Canadian vessels.[5] From this period shipbuilding was carried on briskly, and it formed a leading interest until the breaking out of the War of 1812.

The war put an end to commercial transactions; but the place became the scene of stirring military events. The fort was garrisoned and commanded by Col. Mitchell. On the 5th of May, 1814, the British fleet under Sir James Yeo appeared off the harbor and opened a heavy fire upon the place. The fire was returned by the 4 small guns which constituted the only armament of Fort Ontario, and by a small battery on the w. side of the river. The next morning the British took position still nearer the shore, and under the cover of a heavy fire 2 columns of the enemy effected a landing. After a gallant but vain defense, Col. Mitchell retreated, leaving the fort and town in possession of the enemy.[6] The principal object of the attack was to secure the naval stores destined for the new vessels building at Sackets Harbor; but a large share of these were at Oswego Falls, 12 mi. above, and were not taken. Several cannon and other heavy articles lying upon the wharf were sunk in the river, at the command of Col. Mitchell; these were afterward recovered. On the morning of the 7th the British retired, and the fleet proceeded N. to blockade Sackets Harbor. Lieut. Woolsey, who had charge of the stores, immediately dropped down the river, and, with 19 boats laden with stores, set out on the lake under cover of night, and supported by a body of riflemen and Indians, under Maj. Appling, on shore. The boats were pursued, and took refuge in Sandy Creek, where an action took place, resulting in the capture of the entire attacking party.[7]

Oswego recovered slowly from the effects of the war, and its commercial transactions were comparatively unimportant until the opening of the Oswego and Welland Canals.[8] In the mean time

[1] Five of these mills are located on the harbor, and elevate their grain from lake vessels and discharge flour and grain into canal boats. Six grain warehouses on the harbor elevate and discharge in the same way. The other mills, located above, elevate from and discharge into canal boats. The elevating capacity of the harbor is 37,500 bushels per hour, and the storage room over 2,000,000 bushels of grain,—rendering Oswego the best receiving port on the lakes.

[2] This factory was founded by a stock company, with a capital of $50,000; and, under the supervision of Thos. Kingsford & Sons, its capital has been increased to $450,000, and its main block of buildings have grown to the enormous dimensions of 510 feet front by 250 feet deep, with numerous detached buildings and an extensive box factory. The main establishment works up 500,000 bushels of grain (mostly corn) and makes 12,000,000 pounds of starch per annum. Large quantities of the article are sold and used in London, Liverpool, and the principal cities on the continent of Europe. It gives employment to 200 men.

[3] See page 519.

[4] When Mr. McMullin and his family landed at Oswego they found two American residents,—John Love and Ziba Phillips. They were traders, and left soon after. Capt. Edward O'Conner, of the Revolutionary Army, came in during the same year.

Matthew McNair and Bradner Burt and his father came in 1802; Henry Eagle in 1808; Alvin Bronson in 1810; and Wm. Dolloway in 1811. In 1810 the population numbered 300. Rankin McMullin, son of Neil McMullin, born in 1800, was the first child born within the present limits of the city.

[5] In 1804 all commercial transactions were carried on with unrestricted freedom. No ship papers, licenses, reports, or oaths were required, the keen-scented custom house officers not having yet smelt out the commerce of the lakes.

[6] The British loss in the action was about 200, and the American 60. The British carried off several of the prominent citizens, and kept them prisoners until they were duly discharged. Among the prisoners were Alvin Bronson, Abraham Hugunin, and Eli Stevens.

[7] See page 358.

[8] In 1818, 10 years before the Oswego Canal was completed, 36,000 barrels of Onondaga salt were received at Oswego, of which 26,000 barrels went to Western States by the portages round Niagara Falls. At that period the price of salt at Oswego was $2.50 per barrel, and the cost of transportation from Salina, by Oswego, to Black Rock $1.41 per barrel. In 1856 there were received at Oswego 700,000 barrels, of which over 500,000 went to upper lake ports through the Welland Canal, at a cost of

shipbuilding became a leading pursuit of the people. In 1816, steam navigation was first introduced on Lake Ontario, and its great progress since has been of immense importance to Oswego. In 1829–30, Alvin Bronson and T. S. Morgan erected the first flouring mill. In 1828 the Oswego Canal was finished, and in 1830 the Welland Canal was opened, giving a new impulse to trade and opening to the place an almost boundless commerce in the future. With the advantages of natural position and the stimulus of the lines of internal improvement, both the commerce and manufactures of Oswego have increased in an almost unprecedented manner; and there is every reason to believe that this increase is to continue for many years to come.

OSWEGO (town)—was formed from Hannibal, April 20, 1818. A part of Granby was annexed May 20, 1836. It lies upon the shore of Lake Ontario, on the w. side of the river. Its surface is generally rolling, ending in a bluff shore upon the lake. The streams are the Eight Mile, Rice, Snake, and Minetto Creeks. A fall in Oswego River within the limits of this town affords an abundance of water-power. The underlying rock is principally red sandstone, and the soil a gravelly loam. Boulders and water-worn pebbles are scattered over the surface, making it very stony in places. **Minetto,**[1] (p. v.) situated on Oswego River, 4 mi. from the city, contains 150 inhabitants. **South West Oswego** is a p. o. The first settlement was made in 1797, by Asa Rice, from Conn. Reuben Pixley came in 1800, and Daniel Burt in 1802.[2] There are now in the town 2 churches; M. E. and Bap.

PALERMO—was formed from Volney, April 4, 1832. It is an interior town, lying just s. w. of the center of the co. Its surface is undulating. The large swamp in the E. part of the town is 57 feet above Oneida Lake, and the ridges are about 25 feet above the swamp. The streams are Scotts and Fish Creeks. The soil is generally a sandy loam. Lumber and the products of wood are the principal manufactured products of the town.[3] **Palermo,** (p. v.,) situated near the center of the town, and **Vermillion** (p. v.) each contains 1 church and about 15 dwellings. The first settlement was made in 1806, by David Jennings, Simeon Crandall, and Sylvanus Hopkins.[4] The first settled preacher was Rev. Asaph Graves. There are now 4 churches in town.[5]

PARISH[6]—was formed from Mexico, March 20, 1828. It is an interior town, a little s. E. of the center of the co. Its surface is undulating, but considerably broken by ravines, and in some parts rough and stony. The streams are Salmon Creek and its branches. The valley in the w. part is 246 feet above Lake Ontario, and the E. summits are 25 to 50 feet higher. The soil consists of clay, sand, and gravel, and is moderately fertile. Less than half of the town is under cultivation. There are 12 sawmills, 4 shingle factories, and other manufacturing establishments in town. **Parishville,** (Parish p. o.,) on Salmon Creek, in the w. part, contains 1 church and 34 houses. The first settlement was made in 1804, by Thomas Nutting, Eliada Orton, Jonathan Bedell, Amos Williams, and Rev. Gamaliel Barnes.[7] There are 2 churches in town; M. E. and Bap.

REDFIELD—was taken from Mexico, as part of Oneida co., March 14, 1800.[8] It is the N. E. corner town of the co. Its surface is hilly in the s., but in the N. it spreads out into a high, rolling plateau 800 to 1,000 feet above tide. A wide intervale extends along the course of Salmon River, which stream drains nearly the whole town. The underlying rock is gray limestone, and the soil upon it is generally a thin and moderately fertile gravelly loam. The soil of the intervale is a deep, sandy loam of good quality. The greater part of the town is still unsettled, and the uplands are frosty and forbidding regions. **Center Square,** (Redfield p. o.,) situated on Salmon River, in the s. part of the town, contains 2 churches and about 30 houses. **Greenborough** is a p. o. in the N. w. part. The settlement of the town was commenced in 1798, by immigrants mostly from Conn.[9] The first church (Cong.) was organized with 19 members in 1802, by Rev. Joshua Johnson. There are now 2 churches in the town; Cong. and M. E.

---

transportation ranging from 10 to 20 cents per barrel from Salina to Chicago. This price for freight is much less than it is from St. Clair River to Chicago, less than half the distance, illustrating the fact that the demand for up freights is at the great receiving point of down freights.

[1] A sawmill at this place is one of the largest in the State, and is capable of sawing 20,000 feet per 24 hours.

[2] Among the early settlers were Nathan Nelson and —— Beckwith, in 1804; Eleazur Perry, in 1805; Jonathan Buel and Jacob Thorpe, in 1806; and Daniel Robinson, in 1809. The first birth was that of Thomas Jefferson Rice, in 1801; the first marriage, that of Augustus Ford and Miss Rice, in 1800; and the first death, that of an infant child of Asa Rice, in 1798.

[3] There are in the town 8 sawmills, 3 shingle and stave factories, 2 gristmills, and 2 tanneries.

[4] Among the first settlers were Alvin Walker, Stephen Blake, and Zadock Hopkins. The first birth was that of Alvin Walker, jr.; the first marriage, that of Joseph Jennings and Sally Chapin; and the first death, that of Zadock Hopkins,—all in 1811.

The first inn was opened in 1816, by Stephen Blake; and the first sawmill was built by Phineas Chapin, in 1812. The first school was taught by Harriet Eason, in the summer of 1812.

[5] 2 M. E. and 2 Bap.

[6] Named from David Parish, who purchased the town before its settlement.

[7] Paul Allen settled in town in 1805. The first birth was that of Ransom Orton, in 1805; the first death, that of Jonathan Bedell, killed by the fall of a tree; and the first marriage, that of Nathan Parkhurst and the widow Bedell. John Miller kept the first inn, in 1807; and Martin Way and Paul Allen built the first sawmill, in 1808. The first school was taught at Parishville, in the summer of 1807.

[8] The town of "*Arcadia*," so called, was annexed Feb. 20, 1807. The town of "*Greenboro*" was erected Feb. 21, 1843, and re-annexed March 1, 1848, in consequence of fraudulent practices with regard to assessments upon the lands of non-residents.

[9] Among those who settled in the town in 1798 were Amos Kent, Josiah Tryon, Nathan Sage, Jonathan Harmon, James

RICHLAND—was formed from Williamstown, as part of Oneida co., Feb. 20, 1807. Orwell was taken off in 1817, Sandy Creek and Albion in 1825, a part of Mexico in 1836, and a part of Orwell in 1844. It lies upon the shore of Lake Ontario, N. of the center of the co. The surface is generally level or gently rolling, broken by the deep ravines of the streams. The E. part is 250 feet above Lake Ontario, and Pulaski Village is 131 feet above,—giving to the town a decided westerly inclination. The principal streams are Salmon River,[1] Deer and Sandstone Creeks; and upon each of them are falls, furnishing a large amount of water-power.[2] Spring Brook is a small stream flowing from several large springs in the E. part of the town, and in the course of 3 mi. falls 150 feet. The springs are perpetual, and rather increase than diminish in summer; so that the power furnished is abundant and constant. The mouth of Salmon River furnishes a good harbor. The underlying rock is the Lorraine shales; the soil is a sandy loam, with some clay in the s. w. part, and is generally fertile. **Pulaski,** (p. v.,) on Salmon River, about 3 mi. from its mouth, is the half shire of the co. and was incorp. April 26, 1832. It contains 4 churches, a courthouse, an academy,[3] a newspaper office, a bank, and several manufacturing establishments.[4] Pop. 1,168. **Port Ontario,** (p. v.,) on Salmon River, near its mouth, contains about 50 houses; and **Holmesville** (South Richland p. o.) 1 church and 20 houses; **Selkirk,** at the mouth of Salmon River, contains a church, a U. S. lighthouse, and 30 dwellings. **Richland Station,** on the W. & R. R. R., is in the E. part of the town. The first settlement was made near the mouth of Salmon River, in 1801, by Nathan Tuttle, of Canada, and Nathan Wilcox and Albert Bohannan, from Rome.[5] The first church (Cong.) was organized Jan. 22, 1811; and the Rev. Oliver Leavitt was the first settled pastor. There are 7 churches in town.[6]

SANDY CREEK—was formed from Richland, March 24, 1825. It lies on the shore of Lake Ontario, upon the N. border of the co. Its surface is rolling and has a westerly inclination, its E. border being elevated about 500 feet above the surface of the lake. It is drained by Little Sandy Creek and many smaller streams, all of which have rapid currents and are frequently interrupted by falls, which furnish a good supply of water-power. Little Sandy Pond, a portion of Lake Ontario, nearly landlocked, lies principally within the limits of this town. The soil consists of gravelly loam and disintegrated shale, and is generally productive. Lumber is the principal manufactured product.[7] **Washingtonville,** (Sandy Creek p. o.,) situated on Little Sandy Creek, 4 mi. from its mouth, is a station on the W. & R. R. R. Pop. 423. The first settlement was made in 1804, by Joseph Hurd and Elias Howe, from Oneida co.[8] The first church (Presb.) was organized in 1817, by Rev. Mr. Dunlap. There are now 3 churches in town.[9]

SCHROEPPEL[10]—was taken from Volney, April 4, 1832. It lies in the s. part of the co., in the N. E. angle formed by the junction of Oneida and Oswego Rivers. The surface is level or gently rolling. It is watered by Scott and Fish Creeks and many smaller streams. A swamp extends northward from the mouth of Fish Creek to the N. border of the town, and is a half mile to a mile in width. The soil is a rich sandy loam and clay. The underlying rocks, which belong to the Clinton group, nowhere crop out in the town. There are 10 sawmills, 4 shingle mills, and other manufactures in town. **Phœnix,**[11] (p. v.,) on Oswego River, 2 mi. below Three River Point, was incorp. in 1848. It contains 3 churches and a newspaper office. Pop. 1,164. **Gilbertsville,** (Gilberts Mills p. o.,) in the N. part, contains 2 churches. Pop. 442. **Hinmansville,** (p. v.,) in the extreme w. part, on Oswego River, contains 25 houses; and **Pennelville,**

Drake, Eli Strong, Benj. Austin, Samuel Brooks, Eliakim Simonds, Nathan Cook, Ebenezer Chamberlain, David Harmon, and Elihu Ingraham. The first birth was that of Ezra L. H. Chamberlain; and the first death, that of an infant son of Dr. Alden, in 1801. The first saw and grist mills were built in 1801; and the first inn was opened the same year, by David Butler. The first school was taught in 1802, by Rev. Joshua Johnson.

[1] At the mouth of Salmon River is a harbor admitting vessels of light draught.

[2] There are 19 sawmills, 8 shingle mills, 6 flouring and grist mills, 2 cotton factories, 2 paper mills, a tool factory, and several other manufacturing establishments in the town.

[3] The Pulaski Academy was organized June 4, 1853.

[4] 2 paper mills, 4 flouring and grist mills, 3 sawmills, and 3 tanneries.

[5] Among the early settlers were Hugh Montgomery, in 1801; John Ingersoll, Benj. Bull, Israel Jones, John Farnham, and —— Johnson, in 1804; Jeremiah Matthewson, in 1807; and Ephraim and Justus Fox, in 1808. The first birth was that of Benj. Ingersoll, Aug. 28, 1804; the first marriage, that of Saml. Crippen and Ruth Tuttle, the same year; and the first death, that of a child of Nathan Tuttle. The first inn was kept by

Benj. Winch, in 1806; and the first store, by John Meacham, in 1810. The first sawmill was built by John Hoar, in 1806; and the first gristmill, by Jeremiah Matthewson, in 1808. Milly Ellis taught the first school, in the summer of 1808.

[6] 3 Bap., 2 M. E., Cong.. and Prot. E.

[7] There are 11 sawmills, 2 shingle mills, 2 gristmills, and 2 tanneries in town.

[8] In 1805 Asel Hurd and 5 families from Vt., by the name of Meacham, settled in town. The first sawmill was built by Wm. Skinner and Joseph Hurd, in 1804; and the first gristmill, by James Hinman, in 1806. Simeon Meacham kept the first store and tavern, in 1806; and the first school was taught at the house of George Harding. by his daughter, in 1807–08. The first birth was that of Laura Hurd; the first marriage, that of Henry Patterson and Lucy Meacham, in 1806; and the first death, that of Mrs. Elias Howe, in 1807.

[9] Presb., M. E., and Bap.,—all at Washingtonville.

[10] Pronounced scru'ple; named from Henry W. Schroeppel. His father, Geo. C. Schroeppel, purchased the whole of Township 24 and a large part of 16, of George Scriba. Henry W. settled in the town in 1819, and is still a resident.

[11] Named in honor of Alex. Phœnix.

(p. v.,) near the center, 15. Settlement was commenced by Abram Paddock, in 1800.[1] The first church (M. E.) was organized in 1826. There are now 5 churches in town.[2]

SCRIBA[3]—was taken from "*Fredericksburgh*" (now Volney) as part of Oneida co., April 5, 1811. It lies upon the shore of Lake Ontario and the E. bank of Oswego River. Its surface is rolling, the ridges extending N. and S., and elevated 100 to 180 feet above the lake. It is drained by Black Creek, flowing S., and Nine Mile, Four Mile, and Wine Creeks, flowing N. Upon several of these streams are valuable mill privileges. The soil is a gravelly and sandy loam, stony in places, and only moderately fertile. **Scriba Corners,** (Scriba p. o.,) near the center of the town, contains 1 church and about 40 houses. **North Scriba** is a p. o. The first settlement was made by Henry Everts, in 1798.[4] There are 3 churches in town.[5]

VOLNEY[6]—was formed—by the name of "*Fredericksburgh*"—from Mexico as part of Oneida co., March 21, 1806. Its name was changed April 5, 1811. Scriba was taken off in 1811, and Schroeppel and Palermo in 1832. It lies upon the E. bank of Oswego River, S. W. of the center of the co. Its surface is undulating, with high, steep banks bordering upon the river. The ridges are 50 to 100 feet above the valleys and 100 to 200 feet above Oswego River. The red sandstone crops out on the bank of the river and is extensively quarried for building stone. The falls upon the river furnish an immense water-power.[7] The soil is a sandy and gravelly loam. **Fulton,**[8] (p. v.,) on Oswego River, at the Oswego Falls,[9] was incorp. April 29, 1835. It contains 6 churches, the Falley Seminary,[10] 2 newspaper offices, and a large number of manufacturing establishments. Pop. 3,192. **Seneca Hill,** (p. v.,) on Oswego River, in the N. w. corner of the town, contains 50 dwellings and the largest flouring establishment in the State.[11] **Volney Corners,** (Volney p. o.,) near the center, contains 18 houses. The present village of Fulton became the seat of a floating population in the early part of the eighteenth century; but permanent settlement was not commenced until 1793.[12] The first church (Presb.) was organized in 1814; and the Rev. Mr. Leavitt was the first settled minister. There are 9 churches in town.[13]

WEST MONROE—was formed from Constantia, March 21, 1839. It lies upon the N. shore of Oneida Lake, S. E. of the center of the co. The surface is level and marshy in the S., and rolling, broken, and stony in the N. A marsh on the bank of the lake covers an area of more than 1,000 acres, and a considerable portion of it produces cranberries. In the valleys between the ridges, in the N. part of the town, are several smaller marshes. Red sandstone, the underlying rock, crops out in this town and furnishes a plentiful supply of valuable building stone. Bog iron ore is found in the N. part; and it is said that traces of lead and silver have also been found. The soil is a medium quality of clay, sandy and gravelly loam. **West Monroe** and **Union Settlement** are p. offices. The first settlement was made in 1806, by Martin Owens, Abel and Joseph B. Ames, Ebenezer Loomis, and Sylvanus Allen.[14] The first church (Presb.) was organized in 1843.[15]

WILLIAMSTOWN—was formed from Mexico, as part of Oneida co., March 24, 1804. Richland was taken off in 1807, and Amboy in 1830. It lies near the center of the E. border of the co. The surface is undulating in the S., but broken and stony in the w., and moderately hilly in the E. It is drained by Fish Creek, flowing into Oneida Lake, and the head branches of Salmon

---

[1] Thomas Vickery and —— La Hommedieu settled in 1807; and Wm. Miles in 1808. The first birth was that of Joseph Vickery, Sept. 11, 1807; and the first marriage, that of John Lemanier and Sally Winter. The first sawmill was erected by H. W. Schroeppel, in 1819; and the first gristmill, by A. & H. Gilbert, the same year. The first store was kept by Andrus Gilbert, in 1821; and the first inn, by Alex. Phœnix, in 1828. Horatio Sweet taught the first school, at Three River Point, in 1813.　　[2] 2 M. E., Cong., Bap., and F. W. Bap.

[3] Named in honor of George Scriba, the original proprietor of this and several of the adjoining towns.

[4] Asahel Bush and Samuel Tiffany settled in town in 1801; Wm. Burt and Hiel Stone in 1805; and Dr. Deodatus Clark in 1807. The first birth was that of Henry Everts, jr.; the first marriage, that of John Masters and Eliza Baldwin, in 1806; and the first death, that of a child of Hiram Warner. The first inn was kept by Hiel Stone, in 1806; and the first store, by Orrin Stone and Aaron Parkhurst, in 1819. Benj. Robinson, from Manlius, taught the first school, in 1804.

[5] Bap., M. E., and a Bethel Free and Union.

[6] Named in honor of Volney, the French author, who visited the town in 1808, while on a tour through the U. S.

[7] There are 7 flouring mills in town, having an aggregate of 42 run of stone; also a large number of sawmills and other manufacturing establishments.

[8] Named in honor of Robert Fulton. It was originally called "*Oswego Falls*."

[9] The portage at this place was the only interruption in the

internal water communication between Schenectady and the ports upon Lake Ontario and the St. Lawrence River, after the construction of the canal connecting Wood Creek with the Mohawk River, by the Western Navigation Co., in 1796.

[10] The Fulton Female Seminary was incorp. in 1836, and in 1842 it was changed to the Fulton Academy. In 1849 it received a donation of $3,000 from Mrs. M. E. Falley and assumed the name of the Falley Seminary. At the same time it came under the charge of the Black River Conference of the M. E. Church. It is now a private institution.

[11] This flouring mill has 15 run of stone, with a separate wheel to each run, and a capacity of grinding and packing 1,200 barrels of flour per day.

[12] Daniel Masters settled at Oswego Falls in 1793; Laurence Van Valkenburgh, below the falls, in 1795; and John Van Buren in 1796. John Waterhouse settled in the town in 1797; and Ebenezer Wright in 1800. The first birth after the permanent settlement was in 1795; and the first death, that of John Waterhouse, in Aug. 1799. Daniel Masters kept the first inn, at the falls, in 1794; and he and —— Goodell erected the first sawmill, in 1796. Miss A. Waterhouse taught the first school, in 1800.

[13] 2 M. E., Presb., Prot. E., Cong., Bap., Prot. Meth., Wes. Meth., and Union.

[14] Deacon Smith, from Mass., settled in the town in 1808, and Hiram Nickerson in 1810. The first birth was that of Azariah Ames. The first inn was kept by Deacon Smith, in 1812; and the first school was taught by Caroline Barnes, in 1810.

[15] The census reports 2 churches; Presb. and F. W. Bap.

OSWEGO HARBOR.

River. The surface of Fish Creek at Williamstown Mills, in the S. E. part, is 354 feet above Lake Ontario, and the hills in the N. E. are 200 to 300 feet higher. The greater part of the town is yet unsettled. The soil is a moderately fertile sandy or gravelly loam. Lumber and leather are the principal manufactured products. **Williamstown,** (p. v.,) on Fish Creek, in the S. part, is a station on the W. & R. R. R. Pop. 240. **Kasoag,** (p. v.,) a little W. of the center, is a station on the W. & R. R. R. and contains about 25 houses. The first settlement was made in 1801, by Gilbert Taylor, Solomon Goodwin, Ichabod Comstock, Dennis Orton, Henry Williams, and Henry Filkins.[1] The first church (Cong.) was founded in 1805, by Rev. Wm. Stone.[2]

Acres of Land, Valuation, Population, Dwellings, Families, Freeholders, Schools, Live Stock, Agricultural Products, and Domestic Manufactures, of Oswego County.

Names of Towns.	Acres of Land.		Valuation of 1858.			Population.					Schools.	
	Improved.	Unimproved.	Real Estate.	Personal Property.	Total.	Males.	Females.	No. of Dwellings.	No. of Families.	Freeholders.	No. of Districts.	Children taught.
Albion	9,196¾	16,109	$262,340	$7,750	$270,090	1,147	1,065	413	435	375	14	926
Amboy	6,327½	18,070¼	105,160	5,550	110,710	636	536	215	222	190	7	445
Boylston	5,486	17,379	70,117	1,300	71,417	424	391	144	146	145	6	278
Constantia	6,161	28,660	324,299	15,100	339,399	1,591	1,764	592	632	442	12	1,306
Granby	16,458	13,574¾	608,863	20,270	629,133	1,963	1,784	694	767	458	18	1,520
Hannibal	15,094⅝	12,035	410,170	13,650	423,820	1,555	1,473	590	639	511	17	1,117
Hastings	13,252½	14,010	645,900	44,300	690,200	1,610	1,459	581	608	505	17	1,399
Mexico	20,206¼	8,011	533,030	95,400	628,430	2,015	2,007	782	831	743	19	1,375
New Haven	11,410¼	7,603	283,880	41,195	325,075	1,011	1,001	396	433	344	11	730
Orwell	8,537½	17,345	170,581	7,000	177,581	669	589	241	260	232	9	517
Oswego City	2,042	783½	4,262,372	1,401,410	5,663,782	8,022	7,794	2,618	2,962	1,771	22	5,987
Oswego-Town	12,242½	7,494½	559,736	26,900	586,636	1,428	1,332	523	545	293	15	1,154
Palermo	12,238½	12,777	347,670	18,100	365,770	1,048	975	424	457	277	14	784
Parish	9,010⅛	15,921	241,014	16,975	257,989	875	800	323	337	295	12	752
Redfield	5,988½	51,835	181,547	7,455	189,002	452	346	144	158	139	9	393
Richland	19,632	11,859	709,161	881,950	791,111	2,079	1,933	735	677	520	23	1,660
Sandy Creek	16,738	6,559⅛	410,995	34,300	445,295	1,175	1,098	418	488	337	16	1,019
Schroeppel	13,055½	11,619	603,290	24,100	627,390	1,937	1,810	686	756	443	16	1,459
Scriba	14,398½	8,936	1,417,675	30,800	1,448,475	1,539	1,419	558	587	532	16	1,293
Volney	16,141	12,521½	574,963	44,250	619,213	3,365	3,111	1,166	1,343	855	18	2,310
West Monroe	5,237½	14,663⅛	120.390	5,700	126,090	631	586	224	241	204	9	513
Williamstown	5,271⅛	20,281½	140,161	3,100	143,261	490	463	182	187	170	7	312
Total	244,126	328,047⅝	12,983,314	1,946,555	14,929,869	35,662	33,736	12,649	13,711	9,781	307	27,249

Names of Towns.	Live Stock.					Agricultural Products.							Domestic Cloths, in Yards.
						Bush. of Grain.					Dairy Products.		
	Horses.	Working Oxen and Calves.	Cows.	Sheep.	Swine.	Winter.	Spring.	Tons of Hay.	Bushels of Potatoes.	Bushels of Apples.	Pounds of Butter.	Pounds of Cheese.	
Albion	429	813	769	1,296	705	4,349	42,716½	1,755½	20,454	8,020	83,800	10,550	1,821
Amboy	220	622	464	854	404	1,251	22,193½	1,273½	7,184	6,248	45,822	1,314	1,432
Boylston	169	314	570	460	308	881	19,196	1,063	5,871	2,731	36,860	70,522	1,264
Constantia	392	540	457	996	654	2,767	27,952	1,208	9,000	5,050	47,885	1,050	837
Granby	903	1,381	1,120	3,025	1,600	2,900½	108,261¾	3,409	36,795	25,932	105,210	3,201	1,893
Hannibal	1,097	1,490	1,317	2,215	1,887	3,289½	101,995	3,570	31,255	37,664	127,843	13,756	1,295½
Hastings	669	1,180	956	2,692	1,243	6,258	70,766	2,527¼	18,041	20,016	87,643	5,641	2,549
Mexico	1,007	1,656	2,290	3,170	1,994	4,714½	109,560	5,376	51,244	40,064	204,992	130,915	2,070½
New Haven	531	1,250	1,048	1,878	886	1,558½	47,495¼	2,655½	18,716	35,141	133,550	15,804	1,027
Orwell	278	580	909	582	470	3,572	35,744	1,766	9,631	4,244	105,324	122,780	1,052
Oswego City	596	53	594	194	1,204	292½	4,305½	492	1,910¼	5,225	3,400		
Oswego-Town	748	884	936	1,934	1,060	1,720	48,183	4,054	19,928	16,830	97,306	3,530	363
Palermo	591	1,146	1,005	2,331	1,074	5,037½	64,211	2,874½	24,640	30,885	107,315	12,050	1,444
Parish	403	835	822	1,263	900	2,264	40,613½	1,808¼	14,350	16,099	81,655	15,100	2,242
Redfield	162	420	757	451	176	180	15,218½	2,352	5,786	327	33,980	151,900	284
Richland	866	1,678	2,244	3,042	1,513	2,259	97,019½	5,077	30,962	47,315	174,675	123,970	1,931
Sandy Creek	557	1,134	1,583	2,126	1,139	5,786	64,207	3,346½	14,370	24,873	139,117	167,575	2,220
Schroeppel	760	1,275	1,054	2,768	1,155	2,243	83,548	3,313½	14,689	13,356	81,222	44,555	1,087
Scriba	691	931	1,174	1,302	1,080	2,727	36,261½	4,756½	21,652	33,325	159,514	11,490	906
Volney	904	1,096	1,124	2,185	1,606	1,686	76,339½	4,367	23,235	39,370	102,652	58,451	1,351
West Monroe	249	519	465	907	465	1,183½	25,251	1,403¾	7,142	7,943	47,609	8,357	916
Williamstown	176	392	325	417	313	1,234	17,510	689¼	5,057	5.257	28,800	2,950	632
Total	12,398	20,189	21,983	36,088	21,836	58,153½	1,158,647	58,138	391,912¼	425,915	2,036,174	975,461	28,617

[1] The first marriage was that of Joel Rathburn and Miss P. Alden, in Sept. 1802; and the first death, that of Mrs. Sarah Orton, in the spring of 1804. Isaac Alden opened the first inn, in 1803, built the first sawmill, the same year, and the first gristmill, in 1804. The first store was opened in 1806, by Danl. Furman. The first school was taught by Philander Alden, in 1803.

[2] There are now 2 churches in town; Cong. and M. E.

OTSEGO COUNTY.

THIS county was erected from Montgomery, Feb. 16, 1791, and embraced the 2 original towns of Otsego and Cherry Valley. A part of Schoharie was taken off in 1795, and a part of Delaware in 1797. It lies upon the highlands at the head of Susquehanna River, s. e. of the center of the State. It is centrally distant 66 miles from Albany, and contains 1,038 sq. mi. Its surface is a hilly upland, divided into several ridges separated by deep, broad valleys. The declivities are generally gradual; and the highest summits are 400 to 700 ft. above the valleys and 1,700 to 2,000 ft. above tide. The ridges have a general n. e. and s. w. direction. A high and rocky upland extends into the s. e. corner from Delaware, terminating upon Schenevas Creek in an abrupt and wall-like declivity 300 to 500 ft. high. The other ridges of the co. have a nearly uniform elevation, and generally terminate in steep declivities upon the valleys of the streams. The principal streams are Unadilla River, forming the w. boundary, Wharton and Butternut Creeks, Otego Creek, Susquehanna River, Cherry Valley and Schenevas Creeks. Charlotte River forms a small portion of the s. boundary. Besides these, there are a large number of smaller creeks and brooks, tributaries to the above. A few small streams rise in the n. e. corner and flow into the Mohawk. Otsego Lake, in the n. e. part, is a fine sheet of water 8 mi. long and about 1 mi. broad. It is 1,193 ft. above tide, and is surrounded by hills 400 to 500 ft. high. Its outlet forms the principal head branch of the Susquehanna. Schuyler Lake, n. w. of Otsego, is a similar sheet of water, 3½ mi. long. The other bodies of water in the co. are small ponds. The rocks in the n. e. corner consist of the limestones of the Helderbergh division. The hills in the s. part are composed of the shales of the Hamilton group and the shales and sandstones of the Portage and Chemung groups. The summits in the extreme s. part and s. e. corner are crowned by the red sandstone and shales of the Catskill group. Almost all the valuable quarries of the co. are found in the limestone region of the n. e. The soil in the n. e. is a good quality of gravelly and calcareous loam; but further south it is a clay and shaly loam upon the hills, and a gravelly loam and alluvium in the valleys. The uplands are best adapted to grazing; and the river intervales are well adapted to the cultivation of grain. The people are principally engaged in stock raising and dairying. More hops are raised in this co. than in any other in the State. The manufacturing interests are limited, though the available water-power is very great.

The county seat is located at Cooperstown, in the town of Otsego, at the foot of Otsego Lake.[1] The courthouse is a brick edifice in the w. part of the village.[2] The jail, near by, is built of stone, but has few of the modern improvements or conveniences. The average number of inmates is 8, supported at a weekly cost of $3.00 each. The clerk's office is a fireproof brick building, contiguous to the courthouse. The co. poorhouse is situated upon a farm of 153 acres in Middlefield, 4 mi. s. of Cooperstown. Its average number of inmates is 90. The children attend the district school. The farm yields a revenue of $1,400. The general arrangement and management of this institution are far better than the average. The only work of internal improvement in the co. is the Albany & Susquehanna R. R., now in process of construction. It extends along Susquehanna River and Schenevas Creek, through Unadilla Otego, Oneonta, Milford, Maryland, and Worcester.

Three weekly newspapers are published in the co.[3]

---

[1] Thomas Farrington, of Tioga, Alvin Bronson, of Oswego, and Archibald Campbell, of Dutchess, were the commissioners appointed to locate the co. seat.

[2] The first county officers were Wm. Cooper, *First Judge;* Jacob Morris, *County Clerk;* Richard B. Smith, *Sheriff;* and James Cannon, *Surrogate.*

[3] *The Otsego Herald and Western Advertiser,* the first paper published in the co., and the second in the State w. of Albany, was commenced at Cooperstown, April 3, 1795, by Elihu Phinney, a native of Conn. Mr. Phinney continued its publication until 1803, when he died. It was then published by his sons, E. & H. Phinney, until 1821, when it was discontinued.

The Impartial Observer was established at Cooperstown in 1808

by William Andrews. It soon after passed to John H. Prentiss, who changed its name to

The Cooperstown Federalist, under which title it was published until 1828, when the name was again changed to

The Freeman's Journal. In 1850 it passed into the hands of Samuel M. Shaw, by whom it is now published.

The Otsego Republican was published at Cherry Valley in 1812 by Clark & Crandal.

The Watchtower was established at Cherry Valley in 1813. In 1814 it was removed to Cooperstown, where it was published by Israel W. Clark until May, 1817, when Edward B. Crandal became proprietor, and continued the publication until 1831.

The first settlement in this co. was made at Cherry Valley, in 1740, by John Lindesay, who, with 3 others, held a patent for a tract of 8,000 acres lying in that town.[1] Mr. Lindesay was a Scotch gentleman of some fortune and distinction, and, by his influence, induced a settlement on his lands of several families, comprising about 30 persons, originally from Scotland and Ireland. A few years later, small settlements were made in the present towns of Springfield, Middlefield, Laurens, Otego, and at other points in the valley of the Susquehanna. These settlements then formed the extreme outposts in the advance of civilization west. They increased very slowly, in consequence of the fear of Indian hostilities. In 1765, 25 years after the first settlement, but 40 families had located at Cherry Valley. At the commencement of the Revolution it was still a frontier settlement. On the 11th of Oct. 1778, it was attacked by the tories and Indians, under the lead of Butler and Brant, and a horrible massacre ensued. The family of Robert Wells, father of the late John Wells of New York, consisting of 12 persons, were brutally murdered; and one of the tories boasted that he killed Mr. Wells while at prayer. John Wells, the only member of the family who escaped, was at school in Schenectady at the time. The wife and daughter of Mr. Dunlop were murdered in cold blood, as were also the wife and 4 children of Mr. Mitchell. Thirty-two of the inhabitants, mostly women and children, and 16 Continental officers and soldiers, were killed; the residue of the inhabitants were taken prisoners and carried off, and all the buildings in the place were burned. All the frontier settlements were ravaged, and nearly every building, except those belonging to tories, was burned. These horrible outrages aroused the whole country, and in 1779 Gen. Sullivan, at the head of a large body of troops, was sent against the Western tribes. In Feb. Gen. Clinton, with a force of 1,200 men, marched up the Mohawk, and thence opened a road to Otsego Lake, a distance of 20 mi. At the foot of the lake he halted and built a dam across the outlet, and prepared boats to descend the stream. When the lake was sufficiently high, the boats were launched, the dam was broken down, and the army descended the river on the flood thus produced. The Indians upon the banks, witnessing the extraordinary rise of the river at midsummer without any apparent cause, were struck with superstitious dread, and in the very outset were disheartened at the apparent interposition of the Great Spirit in favor of their foes. Gen. Clinton's forces joined Sullivan on the Chemung. At the close of the war, settlements progressed with great rapidity; and much of the best land in the co. was taken up before the fertile lands in the western part of the State were opened to immigration. In late years the progress of the co. has not been so rapid as that of other sections of the State, from the fact that no great work of public improvement has yet been constructed within its limits, and hence it is comparatively isolated and difficult of access.

BURLINGTON—was formed from Otsego, April 10, 1792. Pittsfield was taken off in 1797, and Edmeston in 1808. It is an interior town, lying N. W. of the center of the co. Its surface is a hilly upland, divided into 3 general ridges extending N. and S. These ridges are about 400 ft. above the valleys, and are arable to their summits. The streams are Butternut Creek, flowing S. through the center, and Wharton Creek, flowing S. W. through the w. part. The soil upon the hills is a slaty loam, in many places underlaid by hardpan, and in the valleys a gravelly loam.

The Tocsin was established at Cooperstown in June, 1829, by Dutton & Hews, and was published by them until 1831, when it took the name of

The Otsego Republican. It was issued by Dutton & Hopkins for about 1 year; by Hopkins alone, 1 year; Hopkins & Clark, a year; by A. W. Clark, about 1 year; and by Andrew W. Barber, 4 or 5 years. In 1845 it was issued by J. K. Williams & Co. Soon after it again came into the possession of A. W. Barber, and was continued by him until his death, in Aug. 1855. In Oct. 1855, the paper was united with The Otsego Democrat, and issued as

The Republican and Democrat, under which title it is now published by James J. Hendrix.

The Otsego Democrat was commenced at Cooperstown in 1846 by James J. Hendrix, and was published by him until it was merged with the Republican in 1855.

The Otsego Examiner was commenced at Cooperstown in 1854 by Robert Shankland, who soon after withdrew, and the publication was continued by B. W. Burditt until 1857.

The Cherry Valley Gazette was started in Oct. 1818, by Wm. McLean, who continued its publication until 1832. It then passed into the hands of Charles McLean, who continued it until Jan. 1, 1847, when A. S. Bottsford became proprietor and continued it until 1851. It then reverted to Charles McLean; and in 1853 it was sold to John B. King, who published it 1 year under the name of

The American Banner, when he sold it to A. S. Bottsford, who changed the name back to

The Cherry Valley Gazette, under which title it is still published.

The Otsego Farmer was published at Cherry Valley in 1841.

The Otsego County Courier was commenced at the village of Louisville, in the town of Morris, by Wm. H. S. Wynans. in 1845. This paper was succeeded by

The Village Advertiser, commenced at the same place in 1851. It was a quarterly publication, conducted, in 1855, by H. S. Avery.

The Oneonta Herald was commenced Feb. 9, 1853, at Oneonta Village, and was published by L. P. Carpenter in 1855.

The Unadilla Advertiser was published at the village of Unadilla for a series of years; but its history is wanting.

[1] During the first winter the snow fell to so great a depth that it was impossible for Mr. Lindesay to go to the nearest settlement, which was 15 mi. distant. His provisions gave out, and his family were in danger of perishing by starvation. In this extremity they were visited by an Indian, who came on snow shoes, and who, on learning their situation, undertook to supply them with food. He went to the Mohawk, and returned with a load of provisions, and continued his visits of mercy until the close of the winter. Mr. Lindesay afterward left the settlement, joined the army, and served for several years.

Burlington Green, (Burlington p. o.,) on Butternut Creek, near the center, contains 3 churches and 118 inhabitants; **Burlington Flats,** (p. v.,) on Wharton Creek, N. W. of the center, 2 churches, a cotton factory, gristmill, sawmill, and about 30 dwellings; and **West Burlington,** (p. v.,) on Wharton Creek, 2 churches and 143 inhabitants. The first settlement was commenced near West Burlington, in 1790, by Robert Garrat, and Eber and Benj. Harrington.[1] The first church (Bap.) was formed at Burlington Green, in 1793; Rev. James Southworth was the first minister.[2]

BUTTERNUTS—was formed from Unadilla, Feb. 5, 1796. Morris was taken off in 1849, and a part of Unadilla was annexed in 1857. It lies upon the w. border of the co., s. w. of the center. Its surface is a hilly upland, divided into several ridges extending N. and S. Unadilla River, forming its w. boundary, is bordered by a narrow intervale, from which the highlands rise in a series of steep bluffs to a height of 500 to 600 ft. Butternut Creek flows s. w. in a deep valley through near the center of the town. A large number of smaller streams, tributaries to these, flow in deep valleys among the hills, dividing the ridges and giving to the region a peculiar broken character. The hills are arable to their summits, and the soil is a good quality of red shale and gravelly loam. **Gilbertsville,** (Butternuts p. o.,) near the center, contains 4 churches, the Gilbertsville Academy and Collegiate Institute, an oil mill, tannery, and various other manufacturing establishments. Pop. 442. Settlements were commenced about 1790, at Gilbertsville, by Gordon and Wyatt Chamberlin and Abijah Gilbert.[3] The first church (Cong.) was formed in 1795–96; Rev. John Stone was the first preacher.[4]

CHERRY VALLEY—was formed from Canajoharie, (Montgomery co.,) Feb. 16, 1791. Middlefield, Springfield, and Worcester were taken off in 1797, and Roseboom in 1854. It is the N. E. corner town in the co. Its surface is a hilly and mountainous upland; and much of it is too rough and rocky for cultivation. Mount Independence, s. E. of the center, is a rocky eminence 1,000 ft. above the valleys and 2,000 ft. above tide. It is the highest summit in the co. A range of highlands extends along the N. W. boundary. The central and s. parts of the town are drained by the head branches of the Susquehanna, and the N. part by tributaries of the Mohawk. The soil upon the uplands is a slaty and gravelly loam, and in the valleys a fine quality of calcareous loam. Upon a small creek in the N. part is the Te-ka-ha-ra-nea Falls, 160 feet in height. In the vicinity are several sulphur springs and quarries of limestone. In the N. E. corner are several springs of weak brine, from which salt was formerly manufactured. **Cherry Valley,**[5] (p. v.,) at the head of the valley of Cherry Valley Creek, was incorp. June 8, 1812. It contains 3 churches, the Cherry Valley Academy,[6] a bank, newspaper office, and gristmill. Pop. 933. **Salt Springs-ville**[7] (p. o.) is a hamlet in the N. E. corner. The first settlement was made on the present site of the village in 1739, by John Lindesay, an emigrant from the Londonderry Colony of Scotch-Irish in N. H.[8] The first religious services were held in 1743, by Rev. Samuel Dunlap, a native of Ireland.[9]

DECATUR[10]—was formed from Worcester, March 25, 1808. It lies upon the E. line of the co., s. of the center. The surface is hilly, and broken by the narrow valleys of several small

---

[1] Paul Gardner settled in 1792, and Benj. Card, Miles Potter, Caleb Gardner, Alexander Parker, Ira Johnson, John Johnson, Lemuel Hubbell, and Sam'l Hubbard, about the same time or soon after, in the vicinity of Burlington Flats. The first school was taught by Jos. Wright, at Burlington Green. Paris Briggs and Willard Church kept the first inns, and Walbridge & Co. the first store, at Burlington Flats. Augustus and Adolphus Walbridge erected the first mill, at the same place.

[2] The census reports 8 churches; 3 Bap., Presb., Cong., Prot. E., Friends, and F. W. Bap.

[3] John Marsh, Joseph Cox, John and Daniel Eastwood were among the first settlers in the w. part of the town, and Wm. Masson and Dr. John Burgess in the s. part. The first child born was Wm. Shaw, and he is supposed to have been the first one that died; the first marriage was that of Jos. Cox and Betsey Gilbert. The first school was taught by Levi Hollibert, at the house of Jos. Cox. Abijah Gilbert kept the first inn, and Wm. Masson the first store, near Gilbertsville. The first mill was erected by Jos. Shaw and Abijah Gilbert.

[4] The census reports 5 churches; Cong., Presb., Prot. E., Bap., and M. E.

[5] This place has been the residence of several of the distinguished political and professional men in the State, among whom were John Mills, Esq., the distinguished lawyer of N. Y. City; Hon. Wm. W. Campbell, author of the "Annals of Tryon Co.;" Rev. Eliphalet Nott; Jabez D. Hammond, Esq., author of "Political History of New York;" Hon. Levi Beardsley, author of "Reminiscences of Otsego;" Alvin Stewart, Esq.; and James C. Morse, Esq.

[6] This institution was incorp. Feb. 8, 1796, and is the oldest academy w. of Schenectady. Its first principal was Rev. Solomon Spaulding, the reputed author of the Book of Mormon; his successor was Rev. Eliphalet Nott, the venerable President of Union College. The institution has maintained a high reputation for more than half a century; and the female department under its present organization has attained a wide celebrity.

[7] Named from the brine springs in the vicinity.

[8] Mr. Lindesay was one of the original proprietors of Cherry Valley, under a patent granted in 1738, by George Clarke, then Lieut. Governor of New York; to John Lindesay, Jacob Roseboom, and others. David Ramsey and James Campbell, from Londonderry, N. H., and Wm. Galt and Wm. Dickson, from Ireland, settled on the patent, in 1742, at and near the village. John Wells, from Ireland, settled at the village, in 1744. From the fear of Indian hostilities, the settlement of Cherry Valley proceeded slowly, there being in 1752, 12 years after the first settlement, but 8 families in the town; and at the breaking out of the Revolution, in 1775, the number of families did not exceed 60. James Ritchie kept the first store and inn, anterior to the war; and James Campbell erected the first gristmill, in 1743–44. John Wells erected the second gristmill. Rev. Samuel Dunlap taught a classical school at his own house, in 1743–44,—the first probably, of the kind w. of the Hudson. The whole settlement was destroyed by the Indians, and the greater part of the inhabitants were murdered and taken prisoners, on the evening of Nov. 11, 1778. See page 531.

[9] The census reports 4 churches; 2 M. E., Presb., and Prot. E

[10] Named in honor of Commodore Stephen Decatur.

streams. The hills generally have gradual slopes and rounded summits, and are elevated 250 to 300 ft. above the valleys. The town is drained s. by Oak and Parker Creeks, flowing into the Schenevas. The soil is a sandy and gravelly loam. **Decatur,** (p. v.,) near the s. w. corner, contains a church and 120 inhabitants. The first settlements were commenced in or about 1790, by Jacob Kinney, originally from New Milford, Conn., at or near the village of Decatur.[1] The first religious association (M. E.) was formed at an early period.[2]

EDMESTON—was formed from Burlington, April 1, 1808. It lies upon the w. border of the co., N. of the center. The surface is an elevated upland, broken by numerous irregular valleys. The highest elevations are 400 to 500 ft. above Unadilla River, which forms the w. boundary Wharton Creek flows across the s. E. corner. Mill Creek and several other small streams take their rise in the town. Smiths Pond is a small sheet of water in the N. E. corner. The soil is a sandy and clayey loam. **Edmeston Center** (Edmeston p. o.) contains 3 churches, a grist and saw mill, and tannery. Pop. 275. **West Edmeston,** (p. v.,) on Unadilla River, and partly in Brookfield, (Madison co.,) contains a church and 35 houses. **South Edmeston** (p. v.,) contains a church and 30 houses. **East Edmeston** is a p. o. Of the first settlement in town, authentic data of the precise date are wanting. It was made, however, on Unadilla River, during the interval between the close of the French War, in 1763, and the commencement of that of the Revolution, in 1775, by Col. Edmeston, an officer of the French War, and Percifer Carr, a faithful soldier who had served under him.[3] The first church (Bap.) was formed at Taylor Hill, March 8, 1794; Rev. Stephen Taylor was the first preacher.[4]

EXETER—was formed from Richfield, March 25, 1799. It is an interior town, lying N. w. of the center of the co. The surface is hilly and broken, consisting mainly of elevated uplands. Angel Cliff and Town Cliff Hills, in the E. part of the town, are 400 to 500 ft. above the valleys. The town is drained E. by several small streams flowing into Schuyler Lake, and s. by Butternut and Wharton Creeks, both of which rise in this town. The soil is a clay and gravelly loam, well adapted to grazing. **Exeter Center** (Exeter p. o.) contains a church and 106 inhabitants. **Schuylers Lake,** (p. v.,) at the outlet of Schuyler Lake, on the E. border of the town, contains 2 churches and 280 inhabitants. **West Exeter** (p. v.) contains 1 church and 100 inhabitants. The first settlements were made by John Tunnicliff, near Schuyler Lake, and William Angel, on Angel Hill, in 1789.[5] The first religious association (Presb.) was formed at Exeter Center, in 1800: Rev. T. W. Duncan was the first regular preacher.[6]

HARTWICK[7]—was formed from Otsego, March 30, 1802. Its N. line was changed in 1803. It is the central town in the co. It is a hilly upland, the highest summits being 200 to 350 ft. above the valleys. Its E. part is drained by the Susquehanna, and its w. part by Otego Creek. The soil is chiefly a sandy and gravelly loam, with an occasional mixture of clay. **Hartwick,** (p. v.,) on Otego Creek, in the w. part, contains 4 churches, 2 iron founderies, several mills, and other manufacturing establishments. Pop. about 400. **Hartwick Seminary,** (p. v.,) in the valley of the Susquehanna, contains the "Hartwick Theological and Classical Seminary,"[8] a church, and 20 dwellings. **South Hartwick** (p. v.) contains a church and 17 houses. **Toddsville,** (p. v.,) upon the line of Otsego, in the N. E. corner of the town, contains the Union Cotton Factory[9] and about a dozen dwellings. **Clintonville,** a hamlet in the s. E. corner, is the seat of the Clinton Cotton Factory.[10] The Hartwick Patent, including the greater part of the area of this town, was granted April 22, 1761; and settlements were made in the town before the

1 Jacob Brown, John and Calvin Seward, and Oliver McIntyre settled soon after; and —— Sloan, from Columbia co., settled near the village, in 1797. Mr. Sloan opened the first tavern and the first store, N. of the village. John Champion erected the first gristmill, and James Stewart the first carding and fulling mill, about 1810. The first school was taught by Samuel Thurber, in 1798. The first death is supposed to have been that of Mr. King, about 1797.

2 The census reports 2 churches; M. E. and Bap.

3 At the close of the war, Col. Edmeston, for his military services, received the grant of a tract of land covering a large portion of the town on which he made the first settlement. At his death the lands fell to heirs and minor children residing in England, from whom no safe title could be obtained for many years,—which greatly retarded the settlement of the town. During the Revolution, the hired men of Mr. Carr were killed while at work, his barn was burned, his property destroyed, and himself and family were taken prisoners by the British and Indians and detained to the close of the war. Abel De Forest and Gideon De Forest were among the early settlers on the Unadilla; Aden Deming and James Kenada, at Edmeston; and Stephen Taylor, on Taylor Hill, where the first school was taught. Rufus

Graves kept the first inn; and James Kenada erected the first gristmill, both at Edmeston Center.

4 The census reports 5 churches; 2 Bap., 7th da. Bap., M. E., and Univ.

5 About the same time, or soon after, Asa Williams settled in the s. part of the town; Joshua and Caleb Angel, on Angel Hill; Seth Tubbs and Bethel Martin, at West Exeter; and M. Cushman, on the Rockdunga. Eliphalet Brockway kept the first inn, at Schuyler Lake; and C. Jones the first store, in 1810. John Hartshorne erected the first gristmill, on Herkimer Creek.

6 The census reports 6 churches; 2 M. E., Cong., Bap., Prot. E., and Union.

7 Named from Christopher Hartwick, the patentee of the Hartwick Patent.

8 This institution, established in 1815, was originally endowed by John Christopher Hartwick with a fund of $80,000.

9 The Union Cotton Factory was erected in 1809, and burned down and rebuilt in 1848. It gives employment to about 40 hands.

10 The Clinton Factory, erected in 1847, gives employment to 35 hands, and turns out 624,000 yards of printed cottons per annum.

Revolution.[1] The first church (Bap.) was formed Aug. 19, 1795; Rev. John Bostwick was the first settled preacher.[2]

LAURENS—was formed from Otsego, April 2, 1810. It is an interior town, lying s. w. of the center of the co. With the exception of the broad valley of Otego Creek, the surface is high and hilly. It is drained s. by Otego Creek and several tributaries, among which are Harrisons and Camps Creeks. The soil is a sandy and gravelly loam, in some parts slaty, and generally productive. One and a half mi. w. of Laurens is a sulphur spring. **Laurens,** (p. v.,) on Otego Creek, in the e. part, was incorp. April 22, 1834. It contains 3 churches, 2 flouring mills, the Otsego Cotton Mills,[3] an iron foundery, and a tannery. Pop. 726. **Jacksonville,** (Mount Vision p. o.,) in the n. e. corner, contains 2 churches, a grist and saw mill, and about 30 houses. **West Laurens** (p. v.) contains about 15 houses. Settlements were made in this town prior to the Revolution, by Joseph Marshall and Richard Smith, a little n. of Laurens Village; by John Sleeper, at the village; and by Wm. Ferguson, a little s. of it.[4] The first religious association was formed by the Friends, who erected a meetinghouse in 1800.[5]

MARYLAND—was formed from Worcester, March 25, 1808. It lies on the s. line of the co., e. of the center. Its surface is a hilly upland, broken by the deep ravines of the streams. Schenevas Creek flows s. w. through near the center and receives several tributaries from the n. South Hill, a steep, unbroken ridge 350 to 500 ft. above the valleys, extends along the s. bank of the creek through the town; and from its summit the surface spreads out into a rocky and broken upland, extending into the s. border. The soil is principally a sandy loam, and is best adapted to grazing. **Maryland,** (p. v.,) near the center of the town, contains a church and 20 houses; **Schenevus,** (p. v.,) near the e. border, a church, tannery, and 383 inhabitants. **Chaseville** is a p. o. The first settlement was made by Thomas Thompson and his son John, from Columbia co., in 1793.[6] The first religious association (Presb.) was formed at an early period; Rev. Mr Ralph was the first preacher.[7]

MIDDLEFIELD—was formed from Cherry Valley, March 3, 1797. It is an interior town, lying n. e. of the center of the co. The surface is a hilly upland, abruptly descending to Otsego Lake and Outlet, which form its w. boundary. The summits of the hills are 400 to 600 ft. above the valleys. Cherry Valley Creek flows s. w. through the e. part of the town. The soil is a gravelly and sandy loam. **Middlefield Center,** (p. v.,) in the n. part of the town, contains 15 dwellings. **Clarksville,**[8] (Middlefield p. o.,) on Cherry Valley Creek, contains 2 churches, a tannery, and 260 inhabitants. The first settlement was made about 1755, by emigrants originally from Ireland and Scotland.[9] The first religious association (Presb.) was formed by Rev. Andrew Oliver, in 1805; the first church edifice was erected in 1808.[10]

MILFORD—was formed from Unadilla, Feb. 5, 1796, as "*Suffrage.*" Its name was changed April 8, 1800. It is an interior town, s. of the center of the co. Its surface is a hilly upland, divided into two distinct ridges by the Susquehanna, which flows s. w. through the town. The valley is deep and bordered by steep hillsides. Crumhorn Mt., on the e. border, is 500 to 600 ft. above the valleys; and the w. hills are 300 to 400 ft. high. Crumhorn Lake, a body of water 3 mi. in circumference, lies upon the summit of Crumhorn Mt. The soil is a sandy and gravelly loam. **Milford Center** (Milford p. o.) contains 1 church and 15 houses; **Collierville** and

---

1 Lot Crosby and Stephen Skiff were among the first settlers at Hartwick Village, and Elijah and Rufus Hawkins and N. Lyon in the n. e. part of the town. James Butterfield kept the first inn, and Daniel Laurens the first store, at what is called White House. The first mill was erected by Samuel Mudge, at Hartwick Village.

2 The census reports 6 churches; 2 Christian, Bap., Luth., Presb., and M. E.

3 This factory was erected in 1846, by an investment of $40,000. It employs 40 persons, and makes sheetings exclusively, to the value of $50,000 per annum.

4 Erastus Crafts kept the first inn, about 1812; and Erastus and Ezra Dean, the first store. John Sleeper erected the first gristmill, and Daniel Johnson the first factory.

5 The census reports 6 churches; 2 M. E., Friends, Bap., Christian, and Presb.

6 In 1794, Josiah Chase, Col. J. Houghton, Ezekiel Rice, and Caleb Byington, from Vt., and Daniel Houghton and Wilder Rice, settled near Schenevus, Daniel Slaver, from Mass., settled at Schenevus, and Joseph Howe on Elk Creek. The first gristmill was built by Israel Spencer, and the first sawmill by Jotham Houghton, in 1795, on Schenevas Creek. Josiah Chase kept the first inn, near Roseville; and Stephen G. Virgil the first fulling and cloth dressing mill. The first death was that of John Rice, killed by the fall of a tree.

7 The census reports 4 churches; 3 M. E., and Bap.

8 About 2 mi. n. of Clarksville is a rock called by the Indians Nis-ka-yu-na, (probably meaning Council Rock,) where various tribes from the s. were accustomed to meet the Mohawks in council. In former days the rock was covered with hieroglyphics, but from its shaly nature all are now obliterated.

9 Among those who settled prior to the Revolutionary War were Wm. Cook, Daniel, Benjamin, and Reuben McCollum, Samuel and Andrew Wilson, Andrew Cochran, Andrew Cameron, and —— Hall, all in the n. part of the town. They came from the n. of Ireland, but were mostly of Scotch descent. Among those who settled near the close of and after the war were Benjamin Gilbert, in the n. part, in 1780; Reuben Beals, in the s. part, in 1786; Wm. Compton, Bernard Temple, —— Rice, Stephen and Thomas Pratt, Whitney Juvill, and Moses Rich, all from Mass., and Wm. Cook, from England, in 1787; —— Dunham, Wm. Temple, and Daniel Moore, from New England, in the s. part of the town, soon after. Hannah Hubbell taught the first school, about 1790. Alexander McCollum and Andrew Cameron kept the first inns, and Benjamin Johnson the first store, in 1790. Mr. McCollum also built the first sawmill, before the war; and Moses Rich the first gristmill, in 1795.

10 The census reports 4 churches in town; 2 Bap., Presb., and M. E.

Portlandville are p. offices. The first settlement was made on the Susquehanna, about 1770, by a squatter named Carr. As the settlements made at that period were broken up by the border wars which followed, little or no progress was made until the close of the Revolution.[1] The first religious services (Cong.) were held near Milford Village, in 1793, by Rev. —— Reed, the first preacher. The census reports 6 churches.[2]

MORRIS—was formed from Butternuts, April 6, 1849. It lies upon the w. border of the co., s. of the center. Its surface is a hilly upland, divided into two principal ridges by Butternut Creek, which flows s. w. through near the center. The w. ridge terminates in a series of steep bluffs bordering upon Unadilla River, which forms the w. boundary of the town. The soil upon the uplands is composed of clay, gravel, and disintegrated slate, and in the valleys of gravelly loam. **Louisville,** (Morris p. o.,) on Butternut Creek, contains 4 churches, 2 cotton factories, 3 tanneries, a gristmill, and several other manufacturing establishments.[3] Pop. about 400. **Maple Grove** is a p. o. The first settlement was made about 1770, by Andre Renouard, at Elm Grove, and Louis and Paschal Franchot, at Louisville, emigrants originally from France.[4] The first church (Bap.) was organized Aug. 28, 1793; Rev. John Lawton was the first preacher.[5]

NEW LISBON—was formed from Pittsfield, April 7, 1806, as *"Lisbon."* Its name was changed April 6, 1808. It is an interior town, lying w. of the center of the co. Its surface is a hilly upland, divided into several ridges by the deep ravines of the streams. The highest summits are 300 to 500 ft. above the valleys. The principal streams are Butternut Creek, flowing s. through the w. part, and Otego Creek, in the E. Gilberts Lake is a small sheet of water on the s. border. The soil upon the uplands is a clay and slaty loam, and in the valleys a gravelly loam. **Garrattsville,** (p. v.,) on Butternut Creek, contains a church, gristmill, sawmill, distillery, and fork factory. Pop. 192. **Noblesville** (New Lisbon p. o.) contains a church, gristmill, and 25 dwellings. **New Lisbon Center** and **Stitsonville** are hamlets. The first settlement was made in 1775, by William Lull and Increase Thurston.[6] The first church (Bap.) was formed at New Lisbon Center, in 1804, by Elder S. Gregory. A Cong. church was formed the same year by Rev. Wm. Stone.[7]

ONEONTA—was formed from Unadilla, Feb. 5, 1796, as *"Otego."* Its name was changed April 17, 1830. It is the central town upon the s. border of the co. Its surface is a hilly upland, broken by the deep valley of the Susquehanna, which extends N. E. and s. w. through the s. part. Otego Creek and several small streams flow into the Susquehanna from the N. A range of hills 500 ft. high extends along the s. E. bank of the Susquehanna. The center and N. part are hilly, and broken by narrow and irregular valleys. The summits are 150 to 300 ft. above the valleys. The soil is gravel, slate, and clay on the uplands, and gravelly loam and alluvium upon the river bottoms. **Oneonta,** (p. v.,) on the Susquehanna, in the s. part of the town, was incorp. Oct. 14, 1848. It contains 3 churches, a woolen factory, an iron foundery, tannery, gristmill, sawmill, and distillery. Pop. 678. **West Oneonta** (p. v.) contains 15 dwellings; **Oneonta Plains,** 2 churches and a dozen houses. Henry Scramlin and —— Youngs settled in town previous to the Revolution.[8] The first religious association (Presb.) was formed at Oneonta Village, in 1786; Rev. Alexander Conkey was the first settled preacher, when the church was built in 1816.[9]

---

[1] Matthew Cully, from Cherry Valley, and George Mumford settled near Milford-Center in 1783. Abraham and Jacob Beals, and a family named Ford, all from Mass., settled at and near Milford Village in 1784. Henry Scott, from Ireland, settled a little N. of the village in 1786. The first child born was David Beals, in Sept. 1786; the first marriage, that of James Brown and Rhoda Marvin, in 1788; and the first death, that of Mrs. Beals, about the same time. Increase Niles taught the first school, in 1790. Matthew Cully and Isaac Collier kept the first inn, below Milford Village, and Isaac Edson the first store, at the village, in 1794. The first gristmill was erected by David Cully, in 1788, and the first sawmill by Matthew Cully, in 1792–93.

[2] 2 M. E., Presb., Bap., Christian, and Friends.

[3] The Butternuts Cotton and Woolen Factory was erected at the village of Louisville in 1812. It employs 40 hands, and manufactures sheetings to the value of $50,000 per annum.

[4] Benjamin, Joseph, Caleb, Benjamin, jr. and Nathan Lull and Jonathan Moore, from Dutchess co., settled at Louisville in 1773. Andrew Cathcart, Jacob Morris, and Ebenezer Knapp were also among the early settlers. The first marriage was that of Joseph Lull and Martha Knapp, in 1776. The first inn was kept by Sturgess Bradley, and the first store by Louis and Paschal Franchot, at Louisville. Louis De Villier erected the first gristmill, on Aldrich Creek, and Paschal Franchot, John C. Morris, and A. G. Washburn the first factory.

[5] The census reports 5 churches; Bap., Friends, Prot. E., M E., and Univ.

[6] Among the other early settlers were S. W. Park, Moses Thurston, Hughey Marks, O. Park, William Pierce, —— Brook, John Johnson, William and John Garratt, all in the vicinity of Garrattsville. Elnathan Nobles was among the first settlers at Noblesville; from him the place derives its name. Joseph Baldwin and John L. Stitson were among the first settlers at Stitsonville. In 1778 the first settlers were driven off by the Indians and tories. Their buildings were burned and their crops destroyed. After the close of the war, all the first settlers returned to their improvements. Sally Thurston was the first child born in town; James McCollum taught the first school; Charles Eldredge kept the first inn, in the s. part of the town; and William Garratt the first store, at Garrattsville. Louis De Villier. a Frenchman, erected the first mill.

[7] The census reports 3 churches in town; Bap., Cong., and M. E.

[8] Aaron Brink, Frederick Brown, and —— McDonald were among the early settlers at Oneonta Village. James Youngs settled at the mouth of Charlotte River; Baltus Himmel, N. of the village; Abraham Houghtaling, Jacob Elias Brewer, and Peter Swartz, in the N. part of the town, in 1786; and Josiah Peck, on Oneonta Creek. The first birth was that of Abraham Houghtaling 2d, in 1786. Baltus Himmel kept the first inn, and Peter Dininey the first store. John Vanderwerker erected the first gristmill.

[9] The census reports 5 churches; 2 M. E., Bap., Presb., and F. W. Bap.

OTEGO—was formed from Franklin (Delaware co.) and Unadilla, April 12, 1822, as "*Hunts-ville.*" A part of Milford was annexed and its name changed April 17, 1830. It lies on the s. border of the co., w. of the center. Its surface is a hilly upland, divided by the Susquehanna, which flows s. w. through the s. part. The N. part is separated into ridges 200 to 400 ft. high, all extending N. and s. The streams are Mill Creek, east and west branches of Otsdawa Creek, Flax Creek, and Center Brook, The soil is a clay and sandy loam. **Otego,** (p. v.,) on the Susquehanna, contains 4 churches and 331 inhabitants; **Otsdawa,** (p. v.,) on Otsdawa Creek, contains a church, tannery, mill, and 20 dwellings. **Center Brook** is a p. o. on the stream of the same name. Settlements were made in this town, along the Susquehanna, soon after the close of the Revolution; but the precise date of the first settlement is not known.[1] The first church (Presb.) was organized at Otego Village, Sept. 17, 1805; Rev. Abner Benedict was the first preacher.[2]

OTSEGO—was formed as a part of Montgomery co., March 7, 1788, and originally included the greater part of Otsego co. Burlington, Richfield, and Unadilla were taken off in 1792, Hart-wick in 1802, and Laurens in 1810. It is an interior town, lying upon the w. bank of Otsego Lake, N. of the center of the co. Its surface is a hilly upland, lying between Otsego and Schuy-ler Lakes and descending abruptly towards each. The summits are 300 to 500 ft. above the water, the uplands being divided into two ridges by Fly Creek, which flows s. through the center. Oak Creek, the outlet of Schuyler Lake, flows s. through the w. part. The soil is clay, gravel, and sandy loam. **Cooperstown,** (p. v.,) at the foot of Otsego Lake, was incorp. April 3, 1807, by the name of "*Otsego.*" Its name was changed to Cooperstown June 12, 1812. Besides the co. buildings, it contains 5 churches, a bank, 3 newspaper offices, an academy,[3] the buildings of the Cooperstown Seminary and Female Collegiate Institute,[4] a flouring mill, and various manu-facturing establishments.[5] The location of the village is pleasant and attractive from its many elegant private residences and historic associations. Pop. about 1,500.[6] **Fly Creek,** (p. v.,) upon the stream of the same name, contains 3 churches, several manufactories,[7] and 30 houses. **Oaksville,** (p. v.,) s. of the center, contains a church, factory, and 15 houses. **Otsego Lake** is a p. o. **Toddsville** (p. v.) is on the line of Hartwick. Settlements were made at Cooperstown and Fly Creek, in 1784–85, by Judge Wm. Cooper, Wm. Jarvis, William Ellison, Israel Guild, John Howard, and Elisha Finney.[8] The first religious association (Presb. and Cong.) was formed Dec. 29, 1798; Rev. Isaac Lewis was the first preacher.[9]

PITTSFIELD—was formed from Burlington, March 24, 1797. New Lisbon was taken off in 1806. It is centrally situated upon the w. line of the co. Its surface is a hilly upland, termi-nating in abrupt declivities upon Unadilla River, which forms its w. boundary. Wharton Creek flows across the N. w. corner, and several small tributaries of Butternut Creek flow through the s. part. The soil is generally a slaty and gravelly loam. **Pittsfield,** (p. o.,) on the Una-dilla, contains 10 houses. The first settlements were made in the valley of the Unadilla, about 1793, by Jacob Lull, Aaron Nobles, Hubbard Goodrich, and Matthew Bennett.[10] The first church (Bap.) was formed at an early period, in the s. E. part of the town. The only church (Union) now in town was organized in the E. part in 1849.

---

[1] Ransom Hunt, Abraham Blakesley, John Birdsall, Benjamin Cummings, Jacob Yates, Joseph Pierce, and Barnard Overhyer, were among the first settlers at Otego Village and along the river. Phineas Cook settled on the E. branch of the Otsdawa in 1800, and built there the first cloth dressing mill, in 1801. Ransom Hunt kept the first inn, and erected the first gristmill in town. Thaddeus R. Austin opened the first store.

[2] The census reports 6 churches; Presb., Prot. E., Bap., F. W. Bap., Christian, and M. E.

[3] The first academy was formed in 1795, and the building burned down March 31, 1809, and was subsequently rebuilt. It has been sustained, and has prospered for most of the time, for half a century.

[4] This institution was established and opened in 1854, and extensive and commodious buildings were erected at a cost of $30,000. It started with J. L. G. McKown as Principal. It suspended operations in 1857, was purchased by R. C. Flack in 1859, and the school is again in operation, with indications of permanent prosperity. See p. 749.

[5] The Hope Cotton Factory, erected in 1813, with an aggregate capital of about $100,000, has through a long series of years given employment to 80 persons. After undergoing various changes in construction, machinery, and proprietorship, the establishment is still continued, with reduced operations.

[6] J. Fenimore Cooper, the novelist, resided here; and his man-sion and grounds were among the finest in Central N. Y.

[7] At this place is a fork factory, with a capital of $75,000, em-ploying 30 men; a pail factory; a manufactory of agricultural

implements and machinery, employing a capital of $25,000; and a foundery and machine shop, employing 25 men.

[8] John Miller, Widow Johnson, Wm. Abbott, and —— Averell settled in 1786. The first child born was Wm. Jarvis, at Fly Creek, in 1787. The first deaths in town were those of two de-serting soldiers, who were shot by order of Gen. Clinton, in 1779, before the settlements were commenced. The first school was taught at Cooperstown, by Joshua Dewey, in 1788. Wm. Ellison opened the first inn, in 1786; and Judge Wm. Cooper the first store, in 1789–90. The first mill was erected by Samuel Tubbs, at Toddsville, in 1790. In 1779, General Clinton, on his way to join Sullivan's expedition, built a dam across the outlet of the lake to raise the waters sufficiently to float down the Susque-hanna the boat, containing his men and military stores. The remains of this dam are still visible. In 1784, Gen. Washing-ton, on a journey of observation, visited the foot of Otsego Lake. In 1786, John Miller felled a large tree across the outlet to serve as a bridge. Judge Cooper removed his family from N. J. in 1790.

[9] The census reports 10 churches; 3 M. E., 2 Presb., 2 Univ., Prot. E., Bap., and R. C.

[10] Seth Harrington and Benj. Eddy settled in the E. part of the town soon after the settlements on the Unadilla. The first school was taught by Benjamin Pendleton, at Pittsfield P. O. Matthew Bennett kept the first inn, in 1797, and Henry Randall the first store, in 1810, at the P. O. Benj. Atwell built the first mill, and the Arkwright Manufacturing Company the first cotton factory, both on the Unadilla.

CHERRY VALLEY FEMALE ACADEMY.

C. G. HAZELTINE } ASSOCIATE PRINCIPALS
J. A. FOWLER.

PLAINFIELD—was formed from Richfield, March 25, 1799. It is the N. W. corner town of the co. Its surface is a broken and hilly upland. Unadilla River, forming the w. boundary, is bordered by steep bluffs rising to the height of 400 to 600 ft. The soil is a clay and sandy loam. **Unadilla Forks,** (p. v.,) at the junction of the E. and w. branches of Unadilla River, contains 2 churches, a hoe factory, flouring mill, sawmill, and machine shop. Pop. 253. **Plainfield Center** contains a church and 15 houses; **Spooners Corners** is a p. o.; **Leonardsville,** (p.v.,) on the Unadilla, in the s. part, is mostly in Madison co. The first settlement was made at and near Plainfield Center, in 1793, by Ruggles Spooner, Elias Wright, and John Kilbourne.[1] The first church (Bap.) was formed and the church erected in 1800; Rev. John Wait the first preacher.[2]

RICHFIELD—was formed from Otsego, April 10, 1792. Exeter and Plainfield were taken off in 1799. It is the extreme northern town of the co. Its surface is rolling and moderately hilly, with a mean elevation of 150 to 200 ft. above Schuyler Lake,—Pray and Nine Hills, on either side of the head of the lake, rising about 200 ft. higher. Schuyler Lake, in the s. E. corner, occupies a deep valley; and into it flow several small streams from the N. and w. The soil is of a diversified character, consisting of gravel, slate, clay, and sandy loam, well cultivated and productive. About 500,000 pounds of cheese are made in the town annually,—being more than double that made in any other town in the co. **Richfield Springs,** (p. v.,) near the head of Schuyler Lake, in the N. E. corner of the town, contains 3 churches, a flouring mill, and 368 inhabitants.[3] **Monticello,** (Richfield p. o.,) near the center, contains a church and 139 inhabitants. **Mayflower** is a p. o; **Brighton** contains about 15 houses. Settlements were made prior to the Revolution; but they were broken up during the war. The first settlers after the war were John Kimball, Richard and Wm. Pray, John Beardsley, Joseph Coats, and Seth Allen, in 1787.[4] The first church (Prot. E.) was formed at Monticello, May 20, 1799; Rev. Daniel Nash was the first pastor.[5]

ROSEBOOM[6]—was formed from Cherry Valley, Nov. 23, 1854. It lies on the E. border of the co., N. of the center. The surface is a hilly upland, broken by the valleys of several streams. The hills are generally rounded, and their summits elevated 300 to 350 ft. above Schoharie Kil. The soil is a gravelly loam. **Roseboom,** (p.v.,) in the N. W. part, on the line of Middlefield, contains a church and 111 inhabitants; and **South Valley,** (p. v.,) in the s. E. part, 2 churches and 175 inhabitants. **Pleasant Brook** (p. o.) is a hamlet.[7] The settlements in this town were commenced about 1800. There are 5 churches in town.[8]

SPRINGFIELD—was formed from Cherry Valley, March 3, 1797. It lies upon the N. line of the co., E. of the center. The surface is a rolling and moderately hilly upland, the hills generally rising about 200 ft. above the valleys. Mt. Wellington, E. of the head of Otsego Lake, in the s. part of the town, is 300 to 400 ft. high. Summit Lake, in the N. part, in high water discharges its waters both N. and s. The streams are small brooks. In the N. part is a deep sink, called "The Chyle," into which a considerable stream of water runs and flows through a subterranean passage to Braman's Factory, where it again appears on the surface. The sink is tunnel-shaped, 240 feet in circumference and 15 ft. deep. After heavy rains it is sometimes filled with water, which, while discharging through the orifice below, often moves round in rapid gyrations. The soil is a black and yellow loam, resting upon limestone and slate. More hops are grown in this town than in any other town in the co. **Springfield Center** (p. v.) contains 2 churches, a tannery, and 15

---

[1] Sam'l Williams settled on the Unadilla, in the N. part, and Benj. and Abel Clark, at the Forks, about the same time. The first school was taught at Spooners Corners, by Jas. Robinson, in 1797–98. Wm. Lincoln kept the first inn at Lloydville, and Luce & Woodward the first store. Capt. Caleb Brown built the first mill, in 1805, on the Unadilla.

[2] The census reports 4 churches; 2 F. W. Bap., Presb., Bap.

[3] Richfield Springs—from which the village derives its name—are celebrated for their medicinal properties in the cure of cutaneous disorders, and large numbers of invalids are annually attracted here. Professor Reid has given the following as the result of an analysis of a wine-gallon of the water of these springs:—

	Grains.
Bicarbonate of magnesia.................................	20
Bicarbonate of lime......................................	10
Chloride of sodium and magnesia....................	1.5
Sulphate of magnesia....................................	30
Hydrosulphate of magnesia and lime.................	2
Sulphate of lime...	20
Solid matter..	153.5
	236.10

Sulphuretted hydrogen gas, 26.9 inches.

[4] Wm. Tunnicliff, Dan'l Hawks, John Hatch, Ebenezer Eaton, and Jos. Rockwell settled at or near Richfield Springs in 1789; Obadiah Beardsley and his son Obadiah, jr., the father and grandfather of the late Levi Beardsley, and Hon. Samuel Beardsley, of Utica, settled near Schuyler Lake in 1790. The first birth was that of Jos. Beardsley; and the first marriage, that of Ebenezer Russell and Mrs. Moore. James S. Palmer taught the first school, at Richfield Springs; Israel Rawson kept the first inn, and Cyrus Robinson the first store, at the Springs; William Tunnicliff erected the first mill, at the same place.

[5] The census reports 7 churches; 3 M. E., 2 Prot. E., Presb., and Univ.

[6] Named from Abram Roseboom, one among the earliest settlers.

[7] Abram Roseboom erected the first sawmill and carding and fulling mill, in 1806, at Lodi; Dan'l Antisdale kept the first inn and the first store, at the same place, in 1832. The first gristmill was erected at Lodi, by Cornelius Law, in 1818.

[8] The census reports 5 churches; 2 M. E., Evan. Luth., Christian, and Bap.

houses; and **East Springfield** (p. v.) a church and 20 houses. **Springfield** is a p. o. near the center. The first settlements were made in 1762, by John Kelly, Richard Ferguson, and James Young, from Ireland, at East Springfield; and Gustavus Klumph and Jacob Tygart, at the head of Otsego Lake. Most of these settlers were driven off during the war.[1] The first church (Bap.) was formed at an early period; Rev. —— Fairman was the first preacher.[2]

UNADILLA—was formed from Otsego, April 10, 1792. Butternuts, "*Suffrage*," (now Milford,) and "*Otego*" (now Oneonta) were taken off in 1796, a part of "*Huntsville*" (now Otego) in 1822, and a part of Butternuts in 1857. It lies at the junction of Unadilla and Susquehanna Rivers, in the s. w. corner of the co. The surface is a rolling and hilly upland, the highest summits being 400 to 500 ft. above the valleys. Unadilla River, forming the w. boundary, Susquehanna River, the E., and Sandy Hill Creek, in the E. part, are the principal streams. The soil on the river bottoms is an alluvial loam, and on the uplands a slaty and gravelly loam. **Unadilla,** (p. v.,) on the Susquehanna, was incorp. April 2, 1827. It contains 3 churches, the Unadilla Academy, a bank, newspaper office, cotton factory, furnace, 2 tanneries, a flouring mill, sawmill, paper mill, and various other manufactories. Pop. 795. **Unadilla Center** (p. v.) contains a church and 15 houses. Settlements were made at Unadilla, along the valley of the Susquehanna, prior to the Revolution; of the precise date, and by whom, no records or tradition inform us.[3] A conference took place between Gen. Herkimer and Brant, the Indian warrior, at Unadilla, in July, 1777. The first church (Prot. E.) was formed Nov. 1, 1809; Rev. Russell Wheeler was the first pastor.[4]

WESTFORD—was formed from Worcester, March 25, 1808. It is an interior town, lying s. E. of the center of the co. Its surface is hilly, the highest summits being 400 to 500 ft. above the valleys. It is drained s. by Elk Creek and w. by tributaries of Cherry Valley Creek. The soil is a sandy loam of good quality. **Westford,** (p. v.,) a little E. of the center of the town, contains 2 churches and 12 houses. **Westville,** (p. v.,) in the w., on the line of Middleford, contains 3 churches and 15 houses. The first settlements were made about 1790, in the s. E. part, by Thomas Sawyer, Benjamin Chase, Oliver Salisbury, Alpheus Earl and father, Artemas, Moses, and David Howe, and Ephraim Smith,—all from Vt.[5] The first religious association (M. E.) was formed in 1791.[6]

WORCESTER—was formed from Cherry Valley, March 3, 1797. Decatur, Maryland, and Westford were taken off in 1808. It is the s. E. corner town in the co. The surface is a hilly and broken upland. The highlands which occupy the s. part of the town descend toward the N. by an abrupt declivity 350 to 400 ft. high. This declivity forms a continuous ridge extending N. E. and s. w. through near the center of the town. The principal streams are Charlotte River and its tributaries and Schenevas Creek. The soil is a sandy loam. **Worcester,** (p. v.,) in the N. w. part, contains 2 churches, 2 gristmills, a tannery, and 40 dwellings; **East Worcester** (p. v.) 2 churches, a gristmill and sawmill, and 25 dwellings; and **South Worcester,** (p. v.,) on Charlotte River, a church, a bank, and 20 dwellings. The first settlements were made on Schenevas Creek, from 1788 to '90. The first church (Presb.) was formed at an early period;[7] Rev. —— Bushnell was the first preacher.[8]

---

[1] Mr. Tygart had two sons, John and Jacob, who were taken prisoners and carried to Canada during the war. Soon after the war, Elisha Dodge, Col. Herrick, and Aaron Bigelow, from Conn., and Eli Parsons, Eliakim Sheldon, and Isaac White, from Mass., settled in the central part of the town. The first inn was kept by Eli Parsons. at East Springfield, and the first store by Thomas and Stacy Horner. Garrat Staats erected the first gristmill and sawmill, before the war.

[2] The census reports 4 churches; Bap., M. E., Presb., and Asso. Presb.

[3] Among the early settlers were Dan'l Bissel, Abijah Beach. and Solomon Martin, at Unadilla, —— Bates, —— Morefield, and Peter Rogers, at Unadilla Center, Abel De Forest and Wm. Buckley, in the E. part of the town. Solomon Martin kept the first store, in 1800. and Sampson Couger the first gristmill.

[4] The census reports 7 churches; 3 M. E., 2 Bap., Prot. E., and Presb.

[5] Among the other early settlers were Luther Seaver and Samuel Babcock, from Mass.; the latter in March, 1793. Wm.

Chase was the first child born in town. Nathaniel Griggs kept the first inn, at Westford Village, in 1795; and David Smith, the first store, about the same time. Capt. Artemas Howe built the first gristmill, in 1794, and also erected the first sawmill.

[6] The census reports 5 churches; 2 M. E., Cong., Prot. E., and Prot. Meth.

[7] Among the early settlers were Silas Crippen and Henry Stever, from Columbia co., Solomon Hartwell, Uriah Bigelow. and Nathaniel Todd, from Mass., and Charles Wilder and Joseph Tainter, from Vt. Philip Crippen, son of Silas Crippen, was the first child born in town. The first school was taught by Joseph Tainter, in 1798. Isaac Puffer kept the first inn, in 1793; and Aaron Kinney, the first store, in 1798. Silas Crippen built the first gristmill, in 1790. and the first sawmill, about the same time. The first clothing and carding works were erected by Rufus Draper.

[8] The census reports 4 churches; 2 Bap., M. E., and Evan. Luth.

Acres of Land, Valuation, Population, Dwellings, Families, Freeholders, Schools, Live Stock, Agricultural Products, and Domestic Manufactures, of Otsego County.

Names of Towns.	Acres of Land.		Valuation of 1858.			Population.		No. of Dwellings.	No. of Families.	Freeholders.	Schools.	
	Improved.	*Unimproved.*	*Real Estate.*	*Personal Property.*	*Total.*	*Males.*	*Females.*				*No. of Districts.*	*Children taught.*
Burlington	20,615½	7,229½	$339,808	$41,400	$381,208	896	912	342	370	292	12	668
Butternuts	21,173	8,766	532,240	110,525	642,765	1,006	1,023	427	435	262	14	695
Cherry Valley	18,012	6,097½	461,930	292,886	754,816	1,367	1,173	427	285	332	11	1,042
Decatur	9,565	3,617	155,565	13,200	168,765	475	438	168	181	159	7	346
Edmeston	18,091½	8,292	419,478	58,830	478,308	888	895	358	384	291	13	604
Exeter	14,135	4,915	295,615	39,116	334,731	757	783	284	305	238	9	622
Hartwick	19,848	5,583	434,454	71,931	506,385	1,038	1,182	449	601	245	17	947
Laurens	19,914½	6,974	420,820	60,500	481,320	1,029	1,077	412	446	346	14	692
Maryland	18,819	13,541½	371,350	39,900	411,250	1,102	1,075	398	432	339	16	835
Middlefield	25,062	11,421½	612,195	98,348	710,543	1,558	1,513	551	571	446	19	1,158
Milford	18,773¼	9,466¾	484,830	122,418	607,248	1,156	1,173	449	483	372	15	689
Morris	17,312	6,756	382,295	77,650	459,945	1,001	1,037	375	434	312	12	837
New Lisbon	20,025	6,481	387,965	39,025	426,990	882	910	339	373	300	16	695
Oneonta	15,238	7,303	373,107	46,568	419,675	1,105	1,062	407	440	327	14	875
Otego	19,393⅝	8,164	373,705	36,650	410,355	914	936	388	394	336	18	667
Otsego	20,374¾	9,619	790,549	563,270	1,353,819	2,115	2,219	738	825	529	18	1,382
Pittsfield	13,201¾	7,072	297,720	27,850	325,570	805	851	317	345	268	10	514
Plainfield	12,857¾	4,103	264,780	21,356	286,136	641	640	294	280	230	10	496
Richfield	15,681	4,213	407,355	84,236	491,591	791	752	252	312	259	10	549
Roseboom	13,366¾	6,730	204,353	62,921	267,274	949	938	345	373	295	12	714
Springfield	22,236½	7,114½	536,045	161,776	697,821	1,235	1,228	426	611	351	14	865
Unadilla	20,543	10,707½	482,337	136,906	619,243	1,393	1,329	516	533	453	14	927
Westford	14,831¾	5,804	298,000	30,650	328,650	678	693	275	314	293	11	415
Worcester	19,862	9,588½	405,245	43,900	449.145	1,055	1,060	387	411	322	15	797
Total	428,932⅝	179,559¼	9,731,741	2,281,812	12,013.553	24,836	24,899	9,324	10,138	7,597	321	18,131

Names of Towns.	Live Stock.					Agricultural Products.							Domestic Cloths in yards.
						Bush. of Grain.					Dairy Products.		
	Horses.	*Working Oxen and Calves.*	*Cows.*	*Sheep.*	*Swine.*	*Winter.*	*Spring.*	*Tons of Hay.*	*Bushels of Potatoes.*	*Bushels of Apples.*	*Pounds Butter.*	*Pounds Cheese.*	
Burlington	565	1,163	1,529	6,704	840	235	53,619½	4,894½	20,585	38,596	122,572	123,086	1,678½
Butternuts	605	1,658	2,003	5,733	1,152	1,326½	50,320	5,977	11,239	46,420	173,046	100,897	792
Cherry Valley	820	1,200	1,250	2,480	968	1,298	101,395	3,984½	17,380	21,107	105,160	22,218	1,176½
Decatur	338	766	855	2,551	710	1,064½	39,236¾	2,125	12,212	12,344	81,985	12,435	882½
Edmeston	664	1,407	1,618	6,355	1,028	557	54,557½	5,500½	18,790	33,133	106,826	157,540	3,146¾
Exeter	478	906	1,167	5,239	619	190	31,249¼	4,856	12,776½	30,911	85,235	156,365	982½
Hartwick	586	1,086	1,255	3,728	850	925½	51,485½	3,170	15,659	26,946	105,280	22,390	811½
Laurens	581	1,153	1,757	5,007	1,108	847	55,501	3,972½	15,333	30.460	195,763	10,530	1,798
Maryland	599	1,413	1,168	4,105	799	3,869	77,198	3,971	24,611	15.899	122,045	3,150	1,755
Middlefield	933	1,657	1,844	3,430	1,284	4,736	116,994½	5,712½	23,672	36.608	153,130	96,415	725
Milford	662	1,138	1,414	3,242	967	3,138¼	75,389¾	3.879½	20,282	20,823	148,017	12,820	23
Morris	514	1,459	1,531	3,719	669	937½	43,125	5,087½	11,581	27.252	134,468	53,625	652
New Lisbon	545	1,132	1,379	7,035	758	54	51,178	3,997	13,000	26,779	144,600	21,022	757½
Oneonta	512	884	1,335	3,956	850	2,637¼	32,309⅛	3,284	16,272	19,990	140,935	5,720	1,110
Otego	594	1,588	1,591	8,453	1,026	3,594½	57,920	5,069½	19,115	24,822	179,195	14,840	2,571¾
Otsego	1,009	1,395	1,854	8,220	1,469	901½	86,709½	6,620½	21,916	36,860	134,801	94.807	1,411
Pittsfield	438	1,137	1,160	4,576	730	1,218	43,534½	4,368¼	15,031	11,780	104,705	22,500	550
Plainfield	410	535	1,223	3,347	665	196	41,366½	4,008	13,405	19,756	57,755	25.710	690½
Richfield	487	817	1,745	2,414	660	138	41,353½	5,248	10,825	26,176	70,375	451.700	239
Roseboom	528	1,005	1,107	1,875	776	1,258	77,682½	3,147	15,044	11,236	115,160	4,010	994
Springfield	1,019	1,268	1,673	3,425	1,083	580	119,843¼	6,011	21,586	25.292	157,430	173,479	5.237½
Unadilla	558	2,054	1,550	7,867	1,212	3,911¾	59,880¾	6,004	19,488	25,741	143,184	31,749	1,099
Westford	534	909	1,118	3,703	880	2,044	57.864	2,930½	16,863	18,310	109,780	19,560	662
Worcester	673	1,355	1,587	2,773	1,265	4,239	66,919½	4,251½	26,038	13,955	183,759	1,925	3,034
Total	14,652	29,086	34,713	109,937	22,368	39,896¼	1,486,632⅞	108,069¾	412,703½	601,196	3,075,206	1,638,493	32,779½

PUTNAM COUNTY.

This county[1] was formed from Dutchess, June 12, 1812. It lies upon the Hudson, between Dutchess and Westchester cos., and extends E. to the Conn. line. It is centrally distant 85 mi. from Albany, and contains 234 sq. mi. It embraces nearly all of The Highlands E. of the Hudson. The mountains consist of several steep, rocky ranges, extending in a N. E. and S. W. direction and separated by deep, narrow valleys, the principal of which are Peekskill Hollow, and Canopus and Pleasant Valleys. The co. is watered by the upper branches of Croton River and several smaller streams. Among the mountain valleys are numerous picturesque lakes, the largest of which are Lakes Mahopac,[2] Canopus,[3] and Gleneida.[4] In the valleys the soil is a productive, sandy loam, but the mountains are bare and rocky, and only valuable for their mines[5] and quarries.[6] Iron ore abounds; and serpentine, magnesian limestone, and several other minerals are also found.[7] The rocks belong chiefly to the primitive and lower sedimentary or metamorphic series, consisting of granite, gneiss, granular quartz, talcose slate, metamorphic limestone, serpentine, greenstone, and hornblende. Peat and marl are found in various localities.[8] In the farming districts the people are principally engaged in dairying and furnishing milk for the New York market. Manufacturing is extensively carried on at Cold Spring. The principal works of internal improvement are the Hudson River R. R., extending through Philipstown, and the Harlem R. R., through Patterson and Southeast. The county seat is located at Carmel.[9] The co. buildings consist of a courthouse,[10] jail,[11] and co. clerk's office.[12] The poorhouse is located on a farm of 196 acres in Kent, about 2½ mi. from Carmel.[13] Two newspapers are published in the co.[14] A strip 580 rods wide along the E. border of the co. constitutes a part of the "*Oblong*" Tract, and was patented by Thomas Hawley and his associates, June 8, 1731.[15] The remaining part of the co., and a small part of Dutchess, are included in the great Highland Patent of Adolph Philipse. At the time of the Revolution this patent was owned by Philip Philipse, and Mary and Susannah, wives of Col. Roger Morris and Beverly Robinson, of the British army. Morris and Robinson, together with their wives, were attainted, and their property was confiscated and sold by the Commissioners of Forfeiture. It was subsequently shown in court that one-third of the patent was vested in the children of Col. Morris and his wife, and was not reached by the bill of attainder. The State was therefore obliged to

---

[1] Named from Maj. Gen. Israel Putnam, who was stationed in the co. a part of the time during the Revolutionary War. In the act of Dec. 16, 1737, the co. was styled "*South Precinct;*" March 24, 1772, it was subdivided into "*Southeast,*" "*Fredericksburgh,*" and "*Philips*" Precincts. The first of these precincts included the present towns of Southeast and Patterson, the second Carmel and Kent, and the third Putnam Valley and Philipsburgh.

[2] On Sauthier's map of 1779 this word is written "*Macookpack.*"

[3] This lake was formerly called "*Hortons Pond.*" It is now frequently called "*Oskawano,*" from an Indian chief said to have resided in this locality.

[4] Formerly called Shaw's Lake.

[5] Magnetic oxyd of iron is the most important of the ores found, although limonite and other varieties are obtained. A bed of magnetic ore was opened several years since on Breakneck Mt.; but it has not been extensively worked. Another bed has been opened on Constitution Island, opposite West Point Foundry. The Simewog vein was formerly worked at the Townsend Mine on Simewog Hill. The Philips vein has been traced at short intervals a distance of 8 mi., and several mines have been opened along its course. The Stewart Mine is the principal of these. Large quantities of iron were obtained from the Denny Mine, in the N. part of Putnam Valley, were formerly used at the Cold Spring Furnace. Coal Grove and Gouverneur Mines are in the neighborhood of the Denny Mine. The "*Harvey Steel and Iron Co.*" have opened several mines in Southeast, from which an excellent quality of ore for the manufacture of steel was obtained; but they are not now worked.

[6] Blunt's Quarry, on the S. side of Breakneck Point, near the line of Dutchess co., affords a bluish gray granite, which has been extensively used for the Delaware Breakwater, Fort Calhoun, and Fortress Monroe. The Highland Granite Co.'s quarry, principally owned by Howard & Holdane, is near the Hudson River, a short distance from Blunt's Quarry. It is elevated about 200 ft. above the river. Stony Point Quarry, on a rocky peninsula extending into the Hudson, Philips Quarry, on an estate of the same name, and other quarries in the co., have been worked. Marble is found in the N. part of Patterson.

[7] Among the minerals of the co. are arsenical and common iron pyrites, arsenite and chromate of iron, pyroxene, tremolite, arragonite, graphite, kerolite, brucite, actynolite hornblende, albite, laumonite stilbite, chabasite, epidote mica, zircon, sphene, and diallage.

[8] The principal localities where peat is found are near Patterson and on the E. side of Lake Mahopac.

[9] The first courts were held at the Baptist Church. The first co. officers were Stephen Barnum, *First Judge;* John Jewett, *Co. Clerk;* Wm. H. Johnston, *Sheriff;* and Joel Frost, *Surrogate.*

[10] The courthouse is a wooden building, erected in 1813, at a cost of $2,500. Joseph Cran, Stephen Barnum, Joel Frost, Jonathan Ferris, and John Jewett were appointed to superintend its erection.

[11] The jail is a stone building, erected in 1844. It adjoins the courthouse on the E.

[12] The clerk's office is a stone fireproof building, located a few rods S. of the courthouse.

[13] The average number of inmates in the poorhouse is 52, supported at a weekly cost of 43 cts. each. The income from the farm is $600 per annum. A school is taught throughout the year.

[14] *The Putnam Co. Courier* was established at Carmel in 1814. It was successively issued as

The Putnam Republican, published by Thos. Smith; and *The Putnam Democrat,* published by W. H. Sloat, and afterward by Elijah Yerks. James D. Little succeeded Yerks, and changed the paper to

The Democratic Courier; and again, in 1852, to

The Putnam Co. Democrat. By this name it is now published.

The Putnam Free Press was commenced at Carmel, June 12, 1858, by Wm. J. Blake, by whom it is still published.   [15] See page 18.

protect the purchasers by settling the claims of these children.[1] During the Revolution the passes through the mountains in this co. were carefully guarded, and at different times large bodies of troops were stationed there. It was the principal scene of the consummation of Arnold's treason, and of many events of minor interest, though no battle took place within its limits. Gen. Putnam had command of the army stationed here most of the time.

CARMEL—was formed from "*Frederickstown,*" March 17, 1795. It lies upon the s. border of the co., between Putnam Valley and Southeast. Its surface is rolling and hilly, with intervening valleys extending in a N. and S. direction. Peekskill Hollow Range and Big Hill are the highest summits.[2] The w. branch of Croton River and Michaels Brook flow through the E. part of the town, and Peekskill Hollow Creek through the N. w. In the town are several beautiful lakes and ponds, the principal of which are Lakes Mahopac,[3] Gleneida,[4] and Gilead, and Kirk and Long Ponds. The soil is a light, sandy and gravelly loam intermixed in some places with clay. **Carmel**, (p. v.,) the co. seat, is situated on Lake Gleneida. It is the seat of the Raymond Collegiate Institute,[5] and contains 3 churches, a bank, and 2 newspaper offices. Pop. 391. **Mahopac** (p. v.) contains 1 church, a bank, and about 40 houses; and **Red Mills,**[6] (p. v.,) contains 1 church and about 20 houses. Settlement was commenced about 1740.[7] Enoch Crosby, the "*Harvey Birch*" of Cooper's Spy, lived in this town till after the Revolution, when he removed to Southeast. A church was organized, and an edifice erected near Gilead Lake, a short time before the commencement of the Revolution. There are now 7 churches in town.[8]

KENT[9]—was formed as "*Frederickstown,*" March 7, 1788. Its name was changed to "*Frederick*" March 17, 1795, and to Kent April 15, 1817. Carmel was taken off in 1795. It is the central town on the N. border of the co. Its surface in the E. part is broken by numerous hills, and in the w. by steep and rocky mountain peaks separated by deep and narrow ravines. Smally Hill is the highest peak. The w. and middle branches of Croton River, and Horse Pound and Pine Pond Brooks, are the principal streams. In the town are several ponds and small lakes, the principal of which are White and Pine Ponds.[10] **Farmers Mills** (p. v.) contains 1 church and several manufacturing establishments.[11] **Coles Mills** (Kent p. o.) and **Ludingtonville** (p. o.) are hamlets. The first settlement was made about 1750, by Zachariah Merritt.[12] The census reports 3 churches in town,—2 Bap. and 1 Union.

PATTERSON[13]—was formed from "*Frederickstown*" and Southeast, as "*Franklin,*" March 17, 1795, and its name was changed April 6, 1808. It is the N. E. corner town of the co. Its surface

---

[1] The Philipse Patent was granted June 17, 1697, to Adolph Philipse, a merchant of New York, who died, in 1749, without issue, leaving his estate to his nephew, Frederick Philipse. The latter had 5 children,—Frederick, Philip, Susannah, Mary, and Margaret. By his will, dated June 6, 1751, Frederick was disinherited, and, Margaret dying young, the property was equally divided among the remaining three. Philip left a widow, who married one Ogilvie; Susannah married Beverly Robinson, and Mary married Col. Roger Morris. On the 7th of Feb. 1754, the patent was divided into 3 lots: 3, each 4 mi. square, bordering upon the Hudson and denominated "water lots;" 3, each 4 mi. wide by 12 long, extending N. and S. across the patent, and denominated "long lots;" and 3, each 4 mi. sq., upon the E. border, denominated "back lots." Philip, Susannah, and Mary Philipse each owned one of each kind of lot. On the 14th of Jan., 1758, previous to the marriage of Mary, a deed of marriage settlement was executed, by which her estate was vested in such children as might be born under the marriage, reserving only to herself and husband a life interest in the property. When Robinson and Morris and their wives were attainted, their property was sold, chiefly to the former tenants. In 1809, John Jacob Astor bought the interest of the heirs of Morris in this property for £20,000. The State, to protect those who held title from the Commissioners of Forfeiture, passed a law, April 16, 1827, directing 5 suits to be prosecuted to judgment in the Circuit Court of the S. Dist. of N. Y., and presented by writs of error to the Supreme Court of the U. S. for review and final decision. If against the defendants, the State agreed to pay $450,000 in 5 per cent. stock, redeemable at pleasure; and if the decision included the improvements that had been made by occupants, $250,000 more. Three suits were tried, each resulting in favor of Astor; upon which the comptroller was, by act of April 5, 1832, directed to issue stock for the full amount, with costs. The amount issued was $561,500. Few suits have been tried in the State involving larger interests to greater numbers, or which were argued with more ability, than this. In the suit against James Carver the counsel for the plaintiff were Messrs. Oakley, J. O. Hoffman, Emmet, Platt, and Ogden; and for the defendant, Talcott, (Attorney Gen.) Webster, Van Buren, Ogden Hoffman, and Cowles. See *Report of Trial*, by E. V. Sparhawk; *Legis. Doc.* 1830, V. 347; *Sen. Doc.* 1831, II. 24, 28; *Assem. Doc.* 1832, 149, 205; *Peters' Reports U. S. Supreme Court*, IV. 1.

[2] Among the principal peaks in town are Round, Turkey, and Comus Mts., and Goose, Barrett, Burned, and Prospect Hills, in the N. part; Pisgah, Watts, Pond, and Drew Hills, in the E.; Ball, Watermelon, Indian, and Round Hills, in the s.; Austin, Golden Root, and Hemlock Hills, in the w.; and Rattle and Hazens Hills, and Adams Ridge, in the central part.

[3] Lake Mahopac is 9 mi. in circumference, and in it are 3 beautiful islands,—Big, Petre, and Goose Islands. Around the lake are several large hotels and boarding houses, which are thronged during the summer season by visitors from New York and Brooklyn. A number of beautiful summer residences have been erected on the surrounding heights.

[4] Lake Gleneida covers an area of 170 acres, and is 130 feet deep.

[5] The Raymond Collegiate Institute was built in 1851, at a cost of about $40,000, by James Raymond. It is a private institution, owned by the heirs of Mr. Raymond.

[6] A gristmill at this place was filled with Government grain at one time during the Revolution, and soldiers were stationed to guard it. When on his way to West Point, André lodged one night at the house of Jas. Cox at this place.

[7] George Hughson settled near Lake Mahopac, and Wm. and Uriah Hill at Red Mills. The first mill was erected at the latter place.

[8] 3 M. E., 2 Bap., and 2 Presb.

[9] "*Frederickstown Precinct*" was formed March 24, 1772, and was named from Frederick Philipse. The town received its present name from the Kent family, who were early settlers.

[10] The other ponds and lakes are Barretts, China Forge, and Drews Ponds, and Lake Sagamore.

[11] A fulling mill, sawmill, gristmill, and tannery.

[12] Families named Boyd, Wixon, Farrington, Burton, Carter, Burrett, Ludington, and others, from Mass. and Westchester, were early settlers.

[13] The town was first named in honor of Dr. Franklin. Its present name was derived from a family of early settlers.

is hilly; but, with a few exceptions, the hills are arable to their summits. The principal streams are the E. branch of Croton River and its tributaries, Quaker, Birch, and Muddy Brooks. Croton Lake is in the W. and Little Pond in the E. part. *"The Great Swamp"* extends along the E. branch of Croton River.[1] The soil is a sandy loam. **Patterson,** (p. v.,) a station on the Harlem R. R., contains 2 churches and 37 houses. **Towners Station** (Towners p. o.) and **Haviland Hollow** (p. o.) are hamlets. The Prot. E. Church at Patterson was built in 1770. There are 4 churches in town.[2]

PHILIPSTOWN[3]—was formed March 7, 1788. A part of Fishkill (Dutchess co.) was taken off in 1806, and Putnam Valley in 1839. It is the most westerly town of the co., and extends about 10 mi. along the Hudson. Its surface is broken by numerous steep and rocky mountain ridges separated by deep and narrow valleys.[4] These mountains constitute the most elevated portion of The Highlands.[5] The ranges have a general N. and S. or N. E. and S. W. direction. Clove Creek flows through the N. part of the town, and Canopus Creek through the N. E. corner. Foundry, Breakneck, Andreas, Indian, and other brooks flow through narrow valleys and rocky ravines into the Hudson. The greater part of the surface is unfit for agricultural purposes. Constitution Island[6] is a promontory opposite West Point, connected with the mainland by a marshy meadow. The *"Sunk Lot"* is a tract of 1300 acres of low and apparently sunken ground. Several mines of magnetic iron ore had been opened in town; but none are now wrought. Granite is extensively quarried, and brick are made at several points along the river. The soil is a gravelly, sandy, and clayey loam. **Coldspring,** (p. v.,) situated on the Hudson, was incorp. April 22, 1846, and includes the suburban villages of Nelsonville and Marysville. It is a station on the Hudson River R. R., and contains 6 churches and an extensive foundry.[7] Pop. 2,237. **Breakneck** and **Griffins Corners** contain each about a dozen houses. **Davenport Corners** contains 1 church and 10 houses. **Continental Village**[8] has 1 church and about 12 houses. **Garrisons,** (p. o.,) on the Hudson, is a station on the Hudson River R. R. The first settlement was made about 1715, by Thos. Davenport.[9] This town was principally settled under Col. Beverly Robinson,[10] who acquired title by marriage with Susannah, daughter of Frederick Philipse. Undercliff, the residence of Gen. Geo. P. Morris, is situated on a high bluff in the N. part of Cold Spring. The census reports 9 churches in town.[11]

PUTNAM VALLEY—was formed from Philipstown, as *"Quincy,"* March 14, 1839. Its

---

1 Pine Island is a rocky ledge 200 ft. high, containing about 30 acres, in the middle of Great Swamp.

2 Prot. E., Bap., Friends, and Presb.

3 Named from Adolph Philipse, patentee of the Philipse Manor. The Philips Precinct was formed March 24, 1772.

4 *"Martlaers Rack,"* or the Martyrs Reach, was a short stretch of the Hudson just above West Point, where early navigators were often retarded by baffling winds. There were 13 racks, or reaches, on the Hudson, known to sailors as *" Horse," " Sailmakers," " Cooks," " High," " Fox," " Bakers," " John Pleasures," " Harts," " Sturgeons," " Fishers," " Fast," " Martlaers,"* and *" Long"* Reaches, the last named extending from Pollepels Island to Krom Elleboogh.—*Benson's Memoir*, p. 42.

5 Among the peaks of The Highlands in this town are Anthonys Nose, Sugar Loaf, and Bull, Hog-Back, Breakneck Mt., Vinegar, Cot, Pine, and Fort Hills. Anthonys Nose is 1228 feet above the Hudson, and Sugar Loaf 800 ft.

6 This promontory was called *"Martlaers Island"* before the Revolution. In July, 1775, a fort was built upon it, under the direction of Bernard Romaine; and in 1778 a heavy chain was stretched across the Hudson from this fort to West Point. Col. Timothy Pickering, appointed to have charge of this work, in March, 1778, contracted with Peter Townsend (at the Sterling Iron Works at Warwick, Orange co.) for the construction of the chain. The task was done in 6 weeks, and the huge chain carted in sections to West Point. The links weighed from 100 to 150 pounds each; and the entire weight was 186 tons, and its length 1,500 ft. It was buoyed up by large spars, a few feet apart, secured by strong timbers framed into them and firmly attached to the rock on both shores. In winter it was drawn on shore by a windlass, and replaced in the spring. It was never disturbed by the enemy, and continued in use until the peace. A similar chain, of half its diameter and 1,800 ft. in length, (made at the Ringwood Iron Works, N. J.,) was stretched across the channel from Anthony's Nose to Fort Montgomery, in Nov. 1776. It parted twice, and the enemy broke and passed it in the fall of 1778. Another, stretched from Pollepels Island to the W. shore, consisted of spars, pointed, and their ends united by iron links. There was also a *chevaux de frize* sunk at the same place to prevent the passage of vessels. Most of these works were constructed and placed under the immediate direction of Capt. Thomas Machin, an engineer in the service. Traces of Fort Constitution and the outworks are still visible.

7 The West Point Foundry is one of the largest establishments of the kind in the country. It was established in 1817, by an association organized for that purpose. A tract of 150 acres was purchased of Frederick Philipse, and a moulding house, boring mill, blacksmith and pattern shops, and drafting and business offices, were erected. An act of incorporation was obtained, April 15, 1818; and in 1839 the finishing or machine, smiths and boiler departments of the establishment were brought from New York. The works now consist of a moulding house, with 3 cupola furnaces; a gun foundry, with 3 air furnaces; 2 boring mills,—one driven by an overshot waterwheel and the other by a steam engine; 3 blacksmith shops; a turning shop; a finishing shop, with a pattern shop on the second floor; a boiler shop, a punching machine house, 5 pattern houses, a fire engine house, an office, and several smaller buildings. A dock on the river belongs to these works, and a branch from the R. R. extends to them. From 400 to 600 men are employed. Shafts 2 ft. in diameter, and of 15 tons' weight, have been forged here.

8 This village, together with barracks for 2000 men, was burned in Oct. 1777, by a detachment of the enemy on their way up the Hudson to co-operate with Gen. Burgoyne. Two small forts were erected here during the Revolution, and traces of them are yet visible.

9 Davenport built the first house at Coldspring, in 1715. David Hurtis, and several families named Haight, Bloomer, and Wilson, settled in the town in 1730. John Meeks was the first settler at Continental Village, and John Rogers settled a little N. of the same place about 1730. Jas. Stanley settled in the town in 1750, and Thos. Sarles in 1756. The first gristmill was built about 1762, by Beverly Robinson, at Continental Village.

10 Col. Robinson's house, situated at the foot of Sugar Loaf Mt., was the headquarters of Gens. Putnam and Parsons in 1778–79, and of Gen. Arnold at the time of his treason. The building is still standing, and is owned by Richard D. Arden, by whom it is carefully preserved in its original character. Col. Robinson granted a glebe to St. Philip's Church in The Highlands, 1 mi. E. of Garrisons, which was confirmed by the act of March 27, 1794. The church was used as a barrack during the Revolution.—*Blake's Hist. Putnam Co.* pp. 180–209; *Sabine's Loyalists*, p. 562.

11 4 M. E., 2 Prot. E., Bap., Presb. and R. C.

name was changed Feb. 13, 1840. It lies on the s. border of the co., between Philipstown and Carmel. Its surface is broken by steep and rocky mountain ridges extending in nearly a N. and S. direction, and separated by narrow valleys. These mountain ranges constitute a part of The Highlands. The principal streams are Canopus Creek, Canopus Lake Creek, and Peekskill Hollow Brook. Canopus Lake is a beautiful sheet of water near the center of the town.[1] The soil in the valleys is a moderately fertile, sandy and gravelly loam. Iron ore has been found in several localities, but in places so difficult of access that it is not mined to any considerable extent. **Oregon,** at the confluence of Peekskill Hollow Brook and Canopus Lake Creek, contains 17 houses, and **Crofts Corners** contains 2 churches and 10 houses. **Tomkins Corners** is a hamlet. Among the early settlers were families named Dusenbury and Adams.[2] The census reports 4 churches in town; 3 M. E. and 1 Bap.

SOUTHEAST—was formed from Frederickstown and "*Southeasttown,*"[3] March 7, 1788. A part of Patterson was taken off, as "*Franklin,*" in 1795. It is the S. E. corner town of the co. Its surface is rolling and hilly. The streams are the E. and middle branches of Croton River and their tributaries. Several small lakes and ponds lie among the hills.[4] The soil is a sandy and gravelly loam. Iron ore abounds, but no mines are wrought at the present time. About 4,000 gals. of milk are sent daily from this town to the New York market. **Brewsters Station,** (p. v.,) on the Harlem R. R., contains 1 church and a bank, and has a pop. of 176. **Heddingville** and **Brush Hollow** are hamlets. **Southeast Center** has 144 inhabitants, and **Milltown** (p.v.) 167. **De Forest Corners, Doanesburgh, Foggingtown,** and **Dykemans Station** (Dykemans p.o.) are hamlets. This was one of the first settled towns in the co.[5] The first religious services were conducted by Rev. Elisha Kent, grandfather of the late Chancellor, about the year 1730.[6]

Acres of Land, Valuation, Population, Dwellings, Families, Freeholders, Schools, Live Stock, Agricultural Products, and Domestic Manufactures, of Putnam County.

Names of Towns.	Acres of Land.		Valuation of 1858.			Population.		No. of Dwellings.	No. of Families.	Freeholders.	Schools.	
	Improved.	Unimproved.	Real Estate.	Personal Property.	Total.	Males.	Females.				No. of Districts.	Children taught.
Carmel	19,300	5,271¼	941,864	362,690	1,304,554	1,169	1,237	470	483	345	11	739
Kent	15,241¾	6,617	425,020	151,175	576,195	755	784	275	308	225	8	572
Patterson	13,789¼	6,523	609,825	100,650	710,475	702	720	266	302	204	9	480
Philipstown	11,505	15,236	761,793	131,300	893,093	2,427	2,382	722	932	433	14	1,760
Putnam Valley	16,313	7,637	365,440	88,500	453,940	826	747	298	312	264	7	735
Southeast	18,056⅞	3,163½	990,179	227,285	1,217,464	1,091	1,094	374	409	268	10	690
Total	94,205⅞	44,447¾	4,094,121	1,061,600	5,155,721	6,970	6,964	2,405	2,746	1,739	59	4.976

Names of Towns.	Live Stock.					Agricultural Products.							Domestic Cloths in yards.
						Bush. of Grain.					Dairy Products.		
	Horses.	Working Oxen and Calves.	Cows.	Sheep.	Swine.	Winter.	Spring.	Tons of Hay.	Bushels of Potatoes.	Bushels of Apples.	Pounds Butter.	Pounds Cheese.	
Carmel	458	1,120	2,113	2,171	1,847	5,326	57,941½	6,040	14,088	8,616	121,479		
Kent	208	1,165	1,493	1,420	766	3,886½	25,288¼	4,261	5,866	4,091	75,856		550
Patterson	268	2,179		539	971	3,148½	22,251¾	4,060¼	9,854	3,321	61,400	3,375	
Philipstown	357	1,145	853	698	1,194	5,393½	23,753	3,370	6,976	3,890	65,591		
Putnam Valley	313	1,081	935	822	1,144	4,505	28,072	3,443	17,649	5,159	73,070	100	646
Southeast	334	966	2,457	154	1,075	4,181¾	40,511¾	6,582½	10,071	2,081	96,300		25
Total	1,938	7,656	7,851	5,804	6,997	26,441¼	197,818¼	27,756¾	64,504	27,158	493,696	3,475	1,221

[1] Canopus Lake is 2 mi. long by 1 wide. Clear, Muddy, Peltons, Salpeu, Owens, Cranberry, Bargers, and Wickopee Ponds are smaller bodies of water in the town.

[2] On the farm of Harry Gillet are the ruins of the Hempstead Huts, built in 1780 by a detachment of the Mass. Line, and one or two companies from Hempstead, L. I.

[3] "*Southeasttown*" was formed as a precinct, Dec. 17, 1737, and confirmed March 24, 1772. The word "*town*" in the name was dropped March 17, 1795.

[4] Tonetta and Kishewana Lakes, and Covils and Peach Ponds.

[5] Among the early settlers were families named Crane, Crosby, Hall, Moody, Paddock, Hane, Howe, Carpenter, and Dickinson, from Mass. and Conn. Joseph Crane built the first mill, at Milltown, about 1730. Chancellor Kent was born in this town, July 31, 1763.

[6] The census reports 3 churches in town; M. E., Presb., and Union.

QUEENS COUNTY.

THIS county was organized Nov. 1, 1683,[1] having previously been included in the North and West Ridings of Yorkshire.[2] Its original bounds have not been changed. It lies upon Long Island, near the w. extremity, is centrally distant 133 mi. from Albany, and contains 410 sq. mi. It extends across the island, bordering both upon Long Island Sound and the ocean. Its coasts are deeply indented by irregular inlets, bays, and harbors. The principal of these upon the sound are Oyster Bay, Cold Spring and Oyster Harbors, Mill Neck Creek, Hempstead Harbor, Manhasset Bay, Little Neck Bay, Little Bay, Powells Cove, Flushing Bay, and Bowery Bay. Upon the East River are Halletts Cove and the narrow passage of Hell Gate, and upon the s. shore, Jamaica, Hempstead, and South Oyster Bays. Along these bays and the creeks that flow into them are wide salt meadows, the most extensive being upon the s. shore. Outside of the bays on the ocean side is a series of beaches and shifting sand-ridges, affording a complete protection from the storms of the ocean. These beaches are divided into distinct parts by several inlets opening into the bays.[3]

Inclosed in the bays within the beaches is a great number of low, marshy islands separated by narrow tidal streams and covered with sedges.[4] A wide strip bordering immediately upon the bays is of the same marshy character. Along the deep bays upon the N. coast are small patches of salt meadow; but the greater part of the land upon the capes, necks, and promontories is of a most excellent character.[5] A range of hills 100 to 300 feet high extends in a general E. and W. direction through the co., a little N. of the center, and irregular spurs extend northward to the sound. From the base of the ridge a wide, unbroken plain extends to the s. to the salt marshes which surround the bays.[6]

The streams of the co. are mostly small, and afford but a limited amount of water-power. At the mouth of several of the creeks on both the N. and s. shores the ebbing tide is used for hydraulic purposes. At the head of several of the streams are little, fresh water ponds,[7] the principal of which is Success Pond,[8] near the top of the high ridge in the s.E. corner of Flushing. The soil upon the N. side is a productive, sandy loam, in some places mixed with clay. The plains have a coarse, sandy soil, which is rendered productive only at considerable cost. Along the borders of the salt meadows is a strip of light, sandy soil, easily cultivated and of moderate fertility.[9]

The people are principally engaged in agriculture and market gardening. Fishing and the taking of oysters afford occupation to a large number of people. An extensive coasting trade is carried on, and the co. each year furnishes a large quota of sailors. Manufactures are extensive and various, and are confined principally to the N. shore.

The co. courthouse is situated upon the plains of North Hempstead, a little N.W. of Mineola station and p.o., and near the geographical center of the co.[10]

---

[1] Named in compliment to the wife of Charles II.

[2] By a convention held at Hempstead in 1665, Long Island, Staten Island, and a part of Westchester co. were erected into a shire called "Yorkshire," for the purpose of holding courts and administering justice. This was subdivided into "Ridings," known as "East Riding," (Suffolk co.;) "West Riding," (Kings co., Staten Island, and Newtown;) and "North Riding," (Queens co. except Newtown.)—Thompson's Hist. L. I., P. 137.

[3] The principal of the inlets are Hog Island, New and Gilgo Inlets, and the entrance into Jamaica Bay; and the principal beaches are Jones, Long, and Rockaway Beaches. The last named is a favorite resort for summer residences and sea-bathing.

[4] These islands are mostly the common property of the towns, and are valued chiefly for their hunting and fishing grounds. Immense numbers of waterfowl frequent them; and a considerable number of persons gain a livelihood by fishing here in summer and hunting in winter. The U.S. Government has erected 5 lifeboat stations upon the s. shore, and the Governor appoints 12 wrecking masters for the co.

[5] A considerable portion of this coast is high, affording beautiful sites for country residences.

[6] The R.R. at Jamaica is 45 feet above sea level. The ascent from Jamaica to Hempstead Junction is 59 feet, and from thence to the Syosset Branch 50 feet, making the latter 154 feet, which is the highest point on the road. The descent of these plains southward is so gradual as scarcely to be apparent.

The Hempstead Branch of the R.R. descends 40 feet in 2¼ mi., and the Syosset Branch rises 66 feet in less than 4 mi. The highest point on the island is Harbor Hill, at the head of Hempstead Harbor, 319 feet above tide.

[7] Several of these ponds have recently been purchased to supply the Brooklyn Waterworks.

[8] Called by the Indians "Sucut," from which the present name is supposed to be derived. The water is clear and cold, with an average depth of 40 feet. The pond is about 500 rods in circumference, is surrounded by a high bank, and has an outlet, but does not usually overflow. It is said to be 100 to 150 feet above tide.—Prime's Hist. L. I., P. 27; Thompson's L. I., II, P. 60.

[9] Extensive tracts in the southern section are devoted to gardening for the city markets. The N. side, originally covered with a heavy growth of timber, is under fine cultivation, and is largely devoted to the raising of fruit. Flushing excels in nurseries of fruit and ornamental trees, for which this co. is second only to Monroe. Locust-timber is raised along the N. shore eastward from Little Neck, in considerable quantities, for treenails and posts. In Oyster Bay large quantities of asparagus are raised for market; and the soil appears to be finely adapted to this crop. Milk is sent to market in large quantities by R.R., especially from near Jericho, Westbury, and Hempstead.

[10] The court of sessions of the "North Riding of Yorkshire" was located at Jamaica in 1683; and a building called the "County

The jail occupies a portion of the courthouse building.[1] The county records are kept in a spacious brick building in the village of Jamaica; and in the same building are offices for the Surrogate and Board of Supervisors.[2] The co. has no poorhouse; but each town provides for the accommodation of its own paupers.

The Brooklyn and Jamaica R. R., extending w. from Jamaica to the co. line, is leased by the Long Island R. R., which extends E. from Jamaica through Hempstead, North Hempstead, and Oyster Bay. The Flushing R. R. extends w. from Flushing Village through Newtown to the mouth of Newtown Creek. The Syosset Branch R. R. connects Hicksville, upon the L. I. R. R., with the village of Syosset, 3¼ mi. N.

There are 7 newspapers published in the co.; 2 at Jamaica, 2 at Hempstead, 2 at Flushing, and 1 at Glen Cove.[3]

The co. was mostly settled by English immigrants, under the authority of the Dutch Government during the last 20 years of its existence. The E. extremity of Long Island was claimed by the English colonies of New England; and the boundary line was the subject of a long and angry dispute, which was never entirely settled until the final subjugation of New York by the British in 1664.[4] The whole of this co. was under the Dutch, except Oyster Bay, which was a disputed territory. The first planters came on in considerable numbers, and were associated in the purchase of the lands from the Indians. They were mostly united by a common religious faith; and they were invested with certain civil rights, which were afterward confirmed by the English Government of New York, and some of which continue to the present time. The people chose a duplicate set of magistrates and municipal officers, from which the Dutch Governor selected such as he pleased.

The people employed their own minister, and enjoyed comparative religious freedom. The Dutch, however, did not faithfully carry out the agreement which they had entered into with the settlers, and, in 1653, delegates were sent to the city to remonstrate against certain abuses. This was not heeded, and when the people again met for a like purpose they were ordered to disperse. The inhabitants rejoiced when the Dutch rule was finally broken and they came under the protection of the English. Gov. Nicoll, the first English Governor, convened deputies from the several towns upon Long Island, who met at Hempstead in the spring of 1665. A code of laws and ordinances was adopted, a shire was erected, the names of towns were changed, boundaries were settled, and affairs were regulated to meet the views of the new government. From this time no land could be taken without purchase from the Indians and patent from the Governor.

During the Revolution considerable numbers of the people joined the loyalists, and the co. was mostly in quiet possession of the enemy. Robberies were common, especially along the N. shore. Presbyterian churches were everywhere used for military purposes. A petty warfare was carried on in whaleboats, and daring exploits were performed by partisans of both sides.

Hall" was erected in 1684. From 1700 to 1708 the courts were held in the Presb. church, when a new co. hall was built, which continued in use until the Revolution, when it was burned. By an act of March 1, 1785, the sum of £2,000 was raised to erect new buildings on the present location under the direction of the co. judge. The building is a half mi. N. of the R. R., and trains stop opposite when courts are in session. Efforts have been made to remove the site to Jamaica, but thus far without success, although most persons will admit that the present site is inconvenient to a majority of the inhabitants.

[1] In the absence of sufficient accommodations in the vicinity, this building is also used as a hotel during the session of the court. The sheriff, who lives upon the premises, usually makes provision for dining a large number, and for furnishing lodgings to a limited extent.

[2] The surrogate's and clerk's offices were kept at the houses of the incumbents until 1833, when they were located at Jamaica. The present clerk's office was erected in 1857.

[3] **The Long Island Farmer** was commenced at Jamaica in 1819 by Henry C. Sleight. It is now published by Charles Welling.

The Union Hall Gazette, semi-mo., was published at Jamaica in 1832 by L. Booth.

The Long Island Democrat was established at Jamaica May 1, 1835, by Jas. J. Brenton, present publisher.

The Journal and Messenger was published about 1843, by S. V. Berry.

The Long Island Telegraph and General Advertiser was started at Hempstead in May, 1830, by Wm. Hutchinson and C. F. Le Fevre. In Nov. 1831 it was changed to

The Hempstead Inquirer. It is now published by Morris Snedeker.

The Queens County Sentinel was established at Hempstead in May, 1858, by John H. Hentz, its present publisher.

The Church Record was started at Flushing in 1840, and continued 3½ years. It was edited by Rev. Dr. F. L. Hawks, and published by C. R. Lincoln.

The Flushing Journal was commenced March 19, 1842, by Chas. R. Lincoln, its present publisher.

The Flushing Pomologist was published in 1848, by William R. Prince.

The Public Voice was started at Flushing in 1852; and in 1855 it was changed to

The Long Island Times. It is now published by W. R. Burling.

The North Hempstead Gazette was started in Dec. 1846, at Manhasset Valley. In 1850 it was removed to Roslyn and changed to

The Plain Dealer. It was subsequently removed to Glen Cove, and was continued until 1855; Jas. L. Crowley was its last publisher.

The Glen Cove Sentinel was published a short time in 1854 by Bright & Perry.

The Glen Cove Gazette was started in May, 1857, by E. M. Lincoln, its present publisher.

The Woodhaven Advertiser was published a short time in 1853.

The Astoria Gazette was started in 1853 by Wm. L. S. Harrison, and continued about 18 months.

The Journal of the Institute was published at Flushing for about 3 years.

[4] Commissioners were appointed to settle these claims in 1650. They were Simon Bradstreet and Thos. Prince on the part of the New England colonies, and Thos. Willett and Geo. Baxter on the part of the Dutch. The boundary was fixed along the w. line of Oyster Bay; but the States General did not ratify the agreement, and the Dutch Governor neglected to carry it into effect. The Dutch subsequently planted a colony at Brookville, (Wolver Hollow,) E. of the line, to assert their claims.

FLUSHING[1]—was first granted by letters patent—issued by the Dutch Governor Keift, Oct. 10, 1645—to a company of English immigrants.[2] This grant was confirmed by Gov. Nicoll, Feb. 1666, and by Gov. Dongan, March 23, 1685.[3] Under the provisions of these charters a considerable amount of land was held in common, to be under the charge of 5 trustees, elected annually.[4] It was recognized as a town under the State Government, March 7, 1788.[5] It lies upon the N. border of the co., w. of the center. Its surface is moderately uneven and has a gentle inclination to the N. A low range of hills extends along its s. border and separates it from Jamaica. Flushing Creek, the principal stream, forms a portion of the w. boundary. The principal indentations upon the coast are Flushing Bay, Powells Cove, Little Bay, and Little Neck Bay. An extensive salt marsh extends along Flushing Creek and the head of Flushing Bay.[6] The soil is a fine quality of productive sandy loam. Gardening, fruit growing,[7] and the nursery business[8] constitute the leading pursuits of the people. The town supports its own poor, and has a house and farm for their accommodation. **Flushing,** (p. v.,) at the head of Flushing Bay, was incorp. April 9, 1813. It contains 8 churches, 2 newspaper offices, several private seminaries,[9] and has a limited amount of manufactures.[10] It is connected with New York by the Flushing R. R. and by a steam ferry from Hunters Point. From its proximity to New York, it has become the residence of many wealthy persons doing business in the city. Pop. 3,488. **College Point,**[11] (p. v.,) on the sound, E. of Flushing Bay, is a modern village, settled mostly by Germans. It contains 2 churches, and an immense manufactory of whalebone, India rubber, and ratan, giving employment to 500 to 700 hands. Pop. 1,150. **Whitestone**[12] (p. v.) is located on the sound, in the extreme N. part of the town. It contains 2 churches, and an extensive tin and sheet ironware manufactory.[13] Pop. 630. **Marathon,** at the head of Little Neck Bay, is a small, straggling village with one church. Several of the neighborhoods in this town are known by distinct local names.[14] **Wilkins Point** has recently been purchased by the U. S. Government for the site of a fort.[15] There are now 13 churches in town.[16] The first settlements were made by English, who probably had first settled in Holland. They arrived at "*New Amsterdam*" in 1645. They were Non-conformists in religion, and settled on the Dutch dominions under the promise of entire religious freedom.[17] But the Dutch soon commenced a series of persecutions that continued until the time of the British conquest in 1664. Several French Protestant families found their way into this town after the revocation of the Edict of Nantes; but few of their descendants are now found. The fruits introduced by these people are said to have given the first direction to the nursery business for which this town is so celebrated. During the Revolution a British force was stationed here.

HEMPSTEAD—was granted by Gov. Keift to several English families, Nov. 14, 1644. This patent was confirmed by Gov. Nicoll, March 6, 1666, and by Gov. Dongan, April 17, 1685.[18]

---

1 Named by the Dutch "*Vlissengen*," from a place in Holland.

2 The first patentees were Thos. Farrington, John Lawrence, John Hicks, John Townsend, Thos. Stiles, Robert Field, Thos. Saul, John Marston, Thos. Applegate, Lawrence Dutch, Wm. Lawrence, Henry Sawtell, Wm. Thorne, Michael Willard, Robt. Firman, and Wm. Widgeon, for themselves and associates.

3 The patentees named in the patent of Gov. Nicoll were John Lawrence, (alderman of New York City,) Richard Cornwell, Chas. Bridges, Wm. Lawrence, Robert Terry, Wm. Noble, John Forbush, Elias Doughty, Robt. Field, Philip Udall, Thos. Stiles, Benj. Field, Wm. Pidgeon, John Adams, John Hinchman, Nicholas Parcell, Tobias Feaks, and John Bowne; and those in the patent of Gov. Dongan were Elias Doughty, Thos. Willett, John Bowne, Matthias Harvey, Thos. Hicks, Richard Cornwell, John Hinchman, Jonathan Wright, and Sam'l Hoyt.—*Patents,* I, 64, V, 222, 325, *Sec. Office.*

4 These lands have since been mostly taken up by individuals, though the trustees are still elected to take charge of the remainder. The town records were burned, Oct. 31, 1797, by a servant girl, who was afterward hung for the deed.

5 By the General Act, establishing towns.

6 A chalybeate spring was discovered near the head of this marsh in 1816. It was named "*Cheltenham Springs*," and for a time attracted much attention.

7 The principal fruit grown are cherries, of which large quantities are annually sent to the New York market.

8 Flushing has a wide reputation for its nurseries, of which there are six, occupying 246 acres and valued at $124,000. The first nursery was commenced about 1750. They now furnish every species of fruit tree, ornamental shrub, and exotic plant cultivated in the country.

9 The principal of these schools are the Flushing Institute, the Flushing Female College, and the Linnean Hill Seminary.

10 The principal manufactories are the Excelsior Emery and Sand Paper Manufactory, a steam planing and saw mill, and a tide gristmill.

11 This place was formerly known as "*Lawrences Neck*." Several farms have been laid out into village plats, each one taking a distinct name. An Episcopal college was incorp. here in 1840; but it has since been abandoned. The location of this institution gave the name to the village.

12 Named from a large boulder near the landing. The place was first called "*Cookie Hill*" and afterward "*Clintonville*."

13 This establishment gives employment to 430 hands.

14 **Bay Side**—the seat of A. G. Mickle, Ex-Mayor of New York—and **Springville** are near Little Neck Bay. **Fresh Meadows, Ireland,** and **Spring Hill** are localities s. E. of Flushing Village. **Rocky Hill** and **Union Place** are farming neighborhoods. Spring Hill was the residence of Cadwallader Colden, who died here Sept. 20, 1776. His son espoused the cause of the Royalists, and his estate was confiscated.—*Onderdonk's Rev. Inc.*

15 When fortified, this point will completely command the channel on the N., and render the approach of ships of war toward New York impossible from that direction.

16 Of these there are at Flushing, 2 Friends, Prot. E., M. E., Ref. Prot. D., R. C., Cong., and Bap.; at College Point, R. C. and Luth.; at Whitestone, Prot. E. and M. E.; and at Marathon, a Prot. E.

17 The religious faith of these people was much the same as that afterward professed by the Quakers, who had not become at that period a distinct sect in England. Their first religious teacher was Francis Doughty, from Taunton. Mass., a Baptist, who became a Quaker in 1657, as did many of the inhabitants. The celebrated Geo. Fox visited America in 1672 and preached in this town. He was entertained at the house of John Bowne, who had particularly suffered from the persecutions of the Dutch; but, his dwelling not being sufficiently large to accommodate the audience, his hearers assembled under the shade of the venerable oaks, one of which is still standing. The Bowne House stands in Parsons & Co.'s Commercial Garden and Nursery, and is in a fine state of preservation.

18 The grantees named in the first patent were Robert Ford-

Upon the erection of North Hempstead, in 1784, its name was changed to South Hempstead; and its present name was re-adopted Feb. 5, 1796. It was recognized as a town March 7, 1788. It lies upon the s. side of the island, extending 20 mi. along the ocean, and embracing about 100 sq. mi. The shore is bordered by a line of beaches and sand hills; and within them are Hempstead and South Oyster Bays, inclosing a large number of low, sedgy islands. West of the bay a long, narrow sandbar, known as Rockaway Beach,[1] extends to the s. w., forming the E. boundary of Jamaica Bay. Wide salt meadows border upon the bays, and from them the land spreads out into an almost perfectly level plain.[2] The soil along the borders of the marshes is moderately fertile, and upon the plain it consists of sand and fine gravel, which is naturally barren, although it may be made productive by the proper application of manures. A considerable portion of the marshes and plain belongs to the town and is used as common property.[3] The people are largely engaged in market gardening. There is no poorhouse; but the paupers are annually put up at auction and struck off to the lowest bidder. **Hempstead**, (p. v.,) near the center of the town, was incorp. June 20, 1853. It contains 3 churches, the Hempstead Seminary,[4] and 1,486 inhabitants. Along the s. shore are several villages, generally scattered and extended over a large territory. They are mostly surrounded by gardens and orchards. **Jerusalem South**, (p. v.,) in the s. E. corner, contains a gristmill and Friends' meetinghouse; next w. are respectively **Bridge Haven**, containing a gristmill and church, **Merrick**,[5] (p. o.,) and **Greenwich Point**, two farming neighborhoods; **Freeport**,[6] (p. v.,) a fishing village, containing 2 churches; **Milburn, Baldwinville**, and **Christian Hook**, hamlets; **Rockville Center**, (p. v.,) containing 1 church; **Near Rockaway**, a hamlet, and **Far Rockaway**, (Rockaway p. o.,) a noted seabathing place.[7] **Valley Stream** and **Fosters Meadow** are two scattered settlements along the E. border. **New Bridge**, (formerly "*Little Neck*,") **Washington Square**, and **Brookfield** are farming neighborhoods. The first settlements were made in 1643, by a colony of English, who had previously settled at Weathersfield and Stamford, in Conn. They founded the first English settlement within the co.[8] The town early acquired a prominent rank, and its records (preserved at North Hempstead) contain a large amount of valuable historical information. Horse races were established here by the Governor in 1690. The first church (Presb.) was started in 1648. There are 18 churches in town.[9]

JAMAICA[10]—was first granted for settlement by Gov. Stuveysant, March 21, 1656; and a more ample patent was granted in 1660. The rights of the town were confirmed by Gov. Nicoll, Feb. 15, 1666, and by Gov. Dongan, March 17, 1686.[11] It was recognized as a town March 7,

---

ham, John Strickland, John Ogden, John Karman, John Lawrence, and Jonas Wood; those in the second patent were John Hicks, J. P., Capt. John Seaman, Richard Gildersleeve, Robert Jackson, John Karman, John Smith, sr. and jr.; and those in the third were Capt. John Seaman. Simon Searing, John Jackson, James Pine. sr., Richard Gildersleeve, sr., and Nath'l Pearsall. —*Thompson's Hist. L.I.*, II, 14; *Patents*, IV, 55. V, 182; *Sec. Office.*

[1] The co. seal presents a view of sea and shore from this beach. The name is of Indian origin. This point was formerly inclosed by a fence from Hempstead to Jamaica Bays, and was used for pasturing cattle, horses, and sheep.

[2] This plain is 15 mi. long and 4 broad. When first known to the Europeans, it was destitute of timber and covered with grass. The annual burning of this grass was prohibited by statute in 1726. It is mostly uninclosed, and used as pasture.

[3] About 16,000 acres of the plain and the salt meadows are common property. The time for cutting the hay is fixed at the annual town meetings, and the first one on the ground has the choice of location. This leads the farmers to the meadows at an early hour on the appointed day, and sometimes during the night previous. where they stand scythe in hand, ready at the first glance of sunrise to strike into the grass before them and mow around as large a piece as they may be able. Several hundred men are often thus employed. Each inhabitant may hire as many laborers as he chooses, and may cut for sale. North Hempstead formerly enjoyed the right of cutting grass upon these meadows, but has been practically deprived of it for many years. See page 545.

[4] This is a private seminary. owned by a joint stock company.

[5] On old documents variously spelled "*Meric*," "*Moroke*," and "*Merikohe*." The name was derived from a tribe of Indians that lived in the vicinity.

[6] First settled by Edward Raynor, and formerly known as "*Raynortown*."

[7] This place contains the Pavilion,—an immense hotel,—and several large summer boarding houses.

[8] Among the early settlers were Rev. Richard Denton, Jonas Wood, Wm. Raynor, Robert Coe, Richard Gildersleeve, Robert Jackson, John Ogden, John Karman, Capt. John Underhill, Andrew Ward, Thurston and Robt. Raynor, Matthew Mitchell,

and Robert Fordham. In 1647 the first eight, with Robt. Ashman, Jeremy, Edmund, and Terry Wood, Benj. and John Coe, Sam'l Strickland, John Topping. John Fordham, Wm. and John Lawrence, Henry Hudson, Thomas Ireland, Richard Valentine, Wm. Thickstone, Nicholas Tanner, Wm., John, sr. and jr., Jas., and Alvin Smith, Richard, jr., Sam'l, Dan'l, and Nath'l Denton, Thos. Armitage, Simon Searing. Thomas Wilson, Henry Pierson, Jos. and Wm. Scott, Henry Whiston, Richard and John Lewis, Thos. Stevenson. John Storge, John and Robert Williams, Wm. Rogers, Richard Ogden, John Foucks, Wm. Washburne, Thos. Sherman, Francis Yates, John Ellison, Wm. Shadding, Thomas and Chas. Foster, Roger Lines, Sam'l Clark, John Hudd, Thos. Pope, Daniel Whitehead, Edward Raynor, John Smith, Samuel Baccus, and John Strickland were freeholders, and shared in the division of the lands. A part of the above locations are now included in North Hempstead. The first child born of white parents in town was Caleb Karman, son of John Karman, Jan. 9, 1645. An order was made at their General Court, Sept. 16, 1650, requiring all persons to "repaire to the publique Meetings and Assemblies on the Lords dayes, and on publique dayes of fastings and thanksgivings, appointed by publique authority, bothe on the forenoons and afternoons," under a penalty of 5 guilders for the first, 10 for the second, and 20 for the third offense. The Rev. Richard Denton, a prominent founder, was their first pastor. He returned to England in 1659, and wrote a historical account of New York, which was published in London in 1670.

[9] 10 M. E., 3 Prot. E., 2 Presb., 2 R. C., and one Friends. Near the M. E. Church in South Hempstead is a monument, erected to the memory of 139 English and Irish immigrants who perished on the ships Bristol and Mexico, wrecked Nov. 21, 1836, and Jan. 2, 1837.

[10] It was first proposed to name this place "*Canorasset*." Many of the first settlers preferred the name of "*Crawford*;" and the Dutch named it "*Rusdorp*," signifying "county town." The present name is by some considered as from the Indian "*Jameco*."

[11] The first patent of confirmation contained the names of Daniel Denton, J. P., Robt. Coe, Capt. Bryan Newton, Wm. Hallet, Andrew Messenger, and Nathaniel Denton; and the second named 24 persons.—*Patents*, I, 66, 91, V, 432; *Sec. Office.*

1788. It is the s. w. corner town of the co. A range of low wooded hills forms its N. boundary; but the remainder of the town consists of an extensive sand plain, and a series of wide salt marshes along the shore. Jamaica Bay, forming its s. boundary, incloses a large number of low, marshy islands. Several small streams take their rise in springs and small ponds among the hills and flow s. to the bay.[1] The soil is light and sandy. A considerable tract immediately bordering upon the marshes is kept in a high state of fertility by artificial means, and is devoted to market gardening. This town has long been celebrated for its race courses.[2] The town poor are annually let to the lowest bidder.[3] **Jamaica,** (p. v.,) near the N. border of the town, was incorp. April 14, 1814. It contains 6 churches, the Union Hall Academy,[4] several private seminaries, a union school, 2 newspaper offices, and several manufactories.[5] Pop. 2,817. **Woodhaven** was organized in 1850 by a number of capitalists for the manufacture of shoes. **Cypress Avenue** is a R. R. station near the line of Kings co. The country in the immediate vicinity is laid out in a village plat, and named **Unionville,** from the Union Race Course; **Clarenceville** is a village plat on the R. R., w. of Jamaica; **Centerville,** a plat adjacent to the trotting course; **Hopedale** and **Jamaica Heights,** two prospective villages in the N. part; **Willow Tree,** a R. R. station, E. of Jamaica; **Queens,**[6] (p. o.,) a R. R. station near the E. line, and **Springfield,** a vicinage 3 mi. long, in the E. part, extending to the bay. The first settlement was made about 1656, by people from Hempstead, who in that year obtained leave of the Dutch Government to purchase lands and erect a town, "according unto their place limited, named Canarise, about midway from Hempstead." In 1702 the civil officers of government removed to this place, on account of prevailing sickness. An attempt was made soon after to appropriate the church to the use of the Episcopalians,—which was resisted, and a controversy commenced, which was not settled until 1728. In 1753 the General Assembly again convened at this place. During the Revolution the town was occupied by the British, and, especially in winter, large bodies of troops were stationed here. The Dutch Church was used as a storehouse. The first church (Presb.) was formed in 1663. The Ref. Prot. D. Church was formed in 1702; and the first Prot. E. services were held during the same year. The Chapel of the Sisters—a neat edifice, built of hewn granite—was erected in the Presb. Cemetery, by Nicholas Ludlum, of New York.[7]

NEWTOWN[8]—was first conveyed by patent, by Gov. Stuyvesant, in 1652. The grant was confirmed by Gov. Nicoll, March 6, 1666, and by Gov. Dongan, Nov. 25, 1683.[9] It was recognized as a town March 7, 1788. It lies upon the East River and Long Island Sound, in the N. w. corner of the co., and includes North and South Brother, Rikers, and Berriens Islands.[10] A range of hills extends along the s. border; but the remaining part of its surface is level or moderately uneven. Flushing Creek forms a portion of the E. boundary, and Newtown Creek a portion of the w. boundary. Extensive salt meadows border upon these creeks and the bays. Hell Gate is a narrow, tortuous passage between Wards Island and Hallets Point, near the N. extremity of the town.[11] The soil is a fine quality of sandy loam. Market gardening and the cultivation of flowers are the most important business. The town poor are let out by contract. **Astoria,**[12] (p. v.,) upon East River, near Hell Gate, was incorp. April 12, 1836. It contains 5 churches, a female seminary, union school, and several extensive manufactories.[13] It is particularly distinguished for its floral gardens

---

[1] Several of these ponds have been purchased by the Brooklyn Water Works Company. The remains of a mastodon were found in excavating at Baisleys Pond, in this town, March 27, 1858. They consisted of six molar teeth and some small fragments of bones, blackened, but not mineralized.

[2] A course was laid out, in colonial times, around the border of Beaver Pond,—a sheet of water adjacent to the village, since drained. Union Course was laid out soon after the passage of the act of 1821, and continued under that of 1834. It is now owned by the "Union Association," formed under general act, Aug. 2, 1858, with a capital of $100,000. It is a few feet over a mile in circuit. There is a trotting course s. E. of the former.

[3] The town elects trustees annually to manage its property. It has a fund—given by Henry Townsend nearly two centuries since—"for the relief of poor widows and children, persons blind, lamed, or aged, and such as should be unable to get a living, or any that should suffer by fire and whose necessities might call for relief."

[4] This institution was incorp. Feb. 29, 1792.

[5] Three carriage factories and the repair shops of the L. I. R. R.

[6] Formerly called "*Brushville.*" The name was changed at a public meeting, Jan. 1, 1857.

[7] There are now 8 churches in the town; 2 M. E., 2 Ref. Prot. D., Presb., Prot. E., Af. Meth., and R. C.

[8] Named "*Middleburg*" under the Dutch.

[9] The first deed of confirmation contained the names of Capt.

Richard Betts, J. P., Capt. Thos. Lawrence, Capt. John Coe, John Burroughs, Ralph Hunt, Dan'l Whitehead, and J. Burger Yost; and the second the names of 108 freeholders. The annual quit-rent was 3£ 4s.—*Patents,* II, 78; *Sec. Office: Thompson's Hist. L. I.,* II, 142.

[10] These islands are cultivated as gardens. Berriens, near Lawrence Point, has an area of 12 acres. Rikers is the largest and most valuable, and was formerly called "*Hewletts Island,*" from its having been the residence of Geo. Hewlett. It is 1 mi. from the mainland, and contains over 50 acres. It was confirmed to Guisbert Riker by Stuyvesant, Dec. 24, 1667, and is still owned by the family.—*Thompson's Hist.,* II, 154.

[11] This name was probably derived from the Dutch "Hellig," angry, and "Gat" a gate. It is often softened down to "*Hurl Gate.*" From the earliest time this has been a difficult strait to navigate, owing to sunken rocks and the strong current of the tide. In 1852 the rocks were mostly removed by a system of submarine blasting and the navigation greatly improved.

[12] This place was formerly known as "*Hallets Cove,*" and was settled by Stephen A. and John C. Halsey. At the time of its incorporation it was proposed to call it "*Sunswick,*" from the Indian name of a stream near by; but the name Astoria was adopted, in hope of securing a gratuity from John Jacob Astor. In this, however, the people were disappointed, as he gave only $100 to the seminary.

[13] The principal manufactories are the chemical works for

and greenhouses.[1] It is connected with New York by ferries, and is inhabited by many persons doing business in the city. Pop. about 3,200. **Ravenswood,** (p. v.,) upon the East River, is a suburban village, and the houses consist mostly of costly residences. The poorhouse farms of New York City were located at this place previous to the purchase of the islands in the river for that purpose.[2] A rifle cartridge factory exploded here about 1850, occasioning a great destruction of life. **Hunters Point**[3] is a newly surveyed and thinly settled village, immediately N. of the mouth of Newtown Creek. It has several manufactories,[4] and is rapidly increasing in business and population. **Newtown,** (p. v.,) near the center, and **Penny Bridge** are stations upon the Flushing R. R.; and **Winfield** and **West Flushing** are village plats upon the same roads. **Maspeth**[5] (p. o.) lies near the head of Newtown Creek; and **Melvina, Columbusville,** and **Winantsville** are village plats in the same vicinity. **Lawrenceville,** N. w. of Winfield, and **Middletown,** s. E. of Astoria, are village plats. **Locust Grove, Linden Hills, New Astoria, Middle Village, and South Williamsburgh** are localities and prospective villages. **Dutch Kills** is a gardening neighborhood. **St. Ronans Well,** a wooded island near the head of Flushing Bay, contains 7 acres, and is a favorite resort for picnic parties. **Calvary Cemetery,** on the Laurel Hills, N. of Newtown Creek, contains 75 acres, and is owned by the R. C. denomination. **The Cemetery of the Evergreens,** in the s. w. corner, is partly in Brooklyn and partly in New Lots, Kings co. It is beautifully situated upon the Cypress Hills, and contains 115 acres, with the privilege of extending its area to 500 acres. **Cypress Hills Cemetery,** E. of the latter, is also situated upon the highlands, and contains 400 acres.[6] **Mount Olivet Cemetery** lies near Maspeth, and the **Lutheran Cemetery** near Middle Village. The National Race Course, incorp. May 31, 1854, is located near the Flushing R. R.[7] The first settlements were made in 1651, by English immigrants, who had first located in New England. The first grant of privileges obtained from the Dutch in 1652 was followed by another more liberal in its character in 1665. The early records of the town were lost during the British occupation in the Revolution. A blockhouse was built at Hell Gate during the Revolution, and a water-battery, named Fort Stevens,[8] during the War of 1812. The first church edifice (Presb.) of which there is any record was erected, in 1670, at Newtown Village; and the first preacher was Rev. John Moore, who was employed from the first settlement until his death, in 1661. The census reports 15 churches in town.[9]

NORTH HEMPSTEAD[10]—was formed from Hempstead, April 6, 1784. It lies upon Long Island Sound, between Hempstead Harbor and Little Neck Bay, and on the s. extends to near the center of Hempstead Plains. A range of hills extends E. and w. through near the center; and from them spurs extend to the Sound, giving to the N. part a moderately hilly character. Hempstead Harbor and Manhasset Bay are irregular bays extending far inland, dividing the coast into "necks" and points,—the principal of which are Cow and Great Necks, Motts, Prospect, Sands,

---

making dry alkalies, the U. S. Vulcanized Gutta Percha Belting and Packing Works, and an extensive carpet factory.

[1] Grant Thorburn, the celebrated seedsman and florist, had a nursery here from 1832 to 1851. There are now 6 floral establishments for supplying the city market, besides many gentlemen's greenhouses, graperies, &c.

[2] About 1834–35, the corporation of New York City erected extensive buildings, about 1¼ mi. s. from Astoria, for a pauper establishment, which were sold at public auction, April 15, 1847, upon the removal of these institutions to the islands in the river. Three large buildings—called the "Boys' Nursery," "School House," and "Infant Nursery," the property of Wm. W. Miles —were leased (May 25) to the Commissioners of Emigration for a ship fever hospital, and other purposes. A public meeting was held immediately after at Astoria, to express indignation at the application of the property to these uses and to remonstrate against it. The people failing to obtain their object, the premises were assailed and destroyed on the night of May 26–27, 1847, by a large mob in disguise. An attempt was made to fasten the expense of these losses upon the town; and, after repeated efforts, the owner recovered $3,000 from the State by act of March 17, 1855.—*Assem. Doc.* 1848, Nos. 19, 161, 164, 186; *Senate Doc.* 1849, No. 31, and 1850, Nos. 62 and 82.

[3] Originally called "*Dominies Hook.*" The place was afterward owned by Geo. Hunter, who died before 1825. It is designated in deeds as "Long Island City." Much of the property given to Union College by Rev. Dr. Nott as an endowment is located here, and consists of graded lots.

[4] The principal manufactories are a flint glass factory, chemical works, paint and varnish factory, foundery for the manufacture of iron pipes, and an oil and locomotive grease factory. Considerable ship-building is also done here.

[5] Sometimes written "*Mespat*," "*Mispat*," &c. It was settled by English, and often designated "*English Kills*," to distinguish

it from Dutch Kills. De Witt Clinton formerly resided here. A foundery for casting metallic burial cases was established here several years since.

[6] The general act forbids cemeteries to hold more than 250 acres in one co.; and hence this was located in two. A special act allows this cemetery to hold 100 acres more in Queens co. The highest point is 219 ft. above tide.

[7] The company that owns this course is incorp., with a capital of $250,000.

[8] Named from Maj. Gen. Ebenezer Stevens, who in his youth was a member of the "Boston Tea Party" and subsequently an officer in the Revolution and the War of 1812.

[9] 4 Prot. E., 3 Prot. Prot. D., 3 M. E., 2 Presb., 2 R. C., and 1 Bap. The Ref. Prot. D. Church at Newtown was formed in 1704, and a Prot. E. church at the same place in 1731. A M. E. church was erected near Middle Village in 1836, chiefly through the liberality of Jos. Harper, father of the Harper Brothers, publishers in New York.

[10] Under the act of organization each town was to enjoy the right of oystering, clamming, and fishing in the other; and both continued to cut grass upon the South Meadows until 1815. They each enjoyed the sole care of the common lands that fell within their several bounds. At the town meeting in Hempstead, April, 1797, a resolution was passed, giving to the people of that town 10 days' precedence of right in cutting grass. A suit was instituted, and was appealed to the Court of Errors, which decided, in Dec. 1828, that North Hempstead had no power to interfere in the regulations of Hempstead.—Opinion of Chancellor Kent, *Johnson's,* II, 320–338; of Chancellor Sanford, *Hopkins,* I, 289–300; Decision of Court of Errors, *Wendell,* II, 109–137. The public lands of the town were sold under an act passed March 25, 1830. Obadiah Townsend, Singleton Mitchell, Benj. Albertson, and Jos. Dodge were appointed commissioners for this purpose.

Barker, and Hewletts Points, and Plum Beach.[1] The soil upon the plains is light and sandy, and in the N. part a sandy and clayey loam, very productive. The town poor are supported by the Jones Fund,[2] at an institution situated at Brookville, in the town of Oyster Bay; and 2 trustees are annually elected to the board having this fund in charge. **Manhasset,**[3] (p. v.,) near the center, a straggling village, contains 4 churches. The neck of land extending eastward of Manhasset Bay is called Manhasset.[4] **Roslyn,** (p. v.,) at the head of Hempstead Harbor, 2 mi. above the steamboat landing, contains 2 churches and several manufactories.[5] Pop. 592. **North Hempstead** (p. o.) is 2 mi. E. of the courthouse; **Mineola** (p. v.) is a scattered village at the junction of the L. I. & Hempstead Branch R. Roads; **Flower Hill** is a farming neighborhood near the center of Manhasset Neck; **Montrose,** a village plat near the country seat of Wm. C. Bryant. **Westbury**[6] is a farming neighborhood, extending from near the courthouse to the E. line of the town. **Carl Place,** near Westbury, and **Clowesville,** near Mineola, are village plats. **Hyde Park,**[7] near the R. R., **Lakeville,**[8] near the line of Flushing, and **Farmers Village,** on the edge of the plains, are farming localities. **Port Washington** (p. o.) is a small village on the w. side of Manhasset Bay. The first settlement was made in the spring of 1640, by a small company of English immigrants from Lynn, Mass., under the lead of Capt. Daniel Howe, who took possession of the head of Cow Bay, under the authority of Farrett, agent of the Earl of Stirling. The Dutch sent a party of soldiers, who captured several of the intruders; but they were released upon promising to quit the place. These persons afterward made the first settlement at Southampton. The necks of land of this town were first used for pasturage in commons. During the Revolution marauding parties committed various depredations upon the people of this town, rendering both property and life insecure. The census reports 9 churches in town.[9]

OYSTER BAY[10]—was patented by Gov. Nicoll, Nov. 29, 1667, and confirmed by Gov. Andross, Sept. 29, 1677.[11] It was recognized as a town March 7, 1788. It occupies the E. extremity of the co., and extends across the island from the sound to the ocean. The N. shore is deeply indented by irregular bays, the principal of which are Oyster Bay, Cold Spring, and Oyster Bay Harbors, Mill Neck Creek, and Mosquito Cove. Cove Neck, Center Island,[12] and Mosquito Neck are long peninsulas formed by these bays;[13] Lloyds Neck is a peninsula extending E. of Cold Spring Harbor. The great indentation of South Oyster Bay, separated from the ocean by Jones Beach, forms the s. boundary. This bay is bordered by salt meadows, and incloses several marshy islands belonging to the town. A range of hills extends through the N. part; and the remainder of the surface is level. The soil is a sandy and clayey loam, and with proper care is very productive. The town poor are supported by the Jones Fund.[14] **Oyster Bay,** (p. v.,) on Oyster Bay Harbor, contains 6 churches and 900 inhabitants;[15] **Glen Cove,**[16] (p. v.,) near Hempstead Harbor, in the N. w. part, contains 3 churches, a printing office, fire insurance office, and a corn starch factory.[17] **South Oyster Bay** (p. o.) is a scattered village on the s. shore. **Farmingdale** (p. o.) is a hamlet and R. R. station near the E. line; **Hicksville**[18] (p. o.) is a R. R. station near the w. line. **Syosset**[19] (p. o.) is the present terminus of a R. R. extending N. E. from

Hicksville, projected to Cold Spring. **Norwich** (East Norwich p. o.) is a farming settlement 3 mi. S. E. of Oyster Bay.[1] **Cedar Swamp,** (p. o.,) S. E. of Glen Cove, and **Locust Valley,**[2] N. E. of the same place, are farming settlements. **Jericho** (p. o.) is a settlement, N. of Hicksville;[3] **Woodbury** (p. o.) is a small village, near the E. border; **Lloyds Neck** is a farming vicinage, in the extreme N. E. part;[4] **Bethphage** is a farming locality, and **Brookville** is a hamlet[5] **Fort Neck** was named from two ancient Indian forts.[6] **Dosoris,**[7] **Lattingtown,** and **Matinicock**[8] are localities N. E. of Glen Cove. An attempt was made by a party of English to make a settlement in this town in 1640; but the settlers were driven off by the Dutch. In 1642 other English parties, who had purchased lands of the Indians, were also driven off. The question of jurisdiction was a matter of debate until 1650, when commissioners were appointed on both sides to settle it. The W. boundary of Oyster Bay was fixed upon as the line of separation of the two colonies; and in 1653 the first permanent English settlement was made, upon land previously purchased of the Indians.[9] In 1662 the town formed a close alliance with Conn. De Lancey's corps of royalists built a small fort on the hill, in the village of Oyster Bay, in 1776; and it was occupied by Simcoe's Queen's Rangers in 1773 and '78. The census reports 16 churches in town.[10]

Acres of Land, Valuation, Population, Dwellings, Families, Freeholders, Schools, Live Stock, Agricultural Products, and Domestic Manufactures, of Queens County.

Names of Towns.	Acres of Land.		Valuation of 1858.			Population.		No. of Dwellings.	No. of Families.	Freeholders.	Schools.	
	Improved.	Unimproved.	Real Estate.	Personal Property.	Total.	Males.	Females.				No. of Districts.	Children taught.
Flushing	11,083	3,813	$3,184,960	$257,110	$3,442,070	3,959	4,011	1,113	1,500	657	8	2,953
Hempstead	25,463	14,888	2,650,760	349,667	3,000,427	5,264	5,213	2,022	2,051	1,409	19	4,056
Jamaica	14,042½	5,555	2,186,430	196,156	2,382,586	2,796	2,836	866	1,005	640	7	2,246
Newtown	10,288¼	2,009	3,146,600	253,290	3,399,890	2,331	2,363	1,518	904	434	10	1,733
North Hempstead	23,150¼	7,989	2,534,400	288,750	2,823,150	4,683	4,763	867	1,766	914	11	3,190
Oyster Bay	35,522	22,950	3,368,695	420,769	3,789,464	4,109	3,938	1,510	1,456	994	21	3,187
Total	119,549	57,204	17,071,845	1,765,742	18,837,587	23,142	23,124	7,896	8,682	5,048	74	17.365

Names of Towns.	Live Stock.					Agricultural Products.							Domestic Cloths, in yards.
						Bush. of Grain.					Dairy Products.		
	Horses.	Working Oxen and Calves.	Cows.	Sheep	Swine.	Winter.	Spring.	Tons of Hay.	Bushels of Potatoes.	Bushels of Apples.	Pounds Butter.	Pounds Cheese.	
Flushing	989	554	878	862	1,924	18,386	65,771	7,105	36,489	955	42,793		
Hempstead	1,651	1,383	2,542	548	2,919	45,844	145,050½	9,179	63,082	100	155,048		
Jamaica	797	325	852		926	23,103	50,515	7,060	64,494	51	46,285		
Newtown	1,397	159	1,163		1,209	7,422	86,677	2,655½	53,983	448	17,416		
North Hempstead	1,236	889	1,611	2,777	2,997	28,670¾	111,309	11,101½	34,438	1,205	61,494½	240	
Oyster Bay	1,884	1,776	2,194	5,527	4,253	49,762½	157,648½	14,294	38,649	587	118,947	525	
Total	7,954	5,086	9,240	9,714	14,228	173,188¼	616,971	51,395	291,135	3,346	441,983½	765	—

1 The town records are usually kept at this place.

2 The p. o. at this place was called "*Buckram*" until recently.

3 Elias Hicks formerly resided here. The first settlement was made by Robert Williams, in 1650; called by the Indians "*Lusum.*"

4 This neck, containing 2,849 acres, is separated from the remainder of the town by Cold Spring Harbor. It is connected with Huntington, Suffolk co., by a narrow isthmus. It is principally devoted to the raising of stock. The Indians called it "*Caum-sett,*" and it is called "*Horse-Neck*" on old documents. It was patented, in 1685, to Jas. Lloyd, of Boston, and erected into a manor. The British maintained a post here during the Revolution; and one of the officers stationed there was the Duke of Clarence, afterward William IV. Daily steamers touch at Lloyd's Dock, on the W. side of the neck.

5 This place was settled by the Dutch, to assert their claim to lands claimed by the English. The Jones Institute is located here.

6 In 1775, Daniel Jones, of this place, gave £300 sterling for a charity school at Oyster Bay.

7 Sometimes written *Desoris*. It is an abbreviation of *dos uxoris*, or "dowry of a wife,"—the property having come to the first settler, Coles, by his wife.

8 A Friends' meetinghouse was erected here in 1682.

9 Peter Wright, Wm. Leveridge, Samuel Mayo, Wm. and John Washburne, Thos. Armitage, Anthony Wright, Robt. Williams, and Richard Holdbrook were joint purchasers. Henry Townsend obtained a grant for a mill Sept. 1661, and erected the first mill, in 1663. There were 53 freeholders in town.

10 4 M. E., 4 Prot. E., 4 Friends, Bap., Ref. Prot. D., Presb., and Af. Meth.

RENSSELAER COUNTY.

This county was formed from Albany, Feb. 7, 1791, and named from the Rensselaer family.[1] It is centrally distant 12 mi. from Albany, and contains an area of 690 sq. mi. Its surface is very broken and hilly. Two distinct ranges of mountains extend through it N. and S., known as the Taghkanick and Petersburgh Mts. The Taghkanick Range occupies the extreme E. borders of the co., and is divided from the Petersburgh Mts. by the long, deep valley through which flow Kinderhook Creek and Little Hoosick and Hoosick Rivers. These mountains are wild, rugged, and rocky, rising to a height of 1000 to 2000 feet above tide, and affording wild and picturesque scenery. Their declivities are usually precipitous, and their summits are crowned with forests or masses of naked rocks. These mountains are composed of the slate, quartz, sandstone, and limestone which constitute the Taconic rocks of Prof. Emmons. The quartz exists in the form of injected veins, and in many places the slate has been decomposed and washed away, leaving the quartz veins in the form of sharp pointed rocks, or of isolated masses. Upon the summits and sides of the mountains the soil is thin and poor; but in the valleys it consists of gravelly loam, and is moderately fertile. The Petersburgh Mts. occupy the whole central part of the co. They are wild, irregular, and broken mountain masses, with precipitous sides on the E., but with more gradual declivities on the w. In some places the summits spread out over a wide surface, constituting a high, sterile plateau broken by hills and rocks. They are composed of the graywacke slates and limestone belonging to the Hudson River group. An extensive tract among these mountains, comprising a portion of Stephentown, Berlin, Sand Lake, and Poestenkill, is still covered with forests. The soil is generally hard and sterile, consisting of a stiff clay and disintegrated slate, largely underlaid by a retentive hardpan.

Hudson River is on the w. boundary of the co.; and along its bank extends an intervale varying from a few rods to a half mile in width, and bounded by a series of bluffs 100 to 200 feet in height. From the summits of the bluffs to the foot of Petersburgh Mts. the country assumes the character of a broken, hilly upland. This region is composed of the drift deposits mixed with disintegrated slates, in some places the clay, and in others the sand, predominating.

The valley of Kinderhook Creek, Little Hoosick and Hoosick Rivers extends through the E. part of the co. The summit level in this valley at S. Berlin, between the waters flowing s. and those flowing N., is 600 feet above tide. The numerous streams that flow from the Petersburgh Mts. westward to the Hudson have worn deep ravines through the clay bluffs, forming lateral valleys, which extend eastward from the valley of the Hudson. Among the wild and rocky regions of the Petersburgh Mts. are numerous small lakes and ponds, forming a peculiar and beautiful feature of the landscape. Several interesting mineral springs are found within the county.

The narrow intervales, and a large portion of the uplands, are adapted to grain, and produce liberal crops, chiefly of corn, oats, spring wheat, potatoes, and flax; but the soil is generally best adapted to grazing and dairying, especially along the E. towns, where these occupations form the leading pursuits. Manufactures are extensively carried on at Troy and in the Hoosick Valley, and commerce has received much attention at Troy, and, at an earlier day, at Lansingburgh.

The principal works of internal improvement in the co. are the Troy & Greenbush R. R., a continuation of the Hudson River R. R. to Troy; the Albany & West Stockbridge R. R., extending from Greenbush in a s. E. direction, through East Greenbush and Schodack, to the s. bounds of the co., 7 mi. from the river; the Troy & Boston R. R., extending from Troy N. E. through Lansingburgh, Schaghticoke, Pittstown, Hoosick, and a corner of Petersburgh, to the Vt. line; the Troy & Bennington R. R., forming a branch ($5\frac{38}{100}$ mi. long) of the Troy & Boston R. R., from Hoosick Fall Junction to the State Line toward Bennington, Vt.; and the Albany, Vt. & Canada R. R., extending through Schaghticoke across the N. w. corner of the co., terminating at Eagle Bridge, where it connects with the Vt. roads. Besides these lines, which are within the co., several others communicate with Troy from the w. side of the river. Among these are the A. V. &

---

[1] This co. included a large share of the Rensselaer Manor E. of the river, and the present towns of Hoosick, Pittstown, Schaghticoke, and a part of Lansingburgh.

C. R. R., which sends a branch to West Troy; a branch of the N. Y. Central R. R., extending to Schenectady;[1] and the Rensselaer & Saratoga R. R., extending from Troy to Saratoga. The Northern and Erie Canals also both connect with the Hudson at Troy, and there is an uninterrupted steamboat navigation to New York.[2]

The first newspaper in the county was established at Lansingburgh, in 1787.[3]

The county seat is the city of Troy, situated at the head of sloop navigation on the Hudson.[4] The courthouse—built at the joint expense of city and co., and containing the courtroom and co. and city offices[5]—is situated on the corner of Congress and Second Sts.[6] The jail is on Ferry, corner of Fifth St. A house of industry, for the support of paupers, located on a farm of 140 acres 2 mi. s. e. of the city, was founded in 1821, on the plan of Count Rumford. In 1857 the co. poorhouse was reported as being located upon a farm of 152 acres. The co. poor were let, by contract, at $1 per week, the contractor having free use of the farm, and the services of the paupers as far as they were able to labor.[7]

The greater part of the co. was included in the patent of Killian Van Rensselaer, in 1630; and the first settlement was made by tenants under him the same year.[8] The lands were held by the same tenure as those in Albany co., and similar difficulties have frequently occurred in endeavoring to enforce the collection of rents. Upon the death of the late Stephen Van Rensselaer the manor was divided, the portion e. of the river passing into the hands of his son William P.; and since that time a considerable portion of the leased land has been conveyed in fee.[9] During

---

[1] A R. R. bridge 1600 feet long, upon this road, crosses the Hudson at Troy. Connected with it is a common road bridge.

[2] These ample facilities for travel are in striking contrast to the condition of things 60 years ago. By an act of March 30, 1798, Alexander J. Turner and Adonijah Skinner, for a period of 5 years, obtained the exclusive right of running a stage wagon, drawn by at least two good horses, at intervals of one week, (unless prevented by badness of roads,) from Troy to Hampton, on the border of Vermont. They were allowed to charge 5 cts. per mi. for passengers, and a like sum for every 150 lbs. of baggage over 14 lbs.

[3] The Northern Centinel and Lansingburgh Advertiser was started at Lansingburgh, May 15, 1787, by Claxton & Babcock; it was subsequently removed to Albany.

The Lansingburgh Gazette, started in 1798, was subsequently for many years published as The Rensselaer County Gazette, but it is now published under its first title by Alexander Kirkpatrick.

The Farmers' Register was started in 1798 at Lansingburgh by Francis Adancourt; it was removed to Troy a few years after, where it was published until 1832.

The Lansingburgh Democrat was commenced in Dec. 1838, by Wm. J. Lamb, by whom it is still published.

The Golden Rule was established at Lansingburgh in 1841 by the Rev. R. W. Smith, and was published several years.

The Juvenile Pearl, of the same place, was started Sept. 1, 1845, by Rev. J. A. Pitman.

The Farmers' Oracle, started at Troy by Luther Pratt in 1796, was of short duration.

The Northern Budget was started at Troy in 1798 by Robert Moffitt and Col. Wells, and has been continued to the present time, with slight changes of name. It is now issued as a daily and weekly by F. L. Hagadorn.

The Troy Gazette was founded in 1802 by Thomas Collier, and was discontinued before 1818.

The Troy Post was commenced Sept. 1, 1812, by Parker & Bliss, and was changed July 15, 1823, to

The Troy Sentinel, semi-w., and continued until Jan. 1, 1833. From May 1, 1830, to Aug. 1831, a daily edition was issued.

The Evangelical Restorationist, semi-mo., was commenced in 1825 by Adolphus Skinner.

The Troy Review, or Religious and Musical Repository, began Jan. 4, 1826, and continued 2 years.

The Evangelical Repository (Univ.) was published in 1828.

The Troy Republican (Anti-Masonic) was started in 1828 by Austin & Wellington, and was continued about a year.

The Northern Watchman (Anti-Masonic) was commenced in 1831 by E. Wellington. In 1832 it was styled The Troy Watchman, and was continued one or two years.

The Gospel Anchor, (Univ.,) started in 1831, was published by John M. Austin, and afterward by H. J. Green; it was continued until 1834.

The Troy Press was started in 1832 by Wm. Yates and Seth Richards, and was continued until July 1, 1834. From 1833 a daily edition was issued.

The Troy Whig, da. and w., was founded in July, 1834, by James M. Stevenson, and is still continued. The weekly since Sept. 1855, has been published as **The Troy American,** by George Abbott.

The Troy Statesman was commenced in 1834, by T. J. Sutherland.

The Botanic Advocate was published in 1834 by Russell Buckley.

The Trojan, da., was started in 1835, and continued a few months.

The State Journal was issued in 1836 by Richards & Mastin, and continued 1 year.

The New York State Journal was published in 1837 by T. Haxtun.

The Troy Daily Mail was started in 1837 by Wellington & Nafew, and was continued until 1841.

The Troy Daily Bulletin was started in Dec. 1841, by R. Thompson.

The Troy Daily Herald was published in 1843 by Isaac D. Ayres.

The Troy Temperance Mirror was issued in 1843 by Bardwell & Kneeland.

The Family Journal was started in 1844 by Fisk & Co. In Sept. 1848, it appeared as **The New York Family Journal,** and it is still continued.

The Troy Post was commenced by Alexander McCall, and in 1845 it was superseded by

The Troy Traveler, da. and w. Fisk & Avery were the publishers, and Wm. L. Avery editor.

The Trojan was started in 1845, and continued several years.

The Rensselaer County Temperance Advocate was begun in 1846 by S. Spicer.

The Daily Telegraph was published at Troy in 1846.

The Journal of Temperance was started in 1846 by Wm. Hager.

The National Watchman was commenced in 1847 by Allen & Garnet, and is still published.

The Troy Daily Times was founded in 1851 by J. M. Francis, and is still published.

La Ruche Canadienne was established at Troy in 1851 by Dorian & Mathiot.

The Nassau Gazette was started in Dec. 1850 by J. M. Geer.

The Lutheran Herald, semi-mo., was started at West Sand Lake by H. L. Dox, in 1844.

The Greenbush Guardian was commenced in Aug. 1856 by A. J. Goodrich. It is now published by J. D. Comstock.

[4] By an act of Jan. 11, 1793, the sum of £600 was appropriated for the erection of a courthouse and jail, to be built under the direction of Cornelius Lansing, Jacob C. Schermerhorn, Abraham Ten Eyck, Mahlon Taylor, and Jacob Vanderheyden, who, with others, had pledged £1000 for that purpose. In 1794 a further sum of £800 was granted; in 1797, $5500; and in 1798, $500.

[5] The first co. officers were Anthony Ten Eyck, Judge; Moss Kent, Surrogate; Nicholas Schuyler, Clerk; and Albert Pawling, Sheriff.

[6] This building was begun in 1828 and finished in 1831. It is in the Grecian style, modeled from the temple of Theseus at Athens, omitting the side columns, and is built of Sing Sing marble. The first building was of brick, on the present courthouse site.

[7] Senate Doc. No. 8, 1857. The committee making this report were very severe in their censure of the manner in which this establishment was kept, the inadequacy of its arrangements, and the treatment of its inmates.

[8] See page 157.

[9] The proportion of leased land in the several towns in 1858 is stated by the agents as follows:—In Stephentown nearly all leased; in Grafton, Nassau, Schodack, E.Greenbush, N.Greenbush, and Brunswick, each about two-thirds leased; Berlin and Petersburgh, each about one-half leased; Poestenkill, nearly all free-leased; and Sand Lake, one-third originally deeded, and one-third of the remainder now leased.

the French wars, the N. border of the co. was repeatedly ravaged by the enemy and the settlements were broken up. Upon the approach of Burgoyne's army, in 1777, the American families hastily fled with such property as could be easily removed, leaving the houses and farms to be plundered by the enemy. Scouting parties of the British penetrated as far s. as Lansingburgh. The battle of Bennington was fought within the limits of the co., Aug. 16, 1777;[1] and from that moment the American cause daily grew brighter.[2] The proprietor of the manor extended every possible assistance to the distressed families flying before the invaders, proving to them a sincere friend in their hour of need.

BERLIN—was formed from Petersburgh, Schodack, and Stephentown, March 21, 1806. A portion of Sand Lake was taken off in 1812. It lies near the center of the E. border of the co. Its surface consists of 2 ranges of mountains separated by a narrow valley extending N. and S. The hilly region is wild and broken, and the declivities are generally precipitous. The principal streams are Kinderhook Creek, flowing S., and Little Hoosick River, flowing N. The headwaters of these streams are but a few rods apart, near S. Berlin. The W. part of the town is covered with forest, in which are several fine lakes. The soil in the valley is a gravelly loam, but among the mountains it is a hard sterile clay intermixed or covered with fragments of rock. **Berlin,** (p. v.,) containing 326 inhabitants, **South Berlin** (p. v.) and **Center Berlin,** (p. v.,) are all situated in the valley of the Little Hoosick. **West Berlin** is a p. o. Godfrey Brimmer located near N. Berlin in 1765.[3] The first church (Seventh Day Bap.) was formed at N. Berlin, in Dec. 1780; Wm. Coon was the first preacher.[4]

BRUNSWICK—was formed from Troy, March 20, 1807. A part of the town was reannexed to Troy, April 15, 1814. It lies a little N. w. of the center of the co., upon the hilly region w. of the summits of the Petersburgh Mts. The most elevated portions of the town, in the extreme E. and in the N. w. parts, are 800 to 1000 feet above tide. The principal streams are Poesten Kil, its tributary Quacken Kil, and Tomhannock Creek. The soil upon the summits of the hills is hard and sterile, but in the valleys and lowlands it consists of a fertile, gravelly loam intermixed with clay. The people are largely engaged in furnishing milk, vegetables, and hay to the Troy market. **Brunswick Center, East Brunswick,**[5] **Millville,** (Eagle Mills p. o.,) and **Cropseyville**[6] (p. o.) are small villages. The first settlement was made about 1760, by a company of Germans.[7] This town suffered greatly upon the approach of Burgoyne in 1777, and after the battle of Saratoga many families of royalists withdrew to Canada, and but few returned. There are 4 churches in town.[8]

EAST GREENBUSH—was formed from Greenbush, as *"Clinton,"* Feb. 23, 1855, and its name was changed April 14, 1858. It lies on the bank of the Hudson, s. w. of the center of the co. The bluffs which border upon the river rise from the edge of the water to an elevation of 100 to 300 feet. The principal one of these, opposite Albany, is known as Pon-o-kose Hill.[9] From the summits of these bluffs the surface spreads out into a rolling upland, rising toward the E. The chief streams are Tierken Kil,[10] or Mill Creek, in the central, and Moordeners Creek in the s. w. part of the town. The soil consists of sand, gravel, and clay, and is very fertile. There are several sulphur springs in town, the principal of which is opposite Albany and is known as "Harrowgate." A large island called Papskanee[11] lies in the river, and belongs to this town. **East Greenbush** (p. o.) is the only village. It contains the Greenbush and Schodack Academy[12] and about a dozen houses. Settlements are supposed to have commenced here as early as

---

1 See p. 556.
2 From this time the timid were emboldened, the secretly dissatisfied overawed, and great numbers before undecided now committed their fortunes to the cause of freedom.
3 Among the other early settlers were Reuben Bonesteel and a family named Richer, who came in soon after Mr. Brimmer. In 1769, Peter Simmons and Jacob O. Cropsey lived at the Hollow, and in the same year Daniel Hull and Joseph Green came into town. Col. Bentley settled near N. Berlin, and Thos. Sweet, a blacksmith, at S. Berlin. Jas. Green, a son of Joseph G., died in 1857, aged 100 years. Daniel Hull kept the first tavern before the Revolution, and Hezekiah Hull opened an inn soon after the war. Caleb Bentley built the first grist mill, and Amos Sweet the first saw-mill, in 1780. Dr. John Forbes, the first physician, located at S. Berlin in 1775. Soon after the battle of Lexington, two companies were formed in this and the adjacent towns, a part of whom were stationed at D. Hull's for local protection; the others were engaged elsewhere in active service.

4 The census reports 3 churches; 2 Bap. and Christian.
5 This village is the seat of a cotton batting and a sash and blind factory.
6 A woolen factory and tannery are located here.
7 Among the early settlers were David Coons, and families named Hardwick, Braunschweiger, Springer, Borck, Hayner, Outhout, Van Arnam, Hogg, Fisher, Benn, Watson, Fret, Quackenboss, Muller, Goeway, and Clum. A man named File kept the first inn, near the Lutheran Church, in 1790, and Henry Clum the first store at Cropseyville. The first factory was erected by a company at "Albia," now a part of Troy. The first mill was built by —— Cross, in 1792, with no tools but an ax, saw, and auger.
8 2 M. E., Ev. Luth., and Presb.
9 Name as given by an aged Stockbridge Indian.
10 Signifying "blustering or noisy creek."
11 Sometimes written "Poepskenekoes" and "Papakenea."
12 This academy is now nearly extinct.

1650.[1] During the war of 1812, extensive barracks were erected on the hills E. of Greenbush Village; and for several years the place was the center of active military preparation, and the rendezvous of large bodies of troops.[2] Edmund C. Genet, Minister of the French Republic to the U. S., was long a resident of this town, and died here July 14, 1834. There is but 1 church (Ref. Prot. D.) in town.

GRAFTON—was formed from Troy and Petersburgh, March 20, 1807. It lies N. of the center of the co., upon the summits of the Petersburgh Mts. Its surface is very rocky and broken, and a large part of it is yet covered with forests. The summits of the hills are 800 to 1200 feet above tide, and many of them are covered with huge and jagged masses of graywacke. Among the hills are 25 ponds, several of which cover an area of several hundred acres each.[3] The Quacken Kil is the principal stream. The soil is chiefly clay, underlaid by hardpan, and is wet, cold, and hard of cultivation. Mineral paint is made from the red argillite at Quackenkill. Considerable quantities of wood, tan bark, and charcoal are sent from this town to Troy. **Grafton**[4] (p. v.) contains 14 houses, **East Grafton** (p. v.) 12, and **Quackenkill** (p. o.) 10. The first settlements were made by tenants under Van Rensselaer; they paid an average annual rent of 10 bushels of wheat per 100 acres.[5] The census reports 2 churches; Bap. and M. E.

GREENBUSH[6]—was formed from *"Rensselaerwyck,"* April 10, 1792. Another act of incorporation is dated March 17, 1795. A part of Sand Lake was set off in 1812, and *"Clinton"* (now E. Greenbush) and N. Greenbush in 1855, leaving but the corporate bounds of the village as defined by the act of April 9, 1852. Its surface consists of the flat intervale on the river and a portion of the adjacent hillsides. The soil is clay mixed with sand and alluvial deposits. **Greenbush** (p. v.) was incorp. April 14, 1815.[7] Pop. about 3303. The upper part of the village, locally known as "East Albany," contains the depôts, freight houses, and machine shops of the several railroads which terminate opposite Albany, and is a place of considerable business.[8] The first settlement was made previous to 1631.[9] A ferry was established at the mouth of Beaver Creek in 1642, and was first kept by Hendrick Albertsen. The country around *"Beverwick"* was thrown into alarm by the news of the Indian massacre at Esopus in June, 1663, and the settlers took refuge in Fort Cralo, on the patroon's farm, and a night watch was established.[10] There are 4 churches in the village.[11]

HOOSICK[12]—was formed as a district, March 24, 1772, and as a town, March 7, 1788. It lies in the N. E. corner of the co. Its surface consists of the narrow valley of Hoosick River, and the wild, rocky regions of the Taghkanick and Petersburgh Mts., rising respectively on the E. and W. The two highest peaks are Fondas Hill in the S. E. and Potters Hill in the S. W. each about 900 feet above tide. The valleys are very narrow, and are bordered by steep hillsides. A belt of dark slate, which is quarried for roofing, extends along the E. bank of the river. East of the river, the rocks consist of a slaty shale and limestone, the latter furnishing lime. The principal streams are Hoosick and Walloomsac[13] Rivers, Punch Kil, White Creek, and Shaw Brook. The soil among the mountains is hard and sterile, but in the valleys it is principally clay, mixed with disintegrated slate. In the S. E. corner are 3 springs, from which issue nitrogen gas.[14] Flax is very extensively cultivated.[15] Considerable attention is also paid to manufactures. **Hoosick**

[1] Among the early settlers were the names of Van Buren, Van Hegen, Staats, Bris, Vandenburgh, Witbeck, Cuyler, and Van Wesipe.

[2] The cantonments contained accommodations for 4000 troops. There were also hospital accommodations for 100. This elevated position, sometimes called "Mount Madison," was supposed to be a very healthy locality; but during the first year of its occupation much sickness occurred, in consequence of the unavoidable exposures of the camp.—See *Mann's Medical Sketches.* Several military executions for desertion took place here during the war. The old barracks have nearly disappeared.

[3] These ponds are noted for the wild beauty of their locality, and they are favorite resorts of sportsmen.

[4] Often called "Grafton Center," and formerly *"Patroons Mills."*

[5] Among the first settlers were families named Coon, Dimmons, and Owens. Stephen McChesney kept the first store and inn, in 1800. A grist mill was built at an early day by the patroon at the Center.

[6] It was named *Greene Bosch* by the Dutch, from the pine woods which originally covered the flats. Called by the Indian names of Pe-tu-qua-poen and Tus-cum-ca-tick in early documents. A part of Sand Lake was annexed in 1843.

[7] The village was purchased and laid out in 1806, and for several years after its growth was quite rapid. During the War of 1812 it contained from 50 to 70 houses.

[8] See page 552.

[9] In that year it is mentioned that Gerrit Teunissen de Reus occupied a well stocked farm. Cornelius Maessen Van Buren, an early settler on the river below, died in 1648. Evert Pels Van Steltyn lived on Mill Creek at an early day.

[10] The following names of persons constituting this watch have been preserved. Chief Officer, Cornelius Van Ness; Cornelius Stephenson Mullen, Adam Dingermans, Gerrit Van Ness, Jan. Juriaensen, Jan. Van Ness, Jacobus Jansen, Tyman Hendricksen, Wm. Bout, (Corporal,) Jan. Outhout, Hendrick Van Nes, Hendrick Maessen, (Van Buren,) Gerret Teunisson, Hans Jacobsen, Hendrick Williamson, and Claes Claessen.

[11] Presb., R. C., (St. Johns,) Prot. E., and M. E.

[12] Variously spelled Hoosack, Hosack, Hoosick, &c. By some it is said to be an Indian name, and by others to be derived from Alexander Hosack, an early settler.

[13] In early maps and documents variously spelled "Wallomsock," "Wallamsock," "Wallomschock," "Walmscock," "Wallamschock," "Wallamsac," "Walmseec," "Walloomscoick," and "Walmsook."

[14] This gas is not combined with the water, but seems to come from the gravel beds beneath. By pressing upon a surface equal to 4 or 5 inches square, a quart of gas can be collected in 10 seconds.—*Eaton's Geol. Survey, Rens. Co.,* p. 29; *Beck's Mineralogy of N. Y.,* p. 134.

[15] In 1854 the product of the flax crop was over 250,000 lbs. of lint and 8300 bush. of seed.

Falls (p. v.) was incorp. April 14, 1827. Pop. 1200. It contains Ball's Seminary, 2 foundries, 2 cotton factories, 2 reaping and mowing machine factories, and 1 establishment for the manufacture of machinery for cotton and woolen factories. **North Hoosick**[1] (p. v.) contains 175 inhabitants, and **Buskirks Bridge** (p. v.) 125; **Hoosick Corners** (Hoosick p.o.) contains 30 houses, **Eagle Bridge** (p. v.) 14, **Walloomsac**[2] 12, **West Hoosick** (p. o.) 10, and **Potter Hill** (p. o.) 7. This town was included in the Hoosick Patent,[3] granted June 3, 1688, and the Walloomsac Patent,[4] granted June 15, 1739. The first settlements were made upon the Hoosick Patent by several Dutch families.[5] A Dutch church was founded, and known as the "Tyoshoke Church," at San Coick, near the N. border of the town. The settlement at Hoosick was entirely broken up by a party of French and Indians on the 28th of Aug. 1754. Two persons were killed, and the houses, barns, and crops were destroyed.[6] The next day the settlement of San Coick, s. of Hoosick, was also destroyed. The battle of Bennington was fought in this town, Aug. 16, 1777.[7] The census reports 6 churches in town.[8]

LANSINGBURGH[9]—was formed from Troy and Petersburgh, March 20, 1807. A tract was annexed from Schaghticoke in 1819. A part of Troy was taken off in 1836, and a part of Brunswick in 1839. It is a narrow strip of land extending along the Hudson. In the s. part the river intervale is one-fourth of a mile in width; but in the N. the bluffs rise directly from the water. In the N. E. is a high, rocky hill, 400 to 600 feet above the river. The high bluff E. of the village is called Diamond Rock. The streams are Deepi Kil and Koola Kil. The soil is a gravelly and clayey loam. The people are largely engaged in the manufacture of brushes, oilcloths, flax cordage, and malt liquors. A lock at Troy admits the passage of sloops up to this place.[10] **Lansingburgh**[11] (p. v.) contains extensive brush, oilcloth, and other manufactories, the Lansingburgh Academy,[12] a Female Seminary,[13] 6 churches, 2 printing offices, and about 4000 inhabitants. A covered bridge

---

[1] On some maps called "McNamarasville." It is the seat of a paper mill and machine shop.

[2] This village contains a paper mill.

[3] This patent was granted to Maria Van Rensselaer, Hendrick Van Ness, Jacobus Van Cortlandt, and Gerrit Finnise. The patent extended from the Schaghticoke Tract, a distance of 2 mi. each side of the river, up to a "certain fall, called Quequick; and from said falls, up the creek, to a place called Nacha-quick-quack."

[4] This patent contained 12,000 acres, on both sides of Walloomsac River, and lying partly in Washington co. and Vt.: it was granted to Edward Collins, James De Lancy, Gerardus Stuyvesant, Stephen Van Rensselaer, Charles Williams, and Frederick Morris.

[5] Among these early settlers were Adam Vrooman, (an Indian trader,) Henry Van Ness, Abraham Fort, Lewis and Peter Viele, John Van Buskirk, Walter Van Vechten, Geo. B. Nichols, Jacob Odekirk, Daniel Bradt, and Reykert Borie.

[6] The invaders were supposed to be Schaghticoke Indians, who a little time before had abandoned their settlements and gone to Canada. The loss of the two settlements was estimated at £4000.— *Smith's Hist. of N. Y.,* Alb. ed., p. 307; *Trans. Ag. Soc.,* 1848, p. 909; *Hall's Hist. Eastern Vt.,* p. 66.

[7] The Battle of Bennington was one of the most important of the military events connected with the expedition of Burgoyne in 1777. About the first of Aug. the British army reached the Hudson and took possession of Fort Edward. For several weeks they had been engaged in repairing the bridges and in clearing the roads from the impediments left by the retreating Americans; and, upon their arrival at the Hudson, Burgoyne congratulated himself that his troubles were at an end. His greatest source of embarrassment was in securing provisions for his army and in obtaining means of transportation. With 15 days' hard labor he was only enabled to bring 10 bateaux and 4 days' provisions from Lake George. Learning that the Americans had collected a large quantity of military stores, cattle, and horses at Bennington, he was persuaded by Maj. Skene, against the advice of his most experienced officers, to send a party to capture them. The detachment consisted of 500 Hessians, Canadians, and tories, under the command of Col. Baum. They were instructed "to try the affections of the county, to mount Reidsel's dragoons, to complete Peters's corps, [of loyalists,] and obtain a large supply of cattle, horses, and carriages." This accomplished, he was to scour the country from Rockingham to Otter Creek, go down as far as Brattleboro, and join the main body by the great road to Albany. The detachment left the camp at Fort Edward, Aug. 13; and on the evening of the same day they surprised and captured 5 Americans at Cambridge. On the 14th they advanced as far as the mill upon Walloomsac River, in the N. E. part of Hoosick and within 12 mi. of Bennington. Gen. Stark, who commanded the American forces at Bennington, learning of the approach of the enemy, took immediate measures for defense. He sent an order to Col. Warner, at Manchester, to march immediately with his regiment of Green Mountain Boys; he rallied the neighboring militia, and on the 13th he sent out an advance guard of 200 men, under Lieut. Col. Gregg, to impede the progress of the enemy. On the

morning of the 14th he marched with his whole force to the support of Gregg, and about 5 mi. from Bennington he met Gregg in full retreat, with the enemy within 1 mi. of him. Both armies chose strong positions and threw up temporary intrenchments. Baum, alarmed at the number of Americans, sent for a reinforcement. On the 15th a heavy rain set in; and the day was spent in skirmishing and in preparing for the battle. Col. Warner's regiment arrived at Bennington in the evening, and there stopped to dry themselves and recruit after their fatiguing march. Stark, fearing the enemy might receive reinforcements, resolved to attack them early on the morning of the 16th. Previous to the signal for attack he made the following laconic speech to his men: "See there, men! there are the red-coats. Before night they are ours, or Molly Stark will be a widow." The attack was at once made simultaneously at all points. The Indians fled at the beginning of the conflict, and the tories were soon driven from their posts, leaving the Hessians to sustain the weight of the engagement. After 2½ hours of hard fighting the enemy gave way at all points, and commenced a disorderly retreat. While the Americans were busy in plundering the abandoned camp of the enemy, and in detached parties were engaged in pursuit, Col. Breyman, with a reinforcement of 500 men, arrived. He met the flying fugitives about 2 mi. from the scene of action, and immediately charged upon the broken ranks of the Americans. The tide of battle now turned, and Stark had the mortification of seeing his army driven helplessly from the field where they had so lately been victorious. At this moment Col. Warner's regiment arrived from Bennington and checked the advance of the British. Stark rallied his broken forces behind the fresh troops, and soon the battle again became general. At sunset the British fled toward the Hoosick and were pursued by the Americans until dark. The Americans lost about 30 killed and 40 wounded. The British loss, in killed, wounded, and prisoners, was 934. The result of this battle was disastrous in the extreme to Burgoyne, and contributed more than any other event to his final surrender at Saratoga.

[8] 2 M. E., Bap., Ref. Prot. D., R. C., and Union.

[9] The town was named from the village, and the latter was named from Abraham Jacob Lansing, its founder.

[10] This lock was completed and opened for use Sept. 10, 1823. About 1800 the State expended large sums for the improvement of navigation to this place, and granted a lottery for that purpose.

[11] Formerly known as "*New City.*" It was once claimed by Vermont as within its jurisdiction. See page 18.

[12] The Lansingburgh Academy, chartered Feb. 8, 1796. By an act passed Feb. 20, 1816, the trustees of this academy were authorized to subscribe 1000 shares to the Bank of Lansingburgh. A. Reed, from New Windsor, Conn., commenced school here in 1793, in a gambrel roofed building, used as the first meeting house. Rev. Dr. Lee taught the languages at the same time.

[13] In Oct. 1857, Rev. Salmon Hatch opened a private female seminary and boarding school. It has about 100 pupils, and employs 9 teachers.

here crosses the Hudson to Waterford. The Troy & Boston R. R. passes through the town. The village was founded by Abraham Jacob Lansing, about 1770. It was first organized under the name of "*Stone Arabia*" in 1771.[1] In May, 1775, 50 of the citizens—at the head of whom was A. J. Lansing, the proprietor—signed articles of association pledging themselves to sustain the measures recommended by the Continental or Provincial Congress. The first act of incorporation under the State government was passed April 5, 1790, at which time the village was included in the town of "*Rensselaerwyck*."[2] In 1791 it was included in the town of Troy. The place rapidly increased in population, and early became an important trading and commercial village. The first church (Ref. Prot. D.) was organized in 1784; and reorganized in 1792 as a Presb. church.[3] **Speigletown** is a village of 15 houses.[4]

NASSAU—was formed from Petersburgh, Stephentown, and Schodack, March 31, 1806, by the name of "*Philipstown*."[5] Its name was changed April 6, 1808. It lies near the center of the s. border of the co. Its surface is very broken. Snake Hill, in the s. w., is about 800 feet above tide. The principal streams are Kinderhook and Tsatsawassa[6] Creeks, and Valatie Kil. There are several fine lakes among the hills, the principal of which are the Tsatsawassa and the Pattawassa. The Psanticoke Swamp, w. of the center, covers several hundred acres. The soil is clay and gravel under-laid by hardpan. Considerable manufacturing is carried on in town.[7] **Nassau**, (p. v.,) incorp. March 12, 1819, is the seat of Nassau Academy. Pop. 300. **West Nassau**[8] has 57 houses, **East Nassau** (p. v.) 45, **Hoags Corner** (p. v.) 25, **Alps** (p. v.) 24, **North Nassau** (p. v.) 15, and **Millers Corners** 10. **Brainards** (p. v.) contains a female seminary and 20 houses.[9] The first settler was Hugh Wilson, who located on the site of Nassau Village in 1760.[10] At that time a few families of the Stockbridge Indians were living where Mr. Hoag's orchard now stands.[11] The Indians conveyed to Joseph Primmer a tract of land N. of Hoags Pond,[12] and another tract s. of it to Hugh Wilson, May 16, 1760.[13] Within the last 20 years a considerable quantity of land has been allowed to produce a second crop of timber. There are 7 churches in town.[14]

NORTH GREENBUSH—was formed from Greenbush, Feb. 23, 1855. It lies upon the Hudson, directly w. of the center of the co. The clay bluffs, 100 to 200 feet high, rise from the edge of the water, leaving little or no intervale. From the summits of the bluffs the surface spreads out into a rolling upland, broken by the deep gulleys of the streams. The principal stream is Wynants Kil, in the N. E. Aries Lake, on the E. border, is a fine sheet of water. The soil is a sandy and gravelly loam interspersed with patches of clay. The people are extensively engaged in supplying the markets of Albany and Troy with garden vegetables and milk. **Bath**,[15] opposite the upper part of Albany, contains about 12 houses, **Defriestville**[16] (p. v.) 12, and **Wynants-kill** (p. v.) 15. The first settlement, made by tenants under Van Rensselaer, was among the first in the manor.[17] There are 3 churches in town.[18]

PETERSBURGH[19]—was formed from Stephentown, March 18, 1791. Its boundary on the line of Berlin was changed, Jan. 4, 1793; parts of Berlin and Lansingburgh were taken off in 1806, and parts of Nassau and Grafton in 1807. It lies upon the E. border of the co., N. of the center. Its surface consists of two precipitous mountain ridges separated by the narrow valley of Little Hoosick River. The highest peaks are 1000 to 2000 feet above tide. The mountain regions are barren and almost inaccessible. The Hoosick River breaks through the Taghkanick Mts. in the N. E. part. The soil in the valley is a gravelly loam. **Petersburgh**, (p. v.,) formerly "*Rens-*

[1] At the first meeting in "*Stone Arabia*," held Jan. 1, 1771, it was voted that A. J. Lansing and his heirs forever should be a committee of the village, with a power equal to each of the four annually chosen by the people.

[2] By an act of 1790, John Van Rensselaer, Charles Tillman, Elijah James, Aaron Ward, Stephen Goreham, Ezra Hickock, and Levinus Lansing, were appointed trustees, to take charge of the waste lands of the village and to perform certain munici-pal duties, their successors to be elected annually.

[3] The census reports 8 churches; 2 M. E., 2 Presb., Bap., Af-rican Meth., Prot. E., and R. C.

[4] The first settlers of this village were Charles W. Douglass and John Follet.

[5] Named from Philip Van Rensselaer.

[6] Sometimes written "Tackawasick."

[7] There are a foundery and machine shop at Nassau Village, a paper mill at Brainards, a carding machine and chair factory at Hoags Corner, and a hoe factory at Dunhams Hollow.

[8] Formerly "*Union Village P. O.*"

[9] Formerly "*Brainards Bridge P. O.*" Transylvania Institute was established here in 1837.

[10] Among the early settlers were Thos. Hicks, Henry Post, John McCagg, Danl. Litz, Titus Hemsted, Abram Holmes, Jas. Marks, John M. Schermerhorn, Maj. A. Brush, Reuben Bateman, Nath'l

Gillet, David Waterbury, —— McNeil, and —— Wiltsie. Wm. Primmer is said to have been the first child born. The first gristmill was built on the outlet of Tsatsawassa Pond, by Mr. Schermerhorn, before the Revolution. The first inn was kept by —— Hicks before, and the first store by Hoag & Vail a little after, the Revolution.

[11] They called their village On-ti-ke-ho-mawck; and their chief was named Kesh-o-mawck.

[12] This pond was called by the early settlers the "*Beaver Dam*."

[13] The former of these deeds is still preserved.

[14] 2 M. E., 2 Presb., Bap., Ref. Prot. D., and Union.

[15] Named from a mineral spring in the vicinity. It was laid out as a village by the Patroon toward the close of the last century. In 1800 the traveller Maude, in his "*Visit to Niagara*," says that it is likely to soon surpass Troy and Lansingburgh in trade, and Ballston and Saratoga as a watering place.

[16] Sometimes called "Blooming Grove." The first settler was Martinus Sharp.

[17] Among the early settlers were John Cranel, Juriah Sharpe, Roinier Van Alstyne, Marte, David, and Philip Defriest, Philip Wendell, Rutger Vandenburgh, Cornelius Van Buren, John Fonda, Ed. Hogg, and Lawrence Rysdorf.

[18] 2 Ref. Prot. D., Free Dutch.

[19] Named from Peter Simmons, one of the first settlers.

selaer Mills," contains 40 houses, and **Petersburgh Four Corners** (p. v.) 12. The first settlers were Dutch, who came in about 1750, as tenants under Van Rensselaer.[1] A few years later, many families came in from Rhode Island. The census reports 3 churches.[2]

PITTSTOWN—was erected as a township by patent, July 23, 1761, and was formed as a town, March 7, 1788. Its boundary was changed Feb. 14, 1793. It lies in the center of the N. part of the co. Its surface is mountainous in the S. and E. and declines into a moderately hilly region in the N. The highest summits, in the S. E., are 800 to 1,000 feet above tide. The soil is principally a gravelly and slaty loam. Flax is extensively cultivated,[3] and there are several manufactories in town.[4] **Johnsonville** (p. v.) contains 35 houses, **Tomhannock** (p. v.) 40, **Raymertown** (p. v.) 27, **Pittstown Corners** (Pittstown p. o.) 22, **Boynton** 20, **Pittstown Station** (Valley Falls p. o.) 16, **North Pittstown** 20, and **Cooksborough** (Haynerville p. o.) 10. **Shermans Mills** is a hamlet. Settlement was commenced about 1650.[5] The first church (Bap.) was formed in 1784; Elder Isaac Webb was the first preacher.[6]

POESTENKILL[7]—named from its principal stream—was formed from Sand Lake, March 2, 1848. It lies near the center of the co., upon the western declivities of the Petersburgh Mts. The central and E. portions are rugged, rocky, and mountainous, and the soil is cold, sterile, and unproductive. The w. part is hilly, with a gravelly loam well adapted to pasturage. Snake Hill, near the center, is one of the principal elevations. Upon the Poesten Kil is a fall of about 80 feet. One mi. w. of the falls is a medicinal spring, with a local celebrity for the cure of eruptions and cutaneous diseases.[8] **Poestenkill** (p. v.) contains 300 inhabitants, **East Poestenkill** (p. o.) 10 houses, and **Barberville** 16. A union academy was formed in this town in 1854, but it is not under the regents. The census reports 4 churches.[9]

SAND LAKE—was formed from Greenbush and Berlin, June 19, 1812. A part of Greenbush was taken off in 1843, and Poestenkill in 1848. It lies a little S. of the center of the co. Its surface is mountainous in the E. and hilly in the w. Perigo Hill, in the N. E. corner, is 900 feet above tide, and Oak Hill, near the center, is but little less in height. The E. part of the town is mostly covered with forest.[10] Wynants Kil, flowing N. w. through the center, and Tsatsawassa Creek, in the E., are the principal streams. Along the valleys of these streams are several fine lakes, the principal of which are Sand, Glass, and Crooked Lakes, and Big Bowmans Pond. The soil among the mountains is a hard, sterile clay, but in the w. it is a good quality of gravelly loam. Three-fourths of a mi. E. of W. Sand Lake is a chalybeate spring. Large quantities of cordwood, charcoal, and tan bark are carried to the Troy and Albany markets. **Sand Lake** (p. v.) contains the Sand Lake Academy, a boarding school,[11] foundery, cotton warp factory, knitting mill, and 300 inhabitants. **West Sand Lake**[12] (p. v.) contains 300 inhabitants, **Sliters Corners** 106, and **Glass House** 200,[13] **South Sand Lake** is a p. o. Settlement commenced before the Revolution.[14] The census reports 7 churches in town.[15]

SCHAGHTICOKE[16]—was formed as a district, March 24, 1772, and as a town, March 7, 1788. Pittstown was taken off, March 7, 1788, and a part of Lansingburgh in 1819. It lies on the Hudson, in the N. w. corner of the co. The surface is principally a rolling upland, about 200 feet above the river. The summits of the hills in the S. are 800 feet above tide. Hoosick River,

---

[1] Among the early settlers were Wm. Prendergast, John Brimmer, Jacob and Godfrey Brimmer, John Spencer, Hans and Peter Bachus, Johannes Ruyter, Henry Litcher, Hans Lautman, Barent Hogg, Jacob Best, Petrus Vosburg, Bastian Deel, Frans. Burn, Juriah Kreiger, Henry Young, Schoolmaster Watson, and Long Andries. John Spencer built a log gristmill before the Revolution, at S. Petersburgh; and Barber & Murray built a carding mill about 1800. Several of the settlers were killed or taken prisoners during the French War,—probably by the same party that destroyed the Hoosick settlements in 1754.

[2] 2 M. E., Seventh Day Bap.

[3] The census of 1855 reports that, in 1854, more than 250,000 lbs. of flax and 7000 bush. of flaxseed were raised, and that there were 13 flax mills in town.

[4] There are two manufactories of cotton bags at Shermans Mills, a paper mill at Valley Falls, and manufactories of cordage and axes at Johnsonville.

[5] Wm. Prendergast, Stephen Hunt, and Edmund Aiken were among the first settlers near Johnsonville; Ludovicus Viele at Valley Falls, in 1772; and Christian Fisher and Michael Vandercook at Cooksborough. In 1770, Wm. Shepard (from New England) settled on 500 acres; in 1778–80, Benj. Aiken (from Dutchess co.) on 950 acres: and in 1785, Alex. Thompson, on 500 acres. Wm. Hammond kept a school at N. Pittstown in 1785, and Rebecca Thompson at Shermans Mills in 1789.

[6] The census reports 15 churches; 6 M. E., 3 Presb., 2 Christian, Bap., Ev. Luth., Friends, Union.

[7] Pronounced "Poos-ten-kill." It is a Dutch word, signifying "puffing or foaming creek."

[8] A bathing establishment erected here was swept away by a freshet.   [9] Bap., F. W. Bap., Disciple, and Ev. Luth.

[10] This town is a favorite resort of hunting and fishing parties.

[11] The Sand Lake Collegiate Institute was established in 1855 by Wm. H. Schram.

[12] Formerly called "*Ulinesville*," from Bernard Uline, who built the first house. His son, of the same name, was first innkeeper.

[13] This village was formerly the seat of an extensive glass factory, and was called "*Rensselaer Village*." The company was organized in 1805, incorp. in 1806, and discontinued in 1852. In 1813 100 men were employed by the co.

[14] Among the early settlers were Abram Frere, Nicholas Fellows, Andreas Barent, Fred. Shaver, Abram Bristol, Eph. Quinby, John Carmichael, Andreas Weatherwax, and Stephen Miller. Joshua Lockwood and Wm. Carpenter built the first grist mill in 1768, at W. Sand Lake.

[15] 2 M. E., 2 Ev. Luth., Ger. Meth., Bap., Presb.

[16] Pron. "Skat-i-kook." In old documents it is variously spelled "Schetekoke," "Schactekoke," "Scahwahook," and "Schagcogue." It is said to be an Algonquin word, signifying "landslide." The Stockbridge Indians called it "Pah-ha-koke."

flowing through the N. part, is bordered on a portion of its course by steep banks 200 feet high. On this stream, at the mouth of Tomhannock Creek, is a beautiful circular valley, three-fourths of a mi. in circumference, and bounded on nearly every side by steep hills.[1] The soil is generally a fertile, sandy or gravelly loam. Considerable manufacturing is carried on in town.[2] **Schaghticoke Point** (Schaghticoke p. o.) contains a pop. of 1148. **Schaghticoke Hill** contains 25 houses, **The Borough** 8, **Junction** (p. v.) 17, and **Old Schaghticoke** 6. About 1670, Gov. Andros settled a remnant of the Pequots and other Eastern tribes, under the name of "Schaghticokes," in this town, on land given them by the Mohawks, as a barrier against the Northern Indians.[3] By the charter of 1686 the city of Albany was allowed to purchase of the natives 500 acres of land in this town; but, neglecting to do so, Hendrick Van Rensselaer obtained the same privilege in 1698. He sold his right to the city the next year, and in 1707 an Indian deed was obtained for a tract 6 mi. square, mostly within the limits of this town. In Oct. 1709, the city conveyed the land to actual settlers.[4] The early settlements suffered greatly from Indian hostilities. A fort was built in 1746 at Old Schaghticoke and garrisoned by 2 companies of soldiers. The whole settlement was abandoned on the approach of Burgoyne; but, through the influence of the royalists, the place was not burned, though held for some time by the British and Hessian outposts.[5] The Schaghticoke Seminary was incorp. May 4, 1836. The first church (Ref. Prot. D.) was formed in 1714.[6]

SCHODACK[7]—was formed March 17, 1795, at the time of the division of "*Rensselaerwyck;*"[8] parts of Berlin and Nassau were taken off in 1806. It lies upon the Hudson, in the S. W. corner of the co. From the river the surface rises in a series of bluffs 200 feet high, from the summits of which it spreads out into an undulating upland inclined toward the w. Bunker Hill, the highest point, is about 500 feet above tide. The surface is intersected by numerous deep gulleys of small streams. The principal streams are Vierdee Kil,[9] Moordeners Kil,[10] Vlockie Kil, Muitzes (Mitch-es) Kil, and Valatie (Vola-she) Kil.[11] The soil in the E. is clay, and in the w. a fertile, sandy and gravelly loam. **Castleton**[12] (p. v.) is a fine village upon the Hudson. Pop. 431. **Schodack Landing** (p. v.) contains 250 inhabitants, **Muitzes Kill** 20 houses, **Schodack Depot** (p. v.) 18, **East Schodack** (p. v.) 15, and **Bunker Hill** 9. **Schodack Center** and **South Schodack** are p. offices. This vicinity seems to have been thickly inhabited by native tribes at the time of Hudson's visit in 1609.[13] The first settlements were made by tenants under Van Rensselaer. Over 40 settlers are mentioned in Bleeker's survey of 1767.[14] The census reports 7 churches.[15]

STEPHENTOWN[16]—was formed from "*Rensselaerwyck*," March 29, 1784. Petersburgh was taken off in 1791, and parts of Berlin and Nassau in 1806. It lies in the S. E. corner of the co. Its surface consists of 2 rocky mountain ranges separated by the valley of Kinderhook Creek. The highest summits are about 1800 feet above tide. The principal peaks are Round Mt., and Whitney and Butternut Hills, E. of the valley, and Brockway Hill and Webster Mt. w. A con-

---

[1] A small stream called the Dwaas Kil (stream running both ways) flows from the Hudson into the mouth of the Hoosick. When Hoosick River suddenly rises, the current of this stream is often changed; and it is not uncommon to see it running N. in the morning and s. at night.—*Fitch's Ag. Surv. Wash. Co.,* 1849, *p.* 939.

[2] The manufactures consist of cotton and linen goods, flax, powder, plaster, and agricultural implements.

[3] A portion of these removed to Kent, Conn., in 1728, and the remainder, numbering 400, joined the French in Canada.

[4] These were Johan de Wandelaer, Jr., John Heermans Vischer, Corset Voeder, Daniel Kittlehuyn, Johan Knickerbacker, Louis Viele, and Derick Van Veghten, who went there to reside, and were joined soon after by Martin de Lamont, Wouter Quackenbosch, Peter Yates, David Schuyler, Wouter Groesbeck, Philip Livingston, Ignace Kip, Cornelius Vandenberg, and many others, whose descendants still reside in the vicinity.

[5] Col. John Knickerbacker, of this town, raised a regiment during the Revolution.

[6] A new church was built in 1760, and Rev. Elias Bunschooten was installed pastor. This quaint edifice was 60 by 40 feet, with low side walls and a high pitched mansard roof and turret, surmounted by a weathercock over the southern gable. There was no burial ground attached, and the oldest is that of the Knickerbacker family, on the site of an Indian cemetery. The first European burial occurred in 1715. A few rods S. E. of this spot is the "Wittenagemote," or "Council Tree," a remarkably vigorous and symmetrical oak, more than 15 feet in circumference. The census reports 8 churches; 2 Ev. Luth., 3 M. E., 1 Presb., 1 Ref. Prot. D., and 1 R. C.

[7] Sometimes written "Shodac" or "Schoddack."

[8] A confirmatory act of incorporation was passed March 17, 1795.

[9] "Fourth Creek," reckoned from Albany.

[10] "Murderers Kil," from an obstinate battle fought between the settlers and a band of robbers at an early day, (traditional.)

[11] "Little Fall Creek." Another small creek in town is named Adams Killetye, (Little Creek,) from Adam Moll, who was taken prisoner by the Indians while drinking of its waters.

[12] Named from an ancient Indian castle on the adjacent hills. It was first settled in 1792, and incorp. April 13, 1827. Formerly called "*Morriches Hastie.*"

[13] "On the evening of the 15th he arrived opposite the mountains which lie from the river side, where he found 'a very loving people and very old men,' and the day following reached the spot hereafter to be honored by his own illustrious name. One day more wafts him up between Schodac and Castleton; and here he landed and passed a day with the natives, greeted with all sorts of barbarous hospitality; the land 'the finest for cultivation he ever set foot on;' the natives so kind and gentle that when they found he would not remain with them over night, and feared that he left them—poor children of nature!—because he was afraid of their weapons,—he, whose quarterdeck was heavy with ordnance!—they 'broke their arrows in pieces and threw them in the fire.'"—*Everett's Address, Inauguration Dudley Observatory, p.* 54.

[14] Among the names of the early settlers are Van Buren, Barhudt, Van Valkenburgh, Springsteen, Schermerhorn, Janze, Ketel, Poel, Miller, Schevers, Lodwick, Huyck, Beekman, Mills, Molls, Salsberg, Witbeck, and Nolton. The first mill was built before the Revolution, below Castleton. —— Barhydt kept the first inn, in 1778. A carding mill was erected on Muitzes Kil in 1800.

[15] 3 Ref. Prot. D., 2 M. E., Bap., and Ev. Luth.

[16] Named from Stephen Van Rensselaer.

siderable portion of the town is covered with forest. The principal streams are Kinderhook and East Creeks, Black River, and Black and Roaring Brooks. The soil is hard and sterile among the mountains, but a gravelly loam in the valleys. **Stephentown** (p. v.) contains 15 houses. **Stephentown Flats** contains a cotton wadding and batting factory, a machine shop, and about 20 houses. **North Stephentown, South Stephentown,** and **West Stephentown** are p. offices. Settlement was commenced here in 1766.[1] The first church (Bap.) formed in 1782, under Rev. Justus Hall. Rev. Robt. Miles was the first pastor.[2]

TROY CITY—was formed as a town from "*Rensselaer-wyck*," March 18, 1791. Brunswick, and parts of Grafton and Lansingburgh, were taken off March 20, 1807, and a part of Greenbush in 1836. A part of Brunswick was annexed in 1814. The first village charter was passed in 1791;[3] and another Feb. 16, 1798. The village was formally incorp. by acts passed April 2, 1801, and April 9, 1805. The city charter was granted April 12, 1816. A portion of Lansingburgh was annexed May 4, 1836. It lies upon the Hudson, near the center of the w. border of the co. Its surface comprises the alluvial flat, three-fourths of a mile wide, upon the river, and the high bluffs which border it on the E. The high land immediately E. of the city is known as Mt. Ida, and that on the N. E. as Mt. Olympus. Mt. Ida is principally clay, and has been the scene of several destructive landslides. Poesten Kil and Wynants Kil both break through these hills in narrow ravines and in a series of cascades, forming an excellent water power.

The first religious meetings were held in a store, and afterward in a schoolhouse, about 1785. The first framed house of worship was erected in 1791, now the First Presb. Church ; Rev. Jonas Coe, of Lansingburgh, was the first pastor. There are now 33 churches in the city.[4]

The *Public Schools* are under the charge of 20 commissioners, elected for two years.[5] In 1857 the city was divided into 25 school districts, and employed 76 teachers,—14 males and 62 females. The number of children, between 4 and 21, was 11,200, of which 7228, or 63 per cent., attended the public schools during some portion of the year.[6]

The *Troy Academy*, incorp. May 5, 1834, and received under the regents Feb. 5, 1839, is located near the center of the city.

The *Troy Female Seminary*,[7] situated on Second Street, between Congress and Ferry Sts., was first established at Middlebury, Vt., in 1813, removed to Waterford in 1819, and to Troy in 1821. It was incorp. May 6, 1837, and received under the regents Jan. 30, 1838. It has gained a national reputation under the charge of Mrs. Emma Willard.

The *Rensselaer Polytechnic Institute*,[8] endowed by Stephen Van Rensselaer, is situated near the head of State St. It was organized in 1824. It was formed for the purpose of teaching the application of mathematics to civil engineering and the natural sciences. It numbers 14 professors and has about 100 students. Next to West Point, this institute has the best reputation, in its special departments, of any school in America.

The *Troy Lyceum of Natural History* was incorp. March 7, 1820. Its cabinet and library are kept in the Troy University.

The *Troy University*[9] is located upon Mt. Ida, a beautiful situati overlooking the city and valley. It is under the charge of the M. E. denomination, and w opened in 1859.

St. Peter's College[10] is under the charge of the R. C. denomination, and is not yet fully organized.

---

[1] Asa Douglas, his son Wm., and his grandson Benj., Nathan Rose, Elnathan Sweet, and Joseph Rogers, settled near the center of the town, Joshua Gardiner in the E. part, Edward Carr near Kinderhook Creek, John Mills, —— Husted, —— Lewis, —— Berry, and others, toward the N. part. The first inhabitants were chiefly from Rhode Island. Wm., grandson of Asa Douglas, was the first child born in town; and he married the first white female born in town. Hon. Stephen A. Douglas is a descendant of the first settler of this town.

[2] The census reports 5 churches; 2 F. W. Bap., Bap., Christ. Cong., and Presb.

[3] The first trustees named in the act of incorp. were Jacob D. Vanderheyden, Benj. Covill, Anthony Goodspeed, John Pease, Ephraim Morgan, Chris. Hutton, and Saml. Gale.

[4] Of these there are 7 M. E., 5 Presb., 4 Prot. E., 3 Bap., 3 R. C., 2 Wes. Meth., 2 Asso. Presb., Ger. Mission, Unit., Univ., Cong., Friends, Disciples, and Jews.

[5] A Lancasterian school was established here at an early period, and continued until superseded by a special school system. The present school law was passed April 4, 1849.

[6] The total receipts and expenditures for 1857 were $38,074 35.

[7] More than 7000 pupils have been educated here, a large number of whom have become teachers. See p. 742.

[8] Rev. Saml. Blatchford was its first President, and Amos Eaton its first senior prof., under whom the school obtained a high and merited reputation.

[9] The grounds of this institution cover 36 acres. The main building is in the Byzantine style of architecture, and is 259 feet long on an average 58 feet broad, and 4 stories high. See p. 741.

[10] The college building, in process of erection, was destroyed by a landslide, March 17, 1859, and is being rebuilt on Mt. St. Vincent.

VIEW OF TROY.

FROM WATERVLIET ARSENAL.

St. Joseph Academy, under the charge of the R. C., was founded, in 1842, as a free school. In 1852 it was enlarged, and a boarding house was annexed.

The *Troy Hospital,* a charitable institution, was incorp. March 1, 1851. It was founded chiefly through the exertions of Rev. P. Havermans, and is supported by the R. C. denomination. The nurses belong to the Sisters of Charity.

Marshall Infirmary was incorp. in 1851. It was founded by Benjamin Marshall. The builling and grounds cost $35,000; which sum was donated by its founder.

Troy Orphan Asylum, incorp. April 10, 1835, is situated on Grand Division between 7th and 8th Streets. The building is of brick, and has about 100 inmates. The Asylum is supported by donations and State appropriations; and children are received between the ages of 3 and 9, and dismissed at 10 if an opportunity offers. At this age they are indentured to farmers until the age of 17. During the first 22 years over 500 had been dismissed; and most of them have since filled respectable stations in life. A school is maintained regularly in the Asylum.

St. Marys Orphan Asylum is an institution connected with St. Marys Church, (R. C.) The male department is under the charge of the "The Brothers of the Christian Schools," and the female, of "The Sisters of Charity."

The *Warren Free Institute,* a school for indigent female children, was incorp. March 19, 1846. It was founded and endowed by the Warren family. A free church, (Prot. E. Church of the Holy Cross,) for the pupils and their parents, is connected with the Institute.

The Troy Water Works were built by the city in 1833–34, and they have been subsequently extended. The water is drawn from Piscawin Creek, and the reservoir is sufficiently high to throw the water to the top of most of the houses. The works are under the charge of water commissioners, and the rents are charged to property owners and collected with the taxes.

The city is 150 miles from New York, with which it is connected by R. R., and, in the season of navigation, by lines of steamers. Its commerce is extensive, and it has a large trade with the region N. and E. The Union R. R. Co. have erected a magnificent depôt in the central part of the city for the accommodation of the various lines of roads that center here.[1]

The manufactures of Troy are extensive and various.[2] Wynants Kil, on the s., furnishes 12 mill sites, with an aggregate of 2000 horse power; Poesten Kil, on the N., has 10 sites, equivalent to 1000 horse power, and the dam across the Hudson furnishes 4000 horse power. Besides these there is an immense amount of steam power in use.

In 1720, Derick Vanderheyden[3] acquired from Van Rensselaer the title to 490 acres of land, now included in Troy, at an annual rent of 3¾ bush. of wheat and 4 fat fowls.[4] The tract was occupied as a farm until about 1786, when a company of New Englanders induced the owners to lay it out as a town. It was surveyed between 1786 and '90, and was variously known as *"Ferry Hook," "Vanderheydens Ferry,"* and *"Ashleys Ferry."* In the spring of 1789 the place contained 5 small stores and about a dozen dwellings. The name, Troy, was adopted at a meeting of the freeholders, Jan. 5, 1789. The first settlers came in soon after the war.[5] The completion of the Erie Canal gave an impulse to this place that speedily raised it from a comparatively obscure village to a large and important city.[6] Several destructive fires have occurred, occasioning great losses.[7]

---

[1] The Troy Union R. R., 214 mi. long, was built by a company, composed of persons chosen by, and representing the interests of, the Hudson R., N. Y. Central, Troy & Boston, and Rensselaer & Saratoga R. Rs. The depôt, built in 1853–54, is 400 by 150 feet, walls 27 feet, and roof a single arch, (Briggs's patent,) supported only by the walls. It is built for 10, and has 7, parallel tracks its entire length. Tower, 115 feet high. Four complete suites of rooms and offices.

[2] The iron manufactures consist of R. R. iron, rolled iron, spikes, nails, stoves, firearms, malleable iron, steam engines, safes, agricultural implements, &c. The business is carried on by more than 30 firms, and gives employment to 2500 men. The Troy nail works are among the most extensive in America. Besides these, there are 6 large flouring mills, 3 grist mills, several breweries and distilleries, and establishments for the manufacture of cotton and woolen goods, hosiery, paper, carriages, clothing, &c., in the aggregate employing about 7000 hands. One establishment for the manufacture of shirts, bosoms, and collars employs 670 hands; 3 others employ 1070 hands, and 17 others 2750 hands. The most extensive mathematical instrument manufactory in the U. S. is located in this city.

[3] A descendant of his was known as the "Patroon of Troy."

[4] Brandt Van Slechtenhorst, director of the "Colonie of Rensselaerwyck," in 1646, purchased for the Patroon two additional tracts of land E. of the Hudson: one, called "Paanpaack," (Field of Corn,) included the site of Troy; and the other, called Panhoosick, farther N.—*Brodhead's Hist. of N. Y.,* pp. 420–534.

[5] The upper part of the city belonged to Jacob Vanderheyden, and the southern to Matthias Vanderheyden. Stephen Ashley and Benjamin Covill were the earliest settlers under the Vanderheydens. They came in about 1786; and the former kept an inn in the old farmhouse of Matthias Vanderheyden for several years. Dr. Saml. Gale, the first physician, came from Guilford, Conn., in 1787. Among the other early settlers were Eph. Morgan, John Boardman, Benj. Smith, Phil. Heartt, Anthony Goodspeed, Mahlon Taylor, Eben'r and Saml. Wilson, Moses Vail, Lewis Richards, Eben'r Jones, Howard Moulton, Amasa Pierce, Jere'h Pierce, Townsend McCoun, Nathan and Steph. Warren, David Buel, and Benj., John, Saml., and Wm. Gale.

[6] The following table shows the increase of the population of Troy for each semi-decade since 1810:—

1810	3,895	1835	16,959
1815	4,841	1840	19,334
1820	5,264	1845	21,709
1825	7,859	1850	28,785
1830	11,556	1855	33,269

[7] The fire of June 20, 1820, destroyed property to the amount of $370,000, and another, Aug. 25, 1854, to the amount of $1,000,000.

Acres of Land, Valuation, Population, Dwellings, Families, Freeholders, Schools, Live Stock, Agricultural Products, and Domestic Manufactures, of Rensselaer County.

Names of Towns.	Acres of Land.		Valuation of 1858.			Population.		No. of Dwellings.	No. of Families.	Freeholders.	Schools.	
	Improved.	Unimproved.	Real Estate.	Personal Property.	Total.	Males.	Females.				No. of Districts.	Children taught.
Berlin	19,437½	16,759	$216,880	$20,050	$236,930	1,089	1,078	397	455	289	10	773
Brunswick	23,512½	4,264	1,050,195	166,119	1,216,314	1,533	1,568	499	570	370	15	1,132
East Greenbush	11,674	2,789½	788,175	111,469	899,644	829	777	286	227	131	6	431
Grafton	15,122½	13,017½	196,427	35,337	231,764	962	926	343	370	254	12	771
Greenbush			841,555	11,100	852,655	1,642	1,661	324	709	299	2	1,374
Hoosick	31,341	8,339	1,374,017	199,877	1,573,894	2,029	2,091	658	736	327	19	1,563
Lansingburgh	3,672½	1,212½	1,012,859	811,713	1,824,572	2,697	3,003	901	1,120	391	3	2,113
Nassau	20,281½	5,754	530,010	156,467	686,477	1,470	1,530	576	587	423	16	1,187
North Greenbush	10,374	2,181	744,020	106,800	850,820	901	911	309	358	137	8	2,217
Petersburgh	17,075	7,388	203,344	28,622	231,966	809	854	316	313	192	12	640
Pittstown	33,857⅞	6,311	1,061,327	237,368	1,298,695	1,762	1,840	652	707	497	18	1,163
Poestenkill	14,206	4,247	255,495	36,332	291,827	965	913	399	403	223	8	710
Sand Lake	15,268½	6,696	356,385	57,805	414,190	1,251	1,337	465	522	291	11	966
Schaghticoke	21,979	4,474	916,133	168,093	1,084,226	1,660	1,643	498	608	318	19	1,217
Schodack	31,531	8,039½	1,623,825	239,786	1,863,611	1,978	1,859	672	757	512	13	1,177
Stephentown	20,982	9,404	258,235	39,150	297,385	1,188	1,209	431	481	323	17	882
Troy City	1,898	126½	7,919,570	4,891,675	12,811,245	16,223	17,046	3,757	6,495	1,482	24	11,428
Total	292,212⅞	101,002½	19,348,452	7,317,763	26,666,215	38,988	40,246	11,683	15,418	6,459	213	29,744

Names of Towns.	Live Stock.					Agricultural Products.							Domestic Cloths in yards.
						Bush. of Grain.					Dairy Products.		
	Horses.	Working Oxen and Calves.	Cows.	Sheep.	Swine.	Winter.	Spring.	Tons of Hay.	Bushels of Potatoes.	Bushels of Apples.	Pounds Butter.	Pounds Cheese.	
Berlin	449	676	1,187	3,630	765	760	38,638	3,280	25,370	15,375	59,071	250,646	296
Brunswick	973	813	1,538	1,269	2,567	36,360	107,400	5,082½	88,688	11,232	112,757	125	454
East Greenbush	492	501	1,101	632	1,128	17,350	47,234	3,469	48,361	4,990	53,765		534
Grafton	368	785	734	1,017	537	728	18,726	3,461¾	25,750	4,780	65,209	4,070	354
Greenbush													
Hoosick	863	1,455	1,243	22,394	2,574	14,305	132,088½	6,356	33,671	5,694	69,325	36,590	299
Lansingburgh	314	178	290	651	690	8,439	20,285	759	9,605	1,550	10,173		
Nassau	644	1,176	1,188	3,458	1,838	22,242	57,110	3,803½	24,135	12,634	124,100	8,725	978
North Greenbush	445	304	999	252	863	19,789	40,265	2,715½	56,125	3,959	64,590		
Petersburgh	505	780	770	5,708	828	627	43,222	2,861	22,643	10,338	45,543	82,820	
Pittstown	1,050	1,504	1,772	11,340	2,983	35,004	157,037	6,630	47,924	6,757	158,529	29,516	361
Poestenkill	428	541	667	804	878	10,238	30,741	2,530	37,261	4,896	65,305	2,780	715
Sand Lake	535	646	997	742	1,218	16,063	41,884	3,224	35,882	10,593	90,848	1,072	333
Schaghticoke	712	1,255	1,137	5,910	3,064	55,055	149,529	3,247½	61,860	4,740	95,098		
Schodack	1,036	935	1,575	3,977	3,111	60,203	106,182½	6,097	43,224	17,682	161,530	3,563	585
Stephentown	472	1,104	1,305	2,707	956	4,071	41,034	4,751	24,716	15,611	107,940	118,555	40
Troy City	898	84	361	118	1,007	1,288	6,979	290	11,344	410	7,955		
Total	10,184	12,737	16,864	64,609	25,007	302,522	1,038,355	58,557¾	596,559	131,241	1,291,738	538,462	4,949

RICHMOND COUNTY.

This county[1] was organized Nov. 1, 1683. It includes Staten Island,[2] Shooters Island,[3] and the islands of the meadow in Staten Island Sound. It is separated from Long Island by New York Bay, the Narrows,[4] and New York Harbor; from Bergen, N. J., by the Kil Van Kull; and from N. J. on the w. by the Arthur Kil, or Staten Island Sound.[5] Staten Island is nearly oval-shaped, its longest diameter extending N. E. and S. W. It is 14 mi. long by 8 broad, has an area of 58½ sq. mi., and is centrally distant 146 mi. from Albany. Princess Bay and Great Kils are small bays upon the S. shore. Fresh Kils is a tidal estuary extending about 3 mi. inland from Staten Island Sound, and during high tide it is navigable nearly its whole extent. The surface of the co. is mostly level or gently undulating. A broad range of hills extends from the Narrows across the island, terminating between the branches of the Fresh Kils. Near Tompkinsville these hills attain an elevation of 310 ft. They are composed of granitic rock upon the N. slope and steatitic rock and serpentine upon the S. Hematitic iron ore[6] and many other interesting minerals are found in the co.[7] Along the Fresh Kils, and along Staten Island Sound, in Northfield, and also around the head of Great Kils and the mouth of New Creek, are extensive salt meadows. The waters of the sound and the bays adjacent to the island abound in oysters; and the oyster trade is the principal industrial pursuit of those inhabitants not engaged in business in New York, Brooklyn, or Jersey City. The right of taking oysters belongs to the owners of the adjoining banks.[8] At Port Richmond, Factoryville, and other places along the N. shore, are extensive manufactories.[9] Market gardening is followed to a limited extent, chiefly to supply the home demand. The erection of forts, hospitals, and other public establishments of the General and State Governments has given employment to great numbers of persons and caused the expenditure among the people of the co. of large sums of money. Since the establishment of regular steam ferries,[10] many wealthy citizens engaged in business in New York City have erected residences upon the island. These country seats are mostly upon the N. shore and upon the heights that overlook the bay and sound. All the villages along the N. shore are lighted by gas furnished by the Richmond Gas Light Works, located near the Quarantine. A company was incorp. in 1836 to build a R. R. across the island to connect with the Camden & Amboy R. R.[11]

The co. seat is located at Richmond.[12] A courthouse and jail, in the same building, was erected pursuant to the act of March 23, 1837, at a cost of $10,000.[13] The co. clerk's office was erected in

---

[1] Named from a natural son of Charles II.

[2] Staten Island was so named by Hudson. The Indian name is "*Matanucke*," "*Monocknong*," or "*Aquehonga Manacknong*."— *Coll. N. J. Hist. Soc.*, I. 17; *N. Y. Common Council Manual*, 1857, p. 545.

[3] A small island at the entrance of Newark Bay.

[4] The width of the Narrows opposite Fort Hamilton, where they are the narrowest, is about 2600 yds., and opposite the Quarantine it is 3700 yds.

[5] The average breadth of Staten Island Sound is about one-third of a mile. It is not usually closed by ice, although in severe winters it has been frozen many weeks together. It is the ordinary route of steamers of the Camden & Amboy R. R. Co.

[6] This ore has a fibrous texture, and is found in botryoidal forms, often with black polished surfaces, and in the granular condition it is known as "shot ore." It is said to be abundant. A gray ore is also found. These ores have never been smelted on the island.

[7] The minerals of the co., beside iron ore, are red and yellow ochre, asbestus, amianthus, marmolite, hydrate and carbonate of magnesia, sulphuret and chromate of iron, quartz, chalcedony, feldspar, and lignite.

[8] This right is often leased. The average annual rent is 75 cts. per ft., measured along the shore. By an act passed May 9, 1846, the taking of oysters from the planted grounds of another is prohibited, under a penalty of $50 for each offense.

[9] The principal articles manufactured are dyed stuffs, and prints, common fire brick, adamantine candles, white lead, and ivory black. A large amount of lager beer is made in Castleton and Southfield, and the island has of late become a Sabbath day resort of the German population of N. Y. City, thousands of whom repair every Sunday to the saloons and gardens attached to the breweries.

[10] The boats of the Staten Island & New York Ferry Co. ply hourly between Whitehall St., in New York, and the island, touching at Port Richmond, Factoryville, New Brighton, Quarantine, Stapleton, and Vanderbilts Landing. This company was organized Oct. 26, 1853, with a capital of $900,000, and now has 7 boats in constant use.

[11] This enterprise was recently revived, and a route surveyed running S. of the hills from Vanderbilts Landing to a point opposite S. Amboy. About $40,000 were expended in purchasing the right of way and grading; but the work is at present suspended.

[12] The first record of an order for the erection of a prison is dated March 4, 1710. It runs as follows:—"Ordered that Mr. Lambart Garisone and Mr. Wm. Tillyer see the prison house built at Cuckols Towne. Ye Demensions Twelve ffot in breadth, ffourteen foot Long, two story high, six foot ye Low Roome from beam to plank, and the uper story, 6 foot: and all to be built with stone." This building was inadequate to the requirements of the co., and a larger one (of brick) was afterward built. The latter building is still standing, and was used as a co. prison until 1837. The first colonial Court of Sessions on Staten Island was held Oct. 4, 1680. The first court after the Revolution convened May 3, 1784; and the first court of Oyer and Terminer under the State Government was held May 22, 1787, Richard Morris, Chief Justice, presiding. The first co. officers under the State Government were David Mersereau, *First Judge*; Cornelius Mersereau, Hendrick Garrison, Peter Rezeau, Anthony Fountain, John Wandle, Gilbert Jackson, and Lambert Merrill, *Judges and Justices*; Abram Bancker, *Sheriff*; John Mersereau, *Clerk*; and Adrian Bancker, *Surrogate*.

[13] The commissioners under whose supervision this building was erected were Richard D. Little, Harman B. Cropsey, and Walter Betts. The jail is reported as without ventilation or means for the classification of prisoners.

1848 and enlarged in 1857. It is a 2 story brick building, and contains the supervisor's room, office for the surrogate and district attorney, and accommodations for the sheriff. The poorhouse is located upon a farm of 105 acres in Northfield.[1] Several of the public schools of Castleton and Southfield have been organized as union schools under a special act, and are in charge of a board of education. The schools of the co. generally are in a flourishing condition.[2] Richmond co. is within the jurisdiction of the Metropolitan Police Commissioners; but no men have hitherto been detailed for ordinary service within its limits.

Two newspapers are published in the co.[3]

Staten Island was visited by Henry Hudson in his celebrated voyage of discovery in 1609. It was purchased from the Indians, Aug. 10, 1630, by Michael Pauw, one of the 4 Patroons of New Netherlands, and formed a part of the tract known as "*Pavonia*" in the early Dutch records.[4] It soon reverted, however, to the West India Co.; and in 1636 a part of the island was granted to D. P. De Vries, by whom a colony was planted upon it in Jan. 1639. The remaining part of the island was granted by the Directors of the West India Co. to Cornelius Melyn in July, 1640. The following year, Melyn with his family settled upon this grant, and in June, 1642, he obtained letters patent. In Sept. 1641, the settlement of De Vries was attacked by the Indians,[5] and hostilities between them and the whites ensued. A peace was concluded in 1642; but in Feb. 1643, under a frivolous pretext, the Indians were attacked opposite Manhattan and at Corlaers Hook and great numbers of them slain. This barbarous measure invoked retaliation, and the white settlements within reach were laid waste. The island was again purchased of the natives, Dec. 6, 1651, by Augustine Herman, and finally quitclaimed to Gov. Lovelace, April 13, 1670.[6] Possession was given on the 1st of May following, and at this time the island was finally abandoned by its primitive inhabitants.

A considerable number of French Huguenots, after the revocation of the Edict of Nantes in 1685, found their way into the English colonies, and a part of them settled upon Staten Island. The family names of these immigrants are still common in this co.[7] The earliest grants upon the island under the English were made to the officers of the ship Elias, immediately after the conquest.[8] Two manors were subsequently granted,—one on the N. shore, styled "*Cassiltown Manor*," to Gov. Dongan,[9] and the other in the s. part, known as "*Billop Manor*." This island was first occupied by British troops in the Revolution, July 4, 1776, and it was held by them until their final removal from the State late in 1783. On the 21st of Aug. 1777, the British posts upon the island were attacked by an American force under Gen. Sullivan. The expedition was well planned, but it failed to accomplish its main object.[10] During the severe winter of 1779–80, while the Americans were encamped near Morristown, (N. J.,) a second expedition was sent out, under Gen. Lord Stirling, to surprise the enemy in the interior of the island. The party, consisting of 2500 men, crossed the sound on the ice from Deharts Point, on the Jersey shore, on the morning of the 15th of Jan.; but the movement was observed in time to prepare for defense. Contrary to expectation, the passage to New York was found to be free from ice, and during the day the British were reinforced from the city. Two or three were killed on each side, and a few prisoners were taken by the Americans. While the party remained, some persons from the mainland passed over and plundered several of the inhabitants; but a strict search was made and the stolen property was recovered and restored to its owners.[11] On the 11th of

[1] The county house consists of 2 stone buildings, each 2 stories high. The Senate Com., in their report of 1857, say that it is "without ventilation and without any provisions for bathing; and a general survey of the house, with its fixtures, as you approach it, is entirely in harmony with its name." The average number of inmates is 80, who are supported at a weekly cost of $1 each. The farm yields an annual revenue of $3000.

[2] In 1817, efforts were made by Gov. Tompkins and other residents to establish a college upon the island. A provisional charter was obtained from the regents, under the name of "*Washington College*," and a subscription of $10,000 for a site and $5,000 for a library was secured. The effort failed; and it was afterward proposed to unite the institution with Columbia College,—but without success. An act was passed, April 18, 1838, incorporating "*Richmond College*" upon condition that $80,000 be raised within 2 years; but the effort failed.

[3] *The Richmond Republican* was established at Tompkinsville in 1828 by C. N. Baldwin, and continued 2 years.
The Richmond Co. Free Press was started at Richmond in 1833 by Wm. Hagadorn, and continued 3 years.
The Staten Islander was established at Stapleton, as a weekly journal, in 1840, by F. L. Hagadorn, and is now published semi-weekly.
The Deutsche Staten Islander was commenced in 1855 at Stapleton by August Fries, but has since been discontinued.

The Staten Island Chronicle was started at Tompkinsville in 1858, and is still published.
[4] *Coll. N. J. Hist. Soc.*, I. 17; *Dunlap's Hist. N. Y.*, I., 48.
[5] *N. Y. Hist. Coll.*, I. 263.
[6] *N. Y. Com. Council Manual*, 1857, p. 544.
[7] Among these are Guion, Mersereau, Dissosway, Ryerss, Michean, Fontaine, Rezeau, Seguine, Crocheron, La Tourrette, &c.
[8] Oct. 4–10, 1684, to Capt. Wm. Hill, 500 acres; Lt. Humphrey Fox, 300; Jas. Coleman, 250; and 7 others, each 200,—*Patents, I. 6–9, Sec. Office;* Jacques Bandoven and Jacques Guion each received 200 acres at the same time.
[9] The greater part of the lands to which existing titles are traced were granted under Dongan's administration. The descendants of Gov. Dongan were living upon the original estate until the close of the last century. Between 30 and 40 grants of land from the colonial governors are upon record in the co. clerk's office.
[10] About 150 British prisoners were taken. The Americans lost 13 killed and 136 in prisoners, and the whole party ran a narrow risk of capture. Gen. Sullivan's conduct was subjected to a court of inquiry by order of Congress; but he was acquitted. A particular account of this affair is given in *Marshall's Life of Washington*, III. 135. See also *Sparks's Life and Writings of Washington*, V. 47, and *Peabody's Life of Sullivan*, 65.
[11] *Coll. N. J. Hist. Soc.*, II. 206; *Sparks's Life and Writings of Washington*, VI. 441–448.

Sept. 1776, a conference between Lord Wm. Howe and a committee of Congress consisting of Dr. Franklin, J. Adams, and E. Rutledge was held at the house of Capt. Billop, opposite Perth Amboy.[1] No events of special interest occurred upon the island during the late war with Great Britain. A brigade of militia, consisting of 2000 men, was stationed here, and remained in camp from Aug. to Dec. 1814. During the troubles that preceded the War of 1812, the Legislature of New York memorialized Congress for the erection of defensive works around the harbor of New York, claiming protection against the arms of a foreign power as no more than an equitable return for the revenues which the State had surrendered to the General Government upon the adoption of the Constitution.[2] Failing in this, the governor was directed to purchase a tract, not to exceed 25 acres, at the Narrows;[3] and upon this tract fortifications were afterward erected. The amount of the appropriation made by the State for the defenses upon Staten Island previous to 1820 was $154,105 46. These works were purchased by the General Government, pursuant to an act of Congress passed Aug. 3, 1846,[4] and they are now being rebuilt at an immense cost. When these and the other contemplated works along the approaches to New York Harbor are completed, the city will be among the best fortified in the world.[5] A quarantine was established by the State, under an act passed Feb. 25, 1799, upon the N. extremity of the island, in the town of Castleton, and maintained until it was destroyed, on the evenings of Sept. 1 and 2, 1858, by an armed mob encouraged and led by prominent citizens.[6]

CASTLETON—was first recognized as a town March 7, 1788. It lies in the N. part of the island, and is the smallest but most populous and wealthy town in the co. The surface is mostly hilly. The people are principally engaged in manufacturing. **Factoryville** (North Shore p. o.) is a populous village in the N. W. part of the town, containing extensive dye and print works[7] and other manufactories. **Elliottsville**[8] is a hamlet. A little E. of this place is the

[1] This conference terminated without any practical results. The old stone house in which it was held is still standing.—*Journal Cong., Sept.* 6–17, 1776; *Sparks's Washington, I.* 198.

[2] *Journal of Senate and Assembly, March* 27, 1807.

[3] Act of Feb. 3, 1810. The erections were chiefly made in 1814.

[4] These defenses consisted of Fort Richmond, a water battery near the water's edge; Fort Tompkins, a heavy fortress on the heights above, and Batteries Hudson and Morton. The last was named from Gen. Jacob Morton, of the N. Y. Artillery. In 1811, the removal of the U. S. Military Academy to this island was proposed, and the governor was empowered to convey to the General Government the jurisdiction of so much territory as might be necessary for this purpose. No further steps toward its removal have been taken.

[5] Additional land was bought in 1857 near Fort Tompkins, and this work is now about to be replaced by one of great strength, at an estimated cost of over $500,000. The aggregate of the appropriations made by the General Government for these works has been as follows: for Fort Richmond, $375,000; for Fort Tompkins, $192,300; for Batteries Hudson and Morton, $10,000. A new fort is to be erected upon Sandy Hook, (N. J.,) which it is estimated will cost $1,500,000, $250,000 of which has been appropriated. For an account of Fort Hamilton and the fortification of the inner harbor, see pp. 373,419. The recent defensive works and those now in progress were chiefly ordered upon the advice of Gen. Totten.

[6] In 1758 an act was passed to prevent the spread of infectious diseases, and a law of similar import was enacted May 4, 1784. By the act of May 4, 1794, Governors Island was assigned as a quarantine; and in March, 1797, a lazaretto was directed to be built upon Bedloes Island. The awful visitation of yellow fever in 1798 led to the passage of an act (Feb. 25, 1799) for the purchase of 30 acres upon Staten Island for a permanent quarantine. Of this lot 5 acres were sold, and ceded (April 1. 1800) to the U. S. for warehouses. The first buildings erected were of materials taken from the Lazaretto on Bedloes Island. In 1819 a long brick building was erected; in 1823, a fever hospital; in 1828–29, a smallpox hospital; and subsequently other buildings as the wants of the institution required. As the surrounding country became thickly settled, the same difficulty arose that led to the removal of quarantine from the vicinity of New York, and for many years an earnest desire had existed among the citizens of this island for its removal. Memorials for this object were met by remonstrances from the importers, and nothing was accomplished. In 1856 the yellow fever appeared, and 769 cases occurred, of which 538 were on Staten Island, between New Brighton and Clifton, 138 in Fort Hamilton and Bay Ridge, 64 on Governors Island, and 29 in Brooklyn. Of those upon Staten Island one-third were fatal. This alarming event convinced the public that new safeguards were necessary, and the citizens of this co. renewed their demand for the removal of the quarantine. An act for the removal of the "*Quarantine Station*" was passed, March 6, 1857, under which George Hall, Egbert Benson, and Obadiah Bowne were appointed commissioners to purchase a new site and erect the necessary buildings. The sum of $150,000 was fixed as the limit of expenditure under this act. After ineffectual efforts to obtain a site on Sandy Hook, the committee purchased a farm of 50 acres, late the property of Joel Wolfe, situated at Seguines Point, in Westfield. The sum paid was $23,000, and the land had upon it farm buildings valued at $15,000. The site was approved, and the purchase completed, May 1, 1857. On the night of the 5th of May all the buildings were burned to the ground by a mob of some 40 persons without disguise. Temporary buildings were erected on the site in June. An attack was made on the 12th of July by a few armed persons, and several shots were fired. The new buildings, consisting of two hospitals and a cook and wash house, were burned on the evening of April 26,1858, and no effort was made to rebuild them, or to bring the incendiaries to justice. The hostility against the old establishment continued unabated, and gained confidence from the approval of many of the leading citizens, some of whom declared their willingness to unite openly, by daylight and without disguise, to destroy the premises that they deemed an insufferable nuisance. In the summer of 1856 a barricade had been erected, by order of the Board of Health of Castleton, to prevent communication with the premises. This was taken down by a party of men from the city under the direction of the Health Office. The occurrence of a few cases of yellow fever outside the walls in Aug. 1858, led to the passage of a series of resolutions by the town Board of Health, declaring the whole quarantine establishment a nuisance too intolerable to be borne any longer, and recommending the citizens of the co. to protect themselves by abating it without delay. Copies of these resolutions were posted up in the village on the 1st of Sept., and on the evening of the same day the walls were broken down and the gates burst open by a mob, the sick carried out upon their mattresses, the family of the resident physician hurried from their dwelling, and every building except the women's hospital was burned. On the following evening the mob completed the ruin by destroying the last building upon the premises. The U. S. stores were saved by a party of marines stationed for the purpose. On the 7th the governor issued a proclamation declaring the co. in a state of insurrection. Temporary quarantine accommodations were soon after erected under the protection of a detachment of the State militia, who were detained in the service till the close of the year. The expenses attending this duty were assumed and paid by Governor King, and reimbursed by a special appropriation soon after. The necessity for a permanent removal of quarantine from Staten Island has been conceded by most persons who have given the subject an investigation; and the practicability of constructing an artificial island upon one of the shoals in the lower bay has been certified by competent engineers. The governor, in his message of 1859, recommended the appointment of a new commission to investigate this difficult but highly important subject and report to the legislature.

[7] The N. Y. Dyeing and Printing Works were established in 1819. They employ from 200 to 250 persons.

[8] Named from Dr. Samuel M. Elliott, oculist.

Sailors' Snug Harbor, an institution established for the support of aged and infirm mariners.[1] An institution for the support and education of the destitute children of seamen is situated near the Sailors' Snug Harbor.[2] **New Brighton** (p. v.) contains 5 churches, several manufactories,[3] 2 large family boarding houses, and the residences of many persons doing business in New York City. **Tompkinsville**[4] (p. v.) contains 4 churches and a number of manufactories. In this village are numerous suburban residences; and near by is the Quarantine. **Centerville** is a hamlet. The census reports 7 churches in town.[5]

NORTHFIELD—was formed March 7, 1788. It is situated in the N. W. part of the co., and includes several small islands in Staten Island Sound and Newark Bay. Its surface is level in the northern and central parts and hilly in the southern. Fresh Kils form the boundary between this town and Westfield. The soil is a clayey loam, under excellent cultivation. Along the W. and S. borders are extensive salt marshes. The town is very thickly settled along the shore of Newark Bay and the Kil Van Kull. **Port Richmond**, (p. v.,) in the N. E. part of the town, is a large manufacturing village,[6] with convenient docks for shipping. Pop. 1,429. **Graniteville,** adjacent to Port Richmond, is a small settlement, with a pop. of 481. Granite was formerly extensively quarried at this place.[7] **Mariners Harbor** is a thickly settled street along the shore of Newark Bay. Pop. 1,142. **Old Place** and **New Springville** (p. o.) are hamlets. **Chelsea** is a small village nearly opposite the mouth of Rahway River. **Southfield** and **Hollins Hook** are hamlets, and **Long Neck** is a p. o. near Fresh Kil. A part of **Richmond** and of **Egbertsville**[8] are in this town. St. Andrews Church, (Prot. E.,) at Richmond, is the oldest on the island, and under the colonial Government it was supported by a co. tax.[9] The census reports 11 churches in town.[10]

SOUTHFIELD—was formed March 7, 1788. It is a long, narrow town extending along New York Bay. Great Kil is a bay in the S. part.[11] Its surface is level or gently undulating, terminating in bluffs upon the E. shore. In the S. part are several small streams bordered by salt meadows. **Stapleton** (p. v.) is a scattered village in the N. part of the town. It contains 4 churches. The Seamen's Retreat[12] and the Mariners' Family Asylum[13] are located here. **Clifton** contains 2 churches and many beautiful residences. **Richmond** (p. v.) is situated

---

[1] This establishment was founded by Robert Richard Randall, of New York. By the provisions of his will, dated June 1, 1801, several annuities and legacies were to be paid, and the residue of his estate conveyed in trust to the State Chancellor, the Mayor and Recorder of New York, the senior minister of the Episcopal and of the Presbyterian churches of the city, the President of the Chamber of Commerce and the President and Vice-President of the Marine Society, and their successors, for the support of aged and infirm sailors. The trustees were incorp. Feb. 6, 1806. The property thus bequeathed lay near Union Square, in New York, and a protracted and expensive lawsuit prevented the trustees from fully executing the intentions of the benefactor until many years after his death. This suit was decided in the U. S. Supreme Court, in Feb. 1830, in favor of the trustees. It was allowed to accumulate until 1830, when the present site (embracing 163 acres) was purchased, and preparations were made for the erection of the necessary buildings. The cornerstone of the edifice was laid Oct. 21, 1831. The buildings consist of a main edifice with two wings, a hospital, (erected in 1853,) a commodious dining and lodging hall, (erected in 1855,) a chapel, (erected in 1856,) the governor, physician, chaplain, and steward's dwellings, a laundry, a gardener's house, and other buildings. The remains of the founder of the institution were interred beneath a monument in front of the main building, Aug. 31, 1834. The officers of the establishment consist of a president, secretary, governor, treasurer, chaplain, physician, assistant governor, steward, and agent, chosen annually by the trustees. Capt. John Whetten was the first governor, and since 1845 Capt. De Peyster has held that office. The total number of inmates received since 1845 has been 477; the present number (Aug. 1858) is 380. Among the inmates the average number of deaths is 25 per annum. The annual income of the institution is $75,000.

[2] " *The Society for the Relief of Destitute Children of Seamen*" was formed in 1846 and incorp. 1851. An annual payment of $2 constitutes a member, and a single payment of $25, a life member. It is managed and chiefly supported by ladies. The yearly expenditures are about $7,000.

[3] A silk handkerchief printing establishment, started here in 1842, gives employment to about 150 persons.

[4] Named from Gov. Daniel D. Tompkins, who resided here from 1814 till his death in 1825.

[5] 2 Prot. E., Bap., Moravian, Ref. Prot. D., R. C., and Unit.

[6] The Damascus Steel Co. employs 50 to 60 hands in the manufacture of iron from the ore, and of steel from iron. At this place are several large brickkilns. The Northfield Brick Co. employ about 30 hands, and the Richmond Co. about 45. White lead is also manufactured to some extent.

[7] The granite obtained at this place is very tough, and consists of hornblende and feldspar intimately blended. It was quarried by the Brick and Granite Co., (organized in May, 1848.) and was largely used in making the Russ pavement of New York City. A R. R. has been built from the quarry to the dock,—a distance of 1 mi.

[8] Named from Jas. Egberts, a former resident.

[9] Elias Duxbury, by will in 1768, devised a certain plantation as a glebe to this church. By the act of Feb. 18, 1814, the trustees were authorized to sell this, and the proceeds were invested for the benefit of the church. A large amount of valuable real estate adjoining the Quarantine Ferry is owned by this society, and is leased for a term of 50 years.

[10] 3 Bap., 2 M. E., Evang. Luth., Cong., Meth., Prot. E., Ref. Prot. D., and R. C.

[11] The waters of the bay S. of this town were selected for the anchorage of infected vessels by the commissioners for the removal of the quarantine, June 9, 1857.

[12] In March, 1801, a tax was imposed upon seamen and passengers entering the port of New York, the proceeds of which were applied to the Quarantine Hospital. But the injustice of devoting a revenue derived from the hard earnings of seamen to objects having no connection with their interests or support led to the passage of a law in 1831, by which this tax was directed to be paid to the Board of Trustees of the Seamen's Fund and Retreat in the city of New York. A surplus that had been paid into the State treasury, amounting to $12,197 68, was also placed in the hands of the trustees. A tract of 40 acres was bought for $10,000, temporary buildings were erected, and, on the 1st of Oct. 1831, 47 patients were admitted. The cornerstone of the present structure was laid July 4, 1835, and the building was finished in 1837. It is built of hammered stone, is 3 stories high, and will accommodate 200 inmates. An insane hospital, nouses for the superintendent and physicians, and other buildings, have been erected. The cost of the main building was $90,000, of the insane hospital $6,000, and the total cost has been $115,000. Up to Jan. 1, 1854, 16,764 patients had been received, of whom 680 had died. By an act passed April 7, 1854, the mayor and health officer of New York, the presidents of the Seamen's Savings Bank and the Marine Society, and 7 other persons, (4 of whom must be masters of vessels, appointed by the governor and Senate,) were constituted trustees of the establishment. The trustees must be residents of New York, Kings, Queens, or Richmond Cos.

[13] By an act passed in 1847, the trustees of the Seamen's Retreat were directed to provide for the support of destitute sick or infirm mothers, wives, sisters, daughters, and widows of seamen, and $10,000 was applied for the erection of suitable build-

on a creek tributary to the Fresh Kils, on the line of Northfield. It is the co. seat, and contains the co. buildings, 1 church, and about 50 houses. **Bay View** is a p. o., and **Egbertsville** (New Dorp p. o.) is a small village. The census reports 5 churches in town.[1]

WESTFIELD—was formed March 7, 1788. It occupies the s. w. extremity of the island, and is the largest town in the co. Its surface is generally level or gently undulating. Princes Bay is an indentation upon the s. coast, to the E. of which is Seguines Point.[2] Fresh Kils forms the boundary between this town and Northfield. Material for fire brick is found in abundance near Staten Island Sound, and considerable quantities of it have been taken to New York for manufacture. Upon the coast, near the w. extremity of Princes Bay, is a lighthouse.[3] The people of this town are principally engaged in fishing and taking oysters. A limited amount of manufactures is carried on.[4] **Tottenville**[5] (Bentley p. o.) is situated on Staten Island Sound, opposite Perth Amboy. Pop. 600. **Kreischerville,** (p. v.,) on Staten Island Sound, contains a large firebrick manufactory, and 1 church. Pop. about 400. In the vicinity are large beds of fire clay, paper clay, fire sand, and kaolin. **Rossville**[6] (p. v.) has a population of 300. The inhabitants are chiefly engaged, directly or indirectly, in the oyster trade. **Lemon Creek** (p. c.) is a hamlet, known as "*Pleasant Plains,*" and **Marshland** is a p. o. **Blooming View**[7] and **Woodrow** are small villages. **Richmond Valley** (p. o.) is a hamlet, and **Southside** a p. o. The census reports 7 churches in town.[8]

Acres of Land, Valuation, Population, Dwellings, Families, Freeholders, Schools, Live Stock, Agricultural Products, and Domestic Manufactures, of Richmond County.

NAMES OF TOWNS.	ACRES OF LAND. Improved.	ACRES OF LAND. Unimproved.	VALUATION OF 1858. Real Estate.	VALUATION OF 1858. Personal Property.	VALUATION OF 1858. Total.	POPULATION. Males.	POPULATION. Females.	No. of Dwellings.	No. of Families.	Freeholders.	SCHOOLS. No. of Districts.	SCHOOLS. Children taught.
Castleton	1,359	$862\frac{1}{8}$	$3,030,090	$325,000	$3,355,090	4,102	4,150	1,154	1,447	623	5	2,638
Northfield	$3,775\frac{1}{2}$	2,932	1,259,095	75,000	1,334,095	2,064	2,123	696	939	518	8	1,790
Southfield	2,752	1,483	1,830,833	17,500	1,848,333	2,654	2,795	759	1,003	473	4	2,409
Westfield	$7,185\frac{7}{8}$	2,325	824,800	75,000	899,800	1,749	1,752	611	667	473	7	1,296
Total	$15,072\frac{3}{8}$	$7,602\frac{1}{8}$	$6,944,818	$492,500	$7,437,318	10,569	10,820	3,220	4,056	2,087	24	8,133

NAMES OF TOWNS.	LIVE STOCK. Horses.	LIVE STOCK. Working Oxen and Calves.	LIVE STOCK. Cows.	LIVE STOCK. Sheep.	LIVE STOCK. Swine.	AGRICULTURAL PRODUCTS. BUSH. OF GRAIN. Winter.	BUSH. OF GRAIN. Spring.	Tons of Hay.	Bushels of Potatoes.	Bushels of Apples.	DAIRY PRODUCTS. Pounds of Butter.	DAIRY PRODUCTS. Pounds of Cheese.	Domestic Manufactures, in Yards.
Castleton	101	137	132	2	183	1,019	5,641	652	4,077		2,595		
Northfield	229	230	399		396	$3,193\frac{1}{2}$	$16,366\frac{1}{2}$	1,501	8,471	28	12,525		
Southfield	135	267	212	25	291	4,970	12,910	1,586	2,972		8,945		
Westfield	380	427	446	30	856	$5,284\frac{3}{4}$	$27,215\frac{1}{4}$	3,293	6,219		300		
Total	845	1,061	1,189	57	1,726	$14,467\frac{1}{4}$	$62,132\frac{3}{4}$	7,032	21,739	28	24,365		

ings. An association of ladies, styled "*The Mariners' Family Industrial Society,*" was incorp. April 9, 1849, having for its object the relief of the destitute families of seamen. The building was completed in Dec. 1853, opened in May, 1855, and dedicated June 9 of the same year. By an act passed March 17, 1851, a board of trustees was created for its management: this board consists of certain *ex-officio* members and the Board of Counsellors of the M. F. I. Soc. Ten per cent. of the receipts by the Trustees of the Seamen's Fund and Retreat was applied to this establishment by a law passed April 12, 1854.

1 2 Prot. E., 2 Ref. Prot. D., and 1 R. C.

2 Pronounced Se-guine. This point was purchased by the State as a site for the quarantine. See page 565.

3 Built in 1828.

4 The Staten Island Oil Co. was organized in July, 1853, and incorp. as the "*Staten Island Oil and Candle Co.*" in Feb. 1857; 30 to 40 hands are employed in the manufacture of adamantine candles and red oil from palm oil and animal fats. On the Fresh Kils is a manufactory of fire brick, and near Rossville a manufactory of bone black.

5 Named from the Totten family, the members of which are numerous in the locality.

6 Named from Wm. E. Ross.

7 A seminary, called the "*Huguenot Institute,*" was formerly located at this place.

8 2 M. E., Bap., Af. Meth., Prot. E., Ref. Prot. D., and R. C.

ROCKLAND COUNTY.

THIS county was formed from Orange, Feb. 23, 1798. It is triangular in form, Hudson River, New Jersey line, and the s. bounds of Orange co. being respectively its E., S. W., and N. W. boundaries. It is centrally distant 105 mi. from Albany, and contains 208 sq. mi. The Ramapo Mts., extending along the N. W. border, are the connecting link between the Blue Ridge of Eastern Penn. and N. J. and the Matteawan Mts. of Putnam co., E. of the Hudson. They are separated into numerous distinct spurs, ridges, and peaks, and occupy more. than one-third of the entire surface of the co. They are generally steep, rocky, and barren, and the valleys between them are narrow, rocky ravines. The Palisade Range from N. J. enters the extreme s. angle of the co., and terminates abruptly s. of Piermont. A broken ridge, known as the Nyack Hills, forming a N. spur of this range, but without its continuous and wall like character, extends N. along the river to the N. part of Clarkstown, where it unites with Verdrieteges Hook, an E. spur of the Ramapo Range. The surface of the central and s. w. portions of the co., lying between these ranges, is rolling or moderately hilly. The highest summits in the N. W. part are 700 to 1,000 feet above tide. The principal streams are Hackensack River, flowing s. through Clarkstown and Orangetown, Ramapo River, in the w. angle of Ramapo, and Minisceongo Creek, Minas Fall Creek, and Spar Kil, tributaries of the Hudson. The rocks of the Ramapo Mts. are principally primitive. Granite, gneiss, and metamorphic limestone abound. The hills along the river and Verdrieteges Hook are composed of red sandstone, known to geologists as the New Red Sandstone; and the central and w. portions of the co. are principally underlaid by limestone. These rocks yield an abundance of most excellent building material,[1] and from the white limestone in the N. E. corner of the co. large quantities of lime are manufactured.[2] Trap rock extends from N. J. into the s. border of the co. The people are largely engaged in fruit growing and gardening. Milk is sent from some parts of the co. in considerable quantities to the New York market. The manufacture of lime and brick and the exportation of ice are important branches of the industry of the co. Large quantities of red sandstone for building are annually quarried and exported. The manufactures of the co. are also important and various, consisting principally of shoes, wooden ware, and woolen yarn.

The co. seat is located at the village of New City, in Clarkstown. A combined courthouse and jail, built of brick, is situated upon a beautiful eminence overlooking the village.[3] The clerk's office is a fireproof brick building adjacent to the courthouse. The poorhouse is located upon a farm of 43 acres at Mechanicsville, in Ramapo, 7 mi. w. of the courthouse. The average number of inmates is 100, supported at a weekly expense of 75 cts. each. The farm yields a revenue of $700. A school is taught during the entire year, and the house is well kept. The N. Y. & Erie R. R. extends through the w. part of Ramapo, and the Piermont Branch of the same road extends from Piermont, on the Hudson, to Sufferns, where it unites with the main track.[4]

Two weekly newspapers are now published in the co.[5]

This co. was included in patents known as the Kakiate Patent, granted to Daniel Honan and Michael Hawdon, June 25, 1696; the Wawayanda Patent, granted to John Bridges, April 29, 1703; and the Cheescocks Patent, granted to Ann Bridges and others, March 20, 1707. The first patent recorded in the co. clerk's office is one granted to Samuel Bayard, bearing date Sept. 16,

---

[1] See page 570.

[2] This lime is used exclusively for agricultural purposes.—See page 569.

[3] The first courthouse after the erection of the co. was built in 1798–99. The present house was erected in 1827, and the jail was added in 1856. The whole cost was about $16,000. The first co. officers were John Suffern, *First Judge;* David Pye, *Co. Clerk;* Jacob Wood, *Sheriff;* Peter Talman, *Surrogate.*

[4] A R. R. extends S. from Piermont to Jersey City. It was finished in 1859, and is intended to continue N. to Warren.

[5] *The Palladium* was started at Warren, about 1812, by Ezekiel Burroughs, and was continued a short time.
The Rockland Register was commenced at Warren, in 1828, by Ezekiel Burroughs; in 1830 it was changed to *The Rockland Gazette,* and in 1834 it was united with The Advertiser.

The Rockland Advertiser was started at Warren, in May, 1823, by John Douglas; and in 1834 it was united with The Gazette, under the name of
The Rockland Advertiser and Family Gazette; and in 1843 it was published as
The Rockland News and General Advertiser, by John L. Burtis.
The North River Times was started at Warren, in 1834, by Alexander H. Wells, and was continued a short time.
The Mirror was published at Warren a short time in 1838.
The Rockland County Messenger was established at Warren, in May, 1846, by Robert Marshall; in 1852 it passed into the hands of Robert Smith, by whom it is still continued.
The Rockland County Journal was commenced in July, 1850, at Nyack, by Wm. G. Haeselbarth, and is still continued by him.

568

1703.[1] The old courthouse, built about 1739 for that part of Orange co. s. of the mountains, was at Tappantown, opposite the old Ref. Prot. D. church, and was burned before the Revolution. The first settlers were Dutch, who located in the s. E. part of the co. from 1690 to 1710.[2]

CLARKSTOWN—was formed from Haverstraw, March 18, 1791. It lies upon the Hudson, and is the central town upon the E. border of the co. Verdrieteges Hook, a rocky ridge 500 to 800 feet above tide, extends along the N. line, and the Nyack Range occupies a considerable portion in the S. E. corner. The remaining parts of the town, comprising four-fifths of its surface, are rolling or moderately hilly. Hackensack River flows s. through near the center, and a narrow swamp extends along the greater part of its course. Rockland Lake, about 1 mi. from the Hudson, is a fine sheet of pure water, 3 mi. in circumference and 160 feet above the river. The soil is a reddish, sandy loam underlaid by clay. Considerable attention is given to fruit growing. **Rockland Lake,**[3] (p. v.,) in the E. part of the town, and extending from the lake to the river, contains a church, a foundry and machine shop, and a ship yard. Pop. 430. An extensive business is carried on at this place in preserving and exporting ice.[4] **New City,** (Clarkstown p. o.,) the co. seat, a little N. w. of the center, contains the co. buildings, a church, and 28 dwellings. **Nanuet,** (p. v.,) formerly "*Clarkstown Station,*" a station upon the Piermont Branch of the Erie R. R., in the s. w. part, contains 1 church and 20 dwellings. **Clarksville,** (Nyack Turnpike p. o.,) in the s. part, contains a church and 18 dwellings. **Dutch Factory,** a hamlet in the w. part, contains a cotton factory and 2 woolen yarn factories. The first settlements were made by the Dutch, at an early period. The first church (Ref. Prot. D.) was formed near Clarksville.[5]

HAVERSTRAW[6]—was formed March 7, 1788.[7] Clarkstown and Ramapo were taken off in 1791. It lies upon the Hudson, in the N. angle of the co. Nearly the entire surface is hilly and mountainous. The Ramapo or Blue Mts., extending through the N. w. part, are divided into numerous precipitous and rocky peaks, and spurs from the principal range extend to the banks of the Hudson.[8] Verdrieteges Hook, a long, rocky ridge, forms a considerable portion of the N. border. The s. E. portion is moderately hilly. The valleys separating these mountains are mostly narrow, rocky ravines. Stony Point is a small rocky peninsula on the river, near the center of the E. border of the town.[9] The principal streams are Minisceonga and Miners Creeks, flowing into the Hudson, and Stony Brook, a tributary of Ramapo River, a branch of the Passaic. The soil is a sandy loam underlaid by clay. Extensive beds of a fine quality of clay border upon the river above Warren, and from them are annually manufactured 150,000,000 of bricks, giving employment to over 1,000 men. Limestone crops out near Tompkins Cove, from which large quantities of lime are manufactured. A gas spring is found 2½ mi. s. of Stony Point.[10] **Warren,**[11] (Haverstraw p. o.,) situated upon the Hudson, in the s. E. angle of the town, was incorp. in 1854.

---

[1] This tract is described as follows:—"A certain tract of vacant land within our county of Orange called by the Indians Whorinims, Peruck, Gemakie, and Nanashunck, and is in several small pieces; and also another parcel of land, beginning at the south bounds of lands lately granted to Daniel Honan and Michael Hawdon, being a small creek that runs into Demaree's Creek to the southward of Nanashunck, and runs from thence by Demaree's said creek as it runs southerly to the lyne parting our said Province from the Jerseys; and soe by the said parting line westward to a small river called Saddle River, thence by the said river northward until an east line due run to the southwest corner of the said Honans and Hawdons land, containing by estimation two thousand acres of improvable land, &c. &c."

Another deed on record commences, "To all X'Tian People," (Christian People,) Johannes Mynne, of Haverstraw, &c. &c. to Albert Mynne, of Haverstraw, &c. &c., and dated 1694.

Witness, Thomas Luirens, Frans Wessel, and Peter Jacobus Maurius.

[2] Among these early settlers were Capt. Cornelius Cuyper, Capt. Cornelius Harring, Johannes Meyer, Gerhardus Clowes, Derrick Straat, Jacobus Swartwout, Jonathan Ross, Thomas Pulling, John Gaile, Cornelius Smith, Jacob King, William Kurtrack, John Ellison, Rinear Kišarike, Col. Vincent Matthews, Hendrick Ten Eyck, Guylbert Crom, Minard Hogon Kamp, Garret Sneideker, Daniel Denton, Petress Decker, Jonathan Seamons, Thos. Maybee, Daniel De Clark, William Wyant, Evert Hombeck, John Van Fliet, Johannes Blauvelt, Nicholas Concklin, Lambert Auriancey, Teunis Van Houten, and Teunis Talman.

[3] The landing at this village is sometimes called Slaughters Landing.

[4] 200,000 tons of ice are annually exported. The business gives employment to 1000 men during the season of securing the ice, and to about 100 men continually.

[5] There are 4 churches in town; 2 M. E., Ref. Prot. D., and Seceders.

[6] Signifying Oat Straw. The name is said to be derived from the quantities of wild oats growing on the borders of the river when the town was first settled.

[7] The date of formation as a precinct was not ascertained. Their distance from Tappan occasioned an act, June 24, 1719, allowing the inhabitants to elect a supervisor, a collector, 2 assessors, a constable, and 2 overseers of highways, on the 1st Tuesday of April annually.

[8] The principal of these peaks are the Dunderbergh and West Mts., in the N. E.; Buchan, Barrack, Bulson, Pine, and Collaberg Hills, near the center; Rock House Hill, Blackmine Ridge, and Horsepond Mts., in the w.; and Hasha Hill and Cheese Coats Hill in the s.

[9] During the Revolution, Stony Point and Verplanks Point, on the opposite side of the Hudson, were strongly fortified, the two fortresses commanding the channel and Kings Ferry, the principal route between New England and the South. On the 1st of June, 1779, Gen. Vaughn, at the head of a considerable British force, made an attack upon these places and captured both. The garrison at Fort La Fayette, on Verplanks Point, consisting of 70 men, were taken prisoners; and that at Stony Point, consisting of 40 men, evacuated the place on the approach of the British. Gen. Clinton immediately ordered the works strengthened, and prepared for permanent occupation. Stony Point was surrounded on 3 sides by water, and on the fourth by a marsh covered at high tide, and crossed by a narrow causeway. On the night of July 16, 1779, this place was stormed and taken by an American force under Gen. Wayne. The loss of the Americans was 15 killed and 83 wounded, and of the British, 63 killed and 543 prisoners. This action was one of the most daring and brilliant that occurred during the war. A light was erected on the site of the fort in 1826.

[10] *Geol. 1st Dist.* p. 107.

[11] Locally known as Haverstraw. The large rolling mill of the Sampson Iron Co., 1¼ mi. w. of this place, usually employing 100 to 150 hands, has suspended operations.

It contains 5 churches, a newspaper office, academy,[1] paper mill, ship yard, foundry, and a silk manufactory. Pop. about 1,700. **Tompkins Cove,** upon the Hudson, is a village grown up around the extensive limeworks of C. Tompkins & Co. It contains a church, a private school supported by the company, and 60 dwellings.[2] **Garnerville,** 2 mi. N. W. of Warren, contains 1 church, the Rockland Print Works,[3] and 40 dwellings. **North Haverstraw,** (p. v.,) upon the Hudson, 3 mi. N. of Warren, contains 2 churches and 28 dwellings. **Thiells Corner,** 4 mi. W. of Warren, contains a needle factory, 2 gristmills, a church, and 15 dwellings. **Montville, Caldwells Landing,**[4] and **Grassy Point** are hamlets. Fort Clinton, the ruins of which are still visible, was situated upon the river, in the N. E. angle of the town. The house in which Arnold and André met to consummate the bargain for the delivery of West Point to the British is still standing, about halfway between Warren and North Haverstraw. There are 11 churches in town.[5]

ORANGETOWN—was formed March 7, 1788, and was named from Orange co., of which it then formed a part. It lies upon the Hudson, in the S. angle of the co. Its surface is broken by abrupt and rocky hills in the E.; but in the center and W. it spreads out into a rolling or moderately hilly region. The Nyack Hills, extending along the river, are 300 to 500 feet high, with steep, rocky declivities upon the E., but more gradual slopes upon the W.[6] Their summits are rocky and covered with a light growth of forest trees. Snake Hill, in the N. E. corner, upon the line of Clarkstown, is one of the principal peaks. The principal stream is Hackensack River, flowing S. through the W. part. Pascack Creek flows through the extreme W. angle, and Spar Kil is a tributary of the Hudson. Near the N. line are several bog or peat meadows, generally well drained and under cultivation. The red sandstone which crops out on the E. declivities of the hills, within a few rods of the river, between Piermont and Nyack, is extensively quarried and exported for building stone.[7] The soil is a reddish, sandy loam intermixed with clay. Fruit growing and furnishing milk for the New York market have become leading pursuits. **Nyack,** (p. v.,) upon the Hudson, in the N. E. corner of the town, contains 5 churches, 5 shoe manufactories,[8] a steam tub and pail factory,[9] the Rockland Female Institute,[10] and a private academy.[11] Pop. 1,458. **Piermont,**[12] (p. v.,) upon the Hudson, in the S. part, was incorp. May 21, 1850. It is the R. terminus of the Piermont Branch of the N. Y. & Erie R. R.,—the one over which the freight is carried. Nearly the whole business of the place is connected with the R. R. establishment. A pier 1 mi. long has been built into the river, where the freight is transferred to and from the cars and barges in the river. Upon each end of the pier are extensive offices for the transaction of the business of the road. At this place the R. R. co. also have a large iron foundry and extensive repair shops. Pop. 2,204. **Tappantown,**[13] (p. v.,) near the N. J. line, contains 2 churches and 30 dwellings. This place was the scene of the trial of André, and for a time in 1780 was the headquarters of Gen. Washington.[14] **Rockland,** (Palisades p. o.,) upon the Hudson, in the S. part

[1] The Haverstraw Mountain Institute, a private institution, was established in 1853. It employs 2 teachers, and has an average of 40 pupils.

[2] This company have 40 limekilns, and manufacture 100,000 bush. of lime annually, giving employment to 100 men. The lime is sent S. and is used for agricultural purposes.

[3] This establishment, incorp. in 1853, with a capital of $100,000, gives employment to 220 hands, and turns out goods to the amount of $700,000 per annum.

[4] This place is just below the Highlands, and opposite Peekskill, with which it is connected by a steam ferry. The day line of steamers between New York and Albany land here. About 15 years since, a company was formed for raising an old wreck at this place, said to be one of the pirate Kidd's vessels laden with treasure! A coffer dam was built, machinery erected, and immense sums were expended in this insane project,—which, it is needless to add, resulted in nothing but a total loss to all concerned.   [5] 4 M. E., 3 Presb., 2 Prot. E., Af. Meth., and R. C.

[6] The valley of Spar Kil forms a break in these hills, through which the Piermont Branch of the Erie R. R. is constructed. In the hill just N. of Piermont is an opening in the rocks, supposed by some to be the shaft of an ancient mine and by others to be a natural cave. It is divided into 2 passages, one extending 70 feet w. s. w. and the other 40 to 50 feet w. by N. The passage is very irregular, 4 to 6 feet in width and 3 to 9 feet high. At the extremity of the longer passage is an immense spring of clear, cold water.

[7] The State House at Albany was built of this stone.

[8] The manufacture of women's and children's shoes at this place is an extensive business. It gives employment to about 600 hands in the vicinity, and 30 sewing machines are kept in constant operation. Goods to the amount of $225,000 are annually produced.

[9] This factory employs 30 hands, and produces $60,000 worth of goods annually.

[10] This institution is beautifully located upon a lot of 10 acres, upon the bank of the Hudson, in the S. part of the village. It is supplied with pure spring water from the mountain, is heated with furnaces and lighted with gas. It has accommodations for 100 boarding pupils. The institution owes its origin to the late Simon V. Sickles, of Nyack, who gave $25,000 toward the erection of the building.

[11] The Nyack Classical School and Commercial Academy, intended to prepare young men for college and commercial pursuits, has recently been established.

[12] Name derived from the *Pier* built by the R. R. company and the *mountain* in rear of the village.

[13] According to Heckewelder, Tappan is from the language of the Delawares, and derived from Thuphane or Tuphánne, "Cold Stream."—*Moulton and Yates's Hist. N. Y.*

[14] The house occupied by Gen. Washington, still standing, is owned and occupied by Dr. Smith. It is a stone house, and is said to have been erected in 1700. The house in which André was confined during his trial is now kept as a tavern, under the name of "The Old '76 House." The trial was held in the old Ref. Prot. D. Church. The scene of André's execution and burial was upon an eminence ¼ mi. w. of the village, and about 20 rods from the N. J. line. In Aug. 1831, his remains were disinterred, under the superintendence of Mr. Buchanan, British Consul at New York, and taken to England. A small cedar tree that stood by the grave was also taken away, and a box was afterward made from its wood, lined with gold, and sent to Rev. Mr. Demarest, of Tappantown, in acknowledgment of the services rendered by him at the disinterment. On the box was the following inscription:—"From his Royal Highness the Duke of York to the Rev. Mr. Demarest." No monument now remains to mark the spot of the execution or the grave. A boulder was formerly placed to mark the spot; but this has been broken up and removed.

of the town, contains 3 churches and 40 dwellings.[1] **Orange Mills, Middletown,** and **Blauveltville,** (p. o.,) a station on the N. Y. & E. R. R., are hamlets. The first settlement is supposed to have been made by the Dutch, as early as 1680.[2] The first church (Ref. Prot. D.) was formed Oct. 24, 1694; and the first preacher was Rev. Guilliam Bartholf.[3] The first church edifice was erected in 1716. There are 16 churches in town.[4]

RAMAPO—was formed from Haverstraw, March 18, 1791, as "*New Hampstead.*" Its name was changed to "*Hampstead*" March 3, 1797, and to Ramapo in 1828. It is the most westerly town in the co. The Ramapo or Blue Mts. extend N. E. and S. W. through the W. part.[5] They are steep and rocky, and the valleys between them are deep and narrow. Ranges of rounded and arable hills extend through the S. E. half of the town and occupy the greater part of its surface. The principal streams are Ramapo River, flowing S. through the W. corner, and its tributaries Maway River and Stony Creek. Niggar and Shepard Ponds, on the line of N. J., in the S. W. angle, are small bodies of water. The people are principally employed in raising vegetables for the New York market. **Ramapo,** (Ramapo Works p. o.,) a station on the N. Y. & E. R. R., in the W. part of the town, contains 1 church, several manufactories, and 50 dwellings.[6] **Sufferns,** (p. v.,) near the line of N. J., in the W. part, contains a rolling mill and 20 dwellings. It lies at the junction of the two branches of the Erie R. R., and is an important station. **Sloatsburgh,** (p. v.,) on the Erie R. R., in the extreme W. part, contains a church, cotton twine factory,[7] hoe factory, and 180 inhabitants. **Spring Valley,** (p. v.,) on the Piermont Branch of the Erie R. R., contains a church and 18 dwellings. **Mechanicsville,** near the center of the town, contains a church and 15 dwellings. **Furmanville** and **Monsey Depot** (Monsey p. o.) are hamlets. The first church (Ref. Prot. D.) was formed near the center of the town, Dec. 4, 1774; Rev. Peter Leyt was the first preacher.[8]

Acres of Land, Valuation, Population, Dwellings, Families, Freeholders, Schools, Live Stock, Agricultural Products, and Domestic Manufactures, of Rockland County.

Names of Towns.	Acres of Land.		Valuation of 1858.			Population.		No. of Dwellings.	No. of Families.	Freeholders.	Schools.	
	Improved.	Unimproved.	Real Estate.	Personal Property.	Total.	Males.	Females.				No. of Districts.	Children taught.
Clarkstown	15,903¼	16,742½	$1,147,673	$227,388	$1,375,061	1,831	1,681	643	743	498	9	1,120
Haverstraw	7,151	14,481	819,105	74,950	894,055	3,706	3,041	974	1,263	348	13	2,386
Orangetown	9,922	3,184	1,692,158	372,994	2,065,152	2,895	2,943	986	1,210	568	7	2,012
Ramapo	13,505½	16,445	896,417	303,300	1,199,717	1,723	1,691	585	644	400	12	1,477
Total	46,481¾	50,852½	$4,555,353	$978,632	$5,533,985	10,155	9,356	3,188	3,860	1,814	41	6,995

Names of Towns.	Live Stock.					Agricultural Products.							Domestic Manufactures, in Yards.
						Bush. of Grain.		Tons of Hay.	Bushels of Potatoes.	Bushels of Apples.	Dairy Products.		
	Horses.	Working Oxen and Calves.	Cows.	Sheep.	Swine.	Winter.	Spring.				Pounds of Butter.	Pounds of Cheese.	
Clarkstown	677	850	1,111	97	876	11,582	30,478	4,824½	7,956½	1,015	80,033	2,500	
Haverstraw	1,873	499	1,647	4	483	4,387½	9,251	2,585	3,974	65	40,070		
Orangetown	418	350	732	82	515	6,055	17,384	3,213	11,726	388	35,328		
Ramapo	747	791	1,218	743	1,311	12,521¾	31,782¼	4,205½	23,567	1,785	110,575		
Total	3,715	2,490	4,708	926	3,185	34,546¼	88,895¼	14,828	47,223½	3,253	266,006	2,500	

[1] Locally known as "Snedens Landing."

[2] Among the early settlers were families named Auriancey, Harring, Blauvelt, Van Houton, and Tallman. These names appear upon the records of the church in 1694. The first baptism on record was that of Derick, (Richard,) son of Cornelius Cooper and Elsie Bogert, his wife, Oct. 13, 1696; and the first marriage, that of Marinus William Flousse Crom and Gertrude Femusse Van Houton, in 1699. The first school was taught by Hermanus Van Huysen, from Holland, soon after the first organization of the church. The first inn is believed to have been kept by Casparus Maybee, in the "Old '76 House," now occupied for the same purpose. Abram Maybee built the first mill: his son, Cornelius Maybee, owned it during the Revolution, but, espousing the cause of the British, his property was confiscated.

[3] A tract of 55 acres was originally donated to this church; but at different times all but 14 or 15 acres have been sold. The records of the church during the Revolution, kept in a small book by the pastor, Rev. Mr. Verbryck, for convenience in carrying when obliged to move from place to place, have been lost.

[4] Ref. Prot. D., Presb., M. E., Af. Meth., and Bap. at Nyack; Prot. E., Ref. Prot. D., M. E., Bap., and R. C. at Piermont; Ref. Prot. D. and M. E. at Tappantown; Bap. at Middletown; and 3 M. E. at Rockland.

[5] Cedar Hill and Table Rock, in the W., Horsepond Mts. and Pine Hill, in the N. W., and High Mt., on the line of N. J., are the highest points, and are 500 to 700 feet above tide.

[6] These establishments, consisting of a cotton factory, file factory, steel works, and car works, are all idle, and only 10 dwellings are occupied. The whole village is rapidly going to decay.

[7] This factory, incorp. in 1854, with a capital of $100,000, gives employment to 150 hands.

[8] There are 7 churches in town; 4 M. E., and 3 Ref. Prot. D.

ST. LAWRENCE COUNTY.

THIS county was formed from Clinton and parts of Montgomery and Herkimer, March 3, 1802.[1] It contains an area of 2,880 sq. mi., and is the largest co. in the State. It is centrally distant 140 mi. from Albany. The surface is broken by a series of parallel ridges extending in a N. E. and S. W. direction, and gradually declining in height from the summits, about 1000 ft. above tide, on the S. border, to the level of the banks of St. Lawrence. The highest summits, in the S. E., are about 2000 ft. above tide. The declivities of the ridges are usually gradual slopes, giving to the surface a rolling character, changing from gentle undulations along the river to a hilly and almost mountainous character in the S. E.

The principal streams are the Indian, Oswegatchie, Grass, Racket, St. Regis, and Deer Rivers.[2] These streams all have their rise upon the highlands, which occupy the center of the great northern wilderness, flow for a considerable distance in a N. W. direction, and most of them gradually bend toward the N. E. and finally traverse the greater part of the co. nearly parallel to the St. Lawrence. They all are frequently interrupted by rapids and cascades in their upper and middle course, but as they approach the St. Lawrence they become sluggish; and most of them are navigable for short distances from their mouths.[3] The southern and central parts of the co. are thus abundantly supplied with water-power. In the S. part are numerous small lakes, the principal of which is Cranberry Lake. Long Lake, the largest body of water in the co., lies along the course of Indian River, near its junction with the Oswegatchie.

The geological formation of the co. is very simple. The whole central and southern portions are underlaid by the primitive formation, consisting of gneiss and white limestone.[4] The northern extremity of this formation may be readily traced, by a line commencing upon the border of Jefferson co., about 2 mi. w. of the Ox Bow, thence extending northerly to near the center of the S. shore of Black Lake, thence bending toward the E., and extending to the E. border of the co. on the N. line of Hopkinton. A belt of country 5 to 10 mi. wide, N. of the primitive region and parallel to it, is underlaid by Potsdam sandstone; and the remainder of the co., comprising a belt 3 to 20 mi. wide bordering upon the St. Lawrence, is underlaid by the calciferous sandrock. The primitive portion of the co. is generally elevated and considerably broken. Its soil is light and sandy; and in some parts are extensive sand plains, entirely unfit for agricultural purposes. A considerable portion of the co. is covered with drift deposits, which go far to neutralize the effect of the underlying rock upon the character of the soil. In this region the intervales along the streams are usually fertile; but the whole is best adapted to grazing. Magnetic iron ores abound in the S. part; but they have never been examined or worked to any considerable extent, owing to their remoteness from settlements.[5] In Rossie rich veins of lead have been found and extensively worked;[6] and the rich specular iron ore found along the w. border of the co. and in the adjacent portions of Jefferson, lies between the gneiss and sandstone.[7] The sandstone region is level or gently undulating, broken in some places by disrupted masses of the underlying rock. In this region are numerous quarries, from which are obtained sheets of sandstone of 2 inches to a foot in thickness and of almost any desirable size. This stone acquires hardness by exposure and is indestructible by atmospheric agencies. The soil in this region is usually thin, but fertile, and is derived principally from drift. The calciferous sandstone region commences as a narrow strip on the St. Lawrence, in the N. part of Hammond, and continually widens to the E. border of the co. The soil, consisting of drift and marine clay, is usually very productive.

---

[1] This co. included the "*Ten Towns;*" and Great Tracts Nos. II and III of Macomb's Purchase were provisionally annexed, and now form part of the co.

[2] These streams are known to the St. Regis Indians by the following names:—Indian, O-tsi-kwa-ke, "where the ash tree grows with knobs;" Oswegatchie, a Huron word, said to signify "black water;" Grass, Ni-kent-si-a-ke, "full of large fishes;" Racket, Ni-ha-na-wa-te, "racket, or noisy river;" St. Regis, Ak-wis-sas-ne, "where the partridge drums;" Deer, Oie-ka-rout-ne, "Trout River."

[3] In severe cold weather the tributaries of the St. Lawrence are liable to a sudden reversal of their currents near their mouths, from the damming up of that stream by ice: the streams in consequence overflow the lowlands, making the maintenance of fences and bridges impossible.

[4] This region is remarkable for the variety and beauty of its minerals, of which 60 species are found.—*Hough's Hist. St. Lawrence and Franklin Cos.,* p. 684.

[5] The Clifton Mine in Pierrepont has furnished 1,500 tons of iron. [6] See p. 582.

[7] In the town of Pierrepont a substance used for red paint has been found in the same relative geological position.

572

Dairying and stock raising are the branches of agriculture most extensively pursued.[1] Grain is also cultivated to some extent.[2] Fruits are not extensively cultivated. Manufactures, consisting of iron,[3] castings, lead,[4] lumber,[5] and articles of wood,[6] are carried on. Commerce to some extent is carried on by means of the St. Lawrence and the various railways.

The chief works of internal improvement in the co. are the Ogdensburgh R. R., extending from Ogdensburgh to Rouses Point, on Lake Champlain;[7] the Potsdam & Watertown R. R.,[8] forming a connection with the O. R. R. on the N. and with the W. & R. R. R. and N. Y. Central on the S. Improvements have been made by the State in the navigation of several of the rivers, for the purpose of floating down logs from the S. forests.[9] Daily lines of steamboats connect Ogdensburgh and other points on the river with Montreal and with the various ports on Lake Ontario.

The county seat is located at the village of Canton,[10] on the P. & W. R. R., 18 mi. S. E. of Ogdensburgh. The courthouse, jail,[11] and clerk's office are in separate buildings, situated adjacent to each other. The co. poorhouse is situated on a farm of 130 acres 1 mi. w. of Canton Village.[12]

Six newspapers are now published in the co.; 3 at Ogdensburgh, 2 at Potsdam, and 1 at Canton.[13]

---

[1] This co. stands first in the State in the value of its stock, amount of pasturage and meadow, and among the first in the amount annually produced of spring wheat, potatoes, peas, and maple sugar.

[2] The marine clay deposits produce fine crops of winter wheat.

[3] Furnaces are or have recently been in operation at Rossie, Wegatchie, Fullersville, and Brasher Iron Works. The supply of ore is inexhaustible, and large quantities of iron are annually made.

[4] The Rossie Lead Mines are now worked by an English company. Lead has also been found in several other localities in the co.

[5] The principal lumber operations are carried on on the Racket River. Since 1851, 10 gang sawmills have been built within 17 mi. In 1855 it was estimated that 120,000 logs were worked up.

[6] Consisting of shingles, staves, lath, heading, boxes, doors, sash and blinds.

[7] Opened to Ogdensburgh Oct. 1, 1850.

[8] Opened through the co. Aug. 23, 1855.

[9] These improvements have been made on the Indian, Oswegatchie, Racket, and Grass Rivers.

[10] The county seat was first located at Ogdensburgh, but was removed to Canton in 1828. The first courts were held in the stone barracks, w. of the Oswegatchie; and a bomb-proof magazine adjacent was used for a jail. The first courthouse stood on the site recently purchased by Government for a customhouse. The first co. officers were Nathan Ford, First Judge; Alex. Turner and Joseph Edsall, Judges; Stillman Foote and John Tibbetts, Assist. Justices; Thos. J. Davies, Sheriff; Lewis Hasbrouck, Co. Clerk; and Matthew Perkins, Surrogate. The present courthouse was located by Joseph Grant, Geo. Brayton, and John E. Hinman, commissioners from Oneida co.; and the buildings were erected under the supervision of Ansel Bailey, David C. Judson, and Asa Sprague, jr. The records of the supervisors previous to 1814 were lost in a fire at Ogdensburgh in 1839.

[11] The jail is a miserable building, poorly adapted to the purposes for which it was erected.

[12] This institution yields an annual revenue of about $1,000. The average number of inmates is about 150. The supplies are furnished by contract. The poorhouse is deficient in necessary conveniences for the health and comfort of its inmates.

[13] At Ogdensburgh the following papers have been published: The Palladium was begun in 1810 by Kip & Strong, sold in 1812 to John P. Sheldon, and continued to 1814.
The St. Lawrence Gazette was begun in 1815 by D. R. Strachan and P. B. Fairchild. In 1830 it was bought by Preston King, and united with
The St. Lawrence Republican, removed to this place from Canton, and continued by him till 1833. It was afterward published by Hitchcock, Tillotson & Stillwell, and is now published by James & Hopkins.
The Northern Light was begun July 7, 1831, by W. B. Rogers, as an anti-masonic organ. In 1834 A. B. James became its publisher, and changed it to
The Times; and at the end of the 4th volume it was enlarged, and called
The Ogdensburgh Times. In 1837 Dr. A. Tyler became associated with James, and the title was changed to
The Times and Advertiser. In March, 1844, it was transferred to H. G. Foote and S. B. Seeley, and changed to
The Frontier Sentinel. In June, 1847, Mr. Foote changed it to
The Ogdensburgh Sentinel, under which name it was published by Stillman Foote until 1858, when it was merged in the Daily Journal.
The Meteorological Register was commenced, and a few numbers issued in 1839; edited by Jas. H. Coffin, now Vice-Pres. of Lafayette Coll., Easton, Penn.
The Ogdensburgh Forum was begun April 24, 1848, by A. Tyler, and discontinued in 1851.
The Daily Sentinel was started April 14, 1848, by S. Foote, and published for 5 months.
The St. Lawrence Budget, a small semi-mo. advertising sheet, was issued from The Sentinel office in 1850-51.

The Daily Morning News was begun in March, 1852, by Wm. N Oswell, publisher, and Fayette Robinson, editor.
The Weekly News was issued from the same office in Sept. 1852. Both were discontinued in the Dec. following.
The St. Lawrence American was begun March 1, 1855, by Wm. Yeaton and E. M. Holbrook, and continued 3 years.
The Boys' Daily Journal was begun May 1, 1855, by H. R. James, J. W. Hopkins, and C. Foster. As lads belonging to the Ogdensburgh Academy, they had previously issued the Morning Glory and Young America. In 1857 Foster withdrew, and the name was changed to
The Daily Journal; the paper is still issued.
The Weekly Journal is made up from the daily. Neither of the publishers is of age (1858.)
The St. Lawrence Democrat was commenced at Canton in the fall of 1855 by H. C. Simpson; and was afterward continued at that place by John F. Ames. It is published by Abbott & O'Brien.
At Potsdam the following have been issued:—
The Potsdam Gazette was begun Jan. 13, 1816, by F. C. Powell, and continued till April, 1823.
The Potsdam American was commenced by F. C. Powell in Jan. 1824, from the old Gazette press, and was continued by Powell & Reddington till April, 1829. In May of the same year it was revived as
The Herald, and published as an anti-masonic organ till Aug.
The St. Lawrence Republican was begun in 1826 by W. H. Wyman, and removed to Canton in 1827.
The Day Star was published 6 months in 1827 by Jonathan Wallace.
The Patriot was commenced in April, 183-, by Wm. Hughes, and published one year.
The Northern Cabinet was removed from Canton in 1845; and from the same office was issued
The Repository in 1846, semi-mo., made up of the literary matter of The Cabinet. This latter was sold to Wm. L. Knowles, and changed to
The St. Lawrence Mercury in 1848. W. H. Wallace became proprietor in 1850; and H. C. Fay in 1851, who changed it to
The St. Lawrence Journal. It was continued till July, 1852, when it was united with The Courier.
The Potsdam Courier was begun in 1851 by V. Harrington, and continued till July, 1852, when it was united with The Journal, and issued as
The Potsdam Courier and Journal was removed to Canton in 1859, and is now published by H. C. Fay & Brother.
The Philomathean was begun in 1852, and a few numbers were issued by students of the St. Lawrence Academy.
The Elementary Republican was begun in 1852, and a few numbers issued from The Journal office.
The Northern Freeman, removed from Gouverneur in 1856, is still published by Doty & Baker.
The Evangelical Herald, mo., was begun in 1856 by Jos. A. Livingston. Printed part of the time at Northfield, Vt. Now published at Boston and Potsdam.
At Canton the following have been published:—
The Canton Advertiser and St. Lawrence Republican, removed from Potsdam in 1827, was published here by Preston King till 1830, when it was removed to Ogdensburgh.
The Northern Telegraph was begun in 1832 by C. C. Bill. It was soon sold to Orlando Squires, and changed to
The Canton Democrat, and continued a short time.
The Luminary of the North, begun in July, 1834, was published a short time.
The St. Lawrence Democrat was begun in Sept. 1840, by E. A. Barber, and continued 2 years.
The Northern Cabinet and Literary Repository, semi-mo., was begun Jan. 2, 1843, by Chas. Boynton, and in 1845 removed to Potsdam.
The Engineer was issued in 1844 by Chas. Boynton.

The first white settlement in this co. was made by Francis Picquet, a French Sulpitian, who established an Indian mission at the mouth of the Oswegatchie in 1749 and styled it "*La Presentation.*"[1] In 1759 the first island below Ogdensburgh, 3 mi. down the St. Lawrence, was taken possession of by the French and strongly fortified.[2] It was named Fort Levi; and here the last French resistance was made against the English, in 1760. During the Revolution it was the rendezvous of scalping parties of tories and Indians, who harassed the frontier settlements on the Mohawk and Hudson. Two expeditions were fitted out against this place during the Revolution; but the English held possession of the fort at Oswegatchie until 1796, when it was surrendered under the provisions of Jay's Treaty.[3] The Oswegatchies collected by Picquet were removed, in 1793, from the vicinity of Johnstown, U. C., to a point opposite, on the s. shore, known as Indian Point. In 1807 they removed to St. Regis and elsewhere.[4]

The co. includes the tract known as the "*Ten Towns,*"[5] Tract No. II,[6] of Macomb's Purchase, containing 821,879 acres, Tract No. III,[7] of the same purchase, containing 640,000 acres,[8] a small portion located by Revolutionary land warrants,[9] and the islands in the St. Lawrence.[10] The first settlement under State authority was made at Ogdensburgh, in 1796, by Nathan Ford, agent of Samuel Ogden. Before 1800, small beginnings had been made at Lisbon, Madrid, and Massena. The "*Ten Towns*" were opened for settlement, under the original purchasers, within the next 5 years, and the adjacent parts of the Macomb Purchase soon after. At the commencement of the War of 1812 there were about 8,000 inhabitants in the co., thinly scattered over nearly the whole territory now settled. Great alarm was felt along the whole frontier, and many families left the river towns. It soon became the theater of stirring military events, and various expeditions were planned and attacks made on both sides of the border.[11]

At the close of the war the co. rapidly filled up with an immigration chiefly from Vt. and the other New England States. The completion of the Erie Canal checked the growth of the co. by opening to emigration the more fertile lands of the West. The price of wild lands greatly fell, and many visions of immense wealth were blighted. For the last twenty years a steady and healthy improvement has been going on, which has been greatly increased by the lines of railroad completed through it.[12] In 1837–40 the whole frontier was greatly excited by the "*Patriot*

The Inquirer and Tariff Advocate, a campaign paper, was issued from The Cabinet press in 1844 by Chas. Boynton.

The Canton Weekly Citizen was begun Jan. 1, 1852, by J. S. Sargeant, and continued 4 weeks.

The Canton Independent was removed from Madrid in 1853, and published by O. L. Ray. It was soon discontinued.

The St. Lawrence Plain Dealer was begun in 1855 by Goodrich & Remmington; it is now published by S. P. Remington.

Young America is now published by C. W. Ames.

The other papers in the co. have been—

The Northern New Yorker, begun April 2, 1849, at Gouverneur, by Wm. Goodrich and M. F. Wilson; and issued a little more than one year.

The St. Lawrence Advertiser was begun in 1850, at Gouverneur, and a few numbers issued.

The Laborer was commenced in July, 1852, at Gouverneur, by M. Mitchel. It was succeeded by

The St. Lawrence Free Press, begun in 1853 by J. J. Emmes, and afterward published by G. K. Lyman. It was removed to Ogdensburgh in the fall of 1854 and united with The Sentinel.

The Progressive Age was begun in June, 1855, at Gouverneur, by G. D. Greenfield. It was removed to Potsdam in 1856, and changed to The Northern Freeman.

The True Democrat was begun in May, 1850, at Madrid, by M. F. Wilson and O. L. Ray. In its 2d year it became

The Columbian Independent; was continued 1 yr., when it was removed to Canton and changed to the Canton Independent.

1 This place became a French military station, and a magazine for supplying expeditions sent to their s. w. posts; and from this point were fitted out many of the parties that ravaged the back settlements of N. Y., Penn., and Va.

2 This island was called by the Indians "*O-ra-co-nen-ton,*" and by the French "*Isle Royal.*" It is now called Chimney Island, from the ruins still visible.

3 Upon the approach of Lord Amherst in 1760, the fort at the mouth of the Oswegatchie was abandoned. The island was invested on the 18th of Aug. Upon Gallop Island the English found a number of scalps, which so exasperated them that they burned the chapel and houses, the ruins of which are still visible. The batteries opened on the 23d, and on the 25th the place, under Pouchot, surrendered. The English named the fortress, Fort Frederick Augustus. On their voyage down the river from this place to Montreal, the English lost in the rapids 46 bateaux, 17 whaleboats, and 84 men. The island was occupied but a short time, and the works soon fell into ruins.—*Knox's Journal; Mante's Hist.; Memoir of Pouchot; Entick's Hist.*

4 These Indians claimed large tracts of land and leased them to parties from Canada, who cut off the most valuable timber and committed other wasteful depredations.

5 The "*Ten Towns*" were sold at auction by the land commissioners in 1787, in quarter sections, except Madrid and Oswegatchie, which were sold in square miles. In each town a mile square was reserved for literature, and another for the gospel and schools.

6 The original townships in this tract were named as follows: —1. Sherwood; 2. Oakham; 3. Mortlake; 4. Harewood; 5. Janestown; 6. Pierrefield; 7. Granshuck; 8. Hollywood; 9. Kildare; 10. Matildavale; 11. Wick; 12. Riversdale; 13. Cookham; 14. Catharineville; 15. Islington; 16. Chesterfield; 17. Grange; 18. Crumack.

7 The original townships of this tract were named as follows: —1. Hammond; 2. Somerville; 3. De Witt; 4. Fitz William; 5. Ballybeen; 6. Clare; 7. Killarney; 8. Edwards; 9. Sarahsburgh; 10. Clifton; 11. Portaferry; 12. Scriba; 13. Chaumont; 14. Bloomfield; 15. Emilyville.

8 These tracts were conveyed to Dan'l McCormack by patent in 1795–98.

9 This town of Massena comprises this portion of the co.

10 The islands were sold in 1823.

11 A regiment of militia was stationed at Ogdensburgh during the summer of 1812. In July, 1812, a fleet of 6 schooners—caught at Ogdensburgh by the war—attempted to reach the lake, but were intercepted: 2 were burned, and the rest hastened back. On the last day of July a bloodless engagement took place between the American schooner, Julia, and the British vessels, Earl of Moira and Duke of Gloucester. In Sept. an attack was made upon a number of bateaux at Toussaint Island, opposite Lisbon, in which the Americans lost one and the British several men. On the 2d of Oct. the British made a show of attacking Ogdensburgh, and on the 4th made a real attack, but were repulsed, with the loss of a gunboat and 2 men killed. In Jan. the Americans surprised and captured Brockville, liberated several prisoners, paroled 50 of the citizens, and took a quantity of stores. On the 22d of Feb. the British, in retaliation, captured Ogdensburgh. carried away the cannon and stores, and paroled a large number of citizens, who were afterward exchanged for those of Brockville. Late in 1813 Gen. Wilkinson's expedition passed down the St. Lawrence, and suffered a disastrous defeat at Chrysler's Field, opposite Louisville. The British followed the retreating Americans and landed at Hamilton, (Waddington.)—*Hough's Hist. St. Law. & Frank. Cos.*

12 The lands in the co. have doubled in value by the completion of the railroads.

War." The battle of Windmill Point, the most memorable event of that ill-concerted movement, was fought within sight of Ogdensburgh, in Nov. 1838.[1] The U. S. Collection Dist. of Oswegatchie was established March 2, 1811, and embraces the whole co. Its chief office is at Ogdensburgh, with subordinate offices at each of the river towns.

BRASHER[2]—was formed from Massena, April 21, 1825. A part of Lawrence was taken off in 1828. It lies on the w. border of the co., N. of the center. Its surface is generally level, with gentle undulations in the w. part. The principal streams are St. Regis and Deer Rivers and Trout Brook. The soil in the w. part is stony and in parts sandy; in the s. E. it is light and sandy; and in the N. it is a clay loam and very productive. Bog iron ore is obtained abundantly in the E. part, in the range where the sand rests upon the clay deposits. **Brasher Falls**[3] (p. v.) is a manufacturing village upon the St. Regis, in the s. w. corner of the town, 1 mi. below the R. R. station. Pop. 257. **Helena**[4] (p. v.) is situated at the mouth of Deer River, and has a limited amount of water-power. Pop. 100. **Brasher Iron Works,** (p. o.,) 2½ mi. above Helena, on Deer River, is the seat of an important furnace. **Brasher Center** is a hamlet on the St. Regis River. The first improvement in town (at Helena) was under the agency of Russell Atwater, in 1817. Stillman Fuller built the furnace at Brasher Iron Works in 1825.[5] The first settlement at Brasher Falls was made in 1826. In 1839 C. T. Hulburd purchased 600 acres, including the village site of Brasher Falls, and in 1841 made the first considerable improvement. On the 26th of May, 1857, a fire in the woods ravaged this town, and destroyed the furnace and nearly the whole village at the "*Iron Works.*"[6] The census reports 6 churches in town.[7]

CANTON[8]—was formed from Lisbon, March 28, 1805. It occupies a nearly central position in the co. Its surface is level or gently undulating. Grass River, flowing through the center, and the Oswegatchie, flowing through the N. w. corner, are the principal streams.[9] It is underlaid by white limestone and gneiss in the s., and by Potsdam sandstone in the central and N. parts. The soil is a deep, fertile, gravelly loam. Iron pyrites, from which copperas (sulphate of iron) has been manufactured, is found in abundance near High Falls, on Grass River.[10] **Canton,**[11] (p. v.,) the county seat, is pleasantly situated on Grass River, a little E. of the center of the town. It is an important station on the P. & W. R. R. It has a number of manufactures,[12] and is the seat of the Canton Academy, founded in 1831, and of the St. Lawrence University,[13] an institution founded under the auspices of the Universalist denomination in 1856. Pop. 1,029. **Morley**[14] (p. v.) is on Grass River, near the N. border of the town. Pop. 350. **Rensselaer Falls**[15] (p. v.) is a small village on the Oswegatchie, in the N. w. corner of the town. It was formerly the seat of an iron forge. **Crarys Mills** (p. o.) is a hamlet on the line of Potsdam. **South Canton** is in the E. part. Daniel Harrington settled on the site of the Agricultural Fair Grounds in Canton Village in 1800. The first permanent settler was Stillman Foote, who bought a mile square where the village now stands, and removed thither in 1801, accompanied by several men. In 1802 he built a mill, and the town began to be rapidly settled.[16] Religious meetings were held as early as 1804. The first church (Presb.) was formed under the Rev. Amos Pettingill, in 1807.[17]

---

[1] The leaders in this movement dared not risk their own lives in the battle, and left the few, consisting mostly of young men and boys, to engage the greatly superior numbers of the British. The battle was short and bloody. Of the 159 patriots taken prisoners, 18 were released without trial, 3 were acquitted, and 129 were sentenced to be hung. Of the last number, 10 were hung, 60 transported to Van Diemens Land, 56 pardoned, 2 sentenced to a 7 years' term in the penitentiary, and 2 died of their wounds.—*Hough's Hist. St. Law. & Frank. Cos.*

[2] Named from Philip Brasher, of Brooklyn, part owner. It embraces the townships of "*Grange*" and "*Crumack,*" or Nos. 17 and 18 of Great Tract No. II, Macomb's Purchase.

[3] Mills, a fork and hoe factory, and an agricultural implement factory, are located here.

[4] Named from Helen, daughter of Joseph Pitcairn, of New York, former owner of a large part of the town.

[5] In 1827 the furnace was purchased by Isaac W. Skinner and R. W. Bush. In 1830 the latter was succeeded by W. H. Alexander, and the business was continued by Alexander & Skinner until the village was destroyed by fire in 1857. The works are about being rebuilt.

[6] The fire desolated nearly the whole town, and for a time threatened Brasher Falls. The country around was also desolated by running fires in 1849.

[7] 2 Presb. and M. E. at Brasher Falls, Presb. at Helena, M. E. at "*Maple Ridge,*" w. part of the town, R. C. near Brasher Falls, and F. W. Bap.

[8] It embraces No. 6 of the "*Ten Towns,*" and is 10 mi. sq.

[9] A natural canal connects the channels of the two streams.

This canal was formerly 3 to 20 rods wide, and was navigable for small boats in high water. It flowed toward the w., and overflowed an alluvial flat of 4500 acres. To reclaim this, both ends of the canal have been closed, and a drain dug along the Oswegatchie to below Rensselaer Falls.

[10] Fruitless explorations for copper have here been made at great expense.

[11] Incorp. May 14, 1845.

[12] Consisting of lumber, shingles, sash, wagons, flour, and leather.

[13] An elegant brick building was erected here in 1857; and in 1858 a theological school was organized by E. Fisher. The collegiate department has not yet been organized.

[14] Formerly "*Long Rapids.*" Named Morley from a relative of the Harrison family. It contains several sawmills, a sash factory, and tannery.

[15] A forge was erected here in 1839, by Tate, Chafee & Co., and the place named "*Tateville.*" It was more generally known as "*Canton Falls*" until the p. o. was established in 1851. The present name was derived from H. Van Rensselaer, who laid out the village in 1846.

[16] Daniel W. Church, the pioneer millwright of the co., erected the first mill here, for S. Foote, in 1801. The summer of that year was very sickly; and in May the father of S. Foote died of the smallpox and was buried in a bark coffin. Wm. Barker taught the first school, in 1804. The first birth was a daughter of L. Johnson.

[17] The census reports 9 churches; 2 M. E., Bap., Univ., Prot. E., (Grace C.,) Wes. Meth., Cong., F. W. Bap., and R. C.

The late Gov. Silas Wright settled in Canton Village as a lawyer in 1819, and continued to reside here until his death, Aug. 27, 1847.

COLTON[1]—was formed from Parishville, April 12, 1843. A small part was annexed from Parishville in 1851. It is a long, narrow town, lying s. e. of the center of the co. and extending to Hamilton co. on the s. Its surface is broken and hilly; and it is nearly all covered with forest. It is crossed by the Racket, Grass, and Oswegatchie Rivers. In the central and s. parts are numerous small lakes, the principal of which is Cranberry Lake. The extreme n. part only is inhabited. The principal business is lumbering. **Colton** (p. v.) is an important lumber station upon Racket River, near the n. w. corner of the town. Several extensive gang sawmills were erected here in 1850–52; but the business has been partially suspended. An extensive tannery for the manufacture of sole-leather was built here in 1857.[2] Pop. 379. **South Colton** is a p. o. at Three Falls. The first settlement was begun in 1824, at Colton Village.[3] There are a M. E. and a Univ. church in town, both built in 1852.

DE KALB[4]—was formed from Oswegatchie, Feb. 21, 1806. A part of De Peyster was taken off in 1825, and a part of Hermon in 1830. It lies on the Oswegatchie, w. of the center of the co. Its surface consists of broken ridges of white limestone and gneiss with narrow valleys between them. The soil is excellent and is generally under a good state of cultivation. **De Kalb**[5] (p. v.) is situated on the Oswegatchie, near the center of the town. Pop. 120. **Richville**[6] (p. v.) is situated on the Oswegatchie, in the s. w. corner of the town. Pop. 250. **East De Kalb** is a p. o. and station on the P. & W. R. R. **Coopers Falls** is a hamlet. The first settlement was made in 1803, under Judge William Cooper, of Cooperstown, as agent. The first settlers were principally from Otsego co. There are 5 churches in town.[7]

DE PEYSTER[8]—was formed from Oswegatchie and De Kalb, March 24, 1825. It lies on the s. shore of Black Lake, n. w. of the center of the co. Its surface is broken in the s. by the parallel primitive ridges, and is level in the n. The principal streams are the Oswegatchie, on the n. border, and Beaver Creek, on the s. Moon Lake lies in the s. part. The soil along the lake is very fertile, in the center of average fertility, and in the s. it is light and sandy. The "*Old State Road,*" the first traveled route through this part of the co., extended through this town. **De Peyster Corners** (De Peyster p. o.) is a small village. **Edenton** is a p. o. The first settlement was made in the fall of 1802, by Sam'l Bristol and others.[9] The census reports 2 churches; a M. E. and a Cong.

EDWARDS[10]—was formed from Fowler, April 7, 1827. A part of Hermon was taken off in 1830, and a part was annexed from Hermon in 1850. It lies on the Oswegatchie, s. w. of the center of the co. Its surface consists of ridges of the primitive formation and the narrow valleys between them. The soil is generally a light, sandy loam, and in the valleys is very productive; but the town is best adapted to grazing. A large number of minerals are found among the primitive rocks.[11] **Edwards** (p. v.) is situated on the Oswegatchie. Pop. 350. **South Edwards**[12] (p. v.) contains a grist and saw mill and several mechanic shops. The first settlement commenced along the St. Lawrence Turnpike, in 1812.[13] Several Scotch families came into town in 1817. There are 5 churches in town.[14]

FINE[15]—was formed from Russell and Pierrepont, March 27, 1844. It lies in the extreme s.

---

1 Named from Jesse Colton Higley, an early settler. It embraces the townships of "*Sherwood,*" "*Harewood,*" "*Granshuck,*" and "*Matildavale,*" or Nos. 1, 4, 7, and 8 of Great Tract No. II, Macomb's Purchase.

2 This establishment employs about 25 men.

3 Among the first settlers were Asahel Lyman, Abel Brown, Wm. Bullard, Horace Garfield, and Sam'l Partridge. Miss Young taught the first school, in 1826. The first death was that of a child of Jas. Brown, in 1829.

4 Named in honor of Baron De Kalb. It originally embraced No. 7 of the "*Ten Towns.*"

5 Originally named "*Williamstown.*"

6 About 30 families came in the first year. Salmon Rich, Jona. Haskins, and Sol. Pratt were among the first settlers of Richville, in 1804. The first child born was Jehiel Dimick; the first marriage, that of Elisha Cook and Lotta Willey; and the first death, that of George Cowdrey. Bela Willis taught the first school at De Kalb, and Jos. Kneeland at Richville. Wm. Cooper built the first hotel, in 1803, and the first mills, at Coopers Falls, in 1804.

7 Bap. and Cong. at Richville, Presb., M. E., and Union (M. E. and Bap.) at East De Kalb.

8 Named from Frederick De Peyster, of New York, former pro-

prietor. Mr. De P. gave the town $300 to assist in building a union church and townhouse; and he also caused a bell to be cast, with an appropriate inscription for its use.

9 Among the first settlers were Thos. Wilson, Joseph Round, Sam'l Barnard, —— Green, Ichabod Arnold, Rott. Hill. Fred. R. Plympton, David Day, Rufus Washburn, and Smith Stillwell. Bela Willis taught the first school and was the first local preacher.

10 Named from Edward McCormack, brother of the proprietor. It embraces most of No. 8 of Great Tract No. III.

11 Among these are iron ore, mica, Rensselaerite, serpentine, and tourmaline.

12 Locally known as "*Shawville,*" from Elijah Shaw, who opened the first store in 1825. *Freemansbush,* in the e. part, was the seat of a large furnace destroyed by fire.

13 Among the first settlers were Asa Brayton, Jos. M. Bonner, S. & E. Jones, and —— Johnson. The first birth was that of John B. Brayton, in 1812; and the first death was that of —— Partridge, accidentally killed in 1812. Orra Shead built the first grist-mill, in 1814. In 1817 a large number of Scotch settlers came in town.

14 M. E., Univ., Cong., Bap., and Union.

15 Named from John Fine, of Ogdensburgh, principal pro-

part of the co. Its surface is elevated and broken, and its soil is a moderately fertile, gravelly loam. It is drained by the Oswegatchie and its branches. It is principally a wilderness, the settlements being confined to the N. part. Iron ore is found in town. **Fine** is a p. o. in the N. There is no village in town. The first clearing was made in 1823, by Elias Teall.[1]

FOWLER[2]—was formed from Rossie and Russell, April 15, 1816. The townships of Edwards and Fitz William (now a part of Hermon) were annexed from Russell in 1818. Edwards was taken off in 1827, a part of Hermon in 1830, and Pitcairn in 1836. It lies upon the Oswegatchie, in the southwesterly part of the co. Its surface is much broken by ridges of gneiss. It is drained by the Oswegatchie and its branches. Silver Lake lies s. of the center of the town. The soil along the streams is a fertile loam, in the N. w. a clayey loam, and in the E. a light sand. Several valuable minerals are found in town.[3] **Hailesborough,** on the Oswegatchie, and **Little York** (Fowler p. o.) are small villages. **Fullerville** (Fullerville Iron Works p. o.) is the seat of an extensive manufactory of iron.[4] **West Fowler** is a p. o. The first settlements were made by Brig. Gen. Haile, at Hailesborough, in 1807,[5] and by Sam'l B. Sprague, at Little York, in 1811. The town did not begin to be settled rapidly until after 1820. The census reports 4 churches in town.[6]

GOUVERNEUR[7]—was formed from Oswegatchie, April 5, 1810. A part of Macomb was taken off in 1841. It lies in the w. part of the co. Its surface is generally level, but somewhat broken in the N. by low ridges of white limestone. It is drained by the Oswegatchie, which twice flows across the town. The town abounds in interesting minerals.[8] The soil is sandy in a few places, but is chiefly clay and loam, and is highly productive. The Kearney Iron Mine, in the s. corner, has furnished an immense quantity of ore. **Gouverneur** (p. v.) was incorp. Dec. 7, 1847. Pop. 785. It is the seat of a flourishing academy,[9] and has a considerable local trade and the only p. o. in town. Riverside Cemetery is beautifully located on the opposite bank of the Oswegatchie, E. of the village. It was consecrated June 23, 1858. It is a station upon the P. & W. R. R. The first settlement was made in the summer of 1805, by Dr. Richard Townsend, agent of Gouverneur Morris, the proprietor.[10] The first church (Bap.) was formed in 1810.[11]

HAMMOND[12]—was formed from Rossie and Morristown, March 30, 1827. A part was annexed to Macomb in 1842, and a part to Rossie in 1844. It lies upon the St. Lawrence, in the extreme w. part of the co., and includes a portion of The Thousand Islands. The surface is generally level, but broken upon its N. and s. borders by low primary ridges. A level terrace of sandstone, forming a continuous and regular mural wall, extends from the N. shore of Black Lake through the center of the town into Jefferson co. Black Brook flows through a stagnant swamp, which borders upon this sandstone terrace. Its soil is generally a deep, fertile loam. **Hammond,** (p. v.,) on the Rossie Plank Road; **South Hammond,** on the *"Old Military Road;"* and **Oak Point,**[13] (p. v.,) a landing on the St. Lawrence, are small villages. **Chippewa** is a hamlet on a bay of the same name. Slight improvements began here in 1812; but settlements did not increase until 1818–21, when a number of Scotch families located just w. of the present site of Hammond Village.[14] There are 4 churches in town.[15]

---

prietor. It embraces *"Scriba,"* *"Bloomfield,"* *"Emilyville,"* and the south half of *"Sarahsburgh,"* or Nos. 12, 14, 15, and 9 of Great Tract No. III, Macomb's Purchase.

[1] Jas. C. Haile built a rude mill in 1828. The settlement was soon after abandoned, but renewed in Feb. 1834, by Amasa J. Brown.

[2] Named from Theodocius Fowler, of New York, former proprietor. It embraces *"Kilkenny,"* or No. 7 of Great Tract No. III, Macomb's Purchase.

[3] Iron ore, white marble, sulphates of lead, copper, and zinc, asbestus, Rensselaerite, mica, and chalcedony.

[4] This village contains a furnace, 2 forges, and several mills.

[5] Gen. H. purchased a mile square, with an agreement to build a mill within a year. Among the other early settlers were Elijah Sackett, Lemuel Arnold, John Ryan, and Ebenezer Parker. The first birth was a child of —— Merrills; the first marriage, that of John Parker and Elizabeth S. Sackett, in 1812.

[6] Univ., Bap., F. W. Bap., and M. E.

[7] Named from Gouverneur Morris, the proprietor of most of the town. It originally embraced the township of *"Cambray,"* or No. 8 of the *"Ten Towns."*

[8] Among the useful minerals are red specular iron ore, marble, limpid calcite, sulphate of barytes, serpentine, Rensselaerite, mica, tourmaline, and fluorspar; and among those interesting to men of science are spinelle, scapolite, tremalite, schorl, sphene, chondvodite, opatite, Babingtonite, and Houghite.

[9] The *"Gouverneur High School"* was opened in 1826, and incorp. April 25, 1828. A new edifice was erected in 1834; and in 1837

it was received under the patronage of the M. E. Black River Conference. The building was burned in 1839, and a new stone edifice erected the next year. The name was changed to the Gouverneur Wesleyan Seminary April 25, 1840. It is a flourishing institution.

[10] The first party of settlers came through the wilderness from the head of Lake George, guided by a compass. They were seven days on the journey. Among the settlers in 1806 were Pardon Babcock, Willard Smith, Eleazar Nichols, and Isaac Austin, who all occupied a small shanty in common. In 1810 there were 50 families in town. A blockhouse was built in 1812, near where the store of Harvey D. Smith now stands. Miss E. S. Sackett taught the first school, in the first shanty; Israel Porter kept the first inn, and John Brown the first store, in 1808. The first religious services were held in 1806, by missionaries. The first child born was Allen Smith; the first marriage, that of Medad Cole and Miss Patterson; and the first death, that of Emily Porter.

[11] There are 5 churches in town; 2 Cong., Univ., Bap., and M. E.; the last hold their meetings in the chapel of the academy.

[12] Named from Abijah Hammond, of New York, proprietor. It embraces the greater part of No. 1 of Great Tract No. III, Macomb's Purchase.

[13] Cross-over-Island Lighthouse was built just above this place in 1847.

[14] The first of these were John and David Gregor, John Baird, John and James Hill, and Peter Allen. James Scott taught the first school, in 1818–19.

[15] Presb., M. E., F. W. Bap., and Prot. E.

HERMON[1]—was formed from Edwards and De Kalb, April 17, 1830, and named "*Depau.*" The name was changed Feb. 28, 1834, and a part was annexed to Edwards in 1850. It lies in the primitive region, s. w. of the center of the co. The surface is generally rolling, but broken and hilly in the s. part. Elm and Cedar Creeks are the principal streams. Trout and Clear Lakes lie near the s. border, and Gardners Pond near the center of the town. The soil is generally a sandy loam interspersed with tracts of sand, and is best adapted to grazing. **Hermon** (p. v.) is situated on Elm Creek, in the N. E. corner of the town. Pop. 346. **Marshville** is a hamlet, 1 mi. s. of Hermon. The first settlement was made by Jas. Taylor, and a few others who came soon after him, previous to 1812.[2] The town did not begin to be settled rapidly until 1822–25. Rev. Mr. Wright was the first preacher.[3]

HOPKINTON[4]—was formed from Massena, March 2, 1805. Russell was taken off in 1807, Parishville in 1818, and a part of Lawrence in 1828. It lies along the E. border of the co., and is the second largest town in the State. Its surface is level in the N., but broken and hilly in the s. It is crossed by the St. Regis and Racket Rivers; and in the central and s. parts are several extensive lakes, the principal of which is Tuppers Lake, on the line of Franklin co. The whole town is a wilderness, except the extreme N. part and a small tract upon Tuppers Lake. The soil is a fertile loam in the N. part. **Hopkinton** (p. v.) contains about 20 houses. **Nicholville** is a small village on the line of Lawrence and mostly in the latter town. **Fort Jackson,** in the N. part, on St. Regis, is a hamlet of a dozen houses. The first settlement in town was made by Roswell Hopkins, in 1802.[5] In 1814 a party of British, consisting of 30 men, under Maj. P. W. De Haven, visited this town and captured a large amount of flour belonging to the U. S., which was here stored in a barn.[6] In the spring of 1858 a company consisting of 13 families located in the vicinity of Tuppers Lake, with the design of forming an agricultural settlement.[7] The township of Mortlake, or No. 3 of Tract II, has been called "*Atherton,*" but it has yet no legal organization. There are 4 religious societies in town.[8]

LAWRENCE[9]—was formed from Hopkinton and Brasher, April 21, 1828. It lies on the E. border of the co., N. of the center. The surface is very level, and the soil is a fertile, sandy loam underlaid by Potsdam sandstone. It is drained by St. Regis and Deer Rivers. **Lawrence-ville** (p. v.) and **North Lawrence** (p. v.) are villages upon Deer River, each with a pop. of about 220. The latter is a station on the Northern R. R. **Nicholville,**[10] (p. v.,) on the line of Hopkinton, contains about 200 inhabitants. The first settlement began in 1806.[11] Since the completion of the R. R. this town has rapidly increased in population. The Quakers held the first meeting in 1808. There are 7 churches in town.[12]

LISBON—was formed March 6, 1801.[13] Madrid and Oswegatchie were taken off in 1802, and Canton in 1805. It lies upon the St. Lawrence, N. w. of the center of the co. Its surface is level or gently undulating. It is drained by Great and Little Sucker Creeks, and several smaller streams. Its soil is a light but fertile loam underlaid by calciferous sandstone. The town includes Gallop[14] Island in the river. **Lisbon Center** (p. o.) is a station on the Ogdensburgh R. R., and contains about a dozen houses. **Flackville**[15] (p. o.) is a hamlet, on the Ogdensburgh & Canton Road. **Red Mills**[16] (Lisbon p. o.) is a hamlet, on the river, opposite Gallop Island. This town was the first one organized in the co. The first settlement was made by Wm. O'Neal, in 1799. Alex. J. Turner came in as agent in Feb. 1800.[17] He was from Salem, N. Y., and induced many families

---

1 Named from Scripture. It embraces "*Fitz William,*" or No. 9 of Great Tract No. III, Macomb's Purchase, and parts of other townships.

2 Among the early settlers were Geo. Davis, Philemon Stuart, Jas. Farr, Ariel Inman, and Rufus Hopkins. William D. Moore taught the first school, in 1817. The first death was that of Thos. Farr.

3 There are 3 churches in town; M. E., Bap., and Christian.

4 Named from Roswell Hopkins, the first settler. It embraces the townships of "*Oakham,*" "*Mortlake,*" "*Jamestown,*" "*Pierce-field,*" "*Hollywood,*" "*Kildare,*" "*Riversdale,*" and "*Islington,*" or Nos. 2, 3, 5, 6, 8, 9, 12, and 15 of Great Tract No. II, Macomb's Purchase.

5 Mr. Hopkins bought a part of Islington. Among the early settlers were Joel and Samuel Goodale, R. W. Hopkins, Jared Dewey, and Eliphalet Branch. The first birth was in the family of —— Sheldon; and the first death, that of an infant, in 1807. Judge Hopkins built the first gristmill, in 1803.

6 There is good reason to believe that on this and other occasions the British received information from a prominent citizen of Franklin co.

7 This township was purchased Oct. 23, 1853, by a company consisting of Chas. G. Atherton, John H. Gage, and Dan'l H. Dear-

born, of Nashua, N. H., Elbridge G. Read and Wm. D. Beason, of Chelsea, Mass., and Moses A. Herrick, of Boston, for its number. The settlement was made under the auspices of this Company.

8 Cong., Bap., M. E., and F. W. Bap.

9 Named from Wm. Lawrence, of New York, proprietor. It embraces "*Chesterfield,*" or No. 16 of Great Tract No. II, Macomb's Purchase.

10 Named from E. S. Nichols, an agent of the proprietors.

11 Mr. Brewer, a sub-agent, came in as early as 1801; J. and S. Tyler, A. Saunders, A. Chandler, J. Allen, and J. and J. Pierce came in 1807. Ephraim Martin built the first sawmill, in 1809; Miss S. Tyler taught the first school, in 1810.

12 2 Cong., 2 M. E., 2 Bap., and F. W. Bap.

13 It originally contained the whole territory of the "*Ten Towns.*" It now includes No. 5 of the "*Ten Towns.*"

14 Pronounced "Gal-loo" Island.

15 Named from John P. Flack, first p. m.

16 Named from the color of the mills erected by Daniel W. Church for the proprietor, Stephen Van Rensselaer, in 1804.

17 Among the first settlers were Peter Sharp, Peter Hinnon, John Tibbets, Reuben Turner, Wm. Shaw, Lemuel Hoskins, Wm. Lyttle, James Aikens, Benj. Stewart, Matthew Perkins, Wesson

to remove from Washington co. A fatal epidemic prevailed in town in 1813. In the fall of 1813 a small party of dragoons stopping at the village were surprised by the Canadians; one was shot, another wounded, and two or three were taken prisoners to Canada. There are 6 churches in town.[1]

LOUISVILLE[2]—was formed from Massena, April 5, 1810. A part of Norfolk was taken off in 1823, and a part of the same town was annexed in 1844. It lies upon the St. Lawrence, in the N. E. part of the co. The surface is level. Grass River, the principal stream, flowing centrally through the town, affords a water-power at the village. The soil is a fertile, sandy loam, underlaid by calciferous sandstone. **Louisville,**[3] (p. o.,) on Grass River, and **Louisville Landing,** (p. o.,) on the St. Lawrence, are hamlets. The water-power at the former place has been somewhat improved; and the latter place is a landing for the American line of steamers. The first settlement was made by Nahum Wilson and Aaron Allen, in 1800.[4] The growth of the town was checked by the war; but it soon revived. There are 2 churches in town; M. E. and Union.

MACOMB[5]—was formed from Gouverneur and Morristown, April 3, 1841. A small tract was annexed from Hammond in 1842. It lies upon the S. shore of Black Lake, in the w. part of the co. Its surface is broken by ridges of gneiss and white limestone parallel to the lake. Fish and Birch Creeks are the principal streams. Pleasant and Yellow or Hickeys Lakes are fine sheets of water, with rocky shores, in the central part of the town. The soil is a light, sandy loam. The ridges are often without vegetation, but the valleys are fertile. Several valuable minerals are found in town.[6] **Macomb,** (p. o.,) on the "*Old State Road,*" and **Popes Mills,** (p. o.,) on Fish Creek, are hamlets. The first settlements were made upon the "*Old State Road,*" about 1805–06.[7] Timothy Pope made the first improvement at Popes Mills, in 1816. There is 1 church (M. E.) in town.

MADRID[8]—was formed from Lisbon, March 3, 1802, and Potsdam was taken off in 1806. It lies upon the St. Lawrence, E. of the center of the co. The surface is level or gently undulating. It is watered by Grass River, and by Great and Little Sucker, Brandy, and Trout Brooks. Upon both the St. Lawrence and Grass Rivers are rapids, from which are derived an immense amount of water-power. The soil is a light, sandy loam, generally fertile. **Waddington**[9] (p. v.) is situated upon the St. Lawrence, opposite Ogdens Island and the "*Rapide Plat.*" The rapids at this place impede the river navigation, but furnish an abundance of water-power.[10] The entire fall is 11 ft. Pop. 705. **Columbia Village** (Madrid p. o.) is situated at the falls of Grass River, 1 mi. from the R. R. station. It is a place of considerable business. Pop. 300. **Chases Mills** (p. o.) is a new settlement, upon Grass River, on the line of Louisville. The first settlement was made along the St. Lawrence, in 1798, under Joseph Edsall, agent of the proprietors.[11] In Jan., 1814, a party of Canadian militia, under Capt. Sherwood, crossed the St. Lawrence at Point Iroquois and marched to Columbia Village, pressed teams, and carried off a quantity of merchandise which had been captured upon bateaux on the preceding Oct. There are 9 churches in town.[12]

MASSENA[13]—was formed March 3, 1802. Hopkinton was taken off in 1805, Stockholm in 1806, Louisville in 1810, and Brasher in 1825. It lies upon the St. Lawrence, in the N. E. corner of the co. The surface is generally level or gently undulating. The principal streams are the Grass[14] and Racket Rivers, which flow through the town in parallel channels 1 to 2 mi. apart. Its soil is a productive, gravelly and sandy loam. **Massena** (p. v.) is situated upon Grass River, at the lower falls. It has a limited amount of manufactures. Pop. 310. **Massena Springs**[15]

Briggs, and Hez. Pierce. The first birth was in the family of J. Tibbets, in 1800. Rev. Alex. Proudfit held the first meetings. Dr. Jos. W. Smith, the first physician in the co., settled here in 1803 and remained two years.

[1] 1 Cong., Asso. Ref. Presb., M. E., Wes. Meth., Ref. Presb., and Prot. E. (St. Luke's.)

[2] It comprises the greater part of No. 1 of the "*Ten Towns.*"

[3] Locally known as "*Millersville,*" from Rev. Levi Miller, of Turin, who came here as agent of McVickar, the proprietor, in 1823.

[4] Among the early settlers were John Wilson, Lyman Bostwick, Elisha W. Barber, and Griffin Place. The first child born was a son of Nahum Wilson; and the first death, that of Philo Barber. Elisha Barber taught the first school, and N. Wilson kept the first inn.

[5] Named from Alex. Macomb, the great land speculator.

[6] Among these are lead, mica, copper pyrites, and blende. Stock companies have been engaged quite extensively in lead mining at Mineral Point, on Black Lake, and elsewhere.

[7] Among the first settlers were Sam'l Bristol, Rufus Washburn, Sam'l and E. Wilson, and Sam'l Peck.

[8] It embraces No. 4 of the "*Ten Towns,*" and is about 10 mi. sq.

[9] Named from Joshua Waddington, proprietor. Formerly called "*Hamilton.*" Incorp. April 26, 1839. A furnace, supplied with bog ore, was established here in 1834; but it was abandoned in 1840. A tract of 1,135 acres on the shore opposite the island, together with the island and water-power, were conveyed in 1811 to Joshua Waddington and Thos. L. and David A. Ogden.

[10] In 1808–11–15, acts were passed to improve the navigation at this place, and a lock was built for the passage of small boats.

[11] Among the early settlers were John Sharpe, Barton Edsall, John Tuttle, Benj. Bartlett, Godfrey Myers, Benj. Campbell, and E. Dimick. Dorothy Fields taught the first school; Seth Roberts built the first mills, at Columbia Village, in 1803. Mills were built at Waddington in 1803–04.

[12] 2 Cong., 2 M. E., Univ., Bap., Prot. E., (St. Paul's,) Asso. Ref., and R. C.

[13] Named from Marshal Massena, of the French army.

[14] This stream near its mouth is liable to a sudden reversal of its current by the damming up of the St. Lawrence by ice in severe cold weather. These back currents have been felt at Massena Village; and no bridges have been made to stand below the lower mills. The water has been known to rise 15 ft. in as many minutes, and to attain a maximum height of 25 ft. The lower dam is built to resist the current both ways.

[15] These springs are saline and sulphurous. Capt. John Polly built the first public house here, in 1822. A spacious brick hotel was erected in 1848, for the accommodation of those who resort here for health or pleasure.

lies upon the Racket, about one mi. distant from Massena. Pop. 120. It is a favorite summer resort. **Massena Center** (p. v.) contains about 25 houses, and **Racket River** (p. v.) about 20. By the treaty of 1796, a mile square at the mouth of Grass River was reserved by the St. Regis Indians; and most of the other lands in the town were located on Revolutionary land warrants before the sale of the rest of the co. Before the treaty the Indians issued unauthorized leases to different parties; and hence arose much annoyance from conflicting claims.[1] The first improvements were made on Grass River, on land leased of the Indians, in 1792. The first settlements on Revolutionary grants were made in 1798, by Amos Lay and others.[2] In 1812 the U. S. Government erected barracks here, which were occupied 3 months by militia. In Sept. 1813, a party of Canadians burned the barracks and carried away several prisoners. There are 5 churches in town.[3]

MORRISTOWN[4]—was formed from Oswegatchie, March 27, 1821. A part of Hammond was taken off in 1827, and a part of Macomb in 1841. It lies between the lower end of Black Lake and the St. Lawrence. Its surface is gently undulating, rising from either side toward the center. Chippewa Creek, flowing though the center, is the principal stream. The soil is a gravelly loam and generally fertile. **Morristown** (p. v.) is situated upon the St. Lawrence. Pop. 254. **Edwardsville**[5] (p. o.) is a small village on Black Lake, at which point a ferry has been established. **Brier Hill** (p. o.) is a hamlet. David Ford—as agent of Gouverneur Morris, the proprietor—made the first settlement on the site of the village, in 1799.[6] John K. Thurbur and Henry Ellenwood made the first improvement in the vicinity of Edwardsville, in 1810. In 1817–18 several English families located at a place still known as the "English Settlement." There are 7 churches in town.[7]

NORFOLK—was formed from Louisville and Stockholm, April 9, 1823. A part was annexed to Louisville in 1844. Its surface is moderately uneven. Racket River, the principal stream, flows diagonally through near the center of the town, and affords a large amount of water-power, partially improved.[8] The soil is generally fertile, resting upon drift deposits of gravel and marine clay, and all underlaid by calciferous sandstone. The E. part is sandy; and a swamp lies between the Racket and Grass Rivers. **Norfolk** (p. v.) is situated upon Racket River. Pop. about 200. It has manufactories of lumber, shingles, and articles of wood. **Raymondville**[9] (p. o.) is a small village on the Racket, below Norfolk. The first settlement was made by Erastus Hall, in 1809, at Raymondsville.[10] The Racket was formerly navigated, to some extent, as far as this place. There are 4 churches in town.[11]

OSWEGATCHIE[12]—was formed from Lisbon, March 3, 1802. De Kalb was taken off in 1806, Gouverneur in 1810, Morristown in 1821, and a part of De Peyster in 1825. The surface is level or gently undulating. Oswegatchie River, the principal stream, affords water-power at Heuvelton and at Ogdensburgh, which is available most of the year. The soil is a fine quality of gravelly loam, and is under a good state of cultivation. **Ogdensburgh,**[13] (p. v.,) situated upon the St. Lawrence, is one of the largest and most important villages in Northern New York. It is the w. terminus of the Ogdensburgh R. R., and stands at the foot of sloop navigation upon the great lakes and St. Lawrence River, giving to it important commercial advantages. A limited amount of manufacturing is also carried on, chiefly on the w. side of the Oswegatchie. It contains the depôts and buildings of the Ogdensburgh R. R.,—among the finest in the co.,—an academy,[14] a townhall,[15] U. S. customhouse,[16] and an armory.[17] Pop. Jan. 1858, 7,308. **Heuvel-**

---

1 Most of the valuable timber was stolen before settlement.

2 Among the first settlers were Manri Victory, Calvin Plumley, Bliss Hoisington, Elijah Bailey, David Lyttle, Seth Read, and Leonard Herrick. Gilbert Read taught the first school, in 1803. Amabel Foucher was a lessee of the first mill, under the Indians.

3 2 Cong., Bap., M. E., and R. C.

4 Named from Gouverneur Morris, principal proprietor. It originally embraced the township of "*Hague*," or No. 9 of the "*Ten Towns.*"

5 Locally known as the "*Narrows.*" Named from Jonathan S. Edwards, the first postmaster. On early maps it was marked "*Marysburgh.*"

6 Arnold Smith and Thomas Hill were first settlers on the river, and H. Harrison, Ephraim Story, and Benj. Tubbs on the lake. Smith kept the first inn, and Ford built the first house.

7 2 M. E., Presb., Cong., Prot. E., Evang. Luth., and Union.

8 There is a dam 1 mi. from the R. R. station, near the S. W. corner of the town, another at Norfolk, and another at Raymondsville.

9 Named from Benj. Raymond, the first agent for this town and Potsdam. First named "*Racketon.*"

10 Among the early settlers, who came in about 1810, were Eben Judson, Martin Barney, J. W. Osborn, C. G. Stowe, and Milo Brewer. The first death was that of E. Judson, in 1813. The first clearing at Norfolk Village was made for Le Ray, in 1811; and the first settlement was begun by Russell Atwater, in 1816.

A furnace was built at the village in 1825, and supplied with bog ore. It was burned in 1844.

11 M. E., Prot. E., and Presb., at Norfolk, and Presb. at Raymondsville.

12 Pronounced Os-we-gotch'ee; named from the river. It embraces most of No. 8 of the "*Ten Towns.*"

13 Named from Sam'l Ogden, the first proprietor. Incorp. in 1817. The unsold lands in and about the village were bought by David Parish in 1808, the owner of large tracts in the co. He built an extensive warehouse and several vessels, and laid plans for a large business, which the war prevented him from realizing.

14 This academy now forms an incorporate part of the public educational system of the village. The schools are all graded, and the pupils are advanced, according to attainment, from the primary schools to the complete academic course. The academy receives the income from the ferry at this place. In 1857 there were 7 schoolhouses and 18 teachers. The average number of pupils on the rolls was 1328, and average daily attendance 755.

15 By special act of 1858 a town hall was erected, at an expense of $10,000, on the corner of Washington and Franklin Sts.

16 The cornerstone of the old French Mission house is placed over one of its entrances.

17 An appropriation of $110,000 was made in 1857 for a customhouse, p. o., and U. S. courtroom. It is to be erected on the site of the old courthouse, corner of State and Knox Sts.

ton[1] (p. v.) lies upon the Oswegatchie, 7 mi. above Ogdensburgh. It has a limited amount of manufactures. Pop. 300. **Black Lake** is a p. o., in the s. w. part of the town. The early history of the town has already been noticed.[2] The first improvement, after Ogdensburgh was abandoned by the British, was made in 1796, by Nathan Ford,[3] and it soon became a place of commercial importance. The war checked the prosperity of the place, and after the return of peace business revived slowly. The opening of the Welland Canal and completion of the Ogdensburgh R. R. greatly increased the trade and added to the population of Ogdensburgh.[4] The completion of the Grand Trunk Railway through Canada has in some measure checked its growth, by diverting business into other channels. The first religious meetings were held while it was a French, and afterward a British, post. The census reports 11 churches.[5]

PARISHVILLE[6]—was formed from Hopkinton, April 15, 1818. Colton was taken off in 1843, and another part of Parishville annexed to it in 1851. It lies upon St. Regis River, s. e. of the center of the co. Its surface is level in the n. and considerably broken in the s. The soil is a deep loam in the n., but in the s. is light and sandy. A large portion of the town is yet a wilderness. **Parishville** (p. v.) is situated upon the w. branch of St. Regis River. Pop. 236. It has a limited amount of manufactures.[7] **Parishville Center**, in the n. part, is a hamlet. Daniel Hoard settled in 1810, as agent for the proprietors.[8] During the war the settlement was greatly increased by immigrants from the frontier towns. The census reports 4 churches.[9]

PIERREPONT[10]—was formed from Russell, April 15, 1818. A part of Fine was taken off in 1844. It occupies a long, narrow strip s. of the center of the co. The surface is quite broken. The three branches of Grass River, e. branch of the Oswegatchie, and Racket River are the principal streams. The soil in the n. is well adapted to grazing, and that in the s. is light and sandy. Settlements are confined to the n. part. Magnetic iron ore and other valuable minerals are found in large quantities. **Pierrepont** (p. o.) is a small village upon the hills, near the center of No. 3. **East Pierrepont**[11] (p. v.) is situated on Racket River. Pop. about 100. Flavius Curtis settled upon the line of Canton in 1806–07. The principal settlement commenced upon the completion of the St. Lawrence Turnpike, in 1811–12.[12] There are 2 churches; M. E. and F. W. Bap.

PITCAIRN[13]—was formed from Fowler, March 29, 1836. It lies on the s. border of the co., w. of the center. Its surface is much broken by ridges, separated by swamps, lakes, and fertile intervales. The soil is light and sandy, with a few alluvial flats along the streams. Iron ore, marble, and lead are found in town. The Jay Iron Ore Bed has been worked; and unprofitable attempts have been made to work some lead mines. The town is thinly settled. **Pitcairn** and **East Pitcairn** are p. offices. Settlement was begun in 1824 by immigrants from Potsdam.[14] There is no church in town.

POTSDAM[15]—was formed from Madrid, Feb. 21, 1806. It lies on Racket River, n. e. of the center of the co. Its surface is rolling; and its soil is a deep, rich loam. The streams are Racket River, affording a large amount of water-power, and Grass River, with a limited amount. Lumber and articles of wood are largely manufactured. There are extensive quarries of sandstone above the village.[16] This is the leading agricultural town in the co., and every part is under improvement. **Potsdam**[17] (p. v.) is located upon Racket River, e. of the center of the town. The river is here divided by islands and broken by rapids, and furnishes an extensive water-power. Pop. in 1st and 4th election districts, 2,123. It has a considerable amount of manufactures, and

---

1 Named from Jacob Van Heuvel, who invested a large sum in a ruinous attempt to establish business here.
2 See p. 574.
3 Among the first settlers were Ezra Fitz Randolph, Thomas Lee, John Lyon, John King, Louis Hasbrouck, Stephen Sloossen, and Powell Davis. The first school was taught by Richard Hubbard, in 1809.
4 A marine railway, constructed here in 1853, has been of great service to the interests of navigation.
5 3 M. E., 2 Presb., Univ., Unitarian, Bap., Cong., Prot. E., and R. C.
6 Named from David and Geo. Parish, proprietors of No. 13. It embraces the most of "*Catharineville*" and "*Wick*," or Nos. 13 and 11 of Great Tract No. II of Macomb's Purchase.
7 The river here descends 125 ft. within a mi., furnishing an abundance of water-power.
8 Among the early settlers were Luke Brown, Isaac Tower, H. Shattuck, and Levi Sawyer, who came in about 1811. During this and the succeeding year the proprietors caused a road to be opened to Carthage, and mills, a distillery, hotel, and forge to be built. The first birth was in the family of Luke Brown, in 1812. Harriet Bronson taught the first school, in the barn of Mr. Hoard.

9 Cong., M. E., Wes. Meth., and Bap.
10 Named from Hezekiah B. Pierrepont, of Brooklyn, proprietor. It embraces the townships of "*Chaumont*," "*Clifton*," "*Clare*," and a part of "*De Witt*," or Nos. 13, 10, 6, and 3 of Great Tract No. III, of Macomb's Purchase.
11 Sometimes called "*Coxes Mills*," from Gardner Coxe, who settled here and built mills in 1817–22. It has a large gang sawmill and a starch factory.
12 Among the early settlers were David Denton, Pet. R. Leonard, Jos. Matthews, and Ebenezer Tupper.
13 Named from Joseph Pitcairn, proprietor. It embraces the township of "*Portaferry*," or No. 11 of Great Tract No. III, Macomb's Purchase.
14 Among the early settlers were Nath'l Dickinson and sons, Levi Gleason, Nathan C. Scovil, and James Streeter. Caroline Dickinson taught the first school. The first birth was in the family of N. C. Scovil; the first marriage, that of Anson Bingham and Caroline Dickinson.
15 It embraces No. 3 of the "*Ten Towns*."
16 From these quarries the city of Hamilton, C. W., is supplied with flagging. The stone also is an excellent building material.
17 Incorp. March 3, 1831.

is the seat of an academy.[1] It also contains a bank and 2 printing offices. **Racketville** (North Potsdam p. o.) lies on Racket River, in the N. corner of the town. Pop. about 150. It has an extensive water-power, and is the Potsdam Junction station on the Ogdensburgh R. R. **Bucks Bridge**[2] is a hamlet upon Grass River, in the W. part of the town. **West Potsdam** (p. o.) is a small village in the midst of an agricultural region. The first settlement commenced in 1803, under Benj. Raymond, agent for the proprietor, and the town rapidly filled up by immigrants from Vt.[3] In Nov. 1804, Wm. Bullard took up 2,427 acres of land, and formed an association, styled "*The Union*," holding the land in common. The association broke up in 2 or 3 years.[4] There are 10 churches in town.[5]

ROSSIE[6]—was formed from Russell, Jan. 27, 1813. A part of Fowler was taken off in 1816, and a part of Hammond in 1827. A part of Hammond was annexed in 1844. It lies on the S. W. border of the co. Its surface is level in the E., and broken by ledges of gneiss, limestone, and sandstone in the remaining parts. It is drained by Oswegatchie and Indian Rivers. Its soil is like that of the adjoining towns. Between the gneiss and limestone, near Indian River, are extensive and valuable mines of lead and iron,[7] and a great variety of valuable minerals.[8] **Rossie** (p. v.) is situated on Indian River, at the head of the Black Lake navigation. Pop. 214. It owes its importance to its iron manufacture, commenced here in 1813. **Churchs Mills,**[9] (Wegatchie p. o.,) situated on the Oswegatchie, is the seat of a furnace. Pop. about 170. **Somerville** (p. v.) contains 20 houses. **Shingle Creek** is a p. o., in the S. E. corner. The first settlement was made in 1807.[10] A number of Scotch families came in about 1810. A blockhouse was built near Somerville in 1812. There are 2 churches in town; Univ. and M. E.

RUSSELL[11]—was formed from Hopkinton, March 27, 1807. Rossie was taken off in 1813, a part of Fowler in 1816, Pierrepont in 1818, and a part of Fine in 1844. It lies upon Grass River, S. of the center of the co. Its surface is much broken, and its S. part is still a wilderness. Its soil is light and sandy, but fertile in the valleys. **Russell** (p. o.) is a small village, upon Grass River, in the central part of the town; **North Russell** is a p. o. The first settlement was made in 1804, under the agency of R. Atwater.[12] A State arsenal was built in the village in 1809;[13] and the St. Lawrence Turnpike was opened the same year. The principal growth of the village was received in 1811 and 1812. A forge was built in 1846, and supplied with bog and magnetic ores. There are 2 churches in town; Bap. and M. E.: the Presb. and Prot. E. each have societies formed.

STOCKHOLM[14]—was formed from Massena, Feb. 21, 1806. A part of Norfolk was taken off in 1823. It lies in the northeasterly part of the co. Its surface is rolling. Its soil is a light, sandy loam, generally productive. It is watered by the two branches of St. Regis River. It is strictly an agricultural town, and one of the most wealthy in the co. **Stockholm Depot** (p. o.) is a small village upon the R. R., in the E. part of the town. **East Stockholm** (Stockholm p. o.) and **Sanfordville** are hamlets of a dozen houses each. **West Stockholm** (p. o.) is a small manufacturing village upon St. Regis River. **Knapps Station** (North Stockholm p. o.) is a R. R. station on the N. W. border of the town; and **Southville** is a p. o. **Skinnerville** is a hamlet on the W. branch of the St. Regis. The first settlement was begun in 1802, by Ebenezer Hulburd and Dr. Luman Pettibone, agents.[15] The census reports 5 churches.[16]

[1] The St. Lawrence Academy was commenced, through the exertions of Benj. Raymond, in 1812. It has long maintained a high reputation among the schools of Northern New York.
[2] Named from Isaac Buck, who settled here in 1807.
[3] Among the early settlers were Wm. and Gurdon Smith, Benj. Stewart, John Delance, David French, Chester Dewey, Joseph Bailey, Bester Pierce, Roswell Parkhurst, Wm. Bullard, Reuben Field, and Abner Royce. The first birth was a daughter of Wm. Smith; and the first death, that of Jas. Chadwick. Mills were built by Raymond.
[4] The members were not professedly united in religious or political views. Spafford, in his Gazetteer, erroneously calls them "Moravians."—*Hough's Hist. St. L. and Frank. Cos., p.435.*
[5] 3 M. E., Presb., Univ., Prot. E., (Trinity,) Bap., Ref. Presb., R. C., and Catholic Apostolic.
[6] Pronounced Ros-seé. Named from a sister of David Parish, the proprietor. It embraces "*Somerville*," or No. 1 of Great Tract No. III, Macomb's Purchase.
[7] The first lead mining operations in this town were unskilfully performed and attended with ruinous results, which led to their abandonment. After 20 years' suspension, the mines were reopened by an English company, (The Rossie & Canada Lead Company,) formed under special act, and working upon a lease of 20 years from June 1, 1856; and they are said to have been successful. The Caledonian and Keene Iron Mines, near the R. R., owned by Parish, have yielded an immense quantity of ore, which has mostly been worked at Rossie Iron Works.

[8] Among these minerals are marble, graphite, heavy spar, phosphate of lime, copper pyrites, calcite, pearl spar, apatite, zircon, tremolite, satin spar, celestine, carbonate of iron, chondrodite, and spinelle.
[9] Formerly called "*Caledonia*," and "*Howards Mills*," from Jas. Howard, former proprietor.
[10] Among the first settlers were Jos. Teall, Reuben Streeter, A. Simmons, O. Malterner, A. Keeney, jr., S. Bonfy, S. Waters, and J. Stearns. The first child born was Wm. Rossie Williams. Reuben Streeter built the first mill.
[11] Named from Russell Atwater, first settler.
[12] Among the early settlers were Nathan, Loren, and David Knox, Heman Morgan, Elias Hayden, Reuben Ashman, Jesse Bunnell, Elihu Morgan, and Joel Clarke, who came in 1805. The first child born was a son of Reuben Ashman, in 1806; the first marriage, that of Calvin Hill and Harriet Knox; and the first death, that of —— Curtis. Rollin Smith taught the first school, and Atwater built the first mills.
[13] Sold for a school building, in 1850.
[14] It originally comprised No. 2 of the "*Ten Towns*," and is nearly 10 mi. sq.
[15] Among the early settlers were Benj. Wright, Isaac Kelsey, Abram Sheldon, and John and Robt. Bisbee. S. Reynolds built the first mill, in 1804. Mrs. Sheldon was the first woman who came into town.
[16] 2 Cong., M. E., Bap., W. Meth.; the Christians and F. W. Bap. have also societies in town.

Acres of Land, Valuation, Population, Dwellings, Families, Freeholders, Schools, Live Stock, Agricultural Products, and Domestic Manufactures, of St. Lawrence County.

NAMES OF TOWNS.	ACRES OF LAND.		VALUATION OF 1858.			POPULATION.		No. of Dwellings.	No. of Families.	Freeholders.	SCHOOLS.	
	Improved.	Unimproved.	Real Estate.	Personal Property.	Total.	Males.	Females.				No. of Districts.	Children taught.
Brasher..............	18,280	40,725	$445,160	$5,250	$450,410	1,514	1,454	487	507	435	13	1,248
Canton	34,101	29,593	1,343,810	148,680	1,492,490	2,497	2,498	874	880	806	27	2,005
Colton	3,460	127,293	166,908	4,750	171,658	546	494	209	212	140	7	492
De Kalb...............	22,658	26,616	473,808	11,200	485,008	1,360	1,316	482	511	319	22	1,065
De Peyster...........	12,334	13,706	327,990	13,550	341,540	599	564	195	196	153	10	502
Edwards.............	7,834	19,285	170,213	12,850	183,063	625	555	208	210	211	9	589
Fine...................	1,824	93,932	55,197		55,197	172	144	57	57	56	4	162
Fowler...............	15,732	12,687	296,498	3,225	299,723	814	806	292	303	241	14	688
Gouverneur.........	25,111	12,157	753,248	43,200	796,448	1,406	1,450	498	512	399	20	1,146
Hammond............	15,701	18,823	339,875	7,300	347,175	970	905	314	320	112	11	705
Hermon..............	12,537	12,258	254,593	4,500	259,093	854	794	289	305	244	10	663
Hopkinton	12,641	36,427	480,803	29,350	518,153	775	779	293	267	241	18	861
Lawrence............	17,338	7,905	421,800	68,900	490,700	1,226	1,139	457	473	407	15	987
Lisbon...............	36,959	24,491	825,780	7,780	833,560	2,622	2,487	907	905	761	33	2,348
Louisville	15,367	23,881	320,216	3,850	324,066	1,087	1,033	345	356	338	14	917
Macomb*.............	10,435	29,765	192,660		192,660	749	717	260	124	221	13	663
Madrid...............	32,788	28,551	1,119,222	69,350	1,188,572	2,435	2,427	844	877	736	25	1,884
Massena..............	19,620	9,037	389,574	63,385	452,959	1,341	1,360	459	468	341	19	1,227
Morristown	19,407	24,691	372,170	21,750	393,920	1,049	1,062	399	399	281	16	889
Norfolk.............	12,286	9,459	359,320	29,550	388,870	882	922	341	350	310	12	758
Oswegatchie........	26,669	12,496	2,416,555	1,149,035	3,565,590	5,033	5,027	1,658	1,474	1,096	24	4,509
Parishville	20,528	42,602	367,230	22,800	390,030	1,054	1,060	395	395	404	15	760
Pierrepont...........	10,339	115,121	274,845	3,200	278,045	906	928	348	347	309	18	781
Pitcairn.............	3,900	20,767	79,960	945	80,905	269	262	106	106	89	6	215
Potsdam..............	40,297	20,521	1,528,405	244,300	1,772,705	3,328	3,303	1,126	1,191	1,015	34	2,238
Rossie................	8,482	12,911	270,419	7,260	277,679	752	728	252	314	153	10	750
Russell...............	12,080	38,068	305,111	10,300	315,411	1,115	993	399	392	262	15	750
Stockholm	30,846	21,763	706,691	25,600	732,291	1,954	1,836	697	726	610	27	1,619
Total...............	499,554	885,531	15,066,061	2,011,860	17,077,921	37,934	37,043	13,191	13,177	10,690	377	10,997

NAMES OF TOWNS.	LIVE STOCK.					AGRICULTURAL PRODUCTS.							Domestic cloths, in Yards.
	Horses.	Working Oxen and Calves.	Cows.	Sheep.	Swine.	BUSH. OF GRAIN.		Tons of Hay.	Bushels of Potatoes.	Bushels of Apples.	DAIRY PRODUCTS.		
						Winter.	Spring.				Pounds Butter.	Pounds Cheese.	
Brasher..............	664	1,745	1,633	2,363	854	1,669	31,450	4,440	26,317	200	135,320	24,982	3,368
Canton..............	1,906	2,991	3,927	6,165	1,802	1,848	61,525	11,192	36,454	3,546	30,840	252,988	4,514
Colton...............	135	218	369	373	131	459	8,221	2,503	8,434		10,340	950	256
De Kalb..............	598	1,961	2,426	1,281	841	1,020	41,927½	6,050	15,495		206,370	233,965	3,889
De Peyster..........	499	836	1,442	4,334	480	738	28,311	2,556	7,985	1,173	136,950	12,200	1,632
Edwards............	320	914	1,017	1,490	446	1,530½	17,877	2,205	12,640	8	92,909	26,023	2,565
Fine.................	32	156	109	147	99	352	3,776	304	3,546		10,900		461
Fowler..............	529	1,228	2,072	1,509	638	1,091	32,324	4,353	9,988	165	159,870	128,004	927
Gouverneur	679	1,486	2,924	2,735	830	1,533	55,052	5,170	16,653	410	278,023	254,561	1,876
Hammond............	770	1,266	1,421	3,441	830	1,702	67,006	3,665	6,576	2,342	112,821	52,750	2,507
Hermon..............	406	1,524	1,753	998	418	164	26,214	3,621	8,057	832	136,615	155,500	2,133
Hopkinton	450	1,031	948	2,919	745	3,256	19,387	2,786	24,046	3,566	82,627	15,190	1,274
Lawrence............	590	1,665	1,621	3,328	655	1,495	29,106	4,776	50,285	1,107	140,525	31,725	1,823
Lisbon...............	1,717	3,057	3,507	7,513	1,904	1,618	50,888	10,681	52,804	9,693	349,863	16,245	12,811
Louisville	724	1,851	1,611	3,974	949	1,556	46,228	4,686	18,053	4,067	148,730	4,880	4,461
Macomb*.............	367	979	981	1,250	444	1,557	18,225	2,536	10,683	194	95,850	7,069	2,379
Madrid...............	1,461	2,805	3,693	7,085	1,820	2,050	86,438	9,454	46,055	8,711	339,082	122,620	9,974
Massena..............	901	2,558	1,817	5,535	1,194	1,997	50,802	6,501	20,542	4,920	148,570	24,940	2,159
Morristown	1,032	1,437	1,861	2,458	1,080	4,154	52,792½	5,133	9,811	7,335	196,289	11,928	5,392
Norfolk..............	477	807	1,066	2,034	605	456	20,631	3,738	16,968	5,798	87,970	24,845	2,268
Oswegatchie........	1,409	2,265	2,616	3,971	1,619	5,826	75,057½	7,704	24,380	8,789	191,901	3,570	5,314
Parishville	735	1,693	1,656	5,389	813	3,979	45,110	4,584	29,110	4,377	168,890	58,307	3,178
Pierrepont..........	399	797	978	1,203	392	2,100	20,106	2,466	12,328	2,141	80,643	17,290	1,846
Pitcairn.............	134	239	300	258	203	146	11,726	554	8,314		3,270	500	699
Potsdam..............	1,505	2,864	4,997	4,554	1,954	1,833	61,419	13,397	50,108	14,553	452,116	44,608	4,443
Rossie................	382	771	1,086	1,290	398	893	25,305½	2,055	8,054	46	110,119	14,880	1,172
Russell...............	358	1,800	1,518	2,046	730	343	30,918	3,912	11,670	2,108	104,170	87,320	2,975
Stockholm	1,082	3,303	2,823	6,811	1,212	5,140	50,521½	8,378	58,667	4,416	257,236	45,119	3,567
Total...............	20,261	44,247	52,161	86,454	24,086	50,505½	1,068,344½	139,400	604,023	90,497	4,268,809	1,672,999	89,863

a The town of WADDINGTON was formed from this town in 1859.

SARATOGA COUNTY.

THIS county[1] was formed from Albany, Feb. 7, 1791. It lies in the N. angle formed by the junction of the Hudson and Mohawk Rivers, centrally distant 31 miles from Albany, and contains 862 sq. mi. Its surface is hilly or undulating in the S. and mountainous in the N. Two ranges of mountains traverse the co. from N. E. to S. W. The Palmertown or Luzerne Mts., the most eastern of these ranges, extend from Warren co., through the W. part of Moreau and Milton and the E. part of Corinth, into Greenfield, where they terminate in a series of low, irregular hills. Hudson River breaks through this range on the N. border of the co. in a deep ravine 3 mi. in extent. The mountains rise abruptly from the water's edge to a height of 800 feet. Their declivities are generally rocky and precipitous, and their summits spread out into a broad, rocky upland covered with forests. The Kayaderosseras Range extend through the N. part of the co. and occupy the greater part of Corinth, Edinburgh, Day, and Hadley. The declivities of these mountains are generally precipitous, and their summits spread out into broad, rocky uplands broken by ledges and craggy peaks. A group of isolated hills, 450 feet high, with rounded summits and terraced declivities, extend through the W. part of Stillwater and Saratoga. A broad intervale extends along the Hudson, bordered by a range of clay bluffs 40 to 200 feet in height. From the summits of these bluffs an extensive sand plain extends westward to the foot of the mountains, covering the greater part of Moreau, Wilton, Northumberland, Saratoga Springs, Malta, and Clifton Park. The S. W. portion of the co. is rolling or moderately hilly.

Hudson River flows nearly 70 mi. along the E. border of the co. It is interrupted by falls and is crossed by several dams and bridges.[2] The Mohawk forms a portion of the S. boundary. The Sacondaga, forming the outlet of the principal lakes in the S. part of Hamilton co., flows in a tortuous channel through Edinburgh, Day, and Hadley. It is navigable for boats and steamboats of light draught from Fish House, on the border of Fulton co., to Conklingville Falls, in Hadley, a distance of 20 mi. Below the falls it flows between high, rocky hills in a series of rapids to the Hudson. Kayaderosseras River drains the central part of the co. and flows into Saratoga Lake. The outlet of the lake takes the name of Fish Creek. The other principal streams are Snook Kil, Anthonys Kil, and Glowegee Creek. Saratoga Lake is a beautiful sheet of water, 6½ mi. long and 2 broad, situated about 4 mi. S. E. of Saratoga Springs. Ballston, Round, and Owl Lakes are small sheets of water in the S. part of the co. Among the mountains and forests in the N. are numerous other small lakes but little known.

The Kayaderosseras and Luzerne Mts. are both principally composed of primary rocks. A stratum of crystalline limestone extends along the foot of the mountains; and this is succeeded by Potsdam sandstone. In these formations iron ore has been obtained; but the beds have been imperfectly explored.[3] The rocks in the S. half of the co. belong to the shales and slates of the Hudson River group. A large part of the co. is covered with drift deposits, consisting of sand and clay. The soil among the mountains is a light, sandy or gravelly loam, and is best adapted to grazing; upon the intervales along the rivers it is a deep, fertile, clayey loam and alluvium; and in the S. W. part it is a heavy, clayey loam. A strip of light sand occupies the greater part of the two eastern tiers of towns. The people are chiefly engaged in grain and stock raising. Lumbering and tanning are extensively carried on in the N. part of the co. Considerable attention is also paid to the manufacture of cotton and woolen goods and paper.[4]

The county seat is located at the village of Ballston Spa, in the town of Milton.[5] The courthouse, a

[1] The origin of the word Saratoga is uncertain. The termination "oga," or "aga," is said to signify "place." The first part of the word has been thought to imply "hillside" by some, and "place of salt springs" by others,—"soragh" in some Indian dialects being the name for salt.

[2] See descriptions of Warren and Washington cos.

[3] Among the other minerals are agate, chalcedony, chrysoberyl, garnet, tourmalin, phosphate of lime, graphite, iron pyrites, and tufa. A full catalogue of minerals is given by Dr. John H. Steele in his geological survey of the co.

[4] Important manufactures have for many years been carried on in Milton, Moreau, Mechanicsville, Schuylerville, and Waterford. The manufacture of lumber is chiefly limited to Glens Falls and Jessups Landing, on the Hudson.

[5] The first courthouse was located 2 mi. s. w. of Ballston Spa. By act of March 26, 1794, the sum of £1500 was appropriated to build a courthouse and jail; and in each of the following two years £600 was added to the amount. John Bradstreet Schuyler, Richard Davis, jr., John Ball, John McClelland, and Jas. Emott, were appointed commissioners to superintend the erection of the

plain brick building, contains the usual rooms and offices and the jail. The co. clerk's office is a small building situated on Main Street. The co. poorhouse is situated on a farm of 112 acres 1½ mi. N. W. of Ballston Spa. The average number of inmates is about 100; and the institution yields an annual revenue of $900.[1]

The Champlain Canal extends along the Hudson from Waterford to the s. border of Northumberland, at which point it crosses the river into Washington co.[2] The Saratoga & Schenectady R. R. extends from Saratoga Springs through Milton, Ballston, and Clifton Park to Schenectady.[3] The Saratoga & Whitehall R. R. extends from Saratoga Springs N. through Wilton and Northumberland to Moreau, where it crosses the Hudson to Fort Edward. The Rensselaer & Saratoga R. R. crosses the Mohawk at Waterford, and passes through that town, Half Moon, Clifton Park, Malta, and Ballston to Ballston Spa. The Albany, Vermont & Canada R. R., crossing the Mohawk at Cohoes, intersects the R. & S. R. R. at Saratoga Junction, and crosses the Hudson at Deepikill into Rensselaer co. The Lake Ontario & Hudson River R. R.[4] has been laid out and partly worked from Saratoga Springs through Greenfield, Corinth, and Hadley.

Eight weekly and 4 daily papers are published in the co.[5]

The greater part of this co. is embraced within the "Half Moon," "Clifton Park" or "Shannondhoi," "Saratoga," "Appel," and "Kayaderosseras" or "Queensborough" Patents.[6] The last named patent includes the greater part of the co. The purchase of the tract was confirmed by the Mohawks, July 26, 1683. The bounds were so loosely defined that disputes arose between the

---

buildings. By an act passed March 14, 1817, Jas. Merrill, Elisha Powell, Isaac Gere, John Gibson, and Gilbert Warring were appointed commissioners to superintend the erection of new buildings in the place of the old ones, which had been burned.

[1] The house is reported as old, ill constructed, and badly out of repair, but generally well kept.—*Report of Senate Com.*, 1857.

[2] The towing path of the canal is constructed across the river on the Fort Miller Bridge.

[3] This was the second R. R. built in the U. S. It is leased and used by the Rensselaer & Saratoga R. R.

[4] Formerly the Saratoga & Sackets Harbor R. R.

[5] *The Waterford Gazette*, the first paper published in the co., was established at Waterford about 1801, by Horace L. Wadsworth, and was continued until after 1816.
The Waterford Reporter was published in 1822 by Wm. L. Fisk.
The Anti Masonic Recorder was published at Waterford in 1830 by J. C. Johnson.
The Waterford Atlas was started Dec. 1, 1832, by Wm. Holland & Co. In 1834 it was changed to
The Waterford Atlas and Manufacturers, Mechanics, and Farmers' Journal. It was soon after discontinued.
The Democratic Champion was published at Waterford in 1840 by H. Wilber.
The Waterford Sentinel was started —— by Andrew Hoffman, and is now published by J. H. Masten.
The Saratoga Advertiser was established at Ballston in 1804 by Samuel B. Brown. It was changed soon after to
The Aurora Borealis and Saratoga Advertiser, and published by Brown & Miller. About 1810 it again passed into the hands of Mr. Brown, and was changed to
The Advertiser, and continued some years.
The Independent American was started Sept. 27, 1808, by Wm. Child. In May, 1818, it appeared as
The People's Watch Tower, published by Jas. Comstock; and in 1820 as
The Saratoga Farmer, published by H. G. Spafford. In 1821 it was changed to
The Ballston Spa Gazette and Saratoga Farmer, and in 1822 to
The Ballston Spa Gazette, published by J. Comstock. April 20, 1847, it appeared as
The Ballston Democratic Whig Journal, edited by J. O. Nodyne. In 1848 it was changed to
The Ballston Journal; and it is now published by Albert A. Moore.
The Saratoga Courier was published at Ballston in 1818 by Ulysses F. Doubleday.
The Saratoga Journal was published at Ballston by Josiah Bunce, in ——.
The Saratoga Recorder and Anti Masonic Democrat was published in 1831 by D. Tehan.
The New York Palladium was published in 1831 by Ansel Warren.
The Schenectady and Saratoga Standard was published at Ballston in 1832–33 by Israel Sackett.
The Ballston Democrat was started in 1843 by Newell Hine. In 1853 it was united with the Northern Mirror as
The Ballston Democrat and Mirror. It is now published as
The Ballston Atlas, by Seymour Chase.
The Northern Mirror was started by S. Chase, and in 1853 it was united with the Ballston Democrat.
The Saratoga Gazette was published at Saratoga Springs in 1810.
The Saratoga Patriot was started by Samuel R. Brown, and in 1812 it was removed to Albany.
The Saratoga Sentinel was commenced in 1819 by G. M. Davidson, and in 1845 it was merged in The Republican.

The Saratoga Whig was started in 1839 by Huling & Watts. Sold to G. W. Spooner in 1840, and afterward to E. G. Huling. In 1851 it was changed to
The Saratoga County Press. A daily edition, started in 1844, was issued in 1855 as
The Saratoga Daily News, Huling & Morehouse, publishers.
The Daily Sentinel was started at Saratoga Springs in 1842 by Wilbur & Palmer. From 1855 to 1857 it was issued as
The Daily Post, and then changed back to The Sentinel. Jan. 1, 1859, it was merged with The Republican.
The Republican, da. and w., was started in 1844 by John A. Corey, and in 1853 it passed into the hands of Thos. G. Young. Jan. 1, 1859, it was united with The Sentinel, under the title of
The Republican & Sentinel, da. and w., Thos. G. Young, publisher.
The Old Settler was pub. at Saratoga in 1849 by A. H. Allen.
The Advent Review and Sabbath Herald, semi-mo., was published in 1850 by Jas. White.
The Temperance Helper was started in Jan. 1853, by the Saratoga Co. Temperance Alliance. In 1855 it was bought by Potter & Judson, and in 1856 it was changed to
The Saratogian. A daily edition is published during the summer season.
The Saratoga Sentinel was started in 1854 by Allen Corey, and sold in May, 1855, to Clark & Thayer.
The Schuylerville Herald was published at Schuylerville in 1844 by J. L. Cramer.
Old Saratoga was started in 1848 at Schuylerville by J. L. Cramer, and continued until 1852.
Battle Ground Herald was published at Schuylerville from Aug. 1853, till July, 1857, by R. N. Atwell & Co.
The Saratoga County American, started in Dec. 1857, is now published at Schuylerville by J. R. Rockwell.
The Stillwater Gazette was commenced at Stillwater in 1845 by Isaac A. Pitman, and was published about 3 years.
The Cold Water Battery was published at Stillwater in 1845 by Isaac A. Pitman.
The Hudson River Chronicle was published at Mechanicsville from Oct. 1856, to March, 1858, by Samuel Heron.
The Crescent Eagle was published in 1852 by C. Ackerman.
The Morning Star was published at Mechanicsville in 1854–55, by C. Smith & Co.

[6] The "Half Moon" Patent, including Waterford and part of Half Moon, was granted to Anthony Van Schaick. The "Saratoga Patent," including the present towns of Easton, Saratoga, and Stillwater, was granted, Nov. 4, 1684, to Cornelius Van Dyck, Jan Jans Bleecker, Peter Phillips Schuyler, Johannes Wendell, Dirk Wessels, David Schuyler, and Robt. Livingston. The "Clifton Park Patent," embracing the E. part of the present town of Clifton Park and the w. part of Half Moon, was granted Sept. 23, 1708. The "Appel Patent," in the w. part of the present town of Clifton Park, was about ¼ mi. wide on the Mohawk and extended back nearly 4½ mi. The "Kayaderosseras Patent" was granted Nov. 2, 1708, to Manning Hermanse, Johannes Beekman, Rip Van Dam, Ann Bridges, May Beckley, Peter Fauconneer, Adrian Hogelandt, Johannes Fisher, John Tuder, Jovis Hogelandt, John Stevens, John Totham, and Samson Broughton. This patent contained 400,000 acres, and embraced nearly all of Saratoga co. N. of the small patents already described, and portions of Montgomery, Fulton, and Warrn cos. The portion of the co. N. of this patent was embraced in the "Palmer" and "Glen" purchases.

proprietors and the owners of the Schenectady, Clifton Park, and Half Moon Patents, which were not settled until after the Revolution.

The first settlements in the co. were made by the Dutch, within a few years after their first colonization of the country about Albany. These settlements commenced near Waterford, on the Mohawk, and gradually extended up the valley of the Hudson. Lying in the great thoroughfare between the English settlements at Albany and the French posts on Lake Champlain, the continual passing of military parties checked the progress of settlement and exposed the few hardy pioneers to all the dangers and anxieties of border warfare. Immediately after the conquest of Canada, in 1760, settlements rapidly extended along the river valleys and to some distance into the interior. During the Revolution, some of the most important events of the war transpired within the limits of this co. Upon the approach of Burgoyne in 1777, Gen. Schuyler retreated from Fort Edward and made a stand first at Saratoga, then at Stillwater, and finally at the mouths of the Mohawk.[1] This last stand he considered the best position for checking the advance of the enemy, which he was expecting both from the N. and W. The inhabitants of the co. above fled in consternation to Albany, leaving their homes and fields of grain to be destroyed by the advancing foe. The islands at the mouth of the Mohawk were fortified about the 1st of August, and Burgoyne took possession of Fort Edward at nearly the same time. While the armies lay in this position, two events took place which served greatly to embarrass Burgoyne and to render sure his final defeat. The first of these was the defeat of Baum at Bennington, and the second the retreat of St. Leger from the siege of Fort Schuyler.[2]

The American army in the mean time, under Gen. Gates, who had superseded Gen. Schuyler, advanced toward the enemy, and about the 1st of September took possession of and fortified the high bluffs known as Bemis Heights, upon the river, in the N. part of Stillwater.[3] Greatly perplexed and embarrassed, Burgoyne finally concluded to continue his march toward Albany. On the 14th of September he crossed the Hudson, above the mouth of the Batten Kil, into the N. part of Saratoga, and continued his march southward. On the 19th the first battle of Stillwater was fought, in front of the American intrenchments at Bemis Heights. The American loss was 315 and the British 500, the former returning to their camp and the latter retaining possession of the battle field. On the 7th of October another severe battle was fought, in which the British lost 700 and the Americans 150. During the succeeding night the British abandoned their camp and retreated northward, and finally took position upon the heights of Saratoga, just W. of the present village of Schuylerville. Here Burgoyne found himself completely hemmed in. A victorious and hourly increasing army was in front; a strong detachment was posted on the E. bank of the river to prevent his crossing that stream; Fort Edward, in his rear, had been taken by the Americans; his bravest officers had fallen in battle; Lord Howe had failed to afford the promised support from New York;[4] and his army was reduced to the last extremity for want of provisions. Under these circumstances, the British commander reluctantly yielded to an imperative necessity, and on the 16th of October signed articles of capitulation. On the 17th the whole British army laid down their arms and were marched eastward to Mass.[5] The close of this campaign left the co. stripped of nearly every evidence of civilized occupation. The fear of continued Indian hostilities prevented the immediate re-occupation of the abandoned lands; but after the close of the war settlements rapidly spread. Since this period few incidents of general interest have occurred, and the history is but the record of the everyday events connected with the conversion of a wilderness into fruitful fields and happy homes.

BALLSTON[6]—was formed from Saratoga as a district, April 1, 1775, and was organized as a town, March 7, 1788. Charlton, Galway, and Milton were taken off in 1792, and the line of Charl-

---

[1] This retreat was occasioned by the limited number of Schuyler's forces and the fact that the militia were every day flocking to his standard. Burgoyne's progress was arrested by felling trees across the roads, breaking down bridges, and by every other possible means of annoyance. Every hour thus gained added to the strength of the Americans and weakened the British forces; so that, when all the obstacles were finally overcome, the American army was in a condition to meet the British in open battle.

[2] Gen. St. Leger, at the head of a body of tories and Canadians, was to co-operate with Burgoyne by marching through the Mohawk Valley and joining the main army at Albany. At Oswego he was joined by a body of Indians under Brant, making his force 1700 strong. On the 2d of Aug. he invested Fort Stanwix, (where Rome, Oneida co., now stands,) and continued the siege until the 22d, when, learning that an American re-enforcement was approaching, he hastily retreated.

[3] The fortifications of the American camp were erected under

the direction of Kosciusko, then holding the office of engineer in the army. They were so constructed as to completely command the passage down the river. The position afterward chosen by the British was about 1 mi. distant, and separated from the American works by a deep ravine.

[4] Instead of co-operating with Burgoyne and sending the promised aid up the Hudson, Lord Howe had marched to Philadelphia, leaving the British forces in N. Y. under the command of Sir Henry Clinton. The latter officer made a diversion in Burgoyne's favor, but too late to be of any service.

[5] The place where the British laid down their arms was a green on the river, N. of the mouth of Fish Creek. It was in front of Fort Hardy, an old fortification erected by Dieskau in 1755. The number of the army at the time of the surrender was 5,792, of whom 2,412 were Germans. The Americans also captured 42 brass cannon, 4,647 muskets, 6,000 dozen of cartridges, and a large amount of carriages and camp equipages.

[6] Named from Rev. Eliphalet Ball, one of the first settlers.

ton was changed March 5, 1795. It lies upon the border of the co., s. w. of the center. The surface is gently rolling. Mourning Kil and the Outlet Creek are the principal streams. Ballston Lake, in the s. e. part, is a long, narrow, and deep body of water, the outlet of which is the principal inlet of Round Lake. The soil s. e. of the lake is generally a light sand, and n. w. it is a clayey and gravelly loam. **Ballston** (p. v.) is situated on the line of Milton. A small portion only of the village is within the limits of this town. **Burnt Hills,**[1] (p. v.,) in the s. part, contains 42 dwellings. **Ballston Center** (p. o.) and **Academy Hill,** near the center, are hamlets. **East Line,** (p. o.,) on the border of Malta, contains 15 houses. It is a station on the R. & S. R. R. **South Ballston** is a p. o. The first settlement was made in 1763, by two brothers named Michael and Nicholas McDonald,[2] who located near the w. bank of Ballston Lake. In 1770, Rev. Eliphalet Ball, with his three sons John, Stephen, and Flamen, and several members of his congregation, removed from Bedford, N. Y., and settled in the vicinity of Academy Hill.[3] Soon after their arrival a large number of settlers came in from New England, N. J., Scotland, and the north of Ireland.[4] The settlements in this town were twice invaded during the Revolution, and several of the inhabitants were carried away prisoners to Canada.[5] The first church (Presb.) was organized Oct. 6, 1792.[6] There are 6 churches in town.

CHARLTON—was formed from Ballston, March 17, 1792. It is the s. w. corner town of the co. Its surface is undulating, with a gentle inclination toward the s. Its streams are the Aalplaats[7] and a branch of the Mourning Kil. The soil is an excellent quality of sandy, gravelly, and clayey loam. Ledges of limestone in the w. part, affording an excellent quality of building stone, are extensively quarried. **Charlton,** (p. v.,) in the s. e. part, contains 3 churches and 38 houses; **West Charlton** (p. v.) contains about 20 houses. The commissioners appointed to divide the Kayaderosseras Patent appropriated 5,000 acres in the s. part of this town to defray the expenses of the division. The first settlement was commenced in 1774, by Thos. Sweetman, who located in the e. part of the town.[8] The first church (Presb.) was incorp. Dec. 11, 1792; Rev. Wm. Schenck was the first pastor.[9]

CLIFTON PARK—was formed from Half Moon, March 3, 1828, as "*Clifton.*" Its name was changed March 31, 1829. The surface is level or undulating, except in the n. e., where it is broken by sand hills and ravines. A line of rugged clay bluffs borders upon the Mohawk Valley. Stony Creek, Swarte and Dwaas Kils are the principal streams. A belt of heavy clay and gravelly loam extends along the river above the bluffs. The soil is alluvial upon the Mohawk flats and a sandy loam in the central and n. parts. **Clifton Park,** (p. v.,) on the border of Half Moon, contains 2 churches and 22 houses; **Amity,** (Visschers Ferry p. o.,) a canal village in the s. part, contains 1 church and 45 houses; **Jonesville,** (p. v.,) in the n. part, 1 church, the Jonesville Academy,[10] and 30 houses; and **Rexfords Flats,**[11] (p. v.,) a canal village in the s. w. corner of the town, 25 houses. **Grooms Corners,** (p. o.,) in the s. w., **Dry Dock,** (p. o.,) in the . e., and **Forts Ferry,** on the Mohawk, are hamlets. Part of this town was included in the 'Clifton Park" or "Shannondhoi" Patent, granted Sept. 23, 1708.[12] Settlements were made in the

---

[1] Named from a tract which had been burned over by the Indians for a deer pasture before white settlements began.

[2] The McDonalds were natives of Ireland. They had been enticed on board a vessel in the Shannon, brought to Philadelphia, and sold for a term of years to pay for their passage.

[3] Mr. Ball was induced to settle by a donation of 500 acres of land from the proprietors of the "Five Mile Square." He was the pastor of the first religious society formed in town. His father and Gen. Washington's mother (Mary Ball) were first cousins. His son, John, was a lieutenant in the army during the Revolution.

[4] Among these early settlers were Judge Beriah Palmer, steward M. C.,) Judge Epenetus White, Edward A. Watrous, Capt. Stephen White, Paul Pierson, Capt. Tyrannus Collins, Hez. Middlebrook, Elisha Benedict, John Higby, Edmund Jennings, Saml. Nash, and Joseph Bettys and his son "Joe," (who was afterward hung as a tory spy,) all from New England; Capt. Kenneth Gordon, and —— McCrea, from N. J.; families named Shearer, McDermids, and Frazers, from Scotland; and Gen. Jas. Gordon, George Scott, Francis Hunter, and 3 brothers Kennedy, from the north of Ireland. The Scotch families settled in "Scotch Bush" and "Paisley Street." Gen. Gordon was a colonel in the army during the Revolution, and afterward a prominent citizen in the town and co. The first death recorded by tombstone in town was that of Gen. Gordon's mother, who died in 1775.

[5] On the 16th of Oct. 1780, a party of 400 regulars and Indians from Canada, under Maj. Munro, a tory from Schenectady, made their appearance in the Ballston settlement. They designed to attack Schenectady; but, after remaining encamped several days, they returned without effecting this object. They pillaged and burned several houses at Ballston, killed one man,

and took 24 prisoners. After crossing the Kayaderosseras, Maj. Munro addressed his men, stating his expectation that they would be pursued, and directing that in case of an attack every prisoner should at once be killed. For this brutal order he was cashiered on his arrival at Montreal. Three aged or infirm prisoners were allowed to return, and the rest reached Bulwaggy Bay on the eighth day, whence they passed into Canada. The notorious Joe Bettys, with about 50 refugees, in May, 1781, captured 5 prisoners; and at the same time Judge White and 4 others were taken on the e. side of Long Lake, by another gang, and marched off to Canada, excepting one, who escaped. Col. Gordon and several others afterward escaped from the Isle of Orleans, and with great hardship made their way through the wilderness to the St. Johns, and thence to the settlements in Maine. They there learned of the peace, and returned home by way of Halifax and Boston.

[6] 2 Christian, Bap., Presb., Prot. E., and R. C.

[7] Pronounced All-Ploss, and signifies "eel-place."

[8] Among the other early settlers were David Maxwell, Joseph La Rue, John McKnight, John Taylor, and Jesse Conde, who came in 1775. Davis & Bostwick kept the first store; —— Harmons the first inn, John Rogers built the first sawmill, and John Holmes the first gristmill.

[9] The census reports 4 churches; 2 Presb., Prot. E., and M. E.

[10] Established in 1841, by Roscius R. Kennedy. It is under the patronage of the Troy (M. E.) Conference.

[11] At this place the canal crosses the river on a fine stone aqueduct.

[12] The patentees were John and Johannes Fort, Gerret and Maas Ryckse, John and Ryerse Quackenboss, and Derick Bratt, most of whom were early settlers.

Mohawk Valley, previous to 1700. The names of the first settlers and the precise date of their settlement are unknown. The first church (Bap.) was organized Sept. 3, 1794; Rev. Abijah Peck was the founder and first pastor.[1]

CORINTH—was formed from Hadley, April 20, 1818. A part of Moreau was annexed Jan. 28, 1848. It lies upon the Hudson, in the N. E. part of the co. The Kayaderosseras Mt. Range occupies the central and N. parts, and the Palmertown Mts. the S. E. corner. The declivities of these mountains are steep, rough, and broken, and their summits are rocky and mostly covered with forests. A valley 4 mi. wide separates the two ranges. The principal streams are the Hudson, forming the N. E. border, and Cole Brook, flowing along the S. foot of the mountains. The Great Falls, in the Hudson, are on the border of this town.[2] Among the mountains in the N. part are several fine lakes, the principal of which are Efnor, Hunt, Jenny, and Black Lakes. The soil is a sandy and clayey loam. Lumbering is extensively carried on, the Hudson River and small streams from the hills furnishing an abundance of water-power. **Jessups Landing,** (Corinth p.o.,) on the Hudson, contains 3 churches and 88 dwellings; and **South Corinth** (p.v.) 1 church and 30 dwellings. The first settlement was made near S. Corinth, in 1790, by Fred. Parkman, Washington Chapman, Jeremiah Eddy, Jephtha Clark, and Jonathan Dewel.[3] The first church (Bap.) was organized June 1, 1822.[4]

DAY—was formed from Edinburgh and Hadley, as "*Concord,*" April 17, 1819. Its name was changed Dec. 3, 1827. It is the N. W. corner town of the co. Its surface is principally occupied by several spurs of the Kayaderosseras Mts. Oak and Bald Mts., the principal peaks, near the center of the town, are 900 feet above the river. The whole mountain region is wild, rugged, and rocky, and scarcely susceptible of cultivation. The Sacondaga River flows in a narrow valley through the S. part. Its course is tortuous, and it is navigable through the town. Paul, Glass House, and Allens Creeks are the other principal streams. Livingston, Sand, and Mud Lakes are small bodies of water in the N. part. The soil is a moderately fertile, sandy and clayey loam. Lumbering is extensively carried on. **Huntsville** (West Day p.o.) is a hamlet in the S. W. part. **Day** is a p.o. The first permanent settlers were Phineas Austin, James Thomas, and Dyer Perry, and families named Clay and Bond. The first religious meetings were held in the barn of Peter Van Vleck, in 1801–02. The first church (Bap.) was formed in 1809. The census reports 2 churches; Christian and Ref. Prot. D.

EDINBURGH—was formed from Providence, March 13, 1801, as "*Northfield,*" and its name was changed April 6, 1808. A part of Day was taken off in 1819. It lies upon the W. border of the co., N. of the center. Its surface is principally occupied by two high mountain ridges separated by the valley of the Sacondaga River. The mountain regions are rocky and broken, with a thin, sandy or gravelly soil, and are covered with forests. Beechers Creek is a small mill stream W. of the river. The soil on the river flats is a good quality of clayey and gravelly loam. Lumbering is the chief occupation of the people. **Batchelerville,** (p.v.,) on the E. bank of the Sacondaga, contains 30 houses; and **Beechers Hollow,** (Edinburgh p.o.,) on the w. side of the river, 12. The first settlers came in about 1790 and located in the valley below "Fish House."[5] The first church (Bap.) was organized in 1798, by Rev. Mr. Munroe, from Galway.[6] Traces of an ancient Indian burial place are visible on the s. bank of the Sacondaga, near the border of Day.[7]

GALWAY[8]—was formed from Ballston, March 7, 1792. Providence was taken off in 1796. It lies on the w. border of the co., s. of the center. Its N. half is occupied by a group of rounded hills forming the southern continuation of the Kayaderosseras Mts. The surface of the s. half is gently undulating. The principal streams are head branches of Feegowesee and Calderwood Creeks and the Mourning Kil. The soil is generally a heavy clay, intermixed in places with sand and gravel. **Galway,** (p.v.,) near the center of the town, was incorp. April 18, 1838. It contains 3 churches, a female seminary,[9] and about 45 houses; **West Galway,** (p.v.,) on the border of Fulton co., contains 1 church and 20 houses. **Yorks Corners,** (E. Galway p.o.,) in the N. E.

---

1 The census reports 6 churches; 4 M. E., Bap., Ref. Prot. D.
2 See description of Warren co., page 675.
8 Among the early settlers were Daniel Boardman and Stephen and Wm. Brayton, at Jessups Landing; Elial Lindsay, at Great Falls; and Ambrose Clothier, in the S. E. part of the town, in 1796. Stephen Ashley kept the first inn, about 1800; and Daniel Boardman kept the first store and built the first gristmill, about 1793.
4 There are 3 churches in town; Bap., Presb., M. E.
5 In 1791 the following persons were living in the valley, viz.: Moses Crane, Jacobis Filkins, Daniel Washburn, John Sumner,

Obadiah Perry, and Saml. Rogers. Daniel Abbott, from Conn., taught the first school, in 1794; —— Chatfield kept the first store, in 1796; Isaac Deming built the first gristmill, in 1793; and Palmer Munroe, the first woolen factory, in 1808.
6 The census reports 3 churches; 2 M. E., Presb.
7 Tradition says that a band of Canadian Indians in canoes, on an expedition against the Mohawks, at this place fell into an ambuscade and were all slain. Bullets are frequently cut out of the trees in this vicinity.
8 Named from the native place of the first Scotch settlers.
9 The Galway Academy.

part, **Mosherville,** (p.o.,) near the N. border, **Whiteside Corners,** (p.o.,) in the N.W., **South Galway** (p.o.) and **North Galway** (p.o.) are hamlets. The first settlers, from Galway, Scotland, located in town in 1774.[1] Rev. Simeon Smith, from Canterhook, came in town in 1778, and located near Yorks Corners.[2] He formed the first religious society (Bap.) during the following year.[3]

GREENFIELD—was formed from Saratoga and Milton, March 12, 1793. A part of Hadley was taken off in 1801. It occupies a position a little N. w. of the center of the co. The Palmerstown Mountain Range extends along the E. border, and the Kayaderosseras Range occupies the w. part of the town. A valley 6 mi. wide separates these ranges. The principal streams are the Kayaderosseras and its branches. The soil is generally a gravelly loam intermixed with clay. Sections of the surface are very stony. Iron ore has been found in the E. part. **Greenfield Center** (p. v.) contains 2 churches. Pop. 85. **Jamesville,** (Middle Grove p.o.,) on the s. border, contains 1 church, 2 paper mills, and 31 houses; **Mount Pleasant,** (p.v.,) in the N.w. corner, a glass factory and 140 inhabitants; and **Porters Corners,** (p.v.,) near the center of the town, 2 churches and 20 houses. **West Greenfield,** (p.o.,) **North Greenfield,** (p.o.,) and **Pages Corners** are hamlets. The first settlers were two men named Haggerty and Root, who located near Haggerty Hill in 1784.[4] The census reports 9 churches in town.[5]

HADLEY—was formed from Greenfield and Northumberland, Feb. 27, 1801. Its boundaries were amended Feb. 28, 1808. Corinth was taken off in 1818, and a part of Day in 1819. It lies upon the Hudson, in the N.E. corner of the co. A large share of its surface is occupied by the peaks and ridges of the Kayaderosseras Mts. Mt. Anthony is an isolated peak in the s.E. part.[6] Sacondaga River flows through the s. part. Its valley is narrow; and below Conklingville its current is rapid and frequently interrupted by falls. The soil generally is a coarse, yellowish, unproductive sand and gravel. Lumbering and tanning are extensively carried on. **Conklingville,** (West Hadley p.o.,) on the Sacondaga, in the w. part of the town, contains 1 church, a large tannery,[7] and 39 houses. **Hadley** (p.o.) is a hamlet at the junction of Sacondaga and Hudson Rivers. Richard Hilton commenced the first settlement, just after the close of the Revolution, on the Hudson.[8] The census reports 2 churches in town; a F. W. Bap. and a Wes. Meth.

HALF MOON[9]—was formed as a district, March 24, 1772, and as a town, March 7, 1788. Its name was changed to "*Orange*" April 17, 1816, and the original name was restored Jan. 16, 1820. Waterford was taken off in 1816, and Clifton Park in 1828. Its surface is undulating and broken by the narrow ravines of small streams. Hudson River forms the E. boundary, and the Mohawk a portion of the s. The river intervales are about ½ mi. wide, and are bordered by a line of steep, clay bluffs 60 to 100 feet high. The other streams are Anthonys, Dwaas, and Steena Kils. The soil is a clayey and gravelly loam upland, and a fine quality of alluvium in the intervales. **Crescent**[10] (p.v.) is a canal village near the center of the s. border of the town. Pop. 593. **Middletown,** (Half Moon p.o.,) 1½ mi. E. of Crescent, has a pop. of 230; **Mechanicsville,** (p. v.,) at the mouth of Anthonys Kil, lies mostly in Stillwater. Pop. in Half Moon, 495. **Clifton Park** (p. v.) is on the w. line. **Newtown, Smithtown,** and **Grays Corners** are hamlets. The first settlements are supposed to have been made between 1680 and '90, by Germans, on the Mohawk Flats.[11] The first church (Ref. Prot. D.) was organized in 1800.[12]

---

[1] Among the early settlers were John and James Major, John McClelland, Wm., Robt., and Alex. Kelsey, and John McHarg, who all came over in the same ship, in 1774. The first death was that of James Major, killed by the fall of a tree, Sept. 11, 1776; John McClelland or —— Prendergast kept the first store, in 1780; Daniel Campbell built the first gristmill.

[2] Mr. Smith was accompanied by his parents and 3 brothers-in-law, Simeon Babcock, Reuben Mattison, and Joseph Bawn.

[3] The census reports 6 churches in town; 2 Bap., Christian, Friends, M. E., and Presb.

[4] Among the other early settlers were —— Brewster, Wm. Scott, a soldier of the Revolution, who came in 1785; Isaac Dennon, John Benedict, Nathl. Seymour, and Benj. Ingham, in 1787; Jas. Vail and Chas. Mirick, in 1789; Isaac and Darius Stephens, —— Reynolds and his sons, in 1790; Eseck Turletot, in 1793; and —— Miner, soon after. Joel Reynolds kept the first inn, in 1789; Gershom Morehouse built the first saw and grist mill, at Middle Grove, the same year. Benj. Clinch kept the first store at Porters Corners, in 1787.

[5] 3 Bap., 2 M. E., 2 Friends, Cong., and Univ.

[6] Iron ore was formerly obtained on the w. side of this mountain, to supply the furnace at Luzerne.

[7] This tannery consumes 5,000 cords of bark and manufactures 50,000 sides of leather per annum.

[8] Alex. Stewart settled on the Hudson in 1788; Elijah Ellis, on the s. side of the Sacondaga, —— Ricard, on the N., and Henry

Walker, at Hadley, in 1790. —— Wilson taught the first school, in 1791-92. Delane & Hazard built the first sawmill, in 1791; and Alex. Stewart, the first gristmill, in 1803. Jonathan Flanders kept the first inn, and Jeremy Rockwell the first store, in 1807. Col. Gordon Conkling built the tannery at Conklingville and placed the first steam tug on the river.

[9] Named from the crescent shape of the land between the Hudson and the Mohawk.

[10] The canal crosses the Mohawk at this place on a stone aqueduct 1,150 feet long and supported by 26 stone piers.

[11] In 1689 it was resolved by the authorities of Albany to remove the fort about the house and barn of Harme Lievese, in Half Moon, to a more convenient place,—from which it is inferred that a considerable settlement existed at that time. In 1714 the precinct of Half Moon contained 101 inhabitants. Among the early settlers were Oldert Onderkirk, on the flats, —— Fort, on the Judge Leland farm, and —— Taylor, at Mechanicsville, before 1763. The ancient stone house on the Dansbach place, in the s. w. corner of the town, was built in 1718, by Killian Van Den Bergh. There was a sawmill on Steena Kil, near Crescent, in 1762. Wm. Bradshaw built a gristmill on Dwaas Kil at the close of the Revolution. A bridge was erected across the Mohawk in 1794, at a cost of $12,000.

[12] The census reports 7 churches in town; 3 M. E., Bap., Wes. Meth., Presb., and Friends.

MALTA—was formed from Stillwater, March 3, 1802, and a part of Saratoga was annexed March 28, 1805. It lies upon the w. bank of Saratoga Lake, s. e. of the center of the co. Its surface is chiefly an undulating upland, 60 to 80 feet above Saratoga Lake, and broken by the deep gulleys of small streams. The streams are Kayaderosseras Creek, forming the n. boundary, Ballston Outlet Creek, an inlet, and Anthonys Kil, the outlet of Round Lake, and Drummonds Brook, flowing into Saratoga Lake. Round Lake, in the s. e., is nearly circular, and 1 mi. in diameter. A swampy region covering an area of several hundred acres lies in the n. e. part of the town, at the mouth of the Kayaderosseras. The soil is principally a light, sandy loam, with clay and muck in the lowlands. **Dunning Street,** (Malta p. o.,) near the center of the town, contains 1 church and 17 houses. **Maltaville,** (p. o.,) in the s. part, **Malta Ridge,** in the n, and **Halls Corners,** are hamlets. The first settlers were two men named Drummond and McKelpin, who came before the Revolution and located w. of the lake.[1] The census reports 5 churches in town.[2]

MILTON—was formed from Ballston, March 7, 1792, and a part of Greenfield was taken off in 1793. It lies a little s. of the center of the co. Its surface is moderately hilly in the n., and undulating in the s., with a slight inclination toward Kayaderosseras Creek, which flows s. e. through the center of the town. This stream has a rapid fall and furnishes a valuable water-power. Glowegee Creek, from the w., is its principal tributary. In the n. part are limestone ridges, extensively quarried for building stone and lime. The Saratoga mineral spring region extends through the s. e. part. The soil is generally a sandy loam. **Ballston Spa,** (Ballston p. o.,) the co. seat, was incorp. March 21, 1807. It is situated on Kayaderosseras Creek, in the s. e. corner of the town. It contains the co. buildings, 2 seminaries,[3] 5 churches, 2 printing offices, and several manufacturing establishments.[4] Pop. 2,285, of which 1,941 are in this town. This village has long been celebrated for its mineral springs.[5] **Rock City Mills** (p. v.) contains 3 paper mills and 34 houses; **West Milton** (p. v.) a church, a paper mill, a shingle mill, a hoe factory, and 40 houses; **Bloodville** a scythe, edge tool, and knitting factories, and 40 houses; and **Factory Village** 2 paper mills and 22 houses. **Milton Center** and **Cranes Village** are hamlets. The first settlement in town was made by David Wood and his sons Stephen, Benj., Elijah, Nathan, and Enoch, who purchased 600 acres and moved into town before the Revolution.[6] The first church (Bap.) was organized Jan. 22, 1793.[7]

MOREAU[8]—was taken from Northumberland, March 28, 1805. A part was annexed to Corinth in 1848. It lies in the great bend of the Hudson, in the n. e. corner of the co. The w. part of the town is occupied by the rocky and precipitous peaks of the Palmertown Mt. Range. The central and e. portions are undulating and broken by the narrow ravines of small streams. The Hudson River forms the n., the e., and a part of the w. boundary of the town. Upon its course are numerous rapids and waterfalls.[9] The Snook Kil and its tributaries drain the s. part of the town. The soil is generally a light, yellow, sandy loam, but in the s. and w. are tracts of clay and gravel. **South Glens Falls,** (p. v.,) on the Hudson, opposite Glens Falls, contains several manufacturing establishments;[10] pop. 513. **Fortsville,** (p. v.,) in the central part, contains 25 houses. **Clarks Corners, Reynolds Corners,** and **State Dam** are hamlets. **Moreau Station** is a p. o., situated on the R. & W. R. R. Settlements are said to have been made before the Revolution; but their history is only a vague tradition.[11] The first church (Bap.) was built in 1795.[12]

---

[1] These men were suspected of toryism and were driven from the co. Michael Dunning, with 6 sons and 3 daughters, from Conn., came into town in 1777–78. John Rhoades and Timothy Shipman were the first settlers on Malta Ridge; Robt. and John Hunter and Jehial Parks located at Maltaville about the commencement of the Revolution.

[2] 2 M. E., Cong., Prot. Meth., and Presb.

[3] The Ballston Spa Institute, for boys, was established in 1846. The Ballston Spa Academy was opened in 1855.

[4] In the village are a cotton, oilcloth, edge tool, 2 seamless bag, and 2 knitting factories, a tannery, and 2 gristmills. A mfg. co. was incorp. here March 10, 1810.

[5] These springs were first discovered in the survey of the Kayaderosseras Patent in 1769. They are situated on the margin of a small stream that flows into Kayaderosseras Creek. The Old Spring, formerly much used, was greatly impaired by the opening of La Fayette Spring, within 30 feet, in 1825. Washington Spring was obtained in 1827, by boring 237 feet in the slate. The Saline, or United States Spring, is considerably impregnated with salt. Besides these are the Fulton and Franklin Springs and the Low Well. In 1817, 4 springs were discovered within 20 feet of each other in the bed of the stream. Their properties were unlike, and after a little time they became fresh. These springs are generally clear, cool, and sparkling. Their average temperature is about 50°. The mineral properties are different in different springs; but generally the water is similar to that of the Saratoga Springs, only less strong. Gas is copiously discharged with these waters.

[6] Benajah Douglas, grandfather of Hon. Stephen A. Douglas, built a log house near the spring, for the accommodation of visitors, in 1792. Silas Adams and Elijah Walbridge located in the n. part of the town in 1784–85. In 1792 Nicholas Low built a tavern close by the spring; and in 1804 he erected the "Sans Souci Hotel."

[7] The census reports 8 churches in town; 2 Bap., 2 M. E., 2 Presb., Prot. E., and R. C.

[8] Named from Marshal Moreau, who visited the U. S. in 1804–05.

[9] See page 690.

[10] In this village are 2 sash and blind factories, a tub and spoke factory, planing mill, broom handle factory, an extensive sawmill, and marble factory. Cheney & Arne's sawmills employ 75 men, run 150 to 190 saws, and manufacture more than 10,000,000 feet of lumber per annum. The marble manufactured is a black variety obtained from the Trenton limestone in the immediate vicinity.

[11] A man named Marvin was the first settler at Fortsville, about 1795; Edward and Elijah Durham and Holly St. John were the first settlers at Clarks Corners; —— Hamilton built the first gristmill, about 1800. Abel Crandall kept the first inn, in 1798.

[12] The census reports 5 churches; Bap., Cong., M. E., Union, and Friends.

NORTHUMBERLAND—was formed from Saratoga, March 16, 1798. A part of Hadley was taken off in 1801, Moreau in 1805, and Wilton in 1818. It lies upon the Hudson, N. of the center of the co. Its surface is level or undulating and broken by deep ravines. A line of clay and slate bluffs, 30 to 100 feet high, extends along the river. Snook Kil and its tributary, Beaver Dam Creek, are the principal streams. The soil is generally a light, sandy loam. This town shares with Fort Edward the Fort Miller Falls.[1] **Gansevoort,**[2] (p.v.,) on Snook Kil, in the N. part of the town, contains 2 churches and a pop. of 162. It is a station on the S. & W. R. R. **Bacon Hill**[3] (p.o.) and **Northumberland,** (p.o.,) in the S.E. part of the town, are hamlets. Fort Miller was built in this town in 1755, under the direction of Col. Miller. It was located upon the flat, above the rapids, and was enclosed on three sides by the river. A blockhouse was built on the heights that commanded the position on the w. The first settlers probably came in before the Revolution. Among them was a man named Munroe,[4] who built the first sawmill, at Gansevoort.[5] There are 4 churches in town.[6]

PROVIDENCE—was formed from Galway, Feb. 5, 1796, and Edinburgh was taken off in 1801. It lies near the center of the w. border of the co. Its surface is mountainous in the N. E. and broken and hilly in the s.w. The high regions along the N. and E. borders are mostly covered with forests. Hagadorns, Hans, Cadmans, and Frenchmans Creeks, small mill streams rising in the mountains and flowing s. w. into Fulton co., are the principal watercourses. The soil is chiefly a coarse, yellow sand or gravel of poor quality. Large tracts are stony and rocky. Wooden ware, leather, and lumber are extensively manufactured. **Barkersville** (p.o.) and **Hagadorns Hollow** are hamlets. **Providence** and **W. Providence** are p. offices. The first settlement was made previous to the Revolution, but the settlers were driven off during the war. Among the first settlers after the war were Nathaniel Wells and Seth Kellogg.[7] There are 3 churches in town; Bap., Christian, and M. E.

SARATOGA[8]—was formed as a district, March 24, 1772, and as a town, March 7, 1788. Easton (Washington co.) was taken off in 1789, a part of Greenfield in 1793, Northumberland in 1798, a part of Malta in 1802, and Saratoga Springs in 1819. It lies upon the Hudson, near the center of the E. border of the co. A range of high, rounded, and sometimes terraced hills extends N. and s. through the central and w. parts. These hills rise 450 feet above the Hudson and slope in every direction. Narrow alluvial flats bordered by high clay bluffs extend along the Hudson. Saratoga Lake forms a portion of the w. boundary. Fish Creek, the outlet of the lake, flowing through the N. part of the town, is the principal stream; and upon it are several fine mill sites. The other streams are small brooks. The soil N. of Fish Creek is light and sandy, and in the remaining parts of the town it is a gravelly and clayey loam. Three mineral springs, known as "Quaker Springs," issue from the Hudson River slate, in a ravine a little S. E. of the center of the town.[9] **Schuylerville,**[10] (p.v.,) incorp. April 16, 1831, is situated on the river, at the mouth of Fish Creek. It contains 4 churches, the Schuylerville Academy, a newspaper office, a bank, cotton factory, and foundery; pop. 1,184. **Victory Mills,** (p.v.,) situated on Fish Creek, contains 1 church, a machine shop, and an extensive cotton factory;[11] pop. 729. **Quaker Springs,** (p.v.,) near the center of the town, contains 1 church and 22 houses. **Grangerville,** (p.o.,) on Fish Creek, is a hamlet. **Deans Corners** (p. o.) and **Coveville** are hamlets. Settlement was begun in the early part of the last century, upon the Hudson.[12] The first church (Ref. Prot. D.) was formed before the Revolution.[13] The census reports 7 churches in town.[14]

SARATOGA SPRINGS—was formed from Saratoga, April 9, 1819. It occupies a nearly central position in the co. Its surface is rolling or moderately hilly. Kayaderosseras Creek

---

[1] See p. 682.
[2] Named from Col. Peter Gansevoort, who located here soon after the war.
[3] Named from Ebenezer Bacon, who came from Conn. in 1794, and opened the first framed tavern the same year. The place has been called "*Fiddletown*" and "*Popes Corners*" at different times.
[4] Munroe was a tory, and fled to Canada, and his property was confiscated.
[5] Gansevoort discovered the irons of Munroe's mill and erected a new sawmill. He soon after built a gristmill. Fort Miller bridge was first erected by a company incorp. March 16, 1803. The present bridge was erected in 1845. It has a single road track and a canal towing path.   [6] Ref. Prot. D., 2 M. E.
[7] —— Corey built the first sawmill, in 1786, and the first gristmill, soon afterward. The first inn was kept by —— Shankland.
[8] Written "Saraghtoga" until about 1793. Upon the old map of the Kayaderosseras Patent this name is spelled "Seraghtogha."

The name was first applied to a settlement on the Hudson, in the vicinity of the present village of Schuylerville. It is said to signify "swift water," and was applied to the rapids in the river, in contradistinction to still water, just below.
[9] The water of these springs contains lime, magnesia, and iron, held in solution by carbonic acid, and a large proportion of common salt and soda.
[10] Named in honor of Gen. Philip Schuyler, who resided here previous to the Revolution. During the war his buildings and mills were burned by order of Burgoyne.
[11] There are 455 looms in this factory. In 1857, 3,565,411 yds. of print cloths and silesias were manufactured.
[12] At the attack upon Old Fort Saratoga, upon the opposite side of the Hudson, in the fall of 1745, several sawmills and other buildings, upon Fish Creek and the river, were burned, and about 30 families were killed or taken prisoners.
[13] The British troops made a riding school of this church during the war.
[14] 3 M. E., Bap., Ref. Prot. D., R. C., and Friends.

and Saratoga Lake, forming the s. boundary, are skirted by a line of low bluffs. The streams are Ellis and Owl Pond Creeks. An extensive tract lying N. of Saratoga Lake and along the course of Owl Pond Creek is low and swampy. The soil is an inferior quality of yellowish, sandy loam. The far famed mineral springs, which give to the town its name, are situated about 3 mi. N. w. of Saratoga Lake. They are near the center of the mineral spring region, which has a radius of nearly 10 mi.[1] **Saratoga Springs** (p. v.) was incorp. April 17, 1826. It contains 2 female seminaries,[2] 7 churches, 2 banks, 5 printing offices, 2 public halls, 22 hotels,[3] and several sanitary institutions.[4] Pop. 5,129. The business of the village is principally connected with the entertainment of strangers during the fashionable watering season. The springs are on that part of the Kayaderosseras Patent that fell to the share of Rip Van Dam. Sir Wm. Johnson is said to have been the first white person who ever used the Saratoga waters for medicinal purposes. In 1767 he was brought to the place on a litter, and, after remaining several days, he was able to return on foot. His example was followed, and the visits of invalids soon became of frequent occurrence. In 1773, Derick Scowton made the first clearing and erected a hut. He was followed soon after by George Arnold and Saml. Norton.[5] In 1783, Gen. Schuyler cut a road through from Fish Creek, and spent several weeks here, living in a tent. The next year he erected a framed house, (the first in town,) and annually afterward until his death he spent a part of the summer here with his family.[6] Several prominent men have resided in the village.[7] The census reports 7 churches in town.[8]

STILLWATER[9]—was formed March 7, 1788. A part of Easton (Washington co.) was

---

[1] *High Rock Spring*, the first discovered of these, was so named from a pyramidal mound of calcareous tufa 3¼ feet high and 24¼ feet in diameter at the base which has been formed around it. An aperture 1 foot in diameter opens from the top of the rock downward, in which the water generally rises 1½ feet above the surface of the ground. It is said that the water once overflowed the top; but at an early day the rock was cracked by the fall of a tree, and the water sunk to its present level. *Congress Spring* was discovered in 1792, by a hunting party, and named in compliment to John Taylor, one of the number, who had been a member of the Continental Congress. The present spring was obtained by sinking a well in the bed of the stream near the original fountain. *The Columbia Spring*, a few rods S. W. of the latter, is chalybeate, and constantly boiling from the escape of gas. It was opened in 1806, by G. Putnam. *The Hamilton Spring*, 50 rods N. E. of Congress, was discovered by G. Putnam, and brought into use by Dr. Clarke. *The Pavilion Fountain*, opened in 1839, has a smart, pungent taste. *The Iodine Spring*, situated a few rods N. of High Rock, was opened in 1839. The water contains a large proportion of iodine and very little iron. This spring has sometimes been called the Walton Spring, from Henry Walton, a large proprietor of lands in the vicinity. *The Empire Spring*, the most northerly in the village, was opened in 1846. It discharges 75 gallons per hour. *The Washington Spring*, 50 rods S. W. of Congress Spring, was opened in 1806. *Putnam Spring* is in the immediate vicinity. *Flat Rock Spring*, 100 rods N. E. from Hamilton, is chalybeate. *Red Spring* is 90 rods N. E. of High Rock; and *Monroe Spring*, 15 rods N. of Flat Rock. *Ten Springs* were discovered in 1814, 1 mi. N. E. of the village. *Ellis Spring* is situated in a ravine 2 mi. S. W. of Congress. There are several other springs in the immediate vicinity. Baths are connected with most of these springs, and an immense trade has sprung up in the bottling and sale of the water. The temperature of the fountains ranges from 48° to 51°, and it is not sensibly affected by the seasons. The following table gives an analysis of several of these springs. The figures show the number of grains in a gallon of water.

INGREDIENTS.	Columbian. (Dr. J. H. Steele.)	Congress. (Dr. J. H. Steele.)	Empire. (Dr. E. Emmons.)	Flat Rock. (Dr. J. H. Steele.)	Hamilton. (Dr. J. H. Steele.)	High Rock. (Dr. J. H. Steele.)	Iodine. (Dr. E. Emmons.)	Magnesian. (Dr. Thomas.)	Pavilion. (Dr. Thomas.)	Putnam. (Jas. R. Chilton.)	Washington. (Dr. J. H. Steele.)
Chloride of sodium	267.00	385.00	269.696	148.87	279.30	189.10	137.00	160.20	226.58	214.00	281.50
Hydriodate of soda	2.56	3.50	12.000	1.33	3.00	2.50		1.70	2.75	2.00	2.75
Bicarbonate of soda	15.40	8.98	30.848	20.79	27.04	17.54					16.50
Carbonate of soda							2.00	10.40	4.70	14.32	
Sulphate of soda										1.68	
Carbonate of magnesia							75.00	44.26	62.50	51.60	
Bicarbonate of magnesia	46.71	95.79	41.984	42.70	35.20	61.59					40.92
Carbonate of lime	68.00	98.10		60.57	92.40	69.29	26.00	48.00	60.24	68.80	92.60
Phosphate of lime			141.824							.21	
Bicarbonate of lime			000								
Carbonate of iron	5.58	5.07		5.39	5.39	5.58	1.00			7.00	3.25
Bicarbonate of iron									4.10		
Silica	2.05	1.50						1.10	.62	.84	1.50
Alumina							3.50	80	.25	.56	
Hydrobromate of potassa	trace.	trace.	trace.	trace.	trace.	trace.					
Total solid contents	407.80	597.943	496.352	279.65	460.33	345.68	244.50	269.10	361.74	361.01	439.12
Carbonic acid gas (inches)	272.06	311.00		287.50	316.00	304.00	360.00	371.00	480.01	348.88	262.50
Atmospheric air	4.50	7.00		6.50	4.00	5.00	4.00	3.25	8.09	6.41	6.80
Total gaseous contents	276.56	318.00	700.00	294.00	320.00	309.00	364.00	374.25	488.10	355.29	269.30

Steele's Analysis, 1838; *Allen's Analysis*, 1858.—*Beck's Mineralogy.* Slightly different results have been obtained from different analyses.

[2] Temple Grove Female Seminary, a boarding school, was established in 1853. The Saratoga Female Seminary.

[3] Several of these hotels are among the most extensive in the country. Union Hall was built in 1802, by G. Putnam; The Columbian, in 1808, by Jotham Holmes; Congress Hall, in 1812, by G. Putnam; The Pavilion, in 1819, by Nathan Lewis; and The United States, in 1824, by Elias Benedict. All of these have been enlarged since their erection.

[4] Among these are the Saratoga Water Cure, and the Medical and Surgical Institute, both established in 1832.

[5] Norton joined the British, and his property was confiscated.

[6] Alexander Bryan and Henry Livingston were the first set-

tlers after the war. Gideon Putnam came in 1789. Mr. P. built the first sawmill, the first large hotels, and opened several of the springs. Dr. Clement Blakely, the first physician, came with Putnam, and remained 3 years. John and Ziba Taylor opened the first store, in 1794; Robt. Ellis and Geo. Peck built the first gristmill, in 1814; and Ward & Rogers, the first clothing works, in 1815. Henry Walton resided here for several years. He was proprietor of the whole village N. of Congress St. Several of the noted springs were on his estate.

[7] Eseck Cowen, Justice of the Supreme Court, and compiler of "*Cowen's Reports*," resided here until his death, in 1844. Chancellor Reuben H. Walworth resides in town.

[8] Bap., M. E., Prot. Meth., Presb., Prot. E., R. C., and Univ.

[9] Named from the "still water" in the Hudson, on the borders of the town.

taken off in 1789, and Malta in 1802. It lies upon the Hudson, s. e. of the center of the co. It is uneven in the s. and moderately hilly in the n. The highest point is about 250 feet above the Hudson. A range of clay bluffs 60 to 100 feet high borders upon intervales of the Hudson and Anthonys Kil. The streams are generally small brooks flowing in deep gulleys worn in the drift deposits.[1] The n. w. corner borders upon Saratoga Lake. The river intervales are alluvial. West of the river bluffs is a wide belt of heavy clay; and in the s. w. part is a sandy tract interspersed with swamps. Upon the lake shore is a sulphur spring.[2] **Stillwater,** (p. v.,) incorp. April 17, 1816, is situated on the Hudson. It contains 4 churches, and manufactories of lumber, paper, woolens, and castings. Pop. 552. **Mechanicsville,** (p. v.,) incorp. July 16, 1859, situated on the Hudson, at the mouth of Anthonys Kil, on the line of Half Moon, is a station on the Rensselaer & Saratoga R. R. It contains 5 churches, a printing office, and an extensive linen thread manufactory.[3] Pop. 1,111,—616 in Stillwater, 495 in Half Moon. **Bemis Heights,**[4] (p. o.,) on the Champlain Canal, near the Hudson, and **Ketchums Corners** (p. o.) are hamlets. This town was included in the Saratoga Patent of 1684; and settlement was commenced about 1750.[5] The first church (Cong.) was established in 1763.[6] There are 8 churches in town.[7]

WATERFORD[8]—was formed from Half Moon, April 17, 1816. It lies at the junction of the Hudson and Mohawk Rivers, in the s. e. corner of the co. Its area is about 7 sq. mi. Its surface is mostly an upland, 50 to 100 feet above the river. The Mohawk is bordered by an almost perpendicular range of slate bluffs, and the Hudson Valley by a range of clay bluffs. The soil is a sandy, clayey, and alluvial loam of great fertility. The falls in the Mohawk furnish a valuable water-power. **Waterford,**[9] (p. v.,) incorp. April 6, 1801,[10] situated on the Champlain Canal, near the confluence of the Hudson[11] and Mohawk Rivers, is a station on the Rensselaer & Saratoga R. R. and the Albany & Northern R. R. It contains 6 churches, a newspaper office, a bank, and several manufacturing establishments.[12] Pop. 3,083. Settlement was commenced by the Dutch at a very early day. The census reports 7 churches in town.[13]

WILTON—was formed from Northumberland, April 20, 1818. It lies a little n. e. of the center of the co. The Palmertown Mts., with their steep, rocky slopes and broken, forest-covered summits, extend across the n. w. corner. The center and s. w. are gently undulating, or broken by low ridges. The principal streams are Snook Kil and Bog Meadow and Cold Brooks. The soil in the e. and s. e. is a yellow, sandy loam resting on clay, and in some places swampy. At the foot of the Palmertown Mts. is a belt of productive gravel and clay loam. A heavy growth of white and yellow pine originally covered the plains, but little woodland now remains. Near Emersons Corners is a spring of acidulous and carbonated water, and in the s. part of the town is a sulphur spring. **Wilton** (p. v.) contains 20 houses; and **Emersons Corners,** in the n. part of the town, is a hamlet. The first settlement was made in 1774 or '75, by Rowland Perry and his sons Samuel, John, Benj., Absalom, Roswell, Artemas, Rowland, and Joseph, from Dutchess co.[14] Near the mill pond on Snook Kil are traces of Indian occupation; pestles, broken pottery, and flint arrow heads have been found in abundance. The census reports 4 churches in town.[15]

---

[1] Upon these streams are several fine cascades.

[2] This spring is called the White Sulphur Spring. A few years since, a hotel and bathing house were erected here, and a small steamer was put upon the lake. The building was burned 2 or 3 years after, and the enterprise was abandoned.

[3] The American Linen Thread Manufacturing Co. was organized in 1852. The number of men employed is 125.

[4] Named from Jonathan Bemis, who during the Revolution kept the only inn worthy of note on the Albany & Fort Edward Road.

[5] Among the first settlers were John Thompson, Geo. Palmer, —— Benjamin, Dirck Swart, —— Ensign, —— Burlinghame, and —— Abeel. The first gristmill was built by Geo. Palmer, before the Revolution.

[6] This church was organized at Litchfield, Conn., in 1752, and in 1763 was removed to Stillwater. Rev. Robt. Campbell was the first pastor.

[7] 3 M. E., 2 Bap., Presb., Prot. E., and R. C.

[8] The Indians called the country around the mouth of the Mohawk "Nach-te-nack." This town was formerly known as Half Moon Point; and the semi-circular tract between the Hudson and the Mohawk was called Half Moon. Its present name originated from the fact that at the village of Waterford a ford crossed to Haver Island.

[9] In 1784 the site of the village was purchased by Col. Jacobus Van Schoon. —— Middlebrook, Ezra Hickock, Judge White, and several others, most of whom were from Conn.; and Flores

Bancker was employed to lay it out into village lots. July 11, 1841, a destructive fire occurred, which destroyed 130 buildings.

[10] On the 25th of March, 1794, Hezekiah Ketchum, Jacobus Van Schoonhoven, Matthew Gregory, Isaac Keeler, John Pettett, Duncan Oliphant, and Thos. Smith were constituted trustees of Half Moon Point.

[11] A bridge across the Hudson at this place was built in 1804, at a cost of $50,000. The present structure, known as the "Union Bridge," was built in 1812, '13, and '14, at a cost of $20,000.

[12] A hydraulic canal ½ mi. in length was constructed in 1828–29, by J. F. King. Upon this canal are 2 stock and die factories, a machine shop, ax factory, twine factory, ink and lampblack factory, soap and candle factory, flouring mill, and a pearling mill. On the Champlain Canal are 3 flouring mills, a foundery and machine shop, an auger factory, and a distillery. The fire engine works at this place were started in 1831. About $60,000 worth of work is turned out per annum, and 40 men are employed.

[13] Bap., Cong., M. E., Presb., Prot. E., Ref. Prot. D., and R. C.

[14] John Stiles, Ebenezer King, John Laing, Peter Johnson, and Jas. and Wm. McGregor settled in town in 1775; and John Boyce, Robt. Milligan, John Kendrick, and Enoch M. Place in 1784. John Laing built the first sawmill, in 1784–85, and Wm. McGregor the first gristmill, soon after the war. Stephen King kept the first inn, and —— Ostrom the first store.

[15] Bap., M. E., Prot. Meth., and Union.

Acres of Land, Valuation, Population, Dwellings, Families, Freeholders, Schools, Live Stock, Agricultural Products, and Domestic Manufactures, of Saratoga County.

Names of Towns.	Acres of Land.		Valuation of 1858.			Population.		No. of Dwellings.	No. of Families.	Freeholders.	Schools.	
	Improved.	Unimproved.	Real Estate.	Personal Property.	Total.	Males.	Females.				No. of Districts.	Children taught.
Ballston	16,177	2,996½	$544,356	$115,110	$659,466	1,058	1,143	385	435	343	12	678
Charlton	15,166	3,156	416,510	104,138	520,648	842	859	318	326	214	10	593
Clifton Park	23,541	5,485	637,750	230,970	868,720	1,502	1,415	429	577	424	16	1,198
Corinth	13,071	10,564	211,166	13,416	224,582	781	753	296	317	131	10	568
Day	7,017	17,047	67,020	4,650	71,670	560	519	197	198	144	11	556
Edinburgh	13,956	25,028	119,540	9,625	129,165	629	689	255	283	283	12	577
Galway	27,760¼	172	420,564	44,909	465,473	1,208	1,233	451	504	401	15	924
Greenfield	28,644½	12,791½	399,410	45,341	444,751	1,432	1,410	579	613	425	21	1,124
Hadley	7,691	13,498	69,811	6,150	75,961	626	546	222	222	112	7	360
Halfmoon	16,550	2,837	707,225	139,600	846,825	1,659	1,656	606	603	231	12	970
Malta	14,434¾	2,983¾	380,570	58,160	438,730	615	621	228	257	222	8	413
Milton	18,366½	3,885	730,685	310,143	1,040,828	2,261	2,408	751	225	261	13	1,772
Moreau	18,291	6,304½	343,106	31,650	374,756	1,079	1,087	360	401	264	12	867
Northumberland	13,133	5,925½	302,880	82,448	385,328	860	808	300	312	244	12	621
Providence	8,694	5,401	91,662	20,921	112,583	678	690	286	295	196	10	512
Saratoga	19,281½	5,089½	788,885	241,458	1,030,343	1,822	2,010	692	701	374	13	1,410
Saratoga Springs	11,740½	6,386	1,346,056	789,887	2,135,943	2,951	3,356	1,013	1,239	694	10	2,399
Stillwater	22,401	3,963	728,017	165.530	893,547	2,468	1,495	498	590	313	13	1,024
Waterford	3,523¾	342	543,652	391,225	934.877	1,569	1,680	498	605	226	2	1,141
Wilton	16,288½	5,994	253,744	24,054	277,798	682	719	267	281	233	10	579
Total	315,728¼	139,849¼	9,102,609	2,829,385	11,931,994	24,282	25,097	8,631	8,984	5,735	229	18,286

Names of Towns.	Live Stock.					Agricultural Products.							Domestic Manufactures, in Yards.
						Bush. of Grain.		Tons of Hay.	Bushels of Potatoes.	Bushels of Apples.	Dairy Products.		
	Horses.	Working Oxen and Calves.	Cows.	Sheep.	Swine.	Winter.	Spring.				Pounds of Butter.	Pounds of Cheese.	
Ballston	654	912	1,020	1,906	2,038	4,241	94,071	3,236½	21,788	40,710	113,463½	18,428¾	104
Charlton	705	882	956	2,276	965	2,338	90,172	3,113	13,912	23,565	65,065	805	142
Clifton Park	897	920	1,270	2,401	2,336	25,244	112,812	3,019	43,846	26,038	101,781	19,285	179
Corinth	421	866	602	1,425	508	1,202	35,164½	1,885½	21,507	4,900	51,580	6,600	604
Day	222	813	380	1,184	335	274	16,977	1,706	11,292	5,761	27,775	100	745
Edinburgh	320	1,290	614	2,591	491	214	31,893	2,902	15,159	7,440	48,495	8,850	1,523
Galway	736	1,320	1,241	3,212	1,379	2,333	113,455	4,817	28,964	31,732	141,903	12,715	922
Greenfield	835	1,602	1,346	3,032	1,590	1,203	83,823	4,515	33,687	26,846	106,990	13,865	1,279
Hadley	190	733	336	961	339	718½	22,120	1,378	10,531	2,595	30,406	1,400	111
Halfmoon	618	785	972	3,414	1,497	19,825½	81,075	2,815½	28,522	12,652	79,735	5,090	179
Malta	474	751	778	3,090	1,456	11,979¾	60,694½	2,427¼	19,083	19,604	77,819	13,314	75
Milton	775	979	1,170	1,416	1,709	8,169¼	89,545	3,075	24,818	28,810	91,657	5,665	302
Moreau	532	655	745	2,350	1,123	5,792	63,675	2,018	13,701	6,131	67,695	15,270	
Northumberland	581	1,057	855	1,989	1,518	5,387	97,394⅞	2,632¼	39,589	5,489	84,705	4,857	197½
Providence	235	793	392	900	484	38	31,161	1,586	15,139	4,538	39,160	3,970	359
Saratoga	832	1,150	1,217	5,776	2,294	17,669	121,896½	4,161	67,541	13,842	103,922	4,440	185
Saratoga Springs	710	457	752	1,023	1,369	6,129	36,847	1,599¾	17,758	4,345	55,710	960	535
Stillwater	862	1,246	1,259	4,848	2,312	22,114	84,523	3,544	32,725	15,734	101,935	13,090	199
Waterford	239	183	248	462	1,205	4,159	23,598	663	5,140	555	16,950	1,250	
Wilton	455	597	625	1,762	1,055	8,580	66,691	1,650	22,970	8,191	61,390	2,947	113
Total	11,293	17,991	16,778	46,018	26,003	147,601	1,357,588⅜	52,743¾	487,672	289,478	1,468,136½	152,901¾	7,753½

SCHENECTADY COUNTY.

This county was formed from Albany, March 7, 1809. It is centrally distant 20 mi. from Albany, and contains 221 sq. mi. The greater part lies between Mohawk River and Schoharie Creek,—one town only lying N. of the Mohawk. The surface consists of the Mohawk Valley and an upland, generally much broken by ridges and isolated hills, 200 to 350 feet above the river. The highlands are the northern continuation of the Helderbergh and Schoharie Mts. The underlying rock is generally the shales of the Hudson River group, which crop out in the valleys and the bottoms of the ravines. In portions of Glenville and Duanesburgh this rock is underlaid by birdseye limestone, from which are obtained both lime and stone for building. The greater part of the surface is covered with a thick deposit of drift, consisting principally of clay in the W. part and sand in the E. The rocks crop out on the banks of the streams and form the declivities of the steeper hills. The soil in the W. part is a tenacious, clayey loam, underlaid by hardpan on the hills, and in the E. a light, unproductive sand. The valley of the Mohawk consists of a deep, rich alluvium, well adapted to tillage, and extensively devoted to the cultivation of broomcorn.[1]

The principal streams are Mohawk River, Schoharie Creek, and Normans Kil, and their branches. The valleys of these streams are generally bordered by the steep declivities of the uplands, rising to a height of about 300 feet. Many of the smaller streams have worn deep gulleys in the loose drift deposits, giving to the surface a very broken character. These small streams are mostly dry in summer. The fine alluvial flats near Schenectady, extending 5 mi. w. on the s. side of the river, were called by the first settlers "The Bouwland."[2] A tract 2 mi. in extent, N. of the river, was called the "Maalwyck;"[3] and a tract on both sides, 4 mi. w. of the city, was known as the "Woestina."[4] A region immediately about Schenectady was called "Oron-nygh-wurrie-gughre;" the hills s. were known as the "Yan-ta-puch-a-berg;"[5] and those on both sides of the river above the city were called "Tou-ar-e-u-ne." The streams of "Woestina" were "Werf Kil,"[6] Zantzee Kil,[7] and "Righelbrigh Kil."[8] The valleys are best adapted to tillage and the hills to pasturage.[9] Manufactures are chiefly limited to the city of Schenectady.[10] In Glenville are about a dozen broom factories, employing 150 persons.

The county seat is located at Schenectady City.[11] The courthouse and clerk's office are both situated on Union St.: the former contains the courtroom, jail, sheriff's and supervisors' rooms,[12] and the latter the clerk's and surrogate's offices. The poorhouse is located on a farm of 116 acres, on the Albany Road, just E. of the city. It has, on an average, about 75 inmates, and the farm yields a revenue of $1,200. There are 4 newspapers published in the co.[13]

---

[1] One-half of the entire broomcorn crop of the State is raised within this co. A considerable portion of the broomcorn land is annually overflowed, rendering it continually fertile; and many tracts have produced this crop alone for many years.
[2] "Arable Land."
[3] "Whirl-back," from the tortuous course of the Mohawk.
[4] "Wilderness."
[5] Mixed Indian and Dutch, signifying "John-ear-of-corn-hill."
[6] "Paint Creek," from the yellow earth along the banks.
[7] "Sea-Sand Creek." [8] "Rail-bridge Creek."
[9] At an early period the Mohawk Valley was celebrated for its large wheat crops; but now very little is raised.
[10] See page 598.
[11] By the terms of the act making Schenectady the co. seat, the courthouse was to be built at the expense of the city. The first county officers were Gerrit S. Veeder, First Judge; Peter V. Veeder, Clerk; Jas. V. S. Rider, Sheriff; and Wm. J. Teller, Surrogate.
[12] The first courts were held in the City Hall, and afterward in the West College.
[13] The following is a nearly complete list of the newspapers in the co.:—
The Western Spectator was issued prior to 1807.
The Schenectady Cabinet was commenced in Jan. 1809, by Isaac Riggs. In 1850 it passed into the hands of S. S. Riggs, who continued it until 1857.
The Western Budget was issued a short time in 1809.
The Mohawk Advertiser was pub. in 1810 by R. Schermerhorn.
The Floriad, 8vo, mo., was published in 1811.

The Schenectady Gazette was published in 1812, by Ryer Schermerhorn.
The Schenectady County Whig was issued in 1830, by C. G. and A. Palmer, and was continued until 1834.
The Schenectady Standard was published in 1831, by T. J. Sutherland.
The Schenectady Democrat was begun in 1828, by C. G. and A. Palmer. T. W. Flagg became its publisher in 1837, and the same year it was changed to
The Reflector and Schenectady Democrat. It has been successively published by G. Yates, E. H. Kincaid, and A. A. Keyser, and is now published by Fred. W. Hoffman.
The Censor was published in 1834, by the students of Union College.
The Parthenon, mo., was published in 1846-47 by the college students.
The Mohawker was published in 1835, by Riggs & Norris.
The Protestant Sentinel was commenced in 1835, by Rev. John Maxson, and continued 2 years.
The Wreath was started in 1835, by W. H. Burleigh, and continued 1 year.
Freedom's Sentinel was issued during the campaign of 1840, by Stephen S. Riggs.
The Antiquarian and General Review, mo., was started in 1845, by Rev. W. Arthur, and continued 2 years.
The Scroll, mo., was published a short time in 1849.
The Schenectady Democrat was founded in 1853, by Wm. M. Colbourne and W. N. Clark, and since 1857 it has been published by Alex. J. Thompson.

The great flat upon the Mohawk w. of "*Fort Orange*," and where the city of Schenectady now stands, was bought of the natives in July, 1661, in the name of Arent Van Corlear;[1] and settlement was commenced during the same year.   It was under the charge of 5 commissioners until Nov. 1, 1684, when Gov. Dongan granted a patent confirming previous rights and extending the territory.[2] On the night between the 8th and 9th of Feb. 1690, N.S.,[3] the settlement—then consisting of about 80 houses—was surprised by a party of about 300 French and Indians, and nearly every house was burned.   Sixty-three persons were killed, and 27 were carried to Canada as prisoners.   The night was intensely cold, and the nearest place of refuge was Albany, to which a few escaped after much suffering.[4]   In 1702 R. Schermerhorn became sole trustee; and in 1705 a new patent was issued, conferring certain township privileges.   On the 23d of Oct. 1765, the place was created a borough, with the rights and immunities incident to these corporations.[5]   From 1726 to the Revolution the township of Schenectady sent a representative to the General Assembly.   During the war the village was fortified and garrisoned at the public expense, and many families from the Upper Mohawk sought protection here from the incursions of the tories and Indians.[6]   For several years after 1779 a large number of friendly Oneida and Tuscarora families, driven from their homes by the hostile tribes, were supported in this vicinity at the expense of the General Government.   At the return of peace the settlement shared in the general prosperity.   A new impulse was given to business by the improvements effected by the Western Inland Navigation Co., which enabled large boats to make longer voyages.[7]   Upon the completion of the Erie Canal the Mohawk navigation was entirely superseded.   For several years after the completion of the R. R. from Albany in 1831, large quantities of merchandise were sent here to be shipped on the canal, saving the delay of the circuitous route and numerous locks on the canal between Schenectady and Troy.[8]   In 1832 a R. R. was built to Saratoga, in 1835, to Utica, and in 1843, to Troy.   In 1849 several plank roads were built, which since have been mostly abandoned.

DUANESBURGH[9]—was erected as a township, by patent, March 13, 1765, and it was first recognized as a town March 22, 1788.   It lies in the s. e. corner of the co.   Its surface consists of an upland, broken by the narrow valleys and gulleys of small streams.   Schoharie Creek forms a portion of its w. boundary, and Normans Kil flows through the s. part.   The hills that border upon these streams are steep, and in some places rocky.   The other principal streams are Corrys Brook, Chuctenunda Creek, and Bozen Kil.   Maria Pond and Featherstons Lake are 2 small bodies of water in the n. e. part, about 250 feet above the canal. The soil is principally a stiff, clay loam, with a slight intermixture of gravel.   It is best adapted to pasturage.   **Duanesburgh** (p. v.) contains about a dozen houses, **Quaker Street**[10] (p. v.) 30, **Mariaville**[11] (p. v.) 20, and **Bramans Corners** (p. v.) 18.   **Eatons Corners** is a hamlet.   Large tracts in this town were purchased by different parties between 1736 and 1770,[12] but no active measures of settlement were taken till about the time of its organization in 1765.   During that year Duane, who had become an extensive proprietor, con-

---

The Schenectady Morning Star, started Feb. 24, 1854, by W. M. Chadbourne and W. N. Clark, was changed in 1854 to **The Evening Star**, da., now published by W. M. Colbourne.

The Schenectady Republican has been published since Sept. 1857, by Colbourne & Landon.

The Schenectady Daily News was started in April, 1859, by Frederic Hoffman.

[1] The grantors were 4 Mohawk chiefs, named Cantuque, Sonareetsie, Aiadane, and Sodachdrasse.   This grant was confirmed the next year, and the tract was surveyed in 1664.   The inhabitants of Fort Orange, wishing to monopolize the Indian trade, presented to the settlers, before the land was received from the surveyor, a written pledge to abstain from trading with the Indians.   A remonstrance against this injustice was signed by the following early settlers, viz.: A. Van Corlear, Philip Hendrickson, Sanders Lendertsen Glen, Simon Volcrertsen, Pieter Soghmaekelyk, Teunis Cornelissen, Marte Cornelise, Willem Teller, Bastiaen De Winter for Catalyn, widow of Arent Andries de Voss, Pieter Jacobse Borsboom, Pieter Danielse Van Olinda, Jan Barentse Wemp, and Jaques Cornelise.   Their resistance occasioned several years' delay in the survey of the lands.

[2] Wm. Teller, Ryer Schermerhorn, Sweer Tunison, Jan Van Eps, and Myndert Wemp were appointed trustees under this grant.   The tract embraced the present city, and the towns of Glenville, Rotterdam, and part of Niskayuna.

[3] Previous to 1752 time was reckoned in England by "Old Style," the year commencing on the 25th of March.   All dates previous to that time, between Jan. 1 and March 25, are reckoned in 1 year by "Old Style," and in the following year by "New Style."

[4] *Colden's Five Nations*, 3d ed., I. p. 120.

[5] This and West Chester were the only boroughs in the colony.

[6] The place was never visited by a hostile army after 1690. The colonial statutes contain frequent provisions for the re-building, repairs, and supplies of this fort.

[7] This company cleared the river of impediments to navigation as much as possible, built a lock at Little Falls, and in 1796 built a short canal connecting the Upper Mohawk with Wood Creek, which flows into Oneida Lake, opening a direct water communication with the chain of lakes in the interior of the State, and with Lake Ontario and the St. Lawrence.   The boats employed, called "*Durham boats*," were propelled up stream by setting poles, and were floated down by the current.

[8] This business was stopped by the repeal of the statute prohibiting the R. R. from carrying freight w. of this place.

[9] Named from James Duane, the principal proprietor.   It was first joined with Schoharie, as "the united district of Duanesburgh and Schoharie."   It was made a separate district, March 24, 1772.   Mr. Duane took an active part in public affairs during the Revolution and the earlier years of the State Government, and was a liberal benefactor of the town.

[10] Boots and shoes, wagons, and sash and blinds, are manufactured here.

[11] Named from a daughter of James Duane.

[12] Among the purchasers were Thos. Freeman, in 1736, Timothy Bagley, in 1737, A. P. and William Cosby, in 1738, Walter Butler, in 1739, and Jonathan Brewer, in 1770.   Wm. North, an officer of the Revolution, married a daughter of Duane and resided several years in this town.

tracted with 20 Germans from Penn., of whom 16 came on and made a permanent settlement.[1] The first church (Christs Ch., Prot. E.) was formed Aug. 3, 1795, and the church edifice was erected by Judge Duane. Rev. David Belden was the first rector.[2]

GLENVILLE[3]—was formed from Schenectady, April 14, 1820. It is the only town in the co. N. of the Mohawk. The central and w. parts are occupied by rugged and wooded hills abruptly rising from the valley of the river to a height of 300 feet. The E. part is nearly level. The streams are Crabbs Kil, Chaugh-ta-noon-da, Aalplaats,[4] and Jan Wemps Creeks, and Verf Kil. The soil among the hills is a stiff clay, underlaid by hardpan, with an occasional outcrop of slate; and in the E. part it is a sandy and gravelly loam. The Mohawk intervales are very fertile, and are chiefly devoted to the culture of broomcorn. **Glenville** (p. v.) contains 2 churches and 20 houses, **Scotia**[5] (p. v.) 2 churches and 266 inhabitants, **Reeseville** 12 houses and a broom factory, and **High Falls** 13 houses, a grist mill, and woolen factory. **Hoffmans Ferry**[6] (p. o.) is a hamlet and station upon the N. Y. C. R. R. **East Glenville** is a p. o. Bridges connect this town with Schenectady and Niskayuna. Settlements were made about 1665, and were among the earliest in the co.[7] The Sanders House, in this town, was spared by the enemy when Schenectady was destroyed.[8] There are 5 churches in town.[9]

NISKAYUNA[10]—was formed from Watervliet, (Albany co.,) March 7, 1809. A part of Schenectady was annexed in 1853. It lies upon the Mohawk, in the E. part of the co. Its surface is mostly upland, terminating in steep bluffs upon the river valley. The intervales are very rich and productive. A strip of land about 1 mi. wide, extending back from the summits of the bluffs, has a hard, clay soil, and a considerable portion of it is swampy and unfit for cultivation. Further s. the soil is sandy. **Watervliet Center** (p. o) is within the limits of this town. **Niskayuna** is a hamlet in the s. E. corner. The first settlements were made about 1640.[11] The canal crosses the Mohawk into this town upon a magnificent stone aqueduct.[12] There is 1 church (Ref. Prot. D.) in town.

PRINCETOWN[13]—was formed from Schenectady, March 26, 1798. It lies a little w. of the center of the co. Its surface consists of a broken upland, gently descending toward the s. E. The streams are Normans Kil in the s. and Zantzee Kil in the N.[14] The soil is a heavy clay loam, underlaid by hardpan, and is best adapted to grazing. **Princetown** (p. o.) is a hamlet. The town was chiefly conveyed to Geo. Ingoldsby and Aaron Bradt, in 1737. Wm. Corry afterward became owner, and formed a settlement, which was long known as "*Corrysbush.*" The town was thinly settled at the time of the Revolution. The Princetown Academy, a Presb. institution, was opened here, on an extensive scale, in 1853, and was discontinued in 1856. There are a Presb. and a Ref. Prot. D. church in town.

ROTTERDAM—was formed from Schenectady, April 14, 1820. A part of the city was annexed in 1853. It lies near the center of the co., upon the s. bank of the Mohawk. The surface consists of a broken, hilly region in the N. W., a level intervale extending from the center toward the s., and a high plain in the E. The soil upon the w. hills is a tough clay, underlaid by shale, which frequently crops out. The central valley or plain, 5 mi. in extent, was called by the Dutch the "*Bouwlandt.*" The soil is a deep alluvium. The E. plateau is sandy and barren. **Rotterdam, Mohawkville,** and **Factoryville** are hamlets.[15] Settlements were first made about 1661.[16] The first church was organized Aug. 29, 1800; Rev. Thos. Romeyn was the first pastor.[17]

---

[1] The tract embraced about 60,000 acres, and the lands were rented at the rate of $15 per 100 acres, on long leases. The agents of Sir Wm. Johnson excited a prejudice against these lands which retarded their settlement.

[2] There are in town 5 other churches; Cameronian, Bap., Univ., Presb., and Quaker.

[3] Named from the original patentee.

[4] "Eel Place."

[5] Locally pronounced "Sco-chy."

[6] Harmanus Vedder established a ferry here about 1790, and it was called Vedders Ferry until 1835, when it was bought by John Hoffman and the name was changed.

[7] In 1665 the country around Scotia was granted to Sanders Lendertsen Glen, a native of Scotland, who removed to Holland in 1645 on account of religious persecutions. After several years there spent in mercantile pursuits, he migrated to "*New Netherlands.*" Van Slycks Island was granted to Jaques Van Slyck, Nov. 13, 1662.—*Barber's Hist. Coll.*

[8] On a former occasion a party of French, sent against the Mohawks, became reduced to the extremity of want, and were obliged to seek assistance of the English. The kindness shown them by Mr. Sanders was remembered, and his house was spared. A stone house built in 1713 is still owned by the Sanders family.

[9] 2 Ref. Prot. D., 2 M. E., and Bap.

[10] Said to be a corruption of Nis-ti-gi-oo-ne, or Co-nis-ti-gio-ne, by which it is known on the old maps. The name is said to signify "extensive corn flats." The term was also applied to portions of Watervliet and Half Moon. Upon the advent of the whites this place was occupied by a tribe of Indians known as the "*Conistigione.*"—*Barber & Howe's Hist. Coll. N. Y.*, p. 508.

[11] Among the early settlers were Clutes, Vedders, Van Vrankens, Groots, Tymesons, Pearces, Jansens, and Van Bockhoovens.

[12] By an act of 1805, Alexander Alexander was authorized to build a dam at this place.

[13] Named from John Prince, a member of the Assembly from Albany co. at the time of the formation of the town.

[14] Upon this stream, on the farm of Eben'r Dougall, is a cascade 60 feet high, and from this point to the Mohawk are numerous rapids and cascades.

[15] Among the early settlers were Wilhelmus Van Otto Van Curazoa, (a native of the island of Curaçoa,) Ryer Schermerhorn, and Simon Veeder. The house of Van Otto stood on the site of the one now occupied by Simon Veeder. At the time of the Revolution there were families living in town by the names of Delemont, Van Pelten, and Brangham.

[16] At this place is a twine and thread factory.

[17] There are 3 churches in town: 2 Ref. Prot. D. and 1 M. E.

SCHENECTADY CITY—was patented, with certain municipal rights, Nov. 4, 1684; chartered as a borough Oct. 23, 1765; incorp. as a district, March 24, 1772, as a town, March 7, 1788, and as a city, March 26, 1798. Princetown was set off in 1798, Rotterdam and Glenville in 1820, and parts of Niskayuna and Rotterdam in 1853.[1] It is situated on the Mohawk, and on the borders of one of the finest intervales in the State. A considerable amount of trade is carried on in the city by means of the canal and the railroads that center here; but the people are more largely engaged in manufactures.[2] The engine houses and repair shops of the N. Y. C. R. R. Co. are very extensive; and one of the largest locomotive manufactories in the country is located here.[3]

This city is especially noted as the seat of Union College. This institution was incorp. by the regents, Feb. 25, 1795, and received its name from the cöoperation and union of several religious denominations in its foundation.[4] A fund was first raised by private subscription to erect the necessary buildings and to defray the expenses of opening the school;[5] and this was increased by the avails of several lotteries authorized by the legislature,[6] by grants of land and money from the State, and by private donations. The total amount received from the State, up to 1822, for permanent investment, was $331,612 13. In a will dated Dec. 28, 1855, Dr. Nott, the president of the college, bequeathed to the trustees $555,000 for specific purposes and an additional fund for miscellaneous expenses.[7] The funds thus bequeathed were derived from the profits of certain investments of college funds, and amounts from other sources, which had been employed for the purpose of creating a fund for the endowment of the institution. The first college building was erected in the city;[8] but in 1814 a tract of land upon an eminence E. of the city was purchased, and the two principal buildings were erected.[9] The site commands an extensive view of the city, the river, and the valley. The faculty of the college now consists of a president, 12 professors, 1 lecturer, and 3 tutors. The total number of students is 420, and has not materially varied from this number for a great number of years, the junior and senior classes being invariably larger than those that preceded them. A considerable number of students derive aid from the State fund, which is extended to students of limited means without reference to the profession they intend to follow. The college has received from E. C. Delavan, Esq., a magnificent donation of minerals and shells, known as the "Wheatley Collection," which was purchased for this purpose at a cost of $10,000. Departments of Civil Engineering and Analytical Chemistry have been organized, and the facilities which they afford are of the most ample kind.

The *Public Schools* are under 8 commissioners, elected once in 2 years. There were, in 1857, 9 school districts, employing 3 male and 22 female teachers. The number of children between 4 and 21, was 3065, of whom 1729, or 56 per cent., attended the public schools.[10]

The first settlement was made in 1661, as already noticed.[11] As this was an advance frontier settlement, the compact part, at an early period, was enclosed by palisades. In 1690 the enclosure

---

[1] An Indian name signifying "beyond the plains." Formerly spelled Schenectada. The city, under its first charter, contained an area of 128 sq. mi.; but the successive changes which have been made have reduced it to a plat of 250 acres.

[2] The manufacturing establishments of the city consist of the R. R. machine shops, locomotive works, a cotton factory, 3 carriage shops, an agricultural implement factory, 3 turning and machine shops. shawl factory, 2 breweries, 1 brick yard, 2 cabinet shops, 4 founderies a planing mill, pump factory, tannery, 2 tool factories, a vice and spring factory, and a great variety of other mechanics' shops.

[3] The Schenectady Locomotive Works Co. was incorp. June 4, 1851, with a capital of $150,000, all of which is actively employed. When in full operation, they employ 600 hands, and can turn out 1 locomotive every 5 days.

[4] Rev. Wm. Andreas opened the first grammar school, in 1771; and before the close of the year he proposed to change it to an academy. The Consistory of the Ref. Prot. D. church erected a small academy in 1785. The Schenectady Academy was incorp. Jan. 29, 1793, and was merged in the college in 1795. Rev. John Blair Smith was the first President. He was succeeded in June, 1799, by Rev. Jonathan Edwards, who remained until his death in Aug. 1801. Rev. Jonathan Maxcy was next elected president, and continued till 1804, when he resigned, and was succeeded by Rev. Eliphalet Nott, the present venerable president of the College.

[5] In 1779, the inhabitants of the northern part of the State petitioned for the incorp. of a college, but without success. The petition was renewed in 1791, but did not succeed. In 1794 another effort was made, and a subscription of $7935 was raised from 99 persons in Albany, and of $3425 from 231 persons in Schenectady, for an endowment. This sum was afterward largely increased by subscription. The location was fixed at Schenectady, it is said, chiefly through the influence of Gen. Schuyler, and because of its then central location.

[6] Lotteries were authorized in 1805, 1814, and 1822.—*Munsell's Ann. of Albany*, VII. 126; *Semi-Centen. Celebration of Union Coll.*

[7] The items of this bequest are as follows:—
$225,000 for 9 professorships, with a salary of $1500 each.
$60,000 for 6 assistant professorships, at $600 each.
$60,000 for an astronomical observatory.
$20,000 for 60 auxiliary scholarships, of $10 and $12 per term.
$60,000 for 60 prize scholarships for undergraduates, of $15 and $18 per term; in certain cases to be increased to $24.
$45,000 for 9 scholarships for graduates or fellows, of $300 each.
$20,000 for a cemetery.
$10,000 for apparatus.
$5,000 for textbooks.
$30,000 for an eclectic library.
$5,000 for a geological and mineralogical cabinet.
$5,000 for a historical cabinet.
$10,000 for a lecture fund.
The miscellaneous fund was left discretionary with the trustees to fill deficiencies and extend the operation of any of the foregoing objects. At the time of this gift the greater part of the funds were invested in real estate in Greenpoint village, opposite N. York City.

[8] This building, formerly known as "*West College*," was sold to the city, and, with an adjoining building, accommodates the 10 departments of the public schools of the city.

[9] Other buildings have since been erected, for library, cabinet, and lecture rooms. The corner stone of the Central Chapel was laid July 28, 1858.

[10] Total receipts, $14,423 06; total expenses, $14,423 06. Volumes in district libraries, 3045.

[11] See page 596.

was in form of an oblong rectangle, with gates at the ends. The people, however, felt so secure that the gates were habitually left open, and no guard was kept; and hence it was easily entered by the enemy on the memorable 9th of Feb. 1690, N. S. The lives of 60 old persons and children were spared from the massacre. The settlement recovered slowly from the disaster, and not until the close of King William's War did it receive any considerable accessions. A new fort was built in May, 1690, which was garrisoned for many years. Another fort was built in 1735, and another in 1780.[1] The old fort stood at the intersection of Ferry and Front Sts. The first church (Ref. Prot. D.) was organized in 1684, and the building was erected on the s. end of Church St. in 1685. It was burned in 1690;[2] and a new building was erected, about 1702, on the site of the present church, corner of Union and Church Sts.[3] St. George's Church (Prot. E.) was organized, in 1735, by Rev. H. Barclay, incorp. in 1766, and an edifice erected in 1768.[4] The first mail was brought to the town April 3, 1763.[5] The first English school was opened, under the care of Rev. Henry Barclay, in 1710.[6] The Vale Cemetery Association was formed Feb. 25, 1858.[7] The population of the city has slowly and steadily increased, although, from the setting off of portions of its territory, the census reports for some periods show an apparent decrease.[8]

Acres of Land, Valuation, Population, Dwellings, Families, Freeholders, Schools, Live Stock, Agricultural Products, and Domestic Manufactures, of Schenectady County.

NAMES OF TOWNS.	ACRES OF LAND. Improved.	Unimproved.	VALUATION OF 1858. Real Estate.	Personal Property.	Total.	POPULATION. Males.	Females.	No. of Dwellings.	No. of Families.	Freeholders.	SCHOOLS. No. of Districts.	Children taught.
Duanesburgh	33,911½	10,827				1,556	1,563	542	395	596	22	1,234
Glenville	22,341½	7,159¼				1,666	1,487	556	417	700	13	1,173
Niskayuna	7,922	2,549				584	536	201	118	217	4	366
Princetown	12,029	3,421				496	460	166	120	172	7	397
Rotterdam	16,729½	7,693				1,537	1,298	440	293	492	13	1,427
Schenectady	515	34				4,012	4,377	1,200	610	1,606	9	3,050
Total	93,448½	31,683¼				9,851	9,721	3,105	1,953	3,783	68	7,647

NAMES OF TOWNS.	LIVE STOCK. Horses.	Working Oxen and Calves.	Cows.	Sheep.	Swine.	BUSH. OF GRAIN. Winter.	Spring.	Tons of Hay.	Bushels of Potatoes.	Bushels of Apples.	DAIRY PRODUCTS. Pounds of Butter.	Pounds of Cheese.	Domestic Manufactures in Yards.
Duanesburgh	1,319	1,872	1,940	5,541	2,097	2,471½	149,507¼	6,233	10,826	25,401	194,591	28,684	1,230¼
Glenville	1,033	1,306	1,482	2,644	2,205	15,324½	135,942½	3,718	41,837	40,628	127,599	5,235	820
Niskayuna	341	271	389	625	557	3,706	32,168	1,716	18,397	8,309	34,521	14,500	
Princetown	404	629	673	1,123	784	7,291	61,160	2,163	1,756	11,826	53,181	13,800	666
Rotterdam	731	720	1,065	826	1,660	20,445	65,049	2,328	30,447	19,042	105,770	9,800	746
Schenectady	391	48	219		424	680	2,291	27½	1,869	345			
Total	4,219	4,846	5,768	10,759	7,727	49,918	446,117¾	16,185½	105,132	105,551	515,662	72,019	3,462¼

[1] By an act of 1780, all the people living within a half mile of the Dutch church were assessed, in labor and materials, for the erection of defensive works—the work to be done under the direction of the field officers and magistrates.

[2] Rev. Peter Tasschemaker, the pastor and first teacher, was killed, and all his papers were destroyed.

[3] On the 27th of Oct. 1701, the Governor granted a special license for the inhabitants, or their agents, "to gather, collect, and receive the free and voluntary offerings and contributions of all and singular his liege subjects, inhabitants of this province, at any time from the day of the date hereof for and during the term of six months then ensuing." The funds raised were restricted to the rebuilding of the church; and all justices of the peace, high sheriffs, and all others his majesty's friends, with all Protestant ministers, were exhorted to use each their utmost diligence to excite and stir up the charities of the inhabitants.—*MSS. Sec. Office.*

[4] Besides these, the census reports 10 churches; 2 Ref. Prot. D.,

[2] Meth. E., Univ., R. C., Presb., Bap., Af. Meth., and a Jewish Synagogue. [5] *Letter of Sir Wm. Johnson.*

[6] A Lancasterian school was incorp. Nov. 12, 1816, and was taught 25 years. It was superseded by the present system of public schools.

[7] The Vale Cemetery, containing 50 acres, is located in a beautiful vale about one-fourth of a mi. from the city. It is covered with pines, and is finely laid out and ornamented.

[8] In 1699, 70 men took the test oath.
In 1710 there were 16 English and 100 Dutch families.
In 1714 the census reported 591 persons.
In 1790 there were s. of the Mohawk (in Schenectady, Prince town, Rotterdam, and a part of Niskayuna) 3472 persons. The fol lowing table shows the progress of population since 1820:—
1820.................. 3939   1840.................. 6784
1825.................. 4068   1845.................. 6555
1830.................. 4268   1850.................. 8921
1835.................. 6272   1855.................. 8389

SCHOHARIE COUNTY.

THIS county was formed from Albany and Otsego, April 6, 1795.[1] A small part of Greene was annexed in 1836. It is an interior co., lying S. E. of the center of the State, is centrally distant 35 mi. from Albany, and contains 675 sq. mi. Its surface is an upland, broken by mountains in the S. and by hills in the center and N. A northerly branch of the Catskill Mts. lies along the S. border, the highest summits of which are 3,000 ft. above tide. From them irregular spurs extend northward, occupying the greater part of the co. Many of the summits along the E. and W. borders are 800 to 1,000 ft. above the valleys and about 2,000 ft. above tide. In the N. the hills are generally rounded and are arable to their summits; but in the center and S. the declivities are steep and in many places precipitous. The high ridge along the E. border, and extending into Albany co., is known as the Hellebark Mts.

The hills derive their general features from the rocks that underlie them. The extreme N. part of the co. is terraced like the limestone region farther W. Toward the S. the hills become more steep; and in the shaly region they are broken by deep, irregular ravines. In many places the hills bordering upon the streams are 1,000 ft. high and in places very steep. Schoharie Creek flows N. E. through the co., a little E. of the center. It receives as tributaries Foxes Creek, Stony Brook, Little Schoharie Creek, Keysers, Platter, and Manor Kils from the E., and Cripplebush, Cobles, Line, Panther, West, and Mine Kils from the W. West and Punch Kils are tributaries of Cobles Kil. Charlotte River, a branch of the Susquehanna, takes its rise in the W. part, and Catskill Creek in the S. E. part, having its source in a marsh called the Vlaie. Utsyanthia[2] and Summit Lakes, two small ponds, are the only bodies of water in the co. The former is 1,900 ft. and the latter 2,150 ft. above tide.

The rocks in the co., commencing upon the N. border and appearing successively toward the S., are those belonging to the Hudson River group, Clinton group, Onondaga salt group, Helderbergh series, Hamilton group, Portage and Chemung group, and the Catskill group. The limestones are cavernous; and the minerals which they afford are particularly interesting to mineralogists.[3] Drift is scattered over the co. to a limited extent. Waterlime is found, but is not now manufactured.

The soils are principally derived from the disintegration of the underlying rocks. In the N. the soil is a productive, clay loam, and in the center and S. it is a clay and sandy loam, the latter predominating upon the S. hills. The alluvial flats along Schoharie Creek are unusually fertile.

The co. is eminently an agricultural region. Spring grains are largely produced. Hops are cultivated in the W. part, and broomcorn upon the Schoharie Flats. Dairying is the principal business in the S. part. Very little manufacturing is done, except such as is customary in an agricultural region.

The county seat is located at the village of Schoharie.[4] The courthouse is a fine edifice built of blue limestone, located near the center of the village. The jail is a stone building, situated in rear of the courthouse. The clerk's office is a small, fireproof building, upon the courthouse lot, nearly in front. The poorhouse is located upon a farm of 160 acres in Middleburgh, 5 mi. s. w. of the courthouse. The average number of inmates is 60, supported at a weekly cost of 75 cents each. This institution seems to be well managed and much above the average of similar institutions in the State.

The Albany & Susquehanna R. R. is located along the valleys of Schoharie Creek and Cobles

---

1 Schoharie is said to signify "drift wood." At a place ¼ mi. above Middleburgh Bridge the Line Kil and Little Schoharie flow into Schoharie Creek from opposite sides; and here drift wood is said to have accumulated in large quantities, forming a natural bridge.—*Brown's Hist. Schoharie.*
The original Indian name was To-wos-scho'her; and it has been written Shoary, Skohary, Schughhorre, &c.

2 Utsyantha was the N. E. corner of the Hardenburgh Patent, and a distinguished landmark in early records.

3 Among the more interesting are stalactites of pure white, translucent and solid, sulphate of barytes, calcite, satin spar, tufa, agaric mineral, bog ore, black oxid of manganese, sulphate and carbonate of strontia, fluor spar, calstronbaryte, carbonate of iron, and arragonite. The co. affords an unusual variety of fossils peculiar to the respective geological formations.

4 The first courts were held in a wagon house of Johannis Ingold, and prisoners were at first sent to the Albany jail. The first meeting of the Judges, Justices, and Supervisors was held Dec. 16, 1795, and it was decided to fix the site for co. buildings 2 mi. w. of their present location. The location was changed before the buildings were erected. The first buildings were erected soon after, and were burned in 1847. The first courthouse was built under the direction of Joost Borst. jr., Jacob Lawyer, Peter Snyder, John H. Shafer, and Wm. Phrall, commissioners. Abraham A. Post, of Ontario, Alexander H. Buel, of Herkimer, and Wm. Duer, of Oswego, were appointed to locate the present site. The first co. officers were Wm. Beekman, *First Judge*, (reappointed constantly till 1838;) Joachim G. Staats, *Clerk*; Jacob Lawyer, jr., *Sheriff*; and Stephen A. Becker, *Surrogate*.

Kil, through Esperance, Schoharie, Cobleskill, and Richmondville.[1] Several turnpikes and lines of plank road extend across the co.[2]

About thirty years previous to the advent of the whites, a number of Indians belonging to the Mohawks, Mohicans, Delawares, Tuscaroras, and Oneidas united together, formed the Schoharie tribe, and took up their abode along Schoharie Creek.[3] Their principal chief was Ka-righ-on-don-tee, who had been a prisoner of the French in Canada and had married a Mohawk woman. This tribe was subordinate to the Six Nations. They could bring into the field about 600 warriors, and in the wars that ensued they steadily espoused the cause of the British. At an early period, with the aid of the Colonial Government, they erected several strongholds to protect themselves from the attacks of the Canada Indians. A band of 200 Indians remained in the valley, at peace with the settlers, until the commencement of the Revolution. Efforts were made to induce them to remain neutral during the war; but the offers of the British were so tempting that at last they took up arms against their neighbors. Previous to this a pestilence had swept off the greater part of the tribe, though the whites were not in the least affected by it.

The first white settlement was made by a colony of German Palatinates, in 1711. These people had previously settled at East and West Camp, on the Hudson. Their number is estimated at 600 to 700. They settled in 7 clusters, or villages, each under a leader or head man, from whom the dorf, or village, was usually named.[4] The Dutch soon after began a settlement at "*Vroomansland*," on the w. side of the creek, 2 or 3 mi. above the German settlement.[5] The Palatinates at first did not secure a patent for the lands they occupied, and a short time after their settlement Nicholas Bayard appeared as agent of the British Government, and offered to give the settlers deeds for their lands; but he was assailed by a mob and was obliged to flee for his life. Upon reaching Schenectady he sent back word that for an ear of corn each he would give a clear title to the lands occupied by each; but this offer was rejected. He returned to Albany and sold the tract to 5 persons at that place.[6] A sheriff, named Adams, was sent to arrest some of the trespassers; but no sooner was his business known than he was assailed by a mob and ridden upon a rail. For a considerable time after this outrage none of the German settlers dared visit Albany; but after a time they ventured to do so, and were at once arrested and thrown into jail. They were at length released on making a written acknowledgment of the outrage they had perpetrated.[7] The settlers at length sent an embassy, consisting of Conrad Weiser, —— Casselman, and another, to England to petition the king for redress. The ship that took them out carried also a statement of the out rages, and the ambassadors were at once imprisoned; but after a time they were set at liberty and permitted to return. Weiser was so chagrined at the result of the controversy that soon after, with about 60 families, he emigrated to Tulpehocton, Berks co., Penn. Other families removed to German Flats and others to Stone Arabia.[8] Peter Vrooman, with several Dutch families,[9] perma-

---

[1] The elevation of this road, where it enters the co. on the E., is 700 ft. above tide; at Schoharie Creek it is 550 ft.; at Cobleskill, 900 ft.; at Richmondville, 1,175 ft.; and at the w. co. line, 1,470 ft.

[2] The principal turnpikes in the co. in early times were the Great Western, extending to Cherry Valley, built in 1802; and the Charlotte River Turnpike, built in 1809. The latter formed the great thoroughfare to the settlements in Delaware co. and adjacent regions. The plank road project was pretty thoroughly tried, and has been abandoned after a sacrifice of nearly all the capital invested.

[3] The Mohicans principally settled near the mouth of the Little Schoharie; and the largest settlement of the others was at "*Vroomansland*," in the present town of Fulton.

[4] Six of these leaders were Conrad Weiser, Hartman Winteker, John Hendrick Kneiskern, Elias Garlock, Johannes George Smidt, and William Fox; and John Lawyer, who came soon after, is supposed to have been the seventh. "*Weisers Dorf*" occupied the present site of Middleburgh Village, and had some 40 dwellings, like the others, built rudely of logs and earth and covered with bark and grass. "*Hartmans Dorf*" was 2 mi. below, and had 65 dwellings. "*Bruns Dorf*," or "*Brunen Dorf*," or "*Fountain Town*," was near the courthouse. "*Smiths Dorf*" was a mi. farther N. "*Foxs Dorf*" was still farther down, about a mi. from Smiths. "*Garlocks Dorf*" was 2 mi. below; and "*Kneiskerns Dorf*" 2 or 3 mi. still farther N. Among these early settlers, besides those above named, were families named Keyser, Bouck, Richard, Richtmeyer, Warner, Weaver, Zimmer, Mattice, Zeh, Bellinger, Borst, Schoolcraft, Crysler, Casselman, Newkirk, Earhart, Brown, Settle, Merckley, Snyder, Ball, Weidman, Deitz, Mann, Sternberg, Stubrach, Enderse, Sidney, Bergh, and Houck. Within a week after their arrival, Catharine Mattice, Elizabeth Lawyer, Wilhelmus Bouck, and Johannes Earhart were born. The first wheat was sown by —— Sternberg, in 1773; and the first skipple planted like corn yielded 83 fold.

[5] Adam Vrooman, from Schenectady, obtained a patent for 1,100 acres, Aug. 26, 1714. His tract was afterward found to contain 1,400 acres. It embraced the flats along the creek in

the present town of Fulton, except Wilder Hook, at which place was an Indian castle and settlement. His son Peter, for whom it was bought, built a house, planted corn, and the first winter left the premises in charge of a man named Truax, and a negro man and his wife. Truax was murdered, and the negro and his wife were arrested, tried at Albany, and burned alive; but years after, one Moore, a resident of "*Weisers Dorf*," confessed that he and the negro man committed the deed, and that the woman was innocent.—*Simm's Schoharie*, p. 56.

[6] The purchasers were Myndert Schuyler, Peter Van Brugh, Robert Livingston, jr., John Schuyler, and Henry Wielman. They received a patent, Nov. 3, 1714, for 10,000 acres, which was designed to include the flats from "*Vroomansland*" to Montgomery co. line; but on being surveyed by Lewis Morris, jr., and Andrus Coeyman, it was found that the flats on Fox Creek and at the mouth of Cobles Kil were not included, and these lands were secured by the surveyors. In a short time Morris and Coeyman joined interest with the five proprietors, and the company became known as the "Seven Partners." Final suits for partition and settlement were adjusted in 1819, '25, '26, '28, and '29.

[7] After this time a large number of settlers took leases of the proprietors, thus abandoning their claims to the lands.

[8] Among those who removed to the Mohawk was Elias Garlock, the first and long the only magistrate in Schoharie.

[9] Among these were families named Swartz, Ecker, Hagadorn, Feeck, and Becker. Lawrence Schoolcraft made the first cider in the Schoharie settlements; —— Brown, in 1752, was the first wagon maker. John Mattice Junk taught the first German school at the Camps, about 1740; and schools were taught in Schoharie soon after. Dutch schools were taught at "*Vroomansland*" at an early period; and about 1760, English was first taught in schools in this region. John Ecker was the first blacksmith. The settlers of the valley resorted to Schenectady to mill, or used stump mortars, until many years after, when a mill was built on Mill Creek, near Fox Creek, by Simeon Laraway. Bolting cloths were first used in this co. about 1760. John Lawyer was the first merchant among the Germans.

nently located upon his patent in 1727. The German and Dutch races long remained distinct. The Dutch were generally wealthier than the more hardy and laborious Germans, and preferred to contract marriages with those of their own class in the older Dutch settlements. They often kept slaves, while the Germans seldom had further assistance than such as their own households, of both sexes, might afford. The Germans, by intermarriage, became a "family of cousins;" and they were united by many ties of common interest. Industry and frugality gradually brought them to a level, and long acquaintance has almost entirely obliterated these hereditary distinctions of society. Upon the approach of the Revolution, a part of the people espoused the cause of the British; but the majority were ardent patriots. In many cases members of the same family were engaged on opposite sides, and the struggle assumed all the horrors of a civil war, aggravated by Indian barbarities. A Council of Safety was organized in 1774, of which Johannes Ball was chairman. During the war several conflicts took place within the limits of the co., and the people were continually exposed to the attacks of small scalping parties of the Indians.[1]

At the close of the war a large number of families removed to Canada, and their property was confiscated.[2] Several tories and Indians who had been active during the war returned at its close and were waylaid and shot. Others, warned by these examples, fled the country.[3] Since that period little of especial interest has occurred in the history of the co. In 1845 and '46, in common with the surrounding regions, this co. partook largely in the anti-rent excitement,— though no actual violence took place within its limits.[4] Within the last ten years, a mania for building large seminaries, far beyond the wants of the people, has spread through the co. The speculation has proved a ruinous one, and the entire amount of capital invested in the enterprises has been sunk.[5]

Three weekly newspapers are now published in the co.[6]

---

[1] The principal events of the Revolution in Schoharie co. were as follows:—
1774.   Council of Safety formed.
1776.   Col. James Huston enlisted tories at Loonenbergh.
1777.   Schoharie militia called into service under Captain Hager. Col. Huston and 20 others were arrested, and Huston was hung.
"   Aug. 10.—Engagement between an American force under Col. John Harper and the tories under Capt. McDonald at Brakabeen. The tories were defeated and fled. Capt. Geo. Mann, one of their number, remained secreted in the vicinity until the succeeding spring, when he delivered himself up to the authorities. He never afterward joined the enemy, and his property was not confiscated.
            In the autumn of this year the middle fort was built, and the upper and lower forts were begun. The lower fort is the old stone church, lately changed to an arsenal.
1778,   May 8.—Battle of Cobles Kil, in which Captain Patrick and 22 men were killed.
"   July.—Lieut. Col. Wm. Butler, with 3 companies of Morgan's Riflemen, was stationed at Schoharie. Several tories recruiting for the British were shot.
1779,   Aug.—Col. Butler joined Sullivan's expedition against the Western Indians.
1780,   Aug. 9.—A party of 73 Indians and 3 tories made an attack upon the settlements at Vroomansland, killed 5, and took 30 prisoners.
"   Oct. 16.—Sir John Johnson, with 500 troops and a large body of tories and Indians, invaded the Schoharie settlements from the s. The upper fort was garrisoned by 100 men, under Capts. Jacob Hager and Joseph Harper; the middle fort by 350 men, under Maj. Woolsey; and the lower fort by 150 men, under Maj. Becker. The middle fort was attacked, and the commander, Major Woolsey, being an arrant coward, wished to surrender it; but a soldier, named Murphy, fired upon the flag which was sent with a summons to surrender; and, after an ineffectual attack, Sir John abandoned the attempt. The dwellings, barns, stacks, and all the property of the inhabitants were destroyed, though but few persons lost their lives.
1781.   Early in the year blockhouses were built at "Kneiskerns Dorf," "Hartmans Dorf," and Cobleskill.
1781,   July 9.—An engagement took place in Sharon, 2 mi. E. of the springs, between a party of tories and Indians under Doxtader, and an American force under Col. Willett, in which the former were defeated, with a loss of 40 killed.

1781,   July.—Several persons at Middleburgh were surprised and taken prisoners while harvesting. One escaped, and the others were carried prisoners to Canada.
"   Oct.—Three men at Christian Myndert's house, in Sharon, were taken prisoners by a small party of Indians, and carried to Canada.
"   Oct. 24.—A party of 60 or 70 Indians, under Brant, entered Vroomansland and commenced their work of plunder. Isaac Vrooman was murdered. A party of Americans, under Capt. Hager, rallied to their assistance, and the Indians retreated. A sharp skirmish took place at Utsyantha Lake; but a part of the American force, under Capt. Hale fled at the commencement, and the remainder were obliged to retreat. Hale was arrested in his retreat by the threat of being shot; but the enemy had escaped.
1782,   July 26.—Several tories and 22 Indians made an incursion into Foxes Creek Valley for the purpose of capturing Maj. Becker; but the Maj. and family defended the house with such vigor that the Indians retreated. Several persons were murdered by the Indians, and several of the latter were shot.
1784,   Dec. 16.—Many persons who had been taken to Canada were released on Lake Champlain, and returned to their homes.

[2] In Canada, opposite St. Lawrence co., are many families who claim relationship to inhabitants of this co. They were refugees to whom grants of land were made by the British Government.

[3] Among these was one Beacraft, who boasted of his feats of villainy. Soon after his return he was surprised by about a dozen whigs, near Blenheim Bridge, led into a grove, stripped, bound, and punished with fifty lashes with hickory gads, the executioners at every ten telling him for what particular offence they were applied. He was then unbound and allowed a very short time to disappear.

[4] In this co. George Clark had then considerable tracts, leased for 3 lives at a rent of 6 pence sterling per acre. Scott's Patent of 56,000 acres was then chiefly owned by the heirs of John Livingston, and leased for 2 lives at a rent of $14 per 100 acres. The Blenheim Patent was also in part leased.

[5] Of 9 academies built in this co., 3 have been burned, 3 are "to let," and 3 are still open.

[6] The American Herald, the first paper published in the co. was commenced at Schoharie in June, 1809, by Derick Van Veghten. In 1812 its name was changed to The Schoharie Herald, and the paper was soon after discontinued.
The True American was commenced at Schoharie in Dec. 1809, by T. M. Tillman. It was discontinued in 1812 or 1813.
The Schoharie Budget was commenced in June, 1817, by Derick Van Veghten. In 1820 its name was changed to

BLENHEIM[1]—was formed from Schoharie, March 17, 1797. Jefferson was taken off in 1803, and a part of Gilboa in 1848. It is an interior town, lying s. w. of the center of the co. Its surface is a hilly upland, broken by the deep ravines of the streams. Schoharie Creek flows N. through the E. part, receiving West Kil and several smaller streams from the w. A wide alluvial flat extends along its course. The streams generally are bordered by steep hills rising to a height of 300 to 500 ft. The soil is principally a clayey loam. **Patchin Hollow,**[2] (North Blenheim p. o.,) upon Schoharie Creek, contains 2 churches, a tannery, and 44 houses. The first settlements were made by Dutch and Palatinates, before 1761; but the settlers were driven out during the Revolution. The present race of settlers came mostly from New England, soon after the close of the war. Rev. Stephen Fenn was the first preacher.[3]

BROOME[4]—was formed March 17, 1797, as "*Bristol.*" Its name was changed April 6, 1808. A part of Conesville was taken off in 1836, a part of Gilboa in 1848, and parts of Middleburgh were annexed Feb. 9 and Oct. 5, 1849. It lies upon the E. border of the co., s. of the center. Its surface is a hilly upland, broken by the deep ravines of the streams. The highest summits are 350 to 500 ft. above the valleys. Catskill Creek takes its rise in the N. part, and several branches of Schoharie Creek drain the N. and w. portions.[5] The soil is a gravelly and clayey loam. **Livingstonville,** (p. v.,) in the E. part, s. of the center, contains 2 churches, a sawmill, gristmill, and sash factory. Pop. 150.[6] **Franklinton,** (p. v.,) in the N. part, contains a church and 100 inhabitants. **Smithton** is a hamlet, near the s. line. The first settlements were made before the Revolution.[7] There are 6 churches in town.[8]

CARLISLE—was formed from Cobleskill and Sharon, March 31, 1807.[9] It is the central town upon the N. border of the co. Its surface consists principally of an immense ridge lying between the valleys of the Mohawk and Cobles Kil, the summit of which is 800 to 1,000 ft. above the former stream.[10] This ridge descends to the N. by a series of terraces formed by the different geological strata, and on the s. by gradual slopes following the general dip of the rocks. The streams are small brooks. The soil is principally a clay loam. Hops are extensively cultivated.

The Schoharie Republican. It soon after passed into the hands of Peter Keyser. Lemuel Cuthbert, A. A. Keyser, Wm. H. Underwood, Wm. H. Gallup, P. D. Lawyer, and —— Rossiter have since been interested in its publication. It is now published by J. B. Hall.

The Observer was commenced at Schoharie in Oct. 1818. In 1819 it passed into the hands of Solomon Baker, in 1820 to Baker & Fish, and in 1822 it was again in the hands of Mr. Baker, and was soon after discontinued.

The Evangelical Luminary was commenced at Schoharie Jan. 1, 1824, by Rev. Geo. A. Lintner and L. Cuthbert. It was continued about 1 year.

The Lutheran Magazine, mo., was commenced in Feb. 1827, by the Western Conference of Lutheran Ministers, L. Cuthbert, printer, and was published for some years.

The Schoharie Free Press was commenced June 9, 1830, by Duncan McDonald. In 1832 it was removed to Esperance and its name changed to

The Esperance Sentinel and Schoharie and Montgomery Reporter. It was discontinued in 1835 or '36.

The Gem was published a short time in 1837.

The Schoharie Patriot was commenced Feb. 13, 1838, by Peter Mix. It is now published by him and his son, S. H. Mix.

The Star was commenced in April, 1838, by S. H. Mix, then a schoolboy.

The Sun was commenced as an opposition paper in May, 1838, by D. L. Underwood, another lad of about the same age. These papers were about 3 by 4 inches. Early in 1839 they were enlarged. On the issue of No. 5 of the Sun it went down never to rise again; and the Star ceased to twinkle after the 12th number.

The Huge Paw, a campaign paper, was published from Aug. 12 1840, to Nov. 11 following, by Wm. H. Gallup.

The Helderbergh Advocate was commenced in 1841 by Wm. H. Gallup. Its name was changed in 1843 to

The Guardian of the Soil, and it was discontinued in 1 year.

The American Christian was commenced at Leesville Jan. 7, 1847, by J. D. Lawyer. It was soon after discontinued.

The Schoharie County Sentinel was commenced at Cobleskill Jan. 22, 1852, by Hiram C. Page. It was published a short time by Chas. Cleveland, and by Wadhams & Knistern, and was soon after purchased by J. B. Hall, who merged it with the Schoharie Republican.

The Charlotteville Journal was commenced at Charlotteville in 1854 by Furman & Brown. In 1855 John Brown became sole proprietor, and removed it to Cobleskill and changed the name to

The Cobleskill Journal. It has since been discontinued.

The Oasis, semi-mo., was commenced at Schoharie by the students of the academy in 1855. It was soon discontinued.

The Schoharie County Jeffersonian was commenced at Cobleskill in 1859 by Matthew Freeman, and is still published.

[1] Named from the Blenheim Patent, a portion of which lies in the N. part of this town.

[2] Hendrick Mattice, the pioneer, built a mill on West Kil, at Patchin Hollow. He became a loyalist and went to Canada. Henry Effner, Lambert Sternberg, Wm. Freeck, Isaac Smith, Banks Morehouse, George Martin, and Henry Hager were early settlers. Freegift Patchin settled in 1798, built the second mill, and gave name to the village. Gen. Patchin had been taken prisoner by the Indians, and suffered extremely at their hands. The first inn was kept by H. Effner; the first store, by Tobias Cuyler, in 1803; and the first tannery was built in 1825, by Jones & Lathrop. Jacob Sutherland, afterward Judge of the U. S. Supreme Court, resided several years at North Blenheim.

[3] There are 4 churches in town; 3 M. E., and Ref. Prot. D.

[4] Named from John Broome, Lieut. Gov. of the State at the time of the formation of the town. Scott's Patent of 37,840 acres, granted Jan. 2, 1770, and a part of Isaac Le Roy's Patent, are within the limits of this town.

[5] On the summit level of the Catskill & Canajoharie R. R. line, between two immense hills, was a "vlaie," or black ash swamp, from which streams issued in opposite directions It was about a mile long and covered many acres. Dams were formerly erected and mills built at each end; and fish placed in the pond thus formed multiplied greatly. It is now drained.

[6] Daniel Shays, the leader of the insurrection in Mass. that bears his name, settled in this town after the dispersion of his forces. David Williams, one of the captors of Andre, removed to this village from South Salem in 1805, bought a farm of Gen. Shays, and resided upon it until his death, Aug. 2, 1831. He left a widow, 4 sons, and 3 daughters. He was the object of much regard, from the interesting historical event with which his name is associated; and the year before his death he became the guest of New York City.—*Simms's Schoharie,* chap. xxi.

[7] Derick Van Dyck settled before the Revolution. John Robbins, —— Guillem, a half-breed, Allen Leet, Joshua and Asa Bushnell, Geo. and Hezekiah Watson, Ebenezer Wickham, Geo. Burtwick, Timothy Kelsey, Joseph Gillet, and Ezra Chapman settled previous to 1796. The first known birth was that of Francis Kelsey, in April, 1794; and the first death, that of Ezra Chapman, Aug. 1794. Griswold, Cardeu & Wells began the erection of a sawmill in 1794, and a gristmill the next season.

[8] 3 M. E., Meth. Prot., Bap., and Presb.

[9] This town embraces portions of New Dorlach, Becker, Livingston's, Van Rensselaer's, Machin's, and the Stone Heap Patents.

[10] A conical elevation near the s. line, early known as O-waere-souere, is one of the highest points in the co., and may be seen from Hamilton co., 50 mi. N.

Several caves are found in the limestone regions in various parts of the town.[1] **Argusville,**[2] (p. v.,) in the N. W. corner, upon the line of Sharon, contains 3 churches, a sawmill, gristmill, tannery, and 35 houses. **Carlisle,** (p. v.,) upon the Western Turnpike, in the N. part, contains a church, boarding school,[3] and foundery. Pop. 107. **Grovenors Corners,** (p. o.,) in the S. E. corner, contains a church and 10 houses. The first settlement was made in the S. W. part, about 1760.[4] The first church was formed by Dr. Simon Hosack, of Johnstown, in 1803 or '04.[5]

COBLESKILL[6]—was formed from Schoharie, March 17, 1797. The line of Sharon was changed March 15, 1799. A part of Carlisle was taken off in 1807, a part of Summit in 1819, and Richmondville in 1845. It is an interior town, lying N. of the center of the co. Its surface is principally a hilly upland, broken by the deep valley of Cobles Kil, which extends E. and W. through the center. The highest points, on the N. and S. borders, are 600 to 900 ft. above the valley. The soil upon the hills is a sandy loam, and in the valley an alluvium. **Cobleskill,** (p. v.,) in the W. part, contains 3 churches, a sawmill, gristmill, planing mill, and tannery. Pop. 364. **Cobleskill Center** (p. v.) contains a church, sawmill, and 20 dwellings. **Lawyersville,**[7] (p. v.,) in the N. W. corner, contains 3 churches, 2 sawmills, and 25 dwellings. **East Cobleskill,**[8] (p. v.,) in the S. E. corner, contains 2 churches and 21 dwellings. **Barnerville,** (p. v.,) near the center, contains a church, gristmill, clothing works, and 16 dwellings. The first settlement was made about 1750.[9] The first land grants were made about 1730. During the Revolution the people mostly espoused the cause of the colonists, and in consequence were subjected to constant incursions from the Indians. A regular engagement took place between a company of militia and a large Indian force under Brant, May 31, 1778. The Americans were defeated, and about one-half of their number were killed.[10] Howe's Cave, near the E. line, is a place of considerable interest.[11] The census reports 7 churches in town.[12]

CONESVILLE[13]—was formed from Broome and Durham, (Greene co.,) March 3, 1836. It is the S. E. corner town of the co. Its surface is generally a hilly upland, mountainous along the E. border. The highest summits are 1,600 to 2,000 ft. above the valleys. Schoharie Creek forms a small portion of the W. boundary; and Manor Kil flows W. through near the center. Upon the latter stream, near its mouth, is a cascade of 60 ft. The valleys of these streams are bordered by high and often nearly precipitous hills. **Strykersville,** (West Conesville p. o.,) upon Manor Kil near its mouth, contains a church, tannery, and 20 houses; and **Stone Bridge,** (Conesville p. o.,) near the center, a church and 10 houses. **Manorkill** (p. o.) is a hamlet. The first settlement was made by Ury Richtmeyer, in 1764.[14] There are 3 churches in town; 2 M. E. and Ref. Prot. D.

ESPERANCE[15]—was formed from Schoharie, April 4, 1846. A small portion was reannexed to Schoharie in 1850. It is the E. town on the N. border of the co. Its surface consists of two ridges, extending E. and W. across the town, separated by the valley of Schoharie Creek. The

---

1 The principal of these caves are known as Young's and Selkirk's caves. Near Carlisle Village is a small cavern, in which it is supposed that Indians found shelter during the Revolution. Fibrous sulphate of barytes, fibrous carbonate of lime, and arragonite are found near Grosvenors Corners.

2 Named from the Albany Argus, at the time the principal paper taken in town. Formerly known as *"Molick's Mills."*

3 The Carlisle Seminary was built by a stock company in 1853, at a cost of $24,000. It is beautifully situated in a grove a little s. of the center of the village. It was opened in Nov. 1853, and closed in March, 1855. It has accommodation for about 300 boarders.

4 Andrew Loucks, Coenradt Engle, Philip Hooker, and Peter Young were among the first that located in town. The late Judge Brown, author of a small local history, settled at an early period. John C. McNeill, Wm. Caldwell, John Sweetman, Aaron Howard, Teunis Van Camp, Mathias Cass, and Lodowyck Primer were also early settlers.

5 There are now 5 churches in town; Bap., Evan. Luth., Presb., Univ., and Union.

6 Named from —— Cobel, who built a mill near Central Bridge at an early period. Cobles Kil was called by the Indians Otsga-ra-gee.

7 Named from Lawrence Lawyer, said to have been the first settler in town.   8 Locally known as "Punchkill."

9 Among the early settlers were families named Shafer, Bouck, Keyser, Warner, Fremyre, Borst, and Brown,—mostly from Schoharie. Capt. Jas. Dana, an early settler, distinguished himself in the battle of Bunker Hill. John Redington, another soldier of much service, also lived in this town.—*Simms's Schoharie, p. 619.* A sawmill, built before the war by Christian Brown, was not destroyed by the Indians, as it was coveted by a tory, who expected to receive it after it was confiscated by the British.

10 The American force of 45 men, under the command of Capts. Brown and Patrick, were drawn into an ambuscade. Upon the retreat, 5 of the soldiers threw themselves into a house, which was surrounded by the Indians and burned, the soldiers perishing in the flames. The delay occasioned by the resistance made at this house gave the remainder of the fugitives and the inhabitants time to escape. The whole number of Americans killed was 22; and it is supposed that the Indians lost about an equal number. Fort Du Bois, a strong blockhouse, stood in this town during the war.

11 This cave was discovered in May, 1842, by Lester Howe, owner. Its entrance is about 50 ft. above Cobles Kil. After passing several spacious rooms, one of which is named "The Chapel," the visitor comes to a crawling place 200 ft. long, beyond which is a limpid sheet of water 30 ft. long, 20 wide, and 10 deep. Beyond this the cavern extends a great distance, much of the way along a brook, and the total length of the passages measures several mi. Many highly interesting stalactital concretions— some of great size—have been found in this locality. It has been named the Otsgaragee Cavern.

12 4 M. E., 2 Ref. Prot. D., and Evan. Luth.

13 Named from Rev. Jonathan Cone, of Durham, Greene co. The town was included in a tract granted to U. Richtmeyer and others, May 6, 1754, known as Dise's Manor; and tracts to Daniel Crane, Samuel Stringer, Walter McFarlane, John Richtmeyer, Christian Patrie, and others.

14 Mr. R. was joint owner of several patents with John Dise and others; and the name is still common in town. During the Revolution the settlers fled for safety to the upper fort. Peter Richtmeyer was twice taken prisoner by the Indians under the tory Jones. After the war, Philip Krinple, Conrad Patrie, John Shew, Barent Stryker, Stephen Scovill, James Allerton, and Hubbard and Judah Luring, the last two from Conn., came into town. The first death was that of Ury Richtmeyer, Aug. 14, 1769. Thomas Canfield taught a school in 1794. Peter Richtmeyer kept the first inn, in 1784. Barent Stryker built the first mill, above the falls of Manor Kil.

15 The town was named from the village. The site of the latter was bought by Gen. Wm. North in 1800, laid out into lots, and named by him from a French word signifying *Hope.*

highest parts are 600 to 800 ft. above the valley. The soil is principally a clayey loam. **Esperance,** (p. v.,) upon the E. line, was incorp. April 21, 1832. It contains 2 churches, a paper mill, gristmill, sawmill, and foundery. Pop. 322. **Sloansville,**[1] (p. v.,) near the center, contains 2 churches, 3 sawmills, and 2 gristmills. Pop. 252. The first settlements were made by Palatinates, about 1711.[2] There are 4 churches in town; 2 Bap., Presb., and M. E.

FULTON[3]—was formed from Middleburgh, April 15, 1828. It is the central town in the co. Its surface is a hilly upland, broken by the ravines of the streams. Schoharie Creek[4] flows N. through the E. part, receiving Panther Creek from the w. The highest summits are 1,000 ft. above the valleys. The hills next to the creek are conical and often precipitous; but farther w. they assume a rounded form and are bounded by more gradual slopes. The soil is a gravelly and clayey loam. **Brakabeen,**[5] (p. v.,) upon Schoharie Creek, in the s. part, contains a church, gristmill, foundery, 2 sawmills, and 200 inhabitants. **Fultonham,** (p. v.,) near the E. line contains a church, gristmill, 2 sawmills, and 25 dwellings; and **West Fulton** (p. v.) a church, sawmill, gristmill, and 16 dwellings. **Watsonville** is a small village, in the E. part; and **Petersburgh** a hamlet, in the N. part. The first settlements were made by Dutch and Palatinates, about 1711. The upper fort of the Schoharie during the Revolution was situated upon the present site of Fultonham. The census reports 5 churches in town.[6] Gov. Wm. C. Bouck was born in this town Jan. 7, 1786, and died here in April, 1859.

GILBOA—was formed from Blenheim and Broome, March 16, 1848. It is the central town upon the s. border of the co. Its surface is a mountainous upland, broken by deep ravines. Schoharie Creek[7] flows N. through the center, receiving Platter Kil from the E. and Mine Kil from the w. The streams are bordered by steep hillsides rising to a height of 2,000 to 3,000 ft. above tide. The soil is a gravelly and clayey loam. **Gilboa,** (p. v.,) upon Schoharie Creek, contains 2 churches, a private seminary, cotton factory,[8] gristmill, tannery, and 566 inhabitants. **South Gilboa,** (p. v.,) in the w. part, contains a church and 20 dwellings. **West Gilboa,** (p. o.,) in the N. w. part, is a hamlet. **Mackies Corners,** (Broome Center p. o.,) in the E. part, contains a church and 15 dwellings. **Mine Kil Falls** is a p. o. Settlement was commenced in 1764, by Matthew and Jacob Dise.[9] The first preacher was Rev. Joel Peebles, settled in 1808.[10]

JEFFERSON—was formed from Blenheim, Feb. 12, 1803. A part of Summit was taken off in 1819. It is on the s. line of the co., near the s. w. corner. Its surface is a hilly upland, the principal summits being about 1,000 ft. above the valleys and 2,000 ft. above tide. Mine Hill, in the extreme s. part, is estimated to be 3,200 ft. above tide. A high ridge extending N. E. and s. w. through near the center forms the watershed between Delaware and Mohawk Rivers. Utsyantha Lake is a small sheet of water on the s. line.[11] The soil is a gravelly and clayey loam. **Jefferson,** (p. v.,) near the center, contains 2 churches and 25 houses. **Morseville,** in the

---

[1] Named from John R. Sloan, an early settler. Many years since, near this place, by the side of a path leading to Fort Hunter, was a stone heap thrown up by the Indians, who, from a superstition among them, never failed to add a stone to the pile who never they passed it. The Rev. Gideon Hawley, who passed it in 1753, relates (1 *Mass. Coll. IV*) that this heap had been accumulating for ages, and that his native guide could give no other reason for the observance than that his father practiced it and enjoined it upon him. He did not like to talk about it; and the missionary believed that the custom was a religious offering to the unknown God. Others state that a tradition fixes this as the spot where a murder was committed. The heap gave name to the "Stone Heap Patent," granted to John Bower and others Sept. 15, 1770. The heap was 4 rods long, 1 or 2 wide, and 10 to 15 ft. high, and consisted of small, flat stones. The covetous owner many years since built the material into a stone wall; and no trace of this curious monument of Indian superstition now remains. Similar stone heaps have been noticed in other sections of the State. The path that led by this pile was that taken by Sir John Johnson and his army from Schoharie to the Mohawk in Oct. 1780.—*Simms's Schoharie*, p. 632.

[2] One of the first settlements was made at "*Kneiskerns Dorf*," opposite the mouth of Cobles Kil. The place was named from John Peter Kneiskern, a prominent settler. The Stubrachs, Enderses, Sidneys, Berghs, and Houcks were also pioneer families. Henry and George Houck built the first gristmill. This town comprises the whole of Jacob Henry Ten Eyck's patent, surveyed Aug. 1761; a part of the Schoharie Patent, and a part of Sawyer & Zimmer's Second Allotment. The Stone Heap Patent lies partly in this town.

[3] This town embraces the whole of several patents and parts of others, the principal of which are Michael Byrne's, of 18,000 acres, granted Dec. 14, 1767; John Butler's, of about 8,000 acres; Wm. Bouck's Patent, of 1,250 acres, E. of the creek, granted May 8, 1755, and another, on the w., of about the same size; Edward Clark's, of 100 acres; Vrooman's Land, granted to Adam Vrooman, Aug. 26, 1714; Wm. Wood's Patent, of 2,000 acres, July

13, 1770; Hendrick Hager's, 900 acres, Dec. 1, 1768; part of John Butler's, of 100 acres, and of Isaac Levy's tract of 4,333 acres, surveyed in July, 1770. Vrooman's Land deeds are still extant, one of which is dated Aug. 22, 1711. Among the early settlers were Peter, son of Adam Vrooman, the patentee; Cornelius and Bartholomew Vrooman, Nicholas Feeck, Adam Brown, Teunis Vrooman, Michael Brown, —— Kriesler, Frere Becker, and Stephen Young, on the w.; and William Bouck, the patentee, with his sons Johannes F., Christian, and William, Nicholas York, and Henry Hager, on the E.

[4] This stream is called by the Indians Ken-ha-na-ga-ra. Upon its course, in a ravine 200 feet deep worn in the Hamilton shales, is a fine cascade, known as "Bouck's Falls."

[5] A German name for the rushes which grew upon the banks of the creek at this place.

[6] 3 Union, Evan. Luth., and Ref. Prot. D.

[7] A fall in the creek at the village was called by the Indians De-was-e-go.

[8] The Gilboa Cotton Mills Co. has a capital of $50,000, and runs 100 looms.

[9] These two settlers joined the British and fled to Canada during the Revolution. Among the early settlers after the war were Richard Stanley, Joseph Desilva, Benoni Frazer, Cornelius Lane, John Breaster, Isaac Van Fort, Daniel Conover, and Jacob Homer,—all from New England. Ruloff Voorhees kept the first inn, in 1785; John Dise built the first mills, in 1764; and Jonah Soper the first tannery, in 1800. This town embraces a part of the Blenheim Patent, with parts of grants to Ury Richtmeyer, David Buffington, (July, 1770,) and —— Scott, with a portion of the "State Lands." The last named tracts comprised the lands escheated to the State by failure of title, and the confiscated estates of tories.

[10] The census reports 8 churches; 4 Bap., 2 M. E., Ref. Prot. D., and Christian.

[11] This lake is 1,800 ft. above tide. It is often mentioned in old documents, and was an angle in the bounds of Albany co. in colonial times. It is the source of the w. branch of the Delaware.

N. part, is a p. o. The first settlements were made, in different parts of the town, in 1794.[1] The first preacher was Rev. Stephen Fenn.[2]

MIDDLEBURGH—was formed from Schoharie, March 17, 1797, as "*Middletown*." Its name was changed in 1801. A part was re-annexed to Schoharie March 26, 1798. Fulton was taken off in 1828, and parts were annexed to Broome in 1849. It is the central town upon the E. border of the co. Its surface is a hilly upland, divided into two ridges by the valley of Schoharie Creek, which extends N. and s. through the town. The highest summits are 600 to 800 ft. above the valley.[3] Schoharie Creek receives Little Schoharie Creek from the E. and Line Kil from the w. The hills bordering upon the streams are usually steep and in many places precipitous. The soil is a clayey loam upon the hills, and a sandy loam in the valleys. Hops and broomcorn are extensively cultivated. **Middleburgh,** (p. v.,) upon Schoharie Creek, contains 4 churches, a private seminary, 2 steam paper mills, a steam gristmill, a foundery, and 110 dwellings. **Hunters Land,** (p. v.,) near the s. E. corner, contains 2 churches, a sawmill, gristmill, foundery, and 101 inhabitants. **Mill Valley,** on the line of Fulton, contains 2 large tanneries, a gristmill, and 25 dwellings. The first settlements were made by Palatinates, in 1711.[4] The middle fort of Schoharie stood a little below the present site of Middleburgh Village during the Revolution. The census reports 5 churches in town.[5]

RICHMONDVILLE—was formed from Cobleskill, April 11, 1845. It lies upon the w. border of the co., a little s. of the center. The surface is a hilly upland, separated into two distinct parts by the valley of Cobles Kil, which extends E. and w. through the center. The highest summits are 500 to 700 ft. above the valley. The soil is generally a clayey loam. Hops are extensively cultivated. **Richmondville,**[6] (p. v.,) near the center, contains 3 churches, a foundery, sawmill, gristmill, and 370 inhabitants. **Warnerville,**[7] (p. v.,) upon Cobles Kil, at the mouth of West Kil, contains 2 churches, a boarding seminary,[8] 2 tanneries, and 44 dwellings. **West Richmondville** is a p. o. The first settlement was made before the Revolution, by George Warner and his sons Nicholas, George, and Daniel, from Schoharie.[9] The census reports 5 churches in town.[10]

SCHOHARIE—was formed as a district March 24, 1772, and as a town March 7, 1788. Sharon, Cobleskill, Middleburgh, and Blenheim were taken off in 1797, and Esperance and Wright in 1846. A part of Middleburgh was re-annexed in 1798, and a part of Esperance in 1850. It lies in the N. E. part of the co., its N. E. corner bordering on Schenectady co. Its surface is a hilly upland, broken by the deep valleys of the streams. The declivities of the hills are generally gradual slopes, and their summits are 400 to 500 ft. above the valleys.[11] Schoharie Creek flows N. through near the center, receiving Foxes Creek from the E. and Cobles Kil from the w. In the limestone region in this town are numerous caverns.[12] The soil upon the hills is a clayey loam, and in the valleys a gravelly loam and alluvium. Hops and broom corn are largely cultivated. **Schoharie,** (p. v.,) the county seat, is situated upon Schoharie Creek, s. of the center of the town. Besides the co. buildings, it contains 3 churches, the Schoharie Academy, 2 newspaper offices, an arsenal, and a bank. Pop. 806. **Central Bridge,** (p. v.,) at the mouth of Cobles Kil, contains a church, sawmill, gristmill, machine shop, and 12 dwellings. **Barton Hill** is a p. o., near the N. E. corner. The first settlement was made in 1711, by a colony of German Palati-

[1] Amos and Caleb Northrop settled in the E. part; Samuel and Noah Judson, near Utsyantha Lake; Henry Shelmerdine and James McKenzie, on West Kil; Stephen Marvin, Erastus Judd, and Aaron Jones, near the village. These were mostly from New England. The first marriage was that of Marvin Judd and Lois Gibbs, Aug. 1800; and the first death, that of Elsie Judd, in June, 1799. Heman Hickok taught the first school, in 1799. Canfield Coe kept the first inn, in 1794; and Roman Lewis the first store, in 1800. Stephen Judd built the first sawmill, in 1796; and Heman Hickok the first gristmill, in 1799. Eli Jones built the first tannery, in 1810.

[2] The census reports 6 churches; 4 M. E. and 2 Bap.

[3] A hill opposite Middleburgh Village was named On-can-ge-na, "Mountain of Snakes." A mountain just above Middleburgh, on the w. side, was called O-nis-ta-gia-wa; the one next w., To-wok-nou-ra, or "Spring Hill;" and the one s. E. of Middleburgh, Mo-he-gou-ter.

[4] This town comprises parts of Schoharie Patent, Lawyer's & Zimmer's 1st Allotment, Thos. Eckerson's, Becker & Eckerson's, Thos. & Cornelius Eckerson's, Clark's, Depeyster's, Vrooman's, John Butler's, Bouck's, Lawrence Lawyer's, Nicholas Mattice's, and the Vlaie Patents.

[5] 2 M. E., Evan. Luth., Ref. Prot. D., and True Dutch.

[6] Richmondville Union Seminary and Female Collegiate Institute was built by a joint stock company in 1852, at a cost of $24,000, including grounds, buildings, and furniture. It was burned Dec. 13, 1853, and was immediately rebuilt at a cost of $34,000, but was again burned June 30, 1854.

[7] Named from Capt. Geo. Warner, the first settler.

[8] Warnerville Seminary was built in 1851, at a cost of about $25,000, grounds and furniture being $3,000 additional. It has accommodations for 200 boarding students. A school was in operation about 3 years, when it was closed and has not since been opened.

[9] Geo. Mann, John and Henry Shafer, Andrew Michael, Elijah Hadsell, John Lick, and John Dingman settled soon after the Revolution. The first school (German) was taught by —— Skinsky. The first inn was kept by —— Bohall; the first store by Geo. Skillmans; the first sawmill was built by a company of settlers; and the first gristmill by David Lawyer, on Cobles Kil. The town is comprised in the Skinner and portions of the Franklin, John F. Bouck, and B. Glazier Patents. Bouck's Patent, of 3,600 acres, was granted March 19, 1754, and Glazier's, of 3,000 acres, July 28, 1772.

[10] 2 M. E., Bap., Evan. Luth., and Christian.

[11] The grade of the Albany & Susquehanna R. R., upon the N. line of this town, is 550 ft. above tide.

[12] Ball's Cave, otherwise called Gebhard's Cave, 4 mi. E. of the courthouse, was first explored in Sept. 1831. It descends about 100 ft. below the surface. A stream of water, with small cascades, flows through it, and a boat is kept for the use of visitors. About 1853, it was purchased by W. H. Knoepfel, of N. Y., with the design of making it a popular place of resort. When first explored, it abounded in magnificent stalactites, of the purest white, translucent and fibrous. Nehtaway's Cave, 2 mi. s. E. of the courthouse, was explored in 1836, by John Gebhard, jr., and John Bouny. A few fine specimens of colored rhombohedral spar were found in it.

nates, who had previously located upon the Hudson.[1] The first church (German) was established soon after the first settlement;[2] Rev. Peter Nicholas Sommer was the first clergyman.

SEWARD[3]—was formed from Sharon, Feb. 11, 1840. It lies on the w. border of the co., N. of the center. Its surface is a hilly and broken upland, the highest summits being 300 to 500 ft. above the valleys.[4] West Kil, the principal stream, flows s. E. through the center. The soil is a clayey loam. Hops are largely cultivated. **Hyndsville,** (p. v.,) upon West Kil, in the s. part, contains a sawmill, gristmill, tannery, and 143 inhabitants. **Seward Valley,**[5] (Seward p. o.,) in the N. W. part, contains a gristmill, sawmill, and 16 houses. **Gardnerville** (p. v.) contains a church and 84 inhabitants. **Clove** is a hamlet. The first settlements were made in the N. part of the town, by a colony of Germans, in 1754.[6] Their settlement was known as "*New Dorlach.*" The census reports 8 churches in town.[7]

SHARON[8]—was formed from Schoharie, March 17, 1797, as "*Dorlach.*" Its name was changed March 17, 1797. Seward was taken off in 1840. It is the N. W. corner town of the co. Its surface is a rolling and hilly upland. The highest summits, in the s. w. corner, are about 500 ft. above the valleys. West Kil, flowing s. through the w. part, is the principal stream. The soil is a gravelly loam. In the underlying limestone are numerous caves. Hops are largely produced. **Sharon Springs,** (p. v.,) a little N. W. of the center, is celebrated for its sulphur and chalybeate springs.[9] It contains 5 large hotels for the accommodation of the visitors to the springs, and 2 churches. Pop. 230. **Rockville,** upon the turnpike, about a quarter of a mi. above the springs, contains 3 churches and 20 dwellings. **Sharon Center** (p. v.) contains 20 dwellings. **Sharon Hill,** (Sharon p. o.,) in the s. E. part, contains a gristmill, sawmill, foundery, and 20 dwellings; **Leesville,** (p. v.,) in the N. w. part, 2 churches and 20 dwellings. **Engellville,** (p. o.,) near the w. line, and **Beekmans Corners,** near the s. line, are hamlets. Col. Calvin Rich, from New England, is said to have been the first settler.[10] July 9, 1781, the tory Doxtader, with a party of 300 Indians, made a descent upon Currytown, Montgomery co.; and on his return, with his plunder and prisoners, he was overtaken by an American force, under Col. Willett. An engagement ensued, in which about 40 Indians were killed, and the remainder fled. The battle ground is about 2 mi. E. of Sharon Springs. The census reports 5 churches in town.[11]

SUMMIT—was formed from Jefferson and Cobleskill, April 13, 1819. It is the s. w. corner town of the co., lying principally on the w. border. Its surface is a broken and hilly upland. The central ridge forms a portion of the watershed between Susquehanna and Mohawk Rivers, the highest summits being 2,000 to 2,300 ft. above tide. Charlotte River, the principal stream, flows s. w. through the w. part. The soil is a gravelly and clayey loam. **Summit,** (p. v.,) upon the ridge, near the center, contains 2 churches and 28 dwellings. It is 2,200 ft. above tide. **Charlotteville,** (p. v.,) upon Charlotte River, in the s. w. part, contains a church, the N. Y. Conference Seminary and Collegiate Institute,[12] 2 sawmills, a gristmill and clothing works, and about 40

---

[1] This town includes parts of the Schoharie, Morris & Coeyman's, Lawyer & Bergh's, and the 2d Allotment of Lawyer & Zimmer's Patents. For particulars of early settlement, see page 601.

[2] A lot of 14 acres in Huntersfield was conveyed, Jan. 3, 1737, by Johannes Sheffer, Hendrick Conradt, and Johannes Ingold, to Jonas Le Roy and Peter Speis, for the support of the Middleburgh and Schoharie high and low Dutch churches. By an act of Feb. 8, 1799, the two congregations were empowered to divide and mutually release this lot. The census reports 4 churches; 2 Evan. Luth., M. E., and Ref. Prot. D.   [3] Named in honor of Gov. Seward.

[4] Upon the s. E. border of the town is a hill, called by the Indians Gogny-ta-nee; and N. of Seward Valley is another, called One-en-ta-dashe.   [5] Locally known as "Neeleys Hollow."

[6] The first settlers were Sebastian France, Michael Merckley, Henry Hynds, and Ernest Fretz. Among the other early settlers were Caleb Crospot, Wm. Ernest Spornhyer, and Conrad Brown, who located near the Luth. church; and Wm. Ripsomah, Henry France, Henry Hanes, Geronimus Chrysler, and John, Peter, and Martin, sons of Rev. Peter Nicholas Sommer, the first Schoharie pastor. The first German school was taught by —— Phawghwer; the first inn was kept by Thos. Almy; the first store by Wm. E. Spornhyer. Wm. Hynds built the first sawmill, and Henry Hanes the first gristmill. The first birth was that of a son of —— France.

[7] 3 Evan. Luth., 3 M. E., Ref. Prot. D., and Bap.

[8] Named from Sharon, Conn.

[9] These springs have a high reputation for the cure of cutaneous disorders, and are a place of resort during the summer. As analyzed by Dr. Chilton, a pint of the water is found to contain,—

Sulphate of magnesia	2.65	grains.
Sulphate of lime	6.98	"
Chloride of sodium	0.14	"
Chloride of magnesium	0.15	"
Hydrosulphuret of sodium }		
Hydrosulphuret of calcium }	0.14	"
Extractive matter }		
	10.06	

Sulphuretted hydrogen gas,—1 cubic inch.

The waters flowing over vegetable substances incrust them with white and flocculent sulphur. The gas from the sulphur spring quickly tarnishes silver, even in the pocket. In the neighborhood is a chalybeate spring. The vicinity derives interest from caves containing stalactites and beautiful crystals of sulphate of lime. A quarter of a mile below the spring is a fine cascade. A copious spring of common water gushes from the rocks a short distance above, in volume sufficient to turn a mill.—*Geol. 1st Dist.*, p. 89; *Beck's Mineralogy of N. Y.*, p. 143; *Simms's Schoharie*, p. 643.

[10] Col. R. was afterward at Sackets Harbor as a Col. of drafted militia in Gen. Richard Dodge's brigade. Calvin Pike, William Vanderwerker, Conrad Fritche, Abraham and John Mereness, John Malick, and Peter Courment were early settlers, and were obliged to flee to Schoharie or Fort Hunter for safety during the war. Wm. Beekman kept the first store; John Hutt built the first sawmill, Omeo Lagrange the first gristmill, John Hutt the first clothing works, and Frederick & Crouck the first tannery. The town comprises a part of Frederick Young's Patent of 20,000 acres, granted Sept. 25, 1761; a tract granted to Bradt & Livingston, of 8,000 acres; a part of Johan D. Gross' Tract; a tract granted to Johannes Lawyer, jr., Jacob Boist, and others, of 7,000 acres, Aug. 14, 1761; and a small part of the New Dorlach Patent. The first owners of New Dorlach Patent were Michael, Johannes, Johannes Jost, and Jacob B. Boist, Johan Braun, Wm. Bauch, Michael Heltzinger, Henrick Hanes, Johannes Shaffer, Johannes and Jacob Lawyer, Christian Zeh, Mathias Baumann, Lambert Sternberg, Barent Keyser, and Peter Nicholas Sommer. The patent provided that any differences that might arise were to be settled by arbitration.

[11] 2 Ev. Luth., Ref. Prot. D., Bap., and Union.

[12] This institution is under the charge of the Methodist Episcopal denomination. It is one of the largest institutions in the State, having accommodations for about 450 boarding students.

dwellings. **Lutheranville,** (p. o.,) in the N. W. part, contains a church and 10 dwellings; and **Eminence,** (p. v.,) on the line of Blenheim, 2 churches and 15 dwellings. The first settlement was made in 1794, by Frederick Prosper, from Dutchess co.[1] Rev. M. Sherman was the first preacher. The census reports 7 churches in town.[2]

WRIGHT[3]—was formed from Schoharie, April 4, 1846. It is the N. town on the E. border of the co. Its surface is a hilly upland. The highest summits, along the S. line, are 600 to 800 ft. above the valleys. The principal stream is Foxes Creek, flowing N. W. through the center. The soil is a clay and gravelly loam. **Gallupville,** (p. v.,) near the center, contains 3 churches, a sawmill, tannery, carding machine, and 40 houses. **Shutters Corners,** (p. o.,) in the W. part, contains a sawmill, gristmill, and 10 houses. **Waldenville** is a p. o., near the E. line. The town comprises the whole of several patents and parts of several others, principally granted from 1760 to 1770. The first settlement was made by Jacob Zimmer, near Gallupville, several years prior to the Revolution.[4] A stone house built by Johannes Becker, an early settler, was used as a fort during the war.[5] There are 5 churches in town.[6]

Acres of Land, Valuation, Population, Dwellings, Families, Freeholders, Schools, Live Stock, Agricultural Products, and Domestic Manufactures, of Schoharie County.

Names of Towns.	Acres of Land.		Valuation of 1858.			Population.		No. of Dwellings.	No. of Families.	Freeholders.	Schools.	
	Improved.	Unimproved.	Real Estate.	Personal Property.	Total.	Males.	Females.				No. of Districts.	Children taught.
Blenheim	9,864	16,102	$186,667	$18,990	$205,657	686	665	225	245	186	12	601
Broome	18,623	8,375	204,346	50,884	255,230	1,071	1,067	421	427	270	19	1,034
Carlisle	14,612	6,243	394,171	42,410	436,581	873	850	311	326	276	9	750
Cobleskill	11,742	6,296	347,926	56,175	404,101	1,096	1,112	373	401	335	9	776
Conesville	12,907	8,552	229,460	27,506	256,966	700	707	262	292	215	13	629
Esperance	7,679½	2,715¼	237,915	71,622	309,537	643	727	239	262	177	8	606
Fulton	17,120⅛	17,192	464,350	58,550	522,900	1,450	1,367	509	530	402	15	1,182
Gilboa	23,139	13,398½	302,308	56,950	359,258	1,306	1,351	478	526	322	18	1,105
Jefferson	15,064	8,045½	278,140	30,478	308,618	820	868	292	321	252	13	683
Middleburgh	14,240⅝	11,609	431,345	53,850	485,195	1,621	1,454	480	547	363	13	1,179
Richmondville	14,207¾	5,475	374,599	32,760	407,359	1,028	999	345	378	291	12	840
Schoharie	9,401	6,429	522,591	222,650	745,241	1,429	1,440	498	495	310	10	1,068
Seward	14,381	5,420	388,128	28,920	417,048	962	963	316	335	247	12	705
Sharon	19,297	4,878	552,188	100,162	652,350	1,360	1,356	460	489	424	15	1,066
Summit	13,027	6,040	320,735	45,065	365,800	940	950	354	374	268	16	687
Wright	12,599	5,276	338,707	62,265	400,972	843	815	283	310	236	10	697
Total	227,904⅜	132,046¼	5,573,576	959,237	6,532,813	16,828	16,691	5,846	6,258	4,574	204	13,808

Names of Towns.	Live Stock.					Agricultural Products.							Domestic Cloths in yards.
						Bush. of Grain.					Dairy Products.		
	Horses.	Working Oxen and Calves.	Cows.	Sheep.	Swine.	Winter.	Spring.	Tons of Hay.	Bushels of Potatoes.	Bushels of Apples.	Pounds of Butter.	Pounds of Cheese.	
Blenheim	252	915	873	1,388	618	3,168	16,109	1,940	5,539	6,746	86,230	608	1,800¼
Broome	608	1,586	1,117	5,438	962	6,469	52,362½	3,315	7,270½	10,481	92,146	2,605	2,092
Carlisle	638	1,338	1,078	3,348	1,137	2,275	61,044¾	2,705	11,349	12,992	115,586	5,379	2,165
Cobleskill	741	1,228	986	2,930	1,463	6,964	63,671	2,745	11,724	14,093	93,725	6,716	2,717½
Conesville	443	1,238	868	3,460	916	2,991	17,185¾	3,130	5,740	10,686	95,550	2,640	848¼
Esperance	379	801	540	1,165	618	2,272	49,561	1,869½	5,889	7,132	53,745	3,025	1,139
Fulton	707	1,867	1,492	3,520	1,484	10,005½	70,860¾	3,436½	18,926	11,847	140,939	869	4,959¾
Gilboa	597	1,903	1,927	3,385	1,229	4,244½	33,427½	5,035½	10,694	13,440	207,265	3,090	2,560
Jefferson	452	1,477	1,753	2,241	791	2,288½	33,261½	4,369	11,164	9,472	183,877		2,593
Middleburgh	838	1,498	750	3,268	1,749	14,499	77,305	2,819¾	16,356	11,108	93,970	500	1,331
Richmondville	601	1,120	1,009	2,182	1,093	6,044½	62,354	3,122	11,761	15,261	98,580	1,883	2,853
Schoharie	758	1,244	1,006	2,241	1,804	19,558	73,555	2,159½	16,754	10,372	72,060	200	1,284
Seward	583	1,072	1,260	2,001	1,444	5,009½	73,296½	3,213	13,206	18,006	136,430	40,661	2,056¼
Sharon	1,001	1,349	1,201	3,923	1,384	4,638	129,765	2,881	16,925	47,182	124,965	2,240	1,976
Summit	506	1,115	1,530	2,030	941	2,151	51,884	4,297	18,971	12,210	150,815	200	3,142
Wright	578	807	823	3,076	1,171	13,660	57,001¼	1,737	8,164	11,154	86,374	400	1,398
Total	9,682	20,558	18,213	45,596	18,804	106,237½	922,644½	48,774¾	190,432½	222,182	1,832,257	71,016	34,915

1 Clement Davis, Samuel Allen, Martin Van Buren, Morris Kiff, Robert and Abraham Van Duser, A. M. Frydenburgh, Joseph L. Barnet, Amos Baldwin, Jonathan Hughes, Baltus Prosper, and James Brown were early settlers. The first birth was that of —— Frydenburgh, and the first marriage that of Clement Davis and Lovina Allen, in 1797. Daniel Harris taught the first school, in 1798. Benj. Rider kept the first inn, James Burns the first store, and —— Van Buren the first sawmill. The town comprises a part of the Strasburgh, Charlotte River, Stephen Skinner, and Walter Franklin Patents.

2 2 Bap., 2 M. E., Ref. Prot. D., Ev. Luth., and Christian.

3 Named in honor of Gov. Silas Wright.

4 Among the early settlers were Johannes Becker, —— Shaffer, Frederick Dening, John Narhold, Frederick Beller, Christopher Shoefelt, and John Hilsley. Jacob Zimmer kept the first inn, John and Henry Becker the first store; Jacob Zimmer built the first gristmill, and Zimmer, Becker & Shaffer the first sawmill.

5 On the morning of July 26, 1782, a band of tories and Indians appeared in the valley of Foxes Creek, murdered several persons, took some prisoners, and attempted to dislodge the inmates of the stone house, but failed. This house is still standing.

6 2 M. E., Ev. Luth., Ref. Prot. D., and Christian.

SCHUYLER COUNTY.

THIS county[1] was formed from Steuben, Chemung, and Tompkins, April 17, 1854. It lies upon both sides of the s. extremity of Seneca Lake; is centrally distant 160 mi. from Albany, and contains 352 sq. mi. Its surface is mostly an undulating and hilly upland, divided into two distinct ridges by the deep valley of Seneca Lake and its inlet. The highest summits are 600 to 1,000 ft. above Seneca Lake and 1,200 to 1,600 ft. above tide. A bluff 100 to 300 ft. high extends along the shores of the lake, too steep for profitable cultivation; but farther inland the hills are bordered by long and gradual slopes and are generally arable to their very summits. The extreme s. part of the co. assumes a more hilly and broken character. Catharines Creek, flowing into the head of Seneca Lake, is the principal stream. Its course is through a deep, narrow, and winding valley bordered by steep hillsides 400 to 600 ft. high. Upon it are numerous falls, affording abundance of water-power; and near its mouth is a marshy region of considerable extent. Meads Creek, a tributary of Chemung River, drains the s. w. corner, and Cayuta Creek the s. E. corner. The other streams are small creeks and brooks, mostly discharging their waters into Seneca Lake. A few streams take their rise along the N. E. border and flow into Cayuga Lake. Little and Mud Lakes, two smaller sheets of water along the w. border, discharge their waters through Mud Creek into Conhocton River. Cayuta Lake is a fine sheet of water, in the E. part of the co. Hector Falls, upon a small stream flowing into Seneca Lake from the E., is one of the finest cascades in the State. The rocks of this co. mostly belong to the Portage and Chemung groups,—the former occupying the N. and the latter the s. part of the co. In the deep valley along the shore of Seneca Lake, in the extreme N. part of the co., are found outcrops of Genesee slate. The only good building stone in the co. is the thin-bedded sandstone separating the thick beds of shale. In many places these rocks are covered deeply with drift deposits. The soil upon the highlands is clayey and gravelly, principally derived from the disintegration of the shales; and in many places this is underlaid by hardpan. In the valleys the soil is a gravelly loam intermixed with alluvium.

Agriculture forms the leading and almost the sole occupation of the people. Spring grains are extensively grown, and stock and wool growing and dairying are largely carried on. The climate and soil are both better adapted to pasturage than to tillage. Fruit is becoming an important article of culture, and all kinds adapted to the climate succeed well. A limited amount of manufacturing is carried on at Watkins and Havana.

In 1854, commissioners appointed to locate the co. buildings fixed upon Havana as the county seat.[2] The action of the commissioners was resisted by the Board of Supervisors, and by them the county seat was located at Watkins, at the head of Seneca Lake. A courthouse was erected at each village; but subsequently the courts decided in favor of the action of the commissioners, and, April 13, 1857, an act was passed by the legislature confirming the location of the county seat at Havana. This act was confirmed by the Supreme Court, April, 1859. The Board of Supervisors soon after changed the location to Watkins, and at this place the co. offices are at present located. The buildings erected at each place for a courthouse, and for a clerk's office and jail at Havana, are fine buildings, embodying nearly all modern improvements. The buildings at Havana were erected at a cost of $30,000. No poorhouse has yet been established.

The public works in the co. are the Chemung Canal, extending from the head of Seneca Lake s. through the valley of Catharines Creek, uniting with Chemung River at Elmira; the Elmira, Jefferson & Canandaigua R. R., extending along the w. shore of Seneca Lake to Watkins; and the Chemung R. R., extending s. from Watkins along Catharines Creek to Elmira. These roads are both leased to the N. Y. & E. R. R. Co.

In 1779, Sullivan's army marched through the defiles along Catharines Creek, closely pursuing the Indians, who were flying from the fatal battle of "*Newtown*," (now Elmira.) So great was the terror of the Indians that they neglected to defend the passes, and the American army

---

[1] Named from Gen. Philip Schuyler.
[2] These commissioners were Delos De Wolf, of Oswego, Edward Dodd, of Washington, and Vivus W. Smith, of Onondaga.

marched unmolested through the only place where successful resistance was practicable. Upon the conclusion of peace, many of the soldiers belonging to the army returned to this region and located upon land which had been first brought to their notice during their march against the Indians. The first settlements in the co. were made on Catharines Creek, near the present site of Havana, in 1788, and on the shores of Seneca Lake, in 1790. The town of Hector belonged to the Military Tract; the towns of Catharines, Dix, and Reading, to the Watkins and Flint Purchase; and Tyrone and Orange, to the Phelps and Gorham Purchase.

Two weekly newspapers are now published in the co.[1]

CATHARINES[2]—was formed from *"Newtown,"* (now Elmira, Chemung co.,) March 15, 1798. Catlin and Veteran (Chemung co.) were taken off in 1823. A part of Newfield (Tompkins co.) was annexed June 4, 1853, and a part was added to Cayuta, April 17, 1854. It lies upon the s. border of the co., E. of the center. Its surface is a hilly upland, broken by the deep valleys of the streams. Catharines Creek, along the w. border, flows in a deep ravine 300 to 700 feet below the summits of the hills. Cayuta Lake lies in the N. E. part; and its outlet, Cayuta Creek, flows s. into the Susquehanna. The soil is principally a gravelly loam mixed with clay. **Havana,** (p.v.,) upon Catharines Creek, on the line of Dix, 3 mi. from Seneca Lake, was incorp. May 13, 1836. It contains a courthouse, jail, clerk's office, the People's College,[3] 3 churches, a newspaper office, 3 flouring mills, and several manufacturing establishments.[4] It is a canal village and a station upon the Chemung R. R. Pop. 1,290. **Odessa,** (p.v.,) near the center of the town, contains 2 churches, a gristmill, several sawmills, and 40 dwellings; and **Catharines,** (p.v.,) in the s. part, 2 churches and 25 dwellings. **Alpine,** (p.v.,) on the s. E. border, is partly in this town. The first settlement in town was made at Havana, in 1788, by Silas Wolcott and —— Wilson.[5] The first religious meeting was held at the house of Mr. P. Bowers, by a Presbyterian minister, in 1794.[6]

CAYUTA—was formed from Spencer, (Tioga co.,) March 20, 1824. Parts of Catharine and Erin (Chemung co.) were annexed in 1854. The town was transferred from Tioga to Tompkins co. March 22, 1822. It is the S. E. corner town in the co. Its surface is a hilly upland. Cayuta Creek flows S. E. through the town, in a narrow valley bordered by steep hillsides 300 to 600 ft. high. The soil is a clayey and gravelly loam. **Cayuta** (West Cayuta p. o.) contains 15 dwellings; **Alpine,** (p.v.,) on the N. line of the town, a flouring mill, sawmill, chair factory, and 25 dwellings. The first settlement was made in the valley of the Cayuta, near West Cayuta, in 1801, by Capt. Gabriel Ogden, Rev. David Janes, and Jos. Thomas,—the first two from Tioga co., and the last from Athens, Penn.[7] The first religious services were held by Rev. Mr. Janes, (Bap.,) at his own house, in 1802. No churches are reported.

---

[1] *The Tioga Patriot* was started at Havana in June, 1828, by L. B. and S. Butler, and was continued a short time.

The Havana Observer was started in 1830 by F. W. Ritter, and was soon discontinued.

The Havana Republican was commenced in 1835 by Nelson Colgrove. It was issued successively by G. Barlow Nye, T. I. Taylor, and W. H. Ongly until 1849, when it was changed to

Life in The Country and Havana Republican. It was discontinued in 1850.

The Chemung Democrat was removed from Horseheads to Havana in 1840, and to *"Jefferson"* (now Watkins) in 1842. Its name was soon after changed to

The Democratic Citizen, and it was issued by J. I. Hendrix until 1850.

The Independent Freeman was started at Watkins, June 15, 1850, by W. B. Slawson & Co.; in 1851 it was changed to

The Jefferson Eagle, and was continued a few months.

The Corona Borealis, a literary paper, was published at *"Jefferson"* about the same time.

The Havana Journal was commenced April 16, 1853, by John B. Look, and its publication is still continued.

The Watkins Republican was established in June, 1854, by S. M. Taylor. It passed into the hands of J. K. Averill, and afterward into those of M. Ells, by whom it is still published.

The Schuyler County Democrat, commenced at Havana, April 25, 1855, by Averill & Baxter, was soon after discontinued.

[2] Named from Catharine Montour, a French woman who married an Indian, was adopted into the Seneca tribe, and exerted a controlling influence among the Indians. She received a small salary from the English Colonial Government, for many years, on account of her influence among the Indians. She resided on the present site of Havana, and was known as Queen Catharine. This town as first formed embraced the N. part of Tps.

[3] and 4 and all of Tps. 2 and 3 of John W. Watkins's Tract.

[3] This institution was incorp. April 13, 1854, and was located at Havana Jan. 8, 1857. The college edifice—the erection of which has been commenced—is to be 320 by 52 feet, 4 stories high, with a basement. At either end is a wing, 206 by 52 ft., 4 stories high; and a wing will project rearward from the center, 68 by 64 ft., 3 stories high. Above the basement the walls are to be erected of brick; the whole at an estimated cost of $175,000. The institution is to afford instruction in some departments of mechanics and manufactures, and students are to be paid for their services. The trustees have resolved to establish 19 professorships.

[4] 2 plaster mills, 2 sawmills, a planing mill, woolen factory, iron foundery, and tannery.

[5] Geo. Mills, Wm. McClure, Phineas Bowers, John King, and 2 families by the name of Stevens, settled in the valley at and near Havana in 1789–90. Anthony Broderick kept the first school, in a house owned by Phineas Bowers, in 1792–93. Silas Wolcott kept the first inn, soon after his settlement, and Isaac Baldwin and George Mills the first store, in 1805, at Havana. Phineas Bowers erected the first grist and saw mills, at or near the village.

[6] The census reports 7 churches; 2 Prot. E., 2 Presb., 2 M. E., and Bap.

[7] Hermon White, Benj. Chambers, and Jeremiah Taylor settled in the same vicinity in 1803; Moses Brown, Langstaff Compton, and others in 1804. The first birth was that of Rosetta, daughter of Jonathan Thomas, in Jan. 1804; the first marriage, that of Ebenezer Edwards and Sarah Ogden, in 1804; and the first death, that of Joseph Thomas, in July, 1802. Robert Lockerby taught the first school, in a house belonging to Elder Janes, in the winter of 1805. Capt. Gabriel Ogden kept the first inn, at West Cayuta, in 1805, and Jesse White the first store, in 1808. John White erected the first sawmill on the E. branch of the Cayuta, in 1816, and John Ennis the first gristmill, 2 mi. below West Cayuta, in 1817.

DIX[1]—was formed from Catlin, (Chemung co.,) April 17, 1835. It lies upon the w. side of Catharines Creek, and extends from the head of Seneca Lake to the s. bounds of the co. The surface is mostly a rolling and hilly upland, the summits being 400 to 700 ft. above the lake. It is drained by Catharines Creek and several smaller streams. The soil is principally a fine quality of gravelly loam. A little s. w. from the head of the lake is a deep glen in the hills, bordered by perpendicular rocks 200 ft. high. A small stream runs through it, forming a series of beautiful cascades. **Watkins,**[2] (p. v.,) upon the line of Reading, at the head of Seneca Lake, was incorp., as *"Jefferson,"* April 11, 1842, and its name was changed April 8, 1852. It contains a courthouse, 5 churches, a newspaper office, and several manufacturing establishments. It is a lake, canal, and R. R. station; a daily steamboat plies upon Seneca Lake between this place and Geneva. Pop. 1,084. **Beaver Dams,** (p. v.,) in the s. w. corner, contains 2 churches, several manufactories, and 28 dwellings; **Townsend,** (p. v.,) near the w. line, contains 1 church, several mills, and 36 dwellings; **Crawford Settlement,** (Moreland p. o.,) near the s. line, contains 2 churches and 26 dwellings. The first settlements were made near the head of the lake and along the valley of Catharines Creek, about the commencement of the present century.[3] The first church edifice (Bap.) was erected in 1833, at Townsend.[4]

HECTOR—was formed from Ovid, (Seneca co.,) March 30, 1802. It is the s. w. corner township of the Military Tract and the N. E. corner town of the co. Its surface is a rolling upland, its highest summits being 500 to 700 ft. above Seneca Lake. The bluffs bordering upon the lake are 100 to 300 ft. high, and nearly perpendicular. It is drained by a large number of small creeks flowing into Seneca and Cayuga Lakes. Hector Falls, upon a small creek in the s. w. part of the town, is a cascade made by the stream flowing down the bluff which borders upon the lake. The soil is a clay, sandy, and gravelly loam, in some places underlaid by hardpan. **Perry City,** (p. v.,) upon the E. line of the town, contains a Friends' meeting house and 120 inhabitants; **Mecklenburgh,** (p. v.,) situated 2 mi. s. w. of Perry City, contains 3 churches, 2 sawmills, a flouring mill, and 338 inhabitants; **Reynoldsville,** (p. v.,) near the center of the town, contains a church and 117 inhabitants; **Bennetsburgh,** (p. v.,) in the s. part, contains a church, 4 saw and shingle mills, 1 gristmill, tannery, and 25 dwellings; **Burdett,** (p. v.,) in the s. w. part, contains 3 churches, a woolen factory, agricultural implement factory, iron foundery, gristmill, sawmill, tannery, and 360 inhabitants; **Peach Orchard,** (Hector p. o.,) in the N. w. part, contains 3 churches and 34 dwellings; **Polkville,** (p. v.,) in the N. w. part, contains a church and 16 dwellings; **Searsburgh** (p. o.) contains 2 churches and 10 dwellings. **North Hector** and **Cayutaville** are p. offices; and **Steamburgh** is a hamlet. John Livingston and Wm. Wickham settled in 1791, in the N. w. part of the town, on the bank of the lake.[5] The first church (Presb.) was formed by Rev. Mr. Stewart, at Peach Orchard, in 1809.[6]

ORANGE—was formed from Wayne, (Steuben co.,) Feb. 12, 1813, as *"Jersey."* Its name was changed Feb. 20, 1836. A part of Hornby (Steuben co.) was annexed April 11, 1842, and a part of Bradford, (Steuben co.,) April 17, 1854. It is the s. w. corner town in the co., and is bounded on the E. by the pre-emption line. Its surface is a rolling and hilly upland, broken by the deep and irregular valleys of the streams. Meads Creek, flowing s. w., forms the principal drainage. The soil is chiefly a gravelly loam. **Monterey** (Orange p. o.) contains 3 churches, a gristmill, and 301 inhabitants. **Sugar Hill** is a p. o. in the N. E. part. The first settlements were made in 1799, by Abraham Rozenback and Samuel Scomp, N. E. of Monterey.[7] The first church (M. E.) was formed by Rev. Peregrine Hallett, the first preacher.[8]

---

[1] Named from Ex-Senator John A. Dix.

[2] Named from Dr. Samuel Watkins, an early settler in the village.

[3] Geo. Mills was among the first settlers in town, and is still living there, at the age of 95 years. Judge John Dowe, David Culver, and John and Wm. Watkins were also among the early settlers. The first settlers at the village of Townsend were Claudius Townsend, Consider B. Evens, Jonas Blower, and Dods Benson, in 1823; Ebenezer Perry was the first settler at Beaver Dams. At this place 2 dams were built across Port Creek by beavers; one of the dams still remains. · A swamp, formed by the lower dam, is an alluvial deposit 400 ft. deep, from which lime is made.

[4] The census reports 10 churches; 3 Bap., 3 M. E., 2 Presb., Prot. E., and Univ.

[5] Reuben Smith and his sons Reuben, Jabez, Sam'l, Harvey, Caleb, and Chauncey W., from Canaan, Conn., settled on Military Lots 20 and 21, in 1794; Richard Ely and Grover Smith, a little N. of Peach Orchard, and Daniel Everts, s. of the same place, in 1795,—all from Salisbury, Conn. The first child born was Polly Everts; the first marriage, that of Stephen Pratt and Betsey Livingston; and the first death, that of Wm. Wickham. The first school was taught at Peach Orchard, by John Livingston. Wm. Wickham kept the first inn, near Peach Orchard, and John B. Seeley the first store, at Hector Falls. The first gristmill and carding machine were put in operation at the same place, by Sam'l B. Seeley.

[6] The census reports 20 churches in town; 7 M. E., 3 Presb., 3 Bap., 2 Wes. Meth., 2 Friends, O. S. Bap., Prot. E., and Chris. Cong.

[7] Henry Switzer, from N. J., settled on Switzer Hill, in 1802, and D. Hewitt, from Rensselaer co., N. Y., was the first settler at Monterey, in 1811. Abner and Thos. Hurd, and Brigham Young, the Mormon leader, were early settlers in the N. E. part of the town. —— Chapman, Wm. Wilkins, Wm. De Witt, Andrew Foot, Danl. Curtiss, and Jedediah Miller settled on Meads Creek in 1811. Elsie Switzer was the first child born. The first school was taught by Dan'l McDougall, in 1819, near Monterey. Thos. Hurd kept the first inn, in 1816, at Monterey, and Walter Hurd the first store, s. w. of the same place.

[8] The census reports 4 churches in town; 2 Bap., Presb., and M. E.

READING—was formed from "*Frederickstown*," (now Wayne, Steuben co.,) Feb. 17, 1806. It lies upon the W. bank of Seneca Lake, and is the central town upon the N. border of the co. Its surface is a rolling upland 400 to 500 ft. above the lake. The bluffs upon the shore are very steep and in many places precipitous. Its streams are small brooks and creeks. The soil is mostly a clay loam. **Reading Center** (p. v.) contains 2 churches and 24 dwellings; **Irelandville** (Reading p. o.) contains 11 dwellings. **North Reading** is a p. o. The Elmira, Jefferson & Canandaigua R. R. traverses the town upon the W. shore of the lake. A settlement was made at Reading Center, by Judge John Dow, from Conn., in 1790.[1] The first church (Bap.) was formed by Elder John Goff, in 1810, at Reading Center.[2]

TYRONE—was formed from Wayne, (Steuben co.,) April 16, 1822. It is the N. W. corner town in the co. Its surface is an elevated upland divided into several ridges by the valleys of streams. Its principal stream is Mud Creek, flowing S. W. Little Lake, upon the W. border, is 3 mi. long and about 1 wide; and Mud Lake, in the S. W. corner, is 1½ mi. long and about one-half mi. wide. These lakes lie in deep valleys, and are bordered by nearly precipitous hills which rise 300 to 400 ft. above them. The soil is a clay loam. **Tyrone,** (p. v.,) a little E. of Mud Lake, contains 2 churches, 1 gristmill, 2 sawmills, 2 tanneries, several manufactories, and 160 inhabitants; **Weston,** (p. v.,) ¾ mi. N. W. of Tyrone, contains 2 churches and 177 inhabitants; **Altay,** (p. v.,) a little E. of the center, contains a church, tannery, 2 sawmills, a steam flouring mill, and 144 inhabitants; **Pine Grove** (p. o.) contains a church and 6 houses. The first settlement was made in 1800, by Gen. Wm. Kernan, on a tract of 4,000 acres, purchased by Thos. O'Conner.[3] The first church edifice (Union) was erected by the Presb. and Bap.; Rev. Joseph Crawford (Presb.) and Rev. Van Rensselaer Wall (Bap.) were the first preachers.[4]

Acres of Land, Valuation, Population, Dwellings, Families, Freeholders, Schools, Live Stock, Agricultural Products, and Domestic Manufactures, of Schuyler County.

Names of Towns.	Acres of Land.		Valuation of 1858.			Population.		No. of Dwellings.	No. of Families.	Freeholders.	Schools.	
	Improved.	Unimproved.	Real Estate.	Personal Property.	Total.	Males.	Females.				No. of Districts.	Children taught.
Catharines	18,160	11,598	$833,291	$157,100	$990,391	1,761	1,756	669	593	421	18	1,390
Cayuta	4,875	7,168¾	74,836	3,840	78,676	324	294	118	119	130	3	208
Dix	15,269	7,326¾	558,503	39,765	598,268	1,447	1,437	545	574	454	13	1,176
Hector	45,904½	15,851	1,520,513	82,600	1,603,113	2,801	2,828	1,090	1,102	988	38	2,126
Orange	20,328¼	11,304½	434,542	47,444	481,986	1,256	1,227	483	483	374	17	885
Reading	12,882½	3,726½	425,073	27,750	452,823	736	716	266	277	237	7	483
Tyrone	16,917	6,023¾	566,555	35,850	602,405	1,083	1,111	409	429	342	16	850
Total	134,336¼	62,999¼	4,413,313	394,349	4,807,662	9,408	9,369	3,582	3,577	2,946	112	7,118

Names of Towns.	Live Stock.					Agricultural Products.							Domestic Cloths, in yards.
						Bush. of Grain.					Dairy Products.		
	Horses.	Working Oxen and Calves.	Cows.	Sheep.	Swine.	Winter.	Spring.	Tons of Hay.	Bushels of Potatoes.	Bushels of Apples.	Pounds Butter.	Pounds Cheese.	
Catharines	755	1,582	1,081	6,216	1,049	12,130	90,038	2,737	11,954	21,358	97,110	8,445	716
Cayuta	176	493	325	1,399	303	1,321½	20,606¾	856½	2,480	7,329	35,085	1,880	897
Dix	661	1,624	938	6,547	1,019	11,617½	86,751½	2,340¾	12,771	12,099	89,611	3,381	1,898½
Hector	2,048	3,512	2,393	15,495	3,562	35,077½	263,492	5,712½	22,829	57,818	258,227	8,988	3,493
Orange	768	1,800	1,168	6,213	1,191	8,007	95,752	3,075	20,460	9,670	119,185	2,363	2,678½
Reading	580	1,052	702	6,261	834	7,129	62,722½	1,301½	9,084	12,374	74,087	3,932	358½
Tyrone	712	1,265	1,069	6,787	1,493	11,317	77,475¼	1,973	1,528	22,581	125,648	3,179	1,304¾
Total	5,700	11,328	7,676	48,918	9,451	86,599½	696,838	17,996¼	81,106	143,229	798,953	32,168	11,346¼

1 David Culver settled near Reading Center, in 1806, and Alexander Hinton, near Watkins, in 1802. The first marriage was that of Elisha Culver and Susan Divins; and the first birth, that of Minor Culver. The first school was taught by Ira Parker, at the Center. David Culver kept the first inn, N. of the Center, and David Culver, jr., the first store, at the same place. Eliadia Parker erected the first sawmill.

2 The census reports 3 churches; Bap., M. E., and R. C.

3 Mr. O'Conner was among the early settlers, and resided for a time in a log house on the shore of Little Lake. He was accompanied by a son and daughter,—the former of whom is Hon. Charles O'Conner, the eminent New York lawyer. Abraham Fleet, sr., from N. J., and Capt. John Seabring, were among the first settlers near Tyrone Village, in 1800; Thaddeus, Gersham, and Abraham Bennett settled about 1801. Simon Fleet was the first child born in town. The first school was taught at Tyrone Village, by Hugh Jameson; the first inn was kept by Capt. Williams, and the first store by Thos. O'Conner, near the N. W. corner of the town. The first mill and factory were erected at Tyrone Village by Ralph Opdyke.

4 The census reports 7 churches; 3 Bap., 2 Presb., and 2 M. E.

SENECA COUNTY.

This county was formed from Cayuga, March 29, 1804. A part of Tompkins was taken off in 1817, and a part of Wayne in 1823. It lies w. of the center of the State, centrally distant 156 mi. from Albany, and contains 420 sq. mi. It occupies the greater part of the land which lies between Seneca and Cayuga Lakes, and extends several mi. N. of Seneca Lake Outlet. A high ridge enters the co. from Tompkins and occupies nearly one-fourth of its surface. The summit of the extreme s. portion of this ridge in this co. is 700 to 800 feet above Seneca Lake and 1,100 to 1,250 feet above tide. Toward the N. it gradually declines to the level of Seneca Lake. The ridge is bordered in some places by steep declivities and in others by gradual slopes, and in the s. part of the co. generally terminates in high bluffs on the shores of the lakes. At the foot of Seneca Lake the bluffs, on an average, are about 20 feet high; but toward the s. they gradually rise to an elevation of 100 to 150 feet. At the foot of Cayuga Lake the shore is low and shelving; but in Romulus a bluff shore commences, which gradually increases in height until on the s. border of the co. it attains an elevation of 150 to 200 feet. From the summits of the bluffs to the central summit of the ridge the land generally rises in beautiful, smooth, gradual slopes, broken in a few places by sharp declivities of a terrace-like formation. From Ovid toward the N. the land abruptly descends about 200 feet, and then by gradual slopes to the level of Seneca River. The region immediately N. of Seneca Lake Outlet and w. of the Cayuga Lake Outlet is level, and some of it is marshy. In the N. w. corner of the co. is a great number of alluvial ridges, composed principally of gravel. These ridges extend in a N. and s. direction and are 30 to 50 feet high. Their declivities are generally very abrupt toward the N., E., and w., but more gradual toward the s.

The geological formation of the co. is very simple. The rocks overlie each other in parallel layers slightly dipping toward the s. The lowest rocks that crop out in the co. are those of the Onondaga salt group, including both the red shales and gypsum. They are found along Seneca River, where the gypsum is extensively quarried. Next above these are heavy, compact masses of the corniferous limestone, occupying a belt of country 2 to 3 mi. wide s. of Seneca River. The intermediate waterlime and Onondaga limestone strata are developed in this co. only in very thin and scarcely noticeable layers. The corniferous limestone furnishes a building stone of great excellence and is extensively quarried. Next in order come the Marcellus and Hamilton shales, occupying a broad belt through the co. and extending nearly to the summits of the ridges; the Tully limestone, a layer of only a few feet in thickness, but valuable from the quantity and quality of lime manufactured from it; and the Genesee slate, a dark, shaly rock which crowns the summits of the southern hills. These rocks throughout the co. are covered with a deep deposit of drift, consisting of clay, sand, gravel, and hardpan, and crop out only along the shores of the lakes, the narrow ravines of the streams, and the steep declivities of the ridges. In the N. w. corner of the co. this drift is arranged in ridges with narrow valleys scooped out between them.[1]

The principal stream is Seneca River, forming the outlet of Seneca Lake. It has a course of about 14 mi. between the two lakes, and in that distance falls 60 feet. The falls are principally at Waterloo and Seneca Falls, furnishing an excellent water-power at each place, but much the greater at the latter. From Cayuga Lake, Seneca River flows N. E. through a marshy region and forms a portion of the E. boundary of the co. Clyde River, a tributary of the Seneca, flows through a portion of the marshy region in the N. E. corner. The other streams are all small brooks and creeks, and for the most part are rapid torrents flowing in deep gulfs worn in the shaly rocks. They are frequently interrupted by waterfalls, are nearly dry in summer, and are subject to severe freshets.

Seneca Lake, the w. border of which forms the greater part of the w. boundary of the co., is 35 mi. long and 1 to 4 mi. broad. It is 216 feet above Lake Ontario and 447 feet above tide. It occupies a deep valley between the hills, and it varies in depth from 300 to 630 feet. Its shores are generally bold; and from their summits the land slopes gently and gracefully upward to a height

---

[1] The position and character of these remarkable ridges seem to indicate that the whole region has been subject to the force of large bodies of running water moving in a southerly direction; and it has been conjectured that at a geological period immediately preceding the present one, the waters of Lake Ontario, then much above its present level, flowed through the valleys of Seneca and Cayuga Lakes and discharged into the Susquehanna.

of 200 to 700 feet above its surface, furnishing some of the most quiet and beautiful scenery 'n the State. This lake is never entirely frozen over. Cayuga Lake occupies a parallel valley on the E. border of the co., and is 38 mi. long and 1 to 3½ mi. wide. It is 60° feet below Seneca, and its greatest depth is 346 feet. Near the foot the lake is very shallow, and a large extent of land, immediately adjoining and lying along the course of its outlet, is swampy.[1] Further s. the shores are bluff and the country is of the same general character as that bordering upon Seneca Lake.

The soil is generally of a very excellent quality. The sandy and gravelly loam of the drift deposits are well adapted to either grain raising or grazing. The lower portions of the ridges are enriched by the disintegration of the rocks above, making the soil very productive. The lowlands bordering upon Seneca River are clayey and in many places mixed with disintegrated gypsum and limestone. North of the river have been found extensive marl deposits of great agricultural value. North of the foot of Seneca Lake is a sandy region once considered worthless; but upon trial the soil has been found susceptible of being made productive at little expense. The marshy regions w. of Cayuga Outlet are covered with thick deposits of marl and muck. Measures have been instituted to drain these marshes; if successful a new and exceedingly fertile region will be added to the productive lands of the State.

The co. is a half-shire, the co. seats being located respectively at Ovid and Waterloo.[2] The courthouse and clerk's office at Ovid are brick buildings, situated in the E. part of the village. The combined courthouse and jail at Waterloo is a brick building, situated near the R. R., fronting the public square, in the w. part of the village. The co. poorhouse is located upon a farm of 126 acres, upon the line between Seneca Falls and Fayette, 4 mi. s. E. of Waterloo.[3]

Four weekly newspapers are now published in the co.[4]

The public works of the co. are the N. Y. Central R. R., extending through Seneca Falls and Waterloo, and the Seneca Canal, extending along Seneca River through the same towns.[5] Above the falls at Waterloo the canal is formed by slackwater navigation upon the river.

The lands in this co. were first brought to the notice of the whites by the expedition of Sullivan, which passed along the banks of Seneca Lake in 1779. Portions of the land at that time had been cleared and were under cultivation. The Indians had a tradition that this whole region had once been occupied by a race that pursued agriculture, but which had long ago disappeared. Many of Sullivan's soldiers, attracted by the beauty and fertility of the lands, after the war settled in various parts of the co. The first settler, Job Smith, who located at Seneca Falls in 1787, and the second, Andrew Dunlap, who located at Ovid in 1789, came in by way of Chemung River. The third settler, Lawrence Van Clief, who settled at Seneca Falls in 1789, came in by way of Oneida Lake and Seneca River.[6] After 1790 settlement progressed rapidly, and the most fertile lands

[1] This swampy region is the southern termination of the noted Montezuma Marshes.

[2] The county seat was located at Ovid upon the erection of the co. in 1804. The courthouse was built in 1806. While a part of Onondaga co., in 1790, courts were held at the barn of Andrew Dunlap. In 1817, upon the erection of Tompkins co., the co. seat was removed to Waterloo; but in 1822 the co. was divided into two jury districts, and the courts have since then been held alternately at Ovid and Waterloo. The first co. officers were Cornelius Humphrey, *First Judge;* Silas Halsey, *Clerk;* William Smith, *Sheriff;* and Jared Sandford, *Surrogate.*

[3] The average number of inmates is 60, supported at a weekly cost of $1.00 each. A school is taught 4 months in the year. The establishment seems to be pretty well arranged and managed.

[4] The *Seneca Patriot,* the first paper published in the co., was started at Ovid in 1815 by Geo. Lewis. In 1816 it was changed to

The *Ovid Gazette.* Upon the change of the co. seat in 1817, it was removed to Waterloo and changed to

The *Waterloo Gazette,* and was continued several years by the original proprietor.

The *Seneca Farmer* was started at Waterloo in 1822 by Wm. Child. In 1832 it was removed to Seneca Falls and united with the Seneca Falls Journal.

The *Waterloo Republican* was issued a short time in 1822.

The *Waterloo Observer* was started in 1824 by Charles Sentell. It was soon after issued a short time as

The *Observer and Union,* and was subsequently changed to

The Seneca Observer, under which title it is still issued by the original proprietor.

The *Wreath and Ladies' Literary Repository* was issued from the Observer office in 1831.

The *Seneca Republican* was established at Ovid in 1827 by Michael Hayes. In 1830 it was changed to

The *Ovid Gazette and Seneca County Register,* and was issued a short time by John Duffy.

The *Seneca Falls Journal* was commenced in 1829 by O. B. Clark. In 1831 it passed into the hands of Wm. N. Brown, and in 1832 it was united with the Seneca Farmer and changed to

The *Seneca Farmer and Seneca Falls Advertiser,* and was issued by Wm. Child until 1835.

The *Western Times* was published at Waterloo in 1830 by Ebenezer P. Mason.

The *Ovid Emporium* was published in 1832 by Bishop Orenshier.

The Seneca County Courier was commenced at Seneca Falls in 1837 by Isaac Fuller & Co. It was successively published by Fuller & Bloomer, Mills & Bloomer, Mills & Davis, John J. Davis, N. J. Milliken, Milliken & Fuller, Milliken & Mumford, Foster & Judd, Fuller & Judd, until 1850, when it passed into the hands of Isaac Fuller, its present publisher.

The Ovid Bee was started in 1838 by David Fairchild & Son. At the end of one year it passed into the hands of the son, Corydon Fairchild, its present publisher.

The *Seneca Falls Democrat* was commenced in 1839 by Josiah T. Miller, and was continued 10 years.

The *Seneca Democrat,* semi-w., was issued a short time from the same office.

The *Seneca Falls Register* was commenced in 1835 by J. K. Brown, and was continued 2 years.

The *Memorial* was commenced at Seneca Falls in 1840 by Ansel Bascom, and was continued until 1846.

The *Water Bucket* was published at Seneca Falls by an association of Washingtonians in 1841.

The *Free-Soil Union* was commenced at Seneca Falls in Aug. 1848, by N. J. Milliken, and continued about 1 year.

The *Lily* was commenced at Seneca Falls in 1849 by Mrs. Amelia Bloomer, and was continued until 1854, when it was removed to Ohio.

The American Reveille was commenced at Seneca Falls in Jan. 1855, by Wilcoxen, Sherman & Baker. In 1856 it was purchased by G. Wilcoxen, and was continued by him until Jan. 1859, when it passed into the hands of Holly & Stowell, the present publishers.

[5] The first locks on this river were made by the Seneca River Navigation Company, in 1815.

[6] Mr. Van Clief was one of the 100 men dispatched by Sullivan under Col. Gansevoort, directly E. from the head of Seneca Lake,

were speedily occupied. In 1791 the State Road, known as the "*Geneva Road*," was built from Whitestown to Geneva; and this soon became the great highway for immigration. This co. formed the extreme w. portion of the Military Tract; and many of the early settlers were old soldiers who had drawn their portion of public land here.

COVERT—was formed from Ovid, April 7, 1817. Lodi was taken off in 1826. It lies upon the w. shore of Cayuga Lake, in the s. e. corner of the co. Its surface is an upland descending from its w. border and terminating in a steep and almost precipitous bluff upon the shore of the lake. This bluff rises 100 to 200 feet above the water, and the summit of the slope is about 400 feet higher. The town is watered by Trumansburg Creek and many smaller streams, flowing into Cayuga Lake. These streams have worn ravines in the slate and shales to the depth of 20 to 40 feet, the sides being nearly precipitous. In summer they are nearly dry, but during heavy rains they become fierce mountain torrents, bounding and seething in their confined channels and leaping from high precipices to mingle with the calm and peaceful waters of the lake. The soil is a gravelly and clayey loam. The whole surface is arable, except the steep declivities of the lake bluffs. **Farmersville,** (Farmer p. o.,) in the N. part, contains 3 churches, a steam sawmill, foundery, and machine shop. Pop. 350. **Covert,** (p. o.,) in the s. E. part, **Halls Corners,** near the center, and **Kellys Corners,** in the N. w., are hamlets. **Port Deposit** (Trumansburg Landing p. o.) is a steamboat landing near the s. E. corner. The first settler was Philip Tremaine, who located at Goodwins Point before 1793.[1] The first religious services were held at the house of Mr. King, by Elder Thomas; the first church (Bap.) was organized in 1805.[2]

FAYETTE—was formed from Romulus, as "*Washington*," March 14, 1800. Its name was changed April 6, 1808. Junius was taken off in 1803. It lies on the s. bank of Seneca River and extends from Seneca to Cayuga Lake. Its surface is rolling and inclined toward the N. From Seneca Lake the land beautifully slopes upward, forming some of the most delightful situations for residences in the co. Upon Cayuga Lake the shores are lower and in some places are marshy. The highest point in town is about 200 feet above Seneca Lake. The streams are mostly small brooks flowing with rapid currents, and at a few places furnishing limited water-power. In some parts the corniferous limestone is extensively quarried, both for lime and for building purposes. The soil is a deep, rich loam, composed of clay, gravel, and sand. Near Canoga Village is an immense spring in a basin 14 feet in diameter, and from it flows sufficient water to form a large and valuable water-power. The spring also emits nitrogen gas. **Canoga,**[3] (p. v.,) in the N. E. part, on Cayuga Lake, contains 2 churches, a gristmill, 2 sawmills, and 197 inhabitants. **South Waterloo,** a suburb of Waterloo, on the s. bank of Seneca River, contains 1 church and 597 inhabitants. **Bearytown,** (Fayette p. o.,) on the line of Varick, is partly in this town. **West Fayette,** in the s. w. corner, and **Rose Hill,** in the w. part, are p. offices. The first settlement was made by James Bennett, from Penn., who located upon the shore of Cayuga Lake in 1789.[4] Red Jacket, the Seneca chief and orator, was born near Canoga Spring. There are 8 churches in town.[5]

JUNIUS—was formed from "*Washington*," (now Fayette,) Feb. 12, 1803; Wolcott (Wayne co.) was taken off in 1807, Galen (Wayne co.) in 1812, and Seneca Falls, Tyre, and Waterloo in 1829. It is the N. w. corner town of the co. In this town are numerous small, isolated gravel and clay ridges 30 to 75 ft. high, all extending in a general N. and s. direction. The numerous small streams that drain the town flow N. into Clyde River. Among the narrow valleys in the E. part is a limited amount of swamp land. The soil is a good quality of gravelly loam. **Dublin,** (Junius p. o.,) N. w. of the center, contains 1 church and 25 dwellings. **West Junius** is a p. o. near the s. w. corner. **Thorntons Corners** is a hamlet. The first settlements were made by Thos. Bedell and Jesse, Sam'l, and David Southwick, about 1795.[6] The first church (Cong.) was formed in 1811; three years after it was changed to a Presb. There are also 2 M. E. churches in town.

LODI—was formed from Covert, Jan. 27, 1826. It borders upon Seneca Lake, and is the s. w.

---

to lay waste the lands of the Cayugas, Onondagas, and Oneidas that had previously escaped destruction.

[1] Among the other early settlers were Nathaniel, Reuben, and Bassler King, from Dutchess co., in 1793; Jonathan Woodworth and sons Nehemiah, Charles, and Oliver, and daughter Deborah, from Norwich, Conn., in 1794; and Miner and Joseph Thomas, in 1795, and Turtellus King, in 1795.

[2] This was the first church formed in the co. The census reports 4 churches; 2 Bap., Univ., and Ref. Prot. D.

[3] The name of the village, derived from that of the spring, is an Indian word said to signify "sweet water."

[4] Samuel Bear settled at "*Schoyes*," now South Waterloo, about 1795. Wm. Watkins kept the first inn, at South Waterloo, and Samuel Bear built the first grist and saw mill, at the same place

[5] 2 Presb., 2 M. E., 2 Lutheran, 2 Ref. Prot. D.

[6] Among the other early settlers were families named Sherman, Chapman, Brownwell, Fisk, Moore, French, Maynard, Thorn, and Hart,—mostly from New England. The first death was that of Mrs. Submit Southwick, wife of Samuel Southwick, in 1802. Joseph Moody kept the first store, at Dublin. He was an Irishman; and hence the name of the village.

corner town in the co. Its surface is mostly inclined toward the w. and n., a small portion only lying E. of the summit. The bluff bordering upon Seneca Lake is 150 to 250 ft. above the surface of the water; and the highest part of the central ridge is 500 ft. higher and about 1,200 ft. above tide. The principal streams are Mill Creek, flowing n. w. through near the center, and Sheldrake Creek, in the n. w. corner. Mill Creek separates the highlands into two distinct ridges, the declivities being very abrupt. Upon this stream are several fine cascades. Lodi Falls, where the creek leaps down the precipitous bluff which borders upon the lake, are 125 ft. high. The water has worn a deep and irregular channel in the shale rocks one mi. back from the face of the bluff. The soil is principally a gravelly loam mixed with the disintegrated rocks. **Lodi**, (p. v.,) in the n. part, contains 2 churches, a gristmill, and 380 inhabitants; **Townsendville**, (p. v.,) in the s. E. part, a church and 20 dwellings. **Lodi Center** (p. o.) is a hamlet. **Lodi Landing** is on Seneca Lake, at the mouth of Mill Creek. The first settlement was made by Geo. Faussett, from Penn., who settled in the s. w. part in 1789.[1] There are 5 churches in town.[2]

OVID—was formed March 5, 1794. Hector (Schuyler co.) was taken off in 1802, and Covert in 1817. It lies s. of the center of the co., and extends from Seneca to Cayuga Lake. Its surface consists of an arable ridge, 600 ft. above Seneca Lake and about 1,100 ft. above tide, descending from w. of the center toward the lakes. The bluffs upon the lakes are 20 to 50 ft. high, and nearly perpendicular. A great number of small streams flow into both Cayuga and Seneca Lakes, the principal of which are Sheldrake, Osborn, Groves, and Barnum Creeks on the E., and Sixteen Falls Creek on the w. These streams have all worn deep, ragged ravines in the yielding shales. They are frequently interrupted by cascades, and in summer are nearly dry. The soil consists principally of clay and gravel intermixed with sand and the disintegrated rocks. **Ovid**, (p. v.,) near the n. line, contains a courthouse, co. clerk's office, 3 churches, the Ovid Academy,[3] a steam mill, and ax factory, and about 650 inhabitants. **Ovid Landing** is just over the town line in Romulus. **Sheldrake Point**, (Sheldrake p. o.,) a steamboat landing upon Cayuga Lake, contains a church, steam sawmill, boat yard, and 168 inhabitants. **Ovid Center** contains 20 houses. **Kidders Ferry**, (p. o.,) near the s. E. corner, and **Scotts Corners**, near the center, are hamlets. The first settlement was made in May, 1789, by Andrew Dunlap, from Penn., who located on Lot 8, in the n. w. part of the town.[4] The first religious services were held at the house of Abraham Covert, in 1794. The first settled preacher (Ref. Prot. D.) was John Lindley, in 1800.[5] The New York State Agricultural College and farm are located on the n. line of this town, w. of the village.[6] In the s. part of the town are the remains of an ancient fortification.[7]

ROMULUS—was formed March 5, 1794. Fayette was taken off in 1800, and Varick in 1830. It lies s. of the center of the co., and extends from Seneca to Cayuga Lake. Its surface is rolling or moderately hilly and has a general northerly inclination. The high bluff from Ovid extends into the s. border of the town, where it drops down abruptly about 200 ft. The land slopes from the center downward to the E. and w. The streams are small and generally flow in deep channels. The surface is smooth, except along the courses of the streams, and is nearly all arable. The soil is a fertile, gravelly and clayey loam. **Romulus**, (p. v.,) on the line of Varick, contains a church, steam sawmill, female seminary, and 36 dwellings. **Hyatts Corners**, in the s. E., contains 20 dwellings. **Romulus Center** is a p. o. **Whitneys Landing** is a station upon Cayuga Lake; and **Cooleys** and **Freleighs Points** and **Ovid Landing** are stations upon Seneca Lake. The first settlement was made by David Wisner, in 1789. There is but one church (Bap.) in town.

---

[1] Mr. Faussett brought in his family in 1790. Jas. Jackson, from Penn., settled in the n. w. part in 1789; Silas Halsey, from L. I., near Lodi, in 1792. The next year his sons and sons-in-law and their families, numbering 18 persons, came in. The first child born was a daughter of Geo. Faussett. Peter Smith kept the first inn, and Silas Halsey built the first gristmill, in 1794.

[2] 3 M. E., Bap., and Ref. Prot. D.

[3] In 1855 the name of this institution was changed to the Seneca Collegiate Institute.

[4] The first settlers, mostly from Penn. and N. J., followed the trail of Sullivan's army and located in the w. part of the town. Among them were Wm. Dunlap and Joseph Wilson, from Penn., Peter Smith, from N. J., and Henry Wharton, in 1789; Abraham Covert and his son Abraham A., from N. J., in 1790; Elijah Kinne, from Dutchess co., and John Seely, from Saratoga co., in 1792; Nicholas and Richard Huff, Peter Hughes, Abraham De Mott and his son James, in 1793; and William and Robert Dunlap and Teunis Covert, in 1794. In the summer of 1795, Jonas C. Baldwin settled on Lot 11, where he remained until 1801, when he sold out and removed to Lysander, Onondaga co., and laid the foundation of Baldwinsville. The first child born was David, son of Andrew Dunlap, Feb. 2, 1793; and the first death was that of George Dunlap, brother of Andrew, Sept. 24, 1791. A

triple marriage in 1793 was the first in town. The parties were Joseph Wilson and Anna Wyckoff; Abraham A. Covert and Catherine Covert; and Enoch Stewart and Jane Covert. They were obliged to cross Seneca Lake to find a justice authorized to perform the ceremony. Benj. Munger taught the first school, in 1795; John McMath kept the first store, in 1797, and the first inn, in 1800; and B. Boardman erected the first mill, in 1793, on Lot 2.

[5] There are now in town 7 churches; 2 Presb., 2 M. E., Ref. Prot. D., Bap., and R. C.

[6] This institution was incorporated in 1853; and the buildings are now in process of erection. They were designed by S. E. Hewes, of Albany, and consist of a main building 90 ft. front and 132 deep, having a wing on each side 84½ by 60, and transverse wings 58 by 128. It is designed to accommodate about 400 students. The farm contains 600 acres.

[7] On Lot 29, within ¼ mi. of the s. line of the town, and exactly on the dividing ridge between the two lakes, once existed a mound or fortification of an irregular, elliptical form, inclosing about 3 acres, and surrounded by an embankment of earth, which in 1801 was about 3 feet in height, with a base 5 to 8 feet in width. The present proprietor, George Bo Dine, with his father, removed here in 1802, and built a house within the inclosed space, where he has since resided until within a few

SENECA FALLS—was formed from Junius, March 26, 1829. It lies upon the w. bank of Cayuga Lake, N. of the center of the co. The surface is nearly flat, and it is elevated 30 to 50 ft. above Cayuga Lake. The shores of the lake are low and shelving, and the N. portion is swampy. Seneca River flows E. and N. through the center of the town, its valley dividing the town into two distinct parts. The river flows over a series of ledges into a deep chasm apparently worn by its waters. Just E. and s. w. of the village are extensive gypsum quarries. The soil is a stiff, hard clay in the s. and E., a sandy loam in the N. w., and a heavy vegetable muck in the N. E. **Seneca Falls,** (p. v.,)[1] upon Seneca River, near the center of the town, was incorp. April 22, 1831. It is a station upon the N. Y. C. R. R. and the Seneca Canal. The total fall is 51 feet, and furnishes an abundance of water-power, which is largely improved. It contains 7 churches, the Seneca Falls Academy, a union school, 2 newspaper offices, extensive manufactories of fire engines, pumps, machinery, iron, and woolen goods, and a great variety of other articles.[2] Pop. about 4,000. The first settlement was made by Job Smith, from Ulster co., upon the present site of the village in 1787; he left in 1793. The first permanent settler was Lawrence Van Clief, in 1789.[3] The first religious services were held by M. E. missionaries, about 1797; and the first regular minister was Rev. Matthew Stewart, (Presb.,) in 1804.[4]

TYRE—was formed from Junius, March 26, 1829. It is the N. E. corner town of the co. The E. half is a swamp, being the s. termination of the Montezuma Marshes. The w. half is occupied by peculiar drift ridges similar to those already described in Junius. These ridges are 30 to 50 feet high, and generally have very steep declivities upon all sides except the s. One of the longest of these, in the w. part of the town, extends nearly two-thirds of the distance from the s. line to the N. Its summit is nearly level; and the road which is located upon it appears as though built upon an artificial embankment. The soil is clay and muck in the E. and a gravelly loam in the w. **Tyre City,** (Tyre p. o.,) near the center, contains 2 churches and 20 dwellings. **Cruso** is a p. o. on the N. line. The first settlement was made by Ezekiel Crane, from N. J., who came in 1794.[5] The first church (Bap.) was formed in 1805. Elder Don Ralph was the first preacher.[6]

VARICK—was formed from Romulus, Feb. 6, 1830. It extends from Seneca to Cayuga Lake, across the center of the co. Its surface is slightly inclined toward the N. The slopes of the ridges are

---

years. The work was evidently of great antiquity,—the timber on the inside being of the same size and apparent age of that in the surrounding forest. Upon the bank and in the ditch large oak trees—the growth of centuries—were standing. In the embankment were several openings a few feet in width, which were once probably used for gates or entrances. In making an excavation for a cellar, on the E. side, 6 skeletons were found at the depth of about 2 feet. This was in 1857. Several had been found previously; and, though all the softer parts of the bones had long since disappeared, the teeth and a few of the larger bones still remained. Inside of the embankment may still be found pieces of a coarse kind of pottery, ornamental pipes, &c. De Witt Clinton visited this place in 1810; and his theory is that this was one of a number of similar works of defense found occupying the most commanding positions in Western New York, and in the valleys of the Ohio and Mississippi, erected by a race more civilized than the Indians, and that they preceded the latter in the occupation of this country: their origin and end are alike a mystery; their annals defy the ken of human research, and their history will remain a sealed book perhaps forever. The Indians were never able to give any account of this fortification, as it was older than their traditions.

[1] Named from the falls in the river, the Indian name, "Sha-se-ounse," signifying rolling water.

[2] Downs & Co.'s manufacturing establishment, commenced in 1840, has a capital, including real estate and machinery, of about $200,000. They are largely engaged in the manufacture of pumps and a great variety of other articles, use annually 3,800 tons of iron, 1,500 tons of coal, and employ 230 hands. Their yearly sales amount to about $400,000. They also manufacture Goffe's Patent Knitting Machine, and are largely engaged in the manufacture of hose, turning out 800 pairs per day; 70 persons are employed in this department. The Island Works of Silsby, Mynderse & Co., commenced in 1848, is engaged in the manufacture of steam fire engines, portable steam engines, and a variety of other machinery. It employs 150 persons, and turns out work to the amount of $200,000 per year. Cowing & Co.'s works commenced about 1840. They are engaged in the manufacture of fire engines, pumps, and various other articles,—employ 140 men, and turn out work yearly to the amount of $125,000. The Phœnix Woolen Mills gives employment to 90 persons, and manufactures goods to the amount of $150,000 per annum. Besides these, there are in the place several flouring mills, having in the aggregate 32 runs of stone, 2 distilleries, a brewery, 2 planing mills, 5 founderies and machine shops, a scythe and fork factory, a woolen factory, and several minor manufactories. About 50 tons of iron are used daily in the several manufactories.—*American Reveille, Seneca Falls,* 1859.

[3] Mr. Smith was the first white settler upon the Military Tract. Mr. Van Clief was a Revolutionary soldier, having been

in the battles of White Plains, with Washington at Valley Forge and with Sullivan in his campaign against the Indians. He settled on the river, and engaged in piloting boats over the rapids until the locks were built in 1815. Among the other early settlers were James Bennett, Col. John Harris, and —— Parker. The first child born was a daughter of Lawrence Van Clief, Nov. 29, 1790; the first marriage, that of —— Ely and Pamela Parkhurst, in 1796; and the first death, that of Mrs. Job Smith, in 1792. The first school was taught by —— Leonard, in 1797. Lawrence Van Clief kept the first inn, in 1794; and Col. Wilhelmus Mynderse kept the first store, in 1795, and built the first saw and grist mill, about the same time. In 1794, Robert Trout, Nicholas Gouverneur, Stephen N. Bayard, and Elkanah Watson, under the title of the Bayard Company, bought of the State 100 acres of land on the N. side of the river, embracing the greater part of the water-power upon that side. In 1798 they purchased 250 acres on the s. side, and in 1809, 650 acres more on the same side, the two purchases embracing all the water-power upon that side of the river. In 1816 they bought 450 acres more on the N. side, completing the purchase of the water-power. In 1795 the company sold a one-fifth interest in their purchase to Col. Mynderse, and constituted him their agent. In 1795 the "Upper Red Mills" were erected under his direction; and in 1807 the "Lower Red Mills" were erected. The Co. refused to sell their land, neglected to improve the immense water-power that they owned, and in 1825 broke down, and the property was sold for about one-fifth of its cost. In 1829-30 the manufacturing interests of the place began to increase. About that time a paper mill was erected by Chauncey Marshall, G. V. Sackett, and Ansel Bascom; a cotton factory, by Judge Sackett; a machine shop, by McClary & Halliday; and a clock factory, by Marshall & Adams. Until the locks were built, in 1815, the most important business of the place was that of transporting goods and boats around the rapids. The "dress reform" movement was commenced in this town by Mrs. Amelia Bloomer, who adopted the dress known as the Bloomer Dress in 1849.

[4] The census reports 7 churches in town; Bap., M. E., Wes. Meth., Prot. E., Presb., Ref. Prot. D., and R. C.

[5] Asher Halsey, from N. J., came in 1798. Among the other early settlers were Stephen Crane, Peter and Ezra Degarmo, Robert Gould, Thos. Susson, Lewis Winans, and Thos. W. Rosevelt. The first child born was Danl. Crane; the first marriage, that of James Cook and Betsey Woodworth; and the first death, that of Ezekiel Crane. Nancy Osman taught the first school, in 1804. Stephen Crane kept the first inn, in 1809; Nicholas Traver built the first sawmill, in 1807, and Noah Davis the first gristmill, in 1817.

[6] There are 4 churches in town; Disciples, Bap., M. E., and Ref. Prot. D.

so gradual that nearly every part is arable. The streams are all small. Near the center of the town is a cranberry swamp, occupying about 800 acres. The soil is a gravelly loam intermixed with clay. **Bearytown,** (Fayette p. o.,) upon the line of Fayette, in the N. E. part, contains 3 churches, a steam sawmill, stave factory, and 128 inhabitants, of whom 51 are in this town. **Romulus** (p. v.) lies on the S. border. **East Varick** (p. o.) is a landing upon Cayuga Lake. **McDuffee Town** is a hamlet in the S. E. corner. **Varick** is a p. o. The first settlement was made by James McKnight, in 1789.[1] There are 3 churches in town; Bap., Presb., and M. E.

WATERLOO—was formed from Junius, March 26, 1829. It lies on the N. bank of Seneca River, N. W. of the center of the co. The surface is almost one unbroken flat. A marsh extends E. and W. through the town S. of the center, and another occupies the N. E. corner.[2] The bed of Seneca River, on the S. boundary, is almost level with the general surface. The soil is muck and clay in the N. and E., gravel along the N. border, and a sandy loam in the center and W. **Waterloo,** (p. v.,) on Seneca River, near the E. border of the town, was incorp. April 9, 1824. It is a station upon the N. Y. C. R. R. and upon the Seneca Canal. A fall of 24½ feet in Seneca River furnishes an excellent water-power, which is mostly improved. It is a half-shire of the co., and contains the courthouse, 6 churches, the Waterloo Union School, a bank, a large shawl factory,[3] 3 distilleries, 2 malt houses, 3 flouring mills, 5 sawmills, 2 founderies and machine shops, 2 oil mills, and numerous other manufactories.[4] Seneca River above the falls, being seldom frozen, is navigable throughout the year. This village is an important depôt of lumber from the S. W. cos., and of coal from the Susquehanna and Blossburg Mines. Pop. 3,050. **South Waterloo,** formerly called "*Schoyes,*" is on the opposite side of Seneca River, in Fayette. Settlement was commenced by John Greene, from R. I., in 1789.[5] The first religious services were held about 1816.[6]

Acres of Land, Valuation, Population, Dwellings, Families, Freeholders, Schools, Live Stock, Agricultural Products, and Domestic Manufactures, of Seneca County.

Names of Towns.	Acres of Land.		Valuation of 1858.			Population.		No. of Dwellings.	No. of Families.	Freeholders.	Schools.	
	Improved.	*Unimproved.*	*Real Estate.*	*Personal Property.*	*Total.*	*Males.*	*Females.*				*No. of Districts.*	*Children taught.*
Covert	15,646¾	3,274½	816,199	160,015	976,214	1,146	1,084	418	432	351	13	894
Fayette	27,105½	6,425	1,437,514	100,615	1,538,129	1,708	1,662	613	653	491	16	1,165
Junius	13,172¾	3,304	706,478	34,250	740,728	713	702	269	295	228	8	590
Lodi	17,112	4,483	696,511	67,770	764,281	1,016	1,002	401	402	298	9	424
Ovid	14,251	3,812¾	916,147	201,393	1,117,540	1,098	1,176	424	439	374	9	1,022
Romulus	17,977⅞	5,600	793,589	148,000	941,589	979	900	342	360	251	12	855
Seneca Falls	11,781½	2,316	1,479,550	481,315	1,960,865	2,511	2,473	836	956	619	10	1,905
Tyre	10,602⅜	8,438⅛	402,243	18,100	420,343	717	702	279	283	212	7	648
Varick	15,606½	4,468	761,251	52,375	813,626	858	865	340	343	271	11	725
Waterloo	8,693½	3,815	1,029,875	359,750	1,389,625	1,964	2,082	747	781	526	7	1,574
Total	151,949¾	45,936⅜	9,039,357	1,623,583	10,662,940	12,710	12,648	4,669	4,944	3,621	102	9,802

Names of Towns.	Live Stock.					Agricultural Products.							Domestic cloths, in Yards.
						Bush. of Grain.					Dairy Products.		
	Horses.	*Working Oxen and Calves.*	*Cows.*	*Sheep.*	*Swine.*	*Winter.*	*Spring.*	*Tons of Hay.*	*Bushels of Potatoes.*	*Bushels of Apples.*	*Pounds Butter.*	*Pounds Cheese.*	
Covert	679	1,207	732	3,576	1,117	16,990	115,334	1,551	3,197	20,648	70,239	1,550	150
Fayette	1,390	1,589	1,311	8,290	3,272	36,082	194,820	4,145	5,205	21,622	140,312	400	685
Junius	731	889	727	5,623	1,410	17,870	97,287	2,049	13,718	11,295	83,500	5,290	471
Lodi	763	1,183	732	3,450	1,611	13,611	101,248	1,988	4,512	17,734	68,295	414	101
Ovid	688	983	803	3,968	1,167	16,129	101,851	1,711½	3,549	26,718	50,068	700	282
Romulus	862	933	758	6,134	1,261	10,682½	143,745½	2,160¾	1,989	20,024	69,136	700	462½
Seneca Falls	560	631	598	4,042	4,245	12,753½	67,435¾	2,029½	4,759	12,966	63,095	1,575	99
Tyre	577	854	629	4,616	1,019	13,533	80,956¾	2,043½	10,023	20,696	72,346	1,793	747½
Varick	755	717	381	4,276	1,350	14,553	112,246	1,570½	1,706	12,809	52,457	70	217
Waterloo	492	874	465	3,559	1,080	7,379	68,097½	1,631	23,886	10,766	36,126	1,320	
Total	7,497	9,860	7,136	47,534	17,532	159,583	1,083,121½	20,879¾	72,544	175,278	705,574	13,812	3,215

[3] The first child born was a son of James McKnight, in 1790.

[4] The waters of Black Brook which flow through the central swampy region are impregnated with earthy and vegetable matter, which gives to them the peculiar quality of clearing the inside of steam boilers of the incrustations of sulphate and carbonate of lime resulting from the use of hard water.

[5] The Waterloo Woolen Manufacturing Co. was organized in 1836, with a capital of $150,000; 200 to 250 hands are employed; 300,000 lbs. of wool are used, and 40,000 long shawls are annually manufactured. This is, next to the Bay State Mills, the largest shawl factory in America.

[6] Among these establishments is a plaster mill, boatyard, and drydock, 4 copper, tin, and sheet iron factories, a fanning mill, and washboard factory, and 2 cabinet and furniture shops.

[7] Among the other early settlers were Jabez Gorham, from Ballston, (Saratoga co.,) who located upon the present site of the village. Salmon Disbrow, from Saratoga co., came in about the same time. The first child born was John Smith, in 1808; the first marriage, that of Job Smith and Miriam Gorham, in 1799; and the first deaths, those of John Gregory and James Hull, two Revolutionary soldiers, who drew lots in this town, settled upon them, and both died about 1808. Isaac Gorham taught the first school, in 1810; Jabez Gorham kept the first inn, about 1795; Charles Swift, the first store, in 1815; and James Bear built the first mill, in 1794.

[8] The census reports 6 churches in town; Presb., Prot. E., Ref. Prot. D., M. E., Disciples, and Friends.

STEUBEN COUNTY.

THIS county was formed from Ontario, March 18, 1796, and named in honor of Baron Steuben. The 7th Range of Townships was annexed to Allegany co. March 11, 1808, the part in the fork of Crooked Lake to Ontario co. Feb. 25, 1814, a part of Dansville to Livingston co. Feb. 15, 1822, and a part to Schuyler co. April 7 1854. It lies upon the s. border of the State, considerably w. of the center, is centrally distant 188 mi. from Albany, and contains 1425 sq. mi. Its surface mostly consists of ridges and high, rolling uplands, forming the northern continuation of the Alleghany Mts. The watershed between Lake Ontario and Susquehanna River extends from Allegany co. eastward across the N. part of the co. The deep valley of Crooked Lake breaks the continuity of the highlands and extends 17 mi. s. w. from the head of the lake, connecting with the Conhocton Valley at Bath, and forming one of the numerous natural passes between the southern valleys and the basin of Lake Ontario. The highlands occupying the s. w. corner of the co. also form a portion of the watershed, being drained by branches of Canisteo River on the E. and of Genesee River on the w. The highest summits in the co. are about 2,500 feet above tide.[1]

The upland region has nearly a uniform elevation, with a slight inclination toward the N. It is intersected by numerous deep valleys, which have evidently been excavated by the action of water.[2] The formation of the steep hillsides which border upon these valleys is such as to prove conclusively that they were once united, and that a wide, rolling plateau spread over the region now so irregular and broken. The principal of these valleys are those of Canisteo and Conhocton Rivers, extending nearly N. W. and S. E. through the co. From these valleys numerous others diverge at nearly right angles and branch off into countless deep, crooked ravines, intersecting the plateau in every direction. The hills that border upon these valleys are usually steep and 300 to 600 feet high.

Conhocton River flows S. E. through near the center of the co. In high water it was once navigable for arks 14 mi. above Bath. It receives from the s. w. Neils, Bennetts, Campbells, Stockton, Michigan, and Stephens Creeks, and from the N. E. Twelve Mile, Ten Mile, Five Mile, (or Kanona,) Mud,[3] and Meads Creeks. Canisteo River flows through a valley s. w. of the Conhocton and nearly parallel to it. In freshets it rises 6 to 8 feet, and is then navigable for boats and arks about 40 mi. Its chief tributaries are Canacadea, Crosby, Purdy, Bennetts, Col. Bills, and Tuscarora Creeks, all from the s. w. Tioga River rises in Penn., flows N. through a deep, wild mountain valley, and unites with the Canisteo at Erwin, and with the Conhocton at Painted Post, from the latter place the combined stream taking the name of Chemung River.[4] Canaseraga Creek, flowing N., drains the N. w. corner of the co.; and several small streams rising in the s. w. corner form branches of Genesee River. Crooked Lake lies along the N. E. border, in a deep valley nearly surrounded by steep hills 500 to 800 feet high. Little Lake lies in a shallow valley along the E. border of the town of Wayne. It discharges its waters s. into Mud Lake, and through Mud Creek into Conhocton River. Loon Lake, in Wayland, lies in a valley which is the southern continuation of the valley of Hemlock Lake in Livingston co. Still further s., in the same valley, is Mud Lake, a small sheet of water, the outlet of which flows s. and empties into the Conhocton.

The shales and sandstones of the Portage group outcrop in all the deep ravines in the N. part of the co. and in the w. bank of Crooked Lake. Elsewhere, the Chemung group composes most of the surface rocks. Near the State Line the highest hills are capped with a coarse, silicious conglomerate, which forms the floor of the coal measures.[5] A feeble brine spring is found at La Grange,

---

[1] The following elevations have been determined, principally by actual surveys: Crooked Lake, 718 feet; Corning, 925; Village of Bath, 1,090; Hornellsville, 1,150; Arkport, 1,194; summit between Mud Lake and Bath, 1,579; summit between Bath and Arkport, 1,840; summit between Arkport and Angelica, 2,062; Troupsburgh Hills, 2,500.

[2] These valleys must have been excavated by more powerful currents of water than now flow through them; and their formation belongs to the drift period of geology.

[3] Mud Creek is the outlet of Mud Lake, in Schuyler co. At the first settlement of the co. this stream was navigable, and arks were floated from Mud Lake down the creek and the Conhocton to the Susquehanna, and thence to the Baltimore market. Since the clearing of the forests, this stream has entirely failed

for purposes of navigation, and now, in summer, it is almost dry.

[4] These streams were all much larger before the destruction of the forests. In time of high water the early settlers describe them as being "full from hill to hill."

[5] The rocks of this co. are generally of a shaly nature and not fit for use. There are a few exceptions, however. One mi. N. of Bath is a stratum, 3 feet thick, of a tough, argillo-calcareous rock, forming an excellent building stone. In Woodhull, Canisteo, and Jasper the sandstone ledges furnish an excellent quality of grindstones. At Arkport, in Dansville, and Troupsburgh are marl beds, from which lime is manufactured.—*Geol. 4th Dist., pp.* 483, 484.

and sulphur springs in Campbell, Jasper, and Urbana. The soil in general is composed of detritus of the adjacent rocks, and is better adapted to grazing than tillage. Upon the intervales along the larger streams the soil is a fertile alluvium. The extensive flats upon the Chemung are among the finest agricultural lands in the State. Agriculture forms the chief occupation of the people. Grain is largely produced on the alluvial lands, and stock is extensively raised on the uplands. Stock and wool growing and dairying are the principal branches of agriculture pursued. Lumbering is still extensively carried on,—though it is gradually decreasing. The manufactures are principally confined to lumber, articles of wood, and the heavier and coarser products necessary to an agricultural region.

The co. is divided into the northern and southern Jury Districts, the co. buildings being respectively situated at Bath and Corning.[1] The courthouse at Bath is a commodious brick building, erected in 1828.[2] The jail is built of wood and closely surrounded by other buildings. The cells for prisoners are in the basement, and are not provided with any means of ventilation. Its arrangements show a culpable neglect and an entire disregard of the general sentiments of the co. and of the age. The co. clerk's office is permanently located at Bath. The courthouse at Corning is a fine brick edifice, erected in 1853–54 at a cost of $14,000. The jail at Corning was erected at the same time. The courts are held alternately at Bath and Corning. The co. poorhouse is located upon a farm of 214 acres about 2 mi. N. E. of Bath Village.[3] The average number of inmates is 75; and they are supported at an average weekly cost of $1.00 each. The farm yields a revenue of about $2,000. No instruction is afforded; but the children of proper age are bound out.

The New York & Erie R. R. enters the co. from Chemung and extends along the valleys of the Chemung, Tioga, and Canisteo Rivers to Hornellsville, and the Canacadea to the w. border of the co. It passes through Corning, Erwin, Addison, Rathbone, Cameron, Canisteo, and Hornellsville.[4] The Buffalo, N. Y. & E. R. R. extends N. w. from Corning up the Conhocton Valley, through Erwin, Campbell, Bath, Avoca, Cohocton, and Wayland, to the N. border of the co. This road intersects the Genesee Valley R. R. at Avon, the N. Y. Central at Batavia, the Buffalo & New York City at Attica, and the N. Y. & Erie at Corning. The Hornellsville Division of the Buffalo, New York & Erie R. R. extends N. w. up the valley of the Canisteo from Hornellsville, passing through that town and the s. w. corner of Dansville. The Blossburg & Corning R. R. extends from Corning, through Erwin and Lindley, s. along the Tioga Valley to the Blossburg coal region. Crooked Lake is navigated by steam and canal boats, and forms a link in the chain of the internal water communication of the State. It is united with the Erie Canal at Montezuma by Crooked Lake Canal, Seneca Lake, and the Cayuga and Seneca Canals. The Chemung Canal navigable feeder extends from Corning E. to Horseheads, in Chemung co. Considerable lumber is floated down the rivers and finds a market at Philadelphia and Baltimore. These various works of internal improvement afford ample facilities for the transportation of goods and passengers, and bring the farm products of the co. into close proximity to the Eastern markets.

Six newspapers are published in the co.[5]

---

[1] Upon the organization of the co., in 1796, the co. buildings were located at Bath. A wood courthouse, one and a half stories high, with two wings, was erected the same year. It was removed in 1828 and the present brick courthouse erected. About the time of the erection of the first courthouse, a jail was built of hewn logs, which was superseded by the erection of the present jail in 1845. By an act of the Legislature, passed July 19, 1853, the co. was divided into two jury districts, and the co. buildings for the southern district were located at Corning.

[2] The first co. officers were William Kersey, First Judge; Abraham Bradley and Eleazur Lindley, Associate Judges; Geo. D. Cooper, Co. Clerk; William Dunn, Sheriff; and Stephen Ross, Surrogate.

[3] This establishment consisted of 3 buildings,—one of brick and two of wood,—containing altogether 31 rooms. In Sept. 1859, the two frame buildings were burned, and 6 persons, inmates of the establishment, perished in the flames.

[4] This road was opened to Corning, Jan. 1, 1850, and to Hornellsville, Sept. 3 of the same year.

[5] The Bath Gazette and Genesee Advertiser, the first paper published in Western New York, was established at Bath by Wm. Kersey and James Eddie in 1796, and was continued several years. In 6 months from its first issue its circulation had reached 1000 copies.

The Steuben and Allegany Patriot was started at Bath in 1815 by Benj. Smead, and was continued until 1822. It was then changed to

The Farmers' Advocate and Steuben Advertiser. In 1849 it passed into the hands of William C. Rhoades, and in 1857 into those of P. S. Donahe, by whom it is now published as

The Steuben Farmers' Advocate.

The Farmers' Gazette was commenced at Bath in 1816 by David Rumsey.

The Steuben Messenger was started at Bath, April 17, 1828, by David Rumsey, and was published by him, Saml. M. Eddie, Wm. P. Agnel, and Chas. Adams successively until 1834, when its name was changed to

The Constitutionalist, and its publication was continued successively by R. L. Underhill, Whitmore & Van Valkenburgh, and Dowe & Richards, and by the last named firm as

The Steuben Democrat, until 1844. The paper was then suspended. In 1848 it was renewed by L. J. Beach, and in 1849 it was transferred to Geo. H. Bidewell, by whom the publication was continued until 1852.

The Steuben Whig was published at Bath during the political campaign of 1828, by William M. Swain.

The Steuben Courier was established at Bath in 1843 by Hull & Whittemore. It is now published by H. H. Hull.

The Temperance Gem was published at Bath in 1854, by Jenny and Caroline Rumsey.

The Addison Record was published in Addison by Isaac D. Booth from 1840 to 1842, and in 1849 by Dryden & Peck.

The Addison Advocate was published by H. D. Dyer in 1848–49.

The Voice of the Nation was commenced at Addison by R. Denton in 1852. In 1855 the paper passed to Anthony L. Underhill, by whom it was published until 1856, when it was removed to Bath and its name changed to

The Steuben American, and its publication continued until May, 1857.

The Canisteo Express was published at Addison in 1850 by T. Messenger.

Steubèn co. was all included in the Phelps and Gorham Purchase. It was sold by Phelps and Gorham to Robert Morris, who conveyed it to Sir Wm. Pulteney and others, in London. The territory was surveyed into townships and lots by Wm. Bull, for the Pulteney estate, in 1792–93. Sales were made by townships, at 18 and 20 cts. per acre. The first settlements were made in 1787–90, by immigrants from Wyoming, Penn., who located upon Chemung River, in the s. e. part of the co. These early settlers were originally from Conn. About 1790, settlements commenced in the w. part, adjoining Yates co. In 1792–93, Capt. Chas. Williamson,[1] agent of the Pulteney estate, commenced a settlement at Bath. He was accompanied by a large number of Scotch and German immigrants; and under his energetic and liberal policy the settlement progressed with great rapidity. The greater part of the early settlers came from Penn. by way of Susquehanna and Chemung Rivers. Subsequently large numbers came from Eastern New York, New England, and New Jersey.[2] The co. was divided by the Court of General Sessions, in 1796, into 6 towns, viz.: Bath, Canisteo, Dansville, Fredericton, Middletown, and Painted Post, comprising the territory now forming 31 towns of this co. and parts of Allegany, Yates, Livingston, and Schuyler cos. In 1790 the population was 168; in 1800 it was 1,788; and in 1855, 62,965. In extent of territory and in agricultural wealth it now ranks among the first cos. in the State.[3]

ADDISON[4]—was formed, as "*Middletown*," in March, 1796. Its name was changed April 6, 1808. A part of Troupsburgh was taken off in 1808, Cameron in 1822, a part of Woodhull in 1828, and a part of Rathbone in 1856. It lies upon the s. border of the co., just e. of the center. The surface is mostly a hilly upland, broken by the valley of the Canisteo and its branches. The principal valley is about 1½ mi. wide and is bordered by steep hillsides 300 to 400 feet high. The principal streams are Canisteo River, and the Tuscarora, Elks Lick, and Goodhue Creeks. Goodhue Lake, covering an area of about 500 acres, lies in the n. w. corner of the town. The soil is principally a clay loam, with strips of gravel and alluvium upon the streams. **Addison,** (p. v.,) situated on Canisteo River, contains 3 churches, a bank, several mills and manufacturing establishments. Pop. about 1,300. **South Addison** (p. v.) contains 18 dwellings. **Addison Hill** is a p. o.

The Addison Journal was started in 1851 by R. Denton, and was removed to Allegany co. in 1852.

The Addison Democrat was commenced by Chas. L. Phelps in 1853, and was merged in The Voice of the Nation in 1854.

The Addison Advertiser, established in 1858 by E. M. Johnson & Henry Baldwin, is still published.

The Corning and Blossburg Advocate was commenced at Corning in 1840 by Chas. Adams. In 1841 it passed into the hands of Henry H. Hull, by whom it was merged, in 1843, in the Steuben Courier, at Bath.

The Corning Journal was commenced by Thomas Messenger in May, 1847. In 1851 it passed to A. W. McDowell and G. W. Pratt, and in 1852 to Dr. Pratt, its present publisher.

The Corning Sun was started in 1853 by M. M. Pomeroy and P. C. Van Gelder. In 1854 Rev. Ira Brown became the publisher, and changed its name to The Elmira Southern Tier Farmer and Corning Sun, and continued it until 1856.

The United States Farmer was published at Corning in the spring of 1856.

The Corning Democrat was established in 1857 by Chas. T. Huston. It is now published by Frank B. Brown.

The Painted Post Gazette was started by —— Fairchild in 1846, and continued 1 year.

The Painted Post Herald was published by Hawley & Bennett from 1848 to 1850.

The Hornellsville Tribune was commenced in Nov. 1851, by Edwin Hough. It is now published by E. Hough & Son.

The National American was established at Hornellsville in 1856 by C. M. Harmon. In Nov. 1858, it was sold to Chas. A. Kinney, and its name changed to the **Canisteo Valley Journal.**

A paper was published for a time at Hammondsport, on Crooked Lake.

[1] Capt. Williamson was a Scotchman, and an officer in the British 24th regiment of infantry during the period of the Revolution; but he did not serve in the war, in consequence of having been made a prisoner by the French while crossing the Atlantic.

[2] "A large proportion of the first settlers upon the Canisteo were from Penn., and had within them a goodly infusion of that boisterous spirit and love of rough play for which the free and manly sons of the backwoods are everywhere famous. On the Susquehanna frontier, before the Revolution, had arisen an athletic, scuffling, wrestling race, lovers of hard blows, sharp shooters, and runners, who delighted in nothing more than in those ancient sports by which the backs and limbs of all stout hearted youths have been tested since the days of Hercules. The eating of bears, the drinking of grog, the devouring of hominy, venison, and all the invigorating diet of the frontiers, the hewing down of forests, the paddling of canoes, the fighting of savages, all combined to form a generation of yeomen and foresters daring, rude, and free. Canisteo was a sprout from this stout stock, and on the generous river flats flourished with amazing vigor. Every thing that could eat, drink, and wrestle was welcome,—Turk or Tuscarora, Anak or Anthropophagus, Blue Beard or Blunderbore. A 'back hold' with a Ghoul would not have been declined, nor a drinking match with a Berserkir. Since the Centaurs never has there been better specimen of a 'half horse' tribe. To many of the settlers in other parts of the country, who emigrated from the decorous civilization of the East and South, these boisterous foreigners were objects of astonishment. When 'Canesteer' went abroad, the public soon found it out. On the Conhocton they were known to some as the Six Nations, and, to the amusement and wonder of young Europeans, would sometimes visit at Bath, being of a social disposition, and sit all day, 'singing, telling stories, and drinking grog, and never got drunk, nayther.' To the staid and devout they were Arabs,—cannibals. Intercourse between the scattered settlements of the colony was, of course, limited mainly to visits of necessity; but rumor took the fair fame of Canisteo in hand, and gave the settlement a notoriety through all the land which few 'rising villages,' even of the present day, enjoy. It was pretty well understood over all the country that beyond the mountains of Steuben, in the midst of the most rugged district of the wilderness, lay a corn growing valley, which had been taken possession of by some vociferous tribe, whether of Mamelukes or Tartars no one could precisely say, whose whooping and obstreperous laughter was heard far and wide, surprising the solitudes."—*McMasters's Hist. Steuben co.,* pp. 66–7–8.

[3] This co. sympathized to some extent in the hostile feeling that prevailed throughout the Holland Land Company's Purchase toward its European proprietors a few years since; but in no instance were the processes of the courts seriously impeded or effectually resisted, and juries have never refused to render for the proprietors as the facts warranted. There was doubtless little interest felt by the foreign owners in this estate beyond the ' of realizing the greatest sum possible from their lands; and the heavy burden of debts, interest, assignments, and back payments, perhaps not always borne with patience, have been gradually discharged, until but a comparatively small amount remains.

[4] Named in honor of Joseph Addison, the English author. Called "*Tuscarora*" by the early settlers.

The first settlement was made by Samuel Rice, in 1791.[1] The first church (M. E.) was organized in 1827, at East Hill.[2]

AVOCA[3]—was formed from Bath, Cohocton, Howard, and Wheeler, April 12, 1843. It is an interior town, lying N. W. of the center of the co. The surface is mostly a broken upland, divided into two ridges by the valley of the Conhocton. The declivities of the hills are steep, and their summits are about 400 feet above the river. The streams are Conhocton River and its tributaries Twelve Mile and Ten Mile Creeks from the N., and Bennetts and Neils Creeks from the S. W. The valley of the river is about 1¼ mile wide. The soil is a clayey and gravelly loam. **Avoca,** (p. v.,) situated in the valley of the Conhocton, is a station on the B., N. Y. & E. R. R. It contains 2 churches, an iron foundery, and a flouring mill. Pop. 301. **Wallace** (p. o.) is a station on the B., N. Y. & E. R. R. The first settlement was made in 1800, by Michael Buchanan.[4] There are 2 churches in town; Bap. and M. E.

BATH[5]—was formed March 18, 1796. Pulteney was taken off in 1808, a part of Howard and Cohocton in 1812, a part of Wheeler in 1820, Urbana in 1822, a part of Avoca in 1843, and a part of Cohocton in 1852. A part of Urbana was annexed April 26, 1839. It lies a little N. E. of the center of the co. Its surface is broken and hilly. The Conhocton Valley, extending S. E. through the center, divides the town into two nearly equal parts. The S. half is a hilly upland, and the N. half consists of a series of wide valleys broken by several steep and isolated hills. The streams are Conhocton River and its tributaries Five Mile and Mud Creeks from the N., and Campbells and Stocktons Creeks from the S. The Crooked Lake Valley extends N. W., and opens into the Conhocton Valley at the village of Bath, 340 feet above the lake. The soil is chiefly a gravelly and clayey loam, with a deep alluvium in the valleys. **Bath,** (p. v.,) incorp. April 12, 1816, is situated upon the N. bank of the Conhocton. It is a half-shire of the co. It commands the trade of a rich agricultural district and has a manufacturing business of considerable importance. It contains the co. buildings, 6 churches, 2 banks, and 2 newspaper offices. Pop. 2,012. **Kanona,**[6] (p. v.,) N. W. of Bath, a station on the B., N. Y. & E. R. R., contains 2 churches and 40 houses; and **Savona,**[7] (p. v.,) S. E. of Bath, a station on the same R. R., contains 2 churches and 232 inhabitants; **Sonora** (p. v.) contains 1 church and 20 houses. The first settlement was made at Bath Village, in 1793, by Charles Williamson, land agent for the Pulteney estate, with 15 families, mostly Scotch and Germans.[8] The first settled minister was Rev. John Niles, who moved to the town in 1807.[9]

BRADFORD[10]—was formed from "*Jersey,*" (now Orange, Schuyler co.,) April 20, 1836. A part was annexed to Orange, April 17, 1854. It lies near the center of the E. border of the co. Its surface is a hilly upland, broken by the valley of Mud Creek. Mud Lake, near the E. border, in Schuyler co., is 1,100 feet above tide, and the summits of the hills are about 600 feet above the lake. The soil is generally a gravelly and clayey loam and best adapted to pasturage. **Bradford,** (p. v.,) on the outlet of Mud Lake, in the N. E. part of the town, contains 1 church and a gristmill and has a pop. of 260. **South Bradford** (p. v.) contains 1 church and 20 houses.

[1] Among the first settlers were Elisha Gilbert, Saml. and Reuben Searls, John and Isaac Martin, Wm. Wombaugh, Wm. B. Jones, Israel Chauncey, Jesse Rowley, Amos Carr, and Amos Towsley. The first birth was that of Stephen Rice; the first marriage, that of Brown Gillespie and Miss Gilbert; and the first death, that of James Martin. Wm. Wombaugh built the first sawmill, in 1805, and the first gristmill, in 1806. The first store was kept by Samuel Smith, and the first inn by Reuben Searls.

[2] The census reports 8 churches in town; 3 M. E., Bap., F. W. Bap., Prot. E., Presb., and R. C.

[3] Probably named from Tom Moore's "Sweet Vale of Avoca." The early settlers called the place "*Buchanan,*" or the "*Eight Mile Tree.*"

[4] James Moore, Joel Collier, Asa Phillips, James McWhorter, Finley McClure, Daniel McKenzie, Abraham Towner, Jonathan Tilton, James Babcock, John Donahe, Richard and John Van Buskirk, Eleazur Tucker, —— Moody, Henry and Allen Smith, James Davis, and Samuel W. Burnham were among the first settlers. Michael Buchanan 2d was born in 1809; Michael Buchanan died in 1811; and James McWhorter and widow Buchanan were married in 1812. Eleazur Tucker built the first sawmill, and Jonathan Tilton the first gristmill, in 1825. Joel Collier kept the first inn, in 1808, and Alonzo Simmons the first store, in 1830.

[5] Named from Lady Bath, only child and heiress of Sir Wm. Pulteney, of London. She was succeeded July 15, 1808, by Sir John L. Johnstone, of Scotland, who appointed Robert Troup agent. Its Indian name was Tanighnaguanda.—*McMasters's Hist. Steuben, pp.* 111, 142.

[6] Formerly "*Kennedyville*" p. o., from a resident named Kennedy.   [7] Formerly "*Mud Creek*" p. o.

[8] Dugald and Charles Cameron, Thos. Metcalf, Hector McKenzie, Andrew Smith, Geo. McClure, James McDonald, Henry McElwee, James Reese; Robert Campbell, and William Dunn settled in the town in 1793; and Wm. Kersey, John Wilson, Geo. D. Cooper, Daniel McKenzie, and Gustavus and Brown Gillespie soon after. Charles Williamson Dunn, born in 1795, was the first male child born in town. The first saw and grist mills were built in 1793, by Charles Williamson; and the first inn was kept the same year, by John Metcalf.

The proprietors of the Pulteney estate indulged in visions of boundless wealth to result from the settlement of their lands. They supposed that the natural avenue to market from the rich "Genesee country" was down the Susquehanna, and that a city might be founded upon some of the headwaters of that stream which would command the entire trade of the West. After a survey of the region, the present site of Bath was selected as the location of the future city. Every inducement was held out to lure settlers; and for several years the markets of Bath proved a mine of wealth to the few who raised more grain than enough for their own use. Williamson erected a theater within a few years after the first settlement, in anticipation of the future metropolitan character of the place. A race course was also established, which for many years attracted sportsmen from all parts of the country. The golden visions of civic grandeur were never realized.

[9] The census reports 9 churches in town; 3 Presb., 2 Bap., 2 M. E., Prot. E., and R. C.   [10] Named from Gen. Bradford.

The first settlement was made in 1793, by Frederick Bartles and John Hervey, from New Jersey.[1] Rev. E. Sanford was the first preacher in town; and Rev. Mr. Lazelle, (Bap.,) who settled in town in 1816, was the first settled minister. There are 2 churches in town; Bap. and M. E.

CAMERON[2]—was formed from Addison, April 16, 1822. Thurston was taken off in 1844, and a part of Rathbone in 1856. It lies a little s. of the center of the co. Its surface is a high, rolling upland, broken by the deep valley of Canisteo River, which flows s. e. through near the center of the town. The soil is a clayey and gravelly loam. **Cameron**, (p. v.,) on the Canisteo, is a station on the Erie R. R. and contains 2 churches and 35 houses; **West Cameron** (p. v.) contains 1 church and 15 houses. **North Cameron** is a p. o. The first settlement was made in 1800, by Richard Hadley, Phones Green, Samuel Baker, and Ira Pratt.[3] Rev. Ira Bronson (M. E.) was the first settled preacher. The census reports 5 churches.[4]

CAMPBELL[5]—was formed from Hornby, April 15, 1831. It is an interior town, lying s. e. of the center of the co. Its surface consists of high, broken ridges, separated by the valleys of the streams. The declivities of the hills are generally steep and their summits are 300 to 500 feet above the valleys. The streams are Conhocton River, flowing s. e. through the w. part of the town, and its tributaries Wolf Run, McNutt Run, Meads Creek, Dry Run, and Stephens and Michigan Creeks. The valley of the river is about 1½ mi. wide. The soil is a clayey and gravelly loam upon the highlands and a rich alluvium in the valleys. **Campbelltown,** (p. v.,) on the Conhocton, is a station on the B., N. Y. & E. R. R., and contains 1 church, 3 sawmills, a flouring mill, 2 tanneries, and about 20 houses. **Curtis** is a station on the same R. R. Settlement was commenced in 1800.[6] The first church (Presb.) was organized in 1831; Rev. B. B. Smith was the first settled pastor. There are 2 churches in town; Presb. and M. E.

CANISTEO—was formed in March, 1796. A part of Troupsburgh was taken off in 1808, Hornellsville in 1820, and parts of Greenwood and Jasper in 1827. A part was annexed to Troupsburgh in 1818. It is an interior town, lying s. w. of the center of the co. The surface is mostly a hilly upland, broken by the deep valleys of the streams. Canisteo River flows eastward through the n. part of the town. Its valley is about ½ mi. wide and is bordered by steep hillsides 400 feet high. From the s. the river receives Bennetts and Col. Bills Creeks, which also flow through deep valleys bordered by steep hills. The soil is generally a clayey and gravelly loam. **Canisteo,** (p. v.,) on Bennetts Creek, in the w. part of the town, is a station on the N. Y. & Erie R. R., and contains 2 churches, a flouring mill, a tannery, and 60 houses; **Crosbyville,** (p. v.,) a station on the Erie R. R., contains 1 church and 20 houses. **Center Canisteo** (p. o.) is a hamlet of 10 houses. **Bennetts Creek** is a p. o. in the s. w. part. The first settlement was made in 1789, by Uriah Stephens, Sen., from Conn.[7] The first preacher—Rev. Geo. Spaulding—settled in town in 1805. There are 3 churches in town.[8]

CATON—was formed from *"Painted Post,"* (now Corning,) as "*Wormly,*" March 28, 1839, and its name was changed April 3, 1840. It is the s. e. corner town of the co. Its surface is a rolling upland, more nearly level than most towns in the co. A considerable portion is yet covered with forests. The streams are small brooks, flowing northward. The soil is a clayey and shaly loam. Lumber is extensively manufactured. **Caton,** (p. v.,) near the center of the town, contains 3 churches and 34 houses. A temporary settlement was made in town in 1814, by Joseph and Charles Wolcott; but the first permanent settlement was made in 1819, by Isaac Rowley, from Bradford co., Penn.[9] The first church (Presb.) was organized in 1832; and the Rev. Benj. Harron was the first settled pastor.[10]

[1] Among the first settlers were John Hemiup, Saml. S. Camp, Abram Rosenburg, Henry Switzer, John Schrinner, Thomas Rolls, Michael Scott, Daniel Bartholomew, Henry Axtelle, Ezekiel Sackett, and —— Smith. The first birth was that of a daughter of John Hervey, in 1799; and the first death, that of Mrs. Thos. Rolls, in Aug. 1803. Frederick Bartles built the first saw and grist mill, about 1795; and Frederick and Charles Bartles opened the first store, about 1800, and the first inn, in 1806. The first school was taught by —— Smith, in 1810.

[2] Named from Dugald Cameron, an agent of the Pulteney estate.—*McMasters's Hist. Steuben, p. 116.*

[3] Joseph Butler, John Sauter, and John Hollet were early settlers. The first gristmill was built by Saml. Baker; the first inn was kept by John Hollet, and the first store, by Andrew G. Erwin.   [4] 3 M. E., Presb., and Christian.

[5] Named from the Campbell family, who were early and prominent settlers.

[6] The first settlers were Samuel Calkins, Elias Williams, Joseph Wolcott, Rev. Robert Campbell and his son Archibald. The first birth was that of Bradford Campbell; the first marriage, that of Asa Milliken and Rachael Campbell; and the first death, that of Frederick Stewart, in 1806. Campbell & Stephens

built the first sawmill, and Campbell & Knox the first gristmill. Robert Campbell kept the first inn, and Frederick Stewart the first store.

[7] Col. John Stevens, Benj. Crosby, Arthur Erwin, Solomon Bennett, Joel Thomas, Uriah Stevens, jr., Jedediah Stephens, Wm. Baker, James Hadley, Joshua Stephens, W. S. Thomas, Isaac and Israel Jones, and Asa Downs were among the early settlers. The first birth was that of Oliver Stephens; the first marriage, that of Richard Crosby and Hannah Baker; and the first death, that of Henry Stephens. Solomon Bennett built the first gristmill and kept the first store; and Jedediah Stephens kept the first inn.

[8] Presb., M. E., and F. W. Bap.

[9] Stephen and Simeon Hurd settled in the town in 1821; Solomon Tabor in 1822; and E. P. Babcock, Edward Robbins, and Henry Miner in 1823. The first birth was that of Shepard Hurd; the first marriage, that of Oliver Woodworth and Elizabeth Hurd; and the first death, that of a child of John Rowe. Bennett Bruce built the first gristmill; Samuel Wormly kept the first inn, and W. D. Gilbert the first store, and Edward Robbins taught the first school.

[10] The census reports 3 churches; Presb., Bap., and M. E.

COHOCTON—was formed from Bath and Dansville, June 18, 1812. A part of Avoca was taken off in 1843, and a part of Wayland in 1848. It lies on the N. border of the co., w. of the center. The surface is mostly a hilly upland, separated into ridges by deep and narrow valleys. The principal streams are Conhocton River, flowing southerly through the center, and its tributaries. The soil is generally a slaty and gravelly loam. **Liberty,** (Cohocton p. o.,) on the Conhocton, is a station on the B., N. Y. & E. R. R. and contains 2 churches. Pop. 200. **North Cohocton** (p. v.) contains 1 church and 30 houses. **Bloods,**[1] a hamlet, is a station on the R. R., 1 mi. from North Cohocton. The first settlement was made in 1796, by Richard Hooker and Joseph Bivin.[2] Rev. Elisha Brownson, (Bap.,) the first settled minister, removed to the town in 1811. The census reports 4 churches in town; 3 M. E. and Presb.

CORNING[3]—was formed, as *"Painted Post,"*[4] March 18, 1796. Its name was changed March 31, 1852. Erwin and Hornby were taken off in 1826, and *"Wormly"* (now Caton) in 1839. A part was annexed to Erwin in 1856. It lies on the E. border of the co., s. of the center. The wide valley of Chemung River, extending N. w. and S. E. through the center of the town, and several lateral valleys, divide the uplands into rounded hills and narrow ridges. Its streams are Borden, Post, Narrows, Clump Foot, and Winfield Creeks, tributaries of Chemung River. The soil upon the hills is a heavy, slaty loam, and in the valleys a fine quality of sandy and gravelly loam, occasionally intermixed with clay. **Corning,** (p. ?.,) incorp. Sept. 6, 1848, is situated on the s. bank of Chemung River, in the w. part of the town. It is a half-shire of the co. The Chemung Canal, the Blossburg & Corning R. R., and the B., N. Y. & E. R. R. terminate here; and the village is an important station on the N. Y. & Erie R. R. It contains 5 churches, 2 newspaper establishments, 2 banks, a State arsenal, and several mills and manufacturing establishments, and commands an extensive and constantly increasing trade.[5] Pop. 3,626. **Knoxville,**[6] opposite Corning, contains 2 churches and a pop. of 628. **Gibson** lies on the N. bank of the Chemung, 1 mi. E. of Corning. Pop. 428. **Centerville** contains 25 houses. **East Painted Post** is a p. o. The first settlement was made near the village of Corning, in 1788, by Frederick Calkins and Benj. Eaton.[7] The first religious services were conducted by John Warren, in 1793. There are 7 churches in town.[8]

DANSVILLE[9]—was formed in March, 1796. Parts of Cohocton and Howard were taken off in 1812, a part of Wayland in 1848, and of Fremont in 1854. A part was annexed to Sparta in 1822, and a part of Cohocton was re-annexed April 26, 1834. It is the N. town upon the w. border of the co. The surface is mostly an upland, divided into ridges by the narrow valleys of small streams. The declivities of the hills are steep and their summits are 300 to 400 feet above the valleys. The streams are head branches of Canaseraga Creek, flowing N., and of Canisteo River, flowing s. The soil is a sandy and gravelly loam in the E. and N., and gravel underlaid by hardpan in the s. w.

---

1 Named from Calvin Blood. This is rendered an important station upon the R. R. from its connection with the Canandaigua Lake Route. A daily line of stages runs to Naples, at the head of the lake, and a steamer plies daily between the latter place and Canandaigua.

2 James and Aruna Woodward settled in the town not long after; Joseph Chamberlain, in 1805; and Saml. Chamberlain, Capt. Jonas Cleland, Joseph Shattuck, Horace Fowler, and —— Eddy, in 1806. Timothy Sherman, James Barnard, Saml. Rhodes, Jesse Atwood, Isaac Morehouse, and Chas. Burlinghame were also early settlers. The first marriage was that of Jos. Bivin and Sarah Hooker, in 1798; and the first birth, that of Bethiah Hooker, their child, in 1800. The first death was that of Richard Hooker, Feb. 10, 1801. Jonas Cleland built the first saw and grist mills, in 1808; and Jos. Shattuck kept the first inn, in 1809. Sophia Trumbull taught the first school, in 1810.

3 Named from Hon. Erastus Corning of Albany.

4 In the summer of 1779, a party of tories and Indians, under the command of a loyalist named McDonald, returned from an incursion into the Susquehanna settlements, bringing with them many of their number wounded. At the confluence of Tioga and Conhocton Rivers, Captain Montour, son of the famous Queen Catharine, a chief of great promise, died of his wounds. " His comrades buried him by the riverside, and planted above his grave a post on which were painted various symbols and rude devices. This monument was known throughout the Genesee Forests as ' *The Painted Post.*' It was a landmark well known to all the Six Nations, and was often visited by their braves and chieftains." This account of the origin of the Painted Post was given to Benj. Patterson, the hunter, by a man named Taggart, who was carried to Fort Niagara a prisoner by McDonald's party, and was a witness of the burial of Capt. Montour, or at least was in the encampment at the mouth of the Tioga at the time of his death. Col. Harper, of Harpersfield, the well known officer of the frontier militia of New York in the Revolution, informed

Judge Knox, of Knoxville, in this co., that the Painted Post was erected over the grave of a chief who was wounded at the battle of the "Hog-Back" and brought in a canoe to the head of the Chemung, where he died. It was well understood by the early settlers that this monument was erected in memory of some distinguished warrior who had been wounded in one of the border battles of the Revolution and afterward died at this place. The post stood for many years after the settlement of the co.; and the story goes that it rotted down at the butt, and was preserved in the bar-room of a tavern till about the year 1810 and then mysteriously disappeared. It is also said to have been swept away in a freshet.—*McMaster's Hist. of Steuben. Simm's Hist. Schoharie, p. 333.*

5 In 1852, 40,000 tons of Blossburg coal, brought by the Blossburg & Corning R. R., were transhipped at this place, and 50,000,000 feet of lumber were exported.

6 Named from Judge John Knox, of this town.

7 Benj. and Peleg Gorton. jr., Ephraim Patterson and his sons Ichabod and Stephen, Bradford Eggleston, Justus Wolcott, Elias, William, and Henry McCormick, Hezekiah Thurber, Jonathan Cook, Samuel Colgrove, and Eli and Eldad Mead settled in the town in 1790-91-92; Jonathan and Warren Rowley in 1794; James Turner and Caleb Wolcott in 1795; George McCullock and Benj. Patterson in 1796; and Nehemiah Hubbell in 1798. The first birth was that of James Calkins, Nov. 24, 1790; the first marriage, that of Benj. Gorton and Rachel Wolcott, in 1794; and the first death, that of Ichabod Patterson, in Aug. 1794. Ichabod Patterson built the first sawmill, and Jas. Henderson the first gristmill, both in 1793; Benj. Eaton kept the first store, in 1791, and Benj. Patterson the first inn, in 1798. The first school was taught by Samuel Colgrove, in 1793.

8 2 Bap., 2 M. E., Prot. E., Presb., and R. C.

9 Named from Daniel P. Faulkner, an early and spirited citizen, known as " Captain Dan."—*McMasters's Hist. Steuben Co., p. 300.*

Rogersville (South Dansville p. o.) contains 2 churches, an academy,[1] and a female seminary.[2] Pop. 200. **Burns,** a station on the B. & N. Y. City R. R., has about 15 houses. **Dotys Corners** is a p. o. The first settlement was made in 1804, by Isaac Sterling and Samuel Gibson.[3] The census reports 6 churches.[4]

ERWIN[5]—was formed from "*Painted Post,*" Jan. 27, 1826. Lindley was taken off in 1837 and a part of Corning was annexed in 1856. It lies w. of Corning, in the s. e. part of the co. Its surface is about equally divided between high, rolling uplands and the low valleys of streams. The summits of the hills are 400 to 600 feet above the valleys. Tioga and Canisteo Rivers unite in the s. e. part of the town, and Tioga and Conhocton Rivers in the n. e., forming the Chemung River. The valleys of these streams are 1 to 2 mi. wide. The soil upon the hills is a shaly and clayey loam, and in the valleys it is a fine quality of alluvium. Nearly three-fourths of the surface is yet covered with forests. The lumber trade is extensively pursued. **Painted Post,** (p. v.,) situated at the junction of Conhocton and Tioga Rivers, is a station on the Erie R. R. and the B., N. Y. & E. R. R. It contains 2 churches, a bank, an iron foundery and machine shop, a tannery, and a flouring mill.[6] Pop. 777. **Coopers Plains** (p. v.) is a station on the B., N. Y. & E. R. R. and contains 1 church. Pop. 293. Wm. Harris, an Indian trader, settled at Painted Post in 1787.[7] The census reports 4 churches.[8]

FREMONT[9]—was formed from Hornellsville, Dansville, Wayland, and Howard, Nov. 17, 1854. It is an interior town, lying n. w. of the center of the co. Its surface is a hilly upland, forming a part of the dividing ridge between Canisteo and Conhocton Rivers. Its streams are small brooks. The soil is chiefly a shaly loam, derived from the disintegration of the surface rocks. **Fremont Center** (Stephens Mills p. o.) and **Haskinville** (p. o.) are hamlets; and **Big Creek** is a p. o. The first settlement was made in 1812, by Job B. Rathbun, Amos Baldwin, and Sylvester Buck.[10] The first religious services were conducted by Rev. Mr. Ford, in 1814. There is but 1 church (M. E.) in town.

GREENWOOD—was formed from Troupsburgh and Canisteo, Jan. 24, 1827. West Union was taken off in 1845, and a part of Jasper was annexed in 1848. It lies upon the w. border of the co., s. of the center. Its surface is mostly a rolling upland. Bennetts Creek flows northerly through the e. part of the town, in a valley 400 to 600 feet below the summits of the hills. The soil is a gravelly and clayey loam. **Greenwood,** (p. v.,) on Bennetts Creek, contains 1 church and 35 houses; and **Rough and Ready** (p. v.) 12 houses. **West Greenwood** is a p. o. The first settlement was made in 1820, by Christian Cobey and John H., Ezra, and Phineas Stephens.[11] The census reports 3 churches.[12]

HARTSVILLE—was formed from Hornellsville, Feb. 7, 1844. It lies on the w. border of the co., s. of the center. The surface is a hilly upland, broken by several deep valleys. Purdy Creek flows e. through the n. part, and the valley of Bennetts Creek extends along the e. border. These creeks are bordered by steep hillsides 400 to 600 feet high. The soil is a shaly and clayey loam. **Hartsville Center,** (Purdy Creek p. o.,) on Purdy Creek, near the center of the town, contains 15 houses. The first settlement was made in 1809, by Benj. Brookins.[13] There is no church in town.

---

[1] The Rogersville Academy was organized in 1849, and the buildings were erected in 1852.

[2] The Rogersville Union Seminary.

[3] Among the first settlers were James, John, and Major Jones, Frederick Fry, William Ganong, Thos. and Nathaniel Brayton, Tisdale Haskin, Thos. and John Root, Joshua Healey, Charles Oliver, Joseph Phelps, Elisha Robinson, William C. Rogers, and Jesse Bridges. Robert Fuller built the first sawmill, in 1820, and Handy & Miller the first gristmill, in 1825. Isaac Sterling kept the first inn, in 1806. The first school was taught by James Jones, in 1811.

[4] 2 Bap., and 1 each Presb., M. E., Univ., and R. C.

[5] Named from Col. Arthur Erwin, of Bucks co., Penn., an officer in the Revolutionary War, by whom the township was purchased of Phelps and Gorham.

[6] One mi. w. of Painted Post is a saw, shingle, and planing mill, that gives employment to 75 men, and turns out 8,000,000 to 11,000,000 feet of lumber per annum.

[7] David Fuller, Eli Mead, and —— Van Nye settled in the town in 1791-92; and Samuel, Frank, and Arthur Erwin, Capt. Howell Bull, and John E. Evans, in 1800-01-02. Samuel Erwin built the first sawmill, in 1820, and the first gristmill, in 1823; and David Fuller kept the first inn, in 1792. The first school was taught by John E. Evans, in 1812.

[8] 2 Bap., Presb., and M. E.

[9] Named in honor of Col. John C. Fremont.

[10] John A. Buck, Joel Everett, and Danl. Atherton settled in the town in 1813-14; —— Taylor and Francis Drake, in 1815; and Solomon and Levi Gates, Robert Kilburg, Danl. Upson, Saml. Sharp, Nehemiah Luther, Lemuel Harding, Stephen Holden, and Edward Markham, in 1816. The first marriage was that of John A. Buck and Rebecca Baldwin, Aug. 24, 1815; the first birth, that of Charles E. Buck, Nov. 12, 1816; and the first death, that of Mrs. Amos Baldwin, Dec. 21, 1815. Danl. Upson built the first sawmill, in 1816, and the first gristmill, in 1819. The first school was taught by Lydia Everett, in 1819.

[11] Eleazar Woodward, John J. Hoyt, H. Carr, and Lewis Ordway settled in town in 1822. The first birth was that of Charles C. Stephens; the first marriage, that of Hiram Putnam and Lucinda Stephens; and the first death, that of Ezra Cobey. The first gristmill was built by Col. John Stephens; and the first inn and store were kept by Levi Davis. Sarah Carr taught the first school.

[12] Presb., Univ., and R. C.

[13] Joseph Purdy settled in the town in 1810; —— Blake in 1815; Thos. Williams, —— Satterlee, Joshua Davis, and —— Neff in 1818; William D. Burdick and Perry Potter in 1819; Daniel P. Carpenter, Frost Powell, Joseph Thompson, John and Robert G. Martin, and —— Hudson in 1822; and Casper Van Buskirk and Wm. Ellison in 1823. The first birth was that of Sarah A. Carpenter; the first marriage, that of Robert G. Martin and Mary A. Gleason; and the first death, that of an infant

HORNBY[1]—was formed from "*Painted Post*," (now·Corning,) Jan. 27, 1826. Campbell was taken off in 1831, and a part was annexed to Orange (Schuyler co.) April 11, 1842. It lies near the center of the **E.** border of the co., and its surface is mostly a high, rolling upland. The streams are Dry Run in the **N. W.**, and Post and Borden Creeks in the **S.**, all flowing in deep, narrow valleys. The soil is a shaly and clayey loam of good quality. **Hornby Forks** (Hornby p. o.) contains 2 churches, several manufactories, and 21 dwellings. The first settlement was made in 1814, by Asa and Uriah Nash, from Otsego co.[2] There are 4 churches in town.[3]

HORNELLSVILLE[4]—was formed from Canisteo, April 1, 1820. Hartsville was taken off in 1844, and a part of Fremont in 1854. It lies near the center of the **W.** border of the co. The surface is mostly a rolling upland, divided into two nearly equal parts by the Canisteo Valley. This valley is 1 to 2 mi. wide and is bordered by steep hills 400 to 500 feet high. Canacadea and Crosby Creeks, flowing through deep valleys from the **W.**, are tributaries of the Canisteo. The soil is generally a clayey and gravelly loam. **Hornellsville,** (p. v.,) situated at the junction of Canisteo River and Canacadea Creek, is an important station on the Erie R. R. and is the southern terminus of the B. & N. Y. C. R. R. It has 4 churches, 2 newspaper offices, a bank, and 2 flouring mills. Pop. 1,519. **Arkport,** (p. v.,) a station on the B. & N. Y. C. R. R., contains 1 church and about 50 houses. **Almond** is partly in this town.[5] The first settlement was made by Benj. Crosby, in 1792.[6] The census reports 6 churches.[7]

HOWARD—was formed from Bath and Dansville, June 18, 1812. A part of Avoca was taken off in 1843, and a part of Fremont in 1854. It is an interior town, lying a little **N. W.** of the center of the co. Its surface is mostly a rolling upland, forming a part of the dividing ridge between Conhocton and Canisteo Rivers. The streams are all small. In the **N. E.** part are 2 small ponds. The soil is generally a heavy clay loam. **Howard** (p. v.) contains 2 churches. Pop. 143. **Towlesville** (p. v.) contains 2 churches and 15 houses. **Buena Vista** (p. o.) and **Goffs Mills** (p. o.) are hamlets, and **South Howard** is a p. o. The first settlement was made in 1806, by Abraham Johnson.[8] There are 5 churches in town.[9]

JASPER[10]—was formed from Troupsburgh and Canisteo, Jan. 24, 1827, and a part was annexed to Greenwood in 1848. It is situated near the **S. W.** corner of the co. Its surface is a hilly and broken upland, the highest summits being nearly 2,000 feet above tide. The streams are small brooks. The soil is a slaty, gravelly, and clayey loam. **Jasper Four Corners** (Jasper p. o.) contains 2 churches. Pop. 222. **Jasper Five Corners** contains 15 houses. **West Jasper** and **South Hill** are p. offices. Settlement was commenced in 1807, by Nicholas Botzman, Ebenezer Spencer, and William Wooley.[11] The first church (Presb.) was organized in 1827; and the Rev. Geo. Howell was the first preacher. The census reports 5 churches.[12]

LINDLEY[13]—was formed from Erwin, May 12, 1837. It lies upon the **S.** border of the co., **E.** of the center. Its surface is a hilly upland, broken by the deep valley of Tioga River, which extends centrally through the town. The summits of the hills are 400 to 600 feet above the valley, and most of them are covered with forests. The valley is about 1 mi. wide and is bordered by steep hillsides. The soil upon the hills is a heavy, shaly loam, and in the valleys a rich alluvium. Three-fourths of the surface is still covered with forests. Lumbering is extensively pursued. **Lindleytown,** (p. v.,) on Tioga River, is a station on the B. & C. R. R. and contains 15 dwell-

---

child of Ebenezer Mather,—all in 1823. Daniel P. Carpenter opened the first store, in 1825, and built the first sawmill, in 1828; and Henry Frisbee kept the first tavern, in 1849. The first school was taught by Miss Z. A. Purdy, in 1826.

[1] Named from John Hornby, an English landholder to a large extent in this and other western cos.

[2] Jesse Platt, John Robbins, and Edward Stubbs settled in the town in 1815; John St. John, Amasa Stanton, James S. and Hiram Gardner, Chester Knowlton, and Aden Palmer in 1815–16; Benj. Gardner, Isaac Goodell, Aaron Harwood, and John Sayer in 1818. The first birth was that of George Stanton; the first marriage, that of John Bidler and Miss Platt, in 1816; and the first death, that of John Stanton. Ezra Shaw kept the first inn; Hon. A. B. Dickinson, the first store; and —— La Fevre built the first mill. James C. Leach taught the first school.

[3] Bap., Christian, Presb., and Wes. Meth.

[4] Named from Hon. Geo. Hornell, one of the early settlers.

[5] See page ——.

[6] Elias Stephens and Geo. Hornell settled in the town in 1793; Elijah Stephens in 1794; Christopher Hurlbut and Nathan Cary in 1795; John and Hugh Carney in 1796; Reuben Crosby in 1797; and James Jones in 1800. The first birth was that of William Stephens, in Dec. 1792; the first marriage, that of Reuben Crosby and Jenny McQueen, in 1799; and the first death,

that of a child of Judge Hornell. Judge Hornell built the first saw and grist mills, and kept the first store and inn. The first school was taught by Abigail Hurlbut, in 1796.

[7] 2 Presb., Prot. E., Bap., M. E., and R. C.

[8] Reuben and Abraham Smith, Abel Bullard, Jacob and Thos. Bennett, Charles McConnell, Simeon McMurty, and —— Colgrove settled in the town in 1808; Samuel Baker, Joel Bullard, Benj. Bennett, Ephraim Rumsey, Wm. Allen, Daniel N. Bennett, Jonas and Seth Rice, and Nathan Cory in 1810–11; and Simeon Bacon, Wm. Goff, Israel Baldwin, and Rufus Halsey in 1812. Arethusa Bullard was born in 1809, and Mrs. Rowley died the same year,—the first birth and death in town. Henry Kennedy built the first sawmill, in 1809; James Vaughn, the first grist-mill, in 1810; and Benj. Bennett kept the first inn, in 1816.

[9] 2 Bap., and 1 each Presb., M. E., and Ref. Presb.

[10] Named from Sergeant Jasper, noted for his courage at the battle of Fort Moultrie, S. C., June 28, 1776.

[11] Adam Botzman and Andrew Craig were also early settlers. The first birth was that of Sally Botzman; and the first marriage, that of Samuel Gray and Polly Simpson. Nicholas Botzman was the first innkeeper. Amanda Smith taught the first school.

[12] Bap., Presb., Christian, M. E., and Wes. Meth.

[13] Named in honor of Col. Eleazur Lindley.

ings. **Erwin Center** is a R. R. station and hamlet upon the river, near the N. border of the town. The first settlement was made in 1790, by Col. Eleazur Lindley, from N. J., the original proprietor of the town, who located upon the Tioga Flats.[1]

PRATTSBURGH[2]—was formed from Pulteney, April 12, 1813, and a part of Wheeler was taken off in 1820. It is centrally situated upon the N. border of the co. Its surface is a hilly upland, broken by the valleys of several small streams flowing in a general s. w. direction. The principal streams are Five Mile, Ten Mile, and Twelve Mile Creeks. The valley at Prattsburgh Village is 1,400 feet above tide, and the hills are 300 to 400 feet higher. The soil is a gravelly and clay loam. **Prattsburgh** (p. v.) was incorp. Dec. 7, 1848. It contains the Franklin Academy,[3] 2 churches, and several manufacturing establishments.[4] Pop. about 600. **Rikers Hollow** (p. o.) is a hamlet. The first settler was Jared Pratt, who came in 1801 and for 2½ years was the only inhabitant.[5] The first religious services were held at the house of Jared Pratt, by Rev. John Niles, in the fall of 1803.[6]

PULTENEY[7]—was formed from Bath, Feb. 12, 1808. Prattsburgh was taken off in 1813, and a part of Urbana in 1848. It lies upon the w. shore of Crooked Lake, and is the N. E. corner town of the co. The surface is a rolling upland, 700 to 900 feet above the level of the lake. The declivities along the lake shore are broken by numerous narrow ravines formed by small streams. The soil is chiefly a shaly and gravelly loam, and in some parts near the lake it is clayey. **Harmonyville** (Pulteney p. o.) contains 2 churches and 20 houses; and **Bluffport** (South Pulteney p. o.) 20 houses. **Peltonville** (p. o.) is a hamlet. **Gulicksville**, a landing on the lake, has a storehouse and 8 houses. Settlement commenced in 1802.[8] Rev. Ephraim Eggleston, the first settled preacher, removed to the town in 1805. The census reports 6 churches.[9]

RATHBONE[10]—was formed from Addison, Cameron, and Woodhull, March 28, 1856. It is an interior town, lying s. of the center of the co. Its surface consists of a high, rolling upland, broken by the valleys of Canisteo River and a branch of Tuscarora Creek. The upland is 300 to 400 feet above the valleys. Naked and precipitous ledges of rock crop out on the hillsides along the valleys. The soil is a clayey and shaly loam, and in the valleys alluvium. **Rathbone-ville**, (p. v.,) on Canisteo River, is a station on the Erie R. R. and contains 1 church, a flouring mill, and 33 houses. **West Addison** (p. o.) and **Cameron Mills** (p. o.) are hamlets. The first settlements were made in 1793–95.[11] There are 2 M. E. churches in town.

THURSTON[12]—was formed from Cameron, Feb. 28, 1844. It is an interior town, lying just s. E. of the center of the co. Its surface is mostly a high, broken upland, forming a portion of the dividing ridge between Conhocton and Canisteo Rivers. The summits of the hills are 500 to 600 feet above the river valleys. The streams are Stocktons Creek, in the N. w., and Michigan Creek, in the s., flowing in deep, narrow ravines bordered by steep hillsides. The soil is a shaly and gravelly loam. **Merchantville**, in the E., **Bonny Hill**, (p. o.,) in the N. E., and **Rising-ville**, (p. o.,) in the w., are hamlets. **Thurston** and **South Thurston** are p. offices. The first settlers were William Smith, Luke Bonny, and Anderson Carpenter, at Bonny Hill, in

---

[1] Col. Lindley served with the Jersey Blues during the Revolutionary War. In his migration to his new home he was accompanied by his two sons Saml. and Eleazur, his son-in-law Ezekiel Mulford and John Seeley, and a man named David Cook. The first child born was Eliza Mulford, Aug. 10, 1792; the first marriage, that of David Cook, jr. and Elizabeth Cady; and the first death, that of Col. Eleazur Lindley, in June, 1794. Joseph Miller taught the first school, near the Penn. line, in 1793; the widow of Col. Lindley kept the first inn, on the w. bank of the river; and John P. Ryers, the first store. The first sawmill was erected by Col. Lindley. There is no church, no hotel, nor place where liquor is sold in the town.

[2] Named from Capt. Joel Pratt, one of the first settlers.

[3] For many years this academy has enjoyed a deservedly high reputation.

[4] A foundery, a tannery and a flouring mill.

[5] Rev. John Niles, David Buell, Saml. Tuthill, and Capt. Joel Pratt came into town in 1803; William P. Curtis, Pomeroy Hull, and Salisbury Burton in 1804; Noah Niles, Cyril Ward, Aaron Bull, Enoch Niles, Harmon Fowler, Rufus Blodgett, and Stephen Hall, in 1805. They were all originally from New England. The first child born was Mariette Pratt, in 1802; the first death, a daughter of Wm. P. Curtis, drowned, in 1804; and the first marriage, that of Isaac Pardee and Patty Waldo, in 1806. The first school was taught in a church by Horace Bull, in 1806–07; the first inn was kept by Aaron Bull, the same year; the first mill was erected on Five Mile Creek, by Robert Porter. Capt. Joel Pratt was a large proprietor of the town; and the first set-

tlement was conducted wholly under his encouragement, advice, and direction.

[6] The census reports 6 churches; 2 Bap., 2 M. E., Cong., and Christian.

[7] Named from Sir Wm. Pulteney, former owner of the Pulteney Tract.

[8] The first settlers were Saml. Miller, John Van Camp, G. F. Fitzsimmons, and John Block. James and George Simms, Henry Hoffman, Abraham Bennett, and Shadrach Norris settled in the town in 1805; and Saml. and Nathaniel Wallis, John Ells, Wm. White, James Daily, Erastus Glass, Harmon Emmons, and Seth Pierce in 1806. The first marriage was that of Christopher Tomer and Jane Miller, in 1809; and the first death, that of a child of Jas. Daily, in 1806. Melchior Waggoner built the first sawmill, in 1810, and the first gristmill, in 1814. Shadrach Norris kept the first inn, in 1807; and Augustus Tyler, the first store, in 1808. The first school was taught by Polly Wentworth, in 1808. [9] 2 Bap., 2 M. E., Cong., and Presb.

[10] Named from Gen. Ransom Rathbone, who settled in the town in 1842.

[11] James Hadley and Wm. Benham were the first settlers Among the early settlers were Isaac and Jonathan Tracy, Martin Young, Wm. Morey, Moses Powers, Zephaniah Townsend, Thos. Maybury, and Saml. Colgrove. Isaac Tracy built the first sawmill, in 1806; Lemuel Benham kept the first inn, in 1804, and Gen. Rathbone the first store in 1842.

[12] Named from Wm. R. Thurston, a landholder residing in N. Y. or vicinity.

1813.[1] The first religious association (M. E.) was formed in 1814; Rev. Parker Buell was the first preacher.[2]

TROUPSBURGH[3]—was formed from "*Middletown*" (now Addison) and Canisteo, Feb. 12, 1808. ~~Parts of Greenwood and Jasper were taken off in 1827, and a part of Woodhull in 1828.~~ A part of Canisteo was annexed April 4, 1818. It lies on the s. border of the co., w. of the center. Its surface is principally a hilly upland, broken by the deep valleys of small streams. The highest summits are 2,500 feet above tide and are the highest points in the co. Troups Creek, flowing s., is the principal stream. The soil is a slaty and clayey loam. **Troupsburgh Center,** (Troups-burgh p. o.,) on Troups Creek, near the center of the town, contains an academy[4] and 20 dwellings; **South Troupsburgh** (p. v.) contains 16 dwellings. **East Troupsburgh,** (p. o.,) **West Troupsburgh,** (p. o.,) and **Young Hickory** (p. o.) are hamlets. The pioneer settler was Samuel B. Rice, from Conn., who located E. of the center of the town in 1805.[5] The first religious association (M. E.) was formed at the house of Samuel Cady, by Rev. Parker Buell, first preacher. The census reports 5 churches.[6]

URBANA—was formed from Bath, April 17, 1822. A part was annexed to Bath in 1839; a part of Wheeler was annexed May 3, 1839, and a part of Pulteney April 12, 1848. It lies at the head of Crooked Lake, N. E. of the center of the co. Its surface is divided by Pleasant Valley (a continuation of Crooked Lake Valley) into two series of highlands, rising 800 to 1,000 feet above the lake. Cold Spring Creek takes its rise in this valley and flows N. E. to the lake. The soil in the valleys is alluvial, and on the hilltops a heavy, gravelly loam. From their sheltered situation, the slopes of the hills descending to the s. and E. are finely adapted to the culture of the grape.[7] The town is noted for the production of a superior quality of fine wool. **Hammondsport,** (Urbana p. o.,) at the head of Crooked Lake, was incorp. June 16, 1856. It contains 2 churches and several manufacturing establishments. A daily line of steamboats plies between this place and Penn Yan. Pop. 560. **North Urbana,** (p. v.,) in the N. E. part of the town, contains 2 churches and 20 houses. **Cold Spring** is a hamlet; and **Mount Washington,** in the S. E., is a p. o. William Aulls and his son Ephraim, from Penn., settled at Pleasant Valley in 1793.[8] Elder Ephraim Sanford (Bap.) preached the first sermon, at the house of Mr. Baker, in 1795.[9]

WAYLAND[10]—was formed from Cohocton and Dansville, April 12, 1848. A part of Fremont was taken off in 1854. It is the most western town upon the N. border of the co. Its surface is an upland, rolling in the N. and moderately hilly in the s. It forms a portion of the watershed between Susquehanna River and Lake Ontario; and its highest summits are 1,600 to 1,800 feet above tide. The streams are small creeks and brooks. Loon and Mud Lakes are situated in a valley in the s. part of the town, and their waters flow in opposite directions. The outlet of the former is subterranean for half a mi.; and where it comes to the surface it is in sufficient volume to form a valuable mill stream. The soil in the N. is gravel and muck, and in the s. a shaly loam. **Way-land,** (Wayland Depôt p. o.,) in the N. E. part of the town, contains 40 dwellings. It is a station on the B., N. Y. & E. R. R. **Perkinsville,** 2 mi. s. w. of Wayland, contains 2 churches and 30 dwellings. **Patchins Mills** is a hamlet. **Loon Lake** is a p. o. The first settlement was made in 1806–07, by Thos. Bowles and John H. Miller.[11] The census reports 3 churches.[12]

---

[1] Amos Dickinson settled in 1814; and Joseph Fluent at Bonny Hill in 1817. The first settlers at Aldrich settlement were William Jack, Samuel Fisk, and Thomas Aldrich, in 1823. The first child born was Irena Smith, in 1813; the first marriage, that of Joseph Fluent and Fanny Dickinson, in 1818; and the first death, that of Anderson Carpenter, killed by the falling of a tree, in 1817. The first school was taught at Bonny Hill, by Caroline Vinan, in 1818; the first store was kept by Harlow Sears, at Merchantville. No tavern was ever kept in the town, and no license was ever granted to sell liquor.

[2] The census reports 4 churches; 2 M. E., Bap., and Christian.

[3] Named from Robert Troup, of N. Y., general agent of the Pulteney estate.—*Turner's Phelps and Gorham Purchase, p.* 279.

[4] This institution has an average attendance of about 60 pupils.

[5] Peter Young and Peter Dalson, from Addison, settled near Mr. Rice, in 1806; Lieut. Reynolds and Jonathan Rogers settled at the same place in 1809, Geo. Martin in 1810, and James Works in 1811. The first child born was Polly Young; the first marriage, that of Zebulon Tubbs and Sarah Rice; and the first death, that of Jeremiah Martin. Abner Thomas taught the first school, a little E. of Troupsburgh Village; Lieut. Reynolds kept the first inn, 4 mi. from the Center, and Ichabod C. Leach the first store, 2 mi. from the Center. Geo. Martin erected the first gristmill, at Troupsburgh Village. [6] 2 Bap., 2 M. E., and F. W. Bap.

[7] In 1857, 30 acres were devoted to vineyards; and the success of the experiment was so great that the number of acres was doubled in 1858. There are about 2,000 acres in town with the S. and E. inclination adapted to this purpose.

[8] Samuel Baker, Eli Read, and William Barney settled in Pleasant Valley in 1794; and Capt. Amos Stone, Capt. John Shether, James Shether, and Richard Daniels in 1795. These settlers were from New England, most of them from Conn. They had served through the Revolutionary War, some of them with distinction as officers; and all were inured to the privations and dangers incident to pioneer settlement. The first child born was Saml. Baker, jr.; the first marriage, that of Jonathan Barney and Polly Aulls, in 1794; and the first death, that of John Phillips, in Sept. of the same year. Eliphalet Norris taught the first school, in 1795, at Pleasant Valley; Caleb Chapman kept the first inn, at N. Urbana; Henry A. Townsend the first store, at Cold Spring, in 1815. John Shether built the first sawmill, in Pleasant Valley, in 1795; and Gen. Geo. McClure, the first gristmill, at Cold Spring, in 1802.

[9] The census reports 6 churches; 2 Bap., and 1 each Presb., M. E., Prot. E., and R. C.

[10] Named from Rev. Dr. Francis Wayland, of R. I.

[11] Among the early settlers were Adam Zimmerman, David Brown, —— Kaizier, Stephen Hicks, Thos. Begole, Solomon, James, and Elisha Brownson, Isaac Willie, Walter and Dr. Warren Patchin, Dennis Hess, Benj. Perkins, and Samuel Draper. The first sawmill was built by Benj. Perkins; and the first gristmill, by Dugald Cameron and Abijah Fowler, in 1816. Saml. Taggart kept the first inn, in 1827; and James L. Monier, the first store, in 1830. The first school was taught by Thos. Wilbur, in 1811.

[12] Evang. Luth., Union, and R. C.

WAYNE[1]—named in honor of Gen. Anthony Wayne—was formed, as "*Frederickstown,*" March 18, 1796. Its name was changed April 6, 1808. Reading (Schuyler co.) was taken off in 1806, Orange (Schuyler co.) in 1813, and Barrington (Yates co.) and Tyrone (Schuyler co.) in 1822. A part was annexed to Tyrone April 17, 1854. It is situated upon Crooked Lake, on the E. border of the co. Its surface is a rolling upland, 400 to 600 feet high, descending abruptly to the lake. Little Lake is a beautiful sheet of water lying along the E. border. The soil is a gravelly and slaty loam underlaid by hardpan. **Wayne,**[2] (p. v.,) on the line of Tyrone, (Schuyler co.,) contains 3 churches and 40 houses. **Wayne Four Corners** is a p. o. The first settlement was made in 1791, by Zephaniah Hoff, Henry Mapes, Widow Jennings, and Solomon Wixson.[3] Rev. Ephraim Sanford (Bap.) was one of the first settlers, and for many years the only clergyman in town. There are 2 churches in town; M. E. and Union.

WEST UNION—was formed from Greenwood, April 25, 1845. It is the s. w. corner town of the co. Its surface is a broken and hilly upland, the highest summits being 2,000 to 2,400 feet above tide. A large part of the town is yet covered with forests. Bennetts Creek is the principal stream. The soil is a heavy, slaty loam. Lumbering is extensively pursued. **Rexville** (p. o.) and **Wileysville** (p. o.) are hamlets. **West Union** is a p. o. The first settler was Abraham V. Olmsted, who located at Rexville in 1822.[4] The first church (M. E.) was formed at Rexville in 1831. There are 2 churches in town; Bap. and M. E.

WHEELER[5]—was formed from Bath and Prattsburgh, Feb. 25, 1820. A part of Avoca was taken off in 1843, and a part of Urbana in 1839. It is an interior town, lying N. E. of the center of the co. Its surface is a high, rolling upland, broken by the valleys of Five Mile and Ten Mile Creeks and of several small lateral streams. The soil is a shaly and clayey loam, well adapted to both grazing and tillage. **Mitchellville** (p. v.) contains 20 houses; and **Wheeler Center** (Wheeler p. o.) 1 church and 15 houses. The first settlement was made in 1799, by Capt. Silas Wheeler, from Albany co.[6] Rev. Ephraim Eggleston (Bap.) conducted the first religious services, in 1802. There are 2 churches in town; Presb. and M. E.

WOODHULL[7]—was formed from Troupsburgh and Addison, Feb. 18, 1828. A part of Rathbone was taken off in 1856. It is the central town upon the s. border of the co. Its surface is a hilly upland, a considerable portion of which is yet covered with forests. Tuscarora Creek, flowing E. through the northerly part of the town, is the principal stream. The soil is a clayey and gravelly loam. Lumbering is carried on to some extent. **Newville,** (Woodhull p. o.,) on Tuscarora Creek, contains 3 churches and several manufacturing establishments. Pop. 215. **Hedgesville** contains 10 houses. The first settlement was made in 1805, by Stephen Dolson, Daniel Johnson, Patrick Breakhill, Bethuel Tubbs, and Samuel B. Rice.[8] The first church (Presb.) was organized in 1830; and the Rev. Mr. Pomeroy was the first pastor. There are 4 churches in town.[9]

---

[1] Its former name was from Frederick Bartles.—*McMasters's Hist. Steuben Co., p.* 181.

[2] Locally known as "Wayne Hotel."

[3] Enos, Joseph, and James Silsbee, Abraham Hendricks, Joshua Smith, John Holdridge, Elijah Reynolds, and Ephraim Tyler were among the early settlers. The first birth was that of Elizabeth Wixson, Nov. 6, 1793; and the first marriage, that of Ephraim Sanford, jr. and Julia Hoff. Jas. Silsbee kept the first store, and Enos Silsbee the first inn. The first school was taught by Nathaniel Frisbee, in 1797.

[4] The late settlement of this town was owing to the fact that a large share of the land was owned in England and by heirs under age. Among the first settlers were Fred. Hauber, Wm. Burger, and Wm. Bray, from Delaware co., who came in 1823 and located near Rexville. John Wiley, Wm. Fisher, and Benj. Wilks settled at Wileyville in 1849. Uriah Stevens taught the first school; Chas. Rexford kept the first inn, and Walter B. Olmsted the first store, at Rexville. John Wiley built the first saw and grist mill, in 1849–50.

[5] Named from Capt. Silas Wheeler, the first settler. Capt. Wheeler served during the Revolutionary War, and was at the attack on Quebec and stood near Montgomery when he fell. He was 4 times taken prisoner during the war. He died in 1828, at the age of 78.

[6] Nathan Rose, Wm. Holmes, and Turner Gardner settled in town in 1799; Col. Jonathan Barney and Thos. Aulls in 1800; Philip Murtle in 1802; and Otto F. Marshall, and others, named Bear, Ferval, and Rifle, in 1803. William, son of Jonathan Barney, was born Nov. 1, 1801, and died Dec. 1, 1802,—the first birth and death in town. Hon. Grattan H. Wheeler was a party to

the first marriage. Capt. Wheeler built the first sawmill, in 1802; and Geo. W. Taylor the first gristmill, in 1803–04. John Beals kept the first inn, in 1820; and Cornelius Younglove, the first store, in 1835. The first school was taught by Uriel Chapin.

"Capt. Wheeler's first trip to mill is worthy of record. There were, at the time when he had occasion to 'go to mill,' three institutions in the neighborhood where grinding was done,—at the Friends' settlement, at Bath, and at Naples. The millstones of Bath had suspended operations,—there being nothing there to grind, as was reported. Capt. Wheeler made a cart, of which the wheels were sawn from the end of a log of curly maple: the box was of corresponding architecture. He started for Naples before the oxen with axes and chopped a road, and the clumsy chariot came floundering through the bushes behind, bouncing over the logs and snubbing the stumps, like a ship working through an ice field. The first day they reached a point a little beyond the present village of Prattsburgh, a distance of six miles from their starting point, and the second moored triumphantly at the mill at Naples."—*McMasters's Hist. Steuben Co., pp.* 195–196.

[7] Named in honor of Gen. Nathaniel Woodhull, of the Revolution.

[8] Caleb Smith settled in the town in 1808. The first birth was that of Polly Smith; the first marriage, that of Levi Rice and Cynthia Tubbs; and the first death, that of Benj. Tubbs. Caleb Smith built the first gristmill, in 1805; Ichabod S. Leach kept the first inn, and Josiah Tubbs the first store. The first school was taught by Abner Thomas.

[9] 2 Bap., Presb., and R. C.

Acres of Land, Valuation, Population, Dwellings, Families, Freeholders, Schools, Live Stock, Agricultural Products, and Domestic Manufactures, of Steuben County.

NAMES OF TOWNS.	ACRES OF LAND.		VALUATION OF 1858.			POPULATION.		No. of Dwellings.	No. of Families.	Freeholders.	SCHOOLS.	
	Improved.	Unimproved.	Real Estate.	Personal Property.	Total.	Males.	Females.				No. of Districts.	Children taught.
Addison...............	9,375	25,862	$428,955	$92,270	$521,225	1,602	1,554	518	565	236	14	1,228
Avoca.................	13,011	8,661	433,627	82,073	515,700	926	860	331	359	286	11	808
Bath..................	30,775	24,319	1,553,476	579,191	2,132,667	3,027	3,004	1,068	984	860	26	2,305
Bradford.............	7,264	5,798	214,087	23,543	237,630	642	643	238	245	189	6	655
Cameron..............	10,871	19,798	219,740	63,257	282,997	916	919	335	343	288	10	590
Campbell.............	8,242	15,297	329,630	6,900	336,530	816	726	287	292	226	7	518
Canisteo.............	9,184	22,300	393,381	41,671	435,052	1,058	927	352	372	271	11	852
Caton.................	7,712	14,453	296,405	21,655	318,060	837	748	274	291	267	11	626
Cohocton.............	11,580	14,441	453,101	64,792	517,893	1,126	1,116	444	444	297	11	875
Corning..............	7,803	26,482	1,308,282	113,689	1,421,971	3,275	3,059	1,037	1,160	514	17	2,162
Dansville............	20,031	12,881	601,936	58,414	660,350	1,077	1,083	401	413	287	14	791
Erwin.................	4,097	18,574	535,668	74,250	609,918	944	875	334	339	174	5	741
Fremont..............	10,733	7,745	247,511	78,624	326,135	571	548	221	233	210	9	457
Greenwood...........	10,065	11,560	176,045	94,231	270,276	622	602	237	237	233	11	557
Hartsville...........	7,189	13,632	158,025	37,143	195,168	584	526	195	212	177	9	467
Hornby...............	13,151	13,177	254,783	40,266	295,049	756	654	262	274	239	12	565
Hornellsville........	8,745½	9,216½	865,680	45,788	911,468	1,950	1,893	689	744	477	13	1,522
Howard...............	20,534½	17,657	410,548	120,476	531,024	1,365	1,304	502	512	458	16	1,083
Jasper................	13,227	15,853	230,172	75,741	305,913	881	887	341	344	299	16	787
Lindsley.............	3,729	19,874	274,701	5,300	280,001	369	335	142	143	59	4	313
Prattsburgh..........	23,136	11,858	556,801	102,270	659,071	1,301	1,281	509	536	440	16	1,072
Pulteney.............	15,730	4,878½	449,787	39,318	489,105	752	808	305	309	275	10	628
Rathbone[a]..........			269,491	28,934	298,425						10	528
Thurston.............	5,408½	15,083	233,276	12,918	246,194	480	445	171	177	157	10	440
Troupsburgh.........	16,545½	17,947	184,531	132,210	316,741	1,042	937	361	373	322	15	967
Urbana...............	17,126	8,656	535,978	30,009	565,987	966	972	361	363	288	12	822
Wayland..............	12,921½	11,364½	210,394	1,200	211,594	1,344	1,307	375	462	332	9	1,060
Wayne................	9,813	3,505	234,142	34,681	268,823	467	461	174	183	143	5	311
West Union...........	7,265	14,268	88,276	11,628	99,904	617	597	214	233	215	9	530
Wheeler..............	14,334	14,246	299,709	59,196	358,905	717	659	253	256	197	10	632
Woodhull.............	11,851½	18,894	240,932	114,785	355,717	1,159	1,046	420	425	294	15	825
Total............	361,450	438,250½	12,689,070	2,286,423	14,975,493	32,189	30,776	11,351	11,823	8,710	354	25,817

NAMES OF TOWNS.	LIVE STOCK.					AGRICULTURAL PRODUCTS.					DAIRY PRODUCTS.		Domestic Cloths in Yards.
	Horses.	Working Oxen and Calves.	Cows.	Sheep.	Swine.	Winter.	Spring.	Tons of Hay.	Bushels of Potatoes.	Bushels of Apples.	Pounds of Butter.	Pounds of Cheese.	
Addison..............	332	937	532	2,448	767	5,979	40,414	2,037	12,004	11,235	56,550	3,640	1,342
Avoca................	600	1,074	854	5,580	1,087	12,595	48,421½	2,044	6,444	23,412	77,063	43,446	773½
Bath.................	1,368	2,578	2,042	12,169	2,350	26,477	100,853½	5,931½	14,379	25,271	118,424	13,630	3,069
Bradford............	330	630	501	3,493	731	4,908½	36,674	1,354	5,726	8,042	37,130	450	978
Cameron.............	418	1,023	639	2,847	619	4,229	22,472½	1,952½	3,864	4,644	69,703	2,100	1,186
Campbell............	326	947	616	2,036	530	5,499	40,412	2,241	5,420	11,896	60,155	1,976	776
Canisteo............	377	1,192	690	1,914	816	13,912½	28,931½	1,884½	6,964	9,893	52,040	500	1,676
Caton...............	341	1,072	627	2,344	610	3,563	60,671	2,242	20,607	6,048	61,156	3,654	736
Cohocton............	536	995	621	3,255	807	13,757	43,334	1,466½	7,531	17,095	67,245	6,231	591
Corning.............	395	570	678	828	901	8,440	52,461	1,684	10,309	8,828	26,316	500	105
Dansville...........	763	1,247	980	5,469	1,358	24,509	50,325	2,064	13,445	14,294	93,541	18,539	1,503
Erwin...............	215	433	385	1,495	553	4,766	35,739½	943	7,185	3,745	29,906	6,000	
Fremont.............	502	683	501	1,715	549	4,172	37,942	1,022	8,985	14,210	50,075	5,775	52
Greenwood...........	300	1,197	788	1,701	420	1,866	31,682	1,049	5,460	3,978	79,900	1,100	1,053
Hartsville..........	229	686	427	3,007	382	3,712	17,254	1,010	3,505	5,525	37,045	3,290	689
Hornby..............	382	1,064	663	3,365	574	3,248	83,162	4,203	22,465	14,201	59,885	1,915	1,461
Hornellsville.......	359	890	530	2,522	646	10,478	24,001½	1,786	5,311	6,217	50,150	1,204	794
Howard..............	810	1,626	1,137	6,998	1,338	6,596	84,977½	2,476¾	13,539	24,461	129,746	13,690	2,689½
Jasper..............	496	1,453	802	3,385	726	2,814	48,078	2,011	7,262	4,298	93,168	3,335	2,435
Lindsley............	121	519	327	967	386	1,326	29,046	948	6,933	5,905	20,962	100	37
Prattsburgh.........	856	1,391	929	8,093	1,022	10,319½	70,342½	2,953½	8,748	14,790	104,620	7,717	1,188
Pulteney............	694	1,272	755	4,968	1,073	9,975	38,218	2,050	5,268	8,347	86,971	5,419	758
Rathbone[a].........													
Thurston............	170	449	295	1,354	331	2,921½	15,416½	1,231	3,055	3,368	32,590	665	1,148
Troupsburgh.........	457	1,984	14	5,340	750	2,519½	38,894½	2,621½	8,170	8,518	103,775	2,816	3,599½
Urbana..............	580	1,117	671	9,946	1,051	11,145	35,587½	2,252	4,626	12,335	62,350	23,500	846
Wayland.............	504	1,031	780	1,805	1,005	12,252	33,755	1,567½	11,604	4,470	55,200	1,816	1,288
Wayne...............	357	583	472	3,553	754	3,354	28,970	1,098	4,711	8,455	55,345	1,816	728
West Union..........	179	929	499	1,206	369	1,242	26,350½	721	7,878	610	41,980	17,700	1,589½
Wheeler.............	496	839	618	5,220	832	7,377	40,777	1,440	4,515	10,024	50,693	4,806	700
Woodhull............	406	1,788	911	2,330	817	5,849½	37,403	2,465	10,025	3,174	112,445	4,745	1,144
Total............	13,899	32,199	20,284	111,353	24,154	229,802	1,282,567	58,749¼	255,938	297,289	1,976,129	203,329	34,935

[a] Formed since 1855.

SUFFOLK COUNTY.

This county[1] was organized Nov. 1, 1683. It occupies the E. part of Long Island, embracing about two-thirds of its area, and includes several smaller islands off the E. and N. coasts. It is centrally distant 138 mi. from Albany, and contains 1,200 sq. mi. The E. extremity of the island is divided by Great and Little Peconic and Gardners Bays into two narrow, unequal branches, between which are Gardners, Shelter, and Robins Islands. A chain of islands extends from the N. branch nearly to the Conn. shore.[2] A beach composed of alluvial sand and shingle, broken only by occasional inlets, skirts the S. shore of the island, enclosing several large, irregular bays, the principal of which are Great South, East, Shinnecock, and Mecox Bays. "This great beach is a line of spits and islands. One of the islands is about 25 mi. long, with a breadth of a few hundred yards. They are all narrow and long; and when above the reach of the surf they are covered by a labyrinth of hillocks of drifted sand, imitating almost all the variety of form which snow drifts present after a storm."

The action of the waves and winds is gradually extending this beach. Off the S. coast the sea is very shallow; 50 mi. from the shore its depth nowhere exceeds 40 fathoms; and sandbars at a considerable distance from the beach approach so near the surface as to break the waves into a surf. The traveler along the beach is seldom out of sight of a wreck.[3] Irregular branches project inland from Long Island Sound, in the W. part of the co., and from the bays upon the S. and E. The peninsulas and points thus formed are locally known as "*necks*." Upon the S. side of the island these necks generally take the name of the stream E. of them. An irregular range of hills extends E. and W. through the co., a little N. of the center. A second range, commencing in Brookhaven, extends into the S. branch of the island, terminating at Canoe Place and reappearing farther E. as the Shinnecock Hills. Along the N. border of the co. the surface is somewhat broken; but in the S. it is very level. In the E. part are several fresh water lakes, and a few in the central and W. parts, the principal of which is Lake Ronkonkoma, on the W. border of Brookhaven. The principal streams are Peconic River, in the E., and the Connecticut, in the central part. The soil is generally a light, sandy loam, moderately fertile along the coasts; but in some parts the surface consists of almost sterile plains or barren sandhills. The interior of the island, from near the foot of the hills to within one or two mi. of South Bay, is occupied by the "*brush plains*," which are sparsely inhabited and hardly susceptible of cultivation. Thousands of acres of these plains were burned over in 1844 and '45; and a thin growth of scrub oak, 3 to 4 feet high, has since sprung up on the burned tract.[4] Along the coast are extensive salt marshes. No native rock is found within this co.; and the whole island, except a few rocks near Hellgate, appears to belong to the drift formation or to have been formed as a strand of the sea. The waters of the sea are slowly encroaching upon the land of the E. and N. parts.

The various branches of agriculture form the leading industrial pursuits.[5] Successful husbandry in this co. involves a large expenditure for fertilizers,[6] which to considerable extent are obtained from the neighboring seas. Immense quantities of bony fish[7] are caught for this pur-

---

[1] Named from a co. in England. From 1665 to 1683 this co. formed the "*East Riding of Yorkshire.*"

[2] These islands appear to have been separated from the mainland and from each other by tidal currents, which flow between them with great force.—*N. Y. Geological Survey*, Mather.

[3] From Nov. 1, 1854, to June 28, 1857, 5 ships, 9 barks, 16 brigs, 25 schooners, and 9 sloops were wrecked, or in distress, off this coast. The Government has established 26 lifeboat stations upon the S. shore, (of which 19 are within this co.,) 1 on Fishers Island, 1 at Orient Point, and 2 upon the sound. Each station is furnished with boats, life-cars, mortars and rockets for throwing lines, and at each a keeper is in constant attendance. Under the provisions of the act of Feb. 16, 1787, "*wreckmasters*" are appointed by the Governor and Senate in and for the several counties bordering upon the seashore. Of these there are 15 in Suffolk co. It is their duty to render every possible aid to distressed vessels. A project has recently been formed of constructing a telegraph line from Montauk Point to Brooklyn, with stations along the beach, so that intelligence may be transmitted in season to admit of aid being sent to vessels in distress.

[4] Some of these tracts are 8 to 10 mi. long and 2 to 4 wide. The fires destroyed not only the forest trees, but every vestige of vegetation, and thousands of cords of wood; hundreds of deer and other animals, perished in them. These lands are valuable only for the timber upon them; and when that is destroyed they become nearly worthless.

[5] Corn and potatoes are the leading agricultural exportations. This co. excels all others in the State in the amount of turnips raised. Wheat is one of the principal crops.

[6] The annual expenditure of this co. for manures is nearly $200,000,—about half as much as is expended for the same purpose by all the rest of the State.

[7] These fish are the *Alosa menhaden*, or "moss bunkers," and are usually called "bunkers" or "skippaugs." They are caught from May to Nov., in seines, in immense quantities; at a single haul, a few years since, 1,400,000 were taken. They are sold at an average price of $1 per M. They are usually strewn upon the surface as a top dressing, or plowed under, but are sometimes rotted with earth, seaweed, and other articles in compost heaps. The stench of these decaying fish is extremely unpleasant and almost overpowering to strangers.

pose, and are used either alone or in connection with seaweed, stable manure, compost, guano, ashes, and other fertilizers. Oysters and clams abound in the bays and seas around the island; and the taking of these, and fishing, form the principal occupations of the inhabitants along the shore. From the first settlement of the co. considerable attention has been given to whaling. This business was originally carried on in open boats from the shore;[1] but large vessels are now sent upon long voyages to the Polar Seas.[2] The preparation of "fish guano," and oil from bunkers,[3] shipbuilding, and brickmaking are the principal manufacturing interests of the co.[4] At Fire Island, Greenport, and Orient, and at most of the villages along the s. county road, are extensive hotels, especially fitted for the accommodation of families from New York City, great numbers of whom spend the summer months at these public houses or in private families.

The county seat is located at Riverhead.[5] The courthouse is a fine two story brick building, situated near the depôt, and contains the usual county offices, and accommodations for the sheriff's family.[6] The jail, situated in rear of the courthouse, is a two story stone octagonal building. The county clerk's office is a fireproof brick building. The co. has no poorhouse.[7]

The first regulation concerning public roads was adopted under authority of an act of General Assembly passed in 1724, and was kept alive by repeated enactments. Commissioners appointed by this authority about 1733 laid out 3 principal roads from w. to e. These were called the North, Middle, and South Country Roads, and upon them the principal villages and settlements are located. The project of opening a navigable communication between the bays upon the s. shore of the island was recommended by Gov. Clinton in 1825, and was subsequently authorized by law, but was never carried into effect.[8] The Long Island R. R. affords the principal avenue of business through the island.[9] Short stage routes connect the several villages along the n. and s. shores with the R. R.

Seven newspapers are published in the co.; 2 at Greenport, 2 at Huntington, 1 at Sag Harbor, 1 at Patchogue, and 1 at Riverhead.[10]

When Long Island first became known, it was inhabited by 13 tribes of Indians, of which all but two resided wholly or in part in this co.[11] Of these the Montauks were the most numerous

---

[1] At present 3 whaleboats at Mastic Point, 2 at Shinnecock, 6 at Southampton, and several at Bridgehampton, Easthampton, and Amaganset, are kept in constant readiness for use upon the beach. They are mounted, bottom upward, upon a staging, and are well supplied with oars, lances, harpoons, and other necessary tackle. During the winter and spring months a lookout is kept, and when a whale appears a signal rallies the neighborhood to the chase. A year seldom passes without one prize; and some years half a dozen are captured.

[2] The whaling interests of this co. received a severe check upon the discovery of gold in California. Many whaleships were fitted out for the trade with that region, and upon the reaction that followed were sold. The number of whaleships now belonging to the co. is 33; and the greatest number at any one time (in 1845-47) was 88.

[3] The manufactories of fish guano and oil are in Southold and ¡upon Shelter Island, and on Napeague Beach. The fish are heated by steam, and the oil is extracted by hydrostatic presses. The residue is dried and ground for guano. Forty tons of fish yield 9 tons of guano and 840 gals. of oil. It is claimed by many that this manufactured article possesses all the valuable properties of the Peruvian guano.

[4] Salt was formerly made from seawater at Sag Harbor. An extensive business was formerly carried on in cutting wood and shipping it to the New York market. Spafford, in his Gazetteer of 1823, says that a great portion of the fuel consumed in the city was furnished by the pine plains, and that 100,000 cords were annually sent from Brookhaven. Since the fires of 1844 and '45 but little wood has been exported.

[5] A small two story frame building, erected in 1725, served for both a courthouse and jail. The first court of Oyer and Terminer under the State Government was held Sept. 4, 1787.

[6] This building was erected in 1854 and '55, at a cost of $17,800. The committee appointed to superintend its erection were Sam'l B. Nicoll, Wm. R. Post, and Sylvester Miller. By an act passed April 9, 1813, the clerk of this co. was authorized to establish his office in two places, and to appoint a deputy to have charge of one. The records migrated between Islip and Southold, and were kept many years at Smithtown. The records of wills in this co. extend back to 1669. The records of the court of General Sessions and Common Pleas have been separately recorded since 1723.

[7] Most of the towns have poorhouses, at which co. paupers are provided for at the co. expense.

[8] The Long Island Canal Company, chartered April 8, 1848, was authorized to effect what in substance was embraced in De Witt Clinton's plan, viz.: communication between Gravesend, Jamaica, Great South, Southampton, and Mecox Bays, and across Canoe Place.

[9] The road was opened to Farmington Oct. 15, 1841, to Yaphank June 26, 1843, and to Greenport July 29, 1844.

[10] *Frothingham's Long Island Herald* was established at Sag Harbor May 10, 1791, by David Frothingham. In 1802 it was sold to Sellick Osborn, and changed to *The Suffolk County Herald.* It was sold in Feb. 1804, to Alden Spooner, and its name was changed to *The Suffolk Gazette,* and in Feb. 1811, it was discontinued. *The Suffolk Co. Recorder* was established at Sag Harbor Oct. 19, 1816, by Sam'l. A. Seabury. In 1817 it was changed to *The American Eagle*; 2 years afterward it was discontinued. **The Corrector** was started at Sag Harbor Aug. 3, 1822, by H. W. Hunt, and is now published by Alex. Hunt. **The Republican Watchman** was commenced at Sag Harbor in Sept. 1826, by Sam'l Phillips. In Sept. 1844, it was removed to Greenport, where it is now published by S. Phillips & Son. **The Suffolk Times** was started at Greenport in Aug. 1857, by John J. Riddell, its present publisher. *The American Eagle* was established at Huntington in 1821 by Sam'l A. Seabury. In May, 1825, it was changed to *The Long Island Journal of Philosophy and Cabinet of Variety,* (mo.,) pub. by Sam. Fleet. In 1827 it was changed to *The Portico,* and was discontinued in 1829. **The Long Islander** was started at Huntington in July, 1838, by Walter Whitman, and is now published by Geo. H. Shepard. **The Suffolk Democrat** was started Feb. 17, 1847, at Huntington, and is now published by Edward Strahan. *The Suffolk Gazette* was commenced at Riverhead in Aug. 1849. After 18 months it was removed to Sag Harbor. In Dec. 1854, it was brought back to Riverhead, and was soon after discontinued. **The Suffolk Herald** was established at Patchogue Aug. 14, 1858, by Van Zandt & Co., its present publishers. **The Suffolk Union** was started at Riverhead in 1859 by Washington Van Zandt. **The Sag Harbor Express** was commenced in 1859, by —— ——.

[11] These tribes were the " *Canarsees,*" occupying Kings co. and a part of Jamaica; the " *Rockaways,*" the country about Rockaway and parts of Jamaica and Newtown; the "*Mattinecocks,*" the w. side of the island, from Flushing to the e. line of Huntington; the "*Nessequogs,*" the country from the e. line of Huntington to Stony Brook; the "*Setaukets,*" that from Stony Brook to Wading River; the "*Corchogues,*" all the n. branch of the island e. of Wading River; the "*Mercokes*" and "*Mureapeques,*" the country upon the s. side of the islands w. of Suffolk co.; the"*Lecatogues,*" the country from the w. line of the co. to the e. part of Islip; the "*Patchogues,*" from the e. line of Islip to the w. part of South ampton; the "*Shinnecocks,*" the country around Canoe Place, and thence e. to Easthampton; the "*Montauks,*" that are now included in the town of Easthampton; and the "*Manhassets,*" occupying Shelter Island. Of all these tribes there now remain

and powerful; and the consent of Wyandance,[1] their grand sachem, was necessary to the validity of all Indian grants of that date upon the island. The earliest settlement within the co. was made in 1639, on Gardners Island, under title derived from James Farrett, agent of the Earl of Stirling, to whom a grant of the whole of Long Island had been made by the Plymouth Company.[2] Southold and Southampton were settled in 1640, Easthampton in 1648, Shelter Island in 1652, Huntington in 1653, Brookhaven in 1655, and Smithtown in 1668, by English immigrants from New England. These settlers were strongly imbued with Puritan doctrines and zealously devoted to their strict observance.[3] They naturally sought alliance with the adjacent New England colonies, to whom they were warmly attached, and with whom they were closely united until they were brought under the government of New York. Among the first measures taken by the colonists was the establishment of religious worship and schools, which in most of the towns date from the first or second year of settlement. These were commonly supported by tax, often levied in kind, and sometimes coupled with privileges and grants that are still recognized.

The patents granted by the New York governors created corporations, with municipal powers and privileges which were liberal for that period. These have never been changed, and are still valid. The rights were of two classes,—one belonging to all who might gain a residence and citizenship within the town, and the other pertaining only to the persons named in the patents and their heirs at law. During the Revolution most of the inhabitants of the co. warmly espoused the cause of the colonists; but after the battle of Long Island the British ascendency was complete, and few opportunities occurred for assisting in the popular movement. Several bold and successful incursions were made by partisan corps; but the armed occupation of the island was at no time interrupted.[4] During the latter part of the War of 1812 an English fleet was stationed off the eastern coast; but few depredations were committed. The history of the co. from that day to the present is only the record of the industrial pursuits of a thriving people.

BROOKHAVEN—was incorp. by patent, under Gov. Nicoll, March 13, 1666, with the usual privileges of a township;[5] and Dec. 27, 1686, the patent was confirmed by Gov. Dongan, and extended privileges were granted.[6] It was recognized as a town March 7, 1788. It occupies the entire width of Long Island, near the center of the co. E. and W. It has 20 mi. of coast on Long Island Sound, 21 on South Bay, and above 30 on Fire Island, which skirts the whole s. coast. Patchogue and Bellport Bays, upon the s. coast, are branches of Great South Bay; and Old Mans Harbor and Port Jefferson, Conscience, Setauket, and Flax Pond Bays, are indentations upon the N. coast from L. I. Sound. The principal capes upon the N. coast are Cranes Neck, Old Field Point,[7] Little Neck,[8] Dyers Neck,[9] Mount Misery, and Rocky Point. A range of low hills extends across the N. part of the town; but elsewhere the surface is level. The principal streams are Peconic River, in the E. part, and the Connecticut, in the central. There are several fresh water ponds of great depth and purity in the town, many of which have no outlet. The soil along the coast, both upon Long Island Sound and South Bay, is a moderately fertile, light, sandy loam, and in the interior it is generally unproductive. Along the streams near their mouths are numerous salt meadows. **Port Jefferson**[10] (p. v.) is situated at the head of Port Jefferson Bay, on the N. coast. It has a good harbor, and shipbuilding is largely carried on.[11] Pop. 1,247. **Setauket,** (p.v.,) on the bay of the same name, contains 2 churches and 4 shipyards and has a pop. of 1,136. **Stony Brook,**[12] (p.v.,) near the line of Smithtown, contains 1 church and has a pop. (in this town) of 542. **Mt. Sinai,**[13] (p. v.,) on Old Mans Harbor, has a pop. of 276. **Millers Place,**[14] (p.o.,) **Rocky Point,** and **Swezys**

---

but a few individuals in Islip and Brookhaven, about 200 at Shinnecock, and 5 families on Montauk Point. They have lost all knowledge of their language, using only the English, and are intelligent and civilized. They have intermarried to a considerable extent with negroes, and are probably of more than half African blood.

[1] Wyandance died in 1659, and the Montauk Indians afterward became tributary to the Narragansetts.

[2] This grant was made in 1635, and, at the request of Charles I, Farrett was appointed agent in 1637.—*Hough's Nantucket Papers, IX.*

[3] Most of the towns were jealous of the admission of strangers, and only allowed them to participate in their privileges upon careful examination of character and motive.

[4] By the act of May 6, 1784, the sum of £10,000 was levied upon this co. as a "*back tax*" for defraying expenses incurred in the wars.

[5] Capt. John Tucker, Dan'l Lane, Richard Woodhull, Henry Perring, and John Jenner were named trustees in this patent. *Patents, I,* 81, Sec. Office.

[6] This instrument provided that 7 trustees should be annually elected, in whom the legal ownership of the property of the town should be vested. John Palmer, Richard Woodhull, Samuel Eburne, Andrew Gibb, Wm. Satterly, Thos. Jenner, and Thos. Helme were named as the first trustees.

[7] The Indian name of this point was "*Co-met-i-co.*"

[8] Called by the Indians "*Mi-nas-se-roke.*"

[9] Its Indian name was "*Po-quott.*"

[10] Formerly known as "*Drowned Meadow,*" and called "*So-was-sett*" by the Indians.

[11] There are 5 shipyards on the E. side of the harbor, and 3 upon the w.

[12] Called by the Indians "*Wopowag.*" The great quantities of shells found near the banks indicate that this was a favorite residence of the natives.

[13] Called by the Indians "*Non-o-wau-tuck.*"

[14] Named from Andrew, son of John Miller, one of the pioneers of Easthampton.

Landing are hamlets on the coast of Long Island Sound. **Patchogue**[1] (p. v.) is situated on Patchogue Bay, in the s. w. part of the town. It contains 4 churches, an academy, and manufactories of twine, paper, cotton, ropes, and flour. Pop. 1,562. **Bellport,** (p. v.,) on the w. side of Bellport Bay, contains 1 church and an academy. Shipbuilding is carried on to a considerable extent. Pop. 383. **Blue Point,**[2] (p. o.,) in the s. w. part, is a hamlet. **Fire Place,** (p. v.,) on Bellport Bay, contains 1 church and about 35 houses; **Moriches,**[3] 4 churches and 50 houses; **East Moriches,** (p. v.,) 40 houses; and **West Moriches** (Moriches p. o.) and **Seatuck,** hamlets, are situated near the coast of East Bay. **Yaphank,**[4] (p. v.,) a station on the Long Island R. R., containing 3 churches and 35 houses, and **South Haven,** (p. v.,) containing 1 church and 20 houses, are situated on Connecticut River. **Mastic**[5] is a hamlet on Mastic River. **Middle Island,** (p. o.,) containing 2 churches, **Selden,** (p. o.,) 1 church, **New Village,** (p. o.,) 1 church, and **Coram,**[6] (Cor-um,) (p. o.,) are hamlets in the central part; and **Wampmissic,**[7] containing 1 church, and **Manorville,**[8] (p. o.,) are hamlets in the e. part. **Center Moriches** is a p. o. **Waverly,** and **Medford,** are hamlets and R. R. stations. The town poorhouse is located near Coram, upon a small farm purchased in 1817 at a cost of $900. The lighthouse on Old Fields Point was built in 1823; and another on Fire Island, near Fire Island Inlet, was built in 1858.[9] The first settlement was made at Setauket,[10] in 1655, by a colony of immigrants from near Boston, Mass.[11] The land was bought from the Setauket Indians, and the sale confirmed by a release from Wyandance, Sachem of Montauk. This settlement was received under the government of Conn. in 1661, and Richard Woodhull and Thos. Pierce were appointed magistrates by the General Court. The tract of land between Islip and Bellport, extending to the center of the island, was purchased of the natives by John Winthrop in 1666, and the title confirmed March 29, 1680.[12] Col. Wm. Smith purchased Little Neck, Oct. 22, 1686, and an extensive tract e. of Connecticut River, extending northward to the center of the co., in May, 1691.[13] Fort St. George, a strongly fortified British post on South Bay, was surprised and taken by a party of 80 men, under Maj. Tallmadge, Nov. 21, 1780. They crossed Long Island Sound from Conn., landing at Old Mans Harbor, marched to Coram, where they destroyed a large amount of forage, and then to Fort St. George, which they captured without the loss of a man. Over 50 men were made prisoners, and a large amount of property was destroyed.[14] Gen. Woodhull,[15] Pres. of the Second and Third Provincial Congresses, Gen. Wm. Floyd, one of the signers of the Declaration of Independence, Col. Richard Floyd,[16] and Maj. Wm. H. Smith, were residents, and Maj. Benj. Tallmadge was a native, of this town. In the infancy of the settlement a building was erected at Setauket, which served the double purpose of a townhall and church.[17] There are now 26 churches in town.[18]

EAST HAMPTON—was incorp. by patent, under Gov. Nicoll, March 13, 1666,[19] and confirmed by Gov. Dongan, Dec. 9, 1686. It was recognized as a town March 7, 1788. It lies at the e. extremity of Long Island, s. of Gardners Bay and Long Island Sound, and includes Gardners Island, lying n. of the mainland. The e. part consists of a narrow peninsula, to which the name, Montauk, is applied. Upon the n. coast are several large bays, some of them nearly landlocked. The principal of these are Northwest, Three Mile, Acabonac, and Napeague Harbors, and Fort Pond Bay. In the central and w. parts the surface is mostly level or gently undulating; but along the coast

---

[1] Named from the *"Po-chough"* Indians, who inhabited this region.

[2] Called by the Indians *"Man-ow-tuss-quott,"* an important oyster bed in Great South Bay, in this vicinity.

[3] An Indian name, pronounced Mo-rich-es. Great quantities of fish and wild fowl are sent from this vicinity to the New York market.

[4] Yaphank is the Indian name of a small tributary of the Connecticut. The place was originally called *"Millville,"* and afterward *"Brookfield."*

[5] This name is applied to a considerable tract of land w. of the river, formerly occupied by the Poos-pa-tuck Indians, a tribe subject to the Pochoughs. Parts of this tract were known as *"Sa-bo-nock," "Ne-com-mack," "Coos-pu-tus," "Pa-ter-quos," "Un-co-houg,"* and *"Mat-te-moy."*

[6] Named from an Indian chief.

[7] This name was given by the Indians to a swamp in the vicinity.

[8] Formerly called *"St. Georges Manor."*

[9] This lighthouse is 150 ft. high and 166 ft. above the sea, and is furnished with a French flashing lens apparatus of superior quality.

[10] Then called *"Cromwell Bay."*

[11] The family names of these settlers were Woodhull, Hawkins, Whitehaire, Jenner, Perring, Gibb, Satterly, Biggs, Tooker, Rogers, Fancy, Longbotham, Lane, Floyd, Muncy, Seward, Wade, Sayler, Smith, Avery, Dayton, Davis, Frost, Thomas, Baylis, Thomson, Ward, Roe, Budd, Brooks, Williams, Woolley, Akerly, Combs, Waring, Mapes, Thorp, Eburne, Brewster, Poole, Sharpe, Burnet, Helme, Garlick, Moger, Pierce, and Ware. Many of these names are still common on the island. By a vote of the inhabitants, taken July 13, 1687, the trustees of the town were directed to establish a school, and Francis Williamson was employed as a teacher, at a salary of £30 per annum. The first mill was erected at Stony Brook in 1690.—*Thompson's Hist. Long Island, 2d Ed.,* I, 408.

[12] A great part of this tract was divided into 36 prizes, and disposed of by lottery for £12,000 in June, 1758.

[13] These purchases were confirmed Oct. 9, 1693, under the title of the *"Manor of -St. George,"* which included all the town as then founded e. of the Connecticut. A large proportion of this tract is still owned by the descendants of Col. Smith.

[14] *Washington's Writings,* VII; *Journal of Congress,* Dec. 6, 1780; *Thompson's Hist. Long Island.*

[15] Gen. Woodhull fell in the battle of Long Island, Sept. 1776, and was buried in this town.—*Onderdonk's Rev. Inc.*

[16] The lands of Col. Richard Floyd located in this town were confiscated by the British.

[17] The early pastors of the church at Setauket were Revs. Nathaniel Brewster, in 1655, Geo. Phillips, in 1697, David Youngs, in 1745, Benj. Tallmadge, in 1754, Noah Wetmore, in 1786, and Zachariah Greene, in 1797.

[18] 9 M. E., 8 Presb., 4 Cong., 2 Prot. E., 2 Af. M. E., Bap.

[19] The trustees named in the patent were John Mulford, Thos. Baker, Thomas Chatfield, Jeremiah Concklyn, Stephen Hedges, Thos. Osborne, sr., and John Osborne.—*Patents,* I, 81, Sec. Office.

upon the s. is a belt of low, shifting sand ridges; and the E. part is broken by low, irregular hills, some of which attain an elevation of 100 ft. above the sea. Near the coast in the s. part of the town and upon the peninsula are several fresh water ponds. The principal of these are Great,[1] Fort,[2] Oyster, Hook, and Georgica Ponds; and their outlets have been closed by sandbars or a beach. Upon the main portion of the peninsula of Montauk the soil is fertile, but its neck is a barren, sandy waste. In the w. part the soil is a light, sandy loam and is kept highly fertile by the use of manures. Stock raising forms the leading occupation; and to that pursuit Gardners Island[3] and Montauk Point are exclusively devoted. A tract of about 9000 acres, embracing the entire E. portion of the town, is devoted wholly to pasturage. It is owned by a company, incorp. as tenants in common, whose affairs are managed by a board of 7 trustees elected annually.[4] Twelve trustees are chosen annually, to whom are committed the management of the town commons, the meadow beaches, and the waters within the bays, the privileges of which are enjoyed by all citizens. A town poor-house is located on a small farm about 2 mi. w. of East Hampton Village. Lighthouses are located upon Cedar Island, at the entrance of Sag Harbor,[5] at the N. extremity of Gardners Island, and upon Montauk Point.[6] **East Hampton,** (p. v.,) about 1 mi. from the beach, in the s. w. part of the town, has 2 churches,[7] an academy,[8] 2 windmills, and about 70 houses. **Amaganset,** (p. v.,) a scattered village about 2 mi. E. of East Hampton, contains 1 church. Pop. 270. **Springs,** (p. o.,) near Acabonac Harbor, and **Wainscott,** in the s. w. corner of the town, are hamlets. **Sag Harbor**[9] (p. v.) is partly in this town. The first settlement in this town, and the first English settlement in the State, was made on Gardners Island in 1639, by Lyon Gardner.[10] Settlement in the w. part of the town was commenced in 1648, upon lands purchased of the Montauk Indians, by a company of English families from Lynn, Mass.[11] The government of the colony was purely democratic. The people met in *"General Court,"* and enacted laws, appointed civil and ministerial officers, and acted upon appeals from the decisions of their magistrates. Three magistrates,[12] a recorder, a secretary, and a constable were annually elected. Lands were allotted to individuals, and could not be alienated without the approval of the General Court. In Dec. 1653, they adopted the laws of Conn.; and from 1657 to 1667 they were united with that colony.[13] The inhabitants sided with the colonists in the disputes which led to the Revolution. In June, 1775, an *"Association"* favoring the measures of the Continental Congress was formed, and its articles were signed by every male inhabitant capable of bearing arms.[14] Rev. Thomas James, the first pastor in the town, settled in 1651.[15] There are now 4 churches in town.[16]

HUNTINGTON—was incorp. by patent, under Gov. Nicoll, Nov. 30, 1666.[17] The patent was renewed Aug. 2, 1688, and again Oct. 5, 1694. It was recognized as a town March 7, 1788, at which time Eatons Neck and Crab Meadow were annexed. The w. line was established Feb. 17,

---

[1] Called by the Indians *"Quaw-no-ti-wock."* This pond contains 500 acres.

[2] The Indian name of this pond is *"Konk-hong-a-nok."* It lies s. of Fort Pond Bay, and nearly divides the isthmus.

[3] Called by the Indians *"Mon-cho-nock,"* or *"Ma-shong-o-muc,"* and mentioned in early records as the *Isle of Wight.* It contains 3,300 acres.

[4] This tract originally belonged to the Montauk Indians, and was conveyed by them to the colonists of East Hampton, Feb. 11, 1661, the natives reserving to themselves the right of living upon and using so much of it as they might need. Its ownership was vested in the colonists in person. The lands were represented at first by 40 shares, valued at £40 each, and were intrusted to the management of the trustees of the town. The shares are now divided into "eighths," of which 36 have been purchased by the corporation and extinguished. These eighths are now worth $350 to $400 each. The tract is divided into large enclosures, of which *"the field"* is reserved for fattening stock. Every share entitles its possessor to the privilege of pasturing for "the season" 48 cattle, 14 of them to be admitted to *"the field."* A horse is rated as 2 "beasts," (cattle,) and 7 sheep as one. "The season" is fixed by the trustees, and generally lasts from June 1 to Oct. 20. About 1400 cattle and 1100 sheep are annually kept within these enclosures. Five Indian families reside upon the tract, who own 50 shares and are entitled to the keeping of 50 cattle. These privileges are usually hired of them for $200 per annum.

[5] Cedar Island Lighthouse (built in 1839) is 34 ft. high.

[6] Montauk Lighthouse, on Turtle Hill, is 85 ft. high, and 160 feet above the level of the sea. It was built in 1795, at a cost of $22,500.

[7] The vane upon this church bears the dates of 1649 and 1717, as those of the first settlement of the village and the erection of the church edifice.

[8] Clinton Academy was founded in 1784, and incorp. by the regents Nov. 17, 1787. A petition of the trustees of this institution suggested to the legislature the propriety of a general system of supervision, and led to the enactment of the law organizing the Board of Regents of the University. This academy and Erasmus Hall, in Flatbush, were incorp. the same day, and are the oldest legally organized academic institutions in the State.

[9] See page 638.

[10] This island was purchased from Jas. Farrett, agent of the Earl of Stirling, March 10, 1639. Elizabeth Gardner—born upon the island, Sept. 14, 1641—was the first child of English parents born within the present limits of this State. The pirate, Kidd, visited the island in 1699 and buried a quantity of gold, silver, and jewels, which were afterward recovered by commissioners sent from Boston for that purpose. A piece of cloth of gold presented by Capt. Kidd to Mrs. Gardner is still preserved.

[11] This purchase was made by the Governors of Conn. and New Haven for the colonists, and was conveyed to them the following year. The tract embraced an area of about 30,000 acres; and the value of the articles given in exchange for it was £30 4s. 8d. The Indians reserved the right of fishing, hunting, and of taking shells for wampum upon the lands sold, and the right to the fins and tails of drift whales.

[12] The first magistrates were John Mulford, Robt. Bond, and Thos. Baker.

[13] The first school was taught by Chas. Barnes, who received a salary of £30 per annum. He was succeeded in 1663 by Peter Benson.

[14] John Chatfield, Col. Abram Gardiner, Burnet Miller, Rev. Sam'l Buell, Thomas Wickham, and 248 others.—*Hedge's 200th Anniversary Address.* In Jan. 1777, the enemy having armed occupation of the island, required the inhabitants to sign a counter declaration, as the condition of their remaining in quiet occupation of their houses. This declaration was signed by 150, of whom 117 had signed the former paper.—*MSS. State Library.*

[15] The succeeding pastors of the same church were Nathaniel Huntting, in 1699, Sam'l Buell, in 1746, Lyman Beecher, in 1799, and Ebenezer Phillips, in 1810.

[16] 2 M. E., Presb., and Af. M. E.

[17] The trustees named in the patent were Jonas Wood, Wm. Leverige, Robt. Seely, John Ketcham, Thos. Scidmore, Isaac Platt, Thos. Jones, and Thos. Wicks.—*Patents, I,* 63, Sec. Office.

1787, and Lloyds Neck was set off to Oyster Bay in 1788. This is the w. town of the co. It extends across the island, and has 10 mi. of coast on Long Island Sound and 6 on Great South Bay. It also includes about half of Oak Island Beach, and Cedar and several smaller islands in Great South Bay. The N. shore is deeply indented by Huntington Bay, from which Lloyds Harbor extends to the w., Huntington Harbor to the s., and Northport Bay to the E. Centerport and Northport Harbors branch off upon the s. of the latter bay, and two smaller arms upon the N. W. Great, Little, and Eatons[1] Necks are peninsulas formed by these bays and harbors. Groups of low hills extend through the center, and the surface 2 to 3 mi. from the sound is broken; but elsewhere it is comparatively level. The soil in the N. and s. is fertile; but in the interior it is unproductive. The industrial pursuits are various; whaling, fishing, and taking oysters and clams are some of the leading occupations. Shipbuilding and manufactures receive considerable attention. At the annual election 7 trustees are chosen, to whose care the management of the town property is committed.[2] The town poorhouse is located near Huntington Village. A lighthouse was built upon the point of Eatons Neck in 1798.[3] **Huntington,** (p. v.,) near the head of Huntington Harbor, contains 5 churches, a flourishing union school,[4] 2 printing offices, and a limited number of manufacturing establishments.[5] Pop. 1,328. **Cold Spring,**[6] (Cold Spring Harbor p. o.,) on the E. side of Cold Spring Harbor, contains 3 churches, 2 shipyards, a woolen factory, and other manufactories. Considerable whaling business is carried on from this port.[7] Pop. 602. **Northport**[8] (p. v.) is on the E. side of Northport Harbor. Shipbuilding is here largely carried on. Pop. 430. **Centerport**[9] (p. v.) contains 1 church and 142 inhabitants; and **Vernon Valley**[10] (p. v.) 1 church and 100 inhabitants. **Babylon,** (p. v.,) near Great South Bay, contains 2 churches and has a pop. of 470. This is a favorite resort for hunting and fishing parties. **Amityville,**[11] (p. v.,) in the s. w. part, contains 1 church and has a pop. of 304; **Deer Park,** (p. v.,) a station on the Long Island R. R., contains 12 houses; **Melville,**[12] in the w. part, 1 church and 108 inhabitants; and **Comac,** (Commack p. o.,) in the E. part, 2 churches and 121 inhabitants. **West Hills,** (p. o.,) containing 1 church, and **Dix Hills,** (p. o.,) are hamlets on the Smithtown turnpike. Settlement began near the N. coast, in 1653, by a company from Sandwich, Mass.[13] In 1660 the settlement was received under the government of Conn.; and in 1663 deputies were elected to the General Court at Hartford. Upon the English conquest, in 1664, the town came reluctantly under the government of New York. During the Revolution, companies of tories were stationed here, and many outrages were committed upon those friendly to the independence of the colonies. There are 22 churches in town.[14]

ISLIP[15]—was first recognized as a town by the Colonial Government, Nov. 25, 1710, and by the State Legislature March 7, 1788.[16] It lies w. of the center of the co., and extends from the s. coast to the middle of the island; it has a coast of about 18 mi. on Great South Bay, and includes Cap Tree, Oak, and several other islands off the s. coast. Numerous narrow inlets from Great South Bay divide the coast into distinct "necks," of which there are 35 within the limits of the town. The Connetquot River, and Sam-po-wans or Thompsons Brook, are the principal streams. The surface is level, except in the N. part, where it is hilly. The brush plains occupy all the central portion; and near the coast are extensive salt meadows. Upon a tract extending along the bay, and varying in width from one to three miles, the soil is fertile. This part of the town is thickly settled; but the remainder is almost uninhabited. The keeping of the town poor is let to the lowest bidders. **Penataquit,**[17] (p. v.,) near the coast, contains 1 church and has a pop. of 292; **Islip,** (p. v.,) 2 mi. E. of Penataquit, contains 3 churches and about 70 houses. **Midroadville,** containing 40 houses, and **Sayville,** (p. v.,) containing 2 churches and 822 inhabitants, are in the s. E. part. **Lake-**

---

1 Named from Gov. Eaton, of New Haven, by whom it was purchased of the Indians in 1646. The names "*Eatons Manor*" and "*Gardners Neck*" have been applied to it.
2 The ferry from this town to Norwalk, Conn., which has been maintained from an early period, is under the control of these trustees. Under their patent—which is still in force—the inhabitants claim the exclusive right of taking oysters and clams in the waters within the jurisdiction of the town. Most of the public lands were sold in 1853, and the proceeds invested, to meet the ordinary expenses of the town. About 3,000 acres were sold, at $5.40 per acre.
3 This lighthouse is 56 ft. high and 138 ft. above tide. It was built at a cost of $9,500.
4 This school has an endowment of $7,400, bequeathed by Nathaniel Potter.
5 E. C. Prime established a thimble factory at this place in 1837. Ten or 12 men are constantly employed, and 5 to 6 gross of gold and silver thimbles are made daily. There is a wind sawmill in this place, erected in 1825.
6 Called by the natives "*Nach-a-qua-tuck.*"
7 Belonging to this port are 5 whaling vessels, with an aggregate of 2,129 tons.

8 Formerly called "*Great Cow Harbor.*"
9 Formerly called "*Little Cow Harbor.*"
10 Formerly "*Red-Hook.*" 11 Formerly "*West Neck.*"
12 Formerly "*Sweet Hollow;*" called by the Indians "*Sunquams.*"
13 The names of some of the families residing in the town at the date of Nicolls Patent were Titus, Wood, Brush, Green, Wickes, Jones, Rogers, Todd, Scudder, Skidmore, Chichester, Whitson, Bagly, Meggs, Mathews, Darling, Baldwin, Harnett, Ludlum, Adams, Smith, Houldsworth, Cranfield, Soper, French, Foster, Platt, Jarvis, Powell, Cory, Leverich, Williams, Westcote, Lynch, Benedict, Conkling, Strickling, Tredwell, Porter, Wheeler, Seely, and Ketcham. The first school was established in 1657.
14 10 M. E., 4 Presb., 2 Meth. Prot., Bap., Prot. E., Union, Univ., R. C. and Af. M. E.
15 Named from Islipe, Oxfordshire, Eng.
16 This act empowered the inhabitants of the district "on the s. side of Long Island, from the westernmost limits of the land of Thos. Willett to the eastermost part of the lands of William Nicoll, near Blue Point," to elect town officers.
17 This name was given by the Indians to a small stream in the neighborhood. The village was formerly called "*Mechanicsville.*"

land[1] (p. v.) is a station on the L. I. R. R., s. of Lake Ronkonkoma. Pop. 215. **Thompsons Station** (p. o.) and **North Islip** (Suffolk Station p. o.) are stations on the Long Island R. R. **Modern Times** is a place of about 20 houses, in the central part.[2] The Patchogue Indians were the original occupants of that part of the town E. of Connetquot River, and the Secatogues, or Secatokets, of that part w. of the river. A large tract of territory, w. of the Connetquot, was purchased by Wm. Nicoll, Nov. 29, 1683, and that part E. of the same stream by Olof, Philip, and Stephen Van Courtlandt, June 1, 1703.[3] During the Revolution the inhabitants were in a constant state of alarm by the frequent passing of British troops to and from New York City. There are 10 churches in town.[4]

RIVERHEAD—was formed from Southold, March 13, 1792. It lies upon the N. side of the island, between Brookhaven and Southold, and has 16½ mi. of coast upon Long Island Sound. Peconic River and Great Peconic Bay form the s. boundary, and Wading River[5] a part of the w. The surface in the s. part is level, but in the N. it is hilly. The shore is lined with high and precipitous bluffs of clay and hardpan. The soil is light and sandy, and in most parts but moderately fertile. The poorhouse is located on a farm of 45 acres. **Riverhead,** (p.v.,) an important station on the L. I. R. R., is situated on Peconic River at the head of boat navigation. It is the county seat, and contains the co. buildings, 3 churches, a seminary,[6] and several manufactories.[7] Pop. 813,—723 in Riverhead and 90 in Southampton. From Riverhead E. to the line of Southold, a distance of about 6 mi. upon the "*South Road*," is a continuous settlement, which has received at different places the names **Upper Aquebogue,** (p. o.,) **Old Aquebogue,** (Jamesport p. o.,) and **Franklinville,** (West Suffolk p. o.) Old Aquebogue and Franklinville are stations on the L. I. R. R. **Jamesport**[8] is situated about one-half mi. s. of Old Aquebogue, on Great Peconic Bay, and contains 1 church; pop. 148. **Northville,** (Success p. o.,) in the N. E. part, contains 1 church and 35 houses; **Bating Hollow,** (p. o.,) in the N. part, in a scattered settlement, has 2 churches; and **Wading River,** (p. v.,) on stream of same name, 1 church and 25 houses. Settlement begun at Riverhead, in 1690, by John Griffing and others. There are 10 churches in town.[9]

SHELTER ISLAND[10]—was incorp. by patent, under Gov. Nicoll, May 31, 1666;[11] but its government was united with that of Southold until 1730. It was recognized as a town March 7, 1788. It lies between the two peninsulas which form the E. extremity of Long Island, and embraces an area of over 8,000 acres. The island is very irregular; upon all sides jutting headlands extend out into the surrounding waters, and branching bays penetrate into the interior. The principal of these inlets are Coeclis, West Neck, and Deerings Harbors. The surface is hilly, and the soil fertile. Grain raising and sheep husbandry form the principal agricultural pursuits. Guano and oil are manufactured in considerable quantities from bony fish caught in the neighboring waters. There is a wind gristmill near the center of the island. **Shelter Island** is a p. o., centrally located. This island was the ancient residence of the Manhassett Indians. It was purchased for the Earl of Sterling by Jas. Farrett, and was afterward sold to Stephen Goodyear, of New Haven. In 1651 it was purchased by Nathaniel and Constant Sylvester, Thos. Middleton, and Thos. Rowe.[12] The first settlement was made in 1652. The first church edifice was built in 1743.[13]

SMITHTOWN[14]—was organized by patent, March 25, 1677, and recognized as a town March 7, 1788. It lies upon the N. side of the island, between Huntington and Brookhaven. Stony Brook and Nissequague Harbors, extending far inland, are separated by the Nissequague Neck. Nissequague River, emptying into the harbor of the same name, divides the town into two nearly equal parts. The surface is considerably broken and hilly. The soil is a light, sandy loam in the s. part, and a clayey loam along the sound. **The Branch,** (Smithtown Branch p. o.,) on Branch Brook, near the center of the town, contains 2 churches and 35 houses; **Smithtown,**[15] (p. v.,) on Nissequague River, 20 houses; and **St. Jamesville,** (St. James p. o.,) at the head of Stony Brook Harbor, 1 church and 25 houses. **Fresh Pond** is a p. o., in the N. w. part. **Hoppogue,**[16] on

---

[1] This place was laid out on a magnificent scale. Large sums were spent in advertising it as a desirable residence for mechanics and others of small means, and many were induced to buy lots. Their investments, however, proved of little value,—their deeds being given by irresponsible parties.

[2] This "*village*" was laid out and built by Stephen Pearl Andrews and others, who held to the doctrine of "the Sovereignty of the Individual," and some of whom were practical believers in the "Free Love" doctrine.

[3] Nicolls's Purchase was confirmed to him by a patent issued by Gov. Dongan Dec. 5, 1684; and the Van Courtlandt Purchase was confirmed to John Mowbray, by whom it had been subsequently bought, by a patent issued in 1708.

[4] 3 M. E., 2 Prot. E., 2 Af. Meth., Cong., Cong. Meth., and Presb.

[5] Called by the Indians "*Pan-qua-cum-suck.*"

[6] Established in 1835.

[7] Upon the river at this place is a fall of 6 ft.; and a hydraulic

canal, connecting two small ponds with the river, has been constructed, in which is a fall of 8¼ ft.

[8] Called by the natives "*Mi-a-mog,*" or "*Mi-an-rogue.*"

[9] 6 Cong., 2 M. E., 2 Swedenborgian.

[10] The Indian name of the island was "*Man-han-sack-a-ha-quash-u-wor-nock,*" signifying "*an island sheltered by islands.*"

[11] This patent was issued to Constant and Nath'l Sylvester.

[12] In 1673 Gov. Anthony Colve proclaimed Middleton and Constant Sylvester "public enemies of Holland," and sold their interests in the island. They were bought by Nath'l Sylvester, and the purchase money was collected by an armed force.—*Thompson's Hist. L. I.*

[13] The census reports 1 church; Presb.

[14] Named from Richard Smith, of R. I., the early proprietor of the town.

[15] Usually called the "*Head of the River.*"

[16] Sometimes written "*Hauppaugs.*" The word is supposed to signify "sweet waters."

the line of Islip, and **Nissequague,** on Nissequague Neck, are hamlets. A tract of land, including the principal part of this town, was, in July, 1659, conveyed to Lyon Gardner as a free gift, by Wyandance, Sachem of the Montauks;[1] and in 1662 the grant was confirmed by the Nessequake tribe, by whom the lands were occupied. In 1663 the tract was sold to Richard Smith, and in 1665 the remaining part of the town was purchased of the Indians by him. Fort Slongo, in the N. W. part of the town, was erected by the British during the Revolution. It was captured by a body of Americans, under Col. Tallmadge, Oct. 3, 1781.[2] There are 6 churches in town.[3]

SOUTHAMPTON[4]—was incorp. by patent, under Gov. Andros, Nov. 1, 1676,[5] confirmed by Gov. Dongan, Dec. 6, 1686, and recognized as a town March 7, 1788. It occupies the greater part of the s. branch of Eastern Long Island, and has 30 mi. of seacoast. The entire s. shore is skirted by a beach which is united in a few places with the mainland, separating the enclosed waters into distinct bays, the principal of which are East, Quantuc, Shinnecock, and Mecox Bays; minor bays, branching from these, divide the surrounding shores into numerous irregular "*necks.*" The beach which separates the waters of these bays from the Atlantic is unbroken except by a single inlet into Shinnecock Bay. The outline of the N. coast is extremely tortuous; ragged and often nearly landlocked bays project inland, and irregular points of land jut out into the surrounding waters. A range of low hills extends along the N. border of the town, and the Shinnecock Hills occupy the central part; elsewhere the surface is level. The soil in the E. and s. parts consists of a light, sandy loam, and is moderately fertile; but in other parts it is of an inferior quality. A large tract s. of Peconic River is covered with extensive pine forests. Stock raising and the other branches of agriculture form the principal industrial pursuits. The lands are enriched by the application of immense quantities of bunkers. Large tracts of meadow and pasturage lands in different parts of the town are owned by 3 companies, who, in common, elect annually a board of 12 trustees, to whose management the lands are committed.[6] Taking clams and oysters, and whaling, form an important part of the business. The town has a small poorhouse, a short distance E. of Bridgehampton. A lighthouse has been recently erected on Ponquogue Beach.[7] **Sag Harbor,** (p. v.,) in the N. E. part, was incorp. as a fire district in 1803, and as a village March 12, 1819. It contains 7 churches, the Sag Harbor Institute, a newspaper office, a bank, a cotton flannel factory,[8] 2 clock factories, and several manufactories of oil casks. This port has long been noted for the extent of its whaling business.[9] It was made a port of entry in 1784, and by itself now constitutes a district of customs. Pop. 2,776,—2,041 in Southampton, and 735 in Easthampton. **Southampton,** (p. v.,) midway between Shinnecock and Mecox Bays, contains 2 churches, an academy,[10] and 65 houses. **Bridgehampton,[11]** (p. v.,) in the E. part, contains 2 churches and about 40 houses; **Shinnecock,** on the E. side of Shinnecock Bay, is an Indian settlement of about 20 houses.[12] **Sagg, Scuttle Hole** and **Watermill** are hamlets, in the E. part. **Flanders,** (p. v.,) in the N. part, contains 2 churches and about 20 houses; **Speonk,** (p. v.,) near East Bay, contains 2 churches and about 40 houses. **Ketchabonec** and **Quogue,** (p. o.,) near Quantuc Bay, and **Goodground** (p. o.) and **Canoe Place,** near Shinnecock Bay, are hamlets. **Riverhead** (p. v.) is partly in this town. The first settlement was made at Southampton, in 1640, by a company of immigrants

---

[1] This gift was made by Wyandance upon the recovery of his daughter, whom Gardner had returned from captivity among the Narragansetts.

[2] The Americans destroyed the fortifications and 2 cannon, took 21 prisoners, and retired without the loss of a man, taking with them 1 brass piece, the British colors, and a quantity of small arms and ammunition.—*Onderdonk's (Revolutionary) Incidents.* [3] 3 M. E., Presb., Prot. E., and R. C.

[4] Named from Southampton, Eng. Called by the Indians "*Ag-wam*," a place abounding in fish.

[5] John Topping, John Howell, Thos. Halsey, sr., Jos. Raynor, Edward Howell, John Jagger, John Foster, Francis Sayre, Jos. Fordham, Henry Pierson, John Cooper, Ellis Cook, Sam'l Clarke, Rich. Post, and John Jennins were named trustees in this patent.

[6] These lands are portions of 3 tracts, severally known as the "*Town Purchase*," the "*Quogue Purchase*," and the "*Topping Purchase*," which are still held by the proprietors in common. The "*Town Purchase*" occupies the E. part of the town. It is divided into 154 shares, called "fifties," worth about $10 each. These fifties are subdivided into sixteenths, and the shares are owned in every conceivable quantity, from 1-40th of a fifty to 10 fifties. The Quogue and Topping Purchases occupy the w. part of the town.

[7] This lighthouse is 150 ft. high, and 160 ft. above the level of the sea. It is furnished with an excellent lens apparatus, and its light can be seen 20 nautical miles distant.

[8] The "*Suffolk Mills*" were built at an expense of $130,000. About 150 hands are employed, and 10,000 to 12,000 yds. of flannel are made per week.

[9] The shipping of this port in 1858 consisted of 5 ships, 11 barks, 2 brigs, and 2 schooners, with an aggregate of 5,927 tons, registered; 15 sloops, 5 schooners, and 1 steamer, in all, 1400 tons, enrolled; and a few small vessels, amounting to about 100 tons, licensed. The total number of vessels belonging to this port at different periods has been as follows: in 1807, 4; in 1832, 20; in 1841, 44; in 1843, 52; in 1845, 61; and in 1847, 63.

[10] This academy was established in 1831, and is unincorporated.

[11] This village is sometimes called "*Bullhead*;" and the name Bridgehampton is applied to a large section of country extending from Easthampton to the w. part of Mecox Bay.

[12] This is the residence of the remnant of the Shinnecock Indians, consisting of about 200 persons. They have learned many of the arts of civilized life, and obtain a subsistence by cultivating the soil, fishing, and taking clams. Many of the young men go on whaling voyages, and the young women are employed as servants in the families of the whites. They have entirely lost their native language, and speak the English fluently. They are frugal, industrious, orderly, and intelligent. They have a small (Cong.) church and a spacious schoolhouse. They receive their proportion of the common school money, and the school commissioner of the district employs a teacher for them. They are exempt from taxation, and are debarred the exercise of the elective franchise. They occupy the lands between Canoe Place and Shinnecock Creek as tenants in common. This tract was conveyed to the trustees of the town by Pompumo, Chico, and Manmanum, the sachems of the Shinnecock Indians, Aug. 16, 1703; and the same day the trustees leased the lands back to the Indians for a term of 1000 years, at an annual rent of one ear of corn. The Indians annually elect 3 trustees, who, with the concurrence of 2 justices, can lease certain of their lands to the whites.

from Lynn, Mass. A grant of the land was obtained from James Farrett, agent of Lord Stirling, in April, and a conveyance from the Indians on the 13th of Dec., 1640. During the first 12 months 47 settlers arrived.[1] In 1644 Southampton was received under the government of Conn., and until 1664[2] was represented in General Court at Hartford. Upon the Dutch invasion in 1673 the town again sought a union with Conn. It was received, and, together with Easthampton and Southold, was erected into a co. Upon the re-establishment of English power, in 1674, the town came under the government of New York. The first settlement at Sag Harbor was made in 1730, by a few fishermen. On the morning of the 24th of May, 1777, Col. Meigs, with 130 men, surprised the British force stationed at Sag Harbor, destroyed 12 brigs and a sloop, besides a large amount of forage, provisions, and merchandise, and returned across the sound without the loss of a man.[3] A body of American troops was stationed at Sag Harbor in 1813, in consequence of the presence of a British fleet in Gardners Bay.[4] The first church was erected at Southampton, in 1641;[5] and the first church in Bridgehampton was built in 1670.[6] There are now 17 churches in town.[7]

SOUTHOLD[8]—was incorp. by patent, under Gov. Andros, Oct. 30, 1676,[9] and recognized as a town March 7, 1788. Riverhead was taken off in 1792. It comprises the principal part of the northern peninsula of Eastern Long Island, and includes Robins Island in Great Peconic Bay, and Plum, Fishers, and several smaller islands in Long Island Sound. Orient[10] is a peninsula upon the E.; and Great and Little Hog Necks are smaller peninsulas in the s. The s. shore is indented by several small, irregular bays; while the outline of the N. coast is unbroken except by 2 or 3 narrow inlets. The surface is elevated and level. The soil is a light, sandy loam, kept highly fertile by the use of manures. Plum Island,[11] separated from the mainland by Plum Gut, contains about 800 acres. Fishers Island, about 8 mi. eastward, is 7 mi. long by 1½ wide and contains about 4000 acres.[12] Great and Little Gull Islands are between Plum and Fishers Islands. Agriculture forms the leading industrial pursuit; potatoes, corn, and wheat are the principal crops.[13] Considerable attention is also given to shipbuilding, whaling, and commerce. A limited amount of manufacturing is carried on.[14] Scattered tracts of lands and beaches, owned by an incorp. company, are intrusted to the management of 3 trustees, elected annually. These lands are represented by 110 shares, valued at $15 each. The town has a poorfarm of 300 acres near Southold Village. Lighthouses are located on Hortons Point, Little Gull Island,[15] and "*The Dumplings*,"—a group of rocks in Fishers Island Sound.[16] **Greenport**,[17] (p. v.,) on Greenport Harbor, was incorp. April 18, 1838. It is a port of considerable whaling and commercial business,[18] and is the E. terminus of the L. I. R. R. It contains 5 churches and 2 printing offices. Pop. 1,665. **Southold**, (p. v.,) near the

---

[1] These were Dan'l and Josiah Howe, Thos. Goldsmith, John Oldfields, Sam'l Dayton, Thos. Burnet, John and Edward Howell, Thos. and Job Sayre, Thos. Topping, John Woodruff, Henry and Abraham Pierson, Richard Post, Obadiah Rogers, John Fordham, Samuel Osman, John Rose, James Herrick, Chris. Foster, Jos. Raynor, Ellis Cook, Edward Needham, Sam'l James, John Gosman, John Bishop, John White, Wm. Payne, John Jessup, Henry Walton, Wm. Harker, Allen Breed, Edmund Farrington, Isaac Hillman. John Cooper, Geo. Woods, John Jagger, Richard Smith, Thos. Hildreth, John Hampton, Josh. Barnes, John Jennings, Benj. Haynes, Geo. Wells, Wm. Odell, and John Lum.

[2] The deputies were John Howell, from 1644 to '51; John Cosmore, from 1651 to '55; Thomas Topping, from 1655 to '58; Alex. Knowles, from 1658 to '59; Thomas Topping, from 1659 to '63; and Edward Howell, from 1663 to '64.

[3] Col. Meigs, with 234 men, crossed from Guildford (Conn.) to Southold, in 13 whaleboats, on the 23d of May, and transported the boats across the peninsula, reaching the s. shore 4 mi. from Sag Harbor at midnight. In the attack the British had 6 men killed and 90 were taken prisoners. The party arrived at Guildford on their return in 25 hours from the time they left. Congress expressed its approbation of this enterprise by presenting Col. Meigs with a sword; and Gen. Washington, in a letter to Gen. Parsons, (by whose command Col. Meigs had undertaken the expedition,) congratulated him upon its successful achievement.—*Onderdonk's Rev. Inc.*

[4] This fleet lay here through the war, making forced levies upon the inhabitants of the adjacent shores, but usually paying for the property taken. A descent was made upon Sag Harbor in June, 1813; but an alarm was raised, and the invaders were repelled without their doing serious injury.

[5] The pastors of the society have been Rev. Abraham Pierson, in 1640; Robt. Fordham, in 1649; Jos. Taylor, in 1680; Joseph Whiting, in 1686; Sam'l Gelston, in 1716; Sylvanus White, in 1727; Josh. Williams, in 1785; Harmon Daggett, in 1792; David S. Bogart, in 1798; John B. Babbitt, in 1817; Peter H. Shaw, in 1821; Dan'l Beers, in 1830; and Hugh N. Wilson, in 1836.

[6] Rev. Ebenezer White, in 1690, Jos. Brown, in 1756, Aaron Woolworth, in 1787, and Amzi Francis, in 1823, have been the pastors of this church.

[7] 6 M. E., 5 Presb., Bap., Cong., Meth. Prot., Prot. E., R. C., and Union.

[8] That part of the town E. of Cutchogue was called by the Indians "*Yen-ne-cock*," and by the English "*Northfleet*."

[9] Isaac Arnold, John and Benj. Youngs, Josh. and Barnabas Horton, Sam'l Glover, and Isaac Corry were named trustees in this patent.

[10] Called by the Indians "*Po-qua-tuck*." It was bought of the Indians by Peter Hallock, in 1641; and the first settlement was made on it soon after, during Hallock's absence in England, by John Tuthill, John Youngs, jr., John King, and Israel, Richard, and Samuel Brown.—*Griffin's Journal*, 19.

[11] Formerly known as the "*Isle of Patmos:*" It was bought of the natives, in 1659, by Sam'l Wyllys.

[12] This island was named "*Vischers Island*" by Capt. Cook, the navigator, in 1614. It was purchased, in 1644, by Gov. Winthrop, of Conn.; and was organized as a township by a patent obtained from Gov. Nicoll, of N. Y., in March, 1688. It was for a time claimed by both N. Y. and Conn. Its surface is undulating; near the w. end is a high sand bluff, and near the middle another still higher. There are two convenient harbors on the coast. The soil is well adapted to grass growing and grazing. Hay, wool, butter, and cheese are exported.

[13] There were nearly as many potatoes raised in this town in 1855 as in all the co. besides. A greater quantity of wheat is raised in Southold than in any other town in the co., and a greater quantity of corn than in any town except Southampton. Immense quantities of fish and seaweed are used as fertilizers.

[14] Brick are made in large quantities near Greenport and upon Robins Island; and oil and guano are extensively manufactured from fish near Southold.

[15] The lighthouse upon Little Gull Island was built in 1806, and is 56 ft. high and 74 ft. above tide. It is supplied with a fog bell, which is rung by machinery.

[16] The lighthouse upon North Dumpling was built in 1848, and is 25 ft. high and 70 ft. above the sea. A red light is used.

[17] Formerly "*Stirling*."

[18] The shipping of this port consists of 7 vessels engaged in whaling; about 100 others, with an aggregate of 6000 tons, enrolled; and 102 small vessels, licensed: mostly engaged in the coasting trade.

center of the town, is a station on the L. I. R. R. It contains 3 churches, the Southold Academy, a savings' bank, and about 80 houses. **Hermitage,** a small settlement, **Cutchogue,** (p. v.,) containing 3 churches and nearly 100 houses, and **Mattituck,** (p. v.,) containing 2 churches and 40 houses, are stations on the L. I. R. R. **New Suffolk,** on Great Peconic Bay, contains 1 church and about 20 houses. **Franklinville** is on the line of Riverhead. **West Southold** is a p. o. **East Marion,**[1] (p. v.,) near the W. side of Orient Harbor, contains a windmill, a tidemill, and 1 church; pop. 300. **Orient,**[2] (p. v.,) on the E. side of the same harbor, contains 2 churches and 60 houses. The first settlement was made about 1640, by Rev. John Youngs and others, from New Haven.[3] The government of this colony, like that of several of the earlier New England settlements, was vested in the church members. None others were allowed to vote or to hold office; and the Mosaic code was adopted as their law. This exclusiveness was of short duration. All citizens were soon admitted to the right of suffrage; and in 1657 the Mosaic code was superseded by one better adapted to the circumstances of the people. Upon the union of New Haven with Conn., in 1662, Southold was united with the latter colony and was represented in General Court. In 1664 the town passed under the jurisdiction of New York. The first church was erected in 1641, in the village of Southold.[4] There are now 17 churches in town.[5]

Acres of Land, Valuation, Population, Dwellings, Families, Freeholders, Schools, Live Stock, Agricultural Products, and Domestic Manufactures, of Suffolk County.

Names of Towns.	Acres of Land.		Valuation of 1858.			Population.		No. of Dwellings.	No. of Families.	Freeholders.	Schools.	
	Improved.	Unimproved.	Real Estate.	Personal Property.	Total.	Males.	Females.				No. of Districts.	Children taught.
Brookhaven	33,696½	90,723½	$1,971,850	$502,000	$2,473,850	4,761	4,935	1,657	1,970	1,431	43	3,773
Easthampton	13,274	14,061	707,200	251,750	958,950	1,050	1,095	402	431	317	7	727
Huntington	30,873½	28,271	1,405,900	374,350	1,780,250	4,153	3,989	1,356	1,584	1,068	28	3,210
Islip	9,969	35,757⅛	771,901	171,800	943,701	1,676	1,606	583	673	418	12	1,372
Riverhead	12,883⅝	20,942¼	609,650	112,750	722,400	1,369	1,365	520	555	519	14	1,113
Shelter Island	4,889½	3,181½	87,800	28,800	116,600	233	250	85	96	70	1	179
Smithtown	12,545½	17,645¾	547,055	146,850	693,905	1,037	1,050	371	410	242	7	608
Southampton	24,447¼	38,506	1,382,000	420,450	1,802,450	3,325	3,336	1,219	1,356	1,064	22	2,279
Southold	21,240	11,482¾	1,203,500	276,500	1,480,000	2,865	2,811	1,048	1,129	964	17	2,040
Total	163,818⅞	260,570⅞	8,686,856	2,285,250	10,972,106	20,469	20,437	7,241	8,204	6,093	151	15,301

Names of Towns.	Live Stock.					Agricultural Products.							Domestic Cloths, in Yards.
						Bush. of Grain.		Tons of Hay.	Bushels of Potatoes.	Bushels of Apples.	Dairy Products.		
	Horses.	Working Oxen and Calves.	Cows.	Sheep.	Swine.	Winter.	Spring.				Pounds of Butter.	Pounds of Cheese.	
Brookhaven	1,281	2,092	1,955	6,069	3,393	36,175½	120,411½	6,425	24,955	6,235	86,047		204
Easthampton	568	1,480	843	4,097	1,076	13,280½	54,793	3,119½	8,973	2,690	37,621	800	225
Huntington	1,583	1,422	1,776	5,847	3,344	39,732½	141,358½	9,255½	28,124½	1,677	114,558		
Islip	407	708	695	610	1,128	10,592	33,043½	2,907½	15,691	1,335	27,095	650	
Riverhead	681	960	1,032	721	2,056	21,432½	71,645	2,386¾	57,234	6,087	71,146		142
Shelter Island	58	373	154	2,422	370	2,866	15,351½	550½	4,840	317	8,694	30	
Smithtown	441	646	662	3,048	1,175	12,376	51,999½	3,091	3,695½	680	40,587		22
Southampton	1,103	3,549	2,037	2,986	4,004	35,728	177,019½	7,968	29,603	2,689	120,675	100	243
Southold	989	2,152	1,679	2,216	3,181	32,550	132,696¾	5,801½	130,947	6,089	127,982		84
Total	7,111	13,382	10,833	28,016	19,727	203,733	798,318¾	41,505¼	304,063	27,799	634,405	1,580	870

1 Formerly "*Rocky Point.*"
2 Formerly "*Oyster Ponds.*"
3 Among these early settlers were Wm. Wells, Barnabas Horton, Thos. Mapes, John Tuthill, and Matthias Corwin.
4 This was the first church edifice erected in the State. The first pastor was Rev. John Youngs. His successors were Joshua Hobart, in 1674, Benj. Wolsey, in 1720, Jas. Davenport, in 1738, and Wm. Throop, in 1748.
5 5 Presb., 5 M. E., 3 Cong., 2 Bap., R. C., and Univ.

SULLIVAN COUNTY.

THIS county was erected from Ulster, March 27, 1809, and was named in honor of Maj. Gen. John Sullivan, of the Revolution. It contains an area of 1,082 sq. mi., and is centrally distant 85 miles from Albany. The surface is generally very hilly, and along the E. border mountainous. In the S. and W. it consists chiefly of ridges separated by narrow ravines; but in the middle and N. it assumes more the character of a rolling plateau. The highlands of this co. may be considered as the S. slope of the Catskills; and near the N. borders of the co. they divide the waters that flow into Hudson and Delaware Rivers. From this elevated portion numerous ridges extend toward the Delaware, giving the co. a general southerly inclination. The Delaware cuts these ridges diagonally, its valley forming the only division between the Catskills and the mountains of Eastern Penn. The highest points in the co. are the hills in the town of Rockland, which are estimated to be 2100 to 2400 feet above tide. Walnut Hill, in Liberty, has an elevation of 1980 feet. The lowest summit of the Shawangunk[1] Mt., between Bloomingburgh and Wurtzboro, is 1271 feet above tide, and the highest summit is about 500 feet higher. This range of mountains at a distance presents a striking uniformity of outline, which is due to the evenness of stratification of the rock composing it. The lowest point in the co. is upon the Delaware, at the mouth of the Mongaup, which has an elevation of 550 feet above tide. The co. line on the Rondout is elevated 773 feet.

With the exception of a small district on its E. border, through which flow the upper waters of Shawangunk Kil and Lackawack Creek, this co. is drained by the Delaware and its branches, the largest of which are Neversink[2] and Mongaup[3] Rivers, Beaver Kil and Bashers Kil, and Callicoon (Caw-li-coon) and Ten Mile Creeks. The Neversink flows entirely across the co., having for its tributaries Bashers Kil, Wyncoop Brook, Bush Kil, Cherry-meadow Brook, and several minor streams. Most of these streams are rapid, and afford at numerous points a great amount of water power. In the valleys and forests of the co. are about 100 small lakes, which form peculiar and often picturesque and highly beautiful features in its scenery. Most of these ponds and streams abound in fish, of which trout is the most common. Pickerel have been introduced into several of them.

The geological formation of the co. is exceedingly simple. The whole surface is underlaid by the red sandstone of the Catskill Group and the Shawangunk Conglomerate. These rocks extend southward into Penn., and form the floor of the coal measures. Of these rocks the latter possesses an economical value for millstones,[4] building stones, and the manufacture of glass. The soil is mostly a reddish loam mixed with gravel, and is generally stony; in the S. E. portion is found some clay. Grass is the staple production, and the hilly character of most of the co. seems to adapt it to grazing rather than to tillage. The facility with which the products of the dairy can now reach the great markets, by means of the N. Y. & E. R. R., has within a few years given an impetus to the prosperity of the co., while the erection of tanneries, which the same thoroughfare has encouraged, has created a home market of great advantage to the farmer. In 1855 there were in the co. about 40 tanneries, producing over $2,000,000 worth of leather annually and employing about 750 laborers. The lumbering interests also employ large amounts of capital and labor. Winter wheat, formerly considered a sure and abundant crop, is found to yield smaller returns and with less certainty as the country becomes older; and other crops, less valuable but more certain, have been substituted to a great extent. The surplus wheat of Sullivan co. was formerly transported by land to the Hudson, where it found a profitable market; but, with the increase of manufactures, there is now less raised than is consumed in the co. Grass seed of a fine quality is raised in considerable quantities. The fruits are limited to apples, pears, plums, cherries, and a few peaches. The timber along the Delaware Valley is mostly hemlock, pine, oak, and chestnut; and on the highlands it is hemlock, beech, maple, birch, ash, and basswood. The climate is cool and bracing, and the co. is remarkably healthy.

---

[1] Pron. Shon-gum; said to signify "white stone."
[2] On Sauthier's Map, 1779, *Mahaickamack,* or *Never-Sink.*
[3] On Sauthier's Map, 1779, *Mangawping,* or *Mingwing.*

[4] Esopus millstones, formerly in high repute, were made from the Shawangunk grit.

The co. seat[1] is located at Monticello, in the town of Thompson. The co. buildings, consisting of a courthouse and jail, are substantial stone edifices, erected in 1844 in place of the original co. buildings, which were burned.[2] The poorhouse is located upon a farm of 100 acres 3 mi. E. of Monticello. The average number of inmates is 56, supported at a weekly cost of 75 cts. each. The farm yields a revenue of $400. A school is kept during 3 mo. in the year. No religious instruction is afforded. The house is too small, is poorly ventilated, is not furnished with water, and will not admit of a proper classification of its inmates.

The 2 great works of internal improvement within the limits of the co. are the Delaware & Hudson Canal,[3] extending through the S. E. part, and the N. Y. & E. R. R., built along the valley of the Delaware.[4] The former opens an easy and direct communication between the Hudson at Rondout and the Penn. coal mines at Carbondale; and the latter forms one link of the great chain of western travel. Several plank roads have been constructed, as auxiliary to this great thoroughfare, greatly benefiting the sections of country through which they pass. The first newspaper in the co. was issued in 1821.[5]

Little is known of the early history of the co. Many traces exist of its occupation long anterior to that by the present race of settlers. Upon the first advent of the present settlers, a road was found to extend S. W. from Esopus, on the Hudson, along the valley N. of the Shawangunk Mts. It was known as the "*Mine Road*," and, according to traditional account, was built by a company of miners from Holland, before the English conquest of 1664.[6] Two mines are said to have been wrought,—one where the mountain approaches the Delaware, near the lower point of Panquaroy Flat; and the other N. of the mountain, about halfway between the Delaware River and Esopus Creek. The Minisink Flat, on the border of Orange and Sullivan cos., is said to have been settled by Hollanders many years before the date of Penn's Charter; and the settlement, which extended 40 mi. or more along both sides of the Delaware, had in a great degree become isolated from the rest of the world. When the present settlements were begun, there was a road from the E., near the central part of the co., called the "*Porter Road;*" and in the N. part was another, called the "*Hunter's Road.*"

With the exception of the vague traditions of early settlement by the Dutch along the Delaware, the first location of a permanent white inhabitant is said to have been made about the year 1700, by Don Manuel Gonzales, a Spaniard, who, having married into a Dutch family in Rochester, (Ulster co.,) removed to Mamakating Hollow, where he erected a house and raised grain. He opened a trade with the neighboring Indians, who were then friendly; and other settlers were induced to follow. Mamakating Precinct was formed in 1743, and until after the Revolution it embraced nearly all of the present co. of Sullivan. About 1750 a number of German families settled upon the w. frontiers of Ulster co. They suffered greatly from Indian hostilities. The first Indian incursion took place in 1777, when the family of Mr. Sprague, in Mamakating, was attacked. The next year the family of Mr. Brooks was attacked, some members were killed, and others taken prisoners.

On the 13th of Oct. 1778, a party of nearly a hundred tories and Indians, under Brant, invaded the settlements, first falling upon the family of Mr. Westfall, and killing one man. They next attacked the house of Mr. Swartwout, who was at home with his sons, (the women having been previously removed to a fort,) and killed all but one, who escaped. The firing alarmed others, who fled to the forts at Gumars and De Witts, where, by a skillful display of force by Capt. Abraham Cuddeback, who commanded at the former, the enemy were deterred from making an attack.

---

[1] By the act of incorporation the Gov. and council were to appoint 3 commissioners to locate the county seat, and the Board of Supervisors 3 others to superintend the erection of the courthouse and jail. Wm. Ross, Jos. Morrell, and Abraham H. Schenck were appointed for the former purpose, and David Hammond, John Linsley, Malachi West, John Newkirk, and Davies Martin successively for the latter.

[2] The first buildings, erected in accordance with an act passed March 22, 1811, were burned Jan. 13, 1844. The first court was held, and the first Board of Supervisors organized, at the house of Curtis Linsley. The county officers first appointed were Wm. A. Thompson, *First Judge;* Samuel F. Jones and Elnathan Sears, *Associate Judges;* John Conklin, Jabez Wakeman, and David Hammond, *Assistant Justices;* James S. Dunning, *Surrogate;* Uriah Lockwood, *Sheriff;* and John P. Jones, *Clerk.*

[3] The Delaware & Hudson Canal Co. was incorp. April 23, 1823. The work was commenced in July, 1825, and completed in Oct. 1828. It was of great importance to the early settlers of the co., as it opened an easy and cheap avenue to market.

[4] This R. R. enters the co. in the town of Tusten from Penn. It having been found difficult to construct the road on the N. Y. side of the river, the right of way for a short distance was solicited from Penn. The petition was granted, and for the sub-

stantial benefit which the R. R. conferred upon that State, the company was subjected to an annual tax of $10,000. This road forms a direct and speedy communication with N. Y., and has been of great value to the co. in stimulating its settlement and developing its resources.

[5] The *Sullivan County Whig* was started at Bloomingburgh in 1821, by John J. Tappan. It was removed to Monticello in 1828, and its name changed to

The Republican Watchman. Frederick A. Devoe and James E. Winslow were successively its editors, and since 1843 it has been published by J. E. Quinlan.

The *Sullivan County Herald* was commenced at Monticello in 1833, and published by M. Smith, S. Phelps, and others, about 4 years.

The *Sullivan County Whig* was published at Bloomingburgh in 1844, by J. S. Brown, and subsequently by John Waller, In 1855 it was changed to the

Sullivan County Democratic Republican, under which title it is now published by Waller.

The *Union Democrat* was established at Monticello in 1854, by F. A. Devoe, and was afterward united with *The Whig.*

[6] See *Eager's Hist. Orange Co.*, p. 50, where will be found a letter from Samuel Preston giving the substance of the tradition. It is from Hazard's Register.

After firing most of the houses and barns of the settlement, the marauders retired, leaving behind them a melancholy scene of havoc and desolation at the verge of an inclement winter. The distress thus occasioned was very great. Major Phillips arrived soon after the incursion with a company of militia; but the enemy had fled beyond reach.

In 1777 or '78, Capt. Graham, with a party of 18 men, went to Chestnut Brook in pursuit of some Indians who had been committing depredations upon the settlements at Pine Bush. Having stopped to drink, Capt. Graham saw an Indian in the path, and the party fired a volley without effect. Upon this the Indians on the opposite banks returned the fire with fatal effect, and but 3 of the party escaped to tell the dismal tale. To deprive the enemy of sustenance and the means for further annoyance, the Legislature, in 1779,[1] enacted a law directing the Governor to cause the destruction of such grain and crops in the w. frontiers of Orange and Ulster cos. as could not be removed to a place of safety. In 1783[2] the precinct of "*Mamacotting*" and the township of Rochester (the district of the regiment of Col. A. Hawke Hay, and that part of the Goshen regiment on the w. side of the Minisink Mts.) were exempted from a levy then made for the defense of the N. and w. frontiers.[3]

Several traces of Indian occupation were found in the first settlement of the co. About 4 mi. from the Delaware, on the Flat, was found a brass or copper tomahawk, with a steel edge, and a handle perforated for smoking. Stone axes, flint arrows, &c. were frequently found. In 1793, an Indian living in Rockland, at a place called "*Pocatocton*," (meaning a river almost spent,) removed to Niagara. He is supposed to have been the last of his race that inhabited the co. Indian trails were found along the Delaware, the Beaver Kil, and in other sections.

The part of this co. s. of the s. bounds of Callicoon and Bethel is comprised in the Neversink Patent, conveyed to Matthew Ling and others Aug. 28, 1704; and the remainder of the co. in the great tract granted to Johannes Hardenbergh and others April 20, 1708, and known as the "Hardenbergh Patent."[4] The Newburgh and Cochecton Turnpike (incorp. March 20, 1801) was opened across the co. in 1808, and gave the first impulse to its prosperity by making it accessible to settlers. This section continued to receive emigrants from New England and the older sections of the State until its growth was checked by the completion of the Erie Canal to the Genesee country and the great lakes, by which emigration was diverted to the new and fertile lands of the West. Real estate in consequence declined materially in value, and many of the early settlers abandoned their locations and joined the westward current. In 1819 or '20 the Orange Branch Turnpike was made, from Montgomery, (Orange co.,) crossing the Shawangunk Mt. at Roses Gap, and extending across the barrens through Wakemans Settlement to the Neversink Falls, and thence to Liberty. The charter of this road was long since given up, but the route is maintained as a district road.

BETHEL—was formed from Lumberland, March 27, 1809. Cochecton was taken off in 1828 It lies upon the high ridges which form the watershed between Delaware and Mongaup Rivers, a little s. w. of the center of the co. Its surface is broken and hilly, and many of the declivities are steep and rocky. It is watered by a large number of small streams, mostly tributary to Mongaup River; and it has many small lakes, which form a beautiful and romantic feature of the landscape. White Lake, near the center,—named from its white sandy shores and bottom,—is noted for the beauty of its scenery.[5] The other principal lakes are Birch Ridge Pond in the N. w., Horse Shoe and Pleasant Ponds in the N., Mallory Pond in the w., Indian Field Pond in the s., Big and Wells Ponds on the s. line, and Chestnut Ridge Pond and Black Lake and Lake Superior near the center. The soil is a sandy and gravelly loam, intermixed in places with clay. The settlements are comparatively new, and the people are chiefly engaged in the raising of neat cattle, dairying, lumbering, and tanning.[6] **Mongaup Valley** (p. v.) contains 35 houses, and **Bethel** 15. **Bashville** and **White Lake** are p. offices. John Fuller was the first settler in the "Fuller Settlement," in 1806–07.[7] The first preacher (Presb.) was the Rev. Mr. Green.[8]

1 October 17.   2 February 21.

3 Incidents connected with these events, and the details of the memorable battle of Minisink in July, 1779, are given in our account of the towns in which they occurred.

4 Portions of the Hardenbergh Patent were settled upon leases of long term; and during the anti rent excitement, a few years since, the clamor against this tenure prevailed extensively, but without acts of open violence. The refusal to pay rents, which this feeling occasioned, led to a great amount of litigation. Although the excitement has subsided, the question is not fully settled.

5 This lake is noticed in one of the poems of Alfred B. Street, by the name of "Kon-ne-on-ga."

6 A tannery at Mongaup Valley, in 1856 manufactured 50,000

sides of leather, valued at $187,000. It consumed about 5000 cords of hemlock bark, and employed 70 men, at a cost of $12,000. There are about 102,000 sides of leather manufactured annually at different tanneries in this town.

7 G. and C. Hurd were the first settlers at the Hurd settlement; Adam and Eve Pentler near Bethel; and Potter and Mattison near White Lake. The first school at Mongaup was taught by G. P. Price, and at Bethel by Dr. Copeland. Gillespie & Hook kept the first store at White Lake, and J. K. Beeman built the first saw and grist mill, on White Lake outlet. The first birth was that of Catharine Fuller, in 1807, and the first death that of a child of Stephen Northrup.

8 The census reports 4 churches; 2 M. E., Presb., and Ref. Presb.

CALLICOON[1]—was formed from Liberty, March 30, 1842. Fremont was taken off in 1851. It lies in the w. part of the co., about the sources of the N. branch of Callicoon Creek. It is watered by numerous streams flowing into the Delaware, the valleys being mostly narrow ravines, and the hills rising in steep declivities 200 to 600 feet above them. In the N. E. are Shandler and Sand Ponds, the latter affording a pure white sand, formerly used in making glass. The soil is mostly a sandy loam, and the hillsides and summits are generally capable of a good degree of cultivation. The settlement is recent, and the people are about equally engaged in lumbering, farming, and tanning.[2] **Jeffersonville,** (p.v.,) on the line of Cochecton, has a population of 433, of which 305 are in this town. **Youngsville,** (p.v.,) **North Branch,** (p.v.,) and **Callicoon Center** (Callicoon p.o.) have each about 30 houses. The first settlers were Wm. Wood and his sons, Gerrett, Edward, and David, who arrived in town May 19, 1814, and lived 15 years in the wilderness.[3] Rev. Mr. McClary, pastor of the Asso. Ref. church of Bethel, was the first preacher.[4]

COCHECTON[5] —was formed from Bethel, March 25, 1828. It is situated upon the bank of the Delaware, in the w. part of the co. Ridges of hills, with narrow valleys between, cover the entire surface of the town. The principal streams are the Callicoon and its branches, and several small tributaries of the Delaware. The mouth of the Callicoon is 777 feet above tide. Pike Pond in the E., Perry Pond in the S., and Mitchells Pond and Lake Huntington in the center, are the principal sheets of water. A large part of the surface is still covered with forests. The soil is mostly a gravelly loam, and best adapted to pasturage. Lumbering and tanning form the leading objects of industry. **Cochecton** (p.v.) contains 269 inhabitants, **Pike Pond** (p.v.) 188, **Callicoon Depot** (p. v.) 207, and **Stevensburgh** (Cochecton p. o.) 209. **Beech Wood** and **Fosterdale** are p. offices. Settlements were begun on the Delaware before the Revolution, but were broken up. The pioneer settler was N. Mitchell, who located near Cochecton Village.[6] The first church (Presb.) was formed in 1839, and the Rev. Mr. Cummings was the first pastor.[7]

FALLSBURGH—was formed from Thompson and Neversink, March 9, 1826. It derives its name from the falls in Neversink River at Fallsburgh Village. Its surface is hilly and rolling. It is drained by the Neversink and its branches. Sheldrake Pond, (named from the wild ducks that formerly frequented its waters,) Smith, Hill, and Brows Ponds in the w., and East Pond, in the E., are the principal lakes. The soil is a gravelly loam. The people are chiefly engaged in lumbering, dairying, and tanning.[8] **Woodbourne** (p.v.) contains 30 houses, **Neversink Falls** (Fallsburgh p. o.) 25, **Hasbrouck** (p. v.) 25, **Loch Sheldrake** (p. v.) 15, and **Sandburgh** (p.v.) 15. It is said that settlement was commenced in this town by Germans previous to the Revolution,[9] but the settlers were driven off during that war. Soon after the peace 3 brothers by the name of Baker located in town and commenced the first permanent settlement.[10] The first church (Ref. Prot. D.) was built at Hasbrouck.[11]

FORESTBURGH—was formed from Thompson and Mamakating, May 2, 1837. It lies principally upon the high ridges between Neversink and Mongaup Rivers, and has a broken surface and an average elevation of 1400 feet above tide. In this town are several small lakes, the principal of which are Ruddicks Pond in the N. W., Beaver Pond in the S., and Panther Pond in the center. The town still retains the character implied by its name. Mongaup Falls, on Mongaup River, 3 mi. above Forestburgh Village, are worthy of note. The river here falls into a chasm 70 feet deep, and the banks below the falls are more than 100 feet high. Lumbering, tan-

---

1 Caw-li-coon. This name is said to signify "Turkey" in both Dutch and Indian. The Dutch for turkey is "Kalkoen." In the statutes and official publications of the State the name is commonly written "Collikoon."—Harper's N. Y. & E. R. R. Guide, p. 84.

2 There are 5 large tanneries in town, which manufacture about 125,000 sides of leather annually.

3 Edward was a cooper; the others were farmers. The first child born was John Wood. Jacob Quick built the first saw-mill, and Samuel Young kept the first store and built the first mill, at Youngsville. In 1833–34 settlers began to come in from Conn. and the N.; and in 1840 Germans began to settle in the town in considerable numbers. The latter class now form about one-third of the population.

4 The census reports 2 churches; Luth., Asso. Ger. Meth.

5 Co-shek-tun. Originally called "Cush-nun-tunk," or low grounds.

6 Among the other early settlers were David Young, at Big Island; John Ross, at Callicoon Creek; Nicholas Conklin and —— Tyler, at Cochecton. Job Jones taught the first school, near Cochecton; Maj. Ebenezer Taylor kept the first tavern and store, at Cochecton; and Mitchell Conklin built the first sawmill, on Mitchells Pond Brook. On Big Island, 2 mi. above Cochecton,

was an extensive Indian burial place, of which traces are occasionally plowed up at the present day. There are about 900 Germans in this town.

7 The census reports 3 churches; M. E., Presb., and Ref. Prot.D.

8 At Fallsburgh is an extensive tannery, that manufactures 40,000 sides of leather annually; and another of the same size is located at Woodbourne.

9 Fruit trees planted by these settlers are said to be still standing.

10 Thomas Rawson came in 1787 or '88; Thomas Grant located in 1789; Samuel Thaddeus, Obadiah Brown, and James Hill settled a little N. of Fallsburgh; and James Nicoll, Peter Ferdon, and Mr. Brush on the site of the village. The first sawmill was built in 1808, and the first grist mill in 1809, by Philo Ruggles. Matthew Seeley kept the first inn, at Hasbrouck, and Robt. Reading the first store, at Fallsburgh. In 1797, the nearest mill was at Napanock, in Ulster co.; and for many years the nearest market was Newburgh. In 1786 or '87 an extraordinary and destructive flood occurred upon this valley.

11 This church was burned in 1837, and was rebuilt at Woodbourne. The census reports 3 churches in town; 2 M. E., and 1 Ref. Prot. D.

ning,[1] and dairying constitute the employments of the people. **Forestburgh** (p. o.) contains 10 houses, **Oakland** 15, and **Hartwood** 10. Settlement commenced before the Revolution, and recommenced in 1795 on the Mongaup River. Zephaniah and Luther Drake were pioneers in the s. w. part of the town, and Elisha Smith near Oakland.[2] Rev. Isaac Thomas (Meth.) was the first preacher.[3]

FREMONT—was formed from Callicoon, Nov. 1, 1851, and named in honor of John C. Fremont. It lies in the extreme w. part of the co., upon the bank of the Delaware. Its surface is broken and hilly, the summits rising 600 to 1000 feet above the valley and 1500 to 1800 feet above tide. Its waters are Basket and Hawkins Creeks, a great number of smaller streams, and numerous small lakes, the principal of which are Long Pond, Round and Basket Ponds in the N., Lox Pond in the E., and Trout Pond near the center. A large share of the surface is still a wilderness and is too rough for tillage. Tanning and lumbering form the principal employments of the people. **Fremont Center** (p. v.) contains 141 inhabitants, and **Obernburgh** (Fremont p. o.) 20 houses. **Long Eddy** (p. o.) is the Basket Station on the N. Y. & E. R. R. **Hankins** is a station on the same R. R. The first settlers were Joseph Green, at Long Eddy, John Hankins, at Hankins Depot, Benj. Misner, at Long Pond, and Zach. Ferdon, at Round Pond.[4]

HIGHLAND—was formed from Lumberland, Dec. 17, 1853. It is an interior town, lying in the s. part of the co. It is named from the character of its surface, which consists of high ridges between Delaware and Mongaup Rivers, 600 to 1,000 feet above the canal at Barryville and 1,200 to 1,600 feet above tide. There are a great number of small lakes in town, the principal of which are Washington and Wells Ponds on the N. line, Mud and Hagan Ponds in the E., York Pond in the s. w., Washington Pond, used as a canal feeder, and Blind, Little, and Montgomery Ponds near the center. The people are chiefly engaged in lumbering and the rudiments of farming. **Barryville,** (p. v.,) a canal village, contains 25 houses, and **Lumberland** (p. v.) 15. The first settler was John Barnes, who located at Narrow Falls.[5] Rev. Isaac Sargent (Cong.) was the first preacher, about 1797.[6] The battle of Neversink, in the Revolution, took place within the limits of this town.[7]

LIBERTY—was formed from Lumberland, March 13, 1807, and Callicoon and a part of Thompson were taken off in 1842. It lies N. of the center of the co., upon the watershed between the Mongaup and Beaver Kil. Its surface is rough and broken. Walnut Hill, s. of Liberty, is 2,000, and Libertyville 1,467, feet above tide. The N. and w. parts of the town are still covered with forests. The principal sheets of water are Lillie Pond in the N., and Broadhead Pond near the center. The soil is good, but stony; and the people are chiefly engaged in lumbering, dairying, and tanning.[8] **Liberty** (p. v.) contains 364 inhabitants, **Parksville** (p. v.) 40 houses, and **Liberty Falls** (p. v.) 25. **Robertsonville** and **Stevensville** are p. offices. The Liberty Normal Institute, at Liberty, is a flourishing academic institution.[9] Stephen Russell (from Conn.) settled near Liberty, in 1793 or '94.[10] Rev. Wm. Randall (Bap.) was the first preacher.[11]

LUMBERLAND—was formed from Mamakating, March 16, 1798, embracing all the co. w. of Mongaup River and s. of the present N. lines of Liberty and Callicoon. From it were erected Liberty in 1807, Bethel in 1809, and Highland and Tusten in 1853. Its surface is rugged and

---

[1] About 100,000 sides of leather are annually manufactured in this town.
[2] Miss Moore taught the first school, at Drakestown; S. Conant kept the first inn, and Thomas Alsop the first store, at Forestburgh. The first sawmill was built at Oakland.
[3] There are no church buildings in town.
[4] Sarah Phillips taught the first school; John Ranfiesen kept the first inn, and John Hawkins kept the first store and built the first sawmill. About one-third of the population are Germans. The census reports 1 church; R. C.
[5] Among the other first settlers were John Carpenter, Wm. Seeley, N. Patterson, and Wm. Randall, at Beaver Brook; and Benj. Hayne at Handsome Eddy. John Carpenter employed Nath'l Wheeler to teach the first school, before the public schools were organized. G. Ferguson kept the first inn, in 1830, and Phineas Terry the first store, in 1828. N. Patterson built the first sawmill, on Beaver Brook.
[6] The census reports 3 churches; Cong., M. E., Union.
[7] This battle took place on the N. side of Beaver Brook, on lot 17 of the 7th div. of the Neversink Patent. The scene of the action is the top of a hill 3 miles from Barryville and half a mile N. W. from Dry Brook. The battle took place between a party of tories and Indians, under Brant,—who were retreating, after having destroyed the settlement of Neversink,—and a party of American militia, who pursued them. The battle was

long and bloody, and resulted in the retreat of the Americans with the loss of 44 killed. In 1822 the bones of the slain were collected and interred beneath a monument at Goshen. An address was delivered on the occasion by Gen. Hathern, who had taken a leading part in the engagement.
[8] About 106,000 sides of leather are annually manufactured in this town.
[9] Incorp. by law, April 12, 1848; the Hon. John D. Watkins, the founder, being sole corporator.
[10] Among the other first settlers were Nathaniel Pinney, Josiah Whipple, and Nathan Staunton, who came from Preston, Conn., in the spring of 1795, and settled on lot 12; John Groton and Edward Swan, who settled on lot 3; Ebenezer Green, on lot 4; Isaiah Whipple, on lot 10, of tract known as the 3000 acre lot; and Stephen Benton, who located at Benton Hollow. Aviar Whipple taught the first school, at Blue Mountain Settlement; Roswell Russell kept the first inn, Stephen Russell the first store; and Chas. Broadhead built the first grist and saw mill, on the mountain, in 1797. The first child born was Sally Staunton, in 1797; the first marriage, that of David Rowland and Aviar Whipple in 1797; and the first death, that of Sally Staunton, or a son of William Aby, in 1798. The first house was erected about half a mile s. of where the Presb. ch. now stands. Most of the first settlers afterward removed west.
[11] The census reports 4 churches; 1 Bap., 2 M. E., and 1 Presb.

broken, and much of it is yet a wilderness. The name of the town still suggests the leading pursuit of the people. A large number of small lakes, with their outlets, form the principal waters. The principal of these lakes are Lebanon Pond in the N., Round, Sand, and Hogais Ponds in the W., and Long Pond in the center. Metauques Pond, in the E., lies about 2 mi. w. of the Mongaup, and 300 feet above it. On its outlet is a beautiful cascade. **Mongaup** and **Pond Eddy** are p. offices. There is but one church, (M. E.) The Delaware & Hudson Canal extends through the town along the course of the river. It is supposed that settlement was commenced before the Revolution; but the names of the first settlers are not preserved.[1] In the survey of the Minisink Patent by Charles Webb in 1762, mention is made of "Reeve's Sawmill."[2]

MAMAKATING,[3] said to have been named in honor of an Indian chief, was erected into a precinct by the General Assembly, Dec. 17, 1743, and embraced all the present territory of Sullivan co. and a portion of Orange. It continued as a precinct until organized as a town, March 7, 1788. It was reduced to its present limits by the erection of Deerpark (Orange co.) and Lumberland in 1798, Thompson in 1803, and a part of Forestburgh in 1837. It lies upon the highlands between Neversink and Shawangunk Creeks. Two parallel ridges, separated by the valley of Bashers Kil, extend through the town in a N. E. and S. W. direction. The eastern of these ridges is known as Shawangunk Mt. The declivities of this mountain are gentle upon the E., but abrupt and broken on the W. It attains an elevation of 1100 feet above the summit level of the canal, and about 1700 feet above tide. In the N. W. part of the town is a mountain of nearly equal elevation, known as Panther Hill. The principal streams are Shawangunk, Bashers, and Pine Kils, the last of which is the outlet of a small lake in the w. part of the town, known as Yankee Pond. The summit level of the Delaware & Hudson Canal, 17 mi. long and 525 feet above tide, is constructed through the valley of Bashers Kil. Masten Pond, in the w. part, is used as a reservoir. About 2 mi. N. of Wurtzboro a vein of lead was discovered several years since, and was worked to a considerable extent. After an abandonment of several years, preparations are again being made to work it. The soil is a sand and gravel loam, in some places intermixed with clay, and best adapted to pasturage. The census of 1855 shows that this town is second only to Thompson in the amount of dairy products. **Bloomingburgh**[4] (p. v.) contains 365 inhabitants, and **Wurtzboro**[5] (p. v.) 491, **Summitville** (Mamakating p. o.) 20 houses, and **Phillipsport** (p. o.) 10; the three last named lie upon the canal. **Burlingham** (p. v.) contains 130 inhabitants. **West Brookville** (p. o.) is a hamlet, and **Homowack** is a p. o. The early settlement of this town has already been noticed,[6] but most of the details have been lost. On the approach of the Revolution the Indians became hostile, and several blockhouses were erected on the frontiers of Ulster co., one of which was at Wurtzboro. On account of the distressed condition of the people by reason of Indian hostilities, they were favored by the supervisors in the apportionment of taxes. Many persons in those days accounted wealthy were reduced to poverty, and but little that could be destroyed remained on the return of peace. Gonzales, the pioneer settler, is said to have built the first sawmill, at Wurtzboro. In 1792 this town contained 182 taxable persons, of whom 34 were in the present towns of Lumberland, Tusten, and Highland. In 1794, Capt. David Dorrance removed from Windham, Conn., and purchased 1000 acres immediately s. of the site of Wurtzboro.[7] John Dorrance, with Elijah Perry, also from Conn., erected the first bark mill in Sullivan co. Rev. Mr. Freleigh was the first pastor of the Ref. Prot. D. Church, built in 1793.[8]

NEVERSINK[9]—was formed from Rochester, (Ulster co.,) March 16, 1798. Rockland was taken off in 1809, and a part of Fallsburgh in 1826. The whole town is elevated, and the surface

---

[1] Among the early settlers since the Revolution were John Showers and Joshua Knight, at Mongaup, S. Gardner and Elnathan Corey, at Pond Eddy, P. Van Vauken, above Mongaup, and John Rinck and Wm. Ryarson, in other parts of the town. The first school was kept in a barn by Mr. Farnham; the first inn was kept by E. Corey, at Pond Eddy.

[2] Mr. Webb lived at Otisville, (Orange co.,) and died at an advanced age in 1814.

[3] Written Mame-Kating, Mame-Cotink, &c. in early records.

[4] This village was settled by J. Newkirk, about 1780, and was incorp. April 26, 1833. It contains 3 churches, 4 hotels, and 5 stores.

[5] Named from Maurice Wurtz, grantee of a canal privilege in Penn., afterward merged in Del. and Hudson Canal Co.

[6] See page 642.

[7] A road was constructed at an early day, by Ananias Sacket, from Mamakating westward, passing about three-fourths of a mi. s. of Lords Pond, and continuing to Nathan Kinne's Flats, from which place Capt. Dorrance made a road to Cochecton for £5 per mi. This road opened a communication from the Hollow to the Delaware River, a distance of about 33 mi. A portion of it is still in use, but the greater part was taken up by the Newburgh & Cochecton Turnpike. The village of Wurtzboro is built upon a tract of 1000 acres bought by Johannes Masten, who cleared the land and erected a sawmill. Westbrookville (formerly "Bashusville") was settled about the same time, and the first house was built of stone and used as a fort to shelter the settlers. Mr. Felton was a pioneer near Burlingham, and J. Newkirk at Bloomingburgh. The early town records have been lost. The first school was kept at Bloomingburgh in 1784, by Mr. Campbell. Wm. Harlow kept the first inn, 2 mi. N. of Bloomingburgh; Wm. Wighton opened the first store, 1 mi. S. of the same place; and H. Newkirk built the first gristmill, on the Shawangunk, within this town.

[8] The census reports 11 churches; 6 M. E., 2 Ref. Prot. D., 1 Bap., 1 R. C., 1 Asso. Ref. Presb.

[9] This name, first applied to the river, is said by some to be derived from the Indian "Ne-wa-sink," or Mad River, and by

is very hilly and to a considerable degree covered with forests. It is watered by the Neversink and its branches, and by the Lackawack, or w. branch of the Rondout, which flows to the Hudson. Denman Hill, 3300 feet, and Thunder Hill, 2500, above tide, are the principal elevations: the latter received its name from the fact that one of the early settlers was frightened away from the place by loud thunder. The soil is generally a gravelly loam, and best adapted to pasturage. The people are chiefly engaged in lumbering, tanning,[1] and dairying. **Grahamsville**[2] (p. v.) contains 40 houses, **Neversink Flats** (Neversink p. o.) 35, and **Claryville** (p. v.) 30. The first settlement was commenced on the Lackawack, 2 mi. below Grahamsville, by the Hornbecks, Clines, Clearwaters, and Lowes, who obtained an Indian title in 1743, and were driven off during the Revolution. Mr. Larrabee, on Thunder Hill, and Benj. Gillett, John Hall, and Wm. Parks, on the 1000 acre lot, were the pioneer settlers after the war.[3] The first church (Meth.) was located at Grahamsville; and the first preacher was Rev. Samuel M. Knapp.[4]

ROCKLAND—was formed from Neversink, March 29, 1809. It lies upon the headwaters of the Popacton, or e. branch of the Delaware, in the extreme n. part of the co. It is a rough, wild region, very hilly and mostly covered with forests. Its principal streams are Beaver Kil and Williwemack Creek. A chain of small lakes extends through the town, the principal of which are Upper, Mongaup, and Hodge Ponds in the e., Big and North Ponds in the s. e., Shaw Pond in the s., Burnt Hill and Jenkins Ponds in the w., and Sand, Mud, and Knapp Ponds in the center. Lumbering, farming, and tanning[5] are the principal pursuits of the people. **Westfield Flats** (Rockland p. o.) contains 28 houses, and **Morsston** (p. v.) about 12. **Beaver Kill, Purvis,** and **Shin Creek** are p. offices. Settlement was begun in 1789, by two families named Stewart and West, from Middletown, Conn.; they located near the middle of the Big Beaver Kil Flat.[6] Rev. Mr. Conkey (Meth.) was the first preacher.[7]

THOMPSON—was formed from Mamakating, March 9, 1803, and named in honor of Wm. A. Thompson, first judge of the co. A part of Fallsburgh was taken off in 1826, and a part of Forestburgh in 1837. It lies principally upon the highlands between Neversink and Mongaup Rivers, and is less hilly than most of the towns of the co. The hills rise 100 to 300 feet above Monticello. Neversink and Mongaup Rivers, with several small lakes and streams, constitute the waters of the town. Kiamesha, or "*Clearwater,*" better known as Pleasant Pond, is a beautiful little lake near Monticello. The other principal ponds are Dutch in the n. e., Lords and Mud in the e., Wolf in the s. e., and Sackets (named from Ananias Sacket, an early settler near it) in the s. w. The quiet scenery of these lakes is becoming appreciated by the lovers of nature and those seeking a retreat from the heat and dust of cities in summer. The soil is a reddish loam. The people are principally engaged in stock raising, lumbering, and tanning.[8] **Monticello,**[9] (p. v.,) the principal village, was incorp. April 20, 1830. Pop. 629. It is beautifully situated upon a ridge of highlands 1387 feet above tide, and is surrounded by hills. It is finely laid out, the main street being 1 mi. long and 8 rods wide, with flagged walks and ornamented with shade trees. It contains a courthouse, jail, co. clerk's and surrogate offices, and a banking house, all of stone; 3 churches, the Monticello Academy, 3 hotels, 10 stores, 3 printing offices, and an iron foundery. **Thompsonville** (p. v.) and **Bridgeville** (p. v.) each contain about a dozen houses. **Gales** and **Glen Wild** are p. offices. The first settlers were Wm. A. Thompson, John Knapp, and Timothy Childs, at Thompsonville.[10] Rev. John Boyd (Presb.) was the first preacher.[11]

TUSTEN—was formed from Lumberland, Dec. 17, 1853, and was named in honor of Col.

---

others to be so named because the stream is less affected by drought than others.

[1] About 95,000 sides of leather are manufactured each year.

[2] Named in honor of Lieut. Graham, who was killed in a skirmish with the Indians near the present site of the village.

[3] The first child born was Elijah Parks. Christopher Darrow taught the first school; Mr. Larrabee kept the first inn, on Thunder Hill; Richard Childs kept the first store; and Wm. Parks built the first gristmill, 3 mi. s. e. of the Flats. There are no town records earlier than 1814.

[4] The census reports 5 churches; 3 M. E., 2 Ref. Prot. D.

[5] One of the most extensive tanneries in the State is in the w. part of the town. About 170,000 sides of leather are manufactured each year in town.

[6] Another account says the first settlers were Robert Cochran, Jehial and Luther Stewart. In the following year, Peter Williams and Cornelius Cochran came in from Mass. Mr. Bascom settled 1 mi. w. of Purvis p. office, and Thomas Nott and James Overton 1 mi. s. of the same. The first child born was Susan Thorn; the first marriage was that of Ebenezer White and Clarissa Field; and the first death was that of Sylvanus Stewart.

Sylvanus Bascom taught the first school, at Westfield Flats; Jehial Stewart kept the first inn, Mr. Loveland the first store; and Luther Stewart built the first mill, at Westfield Flats. The settlers are said to have obtained their first seed corn from the Indians on the Susquehanna Flats, and this stock has been continued till the present time. The lumber trade began in 1798.

[7] The census reports 3 churches; M. E., Presb., and Union.

[8] About 35,000 sides of leather are manufactured annually.

[9] Named by J. P. Jones, from the residence of Thos. Jefferson. The first settlement of this village was made in 1804, by Samuel F. and John P. Jones, from New Lebanon, (Columbia co.,) who located at this place in anticipation of its becoming the co. seat of a new co. to be erected from Ulster. J. P. Jones erected the first house, in 1804, and opened the first store; Curtis Linsley kept the first inn.

[10] A. Sacket and A. D. Kinne were the first settlers in the w. part of the town, and John Wetherlow and John Simson on the Neversink. Asa Hall kept the first school, at Bridgeville; Judge Thompson built the first mill and factory, at Thompsonville.

[11] The census reports 4 churches; M. E., Presb., Prot. E., and Union.

Benjamin Tusten, who was killed in the battle of Minisink, in 1779.[1] This town lies upon the N bank of Delaware River. The W. and S. parts are very hilly, and the E. portions belong to the plateau of rolling lands which comprises the greater part of Tusten, Highland, and Lumberland. The average height of this region is about 750 feet above the Delaware, or 1400 feet above tide. The principal streams are Ten Mile River and its branches: Half Moon and Mill Ponds in the E., and Mill, Davis, and Canfield Ponds in the center, are the principal sheets of water. The soil is a gravelly loam, and best adapted to pasturage. The people are generally engaged in farming and lumbering. **Narrowsburgh,** (p. v.,) containing about 35 houses, is the only village. It derives its name from the fact that the Delaware is here compressed by two points of rock into a deep, narrow channel. Over this is a wooden bridge, with a single span of 184 feet.[2] The place is known to lumbermen by the name of "*Big Eddy.*" Below the narrows the river expands into a wide basin, which in time of a freshet exhibits a stirring scene. **Delaware Bridge** and **Beaver Brook** are p. offices. John Moore kept the first inn and store, and R. Moore built the first mill. The Baptist is the only church in town.

Acres of Land, Valuation, Population, Dwellings, Families, Freeholders, Schools, Live Stock, Agricultural Products, and Domestic Manufactures, of Sullivan County.

Names of Towns.	Acres of Land.		Valuation of 1858.			Population.		No. of Dwellings.	No. of Families.	Freeholders.	Schools.	
	Improved.	Unimproved.	Real Estate.	Personal Property.	Total.	Males.	Females.				No. of Districts.	Children taught.
Bethel	13,468	38,855	$371,920	$42,225	$414,145	1,362	1,249	569	486	301	15	1,136
Cochecton	7,596	33,175	360,170	19,800	379,970	1,640	1,431	523	550	411	15	1,218
Callicoon	5,580	121,475	140,627	6,450	147,077	1,118	974	414	416	328	8	871
Fallsburgh	18,651¼	25,350	316,690	29,200	345,890	1,586	1,443	537	590	414	14	1,271
Forestburgh	1,914	25,049½	117,920	13,900	131,820	468	371	132	140	83	5	325
Fremont	3,170¼	27,852	128,967		128,967	729	572	237	245	184	7	484
Highland	1,454¾	7,449	164,774	5,400	170,174	454	411	158	158	112	6	359
Liberty	15,147½	30,745½	380,945	43,850	424,795	1,477	1,389	520	532	472	17	1,240
Lumberland	1,714½	34,415	191,270	2,200	193,470	497	405	156	162	115	6	398
Mamakating	17,073½	43,652½	612,928	45,850	658,778	2,110	1,974	748	793	511	20	1,616
Neversink	14,366½	24,176	231,551	28,675	260,226	1,136	1,044	413	420	318	18	1,034
Rockland	6,830	47,003¾	106,767	6,817	113,584	674	598	227	237	204	11	618
Thompson	17,436	28,303	515,680	255,800	771,480	1,801	1,749	619	630	514	19	1,445
Tusten	1,087	7,328	131,260	4,950	136,210	439	386	151	158	103	6	315
Total	125,489¼	494,829¼	$3,771,469	$505,117	$4,276,586	15,491	13,996	5,403	5,517	4,070	167	12,330

Names of Towns.	Live Stock.					Agricultural Products.							Domestic Cloths, in yards.
						Bush. of Grain.					Dairy Products.		
	Horses.	Working Oxen and Calves.	Cows.	Sheep.	Swine.	Winter.	Spring.	Tons of Hay.	Bushels of Potatoes.	Bushels of Apples.	Pounds Butter.	Pounds Cheese.	
Bethel	294	1,779	1,042	1,171	844	10,791	36,734½	4,453	8,783	4,210	95,030		1,078
Cochecton	176	1,197	741	228	496	10,214	24,636	2,082	9,861	2,052	48,785	150	235½
Callicoon	78	932	486	166	363	5,565	13,138½	1,520½	5,777	416	24,589		129
Fallsburgh	377	2,448	1,470	1,934	1,099	6,251½	41,686	6,240	13,417	11,045	126,329	228	247
Forestburgh	59	186	161	140	86	983½	2,307½	863½	2,503	877	17,935		73
Fremont	55	490	254	145	152	2,670	7,354½	940	5,321	322	17,515	210	82
Highland	57	277	221	117	225	2,162½	4,409¼	545¼	4,028¾	329	15,501		72
Liberty	396	2,463	1,285	2,131	891	7,491½	36,506½	5,165½	11,569	11,579	105,645	2,935	1,574
Lumberland	55	321	189	31	194	2,613	3,865½	657½	3,818	37	14,155		60
Mamakating	587	1,219	1,553	1,369	1,751	12,886½	33,618½	4,486½	8,030	13,543	127,648		392
Neversink	344	2,099	989	2,450	694	7,370	29,411	4,712	9,720	14,545	110,856	150	3,559
Rockland	168	1,011	559	1,135	297	1,049	12,215	2,474	5,945	4,655	50,814	675	950
Thompson	440	2,025	1,721	1,574	1,095	5,216	30,810½	6,224½	12,314	9,153	168,845	250	984
Tusten	6	124	104		44	1,362	3,373	352	2,102	535	8,280		
Total	3,092	16,571	10,775	12,591	8,231	76,625½	280,066¾	40,716¼	103,188¾	73,298	931,927	4,598	9,435½

[1] See pages 503, 643.

[2] The "Narrowsburgh Bridge Co." was incorp. April 5, 1810, with a capital of $5,000. The bridge was to be 25 feet wide, well covered with plank, and secured by railings.

TIOGA COUNTY.

This county was formed from Montgomery, Feb. 16, 1791. A part of Chenango was taken off in 1798; Broome in 1806; a part of Tompkins in 1822; and Chemung in 1836. It lies near the center of the s. border of the State, centrally distant 135 mi. from Albany, and contains 542 sq. mi. Its surface is broken by a series of ridges extending northerly through the co. from the Penn. line and forming a northerly continuation of the Allegany Mts. The summits of these ridges have a nearly uniform elevation of 1,200 to 1,400 ft. above tide. The valley of the Susquehanna cuts them diagonally and breaks the continuity of the general system of highlands. Numerous lateral valleys extend in a general N. and S. direction from the river, separating the ridges and giving a great variety to the surface. These valleys vary in width from a few rods to a mile and sometimes more, and are generally bordered by steep declivities which rise 250 to 400 ft. above them. The summits of the hills are generally broad and rolling, and in some places are broken and rocky.

The rocks of this co. belong to the Chemung and Catskill groups. The former occupies all the surface N. of the river and forms the underlying rock of the hills s., and the latter crowns all the summits s. of the river. The sandstone of the Chemung group is quarried for flagging; and some of the red sandstone is sufficiently compact to make good building stone. Limestone, from which lime is manufactured, is found along the Penn. border. There are no other minerals of importance. The river valleys, and many of the hills adjoining, are covered deep with drift, consisting of sand, clay, and gravel. This deposit near Factoryville is 80 ft. thick, and a wide belt of it seems to extend northerly in an almost unbroken line from the latter place to Cayuga Lake. The principal streams are Susquehanna River, and Owego, Catatunk, Cayuta, Pipe, and Apalachin Creeks and their branches. These creeks have generally rapid currents, though few waterfalls; and they furnish all necessary water-power for local purposes. Their valleys are usually narrow and rocky in their upper courses, but toward the Susquehanna they expand into broad and beautiful level intervales. The valleys of the Susquehanna and several of its tributaries are celebrated for their beauty.

The soil along the valleys is a rich, deep, gravelly loam, with an occasional intermixture of clay and sand. The intervales along the Susquehanna are especially noted for their fertility. The uplands are gravelly and sandy and moderately fertile. Upon the summits the soil is hard and unproductive, and in many places the rocks are entirely bare. A considerable portion of the uplands is still covered with forests.

The prominent interest of the co. is agricultural, and its various branches are successfully pursued. Winter and spring grains, corn, and the root crops, are mostly cultivated on the lowlands or river bottoms, and the uplands are devoted to stock and wool growing and dairying. Considerable commercial interest has grown up in connection with the rail roads, and manufactures have also been established to a limited extent.[1]

The county seat is located at Owego, upon the Susquehanna.[2] The courthouse, a wooden structure, was erected about 40 years since, at a cost of $8,000. It is in a good state of preservation. The jail, jailor's house, and barn, all of brick, were built in 1851, at a cost of about $6,000. The jail contains 8 double cells. The clerk's office is a fireproof brick building, erected in 1858, at a cost of $2,200. The courthouse, clerk's office, jail, jailor's house, and barn occupy a square in the center of the village.

---

[1] A large lumber and tanning business was formerly carried on; but it has declined, from the scarcity of material.

[2] By the organic act of 1791, Tioga was formed a half-shire county. It provided that the courts should be held alternately at "Chenango," in the town of Union, and at "Newtown Point," in the town of Chemung, the former now Binghamton, Broome co., and the latter Elmira, Chemung co. The half-shire was abolished upon the organization of Broome co. in 1806; Feb. 17, 1810, Nathaniel Locke, Anson Cary, and Samuel Campbell were appointed commissioners to locate the courthouse site, and Joshua Ferris, Isaac Swartwout, and Samuel Westbrook to superintend the erection of the building; and in 1811–12 the county seat was removed from Elmira to Spencer Village. June

8, 1812, the co. was divided into 2 Jury Districts, and the courts were held at Elmira and Spencer. The East Jury District embraced the towns of Tioga, Spencer, Danby, Caroline, Candor, Berkshire, and Owego; and the West, the towns of Cayuta, Catherines, Chemung, and Elmira. The courthouse at Spencer was burned in 1821, and by an act of 1822 the half-shire of the county was re-established, and Owego and Elmira became the half-shire towns. Upon the organization of Chemung co. in 1836, Elmira became its county seat, and Owego the county seat of Tioga. The first county officers were Abram Miller, *First Judge*; Wm. Stuart. *District Attorney*; Thomas Nicholson, *County Clerk*; James McMasters, *Sheriff*; and John Mersereau, *Surrogate.*

The county poorhouse, a stone building, is located near Owego, upon a farm of 62 acres, which yields an annual income of $600. The average number of inmates is 62, and the whole number of rooms for their accommodation is 15. No school is connected with the establishment, and no means are provided for religious instruction.

The principal works of internal improvement are the N. Y. & E. R. R., extending along the river valley through Owego, Tioga, and Barton; and the Cayuga & Susquehanna R. R., extending from Owego northward through Tioga and Candor to Ithaca.[1] These roads furnish ample facilities for transportation, and bring the products of the county into close proximity to the Eastern markets. Three weekly newspapers are now published in the co.[2]

The first settlement in this county was made upon the Susquehanna intervales, soon after the Revolution, by emigrants from the Wyoming Valley in Penn. These settlers originally came from Conn. and Mass., and left Wyoming in consequence of troubles growing out of the Indian hostilities and of controversies in regard to title. They located here before the Indian title to the lands was extinguished. The greater part of the present territory was comprised in the Boston Ten Towns. The title of this tract, comprising 230,400 acres between Chenango River and Owego Creek, was vested in the State of Mass. in 1786, and in 1787 it was sold to a company of 60 persons, mostly residents of that State. The greater part of the proprietors immediately took possession of these lands; and thus it happened that the county was filled up with a New England population while the fertile region of Western New York was yet an unbroken wilderness.

BARTON—was formed from Tioga, March 23, 1824. It lies w. of the Susquehanna, in the s. w. corner of the co. Its surface is generally hilly. A small portion of level land lies along the s. border. The highlands on the w. rise abruptly from the valley of Cayuta Creek, and are divided into two ridges by the valley of Ellis Creek. Their summits are broad and rolling and generally covered with forests. The highest points are 400 to 600 ft. above the river. The soil is a rich alluvium in the valleys and a sandy or gravelly loam upon the hills. A sulphur spring is found on Ellis Creek, near the center of the town. **Waverly,** (p. v.,) situated upon the Erie R. R., in the s. w. part of the town, was incorp. in 1854. It contains the Waverly Academy, 5 churches, and several manufactories. Pop. 1,067. **Factoryville,** (p. v.,) on Cayuta Creek, 1¼ mi. N. of Waverly, contains 180 inhabitants; and **Barton,** (p. v.,) near the N. E. corner, on the Susquehanna, 30 dwellings. **North Barton** is a p. o. **Halsey Valley** (p. o.) is a hamlet in the N. E. part, on the line of Tioga. The first settlement was begun by Ebenezer Ellis and Stephen Mills, who located near the mouth of Ellis Creek in 1791.[3] There are 9 churches in town.[4]

BERKSHIRE—was formed from Tioga, Feb. 12, 1808. Newark was taken off in 1823, and Richford in 1831. It lies upon the E. border of the co., N. of the center. Its surface is mostly a hilly and broken upland, with a mean elevation of 1,200 to 1,400 ft. above tide. A high hill, with steep declivities, lies E. of the center of the town. The streams are the East and West Branches of Owego Creek and their tributaries. The soil in the valleys is a sandy and gravelly loam, and upon the hills it is a tough clay and hardpan. **Berkshire** (p. v.) contains 3 churches and 34 dwellings. **East Berkshire** and **Wilson Creek** are p. offices. The pioneer settlers of the town were Daniel Ball and Isaac Brown, who came in 1791.[5] Rev. Seth Williston conducted the first religious services in town.[6]

---

[1] This road cost $500,000, and it was sold, in 1852, for $4,500.

[2] *The American Farmer* was commenced at Owego in 1810 by Stephen Mack. In 1813 it was sold to Stephen B. Leonard, who changed its name to *The Owego Gazette*, and continued it until 1835, when he sold to J. B. Shurtliff. In 1841 the office was burned, and the paper was discontinued a short time; but soon after it was resuscitated by E. P. Marble, and in 1843 it was sold to Thomas Woods. In 1844 it was changed to *The Tioga Freeman*, John Dow, publisher, and in a few years was discontinued. A local party dispute having arisen, another paper, called *The Owego Gazette*, was started in 1844 by H. A. Beebe, and the two papers were published under the same name for several months. In 1845 Thomas Peasall became proprietor, and in 1846 the paper was sold to David Walter and son. In 1848 it again passed into the hands of H. A. Beebe, by whom it is still published.

The Republican was published 1 year at Owego in 1833 by —— Chatterton.

The Owego Advertiser was commenced in 1836 by Andrew H. Calhoun, and was continued by him until 1852, when he sold to Powell & Barnes, who changed its name to *The Southern Tier Times*. In 1854 Wm. Smyth purchased the establishment and changed the name of the paper to

The Owego Times, under which title he still continues its publication.

The Waverly Advocate was commenced at Waverly Village in 1852 by F. H. Baldwin. It is now published by Baldwin & Polley.

The St. Nicholas, a monthly literary magazine, was published about 1 year in 1853.

[3] Among the other early settlers were —— Aikens, Ezekiel Williams, John Hanna, Wm. Bensley, Luke Saunders, James Swartwood, Charles Bingham, Layton Newell, Lyon C. Hedges, Philip Crans, Justice Lyon, John Manhart, —— Reed, and Silas Wolcott. A number of these were from the Wyoming Valley, and some of them from the adjoining towns of this co. George W. Buttson erected the first sawmill, at Barton Village.

[4] 5 M. E., 2 Bap., Prot. E., and R. C.

[5] Among the first settlers were Stephen and Samuel Ball, Peter Wilson, and Josiah Ball, from Stockbridge, Mass., in 1792–93. John Brown, Capt. Asa Leonard, Eben. Cook, Daniel Carpenter, Consider Lawrence, David Williams, Joseph Waldo, Nathaniel Ford, Abel, Azel, and Nathaniel Hovey, Jeremiah Campbell, and Samuel Collins,—all from Berkshire co., Mass.,—came in soon after. W. H. Moore kept the first inn and store; David Williams erected the first mill; and Miss T. Moore taught the first school.

[6] The census reports 4 churches; 2 M. E., Cong., and Bap.

CANDOR—was formed from Spencer, Feb. 22, 1811. It is a large town, extending from the center to the N. border of the co. Its surface consists of high, broad, rolling uplands, separated into ridges by the narrow valleys of streams flowing in a southerly direction. Their declivities are generally abrupt, and their summits are mostly covered with forests. Catatunk Creek flows through the center of the town, and the West Branch of Owego Creek forms the E. boundary. A western branch of Catatunk Creek enters the town near the center of its W. border and flows E., its valley completely dividing the western ridge into two parts. The soil is a gravelly loam, very fertile in the valleys and moderately so upon the hills. The settlements are mostly confined to the valleys. **Candor** (p. v.) is situated on Catatunk Creek, near the center of the town. It is a station on the C. & S. R. R., and contains 4 churches, a woolen factory, flouring mill, 2 sawmills, and about 70 dwellings. **Candor Center,** ½ mi. w. of Candor, contains 1 church, a flouring mill, 2 sawmills, and 20 dwellings. **Willseyville,** (p. v.,) a station on the C. & S. R. R., in the N. W. part of the town, contains 20 dwellings. **South Candor,** on Catatunk Creek, near the s. border of the town, contains a church and about 20 dwellings. **Weltonville** (p. o.) is a hamlet at the mouth of Doolittle Creek. **East Candor** is a p. o. The first settlers were Thos. Hollister, Job Judd, —— Luddington, and —— Jordan, from Conn., who came into town in 1793.[1] Rev. Daniel Loring was the first preacher. The census reports 10 churches.[2]

NEWARK—was formed from Berkshire, as *"Westville,"* April 12, 1823. Its name was changed March 24, 1824. It lies upon the center of the E. border of the co. Its surface is mostly a hilly, upland region, with a mean elevation of about 1,200 ft. above tide. Its streams are the West Branch of Owego Creek, forming the W. boundary, and the East Branch, flowing S. W. through near the center of the town. The soil in the valleys is a fine, gravelly loam, but upon the hills it is an unproductive hardpan. The greater part of the uplands are yet unsettled. **Newark Valley,** (p. v.,) located in the valley of East Owego Creek, contains 2 churches, mills, an extensive tannery, and 75 dwellings. **Ketchumville,** (p. v.,) in the N. E. corner of the town, 7 mi. N. E. of Newark Valley, contains a church, sawmill, and 26 dwellings. **West Newark** is a p. o. The settlement of the town was commenced in 1791, by emigrants from Berkshire co., Mass.[3] The first religious association (Cong.) was formed in 1798, by Rev. Seth Williston, a missionary from Conn.; Rev. Jeremiah Osborn was the first settled preacher, in 1803.[4]

NICHOLS—was formed from Tioga, March 23, 1824. It lies upon the s. bank of the Susquehanna, near the center of the s. boundary of the co. Its surface is mostly upland, terminating in steep declivities upon the river, and broken by the narrow valleys of small streams. The summits of the hills are broad and 300 to 500 ft. above the river. Many of them are still covered with forests. The soil in the valleys is a gravelly loam and very productive; upon the hills it is a moderately fertile, gravelly and clayey loam, underlaid by red sandstone. **Nichols,** (p. o.,) **Hoopers Valley,** (p. o.,) and **Canfields Corners** (p. o.) are hamlets upon the Susquehanna. The first settlement was made by Ebenezer Ellis, Pelatiah Pierce, Stephen Mills, and James Cole, in 1787. There are 2 churches in town; M. E. and Union.[5]

OWEGO[6]—was organized Feb. 16, 1791. Spencer was taken off in 1806. It is a large town, occupying the s. E. corner of the co. Its surface is mostly upland, separated into two distinct parts by Susquehanna River and broken by the narrow valleys of small creeks. The summits of the ridges are broad and rolling, and 300 to 500 ft. above the river. The intervale along the river in some places is an unbroken flat more than a mile in width. Owego Creek, flowing through a broad and beautiful valley, forms the W. boundary of the town N. of the Susquehanna. The other streams are Nanticoke Creek, from the N., and Apalachin Creek, from the s., and a great number of smaller brooks and creeks. The declivities bordering upon these streams are generally very steep. The soil is a deep, rich, gravelly loam in the valleys, and a less productive, gravelly loam,

---

1 They were followed in 1794 by Joel and Elijah Smith, Israel Mead, and his son Israel,—the former two from Conn, and the latter from Vt. Families named Collins, Sheldon, Marsh, Bates, and Ellis were also among the early settlers. The first inn was kept by Thomas Hollister; the first store by Philip Case; and the first gristmill was erected by Elijah Hart.
2 5 Bap., 2 M. E., Prot. E., Cong., and Union.
3 Among the settlers in 1791 were Elisha Wilson, (living upon the place of his original settlement in 1858, at the age of 87,) Daniel Ball, Isaac and Abram Brown, —— Dean, and —— Norton,—all from Stockbridge, Mass.,—most of them settling in the valley of Owego Creek. The first birth was that of Wm. Ball. Miss E. Moore taught the first school; Enos Slawson kept the first store and inn; and E. Wilson built the first mill.

4 The census reports 5 churches; 3 M. E., Cong., and Presb.
5 Among those who settled later were Judge Emanuel Coryell, Isaiah Jones, —— Bass, and —— Emmons, in 1791; and about the same time Caleb Wright, on the site of Nichols Village, and Stephen Dodd, a short distance below. In 1793 Jonathan Platt and his son Jonathan, Col. Richard Sackett, Lewis Brown, and Miles Forman,—all from Westchester co.,—settled in the valley. Major John Smyth and his sons John, Gilbert, and Nathan, from Monroe co., Penn., Benjamin Lounsbury, Ziba Evans, Jonathan Hunt, Richard Sarles, Asahel Prichard, Jonathan Pettis, Joseph and John Annibal, Joseph Morey, and Daniel Briggs, were also among the pioneer settlers. The first birth was that of Daniel Pierce, in 1787.
6 Owego, "Swift River."—*Annals of Binghamton*, p. 110.

underlaid by hardpan, on the hills. A considerable portion of the hilly regions is yet covered with forests. Manufactures, and commerce to a limited extent, engage the attention of the people. **Owego,** (p. v.,) the co. seat, was incorp. April 4, 1827. It is finely situated upon the Susquehanna, near the mouth of Owego Creek.[1] It is the commercial center of a large agricultural and lumbering district; and since its first settlement it has been one of the most important villages in the southern tier of counties.[2] It contains a the Owego Academy, a female seminary, 7 churches, 2 banks, 2 newspaper offices, and several manufacturing establishments.[3] A bridge 80 rods in length here crosses the Susquehanna. Pop. 3,041. **Apalachin,** (p. v.,) on the s. bank of the Susquehanna, 8 mi. above Owego, contains 1 church and 200 inhabitants. **Campville,** (p. v.,) on the N. bank of the river, 7 mi. above Owego, contains 1 church and 20 dwellings. It is a station on the Erie R. R. **Flemingville** (p. o.) is a hamlet in the N. w. part of the town, on Owego Creek; **Willsboro,** a p. o. on Nanticoke Creek; and **South Owego,** a p. o. near the Penn. line. Amos Draper, an Indian agent and trader, from the Wyoming Valley, erected the first house in town, at Owego Village, in 1786, and moved in his family in 1787.[4] The first religious services were conducted by Rev. Seth Williston. The first religious association (Presb.) was formed in 1810, and a church was organized in 1817; Rev. Horatio I. Lombard was the first settled minister, in 1818. There are 13 churches in town.[5]

RICHFORD—was formed from Berkshire, as "*Arlington,*" April 18, 1831. Its name was changed April 9, 1832. It is the N. E. corner town in the co. Its surface is mostly upland, broken by a few narrow valleys. It contains the highest land in the co., estimated to be 1,400 to 1,600 ft. above tide. Its streams are the head branches of Owego Creek. Its soil is a moderately fertile, gravelly loam. About one third of the surface is yet covered with forests. Leather and lumber are manufactured to some extent. **Richford,** (p. v.,) s. of the center of the town, contains a church and about 60 dwellings. **West Richford** is a p. o. The first settlements, made at a later period than those in Berkshire, from which the town was taken, were since the commencement of the present century;[6] but the exact date could not be ascertained. There is a Presb. church in town.

SPENCER—was formed from Owego, Feb. 28, 1806. Candor, Caroline, Danby, and Newfield (the last three now in Tompkins co.) were taken off Feb. 22, 1811, and Cayuta, March 20, 1824. It is the N. w. corner town of the co. Its surface is an upland, broken by the valleys of small streams. The N. w. portion forms the watershed between Susquehanna River and Cayuga Lake. The ridges have a general N. and s. direction. Their declivities are generally steep and their summits broad and broken. Catatunk Creek, flowing E., breaks through these ridges at nearly right angles, forming a deep and narrow valley. The soil in the valleys is a gravelly loam, and upon the hills it is a hard, shaly loam. **Spencer,**[7] (p. v.,) on Catatunk Creek, w. of the center of the town, contains 3 churches, 2 tanneries, a flouring mill, sawmill, and 75 dwellings. The first settlement was commenced in 1795, by Benj. Drake and Joseph and John Barker.[8] The first religious meeting was held by P. Spaulding, at his own house; and the first religious association (Bap.) was formed by Elder David Jayne.[9]

TIOGA—was formed from Union, (Broome co.,) March 14, 1800. Berkshire was taken off in 1808, a part of Union in 1810, and Barton and Nichols in 1824. It lies on the Susquehanna, s. w. of the center of the co. Its surface is principally upland, terminating in bluffs along the river intervale. The streams are Catatunk and Pipe Creeks and numerous smaller creeks and brooks.

---

[1] Glen Mary, for several years the residence of N. P. Willis, is situated on Owego Creek, near the w. bounds of the village. It was here that his exquisite Rural Letters were written.

[2] For many years the p. o. here was one of the four distributing offices of the State. From this place also were shipped salt, plaster, lumber, and wheat for the Penn. and Md. markets. Sept. 7, 1849, a destructive fire occurred, burning 75 buildings.

[3] The principal of these are manufactories of steam engines and boilers, machinery, castings, sash and blinds, silverware, lumber, leather, flour, and plaster.

[4] John McQuigg and James McMaster, from New England, the original patentees of the half-township on which the village of Owego stands, settled there in 1788. A clearing was made and grain sowed on an Indian improvement at Owego, in the season of 1786, by Wm. McMaster, Wm. Taylor, Robert McMaster, John Nealy, and Wm. Wood, who entered the valley from the E. by way of Otsego Lake and the Susquehanna. The first birth in town was that of Selecta, daughter of Amos Draper, June 19, 1788; the first school was taught by —— Kelly, in 1792; the first store and hotel were kept at Owego, by Wm. Bates.

[5] 5 M. E., 2 Presb., Prot. E., Bap., Cong., Wes. Meth., R. C. and Union.

[6] Among the early settlers were Evan Harris, Samuel Smith, Samuel Gleason, Nathaniel Johnson, —— Stevens, Jeremiah Campbell, Beriah Wells, Caleb and Jesse Gleason,, Ezekiel Rich, and William Dunham,—many of them from the adjoining town of Berkshire.

[7] This village was the co. seat of Tioga co., then including Chemung, from 1812 to 1821.

[8] Among the early settlers at Spencer Village were Joshua Ferris, Henry Miller, Edmund and Rodney Hobart, from Conn., Andrew Purdy, Thos. Mosher, from Westchester co., and George Fisher. The first birth was that of Deborah, daughter of Benjamin Drake; the first marriage, that of John B. Underwood and Polly Spaulding; and the first death, that of Prescott Hobart. The first school was taught by Joseph Barker, in his own house; the first inn was kept by Andrew Purdy; the first store by Samuel Doolittle; and the first gristmill was built by Benj. Drake.

[9] The census reports 3 churches in town; Cong., Bap., and M. E.

The soil is a fine, dark loam in the valleys and a gravelly loam upon the hills. Most of the summits are still covered with forests. **Tioga Center,** (p. v.,) at the mouth of Pipe Creek, contains a church, several mills, and 60 dwellings. It is a station on the N. Y. & Erie R. R. **Smithsboro,** (p. v.,) on the N. Y & E. R. R., contains 230 inhabitants. **Halsey Valley** (p. o.) is a hamlet, in the N. W. corner of the town, on the line of Barton. **Straights Corners** is a p. o. on the N. border. **Jenksville** (p. o.) is a hamlet, near the mouth of Catatunk Creek. The first settlement was made on Pipe Creek, in 1785, by Samuel and Wm. Ransom, —— Primer, and Andrew Alden, from Wyoming, Penn. Col. David Pixley, from Mass., and Abner Turner, from N. H., made the first settlement on the river, in 1791.[1] There are two churches in town; M. E. and Union.

Acres of Land, Valuation, Population, Dwellings, Families, Freeholders, Schools, Live Stock, Agricultural Products, and Domestic Manufactures, of Tioga County.

Names of Towns.	Acres of Land. Improved.	Acres of Land. Unimproved.	Valuation of 1858. Real Estate.	Valuation of 1858. Personal Property.	Valuation of 1858. Total.	Population. Males.	Population. Females.	No. of Dwellings.	No. of Families.	Freeholders.	Schools. No. of Districts.	Schools. Children taught.
Barton	16,629½	15,875½	$713,367	$134,450	$847,817	1,876	1,966	770	775	553	22	1,657
Berkshire	9,283	9,613	145,990	3,655	149,645	533	535	203	219	213	5	376
Candor	30,769	27,521	690,945	37,750	728,695	1,997	1,897	744	787	624	26	1,476
Newark	13,038	16,182	311,586	25,675	337,261	983	962	387	403	365	13	723
Nichols	12,050	7,363½	321,025	29,900	350,925	945	926	319	347	170	13	720
Owego	33,801⅛	26,046½	1,680,121	518,440	2,198,561	4,223	4,105	1,467	1,376	1,115	39	3,440
Richford	8,898	6,947	156,016	11,600	167,616	598	584	231	242	189	9	506
Spencer	13,445	12,367	247,830	16,925	264,755	911	894	357	379	328	12	709
Tioga	16,980½	16,508	548,234	21,350	569,584	1,550	1,477	571	579	369	20	1,268
Total	154,894⅛	138,423½	4,815,114	799,745	5,614,859	13,616	13,346	5,049	5,107	3,926	159	10,875

Names of Towns.	Live Stock. Horses.	Live Stock. Working Oxen and Calves.	Live Stock. Cows.	Live Stock. Sheep.	Live Stock. Swine.	Agricultural Products. Bush. of Grain. Winter.	Agricultural Products. Bush. of Grain. Spring.	Agricultural Products. Tons of Hay.	Agricultural Products. Bushels of Potatoes.	Agricultural Products. Bushels of Apples.	Agricultural Products. Dairy Products. Pounds of Butter.	Agricultural Products. Dairy Products. Pounds of Cheese.	Domestic Cloths, in Yards.
Barton	664	1,850	1,621	3,265	1,414	9,438½	102,007½	4,093	9,907	14,400	167,685	1,610	990
Berkshire	293	1,165	949	2,230	614	426¾	34,334	2,709¼	8,795	17,586	126,340	14,209	699
Candor	1,125	2,905	2,303	7,258	2,019	5,915½	169,266	6,758½	27,519	23,581	287,692	15,996	4,275
Newark	583	1,558	1,386	3,545	907	775	51,789½	4,108	17,191	16,445	145,189	6,210	1,238
Nichols	384	1,372	1,026	2,776	1,202	6,127½	83,848¾	2,907½	12,116	16,896	102,185	1,500	2,395
Owego	1,383	3,680	2,813	8,176	2,837	12,353	185,384¾	8,404	46,528½	29,694	235,444	4,644	3,175½
Richford	284	783	788	2,143	445	775	42,208	2,047	6,009	10,927	84,021	1,625	644
Spencer	426	1,608	913	3,061	673	2,658	68,140	3,078½	9,021	14,197	90,803	2,200	962
Tioga	536	1,789	1,155	3,698	1,137	6,770	91,827	4,296	13,432	25,457	126,424	2,363	2,012
Total	5,678	16,710	12,954	36,152	11,248	45,239¼	828,805½	38,401¾	150,518½	169,183	1,365,783	50,357	16,390½

[1] Among the early settlers were Joel Farnham, Jeremiah White, Abel Stafford, Elizur Wright, Samuel Giles, Hugh E. Fiddis; John Hill, from Mass.; William Taylor, from Saratoga co.; Nathaniel Catlin, Cornelius Taylor, Beriah Mundy, John Smith, James Schoonover, —— Taylor, and —— Hungerford, from Wyoming, Penn.; Daniel Mersereau, from Staten Island; Francis Gragg, Nathaniel Goodspeed, Jesse, Ziba, and Amos Miller, Enos Canfield, Lodowyck Light, —— Lyon, and Ezra Smith, from Westchester co., N. Y.

TOMPKINS COUNTY.

This county was formed from Cayuga and Seneca, April 17, 1817. Three towns were annexed from Tioga, March 22, 1822, and a part of Schuyler co. was taken off in 1854. It lies around the head of Cayuga Lake, s. w. of the center of the State, is centrally distant 141 mi. from Albany, and contains 506 sq. mi. Its surface consists principally of an upland, broken by a series of ridges extending N. and s. The watershed between Cayuga Lake and Tioughnioga River occupies the E. border of the co., and that between the same lake and Susquehanna River the s. border. The deep valley of Cayuga Lake, 700 ft. below the summits of the ridges, separates the N. portions of the co. into two distinct parts. The E. portion, declining toward the N., gradually loses its hilly character and spreads out into the beautifully rolling lands so common in Central N.Y. West of the lake the land does not lessen in height within the limits of the co.; but the rough, broken hills change into smooth ridges, with long, gradual slopes.

The deep valley of Cayuga Lake affords a fine opportunity to examine the geological structure of this region. Upon the shore in the extreme N. part are found the Hamilton shales, the lowest rock in the co. Next above them on the shore appear the Tully limestone, Genesee slate, and Portage or Ithaca shales and sandstones.[1] The summits of all the hills are formed of the rocks belonging to the Chemung group, usually covered deep with drift deposits. The streams, in their course from the table lands to the lake, have worn deep channels into the rocks, and waterfalls which once were, probably, at the face of the bluffs, have receded one to two miles, forming below deep, rocky chasms bordered by perpendicular walls. As the rocks are composed of strata of different degrees of hardness, the water has worn them irregularly,—the soft and yielding shales generally forming a declining surface, while the hard and compact limestone retains its perpendicular forms.[2]

The streams are Salmon, Fall, Cascadilla, Six Mile, and Taughanick Creeks and Cayuga Inlet and their branches, flowing into the lake, and several branches of Owego Creek and other small streams, flowing s. The cascades upon these streams form one of the most peculiar and interesting features of the landscape.

The soil in the N. part is generally a gravelly or clayey loam, formed by the drift deposits; and that in the s. is a gravelly or slaty loam, derived from disintegration. It is all best adapted to grazing. In the N. part the people are generally engaged in grain raising, wheat forming the staple production. In the s. towns the principal branches of agriculture pursued are stock raising and dairying. Considerable manufacturing is carried on at Ithaca and other places.

The co. seat is located at the village of Ithaca. The courthouse is a brick edifice, built upon a fine lot near the center of the village.[3] The jail, contiguous to the courthouse, is a well built stone edifice, with ample accommodations for the health of the prisoners. The cells are clean and well ventilated. The co. clerk's office is a fireproof building, fronting upon Tioga St. The poorhouse is situated upon a farm of 100 acres in Ulysses, 6 mi. N. w. of Ithaca. The average number of inmates is 53, and the revenue derived from the farm is about $1,500. No school is provided for the children, and they are not admitted to the public schools. The house is in bad repair, destitute of ventilation, and entirely unfit for the residence of so many human beings.

The Cayuga & Susquehanna R. R. extends from Ithaca to Owego, connecting with the Erie R. R. at the latter place. Cayuga Lake is navigable and connects with the Erie Canal at Monte-

---

[1] The Tully limestone furnishes an abundance of lime; huge fragments of this rock are found scattered over the land several hundred feet above the regular veins of the rock, showing that some great force had been in operation here at some former period. The Genesee slate is about 100 ft. thick, and the Portage group 300 ft.

[2] The Taughanick Falls, below Trumansburgh, have receded something more than a mile from the lake. "In its passage, the stream first produced a series of falls and rapids, but finally receded so as to form but a single fall. This is caused by the higher strata being so much harder than those below that a firm table is formed of these, while those below are undermined." About 1 mi. N. of these falls is a cascade, where, from

the absence of a resisting stratum at the surface, the rock has been worn down in a continuous slope.—*Geol. IV. Dist.*, p. 378, 379.

[3] The act of incorporation fixed the courthouse at Ithaca, the exact locality to be designated by the Surveyor General, or, if he neglected to do it, by the judges of the co. court. Unless a site was conveyed to the Supervisors and $7,000 secured to be paid, the co. was to be reannexed to the cos. from whence it was taken. Luther Gere, Wm. R. Collins, and Daniel Bates were appointed to superintend the erection of the co. buildings. The first co. officers were Oliver C. Comstock, *First Judge;* Archer Green, *Clerk;* Henry Bloom, *Sheriff;* and Andrew D. W. Bruyn, *Surrogate.*

654

zuma. A daily line of steamers plies between Ithaca and Cayuga Bridge, on the N. Y. C. R. R., touching at all the landings on the lake. The railroad and canal and lake constitute one of the principal routes for supplying the West with the anthracite coal of E. Penn.

Four weekly newspapers are now published in the co.[1]

The three s. towns of this co. were included in the Watkins and Flint's Purchase, and the remainder in the Military Tract. A public road was built from Oxford, on Chenango River, directly through to Ithaca, by Joseph Chaplin, in 1791–92–93, and this became the great highway for immigration in the s. part of the State for many years. As a consequence, the co. immediately bordering upon the road was rapidly settled. The first immigrants were mostly from New England. At the place where Ithaca now stands were found cleared fields which had previously been cultivated by the Indians; and these lands were among the first occupied in the co. The next settlements were made in Ulysses, on the w. bank of the lake, and along Chaplin's road in Dryden. The opening of the rich lands of the Genesee country to settlers diverted immigration from this region, and the co. for many years did not increase in population with the same rapidity as the regions further w. The growth of the co., however, has been gradual and continuous; and now in every element of real prosperity it is fully on an average with the other cos. in the State.

CAROLINE—was formed from Spencer, (Tioga co.,) Feb. 22, 1811, and was transferred to this co. March 22, 1822. A part was annexed to Danby in 1839. It is the s. e. corner town of the co. Its surface is an upland, broken by a series of ridges extending n. w. and s. e. 500 to 700 ft. above the valleys and 1,500 to 1,700 ft. above tide. The summits of the hills are usually rounded and rolling and their declivities steep. The streams are Owego Creek, forming the e. boundary, and Six Mile Creek and their branches. These streams flow in deep, narrow valleys bordered by steep hillsides. The soil is generally a gravelly loam, and is well adapted to grazing. **Caroline Center** (p. v.) contains 2 churches and 14 houses; **Motts Corners,** (p. v.,) on Six Mile Creek, in the n. w. corner of the town, 1 church, several manufacturing establishments,[2] and 40 houses; **Speedsville,** (p. v.,) upon Boyer Creek, in the s. e. corner, contains 3 churches and 30 houses; and **Slaterville,** (p. v.,) near the n. border, 1 church and 30 houses. **Pugsleys Depot** (p. o.) is a station on the C. & S. R. R. **Caroline** (p. o.) is a hamlet in the n. e. corner of the town. **Rawson Hollow,** on the e. line, is a p. o. The first settlement was begun by Capt.

---

[1] The Seneca Republican, the first paper published in the co., was started at Ithaca, July 4, 1815, by Jonathan Ingersoll. In 1816 it was changed to
The Ithaca Journal, and in 1817 Mack & Shepherd became proprietors. It was successively issued by Mack & Searing, Ebenezer Mack, and Mack & Morgan, until 1824, when Wm. Andrus became partner, and the paper was issued by Mack & Andrus. In 1827 the name was changed to
Ithaca Journal, Literary Gazette, and General Advertiser, and about a year afterward a portion of the title was dropped, and it was issued as
The Ithaca Journal and Advertiser. In Dec. 1833, Mack & Andrus sold to Nathan Randall; in 1837 Randall sold to Mattison & Barnaby; and in 1839 A. E. Barnaby became sole proprietor. In 1841 Barnaby sold to Alfred Wells, and soon after Wells sold to J. H. Selkreg, the present publisher.
The Republican Chronicle was started at Ithaca in June, 1820, by Spencer & Stockton. In 1823 David D. Spencer became sole proprietor. In 1826 S. S. Chatterton bought an interest, and in 1828 he became sole proprietor, and soon after changed the name to
The Ithaca Republican. In 1831 or '32 he again changed the name to
The Tompkins American, and in 1834 the paper was discontinued.
The Western Messenger was started at Ithaca in 1826 by A. P. Searing, and was continued about 2 years.
The Philanthropist, a Universalist paper, was started at Ithaca in 1831 by O. A. Brownson, and was continued about 1 year.
The Ithaca Chronicle was started by D. D. & A. Spencer in Feb. 1828, and was continued by them until 1853, when Anson Spencer became sole proprietor. In 1855 it was changed to
The American Citizen, published by A. E. Barnaby & Co. It is now published by Anson Spencer, who has been one of the proprietors from the commencement of the paper in 1828.
The Lake Light was started at Trumansburgh in 1827 by Wm. W. Phelps, and was continued about 2 years.
The Trumansburgh Advertiser was published a short time in 1833 by D. Fairchild.

The Jeffersonian and Tompkins Times was started in 1836 by C. Robbins. He soon after sold to G. G. Freer, who changed the name to
The Ithaca Herald. In 1837 Nathan Randall became proprietor, and merged the paper in the Ithaca Journal and Advertiser.
The Christian Doctrinal Advocate and Spiritual Monitor was started at Motts Corners in 1837, under the auspices of the 7th Day Baptist denomination, and was continued several years.
The Tompkins Volunteer was started at Ithaca by H. C. Goodwin in 1840. He soon after sold to J. Hunt, jr. In 1843 the title was changed to
The Tompkins Democrat, and after a short time the paper was removed to Greene, Chenango co.
The Trumansburgh Gazette was published a short time in 1843 by J. H. Hawes.
The Flag of the Union was started at Ithaca in 1848 by J. B. Gosman. In 1850 it was merged in the Ithaca Journal and Advertiser.
The Templar and Watchman was started at Ithaca in 1853 by Orlando Lund. It afterward passed into the hands of Myron S. Barnes, and was continued a short time.
Rumsey's Companion was started at Dryden in 1856 by H. D. Rumsey. It was soon after changed to
The Fireside Companion, and again in a few months to
The Dryden News. In 1857 it was sold to G. Z. House and changed to
The New York Confederacy, and was soon after discontinued. In 1858 it was resuscitated, as
The Dryden News, by Asahel Clapp, by whom it is still published.
The Tompkins County Democrat was started at Ithaca in Oct. 1856, by Timothy Malony, by whom it is still published.

[2] Two flouring mills, two sawmills, a tannery, and woolen factory. One mile below the village is the extensive gun barrel manufactory of J. & B. Losey, and, with one exception, the only one in the State. This establishment was started 50 years ago, by Abiel Losey, father of the present proprietors, at Otsego; thence it was removed to Fall Creek, near Ithaca; thence to Owego; and thence to its present location.

David Rich, who came from Vt. in 1795 and located near Willow Bridge; Widow Earsley, with four sons and four daughters, from N. J., came in the next year; and for several years these were the only families in town.[1] The first church (Ref. Prot. D.) was formed at an early period; the first pastor was Rev. Garritt Mandeville. The census reports 10 churches in town.[2]

DANBY—was formed from Spencer, (Tioga co.,) Feb. 22, 1811, and was transferred to this co. March 22, 1822. Part of Caroline was annexed April 29, 1839, and a part was annexed to Dryden in 1856. It lies near the center of the s. border of the co. Its surface is broken by ranges of hills extending N. and s. 300 to 400 ft. above the valleys. Their summits are rounded and their declivities generally steep. The valleys are mere ravines. The principal streams are Cayuga Inlet, flowing N., and numerous small streams, the latter being tributaries either to this or to Owego Creek. The soil is a mixed gravelly and shaly loam, with occasional patches of clay, and is well adapted to grazing. **Danby,** (p. v.,) in the N. part, contains 3 churches and 50 houses; **Beers Settlement,** (South Danby p. o.,) near the center, about a dozen houses. **West Danby** is a p. o., near the w. border. The first settlers were Jacob Yaple, Dr. Lewis Beers, Jabez Beers, and Joseph Judson, who located at Beers Settlement in 1797.[3] The first church (Cong.) was formed in 1807; Rev. Daniel Loring was the first pastor. There are 8 churches in town.[4]

DRYDEN[5]—was formed from Ulysses, Feb. 22, 1803. A part of Danby was annexed in 1856. It is a large town, occupying the central portion of the E. border of the co. The surface of the N. half is rolling or moderately hilly, and that of the s. half hilly and broken. The E. border forms the watershed between Tioughnioga River and Cayuga Lake. The highest ridge, in the s. E. part, is 1,700 to 1,800 ft. above tide. The principal stream is Fall Creek, flowing s. w. through near the center of the town, on its course affording several millsites. Several small streams, tributaries to Owego Creek, take their rise in the s. part. Dryden Lake is a small sheet of water 1 mi. long and about ½ mi. wide, lying in an elevated valley near the E. border and 1,500 ft. above tide. A mineral spring, strongly impregnated with sulphur, magnesia, and iron, is situated one mi. w. of Dryden Village, and has a local notoriety for medicinal virtues. In the s. E. part are two swamps, each covering an area of several hundred acres. **Dryden,** (p. v.,) on the s. branch of Fall Creek, in the E. part of the town, is a flourishing inland village. It contains 2 churches, a large gristmill, and several manufacturing establishments. Pop. 522. **Etna,** (p. v.,) on Fall Creek, near the center, contains 2 churches, a grist and saw mill, an iron foundery, and machine shop. Pop. 230. **West Dryden,** (p. v.,) in the N. w. part, contains 93 inhabitants; **Varna,** (p. v.,) on Fall Creek, near the w. border, 170 inhabitants; **Malloryville, Freeville,** and **California** are hamlets. The first settlement was commenced in 1797, by Amos Sweet, on the present site of Dryden Village.[6] Joseph Chaplin built a road from Oxford, Chenango co., to Ithaca, passing through this town, in 1792–93–94. There are 9 churches in town.[7]

ENFIELD[8]—was formed from Ulysses, March 16, 1821. It lies upon the center of the w. border of the co. Its surface is rolling, and it has a mean elevation of 500 to 700 ft. above Cayuga Lake. The principal streams are Ten Mile Creek and the s. branch of Taughanick Creek. Upon the former, in the s. E. tract of the town, is one of the finest of the beautiful cascades so common in this co. It is in a deep gorge, and has a total fall of 230 ft. The soil is principally a gravelly loam. **Enfield Center** (p. v.) contains 2 churches and about 40 dwellings; **Enfield** (p. v.) 25 dwellings. **Enfield Falls** is a hamlet. Among the first settlers were —— Geltner, John Whitlock, Jas. Rumsey, Lewis Owen, and Isaac and John Beech.[9] There are 5 churches in town.[10]

---

[1] Among the other early settlers were Thos. Tracy and Sam'l Yates, from Mass.; Joseph Chambers, Richard Bush, and Hartmore Earnest, from Ulster co., in 1798; Levi Slater, (formerly of Slaterville,) Charles and John Mulks, John Cantine, (first settler at Motts Corners,) and Joseph Bishop, all from Ulster, and John Rounceville, from Mass., in 1801. The first child born was Harriet Rounceville. The first school was taught by John Robinson. Richard Bush kept the first inn, Isaac Miller the first store, and Gen. Cantine built the first gristmill, in 1800.

[2] 4 M. E., Prot. E., Cong., Bap., Ref. Prot. D., F. W. Bap., and Univ.

[3] The first settlers of West Danby were Wm. Hogg and Moses Barker. The first death was an infant son of Lewis Beardsley. Joseph Judson taught the first school, Dr. Beers kept the first inn and store, and Peter Yaple built the first gristmill.

[4] 3 M. E., 2 Bap., Cong., Prot. E., and Swedenborgian.

[5] Named in honor of John Dryden, the English poet.

[6] The next settlers were Ezekiel Sandford, David Fort, and

Ebenezer Chausen, who located at Willow Grove in 1798. A single yoke of oxen, at one load, brought these three families, consisting of 14 persons, and all their household goods, from the Chenango River. Capt. Geo. Robertson (sometimes called the "father of the town") came in the same year, and settled on Lot 53. Among the other early settlers were Lyman Hurd, from Vt., Dr. Sheldon, Dr. Wolf, Irona Peat, Wm. Daley, Joel Hall, and Jas. Wood. The first child born was Robert Robertson; and the first death was that of the mother of Amos Sweet. Daniel Lasey taught the first school, in 1804. Amos Lewis kept the first inn, Joel Hull the first store, and Col. Hopkins, from Homer, built the first mill, in 1800.

[7] 5 M. E., 2 Presb., 2 Bap., and R. C.

[8] Named from Enfield, Ct.

[9] John Applegate kept the first inn, Samuel Ingersoll the first store, and Wm. Ferris built the first mill.

[10] 2 M. E., Christian, Bap., and Presb.

GROTON[1]—was formed from Locke, (Cayuga co.,) as *"Division,"* April 7, 1817, and its name was changed March 13, 1818. It is the N. E. corner town in the co. Its surface is rolling or moderately hilly. From the valleys the land rises by long and gradual slopes to a height of 100 to 300 ft. The highest point in town is about 1,500 ft. above tide. The principal streams are Owasco Inlet and Fall Creek. Bear Swamp, in the E. part, contains an area of several hundred acres. The soil is a fine quality of gravelly loam, underlaid by slate. **Groton,** (p. v.,) on Owasco Inlet, near the center of the town, contains 3 churches, the Groton Academy, and several manufacturing establishments.[2] Pop. 587. **McLean,** (p. v.,) on Fall Creek, in the S. E., contains 5 churches, several factories,[3] and 40 houses. **Peruville,** (p. v.,) near the S. border, contains 2 churches, a saw and grist mill, pail factory, and 30 houses. **Groton City,** (p. v.,) in the N. E. corner, and **West Groton,** (p. v.,) in the N. W., contain about 11 houses each. **Bensons Corners** is a hamlet, in the S. W. corner. Among the first settlers were Saml. Hogg, at West Groton; Ichabod Bowen, John Guthrie, and —— Perrin, at Groton; and J. Williams, J. Houghtaling, and W. S. Clark, at East Groton. The census reports 11 churches.[4]

ITHACA[5]—was formed from Ulysses, March 16, 1821. It is the central town in the co., lying at the head of Cayuga Lake. A tract of land 2 mi. long and 1½ broad, low and nearly level, extends S. from the lake shore; and from this the valley of Cayuga Inlet opens to the S. W. and that of Six Mile Creek to the S. E. Ridges 400 to 700 ft. high, with steep declivities, separate these valleys and surround the low land and the head of the lake. From the summits the surface spreads out into a rolling upland. A marsh ½ mi. wide borders immediately on the lake. The streams are Fall, Cascadilla, Six Mile, Buttermilk, and Ten Mile Creeks, and Cayuga Inlet. In their course from the uplands each of these streams plunges down the wall-like precipices which surround the lake, forming series of cascades which for beauty and variety are scarcely equaled elsewhere.[6] The soil is a fertile, gravelly loam upon the uplands, and a deep, rich alluvium in the valleys. **Ithaca,** (p. v.,) 1½ mi. S. of the head of Cayuga Lake, is the co. seat, and the commercial center of the co. It is beautifully situated upon a fine alluvial plain, bordered on 3 sides by lofty hills, and on the fourth by the lake, with which it is connected by a navigable inlet. It contains the Ithaca Academy,[7] 9 churches,[8] 2 banks, 4 printing offices, and a large number of manufacturing establishments.[9] The commercial interests of the place are extensive and important. A daily line of steamboats on the lake running between this place and Cayuga Bridge, in connection with the C. & S. R. R., serves to connect the Erie R. R. on the S. with the N. Y. Central on the N.[10] The lake is also a link in the great chain of the internal water navigation of the State, and upon it a large amount of canal commerce, centering at Ithaca, is carried on. The transhipment of Scranton and Lackawanna coal brought by the C. & S. R. R. forms an important and constantly growing branch of business. A large proportion of the anthracite coal for the Northern and Western markets is supplied through this avenue.[11] The public schools of the village are graded, and are in a flourishing condition. The annual attendance is about 1,200.[12] The village was incorp. April 2, 1821. Pop. 4,908. The first settlement of the town was made by Jacob Yaple, Isaac

---

[1] Named from Groton, Ct.

[2] Three carriage shops, a foundery, machine shop, and thrashing machine factory.

[3] Thrashing machine factory, pail factory, two furnaces, flouring mills, and 2 sawmills.

[4] 2 Bap., 3 M. E., 3 Cong., Wes. Meth., Prot. E., and Univ.

[5] Name applied by Simeon De Witt, and borrowed from one of the Ionian Isles, the home of Ulysses. It was originally called "The Flats," and its name was brought into use by being placed upon a tavern sign.—*King's Early Hist. of Ithaca.* Mr. De Witt, who for more than 50 years held the office of Surveyor General, became the owner of the site of Ithaca and the surrounding country about the time, or soon after, the first settlement. He died at this place Dec. 3, 1834; his remains have since been removed to the Albany Rural Cemetery.

[6] Upon Fall Creek, within the space of 1 mi., are 5 falls, varying in height from 44 to 125 ft. The deep gorge through which the stream flows is bordered by perpendicular cliffs. A tunnel 200 ft. long, 10 to 12 ft. wide, and 13 ft. high was excavated through the rock for hydraulic purposes in 1831–32, by J. S. Beebe. Upon Cascadilla, Six Mile, and Buttermilk Creeks are also successions of fine cascades, within the limits of the town. At Buttermilk Falls the water rushes down at an angle of about 45 degrees, in a sheet of perfectly white foam, the appearance of the water furnishing a name to both the cascades and the stream.

[7] In 1822 the Genesee Conference of the M. E. Church applied for the incorporation of a college, to be located at Ithaca, and considerable sums were pledged for this object; but the project failed of accomplishment.

[8] 2 M. E., Bap., Presb., Cong., Prot. E., Ref. Prot. D., Af. Meth., and R. C.

[9] The manufactories are as follows:—3 flouring mills, 3 paper mills, 5 plaster mills, 1 oil mill, 1 oilcloth factory, 1 brewery, 1 lead pipe factory, 1 rake factory, 4 carriage shops, 2 tanneries, 2 sewing silk factories, 3 furnaces and machine shops, 2 sawmills, 1 manufactory of collars, bosoms, and neckties, and 8 boatyards; 25 to 30 boats are annually built, at an aggregate cost of $50,000 to $60,000. The silk manufacturies employ 160 persons, and produce 600 lbs. of sewing silk per week.

[10] The Ithaca & Owego R. R.—the second R. R. chartered in the State—was incorp. in 1828, and opened in the spring of 1834. It was 29 mi. long, and had 2 inclined planes ascending from Ithaca. The first was 1,733½ ft. long, with 405 ft. rise, and the second 2,225 ft. long, with a rise of 1 ft. in 21. The total elevation in 8 mi. was 602 ft.,—which was 602 ft. above its s. terminus at Ithaca. A stationary steam engine was used on the first plane, and horses on the other parts of the road. In the first 6 mos. it transported 12,000 tons of freight and 3,300 passengers. The State having a lien upon the road, the Comptroller sold it at auction on the 20th of May, 1842, for $4,500, to Archibald McIntyre and others. For $13,500 it was put in operation, under the name of the Cayuga & Susquehanna R. R. The inclined plane was subsequently changed to a circuitous grade road, and horses were superseded by locomotives. This road is now leased to the Delaware, Lackawanna & Western R. R., and it is extensively used for the transportation of coal.

[11] During the past few years the coal trade has averaged 90,000 tons per annum. This trade will probably largely increase with the increased facilities for moving the coal forward.

[12] A Lancasterian school was early established here, and was continued to within a few years, when it was superseded by the present system of public schools.

42

Dumond, and Peter Hinepaw, who located on the present site of Ithaca Village in 1789. The land that they occupied had previously been partially cultivated by the Indians.[1] The first church (Presb.) was organized in 1804–05, with seven members.

LANSING—was formed from Genoa, (Cayuga co.,) April 7, 1817. It lies upon the E. bank of Cayuga Lake, in the N. part of the co. The surface is principally a rolling upland, 500 ft. above the lake, bordered by steep declivities. Salmon Creek, the principal stream, flows S. through near the center of the town. Its valley is narrow and bordered by steep hillsides. Swartz, Townly, and Hedden Creeks are its principal tributaries. The soil is generally a fertile, gravelly loam. **Ludlowville**, (p. v.,) on Salmon Creek, about 1 mi. from its mouth, contains 3 churches, several factories,[2] and about 50 dwellings. **Lansingville**, (p. v.,) on the ridge w. of Salmon Creek, in the N. part of the town, contains 1 church and 25 dwellings. **North Lansing**, (p. o.,) in the N. E. corner, **Lake Ridge**, (p. o.,) on the bluff above the lake, in the N. w. corner, and **Libertyville** (South Lansing p. o.) are hamlets of about a dozen houses each. **East Lansing** and **Forest City** are p. offices. Forest City Water Cure is finely situated on the bluff overlooking the lake, in the S. part of the town. The first settlement was begun in 1792, by emigrants from N. J.[3] The census reports 7 churches in town.[4]

NEWFIELD—was formed from Spencer, (Tioga co.,) as "*Cayuta*," Feb. 22, 1811. Its name was changed March 29, 1822, and a part was annexed to Catharines (Schuyler co.) in 1853. It is the S. w. corner town in the co. The surface is high and hilly, the ridges being 400 to 600 ft. above the valleys and 1,500 to 1,700 ft. above tide. The streams are Cayuga Inlet and Ten Mile Creek and their branches. The valleys of these streams are usually narrow and bordered by steep hillsides. A portion of the w. part of the town is yet uncultivated. The soil is a shaly and clayey loam, best adapted to grazing. **Newfield**, (p. v.,) in the N. E. part of the town, contains 3 churches, 2 flouring mills, 2 carriage shops, a woolen factory, an oilcloth factory, and about 80 dwellings. **Trumbulls Corners**, (p. v.,) on the N. border, contains 1 church and 20 dwellings. **Poney Hollow** (p. o.) is a hamlet in the S. w. part. The first settler was —— Thomas, who located at Poney Hollow.[5] The census reports 3 churches in town.[6]

ULYSSES—was formed March 5, 1799. Dryden was taken off in 1803, and Ithaca and Enfield in 1821. It lies upon the w. bank of Cayuga Lake, on the N. border of the co. A range of bluffs 600 ft. high, with steep declivities, borders upon the lake; and from their summits the surface spreads out in an undulating upland. The only considerable stream is Taughanick (Ti-kaw-nik) Creek, which crosses the town from the w. In its descent from the plateau to the lake this stream forms a series of cascades, the principal of which is known as Taughanick Falls. These falls have receded about 1 mi. from the shore of the lake, and have worn a deep gorge in the yielding shales, with banks 380 ft. high. The stream now falls, in an unbroken sheet, over a limestone terrace 210 ft. in height. About 1 mi. farther up the gorge is another fall, of 80 ft. The soil is a fine quality of gravelly loam. **Trumansburgh**,[7] (p. v.,) near the N. border of the town, is the second village in the co. in amount of business and population. It contains 4 churches, the Trumansburgh Academy, and several manufacturing establishments.[8] Pop. 1,052. **Jacksonville**, (p. v.,) near the center of the town, contains 1 church and 50 houses. **Waterburgh**, near the w. border, contains 1 church, mills, and 40 dwellings. **Halseyville**[9] is a hamlet. The first settlements were commenced by Samuel Weyburn, at the mouth of Taughanick Creek, and by Abner and Philip Tremaine, on the site of Trumansburgh, in 1792.[10] The first church (Presb.) was formed by Jedediah Chapman, in 1803. There are now 6 churches in town.[11]

---

[1] Among the other early settlers were families named McDowel, Davenport, Bloom, King, Patchin, Star, Conrad, Markle, Sayers, and Brink. The first child born was a daughter of John Dumond, Sept. 1789. The first death was that of Rachel Allen, in 1790. A man named Lightfoot brought a boat load of goods up the lake in 1792, and he continued a kind of itinerating trade for several years. David Quigg opened the first regular store; —— Hartshorn kept the first inn; and Jacob Yaple built the first mill, in 1790. Dr. Frisbee was the first physician, and —— Howe the first teacher. The first families were a month in getting from Kingston (Ulster co.) to Owego, and 19 days from thence to their destination.

[2] Grist and saw mills and an ax helve factory.

[3] Among the early settlers were Wm. Goodwin, Silas Ludlow, Abram Bloom, and families named Beardsley, Depuy, Minier, Allen. At water, and Bowker, who came in 1791; Sam'l Gibbs and —— Holmes, in 1792; and Abram Van Wagner, in 1797. The first marriage was that of Henry Bloom and Miss Goodwin; and the first death, that of the wife of Henry Bloom, in 1798. Wm. Boyse kept the first inn, at Libertyville. The first night of his

stay in the house a rattlesnake crept into the bed and slept with his children. —— Tooker kept the first store; Silas Ludlow, of Ludlowville, built the first mill, in 1798.

[4] 4 M. E., 2 Bap., and Presb.

[5] Among the early settlers were S. Chambers, Elijah Moore, —— Carter, and Dan'l B. Swartwood. Jeremiah Hall kept the first inn, George Dudley the first store; and John Greene built the first mill.

[6] Bap., M. E., and Presb.

[7] Name derived and corrupted from Tremaine, the first family of settlers.

[8] 3 flouring mills and 2 furnaces and machine shops.

[9] Named from Nicoll Halsey, the first settler.

[10] John McLallen, a young man, accompanied the Tremaines in the capacity of teamster. The first child born was Calvin Tremaine, in 1794; and the first marriage, that of John McLallen and Mary King, Dec. 12, 1799. John McLallen kept the first inn, —— Henshaw the first store; Abner Tremaine built the first mill; and Stephen Woodworth taught the first school, all at Trumansburgh. [11] 3 M. E., Bap., Presb., and R. C.

Acres of Land, Valuation, Population, Dwellings, Families, Freeholders, Schools, Live Stock, Agricultural Products, and Domestic Manufactures, of Tompkins County.

Names of Towns.	Acres of Land.		Valuation of 1858.			Population.		No. of Dwellings.	No. of Families.	Freeholders.	Schools.	
	Improved.	Unimproved.	Real Estate.	Personal Property.	Total.	Males.	Females.				No. of Districts.	Children taught.
Caroline	20,120⅛	12,004	$356,246	$23,761	$380,007	1,250	1,216	477	496	456	19	1,065
Danby	21,993½	11,445	393,929	32,850	426,779	1,182	1,149	487	488	424	16	880
Dryden	39,814¾	19,021¾	958,614	132,650	1,091,264	2,497	2,506	968	1,035	918	29	1,790
Enfield	17,611¾	5,257	302,587	16,000	318,587	942	970	392	392	331	15	720
Groton	23,581¾	7,981	612,615	186,950	799,565	1,721	1,683	654	733	486	20	1,215
Ithaca	15,395	3,828¼	1,341,890	841,708	2,183,598	3,485	3,668	1,304	1,322	812	10	2,477
Lansing	29,363	7,912	918,755	135,275	1,054,030	1,636	1,620	616	643	414	20	1,340
Newfield	20,984¾	14,040½	419,731	23,000	442,731	1,440	1,360	557	571	482	22	1,239
Ulysses	16,752	3,474¼	611,250	174,025	785,275	1,566	1,625	596	626	442	14	1,187
Total	205,616⅝	84,963¾	5,915,617	1,566,219	7,481,836	15,719	15,797	6,051	6,306	4,765	165	11,913

Names of Towns.	Live Stock.					Agricultural Products.							Domestic Cloths, in yards.
						Bush. of Grain.					Dairy Products.		
	Horses.	Working Oxen and Calves.	Cows.	Sheep.	Swine.	Winter.	Spring.	Tons of Hay.	Bushels of Potatoes.	Bushels of Apples.	Pounds of Butter.	Pounds of Cheese.	
Caroline	734	1,765	1,676	6,858	1,465	2,332½	135,231¾	3,702¾	9,629½	33,834	191,160	5,343	3,381½
Danby	954	1,946	1,342	7,051	1,467	7,838¾	148,763	3,453	17,791	49,142	130,978	4,019	1,547
Dryden	1,870	3,120	3,316	12,327	2,638	11,629¼	263,805½	7,456½	19,567	85,870	390,214	10,094	4,037½
Enfield	857	1,515	968	5,214	1,435	10,278	141,325	2,380½	13,032	31,721	107,925	495	1,758
Groton	1,152	1,733	2,560	5,246	1,905	2,319	159,884	4,714½	16,343	86,169	326,616	36,001	1,747
Ithaca	919	1,234	871	4,494	1,111	19,310½	85,690½	1,973½	8,420½	23,531	79,625	180	200
Lansing	1,270	1,706	1,617	9,340	1,847	13,675	208,043½	3,063½	7,923	48,677	168,125	1,386	731
Newfield	962	2,024	1,258	5,373	1,367	13,428½	119,267	3,022	13,614	29,758	145,145	1,300	1,407
Ulysses	725	1,232	964	5,133	1,123	21,105	102,177½	2,077½	4,786	29,055	106,159	1,310	38
Total	9,443	16,275	14,572	61,036	14,358	101,916½	1,364,187¾	31,843¾	111,106	417,757	1,645,947	60,128	14,847

ULSTER COUNTY.

This county was formed Nov. 1, 1683,[1] and included the country between the Hudson and the Delaware, bounded N. and S. by due E. and W. lines passing through the mouths of Sawyers and Murderers Creeks. A part of Delaware was taken off in 1797, a part of Greene in 1800, and Sullivan in 1809. A portion was annexed to Orange in 1798, and the town of Catskill was annexed from Albany co. the same year. It lies on the W. bank of the Hudson, centrally distant 68 mi. from Albany, and contains 1,204 sq. mi. Its surface is mostly a hilly and mountainous upland. The Catskill Mts. occupy the N. W. part; and the Shawangunk Mts. extend N. E. from the S. W. corner nearly through the co. The mountain region consists of irregular ridges and isolated peaks with rocky sides and summits too steep and rough for cultivation. The summits are 1,500 to 2,000 ft. above the Hudson. The remaining parts of the co. are generally broken and hilly. Esopus Creek flows in a tortuous course through the N. part and discharges its waters into the Hudson. It receives Platte Kil from the N. Rondout Creek enters the S. W. corner of the co. and flows N. E. along the W. declivity of the Shawangunk Mts. and enters the Hudson at Rondout. It receives as tributaries Sandburgh Creek in the S. W. part of the co., and Wall Kil near its mouth. The latter stream flows along the E. foot of the Shawangunk Mts. The remaining streams are small brooks and creeks.

The rocks of the co. are composed of the Portage and Chemung shales, in the E. part, and the Shawangunk grit or Oneida conglomerate, in the W. part. Drift deposits are found in nearly every part. Lead ore is found to some extent among the Shawangunk Mts.[2]

At an early period the Esopus grit was largely quarried and manufactured into millstones.[3] Water-limestone of an excellent quality is found and largely quarried.[4] The Ulster co. Cement has an excellent reputation throughout the United States, and is used in immense quantities on fortifications and other Government works requiring solidity. It was used on Croton, Brooklyn, Cochituate, Albany, Washington, and other water-works. It finds a ready market in every port on the seaboard from New Brunswick to Texas. It has been exported to California and South America, and is largely used in and around New York, Boston, and Philadelphia, upon public and private buildings. The cement rocks are quarried usually on the hillsides, and these openings often extend in galleries under the overlying rock. The rock outcrops in a belt running N. E. and S. W., first appearing on the Hudson a few miles N. of Kingston Point, and extending 20 to 25 mi. to the town of Rochester, but is lost from view at the surface in several places between these points. In the section occupied by the Portage group of rocks are found extensive outcrops of thin bedded sandstone, yielding a fine quality of flagging, which is largely quarried and exported.[5] The soil is generally a good quality of sandy and gravelly loam, in some places intermixed with clay. Most of the valleys are covered with a deep, rich alluvium.

Most of the land is best adapted to grazing. Dairying is extensively pursued, and spring grain

---

[1] In its charter it is said to "contain the towns of Kingston, Hurley, and Marbletown, Foxhall, and the New Paltz, and all villages, neighborhoods, and Christian habitations on the w. side of the Hudson's River, from the Murderers Creek, near the Highlands, to the Sawyers Creek." It was named from the Irish title of the Duke of York. The boundary of this and Albany cos. were not fully settled at the Revolution. An act was passed in 1774, but nothing was done under it toward a settlement, and it was repealed in 1788. An act was passed in 1774 to run and mark the boundary of this and Orange counties from E. of the Shawangunk Mts. to the Delaware.

[2] A mine was opened near Ellenville more than 40 years ago. It was never worked to profit, and is now abandoned. The Ulster Mine, near Sullivan co. line, was opened in 1837. It is 600 or 700 feet above the valley. The galena in these mines is associated with blende, iron and copper pyrites, calcite, and quartz. There are indications and vague traditions that these mines were worked at a much earlier period and yielded profits beyond computation.

[3] In Smith's History, written in 1732, this co. is said to be noted for fine flour, beer, and a good breed of draft horses. The millstones—then quarried about 10 mi. from the river—had acquired celebrity, and were said to far exceed those from Colen, in Europe, formerly imported at £80 the pair, while Esopus

660

stones did not cost a fourth part of that sum. Small millstones for family use are still made for the Southern market; but the business has lost much of its former importance. A finer quality of these grits, when calcined and crushed, furnishes the silex used in the glass manufacture at Ellenville.

[4] Water-limestone was accidentally discovered on the line of the Erie Canal, by Canvass White, an engineer, in 1818. In 1820 he obtained a patent, and subsequently obtained judgment against one or more of the contractors for using it. The first waterlime or cement made in Ulster co. was about the time the Delaware & Hudson Canal was commenced. Its manufacture has now become a leading and profitable pursuit, employing about $1,000,000 of capital and 1,000 men. In March, 1859, there were 15 establishments in the co., owned by individuals and companies.

[5] The stone is of a bluish gray color and slaty texture, and may be split into slabs of almost any manageable size and from 1 to 4 inches in thickness. The rock is traversed by joints or seams, that divide very smoothly and greatly facilitate the labor of quarrying. It is brought down to the river and shipped in immense quantities at every landing in the co. and transported to New York and other places along the coast. The business employs a large number of hands.

is raised to some extent. Fruit growing is becoming an important branch of business. Manufactures of sole leather and lumber, are located in the western towns,[1] and water-lime in the eastern. The commerce, carried on by means of the river and canal, is large, and is constantly increasing.

The co. seat is located at Kingston.[2] The courthouse is a fine stone edifice, situated upon Wall St.[3] The jail is a stone building in rear of the courthouse. It is well arranged and furnished and is kept in good order.[4] The clerk's office is in a fireproof one story building on the corner of Fair and Main Sts.[5] The poorhouse is located upon a farm of 140 acres, on the s. line of New Paltz, 16 mi. s. w. of Kingston. It is poorly constructed, not ventilated at all, and is entirely unfit for the purposes for which it is used. The average number of inmates is 175, supported at a weekly cost of $1.25 each. A school is taught 6 months in the year.[6] The farm yields a revenue of $500. The Delaware & Hudson Canal is the only important work of internal improvement in the co. It extends from Rondout, on the Hudson, up Rondout and Sandburgh Creeks, through Kingston, Rosendale, Marbletown, Rochester, and Wawarsing. It opens a direct communication between the coal mines of Penn. and the Hudson. The Delaware & Hudson Canal Co. was incorp. April 23, 1823, and the canal was finished in 1828.[7]

One daily and 7 weekly newspapers are now published in the co.[8]

The Dutch established a trading post upon the present site of Rondout in 1614, and probably a few Dutch families settled in the immediate vicinity soon after. This early settlement was broken up by Indian hostilities, and a new one was commenced between 1630 and '40. This was again attacked by the Indians, and in 1655 was abandoned. Before 1660, settlers had again located at Kingston and vicinity. In 1660 a treaty had been concluded with the Indians; and the people were so unsuspicious of danger that they left open the gates to their fort both day and night. In June, 1663, the Indians came into the fort at Wiltwyck in great numbers, apparently to trade, while the greater part of the people were engaged in their usual avocations out of doors. At a given signal the Indians commenced the work of destruction. Recovering from their first panic, the whites rallied, under the leadership of Thomas Chambers, and finally drove the Indians out of the fort; 18 whites were killed, and 42 were carried away prisoners. The out settlements were all destroyed. A destructive war ensued, in which the Ulster Indians were nearly exterminated. During this war the valley of the Wall Kil was discovered, and soon after the peace of 1663 it was occupied by a colony of French Huguenots.[9] The settlements gradually extended along the valleys of Esopus,

---

[1] The principal tanneries are in Shandaken, Olive, Woodstock, Denning, Hardenburgh, and Wawarsing.

[2] A courthouse and jail were built soon after the incorp. of the co., and an appropriation was made for their repair July 21, 1715. These buildings proving inadequate, an act of General Assembly, passed Oct. 14, 1732, allowed the old buildings and lot to be sold and new buildings to be erected. Repairs were authorized in 1745, 1750, 1765, and 1773; and in 1775 a further sum was granted to complete them. The courthouse and jail were burned by the British Oct. 16, 1777, and a lottery was granted 6 months after to raise £2,000 to rebuild them. By act of March 19, 1778, the sheriff's mileage was directed to be computed from the house of Mrs. Ann Dubois, an innkeeper in New Paltz.

[3] The first county officers under State government were Levi Pauling, *First Judge;* Egbert Dumond, *Sheriff;* and Joseph Gasherie, *Surrogate.*

[4] The Senate Committee in 1857 report this jail as one of the best in the State; but, as 15 or 20 prisoners escaped in the winter of 1858 and '59 the correctness of the committee's conclusions may well be questioned.

[5] Dutchess and Ulster cos. were incorp. at the same time, and were united for about 30 years. The records of Dutchess co. for that period are found in the Ulster co. clerk's office.

[6] The Senate Committee of 1857 report that they found 12 cells for lunatics in an old, dilapidated building so open that it was scarcely possible to keep the inmates from perishing.

[7] See page 63. The Canal Company owns a R. R. over the mountain from Honesdale to Carbondale, Penn., and the coal mines at the latter place. It formerly owned most of the boats on the canal, and leased them to boatmen. About 1850 the Penn. Coal Company made an arrangement, by which upon payment of toll they were allowed to transport coal in their own boats from Hawley to Port Ewen.

[8] *The New York Journal and Advertiser*—published by John Holt, and which was removed from New York to Poughkeepsie in 1776 in consequence of British occupation—was published at Kingston from July to Oct. 1777.

The Farmers' Register was commenced at Kingston in 1792 by Nicholas Power and Wm. Copp.

The Rising Sun was commenced at Kingston in 1793 by Wm. Copp and Sam'l S. Freer.

The Ulster Gazette was commenced at Kingston in 1798 by Sam'l S. and A. Freer.

The Plebeian was commenced at Kingston in Nov. 1805, by Jesse Buell, who continued as editor until 1813. In 1827 its name was changed to

The Plebeian and Ulster Co. Advertiser.

The Ulster Sentinel was published at Kingston about 1826-28 by Charles G. De Witt.

The Ulster Republican was commenced at Kingston in 1828 by S. Curtiss, jr. It is now published by Hommell & Lounsbery.

The Ulster Palladium was commenced at Saugerties in 1828 by P. J. Fish and C. Frary. Its name was subsequently changed to

The Ulster Palladium and Manufacturers' Journal.

The National Pioneer was published at Milton in 1830 by Dan'l S. Tuthill.

The Ulster Star was commenced at Saugerties in Jan. 1833, by Wm. Cully.

The Ulster County Whig was commenced at Kingston in 1835 by Wallace & Brown.

The Kingston Democratic Journal was commenced in 1837 by Wm. H. Romeyn, its present publisher.

The Political Reformer was commenced at Kingston in 1840 by H. M. Romeyn.

The Ulster Huguenot was commenced at Kingston in 1843 by J. Cully and T. F. Baldwin.

The Hickory Democrat was issued at Kingston, as a campaign paper, in 1844.

The Ulster Democrat was commenced at Kingston in 1846 by A. A. Bensall. It is now published by S. R. Harlow.

The Kingston Daily Chronicle is issued from the same office.

The Ulster Telegraph was commenced at Saugerties in 1846 by Solomon S. Hommell. Its name was subsequently changed to

The Saugerties Telegraph, and it is now published by R. B. Taylor.

The Rondout Freeman was published in 1845.

The Rondout Courier was commenced in 1847. It is now published by J. P. Hageman.

The Ellenville Journal was commenced in 1847. It is now published by S. Maxwell Taylor.

The People's Press is published at Kingston by Daniel Bradbury.

[9] After the peace of 1660 the Director General of New Netherlands shipped 11 Indians prisoners to Curacoa to be sold as slaves. This outrage led to the attack made in 1663, and the bloody war that followed. Nine days after the retreat of the Indians from the attack upon Wiltwyck, in June, 1663, a rein

Rondout, and Wall Kil Creeks and their tributaries. Besides the manorial grant of Fox Hall,[1] the English made township grants of Kingston, New Paltz, Marbletown, Rochester, Hurley, Shawangunk, and Marlborough. During the Revolution the frontier settlements were exposed to Indian hostilities, and before the close of the war were all destroyed or abandoned. The river towns were taken by the British in 1777, and most of them were pillaged and burned. The Provincial Congress and State Legislature held several sessions at Kingston during the war and soon after. The people were nearly all ardent patriots; and there were probably fewer tories in this co. than in any other section of the State. Since the Revolution the co. has steadily progressed in wealth and population. The completion of the Delaware & Hudson Canal was a marked era in the history of the industry of the co.; and the commencement of the cement manufacture and stone quarrying have greatly added to its permanent prosperity.

DENNING[2]—was formed from Shandaken, March 6, 1849. A part of Hardenburgh was taken off in 1859. It lies in the N. W. part of the co., upon the border of Sullivan. Its surface is a broken and mountainous upland. A spur of the Catskill Mts. extends through the town, with a mean elevation of 1,500 to 2,000 ft. Its streams are head branches of Rondout Creek and Neversink River. The valleys are narrow ravines bordered by steep and rocky hillsides. The soil upon the uplands is a gravelly loam, and in the valleys a sandy loam. The settlements are chiefly confined to the valleys. **Denning** is a p. o. near the center. **Dewittsville** is a hamlet near the s. line. This town, though large, has the least population of any town in the co. Its chief wealth consists in its heavy growth of hemlock and hard wood. Settlements were made at a comparatively recent period.[3]

ESOPUS—was formed from "*Kingston*," April 5, 1811. A part was set off to Kingston, and a part of Hurley was annexed, in 1818, and a part of New Paltz was annexed April 12, 1842. It lies upon the Hudson, and is the central town upon the E. border of the co. Its surface is rolling in the E. and moderately hilly in the W. A range of hills extends N. and S. through near the center of the town, the highest peak being 1,632 ft. above tide. Hussey Hill, s. of Rondout, is 1,000 ft. high. Wall Kil forms the w. and N. boundaries, and Swarte Kil and Black Creek flow through the s. part.[4] The soil is a light, clay loam. Fruit growing is becoming an important branch of business. Cement is largely manufactured, and an extensive commerce is carried on by means of the river and Delaware & Hudson Canal.[5] **Port Ewen,** (p. v.,) upon the Hudson, s. of the mouth of Rondout Creek, is a village built up by the Penn. Coal Co. A large part of the coal brought forward by the canal is here shipped upon barges for the Northern market. Pop. 1,300.[6] **Arnoldton,** (p. v.,) upon Rondout Creek, in the s. part of the town, contains a church, woolen factory, cotton factory, and 150 inhabitants. **South Rondout,** upon Rondout Creek, in the N. part, contains an extensive cement and lime factory, a lager beer brewery, a brickyard, several boatyards, and 568 inhabitants. **Dashville,** upon Rondout Creek, in the s. part, contains a cement factory and 20 houses. **Sleightsburg,** upon the Hudson, at the mouth of Rondout Creek, contains an extensive shipyard and 40 houses. **Ellmores Cove,** (Esopus p. o.,) upon the Hudson, contains a church and 40 houses. **Amesville** (p. o.) and **Atkarton** are hamlets. **Freeville,** in the N. part, contains a gristmill and 20 houses. Settlements were made by the Dutch, soon after their first occupation of the co.[7] The first church (Ref. Prot. D.) of which there is any record was formed in 1751; Rev. G. W. Mancius was the first preacher.[8]

GARDINER[9]—was formed from Rochester, New Paltz, and Shawangunk, April 2, 1853. It is an interior town, lying s. of the center of the co. The surface is rolling in the E. and hilly in the

---

forcement of 40 men, under Ensign Myssen, arrived, and relieved the fort. Capt. Krygier, with a cannon and a force of 210 men, pursued the Indians to their forts and destroyed their grain. In Sept. another expedition surprised an Indian fort, 36 mi. s. w. of Wiltwyck, killed the chief and 20 others, and restored 22 captives. The Indians were effectually broken and scattered, and late in the fall they sued for peace and restored all the remaining prisoners except 3.

[1] Thomas Chambers, the original proprietor of this patent, endeavored by will to entail it in his family; but it passed to strangers before the Revolution.

[2] Named in honor of Wm. H. Denning, former proprietor of a large part of the town.

[3] The first sawmill was built in 1827, and the first tannery in 1850, at Dewittsville, by De Witt & Reynolds.

[4] "*Sopus*," as known by the Dutch, included both Kingston and the country s. of the Rondout. Their descendants still designate Kingston as "*Sopus*," and the corporate town above named as "*Klein Sopus*," or Little Sopus. The word is of Indian

origin. The Esopus Indians—who lived in this region when first known to the whites—were of the Algonquin stock, and were allied to the Mohegan and the other river tribes.

[5] Along the bluffs that overlook the Hudson are several fine country residences. Two lighthouses are built in the river opposite this town.

[6] Named from John Ewen, President of the Penn. Coal Company. The village was laid out in 1851; nearly all of the inhabitants are more or less interested in the coal trade.

[7] Johannes Louw was born in 1681; Baltus Terpening and Tryntje Van Vliet were married in 1682. These, so far as is known, were the first birth and marriage in town. Wm. Hinman taught a school, at the Hook, in 1763. A mill was built on Black Creek prior to 1800. A cotton factory was built at Dashville in 1828, and the one now at Arnoldton in 1830; the former is standing idle.

[8] There are 6 churches in town; 3 Ref. Prot. D., M. E., Prot. E., and Friends.

[9] Named in honor of Addison Gardiner, formerly Lieut. Gov.

center and w. The Shawangunk Mts. extend along the w. border.[1] The Wall Kil flows N. E. through near the center and receives Shawangunk Kil from the S. w. The soil is principally a gravelly loam, with clay and alluvium along the streams. Lumber and leather are manufactured to some extent. **Tuthilltown,** (Tuthill p. o.,) upon Shawangunk Kil, near its mouth, contains 20 dwellings.[2] **Libertyville,** (p. o.,) on the N. line, and **Jenkinstown** are hamlets. The first settlement was made at an early period, by a colony of French Huguenots. The first church was formed in 1833; Rev. Wm. Brush was the first preacher.

HARDENBERGH[3]—was formed from Denning and Shandaken, April 15, 1859. It lies in the extreme w. corner of the co. Its surface is a broken and mountainous upland, the highest summits being 2,000 ft. above tide. It occupies a portion of the watershed between the Hudson and Delaware. Beaver Kil, Mill Brook, and Dry Brook take their rise in the town. **Dry Brook** (West Shandaken p. o.) is a hamlet.

HURLEY[4]—was granted by patent Oct. 19, 1708.[5] A part of the Hardenburgh Patent was released by Margaret Livingston, and was annexed March 3, 1789; and a part of New Paltz was taken off in 1809, a part of Esopus in 1818, a part of Olive in 1823, a part of Rosendale in 1844, and a part of Woodstock in 1853. It is an interior town, lying N. E. of the center of the co. The surface is a rolling and moderately hilly upland, the highest summits being about 700 ft. above tide. Esopus Creek flows N. E. through the S. part. Along its course are extensive fertile flats. The soil is a sandy loam, a considerable portion lying N. of the creek being unfit for cultivation. Stone quarrying is extensively carried on.[6] **Hurley,** (p. v.,) on Esopus Creek, contains a church and 160 inhabitants;[7] and **West Hurley,** (p. v.,) in the N. part, 2 churches and 25 dwellings. The first settlements were made by the Dutch, about 1680.[8] This town became the refuge of the inhabitants of Kingston when the latter place was taken by the British in 1777. The first church (Ref. Prot. D.) was formed in 1800; Rev. Thos. G. Smith was the first pastor.[9]

KINGSTON—was incorp. by patent May 19, 1667, and was recognized as a town May 1, 1702.[10] Fox Hall Patent was annexed March 12, 1787.[11] Esopus and Saugerties were taken off in 1811; a part of Esopus was annexed in 1818, and a part was annexed to Saugerties in 1832. It lies upon the Hudson, N. of the center of the co. Its surface is broken and hilly, the highest summit being Kuykuyt or Lookout Mt., about 600 ft. above tide. Esopus Creek flows N. E. through near the center, receiving Saw Kil from the w. as tributary. Rondout Creek forms the S. boundary. The soil is principally a clayey loam. A large business in coal, ice, and stone is carried on by the canal and river. **Kingston,** (p. v.,) upon Rondout Creek, 2 mi. w. of the Hudson, was incorp. April 6, 1805. Besides the co. buildings, it contains 8 churches, the Kingston Academy, several private seminaries,[12] 3 banks, 1 savings bank, 4 newspaper offices, and several small manufactories.[13] It is the center of an extensive trade upon the river and canal.[14] Pop. 3,971. **Rondout,**[15] (p. v.,) upon the Hudson, at the mouth of Rondout Creek, was incorp. April 4, 1849.

---

[1] *"The Traps"* is a deep pass or gully, 650 ft. wide, extending through these mountains.

[2] A woolen factory was built at this place at an early period.

[3] Named in honor of Johannes Hardenburgh, the patentee of an immense tract in this and adjoining cos. This town has been formed since the statistics for this work were obtained.

[4] Named from Geo. Lovelace's family, who were Barons Hurley in Ireland.—*Benson's Memoir*, p. 49. In early times it was called *"Hurley Common."*

[5] The patentees of this tract were Cornelius Kool, Adrien Garretsie, Matthew Ten Eyck, Jacobus Du Bois, Johannes Schepmoes, Roeloff Swartwout, Cornelius Lammerse, Peter Petersies, Lawrence Osterhout, and Jannetie Newkirk. The successors of the original trustees afterward bought 300 acres for the benefit of the corporation. An act of April 4, 1806, appointed John A. De Witt, Levi Johnston, and a third person, to be named by the freeholders, to sell these lands and make a partition among the owners.

[6] The stone obtained from these quarries is used for building and flagging. The business gives employment to several hundred men.

[7] Some of the buildings at this place are nearly 200 years old. A wire suspension bridge 160 ft. long here crosses the Esopus.

[8] Among the early settlers were families named Crispell, Du Bois, Cole, Newkirk, Schepmoes, Ten Eyck, Wynkoop, Elmendorf, Roosa, Constable, Louw, Delamater, and others,—mostly from Holland and Belgium. In 1719 the following persons held the office of trustees of the corporation:—Cornelius Kool, Adrien Garretsie, Jacob Du Bois, Barnabas Swartwout, Jacob Rutse, Nicolaes Roosa, and Charles Wyle. The first inn of which there is definite knowledge was kept about 1760, by Charles De Witt, at Hurley Village. Two gristmills were erected soon after the first settlement.

[9] There are 3 churches in town; 2 Ref. Prot. D., and M. E.

[10] Called by the Indians *"Atkankarten,"*—said to signify smooth land. It was more commonly called Esopus, from a tribe of Indians that inhabited it. Gov. Stuyvesant granted it a charter, May 16, 1661, under the name of Wiltwyck, (Indian Town,) and relieved it from dependence upon Fort Orange. Its affairs were to be managed by a sheriff and 3 schepens. Roeloff Swartwout was appointed first sheriff, and Evert Pels, Cornelius Barentsen Sleight, and Elbert Heymans Roose, the first schepens. Appeals from their decisions might be made to the Director General and Council in New Netherlands. The sheriff and commissioners were to hold a court every fortnight, except in harvest time, unless occasion or necessity might otherwise require. All criminal cases were to be referred directly to the Director General and Council, except the lesser crimes,—as quarrels, injuries, scolding, kicking, beating, threatenings, simply drawing a knife or sword, without assault or bloodshed,—which might be prosecuted in the lower court.

[11] Fox Hall Patent was issued to Thomas Chambers, May 21, 1667, with manorial privileges. Chambers first settled on the tract now occupied by Troy, as a tenant under Van Rensselaer He removed in 1652 to Esopus, acquired a large estate by trade, and rendered efficient service in the war against the Indians. He died in 1698. The district still bears the name of "Fox Hall."

[12] The Golden Hill Seminary and the Brookside Female Seminary, two private boarding schools, are located at this place.

[13] The Newark Lime and Cement Manufacturing Co., organized in 1848, has 2 manufactories at Newark, N. J., and one 1 at Rondout, N. Y., producing in the aggregate 750,000 barrels annually.

[14] The principal trade is that of stone, obtained from the neigh boring quarries.

[15] Formerly named *"The Strand"* and *"Kingston Landing."* When the canal was located, it was named *"Bolton,"* from the then president of the canal company; but its present name was adopted soon after. It is the Dutch name for *redout.* It was,

It contains 8 churches, a bank, and newspaper office. The people are principally engaged in the coal trade; and a large number of steamers, barges, and sailing vessels are constantly engaged in freighting coal, stone, and cement from this place.[1] The Newark Lime and Cement Manufacturing Co. manufacture a larger amount of waterlime and cement annually than is produced at any similar establishment in the country. Pop. 5,978. **Eddyville,** upon Rondout Creek, 2½ mi. from its mouth, contains a cement factory[2] and about 50 dwellings. It is the N. terminus of the D. & H. Canal. **Wilbur,** (p. v.,) on the Rondout, below Eddyville, contains about 100 houses. It is the center of an immense trade in flagging stones.[3] **Fly Mountain** is a p. o. **Dutch Settlement** is a hamlet in the N. part. **Flatbush** contains a cement factory.[4] The Dutch built a trading and military post here as early as 1614; but every thing was swept away in the wars of 1644-45. Another settlement was commenced in 1652, and abandoned in 1655. The first permanent settlers came in soon after, but suffered much from Indian hostilities for several years.[5] Feb. 19, 1777, the first State Convention adjourned from Fishkill to Kingston. On the 9th of September following, the State Legislature convened here, but dispersed upon the approach of a British force under Sir Henry Clinton on the 7th of Oct. At that time the public records were hastily removed to the back settlements, and the place was burned.[6] The first church (Ref. Prot. D.) was formed May 30, 1658. There are 18 churches in town.[7]

LLOYD—was formed from New Paltz, April 15, 1845. It lies upon the Hudson, s. of the center of the co. Its surface is mostly a rolling and hilly upland, terminating in a bluff upon the river; and the average height of the surface above tide is about 200 ft. Swarte Kil flows N. along its w. boundary and Black Brook N. through the center. The soil is generally a clay and gravelly loam. The bluffs along the river are principally occupied by fine country seats. **New Paltz Landing,** (p. v.,) upon the river, contains 2 churches and 50 houses;[8] **Centerville** (Lloyd p. o.) a church and 17 houses. **Lewisburgh** is a hamlet on the river, s. of New Paltz Landing. **Riverside** is a p. o. in the N. E. part. The date of first settlement in this town is quite ancient; but most of the details of the first years are lost. It was originally named "Paltz." The first church (M. E.) was formed in 1787. There are 3 churches in town; 2 M. E. and Presb.

MARBLETOWN—was formed by patent June 25, 1703.[9] It was first recognized as a town March 7, 1788. A part of Olive was taken off in 1823, and a part of Rosendale in 1844. It is near the geographical center of the co. The surface is a hilly upland, broken by the valleys of the streams. Stone Ridge, near the center, the highest summit, is about 400 ft. above tide. Esopus Creek flows through the N. part, and Rondout Creek through the s. E. corner. The soil is chiefly a clay and sandy loam. A quarry of Shawangunk grit has been opened, and a sulphur spring has been found near the line of Rosendale. **Stone Ridge,** (p. v.,) s. E. of the center, contains 2 churches and 80 houses; **Kripplebush,** (p. v.,) in the s. part, a church and 12 houses. **High Falls**[10] is a hamlet upon the canal. **Marbletown** is a p. o. **Bruceville** (High Falls p. o.) is a small canal village on the line of Rosendale, in the s. E. corner. The first church (Ref. Prot. D.) was formed in 1738.[11]

MARLBOROUGH—was formed as a precinct, from Newburgh Precinct, March 12, 1772,

at an early period of its growth, a maze of crooked lanes, bordered by rude shanties and inhabited by a floating population of Irish laborers. The village still contains a large proportion of Irish, and has a large and increasing number of German inhabitants. Its appearance has much improved within a few years.

[1] About 20 steamers are engaged in the freighting business of this place. Lines of steamers also run regularly to Albany, New York, and intermediate places. A steam ferry connects the place with Rhinebeck, on the E. bank of the Hudson.

[2] The Lawrence Cement Co. manufacture 90,000 barrels of cement annually.

[3] The aggregate amount of this trade is more than $250,000 per annum.

[4] The Kingston and Rosendale Cement Co. manufacture 70,000 barrels of cement annually.

[5] The site of the first Dutch fort is said to be upon a plateau in the w. bounds of Rondout. The locality is still called by its Indian name, Ponkhockie, said to signify "Canoe Harbor." On the 7th of June, 1663, as most of the people were at work in the fields, the Indians made a sudden attack upon the fort, (which was carelessly left open,) killed 18, and carried away 42 as prisoners. Capt. Chambers rallied the men, drove out the Indians, and commenced a war in which the captives were mostly reclaimed and the Indians nearly exterminated. The first marriage on the church record was that of Jan Janse Timmermans and Catharine Mattyson, Oct. 3, 1660.

[6] The British force under Gen. Vaughan, consisting of 3,000 men, was sent up the river to co-operate with Burgoyne. For

10 days after passing the barriers at the Highlands they amused themselves by burning and plundering the places along the river. They took possession of Kingston Oct. 17, and, after plundering it several hours, they burned every house but one. The houses were mostly of stone, and the woodwork was easily replaced after the retreat of the British. Several of the early meetings of the Legislature were held at this place; and the first State Constitution was formed here.

[7] 2 Ref. Prot. D., 2 M. E., Bap., Prot. E., Presb., and Jewish, at Kingston; 2 M. E., Presb., Germ. Evang. Luth., R. C., Bap., Prot. E., Ref. Prot. D., and Jewish, at Rondout; and M. E. at Eddyville.

[8] A ferry connects this place with Poughkeepsie.

[9] This patent was granted to Col. Henry Beekman, Capt. Thos. Gaston, and Capt. Chas. Brodhead, in trust for the inhabitants. Trustees continued to be annually elected until 1808. The records of 1703 contain the names of the following petitioners for grants of land:—Mosys Du Puy, Thomas Vandemarke, Loondart Kool, Richard Wilson, Jeremy Kettell, jr., Gysbert Roosa, Wm. Nottingham, John Cock, sen., and Capt. Richard Brodhead.

[10] The cement works of Delafield & Baxter, at High Falls, employ about 50 men, and produce about 40,000 barrels annually. The falls on the Rondout are here about 50 feet high, affording a great amount of water-power.

[11] The census reports 5 churches in town; 3 Ref. Prot. D. and 2 M. E. Rev. Derick Romeyn and Rev. J. R. Hardenburgh (afterward Pres. of Rutgers College) were both pastors of the Ref. Prot. D. church at Stone Ridge.

and as a town, March 7, 1788. Plattekill was taken off in 1800. It lies upon the Hudson, in the s. e. corner of the co. Its surface is broken and hilly. Marlborough Mt., a rocky ridge along the w. border, is about 1,000 ft. above the river. The streams are principally small brooks flowing directly into the Hudson. The soil is a slaty loam. **Milton,** (p. v.,) upon the Hudson, in the n. part, contains 3 churches and about 75 dwellings. **Marlborough,**[1] (p. v.,) in the s. part, contains 2 churches, several manufactories,[2] and about 50 dwellings. **Lattingtown** is a hamlet. The date and statistics of the early settlement have not been ascertained. The first church (Presb.) was formed Jan. 1, 1764.[3]

NEW PALTZ[4]—was granted by patent by Gov. Andros, Sept. 29, 1677.[5] Its bounds were enlarged April 1, 1775, and a part of Hurley was annexed Feb. 2, 1809. A part of Esopus was taken off in 1842, a part of Rosendale in 1844, Lloyd in 1845, and a part of Gardiner in 1853. It is an interior town, lying s. e. of the center of the co. Its surface is mostly a hilly upland. The Shawangunk Mts. extend along the w. border. Paltz Point, the highest summit, is 700 ft. above tide. Wall Kil flows n. e. through near the center; it is bordered by wide, fertile flats. The soil is generally a fine quality of sandy loam. Hay is one of the principal products and exports. **New Paltz,** (p. v.,) upon Wall Kil, near the center, contains the New Paltz Academy, 2 churches, and 45 dwellings. **Butterville, Ohioville,** and **Springtown** are hamlets. The first settlements were made by a colony of French Huguenots, a few years before the date of the patent.[6] The oldest church record is in French, and bears date of 1683. There are 3 churches in town; Ref. Prot. D., M. E., and Friends.

OLIVE—was formed from Shandaken, Marbletown, and Hurley, April 15, 1823. A part was annexed to Woodstock, and a part of Woodstock was annexed, in 1853. It is an interior town, lying a little n. w. of the center of the co. The surface is mountainous in the n. and w. and hilly in the s. and e.[7] A considerable portion of the mountainous region is too rough for profitable cultivation. Esopus Creek flows s. e. through the town, a little n. of the center. The soil is a sandy, gravelly, and clayey loam. Lumbering and tanning[8] are largely carried on. **Shokan,**[9] (p. v.,) upon the creek, n. of the center, contains 2 churches and 20 houses; **Samsonville,**[10] (p. v.,) on the s. line, a church, tannery, and 30 houses; **Olive,** (p. v.,) in the n. e. corner, a church and 25 houses; and **Olive City,** (Olive Bridge p. o.,) on the creek, near the center, a tannery and 20 houses. The first settlements were made in the Esopus Valley, in 1740.[11] The first church (Ref. Prot. D.) was formed at Shokan, in 1800.[12]

PLATTEKILL[13]—was formed from Marlborough, March 21, 1800. A part of Shawangunk was annexed April 3, 1846, but was restored March 28, 1848. It lies upon the s. border of the co., near the s. e. corner. Its surface is broken by a series of ridges of an average elevation of 300 ft. above the valleys. Its streams are small brooks and creeks. The soil is a fine quality of sandy and gravelly loam. **Plattekill,** (p. v.,) near the s. line, contains a church and 25 dwellings; **Clintondale,** (p. v.,) in the n. part, on the line of Lloyd, a church and 20 dwellings; **Flint,** (New Hurley p. o.,) in the s. w. corner, on the line of Shawangunk, a church and 15 dwellings, and **Modena,** (p. v.,) near the n. w. corner, 16 dwellings. The first settlements were made about

---

[1] This place is situated at the head of a deep, rocky gorge opening toward the Hudson.

[2] About 15,000 wheelbarrows and $40,000 worth of agricultural implements are manufactured annually.

[3] The census reports 9 churches in town; 2 Presb., 2 M. E., 2 Friends, Prot. E., Bap., and Christian.

[4] Pronounced New Pawltz, and named from Pfalz, the German name of the Palatinate.

[5] The patentees of this tract were Lewis Du Bois, Christian Deyo, Abraham Hasbroecq, Andries Le Fevre, Jean Brocq, Pierre Deyo, Lawrens Beverie, Anthony Crespel, Abraham Du Bois, Hugo Frere, Isaac Du Bois, and Simon Le Fevre.

[6] The valley of Wall Kil was discovered by one of the parties engaged in pursuing the destroyers of Wiltwyck, in the summer of 1663. The persecuted exiles from France, who first sought refuge in Germany, and thence emigrated to America, decided upon settling here. They bought the land of the Indians May 26, 1677, and soon after they settled in their new homes. In 1728, the owners of the patent intrusted its care to 12 trustees, known as "The Twelve Men." These trustees were elected annually, until the organization of the town under the State Government. The Twelve Men in 1785 were Simon Du Bois, Jacobus Hasbrouck, Johannis Freer, Jacob Hasbrouck, jr., Abraham Donaldson, Abraham Eltinge, Petris Hasbrouck, Samuel Bevier, Benjamin Deyoe, Isaac Le Fever, Matthew Le Fever, and Abraham Ein. By act of March 31, 1785, the allot-

ments made by the Twelve Men were confirmed. Their "Common Book" was to be retained by the Surveyor General until a convenient time, and then it was to be deposited with the co. clerk of Ulster co., to be forever preserved. Its records are deemed authentic evidence in court.

[7] The towns of Olive, Rochester, and Denning, corner on a hill which is about 2,700 feet above tide. Shokan Point is about 3,100 feet high; and the average elevation of the lowlands is 800 feet above tide.

[8] There are 4 extensive tanneries in town, one of which, owned by Pratt & Samson, is the largest oak tannery in the co. It produces 70,000 sides of sole leather annually.

[9] Pronounced Sho-kan′.

[10] Named from Gen. Henry A. Samson.

[11] Geo. Middagh settled in 1740; Samuel Cox, in 1742; William Nottingham, in 1745,—all near Olive Bridge; John Crispell, in 1747, a little e. of Shokan; Hendrick Crispell, at Shokan, in 1760; John Coons, in 1775; and Thos. Bush, in 1755, s. of Olive City. The first inn was kept at Olive Bridge, by Conrad Du Bois; and the first store, sawmill, and gristmill, by Lemuel Winchell, at Winchells Falls. Two sons of Frederick Bush were carried off by the Indians in 1781. The early history of this town is blended with that of Marbletown.

[12] The census reports 4 churches in town; 2 Ref. Prot. D., Bap., and M. E.

[13] Pronounced Plaw-ta-kill, and signifies "Flat Brook."

the commencement of the last century. The first church (Ref. Prot. D.) was formed in 1770; Rev. Stephen Goetschius was the first pastor.[1]

ROCHESTER[2]—was incorp. by patent June 25, 1703,[3] and organized as a town March 7, 1788. A part of Middletown (Delaware co.) was taken off in 1789, Neversink (Sullivan co.) in 1798, Wawarsing in 1806, and a part of Gardiner in 1853. A part of Wawarsing was annexed March 21, 1823. It is an interior town, lying a little s. w. of the center of the co. Ranges of mountains extend along the e. and w. borders, and a rolling upland occupies the central portions. Rondout Creek flows N. E. through the s. part, and receives as tributaries Sander Kil, Peters Kil, and several other streams. Vernooy Creek flows s. through the w. part. The soil upon the uplands is a gravelly loam, and in the valleys a sandy loam mixed with clay. The Delaware & Hudson Canal extends along the valley of Rondout Creek. Esopus millstones are largely quarried in this town. An extensive cave near Kyserike has been explored about half a mile. **Alligerville** and **Port Jackson** are small villages upon the canal. **Accord** and **Kyserike** are p. offices. The first settlements were made about 1700, by the Dutch.[4] The first church (Ref. Prot. D.) was formed soon after the first settlement. There are now 2 churches in town; Ref. Prot. D. and M. E.

ROSENDALE—was formed from Marbletown, New Paltz, and Hurley, April 26, 1844. It is an interior town, lying e. of the center of the co. Its surface is a rolling and broken upland, the highest summits being 200 to 500 ft. above the valleys. Rondout Creek flows N. E. through near the center, and receives Koxing Kil from the s. and Kottle Kil from the N. The Delaware & Hudson Canal extends along the valley of the Rondout. The soil is principally a sandy loam. The manufacture of cement has become one of the most important branches of business.[5] There is an extensive paper mill in town. **Rosendale**, (p. v.,) upon the creek and canal, contains 2 churches and 450 inhabitants; **Lawrenceville**, 1 mi. w., 40 houses; **Bruceville**, (High Falls p. o.,) upon the line of Marbletown, about 30 houses. **Green Locks**, a canal village, on the e. border, and **Whiteport**, in the N. part, each contain about 20 houses. The first settlements were made by the Dutch, about 1700.[6] The first church (Ref. Prot. D.) was formed in 1797; Rev. Thos. G. Smith was the first preacher.[7]

SAUGERTIES[8]—was formed from Kingston, April 5, 1811. An error in the boundary was corrected June 8, 1812, and a part of Kingston was annexed April 2, 1832. It lies upon the Hudson, in the N. E. corner of the co. The surface is rolling in the e. and hilly in the center and w. The hills upon the river and extending 2 mi. back are underlaid by limestone, from which quicklime and cement are manufactured. Farther w. are quarries of fine flagging stone. Platte Kil flows through the town in a tortuous course and forms the principal drainage. Kaaters Kil flows along the N. border. The soil along the river is a clayey loam, and upon the uplands a sandy and gravelly loam. Quarrying is extensively carried on.[9] **Saugerties**, (p. v.,) upon the Hudson, at the mouth of Esopus Kil, was incorp. April 26, 1831, as "*Ulster.*" Its name was changed April 10, 1855. It contains the Saugerties Academy, 7 churches, a newspaper office, and several extensive manufactories. Pop. 3,334. **Malden**, (p. v.,) upon the Hudson, 2 mi. N. of Saugerties, is the seat of an extensive stone trade. Pop. 350. **Glasco**, (p. v.,) upon the Hudson, 3 mi. s. of Saugerties, is the seat of an extensive brick manufactory and stone trade. Pop.

---

[1] There are 7 churches in town; 3 M. E., Wes. Meth., Ref. Prot. D., Presb., and Friends.

[2] Named in honor of the Earl of Rochester. The Indian name is said to be Mom-bac-cus.

[3] The first trustees under the patent were.Col. Henry Beekman, Joachim Schoonmaker, and Mosys Du Puy.

[4] In 1703 the following persons resided in town:—Van Gerritse Decker, Lodewyck Hornbeck, Leendart Kool, sr., Anthony Hornbeck, Wm. De La Montaigne, Teunis Oosterhout, Jan Cartwright, Gysbert Van Garde, Andries Davies, and David Du Bois. Teunis Oosterhout had a "corne mill" on Mombaccus Kil, in 1743.

[5] More than one-half of the cement made in the co. is manufactured in this town. The water-limestone quarries may be said to constitute the wealth of the town. The cement manufactories are as follows:—

	Barrels.
Newark and Rosendale Lime and Cement Co., at Whiteport. manufactures annually	125,000
Rosendale Cement Co., Rosendale, manufact's annually	40,000
Clearwater & Martin, " " "	40,000
David S. Ogden, " " "	28,000
Luther Hoffman, " " "	8,000

[6] An inn was kept at the old "Rosendale Farm" in 1711.

[7] There are 5 churches in town; 2 Ref. Prot. D., Bap., Friends, and R. C.

[8] This name is said to be derived from the Dutch "Zagger," a sawyer, from a sawmill built by Robert Livingston on Saw Kil. Ebenezer Wooster first used the name in 1749, when surveying the bounds of the Hardenburgh Patent.

In 1826, Henry Barclay, of N. Y., purchased the present site of the village, and the water-power. He built a dam and constructed a race which made a fall of 47 feet. He soon after built a rolling mill, paper mill, and cotton factory. The last named has since been changed to a white lead factory. The Ulster Iron Works employs 300 hands night and day, and manufactures 6,000 tons of bar and hoop iron annually. The paper mill employs 125 hands, and turns out 600 tons of paper annually. The White Lead Works employs 40 men, and manufactures 1,500 tons of paint annually. A steam mill for dressing stone turns out 1½ tons daily. The village is also largely engaged in commerce. About 30 sail-vessels are employed in exporting stone and brick. A steam ferry plies between this place and Tivoli station on the Hudson River R. R., and a daily steamer runs to New York.

[9] It is estimated that 2,000 persons are employed in quarrying, dressing, drawing, and shipping stone from this town. The varieties are chiefly flagging and curb stone; but cut stone for many uses is also sold. About a half million of dollars' worth of stone is shipped annually from Saugerties, Malden, and Glasco.

about 300. **West Camp,** (p. v.,) upon the Hudson, in the N. part, contains a church and 15 houses. **Quarryville,** (p. v.,) in the N. part, and **Unionville,** near the center, each contain about 300 inhabitants, who are mostly engaged in getting out stone from the neighboring quarries. **Glenearie,** upon the s. line, **Van Akens Mills,** near the center, and **Ashbury,** are small villages. The first settlements were made by the Dutch, at an early period; but the largest immigration was that of the German Palatinates,[1] a colony of whom located at West Camp in 1710. The first church (Luth.) was organized at West Camp, in 1711. There are now 15 churches in town.[2]

SHANDAKEN[3]—was formed from Woodstock, April 9, 1804. A part was annexed from Neversink (Sullivan co.) in 1809. A part of Olive was taken off in 1823, Denning in 1849, and a part of Hardenburgh in 1859. It is the N. w. corner town of the co. Its surface is mostly a mountainous upland, broken by deep ravines. The declivities are steep and rocky, and a large share of the surface is too rough for profitable cultivation. The town is not inhabited except along the valleys, the mountain region being left to wild beasts and hunters. The soil in the valleys is a clay and sandy loam. The principal branches of business pursued are lumbering, shingle making, and tanning. **Shandaken,**[4] (p. v.,) in the N. part, contains a church, a large tannery, a sawmill, gristmill, and 20 houses; **Pine Hill,** (p. v.,) in the N. w. part, a sawmill, gristmill, tannery, and 15 houses. **Ladews Corners,** (The Corner p. o.,) in the extreme E. angle of the town; **Phœnicia,** (p. o.,) in the N. E. corner; and **Woodland,** (p. o.,) s. E. of the center, are hamlets. At each of these places, and at several other points in town, are extensive tanneries.[5] The first settlements were made before the Revolution.[6] There are 2 churches in town; Ref. Prot. D. and M.E.

SHAWANGUNK[7]—was formed as a precinct Dec. 17, 1743, and as a town March 7, 1788. A part of Gardiner was taken off in 1853, a part was annexed to Plattekill in 1846 and restored in 1848. It is the central town upon the s. border of the co. The surface is a hilly and broken upland. The Shawangunk Mts., extending along the w. border, are about 2,000 ft. above tide. The Shawangunk River forms about ½ of the s. boundary, and flows N. E. through near the center, receiving Dwaars Kil[8] from the w. Wall Kil flows N. E. through the E. part, receiving Muddy Kil from the E. and Dwaars Kil from the w. The soil is generally a gravelly loam. **Shawangunk,** (p. v.,) in the s. E. part, contains a gristmill, sawmill, spoke factory, and 20 houses; **Ulsterville,** (p. o.,) in the s. w. part, 10 houses; and **Galeville Mills,** (p. o.,) on Wall Kil, a church, sawmill, gristmill, and 10 houses. **Dwaars Kil,** near the center, is a p. o. **Bruynswick,** (p. o.,) on the N. line, contains a church and 10 houses; **Jamesburgh,** (p. v.,) near the extreme w. angle, a church and 12 houses. **New Hurley** (p. o.) is a hamlet, on the line of Plattekill. The first settlements were made along the valley of Shawangunk River, by the Dutch, between 1680 and 1700.[9] New Fort is a locality where two Indian battles were fought in 1663. The first church (Ref. Prot. D.) was formed Oct. 10, 1753; Rev. V. Vrooman was the first pastor.[10]

WAWARSING[11]—was formed from Rochester, March 14, 1806. A part was re-annexed to Rochester in 1823. It is the s. w. corner town in the co. Its surface is mostly a mountainous upland, broken by several deep valleys. The Shawangunk Mts. extend along the E. border; and spurs of the Catskills occupy the central and w. parts. The highest peaks are 2,000 to 3,000 ft. above tide. The mountainous portions in the E. and N. w. corners are rocky and precipitous and

---

[1] Stephen Myers and brothers settled at a place called "Churchland," just w. of Saugerties Village. Martin Snyder settled at the same place, and G. W. Dedrick at West Camp, Aaron Newkirk and Felte Fiero in the same vicinity,—all in 1700, Dedrick Marrtesstock settled at "Kaatsban" in 1728. Peter Winne, Edward Woods, Myndert Mynderse, B. Barham, Jacobus Pearsen, Myndert Schutt, Godfrey Denolfen, and others, were early settlers. On the 18th of May, 1711, there were 14 Palatinates at "Elizabethtown," 111 at "Georgetown," and 321 at "New Village," in this town. The settlers afterward mostly removed to the valleys of the Schoharie and Mohawk.

[2] 4 Ref. Prot. D., 4 M. E., Germ. Meth., Bap., Cong., Prot. E., R. C., Luth., and Presb.

[3] Said to signify "Rapid Water."

[4] The road from Shandaken to Lexington is constructed through a pass 4 mi. long and in some places scarcely 500 feet wide, and abounding in picturesque scenery. It is through the watershed between Esopus and Schoharie Creeks.

[5] 200,000 sides of leather are annually manufactured in this town.

[6] John Longyear, Cornelius Furlough, Jacob Brink, Coonradt Wisner, and Frederick Markle, all settled before the war. —— Witherspoon taught school at The Corner at an early period.

[7] Pronounced Shawn-gum, and said to mean "white rocks." The kil or creek receives this name from large white rocks at its junction with Wall Kil; and it was applied from the stream to the mountain and town. Another version is that it is named from the Shawan, a southern tribe, and gunk, a mountain, or, The mountain that extends toward the south.

[8] The Dutch applied the term Dwaar to streams that flowed sometimes in one direction and sometimes in another. This phenomenon is true of waters at the mouth only of the stream.

[9] Among the early settlers were Jacobus Bruyn, Cornelius Schoonmaker, Abram Schutt, Zachariah Hoffman, Benjamin Smedes, Jacob Decker, John Terwilliger, and Johannes Decker. Along Wall Kil, Robert Kain, Robert Graham, David Davis, Daniel Winfield, Hendrick Van Wegen, and James Penneck settled from 1710 to '30. A school was taught near Bruynswick p. o., between 1730 and '40. The first mill was probably at the junction of Wall and Dwaars Kils, 1 mi. below Shawangunk Village.

[10] There are 4 churches in town; 2 Ref. Prot. D. and 2 M. E.

[11] Usually abbreviated to "War-sink." It is an Indian word, an l said to signify "black bird's nest."

too rough for cultivation. The s. w. portion is a hilly upland. Rondout Creek flows in a deep valley from the w. border s. e. to near the center; thence it turns at nearly right angles and flows n. e. to the e. border. It receives from the s. Sandburgh Creek, a stream which drains the w. declivities of the Shawangunk Mts., Beer Creek, and the outlet of Cape Pond, which flows through near the center and empties into Sandburgh Creek. The Delaware & Hudson Canal extends along the valleys of Rondout and Sandburgh Creeks, at the w. foot of the Shawangunk Mts. The soil in the valleys is principally a sandy loam. Lumber,[1] leather, glass, earthenware, iron, and axes are extensively manufactured in different parts of the town. **Ellenville,** (p. v.,) upon Sandburgh Creek, at the mouth of Beer Kil, was incorp. in Sept. 1858. It is an important canal village, and contains several churches, a high school,[2] newspaper office, and an extensive glass factory.[3] Pop. 1,700. **Napanock,** (p. v.,) upon the Rondout, above its junction with the Sandburgh, contains several churches and manufactories,[4] and a population of about 700. **Homowack,** (p. v.,) a canal village, upon the line of Sullivan co., contains a church, glass factory, woolen factory, and 20 houses. **Kerhonkson,** (p. v.,) a canal village, on the line of Rochester, contains a church and 30 houses. **Lackawack,** (p. v.,) upon the Rondout, in the w. part, contains a church, an extensive tannery, and about 20 houses. **Greenfield,** (p. v.,) in the s. w. part, contains 2 churches, a gristmill, sawmill, tannery, and about 25 houses. **Wawarsing,** (p. v.,) in the n. e., contains a gristmill, sawmill, tannery, and about 25 houses. **Port Benjamin,** a canal village, s. of the Wawarsing, contains about 25 houses. **Port Nixon,** a village upon Rondout Creek and the canal, in the n. e. part, contains a church and about 25 houses. The first settlements were made about the commencement of the last century, principally by the Dutch.[5] During the Revolution the inhabitants were killed, captured, or driven off by the tories and Indians.[6] The first church (Ref. Prot. D.) was formed in 1745; Rev. J. Fryenmoet was the first preacher.[7]

WOODSTOCK—was formed April 11, 1787, from the settlements of Great and Little Shandaken, which had been attached to Hurley. A part of Middletown (Delaware co.) was taken off in 1789, Windham (Greene co.) in 1798, and Shandaken in 1804. A part of Olive was taken off, and parts of Olive and Hurley were annexed, Nov. 25, 1853. It lies upon the n. border of the co., e. of the center. Its surface is mostly a mountainous upland, too rough for profitable cultivation. Several fine valleys extend through the town, separating the upland into several distinct ridges and peaks. Overlook Mt., in the n. e. corner, is 3,500 ft. above tide. Near its summit is Shues Lake, a beautiful sheet of clear water. The scenery in this vicinity is among the finest in Eastern N. Y. Saw Kil and Beaver Kil are the principal streams. The soil is a clay and slaty loam upon the uplands and a gravelly loam in the valleys. **Woodstock,** (p. v.,) in the s. e. part, contains 2 churches, a tannery, and 20 houses; **Bearsville,** (p. o.,) 2 mi. w. of Woodstock, is a hamlet; **Lake Hill** is a p. o., near the center. The first settlements were made just before the commencement of the Revolution.[8] The first church (Luth.) was formed in 1806.[9]

---

[1] About 10,000,000 ft. of lumber are sent from this town annually.

[2] The Ellenville High School, established in 1853. It is a boarding and day school.

[3] The Ellenville Glass Co., incorp. in 1836, turns out more than $100,000 worth of demijohns, bottles, &c. annually. It employs 200 hands.

[4] The Napanock Ax Factory employs about 100 men, and manufactures 150,000 axes annually. The Napanock Iron Works employs 50 or 60 men, and manufactures pig and wrought iron and r. r. car axles.

[5] The first settlers were Abram Bevier, John Bevier, from New Paltz, in 1708, Egbert De Witt, Wm. Nottingham, and Andries De Witt. An inn was kept by Johannes Bevier before the Revolution. The first store at Wawarsing was kept by Abram Vernooy; the first gristmill was built by Cornelius Vernooy.

[6] On the 12th of Aug. 1781, a large party of tories and Indians, under one Caldwell, appeared in this town. They had formed the design of falling upon Napanock, but, being informed that that place was defended by a cannon, they came to Wawarsing before the inhabitants were up in the morning. At this place was a stone fort on the site of B. C. Hornbeck's house. Two men and a young woman discovered the enemy before they reached the fort, and the young woman succeeded in closing the door just in time to prevent it from being burst open by the savages. The latter, finding further attack dangerous, dispersed for burning and plundering the out settlements. Some 5 or 6 dwellings, 7 barns, and a gristmill were burned, and on the next day the enemy withdrew, laden with spoils. Several lives were lost on both sides, and much property was destroyed.—*The Indians; or Narratives of Massacres and Depredations on the Frontiers of Wawarsink and Vicinity,* p. 21.

[7] The census reports 11 churches in town; 4 M. E., 3 Ref. Prot. D., 2 R. C., Bap., and Friends.

[8] Philip Bonesteel, first innkeeper, settled in 1770; Edward Short, in 1776; Peter Short, in 1784; Jacobus Du Bois, Ephraim Van Keuren, Philip Shultis, and Henry Shultis, sen., in 1788; Jno. Hutchens, in 1790; Wm. Elling, in 1786; Mathew Keip, in 1787; and Jacob Montrose at an early day. Robert Livingston built the first sawmill, and J. Montrose the first gristmill. These settlements were much harassed by the Indians during the war.

[9] There are 6 churches in town; 3 M. E., Luth., Bap., and Friends.

Acres of Land, Valuation, Population, Dwellings, Families, Freeholders, Schools, Live Stock, Agricultural Products, and Domestic Manufactures, of Ulster County.

Names of Towns.	Acres of Land.		Valuation of 1858.			Population.		No. of Dwellings.	No. of Families.	Freeholders.	Schools.	
	Improved.	Unimproved.	Real Estate.	Personal Property.	Total.	Males.	Females.				No. of Districts.	Children taught.
Denning	910	76,913½	$71,195	$450	$71,645	385	307	132	131	86	5	327
Esopus	13,044½	8,439	825,450	72,635	898,085	2,252	2,035	679	837	505	16	1,552
Gardiner	18,597	7,281	562,979	73,800	636,779	954	969	337	354	249	9	822
Hardenbergh[a]												
Hurley	7,268¾	9,858	399,254	15,440	414,694	1,094	1,021	380	395	181	8	766
Kingston	8,622½	16,812	3,065,707	1,250,918	4,316,625	7,152	6,822	1,829	2,773	746	15	4,838
Lloyd	12,018	6,513½	483,685	87,350	571,035	1,106	1,086	379	428	269	8	905
Marbletown	17,946¼	14,787	954,530	56,700	1,011,230	1,887	1,840	620	699	639	13	1,546
Marlborough	13,103	2,874½	368,819	58,550	427,369	1,302	1,366	426	514	255	10	981
New Paltz	14,428	5,497½	514,881	165,600	680,481	1,009	1,012	317	326	252	6	698
Olive	14,653¼	22,474	339,120	23,750	362,870	1,496	1,428	516	591	367	14	1,347
Plattekill	15,342¾	4,190½	642,644	45,200	687,844	981	951	348	369	255	9	713
Rochester	18,087	25,966½	800,611	34,488	835,099	1,768	1,707	617	641	391	13	1,301
Rosendale	7,877	3,371	594,460	40,200	634,660	1,333	1,239	375	491	163	6	890
Saugerties	17,815½	14,931¾	1,468,940	372,650	1,841,590	4,812	4,506	1,487	1,788	1,020	22	3,280
Shandaken	12,764	79,891	260,871	7,600	268,471	1,298	1,154	451	454	266	20	1,060
Shawangunk	21,360½	8,097	742,589	77,145	819,734	1,293	1,338	478	484	316	12	1,140
Wawarsing	17,974¼	46,052	871,682	71,555	943,237	3,729	3,498	1,391	1,436	716	30	2,783
Woodstock	8,828¾	24,253	239,881	28,488	268,369	906	900	306	340	218	6	608
Total	240,639⅝	378,202¾	13,207,298	2,482,519	15,689,817	34,757	33,179	11,068	13,051	6,894	222	25,556

Names of Towns.	Live Stock.					Agricultural Products.							Domestic Cloths in yards.
						Bush. of Grain.					Dairy Products.		
	Horses.	Working Oxen and Calves.	Cows.	Sheep.	Swine.	Winter.	Spring.	Tons of Hay.	Bushels of Potatoes.	Bushels of Apples.	Pounds of Butter.	Pounds of Cheese.	
Denning	31	314	142	206	72	529	4,396½	543	2,170	24	15,160		187½
Esopus	549	628	593	453	1,981	13,122	36,195½	3,282	11,662	72,130	63,287		727
Gardiner	504	818	1,665	4,449	2,948	15,452	38,820¾	4,428	3,850	5,692	156,649		459
Hardenbergh[a]													
Hurley	351	565	472	387	913	7,648	22,589	2,006	8,324	3,315	39,081		257½
Kingston	1,018	442	599	3,250	2,977	12,335½	32,296	2,851	12,442	4,460	28,752	100	459
Lloyd	636	554	649	582	1,783	19,709	27,358½	3,868¾	3,564	4,864	84,534		208
Marbletown	718	1,329	1,432	1,662	2,850	23,474½	53,080	4,649½	12,916	18,390	110,870		2,778½
Marlborough	386	684	896	739	1,821	20,306½	30,065½	3,835½	2,940	4,782	99,925		30
New Paltz	448	658	995	1,991	2,056	19,809	38,215	4,419	3,759	8,070	95,785		659
Olive	437	1,304	944	1,147	1,019	11,158½	25,293½	3,727½	7,469	208,996	84,955		3,058
Plattekill	518	767	1,301	1,632	2,678	21,004	36,434	4,974½	8,559	10,024	119,595		90
Rochester	654	1,436	1,295	2,055	2,230	22,610	49,618¾	178¼	8,943	3,051	110,773		1,451¾
Rosendale	317	382	534	262	969	8,252½	17,772	1,805	6,251	5,455	32,715		447
Saugerties	1,211	1,071	1,721	1,216	2,664	14,649¾	41,556¼	6,759	1,162½	11,253	131,887		1,605½
Shandaken	366	1,252	810	1,578	519	2,089	17,070	3,369	8,000	10,616	53,290		2,048
Shawangunk	618	1,294	1,027	4,599	3,671	20,143	46,182	4,979	6,116	11,935	235,000		321
Wawarsing	797	2,129	1,487	2,265	1,840	13,623	59,286½	6,422	20,523	11,613	152,846	230	369
Woodstock	334	1,181	770	1,368	1,034	8,849	16,455	2,698	5,889	3,084	54,527	190	1,291
Total	9,893	16,808	17,332	29,841	34,025	254,764¼	592,785¾	64,795	134,539½	397,754	1,669,631	520	16,446¾

[a] Formed since 1855.

WARREN COUNTY.

THIS county was formed from Washington, March 12, 1813, and was named in honor of Gen. Joseph Warren, of the Revolution. It lies s. and w. of Lake George, near the E. border of the State. It is centrally distant 65 miles from Albany, and contains 968 sq. mi. The surface is very broken and mountainous, less than one-half being susceptible of cultivation. The mountain ranges are continuations of the great mountain masses which culminate in Essex co. The characteristic features of Essex are somewhat softened and subdued in this co. The mountains are broader, less pointed, and generally less precipitous; the valleys are wider and more connected; and there are larger expanses of comparatively level land. With all these modifications, however, a great part of the surface is wild and rugged. High, serrated ridges traverse the entire extent of the co., often rising thousands of feet above the valleys. These mountains, being principally composed of primary rocks, which strongly resist the action of the elements, have a steepness of declivity and sharpness of outline in marked contrast with the gradual slopes and beautifully rounded summits of the highlands of the slate and limestone regions. The soil formed by the exceedingly slow process of disintegration is either washed directly into the valleys, or in the course of ages it collects in thin layers upon the hillsides, giving nutrition to a scanty vegetation. Three of the five mountain ranges N. of the Mohawk Valley extend through this co. The Palmertown Range enters the extreme E. part of Queensbury from Washington co. French Mt., a spur of this range, at the s. E. extremity of Lake George, rises almost precipitously from the lake and attains an elevation of 2,500 to 3,000 ft. above tide. Another spur of this range forms the Luzerne Mts., which extend through the s. part of Luzerne and the E. part of Caldwell,—a N. branch extending N. and forming the whole series of high bluffs which border the w. shore of Lake George. The second or Kayaderosseras Range extends N. E. through Stony Creek, Thurman, Chester, and Horicon, sending spurs both N. and s. Crane Mt., in the s. E. corner of Johnsburgh, the highest peak of this range, has an elevation of 3,000 ft. above the surrounding valleys. The third or Schroon Range occupies the central and northerly part of Johnsburgh and the N. w. angle of Chester. It consists of a great number of rocky peaks rising to a height of 2,500 to 3,000 ft. above tide; most of these have never yet been named. The rocks that compose these great mountain masses are principally gneiss. Granite, white crystaline, limestone, and serpentine are found in considerable quantities in the form of injected veins. A belt of this limestone extends along the course of the Kayaderosseras Mts., and from it a good quality of lime is manufactured. In the valleys and in the s. part of the co. are found layers of Potsdam sandstone, black marble of the Black River limestone strata, Trenton limestone, and Utica slate. Many of these rocks are useful for building materials; and the limestone furnishes an abundance of excellent lime. At the foot of a granite ledge upon Crane Mt. is found a bed of very pure porcelain clay, supposed to have been formed by the slow disintegration of the feldspathic rock. Graphite and magnetic iron ore have also been discovered, but not in sufficient quantities to be profitably worked.

The drainage of the co. is mostly through the Hudson River. This stream enters the co. from Essex, in two branches about 10 mi. apart, and these, after flowing through nearly parallel valleys for about 30 mi., unite in one stream. The E. branch is the outlet of Schroon Lake, and the w. forms the drainage of the Adirondack Mts.[1] This river has a very rapid course; and upon it are several rapids and falls, two of which are worthy of especial note.[2] Lake George[3] is

---

[1] The w. branch of the Hudson was called by the Indians Te-o-ho-ken; the E. branch, At-a-te′ka.

[2] The High Falls are situated just below the great easterly bend of the river in the s. w. corner of Luzerne. The water flows in a series of rapids for three-fourths of a mi. over a declining rocky bottom, and is then compressed into a narrow gorge for 80 rods, at the bottom of which it shoots down a nearly perpendicular descent of 60 ft. The gneiss ledge over which it falls is convex in form, and the water is broken into perfect sheets of snow-white foam. A few rods above the last leap of the water, and where it is rushing with the greatest velocity, the river is spanned by a single plank 13 ft. in length. At Glens Falls the

river flows over a shelving rock with a total descent of 50 ft. The fall is broken into three channels by natural piers of black limestone standing upon the brow of the precipice over which the water flows.

[3] Called by the Indians Can-i-a-de′ri-oit, the tail of the lake. The name "Horicon" has been applied by some modern writers to Lake George, and it is said to be an Indian word meaning "The Lake of Silver Water." However poetic and appropriate this designation may appear, or however euphonious it may sound, it may be questioned whether a term suggested by fancy alone, and never used by the aborigines, will ever find place among the geographical names of the State as one of Indian origin.

670

situated upon the E. border, and receives the drainage of the E. part of the co. It is 36 mi. long and 1 to 3 mi. wide.[1]

The soil of this co. is mostly a thin, sandy loam. The level lands N. of Glens Falls are very sandy, and are known as "*pine plains.*" The declivities of the mountains have a very thin soil, and usually a scanty vegetation. In the valleys is some clay mixed with the sand and disintegrated primitive rocks, forming a deep and excellent soil. Farming and the manufacture of lumber and leather form the leading pursuits of the people. Farming is mostly confined to stock raising and dairying. Immense quantities of logs are floated down the Hudson and manufactured into lumber, shingles, hoops, staves, and heading, at Glens Falls and other places. Black marble is quarried at Glens Falls, and feldspar and kaolin for the manufacture of porcelain, graphite and serpentine are also found in different places. Peat exists in abundance; but it has never been extensively used.

Caldwell, at the head of Lake George, is the county seat.[2] The courthouse was built in 1816–17, with the jail in the basement. The poorhouse is located on a farm of 200 acres in Warrensburgh.[3]

The works of internal improvement are the Glens Falls Navigable Feeder, 7 mi. in length, feeding the summit level of the Champlain Canal, and the improvement in the log navigation of the Hudson. There is no R. R. in the co.[4] Three newspapers are now published in the co.[5]

This co. was the scene of some of the sanguinary battles between the French and English long anterior to its settlement. In 1755, a provincial army of 5,000 men, under Sir. Wm. Johnson, designed to act against the French posts on Lake Champlain, assembled at Albany early in June, and were there joined by a large number of Mohawks under King Hendrick. Forts Lyman (afterward Fort Edward) and Miller were built, and a road was opened to Lake George. The news of Braddock's defeat was received before this army left Albany. The expedition set out on the 8th of Aug., by way of Lake George, for Ticonderoga, with the design of erecting a fort there. Learning that the French had anticipated them and had already fortified Ticonderoga, they encamped near the head of Lake George. About the 1st of Sept., Baron Dieskau, the French commander, with a force of 200 grenadiers, 800 Canadian militia, and 300 Indians, passed up South Bay and across the rocky peninsula, with a view of falling upon the rear of the English and of cutting off their supplies from Fort Lyman. On the 8th, a force of 1000 troops under Col. Ephraim Williams, and of 200 Indians under King Hendrick, were sent out to meet them; but, falling into an ambuscade, the greater part of the troops and the two commanders were killed. The survivors fled, and were immediately followed by the French. The firing alarmed the camp, and a breastwork of logs was immediately thrown up, and 300 men, under Col. Cole, were despatched to cover the retreat of the flying fugitives of the first party. Flushed with victory, the French assailed the English camp with great fury, and a sanguinary conflict ensued, which lasted

---

[1] This lake has long been celebrated for its wild and picturesque beauty. It is almost completely surrounded by precipitous and rocky mountains, and is studded with little, green islands. Its winding course is marked by a panorama of beautiful and distinct views. At some points high rocky bluffs rise precipitously from the very edge of the water, and at others a little basin seems scooped out among the hills. Most of the mountain declivities are covered with verdure; but a few of them are masses of naked rocks. This whole region is full of historic interest. Each mountain, precipice, and cape has its own tales and reminiscences of the olden time. Some of the fiercest conflicts of the last long wars between the French and English colonists took place upon its shores, and the pure and peaceful waters of this beautiful lake were often ensanguined with the blood of fierce combatants. Again during the Revolution war held high carnival here: but since that period its visitors have been principally the lovers of the wild and beautiful in nature. Sabbath-Day Point and Lord Howes Point are two low beaches upon the w. shore, near the foot of the lake; and Rogers Slide is a precipice upon the w. shore, 200 feet high, rising at an angle of about 25 degrees. Tongue Mt., forming a promontory upon the w. shore, Anthonys Nose, upon the E. shore, and French Mt., near the head of the lake, have each an elevation of more than 2,000 feet.

[2] The first courts were held at the "*Lake George Coffee House.*" The clerk's office was located by law within 1 mi. of this place; and this was made the point from which the sheriff's mileage was reckoned. By an act passed March 31, 1815, three commissioners were to be appointed by the governor to locate the site of the courthouse and jail and to superintend its erection. The first co. officers were Wm. Robards, *First Judge;* Henry Spencer, *Sheriff;* John Beebe, *Clerk;* Robert Wilkinson, *Surrogate;* Archibald McMurphy, Wm. Stover, Richard Cameron, and Jirah Skinner. *Coroners.* Thomas Archibald, the present co. clerk, has held the office without interruption since Feb. 1821.

[3] The poorhouse is a two story wooden building. It is 50 years old and in a very dilapidated condition. The annual revenue from the farm is about $800. The average number of inmates

is 54, who are supported at a weekly expense of 90 cts. each.

[4] The Lake Ontario & Hudson River R. R. (late the Sackets Harbor & Saratoga R.R.) is laid out through the co. along the w. side of the Hudson, and a large part of the grading has been done; but the work is now suspended.

[5] *The Warren Co. Patriot,* commenced at Glens Falls about 1813 by John Cunningham, was the first paper in the co.
A newspaper was begun at Caldwell in 1817 or '18 by Timothy Haskins, which in four or five years was changed to
The Guardian. It was a few years after sold to —— Broadwell, its name again changed, and in two years after it was removed to Glens Falls.
The Glens Falls Observer was started in 1828 by E. G. Sidney. In about two years it passed into the hands of Abial Smith, who changed its name to
The Glens Falls Republican, and afterward to
The Warren Co. Messenger. In 1835 it was again changed to
The Warren Co. Messenger and Glens Falls Advertiser, by which name it was continued until 1840, when it appeared as
The Glens Falls Gazette, and in two years after as
The Glens Falls Clarion. In 1850 it passed into the hands of Zabina Ellis, its present publisher, by whom its name was changed to
The Glens Falls Free Press.
The Glens Falls Spectator was published in 1840 by D. Ellis.
The Warren Co. Whig was started by James A. Kellogg, and continued one year.
The Glens Falls Messenger was established by A. D. Milne, and is still continued.
The Glens Falls Republican was established in 1842 by M. & T. J. Strong, who conducted it until 1851. It has passed through several hands, and is now published by H. M. Harris.
The Rechabite and Temperance Bugle, semi-mo., was commenced in 1845 by M. & T. J. Strong, and continued several months.
The Star of Destiny was published in 1855 by A. D. Milne.

from 12 M. to 4 P.M. and resulted in the total defeat of the French.[1]   Col. Blanchard, who commanded at Fort Lyman, learning the result of the first engagement in the morning, sent a party of about 300 N. H. and N. Y. militia to the scene of the conflict.   This party surprised the French camp, and, after dispersing the troops left to guard it, they hastened on to the English camp and arrived in season to assist materially in gaining the victory.   This engagement was the only one fought during the campaign of 1755 that reflected the slightest credit upon the British army.

The remainder of the season was spent in erecting Fort Wm. Henry,[2] on the site of the English camp.   A projected attack upon Ticonderoga during the winter was prevented by the uncommon severity of the season.   In the summer of 1756 a provincial force of 6,000 men assembled here, but too late to effect their purpose.[3]   On the 17th of March, (St. Patrick's day,) 1757, the French, under Longee, a famous partisan officer, attempted to surprise the fort, but were successful only in burning a few buildings and several vessels on the lake.[4]   Soon after, a party of 400 English, under Col. Parker, marched to attack Ticonderoga; but, falling into an ambuscade, only 72 escaped.   Early in the summer of 1757, Montcalm, the French commander, made extensive preparations to capture Fort Wm. Henry.   On the last day of July, Maj. Putnam discovered a large body of the enemy encamped on an island about 18 mi. down the lake.   Gen. Webb, who had immediate command, upon being apprized of the matter, enjoined Putnam to keep the intelligence secret and to prepare to escort him (Webb) back to Fort Edward, leaving Col. Munro in command at Fort Wm. Henry.   The enemy soon landed in force and proceeded to invest the fort.   The garrison consisted of 2,500 men, and the attacking force amounted to nearly 9,000.   Gen. Webb had a force of 4,000 regulars at Fort Edward, only 9 mi. distant, and the militia were rapidly collecting to afford further aid.   Col. Munro sent pressing and repeated messages for relief; but Gen. Webb paid no attention to the request, and appeared totally indifferent to every thing but his own personal safety.   At length, upon the ninth day of the siege, he allowed Gen. Johnson to march with a body of volunteers to the relief of the garrison; but before the party had proceeded 3 mi. they were recalled, and Gen. Webb sent a letter to Col. Munro advising him to surrender on the best terms he could obtain.   This letter was intercepted and given to Col. Munro by Montcalm in person.   Thus cut off from hope, and assured by Montcalm that the garrison should march out with the honors of war, with their arms, and one of the four cannon of the fort, with their baggage and baggage wagons, and an escort of 500 men to Fort Edward, he surrendered.   The Indians soon began to pillage the baggage, and, not being checked, fell upon the sick and wounded, whom they killed and scalped.   Excited by carnage, they next surrounded and attacked the disarmed and defenseless troops; and, although Montcalm was implored to furnish a guard, as promised, the massacre was allowed to proceed until a large number were killed or hurried away prisoners for more deliberate torture.[5]

In the summer of 1758 an army of 7,000 regulars and 10,000 provincials, under Gen. Aber-

---

[1] Gen. Johnson was wounded early in the action, and the command devolved upon Gen. Lyman.   The former in his official report, probably from jealousy, avoided mentioning the name or services of the latter, although they were efficient and valuable.   Popular report stated the French loss at 700 to 800; but Johnson reported it from 300 to 400.   Official accounts place the English loss at 120 killed, 80 wounded, and 62 missing.   Dieskau died in England several years after, from wounds received in the engagement.

[2] Named in honor of the Duke of Cumberland, brother of the heir apparent, afterward George III.

[3] Several incidents worthy of note occurred during this expedition.   At Halfway Brook a party of teamsters were surprised and captured by 600 of the enemy, who immediately retreated down South Bay.   A hundred men, under Capts. Israel Putnam and Robert Rogers, set out from Fort Wm. Henry, crossed over to Lake Champlain, and from an ambuscade poured a destructive fire upon the enemy as they passed.   A number were killed, and the English immediately retreated across to Lake George.   The next morning they embarked on the lake, and at Sabbath-Day Point they were met by a force of French and Indians three times their own number.   The English dashed forward to the attack; and, by reserving their fire until they came into close quarters, they threw the enemy into confusion, and succeeded in escaping, with the loss of one killed and two wounded.   In the winter of 1756-57, Maj. Rogers, with 74 men, went down Lake George, and crossed over to Lake Champlain, where he captured a small party of French.   On his return he was met on the summit of the hill by a party of 200 French; and a desperate conflict ensued.   Maj. Rogers was wounded, and the command devolved upon Capt. Stark, (afterward Gen. Stark of the Revolution.)   The conflict continued until nightfall, when the French retreated, leaving half of their number dead upon the field.   Of the rangers, 48 remained unwounded; and the company pushed forward through deep snows and reached the lake in the morning.   They were now quite exhausted; and Stark, with two others,

pushed on to Fort Wm. Henry, arriving in the evening.   He procured sleds and returned to his suffering comrades, whom he reached the next morning.   The party finally reached the fort, after extreme suffering.—*Rogers's Jour.*, p. 36.

[4] A part of the garrison were Irish, and could not be restrained from celebrating the day by getting drunk.   The fort was defended by the vigilance of the rangers, who repulsed the French while the other troops were coming to their senses.—*Rogers's Jour.*, pp. 43, 109.

[5] Humanity sickens at the revolting scenes of this day, which have stained the memory of Montcalm with the blackest infamy.   A few survivors of the massacre fled for their lives, and succeeded in reaching Fort Edward in safety.   The next day Maj. Putnam was sent with his rangers to watch the motions of the enemy; but he arrived just after they embarked and were beyond reach of pursuit.   As he came to the shore, the demolished fort, the burning buildings, and the ghastly and mangled corpses of the dead and the feeble groans of the dying, quickly told the dismal story of treachery and barbarism, scarcely less chargeable to the cowardice of Webb than to the perfidy of Montcalm.   Writers differ as to the number murdered on this occasion, the estimates varying from 300 to 1,500.   It is probably nearer the latter number.   There was a tendency among the provincials to exaggerate, and among the regulars to palliate, the occurrences above related.   The massacre occurred Aug. 9, 1757.   Among the accounts given by eyewitnesses of the scene, that of Jonathan Carver, the well-known traveler, has perhaps been most frequently quoted.   The feeble attempts that have been made to defend the reputation of Montcalm, under the plea that he exerted himself to restrain the Indian barbarities, find ample refutation in the fact that with five or six times more whites than savages the latter were allowed to proceed unmolested.   If this relatively small number could not be restrained, there must have existed a degree of insubordination incompatible with military success and strangely at variance with the condition of other armies under Montcalm.

crombie, proceeded against Ticonderoga by way of Lake George. On the 5th of July the army embarked on board of 900 bateaux and 135 boats, and passed down the lake with all the pomp and pageantry of war; and four days after they returned, shattered and broken, with a loss of nearly 2,000 in killed and wounded. Such of the latter as admitted of removal were sent to Fort Edward; and the main army lay inactive in camp at the head of the lake during the remainder of the season. In June, 1759, Maj. Gen. Amherst, with an army of 12,000 men, advanced to Lake George, and, while waiting to complete his arrangements, he commenced building Fort George, about half a mile E. from Fort Wm. Henry.[1] As Gen. Amherst advanced to Ticonderoga, the French withdrew to Crown Point, and soon after to the Isle Aux-Noix. Quebec fell soon after, and the conquest of Canada was completed the following year, rendering the vast military works at Fort George, Ticonderoga, and Crown Point of no further utility, and allowing the hardy pioneers of civilization to advance and occupy the fertile valleys which as provincial soldiers they had previously traversed.

BOLTON—was formed from Thurman, March 25, 1799. Hague was taken off in 1807, a part of Caldwell in 1810, and a part of Horicon in 1838. It lies E. of the center of the co., between Schroon River and Lake George. The E. shore of the lake constitutes the E. line, so that more than one-half of the lake is within the limits of this town. The surface is principally occupied by the high mountainous ridges which lie between the lake and Hudson River. There are 3 principal peaks belonging to this range within the limits of the town,—Tongue Mt.,[2] on the peninsula between the lake and North West Bay, 2,000 ft. above tide; Pole Hill, in the N. part, 2,500 ft. high; and Cat Head, in the center, 1,500 to 1,800 ft. above tide. The mountains generally rise precipitously from the lake; but toward the w. the surface assumes the character of a high, rolling upland. High up among the hills are numerous little crystal lakes, the principal of which are Trout Lake, Marsh Pond, and Edgecomb Pond. Trout Lake is 1,000 ft. above Lake George. Not more than one-half of the town is susceptible of cultivation. The soil is a thin, sandy loam.[3] **Bolton,** (p. o.,) situated on Lake George, opposite Green Island,[4] is a small village. The settlement of the town was commenced in 1792, principally by New England people.[5] The improvements are confined mostly to the vicinity of Lake George. The first church (Presb.) was formed in 1804; the Rev. —— Armstrong was the first settled minister. There are 2 churches in town; Bap. and M. E.

CALDWELL[6]—(Col′-well) was formed from Queensbury, Bolton, and Thurman, March 2, 1810. It lies around the s. extremity of Lake George. A range of mountains occupies the extreme w. part. The central portion is a high, hilly region, descending abruptly to the lake. Prospect Hill, w. of the s. extremity of the lake, has an elevation of 2,000 ft. above tide. South of this hill a low valley extends s. w., through Caldwell and Luzerne, to the valley of the Hudson near the mouth of Sacondaga River. This depression seems to be a continuation of the valley in which Lake George is situated, and shows that a change of a few feet in the elevation would cause the waters of the lake to flow into the Hudson. In this valley is a chain of small lakes. A narrow strip of low land lies immediately upon the border of the lake. The soil is a sandy loam among the hills, and a dark, rich, sandy and clayey loam on the lowlands. **Caldwell,** (p. v.,) the county seat, is situated near the head of Lake George. It contains 2 churches, several hotels, and about 50 dwellings. This place is the annual resort of great numbers of tourists and pleasure seekers, who are attracted hither by the beautiful scenery of the lake and the surrounding region. During the summer the steamer Minnehaha plies daily between Caldwell and the foot of the lake. Fort William Henry and Fort George were situated near Caldwell, at the head of Lake George and Bloody Pond, in the s. part. Settlement commenced at the head of Lake George, soon after the conquest of Canada; but its progress was arrested by the Revolution. Soon after the close of the war, settlement was recommenced.[7] There are 2 churches in town; Presb. and Union.

---

[1] Scarcely a vestige of this fort remains, most of the stones of which it was built having been burned for lime.

[2] Indian name, At-al′a-po′sa, a sliding place.

[3] Within the limits of this town is the most beautiful scenery of the lake. Its channel is studded with a multitude of small islands, some of them consisting of barren, desolate rocks, while others are clothed with the richest verdure. Diamond Island, near the s. extremity of the lake, derives its name from the beautiful quartz crystals that have been found upon it.

[4] During the Revolution this island was fortified, and Gen. Burgoyne, when he advanced to the Hudson, left upon it a large amount of public property, guarded by two companies of the 47th regiment, commanded by Capt. Aubrey. After the partial success which attended the attempt upon Ticonderoga in 1777, Cols. Warren and Brown, on the 24th of Sept., made an attack upon this place with the gunboats they had captured. They were repulsed with loss, and retreated to the E. shore. The enemy being in pursuit, they burned their boats, crossed the mountains to Lake Champlain, and returned to Gen. Lincoln's camp at Pawlet, Vt.

[5] Among the first settlers were James Ware, Joseph Tuttle, Rufus Randall, Benj. Pierce, David and Reuben Smith, Eleazer Goodman, Daniel Nims, Frederick Miller, —— Boyd, —— Wright, and Thomas McGee. The first birth was that of Lydia Ware; and the first death, that of Mrs. John Pierce. Sally Boyd taught the first school.

[6] Named from Gen. James Caldwell, a merchant of Albany, who became a patentee of 1,595 acres, in 4 parcels by grants dated Sept. 18–29, 1787.

[7] Among the early settlers were Daniel Shaw, Benoni Burtch,

CHESTER—was formed from Thurman, March 25, 1799. It lies upon the N. border of the co., between Hudson and Schroon Rivers. The surface is broken. The Kayaderosseras Mts. extend through the s. part, and the Schroon Range occupies the N. w. portion. A continuation of the valley of Schroon Lake, extending in a s. w. direction to the w. branch of the Hudson and separating the mountain ranges, contains a chain of small lakes. Loon Lake is the principal one in this valley; and s. of it, among the hills, is another sheet of water, called Friends Lake. Schroon Lake is about 1,000 feet above tide, and the hills that surround it are 500 to 800 feet above its surface. The soil is generally light and sandy. A cave in Moxons Mt. is quite a curiosity, and has some local notoriety. Near the N. border of the town, upon Stone Bridge Creek, is a natural bridge.[1] Feldspar has been quarried to a considerable extent and exported for the manufacture of porcelain. **Chestertown** (p. v.) contains the Chester Academy and 246 inhabitants; and **Pottersville** (p. v.) 126. The settlement of this town commenced toward the close of the last century.[2] The first church (Bap.) was organized in 1796; and the Rev. Jehiel Fox was the first pastor. There are now 6 churches in town.[3]

HAGUE—was formed from Bolton, Feb. 28, 1807, as "*Rochester.*" Its name was changed April 6, 1808, and a part of Horicon was taken off in 1838. It lies upon the shore of Lake George, in the N. E. corner of the co. The surface is very mountainous, not above one-fourth being susceptible of cultivation. The mountains along the lake generally descend abruptly to the very edge of the water. The narrow valleys of Trout and North West Bay Brooks form the line of separation between the two mountain ranges. Ash Grove Hill, upon the w. border, is 2,000 to 2,500 feet above tide; and upon the shore of the lake, in the N. E. corner, is another mountain peak of nearly the same elevation. Rogers Rock is on the lake shore, in the N. E. corner. It rises from the water's edge at an angle of about 45° and attains an elevation of 300 feet.[4] Sabbath-Day Point is a headland projecting into the lake near the s. border.[5] The soil is a light, sandy loam. Iron ore has been found near Seventh Pond; and mines have been worked to some extent, but they are now abandoned. The beauty of the lake and the solitary grandeur of the mountain scenery of this town render it a favorite resort for hunting and fishing parties and the lovers of the beautiful in nature.[6] **Hague,** (p. o.,) on McDonalds Bay, and **Wardboro** (p. o.) are hamlets. The principal improvements are along the lake. The first settlement was made about 1796.[7] There is a union church in the town.

HORICON—was formed from Bolton and Hague, March 29, 1838. It lies upon the N. border of the co., E. of Schroon Lake. The greater part of its surface is occupied by the two branches of the Kayaderosseras Mts., which are here divided by the valley of Brant Lake. In the N. and E. these ranges rise, in numerous sharp, rocky peaks, 1,600 to 2,000 feet above tide; but in the s. and w. they sink into a hilly plateau region. About one-half of the surface is arable. Among the hills are great numbers of small lakes, laving with their crystal waters the base of the huge, rocky masses which tower above them. Brant Lake, the principal of them, is 10 mi. long and is everywhere surrounded by precipitous hills. The soil is a sandy loam. **Horicon,** (p. v.,) situated on Schroon River, in the s. w. part of the town, contains about 20 houses; and **Mill Brook,** (p. v.,) on Schroon Lake, 15 houses. Aaron Harris, Joseph Gregory, Bishop Carpenter, and Timothy Bennett were some of the earliest settlers.[8] The first church (Wes. Meth.) was formed in 1820; Nathaniel Streeter was the first minister. There are 4 churches in town; 2 Bap., M. E., and Wes. Meth.

JOHNSBURGH[9]—was formed from Thurman, April 6, 1805. It lies upon the bank of the

— Tierce, Andrew Edmonds, Reed Wilbur, Obadiah Hunt, Thaddeus Bradley, Elias Prosser, Nathan Burdick, Geo. Van Deusen, —— Butler, and Christopher Potter. The first inn and gristmill were erected by Gen. Caldwell.

[1] The stream, after falling into a basin, enters a passage in two branches under a natural arch 40 feet high and about 80 broad, and emerges in a single stream from under a precipice 54 feet high, 247 feet from its entrance. This bridge is described in Morse's Geography (1796) as follows:—" In the county of Montgomery is a small, rapid stream emptying into Schroon Lake, west of Lake George: it runs under a hill, the base of which is 60 or 70 yards in diameter, forming a most curious and beautiful arch in the rock, as white as snow. The fury of the water and the roughness of the bottom, added to the terrific noise within, have hitherto prevented any person from passing through the chasm."—*Am. Univ. Geog.*, 508.

[2] The first settlers were Titus, James, Levi, Gideon, Enos, Jonathan, Daniel, and Caleb Mead, —— Beman, Isaac Bennett, John Haskins, Obadiah and Benj. Knapp, Noel Wightman, James Storbuck, —— Steward, and D. and J. Punderson. The first birth was that of a son of Caleb Mead; and the first death, that of Martin Wightman.

[3] 3 M. E., Bap., Presb., and Prot. E.

[4] This rock, sometimes called Rogers Slide, receives its name from an incident traditionally related of the escape of Maj. Robert Rogers at this place in the winter of 1758. He was surprised at the top of the rock by a band of Indians, and most of his party were cut off; but he escaped by sliding down the rock to the frozen surface of the lake.

[5] It is generally supposed that this name was derived from the fact that Gen. Amherst and his suite, while passing down the lake on their way to Ticonderoga in the summer of 1759, stopped here to refresh themselves upon the Sabbath; but this derivation of the name is doubtful, for it is mentioned in Rogers's Journal, June 28, 1758,—the season before.

[6] On the 29th of July, 1856, the steamer John Jay, while on her way up the lake, was burned near Garfields. Six persons jumped overboard and were drowned; but the rest were rescued by boats from the shore.

[7] Among the first settlers were Abel Rising, Abner Briggs, Elijah Bailey, Samuel Cook, Ellis Denton, Samuel Patchin, John Holman, Isaac and Urial Balcom, and Uri Waiste.

[8] Howard Waters, Nathan, Benj., and James Hayes, Benj. Hayes 2d, John Robbins, James Frazier, and Benj. Wright were also early settlers. Hannah Reynolds taught the first school.

[9] Named from John Thurman, an early settler.

Hudson, and is the N. W. corner town of the co. Its surface is very broken and mountainous. The Schroon Range occupies the N. and central parts; and a spur of the Kayaderosseras Range extends into the S. Crane Mt.,[1] the highest peak of the latter, is about 3,500 feet above tide. The greater part of the town is too rough and broken for cultivation. The arable land is confined to the narrow valleys. The soil is a sandy and gravelly loam. Kaolin, serpentine iron ore, and other minerals are found. There are 3 large tanneries in town. **Johnsburgh,** (p. v.,) on Mill Creek, contains 20 houses; **Nobles Corners,** on the same stream, 25; **North Creek,** (p. v.,) on the Hudson, at the mouth of North Creek, 15; and **The Glen,** (p. o.,) on the Hudson, in the S. E. corner of the town, 7. The first settlement was made soon after the close of the Revolutionary War, by John Thurman, the proprietor of extensive tracts in this part of the State.[2] The first church (Bap.) was organized in 1793. There are 4 churches in town.[3]

LUZERNE—was formed from Queensbury, April 10, 1792, as "*Fairfield*." Its name was changed April 6, 1808. A strip of territory 1 mi. wide was set off to Queensbury, March 30, 1802. It lies upon the E. bank of Hudson River, in the S. extremity of the co. Two branches of the Luzerne Mts. extend through the town, respectively occupying the N. and S. portions. They are separated by the valley which extends S. W. from the S. end of Lake George. A chain of small lakes lies along its course; and in them two streams take rise, one of which flows to Lake George and the other to the Hudson.[4] About one-half of the surface bordering upon the river is a high, hilly region, but arable. Kettle Bottom, in the S. part, and several peaks of the ridge which extends along the E. border, are 2,000 to 2,500 feet above tide. The soil is a light, sandy loam. **Luzerne** (p. v.) is situated on the Hudson, above its confluence with Sacondaga River. Pop. 280. The first settlements were made about 1770, along the Hudson. Most of the early settlers occupied lands leased from Ebenezer Jessup, the patentee. There are 3 churches in town.[5]

QUEENSBURY—was incorporated by patent[6] as a township, May 20, 1762, and recognized as a town, March 13, 1786. Luzerne was taken off in 1792, and a part of Caldwell in 1810. A strip of territory 1 mi. wide was taken from Luzerne and added to this town in 1802. It lies between Lake George and the Hudson, and is the S. E. corner town of the co. The W part is occupied by the Luzerne Mts., and the extreme N. part by French Mt., a high, rocky bluff which rises precipitously from the surface of Lake George to a height of 2,500 to 3,000 feet above tide. The central and S. parts are rolling, gradually declining toward the S. The soil is a light, sandy loam in the interior, and a deep, tough clay upon the river. The fall in the Hudson at Glens Falls is about 50 feet high, and affords valuable mill privileges. Below the fall is a small island, through which is a cave extending from one channel to the other. The manufacture of lumber is largely carried on.[7] **Glens Falls,**[8] (p. v.,) incorp. April 12, 1839, is situated on the Hudson, in the S. part. It contains 9 churches, the Glens Falls Academy, 3 newspaper offices, 2 banks, and several manufactories.[9] Pop. 3,420. **West Glens Falls,** on the Hudson, contains 25 houses; and **Queensbury,** (p. v.,) in the E. part 20. **French Mountain** (p. o.) is a hamlet. The summit level of the Champlain Canal is fed through the Glens Falls navigable feeder with water taken from the Hudson above the falls. The settlement was commenced in 1766; but its progress was very slow until after the close of the Revolution.[10] The first house of worship was erected by the Society of Friends, in 1786. There are now 11 churches in town.[11]

STONY CREEK—was formed from "*Athol*,"[12] Nov. 3, 1852. It lies upon the W. bank of Hudson River, and is the S. W. corner town of the co. Nearly the whole town is still a wilderness. Through the center of the town extend mountain ranges, several peaks of which attain an elevation of more than 2,000 feet. The valleys of E. and W. Stony Creeks are narrow ravines, forming a natural pass between the valleys of the Hudson and Sacondaga. The soil is a light, sandy loam.

---

[1] There is a small pond near the summit of the mountain which is much frequented by cranes; and from this circumstance it derives its name. Seen from Warrensburgh, 11 mi. distant, the mountain presents a striking resemblance to the profile of the human face.

[2] Among the early settlers were Robt. Woddell, Geo. Hodgson, John Wilkinson, Reuben and Calvin Washburn, and Samuel Somerville. The first birth was that of Polly Woddell; the first marriage, that of Calvin Washburn and Betsey Woddell; and the first death, that of Enos Grover. The first mills were erected in 1789 or '90, by Mr. Thurman. He opened a store and built a distillery; and in 1795 he erected a woolen factory. This was soon after changed to a cotton factory; and as early as 1797 he erected calico printing works, the first, it is believed, in America.

[3] Bap., M. E., Free Will Bap., and Wes. Meth.

[4] Hadley and Jessup Falls, upon the Hudson, are within this town. See page 589.

[5] Bap., M. E., and Union.

[6] This patent embraced 2,300 acres.

[7] An immense number of logs is annually floated down from the pine forests of the Upper Hudson to Glens Falls and Fort Edward. At one mill upon the State dam at the former place are 12 gates and 250 saws.

[8] The Indian name of this place is said to have been Kay-au-do-ros-sa. It was called "*Glenville*" for some time.

[9] This place contains 4 sawmills, a flouring mill, and an establishment for sawing marble.

[10] Among the first settlers were Abraham Wing, Reed Ferris, Asaph and Benajah Putnam, Jeffrey Cooper, Ichabod Merritt, and Caleb Dowell. Immediately after the war, Benj. Wing, Nehemiah Seelice, Phineas Babcock, Wm. Roland, David Bennett, James Houghson, Silas Brown, and Jeremiah Briggs settled in town.

[11] 2 Friends, 2 R. C., Bap., M. E., Presb., Prot. E., Ch. of Messiah, Asso. Presb., and Univ.

[12] See Thurman.

Creek Center (p. o.) and **Stony Creek,** (p. o.,) both upon Stony Creek, are hamlets. The first settlement was made about 1795.[1] The first preacher was Jonathan Paul, a Christian Indian. The first church (Presb.) was formed about 1800.[2]

THURMAN[3]—was formed April 10, 1792. Bolton and Chester were taken off in 1799, Johnsburgh in 1805, and a part of Caldwell in 1810. The town was divided into "*Athol*" and Warrensburgh Feb. 12, 1813; and "*Athol*" was divided into Thurman and Stony Creek, Nov. 13, 1852. It lies upon the w. bank of the Hudson, s. w. of the center of the co. The w. part is a high, broken upland, almost unknown except to hunters. The E. portion, along the Hudson, is a hilly plateau, with several peaks rising 1,000 feet above the valley. Among the hills are numerous small lakes. The soil is a light, sandy loam. **Athol** (p. o.) and **Thurman,** (p. o.,) both in the E. part, are hamlets. Settlement was commenced in the latter part of the last century.[4] A Bap. church was first formed; Elder Jehiel Fox was the first preacher. There are now 4 churches in town.[5]

WARRENSBURGH—was formed from Thurman, Feb. 12, 1813. It lies between the two branches of the Hudson, near the center of the co., and upon the ridges s. of the junction. The peninsular portion is a rolling plateau 600 to 1,000 feet above the river. The s. w. part is occupied by an immense mountain mass with several summits 2,400 to 3,000 feet above tide. Nearly two-thirds of the land in town is arable. The soil is a light, sandy loam among the hills, and upon the river it is nearly the same, mixed with some clay. **Warrensburgh** (p. v.) is on Schroon River, 3 mi. from its junction with the Hudson. Pop. 700. Across the Hudson, below the mouth of Schroon River, is a long bridge connecting this town with Thurman. The first settlement was made a few years after the close of the Revolution.[6] A M. E. church, the first in town, was organized in 1796; and the Rev. Henry Ryan was the first minister. There are 4 churches in town.[7]

Acres of Land, Valuation, Population, Dwellings, Families, Freeholders, Schools, Live Stock, Agricultural Products, and Domestic Manufactures, of Warren County.

Names of Towns.	Acres of Land.		Valuation of 1858.			Population.		No. of Dwellings.	No. of Families.	Freeholders.	Schools.	
	Improved.	Unimproved.	Real Estate.	Personal Property.	Total.	Males.	Females.				No. of Districts.	Children taught.
Bolton	9,583⅜	21,868	113,972	6,050	120,022	625	542	216	232	196	10	449
Caldwell	4,891¾	9,081	75,628	16,325	91,953	452	428	164	170	138	6	378
Chester	16,498	20,428	198,333	13,250	211,583	993	943	359	385	353	20	957
Hague	5,154½	29,655½	59,449	5,259	64,708	309	306	96	110	67	7	277
Horicon	7,492	28,555	101,580	17,275	118,855	678	568	226	335	175	12	551
Johnsburgh	12,954½	80,846½	209,463	5,102	214,565	1,059	924	356	396	293	14	800
Luzerne	10,281⅞	17,187½	91,418	9,350	100,768	666	620	265	265	208	13	622
Queensbury	21,288⅝	16,674½	1,002,430	344,300	1,346,730	3,237	3,201	1,182	1,294	848	24	2,273
Stony Creek	3,618	45,113	55,492	1,450	56,942	491	422	178	180	123	7	359
Thurman	8,595	41,922	63,400	600	64,000	687	572	238	247	168	7	424
Warrensburgh	10,845	20,010	172,485	13,150	185,635	987	959	334	365	238	11	722
Total	111,202⅝	331,341	2,143,650	432,111	2,575,761	10,184	9,485	3,614	3,979	2,807	131	7,812

Names of Towns.	Live Stock.					Agricultural Products.							Domestic cloths, in Yards.
						Bush. of Grain.					Dairy Products.		
	Horses.	Working Oxen and Calves.	Cows.	Sheep.	Swine.	Winter.	Spring.	Tons of Hay.	Bushels of Potatoes.	Bushels of Apples.	Pounds Butter.	Pounds Cheese.	
Bolton	277	1,000	588	2,065	454	706	19,721	2,445	12,416	6,592	48,606	11,171	1,629½
Caldwell	171	288	298	856	347	872	10,683	767	7,187	4,211	27,632		1,294
Chester	450	1,121	709	2,270	694	811	31,855	2,778	25,149	5,705	43,030	4,425	1,405
Hague	132	565	269	501	238	648½	9,601¼	1,123	8,105	6,292	27,300	1,290	151
Horicon	180	728	366	1,094	385	638	20,787½	1,768	13,317	457¾	44,200	1,290	1,291¾
Johnsburgh	358	1,064	913	2,034	734	858½	32,246	2,962	28,175	5,150	63,506	5,940	2,023
Luzerne	282	777	484	930	454	586	20,362½	1,492¼	9,355	3,473	40,600	1,800	616½
Queensbury	960	1,039	1,363	3,154	1,452	6,173	85,908¾	3,720½	35,405	20,744	102,982	30,920	1,505
Stony Creek	143	336	259	601	222	189½	10,165	998	9,437	535	21,470	658	698
Thurman	128	500	308	1,148	220	330	13,075½	2,074	11,847	3,511	26,575	4,700	247
Warrensburgh	260	703	604	1,819	503	352	16,483½	1,961	12,935	2,102	36,885	2,440	574
Total	3,341	8,121	6,161	16,472	5,703	12,164½	270,889	22,088¾	173,328	58,772¾	482,786	64,634	11,434¾

1 The first settlers were James Ferguson, James, John, and Geo. Donald, Wm. Riley, Wm. and Alex. Murray, Hugh McMiller, and John and Jas. E. Cameron. The first birth was that of Anna Murray.

2 The census reports 4 churches; Bap., M. E., Presb., Wes. Meth.

3 Named in honor of John Thurman.

4 Among the early settlers were Thurston Kingston, Wm. Johnson, Zebadiah Burdick, Elisha Kendall, Oliver Brooks, Richardson Moore, Benajah Wells, Amos Bowen, Abial Frost, and John King. The first marriage was that of Duncan McGuen and Miss Cameron; and the first death, that of John Reynolds.

5 Bap., M. E., Prot. Meth., and Wes. Meth.

6 Wm. Bond, Joseph Hutchinson, Wm. Lee, Josiah Woodward, —— Varnum, Richardson Thurman, and Wm. Johnson were some of the first settlers. The first death was that of Wm. Johnson.

7 2 M. E., Wes. Meth., and Presb.

WASHINGTON COUNTY.

This county[1] was formed from Albany as "*Charlotte County*,"[2] March 12, 1772. Its name was changed April 2, 1784; Clinton co. was taken off in 1788; the E. portion was ceded to Vermont in 1790;[3] a strip along its s. border was annexed from Albany Feb. 7, 1791; and Warren co. was taken off in 1813. It lies on the E. border of the State, is centrally distant from Albany 45 miles, and contains an area of 850 sq. mi. The surface consists principally of a series of ridges extending N. E. and s. w., and the valleys between them. The remarkable depression which extends southerly from the s. extremity of Lake Champlain divides these ridges into two distinct groups,—the N. belonging to the Palmertown Mt. Range, and the s. constituting one of the connecting links between the highlands of Southern New York and those of Western Vermont. The s. group is subdivided into three principal ranges, which are all related and of the same general character. The most southerly of these ranges is a northerly continuation of the Taghkanick Range of Rensselaer co., occupying the greater part of White Creek and the E. part of Jackson. The declivities are usually steep, and the summits broad, broken, and rocky. The second—sometimes described as a continuation of the Petersburgh Mts. of Rensselaer—constitutes the highlands of Cambridge, Jackson, Salem, and the E. part of Hebron and Granville. In Salem it spreads out like a fan between the streams. The third comprises the highlands of Easton, Greenwich, Argyle, Hartford, Granville, Hampton, and the E. part of Whitehall. It might with propriety be called Cossayuna Range, from the principal lake which it encloses. The declivities of these ranges are usually steep, and, except where broken by ledges, are arable to their summits. They gradually rise toward the E., reaching their culminating point near the E. border of the co. The highest summits are 1000 to 1200 feet above tide. These three ranges belong to one general group and are of the same geological formation. They are composed of slate rock, ledges of which crop out along their whole extent. Many of these ledges in Granville and Hebron are quarried, and furnish stone much valued for roofing, building, and ornamental purposes. Among the slate quarries are found numerous veins of injected quartz, intersecting the slate strata in every direction, varying from the thickness of paper to several inches. They often present cavities and surfaces beautifully studded with transparent crystals of quartz. The edges of the slate are sometimes bent and distorted by the quartz dikes, showing the extreme heat and great force of the injected veins. The soil in this system of highlands consists chiefly of disintegrated slate, and is very fertile.

The second group of highlands, belonging to the Palmertown Mt. Range, occupy the towns of Fort Ann, Dresden, Putnam, and the E. part of Whitehall. They belong to the primary formation, their rocks consisting principally of gneiss, granite, sandstone, and impure limestone. Their sides are very precipitous and broken, and their summits are wild irregular masses of naked, barren rocks. The valleys between them are narrow and rocky, often bordered by precipices many hundred feet in height. The soil is cold and unproductive, like that of all regions of a similar geological formation. A narrow valley extending s. w. from the s. extremity of South Bay divides the group into two ranges. Saddle Mt., overlooking South Bay and 1000 ft. above tide, is the highest peak in the s. range; and Black Mt., 2878 ft. above tide, is the highest peak in the N. range. Diameter Rock, on the N. shore of South Bay, is 1300 ft. above tide.[4]

[1] The original bounds of this co. were as follows:—All that part of the State N. of the present co. of Saratoga, and of a line extending from the mouth of Stony Creek 510 chains E.; thence s. to the Batten Kil, and along that stream to the s. line of Princetown, and thence to "*Cumberland*" co. Its w. line was the present w. line of Saratoga co. continued to Canada, and its E. line the w. lines of "*Cumberland*" and "*Gloucester*" cos. These limits embraced the w. half of Vermont, N. of the Batten Kil, and the present cos. of Warren, Essex, Clinton, and a part of Franklin.

[2] Named from Princess Charlotte, eldest daughter of Geo. III.

[3] The act of cession, by commissioners appointed for the purpose, was dated Oct. 7, 1790, and the line was finally settled by commissioners from both States in 1812. The N. Y. commis-

sioners were Smith Thompson, Simeon De Witt, and Geo. Tibbitts. See *Notes to N. Y. Session Laws*, April 15, 1814.

[4] The following table of elevations is mostly from Dr. Fitch's Survey of Washington co.:—

	FEET.
Black Mountain, in Dresden, the highest peak............	2,878
Willards Mountain, Easton..	1,605
Bald Mt., Greenwich..	912
Summit between Hudson and Champlain Valleys........	891
Mt. Defiance (Spafford's Gazetteer)..............................	720
Pinnacle, North Granville..	694
Batten Kil, Vt. Line (Sargeant's Canal Survey)............	502
Summit between Lake and Hudson River....................	459
Eagle Bridge R. R. level, above Troy (S. M. Johnson)....	401

The Hudson River forms the s. half of the w. border of the co. A rich intervale, from half a mi. to a mi. in width, bordered by a series of clay bluffs 20 to 60 ft. high, extends along its course. Most of the other streams of the co. are tributaries of the Hudson, and among them are the Hoosick, Batten Kil, Moses and Fort Edward Creeks, and many smaller streams. Wood Creek[1] is a deep, sluggish stream, flowing into Lake Champlain and draining the valley, which here extends from the lake to the Hudson. The soil along the valley is mostly a hard, stiff clay. The Mettowee, or Pawlet, and the Poultney Rivers, from Vt., are tributaries of Wood Creek. In the co. are several other streams important as mill streams.[2] Lake Champlain s. of Ticonderoga is scarcely more than a ship canal through a reedy marsh bordered by rocky cliffs. Lake George lies along the N. W. border of the co. Among the hills in the interior are several small lakes, the principal of which is Cossayuna Lake, in Argyle.[3]

The various branches of agriculture form the leading pursuits of the people. The principal grains raised are rye, spring wheat, oats, buckwheat, and corn. Peas, beans, flax, and potatoes are also extensively cultivated. Stock raising, dairying, and wool growing are also extensively pursued. The manufactures of the co. are principally along the Hudson and Batten Kil.

The county offices are divided among several towns. The courts are held alternately at Salem and Sandy Hill, and the clerk's office and co. poorhouse are located at Argyle.[4] The jail is connected with the courthouse at Salem, and all prisoners sentenced for more than two months are sent to the penitentiary at Albany.

The principal public works in the co. are the Champlain Canal,[5] extending in and along Wood Creek and the Hudson to Greenwich; the Saratoga & Whitehall R. R., extending through Fort Edward, Kingsbury, Fort Ann, and Whitehall, with a branch to Lake Station and another to Castleton, Vt. ; and the Rutland & Washington R. R., extending from Eagle Bridge, through White Creek, Jackson, and Salem, to the State line.

The first newspaper in this co. was established at Salem, in 1788.[6]

Upon the advent of the whites, few Indians were found within the limits of this co.; but Indian

---

	FEET.
Sandy Hill Center, green and street (W. T. Baker)	280
Glens Falls Feeder, summit level "	229
Champlain Canal " (Spafford)	140
Hudson River, Ft. Edward to Ft. Miller "	110
" above Saratoga Dam "	92
Lake Champlain (various authorities)	86 to 93
Lowest point on Hudson in Easton	75
Fort Edward (R. R. Survey)	143
Fort Ann "	121
Comstocks Landing "	114
Whitehall Junction "	121
Lake Champlain "	88.2
State Line "	328

1 *R. du Chicot*, or "*River of Logs*," of the French.

2 At Sandy Hill a dam 8 to 10 ft. high and 1200 ft. long crosses the Hudson, the water setting back to the foot of the rapids below Glens Falls. At Fort Edward a dam 27 ft. high and 900 feet long was built by the State in 1821, as a feeder to the canal, but, the Glens Falls feeder superseding it, it was sold to a company in 1840 and cut down to 16 ft. The Saratoga Dam (where the Champlain Canal crosses the Hudson into Saratoga co.) is 1390 feet long. Batten Kil is crossed by 9 dams. White Creek furnishes a large number of mill sites, once improved, but now mostly abandoned. Black Creek has several valuable and improved mill sites. Mettowee or Pawlet River has also several valuable mill sites.

3 The following estimates are taken from Dr. Fitch's Ag. Survey of Wash. Co. :—

	ACRES.
Surface of Lake Champlain (within the co.)	6,400
" of Hudson River "	1,560
Kingsbury Swamp	9,600
Aggregate amount covered by water or marshes	27,229
" " " by roads	8,200
" " unimproved private lands	188,052
" " lands in cultivation	310,760

4 The first co. officers under the State Government were Wm. Duer, *First Judge*; Ebenezer Clarke, *Co. Clerk*; John Thomas, *Sheriff*; and Richard Hatfield, *Surrogate*.

5 The channel of the Hudson was first used from Saratoga Dam to Fort Edward, except a short canal with locks around the falls at Fort Miller. The summit level is fed by the Glens Falls navigable feeder.

6 The *Times*. It was published by Mr. Gerrish; and in 1795 it was changed to

The *Washington Patriot*. From 1810 to 1818 it bore the name of The *Northern Post*, and was published successively by Dodd & Rumsey and Dodd & Stevenson. About 1827 it appeared as

The Co. Post and North Star; and in 1840 as

The Washington Co. Post. It is now published at North White Creek by R. K. Crocker.

The *Washington Register* was started at Salem in 1802 by John P. Reynolds, and continued several years.

The *Salem Messenger* was commenced about 1819.

The *Salem Press* was issued May 21, 1850, by W. B. Harkness, and is still continued.

The *Whitehall Emporium* was published from 1822 until about 1828.

The *Whitehall Republican* was published in 1832 by J. K. Averill.

The Whitehall Chronicle was started in June, 1840, and is now published by B. B. Smith.

The Whitehall Democrat was founded in 1845, and is now published by H. Dudley and J. B. Wilkins.

The *Whitehall Telegraph* (tri-w.) was commenced in 1847, and continued a short time.

The *Whitehaller* was published by W. S. Southmaid in 1849.

The *American Sentinel* was established in June, 1855, by John E. Watkins.

The Sandy Hill Herald was started in 1824, and is now published by E. D. Baker.

The *Sun* was published at Sandy Hill in 1826 by A. Emmons.

The *Free Press* was issued by the same publisher in 1832.

The *Independent Politician* was published at Sandy Hill in 1832 by C. Y. Haynes & Co.

The *Temperance Advocate* was published at Sandy Hill the same year by S. P. Hines.

The *Anti Masonic Champion* was started at Union Village in 1830 by L. Dewey, and published by him until 1835, when Wells & Lansing became the proprietors.

The *Banner* was published at Union Village in 1836 by Wells & Lansing.

The *Union Village Courant* was published in 1836 by Ormsby & Holmes.

The *Union Village Democrat* was started in 1839 by John W. Lawton, and in 1841 John C. Osborn became the publisher. In 1842 he was succeeded by Joseph Holmes, by whom it was styled

The *Democratic Champion*, and continued until 1846.

The *Washington Co. Sentinel* was published at Union Village in 1840.

The Union Village Journal was founded in 1843 by John W. Curtis, by whom it is still published.

The *Champion* was started at Union Village in 1843, by Joseph Holmes.

The *Eagle* was started by J. L. Cramer in 1845. In 1846 it became The *Union Village Eagle*, and was published about 2 years by McCall & Bailey.

The *Union Village Democratic Standard* was published in 1849 by Wm. A. McCall.

The *Washington Telegraph* was established in 1849, and is now published by C. M. Haven, as

The Granville Register.

The Public Ledger was started at Fort Edward in 1854 by H. F. Blanchard, and is still continued.

The Fort Edward Institute Monthly was started in 1856 by Wm. A. Holley, and is still published.

trails and implements of Indian art frequently found show that it had been inhabited at a former period. The N. portion of the co., lying in the natural channel of communication between Hudson River and Lake Champlain,[1] became the great highway of hostile parties passing between the Five Nations and the Canada Indians, and at a later day by the more formidable armies of disciplined troops in the struggles which ended in the conquest of Canada. The French made incursions upon the English and Five Nations in 1665, 1688, and 1693; and these were returned by attacks upon the French and Indians in Canada in 1691 and 1692. For several years after, the passage of small hostile parties was of frequent occurrence. In 1709, Forts Ann and Nicholson were erected by the English and garrisoned for the protection of the northern frontier; but upon the return of peace they were abandoned.[2] Frequent incursions of small parties were made in the War of 1748, and many persons were murdered,—though no regular engagement took place. Again, during the French War of 1755, forts were built at Ft. Ann, Ft. Edward, and the whole region around the head of Lakes George and Champlain became the theater of stirring military events. The armies that attacked Ticonderoga, and those that finally effected the conquest of all the French posts upon the lakes, marched through this region; and it formed a portion of the great battle-ground between the armies of two nations contending for the sovereignty of a continent. In the summer and fall of 1777, upon the advance of Burgoyne, war again, for a brief space, spread terror and desolation over the whole region "*Skenesborough*" was burned and abandoned on the 7th of July, Fort Ann was taken on the 8th, Fort Edward on the 28th, and the country was overrun by the enemy soon after. On the 13th and 14th of Sept. the British army crossed the Hudson into Saratoga co.; and about the 10th of Oct. Fort Edward was re-taken by the Americans, thus effectually cutting off the retreat of the army, already disheartened by their defeat at Bemis Heights. The surrender of Burgoyne put an end to the war in this section; and the subsequent history of the co. is but the record of the continued and progressive triumphs of peaceful industry.

ARGYLE[3]—was granted by patent, May 21, 1764,[4] and formed as a town, March 23, 1786. Greenwich was taken off in 1803, and Fort Edward in 1818. It lies near the center of the co. Its surface is rolling in the N. and W. and broken and hilly in the S. and E. The highlands are divided into broad ridges with abrupt declivities. In the N. part Tamerack Swamp covers several hundred acres. The principal stream is the Moses Kil,[5] which flows in a s. w. direction through near the center of the town. The other streams are small brooks, which flow into the Hudson, Batten Kil, and Wood Creek. Cossayuna Lake[6] is a beautiful sheet of water, 3 mi. long, situated in a narrow valley in the s. e. part of the town. It is everywhere surrounded by steep hill slopes, and contains several beautiful green islands. To the N. E. of this lake, high up among the hills, is Argyle Lake,[7] a small sheet of water, half a mile in circumference. The soil of the town is generally a productive, slaty or gravelly loam. A mineral spring, 1 mi. N. w. from South Argyle, is said to resemble those at Saratoga. **Argyle** (p. v.) was incorp. March 27, 1838. It is the seat of the Argyle Academy. Pop. 375. **North Argyle** and **South Argyle** (p. offices) each contains about 20 houses, and **The Hook** 10. Argyle was conveyed to 83 families, and in 1765 the first settlement commenced.[8] The family of John Allen, a tory living on Lot 25, was murdered by Indians belonging to Burgoyne's army, July 26, 1777.[9] The first church (Asso. Ref. Presb.) was formed in 1793;[10] Rev. Geo. Mairs was the first preacher.

---

[1] There were three distinct routes,—one from Fort Edward, down Wood Creek, with a portage of 6 to 10 mi., one from Fort Ann to the head of South Bay, and one from Glens Falls to Lake George. [2] See page 682.

[3] Named in honor of the Scottish Duke of Argyle.

[4] This patent was granted to Scotch immigrants (who came over under Laughlin Campbell in 1738–40) and to their descendants. It embraced 47,450 acres, and granted township privileges. Duncan Read, Neal Shaw, Alexander McNachten, (McNaughton,) and Neal Gillespie were appointed trustees. A stately avenue, called "*The Street*," 7 mi. in length and 24 rods in width, was laid out (on paper) and surveyed E. and w. through the center of the township, and lots were laid out on each side. In the rear farm lots were laid out, thus affording accommodations for proprietors and tenants. In the summer of 1764 this tract was surveyed and divided into 141 lots, in accordance with this plan, by Arch. Campbell, of N. J., and Chris. Yates, of Schenectady. The natural impediments in the way, however, precluded the possibility of building the street or in any way realizing the plan.

[5] Formerly "*Moss Kil*," probably from Capt. Moss, who settled opposite its mouth.

[6] Called at different times "*Long*," "*Legbrants*," "*McEachrons*," "*Cowans*," and "*Big Lake*." The name given on the map and in the text, after having gone out of use, was restored by Dr. Fitch in his survey. Cossayuna is said by the St. François Indians to signify "*The Lake at our pines*," and is highly expressive of its original scenery.

[7] Summit Lake is a picturesque sheet of water in the co., upon the very summit of the central range of hills. Two sawmills are supplied by its outlet.

[8] Alex. McNaughton, Arch. Livingston, Duncan Campbell, and Roger Read settled on the Batten Kil; and James Gilles, Duncan Taylor, and George Kilmer, near the center of the town. Many of the lots were never visited or claimed by their proprietors, and they were taken up by squatters. The first death was that of Mrs. Arch. Brown.

[9] This family had been assured of protection by Burgoyne. Their murder, together with that of Jane McCrea, had the tendency to convert many persons who had hitherto been tories into active partisans in the American cause.

[10] The census reports 5 churches; 2 Asso. Presb., M. E., Ref. Presb. or Cong., and Prot. E.

CAMBRIDGE—was incorp. by patent,[1] July 21, 1761. It was formed as a town[2] in Albany co. March 7, 1788, and annexed to Washington co. Feb. 7, 1791. White Creek and Jackson were taken off in 1815. The surface of the town is hilly in the N. and rolling in the S. The summits of the hills are 200 to 300 ft. above the valleys. The E. part embraces a portion of the valley of Owl Kil, which is celebrated for the beauty of its scenery. Upon the W. of this valley are high undulating hills, the broad sweeps of which show alternate patches of green woodland and cultivated farms; and upon the E. rise the Taghkanick Mts., rough and broken, while the valley itself is very smooth and level. The other streams are Wampecack Creek, Whiteside Brook, and several other small brooks. The soil is generally a gravelly and sandy loam. Flax is extensively cultivated. **Cambridge** (p. v.) contains 100 houses and the Cambridge Washington Academy; **Center Cambridge** (p. v.) 13 houses; **North Cambridge** (p. o.) 10; and **Buskirks Bridge**[3] (p. v.) 15. The first settlers consisted of 30 families, who located in 1761, '62, and '63 and who each received 100 acres of land as a gift from the proprietors.[4] Phineas Whiteside,[5] from Penn., settled 8 mi. w. of the Colerain Colony, in 1766. The expedition against Bennington, under Baum, passed through the town Aug. 13, 1777; and the remnant of the fugitives returned on the night of the 16th. The first church (Asso. Presb.) was organized in 1789; Rev. Thos. Beverly was the first pastor.[6]

DRESDEN—was formed from Putnam, as "*South Bay*," March 15, 1822; its present name was adopted April 17, 1822. It lies between Lake George and the S. extremity of Lake Champlain. Nearly its entire surface is covered by steep mountain ridges, several peaks of which are 1500 ft. above the lake. The declivities of the mountains are steep, sometimes forming perpendicular precipices several hundred feet high. Upon the side of Lake George the mountains rise abruptly from the very edge of the water; but upon the borders of Lake Champlain is a narrow strip of arable land. The principal mountain peaks are Black[7] and Sugar Loaf Mts. and Diameter Precipice. Pike Brook and the head branches of Mill Brook take their rise in these mountains. All of the surface in the interior is covered with forests or naked rocky peaks. The soil is hard and sterile, and is unfit for agricultural purposes. The town was principally conveyed to non-commissioned officers and privates of the Colonial British army; and settlement was begun about 1784, by Jos. Phippeny, at the foot of South Bay. Ebenezer Chapman, —— Boggs, and Daniel Ruff came soon after, and settled along the bay and lake. Lumbering has formed a prominent pursuit. In several localities iron and other ores have been noticed, but none worked to any extent. The town is without a p. o. A bridge was built, at the expense of the State, across South Bay, near its outlet, in 1856.

EASTON—was formed from Stillwater and Saratoga, March 3, 1789, while a part of Albany co., and so named from being the E. town in the Saratoga Patent. It was annexed to Washington co. Feb. 7, 1791. It lies upon the E. bank of the Hudson. A broad intervale extends along the course of the river, which is succeeded by a plateau region, embracing the central and S. portions of the town. The E. part is broken by several lofty hills. The principal highlands are Willards Mt.[8] and Harrington Hill. The streams are Hudson River and Batten Kil,[9] forming the w. and N. boundaries of the town, Kidney and Vly Creeks, and a few minor streams. Upon the E. borders of the town is an extensive swamp known as "*The Vly*."[10] The Di-on-on-dah-o-wa Falls,[11] upon

---

1 This patent embraced 31,500 acres, and was nominally conveyed to 60 persons, most of whom resided in Hebron, Conn. The real owners were but 6 in number, and of these 3 only were mentioned in the charter, viz.: Isaac Sawyer and Edward Wells, of Conn., and Jacob Lansing, founder of Lansingburgh. The other three owners—Alex. Colden, Wm. Smith, and Geo. Banyar —were connected with the Colonial Government.

2 The town included a portion of the Hoosick Patent.

3 Named from Martin Van Buskirk, who built the first bridge.

4 The patent was conditional to the settlement of 30 families within 3 years; and to meet this requirement the most inviting portion was surveyed, and 100 acres offered as a gift to each family that would remove thither. These lots lay in a double row, on both sides of Owl Kil, from below the "*Checkered House*" into the present town of Jackson. They embrace the several village precincts from Davis Corners to near Stephensons Corners. Among the settlers were Jas. and Robt., sons of Ephraim Cowan, Jas. and John Cowden, John McClung, Samuel Bell, Col. Blair, Geo. Gilmore, Geo. Duncan, David Harrow, Wm. Clark, John Scott, and Thos. Morrison. A son of the last was the first child born of civilized parents in town. Hugh Kelso, a son of Col. Blair, was the first person who died in town. It is recorded that of these 30 families (who were for a time the most thrifty in town) all but two lost their property and died in poverty, mainly from intemperance. They were mostly from Colerain, Conn.

5 William Whiteside acquired the title to 3 lots, of 400 acres each, of the finest land, and settled his sons (John, Peter,

Thomas, William, and James) upon large farms near him. These estates are all owned by his descendants at the present day. The remaining lands were mostly leased by the six proprietors at an annual rent of one shilling per acre; but, they being generally willing to sell at a sum equal to the present worth of the perpetual rent, most of the settlers have gradually acquired the fee simple of their farms. The first inn was of logs, on the site of the "*Checkered House*," and kept by Jas. Cowden. Philip Van Ness built the first sawmill and gristmill on Gordons Brook, near Buskirks Bridge. This neighborhood was called by the Indians "*Ty-o-shoke*," and by them a field of 12 acres had been cleared there for corn. Other early settlers on the Hoosick Patent were Col. Lewis Van Wort and John Quackenbush.

6 The census reports 4 churches; 3 M. E., 1 Asso. Presb.

7 Black Mt., the highest, is 2,879 ft. above tide.

8 Willards Mt. is said to have derived its name from a Mr. Willard, who from its summit, with a spyglass, reconnoitered the position of Burgoyne's army at Saratoga.

9 Judge Benson, in his work upon the names of places, states that this stream was named from the Christian name of Bartholomew Van Hogeboom, first settler above Stillwater. Bart. is the abbreviation of Bartholomew, and hence *Barts Kil*, or Batten Kil.

10 A term used to denote a marsh overgrown with bog moss and low bushes.

11 Pronounced Di-on-on-dah'o-wa. On a map of Saratoga Patent published in 1709 it is written Di-on-on-de-ho-we.

Batten Kil, below Galesville, are 60 ft. high, and well worthy of note. The soil is an excellent quality of sandy and gravelly loam. Limestone of an excellent quality abounds in this town. Machinery, agricultural implements, and woolen goods are manufactured at Galesville. **Easton Corners** (North Easton p. o.) contains 30 houses; **Easton** (p. v.) 17; **South Easton** (p. v.) 15; and **Crandalls Corners** 8. Parts of **Union Village** and **Galesville**[1] are in this town. The date of the first settlement is unknown, but it was probably several years after the Saratoga Patent[2] was issued. In 1709 a fort[3] was built on the hill top, 1 mi. s. of Galesville, and a few families settled under its shelter; but the dread of Indian hostilities prevented the settlement from spreading. On the 30th of Nov. 1745, the enemy made a descent upon the place, killed 30 persons, and took 60 prisoners, including a portion of the garrison, who were decoyed from the fort by the Indians feigning to be wounded. The remaining part of the garrison burned the fort and unfinished blockhouses and withdrew, leaving the frontier unprotected. Settlers did not return until 1760.[4] At Schuylerville is a bridge across the Hudson 800 ft. long. The first religious meeting (Quaker) was held in 1778. A Ref. Prot. D. church was formed in 1805; Rev. Philip Duryea was the first preacher.[5]

FORT ANN—was formed, as "*Westfield*," March 23, 1786. Hartford was taken off in 1793, and Putnam in 1806. It received its present name, April 6, 1808, from the old fort erected here in 1709. It lies s. of the southern extremity of Lake Champlain, and s. e. of Lake George. Its central and w. parts are occupied by the high and rocky peaks of the Palmertown[6] Mts., here divided into three distinct ranges,—Palmertown Mt., in the w. part, Mt. Putnam, in the center, and Fort Ann Mts., in the e. The extreme e. edge of the town is occupied by uplands belonging to the Cossayuna Range. Diameter Rock and Buck Mt., on the line of Dresden, are the highest peaks, and are 1300 to 2500 ft. above tide. The valleys separating the ranges of the Palmertown Mts. are known as "*Furnace*" and "*Welchs Hollow*." The principal streams are Wood Creek, Halfway Creek, Furnace Hollow Creek, and Podunk Brook. The principal bodies of water are Orebed, Sly, Copeland, Hadlock, and Trout Ponds. The soil in the mountain region is hard and sterile, scarcely strong enough to support the natural growth of forest trees; but in the valleys it is a gravelly loam alternating with a stiff clay.[7] Iron[8] and woolen goods are manufactured to some extent. **Fort Ann**[9] (p. v.) has 608 inhabitants; **Griswolds Mills** (p. v.) about 14 houses. **West Fort Ann**, (p. o.,) **South Bay, Canes Falls**, and **Comstocks Landing** (p. o.) are small villages. Fort Ann was one of a chain of military works erected in 1709, to facilitate the extensive operations then in progress against Canada.[10] It stood upon the w. side of Wood Creek, about half a mile from the present village of Fort Ann, the Champlain Canal passing partly across the spot which it enclosed. It was built at the joint expense of England and the Colonies. Artillery Patent, covering the e. part of this town, was granted Oct. 24, 1764, to Jos. Walton and 23 other Provincial officers, in equal shares, irrespective of grade. Settlement was not generally begun until after the Revolution. An engagement occurred here, July 8, 1777, between the rear guard of the retreating American army, under Col. Long, and the advanced guard of the British, under Col. Hill.[11] In Oct. 1780, a blockhouse in this town was burned by the enemy. The first church (Bap.) was formed in 1789;[12] Rev. Sherman Babcock was the first pastor.

FORT EDWARD—was formed from Argyle, April 10, 1818. It lies upon the e. bank of the Hudson, near the center of the w. border of the co. A wide intervale extends along the

---

1 Formerly called "*Arkansaw*." The present name is derived from John Gale, former proprietor of the village site. See p. 683.

2 This patent was granted Nov. 4, 1684, and renewed Oct. 9, 1708. The part e. of the Hudson was 12 mi. long and 6 mi. broad.

3 This fort was built of thick posts driven into the ground close to each other, in the manner of palisades, forming a square, "the length of whose sides was within the reach of a musket shot." At each corner were houses for officers; and within the palisades were barracks of timbers.—*Kalm's Travels*.

4 Among the first settlers of about this period were Pet. Becker, Elijah Freeman, Thos. and Mishal Beadle, William Thompson, Nathan Potter, John Swain, and William Coffin. A school was taught near Union Village as early as 1787. Gerrit Lansingh kept the first store, in 1794; and John Gale built the first mill, at Galesville, in 1810. The first woolen factory was built in the summer of 1846, by Gale, Rodgers & Reynolds.

5 There are 5 churches in town; 2 M. E., 2 Ref. Prot. D., and 1 Friends.

6 Said to be named from a small remnant of Indians, who were driven from Conn. and settled here.

7 Near Wood Creek, 50 feet above the present surface of the stream, are found pot holes worn by water, evidently by an ancient current flowing southward.

8 A blast furnace was built at Mt. Hope in 1826, which makes

5 tons of pig iron daily. A forge was built at West Fort Ann in 1828, for making anchors and chain cables.

9 Incorp. March 7, 1820.

10 While this fort was in process of erection, a force of 1500 French and Indians were sent to destroy it; but, learning that Col. Nicholson was posted here with a superior force, they returned. While the English were awaiting at this place the opening of a road and the construction of bateaux on Lake Champlain, a fatal sickness broke out in the camp, and great numbers died as if poisoned. In October Col. Nicholson returned with his crippled forces to Albany. Charlevoix states that this sickness was produced by the treachery of the Indians, who threw the skins of their game into the swamp above the camp. It is more probable that it was a malignant dysentery caused by the malaria of the swamps and the extreme heat.

11 The Americans were obliged to retreat in consequence of their ammunition giving out. They destroyed their works, and felled trees across the road and creek, obstructing the route to Fort Edward as much as possible. The removal of these obstructions caused a delay of several weeks, which finally proved fatal to the invading army.

12 The first edifice was built in 1810, 2 mi. e. of Deweys Bridge, and is now used as a schoolhouse. There are 6 churches in town; 3 Bap., M. E., Meth. Prot., and Free.

river, but toward the E. the surface rises to a height of 200 to 300 ft. and spreads out into a beautifully undulating upland. The Hudson, Moses Kil and Dead Creek are the principal streams. The
soil upon the river is a mixture of heavy clay and alluvium, but farther E. it is a sandy or gravelly
loam. In town are several extensive manufacturing establishments.[1] **Fort Edward**[2] (p. v.)
is finely situated on the Hudson. Pop. in 1858, 1,565. The Washington Co. Seminary and Female
Collegiate Institute,[3] one of the largest academic institutions in the State, is located at this village.
Fort Miller (p. v.) is situated on the Hudson, about 7 mi. below Fort Edward. Pop. 225. **Fort
Edward Center** is a p. o., and **Durkeetown** is a hamlet. The first family that located
in the town or co. was that of Col. Lydius, son of Rev. John Lydius, who, having acquired the
title to Delliu's discarded patent, built a house, and engaged in trade with the Indians at what
is now Fort Edward Village.[4] His daughter, Catherine, was born here, and was the first white
child born in the co. Fort Nicholson was built in 1709, but was soon after abandoned. As a
part of the plan of military operations against Canada, about 600 men, under Gen. Lyman, were
sent forward, in June, 1755, to build a fort where Fort Nicholson had formerly stood, at the great
carrying place to Lake Champlain.[5] Fort Edward was a very important depôt for arms and rendezvous for armies in the great expeditions against Canada; and it served as a vast hospital for the
sick and wounded until 1760, when it was allowed to go to decay. During the Revolution it was
again occupied by both British and Americans. Fort Miller is named from the fort built, about
1755, in the bend of the river opposite the village.[6] After the peace this town settled rapidly.
Wm. Duer,[7] son-in-law to Lord Sterling, was the pioneer of Ft. Miller, where he built a large house
and sawmill. There are 6 churches in town.[8]

GRANVILLE—was formed March 23, 1786. It is situated upon the E. border of the co., N.
of the center. Its surface is undulating and hilly. The ridges generally slope gradually to
their summits, which are elevated 300 to 500 ft. above the valleys. Quarries of excellent roofing
slate have been opened in different parts of the town.[9] Wide intervals of excellent land extend
along the course of Mettowee, or Pawlet,[10] and Indian Rivers. The soil is a slaty and gravelly loam,
and is particularly adapted to potatoes, large quantities of which are exported. A limited amount
of manufactures[11] is carried on in town. **Granville**[12] (p. v.) contains an academy and 450 inhabitants; **North Granville** (p. v.) a female seminary and 220 inhabitants; **Middle Granville** (p. v.) 439 inhabitants; and **South Granville** (p. v.) 111. The land in this town is embraced in several grants made to about 30 captains and lieutenants who had served in the French
War.[13] Barnaby Byrnes Patent, of 2000 acres, in the S. E. corner, was sold to Kennith McKennith,
a merchant of New York, who again sold it to Donald Fisher, a tailor of that city. Fisher induced
several relatives of his to remove from Scotland and settle upon his tract. In the Revolution he
withdrew to Canada, and his lands were confiscated and sold; but, owing to some informality, the

---

[1] The dam at Fort Edward furnishes water for 4 gang sawmills,
a machine shop and furnace, a flouring mill, plaster mill, paper
mill, and cotton factory. At Fort Miller Dam are a grist and saw
mill, fulling mill, machine shop, and woolen factory.
[2] Incorp. under Gen. Act of 1847.
[3] The seminary building is 300 ft. long by 40 broad, and 5
stories high, besides an extensive wing. It has accommodations
for 500 pupils. See page 743.
[4] His house was burned by the Indians in 1749, and his son
taken prisoner.
[5] It was named Fort Lyman; but a few years after, the name
was changed to Ft. Edward, in honor of Edward, Duke of York,
grandson of Geo. II., and brother of Geo. III. It stood on the
bank of the river, N. of the creek, and within the present village
limits. It was 4 sided, with bastions on 3 angles, the fourth
being protected by the river. Its ramparts of earth and timber,
16 ft. high and 22 thick, were mounted with 6 cannon and enclosed several large buildings. Storehouses and barracks were
built on Monroes Island, opposite. A band of savages attempted
to surprise it in Aug. 1759, but were repulsed by Maj. Israel Putnam and his rangers. In the winter following, Putnam saved
the fort from destruction by a characteristic exercise of cool in-
trepidity and daring. The fort accidentally took fire, and the
flames spread with great rapidity in the immediate vicinity of
the powder magazine. Putnam placed himself in the path of
the flames, and fought desperately until the fire was subdued;
and when he retired from his post his arms, face, and hands
were entirely skinned, and the frail covering of the magazine was
completely charred.
The murder of Jane McCrea took place July 27, 1777, near a
spring, and beside a venerable pine tree a little E. of the village.
This tragedy was at once reported throughout the country, and
aided greatly to weaken the influence of the British, while it
aroused the patriots to more desperate efforts in resisting the invaders. The old pine tree died in 1849; and in 1853 it was cut

down and made into canes and boxes as mementos of the event.
The remains of Miss McC. are interred in the Union Cemetery.
[6] The flat upon which this fort was erected is protected on three
sides by the river and a narrow bay; it was further defended by
a strong parapet of timber covered with earth, and with a ditch
in front. A blockhouse was built upon the bluff that overlooks
the point; and within the flat storehouses were erected.
[7] He was the first State Senator from this co. Among the
first settlers were Noah Payne, from Warren co., Conn., in 1766;
Timothy Buel, and the Crocker families. Nath'l Gage was living
at Ft. Miller when these families arrived. The Durkee, Saunders, and Bell families settled in the upper part of the town.
The first one of these consisted of a father and 5 sons, from R. I.
These settlers first took out titles under Lydius, but, finding
them invalid, they bought of the Schuyler proprietors. There is
no tradition of loss to the settlers from this cause,—whence it is
inferred that Col. Lydius refunded whatever he may have received. Hugh Monroe, (owner of Monroes Island,) Patrick
Smith, and Dr. Jas. Smith settled at Fort Edward about 1764.
The house of Patrick Smith—still standing, ¼ mi. s. of Canal
Aqueduct—was the headquarters of Burgoyne and Gen. Schuyler at different times during the Revolution; and it was the co.
courthouse.
[8] 2 M. E., 2 Prot. E., Ref. Prot. D., Presb.
[9] The laborers engaged in this business are mostly Welsh.
Extensive arrangements are in preparation for cutting and
dressing this for a variety of ornamental and useful purposes.
[10] This stream, rising among the Green Mts., is subject to sudden and severe freshets, which render the maintenance of
bridges difficult and expensive.
[11] At Granville Village are a paper mill and woolen factory.
[12] Incorp. in 1849; formerly called "Bishops Corners."
[13] These grants became known by the names of the patentees,
as "Grants North and South Patent," "Lakes Patent," "Hutchinsons Patent," "Kelleys Patent," "Dupersons Patent," &c.

State afterward bought off his claim, for $12,000.[1] The first carding machine used in the State was erected at Middle Granville, in 1808.[2] The first church (Presb.) was formed April 16, 1782; the first pastor, Rev. Oliver Hitchcock, was settled in 1786; and the church was erected in 1795.[3]

GREENWICH—was formed from Argyle, March 4, 1803. It lies on the E. border of the co., in the N. angle formed by the junction of the Hudson and Batten Kil. Ranges of hills, 200 to 300 ft. above the valleys, extend through the central and eastern parts of the town. Bald Mt., near Batten Kil, is the principal peak. The declivities of the hills are so gradual that the surface appears to be rolling rather than hilly. Upon Batten Kil are two considerable falls, one of which is 75 ft. in height. The other principal streams are the Cossayuna, Rogers, and Stony Creeks and Livingston Brook. Cossayuna Lake extends into the N. E. corner of the town. The soil is a slaty and gravelly loam interspersed with patches of clay. The town is more extensively engaged in manufactures than any other in the co.[4] **Union Village,**[5] (Greenwich p. o.,) on the line of Easton, contains an academy and 1,173 inhabitants, 888 of whom are in Greenwich; **Bald Mountain**[6] (p. v.) 225 inhabitants; **East Greenwich** (p. v.) and **Center Falls** each about 100 houses; and **North Greenwich** (p. v.) 70. **Galesville** (p. v.) is a manufacturing village of about 40 houses, on the line of Easton. **Battenville,** (p. v.,) in the S. E. corner, contains about 200 inhabitants. **Lakeville** (Lake p. o.) is a hamlet. It is supposed that the first settlement was made by the Dutch, previous to the French War, a few families of them remaining at the time of the Revolution.[7] About 1733 a large number of Scotch emigrants had come over under the promise of grants of land from Government,—which promise was not fulfilled. Jan. 5, 1763, three of these emigrants—Duncan, George, and Jas. Campbell, sons of Laughlin Campbell—petitioned for 100,000 acres; and on the 11th of Nov. following a patent of 10,000 acres was issued to the 3 brothers, their 3 sisters, (Rose Graham, Margaret Eustace, and Lily Murray,) and 4 other persons. This grant embraced about one-third of the town of Greenwich. The first church (Bap.) was organized in 1774; Rev. Leonard Bowers was the first preacher.[8]

HAMPTON—was formed March 3, 1786. It lies upon the E. border of the co., N. of the center. A range of hills, about 500 ft. above the valleys and for the most part covered with forests, extends through the central and eastern parts of the town. Poultney River, separating the town from Vt., is the principal stream. Along its course is a wide intervale of fine land. The soil is a gravelly loam interspersed with clay. The intervale is alike fertilized and desolated by the frequent overflows of the stream. **Hampton Corners** (Hampton p. o.) contains 20 houses, and **Low Hampton**[9] (p. o.) 5. The greater part of this town was included in patents granted to Provincial officers. The N. part embraces about 2000 acres of Skenes Little Patent.[10] The first settlement was made some little time before the Revolution,[11] by Capt. Brooks, Col. Gideon Warren, and —— Webster. The first church (Prot. E.) was built at a very early date;[12] Rev. Stephen Jeweth, from N. J., was the first preacher.

HARTFORD—was formed from "*Westfield,*" (now Fort Ann,) March 12, 1793. It lies near the center of the co. The S. E. section is broken and hilly, and the center and N. w. level or gently undulating. · The summits of the highest hills are 500 to 700 ft. above the level of the Champlain Canal. The principal streams are East Creek and its branches. Slate and limestone of an excellent quality are found among the hills.[13] The soil in the S. E. is a rich, slaty loam, and that in the N. w. a heavy clay. There are several chalybeate springs, the principal of which is

[1] Capt. Dan'l Curtis, from New Lebanon, N. Y., came into town about 1780; Capt. Ebenezer Gould, from Killingly, Conn., Nath'l Spring, Asaph Cook, Tim. Allen, F. S. Hodge, Ebenezer Walker, and David Doane, settled before or about the time of the Revolution. —— Baker kept an inn at North Granville, about 1790, and —— Jenks kept a store as early as 1795. Nath'l Spring erected a gristmill at Granville, about 1787. A school was taught by Jas. Richards, in 1783, at South Granville.

[2] It is said that this carding machine was obtained secretly from England and for some time was worked in private.

[3] The census reports 10 church buildings; 2 Friends, 2 Presb., Bap., Cong., M. E., Meth. Prot., Wes. Meth., and Prot. E.

[4] Batten Kil is improved by a dam of 8 ft. fall at East Greenwich, one of 9 ft. at Battenville, a dam and falls of 25 ft. at Center Falls, a dam of 8 ft. at Union Village, a fall of 40 ft. at Galesville, and a dam near the mouth of the stream. The Di-on-on-dah-o-wa Falls are not improved. There are a woolen factory, a grist, saw, and plaster mill, at East Greenwich, a manufactory of seamless bags at Battenville, a woolen factory, grist, saw, and plaster mill, at Center Falls, and mills near the mouth of the stream.

[5] The first settlement in this village was made in 1781, by Job Whipple, and it was first called "*Whipple City*." It was incorp. March 29, 1809. The first cotton factory in the State was erected here in 1804, by Wm. Mowry, who had received his instruction at the pioneer establishment of Sam'l Slater at Paw-

tucket, R. I. In this village are several mills and machine shops and a large carriage factory.

[6] This village is entirely dependent upon the manufacture of lime widely known as the Bald Mt. lime. At the kilns of R. W. Lowber 100,000 bushels are annually manufactured.

[7] Among the first settlers at Lakeville were Alexander Reid, John McEachron, and Robt. McNaughton; at East Greenwich, Archibald Livingston; at Carters Pond, Asa Carter; near Galesville, Abraham Lansingh, —— Gale, —— White, —— Tefft; and at Center Falls, Thos. McLean, Jas. Conoly, Nathan Rogers, and Smith Barber.

[8] The census reports 9 churches; 3 Bap., 3 M. E., Cong., Ref. Prot. D., and Asso. Presb.

[9] A paper mill here manufactures annually 240,000 lbs. of wrapping paper.

[10] This patent of 9000 acres was granted July 6, 1771.

[11] Among the early settlers were Sam'l Beman, Peter P. French, —— Hyde, Benj. Rice, Rufus Hotchkiss, and Jason Kellogg French & Beman kept the first store, and the former the first inn. Rev. Wm. Miller, originator of the belief that the second advent of Christ would take place in 1843, resided in this town.

[12] The first religious society formed was M. E. The census reports 4 churches; Bap., M. E., Prot. E., and Sec. Advent.

[13] Lime for local use was made in this part of the town.

upon the farm of Alvin Briggs, near the center. Among the limestone ridges in the N. part are several small caves. **North Hartford** (Hartford p. o.) contains about 300 inhabitants; **South Hartford** (p. v.) 150; and **Log Village** 50. This town embraces the Provincial Patent, granted, May 2, 1764, to 26 commissioned officers of the N. Y. Infantry.[1] Settlement was not commenced until after the Revolution.[2] The first church (Bap.) was built in 1789.[3]

HEBRON[4]—was formed March 23, 1786, and named from Hebron, Conn. It lies near the center of the E. border of the co. A broad mountain range extends through the center, occupying nearly one-half of its entire surface, and a series of high hills extends through the E. and W. sections. The summits of the highlands are 300 to 500 ft. above the valleys and are mostly crowned with forests. The ranges of hills are separated by the valleys of Black Creek and its principal W. branch. The soil is a sandy and slaty loam, of a light, porous nature, easy of cultivation, and well adapted to resist the extremes of wet and drouth. In the hilly regions is considerable rocky waste land. In the N. and E. are extensive and valuable quarries of slate. **North Hebron**[5] (p. v.) contains the North Hebron Institute and 12 houses; **East Hebron** (Hebron p. o.) 12 houses; **West Hebron** (p. v.) the West Hebron Classical School and 40 houses; **Belcher**[6] (p. v.) 20 houses; and **Slateville** (p. o.) 8. This town was embraced in patents granted to officers and privates who had served in the French War,—mostly to Scotch Highlanders belonging to the 77th Regt. of Foot. These grants were made so long after the war that those who were entitled to them never appeared to claim them. The first settlements appear to have been made before the Revolution. There are two academic institutions in town. The first church (Asso. Ref. Presb.) was organized in 1780;[7] Rev. Dr. Gray was the first pastor.

JACKSON—was formed from Cambridge, April 17, 1815. It lies on the E. border of the co., S. of the center. The N. branch of the Taghkanick Range occupies the E. portion of the town, and several parallel ranges extend through the central and W. portions, rendering the entire surface very hilly. The summits of the hills are 300 to 800 ft. above the valleys and are generally crowned with forests. The declivities are often steep and rocky. The principal streams are Batten Kil and a branch of Owl Creek. In the valley between the hills that border immediately upon Batten Kil and those farther W. are several small lakes, known as Long, Big, Dead, and Little Ponds. These lakes are beautiful sheets of water, surrounded by hills, forests, and fine cultivated farms. The soil is a slaty loam and very productive. **Jackson Center** (Jackson p. o.) contains 16 houses; **Colla**, (p. v.,) on the line of Cambridge, about 30 houses; and **Anaquassacook** 12. Portions of this town and White Creek were embraced in the Anaquassacook Patent of 10,000 acres, granted May 11, 1762.[8] The first settlers were James Irvine, Peter Magill, and John Miller, all of whom located in the S. part of the town.[9] The only church (Ref. Prot. D.) in town was organized Dec. 31, 1833; Rev. Jas. W. Stewart was the first pastor. Geo. Law, one of the projectors and proprietors of the California line of steamships, was a native of this town.

KINGSBURY—was incorp. by patent May 11, 1762, and recognized as a town by the State Government March 23, 1786. It lies on the W. border of the co., N. of the center. Nearly all of its surface is level or gently undulating. A range of hills, rising about 150 ft. above the valleys, occupies the extreme E. edge of the town. The principal streams are the Hudson, in the S. W. corner; Wood Creek, upon the E. border; Halfway Brook, in the N. W. corner, and Moss Brook. At Bakers Falls,[10] upon the Hudson, the river shoots down a steep descent of ledges, in all 76 ft. in 60 rods, forming a scene of great beauty, and affording an extensive water-power. The soil along the valley of Wood Creek is a hard, stiff clay; in the other parts of the town, a sandy or gravelly loam. There are extensive quarries of limestone in town, furnishing an excellent building material; from these quarries was obtained the stone for the locks on the Champlain & Hudson

---

[1] This patent contained 26,000 acres, each officer receiving 1,000 acres.

[2] Col. John Buck, Manning Bull, Stephen and Asa Bump, John and Edward Ingalls, and Nathan and Sam'l Taylor were among the first settlers. Aaron and Eber Ingoldsbee, from Boylston, Mass., came in 1782, and Timothy Stocking, Ebenezer Smith, and John Paine in 1784. A school was taught in 1790, at North Hartford, by Thos. Paine, from Conn. A gristmill was built of logs at an early date.

[3] The census reports 4 churches in town; M. E. Bap., Cong., and Union.

[4] During the Revolution, and for some time after, the place was known as " Black Creek."

[5] Locally known as " Munros Meadows."

[6] Locally known as " Bedlam."

[7] The census reports 7 churches; 2 M. E., 2 Sec. Advent, Bap., Asso. Presb., and Asso. Ref. Presb.

[8] This patent was granted to Ryer, Jacob, Freeman, and W. M. Schermerhorn, Johannes, Nicholas, and Peter Quackenboss, Thos. and John Smith, and Joseph Jansen, all of Schenectady.

[9] Among the settlers on the Anaquassacook were Hugh Thompson and Ebenezer Billings, and near the ponds John McLean and Jonathan Conger. A schoolhouse was built in 1780, a little w. of Peter Hill's residence. An inn was kept by Isaac Murray about 1790. John McGill built a store of logs, in 1781, on the site of the present residence of Peter Hill.

[10] Named from Albert Baker, the second settler in town.

Canal. Manufacturing is carried on to a considerable extent.[1] **Sandy Hill**[2] (p. v.) has a population of 1,260. **Moss Street** contains 25 houses; **Kingsbury** (p. v.) 25; **Pattens Mills** (p. v.) 20; **Dunhams Basin** 10; **Vaughns Corners** 12; **Adamsville** (p. o.) 12; **Langdons Corners** 5; and **Smiths Basin** (p. o.) 8. Kingsbury Patent, containing 26,000 acres, was granted to Jas. Bradshaw and 22 others, from Conn., May 11, 1762. The first settlers were James Bradshaw, Albert Baker, and his sons Albert and Charles, from New York City.[3] A sawmill was built at Bakers Falls before the Revolution, and a gristmill in 1807. The town was the scene of many an adventure during the French War,[4] and the settlement was entirely broken up during the Revolution. Traces of a road cut by Burgoyne's army are still visible near Kingsbury. The first minister was Francis Baylor, a Moravian, about 1776. Meetings were held by the Prot. Epis. and the Bap. in 1795.[5] Several noted men have been residents of this town.[6]

PUTNAM[7]—was formed from "*Westfield*," (now Fort Ann,) Feb. 28, 1806. Dresden was set off in 1822. This town lies in the extreme N. end of the co., upon the mountainous peninsula between Lakes George and Champlain. The mountains are divided into two separate ranges by the valleys of Mill and Charter Brooks. The w. range of mountains rises abruptly from the surface of Lake George, and in the s. part of the town attains an elevation of 900 to 1,000 ft. above the surface of the lake. The greater part of the surface is rocky, broken, and unfit for cultivation; but sections of arable land extend along the valleys of the small streams and the borders of Lake Champlain. The soil is generally a hard, gravelly loam. Graphite of a fine quality is found in abundance. A small pond lies among the mountains, on the w. side of the town, 300 feet above Lake George. **Putnam Corners,** (Putnam p. o.,) containing about 10 houses, is the only village. The tillable lands were mostly granted to privates of the N. Y. Provincial regiments, and feeble settlements had probably commenced before the Revolution.[8] The first church (Asso. Presb.) was built in 1801;[9] Rev. James Miller, from Scotland, was the first pastor. A private academy at Putnam Corners was established in 1854.

SALEM—was formed by patent Aug. 7, 1764, and was recognized by statute March 23, 1786. It lies on the E. border of the co., s. of the center. Its surface consists of moderately elevated ridges, separated by narrow valleys, all extending in a N. E. and s. w. direction. The hills are usually bordered by gradual slopes and their summits are crowned with forests. There is very little waste land in town. Batten Kil, forming the s. boundary, and Black, White, and Trout Creeks, are the principal streams. Lyttles Pond, in the N. part of the town, is a beautiful sheet of water lying in a basin among the hills and surrounded by forests. The soil is a rich, slaty or gravelly loam. **Salem,** (p. v.,) incorp. April 4, 1803, has 832 inhabitants; **Shushan** (p. v.) about 25 houses; and **Eagleville,** (East Salem p. o.,) **Clapps Mills,** and **Fitches Point** have each 40 to 50 inhabitants. James Turner and Joshua Conkey, from Pelham, Mass., were the first settlers, in 1761. They were joined, the next year, by Hamilton McCollister. In 1764 a patent of 25,000 acres was obtained,—one-half owned by a company of New England settlers and the other by Oliver De Lancey and Peter Du Bois, two Government officials.[10] These last sold their share to Rev. Thos. Clark and his company of Irish and Scotch immigrants at a perpetual rent of one shilling per acre.[11] The Camden Tract, on the E. part of the town, was granted to captains

---

[1] The dam at Sandy Hill, across the Hudson, 1,200 ft. long and 19 ft. high, furnishes water-power for several mills and a woolen factory. At Bakers Falls there are a paper mill and 2 gristmills. The lumber business of the town is very extensive and important, the sawmills being supplied with logs floated down from the Upper Hudson. There are also in town establishments for the manufacture of pianos, steam engines, portable sawmills, &c.

[2] This village has been a half-shire town since 1807. It was incorp. March 9, 1810.

[3] Among the other first settlers were Michael Hoffnagle, Solomon King, Oliver Colvin, and Nehemiah Seely.

[4] At one time 17 soldiers were taken prisoners by the Indians and carried to the present site of Sandy Hill Village. They were seated on a log, in a row, when their captors deliberately began to tomahawk them, taking them in order from one end of the log. When all were killed but one, (John Quackenboss, of Albany,) a squaw claimed him, and his life was spared. He returned after a few years of captivity, and resided near Hoosick, in Cambridge. In Aug. 1758, Majs. Putnam and Rogers encountered a party of French and Indians in this town, during which engagement Putnam was made prisoner. The enemy were finally compelled to withdraw, with a loss of 90 men.

[5] The census reports 9 churches; 3 Bap., 3 M. E., Presb., Prot. E., and R. C.

[6] Gov. Wright received his legal education at the office of

Henry C. Martindale, of Sandy Hill. Lieut. Gov. Pitcher, for some time Acting Governor, was a citizen of this town. Hon. Wm. P. Lee, late Chief Justice and Chancellor of the Sandwich Islands, was a native of Sandy Hill.

[7] Named in honor of Gen. Israel Putnam, who in this vicinity, as major in the colonial service, performed some of his most daring exploits.

[8] The first sawmill was erected by Robt. Cummings, in 1802, on Mill Creek, 1 mi. from Lake Champlain. The first child born was James Jennings, in 1803; the first death was that of Anne Thompson, in 1804. Robt. Patterson kept the first school, in 1804. Many of the first settlers were Scotch, and among them were Obadiah Blake, Robt. Cummings, John Blair, Wm. Hutton, George Easton, Pelatiah Bugbee, John Butterfield, and Josiah Clark.

[9] There are 2 churches; Asso. Presb., and F. W. Bap.

[10] This patent was surveyed into 308 lots, and a large pine lot was reserved for the common benefit, and cut up into small lots for division; 3 lots near the center of the town were set apart to support the minister and schoolmaster.

[11] The New England and Scotch settlers were mixed together in their settlements, and often on alternate farms; and, in consequence of the rivalry between the two parties of proprietors, the town was speedily settled. The New Englanders wished to call the town "*White Creek*," and the Scotch "*New Perth*;" and each name was strongly insisted on.

and lieutenants in the Provincial army.   Rev. Thomas Clark was the first minister.[1]   The Salem Washington Academy was incorp. Feb. 15, 1791.[2]

WHITE CREEK[3]—was formed from Cambridge, April 17, 1815.   It is the s. e. corner town of the co.   The surface of the s. portion is gently rolling, and the central and n. portions are occupied by the Taghkanick Mts.   The summits of these mountains are rocky and broken and covered with forests, and their sides are bounded by abrupt declivities and perpendicular ledges. The principal streams are Hoosick River, Owl Kil, Pumpkin Hook,[4] Center, White, and Little White Creeks.   The upper course of Owl Kil is through a deep and narrow valley abounding with picturesque views.   A small vein of lead has been discovered three-fourths of a mi. e. of Posts Corners. The soil is a fine quality of gravelly loam.   More sheep are raised in this town than in any other in the co.   Garden seeds and flax are largely cultivated.   **North White Creek** (p. v.) adjoins Cambridge.   **White Creek,** (p. o.,) **Posts Corners, Center White Creek,** (p. o.,) **Ash Grove, Dorrs Corners, Pumpkin Hook,** and **Martindale Corners** are hamlets. The Walloomsac Patent, lying partly in this town, on the s., was settled by the Dutch.   Among the other grants were the Bain, Embury, Grant and Campbell, and Lake and Van Cuyler, Patents. A colony of Irish Methodists settled near Ash Grove about 1770 ; and here was organized the second M. E. church in America,[5] by Thos. Ashton (from whom the locality was named) and Rev. Philip Embury.   James and Thos. Morrison made the first settlement, near White Creek.[6]

WHITEHALL[7]—was incorp. by patent Nov. 12, 1763, as *"Skenesborough."*[8]   Its name was changed March 23, 1786.   It lies at the s. extremity of Lake Champlain.   Its surface is mountainous in the w. and level and undulating in the center and e.   Saddle Mt., upon the w. border, is nearly 900 ft. above the surface of the lake.   The principal streams are Wood Creek, Mettowee (or Pawlet) and Poultney Rivers.   Upon Wood Creek, near its mouth, is a fall which furnishes a valuable water-power.   The soil of the greater part of the town is a hard, stiff clay and is best adapted to grazing.   Considerable manufacturing is carried on in town.[9]   **Whitehall** (p. v.) is situated near the mouth of Wood Creek, on Lake Champlain.   The r. r., canal, and lake trade give this place commercial importance.   The Whitehall Academy is in the e. part of the village.   Pop. 3,225.   This town was the scene of stirring military events during the French War.[10]   The first settler was Maj. Skene, who located here, with 30 families, in 1761.   Nominally associating 24 others with himself, he obtained a patent of 25,000 acres, March 13, 1765 ; and a patent of 9,000 acres in the town of Hampton and Whitehall, July 6, 1771, known as Skene's Little Patent. About 1770 he built a massive stone house and barn, a forge, and one or two sawmills.   He also built a sloop upon the lake, and a road, known as *"Skenes Road,"* 30 mi. through the wilderness toward Salem.   He appears to have been a man of great energy of character, and he endeavored to secure solid and permanent advantages to the infant settlement.[11]   Upon the approach of the Revolution, Maj. Skene espoused the royalist cause, and his house was taken by the Americans in May, 1775.[12]   In 1776 an American garrison was stationed here, and a small fleet was fitted

---

[1] Rev. Thos. Clark (Asso. Presb.) was the first minister; and his church, formed in Ireland, was transplanted without reorganization.   In 1769 a Presb. society was formed, Rev. John Harford first pastor.   Their church, then unfinished, was fortified by Capt. Jos. McCracken in 1777, and soon after was burned by the enemy.   There are now 7 churches in town; 2 M. E., Asso. Presb., Asso. Ref. Presb., F. W. Bap., Presb., and Morav.

[2] For a great number of years this school was one of the most noted in Eastern New York.   Among the distinguished persons who have received a portion of their education here were Hon. Samuel Nelson, of the U. S. Supreme Court, Hon. John Savage, formerly Chief Justice of N.Y., and Rev. Dr. Bethune, of Brooklyn.

[3] The creek from which the town was named received its name from the white quartz pebbles that form its bed.

[4] Said to be a corruption of the Indian Pom-pa-nuck, the name of a tribe of Indians who removed hither from Conn.

[5] Embury preached the first Meth. sermon in N. Y., 3 or 4 years before.   The census reports 8 churches in town; 2 Bap., 2 M. E., Friends, Presb., R.C., and Asso. Ref. Presb.

[6] Among the other early settlers were Buel Beebe, Maj. John Porter, Ephraim, James, and Robt. Cowan, Sam'l Clark, John McClung, Geo. Duncan, Robt. and George Gilmore, Wm. Eager, Wm. Selfrage, Sam'l Ball, and John Scott.   The early settlers in the e. part of the town were Thomas Ashton, Edmund Wells, John and Ebenezer Allen, David Sprague, Seth Chase, John Harroun, Thos. McCool, John Woods, Simeon Fowler, John Young, Josiah Dewey, and John Corey.   John Rhodes built the first clothing works, at Pumpkin Hook.

[7] Called by the Indians "Kah-cho-quah-na," *the place where dip fish.*

[8] Named from Maj. Philip Skene, a British half-pay officer, its founder and patentee.

[9] The manufactures consist of lumber, machinery, vessels, boats, carpets, and sash and blinds.   An extensive lumber trade is carried on with Canada and with ports on the Hudson, through Lake Champlain and the Champlain Canal.

[10] Maj. Israel Putnam was stationed here in the summer of 1758, with 35 rangers, to watch the motions of the enemy and prevent the passage of small parties.   A point—now known as Puts Rock—three-fourths of a mi. n. of the village, overlooking South Bay, and completely commanding the passage of Wood Creek, was chosen, and a stone breastwork was built and concealed by bushes.   Soon after the work was finished, a party of 500 French, led by the partisan Molang, upon a secret expedition, attempted to pass up the creek in the night.   They were received by a most destructive fire, and before they could recover from their surprise, one-half of their number were killed. Finding that the enemy had landed below and that he was in danger of being surrounded, Putnam quietly withdrew, with no loss, and but two men wounded.

[11] Maj. Skene became acquainted with this place while accompanying the expedition under Gen. Amherst, in 1755.   Soon after he planted his first settlement, of 30 families, he was obliged to go to the West Indies; and upon his return in 1763 he found but 15 families remaining.   He brought a number of slaves from the West Indies, and employed them and a large number of discharged soldiers upon his works.   His house was 30 by 40 ft. on the ground, and 2½ stories high; and his barn was 130 ft. long, with massive stone walls pierced with portholes.   The other buildings in his settlement were a few frail houses belonging to his tenants.

[12] He was very popular with the settlers, and hence he was an object of both fear and dislike to the patriots.   His place was captured by a party of volunteers under Capt. Herrick, and

out in the harbor and put under the command of Benedict Arnold. Upon the approach of Burgoyne's army, in 1777, the fort was blown up and the houses, mills, &c. were all burned.[1] During the War of 1812 this place became an important depôt of military stores. The first steamboat on the lake was launched here, in 1809. The Champlain Canal was constructed to this point from Fort Edward in 1819, and finished to Troy in 1824.[2] In 1806 Gen. Williams made arrangements for building a church, but died before he could carry them into effect. His son (Col. John Williams) and his widow carried out the design, and presented the building to the Asso. Presb. Soc. It was rebuilt in 1826.[3]

Acres of Land, Valuation, Population, Dwellings, Families, Freeholders, Schools, Live Stock, Agricultural Products, and Domestic Manufactures, of Washington County.

Names of Towns.	Acres of Land. Improved.	Acres of Land. Unimproved.	Valuation of 1858. Real Estate.	Valuation of 1858. Personal Property.	Valuation of 1858. Total.	Population. Males.	Population. Females.	No. of Dwellings.	No. of Families.	Freeholders.	Schools. No. of Districts.	Schools. Children taught.
Argyle	27,186	8,350¾	$1,002,507	$209,232	$1,211,739	1,613	1,631	566	608	484	16	1,078
Cambridge	18,013¼	4,206	902,490	151,804	1,054,294	1,132	1,172	415	459	286	14	990
Dresden	5,500½	21,943½	92,810	4,000	96,810	387	348	146	150	100	11	318
Easton	30,994¼	6,936½	1,366,962	223,330	1,590,292	1,482	1,530	559	614	397	19	976
Fort Ann	22,619¾	27,966¾	657,072	56,137	713,209	1,845	1,699	613	695	327	21	1,310
Fort Edward	12,791½	2,006	500,950	492,150	993,100	1,530	1,434	460	528	350	9	1,112
Granville	27,511¼	6,632	873,565	145,250	1,018,815	1,710	1,653	595	660	469	18	1,235
Greenwich	20,864½	5,349	1,204,115	489,625	1,693,740	1,959	1,929	745	790	473	15	1,442
Hampton	8,725	3,939	231,751	30,845	262,596	429	417	161	161	106	6	282
Hartford	21,978	4,852¾	735,967	82,484	818,451	1,132	1,064	396	416	345	15	807
Hebron	25,515	7,138	779,302	93,390	872,692	1,283	1,266	505	530	379	16	831
Jackson	17,981	4,880	768,170	66,550	834,720	906	864	323	335	242	10	587
Kingsbury	18,440	4,324½	785,406	105,755	891,161	1,736	1,628	552	626	464	16	1,329
Putnam	7,882	12,423	144,580	19,854	164,434	378	346	122	129	101	7	302
Salem	25,104½	7,976	830,385	308,314	1,138,699	1,461	1,464	506	561	410	19	1,016
White Creek	22,683¾	5,616	868,265	333,762	1,202,027	1,257	1,182	462	586	325	13	908
Whitehall	19,240	9,015	1,022,650	396,740	1,419,390	2,299	2,239	749	893	472	15	1,769
Total	333,030¾	143,554¾	12,766,947	3,209,222	15,976,169	22,539	21,866	7,875	8,741	5,730	240	16,292

Names of Towns.	Live Stock. Horses.	Live Stock. Working Oxen and Calves.	Live Stock. Cows.	Live Stock. Sheep.	Live Stock. Swine.	Agricultural Products. Bush. of Grain. Winter.	Agricultural Products. Bush. of Grain. Spring.	Tons of Hay.	Bushels of Potatoes.	Bushels of Apples.	Dairy Products. Pounds Butter.	Dairy Products. Pounds Cheese.	Domestic Cloths in yards.
Argyle	1,196	2,090	1,838	1,515	4,058	18,138	164,446	4,790¼	72,925	29,861	163,321	2,875	215
Cambridge	737	1,085	1,071	982	2,897	14,767	98,283½	4,251	35,211	11,126	109,204	7,420	1,238½
Dresden	150	5,192	300	117	212	802½	13,876¾	1,528	5,096	2,872	23,323	3,105	403
Easton	1,030	1,668	1,577	1,050	3,028	26,848	183,367	5,813½	46,905	14,501	137,864	42,176	1,535
Fort Ann	797	1,652	955	580	1,127	1,625½	63,907½	5,626	27,451	6,812	91,843	44,824	531
Fort Edward	443	947	667	384	933	2,287½	71,573	2,700	11,262	1,525	55,014	2,358	40
Granville	855	1,604	2,023	654	1,581	6,958	80,021	5,428½	107,972	24,697	106,160	334,767	416
Greenwich	913	1,478	1,345	862	2,690	18,928½	140,079	3,539	46,914	14,508	129,495	17,100	212
Hampton	168	602	516	162	330	1,602	22,950	2,169	10,955	5,844	36,210	35,632	
Hartford	697	1,229	1,067	607	1,479	4,284	79,686	4,326¾	87,857	21,422	104,554	18,109	269
Hebron	884	1,612	1,567	808	2,351	4,976	121,047	4,796	109,647	12,877	129,987	26,115	72
Jackson	634	1,052	1,049	966	2,816	14,281	112,987½	3,316	59,570	8,621	106,071	530	278
Kingsbury	634	1,057	971	463	1,184	1,230	63,337	4,717½	38,619	7,075	94,385	30,542	246
Putnam	240	944	468	123	214	1,113	18,507	2,037	4,964	4,652	47,490	440	651
Salem	888	1,606	1,322	1,027	2,963	6,208	134,890½	4,842½	61,934	10,578	143,020	4,635	45
White Creek	559	951	800	628	1,638	3,565½	68,403	4,591	25,994	6,656	67,351	36,150	55
Whitehall	882	1,552	1,153	397	804	2,739½	47,380½	5,409	14,009	5,476	79,846	27,713	92
Total	11,707	21,721	18,689	11,325	30,305	130,354	1,484,742¼	69,881	767,285	189,103	1,625,138	634,491	6,298½

Maj. Skene the younger, 50 tenants, and 12 negroes were taken prisoners. The sloop was sent down the lake to Col. Ethan Allen at Shoreham, Vt. In the cellar of the house was found the body of the wife of the elder Skene, which had been preserved many years to secure to the husband an annuity devised to her "while she remained above ground." The Americans buried the body in the rear of the house.

[1] When Ticonderoga was abandoned to Burgoyne, the public stores were embarked in 200 bateaux and sent up to this point under the convoy of 5 galleys. They were pursued and overtaken, 3 of the galleys were burned, and nearly all of the stores were destroyed. All the works at "*Skenesborough*" were blown up or burned, and the Americans retreated in disorder to Fort Ann. Burgoyne stayed in this place 3 weeks, while opening a road to Fort Ann. The remains of a battery and blockhouse built about this period, overlooking the lake, are still visible.

[2] A company, under the name of the "*Northern Inland Navigation Company*," had previously been formed for the purpose of uniting the waters of Lake Champlain with those of the Hudson. After expending large sums of money, the project was abandoned.

[3] The census reports 7 churches; 2 M. E., Bap., Cong., Presb., Prot. E., and R. C.

WAYNE COUNTY.

This county[1] was formed from Ontario and Seneca, April 11, 1823. It lies upon Lake Ontario, w. of the center of the State; is centrally distant 171 mi. from Albany, and contains 624 sq. mi. A series of bluffs 25 to 75 ft. high extends along the lake shore; and from their summits the surface rises in gradual slopes to the lake ridge, a distance of 4 to 5 mi. This ridge is 50 to 200 ft. wide on the top, and about 200 ft. above the lake. It declines toward the E., and upon the E. border of the co. it can scarcely be traced. The declivity of the ridge upon the s. is 8 to 20 ft.; and from its foot the surface gradually slopes upward to the surface of the limestone ridge, which extends E. and w. through the co. a little N. of the center and forms the watershed between Lake Ontario and Clyde River. The summit of this ridge is 140 feet above the lake ridge, 340 feet above the lake, and is about 3 mi. wide. It is highest upon the w. border of the co., and gradually declines toward the E.[2] From its southern edge the surface gradually declines to Clyde River and slopes upward from the river to the s. line of the co. South of the limestone ridge are numerous drift ridges extending N. and s. and from one-fourth to one and a half miles in length. The declivities are usually very steep, and the summits 40 to 100 ft. above the surrounding surface. They usually end in an abrupt declivity toward the N., but gradually decline toward the s. They are composed of clay, sand, and gravel, and seem to be deposits from great currents of water. Considerable marshy land extends along Clyde and Seneca Rivers, and also through the co. N. of the lake ridge.

Ganargwa, or Mud Creek, enters the s. w. corner of the co. from Ontario, flows in an irregular but generally easterly course to Lyons, where it unites with the Canandaigua Outlet and forms Clyde River,[3] which continues eastward to the E. bounds of the co., where it discharges its waters into Seneca River. These streams receive from the N. West Red Creek, East Red Creek, and Black Creek, and from the s. numerous small brooks. The streams flowing into Lake Ontario are Bear, Deer, Davis, Salmon, Thomas, Wolcott, and Big and Little Red Creeks; First, Second, and Third Creeks flow into Great Sodus Bay. The principal indentations upon Lake Ontario are Great Sodus, East, Port, and Blind Sodus Bays. Great Sodus Bay forms an excellent harbor. Crusoe Lake, in the s. E. corner, is the only considerable body of water. The streams, in their course through the drift deposits and lake ridge, have usually worn deep ravines.

The lowest rock in the co. is the Medina sandstone,[4] appearing upon the lake and in the ravines near it. It occupies a strip with an average width of 2 mi., widest at the w. Next above this is the Clinton group of limestone and shales, extending to the foot of the limestone ridge. Next above is the Niagara limestone, forming the summit ridge and occupying a strip about 3 mi. in width. South of this is the Onondaga salt group of red and green shales and gypsum, extending to the s. border and occupying nearly one-half of the co. The rocks are mostly covered by thick deposits of drift, and are only exposed in the ravines of the streams. Shells, marl, and muck are found in large quantities in the marshy regions. Weak brine and sulphur springs are found in various localities in the Medina sandstone and the red shales of the Onondaga salt group.

The soil derived from the drift deposits is generally a sandy or gravelly loam, with an occasional intermixture of clay. The soil along the lake shore, principally derived from the disintegration of Medina sandstone, is a reddish, sandy loam. At the foot of the mountain ridge, both N. and s., is a strip of very productive clay loam. In the valley of Clyde River the soil is principally a gravelly loam and alluvium. The marsh lands, when drained, are covered deep with a rich vegetable mold, which develops into the most fertile soil in the co.

Agriculture forms the leading pursuit. The branches, in the order of importance, are grain raising, stock growing, dairying, and wool growing. Fruit is extensively cultivated, and is rapidly

---

[1] Named in honor of Gen. Anthony Wayne.

[2] This peculiar formation is accounted for by the theory that the low regions through the N. and central parts of the co. were once covered by the waters of the lake, and that the limestone ridge was a long bar or point extending into the lake from the w.

[3] Named by Wm. McNab, a Scotchman. At an early day it was navigable as far as Lyons, and was a link in the great chain of Western travel.

[4] This stone is extensively quarried for building stone. It is soft when first taken from the quarry, but hardens upon exposure to the atmosphere.

becoming one of the most important agricultural products. Few counties in the State surpass this in the quality or quantity of apples and peaches annually produced. A strip of land bordering upon Lake Ontario, and extending from Niagara River to the Oswego, seems peculiarly adapted to the cultivation of apples and peaches, and is rapidly becoming one of the most important fruit-growing regions in the State. In Wayne co. $25,000 worth of dried fruit is annually prepared. Peppermint and tobacco are raised along the valley of Mud Creek.

The county seat is located at the village of Lyons, near the center of the co. The courthouse is a fine cut stone building, fronting Church St. It has an Ionic portico, and is surmounted by a large dome.[1] The jail is a commodious stone building, in the w. part of the village. It contains rooms for the jailer's residence, and is one of the best arranged and conducted establishments of the kind in the State. The county clerk's office is a fireproof building, fronting Pearl St., a little s. of the courthouse. The poorhouse is situated upon a farm of 130 acres 1½ mi. w. of the court-house. The average number of inmates is 67, supported at a weekly cost of $1.55 each. A school is taught throughout the year. The farm yields a revenue of $1,400. The buildings are insufficient for the accommodation of the inmates; but the institution seems to be well arranged and well kept.

Six weekly newspapers are now published in the co.[2]

The Erie Canal extends through the s. tier of towns; and along its course are the most populous and thriving villages of the co.[3] The direct branch of the N. Y. Central R. R. between Syracuse and Rochester extends, along the course of the canal, through Savannah, Galen, Lyons,

[1] The first courthouse was a brick edifice, erected soon after the organization of the co. It was superseded, in 1854-55, by the present structure, built of Lockport limestone. The building committee of the present courthouse were John Adams, Stephen Marshall, and F. B. Cornwell. The first officers of the co. were John S. Talmadge, *First Judge;* Hugh Jameson, *Sheriff;* Wm. H. Adams, *District Attorney;* Isaiah J. Richardson, *Co. Clerk;* and John S. Talmadge, *Surrogate.*

[2] *The Palmyra Register,* the first paper published in the co., was commenced Nov. 26, 1817, by Timothy C. Strong. It was continued under various titles until 1823, when it was published as
The Western Farmer and Canal Advocate, and passed into the hands of Pomeroy Tucker, who changed its name to
The Wayne Sentinel, under which title it is now published by Wm. N. Cole.
The Lyons Republican was commenced Aug. 3, 1821, by Geo. Lewis. It was discontinued in Feb. 1822.
The Lyons Advertiser was commenced May 31, 1822, by Hiram T. Day. It underwent various changes in name and publishers. It was published as
The Wayne County Gazette, by Ephraim J. Whitney; as
The Lyons Argus, by E. J. & W. W. Whitney;
The Lyons Gazette, by Barker & Chapman;
The Wayne Co. Patriot, and as
The Western Argus, by Chapman & Chapin and Ashley & Co.; and as
The Western Argus, by Charles Poucher. In 1841 it was changed to
The Lyons Republican, and was published by —— Russell from 1849 to 1853, when it was sold to Wm. Van Camp, and in 1855 or '56 it was merged in The Wayne Democratic Press.
The Palmyra Freeman was commenced March 11, 1828, by D. D. Stephenson. It soon after passed into the hands of J. A. Hadley, who removed the press to Lyons and changed the name to
The Countryman. Myron Holley became connected with it as associate editor. In 1831 it was suspended for a time, and afterward resumed as
The Lyons American, by Myron Holley. In 1835 it was published by Wm. H. Childs. In 1836 it was removed to Clyde and published as
The Clyde Gazette, by Dennis Cord, until 1838.
The Reflector, mo., was commenced at Palmyra in 1828 by O. Dogberry, jr. It was discontinued in 1830.
The Newark Republican was commenced at Newark in Nov. 1829, by Jeremiah O. Balch. It was discontinued in 1831.
The Clyde Standard was commenced about 6 mo. in 1830 by E. P. Moon.
The Western Spectator and Wayne Advertiser was commenced at Palmyra Jan. 9, 1830, by Luther Howard and Erastus Shepard. In 1831 its name was changed to
The Spectator and Anti-Masonic Star. It was removed to Rochester the same year and merged in The Anti-Masonic Enquirer.
The Palmyra Whig was commenced in Feb. 1838, by Wm. N. and Sam'l Cole. It was removed to Lyons by Wm. N. Cole, and its name changed to
The Wayne County Whig. In the fall of 1850 it passed into the hands of Williams & Gavitt. In the spring of 1852 they sold it to Silas A. Andrews, who continued it a few months and sold it to Wm. Van Marter; and in

Nov. of the same year it passed into the hands of Rodney L. Adams. In Sept. 1856, its name was changed to
The Lyons Republican; and April 30, 1859, Mr. Adams sold it to W. T. Tinsley & Co., its present publishers.
The Wayne Standard was commenced at Newark in June, 1838, by David M. Keeler. In Aug. 1839, it was sold to Gen. Barney T. Partridge, J. P. Bartle, and S. Culver, who changed its name to
The New Ægis, Stephen Culver, editor. In Jan. 1840, it was sold to —— Norton, and discontinued in May following. In July following it was revived as
The Wayne Standard, by D. M. Keeler, and published until 1843, when it passed into the hands of H. L. Winants, and in about 1 year was discontinued It was revived soon after, as
The Newark Courier, by David Fairfield. It was successively published by Wm. K. Creague and B. F. Jones as
The Newark Journal; and in 1854 by G. D. A. Bridgman, who changed its name to
The Newark Whig. In Sept. 1856, it passed into the hands of C. F. White, who changed its name to
The Newark Weekly Courier, and still continues its publication.
The Palmyra Courier was commenced May 28, 1843, by Frederic Morley. It passed into the hands of J. C. Bennett, who changed its name to
The Palmyra Democrat. It was published again as
The Palmyra Courier, by —— Benedict, from about 1851 to '54. Mr. Benedict sold it to —— Beebe, and, in a short time afterward it passed into the hands of A. E. Averill, who changed its name to
The Palmyra American, and subsequently again to
The Palmyra Courier, under which name Mr. Averill still continues its publication.
The Clyde Eagle was commenced in 1844 by B. Frazee. It was successively published by —— Dryer, Stephen Salisbury, and in 1847 by Rev. Chas. G. Acly and William Tompkins, who changed its name to
The Clyde Telegraph. It afterward passed into the hands of Rev. W. W. Storiker, and soon after to Wm. R. Fowle, and in a short time it was discontinued.
The Clyde Industrial Times was commenced in Feb. 1850, by Payn & Smith. It soon passed into the hands of Jos. A. Payn. Its name was changed in 1851 to
The Clyde Weekly Times, under which title it is now published, by Joseph A. Payn.
The Northern Methodist Protestant was published by an association at Clyde in 1849; Rev. W. W. Storiker, editor.
The Wayne Banner was published at Wolcott in 1850 by John McIntyre, and was removed to Clyde, and merged in The Industrial Times on the first issue of the latter paper.
The Farming Mirror was commenced at Lyons in July, 1853, by R. L. Adams & Co., and was published 1 year.
The Wayne Democratic Press was commenced at Palmyra in 1855. It was removed to Lyons the same year, and is now published by Wm. Van Camp.

[3] The enlarged canal crosses Seneca River on the E. border of the co., on an aqueduct built upon 31 arches of 22 feet span each. It crosses Mud Creek, a little w. of Lyons, upon an aqueduct of 5 arches, and again crosses the same stream, N. of Palmyra, upon an aqueduct of 3 arches.

44

Arcadia, Palmyra, and Macedon. A ship canal[1] route and a R. R. route[2] have,been surveyed, connecting the Erie Canal and Central R. R. with Lake Ontario.

The western 9 towns in this co. belonged to the Pulteney Estate; the E. part, including Savannah, Galen, and portions of Wolcott and Butler, constituted a portion of the Military Tract. The intermediate portion, except the S. 3 tiers of lots in Rose, were compensation lands granted to the Pulteney Estate for the gore between the old and new pre-emption lines. The earliest white inhabitants were hunters and trappers. The first permanent settlements were made in 1789, at Palmyra, under the auspices of General John Swift, agent of a company of settlers from Conn.; and at Lyons, under Charles Williamson, agent for the Pulteney Estate.[3] From 1790 to 1794, colonies came in from R. I., Long Island, and Maryland.[4] The settlements did not progress with great rapidity for several years, owing to the diseases which prevailed. The fear of Indian hostilities and of British invasion during the War of 1812 greatly retarded settlement. On the return of peace, settlers began to arrive in considerable numbers, principally from New England and Eastern N. Y. The completion of the Erie Canal gave a new impulse to immigration; and in a few years the flourishing villages of Lyons, Clyde, Palmyra, and Newark were built up along its course. The N. Y. Central R. R., built through the co. in 1852–53, greatly benefitted the co. and enhanced the value of the lands.

The most notable of the later incidents in the co. have been the rise of Mormonism in Palmyra,[5] and the commencement of spiritual rappings in Arcadia.[6]

ARCADIA—was formed from Lyons, Feb. 15, 1825. It lies on the S. border of the co., a little W. of the center. Its surface is a rolling region, broken by drift ridges. Mud Creek flows E. through the town, N. of the center, and receives several small streams as tributaries. The soil is a sandy, gravelly loam, mixed with clay on the hills. Gypsum is found in the S. W., and marl in the center. **Newark,** (p. v.,) including **Arcadia,** (p. v.,) in the S. part, on the canal, was incorp. July 21, 1853, as Newark. It contains 7 churches, a bank, flouring mill, tannery, 3 furnaces, and several manufactories. It is a flourishing canal village and a station upon the N. Y. C. R. R. Pop. 2,042. **Fairville,** (p. v.,) about 5 mi. N., contains 1 church, a tannery, a limited amount of manufactures, and 159 inhabitants. **Marbletown,** near the S. E. corner, contains a church and 10 houses. **Jessups Corners** and **Hydeville** are hamlets. Settlement was commenced in 1791, by Joseph Winters and B. Franklin.[7] The first church (M. E.) was organized in 1805. J. Wesley Benton was the first settled minister, in 1806.[8] A family named Fox, residing at Hydesville, in Arcadia, first heard the mysterious sounds known as the "rappings" on the night of March 31, 1849. Investigations were made in regard to the origin of the raps, but nothing definite was settled upon. The family soon after removed to Rochester, the "raps" accompanying them; and hence the name "Rochester Rappings." A series of investigations was instituted, and the matter became public, some claiming for it a spiritual origin, but the great majority pronouncing it a humbug or delusion. From this source modern spiritualism originated.

BUTLER—was formed from Wolcott, Feb. 26, 1826. It is the center town on the E. border of the co. Its surface is diversified, level in the S. E. and rising into ridges in the N. W. The highest point is Armstrong Hill. The principal stream is Wolcott Creek, which rises in the N. E. and, flowing in a circuitous course, leaves the town near the N. W. corner. The soil in the valleys is a gravelly loam, and on the hills it is generally clay, with a tenacious subsoil. Lime is manufactured in the N. part to a limited extent. **South Butler,** (p. v.,) on the S. line, contains 5 churches, a classical school, several manufactories, and about 400 inhabitants. **West Butler** (p. o.) contains 10 houses; **Westbury,** (p. v.,) in the N. E. corner, partly in the town of Victory,

---

1 In 1827, a charter was obtained for building a ship canal from the Erie Canal, at Montezuma, to Great Sodus Bay. Surveys were made, but no work was ever done. A new charter was obtained by John Greig, of Canandaigua, in 1836; and another by Gen. Wm. H. Adams, in 1851. The route named in the last charter is from Sodus Bay to the Erie Canal, a little W. of Clyde. Some work has been done on parts of this route.

2 The Sodus Point & Southern R. R. was incorp. in April,1852. The road was to extend from Sodus Bay to Newark. The route has been surveyed, but no work has been done. A survey has also been made for a R. R. route from Clyde to Sodus Bay.

3 Mr. Williamson built roads from Palmyra and Lyons to Sodus Point; upon these the early settlers mostly located. He also laid out a city upon Sodus Bay, which has not yet been built.

4 The Maryland settlers brought with them several slaves; but it was soon found that slave labor was unprofitable.

5 See p. 693.

6 See Arcadia.

7 Gilbert Howell and Paul Reese came in in 1795; Samuel Soverhill in 1798; Humphrey Sherman, Reuben Starks, and John Miller, from Long Island, in 1800; and Ebenezer Smith soon after. The Lusks came in from Columbia co. in 1806. Jacob, Philip, and Isaac Lusk purchased 1 sq. mi., which is now occupied by the village of Newark. Caleb Tibbetts, Stephen Aldridge, Henry Croags, and Cooper Culver settled in 1807; and Dr. A. Hyde, in 1810. The first death was that of a child of B. Franklin, in 1792; the first marriage, that of —— Hess and Amy Tibbetts, in 1798. Stephen Aldridge kept the first inn, and J. P. Bartlett the first store.

8 There are 10 churches in town; 2 Meth. Prot., M. E., Presb., Prot. E., Union, Ref. Prot. D., Bap., R. C., and Christian.

(Cayuga co.,) 1 church and 20 houses. **Butler Center** is a hamlet. The first settlement was commenced in 1802.[1] The first settled minister was —— Mills.[2] Rev. Antoinette L. Brown, the first woman ever regularly ordained in the State, was settled for several years over the Cong. Church at South Butler.

GALEN[3]—was formed from Junius, (Seneca co.,) Feb. 14, 1812. Savannah was taken off in 1824. It lies on the s. border of the co., E. of the center. Its surface is hilly in the E., but more level in the w. In the s. w. is a large tract of swamp land. Clyde River[4] flows through the town from w. to E. in a circuitous course. The soil is a rich, sandy and gravelly loam. **Clyde,**[5] (p. v.,) near the center, on Clyde River, was incorp. May 2, 1835. The canal passes through the village; it is also a station on the N. Y. C. R. R. It contains 6 churches, a high school,[6] 2 banks, a newspaper office, a glass factory, and several other manufactories.[7] Pop. 1,856. **Marengo,** (p. v.,) in the s. part, contains a church and 20 houses; **Lock Berlin,** (p. v.,) in the w. part, on the canal, a church and 30 houses. **Angells Corners,** in the s. E., and **Meadville,** in the E., are hamlets. The first settlement was commenced by Laomi Bedell, in 1800.[8] The first church (Presb.) was organized July 8, 1814.[9] Borings for salt water in the vicinity of Clyde have been made, but without success. One of the wells emitted inflammable gas: the well was soon filled up.

HURON—was formed from Wolcott, as "*Port Bay,*" Feb. 25, 1826. Its name was changed March 17, 1834. It lies on Lake Ontario, E. of the center of the co. A part of Great Sodus Bay lies in the N. w. corner. East Bay, in the N., and a part of Port Bay, in the N. E., extend into the town. Its surface is rolling, with a general northern inclination. In the w. and N. w., near Great Sodus Bay, are several tracts of swamp lands. The lake shore rises in a series of bluffs, the highest of which—Chimney Bluff—is 175 ft. above the lake, and Bay Bluff 120 ft. Several small streams flow N. through the town, the principal of which is Mudge Creek, which empties into East Bay. The soil is a sandy and gravelly loam, intermixed with clay in the s. **North Huron** (p. v.) contains 2 churches, a saw and grist mill, and 40 houses; **South Huron** (Huron p. o.) 1 church, a townhouse, and 20 houses. **Port Glasgow** (p. o.) is a hamlet, at the head of sloop navigation on Great Sodus Bay. The first settlement was commenced by Peregrine Fitzhugh and Wm. Helmus, and some other families from Md., in 1796.[10] The first church (Presb.) was organized in 1813.[11]

LYONS—was formed from Sodus, March 1, 1811. Arcadia was taken off in 1825. It lies on the s. border of the co., a little E. of the center. Its surface is a moderately rolling region, broken by sand ridges. The Canandaigua Outlet from the s., and Mud Creek from the w., join in the s. part and form Clyde River. The soil is a sandy and gravelly loam, with marl upon the creek bottom lands. **Lyons,** (p. v.,) on the canal, at the junction of Canandaigua Outlet and Mud Creek, was incorp. April 18, 1854. It contains the co. buildings, 7 churches, 2 banks, 2 newspaper offices, a union school,[12] and several manufactories;[13] and it is an important R. R. station. Pop. 3,221. **Alloway,** (p. v.,) in the s. part, on Canandaigua Outlet, contains a church, a gristmill, and 30 houses. The first settlement was commenced in 1789, by Nicholas and Wm. Stansell and John Featherly.[14] They settled, with their families, (12 persons in all,) a half mile s. of the

1 John Granby and —— Wellman settled near the center, as early as 1803; Erastus Hubbard and Abijah Moore, in 1805; Capt. Willis, Wm. Hallett, Henry Bunnel, Aaron Hoppin, Mrs. Bunce, and Morris Craw, previous to 1807; and Seth Craw and Roger Olmsted, in 1808. The first birth was a child of —— Winans; the first death was that of Jedediah Wheeler, in April, 1811. —— Vieles built the first sawmill, at the center.
2 There are 7 churches in town; 2 M. E., 2 Christian, Bap., Cong., and 2d Adv.
3 This was Township No. 27 of the Military Tract, and received its name from having been appropriated to the Medical Department.
4 Named by Wm. McNab, agent of the Hornby Estate, Geneva.
5 This location was originally called "*Block House,*" from a blockhouse built here by Indian traders at an early day. It was used during the Revolution by tories as a "station" in smuggling goods from Canada *via* Sodus Bay. It was burned previous to 1800. The village was first called "*Lauraville,*" from Henrietta Laura, Countess of Bath, daughter and heiress of Sir Wm. Pulteney. Its name was changed to Clyde in 1818.
6 It is a union school, formed from Districts 14 and 17. Incorp. April 24, 1834, with special privileges. This was one of the earliest union schools in Western New York. The school employs 6 teachers.
7 2 large distilleries, 2 steam flouring mills, 2 steam sawmills, 2 furnaces and shops for manufacturing agricultural implements, a large cooperage, 1 brewery, 2 malt houses, and a tannery.
8 Among the other early settlers were Nicholas King, David Godfrey, and Isaac Mills, with their families, from Orange co., N. Y., on Lot 70, in the s. w. part of the town, in 1801; —— Creagher, from Md., Elias Austin, —— Payne, and Capt. John

Sherman, in 1804. The first birth was that of Isaac Godfrey, in Feb. 1802; the first death, that of David Godfrey, accidentally killed, Oct. 13, 1801. The first marriage was that of Jabez Reynolds and Polly Mills, in 1805. James B. West kept the first store; Maj. Fred. A. De Zenz built the first saw and grist mill, in 1818.
9 There are 9 churches in town; 2 M. E., 2 Bap., Presb., Prot. E., Germ. Meth., Friends, and R. C.
10 Among the other early settlers were Dr. Zenas Hyde, —— Knox, and several families from Mass. and Conn., in 1807; Josiah Upson, in 1808, and Norman Sheldon, in 1810. The first birth was that of a child of Dr. Hyde; and the first death, that of Mrs. Hale, in 1809. Gardiner Mudge taught the first school, in 1812; Norman Sheldon kept the first inn, in 1810; James Mudge kept the first store; and Elihu Spencer built the first saw and grist mill, in 1809.
11 There are 3 churches in town; M. E., Meth. Prot., and Presb.
12 The Lyons Union School was among the first of the kind established in the State. It employs 12 teachers and has 800 to 900 pupils.
13 Among these are an extensive manufactory of essential oils, (principally peppermint,) a furnace, machine, and agricultural implement shop, a pottery, brewery, tannery, tile manufactory, brickyard, fanning mill factory, and a manufactory of saddle trees. About 10,000 lbs. of peppermint oil are produced annually in the co.,—⅓ of the whole amount in the U. S.—*Trans. Ag. Soc.* 1855, p. 657.
14 John Biggs, Richard Jones, Geo. Carr, Wm. Gibbs, and John Perrine were early settlers. The first marriage was that of Jas.

present village of Lyons. They were piloted up the Mohawk, (where they had previously settled,) and by the usual water route, by Wemple, an Indian trader. Charles Williamson, agent of the Pulteney Estate, commenced a settlement at Lyons Village in 1794, through Charles Cameron, his local agent. Jas. Otto came in 1796. In 1798, Judge Evert Van Winkle and and 40 others came in, from N. J. and Md.; and in 1801, Judge Daniel Dorsey and family, from Md. Judge Dorsey had previously purchased of Mr. Williamson nearly 1,000 acres in the immediate vicinity of the village. Rev. John Cole (Meth.) was the first local preacher.[1]

MACEDON—was formed from Palmyra, Jan. 29, 1823. It is the s. w. corner town of the co. Its surface is rolling and irregular. The valley of Mud Creek extends e. through the s. part. It is drained by Mud and Red Creeks and their tributaries. The soil is a clay and gravelly loam upon a limestone formation. **Macedon,** (p. v.,) a canal village, was incorp. Nov. 1856. It contains 2 churches, a saw and grist mill, furnace, and machine shop, and about 500 inhabitants. **Macedon Center** (p. v.) is incorp., and contains 3 churches, the Macedon Academy, and 20 houses. The first settlement was made as early as 1789, by Webb Harwood and Ebenezer Reed.[2] The first church (Bap.) was organized in 1800.[3]

MARION—was formed from Williamson, as "*Winchester*," April 18, 1825. Its name was changed April 15, 1826. It is an interior town, lying w. of the center of the co. Its surface is broken by sandy hills and gravelly ridges; the Niagara limestone crops out in the n. part. It is drained by East Red Creek, which flows s. into Mud Creek. The soil is a gravelly, calcareous loam, and drift. Limestone is quarried in the n. part, for building purposes and public works. Near Marion Village is a sulphur spring. **Marion,** (p. v.,) in the s. part, contains 4 churches, the Marion Collegiate Institute, a furnace and machine shop, a fanning mill factory, and 390 inhabitants. The first settlement was commenced in 1796, by Daniel Lovell.[4] The first church (Presb.) was organized Nov. 1, 1808.[5]

ONTARIO—was formed from Williamson, as "*Freetown*," March 27, 1807. Its name was changed Feb. 12, 1808. Walworth was taken off in 1829. It is the n. w. corner town of the co., Lake Ontario forming its n. boundary. Its surface is mostly level, with a general inclination toward the lake. It is drained by several streams running n. to the lake, the principal of which are Bear, Deer, and Davis Creeks. The soil is a sandy, gravelly loam, with drift and muck n. of the ridge. Between the lake shore and the ridge road are extensive marshes, heavily timbered. Iron ore, in the form of red oxid, is found in large quantities in the Clinton group, extending e. and w. through the center of the town. Salt was formerly manufactured to some extent. **Ontario,** (p. v.,) in the s. e. part, contains a church, steam sawmill, furnace, and 25 houses; **Ontario Center,** 2 mi. w., a church and 20 houses; **Furnace Village,** near the center, a furnace[6] and 16 houses. **New Boston,** on the lake shore, is a hamlet. The first settlement was commenced by Freeman Hopkins, from Mass., in 1806.[7] The first church (Bap.) was organized in 1811,[8] by Elder Lyon.

PALMYRA—was formed in Jan. 1789. Macedon was taken off in 1823. It lies on the s. border of the co., w. of the center. Its surface is undulating. Mud Creek flows e. through the town, s. of the center. Its tributaries are East and West Red Creeks and several small streams. The soil is a calcareous loam, with marl on the creek bottoms, and drift, sand, and gravel on the hills. **Palmyra,** (p. v.,) in the s. w. part, was incorp. April 9, 1819. It is an important canal village, and is a station on the N. Y. C. R. R. It contains 5 churches, the Palmyra Union School,[9]

Otto and a daughter of Capt. John Dunn. John Biggs kept the first inn, in 1801; Judge Daniel Dorsey, the first store; Henry Tower, agent of Mr. Williamson, built the first mills, at Alloway, in 1796; and Dorsey & Milton, the first carding and cloth dressing mill, in 1807.

[1] There are 8 churches in town; 2 M. E., Presb., Prot. E., Bap., Evan. Luth., Germ. Evan. Ref., and R. C.

[2] Israel Delano, from Mass., and David Comstock, settled in the n. part, and Darius Comstock and Jerome Smith in the central part, in 1790. Jacob Gannett, John Gibson, Barnabas Brown, Abner Hill, Adam Kingman, —— Spear, Jonathan Warren, Constant Southard, —— Reid, Packard Barney, and Philip Woods, from Mass., in 1791. A number of Friends came in 1800 from Penn. and Mass. The first child born was Enoch Gannett, in 1791; the first death was that of David White. Barnabas Reed taught the first school; Wm. Porter kept the first inn, and Jacob Gannett built the first mill.

[3] There are 5 churches in town; 2 Friends, Bap., M. E., and R. C.

[4] —— Blakesley and Ezra Phelps settled in 1796, David and Isaac Sweezy in 1797, and Wm. B. Cogswell, from R. I., in March, 1798. The first birth was in the family of David Lovell; the first

death, that of —— Phelps, in 1800. Widow Stiles kept the first inn, in 1799; and —— —— built the first gristmill, in 1801.

[5] There are 4 churches in town; Cong., M. E., Bap., and Christian.

[6] The "Wayne Co. Iron Co." manufacture about 6 tons of pig iron per day, from ore dug in town.

[7] Among the early settlers were Peter Thatcher and Harry Leavins, who settled on the lake shore, and Noah Fuller, in 1809; Willard Church, Isaac Simmons, John Case, Wm. Middleton, Jared Putnam, David Jennings, and Amos Thayer, from Conn., in 1810. In the s. part settlement commenced in 1808. Daniel Inman settled at the Corners in 1809; John Edmonds, Saml. Sabin, Abraham Smith, Wm. Billings, Lewis Janes, and Geo. Sawyer, near the same place, soon after. Alfred Town, Nathaniel Grant, and Wm. Greenwood located at West Corners. The first child born was Melissa Hopkins, May 7, 1806. Daniel Inman kept the first inn, in 1811, and Freeman Hopkins built the first sawmill.

[8] There are 4 churches in town; 2 M. E., Presb., and Bap.

[9] Incorp. in 1848. Employs 10 teachers and averages about 500 pupils.

a bank, 2 printing offices, and a number of manufactories.[1] Pop. 2,310. **East Palmyra,** (p. v.,) a canal and R. R. station, in the E. part, contains 2 churches, a gristmill, and 20 houses. The first settlement was made by John Swift, in 1789 or '90.[2] In the winter of 1788–89, John Swift and Col. John Jenkins purchased Tp. 12, R. 2, now Palmyra, and commenced the survey of it in March. During the summer, John Swift moved into the town, and erected a log house and storehouse a little N. of the lower end of Main St., Palmyra. Before the close of the year 1789, Webb Harwood and family, Noah Porter, Jonathan Warner, and Bennett Bates, from Mass., came in: Mr. Harwood settled a little w. of the village. David White and family came in in 1790. The first church (Presb.) was formed in 1797 ; Rev. Eleazur Fairbanks was the first pastor.[3] Joseph Smith, the father of the prophet, settled a little s. of Palmyra Village in 1819. The plates of the Mormon Bible were said to have been dug up on a hillside in Manchester, Ontario co., a little s. of the Palmyra line. The Smiths were money diggers, and had previously been digging in this locality for gold. The book was printed at the office of the Wayne Sentinel, Martin Harris, a convert, mortgaging his farm to defray the expense.

ROSE[4]—was formed from Wolcott, Feb. 5, 1826. It lies in the interior, of the co., E. of the center. Its surface is mostly undulating or level, with drift ridges in the s. E. Several small tracts of swamp land lie in different parts of the town. The streams are small; Mudge, Sherman, and Thomas Creeks are the principal. The soil is a gravelly loam, intermixed with clay on the elevations and with muck on the lowlands. The highest point is 140 ft. above Lake Ontario. Limestone approaches the surface in the N. part, and has been quarried to some extent for lime and for building purposes. **Rose Valley,** (Rose p. o.,) near the center, contains 3 churches, a steam sawmill, and tannery. Pop. 218. **Wayne Center,** in the w. part, contains 20 houses ; **Glenmark Falls,**[5] in the N. part, contains 2 gristmills, 2 sawmills, and 10 dwellings. The first settlement was made in 1805, by Caleb Melvin and Alpheus Harman.[6] The first church (M. E.) was organized in 1824.[7]

SAVANNAH[8]—was formed from Galen, Nov. 24, 1824. It is the s. E. corner town of the co. Its surface is broken by drift ridges in the N., and is low and marshy in the s. ; about one-third of the s. part is a woodland marsh, known as Crusoe Island. Seneca River forms the s. part of the E. boundary. Crusoe Lake is a small, shallow body of water near the center ; its outlet, Crusoe Creek, flows into Seneca River. The soil in the N. is a sandy and gravelly loam, and in the s. it is principally composed of muck and shell marl.[9] A tract of about 1,900 acres in the s. E. part is an open marsh, producing coarse grass. **Savannah,** (p. v.,) near the center, is a station upon the N. Y. C. R. R., and contains 20 houses. The first settlement was made by Elias Converse and Joseph Mozier, in 1812.[10] The first preacher was Rev. —— Wiers, (Bap.) There is no church in town.

SODUS[11]—was formed in Jan. 1789. Williamson was taken off in 1802, and Lyons in 1811. It is the central town on the N. border of the co., and is bounded N. by Lake Ontario. A part of Great Sodus Bay lies in the N. E. corner. Its surface in the N. part is mostly level, with a gentle inclination toward the lake. A ridge 140 to 190 ft. higher than the surface of the lake passes through near the center ; and s. of this the surface is broken by several ridges extending N. and s. The lake shore varies in height from a low swamp to bluffs 70 ft. high. Second and Salmon Creeks are the principal streams. The soil in the N. part is a clay and sandy loam, and in the s. gravelly loam. The manufacture of lime is extensively carried on in the s. part ; and red sandstone is quarried in the s. w. Red oxid of iron (argillaceous ore) is found 2 mi. w. of Sodus Point. Salt was manufactured in 1831

---

[1] A machine shop and manufactory of agricultural implements, 2 furnaces, a scale manufactory, distillery, tobacco manufactory, and gas works. About 2 mi. N. E. of the village is an extensive rope and cordage manufactory.

[2] The settlers that followed in 1790–91–92, as near as can be ascertained, were Lemuel Spear, David Jackways, James Galloway, Jonathan Willet, the Mattisons, Gideon Durfee, sr., and his sons, —Gideon, Edward, Job, Pardon, Stephen, and Lemuel,—Isaac Springer. Wm., James, and Thos. Rogers, John Russell, Nathan Harris, David Wilcox, Joel Foster, Abraham Foster, Elias Reeves, and Luther Sanford. In 1791 "The Long Island Co.," through Elias Reeves, A. Foster, Wm. Hopkins, and Luther Sanford, purchased 5,500 acres near East Palmyra, at 25cts. per acre ; and the first wheat harvested sold for 25cts. per bushel. The first birth was that of a child of Webb Harwood, in 1790 ; the first marriage, that of Wm. Wilcox and Ruth Durfee ; and the first death, that of David White. Ira Selby taught the first school, in 1793. Dr. Azel Ensworth kept the first inn, and Samuel Colt the first store, at an early day. Jonah Howell built the first mill, 1 mi. E. of the village.

[3] The census reports 10 churches in town ; 2 Presb., 2 M. E., Prot. E., Bap., Christian, Cong., Friends, and R. C.

[4] Named from Robert L. Rose, Esq., of Geneva.

[5] There is a fall at this place, on Thomas Creek, of 22 ft.

[6] Among the other early settlers were Milton Salisbury, —— Crafts, John Sherman, Joel Bishop, sr., Lott Stuart, Aaron Shepard, Chas. Thomas, —— Pomeroy, and —— Bannister. The first birth was that of a child of Mr. Salisbury, in 1812 ; the first marriage, that of Hosea Gillett and Hannah Burnham, in Jan. 1813 ; and the first death, a child of Harvey Gillett, in 1812. Sally Bishop taught the first school, in 1813 ; and Oliver Wetmore built the first sawmill, in 1812.

[7] There are 3 churches in town ; Presb., M. E., and Bap.

[8] Named from the surface in the s. part.

[9] The Galen Salt Works of an early period were in this town

[10] Among the early settlers were Michael Weatherwax, Benj. Seeley, Garret Burnham, Henry Taylor, Chauncey Yale, John Green, Abner and Ezra Rockway, Henry Myers, David Cushman, Smith Ward, and Sampson McBane, mostly from Eastern N. Y. The first marriage was that of Geo. Fredenburgh and Sally Converse ; the first birth was that of a child of Geo. Fredenburgh ; and the first death, that of —— Sweetman. Lorin Brown taught the first school, in 1817.

[11] Called by the Indians "Assorodus," meaning "silvery water."

and '32. **Sodus** (p. v.) contains 3 churches, the Sodus Academy, and about 300 inhabitants. **Sodus Point,** (p. v.,) on the lake, w. of the entrance to the bay, is a U. S. port of entry in the Genesee District. It has a lighthouse, a church, a steam sawmill, and about 200 inhabitants. **Sodus Center** (p. v.) contains a church, foundery, carding mill, grist and saw mill, and 40 houses; **Alton** (p. v.) a church and 30 houses; **South Sodus** (p. v.) a church and 30 houses; and **Joy** (p. v.) a church, shingle factory, and 30 houses. The first settlement was made in 1794, under the auspices of Charles Williamson, agent of the Pulteney Estate.[1] Mr. Williamson caused a road to be cut through from Palmyra to Sodus Point in the spring of 1794. During the summer the town was surveyed, an extensive city plan laid out between Salmon Creek and the Point, and within two years mills were erected on Salmon Creek. A tavern was built at an expense of $5,000, a pleasure yacht was placed upon the bay; and in roads, surveys, buildings, &c., over $20,000 was expended. Thos. Little and —— Moffat were the local agents of Mr. Williamson. Of all those connected with these premature improvements, but few remained after they were completed. Elijah Brown was an early settler, 4 mi. w. of the Point, and Amos Richards, 7 mi. w. Ammi Ellsworth came from Conn. in 1801, and settled near the Point. Dr. Wm. Nixon Loomis settled at the Point. He built mills and a forge. A daughter of his is Mrs. Elizabeth Ellet, author of the "Women of the Revolution," and "Domestic History of the Revolution." Col. Peregrine Fitzhugh came from Md. in 1803, with his family and slaves,—over 40 persons in all. Dr. Thos. G. Lawson, an Englishman, settled 1 mi. from the Point, in 1803. After expending considerable money in attempting to form a settlement, he abandoned the enterprise in 1805. In 1799, besides those already mentioned, there were 25 families in town on roads leading to Palmyra and Lyons. The first church (Bap.) was organized in 1805; Elder Seba Norton was the first settled minister.[2]

WALWORTH[3]—was formed from Ontario, April 20, 1829. It is the central town on the w. border of the co. Its surface is a high, rolling upland, the ridges being the most elevated land in the co. The Niagara limestone crops out in the N. part, marking its course by a hard, stony surface some rods in width. It is drained N. by several small streams, and s. E. by tributaries of Red Creek. The soil is a rich, sandy loam. **Walworth,** (p. v.,) near the s. E. corner, contains 3 churches, the Walworth Academy, and 230 inhabitants. In the immediate vicinity is an extensive nursery.[4] **West Walworth,** (p. v.,) in the s. w. part, contains a church and 115 inhabitants. The first settlement was begun about 1800.[5] The first church (M. E.) was organized previous to 1809.[6]

WILLIAMSON[7]—was formed from Sodus, Feb. 20, 1802. Ontario was taken off in 1807, and Marion in 1825. It lies on the N. border of the co., w. of the center, Lake Ontario forming its N. boundary. Its surface is level in the N., with a gentle inclination toward the lake. In the s. it rises into low ridges. It is drained by a few small streams that flow N. into Lake Ontario. The soil is a sandy, gravelly loam, mixed with clay near the lake shore. **Pultney-ville,**[8] (p. v.,) on the lake shore, a U. S. port of entry in the Genesee District, contains a church, gristmills, a steam sawmill, and about 450 inhabitants; **Williamson,** (p. v.,) s. of the center, contains 2 churches, a steam flouring mill, and about 300 inhabitants; **East Williamson** contains 2 churches and 20 houses. The first settlement was made in 1803, by Wm. Waters.[9] The census reports 8 churches in town.[10]

WOLCOTT[11]—was formed from Junius, (Seneca co.,) March 24, 1807. Butler, Huron, and Rose were taken off in 1826. It is the N. E. corner town of the co., Lake Ontario forming its N.

[1] Moses and James Sill kept the first inn, at Sodus Point, in the building erected for that purpose by Mr. Williamson. On the evening of June 13, 1813, a party of about 100 English landed at Sodus Point in boats, from the fleet of Sir Jas. Yeo, for the purpose of seizing or destroying what public stores they could find. They were opposed by about 40 Americans, under Capt. Hull, of Lyons. After the first fire the Americans retreated. The enemy burned 5 houses, and the old Williamson Hotel, owned by Capt. Wm. Wickham. The public flour had been secreted in a ravine, and remained undiscovered. The next day a gunboat proceeded up the lake to Nicholas Point and burned a warehouse. The British had 2 killed, and the Americans 1 killed and 1 mortally wounded. The total amount of property destroyed amounted to about $25,000.

[2] The census reports 11 churches in town; 4 M. E., 2 Prot. E., 2 Presb., Bap., Christian, Cong.

[3] Named from Chancellor Walworth.

[4] This nursery—established in 1840—occupies 75 acres, and produces annually 300,000 trees, mostly sent to New England, N. J., Md., and Va.

[5] Among the other early settlers were George Millet, in 1802, Daniel Douglass and George Randolph, at West Walworth, Dr. Hurlbut Crittenden, in 1804, Deacon Gideon Hassett, James and Jonathan Hill, Capt. Gilbert, —— Hinckley, and John and

Marshall Chamberlain. The first death was that of —— Green, killed by the fall of a tree, in 1806. The first store was kept by Thomas F. Kempshall.

[6] There are 5 churches in town; 2 Bap., M. E., Cong., and F. W. Bap.

[7] Named from Charles Williamson, the first agent of the Pulteney Estate.

[8] Named from Sir Wm. Pulteney. On the morning of June 13, 1813, Com. Sir James Yeo, with a British force, made a descent upon this place. Gen. J. Swift, who commanded the Americans, surrendered, with the stipulation that private property and persons should be respected. Most of the U. S. stores had been previously removed to a place of safety. The British had 2 killed and 3 wounded.

[9] Capt. Sam'l Throop, Jeremiah Selby, John Holmes, and Alpheus Curtis, came in 1806, Maj. Wm. Rogers in 1807, and Dan'l Poppins, Timothy Smith, —— Denning, Andrew Connell. Sam'l Ledyard, and Jacob W. Hallett, soon after. The first child born was H. N. Throop, in Nov. 1807. Major Rogers kept the first inn, in 1807; Jos. Colt, the first store. Capt. Sam'l Throop and Jeremiah Selby built the first saw and grist mill.

[10] 2 Presb., M. E., Wes. Meth., Bap., Cong., Ref. Prot. D., and Union.

[11] Named from Gov. Oliver Wolcott, of Conn.

boundary. Its surface is undulating, with a general inclination toward the lake. In several localities are tracts of low marsh land. The streams are Wolcott and Big and Little Red Creeks, and several smaller streams, which flow N. into Lake Ontario. A part of Port Bay, in the N. W., Blind Sodus Bay,[1] in the N. E., and two smaller bays, extend inland from the lake. The soil is a sandy and gravelly loam. Iron ore is found in the N. E. part. **Wolcott,** (p. v.,) near the S. W. corner, was incorp. Feb. 24, 1852. It contains 4 churches, an academy,[2] 2 flouring mills, 2 sawmills, a furnace and agricultural machine shop, carding machine, and carpet and coverlet factory. Pop. 600. **Red Creek,** (p. v.,) in the S. E. part, is incorp., and contains 3 churches, the Red Creek Union Academy, 2 gristmills, 3 sawmills, a woolen factory, furnace, and tannery. Pop. in 1859, 597. **Furnace Village,**[3] in the W. part, contains a furnace, sawmill, and 12 houses. The first settlement was made by Jonathan Melvin, sen., on Lot 50, in 1805.[4] The first settled minister was Daniel S. Buttrick.[5]

Acres of Land, Valuation, Population, Dwellings, Families, Freeholders, Schools, Live Stock, Agricultural Products, and Domestic Manufactures, of Wayne County.

Names of Towns.	Acres of Land. Improved.	Acres of Land. Unimproved.	Valuation of 1858. Real Estate.	Valuation of 1858. Personal Property.	Valuation of 1858. Total.	Population. Males.	Population. Females.	No. of Dwellings.	No. of Families.	Freeholders.	Schools. No. of Districts.	Schools. Children taught.
Arcadia	24,539	5,967¾	$1,421,601	$101,728	$1.523,329	2,832	2,684	987	1,102	796	24	1,993
Butler	15,316	6,920	580,494	21,850	602,344	1,126	1,099	414	438	360	12	815
Galen	24,301¼	10,625	1,381,393	367,578	1,748,971	2,706	2,475	924	995	490	18	1,850
Huron	12,220½	7,692	575,999	31,444	607,443	985	896	386	384	315	12	775
Lyons	15,917	5,230	1,355,531	313,950	1,669,481	2,604	2,601	874	978	676	13	1,849
Macedon	18,674	4,389	951,179	121,670	1,072,849	1,249	1,185	453	493	366	14	815
Marion	14.362¼	3,698	488,585	71,012	559,597	985	952	382	419	366	13	756
Ontario	13,886⅝	5,978¾	464,509	72,588	537,097	1,222	1,101	451	466	371	11	943
Palmyra	17,099½	4,202¼	1,190,524	195,000	1,385,524	2,062	2,053	713	846	527	14	1,319
Rose	13,272⅜	8,577	527,597	35,911	563,508	1,084	1,030	395	419	329	12	791
Savannah	11,250½	7,967¾	455,362	8,000	463,362	951	811	343	349	212	13	719
Sodus	29,963⅝	11,697¾	1,085,811	116,089	1,201,900	2,331	2,207	908	932	777	23	1,880
Walworth	15,858¾	4,605	578,442	82,470	660,912	991	973	390	417	347	11	703
Williamson	14.796	5,802	541,248	69,632	610,880	1,301	1,251	495	529	428	14	791
Wolcott	12,995	8,710	549,749	55,300	605,049	1,535	1,478	593	609	484	15	1,223
Total	254,451⅜	102,062¼	12,308,024	1,364,222	13,512,246	23,964	22.796	8,708	9,376	6,844	219	17,222

Names of Towns.	Live Stock. Horses.	Live Stock. Working Oxen and Calves.	Live Stock. Cows.	Live Stock. Sheep.	Live Stock. Swine.	Agricultural Products. Bush. of Grain. Winter.	Agricultural Products. Bush. of Grain. Spring.	Tons of Hay.	Bushels of Potatoes.	Bushels of Apples.	Dairy Products. Pounds of Butter.	Dairy Products. Pounds of Cheese.	Domestic Cloths, in Yards.
Arcadia	1,453	1,735	1,493	10,821	2,788	44,032	180,099	4,580	23,870	38,424	140,054	5,331	803
Butler	981	1,766	1,024	4,898	1,647	16,462	140,631	2,557	17,906	51.981	97,571	15,112	1,750
Galen	1,373	1.961	1,649	8,814	4.198	31,178	199,092½	3,806	19,546	49,588	140,558	16,278	1,271
Huron	712	1,091	675	3,716	1.438	10,357	113,035	1,910	15,895	20,361	59,850	4,844	1,310
Lyons	1,320	1.322	1,610	7,722	2,406	27.357	134.752½	3,430	17,473	51,526	89,472	4,128	360
Macedon	909	1,329	953	10,288	1,924	25,787	110,899½	3,163	16,777	27,949	77,662	9,900	32
Marion	846	1,084	974	3.763	1,632	12,473	108,744½	2,683½	15,740	34,035	96,550	18,763	592
Ontario	886	1,201	923	4,020	1,286	9,510	83,609¼	2,685½	15,272	17,431	86,375	17,400	1,669
Palmyra	859	1,303	1,193	7,954	1,900	31,073	112,235	3.713	16,701	33,113	105,711	14,816	268
Rose	754	1,286	871	3,727	1,241	9,778	94,200	1,724½	13,246	28,535	66,330	7,075	845
Savannah	675	1,348	761	4.947	1,335	15,925	113,853½	1,904	14,376	14,907	69,216	2,290	1.366
Sodus	1,616	2,516	1,846	15,525	3,149	25,396¼	207,538¾	5,072½	30,847	70,448	177,259	9,755½	779
Walworth	877	1,148	878	6,845	1,644	12,500	113.704¼	3,386	19,065	21,170	68,464	5,444	335
Williamson	994	1,278	1,037	7,509	1,519	8,803	93,427	2,943	13,835	32,702	91,822	30,175	845
Wolcott	673	1,327	882	4,296	1,692	9,103	112,750½	1,713½	10,854	17,456	79,186	2,452	839½
Total	14,928	21,695	16,769	104,845	29,799	289,734¼	1,918,572¼	45,271½	261,403	509,626	1,446,080	163,763½	13,064½

[1] Named from the sandbar which stretches across its mouth from the W. shore.

[2] The Leavenworth Institute, incorp. in 1859; named from Isaac Leavenworth, who contributed one-half the total cost

[3] Wolcott Furnace manufactures about 450 tons of pig iron per annum from ore dug in the N. E. part of the town.

[4] Among the other early settlers were Adonijah Church, from Mass., in 1806, Osgood Church and family, in 1807, Dea. Knapp and Lambert Woodruff, in the vicinity of Red Creek, Noadiah Child, in 1811, and Jacob Snyder, with his family of 10 children, in 1813. The first death was that of a son of George Salmon. Obadiah Adams kept the first inn, and Noadiah Child built the first saw and grist mill, in 1814.

[5] There are 8 churches in town; 2 M. E., 2 Bap., 2 Presb., F. W. Bap., and Meth. Prot.

WESTCHESTER COUNTY.

This county, constituting one of the original divisions of the State under the English rule, soon after the first conquest, was organized Nov. 1, 1683, with its present limits. It lies upon the E. bank of the Hudson, in the S. E. part of the State, and is bounded on the E. by Conn. and on the S. by Long Island Sound. It is centrally distant 105 mi. from Albany, and contains 525 sq. mi. The surface consists of several ridges of hills parallel to the river and separated by wide valleys. The hills are in two general ranges, the first extending along the river and the second along the Conn. line. They are subdivided into a great number of minor ridges and hills, all extending N. and S. The highest summits are 600 to 1,000 ft. above tide. The valleys, extending N. and S., are continuous, affording ample opportunity for the construction of roads and railroads; and they are generally bordered by gradually sloping hillsides.[1] In some localities the hills are abrupt and rocky. The principal streams are Peekskill Creek, Furnace Brook, Croton, Pocantico, and Neperhan Rivers, and Tibbetts Brook, tributaries of the Hudson; Bronx River, Westchester and Hutchinsons Creeks, Mamaroneck and Byram Rivers, flowing into Long Island Sound; Maharness and Stamford Mill Rivers, flowing E. into Conn.; and Muscoot Creek, Plum Brook, and Titicus, Cross, and Kisko Rivers, tributaries of the Croton. The lakes are small bodies of water scattered through the hilly portions. The S. E. portion of the co., along the Sound, is deeply indented with bays and estuaries, which in some places are bordered by extensive marshes. Most of the streams which flow into the Sound afford, by the reflux of the tide, an intermitting hydraulic power, which is employed in several places.

The rocks of the co. consist principally of granite and gneiss, of many dissimilar varieties, and of white crystalline limestone. These rocks crop out upon the declivities and summits of most of the hills, affording an abundance of the best kind of building stone. The marble quarries at Sing Sing and other places are extensively wrought, their products affording one of the most valuable exports of the co. Traces of various kinds of ore have been discovered; but all search for profitable metallic veins has proved unsuccessful. Several mineral springs are found in different sections, the principal of which is the Chappaqua Spring, 3 mi. E. of Sing Sing. It emits sulphuretted hydrogen and is said to possess useful medicinal properties. The soil, derived principally from the disintegration of the primitive rocks, is light, sandy, and, naturally, only moderately productive; but, by a continued process of scientific culture, it has been rendered very fertile. Upon the Hudson and the Sound and in various other localities are drift deposits and alluvium, furnishing a much more productive soil. The people are principally engaged in gardening and fruit raising, fattening cattle, and supplying milk for the New York market. Bricks in immense quantities are manufactured along the Hudson for exportation. Other manufactures are largely carried on in the villages adjacent to New York.

This co. is distinguished for beautiful and picturesque scenery, noticeable in nearly every part. The highlands that border upon the Hudson afford an extended view of that river, the Palisades, and of the hilly country of Rockland and Orange. Along the S. E. border fine views are obtained of the Sound, the numerous green islands along the coast, and the adjacent shores of Long Island. In the interior the landscape is agreeably diversified by hills, dales, and clear, running streams. Many wealthy inhabitants of New York have erected beautiful villas and country residences upon the finest sites; and the hills of the co. are now studded with these splendid specimens of architectural art.

In the vicinity of New York are numerous small villages inhabited by mechanics and working men doing business in the city. These people go back and forth daily on the lines of railroad, or by steamboat, living in the country for the sake of economy. A considerable amount of manufactures is carried on at these suburban villages. A large transient population, mostly from New York, make this co. their residence during the summer months.

---

[1] The roads that cross the co. E. and W. are a constant succession of ascents and descents, while those extending N. and S. through the valleys are nearly level.

The co. is a half-shire, the co. buildings being located respectively at Bedford and White Plains.[1] The courthouse at Bedford is a wooden structure; and attached to it is a jail for the temporary confinement of prisoners. The co. buildings at White Plains are of granite, and are the most commodious and costly buildings of the kind in the State.[2]

The poorhouse is located upon a farm of 173 acres in Mount Pleasant, 5 mi. N. of White Plains. The average number of inmates is 225, supported at a weekly cost of 68½ cts. each. The farm yields a revenue of $2,500. A school is kept throughout the year. The buildings are of stone; and the whole establishment seems to be well arranged.

The Hudson River R. R. extends along the river banks through Yonkers, Greenburgh, Mount Pleasant, Ossining, and Cortlandt. The Harlem R. R. extends N. through the central part of the co., extending through Morrisania, West Farms, Yonkers, East Chester, Scarsdale, Greenburgh, White Plains, Mount Pleasant, New Castle, Bedford, Lewisboro, and North Salem. The New York & New Haven R. R. extends from the Harlem R. R. at East Chester E. through Pelham, New Rochelle, Mamaroneck, Harrison, and Rye. A branch road extends from the Harlem R. R. at Morrisania S. E. about 2 mi. to Port Morris. The other principal public work in the co. is the Croton dam and the great aqueduct which supplies the city of New York with water. Lines of steamers ply between New York and the various ports along the Hudson and East Rivers, affording cheap and easy means of communication with the great city.

Five newspapers are now published in the co.[3]

When first known to the whites, this co. was occupied by the Mohegans, who were divided into several bands or clans with distinctive names.[4] They paid tribute to the Five Nations, and were known in early documents as "River Indians."

---

[1] At the organization of the co. in 1683, the courts were established at Westchester, and were continued there until 1759. A court of sessions was held at East Chester for some time. By act of Dec. 16, 1758, the justices and supervisors were directed to select a new site for a courthouse, which was located at White Plains; and in that year, 1760, and 1762, £2,000 were voted to erect and finish it. It was used until 1776, when it was burned. By an act of May 1, 1786, £1,800 were appropriated for the erection of a courthouse at White Plains and another at Bedford, under the superintendence of Stephen Ward, Ebenezer Lockwood, Jonathan G. Tompkins, Ebenezer Purdy, Thos. Thomas, Richard Hatfield, and Richard Sacket, jr. Prisoners had previously been confined in the New York jail; and courts had for a time been held in the Presbyterian church of Bedford. Both buildings thus erected are still standing, and owned by the co. A clerk's office was built at White Plains, in 1830, adjacent to the courthouse, in the old part of the village. The Provincial Convention held its sessions a few days in July, 1776, at the courthouse in White Plains; and in front of it the Declaration of Independence was publicly read upon its receipt by that body. The building, and what remained of the village, were wantonly burned by a New England major on the night of Nov. 5, 1776.

[2] An act passed March 30, 1855, authorized the county treasurer to loan $35,000 for the erection of a new courthouse, jail, clerk's office, and surrogate's office, upon a site in White Plains, to be selected by the supervisors, and under a committee to be appointed by them. The present buildings were erected in 1856–57, under the superintendence of Abraham Hatfield, States Barton, Wm. Marshall, jr., David Hunt, and Geo. C. Finch, at a cost of $120,000. They are built of granite quarried near the village, and form 3 buildings connected by corridors. The front part is devoted to the records of the clerk and surrogate, is fireproof throughout, and its spacious rooms are furnished with iron cases for books and papers. The records have been recently bound, and put in complete order for preservation. The middle portion is devoted to court and jury rooms, sheriff's office and residence; and the rear building is the jail, connected with the court room only by a verandah. Prisoners may be brought into court without liability to rescue by a crowd. The cells, 36 in number, are built in 2 tiers in a central block. By an act of April 16, 1858, the office of Register of Deeds was created, to be filled by election triennially. The act took effect Jan. 1, 1859.

[3] *The Somers Museum* was published by Milton F. Cushing in 1810.
The Westchester Gazette was published at Peekskill by Robert Crombie about 1810. It was afterward changed to
The Westchester and Putnam Gazette. Several changes of proprietors and perhaps of name, occurred when in 1832 it became
The Westchester and Putnam Sentinel, and was published a short time by Dr. Brewer. It was afterward published about 2 years by Samuel Heustis, as
The Sentinel. It then passed into the hands of Samuel Marks, who continued it as
The Westchester and Putnam Republican. In 1844 it was sold to Wm. Richards, who changed its name to
The Peekskill Republican. In 1852 Joseph J. Chambers became proprietor, and in 1857 the paper was removed to Sing Sing, where it is now published as

The Republican, by J. H. Platt; J. J. Chambers, editor.
The Westchester Patriot was published at West Farms a short time in 1812 by —— Lopez.
The Westchester Herald and Putnam Gazette was published at Sing Sing in 1817. It was subsequently published as
The Westchester Herald, by Caleb Roscoe. The office was burned in 1856, and the publication has not been resumed.
The Westchester Spy was commenced at White Plains in 1832 by —— Harpending. It was continued by William B. Lamphear, S. G. Arnold, John W. Bell, and others, until 1848, when it was discontinued.
The Hudson River Chronicle was commenced at Sing Sing in 1837 by A. H. Wells. It is now published by Wm. C. Howe.
The Protector, a campaign paper, was published in 1844.
The Port Chester Banner was pub. by Wm. A. McMillan in 1845.
The Eastern State Journal was commenced at White Plains in 1845 by Edmund G. Southerland, its present publisher.
The Westchester and Putnam Democrat was commenced at Peekskill in 18— by Bailey & Marks. It was continued by Samuel Marks, and was for a time discontinued. It was revived by G. K. Lyman, and soon after it passed into the hands of J. Arnold, who continued it until 1851, when Ezra J. Horton became proprietor, and changed its name to
The Highland Eagle. In 1855, J. W. Spaight became the publisher, and in 1858 the paper passed into the hands of Dr. Fenelon Hasbrouck, who changed its name to
The Highland Democrat, and still publishes it.
The Westchester Gazette was commenced at Morrisania in 1849. Stephen Angel was for some time editor. It was discontinued about 1856.
The Westchester County Journal was commenced at Morrisania in 1856 by James Stillman, its present publisher.
The Plain Dealer was removed from Roslyn, and afterward to Glen Cove.
The Westchester Gazetteer was commenced at West Farms in 1849, by H. Coggshell; it was removed to Mott Haven July 14, 1851, and discontinued in 1852.
The Yonkers Herald was commenced in 1852 by Thos. Smith, its present proprietor.
The Westchester News was commenced at New Rochelle in 1853 by Thos. Towndrow. It was removed to Yonkers in 1854, and published until Jan. 1856, when it was purchased by M. F. Rowe; and in Feb. following a new paper was issued in its place, called
The Yonkers Examiner, which is still published by M. F. Rowe.
The Mount Vernon Gazette was commenced in 1854 by Egbert A. S. Manning. It was discontinued in 1857.

[4] The *Siwanoys* occupied the shores of the sound from Norwalk to near Hellgate; the *Manhattans* held the island of New York, and as far N. as opposite Tappan; the *Weequashecks* held the shore from the Sint Sink to the Armonck; the *Sint Sinks* occupied the present town of Ossining and its vicinity; the *Kitchawunks* claimed the territory on the Croton, and N. to Anthonys Nose; and the *Puchami* and *Wappingers* the Highlands. The *Tanketenkes* resided in the rear of Sing Sing.— Bolton's W. Chester, I, p. 10.

Settlement began under the Dutch authority, in the southern part, and before the Revolution nearly every part of the co. had been occupied. A large part was embraced by the Cortlandt, Philipsburgh, Pelham, Scarsdale, and Fordham Manors.[1] Of these the first sent a representative to the General Assembly, and the second was forfeited by the attainder of its proprietor in the Revolution. The borough of Westchester, including the present towns of Westchester, West Farms, and Morrisania, was also represented by a member, and had a mayor's court. This co. was the scene of many events of great importance in the Revolution, and, from its occupying the middle ground between the opposing armies, was alternately overrun and pillaged by the refugees of both.[2] The southern part was taxed £2,000, May 6, 1784, to repay Revolutionary expenses.

BEDFORD[3]—was first formed under Connecticut, in May, 1697. Its rights were confirmed by New York in April, 1704; and it was fully organized as a town March 7, 1788. It is an interior town, lying N. E. of thec enter of the co. Its surface is elevated and broken by small hills and valleys, and is almost entirely available for agricultural purposes. Croton River forms part of the N. boundary; Maharness River flows through a small portion of the s. part; and Cross River flows through the N. E. corner. Byram Lake lies on the s. border. The soil is generally a good quality of sandy and gravelly loam, but stony on the hills. **Bedford,** (p. v.,) S. E. of the center, is surrounded by hills, one of which on the N. retains its Indian name of "*Aspetong.*" The village is a half-shire, and contains a courthouse,[4] 2 churches, the Bedford Academy, a Female Institute, and 30 houses. **Bedford Station,** (p. o.,) on the Harlem R. R., contains 10 houses. **Katonah,** (p. v.,) on Cross River, near its junction with the Croton, contains 30 houses. **Mount Kisko,** (p. v.,) a station on the Harlem R. R., on the w. border of the town, contains 200 inhabitants. **Whitlockville** is a station on the Harlem R. R. near the N. border. The town was mostly included in a purchase made July 1, 1640, by Nathan Turner, for New Haven, and sold the same year by the latter to Andrew Ward, Robert Coe, and 20 others, for £33. Other Indian purchases were made, the last of which was July 24, 1703.[5] There are 8 churches in town.[6]

CORTLANDT[7]—was formed March 7, 1788. It lies upon the Hudson, in the N. w. corner of the co. Its surface is broken and hilly. The ranges of hills generally extend N. and s. and are separated by narrow valleys. The declivities are often steep and nearly precipitous. Anthonys Nose,[8] on the N. line, 1,228 ft. above the river, is the highest land in the co. Although very broken, the surface generally is susceptible of cultivation. The principal streams are Croton River, flowing across the s. part, Furnace Brook, Peekskill Hollow Creek, and Gregorys Brook. The soil is generally a sandy and gravelly loam, with a strip of clay along the river. Among the mountains are found a variety of interesting minerals.[9] Brick is extensively manufactured.[10]

---

[1] These patents were granted as follows:—
Cortlandt Patent was granted June 17, 1697, to Stephanus Van Cortlandt, with an annual quitrent of 40 shillings. It included the present towns of Cortlandt, Yorktown, Somers, and North Salem.
Philipsburgh Patent was granted June 12, 1703, to Frederick Philipse, at an annual quitrent of £4 12s. It included the present towns of Greenburgh, Mount Pleasant, and Ossining.
Pelham Patent was granted Oct. 25, 1687, to John Pell, and included the present town of Pelham and a part of New Rochelle.
Fordham Patent was granted in 1671 to John Archer, and included 1,253 acres in the present town of West Farms.
Scarsdale Patent was granted March 21, 1701, to Caleb Heathcote, subject to an annual quitrent of £5. It included the present towns of Scarsdale, New Castle, North Castle, and a part of White Plains.

[2] Two classes of brigands, equally destitute of principle, but professing attachment to opposite interests, infested the co., committing atrocious crimes without punishment, and often preying upon their nominal friends with as little mercy as upon their avowed enemies. Of these, the "Cowboys" professed tory sentiments, while the "Skinners" were ostensibly attached to the American cause. The two parties often operated in concert, the Cowboys bringing contraband goods from New York to exchange for the property plundered by the Skinners; and, when a pretext was necessary, a skirmish would occur, and the goods from the enemy would be openly borne away, as if lawfully captured.—*Bolton's Westchester, I, p.* 211.

[3] Named from Bedfordshire, England, whence many of the early settlers came. It formed part of the territory known as Rippowams. Privilege of plantation was granted under the present name by a court of election held at Hartford, Conn., May 11, 1682. In 1697 a patent was granted by Conn. to the town. In 1700 the royal approval was obtained to the survey

of 1683 and '84, by which Bedford and Rye were included in New York; and in April, 1704, a patent with town privileges was granted by that colony. In 1690 there were 31 proprietors residing in town.

[4] County courts are held alternately here and at White Plains. The village was burned in the Revolution by a party of British light horse, on their route to Fairfield, Conn. By an act passed April 11, 1785, courts were ordered to be held in the Presb. church until the courthouse should be rebuilt, or till the further order of the Legislature.

[5] The title to 5,115 acres of land in this town became invested in Jacobus Van Cortlandt at an early period. This estate was divided in 1743, Frederick Van Cortlandt receiving 1,424, Abram De Peyster 1,110, John Chambers 1,282, and Peter Jay 1,299 acres. Gov. John Jay, a son of Peter Jay, became invested with a large portion of the last mentioned allotment. The estate is still owned by his descendants. On a tract known as "the Hop Grounds" are still living many families of the same name as the first purchasers. Among these are families named Green, Miller, Holme, Roberts, Ambler, Clark, Ayers, Westcott, Simpkin, Mead, Webb, Clason, and Higgins. Tradition locates in this town the scene of a bloody engagement fought in Feb. 1644, between the Dutch and Indians, in which 500 of the latter perished.

[6] 3 M. E., 2 Prot. E., 2 Presb., and Bap.

[7] Named from the original patentee.

[8] Named from Antoine De Hooge, Sec. of Rensselaerwyck.—*Benson's Memoirs, p.* 40.

[9] Among these minerals are epidote, sphene, and sulphate of barytes. In opening the R. R. tunnel through Anthonys Nose, beautiful flat hexagonal crystals of calcite were found.

[10] There were in Aug. 1858, 34 establishments worked as separate yards, 11 of which used steam power and 9 made pressed brick. This business began here about 1812–15, and was most thriving from 1847 to 1854. Large quantities of these brick were used on the Croton Aqueduct. The business gives employ-

Peekskill,[1] (p. v.,) upon Peekskill Bay, in the N. W. part of the town, was incorp. April 17, 1816. It is situated in an elevated valley surrounded by heights which afford extensive views of the river. It contains 10 churches, the Peekskill Academy, 4 boarding schools, a bank, newspaper office, and several manufactories.[2] It is connected by a steam ferry with Caldwells Landing, and by a daily steamer and line of sloops with New York. It is a station upon the H. R. R. R. Pop. 3,538. **Verplancks Point,** (Verplanck p. o.,) upon the Hudson, near the center of the w. border of the town, was laid out in 1836. It contains a church, steamboat landing, several important brick manufactories, and 1,456 inhabitants.[3] **Croton**[4] (Croton Landing p. o.) is a R. R. station, in the s. part of the town. It contains 4 churches, a rolling mill, wire mill, and several brickyards. Pop. 400. **Crugers**[5] (Boscobel p. o.) is a landing and R. R. station, 4 mi. s. of Peekskill. **Annsville,** a small village on Peekskill Creek, contains a church and wire mill.[6] **Cortlandville,** near the Van Cortlandt mansion, contains a church, a planing mill, and about 20 houses. **Oregon,** on the line of Putnam co., contains a rolling mill and a wire mill. **Mount Airy,** E. of Croton, is a hamlet. **Croton Point**[7] is a peninsula in the s. part of the town, devoted chiefly to vineyards. **Montroses Point** is a peninsula s. of Verplancks and separated from it by Meanagh Creek. Daniel Birdsall, Nathaniel Brown, Joseph Travis, and Capt. Isaac Conklin settled at Peekskill, in 1764.[8] There are 18 churches in town.[9]

EAST CHESTER[10]—was recognized as a town March 7, 1788. It is an interior town, lying in the s. part of the co. Its surface is broken by ridges extending N. and s. and separated by narrow valleys. Bronx River,[11] forming the N. boundary, and Hutchinsons or East Chester Creek,[12] forming a portion of the E. boundary, are the principal streams. The soil is a sandy and gravelly loam, with some alluvium along the river intervales. Marble is extensively quarried along the w. border.[13] The Harlem R. R. extends along the valley of the Bronx, and the N. Y. & N. H. R. R. crosses the s. part of the town at nearly right angles to the hills, requiring heavy cuttings and embankments. A portion of the territory of the town is public land, under the management of 3 trustees. **East Chester,** (p. v.,) at the head of sloop navigation on Hutchinson Creek, contains 2 churches and 551 inhabitants. **Mount Vernon,** (p. v.,) a station at the junction of the Harlem and N. H. R. R.s, was incorp. Dec. 13, 1853. It contains 4 churches, several private schools, and 1,161 inhabitants. **West Mount Vernon** contains 630 inhabitants; **East Mount Vernon** 275 inhabitants; and **Waverly** and **Washingtonville** are suburban villages, inhabited principally by mechanics and men doing business in New York. **Bronxville,** (p. v.,) on the line of Yonkers, is a R. R. station, and contains a manufactory of carriage axles. **Tuckahoe** (p. v.) is a R. R. station, near the marble quarries. **Burpos Corners** is a small settlement on the N. border. **Fleetwood** and **Jacksonville** are places projected

ment to 1,350 men, and turns out 80,000,000 to 90,000,000 of bricks annually. The pressed brick made here are known in market as "Croton fronts," and sell at from $8 to $9 per M. There is a small firebrick manufactory at Peekskill, using clay from N. J.

[1] Named from Jan Peek.—*Benson's Mem.* p. 36; *Bolton's West Chester,* I, 62. The vicinity was called Sachus, or Sackhoes, by the natives, and the stream, Magrigaries.

[2] Among the manufactories are 6 iron founderies, chiefly engaged in the manufacture of stoves and plows, and giving employment to 300 men; 2 machine shops, 2 tobacco factories, a pistol and gun factory, tannery, and gin distillery.

[3] Named from the family of Verplancks, former owners. This point lies opposite Stony Point; and upon it Fort La Fayette was erected during the Revolution. King's Ferry, a part of an important military route, was between the two points. The fort was captured by the enemy, under Sir Henry Clinton in person, June 1, 1779, but was abandoned Oct. 21 of that year. Col. Livingston held command of this place in 1780, at the time of Arnold's treason; and the headquarters of Gen. Washington were located here for some time. This locality was called by the Indians "Meanagh," and was sold to Stephanus Van Cortlandt in 1683, with the lands E. called "Appamaghpogh." A small creek N. was called "Tammoesis." The purchase was confirmed by patent, with a quitrent of 2 bushels of wheat. About 1734 it was held by John Lent, at an annual rent of one pepper-corn.—*Bolton's Hist.,* I, 94. The population mentioned in the text is much less in winter.

[4] Formerly called "*Collaberg Landing.*"

[5] Named from Col. John P. Cruger, whose estate, including Oscawana Island, is adjacent. "*Boscobel*" (the original name) was the residence of Staats Morris Dyckman.

[6] Cortlandt Bridge, across the mouth of Peekskill Creek, is 1,496 feet long. Upon the point at the mouth of the creek are the remains of Fort Independence. During the Revolution two British vessels were sunk opposite this point, and about 40 years since several cannon were raised from them by diving bells.

[7] By the Indians called Senasqua Neck, and long known as "*Tellers Point,*" from Wm. Teller and Sarah his wife, first

owners. The ship Vulture anchored opposite this point Sept. 21, 1780, with André's mission.

[8] The first store was built by Daniel Birdsall, in the vicinity of the Middle Dock. Capt. Swim is said to have sailed the first sloop from Pemart's Dock, in 1773.—*Bolton's Westchester,* I, 62. Many stirring events of the Revolution occurred in this vicinity, and the country suffered much from the enemy's incursions. In March, 1777, Col. Bird landed with 500 men, and the few Americans stationed here fired the storehouses and retired. In Sept. 1777, the whole village was sacked and burned. Edmund Palmer, a tory spy, was hanged on Gallows Hill, 2 mi. N. of the village; and Daniel Strang, another spy from the enemy, was executed on a pear tree near the present academy. John Paulding, one of the captors of André, was a native of this village, and received from the State a farm in this town. His remains repose in the Episcopal graveyard, 2 mi. N. of the village, where a neat monument was erected, at the expense of the corporation of New York, in 1827; and the work was completed with imposing ceremonies Nov. 22 of that year. Gen. Pierre Van Cortlandt formerly resided 2 mi. N. of Peekskill; and at this place Gen. McDougal posted his advanced guard when the enemy took possession of Peekskill in March, 1777. East of the Van Cortlandt mansion stands St. Peter's Church, an old, dilapidated building, erected in 1767. The united parishes of St. Peter's and St. Philip's were endowed by Col. Beverly Robinson, and the title was confirmed Mar. 27, 1794. The property has been sold by order of the court of Chancery, and the avails equally divided between the two churches.

[9] 4 Friends, 4 M. E., 3 Prot. E., 2 Presb., Bap., Wes. Meth., Prot. Meth., Ref. Prot. D., and R. C.

[10] Anciently called "*Hutchinsons,*" and afterward "*The Ten Farms.*" Its present name was used as early as 1666.—*Bolton's Westchester,* I, 120.

[11] Named by the Indians "Aquehung."

[12] Named by the Indians "Aqueanounck."

[13] The marble is of the variety called dolomite. The N. Y. Custom House and the City Hall at Brooklyn were built of this material. The Custom House at New Orleans is being constructed of stone from these quarries.

by building associations. This town appears to have been a favorite residence of the natives; and when first settled by the whites it contained traces of former occupation. The Indian title was acquired in 1654 and confirmed in 1654, 1666, and 1700. Thos. Pell, the purchaser, granted it to James Eustis and Philip Pinkney, of Fairfield, Conn., and their associates. In 1665, 26 persons signed a covenant for the security of their mutual rights.[1] The settlers were incorp. by patent, March 9, 1666,[2] and for many years were engaged in a controversy with Westchester concerning the bounds of their grant. A house was fortified in Oct. 1675, as a place of refuge from Indians. The first schoolhouse was agreed upon in 1683; and the site has ever since been occupied for this purpose. A townhouse was voted in 1685. East Chester was celebrated for the interest it took in behalf of Leisler.[3] The Cong. church of this town was formed in 1665; and a place of worship was built about 1700.[4] The town suffered greatly in the Revolution, from its being the middle ground between the opposing armies. A farm of 252½ acres was granted in this town to David Williams, one of the captors of André, June 16, 1783. He afterward removed to Schoharie co., where he died.

GREENBURGH[5]—was formed March 7, 1788. It lies on the w. border of the co., s. of the center. Its surface is much broken by hills parallel to the Hudson, and separated by narrow valleys, through which flow several streams, the principal of which is Neperhan or Sawmill Creek. Hudson River forms the w. boundary, and Bronx River the E. The soil is clay and sandy loam. Several marble quarries are worked near the Hudson. **Hastings,** (Hastings upon Hudson p. o.,) near the s. w. corner, a station on the H. R. R. R. and a steamboat landing, contains 2 churches, steam marble works, limekilns, and a limited number of manufactories. Pop. 1,135. **Dobbs Ferry,**[6] (p. v.,) a station on the H. R. R. R. and a landing on the river, contains 3 churches and 1,040 inhabitants. **Irvington,**[7] (p. v.,) a station on the H. R. R. R. and a landing on the river, contains 2 churches and 599 inhabitants. **Tarrytown,**[8] (p. v.,) on the N. border, a steamboat landing and a station on the H. R. R. R., contains 4 churches, the Pawling Institute, and about 2,000 inhabitants. **Harts Corners,** (Moringville p. o.,) a station on the Harlem R. R., is a hamlet; **Middletown** is a settlement below Tarrytown; **Halls Corners,**[9] a neighborhood in the N. part; **Ashford,** a settlement 3 mi. below; **Abbotsford,** a locality near Dobbs Ferry; and **Greenville,** a neighborhood in the s. part. The first Indian purchase was made in 1649. In 1662 Connecticut bought all the Indian lands w. to the North River, and in 1681-82-84 Frederick Philipse bought the lands now included in this and other towns which, by Patent of 1693, were formed into the Philipsburgh Manor. In 1779 they were forfeited by the attainder of Col. F. Philipse and sold for small sums to the former tenants,[10] under a pre-emption clause in the general act of May 12, 1784, for the sale of confiscated estates. The census reports 6 churches in town.[11]

HARRISON[12]—was formed March 7, 1788. It is an interior town, near the E. border, s. of the center of the co., its N. E. corner touching the line of Conn. Its surface is generally level. Blind

---

[1] Thos. and Richard Shute, Nathaniel and John Tompkins, Thos. and John A. Pinkney, Joseph Joans, John and Moses Hoitt, James Eustis, Daniel Godwin, Wm. Squire, David Osburn, John Goding, Samuel and John Drake, John and Moses Jackson, Nathaniel White, Wm. Haidon, John Gay, Richard Hoadley, Henry Fowler, John Emory, and John Clarke were the signers of this agreement.
[2] Philip Pinkney, James Eustis, and Wm. Haidon were named in this patent; and these persons resigned their trust to the inhabitants soon after.
[3] *Bolton's Westchester,* I, 135.
[4] The census reports 8 churches in town; 3 M. E., 2 Ref. Prot. D., Bap., R. C., and Univ.
[5] In the Dutch "Greinburgh," literally "Grain town." In some early deeds it is called "Lawrence's Plantation;" and by the Indians, Weckquaskeck, Weckquoesqueeck,Wiequoeshook,— in pure Algonquin, Weic-quoes-guck, the place of the bark kettle.—*Bolton's Hist. Westchester Co., I, p.* 163. This town was inhabited by a powerful tribe of Indians known as the Wickquoes-quicks, called by the English Wickers Creeks; and until the middle of the last century the natives were numerous. A cold blooded murder of an Indian was avenged 20 years afterward by his nephew, in Sept. 1691. The Dutch attempted to retaliate, but without success. In Feb. 1641, the Mohawks made a descent upon these Indians, who fled to the Dutch for protection. The soldiers of the fort by night crossed to New Jersey, where the Indians had assembled, and wantonly butchered nearly 100; and 30 were murdered at Corlears Hook. This barbarity aroused 11 tribes to vindictive war, in which the Dutch settlements around Fort Amsterdam were laid waste. A peace was agreed upon April 22, 1643, but was not fully established for many years.

[6] Named from a family of this name who were early settlers and kept a ferry. The first interview between Arnold and André was to have taken place here; but, for some reason, it did not. The British commissioners sent up to obtain André's release had their interview here with Gen. Greene. Gen. Washington and Gov. Clinton here met Gen. Tarleton, at the close of the war, in 1783.
[7] Named from Washington Irving, whose quaint Dutch homestead, "Sunny Side," is a short distance above. The village was formerly called "*Dearmans,*" or "*Dearmans Landing.*"
[8] From "Tarwe," wheat; and, by the natives, Alipconck, or Place of Elms. By an act of May 1, 1786, a tract of 2 acres for a burial place, 100 acres for a glebe to the Ref. Prot. D. church, and 17 acres to the Prot. E. church, were confirmed. The village is pleasantly situated opposite the widest part of the Tappan Zee. The site of André's capture, marked by a handsome monument, dedicated Oct. 7, 1853, is about three-fourths of a mi. N. E. from the station.
[9] Near the Presb. church is the monument to Isaac Van Wart, one of the capturers of Major André,—erected by the citizens of the co., June, 1829.
[10] Among these were families named Van Tassel, Van Wart, Odell, Lawrence, Post, Archer, Hart, Acker, Dyckman, and Requa.
[11] 2 M. E., 2 Ref. Prot. D., Prot. E., and Bap.
[12] Sometimes called "Harrisons Precinct," or "The Purchase." Prior to 1774 it formed one of the six precincts of Rye Parish.—*Bolton's Westchester,* I, 246. It was named from John Harrison, who purchased it from the Indians Feb. 1, 1695, and confirmed to Wm. Nicolls, John Harrison, and others, June 25, 1696. It was made a separate precinct by act of March 9, 1774.

Brook[1] forms a part of the E. boundary, and Mamaroneck Creek a part of the W. Rye Pond[2] lies on the N. border, and St. Mary's Pond on the W. The soil is a fertile, gravelly loam. **Purchase,** (Harrison p. o.,) in the N. part, is a hamlet, containing 2 Friends' meeting houses. The first settlement commenced at an early period. The census reports 2 Friends' meeting houses[3] in town.

LEWISBORO[4]—was formed March 7, 1788, as " *Salem.*" Its name was changed to " *South Salem*" April 6, 1806, and to its present name Feb. 13, 1840. A part of North Salem was annexed April 26, 1844. It lies on the E. border, near the N. E. corner, and forms the eastern angle of the co. Its surface is much broken and in places mountainous. Croton River forms its W. boundary. Cross River flows through a small portion of the central southern part. Waccaback Lake[5] and North and South Ponds are in the N. part, and Cross Pond is on the line of Poundridge. The soil is a clayey and sandy loam. **South Salem,** (p. v.,) in the E. part, is a scattered village, containing a church and 15 houses. **Cross River,** (p. v.,) in the S. corner, contains 2 churches, several manufactories, and 20 houses. **Goldens Bridge** (p. o.) is a station on the Harlem R. R. **Vista,** (p. o.,) in the S. E. corner, is a small settlement. **Lewisboro** (p. o.) is in the S. part. Settlement was commenced under the authority of Connecticut, at an early period. This region was the scene of several Revolutionary incidents.[6] There are 7 churches in town.[7]

MAMARONECK[8]—was recognized as a town March 7, 1788. It lies upon L. I. Sound, in the S. E. part of the co. Its surface is broken by low ridges of gneiss, generally extending N. and S. Mamaroneck Creek, forming the E. boundary, and its tributary, Sheldrake Creek, are the principal streams. The coast is deeply indented by several bays, which divide it into numerous peninsulas and headlands. **Mamaroneck,** (p. v.,) near the head of Mamaroneck Bay, is partly in Rye. It contains 2 churches, (Prot. E. and M. E.,) and several manufactories not at present in operation. **Orienta,**[9] **Washingtonville, Chatsworth,**[10] and **Hickory Grove** are village plats and prospective villages. **Kelloggsville,** on the line of New Rochelle, has an extensive tide mill. The Indian title was obtained in 1640 and in 1662. John Richbell received a ground brief from the Dutch, and letters patent from Gov. Lovelace, Oct. 16, 1668, to three necks of land, at a quitrent of 8 bushels of winter wheat. In 1700 Caleb Heathcote acquired title to most of the eastern neck, with other lands, which was confirmed March 21, 1701. A portion descended in marriage to James De Lancey, afterward Governor of the colony, and ancestor of the present Episcopal Bishop of the Diocese of Western New York. Settlement began about 1660; and the village of Mamaroneck is one of the most ancient in the co. The town records date back to 1697; they were suspended from April, 1776, to April, 1785. During this period numerous events of historical interest occurred in this town. The day before the battle of White Plains, Col. Smallwood surprised and cut off a large body of the enemy under Major Rogers, stationed upon Nelson Hill. Col. White, of the Continental army, was overtaken near this place by Lieut. Hickford, and some thirty stragglers, who had taken refuge upon the ice, were killed.

MORRISANIA[11]—was formed from West Farms, Dec. 7, 1855. It is the S. W. corner town of the co., lying upon Harlem River, contiguous to New York. Its surface is broken by several low ridges which extend N. and S. Most of its surface is occupied by village plats laid out since the extension of railways, and is inhabited by persons doing business in New York. **Morrisania,** (p. v.,) a R. R. station, in the N. E. corner, contains the St. Joseph's Ursuline Convent, an academy and free school, and 2,587 inhabitants. **Mott Haven,** (p. v.,)[12] opposite Harlem, contains 2

---

1 Called by the Indians Mockquams.

2 This pond covers 210 acres, and abounds in pickerel. It discharges into Bronx River; and it was at one time proposed to take this water to supply New York City.

3 One of these was built before the Revolution, and was used by the Americans during the war as a hospital.

4 Named from John Lewis, a prominent citizen. Its northern part formed a portion of Cortlandt Manor; and on its division in 1734 the part in this town fell to the share of Stephen Van Cortlandt, Gertrude Beeckman, Margaret Boyd, and —— Skinner. Its eastern part is included in the Oblong. See p. 269.

5 This lake covers 212 acres, and. with the adjacent ponds, is fed by springs and rivulets from Great Long Pond Mountain. Beavers inhabited its shores as late as 1837.

6 Maj. André was conducted to the headquarters of Col. Jameson, in North Castle, and thence, in charge of Maj. Tallmadge, to Col. Sheldon's quarters, in this town. From this place he addressed Gen. Washington, disclosing his true name and rank. The house where he was detained is still preserved.

7 2 M. E., Meth. Prot., Prot. E., Presb., Bap., and Friends.

8 Pronounced both Mam-a-rō'neck and Mam-âr'ŏ-neck. The latter is more generally used, and is often contracted to "Mor-

neck" or "Mar-neck," in common speech. It has been variously written Momoronack, Mamarinck, Mernnack, and Momoronuck It has been by some supposed to signify "the place of rolling stones."—*Bolton's Westchester, I,* 282. There was an Indian chief of this name, who resided upon the Croton.

9 Formerly called " *Mamaroneck Point,*" " *Great Neck,*" and "*De Lanceys Neck.*" The eastern part of this neck is called Seamans Point, from Giles Seaman, former owner. The natives called it Waumainuck. The modern name " Edgewater" has been applied to this place. The western part is called "Long Beach Point."

10 Near this place is a rocking stone, estimated to weigh 150 tons, which may be moved by the hand.

11 A town of this name was formed March 7, 1788, and annexed to Westchester Feb. 22, 1791. It was named in honor of Gouverneur Morris, whose estate was situated in the town.

12 Named from Jordan L. Mott, principal founder of the works. Steel works have been erected near the rail road bridge. By act of March 31, 1790, Lewis Morris was allowed to build a toll bridge at this place across Harlem River. He assigned his right to John B. Coles, who was allowed, March 24, 1795, to build a dam in Harlem River, with locks, and liability for damages.

churches, an extensive iron foundery, and 843 inhabitants. **Port Morris,**[1] upon the Sound, has a harbor of 60 ft. depth; and it is proposed to land vessels here that draw too much water to enter New York Harbor. A branch of the Harlem R. R. 2⅓ mi. long connects this place with Melrose. **Wilton, Old Morrisania, East Morrisania, West Morrisania, South Melrose, East Melrose, Eltona, Woodstock, Claremont,** and **High Bridgeville,** are suburban village plats. A tract known as Broncks Land,[2] granted by Gov. Nicoll to Jonas Broncks, was sold to Richard Morris in 1668; and on May 8, 1697, Lewis Morris obtained a patent for the township or Manor of Morrisania, with a quitrent of 6 shillings. Prior to the Revolution it formed one of the precincts of Westchester parish. Early in the war a division of the American army was stationed here; but after the disasters of Long Island it retired northward, and British troops were posted there, but not without annoyance from partisan corps. The dwellings at Morrisania were burned the same day as was the courthouse at White Plains.

MOUNT PLEASANT—was formed March 7, 1788. Ossining was taken off in 1845. It lies upon the Hudson, near the center of the w. border of the co. Its surface is broken by high ridges, the principal of which are Buttermilk and Chappequa Hills. Bronx River forms the E. boundary; and Neperhan and Pocantico Rivers flow obliquely across the town. The soil is a clayey and sandy loam, well adapted to cultivation. There are several marble quarries in town.[3] **Pleasantville,**[4] (p. v.,) near the N. line, contains 2 churches and 358 inhabitants. **Unionville,** (Neperhan p. o.,) a station upon the Harlem R. R. contains 97 inhabitants. **Beekmantown,** on Pocantico River, in the s. w. part of the town, is a suburb of Tarrytown. It contains 5 churches, the Irving and Tarrytown Institutes, and about 1,500 inhabitants. **Sleepy Hollow,**[5] **Upper Cross Roads,** and **Lower Cross Roads** are hamlets. This town was included in the Manor of Philipsburgh, granted to Frederick Philipse; and by his will, dated Dec. 9, 1702, he granted to his son Adolph the portion of the manor N. of Dobbs Ferry, including this town. The title descended to his son Frederick, and was forfeited by the attainder of a son of the latter of the same name in 1779. One of the principal grantees under the State was Gerard G. Beeckman. Many Revolutionary associations are connected with this town; and several encounters took place within its limits. The census reports 6 churches in town.[6]

NEW CASTLE[7]—was formed from North Castle, March 18, 1791. A part of Somers was annexed May 12, 1846. It is an interior town, lying N. of the center of the co. Its surface is much broken by hills having a general course a little E. of N., the principal of which are Mount Prospect and the Chappaqua Hills, terminating in Mount Kisko. The Neperhan, Bronx, and Pocantico Rivers rise in this town. Upon the borders are Chappaqua, Wampas,[8] and Kirby Ponds, and Croton Lake. Chappaqua Sulphur Springs, 4 mi. N. E. from Sing Sing, have acquired a local notoriety. The soil is a gravelly clay and sandy loam. **Mount Kisko** (p. o.) is a small village and R. R. station, on the line of Bedford. **New Castle** (p. o.,) is a small scattered village, upon Kirby Pond, near the line of Bedford. **Chappaqua**[9] (p. o.) is a R. R. station, near the s. line. **Sarlesville** is a hamlet, near the center of the town; and here the town business is generally transacted. This town was included within Richbell's purchase of 1660, and, with other lands, was sold to Caleb Heathcote, and was patented to him and 10 associates[10] Feb. 14, 1701. It was afterward known as the "West Patent of Northcastle," or simply "West Patent." Settlement began about 1720, or a little earlier. At the time of the Revolution it formed one of the precincts of Rye parish. It was greatly annoyed by sudden incursions of plundering parties; and St. George's church was for a long time occupied as a guardhouse and hospital by the Continental troops. The census reports 5 churches in town.[11]

NEW ROCHELLE—was recognized as a town March 7, 1788. It lies upon the Sound, in the s. part of the co., and extends northward in a long, narrow strip. The surface is moderately

---

The bridge at Harlem leading to Mott Haven is now free, the charter of its former owners having expired in 1858. The bridge formerly known as Macomb's Bridge is removed, and is about being rebuilt.

[1] Sometimes called "Morrisport." Named from Gouverneur Morris, the principal owner. [2] Called by the natives Ranachque.

[3] The New Orleans Custom House was built of marble from a quarry in the N. E. part of this town.

[4] Formerly called "Clarks Corners."

[5] Sleepy Hollow is noted for being the scene of one of Irving's celebrated legends. The Dutch church at this place was formed in 1697, and the edifice erected in 1699. The communion table and service plate, originally given by the first lord of the manor, are still preserved.

[6] 2 Ref. Prot. D., M. E., Prim. Meth., Prot. E., and R. C.

[7] Called by the Indians Shappaqua, said to signify "a vegetable root."—*Bolton's Westchester, I,* 361.

[8] Named from the sachem, chief proprietor of these lands in 1696, whose residence is said to have been near.

[9] Pronounced Shấp-pa-quaw. It is sometimes written Chapequa.

[10] These patentees were Robt. Walters, Leigh Atwood, Cornelius Depeyster, Caleb Heathcote, Matthew Clarkson, John Caldwell, Richard Slater, Lancaster Simes, Robt. Lusting, and Barne Cosens. It was settled by families named Ward, Conclin, Hyatt, Underhill, Haight, Carpenter, Green, Kirby, Davenport, Van Tassel, Griffen, Tompkins, Kipp, Secor, Brady, Reynolds, Quinly, and Merrith. [11] 2 M. E., 2 Friends, and Prot. E.

uneven and in some parts stony. Davenports Neck,[1] a peninsula containing 200 acres, and several fine islands in the Sound, belong to this town.[2] Crystal Lake, E. of the village, is chiefly celebrated for its ice, large quantities of which are annually "harvested." The soil is fertile and peculiarly adapted to fruit raising.[3] **New Rochelle,** (p. v.,) upon an estuary from the Sound, in the E. part of the town, was incorp. Oct. 5, 1857. It contains 6 churches, several private schools, and about 2,000 inhabitants. A portion of the village and the lands surrounding it are occupied by elegant villas and country residences of persons doing business in New York. The steamboat landing is a half mile s. w. of the village, on a small island connected with the main land by a stone causeway. The village is a station on the N. Y. & N. H. R. R. Beechwood Cemetery, incorp. Jan. 30, 1854, lies a mile w. of the village. **West New Rochelle, Petersville,**[4] and **Upper New Rochelle** are scattered villages, mostly inhabited by Germans. This town was embraced in the Manor of Pelham, and was sold by John Pell, Sept. 20, 1689, to Jacob Leisler, for the settlement of a company of French Huguenots. These people are said to have been brought over in one of the king's ships, and to have landed on the N. E. part of Davenports Neck, then called *"Bauffets"* or *"Bounfoys Point."*[5] They mostly purchased under Leisler in 1690. There were 23 freeholders in town in 1708. The town records commence Nov. 1, 1699, and until 1735 were kept partly in French. They were suspended from April 2, 1776, to June 24, 1783. A French church was organized in 1689, and in 1709 most of the members conformed to the Episcopal faith; and this denomination are now owners of property given by Pell. The Presbyterians also claim succession from the first French church, a part of the members of which did not conform.[6]

NORTH CASTLE[7]—was formed March 7, 1788. New Castle was taken off in 1791. It occupies a long, narrow strip on the E. border of the co., adjoining Stamford and Greenwich, Conn. Its surface is much broken by hills,[8] particularly in the w. part. It is drained by Maharness, Byram, and Bronx Rivers and their branches. Rye Pond lies on the s. border; Byram Pond on the line of Bedford; and Wampus Pond on the line of New Castle. Cobamong Pond, a mile E. of Byram Pond, has no inlet and is very deep. The soil is clay and sandy loam. **North Castle** (p. v.) contains a church and a few houses. **Armonk,**[9] (p. v.,) near the center, contains 3 churches, a woolen factory, and 20 houses. **Kinsico,**[10] (p. v.,) in the s. part, contains several manufactories and 103 inhabitants. **Quarter Station** is on the H. R. R. R., in the extreme s. part. The first settlements commenced at a very early period.[11] The census reports 7 churches in town.[12]

NORTH SALEM[13]—was formed March 7, 1788. A part was annexed to Lewisboro in 1844. It is the N. E. corner town of the co. Its surface is hilly, the summits rising 100 to 300 ft. above the valleys. Croton River forms the w. boundary. Titicus[14] River, a principal branch of the Croton, flows w. from Conn. through near the center. The valley of this stream varies in width from ½ mi. to 1½ mi., and is bordered by steep hills. Peach Pond, on the N. border, covers 400 acres.

---

1 Formerly *"Laylers"* (*"* Leslies") and *"Lecourts"* Neck. Bought in 1786 by Newberry Davenport, and since owned by the Davenport family.

2 Davids or Hewletts Island. Named from Thaddeus Davids, the owner. It contains about 100 acres, and is fitted up for picnic and pleasure parties. Steamboat excursions are occasionally made thither from the city. Goat, Marketts, Whortleberry, Locust, and Van Cleese Islands also belong to this town. Burdens Point, on Davenport Neck, is also a place of resort.

3 From 12 to 20 acres are devoted to raising blackberries,—chiefly the variety known as the "New Rochelle or Lawton blackberry," originally a seedling from the fields, which has proved of much value. There are also extensive nurseries in town.

4 Formerly called *"New Jerusalem."*

5 The purchase included 6,000 acres, to which Pell added 100 acres for the use of the French church. Among the refugees were Francis Le Count, David De Bonrepas, Alexis Allaire, Harvey Beignon, Esaye Valleau, Andrew Thaunet, David Bonnefoy, Louis Guion, Pierre Das, Pierre Palcot, Andrew Naudin and sons Andrew and Louis, Theophile and Chas. Fourrestier, Ambroise Sycard and sons Ambroise, Daniel, and Jacques, Guillaume Laudrie, G. Latteneau, Isaaq Caillard, Marie Cothonneau and her son Guillaume, Jean Newfuille, Estersie Lavigne, and Jean Constant. Thos. Paine, author of "Common Sense," died in this town in 1809, and his remains were taken to England by Cobbett in 1819. His admirers have erected a monument over the spot where he was interred.

6 There are now 8 churches in town; 3 M. E., Prot. E., Presb., Bap., Af. Meth., and R. C.

7 Formerly *"White Fields,"* and afterward designated the *"Liberty of North Castle."*

8 Mt. Misery, in the s. E. angle, 200 to 300 ft. above the valley, is named from the fact that a large party of Indians were cut off here by the Huguenots, in retaliation for a descent upon New Rochelle.—*Bolton's Westchester, I, p.* 447.

9 Formerly *"Mill Square,"* and still often called by that name.

10 Formerly *"Robbins Mills."*

11 The Indian title to this town was obtained by Caleb Heathcote and others between 1660 and 1705, and confirmed by several patents. Of these the "Middle Patent," embracing 1,500 acres, was granted Feb. 17, 1701–02, and the w. portion was confirmed to Anne Bridges and her associates Sept. 25, 1708. A partition of the Middle and West Patents took place June 23, 1766. The allotments were balloted for and sold to numerous persons, of whom many named Brundage, Griffin, Lockland, Sillick, Scofield, Clapp, and others are descendants.—*Bolton's Westchester, I, p.* 455.

Major André immediately after his arrest was sent to Col. Jameson, stationed in this town; and from here he was allowed, through the inadvertence of that officer, to notify Arnold of his arrest.

12 3 M. E., 3 Prot. E., and Friends.

13 This town was mostly purchased by Stephen Van Cortlandt and was embraced within the bounds of his manor. The E. part, within the Oblong, was purchased in 1708 by John Belden, Sam'l Keeler, Matthew Seymour, Matthias St. John, and other inhabitants of Norwalk, Conn. Upon the division of the Manor of Cortlandt in 1734, this town fell to the share of Andrew Miller, John Schuyler, and Stephen De Lancey.

14 Otherwise called Mutighticoss. The name in the text perhaps has been changed from this, and is said to have been derived from an Indian chief.

Beaver Pond is a small sheet of water near the N. line. The soil is better adapted to grazing than to grain raising. Turkey Hill lies in the s. w. part. **North Salem,**[1] (p. v.,) in the E. part, contains 2 churches, a paper mill, and 30 houses. **Salem Center,**[2] (p. o.,) a hamlet, is the seat of the North Salem Academy.[3] **Purdys Station,** (p. o.,) on the Harlem R. R., on the w. border, contains 2 churches and a small woolen factory. **Croton Falls,** (p. o.,) in the N. w. corner, is a station on the Harlem R. R. The first settlement commenced at a very early period, mostly by immigrants from Conn. The census reports 7 churches in town.[4]

OSSINING[5]—was formed from Mount Pleasant, May 2, 1845. It lies upon the Hudson, N. of the center of the co. Its surface is mostly a hilly upland, the ridges extending parallel to the river. Prospect Hill is a commanding eminence on the s. line of the town. Pocantico River forms its E. boundary. Marble is extensively quarried, and traces of several metals have been found.[6] The soil is a productive, gravelly and clayey loam. **Sing Sing,** (p. v.,) upon the Hudson, near the center of the w. border of the town, was incorp. April 2, 1813. It is beautifully situated upon ground gradually rising from the river to the height of 180 ft., and at most points affording fine views of Tappan Bay and the opposite shore of the Hudson. It contains 4 churches, the Mount Pleasant Academy,[7] a female seminary, and several other popular female schools. Pop. about 3,500. This village is chiefly noted for being the seat of one of the N. Y. State prisons. The prison was erected at this place in 1825, with a view of employing the convict labor upon the marble quarries. It receives convicts from certain southern and eastern counties, as specified by statute.[8] **Prospect Hill**[9] is a scattered settlement along the s. border. **Spring Valley,** E. of Sing Sing, and **Sparta,** s. of Sing Sing, are hamlets. This town was included in the Manor of Philipsburgh, and was settled by the Dutch previous to the commencement of the last century. The lands were forfeited by the attainder of Frederick Philipse during the Revolution.[10] The first church was organized at a very early period, but the exact date is lost.[11] The Dale Cemetery, containing 47 acres, ½ mi. N. of Sing Sing, was incorporated January 14, 1851.

PELHAM[12]—was formed March 7, 1788. It lies on Long Island Sound, in the s. part of the co., on the E. border, and it embraces several islands in Long Island Sound.[13] Pelham Neck[14] is a peninsula extending into the Sound; upon it are several elegant country seats. Its surface is undulating, the valleys ranging N. and s. Hutchinsons Creek[15] forms the w. boundary. The soil is mostly of an excellent quality of sandy and gravelly loam. **Pelhamville,** near the N. angle

[1] A granite boulder, weighing 60 tons or over, lies in this village, supported about 3 ft. from the ground upon the points of 5 smaller limestone rocks. There is a chalybeate spring near the village.

[2] About a half mile w. of the village is a natural bridge.

[3] This academy was erected between 1770 and '75 by Stephen De Lancey for a residence, but was not used as such, and in 1786 it was purchased for its present use. It was incorp. Feb. 19, 1790. Among its students have been Dan'l D. Tompkins, Col. N. P. Tallmadge and brother, Hon. James Kent, and several other prominent citizens. Its patronage at present is small.

[4] 2 M. E., Presb., Bap., Prot. E., Union, and Friends.

[5] Originally called "*Ossining.*" It name was changed March 14, 1846. The proper Indian name is said to signify "stone upon stone," and has been written Sin-Sing, and Sink-Sink. A powerful clan of Mohegans of this name inhabited this region when it was first known to the whites.

[6] Small specimens of galena, with several ores of copper, have been obtained. Sulphuret of zinc and oxyd of manganese are occasionally found in the lime rock. [7] See pp. 745, 746.

[8] This prison was erected by the convicts themselves, 100 of whom were sent from Auburn Prison for that purpose under the charge of Capt. Elam Lynds, who had chiefly directed the building of the Auburn Prison. The novel spectacle was exhibited on the 14th of May, 1825, of the arrival of this band on the open ground which was to be the theater of operations, without a place to receive or even a wall to inclose them. * * * The first day sufficed to erect a temporary barrack for shelter at night; and ever after they continued in unpausing labor, watched by a small number of guards, but held under perpetual government of their accustomed discipline and submission to the power whose vigilant eye and unrelaxing hand they felt to be perpetually upon them and around them.—*Introduction to Nat. Hist. N. Y., p.* 186.

The Hudson River R. R. crosses the prison grounds under two broad arches with an intervening walled space. The male prison is 484 by 44 ft. and 5 stories high, and has 1,000 cells. The w. yard is inclosed by 2 buildings 40 ft. wide, 2 stories high, extending from the main prison to the river, and occupied by kitchens, hospital, chapel, and shops. The yard thus formed is 492 by 412 ft., and has a range of shops 40 ft. wide, parallel to the main prison. There are also workshops on the E. The female prison, upon the same premises, but under separate management, is built of rough marble taken from the State quarries. It stands on an elevated site, E. of the R. R., with a

colonnade of the Ionic order across the end fronting the river. It was built in 1835–40, and receives female convicts sentenced to State prison from every co. in the State; it contains 80 cells. By an act of April 18, 1859, the Inspectors of State Prisons were directed to sell such of the premises at this place as are not required for prison purposes, at a price not less than $250 per acre, and to appropriate the moneys thus received to building and repairing such works at the prison as they may deem proper.

[9] Formerly known as "*Long Hill.*"

[10] Families named Ward, Orser, Crank, Bazelie, Acker, Purdy, Merritt, McCord, Bishop, Balyeas, Storm, Jones, Millet, and Ryder, purchased under the Commissioners of Forfeiture.

[11] There are 6 churches in town; 3 Prot. E., Bap., M. E., and Presb.

[12] Named from Thos. Pell, of Fairfield, Conn. A purchase was made of the Indians by Mr. Pell, Nov. 14, 1654; and most of this was confirmed to him by Gov. Nicoll, Oct. 6, 1666. The quitrent reserved in this grant was a lamb annually. Pelham Manor originally embraced 9,166 acres, and was confirmed by Gov. Dongan, Oct. 25, 1687, to John Pell, nephew of the first purchaser. This town is mostly owned by a few wealthy proprietors, and, except Scarsdale, is the least populous in the co. Several acres of berries are cultivated for the city market. Pelham Bridge connects the town with East Chester.

[13] The principal of these is "City Island,"—formerly "*Minneford Island,*" or "*Mulberry Island.*" Its present name is derived from commercial establishments projected at an early colonial period and renewed subsequent to the Revolution. It was supposed that the India trade could be carried on from this place with peculiar advantage. It is now principally occupied by oystermen.

Harts Island, or "*Spectacle Island,*" has an area of 85 acres. Hunters Island, belonging to the estate of E. Desbrosses Hunter, has an area of 250 acres, and was formerly connected with the mainland by a stone causeway and bridge. High Island lies near the s. point of Pelham Neck.

[14] Formerly "*Anne Hooks Neck,*" from an Indian owner; and afterward "*Rodmans Neck.*" It was a favorite place for Indian sepulture; and traces of graves are still seen. A ferry was established to Hempstead Harbor and to Matagarisons Bay in 1755, by Samuel Rodman.

[15] Named from Mrs. Anne Hutchinson, the first settler. Its Indian name was Acqueahounck, from a term descriptive of the red cedar tree.—*Bolton's Westchester, I, p.* 542.

of the town, is a newly surveyed village and station on the N. Y. & N. H. R. R. **Pelham** is a p. o. on the E. border. **Prospect Hill** is a locality near the center. **Pelham Priory**[1] is the seat of a young ladies' seminary, established by the late Rev. Robert Bolton and conducted by his daughters. A settlement was made in this town in 1642,[2] by Mrs. Anne Hutchinson, who was driven from Massachusetts on account of her religious belief. There is 1 church (Prot. E.) in town.

POUNDRIDGE[3]—was formed March 7, 1788. It lies in the E. part of the co., its s. line bordering on Stamford and New Canaan, Conn. Its surface is hilly and much broken. The Stony Hills occupy the N. part and extend 3 or 4 mi. in a N. E. direction, with steep, craggy sides and rocky summits. Cross River flows through the extreme N. corner, Stamford Mill River flows s. through the E. part, and Maharness River forms a part of the s. w. boundary. Cross Pond is on the E. line. The soil is a gravelly loam. **Poundridge**, (p. o.,) near the center, is a small settlement with 2 churches. **Boretontown** is a hamlet, in the N. corner. The first settlement commenced near the center of the town, in 1744, by Capt. Joseph Lockwood and associates, from Stamford, Conn. There are 3 churches in town; M. E., Prot. Meth., and Presb.

RYE[4]—was formed March 7, 1788. It lies on the E. border of the s. part of the co. It is a narrow, irregular strip, bordering on the Sound and Greenwich, Conn. Its surface is broken and rocky. Byram River[5] forms a small part of the E. boundary, and Blind Brook a part of the w. The soil is chiefly clay. There are quarries of hard, blue granite in town. Along the coast are several small islands.[6] The mirage is frequently seen upon the coast, bringing to view the shore of Long Island with great distinctness. **Rye**, (p. v.,) a station on the N. Y. & N. H. R. R., contains 3 churches, a private seminary, and 300 inhabitants. **Milton**, in the s. part, is a hamlet, with 1 church. **Ryebeach** is a place of resort during the hot season. **Port Chester**, (p. v.,) a station on the N. Y. & N. H. R. R., contains 5 churches, several private seminaries, extensive manufactories,[7] and 1,695 inhabitants. **Kingstreet** is a fine agricultural district, extending nearly 7 miles N. of Port Chester. **Glenville** is a hamlet, on Byram River. The first settlement was commenced on Manursing Island.[8] The census reports 9 churches in town.[9]

SCARSDALE[10]—was formed March 7, 1788. It lies in the interior of the s. part of the co. Its surface is broken by ridges and hills. Bronx River forms the w. boundary, and the E. angle borders on the Mamaroneck. Hutchinson and Sheldrake Creeks rise in this town. The soil is a clayey and sandy loam. It has no villages, and is the least populous town in the co. **Scarsdale**, (p. o.,) in the w. part, contains a church and a few houses. **Scarsdale Station**, on the Harlem R. R., is on the w. border of the town. In the s. corner of the town is a Friends meeting house, on a site used for that purpose long before the Revolution. Gov. Tompkins was a native of this town; and Chief Justice Morris and Maj. Wm. Popham—for many years clerk of the Court of Exchequer—resided here. The census reports 2 churches in town; Prot. E. and Friends.

SOMERS[11]—was formed March 7, 1788, as "*Stephentown*." Its name was changed April 6, 1808. A part was annexed to New Castle in 1846. It lies on the N. border of the co., near the

---

[1] Upon these premises is a rocking stone weighing about 20 tons.

[2] This settlement was soon after broken up by the Indians, who killed 18 persons, including the founder.

[3] Named from the ancient Indian pound, or deer trap, which formerly stood at the foot of a high ridge s. of the present village.—*Bolton's Westchester, II, p. 1.* This town was embraced in Turner's Purchase of 1640, and once formed part of Stamford, Conn. The Patent of Stamford, granted May 26, 1685, included a portion of this town. In the settlement of boundaries in 1731, four miles were taken from Conn. A grant was made March 2, 1701, to Robert Walters, John Cholwell, Leigh Atwood, Cornelius De Peyster, Richard Slater, Barne Cosens, Lancaster Symes, Matthew Clarkson, Robert Lurting, Peter Matthews, and Caleb Heathcote. This grant was subsequently known as the "East Patent." It was sold Aug. 7, 1766, under "an act for the more effectual collecting of his Majesty's quitrents." Families named Lockwood, Ambler, Forsher, Bishop, Ferris, Hoyt, Holley, Brown, Sillick, and Scofield were purchasers under this sale. Until 1775 the town formed one of the precincts of Rye. In 1821, 900 acres were sold to satisfy the State claim to quitrents in the East Patent.

[4] Called by the Indians "Poningoe."

[5] Called by the Indians "Armonck." The meadows bordering it were called "Haseco" and "Miosehassaky."

[6] Manursing, called by the Indians "Minnewies," or Pine, Henhawk, Great, Middle, and Little Captains Islands.

[7] These consist of a foundery, edge tool factory, tide gristmill, and a last and shoe factory.

[8] This island was bought by the Dutch W. I. Company, who sold it June 29, 1660, to John Coe, Peter Disbrow, and Thos Studwell. The proprietors proposed to name the place Hastings, and issued a declaration of allegiance to the king, to which was annexed a description of their proposed town, embracing the country between Byram River and Blind Brook. Upon the final annexation to New York it was formed into a market town, with the privilege of holding a fair of four days, beginning on the 2d day of October. Courts of special sessions were also held here. The Dutch made the first Indian purchase in this region, in 1640; and numerous conveyances were afterward made. By the agreement of 1660, this town was included in Conn. In 1683 it was annexed to New York. In 1696 it was again claimed by Conn.; and the present line was fully settled May 14, 1730. The charter of Rye was granted Aug. 12, 1720.

[9] 3 M. E., 2 Prot. E., 2 Presb., Af. Meth., and R. C.

[10] Named from Scarsdale, in England, whence the Heathcote family came. In colonial times this town formed part of the manor of Scarsdale.

[11] Named from Capt. Richard Somers, the intrepid and gallant hero of the Tripolitan War. "*Stephentown*" was named from Stephen Van Cortlandt. Prior to 1788, it formed part of the township of Hanover, within Cortlandt Manor; and under the natives it formed part of the territory of Amapogh, or Ammawalk.—*Bolton's Westchester, II, p. 131.*

center. Its surface is broken by ridges in the s.; in other parts it spreads out into level plains. Croton River forms the s. e. boundary. Muscoot River[1] and Plum Brook flow s. through the town into Croton River. Croton Lake, the fountain head of the Croton Water Works, lies in the s. w. corner, extending into Yorktown. The soil is a sandy and gravelly loam. **Somers,** (p. v.,) in the n. e. part, contains 2 churches, a bank, and 20 houses.[2] **Croton Falls,** (p. v.,) in the n. e. corner, on the line of North Salem, is a small village and station on the Harlem R. R. It has a good water-power. **West Somers** (p. o.) is a hamlet. This town, in the allotment of the manor in 1734, fell to the share of Mrs. Margaret Bayard, Philip and Stephen Van Cortlandt, Andrew Johnston, —— Miller, Stephen De Lancey, and Mrs. Susannah Warren. The census reports 5 churches in town.[3]

WESTCHESTER[4]—was organized as a town, Nov. 7, 1788. West Farms was taken off in 1846. It lies on the Sound, in the extreme s. part of the co. It is bounded on the w. by Bronx River, and on the s. and e. by the Sound. Its surface is generally low and flat along the coast and rolling further inland. Several bays and estuaries extend far inland and divide the land into several peninsulas and necks. The principal of the latter are Classons Point,[5] between Bronx and Westchester Rivers; Zeregors Point, next e.; and Throggs Neck,[6] a long and narrow promontory extending s. e. into the Sound. About 2,500 acres along Westchester River is a salt meadow, a portion of which is held as public property and managed by 3 trustees. The people are principally engaged in gardening and fruit growing. **Westchester,** (p. v.,) at the head of navigation on Westchester Creek, is a scattered village of about 1,000 inhabitants. **Bronxdale,** on the line of West Farms, has an extensive tape factory, a dye and bleach works, and about 400 inhabitants. **Schuylerville,** upon Throggs Neck, is a scattered village of 300 inhabitants. **Integrity,** near Bronxdale, has a tape factory. **Connersville, Wakefield, Center-ville,** and **Unionport** are modern villages. **Fort Schuyler,** upon the extremity of Throggs Neck, was begun in 1833; and in 1851 $848,013 had been expended upon it. The estimated cost of the construction and repairs was then $873,013.[7] The first settlement on Throggs Neck was made in was begun in 1833; and in 1851 $848,013 had been expended upon it. The estimated cost of the construction and repairs was then $873,013.[7] The first settlement on Throggs Neck was made in 1642, by John Throckmorton and 35 associates, from New England, with the consent of the Dutch. The Indian title to the land was extinguished in 1643, by the Dutch, and a land brief was granted in that year, and another in 1652. The English began a settlement at Westchester[8] in 1642; but the Dutch, considering them intruders, arrested several of them, and in 1656 they surrendered themselves to the Dutch Government. The settlement was claimed by Conn. in 1663; but the next year it came under the government of the Duke of York. A patent was granted by Gov. Nicoll, Feb. 13, 1667, and by Gov. Dongan, Jan. 6, 1686. A market was established at West-chester, May 11, 1693, to be held weekly; and the same year an annual fair was established, to meet alternately at this place and Rye. It was made a borough town April 16, 1696, with mayor, aldermen, and common council, "according to the form of the best governed towns and corpora-tions of the realm of England," and the right of holding a mayor's court, and a representation by one delegate in General Assembly. The De Lancey family, prominent officials under the Colonial Government, and loyalists of the Revolution, resided in this town. The first church (Cong.) was formed soon after the arrival of the first settlers.[9]

WEST FARMS—was formed from Westchester, May 13, 1846. Morrisania was taken off in 1855. It lies upon the Sound and along Harlem River, in the s. part of the co. The surface is rolling, the ridges extending n. and s. Bronx River forms its e. boundary, and Sawmill Brook flows through the center. Its soil is a gravelly and sandy loam, rendered very productive by scien-tific farming. **West Farms,** (p. v.,) a large village at the head of navigation on Bronx River,

---

1 This river is said to discharge 3,628,800 gallons of water per day.

2 Hachaliah Bailey, of Somers, about 1815 imported the first elephant brought into the United States. "Old Bet" with other animals soon after imported was formed the first travel-ing menagerie in the country, with which Van Amburgh, the Lion Tamer, was afterward associated. Thaddeus and Gerard Crane, Lewis Titus, and John June, familiar to the public as enterprising showmen, were from this town and North Salem.

3 2 M. E., 2 Presb., and Prot. E.

4 The Dutch called this region "Vreedlandt," or the land of peace, and the village "Oorst Dorp," or East Village.

5 Formerly "Cornhills Neck," and granted to Thos. Cornhill, or Cornell, in 1646.

6 Named from John Throckmorton, the pioneer settler. A lighthouse, 61 feet high and 66 feet above the Sound, was built here in 1826, and refitted in 1855. It has a fog bell struck by machinery 7 times per minute.

7 It was built to accommodate 1,250 men and to mount 318 cannon. With the projected work upon Wilkins Point, in Flushing, Queens co., these fortresses would effectually protect New York against the approach of a hostile fleet from the Sound. The fort is built of granite from Greenwich, Conn.

8 The settlers at "Vreedlandt" at this time were Lieut. Thos Wheeler, Thos. U. Newman, Robert Bassett, John Cloes, Sher-wood Davies, Wm. H. Fenfall, Richard C. Meares, Samuel Havelt, Isaac Holbert, Robert Roes, Jas. Bill, John S. Genner, Richard Osbort, and Wm. Ward. The Dutch released Capt. R. Ponton, Wm. Elet Black, John Gray, and Roger Wheeler, who had been arrested for taking up arms at "Vreedlandt."—Bolton's Westchester, II, p. 160. In 1662 they were allowed to nominate their own magistrates and hold their own courts; "but in dark and dubious matters—especially in witchcraft—the party ag-grieved might appeal to the Governor and Council."

9 There are 7 churches in town; 2 Friends, Cong., Prot. E., M. E., Presb., and Af. Meth.

3 mi. from the Sound, contains 4 churches, a carpet factory, molding mill, and gristmill. **Fordham,** (p. v.,) on the R. R., in the N. part of the town, contains 4 churches and is the seat of St. John's College.[1] **Tremont,**[2] **Central Morrisania,**[3] **Williams Bridge,** (p. o.,) and **Fairmount** are modern villages. The last named is a station upon the Harlem R. R. **Claremont** is a small village on the line of Morrisania. The eastern part of the present town, originally known as "*The West Farms,*" was patented April 25, 1666, to Edward Jessup and John Richardson, Indian purchasers.[4] Fordham was bought by the Dutch in 1639, and in 1646 it was owned by Adrien Van der Donck. In 1671 John Archer, owner of 1,253 acres, obtained a patent under the title of the "Manor of Fordham." It passed to Cornelius Steenwyck, and was conveyed by his widow in 1694 to the Dutch church in New York, in whose possession it remained 60 years.[5] The High Bridge of the Croton Aqueduct connects the s. w. corner of this town with N. Y. City and Macomb's Bridge, in the N. w. corner. Fort No. 8 was built upon the eminence N. w. of the Archer homestead in the Revolution ; and its guns assisted in the capture of Fort Washington in 1776. It was demolished by the enemy Oct. 20, 1782. Fort Independence, on Tetards Hill, was dismantled in 1833. Prince Charles Redoubt and the Negro Fort of the Revolution were on the s. side of Valentines Hill. There are 8 churches in town.[6]

WHITE PLAINS—was formed March 7, 1788. It is an interior town, lying s. of the center of the co. The surface is rolling and hilly. Mamaroneck River forms its E. boundary, and Bronx River its w. St. Marys Lake lies along its E. border. The soil is a clayey and gravelly loam. **White Plains**[7] (p. v.) is situated near the w. line of the town. It contains the old and new co. buildings, 3 churches, and several private seminaries. It is a station upon the Harlem R. R., and contains about 1,000 inhabitants. This town was purchased Nov. 22, 1683, by the inhabitants of Rye, and was settled soon after. In 1720 it was divided among 41 proprietors ;[8] and a charter was granted March 13, 1721, with a quitrent of 2 shillings 6 pence to every 100 acres. It embraced 4,435 acres. Many important historical events occurred in this town during the Revolution. The village was wantonly burned Nov. 5, 1776, by a New England major. The battle of White Plains was fought on Chatterton Hill, in Greenburgh, opposite, and within view of the village. There are 6 churches in town.[9]

YONKERS[10]—was formed as a town March 7, 1788. It is the most southerly town in the co., upon the Hudson. The surface is rugged and broken by several ridges extending N. and s. Valentines Hill,[11] the highest point, is 400 ft. above tide. Tuckahoe Hill, in the E. part, and Thirty Deer Ridge, extending into Greenburgh, are prominent points. The principal streams are Bronx River, forming the E. boundary, Spuyten Duyvil Creek, forming the s. boundary, Neperhan River, flowing through the center, and Sprain River and Tibbetts Brook.[12] The soil is a clayey and gravelly loam. The people are largely engaged in manufactures.[13] The heights along the river are studded with elegant country residences. Many of the inhabitants are engaged in busi-

---

[1] This college, situated on Rose Hill. immediately E. of the Harlem R. R., is under the control of the R. C. denomination. It was incorp. April 10, 1846, having been opened for students June 24, 1841. It is under the direct charge of Jesuits, who, being associated for religious motives, receive no salary beyond personal support. Six other persons are employed as special instructors upon pay. In 1858 it reported to the Regents 59 undergraduates, besides which it has about 100 other pupils. Upon the premises is a large and handsome gothic church, and St. Joseph's Theological Seminary. The main building, of stone, 2 stories high, with an attic, contains the parlor, chapel. and professors' apartments, and is adorned with valuable paintings. Two front wings, of brick, one story each, 90 by 25 feet, contain the refectory, kitchen, study hall for the first division, and general assembly room. A large brick building contains the study hall for the second division, sleeping, play, and wash rooms. At each end of the front wings is a 3 story brick building, for reading hall, music, drawing, and class rooms, and dormitories. A 3 story brick building, 100 by 20 feet, contains the library, museum, wardrobe, and walking hall, for the senior division. The farm and property are valued at $147,000. Its libraries number 12,090 volumes, and it has a valuable cabinet of minerals.

[2] Formerly "*Upper Morrisania,*" "*South Fordham,*" "*Adamsville,*" and "*Mount Hope,*"—all of which are now embraced in one village under the general name of Tremont.

[3] A town hall was authorized to be erected April 15, 1854, and was located E. of Fordham Avenue, in Central Morrisania. It was built at a cost of about $15,000. By the subsequent erection of Morrisania it is brought near the s. border of this town.

[4] This patent was bounded E. by Bronx River, and w. by a little brook called by the natives Sachwrahung,—including a neck of land called Quinnahung. The s. part of the town, or "*Planting Neck,*" was called by the Indians Quinnahung. The w. side of this neck was called the "Debatable Ground," because

it was in dispute between the patentees of West Farms and Morrisania from 1666 to 1740.

[5] An act of General Assembly, Dec. 12, 1753, allowed the Dutch church to sell the Manor of Fordham.—which was done, and the money received is now vested in the city. Three hundred acres were excepted from this sale by Mrs. Steenwyck.

[6] 3 Prot. E., 2 Ref. Prot. D., 3 M. E., Presb., and R. C.

[7] This village is divided into two parts,—the old village, lying about three-fourths of a mile from the R. R., and the new village, lying between the old village and the R. R. station.

[8] Among these were families named Horton, Denham, Purdy, Brown, Lane, Frost, Disbrow, Merritt, Hyatt, Hoyt, Knapp, Pease, Kniffin, Odell, Galpin, Budd, Lounsberry, Travis, Stockham, Fowler, Walter, Cox, Jeffrey, Sherwood, Lyon, and Brondig. Several of these names are still common in town.

[9] 3 M. E., Prot. E., Presb., and R. C.

[10] Pronounced Yunk'ers. It is a Dutch word, signifying "gen tleman," or country nobleman,—a title of respect applied first in this place to Adrien Van der Donck, the patentee and first proprietor. This town and Mile Square formed a township on the great Manor of Philipsburgh, until the Revolution. The Indians called the place Ke-ke-shick.

[11] Named from the family who owned the adjoining property for about 130 years.

[12] Sprain River was called by the natives Ar-men-pe-ral; and Tibbetts Brook, Mos-ho-lu.

[13] There are about 20 manufactories in town, employing, when in full operation, 1,200 to 1,500 persons. Two hat factories each employ near 200 operatives. The foundery at Spuyten Duyvil employs about 300 hands ; and a pickle factory, on the Hudson, a still larger number. The Neperhan, a stream that enters the Hudson in the lower part of Yonkers Village, affords a considerable amount of water-power.

ness in New York. **Yonkers,** (p. v.,) on the Hudson, near the center of the w. border of the town, was incorp. April 12, 1855. It contains 9 churches, several private seminaries,[1] 2 banks, and 2 newspaper offices. Pop. in 1859, 6,800. It is a steamboat landing,[2] and a station on the Hudson River R. R. It has several manufactories and a great number of beautiful suburban villas.[3] **Spuyten Duyvil,** (p. v.,) on the creek separating the town from New York, is the seat of several large founderies, and is principally inhabited by operatives. **Tuckahoe,** (p. o.,) an old settlement in the E. part, is a station upon the Harlem R. R..[4] Near this place are several marble quarries. **Kingsbridge** (p. o.) lies upon Harlem River, and is connected with New York City by a bridge. **Riverdale,** below Yonkers, is a group of villas and a R. R. station. **South Yonkers** is a p. o. The Croton Aqueduct passes through this town from N. to S. A castellated stone mansion, built by Edwin Forrest, the tragedian, on the banks of the Hudson, a mile below Yonkers, has lately been purchased for an educational institution by the Roman Catholics.[5] The country now included in Yonkers, West Farms, and Morrisania, and containing about 24,000 acres, was granted to Adrian Van der Donck in 1646, with the right and title of Patroon. He gave to his estate the title of *"Colen Donck,"* perfected its title by purchase from the Indians, and took measures for its improvement.[6] There are 15 churches in town.[7]

YORKTOWN[8]—was formed March 7, 1788. It lies upon the N. border of the co., w. of the center. Its surface is broken and hilly. The Highlands lie along the N. border; and several points are elevated 600 to 1,000 ft. above tide. The principal stream is Croton River,[9] flowing across the S. part. Moharsic Lake,[10] near the center, Mohegan Lake, in the N. part, and Magriganies Lake, in the N. E. corner, are small bodies of water. **Crompond,** (Yorktown p. o.,) near the center, **Pines Bridge,** (p. o.,) near the E. line, **Jefferson Valley,** (p. o.,) in the N. E. corner, and **Shrub Oak;** (p. o.,) near the N. line, are hamlets. A rolling mill, wire factory, gristmill, and sawmill have been erected 2 mi. w. of Croton dam. This town formed a part of Cortlandt Manor, and in the division of 1734 fell to the shares of Andrew Miller, Gertrude Beeckman, Cornelia and John Schuyler, Gertrude Verplanck, Elizabeth Skinner, John Watts, Philip Verplanck, and Susannah Warren. A Presb. church built at Crompond[10] about 1738 was burned July, 1779, and a committee in Congress in 1839 reported in favor of paying $3,500 for the loss, as the premises had been used as a storehouse by the Continental troops. Col. Green was surprised in this town May 13, 1781, by a party of refugees, in which affair Maj. Flag, 2 subalterns, and 27 men were killed, and many wounded. The census reports 7 churches in town.[11]

---

[1] The principal of these are the Yonkers Collegiate Institute and Gymnasium, conducted on the military system, Starr's Boarding School, several female seminaries, and a public free school.

[2] The steamer Henry Clay was burned not far from this place, on her down trip, July 28, 1852. Of 500 persons on board, nearly 100 perished, among whom was A. J. Downing, the editor and author.

[3] The Manor Hall, near the center of the village, built about 1745, was one of the seats of the Philipse family.

[4] Hodgman's Rubber Goods Manufactory, located at this place, employs about 75 hands.

[5] An edifice of fine architectural proportions and great size was erected, in 1858, in the rear of the mansion. The premises form the institution formerly located on the Central Park in New York, and are under the charge of Sisters of Charity.

[6] Van der Donck subsequently took an active part in representing in Holland the interests of the colonists against the alleged tyranny of the West India Company and its servants, and finally succeeded in his efforts, notwithstanding the enmity of Gov. Stuyvesant and the influence he was able to bring to oppose him. He died in 1655, and his estate was afterward sold in detached portions by his widow. His settlement was laid waste by the Indians, Sept. 15, 1655, and probably remained unoccupied until after the English conquest. In 1672 Frederick Flypsen or Philipse, with Thos. Delaval and Thos. Lewis, bought 8,000 acres of Colen Donck, nearly all in the present town of Yonkers; and subsequently the former became sole owner to Kings Bridge. For one of these thirds he paid £530. These possessions were extended, by further purchase, to Croton and Bronx Rivers; and in June, 1693, the Lordship or Manor of Philipsburgh was erected, with all the rights, honors, or privileges enjoyed by the most favored, excepting that of representation in the General Assembly. He established a drawbridge at Spuyten Duyvil Creek, built a church, still standing, in Sleepy Hollow, and made other improvements. His descendants occupied a prominent position in the colonial government; but, siding with the royal cause, he lost every thing in the Revolution. Col. F. Philipse, the last proprietor of this estate, was paid £62,075 by the British Government, as an equivalent for this

loss; and his estates were sold by the State to his tenants at very moderate rates.
£62,075 by the British Government, as an equivalent for this loss; and his estates were sold by the State to his tenants at very moderate rates.

[7] 4 Prot. E., 3 M. E., 2 Presb., 2 R. C., Bap., Ref. Prot. D., Wes. Meth., and Unita.

[8] The country E. of Cortlandtown was called by the Mohegans Appanraghpogh; and the E. part of Yorktown is still called "Amawalk,"—probably an abbreviation.—*Bolton's Westchester, II, p. 377.*

[9] The Croton dam, at the head of the Croton Aqueduct, is in this town. At the top it is 166 ft. above tide and 55 ft. above the bed of the river; 61 feet wide at low water level, with openings of 90 and 180 feet for the passage of the surplus waters. Between these is a partition, forming the foundation of the gatehouse and sluiceway for relieving the structure from the pressure of the lake, and for the discharge of water during repairs. The water flows over an ogee-curved apron of cut stone laid upon hewn timber, and is received in a pond, formed by a second dam, 300 ft. below. The aqueduct is taken from the lake through a tunnel, on the S. side, 180 ft. long in the solid rock; and the flow of water is regulated by a double set of metal gates. The dam was destroyed while building, in Jan. 1841; but the present structure promises to stand without injury, and almost without repair, to an indefinitely remote period. The surface over which the waste water flows is now much more ample than was intended before the accident in 1841. The pond has a capacity of 500,000,000 gallons.
Croton River was named Kitchawan, signifying a large and swift current. The bend west of Pines Bridge was named Keweghtegnack. The commissioners were obliged to purchase about 900 acres of land overflowed by the dam, at an average cost of $500 per acre.

[10] Often called "Crom Pond," the Dutch term for Crooked Pond. It consists of 2 parts united. Near this pond is French Hill, where the French forces under Rochambeau were encamped in 1781–82. Turkey Mountain is an extensive woodland tract to the s. E.

[11] 2 M. E., 2 Friends, Bap., Cong., and Presb.

Acres of Land, Valuation, Population, Dwellings, Families, Freeholders, Schools, Live Stock, Agricultural Products, and Domestic Manufactures, of Westchester County.

Names of Towns.	Acres of Land.		Valuation of 1858.			Population.		No. of Dwellings.	No. of Families.	Freeholders.	Schools.	
	Improved.	Unimproved.	Real Estate.	Personal Property.	Total.	Males.	Females.				No. of Districts.	Children taught.
Bedford	21,243¼	3,473	$1,326,990	$275,180	$1,602,170	1,706	1,758	615	674	464	14	1,098
Cortlandt	13,614¾	6,966½	2,614,150	502,600	3,116,750	4,500	3,968	1,181	1,576	679	17	3,110
East Chester	4,506½	13,524	1,216,705	243,845	1,460,550	2,425	2,290	774	935	597	5	1,500
Greenburgh	12,702	2,182¼	4,051,057	487,600	4,538,657	3,093	3,342	924	1,192	624	9	2,204
Harrison	8,616¼	1,676	723,550	141,560	865,110	611	660	218	240	152	6	511
Lewisboro	12,840½	4,924	810,785	144,642	955,427	889	886	338	385	288	9	660
Mamaroneck	2,831½	1,051	583,595	46,100	629,695	525	543	172	226	81	2	364
Morrisania[a]			1,768,362	815,500	2,583,862						1	2,748
Mount Pleasant	13,396¼	3,130½	1,584,766	261,979	1,846,745	1,783	1,894	540	704	259	10	1,241
New Castle	11,211	2,781	697,388	148,822	846,210	879	883	317	345	220	8	572
New Rochelle	3,601	1,562	1,350,900	429,800	1,780,700	1,489	1,612	497	607	100	2	1,163
North Castle	11,402¼	4,410½	675,133	119,225	794,358	1,213	1,202	395	467	277	7	830
North Salem	10,970	2,051	801,427	202,750	1,004,177	736	792	289	318	188	8	525
Ossining	5,891	1,304	1,404,033	416,400	1,820,433	3,173	2,585	662	900	615	6	1,513
Pelham	1,901	1,333	533,000	213,750	746,750	391	442	119	122	78	2	246
Poundridge	8,214½	3,894¾	345,734	78,774	424,508	709	730	281	313	250	6	469
Rye	6,090	1,251	1,468,967	528,348	1,997,315	1,651	1,817	531	666	411	5	1,903
Scarsdale	2,801¾	1,132½	334,592	86,820	421,412	205	240	62	74	45	1	137
Somers	17,234½	3,110	1,046,691	319,842	1,366,533	859	885	304	316	157	8	678
Westchester	5,479	2,579½	1,808,915	422,900	2,231,815	1,748	1,716	493	582	303	3	1,215
West Farms	3,235½	992	1,865,274	364,500	2,229,774	6,173	6,263	2,035	2,419	1,445	4	1,928
White Plains	3,276	9,317	771,610	170,755	942,365	627	795	233	262	90	2	448
Yonkers	9,699	4,267	4,072,128	815,540	4,887,668	3,695	3,859	1,368	1,436	568	5	2,521
Yorktown	18,389¼	5,035	1,069,492	176,885	1,246,377	1,156	1,190	410	466	324	9	717
Total	209,146¾	81,947½	32,925,284	7,418,117	40,343,401	40,326	40,352	12,758	15,225	8,215	145	30,301

Names of Towns.	Live Stock.					Agricultural Products.							Domestic Cloths, in Yards.
						Bush. of Grain.		Tons of Hay.	Bushels of Potatoes.	Bushels of Apples.	Dairy Products.		
	Horses.	Working Oxen and Calves.	Cows.	Sheep.	Swine.	Winter.	Spring.				Pounds of Butter.	Pounds of Cheese.	
Bedford	461	922	2,127	655	1,412	9,940	61,833½	8,344	31,432	3,333	76,854	200	40
Cortlandt	725	940	1,635	302	1,491	7,000	36,730	5,100½	18,944	934	85,830		
East Chester	263	238	595	17	684	1,716	15,881	2,572	4,474	145	19,732	140	
Greenburgh	465	832	858	1,949	1,449	5,750½	34,362½	5,127	14,400	430	48,952		
Harrison	221	669	766	175	842	4,226½	20,404	4,187	9,389	2,173	44,515	100	
Lewisboro	319	781	1,386	440	913	3,670	36,990½	4,390⅛	12,205	1,876	62,767	925	25
Mamaroneck	104	154	233	30	257	624	5,576	1,121	2,989	636	16,957		
Morrisania[a]													
Mount Pleasant	389	827	1,058	1,357	1,469	5,073½	49,098½	5,797½	18,987	1,717	60,258		135
New Castle	272	658	1,074	476	763	4,530½	31,251½	4,902	9,117	472	34,260	100	
New Rochelle	166	282	343	88	445	2,340	11,519	2,471	4,343	156	19,500		
North Castle	326	647	898	136	1,156	4,606½	29,335¾	4,600½	17,783	1,609½	92,036		
North Salem	230	634	1,265	417	606	2,442½	26,440½	4,590	7,220	1,447	77,376	120	
Ossining	338	427	685	111	831	2,096	24,847	3,004	8,752	510	22,236		
Pelham	78	108	126		125	563	5,597	968	2,203		7,910		
Poundridge	157	607	92	472	583	2,186	15,969½	2,303¼	6,567	1,346	66,029	100	
Rye	237	397	430	40	584	2,436	15,722½	4,093	7,523	1,731	24,213		
Scarsdale	116	162	213	261	325	1,774	8,552	1,225	2,082	493	17,339		48
Somers	394	1,147	1,705	1,695	1,639	5,883	57,970½	6,675	22,809	5,765	101,278	495	209
Westchester	375	446	675	48	567	1,236	22,835	3,174	10,005	108	20,955		
West Farms	408	241	1,296	24	822	230	7,842	2,786	12,960	118	8,537		
White Plains	167	208	229	246	483	2,367	17,533	2,502	7,948	2,243	21,510	40	
Yonkers	583	503	661	705	1,258	6,243	30,162½	3,327	17,739	29,006	37,644		
Yorktown	538	1,244	1,728	1,677	2,157	8,201½	63,985	7,237	36,378	3,889	149,901		30
Total	7,332	13,074	20,078	11,321	20,861	85,155½	630,438¾	90,496⅞	286,249	60,137½	1,116,589	2,180	487

[a] Formed since the census of 1855. This town is estimated to embrace 7,000 acres, and to contain 4,000 males and 4,150 females.

WYOMING COUNTY.

This county was formed from Genesee, May 14, 1841. Eagle, Pike, and a part of Portage were annexed from Allegany co. in 1846. It is an interior county, in the s. w. part of the State, separated from Lake Erie by Erie co., and from the Penn. line by Cattaraugus and Allegany. It is centrally distant 228 miles from Albany, and contains 590 sq. mi. Its surface is a broad, rolling upland, divided into ridges and broken by ravines worn by the streams. It has a slight inclination toward the N. The summits of the highest ridges are 1,200 to 1,500 ft. above Lake Erie and 1,700 to 2,000 ft. above tide. Several of the ravines in the N. are 1,000 ft. below the summits of the adjacent ridges. In the interior the ridges are broken, and the country begins to assume the hilly character which is more fully developed further s. Genesee River, which forms a portion of the E. boundary, is bordered by steep bluffs 200 to 400 ft. high. Near Portageville the river descends from the plateau, in a series of three falls, to a depth of more than 300 ft. within a distance of 2½ mi. The water has worn a deep and irregular ravine in the shelving rocks, and the nearly perpendicular banks at the foot of the lower falls are 380 ft. high. The deep gorge, with the rapids and falls, form one of the wildest and most picturesque scenes in Western New York.[1]

The other principal streams are Cayuga, Tonawanda, Little Tonawanda, Oatka, East Coy, Wiscoy, Cattaraugus, and Buffalo Creeks. The valley of Oatka Creek, from near the s. border of Warsaw to the N. line of the co., is bordered by steep hills 400 to 1,000 ft. high. Silver Lake, in Castile, (the principal body of water,) is 3 mi. long and about ½ mi. wide. The rocks of this co. consist principally of the shales and sandstones of the Portage group. The summits of the southern hills are covered with the rocks belonging to the Chemung group. Thin layers of compact Portage sandstone are found in many parts of the co. and are extensively quarried for flagging. Upon the ridges little rounded eminences are frequently seen, appearing like drift hills; but upon examination they are found to be shale rock covered with a thin soil. Marl and muck are found in considerable quantities in the swamps. The waters of Silver Lake and of several of the streams are constantly depositing lime in the form of marl. The drift deposits in the co. are very extensive, and the soil in some parts is derived from disintegration. Upon the hills it is mostly a clay loam underlaid by hardpan, and in the valleys it is a fertile, gravelly loam and alluvium. The people are principally engaged in stock and wool growing and in dairying, for which the soil upon the hills is admirably adapted. Wheat, barley, corn, and fruits are largely cultivated in the valleys. Very little attention is paid to manufactures except such as are strictly necessary to an agricultural community.

The county seat is located at Warsaw.[2] The courthouse is a commodious brick edifice, situated in the N. part of the village. The co. clerk's office is a fireproof building, adjacent to the courthouse. The jail is a wood building, arranged so as to enable the keeper to classify the prisoners

---

[1] The Upper or Horse-Shoe Falls are about three-fourths of a mi. below Portageville. The name is derived from the curve in the face of the cliff over which the water flows. For a short distance above the edge of the precipice the water is broken by a succession of steps in the rock, forming a series of rapids. The height of the fall, including the rapids, is about 70 ft. The Middle Falls are about one-half mi. further down the river. For 2 or 3 rods above the edge of the cliff the water is broken into rapids, and then in an unbroken sheet it pours down 110 ft. into a chasm below, bounded by perpendicular ledges. A cave, called the "Devil's Oven," has been worn in the rocks under the w. bank, near the bottom of the falls. In low water 100 persons can be seated within it; but when the river is high it is filled with water, and is only accessible by boats. The Lower Falls consist of a series of rapids one-half mi. in extent. with an aggregate fall of 150 ft. For about 2 mi. below the Middle Falls the river pursues a winding and rapid course between high, perpendicular walls; then descends in a succession of steps almost as regular as a staircase, dives under a shelving rock, shoots out in a narrow pass not more than 15 ft. wide, rushes down a nearly perpendicular descent of 20 ft., strikes against the base of high rocks standing almost directly in its course, whirls back, and, turning at nearly right angles, falls into a deep pool overhung with shelving

rocks. An isolated mass of rocks, 15 ft. in diameter and 100 ft. high, known as "Sugar Loaf," rises from the river bed at the bend of the stream and receives nearly the whole force of the rushing water. It is bordered on one side by the present bed of the stream, and on the other by a deep chasm which separates it from the E. bank of the river. Within the memory of people now living, the river flowed over the precipice on the level of the rock which now forms its w. bank, and Sugar Loaf was an island. These falls are accessible only from the w. The perpendicular bank on the w. side of the river at one point is 380 ft. high.

[2] The commissioners named in the act to select the location were Peter R. Reed, of Onondaga, Davis Hurd, of Niagara, and John Thompson, of Steuben. The building commissioners were John A. McElwaine, Paul Richards, and Jonathan Perry. Trumble Cary, Esq., of Batavia, gave to the co. an ample public square upon which to erect the public buildings. The first courts were held at a public house at East Orangeville, in June, 1841, and the first meeting of the Board of Supervisors was at the same place. The first co. officers were Paul Richards, *First Judge*; James Sprague, Peter Patterson, Jos. Johnson, *Associate Judges*; W. Riley Smith, *District Attorney*; N. Wolcott, *Co. Clerk*; W. R. Groger, *Sheriff*; and Harvey Putnam, *Surrogate*.

according to law.[1] The poorhouse is situated on a farm of 97 acres near the w. border of Orange-ville, 9 mi. w. of Warsaw. The average number of inmates is 73, supported at a cost of 75 cts. per week each. The farm yields a revenue of about $300.[2]

The Buffalo, New York & Erie R. R. extends s. e. through Attica, Middlebury, Warsaw, Gainesville, Castile, and Genesee Falls, crossing the Portage Falls and connecting with the N. Y. & E. R. R. at Hornellsville. A r. r. route has been surveyed, and a road-bed graded, from Attica s. w. to the Allegany River.[3]

There are 5 weekly newspapers published in the co.[4]

The eastern tier of towns in this co., with the exception of a portion of Castile, belonged to the Ogden, Silver Lake, and Cotringer tracts of the Morris Reservation, and the remaining parts of the co. to the Holland Land Purchase. The Gardeau Tract, containing 17,927 acres on both sides of the Genesee, was reserved for Mary Jemison (the "old white woman") by the Seneca Nation in their treaty with Robert Morris in 1797.[5] About one-half of this tract lies in the present town of Castile. Upon this tract Mary Jemison and her descendants continued to reside until 1816, when she sold all but 2 sq. mi. on the w. side of the river to Micah Brooks and Jellis Clute. The remaining 2 mi. she sold in 1831 to Henry B. Gibson and Jellis Clute, and removed to the Cattaraugus Reservation. The first white man that lived within the limits of the co. was a tory, named Ebenezer Allen, who in consequence of his crimes fled from Penn. and joined the Indians about 1780. He located upon the Genesee, and for a time lived upon the lands of Mary Jemison. He afterward built a saw and grist mill on the present site of Rochester, removed thence to Oatka Creek,[6] and thence to Canada.[7] The first permanent white settlers were John Tolles, Jacob Wright, Nathaniel Sprout, and Stephen Crow, in 1802. The settlements increased rapidly, and in a few years most of the best lands of the co. were taken up. Most of the early settlers were from New England; but the later immigrants have principally been Germans.

ATTICA—was formed from Sheldon, April 4, 1811. Orangeville was taken off in 1816. It

---

[1] The courthouse, jail, and clerk's office were erected in 1842, at a cost of $12,000.

[2] The poorhouse contains 22 rooms, and the inmates are provided with good, substantial food; but the house does not admit of proper accommodations for the paupers, or for classification of the insane, of which there are always a number.

[3] The Allegany Valley Railroad.

[4] *The Genesee Register*, the first newspaper in the co., was established at Warsaw in 1828 by L. & W. Walker, and was continued 6 months.

The Warsaw Sentinel was commenced by Andrew W. Young in May, 1830, and continued until Dec. 1831, when it was merged in the Republican Advocate at Batavia.

The Attica Republican was commenced by David Scott in 1833–34. It was soon after changed to

The Attica Republican and Genesee Advertiser. E. A. Cooley became its publisher, and changed it to

The Attica Balance, and subsequently to

The Attica Democrat, and continued it until 1846.

The Genesee Recorder was commenced at Perry by Geo. M. Shipper in 1834, and continued about 2 years.

The American Citizen was commenced at Warsaw in 1836 by J. A. Hadley. After 1 year, it was removed to Perry and published by Mitchell & Warren. Mr. Mitchell continued the publication until Jan. 1841, when it was removed to Rochester.

The Pike Whig was commenced by Thos. Carrier in 1838. Soon after, its name was changed to

The Pike Gazette, and it was continued for about a year.

The Watchtower, a Bap. paper, was issued in 1839 from the office of The American Citizen. It was published 1 year by Ansel Warren.

The Register, a campaign paper, was published at Perry in 1840 by Isaac N. Stoddard and John H. Bailey.

The Perry Democrat was commenced in 1841 by Pet. Lawrence. In 1848 it passed to C. C. Britt, who continued it until 1853.

The Western New Yorker was commenced at Perry in Jan. 1841, by John H. Bailey. In the summer of the same year it passed into the hands of Barlow & Woodward, who removed it to Warsaw. It was successively published by Barlow & Blanchard, Mr. Blanchard, and H. A. Dudley until April 1, 1858, when it passed into the hands of Elijah W. Andrews, and afterward to Andrews & Harrington, by whom it is still published.

The Countryman was commenced at Perry by N. S. Woodward in 1843. It soon passed to Dan'l. S. Curtis, who changed its name to

The Impartial Countryman, and continued it until Aug. 1846, when it passed to Ansel Warren, who changed its name to

The Free Citizen, and continued it until Aug. 1847.

The Wyoming Republican was commenced at Warsaw by E. L. Fuller in 1844; it was published until March, 1847.

The Attica Telegraph was commenced by Abraham Dinsmore in Oct. 1846, and was published about 2 years.

The Old Eighth Whig was commenced at Attica, April 1, 1848, by R. W. Dibble and W. H. Civer. After about 6 mos. Mr. Dibble retired and Mr. Civer continued the paper, as *The Spirit of the Old Eighth,* until 1850.

The Attica Atlas was commenced Jan. 1, 1851, by Silas Folsom, by whom it is still published.

The Christian Investigator was published at the office of the Free Citizen for 1 year. Edited by Wm. Gooddell.

The Wyoming Co. Advertiser was commenced Dec. 22, 1853, and was published 1 year by Horace Wilcox.

The Wyoming Times was commenced at Perry by T. S. Gillet in May, 1855. It was destroyed by fire in 1856, and resuscitated soon after. It is still pub. by Mr. Gillet.

The Wyoming Co. Mirror was commenced at Warsaw in 1848 by A. Holley. In 1856 it passed into the hands of Babbitt & Lewis, in 1858 to Lewis & Merrill, and in 1859 to H. A. Dudley, by whom it is still published.

The Arcade Enterprise was started March 31, 1859, by J. H. Gibson, and is still published.

[5] The parents of Mary Jemison emigrated from Ireland in 1743, and Mary was born during the voyage across the ocean. The family settled upon the western frontiers of Penn., where they remained in peace until the breaking out of the French War in 1754. In 1755 a party of Indians visited the settlement and took the family prisoners, and on their return murdered all but Mary, then a girl of 12 or 13 years. She was carried captive to an Indian settlement on the Ohio, and adopted by two women who had lost a brother in the war. She grew to womanhood among the Indians, adopted their habits and customs, was twice married, and had 8 children,—3 sons and 5 daughters. After the Revolution she had an opportunity to return to her white friends; but she preferred to remain with her husband and children. She was greatly beloved by the Indians, and highly respected by the whites who became acquainted with her. She retained her knowledge of the English language, and to the last remembered the early instructions of her mother, and the last counsel which that mother gave when they were taken captive and the designs of the Indians to murder the father and mother became manifest. She died at the Cattaraugus Reservation, Sept. 19, 1833, aged 90 or 91 years.

[6] This creek is still locally known as Allens Creek.

[7] Few characters mentioned in either history or fiction have approached so near the idea of total depravity as this blood-thirsty monster. He was an open polygamist,—murdered several persons while professing the greatest friendship for them,—and while upon the war-trail with the Indians amused himself by dashing out the brains of infants.

lies upon the N. border of the co., W. of the center. Its surface is a rolling upland, broken by the ravines of the streams. In the E. part are several considerable hills with long gradual slopes. Tonawanda Creek, the principal stream, flows through the N. w. corner, and receives numerous branches from the E., the largest of which is Crow Creek. The soil is a clay and gravelly loam. **Attica,** (p. v.,) upon Tonawanda Creek, in the N. w. part of the town, was incorp. May 2, 1837. It contains a flourishing union school, a bank, a newspaper office, a flouring mill, and 5 churches. Pop. 1,184. **Attica Center** (p. o.) and **Vernal** are hamlets. The first settlement was made in 1802, by Zera Phelps.[1] The first religious services were held Sept. 21, 1809, by Rev. Royal Phelps, at which time the first church (Cong.) was formed, with 5 members.[2]

BENNINGTON—was formed from Sheldon, March 6, 1818. It is the N. w. corner town of the co. Its surface is a rolling upland, broken by the ravines of small streams. Cayuga Creek and its branches drain the central, and Murder Creek the N. part of the town. Tonawanda Creek flows through the S. E. corner. The soil is a clayey, gravelly and sandy loam. **Bennington Center** (Bennington p. o.) contains 3 churches and 30 dwellings; and **Cowlesville**, (p. v.,) in the N. w. part of the town, 2 churches and 206 inhabitants. **Folsomdale** (p. o.) is a hamlet, on Cayuga Creek, and has a valuable water-power. The first settlement was made near the center of the town, in 1802, by John Tolles, Jacob Wright, and William Barber, from Vt.[3] The first religious services were conducted by Rev. Peter B. Root, in 1805. The first church (M. E.) was formed in 1807.[4]

CASTILE (Cas-tíle)—was formed from Perry, Feb. 27, 1821. It is the central town upon the E. border of the co. Its surface is a rolling and terraced upland, broken by the deep valleys of the streams. Genesee River, forming a portion of the E. boundary, is bordered by steep banks 300 to 350 ft. above the water. In some places the faces of the bluffs are perpendicular ledges 200 ft. high. Numerous small tributaries of the river have worn deep lateral channels in these bluffs. The valley of Silver Lake occupies a wide and shallow basin in the N. part of the town.[5] Its outlet is toward the N. Wolf Creek rises in a swamp near the head of the lake and flows S. A wide, level valley, bordered by low terraces, extends from the E. shore of the lake and opens into the valley of Wolf Creek at Castile Village. The soil is a clay and gravelly loam. **Castile** (p. v.) lies on Wolf Creek, in the S. w. part of the town. It is a station on the B. & N. Y. City R. R. Pop. 682. **St. Helena,** (p. v.,) on Genesee River, in the S. E. corner of the town, contains 20 dwellings. The first settlement was made in 1808, by Robert Whalley, from R. I., 1 mi. E. of Castile Village.[6] The first religious services (Bap.) were held near the S. end of Silver Lake, in 1816, by Elder Benj. Luther.[7]

CHINA—was formed from Sheldon, March 6, 1818. Java was taken off in 1832. It is the S. w. corner town of the co. Its surface is a rolling or hilly upland, broken by valleys. Cattaraugus Creek flows S. w. through near the center of the town, and receives several tributaries, the principal of which is Clear Creek, from the S. From the valleys the town spreads out into a rolling region, with long gradual slopes arable to their summits. The highest point is the ridge in the N. E., which is 1,100 ft. above Lake Erie, as determined by actual survey. The soil of the upland is a clayey and in the valleys a gravelly loam. **Arcade** (China p. o.) is situated at the junction of Cattaraugus and Clear Creeks, in the S. w. part of the town. It has a fine

---

[1] Among the other early settlers were Deacon Porter, Nath'l Sprout, and Maj. P. Adams. The first child born was Harriet Phelps, July 25, 1803; the first marriage, that of Stephen Crow and Lucy Elwell; and the first death, that of Thomas Mather, in the winter of 1803. Sophia Williams taught the first school, in 1807; Daniel Stanton kept the first inn, in 1809; —— Fitch, the first store; and Zera Phelps built the first mill, in 1806.

[2] The census reports 6 churches; Cong., Presb., F. W. Bap., Bap., M. E., and R. C.

[3] Among the other early settlers were Chauncey, Justin, and George Loomis, Peletiah Case, Joseph Farnham, George Hoskins, David Tolles, Aaron Clapp, and Ezra Ludden. The first marriage was that of Aaron Whitney and Rachel Truesdale, in 1807; and the first death in town, that of a child of Wm. Barber, in 1803. The first school was taught by Rachel Truesdale, in 1807; the first inn was kept by Joseph Farnham, in 1817. Chauncey Loomis erected the first sawmill, in 1808; he also kept the first store. Quartus Clapp built the first gristmill, at Cowlesville. A son of David Tolles, 8 or 9 years old, was lost in the woods in 1806 and was never found.

[4] The census reports 5 churches; Bap., F. W. Bap., Presb., M. E., and Univ.

[5] Mary Jemison, the "old white woman," with her family, hid

in the alders at the foot of this lake while Gen. Sullivan was laying waste the Indian villages upon the Genesee. In the summer of 1855 it was reported that an immense serpent, 100 ft. long, had been seen in this lake. So well was the story apparently authenticated that thousands of visitors came from all parts of the country to obtain a sight of his snakeship. A burlesque account of the capture of the serpent, which appeared in the *Buffalo Republic*, raised the excitement to the highest pitch; and immediately afterward the whole humbug collapsed.

[6] Soon after, a settlement was made at the foot of the lake, in the w. part of the town, called the "*Tallman Settlement.*" Ziba Hurd and Jonathan Gilbert, from Vt., were the first settlers at Castile Village, in 1816. The first child born was Jane McRay, in 1813; and the first death was that of Laura Wilcox, in 1815. The first school was taught in 1816, by Anna Bennett, from Vt. Robert Whalley kept the first inn, and erected the first sawmill, on Wolf Creek, below Castile Village, in 1811. John Card and Sylvester Lathrop built the first gristmill, on Lot 40, in 1820; the first store was kept by Lemuel Eldridge and M. Frost, in 1815.

[7] The census reports 4 churches; Cong., Bap., M. E., and Christian.

water power, and contains a woolen factory, flouring mill, and 3 churches. Pop. 637. **East China** is a p. o. The first settlement was made in 1808, on Lot 28, by Silas Meech, from New England.[1] The first religious services were conducted by Rev. John Spencer, at Arcade, in 1812. The first church (Cong.) was formed at Arcade, by Jno. Spencer, July 24, 1813.[2]

COVINGTON—named from Gen. Leonard Covington—was formed from Le Roy (Genesee co.) and Perry, Jan. 31, 1817. A part was annexed to York (Livingston co.) in 1823. It is the N. E. corner town of the co. The surface is a moderately hilly upland, broken by the deep ravines of the streams. Oatka Creek flows through the N. W. corner, and receives as tributary Pearl Creek, which flows N. W. through near the center. Wide, fertile alluvial flats extend along Oatka Creek. The soil of the uplands is generally a gravelly loam. **Covington Center,** (Covington p. o.,) in the N. part, contains 20 dwellings; **Pearl Creek,** (p. v.,) in the N. W., contains 15 dwellings; **La Grange,** (p. v.,) near the S. line, a church and 20 dwellings; and **Peoria,** (p. v.,) near the E. line, 15 dwellings. The first settlement was made in 1807, in the W. part, by Jairus Cruttenden, William Miller, and John and William Sprague, all from New England.[3] The first religious services were held at the house of David Norris, in 1814, by Rev. Mark Norris, from Vt.[4]

EAGLE—was formed from Pike, Jan. 21, 1823. It occupies a central position on the S. border of the co. Its surface is a hilly upland, broken by the deep ravines of the streams. Nearly the whole drainage is through Wiscoy Creek and its branches. Cold Creek takes its rise in the S. E. part of the town. The hills bordering upon the streams are very steep, and their summits are 400 to 700 ft. above the valleys. Eagle Lake, a small body of water in the S. W. part, has no visible outlet. The soil is a clayey and gravelly loam. **Eagle Village,** (p. v.,) in the S. W. part of the town, contains a church and 20 dwellings. **Eagle,** (p. o.,) in the N. E. part, is a hamlet. The first settlement was made in town in 1808, on Lot 8, by Silas and Wm. Hodges, from Cayuga co.[5] There are 3 churches in town; M. E., F. W. Bap., and Christian.

GAINESVILLE—named from Gen. E. P. Gaines—was formed from Warsaw, as "*Hebe,*" Feb. 25, 1814. Its name was changed April 17, 1816. It is an interior town, lying S. E. of the center of the co. The surface is an upland, slightly undulating and broken by the valleys of the streams. Oatka Creek flows through the N. E. part, and East Coy Creek through the S. W. The soil on the hills is a thin, dark loam underlaid by hardpan, and in the valleys a fertile, gravelly loam. A good quality of building stone is quarried in the N. part of the town. **Gainesville Creek,** (Gainesville p. o.,) on East Coy Creek, near the center of the town, contains a female seminary,[6] 3 churches, and about 300 inhabitants. **East Gainesville,** (p. v.,) a station on the B. & N. Y. City R. R., contains 20 houses. **Gainesville Center** and **Newburgh** are hamlets. The first settlements were made at Gainesville Creek in 1805, by Wm., Richard, and Chas. Bristol, from Columbia co., and Elnathan George, from Vt.[7] The first religious meeting was held in 1809. The first church (Presb.) was formed in 1815.[8]

GENESEE FALLS—was formed from Pike and Portage, (Livingston co.,) April 1, 1846. It lies on Genesee River, in the S. E. corner of the co. A nearly perpendicular rocky bluff, 100 to 300 ft. high, borders upon the river, and from its summit the country spreads out into an undulating upland. The celebrated Portage Falls, in the Genesee River, are opposite this place.[9] The soil is a sandy and clayey loam. **Portageville,** (p. v.,) on Genesee River, contains 5 churches and several mills. Pop. 561. The B. & N. Y. City R. R. crosses the Genesee, near the village, by a bridge 800 ft. long and 234 ft. above the bed of the river. This bridge was built at a cost of

---

[1] Ichabod Sanders, Samuel Nichols, Silas and Leonard Parker, Jacob Jackson, Wm. Barnes, Amasa and Alfred Kilbourn—most of them from Vt.—settled in the town in 1809. The first child born was a daughter of Jacob Jackson, and the second a son of Samuel Nichols, both in 1810; the first marriage was that of Silas Meech and Lydia Parker; and the first death, that of Mrs. A. Kilbourn, in the spring of 1812. Rebecca Parker taught the first school, in 1811; Silas Parker kept the first inn, in 1812, and the first store, in 1815. Maj. Moses Smith built the first sawmill, in 1811, and Col. Duel Rowley the first gristmill, in 1811.

[2] The census reports 5 churches; Cong., Bap., F. W. Bap., M. E., and R. C.

[3] The first child born was Viola, daughter of Dr. Dan'l White, in 1809; the first marriage was that of Calvin Davis and Sylvia Beardsley, in 1814; and the first death, that of Mrs. Easty, in 1814. Wm. Miller kept the first inn, in 1813; Dan'l Balcom, the first store, in 1812; —— Spaulding built the first gristmill, in 1810; and Sprague and Spaulding the first sawmill, in 1812.

[4] The census reports 3 churches; Presb., Asso. Presb., and M. E.

[5] Alanson, son of Silas Hodges, was the first child born, Oct. 13, 1809. The first inn was kept by Dan Beach, the first store, by Elijah Hyde, and the first sawmill was erected by Amos Huntley.

[6] The Gainesville Female Seminary was established in 1855, by Misses Hardy and Eldridge, and other citizens of this place. The school is on the plan of the Mount Holyoke (Mass.) school. The buildings will accommodate 100 boarding pupils and 150 day scholars.

[7] John Patterson and James Cravath, with others, settled in 1806. Pamela Patterson was the first child born, in 1807. The first school was taught in Dec. 11, by Benj. Cole. The first inn was kept at the Center, by Benj. Hoag, in 1815; and the first store, by Lewis Wood, in the Yates settlement, in 1816. Wheelock Wood erected the first sawmill, in 1809, on Oatka Creek; and John Card and Benj. Mallory, the first gristmill, in 1825, at Gainesville Creek.

[8] The census reports 5 churches; 2 M. E., and 1 each Cong., Bap., and Univ.

[9] See page 710.

$175,000, and is the largest wooden R. R. bridge in the world. The Genesee Valley Canal also crosses the river at this point by an aqueduct built upon stone abutments 40 ft. high; the structure cost $70,000. The first settlements were made on the river, above Portageville, in 1804, by John, Samuel, and Seth Fields.[1] The first religious meeting was held by Rev. John Griffith, (M. E.,) in 1809; and the first church (Bap.) was formed by Rev. Joseph Case, at "*Bigelows Corners*," in 1818.[2]

JAVA—was formed from China, April 20, 1832. It lies on the w. border of the co., s. of the center. Its surface is an elevated region, broken by hills and the deep valleys of the streams. The highest summits are 400 to 600 ft. above the valleys and 1,000 to 1,200 ft. above Lake Erie. Buffalo Creek flows through the w. part, and receives a large number of tributaries. Cattaraugus Creek takes its rise in the E. part. Cattaraugus Lake is a small sheet of water in the s. E. part, nearly surrounded by steep hills. It forms one of the sources of Cattaraugus Creek. The soil upon the hills is a thin, dark loam underlaid by hardpan; in the valleys it is principally a gravelly loam. About 1 mi. E. of Java Village is a quarry of fine building stone. **Java Village** (p. v.) lies upon Buffalo Creek, in the N. w. part of the town. Pop. about 200. **North Java,** (p. v.,) in the N. E. corner of the town, contains a church and about 100 inhabitants. **Java Center,** (p. o.,) **East Java,** (p. o.,) in the S. E. part of the town, **Curriers Corners,** (Java p. o.,) in the s. w., and **Williamsville,** near the E. border, are hamlets. The first settlement was made on Lot 32, in the N. w. part of the town, in 1810, by Wm. Richardson and Timothy Kirby, from Lowell, Mass.[3] The first church (R. C.) was formed in 1838.[4]

MIDDLEBURY—was formed from Warsaw, March 20, 1812. It lies on the N. border of the co., E. of the center. Its surface is a rolling upland, broken by the deep valleys of the streams. Oatka Creek flows through the s. E. corner, and Little Tonawanda Creek through the w. part. A deep ravine extends E. and w. through near the center of the town, forming a natural pass between the valleys of these two streams. The hills that border upon Oatka Creek are steep and 400 to 600 ft. high. The soil is a gravelly and clayey loam. **Wyoming,** (p.v.,) on Oatka Creek, near the E. border of the town, contains the Middlebury Academy,[5] 3 churches, and 378 inhabitants. **West Middlebury,** (Dale p. o.,) a station on the B. & N. Y. City R. R., contains 20 dwellings. The first settlement was made by Jonas Sellick, (from Rutland co., Vt.,) in 1802, near Wrights Corners.[6] There are 5 churches in town.[7]

ORANGEVILLE—was formed from Attica, Feb. 14, 1816. Wethersfield was taken off in 1823. It is an interior town, lying N. w. of the center of the co. Its surface is a rolling upland, broken by deep ravines. The streams are Tonawanda Creek and its branches, draining the w., and small branches of Oatka and East Coy Creeks, draining the E. parts of the town. The summits of the highest hills are 400 to 700 ft. above the valleys. The soil is a gravelly and clayey loam underlaid by hardpan. **Orangeville Center** (Orangeville p. o.) contains 15 houses; **Johnsonburg,** (p. v.,) on Tonawanda Creek, lies partly in Sheldon. Pop. about 100. **Halls Corners** (East Orangeville p. o.) is a hamlet. The first settlement was made in 1805, by John Duncan, on Lot 13, and Elisha Doty, from Cayuga co., on Lot 12.[8] The first church (Presb.) was organized by Rev. John Alexander, July 11, 1812.[9]

1 Nathan and Joseph Dixon, Joseph and Justice Bailey, and Sebetiah Ward settled previous to 1807. The first death was that of Sophia Smith, in 1817. The first school was taught by Maria Bellinger, in 1809. The first inn was kept by Lewis Wood, at Portageville, in 1824; and the first store, by Foot & Martin, the same year. The first sawmill was erected in 1812, and the first gristmill in 1820, on the river, by Mumford, Smith, & McKay.

2 The census reports 5 churches; Bap., M. E., Presb., Univ., and R. C.

3 In 1812 and '14, Chas. Richardson and Daniel H. Worcester settled at Java Village, and Charles Fox at Curriers Corners. The first mill was erected by Daniel H. Worcester, at Java Village, in 1816; the first inn was kept by Chas. Fox, at Curriers Corners, in 1818; and the first store, by Mr. Comstock, at Java Village, in 1820.

4 The census reports 4 churches; Cong., M. E., F. W. Bap., and R. C.

5 This academy was founded mainly by the efforts and liberality of several of the first settlers of the village. Its main building was erected by subscription, in 1817. It now has some endowments, and is under the charge of the Baptist denomination. For many years it was considered the first institution w. of the Genesee River, and still maintains a high reputation.

6 In 1803 a number of immigrants from Vt. settled in the town, among whom were Reuben Chamberlain, Jabez Warren, Frederick Gilbert, Sterling Sterns, and Israel M. Dewey. The first store was kept by Edwin Putnam, in 1810, near Wrights

Corners; the first gristmill was built by Silas Newell, in 1813, near Wyoming Village; the first sawmill, by A. Worden, in 1809, at West Middlebury; Amzi Wright kept the first inn, at Wrights Corners, in 1806. In May, 1817, Artemus Shattuck, a citizen of this town, went into the woods, a distance from home, to chop. While cutting off a log that had been partially split open, his foot was caught in the crack, and he hung for a long time suspended by his foot and partially supported by one hand. Despairing of receiving aid, and entirely unable to extricate himself, he finally unjointed his ankle with his pocket knife, made a crutch of a crooked stick, and started for the house. He was found about dark, and carried to the house, where his leg was amputated by a surgeon. He recovered, became a Bap. minister, and lived many years.

7 2 Bap., and 1 each F. W. Bap., Presb., and M. E.

8 Lemuel Chase and James Sayer settled about the same time, and Seth and Adial Sherwood, Silas Merrifield, and Asahel Ward in 1806; Truman Lewis and a number of other families in 1807. The first child born was a son of Seth Sherwood, in 1807; the first marriage was that of Adial Sherwood and Miss Wood, in 1809; and the first death, that of Mrs. James Sayer. Corinna Lewis and Mary McKnight commenced the first schools, May 1, 1811; Isaac Moore kept the first inn, in 1811, at the Center; and Silas Hubbard the first store, in 1814, at the same place. Robert Hopkins erected the first sawmill, in 1810, and Levi Johnson the first gristmill, in 1817.

9 The census reports 4 churches; Presb., Bap., Ref. Prot. D., and Friends.

PERRY[1]—was formed from Leicester, (Livingston co.,) March 11, 1814. A part of Covington was taken off in 1817, and Castile in 1821. It lies on the E. border of the co., N. of the center. Its surface is level or gently rolling. Its streams are small brooks and creeks. The foot of Silver Lake lies along the s. border. **Perry,** (p. v.,) upon the outlet of Silver Lake, was incorp. in 1829. It contains the Perry Academy,[2] a newspaper office, a bank, a woolen factory, 3 flouring mills, and several churches. Pop. 935. **Perry Center** (p. v.) contains a church and 40 dwellings.[3] **West Perry** is a hamlet. The first settlement was made in 1806, on Lot 28, by Josiah Williams, from Vt.[4] The first religious services were held at Perry Center, in Dec. 1813, by Rev. Mr. Herrick, (Bap.,) when he was retreating from Buffalo. The first church (Presb.) was organized at the Center, by Rev. Oliver Ayer and Silas Hubbard, June 28, 1814.[5]

PIKE[6]—was formed from Nunda, (Livingston co.,) March 6, 1818. Eagle was taken off in 1823, and a part of Genesee Falls in 1846. It lies on the s. border of the co., E. of the center. Its surface is a hilly and broken upland. East Coy Creek flows s. through the E. part, and Wiscoy Creek s. E. through the center. Enory Hill, the highest point, is about 100 ft. above the R. R. at Castile, and the lowest point, in the s. E. corner, is 200 ft. below the R. R. The soil is a gravelly and clayey loam. There are several quarries of building stone in town. **Pike,** (p. v.,) on Wiscoy Creek, near the center, was incorp. Aug. 11, 1848. It contains the Genesee Conference Seminary,[7] an iron foundery, a flouring mill, a woolen factory, and 3 churches. Pop. 581. **East Pike,** (p. v.,) on East Coy Creek, contains a church, a flouring mill, an extensive paper mill, and 50 dwellings. **Pike Five Corners, Griffiths Corners,** and **East Coy** (p. o.) are hamlets. The first settlement was made in 1806, by Peter Granger, Eli Griffith, Asahel Newcomb, Phineas Harvey, and Caleb Powers, all from Whitehall, N. Y.[8] The first church was formed, Sept. 25, 1821, at Pike Village.[9]

SHELDON—was formed from Batavia, (Genesee co.,) March 19, 1808. Attica was taken off in 1811, and Bennington and China in 1818. Its surface is a rolling upland, 400 to 600 ft. above the valleys. Tonawanda Creek flows through the E. and several tributaries of Buffalo Creek through the w. part. The soil upon the hills is a thin, dark loam underlaid by hardpan, and in the valleys a gravelly loam. **Strykersville,** (p. v.,) in the s. w. corner of the town, contains several mills, 2 churches, and about 400 inhabitants. **Varysburgh,**[10] (p. v.,) in the N. E., upon Tonawanda Creek, contains 2 churches and 20 dwellings. **Sheldon** (p. o.) and **North Sheldon** (p. o.) are hamlets. **Johnsonburgh** (p. v.) is on the line of Orangeville. The first settlement was made in the N. part, in 1804, by Roswell Turner, agent of Phelps and Chipman, the original purchasers of the town.[11] The first religious meeting (Bap.) was held at the house of Roswell Turner, by Rev. Mr. Spencer. The first church was formed at the Center, in 1808.[12]

WARSAW—was formed from Batavia, (Genesee co.,) March 19, 1808. Middlebury was taken off in 1812, and Gainesville in 1814. It is an interior town, lying N. E. of the center of the co. Its surface is a broken upland, divided into two ridges by the valley of Oatka Creek. The declivities of the hills are steep, and their summits 700 to 1,000 ft. above the valleys. Upon Mill Brook, a small tributary of Oatka Creek, is a perpendicular fall of 105 ft. **Warsaw,** (p. v.,) the co. seat, was incorp. April 17, 1843. It lies in the valley of Oatka Creek, at the center of the

---

1 Named from Commodore O. H. Perry.
2 The academy buildings were erected by subscription of the inhabitants, and cost $12,000. This school has been offered to the State for a normal school.
3 An academy was sustained here for several years.
4 Among the first settlers were Seth Canfield, Samuel and Nath'l Howard, Amos Smith, Phicol M. Ward, and Amos Otis,— mostly from New England. The first death was that of Nancy Williams, in 1815. The first school was taught at Perry Center, in 1813, by Ann Mann. from Mass. The first inn was kept by Amos Smith, a little E. of the Center, in 1811; the first store, by T. & J. C. Edgerley; and the first mill was erected at Perry Village, by John Hamersley, in 1812.
5 The census reports 7 churches; 2 Bap., 2 M. E., and 1 each Presb., Cong., and Univ.
6 Named from Gen. Zebulon Montgomery Pike.
7 The seminary buildings were erected in 1856, at a cost of $9,000; they have accommodations for 300 students. The property is held by a board of trustees, and is under the patronage of the F. W. Bap. denomination.
8 The first child born was Louisa, daughter of Asahel Newcomb, in Aug. 1806; the first marriage was that of Russell H. Benton and Susannah Olin, Feb. 23, 1809; and the first deaths were those of twin children of Phineas Harvey, in the spring of 1807. Mr. Harvey died the succeeding autumn. The first

school was taught by Miss Beulah Abell, (from Washington co.,) in the summer of 1809. Eli Griffith kept the first inn, at Pike Village, in 1808, and Tilly Parker the first store, in 1810, at the same place. Eli Griffith built the first sawmill, in 1809, and the first gristmill, in 1810, a little above Pike Village.
9 The census reports 4 churches; 2 M. E., and 1 each Cong and Bap.
10 Named from Wm. Vary, one of the first settlers.
11 Mr. Turner was the father of O. Turner, Esq., author of the History of the Holland Purchase, Phelps and Gorhams Purchase, &c. Among the other early settlers were Robert Carr and David Howard, in 1805; Seth Gates, Lemuel Castle, Levi Street, Marvin Brace, Stephen Welton, (from Eastern New York,) and Uriah Persons, (from Penn.,) in 1806. The more recent settlements in the town have been made mostly by German immigrants. The first child born was Chipman Phelps Turner, in 1805; the first marriage was that of Justin Loomis and Polly Rolph, in 1807; and the first death, that of David Hoard, who was killed by the falling of a limb of a tree, in 1805. The first school was taught at North Sheldon, by Polly Rolph, in 1807; the first inn was kept by Roswell Turner, in 1806, at North Sheldon. Wm. Vary built the first sawmill, in 1806, and the first gristmill, in 1808, at Varysburgh.
12 The census reports 8 churches; 2 M. E., and 1 each Presb., Cong., Bap., F. W. Bap., Ref. Prot. D., and R. C.

town. Besides the co. buildings, it contains 5 churches, an academy,[1] 2 newspaper offices, a bank, an insurance company and office, and several important manufactories.[2] Pop. 1,200. **South Warsaw** (p. o.) is a hamlet. **East Warsaw** is a p. o. The first settlement was made at Warsaw Village, by Elizur Webster, in 1803.[3] The first church (Cong.) was organized July 14, 1808; Rev. John Lindsley was the first preacher. Their church edifice was built in 1817, and is still occupied.[4]

WETHERSFIELD—was formed from Orangeville, April 12, 1823. It is an interior town, lying s. w. of the center of the co. Its surface is a rolling upland. Tonawanda, East Coy, and Wiscoy Creeks all take their rise in this town. **Wethersfield Springs,** (p. v.,) in the N. E. corner, contains 3 churches and 25 dwellings. **Hermitage,** (p. v.,) on the E. border of the town, contains 2 churches and 20 dwellings. **Smiths Corners** (Wethersfield p. o.) is a hamlet. The first settlement was made on Lot 11, in 1810, by Lewis Hancock, Guy Morgan, and Calvin Clifford, from Jefferson co.[5] Rev. Mr. Boomer (Bap.) was the first preacher.[6]

Acres of Land, Valuation, Population, Dwellings, Families, Freeholders, Schools, Live Stock, Agricultural Products, and Domestic Manufactures, of Wyoming County.

Names of Towns.	Acres of Land.		Valuation of 1858.			Population.		No. of Dwellings.	No. of Families.	Freeholders.	Schools.	
	Improved.	Unimproved.	Real Estate.	Personal Property.	Total.	Males.	Females.				No. of Districts.	Children taught.
Attica	16,432	8,628	$636,112	$111,350	$747,462	1,327	1,352	500	540	406	13	957
Bennington	22,377	13,110	455,430	18,611	474,041	1,301	1,254	512	545	493	16	941
Castile	17,970½	5,755	771,060	84,303	855,363	1,185	1,158	472	408	374	14	826
China	15,756	13,583	500,246	47,800	548,046	1,051	1,057	345	389	316	13	800
Covington	12,344½	2,980	471,823	31,375	503,198	670	660	248	255	216	10	430
Eagle	12,916	9,923	307,008	7,175	314,183	733	657	264	283	215	10	588
Gainesville	14,128½	6,290	462,024	50,550	512,574	884	869	350	361	312	10	634
Genesee Falls	5,772½	2,925	239,470	9,350	248,820	560	538	218	225	145	4	190
Java	17,996	11,709	423,362	22,315	445,677	1,187	1,108	408	422	383	12	992
Middlebury	15,500	4,603	493,092	75,530	568,622	904	883	351	376	323	15	690
Orangeville	14,336	6,464	300,722	30,098	330,820	730	711	251	244	231	9	459
Perry	17,984	4,771	738,719	126,875	865,594	1,253	1,307	490	532	384	13	801
Pike	11,084	5.930	399,268	23,700	422,968	930	957	351	370	280	10	741
Sheldon	17,795	11,656	382,299	35,400	417,699	1,347	1,319	495	519	432	15	1,225
Warsaw	16,442	4,782	740,790	148,650	889,440	1,393	1,401	510	525	452	16	1,049
Wethersfield	12,820¼	9,655½	330,577	50,150	380,727	734	728	276	291	246	10	549
Total	241,654¼	122,764½	7,652,002	873,232	8,525,234	16,189	15,959	6,041	6,285	5,208	190	11,872

Names of Towns.	Live Stock.					Agricultural Products.							Domestic cloths, in Yards.
						Bush. of Grain.		Tons of Hay.	Bushels of Potatoes.	Bushels of Apples.	Dairy Products.		
	Horses.	Working Oxen and Calves.	Cows.	Sheep.	Swine.	Winter.	Spring.				Pounds Butter.	Pounds Cheese.	
Attica	592	1,318	1,354	5,203	744	10,276	39,212½	5,205	11,364	40,530	54,785	145,950	346
Bennington	806	2,098	1,355	9,743	699	5,981	67,082	6,410	15,261	20,781	90,896	14,618	1,297
Castile	871	1,434	887	6,825	1,281	108,259½	68,278½	2,597	13,027	19,079	97,002	7,171	1,185
China	619	2,164	1,326	4,837	615	208	69,871½	4,683½	15,724	6,694	123,976	25,100	1,761
Covington	585	710	488	7,451	581	60,321	31,589	2,130	5,782	10,735	56,920	3,945	291
Eagle	556	1,317	832	4,708	514	967	68,181½	2,808	17,509	5,790	77,838	16,986	1,130
Gainesville	694	1,235	752	7,522	766	17,788½	62,494½	2,437	13,806	24,396	76,267	15,720	433
Genesee Falls	183	404	261	1,832	299	12,988	24,991	934	4,479	7,449	14,485	100	104
Java	687	2,179	1,470	6,795	927	3,741	90,358½	3,995	16,520	12,962	131,090	42,050	3,747
Middlebury	769	1,168	993	11,531	851	66,078½	53,502½	4,360	9,153	35,499	81,770	74,025	164
Orangeville	501	1,195	1,584	2,303	590	4,298	32,890	4,605	10,902	19,248	63,010	273,150	946
Perry	953	1,349	899	8,551	1,023	60,625	60,955	2,834½	17,203	29,524	105,260	15,718	1,945
Pike	602	1,111	924	4,856	568	6,443	51,971	2,624	14,431	21,016	73,887	28,617	336
Sheldon	623	2,209	1,602	5,607	841	3,611	64,176½	5,859	12,940	25,649	121,962	67,310	1,146
Warsaw	789	1,237	975	2,095	816	18,744	36,800½	4,043	14,700	33,288	88,076	27,505	456
Wethersfield	528	1,183	1,035	3,506	559	4,946½	56,089¾	2,896¼	11,131	10,650	76,724	65,140	1,886
Total	10,358	22,311	16,737	93,365	11,674	385,276	878,444½	58,421¼	203,932	323,290	1,333,948	823,105	17,173

[1] It was incorp. by the regents in 1853, and is under the management of a village board of education.

[2] Sash and blinds, horse rakes, carriages, and waterproof oil blacking.

[3] In the same year, Wm. Webster, Shubael Morris, Amos Kinney, Elijah Cutting, and Joseph Palmer settled in the S. part of the town, and Josiah Hovey in the N. part. The first settlers were mostly from New England. The first child born was Eliza Webster, in 1804; the first marriage was that of Silas C. Fargo and Catharine Whiting; and the first death, that of an infant son of Sterling Stearns, in 1804. The first death of an adult was that of Dwight Noble, in 1808. The first school was taught by Samuel McWhorter, in 1807. Elizur Webster kept the first inn, in 1809; and Absalom Green and Dan'l Shaw, the first store, in the same year. Solomon Morris built the first gristmill, in 1808.

[4] The census reports 6 churches; Presb., Cong., Bap., F. W. Bap., Prot. E., and M. E.

[5] John W. Parry, from Oneida co., settled at Wethersfield Springs in the fall of 1810, and built the first house at that place. The first school was taught by O. Martin. The first gristmill was erected by James Cravath, in 1812, on East Coy Creek; and the first sawmill, by Calvin Clifford, on the same creek, in 1810.

[6] The census reports 6 churches; 2 Bap., and 1 each Cong., Prot. E., M. E., and Christian.

YATES COUNTY.

This county was formed from Ontario, Feb. 5, 1823, and named from Joseph C. Yates, then governor. Barrington and Starkey were added from Steuben, April 6, 1824. It is centrally distant 172 mi. from Albany, and contains an area of 1,370 sq. mi. Its surface consists of a series of ridges extending from Steuben co. in a northerly direction, and gradually declining from a height of about 1,700 ft. above tide, upon the s. border, to a level of the undulating region near the foot of Seneca Lake. The first or most eastern of these ridges lies between Seneca and Crooked Lakes, and occupies the towns of Barrington, Starkey, Milo, Torrey, and a part of Benton. The highest summit is about 900 ft. above Crooked Lake and 1,200 above Seneca. The slopes are generally gradual and the inclination uniform. The second ridge occupies the high peninsula between the two branches of Crooked Lake, and extends N. through Jerusalem, finally losing itself in the rolling upland of Benton. The s. part of this ridge is known as "Bluff Point," from its abrupt termination. It is about 400 ft. above the lake. The third range lies between the w. branch of Crooked Lake and Flint Creek, and occupies the w. part of Jerusalem, the E. part of Italy, and the s. E. part of Potter. The highest summits in the s. are about 700 ft. above the lake. A fourth ridge lies between the valleys of Flint Creek and West River, and extends N. through the w. part of Potter. A fifth range occupies that portion of Middlesex lying between West River Hollow and Canandaigua Lake. The declivities of the last two ranges are mostly very steep; and their summits are 800 to 1,000 ft. above the valleys. The uplands, except in the extreme w. part, are smooth and arable to their summits. The valleys between them are wide and exceedingly fertile, and the N. part of the co. is a fine rolling region.

The lowest rocks in the co. are the upper series of the Hamilton shales, cropping out on the lower course of the Crooked Lake Outlet. Next above these, upon the same stream, appear the Tully limestone, Genesee slate, and Portage groups. The first of the three, furnishing lime, is the most valuable mineral in the co. The Portage group near Penn Yan furnishes a good quality of flagging stone, and is extensively quarried for that purpose. The shales and sandstone of the Chemung group occupy the summits in the s. part of the co.; calcareous tufa is found upon Crooked Lake Outlet, and marl in the swamps near the foot of the lake. Iron pyrites have been found in considerable quantities at Bluff Point. The soil for the most part consists of a fine quality of gravelly loam, intermixed with clay and the disintegrated shales of the Portage group. It is well adapted to either tillage or pasturage.

The principal streams in the co. are Crooked Lake Outlet, Keshong Creek, Big Stream, Rock Stream, Flint Creek, and West River. Seneca Lake, forming the E. boundary of the co., is 447 ft. above tide, and Canandaigua Lake, forming a part of the w. boundary, 668 ft. Crooked Lake,[1] near the center, two-thirds of it lying within the co., is 718 ft. above tide and is 18 mi. in length. Its N. part is divided by Bluff Point into two branches, each of which is from one to two mi. wide. Owing to the depredations of the midge winter wheat is less grown than formerly, while spring grains, root crops, stock, wool, and fruit are much more extensively and profitably produced. The outlet of Crooked Lake affords large water power for manufacturing purposes,—as yet but slightly improved.

The county seat is located at the village of Penn Yan,[2] on the line of Milo and Benton.[3] The first courthouse[4] and jail combined was erected in 1824; and in 1834 it was burned. In 1835 a new brick courthouse was built, on a public square, at a cost of $12,000. A jail, detached, was erected the same season. The latter was destroyed by fire in Feb. 1857, and was rebuilt the same year, at a cost of $10,200. A clerk's office was erected some years previous, upon the public square

---

[1] Called by the Indians O-go-ya-ga, a promontory projecting into the lake.

[2] The commissioners who located the co. seat, were John Sutton, of Tompkins co., George H. Feeter, of Herkimer co., and Joseph B. Walton, of Otsego co.

[3] The first court was held at the house of Asa Cole, in Penn Yan, on the first Tuesday in June, 1823. The first board of supervisors met at the same place. The first co. officers were William M. Oliver, *First Judge*; James Taylor, *Dist. Atty.*; Abraham

H. Bennett, *Co. Clerk*; James P. Robinson, *Sheriff*; and Abraham P. Vosburgh, *Surrogate*.

[4] John Sutton, of Tompkins, Geo. H. Feeter, of Herkimer, and Joseph B. Walton, of Otsego cos., were appointed commissioners to locate the co. buildings, and Wm. Shattuck, of Benton, Geo. Sherman and Samuel Stewart, of Milo, to erect them. The courts were to be held at the house of Asa Cole until the courthouse was finished.

with the other public buildings, near the center of the village. The co. poorhouse is located on a farm of 123 acres in the town of Jerusalem, about 5 mi. s. w. of Penn Yan.[1] The average number of inmates is 86, and they are supported at a weekly cost of $1 40 each. A school is taught in the house during a portion of the year, and religious services are held occasionally. The Crooked Lake Canal extends along the outlet of Crooked Lake, and enters Seneca Lake at Dresden. It opens a direct water communication with Yates co. and the N. portion of Steuben, and affords an easy and cheap means of transportation. The Elmira, Jefferson & Canandaigua R. R. extends through the co., E. of the center, connecting with the N. Y. C. R. R. at the N. terminus and with the N. Y. & E. R. R. at the s. These two works of internal improvement furnish market facilities equal to those generally enjoyed by the interior cos. of the State.

Three newspapers are published in the co.[2]

The early history of this co. is intimately associated with the history of the *"Friends,"* a religious sect founded by Jemima Wilkinson.[3] This singular woman took the name of the *"Universal Friend,"* and was regarded as a prophet by her followers, among whom were persons of respectability, wealth, and influence. At a general meeting of the sect, in Conn., in 1786, it was resolved to emigrate to some unsettled region and found a colony where they might live in peace and in the undisturbed enjoyment of their religious opinions. Three of their number were delegated to seek out a proper location.[4] They proceeded to Penn., went up the Susquehanna River, and followed the route of Gen. Sullivan to Seneca Lake, where they finally determined to locate. In June, 1787, 25 *"Friends"* set out for the land of promise by the way of the Mohawk Valley. They settled about 1 mi. s. of the present village of Dresden, the location being fixed upon from its close proximity to the fine waterfalls upon Crooked Lake Outlet.[5] During the fall they prepared the land, and in the following season sowed it with winter wheat, which they harvested in 1789; and this was the first wheat crop raised in Western N. Y. In 1789, Wm. Potter and Thos. Hathaway, two of their number, purchased of the State 14,000 acres of land lying between Seneca Lake and the Pre-emption Line, and subsequently Thos. Hathaway and Benedict Robinson purchased the town Jerusalem of Phelps and Gorham.[6] In 1789, Jemima and a large number of her followers

---

[1] This building, erected 25 years ago, is 100 ft. by 50, and 3 stories high, including basement. The farm yields a revenue of $1,000.

[2] *The Penn Yan Herald* was established at Penn Yan in May, 1818, by Abraham H. Bennett. In 1820 it appeared as **The Penn Yan Democrat.** In 1835 it was pub. by Bennett & Reed, in 1842 by Reed & Bennett, and in 1847 by Alfred Reed. In 1850 Darius A. Ogden became proprietor, in 1853 Reuben Spicer, and in 1857 Geo. D. A. Bridgman, its present publisher.

The Yates County Republican was started Dec. 16, 1824, by E. J. Fowle, and continued 10 years. He then sold it to John Remmick, who published it as

The Penn Yan Enquirer about 2 years, when it was discontinued.

The Western Star was pub. at Penn Yan in 1833 by H. Gilbert.

The Miscellany was pub. at Penn Yan in 1833 by Thos. H. Bassett.

The Democratic Whig was commenced in 1837 by Wm. Child. About 2 years after it passed into the hands of Nicholas D. Suydam, who changed its name to

The Yates County Whig. In 1845 it passed into the hands of Rodney L. Adams. In 1852 Mr. Adams sold it to Cleveland & Look. Mr. Look soon retired, and in 1856 its name was changed to **The Yates County Chronicle.** It is now published by Stafford C. Cleveland.

The Democratic Organ was commenced in 1844 at Penn Yan by Harvey L. Winants, and published about 2 years.

The Penn Yan Telegraph, da., was issued from the office of The Whig, for 6 mos. in 1846.

The Dundee Record was commenced at Dundee, Jan. 25, 1844, by Gifford J. Booth. Edward Hoagland succeeded to its editorship in 1847, John J. Diefendorf in 1853, and D. S. Bruner, its present publisher, in 1857.

[3] Jemima Wilkinson was the daughter of Jeremiah Wilkinson, a R. I. farmer. She was one of a family of 12 children and had little or no advantages of education. In her 20th year she had a severe attack of fever; and for some time her life was despaired of. Upon her recovery she claimed that she had been raised from the dead,—that her carnal existence was ended and henceforth her life was to be spiritual and divine,—and that she was endowed with the power of prophecy. She soon commenced traveling and exhorting, and succeeded in converting many persons, among whom were several substantial New England farmers. The following description of her person is copied from "The New Haven Gazette and Connecticut Magazine," dated March, 1787. "She is about the middle size of woman, not genteel in her person, rather awkward in her carriage; her complexion good, her eyes remarkably black and brilliant, her hair black and waving with beautiful ringlets upon her neck and shoulders. Her features are regular, and the whole of her face is thought by many to be perfectly beautiful. As she is not to be supposed of either sex, so this neutrality is manifest in her personal appearance. She wears

no cap, letting her hair hang down as has been described. She wears her neckcloth like a man; her chemise is buttoned around the neck and wrists. Her outside garment is a robe, under which it is said she wears an expensive dress, the fashion of which is made to correspond neither with that of man nor woman. Her understanding is not deficient, except touching her religious fanaticism. She is very illiterate, yet her memory is very great; artful in discovering many circumstances which fall out among her disciples. On all occasions she requires the most extraordinary attentions that can be bestowed upon her: one or more of her disciples usually attend upon her and perform the most menial services. Her pronunciation is after the peculiar dialect of the most illiterate of the countrypeople of New England. Her preaching has very little connection, and is very lengthy,—at times cold and languid, but occasionally lively, zealous, and animated." When she first arose from her bed of sickness, she assumed that there was once such a person as Jemima Wilkinson, but that she died and went to heaven, after which the Divine Spirit reanimated that same body and it arose from the dead; now, this divine inhabitant is Christ Jesus our Lord, the Friend to all mankind, and gives his name to the body to which he is united, and therefore body and spirit conjointly is the *"Universal Friend."* She assumed to have two *"Witnesses,"* corresponding in all respects to those prophesied in Rev. chap. xi. from 3d to 13th verses. These were James Parker and Sarah Richards. During her whole life she never yielded the pretensions which she at first made; and her whole career had the merit of consistency. Among the principal peculiar tenets of the sect was the strict enforcement of the Shaker doctrine of celibacy as indispensable to a pure life. The meetings were conducted after the manner of the Quakers, the whole congregation often sitting in perfect silence for an hour or more.—*See Turner's Hist. of The Phelps and Gorham Purchase.*

This extraordinary woman exerted a strong influence over her followers, who gratuitously planted and hoed her corn, sowed and reaped her wheat, and cut and gathered her hay, always having care to be of no trouble or expense to the Friend upon these occasions. On one occasion she addressed, through an interpreter, a band of Oneidas who had encamped near her settlement on their way to a treaty, endeavoring to convince them that she was Christ. They listened with apparent attention, and, when she had finished, one of the chiefs arose and delivered a short address to his countrymen. She requested to have it interpreted to her,—when the savage contemptuously replied, in broken English, that if she were the character she assumed to be, she would have understood the poor Indian as well as any one. She died July 1, 1819, and her heart has long since been broken up.—*Hudson's Life of Jemima Wilkinson.*

[4] Abraham Dayton, Richard Smith, and Thomas Hathaway.

[5] The first gristmill in Western N.Y. was built in 1789, by Rich'd Smith, James Parker, and Abraham Dayton, 2½ mi. from Penn Yan.

[6] "It was a rule at that early period with Messrs. Phelps &

came in. The first framed house in the co. was erected for her, on a farm of 1000 acres set apart for her especial use. For a time the colony flourished; but soon neighbors began to arrive, and jealousies were engendered, and a series of persecutions commenced, which seriously retarded the progress of the colony and embittered the last days of the *"Friend."*[1]

BARRINGTON—was formed from Wayne, (Steuben co.,) April 6, 1822. It lies upon the E. bank of Crooked Lake, in the s. part of the co. Its surface consists principally of a high ridge, sloping gradually upward from Crooked Lake to a height of 600 to 800 ft. Big Stream flows through the s. E. corner, in a deep ravine bordered by steep declivities. From Crooked Lake the ascent is nearly uniform for 2 miles; and the summit of the ridge is rolling. The soil is a slaty gravel mixed with clay, and is generally productive. **Barrington,**[2] (p. v.,) near the center, contains 1 church and 25 houses. The first settlement was made in 1800, by Jacob Teeplis.[3] The Rev. Jas. Osgood (Bap.) was the first preacher. There are two churches in town; Bap. and M. E.

BENTON[4]—was formed from Jerusalem, Feb. 12, 1803, as *"Vernon."* Its name was changed to *"Snell"* April 6, 1808, and to Benton April 2, 1810. Milo was taken off in 1818, and a part of Torrey in 1851. It is the N. E. corner town of the co. Its surface is rolling and gradually descending toward the N. and E. From Seneca Lake the land slopes upward for a mile, and to a height of about 300 ft., where it spreads out in a beautiful undulating region. The valley of Crooked Lake, 200 ft. below the summits of the table land, extends about 1 mi. into the s. part of the town. Keshong Creek passes through the N. E. corner. The soil is clay along the lake, but upon the hills it is a deep, rich, clayey and gravelly loam, well adapted to almost every branch of agriculture. **Bellona,** (Benton p. o.,) situated on Keshong Creek, in the N. E. part, contains 2 churches, (pop. 205;) and **Benton Center** (p. v.) 2 churches and 28 dwellings. **Fergusons Corners** (p. o.) is a hamlet. The village of Penn Yan lies partly within this town. The first settlement was made in the spring of 1789, by Levi Benton, from Catskill, Greene co.[5] The first religious meetings were held in the barn of Levi Benton, in 1792, and were conducted by Ezra Cole. There are now 4 churches in town.[6]

ITALY—was formed from Naples, Feb. 15, 1815. It is the s. w. corner town of the co. Its surface consists of three distinct ridges, each attaining an elevation of about 1000 ft. above Canandaigua Lake. These ridges are divided by the valley of Flint Creek—known as Italy Hollow—and West River Hollow. The valleys are generally narrow and bordered by steep and often precipitous sides. The summits of the ridges are broken uplands. The soil is a slaty and gravelly loam and is best adapted to pasturage. **Italy Hill** (p. v.) is situated in the s. E. corner; and **Italy Hollow** (p. o.) on Flint Creek, s. of the center. The first settlement in the town was made by John Mower, at West Hollow, in 1793.[7] There are 4 churches in town.[8]

JERUSALEM—was organized Jan. 1789, and Benton was taken off in 1803. A small part of Steuben co., in the forks of the lake, was annexed Feb. 25, 1814. It lies on the w. bank of Crooked Lake and is the central town in the co. Its surface is divided into two distinct ridges by the w. branch of the lake and its inlet. The E. ridge terminates on the s. in Bluff Point, a promontory, 8 mi. in extent, lying between the two branches of Crooked Lake; and it extends on the N. into the town of Benton. It is about 400 ft. high and 1½ to 2 mi. wide, and is bordered by steep declivities. The continuity of this ridge is broken by a remarkable depression extending

---

Gorham, in selling a picked township, to require the purchaser to draw for another township at the same price. Robinson and Hathaway, after purchasing Jerusalem, drew what is now the town of Geneseo, Livingston co. The Friend objected to her people 'trading and buying property at a distance,' and, fearing her displeasure, they prevailed upon Mr. Phelps to release them from the bargain, which he was quite willing to do, as he had ascertained the value of the township."—*Turner's Hist.*

[1] She was several times prosecuted for blasphemy, and was harassed by lawsuits, which were chiefly instigated by those who had once been her followers and friends.—*Turner's Hist. of The Phelps and Gorham Purchase.*

[2] Sometimes called *"Warsaw."*

[3] The next settlers were Thomas Bronson, from Conn.; Wm. Coolbaugh, from N. J.; Jonathan Davis, William Ovenshire, Oliver Parker, Matthew Knapp, Joseph Fenton, John Kriss, and Henry Spry. The first school was taught by A. C. West, in 1810. Jacob Teeplis kept the first tavern, in 1804, on the Bath Road; and Elijah Townsend, the first store. John Carr erected the first gristmill, and Wm. Cummins the first sawmill.

[4] Named from Levi Benton, the first settler.

[5] T. Spencer settled at Bellona in 1790; George Wheeler, Robert Chisson, Jas. Scofield, Otis Barden, and Daniel Brown in

1791; and Ezra Cole, Eliphalet Hull, and Samuel and Cyrus Buell, with their families, in 1792. The first birth was that of Matilda Buell, in Sept. 1792; the first marriage, that of Thos. Barden and Olive Benton, in 1791; and the first deaths, those of Ephraim and Samuel Wheeler, who both died in the fall of 1792. The first sawmill was built by Dr. Caleb Benton, in 1790, at Bellona. The first store was kept by Luther Benton and James Stoddard, in 1799, and the first inn by Ezra Cole, in 1800. John Coates taught the first school, at Benton Center, in the winter of 1794. The first town meeting was held at the house of Daniel Brown.

[6] Two M. E., Bap., and Presb.

[7] Josiah Bradish, Seth Sprague, Fisher and Isaac Whitney, William Dunton, Edward Low, William Clark, Archibald Armstrong, Card Knowles, John Armstrong, Morris and Hastings, settled in 1794 and '95, and Nathan Scott and Andrew Robson in 1809. The first birth was that of Polly Mower, in Oct. 1795; and a child of Mr. Mower was the first that died. The first marriage was that of Jabez Metcalf and Nancy Torrey. Nancy Torrey taught the first school, in 1803, at West Hollow. Elias Lee kept the first tavern, at the same place, in 1806; Abraham Maxfield the first store, at Italy Hollow; Asahel Stone, jr., erected the first saw and grist mill, at the same place, at an early date.

[8] Two Bap., M. E., and Presb.

from the head of the w. branch of Crooked Lake E. to the E. branch. The highest point in this valley is about 70 ft. above the lake. The ridge on the w. rises gradually for 3 or 4 mi. and attains a height of about 700 ft. above the lake, where the surface spreads out into a rolling upland. The soil is a gravelly and slaty loam, and is well adapted to both pasturage and tillage. **Branchport,** (p. v.,) situated at the head of the w. branch of Crooked Lake, contains 3 churches and about 55 houses. **Kinneys Corners** (Bluff Point p. o.) is situated in the E. part of the town; **Shermans Hollow** and **Yatesville** are p. offices. The first settlement was made by Jemima Wilkinson, in 1789.[1] In that year crops of wheat were harvested in the town, and a mill was erected that made flour the same season. The first, and for a long time the only, religious services in town were conducted by Jemima, at her own house. There are 4 churches in town.[2]

MIDDLESEX—was formed in 1789, as "*Augusta.*" Its name was changed April 6, 1808. Potter was taken off in 1832, and a part was annexed to Potter in 1856. It is the N. w. corner town, lying upon the E. bank of Canandaigua Lake. Its surface consists chiefly of high ridges separated by narrow valleys. The summits are 500 to 600 ft. above the lake. The valley of West River divides the ridges, and the valley of a small stream known as Boat Brook divides the w. ridge into two peaks, the N. of which is known as "Bare Hill." The soil is clayey on the summits of the hills, and gradually changes to a deep gravelly loam in the valleys. Near Federal Hollow, a mile from Rushville, is an inflammable spring.[3] **Middlesex Center** (Middlesex p. o.) contains 3 churches and 20 dwellings. **Overackers Corners** is a hamlet. The first settlement was made in 1789. Judge Potter, one of the surveyors of Phelps and Gorham's purchase, was the original purchaser of the town, and took an active part in its first settlement.[4] Many of the first settlers were adherents of Jemima Wilkinson; and for a considerable time there was no other religious association in the town. There are now 4 churches.[5]

MILO—was formed from Benton, March 6, 1818. A part of Torrey was taken off in 1851. It lies on the E. border of the co., between Seneca and Crooked Lakes. Its surface rises from Seneca Lake in a gentle and gradual slope for 2 mi., where it attains an elevation of about 400 to 500 ft. From this summit the land spreads out into an undulating region, gradually declining on the w. to the valley of Crooked Lake. The soil is principally a gravelly loam, with some clay in the vicinity of Penn Yan and on the shore of Seneca Lake. **Penn Yan,**[6] (p. v.,) the county seat, was incorp. April 27, 1833. It is situated at the foot of Crooked Lake, and is an important station on the Elmira, Jefferson & Canandaigua R. R. A daily steamer connects it with Hammondsport, at the head of Crooked Lake. It contains 6 churches, a high school,[7] 2 newspaper establishments, and a bank. Pop. 2,277,—2,114 in Milo, 163 in Benton. **Milo Center** (p. v.) contains 150 inhabitants; and **Himrods Corners** (Milo p. v.) 78. The first settlement was commenced in the N. part, by the followers of Jemima Wilkinson, from R. I., in 1788.[8] The first religious services were conducted by Jemima Wilkinson. There are now 10 churches in town.[9]

POTTER[10]—was formed from Middlesex, April 26, 1832, and part of Middlesex was annexed Dec. 18, 1856. It lies near the center of the N. border of the co. Its surface is hilly in the s. w., and rolling in the center and N. Flint Creek, the principal stream, flows northerly through near the center of the town. A swamp of 1 to 1½ mi. wide extends along its course for 8 mi. N. of Potter Center. The soil is a slaty loam in the s. w., and a gravelly and sandy loam, with an intermixture of clay, in the remaining parts. **Rushville** (p. v.) is partly in Gorham, Ontario co., but principally in the N. w. part of this town. Pop. 583,—408 in Potter, 175 in Gorham. **Potter Center** (Potter p. o.) contains 20 houses. **Voak** is a p. o. on the line of Benton. Settlement was begun in 1788, by the followers of Jemima Wilkinson. The most prominent among them were William

---

[1] The first settlers were Thomas Hathaway and Daniel Brown. In 1789, Jemima, "*The Universal Friend,*" as she was called, entered the town with a large retinue, among whom were Sarah Richards and Rachael Malin, her two "Witnesses," Isaac Kinney, Solomon Ingraham, Samuel Doolittle, and Wm. Sandford, as part of her family, all from Rhode Island. They all lived with Jemima in the house previously erected for her,—the first frame house built in Western N. Y. The first gristmill was built by Richard Smith, James Parker, and Abraham Dayton, 2¼ mi. from Penn Yan. David Wagener opened the first public house, at the same place; Daniel Brown built the first sawmill, north of Branchport; and John Noyes taught the first school, in 1794.

[2] Bap., M. E., Presb., Univ.

[3] Beck's *Mineralogy N. Y., p.* 166.

[4] Among the first settlers were Michael Pierce, John Walford, Jabez French, John Blair, James Lewis, and John McNear, all from R. I. William Bassett taught the first school, in 1796; Jesse Gilbert kept the first tavern, near Rushville. and Nelson Wilder the first store. John Walford. jr., built the first sawmill. The first death was that of Mrs. Lucy Walford, in 1791.

[5] Two M. E., Bap., and Free Will Bap.

[6] Among the early settlers of the village were a Pennsylvanian and a Yankee, each of whom wished to name the place. The matter was finally compromised by uniting the first syllable of their respective designations,—Penn and Yan.

[7] The Penn Yan High School was incorporated as an academy in 1857. The building is now in process of erection.

[8] The first settlers were Abraham Dayton, Richard Smith, Jas. Parker, John Lawrence, Stephen Card, Samuel Hartwell, Hezekiah Townsend, David and Peleg Brigg, John Sapplee, Elijah and Micajah Brown, David Wagener, and Adam Hunt and his sons, Abel and Silas. The first death was that of Mrs. Jedediah Holmes, in 1788. As Jemima Wilkinson's creed was the dominant religion of the town at that period and for some time after, there were no marriages, and of course no known births. It was an era in which people died and none were legitimately born. Hezekiah Townsend kept the first inn, a little E. of Penn Yan, and James Hill the first store.

[9] 3 Bap., 2 M. E., Cong., Wes. Meth., Presb., Prot. E., and R. C.

[10] Named from Arnold Potter, an original proprietor and the first settler in town.

Potter and his sons William, Arnold, Simeon, and Edward, who had purchased the whole township.[1] Rev. Mr. Haskill was the first settled preacher, in 1796. There are 11 churches in town.[2]

STARKEY[3]—was formed from Reading, (Schuyler co.,) April 6, 1824. It is the S. E. corner town of the co. Its surface is a gradual slope from the bluffs which border upon Seneca Lake to the W. border of the town, where it attains an elevation of about 700 ft. The bluffs upon the lake in the S. half of the town are 100 to 200 ft. high and nearly perpendicular. In the S. part, a ridge breaks the uniformity of the slope near the center. Big Stream and Rock Stream flow into Seneca Lake, falling several hundred ft. in their course. The soil is clay along the lake, a sandy loam in the S. part, and a gravelly loam in the N. **Dundee,** (p. v.,) incorp. June 26, 1848, situated on Big Stream, in the W. part, contains 4 churches, the Dundee Academy, a bank, and a newspaper office. Pop. 732. **Eddytown** (p. v.) contains a church and the Starkey Seminary.[4] Pop. 123. **Rock Stream** (p. v.) contains 25 houses, and **Starkey** (p. v.) 20. **Big Stream Point** (p. o.) and **Shannons Corners** and **Starkey Corners** are hamlets. Settlement began in 1800.[5] Rev. Mr. Clark conducted the first religious services, in 1808. There are 8 churches in town.[6]

TORREY[7]—was formed from Benton and Milo, Nov. 14, 1851. It lies upon the E. border of the co., on the shore of Seneca Lake. Its surface consists of a slope rising from the lake to the W. borders, to an elevation of 400 to 500 ft. Crooked Lake Outlet flows through a deep, narrow, and rocky valley. Its whole fall from Crooked to Seneca Lake is 271 ft. The soil on the lake shore is clayey, and in the center and W. a sandy and gravelly loam. **West Dresden**[8] (p. v.) is located on Seneca Lake, at the terminus of Crooked Lake Canal. It is a landing for the Seneca Lake steamers. Pop. 365. The town was settled by the followers of Jemima Wilkinson, mostly from New England, in 1788.[9] Jemima was the first preacher. There are now 2 churches in town; Presb. and M. E.

Acres of Land, Valuation, Population, Dwellings, Families, Freeholders, Schools, Live Stock, Agricultural Products, and Domestic Manufactures, of Yates County.

Names of Towns.	Acres of Land. Improved.	Acres of Land. Unimproved.	Valuation of 1858. Real Estate.	Valuation of 1858. Personal Property.	Valuation of 1858. Total.	Population. Males.	Population. Females.	No. of Dwellings.	No. of Families.	Freeholders.	Schools. No. of Districts.	Schools. Children taught.
Barrington	16,888⅝	5,227	$478,775	$12,900	$491,675	760	744	305	216	223	13	593
Benton	19,496	5,009½	988,909	152,678	1,141,587	1,279	1,221	487	504	355	12	797
Italy	15,312⅜	10,156½	295,158	45,656	340,814	783	723	275	289	250	12	697
Jerusalem	26,394½	8,373½	944,497	69,554	1,014,051	1,439	1,358	552	552	456	16	1,019
Middlesex	15,472½	5,172¾	442,815	23,670	466,485	642	663	258	263	223	9	457
Milo	18,026½	4,716	1,421,549	209,750	1,631,299	2,076	2,228	846	610	530	14	1,674
Potter	16,612½	5,599¼	652,673	88,665	741,338	1,083	1,065	402	402	346	13	893
Starkey	15,858½	4,062½	1,060,543	178,550	1,239,093	1,191	1,237	501	527	316	11	914
Torrey	11,481	2,817	540,822	53,400	594,222	647	673	247	258	185	7	492
Total	155,542½	51,134	$6,825,741	$834,823	$7,660,564	9,900	9,912	3,873	3,621	2,884	107	7,536

Names of Towns.	Live Stock. Horses.	Live Stock. Working Oxen and Calves.	Live Stock. Cows.	Live Stock. Sheep.	Live Stock. Swine.	Agricultural Products. Bush. of Grain. Winter.	Agricultural Products. Bush. of Grain. Spring.	Agricultural Products. Tons of Hay.	Agricultural Products. Bushels of Potatoes.	Agricultural Products. Bushels of Apples.	Agricultural Products. Dairy Products. Pounds of Butter.	Agricultural Products. Dairy Products. Pounds of Cheese.	Domestic Cloths, in Yards.
Barrington	651	1,024	780	6,351	1,110	12,726	60,147	1,378	6,889	11,509	73,995	1,523	230
Benton	924	1,249	1,119	12,381	2,025	27,183	117,582	2,435½	8,360	34,626	113,173	6,987	441
Italy	582	855	622	3,848	789	6,061½	20,305¾	1,827	5,311	5,903	65,540	23,470	925½
Jerusalem	1,035	1,639	1,109	9,047	1,832	33,554	61,578½	2,801	7,879	14,814	106,673	8,055	254
Middlesex	620	880	598	5,918	1,141	22,582½	24,088¼	1,522	3,115	7,066	65,885	8,062	412
Milo	959	1,008	970	5,394	1,792	27,348	53,245½	1,392	6,963	15,425	92,705¼	2,010	301
Potter	750	1,186	686	12,203	1,344	21,147½	54,053½	2,046½	3,970	21,139	63,423	5,147	1,163
Starkey	775	1,061	889	4,999	1,507	22,181	85,064¼	1,422¼	11,585½	23,927	91,299	4,123	67
Torrey	477	627	477	4,686	1,046	19,703	54,968	1,026	3,840	9,364	44,566	595	
Total	6,773	9,539	7,250	64,827	12,586	193,486½	531,032¾	15,850¼	57,912½	143,773	717,259¼	59,972	3,793½

[1] Rouse Perry, and Benj., Jesse and Joshua Brown came with the Potters and settled in the E. part of the town. They were followed by Elias Gilbert, Jabez French, Abram, Isaac, and Jacob Lane, Francis and Peleg Briggs, jr., Edward Craft, Amaziah Keyes, M. Sheffield, David Southerland, Nathan and Calvin Loomis, Abial Thomas, and George Green. The first birth was that of Joshua Briggs; the first marriage, that of Amaziah Keyes and a daughter of Major C. Craft, in 1795; and the first death, that of James Lewis, in 1796. Arnold Potter built the first saw and grist mill, in 1792. The first public house was opened in 1792, by Elias Gilbert, and the first store in 1801, by John Griffin.

[2] 4 M. E., 3 Bap., Cong., Ev. Luth., Univ., and R. C.

[3] Named from John Starkey, one of the first settlers.

[4] The seminary building is a 4 story brick edifice. The school is under the control of the Christian denomination.

[5] William Eddy, Archibald Ellis, —— Jacobs, Matthew Royce, —— Gustin, Abner Hurd, and his son Gen. Timothy Hurd were among the first settlers. Andrew Harrison kept the first inn, at Eddytown, in 1808; and Hervey Smith the first store, at the same place, in 1809. The first sawmill was built by Timothy Hurd, in 1807. Rhoda Royce taught the first school, in 1809.

[6] 3 Presb., 2 M. E., Bap., and 2 Christian.

[7] Named from Henry Torrey.

[8] Usually called "*Dresden.*"

[9] The first settlers were Asahel Stone, Abel, Elnathan and Jonathan Botsford, Benedict Robinson, Thos. Hathaway, Jedediah Holmes, Elisha Luther, David Fish, James Brown, Robert Buckley, and Eliphalet Norris. The first marriage was that of Benedict Robinson and Susannah Brown, Sept. 1, 1792; and the first death, that of Mrs. Jedediah Holmes, in 1788. Thomas Hathaway kept the first inn, in 1790; and Eliphalet Norris the first store, in 1792. The first mills were built by Charles Williamson, in 1795

INDEX OF GEOGRAPHICAL NAMES.

ABBREVIATIONS.—*ba.* bay; *br.* brook; *co.* county; *cr.* creek; *h.* hill; *isle,* island; *la.* lake; *lo.* locality or hamlet; *mt.* mountain; *p.* pond; *p. o.* post office; *p. v.* post village; *r.* river; *t.* town; *v.* village.

PAGE

Aalplaats.............cr. 587, 597
Aaronsburgh...............lo. 235
Abbotsford...............lo. 700
Abbotts Corners.........v. 291
Acabonac Harbor........... 634
Academy.............p. o. 495
Academy Hill...........lo. 587
Accord..................p. o. 666
Acra.................p. o. 331
Adam ....mt. 510
Adams.............p. v. 355
Adams ....t. 355
Adams Basin ....p. v. 400
Adams Center.........p. v. 355
Adams Ridge.........h. 541
Adamsville...............lo. 163
Adamsville.............p. o. 377
Addison ....p. v. 621
Addison ....t. 621
Addison Hill.........p. v. 621
Adirondack...mts. 19, 296, 300, 336
Adirondack...............v. 303
Adneys...................h. 510
Adriance.............p. o. 271
Afton.................p. v. 225
Afton.................t. 225
Akron.................p. v. 292
Alabama.............p. o. 324
Alabama..............t. 324
Alabama Center........v. 324
Alabama Springs........... 26
Albany City.........156, 159
Albany..............co. 101, 155
Albion.................p. v. 513
Albion.................t. 520
Alden.................p. v. 282
Alden.................t. 281
Alden Center ....p. v. 282
Alden Station...........lo. 282
Alder Brook...........p. o. 311
Alder Creek...........p. v. 462
Alexander.............p. v. 324
Alexander.............t. 324
Alexandria.............p. v. 355
Alexandria.............t. 355
Alexandria Bay........... 355
Alfred.................p. o. 169
Alfred.................t. 169
Alfred Center.........p. v. 169
Allegany...............co. 168
Allegany ....mts. 19, 178, 649
Allegany.............p. v. 188
Allegany ....r. 21, 23, 186, 187, 188
Allegany ....t. 187
Allen.................p. v. 170
Allen.................t. 170
Allen Center ....p. v. 170
Allens...................cr. 588
Allens Hill ....p. o. 498
Alligerville...............v. 666
Alloway.............p. v. 691
Allyns.................cr. 401
Alma.................p. v. 170
Alma.................t. 170
Almond.............p. v. 170
Almond.................t. 170
Alpina...............lo. 376
Alpine.................p. v. 610
Alps.................p. v. 557
Altay.................p. v. 612
Alton.................p. v. 694
Altona.................t. 235
Amaganset.............p. v. 635
Amber.................p. v. 486
Amboy.................t. 520
Amboy.................v. 481
Amboy Center.........p. v. 520
Amenia.................t. 269
Amenia Union.........p. v. 270
Ameniaville.........p. v. 270
American Falls........... 450
Ames.................p. v. 412
Amesville.............p. o. 662
Amherst.................t. 282
Amity.................p. v. 510
Amity.................t. 170
Amity.................v. 587

PAGE

Amityville..............p. v. 596
Amsterdam..............p. v. 411
Amsterdam ....t. 411
Anaquassacook........v. 684
Ancram.............p. v. 243
Ancram.................t. 242
Ancram Lead Mines...p. o. 243
Andersonville..........p. o. 309
Andes.................p. v. 259
Andes.................t. 259
Andover.............p. v. 171
Andover.................t. 170
Andreas................br. 542
Andrusville.........p. o. 309
Angel Cliff ....h. 533
Angelica................cr. 168
Angelica.............p. v. 171
Angelica.................t. 171
Angells Corners.........lo. 691
Angola......p. v. 289, 290
Annsberg...............lo. 245
Annsville.................t. 461
Annsville........p. v. 503, 699
Ant.................h. 505
Anthony...............mt. 589
Anthonys Kil...........cr. 589
Anthonys Nose....mt. 19, 542, 698
Antwerp.............p. v. 355
Antwerp.................t. 355
Apalachin..........cr. 649, 651
Apalachin.............p. v. 652
Appling...............p. o. 355
Apulia...............p. v. 483
Arcade.................t. 712
Arcadia.............p. v. 690
Arcadia.................t. 690
Argusville.............v. 604
Argyle.................la. 679
Argyle.................p. v. 679
Argyle.................t. 679
Aries.................la. 557
Arietta.................t. 337
Arkport.............p. v. 626
Arkville...............lo. 263
Arkwright.............p. o. 210
Arkwright.................t. 210
Arkwright Summit....p. o. 210
Armonk...............p. v. 703
Armstrong............h. 690
Arnoldton.............p. o. 662
Arthursburgh.........p. o. 272
Ashbel................br. 223
Ashbury.................v. 667
Ashford.................lo. 700
Ashford.............p. v. 188
Ashford.................t. 188
Ash Grove...............v. 686
Ash Grove Hill.........h. 674
Ashland.................h. 131
Ashland.................t. 131
Ash Park.............p. o. 189
Ashville.............p. o. 213
Aspetong................h. 698
Astoria.............p. v. 548
Atkarton...............lo. 662
Athens.............p. v. 331
Athens.................t. 331
Attica.............p. v. 712
Attica.................t. 711
Attica Center.........p. o. 712
Attlebury...........p. o. 277
Auburn City........... 199
Augur.................p. o. 300
Augusta.............p. v. 462
Augusta.................t. 462
Aurelius.............p. v. 200
Aurelius.................t. 200
Auries.............cr. 407, 413
Auriesville...........p. v. 413
Aurora.............p. v. 202
Aurora.................t. 283
Au Sable....mts. 232, 296, 302, 305, 307, 336
Au Sable....r. 21, 232, 235, 236, 238, 296, 300, 302, 303
Au Sable.................t. 235
Au Sable Forks..p. v. 236, 302

PAGE

Austerlitz.............p. v. 243
Austerlitz.................t. 243
Austin...................h. 541
Ava.................p. o. 462
Ava.................t. 462
Ava Corners...............v. 462
Avalanche...........la. 22, 303
Avoca.................p. v. 582
Avoca.................t. 582
Avon.................p. v. 382
Avon.................t. 382
Avon Springs........... 26
Ayreshire.............p. o. 225

Babcock Hill.........p. o. 463
Babylon.............p. v. 596
Bacon Hill.........p. o. 591
Bayleys................br. 261
Baker...........cr. 170, 222
Bakers Bridge...........v. 169
Bakers Falls........... 684
Bakers Falls.............lo. 684
Bakers Mills.........p. o. 248
Bainbridge.........p. v. 225
Bainbridge.................t. 225
Baines Station...........v. 245
Bald................mt. 295, 588, 677
Bald Eagle...............cr. 515
Bald Mountain.........p. v. 683
Baldwin............cr. 220, 222
Baldwin.................p. v. 221
Baldwin..................t. 220
Baldwinville...........lo. 547
Baldwinsville....p. v. 483, 490
Ball.................h. 188, 541
Ball.................p. 507
Ball Hill.................h. 188
Balls Cave...............lo. 606
Ballston...............la. 587
Ballston.............p. o. 590
Ballston.............p. v. 587
Ballston.................t. 586
Ballston Center.........p. o. 587
Ballston Outlet.........cr. 590
Ballston Spa.........p. v. 590
Ballston Spring...........590
Balmville...............lo. 509
Baltimore................v. 254
Bangall.............p. v. 277
Bangor.................t. 308
Baptist Hill...............v. 495
Baquet...............mts. 336
Barberville...............v. 558
Barbourville.........p. o. 265
Barcelona.............p. v. 216
Bare Hill...............h. 720
Bargers.................p. 543
Barker.............p. o. 181
Barker.................t. 181
Barker Point...........lo. 550
Barkersville...........p. o. 591
Barnerville.........p. v. 604
Barnes.................h. 274
Barnes Corners.........p. o. 379
Barnum...............cr. 616
Barrack.................h. 569
Barre.................t. 513
Barre Center...........p. o. 514
Barrett.................t. 541
Barretts.................p. 541
Barrington.........p. v. 719
Barrington.................t. 719
Barrytown.............p. v. 276
Barryville.............p. v. 645
Barton.............p. v. 650
Barton.................t. 650
Barton Hill.........p. o. 606
Bashers Kil...cr. 506, 641, 646
Bashville.............p. o. 643
Basic...........cr. 166, 332
Basket.................cr. 645
Basket.................lo. 645
Basket.................p. 645
Basket Pond............br. 261
Bassitt...............mt. 302
Batavia ....p. v. 324
Batavia.................t. 324
Batavia Kil...263, 264, 331, 334
Batavia Kill...............lo. 264

PAGE

Batchelerville ....p. v. 588
Bath ....isle 450
Bath.................p. v. 622
Bath.................t. 622
Bath ....v. 373, 557
Bating Hollow.........p. o. 637
Batten Kil 680, 683
Battenville ....p. v. 683
Baxters................br. 261
Bay Bluff...............lo. 691
Bay Ridge...............v. 373
Bay Side...............lo. 546
Bay View...............lo. 567
Beach Ridge............... 455
Beacon Hill...............mt. 19
Beacrofts...............mt. 245
Bean...................h. 407, 413
Beanville................v. 176
Bear...........cr. 216, 688, 682
Bear.................la. 216
Bear........mt. 19, 486, 505, 507
Beards...............cr. 381, 384
Beardsley................cr. 222
Bear Kil................ 265
Bearsville.............p. o. 668
Bear Swamp...........br. 204
Bear Trap...............cr. 487
Bearytown.......v. 615, 618
Beaver.....cr. 223, 388, 491, 497
Beaver.................isle 279
Beaver.................la. 190
Beaver.................p. 704
Beaver.................r. 375, 376
Beaver Brook.........p. o. 648
Beaver Dam.......cr. 164, 591
Beaver Dams ....p. v. 611
Beaver Kil.....260, 261, 641, 647, 663
Beaver Kill.........p. o. 647
Beckers Corners.........lo. 163
Bedford.................lo. 367
Bedford.............p. v. 698
Bedford.................t. 698
Bedford Station.........p. o. 698
Bedloes...............isle 418, 419
Beechers.................cr. 588
Beechers Hollow........v. 588
Beechwood Cemetery...lo. 703
Beech Woods.........p. o. 644
Beekman.............p. o. 270
Beekman.................t. 270
Beekman Furnace....lo. 270
Beekmans Corners.....lo. 607
Beekmantown.........p. o. 236
Beekmantown.........t. 236
Beekmantown ....v. 702
Beekmanville ....v. 270
Beer...................cr. 668
Beer Kil............... 668
Beers Settlement........v. 656
Belcher.............p. v. 684
Belle Isle.............p. o. 481
Belfast.............p. v. 171
Belfast.................t. 171
Belfort...............lo. 376
Belgium................v. 481
Belleville.............p. v. 357
Bellmont.................t. 309
Bellona.................v. 119
Bellows.................la. 317
Bellport.............p. v. 634
Bellport Bay.......633, 634
Bellvale.............mts. 501, 510
Bellvale.............p. v. 510
Belvidere.............p. v. 170
Bemis Heights........p. o. 593
Benin Water...........p. 507
Bennett...............h. 164
Bennetts...cr. 225, 622, 623, 625
Bennetts.................p. 303
Bennettsburgh.......p. v. 611
Bennetts Corners .....p. o. 392
Bennetts Creek.......p. o. 623
Bennettsville.........p. v. 225
Bennington.........p. o. 712
Bennington.................t. 712
Bennington Center.......v. 712
Benson...............p. o. 338
Benson Center........p. o. 338

723

PAGE
Bensons Corners...lo. 657
Bentley...p. o. 567
Benton...p. o. 719
Benton...t. 719
Benton Center...p. v. 719
Bergen...p. o. 325
Bergen...t. 325
Bergen Corners...lo. 325
Bergholtz...p. v. 456
Berkshire...p. v. 650
Berkshire...t. 650
Berlin...p. v. 554
Berlin...t. 554
Bern...p. o. 162
Bern...t. 162
Bernhards Bay...p. v. 520
Bernville... 162
Berriens...isle 548
Bethany...p. o. 325
Bethany...t. 325
Bethany Center...lo. 325
Bethel...p. v. 643
Bethel...t. 643
Bethel...v. 346
Bethlehem...t. 163
Bethlehem...v. 505
Bethlehem Center...p. o. 163
Bethphage...lo. 551
Betts Corners...v. 484
Big...isle 541
Big...la. 684
Big...p. 506, 647
Big Alder...cr. 377
Big Bowmans...p. 558
Big Brook...p. o. 471
Big Buffalo...cr. 284, 290, 293
Big Choconut...cr. 179
Big Clear...la. 311
Big Creek...p. o. 625
Bigelow...cr. 325, 327
Big Flats...p. v. 220
Big Flats...t. 220
Big...h. 541
Big Hollow...p. v. 335
Big Red...cr. 688
Big Salmon...cr. 202
Big Sister...cr. 279, 290
Big Stream...cr. 719, 721
Big Stream Point...p. o. 721
Big Tree Corners...p. o. 291
Big Trout...cr. 261
Big Wells...p. 643
Bill...h. 510
Bill Whites...h. 510
Binghamton...p. v. 180
Binghamton...t. 180, 649
Birch...br. 542
Birch...cr. 579
Birch Ridge...p. 643
Birdsall...p. o. 172
Birdsall...t. 171
Birdsall Center...p. o. 172
Birmingham...lo. 300
Birmingham Falls... 235
Birmingham Falls...lo. 300
Birmingham Falls...v. 235
Bisby...la. 349
Black...br. 496, 497, 560, 578
Black...cr. 20, 164, 168, 171, 320, 325, 328, 347, 351, 360, 395, 398, 401, 521, 685, 688
Black...la. 23, 572, 577, 580, 588, 643
Black...mt. 295, 507, 677
Black...p. 271
Black...r. 21, 22, 351, 352, 359, 361, 362, 376, 377, 379, 458, 462, 466, 560.
Black Brook...p. v. 236
Black Brook...t. 236
Black Creek...p. v. 175
Black Cup...h. 507
Black Lake...p. o. 581
Black Meadow...cr. 484, 505
Blackmine Ridge...mt. 569
Black River...bay 352
Black River...p. v. 361
Black River...v. 359
Black Rock...h. 505
Black Rock...p. o. 284, 288
Black Top...h. 507
Black Walnut Island...lo. 510
Blackwells...isle 418, 419
Blanchards Settlement...lo. 376
Blauveltville...lo. 571
Bleecker...p. v. 316
Bleecker...t. 316
Blenheim...t. 603
Blind...br. 700
Blind...p. 645
Blind Sodus Bay.. 206, 688, 695
Blockville...p. v. 213
Blodgets Mills...p. o. 252
Bloods...lo. 624
Bloodville...v. 590
Bloody...p. 255
Bloody Pond...p. 673
Bloomingburgh...p. v. 646
Bloomingdale...lo. 419
Bloomingdale...p. o. 304
Blooming Grove...p. o. 504
Blooming Grove...t. 504
Blooming Grove...v. 504
Blooming View...v. 567
Bloomville...p. v. 262
Blossvale...p. o. 462
Blue...br. 462
Blue Point...p. o. 634
Blue Ridge...mts. 19
Blue Store...lo. 248
Bluff Point...lo. 719
Bluff Point...p. o. 720
Boat...br. 720
Bog Meadow...br. 593
Bog Meadow...cr. 505
Bog Meadow...p. 505
Boght...p. o. 166
Bolivar...p. v. 172
Bolivar...t. 172
Bolton...p. o. 673
Bolton...t. 673
Bolts Corners...lo. 204
Bombay...t. 309
Bombay Corners...p. o. 309
Bonaparte...la. 376
Bone Run...cr. 186
Bonny Hill...p. o. 627
Boonville...p. v. 462
Boonville...t. 462
Booth...p. o. 348
Boquet...mt. 295, 301, 302, 304
Boquet...r. 296, 301, 305
Boquet...v. 301
Borden...cr. 624, 626
Boreas...p. 304
Boretontown...lo. 705
Borodino...p. v. 487
Boston...p. v. 283
Boston...t. 283
Boston Center...v. 283
Boston Corner...p. o. 243
Bosworth...mt. 300
Boucks Falls... 605
Bouckville...p. v. 392
Bovina...p. v. 260
Bovina...t. 259
Bowens...cr. 324
Bowery...cr. 332
Bowery Bay... 544
Bowling Green...lo. 443
Bowmans...cr. 412
Bowmansville...p. v. 291
Boyer...cr. 655
Boylston...p. o. 521
Boylston...t. 521
Boynton...v. 558
Bozen Kil...cr. 164, 596
Brackel...cr. 223, 229
Braddocks...ba. 395
Bradford...p. v. 622
Bradford...t. 622
Bradley...cr. 182
Bradley Brook Reservoir..la. 390
Bradstreets...isle 521
Brag Village...lo. 496
Brainards...p. v. 557
Brakabeen...p. v. 605
Bramans Corners...p. v. 596
Branch...br. 637
Branchport...p. v. 720
Brandon...t. 309
Brandt...p. v. 283
Brandt...t. 283
Brandy...cr. 579
Brant...la. 674
Brantingham...la. 377
Brantingham...p. o. 377
Brasher...t. 575
Brasher Center...lo. 575
Brasher Falls...p. v. 575
Brasher Iron Works...p. o. 575
Bread...cr. 201
Breakneck...br. 542
Breakneck...mt. 19, 540, 542
Breakneck...v. 542
Breesport...p. v. 222
Brewerton...p. v. 481
Brewsters Station...p. v. 543
Brickville...v. 221
Bridge Haven...lo. 547
Bridgehampton...p. v. 638
Bridgeport...p. v. 394
Bridgeville...v. 647
Bridgewater...p. v. 463
Bridgewater...t. 462
Brier Hill...p. o. 580
Brigham...p. o. 215
Brighton...p. v. 398
Brighton...t. 113, 398
Brighton...v. 537
Brinkerhoffville...lo. 272
Brink Street...cr. 332
Bristol...p. o. 495
Bristol...t. 495
Bristol Center...p. v. 495
Broadalbin...p. o. 316
Broadalbin...t. 316
Broadhead...p. 645
Brocken Straw...cr. 211
Brocketts Bridge...p. v. 346
Brockport...p. v. 405
Brockton...p. o. 215
Brockville...lo. 515
Brockway...h. 559
Bronx...r. 23, 696, 699, 700, 702, 703, 705, 706, 707
Bronxdale...v. 706
Bronxville...p. v. 699
Brookfield...lo. 547
Brookfield...p. o. 390
Brookfield...t. 390
Brookhaven...t. 633
Brooklyn...p. o. 367
Brooklyn City... 367
Brooklyn Heights...lo. 367
Brooks Grove...p. v. 385
Brookville...lo. 551
Brookville...p. o. 324
Broome...co. 178
Broome...t. 603
Broome Center...p. o. 605
Brown...cr. 387
Browns...cr. 340
Browns Hollow...cr. 349
Browns Hollow...v. 416
Brownville...lo. 496
Brownville...p. v. 356
Brownville...t. 356
Bruceville...v. 664, 666
Brunswick...t. 554
Brunswick Center...lo. 554
Brushs Mills...p. v. 312
Brush Hollow...lo. 543
Brushland...p. v. 260
Brutus...t. 200
Bruynswick...p. o. 667
Buchan...h. 569
Buck...br. 223
Buck...mt. 681
Buck...p. 395
Buckhorn...isle 279, 449
Bucklins Corners...v. 213
Bucks Bridge...lo. 582
Bucktooth...cr. 188
Bucktooth...p. o. 188
Bucktooth...t. 188
Buel...p. v. 412
Buena Vista...p. o. 626
Buffalo..cr. 20, 22, 279, 293, 714
Buffalo...p. o. 284
Buffalo City... 284
Buffalo Plains...p. o. 284
Bull...h. 542
Bull Hill...mt. 19
Bull Pout...p. 304
Bulls Head...p. o. 270
Bullville...p. v. 506
Bulson...h. 569
Bunker...h. 559
Bunker Hill...lo. 559
Burdens Point...lo. 703
Burdett...p. v. 611
Burdick Settlement...v. 227
Burlingham...p. v. 646
Burlington...p. o. 532
Burlington...t. 531
Burlington Flats...p. v. 532
Burlington Green...v. 532
Burke...p. o. 309
Burke...t. 309
Burke Hollow...v. 309
Burned...h. 507, 541
Burns...p. v. 172
Burns...t. 172
Burns...v. 625
Burnt Hill...p. 647
Burnt Hills...p. v. 587
Burpos Corners...lo. 699
Burralls...br. 491, 498
Burrs Mills...p. o. 362
Burtonsville...p. v. 413
Bush...cr. 175
Bush Kil...263, 641
Bushnells Basin...p. v. 401
Bushnellsville...p. o. 334
Bushville...lo. 325
Bushwick...cr. 367
Bushwick Cross Roads...v. 367
Bushwick Green...v. 367
Buskirks Bridge...p. v. 556, 679
Busti...p. o. 210
Busti...t. 210
Busti Corners...v. 210
Butler...br. 386
Butler...h. 505
Butler...t. 690
Butler Center...lo. 691
Butterfly...cr. 523
Butterfly...p. o. 523
Butter Hill...mt. 19
Buttermilk...cr. 186
Buttermilk...h. 702
Buttermilk...p. 273, 300
Buttermilk Falls...326, 505
Buttermilk Falls...lo. 326
Buttermilk Falls...p. v. 505
Butternut...cr. 474, 481, 484, 530, 532, 533, 535
Butternut...h. 559
Butternut...p. 300
Butternuts...p. o. 532
Butternuts...t. 532
Butterville...lo. 665
Buttonwood...cr. 395
Byersville...p. v. 387
Byram...la. 698
Byram...p. 703
Byram...r. 23, 696, 703
Byron...p. v. 325
Byron...t. 325

Cabin...cr. 334
Cabin Hill...p. o. 259
Cadiz...p. v. 190
Cadmans...cr. 591
Cadosia Valley...p. o. 262
Cadyville...p. v. 239
Cairo...p. v. 331
Cairo...t. 331
Cairo Forge...lo. 331
Calder...cr. 387
Caldwell...cr. 416
Caldwell...p. v. 673
Caldwell...t. 673
Caldwells Landing...lo. 377
Caledonia...p. v. 383
Caledonia...t. 383
Caledonia Spring... 383
Caledonia Springs Outlet cr. 405
California...lo. 482, 656
Callanans Corners...p. v. 163
Callicoon...cr. 641, 644
Callicoon...p. o 644
Callicoon...t. 644
Callicoon Center...v. 644
Callicoon Depôt...p. v. 644
Calvary Cemetery...lo. 549
Cambria...p. o. 453
Cambria...t. 453
Cambridge...p. v. 680
Cambridge...t. 680
Camden...p. v. 463
Camden...t. 463
Cameron...p. v. 623
Cameron...t. 623
Cameron Mills...p. o. 627
Camillus...p. v. 481
Camillus...t. 480
Campbell...t. 623
Campbell Hall...lo. 507
Campbells...cr. 622
Campbelltown...p. v. 623
Campbellville...p. v. 273
Camps...cr. 534
Campville...p. v. 652
Canaan...p. o. 243
Canaan...t. 243

INDEX OF GEOGRAPHICAL NAMES. 725

PAGE
Canaan Four Corners..p. v. 243
Canacadea............cr. 619, 626
Canada..................lo. 201
Canadaway.....cr. 208, 210, 214
Canadice...............la. 20, 495
Canadice......................t. 495
Canadice Corners.......p. o. 495
Canadice Inlet.............cr. 495
Canadice Outlet...........cr. 491
Canajoharie..........cr. 407, 412
Canajoharie...............p. v. 412
Canajoharie.....................t. 412
Canal.........................p. o. 490
Canandaigua.....la. 20, 22, 491, 717, 720
Canandaigua.............p. v. 495
Canandaigua....................t. 495
Canandaigua Inlet.......cr. 497
Canandaigua Outlet.......cr. 21, 491, 497, 688, 691
Canarsie....................p. o. 372
Canasawacta................cr. 223
Canaseraga.......cr. 20, 168, 381, 385, 386, 388, 394, 619
Canaseraga.................p. v. 172
Canaseraga.......................v. 394
Canastota.............cr. 388, 394
Canastota...................p. v. 392
Candor........................p. v. 651
Candor...........................t. 651
Candor Center...............v. 651
Caneadea........cr. 168, 172, 479
Caneadea...................p. v. 172
Caneadea.........................t. 172
Canes Falls....................v. 681
Canfield...........................p. 647
Canfields Corners.......p. o. 651
Canisteo....................p. v. 623
Canisteo......r. 21, 23, 168, 170, 619, 623, 625, 626, 627
Canisteo..........................t. 623
Cannonsville..............p. v. 265
Canoe...............................h. 277
Canoe Place...................lo. 638
Canoga........................p. v. 615
Canopus.........................cr. 542
Canopus..............................l. 540
Canopus Lake.............cr. 543
Canopus Valley...........lo. 540
Canterbury......................v. 504
Canton........................p. v. 575
Canton.............................t. 575
Canton.............................v. 490
Cap................................isle 636
Cape..................................h. 507
Cape Vincent.............p. v. 356
Cape Vincent...................t. 356
Cap Tree.......................isle 636
Cardiff........................p. v. 483
Carlisle.......................p. v. 604
Carlisle.............................t. 603
Carl Place.......................lo. 550
Carlton..........................isle 356
Carlton ....p. o. 514
Carlton..............................t. 514
Carlton Center................lo. 514
Carmansville ....lo. 419
Carmel........................p. v. 541
Carmel...............................t. 541
Caroga..............................t. 317
Caroline.......................p. o. 655
Caroline.............................t. 655
Caroline Center..........p. v. 655
Carpenter...........................h. 277
Carpenters..........................p. 486
Carpenters Point..........lo. 506
Carroll...............................t. 211
Carrolton............................t. 188
Carrs...............................cr. 264
Carterville....................p. v. 521
Cartersville.......................v. 401
Carthage.......................p. v. 363
Carthage Landing......p. v. 272
Carytown........................lo. 413
Caryville.........................lo. 327
Cascadilla.......................cr. 654
Casper.............................cr. 267
Cassadaga......cr. 212, 213, 214, 216
Cassadaga........................la. 216
Cassadaga...................p. v. 216
Cassville.......................p. v. 466
Castile..........................p. v. 712
Castile...............................t. 712
Castle......................br. 491, 498
Castle...................cr. 179, 181
PAGE
Castle...........................isle 163
Castle Creek..............p. v. 181
Castleton...................p. v. 559
Castleton............................t. 565
Castleton............................v. 498
Catatunk.........cr. 649, 651, 652
Catfish.....................cr. 351, 523
Catharine...................cr. 219, 222
Catharines..............cr. 609, 610
Catharines..................p. v. 610
Catharines..........................t. 609
Cathatachua ....cr. 340
Cat Head.............................h. 673
Catlin.................................la. 303
Catlin.................................t. 220
Catlin Center.............p. o. 221
Cato............................p. v. 201
Cato....................................t. 201
Caton..........................p. v. 623
Caton..................................t. 623
Catskill...cr. 156, 165, 329, 331, 332, 600, 603
Catskill...mts. 19, 329, 331, 660
Catskill.......................p. v. 332
Catskill...............................t. 332
Cattaraugus...co. 101, 103, 186
Cattaraugus......cr. 20, 22, 186, 187, 189, 194, 213, 279, 283, 289, 292, 712, 714
Cattaraugus.............la. 22, 714
Cattaraugus..................p. v. 193
Caughnawaga...................lo. 407
Caughdenoy..................p. v. 522
Cayadutta......cr. 314, 407, 415
Cayuga.............................br. 200
Cayuga...................co. 101, 197
Cayuga..........cr. 451, 456, 712
Cayuga..............................isle 449
Cayuga......la. 20, 22, 197, 198, 200, 205, 614, 616
Cayuga.........................p. v. 200
Cayuga Inlet....................cr. 654
Cayuga Outlet..................cr. 197
Cayuta....cr. 219, 222, 609, 610, 649, 650
Cayuta...............................la. 609
Cayuta..........................p. o. 222
Cayuta.................................t. 610
Cayuta.................................v. 610
Cayutaville..................p. o. 611
Cazenove.........cr. 283, 289, 293
Cazenovia..................la. 22, 388
Cazenovia...................p. v. 390
Cazenovia............................t. 390
Cedar.................................cr. 578
Cedar.........................h. 507, 510
Cedar....................................p. 507
Cedar....................................r. 339
Cedar Hill........................lo. 276
Cedar Hill...................p. o. 163
Cedar Island ....isle 635
Cedar Lake..................p. o. 345
Cedar Swamp...............p. o. 551
Cedarville....................p. v. 342
Cemetery of the Evergreens.............lo. 549
Center................................br. 536
Center................................cr. 686
Center Almond ....p. o. 170
Center Berlin..............p. v. 554
Center Brook...............p. o. 536
Center Cambridge......p. v. 680
Center Canisteo ....p. o. 623
Center Falls........................v. 683
Centerfield ....p. o. 495
Center Island ....lo. 550
Center Lisle.................p. v. 182
Center Moriches ....p. o. 634
Center Point.................p. o. 507
Centerport ....p. v. 636
Centerport ....v. 203
Centerport Harbor........... 636
Center Sherman ....p. o. 215
Center Square ....v. 526
Center Village.............p. v. 181
Centerville.....lo. 332, 548, 566, 706
Centerville ....p. v. 172
Centerville............................t. 172
Centerville .....v. 203, 215, 238, 481, 624, 661, 664
Center White Creek ...p. o. 686
Central Bridge............p. v. 606
Central Morrisania ......lo. 707
Central Park...................lo. 423
Central Square ....p. v. 522
PAGE
Ceres.. ....p. v. 174
Chain...................................la. 303
Champion....................p. v. 357
Champion...........................t. 357
Champion South Road..p.o. 357
Champlain...la. 21, 22, 23, 121, 232, 236, 237, 239, 296, 304
Champlain ....p. v. 237
Champlain...........................r. 236
Champlain...........................t. 236
Channingville....................lo. 274
Chapinville..................p. v. 496
Chappaqua ....h. 702
Chappaqua ....p. 702
Chappaqua ....p. o. 702
Chappaqua Springs......696, 702
Charleston ....p. v. 413
Charleston...........................t. 412
Charleston Four Corners p. v. 413
Charlotte ....la. 241, 245
Charlotte ....lo. 454
Charlotte.......................p. v. 399
Charlotte...r. 21, 257, 260, 262, 530, 600, 607
Charlotte ....t. 211
Charlotte Center.........p. v. 211
Charlotteville..............p. v. 607
Charlton ....p. v. 587
Charlton...............................t. 587
Charter ....br. 685
Chases...................la. 316, 379
Chases Mills ....p. o. 579
Chaseville......................p. o. 534
Chateaugay ....p. v. 310
Chateaugay......r. 307, 309, 310
Chateaugay...........................t. 310
Chateaugay Lake.......p. o. 309
Chatham.........................p. v. 244
Chatham...............................t. 244
Chatham Center ....p. v. 244
Chatham Four Corners p. v. 244
Chatsworth ....lo. 701
Chatterdens..........................p. 252
Chatterton ....h. 707
Chaugh-ta-noon-da........cr. 597
Chaumont.....................p. v. 359
Chaumont.................r. 357, 360
Chaumont Bay 124, 352, 359
Chautauqua ....co. 101, 208
Chautauqua ....cr. 211, 216
Chautauqua.....la. 22, 208, 211, 213
Chautauqua.........................t. 211
Chautauqua Valley.....p. o. 174
Chazy...................................la. 237
Chazy ....lo. 235, 682
Chazy...........................p. v. 237
Chazy...........r. 21, 23, 237, 238
Chazy....................................t. 237
Chazy Landing...................lo. 237
Cheese Coats........................h. 569
Chekomiko ....cr. 273
Chelsea ....v. 566
Chemung...........................co. 219
Chemung.......................p. o. 221
Chemung......r. 21, 23, 219, 221, 222, 624, 625
Chemung ....t. 221
Chemung Center...........p. o. 221
Chenango ....co. 101, 223
Chenango ....p. o. 181
Chenango...r. 21, 23, 178, 223, 226, 228, 229, 230, 388, 458
Chenango..............................t. 181
Chenango Forks..p. v. 181, 226
Cheningo ....cr. 250
Chenunda ....cr. 168, 174
Cherry Creek ....p. v. 211
Cherry Creek......................t. 211
Cherry Hill..........................lo. 163
Cherry Meadow...................br. 641
Cherry Valley............cr. 530, 534
Cherry Valley.................p. v. 532
Cherry Valley.........................t. 532
Cherubusco.....................p. o. 237
Cheshire ....p. v. 495
Cheshireville....................p. o. 229
Chester...........................p. o. 505
Chester..........................t. 505, 674
Chester....................................v. 505
Chesterfield...........................t. 300
Chestertown....................p. v. 674
Chesterville............................v. 167
Chestnut Ridge.......................h. 289
PAGE
Chestnut Ridge ....p. 643
Chestnut Ridge ....p. o. 271
Chicktawauga...............p. o. 288
Chicktawauga........................t. 288
Chili..............................p. v. 398
Chili......................................t. 398
Chimney.............................isle 574
Chimney Bluff ....lo. 691
Chimney Point 377
China ....p. o. 712
China......................................t. 712
China Forge ....p. 541
Chippewa...............................cr. 580
Chippewa ....lo. 577
Chittenango...cr. 388, 390, 474, 484
Chittenango ....p. v. 394
Chittenango Falls......p. o. 390
Chittenango Springs........ 26
Chittenango Springs.....lo. 394
Chittendens Falls ....v. 248
Christian Hook ....lo. 547
Chub ....la. 349
Chucks..h. 510
Chuctenunda.......cr. 314, 407, 411, 413, 596
Church Hollow ....p. o. 226
Churchs Mills..........................v. 210
Churchtown.....................p. v. 244
Churchville.......................p. v. 401
Cicero..............................p. o. 481
Cicero..t. 481
Cicero Corners ....v. 481
Cincinnati ....cr. 467
Cincinnatus ....p. v. 251
Cincinnatus.............................t. 251
Circleville........................p. v. 510
Citizens Union Cemetery lo. 371
City..isle 704
City ....p. o. 270
City Park.................................lo. 369
Clapps Mills ....v. 685
Claremont...................lo. 702, 707
Clarence..................................p. o. 289
Clarence.......................................t. 288
Clarence Center...............p. v. 289
Clarence Hollow......................v. 289
Clarenceville ....lo. 548
Clarendon..........................p. v. 514
Clarendon ....t. 514
Clark...mt. 302
Clarksburgh......................p. o. 290
Clarks Corners ....lo. 590
Clarks Factory ....p. o. 263
Clarks Mills...............................v. 464
Clarkson ....p. v. 399
Clarkson......................................t. 398
Clarkson Center..............p. v. 405
Clarkstown......................p. o. 569
Clarkstown..................................t. 569
Clarksville ....p. v. 164
Clarksville...................................t. 173
Clarksville..v. 200, 390, 534, 569
Clarksville Corners..................v. 173
Claryville ....p. v. 647
Classons Point ....lo. 706
Claverack..cr. 241, 244, 245, 247, 248
Claverack ....p. v. 244
Claverack ....t. 244
Clay ....p. o. 481
Clay..t. 481
Clayburgh...................................v. 236
Clayton ....p. v. 357
Clayton...t. 357
Clayton Center................p. o. 357
Clayville ....p. v. 466
Clear.........cr. 190, 212, 289, 712
Clear...la. 190
Clear...................................p. 304, 543
Clear Creek..........p. v. 189, 212
Clearwater............................br. 260
Clendening Valley..................lo. 418
Clermont.............................p. v. 244
Clermont ....t. 244
Cleveland.........................p. v. 521
Clifton ....p. v. 398
Clifton ....v. 566
Clifton Springs...............p. v. 497
Clifton Park ......p. v. 587, 589
Clifton Park..................................t. 587
Clinton......................co. 110, 232
Clinton ....p. v. 464
Clinton ....t. 237
Clinton Corners...............p. v. 270

PAGE
Clintondale....p. v. 665
Clinton Hollow....p. v. 270
Clinton Point....p. o. 270
Clintonville....lo. 485, 533
Clintonville....p. v. 235
Clockville....p. v. 392
Clove....br. 261
Clove....cr. 542
Clove....lo. 607
Clove....p. o. 277
Clove Kil.... 277
Clovesville....p. o. 263
Clowesville....lo. 550
Clump Foot....cr. 624
Clyde....p. v. 691
Clyde....r. 21, 613, 688, 691
Clymer....p. v. 211
Clymer....t. 211
Clymer Center....p. o. 212
Cobamong....p. 703
Cobles Kil....600, 606
Cobleskill....p. v. 604
Cobleskill....t. 604
Cobleskill Center....p. v. 604
Cochecton....p. v. 644
Cochecton....t. 644
Cochecton Center....p. o. 644
Cockburns Gore....lo. 263
Coeclis Harbor....ba. 637
Coeymans....br. 164
Coeymans....cr. 155, 163
Coeymans....p. o. 163
Coeymans....t. 163
Coeymans Hollow....p. o. 163
Coeymans Landing....v. 163
Cohoes....p. v. 166
Coila....p. v. 684
Colchester....p. o. 260
Colchester....t. 260
Cold...br. 223, 250, 253, 254, 593
Cold....cr. 174, 713
Cold....h. 505
Cold Brook....p. v. 348
Cold Creek....v. 174
Colden....la. 22, 302
Colden....p. v. 289
Colden....t. 289
Coldenham....lo. 508
Coldenham....p. o. 508
Cold Spring....br. 201
Cold Spring....cr. 186, 188, 628
Cold Spring....lo. 454, 499, 628
Cold Spring....p. v. 542
Cold Spring....t. 188
Cold Spring....v. 636
Cold Spring Harbor....544, 636
Cold Spring Harbor...p. o. 636
Coldwater....lo. 399
Cole....br. 377, 588
Colemans Mills....lo. 471
Colemans Station....lo. 273
Coles....br. 260
Colesborough....lo. 558
Coles Mills....lo. 541
Colesville....p. o. 181
Colesville....t. 181
Collaberg....h. 506, 569
Collaburgh....p. o. 506
Collamer....p. o. 482
College Point....p. v. 546
Collierville....p. o. 534
Collins....p. o. 292
Collins....t. 289
Collins Center....p. v. 289
Collins Landing....lo. 360
Collinsville....p. v. 380
Col. Bills....cr. 623
Colosse....p. v. 522
Colton....p. v. 526
Colton....t. 526
Columbia....co. 101, 103, 241
Columbia....p. o. 342
Columbia....t. 342
Columbia Center....v. 342
Columbia Springs.... 345
Columbia Village....v. 579
Columbiaville....lo. 248
Columbus....p. o. 472
Columbus....t. 472
Columbus Center....v. 472
Columbusville....lo. 549
Comac....v. 636
Comack....p. o. 636
Comfort....h. 506, 508
Commonsville....v. 385
Comstocks Landing...p. o. 187
Comus....mt. 541
PAGE
Concord....t. 289
Conesus....cr. 20, 381
Conesus....la. 20, 381
Conesus....p. o. 383
Conesus....t. 383
Conesus Center....p. v. 383
Conesville....p. o. 604
Conesville....t. 604
Coney....isle 372
Conhocton....p. o. 624
Conhocton....r. 21, 23, 386, 619, 622, 625
Conhocton....t. 624
Conklin....lo. 182
Conklin....t. 181
Conklin Center....p. v. 182
Conklings....br. 483
Conklingville....v. 589
Conklingville Falls....lo. 584
Connecticut....r. 631, 633
Connery....p. 303
Connetquot....r. 636
Connewango....cr. 23, 186, 189, 208, 210, 211, 214
Connewango....p. o. 189
Connewango....t. 189
Conquest....p. o. 201
Conquest....t. 201
Conquest Center....v. 201
Conscience Bay.... 633
Constable....t. 310
Constable....v. 310
Constableville....p. v. 380
Constantia....t. 521
Constantia Center....p. o. 521
Constitution....isle 540, 542
Continental Village....v. 542
Cooksburgh....p. o. 165
Cooks Corners....p. v. 393
Cooleys Point....lo. 616
Coomer....p. o. 454
Coonsville....lo. 497
Coopers Falls....lo. 576
Coopers Plains....p. v. 625
Cooperstown....p. v. 536
Coopersville....v. 237, 385
Copake....la. 241, 245
Copake....p. o. 245
Copake....t. 244
Copake Flats....v. 245
Copake Iron Works...p. o. 245
Copake Station....v. 245
Copeland....h. 164
Copeland....p. 681
Copenhagen....p. v. 376
Copperas....p. 305
Coram....p. o. 634
Corbeau....cr. 237
Corbetsville....p. o. 182
Corfu....p. o. 327
Corinth....p. o. 218
Corinth....t. 218
Corlaers Hook....lo. 419
Corning....p. v. 624
Corning....t. 624
Cortland....co. 250
Cortland Village....p. v. 252
Cortlandville....t. 252
Cortlandt....t. 698
Cortright....br. 204
Cornwall....p. o. 505
Cornwall....t. 505
Cornwall Landing....v. 505
Cornwallville....p. v. 332
Corrys....br. 596
Coshaqua....cr. 381, 385
Cossayuna....cr. 683
Cossayuna....la. 679
Cossayuna....mts. 677
Cot....h. 542
Cottage....p. o. 189
Coulter....br. 259
County Line....p. o. 456, 516
Cove Neck....lo. 550
Coventry....p. v. 226
Coventry....t. 225
Coventryville....p. v. 226
Covert....p. o. 615
Covert....t. 615
Coveville....lo. 591
Covils....p. 543
Covington....p. o. 713
Covington....t. 713
Covington Center....v. 713
Cowaselon....cr. 388, 394
Cowaselon....p. o. 392
Cow Bay.... 550
PAGE
Cow Neck....lo. 549
Cowilliga....cr. 407, 413
Cowlesville....p. v. 712
Coxcomb....h. 510
Coxsackie....cr. 332
Coxsackie....p. v. 332
Coxsackie....t. 332
Coxsackie Landing....lo. 332
Coxsackie Station....lo. 249
Crab....isle 239
Crabbs Kil.... 597
Craigsville....p. v. 504
Crains Corners....lo. 349
Cranberry....cr. 23, 314, 318
Cranberry....la. 22, 376, 572, 576
Cranberry....p. 395, 505, 543
Cranberry Creek....p. o. 318
Cranberry Island....lo. 510
Crandalls....p. 252
Crandalls Corners....lo. 681
Crane....cr. 200
Crane....mt. 19, 610, 615
Cranes Neck....lo. 633
Cranes Village....lo. 590
Cranesville....p. v. 412
Crarys Mills....p. o. 575
Crawford....t. 506
Crawford Settlement....v. 611
Crescent....p. v. 589
Cripplebush Kil....cr. 600
Crittenden....p. o. 282
Crocker....cr. 182
Crofts Corners....v. 543
Croghan....p. o. 376
Croghan....t. 376
Cromlin....cr. 504
Crompond....lo. 708
Cronks Corners....p. o. 379
Crooked....cr. 326
Crooked....la. 20, 22, 558, 619, 627, 717, 719, 720
Crooked Lake Outlet....cr. 717
Cropseyville....p. o. 554
Crosby....cr. 626
Crosbyville....p. v. 623
Cross....la. 201, 474, 482
Cross....p. 701
Cross....r. 698, 705
Cross River....p. v. 701
Croton....cr. 261
Croton....la. 542, 702, 706
Croton....p. v. 261
Croton....r. 267, 273, 696, 698, 701, 703, 706, 708
Croton....v. 699
Croton Falls....p. v. 704, 706
Croton Landing....p. o. 699
Croton Point....v. 699
Crouse Store....p. o. 277
Crown Point.... 121
Crown Point....p. v. 301
Crown Point....t. 300
Crow....cr. 712
Crow Nest....mt. 19, 505
Crugers....lo. 699
Crum....cr. 416
Crum Elbow...cr. 267, 270, 272
Crum Elbow....p. o. 274
Crumhorn....la. 534
Crumhorn....mt. 534
Cruso....p. o. 617
Crusoe....cr. 693
Crusoe....la. 693
Cryders....cr. 168, 174
Crystal....la. 702, 703
Cuba....p. v. 173
Cuba....t. 173
Cuba Summit....lo. 173
Cuddebackville....p. v. 506
Cumberland Bay.... 239
Cumberland Head....lo. 239
Curriers Corners....lo. 714
Currytown....v. 416
Curtis Station....lo. 623
Cutchogue....p. v. 640
Cuyler....p. v. 255
Cuyler....t. 256
Cuylerville....p. v. 384
Cypress....h. 549
Cypress Avenue....lo. 548
Cypress Hills....h. 549
Cypress Hills....lo. 373
Cypress Hills Cemetery.lo. 549

Da-de-nos-ca-ra....cr. 575
Dalia....p. 303
PAGE
Dale....p. o. 714
Danby....p. v. 656
Danby....t. 656
Dannemora....p. v. 238
Dannemora....t. 237
Dansville....p. v. 385
Dansville....t. 624
Danube....p. o. 343
Danube....t. 342
Darien....p. o. 326
Darien....t. 326
Darien Center....p. v. 326
Darien City....lo. 326
Dashville....v. 662
Davenport....p. v. 260
Davenport....t. 260
Davenport Center....p. v. 260
Davenport Corners....v. 542
Davenports Neck....lo. 703
Davids....isle 703
Davis....cr. 688, 692
Davis....p. 647
Daws Cornerslo.... 326, 686
Day....p. o. 588
Day....t. 588
Dayansville....v. 378
Dayton....p. v. 275
Dayton....t. 275
Dead....cr. 682
Dead....la. 684
Dead Water Iron Works p. o. 304
Deans Corners....p. o. 591
Deansville....p. v. 465
Decatur....p. v. 533
Decatur....t. 532
Decker....h. 510
Deep Clove Kil....cr. 334
Deepi Kil....cr. 556
Deep Spring.... 484
Deer....cr. 168, 173, 527, 688, 692
Deer....h. 505
Deer....l. 339
Deer....r. 307, 308, 309, 310, 375, 376, 377, 572, 575, 578
Deer River....p. v. 376
Deerfield....p. o. 463
Deerfield....t. 463
Deerfield Corners....v. 463
Deering Harbor.... 637
Deer Park....p. v. 636
Deerpark....t. 506
Defiance....mt. 295, 304, 677
De Forest Corners....lo. 543
Defriestville....p. v. 557
De Kalb....p. v. 576
De Kalb....t. 576
De Lancy....p. o. 390
Delanti....v. 216
Delaware....co. 101, 257
Delaware....cr. 283, 290
Delaware....r. 21, 23, 178, 257, 259, 260, 263, 265, 641
Delaware Bridge....p. o. 648
Delhi....p. v. 261
Delhi....t. 260
Delphi....p. v. 486
Delta....p. v. 465
Deming....h. 382
Denman Hill....mt. 647
Denmark....p. v. 376
Denmark....t. 376
Denning....p. o. 662
Denning....t. 662
Dennis....h. 319
Dennison....p. o. 344
Dennisons Corners....lo. 344
Denton....v. 511
Depauville....p. v. 357
De Peyster....p. o. 576
De Peyster....t. 576
De Peyster Corners....v. 576
Deposit....p. v. 183, 265
De Ruyter....p. v. 390
De Ruyter....t. 390
Devereaux....v. 348
De Witt....p. o. 482
De Witt....t. 481
Dewittsville....lo. 662
De Wittville....p. v. 211
Dexter....p. v. 356
Dexterville....lo. 212
Diameter Rock....mt. 677
Diamond Hill....v. 348
Diamond Rock....h. 556
Diana....p. o. 376

PAGE

Diana..............t. 376
Diana Center............p. o. 376
Dickersonville.........p. o. 454
Dickinson............p. o. 310
Dickinson............t. 310
Dickinson Center......p. o. 310
Dickinson Station......lo. 265
Dike..............cr. 168
Dionondahowa Falls.... 680
Discovery...........mt. 296, 302
Ditch..............cr. 505
Dix..............mt. 295
Dix..............t. 611
Dix Hills..........p. o. 636
Dix Peak.........mt. 19, 304
Doanesburgh..........lo. 543
Dobbs Ferry........p. v. 700
Dodges...........cr. 168, 173, 186
Dominies Hook........lo. 419
Doolittle...........cr. 651
Doraville..............p. o. 183
Dormansville.........p. o. 163
Dorrs Corners........lo. 686
Dosoris...........lo. 551
Dotys Corners........p. o. 625
Dover...........p. o. 271
Dover..............t. 270
Dover Plains........v. 271
Downs..............br. 260
Downsville.........p. v. 260
Dresden.............t. 680
Dresserville........p. v. 204
Drew...........h. 541
Drews...........p. 541
Drowned Lands......lo. 501
Drummonds..........br. 590
Dry..............br. 252, 663
Dry Brook............lo. 663
Dry Brook Settlement..lo. 263
Dryden..............la. 656
Dryden..............p. v. 656
Dryden..............t. 656
Dry Dock............p. o. 587
Dry Falls........... 203
Dry Run..............cr. 623
Duane..............p. o. 310
Duane..............t. 310
Duanesburgh.........p. v. 596
Duanesburgh..........t. 596
Dublin..............v. 615
Duck..............p. 201
Duck Cedar..........p. 507
Dudley..............cr. 182
Dug Way............p. o. 520
Dumpling............h. 398
Dunbarton...........v. 479
Dundee..............p. v. 721
Dunderbergh.........mt. 569
Dunhams Basin.......v. 685
Dunkirk..............p. v. 214
Dunning Street......v. 590
Dunnsville..........p. o. 164
Durham..............p. v. 332
Durham..............t. 332
Durhamville.......p. v. 392, 479
Durkeetown..........lo. 682
Dutch..............p. 647
Dutchess..co. 101, 103, 110, 267
Dutch Factory.........lo. 569
Dutch Hills..........lo. 549
Dutch Hollow........br. 204
Dutch Hollow........v. 510
Dutch Settlement......lo. 664
Dwaars Kil........506, 587, 667
Dwaars Kill..........p. o. 667
Dyers Neck..........lo. 633
Dyersville..........v. 256
Dyke..............cr. 169, 171
Dykemans............p. o. 543
Dykemans Station.....lo. 543

Eagle..............la. 713
Eagle..............p. o. 713
Eagle..............t. 713
Eagle Bridge........p. v. 556
Eagle Harbor........p. v. 514
Eagle Mills.........p. o. 554
Eagle Village.......lo. 484
Eagle Village.......p. v. 713
Eagleville..........v. 165
Earlville..........p. v. 230, 391
East..............br. 536
East..............cr. 560, 683
East..........r. 367, 544, 548, 549
East Albany.........lo. 555
East Amherst........p. o. 208
East Ashford........p. o. 188

PAGE

East Ashland........lo. 331
East Aurora.........p. v. 283
East Bainbridge......lo. 225
East Bank..........lo. 260
East Bay.............. 631, 691
East Beekmantown...p. o. 236
East Bergen.........p. o. 325
East Berkshire......p. o. 650
East Bern...........p. v. 162
East Bethany........p. v. 325
East Bloomfield.....p. v. 496
East Bloomfield.....t. 496
East Branch.........cr. 451
East Branch.........p. v. 262
East Branch Potic...cr. 334
East Brook..........br. 265
East Brunswick......lo. 554
East Camp...........v. 245
East Canada...cr. 340, 346, 407, 416, 458
East Candor.........p. o. 651
East Carlton........p. o. 514
East Chatham........p. v. 244
East Chester........p. v. 699
East Chester........t. 699
East Chester........v. 505
East China..........p. o. 713
East Clarkson.......p. v. 399
East Constable......p. v. 325
East Coy.......cr. 713, 714, 716
East Coy..........p. o. 715
East Creek..........v. 346
East De Kalb........p. o. 576
East Dickinson......p. o. 310
East Durham.........p. v. 322
East Eden...........p. o. 290
East Edmeston.......p. o. 533
East Elba...........p. o. 326
East Evans..........p. v. 290
East Farmington.....p. o. 496
East Fish...........la. 317
East Fishkill.......p. v. 271
East Fishkill.......t. 271
East Florence.......p. o. 463
East Gaines.........p. o. 513
East Gainesville....p. v. 713
East Galway.........p. o. 588
East Genoa..........p. o. 202
East German.........p. o. 226
East Glenville......p. o. 597
East Grafton........p. v. 555
East Greenbush......p. o. 555
East Greene.........p. v. 226
East Greenville.....lo. 333
East Greenwich......p. v. 683
East Groveland......p. o. 384
East Guilford.......p. v. 227
East Hamburgh......p. v. 289
East Hamburgh......t. 289
East Hamilton.......p. o. 392
East Hampton........p. v. 635
East Hampton........t. 634
East Hebron.........v. 684
East Henrietta......v. 399
East Hill...........p. o. 385
East Homer..........v. 253
East Hounsfield.....p. o. 358
East Java...........p. o. 714
East Jewett.........p. o. 334
East Kil............ 333
East Lansing........p. o. 658
East Leon...........p. o. 191
East Line...........p. o. 587
East Macdonough....p. v. 227
East Maine..........p. o. 182
East Marion.........p. v. 640
East Melrose........lo. 702
East Moriches.......p. v. 634
East Morrisania.....lo. 702
East Mount Vernon...v. 699
East Nassau.........p. v. 557
East New York.......p. v. 373
East Norwich.......p. o. 551
Easton.............t. 681
Easton..............t. 680
Easton Corners......v. 681
East Orangeville....lo. 714
East Otto...........p. o. 189
East Otto...........t. 189
East Painted Post...p. o. 624
East Palmyra........p. v. 693
East Pembroke.......p. v. 327
East Penfield.......p. o. 401
East Pharsalia......p. v. 229
East Pierrepont.....p. v. 581
East Pike...........p. v. 715
East Pitcairn.......p. o. 581

PAGE

East Poestenkill....p. o. 558
East Porter.........p. o. 456
East Randolph.......p. v. 195
East Red............cr. 688, 692
East Rodman.........p. o. 361
East Rush...........v. 405
East Rushford.......v. 175
East Salem..........p. o. 685
East Sauquoit.......v. 466
East Schodack.......p. v. 559
East Schuyler.......p. v. 348
East Scott..........p. o. 254
East Shelby.........p. o. 516
East Smithville.....v. 230
East Springfield....p. v. 538
East Springwater...p. o. 386
East Stockholm......v. 582
East Stony..........cr. 338, 675
East Township.......lo. 164
East Troupsburgh...p. o. 628
East Varick.........p. o. 618
East Venice.........p. o. 206
East Victor.........lo. 499
East Virgil.........p. v. 255
East Warsaw........p. o. 716
East Williamson.....v. 694
East Wilson.........p. o. 457
East Windham.......p. o. 335
East Winfield.......v. 349
East Worcester......p. v. 538
Eaton..............p. v. 391
Eaton..............t. 390
Eaton Reservoir.....p. 393
Eatons Corners......lo. 596
Eatons Necks........lo. 636
Eatonville..........p. o. 345
Eckford.............la. 22
Eddytown...........p. v. 721
Eddyville...........p. o. 193
Eddyville...........v. 664
Eden..............p. v. 290
Eden..............t. 290
Edenton.............p. o. 576
Eden Valley.........p. v. 290
Edenville...........p. v. 510
Edgecomb Pond.......p. 673
Edinburgh..........p. o. 588
Edinburgh..........t. 588
Edmeston...........p. o. 533
Edmeston...........t. 533
Edmeston Center....v. 533
Edwards...........p. v. 576
Edwards...........t. 576
Edwardsville........p. o. 580
Efnor..............la. 588
Egbertsville........v. 567
Eggertsville........p. o. 283
Egypt..........br. 491, 498
Egypt..............lo. 495
Egypt..............p. v. 401
Eighteen Mile...... 279, 290, 453, 456
Eight Mile....cr. 165, 166, 526
Elba..............p. o. 326
Elba..............t. 326
Elbridge...........p. v. 482
Elbridge...........t. 482
Eleven Mile..cr. 279, 282, 293, 326
Elgin..............p. o. 192
Elizabethtown......p. v. 301
Elizabethtown......t. 301
Elizabethtown......v. 297
Elizaville..........p. o. 248
Elk..............cr. 261
Elks Lick..........cr. 621
Ellenburgh.........p. v. 238
Ellenburgh.........t. 238
Ellenburgh Center..p. v. 238
Ellenburgh Depot...lo. 235, 238
Ellenville..........p. v. 688
Ellery.............p. o. 212
Ellery.............t. 212
Ellery Center......p. v. 212
Ellicott...........p. o. 290
Ellicott...........t. 212
Ellicottville.......p. v. 189
Ellicottville.......t. 189
Ellington..........p. v. 212
Ellington..........t. 212
Elliottsville.......lo. 565
Ellisburgh.........p. o. 357
Ellisburgh.........t. 357
Ellis..............cr. 592, 650
Ellis..........isle 418, 419
Ellis..............v. 357
Ellmores Corners....v. 662
Elm..............cr. 578

PAGE

Elma..............p. v. 290
Elma..............t. 290
Elmira.............v. 221
Elmira.............t. 221, 649
Elmores Cove.......v. 662
Elm Valley.........p. o. 171
Elpis..............lo. 499
Elsinore...........lo. 239
Elton..............p. v. 190
Eltona.............lo. 702
Emersons Corners...lo. 593
Eminence...........p. v. 608
Emmons ....mt. 19, 336
Empeyville.........v. 463
Enfield.............p. v. 656
Enfield.............t. 656
Enfield Center......v. 656
Enfield Falls.......lo. 656
Engellville........p. o. 607
English............r. 232, 238
Enory Hill.........h. 715
Ephratah...........p. v. 317
Ephratah...........t. 317
Erie..............co. 101, 279
Erie.........la. 20, 22, 122, 208, 215, 279, 284
Erieville..........p. v. 393
Erieville Reservoir. p. 393
Erin..............p. o. 222
Erin..............t. 222
Erwin..............t. 625
Erwin Center.......lo. 627
Escopus...........cr. 660, 663
Esopus.............p. o. 662
Esopus.............t. 662
Essex.............co. 110, 295
Essex.............p. v. 301
Essex.............t. 301
Esperance.....p. v. 496, 605
Esperance..........t. 604
Etna..............p. v. 656
Euclid.............p. v. 481
Eureka.............lo. 471
Evans.............p. v. 290
Evans.............t. 290
Evans Mills........v. 359
Evas Kil..........407, 411
Eve..............mt. 510
Exeter.............p. o. 533
Exeter.............t. 533
Exeter Center......v. 533

Fabius.............p. v. 483
Fabius.............t. 482
Factory ....br. 250, 253, 254
Factory Village.....v. 590
Factoryville........lo. 597
Factoryville........p. v. 650
Factoryville........v. 565
Fairfield...........p. v. 343
Fairfield...........t. 343
Fair Haven.........lo. 514
Fair Haven.........p. v. 204
Fairmount..........p. o. 481
Fairport...........p. v. 401
Fairview...........p. o. 190
Fairville..........p. v. 690
Falconer...........p. v. 214
Falkirk............lo. 292
Fall........br. 204, 375, 381, 496
Fall........cr. 253, 267, 332, 383, 461, 491, 497, 654, 655, 656
Fall Kil........... 272, 274
Falls..............h. 346
Fallsburgh.........t. 644
Farmer.............p. o. 615
Farmers Hill.......l. o. 273
Farmers Mills......p. v. 541
Farmers Village.....l. o. 550
Farmersville.......p. v. 190
Farmersville.......t. 190
Farmersville.......v. 615
Farmingdale........p. o. 550
Farmington.........p. o. 496
Farmington.........t. 496
Farmington.........m. 283
Far Rockaway.......r. 547
Fayette........p. o. 615, 618
Fayette............t. 615
Fayetteville.......p. v. 484
Featherstons......la. 596
Federal Hollow....lo. 720
Federal Store......p. o. 273
Felts Mills........p. v. 361
Fenner.............p. o. 391
Fenner.............t. 391
Fentonville........p. o. 211

PAGE
Fergusons Corners......p. o. 719
Fergusonville..... p. v. 260, 262
Feuribush....................lo. 164
Feuri-Spruyt Kil 163
Fields Settlement.........lo. 362
Fillmore ....p. v. 174
Finchville....................lo. 508
Fine...........................p. o. 577
Fine.............................t. 576
Finleys ....la. 214
Finleys Lake ....p. v. 214
Fire............................isle 633
Fire Island..................isle 633
Fire Place ....p. v. 634
First...........................cr. 688
Fish...cr. 22, 349, 375, 451, 456, 458, 461, 465, 491, 496, 526, 527, 529, 591.
Fish............................la. 190
Fish Creek Landing......v. 470
Fishers.......................p. o. 439
Fishers Island............isle 639
Fishkill...............cr. 267, 271
Fishkill.......................mt. 271
Fishkill.......................p. v. 272
Fishkill...........................t. 271
Fishkill Furnace..........lo. 271
Fishkill Landing........p. v. 271
Fishkill Plains...........p. v. 271
Fitchs Point ....v. 685
Five Corners..............p. v. 202
Five Mile..............cr. 186, 622
Five Mile Meadow........lo. 453
Five Mile Run ....p. o. 188
Five Streams...............br. 226
Flanders....................p. v. 638
Flat ....cr. 407, 416
Flat Brook................p. v. 243
Flat Creek..................p. o. 416
Flatbush.....................p. v. 372
Flatbush..........................t. 372
Flatlands...................p. o. 372
Flatlands..........................t. 372
Flax............................cr. 536
Flax Pond Bay.............. 633
Fleetwood ....lo. 699
Fleming.....................p. v. 201
Fleming............................t. 201
Flint ....cr. 491, 498, 719
Flint..............................v. 665
Flint Creek.................p. o. 498
Florence....................p. v. 463
Florence..........................t. 463
Florence Hill................lo. 463
Florida........................p. v. 510
Florida............................t. 413
Flower Hill...................lo. 550
Floyd..........................p. o. 464
Floyd ....t. 463
Floyd Corners..................v. 464
Floyd Road...................lo. 465
Flushing..............cr. 546, 548
Flushing.....................p. v. 546
Flushing...........................t. 546
Flushing Bay............ 544, 546
Fluvanna.....................p. v. 212
Fly..............................br. 223
Fly ....cr. 166
Fly Creek..................p. v. 536
Fly Meadow..........cr. 223, 230
Fly Mountain............p. o. 664
Foggingtown.................lo. 543
Folsomdale.................p. o. 712
Fonda.........................p. v. 415
Fondas..................cr. 314, 316
Fondas.............................h. 555
Fondas Bush.....................v. 316
Foots Corners ....lo. 383
Fordham.....................p. v. 707
Fords ....cr. 168, 176
Fordsborough.....................v. 414
Forestburgh ....p. o. 645
Forest City.................p. o. 658
Forest-of-Dean..............cr. 507
Forest Port........p. v. 462, 466
Forestville..................p. v. 213
Forge Hollow.....................v. 465
Forked......................la. 22, 337
Fort.................................h. 542
Fort.................................p. 635
Fort Ann.......................mts. 681
Fort Ann.....................p. v. 681
Fort Ann...........................t. 681
Fort Brewerton.................v. 522
Fort Clinton....................lo. 570
Fort Covington.........p. v. 311
Fort Covington.............t. 311
Fort Edward.............p. v. 682
Fort Edward....................t. 681
Fort Edward Center...p. o. 682
Fort Hamilton.............p. v. 373
Fort Herkimer..................v. 344
Fort Hill.........................lo. 327
Fort Hill Cemetery............200
Fort Hunter..............p. o. 413
Fort Jackson....................v. 578
Fort Miller..................p. v. 682
Fort Montgomery......p. v. 505
Fort Neck.......................lo. 551
Fort Niagara...................lo. 456
Fort Plain...................p. v. 414
Fort Pond.......................ba. 634
Fort Schuyler..................lo. 706
Forts Ferry......................lo. 587
Fortsville. ....p. v. 590
Fort Tompkins................... 419
Fort Washington ....lo. 419
Fosterdale.................p. o. 644
Fosters Meadow ....lo. 547
Fostertown.....................cr. 509
Fostertown......................lo. 509
Fosterville ....p. v. 200
Foundry.........................br. 542
Four Corners...................lo. 278
Four Mile ......cr. 186, 395, 451, 516, 528
Four Mile Creek.........p. o. 288
Fowler.........................p. o. 577
Fowler...............................t. 577
Fowlerville.........................v. 387
Fox...................cr. 165, 318, 416
Fox...............................isle 356
Foxen Kil 162
Fox's ....cr. 600, 607
Fox Island........................lo. 510
Frankfort.....................p. v. 344
Frankfort...........................t. 344
Frankfort Hill.............p. o. 344
Franklin..................co. 101, 307
Franklin.......................p. v. 261
Franklin ....t. 261, 311
Franklin.............................v. 464
Franklin Falls..............p. v. 311
Franklinton ....p. v. 603
Franklinville....................lo. 640
Franklinville................p. v. 190
Franklinville.......................t. 190
Franklinville........................v. 637
Franks Corners.................lo. 255
Fredonia.......................p. v. 214
Freedom ....p. o. 190
Freedom.............................t. 190
Freedom Plains...........p. v. 272
Freehold.......................p. v. 333
Freemont.....................p. o. 645
Freemont............................t. 645
Freeport........................p. v. 547
Freerville............................v. 662
Freetown ....t. 252
Freetown Corners.......p. v. 252
Freeville.............................lo. 656
Freleighs Point..................lo. 616
Fremont..............................t. 625
Fremont Center.................lo. 625
Freemont Center.........p. v. 645
French..cr. 23, 208, 215, 351, 357
French..................................h. 708
French.....................mt. 670, 675
French Creek..............p. o. 312
French Creek......................t. 312
Frenchmans.......................cr. 591
Frenchmans..........isle 481, 521
French Mills......................lo. 164
French Mountain........p. o. 675
Fresh Kils...............cr. 563, 566
Fresh Meadows.................lo. 546
Fresh Pond....................p. o. 637
Frewsburgh.................p. v. 211
Freysbush....................p. o. 414
Friends ....la. 674
Friends........................p. o. 214
Friends Cemetery.............lo. 371
Friendship...................p. v. 173
Friendship...........................t. 173
Frontier ....p. o. 237
Frost Hill...........................lo. 499
Fullams Basin...................lo. 401
Fullerville...........................lo. 577
FullervilleIronWorks..p.o. 577
Fulmer..............................cr. 344
Fulton...............................co. 314
Fulton...........................p. v. 528
Fulton..................................t. 605
Fultonham.....................p. v. 605
Fulton Lakes........(3, 4, 5) 22
Fulton Lakes........(6, 7, 8) 22
Fulton Lakes.................... 339
Fultonville....................p. v. 413
Furmanville.....................lo. 571
Furnace........................br. 696
Furnace................cr. 340, 461
Furnace Hollow.............cr. 681
Furnace Village......v. 692, 695
Gaines........................p. v. 514
Gaines................................t. 514
Gaines Basin ....lo. 514
Gainesville.......................cr. 713
Gainesville ....p. o. 713
Gainesville..........................t. 713
Gainesville Center.........lo. 713
Gainesville Creek ....v. 713
Galen...................................t. 691
Gales ....p. o. 647
Galesville ....p. v. 683
Galeville Mills............p. o. 667
Gallatin ....t. 245
Gallatinville ....p. v. 245
Gallop ....isle 578
Gallows.................................h. 699
Gallupville...................p. v. 608
Galway........................p. v. 588
Galway................................t. 588
Ganargwa ....cr. 688
Gansevoort..................p. v. 591
Garbuttsville ....v. 406
Gardiner..............................t. 662
Gardners......isle 631, 634, 635
Gardners...............................p. 578
Gardners Bay..................... 631
Gardners Corners ....v. 378
Gardners Island...............lo. 510
Gardnertown ....v. 509
Gardnerville...................p. v. 607
Gardnersville.......................v. 511
Garlick Falls ....p. o. 236
Garnerville ....v. 570
Garoga ... cr. 314, 317, 407, 416
Garoga ....la. 317
Garoga...........................p. v. 317
Garrattsville ....p. v. 535
Garrisons ....p. o. 542
Gasport ....p. v. 456
Gates ....p. o. 399
Gates...................................t. 399
Gates Center ....v. 399
Gay Head.......................p. o. 333
Geddes...........................p. v. 483
Geddes.................................t. 483
Genegantslet.. cr. 223, 227, 230
Genegantslet......................la. 227
Genegantslet............ p. v. 226
Genesee....................co. 101, 320
Genesee ....cr. 174
Genesee.......r. 20, 22, 122, 168, 170, 171, 174, 381, 383, 385, 386, 395, 399, 402, 710, 712, 713.
Genesee ....t. 173
Genesee Falls ....t. 713
Genesee Val. R. R. Junc..lo. 405
Geneseo.........................p. v. 383
Geneseo................................t. 383
Geneva ....p. v. 498
Genoa ....p. v. 202
Genoa ....t. 202
George ....la. 21, 23, 296, 304, 670, 673, 680
Georgetown..................p. v. 391
Georgetown..........................t. 391
Georgica ....p. 635
German...........................p. o. 226
German ....t. 226
German Flats ....t. 344
Germantown..................p. v. 245
Germantown.........................t. 245
Gerry...............................p. o. 211
Gerry ....t. 213
Getzville.........................p. o. 283
Ghent ....p. v. 245
Ghent ....t. 245
Giant of the Valley....mt. 301
Gibson ....v. 624
Gibsonville....................p. v. 384
Gidneys ....cr. 509
Giers.....................................br. 261
Gilberts ....la. 535
Gilberts Mills ....p. o. 527
Gilbertsville ....v. 527, 532
Gilboa ....p. v. 605
Gilboa ....t. 605
Gilderland ....p. o. 164
Gilead ....la. 541
Gilgo Inlet..........................cr. 544
Gill ....cr. 451
Gilman ....p. o. 337
Gilman.....................................t. 337
Glasco ....p. v. 666
Glass ....la. 558
Glass House ....cr. 588
Glass House ....v. 558
Glen...............................p. o. 413
Glen...t. 413
Glen Aubrey.........................lo. 183
Glen Castle......................p. o. 181
Glencoe Mills ....p. v. 248
Glencove.........................p. v. 550
Glenearie...............................v. 667
Gleneida ....la. 540
Glenham..........................p. v. 272
Glen Haven ....p. o. 204
Glenmark Falls ....v. 693
Glen Mary.............................lo. 652
Glenmore ....p. v. 461
Glensdale ....p. o. 378
Glens Falls............................lo. 674
Glens Falls......................p. v. 675
Glenville................................lo. 705
Glenville..........................p. v. 597
Glenville.................................t. 597
Glen Wild ....p. o. 647
Glenwood ....p. v. 289
Gloversville ....p. v. 317
Glowegee....................cr. 584, 590
Goat ....isle 450, 703
Goffs Mills.......................p. o. 626
Golden Hill..............cr. 451, 456
Golden Root............................h. 541
Goldens Bridge ....p. o. 701
Goldsmiths...............cr. 219, 221
Goodground ....p. o. 638
Goodhue..................................cr. 621
Goodhue ....la. 621
Goodwin ....mt. 303
Goose ....cr. 213
Goose ....h. 541
Goose.....................................isle 541
Goose ....la. 339
Goose Pond.............................mt. 505
Goose Neck............................isle 579
Gooseville................................lo. 483
Gorham ....p. v. 496
Gorham......................................t. 496
Goshen.............................p. v. 506
Goshen......................................t. 506
Gouverneur ....p. v. 577
Gouverneur...............................t. 577
Governors................isle 418, 419
Gowanda..........................p. v. 194
Gowanus....................................v. 367
Gowanus Bay.................365, 367
Grafton ....p. v. 555
Grafton......................................t. 555
Grahamsville...................p. v. 647
Grammercy Park ....lo. 423
Granby.......................................t. 521
Granby Center ....p. o. 521
Grand ....isle 279, 449
Grand Island ....p. o. 290
Grand Island..............................t. 290
Grand Sachem ....mt. 271
Granger..............................p. o. 174
Granger ....t. 174
Grangerville.....................p. o. 591
Graniteville...............................v. 566
Grants ....br. 259
Granville ....p. v. 682
Granville ....t. 682
Grass.......v. 572, 575, 579, 581
Grasse ....r. 21
Grassy Point...........................lo. 570
Grassy Swamp........................br. 506
Gravesend.........................p. v. 372
Gravesend...................................t. 372
Gravesend Bay 365, 373
Gravesville ....p. v. 348
Gray Court ....cr. 505
Grays Corners..........................lo. 589
Graysville..........................p. v. 347
Great...........................br. 223, 227
Great......................................isle 705
Great ....p. 635
Great Bend........................p. v. 357
Great Black ....br. 236
Great Chazy..r. 232, 235, 236, 682
Great Gull ....isle 639
Great Hog Neck 639
Great Kils 566

PAGE
Great Long Pond........mt. 701
Great Neck..........lo. 549, 636
Great Peconic Bay......631, 637
Great Sodus................cr. 688
Great Sodus Bay...688, 691, 693
Great South Bay.........631, 636
Great Sucker..................cr. 578
Great Swamp..............lo. 542
Great Valley ....cr. 189, 190
Great Valley.............p. o. 190
Great Valley....................t. 190
Great Valley Station......v. 190
Greece ....p. v. 399
Greece...............................t. 399
Greece Center ....lo. 399
Green...................................h. 510
Green...............................isle 673
Green ....la. 317, 484
Green.....................r. 243, 246
Greenborough ....p. o. 526
Greenburgh......................t. 700
Greenbush...................p. v. 555
Greenbush.........................t. 555
Greene ....co. 329
Greene ....p. v. 226
Greene ....t. 226
Greenfield.........................lo. 372
Greenfield.......................p. v. 668
Greenfield..........................t. 589
Greenfield Center ......p. v. 589
Green Haven ....p. v. 270
Green Island ....p. v. 166
Green Locks....................v. 666
Green Point..............p. o. 367
Greenport...................p. v. 639
Greenport ....t. 245
Green River.................p. v. 246
Greens Corners............lo. 466
Greens Corners ....v. 174
Greenville ....lo. 700
Greenville....................p. v. 332
Greenville.............t. 332, 507
Greenville..........................v. 507
Greenville Center ....v. 333
Greenwich ....lo. 419
Greenwich....................p. o. 683
Greenwich..........................t. 683
Greenwich Point ....lo. 547
Greenwood....... ....la. 510
Greenwood ....p. v. 625
Greenwood.........................t. 625
Greenwood Cemetery ...lo. 371
Greenwood Works .....p. v. 507
Gregorys ....br. 698
Greig..............................p. o. 377
Greig...................................t. 376
Greigsville....................p. v. 387
Grenadier......................isle 356
Gridley ....cr. 255
Griffins Corners.........p. v. 263
Griffins Corners................v. 542
Griffins Mills............p. v. 283
Griffiths Corners..........lo. 715
Griffiths Mills..............lo. 496
Grindstone........................cr. 497
Grindstone ....isle 357
Grippy Hill ....mt. 162
Griswolds Mills.........p. v. 681
Groesbeck.......................lo. 163
Grooms Corners.........p. o. 587
Grosvernors Corners...p. o. 604
Groton..........................p. v. 657
Groton................................t. 657
Groton City..................p. v. 657
Grove ....p. o. 174
Grove ....t. 174
Grove Center.................lo. 174
Groveland..................p. o. 384
Groveland.........................t. 383
Groveland Center......p. o. 384
Groveland Corners.........v. 384
Groves..............................cr. 616
Guilderland........................t. 164
Guilderland Center.....p. v. 164
Guilford..............................t. 227
Guilford Center..........p. v. 227
Guilford Pond............ cr. 227
Gulicksville....................lo. 627
Gulph Summit............p. o. 183
Guy Park.........................lo. 412
Gypsum.........................p. o. 407

Haanakrois..cr.156, 163, 166, 334
Hackensack .....r. 568, 569, 570
Hadley..........................p. o. 589
Hadley.................................t. 589
Hadley Falls 674

PAGE
Hadlock..............................p. 681
Hagadorns.........................cr. 591
Hagadorns Hollow.........lo. 591
Hagamans Mills ....p. v. 412
Hagans ....p. 645
Hagel Kil.............................. 331
Hague............................p. o. 674
Hague..................................t. 674
Hailesborough ....v. 577
Halcott...............................t. 333
Halcottsville.................p. o. 263
Hales Eddy...................p. o. 265
Half Moon........................h. 647
Half Moon..................p. o. 589
Half Moon.........................t. 589
Halfway...................br. 181, 183
Halfway..............................cr. 681
Half Way House ....lo. 587
Hall......................................h. 507
Halletts Cove..............544, 657
Halletts Point...................lo. 669
Halls Corners......lo. 590, 615, 700, 714
Halls Corners...........p. o. 498
Halls Port...................p. v. 176
Halls Station.................lo. 455
Hallsville......................p. o. 414
Halsey Valley......p. o. 650, 653
Halseyville.......................lo. 658
Hamburgh ....p. o. 291
Hamburgh..........................t. 291
Hamburgh-on-the-Lake p. o. 291
Hamden........................p. v. 261
Hamden ....t. 261
Hamilton..........................co. 336
Hamilton ....p. v. 391
Hamilton ....t. 391
Hamilton Square..........lo. 423
Hamiltonville....................v. 164
Hamlin..............................mt. 302
Hamlet..........................p. o. 216
Hammerton......................lo. 274
Hammond......................p. v. 577
Hammond...........................t. 577
Hammonds Corners v. 220, 301
Hammondsport ....v. 628
Hampton......................p. o. 683
Hampton ....t. 683
Hampton...........................v. 471
Hamptonburgh.................lo. 507
Hamptonburgh...................t. 507
Hampton Corners ....v. 683
Hancock.......................p. v. 262
Hancock.............................t. 261
Handsome.........................br. 261
Handsome Eddy ....br. 223
Hanfords Landing......p. v. 399
Hankins Station............lo. 645
Hannibal.......................p. v. 522
Hannibal.............................t. 522
Hannibal Center.........p. v. 522
Hanover............................lo. 213
Hanover...............................t. 213
Hanover..............................v. 465
Hanover Center..............lo. 213
Hans ....cr. 591
Hardenbergh ....t. 663
Harford...........................p. v. 252
Harford................................t. 252
Harkness ....l. 303
Harlem..........................p. o. 419
Harlem.............r. 23, 418, 706
Harlemville ....p. v. 246
Harmony......................p. o. 213
Harmony ....t. 213
Harmonyville.....................v. 627
Harpers ....br. 225
Harpersfield ....t. 262
Harpersfield..................p. v. 262
Harpersville.................p. v. 181
Harrietstown........................t. 311
Harrington..........................h. 680
Harris ....p. 303
Harrisburgh..................p. o. 377
Harrisburgh ....t. 377
Harris Hill....................p. o. 289
Harrison........................p. o. 701
Harrison...............................t. 700
Harrisons...........................cr. 534
Harrisville...........................v. 376
Hartfield.........................p. v. 211
Hartford ....p. v. 684
Hartford...............................t. 683
Hartland........................p. o. 453
Hartland...............................t. 453
Hartland Corners............lo. 453

PAGE
Hart Lot........................p. o. 482
Harts...................................isle 704
Harts Corners...................lo. 700
Harts Village.................p. v. 277
Hartsville...................... lo. 484
Hartsville............................t. 625
Hartsville Center ....v. 625
Hartwick........................p. v. 533
Hartwick..............................t. 533
Hartwick Seminary...p. v. 533
Hartwood............................lo. 645
Harvard ....p. v. 262
Hasenclever......................mts. 340
Hasha.....................................h. 569
Haskel Flat...................p. o. 191
Haskill.....................cr. 186, 194
Haskinville....................p. o. 625
Hastings ....p. v. 522
Hastings...............................t. 522
Hastings ....v. 700
Hastings Center ....p. v. 522
Hastings upon Hudson p. o. 700
Hatch......................................h. 497
Hatchs..................................la. 390
Havana..........................p. v. 610
Haver Island 166
Haverstraw ....p. o. 569
Haverstraw............................t. 569
Haviland........................p. o. 542
Hawkins ....cr. 645
Hawkins Creek ....p. o. 645
Hawkinsville................p. v. 462
Hawks..................................cr. 261
Hawleyton ....p. o. 180
Hay Island Inlet............ 544
Haynerville...................p. o. 558
Haysburgh ....lo. 245
Hazard.....................................p. 507
Hazens.....................................h. 541
Hebron.........................p. o. 684
Hebron..................................t. 684
Hecla Works ....p. v. 471
Hector...........................p. o. 611
Hector ....t. 611
Hector Falls.....................lo. 611
Hedden................................cr. 658
Heddingville......................lo. 543
Hedgesville..........................v. 629
Helderbergh......mts. 19, 155, 332, 595
Helena...........................p. v. 575
Hell Gate...................544, 548
Hellibark.............mts. 19, 600
Hemlock ....cr. 381
Hemlock.....................h. 507, 541
Hemlock ....la. 20, 381
Hemlock Lake.............p. v. 384
Hemlock Outlet.....cr. 491, 498
Hempstead....................p. v. 547
Hempstead Bay.........544, 547
Hempstead Harbor.....544, 549
Hempstead Hook...cr. 367, 368
Henhawk............................isle 705
Henrietta......................p. o. 399
Henrietta...............................t. 399
Henderson..........................bay 358
Henderson................la. 22, 303
Henderson ....mt. 303
Henderson....................p. v. 358
Henderson.............................t. 358
Henderson Harbor.......lo. 358
Hendy ....cr. 218, 221
Herkimer......co. 101, 103, 340
Herkimer ....p. v. 345
Herkimer..............................t. 345
Hermitage.....................p. v. 716
Hermitage.............................v. 640
Hermon..........................p. v. 578
Hermon..................................t. 578
Hess Road.....................p. o. 454
Hessville ....lo. 414
Heusonville...................p. v. 335
Heuvelton......................p. v. 580
Hewletts Point.................lo. 550
Hibernia........................p. o. 270
Hickory Corners........p. o. 454
Hickory Grove..................lo. 701
Hicksville......................p. o. 550
Higginsville..................p. v. 470
High ....isle 704
High Bridge.........................v. 484
High Bridgeville ....lo. 702
High Falls......lo. 376, 575, 664, 670
High Falls ....p. o. 664, 666
High Falls..............................v. 597

PAGE
Highland ....t. 645
Highland Mills ....p. v. 508
Highlands ....mts. 19, 540
High Market ....p. o. 377
High Market........................t. 377
High Peak .....mt. 19, 329, 333
High Point ....h. 497
Hillsborough ....p. o. 463
Hillsdale.......................p. v. 246
Hillsdale...............................t. 246
Hillside ....p. o. 471
Himrods Corners..............v. 720
Hindsburgh..................p. v. 515
Hinmansville.......................v. 527
Hinsdale.......................p. v. 191
Hinsdale................................t. 191
Hitchcocks Corners.......v. 270
Hoag...p. 274
Hoags Corners...........p. v. 557
Hobart...........................p. v. 265
Hoboken City...................lo. 429
Hodge .... p. 647
Hoffmans Ferry.........p. o. 597
Hog..h. 272
Hogais ....p. 646
Hogansburgh...............p. v. 309
Hog Back ....h. 507, 542
Hog Hollow.........cr. 491, 496
Holland ....p. v. 291
Holland..................................t. 291
Holland Patent.........p. v. 467
Holley..........................p. v. 515
Hollins Hook.....................lo. 514
Hollow ....cr. 340
Holman City.........................v. 466
Holmes Pond...................br. 621
Holmesville...........v. 228, 527
Homer...........................p. v. 253
Homer ....t. 252
Homowack.........p. v. 646, 668
Honeoye...cr. 20, 170, 172, 381, 384, 395, 404
Honeoye.....................la. 20, 495
Honeoye ....p. v. 498
Honeoye Corners ....lo. 172
Honeoye Falls...........p. v. 400
Honeoye Inlet......cr. 495, 497
Honeoye Outlet.....cr. 491, 498
Honesville............................v. 506
Hook...p. 635
Hooper..........................p. o. 184
Hoopers Valley.........p. o. 651
Hoosick.........................p. o. 556
Hoosick...r. 21, 552, 555, 557, 558, 686
Hoosick ....t. 555
Hoosick Corners ....v. 556
Hoosick Falls..............p. v. 555
Hope ....mt. 271
Hope ....t. 338
Hope Center...............p. o. 338
Hopedale...........................lo. 548
Hope Falls...................p. o. 338
Hope Ridge......................mt. 402
Hopewell..............lo. 271, 506
Hopewell......................p. o. 497
Hopewell ....t. 496
Hopewell Center........p. v. 496
Hopkinton...................p. v. 578
Hopkinton.............................t. 578
Hoppogue.........................lo. 637
Horicon.........................p. v. 674
Horicon ....t. 674
Hornby ....p. o. 626
Hornby ....t. 626
Hornby Forks ....v. 626
Hornellsville ....p. v. 626
Hornellsville.........................t. 626
Horse ....cr. 172
Horsebone Ledge 344
Horseheads..................p. v. 222
Horseheads ....t. 222
Horsepond.......................mt. 569
Horse Pound......................br. 541
Horse Shoe ....p. 643
Horse Shoe Falls........450, 710
Hortons Point....................lo. 639
Hotchkiss ....cr. 195
Hot Ground.......................lo. 243
Houghton Creek........p. o. 172
Hounsfield..............................t. 358
Houses ....cr. 375
Houseville ....p. v. 379
Howard.........................p. v. 626
Howard ....t. 626
Howards Bush ....lo. 344
Howells Depot.............p. v. 510

PAGE

Howes Cave..............lo. 604
Howlands................isle 201
Howlet Hill ....p. o. 485
Hubbards Run...........cr. 220
Hubbardsville..........p. v. 392
Hudson......r. 21, 23, 155, 267,
274, 276, 296, 329, 540, 542,
552, 568, 569, 570, 584, 588,
589, 590, 591, 593, 662, 665,
670, 674, 676, 700.
Hudson City 246
Hughsonville...........p. v. 272
Huguenot ....b. v. 506

Hulberton..............p. v. 515
Hulls...................h. 510
Hulls Corners..........v. 522
Hume...................p. o. 174
Hume...................t. 174
Humphrey...............p. o. 191
Humphrey ....t. 191
Humphrey Center.......lo. 191
Humphreysville ....p. o. 244
Hunger Kil ....cr. 164
Hungry................bay 351
Hunns..................la. 277
Hunt...................cr. 253
Hunt...................la. 218
Hunter.................p. v. 333
Hunter.................t. 333
Hunters ....isle 704
Hunters Land.........p. v. 606
Hunters Point ....v. 549
Hunterstown...........lo. 245
Huntington............la. 644
Huntington...........p. v. 636
Huntington............t. 635
Huntington Bay 636
Huntington Harbor....ba. 636
Hunts Corners.....lo. 253, 384
Hunts Hollow..........v. 386
Huntsville ....lo. 588
Hurlbutville ....p. o. 462
Hurley ....p. v. 633
Hurley ....t. 663
Huron ....p. o. 691
Huron ....t. 691
Hussey.................h. 662
Hutchinsons...........cr. 696,
699, 704, 705
Hyatts Corners ....p. v. 616
Hyde Park..............lo. 550
Hyde Park.............p. v. 272
Hyde Park..............t. 272
Hydes Brook ....br. 265
Hydeville.............lo. 690
Hyndsville ....p. v. 607

Ida....................mt. 560
Ilion.................p. v. 344
Independence ....cr. 375
Independence ....mt. 532
Independence ....p. o. 174
Independence ....t. 174
Indian................br. 542
Indian ....h. 541
Indian ....la. 273, 339, 376
Indian ....p. 273
Indian ....r. 23, 351,
352, 359, 360, 361, 362,
375, 376, 572, 582, 682
Indian Castle.........lo. 343
Indian Corners........lo. 343
Indian Field ....p. 643
Indian Fields.......p. o. 163
Indian Lake............t. 338
Indian River.........p. o. 376
Inghams Mills.........v. 346
Ingraham ....p. 309
Ingraham.............p. o. 237
Inverness ....p. o. 387
Ionia ....lo. 490
Ira ....t. 202
Ira Center ....p. v. 202
Ireland...............lo. 546
Ireland Corners.....p. o. 166
Irelandville..........v. 612
Irish ....cr. 413
Irish Hill ....mt. 162
Irondale...............v. 301
Irondequoit ....cr. 395, 491
Irondequoit ....p. v. 400
Irondequoit............t. 400
Irondequoit Bay 395, 405
Irving ....p. v. 213
Irvington ....p. v. 700
Ischua.......cr. 186,190,191,192

PAGE

Ischua ....p. v. 191
Ischua ....t. 191
Islip..................p. v. 636
Islip...................t. 636
Italy...................t. 719
Italy Hill.............p. v. 719
Italy Hollow ....p. o. 719
Ithaca................p. v. 657
Ithaca..................t. 657

Jackson................p. o. 684
Jackson.................t. 684
Jacksonburgh..........v. 346
Jackson Center ....v. 684
Jackson Corners......p. v. 245
Jackson Summit.......p. o. 318
Jacksons Corners......lo. 514
Jacksons Corners .....lo. 272
Jacksonville........lo. 332, 699
Jacksonville ....v. 658
Jacksonville .....v. 484, 534
Jacks Reefs..........p. o. 482
Jamaica ....t. 547
Jamaica Bay 365, 544, 548
Jamaica Heights......lo. 548
Jamesburgh..........p. v. 667
Jamesport............p. o. 637
Jamesport ....v. 637
Jamestown............p. v. 212
Jamesville ......v. 482, 589
Janet..................la. 338
Jan Vosent ....cr. 332
Jan Wemps............cr. 597
Jasper................p. o. 626
Jasper ....t. 626
Jasper Five Corners...v. 626
Jasper Four Corners...v. 626
Java....................t. 714
Java..................p. o. 714
Java Center ....p. o. 714
Java Village..........v. 714
Jay................mt. 300, 302
Jay...................p. v. 302
Jay.....................t. 302
Jeddo.................p. v. 515
Jefferson ......co. 101, 103, 315
Jefferson ....t. 605
Jefferson Valley ....p. o. 708
Jeffersonville ....p. v. 644
Jenkins ....p. 647
Jenkinstown ....lo. 633
Jenkinsville ....p. o. 653
Jenny ....la. 588
Jericho ....p. o. 551
Jersey City...........lo. 429
Jerseyfield............la. 339
Jerusalem ....lo. 345
Jerusalem ....t. 719
Jerusalem South .....p. v. 547
Jessup................... t. 339
Jessup Falls.......... 674
Jessups Corners.......lo. 690
Jessups Landing.......v. 588
Jewett................p. v. 333
Jewett ....t. 333
Jewett Center ....p. o. 333
Joe Gee................h. 511
John Browns Tract....lo. 379
John Debackers....cr. 331, 332
Johnsburg.............lo. 457
Johnsburgh...........p. v. 675
Johnsburgh.............t. 674
Johnsonburg.....p. v. 714, 715
Johnsons..cr. 453, 456, 512, 516
Johnsons Creek......v. 453
Johnsonville.........p. v. 558
Johnstown............p. v. 317
Johnstown..............t. 317
Johnstown ....v. 248
Johnsville ....p. v. 271
Jones ....la. 339
Jones Beach..........lo. 544
Jonesville ....p. v. 587
Jordan................p. v. 482
Jordanville ....p. v. 349
Joy...................p. v. 694
Jubilee Springs...... 284
Juhelville..............v. 360
Junction ....lo. 482
Junction ....p. v. 559
Junius................p. o. 615
Junius ....t. 615

Kaaters Kil.. 329, 331, 332, 666
Kahseway.............cr. 245
Kanona...............p. v. 622
Karr Valley.........cr. 168, 170

PAGE

Kasoag................p. v. 528
Katonah..............p. v. 698
Kattel.................cr. 181
Kattelville............lo. 181
Kau-a-da-rauk.........cr. 416
Kayaderosseras.cr. 411, 590, 591
Kayaderosseras....mt. 295, 300,
304, 584, 588, 589, 591, 670
Kayaderosseras.........r. 584

Kecks Center ....p. o. 317
Keefers Corners......p. o. 163
Keene..................p. v. 302
Keene...................t. 302
Keeney Settlement.....lo. 255
Keeseville..........p. v. 235, 300
Kelloggs Mills........lo. 487
Kelloggsville.........p. v. 204
Kelloggsville.........lo. 701
Kellys Corners........lo. 615
Kelsey.................br. 223
Kendall...............p. v. 515
Kendall.................t. 515
Kendall Mills....p. o. 405, 515
Kensico................p. v. 703
Kent...................br. 223
Kent...............cr. 351, 356
Kent...................p. o. 541
Kent....................t. 541
Kenwood................v. 163
Kenyonville...........lo. 514
Kerhonkson...........p. v. 668
Keshong....cr. 491, 498, 719
Ketchabonec...........lo. 638
Ketchamtown..........lo. 505
Ketchums Corners....p. o. 593
Ketchumville.........p. v. 651
Kettle Bottom........mt. 675
Keysers Kil........... 600
Kiantone.............p. o. 214
Kiantone.............p. v. 214
Kiantone...............t. 214
Kidders Ferry........p. o. 616
Kidney................cr. 680
Killawog.............p. o. 182
Killbuck.............p. o. 190
Kil Van Kull.........cr. 566
Kinderhook...cr. 241, 244, 247,
248, 552, 554, 557, 559, 560
Kinderhook...........la. 241, 247
Kinderhook..........p. v. 247
Kinderhook.............t. 247
Kings..................co. 365
Kings Bay.............237
Kingsborough.........p. v. 317
Kingsbridge..........p. o. 708
Kingsbury............p. v. 685
Kingsbury..............t. 684
Kings Falls...........lo. 376
Kings Ferry..........p. o. 202
Kings Garden..........lo. 419
Kings Settlement.....p. o. 228
Kingston.............p. v. 663
Kingston...............t. 663
Kingstreet............lo. 705
Kinneys Corners.......lo. 720
Kinneys Four Corners.p. o. 522
Kirby.................p. 702
Kirk...................p. 351
Kirk...................cr. 168
Kirkland.............p. o. 464
Kirkland...............t. 464
Kirkville.............p. v. 484
Kirkwood.............p. v. 182
Kishewana.............la. 543
Kiskatom.............cr. 332
Kiskatom.............p. o. 332
Kisko...................r. 696
Kleina Kil............ 247
Knapp..................p. 647
Knapps Station........p. v. 582
Knight.................cr. 168
Knights................cr. 203
Knowersville.........p. o. 164
Knowlesville.........p. v. 515
Knox.................p. o. 164
Knox...................t. 164
Knox Corners..........p. v. 462
Knoxville........v. 164, 393, 624
Koola Kil............. 556
Kortright.............p. o. 262
Kortright..............t. 262
Kortright Center .....lo. 262
Kottle Kil............. 666
Koxing Kil............cr. 666
Kripplebush..........p. v. 664
Kyserike.............p. o. 666
Kysorville...........p. v. 386

PAGE

Labrador..............cr. 250
Labrador ....p. 255, 483
Lackawack..........cr. 641, 647
Lackawack............p. v. 668
Ladews Corners ....lo. 667
La Fargeville........p. v. 360
La Fayette...........p. v. 483
La Fayette..............t. 483
La Fayetteville......p. v. 273
La Grange............p. v. 713
La Grange..............t. 272
La Grangeville.......p. v. 272
Lairdsville..........p. v. 471
Lake...................h. 211
Lake..................p. o. 683
Lake Hill............p. o. 668
Lakeland..............t. 636
Lake Pleasant........p. o. 338
Lake Pleasant..........t. 338
Lakeport..............p. o. 394
Lake Ridge..........p. o. 658
Lake Road............p. o. 456
Lakeville.........lo. 550, 683
Lakeville............p. v. 384
Lambs Corners........lo. 167
Lamsons..............p. o. 484
Lancaster............p. v. 291
Lancaster..............t. 291
Landimans..........cr. 267, 276
Landons...............la. 260
Langdons Corners.....lo. 685
Langford..............cr. 222
Langford.............p. o. 292
Langtons Corners......lo. 326
Lansing................t. 658
Lansingburgh ....p. v. 556
Lansingburgh..........t. 556
Lansing Kil... 458, 462, 470
Lansingville........p. v. 658
Lansingville..........v. 261
Lapeer...............p. o. 253
Lapeer.................t. 253
Laphams Mills.........v. 238
Laona................p. v. 215
La Salle.............p. o. 455
Lashers...............cr. 416
Lassellsville........p. v. 317
Lattingtown.......lo. 551, 665
Laurel.................h. 549
Laurens.............p. v. 534
Laurens.................t. 534
Lawrence...........br. 312, 527
Lawrence...............t. 578
Lawrenceville.........lo. 549
Lawrenceville........p. v. 578
Lawrenceville..........v. 666
Laws...................la. 190
Lawsons................la. 163
Lawyers................h. 505
Lawyersville.........p. v. 604
Lazy...................h. 504
Leatherville..........v. 416
Lebanon...............cr. 248
Lebanon................p. 646
Lebanon..............p. v. 392
Lebanon Springs.......v. 248
Ledyard..............p. o. 202
Ledyard.................t. 202
Legiers................la. 376
Lemon Creek.........p. o. 567
Lenox................p. o. 392
Lenox..................t. 392
Lenox Furnace........lo. 392
Lee..................p. v. 465
Lee....................t. 465
Lee Center...........p. v. 465
Leeds................p. v. 332
Leedsville...........p. o. 270
Leesville............p. v. 607
Leicester..............t. 384
Leon.................p. v. 191
Leon...................t. 191
Leonardsville....p. v. 390, 537
Le Ray...............p. v. 359
Le Ray.................t. 359
Le Roy...............p. v. 326
Le Roy.................t. 326
Levana...............p. v. 302
Levant...............p. o. 212
Lewis................p. v. 302
Lewis..................co. 374
Lewis..................cr. 331
Lewis................p. v. 302
Lewis...............t. 302, 377
Lewisboro............p. o. 701
Lewisboro..............t. 701
Lewisburgh...........lo. 664
Lewiston.............p. v. 453

PAGE

Lewiston..............t. 453
Lexington..............p. v. 334
Lexington..............t. 334
Leyden..............p. o. 377
Leyden..............t. 377
Leyden Hill..............v. 377
Liberty..............p. v. 645
Liberty..............t. 645
Liberty..............v. 624
Liberty Falls..............p. v. 645
Libertyville..............mt. 645
Libertyville..............p. o. 663
Libertyville..............v. 658
Lillie..............p. 645
Lima..............p. v. 384
Lima..............t. 384
Lime..............la. 192
Lime Lake..............lo. 192
Limerick..............p. o. 356
Limestone.....cr. 390, 474, 484
Limestone..............p. o. 188
Lincklaen..............p. v. 227
Lincklaen..............t. 227
Linden..............p. v. 325
Linden Hills..............lo. 549
Lindenwald..............lo. 247
Lindley..............t. 626
Lindleytown..............p. v. 626
Line Kil..............cr. 600
Linlithgo..............lo. 248
Linn..............p. o. 483
Lisbon..............lo. 578
Lisbon..............t. 578
Lishas Kil..............p. o. 166
Lisle..............p. v. 182
Lisle..............t. 182
Lispenards Meadows.....lo. 419
Litchfield..............p. v. 345
Litchfield..............t. 345
Lithgow..............p. o. 278
Little..............isle 334
Little..............la. 612, 619, 684
Little......p. 273, 399, 506, 507, 509, 645
Little..............r. 463
Little Alder..............cr. 377
Little Bay..............544, 546
Little Black..............br. 236
Little Black..............cr. 347
Little Britain..............p. o. 510
Little Brocken Straw...cr. 208, 213
Little Buffalo..............cr. 279
Little Bush Kil..............259
Little Captains..............isle 705
Little Cattaraugus..............cr. 208
Little Chautauque..cr. 211, 216
Little Chazy..............r. 232
Little Choconut..............cr. 179
Little Connewango..cr. 189, 194
Little Delaware......r. 259, 261
Little Falls..............lo. 264
Little Falls..............p. v. 346
Little Falls..............t. 345
Little Genesee......cr. 168, 172
Little Genesee..............p. v. 173
Little Gull..............isle 639
Little Hog Neck..............lo. 639
Little Hoosick......r. 552, 554
Little Lakes..............v. 349
Little Long..............la. 338
Little Neck..............lo. 633, 636
Little Neck Bay...544, 546, 549
Little Paughcaugnaugh-
sink..............cr. 506
Little Peconic Bay..............631
Little Pond..............p. 542
Little Red..............cr. 688
Little Rest..............p. v. 278
Little Sable..........cr. 232, 238
Little Salmon....cr. 202, 206, 395, 522
Little Salmon........r. 307, 308, 309, 312
Little Sandy........cr. 446, 527
Little Sandy........p. 517, 527
Little Schoharie..............cr. 600
Little Shawaugunk..... v. 508
Little Snake........cr. 179, 182
Little Sodus......cr. 205, 206
Little Sodus Bay..............205
Little Sprite....cr. 314, 318
Little Stony..............cr. 358
Little Sucker..............cr. 578
Little Tonawanda..cr. 324, 714
Little Trout..........r. 309, 310
Little Utica..............v. 484

PAGE

Little Valley........cr. 186, 192
Little Valley..............t. 192
Littleville..............v. 382
Little White..............cr. 686
Little York..............la. 254
Little York..............p. v. 253
Little York..............v. 577

Livermores Corners.....lo. 226
Liverpool..............p. v. 487
Livingston..............br. 683
Livingston.....co. 101, 103, 381
Livingston..............la. 588
Livingston..............p. o. 248
Livingston..............t. 247
Livingstonville..........p. v. 603
Livonia..............p. o. 384
Livonia..............t. 384
Livonia Center..............v. 384
Livonia Station..........p. v. 384
Lloyd..............p. o. 664
Lloyd..............t. 664
Lloyds..............h. 272
Lloyds Harbor..............ba. 636
Lloyds Neck..........lo. 550, 551
Loch Sheldrake......p. v. 644
Lock Berlin..............p. v. 691
Locke..............p. o. 203
Locke..............t. 202
Lockport..............p. v. 454
Lockport..............t. 454
Locust..............isle 703
Locust Glen..............p. o. 274
Locust Grove..............lo. 549
Locust Tree..............p. o. 456
Locust Valley..............p. o. 551
Lodi..............p. v. 616
Lodi..............t. 616
Lodi Center..............p. o. 616
Lodi Falls..............lo. 616
Lodi Landing..............lo. 616
Log Village..............v. 684
Long..............h. 507
Long..............la. 22, 466, 572, 684
Long........p. 276, 395, 505, 507, 541, 645, 646
Long Beach..............lo. 544
Long Beach Point..............lo. 701
Long Eddy..............p. o. 645
Long Island.101, 121, 365, 544, 631, 633
Long Island Sound... 544, 548, 549, 633, 636, 637, 704, 706
Long Lake..............t. 338
Long Neck..............p. o. 566
Long Pond..............cr. 395
Long Pond..............mt. 302
Longs Corners..............lo. 327
Lookout..............mt. 663
Loon..............la. 619, 674
Looneyville..............p. o. 238
Loon Lake..............p. o. 628
Lords..............br. 261
Lords..............p. 261, 647
Lordsville..............p. o. 262
Lovetts Corners..............p. o. 401
Lorraine..............p. v. 359
Lorraine..............t. 359
Lottville..............p. o. 318
Loudonville..............lo. 166
Louisville..............p. o. 579
Louisville..............t. 579
Louisville..............v. 535
Louisville Landing....p. o. 579
Lowell..............p. v. 471
Lower Black Rock..............284
Lower Chateaugay.....la. 309
Lower Cincinnatus......lo. 250
Lower Cross Roads......lo. 702
Lower Ebenezer..........v. 293
Lower Falls..............v. 304
Lower Genesee Falls..............402
Lower Saranac......la. 22, 311
Lower Smith Clove.....lo. 508
Low Hampton..............p. o. 683
Lowville..............cr. 375
Lowville..............p. v. 378
Lowville..............t. 378
Lox..............p. 645
Luce..............la. 253
Ludingtonville..........p. o. 541
Ludlow..............cr. 223
Ludlowville..............p. v. 658
Lumberland..............p. v. 645
Lumberland..............t. 645
Lumberville..........p. o. 263
Luna..............isle 450

PAGE

Lutheran Cemetery..........549
Lutheranville..............p. o. 608
Luzerne.....mts. 252, 295, 670
Luzerne..............p. v. 675
Luzerne..............t. 675
Lyme..............t. 359
Lyndon..............t. 192
Lyndonville..............p. v. 516
Lyons..............p. v. 691
Lyons..............t. 691
Lyonsdale..............p. o. 377
Lyons Falls..............lo. 379
Lyons Falls..............p. o. 380
Lysander..............p. o. 484
Lysander..............t. 483
Lyttles..............p. 685

Mabbettsville..............p. o. 277
McConnelsville..........lo. 462
McConnelsville........p. v. 470
McDuffee Town..........lo. 618
McEwens Corners.....lo. 317
McGrawville..............p. v. 252
McGrawville..............v. 175
McHenry Valley...cr. 168, 170
McIntyre........mt. 19, 296, 303
McLean..............p. o. 657
McMartin....mt. 19, 296, 303
McNalls Corners......lo. 456
McNutt Run..............cr. 623
Macannon..............h. 507
Macdonough..............p. v. 227
Macdonough..............t. 227
Macedon..............p. v. 692
Macedon..............t. 692
Macedon Center........p. v. 692
Machias..............p. v. 192
Machias..............t. 192
Mackies Corners..........v. 605
Macomb..............p. v. 579
Macomb..............t. 579
Mad..............br. 230
Mad..............r. 463
Madison..............co. 101, 388
Madison..............p. v. 392
Madison..............t. 392
Madison Reservoir.....p. 392
Madison Square..........lo. 423
Madrid..............p. o. 579
Madrid..............t. 579
Magnolia..............p. o. 211
Magriganies..............la. 708
Maharness......r. 696, 698, 703, 705
Mahopac..............la. 540
Mahopac..............p. v. 541
Maine..............p. v. 182
Maine..............t. 182
Malden..............p. v. 666
Malden Bridge..........p. v. 244
Maline..............lo. 523
Mallory..............p. 643
Malloryville..............lo. 656
Malone..............p. v. 312
Malone..............t. 311
Malone..............v. 307
Malta..............p. o. 590
Malta..............t. 590
Malta Ridge..............p. o. 590
Maltaville..............p. o. 590
Mambasha..............p. 547
Mamakating..............p. o. 646
Mamakating..............t. 646
Mamaroneck........cr. 505, 701
Mamaroneck....r. 511, 696, 707
Mamaroneck..............t. 701
Mamaroneck Bay..........701
Manchester..............lo. 274
Manchester..............t. 467
Manchester..............v. 464
Manchester Bridge..p.o.272, 274
Mandana..............p. v. 487
Manhasset..............p. v. 550
Manhasset Bay......544, 549
Manhasset Neck........lo. 550
Manhattan.....isle 418, 437
Manhattan Square......lo. 423
Manhattanville..........p. o. 419
Manheim..............p. o. 346
Manheim Center........p. o. 346
Manilla..............lo. 514
Manlius..............p. v. 484
Manlius..............t. 484
Manlius Center..........v. 484
Manlius Station........p. v. 484
Manns..............br. 637

PAGE

Mannsville..............p. v. 357
Mannys Corners..........lo. 412
Manor Kil..............600, 604
Manorkill..............p. o. 604
Manorville..............p. o. 634
Mansfield..............p. o. 277
Mansfield..............t. 192
Manursing..............isle 705
Maple Grove......p. o. 486, 535
Mapleton..............lo. 107, 412
Mapleton..............p. o. 455
Marathon..............p. v. 253
Marathon..............t. 253
Marathon..............v. 546
Marbletown..............lo. 690
Marbletown..............p. o. 664
Marbletown..............t. 664
Marcellus..............t. 484
Marcellus Falls..........p. v. 485
Marcy..............mt. 19, 295, 296
Marcy..............p. o. 465
Marcy..............t. 465
Marengo..............p. v. 691
Margarettville........p. v. 263
Maria..............p. 596
Mariaville..............p. v. 596
Marietta..............p. v. 485
Marilla..............p. v. 292
Marilla..............t. 292
Mariners Harbor..........v. 566
Marion..............p. v. 692
Marion..............t. 692
Marketts..............isle 703
Marlborough..............mt. 665
Marlborough..............p. v. 665
Marlborough..............t. 664
Marrowback..............h. 383
Marsh..............cr. 514
Marshall..............p. o. 465
Marshall..............t. 465
Marshfield..........p. o. 292, 567
Marsh Pond..............673
Marshville..............lo. 412, 578
Martindale Corners..... lo. 686
Martindale Depot.....p. o. 244
Martins..............cr. 377, 378
Martinsburgh........p. v. 378
Martinsville..............p. o. 456
Martville..............p. o. 205
Marvin..............p. o. 212
Mary..............mt. 302
Maryland..............p. v. 534
Maryland..............t. 534
Marysville..............v. 542
Masonville..............p. v. 263
Masonville..............t. 263
Maspeth..............p. o. 549
Massena..............p. v. 579
Massena..............t. 579
Massena Center......p. v. 580
Massena Springs........v. 580
Masten..............p. 646
Mastic..............lo. 634
Mastic..............t. 634
Mathewson..............p. 227
Matinicock..............lo. 551
Mattahuck..............h. 245
Matteawan........mts. 267, 501
Matteawan..............p. v. 271
Mattituck..............p. v. 640
Maway..............r. 571
Mayfield..............p. v. 318
Mayfield..............p. v. 318
Mayfield..............t. 318
Mayflower..............lo. 537
Maynard..............br. 259
Mayville..............p. v. 211
Meads..............cr. 609, 611, 623
Meadville..............lo. 691
Meanagh..............cr. 699
Mechanic..............lo. 278
Mechanicsville......lo. 327, 571
Mechanicsville......p. v. 593
Mechanic Town..........v. 510
Mecklenburgh........p. v. 611
Mecox Bay..............631
Medford..............lo. 634
Medina..............p. v. 515
Medusa..............p. v. 165
Mellenville..............p. v. 244
Melville..............v. 636
Melvina..............lo. 549
Mendon..............p. v. 400
Mendon..............t. 400
Mendon Center........p. v. 400
Mentz..............t. 203
Merchantville............lo. 627

PAGE
Meredith ... p. o. 263
Meredith ... t. 263
Meredith Square ... v. 263
Meridian ... p. v. 201
Merino Point ... mt. 245
Merrelsville ... lo. 392
Merrick ... p. o. 547
Merrill ... cr. 253
Merrillsville ... p. o. 311
Merritt Island ... lo. 510
Messena Springs ... 26
Messengerville ... p. o. 255
Messina Spring ... 482
Metauques ... p. 646
Mettowee ... r. 682
Mexico ... p. v. 522
Mexico ... t. 522
Michaels Brook ... br. 541
Michigan ... cr. 623, 627
Middle ... br. 262
Middle ... isle 705
Middleburgh ... p. v. 606
Middleburgh ... t. 606
Middlebury ... t. 714
Middle Ebenezer ... v. 293
Middle Falls ... 710
Middlefield ... p. o. 534
Middlefield ... t. 534
Middlefield Center ... p. v. 534
Middle Genesee Falls ... 402
Middle Granville ... p. v. 682
Middle Grove ... p. o. 589
Middle Hope ... p. v. 509
Middle Island ... p. o. 634
Middleport ... lo. 392
Middleport ... p. v. 456
Middlesex ... p. o. 720
Middlesex ... t. 720
Middlesex Center ... v. 720
Middletown ... br. 223
Middletown ... lo. 549, 571, 700
Middletown ... p. v. 510
Middletown ... t. 263
Middletown ... v. 589
Middle Village ... lo. 549
Middleville ... p. v. 343
Midroadville ... v. 636
Midway ... p. o. 334
Milan ... p. o. 273
Milan ... t. 272
Milan ... v. 203
Milanville ... lo. 273
Milburn ... lo. 547
Milford ... p. o. 534
Milford ... t. 534
Milford Center ... v. 534
Military ... p. 236, 238
Mill ... br. 203, 223, 296, 663, 685, 715
Mill ... cr. 186, 211, 263, 375, 536, 554, 616, 675
Mill ... p. 316, 647
Mill Branch ... v. 283
Mill Brook ... p. v. 674
Millburn ... lo. 182
Millens Bay ... p. o. 356
Millers ... br. 204
Millers Corners ... lo. 557
Millers Place ... p. o. 633
Millerton ... lo. 273
Mill Grove ... p. v. 282
Mill Grove ... v. 194
Mill Neck ... cr. 544
Millport ... p. v. 222
Millsburgh ... v. 511
Mills Corners ... lo. 326
Mills Corners ... p. o. 317
Mills Mills ... p. o. 174
Milltown ... p. v. 543
Mill Valley ... v. 606
Millville ... lo. 554
Millville ... p. v. 516
Milo ... t. 720
Milo Center ... p. v. 720
Milton ... lo. 705
Milton ... p. v. 665
Milton ... t. 590
Milton Center ... lo. 590
Mina ... p. o. 214
Mina ... t. 214
Mina Corners ... v. 214
Minas Fall ... cr. 568
Minaville ... p. v. 413
Mine Kil ... 600, 605
Mine Kil Falls ... p. o. 605
Mineola ... p. v. 550
Miners ... cr. 569
Minerva ... p. o. 302
Minerva ... t. 302
Minetto ... cr. 526
Minetto ... p. v. 526
Minden ... p. o. 414
Minden ... t. 414
Mindenville ... p. v. 414
Minisceongo ... cr. 568
Minisink ... p. o. 507
Minisink ... t. 507
Misery ... mt. 703
Mitchells ... p. 644
Mitchellville ... p. v. 629
Mixville ... v. 174
Modena ... p. v. 665
Modern Times ... v. 637
Moffatts Store ... p. v. 248
Moffatville ... v. 359
Mogadore ... lo. 327
Mohawk ... p. v. 344
Mohawk ... r. 21, 23, 155, 165, 340, 343, 344, 345, 407, 458, 462, 463, 465, 466, 584, 589, 593, 595.
Mohawk ... t. 415
Mohawkville ... lo. 597
Mohegan ... la. 708
Moira ... p. o. 312
Moira ... t. 312
Moira Corners ... v. 312
Molly, Mount ... h. 277
Mongaup ... la. 647
Mongaup ... p. o. 646
Mongaup ... r. 506, 641, 647
Mongaup Valley ... p. v. 643
Monhagan ... cr. 510
Monroe ... co. 101, 103, 395
Monroe ... p. v. 507
Monroe ... t. 507
Monroe Works ... p. o. 508
Monsey ... p. o. 571
Monsey Depot ... lo. 571
Montague ... p. o. 378
Montague ... t. 378
Montauk Point ... lo. 635
Monterey ... lo. 277
Monterey ... v. 611
Montezuma ... p. v. 203
Montezuma ... t. 203
Montezuma Marshes ... 197
Montgomery ... co. 101, 103, 407
Montgomery ... p. 645
Montgomery ... p. v. 508
Montgomery ... t. 508
Monticello ... p. v. 647
Monticello ... v. 537
Montrose ... lo. 550
Montrose Point ... lo. 699
Montville ... lo. 570
Montville ... v. 203
Moodna ... p. o. 510
Mooers ... p. v. 238
Mooers ... t. 238
Mooers Forks ... p. o. 238
Moon ... la. 576
Moordeners ... cr. 554
Moordeners Kil ... 559
Moore ... mt. 303
Moose ... cr. 304
Moose ... p. 303
Moose ... r. 375
Moravia ... p. v. 203
Moravia ... t. 203
Moreau ... t. 590
Moreau Station ... p. o. 590
Morehouse ... t. 338
Morehouseville ... p. o. 339
Moreland ... p. o. 611
Moresville ... p. o. 264
Morganville ... p. v. 328
Moriah ... p. v. 303
Moriah ... t. 302
Moriches ... p. v. 634
Moringville ... p. o. 700
Morley ... p. v. 575
Morris ... p. o. 535
Morris ... t. 535
Morrisania ... p. v. 701
Morrisania ... t. 701
Morrisonville ... p. v. 240
Morristown ... p. v. 580
Morristown ... t. 580
Morrisville ... p. v. 390
Morseville ... p. o. 605
Morsston ... p. v. 647
Mortons Corners ... p. v. 289
Mortonville ... p. o. 510
Moscow ... p. v. 384
Moses Kil ... 679
Mosherville ... p. o. 589
Mosquito Cove ... ba. 550
Mosquito Neck ... lo. 550
Moss Street ... v. 685
Mother ... cr. 416
Mott Haven ... p. v. 701
Motts Corners ... p. v. 655
Motts Point ... lo. 549
Mottville ... p. v. 487
Mountain ... br. 259
Mountain Brook ... lo. 260
Mountain Ridge ... mt. 395
Mount Airy ... lo. 699
Mount Hope ... p. v. 508
Mount Hope ... t. 508
Mount Hope Cemetery ... lo. 404
Mount Kisko ... p. o. 702
Mount Kisko ... p. v. 698
Mount Misery ... lo. 633
Mount Morris ... p. v. 385
Mount Morris ... t. 385
Mount Morris Square ... lo. 423
Mount Olivet Cemetery ... lo. 549
Mount Pleasant ... p. v. 589
Mount Pleasant ... t. 702
Mount Rascal ... h. 505
Mount Riga ... p. 273
Mount Ross ... lo. 274
Mount Sinai ... p. v. 633
Mount Upton ... p. v. 227
Mount Vernon ... p. v. 699
Mount Vision ... p. o. 534
Mount Washington ... p. o. 628
Mourning Kil ... 587, 588
Moxons ... mt. 674
Muckle ... h. 277
Mud ... cr. 21, 223, 451, 456, 487, 491, 496, 622, 691, 692
Mud ... la. 190, 210, 349, 483, 588, 612, 619
Mud ... p. 201, 236, 273, 304, 645, 647
Muddy ... br. 542
Muddy ... p. 543
Muddy Kil ... 667
Mudge ... cr. 691
Mud Lick ... cr. 222
Muitzes Kil ... 559
Muitzes Kill ... v. 559
Mumford ... p. v. 406
Muncey ... h. 255
Munnsville ... p. v. 393
Murder ... cr. 279, 292, 326, 327, 712
Murderers Kil ... 501
Murray ... p. o. 515
Murray ... t. 515
Murray Depot ... lo. 515
Muscoot ... cr. 696
Muscoot ... r. 706
Musquito ... h. 504
Muttonville ... v. 495
Myers Corners ... lo. 272
Myersville ... lo. 276

Nanticoke ... cr. 179, 182, 651, 652
Nanticoke ... t. 182
Nanticoke Springs ... p. o. 182
Nannet ... p. v. 569
Napanock ... p. v. 668
Napeague Harbor ... 634
Naples ... p. v. 497
Naples ... t. 497
Napoli ... p. v. 193
Napoli ... t. 193
Narrows ... cr. 624
Narrowsburgh ... p. v. 648
Nashville ... p. v. 213
Nassau ... p. v. 557
Nassau ... t. 557
Natural Bridge ... p. v. 363
Naumburg ... p. o. 376
Navarino ... p. v. 485
Near Rockaway ... lo. 547
Neatahwanta ... la. 521
Nehtaways Cave ... lo. 606
Neils ... cr. 622
Nelson ... p. o. 393
Nelson ... t. 393
Nelson Flats ... v. 393
Nelson Hill ... h. 701
Nelsonville ... v. 542
Neperhan ... cr. 700
Neperhan ... p. o. 702
Neperhan ... r. 696, 702, 707
Neversink ... p. o. 647
Neversink ... r. 21, 501, 506, 641, 647
Neversink ... t. 646
Neversink Flats ... v. 647
New Albion ... p. v. 193
New Albion ... t. 193
Newark ... p. v. 690
Newark ... t. 651
Newark Bay ... 563
Newark Valley ... p. v. 651
New Astoria ... lo. 549
New Baltimore ... p. v. 334
New Baltimore ... t. 334
New Beacon ... mt. 267
New Berlin ... p. v. 228
New Berlin ... t. 227
New Berlin Center ... p. o. 228
New Boston ... lo. 692
New Boston ... p. o. 379
New Bremen ... p. o. 378
New Bremen ... t. 378
New Bridge ... lo. 547
New Brighton ... p. v. 566
New Britain ... p. o. 248
New Brooklyn ... lo. 367
Newburgh ... lo. 713
Newburgh ... p. v. 509
Newburgh ... t. 508
New Castle ... p. o. 702
New Castle ... t. 702
New Centerville ... p. o. 520
New City ... v. 166, 569
Newcomb ... la. 22
Newcomb ... t. 303
New Concord ... v. 244
New Dorp ... p. o. 567
New Ebenezer ... lo. 293
Newfane ... p. o. 454
Newfane ... t. 454
Newfield ... p. v. 658
Newfield ... t. 658
New Forge ... lo 249
New Graefenberg ... p. o. 344
New Hackensack ... p. v. 272
New Hamburgh ... p. v. 274
New Hampton ... p. v. 511
New Hartford ... p. v. 465
New Hartford ... t. 465
New Haven ... p. v. 523
New Haven ... t. 523
New Hope ... v. 204
New Hudson ... p. o. 175
New Hudson Corners ... v. 175
New Hurley ... p. o. 665, 667
New Inlet ... 544
New Kingston ... p. o. 263
Newkirks Mills ... p. v. 317
New Lebanon ... p. o. 248
New Lebanon ... t. 248
New Lebanon Center ... p. v. 248
New Lebanon Springs ... 26
New Lebanon Springs ... p. o. 248
New Lisbon ... p. o. 535
New Lisbon ... t. 535
New Lisbon Center ... lo. 535
New London ... p. v. 470
New Lots ... t. 373
New Milford ... p. v. 510
New Ohio ... p. o. 181
New Oregon ... p. o. 292
New Paltz ... p. v. 665
New Paltz ... t. 665
New Paltz Landing ... p. v. 664
Newport ... p. v. 347
Newport ... t. 347
New Road ... p. o. 265
New Rochelle ... p. v. 702
New Rochelle ... t. 702
New Russia ... p. v. 301
New Salem ... p. v. 164
New Salem ... v. 496
New Scotland ... p. v. 164
New Scotland ... t. 164
New Springville ... p. o. 566
Newstead ... t. 292
New Suffolk ... v. 640
New Sweden ... p. v. 235
Newtonville ... p. o. 166
Newtown ... cr. 219, 221, 222, 365, 367, 548, 549
Newtown Center ... lo. 589
Newtown ... p. v. 549
Newtown ... t. 548
New Utrecht ... p. v. 373
New Utrecht ... t. 373

New Vernon.....v. 508
New Village.....p. o. 634
Newville.....p. v. 343
Newville.....v. 629
New Windsor.....t. 509
New Windsor.....v. 509
New Woodstock.....p. v. 450
New York.....co. 418
New York Bay.....367, 437, 563, 566
New York City.....t. 418
New York Harbor.....563
New York Mills.....p. o. 465
New York Mills.....v. 471
New York Upper Mills...v. 465
Niagara.....co. 101, 449
Niagara.....r. 20, 22, 122, 279, 284, 449, 453, 455
Niagara.....t. 454
Niagara City.....v. 455
Niagara Falls.....450
Niagara Falls.....p. v. 455
Nichols.....p. o. 651
Nichols.....t. 651
Nicholville.....p. v. 578
Niggar.....p. 571
Nile.....p. v. 173
Niles.....p. o. 204
Niles.....t. 204
Nine.....h. 537
Nine Corners.....lo. 204
Nine Mile.....cr. 458, 463, 465, 474, 480, 483, 485, 522, 528
Nineveh.....p. o. 181
Nipple Top.....mt. 19, 296, 304
Niskayuna.....lo. 597
Niskayuna.....t. 597
Nissequague.....lo. 638
Nissequague.....r. 637
Nissequague Harbor.....ba. 637
Nissequague Neck.....637
Niverville.....p. v. 247
Nobles Corners.....v. 675
Noblesville.....v. 535
Norfolk.....p. v. 580
Norfolk.....t. 580
Normans Kil.....155, 163, 164, 595, 596, 597
Normanskill.....p. o. 163
Norrisville.....v. 240
North.....p. 273, 520, 647, 701
North Adams.....p. o. 355
North Albany.....lo. 166
North Almond.....p. o. 170
Northampton.....p. w. 318
Northampton.....t. 318
North Argyle.....p. o. 679
North Bangor.....p. o. 308
North Barton.....p. o. 650
North Bay.....p. v. 470
North Bergen.....p. o. 325
North Blenheim.....p. o. 603
North Bloomfield.....p. v. 500
North Boston.....p. v. 283
North Branch.....p. v. 644
North Bridgewater.....p. v. 463
North Broadalbin.....p. o. 317
North Brookfield.....p. v. 390
North Brother.....isle 548
North Buffalo.....p. o. 284
North Burke.....p. o. 309
North Cambridge.....p. o. 680
North Cameron.....p. o. 623
North Castle.....p. v. 703
North Castle.....t. 703
North Chatham.....v. 244
North Chemung.....p. o. 221
North Chili.....v. 398
North Clarence.....p. o. 289
North Clarkson.....p. o. 405
North Cohocton.....p. v. 624
North Collins.....t. 292
North Collins.....v. 292
North Copake.....p. o. 245
North Creek.....p. v. 675
North Cuba.....v. 173
North Dansville.....t. 385
Northeast.....p. o. 273
Northeast.....t. 273
Northeast Center.....v. 273
North Easton.....p. o. 681
Northeast Station.....p. o. 303
North Elba.....p. o. 303
North Elba.....t. 303
North Evans.....p. v. 290
Northfield.....t. 566
North Franklin.....p. o. 261

North Gage.....p. o. 463
North Galway.....p. o. 589
North Granville.....p. v. 682
North Greece.....p. v. 399
North Greenbush.....t. 557
North Greenfield.....p. o. 589
North Greenwich.....p. v. 683
North Hamden.....p. o. 261
North Harpersfield.....p. o. 262
North Hartford.....p. v. 684
North Haverstraw.....p. v. 570
North Hebron.....p. o. 684
North Hector.....p. o. 611
North Hempstead.....p. o. 550
North Hempstead.....t. 549
North Hill.....h. 211
North Hoosick.....p. v. 556
North Hudson.....p. v. 304
North Hudson.....t. 304
North Huron.....p. v. 691
North Islip.....p. v. 637
North Java.....p. v. 714
North Kortright.....p. v. 262
North Lansing.....p. o. 658
North Lawrence.....p. o. 578
North Lincklaen.....p. o. 227
North Manlius.....p. o. 546
North Nassau.....p. v. 557
North Norwich.....p. v. 228
North Norwich.....t. 228
North Parma.....p. o. 400
North Pembroke.....p. o. 327
North Pharsalia.....p. o. 229
North Pitcher.....p. v. 229
North Pittstown.....v. 558
Northport Bay.....636
Northport Harbor.....636
Northport.....p. v. 636
North Potsdam.....p. o. 582
North Reading.....p. o. 612
North Ridge.....p. o. 453
North Ridgeway.....p. o. 515
North Rome.....lo. 466
North Rush.....p. v. 405
North Russell.....p. o. 582
North Salem.....p. v. 704
North Salem.....t. 703
North Sandy.....cr. 355, 357
North Sanford.....p. o. 183
North Scriba.....p. o. 528
North Sheldon.....p. o. 715
North Shore.....p. o. 565
North Sparta.....p. o. 386
North Stephentown.....p. o. 560
North Sterling.....p. o. 205
North Stockholm.....p. o. 582
Northumberland.....p. o. 591
Northumberland.....t. 591
North Urbana.....p. v. 628
North Valley.....lo. 175
Northville.....p. v. 318
Northville.....v. 202, 637
North West Bay.....673
North West Bay.....br. 674
Northwest Harbor.....ba. 634
North Western.....p. v. 470
North White Creek...p. v. 686
North Wilna.....p. o. 363
North Wilson.....p. o. 457
Norton Hill.....p. v. 332
Nortons Mills.....p. v. 496
Norway.....p. v. 347
Norway.....t. 347
Norwich.....lo. 551
Norwich.....p. v. 228
Norwich.....t. 228
Nowadaga.....cr. 340
Nunda.....p. v. 385
Nunda.....t. 385
Nunda Station.....p. v. 385
Nyack.....p. v. 570
Nyack Hills.....h. 568
Nyack Turnpike.....p. o. 569

Oak.....cr. 533, 536
Oak.....isle 636
Oak.....mt. 588
Oakfield.....lo. 327
Oakfield.....p. o. 327
Oakfield.....t. 327
Oak Hill.....h. 558
Oak Hill.....p. v. 245, 332
Oak Island Beach.....636
Oakland.....p. v. 386
Oakland.....v. 645
Oak Orchard.....cr. 20, 22, 320, 324, 326, 512, 515

Oak Orchard.....p. v. 515
Oak Orchard Acid Springs.....lo. 324
Oak Point.....p. v. 577
Oak Ridge.....lo. 413
Oaks Corners.....p. o. 498
Oaksville.....p. v. 536
Oatka.....cr. 20, 320, 326, 395, 405, 710, 713, 714, 715
Obernburgh.....v. 645
Oblong.....p. v. 570
Oblong.....p. 273
Oblong.....p. o. 273
Odessa.....p. v. 610
Ogden.....p. o. 400
Ogden.....t. 400
Ogden Center.....v. 400
Ogdens.....isle 579
Ogdensburgh.....v. 580
Ohio.....p. o. 347
Ohio.....t. 347
Ohio City.....v. 347
Ohioville.....lo. 665
Oil.....cr. 168, 173, 191
Oil Spring.....173, 186
Okkanum.....cr. 179
Olean.....cr. 191, 193
Olean.....p. v. 193
Olean.....t. 193
Olcott.....p. v. 454
Old Attlebury.....lo. 277
Old Aquebogue.....v. 637
Old Beacon.....mt. 19, 267, 271
Old Castle.....lo. 499
Old Dam Fall.....cr. 506
Old Field Point.....lo. 633
Old Mans Harbor.....633
Old Morrisania.....lo. 702
Old Orchard Shoal....lo. 260
Old Place.....lo. 566
Old Schaghticoke.....lo. 559
Olive.....p. v. 665
Olive.....t. 665
Olive Bridge.....p. o. 665
Olive City.....v. 665
Olmsteadville.....p. v. 302
Olympus.....mt. 560
Omar.....p. o. 360
Omar.....v. 216
Oneida.....co. 101, 103, 110, 458
Oneida.....cr. 388, 458, 469, 470
Oneida.....la. 20, 22, 388, 458, 470, 474, 481, 517
Oneida.....p. v. 392
Oneida.....r. 474, 481, 517
Oneida Castle.....p. v. 469
Oneida Lake.....p. o. 392
Oneida Outlet.....cr. 22
Oneida Valley.....p. v. 392
Oneonta.....p. v. 535
Oneonta.....t. 535
Oneonta Plains.....p. v. 535
One Pine.....h. 510
Oniskethau.....lo. 164
Ontario.....co. 101, 103, 491
Ontario.....la. 20, 22, 122, 197, 204, 395, 517, 526, 688
Ontario.....p. v. 692
Ontario.....t. 692
Ontario Center.....v. 692
Onondaga.....co. 101, 103, 473
Onondaga.....cr. 483, 485, 489
Onondaga...la. 20, 22, 474, 487
Onondaga.....p. o. 485
Onondaga.....t. 485
Onondaga Castle.....p. o. 485
Onondaga Hill.....v. 485
Onondaga Outlet.....cr. 474
Onondaga Reservation.....478
Onondaga Salt Springs...473, 479
Onondaga Valley.....p. v. 485
Onoville.....p. o. 195
Oppenheim.....p. v. 318
Oppenheim.....t. 318
Oquaga.....cr. 179, 183
Oquaga Hill.....mt. 184
Oramel.....v. 172
Oran.....p. v. 486
Orange.....co. 101, 103, 110, 501
Orange.....la. 509
Orange.....p. o. 611
Orange.....t. 611
Orange Lake Outlet.....cr. 509
Orange Mills.....lo. 571
Orangeport.....p. v. 456
Orangetown.....t. 570
Orangeville.....p. o. 714

Orangeville.....t. 714
Orangeville Center.....v. 714
Orebed.....p. 681
Oregon.....p. o. 216
Oregon.....v. 543, 699
Orient.....lo. 639
Orient.....p. v. 640
Orienta.....lo. 701
Orient Harbor.....640
Oriskany.....cr. 393, 392, 458, 462, 464, 465, 471
Oriskany.....p. v. 471
Oriskany Falls.....p. v. 462
Orleans.....co. 103, 512
Orleans.....p. o. 498
Orleans.....p. v. 498
Orleans.....t. 359
Orleans Four Corners..p. o. 360
Orville.....v. 447
Orwell.....p. o. 523
Orwell.....t. 523
Orwell Corners.....v. 523
Osborne.....cr. 616
Osborne Hollow.....p. o. 181
Osborns Bridge.....p. o. 318
Oscawana.....isle 699
Osceola.....p. o. 379
Osceola.....t. 378
Ossian.....p. o. 386
Ossian.....t. 386
Ossian Center.....v. 386
Ossining.....t. 704
Oswago.....cr. 173
Oswaya.....cr. 173, 186, 194
Oswegatchie.....r. 21, 23, 375, 376, 572, 575, 577, 580
Oswegatchie.....t. 580
Oswego.....co. 517
Oswego.....r. 20, 22, 122, 474, 483, 517, 521, 523, 527, 528
Oswego.....t. 526
Oswego City.....t. 523
Oswego Falls.....p. v. 521
Oswego Falls.....521, 524
Oswego Village.....p. o. 277
Otego.....cr. 530, 533, 534, 535
Otego.....p. v. 536
Otego.....t. 536
Otego Lake.....p. o. 536
Otselic.....cr. 228, 229, 388
Otselic.....p. v. 228
Otselic.....r. 178, 183, 223, 250, 251, 255
Otselic.....t. 536
Otsdawa.....cr. 536
Otsdawa.....p. v. 536
Otsego.....co. 101, 103, 530
Otsego.....la. 21, 22, 530
Otsego.....t. 536
Otsego Lake.....p. o. 536
Otsquaga.....cr. 348, 407, 414
Otsquene.....cr. 414
Otter.....br. 252
Otter.....cr. 201, 375, 501, 514
Otter.....la. 201, 466
Otter Kil.....504, 506
Otterkill.....v. 507
Otterville.....p. o. 507
Otto.....p. o. 194
Otto.....t. 193
Otto Corners.....v. 199
Ouaquaga.....p. o. 181
Ouleout.....cr. 257, 261, 264
Ouleout.....p. v. 263
Outlet.....cr. 587
Overackers Corners.....lo. 720
Overlook.....mt. 668
Ovid.....p. v. 616
Ovid.....t. 616
Ovid Center.....v. 616
Ovid Landing.....lo. 616
Owasco...la. 20, 22, 197, 204, 206
Owasco.....p. v. 204
Owasco.....t. 204
Owasco Inlet....cr. 202, 206, 657
Owasco Lake.....p. o. 202
Owasco Outlet.....cr. 199, 203
Owego.....cr. 253, 655
Owego.....h. 250, 252, 255
Owego.....cr. 649, 650, 651, 652
Owego.....p. v. 652
Owego.....t. 649, 651
Owens.....p. 543
Owl Kil.....679, 680

	PAGE
Owl Pond	592
Owls Head	mt. 309
Ox	cr. 521
Ox Bow	p. v. 356
Oxford	p. v. 229
Oxford	t. 228
Oxford Depot	p. o. 505
Oyster	p. 635
Oyster Bay	544
Oyster Bay	p. v. 550
Oyster Bay	t. 550
Oyster Harbor	544
Padgets	br. 223, 377
Pages	br. 223
Pages Corners	lo. 589
Pages Corners	p. v. 349
Paines	cr. 202
Paines Hollow	p. o. 344, 346
Paint	cr. 595
Painted Post	p. v. 625
Painter	la. 520
Palatine	p. o. 416
Palatine	t. 416
Palatine Bridge	v. 416
Palatine Church	lo. 416
Palensville	p. v. 332
Palermo	p. v. 526
Palermo	t. 526
Palisades	p. o. 570
Palmertown	mt. 295, 584, 588, 589, 677, 681
Palmyra	p. v. 692
Palmyra	t. 692
Paltz Point	mt. 665
Pamelia	t. 360
Pamelia Four Corners	p. v. 360
Pamelia Village	v. 360
Panama	p. v. 213
Panther	cr. 605
Panther Hill	mt. 646
Panther Kil	600
Paradox	la. 304
Paris	p. o. 466
Paris	t. 465
Parish	p. o. 526
Parish	t. 526
Paris Hill	v. 466
Parishville	p. v. 581
Parishville	t. 581
Parishville	v. 526
Parishville Center	lo. 581
Parksville	p. v. 645
Parker	cr. 533
Parkers	p. 201
Parma	p. o. 400
Parma	t. 400
Parma Center	p. v. 400
Parma Corners	v. 400
Partridge Island	lo. 262
Pascasck	cr. 570
Patchin	p. o. 283
Patchin Hollow	v. 603
Patchins Mills	lo. 628
Patchogue	bay 633, 634
Patchogue	p. v. 634
Patroon	cr. 155
Pattawassa	la. 557
Patterson	p. v. 542
Patterson	t. 541
Pattens Mills	p. v. 685
Paughcaughnaughsink	cr. 506
Paul	cr. 588
Pavilion	p. v. 327
Pavilion	t. 327
Pavilion Center	p. v. 327
Pawling	p. v. 273
Pawling	t. 273
Peach	p. 543, 703
Peach Orchard	v. 611
Pearl	cr. 713
Pearl Creek	p. v. 713
Peasleville	v. 238
Peat	h. 505
Pecks	cr. 261
Pecksville	lo. 271
Peconic	r. 23, 631, 637
Peddlers	h. 504
Peeks	cr. 261
Peekskill Bay	699
Peekskill	cr. 696
Peekskill	p. v. 699
Peekskill Hollow	br. 698
Peekskill Hollow:	cr. 541
Peekskill Hollow	lo. 540
Peekskill Hollow	mts. 541
Pekin	p. v. 453
Pelham	p. o. 705
Pelham	t. 704
Pelham Neck	704
Pelham Priory	v 705
Pelhamville	lo. 704
Peltons	p. 543
Peltonville	p. o. 627
Pembroke	p. o. 327
Pembroke	t. 327
Penataquit	p. v. 636
Pendleton	p. o. 455
Pendleton	t. 455
Pendleton Center	p. o. 455
Penfield	p. v. 401
Penfield	t. 401
Penfield Center	v. 401
Pennellville	p. v. 527
Penn Yan	p. v. 720
Penny Bridge	lo. 549
Peoria	lo. 164
Peoria	p. v. 713
Peoria	v. 162
Pepacton	p. o. 260
Pepacton	r. 21, 257
Perch	la. 352
Perch	r. 351, 356
Perch River	p. o. 356
Perigo Hill	h. 558
Perinton	t. 401
Perkinsville	v. 628
Perry	p. 644
Perry	p. v. 715
Perry	t. 715
Perry Center	p. v. 715
Perry City	p. v. 611
Perrysburgh	p. v. 194
Perrysburgh	t. 194
Perrys Mills	p. o. 237
Perryville	p. v. 391, 394
Persia	t. 194
Peru	lo. 482
Peru	p. v. 238
Peru	t. 238
Peru Landing	lo. 238
Peruville	p. v. 657
Peterboro	p. v. 393
Petersburgh	lo. 605
Petersburgh	mt. 552, 555, 677
Petersburgh	p. v. 557
Petersburgh	t. 557
Petersburgh Four Corners	p. v. 558
Peters Kil	666
Petersville	v. 703
Peth	v. 190
Petre	isle 541
Pharaoh	la. 304
Pharaoh	mt. 19, 295, 304
Pharsalia	p. v. 229
Pharsalia	t. 229
Phelps	p. v. 498
Phelps	t. 497
Philadelphia	p. v. 360
Philadelphia	t. 360
Philips	cr. 168, 170
Philipsburgh	lo. 510
Philips Creek	p. v. 175
Phillipsport	p. o. 646
Philipstown	p. v. 542
Philipsville	p. v. 170
Philmont	p. v. 244
Phoenicia	p. o. 667
Phoenix	p. v. 527
Pickleville	v. 339
Pierce	cr. 195
Piermont	p. v. 570
Pierrepont	p. o. 581
Pierrepont	t. 581
Pierrepont Manor	p. v. 357
Piffard	p. v. 387
Piffardinia	v. 387
Pike	br. 680
Pike	cr. 290, 309
Pike	p. 644
Pike	p. v. 715
Pike	t. 715
Pike Five Corners	lo. 715
Pike Pond	p. v. 644
Pillar Point	p. o. 356
Pinckney	p. o. 379
Pinckney	t. 379
Pine	h. 505, 507, 542, 569
Pine	isle 705
Pine	la. 317
Pine	p. 541
Pines Bridge	p. o. 708
Pine Bush	lo. 392
Pine Bush	p. v. 506
Pine Grove	p. o. 612
Pine Hill	lo. 326
Pine Hill	p. v. 667
Pine Island	510, 542
Pine Kil	646
Pin Orchard	mt. 19, 329, 333
Pine Plains	p. v. 274
Pine Plains	t. 273
Pine Pond	br. 541
Pine Valley	p. o. 222
Pineville	v. 201, 520
Pine Woods	p. o. 391
Pinnacle	mt. 677
Pipe	cr. 649, 652
Piscawen	cr. 561
Piseco	lo. 337
Pisgah	h. 541
Pisgah	mt. 19, 259
Pitcairn	p. o. 581
Pitcairn	t. 581
Pitcher	p. v. 229
Pitcher	t. 229
Pitcher Springs	p. v. 229
Pitch Off	mt. 302
Pittsfield	p. o. 536
Pittsfield	t. 536
Pittsford	p. v. 401
Pittsford	t. 401
Pittstown	p. o. 558
Pittstown	t. 558
Pittstown Corners	v. 558
Pittstown Station	v. 558
Placid	la. 303
Plainfield	t. 537
Plainfield Center	v. 537
Plainsville	p. o. 497
Plainville	p. v. 484
Plank Road	p. o. 481
Plasterville	lo. 228
Platners	cr. 261
Plato	p. o. 189
Platte Kil	263, 331, 416, 660
Plattekill	p. v. 665
Plattekill	t. 665
Platter Kil	600, 605
Plattsburgh	p. v. 239
Plattsburgh	t. 239
Pleasant	cr. 351, 359
Pleasant	la. 22, 338, 352, 579
Pleasant	br. 223, 230
Pleasant	p. 643, 647
Pleasant Brook	p. o. 537
Pleasant Plains	p. o. 270
Pleasant Ridge	p. o. 277
PleasantValley	lo. 215, 471, 540
Pleasant Valley	p. v. 274
Pleasant Valley	t. 274
Pleasantville	p. v. 702
Plessis	p. v. 355
Plumb	br. 696
Plum	br. 706
Plum	cr. 170
Plum Beach	lo. 550
Plum Gut	639
Plum	isle 639
Plymouth	h. 277
Plymouth	p. v. 229
Plymouth	t. 229
Pocantico	r. 696, 702
Pochuck	cr. 510
Podunk	br. 681
Poesten Kil	554, 558, 560
Poestenkill	p. v. 558
Poestenkill	t. 558
Point-au-Fer	lo. 237
Point-au-Roche	236
Point Orleans	lo. 360
Point Peninsula	p. o. 359
Point Rock	br. 462
Poke-a-Moonshine	mt. 300
Poland	p. v. 348
Poland	t. 214
Poland Center	p. o. 214
Pole Hill	h. 673
Polkville	p. v. 484, 611
Pomfret	t. 214
Pompey	h. 19
Pompey	p. o. 486
Pompey	t. 486
Pompey Center	p. o. 486
Pompey Hill	p. v. 486
Ponchuck	br. 510
Pond	h. 510, 541
Pond Eddy	p. o. 646
Poney Hollow	p. o. 658
Pon-o-kose	h. 554
Pontiac	p. v. 290
Poolville	p. v. 391
Popes Mills	p. o. 579
Poplar Ridge	v. 206
Poplopens	p. 507
Port Bay	688, 691, 695
Portage	t. 386
Portage Falls	710
Portage Station	lo. 386
Portageville	p. v. 713
Port Benjamin	v. 668
Port Byron	p. v. 203
Port Chester	p. v. 705
Port Douglas	lo. 300
Port Crane	t. 183
Port Deposit	lo. 615
Porter	t. 455
Porters Corners	p. v. 589
Port Ewen	p. v. 662
Port Glasgow	p. o. 691
Port Henry	v. 303
Port Jackson	lo. 238
Port Jackson	p. v. 413
Port Jackson	v. 666
Port Jefferson	bay 633
Port Jefferson	p. v. 633
Port Jervis	p. v. 506
Port Kendall	lo. 300
Port Kent	p. v. 300
Portland	p. o. 215
Portland	t. 215
Portlandville	p. o. 535
Port Leyden	p. v. 377
Port Morris	t. 702
Port Nixon	v. 668
Port Ontario	p. v. 527
Port Richmond	p. v. 566
Portville	p. v. 194
Portville	t. 194
Port Washington	p. o. 550
Port Woodhull	lo. 466
Post	cr. 219, 220, 624
Post Creek	p. o. 221
Posts	cr. 332
Posts Corners	v. 686
Potick	cr. 331, 332
Potick	h. 331
Potick Hills	h. 329
Potsdam	p. v. 581
Potter	p. o. 720
Potter	t. 720
Potter Center	v. 720
Potter Hill	p. o. 556
Potters	h. 555
Potters Hollow	p. o. 165
Pottersville	p. v. 674
Potsdam Junction	lo. 582
Potuck	cr. 501
Poughkeepsie	t. 274
Poughkeepsie City	274
Poughkeepsie Rural Cemetery	lo. 275
Poughquag	p. v. 270
Poultney	r. 683
Poundridge	p. v. 705
Poundridge	t. 705
Powells Cove	544, 546
Prairie	la. 317
Pray	h. 537
Prattsburgh	p. v. 627
Prattsburgh	t. 627
Pratts Falls	486
Pratts Hollow	p. o. 391
Prattsville	p. v. 334
Prattsville	t. 334
Preble	t. 254
Preble Corners	p. v. 254
Prendergast	cr. 208
Preston	p. 303
Preston	p. o. 230
Preston	t. 229
Preston Corners	v. 230
Preston Hollow	p. v. 165
Princes Bay	515, 563, 567
Princetown	t. 597
Princetown	t. 597
Prickly Ash	h. 507
Prospect	h. 246, 276, 309, 414, 541, 673
Prospect	lo. 327, 348
Prospect	mt. 264, 702
Prospect	v. 468
Prospect Hill	lo. 705
Prospect Hill	v. 704
Prospect Point	lo. 549
Prospect Station	lo. 468

PAGE
Protection....p. o. 292
Providence....p. o. 591
Providence....t. 591
Psanticoke Swamp.... 557
Pugsleys Depot....p. o. 655
Pulaski....p. v. 527
Pulteney....p. o. 627
Pulteney....t. 627
Pulteneyville....p. v. 694
Pulvers Corners....p. o. 274
Pulvers Station....lo. 245
Pumpkin Hill....lo. 325
Pumpkin Hook....cr. 686
Pumpkin Hook....lo. 686
Punch Kil.... 555, 600
Punsit....cr. 241
Purchase....lo. 703
Purdy....cr. 625
Purdy Creek....p. o. 625
Purdys Station....p. o. 704
Purvis....p. o. 647
Putnam....co. 101, 540
Putnam....cr. 296, 300
Putnam....mt. 681
Putnam....p. o. 685
Putnam....t. 685
Putnam Corners....v. 685
Putnams....cr. 301
Putnam Valley....t. 542

Quacken Kil....554, 555
Quackenkill....p. o. 555
Quaker....br. 542
Quaker....cr. 506, 510
Quaker Hill....lo. 273
Quaker Springs.... 591
Quaker Springs....p. v. 591
Quaker Street....p. v. 596
Quality Hill....v. 392
Quarryville....p. v. 667
Quassaic....cr. 509
Queechy....lo. 243
Queens....co. 103, 544
Queens....p. o. 548
Queensbury....lo. 245
Queensbury....p. v. 675
Queensbury....t. 675
Quincy....v. 215
Quogue....p. o. 638

Racket....la. 22, 337
Racket....r. 21, 23, 307, 309, 338, 572, 576, 580, 581
Racket River....p. v. 580
Racketville....v. 582
Ragged....la. 309
Rahway....r. 566
Rail Bridge....cr. 595
Rainer....h. 504
Ramapo....mts. 568
Ramapo....r. 501, 568, 571
Ramapo....t. 571
Ramapo....v. 571
Ramapo Works....p. o. 571
Rams Head.... 236
Randalls....isle 418, 419
Randolph....p. v. 195
Randolph....t. 194
Randolph Center....p. o. 184
Ransoms....cr. 282, 288
Ransomville....p. v. 456
Rapids....p. o. 454
Rathbone....t. 627
Rathboneville....p. v. 627
Rattle....h. 541
Rattlesnake....h. 454
Rattlesnake....isle 279
Raven Hill....h. 296
Raven Hill....mt. 301
Ravenswood....p. v. 549
Rawson....p. o. 192
Rawson Hollow....p. o. 655
Raymertown....p. v. 558
Raymondville....p. o. 580
Rayville....v. 244
Reading....p. o. 612
Reading....t. 612
Reading Center....p. v. 612
Reads Corners....lo. 399
Red....cr. 206
Red Creek....p. v. 695
Red Falls....p. v. 334
Redfield....p. o. 526
Redfield....t. 526
Redford....p. v. 340
Redhook....p. v. 276
Redhook....t. 276

PAGE
Red Hook.... 419
Red House....cr. 186, 188
Red Kil....263, 264
Red Jacket....p. o. 284
Red Mills....p. v. 541
Red Ridge....h. 504
Red Rock....lo. 243
Redwood....p. v. 355
Reeds Corners....lo. 386
Reeds Corners....p. v. 496
Reeseville....v. 597
Reidsville....p. v. 162
Remsen....p. v. 466
Remsen....t. 466
Rensselaer....co. 101, 103, 552
Rensselaer Falls....p. v. 575
Rensselaerville....p. v. 165
Rensselaerville....t. 165
Rensselaerwyck Manor.... 155
Reserve....p. o. 293
Reservoir....la. 191
Reservoir Square....lo. 423
Rexford Flats....p. v. 587
Reynales Basin....p. v. 456
Reynolds Corners....lo. 590
Reynoldsville....p. v. 611
Rhinebeck....p. v. 277
Rhinebeck....t. 276
Rhinebeck Kil.... 276
Rhinebeck Station....p. v. 277
Rhoda....p. 241, 245
Rhoderic....mt. 254
Rice....cr. 526
Rice....v. 191
Rich....la. 22
Richburgh....p. v. 176
Richfield....p. o. 537
Richfield....t. 537
Richfield Springs.... 26
Richfield Springs....p. v. 537
Richford....p. v. 652
Richford....t. 652
Richland....t. 527
Richland Station....lo. 527
Richmond....co. 563
Richmond....p. v. 566
Richmond....t. 498
Richmond Mills....p. o. 498
Richmond Valley....p. o. 567
Richmondville....p. v. 606
Richmondville....t. 606
Rich's Corners....lo. 514
Richville....lo. 327
Richville....p. v. 576
Ridge....p. 303
Riders Mills....v. 244
Ridge....p. v. 385
Ridgebury....p. v. 511
Ridge Mills....v. 466
Ridgeway....p. v. 515
Ridgeway....t. 515
Rieds....br. 261
Riga....p. o. 401
Riga....t. 401
Riga Center....v. 401
Rikers....isle 548
Rikers Hollow....p. o. 627
Ripley....h. 473
Ripley....p. o. 215
Ripley....t. 215
Risingville....p. o. 627
Riverhead....p. v. 637, 638
Riverhead....t. 637
River Road....lo. 385
River Road Forks....p. o. 385
Riverdale....v. 708
Roanoke....p. v. 328
Roaring....br. 375, 560
Roberts Corners....p. o. 358
Robertsonville....p. o. 645
Robins....isle 631
Robinsons....p. 241, 245
Robins Reef.... 419
Rochdale....lo. 274
Rochester....t. 666
Rochester City.... 402
Rockaway....p. o. 547
Rockaway Beach....lo. 544, 547
Rock City....lo. 173
Rock City....p. v. 273
Rock City Mills....p. v. 590
Rockdale....p. v. 227
Rock House....h. 569
Rockland....co. 101, 568
Rockland....la. 569
Rockland....p. o. 647
Rockland....t. 647

PAGE
Rockland....v. 570
Rockland Lake....p. v. 569
Rockland Mount.... 19
Rocky Point....lo. 633
Rock Stream....cr. 721
Rock Stream....p. v. 721
Rock Stream....r. 721
Rockville....lo. 510
Rockville....p. o. 171
Rockville....v. 607
Rockville Center....p. v. 547
Rockwood....p. v. 317
Rocky....h. 507, 510
Rocky Hill....lo. 546
Rocky Point....lo. 633
Rodman....p. v. 361
Rodman....t. 361
Roeliff Jansens Kil... 241, 233, 244, 245, 247, 248, 267, 272
Rogers....cr. 683
Rogersville....v. 625
Roll Way Bluff....h. 346
Rome....p. v. 466
Rome....t. 466
Romulus....p. v. 616
Romulus....p. v. 618
Romulus....t. 616
Romulus Center....p. o. 616
Rondout...cr. 23, 660, 662, 664, 666, 668
Rondout....p. v. 663
Ronkonkoma....la. 631
Root....p. o. 416
Root....t. 416
Rose....br. 264
Rose....h. 707
Rose....p. o. 693
Rose....t. 693
Roseboom....p. v. 537
Roseboom....t. 537
Rose Hill....p. o. 615
Rosendale....p. v. 666
Rosendale....t. 666
Rose Valley....v. 693
Roslyn....p. v. 550
Rossie....p. v. 582
Rossie....t. 582
Rossville....p. v. 567
Rotterdam....lo. 597
Rotterdam....t. 597
Rough....mts. 501, 510
Rough and Ready....p. v. 625
Round....h. 504, 505, 541
Round....la. 338
Round....mt. 541, 559
Round....p. 225, 273, 303, 309, 399, 507, 645, 646
Round Top....h. 331
Round Top....mt. 19, 329, 333
Rouses Point....p. v. 237
Roxbury....p. v. 264
Roxbury....t. 264
Royalton....p. v. 456
Royalton....t. 456
Rudds....p. 273
Run....cr. 334
Rural Hill....p. o. 358
Rush....cr. 175, 291
Rush....p. o. 405
Rush....t. 404
Rushford....p. v. 175
Rushford....t. 175
Rushville....p. v. 720
Russell....p. o. 582
Russell....t. 582
Russia....p. v. 348
Russia....t. 347
Russia....v. 240
Rutland....p. o. 361
Rutland....t. 361
Rutland Center....v. 361
Rutledge....v. 189
Rye....p. 701, 703
Rye....p. v. 705
Rye....t. 705
Ryebeach....lo. 705

Sabbath Day Point....lo. 674
Sackets....p. 647
Sackets Harbor....p. v. 358
Sacondaga...r. 21, 23, 314, 338, 584, 588, 589
Sacondaga Vlaie....lo. 316
Saddle....mt. 677
Sagamore....la. 541
Sage....cr. 522

PAGE
Sageville....p. v. 338
Sagg....lo. 638
Sag Harbor....p. v. 638
St. Andrews....p. o. 508
St. Armand....t. 304
St. Armands Bay.... 236
St. Helena....p. v. 712
St. James....p. o. 637
St. Jamesville....v. 637
St. Johns Park....lo. 423
St. Johnsville....p. v. 416
St. Johnsville....t. 416
St. Lawrence..co. 101, 103, 572
Saint Lawrence....p. o. 356
St. Lawrence....r. 20, 22, 23, 572, 579
St. Marys....la. 707
St. Marys....p. 701
St. Regis....la. 311
St. Regis....r. 23, 307, 309, 310, 572, 575, 578, 581
St. Regis....v. 309
St. Ronans Well....isle 549
Salem....p. v. 685
Salem....t. 685
Salem....v. 215
Salem Center....p. o. 704
Salina....p. o. 500
Salina....t. 487
Salisbury....p. o. 348
Salisbury....t. 348
Salisbury Center....p. v. 348
Salisbury Corners....v. 348
Salisbury Mills....p. v. 504
Salmon....cr. 22, 395, 405, 526, 654, 658, 688, 694
Salmon...r. 21, 22, 23, 122, 232, 307, 311, 312, 375, 517, 520, 527.
Salmon River....p. o. 520
Salmon River....v. 239
Salmon River Falls.... 523
Salpeu....p. 543
Salt Point....cr. 270
Salt Point....p. v. 274
Salt Springsville....p. o. 532
Sammonsville....p. v. 317
Sam-po-wans....br. 636
Sampson....p. 236
Samsonville....p. v. 665
Sand....la. 558, 588
Sand....p. 646, 647
Sandanona....mt. 19, 296, 303
Sand Bank....p. v. 520
Sandburgh....cr. 660, 668
Sander Kil.... 666
Sandford....la. 22
Sandfordville....v. 582
Sanford....p. 303
Sanford....p. v. 183
Sanfords Corners....p. v. 359
Sand Lake....p. v. 558
Sand Lake....t. 558
Sand Pond....br. 261
Sands....cr. 261
Sands Point....lo. 549, 550
Sandstone....cr. 527
Sandusky....p. v. 190
Sandy....cr. 122, 351, 359, 361, 395, 512, 514
Sandy Creek....p. o. 527
Sandy Creek....t. 527
Sandy Hill....cr. 538
Sandy Hill....p. v. 685
Sandy Hook.... 419
Sangerfield....p. o. 467
Sangerfield....t. 467
Sangerfield Center....v. 467
Saranac....la. 309
Saranac....p. 239
Saranac....p. v. 240
Saranac....r. 21, 232, 236, 239, 240, 303, 304, 307, 311
Saranac Falls.... 239
Saranac Lake....p. o. 303, 311
Saratoga....co. 101, 584
Saratoga....la. 584, 590, 591
Saratoga....t. 591
Saratoga Springs....p. v. 592
Sardinia....p. v. 292
Sardinia....t. 292
Sarlesville....lo. 702
Saugerties....p. v. 666
Saugerties....t. 666
Sauquoit...cr. 458, 465, 466, 471
Savannah....p. v. 693
Savannah....t. 693

	PAGE
Savannah	v. 693
Savil	p. o. 509
Savona	p. v. 622
Saw Kil	267, 276, 663
Saw Mill	br. 706
Sawmill Run	cr. 188
Saw Mill Station	lo. 283
Sawyers	cr. 455, 456
Sayville	p. v. 636
Scajaquady	cr. 284
Scarsdale	p. o. 705
Scarsdale	t. 705
Scarsdale Station	lo. 705
Schaghticoke	p. o. 559
Schaghticoke	t. 558
Schaghticoke Hill	v. 559
Schaghticoke Point	v. 559
Schenectady City	598
Schenectady	co. 409, 595
Schenevas	cr. 530, 533, 534, 538
Schenevus	p. v. 534
Schodack	t. 559
Schodack Center	p. o. 559
Schodack Depot	v. 559
Schodack Landing	p. v. 559
Schoharie	co. 101, 104, 600
Schoharie	cr. 329, 333, 334, 407, 595, 596, 600, 603, 605, 606
Schoharie	mt. 595
Schoharie	p. v. 606
Schoharie	t. 606
Schroeppel	t. 527
Schroon	la. 304, 674
Schroon	mt. 295, 301, 302, 304, 305, 336
Schroon	r. 296, 304, 673, 674, 676
Schroon	t. 304
Schroon Lake	p. v. 304
Schroon River	p. o. 304
Schultzville	p. o. 270
Schunemunk	mts. 501, 507
Schuyler	co. 609
Schuyler	isle 300
Schuyler	la. 22, 530
Schuyler	t. 348
Schuyler Falls	p. v. 340
Schuyler Falls	t. 340
Schuylers Lake	p. v. 533
Schuylerville	p. v. 591
Schuylerville	p. v. 706
Scio	p. v. 175
Scio	t. 175
Sciota	p. v. 237
Scipio	p. o. 204
Scipio	t. 204
Scipio Center	p. v. 204
Scipioville	p. v. 204
Seonondoa	p. v. 470
Scotch Bush	p. o. 413
Scotch Town	p. v. 510
Scotia	p. v. 597
Scott	p. o. 254
Scott	t. 254
Scott Center	v. 254
Scott Corners	lo. 254
Scotts	cr. 526
Scottsburgh	p. v. 386
Scotts Corners	lo. 616
Scotts Corners	v. 191
Scottsville	p. v. 405
Scriba	cr. 521
Scriba	p. o. 528
Scriba	t. 528
Scriba Corners	v. 528
Scrub	cr. 165
Scum	la. 190
Scutters	isle 334
Scuttle Hole	lo. 638
Sea Land	cr. 595
Seamans Point	lo. 701
Searsburgh	p. o. 611
Searsville	p. v. 506
Seatuck	lo. 634
Second	cr. 688
Seely	cr. 219, 222
Seely Creek	p. o. 222
Seguines Point	lo. 567
Selden	p. o. 634
Selkirk	v. 527
Selkirks Cave	lo. 604
Sempronius	p. o. 204
Sempronius	t. 204
Seneca	co. 613

	PAGE
Seneca	la. 20, 22, 498, 609, 613, 616, 717, 720, 721
Seneca	r. 21, 22, 197, 201, 474, 481, 482, 483, 490, 613, 617, 618
Seneca	t. 498
Seneca Castle	p. o. 498
Seneca Falls	p. v. 617
Seneca Falls	t. 617
Seneca Hill	p. v. 528
Seneca River	p. o. 201
Sennett	p. v. 204
Sennett	t. 204
Sepasco	la. 276
Setauket	p. v. 633
Setauket Bay	633
Seventh Pond	v. 674
Seward	mt. 19, 296, 307
Seward	p. o. 607
Seward	t. 607
Seward Valley	v. 607
Seymour	p. o. 173
Shaker Settlement	lo. 166
Shandaken	p. v. 667
Shandaken	t. 667
Shannons Corners	lo. 721
Sharon	p. o. 607
Sharon	t. 607
Sharon Center	p. v. 607
Sharon Hill	v. 607
Sharon Springs	26
Sharon Springs	p. v. 607
Sharon Station	p. o. 270
Shavertown	p. o. 259
Shaw	br. 259, 555
Shaw	p. 277, 647
Shawangunk	cr. 646
Shawangunk	mts. 19, 501, 506, 507, 646, 660
Shawangunk	p. v. 667
Shawangunk	r. 501, 506, 507, 667
Shawangunk	t. 667
Shawangunk Kil	641, 663
Shawler	br. 223
Shawler	cr. 223
Shawnee	p. v. 457
Sheds Corners	p. o. 390
Sheeps Head Bay	365, 372
Shelby	p. o. 516
Shelby	t. 516
Shelby Basin	p. o. 516
Shelby Center	v. 516
Sheldon	p. o. 715
Sheldon	t. 715
Sheldrake	cr. 616, 701, 705
Sheldrake	p. o. 616
Sheldrake Point	v. 616
Shelter	isle 631
Shelter Island	p. o. 637
Shelter Island	t. 637
Shenandoah Corners	p. o. 271
Shepard	p. 571
Shepherd	h. 292
Sherburne	p. v. 230
Sherburne	t. 230
Sheridan	p. v. 215
Sheridan	t. 215
Sheridan Center	p. v. 215
Sherman	cr. 693
Sherman	p. v. 215
Sherman	t. 215
Shermans Hollow	p. o. 720
Shermans Mills	p. o. 558
Sherwood	p. v. 204
Shirley	p. v. 292
Shin Creek	p. o. 647
Shingle	br. 506
Shingle	cr. 331
Shingle Creek	p. o. 582
Shinnecock	h. 638
Shinnecock	v. 638
Shinnecock Bay	631
Shohan	p. v. 161
Shongo	p. v. 176
Shookville	lo. 273
Shooters	isle 563
Short Tract	p. o. 174
Shortsville	p. v. 497
Shoemakers Corners	lo. 171
Shrub Oak	p. o. 708
Shues	la. 668
Shultz	mt. 270
Shultzville	p. o. 270
Shumla	lo. 215
Shushan	p. v. 685
Shutters Corners	p. o. 608

	PAGE
Sibleyville	lo. 400
Sidney	p. v. 264
Sidney	t. 264
Sidney Center	p. v. 264
Sidney Plains	p. v. 264
Siloam	p. o. 393
Silver	cr. 208, 213
Silver	la. 270, 577, 710
Silver Creek	p. v. 213
Simewog	h. 540
Sinclearville	v. 211
Sing Sing	cr. 219, 220
Sing Sing	p. v. 704
Six Mile	cr. 451, 521, 654
Sixteen Falls	cr. 616
Six Town	cr. 168, 172
Skanandoa	cr. 462, 469
Skaneateles	cr. 254
Skaneateles	la. 20, 22, 197, 204, 250, 474, 487
Skaneateles	p. v. 487
Skaneateles	t. 487
Skaneateles Outlet	cr. 474, 482, 599
Skinners	cr. 357, 359
Skinnerville	lo. 582
Slader	cr. 172
Slate Bottom	cr. 288
Slate Hill	p. v. 511
Slate Hills	h. 380
Slateville	p. o. 684
Slaterville	p. v. 655
Slatterleys	cr. 504
Slaughters	p. 507
Slaughters Landing	lo. 569
Sleepy Hollow	lo. 702
Sleightsburg	v. 662
Sliters Corners	v. 558
Sloansville	p. v. 605
Sloatsburgh	p. v. 571
Slush	p. 236
Sly	p. 681
Smally	h. 541
Smithfield	t. 393
Smith Mills	p. v. 213
Smiths	p. 533
Smiths Basin	p. o. 685
Smithsboro	p. v. 653
Smiths Corners	lo. 348, 716
Smiths Corners	v. 507
Smiths Landing	lo. 378
Smiths Mills	v. 522
Smiths Valley	lo. 392
Smithton	lo. 603
Smithtown	lo. 589
Smithtown	p. v. 637
Smithtown	t. 637
Smithtown Branch	p. o. 637
Smithville	lo. 324
Smithville	p. v. 355, 358
Smithville	t. 230
Smithville Flats	p. o. 230
Smokes	cr. 293
Smoky Hollow	p. v. 244
Snook Kil	590
Smyrna	p. v. 230
Smyrna	t. 230
Snake	cr. 182, 526
Snake	h. 505, 509, 557, 558, 570
Snyder	p. 241, 245
Sociality	lo. 189
Sodus	p. v. 122, 694
Sodus	t. 693
Sodus Center	p. v. 694
Sodus Point	p. v. 694
Solitude	lo. 263
Solon	p. o. 254
Solon	p. v. 254
Solon	t. 254
Solsville	p. v. 392
Somers	p. v. 422
Somers	t. 705
Somerset	p. v. 456
Somerset	t. 456
Somerville	p. v. 582
Sonora	p. v. 622
South Melrose	lo. 702
Sour Spring	lo. 325
South	h. 482, 520, 534, 701
South Addison	p. v. 621
South Alabama	p. o. 324
South Albion	p. o. 520
South Amenia	p. o. 270
Southampton	p. v. 638
Southampton	t. 638

	PAGE
South Argyle	p. o. 679
South Avon	p. o. 382
South Ballston	p. o. 587
South Bangor	p. o. 308
South Barre	p. o. 514
South Bay	392, 481, 633, 680
South Bay	v. 681
South Bend Mills	lo. 244
South Berlin	p. v. 554
South Bern	162
South Bethlehem	lo. 163
South Bird	cr. 222
South Bolivar	p. o. 172
South Bombay	lo. 309
South Bradford	p. o. 622
South Branch	cr. 194
South Bristol	p. o. 499
South Bristol	t. 499
South Brookfield	p. o. 390
South Brooklyn	367
South Brother	isle 548
South Butler	p. o. 690
South Byron	p. v. 325
South Cairo	p. o. 331
South Candor	v. 651
South Canton	lo. 575
Southeast Center	v. 543
South Chili	lo. 398
South Colson	p. o. 576
South Columbia	p. o. 342
South Corinth	v. 588
South Cortland	p. v. 252
South Danby	p. o. 656
South Dansville	p. o. 625
South Dickinson	p. o. 310
South Dover	p. v. 271
South Durham	p. o. 332
South Edmeston	p. v. 533
South Edwards	p. v. 576
Southeast	t. 543
South Easton	p. v. 681
South Erin	p. o. 222
Southfield	lo. 508, 566
Southfield	mts. 507
Southfield	t. 566
South Galway	p. o. 589
South Glens Falls	p. v. 590
South Granby	p. o. 521
South Granville	p. v. 682
South Gilboa	p. v. 605
South Greece	p. v. 399
South Hamilton	p. o. 392
South Hammond	v. 577
South Hannibal	p. o. 522
South Harford	v. 252
South Harrisburg	p. o. 377
South Hartford	p. o. 684
South Hartwick	p. v. 533
South Haven	p. v. 634
South Hill	p. o. 626
South Howard	p. o. 626
South Huron	v. 691
South Kortright	p. o. 262
South Lansing	p. o. 658
South Lima	p. v. 384
South Livonia	p. v. 384
South Middle Branch	cr. 186, 189
South New Berlin	p. v. 228
Southold	p. v. 639
Southold	t. 639
South Onondaga	p. v. 485
South Otselic	p. v. 228
South Oxford	p. o. 229
South Oyster Bay	544, 547, 550
South Pekin	p. o. 453
South Pitcher	p. o. 229
South Plattsburgh	p. o. 239
South Plymouth	p. o. 229
Southport	p. v. 222
Southport	t. 222
South Richland	p. o. 527
South Rondout	v. 662
South Royalton	p. o. 456
South Rutland	p. o. 361
South Salem	p. v. 701
South Sandy	cr. 357
South Sand Lake	p. o. 558
South Schodack	p. o. 559
Southside	p. o. 567
South Sodus	p. v. 694
South Stephentown	p. o. 560
South Stockton	p. o. 216
South Thurston	p. o. 627
South Trenton	p. v. 467

	PAGE
South Troupsburgh	p. v. 628
South Valley	p. v. 537
South Valley	t. 195
Southville	p. o. 582
South Wales	p. v. 293
South Warsaw	p. o. 716
South Waterloo	v. 615, 618
South Westerlo	p. o. 167
Southwest Oswego	p. o. 526
South Williamsburgh	lo. 549
South Willsboro	p. o. 652
South Wilson	p. o. 457
South Worcester	p. v. 538
South Yonkers	p. o. 708
Spafford	p. v. 487
Spafford	t. 487
Spafford Hollow	p. o. 487
Spar Kil	568
Sparta	lo. 704
Sparta	p. o. 386
Sparta	t. 386
Sparrow Bush	p. o. 506
Speigletown	v. 557
Spencer	p. v. 652
Spencer	t. 649
Spencer	t. 652
Speedsville	p. v. 655
Spencerport	p. v. 400
Spencerville	lo. 166
Spencers Corners	lo. 273
Spencers Settlement	lo. 471
Spencertown	p. v. 243
Speonk	p. v. 638
Split Rock	295
Split Rock	cr. 186
Split Rock	lo. 485
Spooners Corners	p. o. 537
Spragues Corners	lo. 356
Sprain	r. 707
Sprakers Basin	p. o. 416
Spring	br. 260, 527
Spring	cr. 325
Springs	p. o. 635
Spring Brook	p. v. 290
Springfield	cr. 367, 368
Springfield	lo. 548
Springfield	p. o. 538
Springfield	t. 537
Springfield Center	p. v. 537
Spring Hill	lo. 546
Spring Mills	p. v. 174
Springport	t. 205
Springtown	lo. 665
Spring Valley	lo. 704
Springville	lo. 546
Springville	p. v. 289
Springwater	p. v. 386
Springwater	t. 386
Sprout	cr. 267, 271, 272
Sprout Brook	p. o. 412
Sprout Creek	p. o. 272
Spruce	cr. 348
Spruceville	lo. 263
Spuyten Duyvil	cr. 418, 707
Spuyten Duyvil	p. v. 708
Squaw	isle 279
Stillson Hollow	v. 184
Staatsburgh	p. o. 272
Staceys Basin	lo. 470
Stafford	p. v. 328
Stafford	t. 327
Stamford	p. v. 262, 265
Stamford	t. 264
Stamford Mill	r. 696, 705
Stanford	t. 277
Stanfordville	p. v. 277
Stanleys Corners	p. o. 498
Stanwix	p. v. 466
Stapleton	p. v. 506
Stark	t. 348
Starkey	p. v. 721
Starkey	t. 721
Starkey Corners	lo. 721
Starkville	p. v. 348
Starrs Hill	h. 467
State Bridge	lo. 255
State Bridge	p. v. 470
State Dam	lo. 590
State Line	lo. 215
Staten Island	563, 564
Staten Island Sound	563
State Road	p. o. 222
Steamburgh	lo. 611
Stedman	p. o. 213
Steels	cr. 261
Steena Kil	589
Stephens	cr. 623

	PAGE
Stephens Mills	p. o. 625
Stephensville	lo. 163
Stephentown	p. v. 560
Stephentown	t. 559
Stephentown Flats	v. 560
Sterling	cr. 340
Sterling	mts. 501, 510
Sterling	p. 510
Sterling	p. o. 205
Sterling	t. 205
Sterlingburgh	lo. 356
Sterlingbush	p. v. 376
Sterling Center	v. 205
Sterling Valley	v. 205
Sterlingville	p. v. 360
Sterling Works	lo. 510
Steuben	co. 101, 619
Steuben	cr. 467
Steuben	p. o. 467
Steuben	t. 467
Steuben Corners	v. 467
Stevens	br. 495
Stevensburgh	v. 644
Stevensville	p. o. 645
Stillwater	cr. 214
Stillwater	p. v. 593
Stillwater	t. 592
Stink	la. 317
Stissing	mt. 273
Stissing	p. 273
Stissingville	lo. 277
Stitsonville	lo. 535
Stittsville	p. v. 465, 468
Stockbridge	p. o. 393
Stockbridge	t. 393
Stockholm	p. o. 582
Stockholm	t. 582
Stockholm Depôt	p. o. 582
Stockport	p. v. 248
Stockport	t. 248
Stockport Springs	26
Stockport Station	p. o. 262
Stockton	p. o. 216
Stockton	t. 216
Stocktons	cr. 622, 627
Stockwell Settlement	v. 467
Stokes	p. o. 465
Stony	br. 569, 600, 637
Stony	cr. 314, 351, 355, 358, 376, 587, 683
Stone Arabia	p. v. 416
Stone Bridge	cr. 674
Stone Bridge	lo. 604
Stone Church	lo. 271
Stone Church	p. o. 325
Stone Mills	p. o. 360
Stone Ridge	h. 416
Stone Ridge	mt. 664
Stone Ridge	p. v. 664
Stony Brook	p. v. 633
Stony Brook Harbor	637
Stony Creek	p. 309
Stony Creek	t. 675
Stony Hills	h. 705
Stony Point	lo. 237, 569
Stormville	p. v. 271
Stottsville	v. 248
Stowells Corners	p. o. 358
Stows Square	lo. 378
Straights Corners	p. o. 653
Strattons Falls	p. o. 264
Strawberry	isle 279
Strykers Bay	lo. 419
Strykersville	p. v. 715
Strykersville	v. 604
Stuyvesant	p. o. 248
Stuyvesant	t. 248
Stuyvesant Falls	p. v. 248
Stuyvesant Landing	v. 248
Stuyvesant Square	lo. 423
Success	p. 544
Success	p. o. 639
Sufferns	p. v. 571
Suffolk	co. 631
Suffolk Station	p. o. 637
Sugar	cr. 168, 386
Sugar	r. 375, 377
Sugar Hill	p. o. 611
Sugar Loaf	mt. 505, 542
Sugar Loaf	p. v. 505
Sugar Town	cr. 191
Sugar Town	p. o. 191
Sullivan	co. 641
Sullivan	p. o. 394
Sullivan	t. 393
Sullivanville	p. v. 222
Summer Hill	la. 205

	PAGE
Summer Hill	p. v. 205
Summer Hill	t. 205
Summit	la. 537, 600, 679
Summit	p. v. 607
Summit	t. 607
Summitville	v. 646
Sunken Meadow	isle 419
Sunk Lot	lo. 542
Superior	la. 643
Suspension Bridge	p. o. 455
Susquehanna	r. 21, 23, 178, 223, 225, 257, 530, 538, 649, 651, 652.
Sutherlands	p. 505
Swains	p. 252
Swainsville	p. o. 174
Swamp	r. 267, 270, 273
Swarte Kil	587, 662, 664
Swartz	cr. 658
Swartoutville	lo. 272
Sweden	p. o. 405
Sweden	t. 405
Sweden Center	v. 405
Sweets	la. 376
Swezys Landing	lo. 633
Switz Kil	cr. 162
Syosset	p. o. 550
Syracuse City	488
Taberg	p. v. 461
Taghkanick	cr. 249
Taghkanick	mt. 241, 248, 267, 273, 552, 555, 557, 677, 686.
Taghkanick	p. o. 249
Taghkanick	t. 249
Talcotts Corners	v. 202
Talcotville	v. 377
Tamerack Swamp	679
Tannersville	p. o. 333
Tappan Bay	704
Tappantown	p. v. 570
Tappan Zee	700
Tarrytown	p. v. 700, 702
Taughanick	cr. 654, 658
Taughanick Falls	658
Taylor	mt. 19
Taylor	t. 254
Taylors	p. 236
Taylorville	p. v. 254, 500
Tekaharanea Falls	532
Telards	h. 707
Temple	h. 383
Ten Mile	cr. 165, 622, 641, 655, 656
Ten Mile	r. 267, 270, 273, 647
Teunis	la. 260
Texas	p. v. 522
Texas Valley	p. o. 253
The Battery	lo. 423
The Borough	lo. 559
The Branch	v. 637
The City	p. v. 270
The Corner	p. o. 667
The Cove	lo. 372
The Frontiers	lo. 237
The Glen	p. o. 675
The Gulf	238
The Highlands	mts. 501, 540, 542
The Hook	lo. 679
The Narrows	563
The Noses	h. 19, 416
The Park	lo. 423
Theresa	v. 361
Theresa	t. 361
The Square	p. o. 204
The Union	lo. 236
The Vlaie	lo. 393
The Vly	680
The Wells	lo. 271
Thiells Corner	v. 570
Third	cr. 688
Thomas	cr. 688
Thomasville	lo. 310
Thompson	t. 647
Thompsons	br. 636
Thompsons	la. 162
Thompsons	p. 273, 510
Thompsons Station	p. o. 637
Thompsonville	lo. 191
Thompsonville	p. v. 647
Thorn Hill	p. o. 485
Thorntons Corners	lo. 615
Thornville	lo. 273
Thousand Islands	577
Three Mile Bay	p. v. 359

	PAGE
Three Mile Harbor	ba. 634
Three Falls	lo. 576
Three River Point	p. v. 481
Three Sisters	isles 450
Throggs Neck	lo. 706
Throop	t. 206
Throopsville	p. v. 206
Thurston	p. o. 627
Thurston	t. 627
Thunder Hill	mt. 647
Tibbits	br. 696, 707
Tibbetts Point	122
Ticonderoga	p. v. 304
Ticonderoga	t. 304
Tiger	h. 507
Tildens	v. 248
Tin	br. 508
Tioga	co. 101, 649
Tioga	r. 21, 23. 619, 625, 626
Tioga	p. v. 653
Tioga	t. 652
Tioughnioga	cr. 253
Tioughnioga	r. 178, 182, 250, 388, 489
Tip Top Summit	lo. 169
Ti Street	v. 304
Titicus	r. 696, 703
Titusville	p. o. 312
Tivoli	p. v. 276
Tivoli Hollow	lo. 166
Toddsville	p. o. 536
Toddsville	p. v. 533
Tom	mt. 273
Tomhannock	cr. 554, 559
Tomhannock	p. v. 558
Tom Jones	mt. 507
Tompkins	co. 654
Tompkins	t. 542
Tompkins Corners	lo. 543
Tompkins Cove	lo. 569
Tompkins Cove	v. 570
Tompkins Square	lo. 423
Tompkinsville	p. v. 566
Toms Rocks	h. 504
Tonawanda	cr. 20, 22, 279, 282, 288, 320, 324, 450, 455, 456, 712, 714, 716.
Tonawanda	isle 279, 449
Tonawanda	p. v. 293, 457
Tonawanda	t. 293
Tonawanda Falls	324
Tonawanda Indian Reservation	324
Tonawanda Swamp	320, 450, 513
Tonetta	la. 543
Tongue	mt 295, 673
Toppin	mt. 19, 250, 254
Torn	mt. 507
Torrey	t. 721
Tottenville	v. 567
Towlesville	p. v. 626
Town	br. 264
Town Cliff	h. 533
Towners	p. o. 542
Towners Station	lo. 542
Town House Corners	lo. 166
Town Line	p. o. 292
Townly	cr. 658
Townsend	p. v. 611
Townsend Hill	h. 289
Townsendville	p. v. 616
Townsville	lo. 505
Tracy Creek	p. v. 184
Trammel	cr. 240
Transit	lo. 326
Transit Bridge	p. o. 171
Transparent	la. 349
Tree	isle 636
Trembleau Point	296, 300
Tremont	lo. 707
Trempers Kil	259
Trempers Kill	p. o. 259
Trenton	p. v. 467
Trenton	t. 467
Trenton Falls	347
Trenton Falls	p. v. 467
Triangle	p. v. 183
Triangle	t. 183
Tribes	h. 411
Tribes Hill	p. v. 412, 415
Troups	cr. 628
Troupsburgh	p. o. 628
Troupsburgh	t. 628
Troupsburgh Center	v. 628
Trout	br. 203, 252, 254, 499, 674
Trout	cr. 186, 250, 685

47

738 INDEX OF GEOGRAPHICAL NAMES.

PAGE

Trout ... la. 578, 673
Trout ... p. 645, 681
Trout ... r. 309, 310
Trout Creek ... p. o. 265
Trout River ... p. o. 310
Troy City ... 560
Trumansburg ... cr. 615
Trumansburgh ... p. v. 658
Trumansburg Landing p. o. 615
Trumbulls Corners ... p. v. 658
Truxton ... h. 250, 254, 255
Truxton ... p. v. 255
Truxton ... t. 255
Tsatsawassa ... cr. 557, 558
Tsatsawassa ... la. 557
Tubby Hook ... lo. 419
Tuckahoe ... h. 707
Tuckahoe ... p. o. 699, 708
Tug ... h. 374
Tug ... mt. 189
Tully ... la. 22
Tully ... p. v. 489
Tully ... t. 489
Tully Valley ... p. v. 489
Tuna ... p. o. 188
Tunegawant ... cr. 186, 188
Tunessassa ... cr. 186
Tunesassah ... cr. 186
Tuppers ... la. 22, 578
Turin ... p. v. 379
Turin ... t. 379
Turk ... h. 401
Turkey ... h. 704
Turkey ... mt. 541
Turkey Mountain ... lo. 708
Turkey Street ... lo. 469
Turners ... p. v. 507
Turtle Bay ... lo. 419
Tuscarora ... cr. 621, 629
Tuscarora ... p. v. 385
Tusten ... t. 647
Tuthill ... p. o. 663
Tuthilltown ... v. 663
Twelve Corners ... lo. 204
Twelve Mile ... cr. 451, 622
Twenty Mile ... cr. 208, 215
Two ... p. 507
Tylerville ... v. 361
Tyre ... p. o. 617
Tyre ... t. 617
Tyre City ... v. 617
Tyrone ... p. v. 612
Tyrone ... t. 612

Ulster ... co. 101, 660
Ulsterville ... p. o. 667
Ulysses ... t. 658
Unadilla ... p. v. 538
Unadilla ... r. 21, 23, 223, 225, 227, 228, 388, 458, 530, 532, 535, 536, 538
Unadilla ... t. 538
Unadilla Center ... p. v. 538
Unadilla Forks ... p. v. 537
Union ... p. v. 184
Union ... t. 183, 405
Union Center ... p. v. 184
Union Church ... p. o. 164
Union Corners ... lo. 245, 327, 383
Union Corners ... p. v. 386
Union Falls ... p. o. 236
Union Mills ... p. o. 317
Union Park ... lo. 423
Union Place ... lo. 546
Unionport ... lo. 706
Union Settlement ... p. o. 528
Union Society ... p. o. 335
Union Springs ... p. v. 205
Union Square ... p. o. 522
Union Vale ... t. 277
Union Valley ... p. v. 254
Union Village ... v. 683
Unionville ... lo. 164, 372, 548
Unionville ... p. v. 507
Unionville ... v. 400, 667, 702
Unitaria ... p. o. 181
Upper ... la. 647
Upper Aquebogue ... p. o. 637
Upper Chateaugay ... la. 238
Upper Cross Roads ... lo. 702
Upper Ebenezer ... v. 290
Upper Falls ... v. 304
Upper Hollow ... lo. 163
Upper Genesee Falls ... 402
Upper Green River ... lo. 243
Upper Lisle ... p. v. 183
Upper New Rochelle ... v. 703
Upper Redhook ... p. v. 276
Upper Saranac ... la. 22
Uptons ... p. 277
Urbana ... p. o. 628
Urbana ... t. 628
Utica City ... 468
Utsyanthia ... la. 257, 600, 605

Vails Mills ... p. v. 318
Valatie ... p. v. 247
Valatie Kil ... 557, 559
Valcour ... isle 239
Valcour ... p. o. 238
Valentines ... h. 707
Valley ... cr. 367, 368
Valley Falls ... p. o. 558
Valley Stream ... lo. 547
Valonia Springs ... p. o. 181
Van Aikens Mills ... v. 667
Van Buren ... p. o. 490
Van Buren ... t. 490
Van Buren Center ... p. v. 490
Van Campens ... cr. 168, 170
Van Cleese ... isle 703
Vandemark ... cr. 168
Van Etten ... t. 222
Van Ettenville ... p. v. 222
Van Hornesville ... p. v. 348
Van Leuvens Corners ... lo. 167
Van Schaicks ... isle 166
Vansville ... v. 204
Varick ... p. o. 618
Varick ... t. 617
Varna ... p. v. 656
Varysburgh ... p. v. 715
Vaugans Corners ... v. 685
Venice ... p. v. 206
Venice ... t. 206
Venice Center ... p. o. 206
Verbank ... p. v. 277
Verdrieteges Hook ... h. 568
Verf Kil ... 597
Verona ... p. v. 470
Verona ... t. 470
Verona Depot ... p. o. 470
Verona Mills ... p. v. 470
Verplanck ... p. o. 699
Verplancks Point ... lo. 569
Verplancks Point ... v. 699
Vermillion ... p. v. 526
Vermont ... p. o. 213
Vermontville ... p. v. 311
Vernal ... lo. 712
Vernon ... p. v. 469
Vernon ... t. 469
Vernon Center ... p. v. 469
Vernon Valley ... p. v. 636
Vernooy ... cr. 666
Versailles ... p. v. 194
Vesper ... p. v. 489
Vestal ... p. v. 184
Vestal ... t. 184
Vestal Center ... p. v. 184
Veteran ... p. o. 267
Veteran ... t. 222
Victor ... p. v. 499
Victor ... t. 499
Victory ... p. v. 206
Victory ... t. 206
Victory Mills ... p. v. 591
Vienna ... p. v. 470
Vienna ... t. 470
Vierdee Kil ... 559
Villenova ... p. o. 216
Villenova ... t. 216
Vinegar ... h. 542
Virgil ... cr. 255
Virgil ... p. v. 255
Virgil ... t. 255
Vista ... p. o. 701
Visschers Ferry ... p. o. 587
Vlamans Kil ... 163
Vlamans ... br. 164
Vlomans ... cr. 155
Vlokie Kil ... 559
Vly ... cr. 680
Voak ... p. o. 720
Volney ... p. o. 528
Volney ... t. 528
Volney Corners ... v. 528
Volusia ... p. o. 216
Voorheesville ... v. 413

Waccaback ... la. 701
Waddington ... p. v. 579
Wadhams Mills ... p. v. 305
Wading ... r. 637
Wading River ... p. v. 637
Wainscott ... lo. 635
Waits Corners ... lo. 215
Wakefield ... lo. 706
Walden ... p. v. 508
Waldenville ... p. o. 608
Wales ... p. v. 293
Wales ... t. 293
Wales Center ... p. v. 293
Walesville ... p. o. 471
Wallabout ... lo. 367
Wallabout Bay ... 365, 367
Wallace ... p. o. 622
Wall Kil ... 501, 506, 508, 660, 662, 665
Wallkill ... t. 510
Walloomsac ... r. 555
Walloomsac ... v. 556
Walmore ... p. v. 457
Walnut ... cr. 208, 210, 213
Walnut ... h. 641
Walnut Hill ... mt. 19, 645
Walton ... p. v. 265
Walton ... t. 265
Walworth ... p. v. 694
Walworth ... t. 694
Wampus ... p. 702, 703
Wampecack ... cr. 679
Wampmissic ... lo. 634
Wampsville ... p. v. 392
Wappingers ... cr. 23, 267, 271, 272, 274
Wappingers Falls ... p. v. 272
Ward ... t. 175
Wardboro ... p. o. 674
Wards ... isle 418, 419, 548
Wardville ... lo. 325
Wardwell ... p. o. 358
Warners Station ... v. 490
Warnerville ... p. v. 606
Warren ... co. 670
Warren ... p. o. 349
Warren ... t. 349
Warren ... v. 569
Warrensbush ... lo. 409
Warsaw ... p. v. 715
Warsaw ... t. 715
Warwick ... mts. 501, 510
Warwick ... p. v. 510
Warwick ... t. 510
Washington ... co. 101, 104, 677
Washington ... p. 645
Washington ... p. o. 278
Washington ... t. 277
Washington Heights ... p. o. 419
Washington Hollow ... p. v. 274, 278
Washington Mills ... p. v. 465
Washington Park ... lo. 369
Washington Square ... lo. 423, 547
Washingtonville ... lo. 701
Washingtonville ... v. 504, 527, 699
Wassaic ... p. v. 270
Wassaic ... cr. 269
Waterburgh ... v. 658
Waterford ... p. v. 593
Waterford ... t. 593
Waterloo ... p. v. 618
Waterloo ... t. 618
Waterloo Mills ... p. o. 507
Watermelon ... h. 541
Watermill ... lo. 638
Waterport ... p. o. 514
Watertown ... p. v. 362
Watertown ... t. 362
Watertown Center ... lo. 362
Watervale ... p. v. 486
Water Valley ... p. v. 291
Waterville ... p. v. 467
Watervliet ... t. 165
Watervliet Center ... p. o. 166, 597
Watkins ... p. v. 611
Watson ... p. o. 379
Watson ... t. 379
Watsonville ... v. 605
Watts ... h. 541
Waverly ... lo. 634
Waverly ... p. v. 650
Waverly ... v. 194, 699
Wawarsing ... p. v. 668
Wawarsing ... t. 667
Wawayanda ... cr. 501
Wawayanda ... t. 511
Wayland Depot ... p. o. 628
Wayne Four Corners ... p. o. 629
Wayland ... t. 628
Wayland ... v. 628
Wayne ... co. 101, 104, 688
Wayne ... p. v. 629
Wayne ... t. 629
Wayne Center ... v. 693
Weaver Hollow ... lo. 245
Weavers ... la. 349
Webbs Mills ... p. o. 222
Webster ... mt. 559
Webster ... p. v. 405
Webster ... t. 405
Weedsport ... p. v. 201
Wegatchie ... p. o. 582
Wellington ... mt. 537
Wells ... isle 355, 359
Wells ... p. 645
Wells ... p. o. 339
Wells ... t. 339
Wellsburgh ... p. v. 222
Wells Corners ... p. o. 511
Wellsville ... p. v. 176
Wellsville ... t. 175
Weltonville ... p. o. 651
Wende ... lo. 282
Werners ... la. 162
Wethersfield ... p. o. 716
West ... br. 265, 270, 536
West ... mt. 569
West ... r. 720
West Addison ... p. o. 627
West Albany ... lo. 166
West Amboy ... p. v. 520
West Almond ... p. v. 176
West Almond ... t. 176
West Bainbridge ... p. o. 225
West Bangor ... p. v. 308
West Barre ... p. o. 514
West Bergen ... p. o. 325
West Berlin ... p. o. 554
West Bethany Mills ... p. o. 325
West Bloomfield ... p. v. 499
West Bloomfield ... t. 499
West Branch ... p. v. 465
West Brighton ... p. v. 398
West Brook ... p. o. 265
West Brookville ... p. o. 646
West Burlington ... p. o. 532
Westbury ... lo. 550
Westbury ... p. v. 206, 690
West Bush ... p. o. 317
West Butler ... p. o. 690
West Cameron ... p. v. 623
West Camp ... p. v. 667
West Canada ... cr. 340, 343, 347, 463, 466
West Camden ... p. v. 463
West Carlton ... p. o. 514
West Carthage ... v. 357
West Cayuta ... p. o. 610
West Charlton ... p. v. 587
West Chazy ... p. v. 237
Westchester ... co. 101, 696
Westchester ... p. v. 706
Westchester ... r. 706
Westchester ... t. 706
West Chester ... v. 505
West Clarkson ... v. 399
West Clarksville ... p. o. 173
West Colesville ... p. o. 181
West Constable ... p. o. 312
West Conesville ... p. o. 604
West Danby ... p. o. 656
West Davenport ... p. v. 260
West Day ... p. o. 588
West Dayton ... v. 189
West Dresden ... p. v. 721
West Dryden ... p. v. 656
West Eaton ... p. v. 391
West Edmeston ... p. v. 533
Westerlo ... t. 166
Westerlo ... p. o. 167
Western ... t. 470
Westernville ... p. v. 470
West Exeter ... p. v. 533
West Falls ... p. v. 283
West Farmington ... p. o. 496
West Farms ... p. v. 706
West Farms ... t. 706
West Fayette ... p. o. 615
Westfield ... p. v. 216
Westfield ... t. 567, 216
Westfield Flats ... v. 647
West Fish ... la. 317
West Flushing ... lo. 549

	PAGE
Westford	p. v. 538
Westford	t. 538
West Fort Ann	p. o. 681
West Fowler	p. o. 577
West Fulton	p. v. 605
West Gaines	p. o. 514
West Galway	p. v. 588
West Gates	lo. 399
West Ghent	p. v. 245
West Gilboa	p. o. 605
West Glens Falls	v. 675
West Greece	p. v. 399
West Greenfield	p. o. 589
West Greenwood	p. o. 625
West Groton	p. o. 657
West Hadley	p. o. 589
West Hebron	p. v. 684
West Henrietta	p. v. 399
West Hills	p. o. 636
West Hoosick	p. o. 556
West Hurley	p. o. 663
West Jasper	p. o. 626
West Junius	p. o. 615
West Kendal	p. o. 515
West Kil	334, 600, 607
West Kill	p. v. 334
West Laurens	p. v. 534
West Lexington	p. o. 333
West Leyden	p. v. 377
West Lowville	p. o. 378
West Martinsburgh	p. v. 378
West Meredith	p. o. 263
West Middlebury	p. v. 263
West Milton	p. v. 590
West Monroe	p. o. 528
West Monroe	t. 528
Westmoreland	p. o. 471
Westmoreland	t. 471
West Moriches	lo. 634
West Morrisania	lo. 702
West Mount Vernon	v. 699
West Nassau	v. 557
West Newark	p. o. 651
West Neck Harbor	ba. 637
West New Rochelle	v. 703
West Niles	lo. 204
Weston	p. v. 612
West Oneonta	p. v. 535
West Onondaga	p. o. 485
West Perry	lo. 715
West Plattsburgh	p. o. 239
West Point	p. o. 505
Westport	p. v. 305
Westport	t. 305
West Potsdam	p. o. 582
West Providence	p. o. 591
West Red	cr. 688, 692
West Richford	p. o. 652
West Richmondville	p. o. 606
West Rome	lo. 466
West Rush	p. v. 405
West Sand Lake	p. v. 558
West Sauquoit	v. 466
West Schuyler	p. v. 348
West Seneca	p. o. 293
West Seneca	t. 293
West Seneca Center	p. o. 293
West Shandaken	p. o. 663
West Shelby	p. o. 516
West Somers	p. o. 706
West Somerset	p. o. 456
West Southold	p. o. 640
West Sparta	t. 386

	PAGE
West Stephentown	p. o. 560
West Stockholm	p. o. 582
West Stony Creek	cr. 675
West Suffolk	p. o. 637
West Sweden	v. 405
West Taghkanick	p. v. 470
West Theresa	p. o. 361
West Town	p. v. 507
West Township	p. o. 164
West Troupsburgh	p. o. 628
West Trout	br. 260
West Troy	p. v. 165
West Turin	t. 379
West Union	p. o. 629
West Vienna	p. v. 470
West View	p. v. 386
Westville	p. v. 538
Westville	t. 312
Westville	v. 312
West Walworth	p. o. 694
West Webster	p. v. 405
West Windsor	p. v. 349
West Winfield	p. v. 349
Westwood	p. o. 283
West Yorkshire	p. v. 195
Wethersfield	t. 716
Wethersfield Springs	p. v. 716
Whaleys	p. 273
Whallonsburgh	p. v. 301
Wharton	cr. 530, 532, 533
Wheatfield	t. 456
Wheatland	p. o. 406
Wheatland	t. 405
Wheatland Center	v. 406
Wheatville	p. v. 324
Wheeler	cr. 201
Wheeler	p. o. 629
Wheeler	t. 629
Wheeler Center	v. 629
Wheeler Corners	lo. 522
Whetstone	cr. 375, 378
Whetstone Gulf	lo. 378
White	cr. 168, 347, 381, 555, 685
White	la. 466
White	p. 541
White	r. 643
White Clay Kil	276
White Creek	p. o. 686
White Creek	t. 686
White Face	mt. 19, 296, 306
Whitehall	p. v. 686
Whitehall	t. 686
Whitehall Landing	419
White Lake	p. o. 643
White Plains	p. v. 707
White Plains	t. 707
Whiteport	v. 666
Whitesburgh	p. o. 348
Whitesborough	v. 471
Whites Corners	p. v. 291
Whiteside	br. 679
Whiteside Corners	p. o. 589
Whitestone	p. v. 546
White Store	p. o. 228
Whitestown	p. o. 471
Whitestown	t. 471
White Sulphur Spring	593
Whitesville	p. v. 174
Whitesville	v. 361
Whitings	p. 241, 243
Whitlockville	lo. 698
Whitney	h. 559

	PAGE
Whitneys Crossing	p. o. 172
Whitneys Landing	lo. 616
Whitneys Point	p. v. 183
Whitney Valley	cr. 168, 169
Whortleberry	isle 70, 703
Wiccopee Pass	lo. 271
Wickhams	p. 510
Wickopee	p. 543
Wigwam	cr. 168, 170
Wilbur	p. v. 664
Wildehause Kil	164
Wilkins Point	lo. 546
Willards	mt. 677
Willett	p. o. 256
Willett	t. 255
Williams Bridge	p. o. 707
Williamsburgh	p. o. 367
Williamsburgh	v. 165
Williamson	p. v. 694
Williamson	t. 694
Williamstown	p. v. 528
Williamstown	t. 528
Williamsville	lo. 714
Williamsville	p. v. 282
Willing	t. 176
Willink	p. v. 283
Willow	br. 165
Willow	isle 334
Willow Tree	lo. 548
Willow Vale	v. 465
Willsboro	p. o. 652
Willsborough	p. o. 305
Willsborough	t. 305
Willsborough Falls	v. 305
Willseyville	p. v. 651
Willwemack	cr. 647
Wilmington	p. v. 306
Wilmington	t. 305
Wilmurt	t. 349
Wilna	p. o. 363
Wilna	t. 362
Wilson	p. v. 457
Wilson	t. 457
Wilson Creek	p. o. 650
Wilton	lo. 702
Wilton	p. v. 593
Wilton	t. 593
Winantsville	lo. 549
Windfall	cr. 173, 188
Windham	t. 334
Windham Center	p. v. 335
Windsor	p. v. 184
Windsor	t. 184
Wine	cr. 528
Winfield	cr. 624
Winfield	lo. 549
Winfield	p. o. 349
Winfield	t. 349
Wing Station	p. o. 271
Winspear	p. o. 292
Wirt	p. o. 176
Wirt	t. 176
Wiscoy	cr. 710, 174, 713, 714, 715, 716
Wiscoy	p. o. 174
Wolcott	cr. 688, 690
Wolcott	p. v. 695
Wolcott	t. 694
Wolf	cr. 166, 168, 712
Wolf	p. 647
Wolf Run	cr. 623
Wood	cr. 21, 23, 458, 466, 470, 678, 686

	PAGE
Woodbury	p. o. 551
Woodbury Clove	v. 508
Woodcock	h. 504
Woodhaven	v. 548
Woodhull	la. 349
Woodhull	p. o. 629
Woodhull	t. 629
Woodland	p. o. 567
Woodrow	v. 567
Wood Settlement	lo. 363
Woodstock	lo. 702
Woodstock	p. v. 668
Woodstock	t. 668
Woodville	lo. 387
Woodville	p. v. 357
Woodsville	lo. 507
Woodwards Hollow	p. o. 289
Woodworth	la. 316
Worcester	p. v. 538
Worcester	t. 538
Wortel Kil	271
Worth	t. 363
Worthville	p. o. 363
Wright	t. 608
Wrights	cr. 186
Wrights Corners	p. o. 454
Wrightsville	lo. 237
Wurtzboro	p. v. 646
Wyomanock	cr. 248
Wyoming	co. 101, 710
Wyoming	p. v. 714
Wynants Kil	557, 558, 560
Wynantskill	p. v. 557
Wyncoop	br. 641
Wynkoops	cr. 219, 220, 221, 222
Yankee	p. 646
Yaphank	p. v. 634
Yates	co. 717
Yates	p. o. 516
Yates	t. 516
Yates Center	v. 516
Yatesville	lo. 416
Yatesville	p. o. 720
Yellow	la. 579
Yonkers	p. v. 708
Yonkers	t. 707
York	p. 645
York	p. o. 387
York	t. 387
York Center	v. 387
York Corners	lo. 588
Yorkshire	p. o. 195
Yorkshire	t. 195
Yorkshire	v. 182
Yorkshire Center	p. v. 195
Yorkshire Corners	v. 195
Yorkshire Creek	cr. 182
Yorktown	p. o. 708
Yorktown	t. 708
Yorkville	lo. 419
Yorkville	v. 471
Young Hickory	p. o. 628
Youngs	la. 349
Youngs Cave	lo. 604
Youngstown	p. v. 456
Youngsville	p. v. 644
Zantzee Kil	597
Zeregors Point	lo. 706
Zimmerman	cr. 318, 416
Zoar	v. 361

ADDITIONAL NAMES.

Ambler	lo. 228	Fairmount	v. 707	Moharsic	la. 708
Boscobel	p. o. 699	Integrity	lo. 706	Thirty Deer Ridge	h. 707
Cortlandville	v. 699	Kreischerville	p. v. 567	Waddington	t. 579, 583

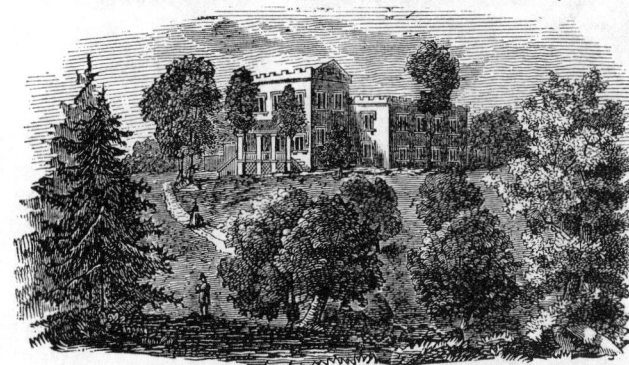
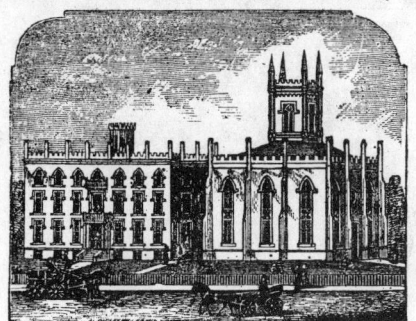
741

TROY FEMALE SEMINARY.

This Institution offers the accumulated advantages of nearly fifty years of successful operation. Every facility is provided for a thorough course of useful and ornamental education, under the direction of a corps of more than twenty professors and teachers. The members of the Institution have the benefit of Lectures of the highest order, on

SCIENCE, HISTORY, LITERATURE, ART, &C. &C.,

And the use of a valuable Library, an extensive Philosophical Apparatus, a well selected Cabinet of Minerals, and Shells, Maps, Charts, and Models.

Superior Music Teachers are constantly employed in the Seminary. Great Attention is given to the French Language.

The teachers reside in the family, and adapt their instructions to its use in conversation.

THE CLASSES IN DRAWING AND PAINTING, IN OIL AND WATER COLORS,

Are under the direction of instructors of long experience and tried ability. A large and choice collection of Pictures is constantly before them for study and for patterns.

The pupils are received into the family of the principals, in which every arrangement is made for their physical education and the improvement of their manners and morals. They occupy private rooms, two in each, the rooms of the female teachers and that of an experienced nurse being among those of the young ladies.

Circulars containing more particular information may be obtained by application to the principals,

Mr. or Mrs. JOHN H. WILLARD, Troy, N. Y.

FORT EDWARD INSTITUTE.
AT FORT EDWARD, WASHINGTON CO., N. Y., ON THE RAILROAD.
REV. JOSEPH E. KING, A.M., PRINCIPAL.

This Institution was opened December, 1854, since which time the Regents' Annual Reports show it to have been the

BEST SUSTAINED BOARDING SEMINARY IN THE STATE.

Nearly every county in the State, and two-thirds of the States of the Union, have been its patrons. The following are some of the grounds of its claim to the popular favor:—

Its substantial brick buildings, well guarded against fire, and which, by the central position of its common Dining Hall, Chapel, and an ample suit of class rooms, accessible respectively to the two separate departments by distinct entrances, are most admirably adapted to the safe and successful co-education of ladies and gentlemen, the two departments being at all hours absolutely under the control of the Faculty. Also its noble Library and Apparatus.

ITS LIBERAL PROVISION FOR THE ABLEST INSTRUCTION

In each branch and department of study; three professors and teachers being devoted *exclusively* to the common English studies, two each to the Mathematics and Classics, one respectively to Commercial Instruction, to Natural Science, to Modern Languages, and to Painting. while no less than four have in charge the department of Music. Rare facilities are thus afforded to prepare for *teaching*; while desirable situations are procured for young ladies who graduate in the prescribed Course of Studies.

It is a part of the well established system of this Christian Institute, to conserve and promote the health, manners, and morals of its pupils. The Principal wishes it distinctly understood that he becomes personally responsible to parents for the moral and social well being of their daughters while in attendance at this Institute.

It provides good, spacious rooms, plainly but suitably furnished; and wholesome and sufficient Board, of a quality and variety satisfactory to its patrons.

ITS REMARKABLY MODERATE RATES.

To many families the difference in the cost of maintaining a son or daughter at home or at this Institute, would be scarcely appreciable. One hundred and three dollars per year, pays for Board, furnished room, fuel, washing and tuition in common English. Extra branches at corresponding rates. A student may enter for a single term, or at any time in the term and pay for the residue only.

There are three terms of fourteen weeks each. Winter Term opens December 1st, 1859; Spring Term opens March 23d, 1860; Fall Term opens August 16th, 1860. For circulars, or for rooms, apply to the Principal.

Turn to the chapter in the Gazetteer descriptive of Fort Edward, also to chapter of statistics of Academies, and notice the Washington Co. Seminary.

TESTIMONIALS OF EXAMINING COMMITTEES.

Rev. Wm. Scott, of Montreal, Secretary, 1855. The Committee found the buildings, in their construction and specific arrangements, better adapted to their purpose than any other ever visited by them.

Rev. S. Washburn, of Troy, Secretary, November, 1856. We were highly gratified with the good order and decorum apparent in every department of the Institute.

Rev. M. Bates, of Schenectady, Secretary, March, 1857. There is, we think, no Institution, not wholly devoted to this object, where equal facilities are afforded for acquiring, at trifling expense, a thorough business education.

Prof. John Newman, A.M., of Union College, Secretary, Nov. 18, 1857. The Committee have found the most satisfactory evidence in its able Board of Instruction and Government, its skilful financial management, as well as in the extent and sterling character of its patronage, that the *Fort Edward Institute* is a *signal success*.

While the Institution is in all departments worthy of entire confidence, the Committee feel called upon to mention the department of Music and that of Painting, as decidedly superior to any thing we have ever heard or seen in any similar Institution.

Rev. J. K. Cheesman, of Schenectady, Secretary, July, 1857.

The *gastronomic department*, under the care of Mr. A. K. Haxtun, the Steward, is finely managed. An abundant supply of well cooked food is provided.

Rev. R. H. Robinson, Secretary, Saratoga Springs, Nov. 25, 1858. The peculiar energy of the Principal pervades every department of instruction, embracing eighteen teachers, a number sufficient to permit a subdivision of classes, so that none need be neglected. Many students have consecrated their young hearts on the altar of Christianity, and will go forth with great *power*, rightly directed, to bless the church and the world.

Prof. C. T. Lewis, A.M., Troy University, March, 1859. The practical drill was admirable. Attention had been given to the powers of ready and neat expression, but the basis lay in a clear comprehension of facts and principles, for which good language was made an ornament, not a substitute. Perhaps no feature of the exercises was more charming than their entire fairness, which was at once transparent and unobtrusive.

Rev. B. Hawley, A.M., Chairman, West Troy, June 23, 1859. In the circle of our large Academies, furnishing the highest advantages at the lowest charges, I know of no one sustaining a better reputation than Fort Edward Institute.   9 *

MOUNT PLEASANT ACADEMY;

A SELECT

Military Boarding School for Boys,

AT SING-SING,

WESTCHESTER COUNTY, NEW YORK.

ASSOCIATE PRINCIPALS.

C. F. MAURICE, A.M.,
Instructor in Ethics, Mental Philosophy, &c.

MAJ. W. W. BENJAMIN,
Instructor in Mathematics and Military Tactics.

Z. M. PHELPS, A.M.,
Instructor in Ancient Languages.

INSTRUCTORS.

H. AYMÈ, M.D.,
Instructor in French, Spanish, and Drawing.

W. MULLER,
Instructor in German and Music.

H. M. WALLACE, A.B.,
Instructor in Historical Studies and Elocution.

CHS. STOCKING,
Instructor in Gymnastics.

R. W. MOORE,
Instructor in Elementary Studies.

J. HYATT,
Lecturer in Chemistry and Philosophy.

This institution, in its plan and arrangements, has regard to the physical as well as the moral and intellectual training of its members.

THE COURSE OF INSTRUCTION

Is liberal and thorough, such as experience has proved to be most effectual for this purpose. By it, students are prepared for any class in college, for the scientific schools, or for commercial life. The

ANCIENT LANGUAGES

are taught critically and with a view to sound scholarship and not to mere superficial acquaintance. The

MATHEMATICAL COURSE

is extensive. The preparation of pupils who have passed through it, and their success elsewhere, gives the best evidence of faithfulness and skill in this very essential department of instruction. Very many are the unsolicited testimonials received on this point. Special attention is given to the

MODERN LANGUAGES:

French, Spanish, and German form an important part of the course of study, and are taught as spoken languages by well qualified masters. The

ENGLISH LANGUAGE,

also, in its elements, as well as in its higher departments, receives more than ordinary notice, and is not made subordinate to any other study.

MORAL AND RELIGIOUS TRAINING

is carefully regarded, as in every well ordered household; but no interference is attempted with the peculiar tenets of any faith. Seats are provided for the pupils in both the Episcopal and Presbyterian Churches.

PHYSICAL EDUCATION.

The complete arrangements made for this generally neglected object, and the success that has attended them, deserve to be specially noticed. Under their influence, we have seen the delicate and almost puny

boy become the robust and enduring youth, able to sustain continued application and to perform in after life an amount of intellectual labor that only a sound and vigorous development could make possible. In connection with the

GYMNASIUM AND THE RIDING SCHOOL

ARE THE

MILITARY EXERCISES,

The infantry and artillery drills; and, while these receive a minuteness of attention not often given to them, and are so used as to produce physically a permanent effect, they have no tendency to create a desire, as experience has shown, for a military life. The system, as here arranged, has been chosen for the great benefits that result from it. But, although a military school, the institution, it must be distinctly understood, is not for the training of those who are vicious or unmanageable under any other system. Should any of this class, by accident or misrepresentation, ever be received, they will, on the manifestation of such character, be at once returned to their parents. The feelings of the principals, not less than their intimate relations with their pupils, look to other associations and other results. Confidence, patience, and kindness on their part, truthfulness, honor, and generous sentiment on the pupil's, are the basis and the bond of union between them. No boy who is insensible to considerations of this kind is desired in the school, nor can he long remain connected with it.

Pupils are received whenever a vacancy occurs; but, as the number is limited and places are usually filled in advance, applications, to prevent disappointment, should be made as early as possible.

Further information may be obtained from the gentlemen named as references, or by addressing the principals.

REFERENCES.

The Faculties of Williams College,
Harvard College,
Yale College,
Columbia College,
Union College,
N. Y. University,
College of New Jersey,
Military Academy, West Point,
and also to the following gentlemen :—

Hon. A. Bruyn Hasbrouck, LL.D., late President Rutgers College, New York City,
Rev. R. W. Dickinson, D.D., New York City,
Samuel Jaudon, Esq., New York City,
S. C. Paxon, Esq., New York City,
George Barrell, Esq., New York City,
Willard Parker, M.D., New York City,
B. R. Winthrop, Esq., New York City,
Doct. E. E. Marcy, New York City,
Rev. John Krebbs, D.D., New York City,
Francis Skiddy, Esq., New York City,
Henry Leverich, Esq., New York City,
Charles Day, Esq., New York City,
Chas. Rockwell, Esq., New York City,
Joseph Bento, Esq., New York City,
D. N. Barney, Esq., New York City,
Rev. J. P. Thompson, D.D., New York City,
McKilop & Wood, Com. Agency, New York City,
John H. Brower, Esq., Brooklyn, L. I.,
H. K. Corning, Esq., Brooklyn, L. I.,
George S. Puffer, Esq., Brooklyn, L. I.,
John Schenck, Esq., Brooklyn, L. I.,
Rev. R. S. Storrs, D.D., Brooklyn, L. I.,
Doct. W. Swift, U.S.N., Brooklyn, L. I.,
Doct. McLellan, Brooklyn, L. I.,
Hon. Aaron Ward, Sing-Sing,
Rev. Wilson Phraner, Sing-Sing,
Thomas Small, Esq., Sing-Sing,
Maj. E. Backus, U.S.A., Governors Island,
Charles L. Schlater, Esq., Ogdensburgh, N. Y.,
Capt. James McIntosh, U.S.N., Sackets Harbor,

Hon. D. B. St. John, Albany,
O. Bronson, M.D., Hudson,
Marcus L. Ward, Esq., Newark,
Cortlandt Parker, Esq., Newark,
Prof. John S. Hart, LL.D., late Principal of High School, Philadelphia, Pa.,
Jacob Sharp, Esq., Philadelphia, Pa.,
Rodolphus Kent, Esq., Philadelphia, Pa.,
Prof. J. Henry, LL.D., Smithsonian Institution, Washington.
Brig. G. S. Churchill, U.S.A., Washington,
Thomas Higham, Jr., Esq., Charleston, S. C.,
J. Izard Pringle, Esq., Georgetown, D. C.,
W. Blake, Esq., Combahee, S. C.,
George Gordon, Esq., Savannah, Ga.,
Henry Roser, Esq., Savannah, Ga.,
G. W. Ludlum, Esq., Rondout,
Col. W. J. Hardee, U.S.A., West Point.
G. T. Hodges, Esq., Rutland, Vt.,
Col. Thomas Williams, Detroit, Mich.,
Wm. Neyle Habersham, Esq., Savannah, Ga.,
Francis Sorrell, Esq., Savannah, Ga.,
J. Clay King, Esq., Waynesville,
J. Emmanuel, Esq., Mobile, Ala.,
R. G. Mays, M.D., Orange Mills, F.A.,
Hon. Thomas Slidell, New Orleans, La.,
J. W. Zacharie, Esq., New Orleans, La.,
Mrs. Clifford Neff, Cincinnati, O.,
R. A. Clay, Esq., Cincinnati, O.,
H. Emerson, Esq., South Reading, Mass.,
Rev. A. Woods, D.D., Providence, R. I.,
P. Hall, Esq., Providence, R. I.,
Edward Pearce, Esq., Providence, R. I.,
Hon. W. C. Gibbs, Newport, R. I.,
Calvin Williams, Esq., Stonington, Conn.,
Giles F. Ward, Esq., Saybrook, Conn.,
Hon. P. D. Vroom, Trenton, N. J.,
Com. Thomas A. Conover, U.S.N., Princeton, N. J.,
Com. Lawrence Kearney, U.S.N., Perth Amboy,
Rev. David Magie, D.D., Elizabethtown.

GARDEN FRONT, LIVINGSTON STREET.

PACKER COLLEGIATE INSTITUTE,

BROOKLYN HEIGHTS, L. I.

This Institution claims to give to females all the advantages for thorough and complete education that are enjoyed by the other sex in our best appointed Colleges.

It is liberally endowed, and is under the patronage of the State.

Its location, in the city of Brooklyn, opposite New York, enables it to command all the educational resources of the metropolis; while no country village is more quiet, beautiful, or healthy.

THE COURSE OF INSTRUCTION

Is under the direction of A. Crittenden, A.M., who has devoted his whole life to female education. He is assisted by twenty-four professors and teachers ; and the course of instruction embraces the modern languages, with Latin, the various branches of Literature, History, Mathematics, Chemistry, Natural, Moral, and Intellectual Philosophy, Music, Drawing, Painting, &c. &c.

THE LABORATORY

Is a model of its kind, and furnished with every necessary article of apparatus.

THE OBSERVATORY

Has an excellent achromatic telescope of six inches object glass. It is equatorially mounted, moved by clockwork, &c.

THE CABINETS

Are amply provided with minerals, shells, &c.   One or two articles of apparatus particularly arrest the attention of the observer,—one of Ross's Compound Microscopes, which magnifies 1800 diameters, also Barlow's large Planetarium, eleven feet in diameter.

The accommodations for pupils from abroad are intended to afford all the comforts of home, and to secure for them social, intellectual, and moral culture.

PACKER COLLEGIATE INSTITUTE, BROOKLYN.

A. CRITTENDEN, A.M., PRINCIPAL.

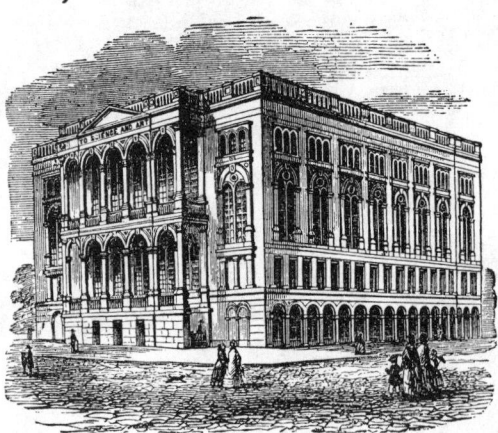
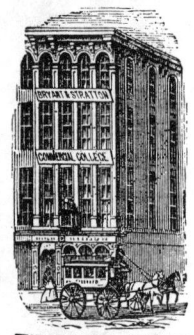

748

Board and Tuition,
Per Year, $120.

COOPERSTOWN SEMINARY AND FEMALE COLLEGIATE INSTITUTE,

(Male and Female.)

Cooperstown, Otsego County, New York.

R. C. FLACK,
Principal and Proprietor

Length of building, 137 feet. Play grounds, 25 acres.
Width of   do.   77 feet. Gymnasium covers 1,900 feet.
The building and grounds cost $75,000.

POUGHKEEPSIE COLLEGIATE SCHOOL.

A BOARDING SCHOOL FOR BOYS OF ALL AGES.

This school was established in 1836. From that time to this there has been but one change in the principalship,—which occurred after the death of the late principal, Charles Bartlett. It has always enjoyed a liberal patronage, drawn from all sections. During the past year pupils have been in attendance from twelve States.

The students prepare their lessons in one large room, where one of the Principals presides.

FRENCH, SPANISH, AND GERMAN

Are each taught by a native teacher.

The principals and their families, the teachers and pupils, all reside in one building and eat at the same table. The pupils are not allowed to leave the premises without permission. The building is lighted with gas, and heated with hot air furnaces. No expense has been spared to attain thorough ventilation. The pupils' rooms are furnished with a carpet, clothes-press, single beds, wash-stand with bowl and pitcher to each pupil.

In short, no effort has been omitted to make this in every respect

A FIRST CLASS SCHOOL.

The annual expense is two hundred and fifty dollars. Spanish and German, Music and Drawing, are the only extras.

We refer to the following gentlemen, most of whom have been patrons of the school :—

Rev. S. H. Weston, Hudson St., New York,
Hon. Gulian C. Verplanck, New York,
Hon. James Emott, Poughkeepsie,
Isaac Roosevelt, M.D., Poughkeepsie,
Prof. Charles Murray Nairne, Columbia College, N. Y.,
Prof. John Foster, Union College, Schenectady,
Prof. Wm. H. Crosby, Poughkeepsie,
O. R. Willis, Freehold, N. J.,
Prof. John Haywood, Westerville, Ohio,
Rev. H. G. Ludlow, Oswego,
Rev. A. D. Traver, Poughkeepsie,
Rev. S. Buel, Poughkeepsie,
J. H. Griscom, M.D., New York,
F. S. Macias, 46 Beaver St., New York,

David F. Hoadly, Office Panama R. R., Wall St., New York,
Hon. John Thompson, Poughkeepsie, N. Y.,
Solomon Jenner, 75 Henry St., N. Y.,
David D. Otis, Watertown, N. Y.,
Thomas R. Smiley, Hamilton, Ohio,
R. C. Crocheron, 1 Park Place, New York,
Col. G. T. M. Davis, 47 Exchange Place, New York,
Hon. E. S. Doughty, Somerville, N. J.,
Capt. James L. Day, Norwich, Conn.,
Joseph A. Eddy, St. Louis, Mo.,
H. H. Hathorn, Saratoga Springs, N. Y.,
Seth Richards, Bentonsport, Iowa,
J. M. Sims, M.D., New York.

Those who may desire further information are invited to visit the school or to address the Principals,

C. B. WARRING, A.M., } Principals.
OTIS BISBEE, A.M., }

YOUNG LADIES' INSTITUTE,

AT TEMPLE GROVE, SARATOGA SPRINGS, N. Y.

REV. L. F. BEECHER, D.D., PRINCIPAL.

Open forty weeks, from the second Monday in September of each year. Every department supplied with experienced teachers. Music taught, singly and in classes, by competent professors, on a new and highly approved plan, by means of which a

MUSICAL EDUCATION

Of the highest grade can be reached at less expense than at any other place in the State.

The French, German, and Spanish Languages receive special attention. Every department is under the special and personal supervision of the Principal. Number of pupils limited to one hundred.

TERMS.

From one hundred and sixty to two hundred dollars, for board and English tuition. Music from forty to fifty dollars per annum. Access to the celebrated Congress Spring daily, free of charge. This privilege alone is often worth the price of a year's residence at the school. Catalogues sent to any address, on application to the Principal.

HIGHLAND ACADEMY,

NEWBURGH, ORANGE Co., N. Y.

DEPARTMENTS.

CLASSICAL STUDIES,
MODERN LANGUAGES,
DRAWING and PAINTING,

ENGLISH BRANCHES,
VOCAL and INSTRUMENTAL MUSIC,
PHYSICAL EDUCATION.

The school year, of forty-two weeks, commences the second Tuesday of September in each year. Accomplished instructors employed in the various departments.
For particulars apply to

WM. N. REID,
Principal and Proprietor.

REFERENCES.

Rev. John Brown, D.D., Newburgh,
Rev. John Forsyth, D.D., Newburgh,
Hon. Nathaniel Jones, Newburgh,
Hon. Jno. W. Brown, Justice Supreme Court, Newburgh,

Hon. John Slosson, Judge of Superior Court, N. Y. City,
Wm. E. Warren, Esq., Deputy Controller of the City of New York,
William Fullerton, Esq., 61 Wall St., New York City.

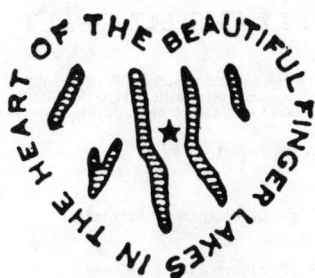

**Heart of the Lakes
Publishing
Interlaken, New York
14847**

Publishers of New York Local and Regional Histories, indexes and atlases.

Send for a complete catalogue of the many items currently available.

Quotations given for publishing of new works or reprinting older works dealing with New York history or genealogy.